Collins

CW00951980

SCRABBLE™
FAMILY
DICTIONARY

Published by Collins
An imprint of HarperCollins Publishers
Westerhill Road
Bishopbriggs
Glasgow G64 2QT

HarperCollins Publishers
1st Floor, Watermarque Building
Ringsend Road, Dublin 4, Ireland

Fifth Edition 2022

10 9 8 7 6 5 4 3 2 1

© HarperCollins Publishers 2008,
2012, 2013, 2016, 2020, 2022

ISBN 978-0-00-852395-4

www.collins.co.uk/scrabble

Typeset by Davidson Publishing
Solutions

Printed in the UK using
100% Renewable Electricity at
CPI Group (UK) Ltd

A catalogue record for this book is
available from the British Library.

If you would like to comment on any
aspect of this book, please contact us
at the given address or online.
E-mail: puzzles@harpercollins.co.uk
 facebook.com/collinsdictionary
 @collinsdict

EDITOR
Mary O'Neill

COMPUTING SUPPORT
Agnieszka Urbanowicz

FOR THE PUBLISHER
Gerry Breslin
Kerry Ferguson

Contents

Abbreviations

adj	adjective
adv	adverb
Brit	British
conj	conjunction
E	East *or* eastern
eg	for example
esp	especially
interj	interjection
n	noun
N	North *or* northern
orig	originally
pl	plural
prep	preposition
pron	pronoun
S	South *or* southern
Scot	Scottish
sing	singular
usu	usually
vb	verb
W	West *or* western

Introduction

The *Collins Scrabble Family Dictionary* is the ideal reference book for people who play Scrabble for enjoyment, in a social or family setting. This dictionary includes words of up to eight letters in length of the 279,000-plus words in *Collins Official Scrabble Words 2022*, the definitive Scrabble word list. The concise definitions in the *Scrabble Family Dictionary* allow players to check the meaning of words, as well as to use the book for settling arguments during games.

Because this dictionary is designed for family play, it does not include vulgar or offensive terms. The complete word list for tournaments and club competitions can be found in *Collins Official Scrabble Words 2022*, along with words of nine to fifteen letters.

How the word list is arranged

Words are listed in alphabetical order, although some inflected forms are included in the base form entry to save space. These appear in bold, after the base form. If the inflected form is created by the simple addition of a letter or letters, then only these letters are shown, for example:

ABET, -S, -TED, -TING

If there is some other spelling change, then the whole inflected form is shown:

ABATE, -D, -S, ABATING

Inflected forms also have a separate entry in the alphabetical list if another word interrupts the alphabetical sequence:

> **AGER, -S** *n* something that ages
> **AGERATUM** *n* tropical American plant with thick clusters of purplish-blue flowers
> **AGERS ▸ager**

Therefore, you should first scan the alphabetical list to check for a word; if the word is not included as a full entry in the alphabetical list, it may well appear as an inflected form beside its base form.

A black triangle symbol (▶) is used to refer readers to another related entry in the dictionary. Inflected, derived and variant forms are referred back to the main entry in this way.

Special Scrabble words

To help family players learn and use some of the most useful words in the game, the *Collins Scrabble Family Dictionary* includes a number of special panel entries, drawing attention to more than 200 words of particular interest or utility. For the most part these are words which are less likely to form part of a novice player's natural vocabulary, and the emphasis is on particularly useful three-letter words, on high-probability seven-letter bonus words, on words that are especially useful when you have either too many vowels on your rack or too many consonants, and on selected shorter words that use the high-value consonants **J**, **K**, **Q**, **X** and **Z**. But just for fun we have also featured a few of the unusual and exciting words of the kind that Scrabble players dream about. Realistically, you may well never get the chance to play words like **ZOOTAXY**, **TZADDIQ** and **QUETZAL**. But imagine the thrill (and the score!) if you did ...

There are also paragraphs at the start of every letter section which offer advice on useful words beginning with that letter.

The *Collins Scrabble Family Dictionary* is designed to be useful to new players and Scrabble veterans alike – we hope you enjoy using it!

Forming words

The key to successful Scrabble is constant awareness of the opportunities for forming words on the board. The obvious way to play a new word is to place it so that it intersects with a word already on the board through a common letter:

The common letter is known as a floater, in this case the floater being **C**. Skilful players are occasionally able to play through two or more floaters, whether the floating letters are adjacent or (even more difficult!) separated. A good deal of Scrabble skill revolves around using floaters, and on denying the use of floaters to your opponent.

Other methods of forming words, however, create more than one new word in the process, giving a higher score. The two main ways of doing this are 'hooking' and 'tagging'.

Hooking

Hooking involves 'hanging' one word on another – the word already on the board acts as a 'hook' on which the other word can be hung – changing the first word in the process. When you form a word by hooking, you add a letter to the beginning or end of a word on the board, transforming it into a longer word as you do so:

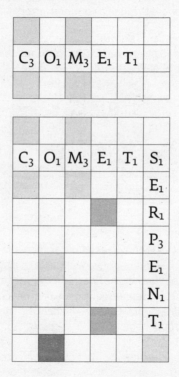

In this example, you get the points for **COMETS** as well as for **SERPENTS**. Plurals ending in **S** provide some of the most obvious – and useful – end-hooks. But there are plenty of other end-hooks as well. There are also lots of useful front-hooks.

Consider the following example:

If you happened to have **C,E,F,I,K** and **L** among the letters on your rack, you could play the following, taking full advantage of the valuable **X** played by your opponent:

Here you get the 13 points for **FOX** as well as those for **FICKLE**. So you can see that hooking is generally a much more profitable method of word-formation than simply playing a word through one that is already on the board.

Obviously, not all words provide hooks. Some words cannot form other words by having a letter added to either their front or their back; these are known as 'blockers', as they prevent other players from adding words by hooking.

Tagging

Playing a word parallel to one already on the board, so that one or more tiles are in contact, is known as tagging. Tagging is more difficult than hooking because you need to form one additional word for each tile in contact with the word on the board. In most circumstances, these will be two-letter words, which is why these words are so vital to the game. The more two-letter words you know, the greater your opportunities for fitting words onto the board through tagging – and of running up some impressive scores! Very skilful players have even been known to make 7-letter parallel plays!

For example, consider the following situation (your opponent has started the game with **SHAM** and you have **E,E,H,I,S,T** and **X** on your rack):

You could play **HEXES** so that it also forms **SH**, **HE**, **AX** and **ME** (all valid two-letter words), thus adding the scores for these three words to the points you make from **HEXES**:

	S_1	H_4	A_1	M_3	
	H_4	E_1	X_8	E_1	S_1

A particular advantage of tagging is that it allows you to benefit from valuable tiles twice in one go, as in the example above where **X** is used in both **HEXES** and **AX**.

Other word-forming techniques

There are other ways of forming new words from letters already on the board. For example, it is sometimes possible to 'infill' between existing letters, or to extend existing words at the front or back by adding more than one letter. Thus, if your opponent opens with **COVER**, placing the **C** on the double-letter square, you may be able to prefix it with **DIS** making **DISCOVER** and earning a triple-word score. But hooking and tagging are by far the most common techniques.

Two-letter words

Where many inexperienced Scrabble players go wrong is that they think the longer a word is, the better it is to know, as it's likely to score more. In fact, the key to a good Scrabble vocabulary is a good knowledge of short words.

The reason for that is you can use the short words to 'hook' the word you want to play on the board, allowing you to play parallel to another word, rather than always going through it crosswise. That way you will usually make more than one word each shot, gaining you a higher score.

8 POINTS = BAD PLAY

25 POINTS = GOOD PLAY

Notice how by using the same letters from your rack, you have scored seventeen more points. But notice also that little word **FA** which enabled you to fit the play in. And there we have the first, essential thing you have to know to improve your game: **all the allowable two-letter words**. Yes, all of them.

There are 127 of these to learn, but to make the list more manageable, you can divide them into three groups:

1 The ones you already know.
2 The ones you already know, but may not have realized were words.
3 The ones you probably don't know.

There are thirty-eight two-letter words which most people would know and which would appear in most dictionaries:

AH	AM	AN	AS	AT	AX	AY	BE	BY	DO	EH
GO	HA	HE	HI	HO	IF	IN	IS	IT	LA	LO
MA	ME	MY	NO	OF	OH	OK	ON	OR	OX	PA
SO	TO	UP	US	WE						

So straight away you only have eighty-nine new ones to learn. But it's not even as bad as that, because now we move on to the second group: the ones you know, but don't know you know.

These include:

Contractions

AD (advertisement)	**PO** (chamberpot)
MO (moment)	**RE** (regarding)
OP (operation)	**TA** (thank you)

Interjections and exclamations

AW	ER	EW	HM	MM	OI	OW
OY	SH	ST	UH	UM	UR	YA
YO						

Letters of the alphabet

AR	EF	EL	EM	EN	ES	EX

Then add in **ID** (a psychiatric term), **PI** (a Greek letter and mathematical term) and **YE** (the old form of **YOU**), and that's another thirty-one taken care of with no trouble at all.

Fifty-eight to go. These are the ones you probably don't know, so let's set them out where you can get the measure of them:

AA	AB	AE	AG	AI	AL	BA	BI	BO	CH	DA
DE	DI	EA	ED	EE	ET	FA	FE	FY	GI	GU
IO	JA	JO	KA	KI	KO	KY	LI	MI	MU	NA
NE	NU	NY	OB	OD	OE	OM	OO	OS	OU	PE
QI	SI	TE	TI	UG	UN	UT	WO	XI	XU	YU
ZA	ZE	ZO								

If all this looks a bit gobbledygookish, you may be surprised to know that even some of these are more familiar to you than you might realize. An **AB** is an abdominal muscle, as in toning up your abs and your pecs. **MU**, **NU** and **XI** are Greek letters. **OM** is a sacred syllable chanted in Hinduism.

Having said that, it can't be denied that some of the definitions are genuinely obscure. To go from start to finish, **AA** is a word from Hawaiian, meaning a rough volcanic rock. And a **ZO** is a Himalayan cross-breed of a yak and a cow, also spelt **ZHO**, **DZO**, **DZHO** or **DSO**.

Now, where else but in Scrabble can you go from Hawaii to the Himalayas in one step? Have a look at the two-letter words every so often. Once you're happy with the first two groups (i.e. the common ones, the contractions, the interjections, the letters, plus **ID**, **PI** and **YE**), have a real go at mastering the unusual ones. They really are the essential first step to improving your game.

Aa

A forms a two-letter word when followed by any one of **A, B, D, E, G, H, I, L, M, N, R, S, T, W, X** and **Y** – 16 letters out of 26 – so it's a really useful tile. There are also a number of short high-scoring words beginning with **A**. **Axe** (10 points) and **adze** (14 points) are good examples, but don't forget their US variants, **ax** (9 points) and **adz** (13 points). Also remember their plurals and the verb form **axed** (12 points). **Aye** (6) and **ay** (5) are handy for tight corners.

AA, -S *n* volcanic rock
AAH, -ED, -ING, -S *vb* exclaim in pleasure
AAL, -S *n* small shrub or tree with yellow fruits

> An **aal** is a South East Asian shrub, useful for getting rid of annoying multiples of A.

AALII, -S *n* bushy shrub

> An **aalii** is a tropical shrub, great for getting rid of surplus As and Is.

AALS ▸ aal
AARDVARK *n* S African anteater with long ears and snout
AARDWOLF *n* nocturnal mammal
AARGH *same as* ▸ argh
AARRGH *same as* ▸ argh
AARRGHH *same as* ▸ argh
AARTI, -S *n* Hindu ceremony
AAS ▸ aa
AASVOGEL *n* South African bird of prey
AB, -S *n* abdominal muscle
ABA, -S *n* type of Syrian cloth
ABAC, -S *n* mathematical diagram
ABACA, -S *n* species of banana
ABACI ▸ abacus
ABACK *adv* towards the back; backwards
ABACS ▸ abac
ABACTOR, -S *n* cattle thief
ABACUS, ABACI, -ES *n* mathematical instrument
ABAFT *adv* by the rear of (a ship) ▸ *adj* closer to the stern
ABAKA, -S *n* abaca
ABALONE, -S *n* edible sea creature

ABAMP, -S *same as* ▸ abampere
ABAMPERE *n* cgs unit of current
ABAMPS ▸ abamp
ABAND, -ED, -ING, -S *vb* abandon
ABANDON, -S *vb* desert or leave ▸ *n* lack of inhibition
ABANDS ▸ aband
ABAPICAL *adj* away from or opposite the apex
ABAS ▸ aba
ABASE, -D, -S, ABASING *vb* humiliate or degrade (oneself)
ABASEDLY ▸ abase
ABASER, -S ▸ abase
ABASES ▸ abase
ABASH, -ES, -ING *vb* cause to feel ill at ease
ABASHED *adj* embarrassed and ashamed
ABASHES ▸ abash
ABASHING ▸ abash
ABASIA, -S *n* disorder affecting ability to walk
ABASING ▸ abase
ABASK *adv* in pleasant warmth
ABATABLE ▸ abate
ABATE, -D, -S, ABATING *vb* make or become less strong
ABATER, -S ▸ abate
ABATES ▸ abate
ABATING ▸ abate
ABATIS, -ES *n* rampart of felled trees
ABATOR, -S *n* person who effects an abatement
ABATTIS *same as* ▸ abatis
ABATTOIR *n* place where animals are killed for food
ABATTU *adj* dejected
ABATURE, -S *n* trail left by hunted stag

ABAXIAL *adj* facing away from the axis
ABAXILE *adj* away from the axis
ABAYA, -S *n* Arab outer garment
ABB, -S *n* yarn used in weaving
ABBA, -S *n* Coptic bishop
ABBACY, ABBACIES *n* office of abbot or abbess
ABBAS ▸ abba
ABBATIAL *adj* relating to abbot, abbess, or abbey
ABBE, -S *n* French abbot
ABBED *adj* displaying strong abdominal muscles
ABBES ▸ abbe
ABBESS, -ES *n* nun in charge of a convent
ABBEY, -S *n* dwelling place of monks or nuns
ABBOT, -S *n* head of an abbey of monks
ABBOTCY ▸ abbot
ABBOTS ▸ abbot
ABBS ▸ abb
ABCEE, -S *n* alphabet
ABDABS *n* highly nervous state
ABDICANT *n* one who abdicates
ABDICATE *vb* give up a responsibility
ABDOMEN, -S, ABDOMINA *n* part of the body
ABDUCE, -D, -S, ABDUCING *vb* abduct
ABDUCENS *n* as in abducens nerve cranial nerve
ABDUCENT *adj* (of a muscle) abducting
ABDUCES ▸ abduce
ABDUCING ▸ abduce
ABDUCT, -ED, -S *vb* carry off, kidnap

ABDUCTEE ▶ abduct
ABDUCTOR ▶ abduct
ABDUCTS ▶ abduct
ABEAM adj at right angles to a ship
ABEAR, -ING, -S, ABORE, ABORNING vb bear or behave
ABED adv in bed
ABEGGING adj in the act of begging
ABEIGH adv aloof
ABELE, -S n white poplar tree
ABELIA, -S n garden plant with pink or white flowers
ABELIAN ▶ abelia
ABELIAS ▶ abelia
ABELMOSK n tropical plant
ABER, -S n estuary
ABERRANT adj showing aberration ▷ n person whose behaviour is aberrant
ABERRATE vb deviate from what is normal
ABERS ▶ aber
ABESSIVE n grammatical case indicating absence
ABET, -S, -TED, -TING vb help in wrongdoing
ABETMENT ▶ abet
ABETS ▶ abet
ABETTAL, -S ▶ abet
ABETTED ▶ abet
ABETTER, -S ▶ abet
ABETTING ▶ abet
ABETTOR, -S ▶ abet
ABEYANCE n state of being suspended
ABEYANCY n abeyance
ABEYANT ▶ abeyance
ABFARAD, -S n unit of capacitance
ABHENRY, -S n unit of inductance
ABHOR, -RED, -S vb detest utterly
ABHORRER ▶ abhor
ABHORS ▶ abhor
ABID ▶ abide
ABIDANCE ▶ abide
ABIDE, ABID, ABIDDEN, -D, -S vb endure, put up with
ABIDER, -S ▶ abide
ABIDES ▶ abide
ABIDING, -S adj lasting ▷ n action of one who abides
ABIES, ABIETES n fir tree
ABIETIC adj as in **abietic acid** yellowish powder
ABIGAIL, -S n a lady's maid
ABILITY n competence, power
ABIOSIS, ABIOSES n absence of life
ABIOTIC ▶ abiosis

ABITUR, -S n German examination
ABJECT, -ED, -S adj utterly miserable ▷ vb throw down
ABJECTLY ▶ abject
ABJECTS ▶ abject
ABJOINT, -S vb cut off
ABJURE, -D, -S, ABJURING vb deny or renounce on oath
ABJURER, -S ▶ abjure
ABJURES ▶ abjure
ABJURING ▶ abjure
ABLATE, -D, -S, ABLATING vb remove by ablation
ABLATION n removal of an organ
ABLATIVE n case of nouns ▷ adj relating to the ablative case
ABLATOR, -S n heat shield of a space craft
ABLAUT, -S n vowel gradation
ABLAZE adj burning fiercely ▷ adv on fire
ABLE, -R, -S, -ST, ABLING adj capable, competent ▷ vb enable
ABLED adj having physical powers
ABLEGATE n papal envoy
ABLEISM, -S n discrimination against disabled people
ABLEIST, -S ▶ ableism
ABLER ▶ able
ABLES ▶ able
ABLEST ▶ able
ABLET, -S n freshwater fish
ABLING ▶ able
ABLINGS adv possibly
ABLINS adv Scots word meaning perhaps
ABLOOM adj in flower
ABLOW adj blooming
ABLUENT, -S n substance used for cleansing
ABLUSH adj blushing
ABLUTED adj washed thoroughly
ABLUTION n ritual washing of a priest's hands
ABLY adv competently or skilfully
ABMHO, -S n unit of electrical conductance
ABNEGATE vb deny to oneself
ABNORMAL adj not normal or usual ▷ n abnormal person or thing
ABOARD adv onto a vehicle ▷ adj onto a vehicle
ABODE, -D, -S, ABODING n home, dwelling ▷ vb forebode

ABOHM, -S n unit of resistance
ABOIDEAU n dyke with sluicegate
ABOIL adj boiling
ABOITEAU same as ▶ aboideau
ABOLISH vb do away with
ABOLLA, -E, -S n Roman cloak
ABOMA, -S n South American snake
ABOMASA ▶ abomasum
ABOMASAL ▶ abomasum
ABOMASI ▶ abomasus
ABOMASUM, ABOMASA n compartment of a stomach
ABOMASUS, ABOMASI n abomasum
ABOON Scots word for ▶ above
ABORAL adj away from the mouth
ABORALLY ▶ aboral
ABORD, -ED, -ING, -S vb accost
ABORE ▶ abear
ABORIGEN n aborigine
ABORIGIN n aborigine
ABORNE adj Shakespearean form of auburn
ABORNING ▶ abear
ABORT, -ED, -ING, -S vb terminate ▷ n termination or failure
ABORTEE, -S n woman having an abortion
ABORTER, -S ▶ abort
ABORTING ▶ abort
ABORTION n operation to end a pregnancy
ABORTIVE adj unsuccessful
ABORTS ▶ abort
ABORTUS n aborted fetus
ABOUGHT ▶ aby
ABOULIA, -S same as ▶ abulia
ABOULIC ▶ aboulia
ABOUND, -ED, -S vb be plentiful
ABOUT adv nearly, approximately
ABOUTS prep about
ABOVE, -S adv higher (than) ▷ n something that is above
ABRACHIA n condition of having no arms
ABRADANT ▶ abrade
ABRADE, -D, -S, ABRADING vb wear down by friction
ABRADER, -S ▶ abrade
ABRADES ▶ abrade
ABRADING ▶ abrade
ABRAID, -ED, -S vb awake
ABRAM adj auburn
ABRASAX same as ▶ abraxas

ABRASION n scraped area on the skin

ABRASIVE adj harsh and unpleasant ▷ n substance for cleaning

ABRAXAS n ancient charm composed of Greek letters

ABRAY, -ED, -ING, -S vb awake

ABRAZO, -S n embrace

ABREACT, -S vb alleviate through abreaction

ABREAST adj side by side

ABREGE, -S n abridgment

ABRI, -S n shelter or place of refuge, esp in wartime

ABRICOCK n apricot

ABRIDGE, -D, -S vb shorten by using fewer words

ABRIDGER ▸ abridge

ABRIDGES ▸ abridge

ABRIM adj full to the brim

ABRIN, -S n poisonous compound

ABRIS ▸ abri

ABROACH adj (of a cask, barrel, etc) tapped

ABROAD, -S adv in a foreign country ▷ adj in general circulation ▷ n foreign place

ABROGATE vb cancel (a law or agreement) formally

ABROOKE, -D, -S vb bear or tolerate

ABROSIA, -S n condition involving refusal to eat

ABRUPT, -ER, -S adj incongruous or ridiculous ▷ n abyss

ABRUPTLY ▸ abrupt

ABRUPTS ▸ abrupt

ABS ▸ ab

ABSCESS n inflamed swelling ▷ vb form a swelling

ABSCIND, -S vb cut off

ABSCISE, -D, -S vb separate or be separated by abscission

ABSCISIC adj as in abscisic acid type of acid

ABSCISIN n plant hormone

ABSCISS same as ▸ abscissa

ABSCISSA n cutting off

ABSCISSE same as ▸ abscissa

ABSCOND, -S vb leave secretly

ABSEIL, -ED, -S vb go down by a rope ▷ n instance of abseiling

ABSEILER n person who abseils

ABSEILS ▸ abseil

ABSENCE, -S n being away

ABSENT, -ED, -S adj not present ▷ vb stay away

ABSENTEE n person who is not present

ABSENTER ▸ absent

ABSENTLY adv in an absent-minded manner

ABSENTS ▸ absent

ABSEY, -S n alphabet

ABSINTH, -S same as ▸ absinthe

ABSINTHE n liqueur

ABSINTHS ▸ absinth

ABSIT, -S n leave from college

ABSOLUTE adj complete, perfect ▷ n something absolute

ABSOLVE, -D, -S vb declare to be free from sin

ABSOLVER ▸ absolve

ABSOLVES ▸ absolve

ABSONANT adj unnatural and unreasonable

ABSORB, -S vb soak up (a liquid)

ABSORBED adj engrossed

ABSORBER n thing that absorbs

ABSORBS ▸ absorb

ABSTAIN, -S vb choose not to do something

ABSTERGE vb cleanse

ABSTRACT adj existing as an idea ▷ n summary ▷ vb summarize

ABSTRICT vb release

ABSTRUSE adj not easy to understand

ABSURD, -ER, -S adj incongruous or ridiculous ▷ n conception of the world

ABSURDLY ▸ absurd

ABSURDS ▸ absurd

ABTHANE, -S n ancient Scottish church territory

ABUBBLE adj bubbling

ABULIA, -S n pathological inability to make decisions

ABULIC ▸ abulia

ABUNA, -S n male head of Ethiopian family

ABUNDANT adj plentiful

ABUNE Scots word for ▸ above

ABURST adj bursting

ABUSABLE ▸ abuse

ABUSAGE, -S n wrong use

ABUSE, -D, -S, ABUSING vb use wrongly ▷ n prolonged ill-treatment

ABUSER, -S ▸ abuse

ABUSES ▸ abuse

ABUSING ▸ abuse

ABUSION, -S n wrong use or deception

ABUSIVE adj rude or insulting

ABUT, -S, -TED, -TING vb be next to or touching

ABUTILON n shrub

ABUTMENT n construction supporting the end of a bridge

ABUTS ▸ abut

ABUTTAL, -S same as ▸ abutment

ABUTTED ▸ abut

ABUTTER, -S n owner of adjoining property

ABUTTING ▸ abut

ABUZZ adj noisy, busy with activity etc

ABVOLT, -S n unit of potential difference in the electromagnetic system

ABWATT, -S n unit of power

ABY, ABOUGHT, -ING, -S vb pay the penalty for

Remember this word can be expanded to **baby** and **gaby** and also to **abye** and **abys**.

ABYE, -ING, -S same as ▸ aby

ABYING ▸ aby

ABYS ▸ aby

ABYSM, -S archaic word for ▸ abyss

ABYSMAL adj extremely bad, awful

ABYSMS ▸ abysm

ABYSS, -ES n very deep hole or chasm

ABYSSAL adj of the ocean depths

ABYSSES ▸ abyss

ACACIA, -S n tree or shrub

ACADEME, -S n place of learning

ACADEMIA n academic world

ACADEMIC adj of a university ▷ n lecturer at a university

ACADEMY n society for arts or sciences

ACAI, -S n berry

ACAJOU, -S n type of mahogany

ACALEPH, -S n invertebrate

ACALEPHE n acaleph

ACALEPHS ▸ acaleph

ACANTH, -S n acanthus

ACANTHA, -E, -S n thorn or prickle

ACANTHI ▸ acanthus

ACANTHIN n organic chemical

ACANTHS ▸ acanth

ACANTHUS, ACANTHI n prickly plant

ACAPNIA, -S n lack of carbon dioxide

ACARBOSE n diabetes medicine

ACARI ▸ acarus

ACARIAN ▸ acarus

ACARID, -S n small arachnid ▷ adj of these arachnids
ACARIDAN same as ▶ acarid
ACARIDS ▶ acarid
ACARINE, -S n acarid
ACAROID adj resembling a mite
ACARPOUS adj producing no fruit
ACARUS, ACARI n type of mite
ACATER, -S n buyer of provisions
ACATES n provisions
ACATOUR, -S n buyer of provisions
ACAUDAL adj having no tail
ACAUDATE same as ▶ acaudal
ACAULINE adj having no stem
ACAULOSE same as ▶ acauline
ACAULOUS adj having a short stem
ACCA, -S n academic
ACCABLE adj dejected or beaten
ACCAS ▶ acca
ACCEDE, -D, -S, ACCEDING vb consent or agree (to)
ACCEDER, -S ▶ accede
ACCEDES ▶ accede
ACCEDING ▶ accede
ACCEND, -ED, -S vb set alight
ACCENT, -ED, -S n style of pronunciation ▷ vb place emphasis on
ACCENTOR n songbird
ACCENTS ▶ accent
ACCEPT, -S vb receive willingly
ACCEPTED adj generally approved
ACCEPTEE n person who has been accepted
ACCEPTER ▶ accept
ACCEPTOR n person signing a bill of exchange
ACCEPTS ▶ accept
ACCESS, -ED, -ES n right to approach ▷ vb obtain data
ACCIDENT n mishap, often causing injury
ACCIDIA, -S same as ▶ accidie
ACCIDIE, -S n spiritual sloth
ACCINGE, -D, -S vb put a belt around
ACCITE, -D, -S, ACCITING vb summon
ACCLAIM, -S vb applaud, praise ▷ n enthusiastic approval
ACCLOY, -ED, -S vb choke or clog

ACCOAST, -S vb accost
ACCOIED ▶ accoy
ACCOIL, -S n welcome ▷ vb gather together
ACCOLADE n award ▷ vb give an award
ACCOMPT, -S vb account
ACCORAGE vb encourage
ACCORD, -ED, -S n agreement, harmony ▷ vb fit in with
ACCORDER ▶ accord
ACCORDS ▶ accord
ACCOST, -ED, -S vb approach and speak to ▷ n greeting
ACCOUNT, -S n report, description ▷ vb judge to be
ACCOURT, -S vb entertain
ACCOUTER same as ▶ accoutre
ACCOUTRE vb provide with equipment
ACCOY, ACCOIED, -ED, -ING, -S vb soothe
ACCOYLD vb past tense of accoil
ACCOYS ▶ accoy
ACCREDIT vb give official recognition to
ACCRETE, -D, -S vb grow together
ACCREW, -ED, -S vb accrue
ACCRUAL, -S n act of accruing
ACCRUE, -D, -S, ACCRUING vb increase gradually
ACCURACY n representation of truth
ACCURATE adj exact, correct
ACCURSE, -S vb curse
ACCURSED adj under a curse
ACCURSES ▶ accurse
ACCURST same as ▶ accursed
ACCUSAL, -S n accusation
ACCUSANT n person who accuses
ACCUSE, -S vb charge with wrongdoing
ACCUSED n person accused of a crime
ACCUSER, -S ▶ accuse
ACCUSES ▶ accuse
ACCUSING ▶ accuse
ACCUSTOM vb make used to
ACE, -D, -S, ACING n playing card with one symbol on it ▷ adj excellent ▷ vb serve an ace in racquet sports
ACEDIA, -S same as ▶ accidie
ACELDAMA n place with ill feeling

ACENTRIC adj without a centre ▷ n acentric chromosome or fragment
ACEQUIA, -S n irrigation ditch
ACER, -S n type of tree
ACERATE same as ▶ acerated
ACERATED adj having sharp points
ACERB, -ER, -EST adj bitter
ACERBATE vb embitter or exasperate
ACERBER ▶ acerb
ACERBEST ▶ acerb
ACERBIC adj harsh or bitter
ACERBITY n bitter speech or temper
ACEROLA, -S n cherry-like fruit
ACEROSE adj shaped like a needle
ACEROUS same as ▶ acerose
ACERS ▶ acer
ACERVATE adj growing in heaps or clusters
ACERVULI ▶ acervulus
ACES ▶ ace
ACESCENT adj slightly sour or turning sour ▷ n something that is turning sour
ACETA ▶ acetum
ACETAL, -S n colourless liquid
ACETAMID same as ▶ acetamide
ACETATE, -S n salt or ester of acetic acid
ACETATED adj combined with acetic acid
ACETATES ▶ acetate
ACETIC adj of or involving vinegar
ACETIFY vb become vinegar
ACETIN, -S n type of acetate
ACETONE, -S n colourless liquid used as a solvent
ACETONIC ▶ acetone
ACETOSE same as ▶ acetous
ACETOUS adj containing acetic acid
ACETOXYL n medicine used to treat acne
ACETUM, ACETA n solution that has dilute acetic acid as solvent
ACETYL, -S n type of monovalent radical
ACETYLIC ▶ acetyl
ACETYLS ▶ acetyl
ACH interj Scots expression of surprise
ACHAENIA ▶ achaenium
ACHAGE, -S n pain
ACHAR, -S n spicy pickle made from mango

ACHARNE adj furiously violent

ACHARS ▸ achar

ACHARYA, -S n religious teacher and spiritual guide

ACHATES same as ▸ **acates**

ACHE, -D, -S n dull continuous pain ▷ vb be in or cause continuous dull pain

ACHENE, -S n type of fruit

ACHENIA ▸ achenium

ACHENIAL ▸ achene

ACHENIUM, ACHENIA n achene

ACHES ▸ ache

ACHIER ▸ achy

ACHIEST ▸ achy

ACHIEVE, -D, -S vb gain by hard work or ability

ACHIEVER ▸ achieve

ACHIEVES ▸ achieve

ACHILLEA n type of plant with white, yellow, or purple flowers, often grown in gardens

ACHINESS ▸ achy

ACHING, -S ▸ ache

ACHINGLY ▸ ache

ACHINGS ▸ aching

ACHIOTE, -S n annatto

ACHIRAL adj of a tuber producing arrowroot

ACHKAN, -S n man's coat in India

ACHOLIA, -S n bile condition

ACHOO, -S n sound of a sneeze

ACHROMAT n lens designed to bring light of two wavelengths to the same focal point

ACHROMIC adj colourless

ACHY, ACHIER, ACHIEST adj affected by a continuous dull pain

ACICULA, -E, -S n needle-shaped part

ACICULAR ▸ acicula

ACICULAS ▸ acicula

ACICULUM n bristle that supports the appendages of some polychaetes

ACID, -ER, -EST, -S n corrosive compound that combines with a base to form a salt ▷ adj containing acid

ACIDEMIA n abnormally high level of acid in blood

ACIDER ▸ acid

ACIDEST ▸ acid

ACIDIC adj containing acid

ACIDIER ▸ acidy

ACIDIEST ▸ acidy

ACIDIFY vb convert into acid

ACIDITY n quality of being acid

ACIDLY ▸ acid

ACIDNESS ▸ acid

ACIDOSIS, ACIDOSES n abnormal increase in the acidity of the blood and bodily fluids

ACIDOTIC ▸ acidosis

ACIDS ▸ acid

ACIDURIA n abnormally high level of acid in urine

ACIDY, ACIDIER, ACIDIEST adj resembling or containing acid

ACIERAGE n iron-plating of metal

ACIERATE vb change (iron) into steel

ACIFORM adj shaped like a needle

ACINAR adj of small sacs

ACING ▸ ace

ACINI ▸ acinus

ACINIC ▸ acinus

ACINOSE ▸ acinus

ACINOUS ▸ acinus

ACINUS, ACINI n part of a gland

ACKEE, -S n tropical tree

ACKER, -S same as ▸ **acca**

ACKNOW, ACKNEW, -N, -S vb recognize

ACKNOWNE adj aware

ACKNOWS ▸ acknow

ACLINIC adj unbending

ACMATIC adj highest or ultimate

ACME, -S n highest point of achievement or excellence

ACMIC same as ▸ **acmatic**

ACMITE, -S n chemical with pyramid-shaped crystals

ACNE, -S n pimply skin disease

ACNED adj marked by acne

ACNES ▸ acne

ACNODAL ▸ acnode

ACNODE, -S n isolated point on the graph of a curve

ACOCK adv cocked

ACOELOUS adj not having a stomach

ACOEMETI n order of monks

ACOLD adj feeling cold

ACOLYTE, -S n follower or attendant

ACOLYTH, -S n acolyte

ACONITE, -S n poisonous plant with hoodlike flowers

ACONITIC ▸ aconite

ACONITUM same as ▸ **aconite**

ACORN, -S n nut of the oak tree

ACORNED adj covered with acorns

ACORNS ▸ acorn

ACOSMISM n belief that no world exists outside the mind

ACOSMIST ▸ acosmism

ACOUCHI, -S n South American rodent with a white-tipped tail

ACOUCHY same as ▸ **acouchi**

ACOUSTIC adj of sound and hearing

ACQUAINT vb make familiar, inform

ACQUEST, -S n something acquired

ACQUIGHT vb acquit

ACQUIRAL ▸ acquire

ACQUIRE, -D, -S vb gain, get

ACQUIREE n one who acquires

ACQUIRER ▸ acquire

ACQUIRES ▸ acquire

ACQUIS n as in **acquis communautaire** European Union laws

ACQUIST, -S n acquisition

ACQUIT, -S vb pronounce (someone) innocent

ACQUITE, -S vb acquit

ACQUITS ▸ acquit

ACRASIA, -S n lack of willpower

ACRASIN, -S n chemical

ACRATIC ▸ acrasia

ACRAWL adv crawling

ACRE, -S n measure of land, 4840 square yards (4046.86 square metres)

ACREAGE, -S n land area in acres ▷ adj of or relating to a large allotment of land, esp in a rural area

ACRED adj having acres of land

ACRES ▸ acre

ACRID, -ER, -EST adj pungent, bitter

ACRIDIN, -S n acridine

ACRIDINE n colourless crystalline solid

ACRIDINS ▸ acridin

ACRIDITY ▸ acrid

ACRIDLY ▸ acrid

ACRIMONY n bitterness and resentment felt about something

ACRO, -S n event where acrobatic skiing moves are performed to music

ACROBAT, -S n person skilled in gymnastic feats requiring agility and balance

ACRODONT adj (of reptile teeth) fused at the base to the jawbones ▷ n acrodont reptile

A

ACROGEN, -S n flowerless plant

ACROLECT n most correct form of language

ACROLEIN n colourless or yellowish flammable poisonous pungent liquid

ACROLITH n wooden sculpture with the head, hands, and feet in stone

ACROMIA ▷ acromion

ACROMIAL ▷ acromion

ACROMION, ACROMIA n outermost edge of the spine of the shoulder blade

ACRONIC adj occurring at sunset

ACRONYM, -S n word formed from the initial letters of other words, such as NASA

ACROS ▷ acro

ACROSOME n structure in reproductive cell

ACROSS adv from side to side (of)

ACROSTIC n lines of writing in which the first or last letters of each line spell a word or saying

ACROTER, -S n plinth

ACROTIC adj of a surface

ACROTISM n absence of pulse

ACRYLATE n chemical compound in plastics and resins

ACRYLIC, -S adj (synthetic fibre, paint, etc) made from acrylic acid ▷ n synthetic fibre used for clothes and blankets

ACRYLYL, -S n type of monovalent group

ACT, -ED, -S n thing done ▷ vb do something

ACTA pl n minutes of meeting

ACTABLE ▷ act

ACTANT, -S n noun phrase functioning as the agent of a verb

ACTED ▷ act

ACTIN, -S n protein

ACTINAL adj having tentacles

ACTING, -S n art of an actor ▷ adj temporarily performing the duties of

ACTINIA, -E, -S n type of sea anemone

ACTINIAN n sea anemone

ACTINIAS ▷ actinia

ACTINIC adj (of radiation) producing a photochemical effect

ACTINIDE n member of the actinide series

ACTINISM ▷ actinic

ACTINIUM n radioactive chemical element

ACTINOID adj having a radiate form, as a sea anemone or starfish ▷ n member of the actinide series

ACTINON, -S same as ▷ actinide

ACTINS ▷ actin

ACTION, -ED, -S n process of doing something ▷ vb put into effect

ACTIONER n film with a fast-moving plot, usually containing scenes of violence

ACTIONS ▷ action

ACTIVATE vb make active

ACTIVE, -ED, -S adj moving, working ▷ n active form of a verb

ACTIVELY ▷ active

ACTIVES ▷ active

ACTIVISE same as ▷ activize

ACTIVISM n taking direct or militant action to achieve a political or social end

ACTIVIST ▷ activism

ACTIVITY n state of being active

ACTIVIZE vb make active

ACTON, -S n jacket

ACTOR, -S n person who acts in a play, film, etc

ACTORISH ▷ actor

ACTORLY adj characteristic of an actor

ACTORS ▷ actor

ACTRESS n woman who acts in a play, film, broadcast, etc

ACTRESSY adj exaggerated and affected in manner

ACTS ▷ act

ACTUAL adj existing in reality

ACTUALLY adv really, indeed

ACTUALS pl n commercial commodities that can be bought and used

ACTUARY n statistician who calculates insurance risks

ACTUATE, -D, -S vb start up (a device)

ACTUATOR ▷ actuate

ACTURE, -S n action

ACUATE, -D, -S, ACUATING adj sharply pointed ▷ vb sharpen

ACUITY, ACUITIES n keenness of vision or thought

ACULEATE adj cutting ▷ n insect, such as a bee, with a sting

ACULEUS, ACULEI n prickle or spine, such as the thorn of a rose

ACUMEN, -S n ability to make good judgments

ACUPOINT n points on the body stimulated with acupuncture or acupressure

ACUSHLA, -S n Irish endearment

ACUTANCE n physical rather than subjective measure of the sharpness of a photographic image

ACUTE, -R, -S, -ST adj severe ▷ n accent over a letter to indicate the quality or length of its sound, as over e in café

ACUTELY ▷ acute

ACUTER ▷ acute

ACUTES ▷ acute

ACUTEST ▷ acute

ACYCLIC adj not cyclic

ACYL, -S n member of the monovalent group of atoms RCO-

ACYLATE, -D, -S vb add acyl group to

ACYLOIN, -S n organic chemical compound

ACYLS ▷ acyl

AD, -S n advertisement

ADAGE, -S n wise saying, proverb

ADAGIAL ▷ adage

ADAGIO, -S adv (to be played) slowly and gracefully ▷ n movement or piece to be performed slowly

ADAMANCE n being adamant

ADAMANCY n being adamant

ADAMANT, -S adj unshakable in determination or purpose ▷ n any extremely hard or apparently unbreakable substance

ADAMSITE n yellow poisonous crystalline solid that readily sublimes

ADAPT, -ED, -ING, -S vb alter for new use or to new conditions

ADAPTER, -S same as ▷ adaptor

ADAPTING ▷ adapt

ADAPTION n adaptation

ADAPTIVE ▷ adapt

ADAPTOR, -S n device for connecting several electrical appliances to a single socket

ADAPTS ▷ adapt

ADAW, -ED, -ING, -S *vb* subdue

ADAXIAL *adj* facing the axis

ADAYS *adv* daily

ADBOT, -S *n* spyware that collects information about a person to display targeted adverts

ADD, -ED, -S *vb* combine (numbers or quantities)

ADDABLE ▶ **add**

ADDAX, -ES *n* antelope

ADDEBTED *adj* indebted

ADDED ▶ **add**

ADDEDLY ▶ **add**

ADDEEM, -ED, -S *vb* adjudge

ADDEND, -S *n* any of a set of numbers that is to be added

ADDENDA ▶ **addendum**

ADDENDS ▶ **addend**

ADDENDUM, ADDENDA *n* addition

ADDER, -S *n* small poisonous snake

ADDIBLE *adj* addable

ADDICT, -ED, -S *n* person who is unable to stop doing or taking something ▷ *vb* cause (someone or oneself) to become dependent (on something)

ADDIES ▶ **addy**

ADDING, -S *n* act or instance of addition ▷ *adj* of, for, or relating to addition

ADDIO, -S *interj* farewell ▷ *n* cry of addio

ADDITION *n* adding

ADDITIVE *n* something added, esp to a foodstuff, to improve it or prevent deterioration ▷ *adj* characterized or produced by addition

ADDITORY *adj* adding to something

ADDLE, -D, -S, ADDLING *vb* become muddled ▷ *adj* indicating a muddled state

ADDOOM, -ED, -S *vb* adjudge

ADDORSED *adj* back to back

ADDRESS, ADDREST *n* place where a person lives ▷ *vb* mark the destination, as on an envelope

ADDS ▶ **add**

ADDUCE, -D, -S, ADDUCING *vb* mention something as evidence or proof

ADDUCENT ▶ **adduce**

ADDUCER, -S ▶ **adduce**

ADDUCES ▶ **adduce**

ADDUCING ▶ **adduce**

ADDUCT, -ED, -S *vb* draw towards medial axis ▷ *n* compound

ADDUCTOR *n* muscle that adducts

ADDUCTS ▶ **adduct**

ADDY, ADDIES *n* email address

ADEEM, -ED, -ING, -S *vb* cancel

ADELGID, -S *n* type of small sap-feeding insect

ADENINE, -S *n* chemical

ADENITIS *n* inflammation of a gland or lymph node

ADENOID *adj* of or resembling a gland

ADENOIDS *pl n* tissue at the back of the throat

ADENOMA, -S *n* tumour occurring in glandular tissue

ADENOSIS, ADENOSES *n* disease of glands

ADENYL, -S *n* enzyme

ADENYLIC *adj* as in **adenylic acid** nucleotide consisting of adenine, ribose or deoxyribose, and a phosphate group

ADENYLS ▶ **adenyl**

ADEPT, -ER, -EST, -S *n* very skilful person ▷ *adj* proficient in something requiring skill

ADEPTLY ▶ **adept**

ADEPTS ▶ **adept**

ADEQUACY ▶ **adequate**

ADEQUATE *adj* sufficient, enough

ADERMIN, -S *n* vitamin

ADESPOTA *n* anonymous writings

ADESSIVE *n* grammatical case denoting place

ADHAN, -S *n* call to prayer

ADHARMA, -S *n* wickedness

ADHERE, -D, -S, ADHERING *vb* stick (to)

ADHEREND *n* something attached by adhesive

ADHERENT *n* devotee, follower ▷ *adj* sticking or attached

ADHERER, -S ▶ **adhere**

ADHERES ▶ **adhere**

ADHERING ▶ **adhere**

ADHESION *n* sticking (to)

ADHESIVE *n* substance used to stick things together ▷ *adj* able to stick to things

ADHIBIT, -S *vb* administer or apply

ADIEU, -S, -X *n* goodbye

Very useful when you want to say goodbye to a surplus of vowels. And remember its plural can be either **adieus** or **adieux**.

ADIOS, -ES *sentence substitute* Spanish for goodbye ▷ *n* goodbye

ADIPIC *adj* as in **adipic acid** crystalline solid used in the preparation of nylon

ADIPOSE *adj* of or containing fat ▷ *n* animal fat

ADIPOSIS, ADIPOSES *n* obesity

ADIPOUS *adj* made of fat

ADIPSIA, -S *n* complete lack of thirst

ADIT, -S *n* shaft into a mine, for access or drainage

ADJACENT *adj* near or next (to) ▷ *n* side lying between a specified angle and a right angle in a right-angled triangle

ADJIGO, -S *n* SW Australian yam plant with edible tubers

ADJOIN, -ED, -S *vb* be next to

ADJOINT, -S *n* type of mathematical matrix

ADJOURN, -S *vb* close (a court) at the end of a session

ADJUDGE, -D, -S *vb* declare (to be)

ADJUNCT, -S *n* something incidental added to something else

ADJURE, -D, -S, ADJURING *vb* command (to do)

ADJURER, -S ▶ **adjure**

ADJURES ▶ **adjure**

ADJURING ▶ **adjure**

ADJUROR, -S ▶ **adjure**

ADJUST, -ED, -S *vb* adapt to new conditions

ADJUSTER ▶ **adjust**

ADJUSTOR ▶ **adjust**

ADJUSTS ▶ **adjust**

ADJUTAGE *n* nozzle

ADJUTANT *n* army officer in charge of routine administration

ADJUVANT *adj* aiding or assisting ▷ *n* something that aids or assists

ADLAND, -S *n* advertising industry and the people who work in it

ADMAN, ADMEN *n* man who works in advertising

ADMASS, -ES *n* mass advertising

ADMEN ▶ **adman**

ADMIN, -S *n* administration

ADMIRAL, -S *n* highest naval rank

ADMIRE, -D, -S *vb* regard with esteem and approval

ADMIRER, -S ▶ **admire**

A

ADMIRES ▸ admire

ADMIRING ▸ admire

ADMIT, -S, -TED vb confess, acknowledge

ADMITTEE n one who admits

ADMITTER ▸ admit

ADMIX, -ED, -ES, -ING, -T vb mix or blend

ADMONISH vb reprove sternly

ADNATE adj growing closely attached to an adjacent part or organ

ADNATION ▸ adnate

ADNEXA pl n organs adjoining the uterus

ADNEXAL ▸ adnexa

ADNOUN, -S n adjective used as a noun

ADO, -S n fuss, trouble

ADOBE, -S n sun-dried brick

ADOBO, -S n Philippine dish

ADONIS n beautiful young man

ADONISE, -D, -S vb adorn

ADONIZE, -D, -S vb adorn

ADOORS adv at the door

ADOPT, -ING, -S vb take (someone else's child) as one's own

ADOPTED adj having been adopted

ADOPTEE, -S n one who has been adopted

ADOPTER, -S n person who adopts

ADOPTING ▸ adopt

ADOPTION ▸ adopt

ADOPTIVE adj related by adoption

ADOPTS ▸ adopt

ADORABLE adj very attractive

ADORABLY ▸ adorable

ADORE, -D, -S vb love intensely

ADORER, -S ▸ adore

ADORES ▸ adore

ADORING adj displaying intense love

ADORN, -ED, -ING, -S vb decorate, embellish

ADORNER, -S ▸ adorn

ADORNING ▸ adorn

ADORNS ▸ adorn

ADOS ▸ ado

ADOWN adv down

ADOZE adv asleep

ADPRESS vb press together

ADRAD adj afraid

ADRATE, -S n price or tariff that businesses pay to advertise

ADREAD, -ED, -S vb dread

ADRED adj filled with dread

ADRENAL, -S adj near the kidneys ▷ n adrenal gland

ADRIFT adv drifting

ADROIT, -ER adj quick and skilful

ADROITLY ▸ adroit

ADRY adj dry

ADS ▸ ad

ADSCRIPT n serf

ADSORB, -ED, -S vb condense to form a thin film

ADSORBER ▸ adsorb

ADSORBS ▸ adsorb

ADSPEAK, -S n kind of language or jargon used in advertising or in advertisements

ADSUKI, -S same as ▸ adzuki

ADSUM sentence substitute I am present

ADUKI, -S same as ▸ adzuki

ADULARIA n white or colourless glassy variety of orthoclase

ADULATE, -D, -S vb flatter or praise obsequiously

ADULATOR ▸ adulate

ADULT, -S adj fully grown, mature ▷ n adult person or animal

ADULTLY ▸ adult

ADULTS ▸ adult

ADUMBRAL adj shadowy

ADUNC adj hooked

ADUNCATE adj hooked

ADUNCITY n quality of being hooked

ADUNCOUS adj hooked

ADUST, -ED, -ING, -S vb dry up or darken by heat

ADVANCE, -S vb go or bring forward ▷ n forward movement ▷ adj done or happening before an event

ADVANCED adj at a late stage in development

ADVANCER ▸ advance

ADVANCES ▸ advance

ADVECT, -ED, -S vb move horizontally in air

ADVENE, -D, -S, ADVENING vb add as extra

ADVENT, -S n arrival

ADVERB, -S n word that adds information about a verb, adjective, or other adverb

ADVERSE, -R adj unfavourable

ADVERT, -ED, -S n advertisement ▷ vb draw attention (to)

ADVEW, -ED, -ING, -S vb look at

ADVICE, -S n recommendation as to what to do

ADVISE, -S vb offer advice to

ADVISED adj considered, thought-out

ADVISEE, -S n person receiving advice

ADVISER, -S n person who offers advice, eg on careers to students or school pupils

ADVISES ▸ advise

ADVISING ▸ advise

ADVISOR, -S same as ▸ adviser

ADVISORY adj giving advice ▷ n statement giving advice or a warning

ADVOCAAT n liqueur with a raw egg base

ADVOCACY n active support of a cause or course of action

ADVOCATE vb propose or recommend ▷ n person who publicly supports a cause

ADVOWSON n right of presentation to a vacant benefice

ADWARD, -ED, -S vb award

ADWARE, -S n computer software

ADWOMAN, ADWOMEN n woman working in advertising

ADYNAMIA n loss of vital power or strength, esp as the result of illness

ADYNAMIC ▸ adynamia

ADYTUM, ADYTA n sacred place in ancient temples

ADZ same as ▸ adze

This is the American spelling of **adze**, and is one of the essential short words to know for using the Z.

ADZE, -D, -S, ADZING n woodworking tool ▷ vb use an adze

ADZELIKE adj like an adze

ADZES ▸ adze

ADZING ▸ adze

ADZUKI, -S n type of plant

AE determiner one

AECIA ▸ aecium

AECIAL ▸ aecium

AECIDIA ▸ aecidium

AECIDIAL ▸ aecidium

AECIDIUM, AECIDIA same as ▸ aecium

AECIUM, AECIA n area of some fungi

AEDES n type of mosquito which transmits yellow fever and dengue

AEDICULE n door or a window framed by columns and a pediment

AEDILE, -S n magistrate of ancient Rome

AEDINE adj of a species of mosquito

AEFALD adj single

AEFAULD adj single

AEGIRINE n green mineral

AEGIRITE n green mineral

AEGIS, -ES n sponsorship, protection

AEGLOGUE n eclogue

AEGROTAT n certificate allowing a candidate to pass an examination missed through illness

AEMULE, -D, -S, AEMULING vb emulate

AENEOUS adj brass-coloured or greenish-gold

AENEUS, -ES n aquarium fish

AEOLIAN adj of or relating to the wind

AEON, -S n immeasurably long period of time

This little word gets played when you have too many vowels. And it has a partner **eoan**, meaning of the dawn: but beware, unlike **aeon**, it does not take a plural S.

AEONIAN adj everlasting

AEONIC ▶ aeon

AEONS ▶ aeon

AEQUORIN n type of protein

This word for a kind of protein secreted by jellyfish is one of the most frequently played 8-letter words using the Q: it's not easy to spot but can give a good score for a difficult-looking rack!

AERADIO, -S n radio system for pilots

AERATE, -D, -S, AERATING vb put gas into (a liquid), as when making a fizzy drink

AERATION ▶ aerate

This means the act of aerating, and while its face value is low, its combination of common letters make it one of the most frequently played of all 8-letter bonus words, scoring you an extra 50 points.

AERATOR, -S ▶ aerate

AERIAL, -S adj in, from, or operating in the air ▷ n metal pole, wire, etc, for receiving or transmitting radio or TV signals

AERIALLY ▶ aerial

AERIALS ▶ aerial

AERIE, -S variant spelling (esp US) of ▶ eyrie

This word for an eagle's nest is a great one for dealing with a surplus of vowels. And it has several variants: **aery, aiery, ayrie, eyrie** and **eyry**.

AERIED adj in a very high place

AERIER ▶ aery

AERIES ▶ aerie

AERIEST ▶ aery

AERIFIED ▶ aerify

AERIFIES ▶ aerify

AERIFORM adj having the form of air

AERIFY, AERIFIED, AERIFIES vb change or cause to change into a gas

AERILY ▶ aery

AERO, -S n aerodynamic vehicle or component

AEROBAT, -S n person who does stunt flying

AEROBE, -S n organism that requires oxygen to survive

AEROBIA ▶ aerobium

AEROBIC adj designed for or relating to aerobics

AEROBICS n exercises designed to increase the amount of oxygen in the blood

AEROBIUM, AEROBIA same as ▶ aerobe

AEROBOMB n bomb dropped from aircraft

AEROBOT, -S n unmanned aircraft used esp in space exploration

AEROBUS n monorail suspended by an overhead cable

AERODART n metal arrow dropped from an aircraft as a weapon

AERODUCT n air duct

AERODYNE n aircraft that derives its lift from aerodynamic forces

AEROFOIL n part of an aircraft, such as the wing, designed to give lift

AEROGEL, -S n colloid

AEROGRAM n airmail letter on a single sheet of paper that seals to form an envelope

AEROLITE n stony meteorite consisting of silicate minerals

An **aerolite** is a type of meteorite, and is important because the chance to play this 8-letter bonus word comes up very frequently.

AEROLITH n meteorite

AEROLOGY n study of the atmosphere, particularly its upper layers

AERONAUT n person who flies in a lighter-than-air craft, esp the pilot or navigator

AERONOMY n science of the earth's upper atmosphere

AEROS ▶ aero

AEROSAT, -S n communications satellite

AEROSOL, -S n pressurized can from which a substance can be dispensed as a fine spray

AEROSTAT n lighter-than-air craft, such as a balloon

AEROTONE n bath incorporating air jets for massage

AERUGO, -S (esp of old bronze) another name for ▶ verdigris

AERY, AERIER, AERIEST adj lofty, insubstantial, or visionary

AESC, -ES n rune

AESCULIN n chemical in horse-chestnut bark

AESIR pl n Norse gods

AESTHETE n person who has or affects an extravagant love of art

AESTIVAL adj of or occurring in summer

AETATIS adj at the age of

AETHER, -S same as ▶ ether

AETHERIC ▶ aether

AETHERS ▶ aether

AFALD adj single

AFAR, -S adv at, from, or to a great distance ▷ n great distance

AFARA, -S n African tree

AFARS ▶ afar

AFAWLD adj single

AFEAR, -ING, -S vb frighten

AFEARD an archaic or dialect word for ▶ afraid

AFEARED same as ▶ afeard

AFEARING ▶ afear

AFEARS ▶ afear

AFEBRILE adj without fever

AFF adv off

AFFABLE adj friendly and easy to talk to

AFFABLY ▶ affable

AFFAIR n event or happening

AFFAIRE, -S n love affair

AFFAIRS pl n personal or business interests

AFFEAR, -D, -ED, -S vb frighten

AFFEARE, -S vb frighten
AFFEARED ▸ affear
AFFEARES ▸ affeare
AFFEARS ▸ affear
AFFECT, -S vb act on, influence ▹ n emotion associated with an idea or set of ideas
AFFECTED adj displaying affectation
AFFECTER ▸ affect
AFFECTS ▸ affect
AFFEER, -ED, -S vb assess
AFFERENT adj directing inwards to a body part, esp the brain or spinal cord ▹ n nerve that conveys impulses towards an organ of the body
AFFIANCE vb bind (a person or oneself) in a promise of marriage ▹ n solemn pledge, esp a marriage contract
AFFIANT, -S n person who makes an affidavit
AFFICHE, -S n poster
AFFIED ▸ affy
AFFIES ▸ affy
AFFINAL ▸ affine
AFFINE, -S adj involving transformations which preserve collinearity ▹ n relation by marriage
AFFINED adj closely related
AFFINELY ▸ affine
AFFINES ▸ affine
AFFINITY n close connection or liking
AFFIRM, -ED, -S vb declare to be true
AFFIRMER ▸ affirm
AFFIRMS ▸ affirm
AFFIX, -ED, -ES, -ING vb attach or fasten ▹ n word or syllable added to a word to change its meaning
AFFIXAL ▸ affix
AFFIXED ▸ affix
AFFIXER, -S ▸ affix
AFFIXES ▸ affix
AFFIXIAL ▸ affix
AFFIXING ▸ affix
AFFLATED adj inspired
AFFLATUS n supposed divine inspiration, esp in poetry
AFFLICT, -S vb give pain or grief to
AFFLUENT adj having plenty of money ▹ n tributary stream
AFFLUX, -ES n flowing towards a point
AFFOGATO n dessert made by pouring espresso over ice cream

AFFOORD, -S vb consent
AFFORCE, -D, -S vb strengthen
AFFORD, -ED, -S vb have enough money to buy
AFFOREST vb plant trees on
AFFRAP, -S vb strike
AFFRAY, -ED, -S n noisy fight, brawl ▹ vb frighten
AFFRAYER ▸ affray
AFFRAYS ▸ affray
AFFRET, -S n furious attack
AFFRIGHT vb frighten ▹ n sudden terror
AFFRONT, -S n insult ▹ vb hurt someone's pride or dignity
AFFRONTE adj facing
AFFRONTS ▸ affront
AFFUSION n baptizing of a person by pouring water onto his or her head
AFFY, AFFIED, AFFIES, -DE, -ING vb trust
AFGHAN, -S n type of blanket
AFGHANI, -S n monetary unit of Afghanistan
AFGHANS ▸ afghan
AFIELD adj away from one's usual surroundings or home
AFIRE adj on fire
AFLAJ ▸ falaj
AFLAME adj burning
AFLOAT adj floating ▹ adv floating
AFLUTTER adv in or into a nervous or excited state
AFOCAL adj relating to a method for transferring an image without bringing it into focus
AFOOT adj happening, in operation ▹ adv happening
AFORE adv before
AFOUL adj in or into a state of difficulty, confusion, or conflict (with)
AFRAID adj frightened
AFREET, -S n powerful evil demon or giant monster
AFRESH adv again, anew
AFRIT, -S same as ▸ afreet
AFRO, -S n full rounded hairstyle
AFRONT adv in front
AFROS ▸ afro
AFT adv at or towards the rear of a ship or aircraft ▹ adj at or towards the rear of a ship or aircraft
AFTER adv at a later time
AFTEREYE vb gaze at someone or something that has passed
AFTERS n sweet course of a meal

AFTERSUN n moisturizing lotion applied to the skin to soothe sunburn and avoid peeling
AFTERTAX adj after tax has been paid
AFTMOST adj furthest towards rear
AFTOSA, -S n foot-and-mouth disease
AG, -S n agriculture
AGA, -S n title of respect
AGACANT adj irritating
AGACANTE adj irritating
AGACERIE n coquetry
AGAIN adv once more
AGAINST prep in opposition or contrast to
AGALLOCH another name for ▸ eaglewood
AGALWOOD n eaglewood
AGAMA, -S n small lizard
AGAMETE, -S n reproductive cell
AGAMI, -S n South American bird
AGAMIC adj asexual
AGAMID, -S same as ▸ agama
AGAMIS ▸ agami
AGAMOID, -S n lizard of the agamid family
AGAMONT, -S another name for ▸ schizont
AGAMOUS adj without sex
AGAPE, AGAPAE, AGAPAI, -S adj (of the mouth) wide open ▹ n love feast among the early Christians
AGAPEIC ▸ agape
AGAPES ▸ agape
AGAR, -S n jelly-like substance obtained from seaweed and used as a thickener in food
AGARIC, -S n type of fungus
AGAROSE, -S n gel used in chemistry
AGARS ▸ agar
AGARWOOD n aromatic wood of an Asian tree
AGAS ▸ aga
AGAST, -ED, -ING, -S adj aghast ▹ vb terrify or be terrified
AGATE, -S n semiprecious form of quartz with striped colouring ▹ adv on the way
AGATISE, -D, -S same as ▸ agatize
AGATIZE, -D, -S vb turn into agate
AGATOID adj like agate
AGAVE, -S n tropical plant
AGAZE adj gazing at something
AGAZED adj amazed

A

AGE, -S n length of time a person or thing has existed ▷ vb make or grow old

AGED adj old

AGEDLY ▷ aged

AGEDNESS ▷ aged

AGEE adj awry, crooked, or ajar ▷ adv awry

AGEING, -S n fact or process of growing old ▷ adj becoming or appearing older

AGEISM, -S n discrimination against people on the grounds of age

AGEIST, -S ▷ ageism

AGELAST, -S n someone who never laughs

AGELESS adj apparently never growing old

AGELONG adj lasting for a very long time

AGEMATE, -S n person the same age as another person

AGEN archaic form of ▷ again

AGENCY, AGENCIES n organization providing a service

AGENDA, -S n list of things to be dealt with, esp at a meeting

AGENDER adj of a person who does not identify with a gender

AGENDUM, -S same as ▷ agenda

AGENE, -S n chemical used to whiten flour

AGENESES ▷ agenesis

AGENESIA n imperfect development

AGENESIS, AGENESES n (of an animal or plant) imperfect development

AGENETIC ▷ agenesis

AGENISE, -D, -S same as ▷ agenize

AGENIZE, -D, -S vb whiten using agene

AGENT, -ED, -S n person acting on behalf of another ▷ vb act as an agent

AGENTIAL ▷ agent

AGENTING ▷ agent

AGENTIVE adj denoting a case of noun etc indicating the agent described by the verb ▷ n agentive case

AGENTRY n activity of an agent

AGENTS ▷ agent

AGER, -S n something that ages

AGERATUM n tropical American plant with thick clusters of purplish-blue flowers

AGERS ▷ ager

AGES ▷ age

AGEUSIA, -S n lack of the sense of taste

AGGADA, -S, AGGADOT, AGGADOTH n explanation in Jewish literature

AGGADAH, -S same as ▷ aggada

AGGADAS ▷ aggada

AGGADIC adj of aggada

AGGADOT ▷ aggada

AGGADOTH ▷ aggada

AGGER n rampart

AGGERS adj aggressive

AGGIE, -S n American agricultural student

AGGRACE, -D, -S, AGRASTE vb add grace to

AGGRADE, -D, -S vb build up by the deposition of sediment

AGGRATE, -D, -S vb gratify

AGGRESS vb attack first or begin a quarrel

AGGRI adj of African beads

AGGRIEVE vb grieve

AGGRO, -S n aggressive behaviour

AGGRY adj of African beads

AGHA, -S same as ▷ aga

AGHAST adj overcome with amazement or horror

AGILA, -S n eaglewood

AGILE, -R, -ST adj nimble, quick-moving

AGILELY ▷ agile

AGILER ▷ agile

AGILEST ▷ agile

AGILITY ▷ agile

AGIN prep against, opposed to

AGING, -S same as ▷ ageing

AGINNER, -S n someone who is against something

AGIO, -S n difference between the nominal and actual values of a currency

AGIOTAGE n business of exchanging currencies

AGISM, -S same as ▷ ageism

AGIST, -ED, -ING, -S vb care for and feed (cattle or horses) for payment

AGISTER, -S n person who grazes cattle for money

AGISTING ▷ agist

AGISTOR, -S n person who grazes cattle for money

AGISTS ▷ agist

AGITA, -S n acid indigestion

AGITABLE ▷ agitate

AGITANS adj as in **paralysis agitans** Parkinson's disease

AGITAS ▷ agita

AGITATE, -D, -S vb disturb or excite

AGITATO adv (to be performed) in an agitated manner

AGITATOR n person who agitates for or against a cause, etc

AGITPOP, -S n use of pop music to promote political propaganda

AGITPROP n political agitation and propaganda

AGLARE adj glaring

AGLEAM adj glowing

AGLEE same as ▷ agley

AGLET, -S n metal tag

AGLEY adj awry

AGLIMMER adj glimmering

AGLITTER adj sparkling, glittering

AGLOO, -S same as ▷ aglu

AGLOSSAL ▷ aglossia

AGLOSSIA n congenital absence of the tongue

AGLOW adj glowing

AGLU, -S n breathing hole made in ice by a seal

AGLY Scots word for ▷ wrong

AGLYCON, -S n chemical compound

AGLYCONE same as ▷ aglycon

AGLYCONS ▷ aglycon

AGMA, -S n symbol used to represent a velar nasal consonant

AGMINATE adj gathered or clustered together

AGNAIL, -S another name for ▷ hangnail

AGNAME, -S n name additional to first name and surname

AGNAMED adj having an agname

AGNAMES ▷ agname

AGNATE, -S adj related through a common male ancestor ▷ n descendant by male links from a common male ancestor

AGNATHAN n type of jawless eel-like aquatic vertebrate

AGNATIC ▷ agnate

AGNATION ▷ agnate

AGNISE, -D, -S, AGNISING vb acknowledge

AGNIZE, -D, -S, AGNIZING vb acknowledge

AGNOMEN, -S, AGNOMINA n name used by ancient Romans

AGNOSIA, -S n loss of power to recognize familiar objects

AGNOSIC ▷ agnosia

A

AGNOSTIC n person who believes that it is impossible to know whether God exists ▷ adj of agnostics

AGO adv in the past

AGOG adj eager or curious

AGOGE, -S n ancient Greek melodic form

AGOGIC, -S n musical accent

AGOING adj moving

AGON, -ES, -S n ancient Greek festival

AGONAL adj of agony

AGONE an archaic word for ▶ ago

AGONES ▶ agon

AGONIC adj forming no angle

AGONIES ▶ agony

AGONISE, -D, -S same as ▶ agonize

AGONISM, -S n struggle between opposing forces

AGONIST, -S n any muscle that is opposed in action by another muscle

AGONIZE, -D, -S vb worry greatly

AGONS ▶ agon

AGONY, AGONIES n extreme physical or mental pain

AGOOD adv seriously or earnestly

AGORA, -E, -S n place of assembly in ancient Greece

AGOROT pl n Israeli coins

AGOROTH same as ▶ agorot

AGOUTA, -S n Haitian rodent

AGOUTI, -ES, -S n rodent

AGOUTY same as ▶ agouti

AGRAFE, -S same as ▶ agraffe

AGRAFFE, -S n loop and hook fastening

AGRAPHA ▶ agraphon

AGRAPHIA n loss of the ability to write, resulting from a brain lesion

AGRAPHIC ▶ agraphia

AGRAPHON, AGRAPHA n saying of Jesus not in Gospels

AGRARIAN adj of land or agriculture ▷ n person who favours the redistribution of landed property

AGRASTE ▶ aggrace

AGRAVIC adj of zero gravity

AGREE, -ING, -S vb be of the same opinion

AGREED adj determined by common consent

AGREEING ▶ agree

AGREES ▶ agree

AGREGE, -S n winner in examination for university teaching post

AGREMENS n amenities

AGREMENT n diplomatic approval of a country

AGRESTAL adj (of uncultivated plants such as weeds) growing on cultivated land

AGRESTIC adj rural

AGRIA, -S n appearance of pustules

AGRIMONY n yellow-flowered plant with bitter-tasting fruits

AGRIN, -S adv grinning ▷ n type of protein

AGRISE, -D, -S, AGRISING vb fill with fear

AGRIZE, -D, -S, AGRIZING vb fill with fear

AGRO, -S n student of agriculture

AGROLOGY n scientific study of soils and their potential productivity

AGRONOMY n science of soil management and crop production

AGROS ▶ agro

AGROUND adv onto the bottom of shallow water ▷ adj on the ground or bottom, as in shallow water

AGRYPNIA n inability to sleep

AGRYZE, -D, -S, AGRYZING vb fill with fear

AGS ▶ ag

AGUACATE n avocado

AGUE, -S n periodic fever with shivering

AGUED adj suffering from fever

AGUELIKE ▶ ague

AGUES ▶ ague

AGUEWEED n N American plant with clusters of pale blue-violet or white flowers

AGUISE, -D, -S, AGUISING vb dress

AGUISH ▶ ague

AGUISHLY ▶ ague

AGUISING ▶ aguise

AGUIZE, -D, -S, AGUIZING vb dress

AGUNA, AGUNOT, AGUNOTH n (in Jewish law) woman whose husband will not grant her a divorce

AGUNAH same as ▶ aguna

AGUNOT ▶ aguna

AGUNOTH ▶ aguna

AGUTI, -S n agouti

AGYRIA, -S n brain disease

AH, -ED, -ING, -S interj exclamation expressing surprise, joy etc ▷ vb say ah

AHA interj exclamation of triumph or surprise

AHCHOO interj sound made by someone sneezing

AHEAD adv in front

AHEAP adv in a heap

AHED ▶ ah

AHEIGHT adv at height

AHEM interj clearing of the throat in order to attract attention

AHEMERAL adj not constituting a full 24-hour day

AHENT adv behind

AHI, -S n yellowfin tuna

A very useful one to catch!

AHIGH adv at height

AHIMSA, -S n the law of reverence for every form of life

AHIND adv behind

AHING ▶ ah

AHINT adv behind

AHIS ▶ ahi

AHOLD adv holding

AHORSE adv on horseback

AHOY interj hail used to call a ship

AHS ▶ ah

AHULL adv with sails furled

AHUNGRY adj very hungry

AHURU, -S n type of small pink cod of SW Pacific waters

AI, -S n shaggy-coated slow-moving animal of South America

AIA, -S n female servant in E Asia

AIBLINS Scots word for ▶ perhaps

AID, -ED, -ING, -S n assistance or support ▷ vb help financially or in other ways

AIDA, -S n cotton fabric with a natural mesh

AIDANCE, -S n help

AIDANT, -S adj helping ▷ n helper

AIDAS ▶ aida

AIDE, -S n assistant

AIDED ▶ aid

AIDER, -S ▶ aid

AIDES ▶ aide

AIDFUL adj helpful

AIDING ▶ aid

AIDLESS adj without help

AIDMAN, AIDMEN n military medical assistant

AIDOI adj of the genitals

AIDOS Greek word for ▶ shame

AIDS ▶ aid

AIERY, AIERIES n eyrie

AIGA, -S n Māori word for family

AIGHT adv all right
AIGLET, -S same as ▷ **aglet**
AIGRET, -S same as ▷ **aigrette**
AIGRETTE n long plume worn on hats or as a headdress, esp one of long egret feathers
AIGUILLE n rock mass or mountain peak shaped like a needle
AIKIDO, -S n Japanese self-defence
AIKONA interj South African expression meaning no
AIL, -ED, -S vb trouble, afflict
AILANTO, -S n Asian tree
AILED ▷ **ail**
AILERON, -S n movable flap on an aircraft wing which controls feathers
AILETTE, -S n shoulder armour
AILING adj sickly
AILMENT, -S n illness
AILS ▷ **ail**
AIM, -ED, -ING, -S vb point (a weapon or missile) or direct (a blow or remark) at a target ▷ n aiming
AIMER, -S ▷ **aim**
AIMFUL adj with purpose or intention
AIMFULLY ▷ **aimful**
AIMING ▷ **aim**
AIMLESS adj having no purpose
AIMS ▷ **aim**
AIN, -S variant of ▷ **ayin**
AINE adj French word for elder (male)

Though it doesn't score much, it is useful to remember when you have too many vowels. And it can be extended to **ainee**, the feminine form.

AINEE adj French word for elder (female)
AINGA, -S n Māori word for village
AINS ▷ **ain**
AINSELL, -S n Scots word meaning own self
AIOLI, -S n garlic mayonnaise
AIR, -ED n mixture of gases forming the earth's atmosphere ▷ vb make known publicly
AIRBAG, -S n safety device in a car
AIRBALL, -S n missed shot in basketball ▷ vb throw an airball

AIRBASE, -S n centre from which military aircraft operate
AIRBOARD n inflatable body board
AIRBOAT, -S n boat for use in swamps
AIRBORNE adj carried by air
AIRBOUND adj heading into the air
AIRBRICK n brick with holes in it, put into the wall of a building for ventilation
AIRBRUSH n atomizer that sprays paint by compressed air ▷ vb paint using an airbrush
AIRBURST n explosion of a bomb, shell, etc, in the air ▷ vb (of a bomb, shell, etc) to explode in the air
AIRBUS, -ES n commercial passenger aircraft
AIRCHECK n recording of a radio broadcast
AIRCOACH n bus travelling to and from an airport
AIRCON, -S n air conditioner
AIRCRAFT n any machine that flies, such as an aeroplane
AIRCREW, -S n crew of an aircraft
AIRDATE, -S n date of a programme broadcast
AIRDRAWN adj imaginary
AIRDROME same as > **aerodrome**
AIRDROP, -S n delivery of supplies by parachute ▷ vb deliver (supplies, etc) by an airdrop
AIRED ▷ **air**
AIRER, -S n device on which clothes are hung to dry
AIRFARE, -S n money for an aircraft ticket
AIRFIELD n place where aircraft can land and take off
AIRFLOW, -S n flow of air past a moving object
AIRFOIL, -S same as ▷ **aerofoil**
AIRFRAME n body of an aircraft, excluding its engines
AIRGAP, -S n gap between parts in an electrical machine
AIRGLOW, -S n faint light in the night sky
AIRGRAPH n photographic reduction of a letter for sending airmail
AIRGUN, -S n gun fired by compressed air

AIRHEAD, -S n stupid person
AIRHOLE, -S n hole that allows the passage of air
AIRIER ▷ **airy**
AIRIEST ▷ **airy**
AIRILY adv in a light-hearted and casual manner
AIRINESS n quality or condition of being fresh, light, or breezy
AIRING, -S n exposure to air for drying or ventilation
AIRLESS adj stuffy
AIRLIFT, -S n transport of troops or cargo by aircraft when other routes are blocked ▷ vb transport by airlift
AIRLIKE ▷ **air**
AIRLINE, -S n company providing scheduled flights for passengers and cargo
AIRLINER n large passenger aircraft
AIRLINES ▷ **airline**
AIRLOCK, -S n air bubble blocking the flow of liquid in a pipe
AIRMAIL, -S n system of sending mail by aircraft ▷ adj of, used for, or concerned with airmail ▷ vb send by airmail
AIRMAN, AIRMEN n member of an air force
AIRN, -ED, -ING, -S Scots word for ▷ **iron**
AIRPARK, -S n car park at airport
AIRPLANE same as > **aeroplane**
AIRPLAY, -S n broadcast performances of a record on radio
AIRPORT, -S n airfield for civilian aircraft, with facilities for aircraft maintenance and passengers
AIRPOST, -S n system of delivering mail by air
AIRPOWER n strength of a nation's air force
AIRPROOF vb make something airtight
AIRPROX n near collision involving aircraft
AIRS pl n manners put on to impress people
AIRSCAPE n picture or view of sky
AIRSCREW n aircraft propeller
AIRSHAFT n shaft for ventilation

A

AIRSHED, -S n air over a particular geographical area

AIRSHIP, -S n lighter-than-air self-propelled aircraft

AIRSHOT, -S n shot that misses the ball completely

AIRSHOW, -S n occasion when an air base is open to the public

AIRSICK adj nauseated from travelling in an aircraft

AIRSIDE, -S n part of an airport nearest the aircraft

AIRSOME adj cold

AIRSPACE n atmosphere above a country, regarded as its territory

AIRSPEED n speed of an aircraft relative to the air in which it moves

AIRSTOP, -S n helicopter landing-place

AIRSTRIP n cleared area where aircraft can take off and land

AIRT, -ED, -ING, -S n point of the compass ▷ vb direct

AIRTH, -ED, -ING, -S same as ▶ airt

AIRTIGHT adj sealed so that air cannot enter

AIRTIME, -S n time period on radio and TV

AIRTING ▶ airt

AIRTRAM, -S n cable car

AIRTS ▶ airt

AIRVAC, -S n evacuation by air ambulance

AIRWARD adj into air

AIRWARDS adv into air

AIRWAVE, -S n radio wave used in radio and television broadcasting

AIRWAY, -S n air route used regularly by aircraft

AIRWISE adv towards the air

AIRWOMAN, AIRWOMEN n member of an air force

AIRY, AIRIER, AIRIEST adj well-ventilated

AIS ▶ ai

AISLE, -S n passageway separating seating areas, rows of shelves, etc

AISLED ▶ aisle

AISLES ▶ aisle

AISLEWAY n aisle

AISLING, -S Irish word for ▶ dream

AIT, -S n islet, esp in a river

AITCH, -ES n letter h or the sound represented by it

AITS ▶ ait

AITU, -S n half-human half-divine being

This demigod is often played to dispose of an excess of vowels.

AIVER, -S n working horse

AIYEE interj expressing alarm

AIZLE, -S n Scots word for hot ashes

AJAR adv (of a door) partly open ▷ adj not in harmony

AJEE same as ▶ agee

This Scots word meaning ajar is often useful for disposing of the J. It has an alternative spelling **agee**.

AJI, -ES, -S n type of spicy pepper

AJIVA, -S n Jainist term for a non-living thing

AJOWAN, -S n plant related to caraway

AJUGA, -S n garden plant

AJUTAGE, -S n nozzle

AJWAN, -S n plant related to caraway

AKA, -S n type of New Zealand vine

One of the key short words when it comes to using the K.

AKARYOTE n cell without a nucleus

AKAS ▶ aka

AKATEA, -S n New Zealand vine with white flowers

AKE, -D, -S, AKING vb old spelling of ache

AKEAKE, -S n New Zealand tree

AKEBIA, -S n E Asian climbing plant

AKED ▶ ake

AKEDAH, -S n binding of Isaac in Bible

AKEE, -S same as ▶ ackee

AKELA, -S n adult leader of a pack of Cub Scouts

AKENE, -S same as ▶ achene

AKENIAL ▶ akene

AKES ▶ ake

AKHARA, -S n (in India) gymnasium

AKIMBO adj as in with arms akimbo with hands on hips and elbows projecting outwards

AKIN adj related by blood

AKINESES ▶ akinesis

AKINESIA n loss of power to move

AKINESIS, AKINESES same as ▶ akinesia

AKINETIC ▶ akinesia

AKING ▶ ake

AKIRAHO, -S n small New Zealand shrub with white flowers

AKITA, -S n large dog

AKKAS slang word for ▶ money

AKRASIA, -S n weakness of will

AKRATIC ▶ akrasia

AKVAVIT, -S same as ▶ aquavit

AL, -S same as ▶ aal

ALA, -E n winglike structure

ALAAP, -S n part of raga in Indian music

ALACHLOR n type of herbicide

ALACK archaic or poetic word for ▶ alas

ALACRITY n speed, eagerness

ALAE ▶ ala

ALAIMENT old spelling of > allayment

ALALIA, -S n complete inability to speak

ALAMEDA, -S n public walk lined with trees

ALAMO, -S n poplar tree

ALAMODE, -S n soft light silk used for shawls and dresses, esp in the 19th century

ALAMORT adj exhausted and downcast

ALAMOS ▶ alamo

ALAN, -S n member of ancient European nomadic people

ALAND, -S vb come onto land

ALANE Scots word for ▶ alone

ALANG, -S n type of grass in Malaysia

ALANIN, -S n alanine

ALANINE, -S n chemical

ALANINS ▶ alanin

ALANNAH, -S interj term of endearment ▷ n cry of alannah

ALANS ▶ alan

ALANT, -S n flowering plant used in herbal medicine

ALANYL, -S n chemical found in proteins

ALAP, -S n Indian vocal music without words

ALAPA, -S n part of raga in Indian music

ALAPS ▶ alap

ALAR adj relating to, resembling, or having wings or alae

ALARM, -ED, -S n sudden fear caused by awareness of danger ▷ vb fill with fear

ALARMING ▸alarm

ALARMISM ▸alarmist

ALARMIST, -S *n* person who alarms others needlessly ▹ *adj* causing needless alarm

ALARMS ▸alarm

ALARUM, -ED, -S *n* alarm, esp a call to arms ▹ *vb* raise the alarm

ALARY *adj* of, relating to, or shaped like wings

ALAS *adv* unfortunately, regrettably

ALASKA, -S *n* dessert made of cake and ice cream

ALASTOR, -S *n* avenging demon

ALASTRIM *n* form of smallpox

ALATE, -S *adj* having wings or winglike extensions ▹ *n* winged insect

ALATED *adj* having wings

ALATES ▸alate

ALATION, -S *n* state of having wings

ALAY, -ED, -ING, -S *vb* allay

ALB, -S *n* long white robe worn by a Christian priest

ALBA, -S *n* song of lament

ALBACORE *n* tuna found in warm seas, eaten for food

ALBAS ▸alba

ALBATA, -S *n* variety of German silver consisting of nickel, copper, and zinc

ALBE *old word for* ▸ **albeit**

ALBEDO, -ES, -S *n* measure of intensity of reflected light

ALBEE *archaic form of* ▸ **albeit**

ALBEIT *conj* even though

ALBERGO, ALBERGHI *n* Italian word for inn

ALBERT, -S *n* watch chain

ALBICORE *n* species of tuna

ALBINAL ▸albino

ALBINESS *n* female albino

ALBINIC ▸albino

ALBINISM ▸albino

ALBINO, -S *n* person or animal with white skin and hair and pink eyes

ALBITE, -S *n* type of mineral

ALBITIC ▸albite

ALBITISE *same as* ▸ **albitize**

ALBITIZE *vb* turn into albite

ALBIZIA, -S *n* mimosa

ALBIZZIA *n* mimosa

ALBS ▸alb

ALBUGO, -S *n* opacity of the cornea

ALBUM, -S *n* book with blank pages for keeping photographs or stamps in

ALBUMEN, -S *same as* ▸ **albumin**

ALBUMIN, -S *n* protein found in blood plasma, egg white, milk, and muscle

ALBUMOSE *the US name for* ▸ **proteose**

ALBUMS ▸album

ALBURNUM *former name for* ▸ **sapwood**

ALCADE, -S *same as* ▸ **alcalde**

ALCAHEST *same as* ▸ **alkahest**

ALCAIC, -S *n* verse consisting of strophes with four tetrametric lines

ALCAIDE, -S *n* commander of a fortress or castle

ALCALDE, -S *n* (in Spain and Spanish America) the mayor or chief magistrate in a town

ALCATRAS *n* pelican

ALCAYDE, -S *n* alcaide

ALCAZAR, -S *n* Moorish palace or fortress

ALCHEMIC ▸alchemy

ALCHEMY *n* medieval form of chemistry

ALCHERA, -S *n* mythical Golden Age

ALCHYMY *old spelling of* ▸ **alchemy**

ALCID, -S *n* bird of the auk family

ALCIDINE *adj* relating to a family of sea birds including the auks, guillemots, and puffins

ALCIDS ▸alcid

ALCO, -S *same as* ▸ **alko**

ALCOHOL, -S *n* colourless flammable liquid present in intoxicating drinks

ALCOLOCK *n* breath-alcohol ignition-interlock device

ALCOOL, -S *n* form of pure grain spirit distilled in Quebec

ALCOPOP, -S *n* alcoholic drink that tastes like a soft drink

ALCORZA, -S *n* Spanish sweet

ALCOS ▸alco

ALCOVE, -S *n* recess in the wall of a room

ALCOVED *adj* with or in an alcove

ALCOVES ▸alcove

ALDEA, -S *n* Spanish village

ALDEHYDE *n* one of a group of chemical compounds derived from alcohol by oxidation

ALDER, -S *n* tree related to the birch

ALDERFLY *n* insect with large broad-based hind wings, which produces aquatic larvae

ALDERMAN, ALDERMEN *n* formerly, senior member of a local council

ALDERN *adj* made of alder wood

ALDERS ▸alder

ALDICARB *n* crystalline compound used as a pesticide

ALDOL, -S *n* colourless or yellowish oily liquid

ALDOLASE *n* enzyme present in the body

ALDOLS ▸aldol

ALDOSE, -S *n* type of sugar

ALDOXIME *n* oxime formed by reaction between hydroxylamine and an aldehyde

ALDRIN, -S *n* brown to white poisonous crystalline solid

ALE, -S *n* kind of beer

ALEATORY *adj* dependent on chance

ALEBENCH *n* bench at alehouse

ALEC, -S *same as* ▸ **aleck**

ALECK, -S *n* irritatingly oversmart person

ALECOST, -S *another name for* ▸ **costmary**

ALECS ▸alec

ALEE *adj* on or towards the lee

ALEF, -S *n* first letter of Hebrew alphabet

ALEFT *adv* at or to left

ALEGAR, -S *n* malt vinegar

ALEGGE, -D, -S, ALEGGING *vb* alleviate

ALEHOUSE *n* public house

ALEMBIC, -S *n* anything that distils

ALENCON, -S *n* elaborate lace worked on a hexagonal mesh

ALENGTH *adv* at length

ALEPH, -S *n* first letter in the Hebrew alphabet

ALEPINE, -S *n* type of cloth

ALERCE, -S *n* wood of the sandarac tree

ALERION, -S *n* eagle in heraldry

ALERT, -ED, -ER, -EST, -ING, -S *adj* watchful, attentive ▹ *n* warning of danger ▹ *vb* warn of danger

ALERTLY ▸alert

ALERTS ▸alert

ALES ▸ale

A

ALETHIC adj of philosophical concepts

ALEURON, -S n outer layer of seeds

ALEURONE same as ▸aleuron

ALEURONS ▸aleuron

ALEVIN, -S n young fish, esp a young salmon or trout

ALEW, -S n cry to call hunting hounds

ALEWIFE, ALEWIVES n North American fish

ALEWS ▸alew

ALEXIA, -S n disorder causing impaired ability to read

ALEXIC ▸alexia

ALEXIN, -S n protein in blood serum

ALEXINE, -S same as ▸alexin

ALEXINIC ▸alexin

ALEXINS ▸alexin

ALEYE, -D, -S, ALEYING vb allay

ALF, -S n uncultivated Australian

ALFA, -S n type of grass

ALFAKI, -S same as ▸alfaqui

ALFALFA, -S n kind of plant used to feed livestock

ALFAQUI, -S n expert in Muslim law

ALFAQUIN same as ▸alfaqui

ALFAQUIS ▸alfaqui

ALFAS ▸alfa

ALFEREZ n Spanish standard-bearer

ALFORJA, -S n saddlebag made of leather or canvas

ALFREDO adj cooked with a cheese and egg sauce

ALFRESCO adj in the open air ▷ adv in the open air

ALFS ▸alf

ALGA, -E, -S n multicellular organism

ALGAL ▸alga

ALGAROBA same as ▸algarroba

ALGAS ▸alga

ALGATE adv anyway

ALGATES adv anyway

ALGEBRA, -S n branch of mathematics using symbols to represent numbers

ALGERINE n soft striped woollen cloth

ALGESES ▸algesis

ALGESIA, -S n capacity to feel pain

ALGESIC ▸algesia

ALGESIS, ALGESES n feeling of pain

ALGETIC ▸algesia

ALGICIDE n any substance that kills algae

ALGID adj chilly or cold

ALGIDITY ▸algid

ALGIN, -S n seaweed solution

ALGINATE n salt or ester of alginic acid

ALGINIC adj as in **alginic acid** powdery substance extracted from kelp

ALGINS ▸algin

ALGOID adj resembling or relating to algae

ALGOLOGY n branch of biology concerned with the study of algae

ALGOR, -S n chill

ALGORISM n Arabic or decimal system of counting

ALGORS ▸algor

ALGUACIL n Spanish law officer

ALGUAZIL n Spanish law officer

ALGUM, -S n type of wood mentioned in Bible

ALIAS, -ED, -ES adv also known as ▷ n false name ▷ vb give or assume an alias

ALIASING n error in a vision or sound signal

ALIBI, -ED, -ES, -ING, -S n plea of being somewhere else when a crime was committed ▷ vb provide someone with an alibi

ALIBLE adj nourishing

ALICANT, -S n wine from Alicante in Spain

ALIDAD, -S same as ▸alidade

ALIDADE, -S n surveying instrument

ALIDADS ▸alidad

ALIEN, -ED, -ING, -S adj foreign ▷ n foreigner ▷ vb transfer (property, etc) to another

ALIENAGE ▸alien

ALIENATE vb cause to become hostile

ALIENED ▸alien

ALIENEE, -S n person to whom a transfer of property is made

ALIENER, -S ▸alien

ALIENING ▸alien

ALIENISM n old term for the study of mental illness

ALIENIST n old term for psychiatrist specializing in the legal aspects of mental illness

ALIENLY ▸alien

ALIENOR, -S n person who transfers property to another

ALIENS ▸alien

ALIF, -S n first letter of Arabic alphabet

ALIFORM adj wing-shaped

ALIFS ▸alif

ALIGARTA n alligator

ALIGHT, -ED, -S vb step out of (a vehicle) ▷ adj on fire ▷ adv on fire

ALIGN, -ED, -ING, -S vb bring (a person or group) into agreement with the policy of another

ALIGNER, -S ▸align

ALIGNING ▸align

ALIGNS ▸align

ALIKE adj like, similar ▷ adv in the same way

ALIMENT, -S n something that nourishes the body ▷ vb support or sustain

ALIMONY n allowance paid under a court order to a separated or divorced spouse

ALINE, -D, -S, ALINING a rare spelling of ▸align

ALINER, -S ▸aline

ALINES ▸aline

ALINING ▸aline

ALIPED, -S n bat-like creature ▷ adj having digits connected by a membrane

ALIQUANT adj denoting or belonging to a number that is not an exact divisor of a given number

ALIQUOT, -S adj of or denoting an exact divisor of a number ▷ n exact divisor

ALISMA, -S n marsh plant

ALISON same as ▸alyssum

ALIST adj leaning over

ALIT rare past tense and past participle of ▸alight

ALIUNDE adj from a source under consideration

ALIVE adj living, in existence

ALIYA, -S same as ▸aliyah

ALIYAH, -S, ALIYOT, ALIYOTH n immigration to the Holy Land

ALIYAS ▸aliya

ALIYOS n remission of sin in Jewish faith

ALIYOT ▸aliyah

ALIYOTH ▸aliyah

ALIZARI, -S n madder plant from the Middle East

ALIZARIN n brownish-yellow powder or orange-red crystalline solid

ALIZARIS ▸alizari

ALKAHEST n hypothetical universal solvent sought by alchemists

ALKALI, -ES, -S *n* substance which combines with acid and neutralizes it to form a salt
ALKALIC *adj* (of rocks) containing large amounts of alkalis
ALKALIES ▶ alkali
ALKALIFY *vb* make or become alkaline
ALKALIN *adj* alkaline
ALKALINE *adj* having the properties of or containing an alkali
ALKALIS ▶ alkali
ALKALISE *same as* ▶ alkalize
ALKALIZE *vb* make alkaline
ALKALOID *n* any of a group of organic compounds containing nitrogen
ALKANE, -S *n* saturated hydrocarbon
ALKANET, -S *n* European plant whose roots yield a red dye
ALKANNIN *same as* ▶ alkanet
ALKENE, -S *n* unsaturated hydrocarbon
ALKIE *same as* ▶ alky
ALKIES ▶ alky
ALKINE, -S *n* alkyne
ALKO, -S *n* slang word for alcoholic
ALKOXIDE *n* chemical compound containing oxygen
ALKOXY *adj* of a type of chemical compound containing oxygen
ALKY, ALKIES *n* slang word for alcoholic
ALKYD, -S *n* synthetic resin
ALKYL, -S *n* type of monovalent radical
ALKYLATE *vb* add alkyl group to a compound
ALKYLIC ▶ alkyl
ALKYLS ▶ alkyl
ALKYNE, -S *n* any unsaturated aliphatic hydrocarbon
ALL, -S *adj* whole quantity or number (of) ▷ *adv* wholly, entirely ▷ *n* entire being, effort, or property
ALLANITE *n* rare black or brown mineral
ALLATIVE *n* word in grammatical case denoting movement towards
ALLAY, -ED, -S *vb* reduce (fear or anger)
ALLAYER, -S ▶ allay
ALLAYING ▶ allay
ALLAYS ▶ allay

ALLEDGE, -D, -S *vb* allege
ALLEE, -S *n* avenue
ALLEGE, -S, ALLEGING *vb* state without proof
ALLEGED *adj* stated but not proved
ALLEGER, -S ▶ allege
ALLEGES ▶ allege
ALLEGGE, -D, -S *vb* alleviate
ALLEGING ▶ allege
ALLEGORY *n* story with an underlying meaning as well as the literal one
ALLEGRO, -S *adv* (to be played) in a brisk lively manner ▷ *n* piece or passage to be performed in a brisk lively manner
ALLEL, -S *n* variant form of a gene
ALLELE, -S *n* variant form of a gene
ALLELIC ▶ allele
ALLELISM ▶ allele
ALLELS ▶ allel
ALLELUIA *n* song of praise to God
ALLERGEN *n* substance capable of causing an allergic reaction
ALLERGIC *adj* having or caused by an allergy ▷ *n* person with an allergy
ALLERGIN *n* allergen
ALLERGY *n* extreme sensitivity to a substance, which causes the body to react to it
ALLERION *n* eagle in heraldry
ALLEY, -S *n* narrow street or path
ALLEYCAT *n* homeless cat that roams in back streets
ALLEYED *adj* having alleys
ALLEYS ▶ alley
ALLEYWAY *n* narrow passage with buildings or walls on both sides
ALLHEAL, -S *n* plant with reputed healing powers
ALLIABLE *adj* able to form an alliance
ALLIAK, -S *n* Inuit sledge
ALLIANCE *n* state of being allied
ALLICE, -S *n* species of fish
ALLICIN, -S *n* chemical found in garlic
ALLIED *adj* joined, as by treaty, agreement, or marriage
ALLIES ▶ ally
ALLIGATE *vb* join together
ALLIS, -ES *n* species of fish
ALLIUM, -S *n* type of plant

ALLNESS *n* being all
ALLNIGHT *adj* lasting all night
ALLOBAR, -S *n* form of an element
ALLOCATE *vb* assign to someone or for a particular purpose
ALLOD, -S *same as* ▶ allodium
ALLODIA ▶ allodium
ALLODIAL *adj* (of land) held as an allodium
ALLODIUM, ALLODIA *n* lands held free from rent or services due to an overlord
ALLODS ▶ allod
ALLOGAMY *n* cross-fertilization in flowering plants
ALLOMONE *n* chemical substance secreted by certain animals
ALLONGE, -D, -S *n* paper extension to bill of exchange ▷ *vb* (in fencing) lunge
ALLONS *interj* French word meaning let's go
ALLONYM, -S *n* name assumed by a person
ALLOPATH *n* person who practises or is skilled in allopathy
ALLOSAUR *n* any large carnivorous bipedal dinosaur common in North America in late Jurassic times
ALLOT, -S, -TED *vb* assign as a share or for a particular purpose
ALLOTTEE *n* person to whom something is allotted
ALLOTTER *n* person who allots
ALLOTYPE *n* type of specimen that differs from the original type
ALLOTYPY *n* existence of allotypes
ALLOVER, -S *n* fabric completely covered with a pattern
ALLOW, -ED, -ING, -S *vb* permit
ALLOXAN, -S *n* chemical found in uric acid
ALLOY, -ED, -ING, -S *n* mixture of two or more metals ▷ *vb* mix (metals)
ALLOZYME *n* different form of an enzyme
ALLS ▶ all
ALLSEED, -S *n* type of plant
ALLSORTS *pl n* assorted sweets

A

ALLSPICE n spice made from the berries of a tropical American tree

ALLUDE, -D, -S, ALLUDING vb refer indirectly to

ALLURE, -D, -S n attractiveness ▷ vb entice or attract

ALLURER, -S ▶ allure

ALLURES ▶ allure

ALLURING adj extremely attractive

ALLUSION n indirect reference

ALLUSIVE adj containing or full of allusions

ALLUVIA ▶ alluvium

ALLUVIAL adj of or relating to alluvium ▷ n soil consisting of alluvium

ALLUVION n wash of the sea or of a river

ALLUVIUM, ALLUVIA n fertile soil deposited by flowing water

ALLY, ALLIES, -ING vb unite or be united, esp formally, as by treaty, confederation, or marriage ▷ n country, person, or group allied with another

ALLYL, -S n type of monovalent hydrocarbon

ALLYLIC ▶ allyl

ALLYLS ▶ allyl

ALLYOU pron all of you

ALMA, -S same as ▶ almah

ALMAGEST n medieval treatise concerning alchemy or astrology

ALMAH, -S n (in Egypt) female entertainer

ALMAIN, -S n German dance

ALMANAC, -S n yearly calendar with detailed information on anniversaries, phases of the moon, etc

ALMANACK same as ▶ almanac

ALMANACS ▶ almanac

ALMAS ▶ alma

ALME, -S same as ▶ almeh

ALMEH, -S n (in Egypt) female entertainer

ALMEMAR, -S n area in a synagogue

ALMERY, ALMERIES n cupboard for church vessels

ALMES ▶ alme

ALMIGHTY adj all-powerful ▷ adv extremely

ALMIRAH, -S n cupboard

ALMNER, -S n almoner

ALMOND, -S n edible oval-shaped nut which grows on a small tree

ALMONDY adj containing or resembling almond

ALMONER, -S n formerly, a hospital social worker

ALMONRY n house of an almoner, usually the place where alms were given

ALMOST adv very nearly

ALMOUS Scots word for ▶ alms

ALMS pl n gifts to the poor

ALMSMAN, ALMSMEN n man who gives or receives alms

ALMUCE, -S n fur-lined hood or cape

ALMUD, -S n Spanish unit of measure

ALMUDE, -S same as ▶ almud

ALMUDS ▶ almud

ALMUG, -S n type of wood mentioned in Bible

ALNAGE, -S n measurement in ells

ALNAGER, -S n inspector of cloth

ALNAGES ▶ alnage

ALNICO, -S n alloy containing iron, nickel, and cobalt

ALOCASIA n type of tropical plant

ALOD, -S n feudal estate with no superior

ALODIA ▶ alodium

ALODIAL ▶ alodium

ALODIUM, ALODIA, -S same as ▶ allodium

ALODS ▶ alod

ALOE n plant with fleshy spiny leaves

ALOED adj containing aloes

ALOES another name for > eaglewood

ALOETIC, -S ▶ aloe

ALOFT adv in the air ▷ adj in or into a high or higher place

ALOGIA, -S n inability to speak

ALOGICAL adj without logic

ALOHA, -S a Hawaiian word for ▶ hello

ALOIN, -S n crystalline compound

ALONE adv without anyone or anything else

ALONELY ▶ alone

ALONG adv forward

ALONGST adv along

ALOO, -S n (in Indian cookery) potato

ALOOF adj distant or haughty in manner

ALOOFLY ▶ aloof

ALOOS ▶ aloo

ALOPECIA n loss of hair

ALOPECIC ▶ alopecia

ALOUD adv in an audible voice ▷ adj in a normal voice

ALOW adj in or into the lower rigging of a vessel, near the deck

ALOWE Scots word for ▶ ablaze

ALP, -S n high mountain

ALPACA, -S n Peruvian llama

ALPACCA, -S same as ▶ alpaca

ALPEEN, -S n Irish cudgel

ALPHA, -S n first letter in the Greek alphabet

ALPHABET n set of letters used in writing a language

ALPHAS ▶ alpha

ALPHORN, -S n wind instrument

ALPHOSIS n absence of skin pigmentation, as in albinism

ALPHYL, -S n univalent radical

ALPINE, -S adj of high mountains ▷ n mountain plant

ALPINELY ▶ alpine

ALPINES ▶ alpine

ALPINISM ▶ alpinist

ALPINIST n mountain climber

ALPS ▶ alp

ALREADY adv before the present time

ALRIGHT adj all right

ALS ▶ al

ALSIKE, -S n clover native to Europe and Asia

ALSO adv in addition, too

ALSOON same as ▶ alsoone

ALSOONE adv as soon

ALT, -S n octave directly above the treble staff

ALTAR, -S n table used for Communion in Christian churches

ALTARAGE n donations placed on altar for priest

ALTARS ▶ altar

ALTER, -ED, -ING, -S vb make or become different

ALTERANT n alternative

ALTERED ▶ alter

ALTERER, -S ▶ alter

ALTERING ▶ alter

ALTERITY n quality of being different

ALTERN adj alternate

ALTERNAT n practice of deciding precedence by lot

ALTERNE, -S n neighbouring but different plant group

ALTERS ▶ alter

ALTESSE, -S n French word for highness

ALTEZA, -S n Spanish word for highness

ALTEZZA, -S n Italian word for highness

ALTHAEA, -S n type of plant

ALTHEA, -S same as ▶althaea

ALTHO conj short form of although

ALTHORN, -S n valved brass musical instrument

ALTHOUGH conj despite the fact that; even though

ALTITUDE n height above sea level

ALTO, -S n (singer with) the highest adult male voice ▷ adj denoting an instrument, singer, or voice with this range

ALTOIST, -S n person who plays the alto saxophone

ALTOS ▶alto

ALTRICES pl n altricial birds

ALTRUISM n unselfish concern for the welfare of others

ALTRUIST ▶altruism

ALTS ▶alt

ALU, -S same as ▶aloo

ALUDEL, -S n pear-shaped vessel

ALULA, -E, -S n tuft of feathers

ALULAR ▶alula

ALULAS ▶alula

ALUM, -S n double sulphate of aluminium and potassium

ALUMIN, -S same as ▶alumina

ALUMINA, -S n aluminium oxide

ALUMINE, -S n French word for alumina

ALUMINIC adj of aluminium

ALUMINS ▶alumin

ALUMINUM same as > aluminium

ALUMISH adj like alum

ALUMIUM, -S old name for > aluminium

ALUMNA, -E n female graduate of a school, college, etc

ALUMNUS, ALUMNI n graduate of a college

ALUMROOT n North American plant

ALUMS ▶alum

ALUNITE, -S n white, grey, or reddish mineral

ALURE, -S n area behind battlements

ALUS ▶alu

ALVAR, -S n area of exposed limestone

ALVEARY n beehive

ALVEATED adj with vaults like beehive

ALVEOLAR adj articulated with the alveoli ▷ n alveolar consonant

ALVEOLE, -S n alveolus

ALVEOLUS, ALVEOLI n sockets in which the roots of teeth are embedded

ALVINE adj of or relating to the intestines or belly

ALWAY same as ▶always

ALWAYS adv at all times

ALYSSUM, -S n garden plant with small yellow or white flowers

AM vb form of the present tense of be

AMA, -S n vessel for water

AMABILE adj sweet

AMADAVAT same as ▶avadavat

AMADODA pl n South African word meaning grown men

AMADOU, -S n spongy substance made from fungi

AMAH, -S n (in East Asia, formerly) a nurse or maidservant

AMAIN adv with great strength, speed, or haste

AMAKHOSI ▶inkhosi

AMAKOSI ▶inkhosi

AMALGAM, -S n blend or combination

AMANDINE n protein found in almonds

AMANDLA, -S n political slogan calling for power to the Black population

AMANITA, -S n type of fungus

AMANITIN n poison from amanita

AMARACUS n marjoram

AMARANT, -S n amaranth

AMARANTH n imaginary flower that never fades

AMARANTS ▶amarant

AMARELLE n variety of sour cherry that has pale red fruit and colourless juice

AMARETTO, AMARETTI n Italian liqueur with a flavour of almonds

AMARNA adj pertaining to the reign of the Pharaoh Akhenaton

AMARONE, -S n strong dry red Italian wine

AMAS ▶ama

AMASS, -ED, -ES, -ING vb collect or accumulate

AMASSER, -S ▶amass

AMASSES ▶amass

AMASSING ▶amass

AMATE, -D, -S, AMATING vb match

AMATEUR, -S n person who engages in a sport or activity as a pastime rather than as a profession ▷ adj not professional

AMATING ▶amate

AMATIVE a rare word for ▶amorous

AMATOL, -S n explosive mixture

AMATORY adj relating to love

AMAUT, -S n hooded coat worn by Inuit women

AMAUTI, -S same as ▶amaut

AMAUTIK, -S same as ▶amaut

AMAUTIS ▶amauti

AMAUTS ▶amaut

AMAZE, -D, -S vb surprise greatly, astound

AMAZEDLY ▶amaze

AMAZES ▶amaze

AMAZING adj causing wonder or astonishment

AMAZON, -S n any tall, strong, or aggressive woman

AMBACH, -ES same as ▶ambatch

AMBAGE, -S n ambiguity

AMBAN, -S n Chinese official

AMBARI, -S same as ▶ambary

AMBARIES ▶ambary

AMBARIS ▶ambari

AMBARY, AMBARIES n tropical Asian plant that yields a fibre similar to jute

AMBASSY n embassy

AMBATCH n tree or shrub

AMBEER, -S n saliva coloured by tobacco juice

AMBER, -S n clear yellowish fossil resin ▷ adj brownish-yellow

AMBERED adj fixed in amber

AMBERIER ▶ambery

AMBERIES ▶ambery

AMBERINA n type of glassware

AMBERITE n powder like amber

AMBEROID n synthetic amber

AMBEROUS adj like amber

AMBERS ▶amber

AMBERY, AMBERIER, AMBERIES adj like amber ▷ n cupboard in the wall of a church

AMBIANCE same as ▶ambience

A

AMBIENCE n atmosphere of a place

AMBIENT, -S adj surrounding ▷ n ambient music

AMBIT, -S n limits or boundary

AMBITION n desire for success

AMBITS ▶ ambit

AMBITTY adj crystalline and brittle

AMBIVERT n person who is intermediate between an extrovert and an introvert

AMBLE, -D, -S vb walk at a leisurely pace ▷ n leisurely walk or pace

AMBLER, -S ▶ amble

AMBLES ▶ amble

AMBLING, -S n walking at a leisurely pace

AMBO, -NES, -S n early Christian pulpit

AMBOINA, -S same as ▶ amboyna

AMBONES ▶ ambo

AMBOS ▶ ambo

AMBOYNA, -S n mottled curly-grained wood

AMBRIES ▶ ambry

AMBROID, -S same as ▶ amberoid

AMBROSIA n anything delightful to taste or smell

AMBRY, AMBRIES n cupboard in the wall of a church

AMBSACE, -S n double ace, the lowest throw at dice

AMBULANT adj moving about from place to place

AMBULATE vb wander about or move from one place to another

AMBUSH, -ED, -ES n act of waiting in a concealed position to make a surprise attack ▷ vb attack from a concealed position

AMBUSHER ▶ ambush

AMBUSHES ▶ ambush

AME, -S n soul

AMEARST old form of ▶ amerce

AMEBA, -E, -S same as ▶ amoeba

AMEBAN ▶ ameba

AMEBAS ▶ ameba

AMEBEAN same as ▶ amoebean

AMEBIC ▶ ameba

AMEBOID same as ▶ amoeboid

AMEER, -S n (formerly) the ruler of Afghanistan

AMEERATE n country ruled by an ameer

AMEERS ▶ ameer

AMEIOSIS, AMEIOSES n absence of pairing of chromosomes during meiosis

AMELCORN n variety of wheat

AMELIA, -S n congenital absence of arms or legs

AMEN, -ED, -ING, -S n term used at the end of a prayer or religious statement ▷ vb say amen

AMENABLE adj likely or willing to cooperate

AMENABLY ▶ amenable

AMENAGE, -D, -S vb tame

AMEND, -ED, -ING vb make small changes

AMENDE, -S n public apology

AMENDED ▶ amend

AMENDER, -S ▶ amend

AMENDES ▶ amende

AMENDING ▶ amend

AMENDS n recompense for injury, insult, etc

AMENE adj pleasant

AMENED ▶ amen

AMENING ▶ amen

AMENITY n useful or enjoyable feature

AMENS ▶ amen

AMENT, -S n catkin

AMENTA ▶ amentum

AMENTAL ▶ amentum

AMENTIA, -S n old word for congenital learning disability

AMENTS ▶ ament

AMENTUM, AMENTA same as ▶ ament

AMERCE, -D, -S, AMERCING vb punish by a fine

AMERCER, -S ▶ amerce

AMERCES ▶ amerce

AMERCING ▶ amerce

AMES ▶ ame

AMESACE, -S same as ▶ ambsace

AMETHYST n bluish-violet variety of quartz used as a gemstone ▷ adj purple or violet

AMI n male friend

AMIA, -S n species of fish

AMIABLE adj friendly, pleasant-natured

AMIABLY ▶ amiable

AMIANTUS n fine silky variety of asbestos

AMIAS ▶ amia

AMICABLE adj friendly

AMICABLY ▶ amicable

AMICE, -S n item of clothing

AMICUS, AMICI n Latin for friend

AMID prep in the middle of, among

AMIDASE, -S n enzyme

AMIDE, -S n type of organic compound

AMIDIC ▶ amide

AMIDIN, -S n form of starch

AMIDINE, -S n crystalline compound

AMIDINS ▶ amidin

AMIDMOST adv in the middle

AMIDO adj containing amide

AMIDOGEN n chemical compound derived from ammonia

AMIDOL, -S n chemical used in developing photographs

AMIDONE, -S n pain-killing drug

AMIDS same as ▶ amid

AMIDSHIP adj in the middle of a ship

AMIDST same as ▶ amid

AMIE, -S n female friend

AMIGA, -S n female friend

AMIGO, -S n friend

AMILDAR, -S n manager in India

AMIN, -S same as ▶ amine

AMINE, -S n chemical

AMINIC ▶ amine

AMINITY n amenity

AMINO, -S n type of organic compound present in amino acids

AMINS ▶ amin

AMIR, -S n (formerly) the ruler of Afghanistan

AMIRATE, -S ▶ amir

AMIRS ▶ amir

AMIS, -ES archaic form of ▶ amice

AMISS, -ES adv wrongly, badly ▷ adj wrong, faulty ▷ n evil deed

AMISSING adj missing

AMITIES ▶ amity

AMITOSIS, AMITOSES n unusual form of cell division

AMITOTIC ▶ amitosis

AMITROLE n pesticide

AMITY, AMITIES n friendship

AMLA, -S n species of Indian tree

AMMAN, -S same as ▶ amtman

AMMETER, -S n instrument for measuring electric current

AMMINE, -S n chemical compound

A

AMMINO adj containing ammonia molecules

AMMIRAL, -S old word for ▸ admiral

AMMO, -S n ammunition

AMMOCETE n ammocoete

AMMOLITE n fossilized ammonite shell

AMMON, -S n Asian wild sheep

AMMONAL, -S n explosive

AMMONATE same as ▸ ammine

AMMONIA, -S n strong-smelling alkaline gas containing hydrogen and nitrogen

AMMONIAC n strong-smelling gum resin obtained from the stems of a N Asian plant

AMMONIAS ▸ ammonia

AMMONIC adj of ammonia

AMMONIFY vb treat or impregnate with ammonia or a compound of ammonia

AMMONITE n fossilized spiral shell of an extinct sea creature

AMMONIUM n type of monovalent chemical group

AMMONO adj using ammonia

AMMONOID n type of fossil

AMMONS ▸ ammon

AMMOS ▸ ammo

AMNESIA, -S n loss of memory

AMNESIAC ▸ amnesia

AMNESIAS ▸ amnesia

AMNESIC, -S ▸ amnesia

AMNESTIC adj relating to amnesia

AMNESTY n general pardon for offences against a government ▸ vb overlook or forget (an offence)

AMNIA ▸ amnion

AMNIC adj relating to amnion

AMNIO, -S n amniocentesis

AMNION, AMNIA, -S n innermost of two membranes enclosing an embryo

AMNIONIC ▸ amnion

AMNIONS ▸ amnion

AMNIOS ▸ amnio

AMNIOTE, -S n group of animals

AMNIOTIC adj of or relating to the amnion

AMOEBA, -E, -S n microscopic single-celled animal able to change its shape

AMOEBAN ▸ amoeba

AMOEBAS ▸ amoeba

AMOEBEAN same as ▸ amoebaean

AMOEBIC ▸ amoeba

AMOEBOID adj of, related to, or resembling amoebae

AMOK, -S n frenzied state

AMOKURA, -S n type of sea bird

AMOLE, -S n American plant

AMOMUM, -S n plant of the ginger family

AMONG prep in the midst of

AMONGST same as ▸ among

AMOOVE, -D, -S, AMOOVING vb stir someone's emotions

AMORAL adj without moral standards

AMORALLY ▸ amoral

AMORANCE n condition of being in love

AMORANT ▸ amorance

AMORCE, -S n small percussion cap

AMORET, -S n sweetheart

AMORETTO, AMORETTI n (esp in painting) a small chubby naked boy representing a cupid

AMORINO, AMORINI same as ▸ amoretto

AMORISM, -S ▸ amorist

AMORIST, -S n lover or a writer about love

AMOROSO, -S adv (to be played) lovingly ▸ n sherry

AMOROUS adj feeling, showing, or relating to love

AMORT adj in low spirits

AMORTISE same as ▸ amortize

AMORTIZE vb pay off (a debt) gradually by periodic transfers to a sinking fund

AMOSITE, -S n form of asbestos

AMOTION, -S n act of removing

AMOUNT, -ED, -S n extent or quantity ▸ vb be equal or add up to

AMOUR, -S n love affair

AMOVE, -D, -S, AMOVING vb stir someone's emotions

AMOWT, -S same as ▸ amaut

AMP, -ED, -ING, -S n ampere ▸ vb excite or become excited

AMPACITY n ampere capacity of a conductor

AMPASSY n ampersand

AMPED ▸ amp

AMPERAGE n strength of an electric current measured in amperes

AMPERE, -S n basic unit of electric current

AMPHIBIA n class of amphibians

AMPHIOXI > amphioxus

AMPHIPOD n type of marine or freshwater crustacean with a flat body

AMPHORA, -E, -S n two-handled ancient Greek or Roman jar

AMPHORAL ▸ amphora

AMPHORAS ▸ amphora

AMPHORIC adj resembling the sound of blowing into a bottle

AMPING ▸ amp

AMPLE, -R, -ST adj more than sufficient

AMPLEXUS n mating in amphibians

AMPLIFY vb increase the strength of (a current or sound signal)

AMPLY adv fully or generously

AMPOULE, -S n small sealed glass vessel

AMPS ▸ amp

AMPUL, -S n ampoule

AMPULE, -S same as ▸ ampoule

AMPULLA, -E n dilated end part of certain tubes in the body

AMPULLAR ▸ ampulla

AMPULS ▸ ampul

AMPUTATE vb cut off (a limb or part of a limb) for medical reasons

AMPUTEE, -S n person who has had a limb amputated

AMREETA, -S same as ▸ amrita

AMRIT, -S n liquid used in the Amrit Ceremony

AMRITA, -S n ambrosia of the gods that bestows immortality

AMRITS ▸ amrit

AMTMAN, -S n magistrate in parts of Europe

AMTRAC, -S n amphibious tracked vehicle

AMTRACK, -S same as ▸ amtrac

AMTRACS ▸ amtrac

AMTRAK, -S same as ▸ amtrac

AMU, -S n unit of mass

AMUCK, -S same as ▸ amok

AMULET, -S n something carried or worn as a protection against evil

AMULETIC ▸ amulet

AMULETS ▸ amulet

A

AMUS ▸ amu
AMUSABLE adj capable of being amused
AMUSE, -D, -S vb cause to laugh or smile
AMUSEDLY ▸ amuse
AMUSER, -S ▸ amuse
AMUSES ▸ amuse
AMUSETTE n type of light cannon
AMUSIA, -S n inability to recognize musical tones
AMUSIC ▸ amusia
AMUSING adj mildly entertaining
AMUSIVE adj deceptive
AMYGDAL, -S n almond
AMYGDALA n almond-shaped part, such as a tonsil or a lobe of the cerebellum
AMYGDALE n small hole in volcanic rock filled with minerals
AMYGDALS ▸ amygdal
AMYGDULE same as ▸ amygdale
AMYL, -S n chemical compound
AMYLASE, -S n enzyme
AMYLENE, -S another name (no longer in technical usage) for ▸ pentene
AMYLIC adj of or derived from amyl
AMYLOGEN n soluble part of starch
AMYLOID, -S n complex protein ▷ adj starchlike
AMYLOSE, -S n type of chemical
AMYLS ▸ amyl
AMYLUM, -S another name for ▸ starch
AMYTAL, -S n as in **sodium amytal** type of sedative
AN adj form of a used before vowels ▷ n additional condition
ANA, -S adv in equal quantities ▷ n collection of reminiscences
ANABAENA n type of freshwater alga
ANABAS n type of fish
ANABASIS, ANABASES n military expedition to the interior of a country
ANABATIC adj (of air currents) rising upwards, esp up slopes
ANABLEPS n type of tropical freshwater fish with eyes adapted for seeing both in air and water
ANABOLIC adj of or relating to anabolism

ANACONDA n large S American snake
ANADEM, -S n garland for the head
ANAEMIA, -S n deficiency in the number of red blood cells
ANAEMIC adj having anaemia
ANAEROBE n organism that does not require oxygen
ANAGEN, -S n phase of hair growth
ANAGLYPH n type of stereoscopic picture
ANAGOGE, -S n allegorical interpretation
ANAGOGIC ▸ anagoge
ANAGOGY same as ▸ anagoge
ANAGRAM, -S n word or phrase made by rearranging the letters of another word or phrase
ANAL adj of the anus
ANALCIME same as ▸ analcite
ANALCITE n white, grey, or colourless zeolite mineral
ANALECTA same as ▸ analects
ANALECTS pl n selected literary passages from one or more works
ANALEMMA n scale shaped like a figure of eight
ANALGIA, -S same as > analgesia
ANALLY ▸ anal
ANALOG, -S same as ▸ analogue
ANALOGA ▸ analogon
ANALOGIC ▸ analogy
ANALOGON, ANALOGA n analogue
ANALOGS ▸ analog
ANALOGUE n something that is similar in some respects to something else ▷ adj displaying information by means of a dial
ANALOGY n similarity in some respects
ANALYSE, -D vb make an analysis of (something)
ANALYSER ▸ analyse
ANALYSIS, ANALYSES n separation of a whole into its parts for study and interpretation
ANALYST, -S n person skilled in analysis
ANALYTE, -S n substance that is being analysed
ANALYTIC adj relating to analysis ▷ n analytical logic
ANALYZE, -D, -S same as ▸ analyse

ANALYZER ▸ analyze
ANALYZES ▸ analyze
ANAN interj expression of failure to understand
ANANA n pineapple

More than two As on your rack is bad news, but there are a number of short words that use three As, of which this word is one.

ANANAS, -ES n plant related to the pineapple
ANANDA, -S n Buddhist principle of extreme happiness
ANANKE, -S n unalterable necessity
ANAPAEST n metrical foot of three syllables, the first two short, the last long
ANAPEST, -S same as ▸ anapaest
ANAPHASE n third stage of mitosis
ANAPHOR, -S n word referring back to a previous word
ANAPHORA n use of a word that has the same reference as a word used previously
ANAPHORS ▸ anaphor
ANARCH, -S n instigator or personification of anarchy
ANARCHAL ▸ anarchy
ANARCHIC ▸ anarchy
ANARCHS ▸ anarch
ANARCHY n lawlessness and disorder
ANAS ▸ ana
ANASARCA n accumulation of fluid within subcutaneous connective tissue
ANATA, -S n Buddhist belief
ANATASE, -S n rare blue or black mineral
ANATEXIS, ANATEXES n partial melting of rocks
ANATHEMA n detested person or thing
ANATMAN, -S same as ▸ anata
ANATOMIC ▸ anatomy
ANATOMY n science of the structure of the body
ANATOXIN n bacterial toxin used in inoculation
ANATROPY n plant ovule inverted by a bending of the stalk
ANATTA, -S n annatto
ANATTO, -S same as ▸ annatto
ANAXIAL adj asymmetrical
ANBURY, ANBURIES n soft spongy tumour occurring in horses and oxen

A

ANCE *dialect form of* ▸ **once**

ANCESTOR, -S *n* person from whom one is descended

ANCESTRY *n* lineage or descent

ANCHO, -S *n* chilli pepper

ANCHOR, -ED *n* heavy hooked device to fasten a ship to the sea bottom ▷ *vb* fasten with or as if with an anchor

ANCHORET *n* anchorite

ANCHORS *pl n* brakes of a motor vehicle

ANCHOS ▸ **ancho**

ANCHOVY *n* small strong-tasting fish

ANCHUSA, -S *n* Eurasian plant

ANCHUSIN *same as* ▸ **alkanet**

ANCIENT, -S *adj* dating from very long ago ▷ *n* member of a civilized nation in the ancient world, esp a Greek, Roman, or Hebrew

ANCILE, ANCILIA *n* mythical Roman shield

ANCILLA, -E, -S *n* Latin word for servant

ANCLE, -S *old spelling of* ▸ **ankle**

ANCOME, -S *n* inflammation

ANCON *n* projecting bracket

ANCONAL ▸ **ancon**

ANCONE, -S *same as* ▸ **ancon**

ANCONEAL ▸ **ancon**

ANCONES ▸ **ancone**

ANCONOID ▸ **ancon**

ANCORA *adv* Italian for encore

ANCRESS *n* female anchorite

AND, -S *n* additional matter or problem

ANDANTE, -S *adv* (to be played) moderately slowly ▷ *n* passage or piece to be performed moderately slowly

ANDESINE *n* feldspar mineral of the plagioclase series

ANDESITE *n* fine-grained tan or grey volcanic rock

ANDESYTE *n* andesite

ANDIRON, -S *n* iron stand for supporting logs in a fireplace

ANDRO, -S *n* type of hormone

ANDROGEN *n* type of steroid

ANDROID, -S *n* robot resembling a human ▷ *adj* resembling a human being

ANDROS ▸ **andro**

ANDS ▸ **and**

ANDVILE, -S *old form of* ▸ **anvil**

ANE, -S *Scots word for* ▸ **one**

ANEAR, -ED, -ING, -S *adv* nearly ▷ *vb* approach

ANEATH *Scots word for* ▸ **beneath**

ANECDOTA *pl n* unpublished writings

ANECDOTE *n* short amusing account of an incident

ANECHOIC *adj* having a low degree of reverberation of sound

ANELACE, -S *same as* ▸ **anlace**

ANELE, -D, -S, ANELING *vb* anoint, esp to give extreme unction to

ANELLI *pl n* pasta shaped like small rings

ANEMIA, -S *n* anaemia

ANEMIC *same as* ▸ **anaemic**

ANEMONE, -S *n* plant with white, purple, or red flowers

ANEMOSIS, ANEMOSES *n* cracking in timber caused by wind affecting growing tree

ANENST *dialect word for* ▸ **against**

ANENT *prep* Scots word meaning alongside

ANERGIA, -S *n* anergy

ANERGIC ▸ **anergy**

ANERGY, ANERGIES *n* lack of energy

ANERLY *Scots word for* ▸ **only**

ANEROID, -S *adj* not containing a liquid ▷ *n* barometer that does not contain liquid

ANES ▸ **ane**

ANESTRA ▸ **anestrum**

ANESTRI ▸ **anestrus**

ANESTRUM, ANESTRA *n* anestrus

ANESTRUS, ANESTRI *same as* > **anoestrus**

ANETHOL, -S *n* substance derived from oil of anise

ANETHOLE *n* white water-soluble crystalline substance with a liquorice-like odour

ANETHOLS ▸ **anethol**

ANETIC *adj* medically soothing

ANEURIN, -S *a less common name for* ▸ **thiamine**

ANEURISM *same as* ▸ **aneurysm**

ANEURYSM *n* permanent swelling of a blood vessel

ANEW *adv* once more

ANGA, -S *n* part in Indian music

ANGAKOK, -S *n* Inuit shaman

ANGARIA, -S *n* species of shellfish

ANGARY, ANGARIES *n* right to use the property of a neutral state during a war

ANGAS ▸ **anga**

ANGEKKOK *n* Inuit shaman

ANGEKOK, -S *n* Inuit shaman

ANGEL, -ED, -ING, -S *n* spiritual being believed to be an attendant or messenger of God ▷ *vb* provide financial support for

ANGELIC *adj* very kind, pure, or beautiful

ANGELICA *n* aromatic plant

ANGELING ▸ **angel**

ANGELS ▸ **angel**

ANGELUS *n* series of prayers

ANGER, -ED, -ING, -S *n* fierce displeasure or extreme annoyance ▷ *vb* make (someone) angry

ANGERLY *adv* old form of angrily

ANGERS ▸ **anger**

ANGICO, -S *n* South American tree

ANGINA, -S *n* heart disorder causing sudden severe chest pains

ANGINAL ▸ **angina**

ANGINAS ▸ **angina**

ANGINOSE ▸ **angina**

ANGINOUS ▸ **angina**

ANGIOMA, -S *n* tumour consisting of a mass of blood vessels or lymphatic vessels

ANGKLUNG *n* Asian musical instrument

ANGLE, -D, -S *n* space between or shape formed by two lines or surfaces that meet ▷ *vb* bend or place (something) at an angle

ANGLEDUG *n* earthworm

ANGLEPOD *n* American wild flower

ANGLER, -S *n* person who fishes with a hook and line

ANGLES ▸ **angle**

ANGLICE *adv* in English

ANGLIFY *same as* > **anglicize**

ANGLING, -S *n* art or sport of fishing with a hook and line

ANGLIST, -S *same as* > **anglicist**

ANGLO, -S *n* White inhabitant of the US not of Latin extraction

ANGOLA *same as* ▸ **angora**

A

ANGORA, -S n variety of goat, cat, or rabbit with long silky hair

ANGRIER ▸ angry

ANGRIES ▸ angry

ANGRIEST ▸ angry

ANGRILY ▸ angry

ANGRY, ANGRIER, ANGRIES, ANGRIEST adj full of anger ▷ n angry person

ANGST, -S n feeling of anxiety

ANGSTIER ▸ angsty

ANGSTROM n unit of length used to measure wavelengths

ANGSTS ▸ angst

ANGSTY, ANGSTIER adj displaying angst

ANGUINE adj of, relating to, or similar to a snake

ANGUIPED adj having snakes for legs ▷ n mythological Persian creature with snakes for legs

ANGUISH n great mental pain ▷ vb afflict or be afflicted with anguish

ANGULAR adj (of a person) lean and bony

ANGULATE adj having angles or an angular shape ▷ vb make or become angular

ANGULOSE same as ▸ angulous

ANGULOUS adj having angles

ANHEDRAL n downward inclination of an aircraft wing in relation to the lateral axis

ANHINGA, -S n type of bird

ANI, -S n tropical bird

ANICCA, -S n Buddhist belief

ANICONIC adj (of images of deities, symbols, etc) not portrayed in a human or animal form

ANICUT, -S n dam in India

ANIGH adv near

ANIGHT adv at night

ANIL, -S n tropical shrub

ANILE adj of or like a feeble old woman

ANILIN, -S n aniline

ANILINE, -S n colourless oily liquid

ANILINS ▸ anilin

ANILITY ▸ anile

ANILS ▸ anil

ANIMA, -S n feminine principle as present in the male unconscious

ANIMACY n state of being animate

ANIMAL, -S n living creature capable of voluntary motion, esp one other than a human being ▷ adj of animals

ANIMALIC ▸ animal

ANIMALLY adv physically

ANIMALS ▸ animal

ANIMAS ▸ anima

ANIMATE, -S vb give life to ▷ adj having life

ANIMATED adj interesting and lively

ANIMATER same as ▸ animator

ANIMATES ▸ animate

ANIMATI ▸ animato

ANIMATIC n animated film sequence

ANIMATO, ANIMATI, -S n piece of music performed in a lively manner

ANIMATOR n person who makes animated cartoons

ANIMATOS ▸ animato

ANIME, -S n type of Japanese animation

ANIMI ▸ animus

ANIMISM, -S n belief that natural objects possess souls

ANIMIST, -S ▸ animism

ANIMUS, ANIMI, -ES n hatred, animosity

ANION, -S n ion with negative charge

ANIONIC ▸ anion

ANIONS ▸ anion

ANIRIDIA n absence of the iris, due to a congenital condition or an injury

ANIRIDIC ▸ aniridia

ANIS ▸ ani

ANISE, -S n plant with liquorice-flavoured seeds

ANISEED, -S n liquorice-flavoured seeds of the anise plant

ANISES ▸ anise

ANISETTE n liquorice-flavoured liqueur made from aniseed

ANISIC ▸ anise

ANISOLE, -S n colourless pleasant-smelling liquid used as a solvent

ANKER, -S n old liquid measure for wine

ANKERITE n greyish to brown mineral that resembles dolomite

ANKERS ▸ anker

ANKH, -S n ancient Egyptian symbol

ANKLE, -D, -S, ANKLING n joint between the foot and leg ▷ vb move

ANKLET, -S n ornamental chain worn round the ankle

ANKLING ▸ ankle

ANKLONG, -S n Asian musical instrument

ANKLUNG, -S n Asian musical instrument

ANKUS, -ES n stick used for goading elephants

ANKUSH, -ES n stick used for goading elephants

ANKYLOSE vb (of bones in a joint, etc) to fuse or stiffen by ankylosis

ANLACE, -S n medieval short dagger with a broad tapering blade

ANLAGE, -N, -S n organ or part in the earliest stage of development

ANLAS, -ES same as ▸ anlace

ANN, -S n old Scots word for a widow's pension

ANNA, -S n former Indian coin worth one sixteenth of a rupee

ANNAL, -S n recorded events of one year

ANNALISE vb record in annals

ANNALIST ▸ annal

ANNALIZE vb record in annals

ANNALS ▸ annal

ANNAS ▸ anna

ANNAT, -S n old Scots word for a widow's pension

ANNATES pl n money paid to the Pope

ANNATS ▸ annat

ANNATTA, -S n annatto

ANNATTO, -S n tropical tree

ANNEAL, -ED, -S vb toughen by heating and slow cooling ▷ n act of annealing

ANNEALER ▸ anneal

ANNEALS ▸ anneal

ANNELID, -S n type of worm with a segmented body

ANNEX, -ED, -ING vb seize (territory)

ANNEXE, -S n extension to a building

ANNEXED ▸ annex

ANNEXES ▸ annexe

ANNEXING ▸ annex

ANNEXION n old form of annexation

ANNEXURE n something that is added

ANNICUT, -S n dam in India

ANNO adv Latin for in the year

ANNONA, -S n American tree or shrub

ANNOTATE vb add notes to (a written work)

ANNOUNCE vb make known publicly

ANNOY, -ED, -S vb irritate or displease

ANNOYER, -S ▶ annoy

ANNOYING adj causing irritation or displeasure

ANNOYS ▶ annoy

ANNS ▶ ann

ANNUAL, -S adj happening once a year ▷ n plant that completes its life cycle in a year

ANNUALLY ▶ annual

ANNUALS ▶ annual

ANNUITY n fixed sum paid every year

ANNUL, -LED, -S vb declare (something, esp a marriage) invalid

ANNULAR, -S adj ring-shaped ▷ n ring finger

ANNULATE adj having, composed of, or marked with rings ▷ n annelid

ANNULET, -S n moulding in the form of a ring

ANNULI ▶ annulus

ANNULLED ▶ annul

ANNULOSE adj having a body formed of a series of rings

ANNULS ▶ annul

ANNULUS, ANNULI n area between two concentric circles

ANOA, -S n type of small cattle

ANOBIID, -S n any type of beetle

ANODAL ▶ anode

ANODALLY ▶ anode

ANODE, -S n positive electrode in a battery, valve, etc

ANODIC ▶ anode

ANODISE, -D, -S same as ▶ anodize

ANODISER same as ▶ anodizer

ANODISES ▶ anodise

ANODIZE, -D, -S vb coat (metal) with a protective oxide film by electrolysis

ANODIZER n something that anodizes

ANODIZES ▶ anodize

ANODYNE, -S n something that relieves pain or distress ▷ adj relieving pain or distress

ANODYNIC ▶ anodyne

ANOESIS, ANOESES n feeling without understanding

ANOESTRA > anoestrus

ANOESTRI > anoestrus

This is the plural of **anoestrus**, a period of inactivity between periods of oestrus. It is one of the most frequently played of all 8-letter bonuses, and the same combination of letters yields no fewer than six other words: **arsonite, notaires, notaries, notarise, rosinate** and **senorita**. It is well worth becoming acquainted with commonly occurring multiple-choice letter combinations like this, as it gives your game great flexibility.

ANOETIC ▶ anoesis

ANOINT, -ED, -S vb smear with oil as a sign of consecration

ANOINTER ▶ anoint

ANOINTS ▶ anoint

ANOLE, -S n type of lizard

ANOLYTE, -S n part of an electrolyte around an anode

ANOMALY n something that deviates from the normal, irregularity

ANOMIC ▶ anomie

ANOMIE, -S n lack of social or moral standards

ANOMY same as ▶ **anomie**

ANON adv in a short time, soon

ANONYM, -S n anonymous person or publication

ANONYMA, -S n main vessel in the arterial network

ANONYMS ▶ anonym

ANOOPSIA n squint in which the eye turns upwards

ANOPIA, -S n inability to see

ANOPSIA, -S n squint in which the eye turns upwards

ANORAK, -S n light waterproof hooded jacket

ANORETIC ▶ anorectic

ANOREXIA n psychological disorder characterized by fear of becoming fat and refusal to eat

ANOREXIC ▶ anorexia

ANOREXY old name for ▶ **anorexia**

ANORTHIC another word for > triclinic

ANOSMIA, -S n loss of the sense of smell

ANOSMIC ▶ anosmia

ANOTHER adj one more

ANOUGH adj old form of enough

ANOUROUS adj having no tail

ANOVULAR adj without ovulation

ANOW adj old form of enough

ANOXEMIA same as > anoxaemia

ANOXEMIC ▶ anoxemia

ANOXIA, -S n lack or absence of oxygen

ANOXIC ▶ anoxia

ANS pl n as in ifs and ans things that might have happened, but which did not

ANSA, -E n either end of Saturn's rings

ANSATE adj having a handle or handle-like part

ANSATED adj ansate

ANSATZ, -ES n (in mathematics) assumption made to help solve a problem

ANSERINE adj of or resembling a goose ▷ n chemical compound

ANSEROUS same as ▶ anserine

ANSWER, -ED, -S n reply to a question, request, letter, etc ▷ vb give an answer (to)

ANSWERER ▶ answer

ANSWERS ▶ answer

ANT, -S n small insect living in highly organized colonies

ANTA, -E, -S n pilaster

ANTACID, -S n substance that counteracts acidity ▷ adj having the properties of this substance

ANTAE ▶ anta

ANTALGIC n pain-relieving drug

ANTAR, -S old word for ▶ **cave**

ANTARA, -S n South American panpipes

ANTARS ▶ antar

ANTAS ▶ anta

ANTBEAR, -S n aardvark

ANTBIRD, -S n South American bird

ANTE, -D, -ED, -ING, -S n player's stake in poker ▷ vb place (one's stake) in poker

ANTEATER n mammal which feeds on ants by means of a long snout

ANTECEDE vb go before, as in time, order, etc

ANTED ▶ ante

ANTEDATE vb precede in time ▷ n earlier date

ANTEED ▶ ante

ANTEFIX, -A n carved ornament

ANTEING ▶ ante

ANTELOPE n deerlike mammal with long legs and horns

A

ANTENATI pl n people born before certain date

ANTENNA, -E, -S n insect's feeler

ANTENNAL ▶ antenna

ANTENNAS ▶ antenna

ANTEPAST n appetizer

ANTERIOR adj the front

ANTEROOM n small room leading into a larger one, often used as a waiting room

ANTES ▶ ante

ANTETYPE n earlier form

ANTEVERT vb displace (an organ or part) by tilting it forward

ANTHELIA > anthelion

ANTHELIX n prominent curved fold of cartilage just inside the outer rim of the external ear

ANTHEM, -ED, -S n song of loyalty, esp to a country ▷ vb provide with an anthem

ANTHEMIA > anthemion

ANTHEMIC ▶ anthem

ANTHEMIS n genus of herbs of Mediterranean and SW Asia

ANTHEMS ▶ anthem

ANTHER, -S n part of a flower's stamen containing pollen

ANTHERAL ▶ anther

ANTHERID n antheridium

ANTHERS ▶ anther

ANTHESIS, ANTHESES n time when a flower begins reproductive cycle

ANTHILL, -S n mound near an ants' nest

ANTHODIA > anthodium

ANTHOID adj resembling a flower

ANTHRAX n dangerous disease of cattle and sheep, communicable to humans

ANTHRO, -S n short for anthropology

ANTI, -S adj opposed (to) ▷ n opponent of a party, policy, or attitude

ANTIACNE adj inhibiting the development of acne

ANTIAIR adj countering attack by aircraft or missile

ANTIAR, -S another name for ▶ upas

ANTIARIN n poison derived from antiar

ANTIARS ▶ antiar

ANTIATOM n atom composed of antiparticles

ANTIBIAS adj countering bias

ANTIBODY n protein produced in the blood, which destroys bacteria

ANTIBOSS adj acting against bosses

ANTIBUG adj acting against computer bugs

ANTIC n actor in a ludicrous or grotesque part ▷ adj fantastic

ANTICAL adj in front of or above another plant part

ANTICAR adj opposed to cars

ANTICISE same as ▶ anticize

ANTICITY adj opposed to cities

ANTICIZE vb play absurdly

ANTICK, -ED, -S vb perform antics

ANTICKE, -S archaic form of ▶ antique

ANTICKED ▶ antick

ANTICKES ▶ anticke

ANTICKS ▶ antick

ANTICLY adv grotesquely

ANTICOLD adj preventing or fighting the common cold

ANTICOUS adj on the part of a flower furthest from the stem

ANTICS pl n absurd acts or postures

ANTICULT n organization that is opposed to religious cults

ANTIDORA > antidoron

ANTIDOTE n substance that counteracts a poison ▷ vb counteract with an antidote

ANTIDRUG adj intended to discourage illegal drug use

ANTIDUNE n type of sand hill or inclined bedding plane

ANTIENT, -S old spelling of ▶ ancient

ANTIFA, -S n antifascist organization

ANTIFAT adj acting to remove or prevent fat

ANTIFLU adj acting against influenza

ANTIFOAM adj allowing gas to escape rather than form foam

ANTIFOG adj preventing the buildup of moisture on a surface

ANTIFUR adj opposed to the wearing of fur garments

ANTIGANG adj designed to restrict the activities of criminal gangs

ANTIGAY adj hostile to gay people

ANTIGEN, -S n substance causing the blood to produce antibodies

ANTIGENE n antigen

ANTIGENS ▶ antigen

ANTIGUN adj opposed to the possession of guns

ANTIHERO n central character in a book, film, etc, who lacks the traditional heroic virtues

ANTIJAM adj preventing jamming

ANTIKING n rival to an established king

ANTILEAK adj preventing leaks

ANTILEFT adj opposed to the left wing in politics

ANTILIFE adj opposed to living in harmony with the natural order

ANTILOCK adj designed to prevent overbraking

ANTILOG, -S n number whose logarithm to a given base is a given number

ANTILOGY n contradiction in terms

ANTIMALE adj opposed to men

ANTIMAN adj hostile to men

ANTIMASK n interlude in a masque

ANTIMEN adj hostile to men

ANTIMERE n body part or organ that mirrors a similar structure on the other side

ANTIMINE adj designed to counteract landmines

ANTIMONY n brittle silvery-white metallic element

ANTIMUON n antiparticle of a muon

ANTING, -S n rubbing of ants by birds on their feathers

ANTINODE n point of amplitude of displacement of opposite value to a node

ANTINOME n opposite

ANTINOMY n contradiction between two laws or principles that are reasonable in themselves

ANTINUKE same as > antinuker

ANTIPHON n hymn sung in alternate parts by two groups of singers

ANTIPILL adj (of a material) not forming pills

ANTIPODE n exact or direct opposite

ANTIPOLE n opposite pole

ANTIPOPE n pope set up in opposition to the one chosen by church laws

ANTIPYIC n drug acting against suppuration

ANTIQUE, -D, -S n object of an earlier period, valued for its beauty, workmanship, or age ▷ adj made in an earlier period ▷ vb give an antique appearance to

ANTIQUER n collector of antiques

ANTIQUES ▸ antique

ANTIQUEY adj having the appearance of an antique

ANTIRED adj of a particular colour of antiquark

ANTIRIOT adj designed for the control of crowds

ANTIROCK adj designed to prevent a vehicle from rocking

ANTIROLL adj designed to prevent a vehicle from tilting

ANTIRUST adj (of a product or procedure) effective against rust ▷ n substance or device that prevents rust

ANTIS ▸ anti

ANTISAG adj preventing sagging

ANTISERA ▸ antiserum

ANTISHIP adj designed for attacking ships

ANTISKID adj intended to prevent skidding

ANTISLIP adj acting to prevent slipping

ANTISMOG adj reducing smog

ANTISNOB n person opposed to snobbery

ANTISPAM adj intended to prevent spam

ANTISTAT n substance preventing static electricity

ANTITANK adj (of weapons) designed to destroy military tanks

ANTITAX adj opposed to taxation

ANTITHET n example of antithesis

ANTITYPE n something foreshadowed by a type or symbol

ANTIVAX adj opposed to vaccination

ANTIWAR adj opposed to war

ANTIWEAR adj preventing wear

ANTIWEED adj killing or preventing weeds

ANTLER, -S n branched horn of a male deer

ANTLERED adj having antlers

ANTLERS ▸ antler

ANTLIA, -E n butterfly proboscis

ANTLIATE adj relating to antlia

ANTLIKE adj of or like an ant or ants

ANTLION, -S n type of insect resembling a dragonfly

ANTONYM, -S n word that means the opposite of another

ANTONYMY n use of antonyms

ANTPITTA n S American bird whose diet consists mainly of ants

ANTRA ▸ antrum

ANTRAL ▸ antrum

ANTRE, -S n cavern or cave

ANTRORSE adj directed or pointing upwards or forwards

ANTRUM, ANTRA, -S n natural cavity, esp in a bone

ANTS ▸ ant

ANTSY, ANTSIER, ANTSIEST adj restless, nervous, and impatient

ANURA pl n order of animals that comprises frogs and toads

ANURAL adj without a tail

ANURAN, -S n type of amphibian

ANURESIS, ANURESES n inability to urinate

ANURETIC ▸ anuresis

ANURIA, -S n result of a kidney disorder

ANURIC ▸ anuria

ANUROUS adj lacking a tail

ANUS, -ES n opening at the end of the alimentary canal, through which faeces are discharged

ANVIL, -ED, -ING, -LED, -S n heavy iron block on which metals are hammered into particular shapes ▷ vb forge on an anvil

ANVILTOP n type of cloud formation

ANXIETY n state of being anxious

ANXIOUS adj worried and tense

ANY adj one or some, no matter which ▷ adv at all

ANYBODY n any person at random

ANYHOW adv anyway

ANYMORE adv at present

ANYON, -S n type of elementary particle

ANYONE, -S pron any person ▷ n any person at random

ANYONS ▸ anyon

ANYPLACE adv in, at, or to any unspecified place

ANYROAD a northern English dialect word for ▸ anyway

ANYTHING pron any object, event, or action whatever ▷ n any thing at random

ANYTIME adv at any time

ANYWAY adv at any rate, nevertheless

ANYWAYS nonstandard word for ▸ anyway

ANYWHEN adv at any time

ANYWHERE adv in, at, or to any place

ANYWISE adv in any way or manner

ANZIANI pl n Italian word for councillors

AORIST, -S n tense of the verb in classical Greek

AORISTIC ▸ aorist

AORISTS ▸ aorist

AORTA, -E, -S n main artery of the body, carrying oxygen-rich blood from the heart

AORTAL ▸ aorta

AORTAS ▸ aorta

AORTIC ▸ aorta

AORTITIS n inflammation of the aorta

AOUDAD, -S n wild mountain sheep

APACE adv swiftly

APACHE, -S n Parisian gangster or ruffian

APADANA, -S n ancient Persian palace hall

APAGE interj Greek word meaning go away

APAGOGE, -S n reduction to absurdity

APAGOGIC ▸ apagoge

APAID ▸ apay

APANAGE, -S same as ▸ appanage

APANAGED adj having apanage

APANAGES ▸ apanage

APAREJO, -S n kind of packsaddle made of stuffed leather cushions

APART adv to pieces or in pieces

APATETIC adj of or relating to coloration that disguises and protects an animal

APATHY, APATHIES n lack of interest or enthusiasm

APATITE, -S n pale green to purple mineral, found in igneous rocks

APAY, APAID, -D, -ING, -S vb old word meaning satisfy

APE, -D, -S, APING n tailless monkey such as the chimpanzee or gorilla ▷ vb imitate

A

APEAK adj in a vertical or almost vertical position

APED ▶ ape

APEDOM, -S n state of being an ape

APEEK adv nautical word meaning vertically

APEHOOD, -S n state of being an ape

APELIKE ▶ ape

APEMAN, APEMEN n primate thought to have been the forerunner of humans

APEPSIA, -S n digestive disorder

APEPSY, APEPSIES n apepsia

APER, -S n person who apes

APERCU, -S n outline

APERIENT adj having a mild laxative effect ▷ n mild laxative

APERIES ▶ apery

APERITIF n alcoholic drink taken before a meal

APERS ▶ aper

APERT adj open

APERTURE n opening or hole

APERY, APERIES n imitative behaviour

APES ▶ ape

APETALY > apetalous

APEX, -ES n highest point

APGAR n as in apgar score system for determining the condition of an infant at birth

APHAGIA, -S n refusal or inability to swallow

APHAKIA, -S n absence of the lens of an eye

APHANITE n type of fine-grained rock, such as a basalt

APHASIA, -S n disorder causing loss of ability to communicate

APHASIAC ▶ aphasia

APHASIAS ▶ aphasia

APHASIC, -S ▶ aphasia

APHELIA ▶ aphelion

APHELIAN ▶ aphelion

APHELION, APHELIA n point of a planet's orbit that is farthest from the sun

APHESIS, APHESES n gradual disappearance of an unstressed vowel at the beginning of a word

APHETIC ▶ aphesis

APHETISE vb lose a vowel at the beginning of a word

APHETIZE vb lose a vowel at the beginning of a word

APHICIDE n substance for killing aphids

APHID, -S n small insect which sucks the sap from plants

APHIDES ▶ aphis

APHIDIAN ▶ aphid

APHIDS ▶ aphid

APHIS, APHIDES n type of aphid such as the blackfly

APHOLATE n type of pesticide

APHONIA, -S n loss of the voice caused by damage to the vocal tract

APHONIC, -S adj affected with aphonia ▷ n person affected with aphonia

APHONIES ▶ aphony

APHONOUS ▶ aphonia

APHONY, APHONIES same as ▶ aphonia

APHORISE same as ▶ aphorize

APHORISM n short clever saying expressing a general truth

APHORIST ▶ aphorism

APHORIZE vb write or speak in aphorisms

APHOTIC adj characterized by or growing in the absence of light

APHTHA, -E n small ulceration

APHTHOUS ▶ aphtha

APHYLLY > aphyllous

APIAN adj of, relating to, or resembling bees

APIARIAN adj of or relating to the breeding and care of bees ▷ n apiarist

APIARIES ▶ apiary

APIARIST n beekeeper

APIARY, APIARIES n place where bees are kept

APICAL, -S adj of, at, or being an apex ▷ n sound made with the tip of the tongue

APICALLY ▶ apical

APICALS ▶ apical

APICES plural of ▶ apex

APICIAN adj of fine or dainty food

APICULUS, APICULI n short sharp point

APIECE adv each

APIEZON adj as in apiezon oil oil left by distillation

APIMANIA n extreme enthusiasm for bees

APING ▶ ape

APIOL, -S n substance derived from parsley seeds

APIOLOGY n study of bees

APIOLS ▶ apiol

APISH adj stupid or foolish

APISHLY ▶ apish

APISM, -S n behaviour like an ape

APLANAT, -S n aplanatic lens

APLASIA, -S n congenital absence of an organ

APLASTIC adj relating to or characterized by aplasia

APLENTY adv in plenty

APLITE, -S n type of igneous rock

APLITIC ▶ aplite

APLOMB, -S n calm self-possession

APLUSTRE n stern ornament on an ancient Greek ship

APNEA, -S same as ▶ apnoea

APNEAL ▶ apnea

APNEAS ▶ apnea

APNEIC ▶ apnea

APNEUSIS, APNEUSES n gasping inhalation followed by short exhalation

APNOEA, -S n temporary inability to breathe

APNOEAL ▶ apnoea

APNOEAS ▶ apnoea

APNOEIC ▶ apnoea

APO, -S n type of protein

APOAPSIS, APOAPSES n point in an orbit furthest from the object orbited

APOCARP, -S n apocarpous gynoecium or fruit

APOCARPY n presence of many carpels

APOCOPE, -S n omission of the final sound or sounds of a word

APOCOPIC ▶ apocope

APOCRINE adj denoting a type of glandular secretion

APOD, -S n animal without feet

APODAL adj (of snakes, eels, etc) without feet

APODE, -S n animal without feet

APODOSIS, APODOSES n consequent of a conditional statement

APODOUS same as ▶ apodal

APODS ▶ apod

APOGAEIC ▶ apogee

APOGAMIC ▶ apogamy

APOGAMY n type of reproduction in some ferns

APOGEAL ▶ apogee

APOGEAN ▶ apogee

APOGEE, -S n point of moon's orbit

APOGEIC ▶ apogee

APOGRAPH n exact copy

APOLLO, -S n strikingly handsome youth

APOLOG, -S same as ▸ apologue

APOLOGAL ▸ apologue

APOLOGIA n formal written defence of a cause

APOLOGS ▸ apolog

APOLOGUE n allegory or moral fable

APOLOGY n expression of regret for wrongdoing

APOLUNE, -S n point in a lunar orbit

APOMICT, -S n organism, esp a plant, produced by apomixis

APOMIXIS, APOMIXES n type of asexual reproduction

APOOP adv on the poop deck

APOPHONY n change in the quality of vowels

APOPHYGE n outward curve at each end of the shaft of a column, adjoining the base or capital

APOPLAST n nonprotoplasmic component of a plant

APOPLEX vb afflict with apoplexy

APOPLEXY n extreme anger

APORETIC ▸ aporia

APORIA, -S n doubt, real or professed, about what to do or say

APORT adj on or towards the port side

APOS ▸ apo

APOSITIA n unwillingness to eat

APOSITIC ▸ apositia

APOSPORY n development of the gametophyte from the sporophyte without the formation of spores

APOSTACY same as ▸ apostasy

APOSTASY n abandonment of one's religious faith or other belief

APOSTATE n person who has abandoned his or her religion, political party, or cause ▸ adj guilty of apostasy

APOSTIL, -S n marginal note

APOSTLE, -S n one of the twelve disciples chosen by Christ to preach His gospel

APOTHECE n obsolete word for shop

APOTHEGM n short cryptic remark containing some general or generally accepted truth; maxim

APOTHEM, -S n line from the centre of a polygon to one of its sides

APOZEM, -S n medicine dissolved in water

APP, -S n application program

APPAID ▸ appay

APPAIR, -ED, -S vb old form of impair

APPAL, -S vb dismay, terrify

APPALL, -ED, -S same as ▸ appal

APPALS ▸ appal

APPALTO, APPALTI n monopoly or contract

APPANAGE n land granted by a king for the support of a younger son

APPARAT, -S n Communist Party organization

APPAREL, -S n clothing ▸ vb clothe, adorn, etc

APPARENT adj readily seen, obvious ▸ n heir apparent

APPAY, APPAID, -D, -ING, -S old word for ▸ satisfy

APPEACH old word for ▸ accuse

APPEAL, -ED, -S vb make an earnest request ▸ n earnest request

APPEALER ▸ appeal

APPEALS ▸ appeal

APPEAR, -ED, -S vb become visible or present

APPEARER ▸ appear

APPEARS ▸ appear

APPEASE, -D, -S vb pacify (a person) by yielding to his or her demands

APPEASER ▸ appease

APPEASES ▸ appease

APPEL, -S n stamp of the foot, used to warn of one's intent to attack

APPELLEE n person who is accused or appealed against

APPELLOR n person initiating a law case

APPELS ▸ appel

APPEND, -ED, -S vb join on, add

APPENDIX n separate additional material at the end of a book

APPENDS ▸ append

APPERIL, -S old word for ▸ peril

APPERILL old word for ▸ peril

APPERILS ▸ apperil

APPESTAT n part of the brain that regulates hunger and satiety

APPETENT adj eager

APPETISE vb stimulate the appetite

APPETITE n desire for food or drink

APPETIZE vb stimulate the appetite

APPLAUD, -S vb show approval of by clapping one's hands

APPLAUSE n approval shown by clapping one's hands

APPLE, -S n round firm fleshy fruit that grows on trees

APPLET, -S n computing program

APPLEY, APPLIEST adj resembling or tasting like an apple

APPLIED adj (of a skill, science, etc) put to practical use

APPLIER, -S ▸ apply

APPLIES ▸ apply

APPLIEST ▸ appley

APPLIQUE n decoration or trimming of one material sewn or otherwise fixed onto another ▸ vb sew or fix (a decoration) on as an appliqué

APPLY, APPLIES, -ING vb make a formal request

APPOINT, -S vb assign to a job or position

APPORT, -S n production of objects at a seance

APPOSE, -D, -S, APPOSING vb place side by side or near to each other

APPOSER, -S ▸ appose

APPOSES ▸ appose

APPOSING ▸ appose

APPOSITE adj suitable, apt

APPRAISE vb estimate the value or quality of

APPRESS vb press together

APPRISE, -D, -S vb make aware (of)

APPRISER ▸ apprise

APPRISES ▸ apprise

APPRIZE, -D, -S same as ▸ apprise

APPRIZER ▸ apprize

APPRIZES ▸ apprize

APPRO, -S n approval

APPROACH vb come near or nearer (to) ▸ n approaching or means of approaching

APPROOF, -S old word for ▸ trial

APPROS ▸ appro

APPROVAL n consent

APPROVE, -D, -S vb consider good or right

APPROVER ▸ approve

APPROVES ▸ approve

APPS ▸ app

A

APPUI, -S *n* support
APPUIED ▸ appuy
APPUIS ▸ appui
APPULSE, -S *n* close approach of two celestial bodies
APPUY, APPUIED, -ED, -ING, -S *vb* support
APRACTIC ▸ apraxia
APRAXIA, -S *n* disorder impairing muscle movement
APRAXIC ▸ apraxia
APRES *prep* French word for after
APRICATE *vb* bask in sun
APRICOCK old word for ▸ apricot
APRICOT, -S *n* yellowish-orange juicy fruit like a small peach ▷ *adj* yellowish-orange
APRON, -ED, -ING, -S *n* garment worn over the front of the body to protect the clothes ▷ *vb* equip with an apron
APRONFUL *n* amount held in an apron
APRONING ▸ apron
APRONS ▸ apron
APROPOS *adj* appropriate
APROTIC *adj* (of solvents) neither accepting nor donating hydrogen ions
APSARAS *n* Hindu water sprite
APSE, -S *n* arched or domed recess, esp in a church
APSIDAL ▸ apsis
APSIS, APSIDES *n* point in the elliptical orbit of a planet or satellite
APSO, -S *n* Tibetan terrier
APT, -ED, -ER, -EST, -ING, -S *adj* having a specified tendency ▷ *vb* be fitting
APTAMER, -S *n* artificially created DNA or RNA molecule
APTED ▸ apt
APTER ▸ apt
APTERAL *adj* (esp of a classical temple) not having columns at the sides
APTERIA ▸ apterium
APTERISM ▸ apterous
APTERIUM, APTERIA *n* bare patch on the skin of a bird
APTEROUS *adj* (of insects) without wings, as silverfish and springtails
APTERYX *n* kiwi (the bird)
APTEST ▸ apt
APTING ▸ apt
APTITUDE *n* natural ability
APTLY ▸ apt

APTNESS ▸ apt
APTOTE, -S *n* noun without inflections
APTOTIC ▸ aptote
APTS ▸ apt
APYRASE, -S *n* enzyme
APYRETIC ▸ apyrexia
APYREXIA *n* absence of fever
AQUA, -E, -S *n* water

This Latin word for water, together with its plural **aquae** or **aquas**, comes up over and over again.

AQUACADE *same as* ▸ aquashow
AQUAE ▸ aqua
AQUAFABA *n* vegan substitute for egg whites
AQUAFARM *vb* cultivate fish or shellfish
AQUAFER, -S *n* aquifer
AQUAFIT, -S *n* type of aerobic exercise done in water
AQUALUNG *n* mouthpiece attached to air cylinders, worn for underwater swimming
AQUANAUT *n* person who lives and works underwater
AQUARIA ▸ aquarium
AQUARIAL ▸ aquarium
AQUARIAN *n* person who keeps an aquarium
AQUARIST *n* curator of an aquarium
AQUARIUM, AQUARIA *n* tank in which fish and other underwater creatures are kept
AQUAS ▸ aqua
AQUASHOW *n* exhibition of swimming and diving, often accompanied by music
AQUATIC *adj* living in or near water ▷ *n* marine or freshwater animal or plant
AQUATICS *pl n* water sports
AQUATINT *n* print like a watercolour, produced by etching copper ▷ *vb* etch (a block, etc) in aquatint
AQUATONE *n* fitness exercise in water
AQUAVIT, -S *n* grain- or potato-based spirit
AQUEDUCT *n* structure carrying water across a valley or river
AQUEOUS *adj* of, like, or containing water
AQUIFER, -S *n* deposit of rock containing water used to supply wells
AQUILINE *adj* (of a nose) curved like an eagle's beak

AQUILON, -S *n* name for the north wind
AQUIVER *adv* quivering
AR, -S *n* letter R
ARAARA, -S *another name for* ▸ trevally
ARABA, -S *n* Asian carriage

This is one of the short words that can help you deal with a surplus of As.

ARABESK, -S *same as* > arabesque
ARABIC *adj* as in gum arabic gum exuded by certain acacia trees
ARABICA, -S *n* high-quality coffee bean
ARABIN, -S *n* essence of gum arabic
ARABIS *n* type of plant
ARABISE, -D, -S *vb* make or become Arab
ARABIZE, -D, -S *vb* make or become Arab
ARABLE, -S *adj* suitable for growing crops on ▷ *n* arable land or farming
ARACEOUS *same as* ▸ aroid
ARACHIS *n* Brazilian plant
ARACHNID *n* eight-legged invertebrate, such as a spider, scorpion, tick, or mite
ARAHUANA *n* tropical freshwater fish
ARAISE, -D, -S, ARAISING *vb* old form of raise
ARAK, -S *same as* ▸ arrack
ARALIA, -S *n* type of plant
ARAME, -S *n* Japanese edible seaweed
ARAMID, -S *n* synthetic fibre
ARANCINI *pl n* fried rice balls with a savoury filling
ARANEID, -S *n* member of the spider family
ARANEOUS *adj* like a spider's web
ARAPAIMA *n* very large primitive freshwater teleost fish that occurs in tropical S America
ARAPONGA *n* South American bird with a bell-like call
ARAPUNGA *same as* ▸ araponga
ARAR, -S *n* African tree
ARAROBA, -S *n* Brazilian leguminous tree
ARARS ▸ arar
ARAWANA, -S *n* tropical freshwater fish
ARAYSE, -D, -S, ARAYSING *vb* old form of raise
ARB, -S *short for* > arbitrage
ARBA, -S *n* Asian carriage

A

ARBALEST n large medieval crossbow, usually cocked by mechanical means

ARBALIST same as ▶arbalest

ARBAS ▶arba

ARBELEST n arbalest

ARBITER, -S n person empowered to judge in a dispute

ARBITRAL adj of or relating to arbitration

ARBLAST, -S n arbalest

ARBOR, -ES, -S n revolving shaft or axle in a machine

ARBOREAL adj of or living in trees

ARBORED adj having arbors

ARBORES ▶arbor

ARBORET, -S n old name for an area planted with shrubs

ARBORETA > arboretum

ARBORETS ▶arboret

ARBORIO, -S n as in arborio rice variety of round-grain rice used for making risotto

ARBORISE same as ▶arborize

ARBORIST n specialist in the cultivation of trees

ARBORIZE vb give or take on a treelike branched appearance

ARBOROUS adj of trees

ARBORS ▶arbor

ARBOUR, -S n glade sheltered by trees

ARBOURED adj having arbours

ARBOURS ▶arbour

ARBS ▶arb

ARBUSCLE n small tree

ARBUTE, -S old name for ▶arbutus

ARBUTEAN ▶arbutus

ARBUTES ▶arbute

ARBUTUS n evergreen shrub with strawberry-like berries

ARC, -ED, -KED, -S n part of a circle or other curve ▷ vb form an arc

ARCADE, -D, -S n covered passageway lined with shops ▷ vb provide with an arcade

ARCADIA, -S n traditional idealized rural setting

ARCADIAN n person who leads a rural life

ARCADIAS ▶arcadia

ARCADING ▶arcade

ARCANA, -S n either of the two divisions of a pack of tarot cards

ARCANE adj mysterious and secret

ARCANELY ▶arcane

ARCANIST n person with secret knowledge

ARCANUM, -S n profound secret or mystery known only to initiates

ARCATURE n small-scale arcade

ARCED ▶arc

ARCH, -ES, -EST n curved structure supporting a bridge or roof ▷ vb (cause to) form an arch ▷ adj superior, knowing

ARCHAEA n order of prokaryotic microorganisms

ARCHAEAL same as ▶archaean

ARCHAEAN n type of microorganism

ARCHAEI ▶archaeus

ARCHAEON same as ▶archaean

ARCHAEUS, ARCHAEI n spirit believed to inhabit a living thing

ARCHAIC adj ancient

ARCHAISE same as ▶archaize

ARCHAISM n archaic word or phrase

ARCHAIST ▶archaism

ARCHAIZE vb give an archaic appearance or character to, as by the use of archaisms

ARCHDUKE n duke of specially high rank

ARCHEAN same as ▶archaean

ARCHED adj provided with or spanned by an arch or arches

ARCHEI ▶archeus

ARCHER, -S n person who shoots with a bow and arrow

ARCHERY n art or sport of shooting with a bow and arrow

ARCHES ▶arch

ARCHEST ▶arch

ARCHEUS, ARCHEI n spirit believed to inhabit a living thing

ARCHFOE, -S n chief enemy

ARCHFOOL n very foolish person

ARCHI ▶arco

ARCHIL, -S variant spelling of ▶orchil

ARCHINE, -S n Russian unit of length

ARCHING, -S n arched part

ARCHIVAL ▶archive

ARCHIVE, -D, -S n collection of records or documents ▷ vb store (documents, data, etc) in an archive or other repository

ARCHLET, -S n small arch

ARCHLIKE adj like an arch

ARCHLUTE n old bass lute

ARCHLY ▶arch

ARCHNESS ▶arch

ARCHON, -S n (in ancient Athens) one of the nine chief magistrates

ARCHWAY, -S n passageway under an arch

ARCHWISE adv like an arch

ARCIFORM adj shaped like an arch

ARCING, -S n formation of an arc

ARCKED ▶arc

ARCKING, -S n formation of an arc

ARCMIN, -S n 1/60 of a degree of an angle

ARCO, ARCHI, -S adv musical direction meaning with bow ▷ n bow of a stringed instrument

ARCOLOGY n architecture blending buildings with the natural environment

ARCOS ▶arco

ARCS ▶arc

ARCSEC, -S n 1/3600 of a degree of an angle

ARCSINE, -S n trigonometrical function

ARCTIC, -S adj very cold ▷ n high waterproof overshoe with buckles

ARCTIID, -S n type of moth

ARCTOID adj like a bear

ARCUATE adj shaped or bent like an arc or bow

ARCUATED same as ▶arcuate

ARCUS, -ES n circle around the cornea of the eye

ARD, -S n primitive plough

ARDEB, -S n unit of dry measure

ARDENCY ▶ardent

ARDENT adj passionate

ARDENTLY ▶ardent

ARDOR, -S same as ▶ardour

ARDOUR, -S n passion

ARDRI, -S n Irish high king

ARDRIGH, -S n Irish high king

ARDRIS ▶ardri

ARDS ▶ard

ARDUOUS adj hard to accomplish, strenuous

ARE, -S n unit of measure, 100 square metres ▷ vb form of the present tense of be

AREA, -E, -S n part or region

A

AREACH, -ED, -ES, ARRAUGHT vb old form of reach

AREAD, -ING, -S, ARED, AREDD vb old word meaning declare

AREAE ▸ area

AREAL ▸ area

AREALLY ▸ area

AREAR, -S n old form of arrear

AREAS ▸ area

AREAWAY, -S n passageway

ARECA, -S n type of palm tree

ARED ▸ aread

AREDD ▸ aread

AREDE, -S, AREDING vb old word meaning declare

AREFY, AREFIED, AREFIES, -ING vb dry up

AREG a plural of ▸ erg

AREIC adj relating to area

ARENA, -S n seated enclosure for sports events

ARENE, -S n aromatic hydrocarbon

ARENITE, -S n any arenaceous rock

ARENITIC ▸ arenite

ARENOSE adj sandy

ARENOUS adj sandy

AREOLA, -E, -S n small circular area

AREOLAR ▸ areola

AREOLAS ▸ areola

AREOLATE ▸ areola

AREOLE, -S n space outlined on a surface

AREOLOGY n study of the planet Mars

AREPA, -S n Colombian cornmeal cake

ARERE adv old word meaning backwards

ARES ▸ are

ARET, -S vb old word meaning entrust

ARETE, -S n sharp ridge separating two glacial valleys

ARETHUSA n N American orchid

ARETS ▸ aret

ARETT, -ED, -ING, -S vb old word meaning entrust

AREW adv old word meaning in a row

ARF, -S n barking sound

ARGAL, -S same as ▸ argali

ARGALA, -S n Indian stork

ARGALI, -S n wild sheep

ARGALS ▸ argal

ARGAN, -S n Moroccan tree

ARGAND, -S n lamp with a hollow circular wick

ARGANS ▸ argan

ARGEMONE n prickly poppy

ARGENT, -S n silver

ARGENTAL adj of or containing silver

ARGENTIC adj of or containing silver in the divalent or trivalent state

ARGENTS ▸ argent

ARGENTUM an obsolete name for ▸ silver

ARGH interj cry of pain

ARGHAN, -S n agave plant

ARGIL, -S n clay, esp potters' clay

ARGINASE n type of enzyme

ARGININE n essential amino acid

ARGLE, -D, -S, ARGLING vb quarrel

ARGOL, -S n chemical compound

ARGON, -S n inert gas found in the air

ARGONAUT n paper nautilus

ARGONON, -S n inert gas

ARGONS ▸ argon

ARGOSY, ARGOSIES n large merchant ship

ARGOT, -S n slang or jargon

ARGOTIC ▸ argot

ARGOTS ▸ argot

ARGUABLE adj capable of being disputed

ARGUABLY adv it can be argued that

ARGUE, -D, -S, ARGUING vb try to prove by giving reasons

ARGUER, -S ▸ argue

ARGUES ▸ argue

ARGUFIED ▸ argufy

ARGUFIER ▸ argufy

ARGUFY, ARGUFIED, ARGUFIES vb argue or quarrel, esp over something trivial

ARGUING ▸ argue

ARGULUS, ARGULI n parasite on fish

ARGUMENT n quarrel

ARGUS, -ES n any of various brown butterflies

ARGUTE adj shrill or keen

ARGUTELY ▸ argute

ARGYLE, -S adj with a diamond-shaped pattern ▹ n sock with this pattern

ARGYLL, -S n sock with diamond pattern

ARGYRIA, -S n staining of skin by exposure to silver

ARGYRITE n mineral containing silver sulphide

ARHAT, -S n Buddhist who has achieved enlightenment

ARIA, -S n elaborate song for solo voice, esp one from an opera

ARIARY, ARIARIES n currency of Madagascar

ARIAS ▸ aria

ARID, -ER, -EST adj parched, dry

ARIDITY ▸ arid

ARIDLY ▸ arid

ARIDNESS ▸ arid

ARIEL, -S n type of Arabian gazelle

ARIETTA, -S n short aria

ARIETTE, -S same as ▸ arietta

ARIGHT adv rightly

ARIKI, -S n Polynesian chief

ARIL, -S n appendage on certain seeds

ARILED adj having an aril

ARILLARY adj having an aril

ARILLATE ▸ arillated

ARILLI ▸ arillus

ARILLODE n structure in certain seeds

ARILLOID adj of or like an aril

ARILLUS, ARILLI n aril

ARILS ▸ aril

ARIOSE adj songlike

ARIOSO, ARIOSI, -S n recitative with the lyrical quality of an aria

ARIOT adv riotously

ARIPPLE adv in ripples

ARISE, -N, -S, ARISING, AROSE vb come about

ARISH, -ES n field that has been mown

ARISING ▸ arise

ARISTA, -E, -S n stiff bristle

ARISTATE ▸ arista

ARISTO, -S n aristocrat

ARK, -ED, -ING, -S n boat built by Noah, which survived the Flood ▹ vb place in an ark

ARKITE, -S n passenger in ark

ARKOSE, -S n type of sandstone

ARKOSIC ▸ arkose

ARKS ▸ ark

ARLE, -D, -S, ARLING vb make a down payment

ARM, -S n limbs from the shoulder to the wrist ▹ vb supply with weapons

ARMADA, -S n large number of warships

ARMAGNAC n dry brown brandy

ARMAMENT n military weapons

ARMATURE n revolving structure in an electric motor or generator

ARMBAND, -S n band worn on the arm

ARMCHAIR n upholstered chair with side supports for the arms ▷ adj taking no active part

ARMED adj equipped with or supported by arms, armour, etc

ARMER, -S ▷ arm

ARMERIA, -S n generic name for the plant thrift

ARMERS ▷ armer

ARMET, -S n close-fitting medieval visored helmet with a neck guard

ARMFUL, -S, ARMSFUL n as much as can be held in the arms

ARMGAUNT adj word in Shakespeare of uncertain meaning

ARMGUARD n covering to protect the arm

ARMHOLE, -S n opening in a garment through which the arm passes

ARMIES ▷ army

ARMIGER, -S n person entitled to bear heraldic arms

ARMIGERO n armiger

ARMIGERS ▷ armiger

ARMIL, -S n bracelet

ARMILLA, -E, -S n bracelet

ARMILS ▷ armil

ARMING, -S n act of taking arms or providing with arms

ARMLESS ▷ arm

ARMLET, -S n band worn round the arm

ARMLIKE ▷ arm

ARMLOAD, -S n amount carried in the arms

ARMLOCK, -S vb grip someone's arm

ARMOIRE, -S n large cabinet

ARMONICA n glass harmonica

ARMOR, -ING, -S same as ▷ armour

ARMORED same as ▷ armoured

ARMORER, -S same as ▷ armourer

ARMORIAL adj of or relating to heraldry or heraldic arms ▷ n book of coats of arms

ARMORIES ▷ armory

ARMORING ▷ armor

ARMORIST n heraldry expert

ARMORS ▷ armor

ARMORY, ARMORIES same as ▷ armoury

ARMOUR, -S n metal clothing formerly worn to protect the body in battle

▷ vb equip or cover with armour

ARMOURED adj having a protective covering

ARMOURER n maker, repairer, or keeper of arms or armour

ARMOURS ▷ armour

ARMOURY n place where weapons are stored

ARMOZEEN n material used for clerical gowns

ARMOZINE n material used for clerical gowns

ARMPIT, -S n hollow under the arm at the shoulder

ARMREST, -S n part of a chair or sofa that supports the arm

ARMS ▷ arm

ARMSFUL ▷ armful

ARMURE, -S n silk or wool fabric with a small cobbled pattern

ARMY, ARMIES n military land forces of a nation

ARMYWORM n caterpillar of a widely distributed noctuid moth

ARNA, -S n Indian water buffalo

ARNATTO, -S n annatto

ARNICA, -S n temperate or Arctic plant

ARNOTTO, -S n annatto

ARNUT, -S n plant with edible tubers

AROBA, -S n Asian carriage

AROHA, -S n love, compassion, or affection

AROID, -S n type of plant

AROINT, -ED, -S vb drive away

AROLLA, -S n European pine tree

AROMA, -S n pleasant smell

AROMATIC adj having a distinctive pleasant smell ▷ n something, such as a plant or drug, that gives off a fragrant smell

AROSE ▷ arise

AROUND adv on all sides (of)

AROUSAL, -S ▷ arouse

AROUSE, -D, -S, AROUSING vb stimulate, make active

AROUSER, -S ▷ arouse

AROUSES ▷ arouse

AROUSING ▷ arouse

AROW adv in a row

AROWANA, -S n tropical freshwater fish

AROYNT, -ED, -S vb old word meaning to drive away

ARPA, -S n website concerned with structure of the internet

ARPEGGIO n notes of a chord played or sung in quick succession

ARPEN, -S n former French unit of length

ARPENT, -S n former French unit of length

ARQUEBUS n portable long-barrelled gun dating from the 15th century

ARRACK, -S n alcoholic drink distilled from grain or rice

ARRAH interj Irish exclamation

ARRAIGN, -S vb bring (a prisoner) before a court to answer a charge

ARRANGE, -D, -S vb plan

ARRANGER ▷ arrange

ARRANGES ▷ arrange

ARRANT adj utter, downright

ARRANTLY ▷ arrant

ARRAS, -ES n tapestry wall-hanging

ARRASED adj having an arras

ARRASENE n material used in embroidery

ARRASES ▷ arras

ARRAUGHT ▷ areach

ARRAY, -ED, -ING, -S n impressive display or collection ▷ vb arrange in order

ARRAYAL, -S ▷ array

ARRAYED ▷ array

ARRAYER, -S ▷ array

ARRAYING ▷ array

ARRAYS ▷ array

ARREAR n singular of arrears

ARREARS pl n money owed

ARRECT adj pricked up

ARREEDE, -S vb old word meaning declare

ARREST, -ED, -S vb take (a person) into custody ▷ n act of taking a person into custody

ARRESTEE n arrested person

ARRESTER n person who arrests

ARRESTOR n person or thing that arrests

ARRESTS ▷ arrest

ARRET, -S n judicial decision

ARRHIZAL adj without roots

ARRIAGE, -S n Scottish feudal service

ARRIBA interj exclamation of pleasure or approval

ARRIDE, -D, -S, ARRIDING vb old word meaning gratify

A

ARRIERE adj French word meaning old-fashioned

ARRIERO, -S n mule driver

ARRIS, -ES n sharp edge at the meeting of two surfaces

ARRISH, -ES n corn stubble

ARRIVAL, -S n arriving

ARRIVE, -D, -S, ARRIVING vb reach a place or destination

ARRIVER, -S ▸ **arrive**

ARRIVES ▸ **arrive**

ARRIVING ▸ **arrive**

ARROBA, -S n unit of weight in Spanish-speaking countries

ARROCES ▸ **arroz**

ARROGANT adj proud and overbearing

ARROGATE vb claim or seize without justification

ARROW, -ING, -S n pointed shaft shot from a bow

ARROWED adj having an arrow pattern

ARROWIER ▸ **arrowy**

ARROWING ▸ **arrow**

ARROWS ▸ **arrow**

ARROWY, ARROWIER adj like an arrow

ARROYO, -S n usually dry stream bed

ARROZ, ARROCES, -ES n Spanish word for rice, used in name of various dishes

ARS ▸ **ar**

ARSENAL, -S n place where arms and ammunition are made or stored

ARSENATE n salt or ester of arsenic acid

ARSENIC, -S n toxic grey element ▹ adj of or containing arsenic

ARSENIDE n compound in which arsenic is the most electronegative element

ARSENITE n salt or ester of arsenous acid

ARSENO adj containing arsenic

ARSENOUS same as ▸ **arsenious**

ARSES ▸ **arsis**

ARSHEEN, -S n old measure of length in Russia

ARSHIN, -S n old measure of length in Russia

ARSHINE, -S n old measure of length in Russia

ARSHINS ▸ **arshin**

ARSINE, -S n colourless poisonous gas

ARSINO adj containing arsine

ARSIS, ARSES n long or stressed syllable in a metrical foot

ARSON, -S n crime of intentionally setting property on fire

ARSONIST ▸ **arson**

ARSONITE n person committing arson

ARSONOUS adj of arson

ARSONS ▸ **arson**

ART, -S n creation of works of beauty, esp paintings or sculpture

ARTAL a plural of ▸ **roti**

ARTEFACT n something made by human beings

ARTEL, -S n cooperative union

ARTERIAL adj of an artery ▹ n major road

ARTERY, ARTERIES n one of the tubes carrying blood from the heart

ARTESIAN adj as in **artesian well** sunken well receiving water from a higher altitude

ARTFUL adj cunning, wily

ARTFULLY ▸ **artful**

ARTHOUSE n cinema which shows artistic films

ARTI, -S n Hindu ritual performed in homes and temples

ARTIC, -S n articulated vehicle

ARTICLE, -D, -S n written piece in a magazine or newspaper ▹ vb bind by a written contract

ARTICS ▸ **artic**

ARTIER ▸ **arty**

ARTIES ▸ **arty**

ARTIEST ▸ **arty**

ARTIFACT same as ▸ **artefact**

ARTIFICE n clever trick

ARTIGI, -S n kind of hooded coat worn in Canada

ARTILY ▸ **arty**

ARTINESS ▸ **arty**

ARTIS ▸ **arti**

ARTISAN, -S n skilled worker, craftsman or craftswoman

ARTIST, -S n person who produces works of art, esp paintings or sculpture

ARTISTE, -S n professional entertainer such as a singer or dancer

ARTISTIC adj of or characteristic of art or artists

ARTISTRY n artistic skill

ARTISTS ▸ **artist**

ARTLESS adj free from deceit or cunning

ARTMAKER n person who creates art

ARTS ▸ **art**

ARTSIE n arts student

ARTSIER ▸ **artsy**

ARTSIES ▸ **artsy**

ARTSIEST ▸ **artsy**

ARTSMAN, ARTSMEN old word for ▸ **craftsman**

ARTSY, ARTSIER, ARTSIES, ARTSIEST adj interested in the arts ▹ n person interested in the arts

ARTWORK, -S n all the photographs and illustrations in a publication

ARTY, ARTIER, ARTIES, ARTIEST adj having an affected interest in art ▹ n person interested in art

ARUANA, -S n tropical freshwater fish

ARUGOLA, -S same as ▸ **arugula**

ARUGULA, -S n salad plant

ARUHE, -S n edible root of a fern

ARUM, -S n type of plant

ARUSPEX variant spelling of ▸ **haruspex**

ARVAL adj of ploughed land

ARVEE, -S n short for recreational vehicle (RV)

ARVICOLE n water rat

ARVO, -S n afternoon

ARY dialect form of ▸ **any**

ARYL, -S n (in chemistry) an aromatic group

ARYTHMIA n any variation

ARYTHMIC ▸ **arythmia**

AS, -AR adv used to indicate amount or extent in comparisons ▹ n ancient Roman unit of weight

ASANA, -S n any of various postures in yoga

ASAR ▸ **as**

ASARUM, -S n dried strong-scented root

ASBESTIC ▸ **asbestos**

ASBESTOS n fibrous mineral which does not burn

ASBESTUS n asbestos

ASCARED adj afraid

ASCARID, -S n type of parasitic nematode

ASCARIS n ascarid

ASCAUNT adv old word meaning slantwise

ASCEND, -ED, -S vb go or move up

ASCENDER n part of some lower-case letters that extends above the body of the letter

ASCENDS ▸ **ascend**

ASCENT, -S n act of ascending

ASCESIS, ASCESES n exercise of self-discipline

ASCETIC, -S adj abstaining from worldly pleasures and comforts ▷ n person who abstains from worldly comforts and pleasures

ASCI ▸ ascus

ASCIAN, -S n person living in the tropics

ASCIDIA ▸ ascidium

ASCIDIAN n type of minute marine invertebrate, such as the sea squirt

ASCIDIUM, ASCIDIA n part of a plant that is shaped like a pitcher

ASCITES n accumulation of serous fluid in the peritoneal cavity

ASCITIC ▸ ascites

ASCOCARP n (in some ascomycetous fungi) a globular structure containing the asci

ASCON, -S n type of sponge having an oval shape and a thin body wall

ASCONCE adv old form of askance

ASCONOID adj like an ascon

ASCONS ▸ ascon

ASCORBIC adj as in ascorbic acid vitamin present in citrus fruits, tomatoes, and green vegetables

ASCOT, -S n type of cravat

ASCRIBE, -D, -S vb attribute, as to a particular origin

ASCUS, ASCI n saclike structure in fungi

ASDIC, -S n early form of sonar

ASEA adv towards the sea

ASEISMIC adj denoting a region free of earthquakes

ASEITY, ASEITIES n existence derived from itself, having no other source

ASEPSIS, ASEPSES n aseptic condition

ASEPTATE adj not divided into cells or sections by septa

ASEPTIC, -S adj free from harmful bacteria ▷ n aseptic substance

ASEXUAL adj without biological sex

ASH, -ED, -ES, -ING n powdery substance left when something is burnt ▷ vb reduce to ashes

ASHAKE adv shaking

ASHAME, -S, ASHAMING vb make ashamed

ASHAMED adj feeling shame

ASHAMES ▸ ashame

ASHAMING ▸ ashame

ASHCAKE, -S n cornmeal bread

ASHCAN, -S n large metal dustbin

ASHED ▸ ash

ASHEN adj pale with shock

ASHERY, ASHERIES n place where ashes are made

ASHES ▸ ash

ASHET, -S n shallow oval dish or large plate

ASHFALL, -S n dropping of ash from a volcano

ASHIER ▸ ashy

ASHIEST ▸ ashy

ASHINE adv old word meaning shining

ASHINESS ▸ ashy

ASHING ▸ ash

ASHIVER adv shivering

ASHKEY, -S n winged fruit of the ash

ASHLAR, -ED, -S n block of hewn stone ▷ vb build with ashlars

ASHLER, -ED, -S same as ▸ ashlar

ASHLESS ▸ ash

ASHMAN, ASHMEN n man who shovels ashes

ASHORE adv towards or on land ▷ adj on land, having come from the water

ASHPAN, -S n pan or tray to catch ashes

ASHPLANT n walking stick made from an ash sapling

ASHRAF pl n descendants of Muhammad

ASHRAM, -S n religious retreat where a Hindu holy man lives

ASHRAMA, -S n stage in Hindu spiritual life

ASHRAMS ▸ ashram

ASHTANGA n type of yoga

ASHTRAY, -S n receptacle for tobacco ash and cigarette butts

ASHY, ASHIER, ASHIEST adj pale greyish

ASIAGO, -S n type of cheese

ASIDE, -S adv one side ▷ n remark not meant to be heard by everyone present

ASINICO, -S n old Spanish word for fool

ASININE adj stupid, idiotic

ASK, -ED, -S vb say (something) in a form that requires an answer

ASKANCE, -D, -S adv with an oblique glance ▷ vb turn aside

ASKANT, -ED, -S same as ▸ askance

ASKARI, -S n (in East Africa) a soldier or police officer

ASKED ▸ ask

ASKER, -S ▸ ask

ASKESIS, ASKESES n practice of self-discipline

ASKEW adj one side, crooked

ASKING, -S ▸ ask

ASKLENT Scots word for ▸ aslant

ASKOS, ASKOI n ancient Greek vase

ASKS ▸ ask

ASLAKE, -D, -S, ASLAKING vb slake

ASLANT adv at a slant (to), slanting (across)

ASLEEP adj sleeping

ASLOPE adj sloping

ASLOSH adj awash

ASMEAR adj smeared

ASOCIAL, -S n person who avoids social contact

ASP, -S n small poisonous snake

ASPARKLE adv sparkling

ASPARTIC adj as in aspartic acid nonessential amino acid that is a component of proteins

ASPECT, -ED, -S n feature or element ▷ vb look at

ASPEN, -S n kind of poplar tree ▷ adj trembling

ASPER, -S n former Turkish monetary unit

ASPERATE adj (of plant parts) having a rough surface due to a covering of short stiff hairs ▷ vb make rough

ASPERGE, -D, -S vb sprinkle

ASPERGER ▸ asperge

ASPERGES ▸ asperge

ASPERITY n roughness of temper

ASPEROUS same as ▸ asperate

ASPERS ▸ asper

ASPERSE, -D, -S vb spread false rumours about

ASPERSER ▸ asperse

ASPERSES ▸ asperse

ASPERSOR ▸ asperse

ASPHALT, -S n black hard tar-like substance used for road surfaces etc ▷ vb cover with asphalt

ASPHERIC adj not spherical ▷ n lens that is not completely spherical

ASPHODEL n plant with clusters of yellow or white flowers

A

ASPHYXIA n suffocation

ASPHYXY vb smother, suffocate

ASPIC, -S n savoury jelly used to coat meat, eggs, fish, etc

ASPICK, -S old word for ▸ asp

ASPICS ▸ aspic

ASPIDIUM, ASPIDIA n variety of fern

ASPINE, -S old word for ▸ aspen

ASPIRANT n person who aspires ▷ adj aspiring or striving

ASPIRATA n rough stop

ASPIRATE vb pronounce with an h sound ▷ n h sound ▷ adj (of a stop) pronounced with a forceful and audible expulsion of breath

ASPIRE, -D, -S vb yearn (for), hope (to do or be)

ASPIRER, -S ▸ aspire

ASPIRES ▸ aspire

ASPIRIN, -S n drug used to relieve pain and fever

ASPIRING ▸ aspire

ASPIRINS ▸ aspirin

ASPIS, -ES n horned viper

ASPISH adj like an asp

ASPORT, -ED, -S vb old word meaning take away

ASPOUT adv spouting

ASPRAWL adv sprawling

ASPREAD adv spreading

ASPRO, -S n associate professor at an academic institution

ASPROUT adv sprouting

ASPS ▸ asp

ASQUAT adv squatting

ASQUINT adj with a glance from the corner of the eye

ASRAMA, -S n stage in Hindu spiritual life

ASS, -ES n donkey

ASSAGAI, -S same as ▸ assegai

ASSAI, -S adv (usually preceded by a musical direction) very ▷ n Brazilian palm tree

ASSAIL, -ED, -S vb attack violently

ASSAILER ▸ assail

ASSAILS ▸ assail

ASSAIS ▸ assai

ASSAM, -S n (in Malaysia) tamarind as used in cooking

ASSART, -ED, -S vb clear ground for cultivation

ASSASSIN n person who murders a prominent person

ASSAULT, -S n violent attack ▷ vb attack violently

ASSAY, -ED, -S n analysis of a substance ▷ vb make such an analysis

ASSAYER, -S ▸ assay

ASSAYING ▸ assay

ASSAYS ▸ assay

ASSEGAAI same as ▸ assegai

ASSEGAI, -S n slender spear used in S Africa ▷ vb spear with an assegai

ASSEMBLE vb collect or congregate

ASSEMBLY n assembled group

ASSENT, -ED, -S n agreement or consent ▷ vb agree or consent

ASSENTER n person supporting another's nomination

ASSENTOR n voter legally required to endorse the nomination of a candidate

ASSENTS ▸ assent

ASSERT, -ED, -S vb declare forcefully

ASSERTER ▸ assert

ASSERTOR ▸ assert

ASSERTS ▸ assert

ASSES ▸ ass

ASSESS, -ED, -ES vb judge the worth or importance of

ASSESSOR n person who values property for taxation or insurance purposes

ASSET, -S n valuable or useful person or thing

ASSEVER, -S vb old form of asseverate

ASSEZ adv (as part of a musical direction) fairly

ASSIEGE, -D, -S vb old form of besiege

ASSIENTO n former slave trade treaty between Britain and Spain

ASSIGN, -ED, -S vb appoint (someone) to a job or task ▷ n person to whom property is assigned

ASSIGNAT n paper money issued in France by the Constituent Assembly in 1789

ASSIGNED ▸ assign

ASSIGNEE n person to whom some right, interest, or property is transferred

ASSIGNER ▸ assign

ASSIGNOR n person who transfers or assigns property

ASSIGNS ▸ assign

ASSIST, -ED, -S vb give help or support ▷ n pass by a player which enables another player to score a goal

ASSISTER ▸ assist

ASSISTOR ▸ assist

ASSISTS ▸ assist

ASSIZE, -D, -S, ASSIZING n sitting of a legislative assembly ▷ vb judge or assess

ASSIZER, -S n weights and measures official

ASSIZES ▸ assize

ASSIZING ▸ assize

ASSLIKE ▸ ass

ASSOIL, -ED, -S vb absolve

ASSONANT > assonance

ASSONATE vb show assonance

ASSORT, -S vb arrange or distribute equally

ASSORTED adj consisting of various types mixed together

ASSORTER ▸ assort

ASSORTS ▸ assort

ASSOT, -S, -TED vb old word meaning make infatuated

ASSOTT adj besotted

ASSOTTED ▸ assot

ASSUAGE, -D, -S vb relieve (pain, grief, thirst, etc)

ASSUAGER ▸ assuage

ASSUAGES ▸ assuage

ASSUME, -S vb take to be true without proof

ASSUMED adj false

ASSUMER, -S ▸ assume

ASSUMES ▸ assume

ASSUMING adj expecting too much ▷ n action of one who assumes

ASSURE, -S, ASSURING vb promise or guarantee

ASSURED, -S adj confident ▷ n beneficiary under a life assurance policy

ASSURER, -S ▸ assure

ASSURES ▸ assure

ASSURING ▸ assure

ASSUROR, -S ▸ assure

ASSWAGE, -D, -S old spelling of ▸ assuage

ASTABLE adj not stable

ASTANGA, -S same as ▸ ashtanga

ASTARE adv staring

ASTART, -ED, -S old word for ▸ start

ASTASIA, -S n inability to stand

ASTATIC adj not static

ASTATIDE n binary compound of astatine with a more electropositive element

ASTATINE n radioactive nonmetallic element

ASTATKI, -S n fuel derived from petroleum

ASTEISM, -S n use of irony

A

ASTELIC ▸ astely
ASTELY, ASTELIES n lack of central cylinder in plants
ASTER, -S n plant with daisy-like flowers
ASTERIA, -S n gemstone with starlike light effect
ASTERID, -S n variety of flowering plant
ASTERISK n star-shaped symbol (*) used in printing or writing to indicate a footnote, etc ▹ vb mark with an asterisk
ASTERISM n three asterisks arranged in a triangle to draw attention to the text that follows
ASTERN adv at or towards the stern of a ship ▹ adj at or towards the stern of a ship
ASTERNAL adj not connected or joined to the sternum
ASTEROID n any of the small planets that orbit the sun between Mars and Jupiter ▹ adj of, relating to, or belonging to the class Asteroidea

Be especially aware of this word because its combination of common letters makes it one of the most often played 8-letter bonus words.

ASTERS ▸ aster
ASTERT, -ED, -S vb start
ASTHANGA n type of yoga
ASTHENIA n abnormal loss of strength
ASTHENIC adj of, relating to, or having asthenia ▹ n person having long limbs and a small trunk
ASTHENY same as ▸ asthenia
ASTHMA, -S n illness causing difficulty in breathing
ASTHORE, -S n Irish endearment
ASTIGMIA n defect of a lens resulting in the formation of distorted images
ASTILBE, -S n type of plant
ASTIR adj out of bed
ASTOMOUS adj having no mouth
ASTONE, -D, -S, ASTONING old form of ▸ astonish
ASTONIED adj stunned
ASTONIES ▸ astony
ASTONING ▸ astone
ASTONISH vb surprise greatly

ASTONY, ASTONIES old form of ▸ astonish
ASTOOP adv stooping
ASTOUND, -S vb overwhelm with amazement
ASTRAGAL n small convex moulding, usually with a semicircular cross section
ASTRAL, -S adj of stars ▹ n oil lamp
ASTRALLY ▸ astral
ASTRALS ▸ astral
ASTRAND adv on the shore
ASTRAY adv off the right path
ASTRICT, -S vb bind, confine, or constrict
ASTRIDE adv with a leg on either side (of) ▹ adj with a leg on either side
ASTRINGE vb cause contraction
ASTROID, -S n hypocycloid having four cusps
ASTRUT adv old word meaning in a protruding way
ASTUCITY n quality of being astute
ASTUN, -NED, -S vb old form of astonish
ASTUTE, -R, -ST adj perceptive or shrewd
ASTUTELY ▸ astute
ASTUTER ▸ astute
ASTUTEST ▸ astute
ASTYLAR adj without columns or pilasters
ASUDDEN adv old form of suddenly
ASUNDER adv into parts or pieces ▹ adj into parts or pieces
ASURA, -S n demon in Hindu mythology
ASWARM adj filled, esp with moving things
ASWAY adv swaying
ASWIM adv floating
ASWING adv swinging
ASWIRL adv swirling
ASWOON adv swooning
ASYLA ▸ asylum
ASYLEE, -S n person who is granted asylum
ASYLUM, ASYLA, -S n refuge or sanctuary
ASYNDETA ▸ asyndeton
ASYNERGY same as > asynergia
ASYSTOLE n absence of heartbeat
AT, -S n Laotian monetary unit worth one hundredth of a kip
ATAATA, -S n grazing marine gastropod

ATABAL, -S n N African drum
ATABEG, -S n Turkish ruler
ATABEK, -S same as ▸ atabeg
ATABRIN, -S n drug formerly used for treating malaria
ATABRINE same as ▸ atabrin
ATABRINS ▸ atabrin
ATACTIC adj attribute of a polymer
ATAGHAN, -S variant of ▸ yataghan
ATALAYA, -S n watchtower in Spain
ATAMAN, -S n elected leader of the Cossacks
ATAMASCO n N American lily
ATAP, -S n palm tree of S Asia
ATARAXIA n calmness or peace of mind
ATARAXIC same as > ataractic
ATARAXY same as ▸ ataraxia
ATAVIC ▸ atavism
ATAVISM, -S n recurrence of a trait present in distant ancestors
ATAVIST, -S ▸ atavism
ATAXIA, -S n lack of muscular coordination
ATAXIC, -S ▸ ataxia
ATAXY, ATAXIES same as ▸ ataxia
ATCHIEVE same as ▸ achieve
ATE ▸ eat
ATEBRIN, -S n drug formerly used to treat malaria
ATECHNIC adj without technical ability ▹ n person with no technical ability
ATELIC adj of action without end
ATELIER, -S n workshop, artist's studio
ATEMOYA, -S n tropical fruit tree
ATENOLOL n type of beta-blocker
ATES n shop selling confectionery
ATHAME, -S n witch's ceremonial knife
ATHANASY n absence of death
ATHANOR, -S n alchemist's furnace
ATHEISE, -D, -S vb speak atheistically
ATHEISM, -S n belief that there is no God
ATHEIST, -S ▸ atheism
ATHEIZE, -D, -S vb speak atheistically
ATHELING n (in Anglo-Saxon England) a prince of any of the royal dynasties

A

ATHENEUM same as
> **athenaeum**

ATHEOUS adj without a
belief in god

ATHERINE n small fish

ATHEROMA n fatty deposit
on or within an artery

ATHETISE vb reject as not
genuine

ATHETIZE vb reject as not
genuine

ATHETOID > **athetosis**

ATHIRST adj having an eager
desire

ATHLETA, -S same as
> **athlete**

ATHLETE, -S n person
trained in or good at athletics

ATHLETIC adj physically fit
or strong

ATHODYD, -S another name
for > **ramjet**

ATHRILL adv feeling thrills

ATHROB adv throbbing

ATHWART adv transversely

ATIGI, -S n type of parka
worn by the Inuit in Canada

ATILT adj in a tilted or
inclined position

ATIMY, ATIMIES n loss of
honour

ATINGLE adv tingling

ATISHOO, -S n sound of a
sneeze

ATLAS, ATLANTES, -ES n
book of maps

ATLATL, -S n Native
American throwing stick

ATMA, -S same as > **atman**

ATMAN, -S n personal soul
or self

ATMAS > **atma**

ATMOLOGY n study of
aqueous vapour

ATMOLYSE vb separate
gases by filtering

ATMOLYZE vb separate
gases by filtering

ATMOS, -ES n (short for)
atmosphere

ATOC, -S n skunk

ATOCIA, -S n inability to
have children

ATOCS > **atoc**

ATOK, -S n skunk

ATOKAL adj having no
children

ATOKE, -S n part of a worm

ATOKOUS adj having no
children

ATOKS > **atok**

ATOLL, -S n ring-shaped
coral reef enclosing a lagoon

ATOM, -S n smallest unit of
matter which can take part
in a chemical reaction

ATOMIC adj of or using
atomic bombs or atomic
energy

ATOMICAL > **atomic**

ATOMICS n science of atoms

ATOMIES > **atomy**

ATOMISE, -D, -S same as
> **atomize**

ATOMISER same as
> **atomizer**

ATOMISES > **atomise**

ATOMISM, -S n ancient
philosophical theory

ATOMIST, -S > **atomism**

ATOMIZE, -D, -S vb reduce
to atoms or small particles

ATOMIZER n device for
discharging a liquid in a fine
spray

ATOMIZES > **atomize**

ATOMS > **atom**

ATOMY, ATOMIES n atom
or minute particle

ATONABLE > **atone**

ATONAL adj (of music) not
written in an established key

ATONALLY > **atonal**

ATONE, -D, -S, ATONING vb
make amends (for sin or
wrongdoing)

ATONER, -S > **atone**

ATONES > **atone**

ATONIA, -S n lack of normal
muscle tone

ATONIC, -S adj carrying no
stress ▷ n unaccented or
unstressed syllable

ATONIES > **atony**

The plural of **atony**, this is
another of the most
frequently played 7-letter
bonus words that it is
essential to know.

ATONING > **atone**

ATONY, ATONIES n lack of
normal tone or tension, as in
muscles

ATOP adv on top

ATOPIC adj of or relating to
hypersensitivity to certain
allergens

ATOPY, ATOPIES n tendency
to be hypersensitive to
certain allergens

ATRAMENT n old word
meaning black liquid

ATRAZINE n white
crystalline compound

ATREMBLE adv trembling

ATRESIA, -S n absence of or
unnatural narrowing of a
body channel

ATRESIC > **atresia**

ATRETIC > **atresia**

ATRIA > **atrium**

ATRIAL > **atrium**

ATRIP adj (of an anchor) no
longer caught at the
bottom

ATRIUM, ATRIA, -S n upper
chamber of either half of the
heart

ATROCITY n wickedness

ATROPHIA n wasting
disease

ATROPHIC > **atrophy**

ATROPHY n wasting away
of an organ or part ▷ vb
(cause to) waste away

ATROPIA, -S same as
> **atropine**

ATROPIN, -S same as
> **atropine**

ATROPINE n poisonous
alkaloid obtained from
deadly nightshade

ATROPINS > **atropin**

ATROPISM n condition
caused by using belladonna

ATROPOUS adj growing
straight

ATS > **at**

ATT n old Siamese coin

ATTABOY, -S sentence
substitute expression of
approval or exhortation

ATTACH, -ES vb join, fasten,
or connect

ATTACHE n specialist
attached to a diplomatic
mission

ATTACHED adj fond of

ATTACHER > **attach**

ATTACHES > **attach**

ATTACK, -ED, -S vb launch a
physical assault (against)
▷ n act of attacking

ATTACKER > **attack**

ATTACKS > **attack**

ATTAGIRL humorous feminine
version of > **attaboy**

ATTAIN, -ED, -S vb achieve
or accomplish (a task or aim)

ATTAINER > **attain**

ATTAINS > **attain**

ATTAINT, -S vb pass
judgment of death ▷ n
dishonour

ATTAP, -S n palm tree of
South Asia

ATTAR, -S n fragrant oil
made from roses

ATTASK, -ED, -S, -T old word
for > **criticize**

ATTEMPER vb modify by
blending

ATTEMPT, -S vb try, make an
effort ▷ n effort or endeavour

ATTEND, -ED, -S vb be
present at

ATTENDEE n person who is
present at a specified event

ATTENDER ▶ attend

ATTENDS ▶ attend

ATTENT, -S old word for > **attention**

ATTENTAT n attempt

ATTENTS ▶ attent

ATTERCOP n spider

ATTEST, -S vb affirm the truth of, be proof of

ATTESTED adj (of cattle) certified to be free from a disease, such as tuberculosis

ATTESTER ▶ attest

ATTESTOR ▶ attest

ATTESTS ▶ attest

ATTIC, -S n space or room within the roof of a house

ATTICISE same as ▶ **atticize**

ATTICISM n elegant, simple, and clear expression

ATTICIST ▶ atticism

ATTICIZE vb conform or adapt to the norms of Attica

ATTICS ▶ attic

ATTIRE, -D, -S n fine or formal clothes ▷ vb dress, esp in fine elegant clothes

ATTIRING ▶ attire

ATTITUDE n way of thinking and behaving

ATTONCE adv old word for at once

ATTONE, -D, -S, ATTONING vb old word meaning appease

ATTORN, -ED, -S vb acknowledge a new owner of land as one's landlord

ATTORNEY n person legally appointed to act for another

ATTORNS ▶ attorn

ATTRACT, -S vb arouse the interest or admiration of

ATTRAP, -S vb adorn

ATTRIST, -S vb old word meaning to sadden

ATTRIT, -S vb wear down or dispose of gradually

ATTRITE, -D, -S vb wear down

ATTRITS ▶ attrit

ATTUENT adj carrying out attuition

ATTUITE, -D, -S vb perceive by attuition

ATTUNE, -D, -S, ATTUNING vb adjust or accustom (a person or thing)

ATUA, -S n spirit or demon

ATWAIN adv old word meaning into two parts

ATWEEL Scots word for ▶ **well**

ATWEEN an archaic or Scots word for ▶ **between**

ATWITTER adv twittering

ATWIXT old word for ▶ **between**

ATYPIC adj not typical

ATYPICAL adj not typical

AUA, -S n yellow-eye mullet

This Māori word for a kind of mullet is very often played to balance a rack by getting rid of a surplus of vowels.

AUBADE, -S n song or poem greeting the dawn

AUBERGE, -S n inn or tavern

AUBRETIA same as > **aubrietia**

AUBRIETA same as > **aubrietia**

AUBURN, -S adj (of hair) reddish-brown ▷ n moderate reddish-brown colour

AUCEPS, -ES n old word for a person who catches hawks

AUCTION, -S n public sale in which articles are sold to the highest bidder ▷ vb sell by auction

AUCUBA, -S n Japanese laurel

AUDACITY > audacious

AUDAD, -S n wild African sheep

AUDIAL adj of sound

AUDIBLE, -D, -S adj loud enough to be heard ▷ n play called in American football by a quarterback ▷ vb call an audible in American football

AUDIBLY ▶ audible

AUDIENCE n group of spectators or listeners

AUDIENT, -S n person who hears

AUDILE, -S n person with a faculty for auditory imagery ▷ adj of or relating to such a person

AUDING, -S n practice of listening to try to understand

AUDIO, -S adj of sound or hearing ▷ n sound

AUDISM, -S n prejudice against deaf people

AUDIST, -S n person prejudiced against deaf people

AUDIT, -ED, -S n official examination of business accounts ▷ vb examine (business accounts) officially

AUDITEE, -S n one who is audited

AUDITING n act of auditing

AUDITION n test of a performer's ability for a particular role or job ▷ vb test or be tested in an audition

AUDITIVE n person who learns primarily by listening

AUDITOR, -S n person qualified to audit accounts

AUDITORY adj of or relating to hearing

AUDITS ▶ audit

AUE interj Māori exclamation

A Māori exclamation, so useful for getting rid of surplus vowels. But, unlike **aua**, it does not take an S.

AUF, -S old word for ▶ **oaf**

AUFGABE, -S n word used in psychology to mean task

AUFS ▶ auf

AUGEND, -S n number to which a number is added

AUGER, -S n tool for boring holes

AUGH interj expressing frustration

AUGHT, -S adv in any least part ▷ n less common word for nought

AUGITE, -S n black or greenish-black mineral

AUGITIC ▶ augite

AUGMENT, -S vb increase or enlarge ▷ n vowel prefix forming a past tense

AUGUR, -ED, -ING, -S vb be a sign of (future events) ▷ n religious official who interpreted omens

AUGURAL ▶ augur

AUGURED ▶ augur

AUGURER, -S old word for ▶ **augur**

AUGURIES ▶ augury

AUGURING ▶ augur

AUGURS ▶ augur

AUGURY, AUGURIES n foretelling of the future

AUGUST, -ER, -S adj dignified and imposing ▷ n auguste

AUGUSTE, -S n type of circus clown

AUGUSTER ▶ august

AUGUSTES ▶ auguste

AUGUSTLY ▶ august

AUGUSTS ▶ august

AUK, -S n sea bird with short wings

AUKLET, -S n type of small auk

AUKS ▶ auk

AULA, -S n hall

AULARIAN n Oxford University student belonging to a hall

AULAS ▶ aula

AULD, -ER, -EST a Scots word for ▶ **old**

AULIC adj relating to a royal court

AULNAGE, -S n measurement in ells

AULNAGER n inspector of cloth

AULNAGES ▶ aulnage

A

AULOS, AULOI n ancient Greek pipe

AUMAIL, -ED, -S old word for ▶ **enamel**

AUMBRY, AUMBRIES same as ▶ **ambry**

AUMIL, -S n manager in India

AUNE, -S n old French measure of length

AUNT, -S n father's or mother's sister

AUNTER, -S old word for > **adventure**

AUNTHOOD ▶ **aunt**

AUNTIE, -S n aunt

AUNTLIER ▶ **auntly**

AUNTLIKE ▶ **aunt**

AUNTLY, AUNTLIER adj of or like an aunt

AUNTS ▶ **aunt**

AUNTY same as ▶ **auntie**

AURA, -E, -S n distinctive air or quality of a person or thing

AURAL adj of or using the ears or hearing

AURALITY ▶ **aural**

AURALLY ▶ **aural**

AURAR plural of ▶ **eyrir**

AURAS ▶ **aura**

AURATE, -S n salt of auric acid

AURATED adj combined with auric acid

AURATES ▶ **aurate**

AUREATE adj covered with gold, gilded

AUREI ▶ **aureus**

AUREITY n attributes of gold

AURELIA, -S n large jellyfish

AURELIAN n person who studies butterflies and moths

AURELIAS ▶ **aurelia**

AUREOLA, -E, -S same as ▶ **aureole**

AUREOLE, -D, -S n halo ▷ vb encircle

AURES ▶ **auris**

AUREUS, AUREI n gold coin of the Roman Empire

AURIC adj of or containing gold in the trivalent state

AURICLE, -S n upper chamber of the heart

AURICLED ▶ **auricle**

AURICLES ▶ **auricle**

AURICULA n alpine primrose with leaves shaped like a bear's ear

AURIFIED ▶ **aurify**

AURIFIES ▶ **aurify**

AURIFORM adj shaped like an ear

AURIFY, AURIFIED, AURIFIES vb turn into gold

AURIS, AURES n medical word for ear

AURIST, -S n former name for an audiologist

AUROCHS n recently extinct European wild ox

AURORA, -E, -S n bands of light seen in the sky

AURORAL ▶ **aurora**

AURORAS ▶ **aurora**

AUROREAN adj of dawn

AUROUS adj of or containing gold, esp in the monovalent state

AURUM, -S n gold

AUSFORM, -S vb temper steel

AUSPEX same as ▶ **augur**

AUSPICE, -S n patronage or guidance

AUSTERE, -R adj stern or severe

AUSTRAL, -S adj southern ▷ n former monetary unit of Argentina

AUSUBO, -S n tropical tree

AUTACOID n any natural internal secretion, esp one that exerts an effect similar to a drug

AUTARCH, -S n absolute ruler

AUTARCHY n absolute power or autocracy

AUTARKIC ▶ **autarky**

AUTARKY n policy of economic self-sufficiency

AUTECISM > **autecious**

AUTEUR, -S n director

AUTHOR, -ED, -S n writer of a book etc ▷ vb write or originate

AUTISM, -S n developmental condition characterized by difficulties with social communication and interaction

AUTIST, -S n autistic person

AUTISTIC ▶ **autism**

AUTISTS ▶ **autist**

AUTO, -ED, -ING, -S n automobile ▷ vb travel in an automobile

AUTOBAHN n German motorway

AUTOBANK n automated teller machine

AUTOBODY n body of a motor vehicle

AUTOBUS n motor bus

AUTOCADE another name for > **motorcade**

AUTOCAR, -S n motor car

AUTOCARP n fruit produced through self-fertilization

AUTOCARS ▶ **autocar**

AUTOCOID n hormone

AUTOCRAT n ruler with absolute authority

AUTOCUE, -S n electronic television prompting device

AUTODIAL vb dial a telephone number automatically

AUTODYNE adj using the same elements and valves as oscillator and detector ▷ n autodyne circuit

AUTOED ▶ **auto**

AUTOGAMY n self-fertilization in flowering plants

AUTOGENY n hypothetical process by which living organisms first arose on earth from nonliving matter

AUTOGIRO n self-propelled aircraft resembling a helicopter but with an unpowered rotor

AUTOGYRO same as ▶ **autogiro**

AUTOHARP n zither-like musical instrument

AUTOING ▶ **auto**

AUTOLOAD vb load automatically

AUTOLOGY n study of oneself

AUTOLYSE vb undergo or cause to undergo autolysis

AUTOLYZE same as ▶ **autolyse**

AUTOMAN, AUTOMEN n car manufacturer

AUTOMAT, -S n vending machine

AUTOMATA > **automaton**

AUTOMATE vb make (a manufacturing process) automatic

AUTOMATS ▶ **automat**

AUTOMEN ▶ **automan**

AUTONOMY n self-government

AUTONYM, -S n writing published under the real name of an author

AUTOPEN, -S n mechanical device used to produce imitation signatures

AUTOPSIA n autopsy

AUTOPSIC ▶ **autopsy**

AUTOPSY n examination of a body to determine the cause of death

AUTOPTIC ▶ **autopsy**

AUTOPUT, -S n motorway in the former Yugoslavia

AUTOS ▶ **auto**

AUTOSAVE n computer facility for automatically

A

saving data ▷ vb save (computer data) automatically

AUTOSOME n type of chromosome

AUTOTEST n motor race in which standard cars are driven round a circuit

AUTOTOMY n casting off by an animal of a part of its body, to facilitate escape when attacked

AUTOTUNE n software that changes a recording of a vocal track

AUTOTYPE n photographic process for producing prints in black and white, using a carbon pigment ▷ vb process using autotype

AUTOTYPY ▶ autotype

AUTOVAC, -S n vacuum pump in a car petrol tank

AUTUMN, -S n season between summer and winter

AUTUMNAL adj of, occurring in, or characteristic of autumn

AUTUMNS ▶ autumn

AUTUMNY adj like autumn

AUTUNITE n yellowish fluorescent radioactive mineral

AUXESIS, AUXESES n increase in cell size without division

AUXETIC, -S n something that promotes growth

AUXILIAR old word for > auxiliary

AUXIN, -S n plant hormone that promotes growth

AUXINIC ▶ auxin

AUXINS ▶ auxin

AUXOCYTE n any cell undergoing meiosis

AVA, -S n Polynesian shrub

AVADAVAT n Asian weaverbird with usu red plumage, often kept as a cagebird

AVAIL, -ED, -ING, -S vb be of use or advantage (to) ▷ n use or advantage

AVAILE, -S old word for ▶ lower

AVAILED ▶ avail

AVAILES ▶ availe

AVAILFUL old word for ▶ useful

AVAILING ▶ avail

AVAILS ▶ avail

AVAL adj of a grandparent

AVALE, -D, -S, AVALING old word for ▶ lower

AVANT prep before

AVANTI interj forward!

AVANTIST n proponent of the avant-garde

AVARICE, -S n greed for wealth

AVAS ▶ ava

AVAST sentence substitute stop! cease!

AVATAR, -S n appearance of a god in animal or human form

AVAUNT, -ED, -S sentence substitute go away! depart! ▷ vb go away; depart

AVE, -S n expression of welcome or farewell

AVEL, -S variant of ▶ ovel

AVELLAN adj of hazelnuts

AVELLANE same as ▶ avellan

AVELS ▶ avel

AVENGE, -D, -S, AVENGING vb take revenge in retaliation for (harm done) or on behalf of (a person harmed)

AVENGER, -S ▶ avenge

AVENGES ▶ avenge

AVENGING ▶ avenge

AVENIR, -S n future

AVENS, -ES n any of several temperate or Arctic rosaceous plants

AVENTAIL n front flap of a helmet

AVENTRE, -D, -S old word for ▶ thrust

AVENTURE old form of > adventure

AVENUE, -S n wide street

AVER, -RED, -RING, -S vb state to be true

AVERAGE, -D, -S n typical or normal amount or quality ▷ adj usual or typical ▷ vb calculate the average of

AVERAGER n average adjuster

AVERAGES ▶ average

AVERMENT ▶ aver

AVERRED ▶ aver

AVERRING ▶ aver

AVERS ▶ aver

AVERSE adj disinclined or unwilling

AVERSELY ▶ averse

AVERSION n strong dislike

AVERSIVE n tool or technique intended to repel animals etc

AVERT, -ED, -ING, -S vb turn away

AVERTER, -S ▶ avert

AVERTING ▶ avert

AVERTS ▶ avert

AVES ▶ ave

AVGAS, -ES, -SES n aviation fuel

AVIAN, -S adj of or like a bird ▷ n bird

AVIANISE same as ▶ avianize

AVIANIZE vb modify microorganisms in a chicken embryo

AVIANS ▶ avian

AVIARIES ▶ aviary

AVIARIST n person who keeps an aviary

AVIARY, AVIARIES n large cage or enclosure for birds

AVIATE, -D, -S, AVIATING vb pilot or fly in an aircraft

AVIATIC adj pertaining to aviation

AVIATING ▶ aviate

AVIATION n art of flying aircraft

AVIATOR, -S n pilot of an aircraft

AVIATRIX ▶ aviator

AVICULAR adj of small birds

AVID, -ER, -EST adj keen or enthusiastic

AVIDIN, -S n protein found in egg white

AVIDITY n quality or state of being avid

AVIDLY ▶ avid

AVIDNESS ▶ avid

AVIETTE, -S n aeroplane driven by human strength

AVIFAUNA n all the birds in a particular region

AVIFORM adj like a bird

AVIGATOR another word for ▶ aviator

AVINE adj of birds

AVION, -S n aeroplane

AVIONIC ▶ avionics

AVIONICS n science and technology of electronics applied to aeronautics and astronautics

AVIONS ▶ avion

AVISE, -D, -S, AVISING old word for ▶ advise

AVISO, -S n boat carrying messages

AVITAL adj of a grandfather

AVIZE, -D, -S, AVIZING old word for ▶ advise

AVO, -S n Macao currency unit

AVOCADO, -S n pear-shaped tropical fruit with a leathery green skin and yellowish-green flesh

AVOCET, -S n long-legged wading bird

AVODIRE, -S n African tree

AVOID, -ED, -ING, -S vb prevent from happening

A

AVOIDANT adj (of behaviour) demonstrating a tendency to avoid intimacy or interaction with others
AVOIDED ▶ avoid
AVOIDER, -S ▶ avoid
AVOIDING ▶ avoid
AVOIDS ▶ avoid
AVOISION n nonpayment of tax
AVOS ▶ avo
AVOSET, -S n avocet
AVOUCH, -ED, -ES vb vouch for
AVOUCHER ▶ avouch
AVOUCHES ▶ avouch
AVOURE, -S old word for ▶ avowal
AVOW, -ING, -S vb state or affirm
AVOWABLE ▶ avow
AVOWABLY ▶ avow
AVOWAL, -S ▶ avow
AVOWED adj openly declared
AVOWEDLY ▶ avowed
AVOWER, -S ▶ avow
AVOWING ▶ avow
AVOWRY, AVOWRIES old word for ▶ avowal
AVOWS ▶ avow
AVOYER, -S n former Swiss magistrate
AVRUGA, -S n herring roe
AVULSE, -D, -S, AVULSING vb take away by force
AVULSION n forcible tearing away of a bodily structure or part
AVYZE, -D, -S, AVYZING old word for ▶ advise
AW variant of ▶ all
AWA adv Scots word for away
AWAIT, -ED, -ING, -S vb wait for
AWAITER, -S ▶ await
AWAITING ▶ await
AWAITS ▶ await
AWAKE, -D, -S, AWOKE, AWOKEN vb emerge or rouse from sleep ▷ adj not sleeping
AWAKEN, -ED, -S vb awake
AWAKENER ▶ awaken
AWAKENS ▶ awaken
AWAKES ▶ awake
AWAKING, -S n emergence from sleep
AWANTING adj missing
AWARD, -ED, -ING, -S vb give (something, such as a prize) formally ▷ n something awarded, such as a prize
AWARDEE, -S ▶ award
AWARDER, -S ▶ award

AWARDING ▶ award
AWARDS ▶ award
AWARE, -R, -ST adj having knowledge, informed
AWARN, -ED, -ING, -S vb old form of warn
AWASH adv washed over by water ▷ adj washed over by water
AWATCH adv watching
AWATO, -S n New Zealand caterpillar
AWAVE adv in waves
AWAY, -S adv from a place ▷ adj not present ▷ n game played or won at an opponent's ground
AWAYDAY, -S n day trip taken for pleasure
AWAYES old word for ▶ away
AWAYNESS ▶ away
AWAYS ▶ away
AWDL, -S n traditional Welsh poem
AWE, -D, -ING, -S, AWING n wonder and respect mixed with dread ▷ vb fill with awe
AWEARIED old word for ▶ weary
AWEARY old form of ▶ weary
AWEATHER adj towards the weather
AWED ▶ awe
AWEE adv Scots word meaning for a short time
AWEEL interj Scots word meaning well
AWEIGH adj (of an anchor) no longer hooked onto the bottom
AWEING ▶ awe
AWELESS ▶ awe
AWES ▶ awe
AWESOME adj inspiring awe
AWETO, -S n New Zealand caterpillar
AWFUL, -LER adj very bad or unpleasant ▷ adv very
AWFULLY adv in an unpleasant way
AWFY adv (Scots) awfully, extremely
AWHAPE, -D, -S, AWHAPING old word for ▶ amaze
AWHATO, -S n New Zealand caterpillar
AWHEEL adv on wheels
AWHEELS same as ▶ awheel
AWHETO, -S n New Zealand caterpillar
AWHILE adv for a brief time
AWHIRL adv whirling
AWING ▶ awe
AWK, -S n type of programming language

This provides a useful high-scoring outlet for what can be the awkward letters W and K.

AWKWARD adj clumsy or ungainly
AWL, -S n pointed tool for piercing wood, leather, etc
AWLBIRD, -S n woodpecker
AWLESS ▶ awe
AWLS ▶ awl
AWLWORT, -S n type of aquatic plant
AWMOUS Scots word for ▶ alms
AWMRIE, -S n cupboard for church vessels
AWMRY n cupboard for church vessels
AWN, -S n bristle on certain grasses
AWNED ▶ awn
AWNER, -S n machine for removing awns
AWNIER ▶ awny
AWNIEST ▶ awny
AWNING, -S n canvas roof supported by a frame to give protection against the weather
AWNINGED adj sheltered with an awning
AWNINGS ▶ awning
AWNLESS ▶ awn
AWNS ▶ awn
AWNY, AWNIER, AWNIEST adj having awns
AWOKE ▶ awake
AWOKEN ▶ awake
AWOL, -S n person who is absent without leave
AWORK adv old word meaning at work
AWRACK adv in wrecked condition
AWRONG adv old word meaning wrongly
AWRY adj with a twist to one side, askew
AWSOME adj old form of awesome
AX same as ▶ axe
AXAL adj of an axis
AXE, -D, AXING n tool with a sharp blade for felling trees or chopping wood ▷ vb dismiss (employees), restrict (expenditure), or terminate (a project)
AXEBIRD, -S n nightjar
AXED ▶ axe
AXEL, -S n ice-skating movement
AXELIKE adj like an axe in form
AXELS ▶ axel

AXEMAN, AXEMEN n man who wields an axe, esp to cut down trees

AXENIC adj (of a biological culture) free from other microorganisms

AXES ▸ axis

AXIAL adj forming or of an axis

AXIALITY ▸ axial

AXIALLY ▸ axial

AXIL, -S n angle where the stalk of a leaf joins a stem

AXILE adj of, relating to, or attached to the axis

AXILEMMA same as ▸ axolemma

AXILLA, -E, -S n area under a bird's wing

AXILLAR, -S same as ▸ axillary

AXILLARY adj of, relating to, or near the armpit ▷ n one of the feathers growing from the axilla of a bird's wing

AXILLAS ▸ axilla

AXILS ▸ axil

AXING ▸ axe

AXINITE, -S n crystalline substance

AXIOLOGY n theory of values, moral or aesthetic

AXIOM, -S n generally accepted principle

AXION, -S n type of hypothetical elementary particle

AXIS, AXES, -ES n imaginary line round which a body can rotate

AXISED adj having an axis

AXISES ▸ axis

AXITE, -S n type of gunpowder

AXLE, -S n shaft on which a wheel or pair of wheels turns

AXLED adj having an axle

AXLES ▸ axle

AXLETREE n bar fixed across the underpart of a wagon or carriage

AXLIKE ▸ ax

AXMAN, AXMEN same as ▸ axeman

AXOID, -S n type of curve

AXOLEMMA n membrane that encloses the axon of a nerve cell

AXOLOTL, -S n aquatic salamander of central America

AXON, -S n threadlike extension of a nerve cell

AXONAL ▸ axon

AXONE, -S same as ▸ axon

AXONEMAL ▸ axoneme

AXONEME, -S n part of a cell consisting of proteins

AXONES ▸ axone

AXONIC ▸ axon

AXONS ▸ axon

AXOPLASM n part of cell

AXSEED, -S n crown vetch

AY, -S adv ever ▷ n expression of agreement

AYAH, -S n Indian or Malay maidservant or nursemaid in former British Empire

AYAYA, -S n type of Inuit singing

AYE, -S n affirmative vote or voter ▷ adv always

AYELP adv yelping

AYENBITE old word for ▸ remorse

AYES ▸ aye

AYGRE old word for ▸ eager

AYIN, -S n 16th letter in the Hebrew alphabet

AYONT adv beyond

AYRE, -S old word for ▸ air

AYRIE, -S old word for ▸ eyrie

AYS ▸ ay

AYU, -S n small Japanese fish

> This comes up quite often, being an extension of both **ay** and **yu**, showing how important it is to know those little 'hook' words.

AYURVEDA n ancient medical treatise on the art of healing and prolonging life

AYUS ▸ ayu

AYWORD, -S n old word meaning byword

AZALEA, -S n garden shrub grown for its showy flowers

AZAN, -S n call to prayer

AZERTY n European version of keyboard

AZIDE, -S n type of chemical compound

AZIDO adj containing an azide

AZIMUTH, -S n arc of the sky between the zenith and the horizon

AZINE, -S n organic compound

AZIONE, -S n musical drama

AZLON, -S n fibre made from protein

AZO adj of the divalent group –N:N–

> **Azo** is a chemical term you will want to play often, but it does not take an S. It takes an N to form **azon**.

AZOIC adj without life

AZOLE, -S n organic compound

AZOLLA, -S n tropical water fern

AZON, -S n type of drawing paper

AZONAL adj not divided into zones

AZONIC adj not confined to a zone

AZONS ▸ azon

AZOTE, -S an obsolete name for ▸ nitrogen

AZOTED adj old word meaning combined with nitrogen

AZOTEMIA same as ▸ azotaemia

AZOTEMIC ▸ azotaemia

AZOTES ▸ azote

AZOTH, -S n panacea postulated by Paracelsus

AZOTIC adj of, containing, or concerned with nitrogen

AZOTISE, -D, -S same as ▸ azotize

AZOTIZE, -D, -S vb combine or treat with nitrogen or a nitrogen compound

AZOTOUS adj containing nitrogen

AZOTURIA n presence of excess nitrogen in urine

AZUKI, -S same as ▸ adzuki

AZULEJO, -S n Spanish porcelain tile

> An **azulejo** is a kind of brightly coloured tile, beautiful in its combination of the J and Z.

AZURE, -S n (of) the colour of a clear blue sky ▷ adj deep blue

AZUREAN adj azure

AZURES ▸ azure

AZURIES ▸ azury

AZURINE, -S n blue dye

AZURITE, -S n azure-blue mineral associated with copper deposits

AZURN old word for ▸ azure

AZURY, AZURIES adj bluish ▷ n bluish colour

AZYGIES ▸ azygy

AZYGOS, -ES n biological structure not in a pair

AZYGOUS adj developing or occurring singly

AZYGY, AZYGIES n state of not being joined in a pair

AZYM, -S n unleavened bread

AZYME, -S same as ▸ azym

AZYMITE, -S n member of a church using unleavened bread in the Eucharist

AZYMOUS adj unleavened

AZYMS ▸ azym

Bb

B forms a two-letter word before every vowel except **U** – and with **Y** as well. With a **B** in your rack, you can play lots of short words that will give you relatively high scores. The best of these are **box** (12 points), **bez** (14 points) and **biz** (14 points), but don't forget **bay** (8), **by** (7), **bow** (8), **boy** (8), **buy** (8) and **bye** (8).

BA, -S *n* symbol for the soul in Ancient Egyptian religion

BAA, -ED, -S *vb* make the characteristic bleating sound of a sheep ▷ *n* cry made by a sheep

BAAING, -S ▶ **baa**

BAAL, -IM, -S *n* any false god or idol

BAALEBOS *n* master of the house

BAALIM ▶ **baal**

BAALISM, -S ▶ **baal**

BAALS ▶ **baal**

BAAS ▶ **baa**

BABA, -S *n* small cake of leavened dough

BABACO, -S *n* greenish-yellow egg-shaped fruit

BABACU, -S *n* type of Brazilian palm tree

BABALAS *adj* South African word for drunk

BABAS ▶ **baba**

BABASSU, -S *n* Brazilian palm tree with hard edible nuts

BABBELAS *same as* ▶ **babalas**

BABBITRY *same as* > **babbittry**

BABBITT, -S *vb* line (a bearing) or face (a surface) with a similar soft alloy

BABBLE, -D, -S *vb* talk excitedly or foolishly ▷ *n* muddled or foolish speech

BABBLER, -S *n* person who babbles

BABBLES ▶ **babble**

BABBLIER ▶ **babbly**

BABBLING ▶ **babble**

BABBLY, BABBLIER ▶ **babble**

BABE, -S *n* baby

BABEL, -S *n* confused mixture of noises or voices

BABELDOM ▶ **babel**

BABELISH ▶ **babel**

BABELISM ▶ **babel**

BABELS ▶ **babel**

BABES ▶ **babe**

BABESIA, -E, -S *n* parasite causing infection in cattle

BABICHE, -S *n* thongs or lacings of rawhide

BABIED ▶ **baby**

BABIER ▶ **baby**

BABIES ▶ **baby**

BABIEST ▶ **baby**

BABIRUSA *n* Indonesian wild pig with an almost hairless skin and huge curved canine teeth

BABKA, -S *n* cake

BABLAH, -S *n* fruit rind used as a dye

BABOO, -S *same as* ▶ **babu**

BABOOL, -S *n* type of acacia

BABOON, -S *n* large monkey with a pointed face and a long tail

BABOOS ▶ **baboo**

BABOOSH *same as* ▶ **babouche**

BABOUCHE *n* Middle-Eastern slipper

BABU, -S *n* title or form of address used in India

BABUCHE, -S *same as* ▶ **babouche**

BABUDOM, -S ▶ **babu**

BABUISM, -S ▶ **babu**

BABUL, -S *n* N African and Indian tree with small yellow flowers

BABUS ▶ **babu**

BABUSHKA *n* headscarf tied under the chin, worn by Russian peasant women

BABY, BABIED, BABIER, BABIES, BABIEST, -ING *n* very young child or animal ▷ *adj* comparatively small of its type ▷ *vb* treat as a baby

BABYCINO *same as* > **babyccino**

BABYDOLL *n* woman's short nightdress

BABYFOOD *n* puréed food for babies

BABYHOOD ▶ **baby**

BABYING ▶ **baby**

BABYISH ▶ **baby**

BABYLIKE *adj* like a baby

BABYMOON *n* early period of new parenthood

BABYSIT, BABYSAT, -S *vb* look after a child in its parents' absence

BAC, -S *n* baccalaureate

BACALAO, -S *n* dried salt cod

BACALHAU *same as* ▶ **bacalao**

BACCA, -E, -S *n* berry

BACCALA, -S *same as* ▶ **bacalao**

BACCARA, -S *same as* ▶ **baccarat**

BACCARAT *n* card game involving gambling

BACCARE *same as* ▶ **backare**

BACCAS ▶ **bacca**

BACCATE, -D *adj* like a berry in form, texture, etc

BACCHANT *n* priest or votary of Bacchus

BACCHIAC ▶ **bacchius**

BACCHIAN *same as* ▶ **bacchic**

BACCHIC *adj* riotously jovial

BACCHIUS, BACCHII *n* metrical foot of one short syllable followed by two long ones

BACCIES ▶ **baccy**

BACCO, -ES, -S *n* tobacco

BACCY, BACCIES *n* tobacco

BACH, -ED, -ES, -ING, -S *same as* ▶ **batch**

BACHA, -S *n* Indian English word for a young child

B

BACHATA, -S n type of dance music originating in the Dominican Republic

BACHCHA, -S n Indian English word for a young child

BACHED ▸ bach

BACHELOR n unmarried man

BACHES ▸ bach

BACHING ▸ bach

BACHS ▸ bach

BACILLAR same as > bacillary

BACILLUS, BACILLI n rod-shaped bacterium

BACK, -S n rear part of the human body, from the neck to the pelvis ▸ vb (cause to) move backwards ▸ adj situated behind ▸ adv at, to, or towards the rear

BACKACHE n ache or pain in one's back

BACKARE interj instruction to keep one's distance; back off

BACKBAND n back support

BACKBAR, -S n area behind a bar where bottles are stored

BACKBEAT n beat in music not usually accented

BACKBEND n gymnastic exercise in which the trunk is bent backwards until the hands touch the floor

BACKBITE, BACKBIT vb talk spitefully about an absent person

BACKBOND n legal document

BACKBONE n spinal column

BACKBURN vb clear an area of bush by creating a fire ▸ n act or result of backburning

BACKCAST n backward casting of fishing rod ▸ vb cast a fishing rod backwards

BACKCHAT n impudent replies

BACKCOMB vb comb (the hair) towards the roots to give more bulk to a hairstyle

BACKDATE vb make (a document) effective from a date earlier than its completion

BACKDOOR adj secret, underhand, or obtained through influence

BACKDOWN n abandonment of an earlier claim

BACKDROP vb provide a backdrop to (something)

BACKED adj having a back or backing

BACKER, -S n person who gives financial support

BACKET, -S n shallow box

BACKFALL n fall onto the back

BACKFAT, -S n layer of fat in animals between the skin and muscle

BACKFILE n archives of a newspaper or magazine

BACKFILL vb refill an excavated trench, esp (in archaeology) at the end of an investigation ▸ n soil used to do this

BACKFIRE vb (of a plan) fail to have the desired effect ▸ n (in an engine) explosion of unburnt gases in the exhaust system

BACKFIT, -S vb overhaul a nuclear power plant

BACKFLIP n backwards somersault

BACKFLOW n reverse flow

BACKHAND n stroke played with the back of the hand facing the direction of the stroke ▸ adv with a backhand stroke ▸ vb play (a shot) backhand

BACKHAUL vb transmit data

BACKHOE, -D, -S n digger ▸ vb dig with a backhoe

BACKIE, -S n ride on the back of someone's bicycle

BACKING, -S n support

BACKLAND n undeveloped land behind a property

BACKLASH n sudden and adverse reaction ▸ vb create a sudden and adverse reaction

BACKLESS adj (of a dress) low-cut at the back

BACKLIFT n backward movement of bat

BACKLINE n defensive players in a sports team as a unit

BACKLIST n publisher's previously published books that are still available ▸ vb put on a backlist

BACKLIT adj illuminated from behind

BACKLOAD n load for lorry on return journey ▸ vb load a lorry for a return journey

BACKLOG, -S n accumulation of things to be dealt with

BACKLOT, -S n area outside a film or television studio used for outdoor filming

BACKMOST adj furthest back

BACKOUT, -S n instance of withdrawing (from an agreement, etc)

BACKPACK n large pack carried on the back ▸ vb go hiking with a backpack

BACKREST n support for the back of something

BACKROOM n place where research or planning is done, esp secret research in wartime

BACKRUSH n seaward return of wave

BACKS ▸ back

BACKSAW, -S n small handsaw

BACKSEAT n seat at the back, esp of a vehicle

BACKSET, -S n reversal ▸ vb attack from the rear

BACKSEY, -S n sirloin

BACKSIDE n buttocks

BACKSLAP vb demonstrate effusive joviality

BACKSLID > backslide

BACKSPIN n backward spin given to a ball to reduce its speed at impact

BACKSTAB vb attack deceitfully

BACKSTAY n stay leading aft from the upper part of a mast to the deck or stern

BACKSTOP n screen or fence to prevent balls leaving the playing area ▸ vb provide with backing or support

BACKTALK n argumentative discourse

BACKUP, -S n support or reinforcement

BACKVELD n (in South Africa) remote sparsely populated area

BACKWALL n rear wall

BACKWARD same as > backwards

BACKWASH n water washed backwards by the motion of a boat ▸ vb remove oil from (combed wool)

BACKWIND vb direct airflow into the back of a sail

BACKWOOD > backwoods

BACKWORD n act or an instance of failing to keep a promise or commitment

BACKWORK n work carried out under the ground

B

BACKWRAP n back support
BACKYARD n yard at the back of a house, etc
BACLAVA, -S same as ▶ **baklava**
BACLOFEN n drug used to treat stroke patients
BACON, -S n salted or smoked pig meat
BACONER, -S n pig that weighs between 83 and 101 kg, from which bacon is cut
BACONS ▶ **bacon**
BACRONYM same as > **backronym**
BACS ▶ **bac**
BACTERIA pl n large group of microorganisms
BACTERIC ▶ **bacteria**
BACTERIN n vaccine prepared from bacteria
BACULA ▶ **baculum**
BACULINE adj relating to flogging
BACULITE n fossil
BACULUM, BACULA, -S n bony support in the penis of certain mammals
BAD, -DER, -DEST, -S adj not good ▷ n unfortunate or unpleasant events collectively ▷ adv badly
BADDIE, -S n bad character in a story, film, etc, esp an opponent of the hero
BADDISH ▶ **bad**
BADDY same as ▶ **baddie**
BADE ▶ **bid**
BADGE, -D, -S, BADGING n emblem worn to show membership, rank, etc ▷ vb put a badge on
BADGER, -ED, -S n nocturnal burrowing mammal ▷ vb pester or harass
BADGERLY adj resembling a badger
BADGERS ▶ **badger**
BADGES ▶ **badge**
BADGING ▶ **badge**
BADINAGE n playful and witty conversation ▷ vb engage in badinage
BADIOUS adj chestnut; brownish-red
BADLAND ▶ **badlands**
BADLANDS pl n any deeply eroded barren area
BADLY adv poorly
BADMAN, BADMEN n hired gunman, outlaw, or criminal
BADMASH n evil-doer ▷ adj naughty or bad
BADMEN ▶ **badman**

BADMOUTH vb speak unfavourably about (someone or something)
BADNESS ▶ **bad**
BADS ▶ **bad**
BADWARE, -S n software designed to harm a computer system
BAE, -S n sweetheart
BAEL, -S n type of spiny Indian tree
BAES ▶ **bae**
BAETYL, -S n magical meteoric stone
BAFF, -ED, -ING, -S vb strike the ground with a golf club
BAFFIES pl n slippers
BAFFING ▶ **baff**
BAFFLE, -D, -S vb perplex or puzzle ▷ n device to limit or regulate the flow of fluid, light, or sound
BAFFLER, -S ▶ **baffle**
BAFFLES ▶ **baffle**
BAFFLING adj impossible to understand
BAFFS ▶ **baff**
BAFFY n obsolete golf club
BAFT, -S n coarse fabric
BAG, -GED, -S n flexible container with an opening at one end ▷ vb put into a bag
BAGARRE, -S n brawl
BAGASS same as ▶ **bagasse**
BAGASSE, -S n pulp of sugar cane or similar plants
BAGEL, -ED, -ING, -LED, -S n hard ring-shaped bread roll ▷ vb win a tennis set by six games to love
BAGFUL, -S, BAGSFUL n amount (of something) that can be held in a bag
BAGGAGE, -S n suitcases packed for a journey
BAGGED ▶ **bag**
BAGGER, -S n person who packs groceries
BAGGIE, -S n plastic bag
BAGGIER ▶ **baggy**
BAGGIES ▶ **baggie**
BAGGIEST ▶ **baggy**
BAGGILY ▶ **baggy**
BAGGING, -S n act of putting in a bag
BAGGIT, -S n salmon which has not yet spawned
BAGGY, BAGGIER, BAGGIEST adj hanging loosely
BAGH, -S n (in India and Pakistan) a garden
BAGHOUSE n dust-filtering chamber
BAGHS ▶ **bagh**

BAGIE, -S n turnip
BAGLESS adj (esp of a vacuum cleaner) not containing a bag
BAGLIKE ▶ **bag**
BAGMAN, BAGMEN n travelling salesman
BAGNETTE variant of ▶ **baguette**
BAGNIO, -S n bathing-house
BAGPIPE, -D vb play the bagpipes
BAGPIPER ▶ **bagpipes**
BAGPIPES pl n musical wind instrument with reed pipes and an inflatable bag
BAGS ▶ **bag**
BAGSFUL ▶ **bagful**
BAGUET, -S same as ▶ **baguette**
BAGUETTE n narrow French stick loaf
BAGUIO, -S n hurricane
BAGWASH n laundry that washes clothes without drying or pressing them
BAGWIG, -S n 18th-century wig with hair pushed back into a bag
BAGWORM, -S n type of moth
BAH interj expression of contempt or disgust
BAHADA, -S same as ▶ **bajada**
BAHADUR, -S n title formerly conferred by the British on distinguished Indians
BAHOOKIE n Scottish informal word for the buttocks
BAHT, -S n standard monetary unit of Thailand, divided into 100 satang
BAHU, -S n (in India) daughter-in-law
BAHUT, -S n decorative cabinet
BAIDAR, -S same as ▶ **baidarka**
BAIDARKA n narrow hunting boat
BAIDARS ▶ **baidar**
BAIL, -ED, -ING, -S n money deposited with a court as security for a person's reappearance ▷ vb pay bail for (a person)
BAILABLE adj eligible for release on bail
BAILBOND n document guaranteeing a prisoner released on bail will attend court
BAILED ▶ **bail**

BAILEE, -S n person to whom the possession of goods is transferred under a bailment

BAILER, -S ▸ **bail**

BAILEY, -S n outermost wall or court of a castle

BAILIE, -S n (in Scotland) a municipal magistrate

BAILIFF, -S n sheriff's officer who serves writs and summonses

BAILING ▸ **bail**

BAILLI, -S same as ▸ **bailie**

BAILLIE, -S same as ▸ **bailie**

BAILLIS ▸ **bailli**

BAILMENT n contractual delivery of goods in trust to a person for a specific purpose

BAILOR, -S n owner of goods entrusted to another under a bailment

BAILOUT, -S n instance of helping (a person, organization, etc) out of a predicament

BAILS ▸ **bail**

BAILSMAN, BAILSMEN n one standing bail for another

BAININ, -S n Irish collarless jacket made of white wool

BAINITE, -S n mixture of iron and iron carbide found in incompletely hardened steels

BAIRN, -S n child

BAIRNISH ▸ **bairn**

BAIRNLY ▸ **bairn**

BAIRNS ▸ **bairn**

BAISA, -S n small unit of currency in Oman

BAIT, -ED, -S n piece of food on a hook or in a trap to attract fish or animals ▸ vb put a piece of food on or in (a hook or trap)

BAITER, -S ▸ **bait**

BAITFISH n small fish used as bait

BAITH adj both

BAITING, -S n act of placing bait

BAITS ▸ **bait**

BAIZA, -S n Omani unit of currency

BAIZE, -D, -S, BAIZING n woollen fabric used to cover billiard and card tables ▸ vb line or cover with such fabric

BAJADA, -S n sloping surface formed from rock deposits

BAJAN, -S n freshman at Aberdeen University

BAJRA, -S n Indian millet

BAJREE, -S variant of ▸ **bajra**

BAJRI, -S variant of ▸ **bajra**

BAJU, -S n Malay jacket

BAKE, -D, -N, -S vb cook by dry heat as in an oven ▸ n party at which the main dish is baked

BAKELITE n tradename for a class of resin

BAKEMEAT n pie

BAKEN ▸ **bake**

BAKEOFF, -S n baking competition

BAKER, -S n person whose business is to make or sell bread, cakes, etc

BAKERIES ▸ **bakery**

BAKERS ▸ **baker**

BAKERY, BAKERIES n place where bread, cakes, etc are baked or sold

BAKES ▸ **bake**

BAKESHOP n bakery

BAKEWARE n dishes for baking

BAKGAT adj fine, excellent, marvellous

BAKING, -S n process of cooking bread, cakes, etc ▸ adj (esp of weather) very hot and dry

BAKKIE, -S n small truck

BAKLAVA, -S n rich pastry of Middle Eastern origin

BAKLAWA, -S same as ▸ **baklava**

BAKSHISH same as ▸ **baksheesh**

BAL, -S n balmoral

BALADIN, -S n dancer

BALADINE n female dancer

BALADINS ▸ **baladin**

BALAFON, -S n type of W African xylophone

BALANCE, -S n stability of mind or body ▸ vb weigh in a balance

BALANCED adj having weight equally distributed

BALANCER n person or thing that balances

BALANCES ▸ **balance**

BALAS, -ES n red variety of spinel, used as a gemstone

BALATA, -S n tropical American tree yielding a latex-like sap

BALAYAGE vb highlight hair by painting dye onto sections

BALBOA, -S n standard currency unit of Panama

BALCONET n small balcony

BALCONY n platform on the outside of a building with a rail along the outer edge

BALD, -ED, -ER, -EST, -S adj having little or no hair on the scalp ▸ vb make bald

BALDHEAD n person with a bald head

BALDIE, -S same as ▸ **baldy**

BALDIER ▸ **baldy**

BALDIES ▸ **baldie**

BALDIEST ▸ **baldy**

BALDING adj becoming bald

BALDISH ▸ **bald**

BALDLY ▸ **bald**

BALDNESS ▸ **bald**

BALDPATE n type of duck

BALDRIC, -S n wide silk sash or leather belt worn across the body

BALDRICK same as ▸ **baldric**

BALDRICS ▸ **baldric**

BALDS ▸ **bald**

BALDY, BALDIER, BALDIEST adj bald ▸ n bald person

BALE, -D, -S same as ▸ **bail**

BALEEN, -S n whalebone

BALEFIRE n bonfire

BALEFUL adj vindictive or menacing

BALER, -S ▸ **bail**

BALES ▸ **bale**

BALING, -S n act of baling

BALISAUR n badger-like animal

BALISE, -S n electronic beacon used on a railway

BALISTA, -E, -S same as ▸ **ballista**

BALK, -ED, -S vb stop short, esp suddenly or unexpectedly ▸ n roughly squared heavy timber beam

BALKER, -S ▸ **balk**

BALKIER ▸ **balky**

BALKIEST ▸ **balky**

BALKILY ▸ **balky**

BALKING, -S ▸ **balk**

BALKLINE n line delimiting the balk area on a snooker table

BALKS ▸ **balk**

BALKY, BALKIER, BALKIEST adj inclined to stop abruptly and unexpectedly

BALL, -ED n round or nearly round object, esp one used in games ▸ vb form into a ball

BALLAD, -ED, -S n narrative poem or song ▸ vb sing or write a ballad

BALLADE, -S n verse form

BALLADED ▸ **ballad**

BALLADES ▸ **ballade**

BALLADIC ▸ **ballad**

BALLADIN same as ▸ **baladin**

BALLADRY n ballad poetry or songs

BALLADS ▸ **ballad**

BALLAN, -S n species of fish

B

BALLANT, -S *vb* write a ballad

BALLAST, -S *n* substance used to stabilize a ship when it is not carrying cargo ▷ *vb* give stability to

BALLAT, -ED, -S *vb* write a ballad

BALLBOY, -S *n* boy who retrieves balls during a tennis, football, etc, match

BALLCLAY *n* clay suitable for ceramics

BALLCOCK *n* device for regulating the flow of a liquid into a tank

BALLED ▸ **ball**

BALLER, -S *n* ball-game player

BALLET, -ED, -S *n* classical style of expressive dancing based on conventional steps ▷ *vb* sing ballads

BALLETIC ▸ **ballet**

BALLETS ▸ **ballet**

BALLGAME *n* any game played with a ball

BALLGIRL *n* girl who retrieves balls during a tennis, football, etc, match

BALLGOWN *n* long formal dress

BALLHAWK *n* skilled basketball player ▷ *vb* act as a ballhawk

BALLIER ▸ **bally**

BALLIES ▸ **bally**

BALLIEST ▸ **bally**

BALLING, -S *n* formation of a ball

BALLISTA *n* ancient catapult for hurling stones, etc

BALLIUM, -S *same as* ▸ **bailey**

BALLON, -S *n* light, graceful quality

BALLONET *n* air or gas compartment in a nonrigid airship

BALLONNE *n* bouncing step

BALLONS ▸ **ballon**

BALLOON, -S *n* inflatable rubber bag used as a plaything or decoration ▷ *vb* fly in a balloon

BALLOT, -ED, -S *n* method of voting ▷ *vb* vote or ask for a vote from

BALLOTEE ▸ **ballot**

BALLOTER ▸ **ballot**

BALLOTS ▸ **ballot**

BALLOW, -S *n* heavy club

BALLPARK *n* stadium used for baseball games

BALLPEEN *adj* as in **ballpeen hammer** type of hammer

BALLROOM *n* large hall for dancing

BALLS *n* plural of ball

BALLUTE, -S *n* inflatable balloon parachute

BALLY, BALLIER, BALLIES, BALLIEST *adj* euphemism for bloody ▷ *n* exaggerated fuss

BALLYARD *n* baseball ground

BALLYHOO *n* exaggerated fuss ▷ *vb* advertise or publicize by sensational or blatant methods

BALLYRAG *same as* ▸ **bullyrag**

BALM, -ED, -ING, -S *n* aromatic substance used for healing and soothing ▷ *vb* apply balm to

BALMIER ▸ **balmy**

BALMIEST ▸ **balmy**

BALMILY ▸ **balmy**

BALMING ▸ **balm**

BALMLIKE ▸ **balm**

BALMORAL *n* laced walking shoe

BALMS ▸ **balm**

BALMY, BALMIER, BALMIEST *adj* (of weather) mild and pleasant

BALNEAL *adj* of or relating to baths or bathing

BALNEARY *same as* ▸ **balneal**

BALONEY, -S *n* foolish talk; nonsense

BALOO, -S *n* bear

BALS ▸ **bal**

BALSA, -S *n* very light wood from a tropical American tree

BALSAM, -ED, -S *n* type of fragrant balm ▷ *vb* embalm

BALSAMIC ▸ **balsam**

BALSAMS ▸ **balsam**

BALSAMY *adj* sweet-smelling

BALSAS ▸ **balsa**

BALTI, -S *n* spicy Indian dish served in a metal dish

BALTIC *adj* very cold

BALTIS ▸ **balti**

BALU, -S *same as* ▸ **baloo**

BALUN, -S *n* electrical device

BALUS ▸ **balu**

BALUSTER *n* set of posts supporting a rail ▷ *adj* (of a shape) swelling at the base and rising in a concave curve to a narrow stem or neck

BAM, -MED, -MING, -S *vb* cheat

BAMBI, -S *n* born-again middle-aged biker

BAMBINO, BAMBINI, -S *n* young child, esp an Italian one

BAMBIS ▸ **bambi**

BAMBOO, -S *n* tall treelike tropical grass with hollow stems

BAMMED ▸ **bam**

BAMMER, -S ▸ **bam**

BAMMING ▸ **bam**

BAMPOT, -S *n* fool

BAMS ▸ **bam**

BAN, -I, -NED *vb* prohibit or forbid officially ▷ *n* unit of currency in Romania and Moldova

BANAK, -S *n* type of Central American tree

BANAL, -ER, -EST *adj* ordinary and unoriginal

BANALISE ▸ **banal**

BANALITY ▸ **banal**

BANALIZE ▸ **banal**

BANALLY ▸ **banal**

BANANA *n* yellow crescent-shaped fruit

BANANAS *adj* crazy

BANAUSIC *adj* merely mechanical

BANC, -S *n* as in **in banc** sitting as a full court

BANCO, -S *n* call made in gambling games

BANCS ▸ **banc**

BAND, -ED, -S *n* group of musicians playing together ▷ *vb* unite

BANDA, -S *n* African thatched hut

BANDAGE, -D, -S *n* piece of material used to cover a wound or wrap an injured limb ▷ *vb* cover with a bandage

BANDAGER ▸ **bandage**

BANDAGES ▸ **bandage**

BANDAID *adj* (of a solution or remedy) temporary

BANDANA, -S *same as* ▸ **bandanna**

BANDANNA *n* large brightly coloured handkerchief or neckerchief

BANDAR, -S *n* species of monkey

BANDARI, -S *n* Indian English word for female monkey

BANDARS ▸ **bandar**

BANDAS ▸ **banda**

BANDBOX *n* lightweight usually cylindrical box for hats

BANDEAU, -S, -X *n* narrow ribbon worn round the head

BANDED ▸ **band**

B

BANDEIRA n 17th-century expedition in search of gold or slaves

BANDELET n moulding round top of column

BANDER, -S ▸ band

BANDEROL same as ▸ banderole

BANDERS ▸ bander

BANDFISH n Mediterranean fish with an elongated body

BANDH, -S n (in India) a general strike

BANDIED ▸ bandy

BANDIER ▸ bandy

BANDIES ▸ bandy

BANDIEST ▸ bandy

BANDING, -S n practice of grouping schoolchildren according to ability

BANDIT, -S, -TI n robber, esp a member of an armed gang

BANDITO, -S n Mexican bandit

BANDITRY ▸ bandit

BANDITS ▸ bandit

BANDITTI ▸ bandit

BANDLIKE adj like a band

BANDMATE n fellow member of band

BANDOG, -S n ferocious dog

BANDOOK, -S same as ▸ bundook

BANDORA, -S same as ▸ bandore

BANDORE, -S n 16th-century musical instrument

BANDPASS n range of frequencies transmitted through a bandpass filter

BANDROL, -S same as ▸ banderole

BANDS ▸ band

BANDSAW, -S n power saw with continuous blade ▷ vb cut with a bandsaw

BANDSMAN, BANDSMEN n player in a musical band

BANDSTER n binder of wheat sheaves

BANDURA, -S n type of lute

BANDY, BANDIED, BANDIER, BANDIES, BANDIEST adj having legs curved outwards at the knees ▷ vb exchange (words) in a heated manner

BANDYING ▸ bandy

BANDYMAN, BANDYMEN n carriage or cart

BANE, -D, -S, BANING n person or thing that causes misery or distress ▷ vb cause harm or distress to (someone)

BANEFUL adj destructive, poisonous, or fatal

BANES ▸ bane

BANG, -ED, -ING, -S vb make a short explosive noise

BANGALAY n Australian tree valued for its hard red wood

BANGALOW n Australian palm tree native to New South Wales and Queensland

BANGED ▸ bang

BANGER, -S n old decrepit car

BANGING ▸ bang

BANGKOK, -S n type of straw hat

BANGLE, -S n bracelet worn round the arm or the ankle

BANGLED ▸ bangle

BANGLES ▸ bangle

BANGS ▸ bang

BANGSTER n ruffian

BANGTAIL n horse's tail cut straight across but not through the bone

BANI ▸ ban

BANIA, -S same as ▸ banyan

BANIAN, -S same as ▸ banyan

BANIAS ▸ bania

BANING ▸ bane

BANISH, -ED, -ES vb send (someone) into exile

BANISHER ▸ banish

BANISHES ▸ banish

BANISTER same as > bannister

BANJAX, -ED, -ES vb ruin; destroy

Meaning to ruin or destroy, this is a great word to remember, with its high-scoring combination of J and X.

BANJO, -ES, -S n guitar-like musical instrument with a circular body

BANJOIST ▸ banjo

BANJOS ▸ banjo

BANK, -ED, -S n institution offering services such as the safekeeping and lending of money ▷ vb deposit (cash or cheques) in a bank

BANKABLE adj likely to ensure financial success

BANKBOOK n record of deposits, withdrawals, and interest held by depositors at certain banks

BANKCARD n card guaranteeing payment of cheque

BANKED ▸ bank

BANKER, -S n manager or owner of a bank

BANKERLY adj like a banker

BANKERS ▸ banker

BANKET n gold-bearing conglomerate found in South Africa

BANKING, -S ▸ bank

BANKIT, -S same as > banquette

BANKNOTE n piece of paper money

BANKROLL n roll of currency notes ▷ vb provide the capital for

BANKRUPT n person declared by a court to be unable to pay his or her debts ▷ adj financially ruined ▷ vb make bankrupt

BANKS ▸ bank

BANKSIA, -S n Australian evergreen tree or shrub

BANKSIDE n riverside

BANKSMAN, BANKSMEN n crane driver's helper

BANKSTER n banker whose illegal practices have been exposed

BANLIEUE n suburb of a city

BANNABLE ▸ ban

BANNED ▸ ban

BANNER, -ED, -S n long strip of cloth displaying a slogan, advertisement, etc ▷ vb (of a newspaper headline) to display (a story) prominently ▷ adj outstandingly successful

BANNERET n small banner

BANNEROL same as > banderole

BANNERS ▸ banner

BANNET, -S n bonnet

BANNING, -S n act of banning

BANNOCK, -S n round flat cake made from oatmeal or barley

BANNS pl n public declaration, esp in a church, of an intended marriage

BANOFFEE n filling for a pie, consisting of toffee and banana

BANOFFI, -S same as ▸ banoffee

BANQUET, -S n elaborate formal dinner ▷ vb hold or take part in a banquet

BANS same as ▸ banns

BANSELA, -S same as ▸ bonsela

BANSHEE, -S n (in Irish folklore) spirit whose wailing warns of a coming death

BANSHIE, -S same as ▸ banshee

B

BANT, -ED, -S *n* string ▷ *vb* tie with string

BANTAM, -S *n* small breed of chicken

BANTED ▸ **bant**

BANTENG, -S *n* wild ox

BANTER, -ED, -S *vb* tease jokingly ▷ *n* teasing or joking conversation

BANTERER ▸ **banter**

BANTERS ▸ **banter**

BANTIES ▸ **banty**

BANTING, -S ▸ **bant**

BANTLING *n* young child

BANTS ▸ **bant**

BANTY, BANTIES *n* bantam

BANXRING *n* tree-shrew

BANYA, -S *n* traditional Russian steam bath

BANYAN, -S *n* Indian tree

BANYAS ▸ **banya**

BANZAI, -S *interj* patriotic cheer, battle cry, or salutation

BAO, -S *n* steamed dumpling

BAOBAB, -S *n* African tree with a thick trunk and angular branches

BAOS ▸ **bao**

BAP, -S *n* large soft bread roll

BAPTISE, -D, -S *same as* ▸ **baptize**

BAPTISER ▸ **baptise**

BAPTISES ▸ **baptise**

BAPTISIA *n* species of wild flower

BAPTISM, -S *n* Christian religious ceremony

BAPTIST, -S *n* one who baptizes

BAPTIZE, -D, -S *vb* perform baptism on

BAPTIZER ▸ **baptize**

BAPTIZES ▸ **baptize**

BAPU, -S *n* spiritual father

BAR, -RED, -S *n* rigid usually straight length of metal, wood, etc, longer than it is wide or thick ▷ *vb* fasten or secure with a bar

BARACAN, -S *same as* ▸ **barracan**

BARATHEA *n* fabric made of silk and wool or cotton and rayon, used esp for coats

BARAZA, -S *n* place where public meetings are held

BARB, -ED, -ING, -S *n* cutting remark ▷ *vb* provide with a barb or barbs

BARBAL *adj* of a beard

BARBARIC *adj* cruel or brutal

BARBASCO *n* S American plant

BARBATE, -D *adj* having tufts of long hairs

BARBE, -S *n* Waldensian missionary

BARBECUE *n* grill on which food is cooked over hot charcoal, usu outdoors ▷ *vb* cook (food) on a barbecue

BARBED ▸ **barb**

BARBEL, -S *n* long thin growth that hangs from the jaws of certain fishes, such as the carp

BARBELL, -S *n* long metal rod to which heavy discs are attached at each end for weightlifting

BARBELS ▸ **barbel**

BARBEQUE *same as* ▸ **barbecue**

BARBER, -ED, -S *n* person who cuts men's hair and shaves beards ▷ *vb* cut the hair of

BARBERRY *n* shrub with orange or red berries

BARBERS ▸ **barber**

BARBES ▸ **barbe**

BARBET, -S *n* type of small tropical bird

BARBETTE *n* earthen platform inside a parapet

BARBICAN *n* walled defence to protect a gate or drawbridge of a fortification

BARBICEL *n* minute hook on the barbule of a feather

BARBIE, -S *short for* ▸ **barbecue**

BARBING ▸ **barb**

BARBITAL *same as* ▸ **barbitone**

BARBLESS ▸ **barb**

BARBOLA, -S *n* creation of small models of flowers, etc from plastic paste

BARBOT, -S *same as* ▸ **burbot**

BARBOTTE *same as* ▸ **burbot**

BARBS ▸ **barb**

BARBULE, -S *n* very small barb

BARBUT, -S *n* open-faced helmet

BARBWIRE *n* barbed wire

BARBY *short for* ▸ **barbecue**

BARCA, -S *n* boat

BARCHAN, -S *n* crescent-shaped shifting sand dune

BARCHANE *same as* ▸ **barchan**

BARCHANS ▸ **barchan**

BARCODE, -S *n* machine-readable code printed on goods

BARCODED *adj* having a barcode

BARCODES ▸ **barcode**

BARD, -ING, -S *n* poet ▷ *vb* place a piece of pork fat on

BARDE, -D, -S *same as* ▸ **bard**

BARDIC ▸ **bard**

BARDIE, -S *n* type of Australian grub

BARDIER ▸ **bardy**

BARDIES ▸ **bardie**

BARDIEST ▸ **bardy**

BARDING ▸ **bard**

BARDISM, -S ▸ **bard**

BARDLING *n* inferior poet

BARDO, -S *n* (in Tibetan Buddhism) the state of the soul between its death and its rebirth

BARDS ▸ **bard**

BARDSHIP ▸ **bard**

BARDY, BARDIER, BARDIEST ▸ **bard**

BARE, -D, -R, -S, -ST, BARING *adj* unclothed, naked ▷ *vb* uncover

BAREBACK *adv* (of horse-riding) without a saddle ▷ *vb* ride bareback

BAREBOAT *n* boat chartered without crew, provisions, etc

BAREBONE *n* computer casing containing bare essentials

BARED ▸ **bare**

BAREFIT *Scots word for* ▸ **barefoot**

BAREFOOT *adv* with the feet uncovered

BAREGE, -S *n* light silky gauze fabric made of wool ▷ *adj* made of such a fabric

BAREGINE *n* curative ingredient in thermal waters

BAREHAND *vb* handle with bare hands

BAREHEAD *adv* with head uncovered

BARELAND *adj* as in bareland croft refers to a croft with no croft house

BARELY *adv* only just

BARENESS ▸ **bare**

BARER ▸ **bare**

BARES ▸ **bare**

BARESARK *another word for* ▸ **berserk**

BAREST ▸ **bare**

BARF, -ED, -ING, -S *vb* vomit ▷ *n* act of vomiting

BARFI, -S *n* type of Indian dessert

BARFING ▸ **barf**

BARFIS ▸ **barfi**

BARFLY, BARFLIES *n* person who frequents bars

BARFS ▸ **barf**

BARFUL *adj* presenting difficulties**

BARGAIN, -S n agreement establishing what each party will give, receive, or perform in a transaction ▷ vb negotiate the terms of an agreement

BARGE, -D, -S, BARGING n flat-bottomed boat used to transport freight ▷ vb push violently

BARGEE, -S n person in charge of a barge

BARGEESE ▶ **bargoose**

BARGELLO n zigzag tapestry stitch

BARGEMAN, BARGEMEN same as ▶ **bargee**

BARGES ▶ **barge**

BARGEST, -S same as ▶ **barghest**

BARGHEST n mythical goblin in the shape of a dog

BARGING ▶ **barge**

BARGOON, -S Canadian word for ▶ **bargain**

BARGOOSE, BARGEESE n type of goose; sheldrake

BARGUEST same as ▶ **barghest**

BARHOP, -S vb visit several bars in succession

BARIC adj of or containing barium

BARILLA, -S n impure mixture of sodium carbonate and sodium sulphate

BARING ▶ **bare**

BARISH adj quite thinly covered

BARISTA, -S n person who makes and sells coffee in a coffee bar

BARITE, -S n colourless or white mineral

BARITONE n (singer with) the second lowest adult male voice ▷ adj relating to or denoting a baritone

BARIUM, -S n soft white metallic element

BARK, -ED, -ING, -S vb (of a dog) make its typical loud abrupt cry

BARKAN, -S same as ▶ **barchan**

BARKED ▶ **bark**

BARKEEP, -S n barkeeper

BARKEN, -ED, -S vb become dry with a bark-like outer layer

BARKER, -S n person at a fairground who calls loudly to passers-by in order to attract customers

BARKHAN, -S same as ▶ **barchan**

BARKIER ▶ **barky**

BARKIEST ▶ **barky**

BARKING ▶ **bark**

BARKLESS ▶ **bark**

BARKLIKE adj like a dog's bark

BARKS ▶ **bark**

BARKY, BARKIER, BARKIEST adj having the texture or appearance of bark

BARLEDUC n French preserve made of currants

BARLESS ▶ **bar**

BARLEY, -S n tall grasslike plant cultivated for grain

BARLOW, -S n type of strong knife

BARM, -S n yeasty froth on fermenting malt liquors

BARMAID, -S n woman who serves in a pub

BARMAN, BARMEN same as > **bartender**

BARMIE same as ▶ **barmy**

BARMIER ▶ **barmy**

BARMIEST ▶ **barmy**

BARMILY ▶ **barmy**

BARMKIN, -S n protective wall around castle

BARMPOT, -S n foolish person

BARMS ▶ **barm**

BARMY, BARMIER, BARMIEST adj mad

BARN, -ED, -ING, -S n large building on a farm used for storing grain ▷ vb keep in a barn

BARNACLE n shellfish that lives attached to rocks, ship bottoms, etc

BARNED ▶ **barn**

BARNET, -S n hair

BARNEY, -ED, -S n noisy fight or argument ▷ vb argue or quarrel

BARNIER ▶ **barny**

BARNIEST ▶ **barny**

BARNING ▶ **barn**

BARNLIKE ▶ **barn**

BARNS ▶ **barn**

BARNWOOD n aged and weathered boards, esp those salvaged from dismantled barns

BARNY, BARNIER, BARNIEST adj reminiscent of a barn

BARNYARD n yard adjoining a barn

BAROCCO, -S same as ▶ **baroque**

BAROCK, -S same as ▶ **baroque**

BAROGRAM n record of atmospheric pressure traced by a barograph or similar instrument

BAROLO, -S n red Italian wine

BAROMETZ n fern whose woolly rhizomes resemble a lamb

BARON, -S n member of the lowest rank of nobility

BARONAGE n barons collectively

BARONESS n woman holding the rank of baron

BARONET, -S n man who holds the lowest hereditary British title

BARONG, -S n broad-bladed cleaver-like knife used in the Philippines

BARONIAL adj of, relating to, or befitting a baron or barons

BARONIES ▶ **barony**

BARONNE, -S n baroness

BARONS ▶ **baron**

BARONY, BARONIES n domain or rank of a baron

BAROQUE, -S n style of art, architecture, or music ▷ adj ornate in style

BAROSAUR n large dinosaur

BAROSTAT n device for maintaining constant pressure, such as one used in an aircraft cabin

BAROUCHE n type of horse-drawn carriage

BARP, -S n hillock or bank of stones

BARQUE, -S n sailing ship, esp one with three masts

BARRA, -S n barramundi

BARRABLE ▶ **bar**

BARRACAN n thick, strong fabric

BARRACE, -S n record of teams entering a sports contest

BARRACK vb criticize loudly or shout against (a team or speaker)

BARRACKS pl n building used to accommodate military personnel

BARRAGE, -D, -S n continuous delivery of questions, complaints, etc ▷ vb attack or confront with a barrage

BARRANCA n ravine or precipice

BARRANCO same as ▶ **barranca**

BARRAS ▶ **barra**

B

BARRAT, -ED, -S n fraudulent dealings ▷ vb quarrel

BARRATER same as ▶ **barrator**

BARRATOR n person guilty of barratry

BARRATRY n (formerly) the vexatious stirring up of quarrels or bringing of lawsuits

BARRATS ▶ **barrat**

BARRE, -ED, -ING, -S n rail at hip height used for ballet practice ▷ vb execute guitar chords by laying the index finger over some or all of the strings ▷ adv by using the barre

BARRED ▶ **bar**

BARREED ▶ **barre**

BARREING ▶ **barre**

BARREL, -ED, -S n cylindrical container with rounded sides and flat ends ▷ vb put in a barrel

BARREN, -ER adj incapable of producing offspring or fruit

BARRENLY ▶ **barren**

BARRENS pl n (in North America) a stretch of land that is sparsely vegetated

BARRES ▶ **barre**

BARRET, -S n small flat cap resembling a biretta

BARRETOR n quarrelsome person

BARRETRY same as ▶ **barratry**

BARRETS ▶ **barret**

BARRETTE n clasp or pin for holding hair in place

BARRICO, -S n small container for liquids

BARRIE adj dialect word for excellent

BARRIER, -S n anything that prevents access, progress, or union ▷ vb create or form a barrier

BARRIES ▶ **barry**

BARRIEST ▶ **barry**

BARRING, -S ▶ **bar**

BARRIO, -S n Spanish-speaking quarter in a town or city, esp in the US

BARRIQUE n wine barrel made of oak

BARRO adj embarrassing

BARROOM, -S n room or building where alcoholic drinks are served over a counter

BARROW, -S n wheelbarrow

BARRULET n narrow band across heraldic shield

BARRY, BARRIES, BARRIEST n mistake or blunder ▷ adj dialect word for excellent

BARS ▶ **bar**

BARSTOOL n high stool in bar

BARTEND, -S vb serve drinks from a bar

BARTER, -ED, -S vb trade (goods) in exchange for other goods ▷ n trade by the exchange of goods

BARTERER ▶ **barter**

BARTERS ▶ **barter**

BARTISAN same as ▶ **bartizan**

BARTIZAN n small turret projecting from a wall, parapet, or tower

BARTON, -S n farmyard

BARTSIA, -S n type of semiparasitic plant

BARWARE, -S n glasses, etc used in a bar

BARWOOD, -S n red wood from a small African tree

BARYE, -S n unit of pressure

BARYON, -S n elementary particle that has a mass greater than or equal to that of the proton

BARYONIC adj of or relating to a baryon

BARYONS ▶ **baryon**

BARYTA, -S same as ▶ **barite**

BARYTE, -S same as ▶ **barite**

BARYTIC ▶ **baryta**

BARYTON, -S n bass viol with sympathetic strings as well as its six main strings

BARYTONE adj having the last syllable unaccented ▷ n word in which the last syllable is unaccented

BARYTONS ▶ **baryton**

BAS ▶ **ba**

BASAL adj of, at, or constituting a base

BASALLY ▶ **basal**

BASALT, -S n dark volcanic rock

BASALTES n unglazed black stoneware

BASALTIC ▶ **basalt**

BASALTS ▶ **basalt**

BASAN, -S n sheepskin tanned in bark

BASANITE n black basaltic rock

BASANS ▶ **basan**

BASANT, -S n Pakistani spring festival

BASCINET same as ▶ **basinet**

BASCULE, -S n drawbridge that operates by a counterbalanced weight

BASE, -D, -R, -ST, BASING n bottom or supporting part of anything ▷ vb use as a basis (for) ▷ adj dishonourable or immoral

BASEBALL n type of team ball game

BASEBAND n transmission using a narrow range of frequencies

BASEBORN adj born of humble parents

BASED ▶ **base**

BASEEJ pl n Iranian volunteer militia

BASELARD n short sword

BASELESS adj not based on fact

BASELINE n value or starting point on an imaginary scale with which other things are compared

BASELOAD n constant part of an electrical power supply

BASELY ▶ **base**

BASEMAN, BASEMEN n fielder positioned near a base

BASEMENT n partly or wholly underground storey of a building

BASEN Spenserian spelling of ▶ **basin**

BASENESS ▶ **base**

BASENJI, -S n small breed of dog

BASEPATH n diamond-shaped path between bases on a baseball field

BASER ▶ **base**

BASES ▶ **basis**

BASEST ▶ **base**

BASH, -ED, -ES vb hit violently or forcefully ▷ n heavy blow

BASHAW, -S n important or pompous person

BASHED ▶ **bash**

BASHER, -S ▶ **bash**

BASHES ▶ **bash**

BASHFUL adj shy or modest

BASHING, -S ▶ **bash**

BASHLESS adj not ashamed

BASHLIK, -S n Caucasian hood

BASHLYK, -S same as ▶ **bashlik**

BASHMENT same as ▷ **dancehall**

BASHO n grand tournament in sumo wrestling

BASHTAG, -S n (on Twitter) hashtag used for abusive comments

BASIC, -S adj of or forming a base or basis ▷ n

B

fundamental principle, fact, etc

BASICITY n state of being a base

BASICS ▸ basic

BASIDIA ▸ basidium

BASIDIAL ▸ basidium

BASIDIUM, BASIDIA n spore-forming structure in fungi

BASIFIED ▸ basify

BASIFIER ▸ basify

BASIFY, BASIFIED, BASIFIES vb make basic

BASIJ same as ▸ baseej

BASIL, -S n aromatic herb used in cooking

BASILAR adj of or situated at a base

BASILARY same as ▸ basilar

BASILECT n debased dialect

BASILIC ▸ basilica

BASILICA n rectangular church with a rounded end and two aisles

BASILISK n legendary serpent said to kill by its breath or glance

BASILS ▸ basil

BASIN, -S n round open container

BASINAL ▸ basin

BASINED ▸ basin

BASINET, -S n close-fitting medieval helmet of light steel usually with a visor

BASINFUL n amount a basin will hold

BASING ▸ base

BASINS ▸ basin

BASION, -S n (in anatomy) midpoint on the forward border of the foramen magnum

BASIS, BASES n fundamental principles etc from which something is started or developed

BASK, -ED, -ING, -S vb lie in or be exposed to something, esp pleasant warmth

BASKET, -S n container made of interwoven strips of wood or cane

BASKETRY n art or practice of making baskets

BASKETS ▸ basket

BASKING ▸ bask

BASKS ▸ bask

BASMATI, -S n variety of long-grain rice with slender aromatic grains

BASNET, -S same as ▸ basinet

BASOCHE, -S n society of medieval French lawyers who performed comic plays

BASON, -S same as ▸ basin

BASOPHIL adj (of cells or cell contents) easily stained by basic dyes ▷ n basophil cell, esp a leucocyte

BASQUE, -D, -S n tight-fitting bodice

BASQUINE n tight-fitting bodice

BASS, -ED, -ES, -EST, -ING n (singer with) the lowest adult male voice ▷ adj relating to or denoting a bass ▷ vb speak or sing in a low pitch

BASSE same as ▸ bass

BASSED ▸ bass

BASSER, -S n someone who plays bass guitar or double bass

BASSES ▸ bass

BASSEST ▸ bass

BASSET, -ED, -S n breed of hound ▷ vb (of rock) protrude through earth's surface

BASSETT, -S same as ▸ basset

BASSI ▸ basso

BASSIER ▸ bassy

BASSIEST ▸ bassy

BASSINET n wickerwork or wooden cradle or pram, usually hooded

BASSING ▸ bass

BASSIST, -S n player of a double bass, esp in a jazz band

BASSLINE n (in jazz, rock, and pop music) part played by the bass guitar

BASSLY ▸ bass

BASSNESS ▸ bass

BASSO, BASSI, -S n singer with a bass voice

BASSOON, -S n low-pitched woodwind instrument

BASSOS ▸ basso

BASSWOOD n N American linden tree

BASSY, BASSIER, BASSIEST adj manifesting strong bass tones

BAST, -S n fibrous material used for making rope, matting, etc

BASTA interj enough; stop

BASTE, -D, -S vb moisten (meat) during cooking with hot fat

BASTER, -S ▸ baste

BASTES ▸ baste

BASTI, -S n (in India) a slum inhabited by poor people

BASTIDE, -S n small isolated house in France

BASTILE, -S same as ▸ bastille

BASTILLE n prison

BASTING, -S n loose temporary stitches

BASTION, -S n projecting part of a fortification

BASTIS ▸ basti

BASTLE, -S n fortified house

BASTO, -S n ace of clubs in certain card games

BASTS ▸ bast

BASUCO, -S n illegal cocaine-based drug

BAT, -S, -TED n any of various types of club used to hit the ball in certain sports ▷ vb strike with or as if with a bat

BATABLE ▸ bat

BATARD, -S n canoe made of birchbark

BATATA, -S n sweet potato

BATAVIA, -S n variety of lettuce with smooth pale green leaves

BATBOY, -S n boy who works at baseball games

BATCH, -ED, -ES n group of people or things dealt with at the same time ▷ vb group (items) for efficient processing

BATCHER, -S ▸ batch

BATCHES ▸ batch

BATCHING ▸ batch

BATE, -D, -S, BATING vb (of hawks) to jump violently from a perch or the falconer's fist

BATEAU, -X n light flat-bottomed boat used on rivers in Canada and the northern US

BATED ▸ bate

BATELESS ▸ bate

BATELEUR n African bird of prey with a short tail and long wings

BATEMENT n reduction

BATES ▸ bate

BATFISH n type of angler fish with a flattened scaleless body

BATFOWL, -S vb catch birds by temporarily blinding them with light

BATGIRL, -S n girl who works at baseball games

BATH, -S n large container in which to wash the body ▷ vb wash in a bath

BATHCUBE n cube of soluble scented material for use in a bath

BATHE, -D, -S vb swim in open water for pleasure

B

BATHER ▸ bathe

BATHERS pl n swimming costume

BATHES ▸ bathe

BATHETIC adj containing or displaying bathos

BATHING, -S n act of bathing

BATHLESS ▸ bath

BATHMAT, -S n mat to stand on after a bath

BATHMIC ▸ bathmism

BATHMISM n growth-force

BATHORSE n officer's packhorse

BATHOS, -ES n sudden change from a serious subject to a trivial one

BATHROBE n loose-fitting garment for wear before or after a bath or swimming

BATHROOM n room with a bath, sink, and usu a toilet

BATHS ▸ bath

BATHTUB, -S n bath, esp one not permanently fixed

BATHYAL adj relating to an ocean depth of between 200 and 2000 metres

BATIK, -ED, -ING, -S n process of printing fabric using wax to cover areas not to be dyed ▷ vb treat material with this process

BATING ▸ bate

BATISTE, -S n fine plain-weave cotton fabric

BATLER, -S n flat piece of wood for beating clothes, etc before washing

BATLET, -S same as ▸ batler

BATLIKE ▸ bat

BATMAN, BATMEN n male servant in the armed forces

BATOLOGY n study of brambles

BATON, -ED, -ING, -S n thin stick used by the conductor of an orchestra ▷ vb carry or wave a baton

BATOON, -ED, -S same as ▸ baton

BATS ▸ bat

BATSMAN, BATSMEN n man who bats or specializes in batting

BATSWING adj in the form of the wing of a bat

BATT, -S same as ▸ bat

BATTA, -S n soldier's allowance

BATTALIA n arrangement of army prepared for battle

BATTAS ▸ batta

BATTEAU, -X same as ▸ bateau

BATTED ▸ bat

BATTEL, -ED, -S vb make fertile

BATTELER ▸ battel

BATTELS ▸ battel

BATTEN, -ED, -S n strip of wood fixed to something, esp to hold it in place ▷ vb strengthen or fasten with battens

BATTENER ▸ batten

BATTENS ▸ batten

BATTER, -S vb hit repeatedly ▷ n mixture of flour, eggs, and milk, used in cooking

BATTERED adj subjected to persistent physical violence

BATTERER n person who batters someone

BATTERIE n movement in ballet involving the legs beating together

BATTERO, -S n heavy club

BATTERS ▸ batter

BATTERY n device that produces electricity in a torch, radio, etc ▷ adj kept in series of cages for intensive rearing

BATTIER ▸ batty

BATTIES ▸ batty

BATTIEST ▸ batty

BATTIK, -S same as ▸ batik

BATTILL, -S vb fatten an animal

BATTILY adv in an eccentric or crazy manner

BATTING, -S n act of hitting with a bat

BATTLE, -D, -S, BATTLING n fight between large armed forces ▷ vb struggle

BATTLEAX same as ▸ battleaxe

BATTLED ▸ battle

BATTLER, -S ▸ battle

BATTLES ▸ battle

BATTLING ▸ battle

BATTS ▸ batt

BATTU adj (in ballet) involving a beating movement

BATTUE, -S n beating of woodland or cover to force game to flee in the direction of hunters

BATTUTA, -S n (in music) a beat

BATTUTO, -S n (in Italian cookery) selection of chopped herbs

BATTY, BATTIER, BATTIES, BATTIEST adj eccentric or crazy ▷ n person's bottom

BATWING adj shaped like the wings of a bat, as a black tie, collar, etc

BATWOMAN, BATWOMEN n female servant in any of the armed forces

BAUBEE, -S same as ▸ bawbee

BAUBLE, -S, BAUBLING n trinket of little value

BAUCHLE, -D, -S vb shuffle along

BAUD, -S n unit used to measure the speed of transmission of electronic data

BAUDEKIN old variant of ▸ baldachin

BAUDRIC, -S same as ▸ baldric

BAUDRICK same as ▸ baldric

BAUDRICS ▸ baudric

BAUDRONS n name for a cat

BAUDS ▸ baud

BAUERA, -S n small evergreen Australian shrub

BAUHINIA n type of climbing or shrubby plant

BAUK, -ED, -ING, -S same as ▸ balk

BAULK, -ED, -ING, -S same as ▸ balk

BAULKER, -S ▸ baulk

BAULKIER ▸ baulky

BAULKILY ▸ baulky

BAULKING ▸ baulk

BAULKS ▸ baulk

BAULKY, BAULKIER same as ▸ balky

BAUR, -S n humorous anecdote; joke

BAUSOND adj (of animal) dappled with white spots

BAUXITE, -S n claylike substance that is the chief source of aluminium

BAUXITIC ▸ bauxite

BAVAROIS n cold dessert consisting of a rich custard set with gelatine

BAVIN, -ED, -ING, -S n bundle of brushwood or firewood ▷ vb bind (brushwood or firewood) into bavins

BAWBEE, -S n former Scottish silver coin

BAWBLE, -S same as ▸ bauble

BAWCOCK, -S n fine fellow

BAWDKIN, -S same as ▸ baldachin

BAWDRIC, -S n heavy belt to support sword

BAWK, -S n type of Atlantic seabird

BAWL, -ED, -S vb shout or weep noisily ▷ n loud shout or cry

BAWLER, -S ▸ bawl

BAWLEY, -S n small fishing boat

BAWLING, -S ▸ bawl

BAWLS ▸ bawl

BAWN, -S n fortified enclosure

BAWNEEN, -S same as ▸ bainin

BAWNS ▸ bawn

BAWR, -S same as ▸ baur

BAWSUNT adj black and white in colour

BAWTIE, -S n Scots word for a dog

BAWTY same as ▸ bawtie

BAXTER, -S old variant of ▸ baker

BAY, -ED, -ER, -EST, -ING, -S n wide semicircular indentation of a shoreline ▷ vb howl in deep tones ▷ adj (esp of horses) of a reddish brown colour

BAYADEER same as ▸ bayadere

BAYADERE n female dancer, esp one serving in a Hindu temple ▷ adj (of fabric, etc) having horizontal stripes

BAYAMO, -S n Cuban strong wind

BAYARD, -S n bay horse

BAYBERRY n tropical American tree that yields an oil used in making bay rum

BAYE, -S vb bathe

BAYED ▸ bay

BAYER ▸ bay

BAYES ▸ baye

BAYEST ▸ bay

BAYFRONT n shoreline of a bay

BAYING ▸ bay

BAYLE, -S n barrier

BAYMAN, BAYMEN n fisherman

BAYNODDY n person who fishes in a bay

BAYONET, -S n sharp blade that can be fixed to the end of a rifle ▷ vb stab with a bayonet

BAYOU, -S n (in the southern US) a sluggish marshy tributary of a lake or river

BAYS ▸ bay

BAYSIDE, -S n shore of a bay

BAYT, -ED, -ING, -S same as ▸ bate

BAYWOOD, -S n light soft wood of a tropical American mahogany tree

BAYYAN, -S n Islamic declaration

BAZAAR, -S n sale in aid of charity

BAZAR, -S same as ▸ bazaar

BAZAZZ, -ES same as ▸ pizzazz

BAZOO, -S a US slang word for ▸ mouth

BAZOOKA, -S n portable rocket launcher that fires an armour-piercing projectile

BAZOOS ▸ bazoo

BAZOUKI, -S same as ▸ bouzouki

BAZZ, -ED, -ES, -ING vb throw (an object)

BAZZAZZ same as ▸ pizzazz

BAZZED ▸ bazz

BAZZES ▸ bazz

BAZZING ▸ bazz

BDELLIUM n African or W Asian tree that yields a gum resin

BE vb exist or live

BEACH, -ED, -ES, -ING n area of sand or pebbles on a shore ▷ vb run or haul (a boat) onto a beach

BEACHBOY n male lifeguard on beach

BEACHED ▸ beach

BEACHES ▸ beach

BEACHIER ▸ beachy

BEACHING ▸ beach

BEACHY, BEACHIER adj with gentle sandy slopes

BEACON, -ED, -S n fire or light on a hill or tower, used as a warning ▷ vb guide or warn

BEAD, -ED, -S n small piece of plastic, wood, etc, pierced for threading ▷ vb decorate with beads

BEADER, -S n person making things with beads

BEADIER ▸ beady

BEADIEST ▸ beady

BEADILY ▸ beady

BEADING, -S n strip of moulding used for edging furniture

BEADLE, -S n (formerly) a minor parish official who acted as an usher

BEADLIKE ▸ bead

BEADMAN, BEADMEN same as ▸ beadsman

BEADROLL n list of persons for whom prayers are to be offered

BEADS ▸ bead

BEADSMAN, BEADSMEN n man who prays for another's soul

BEADWORK same as ▸ beading

BEADY, BEADIER, BEADIEST adj small, round, and glittering

BEAGLE, -D, -S n small hound with short legs and drooping ears ▷ vb hunt with beagles, normally on foot

BEAGLER, -S n person who hunts with beagles

BEAGLES ▸ beagle

BEAGLING ▸ beagle

BEAK, -S n projecting horny jaws of a bird

BEAKED ▸ beak

BEAKER, -S n large drinking cup

BEAKIER ▸ beaky

BEAKIEST ▸ beaky

BEAKLESS ▸ beak

BEAKLIKE ▸ beak

BEAKS ▸ beak

BEAKY, BEAKIER, BEAKIEST ▸ beak

BEAL, -S n infected sore

BEALING, -S n infected sore

BEALS ▸ beal

BEAM, -ED, -S n broad smile ▷ vb smile broadly

BEAMER, -S n full-pitched ball bowled at the batsman's head

BEAMIER ▸ beamy

BEAMIEST ▸ beamy

BEAMILY ▸ beam

BEAMING, -S ▸ beam

BEAMISH adj smiling

BEAMLESS ▸ beam

BEAMLET, -S n small beam

BEAMLIKE ▸ beam

BEAMS ▸ beam

BEAMY, BEAMIER, BEAMIEST ▸ beam

BEAN, -ED, -ING, -S n seed or pod of various plants, eaten as a vegetable or used to make coffee etc ▷ vb strike on the head

BEANBAG, -S n small cloth bag filled with dried beans and thrown in games

BEANBALL n baseball intended to hit batter's head

BEANED ▸ bean

BEANERY n cheap restaurant

BEANIE, -S n close-fitting woollen hat

BEANING ▸ bean

BEANLIKE ▸ bean

BEANO, -S n celebration or party

BEANPOLE n pole used to support bean plants

BEANS ▸ bean

BEANY same as ▸ beanie

B

BEAR, -ED, -S, BORNE vb support or hold up (something) ▷ vb lower the price of (a security) ▷ n type of omnivorous mammal
BEARABLE adj endurable
BEARABLY ▶ bearable
BEARBINE n type of bindweed
BEARCAT, -S n lesser panda
BEARD, -ED, -ING, -S n hair growing on the lower parts of a person's face ▷ vb oppose boldly
BEARDIE, -S n another name for bearded loach
BEARDIER ▶ beardy
BEARDIES ▶ beardie
BEARDING ▶ beard
BEARDS ▶ beard
BEARDY, BEARDIER adj having a beard
BEARE, -S same as ▶ bear
BEARED ▶ bear
BEARER, -S n person who carries, presents, or upholds something
BEARES ▶ beare
BEARHUG, -S n wrestling hold in which the arms are locked tightly round an opponent's chest and arms ▷ vb hold an opponent in a bearhug
BEARING, -S ▶ bear
BEARISH adj like a bear
BEARLIKE ▶ bear
BEARPAW, -S n paw of a bear
BEARS ▶ bear
BEARSKIN n tall fur helmet worn by some British soldiers
BEARWARD n bear keeper
BEARWOOD another name for ▶ cascara
BEAST, -ED, -ING, -S n large wild animal ▷ vb torture someone using excessive physical exercise
BEASTIE, -S n small animal
BEASTILY same as > **bestially**
BEASTING ▶ beast
BEASTLY adj unpleasant or disagreeable ▷ adv extremely
BEASTS ▶ beast
BEAT, -EN, -S vb strike with a series of violent blows ▷ n stroke or blow ▷ adj totally exhausted
BEATABLE ▶ beat
BEATBOX n drum machine simulated by a human voice ▷ vb simulate a drum machine with a human voice

BEATDOWN n heavy defeat
BEATEN ▶ beat
BEATER, -S n device used for beating
BEATH, -ED, -ING, -S vb dry; heat
BEATIER ▶ beaty
BEATIEST ▶ beaty
BEATIFIC adj displaying great happiness
BEATIFY vb take first step towards making (a dead person) a saint
BEATING, -S ▶ beat
BEATLESS ▶ beat
BEATNIK, -S n young person in the late 1950s who rebelled against conventional attitudes etc
BEATS ▶ beat
BEATY, BEATIER, BEATIEST adj (of music) having a strong rhythm
BEAU, -S, -X n boyfriend or admirer
BEAUCOUP n large amount
BEAUFET, -S same as ▶ buffet
BEAUFFET same as ▶ buffet
BEAUFIN, -S same as ▶ biffin
BEAUISH adj vain and showy
BEAUS ▶ beau
BEAUT, -ER, -EST, -S n person or thing that is outstanding or distinctive ▷ adj good or excellent ▷ interj exclamation of joy or pleasure
BEAUTIED ▶ beauty
BEAUTIES ▶ beauty
BEAUTIFY vb make beautiful
BEAUTS ▶ beaut
BEAUTY, BEAUTIED, BEAUTIES n combination of all the qualities of a person or thing that delight the senses and mind ▷ interj expression of approval or agreement ▷ vb make beautiful
BEAUX ▶ beau
BEAUXITE same as ▶ bauxite
BEAVER, -ED, -S n amphibious rodent with a big flat tail ▷ vb work steadily or assiduously
BEAVERY n place for keeping beavers
BEBEERU, -S n tropical American tree
BEBLOOD, -S vb stain with blood
BEBOP, -PED, -S same as ▶ bop
BEBOPPER ▶ bebop
BEBOPS ▶ bebop

BEBUNG, -S n vibrato effect on clavichord
BECALL, -ED, -S vb use insulting words about someone
BECALM, -S vb make calm
BECALMED adj (of a sailing ship) motionless through lack of wind
BECALMS ▶ becalm
BECAME ▶ become
BECAP, -PED, -S vb put a cap on
BECARPET vb lay carpet on
BECASSE, -S n woodcock
BECAUSE conj on account of the fact that; on account of being; since
BECHALK, -S vb mark with chalk
BECHAMEL n thick white sauce flavoured with onion and seasoning
BECHANCE vb happen (to)
BECHARM, -S vb delight
BECK, -ED, -ING, -S n stream ▷ vb attract someone's attention by nodding or gesturing
BECKE, -S same as ▶ beak
BECKED ▶ beck
BECKES ▶ becke
BECKET, -S n clevis forming part of one end of a sheave
BECKING ▶ beck
BECKON, -ED, -S vb summon with a gesture ▷ n summoning gesture
BECKONER ▶ beckon
BECKONS ▶ beckon
BECKS ▶ beck
BECLAMOR vb clamour excessively
BECLASP, -S vb embrace
BECLOAK, -S vb dress in cloak
BECLOG, -S vb put clogs on
BECLOTHE vb put clothes on
BECLOUD, -S vb cover or obscure with a cloud
BECLOWN, -S vb clown around
BECOME, BECAME, -S vb come to be
BECOMING adj attractive or pleasing ▷ n any process of change
BECOWARD vb make cowardly
BECRAWL, -S vb crawl all over
BECRIME, -D, -S vb make someone guilty of a crime
BECROWD, -S vb crowd with something
BECRUST, -S vb cover with crust

B

BECUDGEL vb arm with cudgel

BECURL, -ED, -S vb curl

BECURSE, -D, -S, BECURST vb curse

BED, -DED, -S n piece of furniture on which to sleep ▷ vb plant in a bed

BEDABBLE vb dabble; moisten

BEDAD interj exclamation of affirmation

BEDAGGLE vb soil by trailing through dirt

BEDAMN, -ED, -S vb damn

BEDARKEN vb make dark

BEDASH, -ED, -ES vb sprinkle with liquid

BEDAUB, -ED, -S vb smear with something sticky or dirty

BEDAWIN, -S same as ▸ bedouin

BEDAZE, -D, -S, BEDAZING vb daze

BEDAZZLE vb dazzle or confuse, as with brilliance

BEDBATH, -S n washing of a sick person in bed

BEDBOARD n base of bed

BEDBUG, -S n small blood-sucking wingless insect that infests dirty houses

BEDCHAIR n adjustable chair to support invalid in bed

BEDCOVER n cover for bed

BEDDED ▸ bed

BEDDER, -S n (at some universities) college servant employed to keep students' rooms in order

BEDDING, -S ▸ bed

BEDE, -S n prayer

BEDEAFEN vb deafen

BEDECK, -ED, -S vb cover with decorations

BEDEGUAR n growth found on rosebushes

BEDEL, -S archaic spelling of ▸ beadle

BEDELL, -S same as ▸ beadle

BEDELS ▸ bedel

BEDEMAN, BEDEMEN same as ▸ beadsman

BEDERAL, -S same as ▸ bedral

BEDES ▸ bede

BEDESMAN, BEDESMEN same as ▸ beadsman

BEDEVIL, -S vb harass, confuse, or torment

BEDEW, -ED, -ING, -S vb wet or cover with or as if with drops of dew

BEDFAST an archaic word for ▸ bedridden

BEDFRAME n framework of bed

BEDGOWN, -S n night dress

BEDHEAD, -S n untidy state of the hair, esp caused by sleeping

BEDIAPER vb put a nappy on

BEDIDE ▸ bedye

BEDIGHT, -S vb array or adorn ▷ adj adorned or bedecked

BEDIM, -MED, -S vb make dim

BEDIMPLE vb form dimples in

BEDIMS ▸ bedim

BEDIRTY vb make dirty

BEDIZEN, -S vb dress or decorate gaudily

BEDLAM, -S n noisy confused situation

BEDLAMER n young harp seal

BEDLAMP, -S n bedside light

BEDLAMS ▸ bedlam

BEDLESS ▸ bed

BEDLIKE adj like a bed

BEDLINER n lining for the bed of a truck

BEDMAKER n person who makes beds

BEDMATE, -S n person who shares a bed

BEDOTTED adj scattered; strewn

BEDOUIN, -S n member of any of the nomadic tribes of Arabs

BEDPAN, -S n shallow bowl used as a toilet by bedridden people

BEDPLATE n heavy metal platform or frame to which an engine or machine is attached

BEDPOST, -S n vertical support on a bedstead

BEDQUILT n padded bed cover

BEDRAIL, -S n rail along the side of a bed connecting the headboard with the footboard

BEDRAL, -S n minor church official

BEDRAPE, -D, -S vb adorn

BEDRENCH vb drench

BEDREST, -S n rest in bed, eg to recover from illness

BEDRID same as ▸ bedridden

BEDRITES ▸ bedrite

BEDRIVEL vb drivel around

BEDROCK, -S n solid rock beneath the surface soil

BEDROLL, -S n portable roll of bedding

BEDROOM, -S n room used for sleeping

BEDROP, -S, -T vb drop on

BEDRUG, -S vb drug excessively

BEDS ▸ bed

BEDSHEET n sheet for bed

BEDSIDE, -S n area beside a bed ▷ adj placed at or near the side of the bed

BEDSIT, -S n furnished sitting room with a bed

BEDSKIRT n drapery round the edge of a bed

BEDSOCK, -S n sock worn in bed

BEDSONIA n bacterium causing diseases such as trachoma

BEDSORE, -S n ulcer on the skin, caused by a lengthy period of lying in bed due to illness

BEDSTAND n bedside table

BEDSTEAD n framework of a bed

BEDSTRAW n plant with small white or yellow flowers

BEDTICK, -S n case containing stuffing in mattress

BEDTIME, -S n time when one usually goes to bed

BEDU adj relating to beduins

BEDUCK, -ED, -S vb duck under water

BEDUIN, -S variant of ▸ bedouin

BEDUMB, -ED, -S vb make dumb

BEDUNCE, -D, -S vb cause to look or feel foolish

BEDUNG, -ED, -S vb spread with dung

BEDUST, -ED, -S vb cover with dust

BEDWARD adj towards bed

BEDWARDS adv towards bed

BEDWARF, -S vb hamper growth of

BEDYE, BEDYDE, -D, -ING, -S vb dye

BEE, -S n insect that makes wax and honey

BEEBEE, -S n air rifle

BEEBREAD n mixture of pollen and nectar prepared by worker bees and fed to the larvae

BEECH, -ES n tree with a smooth greyish bark

BEECHEN ▸ beech

B

BEECHES ▸ beech
BEECHIER ▸ beechy
BEECHNUT n small brown triangular edible nut of the beech tree
BEECHY, BEECHIER ▸ beech
BEEDI n Indian cigarette
BEEDIE, -S same as ▸ beedi
BEEF, -ED, -ING, -S, BEEVES n flesh of a cow, bull, or ox ▷ vb complain
BEEFALO, -S n cross between cow and buffalo
BEEFCAKE n muscular man as displayed in photographs
BEEFED ▸ beef
BEEFIER ▸ beefy
BEEFIEST ▸ beefy
BEEFILY ▸ beefy
BEEFING ▸ beef
BEEFLESS ▸ beef
BEEFS ▸ beef
BEEFWOOD n any of various trees that produce very hard wood
BEEFY, BEEFIER, BEEFIEST adj like beef
BEEGAH, -S same as ▸ bigha
BEEHIVE, -S n structure in which bees live
BEEHIVED adj (esp of a hairstyle) shaped like a beehive
BEEHIVES ▸ beehive
BEELIKE ▸ bee
BEELINE, -D, -S n most direct route between two places ▷ vb make a beeline for (something)
BEEN vb past participle of be
BEENAH, -S n understanding; insight
BEENTO, -S n W African word for a person who has lived in Britain ▷ adj of or relating to such a person
BEEP, -ED, -ING, -S n high-pitched sound, like that of a car horn ▷ vb (cause to) make this noise
BEEPER, -S ▸ beep
BEEPING ▸ beep
BEEPS ▸ beep
BEER, -S n alcoholic drink brewed from malt and hops
BEERAGE, -S n brewing industry
BEERFEST n beer festival
BEERHALL n large public room where beer is consumed
BEERIER ▸ beery
BEERIEST ▸ beery
BEERILY ▸ beery
BEERMAT, -S n small mat put under a glass of beer

BEERNUT, -S n coated peanut eaten as a snack
BEERS ▸ beer
BEERSIES pl n New Zealand informal word for beers
BEERY, BEERIER, BEERIEST adj smelling or tasting of beer
BEES ▸ bee
BEESOME same as ▸ bisson
BEESTING adj as in **beesting lips**, pouting
BEESTUNG adj as in **beestung lips** of lips, pouting
BEESWAX n wax secreted by bees, used in polishes etc ▷ vb polish with such wax
BEESWING n light filmy crust that forms in port wine
BEET, -ED, -ING, -S n plant with an edible root and leaves ▷ vb improve or make better
BEETFLY n type of fly which is a common pest of beets and mangel-wurzels
BEETING ▸ beet
BEETLE, -D, -S n insect with a hard wing cover on its back ▷ vb scuttle or scurry
BEETLER, -S n one who operates a beetling machine
BEETLES ▸ beetle
BEETLING ▸ beetle
BEETROOT n type of beet plant with a dark red root
BEETS ▸ beet
BEEVES ▸ beef
BEEYARD, -S n place where bees are kept
BEEZER, -S n person or chap ▷ adj excellent
BEFALL, -EN, -S, BEFELL vb happen to (someone)
BEFANA, -S n Italian gift-bearing good fairy
BEFELD archaic past participle of ▸ befall
BEFELL ▸ befall
BEFFANA, -S same as ▸ befana
BEFINGER vb mark by handling
BEFINNED adj with fins
BEFIT, -S, -TED vb be appropriate or suitable for
BEFLAG, -S vb decorate with flags
BEFLEA, -ED, -S vb infest with fleas
BEFLECK, -S vb fleck
BEFLOWER vb decorate with flowers
BEFLUM, -S vb fool; deceive
BEFOAM, -ED, -S vb cover with foam

BEFOG, -GED, -S vb surround with fog
BEFOOL, -S vb make a fool of
BEFORE adv indicating something earlier in time, in front of, or preferred to ▷ prep preceding in space or time
BEFOUL, -ED, -S vb make dirty or foul
BEFOULER ▸ befoul
BEFOULS ▸ befoul
BEFRET, -S vb fret about something
BEFRIEND vb become friends with
BEFRINGE vb decorate with fringe
BEFUDDLE vb confuse, muddle, or perplex
BEG, -GED, -S vb solicit (money, food, etc), esp in the street
BEGAD interj emphatic exclamation
BEGALL, -ED, -S vb make sore by rubbing
BEGAN ▸ begin
BEGAR, -S n compulsory labour
BEGAT archaic past tense of ▸ beget
BEGAZE, -D, -S, BEGAZING vb gaze about or around
BEGEM, -MED, -S vb decorate with gems
BEGET, -S, BEGOT, BEGOTTEN vb cause or create
BEGETTER ▸ beget
BEGGAR, -ED, -S n person who begs, esp one who lives by begging ▷ vb be beyond the resources of
BEGGARLY adj meanly inadequate
BEGGARS ▸ beggar
BEGGARY n extreme poverty or need
BEGGED ▸ beg
BEGGING, -S ▸ beg
BEGHARD, -S n member of a 13th century Christian brotherhood
BEGIFT, -ED, -S vb give a gift or gifts to
BEGILD, -ED, -S, BEGILT vb gild
BEGIN, BEGAN, -S, BEGUN vb start
BEGINNE, -S same as ▸ **beginning**
BEGINNER n person who has just started learning to do something

BEGINNES ▸ beginne
BEGINS ▸ begin
BEGIRD, -ED, -S, BEGIRT vb surround
BEGIRDLE vb surround with girdle
BEGIRDS ▸ begird
BEGIRT ▸ begird
BEGLAD, -S vb make glad
BEGLAMOR same as > beglamour
BEGLOOM, -S vb make gloomy
BEGNAW, -ED, -S vb gnaw at
BEGO, -ES, -ING, -NE, BEWENT vb harass; beset
BEGONIA, -S n tropical plant with waxy flowers
BEGORAH same as ▸ begorra
BEGORED adj smeared with gore
BEGORRA interj emphatic exclamation, regarded as a characteristic utterance of Irish people
BEGORRAH same as ▸ begorra
BEGOT ▸ beget
BEGOTTEN ▸ beget
BEGRIM, -S same as ▸ begrime
BEGRIME, -D, -S vb make dirty
BEGRIMS ▸ begrim
BEGROAN, -S vb groan at
BEGRUDGE vb envy (someone) the possession of something
BEGS ▸ beg
BEGUILE, -D, -S vb cheat or mislead
BEGUILER ▸ beguile
BEGUILES ▸ beguile
BEGUIN, -S another name for ▸ beghard
BEGUINE, -S n S American dance
BEGUINS ▸ beguin
BEGULF, -ED, -S vb overwhelm
BEGUM, -S n Muslim woman of high rank
BEGUN ▸ begin
BEGUNK, -ED, -S vb delude; trick
BEHALF, BEHALVES n interest, part, benefit, or respect
BEHAPPEN vb befall
BEHATTED adj wearing a hat
BEHAVE, -D, -S, BEHAVING vb act or function in a particular way
BEHAVER, -S ▸ behave
BEHAVES ▸ behave

BEHAVING ▸ behave
BEHAVIOR same as > behaviour
BEHEAD, -ED, -S vb remove the head from
BEHEADAL ▸ behead
BEHEADED ▸ behead
BEHEADER ▸ behead
BEHEADS ▸ behead
BEHELD ▸ behold
BEHEMOTH n huge person or thing
BEHEST, -S n order or earnest request
BEHIGHT, -S vb entrust
BEHIND, -S adv indicating position to the rear, lateness, responsibility, etc ▹ n buttocks ▹ prep in or to a position further back than ▹ adj in a position further back
BEHOLD, BEHELD, -S vb look (at)
BEHOLDEN adj indebted or obliged
BEHOLDER ▸ behold
BEHOLDS ▸ behold
BEHOOF, -S n advantage or profit
BEHOOVE, -D, -S same as ▸ behove
BEHOTE, -S, BEHOTING same as ▸ behight
BEHOVE, -D, -S, BEHOVING vb be necessary or fitting for
BEHOVELY adj useful
BEHOVES ▸ behove
BEHOVING ▸ behove
BEHOWL, -ED, -S vb howl at
BEIGE, -R, -S, -ST adj pale brown ▹ n very light brown
BEIGEL, -S same as ▸ bagel
BEIGER ▸ beige
BEIGES ▸ beige
BEIGEST ▸ beige
BEIGIER ▸ beigy
BEIGIEST ▸ beigy
BEIGNE, -S variant of ▸ beignet
BEIGNET, -S n square deep-fried pastry served hot and sprinkled with icing sugar
BEIGY, BEIGIER, BEIGIEST ▸ beige
BEIN, -ED, -ING, -S adj financially comfortable ▹ vb fill
BEING, -S ▸ be
BEINING ▸ bein
BEINKED adj daubed with ink
BEINNESS ▸ bein
BEINS ▸ bein
BEJADE, -D, -S, BEJADING vb jade; tire

BEJANT, -S same as ▸ bajan
BEJESUIT vb convert to Jesuitism
BEJEWEL, -S vb decorate with or as if with jewels
BEJUMBLE vb jumble up
BEKAH, -S n half shekel
BEKISS, -ED, -ES vb smother with kisses
BEKNAVE, -D, -S vb treat as a knave
BEKNIGHT vb esteem
BEKNOT, -S vb tie a knot or knots in
BEKNOWN adj known about
BEL, -S n unit for comparing two power levels or measuring the intensity of a sound
BELABOR, -S same as ▸ belabour
BELABOUR vb attack verbally or physically
BELACE, -D, -S, BELACING vb decorate with lace
BELADY, BELADIED, BELADIES vb call a lady
BELAH, -S n Australian tree which yields a useful timber
BELAMIES ▸ belamy
BELAMOUR n beloved person
BELAMY, BELAMIES n close friend
BELAR, -S same as ▸ belah
BELATE, -S, BELATING vb cause to be late
BELATED adj late or too late
BELATES ▸ belate
BELATING ▸ belate
BELAUD, -ED, -S vb praise highly
BELAY, -ED, -ING, -S vb secure a line to a pin or cleat ▹ n attachment (of a climber) to a mountain
BELAYER, -S ▸ belay
BELAYING ▸ belay
BELAYS ▸ belay
BELCH, -ED, -ES, -ING vb expel wind from the stomach noisily through the mouth ▹ n act of belching
BELCHER, -S ▸ belch
BELCHES ▸ belch
BELCHING ▸ belch
BELDAM, -S n old woman, esp an ugly or malicious one
BELDAME, -S same as ▸ beldam
BELDAMS ▸ beldam
BELEAP, -ED, -S, -T vb leap over
BELEE, -D, -ING, -S vb put on sheltered side
BELFRIED adj with a belfry

B

BELFRY, BELFRIES *n* part of a tower where bells are hung

BELGA, -S *n* former Belgian monetary unit worth five francs

BELGARD, -S *n* kind gaze

BELGAS ▸ belga

BELIE, -D, -S, BELYING *vb* show to be untrue

BELIEF, -S *n* faith or confidence

BELIER, -S ▸ belie

BELIES ▸ belie

BELIEVE, -D, -S *vb* accept as true or real

BELIEVER ▸ believe

BELIEVES ▸ believe

BELIKE *adv* perhaps

BELIQUOR *vb* cause to be drunk

BELITTLE *vb* treat as having little value or importance

BELIVE *adv* speedily

BELL, -ED, -S *n* hollow cup-shaped instrument that emits a ringing sound when struck ▷ *vb* utter (such a sound)

BELLBIND *n* bindweed-type climber

BELLBIRD *n* Australasian bird with bell-like call

BELLBOY, -S *n* man or boy employed to carry luggage and answer calls for service

BELLBUOY *n* buoy with a bell

BELLCAST *adj* relating to a style of roof with a bell shape

BELLCOTE *n* small roofed structure for bell

BELLE, -S *n* beautiful woman, esp the most attractive woman at a function

BELLED ▸ bell

BELLEEK, -S *n* kind of thin fragile porcelain with a lustrous glaze

BELLES ▸ belle

BELLETER *n* person who makes bells

BELLHOP, -S *same as* ▸ bellboy

BELLIED ▸ belly

BELLIES ▸ belly

BELLING, -S ▸ bell

BELLINI, -S *n* Prosecco and peach cocktail

BELLMAN, BELLMEN *n* man who rings a bell, esp (formerly) a town crier

BELLOCK, -S *vb* shout

BELLOW, -ED *vb* make a low deep cry like that of a bull ▷ *n* loud deep roar

BELLOWER ▸ bellow

BELLOWS *pl n* instrument for pumping a stream of air into something

BELLPULL *n* handle, rope, or cord pulled to operate a doorbell or servant's bell

BELLS ▸ bell

BELLWORT *n* N American plant with slender bell-shaped yellow flowers

BELLY, BELLIED, BELLIES *n* part of the body of a vertebrate which contains the intestines ▷ *vb* (cause to) swell out

BELLYFUL *n* more than one can tolerate

BELLYING ▸ belly

BELON, -S *n* type of oyster

BELONG, -ED, -S *vb* be the property of

BELONGER *n* native-born Caribbean

BELONGS ▸ belong

BELONS ▸ belon

BELOVE, -S, BELOVING *vb* love

BELOVED, -S *adj* dearly loved ▷ *n* person dearly loved

BELOVES ▸ belove

BELOVING ▸ belove

BELOW *adv* at or to a position lower than, under ▷ *prep* at or to a position lower than

BELOWS *same as* ▸ bellows

BELS ▸ bel

BELT, -ED, -S *n* band of cloth, leather, etc, worn usu around the waist ▷ *vb* fasten with a belt

BELTER, -S *n* outstanding person or event

BELTING, -S *n* material used to make a belt or belts ▷ *adj* excellent

BELTLESS ▸ belt

BELTLIKE *adj* like a belt

BELTLINE *n* line separating car's windows from main body

BELTMAN, BELTMEN *n* (formerly) a member of a beach life-saving team

BELTS ▸ belt

BELTWAY, -S *n* people and institutions located in the area bounded by the Washington Beltway

BELUGA, -S *n* large white sturgeon

BELYING ▸ belie

BEMA, -S, -TA *n* speaker's platform in the assembly in ancient Athens

BEMAD, -DED, -S *vb* old word meaning cause to become mad

BEMADAM, -S *vb* call a person madam

BEMADDED ▸ bemad

BEMADDEN *vb* old word meaning cause to become mad

BEMADS ▸ bemad

BEMAS ▸ bema

BEMATA ▸ bema

BEMAUL, -ED, -S *vb* maul

BEMAZED *adj* amazed

BEMBEX, -ES *n* type of wasp

BEMBIX, -ES *same as* ▸ bembex

BEMEAN, -ED, -S, -T *a less common word for* ▸ demean

BEMEDAL, -S *vb* decorate with medals

BEMETE, -D, -S, BEMETING *vb* measure

BEMINGLE *vb* mingle

BEMIRE, -D, -S, BEMIRING *vb* soil with or as if with mire

BEMIST, -ED, -S *vb* cloud with mist

BEMIX, -ED, -ES, -ING, -T *vb* mix thoroughly

BEMOAN, -ED, -S *vb* express sorrow or dissatisfaction about

BEMOANER ▸ bemoan

BEMOANS ▸ bemoan

BEMOCK, -ED, -S *vb* mock

BEMOIL, -ED, -S *vb* soil with mud

BEMOUTH, -S *vb* endow with a mouth

BEMUD, -DED, -S *vb* cover with mud

BEMUDDLE *vb* confound

BEMUDS ▸ bemud

BEMUFFLE *vb* muffle up

BEMURMUR *vb* murmur at

BEMUSE, -S *vb* confuse

BEMUSED *adj* puzzled or confused

BEMUSES ▸ bemuse

BEMUSING ▸ bemuse

BEMUZZLE *vb* put muzzle on

BEN, -S *n* mountain peak ▷ *adv* in ▷ *adj* inner

BENADRYL *n* tradename of an antihistamine drug used in sleeping tablets

BENAME, -D, -S, BENAMING *an archaic word for* ▸ name

BENCH, -ED, -ES, -ING *n* long seat ▷ *vb* put a person on a bench

BENCHER, -S *n* member of the governing body of one of the Inns of Court

BENCHES ▸ bench

BENCHIER ▶ benchy
BENCHING ▶ bench
BENCHTOP adj for use at bench ▷ n flat surface area
BENCHY, BENCHIER, BENCHIEST adj (of a hillside) hollowed out in benches
BEND, -ED, -S vb (cause to) form a curve ▷ n curved part
BENDABLE ▶ bend
BENDAY, -ED, -S vb (printing) reproduce using the Benday technique
BENDED ▶ bend
BENDEE, -S same as ▶ bendy
BENDER, -S n makeshift shelter
BENDIER ▶ bendy
BENDIEST ▶ bendy
BENDING, -S n curving action
BENDLET, -S n narrow diagonal stripe on heraldic shield
BENDS ▶ bend
BENDWAYS same as ▶ bendwise
BENDWISE adv diagonally
BENDY, BENDIER, BENDIEST, -S adj flexible or pliable ▷ n okra
BENE, -S n blessing
BENEATH prep below ▷ adv below
BENEDICK n recently married man
BENEDICT n newly married man
BENEFACT vb be benefactor to
BENEFIC adj rare word for beneficent
BENEFICE n church office providing its holder with an income ▷ vb provide with a benefice
BENEFIT, -S n something that improves or promotes ▷ vb do or receive good
BENEMPT a past participle of ▶ bename
BENES ▶ bene
BENET, -S, -TED vb trap (something) in a net
BENGA, -S n type of Kenyan popular music featuring guitars
BENI, -S n sesame plant
BENIGHT, -S vb shroud in darkness
BENIGN, -ER adj showing kindliness
BENIGNLY ▶ benign
BENIS ▶ beni
BENISEED n sesame
BENISON, -S n blessing, esp a spoken one

BENITIER n basin for holy water
BENJ, -ES another word for ▶ bhang
BENJAMIN same as ▶ benzoin
BENJES ▶ benj
BENNE, -S another name for ▶ sesame
BENNET, -S n Eurasian and N African plant with yellow flowers
BENNI, -S n sesame
BENNIES ▶ benny
BENNIS ▶ benni
BENNY, BENNIES n US word for a man's overcoat
BENOMYL, -S n fungicide
BENS ▶ ben
BENT, -S adj not straight ▷ n personal inclination, propensity, or aptitude
BENTHAL ▶ benthos
BENTHIC ▶ benthos
BENTHOAL ▶ benthos
BENTHON, -S same as ▶ benthos
BENTHOS n animals and plants living at the bottom of a sea or lake
BENTIER ▶ benty
BENTIEST ▶ benty
BENTO, -S n thin lightweight box used in Japanese cuisine
BENTS ▶ bent
BENTWOOD n wood bent in moulds, used mainly for furniture ▷ adj made from such wood
BENTY, BENTIER, BENTIEST adj covered with bentgrass
BENUMB, -ED, -S vb make numb or powerless
BENZAL, -S n transparent crystalline substance
BENZENE, -S n flammable poisonous liquid used as a solvent, insecticide, etc
BENZIDIN same as > benzidine
BENZIL, -S n yellow compound radical
BENZIN, -S same as ▶ benzine
BENZINE, -S n volatile liquid used as a solvent
BENZINS ▶ benzin
BENZOATE n any salt or ester of benzoic acid
BENZOIC adj of, containing, or derived from benzoic acid or benzoin
BENZOIN, -S n gum resin used in ointments, perfume, etc
BENZOL, -S n crude form of benzene

BENZOLE, -S same as ▶ benzol
BENZOLS ▶ benzol
BENZOYL, -S n type of monovalent radical
BENZYL, -S n molecular fragment of certain alcohols and solvents
BENZYLIC ▶ benzyl
BENZYLS ▶ benzyl
BEPAINT, -S vb dye; paint
BEPAT, -S, -TED vb pat
BEPEARL, -S vb decorate with pearls
BEPELT, -ED, -S vb pelt energetically
BEPEPPER vb shower with small missiles
BEPESTER vb pester persistently
BEPIMPLE vb form pimples on
BEPITY, BEPITIED, BEPITIES vb feel great pity for
BEPLUMED adj decorated with feathers
BEPOMMEL vb beat vigorously
BEPOWDER vb cover with powder
BEPRAISE vb praise highly
BEPROSE, -D, -S vb (of poetry) reduce to prose
BEPUFF, -ED, -S vb puff up
BEQUEATH vb dispose of (property) as in a will
BEQUEST, -S n legal gift of money or property by someone who has died
BERAKE, -D, -S, BERAKING vb rake thoroughly
BERASCAL vb accuse of being rascal
BERATE, -D, -S, BERATING vb scold harshly
BERAY, -ED, -ING, -S vb soil; defile
BERBER, -S same as ▶ berbere
BERBERE, -S n hot-tasting Ethiopian paste
BERBERIN same as > berberine
BERBERIS n shrub with red berries
BERBERS ▶ berber
BERBICE n as in berbice chair large armchair with long arms that can be folded inwards to act as leg rests
BERCEAU, -X n arched trellis for climbing plants
BERCEUSE n lullaby
BERE, -S n barley
BEREAVE, -N, -S vb deprive (of) something or someone valued, esp through death

B

BEREAVED adj having recently lost a close friend or relative through death
BEREAVEN ▶ bereave
BEREAVER ▶ bereave
BEREAVES ▶ bereave
BEREFT adj deprived
BERES ▶ bere
BERET, -S n round flat close-fitting brimless cap
BERETTA, -S n type of pistol
BERG, -S n iceberg
BERGALL, -S n fish of the wrasse family
BERGAMA, -S n type of Turkish rug
BERGAMOT n small Asian tree, the fruit of which yields an oil used in perfumery
BERGEN, -S n large rucksack with a capacity of over 50 litres
BERGENIA n evergreen ground-covering plant
BERGENS ▶ bergen
BERGERE, -S n type of French armchair
BERGFALL n avalanche
BERGHAAN same as ▶ bergmehl
BERGMEHL n light powdery variety of calcite
BERGS ▶ berg
BERGYLT, -S n large northern marine food fish
BERHYME, -D, -S vb mention in poetry
BERIBERI n disease caused by dietary deficiency of thiamine
BERIMBAU n Brazilian single-stringed bowed instrument, used to accompany capoeira
BERIME, -D, -S, BERIMING same as ▶ berhyme
BERINGED adj wearing a ring or rings
BERK, -S n stupid person
BERKO adj berserk
BERKS ▶ berk
BERLEY, -ED, -S n bait scattered on water to attract fish ▷ vb scatter (bait) on water
BERLIN, -S n fine wool yarn used for tapestry work, etc
BERLINE, -S same as ▶ berlin
BERLINS ▶ berlin
BERM, -ED, -ING, -S n narrow grass strip between the road and the footpath in a residential area ▷ vb create a berm
BERME, -S same as ▶ berm
BERMED ▶ berm

BERMES ▶ berme
BERMING ▶ berm
BERMS ▶ berm
BERMUDAS pl n close-fitting shorts that come down to the knees
BERNICLE n barnacle goose
BEROB, -BED, -S vb rob
BEROBED adj wearing a robe
BEROBS ▶ berob
BEROUGED adj wearing rouge
BERRET, -S same as ▶ beret
BERRETTA same as ▶ biretta
BERRIED ▶ berry
BERRIES ▶ berry
BERRIGAN n Australian tree with hanging branches
BERRY, BERRIED, BERRIES n small soft stoneless fruit ▷ vb bear or produce berries
BERRYING ▶ berry
BERSEEM, -S n Mediterranean clover grown as a forage crop and to improve the soil
BERSERK, -S adj frenziedly violent or destructive ▷ n fearsome Norse warrior
BERTH, -ED, -S n bunk in a ship or train ▷ vb dock (a ship)
BERTHA, -S n type of lace collar
BERTHAGE n place for mooring boats
BERTHAS ▶ bertha
BERTHE, -S n type of lace collar
BERTHED ▶ berth
BERTHES ▶ berthe
BERTHING n act of berthing
BERTHS ▶ berth
BERYL, -S n hard transparent mineral
BERYLINE ▶ beryl
BERYLLIA n beryllium oxide
BERYLS ▶ beryl
BES, -ES variant of ▶ beth
BESAINT, -S vb give saint status to
BESANG ▶ besing
BESAT ▶ besit
BESAW ▶ besee
BESCORCH vb scorch badly
BESCOUR, -S vb scour thoroughly
BESCRAWL vb cover with scrawls
BESCREEN vb conceal with screen
BESEE, BESAW, -ING, -N, -S vb provide for; mind
BESEECH, BESOUGHT vb ask earnestly
BESEEING ▶ besee

BESEEKE, -S archaic form of ▶ beseech
BESEEM, -ED, -S vb be suitable for
BESEEMLY adj becoming; suitable
BESEEMS ▶ beseem
BESEEN ▶ besee
BESEES ▶ besee
BESES ▶ bes
BESET, -S vb trouble or harass constantly
BESETTER ▶ beset
BESHADOW vb darken with shadow
BESHAME, -D, -S vb cause to feel shame
BESHINE, -S, BESHONE vb illuminate
BESHIVER vb shatter
BESHONE ▶ beshine
BESHOUT, -S vb shout about
BESHREW, -S vb wish evil on
BESHROUD vb cover with a shroud
BESIDE prep at, by, or to the side of
BESIDES prep in addition ▷ adv in addition
BESIEGE, -D, -S vb surround with military forces
BESIEGER ▶ besiege
BESIEGES ▶ besiege
BESIGH, -ED, -S vb sigh for
BESING, BESANG, -S, BESUNG vb sing about joyfully
BESIT, BESAT, -S vb suit; fit
BESLAVE, -D, -S vb treat as slave
BESLAVER vb fawn over
BESLAVES ▶ beslave
BESLIME, -D, -S vb cover with slime
BESMEAR, -S vb smear over
BESMILE, -D, -S vb smile on
BESMIRCH vb tarnish (someone's name or reputation)
BESMOKE, -D, -S vb blacken with smoke
BESMOOTH vb smooth
BESMUDGE vb blacken
BESMUT, -S vb blacken with smut
BESMUTCH same as ▶ besmirch
BESMUTS ▶ besmut
BESNOW, -ED, -S vb cover with snow
BESOGNIO n worthless person
BESOIN, -S n need
BESOM, -ED, -ING, -S n broom made of twigs ▷ vb sweep with a besom

BESONIAN same as
▸ **bezonian**
BESOOTHE vb soothe
BESORT, -ED, -S vb fit
BESOT, -S vb make stupid or
muddled
BESOTTED adj infatuated
BESOUGHT ▸ **beseech**
BESOULED adj having a soul
BESPAKE ▸ **bespeak**
BESPAT ▸ **bespit**
BESPATE ▸ **bespit**
BESPEAK, BESPAKE, -S,
BESPOKEN vb indicate or
suggest
BESPEED, BESPED, -S vb get
on with (doing something)
BESPICE, -D, -S vb flavour
with spices
BESPIT, BESPAT, BESPATE,
-S vb cover with spittle
BESPOKE adj (esp a suit)
made to the customer's
specifications
BESPOKEN ▸ **bespeak**
BESPORT, -S vb amuse
oneself
BESPOT, -S vb mark with spots
BESPOUSE vb marry
BESPOUT, -S vb speak
pretentiously
BESPREAD vb cover (a
surface) with something
BESPRENT adj sprinkled
over
BEST, -ED, -ING, -S adj most
excellent of a particular
group etc ▸ adv in a manner
surpassing all others ▸ n
utmost effort ▸ vb defeat
BESTAD Spenserian form of
▸ **bestead**
BESTADDE Spenserian form of
▸ **bestead**
BESTAIN, -S vb stain
BESTAR, -S vb decorate with
stars
BESTEAD, -S vb serve; assist
▸ adj beset (by)
BESTED ▸ **best**
BESTEST adj best
BESTI, -S Indian English word
for ▸ **shame**
BESTIAL, -S adj brutal or
savage
BESTIARY n medieval
collection of descriptions of
animals
BESTICK, -S, BESTUCK vb
cover with sharp points
BESTIE, -S n best friend
BESTILL, -S vb cause to be
still
BESTING ▸ **best**
BESTIR, -S vb cause (oneself)
to become active

BESTIS ▸ **besti**
BESTORM, -S vb assault
BESTOW, -ED, -S vb present
(a gift) or confer (an honour)
BESTOWAL ▸ **bestow**
BESTOWED ▸ **bestow**
BESTOWER ▸ **bestow**
BESTOWS ▸ **bestow**
BESTREAK vb streak
BESTREW, -N, -S vb scatter
or lie scattered over (a
surface)
BESTRIDE, BESTRID,
BESTRODE vb have or put a
leg on either side of
BESTROW, -N, -S same as
▸ **bestrew**
BESTS ▸ **best**
BESTUCK ▸ **bestick**
BESTUD, -S vb set with, or as
with studs
BESUITED adj wearing a suit
BESUNG ▸ **besing**
BESWARM, -S vb swarm
over
BET, -S, -TED n wager
between two parties
predicting different
outcomes of an event ▸ vb
predict
BETA, -S n second letter in
the Greek alphabet, a
consonant, transliterated
as b
BETACISM n type of speech
impediment
BETAINE, -S n sweet-tasting
alkaloid that occurs in the
sugar beet
BETAKE, -N, -S, BETAKING,
BETOOK vb as in **betake**
oneself go
BETAS ▸ **beta**
BETATRON n type of particle
accelerator for producing
high-energy beams of
electrons
BETATTER vb make ragged
BETAXED adj burdened with
taxes
BETCHA interj bet you
BETE, -D, -S, BETING same as
▸ **beet**
BETEEM, -ED, -S vb accord
BETEEME, -S same as
▸ **beteem**
BETEEMED ▸ **beteem**
BETEEMES ▸ **beteeme**
BETEEMS ▸ **beteem**
BETEL, -S n Asian climbing
plant, the leaves and nuts of
which can be chewed
BETELNUT n seed of the
betel palm
BETELS ▸ **betel**
BETES ▸ **bete**

BETH, -S n second letter of
the Hebrew alphabet,
transliterated as b
BETHANK, -S vb thank
BETHEL, -S n seaman's
chapel
BETHESDA n church
building of certain Christian
denominations
BETHINK, -S vb cause
(oneself) to consider or
meditate
BETHORN, -S vb cover with
thorns
BETHRALL vb make a slave
of
BETHS ▸ **beth**
BETHUMB, -S vb (of books)
wear by handling
BETHUMP, -S vb thump hard
BETHWACK vb strike hard
with flat object
BETIDE, BETID, -D, -S,
BETIDING, BETIGHT vb
happen (to)
BETIME, -D, -S, BETIMING
vb befall
BETING ▸ **bete**
BETISE, -S n folly or lack of
perception
BETITLE, -D, -S vb give title
to
BETOIL, -ED, -S vb tire
through hard work
BETOKEN, -S vb indicate or
signify
BETON, -S n concrete
BETONIES ▸ **betony**
BETONS ▸ **beton**
BETONY, BETONIES n
North American plant
BETOOK ▸ **betake**
BETOSS, -ED, -ES vb toss
about
BETRAY, -ED, -S vb hand
over or expose (one's nation,
friend, etc) treacherously to
an enemy
BETRAYAL ▸ **betray**
BETRAYED ▸ **betray**
BETRAYER ▸ **betray**
BETRAYS ▸ **betray**
BETREAD, -S, BETROD vb
tread over
BETRIM, -S vb decorate
BETROD ▸ **betread**
BETROTH, -S vb promise to
marry or to give in marriage
BETS ▸ **bet**
BETTA, -S n fighting fish
BETTED ▸ **bet**
BETTER, -ED, -S adj more
excellent than others ▸ adv
in a more excellent manner
▸ vb improve upon
BETTIES ▸ **betty**

B

BETTING, -S ▶ bet

BETTONG, -S *n* short-nosed rat kangaroo

BETTOR, -S *n* person who bets

BETTY, BETTIES *n* type of short crowbar

BETWEEN *adv* indicating position in the middle, alternatives, etc ▷ *prep* at a point intermediate to two other points in space, time, etc

BETWIXT *adv* between

BEUNCLED *adj* having many uncles

BEURRE, -S *n* butter

BEVATRON *n* proton synchrotron at the University of California

BEVEL, -ED, -ING, -LED, -S *n* slanting edge ▷ *vb* slope

BEVELER, -S ▶ bevel

BEVELING ▶ bevel

BEVELLED ▶ bevel

BEVELLER ▶ bevel

BEVELS ▶ bevel

BEVER, -ED, -ING, -S *n* snack ▷ *vb* have a snack

BEVERAGE *n* drink

BEVERED ▶ bever

BEVERING ▶ bever

BEVERS ▶ bever

BEVIES ▶ bevy

BEVOMIT, -S *vb* vomit over

BEVOR, -S *n* armour protecting lower part of face

BEVUE, -S *n* careless error

BEVVY, BEVVIED, BEVVIES, -ING *n* alcoholic drink ▷ *vb* drink alcohol

BEVY, BEVIES *n* flock or group

BEWAIL, -ED, -S *vb* express great sorrow over

BEWAILER ▶ bewail

BEWAILS ▶ bewail

BEWARE, -D, -S, BEWARING *vb* be on one's guard (against)

BEWEARY *vb* cause to be weary

BEWEEP, -S, BEWEPT *vb* express grief through weeping

BEWENT ▶ bego

BEWEPT ▶ beweep

BEWET, -S, -TED *vb* make wet

BEWIG, -GED, -S *vb* adorn with a wig

BEWILDER *vb* confuse utterly

BEWINGED *adj* having wings

BEWITCH *vb* attract and fascinate

BEWORM, -ED, -S *vb* fill with worms

BEWORRY *vb* beset with worry

BEWRAP, -S, -T *vb* wrap up

BEWRAY, -ED, -S *an obsolete word for* ▶ betray

BEWRAYER ▶ bewray

BEWRAYS ▶ bewray

BEY, -S *n* title in the Ottoman Empire

A **bey** was an official in the Ottoman empire. If someone plays this remember that you can of course put an O in front of it to make **obey**.

BEYLIC, -S *n* province ruled over by a bey

BEYLIK, -S *same as* ▶ beylic

BEYOND, -S *prep* at or to a point on the other side of ▷ *adv* at or to the far side of something ▷ *n* unknown, esp life after death

BEYS ▶ bey

BEZ, -ES *n* part of a deer's horn

This word for the tine of a deer's horn is one of the essential short words for using the Z.

BEZANT, -S *n* medieval Byzantine gold coin

BEZAZZ, -ES *another word for* ▶ pizzazz

BEZEL, -S *n* sloping edge of a cutting tool

BEZES ▶ bez

BEZIL, -S *archaic word for* > alcoholic

BEZIQUE, -S *n* card game for two or more players

This card game played with two decks of cards combines the Q and Z and would make a wonderful bonus word.

BEZOAR, -S *n* hard mass, such as a stone or hairball, in the stomach and intestines of animals

BEZONIAN *n* knave or rascal

BEZZANT, -S *same as* ▶ bezant

BEZZAZZ *same as* ▶ bezazz

BEZZIE, -S *n* best friend

BEZZLE, -D, -S, BEZZLING *vb* waste (money)

BEZZY *same as* ▶ bezzie

BHAGEE, -S *same as* ▶ bhaji

BHAI, -S *n* Indian form of address for a man

BHAJAN, -S *n* singing of devotional songs and hymns

BHAJEE, -S *same as* ▶ bhaji

BHAJI, -A, -S *n* Indian deep-fried savoury of chopped vegetables in spiced batter

BHAKTA, -S *n* Hindu term for a devotee of God

BHAKTI, -S *n* loving devotion to God leading to nirvana

BHANG, -S *n* preparation of Indian hemp

BHANGRA, -S *n* Punjabi folk music combined with elements of Western pop music

BHANGS ▶ bhang

BHARAL, -S *n* wild Himalayan sheep

BHAT, -S *n* currency of Thailand

BHAVAN, -S *n* (in India) a large house or building

BHAWAN, -S *same as* ▶ bhavan

BHEESTIE *same as* ▶ bhishti

BHEESTY *same as* ▶ bhishti

BHEL, -S *same as* ▶ bael

BHELPURI *n* Indian dish of puffed rice and vegetables

BHELS ▶ bhel

BHIKHU, -S *n* fully ordained Buddhist monk

BHINDI, -S *same as* ▶ bindhi

BHISHTI, -S *n* (formerly in India) a water-carrier

BHISTEE, -S *same as* ▶ bhishti

BHISTI, -S *same as* ▶ bhishti

BHISTIE, -S *same as* ▶ bhishti

BHISTIS ▶ bhisti

BHOONA, -S *same as* ▶ bhuna

BHOOT, -S *same as* ▶ bhut

BHUNA, -S *n* Indian sauce

BHUT, -S *n* Hindu term for a type of ghost

BI *short for* ▶ bisexual

BIACETYL *n* liquid with strong odour

BIALI, -S *same as* ▶ bialy

BIALIES ▶ bialy

BIALIS ▶ biali

BIALY, BIALIES, -S *n* type of bagel

BIANNUAL *adj* occurring twice a year ▷ *n* something that happens biannually

BIAS, -ES *n* mental tendency, esp prejudice ▷ *vb* cause to have a bias ▷ *adj* slanting obliquely ▷ *adv* obliquely

BIASED ▶ bias

BIASEDLY ▶ bias

BIASES ▶ bias

BIASING, -S ▶ bias

B

BIASNESS ▸ bias

BIASSED same as ▸ biased

BIASSES same as ▸ biases

BIASSING same as ▸ biasing

BIATHLON n contest combining skiing with rifle shooting

BIAXAL same as ▸ biaxial

BIAXIAL adj (esp of a crystal) having two axes

BIB, -BED, -S vb drink

BIBASIC adj with two bases

BIBATION n drinking to excess

BIBB, -S n wooden support on a mast for the trestletrees

BIBBED ▸ bib

BIBBER, -S n drinker

BIBBERY n drinking to excess

BIBBING, -S n act of bibbing

BIBBLE, -S n pebble

BIBBS ▸ bibb

BIBCOCK, -S n tap with a nozzle bent downwards

BIBE, -S n (in Newfoundland folklore) spirit whose wailing warns of a coming death

BIBELOT, -S n attractive or curious trinket

BIBES ▸ bibe

BIBFUL, -S n as in spill a bibful divulge secrets

BIBIMBAP n Korean rice dish

BIBLE, -S n any book containing the sacred writings of a religion

BIBLESS ▸ bib

BIBLICAL adj of, occurring in, or referring to the Bible

BIBLIKE ▸ bib

BIBLIST, -S same as > biblicist

BIBS ▸ bib

BIBULOUS adj addicted to alcohol

BICARB, -S n bicarbonate of soda

BICAUDAL adj having two tails

BICCY, BICCIES n biscuit

BICE, -S n medium blue colour

BICEP same as ▸ biceps

BICEPS, -ES n muscle with two origins, esp the muscle that flexes the forearm

BICES ▸ bice

BICHIR, -S n African freshwater fish with an elongated body

BICHORD adj having two strings for each note

BICHROME adj having two colours

BICKER, -ED, -S vb argue over petty matters ▷ n petty squabble

BICKERER ▸ bicker

BICKERS ▸ bicker

BICKIE, -S short for ▸ biscuit

BICOLOR, -S same as ▸ bicolour

BICOLOUR adj two-coloured

BICONVEX adj (of a lens) having convex faces on both sides

BICORN, -S adj having two horns or hornlike parts

BICORNE, -S same as ▸ bicorn

BICORNS ▸ bicorn

BICRON, -S n billionth part of a metre

BICUSPID adj having two points ▷ n bicuspid tooth

BICYCLE, -D, -S n vehicle with two wheels, one behind the other, pedalled by the rider ▷ vb ride a bicycle

BICYCLER ▸ bicycle

BICYCLES ▸ bicycle

BICYCLIC adj of, forming, or formed by two circles, cycles, etc

BID, BADE, -DEN, -S vb offer (an amount) in attempting to buy something ▷ n offer of a specified amount, as at an auction

BIDARKA, -S same as ▸ baidarka

BIDARKEE same as ▸ bidarka

BIDDABLE adj obedient

BIDDABLY ▸ biddable

BIDDEN ▸ bid

BIDDER, -S ▸ bid

BIDDIES ▸ biddy

BIDDING, -S ▸ bid

BIDDY, BIDDIES n woman, esp an old gossipy one

BIDE, -D, -S vb stay or continue

BIDENT, -S n instrument with two prongs

BIDENTAL n sacred place where lightning has struck

BIDENTS ▸ bident

BIDER, -S ▸ bide

BIDES ▸ bide

BIDET, -S n low basin for washing the genital area

BIDI, -S same as ▸ beedi

BIDING, -S ▸ bide

BIDIS ▸ bidi

BIDON, -S n oil drum

BIDS ▸ bid

BIELD, -ED, -ING, -S n shelter ▷ vb shelter or take shelter

BIELDIER ▸ bieldy

BIELDING ▸ bield

BIELDS ▸ bield

BIELDY, BIELDIER adj sheltered

BIEN adv well

BIENNALE n event occurring every two years

BIENNIA ▸ biennium

BIENNIAL adj occurring every two years ▷ n plant that completes its life cycle in two years

BIENNIUM, BIENNIA n period of two years

BIER, -S n stand on which a body or coffin rests before burial

BIFACE, -S n prehistoric stone tool

BIFACIAL adj having two faces or surfaces

BIFF, -ED, -ING, -S n blow with the fist ▷ vb give (someone) such a blow

BIFFER, -S n someone, such as a sportsperson, who has a reputation for hitting hard

BIFFIES ▸ biffy

BIFFIN, -S n variety of red cooking apple

BIFFING ▸ biff

BIFFINS ▸ biffin

BIFFO, -S n fighting or aggressive behaviour ▷ adj aggressive

BIFFS ▸ biff

BIFFY, BIFFIES n outdoor toilet

BIFID adj divided into two by a cleft in the middle

BIFIDA ▸ bifidum

BIFIDITY ▸ bifid

BIFIDLY ▸ bifid

BIFIDUM, BIFIDA, -S n type of bacterium

BIFIDUS n bacterium of the human digestive system

BIFILAR adj having two parallel threads, as in the suspension of certain measuring instruments

BIFLEX adj bent or flexed in two places

BIFOCAL adj having two different focuses

BIFOCALS pl n spectacles with lenses permitting near and distant vision

BIFOLD, -S n something folded in two places

BIFORATE adj having two openings, pores, or perforations

BIFORKED adj two-pronged

B

BIFORM adj having or combining the characteristics of two forms, as a centaur

BIFORMED same as ▶ **biform**

BIFTAH, -S same as ▶ **bifter**

BIFTER, -S n cigarette

BIG, -GED, -GER, -GEST, -S adj of considerable size, height, number, or capacity ▷ adv on a grand scale ▷ vb build

BIGA, -E n chariot drawn by two horses

BIGAMIES ▶ **bigamy**

BIGAMIST ▶ **bigamy**

BIGAMOUS ▶ **bigamy**

BIGAMY, BIGAMIES n crime of marrying a person while still legally married to someone else

BIGARADE n Seville orange

BIGAROON same as ▷ **bigarreau**

BIGEMINY n heart complaint

BIGENER, -S n hybrid between individuals of different genera

BIGEYE, -S n type of red marine fish

BIGFOOT, BIGFEET, -S n yeti ▷ vb throw one's weight around

BIGG, -S n type of barley

BIGGED ▶ **big**

BIGGER ▶ **big**

BIGGEST ▶ **big**

BIGGETY adj conceited

BIGGIE, -S n something big or important

BIGGIN, -S n plain close-fitting cap

BIGGING, -S ▶ **big**

BIGGINS ▶ **biggin**

BIGGISH ▶ **big**

BIGGITY adj conceited

BIGGON, -S same as ▶ **biggin**

BIGGS ▶ **bigg**

BIGGY same as ▶ **biggie**

BIGHA, -S n in India, unit for measuring land

BIGHEAD, -S n conceited person

BIGHORN, -S n large wild mountain sheep

BIGHT, -ED, -ING, -S n long curved shoreline ▷ vb fasten or bind with a loop of rope

BIGLY ▶ **big**

BIGMOUTH n noisy, indiscreet, or boastful person

BIGNESS ▶ **big**

BIGNONIA n tropical American climbing shrub

BIGOS, -ES n Polish stew

BIGOT, -S n person who is intolerant of ideas other than their own

BIGOTED ▶ **bigot**

BIGOTRY n attitudes, behaviour, or way of thinking of a bigot

BIGOTS ▶ **bigot**

BIGS ▶ **big**

BIGSTICK adj of or relating to irresistible military strength

BIGTIME adj important

BIGUINE, -S same as ▶ **beguine**

BIGWIG, -S n important person

BIHOURLY adj occurring every two hours

BIJOU, -S, -X adj (of a house) small but elegant ▷ n something small and delicately worked

A **bijou** is a French word for a jewel, and it is indeed a jewel to play, getting rid of awkward letters for a good score. And remember that the plural can be **bijous** or **bijoux**.

BIJUGATE adj (of compound leaves) having two pairs of leaflets

BIJUGOUS same as ▶ **bijugate**

BIJURAL adj relating to two coexisting legal systems

BIJWONER same as ▶ **bywoner**

BIKE, -D, -S same as ▶ **bicycle**

BIKER, -S n person who rides a motorcycle

BIKES ▶ **bike**

BIKEWAY, -S n cycle lane

BIKIE, -S n member of a motorcycle gang

BIKING, -S ▶ **bike**

BIKINI, -S n woman's brief two-piece swimming costume

BIKINIED ▶ **bikini**

BIKINIS ▶ **bikini**

BIKKIE, -S short for ▶ **biscuit**

BILABIAL adj of, relating to, or denoting a speech sound articulated using both lips ▷ n bilabial speech sound

BILANDER n small two-masted cargo ship

BILAYER, -S n part of a cell membrane

BILBERRY n bluish-black edible berry

BILBIES ▶ **bilby**

BILBO, -ES, -S n (formerly) a sword with a marked temper and elasticity

BILBOA, -S same as ▶ **bilbo**

BILBOES ▶ **bilbo**

BILBOS ▶ **bilbo**

BILBY, BILBIES n Australian marsupial with long pointed ears and grey fur

BILE, -D, -S, BILING n bitter yellow fluid secreted by the liver ▷ vb Scots word for boil

BILEVEL, -S n hairstyle with two different lengths

BILGE, -D, -S, BILGING n nonsense ▷ vb (of a vessel) to take in water at the bilge

BILGIER ▶ **bilgy**

BILGIEST ▶ **bilgy**

BILGING ▶ **bilge**

BILGY, BILGIER, BILGIEST ▶ **bilge**

BILIAN, -S n type of tree used for its wood

BILIARY adj of bile, the ducts that convey bile, or the gall bladder ▷ n disease found in dogs

BILIMBI, -S n type of fruit-bearing tree

BILINEAR adj of or referring to two lines

BILING ▶ **bile**

BILIOUS adj sick, nauseous

BILK, -ED, -ING, -S vb cheat, esp by not paying ▷ n swindle or cheat

BILKER, -S ▶ **bilk**

BILKING ▶ **bilk**

BILKS ▶ **bilk**

BILL, -ED, -S n money owed for goods or services supplied ▷ vb send or present an account for payment to (a person)

BILLABLE adj that can be charged to a client

BILLBOOK n business record of bills received, paid, etc

BILLBUG, -S n type of weevil

BILLED ▶ **bill**

BILLER, -S n stem of a plant

BILLET, -ED, -S vb assign a lodging to (a soldier) ▷ n accommodation for a soldier in civil lodgings

BILLETEE ▶ **billet**

BILLETER ▶ **billet**

BILLETS ▶ **billet**

BILLFISH n type of fish with elongated jaws, such as the spearfish and marlin

BILLFOLD n small folding case, usually of leather, for holding paper money, documents, etc

BILLHEAD n printed form for making out bills

BILLHOOK n tool with a hooked blade, used for chopping etc

BILLIARD n (modifier) of or relating to billiards

BILLIE same as ▶ **billy**

BILLIES ▶ **billy**

BILLING, -S n prominence given in programmes, advertisements, etc, to performers or acts

BILLION, -S n one thousand million ▷ determiner amounting to a billion

BILLMAN, BILLMEN n person who uses a billhook

BILLON, -S n alloy consisting of gold or silver and a base metal

BILLOW, -ED, -S n large sea wave ▷ vb rise up or swell out

BILLOWY adj full of or forming billows

BILLS ▶ **bill**

BILLY, BILLIES n metal can or pot for cooking on a camp fire

BILLYBOY n type of river barge

BILLYCAN same as ▶ **billy**

BILLYO n as in **like billyo** phrase used to emphasize or intensify something

BILLYOH same as ▶ **billyo**

BILOBAR same as ▶ **bilobate**

BILOBATE adj divided into or having two lobes

BILOBED same as ▶ **bilobate**

BILSTED, -S n American gum tree

BILTONG, -S n strips of dried meat

BIMA, -S same as ▶ **bema**

BIMAH, -S same as ▶ **bema**

BIMANAL same as ▶ **bimanous**

BIMANOUS adj having two hands as opposed to four feet

BIMANUAL adj using or requiring both hands

BIMAS ▶ **bima**

BIMBASHI n Turkish military official

BIMBETTE n derogatory term for an attractive but empty-headed young woman

BIMBLE n as in **bimble box** type of dense Australian tree

BIMBO, -ES, -S n derogatory term for an attractive but empty-headed young person

BIMENSAL adj occurring every two months

BIMESTER n period of two months

BIMETAL, -S n material made from two sheets of metal

BIMETHYL another word for ▶ **ethane**

BIMINI, -S n type of awning for a yacht

BIMODAL adj having two modes

BIMORPH, -S n assembly of piezoelectric crystals

BIN, -NED, -NING, -S n container for rubbish or for storing grain, coal, etc ▷ vb put in a rubbish bin

BINAL adj twofold

BINARIES ▶ **binary**

BINARISM n state of being binary

BINARY, BINARIES adj composed of, relating to, or involving two ▷ n something composed of two parts or things

BINATE adj occurring in two parts or in pairs

BINATELY ▶ **binate**

BINAURAL adj relating to, having, or hearing with both ears

BIND, -S vb make secure with or as if with a rope ▷ n annoying situation

BINDABLE ▶ **bind**

BINDER, -S n firm cover for holding loose sheets of paper together

BINDERY n bookbindery

BINDHI, -S same as ▶ **bindi**

BINDI, -S n decorative dot worn in the middle of the forehead, esp by Hindu women

BINDING, -S ▶ **bind**

BINDIS ▶ **bindi**

BINDLE, -S n small packet

BINDS ▶ **bind**

BINDWEED n plant that twines around a support

BINE, -S n climbing or twining stem of various plants

BINER, -S n clip used by climbers

BINES ▶ **bine**

BING, -S n heap or pile, esp of spoil from a mine

BINGE, -D, -S n bout of excessive indulgence ▷ vb indulge in a binge

BINGEING n act of indulging in a binge

BINGER, -S ▶ **binge**

BINGES ▶ **binge**

BINGIES ▶ **bingy**

BINGING, -S n act of indulging in a binge

BINGLE, -D, -S, BINGLING n minor crash or upset, as in a car or on a surfboard ▷ vb layer (hair)

BINGO, -ED, -ES, -ING, -S n gambling game ▷ sentence substitute cry by the winner of a game of bingo ▷ vb (in Scrabble) play all seven of one's tiles in a single turn

BINGS ▶ **bing**

BINGY, BINGIES Australian slang for ▶ **stomach**

BINIOU, -S n small high-pitched Breton bagpipe

BINIT, -S n (computing) early form of bit

BINK, -S n ledge

BINMAN, BINMEN another name for ▶ **dustman**

BINNACLE n box holding a ship's compass

BINNED ▶ **bin**

BINNING ▶ **bin**

BINOCLE, -S n binocular-style telescope

BINOCS > **binocular**

BINOMIAL adj consisting of two terms ▷ n mathematical expression consisting of two terms, such as $3x + 2y$

BINS ▶ **bin**

BIO, -S short for > **biography**

BIOASSAY n method of determining the effect of a change to substance ▷ vb subject to a bioassay

BIOBANK, -S n large store of human samples for medical research

BIOBLAST same as ▶ **bioplast**

BIOCHIP, -S n small glass or silicon plate containing an array of biochemical molecules or structures

BIOCIDAL ▶ **biocide**

BIOCIDE, -S n substance used to destroy living things

BIOCLEAN adj free from harmful bacteria

BIOCYCLE n cycling of chemicals through the biosphere

BIODATA n information regarding an individual's education and work history

BIODOT, -S n temperature-sensitive device stuck to the skin in order to monitor stress

BIOETHIC > **bioethics**

B

BIOFACT, -S *n* item of biological information

BIOFILM, -S *n* thin layer of living organisms

BIOFUEL, -S *n* gaseous, liquid, or solid substance of biological origin used as a fuel ▷ *vb* fuel (a vehicle, etc) using biofuel

BIOG, -S *short form of* > biography

BIOGAS, -ES *n* gaseous fuel produced by the fermentation of organic waste

BIOGEN, -S *n* hypothetical protein

BIOGENIC *adj* originating from a living organism

BIOGENS ▶ biogen

BIOGENY *n* principle that a living organism must originate from a parent form similar to itself

BIOGRAPH *vb* write biography of

BIOGS ▶ biog

BIOHERM, -S *n* mound of material laid down by sedentary marine organisms

BIOLOGIC *adj* of or relating to biology ▷ *n* drug that is derived from a living organism

BIOLOGY *n* study of living organisms

BIOLYSIS, BIOLYSES *n* death and dissolution of a living organism

BIOLYTIC ▶ biolysis

BIOMASS *n* total number of living organisms in a given area

BIOME, -S *n* major ecological community

BIOMETER *n* device for measuring natural radiation

BIOMETRY *n* analysis of biological data

BIOMORPH *n* form or pattern resembling living thing

BIONIC *adj* having a part of the body that is operated electronically

BIONICS *n* study of biological functions to create electronic versions

BIONOMIC > bionomics

BIONOMY *n* laws of life

BIONT, -S *n* living thing

BIONTIC ▶ biont

BIONTS ▶ biont

BIOPHOR, -S *n* hypothetical material particle

BIOPHORE *same as* ▶ biophor

BIOPHORS ▶ biophor

BIOPIC, -S *n* film based on the life of a famous person

BIOPLASM *n* living matter

BIOPLAST *n* very small unit of bioplasm

BIOPLAY, -S *n* play based on the life of a famous person

BIOPSIC ▶ biopsy

BIOPSY, BIOPSIED, BIOPSIES *n* examination of tissue from a living body ▷ *vb* perform a biopsy on

BIOPTIC ▶ biopsy

BIOS ▶ bio

BIOSCOPE *n* kind of early film projector

BIOSCOPY *n* examination of a body to determine whether it is alive

BIOSOLID *n* residue from treated sewage

BIOTA, -S *n* plant and animal life of a particular region or period

BIOTECH, -S *n* biotechnology

BIOTIC, -S *adj* of or relating to living organisms ▷ *n* living organism

BIOTICAL *same as* ▶ biotic

BIOTICS ▶ biotic

BIOTIN, -S *n* vitamin of the B complex, abundant in egg yolk and liver

BIOTITE, -S *n* black or dark green mineral of the mica group

BIOTITIC ▶ biotite

BIOTOPE, -S *n* small area that supports its own distinctive community

BIOTOXIN, -S *n* toxic substance produced by a living organism

BIOTRON, -S *n* climate-control chamber

BIOTROPH *n* parasitic organism, esp a fungus

BIOTYPE, -S *n* group of genetically identical plants within a species, produced by apomixis

BIOTYPIC ▶ biotype

BIOVULAR *adj* (of twins) from two separate eggs

BIOWASTE *n* organic or biodegradable waste

BIPACK, -S *n* obsolete filming process

BIPAROUS *adj* producing offspring in pairs

BIPARTED *adj* divided into two parts

BIPARTY *adj* involving two parties

BIPED, -S *n* animal with two feet ▷ *adj* having two feet

BIPEDAL *adj* having two feet

BIPEDS ▶ biped

BIPHASIC *adj* having two phases

BIPHENYL *n* white or colourless crystalline solid used as a heat-transfer agent

BIPLANE, -S *n* aeroplane with two sets of wings, one above the other

BIPOD, -S *n* two-legged support or stand

BIPOLAR *adj* having two poles

BIPRISM, -S *n* prism having a highly obtuse angle to facilitate beam splitting

BIRACIAL *adj* involving two races or ethnic groups

BIRADIAL *adj* showing both bilateral and radial symmetry, as certain sea anemones

BIRAMOSE *same as* ▶ biramous

BIRAMOUS *adj* divided into two parts, as the appendages of crustaceans

BIRCH, -ED, -ES *n* tree with thin peeling bark ▷ *vb* flog with a birch

BIRCHEN ▶ birch

BIRCHES ▶ birch

BIRCHING *n* act of birching

BIRCHIR, -S *same as* ▶ bichir

BIRD, -ED, -S *n* creature with feathers and wings, most types of which can fly ▷ *vb* hunt for birds

BIRDBATH *n* small basin or trough for birds to bathe in, usually in a garden

BIRDCAGE *n* wire or wicker cage in which captive birds are kept

BIRDCALL *n* characteristic call or song of a bird

BIRDDOG, -S *n* dog used or trained to retrieve game birds

BIRDED ▶ bird

BIRDER, -S *n* birdwatcher

BIRDFARM *n* place where birds are kept

BIRDFEED *n* food for birds

BIRDIE, -D, -S *n* score of one stroke under par for a hole ▷ *vb* play (a hole) in one stroke under par

BIRDING, -S ▶ bird

BIRDLIFE *n* birds collectively

BIRDLIKE ▶ bird

BIRDLIME n sticky substance smeared on twigs to catch small birds ▷ vb smear (twigs) with birdlime to catch (small birds)

BIRDMAN, BIRDMEN n man concerned with birds, such as a fowler or ornithologist

BIRDS ▶ bird

BIRDSEED n mixture of various kinds of seeds for feeding cage birds

BIRDSEYE n type of primrose

BIRDSHOT n small pellets designed for shooting birds

BIRDSONG n musical call of a bird or birds

BIRDWING n type of butterfly

BIREME, -S n ancient galley having two banks of oars

BIRETTA, -S n stiff square cap worn by the Catholic clergy

BIRIANI, -S same as ▶ biryani

BIRIYANI same as ▶ biriani

BIRK, -S n birch tree ▷ adj consisting or made of birch

BIRKEN adj relating to the birch tree

BIRKIE, -R, -S, -ST n spirited or lively person ▷ adj lively

BIRKS ▶ birk

BIRL, -ED, -S same as ▶ burl

BIRLE, -S same as ▶ burl

BIRLED ▶ birl

BIRLER, -S ▶ birl

BIRLES ▶ birle

BIRLING, -S ▶ birl

BIRLINN, -S n small Scottish book

BIRLS ▶ birl

BIRO, -S n tradename of a kind of ballpoint pen

BIRR, -ED, -ING, -S vb make or cause to make a whirring sound ▷ n whirring sound

BIRRETTA same as ▶ biretta

BIRRING ▶ birr

BIRROTCH n plural of birr, Ethiopian monetary unit

BIRRS ▶ birr

BIRSE, -D, -S, BIRSING n bristle ▷ vb bruise

BIRSIER ▶ birsy

BIRSIEST ▶ birsy

BIRSING ▶ birse

BIRSLE, -D, -S, BIRSLING vb roast

BIRSY, BIRSIER, BIRSIEST adj bristly

BIRTH, -ED, -S n process of bearing young ▷ vb give birth to

BIRTHDAY n anniversary of the day of one's birth

BIRTHDOM n birthright

BIRTHED ▶ birth

BIRTHER, -S n person who believes Barack Obama was not born in the USA

BIRTHING ▶ birth

BIRTHS ▶ birth

BIRYANI, -S n Indian rice-based dish

BIS adv twice ▷ sentence substitute encore! again!

BISCACHA same as ▶ viscacha

BISCOTTO, BISCOTTI n small Italian biscuit

BISCUIT, -S n small flat dry sweet or plain cake ▷ adj pale brown

BISCUITY adj reminiscent of biscuit

BISE, -S n cold dry northerly wind

BISECT, -ED, -S vb divide into two equal parts

BISECTOR n straight line or plane that bisects an angle

BISECTS ▶ bisect

BISERIAL adj in two rows

BISES ▶ bise

BISEXUAL adj attracted to more than one sex or gender identity ▷ n bisexual person

BISH, -ES n mistake

BISHOP, -ED, -S n clergyman or clergywoman who governs a diocese ▷ vb make a bishop

BISK, -S a less common spelling of ▶ bisque

BISMAR, -S n type of weighing scale

BISMARCK n type of pastry

BISMARS ▶ bismar

BISMUTH, -S n pinkish-white metallic element

BISNAGA, -S n type of cactus

BISOM, -S same as ▶ besom

BISON, -S same as ▶ buffalo

BISQUE, -S n thick rich soup made from shellfish

BISSON, -ED, -S adj blind ▷ vb cause to be blind

BIST a form of the second person singular of ▶ be

BISTABLE adj (of an electronic system) having two stable states ▷ n bistable system

BISTATE adj involving two states

BISTER, -S same as ▶ bistre

BISTERED ▶ bister

BISTERS ▶ bister

BISTORT, -S n Eurasian plant with a spike of small pink flowers

BISTOURY n long surgical knife with a narrow blade

BISTRE, -S n water-soluble pigment

BISTRED ▶ bistre

BISTRES ▶ bistre

BISTRO, -S n small restaurant

BISTROIC ▶ bistro

BISTROS ▶ bistro

BIT, -S n small piece, portion, or quantity

BITABLE ▶ bite

BITCH, -ED, -ES n female dog, fox, or wolf ▷ vb complain or grumble

BITCHEN same as ▶ bitching

BITCHERY n spiteful talk

BITCHES ▶ bitch

BITCHIER ▶ bitchy

BITCHILY ▶ bitchy

BITCHING adj wonderful or excellent

BITCHY, BITCHIER adj spiteful or malicious

BITCOIN, -S n type of digital currency

BITE, -S, BITTEN vb grip, tear, or puncture the skin, as with the teeth or jaws ▷ n act of biting

BITEABLE ▶ bite

BITER, -S ▶ bite

BITES ▶ bite

BITESIZE adj small enough to put in the mouth whole

BITEWING n dental X-ray film

BITING, -S ▶ bite

BITINGLY ▶ bite

BITINGS ▶ biting

BITLESS adj without a bit

BITMAP, -S n picture created by colour or shading on a visual display unit ▷ vb create a bitmap of

BITO, -S n African and Asian tree

BITONAL adj consisting of black and white tones

BITOS ▶ bito

BITOU n as in bitou bush type of sprawling woody shrub

BITRATE, -S n rate of data processing

BITS ▶ bit

BITSER, -S n mongrel dog

BITSIER ▶ bitsy

BITSIEST ▶ bitsy

BITSTOCK n handle or stock of a tool into which a drilling bit is fixed

B

BITSY, BITSIER, BITSIEST adj very small

BITT, -ED, -S n strong post on the deck of a ship for securing lines ▷ vb secure (a line) by means of a bitt

BITTACLE same as ▶ binnacle

BITTE interj you're welcome

BITTED ▶ bitt

BITTEN ▶ bite

BITTER, -ED, -ER adj having a sharp unpleasant taste ▷ n beer with a slightly bitter taste ▷ adv very ▷ vb make or become bitter

BITTERLY ▶ bitter

BITTERN, -S n wading marsh bird with a booming call

BITTERS pl n bitter-tasting spirits flavoured with plant extracts

BITTIE, -S n small piece

BITTIER ▶ bitty

BITTIES ▶ bittie

BITTIEST ▶ bitty

BITTILY adv in a disjointed way

BITTING, -S ▶ bitt

BITTOCK, -S n small amount

BITTOR, -S n bittern

BITTOUR, -S same as ▶ bittor

BITTS ▶ bitt

BITTUR, -S same as ▶ bittor

BITTY, BITTIER, BITTIEST adj lacking unity, disjointed

BITUMED adj covered with bitumen

BITUMEN, -S n black sticky substance obtained from tar or petrol

BITURBO, -S n engine with two turbochargers

BITWISE adj relating to an operator in a programming language that manipulates bits

BIUNIQUE adj relating to a one-to-one correspondence

BIVALENT adj associated together in pairs ▷ n structure consisting of two homologous chromosomes

BIVALVE, -S adj (of a marine mollusc) with two hinged segments to its shell ▷ n sea creature with a shell consisting of two hinged segments

BIVALVED ▶ bivalve

BIVALVES ▶ bivalve

BIVIA ▶ bivium

BIVINYL, -S another word for > butadiene

BIVIOUS adj offering a choice of two different ways

BIVIUM, BIVIA n parting of ways

BIVOUAC, -S n temporary camp in the open air ▷ vb camp in a bivouac

BIVVY, BIVVIED, BIVVIES, -ING n small tent or shelter ▷ vb camp in a bivouac

BIWEEKLY adv every two weeks ▷ n periodical published every two weeks

BIYEARLY adv every two years

BIZ, -ZES n business

BIZARRE, -S adj odd or unusual ▷ n bizarre thing

BIZARRO, -S n bizarre person

BIZAZZ, -ES same as ▶ pizazz

BIZCACHA same as ▶ viscacha

BIZE, -S n dry, cold wind in France

BIZJET, -S n small jet plane used by businesspeople

BIZNAGA, -S same as ▶ bisnaga

BIZONAL ▶ bizone

BIZONE, -S n place comprising two zones

BIZZAZZ n combination of energy and style

BIZZES ▶ biz

BIZZIES ▶ bizzy

BIZZO, -S n empty and irrelevant talk or ideas

BIZZY, BIZZIES n slang word for a police officer

BLAB, -BED, -S vb reveal (secrets) indiscreetly

BLABBER, -S vb talk without thinking ▷ n person who blabs

BLABBIER ▶ blabby

BLABBING ▶ blab

BLABBY, BLABBIER adj talking too much; indiscreet

BLABS ▶ blab

BLACK, -ED, -ER, -EST, -S adj of the darkest colour, like coal ▷ n darkest colour ▷ vb make black

BLACKBOY n grass tree

BLACKCAP n brownish-grey warbler, the male of which has a black crown

BLACKED ▶ black

BLACKEN, -S vb make or become black

BLACKER ▶ black

BLACKEST ▶ black

BLACKFIN n type of tuna

BLACKFLY n type of black aphid that infests beans, sugar beet, and other plants

BLACKGUM n US tree

BLACKING n preparation for giving a black finish to shoes, metals, etc

BLACKISH ▶ black

BLACKLEG n person who continues to work during a strike ▷ vb refuse to join a strike

BLACKLY ▶ black

BLACKOUT n extinguishing of all light as a precaution against an air attack

BLACKS ▶ black

BLACKTIP n shark of coastal tropical waters

BLACKTOP n bituminous mixture used for paving

BLAD, -DED, -DING, -S same as ▶ blaud

BLADDER, -S n sac in the body where urine is held

BLADDERY adj like a bladder

BLADDING ▶ blad

BLADE, -S n cutting edge of a weapon or tool

BLADED ▶ blade

BLADER, -S n person skating with in-line skates

BLADES ▶ blade

BLADIER ▶ blady

BLADIEST ▶ blady

BLADING, -S n act or instance of skating with in-line skates

BLADS ▶ blad

BLADY, BLADIER, BLADIEST adj as in blady grass coarse leafy Australasian grass

BLAE, -R, -ST adj bluish-grey

BLAES n hardened clay or shale

BLAEST ▶ blae

BLAFF, -ED, -ING, -S n fish stew of the Caribbean ▷ vb make a barking noise

BLAG, -GED, -S vb obtain by wheedling or cadging ▷ n robbery, esp with violence

BLAGGER, -S ▶ blag

BLAGGING ▶ blag

BLAGS ▶ blag

BLAGUE, -S n pretentious but empty talk

BLAGUER, -S ▶ blague

BLAGUES ▶ blague

BLAGUEUR n bluffer

BLAH, -ED, -ER, -EST, -ING, -S n worthless or silly talk ▷ adj uninteresting ▷ vb talk nonsense or boringly

BLAIN, -S n blister, blotch, or sore on the skin

BLAISE same as ▶ blaes

BLAIZE same as ▶ blaes

B

BLAM, -MED, -MING, -S *n* representation of the sound of a bullet being fired ▷ *vb* make the noise of a bullet being fired
BLAMABLE ▸ blame
BLAMABLY ▸ blame
BLAME, -S, BLAMING *vb* consider (someone) responsible ▷ *n* responsibility for something that is wrong
BLAMED euphemistic word for ▸ damned
BLAMEFUL *adj* deserving blame
BLAMER, -S ▸ blame
BLAMES ▸ blame
BLAMING ▸ blame
BLAMMED ▸ blam
BLAMMING ▸ blam
BLAMS ▸ blam
BLANCH, -ED, -ES *vb* become white or pale
BLANCHER ▸ blanch
BLANCHES ▸ blanch
BLANCO, -ED, -S *n* whitening substance ▷ *vb* whiten (something) with blanco
BLAND, -ED, -ER, -EST, -ING, -S *adj* dull and uninteresting ▷ *n* bland thing ▷ *vb* as in **bland out** become bland
BLANDISH *vb* persuade by mild flattery
BLANDLY ▸ bland
BLANDS ▸ bland
BLANK, -ED, -ER, -EST, -S *adj* not written on ▷ *n* empty space ▷ *vb* cross out, blot, or obscure
BLANKET, -S *n* large thick cloth used as covering for a bed ▷ *adj* applying to a wide group of people, situations, conditions, etc ▷ *vb* cover as with a blanket
BLANKETY *n* euphemism for any taboo word
BLANKIE, -S *n* child's security blanket
BLANKING ▸ blank
BLANKLY ▸ blank
BLANKS ▸ blank
BLANKY same as ▸ blankie
BLANQUET *n* variety of pear
BLARE, -D, -S, BLARING *vb* sound loudly and harshly ▷ *n* loud harsh noise
BLARNEY, -S *n* flattering talk ▷ *vb* cajole with flattery
BLART, -ED, -ING, -S *vb* sound loudly and harshly
BLASE *adj* indifferent or bored through familiarity

BLASH, -ED, -ES, -ING *n* splash ▷ *vb* splash (something) with liquid
BLASHIER ▸ blashy
BLASHING ▸ blash
BLASHY, BLASHIER *adj* windy and rainy
BLAST, -S *n* explosion ▷ *vb* blow up (a rock etc) with explosives ▷ *interj* expression of annoyance
BLASTED *adv* extremely ▷ *adj* blighted or withered
BLASTEMA *n* mass of animal cells that will regenerate a lost organ or tissue
BLASTER, -S ▸ blast
BLASTIE, -S *n* ugly creature
BLASTIER ▸ blasty
BLASTIES ▸ blastie
BLASTING *n* distortion of sound caused by overloading certain components of a radio system
BLASTOFF *n* launching of a rocket
BLASTOID *n* extinct echinoderm found in fossil form
BLASTOMA *n* tumour composed of embryonic tissue that has not yet developed a specialized function
BLASTS ▸ blast
BLASTULA *n* early form of an animal embryo
BLASTY, BLASTIER *adj* gusty
BLAT, -S, -TED, -TING *vb* cry out or bleat like a sheep
BLATANCY ▸ blatant
BLATANT *adj* glaringly obvious
BLATE, -D, -R, -S, -ST, BLATING *adj* shy; ill at ease ▷ *vb* babble (something)
BLATHER, -S *vb* speak foolishly ▷ *n* foolish talk
BLATING ▸ blate
BLATS ▸ blat
BLATT, -S *n* newspaper
BLATTANT same as ▸ blatant
BLATTED ▸ blat
BLATTER, -S *vb* prattle
BLATTING ▸ blat
BLATTS ▸ blatt
BLAUBOK, -S *n* South African antelope
BLAUD, -ED, -ING, -S *vb* slap
BLAW, -ED, -ING, -N, -S *vb* Scots word for blow
BLAWORT, -S *n* harebell
BLAWS ▸ blaw
BLAY, -S *n* small river fish

BLAZAR, -S *n* type of active galaxy
BLAZE, -D, BLAZING *n* strong fire or flame ▷ *vb* burn or shine brightly
BLAZER, -S *n* lightweight jacket, often in the colours of a school etc
BLAZERED ▸ blazer
BLAZERS ▸ blazer
BLAZES *pl n* hell
BLAZING ▸ blaze
BLAZON, -ED, -S *vb* proclaim publicly ▷ *n* coat of arms
BLAZONER ▸ blazon
BLAZONRY *n* art or process of describing heraldic arms in proper form
BLAZONS ▸ blazon
BLEACH, -ED, -ES *vb* make or become white or colourless ▷ *n* bleaching agent
BLEACHER ▸ bleach
BLEACHES ▸ bleach
BLEAK, -ER, -EST, -S *adj* exposed and barren ▷ *n* type of fish found in slow-flowing rivers
BLEAKISH ▸ bleak
BLEAKLY ▸ bleak
BLEAKS ▸ bleak
BLEAKY same as ▸ bleak
BLEAR, -ED, -ER, -EST, -ING, -S *vb* make (eyes or sight) dim with or as if with tears ▷ *adj* bleary
BLEARIER ▸ bleary
BLEARILY ▸ bleary
BLEARING ▸ blear
BLEARS ▸ blear
BLEARY, BLEARIER *adj* with eyes dimmed, as by tears or tiredness
BLEAT, -ED, -S *vb* (of a sheep, goat, or calf) utter its plaintive cry ▷ *n* cry of sheep, goats, and calves
BLEATER, -S ▸ bleat
BLEATING ▸ bleat
BLEATS ▸ bleat
BLEB, -S *n* fluid-filled blister on the skin
BLEBBIER ▸ blebby
BLEBBING *n* formation of bleb
BLEBBY, BLEBBIER ▸ bleb
BLEBS ▸ bleb
BLECH *interj* expressing disgust
BLED ▸ bleed
BLEE, -S *n* complexion; hue
BLEED, BLED, -S *vb* lose or emit blood
BLEEDER, -S *n* despicable person

B

BLEEDING ▷ bleed

BLEES ▷ bleed

BLEEP, -ED, -ING, -S n high-pitched signal or beep ▷ vb make such a noise

BLEEPER, -S n small portable radio receiver that makes a bleeping signal

BLEEPING ▷ bleep

BLEEPS ▷ bleep

BLEES ▷ blee

BLELLUM, -S n babbler; blusterer

BLEMISH n defect or stain ▷ vb spoil or tarnish

BLENCH, -ED, -ES vb shy away, as in fear

BLENCHER ▷ blench

BLENCHES ▷ blench

BLEND, -ED, -S vb mix or mingle (components or ingredients) ▷ n mixture

BLENDE, -S n mineral consisting mainly of zinc sulphide

BLENDED ▷ blend

BLENDER, -S n electrical appliance for puréeing vegetables etc

BLENDES ▷ blende

BLENDING ▷ blend

BLENDS ▷ blend

BLENNY, BLENNIES n small fish with a tapering scaleless body

BLENT a past participle of ▷ blend

BLERT, -S n foolish person

BLESBOK, -S n S African antelope

BLESBUCK same as ▷ blesbok

BLESS, -ES, BLEST vb make holy by means of a religious rite

BLESSED adj made holy

BLESSER, -S ▷ bless

BLESSES ▷ bless

BLESSING ▷ bless

BLEST ▷ bless

BLET, -S, -TED, -TING n state of decay in certain fruits, due to overripening ▷ vb go soft

BLETHER, -S same as ▷ blather

BLETS ▷ blet

BLETTED ▷ blet

BLETTING ▷ blet

BLEUATRE adj blueish

BLEW ▷ blow

BLEWART, -S same as ▷ blawort

BLEWITS n type of edible fungus with a pale brown cap and a bluish stalk

BLEY, -S same as ▷ blay

BLIGHT, -ED, -S n person or thing that spoils or prevents growth ▷ vb cause to suffer a blight

BLIGHTER n irritating person

BLIGHTS ▷ blight

BLIGHTY n home country; home leave

BLIKSEM interj South African expression of surprise

BLIMBING same as ▷ bilimbi

BLIMEY interj exclamation of surprise or annoyance

BLIMP, -ED, -ING, -S n small airship ▷ vb swell out

BLIMPERY n complacent or reactionary behaviour

BLIMPING ▷ blimp

BLIMPISH adj complacent and reactionary

BLIMPS ▷ blimp

BLIMY same as ▷ blimey

BLIN, -NED, -NING, -S Scots word for ▷ blind

BLIND, -ED, -EST, -S adj unable to see ▷ vb deprive of sight ▷ n covering for a window

BLINDAGE n (esp formerly) a protective screen or structure, as over a trench

BLINDED ▷ blind

BLINDER, -S n outstanding performance

BLINDEST ▷ blind

BLINDGUT same as ▷ caecum

BLINDING n sand or grit spread over a road surface to fill up cracks ▷ adj making one blind or as if blind

BLINDLY ▷ blind

BLINDS ▷ blind

BLING, -ED, -ER, -EST, -S adj flashy ▷ n ostentatious jewellery ▷ vb make ostentatious or flashy

BLINGIER ▷ blingy

BLINGING adj flashy and expensive

BLINGS ▷ bling

BLINGY, BLINGIER same as ▷ bling

BLINI pl n Russian pancakes made of buckwheat flour and yeast

BLINIS same as ▷ blini

BLINK, -ED, -S vb close and immediately reopen (the eyes) ▷ n act of blinking

BLINKARD n something that twinkles

BLINKED ▷ blink

BLINKER vb provide (a horse) with blinkers ▷ n flashing light for sending messages

BLINKERS same as ▷ blinker

BLINKING ▷ blink

BLINKS ▷ blink

BLINNED ▷ blin

BLINNING ▷ blin

BLINS ▷ blin

BLINTZ n thin pancake folded over a filling usually of apple, cream cheese, or meat

BLINTZE, -S same as ▷ blintz

BLINY same as ▷ blini

BLIP, -PED, -PING, -S n spot of light on a radar screen indicating the position of an object ▷ vb produce such a noise

BLIPVERT n very short television advertisement

BLISS, -ED, -ES, -ING n perfect happiness ▷ vb make or become perfectly happy

BLISSFUL adj serenely joyful or glad

BLISSING ▷ bliss

BLIST archaic form of ▷ blessed

BLISTER, -S n small bubble on the skin ▷ vb (cause to) have blisters

BLISTERY ▷ blister

BLIT, -S, -TED, -TING vb move (a block of data) in a computer's memory

BLITE, -S n type of herb

BLITHE, -ST adj casual and indifferent

BLITHELY ▷ blithe

BLITHER, -S same as ▷ blather

BLITHEST ▷ blithe

BLITS ▷ blit

BLITTED ▷ blit

BLITTER, -S n circuit that transfers large amounts of data within a computer's memory

BLITTING ▷ blit

BLITZ, -ED, -ES, -ING n violent and sustained attack by aircraft ▷ vb attack suddenly and intensively

BLITZER, -S ▷ blitz

BLITZES ▷ blitz

BLITZING ▷ blitz

BLIVE same as ▷ belive

BLIZZARD n blinding storm of wind and snow ▷ vb (of weather) be stormy with wind and snow

BLOAT, -ING, -S vb cause to swell, as with liquid or air ▷ n abnormal distention of the abdomen in cattle, sheep, etc

BLOATED adj swollen, as with a liquid, air, or wind

BLOATER, -S n salted smoked herring

BLOATING ▶ bloat

BLOATS ▶ bloat

BLOB, -BED, -BING, -S n soft mass or drop ▷ vb put blobs, as of ink or paint, on

BLOBBIER ▶ blob

BLOBBING ▶ blob

BLOBBY ▶ blob

BLOBS ▶ blob

BLOC, -S n people or countries combined by a common interest

BLOCK, -ED, -S n large solid piece of wood, stone, etc ▷ vb obstruct or impede by introducing an obstacle

BLOCKADE n sealing off of a place to prevent the passage of goods ▷ vb impose a blockade on

BLOCKAGE n act of blocking or state of being blocked

BLOCKED ▶ block

BLOCKER, -S n person or thing that blocks

BLOCKIE, -S n owner of a small property, esp a farm

BLOCKIER ▶ blocky

BLOCKIES ▶ blockie

BLOCKING n interruption of anode current in a valve

BLOCKISH adj lacking vivacity or imagination

BLOCKS ▶ block

BLOCKY, BLOCKIER adj like a block, esp in shape and solidity

BLOCS ▶ bloc

BLOG, -GED, -S n journal written online and accessible to users of the internet ▷ vb write a blog

BLOGGER, -S ▶ blog

BLOGGIER ▶ bloggy

BLOGGING ▶ blog

BLOGGY, BLOGGIER adj characteristic of a blog

BLOGPOST n single posting made as part of a blog

BLOGRING n group of blogs joined in a ring

BLOGROLL n list of blogs

BLOGS ▶ blog

BLOKART, -S n single-seat three-wheeled vehicle propelled by the wind

BLOKE, -S n man

BLOKEDOM n state of being a bloke

BLOKEISH adj denoting or exhibiting the characteristics believed typical of an ordinary man

BLOKES ▶ bloke

BLOKEY, BLOKIER, BLOKIEST same as ▶ blokeish

BLOKISH same as ▶ blokeish

BLONCKET adj blue-grey

BLOND, -S adj (of hair) light-coloured ▷ n person with light-coloured hair

BLONDE, -R, -S, -ST adj (of hair) light-coloured ▷ n person with light-coloured hair

BLONDINE vb dye hair blonde

BLONDING n act or an instance of dyeing hair blonde

BLONDISH ▶ blond

BLONDS ▶ blond

BLOOD, -S n red fluid that flows around the body ▷ vb initiate (a person) to war or hunting

BLOODED adj (of horses, cattle, etc) of good breeding

BLOODFIN n silvery red-finned S American freshwater fish, popular in aquariums

BLOODIED ▶ bloody

BLOODIER ▶ bloody

BLOODIES ▶ bloody

BLOODILY ▶ bloody

BLOODING ▶ blood

BLOODRED adj having a deep red colour

BLOODS ▶ blood

BLOODY, BLOODIED, BLOODIER, BLOODIES adj covered with blood ▷ adv extreme or extremely ▷ vb stain with blood

BLOOEY adj out of order; faulty

BLOOIE same as ▶ blooey

BLOOK, -S n book published on a blog

BLOOM, -S n blossom on a flowering plant ▷ vb (of flowers) open

BLOOMED adj (of a lens) coated to reduce light lost by reflection

BLOOMER n stupid mistake

BLOOMERS pl n woman's baggy underwear

BLOOMERY n place in which malleable iron is produced directly from iron ore

BLOOMIER ▶ bloomy

BLOOMING n act of blooming

BLOOMS ▶ bloom

BLOOMY, BLOOMIER adj having a fine whitish coating on the surface

BLOOP, -ED, -ING, -S vb (baseball) hit a ball into the air beyond the infield

BLOOPER, -S n stupid mistake

BLOOPIER ▶ bloopy

BLOOPING ▶ bloop

BLOOPS ▶ bloop

BLOOPY, BLOOPIER adj (in baseball) relating to a ball hit into the air beyond the infield

BLOOSME, -D, -S archaic form of ▶ blossom

BLORE, -S n strong blast of wind

BLOSSOM, -S n flowers of a plant ▷ vb (of plants) flower

BLOSSOMY adj full of blossoms

BLOT, -S, -TED n spot or stain ▷ vb cause a blemish in or on

BLOTCH, -ED, -ES n discoloured area or stain ▷ vb become or cause to become marked by such discoloration

BLOTCHY adj covered in or marked by blotches

BLOTLESS ▶ blot

BLOTS ▶ blot

BLOTTED ▶ blot

BLOTTER, -S n sheet of blotting paper

BLOTTIER ▶ blotty

BLOTTING n blot analysis

BLOTTO adj extremely drunk

BLOTTY, BLOTTIER adj covered in blots

BLOUBOK, -S same as ▶ blaubok

BLOUSE, -D, -S, BLOUSING n woman's shirtlike garment ▷ vb hang or cause to hang in full loose folds

BLOUSIER ▶ blousy

BLOUSILY ▶ blousy

BLOUSING ▶ blouse

BLOUSON, -S n short loose jacket with a tight waist

BLOUSY, BLOUSIER adj loose; blouse-like

BLOVIATE vb discourse at length

BLOW, BLEW, -ED, -N, -S vb (of air, the wind, etc) move ▷ n hard hit

BLOWBACK n gases escaping to the rear

BLOWBALL n dandelion seed head

B

BLOWBY, -S n leakage of gas past the piston of an engine at maximum pressure

BLOWDART n dart from a blowpipe

BLOWDOWN n accidental burst of a cooling pipe in a nuclear reactor

BLOWED ▸ **blow**

BLOWER, -S n mechanical device, such as a fan, that blows

BLOWFISH a popular name for ▸ **puffer**

BLOWFLY n fly that lays its eggs in meat

BLOWGUN, -S same as ▸ **blowpipe**

BLOWHARD n boastful person ▹ adj blustering or boastful

BLOWHOLE n nostril of a whale

BLOWIE, -S n bluebottle

BLOWIER ▸ **blowy**

BLOWIES ▸ **blowie**

BLOWIEST ▸ **blowy**

BLOWING, -S n moving of air

BLOWKART n land vehicle with a sail

BLOWLAMP another name for > **blowtorch**

BLOWN ▸ **blow**

BLOWOFF, -S n discharge of a surplus fluid

BLOWOUT, -S n sudden loss of air in a tyre

BLOWPIPE n long tube from which darts etc are shot by blowing

BLOWS ▸ **blow**

BLOWSE, -S n large, red-faced woman

BLOWSED same as ▸ **blowsy**

BLOWSES ▸ **blowse**

BLOWSIER ▸ **blowsy**

BLOWSILY ▸ **blowsy**

BLOWSY, BLOWSIER adj fat, untidy, and red-faced

BLOWTUBE n tube for blowing air or oxygen into a flame to intensify its heat

BLOWUP, -S n fit of temper

BLOWY, BLOWIER, BLOWIEST adj windy

BLOWZE, -S variant of ▸ **blowse**

BLOWZED same as ▸ **blowsy**

BLOWZES ▸ **blowze**

BLOWZIER ▸ **blowzy**

BLOWZILY ▸ **blowzy**

BLOWZY, BLOWZIER same as ▸ **blowsy**

BLUB, -BED, -BING, -S a slang word for ▸ **blubber**

BLUBBER, -S vb sob without restraint ▹ adj swollen or fleshy ▹ n fat of whales, seals, etc

BLUBBERY adj of, containing, or like blubber

BLUBBING ▸ **blub**

BLUBS ▸ **blub**

BLUCHER, -S n high shoe with laces over the tongue

BLUD, -S n slang term for a friend

BLUDE, -S Scots form of ▸ **blood**

BLUDGE, -D, -S, BLUDGING vb evade work ▹ n easy task

BLUDGEON n short thick club ▹ vb hit with a bludgeon

BLUDGER, -S n person who scrounges

BLUDGES ▸ **bludge**

BLUDGING ▸ **bludge**

BLUDIE, -R, -ST Scots form of ▸ **bloody**

BLUDS ▸ **blud**

BLUDY same as ▸ **bludie**

BLUE, -D, -R, -ST n colour of a clear unclouded sky ▹ adj of the colour blue ▹ vb make or become blue

BLUEBACK n type of salmon

BLUEBALL n type of European herb

BLUEBEAT n type of Jamaican pop music of the 1960s

BLUEBELL n flower with blue bell-shaped flowers

BLUEBILL another name for ▸ **scaup**

BLUEBIRD n North American songbird with a blue plumage

BLUEBOOK n (in Britain) a government publication, usually the report of a commission

BLUEBUCK same as ▸ **blaubok**

BLUEBUSH n blue-grey herbaceous Australian shrub

BLUECAP, -S another name for ▸ **bluetit**

BLUECOAT n person who wears blue uniform

BLUED ▸ **blue**

BLUEFIN, -S another name for ▸ **tunny**

BLUEFISH n type of bluish marine food and game fish

BLUEGILL n common N American sunfish, an important freshwater food and game fish

BLUEGOWN n in past, pauper, recipient of blue gown on king's birthday

BLUEGUM, -S n widely cultivated Australian tree

BLUEHEAD n type of fish

BLUEING, -S ▸ **blue**

BLUEISH same as ▸ **bluish**

BLUEJACK n type of oak tree

BLUEJAY, -S n N American jay

BLUELINE n blue-toned photographic proof

BLUELY ▸ **blue**

BLUENESS ▸ **blue**

BLUENOSE n puritanical or prudish person

BLUER ▸ **blue**

BLUES pl n type of music

BLUESIER ▸ **bluesy**

BLUESMAN, BLUESMEN n blues musician

BLUEST ▸ **blue**

BLUESTEM n type of tall grass

BLUESY, BLUESIER ▸ **blues**

BLUET, -S n N American plant with small four-petalled blue flowers

BLUETICK n fast-running dog

BLUETIT, -S n small European bird

BLUETS ▸ **bluet**

BLUETTE, -S n short, brilliant piece of music

BLUEWEED n Eurasian weed with blue flowers and pink buds

BLUEWING n type of duck

BLUEWOOD n type of Mexican shrub

BLUEY, -S, BLUIER, BLUIEST adj bluish ▹ n informal Australian word meaning blanket

BLUFF, -ED, -EST, -ING, -S vb pretend to be confident in order to influence (someone) ▹ n act of bluffing ▹ adj good-naturedly frank and hearty

BLUFFER, -S ▸ **bluff**

BLUFFEST ▸ **bluff**

BLUFFING ▸ **bluff**

BLUFFLY ▸ **bluff**

BLUFFS ▸ **bluff**

BLUGGY, BLUGGIER same as ▸ **bloody**

BLUID, -S Scots word for ▸ **blood**

BLUIDIER ▸ **bluidy**

BLUIDS ▸ **bluid**

BLUIDY, BLUIDIER ▸ **bluid**

BLUIER ▸ **bluey**

BLUIEST ▸ **bluey**

BLUING, -S ►blue

BLUISH adj slightly blue

BLUME, -D, -S, BLUMING Scots word for ►bloom

BLUNDER, -S n clumsy mistake ▷vb make a blunder

BLUNGE, -D, -S, BLUNGING vb mix clay with water

BLUNGER, -S n large vat in which the contents are mixed by rotating arms

BLUNGES ►blunge

BLUNGING ►blunge

BLUNK, -ED, -ING, -S vb ruin; botch

BLUNKER, -S ►blunk

BLUNKING ►blunk

BLUNKS ►blunk

BLUNT, -ED, -ER, -EST, -ING, -S adj not having a sharp edge or point ▷vb make less sharp

BLUNTISH ►blunt

BLUNTLY ►blunt

BLUNTS ►blunt

BLUR, -RED, -RING, -S vb make or become vague or less distinct ▷n something vague, hazy, or indistinct

BLURB, -ED, -ING, -S n promotional description, as on the jacket of a book ▷vb describe or recommend in a blurb

BLURBIST n writer of blurbs

BLURBS ►blurb

BLURRED ►blur

BLURRIER ►blurry

BLURRILY ►blur

BLURRING ►blur

BLURRY, BLURRIER ►blur

BLURS ►blur

BLURT, -ED, -S vb utter suddenly and involuntarily

BLURTER, -S ►blurt

BLURTING ►blurt

BLURTS ►blurt

BLUSH, -ED, -ES vb become red in the face, esp from embarrassment or shame ▷n reddening of the face

BLUSHER, -S n cosmetic for giving the cheeks a rosy colour

BLUSHES ►blush

BLUSHET, -S n modest young woman

BLUSHFUL ►blush

BLUSHING ►blush

BLUSTER, -S vb speak loudly or in a bullying way ▷n empty threats or protests

BLUSTERY adj (of wind) noisy or gusty

BLYPE, -S n piece of skin peeled off after sunburn

BO, -S interj exclamation uttered to startle or surprise someone ▷n fellow, buddy

BOA, -S n large nonvenomous snake

BOAB, -S short for ►baobab

BOAK, -ED, -ING, -S same as ►boke

BOAR, -S n uncastrated male pig

BOARD, -ED, -S n long flat piece of sawn timber ▷vb go aboard (a train, aeroplane, etc)

BOARDER, -S n person who pays rent for accommodation in someone else's home

BOARDIES pl n board shorts

BOARDING n act of embarking on an aircraft, train, ship, etc

BOARDMAN, BOARDMEN n man who carries a sandwich board

BOARDS ►board

BOARFISH n type of spiny-finned marine fish with a compressed body, a long snout, and large eyes

BOARISH adj coarse, cruel, or sensual

BOARS ►boar

BOART, -S same as ►bort

BOAS ►boa

BOAST, -ED, -S vb speak too proudly about one's talents etc ▷n bragging statement

BOASTER, -S ►boast

BOASTFUL adj tending to boast

BOASTING ►boast

BOASTS ►boast

BOAT, -ED, -S n small vehicle for travelling across water ▷vb travel in a boat

BOATABLE adj able to be carried by boat

BOATBILL n nocturnal tropical American wading bird with a broad flattened bill

BOATED ►boat

BOATEL, -S n waterside hotel catering for boating people

BOATER, -S n flat straw hat

BOATFUL, -S ►boat

BOATHOOK n hooked pole used for fending off other vessels or obstacles

BOATIE, -S n boating enthusiast

BOATING, -S n rowing, sailing, or cruising in boats as a form of recreation

BOATLIFT n evacuation by boat

BOATLIKE ►boat

BOATLOAD n amount of cargo or number of people held by a boat or ship

BOATMAN, BOATMEN n man who works on, hires out, or repairs boats

BOATNECK n wide open neck on garment

BOATPORT n enclosure for boats

BOATS ►boat

BOATSMAN, BOATSMEN same as ►boatman

BOATTAIL n type of blackbird

BOATYARD n place where boats are kept, repaired, etc

BOB, -BED, -BING, -S vb move or cause to move up and down repeatedly ▷n short abrupt movement, as of the head

BOBA, -S n type of Chinese tea

BOBAC, -S same as ►bobak

BOBAK, -S n type of marmot

BOBAS ►boba

BOBBED ►bob

BOBBER, -S n type of float for fishing

BOBBERY n mixed pack of hunting dogs ▷adj noisy or excitable

BOBBIES ►bobby

BOBBIN, -S n reel on which thread is wound

BOBBINET n netted fabric of hexagonal mesh, made on a lace machine

BOBBING ►bob

BOBBINS ►bobbin

BOBBISH adj cheery

BOBBLE, -D, -S, BOBBLING n small ball of material, usu for decoration ▷vb (of a ball) to bounce erratically because of an uneven playing surface

BOBBLIER ►bobbly

BOBBLING ►bobble

BOBBLY, BOBBLIER adj (of fabric) covered in small balls; worn

BOBBY, BOBBIES n slang word for a police officer

BOBBYSOX pl n bobbysocks

BOBCAT, -S n N American feline

BOBECHE, -S n candle drip-catcher

BOBFLOAT n small buoyant float, usually consisting of a quill stuck through a piece of cork

B

BOBLET, -S n two-person bobsleigh

BOBO, -S n rich person who holds bohemian values

BOBOL, -LED, -S n type of fraud ▷ vb commit a bobol

BOBOLINK n American songbird

BOBOLLED ▶ bobol

BOBOLS ▶ bobol

BOBOS ▶ bobo

BOBOTIE, -S n dish of curried mince

BOBOWLER n large moth

BOBS ▶ bob

BOBSKATE n child's skate with two parallel blades

BOBSLED, -S same as ▶ bobsleigh

BOBSTAY, -S n stay between a bowsprit and the stem of a vessel

BOBTAIL, -S n docked tail ▷ adj having the tail cut short ▷ vb dock the tail of

BOBWHEEL n poetic device

BOBWHITE n brown N American quail

BOBWIG, -S n type of short wig

BOCACCIO n edible American fish

BOCAGE, -S n wooded countryside characteristic of northern France

BOCCA, -S n round opening of a glass-furnace

BOCCE, -S same as ▶ boccie

BOCCI, -S same as ▶ boccie

BOCCIA, -S same as ▶ boccie

BOCCIE, -S n Italian version of bowls

BOCCIS ▶ bocci

BOCK, -ED, -ING, -S variant spelling of ▶ boke

BOCKEDY adj (of a structure, piece of furniture, etc) unsteady

BOCKING ▶ bock

BOCKS ▶ bock

BOD, -S n person

BODACH, -S n old man

BODDLE, -S same as ▶ bodle

BODE, -D, -S vb portend or presage

BODEFUL adj portentous

BODEGA, -S n shop in a Spanish-speaking country that sells wine

BODEMENT ▶ bode

BODES ▶ bode

BODGE, -D, -S, BODGING vb make a mess of

BODGER, -S n labourer who made chairs from felled trees

BODGES ▶ bodge

BODGIE, -R, -S, -ST n unruly or uncouth young man, esp in the 1950s ▷ adj inferior

BODGING ▶ bodge

BODHI, -S n as in bodhi tree holy tree of Buddhists

BODHRAN, -S n shallow one-sided drum popular in Irish and Scottish folk music

BODICE, -S n upper part of a dress

BODIED ▶ body

BODIES ▶ body

BODIKIN, -S n little body

BODILESS adj having no body or substance

BODILY adj relating to the body ▷ adv by taking hold of the body

BODING, -S ▶ bode

BODINGLY ▶ bode

BODINGS ▶ boding

BODKIN, -S n blunt large-eyed needle

BODLE, -S n small obsolete Scottish coin

BODRAG, -S n enemy attack

BODS ▶ bod

BODY, BODIED, BODIES, -ING n entire physical structure of an animal or human ▷ vb give form to

BODYLINE n (in cricket) fast bowling aimed at the batsman's body

BODYMAN, BODYMEN n person who repairs car bodies

BODYSIDE n side of a body of a vehicle

BODYSUIT n one-piece undergarment for a baby

BODYSURF vb ride a wave by lying on it without a surfboard

BODYWASH n liquid soap for use in the shower or bath

BODYWORK n outer shell of a motor vehicle

BOEHMITE n type of grey, red, or brown mineral

BOEP, -S n S African word for a big belly

BOERBUL, -S n crossbred mastiff used esp as a watchdog

BOERBULL same as ▶ boerbul

BOERBULS ▶ boerbul

BOERTJIE South African word for ▶ friend

BOET, -S n brother

BOEUF, -S n as in boeuf bourguignon type of beef casserole

BOFF, -ED, -ING, -S n boffin ▷ vb hit

BOFFIN, -S n scientist or expert

BOFFING ▶ boff

BOFFINS ▶ boffin

BOFFINY adj like a boffin

BOFFO, -S n boffin

BOFFOLA, -S n great success

BOFFOS ▶ boffo

BOFFS ▶ boff

BOG, -GED, -GING, -S n wet spongy ground ▷ vb mire or delay

BOGAN, -S n youth who dresses and behaves rebelliously

BOGART, -ED, -S vb monopolize or keep to oneself selfishly

BOGBEAN, -S same as ▶ buckbean

BOGEY, -ED, -ING, -S n evil or mischievous spirit ▷ vb play (a hole) in one stroke over par

BOGEYISM n demonization

BOGEYMAN, BOGEYMEN n frightening person, real or imaginary, used as a threat, esp to children

BOGEYS ▶ bogey

BOGGARD, -S same as ▶ boggart

BOGGART, -S n ghost or poltergeist

BOGGED ▶ bog

BOGGER, -S n lavatory

BOGGIER ▶ boggy

BOGGIEST ▶ boggy

BOGGING ▶ bog

BOGGISH ▶ bog

BOGGLE, -D, -S, BOGGLING vb be surprised, confused, or alarmed

BOGGLER, -S ▶ boggle

BOGGLES ▶ boggle

BOGGLING ▶ boggle

BOGGY, BOGGIER, BOGGIEST ▶ bog

BOGHEAD adj relating to variety of coal from which paraffin can be derived

BOGHOLE, -S n natural hole of wet spongy ground

BOGIE, -D, -ING, -S same as ▶ bogey

BOGLAND, -S n area of wetland

BOGLE, -D, -S, BOGLING n rhythmic dance performed to ragga music ▷ vb perform such a dance

BOGMAN, BOGMEN n body of a person found preserved in a peat bog

BOGOAK, -S *n* oak or other wood found preserved in peat bogs

BOGONG, -S *n* large nocturnal Australian moth

BOGS ▸ bog

BOGUE, -S *n* type of Mediterranean fish

BOGUS *adj* not genuine

BOGUSLY ▸ bogus

BOGWOOD, -S *same as* ▸ bogoak

BOGY *same as* ▸ bogey

BOGYISM, -S *same as* ▸ bogeyism

BOGYMAN, BOGYMEN *same as* ▸ bogeyman

BOH, -S *same as* ▸ bo

BOHEA, -S *n* black Chinese tea

BOHEMIA, -S *n* area frequented by unconventional (esp creative) people

BOHEMIAN *adj* unconventional in lifestyle or appearance ▷ *n* person, esp an artist or writer, who lives an unconventional life

BOHEMIAS ▸ bohemia

BOHO, -S *short for* ▸ bohemian

BOHRIUM, -S *n* element artificially produced in minute quantities

BOHS ▸ boh

BOIL, -ED, -S *vb* change from a liquid to a vapour so quickly that bubbles are formed ▷ *n* state or action of boiling

BOILABLE ▸ boil

BOILED ▸ boil

BOILER, -S *n* piece of equipment which provides hot water

BOILERY *n* place where water is boiled to extract salt

BOILING, -S *adj* very hot ▷ *n* sweet

BOILOFF, -S *n* quantity of liquefied gases lost in evaporation

BOILOVER *n* surprising result in a sporting event, esp in a horse race

BOILS ▸ boil

BOING, -ED, -ING, -S *vb* rebound making a noise

BOINK, -ED, -ING, -S *same as* ▸ boing

BOISERIE *n* finely crafted wood-carving

BOITE, -S *n* artist's portfolio

BOK, -S *n* S African antelope

This useful K word, meaning an antelope, can take quite a number of front extensions, forming words like **blesbok, bontbok, reitbok, rhebok**, and even, if you are lucky, **jambok** or **sjambok**.

BOKE, -D, -S, BOKING *vb* retch or vomit ▷ *n* retch

BOKEH, -S *n* blurred area of an image

BOKES ▸ boke

BOKING ▸ boke

BOKKEN, -S *n* wooden practice sword in kendo

BOKO, -S *slang word for* ▸ nose

BOKS ▸ bok

BOLA *n* missile used by gauchos and Indians of South America

BOLAR *adj* relating to clay

BOLAS, -ES *same as* ▸ bola

BOLD, -ED, -ER, -EST, -ING, -S *adj* confident and fearless ▷ *n* boldface ▷ *vb* be or make bold

BOLDEN, -ED, -S *vb* make bold

BOLDER ▸ bold

BOLDEST ▸ bold

BOLDFACE *n* weight of type characterized by thick heavy lines ▷ *vb* print in boldface

BOLDING ▸ bold

BOLDLY ▸ bold

BOLDNESS ▸ bold

BOLDS ▸ bold

BOLE, -S *n* tree trunk

BOLERO, -S *n* (music for) traditional Spanish dance

BOLES ▸ bole

BOLETE, -S *same as* ▸ boletus

BOLETUS, BOLETI *n* type of fungus

BOLIDE, -S *n* large exceptionally bright meteor that often explodes

BOLINE, -S *n* (in Wicca) a knife

BOLIVAR, -S *n* standard monetary unit of Venezuela, equal to 100 céntimos

BOLIVIA, -S *n* type of woollen fabric

BOLL, -ED, -EN, -ING, -S *n* rounded seed capsule of cotton, flax, etc ▷ *vb* form into a boll

BOLLARD, -S *n* short thick post used to prevent the passage of motor vehicles

BOLLED ▸ boll

BOLLEN ▸ boll

BOLLING ▸ boll

BOLLS ▸ boll

BOLLWORM *n* any of various moth caterpillars that feed on and destroy cotton bolls

BOLO, -S *n* large single-edged knife, originating in the Philippines

BOLOGNA, -S *n* type of sausage

BOLONEY, -S *variant spelling of* ▸ baloney

BOLOS ▸ bolo

BOLSHIE, -R, -S *adj* difficult or rebellious ▷ *n* any political radical

BOLSHY *same as* ▸ bolshie

BOLSON, -S *n* desert valley surrounded by mountains, with a shallow lake at the centre

BOLSTER, -S *vb* support or strengthen ▷ *n* long narrow pillow

BOLT, -ED, -S, BOULTERS *n* sliding metal bar for fastening a door etc ▷ *vb* run away suddenly

BOLTER, -S ▸ bolt

BOLTHEAD *n* glass receptacle used in chemistry

BOLTHOLE *n* place of escape from danger

BOLTING, -S ▸ bolt

BOLTLESS ▸ bolt

BOLTLIKE ▸ bolt

BOLTONIA *n* N American plant with daisy-like flowers with white, violet, or pinkish rays

BOLTROPE *n* rope sewn to the foot or luff of a sail to strengthen it

BOLTS ▸ bolt

BOLUS, -ES *same as* ▸ bole

BOMA, -S *n* enclosure set up to protect a camp, herd of animals, etc

BOMB, -ED, -S *n* container fitted with explosive material ▷ *vb* attack with bombs

BOMBABLE ▸ bomb

BOMBARD, -S *vb* attack with heavy gunfire or bombs ▷ *n* ancient type of cannon that threw stone balls

BOMBARDE *n* alto wind instrument similar to the oboe

BOMBARDS ▸ bombard

BOMBAST, -S *n* pompous language ▷ *vb* speak pompous language

B

BOMBAX, -ES *n* type of S American tree

BOMBE, -S *n* dessert of ice cream lined or filled with custard, cake crumbs, etc ▷ *adj* (of furniture) having a projecting swollen shape

BOMBED ▶ **bomb**

BOMBER, -S *n* aircraft that drops bombs

BOMBES ▶ **bombe**

BOMBESIN *n* hormone found in brain

BOMBING, -S ▶ **bomb**

BOMBLET, -S *n* small bomb

BOMBLOAD *n* quantity of bombs carried at one time

BOMBO, -S *same as* ▶ **bumbo**

BOMBORA, -S *n* submerged reef

BOMBOS ▶ **bombo**

BOMBS ▶ **bomb**

BOMBSITE *n* area where the buildings have been destroyed by bombs

BOMBYCID *n* type of moth of the silkworm family

BOMBYX, -ES *n* type of moth

BOMMIE, -S *n* outcrop of coral reef

BON *adj* good

BONA *pl n* goods

BONACI, -S *n* type of fish

BONAMANO, BONAMANI *n* gratuity

BONAMIA, -S *n* parasite

BONANZA, -S *n* sudden good luck or wealth

BONASSUS *same as* ▶ **bonasus**

BONASUS *n* European bison

BONBON, -S *n* sweet

BONCE, -S *n* head

BOND, -S *n* something that binds, fastens or holds together ▷ *vb* bind

BONDABLE ▶ **bond**

BONDAGE, -S *n* slavery

BONDAGER ▶ **bondage**

BONDAGES ▶ **bondage**

BONDED *adj* consisting of, secured by, or operating under a bond or bonds

BONDER, -S *same as* > **bondstone**

BONDING, -S *n* process by which individuals become emotionally attached to one another

BONDLESS ▶ **bond**

BONDMAID *n* unmarried female servant

BONDMAN, BONDMEN *same as* ▶ **bondsman**

BONDS ▶ **bond**

BONDSMAN, BONDSMEN *n* person bound by bond to act as surety for another

BONDUC, -S *n* type of North American tree

BONE, -D, -S *n* any of the hard parts in the body that form the skeleton ▷ *vb* remove the bones from (meat for cooking etc)

BONEBED, -S *n* site where dinosaur fossils are found

BONED ▶ **bone**

BONEFISH *n* type of silvery marine game fish occurring in warm shallow waters

BONEHEAD *n* stupid or obstinate person

BONELESS ▶ **bone**

BONELIKE *adj* like bone

BONEMEAL *n* product of dried and ground animal bones, used as a fertilizer or in stock feeds

BONER, -S *n* blunder

BONES ▶ **bone**

BONESET, -S *n* N American plant with flat clusters of small white flowers

BONEY, -ER, -EST *same as* ▶ **bony**

BONEYARD *an informal name for a* ▶ **cemetery**

BONEYER ▶ **boney**

BONEYEST ▶ **boney**

BONFIRE, -S *n* large outdoor fire

BONG, -ED, -ING, -S *n* deep reverberating sound, as of a large bell ▷ *vb* make a deep reverberating sound

BONGO, -ES, -S *n* small drum played with the fingers

BONGOIST *n* bongo player

BONGOS ▶ **bongo**

BONGRACE *n* shade for face

BONGS ▶ **bong**

BONHAM, -S *n* piglet

BONHOMIE *n* cheerful friendliness

BONIATO, -S *n* sweet potato

BONIBELL *same as* > **bonnibell**

BONIE *same as* ▶ **bonny**

BONIER ▶ **bony**

BONIEST ▶ **bony**

BONIFACE *n* pub landlord

BONINESS ▶ **bony**

BONING, -S ▶ **bone**

BONISM, -S *n* doctrine that the world is good, although not the best of all possible worlds

BONIST, -S ▶ **bonism**

BONITO, -ES, -S *n* small tuna-like marine food fish

BONJOUR *interj* hello

BONK, -ED, -S *vb* hit

BONKERS *adj* crazy

BONKING, -S ▶ **bonk**

BONKS ▶ **bonk**

BONNE, -S *n* housemaid or female servant

BONNET, -ED, -S *n* metal cover over a vehicle's engine ▷ *vb* place a bonnet on

BONNIE *same as* ▶ **bonny**

BONNIER ▶ **bonny**

BONNIES ▶ **bonny**

BONNIEST ▶ **bonny**

BONNILY ▶ **bonny**

BONNOCK, -S *n* thick oatmeal cake

BONNY, BONNIER, BONNIES, BONNIEST *adj* beautiful ▷ *adv* agreeably or well ▷ *n* beautiful person

BONOBO, -S *n* type of anthropoid ape of central W Africa

BONSAI *n* ornamental miniature tree or shrub

BONSELA, -S *n* small gift of money

BONSELLA *same as* > **bonsela**

BONSOIR *interj* good evening

BONSPELL *same as* > **bonspiel**

BONSPIEL *n* curling match

BONTBOK, -S *n* antelope found in S Africa

BONTEBOK *n* S African antelope

BONUS, -ED, -ES, -SED, -SES *n* something given, paid, or received above what is due or expected ▷ *vb* (in Scrabble) play all seven of one's tiles in a single turn

BONUSING *n* (in Scrabble) act of playing all seven of one's tiles in a single turn

BONUSSED ▶ **bonus**

BONUSSES ▶ **bonus**

BONXIE, -S *n* great skua

BONY, BONIER, BONIEST *adj* having many bones

BONZA *same as* ▶ **bonzer**

BONZE, -S *n* Chinese or Japanese Buddhist priest or monk

BONZER *adj* excellent

BONZES ▶ **bonze**

BOO, -ED, -S *interj* shout of disapproval ▷ *vb* shout 'boo' to show disapproval

BOOAI, -S *same as* ▶ **boohai**

BOOAY, -S *same as* ▶ **boohai**

BOOB, -ED, -ING, -S *n* foolish mistake ▷ *vb* make a

foolish mistake ▷ *adj* of poor quality, similar to that provided in a prison

BOOBHEAD *n* repeat offender in a prison

BOOBIE *same as* ▸ **booby**

BOOBIES ▸ **booby**

BOOBING ▸ **boob**

BOOBIRD, -S *n* person who boos

BOOBISH *adj* doltish

BOOBOO, -S *n* blunder

BOOBOOK, -S *n* small spotted Australian brown owl

BOOBOOS ▸ **booboo**

BOOBS ▸ **boob**

BOOBY, BOOBIES *n* foolish person

BOOBYISH ▸ **booby**

BOOBYISM ▸ **booby**

BOOCOO, -S *same as* ▸ **beaucoup**

BOODIE *n* type of kangaroo

BOODIED ▸ **boody**

BOODIES ▸ **boody**

BOODLE, -D, -S, BOODLING *n* money or valuables that are counterfeit or used as a bribe ▷ *vb* give or receive money corruptly or illegally

BOODLER, -S ▸ **boodle**

BOODLES ▸ **boodle**

BOODLING ▸ **boodle**

BOODY, BOODIED, BOODIES, -ING *vb* sulk

BOOED ▸ **boo**

BOOFHEAD *n* stupid person

BOOFY, BOOFIER, BOOFIEST *adj* muscular and strong but stupid

BOOGALOO *n* type of dance performed to rock and roll music ▷ *vb* dance a boogaloo

BOOGER, -S *n* piece of dried mucus from the nose

BOOGEY, -ED, -S *same as* ▸ **boogie**

BOOGIE, -D, -S *vb* dance to fast pop music ▷ *n* session of dancing to pop music

BOOGY, -ING *same as* ▸ **boogie**

BOOGYMAN, BOOGYMEN *same as* ▸ **bogeyman**

BOOH, -ED, -ING, -S *same as* ▸ **boo**

BOOHAI, -S *n* as in up the boohai thoroughly lost

BOOHED ▸ **booh**

BOOHING ▸ **booh**

BOOHOO, -ED, -S *vb* sob or pretend to sob noisily ▷ *n* distressed or pretended sobbing

BOOHS ▸ **booh**

BOOING, -S *n* act of booing

BOOJUM, -S *n* American tree

BOOK, -ED, -S *n* number of pages bound together between covers ▷ *vb* reserve (a place, passage, etc) in advance

BOOKABLE ▸ **book**

BOOKBAG, -S *n* bag for books

BOOKCASE *n* piece of furniture containing shelves for books

BOOKED ▸ **book**

BOOKEND, -S *n* one of a pair of supports for holding books upright ▷ *vb* occur or be located on either side (of something)

BOOKER, -S ▸ **book**

BOOKFUL, -S ▸ **book**

BOOKIE, -S *short for* > **bookmaker**

BOOKIER ▸ **booky**

BOOKIES ▸ **bookie**

BOOKIEST ▸ **booky**

BOOKING, -S *n*. reservation, as of a table or seat

BOOKISH *adj* fond of reading

BOOKLAND *n* common land given to private owner

BOOKLESS ▸ **book**

BOOKLET, -S *n* thin book with paper covers

BOOKLICE > **booklouse**

BOOKLIKE *adj* like a book

BOOKLORE *n* knowledge or beliefs gleaned from books

BOOKMAN, BOOKMEN *n* learned person

BOOKMARK *n* address for a website stored on a computer so that the user can easily return to the site ▷ *vb* identify and store (a website) so that one can return to it quickly and easily

BOOKMEN ▸ **bookman**

BOOKOO, -S *same as* ▸ **boocoo**

BOOKRACK *n* rack for holding books

BOOKREST *n* stand for supporting open book

BOOKS ▸ **book**

BOOKSHOP *n* shop where books are sold

BOOKSIE *same as* ▸ **booksy**

BOOKSY, BOOKSIER *adj* inclined to be bookish or literary

BOOKWORK *n* academic study

BOOKWORM *n* person devoted to reading

BOOKY, BOOKIER, BOOKIEST *adj* bookish

BOOL, -ED, -ING, -S *n* bowling ball ▷ *vb* play bowls

BOOM, -ED, -S *vb* make a loud deep echoing sound ▷ *n* loud deep echoing sound

BOOMBOX *n* portable stereo system

BOOMBURB *n* large suburb that is growing quickly

BOOMED ▸ **boom**

BOOMER, -S *n* large male kangaroo

BOOMIER ▸ **boomy**

BOOMIEST ▸ **boomy**

BOOMING, -S ▸ **boom**

BOOMKIN, -S *n* short boom projecting from the deck of a ship

BOOMLET, -S *n* small boom in business, birth rate, etc

BOOMS ▸ **boom**

BOOMTOWN *n* town that is enjoying sudden prosperity or has grown rapidly

BOOMY, BOOMIER, BOOMIEST *adj* characterized by heavy bass sound

BOON, -EST, -S *n* something useful, helpful, or beneficial ▷ *adj* useful, helpful, or beneficial

BOONDOCK *adj* of or relating to the boondocks

BOONER, -S *n* derogatory term for a young working-class person from Canberra

BOONEST ▸ **boon**

BOONGARY *n* tree kangaroo of NE Queensland, Australia

BOONIES *short form of* > **boondocks**

BOONLESS ▸ **boon**

BOONS ▸ **boon**

BOOR, -S *n* rude or insensitive person

BOORD, -S *obsolete spelling of* ▸ **board**

BOORDE, -S *obsolete spelling of* ▸ **board**

BOORDS ▸ **boord**

BOORISH *adj* ill-mannered, clumsy, or insensitive

BOORKA, -S *same as* ▸ **burka**

BOORS ▸ **boor**

BOORTREE *same as* ▸ **bourtree**

BOOS ▸ **boo**

BOOSE, -D, -S, BOOSING *same as* ▸ **booze**

BOOST, -ED, -ING, -S *n* encouragement or help ▷ *vb* improve

B

B

BOOSTER, -S n small additional injection of a vaccine

BOOSTING ▸ boost

BOOSTS ▸ boost

BOOT, -ING, -S n outer covering for the foot that extends above the ankle ▸ vb kick

BOOTABLE ▸ boot

BOOTCUT adj (of trousers) slightly flared at the bottom of the legs

BOOTED adj wearing boots

BOOTEE, -S n baby's soft shoe

BOOTERY n shop where boots and shoes are sold

BOOTH, -S n small partly enclosed cubicle

BOOTHOSE n stocking worn with boots

BOOTHS ▸ booth

BOOTIE n Royal Marine

BOOTIES ▸ booty

BOOTIKIN n small boot

BOOTING ▸ boot

BOOTJACK n device that grips the heel of a boot to enable the foot to be withdrawn easily

BOOTLACE n strong lace for fastening a boot

BOOTLAST n foot shape placed in boots or shoes to keep their shape

BOOTLEG, -S adj produced, distributed, or sold illicitly ▸ vb make, carry, or sell (illicit goods) ▸ n something made or sold illicitly

BOOTLESS adj of little or no use

BOOTLICK vb seek favour by servile or ingratiating behaviour

BOOTS ▸ boot

BOOTY, BOOTIES n valuable articles obtained as plunder

BOOZE, -D, -S n alcoholic drink ▸ vb drink alcohol, esp in excess

BOOZER, -S n person who is fond of drinking

BOOZES ▸ booze

BOOZEY same as ▸ boozy

BOOZIER ▸ boozy

BOOZIEST ▸ boozy

BOOZILY ▸ boozy

BOOZING, -S ▸ booze

BOOZY, BOOZIER, BOOZIEST adj inclined to or involving excessive drinking of alcohol

BOP, -PED, -PING, -S vb dance to pop music ▸ n form of jazz with complex rhythms and harmonies

BOPEEP, -S n quick look; peek

BOPPED ▸ bop

BOPPER, -S ▸ bop

BOPPIER ▸ boppy

BOPPIEST ▸ boppy

BOPPING ▸ bop

BOPPISH same as ▸ boppy

BOPPY, BOPPIER, BOPPIEST adj resembling or suggesting bebop

BOPS ▸ bop

BOR, -S n neighbour

BORA, -S n Aboriginal Australian initiation ceremony

BORACES ▸ borax

BORACHIO n pig's skin wine carrier

BORACIC same as ▸ boric

BORACITE n white mineral that forms salt deposits of magnesium borate

BORAGE, -S n Mediterranean plant with star-shaped blue flowers

BORAK, -S n rubbish

BORAL, -S n type of fine powder

BORANE, -S n any compound of boron and hydrogen

BORAS ▸ bora

BORATE, -D, -S, BORATING n salt or ester of boric acid ▸ vb treat with borax, boric acid, or borate

BORAX, BORACES, -ES n soluble white mineral occurring in alkaline soils and salt deposits

BORAZON, -S n extremely hard form of boron nitride

BORD, -S obsolete spelling of ▸ board

BORDAR, -S n smallholder who held cottage in return for menial work

BORDE, -S obsolete spelling of ▸ board

BORDEAUX n any of several wines produced around Bordeaux

BORDER, -ED, -S n dividing line between political or geographical regions ▸ vb provide with a border

BORDERER n person who lives in a border area, esp the border between England and Scotland

BORDERS ▸ border

BORDES ▸ borde

BORDS ▸ bord

BORDURE, -S n outer edge of a shield, esp when decorated distinctively

BORE, -D, -S vb make (someone) weary by being dull

BOREAL adj of or relating to the north or the north wind

BOREALIS adj as in aurora borealis lights seen around the North Pole

BOREAS, -ES n name for the north wind

BORECOLE another name for ▸ kale

BORED ▸ bore

BOREDOM, -S n state of being bored

BOREE, -S same as ▸ myall

BOREEN, -S n country lane or narrow road

BOREES ▸ boree

BOREHOLE n hole driven into the ground to obtain geological information, release water, etc

BOREL, -S adj unlearned ▸ n boring tool

BORER, -S n machine or hand tool for boring holes

BORES ▸ bore

BORESOME adj boring

BORGO, -S n small attractive medieval village

BORIC adj of or containing boron

BORIDE, -S n compound in which boron is the most electronegative element

BORING, -S n act or process of making or enlarging a hole ▸ adj dull

BORINGLY ▸ boring

BORINGS ▸ boring

BORK, -ED, -S vb dismiss from a job unfairly

BORKING, -S n act of incorrectly configuring a device

BORKS ▸ bork

BORLOTTI pl n as in borlotti bean variety of kidney bean

BORM, -ED, -ING, -S vb smear with paint, oil, etc

BORN adj possessing certain qualities from birth

BORNA n as in borna disease viral disease found in mammals, esp horses

BORNE ▸ bear

BORNEOL, -S n white solid terpene alcohol

BORNITE, -S n type of mineral

BORNITIC ▶ bornite
BORNYL, -S n as in bornyl alcohol white solid alcohol from a Malaysian tree
BORON, -S n element used in hardening steel
BORONIA, -S n Australian aromatic flowering shrub
BORONIC ▶ boron
BORONS ▶ boron
BOROUGH, -S n town or district with its own council
BORREL adj ignorant
BORRELIA n type of bacterium
BORRELL same as ▶ borrel
BORROW, -ED, -S vb obtain (something) temporarily
BORROWER ▶ borrow
BORROWS ▶ borrow
BORS ▶ bor
BORSCH, -ES same as ▶ borscht
BORSCHT, -S n Russian soup based on beetroot
BORSHCH same as ▶ borscht
BORSHT, -S same as ▶ borscht
BORSIC, -S n composite material used in aviation
BORSTAL, -S n (formerly in Britain) prison for young criminals
BORSTALL same as ▶ borstal
BORSTALS ▶ borstal
BORT, -S n inferior grade of diamond used for cutting and drilling
BORTIER ▶ borty
BORTIEST ▶ borty
BORTS ▶ bort
BORTSCH same as ▶ borscht
BORTY, BORTIER, BORTIEST ▶ bort
BORTZ, -ES same as ▶ bort
BORZOI, -S n tall dog with a long silky coat
BOS ▶ bo
BOSBOK, -S same as ▶ bushbuck
BOSCAGE, -S n mass of trees and shrubs
BOSCHBOK same as ▶ bushbuck
BOSH, -ES n empty talk, nonsense
BOSHBOK, -S same as ▶ bushbuck
BOSHES ▶ bosh
BOSHTA same as ▶ boshter
BOSHTER adj excellent
BOSHVARK same as > boschvark
BOSIE, -S n (in cricket) another term for googly

BOSK, -S n small wood of bushes and small trees
BOSKAGE, -S same as ▶ boscage
BOSKER adj excellent
BOSKET, -S n clump of small trees or bushes
BOSKIER ▶ bosky
BOSKIEST ▶ bosky
BOSKS ▶ bosk
BOSKY, BOSKIER, BOSKIEST adj containing or consisting of bushes or thickets
BOSOM, -ED, -ING, -S n chest of a person ▷ adj very dear ▷ vb embrace
BOSOMIER ▶ bosomy
BOSOMING ▶ bosom
BOSOMS ▶ bosom
BOSOMY, BOSOMIER adj (of a woman) having large breasts
BOSON, -S n type of elementary particle
BOSONIC ▶ boson
BOSONS ▶ boson
BOSQUE, -S same as ▶ bosk
BOSQUET, -S same as ▶ bosket
BOSS, -ED, -ER, -ES, -EST n raised knob or stud ▷ vb employ, supervise, or be in charge of ▷ adj excellent
BOSSDOM, -S n bosses collectively
BOSSED ▶ boss
BOSSER ▶ boss
BOSSES ▶ boss
BOSSEST ▶ boss
BOSSET, -S n either of the rudimentary antlers found in young deer
BOSSIER ▶ bossy
BOSSIES ▶ bossy
BOSSIEST ▶ bossy
BOSSILY ▶ bossy
BOSSING, -S n act of shaping malleable metal
BOSSISM, -S n domination of political organizations by bosses
BOSSY, BOSSIER, BOSSIES, BOSSIEST adj domineering or overbearing ▷ n US pet name for a cow
BOSTANGI n imperial Turkish guard
BOSTHOON n boor
BOSTON, -S n card game for four, played with two packs
BOSTRYX n phenomenon in which flowers develop on one side only
BOSUN, -S same as > boatswain

BOT, -TED, -TING vb scrounge
BOTA, -S n leather container
BOTANIC, -S same as > botanical
BOTANICA n botany
BOTANICS ▶ botanic
BOTANIES ▶ botany
BOTANISE same as ▶ botanize
BOTANIST ▶ botany
BOTANIZE vb collect or study plants
BOTANY, BOTANIES n study of plants
BOTARGO, -S n relish consisting of the roe of mullet or tuna, salted and pressed into rolls
BOTAS ▶ bota
BOTCH, -ED, -ES vb spoil through clumsiness ▷ n badly done piece of work or repair
BOTCHER, -S ▶ botch
BOTCHERY n instance of botching
BOTCHES ▶ botch
BOTCHIER ▶ botchy
BOTCHILY ▶ botchy
BOTCHING ▶ botch
BOTCHY, BOTCHIER adj clumsily done or made
BOTE, -S n compensation given for injury or damage to property
BOTEL, -S same as ▶ boatel
BOTES ▶ bote
BOTFLY, BOTFLIES n type of stout-bodied hairy fly
BOTH pron two considered together ▷ adj two considered together ▷ determiner two
BOTHAN, -S n unlicensed drinking house
BOTHER, -ED, -S vb take the time or trouble ▷ n trouble, fuss, or difficulty ▷ interj exclamation of slight annoyance
BOTHIE same as ▶ bothy
BOTHIES ▶ bothy
BOTHOLE, -S n hole made by the larva of the botfly
BOTHRIUM, BOTHRIA n groove-shaped sucker on tapeworm
BOTHY, BOTHIES n hut used for temporary shelter
BOTHYMAN, BOTHYMEN n man who lives in bothy
BOTNET, -S n network of infected computers
BOTONE adj having lobes at the ends

B

BOTONEE same as ▶ **botone**

BOTONNEE same as ▶ **botone**

BOTOXED adj having had Botox treatment

BOTRYOID adj shaped like a bunch of grapes

BOTRYOSE same as ▶ **botryoid**

BOTRYTIS n type of fungus which causes plant diseases

BOTS n digestive disease of horses and some other animals

BOTT, -S same as ▶ **bot**

BOTTARGA same as ▶ **botargo**

BOTTE, -S n thrust or hit

BOTTED ▶ **bot**

BOTTEGA, -S n workshop; studio

BOTTES ▶ **botte**

BOTTIES ▶ **botty**

BOTTINE, -S n light boot for women or children

BOTTING ▶ **bot**

BOTTLE, -D, -S n container for holding liquids ▷ vb put in a bottle

BOTTLER, -S n exceptional person or thing

BOTTLES ▶ **bottle**

BOTTLING ▶ **bottle**

BOTTOM, -ED, -S n lowest, deepest, or farthest removed part of a thing ▷ adj lowest or last ▷ vb provide with a bottom

BOTTOMER n pit worker

BOTTOMRY n loan in which a ship's owner pledges the ship as security

BOTTOMS ▶ **bottom**

BOTTONY same as ▶ **botone**

BOTTS ▶ **bott**

BOTTY, BOTTIES n diminutive for bottom

BOTULIN, -S n potent toxin which causes botulism

BOTULISM n severe food poisoning

BOUBOU, -S n long flowing garment

BOUCHE, -S n notch cut in the top corner of a shield

BOUCHEE, -S n small pastry case filled with a savoury mixture

BOUCHES ▶ **bouche**

BOUCLE, -S n looped yarn giving a knobbly effect ▷ adj of or designating such a yarn or fabric

BOUCLEE, -S n support for a cue in billiards using the hand

BOUCLES ▶ **boucle**

BOUDERIE n sulkiness

BOUDIN, -S n French version of a black pudding

BOUDOIR, -S n woman's bedroom or private sitting room

BOUFFANT adj (of a hairstyle) having extra height through backcombing ▷ n bouffant hair style

BOUFFE, -S n type of light or satirical opera common in France during the 19th century

BOUGE, -D, -S, BOUGING vb move

BOUGET, -S n budget

BOUGH, -S n large branch of a tree

BOUGHED ▶ **bough**

BOUGHPOT n container for displaying boughs

BOUGHS ▶ **bough**

BOUGHT, -S n curve

BOUGHTEN archaic past participle of ▶ **buy**

BOUGHTS ▶ **bought**

BOUGIE, -S n medical instrument

BOUGING ▶ **bouge**

BOUILLI, -S n stew

BOUILLON n thin clear broth or stock

BOUK, -S n bulk; volume

BOULDER, -S n large rounded rock ▷ vb convert into boulders

BOULDERY adj covered in boulders

BOULE same as ▶ **boulle**

BOULES n game popular in France

BOULLE, -S adj relating to a type of marquetry much used on French furniture from the 17th century ▷ n something ornamented with such marquetry

BOULT, -ED, -S same as ▶ **bolt**

BOULTER ▶ **boult**

BOULTERS ▶ **boult**

BOULTING ▶ **boult**

BOULTS ▶ **boult**

BOUN, -ED, -ING, -S vb prepare to go out

BOUNCE, -D, -S vb (of a ball etc) rebound from an impact ▷ n act of rebounding

BOUNCER, -S n person employed at a nightclub etc to remove unwanted people

BOUNCES ▶ **bounce**

BOUNCIER ▶ **bouncy**

BOUNCILY ▶ **bouncy**

BOUNCING adj vigorous and robust

BOUNCY, BOUNCIER adj lively, exuberant, or self-confident

BOUND, -ING vb jump suddenly ▷ n sudden jump ▷ adj certain

BOUNDARY n dividing line that indicates the farthest limit

BOUNDED adj (of a set) having a bound

BOUNDEN adj morally obligatory

BOUNDER, -S n morally reprehensible person

BOUNDING ▶ **bound**

BOUNDS pl n limit

BOUNED ▶ **boun**

BOUNING ▶ **boun**

BOUNS ▶ **boun**

BOUNTIED ▶ **bounty**

BOUNTIES ▶ **bounty**

BOUNTREE another name for ▶ **bourtree**

BOUNTY, BOUNTIES n generosity

BOUQUET, -S n bunch of flowers

BOURBON, -S n whiskey made from maize

BOURD, -ED, -ING, -S n prank ▷ vb jest or joke

BOURDER, -S n prankster

BOURDING ▶ **bourd**

BOURDON, -S n 16-foot organ stop of the stopped diapason type

BOURDS ▶ **bourd**

BOURG, -S n French market town, esp one beside a castle

BOURGEON same as ▶ **burgeon**

BOURGS ▶ **bourg**

BOURKHA, -S same as ▶ **burka**

BOURLAW, -S same as ▶ **byrlaw**

BOURN, -S n (in S Britain) stream

BOURNE, -S same as ▶ **bourn**

BOURNS ▶ **bourn**

BOURREE, -S n traditional French dance in fast duple time

BOURRIDE n Mediterranean fish soup

BOURSE, -S n stock exchange of continental Europe, esp Paris

BOURSIER n stock-exchange worker

BOURSIN, -S n tradename of a smooth white creamy cheese, often flavoured with garlic

BOURTREE n elder tree

BOUSE, -D, -S, BOUSING vb raise or haul with a tackle

BOUSIER ▶ bousy

BOUSIEST ▶ bousy

BOUSING ▶ bouse

BOUSOUKI same as ▶ bouzouki

BOUSY, BOUSIER, BOUSIEST adj drunken; boozy

BOUT, -S n period of activity or illness

BOUTADE, -S n outburst

BOUTIQUE n small clothes shop

BOUTON, -S n knob-shaped contact between nerve fibres

BOUTONNE adj reserved or inhibited

BOUTONS ▶ bouton

BOUTS ▶ bout

BOUVIER, -S n large powerful dog

BOUZOUKI n Greek stringed musical instrument

BOVATE, -S n obsolete measure of land

BOVID, -S n type of ruminant

BOVINE, -S n domesticated bovid mammal

BOVINELY ▶ bovine

BOVINES ▶ bovine

BOVINITY ▶ bovine

BOVVER, -S n rowdiness, esp caused by gangs of teenage youths

BOW, -S vb lower (one's head) or bend (one's knee or body) as a sign of respect or shame ▷ n movement made when bowing

BOWAT, -S n lamp

BOWBENT adj bent; bow-like

BOWED adj lowered, bent forward, or curved

BOWEL, -ED, -ING, -LED, -S n intestine, esp the large intestine ▷ vb remove the bowels

BOWER, -ED, -ING, -S n shady leafy retreat ▷ vb surround as with a bower

BOWERIES ▶ bowery

BOWERING ▶ bower

BOWERS ▶ bower

BOWERY, BOWERIES n farm

BOWES poetic plural form of ▶ bough

BOWET, -S same as ▶ bowat

BOWFIN, -S n N American freshwater fish

BOWFRONT adj having a front that curves outwards

BOWGET, -S obsolete variant of ▶ budget

BOWHEAD, -S n type of large-mouthed Arctic whale

BOWHUNT, -S vb hunt using a bow and arrows

BOWIE n as in bowie knife type of hunting knife

BOWING, -S n musical technique

BOWINGLY ▶ bowing

BOWINGS ▶ bowing

BOWKNOT, -S n decorative knot usually having two loops and two loose ends

BOWL, -ED n round container with an open top ▷ vb roll smoothly along the ground

BOWLDER, -S same as ▶ boulder

BOWLED ▶ bowl

BOWLEG, -S n leg curving outwards like a bow between the ankle and the thigh

BOWLER, -S n player who sends a ball towards a batter

BOWLESS ▶ bow

BOWLFUL, -S same as ▶ bowl

BOWLIKE ▶ bow

BOWLINE, -S n line used to keep the sail taut against the wind

BOWLING, -S n game in which bowls are rolled at a group of pins

BOWLLIKE ▶ bowl

BOWLS n game involving biased wooden bowls and a small bowl (the jack)

BOWMAN, BOWMEN n archer

BOWNE, -D, -S, BOWNING same as ▶ boun

BOWPOT, -S same as ▶ boughpot

BOWR, -S n muscle

BOWS ▶ bow

BOWSAW, -S n saw with a thin blade in a bow-shaped frame

BOWSE, -D, -S, BOWSING same as ▶ bouse

BOWSER, -S n tanker containing fuel for aircraft, military vehicles, etc

BOWSES ▶ bowse

BOWSEY same as ▶ bowsie

BOWSHOT, -S n distance an arrow travels from the bow

BOWSIE, -S n low-class, mean or obstreperous person

BOWSING ▶ bowse

BOWSMAN, BOWSMEN n man who hunts using a bow and arrows

BOWSPRIT n spar projecting from the bow of a sailing ship

BOWWOOD, -S n tree of the mulberry family, native to south-central US

BOWWOW, -ED, -S n imitation of the bark of a dog ▷ vb make a noise like a dog

BOWYANG, -S n band worn round a trouser leg below the knee

BOWYER, -S n person who makes or sells archery bows

BOX, -ED, -ES n container with a firm flat base and sides ▷ vb put into a box

BOXBALL, -S n street ball game

BOXBERRY n fruit of the partridgeberry or wintergreen

BOXBOARD n tough paperboard made from wood and wastepaper pulp: used for making boxes, etc

BOXCAR, -S n closed railway freight van

BOXED ▶ box

BOXEN adj made of boxwood

BOXER, -S n person who participates in the sport of boxing

BOXES ▶ box

BOXFISH another name for ▷ trunkfish

BOXFUL, -S same as ▶ box

BOXHAUL, -S vb method for bringing a square-rigged ship onto a new tack

BOXIER ▶ boxy

BOXIEST ▶ boxy

BOXILY ▶ boxy

BOXINESS ▶ boxy

BOXING, -S n sport of fighting with the fists

BOXLA, -S n type of lacrosse played indoors

BOXLIKE ▶ box

BOXPLOT, -S n (in statistics) type of graph

BOXROOM, -S n small room in which boxes, cases, etc may be stored

BOXTHORN n matrimony vine

BOXTY, BOXTIES n type of Irish potato pancake

BOXWOOD, -S n hard yellow wood of the box tree, used to make tool handles, etc

B

BOXY, BOXIER, BOXIEST *adj* squarish or chunky

BOY, -ED, -ING, -S *n* male child ▷ *vb* act the part of a boy in a play

BOYAR, -S *n* member of an old order of Russian nobility

BOYARD, -S *same as* ▶ **boyar**

BOYARISM ▶ **boyar**

BOYARS ▶ **boyar**

BOYAU, -X *n* connecting trench

BOYCHICK *same as* ▶ **boychik**

BOYCHIK, -S *n* young boy

BOYCOTT, -S *vb* refuse to deal with (an organization or country) ▷ *n* instance of boycotting

BOYED ▶ **boy**

BOYF, -S *n* boyfriend

BOYG, -S *n* troll-like mythical creature

BOYHOOD, -S *n* state or time of being a boy

BOYING ▶ **boy**

BOYISH *adj* of or like a boy in looks, behaviour, or character

BOYISHLY ▶ **boyish**

BOYKIE, -S *n* chap or fellow

BOYLA, -S *n* Aboriginal Australian magician or medicine-man

BOYO, -S *n* boy or young man: often used in direct address

BOYS ▶ **boy**

BOYSY, BOYSIER, BOYSIEST *adj* suited to or typical of boys or young men

BOZO, -S *n* man, esp a stupid one

BOZZETTO, BOZZETTI *n* small sketch of planned work

BRA *n* women's undergarment

BRAAI, -ED, -ING, -S *vb* grill or roast (meat) over open coals

BRAATA *n* small portion added to a purchase to encourage the customer to return

BRAATAS *same as* ▶ **braata**

BRABBLE, -D, -S *rare word for* ▶ **squabble**

BRABBLER ▶ **brabble**

BRABBLES ▶ **brabble**

BRACCATE *adj* (of birds) having feathered legs

BRACCIO, BRACCIA *n* former unit of measurement of length

BRACE, -D *n* object fastened to something to straighten or support it ▷ *vb* steady or prepare (oneself) for something unpleasant

BRACELET *n* ornamental chain or band for the wrist

BRACER, -S *n* person or thing that braces

BRACERO, -S *n* Mexican World War II labourer

BRACERS ▶ **bracer**

BRACES *pl n* pair of straps worn over the shoulders for holding up the trousers

BRACH, -ES, -S *n* female dog

BRACHAH, -S, BRACHOT *n* blessing

BRACHES ▶ **brach**

BRACHET, -S *same as* ▶ **brach**

BRACHIA ▶ **brachium**

BRACHIAL *adj* of or relating to the arm or to an armlike part or structure ▷ *n* brachial part or structure

BRACHIUM, BRACHIA *n* arm, esp the upper part

BRACHOT ▶ **brachah**

BRACHS ▶ **brach**

BRACING, -S *adj* refreshing and invigorating ▷ *n* system of braces used to strengthen or support

BRACIOLA, BRACIOLE *n* Italian meat roulade

BRACK, -S *same as* > **barmbrack**

BRACKEN, -S *n* large fern

BRACKET, -S *n* pair of characters used to enclose a section of writing ▷ *vb* put in brackets

BRACKISH *adj* (of water) slightly salty

BRACKS ▶ **brack**

BRACONID *n* type of fly with parasitic larva

BRACT, -S *n* leaf at the base of a flower

BRACTEAL ▶ **bract**

BRACTED ▶ **bract**

BRACTLET *variant of* > **bracteole**

BRACTS ▶ **bract**

BRAD, -DED, -DING, -S *n* small tapered nail with a small head

BRADAWL, -S *n* small boring tool

BRADDED ▶ **brad**

BRADDING ▶ **brad**

BRADOON, -S *same as* ▶ **bridoon**

BRADS ▶ **brad**

BRAE, -S *n* hill or slope

BRAEHEID *n* summit of a hill or slope

BRAES ▶ **brae**

BRAG, -GED, -GEST, -S *vb* speak arrogantly and boastfully ▷ *n* boastful talk or behaviour ▷ *adj* boastful

BRAGGART *n* person who boasts loudly ▷ *adj* boastful

BRAGGED ▶ **brag**

BRAGGER, -S ▶ **brag**

BRAGGEST ▶ **brag**

BRAGGIER ▶ **braggy**

BRAGGING ▶ **brag**

BRAGGY, BRAGGIER *adj* boastful

BRAGLY ▶ **brag**

BRAGS ▶ **brag**

BRAHMA, -S *n* breed of domestic fowl

BRAHMAN, -S *n* member of the highest Hindu caste

BRAHMANI *n* woman of the highest Hindu caste

BRAHMANS ▶ **brahman**

BRAHMAS ▶ **brahma**

BRAHMIN, -S *same as* ▶ **brahman**

BRAID, -EST, -S *vb* interweave (hair, thread, etc) ▷ *n* length of hair etc that has been braided ▷ *adj* broad ▷ *adv* broadly

BRAIDE *adj* given to deceit

BRAIDED *adj* flowing in several shallow interconnected channels

BRAIDER, -S ▶ **braid**

BRAIDEST ▶ **braid**

BRAIDING *n* braids collectively

BRAIDS ▶ **braid**

BRAIL, -ED, -ING, -S *n* one of several lines fastened to a fore-and-aft sail to aid in furling it ▷ *vb* furl (a fore-and-aft sail) using brails

BRAILLE, -D, -S *n* system of writing consisting of raised dots ▷ *vb* print or write using this method

BRAILLER *n* device for producing text in braille

BRAILLES ▶ **braille**

BRAILS ▶ **brail**

BRAIN, -ED, -ING, -S *n* soft mass of nervous tissue in the head ▷ *vb* hit (someone) hard on the head

BRAINBOX *n* skull

BRAINED ▶ **brain**

BRAINIAC *n* highly intelligent person

BRAINIER ▶ **brainy**

BRAINILY ▶ **brainy**

BRAINING ▶ **brain**

BRAINISH adj impulsive
BRAINPAN n skull
BRAINS ▸ brain
BRAINY, BRAINIER adj clever
BRAIRD, -ED, -S vb appear as shoots
BRAISE, -D, -S, BRAISING vb cook slowly in a covered pan with a little liquid
BRAIZE, -S n sea bream
BRAK, -S n crossbred dog ▷ adj (of water) slightly salty
BRAKE, -D, -S n device for slowing a vehicle ▷ vb apply a brake
BRAKEAGE ▸ brake
BRAKED ▸ brake
BRAKEMAN, BRAKEMEN n crew member of a goods or passenger train
BRAKES ▸ brake
BRAKIER ▸ braky
BRAKIEST ▸ braky
BRAKING, -S n act of braking
BRAKS ▸ brak
BRAKY, BRAKIER, BRAKIEST adj brambly
BRALESS ▸ bra
BRAMBLE, -D, -S n Scots word for blackberry ▷ vb pick blackberries
BRAMBLY ▸ bramble
BRAME, -S n powerful feeling of emotion
BRAN, -NED, -NING, -S n husks of cereal grain ▷ vb clean with water in which bran has been boiled
BRANCARD n couch on shafts, carried between two horses
BRANCH, -ED, -ES n secondary stem of a tree ▷ vb (of stems, roots, etc) divide, then develop in different directions
BRANCHER n young bird learning to fly
BRANCHES ▸ branch
BRANCHIA n gill in aquatic animals
BRANCHY ▸ branch
BRAND, -S n particular product ▷ vb mark with a brand
BRANDADE n French puréed fish dish
BRANDED adj identifiable as being the product of a particular company
BRANDER, -S ▸ brand
BRANDIED ▸ brandy
BRANDIES ▸ brandy
BRANDING ▸ brand
BRANDISE n three-legged metal stand for cooking pots

BRANDISH vb wave (a weapon etc) in a threatening way ▷ n threatening or defiant flourish
BRANDS ▸ brand
BRANDY, BRANDIED, BRANDIES n alcoholic spirit distilled from wine ▷ vb give brandy to
BRANE, -S n hypothetical component of string theory
BRANGLE, -D, -S vb quarrel noisily
BRANK, -ED, -ING vb walk with a swaggering gait
BRANKIER ▸ branky
BRANKING ▸ brank
BRANKS pl n (formerly) iron bridle used to restrain scolding women
BRANKY, BRANKIER adj ostentatious
BRANLE, -S n old French country dance performed in a linked circle
BRANNED ▸ bran
BRANNER, -S n person or machine that treats metal with bran
BRANNIER ▸ branny
BRANNING ▸ bran
BRANNY, BRANNIER adj having the appearance or texture of bran
BRANS ▸ bran
BRANSLE, -S another word for ▸ brantle
BRANT, -S n type of small goose
BRANTAIL n singing bird with red tail
BRANTLE, -S n French country dance
BRANTS ▸ brant
BRAP interj exclamation used to imitate a burst of gunfire
BRAS, -ES archaic form of ▸ brass
BRASCO, -S n lavatory
BRASERO, -S n metal grid for burning coals
BRASES ▸ bras
BRASH, -ED, -ER, -ES, -EST, -ING adj offensively loud, showy, or self-confident ▷ n loose rubbish, such as broken rock, hedge clippings, etc ▷ vb assault
BRASHIER ▸ brashy
BRASHING ▸ brash
BRASHLY ▸ brash
BRASHY, BRASHIER adj loosely fragmented
BRASIER, -S same as ▸ brazier

BRASIL, -S same as ▸ brazil
BRASILIN same as ▸ brazilin
BRASILS ▸ brasil
BRASS, -ED, -ES, -ING n alloy of copper and zinc ▷ vb make irritated or annoyed
BRASSAGE n amount charged by government for making coins
BRASSARD n identifying armband or badge
BRASSART same as ▸ brassard
BRASSED ▸ brass
BRASSES ▸ brass
BRASSET, -S same as ▸ brassart
BRASSICA n any plant of the cabbage and turnip family
BRASSIE, -S n former type of golf club
BRASSIER ▸ brassy
BRASSIES ▸ brassie
BRASSILY ▸ brassy
BRASSING ▸ brass
BRASSISH ▸ brass
BRASSY, BRASSIER adj showy and vulgar
BRAST, -ING, -S same as ▸ burst
BRAT, -S n unruly child
BRATCHET n hunting dog
BRATLING n small badly behaved child
BRATPACK n group of precocious and successful young actors, writers, etc
BRATS ▸ brat
BRATTICE n partition of wood or treated cloth used to control ventilation in a mine ▷ vb fit with a brattice
BRATTIER ▸ bratty
BRATTISH same as ▸ brattice
BRATTLE, -D, -S vb make a rattling sound
BRATTY, BRATTIER ▸ brat
BRAUNCH old variant of ▸ branch
BRAUNITE n brown or black mineral
BRAVA, -S n professional assassin
BRAVADO, -S n showy display of self-confidence ▷ vb behave with bravado
BRAVAS ▸ brava
BRAVE, -D, -S, -ST, BRAVING adj having or showing courage, resolution, and daring ▷ n Native American warrior ▷ vb confront with resolution or courage
BRAVELY ▸ brave
BRAVER, -S ▸ brave
BRAVERY ▸ brave

B

BRAVES ▸ brave
BRAVEST ▸ brave
BRAVI ▸ bravo
BRAVING ▸ brave
BRAVO, BRAVI, -ED, -ES, -ING, -S interj well done! ▹ n cry of 'bravo' ▹ vb cry or shout 'bravo'
BRAVURA, -S, BRAVURE n display of boldness or daring
BRAW, -ER, -EST adj fine or excellent, esp in appearance or dress
BRAWL, -ED, -S n noisy fight ▹ vb fight noisily
BRAWLER, -S ▸ brawl
BRAWLIE, -R adj in good health
BRAWLING ▸ brawl
BRAWLS ▸ brawl
BRAWLY ▸ braw
BRAWN, -S n physical strength
BRAWNED ▸ brawn
BRAWNIER ▸ brawny
BRAWNILY ▸ brawny
BRAWNS ▸ brawn
BRAWNY, BRAWNIER adj muscular and strong
BRAWS pl n fine apparel
BRAXY, BRAXIES n acute and usually fatal bacterial disease of sheep
BRAY, -ED, -ING, -S vb (of a donkey) utter its loud harsh sound ▹ n donkey's loud harsh sound
BRAYER, -S ▸ bray
BRAYING ▸ bray
BRAYS ▸ bray
BRAZA, -S n Spanish unit of measurement
BRAZE, -D, -S, BRAZING vb join (two metal surfaces) with brass ▹ n high-melting solder or alloy used in brazing
BRAZEN, -ED, -S adj shameless and bold ▹ vb face and overcome boldly or shamelessly
BRAZENLY ▸ brazen
BRAZENRY n audacity
BRAZENS ▸ brazen
BRAZER, -S ▸ braze
BRAZES ▸ braze
BRAZIER, -S n portable container for burning charcoal or coal
BRAZIERY ▸ brazier
BRAZIL, -S n red wood used for cabinetwork
BRAZILIN n pale yellow soluble crystalline solid
BRAZILS ▸ brazil
BRAZING ▸ braze

BREACH, -ED, -ES n breaking of a promise, obligation, etc ▹ vb break (a promise, law, etc)
BREACHER ▸ breach
BREACHES ▸ breach
BREAD, -ED, -ING, -S n food made by baking a mixture of flour and water or milk ▹ vb cover (food) with breadcrumbs before cooking
BREADBIN n container for bread
BREADBOX n airtight container for bread, cakes, etc
BREADED ▸ bread
BREADIER ▸ bready
BREADING ▸ bread
BREADNUT n type of Central American and Caribbean tree
BREADS ▸ bread
BREADTH, -S n extent of something from side to side
BREADY, BREADIER adj having the appearance or texture of bread
BREAK, -S, BROKEN vb separate into pieces ▹ n act of breaking
BREAKAGE n act or result of breaking
BREAKER, -S n large wave
BREAKING ▸ break
BREAKOFF n act or an instance of breaking off or stopping
BREAKOUT n escape, esp from prison or confinement
BREAKS ▸ break
BREAKUP, -S n separation or disintegration
BREAM, -ED, -ING, -S n Eurasian freshwater fish ▹ vb clean debris (from the bottom of a vessel)
BREARE, -S same as ▸ brier
BREASKIT same as ▸ brisket
BREAST, -ED, -S n front part of the body from the neck to the abdomen ▹ vb reach the summit of
BREATH, -S n taking in and letting out of air during breathing
BREATHED adj denoting a speech sound in which the vocal cords do not vibrate
BREATHER n short rest
BREATHES ▸ breathe
BREATHS ▸ breath

BREATHY adj (of the speaking voice) accompanied by an audible emission of breath
BRECCIA, -S n type of rock
BRECCIAL ▸ breccia
BRECCIAS ▸ breccia
BRECHAM, -S n straw horse-collar
BRECHAN, -S same as ▸ brecham
BRED, -S n person who lives in a small remote place
BREDE, -D, -S, BREDING archaic spelling of ▸ braid
BREDIE, -S n meat and vegetable stew
BREDING ▸ brede
BREDREN, -S same as ▸ brethren
BREDRIN, -S same as ▸ brethren
BREDS ▸ bred
BREE, -S n broth, stock, or juice
BREECH, -ED n lower part ▹ vb fit (a gun) with a breech
BREECHES pl n trousers extending to just below the knee
BREED, -S vb produce new or improved strains of (domestic animals or plants) ▹ n group of animals etc within a species that have certain clearly defined characteristics
BREEDER, -S n person who breeds plants or animals
BREEDING ▸ breed
BREEDS ▸ breed
BREEKS pl n trousers
BREEM same as ▸ breme
BREENGE, -D, -S vb lunge forward ▹ n violent movement
BREER, -ED, -ING, -S another word for ▸ braird
BREES ▸ bree
BREESE same as ▸ breeze
BREEST, -S Scot word for ▸ breast
BREEZE, -D, -S, BREEZING n gentle wind ▹ vb move quickly or casually
BREEZIER ▸ breezy
BREEZILY ▸ breezy
BREEZING ▸ breeze
BREEZY, BREEZIER adj windy
BREGMA, -S, -TA, -TE n point on the top of the skull
BREHON, -S n (formerly) judge in Ireland
BREI, -ING, -S vb speak with a uvular r, esp in Afrikaans
BREID, -S n bread

BREIING ▸ brei
BREINGE, -D, -S same as ▸ **breenge**
BREIS ▸ brei
BREIST, -S Scot word for ▸ **breast**
BREKKIE same as ▸ **brekky**
BREKKY, BREKKIES slang word for > **breakfast**
BRELOQUE n charm attached to watch chain
BREME adj well-known
BREN, -NING, -S n type of machine gun ▷ vb burn
BRENNE, -S vb burn
BRENNING ▸ bren
BRENS ▸ bren
BRENT, -ER, -EST, -S n type of goose ▷ adj steep
BRER, -S n brother: usually prefixed to a name
BRERE, -S same as ▸ **brier**
BRERS ▸ brer
BRESAOLA n (in Italian cookery) air-dried, salted beef
BRETESSE another word for ▸ **brattice**
BRETHREN ▸ brother
BRETON, -S n hat with an upturned brim and a rounded crown
BRETTICE same as ▸ **brattice**
BREVE, -S n accent placed over a vowel to indicate shortness
BREVET, -ED, -S n document entitling a commissioned officer to hold temporarily a higher military rank ▷ vb promote by brevet
BREVETCY ▸ brevet
BREVETE adj patented
BREVETED ▸ brevet
BREVETS ▸ brevet
BREVIARY n book of prayers to be recited daily by a Roman Catholic priest
BREVIATE n summary
BREVIER, -S n (formerly) size of printer's type approximately equal to 8 point
BREVIS, -ES same as ▸ **brewis**
BREVITY n shortness
BREW, -ED, -S vb make (beer etc) by steeping, boiling, and fermentation ▷ n beverage produced by brewing
BREWAGE, -S n product of brewing
BREWED ▸ brew
BREWER, -S ▸ brew
BREWERY n place where beer, etc is brewed

BREWING, -S n quantity of a beverage brewed at one time
BREWIS, -ES n bread soaked in broth, gravy, etc
BREWPUB, -S n pub that incorporates a brewery on its premises
BREWS ▸ brew
BREWSKI, -S n beer
BREWSTER n person, particularly a woman, who brews
BREY, -ED, -ING, -S same as ▸ **brei**
BRIAR, -S n S European shrub with a hard woody root (briarroot)
BRIARD, -S n medium-sized dog
BRIARED ▸ briar
BRIARIER ▸ briary
BRIARS ▸ briar
BRIARY, BRIARIER adj resembling or containing briar
BRIBABLE ▸ bribe
BRIBE, -D, -S, BRIBING vb offer or give something to someone to gain favour, influence, etc ▷ n something given or offered as a bribe
BRIBEE, -S n one who is bribed
BRIBER, -S ▸ bribe
BRIBERY n process of giving or taking bribes
BRIBES ▸ bribe
BRIBING ▸ bribe
BRICHT, -ER Scot word for ▸ **bright**
BRICK, -ED, -S n (rectangular block of) baked clay used in building ▷ vb build, enclose, or fill with bricks
BRICKBAT n blunt criticism
BRICKED ▸ brick
BRICKEN adj made of brick
BRICKIE, -S n bricklayer
BRICKIER ▸ bricky
BRICKIES ▸ brickie
BRICKING ▸ brick
BRICKLE, -S variant of ▸ **brittle**
BRICKS ▸ brick
BRICKY, BRICKIER adj resembling brick
BRICOLE, -S n billiards shot
BRIDAL, -S adj of a bride or a wedding ▷ n wedding or wedding feast
BRIDALLY ▸ bridal
BRIDALS ▸ bridal
BRIDE, -D, -S, BRIDING n woman who has just been or

is about to be married ▷ vb act as a bride
BRIDEMAN, BRIDEMEN n bridegroom's attendant
BRIDES ▸ bride
BRIDGE, -D, -S n structure for crossing a river etc ▷ vb build a bridge over (something)
BRIDGING n timber struts fixed between floor or roof joists
BRIDIE, -S n semicircular pie containing meat and onions
BRIDING ▸ bride
BRIDLE, -D, -S, BRIDLING n headgear for controlling a horse ▷ vb show anger or indignation
BRIDLER, -S ▸ bridle
BRIDLES ▸ bridle
BRIDLING ▸ bridle
BRIDOON, -S n horse's bit
BRIE, -S same as ▸ **bree**
BRIEF, -ED, -EST adj short in duration ▷ n condensed statement or written synopsis ▷ vb give information and instructions to (a person)
BRIEFER, -S ▸ brief
BRIEFEST ▸ brief
BRIEFING n meeting for giving out detailed information or instructions
BRIEFLY ▸ brief
BRIEFS pl n men's or women's underpants without legs
BRIER, -S same as ▸ **briar**
BRIERED ▸ brier
BRIERIER ▸ briery
BRIERS ▸ brier
BRIERY, BRIERIER ▸ brier
BRIES ▸ brie
BRIG, -S n two-masted square-rigged ship
BRIGADE, -D, -S n army unit smaller than a division ▷ vb organize into a brigade
BRIGALOW n type of acacia tree
BRIGAND, -S n bandit
BRIGHT, -ER adj emitting or reflecting much light ▷ adv brightly
BRIGHTEN vb make or become bright or brighter
BRIGHTER ▸ bright
BRIGHTLY ▸ bright
BRIGHTS pl n high beam of the headlights of a motor vehicle
BRIGS ▸ brig
BRIGUE, -D, -S vb solicit
BRIGUING ▸ brigue

B

B

BRIK, -S n Tunisian pastry
BRIKI, -S same as ▶ **cezve**
BRIKS ▶ **brik**
BRILL, -ER, -EST, -S n type of European flatfish popular as a food fish ▷ adj brilliant
BRILLO, -S n tradename for a type of scouring pad impregnated with a detergent
BRILLS ▶ **brill**
BRIM, -MED, -MING, -S n upper rim of a vessel ▷ vb fill or be full to the brim
BRIMFUL adj completely filled with
BRIMFULL same as ▶ **brimful**
BRIMING, -S n phosphorescence of sea
BRIMLESS ▶ **brim**
BRIMMED ▶ **brim**
BRIMMER, -S n vessel, such as a glass or bowl, filled to the brim
BRIMMING ▶ **brim**
BRIMS ▶ **brim**
BRIN, -S n thread of silk from silkworm
BRINDED adj streaky or patchy
BRINDISI n song sung in celebration
BRINDLE, -S n brindled animal
BRINDLED adj brown or grey streaked with a darker colour
BRINDLES ▶ **brindle**
BRINE, -D, -S, BRINING n salt water ▷ vb soak in or treat with brine
BRINER, -S ▶ **brine**
BRINES ▶ **brine**
BRING, -S, BROUGHT, BRUNG vb carry, convey, or take to a designated place or person
BRINGER, -S ▶ **bring**
BRINGING ▶ **bring**
BRINGS ▶ **bring**
BRINIER ▶ **briny**
BRINIES ▶ **briny**
BRINIEST ▶ **briny**
BRINING ▶ **brine**
BRINISH ▶ **brine**
BRINJAL, -S n dark purple tropical fruit, cooked and eaten as a vegetable
BRINK, -S n edge of a steep place
BRINKMAN, BRINKMEN n one who goes in for brinkmanship
BRINKS ▶ **brink**
BRINNY, BRINNIES n stone, esp when thrown

BRINS ▶ **brin**
BRINY, BRINIER, BRINIES, BRINIEST adj very salty ▷ n sea
BRIO, -S n liveliness
BRIOCHE, -S n soft roll or loaf made from a very light yeast dough, sometimes mixed with currants
BRIONY, BRIONIES same as ▶ **bryony**
BRIOS ▶ **brio**
BRIQUET, -S same as ▷ **briquette**
BRIS, -ES, -SES n ritual circumcision of male babies
BRISANCE n shattering effect or power of an explosion or explosive
BRISANT ▶ **brisance**
BRISE n type of jump
BRISES ▶ **bris**
BRISK, -ED, -ER, -EST, -ING, -S adj lively and quick ▷ vb enliven
BRISKEN, -S vb make or become more lively or brisk
BRISKER ▶ **brisk**
BRISKEST ▶ **brisk**
BRISKET, -S n beef from the breast of a cow
BRISKIER ▶ **brisky**
BRISKING ▶ **brisk**
BRISKISH ▶ **brisk**
BRISKLY ▶ **brisk**
BRISKS ▶ **brisk**
BRISKY, BRISKIER another word for ▶ **brisk**
BRISLING same as ▶ **sprat**
BRISS same as ▶ **bris**
BRISSES ▶ **bris**
BRISTLE, -D, -S n short stiff hair ▷ vb (cause to) stand up like bristles
BRISTLY ▶ **bristle**
BRISTOL n as in **bristol board** type of heavy cardboard
BRISURE, -S n mark of cadency in heraldry
BRIT, -S n young of a herring, sprat, or similar fish
BRITCHES same as ▷ **breeches**
BRITH, -S same as ▶ **bris**
BRITS ▶ **brit**
BRITSKA, -S same as ▷ **britzka**
BRITT, -S n young herring or sprat
BRITTLE, -D, -R, -S adj hard but easily broken ▷ vb make brittle ▷ n crunchy sweet made with treacle and nuts
BRITTLY ▶ **brittle**
BRITTS ▶ **britt**

BRITZKA, -S n long horse-drawn carriage
BRITZSKA same as ▶ **britzka**
BRIZE, -S same as ▶ **breeze**
BRO, -S n close male associate
BROACH, -ED, -ES vb introduce (a topic) for discussion ▷ n spit for roasting meat
BROACHER ▶ **broach**
BROACHES ▶ **broach**
BROAD, -ER, -EST, -S adj having great breadth or width ▷ n broad part of something
BROADAX same as ▶ **broadaxe**
BROADAXE n broad-bladed axe
BROADEN, -S vb make or become broad or broader
BROADER ▶ **broad**
BROADEST ▶ **broad**
BROADISH ▶ **broad**
BROADLY ▶ **broad**
BROADS ▶ **broad**
BROADWAY n wide road
BROAST, -ED, -S vb cook by broiling and roasting
BROCADE, -D, -S n rich fabric woven with a raised design ▷ vb weave with such a design
BROCAGE, -S another word for ▷ **brokerage**
BROCARD, -S n basic principle of civil law
BROCATEL n heavy upholstery brocade
BROCCOLI n type of cabbage with greenish flower heads
BROCH, -S n (in Scotland) a circular dry-stone tower large enough to serve as a fortified home
BROCHAN, -S n type of thin porridge
BROCHE, -D, -S, BROCHING adj woven with a raised design, as brocade
BROCHO, -S same as ▷ **brachah**
BROCHS ▶ **broch**
BROCHURE n booklet that contains information about a product or service
BROCK, -S n badger
BROCKAGE same as ▷ **brokerage**
BROCKED adj having different colours
BROCKET, -S n small tropical American deer with small unbranched antlers

BROCKIT same as ▸ brocked

BROCKRAM another word for ▸ breccia

BROCKS ▸ brock

BROCOLI, -S same as ▸ broccoli

BROD, -DED, -DING, -S vb prod

BRODDLE, -D, -S vb poke or pierce (something)

BRODEKIN another word for ▸ buskin

BRODKIN, -S same as ▸ brodekin

BRODS ▸ brod

BROEKIES pl n underpants

BROG, -GED, -GING, -S vb prick with an awl

BROGAN, -S n heavy laced, usually ankle-high, work boot

BROGGED ▸ brog

BROGGING ▸ brog

BROGH, -S same as ▸ broch

BROGS ▸ brog

BROGUE, -S n gentle accent

BROGUERY ▸ brogue

BROGUES ▸ brogue

BROGUISH ▸ brogue

BROIDER, -S archaic word for > embroider

BROIDERY n old form of embroidery

BROIL, -ED, -ING, -S vb cook by direct heat under a grill ▷ n process of broiling

BROILER, -S n young tender chicken for roasting

BROILING ▸ broil

BROILS ▸ broil

BROKAGE, -S another word for ▸ brokerage

BROKE, -D, -S vb negotiate or deal

BROKEN ▸ break

BROKENLY ▸ break

BROKER, -ED, -S n agent who buys or sells goods, securities, etc ▷ vb act as a broker (in)

BROKERY n work done by a broker

BROKES ▸ broke

BROKING, -S ▸ broke

BROLGA, -S n large grey Australian crane with a trumpeting call

BROLLY, BROLLIES n umbrella

BROMAL, -S n synthetic liquid formerly used medicinally

BROMANCE n close friendship between two men

BROMATE, -D, -S same as > brominate

BROME, -S n type of grass

BROMELIA n type of plant

BROMELIN n protein-digesting enzyme found in pineapple

BROMES ▸ brome

BROMIC adj of or containing bromine in the trivalent or pentavalent state

BROMID, -S same as ▸ bromide

BROMIDE, -S n chemical compound used in medicine and pharmacy

BROMIDIC adj ordinary

BROMIDS ▸ bromid

BROMIN, -S same as ▸ bromine

BROMINE, -S n dark red liquid element that gives off a pungent vapour

BROMINS ▸ bromin

BROMISE, -D, -S same as ▸ bromize

BROMISM, -S n bromine poisoning

BROMIZE, -D, -S vb treat with bromine

BROMMER, -S n S African word for bluebottle

BROMO, -S n something that contains bromide

BRONC, -S same as ▸ bronco

BRONCHI ▸ bronchus

BRONCHIA pl n bronchial tubes

BRONCHO, -S same as ▸ bronco

BRONCHUS, BRONCHI n either of the two branches of the windpipe

BRONCO, -S n (in the US) wild or partially tamed pony

BRONCS ▸ bronc

BROND, -S n piece of burning wood

BRONDE, -R, -S, -ST adj in a shade between blonde and brunette ▷ n woman with bronde hair

BRONDS ▸ brond

BRONZE, -D, -S n alloy of copper and tin ▷ adj made of, or coloured like, bronze ▷ vb (esp of the skin) make or become brown

BRONZEN adj made of or the colour of bronze

BRONZER, -S n cosmetic applied to the skin to simulate a sun tan

BRONZES ▸ bronze

BRONZIER ▸ bronzy

BRONZIFY vb cause to become colour of bronze

BRONZING n blue pigment

BRONZITE n type of orthopyroxene often having a metallic or pearly sheen

BRONZY, BRONZIER ▸ bronze

BROO, -S n brow of hill

BROOCH, -ED, -ES n ornament with a pin, worn fastened to clothes ▷ vb decorate with a brooch

BROOD, -ED, -S n number of birds produced at one hatching ▷ vb (of a bird) sit on or hatch eggs

BROODER, -S n structure used for rearing young chickens or other fowl

BROODIER ▸ broody

BROODILY ▸ broody

BROODING ▸ brood

BROODS ▸ brood

BROODY, BROODIER adj moody and sullen

BROOK, -ED, -ING, -S n small stream ▷ vb bear or tolerate

BROOKIE, -S n brook trout

BROOKING ▸ brook

BROOKITE n reddish-brown to black mineral

BROOKLET n small brook

BROOKS ▸ brook

BROOL, -S n low roar

BROOM, -ED, -ING, -S n long-handled sweeping brush ▷ vb sweep with a broom

BROOMIER ▸ broomy

BROOMING ▸ broom

BROOMS ▸ broom

BROOMY, BROOMIER adj covered with a growth of broom

BROOS ▸ broo

BROOSE, -S n race at a country wedding

BROS ▸ bro

BROSE, -S n oatmeal or pease porridge, sometimes with butter or fat added

BROSY, BROSIER, BROSIEST adj smeared with porridge

BROTH, -S n soup, usu containing vegetables

BROTHA, -S n informal term for an African-American man

BROTHER, BRETHREN, -S n boy or man with the same parents as another person ▷ interj exclamation of amazement, disgust, surprise, disappointment, etc ▷ vb treat someone like a brother

BROTHIER ▸ brothy

BROTHS ▸ broth

BROTHY, BROTHIER *adj* having the appearance or texture of broth

BROUGH, -S *same as* ▸ **broch**

BROUGHAM *n* horse-drawn closed carriage with a raised open driver's seat in front

BROUGHS ▸ brough

BROUGHT ▸ bring

BROUGHTA *same as* ▸ **braata**

BROUHAHA *n* loud confused noise

BROUZE, -S *same as* ▸ **brooze**

BROW, -S *n* part of the face (from the eyes to the hairline)

BROWBAND *n* strap of a horse's bridle that goes across the forehead

BROWBEAT *vb* frighten (someone) with threats

BROWBONE *n* bone of the brow

BROWED *adj* having a brow

BROWLESS ▸ brow

BROWN, -ED, -EST, -S *n* colour of earth or wood ▷ *adj* (of bread) made from wheatmeal or wholemeal flour ▷ *vb* make or become brown

BROWNER, -S *n* brown object

BROWNEST ▸ brown

BROWNIE, -S *n* small square nutty chocolate cake

BROWNIER ▸ browny

BROWNIES ▸ brownie

BROWNING *n* substance used to darken gravies

BROWNISH ▸ brown

BROWNOUT *n* dimming or reduction in the use of electric lights in a city

BROWNS ▸ brown

BROWNY, BROWNIER ▸ **brown**

BROWS ▸ brow

BROWSE, -D, -S *vb* look through in a casual manner ▷ *n* instance of browsing

BROWSER, -S *n* software package that enables a user to read hypertext, esp on the internet

BROWSES ▸ browse

BROWSIER ▸ browsy

BROWSING ▸ browse

BROWST, -S *n* brewing (of ale, tea)

BROWSY, BROWSIER ▸ **browse**

BRR *same as* ▸ **brrr**

This is useful if your consonant-heavy rack is giving you the shivers. And if you are even colder, **brrr** is available.

BRRR *interj* used to suggest shivering

BRU, -S *South African word for* ▸ **friend**

BRUCELLA *n* type of bacterium

BRUCHID, -S *n* type of beetle

BRUCIN, -S *same as* ▸ **brucine**

BRUCINE, -S *n* bitter poisonous alkaloid resembling strychnine

BRUCINS ▸ brucin

BRUCITE, -S *n* white translucent mineral

BRUCKLE *adj* brittle

BRUGH, -S *n* large house

BRUHAHA, -S *same as* ▸ **brouhaha**

BRUILZIE *same as* ▸ **brulzie**

BRUIN, -S *n* name for a bear, used in children's tales, fables, etc

BRUISE, -D, -S *n* discoloured area on the skin caused by an injury ▷ *vb* cause a bruise on

BRUISER, -S *n* strong tough person

BRUISES ▸ bruise

BRUISING *adj* causing bruises, as by a blow ▷ *n* bruise or bruises

BRUIT, -ED, -ING, -S *vb* report ▷ *n* abnormal sound heard within the body

BRUITER, -S ▸ bruit

BRUITING ▸ bruit

BRUITS ▸ bruit

BRULE, -S *n* person of Native Canadian and French Canadian ancestry

BRULOT, -S *n* coffee-based alcoholic drink, served flaming

BRULYIE, -S *same as* ▸ **brulzie**

BRULZIE, -S *n* noisy dispute

BRUMAL *adj* of, characteristic of, or relating to winter

BRUMBY, BRUMBIES *n* wild horse

BRUME, -S *n* heavy mist or fog

BRUMMER, -S *same as* ▸ **brommer**

BRUMOUS ▸ brume

BRUNCH, -ED, -ES *n* breakfast and lunch combined ▷ *vb* eat brunch

BRUNCHER ▸ brunch

BRUNCHES ▸ brunch

BRUNET, -S *n* boy or man with dark brown hair

BRUNETTE *n* girl or woman with dark brown hair

BRUNG ▸ bring

BRUNIZEM *n* prairie soil

BRUNT, -ED, -ING, -S *n* main force or shock of a blow, attack, etc ▷ *vb* suffer the main force or shock of a blow, attack, etc

BRUS ▸ bru

BRUSH, -ES *n* device made of bristles, wires, etc ▷ *vb* clean, scrub, or paint with a brush

BRUSHED *adj* treated with a brushing process

BRUSHER, -S ▸ brush

BRUSHES ▸ brush

BRUSHIER ▸ brushy

BRUSHING ▸ brush

BRUSHOFF *n* abrupt dismissal or rejection

BRUSHUP, -S *n* the act or an instance of tidying one's appearance

BRUSHY, BRUSHIER *adj* like a brush

BRUSK, -ER, -EST *same as* ▸ **brusque**

BRUSQUE, -R *adj* blunt or curt in manner or speech

BRUSSELS *adj* as in **brussels sprout** small cabbage-like vegetable

BRUSSEN *adj* bold

BRUST, -ING, -S *same as* ▸ **burst**

BRUT, -S *adj* (of champagne or sparkling wine) very dry ▷ *n* very dry champagne

BRUTAL *adj* cruel and vicious

BRUTALLY ▸ brutal

BRUTE, -S, -ST *n* brutal person ▷ *adj* wholly instinctive or physical, like an animal

BRUTED ▸ bruting

BRUTELY ▸ brute

BRUTER, -S *n* diamond cutter

BRUTES ▸ brute

BRUTEST ▸ brute

BRUTIFY *less common word for* ▸ **brutalize**

BRUTING, -S *n* diamond cutting

BRUTISH *adj* of or like an animal

BRUTISM, -S *n* stupidity; vulgarity

BRUTS ▸ brut

BRUX, -ED, -ES, -ING *vb* grind one's teeth

BRUXISM, -S *n* habit of grinding the teeth, esp unconsciously

BRYOLOGY *n* branch of botany concerned with the study of bryophytes

BRYONY, BRYONIES *n* wild climbing hedge plant

BRYOZOAN *n* type of aquatic invertebrate which forms colonies of polyps

BUAT, -S *same as* ▸ **bowat**

BUAZE, -S *n* fibrous African plant

BUB, -S *n* youngster

BUBA, -S *another name for* ▸ **yaws**

BUBAL, -S *n* type of antelope

BUBALE, -S *n* type of antelope

BUBALINE *adj* (of antelopes) related to or resembling the bubal

BUBALIS *same as* ▸ **bubal**

BUBALS ▸ **bubal**

BUBAS ▸ **buba**

BUBBE, -S *n* Yiddish word for grandmother

BUBBIE *same as* ▸ **bubbe**

BUBBLE, -D, -S, BUBBLING *n* ball of air in a liquid or solid ▸ *vb* form bubbles

BUBBLER, -S *n* drinking fountain

BUBBLES ▸ **bubble**

BUBBLIER ▸ **bubbly**

BUBBLIES ▸ **bubbly**

BUBBLING ▸ **bubble**

BUBBLY, BUBBLIER, BUBBLIES *adj* excited and lively ▸ *n* champagne

BUBINGA, -S *n* reddish-brown wood from African tree

BUBKES *same as* ▸ **bubkis**

BUBKIS *n* nothing

BUBO, -ES *n* inflammation and swelling of a lymph node, esp in the armpit or groin

BUBOED ▸ **bubo**

BUBOES ▸ **bubo**

BUBONIC ▸ **bubo**

BUBS ▸ **bub**

BUBU, -S *same as* ▸ **boubou**

BUBUKLE, -S *n* red spot on skin

BUBUS ▸ **bubu**

BUCARDO, -S *n* type of Spanish mountain goat, recently extinct

BUCATINI *pl n* pasta in the shape of long tubes

BUCCAL *adj* of or relating to the cheek

BUCCALLY ▸ **buccal**

BUCCINA, -S *n* curved Roman horn

BUCELLAS *n* type of Portuguese white wine

BUCHU, -S *n* S African shrub whose leaves are used as an antiseptic and diuretic

BUCK, -ED, -S *n* male of the goat, hare, kangaroo, rabbit, and reindeer ▸ *vb* (of a horse etc) jump with legs stiff and back arched

BUCKAROO *n* cowboy

BUCKAYRO *same as* ▸ **buckaroo**

BUCKBEAN *n* type of marsh plant with white or pink flowers

BUCKED ▸ **buck**

BUCKEEN, -S *n* (in Ireland) poor young man who aspires to the habits and dress of the wealthy

BUCKER, -S ▸ **buck**

BUCKEROO *same as* ▸ **buckaroo**

BUCKERS ▸ **bucker**

BUCKET, -ED, -S *n* open-topped roughly cylindrical container ▸ *vb* rain heavily

BUCKEYE, -S *n* N American tree with erect clusters of white or red flowers and prickly fruits

BUCKHORN *n* horn from a buck, used for knife handles, etc

BUCKIE, -S *n* whelk or its shell

BUCKING, -S ▸ **buck**

BUCKISH ▸ **buck**

BUCKLE, -D, -S *n* clasp for fastening a belt or strap ▸ *vb* fasten or be fastened with a buckle

BUCKLER, -S *n* small round shield worn on the forearm ▸ *vb* defend

BUCKLES ▸ **buckle**

BUCKLING *another name for* ▸ **bloater**

BUCKO, -ES, -S *n* lively young fellow: often a term of address

BUCKRAKE *n* large rake attached to tractor

BUCKRAM, -S *n* cotton or linen cloth stiffened with size, etc ▸ *vb* stiffen with buckram

BUCKS ▸ **buck**

BUCKSAW, -S *n* woodcutting saw

BUCKSHEE *adj* free

BUCKSHOT *n* large lead pellets used for shooting game

BUCKSKIN *n* skin of a male deer ▸ *adj* greyish-yellow

BUCKSOM *same as* ▸ **buxom**

BUCKTAIL *n* in fishing, fly with appearance of minnow

BUCKU, -S *same as* ▸ **buchu**

BUCOLIC, -S *adj* of the countryside or country life ▸ *n* pastoral poem

BUD, -DED, -S *n* swelling on a plant that develops into a leaf or flower ▸ *vb* produce buds

BUDDER, -S ▸ **bud**

BUDDHA, -S *n* person who has achieved a state of perfect enlightenment

BUDDIED ▸ **buddy**

BUDDIER ▸ **buddy**

BUDDIES ▸ **buddy**

BUDDIEST ▸ **buddy**

BUDDING, -S ▸ **bud**

BUDDLE, -D, -S, BUDDLING *n* sloping trough in which ore is washed ▸ *vb* wash (ore) in a buddle

BUDDLEIA *n* shrub with long spikes of purple flowers

BUDDLES ▸ **buddle**

BUDDLING ▸ **buddle**

BUDDY, BUDDIED, BUDDIER, BUDDIES, BUDDIEST, -ING *n* friend ▸ *vb* act as a friend to ▸ *adj* friendly

BUDGE, -D, -S, BUDGING *vb* move slightly ▸ *n* lambskin dressed for the fur to be worn on the outer side

BUDGER, -S ▸ **budge**

BUDGEREE *adj* good

BUDGERO, -S *same as* ▸ **budgerow**

BUDGEROW *n* barge used on the Ganges

BUDGERS ▸ **budger**

BUDGES ▸ **budge**

BUDGET, -ED, -S *n* financial plan for a period of time ▸ *vb* plan the expenditure of (money or time) ▸ *adj* cheap

BUDGETER ▸ **budget**

BUDGETS ▸ **budget**

BUDGIE, -S *n* short form of budgerigar

BUDGING ▸ **budge**

BUDLESS ▸ **bud**

BUDLIKE ▸ **bud**

BUDMASH *same as* ▸ **badmash**

BUDO, -S *n* combat and spirit in martial arts

BUDS ▸ **bud**

B

BUDWOOD, -S *n* branch with buds that is used for grafting

BUDWORM, -S *n* pest that eats tree leaves and buds

BUFF, -ED, -EST, -S *n* soft flexible undyed leather ▷ *adj* dull yellowish-brown ▷ *vb* clean or polish with soft material

BUFFA, -S *n* female comic part in an opera

BUFFABLE ▶ **buff**

BUFFALO, -S *n* member of the cattle tribe ▷ *vb* confuse

BUFFAS ▶ **buffa**

BUFFE ▶ **buffo**

BUFFED ▶ **buff**

BUFFEL *adj* as in **buffel grass** grass used for pasture in Africa, India, and Australia

BUFFER, -ED, -S *vb* protect from shock

BUFFEST ▶ **buff**

BUFFET, -ED, -S *n* counter where drinks and snacks are served ▷ *vb* knock against or about

BUFFETER ▶ **buffet**

BUFFETS ▶ **buffet**

BUFFI ▶ **buffo**

BUFFIER ▶ **buffy**

BUFFIEST ▶ **buffy**

BUFFING, -S *n* act of polishing

BUFFO, BUFFE, BUFFI, -S *n* (in Italian opera of the 18th century) comic part, esp one for a bass

BUFFOON, -S *n* clown or fool

BUFFOS ▶ **buffo**

BUFFS ▶ **buff**

BUFFY, BUFFIER, BUFFIEST *adj* having appearance or texture of buff

BUFO, -S *n* type of toad

BUG, -GED, -S *n* insect ▷ *vb* irritate

BUGABOO, -S *n* imaginary source of fear

BUGBANE, -S *n* European plant whose flowers are reputed to repel insects

BUGBEAR, -S *n* thing that causes obsessive anxiety

BUGEYE, -S *n* oyster-dredging boat

BUGGAN, -S *n* evil spirit

BUGGANE, -S *same as* ▶ **buggan**

BUGGANS ▶ **buggan**

BUGGED ▶ **bug**

BUGGIER ▶ **buggy**

BUGGIES ▶ **buggy**

BUGGIEST ▶ **buggy**

BUGGIN, -S *same as* ▶ **buggan**

BUGGING, -S ▶ **bug**

BUGGINS ▶ **buggin**

BUGGY, BUGGIER, BUGGIES, BUGGIEST *n* light horse-drawn carriage ▷ *adj* infested with bugs

BUGLE, -D, -S, BUGLING *n* instrument like a small trumpet ▷ *vb* play or sound (on) a bugle

BUGLER, -S ▶ **bugle**

BUGLES ▶ **bugle**

BUGLET, -S *n* small bugle

BUGLING ▶ **bugle**

BUGLOSS *n* hairy Eurasian plant with clusters of blue flowers

BUGONG, -S *same as* ▶ **bogong**

BUGOUT, -S *n* act of running away

BUGS ▶ **bug**

BUGSEED, -S *n* form of tumbleweed

BUGSHA, -S *same as* ▶ **buqsha**

BUGWORT, -S *another name for* ▶ **bugbane**

BUHL, -S *same as* ▶ **boulle**

BUHLWORK *n* woodwork with decorative inlay

BUHR, -S *same as* ▶ **burr**

BUHUND, -S *n* type of Norwegian dog

BUIBUI, -S *n* black robe worn by Muslim women in E Africa

BUIK, -S *same as* ▶ **book**

BUILD, -ED, -S, BUILT *vb* make, construct, or form by joining parts or materials ▷ *n* shape of the body

BUILDER, -S *n* person who constructs houses and other buildings

BUILDING ▶ **build**

BUILDOUT *n* expansion, development, or growth

BUILDS ▶ **build**

BUILDUP, -S *n* gradual approach to a climax or critical point

BUILT ▶ **build**

BUIRDLY *adj* well-built

BUIST, -ED, -ING, -S *vb* brand sheep with an identification mark

BUKE, -S *same as* ▶ **book**

BUKSHEE, -S *n* person in charge of paying wages

BUKSHI, -S *same as* ▶ **bukshee**

BULB, -ED, -ING, -S *n* onion-shaped root which grows into a flower or plant ▷ *vb* form into the shape of a bulb

BULBAR *adj* of or relating to a bulb, esp the medulla oblongata

BULBED ▶ **bulb**

BULBEL, -S *same as* ▶ **bulbil**

BULBIL, -S *n* small bulblike organ growing on plants such as the onion and tiger lily

BULBING ▶ **bulb**

BULBLET, -S *n* small bulb at the base of a main bulb

BULBOUS *adj* round and fat

BULBS ▶ **bulb**

BULBUL, -S *n* songbird of tropical Africa and Asia

BULGAR, -S *same as* ▶ **bulgur**

BULGE, -D, -S *n* swelling on a normally flat surface ▷ *vb* swell outwards

BULGER, -S ▶ **bulge**

BULGES ▶ **bulge**

BULGHUR, -S *same as* ▶ **bulgur**

BULGIER ▶ **bulgy**

BULGIEST ▶ **bulgy**

BULGINE, -S *same as* ▶ **bullgine**

BULGING *adj* curving outwards

BULGUR, -S *n* kind of dried cracked wheat

BULGY, BULGIER, BULGIEST ▶ **bulge**

BULIMIA, -S *n* eating disorder

BULIMIAC *n* person who has bulimia

BULIMIAS ▶ **bulimia**

BULIMIC, -S ▶ **bulimia**

BULIMIES ▶ **bulimy**

BULIMUS *n* terrestrial mollusc

BULIMY, BULIMIES *same as* ▶ **bulimia**

BULK, -ED, -S *n* volume, size, or magnitude of something ▷ *vb* cohere or cause to cohere in a mass

BULKAGE, -S ▶ **bulk**

BULKED ▶ **bulk**

BULKER, -S *n* ship that carries bulk cargo

BULKHEAD *n* partition in a ship or aeroplane

BULKIER ▶ **bulky**

BULKIEST ▶ **bulky**

BULKILY ▶ **bulky**

BULKING, -S *n* expansion of excavated material to a greater volume

BULKS ▶ **bulk**

BULKY, BULKIER, BULKIEST adj very large and massive, esp so as to be unwieldy

BULL, -ED, -S n male bovine animal ▷ vb raise the price of (a security)

BULLA, -E n leaden seal affixed to a papal bull

BULLACE, -S n small Eurasian tree of which the damson is the cultivated form

BULLAE ▸ bulla

BULLARY n boilery for preparing salt

BULLATE adj puckered or blistered in appearance

BULLBARS pl n large protective metal grille on the front of some vehicles

BULLBAT, -S another name for > nighthawk

BULLCOOK n casual or odd job worker in a camp

BULLDOG, -S n thickset dog with a broad head and a muscular body

BULLDOZE vb demolish or flatten with a bulldozer

BULLDUST n fine dust

BULLED ▸ bull

BULLER, -ED, -S vb make bubbling sound

BULLET, -ED, -S n small piece of metal fired from a gun ▷ vb move extremely quickly

BULLETIN n short official report or announcement ▷ vb make known by bulletin

BULLETS ▸ bullet

BULLEY, -S n fishing boat with two masts

BULLFROG n large American frog with a deep croak

BULLGINE n steam locomotive

BULLHEAD n type of small northern mainly marine fish

BULLHORN n portable loudspeaker having a built-in amplifier and microphone

BULLIED ▸ bully

BULLIER ▸ bully

BULLIES ▸ bully

BULLIEST ▸ bully

BULLING, -S n act of raising the price of a security

BULLION, -S n gold or silver in the form of bars

BULLISH adj like a bull

BULLNECK n enlarged neck

BULLNOSE n rounded exterior angle, as where two walls meet

BULLOCK, -S n young bull ▷ vb work hard and long

BULLOCKY n driver of a team of bullocks ▷ adj resembling a bullock

BULLOSA adj as in **epidermolysis bullosa** type of genetic skin disorder

BULLOUS adj blistered

BULLPEN, -S n large cell where prisoners are confined together temporarily

BULLPOUT n type of fish

BULLRING n arena for staging bullfights

BULLRUSH same as ▸ bulrush

BULLS ▸ bull

BULLSEYE n central disc of a target

BULLSHOT n cocktail of vodka and beef stock

BULLWEED n knapweed

BULLWHIP n long tapering heavy whip, esp one of plaited rawhide ▷ vb whip with a bullwhip

BULLY, BULLIED, BULLIER, BULLIES, BULLIEST n person who repeatedly intimidates another person ▷ vb repeatedly intimidate another person ▷ adj dashing

BULLYBOY n ruffian or tough, esp a hired one

BULLYING n act of threatening another person

BULLYISM ▸ bully

BULLYRAG vb bully, esp by means of cruel practical jokes

BULNBULN another name for ▸ lyrebird

BULRUSH n tall stiff reed

BULRUSHY adj full of bulrushes

BULSE, -S n purse or bag for diamonds

BULWADDY same as > bullwaddy

BULWARK, -S n wall used as a fortification ▷ vb defend or fortify with or as if with a bulwark

BUM, -MED, -MEST, -MING, -S n loafer or idler ▷ vb get by begging ▷ adj of poor quality

BUMALO same as ▸ bummalo

BUMALOTI same as > bummaloti

BUMBAG, -S n small bag attached to a belt and worn round the waist

BUMBAZE, -D, -S vb confuse; bewilder

BUMBLE, -D, -S vb speak, do, or move in a clumsy way ▷ n blunder or botch

BUMBLER, -S ▸ bumble

BUMBLES ▸ bumble

BUMBLING ▸ bumble

BUMBO, -S n African tree

BUMBOAT, -S n any small boat used for ferrying goods to a ship at anchor or at a mooring

BUMBOS ▸ bumbo

BUMELIA, -S n thorny shrub

BUMF, -S n official documents or forms

BUMFLUFF n soft and fluffy growth of hair on the chin of an adolescent

BUMFS ▸ bumf

BUMKIN, -S same as ▸ bumpkin

BUMMALO, -S n Bombay duck

BUMMAREE n dealer at Billingsgate fish market

BUMMED ▸ bum

BUMMEL, -S n stroll

BUMMER, -S n unpleasant or disappointing experience

BUMMEST ▸ bum

BUMMING ▸ bum

BUMMLE, -D, -S, BUMMLING Scots variant of ▸ bumble

BUMMOCK, -S n submerged mass of ice projecting downwards

BUMP, -ED, -S vb knock or strike with a jolt ▷ n dull thud from an impact or collision

BUMPER, -ED, -S n bar on the front and back of a vehicle ▷ adj unusually large or abundant ▷ vb toast with a full drinking glass

BUMPH, -S same as ▸ bumf

BUMPIER ▸ bumpy

BUMPIEST ▸ bumpy

BUMPILY ▸ bumpy

BUMPING, -S ▸ bump

BUMPKIN, -S n awkward simple country person

BUMPS ▸ bump

BUMPY, BUMPIER, BUMPIEST adj having an uneven surface

BUMS ▸ bum

BUMSTER adj (of trousers) cut very low at the hips

BUMSTERS pl n trousers cut very low at the hips

BUMWAD, -S n type of sketching paper

B

BUN, -S n small sweet bread roll or cake

BUNA, -S n synthetic rubber

BUNBURY vb make up a story to avoid an unwanted engagement

BUNCE, -D, -S, BUNCING n windfall; boom ▷ vb charge someone too much money

BUNCH, -ED n number of things growing, fastened, or grouped together ▷ vb group or be grouped together in a bunch

BUNCHER, -S n person who groups things together

BUNCHES pl n hair tied into two sections

BUNCHIER ▷ bunchy

BUNCHILY ▷ bunchy

BUNCHING ▷ bunch

BUNCHY, BUNCHIER adj composed of or resembling bunches

BUNCING ▷ bunce

BUNCO, -ED, -ES, -ING, -S n swindle, esp one by confidence tricksters ▷ vb swindle

BUNCOMBE same as ▷ bunkum

BUNCOS ▷ bunco

BUND, -E, -ED, -ING, -S n (in Germany) confederation ▷ vb form into an embankment

BUNDH, -S same as ▷ bandh

BUNDIED ▷ bundy

BUNDIES ▷ bundy

BUNDING ▷ bund

BUNDIST, -S ▷ bund

BUNDLE, -D, -S n number of things gathered loosely together ▷ vb cause to go roughly and unceremoniously

BUNDLER, -S ▷ bundle

BUNDLES ▷ bundle

BUNDLING ▷ bundle

BUNDOOK, -S n rifle

BUNDS ▷ bund

BUNDT, -S n type of sweet cake

BUNDU, -S n largely uninhabited wild region far from towns

BUNDWALL n concrete or earth wall surrounding a storage tank

BUNDY, BUNDIED, BUNDIES, -ING n time clock at work ▷ vb register arrival or departure from work on a time clock

BUNFIGHT n tea party

BUNG, -ED, -ING, -S n stopper for a cask etc ▷ vb close with a bung

BUNGALOW n one-storey house

BUNGED ▷ bung

BUNGEE, -S n strong elastic cable

BUNGER, -S n firework

BUNGEY, -S same as ▷ bungee

BUNGHOLE n hole in a cask or barrel through which liquid can be drained

BUNGIE, -S same as ▷ bungee

BUNGING ▷ bung

BUNGLE, -D, -S vb spoil through incompetence ▷ n blunder or muddle

BUNGLER, -S ▷ bungle

BUNGLES ▷ bungle

BUNGLING ▷ bungle

BUNGS ▷ bung

BUNGWALL n Australian fern with an edible rhizome

BUNGY same as ▷ bungee

BUNHEAD, -S n ballerina

BUNIA, -S same as ▷ bunnia

BUNION, -S n inflamed swelling on the big toe

BUNJE, -S same as ▷ bungee

BUNJEE, -S same as ▷ bungee

BUNJES ▷ bunje

BUNJIE, -S same as ▷ bungee

BUNJY same as ▷ bungee

BUNK, -ED, -ING, -S n narrow shelflike bed ▷ vb prepare to sleep

BUNKER, -ED, -S n sand-filled hollow forming an obstacle on a golf course ▷ vb drive (the ball) into a bunker

BUNKIE, -S n short for bunkhouse

BUNKING ▷ bunk

BUNKMATE n person who sleeps in the same quarters as another

BUNKO, -ED, -ING, -S same as ▷ bunco

BUNKS ▷ bunk

BUNKUM, -S n nonsense

BUNN, -S same as ▷ bun

BUNNET, -S same as ▷ bonnet

BUNNIA, -S n Hindu shopkeeper

BUNNIES ▷ bunny

BUNNS ▷ bunn

BUNNY, BUNNIES n child's word for a rabbit

BUNODONT adj (of the teeth of certain mammals) having cusps that are separate and rounded

BUNRAKU, -S n Japanese puppet theatre

BUNS ▷ bun

BUNSEN, -S n as in bunsen burner gas burner used in scientific labs

BUNT, -ED, -S vb (of an animal) butt (something) with the head or horns ▷ n act or an instance of bunting

BUNTAL, -S n straw obtained from leaves of the talipot palm

BUNTED ▷ bunt

BUNTER, -S n batter who deliberately taps ball lightly

BUNTIER ▷ bunty

BUNTIEST ▷ bunty

BUNTING, -S n decorative flags

BUNTLINE n one of several lines fastened to the foot of a square sail

BUNTS ▷ bunt

BUNTY, BUNTIER, BUNTIEST ▷ bunt

BUNYA, -S n tall dome-shaped Australian coniferous tree

BUNYIP, -S n legendary monster said to live in swamps and lakes

BUOY, -ED, -ING, -S n floating marker anchored in the sea ▷ vb prevent from sinking

BUOYAGE, -S n system of buoys

BUOYANCE same as ▷ buoyancy

BUOYANCY n ability to float in a liquid or to rise in a fluid

BUOYANT adj able to float

BUOYED ▷ buoy

BUOYING ▷ buoy

BUOYS ▷ buoy

BUPKES same as ▷ bupkis

BUPKIS n nothing

BUPKUS same as ▷ bupkis

BUPLEVER n type of plant

BUPPIE, -S n affluent young Black person

BUPPY variant of ▷ buppie

BUQSHA, -S n former Yemeni coin

BUR, -S same as ▷ burr

BURA, -S same as ▷ buran

BURAN, -S n blizzard, with the wind blowing from the north and reaching gale force

BURAS ▷ bura

BURB, -S n suburb

BURBLE, -D, -S vb make a bubbling sound ▷ n bubbling or gurgling sound

BURBLER, -S ▷ burble

BURBLES ▷ burble

BURBLIER ▸ burbly

BURBLING ▸ burble

BURBLY, BURBLIER *adj* burbling

BURBOT, -S *n* freshwater fish of the cod family that has barbels around its mouth

BURBS ▸ burb

BURD, -S *Scots form of* ▸ **bird**

BURDASH *n* fringed sash worn over a coat

BURDEN, -ED, -S *n* heavy load ▹ *vb* put a burden on

BURDENER ▸ burden

BURDENS ▸ burden

BURDIE, -S *Scots form of* ▸ **birdie**

BURDIZZO *n* surgical instrument

BURDOCK, -S *n* weed with prickly burrs

BURDS ▸ burd

BUREAU, -S, -X *n* office that provides a service

BURET, -S *same as* ▸ **burette**

BURETTE, -S *n* glass tube for dispensing known volumes of fluids

BURFI, -S *same as* ▸ **barfi**

BURG, -S *n* fortified town

BURGAGE, -S *n* type of tenure of land or tenement in a town or city

BURGANET *same as* ▸ **burgonet**

BURGEE, -S *n* triangular or swallow-tailed flag flown from the mast of a merchant ship

BURGEON, -S *vb* develop or grow rapidly ▹ *n* bud of a plant

BURGER, -S *n* hamburger

BURGESS *n* (in England) citizen of a borough

BURGH, -S *n* Scottish borough

BURGHAL ▸ burgh

BURGHER, -S *n* citizen

BURGHS ▸ burgh

BURGHUL, -S *same as* ▸ **bulgur**

BURGLAR, -S *n* person who enters a building to commit a crime, esp theft ▹ *vb* burgle

BURGLARY *n* crime of entering a building as a trespasser to commit theft or another offence

BURGLE, -D, -S, BURGLING *vb* break into (a house, shop, etc)

BURGONET *n* light 16th-century helmet, usually made of steel, with hinged cheekpieces

BURGOO, -S *n* porridge

BURGOUT, -S *same as* ▸ **burgoo**

BURGRAVE *n* military governor of a German town or castle, esp in the 12th and 13th centuries

BURGS ▸ burg

BURGUNDY *adj* dark-purplish red

BURHEL, -S *same as* ▸ **bharal**

BURIAL, -S *n* burying of a dead body

BURIED ▸ bury

BURIER, -S *n* person or thing that buries

BURIES ▸ bury

BURIN, -S *n* steel chisel used for engraving metal, wood, or marble

BURINIST ▸ burin

BURINS ▸ burin

BURITI, -S *n* type of palm tree

BURK, -S *same as* ▸ **berk**

BURKA, -S *same as* ▸ **burqa**

BURKE, -D, -S, BURKING *vb* suppress or silence

BURKER, -S ▸ burke

BURKES ▸ burke

BURKHA, -S *same as* ▸ **burqa**

BURKING ▸ burke

BURKINI, -S *n* swimming costume covering the whole body apart from the face, hands, and feet

BURKITE, -S *n* murderer

BURKS ▸ burk

BURL, -ED, -ING, -S *n* small knot or lump in wool ▹ *vb* remove the burls from (cloth)

BURLAP, -S *n* coarse fabric woven from jute, hemp, or the like

BURLED ▸ burl

BURLER, -S ▸ burl

BURLESK, -S *same as* ▸ **burlesque**

BURLETTA *n* type of comic opera

BURLEY, -ED, -S *same as* ▸ **berley**

BURLIER ▸ burly

BURLIEST ▸ burly

BURLIKE *adj* like a bur

BURLILY ▸ burly

BURLING ▸ burl

BURLS ▸ burl

BURLY, BURLIER, BURLIEST *adj* (of a person) broad and strong

BURN, -ED, -S, -T *vb* be or set on fire ▹ *n* injury or mark

caused by fire or exposure to heat

BURNABLE ▸ burn

BURNED ▸ burn

BURNER, -S *n* part of a stove or lamp that produces the flame

BURNET, -S *n* type of rose

BURNIE, -S *n* sideburn

BURNING, -S ▸ burn

BURNISH *vb* make smooth and shiny by rubbing ▹ *n* shiny finish

BURNOOSE *same as* ▸ **burnous**

BURNOUS *n* long circular cloak with a hood, worn esp by Arabs

BURNOUSE *same as* ▸ **burnous**

BURNOUT, -S *n* failure of a mechanical device from excessive heating

BURNS ▸ burn

BURNSIDE *n* land along side of burn

BURNT ▸ burn

BUROO, -S *n* informal Scottish or Irish name for an unemployment benefit office

BURP, -ED, -ING, -S *n* belch ▹ *vb* belch

BURPEE, -S *n* type of physical exercise movement

BURPING ▸ burp

BURPS ▸ burp

BURQA, -S *n* garment worn by some Muslim women in public

This garment illustrates the fact that Q doesn't always have to be followed by U. It has several variants including **burka** and **burkha**.

BURQUINI *n* swimming costume covering the whole body apart from the face, hands, and feet

BURR, -ED, -ING, -S *n* small rotary file ▹ *vb* form a rough edge on (a workpiece)

BURRAMYS *n* very rare Australian mountain pigmy possum

BURRATA, -S *n* type of Italian cheese

BURRED ▸ burr

BURREL, -S *same as* ▸ **bharal**

BURRELL, -S *variant of* ▸ **bharal**

BURRELS ▸ burrel

BURRER, -S *n* person who removes burrs**

BURRFISH n type of fish with sharp spines

BURRHEL, -S same as ▸ **bharal**

BURRIER ▸ **burry**

BURRIEST ▸ **burry**

BURRING ▸ **burr**

BURRITO, -S n tortilla folded over a filling of minced beef, chicken, cheese, or beans

BURRO, -S n donkey, esp one used as a pack animal

BURROW, -ED, -S n hole dug in the ground by a rabbit etc ▹ vb dig holes in the ground

BURROWER ▸ **burrow**

BURROWS ▸ **burrow**

BURRS ▸ **burr**

BURRY, BURRIER, BURRIEST adj full of or covered in burs

BURS ▸ **bur**

BURSA, -E, -S n small fluid-filled sac that reduces friction between movable parts of the body

BURSAL ▸ **bursa**

BURSAR, -S n treasurer of a school, college, or university

BURSARY n scholarship

BURSAS ▸ **bursa**

BURSATE ▸ **bursa**

BURSE, -S n flat case used at Mass as a container for the corporal

BURSEED, -S n type of plant

BURSERA adj of a type of gum tree

BURSES ▸ **burse**

BURSICON n hormone produced by the insect brain

BURSITIS n inflammation of a bursa, esp one in the shoulder joint

BURST, -ED, -EN, -ING, -S vb break or cause to break open or apart suddenly and noisily ▹ n sudden breaking open or apart ▹ adj broken apart

BURSTER, -S ▸ **burst**

BURSTIER ▸ **bursty**

BURSTING ▸ **burst**

BURSTONE same as > **buhrstone**

BURSTS ▸ **burst**

BURSTY, BURSTIER adj occurring or happening in sudden bursts; irregular

BURTHEN, -S archaic word for ▸ **burden**

BURTON, -S n type of hoisting tackle

BURWEED, -S n any of various plants that bear burs, such as the burdock

BURY, BURIED, BURIES, -ING vb place in a grave

BUS, -ED, -ES, -SED, -SES n large motor vehicle for carrying passengers between stops ▹ vb travel by bus

BUSBAR, -S n electrical conductor

BUSBIES ▸ **busby**

BUSBOY, -S n waiter's assistant

BUSBY, BUSBIES n tail fur hat worn by some soldiers

BUSED ▸ **bus**

BUSERA, -S n Ugandan alcoholic drink made from millet

BUSES ▸ **bus**

BUSGIRL, -S n waiter's assistant

BUSH, -ES n dense woody plant, smaller than a tree ▹ vb fit a bush to (a casing or bearing)

BUSHBABY n small African tree-living mammal with large eyes

BUSHBUCK n small nocturnal spiral-horned antelope of Africa

BUSHED adj extremely tired

BUSHEL, -ED, -S n obsolete unit of measure equal to 8 gallons ▹ vb alter or mend (a garment)

BUSHELER ▸ **bushel**

BUSHELS ▸ **bushel**

BUSHER, -S ▸ **bush**

BUSHES ▸ **bush**

BUSHFIRE n uncontrolled fire in the bush

BUSHFLY n small black Australian fly

BUSHGOAT n S African antelope

BUSHIDO, -S n feudal code of the Japanese samurai

BUSHIE same as ▸ **bushy**

BUSHIER ▸ **bushy**

BUSHIES ▸ **bushy**

BUSHIEST ▸ **bushy**

BUSHILY ▸ **bushy**

BUSHING, -S same as ▸ **bush**

BUSHLAND n land characterized by natural vegetation

BUSHLESS ▸ **bush**

BUSHLIKE ▸ **bush**

BUSHLOT, -S n small wooded area of land

BUSHMAN, BUSHMEN n person who lives or travels in the bush

BUSHMEAT n meat taken from any animal native to African forests

BUSHMEN ▸ **bushman**

BUSHPIG, -S n wild brown or black forest pig of tropical Africa and Madagascar

BUSHTIT, -S n small grey active North American songbird

BUSHVELD n bushy countryside

BUSHWA, -S n nonsense

BUSHWAH, -S same as ▸ **bushwa**

BUSHWALK vb hike through bushland

BUSHWAS ▸ **bushwa**

BUSHY, BUSHIER, BUSHIES, BUSHIEST adj (of hair) thick and shaggy ▹ n person who lives in the bush

BUSIED ▸ **busy**

BUSIER ▸ **busy**

BUSIES ▸ **busy**

BUSIEST ▸ **busy**

BUSILY adv in a busy manner

BUSINESS n purchase and sale of goods and services

BUSING, -S n act of transporting by bus from one area to another

BUSK, -ED, -S vb act as a busker ▹ n strip of whalebone, wood, steel, etc, inserted into the front of a corset

BUSKER, -S ▸ **busk**

BUSKET, -S n bouquet

BUSKIN, -S n (formerly) sandal-like covering

BUSKINED adj relating to tragedy

BUSKING, -S ▸ **busk**

BUSKINS ▸ **buskin**

BUSKS ▸ **busk**

BUSKY same as ▸ **bosky**

BUSLOAD, -S n number of people bus carries

BUSMAN, BUSMEN n person who drives a bus

BUSS archaic or dialect word for ▸ **kiss**

BUSSED ▸ **bus**

BUSSES ▸ **bus**

BUSSING, -S n act of transporting by bus from one area to another

BUSSU, -S n type of palm tree

BUST, -ED, -S n chest of a human being ▹ adj broken ▹ vb burst or break

BUSTARD, -S n type of bird

BUSTED ▸ **bust**

BUSTEE, -S same as ▸ **basti**

BUSTER, -S n person or thing destroying something as specified

B

BUSTI, -S same as ▶ **basti**

BUSTIC, -S n type of small American tree

BUSTIER, -S n close-fitting strapless women's top

BUSTIEST ▶ **busty**

BUSTING, -S ▶ **bust**

BUSTIS ▶ **busti**

BUSTLE, -D, -S vb hurry with a show of activity or energy ▷ n energetic and noisy activity

BUSTLER, -S ▶ **bustle**

BUSTLES ▶ **bustle**

BUSTLINE n shape or size of woman's bust

BUSTLING ▶ **bustle**

BUSTS ▶ **bust**

BUSTY, BUSTIEST adj (of a woman) having a prominent bust

BUSULFAN n drug used to treat cancer

BUSUUTI, -S n garment worn by Ugandan women

BUSY, BUSIED, BUSIER, BUSIES, BUSIEST, -ING adj actively employed ▷ vb keep (someone, esp oneself) busy

BUSYBODY n meddlesome or nosy person

BUSYING ▶ **busy**

BUSYNESS ▶ **busy**

BUSYWORK n unproductive work

BUT, -S prep except ▷ adv only ▷ n outer room of a two-roomed cottage: usually the kitchen

BUTANE, -S n gas used for fuel

BUTANOIC adj as in **butanoic acid** kind of acid

BUTANOL, -S n colourless substance

BUTANONE n colourless soluble flammable liquid used mainly as a solvent for resins

BUTCH, -ES, -EST adj markedly or aggressively masculine ▷ n strong, rugged man

BUTCHER, -S n person who slaughters animals or sells their meat ▷ vb kill and prepare (animals) for meat

BUTCHERY n senseless slaughter

BUTCHES ▶ **butch**

BUTCHEST ▶ **butch**

BUTCHING n dialect word for butchering

BUTE, -S n drug used in veterinary medicine

BUTENE, -S n pungent colourless gas

BUTEO, -S n type of American hawk

BUTES ▶ **bute**

BUTLE, -D, -S, BUTLING vb act as butler

BUTLER, -ED, -S n chief male servant ▷ vb act as a butler

BUTLERY n butler's room

BUTLES ▶ **butle**

BUTLING ▶ **butle**

BUTMENT, -S same as ▶ **abutment**

BUTOH, -S n style of contemporary Japanese dance

BUTS ▶ **but**

BUTSUDAN n (in Buddhism) small household altar

BUTT, -ED, -ING, -S n thicker or blunt end of something, such as the end of the stock of a rifle ▷ vb strike or push with the head or horns

BUTTALS pl n abuttals

BUTTE, -S n isolated steep flat-topped hill

BUTTED ▶ **butt**

BUTTER, -ED, -S n edible fatty yellow solid made form cream ▷ vb put butter on

BUTTERY n (in some universities) room in which food and drink are sold to students ▷ adj containing, like, or coated with butter

BUTTES ▶ **butte**

BUTTIES ▶ **butty**

BUTTING ▶ **butt**

BUTTLE, -D, -S, BUTTLING vb act as butler

BUTTOCK, -S n either of the two fleshy masses that form the human rump ▷ vb perform a kind of wrestling manoeuvre on a person

BUTTON, -ED n small disc or knob sewn to clothing ▷ vb fasten with buttons

BUTTONER ▶ **button**

BUTTONS n page boy

BUTTONY adj having a lot of buttons

BUTTRESS n structure to support a wall ▷ vb support with, or as if with, a buttress

BUTTS ▶ **butt**

BUTTY, BUTTIES n sandwich

BUTTYMAN, BUTTYMEN n coalmine worker

BUTUT, -S n Gambian monetary unit worth one hundredth of a dalasi

BUTYL, -S n substituent group of a certain carbon compound

BUTYLATE vb introduce butyl into (compound)

BUTYLENE same as ▶ **butene**

BUTYLS ▶ **butyl**

BUTYRAL, -S n type of resin

BUTYRATE n any salt or ester of butyric acid

BUTYRIC adj as in **butyric acid** type of acid

BUTYRIN, -S n colourless liquid found in butter

BUTYROUS adj butyraceous

BUTYRYL, -S n radical of butyric acid

BUVETTE, -S n roadside café

BUXOM, -ER, -EST adj (of a woman) healthily plump

BUXOMLY ▶ **buxom**

BUY, -S vb acquire by paying money for ▷ n thing acquired through payment

BUYABLE, -S ▶ **buy**

BUYBACK, -S n repurchase by a company of some or all of its shares from an early investor

BUYER, -S n customer

BUYING, -S n act or instance of purchasing something

BUYOFF, -S n purchase

BUYOUT, -S n purchase of a company

BUYS ▶ **buy**

BUZKASHI n team sport played in Afghanistan

BUZUKI, -A, -S same as ▶ **bouzouki**

BUZZ, -ED, -ES n rapidly vibrating humming sound ▷ vb make a humming sound

BUZZARD, -S n bird of prey of the hawk family

BUZZBAIT n fishing lure with small blades that stir the water

BUZZCUT, -S n very short haircut

BUZZED ▶ **buzz**

BUZZER, -S n electronic device that produces a buzzing sound as a signal

BUZZES ▶ **buzz**

BUZZIER ▶ **buzzy**

BUZZIEST ▶ **buzzy**

BUZZING, -S ▶ **buzz**

BUZZKILL n someone or something that spoils the enjoyment of others

BUZZSAW, -S n power-operated circular saw

BUZZWIG, -S n bushy wig

BUZZWORD n vogue word in a certain community or among a particular group

B

BUZZY, BUZZIER, BUZZIEST
adj making a buzzing sound

BWANA, -S n (in E Africa)
master, often used as a
respectful form of address

BWAZI, -S same as ▶ **buaze**

BY, -S prep indicating agent,
nearness, movement past,
etc ▷ adv near ▷ n pass to
the next round

BYCATCH n unwanted fish
and sea animals caught
along with the desired kind

BYCOKET, -S n former Italian
high-crowned hat

BYDE, -D, -S, BYDING same
as ▶ **bide**

BYE, -S n situation where a
player or team wins a round
by having no opponent
▷ interj goodbye

BYELAW, -S n rule made by a
local authority

BYES ▶ bye

BYGONE, -S adj past ▷ n
article from a former time

BYKE, -D, -S, BYKING n
wasp's nest ▷ vb swarm

BYLANDER same as
▶ bilander

BYLANE, -S n side lane or
alley off a road

BYLAW, -S n rule made by a
local authority

BYLINE, -D, -S, BYLINING n
line under the title of a
newspaper or magazine
article giving the author's
name ▷ vb give a byline to

BYLINER, -S ▶ byline

BYLINES ▶ byline

BYLINING ▶ byline

BYLIVE same as ▶ **belive**

BYNAME, -S n nickname

BYNEMPT archaic past
participle of ▶ **bename**

BYPASS, -ED, -ES, BYPAST n
main road built to avoid a
city ▷ vb go round or avoid

BYPATH, -S n little-used
path or track, esp in the
country

BYPLACE, -S n private place

BYPLAY, -S n secondary
action or talking carried on
apart while the main action
proceeds

BYRE, -S n shelter for cows

BYREMAN, BYREMEN n
man who works in a byre

BYRES ▶ byre

BYRL, -ED, -ING, -S same as
▶ birl

BYRLADY interj archaic
exclamation of surprise

BYRLAKIN interj By Our
Ladykin

BYRLAW, -S same as ▶ bylaw

BYRLED ▶ byrl

BYRLING ▶ byrl

BYRLS ▶ byrl

BYRNIE, -S n archaic word
for coat of mail

BYROAD, -S n secondary or
side road

BYROOM, -S n private room

BYS ▶ by

BYSSAL adj of mollusc's
byssus

BYSSI ▶ byssus

BYSSINE adj made from flax

BYSSOID adj consisting of
fine fibres

BYSSUS, BYSSI, -ES n mass
of threads that attaches an
animal to a hard surface

BYSTREET n obscure or
secondary street

BYTALK, -S n trivial
conversation

BYTE, -S n group of bits
processed as one unit of
data

BYWAY, -S n minor road

BYWONER, -S n poor
tenant-farmer

BYWORD, -S n person or
thing regarded as a perfect
example of something

BYWORK, -S n work done
outside usual working hours

BYZANT, -S same as ▶ bezant

Cc

C

C can be a tricky letter to use, especially as it only forms a single two-letter word **ch**. But if you remember this, you won't waste time racking your brains for two-letter words. There are, however, plenty of good three-letter words beginning with **C**. **Cox** scores 12 points, while **caw**, **cow** and **coy** are each worth 8 and **caz**, **coz** and **cuz** are worth 14. It's also a good idea to remember the short words starting with **C** that don't contain any vowels: **cly** and **cwm** as well as **ch**.

CAA, -ED, -ING, -S *a Scot word for* ▸ **call**

CAATINGA *n* Brazilian semi-arid scrub forest

CAB, -BED, -BING, -S *n* taxi ▸ *vb* take a taxi

CABA *same as* ▸ **cabas**

CABAL, -LED, -S *n* small group of political plotters ▸ *vb* form a cabal

CABALA, -S *variant spelling of* ▸ **kabbalah**

CABALISM ▸ **cabala**

CABALIST ▸ **cabala**

CABALLED ▸ **cabal**

CABALLER ▸ **cabal**

CABALS ▸ **cabal**

CABANA, -S *n* tent used as a dressing room by the sea

CABARET, -S *n* dancing and singing show in a nightclub

CABAS *n* small bag

CABBAGE, -D, -S *n* vegetable with a large head of green leaves ▸ *vb* steal

CABBAGEY ▸ **cabbage**

CABBAGY *adj* resembling cabbage

CABBALA, -S *variant spelling of* ▸ **kabbalah**

CABBALAH *same as* ▸ **cabbala**

CABBALAS ▸ **cabbala**

CABBED ▸ **cab**

CABBIE, -S *n* taxi driver

CABBING ▸ **cab**

CABBY *same as* ▸ **cabbie**

CABER, -S *n* tree trunk tossed in competition at Highland games

CABERNET *n* type of grape, or the red wine made from it

CABERS ▸ **caber**

CABESTRO *n* halter made from horsehair

CABEZON, -S *n* large fish

CABEZONE *same as* ▸ **cabezon**

CABEZONS ▸ **cabezon**

CABILDO, -S *n* Spanish municipal council

CABIN, -ED, -ING, -S *n* compartment in a ship or aircraft ▸ *vb* confine in a small space

CABINET, -S *n* piece of furniture with drawers or shelves

CABINING ▸ **cabin**

CABINS ▸ **cabin**

CABLE, -D, -S *n* strong thick rope; a wire or bundle of wires that conduct electricity ▸ *vb* (esp formerly) send (someone) a message by cable

CABLER, -S *n* cable broadcasting company

CABLES ▸ **cable**

CABLET, -S *n* small cable

CABLEWAY *n* transport system involving cars, buckets, etc, suspended on cables

CABLING, -S ▸ **cable**

CABMAN, CABMEN *n* driver of a cab

CABOB, -BED, -S *vb* roast on a skewer

CABOC, -S *n* type of Scottish cheese

CABOCEER *n* (formerly) African appointed to deal with European slave traders

CABOCHED *adj* in heraldry, with the face exposed, but neck concealed

CABOCHON *n* smooth domed gem, polished but unfaceted

CABOCS ▸ **caboc**

CABOMBA, -S *n* type of aquatic plant

CABOODLE *n* lot, bunch, or group

CABOOSE, -S *n* guard's van on a train

CABOSHED *same as* ▸ **caboched**

CABOTAGE *n* coastal navigation or shipping, esp within the borders of one country

CABOVER, -S *n* truck or lorry in which the cab is over the engine

CABRE *adj* heraldic term designating an animal rearing

CABRESTA *variant of* ▸ **cabestro**

CABRESTO *variant of* ▸ **cabestro**

CABRETTA *n* soft leather obtained from the skins of certain South American or African sheep

CABRIE, -S *n* pronghorn antelope

CABRILLA *n* type of food fish occurring in warm seas around Florida and the Caribbean

CABRIO, -S *short for* > **cabriolet**

CABRIOLE *n* type of furniture leg featuring a tapering curve

CABRIOS ▸ **cabrio**

CABRIT, -S *n* pronghorn antelope

CABS ▸ **cab**

CABSTAND *n* taxi-rank

CACAFOGO *same as* > **cacafuego**

CACAO, -S *same as* ▸ **cocoa**

CACHACA, -S *n* white Brazilian rum made from sugar cane

CACHALOT n sperm whale

CACHE, -D, -S, CACHING n hidden store of weapons or treasure ▷ vb store in a cache

CACHEPOT n ornamental container for a flowerpot

CACHES ▸ cache

CACHET, -ED, -S n prestige, distinction ▷ vb apply a commemorative design to an envelope, as a first-day cover

CACHEXIA n generally weakened condition of body or mind

CACHEXIC ▸ cachexia

CACHEXY same as ▸ cachexia

CACHING ▸ cache

CACHOLOT same as ▸ cachalot

CACHOU, -S same as ▸ catechu

CACHUCHA n graceful Spanish solo dance in triple time

CACIQUE, -S n Native American chief in a Spanish-speaking region

CACK, -ED, -ING, -S n slang word for nonsense ▷ vb slang word for defecate

CACKIER ▸ cacky

CACKIEST ▸ cacky

CACKING ▸ cack

CACKLE, -D, -S, CACKLING vb laugh shrilly ▷ n cackling noise

CACKLER, -S ▸ cackle

CACKLES ▸ cackle

CACKLING ▸ cackle

CACKS ▸ cack

CACKY, CACKIER, CACKIEST adj dirty or worthless

CACODOXY n heterodoxy

CACODYL, -S n oily poisonous liquid with a strong garlic smell

CACOEPY n bad or mistaken pronunciation

CACOLET, -S n seat fitted to the back of a mule

CACOLOGY n bad choice of words

CACOMIXL n carnivorous mammal

CACONYM, -S n erroneous name

CACONYMY ▸ caconym

CACOON, -S n large seed of the sword-bean

CACTI ▸ cactus

CACTOID adj resembling a cactus

CACTUS, CACTI, -ES n fleshy desert plant with spines but no leaves

CACUMEN, -S, CACUMINA n apex

CAD, -S n dishonourable man

CADAGA, -S n eucalyptus tree

CADAGI same as ▸ cadaga

CADASTER n register of ownership, boundaries, and value of property

CADASTRE same as ▸ cadaster

CADAVER, -S n corpse

CADDICE, -S same as ▸ caddis

CADDIE, -D, -S, CADDYING n person who carries a golfer's clubs ▷ vb act as a caddie

CADDIS, -ES n type of coarse woollen yarn, braid, or fabric

CADDISED adj trimmed with a type of ribbon

CADDISES ▸ caddis

CADDISH ▸ cad

CADDY same as ▸ caddie

CADDYING ▸ caddie

CADDYSS same as ▸ caddis

CADE, -S n juniper tree ▷ adj (of a young animal) left by its mother and reared by humans

CADEAU, -X n present

CADEE, -S old form of ▸ cadet

CADELLE, -S n type of beetle that feeds on flour, grain, and other stored foods

CADENCE, -D, -S n rise and fall in the pitch of the voice ▷ vb modulate musically

CADENCY same as ▸ cadence

CADENT adj having cadence

CADENZA, -S n complex solo passage in a piece of music

CADES ▸ cade

CADET, -S n young person training for the armed forces or police

CADGE, -D, -S, CADGING vb get (something) by taking advantage of someone's generosity

CADGER, -S n person who cadges

CADGES ▸ cadge

CADGIER ▸ cadgy

CADGIEST ▸ cadgy

CADGING ▸ cadge

CADGY, CADGIER, CADGIEST adj cheerful

CADI, -S n judge in a Muslim community

CADIE, -S n messenger

CADIS ▸ cadi

CADMIC ▸ cadmium

CADMIUM, -S n bluish-white metallic element used in alloys

CADRANS n instrument used in gem cutting

CADRE, -S n group of people trained to form the core of a political or military unit

CADS ▸ cad

CADUAC, -S n windfall

CADUCEAN ▸ caduceus

CADUCEUS, CADUCEI n mythical staff carried by Hermes (Mercury)

CADUCITY n perishableness

CADUCOUS adj (of parts of a plant or animal) shed during the life of the organism

CAECA ▸ caecum

CAECAL ▸ caecum

CAECALLY ▸ caecum

CAECITIS n inflammation of the caecum

CAECUM, CAECA n pouch at the beginning of the large intestine

CAEOMA, -S n aecium in some rust fungi that has no surrounding membrane

CAERULE same as ▸ cerule

CAESAR, -S n any emperor, autocrat, dictator, or other powerful ruler

CAESE interj Shakespearean interjection

CAESIOUS adj having a waxy bluish-grey coating

CAESIUM, -S n silvery-white metallic element used in photocells

CAESTUS same as ▸ cestus

CAESURA, -E, -S n pause in a line of verse

CAESURAL ▸ caesura

CAESURAS ▸ caesura

CAESURIC ▸ caesura

CAF, -S n short for cafeteria

CAFARD, -S n feeling of severe depression

CAFE, -S n small or inexpensive restaurant serving light refreshments

CAFF, -S n café

CAFFEIN, -S same as ▸ caffeine

CAFFEINE n stimulant found in tea and coffee

CAFFEINS ▸ caffein

CAFFEISM n addiction to caffeine

CAFFILA, -S n caravan train

CAFFS ▸ caff

CAFILA, -S same as ▸ caffila

:AFS ▸ caf

:AFTAN, -S same as ▸ kaftan

:AFTANED adj wearing caftan

:AFTANS ▸ caftan

:AG, -S same as ▸ cagoule

:AGANER, -S n figure of a squatting defecating person

:AGE, -D, -S, CAGING n enclosure of bars or wires, for keeping animals or birds ▸ vb confine in a cage

:AGEFUL, -S n amount which fills a cage to capacity

:AGELIKE ▸ cage

:AGELING n bird kept in a cage

:AGER, -S n basketball player

:AGES ▸ cage

:AGEWORK n something constructed as if from the bars of a cage

CAGEY, CAGIER, CAGIEST adj reluctant to go into details

CAGILY ▸ cagey

CAGINESS ▸ cagy

CAGING ▸ cage

CAGMAG, -S adj done shoddily ▸ vb chat idly

CAGOT, -S n member of a class of French outcasts

CAGOUL, -S same as ▸ cagoule

CAGOULE, -S n lightweight hooded waterproof jacket

CAGOULS ▸ cagoul

CAGS ▸ cag

CAGY same as ▸ cagey

CAGYNESS ▸ cagy

CAHIER, -S n notebook

CAHOOT, -S n partnership

CAHOUN, -S n type of S American palm tree

CAHOW, -S n Bermuda petrel

CAID, -S n Moroccan district administrator

CAILLACH same as ▸ cailleach

CAILLE, -S n quail

CAIMAC, -S same as ▸ caimacam

CAIMACAM n Turkish governor of a sanjak

CAIMACS ▸ caimac

CAIMAN, -S same as ▸ cayman

CAIN, -S n (in Scotland and Ireland) payment in kind

CAIQUE, -S n long narrow light rowing skiff used on the Bosporus

CAIRD, -S n travelling tinker

CAIRN, -S n mound of stones erected as a memorial or marker

CAIRNED adj marked by a cairn

CAIRNIER ▸ cairny

CAIRNS ▸ cairn

CAIRNY, CAIRNIER adj covered with cairns

CAISSON, -S n watertight enclosure pumped dry to enable construction work to be done

CAITIFF, -S n cowardly or base person ▸ adj cowardly

CAITIVE, -S n captive

CAJAPUT, -S same as ▸ cajuput

CAJEPUT, -S same as ▸ cajuput

CAJOLE, -D, -S, CAJOLING vb persuade by flattery

CAJOLER, -S ▸ cajole

CAJOLERY ▸ cajole

CAJOLES ▸ cajole

CAJOLING ▸ cajole

CAJON, -ES n Peruvian wooden box used as a drum

CAJUN n music of the Cajun people

CAJUPUT, -S n small tree or shrub

CAKE, -D, -S n sweet food baked from a mixture of flour, eggs, etc ▸ vb form into a hardened mass or crust

CAKEAGE, -S n charge in a restaurant for serving cake brought in from outside

CAKEBOX n box for a cake

CAKED ▸ cake

CAKEHOLE n slang word for mouth

CAKES ▸ cake

CAKEWALK n dance based on a march with the prize of a cake for the best performers ▸ vb perform the cakewalk

CAKEY ▸ cake

CAKIER ▸ caky

CAKIEST ▸ caky

CAKINESS ▸ cake

CAKING, -S ▸ cake

CAKY, CAKIER, CAKIEST ▸ cake

CAL, -S n short for calorie

CALABASH n type of large round gourd

CALABAZA n variety of squash

CALADIUM n type of tropical plant

CALALOO, -S same as ▸ calalu

CALALU, -S n edible leaves of various plants

CALAMAR, -S n any member of the squid family

CALAMARI n squid cooked for eating, esp cut into rings and fried in batter

CALAMARS ▸ calamar

CALAMARY variant of ▸ calamari

CALAMATA same as ▸ kalamata

CALAMI ▸ calamus

CALAMINE n pink powder consisting chiefly of zinc oxide, used in skin lotions and ointments ▸ vb apply calamine

CALAMINT n aromatic Eurasian plant with clusters of purple or pink flowers

CALAMITE n type of extinct treelike plant related to the horsetails

CALAMITY n disaster

CALAMUS, CALAMI n tropical Asian palm

CALANDO adv (to be performed) with gradually decreasing tone and speed

CALANTHE n type of orchid

CALASH, -ES n horse-drawn carriage with low wheels and a folding top

CALATHEA n S American plant often grown as a greenhouse or house plant for its variegated leaves

CALATHI ▸ calathus

CALATHOS same as ▸ calathus

CALATHUS, CALATHI n vase-shaped basket represented in ancient Greek art, used as a symbol of fruitfulness

CALCANEA > calcaneum

CALCANEI > calcaneus

CALCAR, -IA, -S n spur or spurlike process

CALCEATE vb to shoe

CALCED adj wearing shoes

CALCES ▸ calx

CALCIC adj of, containing, or concerned with lime or calcium

CALCIFIC adj forming or causing to form lime or chalk

CALCIFY vb harden by the depositing of calcium salts

CALCINE, -D, -S vb oxidize (a substance) by heating

CALCITE, -S n colourless or white form of calcium carbonate

CALCITIC ▸ calcite

CALCIUM, -S n silvery-white metallic element

CALCRETE another name for ▸ caliche

CALCSPAR another name for
▶ **calcite**
CALCTUFA another name for
▶ **tufa**
CALCTUFF another name for
▶ **tufa**
CALCULAR adj relating to
calculus
CALCULUS, CALCULI n
branch of mathematics
dealing with infinitesimal
changes to a variable
number or quantity
CALDARIA > **caldarium**
CALDERA, -S n large
basin-shaped crater at the
top of a volcano
CALDRON, -S same as
▶ **cauldron**
CALECHE, -S variant of
▶ **calash**
**CALEFY, CALEFIED,
CALEFIES** vb make warm
CALENDAL ▶ **calends**
CALENDAR n chart showing
a year divided up into
months, weeks, and days
▷ vb enter in a calendar
CALENDER n machine in
which paper or cloth is
smoothed by passing it
between rollers ▷ vb smooth
in such a machine
CALENDRY n place where
calendering is carried out
CALENDS pl n first day of
each month in the ancient
Roman calendar
CALESA, -S n horse-drawn
buggy
CALF, -S, CALVES n young
cow, bull, elephant, whale,
or seal
CALFHOOD n state of being
a calf
CALFLESS ▶ **calf**
CALFLICK another word for
▶ **cowlick**
CALFLIKE ▶ **calf**
CALFS ▶ **calf**
CALFSKIN n fine leather
made from the skin of a calf
CALIBER, -S same as
▶ **calibre**
CALIBRE, -S n person's
ability or worth
CALIBRED ▶ **calibre**
CALIBRES ▶ **calibre**
CALICES ▶ **calix**
CALICHE, -S n bed of sand or
clay in arid regions
CALICLE, -S same as
▶ **calycle**
CALICO, -ES, -S n white
cotton fabric
CALID adj warm

CALIDITY ▶ **calid**
CALIF, -S same as ▶ **caliph**
CALIFATE same as > **caliphate**
CALIFONT n gas water
heater
CALIFS ▶ **calif**
CALIGO, -ES, -S n speck on
the cornea causing poor
vision
CALIMA, -S n Saharan
dust-storm
CALIPASH n greenish
glutinous edible part of the
turtle
CALIPEE, -S n edible part of
the turtle found next to the
lower shell
CALIPER, -S same as
▶ **calliper**
CALIPH, -S n Muslim ruler
CALIPHAL ▶ **caliph**
CALIPHS ▶ **caliph**
CALISAYA n bark of a type of
tropical tree from which
quinine is extracted
CALIVER, -S n type of
musket
CALIX, CALICES, -ES n cup
CALK, -ED, -S same as
▶ **caulk**
CALKER, -S ▶ **calk**
CALKIN, -S same as ▶ **calk**
CALKING, -S ▶ **calk**
CALKINS ▶ **calkin**
CALKS ▶ **calk**
CALL, -ED, -S vb name ▷ n
cry, shout
CALLA, -S n S African plant
with a white funnel-shaped
spathe enclosing a yellow
spadix
CALLABLE adj (of a security)
subject to redemption
before maturity
CALLAIS n type of green
stone
CALLALOO n leafy green
vegetable
CALLALOU n crabmeat soup
CALLAN, -S same as ▶ **callant**
CALLANT, -S n youth
CALLAS ▶ **calla**
CALLBACK n telephone call
made in response to an
earlier call
CALLBOY, -S n person who
notifies actors when it is
time to go on stage
CALLED ▶ **call**
CALLEE, -S n computer
function being used
CALLER, -S n person or thing
that calls, esp a person who
makes a brief visit ▷ adj (of
food, esp fish) fresh
CALLET, -S n scold

CALLID adj cunning
CALLING, -S n vocation,
profession
CALLIOPE n steam organ
CALLIPEE same as ▶ **calipee**
CALLIPER n metal splint for
supporting the leg ▷ vb
measure the dimensions of
(an object) with callipers
CALLOP, -S n edible
Australian freshwater fish
CALLOSE, -S n carbohydrate
found in plants
CALLOUS adj showing no
concern for other people's
feelings ▷ vb make or
become callous
CALLOUT, -S n inset text
within a printed article
CALLOW, -ER, -S adj young
and inexperienced ▷ n
someone young and
inexperienced
CALLOWLY adv in a manner
suggesting immaturity or
inexperience
CALLOWS ▶ **callow**
CALLS ▶ **call**
CALLTIME n time available
for making calls on a mobile
phone
CALLUNA, -S n type of
heather
CALLUS, -ED, -ES n area of
thick hardened skin ▷ vb
produce or cause to produce
a callus
CALM, -ED, -ER, -EST, -S adj
not agitated or excited ▷ n
peaceful state ▷ vb make or
become calm
CALMANT, -S n sedative
CALMED ▶ **calm**
CALMER ▶ **calm**
CALMEST ▶ **calm**
CALMIER ▶ **calmy**
CALMIEST ▶ **calmy**
CALMING, -S ▶ **calm**
CALMLY ▶ **calm**
CALMNESS ▶ **calm**
CALMS ▶ **calm**
**CALMY, CALMIER,
CALMIEST** adj tranquil
CALO, -S n military servant
CALOMEL, -S n colourless
tasteless powder
CALORIC, -S adj of heat or
calories ▷ n hypothetical
fluid formerly postulated as
the embodiment of heat
CALORIE, -S n unit of
measurement for the energy
value of food
CALORISE same as ▶ **calorize**
CALORIST n believer in
caloric theory

CALORIZE vb coat (a ferrous metal) by spraying with aluminium powder and then heating

CALORY same as ▶ calorie

CALOS ▶ calo

CALOTTE, -S n skullcap worn by Roman Catholic clergy

CALOTYPE n early photographic process

CALOYER, -S n monk of the Greek Orthodox Church, esp of the Basilian Order

CALP, -S n type of limestone

CALPA, -S n Hindu unit of time

CALPAC, -S n large black brimless hat

CALPACK, -S same as ▶ calpac

CALPACS ▶ calpac

CALPAIN, -S n type of enzyme

CALPAS ▶ calpa

CALPS ▶ calp

CALQUE, -D, -S, CALQUING same as ▶ caulk

CALS ▶ cal

CALTHA, -S n marsh marigold

CALTHROP same as ▶ caltrop

CALTRAP, -S same as ▶ caltrop

CALTROP, -S n floating Asian plant

CALUMBA, -S n Mozambiquan root used for medicinal purposes

CALUMET, -S n peace pipe

CALUMNY n false or malicious statement ▷ vb make a false or malicious statement about (a person)

CALUTRON n device used for the separation of isotopes

CALVADOS n type of apple brandy

CALVARIA n top part of the skull of vertebrates

CALVARY n representation of Christ's crucifixion

CALVE, -D, CALVING vb give birth to a calf

CALVER, -ED, -S vb prepare fish for cooking

CALVES ▶ calf

CALVING ▶ calve

CALX, CALCES, -ES n powdery metallic oxide formed when an ore or mineral is roasted

CALYCATE ▶ calyx

CALYCEAL adj resembling a calyx

CALYCES ▶ calyx

CALYCINE adj relating to, belonging to, or resembling a calyx

CALYCLE, -S n cup-shaped structure, as in the coral skeleton

CALYCLED ▶ calycle

CALYCLES ▶ calycle

CALYCOID adj resembling a calyx

CALYCULE n bracts surrounding the base of the calyx

CALYCULI ▶ calyculus

CALYPSO, -S n Trinidadian song with improvised topical lyrics

CALYPTER n alula

CALYPTRA n membranous hood covering the spore-bearing capsule of mosses and liverworts

CALYX, CALYCES, -ES n outer leaves that protect a flower bud

CALZONE, -S, CALZONI n folded pizza filled with cheese, tomatoes, etc

CAM, -MED, -MING, -S n device that converts a circular motion to a to-and-fro motion ▷ vb furnish (a machine) with a cam

CAMA n hybrid offspring of a camel and a llama

CAMAIEU, -X n cameo

CAMAIL, -S n covering of chain mail

CAMAILED ▶ camail

CAMAILS ▶ camail

CAMAN, -S n wooden stick used to hit the ball in shinty

CAMARON, -S n shrimp

CAMAS, -ES same as ▶ camass

CAMASH, -ES same as ▶ camass

CAMASS, -ES n type of North American plant

CAMBER, -ED, -S n slight upward curve to the centre of a surface ▷ vb form or be formed with a surface that curves upwards to its centre

CAMBIA ▶ cambium

CAMBIAL ▶ cambium

CAMBISM, -S ▶ cambist

CAMBIST, -S n dealer or expert in foreign exchange

CAMBIUM, CAMBIA, -S n meristem that increases the girth of stems and roots

CAMBOGE, -S n type of gum resin

CAMBOGIA another name for ▶ gamboge

CAMBOOSE n cabin built as living quarters for a gang of lumber workers

CAMBREL, -S variant of ▶ gambrel

CAMBRIC, -S n fine white linen fabric

CAMCORD, -S vb film with a camcorder

CAME ▶ come

CAMEL, -S n humped mammal

CAMELEER n camel-driver

CAMELEON same as > chameleon

CAMELIA, -S same as ▶ camellia

CAMELID, -S adj of or relating to camels ▷ n any animal of the camel family

CAMELINE n material made from camel hair

CAMELISH ▶ camel

CAMELLIA n evergreen ornamental shrub with white, pink, or red flowers

CAMELOID n member of the camel family

CAMELOT, -S n supposedly idyllic period or age

CAMELRY n troops mounted on camels

CAMELS ▶ camel

CAMEO, -ED, -ING, -S n brooch or ring with a profile head carved in relief ▷ vb appear in a brief role

CAMERA, -E, -S n apparatus used for taking still or moving images

CAMERAL adj of or relating to a judicial or legislative chamber

CAMERAS ▶ camera

CAMES pl n pieces of lead used in lattice windows

CAMESE, -S same as ▶ camise

CAMI n camisole

CAMION, -S n lorry, or, esp formerly, a large dray

CAMIS n light robe

CAMISA, -S n smock

CAMISADE same as ▶ camisado

CAMISADO n (formerly) an attack made under cover of darkness

CAMISAS ▶ camisa

CAMISE, -S n loose light shirt, smock, or tunic originally worn in the Middle Ages

CAMISIA, -S n surplice

CAMISOLE n woman's bodice-like garment

CAMLET, -S n tough waterproof cloth

CAMMED ▶ **cam**

CAMMIE, -S n webcam award

CAMMING ▶ **cam**

CAMO, -S n short for camouflage

CAMOGIE, -S n form of hurling played by women

CAMOMILE n aromatic plant, used to make herbal tea

CAMOODI, -S a Caribbean name for ▶ **anaconda**

CAMORRA, -S n secret criminal group

CAMOS ▶ **camo**

CAMOTE, -S n type of sweet potato

CAMP, -ED, -EST, -S vb stay in a camp ▷ adj consciously artificial ▷ n (place for) temporary lodgings consisting of tents, huts, or cabins

CAMPAGNA, CAMPAGNE same as > **champaign**

CAMPAIGN n series of coordinated activities designed to achieve a goal ▷ vb take part in a campaign

CAMPANA, -S n bell or bell shape

CAMPED ▶ **camp**

CAMPER, -S n person who lives or temporarily stays in a tent, cabin, etc

CAMPERY n campness

CAMPEST ▶ **camp**

CAMPFIRE n outdoor fire in a camp

CAMPHANE n one of the terpene hydrocarbons

CAMPHENE n colourless crystalline insoluble terpene

CAMPHINE n type of solvent

CAMPHIRE an archaic name for ▶ **henna**

CAMPHOL, -S another word for ▶ **borneol**

CAMPHONE n combined mobile phone and digital camera

CAMPHOR, -S n aromatic crystalline substance

CAMPI ▶ **campo**

CAMPIER ▶ **campy**

CAMPIEST ▶ **campy**

CAMPILY ▶ **campy**

CAMPING ▶ **camp**

CAMPINGS ▶ **camp**

CAMPION, -S n red, pink, or white wild flower

CAMPLE, -D, -S, CAMPLING vb argue

CAMPLY ▶ **camp**

CAMPNESS ▶ **camp**

CAMPO, CAMPI, -S n level or undulating savanna country

CAMPONG, -S n in Malaysia, a village

CAMPOREE n local meeting or assembly of Scouts

CAMPOS ▶ **campo**

CAMPOUT, -S n camping trip

CAMPS ▶ **camp**

CAMPSITE n area on which holiday makers may pitch a tent

CAMPUS, -ED, -ES n grounds of a university or college ▷ vb restrict a student to campus, as a punishment

CAMPY, CAMPIER, CAMPIEST adj consciously artificial

CAMS ▶ **cam**

CAMSHAFT n part of an engine consisting of a rod to which cams are fixed

CAMSHO adj crooked

CAMSHOCH same as ▶ **camsho**

CAMSTANE same as ▶ **camstone**

CAMSTONE n limestone used for whitening stone doorsteps

CAMUS, -ES n type of loose robe

CAMWOOD, -S n W African leguminous tree

CAN, -NED, -S, COULD vb be able to ▷ vb put (food etc) into a can ▷ n metal container for food or liquids

CANADA, -S n canada goose

CANAIGRE n southern US dock, the root of which yields a substance used in tanning

CANAILLE n masses or rabble

CANAKIN, -S same as ▶ **cannikin**

CANAL, -ED, -ING, -LED, -S n artificial waterway ▷ vb dig a canal through

CANALISE same as ▶ **canalize**

CANALIZE vb give direction to

CANALLED ▶ **canal**

CANALLER n canal boat worker

CANALS ▶ **canal**

CANAPE, -S n small piece of bread or toast with a savoury topping

CANARD, -S n false report

CANARY, CANARIED, CANARIES n small yellow songbird often kept as a pet ▷ vb perform a dance called the canary

CANASTA, -S n card game like rummy, played with two packs

CANASTER n coarsely broken dried tobacco leaves

CANBANK, -S n container for receiving cans for recycling

CANCAN, -S n lively high-kicking dance performed by a female group

CANCEL, -ED, -S vb stop (something that has been arranged) from taking place ▷ n new leaf or section of a book replacing a defective one

CANCELER ▶ **cancel**

CANCELLI pl n any lattice-like structures

CANCELS ▶ **cancel**

CANCER, -S n serious disease resulting from a malignant growth or tumour

CANCERED adj affected by cancer

CANCERS ▶ **cancer**

CANCHA, -S n toasted maize

CANCRINE adj crab-like

CANCROID adj resembling a cancerous growth ▷ n skin cancer, esp one of only moderate malignancy

CANDELA, -S n unit of luminous intensity

CANDENT adj emitting light as a result of being heated to a high temperature

CANDID, -ER, -S adj honest and straightforward ▷ n unposed photograph

CANDIDA, -S n yeastlike parasitic fungus

CANDIDAL ▶ **candida**

CANDIDAS ▶ **candida**

CANDIDER ▶ **candid**

CANDIDLY ▶ **candid**

CANDIDS ▶ **candid**

CANDIE n South Indian unit of weight

CANDIED adj coated with sugar

CANDIES ▶ **candy**

CANDIRU, -S n parasitic freshwater catfish of the Amazon region

CANDLE, -D, -S, CANDLING n stick of wax enclosing a wick, burned to produce light ▷ vb test by holding up to a candle

CANDLER, -S ▸ candle

CANDLES ▸ candle

CANDLING ▸ candle

CANDOCK, -S n type of water lily

CANDOR, -S same as ▸ candour

CANDOUR, -S n honesty and straightforwardness

CANDY, CANDIES, -ING n sweet or sweets ▷ vb make sweet

CANDYMAN, CANDYMEN n itinerant seller of toffee

CANE, -D, -S n stem of the bamboo or similar plant ▷ vb beat with a cane

CANEGRUB n Australian grub that feeds on sugarcane

CANEH, -S n Hebrew unit of length

CANELLA, -S n fragrant cinnamon-like inner bark of a Caribbean tree

CANEPHOR n sculpted figure carrying a basket on its head

CANER, -S ▸ cane

CANES ▸ cane

CANEWARE n type of unglazed stoneware

CANFIELD, -S n gambling game adapted from a type of patience

CANFUL, -S, CANSFUL n amount a can will hold

CANG, -S same as ▸ cangue

CANGLE, -D, -S, CANGLING vb wrangle

CANGS ▸ cang

CANGUE, -S n (formerly in China) a wooden collar worn as a punishment

CANID, -S n animal of the dog family

CANIER ▸ cany

CANIEST ▸ cany

CANIKIN, -S same as ▸ cannikin

CANINE, -S adj of or like a dog ▷ n sharp pointed tooth between the incisors and the molars

CANING, -S n beating with a cane as a punishment

CANINITY ▸ canine

CANISTEL n Caribbean fruit

CANISTER n metal container ▷ vb put into canisters

CANITIES n grey hair

CANKER, -ED, -S n ulceration ▷ vb infect or become infected with or as if with canker

CANKERY adj like a canker

CANKLE, -S n thickened ankle on an overweight person

CANN, -S vb direct a ship's steering

CANNA, -S n type of tropical plant

CANNABIC ▸ cannabis

CANNABIN n greenish-black poisonous resin obtained from the Indian hemp plant

CANNABIS n Asian plant with tough fibres

CANNACH, -S n cotton grass

CANNAE vb Scottish form of 'cannot'

CANNAS ▸ canna

CANNED ▸ can

CANNEL, -S n type of dull coal

CANNELON n type of meat loaf

CANNELS ▸ cannel

CANNER, -S n person or organization whose job is to can foods

CANNERY n factory where food is canned

CANNIBAL n person who eats human flesh

CANNIE same as ▸ canny

CANNIER ▸ canny

CANNIEST ▸ canny

CANNIKIN n small can, esp one used as a drinking vessel

CANNILY ▸ canny

CANNING, -S n act of putting food in a can

CANNOLI, -S n Sicilian pudding of pasta shells filled with sweetened ricotta

CANNON, -ED, -S n gun of large calibre ▷ vb collide (with)

CANNONRY n volley of artillery fire

CANNONS ▸ cannon

CANNOT vb can not

CANNS ▸ cann

CANNULA, -E, -S n narrow tube for insertion into a bodily cavity

CANNULAR adj shaped like a cannula

CANNULAS ▸ cannula

CANNY, CANNIER, CANNIEST adj shrewd, cautious ▷ adv quite

CANOE, -D, -S n light narrow open boat propelled by a paddle or paddles ▷ vb use a canoe

CANOEING ▸ canoe

CANOEIST ▸ canoe

CANOEMAN, CANOEMEN n man who canoes

CANOER, -S ▸ canoe

CANOES ▸ canoe

CANOLA, -S n cooking oil extracted from a variety of rapeseed

CANON, -S n priest serving in a cathedral

CANONESS n woman belonging to any one of several religious orders

CANONIC same as ▸ canonical

CANONISE same as ▸ canonize

CANONIST n specialist in canon law

CANONIZE vb declare (a person) officially to be a saint

CANONRY n office, benefice, or status of a canon

CANONS ▸ canon

CANOODLE vb kiss and cuddle

CANOPIC adj of a type of ancient Egyptian vase

CANOPY, CANOPIED, CANOPIES n covering above a bed, door, etc ▷ vb cover with or as if with a canopy

CANOROUS adj tuneful

CANS ▸ can

CANSFUL ▸ canful

CANSO, -S n love song

CANST vb form of 'can' used with the pronoun thou or its relative form

CANSTICK n candlestick

CANT, -ED, -EST, -S n insincere talk ▷ vb use cant ▷ adj oblique

CANTAL, -S n French cheese

CANTALA, -S n tropical American plant, the agave

CANTALS ▸ cantal

CANTAR, -S variant form of ▸ kantar

CANTATA, -S n musical work consisting of arias, duets, and choruses

CANTATE, -S n 98th psalm sung as a nonmetrical hymn

CANTDOG, -S same as ▸ canthook

CANTED ▸ cant

CANTEEN, -S n restaurant attached to a workplace or school

CANTER, -ED, -S vb move at gait between trot and gallop

C

CANTEST ▸ cant

CANTHAL ▸ canthus

CANTHARI ▸ cantharus

CANTHI ▸ canthus

CANTHIC adj relating to the canthus

CANTHOOK n wooden pole with a hook used for handling logs

CANTHUS, CANTHI n inner or outer corner or angle of the eye

CANTIC ▸ cant

CANTICLE n short hymn with words from the Bible

CANTICO, -S vb dance as part of an act of worship

CANTICOY same as ▸ cantico

CANTICUM n canticle

CANTIER ▸ canty

CANTIEST ▸ canty

CANTILY ▸ canty

CANTINA, -S n bar or wine shop, esp in a Spanish-speaking country

CANTING, -S ▸ cant

CANTION, -S n song

CANTLE, -D, -S, CANTLING n back part of a saddle that slopes upwards ▸ vb set up, or stand, on high

CANTLET, -S n piece

CANTLING ▸ cantle

CANTO, -S same as ▸ cantus

CANTON, -ED, -S n political division of a country, esp Switzerland ▸ vb divide into cantons

CANTONAL ▸ canton

CANTONED ▸ canton

CANTONS ▸ canton

CANTOR, -S n man employed to lead services in a synagogue

CANTORIS adj (in antiphonal music) to be sung by the cantorial side of a choir

CANTORS ▸ cantor

CANTOS ▸ canto

CANTRAIP n witch's spell or charm

CANTRAP, -S same as ▸ cantraip

CANTRED, -S n district comprising a hundred villages

CANTREF, -S same as ▸ cantred

CANTRIP, -S n magic spell ▸ adj (of an effect) produced by black magic

CANTS ▸ cant

CANTUS, -ES n medieval form of church singing

CANTY, CANTIER, CANTIEST adj lively

CANULA, -E, -S same as ▸ cannula

CANULAR adj shaped like a cannula

CANULAS ▸ canula

CANULATE same as ▸ cannulate

CANVAS, -ED, -ES n heavy coarse cloth ▸ vb cover with, or be applied to, canvas

CANVASER ▸ canvas

CANVASES ▸ canvas

CANVASS vb try to get votes or support (from) ▸ n canvassing

CANY, CANIER, CANIEST adj cane-like

CANYON, -S n deep narrow valley

CANZONA, -S n type of 16th- or 17th-century contrapuntal music

CANZONE, -S, CANZONI n Provençal or Italian lyric, often in praise of love or beauty

CANZONET n short, cheery, or lively Italian song

CANZONI ▸ canzone

CAP, -PED, -S n soft close-fitting covering for the head ▸ vb cover or top with something

CAPA, -S n type of Spanish cloak

CAPABLE, -R adj having the ability (for)

CAPABLY ▸ capable

CAPACITY n ability to contain, absorb, or hold ▸ adj of the maximum amount or number possible

CAPAS ▸ capa

CAPCOM, -S n flight controller who communicates with the crew of a spacecraft

CAPE, -D, -S, CAPING n short cloak ▸ vb cut and remove the hide of an animal

CAPEESH same as ▸ capisce

CAPELAN, -S another word for ▸ capelin

CAPELET, -S n small cape

CAPELIKE adj like a cape

CAPELIN, -S n type of small marine food fish

CAPELINE n cap-shaped bandage to cover the head or an amputation stump

CAPELINS ▸ capelin

CAPELLET n wen-like swelling on a horse

CAPER, -ED, -ING n high-spirited prank ▸ vb skip about

CAPERER, -S ▸ caper

CAPERING ▸ caper

CAPERS pl n pickled flower buds of a Mediterranean shrub used in sauces

CAPES ▸ cape

CAPESKIN n soft leather obtained from the skins of a type of lamb or sheep having hairlike wool ▸ adj made of this leather

CAPEWORK n use of the cape by the matador in bullfighting

CAPEX, -ES n capital expenditure

CAPFUL, -S n quantity held by a (usually bottle) cap

CAPH, -S n letter of the Hebrew alphabet

CAPI ▸ capo

CAPIAS, -ES n (formerly) a writ directing the arrest of a named person

CAPICHE interj do you understand?

CAPING ▸ cape

CAPISCE interj expression meaning do you understand?

CAPISH interj do you understand?

CAPITA ▸ caput

CAPITAL, -S n chief city of a country ▸ adj involving or punishable by death

CAPITAN, -S another name for ▸ hogfish

CAPITANO, CAPITANI n chief; captain

CAPITANS ▸ capitan

CAPITATE n largest of the bones of the human wrist

CAPITAYN n captain

CAPITOL, -S n (in America) building housing the state legislature

CAPITULA ▸ capitulum

CAPIZ, -ES n bivalve shell of a mollusc

CAPLE, -S n horse

CAPLESS ▸ cap

CAPLET, -S n medicinal tablet, usually oval in shape, coated in a soluble substance

CAPLIKE adj like a cap

CAPLIN, -S same as ▸ capelin

CAPMAKER ▸ cap

CAPO, CAPI, -S n device used to raise the pitch of a stringed instrument

CAPOEIRA n Brazilian combination of martial art and dance

CAPON, -S n cock fowl fattened for eating

CAPONATA n Sicilian antipasto relish

CAPONIER n covered passageway built across a ditch as a military defence

CAPONISE same as ▸ **caponize**

CAPONIZE vb make (a cock) into a capon

CAPONS ▸ **capon**

CAPORAL, -S n strong coarse dark tobacco

CAPOS ▸ **capo**

CAPOT, -S, -TED n winning of all the tricks by one player ▹ vb score a capot (against)

CAPOTE, -S n long cloak or soldier's coat, usually with a hood

CAPOTS ▸ **capot**

CAPOTTED ▸ **capot**

CAPOUCH same as ▸ **capuche**

CAPPED ▸ **cap**

CAPPER, -S ▸ **cap**

CAPPING, -S ▸ **cap**

CAPRATE, -S n any salt of capric acid

CAPRESE, -S n salad of mozzarella, basil, and tomatoes

CAPRI adj as in **capri pants** women's tight-fitting trousers

CAPRIC adj (of a type of acid) smelling of goats

CAPRICCI > **capriccio**

CAPRICE, -S n whim

CAPRID, -S n any member of the goat family

CAPRIFIG n wild variety of fig of S Europe and SW Asia

CAPRIFY vb induce figs to ripen

CAPRINE adj of or resembling a goat

CAPRIOLE n upward but not forward leap made by a horse ▹ vb perform a capriole

CAPRIS pl n women's tight-fitting trousers

CAPROATE n any salt of caproic acid

CAPROCK, -S n layer of rock that overlies a salt dome

CAPROIC adj as in **caproic acid** oily acid found in milk

CAPRYLIC variant of ▸ **capric**

CAPS ▸ **cap**

CAPSICIN n liquid or resin extracted from capsicum

CAPSICUM n kind of pepper used as a vegetable or as a spice

CAPSID, -S n outer protein coat of a mature virus

CAPSIDAL ▸ **capsid**

CAPSIDS ▸ **capsid**

CAPSIZAL ▸ **capsize**

CAPSIZE, -D, -S vb (of a boat) overturn accidentally

CAPSOMER n one of the units making up a viral capsid

CAPSTAN, -S n rotating cylinder round which a ship's rope is wound

CAPSTONE n one of a set of slabs on the top of a wall, building, etc

CAPSULAR adj relating to a capsule

CAPSULE, -D, -S n soluble gelatine case containing a dose of medicine ▹ adj very concise ▹ vb contain within a capsule

CAPTAIN, -S n commander of a ship or civil aircraft ▹ vb be captain of

CAPTAN, -S n type of fungicide

CAPTCHA, -S n test in which the user of a website has to decipher a distorted image

CAPTION, -S n title or explanation accompanying an illustration ▹ vb provide with a caption

CAPTIOUS adj tending to make trivial criticisms

CAPTIVE, -D, -S n person kept in confinement ▹ adj kept in confinement ▹ vb take prisoner

CAPTOR, -S n person who captures a person or animal

CAPTURE, -D, -S vb take by force ▹ n capturing

CAPTURER ▸ **capture**

CAPTURES ▸ **capture**

CAPUCCIO n hood

CAPUCHE, -S n large hood or cowl, esp that worn by Capuchin friars

CAPUCHED adj hooded

CAPUCHES ▸ **capuche**

CAPUCHIN n S American monkey with thick hair on the top of its head

CAPUERA, -S variant of ▸ **capoeira**

CAPUL, -S same as ▸ **caple**

CAPUT, CAPITA n main or most prominent part of an organ or structure

CAPYBARA n very large S American rodent

CAR, -S n motor vehicle designed to carry a small number of people

CARABAO, -S n water buffalo

CARABID, -S n type of beetle

CARABIN, -S same as ▸ **carbine**

CARABINE same as ▸ **carbine**

CARABINS ▸ **carabin**

CARACAL, -S n lynx with reddish fur, which inhabits deserts of N Africa and S Asia

CARACARA n carrion-eating bird of S North, Central, and S America

CARACK, -S same as ▸ **carrack**

CARACOL, -S same as ▸ **caracole**

CARACOLE n half turn to the right or left ▹ vb execute a half turn to the right or left

CARACOLS ▸ **caracol**

CARACT, -S n sign or symbol

CARACUL, -S n fur from the skins of newly born lambs of the karakul sheep

CARAFE, -S n glass bottle

CARAGANA n pea tree

CARAGEEN same as > **carrageen**

CARAMBA interj Spanish interjection similar to 'wow!'

CARAMEL, -S n chewy sweet made from sugar and milk ▹ vb turn into caramel

CARANGID n type of marine fish

CARANNA, -S n gumlike substance

CARAP, -S n crabwood

CARAPACE n hard upper shell of tortoises and crustaceans

CARAPAX n carapace

CARAPS ▸ **carap**

CARASSOW same as ▸ **curassow**

CARAT, -S n unit of weight of precious stones

CARATE, -S n tropical disease

CARATS ▸ **carat**

CARAUNA, -S same as ▸ **caranna**

CARAVAN, -S n large enclosed vehicle for living in ▹ vb travel or have a holiday in a caravan

CARAVEL, -S n two- or three-masted sailing ship

CARAWAY, -S n plant whose seeds are used as a spice

CARB, -S n carbohydrate

CARBAMIC adj as in **carbamic acid** hypothetical compound known only in carbamate salts

CARBAMYL n radical from carbamic acid

CARBARN, -S n streetcar depot

CARBARYL n organic compound of the carbamate group

CARBEEN, -S n Australian eucalyptus tree

CARBENE, -S n type of divalent free radical

CARBIDE, -S n compound of carbon with a metal

CARBIES ▸ carby

CARBINE, -S n light automatic rifle

CARBINOL same as ▸ **methanol**

CARBO, -S n carbohydrate

CARBOLIC adj as in **carbolic acid** phenol, when it is used as a disinfectant

CARBON, -S n nonmetallic element

CARBONIC adj containing carbon

CARBONS ▸ carbon

CARBONYL n the divalent group =CO

CARBORA, -S n former name for the koala

CARBORNE adj travelling by car

CARBOS ▸ carbo

CARBOXYL adj as in **carboxyl group** functional group in organic acids

CARBOY, -S n large bottle with a protective casing

CARBOYED ▸ carboy

CARBOYS ▸ carboy

CARBS ▸ carb

CARBURET vb combine with carbon

CARBY, CARBIES n short for carburettor

CARCAJOU a North American name for ▸ **wolverine**

CARCAKE, -S n (formerly, in Scotland) a cake traditionally made for Shrove Tuesday

CARCANET n jewelled collar or necklace

CARCASE, -D, -S same as ▸ **carcass**

CARCASS n dead body of an animal ▷ vb make a carcass of

CARCEL, -S n French unit of light

CARCERAL adj relating to prison

CARD, -ED, -S n piece of thick stiff paper or cardboard ▷ vb comb out fibres of wool or cotton before spinning

CARDAMOM n spice obtained from the seeds of a tropical plant

CARDAMON same as ▸ **cardamom**

CARDAMUM same as ▸ **cardamom**

CARDAN n as in **cardan joint** type of universal joint

CARDCASE n small case for holding business cards

CARDECU, -S n old French coin (a quarter of a crown)

CARDECUE same as ▸ **cardecu**

CARDECUS ▸ cardecu

CARDED ▸ card

CARDER, -S ▸ card

CARDI, -S n cardigan

CARDIA, -E, -S n lower oesophageal sphincter

CARDIAC, -S adj of the heart ▷ n person with a heart disorder

CARDIAE ▸ cardia

CARDIAS ▸ cardia

CARDIE, -S short for ▸ **cardigan**

CARDIGAN n knitted jacket

CARDINAL n high-ranking clergyman of the RC Church ▷ adj fundamentally important

CARDING, -S ▸ card

CARDIO, -S adj exercising heart ▷ n cardiovascular exercise

CARDIOID n heart-shaped curve

CARDIOS ▸ cardio

CARDIS ▸ cardi

CARDITIC ▸ carditis

CARDITIS n inflammation of the heart

CARDON, -S n variety of cactus

CARDOON, -S n thistle-like S European plant

CARDS ▸ card

CARDUUS n thistle

CARDY short for ▸ **cardigan**

CARE, -D, -S vb be concerned ▷ n careful attention, caution

CAREEN, -ED, -S vb tilt over to one side

CAREENER ▸ careen

CAREENS ▸ careen

CAREER, -ED, -S n series of jobs that a person has through their life ▷ vb rush in an uncontrolled way ▷ adj having chosen to dedicate his or her life to a particular occupation

CAREERER ▸ career

CAREERS ▸ career

CAREFREE adj without worry or responsibility

CAREFUL adj cautious in attitude or action

CARELESS adj done or acting with insufficient attention

CARELINE n telephone service set up by a company or other organization

CAREME, -S n period of Lent

CARER, -S n person who looks after someone who is ill or old, often a relative

CARES ▸ care

CARESS, -ED, -ES n gentle affectionate touch or embrace ▷ vb touch gently and affectionately

CARESSER ▸ caress

CARESSES ▸ caress

CARET, -S n proofreading symbol

CARETAKE, CARETOOK vb work as a caretaker

CARETS ▸ caret

CAREWARE n computer software licensed in exchange for a donation to charity

CAREWORN adj showing signs of worry

CAREX, CARICES n any member of the sedge family

CARFARE, -S n fare that a passenger is charged for a ride on a bus, etc

CARFAX, -ES n place where principal roads or streets intersect

CARFOX, -ES same as ▸ **carfax**

CARFUL, -S n maximum number of people a car will hold

CARGEESE ▸ cargoose

CARGO, -ED, -ES, -ING, -S n goods carried by a ship, aircraft, etc ▷ vb load

CARGOOSE, CARGEESE n crested grebe

CARGOS ▸ cargo

CARHOP, -S n waiter or waitress at a drive-in restaurant ▷ vb work as a carhop

CARIACOU n type of deer

CARIAMA, -S another word for ▸ **seriema**

CARIBE, -S n piranha

CARIBOO, -S same as ▸ **caribou**

CARIBOU, -S n large N American reindeer

CARICES ▸ carex

CARIED adj (of teeth) decayed

CARIERE, -S obsolete word for ▸ **career**

CARIES n tooth decay

CARILLON n set of bells played by keyboard or mechanically ▷ vb play a carillon

CARINA, -E, -S n keel-like part or ridge

CARINAL adj keel-like

CARINAS ▶ carina

CARINATE adj having a keel or ridge

CARING, -S adj feeling or showing care and compassion for other people ▷ n practice or profession of providing social or medical care

CARINGLY ▶ caring

CARINGS ▶ caring

CARIOCA, -S n Brazilian dance similar to the samba

CARIOLE, -S n small open two-wheeled horse-drawn vehicle

CARIOSE same as ▶ carious

CARIOUS adj (of teeth or bone) affected with caries

CARITAS n divine love; charity

CARJACK, -S vb attack (a car driver) to rob them or to steal the car

CARJACOU variation of ▶ cariacou

CARK, -ED, -ING, -S vb break down

CARL, -S another word for ▶ churl

CARLE, -S same as ▶ carl

CARLESS adj

CARLIN, -S same as ▶ carling

CARLINE, -S same as ▶ carling

CARLING, -S n fore-and-aft beam in a vessel

CARLINS ▶ carlin

CARLISH adj churlish

CARLOAD, -S n amount that can be carried by a car

CARLOCK, -S n type of Russian isinglass

CARLOT, -S n boor

CARLS ▶ carl

CARMAKER n car manufacturing company

CARMAN, CARMEN n man who drives a car or cart

CARMINE, -S adj vivid red ▷ n vivid red colour, sometimes with a purplish tinge

CARN, -S n cairn

CARNAGE, -S n extensive slaughter of people

CARNAL, -S adj of a physical or sensual nature ▷ vb act in a carnal manner

CARNALLY ▶ carnal

CARNALS ▶ carnal

CARNAUBA n Brazilian fan palm tree

CARNEOUS adj fleshy

CARNET, -S n type of customs licence

CARNEY, -ED, -S same as ▶ carny

CARNIE same as ▶ carny

CARNIED ▶ carny

CARNIER ▶ carny

CARNIES ▶ carny

CARNIEST ▶ carny

CARNIFEX n executioner

CARNIFY vb be altered so as to resemble skeletal muscle

CARNIVAL n festive period with processions, music, and dancing in the street

CARNOSE adj fleshy

CARNS ▶ carn

CARNY, CARNIED, CARNIER, CARNIES, CARNIEST, -ING vb coax or cajole or act in a wheedling manner ▷ n person who works in a carnival ▷ adj sly

CARNYX, -ES n bronze Celtic war trumpet

CAROACH same as ▶ caroche

CAROB, -S n pod of a Mediterranean tree, used as a chocolate substitute

CAROCH same as ▶ caroche

CAROCHE, -S n stately ceremonial carriage used in the 16th and 17th centuries

CAROL, -ED, -LED, -S n joyful Christmas hymn ▷ vb sing carols

CAROLER, -S ▶ carol

CAROLI ▶ carolus

CAROLING ▶ carol

CAROLLED ▶ carol

CAROLLER ▶ carol

CAROLS ▶ carol

CAROLUS, CAROLI n any of several coins struck in the reign of a king called Charles

CAROM, -ED, -ING, -S n shot in which the cue ball is caused to contact one object ball after another ▷ vb carambole

CAROMEL, -S vb turn into caramel

CAROMING ▶ carom

CAROMS ▶ carom

CARON, -S n inverted circumflex

CAROTENE n orange-red hydrocarbons found in many plants

CAROTID, -S n either of the two arteries supplying blood to the head ▷ adj of either of these arteries

CAROTIN, -S same as ▶ carotene

CAROUSAL n merry drinking party

CAROUSE, -D, -S vb have a merry drinking party

CAROUSEL n revolving conveyor belt for luggage or photographic slides

CAROUSER ▶ carouse

CAROUSES ▶ carouse

CARP, -ED, -S n large freshwater fish ▷ vb complain, find fault

CARPAL, -IA, -S n wrist bone

CARPALE, -S same as ▶ carpal

CARPALIA ▶ carpal

CARPALS ▶ carpal

CARPED ▶ carp

CARPEL, -S n female reproductive organ of a flowering plant

CARPER, -S ▶ carp

CARPET, -ED, -S n heavy fabric for covering floors ▷ vb cover with a carpet

CARPHONE n (formerly) phone designed for use in a car

CARPI ▶ carpus

CARPING, -S adj tending to make petty complaints ▷ n petty complaint

CARPLIKE adj like a carp

CARPOOL, -S vb share the use of a single car to travel to work or school

CARPORT, -S n shelter for a car, consisting of a roof supported by posts

CARPS ▶ carp

CARPUS, CARPI n set of eight bones of the wrist

CARR, -S n area of bog or fen in which scrub has become established

CARRACK, -S n galleon used as a merchantman

CARRACT, -S same as ▶ carrack

CARRAT, -S same as ▶ carat

CARRAWAY same as ▶ caraway

CARRECT, -S same as ▶ carrack

CARREL, -S n small individual study room or private desk

CARRELL, -S same as ▶ carrel

CARRELS ▶ carrel

CARRIAGE n one of the sections of a train for passengers

CARRICK n as in **carrick bend** type of knot

CARRIED ▶ carry

CARRIER, -S n person or thing that carries something

CARRIES ▶ carry

CARRIOLE same as ▶ cariole

CARRION, -S n dead and rotting flesh

CARRITCH n catechism

CARROCH variant of ▶ caroche

CARROM, -ED, -S same as ▶ carom

CARRON n as in **carron oil** ointment of limewater and linseed oil

CARROT, -S n long tapering orange root vegetable

CARROTIN n carotene

CARROTS ▶ carrot

CARROTY adj (of hair) reddish-orange

CARRS ▶ carr

CARRY, CARRIED, CARRIES, -ING vb take from one place to another

CARRYALL n light four-wheeled horse-drawn carriage usually designed to carry four passengers

CARRYCOT n light portable bed for a baby, with handles and a hood

CARRYING ▶ carry

CARRYON, -S n fuss or commotion

CARRYOUT n hot cooked food bought in a shop for consumption elsewhere

CARS ▶ car

CARSE, -S n riverside area of flat fertile alluvium

CARSEY, -S slang word for ▶ toilet

CARSHARE same as ▶ carpool

CARSICK adj nauseated from riding in a car

CARSPIEL n curling match which has a car as a prize

CART, -ED, -ING, -S n open two-wheeled horse-drawn vehicle ▷ vb carry, usu with some effort

CARTA, -S n charter

CARTABLE ▶ cart

CARTAGE, -S n process or cost of carting

CARTAS ▶ carta

CARTE, -S n fencing position

CARTED ▶ cart

CARTEL, -S n association of competing firms formed to fix prices

CARTER, -S ▶ cart

CARTES ▶ carte

CARTFUL, -S n amount a cart can hold

CARTING ▶ cart

CARTLOAD n amount a cart can hold

CARTON, -ED, -S n container made of cardboard or waxed paper ▷ vb enclose (goods) in a carton

CARTOON, -S n humorous or satirical drawing ▷ vb depict in a cartoon

CARTOONY adj of or like a cartoon

CARTOP adj designed to be transported on top of a vehicle

CARTOUCH same as > cartouche

CARTROAD n road for carts to drive on

CARTS ▶ cart

CARTWAY, -S n way by which carts travel

CARUCAGE n tax due on a carucate

CARUCATE n area of land an oxen team could plough in a year

CARUNCLE n fleshy outgrowth on the heads of certain birds, such as a cock's comb

CARVE, -D, -S vb cut to form an object

CARVEL, -S same as ▶ caravel

CARVEN an archaic or literary past participle of ▶ carve

CARVER, -S n carving knife

CARVERY n restaurant where customers pay a set price for unrestricted helpings

CARVES ▶ carve

CARVIES ▶ carvy

CARVING, -S n figure or design produced by carving stone or wood

CARVY, CARVIES n caraway seed

CARWASH n drive-through structure containing automated equipment for washing cars

CARYATIC ▶ caryatid

CARYATID n supporting column in the shape of a female figure

CARYOTIN variant of ▶ karyotin

CASA, -S n house

CASABA, -S n kind of winter muskmelon

CASAS ▶ casa

CASAVA, -S same as ▶ cassava

CASBAH, -S n citadel of a N African city

CASCABEL n knoblike protrusion on a type of cannon

CASCABLE same as ▶ cascabel

CASCADE, -D, -S n waterfall ▷ vb flow or fall in a cascade

CASCARA, -S n bark of a N American shrub, used as a laxative

CASCHROM n wooden hand-plough

CASCO, -S n Argentinian homestead

CASE, -D, -S n instance, example ▷ vb inspect (a building) with the intention of burgling it

CASEASE, -S n proteolytic enzyme

CASEATE, -D, -S vb undergo caseation

CASEBOOK n book in which records of legal or medical cases are kept

CASED ▶ case

CASEFY, CASEFIED, CASEFIES vb make or become similar to cheese

CASEIC adj relating to cheese

CASEIN, -S n phosphoprotein forming the basis of cheese

CASELAW, -S n law established by previous cases

CASELOAD n number of cases that a worker deals with at any one time

CASEMAN, CASEMEN n in printing, a person who sets and corrects type

CASEMATE n armoured compartment in a ship or fortification in which guns are mounted

CASEMEN ▶ caseman

CASEMENT n window that is hinged on one side

CASEMIX n mix or type of patients treated by a hospital or medical unit

CASEOSE, -S n peptide produced by the peptic digestion of casein

CASEOUS adj of or like cheese

C

CASERN, -S n (formerly) a billet or accommodation for soldiers in a town

CASERNE, -S same as ▶ casern

CASERNS ▶ casern

CASES ▶ case

CASETTE, -S variant of ▶ cassette

CASEVAC, -S vb evacuate (a casualty) from a combat zone, usu by air

CASEWORK n social work based on close study

CASEWORM n caddis worm

CASH, -ED, -ES, -ING n banknotes and coins ▷ adj of, for, or paid in cash ▷ vb obtain cash for

CASHABLE ▶ cash

CASHAW, -S n winter squash

CASHBACK n discount offered in return for immediate payment

CASHBOOK n journal in which cash receipts and payments are recorded

CASHBOX n box for holding cash

CASHED ▶ cash

CASHES ▶ cash

CASHEW, -S n edible kidney-shaped nut

CASHIER, -S n person responsible for handling cash in a bank, shop, etc ▷ vb dismiss with dishonour from the armed forces

CASHING ▶ cash

CASHLESS adj using credit cards or electronic money transfers instead of coins or banknotes

CASHMERE n fine soft wool obtained from goats

CASHOO, -S n catechu

CASIMERE same as > cassimere

CASIMIRE variant of > cassimere

CASING, -S n protective case, covering

CASINO, CASINI, -S n public building or room where gambling games are played

CASITA, -S n small house

CASK, -ED, -ING, -S n large barrel ▷ vb put into a cask

CASKET, -ED, -S n small box for valuables ▷ vb put into a casket

CASKIER ▶ casky

CASKIEST ▶ casky

CASKING ▶ cask

CASKS ▶ cask

CASKY, CASKIER,

CASKIEST adj (of wine) having a musty smell due to resting too long in the cask

CASPASE, -S n type of enzyme

CASQUE, -S n helmet or a helmet-like process or structure

CASQUED ▶ casque

CASQUES ▶ casque

CASSABA, -S same as ▶ casaba

CASSATA, -S n ice cream usually containing nuts and candied fruit

CASSAVA, -S n starch obtained from the roots of a tropical American plant, used to make tapioca

CASSENA, -S same as ▶ cassina

CASSENE, -S same as ▶ cassina

CASSETTE n (formerly) plastic container for magnetic tape

CASSIA, -S n tropical plant whose pods yield a mild laxative

CASSIE, -S n type of thorny shrub

CASSINA, -S n American tree

CASSINE, -S same as ▶ cassina

CASSINO, -S n card game for two to four players

CASSIOPE n type of evergreen shrub

CASSIS, -ES n blackcurrant cordial

CASSOCK, -S n long tunic, usu black, worn by priests

CASSONE, -S n highly decorated Italian dowry chest

CASSPIR, -S n armoured military vehicle

CAST, -S n actors in a play or film collectively ▷ vb select (an actor) to play a part in a play or film

CASTABLE adj able to be cast

CASTANET > castanets

CASTAWAY n shipwrecked person ▷ adj shipwrecked or put adrift ▷ vb cause (a ship, person, etc) to be shipwrecked or abandoned

CASTE, -S n any of the hereditary classes into which Hindu society is divided

CASTED adj having a caste

CASTEISM n belief in, and adherence to, the caste system

CASTELLA > castellum

CASTER, -S n person or thing that casts

CASTERED adj having casters

CASTERS ▶ caster

CASTES ▶ caste

CASTING, -S ▶ cast

CASTLE, -S n large fortified building ▷ vb (in chess) make a move involving king and rook

CASTLED adj like a castle in construction

CASTLES ▶ castle

CASTLING n (in chess) act of castling

CASTOCK, -S n kale stalk

CASTOFF, -S n person or thing that has been discarded or abandoned

CASTOR, -S same as ▶ caster

CASTORY n dye derived from beaver pelts

CASTRAL adj relating to camps

CASTRATE vb remove the testicles of

CASTRATO, CASTRATI n male singer who retains a soprano or alto voice

CASTS ▶ cast

CASUAL, -S adj careless, nonchalant ▷ n occasional worker

CASUALLY ▶ casual

CASUALS ▶ casual

CASUALTY n person killed or injured in an accident or war

CASUIST, -S n person who attempts to resolve moral dilemmas

CASUS n event

CAT, -S, -TED, -TING n small domesticated furry mammal ▷ vb flog with a cat-o'-nine-tails

CATACOMB n underground burial place

CATAGEN, -S n phase of hair growth

CATALASE n enzyme that catalyses the decomposition of hydrogen peroxide

CATALO, -ES, -S same as ▶ cattalo

CATALOG, -S same as > catalogue

CATALOS ▶ catalo

CATALPA, -S n tree of N America and Asia with bell-shaped whitish flowers

CATALYSE vb speed up (a chemical reaction) by a catalyst

CATALYST n substance that speeds up a chemical reaction without itself changing

CATALYZE same as ▸ catalyse

CATAPAN, -S n governor in the Byzantine Empire

CATAPHOR n word that refers to or stands for another word used later

CATAPULT n Y-shaped device with a loop of elastic, used by children for firing stones ▸ vb shoot forwards or upwards violently

CATARACT n eye disease in which the lens becomes opaque

CATARRH, -S n excessive mucus in the nose and throat, during or following a cold

CATASTA, -S n platform on which slaves were presented for sale

CATATONY another word for ▸ catatonia

CATAWBA, -S n type of red North American grape

CATBIRD, -S n North American songbird

CATBOAT, -S n sailing vessel

CATBRIAR same as ▸ catbrier

CATBRIER n greenbrier

CATCALL, -S n derisive whistle or cry ▸ vb utter such a call (at)

CATCH, -ES, CAUGHT vb seize, capture ▸ n device for fastening a door, window, etc

CATCHALL n something designed to cover a variety of situations

CATCHCRY n well-known much-used phrase, perhaps associated with a particular group

CATCHED rarely used past tense of ▸ catch

CATCHEN archaic form of ▸ catch

CATCHER, -S n person or thing that catches, esp in a game or sport

CATCHES ▸ catch

CATCHFLY n type of plant with sticky calyxes and stems on which insects are trapped

CATCHIER ▸ catchy

CATCHILY adv in a pleasant or catchy way

CATCHING ▸ catch

CATCHT same as ▸ catched

CATCHUP, -S variant spelling (esp US) of ▸ ketchup

CATCHY, CATCHIER adj (of a tune) pleasant and easily remembered

CATCLAW, -S n type of shrub; black bead

CATCON, -S n catalytic converter

CATE n delicacy

CATECHIN n soluble yellow solid substance found in mahogany wood

CATECHOL n colourless crystalline phenol found in resins and lignins

CATECHU n astringent resinous substance

CATEGORY n class, group

CATELOG, -S old form of ▸ catalogue

CATENA, -E, -S n connected series, esp of patristic comments on the Bible

CATENANE n type of chemical compound

CATENARY n curve assumed by a heavy uniform flexible cord hanging freely from two points ▸ adj of, resembling, relating to, or constructed using a catenary or suspended chain

CATENAS ▸ catena

CATENATE vb arrange or be arranged in a series of chains or rings

CATENOID n geometrical surface generated by rotating a catenary about its axis

CATER, -ED, -S vb provide what is needed or wanted, esp food or services

CATERAN, -S n (formerly) a member of a band of brigands in the Scottish highlands

CATERED ▸ cater

CATERER, -S n person whose job is to provide food for social events

CATERESS n female caterer

CATERING n supplying of food for a social event

CATERS ▸ cater

CATES pl n choice dainty food

CATFACE, -S n deformity of the surface of a tree trunk, caused by fire or disease

CATFALL, -S n line used as a tackle for hoisting an anchor to the cathead

CATFIGHT n fight, especially between two women

CATFISH vb create a false identity online to lure someone into a relationship

CATFLAP, -S n small flap in a door to let a cat go through

CATFOOD, -S n food for cats

CATGUT, -S n strong cord used to string musical instruments and sports rackets

CATHEAD, -S n fitting at the bow of a vessel for securing the anchor when raised

CATHECT, -S vb invest mental or emotional energy in

CATHEDRA n bishop's throne

CATHETER n tube inserted into a body cavity to drain fluid

CATHETUS n straight line or radius perpendicular to another line or radius

CATHEXIS, CATHEXES n concentration of psychic energy on a single goal

CATHISMA n short hymn used as a response

CATHODAL ▸ cathode

CATHODE, -S n negative electrode, by which electrons leave a circuit

CATHODIC ▸ cathode

CATHOLE, -S n hole in a ship through which ropes are passed

CATHOLIC adj (of tastes or interests) covering a wide range ▸ n member of the Roman Catholic Church

CATHOOD, -S n state of being a cat

CATION, -S n positively charged ion

CATIONIC ▸ cation

CATIONS ▸ cation

CATJANG, -S n tropical shrub

CATKIN, -S n drooping flower spike of certain trees

CATLIKE ▸ cat

CATLIN, -S same as ▸ catling

CATLING, -S n long double-edged surgical knife for amputations

CATLINS ▸ catlin

CATMINT, -S n Eurasian plant with scented leaves that attract cats

CATNAP, -S vb doze ▸ n short sleep or doze

CATNAPER ▸ catnap

CATNAPS ▸ catnap

CATNEP, -S same as ▸ catmint

CATNIP, -S same as ▸ catmint

CATOLYTE n part of the electrolyte that surrounds the cathode in an electrolytic cell

CATS ▸ cat

CATSKIN, -S n skin or fur of a cat

CATSPAW, -S n person used by another as a tool

CATSUIT, -S n one-piece usually close-fitting trouser suit

CATSUP, -S variant (esp US) of ▸ **ketchup**

CATTABU, -S n cross between common cattle and zebu

CATTAIL, -S n reed mace

CATTALO, -S n hardy breed of cattle

CATTED ▸ cat

CATTERY n place where cats are bred or looked after

CATTIE same as ▸ **catty**

CATTIER ▸ catty

CATTIES ▸ catty

CATTIEST ▸ catty

CATTILY ▸ catty

CATTING ▸ cat

CATTISH ▸ cat

CATTLE pl n domesticated cows and bulls

CATTLEYA n tropical American orchid cultivated for its purplish-pink or white showy flowers

CATTY, CATTIER, CATTIES, CATTIEST adj spiteful ▸ n unit of weight, used esp in China

CATWALK, -S n narrow pathway or platform

CATWORKS n machinery on a drilling platform

CATWORM, -S n type of carnivorous worm

CAUCUS, -ED, -ES n local committee or faction of a political party ▸ vb hold a caucus

CAUDA, -E n tail of an animal

CAUDAD adv towards the tail or posterior part

CAUDAE ▸ cauda

CAUDAL adj at or near an animal's tail

CAUDALLY ▸ caudal

CAUDATE, -S adj having a tail or a tail-like appendage ▸ n lizard-like amphibian

CAUDATED same as ▸ **caudate**

CAUDATES ▸ caudate

CAUDEX, -ES, CAUDICES n thickened persistent stem

base of some herbaceous perennial plants

CAUDICLE n stalk to which an orchid's pollen masses are attached

CAUDILLO n (in Spanish-speaking countries) a military or political leader

CAUDLE, -D, -S, CAUDLING n hot spiced wine drink made with gruel, formerly used medicinally ▸ vb make such a drink

CAUDRON, -S Spenserian spelling of ▸ **cauldron**

CAUF, CAUVES n cage for holding live fish in the water

CAUGHT ▸ catch

CAUK, -S n type of barite

CAUKER, -S n one who caulks

CAUKS ▸ cauk

CAUL, -S n membrane sometimes covering a child's head at birth

CAULD, -ER, -EST, -S a Scot word for ▸ **cold**

CAULDRON n large pot used for boiling

CAULDS ▸ cauld

CAULES ▸ caulis

CAULICLE n small stalk or stem

CAULINE adj relating to or growing from a plant stem

CAULIS, CAULES n main stem of a plant

CAULK, -ED, -S vb fill in (cracks) with paste etc

CAULKER, -S ▸ caulk

CAULKING ▸ caulk

CAULKS ▸ caulk

CAULOME, -S n plant's stem structure, considered as a whole

CAULS ▸ caul

CAUM, -ED, -ING, -S same as ▸ **cam**

CAUP, -S n type of quaich

CAURI, -S n former coin of Guinea

CAUSA, -E n reason or cause

CAUSABLE ▸ cause

CAUSAE ▸ causa

CAUSAL, -S adj of or being a cause ▸ n something that suggests a cause

CAUSALLY ▸ causal

CAUSALS ▸ causal

CAUSE, -D, -S, CAUSING n something that produces a particular effect ▸ vb be the cause of

CAUSEN old infinitive of ▸ **cause**

CAUSER, -S ▸ cause

CAUSERIE n informal talk or conversational piece of writing

CAUSERS ▸ causer

CAUSES ▸ cause

CAUSEWAY n raised path or road across water or marshland

CAUSEY, -S n cobbled street ▸ vb cobble

CAUSEYED ▸ causey

CAUSEYS ▸ causey

CAUSING ▸ cause

CAUSTIC, -S adj capable of burning by chemical action ▸ n caustic substance

CAUTEL, -S n craftiness

CAUTER, -S n cauterizing instrument

CAUTERY n coagulation of blood or destruction of body tissue by cauterizing

CAUTION, -S n care, esp in the face of danger ▸ vb warn, advise

CAUTIOUS adj showing caution

CAUVES ▸ cauf

CAVA, -S n Spanish sparkling wine

CAVALERO n cavalier

CAVALIER adj showing haughty disregard ▸ n gallant gentleman

CAVALLA, -S n type of tropical fish

CAVALLY same as ▸ **cavalla**

CAVALRY n part of the army

CAVAS ▸ cava

CAVASS, -ES n Turkish armed police officer

CAVATINA, CAVATINE n solo song resembling a simple aria

CAVE, -D, -S n hollow in the side of a hill or cliff ▸ vb hollow out

CAVEAT, -ED, -S n warning ▸ vb introduce a caveat

CAVEATOR n person who enters a caveat

CAVEATS ▸ caveat

CAVED ▸ cave

CAVEFISH n small N American freshwater fish

CAVEL, -S n drawing of lots among miners for an easy and profitable place at the coalface

CAVELIKE adj resembling a cave

CAVELS ▸ cavel

CAVEMAN, CAVEMEN n prehistoric cave dweller

CAVEOLA, -E n pit in a cell membrane

CAVEOLAR ▶ caveola
CAVER, -S ▶ cave
CAVERN, -ED, -S n large cave ▷ vb shut in or as if in a cavern
CAVERS ▶ caver
CAVES ▶ cave
CAVESSON n kind of hard noseband, used (esp formerly) in breaking a horse in
CAVETTO, CAVETTI, -S n concave moulding, shaped to a quarter circle in cross section
CAVIAR, -S n salted sturgeon roe, regarded as a delicacy
CAVIARE, -S same as ▶ caviar
CAVIARIE same as ▶ caviar
CAVIARS ▶ caviar
CAVICORN adj (of sheep, goats, etc) having hollow horns as distinct from the solid antlers of deer ▷ n sheep, goat, etc with hollow horns
CAVIE n hen coop
CAVIER, -S same as ▶ caviar
CAVIES ▶ cavy
CAVIL, -ED, -ING, -LED, -S vb make petty objections ▷ n petty objection
CAVILER, -S ▶ cavil
CAVILING ▶ cavil
CAVILLED ▶ cavil
CAVILLER ▶ cavil
CAVILS ▶ cavil
CAVING, -S n sport of exploring caves
CAVITARY adj containing cavities
CAVITATE vb form cavities or bubbles
CAVITIED ▶ cavity
CAVITY, CAVITIES n hollow space
CAVORT, -ED, -S vb skip about
CAVORTER ▶ cavort
CAVORTS ▶ cavort
CAVY, CAVIES n type of small rodent
CAW, -ED, -S n cry of a crow, rook, or raven ▷ vb make this cry
CAWING, -S ▶ caw
CAWK, -S same as ▶ cauk
CAWKER, -S n metal projection on a horse's shoe to prevent slipping
CAWKS ▶ cawk
CAWS ▶ caw
CAXON, -S n type of wig
CAY, -S n low island or bank composed of sand and coral fragments

CAYENNE, -S n very hot condiment
CAYENNED adj seasoned with cayenne
CAYENNES ▶ cayenne
CAYMAN, -S n S American reptile similar to an alligator
CAYS ▶ cay
CAYUSE, -S n small pony used by Native Americans
CAZ short for ▶ casual

Caz is slang for casual, and is one of the essential short words for using the Z.

CAZH adj casual
CAZIQUE, -S same as ▶ cacique

This word means a Native American chief, and its plural **caziques** was once played as a 9-timer (that is, a word spanning two triple-word squares) earning the highest score for a single word ever officially recorded in a game of Scrabble, 392 points.

CEAS same as ▶ caese
CEASE, -D, -S vb bring or come to an end
CEASING, -S ▶ cease
CEAZE, -D, -S, CEAZING obsolete spelling of ▶ seize
CEBID, -S n any member of the Cebidae family of New World monkeys
CEBOID, -S same as ▶ cebid
CECA ▶ cecum
CECAL ▶ cecum
CECALLY ▶ cecum
CECILS pl n fried meatballs
CECITIES ▶ cecity
CECITIS n inflammation of the c(a)ecum
CECITY, CECITIES n rare word for blindness
CECROPIA n large North American moth
CECROPIN n antimicrobial peptide originally derived from the cecropia moth
CECUM, CECA same as ▶ caecum
CEDAR, -S n evergreen coniferous tree ▷ adj made of the wood of a cedar tree
CEDARED adj covered with cedars
CEDARIER ▶ cedary
CEDARN adj relating to cedar
CEDARS ▶ cedar
CEDARY, CEDARIER adj like cedar
CEDE, -D, -S, CEDING vb surrender (territory or legal rights)

CEDER, -S ▶ cede
CEDES ▶ cede
CEDI, -S n standard monetary unit of Ghana, divided into 100 pesewas
CEDILLA, -S n character placed under a c in some languages
CEDING ▶ cede
CEDIS ▶ cedi
CEDRATE, -S n citron
CEDRINE adj relating to cedar
CEDULA, -S n form of identification in Spanish-speaking countries
CEE, -S n third letter of the alphabet
CEIBA, -S n type of tropical tree
CEIL, -ED, -S vb line (a ceiling) with plaster, boarding, etc
CEILER, -S ▶ ceil
CEILI, -S variant spelling of ▶ ceilidh
CEILIDH, -S n social gathering for singing and dancing
CEILING, -S n inner upper surface of a room ▷ vb make a ceiling
CEILIS ▶ ceili
CEILS ▶ ceil
CEINTURE n belt
CEL, -S short for ▶ celluloid
CELADON, -S n type of porcelain having a greyish-green glaze: mainly Chinese
CELEB, -S n celebrity
CELERIAC n variety of celery with a large turnip-like root
CELERIES ▶ celery
CELERITY n swiftness
CELERY, CELERIES n vegetable with long green crisp edible stalks
CELESTA, -S n instrument like a small piano
CELESTE, -S same as ▶ celesta
CELIAC, -S same as ▶ coeliac
CELIBACY ▶ celibate
CELIBATE adj unmarried, esp because of a religious vow ▷ n celibate person
CELL, -S n smallest unit of an organism that is able to function independently
CELLA, -E n inner room of a classical temple
CELLAR, -ED, -S n underground room for storage ▷ vb store in a cellar
CELLARER n monastic official responsible for food, drink, etc

CELLARET *n* case, cabinet, or sideboard with compartments for holding wine bottles

CELLARS ▸ **cellar**

CELLED *adj* cellular

CELLI ▸ **cello**

CELLING, -S *n* formation of cells

CELLIST, -S ▸ **cello**

CELLMATE *n* person with whom a prisoner shares a prison cell

CELLO, CELLI, -S *n* large low-pitched instrument of the violin family

CELLOSE, -S *n* disaccharide obtained by the hydrolysis of cellulose by cellulase

CELLS ▸ **cell**

CELLULAR *adj* of or consisting of cells ▷ *n* cellular phone

CELLULE, -S *n* very small cell

CELOM, -ATA, -S *same as* ▸ **coelom**

CELOMIC ▸ **celom**

CELOMS ▸ **celom**

CELOSIA, -S *same as* > **cockscomb**

CELOTEX *n* tradename for a type of insulation board

CELS ▸ **cel**

CELT, -S *n* stone or metal axelike instrument with a bevelled edge

CEMBALO, CEMBALI, -S *n* harpsichord

CEMBRA, -S *n* Swiss pine

CEMENT, -ED, -S *n* powder mixed with water and sand to make mortar or concrete ▷ *vb* join, bind, or cover with cement

CEMENTA ▸ **cementum**

CEMENTED ▸ **cement**

CEMENTER ▸ **cement**

CEMENTS ▸ **cement**

CEMENTUM, CEMENTA *n* thin bonelike tissue that covers the dentine in the root of a tooth

CEMETERY *n* place where dead people are buried

CEMITARE *obsolete spelling of* ▸ **scimitar**

CENACLE, -S *n* supper room, esp one on an upper floor

CENDRE *adj* ash-blond

CENOBITE *same as* > **coenobite**

CENOTAPH *n* monument honouring soldiers who died in a war

CENOTE, -S *n* natural well formed by the collapse of an overlying limestone crust

CENOZOIC *adj* of or relating to the most recent geological era

CENS *n* type of annual property rent

CENSE, -D, -S, CENSING *vb* burn incense near or before (an altar, shrine, etc)

CENSER, -S *n* container for burning incense

CENSES ▸ **cense**

CENSING ▸ **cense**

CENSOR, -ED, -S *n* person authorized to prohibit anything considered obscene or objectionable ▷ *vb* ban or cut parts of (a film, book, etc)

CENSUAL ▸ **census**

CENSURE, -D, -S *n* severe disapproval ▷ *vb* criticize severely

CENSURER ▸ **censure**

CENSURES ▸ **censure**

CENSUS, -ED, -ES *n* official count of a population ▷ *vb* conduct a census

CENT, -S *n* hundredth part of a monetary unit such as the dollar or euro

CENTAGE, -S *n* rate per hundred

CENTAI ▸ **centas**

CENTAL, -S *n* unit of weight equal to 100 pounds (45.3 kilograms)

CENTARE, -S *same as* ▸ **centiare**

CENTAS, CENTAI, CENTU *n* former monetary unit of Lithuania

CENTAUR, -S *n* mythical creature

CENTAURY *n* plant with purplish-pink flowers

CENTAVO, -S *n* monetary unit in many Latin American countries

CENTER, -ED, -S *same as* ▸ **centre**

CENTESIS, CENTESES *n* surgical puncturing of part of the body with a hollow needle, to extract fluid

CENTIARE *n* unit of area equal to one square metre

CENTILE, -S *n* (in statistics) another word for percentile

CENTIME, -S *n* monetary unit worth one hundredth of a franc

CENTIMO, -S *n* monetary unit of Costa Rica, Paraguay, Peru, and Venezuela

CENTINEL *obsolete variant of* ▸ **sentinel**

CENTNER, -S *n* unit of weight equivalent to 100 pounds (45.3 kilograms)

CENTO, -NES, -S *n* piece of writing composed of quotations from other authors

CENTOIST *n* one who composes centos

CENTONEL *obsolete variant of* ▸ **sentinel**

CENTONES ▸ **cento**

CENTOS ▸ **cento**

CENTRA ▸ **centrum**

CENTRAL, -S *adj* of, at, or forming the centre ▷ *n* workplace serving as a telecommunications facility

CENTRE, -S *n* middle point or part ▷ *vb* put in the centre of something

CENTRED *adj* mentally and emotionally confident, focused, and well-balanced

CENTRES ▸ **centre**

CENTRIC *adj* being central or having a centre

CENTRIES ▸ **centry**

CENTRING *n* temporary structure used to support an arch during construction

CENTRISM ▸ **centrist**

CENTRIST *n* person favouring political moderation

CENTRODE *n* locus produced by plotting the course of two bodies in relative motion

CENTROID *n* centre of mass of an object of uniform density, esp of a geometric figure

CENTRUM, CENTRA, -S *n* main part or body of a vertebra

CENTRY, CENTRIES *obsolete variant of* ▸ **sentry**

CENTS ▸ **cent**

CENTU ▸ **centas**

CENTUM, -S *adj* denoting or belonging to certain Indo-European languages ▷ *n* hundred

CENTUPLE *n* one hundredfold

CENTURY *n* period of 100 years

CEORL, -S *n* freeman of the lowest class in Anglo-Saxon England

CEORLISH ▸ ceorl

CEORLS ▸ ceorl

CEP, -S another name for ▸ porcino

CEPAGE, -S n grape variety or type of wine

CEPE, -S another spelling of ▸ cep

CEPHALAD adv towards the head or anterior part

CEPHALIC adj of or relating to the head ▷ n remedy for pains in the head

CEPHALIN n phospholipid, similar to lecithin, that occurs in the nerve tissue and brain

CEPHEID, -S n type of variable star with a regular cycle of variations in luminosity

CEPS ▸ cep

CERAMAL, -S same as ▸ cermet

CERAMIC n hard brittle material ▷ adj made of ceramic

CERAMICS n art of producing ceramic objects

CERAMIDE n class of compounds used as moisturizers

CERAMIST ▸ ceramics

CERASIN, -S n meta-arabinic acid

CERASTES n type of venomous snake, esp the horned viper

CERATE, -S n hard ointment or medicated paste

CERATED adj (of certain birds, such as the falcon) having a cere

CERATES ▸ cerate

CERATIN, -S same as ▸ keratin

CERATOID adj having the shape or texture of animal horn

CERCAL adj of or relating to a tail

CERCARIA n one of the larval forms of trematode worms

CERCI ▸ cercus

CERCIS, -ES n type of tree or shrub

CERCOPID n froghopper or spittlebug

CERCUS, CERCI n one of a pair of sensory appendages on some insects and other arthropods

CERE, -D, -S, CERING n soft waxy swelling at the base of the upper beak of a parrot ▷ vb wrap in a cerecloth

CEREAL, -S n grass plant with edible grain, such as oat or wheat

CEREBRA ▸ cerebrum

CEREBRAL same as > cacuminal

CEREBRIC ▸ cerebrum

CEREBRUM, CEREBRA n main part of the brain

CERED ▸ cere

CEREMENT n any burial clothes

CEREMONY n formal act or ritual

CEREOUS adj waxlike

CERES ▸ cere

CERESIN, -S n white wax extracted from ozocerite

CERESINE same as ▸ ceresin

CERESINS ▸ ceresin

CEREUS, -ES n type of tropical American cactus

CERGE, -S n large altar candle

CERIA, -S n ceric oxide

CERIC adj of or containing cerium in the tetravalent state

CERING ▸ cere

CERIPH, -S same as ▸ serif

CERISE, -S adj cherry-red ▷ n moderate to dark red colour

CERITE, -S n hydrous silicate of cerium

CERIUM, -S n steel-grey metallic element

CERMET, -S n material consisting of a metal matrix with ceramic particles disseminated through it

CERNE, -D, -S, CERNING obsolete variant of ▸ encircle

CERNUOUS adj (of some flowers or buds) drooping

CERO, -S n type of large food fish

CEROC, -S n dance combining many styles, including jive and salsa

CEROON, -S n hide-covered bale

CEROS ▸ cero

CEROTIC adj as in cerotic acid white insoluble odourless wax

CEROTYPE n process for preparing a printing plate

CEROUS adj of or containing cerium in the trivalent state

CERRADO, -S n vast area of tropical savanna in Brazil

CERRIAL adj relating to the cerris

CERRIS, -ES n Turkey oak

CERT, -S n certainty

CERTAIN adj positive and confident

CERTES adv with certainty

CERTIE n as in by my certie assuredly

CERTIFY vb confirm, attest to

CERTS ▸ cert

CERTY n as in by my certy assuredly

CERULE adj sky-blue

CERULEAN n deep blue colour

CERULEIN n type of dyestuff

CERUMEN, -S n wax secreted by glands in the external ear

CERUSE, -S n white lead

CERUSITE same as > cerussite

CERVELAS n French garlicky pork sausage

CERVELAT n smoked sausage made from pork and beef

CERVEZA, -S n Spanish word for beer

CERVICAL adj of or relating to the neck or cervix

CERVICES ▸ cervix

CERVICUM n flexible region between the prothorax and head in insects

CERVID, -S n type of ruminant mammal characterized by the presence of antlers

CERVINE adj resembling or relating to a deer

CERVIX, CERVICES, -ES n narrow entrance of the womb

CESAREAN variant of > caesarean

CESARIAN US variant of > caesarean

CESIOUS same as ▸ caesious

CESIUM, -S same as ▸ caesium

CESS, -ED, -ES, -ING n any of several special taxes, such as a land tax in Scotland ▷ vb tax or assess for taxation

CESSE obsolete variant of ▸ cease

CESSED ▸ cess

CESSER, -S n coming to an end of a term interest or annuity

CESSES ▸ cess

CESSING ▸ cess

CESSION, -S n ceding

CESSPIT, -S same as ▸ cesspool

CESSPOOL n covered tank or pit for collecting and storing sewage or waste water

CESTA, -S *n* in jai alai, the basket used to throw and catch the pelota
CESTI ▶ **cestus**
CESTODE, -S *n* type of parasitic flatworm such as the tapeworms
CESTOI ▶ **cestos**
CESTOID, -S *adj* (esp of tapeworms and similar animals) ribbon-like in form ▷ *n* ribbon-like worm
CESTOS, CESTOI, -ES *same as* ▶ **cestus**
CESTUI, -S *n* legal term to designate a person
CESTUS, CESTI, -ES *n* girdle of Aphrodite
CESURA, -E, -S *variant spelling of* ▶ **caesura**
CESURAL ▶ **cesura**
CESURAS ▶ **cesura**
CESURE, -S *same as* ▶ **caesura**
CETACEAN *n* fish-shaped sea mammal such as a whale or dolphin ▷ *adj* relating to these mammals
CETANE, -S *n* colourless liquid hydrocarbon, used as a solvent
CETE, -S *n* group of badgers
CETERACH *n* scale-fern
CETES ▶ **cete**
CETOLOGY *n* branch of zoology concerned with the study of whales (cetaceans)
CETYL, -S *n* univalent alcohol radical
CETYWALL *n* valerian
CEVICHE, -S *n* Peruvian seafood dish
CEZVE, -S *n* small metal pot for brewing coffee
CH *pron* obsolete form of I
CHA, -S *n* tea
CHABLIS *n* dry white French wine
CHABOUK, -S *n* type of whip
CHABUK, -S *same as* ▶ **chabouk**
CHACE, -D, -S, CHACING *obsolete variant of* ▶ **chase**
CHACHKA, -S *n* cheap trinket
CHACING ▶ **chace**
CHACK, -ED, -ING, -S *vb* bite
CHACMA, -S *n* type of baboon with coarse greyish hair, living in S and E Africa
CHACO, -ES, -S *same as* ▶ **shako**
CHACONNE *n* musical form consisting of a set of variations on a repeated melodic bass line

CHACOS ▶ **chaco**
CHAD, -S *n* small pieces removed during the punching of holes in punch cards, printer paper, etc
CHADAR, -S *same as* ▶ **chuddar**
CHADARIM ▶ **cheder**
CHADARS ▶ **chadar**
CHADDAR, -S *same as* ▶ **chuddar**
CHADDOR, -S *same as* ▶ **chuddar**
CHADLESS *adj* (of a keypunch) not producing chads
CHADO, -S *n* Japanese tea ceremony
CHADOR, -S *same as* ▶ **chuddar**
CHADOS ▶ **chado**
CHADRI *n* shroud which covers the body from head to foot
CHADS ▶ **chad**
CHAEBOL, -S *n* large, usually family-owned, business group in South Korea
CHAETA, -E *n* a bristle on the body of an annelid
CHAETAL ▶ **chaeta**
CHAFE, -D, -S, CHAFING *vb* make sore or worn by rubbing
CHAFER, -S *n* large beetle
CHAFES ▶ **chafe**
CHAFF, -ED, -S *n* grain husks ▷ *vb* tease good-naturedly
CHAFFER, -S *vb* haggle
CHAFFERY *n* bargaining
CHAFFIER ▶ **chaffy**
CHAFFING ▶ **chaff**
CHAFFRON *same as* ▶ **chamfron**
CHAFFS ▶ **chaff**
CHAFFY, CHAFFIER ▶ **chaff**
CHAFING ▶ **chafe**
CHAFT, -S *n* jaw
CHAGAN, -S *n* Mongolian royal or imperial title
CHAGRIN, -S *n* annoyance and disappointment ▷ *vb* embarrass and annoy
CHAI, -S *n* tea, esp as made in India with added spices
CHAIN, -ED, -ING, -S *n* flexible length of connected metal links ▷ *vb* restrict or fasten with or as if with a chain
CHAINE, -S *adj* (of a dance turn) producing a full rotation for every two steps taken ▷ *vb* produce a full rotation for every two steps taken

CHAINED ▶ **chain**
CHAINER, -S *n* person who chains
CHAINES ▶ **chaine**
CHAINING ▶ **chain**
CHAINLET *n* small chain
CHAINMAN, CHAINMEN *n* person who does the chaining in a survey
CHAINS ▶ **chain**
CHAINSAW *n* motor-driven saw with teeth linked in a continuous chain ▷ *vb* operate a chainsaw
CHAIR, -ED, -ING, -S *n* seat with a back, for one person ▷ *vb* preside over (a meeting)
CHAIRMAN, CHAIRMEN *n* man in charge of a company or a meeting ▷ *vb* act as chairman of
CHAIRS ▶ **chair**
CHAIS ▶ **chai**
CHAISE, -S *n* light horse-drawn carriage
CHAKRA, -S *n* (in yoga) any of the seven major energy centres in the body
CHAL, -S *n* in Romany, person or fellow
CHALAH, -S, CHALOT, CHALOTH *same as* ▶ **challah**
CHALAN, -ED, -S *vb* (in India) to cause an accused person to appear before a magistrate ▷ *n* invoice, pass, or voucher
CHALAZA, -E, -S *n* one of a pair of spiral threads holding the yolk of a bird's egg in position
CHALAZAL ▶ **chalaza**
CHALAZAS ▶ **chalaza**
CHALAZIA ▶ **chalazion**
CHALCID, -S *n* type of tiny insect
CHALDER, -S *n* former Scottish dry measure
CHALDRON *n* unit of capacity equal to 36 bushels
CHALEH, -S *same as* ▶ **challah**
CHALET, -S *n* kind of Swiss wooden house with a steeply sloping roof
CHALICE, -S *n* large goblet
CHALICED *adj* (of plants) having cup-shaped flowers
CHALICES ▶ **chalice**
CHALK, -ED, -ING, -S *n* soft white rock consisting of calcium carbonate ▷ *vb* draw or mark with chalk
CHALKIER ▶ **chalky**
CHALKING ▶ **chalk**

CHALKPIT n quarry for chalk

CHALKS ▸ **chalk**

CHALKY, CHALKIER ▸ **chalk**

CHALLA, -S same as ▸ **challah**

CHALLAH, -S, CHALLOT, CHALLOTH n type of bread

CHALLAN, -S same as ▸ **chalan**

CHALLAS ▸ **challa**

CHALLIE, -S same as ▸ **challis**

CHALLIS n lightweight plain-weave fabric

CHALLOT ▸ **challah**

CHALLOTH ▸ **challah**

CHALLY same as ▸ **challis**

CHALONE, -S n any internal secretion that inhibits a physiological process or function

CHALONIC ▸ **chalone**

CHALOT ▸ **chalah**

CHALOTH ▸ **chalah**

CHALS ▸ **chal**

CHALUPA, -S n Mexican dish

CHALUTZ n member of an organization of immigrants to Israeli agricultural settlements

CHAM, -S an archaic word for ▸ **khan**

CHAMADE, -S n (formerly) a signal by drum or trumpet inviting an enemy to a parley

CHAMBER n hall used for formal meetings ▸ vb act lasciviously

CHAMBERS pl n a judge's room for hearing private cases not taken in open court

CHAMBRAY n smooth light fabric of cotton, linen, etc, with white weft and a coloured warp

CHAMBRE adj (of wine) at room temperature

CHAMELOT same as ▸ **camlet**

CHAMETZ n leavened food which may not be eaten during Passover

CHAMFER, -S same as ▸ **chase**

CHAMFRON n piece of armour for a horse's head

CHAMISA, -S n American shrub

CHAMISAL n place overgrown with chamiso

CHAMISAS ▸ **chamisa**

CHAMISE, -S same as ▸ **chamiso**

CHAMISO, -S n four-wing saltbush

CHAMLET, -S same as ▸ **camlet**

CHAMMY, CHAMMIED, CHAMMIES same as ▸ **chamois**

CHAMOIS n small mountain antelope or a piece of leather from its skin, used for polishing ▸ vb polish with a chamois

CHAMOIX same as ▸ **chamois**

CHAMP, -ED, -ING, -S vb chew noisily

CHAMPAC, -S n type of tree

CHAMPACA same as ▸ **champac**

CHAMPACS ▸ **champac**

CHAMPAK, -S same as ▸ **champac**

CHAMPART n granting of land to a person for a portion of the crops

CHAMPAS n champagne

CHAMPED ▸ **champ**

CHAMPER ▸ **champ**

CHAMPERS n champagne

CHAMPIER ▸ **champy**

CHAMPING ▸ **champ**

CHAMPION n overall winner of a competition ▸ vb support ▸ adj excellent ▸ adv very well

CHAMPS ▸ **champ**

CHAMPY, CHAMPIER adj (of earth) churned up (by cattle, for example)

CHAMS ▸ **cham**

CHANA, -S n (in Indian cookery) chickpeas

CHANCE, -D, -S, CHANCING n likelihood, probability ▸ vb risk, hazard

CHANCEL, -S n part of a church containing the altar and choir

CHANCER, -S n unscrupulous or dishonest opportunist

CHANCERY n Lord Chancellor's court, now a division of the High Court of Justice

CHANCES ▸ **chance**

CHANCEY same as ▸ **chancy**

CHANCIER ▸ **chancy**

CHANCILY ▸ **chancy**

CHANCING ▸ **chance**

CHANCRE, -S n small hard growth

CHANCY, CHANCIER adj uncertain, risky

CHANDLER n dealer, esp in ships' supplies

CHANFRON same as ▸ **chamfron**

CHANG, -S n loud discordant noise

CHANGA interj in Indian English, an expression of approval or agreement

CHANGE, -D, -S, CHANGING n becoming different ▸ vb make or become different

CHANGER, -S ▸ **change**

CHANGES ▸ **change**

CHANGEUP n type of baseball pitch

CHANGING ▸ **change**

CHANGS ▸ **chang**

CHANK, -S n shell of several types of sea conch, used to make bracelets

CHANNEL, -S n band of broadcasting frequencies ▸ vb direct or convey through a channel

CHANNER, -S n gravel

CHANOYO, -S variant of ▸ **chado**

CHANOYU, -S same as ▸ **chado**

CHANSON, -S n song

CHANT, -ED, -ING, -S vb utter or sing (a slogan or psalm) ▸ n rhythmic or repetitious slogan

CHANTAGE n blackmail

CHANTED ▸ **chant**

CHANTER, -S n (on bagpipes) pipe on which the melody is played

CHANTEY, -S the usual US spelling of ▸ **shanty**

CHANTIE n chamber pot

CHANTIES ▸ **chanty**

CHANTING ▸ **chant**

CHANTOR, -S same as ▸ **chanter**

CHANTRY n endowment for the singing of Masses for the founder

CHANTS ▸ **chant**

CHANTY, CHANTIES same as ▸ **shanty**

CHAO n Vietnamese rice porridge

CHAOLOGY n study of chaos theory

CHAORDIC adj combining elements of chaos and order

CHAOS, -ES n complete disorder or confusion

CHAOTIC ▸ **chaos**

CHAP, -PED, -PING, -S n man or boy ▸ vb (of the skin) to make or become raw and cracked, esp by exposure to cold

CHAPATI, -S n (in Indian cookery) flat thin unleavened bread

CHAPATTI same as ▸ **chapati**

CHAPBOOK n book of popular ballads, stories, etc, formerly sold by chapmen or pedlars

CHAPE, -S n metal tip or trimming for a scabbard

CHAPEAU, -S, -X n hat

CHAPEL, -S n place of worship with its own altar, within a church

CHAPELRY n district legally assigned to and served by an Anglican chapel

CHAPELS ▸ **chapel**

CHAPERON n older or married woman who supervises a young unmarried woman ▷ vb act as a chaperon to

CHAPES ▸ **chape**

CHAPESS n woman

CHAPITER same as ▸ **capital**

CHAPKA, -S same as ▸ **czapka**

CHAPLAIN n clergyman or clergywoman attached to a chapel, military body, or institution

CHAPLESS adj lacking a lower jaw

CHAPLET, -S n garland for the head ▷ vb create a garland

CHAPMAN, CHAPMEN n travelling pedlar

CHAPPAL, -S n one of a pair of sandals, usually of leather, worn in India

CHAPPATI same as ▸ **chapati**

CHAPPED ▸ **chap**

CHAPPESS same as ▸ **chapess**

CHAPPIE, -S n man or boy

CHAPPIER ▸ **chappy**

CHAPPIES ▸ **chappie**

CHAPPING ▸ **chap**

CHAPPY, CHAPPIER adj (of skin) chapped

CHAPS ▸ **chap**

CHAPT adj chapped

CHAPTER, -S n division of a book ▷ vb divide into chapters

CHAPTREL n capital of a pillar supporting an arch

CHAQUETA n South American cowboy jacket

CHAR, -RED, -RING, -S vb blacken by partial burning ▷ n charwoman

CHARA n type of green freshwater algae

CHARACID same as ▸ **characin**

CHARACIN n type of small carnivorous freshwater fish of Central and S America and Africa

CHARACT, -S n distinctive mark

CHARADE n absurd pretence

CHARADES n game in which teams act out each syllable of a word or phrase

CHARANGA n type of orchestra used in performing traditional Cuban music

CHARANGO n Andean ten-stringed mandolin

CHARAS, -ES another name for ▸ **hashish**

CHARCOAL n black substance formed by partially burning wood ▷ adj very dark grey ▷ vb write, draw, or blacken with charcoal

CHARD, -S n variety of beet

CHARE, -D, -S, CHARING same as ▸ **char**

CHARET, -S obsolete variant of ▸ **chariot**

CHARETTE n public brainstorming session

CHARGE, -D, -S vb ask as a price ▷ n price charged

CHARGER, -S n device for charging an accumulator

CHARGES ▸ **charge**

CHARGING n act of charging

CHARIDEE n jocular spelling of charity, as pronounced in a mid-Atlantic accent

CHARIER ▸ **chary**

CHARIEST ▸ **chary**

CHARILY adv cautiously

CHARING ▸ **chare**

CHARIOT, -S n two-wheeled horse-drawn vehicle ▷ vb ride in a chariot

CHARISM, -S same as ▸ **charisma**

CHARISMA n person's power to attract or influence people

CHARISMS ▸ **charism**

CHARITY n organization that gives help, such as money or food, to those in need

CHARK, -ED, -ING, -S vb char

CHARKA, -S same as ▸ **charkha**

CHARKED ▸ **chark**

CHARKHA, -S n (in India) a spinning wheel, esp for cotton

CHARKING ▸ **chark**

CHARKS ▸ **chark**

CHARLADY same as > **charwoman**

CHARLEY, -S n as in **charley horse** muscle stiffness after strenuous exercise

CHARLIE, -S n fool

CHARLIER n as in **charlier shoe** special light horseshoe

CHARLIES ▸ **charlie**

CHARLOCK n weed with hairy leaves and yellow flowers

CHARM, -S n attractive quality ▷ vb attract, delight

CHARMED adj delighted or fascinated

CHARMER, -S n attractive person

CHARMFUL adj highly charming or enchanting

CHARMING adj attractive

CHARMS ▸ **charm**

CHARNECO n type of sweet wine

CHARNEL, -S adj ghastly ▷ n ghastly thing

CHAROSET n dish eaten at Passover

CHARPAI, -S same as ▸ **charpoy**

CHARPIE, -S n lint pieces used to make surgical dressings

CHARPOY, -S n type of bedstead

CHARQUI, -S n meat, esp beef, cut into strips and dried

CHARQUID ▸ **charqui**

CHARQUIS ▸ **charqui**

CHARR, -S same as ▸ **char**

CHARRED ▸ **char**

CHARRIER ▸ **charry**

CHARRING ▸ **char**

CHARRO, -S n Mexican cowboy

CHARRS ▸ **charr**

CHARRY, CHARRIER adj of or relating to charcoal

CHARS ▸ **char**

CHART, -ED, -ING, -S n graph, table, or diagram showing information ▷ vb plot the course of

CHARTA, -S n charter

CHARTED ▸ **chart**

CHARTER, -S n document granting or demanding certain rights ▷ vb hire by charter

CHARTING ▸ **chart**

CHARTISM n historical reform movement in Britain

CHARTIST n supporter of chartism

CHARTS ▸ chart

CHARY, CHARIER, CHARIEST adj wary, careful

CHAS ▸ cha

CHASE, -D, -S vb run after quickly in order to catch or drive away ▷ n chasing, pursuit

CHASER, -S ▸ chase

CHASES ▸ chase

CHASING, -S ▸ chase

CHASM, -S n deep crack in the earth

CHASMAL ▸ chasm

CHASMED ▸ chasm

CHASMIC ▸ chasm

CHASMIER ▸ chasmy

CHASMS ▸ chasm

CHASMY, CHASMIER adj full of chasms

CHASSE, -D, -ED, -S n one of a series of gliding steps in ballet ▷ vb perform either of these steps

CHASSEUR n member of a unit specially trained and equipped for swift deployment ▷ adj designating or cooked in a sauce consisting of white wine and mushrooms

CHASSIS n frame, wheels, and mechanical parts of a vehicle

CHASTE, -R, -ST adj pure and modest

CHASTELY ▸ chaste

CHASTEN, -S vb subdue by criticism

CHASTER ▸ chaste

CHASTEST ▸ chaste

CHASTISE vb scold severely

CHASTITY n state of being chaste

CHASUBLE n long sleeveless robe worn by a priest when celebrating Mass

CHAT, -S, -TED, -TING n informal conversation ▷ vb have an informal conversation

CHATBOT, -S n computer program that simulates conversation with human users over the internet

CHATCHKA variant of > tchotchke

CHATCHKE same as > tchotchke

CHATEAU, -S, -X n French castle

CHATLINE n telephone service enabling callers to join in general conversation with each other

CHATON, -S n in jewellery, a stone with a reflective metal foil backing

CHATROOM n site on the internet where users have group discussions by email

CHATS ▸ chat

CHATTA, -S n umbrella

CHATTED ▸ chat

CHATTEL, -S n item of movable personal property

CHATTER, -S vb speak quickly and continuously about unimportant things ▷ n idle talk

CHATTERY adj tending to chatter

CHATTI, -S n (in India) earthenware pot

CHATTIER ▸ chatty

CHATTIES ▸ chatty

CHATTILY ▸ chatty

CHATTING ▸ chat

CHATTIS ▸ chatti

CHATTY, CHATTIER, CHATTIES adj (of a person) fond of friendly, informal conversation ▷ n (in India) earthenware pot

CHAUFE, -D, -S, CHAUFING obsolete variant of ▸ chafe

CHAUFER, -S same as ▸ chauffer

CHAUFES ▸ chaufe

CHAUFF, -ED, -S obsolete variant of ▸ chafe

CHAUFFER n small portable heater or stove

CHAUFFS ▸ chauff

CHAUFING ▸ chaufe

CHAUMER, -S n chamber

CHAUNCE, -D, -S archaic variant of ▸ chance

CHAUNGE, -D, -S archaic variant of ▸ change

CHAUNT, -ED, -S a less common variant of ▸ chant

CHAUNTER ▸ chaunt

CHAUNTRY same as ▸ chantry

CHAUNTS ▸ chaunt

CHAUSSES n tight-fitting medieval garment covering the feet and legs, usually made of chain mail

CHAUVIN, -S n chauvinist

CHAV, -S n insulting word for a young working-class person who wears casual sports clothes

CHAVE vb old dialect term for 'I have'

CHAVETTE n insulting word for a young working-class woman who wears casual sports clothes

CHAVISH ▸ chav

CHAVS ▸ chav

CHAVVY, CHAVVIER adj relating to or like a chav

CHAW, -ED, -ING, -S vb chew (tobacco), esp without swallowing it ▷ n something chewed, esp a plug of tobacco

CHAWDRON n entrails

CHAWED ▸ chaw

CHAWER, -S ▸ chaw

CHAWING ▸ chaw

CHAWK, -S n jackdaw

CHAWS ▸ chaw

CHAY, -S n plant of the madder family

CHAYA, -S same as ▸ chay

CHAYOTE, -S n tropical climbing plant

CHAYROOT n root of the chay plant

CHAYS ▸ chay

CHAZAN, -IM, -S n man employed to lead services in a synagogue

CHAZZAN, -S variant of ▸ chazan

CHAZZEN, -S same as ▸ chazzan

CHE pron dialectal form meaning 'I'

CHEAP, -ED, -ER, -EST, -ING, -S adj costing relatively little ▷ adv at very little cost ▷ n bargain ▷ vb take the cheapest option

CHEAPEN, -S vb lower the reputation of

CHEAPER ▸ cheap

CHEAPEST ▸ cheap

CHEAPIE, -S n something inexpensive

CHEAPING ▸ cheap

CHEAPISH ▸ cheap

CHEAPLY ▸ cheap

CHEAPO, -S n very cheap and possibly shoddy thing

CHEAPS ▸ cheap

CHEAPY same as ▸ cheapie

CHEAT, -ED, -S vb act dishonestly to gain profit or advantage ▷ n person who cheats

CHEATER, -S ▸ cheat

CHEATERY n cheating

CHEATING ▸ cheat

CHEATS ▸ cheat

CHEBEC, -S n type of boat

CHECHAKO same as > cheechako

CHECHIA, -S n Berber skullcap

CHECK, -ED, -S vb examine or investigate ▷ n control designed to ensure accuracy

CHECKBOX n small clickable box on a computer screen

CHECKED ▸ check

CHECKER same as ▸ chequer

CHECKERS n game for two players using a checkerboard and small pieces

CHECKIER ▸ checky

CHECKING n act of checking

CHECKOFF n paying of an employee's union dues straight from their salary

CHECKOUT n counter in a supermarket, where customers pay

CHECKROW n row of plants, esp. corn ▷ vb plant in checkrows

CHECKS ▸ check

CHECKSUM n digit attached to the end of a message to verify data

CHECKUP, -S n thorough medical examination

CHECKY, CHECKIER adj having squares of alternating tinctures or furs

CHEDARIM same as ▸ chadarim

CHEDDAR, -S n type of smooth hard yellow or whitish cheese

CHEDDARY adj like cheddar cheese

CHEDDITE n type of explosive

CHEDER, CHADARIM, -S n Jewish religious education

CHEDITE, -S same as ▸ cheddite

CHEEK, -ED, -ING, -S n either side of the face below the eye ▷ vb speak impudently to

CHEEKFUL n quantity that can be held in a cheek

CHEEKIER ▸ cheeky

CHEEKILY ▸ cheeky

CHEEKING ▸ cheek

CHEEKS ▸ cheek

CHEEKY, CHEEKIER adj impudent, disrespectful

CHEEP, -ED, -ING, -S n young bird's high-pitched cry ▷ vb utter a cheep

CHEEPER, -S ▸ cheep

CHEEPING ▸ cheep

CHEEPS ▸ cheep

CHEER, -ED vb applaud or encourage with shouts ▷ n shout of applause or encouragement

CHEERER, -S ▸ cheer

CHEERFUL adj having a happy disposition

CHEERIER ▸ cheery

CHEERILY ▸ cheery

CHEERING n act of cheering

CHEERIO, -S interj goodbye ▷ n small red cocktail sausage ▷ sentence substitute farewell greeting

CHEERLED > cheerlead

CHEERLY adv cheerfully

CHEERO, -S same as ▸ cheerio

CHEERS interj drinking toast

CHEERY, CHEERIER adj cheerful

CHEESE, -D, -S, CHEESING n food made from coagulated milk curd ▷ vb stop

CHEESIER ▸ cheesy

CHEESILY ▸ cheesy

CHEESING ▸ cheese

CHEESY, CHEESIER adj like cheese

CHEETAH, -S n large fast-running spotted African wild cat

CHEEWINK same as ▸ chewink

CHEF, -ED, -FED, -FING, -ING, -S n cook in a restaurant ▷ vb work as a chef

CHEFDOM, -S n state or condition of being a chef

CHEFED ▸ chef

CHEFFED ▸ chef

CHEFFIER ▸ cheffy

CHEFFING ▸ chef

CHEFFY, CHEFFIER adj relating to or characteristic of chefs

CHEFING ▸ chef

CHEFS ▸ chef

CHEGOE, -S same as ▸ chigger

CHEKA, -S n secret police set up in Russia in 1917

CHEKIST, -S n member of the cheka

CHELA, -E, -S n disciple of a religious teacher

CHELATE, -D, -S n coordination compound ▷ adj of or possessing chelae ▷ vb form a chelate

CHELATOR ▸ chelate

CHELIPED n (on a arthropod) either of two legs which each carry a claw

CHELLUP, -S n noise

CHELOID, -S variant spelling of ▸ keloid

CHELONE, -S n hardy N American plant

CHELP, -ED, -ING, -S vb to chatter or speak out of turn

CHEM, -S n chemistry

CHEMIC, -S vb bleach ▷ n chemist

CHEMICAL n substance used in or resulting from a reaction involving changes to atoms or molecules ▷ adj of chemistry or chemicals

CHEMICS ▸ chemic

CHEMISE, -S n woman's loose-fitting slip

CHEMISM, -S n chemical action

CHEMIST, -S n shop selling medicines and cosmetics

CHEMMY, CHEMMIES n gambling card game

CHEMO, -S n short form of chemotherapy

CHEMS ▸ chem

CHEMURGY n branch of chemistry

CHENAR, -S n oriental plane tree

CHENET, -S another word for ▸ genip

CHENILLE n (fabric of) thick tufty yarn

CHENIX, -ES n ancient measure, slightly more than a quart

CHENOPOD n plant of the beetroot family

CHEQUE, -S n written order to one's bank to pay money from one's account

CHEQUER n piece used in Chinese chequers ▷ vb make irregular in colour or character

CHEQUERS n game of draughts

CHEQUES ▸ cheque

CHEQUIER ▸ chequy

CHEQUING adj as in chequing account (in Canada) account against which cheques can be drawn

CHEQUY, CHEQUIER same as ▸ checky

CHER adj dear or expensive

CHERE feminine variant of ▸ cher

CHERISH vb cling to (an idea or feeling)

CHEROOT, -S n cigar with both ends cut flat

CHERRY, CHERRIED, CHERRIER, CHERRIES n small red or black fruit with a stone ▷ adj deep red ▷ vb cheer

CHERT, -S n microcrystalline form of silica

CHERTIER ▸ cherty

CHERTS ▸ chert

CHERTY, CHERTIER ▸ chert

CHERUB, -IM, -S n angel, often represented as a winged child

CHERUBIC ▸ **cherub**
CHERUBIM ▸ **cherub**
CHERUBIN n cherub ▹ adj cherubic
CHERUBS ▸ **cherub**
CHERUP, -ED, -S same as ▸ **chirrup**
CHERVIL, -S n aniseed-flavoured herb
CHESHIRE n breed of American pig
CHESIL, -S n gravel or shingle
CHESNUT, -S rare variant of ▸ **chestnut**
CHESS, -ES n board game for two players
CHESSEL, -S n mould used in cheese-making
CHESSES ▸ **chess**
CHESSMAN, CHESSMEN n piece used in chess
CHEST, -ED, -ING, -S n front of the body, from neck to waist ▹ vb hit with the chest, as with a ball in football
CHESTFUL n amount a chest will hold
CHESTIER ▸ **chesty**
CHESTILY ▸ **chesty**
CHESTING ▸ **chest**
CHESTNUT n reddish-brown edible nut ▹ adj (of hair or a horse) reddish-brown
CHESTS ▸ **chest**
CHESTY, CHESTIER adj symptomatic of chest disease
CHETAH, -S same as ▸ **cheetah**
CHETH, -S same as ▸ **heth**
CHETNIK, -S n member of a Serbian nationalist paramilitary group
CHETRUM, -S n monetary unit in Bhutan
CHEVAL n as in **cheval glass** full-length mirror that can swivel
CHEVALET n bridge of a stringed musical instrument
CHEVEN, -S n chub
CHEVEREL n kid or goatskin leather
CHEVERIL same as ▸ **cheverel**
CHEVERON same as ▸ **chevron**
CHEVERYE same as ▸ **chiefery**
CHEVET, -S n semicircular or polygonal east end of a church
CHEVIED ▸ **chevy**
CHEVIES ▸ **chevy**

CHEVILLE n peg of a stringed musical instrument
CHEVIN, -S same as ▸ **cheven**
CHEVIOT, -S n type of British sheep reared for its wool
CHEVRE, -S n any cheese made from goats' milk
CHEVRET, -S n type of goats' cheese
CHEVRON, -S n V-shaped pattern ▹ vb make a chevron
CHEVRONY adj in heraldry, bearing chevrons
CHEVY, CHEVIED, CHEVIES, -ING same as ▸ **chivy**
CHEW, -ED, -ING, -S vb grind (food) between the teeth ▹ n act of chewing
CHEWABLE ▸ **chew**
CHEWED ▸ **chew**
CHEWER, -S ▸ **chew**
CHEWET, -S n type of meat pie
CHEWIE n chewing gum
CHEWIER ▸ **chewy**
CHEWIES ▸ **chewy**
CHEWIEST ▸ **chewy**
CHEWING ▸ **chew**
CHEWINK, -S n towhee
CHEWS ▸ **chew**
CHEWY, CHEWIER, CHEWIES, CHEWIEST adj requiring a lot of chewing ▹ n dog's rubber toy
CHEZ prep at the home of
CHHERTUM same as ▸ **chetrum**
CHI, -S n 22nd letter of the Greek alphabet

Chi is a letter of the Greek alphabet. It can also be spelt **khi**.

CHIA, -S n plant of the mint family
CHIACK, -ED, -S vb tease or banter ▹ n good-humoured banter
CHIANTI, -S n dry red Italian wine
CHIAO, -S n Chinese coin equal to one tenth of one yuan
CHIAS ▸ **chia**
CHIASM, -S same as ▸ **chiasma**
CHIASMA, -S n crossing over of two anatomical structures
CHIASMAL ▸ **chiasma**
CHIASMAS ▸ **chiasma**
CHIASMI ▸ **chiasmus**
CHIASMIC ▸ **chiasma**
CHIASMS ▸ **chiasm**
CHIASMUS, CHIASMI n reversal of the order of words in the second of two parallel phrases

CHIASTIC ▸ **chiasmus**
CHIAUS, -ED, -ES same as ▸ **chouse**
CHIB, -BED, -BING, -S vb in Scots English, stab or slash with a sharp weapon ▹ n sharp weapon
CHIBOL, -S n spring onion
CHIBOUK, -S n Turkish tobacco pipe with an extremely long stem
CHIBS ▸ **chib**
CHIC, -ER, -EST, -S adj stylish, elegant ▹ n stylishness, elegance
CHICA, -S n Spanish girl or young woman
CHICANA, -S n American female citizen of Mexican origin
CHICANE, -D, -S n obstacle in a motor-racing circuit ▹ vb deceive or trick by chicanery
CHICANER ▸ **chicane**
CHICANES ▸ **chicane**
CHICANO, -S n American male citizen of Mexican origin
CHICAS ▸ **chica**
CHICCORY variant spelling of ▸ **chicory**
CHICER ▸ **chic**
CHICEST ▸ **chic**
CHICH, -ES another word for ▸ **chickpea**
CHICHA, -S n Andean drink made from fermented maize
CHICHES ▸ **chich**
CHICHI, -ER, -ES adj affectedly pretty or stylish ▹ n quality of being affectedly pretty or stylish
CHICK, -S n baby bird
CHICKEE, -S n open-sided, thatched building on stilts
CHICKEN, -S n domestic fowl ▹ adj cowardly ▹ vb lose one's nerve
CHICKORY same as ▸ **chicory**
CHICKPEA n edible yellow pealike seed
CHICKS ▸ **chick**
CHICLE, -S n gumlike substance obtained from the sapodilla
CHICLY ▸ **chic**
CHICNESS ▸ **chic**
CHICO, -S n spiny chenopodiaceous shrub
CHICON, -S same as ▸ **chicory**
CHICORY n plant whose leaves are used in salads
CHICOS ▸ **chico**
CHICOT, -S n dead tree

CHICS ▸ chic

CHIDE, CHID, CHIDDEN, -D, -S, CHODE vb rebuke, scold

CHIDER, -S ▸ chide

CHIDES ▸ chide

CHIDING, -S ▸ chide

CHIEF, -ER, -EST, -S n head of a group of people ▷ adj most important

CHIEFDOM n any tribal social group led by a chief

CHIEFER ▸ chief

CHIEFERY n lands belonging to a chief

CHIEFESS n female chief

CHIEFEST ▸ chief

CHIEFLY adv especially ▷ adj of or relating to a chief or chieftain

CHIEFRY same as ▸ chiefery

CHIEFS ▸ chief

CHIEL, -S n young man

CHIELD, -S same as ▸ chiel

CHIELS ▸ chiel

CHIFFON, -S n fine see-through fabric ▷ adj made of chiffon

CHIFFONY adj like chiffon

CHIGETAI n variety of the Asiatic wild ass of Mongolia

CHIGGER, -S n parasitic larva of various mites

CHIGNON, -S n knot of hair pinned up at the back of the head ▷ vb make a chignon

CHIGOE, -S same as ▸ chigger

CHIGRE, -S same as ▸ chigger

CHIK, -S n slatted blind

CHIKARA, -S n Indian seven-stringed musical instrument

CHIKHOR, -S same as ▸ chukar

CHIKOR, -S same as ▸ chukar

CHIKS ▸ chik

CHILD, -ED, -ING, -REN, -S n young human being ▷ vb give birth

CHILDBED n condition of giving birth to a child

CHILDE, -S n young man of noble birth

CHILDED ▸ child

CHILDER dialect variant of ▸ children

CHILDES ▸ childe

CHILDING ▸ child

CHILDISH adj immature, silly

CHILDLY ▸ child

CHILDREN ▸ child

CHILDS ▸ child

CHILE, -S variant spelling of ▸ chilli

CHILI, -ES, -S same as ▸ chilli

CHILIAD, -S n group of one thousand

CHILIASM n belief in the Second Coming of Christ

CHILIAST ▸ chiliasm

CHILIDOG n hot dog served with chilli sauce

CHILIES ▸ chili

CHILIS ▸ chili

CHILL, -ED, -EST, -S n feverish cold ▷ vb make (something) cool or cold ▷ adj unpleasantly cold

CHILLADA n spicy Mexican dish made of fried vegetables and pulses

CHILLAX vb take rest or recreation, as from work

CHILLED ▸ chill

CHILLER, -S n cooling or refrigerating device

CHILLEST ▸ chill

CHILLI, -ES, -S n small red or green hot-tasting capsicum pod, used in cooking

CHILLIER ▸ chilly

CHILLIES ▸ chilli

CHILLILY ▸ chilly

CHILLING ▸ chill

CHILLIS ▸ chilli

CHILLS ▸ chill

CHILLUM, -S n short pipe used for smoking

CHILLY, CHILLIER adj moderately cold

CHILOPOD n type of arthropod of the class which includes the centipedes

CHIMAERA same as ▸ chimera

CHIMAR, -S same as ▸ chimere

CHIMB, -S same as ▸ chime

CHIMBLEY same as ▸ chimney

CHIMBLY same as ▸ chimney

CHIMBS ▸ chimb

CHIME, -D, -S, CHIMING n musical ringing sound of a bell or clock ▷ vb make a musical ringing sound

CHIMENEA n freestanding outdoor fireplace

CHIMER, -S ▸ chime

CHIMERA, -S n unrealistic hope or idea

CHIMERE, -S n gown worn by bishops

CHIMERIC same as ▸ chimera

CHIMERID n fish of the genus Chimaera

CHIMERS ▸ chimer

CHIMES ▸ chime

CHIMINEA n free-standing outdoor fireplace with a rounded body

CHIMING ▸ chime

CHIMLA, -S same as ▸ chimney

CHIMLEY, -S same as ▸ chimney

CHIMNEY, -S n hollow vertical structure for carrying away smoke from a fire ▷ vb climb two vertical, parallel, chimney-like rock faces

CHIMO interj Inuit greeting and toast

CHIMP, -S n chimpanzee

CHIN, -NED, -NING, -S n part of the face below the mouth ▷ vb hit someone in the chin

CHINA, -S n fine earthenware or porcelain

CHINAMAN, CHINAMEN n type of ball bowled in cricket

CHINAMPA n in Mesoamerican agriculture, an artificially created island used for growing crops

CHINAR, -S same as ▸ chenar

CHINAS ▸ china

CHINBONE n front part of the mandible which forms the chin

CHINCH, -ED, -ES n (S US) bedbug ▷ vb be frugal or miserly

CHINCHY adj tightfisted

CHINDIT, -S n Allied soldier fighting behind the Japanese lines in Burma during World War II

CHINE, -D, -S, CHINING same as ▸ chime

CHINESE adj of or relating to China

CHING, -S n high-pitched ring or chime

CHINING ▸ chine

CHINK, -ED, -ING, -S n small narrow opening ▷ vb make a light ringing sound

CHINKARA n Indian gazelle

CHINKED ▸ chink

CHINKING ▸ chink

CHINKS ▸ chink

CHINLESS adj having a receding chin

CHINNED ▸ chin

CHINNING ▸ chin

CHINO n durable cotton twill cloth

CHINOIS n conical sieve

CHINONE, -S n benzoquinone

CHINOOK, -S n wind found in the Rocky Mountains**

C

CHINOS pl n trousers made of a kind of hard-wearing cotton

CHINS ▸ chin

CHINSE, -D, -S, CHINSING vb fill the seams of a boat

CHINTS, -ES obsolete variant of ▸ chintz

CHINTZ, -ES n printed cotton fabric with a glazed finish

CHINTZY adj of or covered with chintz

CHINWAG, -S n chat

CHIP, -PED, -S n strip of potato, fried in deep fat ▸ vb break small pieces from

CHIPMUCK another word for ▸ chipmunk

CHIPMUNK n small squirrel-like N American rodent with a striped back

CHIPOTLE n dried chilli pepper

CHIPPED ▸ chip

CHIPPER, -S vb chirp or chatter ▸ adj cheerful, lively

CHIPPIE same as ▸ chippy

CHIPPIER ▸ chippy

CHIPPIES ▸ chippy

CHIPPING ▸ chip

CHIPPY, CHIPPIER, CHIPPIES n fish-and-chip shop ▸ adj resentful or oversensitive about being perceived as inferior

CHIPS ▸ chip

CHIPSET, -S n highly integrated circuit on the motherboard of a computer

CHIRAGRA n gout occurring in the hands

CHIRAL ▸ chirality

CHIRK, -ED, -ER, -EST, -ING, -S vb creak, like a door ▸ adj high-spirited

CHIRL, -ED, -ING, -S vb warble

CHIRM, -ED, -ING, -S n chirping of birds ▸ vb (esp of a bird) to chirp

CHIRO, -S n informal name for chiropractor

CHIRP, -ED, -ING, -S vb (of a bird or insect) make a short high-pitched sound ▸ n chirping sound

CHIRPER, -S ▸ chirp

CHIRPIER ▸ chirpy

CHIRPILY ▸ chirpy

CHIRPING n act of chirping

CHIRPS ▸ chirp

CHIRPY, CHIRPIER adj lively and cheerful

CHIRR, -ED, -ING, -S vb (esp of certain insects, such as crickets) to make a shrill trilled sound ▸ n sound of chirring

CHIRRE, -S same as ▸ chirr

CHIRRED ▸ chirr

CHIRREN pl n dialect form of children

CHIRRES ▸ chirre

CHIRRING ▸ chirr

CHIRRS ▸ chirr

CHIRRUP, -S vb (of some birds) to chirp repeatedly ▸ n chirruping sound

CHIRRUPY adj making chirping sounds

CHIRT, -ED, -ING, -S vb squirt

CHIRU, -S n Tibetan antelope

CHIS ▸ chi

CHISEL, -S n metal tool with a sharp end for shaping wood or stone ▸ vb carve or form with a chisel

CHISELED same as > chiselled

CHISELER ▸ chisel

CHISELS ▸ chisel

CHIT, -S, -TED, -TING n short official note, such as a receipt ▸ vb sprout

CHITAL, -S n type of deer

CHITCHAT n chat, gossip ▸ vb gossip

CHITIN, -S n outer layer of the bodies of arthropods

CHITLIN, -S n pig intestine cooked and served as a dish

CHITLING > chitlins

CHITLINS ▸ chitlin

CHITON, -S n (in ancient Greece and Rome) a loose woollen tunic

CHITOSAN n polysaccharide derived from chitin

CHITS ▸ chit

CHITTED ▸ chit

CHITTER, -S vb twitter or chirp

CHITTIER ▸ chitty

CHITTIES ▸ chitty

CHITTING ▸ chit

CHITTY, CHITTIER, CHITTIES adj childish ▸ vb sprout

CHIV, -S, -VED, -VING n knife ▸ vb stab (someone)

CHIVALRY n courteous behaviour, esp by men towards women

CHIVAREE n charivari ▸ vb perform a chivaree

CHIVARI same as ▸ charivari

CHIVE, -D, CHIVING n small Eurasian plant ▸ vb file or cut off

CHIVES same as ▸ chive

CHIVIED ▸ chivy

CHIVIES ▸ chivy

CHIVING ▸ chive

CHIVS ▸ chiv

CHIVVED ▸ chiv

CHIVVIED ▸ chivvy

CHIVVIES ▸ chivvy

CHIVVING ▸ chiv

CHIVVY, CHIVVIED, CHIVVIES same as ▸ chivy

CHIVY, CHIVIED, CHIVIES, -ING vb harass or nag ▸ n hunt

CHIZ, -ZED, -ZES, -ZING n cheat ▸ vb cheat

CHIZZ same as ▸ chiz

CHIZZED ▸ chiz

CHIZZES ▸ chiz

CHIZZING ▸ chiz

CHLAMYS n woollen cloak worn by ancient Greek soldiers

CHLOASMA n patches of darker colour on a person's skin

CHLORAL, -S n colourless oily liquid with a pungent odour

CHLORATE n type of chemical salt

CHLORDAN same as > chlordane

CHLORIC adj of or containing chlorine in the pentavalent state

CHLORID, -S n type of chlorine compound

CHLORIDE n compound of chlorine and another substance

CHLORIDS ▸ chlorid

CHLORIN, -S same as ▸ chlorine

CHLORINE n strong-smelling greenish-yellow gaseous element, used to disinfect water

CHLORINS ▸ chlorin

CHLORITE n any of a group of green soft secondary minerals

CHLOROUS adj of or containing chlorine in the trivalent state

CHOANA, -E n posterior nasal aperture

CHOBDAR, -S n in India and Nepal, king's macebearer or attendant

CHOC, -S short form of > chocolate

CHOCCY, CHOCCIER, CHOCCIES n chocolate ▸ adj made of, tasting of, smelling of, or resembling chocolate

CHOCHO, -S *same as* ▸ **chayote**

CHOCK, -ED, -ING, -S *n* block or wedge used to prevent a heavy object from moving ▹ *vb* secure by a chock ▹ *adv* as closely or tightly as possible

CHOCKER *adj* full up

CHOCKERS *adj* Australian term meaning full up, packed

CHOCKFUL *adj* filled to capacity

CHOCKIE, -R, -S *n* chocolate ▹ *adj* like chocolate

CHOCKING ▸ **chock**

CHOCKO, -S *same as* ▸ **choco**

CHOCKS ▸ **chock**

CHOCKY *n* chocolate ▹ *adj* like chocolate

CHOCO, -S *n* member of the Australian army

CHOCS ▸ **choc**

CHOCTAW, -S *n* movement in ice-skating

CHODE ▸ **chide**

CHOENIX *same as* ▸ **chenix**

CHOG, -S *n* core of a piece of fruit

CHOICE, -R, -S, -ST *n* choosing ▹ *adj* of high quality

CHOICELY ▸ **choice**

CHOICER ▸ **choice**

CHOICES ▸ **choice**

CHOICEST ▸ **choice**

CHOIL, -S *n* end of a knife blade next to the handle

CHOIR, -ED, -ING, -S *n* organized group of singers, esp in church ▹ *vb* sing in chorus

CHOIRBOY *n* boy who sings in a church choir

CHOIRED ▸ **choir**

CHOIRING ▸ **choir**

CHOIRMAN, CHOIRMEN *n* man who sings in a choir

CHOIRS ▸ **choir**

CHOKE, -S, CHOKING *vb* hinder or stop the breathing of (a person) by strangling or smothering ▹ *n* device found in a petrol engine

CHOKED *adj* disappointed or angry

CHOKER, -S *n* tight-fitting necklace

CHOKES ▸ **choke**

CHOKEY, -S, CHOKIER, CHOKIEST *n* slang word for prison ▹ *adj* involving, caused by, or causing choking

CHOKIDAR *n* in India, a gatekeeper

CHOKIER ▸ **chokey**

CHOKIES ▸ **choky**

CHOKIEST ▸ **chokey**

CHOKING ▸ **choke**

CHOKO, -S *n* pear-shaped fruit of a tropical American vine, eaten as a vegetable

CHOKRA, -S *n* in India, a boy or young man

CHOKRI, -S *n* in India, a girl or young woman

CHOKY, CHOKIES *same as* ▸ **chokey**

CHOLA, -S *n* long, loose Sikh robe

CHOLATE, -S *n* salt of cholic acid

CHOLEMIA *same as* > **cholaemia**

CHOLENT, -S *n* meal prepared on Friday and left to cook until eaten for Sabbath lunch

CHOLER, -S *n* bad temper

CHOLERA, -S *n* serious infectious disease

CHOLERIC *adj* bad-tempered

CHOLERS ▸ **choler**

CHOLI, -S *n* short-sleeved bodice, as worn by Indian women

CHOLIAMB *n* imperfect iambic trimeter, with a spondee as the last foot

CHOLIC *adj* as in **cholic acid** crystalline acid found in bile

CHOLINE, -S *n* colourless viscous soluble alkaline substance present in animal tissues

CHOLIS ▸ **choli**

CHOLLA, -S *n* type of spiny cactus

CHOLLERS *pl n* jowls or cheeks

CHOLTRY *n* caravanserai

CHOMETZ *same as* ▸ **chametz**

CHOMMIE, -S *n* (in informal South African English) friend

CHOMP, -ED, -ING, -S *vb* chew noisily ▹ *n* act or sound of chewing in this manner

CHOMPER, -S ▸ **chomp**

CHOMPING ▸ **chomp**

CHOMPS ▸ **chomp**

CHON, -S *n* North and South Korean monetary unit

CHONDRAL *adj* of or relating to cartilage

CHONDRE, -S *another word for* > **chondrule**

CHONDRI ▸ **chondrus**

CHONDRIN *n* resilient translucent bluish-white substance that forms the matrix of cartilage

CHONDRUS, CHONDRI *n* cartilage

CHONS ▸ **chon**

CHOOF, -ED, -ING, -S *vb* go away

CHOOK, -ED, -ING, -S *n* hen or chicken ▹ *vb* make the sound of a hen of chicken

CHOOKIE, -S *same as* ▸ **chook**

CHOOKING ▸ **chook**

CHOOKS ▸ **chook**

CHOOM, -S *n* Englishman

CHOON, -S *n* slang term for music that one likes

CHOOSE, -S, CHOOSING, CHOSEN *vb* select from a number of alternatives

CHOOSER, -S ▸ **choose**

CHOOSES ▸ **choose**

CHOOSEY *same as* ▸ **choosy**

CHOOSIER ▸ **choosy**

CHOOSILY *adv* in a fussy or choosy way

CHOOSING ▸ **choose**

CHOOSY, CHOOSIER *adj* fussy, hard to please

CHOP, -PED, -S *vb* cut with a blow from an axe or knife ▹ *n* cutting or sharp blow

CHOPIN, -S *same as* ▸ **chopine**

CHOPINE, -S *n* sandal-like shoe popular in the 18th century

CHOPINS ▸ **chopin**

CHOPPED ▸ **chop**

CHOPPER, -S *n* helicopter ▹ *vb* travel by helicopter

CHOPPIER ▸ **choppy**

CHOPPILY ▸ **choppy**

CHOPPING ▸ **chop**

CHOPPY, CHOPPIER *adj* (of the sea) fairly rough

CHOPS ▸ **chop**

CHORAGI ▸ **choragus**

CHORAGIC ▸ **choragus**

CHORAGUS, CHORAGI *n* leader of a chorus

CHORAL, -S *adj* of a choir ▹ *n* slow stately hymn tune

CHORALE, -S *n* slow stately hymn tune

CHORALLY ▸ **choral**

CHORALS ▸ **choral**

CHORD, -S *n* straight line joining two points on a curve ▹ *vb* provide (a melodic line) with chords

CHORDA, -E *n* in anatomy, a cord

CHORDAL ▸ **chord**

CHORDATE *n* type of animal which includes the vertebrates

CHORDED ▸ chord

CHORDING n distribution of chords throughout a piece of harmony

CHORDS ▸ chord

CHORE, -D, -S, CHORING n routine task ▷ vb carry out chores

CHOREA, -S n disorder of the nervous system

CHOREAL ▸ chorea

CHOREAS ▸ chorea

CHOREBOY n boy who does chores

CHORED ▸ chore

CHOREE, -S n trochee

CHOREGI ▸ choregus

CHOREGIC ▸ choregus

CHOREGUS, CHOREGI n in ancient Greece, the producer and financier of a dramatist's works

CHOREIC ▸ chorea

CHOREMAN, CHOREMEN n handyman

CHOREOID adj resembling chorea

CHORES ▸ chore

CHOREUS same as ▸ choree

CHORIA ▸ chorion

CHORIAL ▸ chorion

CHORIAMB n metrical foot used in classical verse

CHORIC adj in the manner of a chorus

CHORINE, -S n young woman in a chorus line

CHORING ▸ chore

CHORIOID same as ▸ choroid

CHORION, CHORIA, -S n outer membrane forming a sac around an embryo

CHORISIS, CHORISES n multiplication of leaves etc by branching or splitting

CHORISM, -S ▸ chorisis

CHORIST, -S n choir member

CHORIZO, -S n kind of highly seasoned pork sausage of Spain or Mexico

CHOROID, -S adj resembling the chorion, esp in being vascular ▷ n vascular membrane of the eyeball

CHORRIE, -S n dilapidated old car

CHORTEN, -S n Buddhist shrine

CHORTLE, -D, -S vb chuckle in amusement ▷ n amused chuckle

CHORTLER ▸ chortle

CHORTLES ▸ chortle

CHORUS, -ED, -ES n large choir ▷ vb sing or say together

CHOSE, -S n item of property

CHOSEN ▸ choose

CHOSES ▸ chose

CHOTA adj (in British Empire Indian usage) small

CHOTT, -S variant spelling of ▸ shott

CHOU, -X n type of cabbage

CHOUGH, -S n large black Eurasian and N African bird of the crow family

CHOULTRY same as ▸ choltry

CHOUNTER same as ▸ chunter

CHOUSE, -D, -S, CHOUSING vb cheat

CHOUSER, -S ▸ chouse

CHOUSES ▸ chouse

CHOUSH, -ES n Turkish messenger

CHOUSING ▸ chouse

CHOUT, -S n blackmail

CHOUX ▸ chou

CHOW, -ED, -ING, -S n thick-coated dog with a curled tail, orig from China ▷ vb eat

CHOWCHOW same as ▸ chow

CHOWDER, -S n thick soup containing clams or fish ▷ vb make a chowder of

CHOWDOWN n act of eating a lot of food

CHOWED ▸ chow

CHOWING ▸ chow

CHOWK, -S n marketplace or market area

CHOWRI, -ES, -S n fly-whisk

CHOWRY same as ▸ chowri

CHOWS ▸ chow

CHOWSE, -D, -S, CHOWSING same as ▸ chouse

CHOWTIME n mealtime

CHRESARD n amount of water present in the soil that is available to plants

CHRISM, -S n consecrated oil used for anointing in some churches

CHRISMA ▸ chrismon

CHRISMAL n chrism container

CHRISMON, CHRISMA n monogram and symbol of Christ's name

CHRISMS ▸ chrism

CHRISOM, -S same as ▸ chrism

CHRISTEN vb baptize

CHRISTIE same as ▸ christy

CHRISTOM same as ▸ chrisom

CHRISTY n skiing turn for stopping or changing direction quickly

CHROMA, -S n attribute of a colour

CHROMATE n any salt or ester of chromic acid

CHROME, -D, -S, -ING n anything plated with chromium ▷ vb plate with chromium ▷ adj of or having the appearance of chrome

CHROMEL, -S n nickel-based alloy

CHROMENE n chemical compound

CHROMES ▸ chrome

CHROMIC adj of or containing chromium in the trivalent state

CHROMIDE n any member of the cichlid family of fish

CHROMIER ▸ chromy

CHROMING ▸ chrome

CHROMISE same as ▸ chromize

CHROMITE n brownish-black mineral which is the only commercial source of chromium

CHROMIUM n grey metallic element used in steel alloys and for electroplating

CHROMIZE vb chrome-plate

CHROMO, -S n picture produced by lithography

CHROMOLY n type of steel alloy

CHROMOS ▸ chromo

CHROMOUS adj of or containing chromium in the divalent state

CHROMY, CHROMIER ▸ chrome

CHROMYL, -S n type of divalent radical

CHRONAXY same as > chronaxie

CHRONIC, -S adj (of an illness) lasting a long time ▷ n chronically ill patient

CHRONON, -S n unit of time

CHTHONIC same as > chthonian

CHUB, -S n European freshwater fish of the carp family

CHUBASCO n in Mexico, a hurricane

CHUBBIER ▸ chubby

CHUBBILY ▸ chubby

CHUBBY, CHUBBIER adj plump and round

CHUBS ▸ chub

CHUCK, -ED, -ING, -S vb throw ▷ n cut of beef from the neck to the shoulder

CHUCKER, -S n person who throws something

CHUCKIE, -S *n* small stone

CHUCKING ▸ chuck

CHUCKLE, -D, -S *vb* laugh softly ▷ *n* soft laugh

CHUCKLER ▸ chuckle

CHUCKLES ▸ chuckle

CHUCKS ▸ chuck

CHUCKY *same as* ▸ chuckie

CHUDDAH, -S *same as* ▸ chuddar

CHUDDAR, -S *n* large shawl or veil

CHUDDER, -S *same as* ▸ chuddar

CHUDDIES *pl n* underpants

CHUDDY *n* chewing gum

CHUFA, -S *n* type of sedge

CHUFF, -ER, -EST, -ING, -S *vb* (of a steam engine) move while making a puffing sound ▷ *n* puffing sound of or as if of a steam engine ▷ *adj* boorish

CHUFFED *adj* very pleased

CHUFFER ▸ chuff

CHUFFEST ▸ chuff

CHUFFIER ▸ chuffy

CHUFFING ▸ chuff

CHUFFS ▸ chuff

CHUFFY, CHUFFIER *adj* boorish and heavy

CHUG, -GED, -S *n* short dull sound like the noise of an engine ▷ *vb* operate or move with this sound

CHUGALUG *vb* gulp down a drink in one go

CHUGGED ▸ chug

CHUGGER, -S ▸ chug

CHUGGING *n* act of drinking a liquid quickly

CHUGS ▸ chug

CHUKAR, -S *n* common Indian partridge

CHUKKA, -S *n* period of play in polo

CHUKKAR, -S *same as* ▸ chukka

CHUKKAS ▸ chukka

CHUKKER, -S *same as* ▸ chukka

CHUKOR, -S *same as* ▸ chukar

CHUM, -MED, -MING, -S *n* close friend ▷ *vb* be or become an intimate friend (of)

CHUMASH *n* printed book containing one of the Five Books of Moses

CHUMLEY, -S *same as* ▸ chimney

CHUMMAGE *n* formerly, fee paid by a prisoner for sole occupancy of a cell

CHUMMED ▸ chum

CHUMMIER ▸ chummy

CHUMMIES ▸ chummy

CHUMMILY ▸ chummy

CHUMMING ▸ chum

CHUMMY, CHUMMIER, CHUMMIES *adj* friendly ▷ *n* chum

CHUMP, -ED, -S *n* stupid person ▷ *vb* chew noisily

CHUMPING *n* collecting wood for bonfires on Guy Fawkes Day

CHUMPS ▸ chump

CHUMS ▸ chum

CHUMSHIP *n* friendship

CHUNDER, -S *vb* slang word for vomit

CHUNK, -ED, -S *n* thick solid piece ▷ *vb* break up into chunks

CHUNKIER ▸ chunky

CHUNKILY ▸ chunky

CHUNKING *n* mnemonic technique involving grouping together of a number of items

CHUNKS ▸ chunk

CHUNKY, CHUNKIER *adj* (of a person) broad and heavy

CHUNNEL, -S *n* rail tunnel linking England and France

CHUNNER, -S *same as* ▸ chunter

CHUNTER, -S *vb* mutter or grumble incessantly in a meaningless fashion

CHUPATI, -S *same as* ▸ chupatti

CHUPATTI *variant spelling of* ▸ chapati

CHUPATTY *same as* ▸ chupatti

CHUPPA, -S *variant of* ▸ chuppah

CHUPPAH, -S, CHUPPOT, CHUPPOTH *n* canopy under which a marriage is performed

CHUPPAS ▸ chuppa

CHUPPOT ▸ chuppah

CHUPPOTH ▸ chuppah

CHUR *interj* expression of agreement

CHURCH, -ED, -ES *n* building for public Christian worship ▷ *vb* bring someone to church for special ceremonies

CHURCHLY *adj* appropriate to, associated with, or suggestive of church life and customs

CHURCHY *adj* like a church, church service, etc

CHURIDAR *n* as in churidar pyjamas long tight-fitting

trousers, worn by Indian men and women

CHURINGA *n* sacred amulet of the native Australians

CHURL, -S *n* surly ill-bred person

CHURLISH *adj* surly and rude

CHURLS ▸ churl

CHURN, -ED, -S *n* machine in which cream is shaken to make butter ▷ *vb* stir (cream) vigorously to make butter

CHURNER, -S ▸ churn

CHURNING *n* quantity of butter churned at any one time

CHURNS ▸ churn

CHURR, -ED, -ING, -S *same as* ▸ chirr

CHURRO, -S *n* Spanish dough stick snack

CHURRS ▸ churr

CHURRUS *n* hemp resin

CHUSE, -D, -S, CHUSING *obsolete variant of* ▸ choose

CHUT, -S *interj* expression of surprise or annoyance ▷ *n* such an expression

CHUTE, -D, -S, CHUTING *n* steep slope down which things may be slid ▷ *vb* descend by a chute

CHUTIST, -S ▸ chute

CHUTNEE, -S *same as* ▸ chutney

CHUTNEY, -S *n* pickle made from fruit, vinegar, spices, and sugar

CHUTS ▸ chut

CHUTZPA, -S *same as* ▸ chutzpah

CHUTZPAH *n* unashamed self-confidence

CHUTZPAS ▸ chutzpa

CHYACK, -ED, -S *same as* ▸ chiack

CHYLDE *archaic word for* ▸ child

CHYLE, -S *n* milky fluid formed in the small intestine during digestion

CHYLIFY *vb* be turned into chyle

CHYLOUS ▸ chyle

CHYLURIA *n* presence of chyle in urine

CHYME, -S *n* partially digested food that leaves the stomach

CHYMIC, -S *same as* ▸ chemic

CHYMIFY *vb* form into chyme

CHYMIST, -S *same as* ▸ chemist

CHYMOSIN *another name for* ▸ **rennin**

CHYMOUS ▸ **chyme**

CHYND *adj* chined

CHYPRE, -S *n* perfume made from sandalwood

CHYRON, -S *n* caption superimposed on a TV screen

CHYTRID, -S *n* variety of fungus

CIABATTA, CIABATTE *n* type of bread made with olive oil

CIAO *an informal word for* ▸ **hello**

CIBATION *n* feeding

CIBOL, -S *same as* ▸ **chibol**

CIBORIUM, CIBORIA *n* goblet-shaped lidded vessel used to hold consecrated wafers in Holy Communion

CIBOULE, -S *same as* ▸ **chibol**

CICADA, -E, -S *n* large insect that makes a high-pitched drone

CICALA, -S, CICALE *same as* ▸ **cicada**

CICATRIX *n* scar

CICELY, CICELIES *n* type of plant

CICERO, -S *n* measure for type that is somewhat larger than the pica

CICERONE, CICERONI *n* person who guides and informs sightseers ▷ *vb* act as a cicerone

CICEROS ▸ **cicero**

CICHLID, -S *n* type of tropical freshwater fish popular in aquariums

CICHLOID ▸ **cichlid**

CICINNUS *n* scorpioid cyme

CICLATON *n* rich material of silk and gold

CICOREE, -S *same as* ▸ **chicory**

CICUTA, -S *n* spotted hemlock

CICUTINE *same as* ▸ **coniine**

CID, -S *n* leader

CIDARIS *n* sea urchin

CIDE, -D, -S, CIDING *Shakespearean variant of* ▸ **decide**

CIDER, -S *n* alcoholic drink made from fermented apple juice

CIDERIER ▸ **cidery**

CIDERKIN *n* weak type of cider

CIDERS ▸ **cider**

CIDERY, CIDERIER *adj* like cider

CIDES ▸ **cide**

CIDING ▸ **cide**

CIDS ▸ **cid**

CIEL, -ED, -INGS, -S *same as* ▸ **ceil**

CIELING *same as* ▸ **ceiling**

CIELINGS ▸ **ciel**

CIELS ▸ **ciel**

CIERGE, -S *same as* ▸ **cerge**

CIG, -S *same as* > **cigarette**

CIGAR, -S *n* roll of cured tobacco leaves for smoking

CIGARET, -S *same as* > **cigarette**

CIGARS ▸ **cigar**

CIGGIE, -S *same as* > **cigarette**

CIGGY *same as* > **cigarette**

CIGS ▸ **cig**

CILANTRO *same as* > **coriander**

CILIA ▸ **cilium**

CILIARY *adj* of or relating to cilia

CILIATE, -S *n* type of protozoan

CILIATED ▸ **ciliate**

CILIATES ▸ **ciliate**

CILICE, -S *n* haircloth fabric or garment

CILIUM, CILIA *n* short thread projecting from a cell that causes movement

CILL, -S *variant spelling (used in the building industry) of* ▸ **sill**

CIMAR, -S *same as* ▸ **cymar**

CIMBALOM *n* type of dulcimer, esp of Hungary

CIMELIA *pl n* (especially, ecclesiastical) treasures

CIMEX, CIMICES *n* type of heteropterous insect, esp the bedbug

CIMIER, -S *n* crest of a helmet

CIMINITE *n* type of igneous rock

CIMOLITE *n* clayey, whitish mineral

CINCH, -ED, -ES *n* easy task ▷ *vb* fasten a girth around (a horse)

CINCHING ▸ **cinch**

CINCHONA *same as* ▸ **calisaya**

CINCT *adj* encircled

CINCTURE *n* something, such as a belt or girdle, that goes around another thing ▷ *vb* encircle

CINDER, -ED, -S *n* piece of material that will not burn, left after burning coal ▷ *vb* burn to cinders

CINDERY *adj* covered in cinders

CINE, -S *n* as in **cine camera** camera able to film moving pictures

CINEAST, -S *same as* ▸ **cineaste**

CINEASTE *n* enthusiast for films

CINEASTS ▸ **cineast**

CINEMA, -S *n* place for showing films

CINEOL, -S *n* colourless oily liquid with a camphor-like odour and a spicy taste

CINEOLE, -S *same as* ▸ **cineol**

CINEOLS ▸ **cineol**

CINEPLEX *n* large cinema complex

CINERARY *adj* of (someone's) ashes

CINEREA, -S *n* grey matter of the brain and nervous system

CINEREAL *adj* ashy

CINEREAS ▸ **cinerea**

CINERIN, -S *n* either of two organic compounds used as insecticides

CINES ▸ **cine**

CINGULA ▸ **cingulum**

CINGULAR *adj* ring-shaped

CINGULUM, CINGULA *n* girdle-like part of certain structures

CINNABAR *n* heavy red mineral containing mercury

CINNAMIC ▸ **cinnamon**

CINNAMON *n* spice obtained from the bark of an Asian tree

CINNAMYL *n* univalent radical of cinnamic compounds

CINQ, -S *n* number five

CINQUAIN *n* stanza of five lines

CINQUE, -S *n* number five in cards, dice, etc

CION, -S *same as* ▸ **scion**

CIOPPINO *n* Italian rich fish stew

CIPAILLE *n* type of pie traditional in Quebec

CIPHER, -ED, -S *n* system of secret writing ▷ *vb* put (a message) into secret writing

CIPHERER ▸ **cipher**

CIPHERS ▸ **cipher**

CIPHONY *n* ciphered telephony

CIPOLIN, -S *n* Italian marble with alternating white and green streaks

CIPPUS, CIPPI *n* pillar bearing an inscription

CIRCA *prep* approximately, about

CIRCAR, -S *n* in India, part of a province

CIRCITER *prep* around, about

CIRCLE, -D, -S n perfectly round geometric figure, line, or shape ▷ vb move in a circle (round)
CIRCLER, -S ▷ circle
CIRCLES ▷ circle
CIRCLET, -S n circular ornament worn on the head
CIRCLING ▷ circle
CIRCLIP, -S n type of fastener
CIRCS pl n circumstances
CIRCUIT, -S n complete route or course, esp a circular one ▷ vb make or travel in a circuit around (something)
CIRCUITY n (of speech, reasoning, etc) a roundabout or devious quality
CIRCULAR adj in the shape of a circle ▷ n letter for general distribution
CIRCUS, -ES n travelling company of acrobats, clowns, performing animals, etc
CIRCUSSY adj like a circus
CIRCUSY adj like a circus
CIRE, -S adj (of fabric) treated with a heat or wax process to make it smooth ▷ n such a surface on a fabric
CIRL, -S n bird belonging to the bunting family
CIRQUE, -S n steep-sided semicircular hollow found in mountainous areas
CIRRATE adj bearing or resembling cirri
CIRRI ▷ cirrus
CIRRIPED same as ▷ cirripede
CIRROSE same as ▷ cirrate
CIRROUS same as ▷ cirrate
CIRRUS, CIRRI, -ES n high wispy cloud
CIRSOID adj resembling a varix
CIS adj having two groups of atoms on the same side of a double bond
CISCO, -ES, -S n whitefish, esp the lake herring of cold deep lakes of North America
CISELEUR n person who is expert in ciselure
CISELURE n art or process of chasing metal
CISLUNAR adj of or relating to the space between the earth and the moon
CISSIER ▷ cissy
CISSIES ▷ cissy
CISSIEST ▷ cissy
CISSING, -S n appearance of pinholes, craters, etc, in paintwork

CISSOID, -S n type of geometric curve
CISSUS, -ES n type of climbing plant
CISSY, CISSIER, CISSIES, CISSIEST same as ▷ sissy
CIST, -S n wooden box for holding ritual objects used in ancient Rome and Greece
CISTED ▷ cist
CISTERN, -S n water tank, esp one that holds water for flushing a toilet
CISTERNA n sac or partially closed space containing body fluid, esp lymph or cerebrospinal fluid
CISTERNS ▷ cistern
CISTIC adj cist-like
CISTRON, -S n section of a chromosome that encodes a single polypeptide chain
CISTS ▷ cist
CISTUS, -ES n type of plant
CISTVAEN n pre-Christian stone coffin or burial chamber
CIT, -S n pejorative term for a town dweller
CITABLE ▷ cite
CITADEL, -S n fortress in a city
CITAL, -S n court summons
CITATION n commendation for bravery
CITATOR, -S n legal publication
CITATORY ▷ citation
CITE, -D, -S, CITING vb quote, refer to
CITEABLE ▷ cite
CITED ▷ cite
CITER, -S ▷ cite
CITES ▷ cite
CITESS, -ES n female cit
CITHARA, -S n ancient stringed musical instrument
CITHER, -S same as ▷ cittern
CITHERN, -S same as ▷ cittern
CITHERS ▷ cither
CITHREN, -S same as ▷ cithara
CITIED adj having cities
CITIES ▷ city
CITIFY, CITIFIED, CITIFIES vb cause to conform to or adopt the customs, habits, or dress of city people
CITING ▷ cite
CITIZEN, -S n native or naturalized member of a state or nation
CITO adv swiftly
CITOLA, -S same as ▷ citole
CITOLE, -S n type of medieval stringed instrument

CITRAL, -S n volatile liquid with a lemon-like odour
CITRANGE n type of acidic and aromatic orange
CITRATE, -S n any salt or ester of citric acid
CITRATED adj treated with a citrate
CITRATES ▷ citrate
CITREOUS adj of a greenish-yellow colour
CITRIC adj of or derived from citrus fruits or citric acid
CITRIN, -S n vitamin P
CITRINE, -S n brownish-yellow variety of quartz: a gemstone
CITRININ n type of mycotoxin
CITRINS ▷ citrin
CITRON, -S n lemon-like fruit of a small Asian tree
CITROUS same as ▷ citrus
CITRUS, -ES n type of tropical or subtropical tree or shrub
CITRUSSY adj having or resembling the taste or colour of a citrus fruit
CITRUSY same as ▷ citrussy
CITS ▷ cit
CITTERN, -S n medieval stringed instrument
CITY, CITIES n large or important town
CITYFY, CITYFIED, CITYFIES same as ▷ citify
CITYWARD adv towards a city
CITYWIDE adj occurring throughout a city
CIVE, -S same as ▷ chive
CIVET, -S n spotted catlike African mammal
CIVIC adj of a city or citizens
CIVICISM n principle of civil government
CIVICS n study of the rights and responsibilities of citizenship
CIVIE, -S same as ▷ civvy
CIVIL adj relating to the citizens of a state
CIVILIAN adj not belonging to the armed forces ▷ n person who is not a member of the armed forces or police
CIVILISE same as ▷ civilize
CIVILIST n civilian
CIVILITY n polite or courteous behaviour
CIVILIZE vb refine or educate (a person)
CIVILLY ▷ civil
CIVILS n civil engineering
CIVISM, -S n good citizenship

CIVVY, CIVVIES n civilian

CIZERS archaic spelling of ▶scissors

CLABBER, -S vb cover with mud

CLACH, -ED, -ES, -ING, -S n stone ▷ vb kill by stoning

CLACHAN, -S n small village

CLACHED ▶clach

CLACHES ▶clach

CLACHING ▶clach

CLACHS ▶clach

CLACK, -ED, -ING, -S n sound made by two hard objects striking each other ▷ vb make this sound

CLACKBOX n casing enclosing a clack

CLACKED ▶clack

CLACKER, -S n object that makes a clacking sound

CLACKING ▶clack

CLACKS ▶clack

CLAD, -S vb bond a metal to (another metal), esp to form a protective coat

CLADDAGH n Irish ring

CLADDED adj covered with cladding

CLADDER, -S ▶clad

CLADDIE, -S another name for ▶korari

CLADDING ▶clad

CLADE, -S n group of organisms sharing a common ancestor

CLADISM, -S ▶cladist

CLADIST, -S n proponent of cladistics

CLADODE, -S n stem resembling and functioning as a leaf

CLADS ▶clad

CLAES Scots word for ▶clothes

CLAFOUTI same as > clafoutis

CLAG, -GED, -GING, -S n sticky mud ▷ vb stick, as mud

CLAGGIER ▶claggy

CLAGGING ▶clag

CLAGGY, CLAGGIER adj stickily clinging, as mud

CLAGS ▶clag

CLAIM, -ED, -ING, -S vb assert as a fact ▷ n assertion that something is true

CLAIMANT n person who makes a claim

CLAIMED ▶claim

CLAIMER, -S ▶claim

CLAIMING ▶claim

CLAIMS ▶claim

CLAM, -MED, -MING, -S n edible shellfish with a hinged shell ▷ vb gather clams

CLAMANCY n urgency

CLAMANT adj noisy

CLAMBAKE n picnic, often by the sea, at which clams, etc, are baked

CLAMBE old variant of ▶climb

CLAMBER, -S vb climb awkwardly ▷ n climb performed in this manner

CLAME, -S archaic variant of ▶claim

CLAMLIKE ▶clam

CLAMMED ▶clam

CLAMMER, -S n person who gathers clams

CLAMMIER ▶clammy

CLAMMILY ▶clammy

CLAMMING ▶clam

CLAMMY, CLAMMIER adj unpleasantly moist and sticky

CLAMOR, -ED, -S same as ▶clamour

CLAMORER ▶clamor

CLAMORS ▶clamor

CLAMOUR, -S n loud protest ▷ vb make a loud noise or outcry

CLAMP, -ED, -S n tool with movable jaws for holding things together tightly ▷ vb fasten with a clamp

CLAMPER, -S n spiked metal frame fastened to the sole of a shoe ▷ vb tread heavily

CLAMPING n act of clamping

CLAMPS ▶clamp

CLAMS ▶clam

CLAMWORM the US name for the ▶ragworm

CLAN, -S n group of families with a common ancestor

CLANG, -ED, -S vb make a loud ringing metallic sound ▷ n ringing metallic sound

CLANGBOX n device fitted to a jet-engine to change the direction of thrust

CLANGED ▶clang

CLANGER, -S n obvious mistake

CLANGING ▶clang

CLANGOR, -S same as ▶clangour

CLANGOUR n loud continuous clanging sound ▷ vb make or produce a loud resonant noise

CLANGS ▶clang

CLANK, -ED, -S n harsh metallic sound ▷ vb make such a sound

CLANKIER ▶clanky

CLANKING ▶clank

CLANKS ▶clank

CLANKY, CLANKIER adj making clanking sounds

CLANNISH adj (of a group) tending to exclude outsiders

CLANS ▶clan

CLANSHIP n association of families under the leadership of a chieftain

CLANSMAN, CLANSMEN n man belonging to a clan

CLAP, -PED, -S, -T vb applaud by hitting the palms of one's hands sharply together ▷ n act or sound of clapping

CLAPDISH same as > clackdish

CLAPNET, -S n net that can be closed instantly by pulling a string

CLAPPED ▶clap

CLAPPER, -S n piece of metal inside a bell ▷ vb make a sound like a clapper

CLAPPING ▶clap

CLAPS ▶clap

CLAPT ▶clap

CLAPTRAP n foolish or pretentious talk

CLAQUE, -S n group of people hired to applaud

CLAQUER, -S same as ▶claqueur

CLAQUES ▶claque

CLAQUEUR n member of a claque

CLARAIN, -S n one of the four major lithotypes of banded coal

CLARENCE n closed four-wheeled horse-drawn carriage, having a glass front

CLARET, -ED, -S n dry red wine from Bordeaux ▷ adj purplish-red ▷ vb drink claret

CLARIES ▶clary

CLARIFY vb make (a matter) clear and unambiguous

CLARINET n keyed woodwind instrument with a single reed

CLARINO, CLARINI, -S adj relating to a high passage for the trumpet in 18th-century music ▷ n high register of the trumpet

CLARION, -S n obsolete high-pitched trumpet ▷ adj clear and ringing ▷ vb proclaim loudly

CLARITY n clearness

CLARKIA, -S n N American plant cultivated for its red, purple, or pink flowers

CLARO, -ES, -S n mild light-coloured cigar

CLARSACH n Celtic harp of Scotland and Ireland

CLART, -ED, -ING vb to dirty

CLARTIER ▸ **clarty**

CLARTING ▸ **clart**

CLARTS pl n lumps of mud, esp on shoes

CLARTY, CLARTIER adj dirty, esp covered in mud

CLARY, CLARIES n European plant with aromatic leaves and blue flowers

CLASH, -ED, -ES vb come into conflict ▷ n fight, argument

CLASHER, -S ▸ **clash**

CLASHES ▸ **clash**

CLASHING ▸ **clash**

CLASP, -ED, -S n device for fastening things ▷ vb grasp or embrace firmly

CLASPER, -S ▸ **clasp**

CLASPING ▸ **clasp**

CLASPS ▸ **clasp**

CLASPT old inflection of ▸ **clasp**

CLASS, -ED n group of people sharing a similar social position ▷ vb place in a class

CLASSER, -S ▸ **class**

CLASSES ▸ **classis**

CLASSIC, -S adj being a typical example of something ▷ n author, artist, or work of art of recognized excellence

CLASSICO adj (of Italian wines) coming from the centre of a specific wine-growing region

CLASSICS ▸ **classic**

CLASSIER ▸ **classy**

CLASSIFY vb divide into groups with similar characteristics

CLASSILY ▸ **classy**

CLASSING ▸ **class**

CLASSIS, CLASSES n governing body of elders or pastors

CLASSISM n belief that people from certain social or economic classes are superior to others

CLASSIST ▸ **classism**

CLASSMAN, CLASSMEN n graduate of Oxford University with a classed honours degree

CLASSON, -S n elementary atomic particle

CLASSY, CLASSIER adj stylish and elegant

CLAST, -S n fragment of a clastic rock

CLASTIC, -S adj composed of fragments ▷ n clast

CLASTS ▸ **clast**

CLAT, -S, -TED, -TING n irksome or troublesome task ▷ vb scrape

CLATCH, -ED, -ES vb move making a squelching sound

CLATS ▸ **clat**

CLATTED ▸ **clat**

CLATTER, -S n rattling noise ▷ vb make a rattling noise, as when hard objects hit each other

CLATTERY adj making a clattering sound

CLATTING ▸ **clat**

CLAUCHT, -S vb seize by force

CLAUGHT, -S same as ▸ **claucht**

CLAUSAL ▸ **clause**

CLAUSE, -S n section of a legal document

CLAUSTRA > **claustrum**

CLAUSULA n type of cadence in polyphony

CLAUT, -ED, -ING, -S same as ▸ **clat**

CLAVATE adj shaped like a club with the thicker end uppermost

CLAVATED same as ▸ **clavate**

CLAVE, -S n one of a pair of hardwood sticks struck together to make a hollow sound

CLAVECIN n harpsichord

CLAVER, -ED, -S vb talk idly ▷ n idle talk

CLAVES ▸ **clave**

CLAVI ▸ **clavus**

CLAVICLE n bone connecting the shoulder blade to the breastbone

CLAVIE, -S n tar-barrel traditionally set alight in Moray in Scotland on Hogmanay

CLAVIER, -S n any keyboard instrument

CLAVIES ▸ **clavie**

CLAVIGER n key- or club-bearer

CLAVIS n key

CLAVUS, CLAVI n corn on the toe

CLAW, -ED, -ING, -S n sharp hooked nail of a bird or beast ▷ vb tear with claws or nails

CLAWBACK n recovery of a sum of money

CLAWED ▸ **claw**

CLAWER, -S ▸ **claw**

CLAWING ▸ **claw**

CLAWLESS ▸ **claw**

CLAWLIKE adj resembling a claw or claws

CLAWS ▸ **claw**

CLAXON, -S same as ▸ **klaxon**

CLAY, -ED, -ING, -S n fine-grained earth used to make bricks and pottery ▷ vb cover or mix with clay

CLAYBANK n dull brownish-orange colour

CLAYED ▸ **clay**

CLAYEY, CLAYIER, CLAYIEST ▸ **clay**

CLAYING ▸ **clay**

CLAYISH ▸ **clay**

CLAYLIKE ▸ **clay**

CLAYMORE n large two-edged sword formerly used by Scottish Highlanders

CLAYPAN, -S n layer of stiff impervious clay situated just below the surface of the ground

CLAYS ▸ **clay**

CLAYWARE n pottery

CLEAN, -ED, -EST, -S adj free from dirt or impurities ▷ vb make (something) free from dirt ▷ adv completely

CLEANER, -S n person or thing that removes dirt

CLEANEST ▸ **clean**

CLEANING n act of cleaning something

CLEANISH adj quite clean

CLEANLY adv easily or smoothly ▷ adj habitually clean or neat

CLEANOUT n act or instance of cleaning (something) out

CLEANS ▸ **clean**

CLEANSE, -D, -S vb make clean

CLEANSER n cleansing agent, such as a detergent

CLEANSES ▸ **cleanse**

CLEANUP, -S n process of cleaning up or eliminating something

CLEAR, -ED, -EST, -S adj free from doubt or confusion ▷ adv in a clear or distinct manner ▷ vb make or become clear

CLEARAGE n clearance

CLEARCUT n act of felling all trees in area

CLEARED ▸ **clear**

CLEARER, -S ▸ **clear**

CLEAREST ▸ **clear**

CLEARING n treeless area in a wood

CLEARLY adv in a clear, distinct, or obvious manner

CLEAROUT n act or instance of removing (things or material)

CLEARS ▸ clear

CLEARWAY n stretch of road on which motorists may stop in an emergency

CLEAT, -ED, -ING, -S n wedge ▷ vb supply or support with a cleat or cleats

CLEAVAGE n division or split

CLEAVE, -D, -S, CLOVEN vb split apart ▷ n split

CLEAVER n butcher's heavy knife with a square blade

CLEAVERS n plant with small white flowers and sticky fruits

CLEAVES ▸ cleave

CLEAVING ▸ cleave

CLECHE adj (in heraldry) voided so that only a narrow border is visible

CLECK, -ED, -S vb (of birds) to hatch ▷ n piece of gossip

CLECKIER ▸ clecky

CLECKING ▸ cleck

CLECKS ▸ cleck

CLECKY, CLECKIER ▸ clecky

CLEEK, -ED, -ING, -IT, -S n large hook, such as one used to land fish ▷ vb seize

CLEEP, -ED, -ING, -S same as ▸ clepe

CLEEVE, -S n cliff

CLEF, -S n symbol at the beginning of a stave to show the pitch

CLEFT, -ED, -ING, -S vb split ▷ n opening

CLEG, -S another name for a ▸ horsefly

CLEIDOIC adj as in cleidoic egg egg of birds and insects

CLEIK, -S same as ▸ cleek

CLEM, -MED, -MING, -S vb be hungry or cause to be hungry

CLEMATIS n climbing plant with large colourful flowers

CLEMENCY n kind or lenient treatment

CLEMENT adj (of weather) mild

CLEMMED ▸ clem

CLEMMING ▸ clem

CLEMS ▸ clem

CLENCH, -ED, -ES vb close or squeeze (one's teeth or fist) tightly ▷ n firm grasp or grip

CLENCHER ▸ clench

CLENCHES ▸ clench

CLEOME, -S n type of herbaceous or shrubby plant

CLEPE, -D, -S, CLEPING, CLEPT vb call by the name of

CLERGY, CLERGIES n priests and ministers as a group

CLERIC, -S n member of the clergy

CLERICAL adj of clerks or office work

CLERICS ▸ cleric

CLERID, -S n beetle that preys on other insects

CLERIHEW n form of comic or satiric verse

CLERISY n learned or educated people

CLERK, -ED, -ING, -S n employee who keeps records, files, and accounts ▷ vb work as a clerk

CLERKDOM ▸ clerk

CLERKED ▸ clerk

CLERKESS n female office clerk

CLERKING ▸ clerk

CLERKISH ▸ clerk

CLERKLY adj of or like a clerk ▷ adv in the manner of a clerk

CLERKS ▸ clerk

CLERUCH, -S n settler in a cleruchy

CLERUCHY n type of colony of ancient Athens

CLEUCH, -S same as ▸ clough

CLEUGH, -S same as ▸ clough

CLEVE, -S same as ▸ cleeve

CLEVEITE n crystalline variety of the mineral uraninite

CLEVER, -ER adj intelligent, quick at learning

CLEVERLY ▸ clever

CLEVES ▸ cleve

CLEVIS, -ES n type of fastening used in agriculture

CLEW, -ED, -ING, -S n ball of thread, yarn, or twine ▷ vb coil or roll into a ball

CLICHE, -S n expression or idea that is no longer effective because of overuse ▷ vb use a cliché (in speech or writing)

CLICHED ▸ cliche

CLICHEED ▸ cliche

CLICHES ▸ cliche

CLICK, -ED, -S n short sharp sound ▷ vb make this sound

CLICKER, -S ▸ click

CLICKET, -S vb make a click

CLICKING ▸ click

CLICKS ▸ click

CLIED ▸ cly

CLIENT, -S n person who uses the services of a professional person or company

CLIENTAL ▸ client

CLIENTS ▸ client

CLIES ▸ cly

CLIFF, -S n steep rock face, esp along the sea shore ▷ vb scale a cliff

CLIFFED ▸ cliff

CLIFFIER ▸ cliffy

CLIFFS ▸ cliff

CLIFFTOP n top of a cliff

CLIFFY, CLIFFIER ▸ cliff

CLIFT, -S same as ▸ cliff

CLIFTED ▸ clift

CLIFTIER ▸ clifty

CLIFTS ▸ clift

CLIFTY, CLIFTIER ▸ clift

CLIMATAL ▸ climate

CLIMATE, -D, -S n typical weather conditions of an area ▷ vb acclimatize

CLIMATIC ▸ climate

CLIMAX, -ED, -ES n most intense point of an experience, series of events, or story ▷ vb reach a climax

CLIMB, -ED, -S vb go up, ascend ▷ n climbing

CLIMBER, -S n person or thing that climbs

CLIMBING ▸ climb

CLIMBS ▸ climb

CLIME, -S n place or its climate

CLINAL ▸ cline

CLINALLY ▸ cline

CLINAMEN n bias

CLINCH, -ED, -ES vb settle (an argument or agreement) decisively ▷ n movement in which one competitor holds on to the other to avoid punches

CLINCHER n something decisive

CLINCHES ▸ clinch

CLINE, -S n variation within a species

CLING, -ED, -ING, -S, CLUNG vb hold tightly or stick closely ▷ n tendency of cotton fibres in a sample to stick to each other

CLINGER, -S ▸ cling

CLINGIER ▸ clingy

CLINGING ▸ cling

CLINGS ▸ cling

CLINGY, CLINGIER ▸ cling

CLINIC, -S n building where outpatients receive medical treatment or advice

CLINICAL adj of a clinic

CLINICS ▸ clinic

CLINIQUE same as ▸ clinic

CLINK, -ED, -ING, -S n light sharp metallic sound ▷ vb make a light sharp metallic sound

CLINKER, -S n fused coal left over in a fire or furnace ▷ vb form clinker during burning

CLINKING ▸ clink

CLINKS ▸ clink

CLINT, -S n section of a limestone pavement separated from others by fissures

CLIP, -PED, -S vb cut with shears or scissors ▷ n short extract of a film

CLIPART, -S n large collection of simple drawings stored in a computer

CLIPE, -D, -S, CLIPING same as ▸ clype

CLIPPED ▸ clip

CLIPPER n fast commercial sailing ship

CLIPPERS pl n tool for clipping

CLIPPIE, -S n bus conductress

CLIPPING ▸ clip

CLIPS ▸ clip

CLIPT old inflection of ▸ clip

CLIQUE, -D, -S, CLIQUING n small exclusive group ▷ vb form a clique

CLIQUEY, CLIQUIER adj exclusive, confined to a small group

CLIQUING ▸ clique

CLIQUISH ▸ clique

CLIQUISM ▸ clique

CLIQUY same as ▸ cliquey

CLITELLA > clitellum

CLITHRAL same as > cleithral

CLITIC, -S adj (of a word) incapable of being stressed ▷ n clitic word

CLITORAL ▸ clitoris

CLITORIC ▸ clitoris

CLITORIS n small sensitive organ at the front of the vulva

CLITTER, -S vb make a shrill noise

CLIVERS same as ▸ cleavers

CLIVIA, -S n plant belonging to the Amaryllid family

CLOACA, -E, -S n body cavity in most animals

CLOACAL ▸ cloaca

CLOACAS ▸ cloaca

CLOAK, -ED, -ING, -S n loose sleeveless outer garment ▷ vb cover or conceal

CLOAM, -S adj made of clay or earthenware ▷ n clay or earthenware pots, dishes, etc, collectively

CLOBBER, -S vb hit ▷ n belongings, esp clothes

CLOCHARD n tramp

CLOCHE, -S n cover to protect young plants

CLOCK, -ED, -S n instrument for showing the time ▷ vb record (time) with a stopwatch

CLOCKER, -S ▸ clock

CLOCKING ▸ clock

CLOCKS ▸ clock

CLOD, -DED, -DING, -S n lump of earth ▷ vb pelt with clods

CLODDIER ▸ cloddy

CLODDING ▸ clod

CLODDISH ▸ clod

CLODDY, CLODDIER ▸ clod

CLODLY ▸ clod

CLODPATE n dull or stupid person

CLODPOLE same as ▸ clodpate

CLODPOLL same as ▸ clodpate

CLODS ▸ clod

CLOFF, -S n cleft of a tree

CLOG, -GED, -S vb obstruct ▷ n wooden or wooden-soled shoe

CLOGGER, -S n clogmaker

CLOGGIER ▸ cloggy

CLOGGILY ▸ clog

CLOGGING ▸ clog

CLOGGY, CLOGGIER ▸ clog

CLOGS ▸ clog

CLOISON, -S n partition

CLOISTER n covered pillared arcade, usu in a monastery ▷ vb confine or seclude in or as if in a monastery

CLOKE, -D, -S, CLOKING same as ▸ cloak

CLOMB a past tense and past participle of ▸ climb

CLOMP, -ED, -ING, -S same as ▸ clump

CLON, -S same as ▸ clone

CLONAL ▸ clone

CLONALLY ▸ clone

CLONE, -D, -S n animal or plant produced artificially from the cells of another animal or plant ▷ vb produce as a clone

CLONER, -S ▸ clone

CLONES ▸ clone

CLONIC ▸ clonus

CLONING, -S ▸ clone

CLONISM, -S n series of clonic spasms

CLONK, -ED, -ING, -S vb make a loud dull thud ▷ n loud thud

CLONKIER ▸ clonky

CLONKING ▸ clonk

CLONKS ▸ clonk

CLONKY, CLONKIER same as ▸ clunky

CLONS ▸ clon

CLONUS, -ES n type of convulsion

CLOOP, -S n sound made when a cork is drawn from a bottle

CLOOT, -S n hoof

CLOOTIE adj as in **clootie dumpling** kind of dumpling

CLOOTS ▸ cloot

CLOP, -PED, -PING, -S vb make a sound as of a horse's hooves ▷ n sound of this nature

CLOQUE, -S n fabric with an embossed surface

CLOSABLE ▸ close

CLOSE, -D, -S, -ST vb shut ▷ n end, conclusion ▷ adj near ▷ adv closely, tightly

CLOSELY ▸ close

CLOSEOUT n termination of an account on which the margin is exhausted

CLOSER, -S ▸ close

CLOSES ▸ close

CLOSEST ▸ close

CLOSET, -ED, -S n cupboard ▷ adj private, secret ▷ vb shut (oneself) away in private

CLOSEUP, -S n photo taken close to a subject

CLOSING, -S ▸ close

CLOSURE, -D, -S n closing ▷ vb (in a deliberative body) to end (debate) by closure

CLOT, -S, -TED n soft thick lump formed from liquid ▷ vb form soft thick lumps

CLOTBUR, -S n burdock

CLOTE, -S n burdock

CLOTH, -S n (piece of) woven fabric

CLOTHE, -D vb put clothes on

CLOTHES pl n garments

CLOTHIER n maker or seller of clothes or cloth

CLOTHING ▸ clothe

CLOTHS ▸ cloth

CLOTPOLL same as ▸ clodpoll

CLOTS ▸ clot

CLOTTED ▸ clot

CLOTTER, -S vb to clot

CLOTTIER ▸ clotty

CLOTTING ▸ clot

CLOTTISH ▸ clot

CLOTTY, CLOTTIER adj full of clots

CLOTURE, -D, -S n closure in the US Senate ▷ vb end (debate) in the US Senate by cloture

CLOU, -S n crux; focus

CLONKY, CLONKIER same as ▸ clunky

CLONS ▸ clon

CLOUD, -ED, -S *n* mass of condensed water vapour floating in the sky ▷ *vb* become cloudy

CLOUDAGE *n* mass of clouds

CLOUDED ▸ cloud

CLOUDIER ▸ cloudy

CLOUDILY ▸ cloudy

CLOUDING ▸ cloud

CLOUDLET *n* small cloud

CLOUDS ▸ cloud

CLOUDY, CLOUDIER *adj* having a lot of clouds

CLOUGH, -S *n* gorge or narrow ravine

CLOUR, -ED, -ING, -S *vb* to thump or dent

CLOUS ▸ clou

CLOUT, -ED, -ING, -S *n* hard blow ▷ *vb* hit hard

CLOUTER, -S ▸ clout

CLOUTING ▸ clout

CLOUTS ▸ clout

CLOVE, -S *n* tropical evergreen myrtaceous tree

CLOVEN ▸ cleave

CLOVER, -S *n* plant with three-lobed leaves

CLOVERED *adj* covered with clover

CLOVERS ▸ clover

CLOVERY *adj* like clover

CLOVES ▸ clove

CLOVIS *n* as in clovis point flint projectile dating from the 10th millennium BC

CLOW, -ED, -ING, -S *n* clove ▷ *vb* rake with a fork

CLOWDER, -S *n* collective term for a group of cats

CLOWED ▸ clow

CLOWING ▸ clow

CLOWN, -ED, -S *n* comic entertainer in a circus ▷ *vb* behave foolishly

CLOWNERY ▸ clown

CLOWNING ▸ clown

CLOWNISH ▸ clown

CLOWNS ▸ clown

CLOWS ▸ clow

CLOY, -ED, -S *vb* cause weariness through an excess of something initially pleasurable

CLOYE, -S *vb* to claw

CLOYED ▸ cloy

CLOYES ▸ cloye

CLOYING *adj* sickeningly sweet

CLOYLESS *adj* not cloying

CLOYMENT *n* satiety

CLOYS ▸ cloy

CLOYSOME *adj* cloying

CLOZE, -S *adj* as in cloze test test of the ability to understand text

CLUB, -BED, -S *n* association of people with common interests ▷ *vb* hit with a club

CLUBABLE *same as* > clubbable

CLUBBED ▸ club

CLUBBER, -S *n* person who regularly frequents nightclubs

CLUBBIER ▸ clubby

CLUBBILY ▸ clubby

CLUBBING ▸ club

CLUBBISH *adj* clubby

CLUBBISM *n* advantage gained through membership of a club or clubs

CLUBBIST ▸ clubbism

CLUBBY, CLUBBIER *adj* sociable, esp effusively so

CLUBFACE *n* face of golf club

CLUBFOOT, CLUBFEET *n* congenital deformity of the foot

CLUBHAND *n* congenital deformity of the hand

CLUBHAUL *vb* force (a sailing vessel) onto a new tack, esp in an emergency

CLUBHEAD *n* head of golf club

CLUBLAND *n* area of London which contains most of the famous clubs

CLUBLIKE *adj* like a club

CLUBMAN, CLUBMEN *n* man who is an enthusiastic member of a club or clubs

CLUBMATE *n* friend or contemporary in the same club

CLUBMEN ▸ clubman

CLUBMOSS *n* type of green moss-like plant

CLUBROOM *n* room in which a club meets

CLUBROOT *n* disease of cabbages

CLUBRUSH *n* any rush of the genus Scirpus

CLUBS ▸ club

CLUCK, -ED, -ING, -S *n* low clicking noise made by a hen ▷ *vb* make this noise

CLUCKER, -S *n* chicken

CLUCKIER ▸ clucky

CLUCKING ▸ cluck

CLUCKS ▸ cluck

CLUCKY, CLUCKIER *adj* wishing to have a baby

CLUDGIE, -S *n* toilet

CLUE, -D, -ING, -S, CLUING *n* something that helps to solve a mystery or puzzle ▷ *vb* help solve a mystery or puzzle

CLUELESS *adj* stupid

CLUES ▸ clue

CLUEY, CLUIER, CLUIEST *adj* (Australian) well-informed and adroit

CLUING ▸ clue

CLUMBER, -S *n* type of thickset spaniel

CLUMP, -ED, -ERS, -ING, -S *n* small group of things or people ▷ *vb* walk heavily

CLUMPER *vb* walk heavily

CLUMPERS ▸ clump

CLUMPET, -S *n* large chunk of floating ice

CLUMPIER ▸ clumpy

CLUMPING ▸ clump

CLUMPISH ▸ clump

CLUMPS ▸ clump

CLUMPY, CLUMPIER ▸ clump

CLUMSIER ▸ clumsy

CLUMSILY ▸ clumsy

CLUMSY, CLUMSIER *adj* lacking skill or physical coordination

CLUNCH, -ES *n* hardened clay

CLUNG ▸ cling

CLUNK, -ED, -ING, -S *n* dull metallic sound ▷ *vb* make such a sound

CLUNKER, -S *n* dilapidated old car or other machine

CLUNKIER ▸ clunky

CLUNKING ▸ clunk

CLUNKS ▸ clunk

CLUNKY, CLUNKIER *adj* making a clunking noise

CLUPEID, -S *n* type of fish

CLUPEOID *n* type of soft-finned fish

CLUSIA, -S *n* tree of the tropical American genus Clusia

CLUSTER, -S *n* small close group ▷ *vb* gather in clusters

CLUSTERY *adj* full of clusters

CLUTCH, -ED, -ES *vb* grasp tightly ▷ *n* mechanical device

CLUTCHY *adj* (of a person) tending to cling

CLUTTER, -S *vb* scatter objects about (a place) untidily ▷ *n* untidy mess

CLUTTERY *adj* full of clutter

CLY, CLIED, CLIES, -ING *vb* steal or seize

A little word meaning to seize or steal, this can be useful when you are short of vowels.

CLYPE, -D, -S, CLYPING *vb* tell tales ▷ *n* person who tells tales

CLYPEAL ▸ clypeus

CLYPEATE ▷ **clypeus**

CLYPED ▷ **clype**

CLYPEI ▷ **clypeus**

CLYPES ▷ **clype**

CLYPEUS, CLYPEI *n* cuticular plate on the head of some insects

CLYPING ▷ **clype**

CLYSTER, -S *a former name for an* ▷ **enema**

CNEMIAL ▷ **cnemis**

CNEMIS, CNEMIDES *n* shin or tibia

CNIDA, -E *n* stinging organ in jellyfish

COACH, -ED, -ES *n* long-distance bus ▷ *vb* train, teach

COACHDOG *n* Dalmatian dog

COACHED ▷ **coach**

COACHEE, -S *n* person who receives training from a coach

COACHER, -S ▷ **coach**

COACHES ▷ **coach**

COACHIER ▷ **coachy**

COACHIES ▷ **coachy**

COACHING ▷ **coach**

COACHMAN, COACHMEN *n* driver of a horse-drawn coach or carriage

COACHY, COACHIER, COACHIES *n* coachman ▷ *adj* resembling or pertaining to a coach

COACT, -ED, -ING, -S *vb* act together

COACTION *n* any relationship between organisms within a community

COACTIVE ▷ **coaction**

COACTOR, -S ▷ **coact**

COACTS ▷ **coact**

COADIES ▷ **coady**

COADMIRE *vb* admire together

COADMIT, -S *vb* admit together

COADY, COADIES *n* sauce made from molasses

COAEVAL, -S *n* contemporary

COAGENCY *n* joint agency

COAGENT, -S ▷ **coagency**

COAGULUM, COAGULA *n* any coagulated mass

COAITA, -S *n* spider monkey

COAL, -ED, -ING, -S *n* black rock consisting mainly of carbon, used as fuel ▷ *vb* take in, or turn into coal

COALA, -S *same as* ▷ **koala**

COALBALL *n* in coal, nodule containing petrified plant or animal remains

COALBIN, -S *n* bin for holding coal

COALBOX *n* box for holding coal

COALDUST *n* dust from coal

COALED ▷ **coal**

COALER, -S *n* ship, train, etc, used to carry or supply coal

COALESCE *vb* come together, merge

COALFACE *n* exposed seam of coal in a mine

COALFISH *n* type of dark-coloured food fish occurring in northern seas

COALHOLE *n* small coal cellar

COALIER ▷ **coaly**

COALIEST ▷ **coaly**

COALIFY *vb* turn into coal

COALING ▷ **coal**

COALISE, -D, -S *vb* form a coalition

COALIZE, -D, -S *same as* ▷ **coalise**

COALLESS *adj* without coal

COALMAN, COALMEN *n* man who delivers coal

COALMINE *n* mine from which coal is extracted

COALPIT, -S *n* pit from which coal is extracted

COALS ▷ **coal**

COALSACK *n* dark nebula near the constellation Cygnus

COALSHED *n* shed in which coal is stored

COALY, COALIER, COALIEST ▷ **coal**

COALYARD *n* yard in which coal is stored

COAMING, -S *n* raised frame round a ship's hatchway for keeping out water

COANCHOR *vb* co-present a TV programme

COANNEX *vb* annex with something else

COAPPEAR *vb* appear jointly

COAPT, -ED, -ING, -S *vb* secure

COARB, -S *n* spiritual successor

COARSE, -R, -ST *adj* rough in texture

COARSELY ▷ **coarse**

COARSEN, -S *vb* make or become coarse

COARSER ▷ **coarse**

COARSEST ▷ **coarse**

COARSISH ▷ **coarse**

COASSIST *vb* assist jointly

COASSUME *vb* assume jointly

COAST, -ED, -S *n* place where the land meets the sea ▷ *vb* move by momentum, without the use of power

COASTAL ▷ **coast**

COASTED ▷ **coast**

COASTER, -S *n* small mat placed under a glass

COASTING ▷ **coast**

COASTS ▷ **coast**

COAT, -S *n* outer garment with long sleeves ▷ *vb* cover with a layer

COATE, -S *same as* ▷ **quote**

COATED *adj* covered with an outer layer, film, etc

COATEE, -S *n* short coat, esp for a baby

COATER, -S *n* machine that applies a coating to something

COATES ▷ **coate**

COATI, -S *n* type of omnivorous mammal

COATING, -S *n* covering layer

COATIS ▷ **coati**

COATLESS *adj* without a coat

COATLIKE *adj* like a coat

COATRACK *n* rack for hanging coats on

COATROOM *n* cloakroom

COATS ▷ **coat**

COATTAIL *n* long tapering tail at the back of a man's tailored coat

COATTEND *vb* attend jointly

COATTEST *vb* attest jointly

COAUTHOR *n* person who shares the writing of a book, article, etc, with another ▷ *vb* be the joint author of (a book, article, etc)

COAX, -ED, -ES *vb* persuade gently

COAXAL *same as* ▷ **coaxial**

COAXED ▷ **coax**

COAXER, -S ▷ **coax**

COAXES ▷ **coax**

COAXIAL *adj* (of a cable) transmitting by means of two concentric conductors separated by an insulator

COAXING, -S *n* act of coaxing

COB, -BED, -BING, -S *n* stalk of an ear of maize ▷ *vb* beat

COBAEA, -S *n* tropical climbing shrub

COBALT, -S *n* brittle silvery-white metallic element

COBALTIC *adj* of or containing cobalt, esp in the trivalent state

COBALTS ▶ cobalt
COBB, -S same as ▶ **cob**
COBBED ▶ cob
COBBER, -S n friend
COBBIER ▶ cobby
COBBIEST ▶ cobby
COBBING ▶ cob
COBBLE, -D, -S n cobblestone ▷vb pave (a road) with cobblestones
COBBLER, -S n shoe mender
COBBLERY n shoemaking or shoemending
COBBLES ▶ cobble
COBBLING ▶ cobble
COBBS ▶ cobb
COBBY, COBBIER, COBBIEST adj short and stocky
COBIA, -S n large dark-striped game fish
COBLE, -S n small single-masted flat-bottomed fishing boat
COBLOAF n round loaf of bread
COBNUT, -S another name for ▶ **hazelnut**
COBRA, -S n venomous hooded snake of Asia and Africa
COBRIC ▶ cobra
COBS ▶ cob
COBURG, -S n rounded loaf with a cross cut on the top
COBWEB, -S n spider's web
COBWEBBY ▶ cobweb
COBWEBS ▶ cobweb
COBZA, -S n Romanian lute
COCA, -S n S American shrub
COCAIN, -S same as ▶ **cocaine**
COCAINE, -S n drug used illegally as a narcotic and as an anaesthetic
COCAINS ▶ cocain
COCAS ▶ coca
COCCAL ▶ coccus
COCCI ▶ coccus
COCCIC ▶ coccus
COCCID, -S n type of homopterous insect
COCCIDIA ▶ coccidium
COCCIDS ▶ coccid
COCCO, -S n taro
COCCOID, -S ▶ coccus
COCCOS ▶ cocco
COCCOUS ▶ coccus
COCCUS, COCCI n any spherical or nearly spherical bacterium
COCCYX, COCCYGES, -ES n bone at the base of the spinal column
COCH, -ES obsolete variant of ▶ **coach**

COCHAIR, -S vb chair jointly
COCHES ▶ coch
COCHIN, -S n large breed of domestic fowl
COCHLEA, -E, -S n spiral tube in the internal ear
COCHLEAR adj of or relating to the cochlea ▷n spoonful
COCHLEAS ▶ cochlea
COCINERA n in Mexico, a female cook
COCK, -ED, -ING, -S n male bird, esp of domestic fowl ▷vb draw back (the hammer of a gun) to firing position
COCKADE, -S n feather or rosette worn on a hat as a badge
COCKADED ▶ cockade
COCKADES ▶ cockade
COCKAPOO n cross between a cocker spaniel and a poodle
COCKATOO n crested parrot of Australia or Indonesia
COCKBILL vb tilt up one end of
COCKBIRD n male bird
COCKBOAT n any small boat
COCKCROW n daybreak
COCKED ▶ cock
COCKER, -ED, -S n devotee of cockfighting ▷vb pamper or spoil by indulgence
COCKEREL n young domestic cock
COCKERS ▶ cocker
COCKET, -S n document issued by a customs officer
COCKEYE, -S n eye affected with strabismus or one that squints
COCKEYED adj crooked, askew
COCKEYES ▶ cockeye
COCKIER ▶ cocky
COCKIES ▶ cocky
COCKIEST ▶ cocky
COCKILY ▶ cocky
COCKING ▶ cock
COCKISH adj wanton
COCKLE, -D, -S, COCKLING n edible shellfish ▷vb fish for cockles
COCKLER, -S n person employed to gather cockles
COCKLES ▶ cockle
COCKLIKE adj resembling a cock
COCKLING ▶ cockle
COCKLOFT n small loft, garret, or attic
COCKNEY, -S n native of London, esp of its East End ▷adj characteristic of cockneys or their dialect

COCKNIFY same as ▶ **cockneyfy**
COCKPIT, -S n pilot's compartment in an aircraft
COCKS ▶ cock
COCKSHOT another name for ▶ **cockshy**
COCKSHUT n dusk
COCKSHY n target aimed at in throwing games
COCKSIER ▶ cocksy
COCKSPUR n spur on the leg of a cock
COCKSURE adj overconfident, arrogant
COCKSY, COCKSIER adj cocky
COCKTAIL n mixed alcoholic drink
COCKY, COCKIER, COCKIES, COCKIEST adj conceited and overconfident ▷n farmer whose farm is regarded as small or of little account
COCO, -S n coconut palm
COCOA, -S n powder made from the seed of the cacao tree
COCOANUT same as ▶ **coconut**
COCOAS ▶ cocoa
COCOBOLA n type of rosewood
COCOBOLO same as ▶ **cocobola**
COCOMAT, -S n mat made from coconut fibre
COCONUT, -S n large hard fruit of a type of palm tree
COCOON, -ED, -S n silky protective covering of a silkworm ▷vb wrap up tightly for protection
COCOONER n person who retreats to a secure family environment
COCOONS ▶ cocoon
COCOPAN, -S n (in South Africa) a small wagon running on narrow-gauge railway lines used in mines
COCOPLUM n tropical shrub or its fruit
COCOS ▶ coco
COCOTTE, -S n small fireproof dish in which individual portions of food are cooked
COCOYAM, -S n food plant of West Africa with edible underground stem
COCREATE vb create jointly
COCTILE adj made by exposing to heat
COCTION, -S n boiling

COCURATE vb curate jointly

COD, -DED, -DING, -S n large food fish of the North Atlantic ▷ adj having the character of an imitation or parody ▷ vb make fun of

CODA, -S n final part of a musical composition

CODABLE adj capable of being coded

CODAS ▸ coda

CODDED ▸ cod

CODDER, -S n cod fisherman or fishing boat

CODDING ▸ cod

CODDLE, -D, -S, CODDLING vb pamper, overprotect ▷ n stew made from ham and bacon scraps

CODDLER, -S ▸ coddle

CODDLES ▸ coddle

CODDLING ▸ coddle

CODE, -D, -S n system by which messages can be communicated secretly or briefly ▷ vb put into code

CODEBOOK n book containing the means to decipher a code

CODEBTOR n fellow debtor

CODEC, -S n set of electrical equipment

CODED ▸ code

CODEIA, -S n codeine

CODEIN, -S same as ▸ codeine

CODEINA, -S obsolete variant of ▸ codeine

CODEINE, -S n drug used as a painkiller

CODEINS ▸ codein

CODELESS adj lacking a code

CODEN, -S n identification code assigned to a publication

CODENAME same as ▸ codeword

CODENS ▸ coden

CODER, -S n person or thing that codes

CODERIVE vb derive jointly

CODERS ▸ coder

CODES ▸ code

CODESIGN vb design jointly

CODETTA, -S n short coda

CODEWORD n (esp in military use) a word used to identify a classified plan, operation, etc

CODEX, -ES, CODICES n volume of manuscripts of an ancient text

CODFISH n cod

CODGER, -S n old man

CODICES ▸ codex

CODICIL, -S n addition to a will

CODIFIED ▸ codify

CODIFIER ▸ codify

CODIFY, CODIFIED, CODIFIES vb organize (rules or procedures) systematically

CODILLA, -S n coarse tow of hemp and flax

CODILLE, -S n in the card game ombre, term indicating that the game is won

CODING, -S ▸ code

CODIRECT vb direct jointly

CODIST, -S n codifier

CODLIN, -S same as ▸ codling

CODLING, -S n young cod

CODLINS ▸ codlin

CODOLOGY n art or practice of bluffing or deception

CODOMAIN n set of values that a function is allowed to take

CODON, -S n part of a DNA molecule

CODPIECE n bag covering the male genitals, attached to the breeches

CODRIVE, -N, -S, CODROVE vb take alternate turns driving a car with another person

CODRIVER n one of two drivers who take turns to drive a car

CODRIVES ▸ codrive

CODROVE ▸ codrive

CODS ▸ cod

COED, -S adj educating boys and girls together ▷ n school or college that educates boys and girls together

COEDIT, -ED, -S vb edit (a book, newspaper, etc) jointly

COEDITOR ▸ coedit

COEDITS ▸ coedit

COEDS ▸ coed

COEFFECT n secondary effect

COEHORN, -S n type of small artillery mortar

COELIAC, -S adj of or relating to the abdomen ▷ n person who has coeliac disease

COELOM, -S n body cavity of many multicellular animals

COELOME, -S same as ▸ coelom

COELOMIC ▸ coelom

COELOMS ▸ coelom

COEMBODY vb embody jointly

COEMPLOY vb employ together

COEMPT, -ED, -S vb buy up something in its entirety

COENACLE same as ▸ cenacle

COENACT, -S vb enact jointly

COENAMOR vb enamour jointly

COENDURE vb endure together

COENOBIA > coenobium

COENURE, -S variant form of ▸ coenurus

COENURUS, COENURI n encysted larval form of a type of tapeworm with many encapsulated heads

COENZYME n type of nonprotein organic molecule

COEQUAL, -S n equal ▷ adj of the same size, rank, etc

COEQUATE vb equate together

COERCE, -D, -S, COERCING vb compel, force

COERCER, -S ▸ coerce

COERCES ▸ coerce

COERCING ▸ coerce

COERCION n act or power of coercing

COERCIVE ▸ coerce

COERECT, -S vb erect together

COESITE, -S n polymorph of silicon dioxide

COEVAL, -S n contemporary ▷ adj contemporary

COEVALLY ▸ coeval

COEVALS ▸ coeval

COEVOLVE vb evolve together

COEXERT, -S vb exert together

COEXIST, -S vb exist together, esp peacefully despite differences

COEXTEND vb extend or cause to extend equally in space or time

COFACTOR n type of nonprotein substance

COFF, -ED, -ING, -S, COFT vb buy

COFFEE, -S n drink made from the roasted and ground seeds of a tropical shrub ▷ adj medium-brown

COFFER, -ED, -S n chest, esp for storing valuables ▷ vb store

COFFIN, -ED, -S n box in which a corpse is buried or cremated ▷ vb place in or as in a coffin

COFFING ▸ coff
COFFINS ▸ coffin
COFFLE, -D, -S, COFFLING n (esp formerly) line of slaves, beasts, etc, fastened together ▸ vb fasten together in a coffle
COFFRET, -S n small coffer
COFFS ▸ coff
COFIRING n combustion of two different types of fuel at the same time
COFOUND, -S vb found jointly
COFT ▸ coff
COG, -GED, -S n one of the teeth on the rim of a gearwheel ▸ vb roll (cast-steel ingots) to convert them into blooms
COGENCE, -S ▸ cogent
COGENCY ▸ cogent
COGENER, -S n thing of the same kind
COGENT adj forcefully convincing
COGENTLY ▸ cogent
COGGED ▸ cog
COGGER, -S n deceiver
COGGIE, -S n quaich or drinking cup
COGGING, -S ▸ cog
COGGLE, -D, -S, COGGLING vb wobble or rock
COGGLIER ▸ coggly
COGGLING ▸ coggle
COGGLY, COGGLIER ▸ coggle
COGIE, -S same as ▸ coggie
COGITATE vb think deeply about
COGITO, -S n philosophical theory
COGNAC, -S n French brandy
COGNATE, -S adj derived from a common original form ▸ n cognate word or language
COGNISE, -D, -S same as ▸ cognize
COGNISER ▸ cognise
COGNISES ▸ cognise
COGNIZE, -D, -S vb perceive, become aware of, or know
COGNIZER ▸ cognize
COGNIZES ▸ cognize
COGNOMEN n nickname
COGNOSCE vb in Scots law, to give judgment upon
COGNOVIT n in law, a defendant's confession that the case against him or her is just
COGON, -S n type of coarse tropical grass used for thatching

COGS ▸ cog
COGUE, -S n wooden pail or drinking vessel
COGWAY, -S n rack railway
COGWHEEL same as > gearwheel
COHAB, -S n cohabitor
COHABIT, -S vb live together as spouses without being married
COHABS ▸ cohab
COHEAD, -ED, -S vb head jointly
COHEIR, -S n person who inherits jointly with others
COHEN, -S same as ▸ kohen
COHERE, -D, -S, COHERING vb hold or stick together
COHERENT adj logical and consistent
COHERER, -S n electrical component
COHERES ▸ cohere
COHERING ▸ cohere
COHESION n sticking together
COHESIVE adj sticking together to form a whole
COHIBIT, -S vb restrain
COHO, -ES, -S n type of Pacific salmon
COHOBATE vb redistil (a distiller), esp by allowing it to mingle with the remaining matter
COHOE same as ▸ coho
COHOES ▸ coho
COHOG, -S n quahog, an edible clam
COHOLDER n joint holder
COHORN, -S same as ▸ coehorn
COHORT, -S n band of associates
COHOS ▸ coho
COHOSH, -ES n type of North American plant
COHOST, -ED, -S vb host jointly
COHUNE, -S n tropical feather palm
COIF, -FED, -FING, -ING, -S vb arrange the hair of ▸ n close-fitting cap worn in the Middle Ages
COIFED adj wearing a coif
COIFFE, -S vb coiffure
COIFFED ▸ coif
COIFFES ▸ coiffe
COIFFEUR n hairdresser
COIFFING ▸ coif
COIFFURE n hairstyle ▸ vb dress or arrange (the hair)
COIFING ▸ coif
COIFS ▸ coif

COIGN, -ED, -ING, -S vb wedge ▸ n quoin
COIGNE, -S same as ▸ coign
COIGNED ▸ coign
COIGNES ▸ coigne
COIGNING ▸ coign
COIGNS ▸ coign
COIL, -ED, -ING, -S vb wind in loops ▸ n something coiled
COILER, -S ▸ coil
COILING ▸ coil
COILS ▸ coil
COIN, -ED, -S n piece of metal money ▸ vb invent (a word or phrase)
COINABLE ▸ coin
COINAGE, -S n coins collectively
COINCIDE vb happen at the same time
COINED ▸ coin
COINER, -S ▸ coin
COINFECT vb infect at same time as other infection
COINFER, -S vb infer jointly
COINHERE vb inhere together
COINING, -S ▸ coin
COINMATE n fellow inmate
COINOP adj (of a machine) operated by putting a coin in a slot
COINS ▸ coin
COINSURE vb insure jointly
COINTER, -S vb inter together
COINVENT vb invent jointly
COINVEST vb invest jointly
COIR, -S n coconut fibre, used for matting
COISTREL n knave
COISTRIL same as ▸ coistrel
COIT, -S n buttocks
COJOIN, -ED, -S vb conjoin
COKE, -D n solid fuel left after gas has been distilled from coal ▸ vb become or convert into coke
COKELIKE ▸ coke
COKERNUT same as ▸ coconut
COKES, -ES n fool
COKIER ▸ coky
COKIEST ▸ coky
COKING, -S n act of coking
COKY, COKIER, COKIEST adj like coke
COL, -S n high mountain pass
COLA, -S n dark brown fizzy soft drink
COLANDER n perforated bowl for straining or rinsing foods
COLAS ▸ cola

COLBY, COLBIES, -S *n* type of mild-tasting hard cheese

COLCHICA ▸ colchicum

COLD, -ER, -EST, -S *adj* lacking heat ▷ *n* lack of heat

COLDCOCK *vb* knock to the ground

COLDER ▸ cold

COLDEST ▸ cold

COLDIE, -S *n* cold can or bottle of beer

COLDISH ▸ cold

COLDLY ▸ cold

COLDNESS ▸ cold

COLDS ▸ cold

COLE, -S *same as* ▸ **cabbage**

COLEAD, -S, COLED *vb* lead together

COLEADER ▸ colead

COLEADS ▸ colead

COLED ▸ colead

COLES ▸ cole

COLESEED *n* seeds or plants of the cole

COLESLAW *n* salad dish of shredded raw cabbage in a dressing

COLESSEE *n* joint lessee

COLESSOR *n* joint lessor

COLETIT, -S *n* coal tit

COLEUS, -ES *n* Old World plant

COLEWORT *same as* ▸ **cabbage**

COLEY, -S *same as* ▸ **coalfish**

COLIBRI, -S *n* hummingbird

COLIC, -S *n* severe pains in the stomach and bowels

COLICIN, -S *n* bactericidal protein

COLICINE *n* antibacterial protein

COLICINS ▸ colicin

COLICKY *adj* relating to or suffering from colic

COLICS ▸ colic

COLIES ▸ coly

COLIFORM *n* type of bacteria of the intestinal tract

COLIN, -S *n* quail

COLINEAR *same as* > **collinear**

COLINS ▸ colin

COLISEUM *n* large building, such as a stadium or theatre, used for entertainments, sports, etc

COLISTIN *n* polymyxin antibiotic

COLITIC ▸ colitis

COLITIS *n* inflammation of the colon

COLL, -ED, -S *vb* embrace

COLLAB, -S *n* collaboration

COLLAGE, -D, -S *n* type of art form ▷ *vb* make a collage

COLLAGEN *n* protein found in cartilage and bone that yields gelatine when boiled

COLLAGES ▸ collage

COLLAPSE *vb* fall down suddenly ▷ *n* collapsing

COLLAR, -ED, -S *n* part of a garment round the neck ▷ *vb* seize, arrest

COLLARD, -S *n* variety of cabbage with a crown of edible leaves

COLLARED ▸ collar

COLLARET *n* small collar

COLLARS ▸ collar

COLLATE, -D, -S *vb* gather together, examine, and put in order

COLLATOR *n* person or machine that collates texts or manuscripts

COLLECT, -S *vb* gather together ▷ *n* short prayer

COLLED ▸ coll

COLLEEN, -S *n* girl or young woman

COLLEGE, -S *n* place of higher education

COLLEGER *n* member of a college

COLLEGES ▸ college

COLLEGIA > collegium

COLLET, -ED, -S *n* (in a jewellery setting) a band or coronet-shaped claw that holds an individual stone ▷ *vb* mount in a collet

COLLIDE, -D, -S *vb* crash together violently

COLLIDER *n* particle accelerator in which beams of particles are made to collide

COLLIDES ▸ collide

COLLIE *n* silky-haired sheepdog

COLLIED ▸ colly

COLLIER, -S *n* coal miner

COLLIERY *n* coal mine

COLLIES ▸ colly

COLLING, -S *n* embrace

COLLINS *n* type of cocktail

COLLOGUE *vb* confer confidentially

COLLOID, -S *n* suspension of particles in a solution ▷ *adj* relating to the gluelike material found in certain degenerating tissues

COLLOP, -S *n* small slice of meat

COLLOQUE *vb* converse

COLLOQUY *n* conversation or conference

COLLS ▸ coll

COLLUDE, -D, -S *vb* act in collusion

COLLUDER ▸ collude

COLLUDES ▸ collude

COLLUVIA > colluvium

COLLY, COLLIED, COLLIES, -ING *n* soot or grime, such as coal dust ▷ *vb* begrime

COLLYRIA > collyrium

COLOBI ▸ colobus

COLOBID, -S *n* type of African monkey

COLOBOMA *n* structural defect of the eye, esp in the choroid, retina, or iris

COLOBUS, COLOBI *n* type of Old World monkey

COLOCATE *vb* locate together

COLOG, -S *n* logarithm of the reciprocal of a number

COLOGNE, -S *n* mild perfume

COLOGNED ▸ cologne

COLOGNES ▸ cologne

COLOGS ▸ colog

COLON, -S *n* punctuation mark (:)

COLONE, -S *variant of* ▸ **colon**

COLONEL, -S *n* senior commissioned army or air-force officer

COLONES ▸ colone

COLONI ▸ colonus

COLONIAL *n* inhabitant of a colony ▷ *adj* of or inhabiting a colony or colonies

COLONIC, -S *adj* of or relating to the colon ▷ *n* irrigation of the colon

COLONIES ▸ colony

COLONISE *same as* ▸ **colonize**

COLONIST *n* settler in a colony

COLONIZE *vb* make into a colony

COLONS ▸ colon

COLONUS, COLONI *n* ancient Roman farmer

COLONY, COLONIES *n* people who settle in a new country but remain ruled by their homeland

COLOPHON *n* publisher's symbol on a book

COLOR, -S *same as* ▸ **colour**

COLORADO *adj* (of a cigar) of middling colour and strength

COLORANT *n* any substance that imparts colour, such as a pigment, dye, or ink

COLORED *same as* ▸ **coloured**

C

COLOREDS same as
> **coloureds**
COLORER, -S ► color
COLORFUL ► color
COLORIER ► colory
COLORING same as
> **colouring**
COLORISM ► color
COLORIST ► color
COLORIZE same as
> **colourize**
COLORMAN, COLORMEN
same as > **colourman**
COLORS ► color
COLORWAY variant of
> **colourway**
COLORY, COLORIER adj full
of color
COLOSSAL adj very large
COLOSSUS, COLOSSI n
huge statue
COLOTOMY n colonic
incision
COLOUR, -S n appearance of
things as a result of
reflecting light ▷ vb apply
colour to
COLOURED adj having
colour
COLOURER ► colour
COLOURS ► colour
COLOURY adj possessing
colour
COLS ► col
COLT, -ED, -ING, -S n young
male horse ▷ vb to fool
COLTAN, -S n metallic ore
COLTED ► colt
COLTER, -S same as ► **coulter**
COLTHOOD n state of being
a colt
COLTING ► colt
COLTISH adj inexperienced
COLTS ► colt
COLTWOOD n plant
mentioned in Spenser's
Faerie Queene
COLUBRID n type of snake
such as the grass snake and
whip snakes
COLUGO, -S n flying lemur
COLUMBIC another word for
► **niobic**
COLUMEL, -S n in botany,
the central column in a
capsule
COLUMN, -S n pillar ▷ vb
create a column
COLUMNAL n part of the
stem of a crinoid
COLUMNAR ► column
COLUMNEA n flowering
plant
COLUMNED ► column

COLUMNS ► column
COLURE, -S n either of two
great circles on the celestial
sphere
COLY, COLIES n S African
arboreal bird
COLZA, -S n Eurasian plant
with bright yellow flowers
COMA, -E, -S n state of deep
unconsciousness
COMADE ► comake
COMAE ► coma
COMAKE, COMADE, -S,
COMAKING vb make
together
COMAKER, -S ► comake
COMAKES ► comake
COMAKING ► comake
COMAL ► coma
COMARB, -S same as ► **coarb**
COMART, -S n covenant
COMAS ► coma
COMATE, -S adj having tufts
of hair ▷ n companion
COMATIC ► coma
COMATIK, -S variant of
► **komatik**
COMATOSE adj in a coma
COMATULA same as
> **comatulid**
COMB, -ED, -ING, -S n
toothed implement for
arranging the hair ▷ vb use a
comb on
COMBAT, -ED, -S vb fight,
struggle ▷ n fight or
struggle
COMBATER ► combat
COMBATS ► combat
COMBE, -S same as ► **comb**
COMBED ► comb
COMBER, -S n long curling
wave
COMBES ► combe
COMBI, -S n combination
boiler
COMBIER ► comby
COMBIES ► comby
COMBIEST ► comby
COMBINE, -S vb join
together ▷ n association of
people or firms for a
common purpose
COMBINED n competitive
event consisting of two
skiing competitions
COMBINER ► combine
COMBINES ► combine
COMBING ► comb
COMBINGS pl n loose hair or
fibres removed by combing,
esp from animals
COMBIS ► combi
COMBLE, -S n apex; zenith

COMBLESS adj without a
comb
COMBLIKE adj resembling a
comb
COMBO, -S n small group of
jazz musicians
COMBOVER n hairstyle in
which thinning hair is
combed over the scalp
COMBS ► comb
COMBUST, -S vb burn
COMBWISE adv in the
manner of a comb
COMBY, COMBIER,
COMBIES, COMBIEST adj
comb-like ▷ n combination
boiler
COME, CAME, -S, -TH vb
move towards a place,
arrive
COMEBACK n return to a
former position ▷ vb return,
esp to the memory
COMEDDLE vb mix
COMEDIAN n entertainer
who tells jokes
COMEDIC adj of or relating
to comedy
COMEDIES ► comedy
COMEDIST n writer of
comedies
COMEDO, -S the technical
name for ► **blackhead**
COMEDOWN n decline in
status ▷ vb come to a place
regarded as lower
COMEDY, COMEDIES n
humorous play, film, or
programme
COMELIER ► comely
COMELILY ► comely
COMELY, COMELIER adj
nice-looking
COMEMBER n fellow
member
COMEOVER n person who
has come from Britain to the
Isle of Man to settle
COMER, -S n person who
comes
COMES ► come
COMET, -S n heavenly body
with a long luminous tail
COMETARY ► comet
COMETH ► come
COMETHER n coaxing;
allure
COMETIC ► comet
COMETS ► comet
COMFIER ► comfy
COMFIEST ► comfy
COMFILY adv in a manner
suggestive of or promoting
comfort
COMFIT, -S n sugar-coated
sweet

COMFORT, -S n physical ease or wellbeing ▷ vb soothe, console

COMFREY, -S n tall plant with bell-shaped flowers

COMFY, COMFIER, COMFIEST adj comfortable

COMIC, -S adj humorous, funny ▷ n comedian

COMICAL adj amusing

COMICE, -S n kind of pear

COMICS ▸ comic

COMING, -S ▸ come

COMINGLE same as > commingle

COMINGS ▸ coming

COMIQUE, -S n comic actor

COMITAL adj relating to a count or earl

COMITIA, -S n ancient Roman assembly

COMITIAL ▸ comitia

COMITIAS ▸ comitia

COMITY, COMITIES n friendly politeness, esp between different countries

COMIX n comic books in general

COMM n as in **comm badge** small wearable badge-shaped radio transmitter and receiver

COMMA, -S, -TA n punctuation mark (,)

COMMAND, -S vb order ▷ n authoritative instruction that something must be done

COMMANDO n (member of) a military unit trained for swift raids in enemy territory

COMMANDS ▸ command

COMMAS ▸ comma

COMMATA ▸ comma

COMMENCE vb begin

COMMEND, -S vb praise

COMMENT, -S n remark ▷ vb make a comment

COMMER, -S same as ▸ comer

COMMERCE n buying and selling, trade ▷ vb to trade

COMMERE, -S n female compere

COMMERGE vb merge together

COMMERS ▸ commer

COMMIE, -S n communist

COMMIS n apprentice waiter or chef ▷ adj (of a waiter or chef) apprentice

COMMISH n commissioner

COMMIT, -S vb perform (a crime or error)

COMMIX, -ED, -ES, -T a rare word for ▸ mix

COMMO, -S short for > communist

COMMODE, -S n seat with a hinged flap concealing a chamber pot

COMMODO same as ▸ comodo

COMMON, -ED adj occurring often ▷ n area of grassy land belonging to a community ▷ vb sit at table with strangers

COMMONER n person who does not belong to the nobility

COMMONEY n playing marble of a common sort

COMMONLY adv usually

COMMONS n people not of noble birth viewed as forming a political order

COMMOS ▸ commo

COMMOT, -S n in medieval Wales, a division of land

COMMOTE, -S same as ▸ commot

COMMOTS ▸ commot

COMMOVE, -D, -S vb disturb

COMMS pl n communications

COMMUNAL adj shared

COMMUNE, -D, -S n group of people who live together and share everything ▷ vb feel very close (to)

COMMUNER ▸ commune

COMMUNES ▸ commune

COMMUTE, -D, -S vb travel daily to and from work ▷ n journey made by commuting

COMMUTER n person who commutes to and from work

COMMUTES ▸ commute

COMMY same as ▸ commie

COMODO adv (to be performed) at a convenient relaxed speed

COMORBID adj (of illness) happening at same time as other illness

COMOSE another word for ▸ comate

COMOUS adj hairy

COMP, -ED, -S n person who sets and corrects type ▷ vb set or correct type

COMPACT, -S adj closely packed ▷ n small flat case containing a mirror and face powder ▷ vb pack closely together

COMPADRE n masculine friend

COMPAGE obsolete form of ▸ compages

COMPAGES n structure or framework

COMPAND, -S vb (of a transmitter signal) to compress before, and expand after, transmission

COMPANY n business organization ▷ vb associate or keep company with someone

COMPARE, -D, -S vb examine (things) and point out the resemblances or differences

COMPARER ▸ compare

COMPARES ▸ compare

COMPART, -S vb divide into parts

COMPAS n rhythm in flamenco

COMPASS n instrument for showing direction ▷ vb encircle or surround

COMPAST adj rounded

COMPEAR, -S vb in Scots law, to appear in court

COMPED ▸ comp

COMPEER, -S n person of equal rank, status, or ability ▷ vb to equal

COMPEL, -S vb force (to be or do)

COMPEND, -S n compendium

COMPER, -S n person who regularly enters competitions

COMPERE, -D, -S n person who presents a stage, radio, or television show ▷ vb be the compere of

COMPERS ▸ comper

COMPESCE vb curb

COMPETE, -D, -S vb try to win or achieve (a prize, profit, etc)

COMPILE, -D, -S vb collect and arrange (information), esp to make a book

COMPILER n person who compiles information

COMPILES ▸ compile

COMPING, -S n act of comping

COMPITAL adj pertaining to crossroads

COMPLAIN vb express resentment or displeasure

COMPLEAT an archaic spelling of ▸ complete

COMPLECT vb interweave or entwine

COMPLETE adj thorough, absolute ▷ vb finish

COMPLEX adj made up of parts ▷ n whole made up of parts ▷ vb form a complex

COMPLICE *n* associate or accomplice

COMPLIED ▸ comply

COMPLIER ▸ comply

COMPLIES ▸ comply

COMPLIN, -S *same as* ▸ compline

COMPLINE *n* last service of the day in the Roman Catholic Church

COMPLINS ▸ complin

COMPLISH *vb* accomplish

COMPLOT, -S *n* plot or conspiracy ▷ *vb* plot together

COMPLY, COMPLIED, COMPLIES *vb* act in accordance (with)

COMPO, -S *n* mixture of materials, such as mortar, plaster, etc ▷ *adj* intended to last for several days

COMPONE *same as* ▸ compony

COMPONY *adj* made up of alternating metal and colour, colour and fur, or fur and metal

COMPORT, -S *vb* behave (oneself) in a specified way

COMPOS ▸ compo

COMPOSE, -S *vb* put together

COMPOSED *adj* calm

COMPOSER *n* person who writes music

COMPOSES ▸ compose

COMPOST, -S *n* decayed plants used as a fertilizer ▷ *vb* make (vegetable matter) into compost

COMPOT, -S *same as* ▸ compote

COMPOTE, -S *n* fruit stewed with sugar

COMPOTS ▸ compot

COMPOUND *adj* (thing, esp chemical) made up of two or more combined parts or elements ▷ *vb* combine or make by combining ▷ *n* fenced enclosure containing buildings

COMPRESS *vb* squeeze together ▷ *n* pad applied to stop bleeding or cool inflammation

COMPRINT *vb* print jointly

COMPRISE *vb* be made up of or make up

COMPRIZE *same as* ▸ comprise

COMPS ▸ comp

COMPT, -ED, -ING, -S *obsolete variant of* ▸ count

COMPTER, -S *n* formerly, a prison

COMPTING ▸ compt

COMPTS ▸ compt

COMPULSE *vb* compel

COMPUTE, -D, -S *vb* calculate, work out using a computer ▷ *n* calculation

COMPUTER *n* electronic machine that stores and processes data

COMPUTES ▸ compute

COMRADE, -S *n* fellow member of a union or socialist political party

COMS *pl n* one-piece woollen undergarment with long sleeves and legs

COMSAT, -S *n* communications satellite

COMSYMP, -S *n* disparaging term for a person sympathetic to communism

COMTE, -S *n* European noble

COMUS, -ES *n* wild party

CON, -NED, -S *vb* deceive, swindle ▷ *n* convict ▷ *prep* with

CONACRE, -D, -S *n* farming land let for a season or for eleven months ▷ *vb* let conacre

CONARIA ▸ conarium

CONARIAL ▸ conarium

CONARIUM, CONARIA *n* pineal gland

CONATION *n* psychological element that tends towards activity or change

CONATIVE *adj* aspect of some verbs indicating the effort of the agent in performing the verb

CONATUS *n* effort or striving of natural impulse

CONCAUSE *n* shared cause

CONCAVE, -D, -S *adj* curving inwards ▷ *vb* make concave

CONCEAL, -S *vb* cover and hide

CONCEDE, -D, -S *vb* admit to be true

CONCEDER ▸ concede

CONCEDES ▸ concede

CONCEDO *interj* I allow; I concede (a point)

CONCEIT, -S *n* too high an opinion of oneself ▷ *vb* like or be able to bear (something, such as food or drink)

CONCEITY *adj* full of conceit

CONCEIVE *vb* imagine, think

CONCENT, -S *n* concord, as of sounds, voices, etc

CONCEPT, -S *n* abstract or general idea

CONCEPTI > conceptus

CONCEPTS ▸ concept

CONCERN, -S *n* anxiety, worry ▷ *vb* worry (someone)

CONCERT, -S *n* musical entertainment

CONCERTO, CONCERTI *n* large-scale composition for a solo instrument and orchestra

CONCERTS ▸ concert

CONCETTO, CONCETTI *n* conceit, ingenious thought

CONCH, -S *same as* ▸ concha

CONCHA, -E, -S *n* any bodily organ or part resembling a shell in shape

CONCHAL ▸ concha

CONCHAS ▸ concha

CONCHATE *adj* shell-shaped

CONCHE, -D, -S, CONCHING *n* machine used to make chocolate ▷ *vb* use a conche

CONCHIE, -S *n* conscientious objector

CONCHING ▸ conche

CONCHO, -S *n* American metal ornament

CONCHOID *n* type of plane curve

CONCHOS ▸ concho

CONCHS ▸ conch

CONCHY *same as* ▸ conchie

CONCISE, -D, -R, -S *adj* brief and to the point ▷ *vb* mutilate

CONCLAVE *n* secret meeting

CONCLUDE *vb* decide by reasoning

CONCOCT, -S *vb* make up (a story or plan)

CONCOLOR *adj* of a single colour

CONCORD, -S *n* state of peaceful agreement, harmony ▷ *vb* agree

CONCOURS *n* contest

CONCRETE *n* mixture of cement, sand, stone, and water, used in building ▷ *vb* cover with concrete ▷ *adj* made of concrete

CONCREW, -S *vb* grow together

CONCUPY *n* concupiscence

CONCUR, -S *vb* agree

CONCUSS *vb* injure (the brain) by a fall or blow

COND *old inflection of* ▸ con

CONDEMN, -S *vb* express disapproval of

CONDENSE *vb* make shorter

CONDER, -S *n* person who directs the steering of a vessel

CONDIE, -S *n* culvert; tunnel

CONDIGN *adj* (esp of a punishment) fitting

CONDO, -ES, -S *n* condominium

CONDOLE, -D, -S *vb* express sympathy with someone in grief, pain, etc

CONDOLER ▸ condole

CONDOLES ▸ condole

CONDONE, -D, -S *vb* overlook or forgive (wrongdoing)

CONDONER ▸ condone

CONDONES ▸ condone

CONDOR, -ES, -S *n* large vulture of S America

CONDOS ▸ condo

CONDUCE, -D, -S *vb* lead or contribute (to a result)

CONDUCER ▸ conduce

CONDUCES ▸ conduce

CONDUCT, -S *n* management of an activity ▷ *vb* carry out (a task)

CONDUCTI > conductus

CONDUCTS ▸ conduct

CONDUIT, -S *n* channel or tube for fluid or cables

CONDYLAR ▸ condyle

CONDYLE, -S *n* rounded projection on the articulating end of a bone

CONE, -D, -S, CONING *n* object with a circular base, tapering to a point ▷ *vb* shape like a cone or part of a cone

CONELESS *adj* not bearing cones

CONELIKE *adj* like a cone

CONELRAD *n* US defence and information system for use in the event of air attack

CONENOSE *n* bloodsucking bug of the genus Triatoma

CONEPATE *same as* ▸ **conepatl**

CONEPATL *n* skunk

CONES ▸ cone

CONEY, -S *same as* ▸ **cony**

CONF, -S *n* online forum

CONFAB, -S *n* conversation ▷ *vb* converse

CONFECT, -S *vb* prepare by combining ingredients

CONFER, -S *vb* discuss together

CONFEREE *n* person who takes part in a conference

CONFERS ▸ confer

CONFERVA *n* type of threadlike green alga typically occurring in fresh water

CONFESS *vb* admit (a fault or crime)

CONFEST *adj* admitted

CONFETTI *n* small pieces of coloured paper thrown at weddings

CONFETTO *n* sweetmeat

CONFIDE, -D, -S *vb* tell someone (a secret)

CONFIDER ▸ confide

CONFIDES ▸ confide

CONFINE, -S *vb* keep within bounds ▷ *n* limit

CONFINED *adj* enclosed or restricted

CONFINER ▸ confine

CONFINES ▸ confine

CONFIRM, -S *vb* prove to be true

CONFIT, -S *n* preserve

CONFIX, -ED, -ES *vb* fasten

CONFLATE *vb* combine or blend into a whole

CONFLICT *n* disagreement ▷ *vb* be incompatible

CONFLUX *n* merging or following together, especially of rivers

CONFOCAL *adj* having a common focus or common foci

CONFORM, -S *vb* comply with accepted standards or customs

CONFOUND *vb* astound, bewilder

CONFRERE *n* colleague

CONFRONT *vb* come face to face with

CONFS ▸ conf

CONFUSE, -S *vb* mix up

CONFUSED *adj* lacking a clear understanding of something

CONFUSES ▸ confuse

CONFUTE, -D, -S *vb* prove wrong

CONFUTER ▸ confute

CONFUTES ▸ confute

CONGA, -ED, -ING, -S *n* dance performed by a number of people in single file ▷ *vb* dance the conga

CONGE, -D, -ING, -S *n* permission to depart or dismissal, esp when formal ▷ *vb* take one's leave

CONGEAL, -S *vb* (of a liquid) become thick and sticky

CONGED ▸ conge

CONGEE, -D, -S *same as* ▸ **conge**

CONGEING ▸ conge

CONGENER *n* member of a class, group, or other category, esp any animal of a specified genus

CONGENIC *adj* (of inbred animal cells) genetically

identical except for a single gene locus

CONGER, -S *n* large sea eel

CONGES ▸ conge

CONGEST, -S *vb* crowd or become crowded to excess

CONGIARY *n* Roman emperor's gift to the people or soldiers

CONGIUS, CONGII *n* unit of liquid measure equal to 1 imperial gallon

CONGLOBE *vb* gather into a globe or ball

CONGO, -ES, -S *same as* ▸ **congou**

CONGOU, -S *n* kind of black tea from China

CONGRATS *sentence substitute* congratulations

CONGREE, -D, -S *vb* agree

CONGREET *vb* (of two or more people) to greet one another

CONGRESS *n* formal meeting for discussion

CONGRUE, -D, -S *vb* agree

CONI ▸ conus

CONIA, -S *same as* ▸ **coniine**

CONIC *adj* having the shape of a cone

CONICAL *adj* cone-shaped

CONICINE *same as* ▸ **coniine**

CONICITY ▸ conical

CONICS *n* branch of geometry

CONIDIA ▸ conidium

CONIDIAL ▸ conidium

CONIDIAN ▸ conidium

CONIDIUM, CONIDIA *n* asexual spore formed at the tip of a specialized filament in certain types of fungi

CONIES ▸ cony

CONIFER, -S *n* cone-bearing tree, such as the fir or pine

CONIFORM *adj* cone-shaped

CONIINE, -S *n* colourless poisonous soluble liquid alkaloid found in hemlock

CONIMA, -S *n* gum resin from the conium hemlock tree

CONIN, -S *same as* ▸ **coniine**

CONINE, -S *same as* ▸ **coniine**

CONING ▸ cone

CONINS ▸ conin

CONIOSIS, CONIOSES *n* any disease or condition caused by dust inhalation

CONIUM, -S *n* umbelliferous plant, esp hemlock

CONJECT, -S *vb* conjecture

C

CONJEE, -D, -S n gruel of boiled rice and water ▷ vb prepare as, or in, a conjee

CONJOIN, -S vb join or become joined

CONJOINT adj united, joint, or associated

CONJUGAL adj of marriage

CONJUNCT adj joined ▷ n one of the propositions or formulas in a conjunction

CONJUNTO n style of Mexican music

CONJURE, -D, -S vb perform tricks that appear to be magic

CONJURER same as ▶ conjuror

CONJURES ▶ conjure

CONJUROR n person who performs magic tricks for people's entertainment

CONJURY n magic

CONK, -ED, -ING, -S n nose ▷ vb strike (someone) on the head or nose

CONKER n nut of the horse chestnut

CONKERS n game played with conkers tied on strings

CONKIER ▶ conky

CONKIEST ▶ conky

CONKING ▶ conk

CONKOUT, -S n time when a machine stops working

CONKS ▶ conk

CONKY, CONKIER, CONKIEST adj affected by the timber disease, conk

CONLANG, -S n artificially constructed language

CONMAN, CONMEN n man who uses confidence tricks to swindle or defraud

CONN, -S same as ▶ con

CONNATE adj existing in a person or thing from birth

CONNE, -S same as ▶ con

CONNECT, -S vb join together

CONNED ▶ con

CONNER, -S same as ▶ conder

CONNES ▶ conne

CONNIE, -S n tram or bus conductor

CONNING, -S ▶ con

CONNIVE, -D, -S vb allow (wrongdoing) by ignoring it

CONNIVER ▶ connive

CONNIVES ▶ connive

CONNOR, -S n type of saltwater fish

CONNOTE, -D, -S vb imply or suggest

CONNS ▶ conn

CONODONT n toothlike fossil derived from an eel-like animal

CONOID, -S n geometric surface ▷ adj conical, cone-shaped

CONOIDAL same as ▶ conoid

CONOIDIC ▶ conoid

CONOIDS ▶ conoid

CONQUER, -S vb defeat

CONQUEST n conquering

CONQUIAN same as ▶ cooncan

CONS ▶ con

CONSEIL, -S n advice

CONSENT, -S n agreement, permission ▷ vb permit, agree to

CONSERVE vb protect from harm, decay, or loss ▷ n jam containing large pieces of fruit

CONSIDER vb regard as

CONSIGN, -S vb put somewhere

CONSIST, -S vb be composed (of)

CONSOL n consolidated annuity, a former British government security

CONSOLE, -D, -S vb comfort in distress ▷ n panel of controls for electronic equipment

CONSOLER ▶ console

CONSOLES ▶ console

CONSOLS ▶ consol

CONSOMME n thin clear meat soup

CONSORT, -S vb keep company (with) ▷ n spouse of a monarch

CONSPIRE vb plan a crime together in secret

CONSPUE, -D, -S vb spit on with contempt

CONSTANT adj continuous ▷ n unvarying quantity

CONSTATE vb affirm

CONSTER, -S obsolete variant of ▶ construe

CONSTRUE vb interpret ▷ n something that is construed, such as a piece of translation

CONSUL, -S n official representing a state in a foreign country

CONSULAR n anyone of consular rank

CONSULS ▶ consul

CONSULT, -S vb go to for advice or information

CONSULTA n official planning meeting

CONSULTS ▶ consult

CONSUME, -D, -S vb eat or drink

CONSUMER n person who buys goods or uses services

CONSUMES ▶ consume

CONSUMPT n quantity used up; consumption

CONTACT, -S n communicating ▷ vb get in touch with ▷ interj (formerly) call made by the pilot to indicate the engine is ready for starting

CONTAGIA ▶ contagium

CONTAIN, -S vb hold or be capable of holding

CONTANGO n postponement of payment for and delivery of stock ▷ vb arrange such a postponement of payment

CONTE, -S n tale or short story, esp of adventure

CONTECK, -S n contention

CONTEMN, -S vb regard with contempt

CONTEMPO adj contemporary

CONTEMPT n dislike and disregard

CONTEND, -S vb deal with

CONTENT, -S n meaning or substance of a piece of writing ▷ adj satisfied with things as they are ▷ vb make (someone) content

CONTES ▶ conte

CONTESSA n Italian countess

CONTEST, -S n competition or struggle ▷ vb dispute, object to

CONTEXT, -S n circumstances of an event or fact

CONTINUA > continuum

CONTINUE vb (cause to) remain in a condition or place

CONTINUO n continuous bass part, usu played on a keyboard instrument

CONTLINE n space between the bilges of stowed casks

CONTO, -S n former Portuguese monetary unit worth 1000 escudos

CONTORNO, CONTORNI n in Italy, side dish of salad or vegetables

CONTORT, -S vb twist out of shape

CONTOS ▶ conto

CONTOUR, -S n outline ▷ vb shape so as to form or follow the contour of something

CONTRA, -S n counter-argument

CONTRACT n (document setting out) a formal agreement ▷ vb make a formal agreement (to do something)

CONTRAIL n aeroplane's vapour trail

CONTRAIR adj contrary

CONTRARY n complete opposite ▷ adj opposed, completely different ▷ adv in opposition

CONTRAS ▶ contra

CONTRAST n obvious difference ▷ vb compare in order to show differences

CONTRAT, -S old form of ▶ contract

CONTRATE adj (of gears) having teeth set at a right angle to the axis

CONTRATS ▶ contrat

CONTRIST vb make sad

CONTRITE adj sorry and apologetic

CONTRIVE vb make happen

CONTROL, -S n power to direct something ▷ vb have power over

CONTROLE adj officially registered

CONTROLS ▶ control

CONTROUL obsolete variant of ▶ control

CONTUND, -S vb pummel

CONTUSE, -D, -S vb injure (the body) without breaking the skin

CONURBAN adj relating to an urban region

CONURBIA n conurbations considered collectively

CONURE, -S n small American parrot

CONUS, CONI n any of several cone-shaped structures

CONVECT, -S vb circulate hot air by convection

CONVENE, -D, -S vb gather or summon for a formal meeting

CONVENER n person who calls a meeting

CONVENES ▶ convene

CONVENOR same as ▶ convener

CONVENT, -S n building where nuns live ▷ vb summon

CONVERGE vb meet or join

CONVERSE vb have a conversation ▷ n opposite or contrary ▷ adj reversed or opposite

CONVERSO n medieval Spanish Jew converting to Catholicism

CONVERT, -S vb change in form, character, or function ▷ n person who has converted to a different belief or religion

CONVEX, -ED, -ES adj curving outwards ▷ vb make convex

CONVEXLY ▶ convex

CONVEY, -ED, -S vb communicate (information)

CONVEYAL n act or means of conveying

CONVEYED ▶ convey

CONVEYER same as ▶ conveyor

CONVEYOR n person or thing that conveys

CONVEYS ▶ convey

CONVICT, -S vb declare guilty ▷ n person serving a prison sentence ▷ adj convicted

CONVINCE vb persuade by argument or evidence

CONVIVE, -D, -S vb feast together

CONVO, -S n conversation

CONVOKE, -D, -S vb call together

CONVOKER ▶ convoke

CONVOKES ▶ convoke

CONVOLVE vb wind or roll together

CONVOS ▶ convo

CONVOY, -ED, -S n group of vehicles or ships travelling together ▷ vb escort while in transit

CONVULSE vb (of part of the body) undergo violent spasms

CONWOMAN, CONWOMEN n woman who uses confidence tricks to swindle or defraud

CONY, CONIES n rabbit

COO, -ED, -S vb (of a dove or pigeon) make a soft murmuring sound ▷ n sound of cooing ▷ interj exclamation of surprise, awe, etc

COOCOO old spelling of ▶ cuckoo

COOED ▶ coo

COOEE, -D, -ING, -S interj call to attract attention ▷ vb utter this call ▷ n calling distance

COOER, -S ▶ coo

COOEY, -ED, -ING, -S same as ▶ cooee

COOF, -S n unintelligent person

COOING, -S ▶ coo

COOINGLY ▶ coo

COOINGS ▶ cooing

COOK, -ED, -S vb prepare (food) by heating ▷ n person who cooks food

COOKABLE adj able to be cooked ▷ n something that can be cooked

COOKBOOK n book containing recipes and instructions for cooking

COOKED ▶ cook

COOKER, -S n apparatus for cooking heated by gas or electricity

COOKERY n art of cooking

COOKEY, -S same as ▶ cookie

COOKIE, -S n biscuit

COOKING, -S ▶ cook

COOKLESS adj devoid of a cook

COOKMAID n maid who assists a cook

COOKOFF, -S n cookery competition

COOKOUT, -S n party where a meal is cooked and eaten out of doors

COOKROOM n room in which food is cooked

COOKS ▶ cook

COOKSHOP n shop that sells cookery equipment

COOKTOP, -S n flat unit for cooking in saucepans or the top part of a stove

COOKWARE n cooking utensils

COOKY same as ▶ cookie

COOL, -ED, -EST, -S adj moderately cold ▷ vb make or become cool ▷ n coolness

COOLABAH n Australian tree that grows along rivers, with smooth bark and long narrow leaves

COOLAMON n shallow dish of wood or bark, used for carrying water

COOLANT, -S n fluid used to cool machinery while it is working

COOLDOWN n gentle stretching exercises after strenuous activity

COOLED ▶ cool

COOLER, -S n container for making or keeping things cool

COOLEST ▶ cool

COOLIBAH same as ▶ coolabah

COOLIBAR same as ▶ **coolabah**

COOLING, -S n as in **regenerative cooling** method of cooling rocket combustion chambers

COOLISH ▶ **cool**

COOLIST, -S n person who does not believe in global warming

COOLLY ▶ **cool**

COOLNESS ▶ **cool**

COOLS ▶ **cool**

COOLTH, -S n coolness

COOM, -ED, -ING, -S n waste material ▷ vb blacken

COOMB, -S n short valley or deep hollow

COOMBE, -S same as ▶ **coomb**

COOMBS ▶ **coomb**

COOMED ▶ **coom**

COOMIER ▶ **coomy**

COOMIEST ▶ **coomy**

COOMING ▶ **coom**

COOMS ▶ **coom**

COOMY, COOMIER, COOMIEST adj grimy

COONCAN, -S n card game for two players, similar to rummy

COONDOG, -S n dog trained to hunt raccoons

COONSKIN n pelt of a raccoon

COONTIE, -S n evergreen plant of S Florida

COONTY same as ▶ **coontie**

COOP, -ED, -ING, -S n cage or pen for poultry ▷ vb confine in a restricted area

COOPER, -ED, -S n person who makes or repairs barrels ▷ vb make or mend (barrels, casks, etc)

COOPERY same as > **cooperage**

COOPING ▶ **coop**

COOPS ▶ **coop**

COOPT, -ED, -ING, -S vb add (someone) to a group by the agreement of the existing members

COOPTION ▶ **coopt**

COOPTS ▶ **coopt**

COORIE, -D, -S same as ▶ **courie**

COOS ▶ **coo**

COOSEN, -ED, -S same as ▶ **cozen**

COOSER, -S n stallion

COOSIN, -ED, -S same as ▶ **cozen**

COOST Scots form of ▶ **cast**

COOT, -S n small black water bird

COOTCH, -ED, -ES n hiding place ▷ vb hide

COOTER, -S n type of freshwater turtle

COOTIE, -S n body louse

COOTIKIN n gaiter

COOTS ▶ **coot**

COP, -PED, -PING, -S same as ▶ **copper**

COPAIBA, -S n resin obtained from certain tropical trees

COPAIVA, -S same as ▶ **copaiba**

COPAL, -S n resin used in varnishes

COPALM, -S n aromatic resin

COPALS ▶ **copal**

COPARENT n fellow parent

COPASTOR n fellow pastor

COPATRON n fellow patron

COPAY, -S n amount payable for treatment by person with medical insurance

COPE, -D, -S vb deal successfully (with) ▷ n large ceremonial cloak worn by some Christian priests

COPECK, -S same as ▶ **kopeck**

COPED ▶ **cope**

COPEMATE n partner

COPEN, -S n shade of blue

COPEPOD, -S n type of minute crustacean

COPER, -ED, -ING, -S n horse-dealer ▷ vb smuggle liquor to deep-sea fishermen

COPES ▶ **cope**

COPIABLE adj able to be copied

COPIED ▶ **copy**

COPIER, -S n machine that copies

COPIES ▶ **copy**

COPIHUE, -S n Chilean bellflower

COPILOT, -S n second pilot of an aircraft ▷ vb act as a copilot

COPING, -S n sloping top row of a wall

COPIOUS adj abundant, plentiful

COPITA, -S n tulip-shaped sherry glass

COPLANAR adj lying in the same plane

COPLOT, -S vb plot together

COPOUT, -S n act of avoiding responsibility

COPPED ▶ **cop**

COPPER, -ED, -S n soft reddish-brown metal ▷ adj reddish-brown ▷ vb coat or cover with copper

COPPERAH same as ▶ **copra**

COPPERAS n ferrous sulphate

COPPERED ▶ **copper**

COPPERS ▶ **copper**

COPPERY adj like copper

COPPICE, -S n small group of trees growing close together ▷ vb trim back (trees or bushes) to form a coppice

COPPICED ▶ **coppice**

COPPICES ▶ **coppice**

COPPIES ▶ **coppy**

COPPIN, -S n ball of thread

COPPING ▶ **cop**

COPPINS ▶ **coppin**

COPPLE, -S n hill rising to a point

COPPRA, -S same as ▶ **copra**

COPPY, COPPIES n small wooden stool

COPRA, -S n dried oil-yielding kernel of the coconut

COPRAH, -S same as ▶ **copra**

COPRAS ▶ **copra**

COPREMIA same as > **copraemia**

COPREMIC same as > **copraemic**

COPRINCE n fellow prince

COPROSMA n Australasian shrub sometimes planted for ornament

COPS ▶ **cop**

COPSE, -D, -S, COPSING same as ▶ **coppice**

COPSHOP, -S n police station

COPSIER ▶ **copsy**

COPSIEST ▶ **copsy**

COPSING ▶ **copse**

COPSY, COPSIER, COPSIEST adj having copses

COPTER, -S n helicopter

COPULA, -E, -S n verb used to link the subject and complement of a sentence

COPULAR ▶ **copula**

COPULAS ▶ **copula**

COPURIFY vb purify together

COPY, COPIED, COPIES n thing made to look exactly like another ▷ vb make a copy of

COPYABLE ▶ **copy**

COPYBOOK n book of specimens for imitation

COPYBOY, -S n formerly, in journalism, young man who carried copy and ran errands

COPYCAT, -S n person who imitates or copies someone ▷ vb imitate with great attention to detail

COPYDESK n desk where newspaper copy is edited

COPYEDIT vb prepare text for printing by styling, correcting, etc

COPYGIRL n formerly, in journalism, young woman who carried copy and ran errands

COPYHOLD n tenure less than freehold of land in England evidenced by a copy of the Court roll

COPYING, -S n act of copying

COPYISM, -S n slavish copying

COPYIST, -S n person who makes written copies

COPYLEFT n permission to use something free of charge ▷ vb use copyright law to make (work, esp software) free to use

COPYREAD vb subedit

COQUET, -S vb behave flirtatiously

COQUETRY n flirtation

COQUETS ▸ coquet

COQUETTE n woman who flirts

COQUI, -S n type of tree-dwelling frog

COQUILLA n type of South American nut

COQUILLE n any dish, esp seafood, served in a scallop shell

COQUINA, -S n soft limestone

COQUIS ▸ coqui

COQUITO, -S n Chilean palm tree yielding edible nuts and a syrup

COR, -S interj exclamation of surprise, amazement, or admiration ▷ n Hebrew measure of dry weight

CORACLE, -S n small round boat of wicker covered with skins

CORACOID n paired ventral bone of the pectoral girdle in vertebrates

CORAGGIO interj exhortation to hold one's nerve

CORAL, -S n hard substance formed from the skeletons of very small sea animals ▷ adj orange-pink

CORALLUM, CORALLA n skeleton of any zoophyte

CORALS ▸ coral

CORAM prep before, in the presence of

CORAMINE n type of stimulant

CORANACH same as ▸ coronach

CORANTO, -S same as ▸ courante

CORBAN, -S n gift to God

CORBE, -S obsolete variant of ▸ corbel

CORBEAU, -S n blackish green colour

CORBEIL, -S n carved ornament in the form of a basket of fruit, flowers, etc

CORBEL, -ED, -S n stone or timber support sticking out of a wall ▷ vb lay (a stone or brick) so that it forms a corbel

CORBES ▸ corbe

CORBIE, -S n raven or crow

CORBINA, -S n type of North American whiting

CORBY same as ▸ corbie

CORCASS n in Ireland, marshland

CORD n thin rope or thick string ▷ adj (of fabric) ribbed ▷ vb bind or furnish with a cord or cords

CORDAGE, -S n lines and rigging of a vessel

CORDATE adj heart-shaped

CORDED adj tied or fastened with cord

CORDELLE vb to tow

CORDER, -S ▸ cord

CORDIAL, -S adj warm and friendly ▷ n drink with a fruit base

CORDINER n shoemaker

CORDING, -S ▸ cord

CORDITE, -S n explosive used in guns and bombs

CORDLESS adj powered by an internal battery rather than a power cable

CORDLIKE ▸ cord

CORDOBA, -S n standard monetary unit of Nicaragua

CORDON, -ED, -S n chain of police, soldiers, etc, guarding an area ▷ vb put or form a cordon (around)

CORDOVAN n fine leather made principally from horsehide

CORDS pl n trousers made of corduroy

CORDUROY n cotton fabric with a velvety ribbed surface

CORDWAIN an archaic name for ▸ cordovan

CORDWOOD n wood that has been cut into lengths of four feet so that it can be stacked in cords

CORE, -D, -S, CORING n central part of certain fruits, containing the seeds ▷ vb remove the core from

COREDEEM vb redeem together

COREGENT n joint regent

COREIGN, -S vb reign jointly

CORELATE same as > correlate

CORELESS ▸ core

CORELLA, -S n white Australian cockatoo

COREMIUM, COREMIA n spore-producing organ of certain fungi

CORER, -S ▸ core

CORES ▸ core

CORF, CORVES n wagon or basket used formerly in mines

CORGI, -S n short-legged sturdy dog

CORIA ▸ corium

CORIES ▸ cory

CORING ▸ core

CORIOUS adj leathery

CORIUM, CORIA, -S n deep inner layer of the skin

CORIVAL, -S same as ▸ corrival

CORIXID, -S n type of water bug

CORK, -S n thick light bark of a Mediterranean oak ▷ vb seal with a cork ▷ adj made of cork

CORKAGE, -S n restaurant's charge for serving wine bought elsewhere

CORKED adj (of wine) spoiled through having a decayed cork

CORKER, -S n splendid or outstanding person or thing

CORKIER ▸ corky

CORKIEST ▸ corky

CORKING adj excellent

CORKIR, -S n lichen from which red or purple dye is made

CORKLIKE ▸ cork

CORKS ▸ cork

CORKTREE n type of evergreen oak tree

CORKWING n type of greenish or bluish European fish

CORKWOOD n type of small tree of the southeastern US, with very lightweight porous wood

CORKY, CORKIER, CORKIEST same as ▸ corked

CORM, -S n bulblike underground stem of certain plants

C

CORMEL, -S n new small corm arising from the base of a fully developed one

CORMIDIA ▷ **cormidium**

CORMLET, -S n small corm

CORMLIKE adj resembling a corm

CORMOID adj like a corm

CORMOUS ▷ **corm**

CORMS ▷ **corm**

CORMUS, -ES n corm

CORN, -ING, -S n cereal plant such as wheat or oats ▷ vb feed (animals) with corn, esp oats

CORNACRE same as ▷ **conacre**

CORNAGE, -S n rent fixed according to the number of horned cattle pastured

CORNBALL n person given to mawkish or unsophisticated behaviour

CORNCAKE n kind of cornmeal flatbread

CORNCOB, -S n core of an ear of maize, to which the kernels are attached

CORNCRIB n ventilated building for the storage of unhusked maize

CORNEA, -E, -S n transparent membrane covering the eyeball

CORNEAL ▷ **cornea**

CORNEAS ▷ **cornea**

CORNED adj preserved in salt or brine

CORNEL, -S n type of plant such as the dogwood and dwarf cornel

CORNEOUS adj horny

CORNER, -ED, -S n area or angle where two converging lines or surfaces meet ▷ vb force into a difficult or inescapable position

CORNET, -S n former cavalry officer

CORNETCY n commission or rank of a cornet

CORNETS ▷ **cornet**

CORNETT, -S n musical instrument

CORNETTO, CORNETTI same as ▷ **cornett**

CORNETTS ▷ **cornett**

CORNFED adj fed on corn

CORNFLAG n gladiolus

CORNFLY n small fly

CORNHUSK n outer protective covering of an ear of maize

CORNI ▷ **corno**

CORNICE, -D, -S n decorative moulding round

the top of a wall ▷ vb furnish or decorate with or as if with a cornice

CORNICHE n coastal road, esp one built into the face of a cliff

CORNICLE n wax-secreting organ on an aphid's abdomen

CORNIER ▷ **corny**

CORNIEST ▷ **corny**

CORNIFIC adj producing horns

CORNIFY vb turn soft tissue hard

CORNILY ▷ **corny**

CORNING ▷ **corn**

CORNIST, -S n horn-player

CORNLAND n land suitable for growing corn or grain

CORNLOFT n loft for storing corn

CORNMEAL n meal made from maize

CORNMILL n flour mill

CORNMOTH n moth whose larvae feed on grain

CORNO, CORNI n French horn

CORNPIPE n musical instrument made from a stalk of corn etc

CORNPONE n American corn bread

CORNRENT n rent for land that is paid in corn

CORNROW, -S n hairstyle in which the hair is plaited in close parallel rows ▷ vb style the hair in a cornrow

CORNS ▷ **corn**

CORNSILK n threads on an ear of maize

CORNU, -A n part or structure resembling a horn or having a hornlike pattern

CORNUAL ▷ **cornu**

CORNUS, -ES n any member of the genus Cornus, such as dogwood

CORNUTE adj having or resembling cornua

CORNUTED same as ▷ **cornute**

CORNWORM n cornmoth larva

CORNY, CORNIER, CORNIEST adj unoriginal or excessively sentimental

COROCORE same as ▷ **corocoro**

COROCORO n South Asian vessel fitted with outriggers

CORODY, CORODIES n feudal law

COROLLA, -S n petals of a flower collectively

CORONA, -E, -S n ring of light round the moon or sun

CORONACH n dirge or lamentation for the dead

CORONAE ▷ **corona**

CORONAL, -S n circlet for the head ▷ adj of or relating to a corona or coronal

CORONARY adj of the arteries surrounding the heart ▷ n coronary thrombosis

CORONAS ▷ **corona**

CORONATE vb to crown

CORONEL, -S n iron head of a tilting spear

CORONER, -S n official responsible for the investigation of deaths

CORONET, -S n small crown

CORONIAL adj relating to a coroner

CORONIS n symbol used in Greek writing

CORONIUM n highly ionized iron and nickel seen as a green line in the solar coronal spectrum

CORONOID adj crown-shaped

COROTATE vb rotate together

COROZO, -S n tropical American palm whose seeds yield a useful oil

CORPORA ▷ **corpus**

CORPORAL n noncommissioned officer in an army ▷ adj of the body

CORPORAS n communion cloth

CORPS n military unit with a specific function

CORPSE, -D, -S, CORPSING n dead body ▷ vb laugh or cause to laugh involuntarily or inopportunely while on stage

CORPSMAN, CORPSMEN n medical orderly or stretcher-bearer

CORPUS, CORPORA, -ES n collection of writings, esp by a single author

CORRADE, -D, -S vb erode by the abrasive action of rock particles

CORRAL, -S n enclosure for cattle or horses ▷ vb put in a corral

CORREA, -S n Australian evergreen shrub with large showy tubular flowers

CORRECT, -S adj free from error, true ▷ vb put right

CORRETTO n espresso containing alcohol

CORRIDA, -S the Spanish word for ▶ **bullfight**

CORRIDOR n passage in a building or train

CORRIE, -S same as ▶ **cirque**

CORRIVAL a rare word for ▶ **rival**

CORRODE, -D, -S vb eat or be eaten away by chemical action or rust

CORRODER ▶ **corrode**

CORRODES ▶ **corrode**

CORRODY same as ▶ **corody**

CORRUPT, -S adj open to or involving bribery ▷ vb make corrupt

CORS ▶ **cor**

CORSAC, -S n type of fox of central Asia

CORSAGE, -S n small bouquet worn on the bodice of a dress

CORSAIR, -S n pirate

CORSE, -S n archaic word for corpse

CORSELET n one-piece undergarment combining a corset and bra

CORSES ▶ **corse**

CORSET, -ED, -S n women's undergarment ▷ vb dress or enclose in, or as in, a corset

CORSETRY n making of or dealing in corsets

CORSETS ▶ **corset**

CORSEY, -S n pavement or pathway

CORSITE, -S n type of rock

CORSIVE, -S n corrodent

CORSLET, -S same as ▶ **corselet**

CORSNED, -S n ordeal to discover innocence or guilt

CORSO, -S n promenade

CORTEGE, -S n funeral procession

CORTEX, -ES, CORTICES n outer layer of the brain or other internal organ

CORTICAL ▶ **cortex**

CORTICES ▶ **cortex**

CORTILE, CORTILI n open, internal courtyard

CORTIN, -S n adrenal cortex extract

CORTINA, -S n weblike part of certain mushrooms

CORTINS ▶ **cortin**

CORTISOL n principal glucocorticoid secreted by the adrenal cortex

CORULER, -S n joint ruler

CORUNDUM n hard mineral used as an abrasive

CORVEE, -S n day's unpaid labour owed by a feudal vassal to their lord

CORVES ▶ **corf**

CORVET, -ED, -S same as ▶ **curvet**

CORVETTE n lightly armed escort warship ▷ vb participate in social activities with fellow Corvette car enthusiasts

CORVID, -S n any member of the crow family

CORVINA, -S same as ▶ **corbina**

CORVINE adj of, relating to, or resembling a crow

CORVUS, -ES n type of ancient hook

CORY, CORIES n catfish belonging to the South American Corydoras genus

CORYBANT n wild attendant of the goddess Cybele

CORYLUS n hazel genus

CORYMB, -S n flat-topped flower cluster

CORYMBED ▶ **corymb**

CORYMBS ▶ **corymb**

CORYPHE, -S n leader of a Greek chorus

CORYPHEE n leading dancer of a corps de ballet

CORYPHES ▶ **coryphe**

CORYZA, -S n acute inflammation in the nose

CORYZAL ▶ **coryza**

CORYZAS ▶ **coryza**

COS same as ▶ **cosine**

COSCRIPT vb script jointly

COSE, -D, -S, COSING vb get cosy

COSEC, -S same as ▶ **cosecant**

COSECANT n ratio of the hypotenuse to the opposite side in a right-angled triangle

COSECH, -S n hyperbolic cosecant

COSECS ▶ **cosec**

COSED ▶ **cose**

COSES ▶ **cose**

COSET, -S n mathematical set

COSEY, -S n tea cosy

COSH, -ED, -ES, -ING n heavy blunt weapon ▷ vb hit with a cosh

COSHER, -ED, -S vb pamper or coddle

COSHERER ▶ **cosher**

COSHERS ▶ **cosher**

COSHERY n Irish chief's right to lodge at their tenants' houses

COSHES ▶ **cosh**

COSHING ▶ **cosh**

COSIE same as ▶ **cosy**

COSIED ▶ **cosy**

COSIER, -S n cobbler

COSIES ▶ **cosy**

COSIEST ▶ **cosy**

COSIGN, -ED, -S vb sign jointly

COSIGNER ▶ **cosign**

COSIGNS ▶ **cosign**

COSILY ▶ **cosy**

COSINE, -S n trigonometric function

COSINESS ▶ **cosy**

COSING ▶ **cose**

COSMEA, -S n plant of the genus Cosmos

COSMESIS, COSMESES n aesthetic covering on a prosthesis to make it look more natural

COSMETIC n preparation used to improve the appearance of a person's skin ▷ adj improving the appearance only

COSMIC adj of the whole universe

COSMICAL same as ▶ **cosmic**

COSMID, -S n segment of DNA

COSMIN, -S same as ▶ **cosmine**

COSMINE, -S n substance resembling dentine

COSMINS ▶ **cosmin**

COSMISM, -S n Russian cultural and philosophical movement

COSMIST, -S ▶ **cosmism**

COSMOID adj having two inner bony layers and a cosmine outer layer

COSMOS, -ES n universe

COSPLAY, -S n recreational activity in which people interact while dressed as fictional characters

COSS, -ES another name for ▶ **kos**

COSSACK, -S n Slavonic warrior-peasant

COSSES ▶ **coss**

COSSET, -ED, -S vb pamper ▷ n any pet animal, esp a lamb

COSSIE, -S n informal name for a swimming costume

COST, -ED, -S n amount of money, time, labour, etc, required for something ▷ vb have as its cost

COSTA, -E n riblike part, such as the midrib of a plant leaf

COSTAL, -S n strengthening rib of an insect's wing

COSTALLY ▶ costal

COSTALS ▶ costal

COSTAR, -S n actor who shares the billing with another ▷ vb share the billing with another actor

COSTARD, -S n English variety of apple tree

COSTARS ▶ costar

COSTATE adj having ribs

COSTATED same as ▶ costate

COSTE, -S vb draw near

COSTEAN, -S vb mine for lodes

COSTED ▶ cost

COSTER, -S n person who sells fruit, vegetables etc from a barrow

COSTES ▶ coste

COSTING, -S n as in marginal costing method of cost accounting

COSTIVE adj having or causing constipation

COSTLESS ▶ cost

COSTLY, COSTLIER adj expensive

COSTMARY n herbaceous Asian plant

COSTREL, -S n flask, usually of earthenware or leather

COSTS ▶ cost

COSTUME, -D, -S n style of dress of a particular place or time, or for a particular activity ▷ vb provide with a costume

COSTUMER same as ▷ costumier

COSTUMES ▶ costume

COSTUMEY adj (stage) costume-like; unrealistic

COSTUS, -ES n Himalayan herb with an aromatic root

COSY, COSIED, COSIES, COSIEST, -ING adj warm and snug ▷ n cover for keeping things warm ▷ vb make oneself snug and warm

COT, -S, -TED, -TING n baby's bed with high sides ▷ vb entangle or become entangled

COTAN, -S same as ▷ cotangent

COTE, -D, -S, COTING same as ▶ cot

COTEAU, -S, -X n hillside

COTED ▶ cote

COTELINE n kind of muslin

COTENANT n person who holds property jointly or in common with others

COTERIE, -S n exclusive group, clique

COTES ▶ cote

COTH, -S n hyperbolic cotangent

COTHURN, -S same as ▷ cothurnus

COTHURNI > cothurnus

COTHURNS ▶ cothurn

COTIDAL adj (of a line on a tidal chart) joining points at which high tide occurs simultaneously

COTIJA, -S n salty Mexican cheese

COTILLON same as ▷ cotillion

COTING ▶ cote

COTINGA, -S n tropical bird

COTININE n substance used to indicate presence of nicotine

COTISE, -D, -S, COTISING same as ▶ cottise

COTLAND, -S n grounds that belong to a cotter

COTQUEAN n coarse woman

COTS ▶ cot

COTT, -S same as ▶ cot

COTTA, -E, -S n short surplice

COTTABUS n ancient Greek game involving throwing wine into a vessel

COTTAE ▶ cotta

COTTAGE, -S n small house in the country

COTTAGER n person who lives in a cottage

COTTAGES ▶ cottage

COTTAGEY adj resembling a cottage

COTTAR, -S n cottage-dwelling peasant

COTTAS ▶ cotta

COTTED ▶ cot

COTTER, -ED, -S n pin or wedge used to secure machine parts ▷ vb secure (two parts) with a cotter

COTTID, -S n type of fish typically with a large head, tapering body, and spiny fins

COTTIER, -S same as ▶ cottar

COTTING ▶ cot

COTTISE, -D, -S n type of heraldic decoration ▷ vb (in heraldry) decorate with a cottise

COTTOID adj resembling a fish of the genus Cottus

COTTON, -ED, -S n white downy fibre covering the seeds of a tropical plant ▷ vb take a liking

COTTONY adj like cotton

COTTOWN, -S Scots variant of ▶ cotton

COTTS ▶ cott

COTTUS, -ES n type of fish with four yellowish knobs on its head

COTURNIX n variety of quail

COTWAL, -S n Indian police officer

COTYLE, COTYLAE, -S n cuplike cavity

COTYLOID adj shaped like a cup ▷ n small bone forming part of the acetabular cavity in some mammals

COTYPE, -S n additional specimen in biological study

COUCAL, -S n type of ground-living bird of Africa, S Asia, and Australia, with long strong legs

COUCH, -ED, -ES n piece of upholstered furniture for seating more than one person ▷ vb express in a particular way

COUCHANT adj in a lying position

COUCHE adj in heraldry (of a shield), tilted

COUCHED ▶ couch

COUCHEE, -S n reception held late at night

COUCHER, -S ▶ couch

COUCHES ▶ couch

COUCHING n method of embroidery

COUDE, -S adj relating to the construction of a reflecting telescope ▷ n type of reflecting telescope

COUGAN, -S n drunk and rowdy person

COUGAR, -S n puma

COUGH, -ED, -ING, -S vb expel air from the lungs abruptly and noisily ▷ n act or sound of coughing

COUGHER, -S ▶ cough

COUGHING ▶ cough

COUGHS ▶ cough

COUGUAR, -S same as ▶ cougar

COULD ▶ can

COULDEST same as ▶ couldst

COULDST vb form of 'could' used with the pronoun thou or its relative form

COULEE, -S n flow of molten lava

COULIS n thin purée of vegetables or fruit
COULISSE n timber grooved to take a sliding panel
COULOIR, -S n deep gully on a mountain side, esp in the French Alps
COULOMB, -S n SI unit of electric charge
COULTER, -S n blade at the front of a ploughshare
COUMARIC ▶ **coumarin**
COUMARIN n white vanilla-scented crystalline ester
COUMAROU n tonka bean tree, or its seed
COUNCIL, -S n group meeting for discussion or consultation ▷ adj of or by a council
COUNSEL, -S n advice or guidance ▷ vb give guidance to
COUNT, -ED, -S vb say numbers in order ▷ n counting
COUNTER, -S n long flat surface in a bank or shop ▷ vb oppose, retaliate against ▷ adv in the opposite direction
COUNTESS n woman holding the rank of count or earl
COUNTIAN n dweller in a given county
COUNTIES ▶ **county**
COUNTING n act or instance of saying numbers in order
COUNTROL obsolete variant of ▶ **control**
COUNTRY n nation
COUNTS ▶ **count**
COUNTY, COUNTIES n (in some countries) division of a country ▷ adj upper-class
COUP, -ED, -ING, -S n successful action ▷ vb turn or fall over
COUPE, -S n sports car with two doors and a sloping fixed roof
COUPED ▶ **coup**
COUPEE, -S n dance movement
COUPER, -S n dealer
COUPES ▶ **coupe**
COUPING ▶ **coup**
COUPLE, -D, -S n two people who are married or romantically involved ▷ vb connect, associate
COUPLER, -S n mechanical device
COUPLES ▶ **couple**

COUPLET, -S n two consecutive lines of verse
COUPLING n device for connecting things, such as railway carriages
COUPON, -S n piece of paper entitling the holder to a discount or gift
COUPS ▶ **coup**
COUPURE, -S n entrenchment made by besieged forces behind a breach
COUR, -ING, -S obsolete variant of ▶ **cover**
COURAGE, -S n ability to face danger or pain without fear
COURANT, -S n old dance in quick triple time ▷ adj (of an animal) running
COURANTE n old dance in quick triple time
COURANTO same as ▶ **courante**
COURANTS ▶ **courant**
COURB, -ED, -ING, -S vb to bend
COURD obsolete variant of ▶ **covered**
COURE, -D, -S obsolete variant of ▶ **cover**
COURIE, -D, -S vb nestle or snuggle
COURIER, -S n person employed to look after holidaymakers ▷ vb send (a parcel, letter, etc) by courier
COURIES ▶ **courie**
COURING ▶ **cour**
COURLAN, -S another name for ▶ **limpkin**
COURS ▶ **cour**
COURSE, -D n series of lessons or medical treatment ▷ vb (of liquid) run swiftly
COURSER, -S n swift horse
COURSES another word for ▶ **menses**
COURSING n hunting with hounds trained to hunt game by sight
COURT, -ED, -ING, -S n body which decides legal cases ▷ vb try to gain the love of
COURTER, -S n suitor
COURTESY n politeness, good manners
COURTIER n attendant at a royal court
COURTING ▶ **court**
COURTLET n small court
COURTLY adj ceremoniously polite
COURTS ▶ **court**

COUSCOUS n type of semolina used in North African cookery
COUSIN, -S n child of one's uncle or aunt
COUSINLY ▶ **cousin**
COUSINRY n collective term for cousins
COUSINS ▶ **cousin**
COUTA, -S n traditional Australian sailing boat
COUTEAU, -X n large two-edged knife used formerly as a weapon
COUTER, -S n armour designed to protect the elbow
COUTH, -ER, -EST, -S adj refined or refinement
COUTHIE, -R adj sociable
COUTHS ▶ **couth**
COUTHY same as ▶ **couthie**
COUTIL, -S n type of tightly woven twill cloth
COUTILLE same as ▶ **coutil**
COUTILS ▶ **coutil**
COUTURE, -S n high-fashion designing and dressmaking ▷ adj relating to high fashion design and dress-making
COUVADE n custom in certain cultures relating to childbirth
COUVERT, -S another word for ▶ **cover**
COUZIN, -S n South African word for a friend
COVALENT > **covalency**
COVARY, COVARIED, COVARIES vb vary together maintaining a certain mathematical relationship
COVE, -D, -S n small bay or inlet ▷ vb form an architectural cove in
COVELET, -S n small cove
COVEN, -S n meeting of witches
COVENANT n contract ▷ vb agree by a covenant
COVENS ▶ **coven**
COVENT, -S same as ▶ **convent**
COVER, -ED, -S vb place something over, to protect or conceal ▷ n anything that covers
COVERAGE n amount or extent covered
COVERALL n thing that covers something entirely
COVERED ▶ **cover**
COVERER, -S ▶ **cover**
COVERING another word for ▶ **cover**
COVERLET n bed cover

COVERLID same as ▸coverlet

COVERS ▸cover

COVERSED adj as in coversed sine obsolete function in trigonometry

COVERT, -ER, -S adj concealed, secret ▷ n thicket giving shelter to game birds or animals

COVERTLY ▸covert

COVERTS ▸covert

COVERUP, -S n concealment of a mistake, crime, etc

COVES ▸cove

COVET, -ED, -ING, -S vb long to possess (what belongs to someone else)

COVETER, -S ▸covet

COVETING ▸covet

COVETISE n covetousness

COVETOUS adj jealously longing to possess something

COVETS ▸covet

COVEY, -S n small flock of grouse or partridge

COVIN, -S n conspiracy between two or more persons

COVINE, -S n conspiracy between two or more persons

COVING, -S same as ▸cove

COVINOUS adj deceitful

COVINS ▸covin

COVYNE, -S same as ▸covin

COW, -ED, -ING, -S n mature female of certain mammals ▷ vb intimidate, subdue

COWAGE, -S n tropical climbing plant

COWAL, -S n shallow lake or swampy depression supporting vegetation

COWAN, -S n drystone waller

COWARD, -ED, -S n person who lacks courage ▷ vb show (someone) up to be a coward

COWARDLY adj of or characteristic of a coward

COWARDRY n cowardice

COWARDS ▸coward

COWBANE, -S n poisonous marsh plant

COWBELL, -S n bell hung around a cow's neck

COWBERRY n evergreen shrub of N temperate and Arctic regions

COWBIND, -S n any of various bryony plants, esp the white bryony

COWBIRD, -S n American oriole with a dark plumage and short bill

COWBOY, -ED, -S n (in the US) man who herds and tends cattle on a ranch ▷ vb work or behave as a cowboy

COWED ▸cow

COWEDLY ▸cow

COWER, -ED, -ING, -S vb cringe in fear

COWFISH n type of trunkfish with hornlike spines over the eyes

COWFLAP, -S n cow dung

COWFLOP, -S n foxglove

COWGIRL, -S n (in the US) woman who herds and tends cattle on a ranch

COWGRASS n red clover

COWHAGE, -S same as ▸cowage

COWHAND, -S same as ▸cowboy

COWHEARD same as ▸cowherd

COWHEEL, -S n heel of a cow, used as a cooking ingredient

COWHERB, -S n European plant with clusters of pink flowers

COWHERD, -S n person employed to tend cattle

COWHIDE, -D, -S n hide of a cow ▷ vb lash with a cowhide whip

COWHOUSE n byre

COWIER ▸cowy

COWIEST ▸cowy

COWING ▸cow

COWINNER n joint winner

COWISH, -ES adj cowardly ▷ n N American plant with an edible root

COWITCH another name for ▸cowage

COWK, -ED, -ING, -S vb retch or feel nauseated

COWL, -S same as ▸cowling

COWLED adj wearing a cowl

COWLICK, -S n tuft of hair over the forehead

COWLIKE adj like a cow

COWLING, -S n cover on an engine

COWLS ▸cowl

COWMAN, COWMEN n man who owns cattle

COWORKER n fellow worker

COWP, -ED, -ING, -S same as ▸coup

COWPAT, -S n pool of cow dung

COWPEA, -S n type of tropical climbing plant

COWPED ▸cowp

COWPIE, -S n cowpat

COWPING ▸cowp

COWPLOP, -S n cow dung

COWPOKE, -S n cowboy

COWPOX, -ES n disease of cows

COWPS ▸cowp

COWPUNK, -S n music that combines country music and punk

COWRIE, -S n brightly marked sea shell

COWRITE, -S, COWROTE vb write jointly

COWRITER ▸cowrite

COWRITES ▸cowrite

COWROTE ▸cowrite

COWRY same as ▸cowrie

COWS ▸cow

COWSHED, -S n byre

COWSKIN, -S same as ▸cowhide

COWSLIP, -S n small yellow European wild flower

COWTOWN, -S n rural town in a cattle-raising area

COWTREE, -S n South American tree that produces latex

COWY, COWIER, COWIEST adj cowlike

COX, -ED, -ES, -ING n coxswain ▷ vb act as cox of (a boat)

COXA, -E n technical name for the hipbone or hip joint

COXAL ▸coxa

COXALGIA n pain in the hip joint

COXALGIC ▸coxalgia

COXALGY same as ▸coxalgia

COXCOMB, -S same as ▸cockscomb

COXED ▸cox

COXES ▸cox

COXIB, -S n anti-inflammatory drug

COXIER ▸coxy

COXIEST ▸coxy

COXINESS ▸coxy

COXING ▸cox

COXITIS n inflammation of the hip joint

COXLESS ▸cox

COXSWAIN n person who steers a rowing boat

COXY, COXIER, COXIEST adj cocky

COY, -ED, -ER, -EST, -ING, -S adj affectedly shy or modest ▷ vb caress

COYAU, -S n type of steep roof

COYDOG, -S n cross between a coyote and a dog

COYED ▸ coy

COYER ▸ coy

COYEST ▸ coy

COYING ▸ coy

COYISH ▸ coy

COYISHLY ▸ coy

COYLY ▸ coy

COYNESS ▸ coy

COYOTE, -S *n* prairie wolf of N America

COYPOU, -S *same as* ▸ coypu

COYPU, -S *n* beaver-like aquatic rodent

COYS ▸ coy

COYSTREL *same as* ▸ coistrel

COYSTRIL *same as* ▸ coistrel

COZ, -ZES *archaic word for* ▸ cousin

> **Coz** is an old word for **cousin**, and a good one to know for using the Z.

COZE, -D, -S, COZING *vb* to chat

COZEN, -ED, -ING, -S *vb* cheat, trick

COZENAGE ▸ cozen

COZENED ▸ cozen

COZENER, -S ▸ cozen

COZENING ▸ cozen

COZENS ▸ cozen

COZES ▸ coze

COZEY, -S *n* tea cosy

COZIE *same as* ▸ cozey

COZIED ▸ cozy

COZIER, -S *n* cobbler

COZIES ▸ cozy

COZIEST ▸ cozy

COZILY ▸ cozy

COZINESS ▸ cozy

COZING ▸ coze

COZY, COZIED, COZIES, COZIEST, -ING *same as* ▸ cosy

COZZES ▸ coz

COZZIE, -S *n* swimming costume

CRAAL, -ED, -ING, -S *n* enclosure for livestock ▷ *vb* enclose in a craal

CRAB, -BED, -BING, -S *n* edible shellfish with ten legs, the first pair modified into pincers ▷ *vb* catch crabs

CRABBER, -S *n* crab fisherman

CRABBIER ▸ crabby

CRABBILY ▸ crabby

CRABBING ▸ crab

CRABBIT *Scots word meaning bad-tempered*

CRABBY, CRABBIER *adj* bad-tempered

CRABLIKE *adj* resembling a crab

CRABMEAT *n* edible flesh of a crab

CRABS ▸ crab

CRABWISE *adv* (of motion) sideways

CRABWOOD *n* tropical American tree

CRACHACH *pl n* (in Wales) elitists

CRACK, -S *vb* break or split partially ▷ *n* sudden sharp noise ▷ *adj* first-rate, excellent

CRACKED *adj* damaged by cracking

CRACKER *n* thin dry biscuit

CRACKERS *adj* mad

CRACKET, -S *n* low stool, often one with three legs

CRACKIE *n* small mongrel dog

CRACKIER ▸ cracky

CRACKIES ▸ cracky

CRACKING *adj* very fast

CRACKJAW *adj* difficult to pronounce ▷ *n* word or phrase that is difficult to pronounce

CRACKLE, -D, -S *vb* make small sharp popping noises ▷ *n* crackling sound

CRACKLY *adj* making a crackling sound

CRACKNEL *n* type of hard plain biscuit

CRACKPOT *adj* eccentric ▷ *n* eccentric person

CRACKS ▸ crack

CRACKUP, -S *n* collapse

CRACKY, CRACKIER, CRACKIES *adj* full of cracks ▷ *n* something that is full of cracks

CRACOWE, -S *n* medieval shoe with a sharply pointed toe

CRADLE, -D, -S *n* baby's bed on rockers ▷ *vb* hold gently as if in a cradle

CRADLER, -S ▸ cradle

CRADLES ▸ cradle

CRADLING *n* framework of iron or wood, esp as used in the construction of a ceiling

CRAFT, -ED, -ING, -S *n* occupation requiring skill with the hands ▷ *vb* make skilfully

CRAFTER, -S *n* person doing craftwork

CRAFTIER ▸ crafty

CRAFTILY ▸ crafty

CRAFTING ▸ craft

CRAFTS ▸ craft

CRAFTY, CRAFTIER *adj* skilled in deception

CRAG, -S *n* steep rugged rock

CRAGFAST *adj* stranded on a crag

CRAGGED *same as* ▸ craggy

CRAGGER, -S *n* member of a carbon reduction action group

CRAGGIER ▸ craggy

CRAGGILY ▸ craggy

CRAGGY, CRAGGIER *adj* having many crags

CRAGS ▸ crag

CRAGSMAN, CRAGSMEN *n* rock climber

CRAIC, -S *n* Irish word meaning fun

CRAIG, -S *a Scot word for* ▸ crag

CRAKE, -D, -S, CRAKING *n* bird of the rail family, such as the corncrake ▷ *vb* to boast

CRAM, -MED, -S *vb* force into too small a space ▷ *n* act or condition of cramming

CRAMBE, -S *n* any plant of the genus Crambe

CRAMBO, -ES, -S *n* word game

CRAME, -S *n* merchant's booth or stall

CRAMESY *same as* ▸ cramoisy

CRAMFULL *adj* very full

CRAMMED ▸ cram

CRAMMER, -S *n* person or school that prepares pupils for an examination

CRAMMING *n* act of cramming

CRAMOISY *adj* of a crimson colour ▷ *n* crimson cloth

CRAMP, -ING, -S *n* painful muscular contraction ▷ *vb* affect with a cramp

CRAMPED *adj* closed in

CRAMPER, -S *n* brace for the feet in the sport of curling

CRAMPET, -S *n* cramp iron

CRAMPIER ▸ crampy

CRAMPING ▸ cramp

CRAMPIT, -S *same as* ▸ crampet

CRAMPON, -S *n* spiked plate strapped to a boot for climbing on ice ▷ *vb* climb using crampons

CRAMPOON *same as* ▸ crampon

CRAMPS ▸ cramp

CRAMPY, CRAMPIER *adj* affected with cramp

CRAMS ▸ cram

CRAN, -S *n* unit of capacity used for measuring fresh herring, equal to 37.5 gallons

CRANAGE, -S *n* use of a crane

C

CRANCH, -ED, -ES vb to crunch

CRANE, -D, -S, CRANING n machine for lifting and moving heavy weights ▷ vb stretch (one's neck) to see something

CRANEFLY n fly with long legs, slender wings, and a narrow body

CRANES ▶ crane

CRANIA ▶ cranium

CRANIAL adj of or relating to the skull

CRANIATE adj having a skull or cranium ▷ n vertebrate

CRANING ▶ crane

CRANIUM, CRANIA, -S n skull

CRANK, -ED, -ER, -EST, -ING, -S n arm projecting at right angles from a shaft ▷ vb turn with a crank ▷ adj (of a sailing vessel) easily keeled over by the wind

CRANKIER ▶ cranky

CRANKILY ▶ cranky

CRANKING ▶ crank

CRANKISH adj somewhat eccentric or bad-tempered

CRANKLE, -D, -S vb bend or wind

CRANKLY adj vigorously

CRANKOUS adj fretful

CRANKPIN n short cylindrical pin in a crankshaft, to which the connecting rod is attached

CRANKS ▶ crank

CRANKY, CRANKIER same as ▶ crankish

CRANNIED ▶ cranny

CRANNIES ▶ cranny

CRANNOG, -S n ancient Celtic lake or bog dwelling

CRANNOGE same as ▶ crannog

CRANNOGS ▶ crannog

CRANNY, CRANNIED, CRANNIES n narrow opening ▷ vb become full of crannies

CRANS ▶ cran

CRANTS, -ES n garland carried in front of a maiden's bier

CRAP n slang word for rubbish, nonsense

CRAPAUD, -S n frog or toad

CRAPE, -D, -S, CRAPING same as ▶ crepe

CRAPIER ▶ crapy

CRAPIEST ▶ crapy

CRAPING ▶ crape

CRAPLE, -S same as ▶ grapple

CRAPOLA, -S n slang word for rubbish, nonsense

CRAPPIE, -S n N American freshwater fish

CRAPPIER ▶ crappy

CRAPPIES ▶ crappie

CRAPPY, CRAPPIER adj slang word for worthless, of poor quality

CRAPS pl n game using two dice

CRAPY, CRAPIER, CRAPIEST ▶ crape

CRARE, -S n type of trading vessel

CRASES ▶ crasis

CRASH, -ED, -ES n collision involving a vehicle or vehicles ▷ vb (cause to) collide violently with a vehicle, a stationary object, or the ground ▷ adj requiring or using great effort in order to achieve results quickly

CRASHER, -S ▶ crash

CRASHES ▶ crash

CRASHING adj extreme

CRASHPAD n place to sleep or live temporarily

CRASIS, CRASES n fusion or contraction of two adjacent vowels into one

CRASS, -ER, -EST adj stupid and insensitive

CRASSLY ▶ crass

CRATCH, -ES n rack for holding fodder for cattle, etc

CRATE, -D, -S, CRATING n large wooden container for packing goods ▷ vb put in a crate

CRATEFUL ▶ crate

CRATER, -ED, -S n bowl-shaped opening at the top of a volcano ▷ vb make or form craters

CRATES ▶ crate

CRATHUR, -S same as ▶ cratur

CRATING ▶ crate

CRATON, -S n stable part of the earth's continental crust

CRATONIC ▶ craton

CRATONS ▶ craton

CRATUR, -S n whisky or whiskey

CRAUNCH same as ▶ crunch

CRAUNCHY ▶ craunch

CRAVAT, -S n man's scarf worn like a tie ▷ vb wear a cravat

CRAVATE, -S same as ▶ cravat

CRAVATS ▶ cravat

CRAVE, -D, -S vb desire intensely

CRAVEN, -ED, -ER, -S adj cowardly ▷ n coward ▷ vb make cowardly

CRAVENLY ▶ craven

CRAVENS ▶ craven

CRAVER, -S ▶ crave

CRAVES ▶ crave

CRAVING, -S n intense desire or longing

CRAW, -S n pouchlike part of a bird's oesophagus

CRAWDAD, -S n crayfish

CRAWFISH same as ▶ crayfish

CRAWL, -ED, -S vb move on one's hands and knees ▷ n crawling motion or pace

CRAWLER, -S n servile flatterer

CRAWLIER ▶ crawly

CRAWLING n defect in freshly applied paint or varnish characterized by bare patches and ridging

CRAWLS ▶ crawl

CRAWLWAY n in a mine, low passageway that can only be negotiated by crawling

CRAWLY, CRAWLIER adj feeling like creatures are crawling on one's skin

CRAWS ▶ craw

CRAY, -EST, -S n crayfish ▷ adj crazy

CRAYER, -S same as ▶ crare

CRAYEST ▶ cray

CRAYFISH n edible shellfish like a lobster

CRAYON, -ED, -S n stick or pencil of coloured wax or clay ▷ vb draw or colour with a crayon

CRAYONER ▶ crayon

CRAYONS ▶ crayon

CRAYS ▶ cray

CRAYTHUR variant of ▶ cratur

CRAZE, -S n short-lived fashion or enthusiasm ▷ vb make mad

CRAZED adj wild and uncontrolled

CRAZES ▶ craze

CRAZIER ▶ crazy

CRAZIES ▶ crazy

CRAZIEST ▶ crazy

CRAZILY ▶ crazy

CRAZING, -S n act of crazing

CRAZY, CRAZIER, CRAZIES, CRAZIEST adj ridiculous ▷ n crazy person

CREACH, -S same as ▶ creagh

CREAGH, -S n foray

CREAK, -ED, -ING, -S *n* harsh squeaking sound ▷ *vb* make or move with a harsh squeaking sound
CREAKIER ▸ creaky
CREAKILY ▸ creak
CREAKING ▸ creak
CREAKS ▸ creak
CREAKY, CREAKIER ▸ creak
CREAM, -ED, -ING, -S *n* fatty part of milk ▷ *vb* beat to a creamy consistency
CREAMER, -S *n* powdered milk substitute for use in coffee
CREAMERY *n* place where dairy products are made or sold
CREAMIER ▸ creamy
CREAMILY ▸ creamy
CREAMING ▸ cream
CREAMS ▸ cream
CREAMY, CREAMIER *adj* resembling cream in colour, taste, or consistency
CREANCE, -S *n* long light cord used in falconry
CREANT *adj* formative
CREASE, -D, -S, CREASING *n* line made by folding or pressing ▷ *vb* crush or line
CREASER, -S ▸ crease
CREASES ▸ crease
CREASIER ▸ creasy
CREASING ▸ crease
CREASOTE *same as* ▸ **creosote**
CREASY, CREASIER ▸ crease
CREATE, -D, -S, CREATING *vb* make, cause to exist
CREATIC *adj* relating to flesh or meat
CREATIN, -S *same as* ▸ **creatine**
CREATINE *n* metabolite involved in biochemical reactions
CREATING ▸ create
CREATINS ▸ creatin
CREATION *n* creating or being created
CREATIVE *adj* imaginative or inventive ▷ *n* person who is creative professionally
CREATOR, -S *n* person who creates
CREATRIX ▸ creator
CREATURE *n* animal, person, or other being
CRECHE, -S *n* place where small children are looked after
CRED, -S *n* short for credibility

CREDAL ▸ creed
CREDENCE *n* belief in the truth or accuracy of a statement
CREDENDA > credendum
CREDENT *adj* believing or believable
CREDENZA *n* type of small sideboard
CREDIBLE *adj* believable
CREDIBLY ▸ credible
CREDIT, -ED *n* system of allowing customers to receive goods and pay later ▷ *vb* enter as a credit in an account
CREDITOR *n* person to whom money is owed
CREDITS *pl n* list of people responsible for the production of a film or TV programme
CREDO, -S *n* creed
CREDS ▸ cred
CREE, -ING, -S *vb* soften grain by boiling or soaking
CREED, -S *n* statement or system of (Christian) beliefs or principles
CREEDAL ▸ creed
CREEDS ▸ creed
CREEING ▸ cree
CREEK, -S *n* narrow inlet or bay
CREEKIER ▸ creeky
CREEKS ▸ creek
CREEKY, CREEKIER *adj* abounding in creeks
CREEL, -ED, -ING, -S *n* wicker basket used by anglers ▷ *vb* to fish using creels
CREEP, -ED, -ING, -S, CREPT *vb* move quietly and cautiously ▷ *n* creeping movement
CREEPAGE *n* imperceptible movement
CREEPED ▸ creep
CREEPER, -S *n* creeping plant ▷ *vb* train a plant to creep
CREEPIE, -S *n* low stool
CREEPIER ▸ creepy
CREEPIES ▸ creepie
CREEPILY ▸ creepy
CREEPING ▸ creep
CREEPS ▸ creep
CREEPY, CREEPIER *adj* causing a feeling of fear or disgust
CREES ▸ cree
CREESE, -D, -S, CREESING *same as* ▸ **kris**
CREESH, -ED, -ES *vb* lubricate

CREESHY *adj* greasy
CREESING ▸ creese
CREM, -S *n* crematorium
CREMAINS *pl n* cremated remains of a body
CREMANT *adj* (of wine) moderately sparkling
CREMATE, -D, -S *vb* burn (a corpse) to ash
CREMATOR *n* furnace for cremating corpses
CREME, -S *n* cream
CREMINI, -S *n* variety of mushroom
CREMONA, -S *same as* ▸ **cromorna**
CREMOR, -S *n* thick creamy liquid
CREMOSIN *adj* crimson
CREMS ▸ crem
CREMSIN *same as* ▸ **cremosin**
CRENA, -S *n* cleft or notch
CRENATE *adj* having a scalloped margin, as certain leaves
CRENATED *same as* ▸ **crenate**
CRENEL, -ED, -S *n* opening formed in the top of a wall having slanting sides ▷ *vb* crenellate
CRENELLE *same as* ▸ **crenel**
CRENELS ▸ crenel
CRENSHAW *n* variety of melon
CREODONT *n* type of extinct Tertiary mammal, the ancestor of modern carnivores
CREOLE, -S *n* language developed from a mixture of languages ▷ *adj* of or relating to a creole
CREOLIAN *n* Creole
CREOLISE *vb* (of a pidgin language) to become the native language of a speech community
CREOLIST *n* student of creole languages
CREOLIZE *same as* ▸ **creolise**
CREOSOL, -S *n* insoluble oily liquid
CREOSOTE *n* dark oily liquid made from coal tar and used for preserving wood ▷ *vb* treat with creosote
CREPANCE *n* injury to a horse's hind leg caused by being struck by the shoe of the other hind foot
CREPE, -D, -S, CREPING *n* fabric or rubber with a crinkled texture ▷ *vb* crimp or frizz

CREPERIE n eating establishment that specializes in pancakes

CREPES ▶ crepe

CREPEY same as ▶ crepy

CREPIER ▶ crepy

CREPIEST ▶ crepy

CREPING ▶ crepe

CREPITUS n crackling chest sound heard in pneumonia and other lung diseases

CREPON, -S n thin material made of fine wool and/or silk

CREPS pl n slang term for training shoes

CREPT ▶ creep

CREPY, CREPIER, CREPIEST adj (esp of the skin) having a dry wrinkled appearance like crepe

CRESCENT n (curved shape of) the moon as seen in its first or last quarter ▷ adj crescent-shaped

CRESCIVE adj increasing

CRESOL, -S n aromatic compound

CRESS, -ES n plant with strong-tasting leaves, used in salads

CRESSET, -S n metal basket mounted on a pole

CRESSY, CRESSIER ▶ cress

CREST, -ED, -S n top of a mountain, hill, or wave ▷ vb come to or be at the top of

CRESTA adj as in cresta run high-speed tobogganing down a steep narrow passage

CRESTAL, -S ▶ crystal

CRESTED ▶ crest

CRESTING same as ▶ crest

CRESTON, -S n hogback

CRESTS ▶ crest

CRESYL, -S n tolyl

CRESYLIC adj of, concerned with, or containing creosote or cresol

CRESYLS ▶ cresyl

CRETIC, -S n metrical foot

CRETIN, -S n insulting term for a stupid person

CRETISM, -S n lying

CRETONNE n heavy printed cotton fabric used in furnishings

CRETONS pl n spread made from pork fat and onions

CREUTZER n former copper and silver coin of Germany or Austria

CREVALLE n any fish of the family Carangidae

CREVASSE n deep open crack in a glacier ▷ vb make a break or fissure in (a dyke, wall, etc)

CREVETTE n shrimp

CREVICE, -S n narrow crack or gap in rock

CREVICED ▶ crevice

CREVICES ▶ crevice

CREW, -ED, -ING, -S n people who work on a ship or aircraft ▷ vb serve as a crew member (on)

CREWCUT, -S n very short haircut

CREWE, -S n type of pot

CREWED ▶ crew

CREWEL, -S n fine worsted yarn used in embroidery ▷ vb embroider in crewel

CREWES ▶ crewe

CREWING ▶ crew

CREWLESS adj lacking a crew

CREWMAN, CREWMEN n member of a ship's crew

CREWMATE n colleague on the crew of a boat or ship

CREWMEN ▶ crewman

CREWNECK n plain round neckline in sweaters

CREWS ▶ crew

CRIA, -S n baby llama or alpaca

CRIANT adj garish

CRIAS ▶ cria

CRIB, -BED, -BING, -S n piece of writing stolen from elsewhere ▷ vb copy (someone's work) dishonestly

CRIBBAGE n card game for two to four players

CRIBBED ▶ crib

CRIBBER, -S ▶ crib

CRIBBING ▶ crib

CRIBBLE, -D, -S vb to sift

CRIBELLA ▶ cribellum

CRIBLE, -S adj dotted ▷ n method of engraving with holes or dots

CRIBRATE adj sievelike

CRIBROSE adj pierced with holes

CRIBROUS same as ▶ cribrose

CRIBS ▶ crib

CRIBWORK same as ▶ crib

CRICETID n any member of the family Cricetidae, such as the hamster and vole

CRICK, -ED, -ING, -S n muscle spasm or cramp in the back or neck ▷ vb cause a crick in

CRICKET, -S n outdoor sport ▷ vb play cricket

CRICKEY same as ▶ crikey

CRICKING ▶ crick

CRICKS ▶ crick

CRICKY same as ▶ crikey

CRICOID, -S adj of or relating to part of the larynx ▷ n this cartilage

CRIED ▶ cry

CRIER, -S n (formerly) official who made public announcements

CRIES ▶ cry

CRIKEY interj expression of surprise

CRIM, -S short for ▶ criminal

CRIME, -D, -S, CRIMING n unlawful act ▷ vb charge with a crime

CRIMEFUL adj criminal

CRIMEN, CRIMINA n crime

CRIMES ▶ crime

CRIMINA ▶ crimen

CRIMINAL n person guilty of a crime ▷ adj of crime

CRIMINE interj expression of surprise

CRIMING ▶ crime

CRIMINI same as ▶ crimine

CRIMINIS n as in particeps criminis accomplice in crime

CRIMINY same as ▶ crimine

CRIMMER, -S variant spelling of ▶ krimmer

CRIMP, -ED, -ING, -S vb fold or press into ridges ▷ n act or result of crimping

CRIMPER, -S ▶ crimp

CRIMPIER ▶ crimpy

CRIMPING ▶ crimp

CRIMPLE, -D, -S vb crumple, wrinkle, or curl

CRIMPS ▶ crimp

CRIMPY, CRIMPIER ▶ crimp

CRIMS ▶ crim

CRIMSON, -S adj deep purplish-red ▷ n deep or vivid red colour ▷ vb make or become crimson

CRINAL adj relating to the hair

CRINATE adj having hair

CRINATED same as ▶ crinate

CRINE, -D, -S, CRINING vb to shrivel

CRINGE, -D, -S, CRINGING vb flinch in fear ▷ n act of cringing

CRINGER, -S ▶ cringe

CRINGES ▶ cringe

CRINGEY, CRINGIER adj causing the urge to cringe

CRINGING ▶ cringe

CRINGLE, -S n eye at the edge of a sail

CRINGY same as ▶ cringey

CRINING ▶ crine

CRINITE, -S adj covered with soft hairs or tufts ▷ n sedimentary rock
CRINKLE, -D, -S n wrinkle, crease, or fold ▷ vb become slightly creased or folded
CRINKLY adj wrinkled ▷ n derogatory term for an old person
CRINOID, -S n type of primitive echinoderm
CRINOSE adj hairy
CRINUM, -S n type of mostly tropical plant
CRIOLLO, -S n native or inhabitant of Latin America of European descent ▷ adj of, relating to, or characteristic of a criollo or criollos
CRIOS, -ES n multicoloured woven woollen belt
CRIPE variant of ▷ cripes
CRIPES interj expression of surprise
CRIPPLE, -D, -S vb make lame or disabled
CRIPPLER ▷ cripple
CRIPPLES ▷ cripple
CRIS variant of ▷ kris
CRISE n crisis
CRISES ▷ crisis
CRISIC adj relating to a crisis
CRISIS, CRISES n crucial stage, turning point
CRISP, -EST, -ING, -S adj fresh and firm ▷ n very thin slice of potato fried till crunchy ▷ vb make or become crisp
CRISPATE adj having a curled or waved appearance
CRISPED same as ▷ crispate
CRISPEN, -S vb make crisp
CRISPER, -S n compartment in a refrigerator
CRISPEST ▷ crisp
CRISPIER ▷ crispy
CRISPIES pl n as in rice crispies puffed grains of rice, eaten esp as breakfast cereal
CRISPILY ▷ crispy
CRISPIN, -S n cobbler
CRISPING ▷ crisp
CRISPINS ▷ crispin
CRISPLY ▷ crisp
CRISPS ▷ crisp
CRISPY, CRISPIER adj hard and crunchy
CRISSA ▷ crissum
CRISSAL ▷ crissum
CRISSUM, CRISSA n area or feathers surrounding the cloaca of a bird
CRISTA, -E n structure resembling a ridge or crest

CRISTATE adj having a crest
CRIT, -S short for > criticism
CRITERIA > criterion
CRITH, -S n unit of weight for gases
CRITIC, -S n professional judge of any of the arts
CRITICAL adj very important or dangerous
CRITICS ▷ critic
CRITIQUE n critical essay ▷ vb review critically
CRITS ▷ crit
CRITTER, -S a dialect word for ▷ creature
CRITTUR, -S same as ▷ critter
CRIVENS interj expression of surprise
CRIVVENS same as ▷ crivens
CROAK, -ED, -ING, -S vb (of a frog or crow) give a low hoarse cry ▷ n low hoarse sound
CROAKER, -S n animal, bird, etc, that croaks
CROAKIER ▷ croaky
CROAKILY ▷ croak
CROAKING ▷ croak
CROAKS ▷ croak
CROAKY, CROAKIER ▷ croak
CROC, -S short for > crocodile
CROCEATE adj saffron-coloured
CROCEIN, -S n any one of a group of red or orange acid azo dyes
CROCEINE same as ▷ crocein
CROCEINS ▷ crocein
CROCEOUS adj saffron-coloured
CROCHE, -S n knob at the top of a deer's horn
CROCHET, -S vb make by looping and intertwining yarn with a hooked needle ▷ n work made in this way
CROCI ▷ crocus
CROCINE adj relating to the crocus
CROCK, -ING, -S n earthenware pot or jar ▷ vb injure or cause to become weak
CROCKED adj injured
CROCKERY n dishes
CROCKET, -S n carved ornament in the form of a curled leaf or cusp
CROCKING ▷ crock
CROCKPOT n tradename for a brand of slow cooker
CROCKS ▷ crock
CROCOITE n rare orange secondary mineral

CROCS ▷ croc
CROCUS, CROCI, -ES n flowering plant
CROFT, -ED, -S n small farm worked by one family in Scotland ▷ vb farm land as a croft
CROFTER, -S n owner or tenant of a small farm, esp in Scotland or northern England
CROFTING n system or occupation of working land in crofts
CROFTS ▷ croft
CROG, -GED, -GING, -S vb ride on a bicycle as a passenger
CROGGIES ▷ croggy
CROGGING ▷ crog
CROGGY, CROGGIES n ride on a bicycle as a passenger
CROGS ▷ crog
CROJIK, -S n triangular sail
CROMACK, -S same as ▷ crummock
CROMB, -ED, -ING, -S same as ▷ crome
CROMBEC, -S n African bird with colourful plumage
CROMBED ▷ cromb
CROMBING ▷ cromb
CROMBS ▷ cromb
CROME, -D, -S, CROMING n hook ▷ vb use a crome
CROMLECH n circle of prehistoric standing stones
CROMORNA n one of the reed stops in an organ
CROMORNE variant of ▷ cromorna
CRON, -S n computer application that schedules tasks chronologically
CRONE, -S n witchlike old woman
CRONET, -S n hair which grows over the top of a horse's hoof
CRONIES ▷ crony
CRONISH ▷ crone
CRONK, -ER, -EST adj unfit
CRONS ▷ cron
CRONY, CRONIES n close friend
CRONYISM n appointing friends to high-level posts
CROODLE, -D, -S vb nestle close
CROOK, -ER, -EST, -ING, -S n dishonest person ▷ vb bend or curve ▷ adj informal Australian word meaning ill
CROOKED adj bent or twisted
CROOKER ▷ crook

CROOKERY n illegal or dishonest activity

CROOKEST ▸ crook

CROOKING ▸ crook

CROOKS ▸ crook

CROOL, -ED, -ING, -S vb spoil

CROON, -ED, -ING, -S vb sing, hum, or speak in a soft low tone ▹ n soft low singing or humming

CROONER, -S ▸ croon

CROONIER ▸ croony

CROONING ▸ croon

CROONS ▸ croon

CROONY, CROONIER adj singing like a crooner

CROOVE, -S n animal enclosure

CROP, -PED, -PING, -S n cultivated plant ▹ vb cut very short

CROPFUL, -S n quantity that can be held in the craw

CROPFULL adj satiated ▹ n amount that a crop can take

CROPFULS ▸ cropful

CROPLAND n land on which crops are grown

CROPLESS adj without crops

CROPPED ▸ crop

CROPPER, -S n person who cultivates or harvests a crop

CROPPIE same as ▸ croppy

CROPPIES ▸ croppy

CROPPING ▸ crop

CROPPY, CROPPIES n rebel in the Irish rising of 1798

CROPS ▸ crop

CROPSICK adj sick from excessive food or drink

CROQUET, -S n game played on a lawn in which balls are hit through hoops ▹ vb drive away a ball by hitting one's own when the two are in contact

CROQUIS n rough sketch

CRORE, -S n (in Indian English) ten million

CROSIER, -S n staff carried by bishops as a symbol of pastoral office ▹ vb bear or carry such a staff

CROSS, -ED, -ES, -EST, CROST vb move or go across (something) ▹ n structure, symbol, or mark of two intersecting lines ▹ adj angry, annoyed

CROSSARM n in mining, horizontal bar on which a drill is mounted

CROSSBAR n horizontal bar across goalposts or on a bicycle ▹ vb provide with crossbars

CROSSBIT ▸ crossbite

CROSSBOW n weapon consisting of a bow fixed across a wooden stock

CROSSCUT vb cut across ▹ adj cut across ▹ n transverse cut or course

CROSSE n light staff used in playing lacrosse

CROSSED ▸ cross

CROSSER, -S ▸ cross

CROSSES ▸ cross

CROSSEST ▸ cross

CROSSING n place where a street may be crossed safely

CROSSISH ▸ cross

CROSSLET n cross having a smaller cross near the end of each arm

CROSSLY ▸ cross

CROSSPLY adj having layers of fabric with cords running diagonally

CROSSTIE n railway sleeper

CROSSWAY same as > crossroad

CROST ▸ cross

CROSTATA n type of fruit tart

CROSTINO, CROSTINI n piece of toasted bread served with a savoury topping

CROTAL, -S n any of various lichens used in dyeing wool

CROTALA ▸ crotalum

CROTALE, -S n type of small cymbal

CROTALS ▸ crotal

CROTALUM, CROTALA n ancient castanet-like percussion instrument

CROTCH, -ES n part of the body between the tops of the legs

CROTCHED ▸ crotch

CROTCHES ▸ crotch

CROTCHET n musical note half the length of a minim

CROTON, -S n type of shrub or tree, the seeds of which yield croton oil

CROTONIC adj as in **crotonic acid** type of colourless acid

CROTONS ▸ croton

CROTTLE, -S same as ▸ crotal

CROUCH, -ED, -ES vb bend low with the legs and body close ▹ n this position

CROUP, -ED, -ING, -S n throat disease of children, with a cough ▹ vb have croup

CROUPADE n leap by a horse, pulling the hind legs towards the belly

CROUPE, -S same as ▸ croup

CROUPED ▸ croup

CROUPER, -S obsolete variant of ▸ crupper

CROUPES ▸ croupe

CROUPIER n person who collects bets and pays out winnings at a gambling table in a casino

CROUPILY ▸ croup

CROUPING ▸ croup

CROUPON, -S n type of highly polished flexible leather

CROUPOUS ▸ croup

CROUPS ▸ croup

CROUPY ▸ croup

CROUSE adj lively, confident, or saucy

CROUSELY ▸ crouse

CROUT, -S n sauerkraut

CROUTE, -S n small round of toasted bread on which a savoury mixture is served

CROUTON, -S n small piece of fried or toasted bread served in soup

CROUTS ▸ crout

CROW, -ED, -S n large black bird with a harsh call ▹ vb (of a cock) make a shrill squawking sound

CROWBAIT n worn-out horse

CROWBAR, -S n iron bar used as a lever ▹ vb use a crowbar to lever (something)

CROWBOOT n type of Inuit boot made of fur and leather

CROWD, -ED, -ING, -S n large group of people or things ▹ vb gather together in large numbers

CROWDER, -S ▸ crowd

CROWDIE, -S n porridge of meal and water

CROWDING ▸ crowd

CROWDS ▸ crowd

CROWDY same as ▸ crowdie

CROWEA, -S n Australian shrub with pink flowers

CROWED ▸ crow

CROWER, -S ▸ crow

CROWFOOT, CROWFEET n type of plant

CROWING, -S n act of crowing

CROWLIKE adj like a crow

CROWN, -ED, -S n monarch's headdress of gold and jewels ▹ vb put a crown on the head of (someone) to proclaim him or her monarch

CROWNER, -S n promotional label

CROWNET, -S n coronet

CROWNING n coronation

CROWNLET n small crown

CROWNS ▶ crown

CROWS ▶ crow

CROWSTEP n set of steps to the top of a gable on a building

CROZE, -S n recess cut at the end of a barrel or cask to receive the head

CROZER, -S n machine which cuts grooves in cask staves

CROZES ▶ croze

CROZIER, -S same as ▶ crosier

CROZZLED adj blackened or burnt at the edges

CRU n (in France) a vineyard, group of vineyards, or wine-producing region

CRUBEEN, -S n pig's trotter

CRUCES ▶ crux

CRUCIAL adj very important

CRUCIAN, -S n European fish

CRUCIATE adj shaped or arranged like a cross ▷ n cruciate ligament

CRUCIBLE n pot in which metals are melted

CRUCIFER n type of plant with four petals arranged like a cross

CRUCIFIX n model of Christ on the Cross

CRUCIFY vb put to death by fastening to a cross

CRUCK, -S n wooden timber supporting the end of certain roofs

CRUD, -DED, -DING, -S n sticky or encrusted substance ▷ interj expression of disgust, disappointment, etc ▷ vb cover with a sticky or encrusted substance

CRUDDIER ▶ cruddy

CRUDDING ▶ crud

CRUDDLE, -D, -S vb curdle

CRUDDY, CRUDDIER adj dirty or unpleasant

CRUDE, -R, -S, -ST adj rough and simple ▷ n crude oil

CRUDELY ▶ crude

CRUDER ▶ crude

CRUDES ▶ crude

CRUDEST ▶ crude

CRUDIER ▶ crudy

CRUDIEST ▶ crudy

CRUDITES pl n selection of raw vegetables often served with a variety of dips before a meal

CRUDITY ▶ crude

CRUDO, -S n sliced raw seafood

CRUDS ▶ crud

CRUDY, CRUDIER, CRUDIEST adj raw

CRUE, -S obsolete variant of ▶ crew

CRUEL, -ER, -EST, -LER adj delighting in others' pain

CRUELLS same as ▶ cruels

CRUELLY ▶ cruel

CRUELS n disease of cattle and sheep

CRUELTY n deliberate infliction of pain or suffering

CRUES ▶ crue

CRUET, -S n small container for salt, pepper, etc, at table

CRUFT, -S n redundant technical hardware

CRUISE, -D, -S, CRUISING n sea trip for pleasure ▷ vb sail from place to place for pleasure

CRUISER, -S n fast warship

CRUISES ▶ cruise

CRUISEY same as ▶ cruisy

CRUISIE, -S same as ▶ cruizie

CRUISIER ▶ cruisy

CRUISIES ▶ cruisie

CRUISING ▶ cruise

CRUISY, CRUISIER adj relaxed or easy-going

CRUIVE, -S n animal enclosure

CRUIZIE, -S n oil lamp

CRULLER, -S n light sweet ring-shaped cake, fried in deep fat

CRUMB, -ED, -ING n small fragment of bread or other dry food ▷ vb prepare or cover (food) with breadcrumbs ▷ adj (esp of pie crusts) made with a mixture of biscuit crumbs, sugar, etc

CRUMBER, -S ▶ crumb

CRUMBIER ▶ crumby

CRUMBING ▶ crumb

CRUMBLE, -D, -S vb break into fragments ▷ n pudding of stewed fruit with a crumbly topping

CRUMBLY adj easily crumbled or crumbling

CRUMBS interj expression of dismay or surprise

CRUMBUM, -S n rogue

CRUMBY, CRUMBIER adj full of crumbs

CRUMEN, -S n deer's larmier or tear-pit

CRUMENAL n purse

CRUMENS ▶ crumen

CRUMHORN n medieval woodwind instrument of bass pitch

CRUMMACK same as ▶ crummock

CRUMMIE n cow with a crumpled horn

CRUMMIER ▶ crummy

CRUMMIES ▶ crummy

CRUMMILY adv in a manner suggestive of or indicating poor quality

CRUMMOCK n stick with a crooked head

CRUMMY, CRUMMIER, CRUMMIES adj of poor quality ▷ n lorry that carries loggers to work from their camp

CRUMP, -ED, -ER, -EST, -ING, -S vb thud or explode with a loud dull sound ▷ n crunching, thudding, or exploding noise ▷ adj crooked

CRUMPET, -S n round soft yeast cake, eaten buttered

CRUMPIER ▶ crumpy

CRUMPING ▶ crump

CRUMPLE, -D, -S vb crush, crease ▷ n untidy crease or wrinkle

CRUMPLY ▶ crumple

CRUMPS ▶ crump

CRUMPY, CRUMPIER adj crisp

CRUNCH, -ED, -ES vb bite or chew with a noisy crushing sound ▷ n crunching sound

CRUNCHER ▶ crunch

CRUNCHES ▶ crunch

CRUNCHIE n type of crunchy oat biscuit

CRUNCHY ▶ crunch

CRUNK, -S n form of hip-hop music originating in the Southern US

CRUNKED adj excited or intoxicated

CRUNKLE, -D, -S Scots variant of ▶ crinkle

CRUNKS ▶ crunk

CRUNODAL ▶ crunode

CRUNODE, -S n point at which two branches of a curve intersect

CRUOR, -ES, -S n blood clot

CRUPPER, -S n strap that passes from the back of a saddle under a horse's tail

CRURA ▶ crus

CRURAL adj of or relating to the leg or thigh

CRUS, CRURA n leg, esp from the knee to the foot

C

CRUSADE, -D, -S n medieval Christian war to recover the Holy Land from the Muslims ▷ vb take part in a crusade
CRUSADER ▸ crusade
CRUSADES ▸ crusade
CRUSADO, -S n former gold or silver coin of Portugal
CRUSE, -S n small earthenware jug or pot
CRUSET, -S n goldsmith's crucible
CRUSH, -ED, -ES vb compress so as to injure, break, or crumple ▷ n dense crowd
CRUSHER, -S ▸ crush
CRUSHES ▸ crush
CRUSHING n act or instance of compressing so as to injure or break
CRUSIAN, -S variant of ▸ crucian
CRUSIE, -S same as ▸ cruizie
CRUSILY adj (in heraldry) strewn with crosses
CRUST, -ED, -ING, -S n hard outer part of something, esp bread ▷ vb cover with or form a crust
CRUSTA, -E, -S n hard outer layer
CRUSTAL adj of or relating to the earth's crust
CRUSTAS ▸ crusta
CRUSTATE adj covered with a crust
CRUSTED ▸ crust
CRUSTIER ▸ crusty
CRUSTIES ▸ crusty
CRUSTILY ▸ crusty
CRUSTING ▸ crust
CRUSTOSE adj having a crustlike appearance
CRUSTS ▸ crust
CRUSTY, CRUSTIER, CRUSTIES adj having a crust ▷ n scruffy type of punk or hippy whose lifestyle involves travelling and squatting
CRUSY same as ▸ cruizie
CRUTCH, -ED, -ES n long sticklike support with a rest for the armpit ▷ vb support or sustain (a person or thing) as with a crutch
CRUVE, -S same as ▸ cruive
CRUX, CRUCES, -ES n crucial or decisive point
CRUZADO, -S same as ▸ crusado
CRUZEIRO n former monetary unit of Brazil, replaced by the cruzeiro real

CRUZIE, -S same as ▸ cruizie
CRWTH, -S n ancient stringed instrument of Celtic origin

This old Celtic musical instrument makes a fine tune when your rack is all consonants.

CRY, CRIED, CRIES vb shed tears ▷ n fit of weeping
CRYBABY n person, esp a child, who cries too readily
CRYER, -S same as ▸ crier
CRYING, -S ▸ cry
CRYINGLY ▸ cry
CRYINGS ▸ crying
CRYOBANK n place for storing genetic material at low temperature
CRYOGEN, -S n substance used to produce low temperatures
CRYOGENY n cryogenic science
CRYOLITE n white or colourless mineral
CRYONIC adj relating to or involving cryonics
CRYONICS n practice of freezing a human corpse in the hope of restoring it to life in the future
CRYOSTAT n apparatus for maintaining a constant low temperature
CRYOTRON n switch working at the temperature of liquid helium
CRYPT, -S n vault under a church, esp one used as a burial place
CRYPTAL ▸ crypt
CRYPTIC adj obscure in meaning, secret
CRYPTO, -S n person who is a secret member of an organization or sect
CRYPTON, -S n hypothetical particle
CRYPTOS ▸ crypto
CRYPTS ▸ crypt
CRYSTAL, -S n symmetrically shaped solid formed naturally ▷ adj bright and clear
CSARDAS n type of Hungarian folk dance
CTENE, -S n locomotor organ found in ctenophores (or comb jellies)
CTENIDIA > ctenidium
CTENOID adj toothed like a comb, as the scales of perches
CUATRO, -S n four-stringed guitar

CUB, -BED, -S n young wild animal such as a bear or fox ▷ adj young or inexperienced ▷ vb give birth to cubs
CUBAGE, -S same as ▸ cubature
CUBANE, -S n rare octahedral hydrocarbon
CUBATURE n determination of the cubic contents of something
CUBBED ▸ cub
CUBBIER ▸ cubby
CUBBIES ▸ cubby
CUBBIEST ▸ cubby
CUBBING, -S ▸ cub
CUBBISH ▸ cub
CUBBY, CUBBIER, CUBBIES, CUBBIEST n cubbyhole ▷ adj short and plump
CUBE, -D, -S, CUBING n object with six equal square sides ▷ vb cut into cubes
CUBEB, -S n SE Asian woody climbing plant with brownish berries
CUBED ▸ cube
CUBELIKE adj like a cube
CUBER, -S ▸ cube
CUBES ▸ cube
CUBHOOD, -S n state of being a cub
CUBIC, -S adj having three dimensions ▷ n cubic equation
CUBICA, -S n fine shalloon-like fabric
CUBICAL adj of or related to volume
CUBICAS ▸ cubica
CUBICITY n property of being cubelike
CUBICLE, -S n enclosed part of a large room, screened for privacy
CUBICLY ▸ cubic
CUBICS ▸ cubic
CUBICULA > cubiculum
CUBIFORM adj having the shape of a cube
CUBING ▸ cube
CUBISM, -S n style of art in which objects are represented by geometrical shapes
CUBIST, -S ▸ cubism
CUBISTIC ▸ cubism
CUBISTS ▸ cubist
CUBIT, -S n old measure of length based on the length of the forearm
CUBITAL adj of or relating to the forearm
CUBITI ▸ cubitus
CUBITS ▸ cubit
CUBITUS, CUBITI n elbow

CUBLESS *adj* having no cubs

CUBOID, -S *adj* shaped like a cube ▷ *n* geometric solid whose six faces are rectangles

CUBOIDAL *same as* ▶ **cuboid**

CUBOIDS ▶ **cuboid**

CUBS ▶ **cub**

CUCKING *adj* as in **cucking stool** stool in which suspected witches were tested

CUCKOO, -ED, -S *n* migratory bird ▷ *vb* repeat over and over

CUCUMBER *n* long green-skinned fleshy fruit used in salads

CUCURBIT *n* type of tropical or subtropical creeping plant

CUD, -S *n* partially digested food chewed by a ruminant

CUDBEAR, -S *another name for* ▶ **orchil**

CUDDEN, -S *n* young coalfish

CUDDIE *same as* ▶ **cuddy**

CUDDIES ▶ **cuddy**

CUDDIN, -S *same as* ▶ **cudden**

CUDDLE, -D, -S, CUDDLING *n* hug ▷ *vb* hold close

CUDDLER, -S ▶ **cuddle**

CUDDLES ▶ **cuddle**

CUDDLIER ▶ **cuddly**

CUDDLING ▶ **cuddle**

CUDDLY, CUDDLIER ▶ **cuddle**

CUDDY, CUDDIES *n* small cabin in a boat

CUDGEL, -ED, -S *n* short thick stick used as a weapon ▷ *vb* use a cudgel

CUDGELER ▶ **cudgel**

CUDGELS ▶ **cudgel**

CUDGERIE *n* type of large tropical tree with light-coloured wood

CUDS ▶ **cud**

CUDWEED, -S *n* type of temperate plant

CUE, -D, -S, CUING *n* signal to an actor or musician to begin speaking or playing ▷ *vb* give a cue to

CUEING, -S ▶ **cue**

CUEIST, -S *n* snooker or billiards player

CUES ▶ **cue**

CUESTA, -S *n* long low ridge with a steep scarp slope and a gentle back slope

CUFF, -ED, -ING, -S *n* end of a sleeve ▷ *vb* hit with an open hand

CUFFABLE *adj* able to be folded down at the ankle

CUFFED ▶ **cuff**

CUFFIN, -S *n* man

CUFFING ▶ **cuff**

CUFFINS ▶ **cuffin**

CUFFLE, -D, -S, CUFFLING *vb* scuffle

CUFFLESS *adj* having no cuff(s)

CUFFLING ▶ **cuffle**

CUFFLINK *n* detachable fastener for shirt cuff

CUFFO *adv* free of charge

CUFFS ▶ **cuff**

CUIF, -S *same as* ▶ **coof**

CUING ▶ **cue**

CUIRASS *n* piece of armour covering the chest and back ▷ *vb* equip with a cuirass

CUISH, -ES *same as* ▶ **cuisse**

CUISINE, -S *n* style of cooking

CUISSE, -S *n* piece of armour for the thigh

CUISSER, -S *same as* ▶ **cooser**

CUISSES ▶ **cuisse**

CUIT, -S *n* ankle

CUITER, -ED, -S *vb* pamper

CUITIKIN *n* gaiter

CUITS ▶ **cuit**

CUITTLE, -D, -S *vb* wheedle

CUKE, -S *n* cucumber

CULCH, -ES *n* the basis of an oyster bed

CULCHIE, -R, -S *n* mildly derogatory Irish term for a country-dweller ▷ *adj* rough or unsophisticated

CULET, -S *n* flat face at the bottom of a gem

CULEX, -ES, CULICES *n* type of mosquito

CULICID, -S *n* type of dipterous insect

CULICINE *n* any member of the genus Culex containing mosquitoes

CULINARY *adj* of kitchens or cookery

CULL, -ED, -S *vb* choose, gather ▷ *n* culling

CULLAY, -S *n* soapbark tree

CULLED ▶ **cull**

CULLER, -S *n* person employed to cull animals

CULLET, -S *n* waste glass for melting down to be reused

CULLIED ▶ **cully**

CULLIES ▶ **cully**

CULLING, -S ▶ **cull**

CULLION, -S *n* rascal

CULLIS, -ES *same as* ▶ **coulisse**

CULLS ▶ **cull**

CULLY, CULLIED, CULLIES, -ING *n* pal ▷ *vb* to trick

CULLYISM *n* state of being a dupe

CULM, -ED, -ING, -S *n* coal-mine waste ▷ *vb* form a stalk or stem

CULMEN, CULMINA *n* summit

CULMING ▶ **culm**

CULMS ▶ **culm**

CULOTTE ▶ **culottes**

CULOTTES *pl n* women's knee-length trousers cut to look like a skirt

CULPA, -E *n* act of neglect

CULPABLE *adj* deserving blame

CULPABLY ▶ **culpable**

CULPAE ▶ **culpa**

CULPRIT, -S *n* person guilty of an offence or misdeed

CULSHIE, -R, -S *n* mildly derogatory Irish term for a country-dweller ▷ *adj* rough or unsophisticated

CULT, -S *n* specific system of worship ▷ *adj* very popular among a limited group of people

CULTCH, -ES *same as* ▶ **culch**

CULTER, -S *same as* ▶ **coulter**

CULTI ▶ **cultus**

CULTIC *adj* of or relating to a religious cult

CULTIER ▶ **culty**

CULTIEST ▶ **culty**

CULTIGEN *n* cultivated species of plant that did not come from a wild type

CULTISH *adj* intended to appeal to a small group of fashionable people

CULTISM, -S ▶ **cult**

CULTIST, -S ▶ **cult**

CULTIVAR *n* cultivated plant produced from a natural species

CULTLIKE *adj* resembling a cult

CULTRATE *adj* shaped like a knife blade

CULTS ▶ **cult**

CULTURAL *adj* of or relating to artistic or social pursuits

CULTURE, -S *n* ideas, customs, and art of a particular society ▷ *vb* grow (bacteria) for study

CULTURED *adj* showing good taste or manners

CULTURES ▶ **culture**

CULTUS, CULTI, -ES *another word for* ▶ **cult**

CULTY, CULTIER, CULTIEST *same as* ▶ **cultish**

CULVER, -S *an archaic or poetic name for* ▶ **pigeon**

CULVERIN n long-range medium to heavy cannon used during the 15th, 16th, and 17th centuries

CULVERS ▶ culver

CULVERT, -S n drain under a road or railway ▷ vb direct water through a culvert

CUM prep with

CUMACEAN n type of small marine crustacea

CUMARIC ▶ cumarin

CUMARIN, -S same as ▶ coumarin

CUMARONE variant spelling of ▷ coumarone

CUMBENT adj lying down

CUMBER, -ED, -S vb obstruct or hinder ▷ n hindrance or burden

CUMBERER ▶ cumber

CUMBERS ▶ cumber

CUMBIA, -S n Colombian style of music

CUMBROUS adj awkward because of size, weight, or height

CUMBUNGI n type of tall Australian marsh plant

CUMEC, -S n unit of volumetric rate of flow

CUMIN, -S n sweet-smelling seeds of a Mediterranean plant, used in cooking

CUMMER, -S n gossip

CUMMIN, -S same as ▶ cumin

CUMQUAT, -S same as ▶ kumquat

CUMSHAW, -S n (used, esp formerly, by beggars in Chinese ports) a present or tip

CUMULATE vb accumulate ▷ adj heaped up

CUMULET, -S n variety of domestic fancy pigeon

CUMULI ▶ cumulus

CUMULOSE adj full of heaps

CUMULOUS adj resembling or consisting of cumulus clouds

CUMULUS, CUMULI n thick white or dark grey cloud

CUNABULA n cradle

CUNDY, CUNDIES n sewer

CUNEAL same as ▷ cuneiform

CUNEATE adj wedge-shaped

CUNEATED same as ▶ cuneate

CUNEATIC adj cuneiform

CUNEI ▶ cuneus

CUNETTE, -S n small trench dug in the main ditch of a fortification

CUNEUS, CUNEI n small wedge-shaped area of the cerebral cortex

CUNIFORM same as ▷ cuneiform

CUNIT, -S n one hundred cubic feet

CUNJEVOI n plant of tropical Asia and Australia

CUNNER, -S n fish of the wrasse family

CUNNING, -S adj clever at deceiving ▷ n cleverness at deceiving

CUP, -PED, -S n small bowl-shaped drinking container with a handle ▷ vb form (one's hands) into the shape of a cup

CUPBOARD n piece of furniture or alcove with a door, for storage ▷ vb store in a cupboard

CUPCAKE, -S n small cake baked in a cup-shaped foil or paper case

CUPEL, -ED, -ING, -LED, -S n refractory pot in which gold or silver is refined ▷ vb refine (gold or silver) by means of cupellation

CUPELER, -S ▶ cupel

CUPELING ▶ cupel

CUPELLED ▶ cupel

CUPELLER ▶ cupel

CUPELS ▶ cupel

CUPFUL, -S, CUPSFUL n amount a cup will hold

CUPGALL, -S n gall found on oakleaves

CUPHEAD, -S n type of bolt or rivet with a cup-shaped head

CUPID, -S n figure representing the Roman god of love

CUPIDITY n greed for money or possessions

CUPIDS ▶ cupid

CUPLIKE ▶ cup

CUPMAN, CUPMEN n drinking companion

CUPOLA, -ED, -S n domed roof or ceiling ▷ vb provide with a cupola

CUPOLAR ▶ cupola

CUPOLAS ▶ cupola

CUPPA, -S n cup of tea

CUPPED ▶ cup

CUPPER, -S same as ▶ cuppa

CUPPIER ▶ cuppy

CUPPIEST ▶ cuppy

CUPPING, -S ▶ cup

CUPPY, CUPPIER, CUPPIEST adj cup-shaped

CUPREOUS adj of copper

CUPRIC adj of or containing copper in the divalent state

CUPRITE, -S n red secondary mineral

CUPROUS adj of or containing copper in the monovalent state

CUPRUM, -S an obsolete name for ▶ copper

CUPS ▶ cup

CUPSFUL ▶ cupful

CUPULA, -E n dome-shaped structure

CUPULAR same as ▶ cupulate

CUPULATE adj shaped like a small cup

CUPULE, -S n cup-shaped part or structure

CUR, -S n mongrel dog

CURABLE adj capable of being cured

CURABLY ▶ curable

CURACAO, -S n orange-flavoured liqueur

CURACIES ▶ curacy

CURACOA, -S same as ▶ curacao

CURACY, CURACIES n work or position of a curate

CURAGH, -S same as ▶ currach

CURARA, -S same as ▶ curare

CURARE, -S n poisonous resin of a S American tree

CURARI, -S same as ▶ curare

CURARINE n alkaloid extracted from curare, used as a muscle relaxant in surgery

CURARIS ▶ curari

CURARISE same as ▶ curarize

CURARIZE vb paralyse or treat with curare

CURASSOW n gallinaceous ground-nesting bird

CURAT, -S n cuirass

CURATE, -D, -S, CURATING n clergyman or clergywoman who assists a parish priest ▷ vb be in charge of (an art exhibition or museum)

CURATION n work of a curator

CURATIVE n something able to cure ▷ adj able to cure

CURATOR, -S n person in charge of a museum or art gallery

CURATORY ▶ curator

CURATRIX n female curator

CURATS ▶ curat

CURB, -ED, -S n something that restrains ▷ vb control, restrain

CURBABLE adj capable of being restrained

CURBED ▶ curb

CURBER, -S ▶ curb

CURBING, -S the US spelling of ▶ kerbing

CURBLESS adj having no restraint

CURBS ▶ curb

CURBSIDE n pavement

CURCH, -ES n woman's plain cap or kerchief

CURCHEF, -S same as ▶ curch

CURCHES ▶ curch

CURCULIO n type of American weevil

CURCUMA, -S n type of tropical Asian tuberous plant

CURCUMIN n yellow dye derived from turmeric

CURD, -ED, -ING, -S n coagulated milk, used to make cheese ▷ vb turn into or become curd

CURDIER ▶ curdy

CURDIEST ▶ curdy

CURDING ▶ curd

CURDLE, -D, -S, CURDLING vb turn into curd, coagulate

CURDLER, -S ▶ curdle

CURDLES ▶ curdle

CURDLING ▶ curdle

CURDS ▶ curd

CURDY, CURDIER, CURDIEST ▶ curd

CURE, -D, -S vb get rid of (an illness or problem) ▷ n (treatment causing) curing of an illness or person

CURELESS ▶ cure

CURER, -S ▶ cure

CURES ▶ cure

CURET, -S same as ▶ curette

CURETTE, -D, -S n surgical instrument for scraping tissue from body cavities ▷ vb scrape with a curette

CURF, -S n type of limestone

CURFEW, -S n law ordering people to stay inside after a specific time

CURFS ▶ curf

CURIA, -E, -S n papal court and government of the Roman Catholic Church

CURIAL ▶ curia

CURIAS ▶ curia

CURIE, -S n standard unit of radioactivity

CURIET, -S n cuirass

CURING, -S n act of curing

CURIO, -S n rare or unusual object valued as a collector's item

CURIOSA pl n curiosities

CURIOUS adj eager to learn or know

CURITE, -S n oxide of uranium and lead

CURIUM, -S n radioactive element artificially produced from plutonium

CURL, -ED, -S n curved piece of hair ▷ vb make (hair) into curls or (of hair) grow in curls

CURLER, -S n pin or small tube for curling hair

CURLEW, -S n long-billed wading bird

CURLI pl n curled hairlike processes on the surface of the E. coli bacterium

CURLICUE n ornamental curl or twist ▷ vb curl or twist elaborately, as in curlicues

CURLIER ▶ curly

CURLIES pl n as in **have by the short and curlies** have completely in one's power

CURLIEST ▶ curly

CURLILY ▶ curly

CURLING, -S n game like bowls, played with heavy stones on ice

CURLS ▶ curl

CURLY, CURLIER, CURLIEST adj tending to curl

CURLYCUE same as ▶ curlicue

CURN, -S n grain (of corn etc)

CURNEY same as ▶ curny

CURNIER ▶ curny

CURNIEST ▶ curny

CURNS ▶ curn

CURNY, CURNIER, CURNIEST adj granular

CURPEL, -S same as ▶ crupper

CURR, -ED, -ING, -S vb purr

CURRACH, -S a Scot or Irish name for ▶ coracle

CURRAGH, -S same as ▶ currach

CURRAN, -S n black bun

CURRANT, -S n small dried grape

CURRANTY ▶ currant

CURRED ▶ curr

CURRENCY n money in use in a particular country

CURRENT, -S adj of the immediate present ▷ n flow of water or air in one direction

CURRICLE n two-wheeled open carriage drawn by two horses side by side

CURRIE same as ▶ curry

CURRIED ▶ curry

CURRIER, -S n person who curries leather

CURRIERY n trade, work, or place of occupation of a currier

CURRIES ▶ curry

CURRING ▶ curr

CURRISH adj of or like a cur

CURRS ▶ curr

CURRY, CURRIED, CURRIES, -ING n Indian dish of meat or vegetables in a hot spicy sauce ▷ vb prepare (food) with curry powder

CURS ▶ cur

CURSAL ▶ cursus

CURSE, -S vb swear (at) ▷ n swearword

CURSED, -ER ▶ curse

CURSEDLY ▶ curse

CURSER, -S ▶ curse

CURSES ▶ curse

CURSI ▶ cursus

CURSILLO n short religious retreat

CURSING, -S ▶ curse

CURSITOR n clerk in the Court of Chancery

CURSIVE, -S n handwriting done with joined letters ▷ adj of handwriting or print in which letters are joined in a flowing style

CURSOR, -ES, -S n movable point of light that shows a specific position on a visual display unit

CURSORY adj quick and superficial

CURST same as ▶ cursed

CURSUS, CURSI n Neolithic parallel earthworks

CURT, -ER, -EST adj brief and rather rude

CURTAIL, -S vb cut short

CURTAIN n piece of cloth hung at a window or opening as a screen ▷ vb provide with curtains

CURTAINS pl n death or ruin

CURTAL, -S adj cut short ▷ n animal whose tail has been docked

CURTALAX same as > curtalaxe

CURTALS ▶ curtal

CURTANA, -S n unpointed sword displayed at a coronation as an emblem of mercy

CURTATE adj shortened

CURTAXE, -S same as
> **curtalaxe**

CURTER ▸ **curt**

CURTEST ▸ **curt**

CURTESY n widower's life interest in his wife's estate

CURTLY ▸ **curt**

CURTNESS ▸ **curt**

CURTSEY, -S same as ▸ **curtsy**

**CURTSY, CURTSIED,
CURTSIES** n woman's
gesture of respect ▹ vb
make a curtsy

CURULE adj (in ancient
Rome) of the highest rank,
esp one entitled to use a
curule chair

CURVATE adj curved

CURVATED same as
▸ **curvate**

CURVE, -D, -S, CURVING n
continuously bending line
with no straight parts ▹ vb
form or move in a curve

CURVEDLY ▸ **curve**

CURVES ▸ **curve**

CURVET, -ED, -S n horse's
low leap with all four feet off
the ground ▹ vb make such
a leap

CURVEY same as ▸ **curvy**

CURVIER ▸ **curvy**

CURVIEST ▸ **curvy**

CURVING ▸ **curve**

CURVITAL adj relating to
curvature

CURVITY n curvedness

**CURVY, CURVIER,
CURVIEST** ▸ **curve**

CUSCUS, -ES n large
Australian nocturnal
possum

CUSEC, -S n unit of flow
equal to 1 cubic foot per
second

CUSH, -ES n cushion

CUSHAT, -S n wood pigeon

CUSHAW, -S same as
▸ **cashaw**

CUSHES ▸ **cush**

CUSHIE, -S same as ▸ **cushat**

CUSHIER ▸ **cushy**

CUSHIES ▸ **cushie**

CUSHIEST ▸ **cushy**

CUSHILY ▸ **cushy**

CUSHION, -S n bag filled
with soft material, to make a
seat more comfortable ▹ vb
lessen the effects of

CUSHIONY adj like a cushion

CUSHTY interj exclamation
of pleasure, agreement,
approval, etc

**CUSHY, CUSHIER,
CUSHIEST** adj easy

CUSK, -S n type of food fish
of northern coastal waters,
with a single long dorsal fin

CUSP, -S n pointed end, esp
on a tooth

CUSPAL ▸ **cusp**

CUSPATE adj having a cusp
or cusps

CUSPATED same as ▸ **cuspate**

CUSPED same as ▸ **cuspate**

CUSPID, -S n tooth having
one point

CUSPIDAL same as
> **cuspidate**

CUSPIDES ▸ **cuspis**

CUSPIDOR another word (esp
US) for ▸ **spittoon**

CUSPIDS ▸ **cuspid**

CUSPIER ▸ **cuspy**

CUSPIEST ▸ **cuspy**

CUSPIS, CUSPIDES n in
anatomy, a tapering
structure

CUSPLIKE adj like a cusp

CUSPS ▸ **cusp**

CUSPY, CUSPIER, CUSPIEST
adj (of a computer program)
well-designed and
user-friendly

CUSS, -ES, -ING n curse,
oath ▹ vb swear (at)

CUSSED adj obstinate

CUSSEDLY ▸ **cussed**

CUSSER, -S same as ▸ **cooser**

CUSSES ▸ **cuss**

CUSSING ▸ **cuss**

CUSSO, -S n tree of the rose
family

CUSSWORD n swearword

CUSTARD, -S n sweet yellow
sauce made from milk and
eggs

CUSTARDY adj like custard

CUSTOCK, -S same as
▸ **castock**

CUSTODE, -S n custodian

CUSTODY n protective care

CUSTOM n long-established
activity or action ▹ adj made
to the specifications of an
individual customer

CUSTOMED adj accustomed

CUSTOMER n person who
buys goods or services

CUSTOMS n duty charged
on imports or exports

CUSTOS n superior in the
Franciscan religious order

CUSTREL, -S n knave

CUSTUMAL another word for
> **customary**

CUSUM, -S n analysis
technique used in statistics

CUT, -S vb open up,
penetrate, wound, or divide
with a sharp instrument

CUTAWAY, -S adj (of a
drawing or model) having
part of the outside omitted
to reveal the inside ▹ n
man's coat cut diagonally
from the front waist to the
back of the knees

CUTBACK, -S n decrease or
reduction

CUTBANK, -S n steep
banking at a bend in a river

CUTBLOCK n area where
logging is permitted

CUTCH, -ES same as
▸ **catechu**

CUTCHA adj crude

CUTCHERY same as
> **cutchery**

CUTCHES ▸ **cutch**

CUTDOWN, -S n decrease

CUTE, -R, -ST adj appealing
or attractive

CUTELY ▸ **cute**

CUTENESS ▸ **cute**

CUTER ▸ **cute**

CUTES ▸ **cutis**

CUTESIE same as ▸ **cutesy**

CUTESIER ▸ **cutesy**

CUTEST ▸ **cute**

CUTESY, CUTESIER, CUTESIEST
affectedly cute or coy

CUTEY, -S same as ▸ **cutie**

CUTGLASS adj (of an accent)
upper-class

CUTGRASS n any grass of
the genus Leersia

CUTICLE, -S n skin at the
base of a fingernail or toenail

CUTICULA n cuticle

CUTIE, -S n person regarded
as appealing or attractive

CUTIKIN, -S same as
▸ **cuitikin**

CUTIN, -S n waxy
waterproof substance

CUTINISE same as ▸ **cutinize**

CUTINIZE vb become or
cause to become covered or
impregnated with cutin

CUTINS ▸ **cutin**

CUTIS, CUTES, -ES a
technical name for the ▸ **skin**

CUTLAS, -ES same as
▸ **cutlass**

CUTLASS n curved
one-edged sword formerly
used by sailors

CUTLER, -S n maker of
cutlery

CUTLERY n knives, forks,
and spoons

CUTLET, -S n small piece of
meat like a chop

CUTLETTE n flat croquette
of minced meat

CUTLINE, -S n caption

CUTOFF, -S n limit or termination

CUTOUT, -S n something that has been cut out from something else

CUTOVER, -S n transitional period in an IT system changeover

CUTPURSE n pickpocket

CUTS ▶ cut

CUTSCENE n non-interactive scene in a computer game

CUTTABLE adj capable of being cut

CUTTAGE, -S n propagation by using parts taken from growing plants

CUTTER, -S n person or tool that cuts

CUTTIER ▶ cutty

CUTTIES ▶ cutty

CUTTIEST ▶ cutty

CUTTING, -S ▶ cut

CUTTLE, -D, -S, CUTTLING vb to whisper

CUTTO, -ES n large knife

CUTTOE same as ▶ **cutto**

CUTTOES ▶ cutto

CUTTY, CUTTIER, CUTTIES, CUTTIEST adj short or cut short ▷ n something cut short

CUTUP, -S n joker or prankster

CUTWATER n forward part of the stem of a vessel, which cuts through the water

CUTWORK, -S n type of openwork embroidery

CUTWORM, -S n caterpillar of various types of moth

CUVEE, -S n individual batch or blend of wine

CUVETTE, -S n shallow dish or vessel for holding liquid

CUZ, -ES, -ZES n cousin

Cuz is another word for **cousin**, great for using the Z.

CUZZIE, -S n close friend or family member

CWM, -S same as ▶ **cirque**

Cwm is a Welsh word meaning a valley, a useful one to remember because it doesn't contain any vowels.

CWTCH, -ED, -ES, -ING vb cuddle or be cuddled

This delightful Welsh word meaning to cuddle is not likely to come up, but it might just help you out of a tight spot one day when your rack is all consonants.

CYAN, -S n highly saturated green-blue ▷ adj of this colour

CYANAMID same as ▶ **cyanamide**

CYANATE, -S n any salt or ester of cyanic acid

CYANIC adj as in **cyanic acid** colourless poisonous volatile liquid acid

CYANID, -S same as ▶ **cyanide**

CYANIDE, -D, -S n extremely poisonous chemical compound ▷ vb treat with cyanide

CYANIDS ▶ cyanid

CYANIN, -S same as ▶ **cyanine**

CYANINE, -S n blue dye used in photography

CYANINS ▶ cyanin

CYANISE, -D, -S same as ▶ **cyanize**

CYANITE, -S variant spelling of ▶ **kyanite**

CYANITIC ▶ cyanite

CYANIZE, -D, -S vb turn into cyanide

CYANO adj containing cyanogen

CYANOGEN n poisonous colourless flammable gas

CYANOSE same as ▶ **cyanosis**

CYANOSED adj affected by cyanosis

CYANOSIS, CYANOSES n blueness of the skin, caused by a deficiency of oxygen in the blood

CYANOTIC ▶ cyanosis

CYANS ▶ cyan

CYANURET n cyanide

CYANURIC adj as in **cyanuric acid** type of acid

CYATHI ▶ cyathus

CYATHIUM, CYATHIA n inflorescence of the type found in the poinsettia

CYATHUS, CYATHI n ancient measure of wine

CYBER adj involving computers

CYBERPET n electronic toy that simulates the activities of a pet

CYBERWAR n information warfare

CYBORG, -S n (in science fiction) a living being enhanced by computer implants

CYBRID, -S n cytoplasmic hybrid

CYCAD, -S n type of tropical or subtropical plant

CYCAS, -ES n palm tree of the genus Cycas

CYCASIN, -S n glucoside, toxic to mammals, occurring in cycads

CYCLAMEN n plant with red, pink, or white flowers ▷ adj of a dark reddish-purple colour

CYCLAMIC adj as in **cyclamic acid** type of acid

CYCLASE, -S n enzyme which acts as a catalyst in the formation of a cyclic compound

CYCLE, -D, -S vb ride a bicycle ▷ n bicycle

CYCLECAR n any light car with an engine capacity of 1100cc or less

CYCLED ▶ cycle

CYCLER, -S same as ▶ **cyclist**

CYCLERY n business dealing in bicycles and bicycle accessories

CYCLES ▶ cycle

CYCLEWAY n path or way designed, and reserved for, cyclists

CYCLIC adj recurring or revolving in cycles

CYCLICAL n short-term trend, of which reversal is expected ▷ adj cyclic

CYCLICLY ▶ cyclic

CYCLIN, -S n type of protein

CYCLING, -S ▶ cycle

CYCLINS ▶ cyclin

CYCLISE, -D, -S same as ▶ **cyclize**

CYCLIST, -S n person who rides a bicycle

CYCLITOL n alicyclic compound

CYCLIZE, -D, -S vb be cyclical

CYCLO, -S n type of rickshaw

CYCLOID, -S adj resembling a circle ▷ n mathematical curve

CYCLONAL ▶ cyclone

CYCLONE, -S n violent wind moving round a central area

CYCLONIC ▶ cyclone

CYCLOPES ▶ cyclops

CYCLOPIC ▶ cyclops

CYCLOPS, CYCLOPES n type of copepod characterized by having one eye

CYCLOS ▶ cyclo

CYCLOSIS, CYCLOSES n circulation of cytoplasm or cell organelles, such as food vacuoles in some protozoans

CYCLUS, -ES n cycle

CYDER, -S same as ▶ **cider**

CYESIS, CYESES *the technical name for* ▸ **pregnancy**
CYGNET, -S *n* young swan
CYLICES ▸ **cylix**
CYLIKES ▸ **cylix**
CYLINDER *n* solid or hollow body with straight sides and circular ends
CYLIX, CYLICES, CYLIKES *variant of* ▸ **kylix**
CYMA, -E, -S *n* moulding with a double curve, part concave and part convex
CYMAR, -S *n* woman's short fur-trimmed jacket, popular in the 17th and 18th centuries
CYMAS ▸ **cyma**
CYMATIA ▸ **cymatium**
CYMATICS *n* therapy involving sound waves directed at the body
CYMATIUM, CYMATIA *n* top moulding of a classical cornice or entablature
CYMBAL, -S *n* percussion instrument
CYMBALER ▸ **cymbal**
CYMBALO, -S *another name for* ▸ **dulcimer**
CYMBALOM *same as* ▸ **cimbalom**
CYMBALOS ▸ **cymbalo**
CYMBALS ▸ **cymbal**
CYMBIDIA > **cymbidium**
CYMBLING *same as* ▸ **cymling**
CYME, -S *n* type of flower cluster
CYMENE, -S *n* colourless insoluble liquid
CYMES ▸ **cyme**
CYMLIN, -S *same as* ▸ **cymling**
CYMLING, -S *n* pattypan squash
CYMLINS ▸ **cymlin**
CYMOGENE *n* mixture of volatile flammable hydrocarbons
CYMOID *adj* resembling a cyme or cyma
CYMOL, -S *same as* ▸ **cymene**
CYMOSE *adj* having the characteristics of a cyme
CYMOSELY ▸ **cymose**
CYMOUS *adj* relating to a cyme
CYNANCHE *n* any disease characterized by

inflammation and swelling of the throat
CYNIC, -S *n* person who believes that people always act selfishly ▷ *adj* of or relating to Sirius, the Dog Star
CYNICAL *adj* believing that people always act selfishly
CYNICISM *n* attitude or beliefs of a cynic
CYNICS ▸ **cynic**
CYNODONT *n* carnivorous mammal-like reptile
CYNOSURE *n* centre of attention
CYPHER, -ED, -S *same as* ▸ **cipher**
CYPRES, -ES *n* legal doctrine
CYPRESS *n* evergreen tree with dark green leaves
CYPRIAN, -S *n* licentious or profligate person
CYPRID, -S *n* small bivalve freshwater crustacean
CYPRIDES ▸ **cypris**
CYPRIDS ▸ **cyprid**
CYPRINE *adj* relating to carp ▷ *n* type of silicate mineral
CYPRINID *n* type of mainly freshwater fish, usu with toothless jaws
CYPRIS, CYPRIDES *n* small bivalve freshwater crustacean
CYPRUS, -ES *same as* ▸ **cypress**
CYPSELA, -E *n* dry one-seeded fruit of the daisy and related plants
CYST, -S *n* (abnormal) sac in the body containing fluid or soft matter
CYSTEIN, -S *same as* ▸ **cysteine**
CYSTEINE *n* sulphur-containing amino acid
CYSTEINS ▸ **cystein**
CYSTIC *adj* of, relating to, or resembling a cyst
CYSTID, -S *n* fossil echinoderm of an extinct order of sea lilies
CYSTINE, -S *n* sulphur-containing amino acid
CYSTITIS *n* inflammation of the bladder
CYSTOID, -S *adj* resembling a cyst or bladder ▷ *n* tissue

mass that resembles a cyst but lacks an outer membrane
CYSTS ▸ **cyst**
CYTASE, -S *n* cellulose-dissolving enzyme
CYTASTER *another word for* ▸ **aster**
CYTE, -S *n* biological cell
CYTIDINE *n* nucleoside formed by the condensation of cytosine and ribose
CYTISI ▸ **cytisus**
CYTISINE *n* poisonous alkaloid found in laburnum seeds
CYTISUS, CYTISI *n* any plant of the broom genus, Cytisus
CYTODE, -S *n* mass of protoplasm without a nucleus
CYTOGENY *n* origin and development of plant cells
CYTOID *adj* resembling a cell
CYTOKINE *n* type of protein that carries signals to neighbouring cells
CYTOLOGY *n* study of plant and animal cells
CYTON, -S *n* main part of a neuron
CYTOSINE *n* white crystalline pyrimidine occurring in nucleic acids
CYTOSOL, -S *n* solution in a biological cell
CYTOSOME *n* body of a cell excluding its nucleus
CZAPKA, -S *n* leather and felt peaked military helmet of Polish origin
CZAR, -S *n* Russian emperor
CZARDAS *n* Hungarian national dance of alternating slow and fast sections
CZARDOM, -S ▸ **czar**
CZAREVNA *n* daughter of a czar
CZARINA, -S *n* wife of a czar
CZARISM, -S *n* system of government by a czar
CZARIST, -S *n* supporter of a czar
CZARITSA *n* wife of a czar
CZARITZA *same as* ▸ **czaritsa**
CZARS ▸ **czar**

Dd

D forms a two-letter word before every vowel except **U**. There are plenty of good three-letter words beginning with **D**, particularly those with a **Y** or **W**: **day**, **dye** and **dew** are worth 7 points each, for example. And don't forget **dex**, **dox** and **dux** for 11 points each and the invaluable **dzo** for 13 points.

DA, -S n Burmese knife

DAAL, -S n (in Indian cookery) split pulses

DAB, -BED, -BING, -S vb pat lightly ▷ n small amount of something soft or moist

DABBA, -S n in Indian cookery, a round metal box used to transport hot food

DABBED ▷ dab

DABBER, -S n pad used by printers for applying ink by hand

DABBING ▷ dab

DABBITY n temporary tattoo

DABBLE, -D, -S, DABBLING vb be involved in something superficially

DABBLER, -S ▷ dabble

DABBLES ▷ dabble

DABBLING ▷ dabble

DABCHICK n type of small grebe

DABS ▷ dab

DABSTER, -S n incompetent or amateurish worker

DACE, -S n small European freshwater fish

DACHA, -S n country cottage in Russia

DACITE, -S n volcanic rock

DACK, -ED, -ING, -S vb remove the trousers from (someone) by force

DACKER, -ED, -S vb walk slowly

DACKING ▷ dack

DACKS ▷ dack

DACOIT, -S n (in India and Myanmar) a member of a gang of armed robbers

DACOITY n (in India and Myanmar) robbery by an armed gang

DACRON, -S n US tradename for a synthetic polyester fibre or fabric

DACTYL, -S n metrical foot of three syllables, one long followed by two short

DACTYLAR adj of or relating to a dactyl

DACTYLI ▷ dactylus

DACTYLIC same as ▷ dactyl

DACTYLS ▷ dactyl

DACTYLUS, DACTYLI n tip of a squid's tentacular club

DAD, -DED, -DING, -S n father ▷ vb act or treat as a father

DADA, -S n nihilistic artistic movement of the early 20th century

DADAISM, -S same as ▷ dada

DADAIST, -S ▷ dada

DADAS ▷ dada

DADBOD, -S n untoned male physique

DADDED ▷ dad

DADDIES ▷ daddy

DADDING ▷ dad

DADDLE, -D, -S, DADDLING vb walk unsteadily

DADDOCK, -S n core of a dead tree

DADDY, DADDIES n father

DADGUM mild form of ▷ damned

DADO, -ED, -ES, -ING, -S n lower part of an interior wall decorated differently from the upper part ▷ vb provide with a dado

DADS ▷ dad

DAE, -ING, -S a Scot word for ▷ do

DAEDAL adj skilful or intricate

DAEDALIC same as > daedalian

DAEING ▷ dae

DAEMON, -ES, -S same as ▷ demon

DAEMONIC ▷ daemon

DAEMONS ▷ daemon

DAES ▷ dae

DAFF, -ED, -S vb frolic

DAFFIER ▷ daffy

DAFFIES ▷ daffy

DAFFIEST ▷ daffy

DAFFILY ▷ daffy

DAFFING, -S ▷ daff

DAFFODIL n yellow trumpet-shaped flower that blooms in spring ▷ adj brilliant yellow

DAFFS ▷ daff

DAFFY, DAFFIER, DAFFIES, DAFFIEST adj daft ▷ n daffodil

DAFT, -ER, -EST adj foolish or crazy

DAFTAR, -S Indian word for ▷ office

DAFTER ▷ daft

DAFTEST ▷ daft

DAFTIE, -S n foolish person

DAFTLY ▷ daft

DAFTNESS ▷ daft

DAG, -GED, -S n daglock ▷ vb cut daglocks from sheep

DAGABA, -S n dome-shaped Buddhist shrine

DAGGED ▷ dag

DAGGER, -ED, -S n short weapon with pointed blade ▷ vb stab with a dagger

DAGGIER ▷ daggy

DAGGIEST ▷ daggy

DAGGING, -S ▷ dag

DAGGLE, -D, -S, DAGGLING vb trail through water

DAGGY, DAGGIER, DAGGIEST adj amusing

DAGLOCK, -S n dung-caked lock of wool around the hindquarters of a sheep

DAGOBA, -S n dome-shaped Buddhist shrine

DAGS ▷ dag

DAGWOOD, -S n European shrub

DAH, -S n long sound used in Morse code

D

DAHABEAH n houseboat used on the Nile

DAHABIAH same as ▸**dahabeah**

DAHABIEH n Egyptian houseboat

DAHABIYA n Egyptian houseboat

DAHL, -S same as ▸ **dhal**

DAHLIA, -S n brightly coloured garden flower

DAHLS ▸ **dahl**

DAHOON, -S n evergreen shrub

DAHS ▸ **dah**

DAIDLE, -D, -S, DAIDLING vb waddle about

DAIDZEIN n type of protein

DAIKER, -ED, -S vb walk slowly

DAIKO, -S n Japanese drum

DAIKON, -S another name for ▸ **mooli**

DAIKOS ▸ **daiko**

DAILY, DAILIES adj occurring every day or every weekday ▹ adv every day ▹ n daily newspaper

DAIMEN adj occasional

DAIMIO, -S same as ▸ **daimyo**

DAIMOKU, -S n Nichiren Buddhist chant

DAIMON, -S same as ▸ **demon**

DAIMONES pl n disembodied souls

DAIMONIC ▸ **daimon**

DAIMONS ▸ **daimon**

DAIMYO, -S n magnate in Japan from the 11th to the 19th century

DAINE, -D, -S, DAINING vb condescend

DAINT, -S adj dainty ▹ n dainty

DAINTIER ▸ **dainty**

DAINTIES ▸ **dainty**

DAINTILY ▸ **dainty**

DAINTS ▸ **daint**

DAINTY, DAINTIER, DAINTIES adj delicate or elegant ▹ n small cake or sweet

DAIQUIRI n iced drink containing rum, lime juice, and sugar

DAIRY, DAIRIES n place for the processing or sale of milk and its products ▹ adj of milk or its products

DAIRYING n business of producing, processing, and selling dairy products

DAIRYMAN, DAIRYMEN n man employed to look after cows

DAIS, -ES n raised platform in a hall, used by a speaker

DAISHIKI n upper garment

DAISIED ▸ **daisy**

DAISY, DAISIES n small wild flower with a yellow centre and white petals

DAK n system of mail delivery or passenger transport

A **dak** is an old mail or transport system, often useful for disposing of the K.

DAKER, -ED, -ING, -S vb walk slowly

DAKERHEN n European bird

DAKERING ▸ **daker**

DAKERS ▸ **daker**

DAKOIT, -S same as ▸ **dacoit**

DAKOITI, -S same as ▸ **dakoit**

DAKOITS ▸ **dakoit**

DAKOITY n armed robbery

DAKS an informal name for ▸ **trousers**

DAL, -S same as ▹ **decalitre**

DALAPON, -S n herbicide

DALASI, -S n standard monetary unit of The Gambia, divided into 100 bututs

DALE, -S n (esp in N England) valley

DALED, -S same as ▸ **daleth**

DALEDH, -S n letter of the Hebrew alphabet

DALEDS ▸ **daled**

DALES ▸ **dale**

DALESMAN, DALESMEN n person living in a dale, esp in the dales of N England

DALETH, -S n fourth letter of the Hebrew alphabet

DALGYTE, -S another name for ▸ **bilby**

DALI, -S n type of tree

DALLES, DALLE pl n stretch of a river between high rock walls, with rapids and dangerous currents

DALLIED ▸ **dally**

DALLIER, -S ▸ **dally**

DALLIES ▸ **dally**

DALLOP, -S n semisolid lump

DALLY, DALLIED, DALLIES, -ING vb waste time

DALMAHOY n bushy wig

DALMATIC n wide-sleeved tunic-like vestment open at the sides, worn by deacons and bishops

DALS ▸ **dal**

DALT, -S n foster child

DALTON, -S n atomic mass unit

DALTONIC > **daltonism**

DALTONS ▸ **dalton**

DALTS ▸ **dalt**

DAM, -MED, -MING, -S n barrier built across a river to create a lake ▹ vb build a dam across (a river)

DAMAGE, -D vb harm, spoil ▹ n harm to a person or thing

DAMAGER, -S ▸ **damage**

DAMAGES pl n money awarded as compensation for injury or loss

DAMAGING ▸ **damage**

DAMAN, -S n the Syrian rock hyrax

DAMAR, -S same as ▸ **dammar**

DAMASK, -ED, -S n fabric with a pattern woven into it, used for tablecloths etc ▹ vb ornament (metal) by etching or inlaying, usually with gold or silver

DAMASKIN vb decorate metal

DAMASKS ▸ **damask**

DAMASSIN n patterned damask

DAMBOARD n draughtboard

DAMBROD, -S n draughtboard

DAME, -S n woman

DAMEHOOD n state of being a dame

DAMES ▸ **dame**

DAMEWORT n sweet-scented perennial plant with mauve or white flowers

DAMFOOL, -S adj foolish ▹ n foolish person

DAMIANA, -S n herbal medicine

DAMMAR, -S n any of various resins obtained from SE Asian trees

DAMME interj exclamation of surprise

DAMMED ▸ **dam**

DAMMER, -S same as ▸ **dammar**

DAMMING ▸ **dam**

DAMMIT interj exclamation of surprise

DAMN, -ING, -S interj exclamation of annoyance ▹ adj extreme ▹ adv extremely ▹ vb condemn as bad or worthless

DAMNABLE adj annoying

DAMNABLY adv in a detestable manner

DAMNDEST n utmost

DAMNED, -ER adj condemned to hell ▹ adv extremely

DAMNER, -S n person who damns

DAMNEST, -S same as > damnedest

DAMNIFY vb cause loss or damage to (a person)

DAMNING ► damn

DAMNS ► damn

DAMOISEL same as ► damsel

DAMOSEL, -S same as ► damsel

DAMOZEL, -S n young woman

DAMP, -ED, -EST, -S adj slightly wet ▷ n slight wetness, moisture ▷ vb make damp

DAMPEN, -ED, -S vb reduce the intensity of

DAMPENER ► dampen

DAMPENS ► dampen

DAMPER, -S n movable plate to regulate the draught in a fire

DAMPEST ► damp

DAMPIER ► dampy

DAMPIEST ► dampy

DAMPING, -S n act of moistening

DAMPISH ► damp

DAMPLY ► damp

DAMPNESS ► damp

DAMPS ► damp

DAMPY, DAMPIER, DAMPIEST adj damp

DAMS ► dam

DAMSEL, -S n young woman

DAMSON, -S n small blue-black plumlike fruit

DAN, -S n in judo, any of the 10 black-belt grades of proficiency

DANAZOL, -S n synthetic male hormone

DANCE, -D, -S vb move the feet and body rhythmically in time to music ▷ n series of steps and movements in time to music

DANCER, -S ► dance

DANCES ► dance

DANCETTE another name for ► chevron

DANCETTY adj having a zigzag pattern

DANCEY, DANCIER, DANCIEST adj of, relating to, or resembling dance music

DANCICAL n type of dance show set to pop music

DANCIER ► dancey

DANCIEST ► dancey

DANCING, -S ► dance

DANCY adj (of music) appropriate for dancing

DANDER, -ED, -S n stroll ▷ vb stroll

DANDIER ► dandy

DANDIES ► dandy

DANDIEST ► dandy

DANDIFY vb dress like or cause to resemble a dandy

DANDILY ► dandy

DANDLE, -D, -S, DANDLING vb move (a child) up and down on one's knee

DANDLER, -S ► dandle

DANDLES ► dandle

DANDLING ► dandle

DANDRIFF same as ► dandruff

DANDRUFF n loose scales of dry dead skin shed from the scalp

DANDY, DANDIER, DANDIES, DANDIEST n man who is overconcerned with the elegance of his appearance ▷ adj very good

DANDYISH ► dandy

DANDYISM ► dandy

DANEGELD n tax levied in Anglo-Saxon England to provide protection from Viking invaders

DANEGELT same as ► danegeld

DANELAGH same as ► danelaw

DANELAW, -S n Danish law in parts of Anglo-Saxon England

DANEWEED n dwarf elder

DANEWORT n dwarf elder

DANG, -ED, -EST, -ING, -S vb euphemism for damn, meaning condemn ▷ adj euphemism for damn, meaning extreme

DANGER, -ED, -S n state of being vulnerable to injury, loss, or evil ▷ vb in archaic usage, endanger

DANGEST ► dang

DANGING ► dang

DANGLE, -D, -S, DANGLING vb hang loosely ▷ n act of dangling or something that dangles

DANGLER, -S ► dangle

DANGLES ► dangle

DANGLIER ► dangly

DANGLING ► dangle

DANGLY, DANGLIER ► dangle

DANGS ► dang

DANIO, -S n type of tropical freshwater fish

DANISH, -ES n sweet pastry

DANK, -ER, -EST, -S adj unpleasantly damp and

chilly ▷ n unpleasant damp and chilliness

DANKISH ► dank

DANKLY ► dank

DANKNESS ► dank

DANKS ► dank

DANNY, DANNIES n hand (used esp when addressing children)

DANS ► dan

DANSAK, -S n type of Indian dish

DANSEUR, -S n male ballet dancer

DANSEUSE n female ballet dancer

DANT, -ED, -ING, -S vb intimidate

DANTON, -ED, -S same as ► daunton

DANTS ► dant

DAP, -PED, -PING, -S vb engage in a type of fly fishing

DAPHNE, -S n ornamental Eurasian shrub

DAPHNIA, -S n type of water flea

DAPHNID, -S n water flea

DAPPED ► dap

DAPPER, -ER, -S adj (of a man) neat in appearance ▷ n fisherman or -woman who uses a bobbing bait

DAPPERLY ► dapper

DAPPERS ► dapper

DAPPING ► dap

DAPPLE, -D, -S, DAPPLING vb mark or become marked with spots or patches of a different colour ▷ n mottled or spotted markings ▷ adj marked with dapples or spots

DAPS ► dap

DAPSONE, -S n antimicrobial drug

DAQUIRI, -S n rum cocktail

DARAF, -S n unit of elastance equal to a reciprocal farad

DARB, -S n something excellent

DARBAR, -S n hall in a Sikh temple

DARBIES pl n handcuffs

DARBS ► darb

DARCY, DARCIES, -S n unit expressing the permeability coefficient of rock

DARE, -D, -S vb be courageous enough to try (to do something) ▷ n challenge to do something risky

DAREFUL adj daring

DARER, -S ► dare

DARES ▶ dare
DARESAY vb venture to say
DARG, -S n day's work
DARGA, -S same as ▶ dargah
DARGAH, -S n tomb of a Muslim saint
DARGAS ▶ darga
DARGLE, -S n wooded hollow
DARGS ▶ darg
DARI, -S n variety of sorghum
DARIC, -S n gold coin of ancient Persia
DARING, -S adj willing to take risks ▷ n courage to do dangerous things
DARINGLY ▶ daring
DARINGS ▶ daring
DARIOLE, -S n small cup-shaped mould
DARIS ▶ dari
DARK, -ED, -ER, -EST, -ING, -S adj having little or no light ▷ n absence of light ▷ vb in archaic usage, darken
DARKEN, -ED, -S vb make or become dark or darker
DARKENER ▶ darken
DARKENS ▶ darken
DARKER ▶ dark
DARKEST ▶ dark
DARKING ▶ dark
DARKISH ▶ dark
DARKLE, -D, -S vb grow dark
DARKLIER ▶ darkly
DARKLING adj in the dark or night
DARKLY, DARKLIER ▶ dark
DARKMANS n slang term for night-time
DARKNESS ▶ dark
DARKNET, -S n covert communication network on the internet
DARKROOM n darkened room for processing photographic film
DARKS ▶ dark
DARKSOME adj dark or darkish
DARLING, -S n much-loved person ▷ adj much-loved
DARN, -S vb mend (a garment) with a series of interwoven stitches ▷ n patch of darned work
DARNDEST n utmost
DARNED, -ER adj damned
DARNEL, -S n weed that grows in grain fields
DARNER, -S ▶ darn
DARNEST, -S same as ▶ darndest
DARNING, -S ▶ darn
DARNS ▶ darn

DAROGHA, -S n in India, a manager
DARRAIGN same as ▶ deraign
DARRAIN, -S vb clear of guilt
DARRAINE vb clear of guilt
DARRAINS ▶ darrain
DARRAYN, -S vb clear of guilt
DARRE, -D, -S, DARRING vb archaic spelling of dare
DARSHAN, -S n Hindu blessing
DART, -ED n small narrow pointed missile ▷ vb move or direct quickly and suddenly
DARTER, -S n type of aquatic bird
DARTING ▶ dart
DARTITIS n nervous twitching while playing darts
DARTLE, -D, -S, DARTLING vb move swiftly
DARTRE, -S n skin disease
DARTROUS adj having a skin disease
DARTS n game in which darts are thrown at a dartboard
DARZI, -S n tailor in India
DAS ▶ da
DASH, -ED, -ES vb move quickly ▷ n sudden quick movement
DASHCAM, -S n video camera on a vehicle's dashboard
DASHED ▶ dash
DASHEEN, -S another name for ▶ taro
DASHEKI, -S same as ▶ dashiki
DASHER, -S n one of the boards surrounding an ice-hockey rink
DASHES ▶ dash
DASHI, -S n clear stock made from dried fish and kelp
DASHIER ▶ dashy
DASHIEST ▶ dashy
DASHIKI, -S n large loose-fitting buttonless upper garment
DASHING adj stylish and attractive
DASHIS ▶ dashi
DASHPOT, -S n device for damping vibrations
DASHY, DASHIER, DASHIEST adj showy
DASSIE, -S n type of hoofed rodent-like animal
DASTARD, -S n contemptible sneaking coward

DASTARDY n cowardice
DASYPOD, -S n armadillo
DASYURE, -S n small marsupial of Australia, New Guinea, and adjacent islands
DATA n information consisting of observations, measurements, or facts
DATABANK n store of a large amount of information
DATABASE n store of information in a form that can be easily handled by a computer ▷ vb put data into a database
DATABLE ▶ date
DATABUS n pathway transferring data between computer parts
DATACARD n smart card
DATAFLOW n as in dataflow architecture means of arranging computer data processing
DATAGRAM n (in computing) self-contained unit of data transmitted in a packet-switched network
DATAL, -S adj slow-witted ▷ n day labour
DATALLER n worker paid by the day
DATALS ▶ datal
DATARIA, -S n Roman Catholic office
DATARY, DATARIES n head of the dataria
DATCHA, -S same as ▶ dacha
DATE, -S n specified day of the month ▷ vb mark with the date
DATEABLE ▶ date
DATEBOOK n list of forthcoming events
DATED adj old-fashioned
DATEDLY ▶ dated
DATELESS ▶ date
DATELINE n information about the place and time an article was written
DATER, -S n person who dates
DATES ▶ date
DATING, -S n any of several techniques for establishing the age of objects
DATIVAL ▶ dative
DATIVE, -S adj denoting a grammatical case ▷ n grammatical case
DATIVELY ▶ dative
DATIVES ▶ dative
DATO, -S n chief of any of certain Muslim tribes in the Philippine Islands
DATOLITE n colourless mineral

DATOS ▸ dato

DATTO, -S n Datsun car

DATUM, -S n single piece of information in the form of a fact or statistic

DATURA, -S n type of plant

DATURIC ▸ datura

DATURINE n poisonous alkaloid

DAUB, -ED, -S vb smear or spread quickly or clumsily ▸ n crude or badly done painting

DAUBE, -S n braised meat stew

DAUBED ▸ daub

DAUBER, -S ▸ daub

DAUBERY n act or an instance of daubing

DAUBES ▸ daube

DAUBIER ▸ dauby

DAUBIEST ▸ dauby

DAUBING, -S ▸ daub

DAUBRY, DAUBRIES n unskilful painting

DAUBS ▸ daub

DAUBY, DAUBIER, DAUBIEST ▸ daub

DAUD, -ED, -ING, -S n lump or chunk of something ▸ vb (in dialect) whack

DAUGHTER n female child ▸ adj denoting a cell, chromosome, etc produced by the division of one of its own kind

DAULT, -S n foster child

DAUNDER, -S vb stroll

DAUNER, -ED, -S vb stroll

DAUNT, -ED, -S vb intimidate

DAUNTER, -S ▸ daunt

DAUNTING adj intimidating or worrying

DAUNTON, -S vb dishearten

DAUNTS ▸ daunt

DAUPHIN, -S n (formerly) eldest son of the king of France

DAUPHINE n wife of a dauphin

DAUPHINS ▸ dauphin

DAUR, -ED, -ING, -S a Scot word for ▸ dare

DAUT, -ED, -ING, -S vb fondle

DAUTIE, -S n darling

DAUTING ▸ daut

DAUTS ▸ daut

DAVEN, -ED, -ING, -S vb pray

DAVIDIA, -S n Chinese shrub

DAVIES ▸ davy

DAVIT, -S n crane, usu one of a pair, at a ship's side, for lowering and hoisting a lifeboat

DAVY, DAVIES n miner's safety lamp

DAW, -ED, -EN, -ING, -S n archaic, dialect, or poetic name for a jackdaw ▸ vb old word for dawn

This is another name for a **jackdaw**. It is worth remembering that not only does this little word take D, K, N, S and T at the back, to make **dawd, dawk, dawn, daws** and **dawt**, but you can put an A on the front of it to make **adaw**.

DAWAH, -S n practice of educating non-Muslims about the message of Islam

DAWBAKE, -S n foolish or slow-witted person

DAWBRY, DAWBRIES n unskilful painting

DAWCOCK, -S n male jackdaw

DAWD, -ED, -ING, -S vb thump

DAWDLE, -D, -S vb walk slowly, lag behind

DAWDLER, -S ▸ dawdle

DAWDLES ▸ dawdle

DAWDLING n act or instance of lagging behind

DAWDS ▸ dawd

DAWED ▸ daw

DAWEN ▸ daw

DAWING ▸ daw

DAWISH ▸ daw

DAWK, -S same as ▸ dak

DAWN, -ED, -S n daybreak ▸ vb begin to grow light

DAWNER, -ED, -S vb stroll

DAWNEY adj (of a person) dull or slow

DAWNING, -S ▸ dawn

DAWNLIKE ▸ dawn

DAWNS ▸ dawn

DAWS ▸ daw

DAWT, -ED, -ING, -S vb fondle

DAWTIE, -S n darling

DAWTING ▸ dawt

DAWTS ▸ dawt

DAY n period of 24 hours

DAYAN, -IM, -S n senior rabbi, esp one who sits in a religious court

DAYBED, -S n narrow bed for day use

DAYBOAT, -S n small sailing boat with no sleeping accommodation

DAYBOOK, -S n book in which transactions are recorded as they occur

DAYBOY, -S n boy who attends a boarding school but returns home each evening

DAYBREAK n time in the morning when light first appears

DAYCARE, -S n care provided during the working day for people who might be at risk if left on their own

DAYCH, -ED, -ES, -ING vb thatch

DAYDREAM n pleasant fantasy indulged in while awake ▸ vb indulge in idle fantasy

DAYFLY, DAYFLIES another name for ▸ mayfly

DAYGIRL, -S n girl who attends a boarding school but returns home each evening

DAYGLO n fluorescent colours

DAYGLOW, -S n fluorescent colours

DAYLIGHT n light from the sun

DAYLILY n any of various plants having lily-like flowers

DAYLIT ▸ daylight

DAYLONG adv lasting the entire day

DAYMARE, -S n bad dream during the day

DAYMARK, -S n navigation aid

DAYNT, -S adj dainty ▸ n thing or condition that is extravagant or best

DAYPACK, -S n small rucksack

DAYROOM, -S n communal living room in a residential institution

DAYS adv during the day, esp regularly

DAYSACK, -S n rucksack

DAYSAIL, -S vb take a day trip on a sailing boat or yacht

DAYSHELL n thistle

DAYSIDE, -S n side of a planet nearest the sun

DAYSMAN, DAYSMEN n umpire

DAYSTAR, -S a poetic word for ▸ sun

DAYTALE, -S n day labour

DAYTALER n worker paid by the day

DAYTALES ▸ daytale

DAYTIME, -S n time from sunrise to sunset

DAYWEAR, -S n clothes for everyday or informal wear

DAYWORK, -S n daytime work

DAZE, -D, -S, DAZING vb stun, by a blow or shock ▷ n state of confusion or shock

DAZEDLY ▸ daze

DAZER, -S ▸ daze

DAZES ▸ daze

DAZING ▸ daze

DAZZLE, -D, -S, DAZZLING vb impress greatly ▷ n bright light that dazzles

DAZZLER, -S ▸ dazzle

DAZZLES ▸ dazzle

DAZZLING ▸ dazzle

DE prep of or from

DEACON, -ED, -S n ordained minister ranking immediately below a priest ▷ vb make a deacon of

DEACONRY n office or status of a deacon

DEACONS ▸ deacon

DEAD, -ED, -ERS, -EST, -ING, -S adj no longer alive ▷ n period during which coldness or darkness is most intense ▷ adv extremely ▷ vb in archaic usage, die or kill

DEADBEAT n lazy useless person

DEADBOLT n bolt operated without a spring

DEADBOY, -S same as ▸ deadman

DEADED ▸ dead

DEADEN, -ED, -S vb make less intense

DEADENER ▸ deaden

DEADENS ▸ deaden

DEADER n dead person

DEADERS ▸ dead

DEADEST ▸ dead

DEADEYE, -S n either of two disclike blocks used to tighten a shroud on a boat

DEADFALL n type of trap using a heavy weight to crush prey

DEADHEAD n person who does not pay on a bus, at a game, etc ▷ vb cut off withered flowers from (a plant)

DEADING ▸ dead

DEADLIER ▸ deadly

DEADLIFT vb (weightlifting) lift a weight off the ground and stand up straight

DEADLINE n time limit ▷ vb put a time limit on an action, decision, etc

DEADLOCK n point in a dispute at which no agreement can be reached ▷ vb bring or come to a deadlock

DEADLY, DEADLIER adj likely to cause death ▷ adv extremely

DEADMAN, DEADMEN n item used in construction

DEADNESS ▸ dead

DEADPAN, -S adv showing no emotion or expression ▷ adj deliberately emotionless ▷ n deadpan expression or manner

DEADS ▸ dead

DEADWOOD n dead trees or branches

DEAERATE vb remove air from

DEAF, -ER, -EST adj unable to hear

DEAFEN, -ED, -S vb make deaf, esp temporarily

DEAFER ▸ deaf

DEAFEST ▸ deaf

DEAFISH ▸ deaf

DEAFLY ▸ deaf

DEAFNESS ▸ deaf

DEAIR, -ED, -ING, -S vb remove air from

DEAL, -ING, -S, -T n agreement or transaction ▷ vb inflict (a blow) on ▷ adj of fir or pine

DEALATE, -S adj (of insects) having lost their wings after mating ▷ n insect that has shed its wings

DEALATED same as ▸ dealate

DEALATES ▸ dealate

DEALBATE adj bleached

DEALER, -S n person whose business involves buying and selling

DEALFISH n long thin fish

DEALIGN, -S vb fall out of agreement with (a political party)

DEALING ▸ deal

DEALINGS pl n transactions or business relations

DEALS ▸ deal

DEALT ▸ deal

DEAN, -ED, -ING, -S n chief administrative official of a college or university faculty ▷ vb punish (a student) by sending them to the dean

DEANER, -S n shilling

DEANERY n office or residence of a dean

DEANING ▸ dean

DEANS ▸ dean

DEANSHIP ▸ dean

DEAR, -ER, -S n someone regarded with affection ▷ adj much-loved

DEARE, -D, -S, DEARING vb harm

DEARER ▸ dear

DEARES ▸ deare

DEAREST, -S n term of affection

DEARIE same as ▸ deary

DEARIES ▸ deary

DEARING ▸ deare

DEARLING n darling

DEARLY adv very much

DEARN, -ED, -ING, -S vb hide

DEARNESS ▸ dear

DEARNFUL adj secret

DEARNING ▸ dearn

DEARNLY ▸ dearn

DEARNS ▸ dearn

DEARS ▸ dear

DEARTH, -S n inadequate amount, scarcity

DEARY, DEARIES n term of affection: now often sarcastic or facetious

DEASH, -ED, -ES, -ING vb remove ash from

DEASIL, -S n motion towards the sun

DEASIUL, -S n motion towards the sun

DEASOIL, -S n motion towards the sun

DEATH, -S n permanent end of life in a person or animal

DEATHBED n bed where a person is about to die or has just died

DEATHCUP n poisonous fungus

DEATHFUL adj murderous

DEATHIER ▸ deathy

DEATHLY adv like death ▷ adj resembling death

DEATHS ▸ death

DEATHY, DEATHIER ▸ death

DEAVE, -D, -S, DEAVING vb deafen

DEAW, -ED, -ING, -S n archaic spelling of dew ▷ vb cover with dew

DEAWIE ▸ deaw

DEAWING ▸ deaw

DEAWS ▸ deaw

DEAWY ▸ deaw

DEB, -S n debutante

DEBACLE, -S n disastrous failure

DEBAG, -GED, -S vb remove the trousers from (someone) by force

DEBAR, -RED, -S vb prevent, bar

DEBARK, -ED, -S vb remove the bark from (a tree)

DEBARKER ▸ debark

DEBARKS ▸ debark

DEBARRED ▸ debar

DEBARS ▸ debar

DEBASE, -D, -S, DEBASING vb lower in value, quality, or character

DEBASER, -S ▸ debase

DEBASES ▸ debase

DEBASING ▸ debase

DEBATE, -D, -S n discussion ▷ vb discuss formally

DEBATER, -S ▸ debate

DEBATES ▸ debate

DEBATING n act of debating

DEBAUCH vb make (someone) bad or corrupt ▷ n instance or period of extreme dissipation

DEBBY, DEBBIER, DEBBIES, DEBBIEST n debutante ▷ adj of, or resembling a debutante

DEBE, -S n tin

DEBEAK, -ED, -S vb remove part of the beak of poultry

DEBEARD, -S vb remove the beard from a mussel

DEBEL, -LED, -S vb beat in war

DEBES ▸ debe

DEBILE adj lacking strength

DEBILITY n weakness, infirmity

DEBIT, -ED, -ING, -S n sum owing entered on the left side of an account ▷ vb charge (an account) with a debt

DEBITOR, -S n person in debt

DEBITS ▸ debit

DEBONAIR adj charming and refined

DEBONE, -D, -S, DEBONING vb remove bones from

DEBONER, -S ▸ debone

DEBONES ▸ debone

DEBONING ▸ debone

DEBOSH, -ED, -ES vb debauch

DEBOSS, -ED, -ES vb carve a design into

DEBOUCH vb move out from a narrow place to a wider one ▷ n outlet or passage, as for the exit of troops

DEBOUCHE same as ▸ debouch

DEBRIDE, -D, -S vb remove dead tissue from

DEBRIEF, -S vb receive a report from (a soldier, diplomat, etc) after an event

DEBRIS n fragments of something destroyed

DEBRUISE vb (in heraldry) overlay or partly cover

DEBS ▸ deb

DEBT, -S n something owed, esp money

DEBTED adj in debt

DEBTEE, -S n person owed a debt

DEBTLESS ▸ debt

DEBTOR, -S n person who owes money

DEBTS ▸ debt

DEBUD, -DED, -S same as ▸ disbud

DEBUG, -GED, -S vb find and remove defects in (a computer program) ▷ n something that locates and removes defects in a device, system, etc

DEBUGGER ▸ debug

DEBUGS ▸ debug

DEBUNK, -ED, -S vb expose the falseness of

DEBUNKER ▸ debunk

DEBUNKS ▸ debunk

DEBUR, -S vb remove burs from

DEBURR, -ED, -S vb remove burrs from

DEBURS ▸ debur

DEBUS, -ED, -ES, -ING, -SED, -SES vb unload (goods) or (esp of troops) to alight from a motor vehicle

DEBUT, -ED, -ING, -S n first public appearance of a performer ▷ vb make a debut

DEBUTANT n person making a first appearance in a particular capacity

DEBUTED ▸ debut

DEBUTING ▸ debut

DEBUTS ▸ debut

DEBYE, -S n unit of electric dipole moment

DECAD, -S n ten years

DECADAL ▸ decade

DECADE, -S n period of ten years

DECADENT adj characterized by decay or decline, as in being self-indulgent or morally corrupt ▷ n decadent person

DECADES ▸ decade

DECADS ▸ decad

DECAF, -S n decaffeinated coffee ▷ adj decaffeinated

DECAFF, -S n decaffeinated coffee

DECAFS ▸ decaf

DECAGON, -S n geometric figure with ten sides

DECAGRAM n ten grams

DECAL, -ED, -ING, -LED, -S vb transfer (a design) by decalcomania

DECALOG, -S same as ▸ decalogue

DECALS ▸ decal

DECAMP, -ED, -S vb depart secretly or suddenly

DECAN, -S n one of three divisions of a sign of the zodiac

DECANAL adj of or relating to a dean or deanery

DECANE, -S n liquid alkane hydrocarbon

DECANI adj to be sung by the decanal side of a choir

DECANOIC adj as in decanoic acid white crystalline insoluble carboxylic acid

DECANS ▸ decan

DECANT, -ED, -S vb pour (a liquid) from one container to another

DECANTER n stoppered bottle for wine or spirits

DECANTS ▸ decant

DECAPOD, -S n creature, such as a crab, with five pairs of walking limbs ▷ adj of, relating to, or belonging to these creatures

DECARB, -ED, -S vb decarbonize

DECARE, -S n ten ares or 1000 square metres

DECAY, -ED, -ING, -S vb become weaker or more corrupt ▷ n process of decaying

DECAYER, -S ▸ decay

DECAYING ▸ decay

DECAYS ▸ decay

DECCIE, -S n decoration

DECEASE, -S n death

DECEASED adj dead ▷ n dead person

DECEASES ▸ decease

DECEDENT n deceased person

DECEIT, -S n behaviour intended to deceive

DECEIVE, -D, -S vb mislead by lying

DECEIVER ▸ deceive

DECEIVES ▸ deceive

DECEMVIR n member of a board of ten magistrates in Ancient Rome

DECENARY adj of or relating to a tithing

DECENCY n conformity to the prevailing standards of what is right

DECENNIA > decennium

DECENT adj (of a person) polite and morally acceptable

D

DECENTER vb put out of centre

DECENTLY ▸ decent

DECENTRE vb put out of centre

DECERN, -ED, -S vb decree or adjudge

DECIARE, -S n one tenth of an are or 10 square metres

DECIBEL, -S n unit for measuring the intensity of sound

DECIDE, -S, DECIDING vb (cause to) reach a decision

DECIDED adj unmistakable

DECIDER, -S n thing that determines who wins a match or championship

DECIDES ▸ decide

DECIDING ▸ decide

DECIDUA, -E, -S n membrane lining the uterus of some mammals during pregnancy

DECIDUAL ▸ decidua

DECIDUAS ▸ decidua

DECIGRAM n tenth of a gram

DECILE, -S n one of nine values of a variable divided into ten equal groups

DECIMAL, -S n fraction written in the form of a dot followed by one or more numbers ▸ adj relating to or using powers of ten

DECIMATE vb destroy or kill a large proportion of

DECIME, -S n former French coin

DECIPHER vb work out the meaning of (something illegible or in code)

DECISION n judgment, conclusion, or resolution

DECISIVE adj having a definite influence

DECISORY adj deciding

DECK, -S n area of a ship that forms a floor ▸ vb dress or decorate

DECKED adj having a wooden deck or platform

DECKEL, -S same as ▸ deckle

DECKER, -S ▸ deck

DECKHAND n seafarer assigned various duties on the deck of a ship

DECKING, -S n wooden platform in a garden

DECKLE, -D, -S n frame used to contain pulp on the mould in the making of handmade paper

DECKLESS adj without a deck

DECKO, -ED, -ING, -S n look ▸ vb have a look

DECKS ▸ deck

DECLAIM, -S vb speak loudly and dramatically

DECLARE, -D, -S vb state firmly and forcefully

DECLARER n person who declares

DECLARES ▸ declare

DECLASS vb lower in social status or position

DECLASSE adj having lost social standing or status

DECLAW, -ED, -S vb remove claws from

DECLINAL adj bending down ▸ n action of politely refusing or declining

DECLINE, -D, -S vb become smaller, weaker, or less important ▸ n gradual weakening or loss

DECLINER ▸ decline

DECLINES ▸ decline

DECLUTCH vb disengage the clutch of a motor vehicle

DECO adj as in art deco style of art, jewellery, design, etc

DECOCT, -ED, -S vb extract the essence from (a substance) by boiling

DECODE, -D, -S vb convert from code into ordinary language

DECODER, -S ▸ decode

DECODES ▸ decode

DECODING n act of decoding

DECOKE, -D, -S, DECOKING n decarbonize

DECOLOR, -S vb bleach

DECOLOUR vb deprive of colour, as by bleaching

DECOMMIT vb withdraw from a commitment or agreed course of action

DECOR, -S n style in which a room or house is decorated

DECORATE vb make more attractive by adding something ornamental

DECOROUS adj polite, calm, and sensible in behaviour

DECORS ▸ decor

DECORUM, -S n polite and socially correct behaviour

DECOS pl n decorations

DECOUPLE vb separate two joined entities or subsystems

DECOY, -ED, -ING, -S n person or thing used to lure someone into danger ▸ vb lure away by means of a trick

DECOYER, -S ▸ decoy

DECOYING ▸ decoy

DECOYS ▸ decoy

DECREASE vb make or become less ▸ n lessening, reduction

DECREE, -D, -S n law made by someone in authority ▸ vb order by decree

DECREER, -S ▸ decree

DECREES ▸ decree

DECREET, -S n final judgment or sentence of a court

DECREPIT adj weakened or worn out by age or long use

DECRETAL n papal decree ▸ adj of or relating to a decretal or a decree

DECREW, -ED, -S vb archaic word for decrease

DECRIAL, -S ▸ decry

DECRIED ▸ decry

DECRIER, -S ▸ decry

DECRIES ▸ decry

DECROWN, -S vb depose

DECRY, DECRIED, DECRIES, -ING vb express disapproval of

DECRYPT, -S vb decode (a message)

DECTET, -S n group of ten musicians

DECUBITI > decubitus

DECUMAN, -S n large wave

DECUPLE, -D, -S vb increase by ten times ▸ n amount ten times as large as a given reference ▸ adj increasing tenfold

DECURIA, -S n group of ten

DECURIES ▸ decury

DECURION n local councillor

DECURVE, -S vb curve downwards

DECURVED adj bent or curved downwards

DECURVES ▸ decurve

DECURY, DECURIES n (in ancient Rome) a body of ten men

DEDAL same as ▸ daedal

DEDALIAN adj of Daedalus

DEDANS n open gallery at the server's end of a real tennis court

DEDENDUM, DEDENDA n radial distance between the pitch circle and root of a gear tooth

DEDICANT n person who dedicates

DEDICATE vb commit (oneself or one's time) wholly to a special purpose or cause

DEDIMUS n document authorizing a person to act as a judge

DEDUCE, -D, -S, DEDUCING vb reach (a conclusion) by reasoning from evidence

DEDUCT, -ED, -S vb subtract

DEE, -ING, -S a Scot word for ▸ **die**

DEED, -ED, -ER, -EST, -ING, -S n something that is done ▷ vb convey or transfer (property) by deed ▷ adj Scots form of dead

DEEDFUL adj full of exploits

DEEDIER ▸ **deedy**

DEEDIEST ▸ **deedy**

DEEDILY ▸ **deedy**

DEEDING ▸ **deed**

DEEDLESS adj without exploits

DEEDS ▸ **deed**

DEEDY, DEEDIER, DEEDIEST adj hard-working

DEEING ▸ **dee**

DEEJAY, -ED, -S n disc jockey ▷ vb work or act as a disc jockey

DEEK interj look at!

DEELY adj as in **deely boppers** hairband with two bobbing antennae-like attachments

DEEM, -ED, -ING, -S, DEMPT vb consider, judge

DEEMSTER n title of one of the two justices in the Isle of Man

DEEN, -S n din

DEEP, -ER, -EST, -S adj extending or situated far down, inwards, backwards, or sideways ▷ n any deep place on land or under water

DEEPEN, -ED, -S vb make or become deeper or more intense

DEEPENER ▸ **deepen**

DEEPENS ▸ **deepen**

DEEPER ▸ **deep**

DEEPEST ▸ **deep**

DEEPFELT adj sincere

DEEPIE, -S n 3D film

DEEPLY ▸ **deep**

DEEPMOST adj deepest

DEEPNESS ▸ **deep**

DEEPS ▸ **deep**

DEER, -S n large wild animal, the male of which has antlers

DEERE, -S adj serious ▷ n deer

DEERFLY n insect related to the horsefly

DEERHORN n horn of a deer

DEERLET, -S n small deer

DEERLIKE adj like a deer

DEERS ▸ **deer**

DEERSKIN n hide of a deer

DEERWEED n forage plant

DEERYARD n gathering place for deer

DEES ▸ **dee**

DEET, -S n insect repellent

DEEV, -S n mythical monster

DEEVE, -D, -S, DEEVING vb deafen

DEEVS ▸ **deev**

DEEWAN, -S n chief of a village in India

DEF, -FER, -FEST adj very good

DEFACE, -D, -S, DEFACING vb deliberately spoil the appearance of

DEFACER, -S ▸ **deface**

DEFACES ▸ **deface**

DEFACING ▸ **deface**

DEFAME, -D, -S, DEFAMING vb attack the good reputation of

DEFAMER, -S ▸ **defame**

DEFAMES ▸ **defame**

DEFAMING ▸ **defame**

DEFANG, -ED, -S vb remove the fangs of

DEFAST adj old form of defaced

DEFASTE adj old form of defaced

DEFAT, -S, -TED vb remove fat from

DEFAULT, -S n failure to do something ▷ vb fail to fulfil an obligation

DEFEAT, -ED, -S vb win a victory over ▷ n defeating

DEFEATER ▸ **defeat**

DEFEATS ▸ **defeat**

DEFECATE vb discharge waste from the body

DEFECT, -ED, -S n imperfection, blemish ▷ vb desert one's cause or country to join the opposing forces

DEFECTOR ▸ **defect**

DEFECTS ▸ **defect**

DEFENCE, -D, -S n resistance against attack ▷ vb provide with defence

DEFEND, -ED, -S vb protect from harm or danger

DEFENDER ▸ **defend**

DEFENDS ▸ **defend**

DEFENSE, -D, -S same as ▸ **defence**

DEFER, -S vb delay (something) until a future time

DEFERENT adj conveying outwards, down, or away ▷ n type of circle in the Ptolemaic system

DEFERRAL same as ▸ **deferment**

DEFERRED adj withheld over a certain period

DEFERRER ▸ **defer**

DEFERS ▸ **defer**

DEFFER ▸ **def**

DEFFEST ▸ **def**

DEFFLY archaic form of ▸ **deftly**

DEFFO interj informal word meaning definitely

DEFI, -S n challenge

DEFIANCE n open resistance or disobedience

DEFIANT adj marked by resistance or bold opposition, as to authority

DEFICIT, -S n amount by which a sum of money is too small

DEFIED ▸ **defy**

DEFIER, -S ▸ **defy**

DEFIES ▸ **defy**

DEFILADE n protection provided by obstacles against enemy crossfire from the rear, or observation ▷ vb provide protection for by defilade

DEFILE, -D, -S, DEFILING vb treat (something sacred or important) without respect ▷ n narrow valley or pass

DEFILER, -S ▸ **defile**

DEFILES ▸ **defile**

DEFILING ▸ **defile**

DEFINE, -D, -S, DEFINING vb state precisely the meaning of

DEFINER, -S ▸ **define**

DEFINES ▸ **define**

DEFINING ▸ **define**

DEFINITE adj firm, clear, and precise ▷ n something that is firm, clear, and precise

DEFIS ▸ **defi**

DEFLATE, -D, -S vb (cause to) collapse through the release of air

DEFLATER ▸ **deflate**

DEFLATES ▸ **deflate**

DEFLATOR ▸ **deflate**

DEFLEA, -ED, -S vb remove fleas from

DEFLECT, -S vb (cause to) turn aside from a course

DEFLEX, -ED, -ES vb turn downwards

DEFLUENT adj running downwards

DEFO interj informal word meaning definitely

DEFOAM, -ED, -S vb remove foam from

DEFOAMER ▸ **defoam**

D

D

DEFOAMS ▸ defoam
DEFOCUS vb put out of focus
DEFOG, -GED, -S vb clear of vapour
DEFOGGER ▸ defog
DEFOGS ▸ defog
DEFORCE, -D, -S vb withhold (property, esp land) wrongfully or by force from the rightful owner
DEFORCER ▸ deforce
DEFORCES ▸ deforce
DEFOREST vb clear of trees
DEFORM, -S vb put out of shape or spoil the appearance of
DEFORMED adj disfigured or misshapen
DEFORMER ▸ deform
DEFORMS ▸ deform
DEFOUL, -ED, -S vb defile
DEFRAG, -S vb defragment
DEFRAUD, -S vb cheat out of money, property, etc
DEFRAY, -ED, -S vb provide money for (costs or expenses)
DEFRAYAL ▸ defray
DEFRAYED ▸ defray
DEFRAYER ▸ defray
DEFRAYS ▸ defray
DEFREEZE, DEFROZE, DEFROZEN vb defrost
DEFRIEND vb remove (a person) from the list of one's friends on a social networking website
DEFROCK, -S vb deprive (a priest) of priestly status
DEFROST, -S vb make or become free of ice
DEFROZE ▸ defreeze
DEFROZEN ▸ defreeze
DEFT, -ER, -EST adj quick and skilful in movement
DEFTLY ▸ deft
DEFTNESS ▸ deft
DEFUEL, -ED, -S vb remove fuel from
DEFUNCT, -S adj no longer existing or operative ▷ n deceased person
DEFUND, -ED, -S vb stop funds to
DEFUSE, -D, -S, DEFUSING vb remove the fuse of (an explosive device)
DEFUSER, -S ▸ defuse
DEFUSES ▸ defuse
DEFUSING ▸ defuse
DEFUZE, -D, -S, DEFUZING same as ▸ defuse
DEFY, DEFIED, DEFIES, -ING vb resist openly and boldly
DEG, -GED, -GING, -S vb water (a plant, etc)

DEGAGE adj unconstrained in manner
DEGAME, -S n tree of South and Central America
DEGAMI, -S same as ▸ degame
DEGAS, -ES, -SED, -SES vb remove gas from (a container, vacuum tube, liquid, adsorbent, etc)
DEGASSER ▸ degas
DEGASSES ▸ degas
DEGAUSS vb demagnetize
DEGENDER vb remove reference to gender from
DEGERM, -ED, -S vb remove germs from
DEGGED ▸ deg
DEGGING ▸ deg
DEGLAZE, -D, -S vb dilute meat sediments in (a pan) in order to make a sauce or gravy
DEGOUT, -ED, -S n disgust ▷ vb cover (something) with gouts or drops of something
DEGRADE, -D, -S vb reduce to dishonour or disgrace
DEGRADER ▸ degrade
DEGRADES ▸ degrade
DEGRAS n emulsion used for dressing hides
DEGREASE vb remove grease from
DEGREE, -S n stage in a scale of relative amount or intensity
DEGREED adj having a degree
DEGREES ▸ degree
DEGS ▸ deg
DEGU, -S n small S American rodent
DEGUM, -MED, -S vb remove gum from
DEGUS ▸ degu
DEGUST, -ED, -S vb taste, esp with care or relish
DEHAIR, -ED, -S vb remove hair
DEHISCE, -D, -S vb (of the seed capsules of some plants) to burst open spontaneously
DEHORN, -ED, -S vb remove or prevent the growth of the horns of (cattle, sheep, or goats)
DEHORNER ▸ dehorn
DEHORNS ▸ dehorn
DEHORS prep apart from
DEHORT, -ED, -S vb dissuade
DEHORTER ▸ dehort
DEHORTS ▸ dehort
DEI ▸ deus

DEICE, -D, -S, DEICING vb free or be freed of ice
DEICER, -S ▸ deice
DEICES ▸ deice
DEICIDAL ▸ deicide
DEICIDE, -S n act of killing a god
DEICING ▸ deice
DEICTIC, -S adj proving by direct argument ▷ n term whose reference depends on the context
DEID, -ER, -EST, -S a Scot word for ▸ dead
DEIF, -ER, -EST a Scot word for ▸ deaf
DEIFIC adj making divine or exalting to the position of a god
DEIFICAL adj divine
DEIFIED ▸ deify
DEIFIER, -S ▸ deify
DEIFIES ▸ deify
DEIFORM adj having the form or appearance of a god
DEIFY, DEIFIED, DEIFIES, -ING vb treat or worship as a god
DEIGN, -ED, -ING, -S vb agree (to do something), but as if doing someone a favour
DEIL, -S a Scot word for ▸ devil
DEINDEX vb cause to become no longer index-linked
DEIONISE same as ▸ deionize
DEIONIZE vb remove ions from (water, etc), esp by ion exchange
DEISEAL, -S n motion towards the sun
DEISHEAL n clockwise motion
DEISM, -S n belief in God but not in divine revelation
DEIST, -S ▸ deism
DEISTIC ▸ deism
DEISTS ▸ deist
DEITY, DEITIES n god or goddess
DEIXIS, DEIXES, -ES n use or reference of a deictic word
DEJECT, -S vb dispirit; dishearten ▷ adj downcast
DEJECTA pl n waste products excreted from the body
DEJECTED adj unhappy
DEJECTS ▸ deject
DEJEUNE, -S n lunch
DEJEUNER n lunch
DEJEUNES ▸ dejeune
DEKAGRAM n ten grams
DEKALOGY n series of ten related works**

DEKARE, -S n unit of measurement equal to ten ares

DEKE, -D, -ING, -S, DEKING vb make a deceptive movement ▷ n deceptive movement

DEKKO, -ED, -ING, -S n look ▷ vb have a look

DEL, -S n differential operator

DELAINE, -S n sheer wool or wool and cotton fabric

DELAPSE, -D, -S vb be inherited

DELATE, -D, -S, DELATING vb (formerly) to bring a charge against

DELATION ▶ delate

This means the act of informing against someone, and is an important word to know because its combination of common letters make it one of the 8-letter bonus words that come up most often.

DELATOR, -S ▶ delate

DELAY, -ED, -ING, -S vb put off to a later time ▷ n act of delaying

DELAYER, -S ▶ delay

DELAYING ▶ delay

DELAYS ▶ delay

DELE, -D, -ING, -S n sign indicating that typeset matter is to be deleted ▷ vb mark (matter to be deleted) with a dele

DELEAD, -ED, -S vb remove lead from

DELEAVE, -D, -S vb separate copies

DELEBLE adj able to be deleted

DELED ▶ dele

DELEGACY n elected standing committee at some British universities

DELEGATE n person chosen to represent others, esp at a meeting ▷ vb entrust (duties or powers) to someone

DELEING ▶ dele

DELENDA pl n items for deleting

DELES ▶ dele

DELETE, -D, -S, DELETING vb remove (something written or printed)

DELETION n act of deleting or fact of being deleted

DELETIVE ▶ delete

DELETORY ▶ delete

DELF, -S n kind of earthenware

DELFT, -S n type of earthenware

DELI, -S n delicatessen

DELIBATE vb taste

DELIBLE adj able to be deleted

DELICACY n being delicate

DELICATE adj fine or subtle in quality ▷ n delicacy

DELICE, -S n delicacy

DELICT, -S n wrongful act for which the person injured has the right to a civil remedy

DELIGHT, -S n (source of) great pleasure ▷ vb please greatly

DELIME, -D, -S, DELIMING vb remove lime from

DELIMIT, -S vb mark or lay down the limits of

DELINK, -ED, -S vb remove or break a link

DELIRIUM, DELIRIA n state of excitement and confusion

DELIS ▶ deli

DELISH adj delicious

DELIST, -ED, -S vb remove from a list

DELIVER, -S vb carry (goods etc) to a destination

DELIVERY n delivering

DELL, -S n small wooded hollow

DELLIER ▶ delly

DELLIES ▶ delly

DELLIEST ▶ delly

DELLS ▶ dell

DELLY, DELLIER, DELLIES, DELLIEST n delicatessen ▷ adj full of dells

DELO, -S an informal word for ▶ delegate

DELOPE, -D, -S, DELOPING vb shoot into the air

DELOS ▶ delo

DELOUSE, -D, -S vb rid (a person or animal) of lice

DELOUSER ▶ delouse

DELOUSES ▶ delouse

DELPH, -S n kind of earthenware

DELPHIC adj obscure or ambiguous

DELPHIN, -S n fatty substance from dolphin oil

DELPHS ▶ delph

DELS ▶ del

DELT, -S n deltoid muscle

DELTA, -S n fourth letter in the Greek alphabet

DELTAIC ▶ delta

DELTAS ▶ delta

DELTIC ▶ delta

DELTOID, -S n muscle acting to raise the arm ▷ adj shaped like a Greek capital delta

DELTS ▶ delt

DELUBRUM, DELUBRA n shrine

DELUDE, -D, -S, DELUDING vb deceive

DELUDER, -S ▶ delude

DELUDES ▶ delude

DELUDING ▶ delude

DELUGE, -D, -S, DELUGING n great flood ▷ vb flood

DELUSION n mistaken idea or belief

DELUSIVE ▶ delusion

DELUSORY ▶ delusion

DELUSTER same as ▶ delustre

DELUSTRE vb remove the lustre from

DELUXE adj rich, elegant, superior, or sumptuous

DELVE, -D, -S, DELVING vb research deeply (for information)

DELVER, -S ▶ delve

DELVES ▶ delve

DELVING ▶ delve

DEMAGOG, -S same as ▷ demagogue

DEMAGOGY n demagoguery

DEMAIN, -S n demesne

DEMAINE, -S n demesne

DEMAINS ▶ demain

DEMAN, -NED, -S vb reduce the workforce of (a plant, industry, etc)

DEMAND, -ED, -S vb request forcefully ▷ n forceful request

DEMANDER ▶ demand

DEMANDS ▶ demand

DEMANNED ▶ deman

DEMANS ▶ deman

DEMARCHE n move, step, or manoeuvre, esp in diplomatic affairs

DEMARK, -ED, -S vb demarcate

DEMARKET vb discourage consumers from buying

DEMARKS ▶ demark

DEMAST, -ED, -S vb remove the mast from

DEMAYNE, -S n demesne

DEME, -S n (in preclassical Greece) the territory inhabited by a tribe

DEMEAN, -ED, -S vb lower (oneself) in dignity, status, or character

DEMEANE n demesne

DEMEANED ▶ demean

DEMEANES n demesne

DEMEANOR same as ▷ demeanour

DEMEANS ▶ demean

DEMENT, -S vb deteriorate mentally, esp because of old age

DEMENTED adj driven mad

DEMENTI, -S n denial

DEMENTIA n state of serious mental deterioration

DEMENTIS ▸ dementi

DEMENTS ▸ dement

DEMERARA n brown crystallized cane sugar from the Caribbean and nearby countries

DEMERGE, -D, -S vb separate a company from another

DEMERGER n separation of two or more companies which have previously been merged

DEMERGES ▸ demerge

DEMERIT, -S n fault, disadvantage ▷ vb deserve

DEMERSAL adj living or occurring on the bottom of a sea or a lake

DEMERSE, -D, -S vb immerse

DEMES ▸ deme

DEMESNE, -S n land surrounding a house

DEMETON, -S n insecticide

DEMIC adj of population

DEMIES ▸ demy

DEMIGOD, -S n being who is part mortal, part god

DEMIJOHN n large bottle with a short neck, often encased in wicker

DEMILUNE n outwork in front of a fort, shaped like a crescent moon

DEMINER, -S n person who removes mines

DEMINING n act of removing mines

DEMISE, -D, -S, DEMISING n eventual failure (of something successful) ▷ vb transfer for a limited period

DEMISS adj humble

DEMISSLY ▸ demiss

DEMIST, -ED, -S vb remove condensation from (a windscreen)

DEMISTER n device in a motor vehicle to free the windscreen of condensation

DEMISTS ▸ demist

DEMIT, -S, -TED vb resign (an office, position, etc)

DEMIURGE n (in the philosophy of Plato) the creator of the universe

DEMIVEG n person who eats poultry and fish, but no red meat ▷ adj denoting a

person who eats poultry and fish, but no red meat

DEMIVOLT n half turn on the hind legs

DEMO, -ED, -ING n demonstration, organized expression of public opinion ▷ vb demonstrate

DEMOB, -BED, -S vb demobilize

DEMOCRAT n advocate of democracy

DEMODE adj out of fashion

DEMODED adj out of fashion

DEMOED ▸ demo

DEMOI ▸ demos

DEMOING ▸ demo

DEMOLISH vb knock down or destroy (a building)

DEMOLOGY n demography

DEMON, -S n evil spirit

DEMONESS n female demon

DEMONIAC adj appearing to be possessed by a devil ▷ n person possessed by an evil spirit or demon

DEMONIAN adj of a demon

DEMONIC adj evil

DEMONISE same as ▸ demonize

DEMONISM n study of demons

DEMONIST ▸ demonism

DEMONIZE vb make into a demon

DEMONRY ▸ demon

DEMONS ▸ demon

DEMONYM, -S n name for the inhabitants of a place

DEMOS, DEMOI, -ES n people of a nation regarded as a political unit

DEMOTE, -D, -S, DEMOTING vb reduce in status or rank

DEMOTIC, -S adj of the common people ▷ n demotic script of ancient Egypt

DEMOTING ▸ demote

DEMOTION ▸ demote

DEMOTIST ▸ demotic

DEMOUNT, -S vb remove (a motor, gun, etc) from its mounting or setting

DEMPSTER same as ▸ deemster

DEMPT ▸ deem

DEMUR, -RED, -S vb raise objections or show reluctance ▷ n act of demurring

DEMURE, -D, -R, -S, -ST, DEMURING adj quiet, reserved, and rather shy ▷ vb archaic word meaning to look demure

DEMURELY ▸ demure

DEMURER ▸ demure

DEMURES ▸ demure

DEMUREST ▸ demure

DEMURING ▸ demure

DEMURRAL n act of demurring

DEMURRED ▸ demur

DEMURRER n any objection raised

DEMURS ▸ demur

DEMY, DEMIES n size of printing paper, 17½ by 22½ inches (444.5 × 571.5 mm)

DEMYSHIP n scholarship at Oxford University

DEN, -NED, -NING, -S n home of a wild animal ▷ vb live in or as if in a den

DENAR, -I, -S n monetary unit of North Macedonia, divided into 100 deni

DENARIES ▸ denary

DENARIUS, DENARII n ancient Roman silver coin, often called a penny in translation

DENARS ▸ denar

DENARY, DENARIES same as ▸ denarius

DENATURE vb change the nature of

DENAY, -ED, -ING, -S vb old form of deny

DENAZIFY vb free or declare (people, institutions, etc) freed from Nazi influence or ideology

DENCH adj excellent

DENDRITE n threadlike extension of a nerve cell

DENDROID adj freely branching ▷ n something that branches freely

DENDRON, -S same as ▸ dendrite

DENE, -S n narrow wooded valley

DENET, -S, -TED vb remove from the former Net Book Agreement

DENGUE, -S n viral disease transmitted by mosquitoes

DENI, -S n monetary unit of North Macedonia

DENIABLE adj able to be denied

DENIABLY ▸ deniable

DENIAL, -S n statement that something is not true

DENIED ▸ deny

DENIER, -S n unit of weight used to measure the fineness of nylon or silk

DENIES ▸ deny

DENIM, -S n hard-wearing cotton fabric, usu blue

DENIMED adj wearing denim

DENIMS pl n jeans or overalls made of denim

DENIS ▸ deni

DENIZEN, -S n inhabitant ▷ vb make a denizen

DENNED ▸ den

DENNET, -S n carriage for one horse

DENNING ▸ den

DENOTATE vb denote

DENOTE, -D, -S, DENOTING vb be a sign of

DENOTIVE ▸ denote

DENOUNCE vb speak vehemently against

DENS ▸ den

DENSE, -R, -ST adj closely packed

DENSELY ▸ dense

DENSER ▸ dense

DENSEST ▸ dense

DENSIFY vb make or become dense

DENSITY n degree to which something is filled or occupied

DENT, -ED, -ING, -S n hollow in the surface of something, made by hitting it ▷ vb make a dent in

DENTAL, -S adj of teeth or dentistry ▷ n dental consonant

DENTALIA > dentalium

DENTALLY ▸ dental

DENTALS ▸ dental

DENTARIA n plant of the crucifer family

DENTARY n lower jawbone with teeth

DENTATE adj having teeth or toothlike notches

DENTATED adj having teeth

DENTED ▸ dent

DENTEL, -S n architectural ornament

DENTELLE n lacelike ornamentation on a book

DENTELS ▸ dentel

DENTEX, -ES n large predatory fish

DENTICLE n small tooth or toothlike part, such as any of the placoid scales of sharks

DENTIL, -S n architectural ornament

DENTILED ▸ dentil

DENTILS ▸ dentil

DENTIN, -S same as ▸ dentine

DENTINAL ▸ dentine

DENTINE, -S n hard dense tissue forming the bulk of a tooth

DENTING ▸ dent

DENTINS ▸ dentin

DENTIST, -S n person qualified to practise dentistry

DENTOID adj resembling a tooth

DENTS ▸ dent

DENTURAL ▸ denture

DENTURE, -S n false tooth

DENUDATE adj denuded ▷ vb denude

DENUDE, -D, -S, DENUDING vb remove the covering or protection from

DENUDER, -S ▸ denude

DENUDES ▸ denude

DENUDING ▸ denude

DENY, DENIED, DENIES, -ING vb declare to be untrue

DEODAND, -S n thing forfeited to charity because it has caused a death

DEODAR, -S n Himalayan cedar with drooping branches

DEODARA, -S same as ▸ deodar

DEODARS ▸ deodar

DEODATE, -S n offering to God

DEONTIC n ethical concept such as obligation or permissibility

DEONTICS ▸ deontic

DEORBIT, -S vb go out of orbit

DEOXY adj having less oxygen than a specified related compound

DEP, -S n small shop where newspapers, sweets, soft drinks, etc are sold

DEPAINT, -S vb depict

DEPART, -S vb leave

DEPARTED adj dead ▷ n dead person

DEPARTEE ▸ depart

DEPARTER ▸ depart

DEPARTS ▸ depart

DEPECHE, -D, -S n message ▷ vb dispatch; rid oneself of

DEPEINCT vb paint

DEPEND, -ED, -S vb put trust (in)

DEPEOPLE vb reduce population

DEPERM, -ED, -S vb demagnetize (a ship or submarine)

DEPICT, -ED, -S vb produce a picture of

DEPICTER ▸ depict

DEPICTOR ▸ depict

DEPICTS ▸ depict

DEPILATE vb remove the hair from

DEPLANE, -D, -S vb disembark from an aeroplane

DEPLETE, -D, -S vb use up

DEPLETER ▸ deplete

DEPLETES ▸ deplete

DEPLORE, -D, -S vb condemn strongly

DEPLORER ▸ deplore

DEPLORES ▸ deplore

DEPLOY, -ED, -S vb get (troops or resources) ready for immediate action

DEPLOYER ▸ deploy

DEPLOYS ▸ deploy

DEPLUME, -D, -S vb deprive of feathers

DEPOLISH vb remove the polish from

DEPONE, -D, -S, DEPONING vb declare (something) under oath

DEPONENT n person who makes a statement on oath ▷ adj having a passive form but active meaning

DEPONES ▸ depone

DEPONING ▸ depone

DEPORT, -ED, -S vb remove forcibly from a country

DEPORTEE n person deported or awaiting deportation

DEPORTER ▸ deport

DEPORTS ▸ deport

DEPOSAL, -S n deposition; giving of testimony under oath

DEPOSE, -D, -S, DEPOSING vb remove from an office or position of power

DEPOSER, -S ▸ depose

DEPOSES ▸ depose

DEPOSING ▸ depose

DEPOSIT, -S vb put down ▷ n sum of money paid into a bank account

DEPOT, -S n building where goods or vehicles are kept when not in use ▷ adj (of a drug) designed for gradual release

DEPRAVE, -S vb make morally bad

DEPRAVED adj morally bad

DEPRAVER ▸ deprave

DEPRAVES ▸ deprave

DEPRENYL n drug combating effects of ageing

DEPRESS vb make sad

DEPRIME, -D, -S vb remove the primer from a device

DEPRIVAL ▸ deprive

DEPRIVE, -S vb prevent from (having or enjoying)

D

D

DEPRIVED adj lacking adequate living conditions, education, etc

DEPRIVER ▸ deprive

DEPRIVES ▸ deprive

DEPS ▸ dep

DEPSIDE, -S n organic chemical compound

DEPTH, -S n distance downwards, backwards, or inwards

DEPURANT adj purifying

DEPURATE vb cleanse or purify or to be cleansed or purified

DEPUTE, -D, -S, DEPUTING vb appoint (someone) to act on one's behalf ▷ n deputy

DEPUTIES ▸ deputy

DEPUTING ▸ depute

DEPUTISE same as ▸ deputize

DEPUTIZE vb act as deputy

DEPUTY, DEPUTIES n person appointed to act on behalf of another

DEQUEUE, -D, -S vb remove (an item) from a queue of computing tasks

DERACINE adj uprooted from their usual environment ▷ n person who has been uprooted from their usual environment

DERAIGN, -S vb contest (a claim, suit, etc)

DERAIL, -ED, -S vb cause (a train) to go off the rails

DERAILER same as ▸ derail

DERAILS ▸ derail

DERANGE, -D, -S vb disturb the order or arrangement of

DERANGER ▸ derange

DERANGES ▸ derange

DERAT, -S, -TED vb remove rats from

DERATE, -D, -S vb assess the value of some types of property at a lower rate than others for local taxation

DERATING ▸ derate

DERATION vb end rationing of (food, petrol, etc)

DERATS ▸ derat

DERATTED ▸ derat

DERAY, -ED, -ING, -S vb old word meanng go mad

DERBY, DERBIES n bowler hat

DERE, -D, -S, DERING vb injure

DERECHO, -S n long, fast-moving line of severe storms

DERED ▸ dere

DERELICT adj unused and falling into ruins ▷ n social outcast, vagrant

DERES ▸ dere

DERHAM, -S same as ▸ dirham

DERIDE, -D, -S, DERIDING vb treat with contempt or ridicule

DERIDER, -S ▸ deride

DERIDES ▸ deride

DERIDING ▸ deride

DERIG, -GED, -S vb remove equipment from

DERING ▸ dere

DERINGER same as ▸ derringer

DERISION n act of deriding

DERISIVE adj mocking, scornful

DERISORY adj too small or inadequate to be considered seriously

DERIVATE n derivative ▷ vb derive (something)

DERIVE, -D, -S, DERIVING vb take or develop (from)

DERIVER, -S ▸ derive

DERIVES ▸ derive

DERIVING ▸ derive

DERM, -S same as ▸ derma

DERMA, -S n beef or fowl intestine used as a casing for certain dishes, esp kishke

DERMAL adj of or relating to the skin

DERMAS ▸ derma

DERMATIC adj of skin

DERMIC ▸ dermis

DERMIS, -ES another name for ▸ corium

DERMOID, -S adj of or resembling skin ▷ n congenital cystic tumour whose walls are lined with epithelium

DERMS ▸ derm

DERN, -ED, -ING, -S n concealment ▷ vb keep hidden

DERNFUL adj sorrowful

DERNIER adj last

DERNIES ▸ derny

DERNING ▸ dern

DERNLY adv sorrowfully

DERNS ▸ dern

DERNY, DERNIES, -S n bicycle with a small motor

DERO, -S n vagrant or derelict

DEROGATE vb detract from ▷ adj debased or degraded

DEROS ▸ dero

DERRICK, -S n simple crane ▷ vb raise or lower the jib of (a crane)

DERRIERE n backside

DERRIES ▸ derry

DERRIS, -ES n woody climbing plant

DERRO, -S n vagrant or derelict

DERRY, DERRIES n derelict house, esp one used by tramps

DERTH, -S same as ▸ dearth

DERV, -S n diesel oil, when used for road transport

DERVISH n member of a Muslim religious order noted for a frenzied whirling dance

DERVS ▸ derv

DESALT, -ED, -S vb desalinate

DESALTER ▸ desalt

DESALTS ▸ desalt

DESAND, -ED, -S vb remove sand from

DESCALE, -D, -S vb remove a hard coating from inside (a kettle or pipe)

DESCALER n something that removes limescale

DESCALES ▸ descale

DESCANT, -S n tune played or sung above a basic melody ▷ adj denoting the highest member in a family of musical instruments ▷ vb compose or perform a descant (for a piece of music)

DESCEND, -S vb move down (a slope etc)

DESCENT, -S n descending

DESCHOOL vb educate by means other than a school

DESCRIBE vb give an account of (something or someone) in words

DESCRIED ▸ descry

DESCRIER ▸ descry

DESCRIES ▸ descry

DESCRIVE vb describe

DESCRY, DESCRIED, DESCRIES vb catch sight of

DESEED, -ED, -S vb remove the seeds from (eg a fruit)

DESEEDER n person who deseeds

DESEEDS ▸ deseed

DESELECT vb refuse to select (an MP) for re-election

DESERT, -ED, -S n region with little or no vegetation because of low rainfall ▷ vb abandon (a person or place) without intending to return

DESERTER ▸ desert

DESERTIC adj (of soil) developing in hot climates

DESERTS ▸ desert

DESERVE, -D, -S vb be entitled to or worthy of

DESERVER ▸ deserve

DESERVES ▸ deserve

DESHI, -S same as ▸ desi

DESI, -S adj (in Indian English) indigenous or local ▷ n (in Indian English) indigenous or local person

DESIGN, -ED, -S vb work out the structure or form of (something), by making a sketch or plans ▷ n preliminary drawing

DESIGNEE n person designated to do something

DESIGNER n person who draws up original sketches or plans from which things are made ▷ adj designed by a well-known designer

DESIGNS ▸ design

DESILVER vb remove silver from

DESINE, -D, -S, DESINING same as ▸ design

DESINENT > desinence

DESINES ▸ desine

DESINING ▸ desine

DESIRE, -D, -S, DESIRING vb want very much ▷ n wish, longing

DESIRER, -S ▸ desire

DESIRES ▸ desire

DESIRING ▸ desire

DESIROUS adj having a desire for

DESIS ▸ desi

DESIST, -ED, -S vb stop (doing something)

DESK, -S n piece of furniture with a writing surface and drawers

DESKFAST n breakfast eaten at one's desk at work

DESKILL, -S vb mechanize or computerize (a job) thereby reducing the skill required to do it

DESKING, -S n desks and related furnishings in a given space, eg an office

DESKMAN, DESKMEN n police officer in charge in police station

DESKNOTE n small computer

DESKS ▸ desk

DESKTOP, -S adj (of a computer) small enough to use at a desk ▷ n computer small enough to use at a desk

DESMAN, -S n either of two molelike amphibious mammals

DESMID, -S n type of mainly unicellular freshwater green alga

DESMINE, -S n type of mineral

DESMOID, -S adj resembling a tendon or ligament ▷ n very firm tumour of connective tissue

DESNOOD, -S vb remove the snood of a turkey poult to reduce the risk of cannibalism

DESOLATE adj uninhabited and bleak ▷ vb deprive of inhabitants

DESORB, -ED, -S vb change from an adsorbed state to a gaseous or liquid state

DESORBER n something that desorbs

DESORBS ▸ desorb

DESOXY same as ▸ deoxy

DESPAIR, -S n total loss of hope ▷ vb lose hope

DESPATCH same as ▸ dispatch

DESPIGHT obsolete form of ▸ despite

DESPISAL ▸ despise

DESPISE, -D, -S vb regard with contempt

DESPISER ▸ despise

DESPISES ▸ despise

DESPITE, -D, -S prep in spite of ▷ n contempt ▷ vb show contempt for

DESPOIL, -S vb plunder

DESPOND, -S vb lose heart or hope

DESPOT, -S n person in power who acts unfairly or cruelly

DESPOTAT n despot's domain

DESPOTIC ▸ despot

DESPOTS ▸ despot

DESSE, -S n old word for desk

DESSERT, -S n sweet course served at the end of a meal

DESSES ▸ desse

DESTAIN, -S vb remove stain from

DESTINE, -S vb set apart or appoint

DESTINED adj certain to be or to do something

DESTINES ▸ destine

DESTINY n future marked out for a person or thing

DESTOCK, -S vb reduce the amount of stock

DESTREAM vb take (pupils) out of classes that are organized by ability

DESTRESS vb make or become less stressed

DESTRIER an archaic word for ▸ warhorse

DESTROY, -S vb ruin, demolish

DESTRUCT vb destroy intentionally for safety ▷ n act of destructing ▷ adj capable of self-destruction

DESUGAR, -S vb remove sugar from

DESULFUR same as > desulphur

DESYATIN n Russian unit of area

DESYNE, -D, -S, DESYNING same as ▸ design

DETACH, -ES vb disengage and separate

DETACHED adj (of a house) not joined to another house

DETACHER ▸ detach

DETACHES ▸ detach

DETAIL, -S n individual piece of information ▷ vb list fully

DETAILED adj having many details

DETAILER ▸ detail

DETAILS ▸ detail

DETAIN, -ED, -S vb delay (someone)

DETAINEE ▸ detain

DETAINER n wrongful withholding of the property of another person

DETAINS ▸ detain

DETANGLE vb remove tangles from (esp hair)

DETASSEL vb remove top part of corn plant

DETECT, -ED, -S vb notice

DETECTER ▸ detect

DETECTOR n instrument used to find something

DETECTS ▸ detect

DETENT, -S n mechanism to check movement in one direction only

DETENTE, -S n easing of tension between nations

DETENTS ▸ detent

DETENU, -S n prisoner

DETENUE, -S n female prisoner

DETENUS ▸ detenu

DETER, -RED, -S vb discourage (someone) from doing something by instilling fear or doubt

DETERGE, -D, -S vb wash or wipe away

DETERGER n detergent

DETERGES ▸ deterge

DETERRED ▸ deter

DETERRER ▸ deter

DETERS ▸ deter

DETEST, -ED, -S vb dislike intensely

DETESTER ▸ detest

DETESTS ▸ detest

DETHATCH vb remove dead grass from lawn

DETHRONE vb remove from a throne or position of power

DETICK, -ED, -S vb remove ticks from

DETICKER ▶ **detick**

DETICKS ▶ **detick**

DETINUE, -S n action brought by a plaintiff to recover goods wrongfully detained

DETONATE vb explode

DETORT, -ED, -S vb twist or distort

DETOUR, -ED, -S n route that is not the most direct one ▷ vb deviate or cause to deviate from a direct route or course of action

DETOX, -ED, -ES, -ING n treatment to rid the body of poisonous substances ▷ vb undergo treatment to rid the body of poisonous substances

DETOXIFY vb remove poison from

DETOXING ▶ **detox**

DETRACT, -S vb make (something) seem less good

DETRAIN, -S vb leave or cause to leave a railway train, as passengers, etc

DETRAQUE n insane person

DETRITAL ▶ **detritus**

DETRITUS n loose mass of stones and silt worn away from rocks

DETRUDE, -D, -S vb force down or thrust away or out

DETRUSOR n muscle in the wall of the bladder

DETUNE, -D, -S, DETUNING vb change pitch of (stringed instrument)

DEUCE, -S, DEUCING vb score deuce in tennis ▷ n score of forty all

DEUCED adj damned

DEUCEDLY ▶ **deuced**

DEUCES ▶ **deuce**

DEUCING ▶ **deuce**

DEUDDARN n two-tiered Welsh dresser

DEUS, DEI, DI n god

DEUTERIC adj (of mineral) formed by metasomatic changes

DEUTERON n nucleus of a deuterium atom, consisting of one proton and one neutron

DEUTON n old form of ▶ **deuteron**

DEUTZIA, -S n shrub with clusters of pink or white flowers

DEV, -S same as ▶ **deva**

Dev is a Sanskrit word for a deity; related words are **deev** and **deva**

DEVA, -S n (in Hinduism and Buddhism) divine being or god

DEVALL, -ED, -S vb Scots word meaning stop

DEVALUE, -D, -S vb reduce the exchange value of (a currency)

DEVAS ▶ **deva**

DEVEIN, -ED, -S vb remove vein from

DEVEL, -ED, -ING, -LED, -S same as ▶ **devvel**

DEVELOP, -S vb grow or bring to a later, more elaborate, or more advanced stage

DEVELOPE old form of ▶ **develop**

DEVELOPS ▶ **develop**

DEVELS ▶ **devel**

DEVERBAL n word deriving from verb

DEVEST, -ED, -S variant spelling of ▶ **divest**

DEVI, -S n Hindu goddess

DEVIANCE n act or state of being deviant

DEVIANCY same as ▶ **deviance**

DEVIANT, -S adj (person) deviating from what is considered acceptable behaviour ▷ n person whose behaviour deviates from what is considered to be acceptable

DEVIATE, -D, -S vb differ from others in belief or thought

DEVIATOR ▶ **deviate**

DEVICE, -S n machine or tool used for a specific task

DEVIL, -ED, -ING, -LED, -S n evil spirit ▷ vb prepare (food) with a highly flavoured spiced mixture

DEVILDOM n domain of evil spirits

DEVILED ▶ **devil**

DEVILESS n female devil

DEVILET, -S n young devil

DEVILING ▶ **devil**

DEVILISH adj cruel or unpleasant ▷ adv extremely

DEVILISM n doctrine of devil

DEVILKIN n small devil

DEVILLED ▶ **devil**

DEVILRY n mischievousness

DEVILS ▶ **devil**

DEVILTRY same as ▶ **devilry**

DEVIOUS adj insincere and dishonest

DEVIS ▶ **devi**

DEVISAL, -S n act of inventing, contriving, or devising

DEVISE, -D, -S, DEVISING vb work out (something) in one's mind ▷ n disposition of property by will

DEVISEE, -S n person to whom property, esp realty, is devised by will

DEVISER, -S ▶ **devise**

DEVISES ▶ **devise**

DEVISING ▶ **devise**

DEVISOR, -S n person who devises property, esp realty, by will

DEVLING, -S n young devil

DEVO, -S n short for devolution

DEVOICE, -D, -S vb make (a voiced speech sound) voiceless

DEVOID adj completely lacking (in)

DEVOIR, -S n duty

DEVOLVE, -D, -S vb pass to a successor or substitute

DEVON, -S n bland processed meat in sausage form, eaten cold in slices

DEVONIAN adj denoting the fourth period of the Palaeozoic era

DEVONS ▶ **devon**

DEVORE, -S n velvet fabric with a raised pattern

DEVOS ▶ **devo**

DEVOT, -S n devotee

DEVOTE, -S, DEVOTING vb apply or dedicate to a particular purpose

DEVOTED adj showing loyalty or devotion

DEVOTEE, -S n person who is very enthusiastic about something

DEVOTES ▶ **devote**

DEVOTING ▶ **devote**

DEVOTION n strong affection for or loyalty to someone or something

DEVOTS ▶ **devot**

DEVOUR, -ED, -S vb eat greedily

DEVOURER ▶ **devour**

DEVOURS ▶ **devour**

DEVOUT, -ER adj deeply religious

DEVOUTLY ▶ **devout**

DEVS ▶ **dev**

DEVVEL, -S vb strike with blow

DEW, -ED, -ING, -S n drops of water that form on the ground at night from vapour in the air ▷ vb moisten with or as with dew

DEWAN, -S n (formerly in India) the chief or finance minister of a state ruled by an Indian prince

DEWANI, -S n post of a dewan

DEWANNY same as ▶ **dewani**

DEWANS ▶ **dewan**

DEWAR, -S n type of vacuum flask

DEWATER, -S vb remove water from

DEWAX, -ED, -ES, -ING vb remove wax from

DEWBERRY n type of bramble with blue-black fruits

DEWCLAW, -S n nonfunctional claw on a dog's leg

DEWDROP, -S n drop of dew

DEWED ▶ **dew**

DEWFALL, -S n formation of dew

DEWFULL obsolete form of ▶ **due**

DEWIER ▶ **dewy**

DEWIEST ▶ **dewy**

DEWILY ▶ **dewy**

DEWINESS ▶ **dewy**

DEWING ▶ **dew**

DEWITT, -ED, -S vb kill, esp hang unlawfully

DEWLAP, -S n loose fold of skin hanging under the throat in dogs, cattle, etc

DEWLAPT ▶ **dewlap**

DEWLESS ▶ **dew**

DEWOOL, -ED, -S vb remove wool from

DEWORM, -ED, -S vb rid of worms

DEWORMER ▶ **deworm**

DEWORMS ▶ **deworm**

DEWPOINT n temperature at which water droplets form in the air

DEWS ▶ **dew**

DEWY, DEWIER, DEWIEST adj moist with or as with dew

DEX, -ES n dextroamphetamine

DEXTER, -S adj of or on the right side of a shield, etc, from the bearer's point of view ▷ n small breed of beef cattle

DEXTRAL, -S n right-handed person

DEXTRAN, -S n polysaccharide compound

DEXTRIN, -S n sticky substance obtained from starch

DEXTRINE same as ▶ **dextrin**

DEXTRINS ▶ **dextrin**

DEXTRO adj dextrorotatory or rotating to the right

DEXTROSE n glucose occurring in fruit, honey, and the blood of animals

DEXTROUS same as ▷ **dexterous**

DEY, -S n title given to commanders or governors of the Janissaries of Algiers

DEZINC, -ED, -S vb remove zinc from

DHABA, -S n roadside café in India

DHAK, -S n tropical Asian tree

DHAL, -S n curry made from lentils or beans

DHAMMA, -S variant of ▶ **dharma**

DHANSAK, -S n any of a variety of Indian dishes

DHARMA, -S n moral law or behaviour

DHARMIC ▶ **dharma**

DHARNA, -S n (in India) a method of obtaining justice

DHIKR, -S n Sufi religious ceremony

DHIMMI, -S n non-Muslim living in a state governed by sharia law

DHOBI, -S n (in India, Malaya, East Africa, etc, esp formerly) a washerman

DHOL, -S n type of Indian drum

DHOLAK, -S n type of two-headed drum

DHOLE, -S n fierce canine mammal

DHOLL, -S same as ▶ **dhal**

DHOLS ▶ **dhol**

DHOOLY, DHOOLIES same as ▶ **doolie**

DHOORA, -S same as ▶ **durra**

DHOOTI, -S same as ▶ **dhoti**

DHOOTIE, -S same as ▶ **dhoti**

DHOOTIS ▶ **dhooti**

DHOTI, -S n long loincloth worn by men in India

DHOURRA, -S same as ▶ **durra**

DHOW, -S n Arab sailing ship

DHURNA, -S same as ▶ **dharna**

DHURRA, -S same as ▶ **durra**

DHURRIE, -S same as ▶ **durrie**

DHUTI, -S same as ▶ **dhoti**

DHYANA, -S n type of Hindu meditation

DI ▶ **deus**

DIABASE, -S n altered dolerite

DIABASIC ▶ **diabase**

DIABETES n disorder in which an abnormal amount of urine containing an excess of sugar is excreted

DIABETIC n person who has diabetes ▷ adj of or having diabetes

DIABLE, -S n type of sauce

DIABLERY same as ▷ **diablerie**

DIABLES ▶ **diable**

DIABOLIC adj of the Devil

DIABOLO, -S n game using a spinning top and a cord fastened to two sticks

DIACETYL n aromatic compound

DIACID, -S n lead plaster

DIACIDIC adj capable of neutralizing two protons with one molecule

DIACIDS ▶ **diacid**

DIACONAL adj of or associated with a deacon or the diaconate

DIACT, -S same as ▶ **diactine**

DIACTINE adj two-rayed ▷ n two-rayed sponge spicule

DIACTS ▶ **diact**

DIADEM, -ED, -S n crown ▷ vb adorn or crown with or as with a diadem

DIADOCHI pl n six generals who fought for control of the Alexandrian Empire

DIADOCHY n replacement of one element in a crystal by another

DIADROM, -S n complete course of pendulum

DIAGLYPH n figure cut into stone

DIAGNOSE vb determine by diagnosis

DIAGONAL adj from corner to corner ▷ n diagonal line

DIAGRAM, -S n sketch showing the form or workings of something ▷ vb show in or as if in a diagram

DIAGRAPH n device for enlarging or reducing maps, plans, etc

DIAGRID, -S n diagonal structure network

DIAL, -ED, -LED, -S n face of a clock or watch ▷ vb operate the dial or buttons on a telephone in order to contact (a number)

DIALECT, -S n form of a language spoken in a particular area

DIALED ▶ **dial**

DIALER, -S ▶ **dial**

D

DIALING, -S ▸ **dial**
DIALIST, -S n dial-maker
DIALLAGE n green or brownish-black variety of the mineral augite
DIALLED ▸ **dial**
DIALLEL, -S n interbreeding among a group of parents ▷ adj (of lines) not parallel, meeting, or intersecting
DIALLER, -S ▸ **dial**
DIALLING ▸ **dial**
DIALLIST same as ▸ **dialist**
DIALOG, -ED, -S same as ▸ **dialogue**
DIALOGER ▸ **dialog**
DIALOGIC ▸ **dialogue**
DIALOGS ▸ **dialog**
DIALOGUE n conversation between two people, esp in a book, film, or play ▷ vb put into the form of a dialogue
DIALS ▸ **dial**
DIALYSE, -D vb separate by dialysis
DIALYSER n machine that performs dialysis
DIALYSIS, DIALYSES n filtering of blood through a membrane to remove waste products
DIALYTIC ▸ **dialysis**
DIALYZE, -D, -S same as ▸ **dialyse**
DIALYZES same as ▸ **dialyser**
DIALYZES ▸ **dialyze**
DIAMANTE adj decorated with artificial jewels or sequins ▷ n fabric so covered
DIAMETER n (length of) a straight line through the centre of a circle or sphere
DIAMIDE, -S n compound containing two amido groups
DIAMIN, -S same as ▸ **diamine**
DIAMINE, -S n any chemical compound containing two amino groups in its molecules
DIAMINS ▸ **diamin**
DIAMOND, -S n exceptionally hard precious stone ▷ adj (of an anniversary) the sixtieth ▷ vb stud or decorate with diamonds
DIAMYL adj with two amyl groups
DIANDRY n practice of having two husbands
DIANE adj as in steak diane steak served in a rich sauce
DIANODAL adj going through a node

DIANOIA, -S n perception and experience regarded as lower modes of knowledge
DIANTHUS n type of widely cultivated Eurasian plant
DIAPASE, -S same as ▸ **diapason**
DIAPASON n either of two stops found throughout the range of a pipe organ
DIAPAUSE vb undergo diapause ▷ n period of suspended development and growth
DIAPENTE n (in classical Greece) the interval of a perfect fifth
DIAPER, -ED, -S n nappy ▷ vb decorate with a geometric pattern
DIAPHONE n set of all realizations of a given phoneme in a language
DIAPHONY n style of two-part polyphonic singing
DIAPIR, -S n type of geological formation
DIAPIRIC ▸ **diapir**
DIAPIRS ▸ **diapir**
DIAPSID, -S n reptile with two holes in rear of skull
DIARCH adj (of a vascular bundle) having two strands of xylem
DIARCHAL ▸ **diarchy**
DIARCHIC ▸ **diarchy**
DIARCHY n government by two states, individuals, etc
DIARIAL ▸ **diary**
DIARIAN ▸ **diary**
DIARIES ▸ **diary**
DIARISE, -D, -S same as ▸ **diarize**
DIARIST, -S n person who writes a diary
DIARIZE, -D, -S vb record in diary
DIARRHEA same as > **diarrhoea**
DIARY, DIARIES n (book for) a record of daily events, appointments, or observations
DIASCIA, -S n S African plant, usu with pink flowers
DIASCOPE n optical projector used to display transparencies
DIASPORA n dispersion or spreading of a people
DIASPORE n white, yellowish, or grey mineral
DIASTASE n enzyme that converts starch into sugar
DIASTEM, -S same as ▸ **diastema**

DIASTEMA n abnormal space, fissure, or cleft in a bodily organ or part
DIASTEMS ▸ **diastem**
DIASTER, -S n stage in cell division
DIASTOLE n dilation of the chambers of the heart
DIASTRAL ▸ **diaster**
DIASTYLE adj having columns about three diameters apart ▷ n diastyle building
DIATOM, -S n microscopic unicellular alga
DIATOMIC adj containing two atoms
DIATOMS ▸ **diatom**
DIATONIC adj of a regular major or minor scale
DIATREME n volcanic vent produced by an eruption of gas
DIATRETA > **diatretum**
DIATRIBE n bitter critical attack
DIATRON, -S n circuit that uses diodes
DIAXON, -S n bipolar cell
DIAZEPAM n minor tranquillizer used to treat epilepsy
DIAZIN, -S same as ▸ **diazine**
DIAZINE, -S n organic compound
DIAZINON n type of insecticide
DIAZINS ▸ **diazin**
DIAZO, -ES, -S adj relating to a method for reproducing documents ▷ n document produced by this method
DIAZOLE, -S n type of organic compound
DIAZOS ▸ **diazo**
DIB, -BED, -BING, -S vb fish by allowing the bait to bob and dip on the surface
DIBASIC adj (of an acid) containing two acidic hydrogen atoms
DIBBED ▸ **dib**
DIBBER, -S same as ▸ **dibble**
DIBBING ▸ **dib**
DIBBLE, -D, -S, DIBBLING n small gardening tool ▷ vb make a hole in (the ground) with a dibble
DIBBLER, -S ▸ **dibble**
DIBBLES ▸ **dibble**
DIBBLING ▸ **dibble**
DIBBS ▸ **dib**
DIBBUK, -IM, -S variant spelling of ▸ **dybbuk**
DIBS ▸ **dib**
DIBUTYL adj with two butyl groups

DICACITY n playful teasing
DICAMBA, -S n type of weedkiller
DICAST, -S n juror in ancient Athens
DICASTIC ▶ dicast
DICASTS ▶ dicast
DICE, -D, -S n small cube with numbered sides ▷ vb cut (food) into small cubes
DICELIKE adj like dice
DICENTRA n Asian or N American ornamental plant
DICER, -S ▶ dice
DICES ▶ dice
DICEY, DICIER, DICIEST adj dangerous or risky
DICH interj archaic expression meaning 'may it do'
DICHASIA ▶ dichasium
DICHORD, -S n two-stringed musical instrument
DICHOTIC adj relating to or involving the stimulation of each ear simultaneously by different sounds
DICHROIC adj having or consisting of only two colours
DICHT, -ED, -ING, -S vb wipe
DICIER ▶ dicey
DICIEST ▶ dicey
DICING, -S ▶ dice
DICK, -S n fellow
DICKENS n euphemism for devil
DICKER, -ED, -S vb trade (goods) by bargaining ▷ n petty bargain or barter
DICKERER n person who dickers
DICKERS ▶ dicker
DICKEY, -S same as ▶ dicky
DICKIE same as ▶ dicky
DICKIER ▶ dicky
DICKIES ▶ dicky
DICKIEST ▶ dicky
DICKS ▶ dick
DICKTY, DICKTIER same as ▶ dicty
DICKY, DICKIER, DICKIES, DICKIEST n false shirt front ▷ adj shaky or weak
DICLINY ▷ diclinous
DICOT, -S n type of flowering plant
DICOTYL, -S n type of flowering plant
DICROTAL same as ▶ dicrotic
DICROTIC adj having or relating to a double pulse for each heartbeat
DICT, -ED, -ING, -S vb dictate
DICTA ▶ dictum
DICTATE, -D, -S vb say aloud for someone else to write

down ▷ n authoritative command
DICTATOR n ruler who has complete power
DICTED ▶ dict
DICTIER ▶ dicty
DICTIEST ▶ dicty
DICTING ▶ dict
DICTION, -S n manner of pronouncing words and sounds
DICTS ▶ dict
DICTUM, DICTA, -S n formal statement
DICTY, DICTIER, DICTIEST adj conceited; snobbish
DICYCLIC adj having the perianth arranged in two whorls
DICYCLY ▶ dicyclic
DID ▶ do
DIDACT, -S n instructive person
DIDACTIC adj intended to instruct
DIDACTS ▶ didact
DIDACTYL adj having only two toes on each foot ▷ n animal with only two toes on each foot
DIDAKAI, -S same as ▶ didicoy
DIDAKEI, -S same as ▶ didicoy
DIDAPPER n small grebe
DIDDER, -ED, -S vb shake with fear
DIDDICOY same as ▶ didicoy
DIDDIER ▶ diddy
DIDDIES ▶ diddy
DIDDIEST ▶ diddy
DIDDLE, -D, -S, DIDDLING vb swindle
DIDDLER, -S ▶ diddle
DIDDLES ▶ diddle
DIDDLEY, -S n worthless amount
DIDDLIES ▶ diddly
DIDDLING ▶ diddle
DIDDLY, DIDDLIES n worthless amount
DIDDUMS interj expression of sympathy, esp to a child
DIDDY, DIDDIER, DIDDIES, DIDDIEST n Scots word for a foolish person ▷ adj foolish
DIDICOI, -S same as ▶ didicoy
DIDICOY, -S n (in Britain) a person who lives like a Roma but is not a true one
DIDIE same as ▶ didy
DIDIES ▶ didy
DIDO, -ES, -S n antic
DIDRACHM n two-drachma piece

DIDST form of the past tense of ▶ do
DIDY, DIDIES n (US) child's word for nappy
DIDYMIUM n metallic mixture once thought to be an element
DIDYMO, -S n class of algae
DIDYMOUS adj in pairs or in two parts
DIDYNAMY n (of stamens) being in two unequal pairs
DIE, -D, -ING, -S vb cease all biological activity permanently ▷ n shaped block used to cut or form metal
DIEB, -S n N African jackal
DIEBACK, -S n disease of trees and shrubs ▷ vb (of plants) to suffer from dieback
DIEBS ▶ dieb
DIECIOUS same as ▷ dioecious
DIED ▶ die
DIEDRAL, -S same as ▷ dihedral
DIEDRE, -S n large shallow groove or corner in a rock face
DIEGESIS, DIEGESES n utterance of fact
DIEGETIC adj relating to a factual narrative
DIEHARD, -S n person who resists change
DIEING ▶ die
DIEL, -S n 24-hour period ▷ adj of or lasting for any 24-hour period
DIELDRIN n highly toxic insecticide
DIELS ▶ diel
DIELYTRA n genus of herbaceous plants
DIEMAKER n one who makes dies
DIENE, -S n type of hydrocarbon
DIEOFF, -S n process of dying in large numbers
DIERESIS, DIERESES same as ▷ diaeresis
DIERETIC ▶ dieresis
DIES ▶ die
DIESEL, -ED, -S vb drive diesel-fuelled vehicle ▷ n diesel engine
DIESIS, DIESES n printed symbol indicating a footnote
DIESTER, -S n synthetic lubricant
DIESTOCK n device holding the dies used to cut an external screw thread

D

DIESTRUM another word for
> **dioestrus**

DIESTRUS same as
> **dioestrus**

DIET, -ED, -S n food that a
person or animal regularly
eats ▷ vb follow a special
diet so as to lose weight
▷ adj (of food) suitable for a
weight-reduction diet

DIETARY adj of or relating to
a diet ▷ n regulated diet

DIETED ▶ **diet**

DIETER, -S ▶ **diet**

DIETETIC adj prepared for
special dietary requirements

DIETHER, -S n chemical
compound

DIETHYL, -S adj as in **diethyl
ether** ether

DIETINE, -S n low-ranking
diet or assembly

DIETING, -S ▶ **diet**

DIETIST, -S another word for
> **dietitian**

DIETS ▶ **diet**

DIF, -S same as ▶ **diff**

DIFF, -S n informal word
meaning difference

DIFFER, -ED, -S vb be unlike

DIFFORM adj irregular in
form

DIFFRACT vb cause to
undergo diffraction

DIFFS ▶ **diff**

DIFFUSE, -D, -S vb spread
over a wide area ▷ adj widely
spread

DIFFUSER n person or thing
that diffuses

DIFFUSES ▶ **diffuse**

DIFFUSOR same as ▶ **diffuser**

DIFS ▶ **dif**

DIG, -GING, -S vb cut into,
break up, and turn over or
remove (earth), esp with a
spade ▷ n digging

DIGAMIES ▶ **digamy**

DIGAMIST ▶ **digamy**

DIGAMMA, -S n obsolete
letter of the Greek alphabet

DIGAMOUS ▶ **digamy**

DIGAMY, DIGAMIES n
second marriage

DIGERATI pl n people who
earn large amounts of
money through
internet-related business

DIGEST, -ED, -S vb subject to
a process of digestion ▷ n
shortened version of a book,
report, or article

DIGESTER n apparatus or
vessel, such as an autoclave,
in which digestion is
carried out

DIGESTIF n something, esp a
drink, taken as an aid to
digestion, either before or
after a meal

DIGESTOR same as
▶ **digester**

DIGESTS ▶ **digest**

DIGGABLE adj that can be
dug

DIGGED a past tense of ▶ **dig**

DIGGER, -S n machine used
for digging

DIGGING ▶ **dig**

DIGGINGS pl n material that
has been dug out

DIGHT, -ED, -ING, -S vb
adorn or equip, as for battle

DIGICAM, -S n digital
camera

DIGIPACK n (esp formerly)
type of packaging for a CD or
DVD

DIGIT, -S n finger or toe

DIGITAL, -S adj displaying
information as numbers ▷ n
one of the keys on the
manuals of an organ or
piano, etc

DIGITATE adj (of leaves)
having leaflets in the form of
a spread hand

DIGITISE same as ▶ **digitize**

DIGITIZE vb transcribe (data)
into a digital form for
processing by a computer

DIGITRON n type of tube for
displaying information

DIGITS ▶ **digit**

DIGITULE n any small
finger-like process

DIGLOT, -S n bilingual book

DIGLYPH, -S n ornament in a
Doric frieze with two
grooves

DIGNIFY vb add distinction
to

DIGNITY n serious, calm,
and controlled behaviour or
manner

DIGONAL adj of or relating
to a symmetry operation

DIGOXIN, -S n glycoside
extracted from the leaves of
the woolly foxglove

DIGRAPH, -S n two letters
used to represent a single
sound

DIGRESS vb depart from the
main subject in speech or
writing

DIGS ▶ **dig**

DIGYNIAN adj relating to
plant class Digynia

DIGYNOUS another word for
▶ **digynian**

DIHEDRA ▶ **dihedron**

DIHEDRAL adj having or
formed by two intersecting
planes ▷ n figure formed by
two intersecting planes

DIHEDRON, DIHEDRA n
figure formed by two
intersecting planes

DIHYBRID n offspring of two
individuals that differ with
respect to two pairs of genes

DIHYDRIC adj (of an alcohol)
containing two hydroxyl
groups per molecule

DIKA, -S n wild mango

DIKAST, -S same as ▶ **dicast**

DIKDIK, -S n small African
antelope

DIKE, -D, -S, DIKING same as
▶ **dyke**

DIKER, -S n builder of dikes

DIKES ▶ **dike**

DIKETONE n as in
diphenylene diketone
compound used in dye
manufacture, aka
anthraquinone

DIKING ▶ **dike**

DIKKOP, -S n type of
brownish shore bird with a
large head and eyes

DIKTAT, -S n dictatorial
decree

DILATANT adj tending to
dilate ▷ n something, such
as a catheter, that causes
dilation

DILATATE same as ▶ **dilate**

DILATE, -D, -S, DILATING vb
make or become wider or
larger

DILATER, -S same as
▶ **dilator**

DILATES ▶ **dilate**

DILATING ▶ **dilate**

DILATION ▶ **dilate**

DILATIVE ▶ **dilate**

DILATOR, -S n something
that dilates an object

DILATORY adj tending or
intended to waste time

DILEMMA, -S n situation
offering a choice between
two undesirable alternatives

DILEMMIC ▶ **dilemma**

DILIGENT adj careful and
persevering in carrying out
duties

DILL, -ED, -S n sweet-
smelling herb ▷ vb flavour
with dill

DILLI, -S n small bag, esp one
made of plaited grass

DILLIER ▶ **dilly**

DILLIES ▶ **dilly**

DILLIEST ▶ **dilly**

DILLING, -S ▶ **dill**

DILLIS ▸ dilli

DILLS ▸ dill

DILLWEED n dill plant or its foliage

DILLY, DILLIER, DILLIES, DILLIEST adj foolish ▸ n person or thing that is remarkable

DILSCOOP n type of shot in cricket in which the ball goes over the wicketkeeper's head

DILUENT, -S adj causing dilution or serving to dilute ▸ n substance used for or causing dilution

DILUTE, -D, -S, DILUTING vb make (a liquid) less concentrated, esp by adding water ▸ adj (of a liquid) thin and watery

DILUTEE, -S ▸ dilute

DILUTER, -S ▸ dilute

DILUTES ▸ dilute

DILUTING ▸ dilute

DILUTION n act of diluting or state of being diluted

DILUTIVE adj having effect of decreasing earnings per share

DILUTOR, -S n thing intended to have a diluting effect

DILUVIA ▸ diluvium

DILUVIAL adj of a flood, esp the great Flood described in the Old Testament

DILUVIAN same as ▸ diluvial

DILUVION same as ▸ diluvium

DILUVIUM, DILUVIA n glacial drift

DIM, -MED, -MEST, -S adj badly lit ▸ vb make or become dim

DIMBLE, -S n wooded hollow; dingle

DIMBO, -ES, -S n unintelligent person

DIME, -S n coin of the US and Canada, worth ten cents

DIMER, -S n type of molecule

DIMERIC adj of a dimer

DIMERISE same as ▸ dimerize

DIMERISM ▸ dimerous

DIMERISM vb react or cause to react to form a dimer

DIMEROUS adj consisting of or divided into two segments, as the tarsi of some insects

DIMERS ▸ dimer

DIMES ▸ dime

DIMETER, -S n type of verse

DIMETHYL n ethane

DIMETRIC adj of, relating to, or shaped like a quadrilateral

DIMINISH vb make or become smaller, fewer, or less

DIMITY, DIMITIES n light strong cotton fabric with woven stripes or squares

DIMLY ▸ dim

DIMMABLE adj that can be dimmed

DIMMED ▸ dim

DIMMER, -S ▸ dim

DIMMEST ▸ dim

DIMMING, -S n as in **global dimming** decrease in the amount of sunlight reaching the earth

DIMMISH ▸ dim

DIMNESS ▸ dim

DIMORPH, -S n either of two forms of a substance that exhibits dimorphism

DIMOUT, -S n reduction of lighting

DIMP, -S n in Northern English dialect, a cigarette butt

DIMPLE, -D, -S, DIMPLING n small natural dent, esp in the cheeks or chin ▸ vb produce dimples by smiling

DIMPLIER ▸ dimply

DIMPLING ▸ dimple

DIMPLY, DIMPLIER ▸ dimple

DIMPS ▸ dimp

DIMPSY, DIMPSIES n twilight

DIMS ▸ dim

DIMWIT, -S n stupid person

DIMYARY adj with two adductor muscles

DIN, -NED, -NING, -S n loud unpleasant confused noise ▸ vb instil (something) into someone by constant repetition

DINAR, -S n monetary unit

DINARCHY same as ▸ diarchy

DINARS ▸ dinar

DINDLE, -D, -S, DINDLING another word for ▸ dinnle

DINE, -D, -S vb eat dinner

DINER, -S n person eating a meal

DINERIC adj of or concerned with the interface between immiscible liquids

DINERO, -S n money

DINERS ▸ diner

DINES ▸ dine

DINETTE, -S n alcove or small area for use as a dining room

DINFUL adj noisy

DING, -S n small dent in a vehicle ▸ vb ring or cause to ring, esp with tedious repetition

DINGBAT, -S n any unnamed object

DINGDONG n sound of a bell or bells ▸ vb make such a sound

DINGE, -D, -DINGING n dent ▸ vb make a dent in (something)

DINGER, -S n (in baseball) home run

DINGES, -ES n jocular word for something whose name is unknown or forgotten

DINGEY, -S same as ▸ dinghy

DINGHY, DINGHIES n small boat, powered by sails, oars, or a motor ▸ vb ignore or avoid a person or event

DINGIED ▸ dingy

DINGIER ▸ dingy

DINGIES ▸ dingy

DINGIEST ▸ dingy

DINGILY ▸ dingy

DINGING ▸ dinge

DINGLE, -S n small wooded hollow or valley

DINGO, -ED, -ES, -ING, -S n Australian wild dog ▸ vb act in a cowardly manner

DINGS ▸ ding

DINGUS, -ES same as ▸ dinges

DINGY, DINGIED, DINGIER, DINGIES, DINGIEST, -ING adj lacking light ▸ vb ignore or avoid a person or event

DINIC, -S n remedy for vertigo

DINING, -S n act of dining

DINITRO adj containing two nitro groups

DINK, -ED, -ER, -EST, -ING, -S adj neat or neatly dressed ▸ vb carry (a second person) on a horse, bicycle, etc ▸ n ball struck delicately

DINKEY, -S n small locomotive

DINKIE, -S n affluent married childless person ▸ adj designed for or appealing to dinkies

DINKIER ▸ dinky

DINKIES ▸ dinkie

DINKIEST ▸ dinky

DINKING ▸ dink

DINKLY, DINKLIER adj neat

DINKS ▸ dink

DINKUM, -S n truth or genuineness

DINKY, DINKIER, DINKIEST adj small and neat

D

D

DINMONT, -S n neutered sheep

DINNA vb a Scots word for do not

DINNAE vb (Scots) do not

DINNED ▸ din

DINNER, -ED, -S vb dine ▹ n main meal of the day

DINNING ▸ din

DINNLE, -D, -S, DINNLING vb shake

DINO, -S n dinosaur

DINOSAUR n type of extinct prehistoric reptile, many of which were of gigantic size

DINS ▸ din

DINT, -ED, -ING, -S variant of ▸ dent

DINTLESS ▸ dint

DINTS ▸ dint

DIOBOL, -S n ancient Greek coin

DIOBOLON same as ▸ diobol

DIOBOLS ▸ diobol

DIOCESAN adj of or relating to a diocese ▹ n bishop of a diocese

DIOCESE, -S n district over which a bishop has control

DIODE, -S n semiconductor device

DIOECIES ▸ dioecy

DIOECISM > dioecious

DIOECY, DIOECIES n state of being dioecious

DIOICOUS same as > dioecious

DIOL, -S n any of a class of alcohols that have two hydroxyl groups in each molecule

DIOLEFIN n type of polymer

DIOLS ▸ diol

DIOPSIDE n colourless or pale-green pyroxene mineral

DIOPTASE n green glassy mineral

DIOPTER, -S same as ▸ dioptre

DIOPTRAL ▸ dioptre

DIOPTRE, -S n unit for measuring the refractive power of a lens

DIOPTRIC adj of or concerned with dioptrics

DIORAMA, -S n miniature three-dimensional scene

DIORAMIC ▸ diorama

DIORISM, -S n definition; clarity

DIORITE, -S n dark coarse-grained igneous plutonic rock

DIORITIC ▸ diorite

DIOTA, -S n type of ancient vase

DIOXAN, -S n colourless insoluble toxic liquid

DIOXANE, -S same as ▸ dioxan

DIOXANS ▸ dioxan

DIOXID, -S same as ▸ dioxide

DIOXIDE, -S n oxide containing two oxygen atoms per molecule

DIOXIDS ▸ dioxid

DIOXIN, -S n poisonous chemical by-product of certain weedkillers

DIP, -PED, -S, -T vb plunge quickly or briefly into a liquid ▹ n dipping

DIPCHICK same as ▸ dabchick

DIPHASE adj of, having, or concerned with two phases

DIPHASIC same as ▸ diphase

DIPHENYL another name for ▸ biphenyl

DIPHONE, -S n combination of two speech sounds

DIPLEGIA n paralysis of corresponding parts on both sides of the body

DIPLEGIC ▸ diplegia

DIPLEX adj permitting simultaneous transmission in both directions

DIPLEXER n device that enables the simultaneous transmission of more than one signal

DIPLOE, -S n spongy bone separating the two layers of compact bone of the skull

DIPLOGEN n heavy hydrogen

DIPLOIC adj relating to a diploe

DIPLOID, -S adj denoting a cell or organism with pairs of homologous chromosomes ▹ n diploid cell or organism

DIPLOIDY ▸ diploid

DIPLOMA, -S vb bestow diploma on ▹ n qualification awarded by a college on successful completion of a course

DIPLOMAT n official engaged in diplomacy

DIPLON, -S another name for ▸ deuteron

DIPLONT, -S n animal or plant that has the diploid number of chromosomes in its somatic cells

DIPLOPIA n visual defect in which a single object is seen in duplicate

DIPLOPIC ▸ diplopia

DIPLOPOD n type of arthropod such as the millipede

DIPLOSIS, DIPLOSES n doubling of the haploid number of chromosomes

DIPLOZOA n type of parasitic worm

DIPNET, -S vb fish using a fishing net on a pole

DIPNOAN, -S n lungfish

DIPNOOUS adj having lungs and gills

DIPODIC ▸ dipody

DIPODY, DIPODIES n metrical unit consisting of two feet

DIPOLAR ▸ dipole

DIPOLE, -S n two equal but opposite electric charges or magnetic poles separated by a small distance

DIPPABLE ▸ dip

DIPPED ▸ dip

DIPPER, -S n ladle used for dipping

DIPPIER ▸ dippy

DIPPIEST ▸ dippy

DIPPING, -S ▸ dip

DIPPY, DIPPIER, DIPPIEST adj odd, eccentric, or crazy

DIPROTIC adj having two hydrogen atoms

DIPS ▸ dip

DIPSAS, DIPSADES n type of snake

DIPSO, -S n dipsomaniac

DIPSTICK n notched rod dipped into a container to measure the level of a liquid

DIPT ▸ dip

DIPTERA, -S n order of insects with two wings

DIPTERAL adj having a double row of columns

DIPTERAN n dipterous insect ▹ adj having two wings or winglike parts

DIPTERAS ▸ diptera

DIPTEROI ▸ dipteros

DIPTERON same as ▸ dipteran

DIPTEROS, DIPTEROI n Greek building with double columns

DIPTYCA, -S same as ▸ diptych

DIPTYCH, -S n painting on two hinged panels

DIQUARK, -S n particle in physics

DIQUAT, -S n type of herbicide

DIRAM, -S n money unit of Tajikistan

DIRDAM, -S same as ▸ dirdum

DIRDUM, -S n tumult

DIRE, -R, -ST adj disastrous, urgent, or terrible

DIRECT, -ED, -ER, -S adj (of a route) shortest, straight ▷ adv in a direct manner ▷ vb lead and organize
DIRECTLY adv in a direct manner
DIRECTOR n person or thing that directs or controls
DIRECTS ▶ direct
DIREFUL same as ▶ dire
DIRELY ▶ dire
DIREMPT, -S vb separate with force
DIRENESS ▶ dire
DIRER ▶ dire
DIREST ▶ dire
DIRGE, -S n slow sad song of mourning
DIRGEFUL ▶ dirge
DIRGES ▶ dirge
DIRHAM, -S n standard monetary unit of Morocco
DIRHEM, -S same as ▶ dirham
DIRIGE, -S n dirge
DIRIGENT adj directing
DIRIGES ▶ dirige
DIRIGISM same as > dirigisme
DIRIMENT adj (of an impediment to marriage in canon law) totally invalidating
DIRK, -ED, -ING, -S n dagger, formerly worn by Scottish Highlanders ▷ vb stab with a dirk
DIRKE, -S variant of ▶ dirk
DIRKED ▶ dirk
DIRKES ▶ dirke
DIRKING ▶ dirk
DIRKS ▶ dirk
DIRL, -ED, -ING, -S vb tingle; vibrate
DIRNDL, -S n full gathered skirt
DIRT, -ED, -ING, -S vb soil ▷ n unclean substance, filth
DIRTBAG, -S n filthy person
DIRTBALL n insulting word for a contemptible person
DIRTED ▶ dirt
DIRTIED ▶ dirty
DIRTIER ▶ dirty
DIRTIES ▶ dirty
DIRTIEST ▶ dirty
DIRTILY ▶ dirty
DIRTING ▶ dirt
DIRTS ▶ dirt
DIRTY, DIRTIED, DIRTIER, DIRTIES, DIRTIEST, -ING adj covered or marked with dirt ▷ vb make dirty
DIS same as ▶ diss
DISA, -S n type of orchid
DISABLE, -S vb make ineffective, unfit, or incapable

DISABLED adj restricted in ability to move or use a sense
DISABLER ▶ disable
DISABLES ▶ disable
DISABUSE vb rid (someone) of a mistaken idea
DISADORN vb deprive of ornamentation
DISAGREE vb argue or have different opinions
DISALLOW vb reject as untrue or invalid
DISALLY vb separate
DISANNEX vb disunite
DISANNUL vb cancel
DISAPPLY vb make (law) invalid
DISARM, -ED, -S vb deprive of weapons
DISARMER ▶ disarm
DISARMS ▶ disarm
DISARRAY n confusion and lack of discipline ▷ vb throw into confusion
DISAS ▶ disa
DISASTER n occurrence that causes great distress or destruction
DISAVOW, -S vb deny connection with or responsibility for
DISBAND, -S vb (cause to) cease to function as a group
DISBAR, -S vb deprive (a barrister) of the right to practise
DISBARK, -S same as > disembark
DISBARS ▶ disbar
DISBENCH vb remove from bench
DISBOSOM vb disclose
DISBOUND adj unbound
DISBOWEL vb disembowel
DISBUD, -S vb remove superfluous buds from (a plant, esp a fruit tree)
DISBURSE vb pay out
DISC, -ED, -ING, -S n flat circular object ▷ vb work (land) with a disc harrow
DISCAGE, -D, -S vb release from cage
DISCAL adj relating to or resembling a disc
DISCANDY vb melt; dissolve
DISCANT, -S same as ▶ descant
DISCARD, -S vb get rid of (something or someone) as useless or undesirable ▷ n person or thing that has been cast aside
DISCASE, -D, -S vb remove the case from
DISCED ▶ disc

DISCEPT, -S vb discuss
DISCERN, -S vb see or be aware of (something) clearly
DISCERP, -S vb divide
DISCI ▶ discus
DISCIDE, -D, -S vb split
DISCINCT adj loosely dressed, without belt
DISCING ▶ disc
DISCIPLE vb teach ▷ n follower of the doctrines of a teacher, esp Jesus Christ
DISCLAIM vb deny (responsibility for or knowledge of something)
DISCLESS adj having no disc
DISCLIKE ▶ disc
DISCLOSE, DISCLOST vb make known
DISCO, -ED, -ES, -ING, -S vb go to a disco ▷ n nightclub where people dance to amplified pop records
DISCOER, -S ▶ disco
DISCOES ▶ disco
DISCOID, -S adj like a disc ▷ n dislike object
DISCOING ▶ disco
DISCOLOR same as > discolour
DISCORD, -S n lack of agreement or harmony between people ▷ vb disagree
DISCOS ▶ disco
DISCOUNT vb take no account of something ▷ n deduction from the full price of something
DISCOURE vb discover
DISCOVER vb be the first to find or to find out about
DISCREET adj careful to avoid embarrassment, esp by keeping confidences secret
DISCRETE adj separate, distinct
DISCROWN vb deprive of a crown
DISCS ▶ disc
DISCURE, -D, -S old form of ▶ discover
DISCUS, DISCI, -ES n object thrown in sports competitions
DISCUSS vb consider (something) by talking it over
DISDAIN, -S n feeling of superiority and dislike ▷ vb refuse with disdain
DISEASE, -S vb make uneasy ▷ n illness, sickness
DISEASED adj having or affected with disease

D

DISEASES ▶ disease

DISEDGE, -D, -S vb render blunt

DISENDOW vb take away an endowment from

DISENROL vb remove from register

DISEUR, -S n (esp formerly) an actor who presents dramatic recitals

DISEUSE, -S n (esp formerly) an actress who presents dramatic recitals

DISFAME, -D, -S n discredit ▷ vb throw into disrepute or remove fame (from)

DISFAVOR same as ▶ disfavour

DISFLESH vb reduce flesh of

DISFORM, -S vb change form of

DISFROCK another word for ▶ unfrock

DISGAVEL vb deprive of quality of gavelkind

DISGEST, -S vb digest

DISGORGE vb empty out, discharge

DISGOWN, -S vb remove a gown from

DISGRACE n condition of shame, loss of reputation, or dishonour ▷ vb bring shame upon (oneself or others)

DISGRADE vb degrade

DISGUISE vb change the appearance to conceal the identity ▷ n mask, costume, or manner that disguises

DISGUST, -S n great loathing or distaste ▷ vb sicken, fill with loathing

DISH, -ES n shallow container used for holding or serving food ▷ vb put into a dish

DISHABIT vb dislodge

DISHABLE obsolete form of ▶ disable

DISHDASH same as ▶ dishdasha

DISHED adj shaped like a dish

DISHELM, -S vb remove a helmet from

DISHERIT vb disinherit

DISHES ▶ dish

DISHEVEL vb disarrange (the hair or clothes) of (someone)

DISHFUL, -S n the amount that a dish is able to hold

DISHIER ▶ dishy

DISHIEST ▶ dishy

DISHING, -S ▶ dish

DISHLIKE ▶ dish

DISHMOP, -S n mop for cleaning dishes

DISHOARD vb put previously withheld (money) into circulation

DISHOME, -D, -S vb deprive of home

DISHONOR same as ▶ dishonour

DISHORN, -S vb remove the horns from

DISHORSE vb dismount

DISHOUSE vb deprive of home

DISHPAN, -S n large pan for washing dishes, pots, etc

DISHRAG, -S n dishcloth

DISHWARE n tableware

DISHY, DISHIER, DISHIEST adj good-looking

DISINTER vb dig up

DISINURE vb render unaccustomed

DISJECT, -S vb break apart

DISJOIN, -S vb disconnect or become disconnected

DISJOINT vb take apart or come apart at the joints ▷ adj (of two sets) having no members in common

DISJUNCT adj not united or joined ▷ n one of the propositions or formulas in a disjunction

DISJUNE, -D, -S n breakfast ▷ vb breakfast

DISK, -ED, -ING, -S same as ▶ disc

DISKER, -S n person who breaks up earth with a type of farm implement

DISKETTE n floppy disk

DISKING ▶ disk

DISKLESS ▶ disk

DISKLIKE ▶ disk

DISKS ▶ disk

DISLEAF, -S vb remove a leaf or leaves from

DISLEAL archaic form of ▶ disloyal

DISLEAVE variant of ▶ disleaf

DISLIKE, -D, -S vb consider unpleasant or disagreeable ▷ n feeling of not liking something or someone

DISLIKEN vb render dissimilar to

DISLIKER ▶ dislike

DISLIKES ▶ dislike

DISLIMB, -S vb remove limbs from

DISLIMN, -S vb efface

DISLINK, -S vb disunite

DISLOAD, -S vb unload

DISLODGE vb remove (something) from a previously fixed position

DISLOIGN vb put at a distance

DISLOYAL adj not loyal, deserting one's allegiance

DISMAL, -ER adj gloomy

DISMALLY ▶ dismal

DISMALS pl n gloomy state of mind

DISMAN, -S vb remove men from

DISMASK, -S vb remove a mask from

DISMAST, -S vb break off the mast or masts of (a sailing vessel)

DISMAY, -ED, -S vb fill with alarm or sadness ▷ n alarm mixed with sadness

DISMAYD word used by Spenser meaning misshapen

DISMAYED ▶ dismay

DISMAYL, -S vb remove a coat of mail from

DISMAYS ▶ dismay

DISME, -S old form of ▶ dime

DISMISS vb remove (an employee) from a job ▷ sentence substitute order to end an activity or give permission to disperse

DISMODED adj no longer fashionable

DISMOUNT vb get off a horse or bicycle ▷ n act of dismounting

DISNEST, -S vb remove from a nest

DISOBEY, -S vb neglect or refuse to obey

DISODIUM n compound containing two sodium atoms

DISOMIC adj having an extra chromosome in the haploid state

DISOMY, DISOMIES ▶ disomic

DISORBED adj thrown out of orbit

DISORDER n state of untidiness and disorganization ▷ vb upset the order of

DISOWN, -ED, -S vb deny any connection with (someone)

DISOWNER ▶ disown

DISOWNS ▶ disown

DISPACE, -D, -S vb move or travel about

DISPARK, -S vb release

DISPART, -S vb separate

DISPATCH vb send off to a destination or to perform a task ▷ n official communication or report, sent in haste

DISPATHY obsolete spelling of ▸ **dyspathy**

DISPEACE n absence of peace

DISPEL, -S vb destroy or remove

DISPENCE same as ▸ **dispense**

DISPEND, -S vb spend

DISPENSE vb distribute in portions

DISPERSE vb scatter over a wide area ▷ adj of or consisting of the particles in a colloid or suspension

DISPIRIT vb make downhearted

DISPLACE vb move from the usual location

DISPLANT vb displace

DISPLAY, -S vb make visible or noticeable ▷ n displaying

DISPLE, -D, -S, DISPLING vb punish

DISPLODE obsolete word for ▸ **explode**

DISPLUME vb remove feathers from

DISPONE, -D, -S vb transfer ownership

DISPONEE n person whom something is disponed to

DISPONER ▸ **dispone**

DISPONES ▸ **dispone**

DISPONGE same as ▸ **dispunge**

DISPORT, -S vb indulge (oneself) in pleasure ▷ n amusement

DISPOSAL n getting rid of something

DISPOSE, -S vb place in a certain order

DISPOSED adj willing or eager

DISPOSER ▸ **dispose**

DISPOSES ▸ **dispose**

DISPOST, -S vb remove from a post

DISPRAD old form of ▸ **dispread**

DISPREAD vb spread out

DISPRED, -S old spelling of ▸ **dispread**

DISPRIZE vb scorn

DISPROOF n facts that disprove something

DISPROVE vb show (an assertion or claim) to be incorrect

DISPUNGE vb expunge

DISPURSE another word for ▸ **disburse**

DISPUTE, -D, -S n disagreement, argument ▷ vb argue about (something)

DISPUTER ▸ **dispute**

DISPUTES ▸ **dispute**

DISQUIET n feeling of anxiety ▷ vb make (someone) anxious ▷ adj uneasy or anxious

DISRANK, -S vb demote

DISRATE, -D, -S vb punish (an officer) by lowering in rank

DISROBE, -D, -S vb undress

DISROBER ▸ **disrobe**

DISROBES ▸ **disrobe**

DISROOT, -S vb uproot

DISRUPT, -S vb interrupt the progress of

DISS, -ED, -ES, -ING vb treat (a person) with contempt

DISSAVE, -D, -S vb spend savings

DISSAVER n person who dissaves

DISSAVES ▸ **dissave**

DISSEAT, -S vb unseat

DISSECT, -S vb cut something open to examine it

DISSED ▸ **diss**

DISSEISE vb deprive of seisin

DISSEIZE same as ▸ **disseise**

DISSENT, -S vb disagree ▷ n disagreement

DISSERT, -S vb give or make a dissertation; dissertate

DISSERVE vb do a disservice to

DISSES ▸ **diss**

DISSEVER vb break off or become broken off

DISSIGHT n eyesore

DISSING ▸ **diss**

DISSOLVE vb (cause to) become liquid ▷ n scene filmed or televised by dissolving

DISSUADE vb deter (someone) by persuasion from doing something

DISTAFF, -S, DISTAVES n rod on which wool etc is wound for spinning

DISTAIN, -S vb stain; tarnish

DISTAL adj (of a bone, limb, etc) situated farthest from the point of attachment

DISTALLY ▸ **distal**

DISTANCE n space between two points

DISTANT adj far apart

DISTASTE n dislike, disgust

DISTAVES ▸ **distaff**

DISTEND, -S vb (of part of the body) swell

DISTENT, -S adj bloated; swollen ▷ n breadth; distension

DISTHENE n bluish-green mineral

DISTICH, -S n unit of two verse lines

DISTIL, -S vb subject to or obtain by distillation

DISTILL, -S same as ▸ **distil**

DISTILS ▸ **distil**

DISTINCT adj not the same

DISTOME, -S n parasitic flatworm

DISTORT, -S vb misrepresent (the truth or facts)

DISTRACT vb draw the attention of (a person) away from something

DISTRAIL n trail made by aircraft flying through cloud

DISTRAIN vb seize (personal property) to enforce payment of a debt

DISTRAIT adj absent-minded or preoccupied

DISTRESS n extreme unhappiness ▷ vb upset badly

DISTRICT n area of land regarded as an administrative or geographical unit ▷ vb divide into districts

DISTRIX n splitting of the ends of hairs

DISTRUST vb regard as untrustworthy ▷ n feeling of suspicion or doubt

DISTUNE, -D, -S vb cause to be out of tune

DISTURB, -S vb intrude on

DISTYLE, -S n temple with two columns

DISULFID same as > **disulfide**

DISUNION ▸ **disunite**

DISUNITE vb cause disagreement among

DISUNITY n dissension or disagreement

DISUSAGE n disuse

DISUSE, -S, DISUSING vb stop using ▷ n state of being no longer used

DISUSED adj no longer used

DISUSES ▸ **disuse**

DISUSING ▸ **disuse**

DISVALUE vb belittle

DISVOUCH vb dissociate oneself from

DISYOKE, -D, -S vb unyoke

DIT, -S, -TED, -TING, -TIT vb stop something happening ▷ n short sound used in the spoken representation of telegraphic codes

DITA, -S n tropical shrub

DITAL, -S n key for raising the pitch of a lute string

DITAS ▸ **dita**

DITCH, -ED, -ES, -ING *n* narrow channel dug in the earth for drainage or irrigation ▹ *vb* abandon

DITCHER, -S ▸ **ditch**

DITCHES ▸ **ditch**

DITCHING ▸ **ditch**

DITE, -D, -S, DITING *vb* set down in writing

DITHECAL *adj* having two thecae

DITHEISM *n* belief in two equal gods

DITHEIST ▸ **ditheism**

DITHER, -ED, -S *vb* be uncertain or indecisive ▹ *n* state of indecision or agitation

DITHERER ▸ **dither**

DITHERS ▸ **dither**

DITHERY ▸ **dither**

DITHIOL, -S *n* chemical compound

DITING ▸ **dite**

DITOKOUS *adj* producing two eggs

DITONE, -S *n* interval of two tones

DITS ▸ **dit**

DITSY, DITSIER, DITSIEST *same as* ▸ **ditzy**

DITT, -S *same as* ▸ **dit**

DITTANY *n* aromatic plant

DITTAY, -S *n* accusation; charge

DITTED ▸ **dit**

DITTIED ▸ **ditty**

DITTIES ▸ **ditty**

DITTING ▸ **dit**

DITTIT ▸ **dit**

DITTO, -ED, -ING, -S *n* same ▹ *adv* in the same way ▹ *sentence substitute* used to avoid repeating or to confirm agreement with an immediately preceding sentence ▹ *vb* copy

DITTS ▸ **ditt**

DITTY, DITTIED, DITTIES, -ING *vb* set to music ▹ *n* short simple poem or song

DITZ, -ES *n* silly scatterbrained person

DITZY, DITZIER, DITZIEST *adj* silly and scatterbrained

DIURESIS, DIURESES *n* excretion of an unusually large quantity of urine

DIURETIC *n* drug that increases the flow of urine ▹ *adj* acting to increase the flow of urine

DIURNAL, -S *adj* happening during the day or daily ▹ *n* service book containing all the canonical hours except matins

DIURON, -S *n* type of herbicide

DIV, -S *n* dividend

DIVA, -S *n* distinguished female singer

DIVAGATE *vb* digress or wander

DIVALENT *n* element that can unite with two atoms ▹ *adj* having two valencies or a valency of two

DIVAN, -S *n* low backless bed

DIVAS ▸ **diva**

DIVE, -D, -S *vb* plunge headfirst into water ▹ *n* diving

DIVEBOMB *vb* bomb while making steep dives

DIVED ▸ **dive**

DIVER *n* person who works or explores underwater

DIVERGE, -D, -S *vb* separate and go in different directions

DIVERS *adj* various ▹ *determiner* various

DIVERSE, -D, -S *vb* turn away ▹ *adj* having variety, assorted

DIVERSLY ▸ **divers**

DIVERT, -ED, -S *vb* change the direction of

DIVERTER ▸ **divert**

DIVERTS ▸ **divert**

DIVES ▸ **dive**

DIVEST, -ED, -S *vb* strip (of clothes)

DIVI, -ED, -S *alternative spelling of* ▸ **divvy**

DIVIDANT *adj* distinct

DIVIDE, -S, DIVIDING *vb* separate into parts ▹ *n* division, split

DIVIDED *adj* split

DIVIDEND *n* sum of money representing part of the profit made, paid by a company to its shareholders

DIVIDER *n* screen used to divide a room into separate areas

DIVIDERS *pl n* compasses with two pointed arms, used for measuring or dividing lines

DIVIDES ▸ **divide**

DIVIDING ▸ **divide**

DIVIDIVI *n* tropical tree

DIVIDUAL *adj* divisible

DIVIED ▸ **divi**

DIVINE, -D, -S, -ST, DIVINING *adj* of God or a god ▹ *vb* discover (something) by intuition or guessing ▹ *n* priest who is learned in theology

DIVINELY ▸ **divine**

DIVINER, -S ▸ **divine**

DIVINES ▸ **divine**

DIVINEST ▸ **divine**

DIVING, -S ▸ **dive**

DIVINIFY *vb* give divine status to

DIVINING ▸ **divine**

DIVINISE *same as* ▸ **divinize**

DIVINITY *n* study of religion

DIVINIZE *vb* make divine

DIVIS ▸ **divi**

DIVISIM *adv* separately

DIVISION *n* dividing, sharing out

DIVISIVE *adj* tending to cause disagreement

DIVISOR, -S *n* number to be divided into another number

DIVNA *vb* do not

DIVO, -S *n* male diva

DIVORCE, -D, -S *n* legal ending of a marriage ▹ *vb* legally end one's marriage (to)

DIVORCEE *n* person who is divorced

DIVORCER ▸ **divorce**

DIVORCES ▸ **divorce**

DIVOS ▸ **divo**

DIVOT, -S *n* small piece of turf

DIVS ▸ **div**

DIVULGE, -D, -S *vb* make known, disclose

DIVULGER ▸ **divulge**

DIVULGES ▸ **divulge**

DIVULSE, -D, -S *vb* tear apart

DIVVY, DIVVIED, DIVVIER, DIVVIES, DIVVIEST, -ING *vb* divide and share ▹ *adj* dialect word for stupid

DIVVYING *alternative present participle of* ▸ **divvy**

DIWAN, -S *same as* ▸ **dewan**

DIXI *interj* I have spoken

DIXIE, -S *n* large metal pot for cooking, brewing tea, etc

DIXIT, -S *n* statement

DIXY *same as* ▸ **dixie**

DIYA, -S *n* small oil lamp, usu made from clay

DIZAIN, -S *n* ten-line poem

DIZEN, -ED, -ING, -S *archaic word for* ▸ **bedizen**

DIZYGOUS *another word for* > **dizygotic**

DIZZARD, -S *n* dunce

DIZZIED ▸ **dizzy**

DIZZIER ▸ **dizzy**

DIZZIES ▸ **dizzy**

DIZZIEST ▸ **dizzy**

DIZZILY ▸ **dizzy**

DIZZY, DIZZIED, DIZZIER, DIZZIES, DIZZIEST, -ING *adj* having or causing a whirling sensation ▹ *vb* make dizzy

DJEBEL, -S variant spelling of ▸jebel

DJELLABA n kind of loose cloak with a hood, worn by men esp in North Africa and the Middle East

DJEMBE, -S n W African drum

DJIBBA, -S same as ▸jubbah

DJIBBAH, -S same as ▸jubbah

DJIBBAS ▸djibba

DJIN, -S same as ▸jinn

DJINNI, DJINN, DJINNS same as ▸jinni

DJINNY same as ▸jinni

DJINS ▸djin

DO, DID, -EN, -ES, -EST, -ETH, -ING, -NE, -S vb perform or complete (a deed or action) ▷ n party, celebration

DOAB, -S n alluvial land between two converging rivers

DOABLE adj capable of being done

DOABS ▸doab

DOAT, -ED, -S same as ▸dote

DOATER, -S ▸doat

DOATING, -S ▸doat

DOATS ▸doat

DOB, -BED, -BING, -S vb as in **dob in** inform against or report

DOBBER, -S n informant or traitor

DOBBIE same as ▸dobby

DOBBIES ▸dobby

DOBBIN, -S n name for a horse

DOBBING ▸dob

DOBBINS ▸dobbin

DOBBY, DOBBIES n attachment to a loom, used in weaving small figures

DOBCHICK same as ▸dabchick

DOBE, -S same as ▸adobe

DOBHASH n interpreter

DOBLA, -S n medieval Spanish gold coin, probably worth 20 maravedis

DOBLON, -ES, -S variant spelling of ▸doubloon

DOBRA, -S n standard monetary unit of São Tomé e Principe

DOBRO, -S n type of acoustic guitar

DOBS ▸dob

DOBSON, -S n larva of a dobsonfly

DOC, -S same as ▸doctor

DOCENT, -S n voluntary worker who acts as a guide

DOCETIC adj believing that the humanity of Christ was apparent and not real

DOCHMIAC ▸dochmius

DOCHMIUS, DOCHMII n five-syllable foot

DOCHT ▸dow

DOCIBLE adj easily tamed

DOCILE, -R, -ST adj (of a person or animal) easily controlled

DOCILELY ▸docile

DOCILER ▸docile

DOCILEST ▸docile

DOCILITY ▸docile

DOCIMASY n close examination

DOCK, -ED, -S n enclosed area of water where ships are loaded, unloaded, or repaired ▷ vb bring or be brought into dock

DOCKAGE, -S n charge levied upon a vessel for using a dock

DOCKED ▸dock

DOCKEN, -S n something of no value or importance

DOCKER, -S n person employed to load and unload ships

DOCKET, -ED, -S n label on a delivery, stating contents, delivery instructions, etc ▷ vb fix a docket to (a package or other delivery)

DOCKHAND n dock labourer

DOCKING, -S ▸dock

DOCKISE, -D, -S same as ▸dockize

DOCKIZE, -D, -S vb convert into docks

DOCKLAND n area around the docks

DOCKS ▸dock

DOCKSIDE n area next to dock

DOCKYARD n place where ships are built or repaired

DOCO, -S n documentary

DOCQUET, -S same as ▸docket

DOCS ▸doc

DOCTOR, -ED, -S n person licensed to practise medicine ▷ vb alter in order to deceive

DOCTORAL ▸doctor

DOCTORED ▸doctor

DOCTORLY ▸doctor

DOCTORS ▸doctor

DOCTRESS same as >doctoress

DOCTRINE n body of teachings of a religious, political, or philosophical group

DOCU, -S n documentary film

DOCUMENT n piece of paper providing an official record of something ▷ vb record or report (something) in detail

DOCUS ▸docu

DOCUSOAP n reality television programme in the style of a documentary

DOD, -DED, -DING, -S vb clip

DODDARD, -S adj archaic word for missing branches; rotten ▷ n tree missing its top branches through rot

DODDED ▸dod

DODDER, -ED, -S vb move unsteadily ▷ n type of rootless parasitic plant

DODDERER ▸dodder

DODDERS ▸dodder

DODDERY ▸dodder

DODDIER ▸doddy

DODDIES ▸doddy

DODDIEST ▸doddy

DODDING ▸dod

DODDLE, -S n something easily accomplished

DODDY, DODDIER, DODDIES, DODDIEST n bad mood ▷ adj sulky

DODGE, -D, -S vb avoid (a blow, being seen, etc) by moving suddenly ▷ n cunning or deceitful trick

DODGEM, -S n bumper car

DODGER, -S n person who evades a responsibility or duty

DODGERY n deception

DODGES ▸dodge

DODGIER ▸dodgy

DODGIEST ▸dodgy

DODGING, -S ▸dodge

DODGY, DODGIER, DODGIEST adj dangerous, risky

DODKIN, -S n coin of little value

DODMAN, -S n snail

DODO, -ES, -S n large flightless extinct bird

DODOISM, -S ▸dodo

DODOS ▸dodo

DODS ▸dod

DOE n female deer, hare, or rabbit

DOEK, -S n square of cloth worn on the head by some African women

DOEN ▸do

DOER, -S n active or energetic person

DOES ▸do

DOESKIN, -S n skin of a deer, lamb, or sheep

D

DOEST ▸ do

DOETH ▸ do

DOF informal South African word for ▸ stupid

DOFF, -ED, -ING, -S vb take off or lift (one's hat) in polite greeting

DOFFER, -S ▸ doff

DOFFING ▸ doff

DOFFS ▸ doff

DOG, -S n domesticated four-legged mammal ▷ vb follow (someone) closely

DOGATE, -S n office of doge

DOGBANE, -S n N American plant

DOGBERRY n any of certain plants that have berry-like fruits

DOGBOLT, -S n bolt on a cannon

DOGCART, -S n light horse-drawn two-wheeled cart

DOGDOM, -S n world of dogs

DOGE, -S n (formerly) chief magistrate of Venice or Genoa

DOGEAR, -ED, -S vb fold down the corner of (a page) ▷ n folded-down corner of a page

DOGEATE, -S n office of doge

DOGEDOM, -S n domain of a doge

DOGES ▸ doge

DOGESHIP ▸ doge

DOGEY, -S same as ▸ dogie

DOGFACE, -S n WW2 US soldier

DOGFIGHT vb fight in confused way ▷ n close-quarters combat between fighter aircraft

DOGFISH n small shark

DOGFOOD, -S n food for a dog

DOGFOX, -ES n male fox

DOGGED, -ER adj stubbornly determined

DOGGEDLY ▸ dogged

DOGGER, -S n Dutch fishing vessel with two masts

DOGGEREL ▸ doggerel

DOGGERY n surly behaviour

DOGGESS n female dog

DOGGIE same as ▸ doggy

DOGGIER ▸ doggy

DOGGIES ▸ doggy

DOGGIEST ▸ doggy

DOGGING, -S ▸ dog

DOGGISH adj of or like a dog

DOGGO adv in hiding and keeping quiet

DOGGONE, -D, -R, -S interj exclamation of annoyance, disappointment, etc ▷ vb damn ▷ adj damnedest

DOGGREL, -S same as ▸ doggerel

DOGGY, DOGGIER, DOGGIES, DOGGIEST n child's word for a dog ▷ adj of or like a dog

DOGHOLE, -S n squalid dwelling place

DOGHOUSE n kennel

DOGIE, -S n motherless calf

DOGLEG, -S n sharp bend ▷ vb go off at an angle ▷ adj of or with the shape of a dogleg

DOGLIKE ▸ dog

DOGMA, -S, -TA n doctrine or system of doctrines proclaimed by authority as true

DOGMAN, DOGMEN n person who directs a crane whilst riding on an object being lifted by it

DOGMAS ▸ dogma

DOGMATA ▸ dogma

DOGMATIC adj habitually stating one's opinions forcefully or arrogantly

DOGMEN ▸ dogman

DOGNAP, -ED, -S vb carry off and hold (a dog), usually for ransom

DOGNAPER ▸ dognap

DOGNAPS ▸ dognap

DOGPILE, -S n pile of bodies formed by people jumping on top of each other

DOGREL, -S n doggerel

DOGS ▸ dog

DOGSBODY n person who carries out boring tasks for others ▷ vb act as a dogsbody

DOGSHIP, -S n condition of being a dog

DOGSHOW, -S n competition in which dogs are judged

DOGSKIN, -S n leather from a dog's skin

DOGSLED, -S n sleigh drawn by dogs

DOGSLEEP n feigned sleep

DOGSTAIL n type of grass

DOGTAIL, -S same as ▸ dogstail

DOGTOOTH, DOGTEETH n medieval carved ornament

DOGTOWN, -S n community of prairie dogs

DOGTROT, -S n gently paced trot

DOGVANE, -S n light windvane mounted on the side of a vessel

DOGWATCH n either of two watches aboard ship, from four to six pm or from six to eight pm

DOGWOOD, -S n type of tree or shrub

DOGY same as ▸ dogie

DOH, -S n in tonic sol-fa, the first degree of any major scale ▷ interj exclamation of annoyance when something goes wrong

This is one of the very useful short words denoting a note of the musical scale.

DOHYO, -S n sumo wrestling ring

DOILED same as ▸ doilt

DOILIED adj having a doily

DOILIES ▸ doily

DOILT, -ER, -EST adj foolish

DOILY, DOILIES n decorative lacy paper mat, laid on a plate

DOING ▸ do

DOINGS pl n deeds or actions

DOIT, -S n former small copper coin of the Netherlands

DOITED adj foolish or childish, as from senility

DOITIT same as ▸ doited

DOITKIN, -S same as ▸ doit

DOITS ▸ doit

DOJO, -S n room or hall for the practice of martial arts

DOL, -S n unit of pain intensity, as measured by dolorimetry

DOLCE, -S, DOLCI n dessert ▷ adv (to be performed) gently and sweetly

DOLCETTO n variety of grape

DOLCI ▸ dolce

DOLDRUMS pl n unhappy state of mind

DOLE, -D, -S, DOLING n money received from the state while unemployed ▷ vb distribute in small quantities

DOLEFUL adj dreary, unhappy

DOLENT adj sad

DOLENTE adv (to be performed) in a sorrowful manner

DOLERITE n dark igneous rock such as augite

DOLES ▸ dole

DOLESOME same as ▸ doleful

DOLIA ▸ dolium

DOLICHOS n tropical vine

DOLINA, -S same as ▸ **doline**

DOLINE, -S n depression of the ground surface formed in limestone regions

DOLING ▸ **dole**

DOLIUM, DOLIA n genus of molluscs

DOLL, -ED, -ING, -S n small model of a human being, used as a toy ▸ vb as in **doll up** dress up

DOLLAR, -S n standard monetary unit of many countries

DOLLARED adj flagged with a dollar sign

DOLLARS ▸ **dollar**

DOLLDOM, -S ▸ **doll**

DOLLED ▸ **doll**

DOLLHOOD ▸ **doll**

DOLLIED ▸ **dolly**

DOLLIER, -S n person who operates a dolly

DOLLIES ▸ **dolly**

DOLLING ▸ **doll**

DOLLISH ▸ **doll**

DOLLOP, -ED, -S n lump (of food) ▸ vb serve out (food)

DOLLS ▸ **doll**

DOLLY, DOLLIED, DOLLIES, -ING adj attractive and unintelligent ▸ n wheeled support for a camera ▸ vb wheel a camera on a dolly

DOLMA, -DES, -S n vine leaf stuffed with a filling of meat and rice

DOLMAN, -S n long Turkish outer robe

DOLMAS ▸ **dolma**

DOLMEN, -S n prehistoric monument

DOLMENIC ▸ **dolmen**

DOLMENS ▸ **dolmen**

DOLOMITE n mineral consisting of calcium magnesium carbonate

DOLOR, -S same as ▸ **dolour**

DOLOROSO adv (to be performed) in a sorrowful manner

DOLOROUS adj sad, mournful

DOLORS ▸ **dolor**

DOLOS, -SE n knucklebone of a sheep, buck, etc, used esp by diviners

DOLOUR, -S n grief or sorrow

DOLPHIN, -S n sea mammal of the whale family .

DOLS ▸ **dol**

DOLT, -S n stupid person

DOLTISH ▸ **dolt**

DOLTS ▸ **dolt**

DOM, -S n title given to various monks and to certain of the canons regular

DOMAIN, -S n field of knowledge or activity

DOMAINAL ▸ **domain**

DOMAINE, -S n French estate

DOMAINS ▸ **domain**

DOMAL adj of a house

DOMANIAL ▸ **domain**

DOMATIUM, DOMATIA n plant cavity inhabited by commensal insects or mites or, occasionally, microorganisms

DOME, -D, -S, DOMING n rounded roof built on a circular base ▸ vb cover with or as if with a dome

DOMELIKE ▸ **dome**

DOMES ▸ **dome**

DOMESDAY same as ▸ **doomsday**

DOMESTIC adj of one's own country or a specific country ▸ n person whose job is to do housework in someone else's house

DOMETT, -S n wool and cotton cloth

DOMIC adj dome-shaped

DOMICAL ▸ **dome**

DOMICIL, -S same as ▸ **domicile**

DOMICILE n place where one lives ▸ vb establish or be established in a dwelling place

DOMICILS ▸ **domicil**

DOMIER ▸ **domy**

DOMIEST ▸ **domy**

DOMINANT adj having authority or influence ▸ n dominant allele or character

DOMINATE vb control or govern

DOMINE, -S n clergyman or clergywoman

DOMINEE, -S n minister of the Dutch Reformed Church

DOMINEER vb act with arrogance or tyranny

DOMINEES ▸ **dominee**

DOMINES ▸ **domine**

DOMING ▸ **dome**

DOMINICK n breed of chicken

DOMINIE, -S n minister, clergyman or clergywoman: also used as a term of address

DOMINION same as ▸ **dominium**

DOMINIUM n ownership or right to possession of property, esp realty

DOMINO, -S n small rectangular block marked with dots, used in dominoes

DOMINOES n game in which dominoes with matching halves are laid together

DOMINOS ▸ **domino**

DOMOIC adj as in **domoic acid** kind of amino acid

DOMS ▸ **dom**

DOMY, DOMIER, DOMIEST adj having a dome or domes

DON, -NED, -NING, -S vb put on (clothing) ▸ n member of the teaching staff at a university or college

DONA, -S n Spanish woman

DONAH, -S n woman

DONAIR, -S same as ▸ **doner**

DONARY, DONARIES n thing given for holy use

DONAS ▸ **dona**

DONATARY n recipient

DONATE, -D, -S, DONATING vb give, esp to a charity or organization

DONATION n donating

DONATISM n doctrine and beliefs relating to an early Christian sect

DONATIVE n gift or donation ▸ adj of or like a donation

DONATOR, -S ▸ **donate**

DONATORY n recipient

DONDER, -ED, -S vb beat (someone) up ▸ n wretch

DONE ▸ **do**

DONEE, -S n person who receives a gift

DONEGAL, -S n type of tweed

DONENESS n extent to which something is cooked

DONER, -S n kebab of grilled meat served in pitta bread

DONG, -ED, -ING, -S n deep reverberating sound of a large bell ▸ vb (of a bell) to make a deep reverberating sound

DONGA, -S n steep-sided gully created by soil erosion

DONGED ▸ **dong**

DONGING ▸ **dong**

DONGLE, -S n electronic device

DONGOLA, -S n leather tanned using a particular method

DONGS ▸ **dong**

DONING, -S n act of giving blood

DONJON, -S n heavily fortified central tower of a castle

DONKEY, -S n long-eared member of the horse family

DONKO, -S n tearoom or cafeteria in a factory, wharf area, etc

DONNA, -S n Italian woman

DONNARD same as ▶ donnert

DONNART same as ▶ donnert

DONNAS ▶ donna

DONNAT, -S n lazy person

DONNE, -S same as ▶ donnee

DONNED ▶ don

DONNEE, -S n subject or theme

DONNERD adj stunned

DONNERED same as ▶ donnert

DONNERT adj stunned

DONNES ▶ donne

DONNIES ▶ donny

DONNIKER same as > donnicker

DONNING ▶ don

DONNISH adj serious and academic

DONNISM, -S n loftiness

DONNOT, -S n lazy person

DONNY, DONNIES same as ▶ danny

DONOR, -S n person who gives blood or organs for medical use

DONS ▶ don

DONSHIP, -S n state or condition of being a don

DONSIE, -R, -ST adj rather unwell

DONSY same as ▶ donsie

DONUT, -S, -TED same as ▶ doughnut

DONZEL, -S n man of high birth

DOO, -S a Scot word for ▶ dove

DOOB, -S n type of Indian grass

DOOBIE, -S same as ▶ doob

DOOBREY, -S n thingumabob

DOOBRIE, -S same as ▶ doobrey

DOOBRY n thing whose name is unknown or forgotten

DOOBS ▶ doob

DOOCE, -D, -S, DOOCING vb dismiss (an employee) because of comments they have posted on the internet

DOOCOT, -S n dovecote

DOODAD, -S same as ▶ doodah

DOODAH, -S n unnamed thing

DOODIES ▶ doody

DOODLE, -D, -S, DOODLING vb scribble or draw aimlessly ▷ n shape or picture drawn aimlessly

DOODLER, -S ▶ doodle

DOODLES ▶ doodle

DOODLING ▶ doodle

DOODOO, -S n excrement

DOODY, DOODIES same as ▶ doodoo

DOOFER, -S n thingamajig

DOOFUS, -ES n slow-witted or stupid person

DOOK, -ED, -ING, -S n wooden plug driven into a wall to hold a nail, screw, etc ▷ vb dip or plunge

DOOKET, -S n dovecote

DOOKING ▶ dook

DOOKS ▶ dook

DOOL, -S n boundary marker

DOOLALLY adj out of one's mind

DOOLAN, -S n New Zealand informal term for a Roman Catholic

DOOLE, -S same as ▶ dool

DOOLEE, -S same as ▶ doolie

DOOLES ▶ doole

DOOLIE, -S n enclosed couch on poles for carrying passengers

DOOLS ▶ dool

DOOLY same as ▶ doolie

DOOM, -ED, -ING, -S n death or a terrible fate ▷ vb destine or condemn to death or a terrible fate

DOOMFUL ▶ doom

DOOMIER ▶ doomy

DOOMIEST ▶ doomy

DOOMILY ▶ doomy

DOOMING ▶ doom

DOOMS ▶ doom

DOOMSDAY n day on which the Last Judgment will occur

DOOMSMAN, DOOMSMEN n pessimist

DOOMSTER n person habitually given to predictions of impending disaster or doom

DOOMY, DOOMIER, DOOMIEST adj despondent or pessimistic

DOON same as ▶ down

DOONA, -S n large quilt used as a bed cover

DOOR, -S n hinged or sliding panel for closing the entrance to a building, room, etc

DOORBELL n device for visitors to announce presence at a door

DOORCASE same as > doorframe

DOORED adj having a door

DOORJAMB n vertical post forming one side of a door frame

DOORKNOB n knob for opening and closing a door

DOORLESS ▶ door

DOORLIKE adj like a door

DOORMAN, DOORMEN n man employed to be on duty at the entrance to a large public building

DOORMAT, -S n mat for wiping dirt from shoes before going indoors

DOORMEN ▶ doorman

DOORN, -S n thorn

DOORNAIL n as in dead as a doornail dead beyond any doubt

DOORNS ▶ doorn

DOORPOST same as ▶ doorjamb

DOORS ▶ door

DOORSILL n horizontal member of wood, stone, etc, forming the bottom of a doorframe

DOORSMAN, DOORSMEN n doorkeeper

DOORSTEP n step in front of a door

DOORSTOP n object which prevents a door from closing or striking a wall

DOORWAY, -S n opening into a building or room

DOORYARD n yard in front of the front or back door of a house

DOOS, -ES ▶ doo

DOOSRA, -S n type of delivery in cricket

DOOWOP, -S n style of singing in harmony

DOOZER, -S same as ▶ doozy

DOOZIE, -S same as ▶ doozy

DOOZY n something excellent

DOP, -PED, -S n small drink ▷ vb fail to reach the required standard in (an examination, course, etc)

DOPA, -S n precursor to dopamine

DOPAMINE n chemical found in the brain that acts as a neurotransmitter

DOPANT, -S n element or compound used to produce an effect in a semiconductor

DOPAS ▶ dopa

DOPATTA, -S n headscarf

DOPE, -D, -S, -ST n additive used to improve the properties of something ▷ vb apply a dopant ▷ adj excellent

DOPER, -S n person who administers dope

DOPES ▶ dope

DOPEST ▶ dope

DOPESTER n person who makes predictions, esp in sport or politics

DOPEY, DOPIER, DOPIEST adj half-asleep, drowsy

DOPIAZA, -S n Indian meat or fish dish cooked in onion sauce

DOPIER ▶ dopey

DOPIEST ▶ dopey

DOPILY ▶ dopey

DOPINESS ▶ dopey

DOPING, -S ▶ dope

DOPPED ▶ dop

DOPPER, -S n member of an Afrikaner church which practises a strict Calvinism

DOPPIE, -S n cartridge case

DOPPING, -S ▶ dop

DOPPIO, -S n double measure, esp of espresso coffee

DOPS ▶ dop

DOPY same as ▶ dopey

DOR, -RED, -RING, -S n European dung beetle ▷ vb mock

DORAD, -S n South American river fish

DORADO, -S n large marine percoid fish

DORADS ▶ dorad

DORB, -S same as ▶ dorba

DORBA, -S n stupid, inept, or clumsy person

DORBS ▶ dorb

DORBUG, -S n type of beetle

DORE, -S n walleye fish

DOREE, -S n walleye fish

DORES ▶ dore

DORHAWK, -S n nightjar

DORIC adj rustic

DORIDOID n shell-less mollusc

DORIES ▶ dory

DORIS n woman

DORISE, -D, -S, DORISING same as ▶ dorize

DORIZE, -D, -S, DORIZING vb become Doric

DORK, -S n stupid person

DORKIER ▶ dorky

DORKIEST ▶ dorky

DORKISH adj stupid or contemptible

DORKS ▶ dork

DORKY, DORKIER, DORKIEST ▶ dork

DORLACH, -S n quiver of arrows

DORM, -S same as > dormitory

DORMANCY ▶ dormant

DORMANT, -S n supporting beam ▷ adj temporarily quiet, inactive, or not being used

DORMER, -S n window that sticks out from a sloping roof

DORMERED adj having dormer windows

DORMERS ▶ dormer

DORMICE ▶ dormouse

DORMIE adj (in golf) leading by as many holes as there are left

DORMIENT adj dormant

DORMIN, -S n hormone found in plants

DORMOUSE, DORMICE n small mouselike rodent with a furry tail

DORMS ▶ dorm

DORMY same as ▶ dormie

DORNECK, -S same as ▶ dornick

DORNICK, -S n heavy damask cloth

DORNOCK, -S same as ▶ dornick

DORP, -S n small town

DORPER, -S n breed of sheep

DORPS ▶ dorp

DORR, -S same as ▶ dor

DORRED ▶ dor

DORRING ▶ dor

DORRS ▶ dorr

DORS ▶ dor

DORSA ▶ dorsum

DORSAD adj towards the back or dorsal aspect

DORSAL, -S adj of or on the back ▷ n dorsal fin

DORSALLY ▶ dorsal

DORSALS ▶ dorsal

DORSE, -S n type of small fish

DORSEL, -S another word for ▶ dossal

DORSER, -S n hanging tapestry

DORSES ▶ dorse

DORSUM, DORSA n the back

DORT, -ED, -ING, -S vb sulk

DORTER, -S n dormitory

DORTIER ▶ dorty

DORTIEST ▶ dorty

DORTING ▶ dort

DORTOUR, -S same as ▶ dorter

DORTS ▶ dort

DORTY, DORTIER, DORTIEST adj haughty, or sullen

DORY, DORIES n spiny-finned edible sea fish

DORYMAN, DORYMEN n person who fishes from a small boat called a dory

DOS ▶ do

DOSA, -I, -S n Indian pancake made from rice flour

DOSAGE, -S same as ▶ dose

DOSAI ▶ dosa

DOSAS ▶ dosa

DOSE, -D, -S, DOSING n specific quantity of a medicine taken at one time ▷ vb give a dose to

DOSEH, -S n former Egyptian religious ceremony

DOSER, -S ▶ dose

DOSES ▶ dose

DOSH, -ES n money

DOSHA, -S n (in Hinduism) any of the three energies believed to be in the body

DOSHES ▶ dosh

DOSING ▶ dose

DOSOLOGY same as > dosiology

DOSS, -ED, -ES, -ING vb sleep, esp in a dosshouse ▷ n bed, esp in a dosshouse

DOSSAL, -S n ornamental hanging used in churches

DOSSED ▶ doss

DOSSEL, -S same as ▶ dossal

DOSSER, -S n bag or basket for carrying objects on the back

DOSSERET n stone above column supporting an arch

DOSSERS ▶ dosser

DOSSES ▶ doss

DOSSIER, -S n collection of documents about a subject or person

DOSSIL, -S n lint for dressing wound

DOSSING ▶ doss

DOST a singular form of the present tense (indicative mood) of ▶ do

DOT, -S, -TED, -TING n small round mark ▷ vb mark with a dot

DOTAGE, -S n weakness as a result of old age

DOTAL adj of a dowry

DOTANT, -S another word for ▶ dotard

DOTARD, -S n person who is feeble-minded through old age

DOTARDLY adj like a dotard

DOTARDS ▶ dotard

DOTATION n act of giving a dowry

DOTCOM, -S n company that does most of its business on the internet

DOTE, -D, -S vb love to an excessive or foolish degree

DOTER, -S ▶ dote

DOTES ▶ dote

DOTH a singular form of the present tense of ▶ do

DOTIER ▶ doty

DOTIEST ▶ doty

DOTING, -S ▶ dote

DOTINGLY ▶ dote

DOTINGS ▶ doting

DOTISH adj foolish

DOTS ▶ dot

DOTTED ▶ dot

DOTTEL, -S same as ▶ dottle

DOTTER, -S ▶ dot

DOTTEREL n rare kind of plover

DOTTERS ▶ dotter

DOTTIER ▶ dotty

DOTTIEST ▶ dotty

DOTTILY ▶ dotty

DOTTING ▶ dot

DOTTLE, -R, -S, -ST n tobacco left in a pipe after smoking ▷ adj relating to dottle

DOTTLED adj foolish

DOTTLER ▶ dottle

DOTTLES ▶ dottle

DOTTLEST ▶ dottle

DOTTREL, -S same as ▶ dotterel

DOTTY, DOTTIER, DOTTIEST adj rather eccentric

DOTY, DOTIER, DOTIEST adj (of wood) rotten

DOUANE, -S n customs house

DOUANIER n customs officer

This is a French word for a customs official; it's not easy to see in play, but its combination of common letters makes it one of the 8-letter bonus words that come up most often.

DOUAR, -S same as ▶ duar

DOUBLE, -D, -S, DOUBLING adj as much again in number, amount, size, etc ▷ adv twice over ▷ n twice the number, amount, size, etc ▷ vb make or become twice as much or as many

DOUBLER, -S ▶ double

DOUBLES ▶ double

DOUBLET, -S n man's close-fitting jacket, with or without sleeves

DOUBLING ▶ double

DOUBLOON n former Spanish gold coin

DOUBLURE n decorative lining of vellum or leather, etc, on the inside of a book cover

DOUBLY adv in a greater degree, quantity, or measure

DOUBT, -ED, -ING, -S n uncertainty about the truth, facts, or existence of something ▷ vb question the truth of

DOUBTER, -S ▶ doubt

DOUBTFUL adj unlikely ▷ n person who is undecided or uncertain about an issue

DOUBTING ▶ doubt

DOUBTS ▶ doubt

DOUC, -S n Old World monkey

DOUCE, -R, -ST adj quiet

DOUCELY ▶ douce

DOUCER ▶ douce

DOUCEST ▶ douce

DOUCET, -S n former flute-like instrument

DOUCEUR, -S n gratuity, tip, or bribe

DOUCHE, -D, -S n stream of water onto or into the body ▷ vb cleanse or treat by means of a douche

DOUCHING n act of douching

DOUCINE, -S n type of moulding for a cornice

DOUCS ▶ douc

DOUGH, -S n thick mixture used for making bread etc

DOUGHBOY n infantryman, esp in World War I

DOUGHIER ▶ doughy

DOUGHNUT n small cake of sweetened dough fried in deep fat ▷ vb surround a speaker to give the impression that Parliament is crowded

DOUGHS ▶ dough

DOUGHT ▶ dow

DOUGHTY adj brave and determined

DOUGHY, DOUGHIER adj resembling dough in consistency, colour, etc

DOUK, -ED, -ING, -S same as ▶ dook

DOULA, -S n woman who supports families during pregnancy and childbirth

DOULEIA, -S same as ▶ dulia

This word refers to the inferior veneration accorded to saints and angels, as distinct from **latria**, the veneration accorded to God alone, and is another of the few 7-letter words that use all five vowels. It's surprising how often you want to do this!

DOUM, -S n as in doum palm variety of palm tree

DOUMA, -S same as ▶ duma

DOUMS ▶ doum

DOUN same as ▶ down

DOUP, -S n bottom

DOUPIONI n type of fabric

DOUPS ▶ doup

DOUR, -ER, -EST adj sullen and unfriendly

DOURA, -S same as ▶ durra

DOURAH, -S same as ▶ durra

DOURAS ▶ doura

DOURER ▶ dour

DOUREST ▶ dour

DOURINE, -S n infectious disease of horses

DOURLY ▶ dour

DOURNESS ▶ dour

DOUSE, -D, -S, DOUSING vb drench with water or other liquid ▷ n immersion

DOUSER, -S ▶ douse

DOUSES ▶ douse

DOUSING ▶ douse

DOUT, -ED, -ING, -S vb extinguish

DOUTER, -S ▶ dout

DOUTING ▶ dout

DOUTS ▶ dout

DOUX adj sweet

DOUZEPER n distinguished person

DOVE, -D, -S, DOVING vb be semi-conscious ▷ n bird with a heavy body, small head, and short legs

DOVECOT, -S same as ▶ dovecote

DOVECOTE n structure for housing pigeons

DOVECOTS ▶ dovecot

DOVED ▶ dove

DOVEISH adj dovelike

DOVEKEY, -S same as ▶ dovekie

DOVEKIE, -S n small short-billed auk

DOVELET, -S n small dove

DOVELIKE ▶ dove

DOVEN, -ED, -ING, -S vb pray

DOVER, -ED, -ING, -S vb doze ▷ n doze

DOVES ▶ dove

DOVETAIL n joint containing wedge-shaped tenons ▷ vb fit together neatly

DOVIE, -R, -ST Scots word for ▶ stupid

DOVING ▶ dove

DOVISH, -LY ▸ dove

DOW, DOCHT, DOUGHT, -ED, -ING, -S vb archaic word meaning be of worth

DOWABLE adj capable of being endowed

DOWAGER, -S n widow possessing property or a title obtained from her husband

DOWAR, -S same as ▸ duar

DOWD, -S n person who wears unfashionable clothes

DOWDIER ▸ dowdy

DOWDIES ▸ dowdy

DOWDIEST ▸ dowdy

DOWDILY ▸ dowdy

DOWDS ▸ dowd

DOWDY, DOWDIER, DOWDIES, DOWDIEST adj dull and old-fashioned ▷ n dowdy person

DOWDYISH ▸ dowdy

DOWDYISM ▸ dowdy

DOWED ▸ dow

DOWEL, -ED, -LED, -S n wooden or metal peg used as a fastener ▷ vb join pieces of wood using dowels

DOWELING n joining of two pieces of wood using dowels

DOWELLED ▸ dowel

DOWELS ▸ dowel

DOWER, -ED, -ING, -S n life interest in a part of her husband's estate allotted to a widow by law ▷ vb endow

DOWERIES ▸ dowery

DOWERING ▸ dower

DOWERS ▸ dower

DOWERY, DOWERIES same as ▸ dowry

DOWF adj dull; listless

DOWFNESS ▸ dowf

DOWIE, -R, -ST adj dull and dreary

DOWING ▸ dow

DOWL, -S n fluff

DOWLAS, -ES n coarse fabric

DOWLE, -S same as ▸ dowl

DOWLIER ▸ dowly

DOWLIEST ▸ dowly

DOWLNE, -S n obsolete word meaning down (feathers)

DOWLNEY ▸ dowlne

DOWLS ▸ dowl

DOWLY, DOWLIER, DOWLIEST adj dull

DOWN, -ED, -ING adv indicating movement to or position in a lower place ▷ adj unhappy ▷ vb drink quickly ▷ n soft fine feathers

DOWNA obsolete Scots form of ▸ cannot

DOWNBEAT adj gloomy ▷ n first beat of a bar

DOWNBOW, -S n (in music) a downward stroke of the bow across the strings

DOWNCAST adj sad, dejected ▷ n ventilation shaft

DOWNCOME same as > downcomer

DOWNCRY vb denigrate or disparage

DOWNED ▸ down

DOWNER, -S n dispiriting experience

DOWNFALL n sudden loss of success or power

DOWNFLOW n something that flows down

DOWNHAUL n line for hauling down a sail or for increasing the tension at its luff

DOWNHILL adj going or sloping down ▷ adv towards the bottom of a hill ▷ n downward slope

DOWNHOLE adj (in the oil industry) denoting any piece of equipment that is used in the well itself

DOWNIER ▸ downy

DOWNIES ▸ downy

DOWNIEST ▸ downy

DOWNILY adv in a manner resembling or indicating a layer of soft fine feathers or hairs

DOWNING ▸ down

DOWNLAND same as ▸ downs

DOWNLESS ▸ down

DOWNLIKE ▸ down

DOWNLINK n satellite transmission channel

DOWNLOAD vb transfer data from one computer to another ▷ n file transferred in such a way

DOWNLOW, -S n as in on the downlow not widely known

DOWNMOST adj lowest

DOWNPIPE n pipe for carrying rainwater from a roof gutter to the ground or to a drain

DOWNPLAY vb play down

DOWNPOUR n heavy fall of rain

DOWNRATE vb reduce in value or importance

DOWNRUSH n instance of rushing down

DOWNS pl n low grassy hills, esp in S England

DOWNSIDE n disadvantageous aspect of a situation

DOWNSIZE vb reduce the number of people employed by (a company)

DOWNSPIN n sudden downturn

DOWNTICK n small decrease

DOWNTIME n time during which a computer or other machine is not working

DOWNTOWN n central or lower part of a city, esp the main commercial area ▷ adv towards, to, or into this area ▷ adj of, relating to, or situated in the downtown area

DOWNTROD adj downtrodden

DOWNTURN n drop in the success of an economy or a business

DOWNVOTE vb publicly disapprove of a social media post

DOWNWARD same as > downwards

DOWNWARP n wide depression in the earth's surface

DOWNWASH n downward deflection of an airflow, esp one caused by an aircraft wing

DOWNWIND adj in the same direction towards which the wind is blowing

DOWNY, DOWNIER, DOWNIES, DOWNIEST adj covered with soft fine hair or feathers ▷ n bed

DOWNZONE vb reduce density of housing in area

DOWP, -S same as ▸ doup

DOWRY, DOWRIES n property brought by a woman to her husband at marriage

DOWS ▸ dow

DOWSABEL n sweetheart

DOWSE, -D, -S same as ▸ douse

DOWSER, -S ▸ dowse

DOWSES ▸ dowse

DOWSET, -S same as ▸ doucet

DOWSING, -S n act of dowsing

DOWT, -S n cigarette butt

DOX, -ED, -ES, -ING vb publish someone's personal information on the internet

DOXAPRAM n drug used to stimulate the respiration

DOXASTIC adj of or relating to belief ▷ n branch of logic that studies the concept of belief

DOXED ▸ dox

DOXES ▸ dox

DOXIE same as ▸ doxy

DOXIES ▸ doxy

DOXING ▸ dox

DOXOLOGY n short hymn of praise to God

DOXY, DOXIES n opinion or doctrine, esp concerning religious matters

DOY, -S n beloved person: used esp as an endearment

DOYEN, -S n senior member of a group, profession, or society

DOYENNE, -S ▸ doyen

DOYENS ▸ doyen

DOYLEY, -S same as ▸ doily

DOYLY, DOYLIES same as ▸ doily

DOYS ▸ doy

DOZE, -S vb sleep lightly or briefly ▷ n short sleep

DOZED adj (of timber or rubber) rotten or decayed

DOZEN, -ED, -ING, -S n set of twelve ▷ vb stun

DOZENTH, -S ▸ dozen

DOZER, -S ▸ doze

DOZES ▸ doze

DOZIER ▸ dozy

DOZIEST ▸ dozy

DOZILY ▸ dozy

DOZINESS ▸ dozy

DOZING, -S ▸ doze

DOZY, DOZIER, DOZIEST adj feeling sleepy

DRAB, -BEST, -S adj dull and dreary ▷ n light olive-brown colour

DRABBER adj more drab

DRABBEST ▸ drab

DRABBET, -S n yellowish-brown fabric of coarse linen

DRABBIER ▸ drabby

DRABBISH adj slightly drab

DRABBLE, -D, -S vb make or become wet or dirty

DRABBLER n part fixed to bottom of sail

DRABBLES ▸ drabble

DRABBY, DRABBIER adj slightly drab

DRABETTE n type of rough linen fabric

DRABLER, -S same as ▸ drabbler

DRABLY ▸ drab

DRABNESS ▸ drab

DRABS ▸ drab

DRAC same as ▸ drack

DRACAENA n type of tropical plant often cultivated as a house plant for its decorative foliage

DRACENA, -S same as ▸ dracaena

DRACHM, -S n unit of liquid measure

DRACHMA, -E, -I, -S n former monetary unit of Greece

DRACHMS ▸ drachm

DRACK adj unattractive

DRACO n as in draco lizard flying lizard

DRACONE, -S n large container towed by a ship

DRACONIC same as ▸ draconian

DRAD archaic past of ▸ dread

DRAFF, -S n residue of husks used as a food for cattle

DRAFFIER ▸ draffy

DRAFFISH adj worthless

DRAFFS ▸ draff

DRAFFY, DRAFFIER ▸ draff

DRAFT, -ED, -ING, -S same as ▸ draught

DRAFTEE, -S n conscript

DRAFTER, -S ▸ draft

DRAFTIER ▸ drafty

DRAFTILY ▸ drafty

DRAFTING ▸ draft

DRAFTS ▸ draft

DRAFTY, DRAFTIER same as ▸ draughty

DRAG, -GED, -GING, -S vb pull with force, esp along the ground ▷ n person or thing that slows up progress

DRAGEE, -S n sweet made of a nut, fruit, etc, coated with a hard sugar icing

DRAGGED ▸ drag

DRAGGER, -S ▸ drag

DRAGGIER ▸ draggy

DRAGGING ▸ drag

DRAGGLE, -D, -S vb make or become wet or dirty by trailing on the ground

DRAGGY, DRAGGIER adj slow or boring

DRAGLINE same as ▸ dragrope

DRAGNET, -S n net used to scour the bottom of a pond or river

DRAGOMAN, DRAGOMEN n (in some Middle Eastern countries) professional interpreter or guide

DRAGON, -S n mythical fire-breathing monster like a huge lizard

DRAGONET n type of small spiny-finned fish with a flat head and a slender brightly coloured body

DRAGONNE adj dragonlike

DRAGONS ▸ dragon

DRAGOON, -S n heavily armed cavalryman ▷ vb coerce, force

DRAGROPE n rope used to drag military equipment, esp artillery

DRAGS ▸ drag

DRAGSMAN, DRAGSMEN n carriage driver

DRAGSTER n car specially built or modified for drag racing

DRAGWAY, -S n race course for drag racing

DRAIL, -ED, -ING, -S n weighted hook used in trolling ▷ vb fish with a drail

DRAIN, -ED, -ING, -S n pipe or channel that carries off water or sewage ▷ vb draw off or remove liquid from

DRAINAGE n system of drains

DRAINED ▸ drain

DRAINER, -S n person or thing that drains

DRAINING ▸ drain

DRAINS ▸ drain

DRAISENE same as ▸ draisine

DRAISINE n light rail vehicle

DRAKE, -S n male duck

DRAM, -MED, -MING, -S n small amount of a strong alcoholic drink, esp whisky ▷ vb drink a dram

DRAMA, -S n serious play for theatre, television, or radio

DRAMADY same as ▸ dramedy

DRAMAS ▸ drama

DRAMATIC adj of or like drama

DRAMEDY n television or film drama in which there are important elements of comedy

DRAMMACH n oatmeal mixed with cold water

DRAMMED ▸ dram

DRAMMING ▸ dram

DRAMMOCK same as ▸ drammach

DRAMS ▸ dram

DRAMSHOP n bar

DRANGWAY n narrow lane

DRANK ▸ drink

DRANT, -ED, -ING, -S vb drone

DRAP, -PED, -PING, -S a Scot word for ▸ drop

DRAPABLE ▸ drape

DRAPE, -D, DRAPING vb cover with material, usu in folds ▷ n piece of cloth hung at a window or opening as a screen

DRAPER, -S n person who sells fabrics and sewing materials

DRAPERY n fabric or clothing arranged and draped

DRAPES pl n material hung at an opening or window to shut out light or to provide privacy

DRAPET, -S n cloth

DRAPEY, DRAPIEST adj hanging in loose folds

DRAPIER, -S n draper

DRAPIEST ▶ drapey

DRAPING ▶ drape

DRAPPED ▶ drap

DRAPPIE, -S n little drop

DRAPPING ▶ drap

DRAPPY n drop (of liquid)

DRAPS ▶ drap

DRASTIC, -S n strong purgative ▷ adj strong and severe

DRAT, -S, -TING interj exclamation of annoyance ▷ vb curse

DRATTED adj wretched

DRATTING ▶ drat

DRAUGHT vb make preliminary plan ▷ n current of cold air, esp in an enclosed space ▷ adj (of an animal) used for pulling heavy loads

DRAUGHTS n game for two players using a draughtboard and 12 draughtsmen each

DRAUGHTY adj exposed to draughts of air

DRAUNT, -ED, -S same as ▶ drant

DRAVE archaic past of ▶ drive

DRAW, -N, -S, DREW vb sketch (a figure, picture, etc) with a pencil or pen ▷ n attraction

DRAWABLE ▶ draw

DRAWBACK n disadvantage ▷ vb move backwards

DRAWBAR, -S n strong metal bar on a tractor, locomotive, etc

DRAWBORE n hole bored through tenon

DRAWCARD n performer certain to attract a large audience

DRAWCORD n cord for drawing tight eg round a hood

DRAWDOWN n decrease

DRAWEE, -S n person or organization on which payment is drawn

DRAWER n sliding box-shaped part of a piece of furniture, used for storage

DRAWERS pl n undergarment worn on the lower part of the body

DRAWING, -S ▶ draw

DRAWL, -ED, -S vb speak slowly, with long vowel sounds ▷ n drawling manner of speech

DRAWLER, -S ▶ drawl

DRAWLIER ▶ drawly

DRAWLING ▶ drawl

DRAWLS ▶ drawl

DRAWLY, DRAWLIER ▶ drawl

DRAWN ▶ draw

DRAWS ▶ draw

DRAWTUBE n type of tube used in a telescope

DRAY, -ED, -ING, -S vb pull using cart ▷ n low cart used for carrying heavy loads

DRAYAGE, -S n act of transporting something a short distance

DRAYED ▶ dray

DRAYING ▶ dray

DRAYMAN, DRAYMEN n driver of a dray

DRAYS ▶ dray

DREAD, -ED, -EST, -ING, -S vb anticipate with apprehension or fear ▷ n great fear ▷ adj awesome

DREADER, -S ▶ dread

DREADEST ▶ dread

DREADFUL n cheap, often lurid or sensational book or magazine ▷ adj very disagreeable or shocking

DREADING ▶ dread

DREADLY ▶ dread

DREADS ▶ dread

DREAM, -ED, -S, -T n imagined events experienced while asleep ▷ vb see imaginary pictures in the mind while asleep ▷ adj ideal

DREAMER, -S n person who dreams habitually

DREAMERY n dream world

DREAMFUL ▶ dream

DREAMIER ▶ dreamy

DREAMILY ▶ dreamy

DREAMING ▶ dream

DREAMS ▶ dream

DREAMT ▶ dream

DREAMY, DREAMIER adj vague or impractical

DREAR, -ER, -EST, -S same as ▶ dreary

DREARE, -S obsolete form of ▶ drear

DREARER ▶ drear

DREARES ▶ dreare

DREAREST ▶ drear

DREARIER ▶ dreary

DREARIES ▶ dreary

DREARILY ▶ dreary

DREARING n sorrow

DREARS ▶ drear

DREARY, DREARIER, DREARIES adj dull, boring ▷ n dreary thing or person

DRECK, -S n rubbish

DRECKIER ▶ drecky

DRECKISH adj like rubbish

DRECKS ▶ dreck

DRECKY, DRECKIER ▶ dreck

DREDGE, -D, -S, DREDGING vb clear or search (a river bed or harbour) by removing silt or mud

DREDGER, -S n machine used to remove mud from a river bed or harbour

DREDGES ▶ dredge

DREDGING ▶ dredge

DREE, -D, -ING, -R, -S, -ST vb endure ▷ adj dreary

DREG n small quantity

DREGGIER ▶ dreggy

DREGGISH adj foul

DREGGY, DREGGIER adj like or full of dregs

DREGS pl n solid particles that settle at the bottom of some liquids

DREICH, -ER adj dreary

DREIDEL, -S n spinning top

DREIDL, -S same as ▶ dreidel

DREIGH, -ER same as ▶ dreich

DREK, -S same as ▶ dreck

DREKKY, DREKKIER ▶ drek

DREKS ▶ drek

DRENCH, -ED, -ES vb make completely wet ▷ n act or an instance of drenching

DRENCHER ▶ drench

DRENCHES ▶ drench

DRENT obsolete word for ▶ drenched

DREPANID n type of moth of the superfamily which comprises the hook-tip moths

DRERE, -S obsolete form of ▶ drear

DRESS, -ED, -ES, DREST n one-piece consisting of a skirt and bodice ▷ vb put clothes on ▷ adj suitable for a formal occasion

DRESSAGE n training of a horse to perform manoeuvres in response to the rider's body signals

DRESSED ▸ dress

DRESSER, -S n piece of furniture with shelves and cupboards

DRESSES ▸ dress

DRESSIER ▸ dressy

DRESSILY ▸ dressy

DRESSING n sauce for salad

DRESSY, DRESSIER adj (of clothes) elegant

DREST ▸ dress

DREVILL, -S n offensive person

DREW ▸ draw

DREY, -S n squirrel's nest

DRIB, -BED, -BING, -S vb flow in drops

DRIBBER, -S ▸ drib

DRIBBING ▸ drib

DRIBBLE, -D, -S vb (allow to) flow in drops ▷ n small quantity of liquid falling in drops

DRIBBLER ▸ dribble

DRIBBLES ▸ dribble

DRIBBLET same as ▸ driblet

DRIBBLY ▸ dribble

DRIBLET, -S n small amount

DRIBS ▸ drib

DRICE, -S n pellets of frozen carbon dioxide

DRICKSIE same as ▸ druxy

DRIED ▸ dry

DRIEGH adj dreary

DRIER, -S ▸ dry

DRIES ▸ dry

DRIEST ▸ dry

DRIFT, -ED, -S vb be carried along by currents of air or water ▷ n something piled up by the wind or current

DRIFTAGE n act of drifting

DRIFTED ▸ drift

DRIFTER, -S n person who moves aimlessly from place to place or job to job

DRIFTIER ▸ drifty

DRIFTING n act of drifting

DRIFTNET n fishing net that drifts with the tide

DRIFTPIN same as ▸ drift

DRIFTS ▸ drift

DRIFTY, DRIFTIER ▸ drift

DRILL, -ED, -S n tool or machine for boring holes ▷ vb bore a hole in (something) with or as if with a drill

DRILLER, -S ▸ drill

DRILLING n type of hard-wearing cloth

DRILLS ▸ drill

DRILY adv in a dry manner

DRINK, DRANK, -ING, -S vb swallow (a liquid) ▷ n (portion of) a liquid suitable for drinking

DRINKER, -S n person who drinks

DRINKING ▸ drink

DRINKS ▸ drink

DRIP, -PED, -PING, -S, -T vb (let) fall in drops ▷ n falling of drops of liquid

DRIPLESS ▸ drip

DRIPPED ▸ drip

DRIPPER, -S ▸ drip

DRIPPIER ▸ drippy

DRIPPILY ▸ drippy

DRIPPING ▸ drip

DRIPPY, DRIPPIER adj mawkish, insipid, or inane

DRIPS ▸ drip

DRIPT ▸ drip

DRISHEEN n pudding made of sheep's intestines filled with meal and sheep's blood

DRIVABLE ▸ drive

DRIVE, -N, -S vb guide the movement of (a vehicle) ▷ n journey by car, van, etc

DRIVEL, -ED, -S n foolish talk ▷ vb speak foolishly

DRIVELER ▸ drivel

DRIVELS ▸ drivel

DRIVEN ▸ drive

DRIVER, -S n person who drives a vehicle

DRIVES ▸ drive

DRIVEWAY n path for vehicles connecting a building to a public road

DRIVING, -S ▸ drive

DRIZZLE, -D, -S n very light rain ▷ vb rain lightly

DRIZZLY ▸ drizzle

DROGER, -S n long-masted boat

DROGHER, -S same as ▸ droger

DROGUE, -S n any funnel-like device used as a sea anchor

DROGUET, -S n woollen fabric

DROICH, -S n dwarf

DROICHY adj dwarfish

DROID, -S same as ▸ android

DROIL, -ED, -ING, -S vb carry out boring menial work

DROIT, -S n legal or moral right or claim

DROKE, -S n small group of trees

DROLE, -R, -S, -ST adj amusing ▷ n scoundrel

DROLL, -ED, -ER, -EST, -ING, -S vb speak wittily ▷ adj quaintly amusing

DROLLERY n humour

DROLLEST ▸ droll

DROLLING ▸ droll

DROLLISH adj somewhat droll

DROLLS ▸ droll

DROLLY ▸ droll

DROME, -S same as ▸ aerodrome

DROMIC adj relating to a running track

DROMICAL same as ▸ dromic

DROMOI ▸ dromos

DROMON, -S same as ▸ dromond

DROMOND, -S n sailing vessel of the 12th to 15th centuries

DROMONS ▸ dromon

DROMOS, DROMOI n Greek passageway

DRONE, -D, -S, DRONING n male bee ▷ vb make a monotonous low dull sound

DRONER, -S ▸ drone

DRONES ▸ drone

DRONGO, -ES, -S n tropical songbird

DRONIER ▸ drony

DRONIEST ▸ drony

DRONING ▸ drone

DRONISH ▸ drone

DRONKLAP n South African word for a drunkard

DRONY, DRONIER, DRONIEST adj monotonous

DROOB, -S n pathetic person

DROOG, -S n ruffian

DROOGISH ▸ droog

DROOGS ▸ droog

DROOK, -ED, -ING, -S same as ▸ drouk

DROOKIT same as ▸ droukit

DROOKS ▸ drook

DROOL, -ED, -ING, -S vb show excessive enthusiasm (for)

DROOLIER ▸ drooly

DROOLING ▸ drool

DROOLS ▸ drool

DROOLY, DROOLIER adj tending to drool

DROOME, -S obsolete form of ▸ drum

DROOP, -ED, -S vb hang downwards loosely ▷ n act or state of drooping

DROOPIER ▸ droopy

DROOPILY ▸ droopy

DROOPING ▸ droop

DROOPS ▸ droop

DROOPY, DROOPIER adj hanging or sagging downwards

DROP, -PED, -PING, -S, -T *vb* (allow to) fall vertically ▷ *n* small quantity of liquid forming a round shape

DROPDOWN *n* menu on a computer screen, beneath a selected item

DROPFLY *n* (in angling) an artificial fly

DROPHEAD *adj* as in **drophead coupe** two-door car with a folding roof and sloping back

DROPKICK *n* kick in which a ball is dropped and then kicked

DROPLET, -S *n* very small drop of liquid

DROPLIKE *adj* like a drop

DROPLOCK *adj* as in **droplock loan** type of bank loan ▷ *n* type of bank loan

DROPOUT, -S *n* person who rejects conventional society

DROPPED ▸ drop

DROPPER, -S *n* small tube with a rubber part at one end

DROPPING ▸ drop

DROPPLE, -S *n* trickle

DROPS ▸ drop

DROPSEED *n* type of grass

DROPSHOT *n* type of tennis shot

DROPSIED ▸ dropsy

DROPSY, DROPSIES *n* illness in which watery fluid collects in the body

DROPT ▸ drop

DROPTOP, -S *n* convertible car

DROPWISE *adv* in form of a drop

DROPWORT *n* Eurasian plant with cream-coloured flowers, related to the rose

DROSERA, -S *n* insectivorous plant

DROSHKY *n* four-wheeled carriage, formerly used in Russia

DROSKY, DROSKIES *same as* ▸ **droshky**

DROSS, -ES *n* scum formed on the surfaces of molten metals

DROSSY, DROSSIER ▸ **dross**

DROSTDY, -S *n* office of landdrost

DROUGHT, -S *n* prolonged shortage of rainfall

DROUGHTY ▸ drought

DROUK, -ED, -ING, -S *vb* drench

DROUKIT *adj* drenched

DROUKS ▸ drouk

DROUTH, -S *same as* ▸ **drought**

DROUTHY *adj* thirsty or dry

DROVE, -D, -S *vb* drive livestock ▷ *n* moving crowd

DROVER, -S *n* person who drives sheep or cattle

DROVES ▸ drove

DROVING, -S ▸ drove

DROW, -S *n* sea fog

DROWN, -ED, -ING, -S *vb* die or kill by immersion in liquid

DROWND, -ED, -S *dialect form of* ▸ **drown**

DROWNED ▸ drown

DROWNER, -S ▸ drown

DROWNING ▸ drown

DROWNS ▸ drown

DROWS ▸ drow

DROWSE, -D, -S, DROWSING *vb* be sleepy, dull, or sluggish ▷ *n* state of being drowsy

DROWSIER ▸ drowsy

DROWSILY ▸ drowsy

DROWSING ▸ drowse

DROWSY, DROWSIER *adj* feeling sleepy

DRUB, -BED, -BING, -S *vb* beat as with a stick ▷ *n* blow, as from a stick

DRUBBER, -S ▸ drub

DRUBBING ▸ drub

DRUBS ▸ drub

DRUCKEN *adj* old word meaning drunken

DRUDGE, -D, -S, DRUDGING *n* person who works hard at uninteresting tasks ▷ *vb* work at such tasks

DRUDGER, -S ▸ drudge

DRUDGERY *n* uninteresting work that must be done

DRUDGES ▸ drudge

DRUDGING ▸ drudge

DRUDGISM ▸ drudge

DRUG, -GED, -GING, -S *n* substance used in the treatment or prevention of disease ▷ *vb* give a drug to (a person or animal) to cause sleepiness or unconsciousness

DRUGGER, -S *n* druggist

DRUGGET, -S *n* coarse fabric used as a protective floor-covering, etc

DRUGGIER ▸ druggy

DRUGGING ▸ drug

DRUGGIST *n* pharmacist

DRUGGY, DRUGGIER ▸ **drug**

DRUGLESS *adj* having no drugs

DRUGS ▸ drug

DRUID, -S *n* member of an ancient order of priests in the pre-Christian era

DRUIDESS ▸ druid

DRUIDIC ▸ druid

DRUIDISM ▸ druid

DRUIDRY ▸ druid

DRUIDS ▸ druid

DRUM, -MED, -S *n* percussion instrument ▷ *vb* play (music) on a drum

DRUMBEAT *n* sound made by beating a drum

DRUMBLE, -D, -S *vb* be inactive

DRUMFIRE *n* heavy, rapid, and continuous gunfire, the sound of which resembles rapid drumbeats

DRUMFISH *n* one of several types of fish that make a drumming sound

DRUMHEAD *n* part of a drum that is struck

DRUMLIER ▸ drumly

DRUMLIKE ▸ drum

DRUMLIN, -S *n* streamlined mound of glacial drift

DRUMLY, DRUMLIER *adj* dismal; dreary

DRUMMED ▸ drum

DRUMMER, -S *n* person who plays a drum or drums

DRUMMIES ▸ drummy

DRUMMING *n* act of drumming

DRUMMOCK *same as* ▸ **drammock**

DRUMMY, DRUMMIES *n* (in South Africa) drum majorette

DRUMROLL *n* continued repeated sound of drum

DRUMS ▸ drum

DRUNK, -ER, -EST, -S *adj* intoxicated with alcoholic drink ▷ *n* drunk person

DRUNKARD *n* person who frequently gets drunk

DRUNKEN *adj* drunk or frequently drunk

DRUNKER ▸ drunk

DRUNKEST ▸ drunk

DRUNKISH *adj* rather drunk

DRUNKS ▸ drunk

DRUPE, -S *n* fleshy fruit with a stone, such as the peach or cherry

DRUPEL, -S *same as* ▸ **drupelet**

DRUPELET *n* small drupe, usually one of a number forming a compound fruit

DRUPELS ▸ drupel

DRUPES ▸ drupe

DRUSE, -S *n* aggregate of small crystals within a cavity

D

DRUSEN pl n small deposits of material on the retina

DRUSES ▸ druse

DRUSY, DRUSIER, DRUSIEST adj made of tiny crystals

DRUTHER n preference

DRUTHERS n preference

DRUXY, DRUXIER, DRUXIEST adj (of wood) having decayed white spots

DRY, DRIED, DRIES, DRIEST, -EST, -S adj lacking moisture ▷ vb make or become dry

DRYABLE ▸ dry

DRYAD, -ES, -S n wood nymph

DRYADIC ▸ dryad

DRYADS ▸ dryad

DRYAS n alpine plant with white flowers

DRYBEAT, -S vb beat severely

DRYER, -S ▸ dry

DRYEST ▸ dry

DRYING, -S ▸ dry

DRYISH adj fairly dry

DRYLAND, -S n arid area

DRYLOT, -S n livestock enclosure

DRYLY same as ▸ drily

DRYMOUTH n condition of insufficient saliva

DRYNESS ▸ dry

DRYPOINT n copper engraving technique using a hard steel needle

DRYS ▸ dry

DRYSTONE adj (of a wall) made without mortar

DRYSUIT, -S n waterproof rubber suit worn by divers

DRYWALL, -S n wall built without mortar ▷ vb build a wall without mortar

DRYWELL, -S n type of sewage disposal system

DSO, -S same as ▸ zho

A **dso** is a kind of Himalayan ox; the other forms are **dzo, zho, dzho** and **zo** and it's worth remembering all of them.

DSOBO, -S same as ▸ zobo

DSOMO, -S same as ▸ zhomo

DSOS ▸ dso

DUAD, -S a rare word for ▸ pair

DUAL, -LED, -LING, -S adj having two parts, functions, or aspects ▷ n dual number ▷ vb make (a road) into a dual carriageway

DUALIN, -S n explosive substance

DUALISE, -D, -S same as ▸ dualize

DUALISM, -S n state of having two distinct parts

DUALIST, -S ▸ dualism

DUALITY n state or quality of being two or in two parts

DUALIZE, -D, -S vb cause to have two parts

DUALLED ▸ dual

DUALLIE, -S n pickup truck with dual rear tyres

DUALLING ▸ dual

DUALLY ▸ dual

DUALS ▸ dual

DUAN, -S n poem

DUAR, -S n Arab camp

DUARCHY same as ▸ diarchy

DUARS ▸ duar

DUATHLON n athletic contest in which each athlete competes in running and cycling events

DUB, -BED, -S vb give (a person or place) a name or nickname ▷ n style of reggae record production

DUBBER, -S ▸ dub

DUBBIN, -ED, -S n thick grease applied to leather to soften and waterproof it ▷ vb apply dubbin to

DUBBING, -S ▸ dub

DUBBINS ▸ dubbin

DUBBO, -S adj stupid ▷ n stupid person

DUBIETY n state of being doubtful

DUBIOUS adj feeling or causing doubt

DUBITATE vb doubt

DUBNIUM, -S n chemical element

DUBONNET n dark purplish-red colour

DUBS ▸ dub

DUBSTEP, -S n genre of electronic music

DUCAL adj of a duke

DUCALLY ▸ ducal

DUCAT, -S n former European gold or silver coin

DUCATOON n former silver coin

DUCATS ▸ ducat

DUCDAME interj Shakespearean nonsense word

DUCE, -S, DUCI n leader

DUCHESS n woman who holds the rank of duke ▷ vb overwhelm with flattering attention

DUCHESSE n type of satin

DUCHY, DUCHIES n territory of a duke or duchess

DUCI ▸ duce

DUCK, -ED, -S n water bird ▷ vb move (the head or body) quickly downwards

DUCKBILL n duck-billed platypus

DUCKED ▸ duck

DUCKER, -S ▸ duck

DUCKFOOT adj as in duckfoot quote chevron-shaped quotation mark

DUCKIE same as ▸ ducky

DUCKIER ▸ ducky

DUCKIES ▸ ducky

DUCKIEST ▸ ducky

DUCKING, -S ▸ duck

DUCKISH n twilight

DUCKLING n baby duck

DUCKMOLE another word for ▸ duckbill

DUCKPIN, -S n short bowling pin

DUCKS ▸ duck

DUCKTAIL n Teddy boy's hairstyle

DUCKWALK vb walk in a squatting posture

DUCKWEED n type of small stemless aquatic plant

DUCKY, DUCKIER, DUCKIES, DUCKIEST n darling or dear ▷ adj delightful

DUCT, -ED, -S vb convey via a duct ▷ n tube, pipe, or channel through which liquid or gas is conveyed

DUCTAL ▸ duct

DUCTED ▸ duct

DUCTILE adj (of a metal) able to be shaped into sheets or wires

DUCTING, -S ▸ duct

DUCTLESS ▸ duct

DUCTS ▸ duct

DUCTULE, -S n small duct

DUCTWORK n system of ducts

DUD, -S n ineffectual person or thing ▷ adj bad or useless

DUDDER, -ED, -S n door-to-door salesperson ▷ vb tremble or shudder

DUDDERY n place where old clothes are sold

DUDDIE, -R, -S, -ST adj ragged ▷ n friend or a chum

DUDDY same as ▸ duddie

DUDE, -D, -S, DUDING vb dress fashionably ▷ n man

DUDEEN, -S n clay pipe with a short stem

DUDENESS n state of being a dude

DUDES ▸ dude

DUDETTE, -S *n* woman who behaves like a dude

DUDGEON, -S *n* anger or resentment

DUDHEEN, -S *n* type of pipe

DUDING ▶ **dude**

DUDISH ▶ **dude**

DUDISHLY ▶ **dude**

DUDISM, -S *n* being a dude

DUDS ▶ **dud**

DUE, -D, DUING *vb* supply with ▷ *adj* expected or scheduled to be present or arrive ▷ *n* something that is owed or required ▷ *adv* directly or exactly

DUECENTO *n* thirteenth century (in Italian art)

DUED ▶ **due**

DUEFUL *adj* proper

DUEL, -ED, -LED, -S *n* formal fight with deadly weapons between two people ▷ *vb* fight in a duel

DUELER, -S ▶ **duel**

DUELING, -S ▶ **duel**

DUELIST, -S ▶ **duel**

DUELLED ▶ **duel**

DUELLER, -S ▶ **duel**

DUELLI ▶ **duello**

DUELLING ▶ **duel**

DUELLIST ▶ **duel**

DUELLO, DUELLI, -S *n* art of duelling

DUELS ▶ **duel**

DUELSOME *adj* given to duelling

DUENDE, -S *n* Spanish goblin

DUENESS ▶ **due**

DUENNA, -S *n* (esp in Spain) woman acting as a chaperone to a young woman

DUES *pl n* membership fees

DUET, -ED, -ING, -S, -TED, -TING *n* piece of music for two performers ▷ *vb* perform a duet

DUETT, -S *same as* ▶ **duet**

DUETTED ▶ **duet**

DUETTI ▶ **duetto**

DUETTING ▶ **duet**

DUETTINO *n* simple duet

DUETTIST ▶ **duet**

DUETTO, DUETTI, -S *same as* ▶ **duet**

DUETTS ▶ **duett**

DUFF, -ED, -EST, -S *adj* broken or useless ▷ *vb* change the appearance of or give a false appearance to (old or stolen goods) ▷ *n* mishit golf shot

DUFFEL, -S *n* heavy woollen cloth with a thick nap

DUFFER, -S *n* dull or incompetent person

DUFFEST ▶ **duff**

DUFFING, -S ▶ **duff**

DUFFLE, -S *same as* ▶ **duffel**

DUFFS ▶ **duff**

DUFUS, -ES *same as* ▶ **doofus**

DUG, -S Scottish word for ▶ **dog**

DUGITE, -S *n* medium-sized Australian venomous snake

DUGONG, -S *n* whalelike mammal of tropical waters

DUGOUT, -S *n* (at a sports ground) covered bench where managers and substitutes sit

DUGS ▶ **dug**

DUH *interj* ironic response to a question or statement

This word provides a useful front hook to **uh**.

DUHKHA, -S *same as* ▶ **dukkha**

DUI ▶ **duo**

DUIKER, -S *n* small African antelope

DUING ▶ **due**

DUIT, -S *n* former Dutch coin

DUKA, -S *n* shop

DUKE, -D, DUKING *vb* fight with fists ▷ *n* nobleman of the highest rank

DUKEDOM, -S *n* title, rank, or position of a duke

DUKELING *n* low-ranking duke

DUKERY, DUKERIES *n* duke's domain

DUKES *pl n* fists

DUKESHIP ▶ **duke**

DUKING ▶ **duke**

DUKKA, -S *n* mix of ground roast nuts and spices

DUKKAH, -S *same as* ▶ **dukka**

DUKKAS ▶ **dukka**

DUKKHA, -S *n* Buddhist belief that all things are suffering

DULCE, -S *n* sweet food or drink

DULCET, -S *adj* (of a sound) soothing or pleasant ▷ *n* soft organ stop

DULCETLY ▶ **dulcet**

DULCETS ▶ **dulcet**

DULCIAN, -S *n* precursor to the bassoon

DULCIANA *n* sweet-toned organ stop, controlling metal pipes of narrow scale

DULCIANS ▶ **dulcian**

DULCIFY *vb* make pleasant or agreeable

DULCIMER *n* tuned percussion instrument

DULCINEA *n* female sweetheart

DULCITE, -S *n* sweet substance

DULCITOL *another word for* ▶ **dulcite**

DULCOSE, -S *another word for* ▶ **dulcite**

DULE, -S *n* suffering; misery

DULIA, -S *n* veneration accorded to saints

DULL, -ED, -ER, -EST, -ING, -S *adj* not interesting ▷ *vb* make or become dull

DULLARD, -S *n* dull or stupid person

DULLED ▶ **dull**

DULLER ▶ **dull**

DULLEST ▶ **dull**

DULLIER ▶ **dully**

DULLIEST ▶ **dully**

DULLING ▶ **dull**

DULLISH ▶ **dull**

DULLNESS ▶ **dull**

DULLS ▶ **dull**

DULLY, DULLIER, DULLIEST ▶ **dull**

DULNESS ▶ **dull**

DULOSIS, DULOSES *n* behaviour where one species of ant forces members of another to work for them

DULOTIC ▶ **dulosis**

DULSE, -S *n* seaweed with large red edible fronds

DULY *adv* in a proper manner

DUM *adj* steamed

DUMA, -S *n* elective legislative assembly established by Tsar Nicholas II

DUMAIST, -S *n* member of duma

DUMAS ▶ **duma**

DUMB, -ED, -ER, -EST, -ING, -S *vb* silence ▷ *adj* temporarily bereft of speech

DUMBBELL *n* short bar with a heavy ball or disc at each end, used for physical exercise

DUMBCANE *n* tropical aroid plant

DUMBED ▶ **dumb**

DUMBER ▶ **dumb**

DUMBEST ▶ **dumb**

DUMBHEAD *n* dunce

DUMBING ▶ **dumb**

DUMBLY ▶ **dumb**

DUMBNESS ▶ **dumb**

DUMBO, -S *n* unintelligent person

DUMBS ▶ **dumb**

DUMBSHOW *n* actions performed without words in a play

DUMBSIZE vb reduce the number in a workforce to the point it becomes ineffective

DUMDUM, -S n soft-nosed bullet

DUMELA sentence substitute hello

DUMFOUND same as > **dumbfound**

DUMKA, -S, DUMKY n Slavonic lyrical song

DUMMERER n archaic word for a person who pretends they cannot speak

DUMMIED ▸ **dummy**

DUMMIER ▸ **dummy**

DUMMIES ▸ **dummy**

DUMMIEST ▸ **dummy**

DUMMKOPF n stupid person

DUMMY, DUMMIED, DUMMIER, DUMMIES, DUMMIEST, -ING n figure representing the human form ▷ adj imitation, substitute ▷ vb prepare an imitation of (a proposed book, page, etc)

DUMOSE adj bushlike

DUMOSITY ▸ **dumose**

DUMOUS same as ▸ **dumose**

DUMP, -ED vb drop or let fall in a careless manner ▷ n place where waste materials are left

DUMPBIN, -S n unit in a bookshop displaying a particular publisher's books

DUMPCART n cart for dumping without handling

DUMPED ▸ **dump**

DUMPEE, -S n person dumped from a relationship

DUMPER, -S ▸ **dump**

DUMPIER ▸ **dumpy**

DUMPIES ▸ **dumpy**

DUMPIEST ▸ **dumpy**

DUMPILY ▸ **dumpy**

DUMPING, -S ▸ **dump**

DUMPISH same as ▸ **dumpy**

DUMPLE, -D, -S vb form into a dumpling shape

DUMPLING n small ball of dough cooked and served with stew

DUMPS pl n state of melancholy

DUMPSITE n location of dump

DUMPSTER n refuse skip

DUMPY, DUMPIER, DUMPIES, DUMPIEST adj short and plump ▷ n short, plump person

DUN, -NED, -NER, -NEST, -NING, -S adj brownish-grey ▷ vb demand payment from

(a debtor) ▷ n demand for payment

DUNAM, -S n unit of area measurement

DUNCE, -S n person who is stupid or slow to learn

DUNCEDOM ▸ **dunce**

DUNCERY n duncelike behaviour

DUNCES ▸ **dunce**

DUNCH, -ED, -ES, -ING vb push against gently

DUNCICAL adj duncelike

DUNCISH adj duncelike

DUNDER, -S n cane juice lees

DUNE, -S n mound or ridge of drifted sand

DUNELAND n land characterized by dunes

DUNELIKE ▸ **dune**

DUNES ▸ **dune**

DUNG, -ED, -ING, -S n faeces from animals such as cattle ▷ vb cover (ground) with manure

DUNGAREE n coarse cotton fabric used chiefly for work clothes, etc

DUNGED ▸ **dung**

DUNGEON, -S n hold captive in dungeon ▷ n underground prison cell

DUNGER, -S n old decrepit car

DUNGHEAP n pile of dung

DUNGHILL n heap of dung

DUNGIER ▸ **dungy**

DUNGIEST ▸ **dungy**

DUNGING ▸ **dung**

DUNGMERE n cesspool

DUNGS ▸ **dung**

DUNGY, DUNGIER, DUNGIEST ▸ **dung**

DUNITE, -S n ultrabasic igneous rock

DUNITIC ▸ **dunite**

DUNK, -ED, -S vb dip (a biscuit or bread) in a drink or soup before eating it

DUNKER, -S ▸ **dunk**

DUNKING, -S n act of dunking

DUNKS ▸ **dunk**

DUNLIN, -S n small sandpiper

DUNNAGE, -S n loose material used for packing cargo

DUNNAKIN n lavatory

DUNNART, -S n type of insectivorous marsupial

DUNNED ▸ **dun**

DUNNER ▸ **dun**

DUNNESS ▸ **dun**

DUNNEST ▸ **dun**

DUNNIER ▸ **dunny**

DUNNIES ▸ **dunny**

DUNNIEST ▸ **dunny**

DUNNING ▸ **dun**

DUNNINGS ▸ **dunning**

DUNNISH ▸ **dun**

DUNNITE, -S n explosive containing ammonium picrate

DUNNO vb slang for don't know

DUNNOCK, -S n hedge sparrow

DUNNY, DUNNIER, DUNNIES, DUNNIEST n in Australia, toilet ▷ adj like or relating to a dunny

DUNS ▸ **dun**

DUNSH, -ED, -ES, -ING same as ▸ **dunch**

DUNT, -ED, -ING, -S n blow ▷ vb strike or hit

DUO, DUI, -S same as ▸ **duet**

DUODENA ▸ **duodenum**

DUODENAL ▸ **duodenum**

DUODENUM, DUODENA n first part of the small intestine, just below the stomach

DUOLOG, -S same as ▸ **duologue**

DUOLOGUE n (in drama) conversation between only two speakers

DUOMO, DUOMI, -S n cathedral in Italy

DUOPOLY n situation when control of a commodity is vested in two producers or suppliers

DUOPSONY n two rival buyers controlling sellers

DUOS ▸ **duo**

DUOTONE, -S n process for producing halftone illustrations

DUP, -PED, -PING, -S vb open

DUPABLE ▸ **dupe**

DUPATTA, -S n scarf worn in India

DUPE, -D, -S vb deceive or cheat ▷ n person who is easily deceived

DUPER, -S ▸ **dupe**

DUPERIES ▸ **dupery**

DUPERS ▸ **duper**

DUPERY, DUPERIES ▸ **dupe**

DUPES ▸ **dupe**

DUPING, -S n act of duping

DUPION, -S n silk fabric made from the threads of double cocoons

DUPLE adj having two beats in a bar

DUPLET, -S n pair of electrons shared between

two atoms in a covalent bond

DUPLEX, -ED, -ES *vb* duplicate ▷ *n* apartment on two floors ▷ *adj* having two parts

DUPLEXER *n* telecommunications system

DUPLEXES ▶ duplex

DUPLY, DUPLIED, DUPLIES, -ING *vb* give a second reply

DUPONDII ▷ dupondius

DUPPED ▶ dup

DUPPIES ▶ duppy

DUPPING ▶ dup

DUPPY, DUPPIES *n* spirit or ghost

DUPS ▶ dup

DURA, -S *same as* ▶ **durra**

DURABLE *adj* long-lasting

DURABLES *pl n* goods that require infrequent replacement

DURABLY ▶ durable

DURAL, -S *n* alloy of aluminium and copper

DURAMEN, -S *another name for* ▷ **heartwood**

DURANCE, -S *n* imprisonment

DURANT, -S *n* tough, leathery cloth

DURAS ▶ dura

DURATION *n* length of time that something lasts

DURATIVE *adj* denoting an aspect of verbs that includes the imperfective and the progressive ▷ *n* durative aspect of a verb

DURBAR, -S *n* (formerly) the court of a native ruler or a governor in India

DURDUM, -S *same as* ▷ **dirdum**

DURE, -D, -S *vb* endure

DUREFUL *adj* lasting

DURES ▶ dure

DURESS, -ES *n* compulsion by use of force or threats

DURESSE *same as* ▶ **duress**

DURESSES ▶ duress

DURGAH, -S *same as* ▷ **dargah**

DURGAN, -S *n* dwarf

DURGY, DURGIER, DURGIEST *adj* dwarflike

DURIAN, -S *n* SE Asian tree with very large oval fruits

DURING *prep* throughout or within the limit of (a period of time)

DURION, -S *same as* ▶ **durian**

DURMAST, -S *n* large Eurasian oak tree with lobed leaves

DURN, -ING, -S *same as* ▷ **darn**

DURNDEST *same as* > **darnedest**

DURNED, -ER ▶ durn

DURNING ▶ durn

DURNS ▶ durn

DURO, -S *n* silver peso of Spain or Spanish America

DUROC, -S *n* breed of pig

DUROS ▶ duro

DUROY, -S *n* coarse woollen fabric

DURR, -S *same as* ▶ **durra**

DURRA, -S *n* Old World variety of sorghum

DURRIE *n* cotton carpet made in India, often in rectangular pieces fringed at the ends

DURRIES ▶ durry

DURRS ▶ durr

DURRY, DURRIES *n* cigarette

DURST *a past tense of* ▶ **dare**

DURUKULI *n* S American monkey

DURUM, -S *n* variety of wheat

DURZI, -S *n* Indian tailor

DUSH, -ED, -ES, -ING *vb* strike hard

DUSK, -ED, -ER, -EST, -ING, -S *n* time just before nightfall, when it is almost dark ▷ *adj* shady ▷ *vb* make or become dark

DUSKEN, -ED, -S *vb* grow dark

DUSKER ▶ dusk

DUSKEST ▶ dusk

DUSKIER ▶ dusky

DUSKIEST ▶ dusky

DUSKILY ▶ dusky

DUSKING ▶ dusk

DUSKISH ▶ dusk

DUSKLY ▶ dusk

DUSKNESS ▶ dusk

DUSKS ▶ dusk

DUSKY, DUSKIER, DUSKIEST *adj* dark in colour

DUST, -ED, -S *n* small dry particles of earth, sand, or dirt ▷ *vb* remove dust from (furniture) by wiping

DUSTBALL *n* ball of dust

DUSTBIN, -S *n* large container for household rubbish

DUSTCART *n* truck for collecting household rubbish

DUSTCOAT *n* light, loose-fitting long coat

DUSTED ▶ dust

DUSTER, -S *n* cloth used for dusting

DUSTHEAP *n* accumulation of refuse

DUSTIER ▶ dusty

DUSTIEST ▶ dusty

DUSTILY ▶ dusty

DUSTING, -S ▶ dust

DUSTLESS ▶ dust

DUSTLIKE ▶ dust

DUSTMAN, DUSTMEN *n* man whose job is to collect household rubbish

DUSTOFF, -S *n* casualty evacuation helicopter

DUSTPAN, -S *n* short-handled shovel

DUSTRAG, -S *n* cloth for dusting

DUSTS ▶ dust

DUSTUP, -S *n* quarrel, fight, or argument

DUSTY, DUSTIER, DUSTIEST *adj* covered with dust

DUTCH, -ES *n* wife

DUTCHMAN, DUTCHMEN *n* piece of wood, metal, etc, used to repair or patch faulty workmanship

DUTEOUS *adj* dutiful or obedient

DUTIABLE *adj* (of goods) requiring payment of duty

DUTIED *adj* liable for duty

DUTIES ▶ duty

DUTIFUL *adj* doing what is expected

DUTY, DUTIES *n* work or a task performed as part of one's job

DUUMVIR, -I, -S *n* one of two coequal magistrates or officers

DUVET, -S *n* large quilt used as a bed cover

DUVETINE *same as* ▶ **duvetyn**

DUVETS ▶ duvet

DUVETYN, -S *n* soft napped velvety fabric of cotton, silk, wool, or rayon

DUVETYNE *same as* ▶ **duvetyn**

DUVETYNS ▶ duvetyn

DUX, -ES *n* (in Scottish and certain other schools) the top pupil in a class or school

A **dux** is a leader or top student, and is often useful for disposing of the X.

DUXELLES *n* paste of mushrooms and onions

DUXES ▶ dux

DUYKER, -S *same as* ▶ **duiker**

DVANDVA, -S *n* class of compound words

DVORNIK, -S n Russian doorkeeper

DWAAL, -S n state of absent-mindedness

DWALE, -S n deadly nightshade

DWALM, -ED, -ING, -S same as ▸ dwam

DWAM, -MED, -MING, -S n stupor or daydream ▸ vb faint or fall ill

DWANG, -S n short piece of wood inserted in a timber-framed wall

DWARF, -ED, -ER, -EST, -ING, -S, DWARVES adj undersized ▸ n person who is smaller than average ▸ vb cause (someone or something) to seem small by being much larger

DWARFISH ▸ dwarf

DWARFISM n condition of being a dwarf

DWARFS ▸ dwarf

DWARVES ▸ dwarf

DWAUM, -ED, -ING, -S same as ▸ dwam

DWEEB, -S n stupid or uninteresting person

DWEEBIER ▸ dweeby

DWEEBISH ▸ dweeb

DWEEBS ▸ dweeb

DWEEBY, DWEEBIER adj like or typical of a dweeb

DWELL, -ED, -ING, -S, DWELT vb live, reside ▸ n regular pause in the operation of a machine

DWELLER, -S ▸ dwell

DWELLING ▸ dwell

DWELLS ▸ dwell

DWELT ▸ dwell

DWILE, -S n floor cloth

DWINDLE, -D, -S vb grow less in size, strength, or number

DWINE, -D, -S, DWINING vb languish

DYABLE ▸ dye

DYAD, -S n operator that is the unspecified product of two vectors

DYADIC, -S adj of or relating to a dyad ▸ n sum of a particular number of dyads

DYADS ▸ dyad

DYARCHAL ▸ dyarchy

DYARCHIC ▸ dyarchy

DYARCHY same as ▸ diarchy

DYBBUK, -IM, -S n (in Jewish folklore) the soul of a dead sinner possessing a living person's body

DYE, -D, -S n colouring substance ▸ vb colour (hair or fabric) by applying a dye

DYEABLE ▸ dye

DYED ▸ dye

DYEING, -S ▸ dye

DYELINE, -S same as ▸ diazo

DYER, -S ▸ dye

DYES ▸ dye

DYESTER, -S n dyer

DYESTUFF n substance that can be used as a dye or from which a dye can be obtained

DYEWEED, -S n plant that produces dye

DYEWOOD, -S n any wood from which dyes and pigments can be obtained

DYEWORKS n place where dye is made

DYING, -S ▸ die

DYINGLY ▸ die

DYINGS ▸ dying

DYKE, -D, -S, DYKING n wall built to prevent flooding ▸ vb protect with a dyke

DYNAMIC adj full of energy, ambition, and new ideas ▸ n energetic or driving force

DYNAMICS n branch of mechanics concerned with motions of bodies

DYNAMISE same as ▸ dynamize

DYNAMISM n great energy and enthusiasm

DYNAMIST ▸ dynamism

DYNAMITE n explosive made of nitroglycerine ▸ vb blow (something) up with dynamite

DYNAMIZE vb cause to be dynamic

DYNAMO, -S n device for converting mechanical energy into electrical energy

DYNAST, -S n hereditary ruler

DYNASTIC ▸ dynasty

DYNASTS ▸ dynast

DYNASTY n sequence of hereditary rulers

DYNATRON n as in **dynatron oscillator** type of oscillator

DYNE, -S n unit of force

DYNEIN, -S n class of proteins

DYNEL, -S n trade name for a synthetic fibre

DYNES ▸ dyne

DYNODE, -S n electrical component

DYSCHROA n discolouration of skin

DYSGENIC adj referring to the degeneration of the human race

DYSLALIA n defective speech

DYSLEXIA n disorder causing impaired ability to read

DYSLEXIC ▸ dyslexia

DYSLOGY n uncomplimentary remarks

DYSMELIA n condition of missing or stunted limbs

DYSMELIC ▸ dysmelia

DYSODIL, -S n yellow or green mineral

DYSODILE same as ▸ dysodil

DYSODILS ▸ dysodil

DYSODYLE same as ▸ dysodil

DYSPATHY n dislike

DYSPEPSY same as > dyspepsia

DYSPHAGY same as ▸ dysphagia

DYSPNEA, -S same as ▸ dyspnoea

DYSPNEAL ▸ dyspnea

DYSPNEAS ▸ dyspnea

DYSPNEIC ▸ dyspnea

DYSPNOEA n difficulty in breathing or in catching the breath

DYSPNOIC ▸ dyspnoea

DYSTAXIA n lack of muscular coordination resulting in shaky limb movements and unsteady gait

DYSTAXIC adj relating to or affected by dystaxia

DYSTOCIA n abnormal, slow, or difficult childbirth

DYSTONIA n neurological disorder

DYSTONIC ▸ dystonia

DYSTOPIA n imaginary place where everything is as bad as it can be

DYSURIA, -S n difficult or painful urination

DYSURIC ▸ dysuria

DYSURY, DYSURIES same as ▸ dysuria

DYTISCID n type of carnivorous aquatic beetle with large flattened back legs used for swimming

DYVOUR, -S n debtor

DYVOURY n bankruptcy

DZEREN, -S n Chinese yellow antelope

DZHO, -S same as ▸ zho

DZO, -S variant spelling of ▸ zo

Ee

E is the most common tile in the game and, while it is only worth one point, as the most frequent letter in English it is extremely useful, especially when it comes to forming bonus words scoring an extra 50 points. Many words contain two or more **E**s, so, unlike many tiles, it does no harm to have two **E**s on your rack and even three can be manageable. Keep in mind three-letter words formed by an **E** on either side of a consonant, like **eye**, **ewe** and **eve** (6 points each), and **eke** (7). **E** can also be handy for getting rid of double consonants: think of words like **egg** or **ebb** (each 5 points). **E** also combines well with **K**: as well as **eke**, we have **elk** and **eek** (both 7), and **ewk** (10). If you have an **X** on your rack, **E** offers you all kinds of options: just think of all the words that begin with **ex-**, like **exhaust** (17), which will give you a 50-point bonus if you use all of your tiles to form it. And don't forget **ex** itself, a nice little word that earns you 9 points, and also the very useful **exo** for 10 points. Just as important are **jee** for 10 points, **zee** for 12 points and **zed** for 13 points.

EA, -S *n* river

EACH *pron* every (one) taken separately ▷ *determiner* every (one) of two or more considered individually ▷ *adv* for, to, or from each one

EADISH, -ES *n* aftermath

EAGER, -ER, -EST, -S *adj* showing or feeling great desire, keen ▷ *n* eagre

EAGERLY ▶ eager

EAGERS ▶ eager

EAGLE, -D, -S, EAGLING *n* bird of prey ▷ *vb* in golf, score two strokes under par for a hole

EAGLET, -S *n* young eagle

EAGLING ▶ eagle

EAGRE, -S *n* tidal bore, esp of the Humber or Severn estuaries

EALE, -D, -S, EALING *n* beast in Roman legend ▷ *vb* to ail

EAN, -ED, -ING, -S *vb* give birth

EANLING, -S *n* newborn lamb

EANS ▶ ean

EAR, -S *n* organ of hearing, esp the external part of it ▷ *vb* (of cereal plants) to develop such parts

EARACHE, -S *n* pain in the ear

EARBALL, -S *n* device used in acupressure

EARBASH *vb* talk incessantly

EARBOB, -S *n* earring

EARBUD, -S *n* small earphone

EARCON, -S *n* sound representing an object or event

EARD, -ED, -ING, -S *vb* bury

EARDROP *n* pendant earring

EARDROPS *pl n* liquid medication for inserting into the external ear

EARDRUM, -S *n* part of the ear which enables one to hear sounds

EARDS ▶ eard

EARED *adj* having an ear or ears

EARFLAP, -S *n* either of two pieces of fabric or fur attached to a cap

EARFUL, -S *n* scolding or telling-off

EARHOLE, -S *n* the external opening of the ear

EARING, -S *n* line fastened to a corner of a sail for reefing

EARL, -S *n* British nobleman ranking next below a marquess

EARLAP, -S *same as* ▶ earflap

EARLDOM, -S *n* rank, title, or dignity of an earl or countess

EARLESS ▶ ear

EARLIER ▶ early

EARLIES ▶ early

EARLIEST ▶ early

EARLIKE ▶ ear

EARLOBE, -S *n* fleshy lower part of the outer ear

EARLOCK, -S *n* curl of hair close to ear

EARLS ▶ earl

EARLSHIP *n* title or position of earl

EARLY, EARLIER, EARLIES, EARLIEST *adv* before the expected or usual time ▷ *adj* occurring or arriving before the correct or expected time ▷ *n* something which is early

EARMARK, -S *vb* set (something) aside for a specific purpose ▷ *n* distinguishing mark

EARMUFF, -S *n* item of clothing for keeping the ears warm

EARN, -ED, -ING, -S, -T *vb* obtain by work or merit

EARNER, -S ▶ earn

EARNEST, -S *adj* serious and sincere ▷ *n* part payment given in advance

EARNING ▸ earn

EARNINGS pl n money earned

EARNS ▸ earn

EARNT ▸ earn

EARPHONE n receiver for a radio etc, held to or put in the ear

EARPICK, -S n instrument for removing ear wax

EARPIECE n earphone in a telephone receiver

EARPLUG, -S n piece of soft material placed in the ear to keep out water or noise

EARRING, -S n ornament for the lobe of the ear

EARS ▸ ear

EARSHOT, -S n hearing range

EARST adv first; previously

EARSTONE n calcium carbonate crystal in the ear

EARTH, -ED, -ING, -S n planet that we live on ▷ vb connect (a circuit) to earth

EARTHEN adj made of baked clay or earth

EARTHIER ▸ earthy

EARTHILY ▸ earthy

EARTHING ▸ earth

EARTHLY adj conceivable or possible ▷ n chance

EARTHMAN, EARTHMEN n (esp in science fiction) an inhabitant or native of the earth

EARTHNUT n perennial umbelliferous plant of Europe and Asia, with edible dark brown tubers

EARTHPEA n peanut; groundnut

EARTHS ▸ earth

EARTHSET n setting of the earth below the lunar horizon

EARTHWAX n ozocerite

EARTHY, EARTHIER adj coarse or crude

EARWAX, -ES nontechnical name for ▸ cerumen

EARWIG, -S n small insect with a pincer-like tail ▷ vb eavesdrop

EARWIGGY adj like an earwig

EARWIGS ▸ earwig

EARWORM, -S n irritatingly catchy tune

EAS ▸ ea

EASE, -D, -S n freedom from difficulty, discomfort, or worry ▷ vb give bodily or mental ease to

EASEFUL adj characterized by or bringing ease

EASEL, -S n frame to support an artist's canvas or a blackboard

EASELED adj mounted on an easel

EASELESS ▸ ease

EASELS ▸ easel

EASEMENT n right of a landowner to make limited use of a neighbour's land

EASER, -S ▸ ease

EASES ▸ ease

EASIED ▸ easy

EASIER ▸ easy

EASIES ▸ easy

EASIEST ▸ easy

EASILY adv without difficulty

EASINESS n quality or condition of being easy to accomplish, do, obtain, etc

EASING, -S n as in **quantitative easing** increasing the supply of money to stimulate the economy

EASLE, -S n hot ash

EASSEL adv easterly

EASSIL adv easterly

EAST, -ED, -S n (direction towards) the part of the horizon where the sun rises ▷ adj in the east ▷ adv in, to, or towards the east ▷ vb move or turn east

EASTER, -S n most important festival of the Christian Church

EASTERLY adj of or in the east ▷ adv towards the east ▷ n wind from the east

EASTERN adj situated in or towards the east

EASTERS ▸ easter

EASTING, -S n net distance eastwards made by a vessel moving towards the east

EASTLAND n land in east

EASTLIN adj easterly

EASTLING adj easterly

EASTLINS adv eastward

EASTMOST adj furthest east

EASTS ▸ east

EASTWARD same as ▸ eastwards

EASY, EASIED, EASIER, EASIES, EASIEST, -ING adj not needing much work or effort ▷ vb stop rowing

EAT, ATE, -EN, -S vb take (food) into the mouth and swallow it

EATABLE adj fit or suitable for eating

EATABLES pl n food

EATAGE, -S n grazing rights

EATCHE, -S n adze

EATEN ▸ eat

EATER, -S ▸ eat

EATERIE same as ▸ eatery

EATERIES ▸ eatery

EATERS ▸ eater

EATERY, EATERIES n restaurant or eating house

EATH adj easy

EATHE same as ▸ eath

EATHLY ▸ eath

EATING, -S ▸ eat

EATS ▸ eat

EAU, -S, -X same as ▸ ea

EAVE, -S, EAVING vb give cover under the eaves of a building

EAVED adj having eaves

EAVES ▸ eave

EAVING ▸ eave

EBAUCHE, -S n rough sketch

EBAYER, -S n any person who uses eBay

EBAYING, -S n buying or selling using eBay

EBB, -ED, -ING, -S vb (of tide water) flow back ▷ n flowing back of the tide

EBBET, -S n type of newt

EBBING ▸ ebb

EBBLESS ▸ ebb

EBBS ▸ ebb

EBENEZER n chapel

EBENISTE n cabinetmaker

EBIONISE same as ▸ ebionize

EBIONISM n doctrine that the poor shall be saved

EBIONIZE vb preach ebionism

EBON, -S poetic word for ▸ ebony

EBONICS n dialect used by African-Americans

EBONIES ▸ ebony

EBONISE, -D, -S same as ▸ ebonize

EBONIST, -S n carver of ebony

EBONITE, -S another name for > vulcanite

EBONIZE, -D, -S vb stain or otherwise finish in imitation of ebony

EBONS ▸ ebon

EBONY, EBONIES n hard black wood ▷ adj deep black

EBOOK, -S n book in electronic form

EBRIATE adj drunk

EBRIATED same as ▸ ebriate

EBRIETY n drunkenness

EBRIOSE adj drunk

EBURNEAN adj made of ivory

ECAD, -S n organism whose form has been affected by its environment

ECARTE, -S n card game for two, played with 32 cards and king high

ECAUDATE adj tailless

ECBOLE, -S n digression

ECBOLIC, -S adj inducing labour ▷ n drug or agent that induces labour

ECCE interj behold

ECCLESIA n (in formal Church usage) a congregation

ECCO interj look there

ECCRINE adj of or denoting glands that secrete externally

ECCRISIS, ECCRISES n excrement

ECCRITIC n purgative

ECDEMIC adj not indigenous or endemic

ECDYSES ▶ ecdysis

ECDYSIAL ▶ ecdysis

ECDYSIS, ECDYSES n shedding of the cuticle in arthropods or the outer epidermal layer in reptiles

ECDYSON, -S same as ▶ ecdysone

ECDYSONE n hormone secreted by the prothoracic gland of insects

ECDYSONS ▶ ecdyson

ECESIC ▶ ecesis

ECESIS, -ES n establishment of a plant in a new environment

ECH same as ▶ eche

ECHAPPE, -S n leap in ballet

ECHARD, -S n water that is present in the soil but cannot be utilized by plants

ECHE, -D, -S, ECHING vb eke out

ECHELLE, -S n ladder; scale

ECHELON, -S n level of power or responsibility ▷ vb assemble soldiers in rows

ECHES ▶ eche

ECHIDNA, -E, -S n spiny egg-laying mammal

ECHINATE adj covered with spines, bristles, or bristle-like outgrowths

ECHING ▶ eche

ECHINI ▶ echinus

ECHINOID n type of echinoderm of the class which includes the sea urchins and sand dollars

ECHINUS, ECHINI n ovolo moulding between the shaft and the abacus of a Doric column

ECHIUM, -S n type of Eurasian and African plant

ECHIURAN n spoonworm

ECHO, -ED, -ES, -ING, -S n repetition of sounds by reflection of sound waves off a surface ▷ vb repeat or be repeated as an echo

ECHOER, -S ▶ echo

ECHOES ▶ echo

ECHOEY, ECHOIER, ECHOIEST adj producing echoes

ECHOGRAM n record made by echography

ECHOIC adj characteristic of or resembling an echo

ECHOIER ▶ echoey

ECHOIEST ▶ echoey

ECHOING ▶ echo

ECHOISE, -D, -S same as ▶ echoize

ECHOISM, -S n onomatopoeia as a source of word formation

ECHOIST, -S ▶ echoism

ECHOIZE, -D, -S vb repeat like an echo

ECHOLESS ▶ echo

ECHOS ▶ echo

ECHT adj real

ECLAIR, -S n finger-shaped pastry filled with cream and covered with chocolate

ECLAMPSY same as > eclampsia

ECLAT, -S n brilliant success

ECLECTIC adj selecting from various styles, ideas, or sources ▷ n person who takes an eclectic approach

ECLIPSE, -D n temporary obscuring of one star or planet by another ▷ vb surpass or outclass

ECLIPSER ▶ eclipse

ECLIPSIS, ECLIPSES same as ▶ ellipsis

ECLIPTIC n apparent path of the sun ▷ adj of or relating to an eclipse

ECLOGITE n rare coarse-grained basic rock

ECLOGUE, -S n pastoral or idyllic poem, usually in the form of a conversation or soliloquy

ECLOSE, -D, -S, ECLOSING vb emerge

ECLOSION n emergence of an insect larva from the egg or an adult from the pupal case

ECO, -S n ecology activist

ECOCIDAL ▶ ecocide

ECOCIDE, -S n total destruction of an area of the natural environment

ECOD same as ▶ egad

ECOFREAK n environmentalist

ECOGIFT, -S n donation of land for environmental purposes

ECOLODGE n eco-friendly tourist accommodation

ECOLOGIC ▶ ecology

ECOLOGY n study of the links between living things and their environment

ECOMAP, -S n diagram showing the links between an individual and their community

ECONOBOX n fuel efficient utility vehicle

ECONOMIC adj of economics

ECONOMY n system of interrelationship of money, industry, and employment in a country ▷ adj denoting a class of air travel that is cheaper than first-class

ECONUT, -S n derogatory term for a keen environmentalist

ECORCHE, -S n anatomical figure without the skin

ECOS ▶ eco

ECOSTATE adj with no ribs or nerves

ECOTAGE, -S n sabotage for ecological motives

ECOTONAL ▶ ecotone

ECOTONE, -S n zone between two major ecological communities

ECOTOPIA n ecologically ideal area or society

ECOTOUR, -S n holiday taking care not to damage environment ▷ vb take an ecotour

ECOTOXIC adj harmful to animals, plants or the environment

ECOTYPE, -S n group of organisms in a species that have adapted to a particular environment

ECOTYPIC ▶ ecotype

ECOZONE, -S n large area with an ecosystem

ECRASEUR n surgical device consisting of a heavy wire loop

ECRU, -S n greyish-yellow colour

ECSTASIS, ECSTASES same as ▶ ecstasy

ECSTASY n state of intense delight

E

E

ECSTATIC adj in a trancelike state of great rapture or delight ▷ n person who has periods of intense trancelike joy

ECTASES ▷ ectasis

ECTASIA, -S n distension or dilation of a duct, vessel, or hollow viscus

ECTASIS, ECTASES same as ▷ ectasia

ECTATIC ▷ ectasia

ECTHYMA, -S n local inflammation of the skin

ECTODERM n outer germ layer of an animal embryo

ECTOGENE n type of gene

ECTOGENY n (of bacteria, etc) development outside the host

ECTOMERE n any of the blastomeres that later develop into ectoderm

ECTOPIA, -S n congenital displacement of an organ or part

ECTOPIC ▷ ectopia

ECTOPY, ECTOPIES same as ▷ ectopia

ECTOSARC n ectoplasm of an amoeba or any other protozoan

ECTOZOA ▷ ectozoon

ECTOZOAN same as ▷ ectozoon

ECTOZOIC ▷ ectozoon

ECTOZOON, ECTOZOA n parasitic organism that lives on the outside of its host

ECTROPIC ▷ ectropion

ECTYPAL ▷ ectype

ECTYPE, -S n copy

ECU, -S n any of various former French gold or silver coins

ECUELLE, -S n covered soup bowl with handles

ECUMENE, -S n inhabited area of the world

ECUMENIC adj tending to promote unity among Churches

ECURIE, -S n team of motor-racing cars

ECUS ▷ ecu

ECZEMA, -S n skin disease causing intense itching

ED, -S n editor

EDACIOUS adj devoted to eating

EDACITY ▷ edacious

EDAMAME, -S n Japanese dish of salted green soya beans

EDAPHIC adj of or relating to the physical and chemical conditions of the soil

EDDIED ▷ eddy

EDDIES ▷ eddy

EDDISH, -ES n pasture grass

EDDO, -ES same as ▷ taro

EDDY, EDDIED, EDDIES, -ING n circular movement of air, water, etc ▷ vb move with a circular motion

EDEMA, -S, -TA same as ▷ oedema

EDENIC adj delightful, like the Garden of Eden

EDENTAL adj having few or no teeth

EDENTATE n mammal with few or no teeth, such as an armadillo or a sloth ▷ adj denoting such a mammal

EDGE, -D, -S n border or line where something ends or begins ▷ vb provide an edge or border for

EDGEBONE n aitchbone

EDGED ▷ edge

EDGELESS ▷ edge

EDGER, -S ▷ edge

EDGES ▷ edge

EDGEWAYS adv with the edge forwards or uppermost

EDGEWISE same as ▷ edgeways

EDGIER ▷ edgy

EDGIEST ▷ edgy

EDGILY ▷ edgy

EDGINESS ▷ edgy

EDGING, -S n anything placed along an edge to finish it ▷ adj relating to or used for making an edge

EDGY, EDGIER, EDGIEST adj nervous or irritable

EDH, -S n character of the runic alphabet

EDIBLE adj fit to be eaten

EDIBLES pl n articles fit to eat

EDICT, -S n order issued by an authority

EDICTAL ▷ edict

EDICTS ▷ edict

EDIFICE, -S n large building

EDIFIED ▷ edify

EDIFIER, -S ▷ edify

EDIFY, EDIFIED, EDIFIES vb improve morally by instruction

EDIFYING ▷ edify

EDILE, -S variant spelling of ▷ aedile

EDIT, -ED, -S vb prepare (a book, film, etc) for publication or broadcast ▷ n act of editing

EDITABLE ▷ edit

EDITED ▷ edit

EDITING, -S ▷ edit

EDITION, -S n number of copies of a new publication printed at one time ▷ vb produce multiple copies of (an original work of art)

EDITOR, -S n person who edits

EDITRESS n female editor

EDITRIX n female editor

EDITS ▷ edit

EDS ▷ ed

EDUCABLE adj capable of being trained or educated ▷ n person who is capable of being educated

EDUCATE, -S vb teach

EDUCATED adj having had an education

EDUCATES ▷ educate

EDUCATOR n person who educates

EDUCE, -D, -S, EDUCING vb evolve or develop

EDUCIBLE ▷ educe

EDUCING ▷ educe

EDUCT, -S n substance separated from a mixture without chemical change

EDUCTION n something educed

EDUCTIVE ▷ educe

EDUCTOR, -S ▷ educe

EDUCTS ▷ educe

EE, -N Scots word for ▷ eye

EECH, -ED, -ES, -ING same as ▷ eche

EEEW interj exclamation of disgust

EEJIT, -S Scots and Irish word for ▷ idiot

EEK interj indicating shock or fright

EEL, -S n snakelike fish

EELFARE, -S n young eel

EELGRASS n type of submerged marine plant with grasslike leaves

EELIER ▷ eely

EELIEST ▷ eely

EELING, -S n practice of catching eels

EELLIKE adj resembling an eel

EELPOUT, -S n marine eel-like blennioid fish

EELS ▷ eel

EELWORM, -S n any of various nematode worms

EELWRACK n grasslike plant growing in seawater

EELY, EELIER, EELIEST ▷ eel

EEN ▷ ee

EENSY, EENSIER, EENSIEST adj very small

EERIE, -R, -ST adj uncannily frightening or disturbing

EERILY ▸ eerie

EERINESS ▸ eerie

EERY *same as* ▸ **eerie**

EEVEN, -S *n* old form of evening

EEVN, -S *same as* ▸ **eeven**

EEVNING, -S *n* old form of evening

EEVNS ▸ eevn

EEW *interj* exclamation of disgust

EF, -S *n* letter F

EFF, -ED, -S *vb* use bad language

EFFABLE *adj* capable of being expressed in words

EFFACE, -D, -S, EFFACING *vb* remove by rubbing

EFFACER, -S ▸ efface

EFFACES ▸ efface

EFFACING ▸ efface

EFFECT, -ED *n* change or result caused by someone or something ▷ *vb* cause to happen, accomplish

EFFECTER ▸ effect

EFFECTOR *n* nerve ending that terminates in a muscle or gland

EFFECTS *pl n* personal belongings

EFFED ▸ eff

EFFEIR, -ED, -S *vb* suit

EFFENDI, -S *n* (in the Ottoman Empire) a title of respect

EFFERE, -D, -S, EFFERING *same as* ▸ **effeir**

EFFERENT *adj* carrying or conducting outwards ▷ *n* type of nerve

EFFERES ▸ effere

EFFERING ▸ effere

EFFETE *adj* powerless, feeble

EFFETELY ▸ effete

EFFICACY *n* quality of being successful in producing an intended result

EFFIERCE *vb* archaic word meaning make fierce

EFFIGIAL ▸ effigy

EFFIGY, EFFIGIES *n* image or likeness of a person

EFFING, -S ▸ eff

EFFLUENT *n* liquid discharged as waste ▷ *adj* flowing out or forth

EFFLUVIA > effluvium

EFFLUX, -ES *same as* > **effluence**

EFFORCE, -D, -S *vb* old word for force

EFFORT, -S *n* physical or mental exertion

EFFRAIDE *archaic form of* ▸ **afraid**

EFFRAY, -S *archaic form of* ▸ **affray**

EFFS ▸ eff

EFFULGE, -D, -S *vb* radiate

EFFUSE, -D, -S, EFFUSING *vb* pour or flow out ▷ *adj* (esp of an inflorescence) spreading out loosely

EFFUSION *n* unrestrained outburst

EFFUSIVE *adj* openly emotional, demonstrative

EFS ▸ ef

EFT, -S *n* dialect or archaic name for a newt ▷ *adv* again

EFTEST *adj* nearest at hand

EFTS ▸ eft

EFTSOONS, EFTSOON *adv* soon afterwards

EGAD, -S *n* mild oath or expression of surprise

EGAL *adj* equal

EGALITE, -S *n* equality

EGALITY *n* equality

EGALLY ▸ egal

EGENCE, -S *n* need

EGENCY, EGENCIES *same as* ▸ **egence**

EGER, -S *same as* ▸ **eagre**

EGEST, -ED, -ING, -S *vb* excrete (waste material)

EGESTA *pl n* anything egested, as waste material from the body

EGESTED ▸ egest

EGESTING ▸ egest

EGESTION ▸ egest

EGESTIVE ▸ egest

EGESTS ▸ egest

EGG, -ED, -ING, -S *n* object laid by birds and other creatures, containing a developing embryo ▷ *vb* urge or incite, esp to daring or foolish acts

EGGAR, -S *same as* ▸ **egger**

EGGCORN, -S *n* misspelling caused by the mishearing of a word

EGGCUP, -S *n* cup for holding a boiled egg

EGGED ▸ egg

EGGER, -S *n* moth with brown body and wings

EGGERIES ▸ eggery

EGGERS ▸ egger

EGGERY, EGGERIES *n* place where eggs are laid

EGGFRUIT *n* fruit of eggplant

EGGHEAD, -S *n* intellectual person

EGGIER ▸ eggy

EGGIEST ▸ eggy

EGGING ▸ egg

EGGLER, -S *n* egg dealer: sometimes itinerant

EGGLESS ▸ egg

EGGLIKE *adj* like an egg

EGGMASS *n* intelligentsia

EGGNOG, -S *n* drink made of raw eggs, milk, sugar, spice, and brandy or rum

EGGPLANT *n* dark purple tropical fruit, cooked and eaten as a vegetable

EGGS ▸ egg

EGGSHELL *n* hard covering round the egg of a bird or animal ▷ *adj* (of paint) having a very slight sheen

EGGWASH *n* beaten egg for brushing on pastry

EGGWHISK *same as* > **eggbeater**

EGGY, EGGIER, EGGIEST *adj* soaked in or tasting of egg

EGIS, -ES *rare spelling of* ▸ **aegis**

EGLATERE *archaic name for* > **eglantine**

EGLOMISE *n* gilding

EGMA, -S *mispronunciation of* ▸ **enigma**

EGO, -S *n* conscious mind of an individual

EGOISM, -S *n* excessive concern for one's own interests

EGOIST, -S *n* person who is preoccupied with their own interests

EGOISTIC ▸ egoist

EGOISTS ▸ egoist

EGOITY, EGOITIES *n* essence of the ego

EGOLESS *adj* without an ego

EGOMANIA *n* obsessive concern with one's own needs and desires

EGOS ▸ ego

EGOSURF, -S *vb* search for one's own name on the internet

EGOTISE, -D, -S *same as* ▸ **egotize**

EGOTISM, -S *n* concern only for one's own interests and feelings

EGOTIST, -S *n* conceited boastful person

EGOTIZE, -D, -S *vb* talk or write in a self-important way

EGRESS, -ED, -ES *same as* ▸ **emersion**

EGRET, -S *n* lesser white heron

EGYPTIAN *n* type of typeface

EH, -ED, -ING, -S *interj* exclamation of surprise or inquiry ▷ *vb* say 'eh'

EIDE ▸ eidos

EIDENT adj diligent

EIDER, -S n Arctic duck

EIDETIC, -S adj (of images) exceptionally vivid, allowing detailed recall of something ▷ n person with eidetic ability

EIDOLA ▶ eidolon

EIDOLIC ▶ eidolon

EIDOLON, EIDOLA, -S n unsubstantial image

EIDOS, EIDE n intellectual character of a culture or a social group

EIGHT, -S n one more than seven

EIGHTEEN n eight and ten

EIGHTH, -S n number eight in a series ▷ adj coming after the seventh and before the ninth

EIGHTHLY adv in the eighth place or position

EIGHTHS ▶ eighth

EIGHTIES ▶ eighty

EIGHTS ▶ eight

EIGHTVO, -S another word for ▶ octavo

EIGHTY, EIGHTIES n eight times ten

EIGNE adj firstborn

EIK, -ED, -ING, -S variant form of ▶ eke

EIKON, -ES, -S variant spelling of ▶ icon

EIKS ▶ eik

EILD, -S n old age

EILDING, -S n fuel

EILDS ▶ eild

EINA interj exclamation of pain

EINE pl n eyes

EINKORN, -S n variety of wheat of Greece and SW Asia

EINSTEIN n scientific genius

EIRACK, -S n young hen

EIRENIC variant spelling of ▶ irenic

EIRENICS n theology concerned with unity among churches

EISEL, -S n vinegar

EISELL, -S same as ▶ eisel

EISELS ▶ eisel

EISH interj South African exclamation

EISWEIN, -S n wine made from grapes frozen on the vine

EITHER pron one or the other (of two) ▷ adv likewise ▷ determiner one or the other (of two)

EJECT, -ED, -ING, -S vb force out, expel

EJECTA pl n matter thrown out by a volcano or during a meteorite impact

EJECTED ▶ eject

EJECTING ▶ eject

EJECTION ▶ eject

EJECTIVE adj relating to or causing ejection ▷ n ejective consonant

EJECTOR, -S n person or thing that ejects

EJECTS ▶ eject

EJIDO, -S n communal farmland in Mexico

EKE, -D, -S, EKING vb increase, enlarge, or lengthen

EKISTIC ▶ ekistics

EKISTICS n science or study of human settlements

EKKA, -S n type of one-horse carriage

EKLOGITE same as ▶ eclogite

EKPWELE, -S n former monetary unit of Equatorial Guinea

EKTEXINE n in pollen and spores, the outer of the two layers that make up the exine

EKUELE same as ▶ ekpwele

EL, -S n American elevated railway

ELAIN, -S same as ▶ triolein

ELAN, -S n style and vigour

ELANCE, -D, -S, ELANCING vb throw a lance

ELAND, -S n large antelope of southern Africa

ELANET, -S n bird of prey

ELANS ▶ elan

ELAPHINE adj of or like a red deer

ELAPID, -S n mostly tropical type of venomous snake

ELAPINE adj of or like an elapid

ELAPSE, -D, -S, ELAPSING vb (of time) pass by

ELASTANE n synthetic fibre that is able to return to its original shape after being stretched

ELASTASE n enzyme that digests elastin

ELASTIC, -S adj resuming normal shape after distortion ▷ n tape or fabric containing interwoven strands of flexible rubber

ELASTIN, -S n fibrous scleroprotein

ELATE, -S, ELATING vb fill with high spirits, exhilaration, pride or optimism

ELATED adj extremely happy and excited

ELATEDLY ▶ elated

ELATER, -S n elaterid beetle

ELATERID n type of beetle of the family which constitutes the click beetles

ELATERIN n white crystalline substance found in elaterium, used as a purgative

ELATERS ▶ elater

ELATES ▶ elate

ELATING ▶ elate

ELATION, -S n feeling of great happiness and excitement

ELATIVE, -S adj denoting a grammatical case in Finnish and other languages ▷ n elative case

ELBOW, -ED, -S n joint between the upper arm and the forearm ▷ vb shove or strike with the elbow

ELBOWING n act of elbowing

ELBOWS ▶ elbow

ELCHEE, -S n ambassador

ELCHI, -S same as ▶ elchee

ELD, -S n old age

ELDER, -S adj older ▷ n older person

ELDERLY adj (fairly) old

ELDERS ▶ elder

ELDEST, -S n oldest child

ELDIN, -S n fuel

ELDING, -S same as ▶ eldin

ELDINS ▶ eldin

ELDORADO n place of great riches or fabulous opportunity

ELDRESS n woman elder

ELDRICH same as ▶ eldritch

ELDRITCH adj weird, uncanny

ELDS ▶ eld

ELECT, -ED, -ING, -S vb choose by voting ▷ adj appointed but not yet in office

ELECTEE, -S n someone who is elected

ELECTING ▶ elect

ELECTION n choosing of representatives by voting

ELECTIVE adj chosen by election ▷ n optional course or hospital placement undertaken by a medical student

ELECTOR, -S n someone who has the right to vote in an election

ELECTRET n permanently polarized dielectric material

ELECTRIC adj produced by, transmitting, or powered by electricity ▷ n electric train, car, etc

ELECTRO, -S vb (in printing) make a metallic copy of a page

ELECTRON n elementary particle in all atoms that has a negative electrical charge

ELECTROS ► electro

ELECTRUM n alloy of gold (55–88 per cent) and silver used for jewellery and ornaments

ELECTS ► elect

ELEGANCE n dignified grace in appearance, movement, or behaviour

ELEGANCY same as **► elegance**

ELEGANT adj pleasing or graceful in dress, style, or design

ELEGIAC, -S adj mournful or plaintive ▷ n elegiac couplet or stanza

ELEGIAST n writer of elegies

ELEGIES ► elegy

ELEGISE, -D, -S same as **► elegize**

ELEGIST, -S ► elegize

ELEGIT, -S n writ delivering debtor's property to plaintiff

ELEGIZE, -D, -S vb compose an elegy or elegies (in memory of)

ELEGY, ELEGIES n mournful poem, esp a lament for the dead

ELEMENT, -S n component part

ELEMI, -S n fragrant resin obtained from various tropical trees

ELENCH, -S n refutation in logic

ELENCHI ► elenchus

ELENCHIC ► elenchus

ELENCHS ► elench

ELENCHUS, ELENCHI n refutation of an argument by proving the contrary of its conclusion

ELENCTIC adj refuting an argument by proving the falsehood of its conclusion

ELEPHANT n huge four-footed thick-skinned animal with ivory tusks and a long trunk

ELEVATE, -S vb raise in rank or status

ELEVATED adj higher than normal ▷ n railway that runs on an elevated structure

ELEVATES ► elevate

ELEVATOR n lift for carrying people

ELEVEN, -S n one more than ten

ELEVENTH n number eleven in a series ▷ adj coming after the tenth in numbering or counting order, position, time, etc

ELEVON, -S n aircraft control surface usually fitted to tailless or delta-wing aircraft

ELF, -ED, -ING, -S, ELVES n (in folklore) small mischievous fairy ▷ vb entangle (esp hair)

ELFHOOD, -S ► elf

ELFIN, -S adj small and delicate ▷ n young elf

ELFING ► elf

ELFINS ► elfin

ELFISH, -ES adj of, relating to, or like an elf or elves ▷ n supposed language of elves

ELFISHLY ► elfish

ELFLAND, -S another name for **> fairyland**

ELFLIKE ► elf

ELFLOCK, -S n lock of hair

ELFS ► elf

ELHI adj informal US word meaning relating to elementary or high school

ELIAD, -S n glance

ELICHE, -S n pasta in the form of spirals

ELICIT, -ED, -S vb bring about (a response or reaction)

ELICITOR ► elicit

ELICITS ► elicit

ELIDE, -D, -S, ELIDING vb omit (a vowel or syllable) from a word

ELIDIBLE ► elide

ELIDING ► elide

ELIGIBLE adj meeting the requirements or qualifications needed ▷ n eligible person or thing

ELIGIBLY ► eligible

ELINT, -S n electronic intelligence

ELISION, -S n omission of a vowel or syllable from a word

ELITE, -S n most powerful, rich, or gifted members of a group ▷ adj of, relating to, or suitable for an elite

ELITISM, -S n belief that society should be ruled by a small group of superior people

ELITIST, -S ► elitism

ELIXIR, -S n legendary liquid

ELK, -S n large deer of N Europe and Asia

ELKHORN n as in **elkhorn fern** fern with a large leaf like an elk's horn

ELKHOUND n powerful breed of dog

ELKS ► elk

ELL, -S n obsolete unit of length

ELLAGIC adj of an acid derived from gallnuts

ELLIPSE n oval shape

ELLIPSIS, ELLIPSES n omission of letters or words in a sentence

ELLIPTIC adj relating to or having the shape of an ellipse

ELLOPS, -ES same as **► elops**

ELLS ► ell

ELLWAND, -S n stick for measuring lengths

ELM, -S n tree with serrated leaves

ELMEN adj of or relating to elm trees

ELMIER ► elmy

ELMIEST ► elmy

ELMS ► elm

ELMWOOD, -S n wood from an elm tree

ELMY, ELMIER, ELMIEST adj of or relating to elm trees

ELOCUTE, -D, -S vb speak as if practising elocution

ELODEA, -S n type of American plant

ELOGE, -S same as **► eulogy**

ELOGIES ► elogy

ELOGIST, -S ► elogy

ELOGIUM, -S same as **► eulogy**

ELOGY, ELOGIES same as **► eulogy**

ELOIGN, -ED, -S vb remove (oneself, one's property, etc) to a distant place

ELOIGNER ► eloign

ELOIGNS ► eloign

ELOIN, -ED, -ING, -S same as **► eloign**

ELOINER, -S ► eloin

ELOINING ► eloin

ELOINS ► eloin

ELOPS, -ES n type of fish

ELOQUENT adj (of speech or writing) fluent and persuasive

ELPEE, -S n LP, long-playing record

ELS ▸ el

ELSE adv in addition or more

ELSEWISE adv otherwise

ELSHIN, -S n cobbler's awl

ELSIN, -S variant of ▸ elshin

ELT, -S n young female pig

ELTCHI, -S variant of ▸ elchee

ELTS ▸ elt

ELUANT, -S same as ▸ eluent

ELUATE, -S n solution of adsorbed material obtained during the process of elution

ELUDE, -D, -S, ELUDING vb escape from by cleverness or quickness

ELUDER, -S ▸ elude

ELUDES ▸ elude

ELUDIBLE adj able to be eluded

ELUDING ▸ elude

ELUENT, -S n solvent used for eluting

ELUSION, -S ▸ elude

ELUSIVE adj difficult to catch or remember

ELUSORY adj avoiding the issue

ELUTE, -D, -S, ELUTING vb wash out (a substance) by the action of a solvent

ELUTION, -S ▸ elute

ELUTOR, -S ▸ elute

ELUVIA ▸ eluvium

ELUVIAL ▸ eluvium

ELUVIATE vb remove material suspended in water in a layer of soil by the action of rainfall

ELUVIUM, ELUVIA, -S n mass of sand, silt, etc

ELVAN, -S n type of rock

ELVANITE variant of ▸ elvan

ELVANS ▸ elvan

ELVEN adj like an elf

ELVER, -S n young eel

ELVES ▸ elf

ELVISH, -ES same as ▸ elfish

ELVISHLY ▸ elvish

ELYSIAN adj delightful, blissful

ELYTRA ▸ elytron

ELYTRAL ▸ elytron

ELYTROID ▸ elytron

ELYTRON, ELYTRA n either of the horny front wings of beetles and some other insects

ELYTROUS ▸ elytron

ELYTRUM same as ▸ elytron

EM, -S n square of a body of any size of type, used as a unit of measurement

EMACIATE vb become or cause to become abnormally thin

EMACS, -EN n powerful computer program

EMAIL, -ED, -S n electronic mail ▷ vb send a message by electronic mail

EMAILER, -S ▸ email

EMAILING ▸ email

EMAILS ▸ email

EMANANT ▸ emanate

EMANATE, -D, -S vb issue, proceed from a source

EMANATOR ▸ emanate

EMBACE, -S, EMBACING variant of ▸ embase

EMBAIL, -ED, -S vb enclose in a circle

EMBALE, -D, -S, EMBALING vb bind

EMBALL, -ED, -S vb· enclose in a circle

EMBALM, -ED, -S vb preserve (a corpse) from decay by the use of chemicals etc

EMBALMER ▸ embalm

EMBALMS ▸ embalm

EMBANK, -ED, -S vb protect, enclose, or confine with an embankment

EMBANKER ▸ embank

EMBANKS ▸ embank

EMBAR, -RED, -S vb close in with bars

EMBARGO n order by a government prohibiting trade with a country ▷ vb put an embargo on

EMBARK, -ED, -S vb board a ship or aircraft

EMBARRAS n embarrassment

EMBARRED ▸ embar

EMBARS ▸ embar

EMBASE, -D, -S, EMBASING, EMBASTE vb degrade or debase

EMBASSY n offices or official residence of an ambassador

EMBASTE ▸ embase

EMBATHE, -D, -S vb bathe with water

EMBATTLE vb deploy (troops) for battle

EMBAY, -ED, -ING, -S vb form into a bay

EMBAYLD archaic past form of ▸ embail

EMBAYS ▸ embay

EMBED, -DED, -S vb fix firmly in something solid ▷ n journalist accompanying an active military unit

EMBER, -S n glowing piece of wood or coal in a dying fire

EMBEZZLE vb steal money that has been entrusted to one

EMBIGGEN vb make bigger

EMBITTER vb make (a person) resentful or bitter

EMBLAZE, -D, -S vb cause to light up

EMBLAZER ▸ emblaze

EMBLAZES ▸ emblaze

EMBLAZON vb decorate with bright colours

EMBLEM, -ED, -S n object or design that symbolizes a quality, type, or group ▷ vb represent or signify

EMBLEMA n mosaic decoration

EMBLEMED ▸ emblem

EMBLEMS ▸ emblem

EMBLIC, -S n type of Indian tree

EMBLOOM, -S vb adorn with blooms

EMBODIED ▸ embody

EMBODIER ▸ embody

EMBODY, EMBODIED, EMBODIES vb be an example or expression of

EMBOG, -GED, -S vb sink down into a bog

EMBOGUE, -D, -S vb go out through a narrow channel or passage

EMBOIL, -ED, -S vb enrage or be enraged

EMBOLDEN vb encourage (someone)

EMBOLI ▸ embolus

EMBOLIC adj of or relating to an embolus or embolism

EMBOLIES ▸ emboly

EMBOLISE same as ▸ embolize

EMBOLISM n blocking of a blood vessel by a blood clot or air bubble

EMBOLIZE vb cause embolism in (a blood vessel)

EMBOLUS, EMBOLI n material that blocks a blood vessel

EMBOLY, EMBOLIES n infolding of an outer layer of cells so as to form a pocket in the surface

EMBORDER vb edge or border

EMBOSK, -ED, -S vb hide or cover

EMBOSOM, -S vb enclose or envelop, esp protectively

EMBOSS, -ES, EMBOST vb create a decoration that stands out on (a surface)

EMBOSSED adj (of a design or pattern) standing out from a surface

EMBOSSER ▸ emboss

EMBOSSES ▸ emboss

EMBOST ▸ emboss

EMBOUND, -S vb surround or encircle

EMBOW, -ED, -ING, -S vb design or create (a structure) in the form of an arch or vault

EMBOWEL, -S vb bury or embed deeply

EMBOWER, -S vb enclose in or as in a bower

EMBOWING ▸ embow

EMBOWS ▸ embow

EMBOX, -ED, -ES, -ING vb put in a box

EMBRACE, -D, -S vb clasp in the arms, hug ▷ n act of embracing

EMBRACER ▸ embrace

EMBRACES ▸ embrace

EMBRAID, -S vb braid or interweave

EMBRASOR n one who embraces

EMBRAVE, -D, -S vb adorn or decorate

EMBREAD, -S vb braid

EMBROIL, -S vb involve (a person) in problems

EMBROWN, -S vb make or become brown

EMBRUE, -D, -S, EMBRUING variant spelling of ▸ imbrue

EMBRUTE, -D, -S variant of ▸ imbrute

EMBRYO, -S n unborn creature in the early stages of development

EMBRYOID ▸ embryo

EMBRYON, -S variant of ▸ embryo

EMBRYOS ▸ embryo

EMBUS, -ED, -ES, -ING, -SED, -SES vb cause (troops) to board a transport vehicle

EMBUSIED ▸ embusy

EMBUSIES ▸ embusy

EMBUSING ▸ embus

EMBUSQUE n man who avoids military conscription by obtaining a government job

EMBUSSED ▸ embus

EMBUSSES ▸ embus

EMBUSY, EMBUSIED, EMBUSIES vb keep occupied

EMCEE, -D, -ING, -S n master of ceremonies ▷ vb act as master of ceremonies (for or at)

EMDASH, -ES n long dash in punctuation

EME, -S n uncle

EMEER, -S variant of ▸ emir

EMEERATE variant of ▸ emirate

EMEERS ▸ emeer

EMEND, -ED, -ING, -S vb remove errors from

EMENDALS pl n funds put aside for repairs

EMENDATE vb make corrections

EMENDED ▸ emend

EMENDER, -S ▸ emend

EMENDING ▸ emend

EMENDS ▸ emend

EMERALD, -S n bright green precious stone ▷ adj bright green

EMERAUDE archaic variant of ▸ emerald

EMERG, -S n part of a hospital dealing with emergencies

EMERGE, -D, -S vb come into view

EMERGENT adj coming into being or notice ▷ n aquatic plant with stem and leaves above the water

EMERGES ▸ emerge

EMERGING ▸ emerge

EMERGS ▸ emerg

EMERIED ▸ emery

EMERIES ▸ emery

EMERITA, -E, -S adj retired, but retaining an honorary title ▷ n woman who is retired, but retains an honorary title

EMERITUS, EMERITI adj retired, but retaining an honorary title ▷ n person who is retired, but retains an honorary title

EMEROD, -S n haemorrhoid

EMEROID, -S variant of ▸ emerod

EMERSE same as ▸ emersed

EMERSED adj protruding above the surface of the water

EMERSION n act or an instance of emerging

EMERY, EMERIED, EMERIES, -ING n hard mineral used for smoothing and polishing ▷ vb apply emery to

EMES ▸ eme

EMESIS, EMESES, -ES technical name for ▸ vomiting

EMETIC, -S n substance that causes vomiting ▷ adj causing vomiting

EMETICAL same as ▸ emetic

EMETICS ▸ emetic

EMETIN, -S same as ▸ emetine

EMETINE, -S n white bitter poisonous alkaloid

EMETINS ▸ emetin

EMEU, -S variant of ▸ emu

EMEUTE, -S n uprising or rebellion

EMIC, -S adj of or relating to a significant linguistic unit ▷ n emic viewpoint or approach

EMICANT ▸ emicate

EMICATE, -D, -S vb twinkle

EMICS ▸ emic

EMICTION n passing of urine

EMICTORY ▸ emiction

EMIGRANT n person who leaves one place or country, esp a native country, to settle in another

EMIGRATE vb go and settle in another country

EMIGRE, -S n someone who has left his or her native country for political reasons

EMIGREE, -S n female emigre

EMIGRES ▸ emigre

EMINENCE n position of superiority or fame

EMINENCY same as ▸ eminence

EMINENT adj distinguished, well-known

EMIR, -S n Muslim ruler

EMIRATE, -S n emir's country

EMIRS ▸ emir

EMISSARY n agent sent on a mission by a government ▷ adj (of veins) draining blood from sinuses in the dura mater to veins outside the skull

EMISSILE adj able to be emitted

EMISSION n act of giving out heat, light, a smell, etc

EMISSIVE ▸ emission

EMIT, -S, -TED, -TING vb give out

EMITTER, -S n person or thing that emits

EMITTING ▸ emit

EMLETS pl n as in **blood-drop emlets** Chilean plant

EMMA, -S n former communications code for the letter M

EMMARBLE vb decorate with marble

EMMAS ▸ emma

EMMER, -S n variety of wheat

EMMESH, -ED, -ES variant of ▸ enmesh

EMMET, -S n tourist or holidaymaker

EMMEW, -ED, -ING, -S vb restrict

EMMOVE, -D, -S, EMMOVING vb cause emotion in

EMMY, -S n award for outstanding television performances and productions

EMO, -S n type of music combining rock with emotional lyrics

EMOCORE, -S same as ▶ emo

EMODIN, -S n chemical compound obtained from rhubarb root

EMOJI, -S n digital icon used in electronic communication

EMONG variant of ▶ among

EMONGES variant of ▶ among

EMONGEST variant of ▶ amongst

EMONGST variant of ▶ amongst

EMOS ▶ emo

EMOTE, -D, -S, EMOTING vb display exaggerated emotion, as if acting

EMOTER, -S ▶ emote

EMOTES ▶ emote

EMOTICON n any of several combinations of symbols used in email and texting

EMOTING ▶ emote

EMOTION, -S n strong feeling

EMOTIVE adj tending to arouse emotion

EMOVE, -D, -S, EMOVING vb cause to feel emotion

EMPACKET vb wrap up

EMPAIRE, -D, -S variant of ▶ impair

EMPALE, -D, -S, EMPALING less common spelling of ▶ impale

EMPALER, -S ▶ empale

EMPALES ▶ empale

EMPALING ▶ empale

EMPANADA n Spanish meat-filled pastry

EMPANEL, -S vb enter on a list (names of persons to be summoned for jury service)

EMPARE, -D, -S, EMPARING archaic variant of ▶ impair

EMPARL, -ED, -S variant of ▶ imparl

EMPART, -ED, -S variant of ▶ impart

EMPATHIC adj of or relating to empathy

EMPATHY n ability to understand someone else's feelings

EMPATRON vb treat in the manner of a patron

EMPAYRE, -D, -S archaic variant of ▶ impair

EMPEACH variant of ▶ impeach

EMPEOPLE vb bring people into

EMPERCE, -D, -S archaic variant of ▶ empierce

EMPERIES ▶ empery

EMPERISE variant of ▶ emperize

EMPERISH vb damage or harm

EMPERIZE vb act like an emperor

EMPEROR, -S n ruler of an empire

EMPERY, EMPERIES n dominion or power

EMPHASIS, EMPHASES n special importance or significance

EMPHATIC adj showing emphasis ▷ n emphatic consonant, as used in Arabic

EMPIERCE vb pierce or cut

EMPIGHT, -S adj attached or positioned ▷ vb attach or position

EMPIRE, -S n group of territories under the rule of one state or person

EMPIRIC, -S n person who relies on empirical methods

EMPLACE, -D, -S vb put in place or position

EMPLANE, -D, -S vb board or put on board an aeroplane

EMPLEACH variant of ▶ impleach

EMPLONGE variant of ▶ implunge

EMPLOY, -ED, -S vb engage or make use of the services of (a person) in return for money ▷ n state of being employed

EMPLOYE, -S same as ▶ employee

EMPLOYED ▶ employ

EMPLOYEE n person who is hired to work for someone in return for payment

EMPLOYER n person or organization that employs someone

EMPLOYES ▶ employe

EMPLOYS ▶ employ

EMPLUME, -D, -S vb put a plume on

EMPOISON vb embitter or corrupt

EMPOLDER variant spelling of ▶ impolder

EMPORIUM, EMPORIA n large general shop

EMPOWER, -S vb enable, authorize

EMPRESS n woman who rules an empire

EMPRESSE adj keen; zealous

EMPRISE, -S n chivalrous or daring enterprise

EMPRIZE, -S variant of ▶ emprise

EMPT, -ED, -ING, -S vb empty

EMPTIED ▶ empty

EMPTIER, -S ▶ empty

EMPTIES ▶ empty

EMPTIEST ▶ empty

EMPTILY ▶ empty

EMPTING ▶ empt

EMPTINGS variant of ▶ emptins

EMPTINS pl n liquid leavening agent made from potatoes

EMPTION, -S n process of buying something

EMPTS ▶ empt

EMPTY, EMPTIED, EMPTIES, EMPTIEST adj containing nothing ▷ vb make or become empty ▷ n empty container, esp a bottle

EMPTYING ▶ empty

EMPTYSIS, EMPTYSES n act of spitting up blood

EMPURPLE vb make or become purple

EMPUSA, -S n goblin in Greek mythology

EMPUSE, -S variant of ▶ empusa

EMPYEMA, -S n collection of pus in a body cavity

EMPYEMIC ▶ empyema

EMPYESIS, EMPYESES n pus-filled boil on the skin

EMPYREAL variant of ▶ empyrean

EMPYREAN n heavens or sky ▷ adj of or relating to the sky or the heavens

EMS ▶ em

EMU, -S n large Australian flightless bird with long legs

EMULATE, -D, -S vb attempt to equal or surpass by imitating

EMULATOR ▶ emulate

EMULE, -D, -S, EMULING variant of ▶ emulate

EMULGE, -D, -S, EMULGING vb remove liquid from

EMULGENT ▶ emulge

EMULGES ▶ emulge

EMULGING ▶ emulge

EMULING ▸ emule
EMULOUS adj desiring or aiming to equal or surpass another
EMULSIFY vb (of two liquids) join together
EMULSIN, -S n enzyme that is found in almonds
EMULSION n light-sensitive coating on photographic film ▷ vb paint with emulsion paint
EMULSIVE ▸ emulsion
EMULSOID n sol with a liquid disperse phase
EMULSOR, -S n device that emulsifies
EMUNGE, -D, -S, EMUNGING vb clean or clear out
EMURE, -D, -S, EMURING variant of ▸ immure
EMUS ▸ emu
EMYD, -S n freshwater tortoise or terrapin
EMYDE, -S same as ▸ emyd
EMYDS ▸ emyd
EMYS n freshwater tortoise or terrapin
EN n unit of measurement, half the width of an em
ENABLE, -D, -S, ENABLING vb provide (a person) with the means (to do something)
ENABLER, -S ▸ enable
ENABLES ▸ enable
ENABLING ▸ enable
ENACT, -ED, -ING, -S vb establish by law
ENACTION ▸ enact
ENACTIVE ▸ enact
ENACTOR, -S ▸ enact
ENACTORY ▸ enact
ENACTS ▸ enact
ENACTURE ▸ enact
ENALLAGE n act of using one grammatical form in the place of another
ENAMEL, -ED, -S n glasslike coating applied to metal etc to preserve the surface ▷ vb cover with enamel
ENAMELER ▸ enamel
ENAMELS ▸ enamel
ENAMINE, -S n type of unsaturated compound
ENAMOR, -S same as ▸ enamour
ENAMORED same as > enamoured
ENAMORS ▸ enamor
ENAMOUR, -S vb inspire with love
ENARCH, -ED, -ES variant of ▸ inarch

ENARGITE n sulphide of copper and arsenic
ENARM, -ED, -ING, -S vb provide with arms
ENATE, -S adj growing out or outwards ▷ n relative on the mother's side
ENATIC adj related on one's mother's side
ENATION, -S ▸ enate
ENAUNTER conj in case that
ENCAENIA n festival of dedication or commemoration
ENCAGE, -D, -S, ENCAGING vb confine in or as in a cage
ENCALM, -ED, -S vb becalm, settle
ENCAMP, -ED, -S vb set up in a camp
ENCARPUS n decoration of fruit or flowers on a frieze
ENCASE, -D, -S, ENCASING vb enclose or cover completely
ENCASH, -ED, -ES vb exchange (a cheque) for cash
ENCASING ▸ encase
ENCASTRE adj (of a beam) fixed at the ends
ENCAVE, -D, -S, ENCAVING variant of ▸ incave
ENCEINTE n boundary wall enclosing a defended area
ENCHAFE, -D, -S vb heat up
ENCHAIN, -S vb bind with chains
ENCHANT, -S vb delight and fascinate
ENCHARGE vb give into the custody of
ENCHARM, -S vb enchant
ENCHASE, -D, -S less common word for ▸ chase
ENCHASER ▸ enchase
ENCHASES ▸ enchase
ENCHEER, -S vb cheer up
ENCHORIC same as > enchorial
ENCIERRO n Spanish bull run
ENCINA, -S n type of oak
ENCINAL ▸ encina
ENCINAS ▸ encina
ENCIPHER vb convert (a message, document, etc) from plain text into code or cipher
ENCIRCLE vb form a circle around
ENCLASP, -S vb clasp
ENCLAVE, -D, -S n part of a country entirely surrounded by another ▷ vb hold in an enclave
ENCLISIS, ENCLISES n state of being enclitic

ENCLITIC adj relating to a monosyllabic word treated as a suffix ▷ n enclitic word or linguistic form
ENCLOSE, -D, -S vb surround completely
ENCLOSER ▸ enclose
ENCLOSES ▸ enclose
ENCLOTHE vb clothe
ENCLOUD, -S vb hide with clouds
ENCODE, -D, -S vb convert (a message) into code
ENCODER, -S ▸ encode
ENCODES ▸ encode
ENCODING n act of encoding
ENCOLOUR vb give a colour to
ENCOLPIA > encolpion
ENCOLURE n mane of a horse
ENCOMIA ▸ encomium
ENCOMION variant of ▸ encomium
ENCOMIUM, ENCOMIA n formal expression of praise
ENCORE, -D, -S, ENCORING interj again, once more ▷ n extra performance due to enthusiastic demand ▷ vb demand an extra or repeated performance
ENCRADLE vb put in a cradle
ENCRATY n control of one's desires, actions, etc
ENCREASE variant form of ▸ increase
ENCRINAL ▸ encrinite
ENCRINIC > encrinite
ENCROACH vb intrude gradually on a person's rights or land
ENCRUST, -S vb cover with a layer of something
ENCRYPT, -S vb put (a message) into code
ENCUMBER vb hinder or impede
ENCYCLIC n letter sent by the Pope to all bishops
ENCYST, -S vb enclose or become enclosed by a cyst, thick membrane, or shell
ENCYSTED ▸ encyst
ENCYSTS ▸ encyst
END, -ED, -S n furthest point or part ▷ vb bring or come to a finish
ENDAMAGE vb cause injury to
ENDAMEBA same as > endamoeba
ENDANGER vb put in danger
ENDARCH adj having the first-formed xylem internal to that formed later

E

ENDARCHY n state of being endarch

ENDART, -ED, -S variant of ▸indart

ENDASH, -ES n short dash in punctuation

ENDBRAIN n part of the brain

ENDCAP, -S n display placed at the end of a shop aisle

ENDEAR, -ED, -S vb cause to be liked

ENDEAVOR same as ▸endeavour

ENDED ▸end

ENDEIXIS, ENDEIXES n sign or mark

ENDEMIAL same as ▸endemic

ENDEMIC, -S adj present within a particular area or group of people ▷ n endemic disease or plant

ENDEMISM ▸endemic

ENDER, -S ▸end

ENDERMIC adj (of a medicine) acting by absorption through the skin

ENDERON, -S variant of ▸andiron

ENDERS ▸ender

ENDEW, -ED, -ING, -S variant of ▸endue

ENDEXINE n inner layer of an exine

ENDGAME, -S n closing stage of a game of chess

ENDGATE, -S n tailboard of a vehicle

ENDING, -S n last part or conclusion of something

ENDIRON, -S variant of ▸andiron

ENDITE, -D, -S, ENDITING variant of ▸indict

ENDIVE, -S n curly-leaved plant used in salads

ENDLANG variant of ▸endlong

ENDLEAF, -S n endpaper in a book

ENDLESS adj having no end

ENDLONG adv lengthways or on end

ENDMOST adj nearest the end

ENDNOTE, -S n note at the end of a section of writing

ENDOCARP n inner layer of a fruit

ENDOCAST n cast made of the inside of a cranial cavity to show the size and shape of a brain

ENDODERM n inner germ layer of an animal embryo

ENDODYNE same as ▸autodyne

ENDOGAMY n marriage within one's own tribe or similar unit

ENDOGEN, -S n plant that increases in size by internal growth

ENDOGENY n development by internal growth

ENDOPOD, -S n inner branch of a two-branched crustacean

ENDORSE, -D, -S vb give approval to

ENDORSEE n person in whose favour a negotiable instrument is endorsed

ENDORSER ▸endorse

ENDORSES ▸endorse

ENDORSOR ▸endorse

ENDOSARC same as ▸endoplasm

ENDOSMOS same as ▸endosmose

ENDOSOME n sac within a biological cell

ENDOSS, -ED, -ES vb endorse

ENDOSTEA ▸endosteum

ENDOW, -ED, -ING, -S vb provide permanent income for

ENDOWER, -S ▸endow

ENDOWING ▸endow

ENDOWS ▸endow

ENDOZOA ▸endozoon

ENDOZOIC adj (of a plant) living within an animal

ENDOZOON, ENDOZOA variant of ▸entozoon

ENDPAPER n either of two leaves pasted to the inside of the cover of a book

ENDPLATE n any usually flat platelike structure at the end of something

ENDPLAY, -S n technique in card games ▷vb force (an opponent) to make a particular lead near the end of a hand

ENDPOINT n point at which anything is complete

ENDRIN, -S n type of insecticide

ENDS ▸end

ENDSHIP, -S n small village

ENDUE, -D, -S, ENDUING vb invest or provide, as with some quality or trait

ENDURE, -D, -S vb bear (hardship) patiently

ENDURER, -S ▸endure

ENDURES ▸endure

ENDURING adj long-lasting

ENDURO, -S n long-distance race for vehicles

ENDWAYS adv having the end forwards or upwards ▷adj vertical or upright

ENDWISE same as ▸endways

ENDYSIS, ENDYSES n formation of new layers of integument after ecdysis

ENDZONE, -S n (in American football) area at either end of the playing field

ENE, -S variant of ▸even

ENEMA, -S, -TA n medicine that helps to empty the bowels

ENEMY, ENEMIES n hostile person or nation, opponent ▷adj of or belonging to an enemy

ENERGIC ▸energy

ENERGID, -S n nucleus and cytoplasm in a syncytium

ENERGIES ▸energy

ENERGISE same as ▸energize

ENERGIZE vb give vigour to

ENERGY, ENERGIES n capacity for intense activity

ENERVATE vb deprive of strength or vitality ▷adj deprived of strength or vitality

ENERVE, -D, -S, ENERVING vb enervate

ENES ▸ene

ENEW, -ED, -ING, -S vb force a bird into water

ENFACE, -D, -S, ENFACING vb write, print, or stamp (something) on the face of (a document)

ENFANT, -S n French child

ENFEEBLE vb weaken

ENFELON, -S vb infuriate

ENFEOFF, -S vb invest (a person) with possession of a freehold estate in land

ENFESTED adj made bitter

ENFETTER vb fetter

ENFEVER, -S vb make feverish

ENFIERCE vb make ferocious

ENFILADE n burst of gunfire sweeping from end to end along a line of troops ▷vb attack with an enfilade

ENFILED adj passed through

ENFIRE, -D, -S, ENFIRING vb set alight

ENFIX, -ED, -ES, -ING variant of ▸infix

ENFLAME, -D, -S variant of ▸inflame

ENFLESH vb make flesh

ENFLOWER vb put flowers on

ENFOLD, -ED, -S vb cover by wrapping something around

ENFOLDER ▸ enfold

ENFOLDS ▸ enfold

ENFORCE, -D, -S vb impose obedience (to a law etc)

ENFORCER ▸ enforce

ENFORCES ▸ enforce

ENFOREST vb make into a forest

ENFORM, -ED, -S variant of ▸ inform

ENFRAME, -D, -S vb put inside a frame

ENFREE, -D, -S vb release, make free

ENFREEZE, ENFROZE, ENFROZEN vb freeze

ENFROSEN archaic past participle of ▸ enfreeze

ENFROZE ▸ enfreeze

ENFROZEN ▸ enfreeze

ENG, -S another name for ▸ agma

ENGAGE, -S vb take part, participate ▷ adj (of an artist) morally or politically committed to some ideology

ENGAGED adj pledged to be married

ENGAGEE adj (of a female artist) morally or politically committed to some ideology

ENGAGER, -S ▸ engage

ENGAGES ▸ engage

ENGAGING adj charming

ENGAOL, -ED, -S vb put into gaol

ENGENDER vb produce, cause to occur

ENGILD, -ED, -S, ENGILT vb cover with or as if with gold

ENGINE, -D, -S, ENGINING n any machine which converts energy into mechanical work ▷ vb put an engine in

ENGINEER n person trained in any branch of engineering ▷ vb plan in a clever manner

ENGINER, -S ▸ engine

ENGINERY n collection or assembly of engines

ENGINES ▸ engine

ENGINING ▸ engine

ENGINOUS adj ingenious or clever

ENGIRD, -ED, -S, ENGIRT vb surround

ENGIRDLE variant of ▸ engird

ENGIRDS ▸ engird

ENGIRT ▸ engird

ENGLISH vb put spin on a billiard ball

ENGLOBE, -D, -S vb surround as if in a globe

ENGLOOM, -S vb make dull or dismal

ENGLUT, -S vb devour ravenously

ENGOBE, -S n liquid put on pottery before glazing

ENGORE, -D, -S, ENGORING vb pierce or wound

ENGORGE, -D, -S vb clog with blood

ENGORING ▸ engore

ENGOULED adj (in heraldry) with ends coming from the mouths of animals

ENGRACE, -D, -S vb give grace to

ENGRAFF, -S variant of ▸ engraft

ENGRAFT, -S vb graft (a shoot, bud, etc) onto a stock

ENGRAIL, -S vb decorate or mark with small carved notches

ENGRAIN, -S variant spelling of ▸ ingrain

ENGRAM, -S n physical basis of an individual memory in the brain

ENGRAMMA variant of ▸ engram

ENGRAMME variant of ▸ engram

ENGRAMS ▸ engram

ENGRASP, -S vb grasp or seize

ENGRAVE, -D, -N, -S vb carve (a design) onto a hard surface

ENGRAVER ▸ engrave

ENGRAVES ▸ engrave

ENGRIEVE vb grieve

ENGROOVE vb put a groove in

ENGROSS vb occupy the attention of (a person) completely

ENGS ▸ eng

ENGUARD, -S vb protect or defend

ENGULF, -ED, -S vb cover or surround completely

ENGULPH, -S variant of ▸ engulf

ENHALO, -ED, -ES, -S vb surround with or as if with a halo

ENHANCE, -D, -S vb increase in quality, value, or attractiveness

ENHANCER ▸ enhance

ENHANCES ▸ enhance

ENHEARSE variant of ▸ inhearse

ENHUNGER vb cause to be hungry

ENHYDROS n piece of chalcedony that contains water

ENIAC, -S n early type of computer built in the 1940s

ENIGMA, -S, -TA n puzzling thing or person

ENISLE, -D, -S, ENISLING vb put on or make into an island

ENJAMB, -ED, -S vb (of a line of verse) run over into the next line

ENJOIN, -ED, -S vb order (someone) to do something

ENJOINER ▸ enjoin

ENJOINS ▸ enjoin

ENJOY, -ED, -ING, -S vb take joy in

ENJOYER, -S ▸ enjoy

ENJOYING ▸ enjoy

ENJOYS ▸ enjoy

ENKERNEL vb put inside a kernel

ENKINDLE vb set on fire

ENLACE, -D, -S, ENLACING vb bind or encircle with or as with laces

ENLARD, -ED, -S vb put lard on

ENLARGE, -D, -S vb make or grow larger

ENLARGEN variant of ▸ enlarge

ENLARGER n optical instrument for making enlarged photographs

ENLARGES ▸ enlarge

ENLEVE adj having been abducted

ENLIGHT, -S, ENLIT vb light up

ENLINK, -ED, -S vb link together

ENLIST, -ED, -S vb enter the armed forces

ENLISTEE ▸ enlist

ENLISTER ▸ enlist

ENLISTS ▸ enlist

ENLIT ▸ enlight

ENLIVEN, -S vb make lively or cheerful

ENLOCK, -ED, -S vb lock or secure

ENLUMINE vb illuminate

ENMESH, -ED, -ES vb catch or involve in or as if in a net or snare

ENMEW, -ED, -ING, -S variant of ▸ emmew

ENMITY, ENMITIES n ill will, hatred

ENMOSSED adj having a covering of moss

ENMOVE, -D, -S, ENMOVING variant of ▸ emmove

ENNAGE, -S n number of ens in printed matter

ENNEAD, -S n group or series of nine

ENNEADIC ▸ ennead

ENNEADS ▸ ennead

ENNEAGON another name for ▸ **nonagon**

ENNOBLE, -D, -S vb make noble, elevate

ENNOBLER ▸ ennoble

ENNOBLES ▸ ennoble

ENNOG, -S n back alley

ENNUI, -ED, -S, ENNUYED, ENNUYING n boredom, dissatisfaction ▷ vb bore

ENNUYE adj bored

ENNUYED ▸ ennui

ENNUYEE same as ▸ **ennuye**

ENNUYING ▸ ennui

ENODAL adj having no nodes

ENOKI, -S variant of > **enokitake**

ENOL, -S n type of organic compound

ENOLASE, -S n type of enzyme

ENOLIC ▸ enol

ENOLOGY usual US spelling of ▸ **oenology**

ENOLS ▸ enol

ENOMOTY n division of the Spartan army in ancient Greece

ENOPHILE n lover of wine

ENORM variant of ▸ **enormous**

ENORMITY n great wickedness

ENORMOUS adj very big, vast

ENOSIS, ENOSES, -ES n union of Greece and Cyprus

ENOUGH, -S adj as much or as many as necessary ▷ n sufficient quantity ▷ adv sufficiently

ENOUNCE, -D, -S vb enunciate

ENOW, -S archaic word for ▸ **enough**

ENPLANE, -D, -S vb board an aircraft

ENPRINT, -S n standard photographic print

ENQUEUE, -D, -S vb add (an item) to a queue of computing tasks

ENQUIRE, -D, -S same as ▸ **inquire**

ENQUIRER ▸ enquire

ENQUIRES ▸ enquire

ENQUIRY ▸ enquire

ENRACE, -D, -S, ENRACING vb archaic word meaning to bring into a race (of people)

ENRAGE, -D, -S, ENRAGING vb make extremely angry

ENRANGE, -D, -S vb arrange, organize

ENRANK, -ED, -S vb put in a row

ENRAPT > enrapture

ENRAUNGE archaic variant of ▸ **enrange**

ENRAVISH vb enchant

ENRHEUM, -S vb pass a cold on to

ENRICH, -ED, -ES vb improve in quality

ENRICHER ▸ enrich

ENRICHES ▸ enrich

ENRIDGED adj ridged

ENRING, -ED, -S vb put a ring round

ENRIVEN adj ripped

ENROBE, -D, -S, ENROBING vb dress in or as if in a robe

ENROBER, -S ▸ enrobe

ENROBES ▸ enrobe

ENROBING ▸ enrobe

ENROL, -S vb (cause to) become a member

ENROLL, -ED, -S same as ▸ **enrol**

ENROLLEE ▸ enrol

ENROLLER ▸ enrol

ENROLLS ▸ enroll

ENROLS ▸ enrol

ENROOT, -ED, -S vb establish (plants) by fixing their roots in the earth

ENROUGH, -S vb roughen

ENROUND, -S vb encircle

ENS, ENTIA n entity

ENSAMPLE n example ▷ vb make an example

ENSATE adj shaped like a sword

ENSCONCE vb settle firmly or comfortably

ENSCROLL variant of ▸ **inscroll**

ENSEAL, -ED, -S vb seal up

ENSEAM, -ED, -S vb put a seam on

ENSEAR, -ED, -S vb dry

ENSEMBLE n all the parts of something taken together ▷ adv all together or at once ▷ adj (of a film or play) involving several separate but often interrelated story lines

ENSERF, -ED, -S vb enslave

ENSEW, -ED, -ING, -S variant of ▸ **ensue**

ENSHEATH variant of > **insheathe**

ENSHELL, -S variant of ▸ **inshell**

ENSHIELD vb protect

ENSHRINE vb cherish or treasure

ENSHROUD vb cover or hide as with a shroud

ENSIFORM adj shaped like a sword blade

ENSIGN, -ED, -S n military officer ▷ vb mark with a sign

ENSIGNCY ▸ ensign

ENSIGNED ▸ ensign

ENSIGNS ▸ ensign

ENSILAGE n process of ensiling green fodder ▷ vb make into silage

ENSILE, -D, -S, ENSILING vb store and preserve (green fodder) in an enclosed pit or silo

ENSKY, ENSKIED, ENSKIES, -ED, -ING vb put in the sky

ENSLAVE, -D, -S vb make a slave of (someone)

ENSLAVER ▸ enslave

ENSLAVES ▸ enslave

ENSNARE, -D, -S vb catch in or as if in a snare

ENSNARER ▸ ensnare

ENSNARES ▸ ensnare

ENSNARL, -S vb catch in or as if in a snarl

ENSORCEL vb enchant

ENSOUL, -ED, -S vb endow with a soul

ENSPHERE vb enclose in or as if in a sphere

ENSTAMP, -S vb imprint with a stamp

ENSTEEP, -S vb soak in water

ENSTYLE, -D, -S vb give a name to

ENSUE, -D, -S vb come next, result

ENSUING adj following subsequently or in order

ENSUITE, -S n bathroom attached to another room

ENSURE, -D, -S, ENSURING vb make certain or sure

ENSURER, -S ▸ ensure

ENSURES ▸ ensure

ENSURING ▸ ensure

ENSWATHE vb bind or wrap

ENSWEEP, -S, ENSWEPT vb sweep across

ENTAIL, -ED, -S vb bring about or impose inevitably ▷ n restriction imposed by entailing an estate

ENTAILER ▸ entail

ENTAILS ▸ entail

ENTAME, -D, -S, ENTAMING vb make tame

ENTAMEBA same as > **entamoeba**

ENTAMED ▸ entame

ENTAMES ▸ entame

ENTAMING ▸ entame

ENTANGLE vb catch or involve in or as if in a tangle

ENTASES ▸ entasis

ENTASIA, -S same as ▸ entasis

ENTASIS, ENTASES n slightly convex curve given to the shaft of a structure

ENTASTIC adj (of a disease) characterized by spasms

ENTAYLE, -D, -S variant of ▸ entail

ENTELLUS n langur of S Asia

ENTENDER vb make more tender

ENTENTE, -S n friendly understanding between nations

ENTER, -ED, -S vb come or go in

ENTERA ▸ enteron

ENTERAL same as ▸ enteric

ENTERATE adj with an intestine separate from the outer wall of the body

ENTERED ▸ enter

ENTERER, -S ▸ enter

ENTERIC, -S adj intestinal ▷ n infectious disease of the intestines

ENTERING ▸ enter

ENTERON, ENTERA, -S n alimentary canal

ENTERS ▸ enter

ENTETE adj obsessed

ENTETEE variant of ▸ entete

ENTHALPY n property of a thermodynamic system

ENTHETIC adj (esp of infectious diseases) introduced into the body from without

ENTHRAL, -S vb hold the attention of

ENTHRALL same as ▸ enthral

ENTHRALS ▸ enthral

ENTHRONE vb place (someone) on a throne

ENTHUSE, -D, -S vb (cause to) show enthusiasm

ENTIA ▸ ens

This means entities, and because of the common letters it uses is one of the most frequently played 5-letter words, at least towards the end of the game.

ENTICE, -D, -S vb attract by exciting hope or desire, tempt

ENTICER, -S ▸ entice

ENTICES ▸ entice

ENTICING ▸ entice

ENTIRE, -S adj including every detail, part, or aspect of something ▷ n state of being entire

ENTIRELY adv without reservation or exception

ENTIRES ▸ entire

ENTIRETY n state of being entire or whole

ENTITIES ▸ entity

ENTITLE, -D, -S vb give a right to

ENTITY, ENTITIES n separate distinct thing

ENTODERM same as ▸ endoderm

ENTOIL, -ED, -S archaic word for ▸ ensnare

ENTOMB, -ED, -S vb place (a corpse) in a tomb

ENTOMIC adj denoting or relating to insects

ENTOPIC adj situated in its normal place or position

ENTOPTIC adj (of visual sensation) resulting from structures within the eye itself

ENTOTIC adj of or relating to the inner ear

ENTOZOA ▸ entozoon

ENTOZOAL ▸ entozoon

ENTOZOAN same as ▸ entozoon

ENTOZOIC adj of or relating to an entozoon

ENTOZOON, ENTOZOA n internal parasite

ENTRAIL vb twist or entangle

ENTRAILS pl n intestines

ENTRAIN, -S vb board or put aboard a train

ENTRALL old variant of ▸ entrails

ENTRANCE n way into a place ▷ vb delight ▷ adj necessary in order to enter something

ENTRANT, -S n person who enters a university, contest, etc

ENTRAP, -S vb trick into difficulty etc

ENTREAT, -S vb ask earnestly

ENTREATY n earnest request

ENTREE, -S n dish served before a main course

ENTREMES variant of > entremets

ENTRENCH vb establish firmly

ENTREPOT n warehouse for commercial goods

ENTRESOL another name for > mezzanine

ENTREZ interj enter

ENTRIES ▸ entry

ENTRISM, -S variant of ▸ entryism

ENTRIST, -S ▸ entrism

ENTROLD adj word used by Spenser meaning surrounded

ENTROPIC ▸ entropy

ENTROPY n lack of organization

ENTRUST, -S vb put into the care or protection of

ENTRY, ENTRIES n entrance ▷ adj necessary in order to enter something

ENTRYISM n joining a political party to change its principles

ENTRYIST ▸ entryism

ENTRYWAY n entrance passage

ENTS pl n (college) entertainments

ENTWINE, -D, -S vb twist together or around

ENTWIST, -S vb twist together or around

ENUF common intentional literary misspelling of ▸ enough

ENURE, -D, -S, ENURING variant spelling of ▸ inure

ENURESIS, ENURESES n involuntary discharge of urine, esp during sleep

ENURETIC ▸ enuresis

ENURING ▸ enure

ENURN same as ▸ inurn

ENURNED same as ▸ inurned

ENURNING same as ▸ inurning

ENURNS same as ▸ inurns

ENVASSAL vb make a vassal of

ENVAULT, -S vb enclose in a vault; entomb

ENVEIGLE same as ▸ inveigle

ENVELOP, -S vb wrap up, enclose

ENVELOPE n folded gummed paper cover for a letter

ENVELOPS ▸ envelop

ENVENOM, -S vb fill or impregnate with venom

ENVIABLE adj arousing envy, fortunate

ENVIABLY ▸ enviable

ENVIED ▸ envy

ENVIER, -S ▸ envy

ENVIES ▸ envy

ENVIOUS adj full of envy

ENVIRO, -S n environmentalist

E

ENVIRON vb encircle or surround

ENVIRONS pl n surrounding area, esp of a town

ENVIROS ▸ enviro

ENVISAGE vb conceive of as a possibility

ENVISION vb conceive of as a possibility, esp in the future

ENVOI, -S same as ▸ envoy

ENVOY, -S n messenger

ENVY, ENVIED, ENVIES n feeling of discontent aroused by another's good fortune ▹ vb grudge (another's good fortune, success, or qualities)

ENVYING, -S ▸ envy

ENWALL, -ED, -S n wall in

ENWALLOW vb sink or plunge

ENWALLS ▸ enwall

ENWHEEL, -S archaic word for ▸ encircle

ENWIND, -S, ENWOUND vb wind or coil around

ENWOMB, -ED, -S vb enclose in or as if in a womb

ENWOUND ▸ enwind

ENWRAP, -S, -T vb wrap or cover up

ENWREATH vb surround or encircle with or as with a wreath or wreaths

ENZIAN, -S n gentian violet

ENZONE, -D, -S, ENZONING vb enclose in a zone

ENZOOTIC adj (of diseases) affecting animals within a limited region ▹ n enzootic disease

ENZYM, -S same as ▸ enzyme

ENZYME, -S n complex protein that acts as a catalyst

ENZYMIC ▸ enzyme

ENZYMS ▸ enzym

EOAN adj of or relating to the dawn

EOBIONT, -S n hypothetical chemical precursor of a living cell

EOCENE adj of, denoting, or formed in the second epoch of the Tertiary period

EOHIPPUS n extinct dog-sized ancestor of the horse

EOLIAN adj of or relating to the wind

6-letter words tend to be among the least known and least used, because they leave you at the mercy of the tile bag without scoring

that extra 50 points you would get for using all 7 letters. This word, meaning relating to the wind, often comes in useful for dumping a surplus of vowels. Its alternative spelling **aeolian** is even better for this, and what's more will get you a bonus!

EOLIENNE n type of fine cloth

EOLIPILE variant of > aeolipile

EOLITH, -S n stone used as a primitive tool in Eolithic times

EOLITHIC ▸ eolith

EOLITHS ▸ eolith

EOLOPILE variant of > aeolipile

EON, -S n immeasurably long period of time

EONIAN adj everlasting

EONISM, -S n adoption of female dress and behaviour by a male

EONS ▸ eon

EORL, -S n Anglo-Saxon nobleman

EOSIN, -S n red crystalline water-insoluble derivative of fluorescein

EOSINE, -S same as ▸ eosin

EOSINIC ▸ eosin

EOSINS ▸ eosin

EOTHEN adv from the East

EPACRID, -S n type of heath-like plant

EPACRIS n genus of the epacrids

EPACT, -S n difference in time between the solar year and the lunar year

EPAGOGE, -S n inductive reasoning

EPAGOGIC ▸ epagoge

EPANODOS n return to main theme after a digression

EPARCH, -S n bishop or metropolitan in charge of an eparchy

EPARCHY n diocese of the Eastern Christian Church

EPATANT adj startling or shocking

EPATER, -ED, -S vb startle or shock

EPAULE, -S n shoulder of a fortification

EPAULET, -S same as > epaulette

EPAXIAL adj above the axis

EPAZOTE, -S n type of herb

EPEE, -S n straight-bladed sword used in fencing

EPEEIST, -S n one who uses or specializes in using an epee

EPEES ▸ epee

EPEIRA, -S same as ▸ epeirid

EPEIRIC adj in, of, or relating to a continent

EPEIRID, -S n type of spider

EPENDYMA n membrane lining the ventricles of the brain and the central canal of the spinal cord

EPERDU adj distracted

EPERDUE adj distracted

EPERGNE, -S n ornamental centrepiece for a table

EPHA, -S same as ▸ ephah

EPHAH, -S n Hebrew unit of dry measure

EPHAS ▸ epha

EPHEBE, -S n (in ancient Greece) youth about to enter full citizenship

EPHEBI ▸ ephebus

EPHEBIC ▸ ephebe

EPHEBOS, EPHEBOI same as ▸ ephebe

EPHEBUS, EPHEBI same as ▸ ephebe

EPHEDRA, -S n gymnosperm shrub

EPHEDRIN same as > ephedrine

EPHELIS n freckle

EPHEMERA n something transitory or short-lived

EPHOD, -S n embroidered vestment worn by priests

EPHOR, -I, -S n one of a board of senior magistrates in several ancient Greek states

EPHORAL ▸ ephor

EPHORATE ▸ ephor

EPHORI ▸ ephor

EPHORS ▸ ephor

EPIBLAST n outermost layer of an embryo, which becomes the ectoderm at gastrulation

EPIBLEM, -S n outermost cell layer of a root

EPIBOLIC ▸ epiboly

EPIBOLY n process that occurs during gastrulation in vertebrates

EPIC, -S n long poem, book, or film about heroic events or actions ▹ adj very impressive or ambitious

EPICAL ▸ epic

EPICALLY ▸ epic

EPICALYX n small sepal-like bracts in some flowers

EPICARP, -S n outermost layer of the pericarp of fruits

EPICEDE, -S same as
> epicedium
EPICEDIA > epicedium
EPICENE, -S adj having the
characteristics of both
sexes; hermaphroditic ▷ n
epicene person or creature
EPICIER, -S n grocer
EPICISM, -S n style or trope
characteristic of epics
EPICIST, -S n writer of epics
EPICLIKE adj resembling or
reminiscent of an epic
EPICOTYL n part of an
embryo plant stem above
the cotyledons but beneath
the terminal bud
EPICS ▸ epic
EPICURE, -S n person who
enjoys good food and drink
EPICYCLE n (in the
Ptolemaic system) a small
circle, around which a planet
was thought to revolve
EPIDEMIC n widespread
occurrence of a disease ▷ adj
(esp of a disease) affecting
many people in an area
EPIDERM, -S same as
> epidermis
EPIDOTE, -S n green mineral
EPIDOTIC ▸ epidote
EPIDURAL n spinal
anaesthetic injected to
relieve pain during childbirth
▷ adj on or over the
outermost membrane
covering the brain and spinal
cord
EPIFAUNA n animals that
live on the surface of the
seabed
EPIFOCAL adj situated or
occurring at an epicentre
EPIGAEAL same as ▸ epigeal
EPIGAEAN same as ▸ epigeal
EPIGAMIC adj denoting an
animal feature that attracts
the opposite sex
EPIGEAL adj of or relating to
a form of seed germination
EPIGEAN same as ▸ epigeal
EPIGEIC same as ▸ epigeal
EPIGENE adj formed or
taking place at or near the
surface of the earth
EPIGENIC adj pertaining to
the theory of the gradual
development of the embryo
EPIGEOUS same as ▸ epigeal
EPIGON, -S same as
▸ epigone
EPIGONE, -S, EPIGONI n
inferior follower or imitator
EPIGONIC ▸ epigone
EPIGONS ▸ epigon

EPIGONUS same as
▸ epigone
EPIGRAM, -S n short witty
remark or poem
EPIGRAPH n quotation at
the start of a book
EPIGYNY > epigynous
EPILATE, -D, -S vb remove
hair from
EPILATOR n electrical
appliance for plucking
unwanted hair
EPILEPSY n disorder of the
nervous system causing loss
of consciousness and
sometimes convulsions
EPILOG, -S same as
▸ epilogue
EPILOGIC ▸ epilogue
EPILOGS ▸ epilog
EPILOGUE n short speech or
poem at the end of a literary
work, esp a play
EPIMER, -S n isomer
EPIMERE, -S n dorsal part of
the mesoderm of a
vertebrate embryo
EPIMERIC ▸ epimerism
EPIMERS ▸ epimer
EPIMYSIA > epimysium
EPINAOS, EPINAOI n rear
vestibule
EPINASTY n increased
growth of the upper surface
of a plant part
EPINOSIC adj unhealthy
EPIPHANY n moment of
great or sudden revelation
EPIPHYTE n plant that
grows on another plant but
is not parasitic on it
EPIPLOA ▸ epiploon
EPIPLOIC ▸ epiploon
EPIPLOON, EPIPLOA n
greater omentum
EPIPOLIC > epipolism
EPISCIA, -S n creeping plant
EPISCOPE n optical device
that projects an enlarged
image
EPISCOPY n area overseen
EPISEMON n emblem
EPISODAL same as
▸ episodic
EPISODE, -S n incident in a
series of incidents
EPISODIC adj occurring at
irregular intervals
EPISOMAL adj of or like an
episome
EPISOME, -S n unit of
genetic material (DNA) in
bacteria that can be
replicated
EPISPERM n protective
outer layer of certain seeds

EPISPORE n outer layer of
certain spores
EPISTASY same as
> epistasis
EPISTLE, -D, -S n letter, esp
of an apostle ▷ vb preface
EPISTLER n writer of an
epistle or epistles
EPISTLES ▸ epistle
EPISTOME n area between
the mouth and antennae of
crustaceans
EPISTYLE n lowest part of an
entablature that bears on
the columns
EPITAPH, -S n
commemorative inscription
on a tomb ▷ vb compose an
epitaph
EPITASIS, EPITASES n (in
classical drama) part of a
play in which the main
action develops
EPITAXES ▸ epitaxis
EPITAXIC ▸ epitaxy
EPITAXIS, EPITAXES same as
▸ epitaxy
EPITAXY n growth of a thin
layer on the surface of a
crystal
EPITHECA n outer and older
layer of the cell wall of a
diatom
EPITHEM, -A, -S n external
topical application
EPITHET, -S n descriptive
word or name ▷ vb name
EPITOME, -S n typical
example
EPITOMIC ▸ epitome
EPITONIC adj undergoing
too great a strain
EPITOPE, -S n site on an
antigen at which a specific
antibody becomes attached
EPITRITE n metrical foot
with three long syllables and
one short one
EPIZOA ▸ epizoon
EPIZOAN, -S same as
▸ epizoon
EPIZOIC adj (of an animal or
plant) growing or living on
the exterior of a living animal
EPIZOISM ▸ epizoic
EPIZOITE n organism that
lives on an animal but is not
parasitic on it
EPIZOON, EPIZOA n animal
that lives on the body of
another animal
EPIZOOTY n animal disease
EPOCH, -S n period of
notable events
EPOCHA, -S same as ▸ epoch
EPOCHAL ▸ epoch

E

EPOCHAS ▸ epocha
EPOCHS ▸ epoch
EPODE, -S n part of a lyric ode that follows the strophe and the antistrophe
EPODIC ▸ epode
EPONYM, -S n name derived from the name of a real or mythical person
EPONYMIC ▸ eponym
EPONYMS ▸ eponym
EPONYMY n derivation of names of places, etc, from those of persons
EPOPEE, -S n epic poem
EPOPOEIA same as ▸ epopee
EPOPT, -S n one initiated into the Eleusinian mysteries, an ancient Greek festival
EPOS, -ES n body of poetry in which the tradition of a people is conveyed
EPOXIDE, -S n chemical compound
EPOXY, EPOXIED, EPOXIES, -ED, -ING adj of or containing a specific type of chemical compound ▷ n epoxy resin ▷ vb glue with epoxy resin
EPRIS adj enamoured
EPRISE feminine form of ▸ epris
EPSILON, -S n fifth letter of the Greek alphabet
EPSOMITE n sulphate of magnesium
EPUISE adj exhausted
EPUISEE feminine form of ▸ epuise
EPULARY adj of or relating to feasting
EPULIS, EPULIDES, -ES n swelling of the gum
EPULOTIC n scarring
EPURATE, -D, -S vb purify
EPYLLION, EPYLLIA n miniature epic
EQUABLE adj even-tempered
EQUABLY ▸ equable
EQUAL, -ED, -ING, -LED, -S adj identical in size, quantity, degree, etc ▷ n person or thing equal to another ▷ vb be equal to
EQUALI pl n pieces for a group of instruments of the same kind
EQUALING ▸ equal
EQUALISE same as ▸ equalize
EQUALITY n state of being equal
EQUALIZE vb make or become equal

EQUALLED ▸ equal
EQUALLY ▸ equal
EQUALS ▸ equal
EQUANT, -S n circle in which a planet was formerly believed to move
EQUATE, -D, -S, EQUATING vb make or regard as equivalent
EQUATION n mathematical statement that two expressions are equal

A rack that contains Q and a jumble of vowels can look unpromising, but if you mentally affix the U to the Q and then look for likely letter strings you will soon arrive at ATION, from where it is only a short step to this useful 8-letter word, one of the most frequently played bonuses containing Q.

EQUATIVE adj (in grammar) denoting the equivalence or identity of two terms
EQUATOR, -S n imaginary circle round the earth
EQUERRY n attendant to a member of a royal family
EQUES n (in ancient Rome) horseman
EQUID, -S n any animal of the horse family
EQUINAL same as ▸ equine
EQUINE, -S adj of or like a horse ▷ n any animal of the horse family
EQUINELY ▸ equine
EQUINES ▸ equine
EQUINIA, -S n glanders
EQUINITY n horse-like nature
EQUINOX n time of year when day and night are of equal length
EQUIP, -PED, -S vb provide with supplies, components, etc
EQUIPAGE n horse-drawn carriage, esp one elegantly equipped and attended by liveried footmen ▷ vb equip
EQUIPE, -S n (esp in motor racing) team
EQUIPPED ▸ equip
EQUIPPER ▸ equip
EQUIPS ▸ equip
EQUISETA > equisetum
EQUITANT adj having the base folded around the stem
EQUITES pl n cavalry
EQUITY, EQUITIES n fairness
EQUIVOKE same as > equivoque

ER interj sound made when hesitating in speech
ERA, -S n period of time considered as distinctive
ERADIATE less common word for ▸ radiate
ERAS ▸ era
ERASABLE ▸ erase
ERASE, -D, -S, ERASING vb destroy all traces of
ERASER, -S n object for erasing something written
ERASES ▸ erase
ERASING ▸ erase
ERASION, -S n act of erasing

This means the act of erasing: not an exciting word, but its combination of common letters makes it one of the most frequently played 7-letter bonus words.

ERASURE, -S n erasing
ERATHEM, -S n stratum of rocks representing a specific geological era
ERBIA, -S n oxide of erbium
ERBIUM, -S n metallic element of the lanthanide series
ERE, -D, -S, ERING prep before ▷ vb plough
ERECT, -ED, -ING, -S vb build ▷ adj upright
ERECTER, -S same as ▸ erector
ERECTILE adj capable of becoming erect
ERECTING ▸ erect
ERECTION n act of erecting or the state of being erected
ERECTIVE adj tending to erect
ERECTLY ▸ erect
ERECTOR, -S n any muscle that raises a part or makes it erect
ERECTS ▸ erect
ERED ▸ ere
ERELONG adv before long
EREMIC adj of or relating to deserts
EREMITAL ▸ eremite
EREMITE, -S n Christian hermit
EREMITIC ▸ eremite
EREMURUS, EREMURI n type of herb
ERENOW adv long before the present
EREPSIN, -S n mixture of proteolytic enzymes secreted by the small intestine
ERES ▸ ere
ERETHIC ▸ erethism

ERETHISM n abnormally high degree of irritability or sensitivity in any part of the body

EREV, -S n day before

EREWHILE adv short time ago

ERF, ERVEN n plot of land marked off for building purposes

ERG, -S same as > ergometer

ERGASTIC adj consisting of the non-living by-products of protoplasmic activity

ERGATE, -S n worker ant

ERGATIVE adj denoting a verb that takes the same noun as either direct object or subject ▷ n ergative verb

ERGATOID ▶ ergate

ERGO, -S same as > ergometer

ERGODIC adj of or relating to the probability that any state will recur

ERGOGRAM n tracing produced by an ergograph

ERGON, -S n work

ERGOS ▶ ergo

ERGOT, -S n fungal disease of cereal

ERGOTIC ▶ ergot

ERGOTISE same as ▶ ergotize

ERGOTISM n ergot poisoning

ERGOTIZE vb inflict ergotism upon

ERGOTS ▶ ergot

ERGS ▶ erg

ERHU, -S n Chinese two-stringed violin

ERIACH, -S same as ▶ eric

ERIC, -S n (in old Irish law) fine paid by a murderer to the family of his or her victim

ERICA, -S n genus of plants including heathers

ERICK, -S same as ▶ eric

ERICOID adj (of leaves) small and tough, resembling those of heather

ERICS ▶ eric

ERIGERON n type of plant

ERING ▶ ere

ERINGO, -ES, -S same as ▶ eryngo

ERINITE, -S n arsenate of copper

ERINUS, -ES n type of plant

ERIONITE n common form of zeolite

ERISTIC, -S adj of, relating, or given to controversy or logical disputation ▷ n person who engages in logical disputes

ERK, -S n aircraftman or naval rating

ERLANG, -S n unit of traffic intensity in a telephone system

ERLKING, -S n malevolent spirit who carries off children

ERM interj expression of hesitation

ERMELIN, -S n ermine

ERMINE, -S n stoat in northern regions

ERMINED adj clad in the fur of the ermine

ERMINES ▶ ermine

ERN, -ED, -ING, -S archaic variant of ▶ earn

ERNE, -S n fish-eating (European) sea eagle

ERNED ▶ ern

ERNES ▶ erne

ERNING ▶ ern

ERNS ▶ ern

ERODABLE ▶ erode

ERODE, -D, -S, ERODING vb wear away

ERODENT, -S ▶ erode

ERODES ▶ erode

ERODIBLE ▶ erode

ERODING ▶ erode

ERODIUM, -S n type of geranium

EROS, -ES n love

EROSE adj jagged or uneven, as though gnawed or bitten

EROSELY ▶ erose

EROSES ▶ eros

EROSIBLE adj able to be eroded

EROSION, -S n wearing away of rocks or soil

EROSIVE ▶ erosion

EROTEMA, -S n rhetorical question

EROTEME, -S same as ▶ erotema

EROTESIS, EROTESES same as ▶ erotema

EROTETIC adj pertaining to a rhetorical question

ERR, -ED, -S vb make a mistake

ERRABLE adj capable of making a mistake

ERRANCY n state or an instance of erring or a tendency to err

ERRAND, -S n short trip to do something for someone

ERRANT, -S adj behaving in a manner considered to be unacceptable ▷ n knight-errant

ERRANTLY ▶ errant

ERRANTRY n way of life of a knight errant

ERRANTS ▶ errant

ERRATA ▶ erratum

ERRATIC, -S adj irregular or unpredictable ▷ n rock that has been transported by glacial action

ERRATUM, ERRATA n error in writing or printing

ERRED ▶ err

ERRHINE, -S adj causing nasal secretion ▷ n errhine drug or agent

ERRING, -S ▶ err

ERRINGLY ▶ err

ERRINGS ▶ erring

ERROR, -S n mistake, inaccuracy, or misjudgment

ERRORIST n one who makes errors

ERRORS ▶ error

ERRS ▶ err

ERS, -ES same as ▶ ervil

ERSATZ, -ES adj made in imitation ▷ n ersatz substance or article

ERSES ▶ ers

ERST adv long ago

ERUCIC adj as in erucic acid crystalline fatty acid

ERUCT, -ED, -ING, -S vb belch

ERUCTATE same as ▶ eruct

ERUCTED ▶ eruct

ERUCTING ▶ eruct

ERUCTS ▶ eruct

ERUDITE, -S adj having great academic knowledge ▷ n erudite person

ERUGO, -S n verdigris

ERUMPENT adj bursting out or developing as though bursting through

ERUPT, -ED, -ING, -S vb eject (steam, water, or volcanic material) violently

ERUPTION ▶ erupt

ERUPTIVE adj erupting or tending to erupt ▷ n type of volcanic rock

ERUPTS ▶ erupt

ERUV, -IM, -IN, -S n area within which certain activities forbidden to be done on the Sabbath are permitted

ERVEN ▶ erf

ERVIL, -S n type of vetch

ERYNGIUM n type of temperate and subtropical plant

ERYNGO, -ES, -S n type of plant with toothed or lobed leaves

ERYTHEMA n patchy inflammation of the skin

ERYTHRON n red blood cells and their related tissues

ES, -ES n letter S

ESCALADE n assault by the use of ladders, esp on a fortification ▷ vb gain access to (a place) by the use of ladders

ESCALADO n escalade

ESCALATE vb increase in extent or intensity

ESCALIER n staircase

ESCALLOP another word for ▷ scallop

ESCALOP, -S another word for ▷ scallop

ESCALOPE n thin slice of meat, esp veal

ESCALOPS ▷ escalop

ESCAPADE n mischievous adventure

ESCAPADO n escaped criminal

ESCAPE, -D, -S, ESCAPING vb get free (of) ▷ n act of escaping

ESCAPEE, -S n person who has escaped

ESCAPER, -S ▷ escape

ESCAPES ▷ escape

ESCAPING ▷ escape

ESCAPISM n taking refuge in fantasy to avoid unpleasant reality

ESCAPIST ▷ escapism

ESCAR, -S same as ▷ esker

ESCARGOT n variety of edible snail, usually eaten with a sauce made of melted butter and garlic

ESCAROLE n variety of endive with broad leaves, used in salads

ESCARP, -ED, -S n inner side of a ditch separating besiegers and besieged ▷ vb make into a slope

ESCARS ▷ escar

ESCHALOT another name for a ▷ shallot

ESCHAR, -S n dry scab or slough

ESCHEAT, -S n possessions that become state property in the absence of an heir ▷ vb take such property

ESCHEW, -ED, -S vb abstain from, avoid

ESCHEWAL ▷ eschew

ESCHEWED ▷ eschew

ESCHEWER ▷ eschew

ESCHEWS ▷ eschew

ESCOLAR, -S n slender spiny-finned fish

ESCORT, -ED, -S n people following another person for protection or as an honour ▷ vb act as an escort to

ESCOT, -ED, -ING, -S, -TED vb maintain

ESCRIBE, -D, -S vb make a mathematical drawing

ESCROC, -S n conman

ESCROL, -S same as ▷ escroll

ESCROLL, -S n scroll

ESCROLS ▷ escrol

ESCROW, -ED, -S n item delivered to a third party pending fulfilment of a condition ▷ vb place (money, a document, etc) in escrow

ESCUAGE, -S (in medieval Europe) another word for ▷ scutage

ESCUDO, -S n former monetary unit of Portugal

ESCULENT adj edible ▷ n any edible substance

ESERINE, -S n crystalline alkaloid

ESES ▷ es

ESILE, -S n vinegar

ESKAR, -S same as ▷ esker

ESKER, -S n long ridge of gravel, sand, etc

ESKY, ESKIES n portable insulated container

ESLOIN, -ED, -S same as ▷ eloign

ESLOYNE, -D, -S same as ▷ eloign

ESNE, -S n household slave

ESNECY, ESNECIES n inheritance law

ESNES ▷ esne

ESOPHAGI ▷ esophagus

ESOTERIC adj understood by only a small number of people with special knowledge

ESOTERY ▷ esoteric

ESPADA, -S n sword

ESPALIER n shrub or fruit tree trained to grow flat ▷ vb train (a plant) on an espalier

ESPANOL n Spanish person

ESPARTO, -S n grass of S Europe and N Africa

ESPECIAL adj special

ESPIAL, -S n act or fact of being seen or discovered

ESPIED ▷ espy

ESPIEGLE adj playful

ESPIER, -S ▷ espy

ESPIES ▷ espy

ESPOIR, -S n category of wrestler

ESPOUSAL n adoption or support

ESPOUSE, -D, -S vb adopt or give support to (a cause etc)

ESPOUSER ▷ espouse

ESPOUSES ▷ espouse

ESPRESSO n strong coffee made by forcing steam or boiling water through ground coffee beans

ESPRIT, -S n spirit, liveliness, or wit

ESPUMOSO n sparkling wine

ESPY, ESPIED, ESPIES, -ING vb catch sight of

ESQUIRE, -D, -S n courtesy title placed after a man's name ▷ vb escort

ESQUISSE n sketch

ESS, -ES n letter S

ESSAY, -ED, -ING, -S n short literary composition ▷ vb attempt

ESSAYER, -S ▷ essay

ESSAYING ▷ essay

ESSAYISH ▷ essay

ESSAYIST n person who writes essays

ESSAYS ▷ essay

ESSE n existence

ESSENCE, -S n most important feature of a thing which determines its identity

ESSES ▷ ess

ESSIVE, -S n grammatical case

ESSOIN, -ED, -S n excuse ▷ vb excuse for not appearing in court

ESSOINER ▷ essoin

ESSOINS ▷ essoin

ESSONITE variant spelling of > hessonite

ESSOYNE, -S same as ▷ essoin

EST, -S n treatment intended to help people towards psychological growth

ESTACADE n defensive arrangement of stakes

ESTANCIA n (in Spanish America) a large estate or cattle ranch

ESTATE, -D, -S, ESTATING n landed property ▷ vb provide with an estate

ESTEEM, -ED, -S n high regard ▷ vb think highly of

ESTER, -S n chemical compound

ESTERASE n any of a group of enzymes that hydrolyse esters

ESTERIFY vb change or cause to change into an ester

ESTERS ▷ ester

ESTHESES ▷ esthesis

ESTHESIA US spelling of > aesthesia

ESTHESIS, ESTHESES *n* esthesia

ESTHETE, -S US spelling of ▸**aesthete**

ESTHETIC ▸**esthete**

ESTIMATE *vb* calculate roughly ▸ *n* approximate calculation

ESTIVAL usual US spelling of ▸**aestival**

ESTIVATE usual US spelling of >**aestivate**

ESTOC, -S *n* short stabbing sword

ESTOILE, -S *n* heraldic star with wavy points

ESTOP, -PED, -S *vb* preclude by estoppel

ESTOPPEL *n* rule precluding a person from denying the truth of a statement of facts

ESTOPS ▸**estop**

ESTOVER same as ▸**estovers**

ESTOVERS *pl n* right allowed by law to tenants of land to cut timber, esp for fuel and repairs

ESTRADE, -S *n* dais or raised platform

ESTRAGON another name for ▸**tarragon**

ESTRAL US spelling of ▸**oestral**

ESTRANGE *vb* separate and live apart from (one's spouse)

ESTRAY, -ED, -S *n* stray domestic animal of unknown ownership ▸ *vb* stray

ESTREAT, -S *n* extract from a court record ▸ *vb* send an extract of a court record

ESTREPE, -D, -S *vb* lay waste

ESTRICH *n* obsolete word for ostrich

ESTRIDGE same as ▸**estrich**

ESTRIN, -S US spelling of ▸**oestrin**

ESTRIOL, -S usual US spelling of ▸**oestriol**

ESTRO, -S *n* poetic inspiration

ESTROGEN usual US spelling of >**oestrogen**

ESTRONE, -S usual US spelling of ▸**oestrone**

ESTROS ▸**estro**

ESTROUS ▸**estrus**

ESTRUAL ▸**estrus**

ESTRUM, -S usual US spelling of ▸**oestrum**

ESTRUS, -ES usual US spelling of ▸**oestrus**

ESTS ▸**est**

ESTUARY *n* mouth of a river

ESURIENT *adj* greedy

ET dialect past tense of ▸**eat**

ETA, -S *n* seventh letter in the Greek alphabet

ETACISM, -S *n* pronunciation of eta as a long vowel sound

ETAERIO, -S *n* aggregate fruit

This strange-looking word is a type of fruit, and because it uses the commonest letters it is, along with **otarine**, the most frequently played of all bonus words.

ETAGE, -S *n* floor in a multi-storey building

ETAGERE, -S *n* stand with open shelves for displaying ornaments, etc

ETAGES ▸**etage**

ETALAGE, -S *n* display

ETALON, -S *n* device used in spectroscopy

ETAMIN, -S same as ▸**etamine**

ETAMINE, -S *n* cotton or worsted fabric of loose weave

ETAMINS ▸**etamin**

ETAPE, -S *n* public storehouse

ETAS ▸**eta**

ETAT, -S *n* state

ETATISM, -S same as ▸**etatisme**

ETATISME *n* authoritarian control by the state

ETATISMS ▸**etatism**

ETATIST ▸**etatisme**

ETATISTE ▸**etatisme**

ETATS ▸**etat**

ETCETERA *n* number of other items

ETCH, -ED, -ES *vb* wear away or cut the surface of (metal, glass, etc) with acid

ETCHANT, -S *n* any acid or corrosive used for etching

ETCHED ▸**etch**

ETCHER, -S ▸**etch**

ETCHES ▸**etch**

ETCHING, -S *n* picture printed from an etched metal plate

ETEN, -S *n* giant

ETERNAL, -S *adj* without beginning or end ▸ *n* eternal thing

ETERNE archaic or poetic word for ▸**eternal**

ETERNISE same as ▸**eternize**

ETERNITY *n* infinite time

ETERNIZE *vb* make eternal

ETESIAN, -S *adj* (of NW winds) recurring annually in the summer in the E Mediterranean ▸ *n* etesian wind

ETH, -S same as ▸**edh**

ETHAL, -S *n* cetyl alcohol

ETHANAL, -S *n* colourless volatile pungent liquid

ETHANE, -S *n* odourless flammable gas

ETHANOIC *adj* as in ethanoic acid acetic acid

ETHANOL, -S same as ▸**alcohol**

ETHANOYL *n* type of acyl group or radical

ETHE *adj* easy

ETHENE, -S same as ▸**ethylene**

ETHEPHON *n* synthetic plant-growth regulator

ETHER, -S *n* colourless anaesthetic

ETHERCAP *n* spider

ETHEREAL *adj* extremely delicate

ETHERIAL same as ▸**ethereal**

ETHERIC ▸**ether**

ETHERIFY *vb* change (a compound, such as an alcohol) into an ether

ETHERION *n* gas formerly believed to exist in air

ETHERISE same as ▸**etherize**

ETHERISH ▸**ether**

ETHERISM *n* addiction to ether

ETHERIST ▸**etherism**

ETHERIZE *vb* subject (a person) to the anaesthetic influence of ether fumes

ETHERS ▸**ether**

ETHIC *n* moral principle

ETHICAL, -S *adj* of or based on a system of moral beliefs ▸ *n* drug available only by prescription

ETHICIAN ▸**ethics**

ETHICISE same as ▸**ethicize**

ETHICISM ▸**ethics**

ETHICIST ▸**ethics**

ETHICIZE *vb* make or consider as ethical

ETHICS *n* code of behaviour

ETHINYL, -S same as ▸**ethynyl**

ETHION, -S *n* type of pesticide

ETHIOPS *n* dark-coloured chemical compound

ETHMOID, -S *adj* denoting or relating to a specific bone of the skull ▸ *n* ethmoid bone

E

E

ETHNARCH n ruler of a people or province, as in parts of the Roman and Byzantine Empires

ETHNE ▸ ethnos

ETHNIC adj relating to a people or group that shares a culture, religion, or language ▹ n member of an ethnic group

ETHNICAL same as ▸ ethnic

ETHNICS ▸ ethnic

ETHNONYM n name of ethnic group

ETHNOS, ETHNE, -ES n ethnic group

ETHOGRAM n description of animal's behaviour

ETHOLOGY n study of the behaviour of animals in their normal environment

ETHONONE another name for ▸ ketene

ETHOS, -ES n distinctive spirit and attitudes of a people, culture, etc

ETHOXIDE n any of a class of saltlike compounds

ETHOXY, ETHOXIES same as ▸ ethoxyl

ETHOXYL, -S n univalent radical

ETHS ▸ eth

ETHYL, -S adj type of chemical hydrocarbon group

ETHYLATE same as ▸ ethoxide

ETHYLENE n poisonous gas used as an anaesthetic and as fuel

ETHYLIC ▸ ethyl

ETHYLS ▸ ethyl

ETHYNE, -S another name for ▹ acetylene

ETHYNYL, -S n univalent radical

ETIC, -S adj relating to linguistic terms analysed without regard to structural function ▹ n etic approach or viewpoint

ETIOLATE vb become pale and weak

ETIOLIN, -S n yellow pigment

ETIOLOGY n study of the causes of diseases

ETNA, -S n container used to heat liquids

ETOILE, -S n star

ETOUFFEE n spicy Cajun stew

ETOURDI adj foolish

ETOURDIE feminine form of ▸ etourdi

ETRANGER n foreigner

ETRENNE, -S n New Year's gift

ETRIER, -S n short portable ladder or set of webbing loops

ETTERCAP n spider

ETTIN, -S n giant

ETTLE, -D, -S, ETTLING vb intend

ETUDE, -S n short musical composition for a solo instrument

ETUI, -S n small usually ornamented case

ETWEE, -S same as ▸ etui

E is a very desirable letter, but sometimes you can have too much of even this good thing. This word for a needle-case, a variant of **etui**, can help you dispose of a few of them.

ETYMA ▸ etymon

ETYMIC ▸ etymon

ETYMON, ETYMA, -S n earliest form of a word or morpheme from which another is derived

ETYPIC adj unable to conform to type

ETYPICAL same as ▸ etypic

EUCAIN, -S same as ▸ eucaine

EUCAINE, -S n crystalline optically active substance

EUCAINS ▸ eucain

EUCALYPT n myrtaceous tree

EUCARYON same as > eukaryote

EUCARYOT same as > eukaryote

EUCHARIS n S American plant cultivated for its large white fragrant flowers

EUCHRE, -D, -S, EUCHRING n US and Canadian card game ▹ vb prevent (a player) from making their contracted tricks

EUCLASE, -S n brittle green gem

EUCRITE, -S n type of stony meteorite

EUCRITIC ▸ eucrite

EUCYCLIC adj (of plants) having the same number of leaves in each whorl

EUDAEMON same as ▸ eudemon

EUDAIMON same as ▸ eudaemon

This word for a benevolent spirit is difficult to spot in play, but it is one of those high-probability 8-letter bonus words using many vowels that are well worth special attention. It has variant spellings **eudaemon** and **eudemon**.

EUDEMON, -S n benevolent spirit or demon

EUGARIE, -S another name for ▸ pipi

EUGE interj well done!

EUGENIA, -S n plant of the clove family

EUGENIC ▸ eugenics

EUGENICS n study of methods of improving the human race

EUGENISM ▸ eugenics

EUGENIST ▸ eugenics

EUGENOL, -S n oily liquid used in perfumery

EUGH, -S archaic form of ▸ yew

EUGHEN archaic form of ▸ yew

EUGHS ▸ eugh

EUGLENA, -S n type of freshwater unicellular organism

EUGLENID same as ▸ euglena

EUK, -ED, -ING, -S vb itch

EUKARYON same as > eukaryote

EUKARYOT same as > eukaryote

EUKED ▸ euk

EUKING ▸ euk

EUKS ▸ euk

EULACHAN same as ▸ eulachon

EULACHON n salmonoid food fish

EULOGIA, -E, -S n blessed bread

This is one of the few 7-letter words using all the vowels. What's more, it can take a plural in E as well as S, giving **eulogiae**, which can be great for getting you out of vowel trouble.

EULOGIES ▸ eulogy

EULOGISE same as ▸ eulogize

EULOGIST ▸ eulogize

EULOGIUM same as ▸ eulogy

EULOGIZE vb praise (a person or thing) highly in speech or writing

EULOGY, EULOGIES n speech or writing in praise of a person

EUMERISM n collection of similar parts

EUMONG, -S same as ▸ **eumung**

EUMUNG, -S n any of various Australian acacias

EUNUCH, -S n castrated man

EUOI n cry of Bacchic frenzy

> This is a cry expressing Bacchic frenzy, and is forever coming in useful to dispose of a surplus of vowels. It has the less commonly played but still useful variants **evoe, evhoe** and **evohe**.

EUONYMIN n extract derived from the bark of the euonymus

EUONYMUS n type of N temperate tree or shrub

EUOUAE, -S n mnemonic used in medieval music

> This word is remarkable in that it contains no consonants. You will be surprised at how often you will be glad to play it!

EUPAD, -S n antiseptic powder

EUPATRID n (in ancient Greece) hereditary noble or landowner

EUPEPSIA n good digestion

EUPEPSY same as ▸ **eupepsia**

EUPEPTIC ▸ **eupepsia**

EUPHENIC adj of or pertaining to biological improvement

EUPHOBIA n fear of good news

EUPHON, -S n glass harmonica

EUPHONIA same as ▸ **euphony**

EUPHONIC adj denoting or relating to euphony

EUPHONS ▸ **euphon**

EUPHONY n pleasing sound

EUPHORIA n sense of elation

EUPHORIC ▸ **euphoria**

EUPHORY same as ▸ **euphoria**

EUPHOTIC adj denoting the part of a sea or lake with enough light to enable photosynthesis

EUPHRASY same as > **eyebright**

EUPHROE, -S n wooden block through which the lines of a crowfoot are rove

EUPHUISE same as ▸ **euphuize**

EUPHUISM n artificial prose style of the Elizabethan period

EUPHUIST ▸ **euphuism**

EUPHUIZE vb write in euphuism

EUPLOID, -S adj having chromosomes in an exact multiple of the haploid number ▸ n euploid cell or individual

EUPLOIDY ▸ **euploid**

EUPNEA, -S same as ▸ **eupnoea**

EUPNEIC ▸ **eupnea**

EUPNOEA, -S n normal relaxed breathing

EUPNOEIC ▸ **eupnoea**

EUREKA, -S n exclamation of triumph at finding something

EURIPUS, EURIPI n strait or channel with a strong current or tide

EURO, -S n unit of the single currency of the European Union

EUROBOND n bond issued in a eurocurrency

EUROCRAT n member, esp a senior member, of the administration of the European Union

EUROKIES ▸ **euroky**

EUROKOUS ▸ **euroky**

EUROKY, EUROKIES n ability of an organism to live under different conditions

EUROLAND n area containing the countries using the euro

EURONOTE n form of euro-commercial paper consisting of short-term negotiable bearer notes

EUROPIUM n silvery-white element of the lanthanide series

EUROPOP, -S n type of pop music by European artists

EUROS ▸ **euro**

EUROZONE n area containing the countries using the euro

EURYBATH n organism that can live at different depths underwater

EURYOKY same as ▸ **euroky**

EURYTHMY n dancing style in which the rhythm of music is expressed through body movements

EUSOCIAL adj using division of labour

EUSOL, -S n solution of eupad in water

EUSTACY ▸ **eustatic**

EUSTASY ▸ **eustatic**

EUSTATIC adj denoting worldwide changes in sea level

EUSTELE, -S n central cylinder of a seed plant

EUSTRESS n type of stress that is beneficial

EUSTYLE, -S n building with columns optimally spaced

EUTAXIA, -S n condition of being easily melted

EUTAXIES ▸ **eutaxy**

EUTAXITE n banded volcanic rock

EUTAXY, EUTAXIES n good order

EUTECTIC adj having the lowest freezing point possible for the mixture ▸ n eutectic mixture

EUTEXIA, -S same as ▸ **eutaxia**

EUTHYMIA n pleasant state of mind

EUTROPHY > **eutrophic**

EUTROPIC ▸ **eutropy**

EUTROPY n chemical structure

EUXENITE n rare brownish-black mineral

EVACUANT adj serving to promote excretion ▸ n evacuant agent

EVACUATE vb send (someone) away from a place of danger

EVACUEE, -S n person evacuated from a place of danger

EVADABLE ▸ **evade**

EVADE, -D, -S, EVADING vb get away from or avoid

EVADER, -S ▸ **evade**

EVADES ▸ **evade**

EVADIBLE ▸ **evade**

EVADING ▸ **evade**

EVALUATE vb find or judge the value of

EVANESCE vb fade gradually from sight

EVANGEL, -S n gospel of Christianity

EVANGELY n gospel

EVANISH poetic word for ▸ **vanish**

EVASIBLE ▸ **evasion**

EVASION, -S n act of evading something by cunning or illegal means

EVASIVE adj not straightforward

EVE, -S n evening or day before some special event

EVECTION n irregularity in the moon's motion caused

E

by perturbations of the sun and planets

EVEJAR, -S n nightjar

EVEN, -ED, -EST adj flat or smooth ▷ adv equally ▷ vb make even ▷ n eve

EVENER, -S ▶ even

EVENEST ▶ even

EVENFALL n early evening

EVENING n end of the day or early part of the night ▷ adj of or in the evening

EVENINGS adv in the evening, esp regularly

EVENLY ▶ even

EVENNESS ▶ even

EVENS adv (of a bet) winning the same as the amount staked if successful

EVENSONG n evening prayer

EVENT, -ED, -S n anything that takes place ▷ vb take part in or ride (a horse) in eventing

EVENTER, -S ▶ eventing

EVENTFUL adj full of exciting incidents

EVENTIDE n evening

EVENTING n riding competitions, usu involving cross-country, jumping, and dressage

EVENTIVE adj relating to an event

EVENTS ▶ event

EVENTUAL adj ultimate

EVER adv at any time

EVERMORE adv for all time to come

EVERNET, -S n hypothetical form of internet

EVERSION ▶ evert

EVERT, -ED, -ING, -S vb turn (some bodily part) outwards or inside out

EVERTOR, -S n any muscle that turns a part outwards

EVERTS ▶ evert

EVERY adj each without exception

EVERYDAY adj usual or ordinary ▷ n ordinary day

EVERYMAN, EVERYMEN n ordinary person; common person

EVERYONE pron every person

EVERYWAY adv in every way

EVES ▶ eve

EVET, -S n eft

EVHOE interj cry of Bacchic frenzy

EVICT, -ED, -ING, -S vb legally expel (someone) from his or her home

EVICTEE, -S ▶ evict

EVICTING ▶ evict

EVICTION ▶ evict

EVICTOR, -S ▶ evict

EVICTS ▶ evict

EVIDENCE n ground for belief ▷ vb demonstrate, prove

EVIDENT, -S adj easily seen or understood ▷ n item of evidence

EVIL, -ER, -EST, -LER, -LEST, -S n wickedness ▷ adj harmful ▷ adv in an evil manner

EVILDOER n wicked person

EVILER ▶ evil

EVILEST ▶ evil

EVILLER ▶ evil

EVILLEST ▶ evil

EVILLY ▶ evil

EVILNESS ▶ evil

EVILS ▶ evil

EVINCE, -D, -S, EVINCING vb make evident

EVINCIVE ▶ evince

EVIRATE, -D, -S vb deprive of strength or vigour

EVITABLE adj able to be avoided

EVITATE, -D, -S archaic word for ▶ avoid

EVITE, -D, -S, EVITING archaic word for ▶ avoid

EVO, -S informal word for ▶ evening

EVOCABLE ▶ evoke

EVOCATE, -D, -S vb evoke

EVOCATOR n person or thing that evokes

EVOE interj cry of Bacchic frenzy

EVOHE interj cry of Bacchic frenzy

EVOKE, -D, -S, EVOKING vb call or summon up (a memory, feeling, etc)

EVOKER, -S ▶ evoke

EVOKES ▶ evoke

EVOKING ▶ evoke

EVOLUE, -S n colonial term for an African educated according to European principles

EVOLUTE, -D, -S n geometric curve ▷ adj having the margins rolled outwards ▷ vb evolve

EVOLVE, -D, -S, EVOLVING vb develop gradually

EVOLVENT adj evolving ▷ n involute curve

EVOLVER, -S ▶ evolve

EVOLVES ▶ evolve

EVOLVING ▶ evolve

EVONYMUS same as ▶ euonymus

EVOS ▶ evo

EVOVAE, -S n mnemonic used in medieval music

EVULGATE vb make public

EVULSE, -D, -S, EVULSING vb extract by force

EVULSION n act of extracting by force

EVZONE, -S n soldier in an elite Greek infantry regiment

EW interj expression of disgust

EWE, -S n female sheep

EWER, -S n large jug with a wide mouth

EWES ▶ ewe

EWEST Scots word for ▶ near

EWFTES Spenserian plural of ▶ eft

EWGHEN archaic form of ▶ yew

EWHOW interj expression of pity or regret

EWK, -ED, -ING, -S vb itch

Ewk is a dialect word for itch. It's a handy little word and a good one to remember in case you end up with both K and W, and remember that as a verb, so you can have **ewks, ewked** and **ewking**. It's also worth knowing its variants **euk, yeuk, youk, yuck** and **yuke**!

EWT, -S archaic form of ▶ newt

EX, -ED, -ES, -ING prep not including ▷ n former spouse, significant other, etc ▷ vb cross out or delete

EXABYTE, -S n very large unit of computer memory

EXACT, -ED, -EST, -S adj correct and complete in every detail ▷ vb demand (payment or obedience)

EXACTA, -S n horse-racing bet

EXACTED ▶ exact

EXACTER, -S ▶ exact

EXACTEST ▶ exact

EXACTING adj making rigorous or excessive demands

EXACTION n act of obtaining or demanding money as a right

EXACTLY adv precisely, in every respect ▷ interj just so! precisely!

EXACTOR, -S ▶ exact

EXACTS ▶ exact

EXACUM, -S n type of tropical plant

EXAHERTZ n very large unit of frequency

EXALT, -ING, -S vb praise highly

EXALTED adj high or elevated in rank, position, dignity, etc

EXALTER, -S ▸ exalt

EXALTING ▸ exalt

EXALTS ▸ exalt

EXAM, -S n examination

EXAMEN, -S n examination of conscience

EXAMETRE n ten to the power of eighteen metres

EXAMINE, -D, -S vb look at closely

EXAMINEE n person who sits an exam

EXAMINER ▸ examine

EXAMINES ▸ examine

EXAMPLAR archaic form of ▸ exemplar

EXAMPLE, -D, -S n specimen typical of its group

EXAMS ▸ exam

EXANTHEM same as > exanthema

EXAPTED adj biologically adapted

EXAPTIVE adj involving biological adaptation

EXARATE adj (of the pupa of some insects) having legs, wings, antennae, etc, free and movable

EXARCH, -S n head of certain autonomous Orthodox Christian Churches ▹ adj (of a xylem strand) having the first-formed xylem external to that formed later

EXARCHAL ▸ exarch

EXARCHS ▸ exarch

EXARCHY same as > exarchate

EXCAMB, -ED, -S vb exchange

EXCAVATE vb unearth buried objects from (a piece of land) methodically to learn about the past

EXCEED, -ED, -S vb be greater than

EXCEEDER ▸ exceed

EXCEEDS ▸ exceed

EXCEL, -LED, -S vb be superior to

EXCEPT, -ED, -S prep other than, not including ▹ vb leave out; omit; exclude

EXCEPTOR ▸ except

EXCEPTS ▸ except

EXCERPT, -S n passage taken from a book, speech, etc ▹ vb take a passage from a book, speech, etc

EXCERPTA > excerptum

EXCERPTS ▸ excerpt

EXCESS, -ED, -ES n state or act of exceeding the permitted limits ▹ vb make (a position) redundant

EXCHANGE vb give or receive (something) in return for something else ▹ n act of exchanging

EXCHEAT, -S same as ▸ escheat

EXCIDE, -D, -S, EXCIDING vb cut out

EXCIMER, -S n excited dimer which would remain dissociated in the ground state

EXCIPLE, -S n part of a lichen

EXCISE, -D, -S, EXCISING n tax on goods produced for the home market ▹ vb cut out or away

EXCISION ▸ excise

EXCITANT adj able to excite or stimulate ▹ n something able to excite

EXCITE, -S vb arouse to strong emotion

EXCITED adj emotionally aroused, esp to pleasure or agitation

EXCITER, -S n person or thing that excites

EXCITES ▸ excite

EXCITING adj causing excitement

EXCITON, -S n excited electron bound to the hole produced by its excitation

EXCITOR, -S n type of nerve

EXCLAIM, -S vb speak suddenly, cry out

EXCLAVE, -S n territory owned by a country, but surrounded by another

EXCLUDE, -D, -S vb keep out, leave out

EXCLUDEE ▸ exclude

EXCLUDER ▸ exclude

EXCLUDES ▸ exclude

EXCRETA pl n excrement

EXCRETAL ▸ excreta

EXCRETE, -D, -S vb discharge (waste matter) from the body

EXCRETER ▸ excrete

EXCRETES ▸ excrete

EXCUBANT adj keeping guard

EXCUDIT sentence substitute (named person) made this

EXCURSE, -D, -S vb wander

EXCURSUS n incidental digression from the main topic

EXCUSAL, -S ▸ excuse

EXCUSE, -D, -S, EXCUSING n explanation offered to justify (a fault etc) ▹ vb put forward a reason or justification for (a fault etc)

EXCUSER, -S ▸ excuse

EXCUSES ▸ excuse

EXCUSING ▸ excuse

EXCUSIVE adj excusing

EXEAT, -S n leave of absence from school or some other institution

EXEC, -S n executive

EXECRATE vb feel and express loathing and hatred of (someone or something)

EXECS ▸ exec

EXECUTE, -D, -S vb put (a condemned person) to death

EXECUTER ▸ execute

EXECUTES ▸ execute

EXECUTOR n person appointed to perform the instructions of a will

EXECUTRY n condition of being an executor

EXED ▸ ex

EXEDRA, -E, -S n building, room, portico, or apse containing a continuous bench

EXEEM, -ED, -ING, -S same as ▸ exeme

EXEGESIS, EXEGESES n explanation of a text, esp of the Bible

EXEGETE, -S n person who practises exegesis

EXEGETIC adj of or relating to exegesis

EXEME, -D, -S, EXEMING vb set free

EXEMPLA ▸ exemplum

EXEMPLAR n person or thing to be copied, model

EXEMPLE, -S same as ▸ example

EXEMPLUM, EXEMPLA n anecdote that supports a moral point

EXEMPT, -ED, -S adj not subject to an obligation etc ▹ vb release from an obligation etc ▹ n person who is exempt from an obligation, tax, etc

EXEQUIAL ▸ exequy

EXEQUY, EXEQUIES n funeral rite

Meaning a funeral rite, this word combines X and Q. Even better is its plural **exequies**, which would earn an extra 50 points for using all your tiles.

E

EXERCISE n activity to train the body or mind ▷ vb make use of

EXERGIES ▶ exergy

EXERGUAL ▶ exergue

EXERGUE, -S n space on the reverse of a coin or medal

EXERGY, EXERGIES n maximum amount of useful work obtainable from a system

EXERT, -ED, -ING, -S vb use (influence, authority, etc) forcefully or effectively

EXERTION ▶ exert

EXERTIVE ▶ exert

EXERTS ▶ exert

EXES ▶ ex

EXEUNT vb (they) go out

EXFIL, -LED, -S vb exfiltrate

EXHALANT adj emitting a vapour or liquid ▷ n organ or vessel that emits a vapour or liquid

EXHALE, -D, -S, EXHALING vb breathe out

EXHALENT same as ▶ exhalant

EXHALES ▶ exhale

EXHALING ▶ exhale

EXHAUST, -S vb tire out ▷ n gases ejected from an engine as waste products

EXHEDRA, -E same as ▶ exedra

EXHIBIT, -S vb display to the public ▷ n object exhibited to the public

EXHORT, -ED, -S vb urge earnestly

EXHORTER ▶ exhort

EXHORTS ▶ exhort

EXHUMATE same as ▶ exhume

EXHUME, -D, -S, EXHUMING vb dig up (something buried, esp a corpse)

EXHUMER, -S ▶ exhume

EXHUMES ▶ exhume

EXHUMING ▶ exhume

EXIES n hysterics

EXIGEANT adj exacting

EXIGENCE same as ▶ exigency

EXIGENCY n urgent demand or need

EXIGENT, -S adj urgent ▷ n emergency

EXIGIBLE adj liable to be exacted or required

EXIGUITY ▶ exiguous

EXIGUOUS adj scanty or meagre

EXILABLE ▶ exile

EXILE, -D, -S, EXILING n prolonged, usu enforced, absence from one's country ▷ vb expel from one's country

EXILER, -S ▶ exile

EXILES ▶ exile

EXILIAN ▶ exile

EXILIC ▶ exile

EXILING ▶ exile

EXILITY n poverty or meagreness

EXIMIOUS adj select and distinguished

EXINE, -S n outermost coat of a pollen grain or a spore

EXING ▶ ex

EXIST, -ED, -S vb have being or reality

EXISTENT adj in existence ▷ n person or a thing that exists

EXISTING ▶ exist

EXISTS ▶ exist

EXIT, -ED, -ING, -S n way out ▷ vb go out

EXITANCE n measure of the ability of a surface to emit radiation

EXITED ▶ exit

EXITING ▶ exit

EXITLESS ▶ exit

EXITS ▶ exit

EXO informal word for > excellent

> Exo is an informal Australian way of saying excellent. This is a great little word as it allows you to combine X with two of the most common tiles in the game, E and O.

EXOCARP, -S same as ▶ epicarp

EXOCRINE adj relating to a gland, such as the sweat gland, that secretes externally through a duct ▷ n exocrine gland

EXOCYTIC adj outside biological cell

EXODE, -S n exodus

EXODERM, -S same as ▶ ectoderm

EXODES ▶ exode

EXODIC ▶ exodus

EXODIST, -S ▶ exodus

EXODOS, EXODOI n (in Greek drama) concluding scene

EXODUS, -ES n departure of a large number of people

EXOERGIC adj (of a nuclear reaction) occurring with evolution of energy

EXOGAMIC ▶ exogamy

EXOGAMY n act of marrying a person from another tribe, clan, etc

EXOGEN, -S n type of plant

EXOGENIC adj formed or occurring on the earth's surface

EXOGENS ▶ exogen

EXOME, -S n part of the genome consisting of exons

EXOMION, -S same as ▶ exomis

EXOMIS, -ES n sleeveless jacket

EXON, -S n one of the officers who command the Yeomen of the Guard

EXONEREE n person who has been exonerated

EXONIC ▶ exon

EXONS ▶ exon

EXONUMIA n objects of interest to numismatists that are not coins, such as medals and tokens

EXONYM, -S n name given to a place by foreigners

EXOPHAGY n (among cannibals) custom of eating only members of other tribes

EXOPLASM another name for > ectoplasm

EXOPOD, -S same as > exopodite

EXORABLE adj able to be persuaded or moved by pleading

EXORCISE same as ▶ exorcize

EXORCISM ▶ exorcize

EXORCIST ▶ exorcize

EXORCIZE vb expel (evil spirits) by prayers and religious rites

EXORDIA ▶ exordium

EXORDIAL ▶ exordium

EXORDIUM, EXORDIA n introductory part or beginning, esp of an oration or discourse

EXOSMIC > exosmosis

EXOSMOSE same as > exosmosis

EXOSPORE n outer layer of the spores of some algae and fungi

EXOTERIC adj intelligible to or intended for more than a select or initiated minority

EXOTIC, -S adj having a strange allure or beauty ▷ n non-native plant

EXOTICA pl n (collection of) exotic objects

EXOTICS ▶ exotic

EXOTISM, -S n something exotic

EXOTOXIC ▸ exotoxin

EXOTOXIN n toxin produced by a microorganism and secreted into the surrounding medium

EXPAND, -S vb make or become larger

EXPANDED adj (of printer's type) wider than usual for a particular height

EXPANDER n device for exercising and developing the muscles of the body

EXPANDOR same as ▸ expander

EXPANDS ▸ expand

EXPANSE, -S n uninterrupted wide area

EXPAT, -S n short for expatriate

EXPECT, -ED, -S vb regard as probable

EXPECTER n person who expects

EXPECTS ▸ expect

EXPEDITE vb hasten the progress of ▸ adj unimpeded or prompt

EXPEL, -LED, -S vb drive out with force

EXPELLEE ▸ expel

EXPELLER ▸ expel

EXPELS ▸ expel

EXPEND, -ED, -S vb spend, use up

EXPENDER ▸ expend

EXPENDS ▸ expend

EXPENSE, -D, -S n cost ▸ vb treat as an expense

EXPERT, -ED, -S n person with extensive skill or knowledge in a particular field ▸ adj skilful or knowledgeable ▸ vb experience

EXPERTLY ▸ expert

EXPERTS ▸ expert

EXPIABLE adj capable of being expiated or atoned for

EXPIATE, -D, -S vb make amends for

EXPIATOR ▸ expiate

EXPIRANT n one who expires

EXPIRE, -D, -S, EXPIRING vb finish or run out

EXPIRER, -S ▸ expire

EXPIRES ▸ expire

EXPIRIES ▸ expiry

EXPIRING ▸ expire

EXPIRY, EXPIRIES n end, esp of a contract period

EXPLAIN, -S vb make clear and intelligible

EXPLANT, -S vb transfer (living tissue) from its natural site to a new site or to a culture medium ▸ n piece of tissue treated in this way

EXPLICIT adj precisely and clearly expressed ▸ n word used to indicate the end of a book

EXPLODE, -D, -S vb burst with great violence, blow up

EXPLODER ▸ explore

EXPLODES ▸ explode

EXPLOIT, -S vb take advantage of for one's own purposes ▸ n notable feat or deed

EXPLORE, -D, -S vb investigate

EXPLORER ▸ explore

EXPLORES ▸ explore

EXPO, -S n exposition, large public exhibition

EXPONENT n person who advocates an idea, cause, etc ▸ adj offering a declaration, explanation, or interpretation

EXPORT, -ED, -S n selling or shipping of goods to a foreign country ▸ vb sell or ship (goods) to a foreign country

EXPORTER ▸ export

EXPORTS ▸ export

EXPOS ▸ expo

EXPOSAL, -S ▸ expose

EXPOSE, -S, EXPOSING vb uncover or reveal ▸ n bringing of a crime, scandal, etc to public notice

EXPOSED adj not concealed

EXPOSER, -S ▸ expose

EXPOSES ▸ expose

EXPOSING ▸ expose

EXPOSIT, -S vb state

EXPOSOME n collection of environmental factors which can affect a person's health

EXPOSURE n exposing

EXPOUND, -S vb explain in detail

EXPRESS vb put into words ▸ adj explicitly stated ▸ n fast train or bus stopping at only a few stations ▸ adv by express delivery

EXPRESSO variant of ▸ espresso

EXPUGN, -ED, -S vb storm

EXPULSE, -D, -S vb expel

EXPUNCT, -S vb expunge

EXPUNGE, -D, -S vb delete, erase, blot out

EXPUNGER ▸ expunge

EXPUNGES ▸ expunge

EXPURGE, -D, -S vb purge

EXSCIND, -S vb cut off or out

EXSECANT n trigonometric function

EXSECT, -ED, -S vb cut out

EXSERT, -ED, -S vb thrust out ▸ adj protruded or stretched out from (something)

EXTANT adj still existing

EXTASY, EXTASIES same as ▸ ecstasy

EXTATIC same as ▸ ecstatic

EXTEND, -ED, -S vb draw out or be drawn out, stretch

EXTENDER n person or thing that extends

EXTENDS ▸ extend

EXTENSE, -S adj extensive ▸ n extension; expanse

EXTENSOR n muscle that extends a part of the body

EXTENT, -S n range over which something extends, area

EXTERIOR n part or surface on the outside ▸ adj of, on, or coming from the outside

EXTERN, -S n person with an official connection to an institution but not residing in it

EXTERNAL adj of, situated on, or coming from the outside ▸ n external circumstance or aspect, esp one that is superficial or inessential

EXTERNAT n day school

EXTERNE, -S same as ▸ extern

EXTERNS ▸ extern

EXTINCT, -S adj having died out ▸ vb extinguish

EXTINE, -S same as ▸ exine

EXTIRP, -ED, -S vb extirpate

EXTOL, -S vb praise highly

EXTOLD archaic past participle of ▸ extol

EXTOLL, -ED, -S same as ▸ extol

EXTOLLER ▸ extol

EXTOLLS ▸ extoll

EXTOLS ▸ extol

EXTORT, -ED, -S vb get (something) by force or threats

EXTORTER ▸ extort

EXTORTS ▸ extort

EXTRA, -S adj more than is usual, expected or needed ▸ n additional person or thing ▸ adv unusually or exceptionally

E

EXTRACT, -S vb pull out by force ▷ n something extracted, such as a passage from a book etc

EXTRADOS n outer curve or surface of an arch or vault

EXTRAIT, -S n extract

EXTRANET n intranet modified to allow outside access

EXTRAS ▸ extra

EXTREAT, -S n extraction ▷ vb extract or eliminate (something)

EXTREMA ▸ extremum

EXTREMAL n clause in a recursive definition

EXTREME, -R, -S adj of a high or the highest degree or intensity ▷ n either of the two limits of a scale or range

EXTREMUM, EXTREMA n extreme point

EXTROPY n supposition that human life will expand throughout the universe via technology

EXTRORSE adj turned or opening outwards or away from the axis

EXTRUDE, -D, -S vb squeeze or force out

EXTRUDER ▸ extrude

EXTRUDES ▸ extrude

EXTUBATE vb remove tube from hollow organ

EXUDATE, -S same as > exudation

EXUDE, -D, -S, EXUDING vb (of a liquid or smell) seep or flow out slowly and steadily

EXUL, -LED, -LING, -S vb exile; banish

EXULT, -ED, -ING, -S vb be joyful or jubilant

EXULTANT adj elated or jubilant, esp because of triumph or success

EXULTED ▸ exult

EXULTING ▸ exult

EXULTS ▸ exult

EXURB, -S n residential area beyond suburbs

EXURBAN ▸ exurbia

EXURBIA, -S n region outside the suburbs of a city

EXURBS ▸ exurb

EXUVIA, -E n something cast off

EXUVIAL ▸ exuvia

EXUVIATE vb shed (a skin or similar outer covering)

EXUVIUM n something cast off

EYALET, -S n province of Ottoman Empire

EYAS, -ES n nestling hawk or falcon

EYASS, -ES same as ▸ eyas

EYE, -D, -ING, -S, EYING n organ of sight ▷ vb look at carefully or warily

EYEABLE adj pleasant to look at

EYEBALL, -S n ball-shaped part of the eye ▷ vb eye

EYEBANK, -S n place in which corneas are stored

EYEBAR, -S n bar with flattened ends with holes for connecting pins

EYEBATH, -S n small cup for applying medication to the eye

EYEBEAM, -S n glance

EYEBLACK another name for ▸ mascara

EYEBLINK n very small amount of time

EYEBOLT, -S n type of threaded bolt

EYEBROW, -S n line of hair on the bony ridge above the eye ▷ vb equip with artificial eyebrows

EYECUP, -S same as ▸ eyebath

EYED ▸ eye

EYEDNESS ▸ eye

EYEDROPS n medicine applied to the eyes in drops

EYEFOLD, -S n fold of skin above eye

EYEFUL, -S n view

EYEGLASS n lens for aiding defective vision

EYEHOLE, -S n hole through which something is passed

EYEHOOK, -S n hook attached to a ring at the extremity of a rope or chain

EYEING ▸ eye

EYELASH n short hair that grows out from the eyelid

EYELESS ▸ eye

EYELET, -ED, -S n small hole for a lace or cord to be passed through ▷ vb supply with an eyelet or eyelets

EYELIAD, -S same as ▸ oeillade

EYELID, -S n fold of skin that covers the eye when it is closed

EYELIFT, -S n cosmetic surgery for eyes

EYELIKE ▸ eye

EYELINE, -S n line of sight

EYELINER n cosmetic used to outline the eyes

EYELINES ▸ eyeline

EYEN pl n eyes

EYEPATCH n material worn over an injured eye

EYEPIECE n lens in a microscope, telescope, etc, into which the person using it looks

EYEPOINT n position of a lens at which the sharpest image is obtained

EYER, -S n someone who eyes

EYES ▸ eye

EYESHADE n opaque or tinted translucent visor

EYESHINE n reflection of light from animal eye at night

EYESHOT, -S n range of vision

EYESIGHT n ability to see

EYESOME adj attractive

EYESORE, -S n ugly object

EYESPOT, -S n small area of pigment

EYESTALK n movable stalk bearing a compound eye at its tip

EYESTONE n device for removing foreign body from eye

EYETOOTH, EYETEETH n either of the two canine teeth in the upper jaw

EYEWASH n nonsense

EYEWATER n lotion for the eyes

EYEWEAR, -S n spectacles; glasses

EYEWINK, -S n wink of the eye; instant

EYING ▸ eye

EYLIAD, -S same as ▸ oeillade

EYNE poetic plural of ▸ eye

EYOT, -S n island

EYRA, -S n reddish-brown variety of the jaguarondi

EYRE, -S n obsolete circuit court

EYRIE, -S n nest of an eagle

EYRIR n Icelandic monetary unit

EYRY same as ▸ eyrie

EZINE, -S n magazine available only in electronic form

Ff

F is a useful letter in Scrabble: it begins three two-letter words (**fa**, **fe** and **fy**). There are also quite a few words that combine **F** with **X** or **Z**, allowing high scores, particularly if you can hit a bonus square with them. **Fax**, **fix** and **fox** are good examples (13 points each), and don't forget **fez** and **fiz** (15 points each). **Fay**, **fey**, **fly**, **foy** and **fry** can also be useful (9 each).

FA, -S same as ▶ **fah**

FAA, -ING, -N, -S Scot word for ▶ **fall**

FAB, -BER, -BEST, -S adj excellent ▷ n fabrication

FABBY, FABBIER, FABBIEST same as ▶ **fab**

FABLE, -S n story with a moral ▷ vb relate or tell (fables)

FABLED adj made famous in legend

FABLER, -S ▶ **fable**

FABLES ▶ **fable**

FABLET, -S n large smartphone able to perform many of the functions of a tablet computer

FABLIAU, -X n comic, usually ribald verse tale

FABLING, -S ▶ **fable**

FABRIC, -S n knitted or woven cloth ▷ vb build

FABRIQUE n (in Quebec) group of laypersons who hold church property in trust for the parish

FABS ▶ **fab**

FABULAR adj relating to fables

FABULATE vb make up fables

FABULISE vb make up fables

FABULISM n literary technique of placing fantastical elements in mundane settings

FABULIST n person who invents or recounts fables

FABULIZE vb make up fables

FABULOUS adj excellent

FABURDEN n early form of counterpoint

FACADE, -S n front of a building

FACE, -D, -S n front of the head ▷ vb look or turn towards

FACEABLE ▶ **face**

FACEBAR, -S n wrestling hold

FACEBOOK vb search for (someone) on the Facebook website

FACED ▶ **face**

FACEDOWN vb confront and force (someone or something) to back down

FACELESS adj impersonal, anonymous

FACELIFT n cosmetic surgery for the face

FACEMAIL n computer-generated face that delivers messages on screen

FACEMAN, FACEMEN n miner who works at the coalface

FACEMASK n protective mask for the face

FACEMEN ▶ **faceman**

FACEOFF, -S n confrontation

FACEPALM vb bring one's palm to one's face in dismay

FACER, -S n difficulty or problem

FACES ▶ **face**

FACET, -ED, -S, -TED n aspect ▷ vb cut facets in (a gemstone)

FACETE adj witty and humorous

FACETED ▶ **facet**

FACETELY ▶ **facete**

FACETIAE pl n humorous or witty sayings

FACETIME vb talk with (someone) via the FaceTime application

FACETING n act of faceting

FACETS ▶ **facet**

FACETTED ▶ **facet**

FACEUP adj with the face or surface exposed

FACIA, -E, -S same as ▶ **fascia**

FACIAL, -S adj of or relating to the face ▷ n beauty treatment for the face

FACIALLY ▶ **facial**

FACIALS ▶ **facial**

FACIAS ▶ **facia**

FACIEND, -S n multiplicand

FACIES n general form and appearance

FACILE adj (of a remark, argument, etc) lacking depth

FACILELY ▶ **facile**

FACILITY n skill

FACING, -S n lining or covering for decoration or reinforcement

FACONNE, -S adj denoting a fabric with the design woven in ▷ n such a fabric

FACT, -S n event or thing known to have happened or existed

FACTA ▶ **factum**

FACTFUL ▶ **fact**

FACTICE, -S n soft rubbery material

FACTION, -S n (dissenting) minority group within a larger body

FACTIOUS adj of or producing factions

FACTIS, -ES variant of ▶ **factice**

FACTIVE adj giving rise to the presupposition that a sentence is true

FACTOID, -S n piece of unreliable information believed to be true

FACTOR, -ED, -S n element contributing to a result ▷ vb engage in the business of a factor

FACTORY n building where goods are manufactured

FACTOTUM n person employed to do all sorts of work

FACTS ▶ **fact**

FACTUAL adj concerning facts rather than opinions or theories

FACTUM, FACTA, -S n something done, deed

FACTURE, -S n construction

FACULA, -E n any of the bright areas on the sun's surface

FACULAR ▶ facula

FACULTY n physical or mental ability

FAD, -S n short-lived fashion

FADABLE ▶ fade

FADAISE, -S n silly remark

FADDIER ▶ faddy

FADDIEST ▶ faddy

FADDISH ▶ fad

FADDISM, -S ▶ fad

FADDIST, -S ▶ fad

FADDLE, -D, -S, FADDLING vb mess around, toy with

FADDY, FADDIER, FADDIEST adj unreasonably fussy, particularly about food

FADE, -D, -S vb (cause to) lose brightness, colour, or strength ▷ n act or an instance of fading

FADEAWAY n fading to the point of disappearance

FADED ▶ fade

FADEDLY ▶ fade

FADEIN, -S n gradual appearance of an image on film

FADELESS adj not subject to fading

FADEOUT, -S n gradual disappearance of an image on film

FADER, -S ▶ fade

FADES ▶ fade

FADEUR, -S n blandness, insipidness

FADGE, -D, -S, FADGING vb agree ▷ n package of wool in a wool-bale

FADIER ▶ fady

FADIEST ▶ fady

FADING, -S n variation in strength of received radio signals

FADLIKE ▶ fad

FADO, -S n type of melancholy Portuguese folk song

FADS ▶ fad

FADY, FADIER, FADIEST adj faded

FAE Scot word for ▶ from

FAECAL adj of, relating to, or consisting of faeces

FAECES pl n waste matter discharged from the body

FAENA, -S n matador's final actions before the kill

FAERIE, -S n land of fairies

FAERY same as ▶ faerie

FAFF, -ED, -ING, -S vb dither or fuss

FAFFIER ▶ faffy

FAFFIEST ▶ faffy

FAFFING ▶ faff

FAFFS ▶ faff

FAFFY, FAFFIER, FAFFIEST adj awkward and time-consuming to do or use

FAG, -GED, -S n tiresome work ▷ vb work hard

FAGGING, -S ▶ fag

FAGIN, -S n criminal

FAGOTING same as > faggoting

FAGOTTO, FAGOTTI, -S n bassoon

FAGS ▶ fag

FAH, -S n (in tonic sol-fa) fourth degree of any major scale

FAHLBAND n thin bed of schistose rock impregnated with metallic sulphides

FAHLERZ n copper ore

FAHLORE, -S n copper ore

FAHS ▶ fah

FAIBLE, -S variant of ▶ foible

FAIENCE, -S n tin-glazed earthenware

FAIK, -ED, -ING, -S vb Scots word meaning fold

FAIKES n sandy rock

FAIKING ▶ faik

FAIKS ▶ faik

FAIL, -ED, -S vb be unsuccessful ▷ n instance of not passing an exam or test

FAILING, -S n weak point ▷ prep in the absence of

FAILLE, -S n soft light ribbed fabric of silk, rayon, or taffeta

FAILOVER n automatic transfer to a backup computer system in the event of a primary system failure

FAILS ▶ fail

FAILURE, -S n act or instance of failing

FAIN, -ED, -ER, -EST, -ING, -S adv gladly ▷ adj willing or eager ▷ vb desire

FAINE, -S variant of ▶ fain

FAINEANT n lazy person ▷ adj indolent

FAINED ▶ fain

FAINER ▶ fain

FAINES ▶ faine

FAINEST ▶ fain

FAINING ▶ fain

FAINITES interj cry for truce or respite from the rules of a game

FAINLY ▶ fain

FAINNE, -S n badge worn by advocates of the Irish language

FAINNESS ▶ fain

FAINS ▶ fain

FAINT, -ED, -EST, -ING, -S adj lacking clarity, brightness, or volume ▷ vb lose consciousness temporarily ▷ n temporary loss of consciousness

FAINTER, -S ▶ faint

FAINTEST ▶ faint

FAINTIER ▶ fainty

FAINTING ▶ faint

FAINTISH ▶ faint

FAINTLY ▶ faint

FAINTS ▶ faint

FAINTY, FAINTIER ▶ faint

FAIR, -ED, -ER, -EST, -S adj unbiased and reasonable ▷ adv fairly ▷ n travelling entertainment ▷ vb join together to form a smooth shape

FAIRGOER n person attending fair

FAIRIER ▶ fairy

FAIRIES ▶ fairy

FAIRIEST ▶ fairy

FAIRILY ▶ fairy

FAIRING, -S n structure fitted round part of a vehicle to reduce drag

FAIRISH adj moderately good, well, etc

FAIRLEAD n block or ring through which a line is rove

FAIRLY adv moderately

FAIRNESS ▶ fair

FAIRS ▶ fair

FAIRWAY, -S n area between the tee and the green

FAIRY, FAIRIER, FAIRIES, FAIRIEST n imaginary small creature ▷ adj of or relating to a fairy or fairies

FAIRYDOM ▶ fairy

FAIRYISM ▶ fairy

FAITH, -S n strong belief, esp without proof

FAITHED adj having faith or a faith

FAITHER, -S Scot word for ▶ father

FAITHFUL adj loyal

FAITHING n practising a faith

FAITHS ▶ faith

FAITOR, -S n impostor

FAITOUR, -S n impostor

FAIX interj have faith

FAJITAS, FAJITA pl n Mexican dish

FAKE, -D, -S, -ST, FAKING vb cause something not genuine to appear so by fraud ▷ n person, thing, or act that is not genuine ▷ adj not genuine

FAKEER, -S same as ▶ fakir

FAKEMENT n something false, counterfeit

FAKER, -S ▶ fake

FAKERIES ▶ fakery

FAKERS ▶ faker

FAKERY, FAKERIES ▶ fake

FAKES ▶ fake

FAKEST ▶ fake

FAKEY, -S, FAKIER, FAKIEST adj (of a skateboarding manoeuvre) travelling backwards ▷ n skateboarding position in which the skateboarder faces backwards

FAKIE, -S same as ▶ fakey

FAKIER ▶ fakey

FAKIES ▶ fakie

FAKIEST ▶ fakey

FAKING ▶ fake

FAKIR, -S n Muslim who spurns worldly possessions

FAKIRISM ▶ fakir

FAKIRS ▶ fakir

FALAFEL, -S n ball or cake made from chickpeas

FALAJ, AFLAJ n kind of irrigation channel in ancient Oman

FALBALA, -S n gathered flounce, frill, or ruffle

FALCADE, -S n movement of a horse

FALCATE adj shaped like a sickle

FALCATED same as ▶ falcate

FALCES ▶ falx

FALCHION n short and slightly curved medieval sword broader towards the point

FALCON, -S n small bird of prey

FALCONER n person who breeds or trains hawks or who follows the sport of falconry

FALCONET n type of small falcon

FALCONRY n art of training falcons

FALCONS ▶ falcon

FALCULA, -E, -S n sharp curved claw, esp of a bird

FALDAGE, -S n feudal right

FALDERAL n showy but worthless trifle ▷ vb sing nonsense words

FALDEROL same as ▶ falderal

FALDETTA n Maltese woman's garment with a stiffened hood

FALL, -EN, -S vb drop through the force of gravity ▷ n falling

FALLACY n false belief

FALLAL, -S n showy ornament, trinket, or article of dress

FALLAWAY n friendship that has been withdrawn

FALLBACK n something that recedes or retreats

FALLEN ▶ fall

FALLER, -S n any device that falls or operates machinery by falling

FALLFISH n large N American freshwater fish resembling the chub

FALLIBLE adj (of a person) liable to make mistakes

FALLIBLY ▶ fallible

FALLING, -S ▶ fall

FALLOFF, -S n decline or drop

FALLOUT, -S n descent of solid material in the atmosphere onto the earth

FALLOW, -ED, -ER, -S adj (of land) ploughed but left unseeded to regain fertility ▷ n land treated in this way ▷ vb leave (land) unseeded after ploughing and harrowing it

FALLS ▶ fall

FALSE, -D, -R, -S, -ST, FALSING adj not true or correct ▷ adv in a false or dishonest manner ▷ vb falsify

FALSELY ▶ false

FALSER ▶ false

FALSERS pl n colloquial term for false teeth

FALSES ▶ false

FALSEST ▶ false

FALSETTO n voice pitched higher than one's natural range

FALSIE, -S n pad used to enlarge breast shape

FALSIFY vb alter fraudulently

FALSING ▶ false

FALSISH ▶ false

FALSISM, -S ▶ false

FALSITY n state of being false

FALTBOAT n collapsible boat made of waterproof material stretched over a light framework

FALTER, -ED, -S vb be hesitant, weak, or unsure ▷ n uncertainty or hesitancy in speech or action

FALTERER ▶ falter

FALTERS ▶ falter

FALX, FALCES n sickle-shaped anatomical structure

FAME, -D, -S, FAMING n state of being widely recognized ▷ vb make known or famous

FAMELESS ▶ fame

FAMES ▶ fame

FAMILIAL adj of or relating to the family

FAMILIAR adj well-known ▷ n demon supposed to attend a witch

FAMILIES ▶ family

FAMILISM n beliefs of a mystical Christian religious sect

FAMILIST adj relating to familism

FAMILLE, -S n type of Chinese porcelain

FAMILY, FAMILIES n group of parents and their children ▷ adj suitable for parents and children together

FAMINE, -S n severe shortage of food

FAMING ▶ fame

FAMISH, -ES vb be or make very hungry or weak

FAMISHED adj very hungry

FAMISHES ▶ famish

FAMOUS, -ED, -ES adj very well-known ▷ vb make famous

FAMOUSLY adv excellently

FAMULUS, FAMULI n (formerly) the attendant of a sorcerer or scholar

FAN, -NED, -S n object used to create a current of air ▷ vb blow or cool with a fan

FANAL, -S n lighthouse

FANATIC, -S n person who is excessively enthusiastic about something ▷ adj excessively enthusiastic

FANBASE, -S n body of admirers

FANBOY, -S n obsessive fan of a subject or hobby

FANCIED adj imaginary

FANCIER, -S n person interested in plants or animals

FANCIES ▶ fancy

FANCIEST ▶ fancy

FANCIFUL adj not based on fact

FANCIFY vb make more beautiful

FANCILY ▸ fancy

FANCY, FANCIES, FANCIEST, -ING adj elaborate, not plain ▷ n sudden irrational liking or desire ▷ vb suppose; imagine

FAND, -ED, -ING, -S vb old word meaning try

FANDANGO n lively Spanish dance

FANDED ▸ fand

FANDING ▸ fand

FANDOM, -S n collectively, the fans of a sport, pastime or person

FANDS ▸ fand

FANE, -S n temple or shrine

FANEGA, -S n Spanish unit of measurement

FANEGADA n Spanish unit of land area

FANEGAS ▸ fanega

FANES ▸ fane

FANFARE, -D, -S n tune played on brass instruments ▷ vb perform a fanfare

FANFARON n braggart

FANFIC, -S n fiction based on work by other authors

FANFOLD, -S vb fold (paper) like a fan

FANG, -ED, -ING, -S n snake's tooth which injects poison ▷ vb dialect word meaning seize

FANGA, -S same as ▸ fanega

FANGED ▸ fang

FANGING ▸ fang

FANGIRL, -S n enthusiastic female devotee of something

FANGLE, -D, -S, FANGLING vb fashion

FANGLESS ▸ fang

FANGLIKE ▸ fang

FANGLING ▸ fangle

FANGO, -S n mud from thermal springs in Italy

FANGS ▸ fang

FANION, -S n small flag used by surveyors

FANJET, -S same as ▸ turbofan

FANK, -ED, -ING, -S n sheep pen ▷ vb put sheep in a pen

FANKLE, -D, -S, FANKLING vb entangle ▷ n tangle

FANKS ▸ fank

FANLIGHT n semicircular window over a door or window

FANLIKE ▸ fan

FANNED ▸ fan

FANNEL, -S n ecclesiastical vestment

FANNELL, -S variant of ▸ fannel

FANNELS ▸ fannel

FANNER, -S ▸ fan

FANNING, -S ▸ fan

FANO, -S same as ▸ fanon

FANON, -S n collar-shaped vestment

FANOS ▸ fano

FANS ▸ fan

FANSITE, -S n website aimed at fans of a celebrity, film, etc

FANSUB, -S n fan-produced subtitling of films

FANTAD, -S n nervous, agitated state

FANTAIL, -S n small New Zealand bird with a tail like a fan

FANTASIA n musical composition of an improvised nature

FANTASIE same as ▸ fantasy

FANTASM, -S archaic spelling of ▸ phantasm

FANTAST, -S n dreamer or visionary

FANTASY n far-fetched notion ▷ adj of a type of competition ▷ vb fantasize

FANTEEG, -S n nervous, agitated state

FANTIGUE variant of ▸ fanteeg

FANTOD, -S n crotchety or faddish behaviour

FANTOM, -S archaic spelling of ▸ phantom

FANTOOSH adj pretentious

FANUM, -S n temple

FANWISE adj like a fan

FANWORT, -S n aquatic plant

FANZINE, -S n magazine produced by fans

FAP adj drunk

FAQIR, -S same as ▸ fakir

Meaning a Hindu ascetic, this is one of those invaluable words allowing you to play the Q without a U. It can also be spelt **fakeer, fakir** and **faquir**.

FAQUIR, -S variant of ▸ faqir

FAR, -RED, -RING, -S, -THER, -THEST adv at, to, or from a great distance ▷ adj remote in space or time ▷ vb go far

FARAD, -S n unit of electrical capacitance

FARADAIC same as ▸ faradic

FARADAY, -S n quantity of electricity

FARADIC adj of an intermittent asymmetric alternating current

FARADISE same as ▸ faradize

FARADISM n therapeutic use of faradic currents

FARADIZE vb treat (an organ or part) with faradic currents

FARADS ▸ farad

FARAND adj pleasant or attractive in manner or appearance

FARANG, -S n (in Thailand) a foreigner

FARAWAY adj very distant

FARAWAYS same as ▸ faraway

FARCE, -D, -S n boisterous comedy ▷ vb enliven (a speech, etc) with jokes

FARCER, -S same as ▸ farceur

FARCES ▸ farce

FARCEUR, -S n writer of or performer in farces

FARCEUSE n female farceur

FARCI adj (of food) stuffed

FARCICAL adj ludicrous

FARCIE same as ▸ farci

FARCIED adj afflicted with farcy

FARCIES ▸ farcy

FARCIFY vb turn into a farce

FARCIN, -S n bacterial disease of horses

FARCING, -S ▸ farce

FARCINS ▸ farcin

FARCY, FARCIES n bacterial disease of horses

FARD, -ED, -S n paint for the face, esp white paint ▷ vb paint (the face) with fard

FARDAGE, -S n material laid beneath or between cargo

FARDED ▸ fard

FARDEL, -S n bundle or burden

FARDEN, -S n farthing

FARDING, -S ▸ fard

FARDS ▸ fard

FARE, -D, -S, FARING n charge for a passenger's journey ▷ vb get on (as specified)

FAREBOX n box where money for bus fares is placed

FARED ▸ fare

FARER, -S ▸ fare

FARES ▸ fare

FAREWELL interj goodbye ▷ n act of saying goodbye and leaving ▷ vb say goodbye ▷ adj parting or closing

FARFAL, -S same as ▸ falafel

FARFALLE *n* pasta in bow shapes
FARFALS ▶ farfal
FARFEL, -S same as ▶ falafel
FARFET *adj* far-fetched
FARINA, -S *n* flour or meal made from any kind of cereal grain
FARING ▶ fare
FARINHA, -S *n* cassava meal
FARINOSE *adj* similar to or yielding farina
FARL, -S *n* thin cake of oatmeal, often triangular in shape
FARLE, -S same as ▶ farl
FARLS ▶ farl
FARM, -S *n* area of land for growing crops or rearing livestock ▷ *vb* cultivate (land)
FARMABLE ▶ farm
FARMED *adj* (of fish or game) reared on a farm
FARMER, -S *n* person who owns or runs a farm
FARMERY *n* farm buildings
FARMHAND *n* person who is hired to work on a farm
FARMING, -S *n* business or skill of agriculture
FARMLAND *n* land that is used for or suitable for farming
FARMOST *adj* most distant
FARMS ▶ farm
FARMWIFE *n* woman who works on a farm
FARMWORK *n* tasks carried out on a farm
FARMYARD *n* small area of land enclosed by or around the farm buildings
FARNESOL *n* type of alcohol
FARNESS ▶ far
FARO, -S *n* gambling game
FAROLITO *n* votive candle
FAROS ▶ faro
FAROUCHE *adj* sullen or shy
FARRAGO, -S *n* jumbled mixture of things
FARRAND variant of ▶ farand
FARRANT variant of ▶ farand
FARRED ▶ far
FARREN, -S *n* allotted ground
FARRIER, -S *n* person who shoes horses
FARRIERY *n* art, work, or establishment of a farrier
FARRING ▶ far
FARRO, -S *n* variety of wheat
FARROW, -ED, -S *n* litter of piglets ▷ *vb* (of a sow) give birth ▷ *adj* (of a cow) not calving in a given year

FARRUCA, -S *n* flamenco dance performed by men
FARS ▶ far
FARSE, -D, -S, FARSING *vb* insert into
FARSIDE, -S *n* part of the Moon facing away from the Earth
FARSING ▶ farse
FART, -ED, -ING, -S *n* emission of gas from the anus ▷ *vb* emit gas from the anus
FARTHEL, -S same as ▶ farl
FARTHER ▶ far
FARTHEST ▶ far
FARTHING *n* former British coin equivalent to a quarter of a penny
FARTING ▶ fart
FARTLEK, -S *n* in sport, another name for interval training
FARTS ▶ fart
FAS ▶ fa
FASCES *pl n* (in ancient Rome) a bundle of rods containing an axe
FASCI ▶ fascio
FASCIA, -E, -S *n* outer surface of a dashboard
FASCIAL ▶ fascia
FASCIAS ▶ fascia
FASCIATE *adj* (of stems and branches) abnormally flattened due to coalescence
FASCICLE same as ▶ fascicule
FASCINE, -S *n* bundle of long sticks used in construction
FASCIO, FASCI *n* political group
FASCIOLA *n* band
FASCIOLE *n* band
FASCISM, -S *n* right-wing totalitarian political system
FASCISMO, FASCISMI Italian word for ▶ fascism
FASCISMS ▶ fascism
FASCIST, -S *n* adherent or practitioner of fascism ▷ *adj* characteristic of or relating to fascism
FASCISTA, FASCISTI Italian word for ▶ fascist
FASCISTS ▶ fascist
FASCIITIS same as ▶ fasciitis
FASH, -ED, -ES, -ING *n* worry ▷ *vb* trouble
FASHERY *n* difficulty, trouble
FASHES ▶ fash
FASHING ▶ fash
FASHION, -S *n* style popular at a particular time ▷ *vb* form or make into a particular shape

FASHIONY *adj* fashionable, trendy
FASHIOUS *adj* troublesome
FAST, -ED, -EST, -S *adj* (capable of) acting or moving quickly ▷ *adv* quickly ▷ *vb* go without food, esp for religious reasons ▷ *n* period of fasting
FASTBACK *n* car having a back that forms one continuous slope from roof to rear
FASTBALL *n* ball pitched at the pitcher's top speed
FASTED ▶ fast
FASTEN, -ED, -S *vb* make or become firmly fixed or joined
FASTENER ▶ fasten
FASTENS ▶ fasten
FASTER, -S ▶ fast
FASTEST ▶ fast
FASTI *pl n* in ancient Rome, business days
FASTIE, -S *n* deceitful act
FASTING, -S ▶ fast
FASTISH ▶ fast
FASTLY ▶ fast
FASTNESS *n* fortress, safe place
FASTS ▶ fast
FASTUOUS *adj* arrogant
FAT, -S, -TED, -TER, -TEST, -TING *adj* having excess flesh on the body ▷ *n* extra flesh on the body ▷ *vb* fatten
FATAL *adj* causing death or ruin
FATALISM *n* belief that all events are predetermined
FATALIST ▶ fatalism
FATALITY *n* death caused by an accident or disaster
FATALLY *adv* resulting in death or disaster
FATBACK, -S *n* fat from the upper part of a side of pork
FATBERG, -S *n* large mass of fat in a sewer
FATBIRD, -S *n* nocturnal bird
FATE, -S, FATING *n* power supposed to predetermine events ▷ *vb* predetermine
FATED *adj* destined
FATEFUL *adj* having important, usu disastrous, consequences
FATES ▶ fate
FATHEAD, -S *n* stupid person
FATHER, -ED, -S *n* male parent ▷ *vb* be the father of (offspring)
FATHERLY *adj* kind or protective, like a father
FATHERS ▶ father

F

FATHOM, -ED, -S *n* unit of length ▷ *vb* understand
FATHOMER ▸ fathom
FATHOMS ▸ fathom
FATIDIC *adj* prophetic
FATIGATE *vb* fatigue
FATIGUE, -D, -S *n* extreme physical or mental tiredness ▷ *vb* tire out
FATING ▸ fate
FATLESS ▸ fat
FATLIKE ▸ fat
FATLING, -S *n* young farm animal fattened for killing
FATLY ▸ fat
FATNESS ▸ fat
FATS ▸ fat
FATSIA, -S *n* type of shrub
FATSO, -ES, -S *n* disparaging term for a fat person
FATSTOCK *n* livestock fattened and ready for market
FATTED ▸ fat
FATTEN, -ED, -S *vb* (cause to) become fat
FATTENER ▸ fatten
FATTENS ▸ fatten
FATTER ▸ fat
FATTEST ▸ fat
FATTIER ▸ fatty
FATTIES ▸ fatty
FATTIEST ▸ fatty
FATTILY ▸ fatty
FATTING ▸ fat
FATTISH ▸ fat
FATTISM, -S *n* discrimination on the basis of weight
FATTIST, -S ▸ fattism
FATTRELS *n* ends of ribbon
FATTY, FATTIER, FATTIES, FATTIEST *adj* containing fat ▷ *n* insulting word for a fat person
FATUITY *n* foolish thoughtlessness
FATUOUS *adj* foolish
FATWA, -ED, -ING, -S *n* religious decree issued by a Muslim leader ▷ *vb* issue a fatwa
FATWAH, -ED, -S *same as* ▸ fatwa
FATWAING ▸ fatwa
FATWAS ▸ fatwa
FATWOOD, -S *n* wood used for kindling
FAUBOURG *n* suburb or quarter, esp of a French city
FAUCAL, -S *adj* of or relating to the fauces
FAUCES *n* area of the mouth
FAUCET, -S *n* tap
FAUCETRY *n* art or practice of making faucets
FAUCETS ▸ faucet

FAUCHION *n* short sword
FAUCHON, -S *variant of* ▸ fauchion
FAUCIAL *same as* ▸ faucal
FAUGH *interj* exclamation of disgust, scorn, etc
FAULD, -S *n* piece of armour
FAULT, -ED, -ING, -S *n* responsibility for something wrong ▷ *vb* criticize or blame
FAULTFUL ▸ fault
FAULTIER ▸ faulty
FAULTILY ▸ faulty
FAULTING ▸ fault
FAULTS ▸ fault
FAULTY, FAULTIER *adj* badly designed or not working properly
FAUN, -S *n* (in Roman legend) mythological creature
FAUNA, -E, -S *n* animals of a given place or time
FAUNAL ▸ fauna
FAUNALLY ▸ fauna
FAUNAS ▸ fauna
FAUNIST, -S ▸ fauna
FAUNLIKE ▸ faun
FAUNS ▸ faun
FAUNULA, -E *n* fauna of a small single environment
FAUNULE, -S *same as* ▸ faunula
FAUR, -ER, -EST *Scot word for* ▸ far
FAURD *adj* favoured
FAURER ▸ faur
FAUREST ▸ faur
FAUSTIAN *adj* of or relating to Faust, esp reminiscent of his bargain with the devil
FAUT, -ED, -ING, -S *Scot word for* ▸ fault
FAUTEUIL *n* armchair, the sides of which are not upholstered
FAUTING ▸ faut
FAUTOR, -S *n* patron
FAUTS ▸ faut
FAUVE, -S *adj* of the style of the Fauve art movement ▷ *n* member of the Fauve art movement
FAUVETTE *n* singing bird, warbler
FAUVISM, -S ▸ fauve
FAUVIST, -S *n* artist following the Fauve style of painting
FAUX *adj* false
FAVA, -S *n* type of bean
FAVE, -R, -S, -ST *short for* ▸ favourite
FAVEL, -S *adj* (of a horse) fallow-coloured ▷ *n* fallow-coloured horse

FAVELA, -S *n* (in Brazil) a shanty or shantytown
FAVELL *variant of* ▸ favel
FAVELLA, -S *n* group of spores
FAVELS ▸ favel
FAVER ▸ fave
FAVES ▸ fave
FAVEST ▸ fave
FAVICON, -S *n* icon displayed before a website's URL
FAVISM, -S *n* type of anaemia
FAVONIAN *adj* of or relating to the west wind
FAVOR, -ED, -ING, -S *same as* ▸ favour
FAVORER, -S ▸ favour
FAVORING ▸ favor
FAVORITE *same as* > favourite
FAVORS ▸ favor
FAVOSE *same as* > faveolate
FAVOUR, -ED, -S *n* approving attitude ▷ *vb* prefer
FAVOURER ▸ favour
FAVOURS ▸ favour
FAVOUS *adj* resembling honeycomb
FAVRILE, -S *n* type of iridescent glass
FAVUS, -ES *n* infectious fungal skin disease
FAW, -S *n* old word for an itinerant person

> A **faw** is a person with an itinerant lifestyle, a good word for taking advantage of a nearby bonus square.

FAWN, -ED, -S *n* young deer ▷ *adj* light yellowish-brown ▷ *vb* seek attention from (someone) by insincere flattery
FAWNER, -S ▸ fawn
FAWNIER ▸ fawny
FAWNIEST ▸ fawny
FAWNING, -S ▸ fawn
FAWNLIKE ▸ fawn
FAWNS ▸ fawn
FAWNY, FAWNIER, FAWNIEST *adj* of a fawn colour
FAWS ▸ faw
FAX, -ED, -ES, -ING *n* electronic system ▷ *vb* send (a document) by this system
FAXABLE *adj* able to be faxed
FAXED ▸ fax
FAXES ▸ fax
FAXING ▸ fax
FAY, -ED, -ER, -EST, -ING, -S *n* fairy or sprite ▷ *adj* of or resembling a fay ▷ *vb* fit or

be fitted closely or tightly

A **fay** is a fairy, but it can also be a verb meaning to fit closely. It has an older variant **fey**. Both are useful high-scoring short words.

FAYALITE n rare brown or black mineral
FAYED ▸ fay
FAYENCE, -S variant of ▸ faience
FAYER ▸ fay
FAYEST ▸ fay
FAYING ▸ fay
FAYNE, -D, -S, FAYNING archaic spelling of ▸ feign
FAYRE, -S pseudo-archaic spelling of ▸ fair
FAYS ▸ fay
FAZE, -S, FAZING vb disconcert or fluster
FAZED ▸ faze
FAZENDA, -S n large estate or ranch
FAZES ▸ faze
FAZING ▸ faze
FE, -S n variant of Hebrew letter pe, transliterated as f
FEAGUE, -D, -S, FEAGUING vb whip or beat
FEAL, -ED, -ING, -S vb conceal
FEALTY, FEALTIES n (in feudal society) subordinate's loyalty
FEAR, -ED, -ING, -S n distress or alarm caused by impending danger or pain ▷ vb be afraid of (something or someone)
FEARE, -S n companion
FEARED ▸ fear
FEARER, -S ▸ fear
FEARES ▸ feare
FEARFUL adj feeling fear
FEARING ▸ fear
FEARLESS ▸ fear
FEARS ▸ fear
FEARSOME adj terrifying
FEART adj (Scots) afraid
FEASANCE n performance of an act
FEASE, -D, -S, FEASING vb perform an act
FEASIBLE adj able to be done, possible
FEASIBLY ▸ feasible
FEASING ▸ fease
FEAST, -ED, -ING, -S n lavish meal ▷ vb eat a feast
FEASTER, -S ▸ feast
FEASTFUL adj festive
FEASTING ▸ feast
FEASTS ▸ feast
FEAT, -ED, -ER, -EST, -ING, -S n remarkable, skilful, or

daring action ▷ adj neat ▷ vb make neat
FEATEOUS adj neat
FEATER ▸ feat
FEATEST ▸ feat
FEATHER, -S n one of the barbed shafts forming the plumage of birds ▷ vb fit or cover with feathers
FEATHERY ▸ feather
FEATING ▸ feat
FEATLY, FEATLIER ▸ feat
FEATOUS variant of ▸ feateous
FEATS ▸ feat
FEATUOUS variant of ▸ feateous
FEATURE, -S n part of the face, such as the eyes ▷ vb have as a feature or be a feature in
FEATURED adj having features as specified
FEATURES ▸ feature
FEAZE, -D, -S, FEAZING same as ▸ feeze
FEBLESSE n feebleness
FEBRIFIC adj causing or having a fever
FEBRILE adj very active and nervous
FECAL same as ▸ faecal
FECES same as ▸ faeces
FECHT, -ING, -S Scot word for ▸ fight
FECHTER, -S ▸ fecht
FECHTING ▸ fecht
FECHTS ▸ fecht
FECIAL, -S adj heraldic
FECIT vb (he or she) made it
FECKLESS adj ineffectual or irresponsible
FECKLY adv dialect word meaning mostly
FECULA, -E, -S n type of starch
FECULENT adj filthy, scummy, muddy, or foul
FECUND adj fertile
FED, -S n FBI agent
FEDARIE, -S n old word for an accomplice
FEDAYEE, -N n (in Arab states) a commando
FEDELINI n type of pasta
FEDERACY n alliance
FEDERAL, -S adj of a system of governance ▷ n supporter of federal union or federation
FEDERARY variant of ▸ fedarie
FEDERATE vb unite in a federation ▷ adj federal
FEDEX, -ED, -ES, -ING vb send by FedEx

FEDORA, -S n soft hat with a brim
FEDS ▸ fed
FEE, -ING, -S n charge paid to be allowed to do something ▷ vb pay a fee to
FEEB, -S n contemptible person
FEEBLE, -D, -R, -S, -ST, FEEBLING adj lacking physical or mental power ▷ vb make feeble
FEEBLISH ▸ feeble
FEEBLY ▸ feeble
FEEBS ▸ feeb
FEED, -ING, -INGS, -S vb give food to ▷ n act of feeding
FEEDABLE ▸ feed
FEEDBACK n information received in response to something done
FEEDBAG, -S n any bag in which feed for livestock is sacked
FEEDBOX n trough, manger
FEEDER, -S n baby's bib
FEEDHOLE n small hole through which cable etc is inserted
FEEDING ▸ feed
FEEDINGS ▸ feed
FEEDLOT, -S n area where livestock are fattened rapidly
FEEDPIPE n pipe through which something is supplied to a machine or system
FEEDS ▸ feed
FEEDYARD n place where cattle are kept and fed
FEEING ▸ fee
FEEL, -S vb have a physical or emotional sensation of ▷ n act of feeling
FEELBAD adj inducing feelings of unhappiness
FEELER, -S n organ of touch in some animals
FEELESS ▸ fee
FEELGOOD adj causing or characterized by a feeling of self-satisfaction
FEELING, -S ▸ feel
FEELS ▸ feel
FEEN, -S n in Irish dialect, an informal word for 'man'
FEER, -ED, -S vb make a furrow
FEERIE, -S n fairyland
FEERIN, -S n furrow
FEERING, -S ▸ feer
FEERINS ▸ feerin
FEERS ▸ feer
FEES ▸ fee
FEESE, -D, -S, FEESING vb perturb

F

FEET ▸ foot

FEETLESS ▸ foot

FEEZE, -D, -S, FEEZING vb beat ▷ n rush

FEG, -S same as ▸ fig

FEGARY, FEGARIES variant of ▸ vagary

FEGS ▸ feg

FEH, -S same as ▸ fe

FEHM, -E n medieval German court

FEHMIC ▸ fehm

FEHS ▸ feh

FEIGN, -ED, -ING, -S vb pretend

FEIGNER, -S ▸ feign

FEIGNING ▸ feign

FEIGNS ▸ feign

FEIJOA, -S n evergreen myrtaceous shrub of S America

FEIJOADA n Brazilian stew of black beans, meat and vegetables

FEIJOAS ▸ feijoa

FEINT, -ED, -ER, -EST, -ING n sham attack meant to distract an opponent ▷ vb make a feint ▷ adj printing term meaning ruled with faint lines

FEINTS pl n leavings of the second distillation of Scotch malt whisky

FEIRIE, -R, -ST adj nimble

FEIS n Irish music and dance festival

FEIST, -S n small aggressive dog

FEISTIER ▸ feisty

FEISTILY ▸ feisty

FEISTS ▸ feist

FEISTY, FEISTIER adj showing courage or spirit

FELAFEL, -S same as ▸ falafel

FELDGRAU n ordinary German soldier (from uniform colour)

FELDSHER n (in Russia) a medical doctor's assistant

FELDSPAR n hard mineral that is the main constituent of igneous rocks

FELICIA, -S n type of African herb

FELICITY n happiness

FELID, -S n any animal belonging to the cat family

FELINE, -S adj of cats ▷ n member of the cat family

FELINELY ▸ feline

FELINES ▸ feline

FELINITY ▸ feline

FELL, -ED, -EST, -S vb cut or knock down ▷ adj cruel or deadly

FELLA, -S nonstandard variant of ▸ fellow

FELLABLE ▸ fell

FELLAH, -IN, -S n peasant in Arab countries

FELLAS ▸ fella

FELLED ▸ fell

FELLER, -S n person or thing that fells

FELLEST ▸ fell

FELLIES ▸ felly

FELLING, -S ▸ fell

FELLNESS ▸ fell

FELLOE, -S n (segment of) the rim of a wheel

FELLOW, -ED, -S n man or boy ▷ adj in the same group or condition ▷ vb join as a companion

FELLOWLY adj friendly, companionable

FELLOWS ▸ fellow

FELLS ▸ fell

FELLY, FELLIES same as ▸ felloe

FELON, -S n (formerly) person guilty of a felony ▷ adj evil

FELONIES ▸ felony

FELONOUS adj wicked

FELONRY n felons collectively

FELONS ▸ felon

FELONY, FELONIES n serious crime

FELSIC adj relating to igneous rock

FELSITE, -S n any fine-grained igneous rock

FELSITIC ▸ felsite

FELSPAR, -S same as ▸ feldspar

FELSTONE same as ▸ felsite

FELT, -ED, -S n matted fabric ▷ vb become matted

FELTER, -ED, -S vb mat together

FELTIER ▸ felty

FELTIEST ▸ felty

FELTING, -S n felted material

FELTLIKE ▸ felt

FELTS ▸ felt

FELTY, FELTIER, FELTIEST ▸ felt

FELUCCA, -S n narrow lateen-rigged vessel

FELWORT, -S n type of plant

FEM, -S n type of igneous rock

FEMAL, -S archaic variant of ▸ female

FEMALE, -S adj of the sex which bears offspring ▷ n female person or animal

FEMALITY ▸ female

FEMALS ▸ femal

FEME, -S n woman or wife

FEMERALL n ventilator or smoke outlet on a roof

FEMERELL n ventilator or smoke outlet in a roof

FEMES ▸ feme

FEMETARY variant of ▸ fumitory

FEMICIDE n killing of a woman or girl

FEMINACY n feminine character

FEMINAL adj feminine, female

FEMINIE, -S n women collectively

FEMININE adj relating to females ▷ n short for feminine noun

FEMINISE same as ▸ feminize

FEMINISM n advocacy of equal rights for women

FEMINIST n person who advocates equal rights for women ▷ adj of, relating to, or advocating feminism

FEMINITY ▸ feminal

FEMINIZE vb make or become feminine

FEMITER, -S variant of ▸ fumitory

FEMME, -S n woman or wife

FEMMY, FEMMIER, FEMMIEST adj markedly or exaggeratedly feminine

FEMORA ▸ femur

FEMORAL adj of the thigh

FEMS ▸ fem

FEMUR, FEMORA, -S n thighbone

FEN, -S n low-lying flat marshy land

FENAGLE, -D, -S variant of ▸ finagle

FENCE, -D, -S n barrier of posts linked by wire or wood ▷ vb enclose with or as if with a fence

FENCER, -S n person who fights with a sword

FENCEROW n uncultivated land flanking a fence

FENCERS ▸ fencer

FENCES ▸ fence

FENCIBLE n person who undertook military service in defence of their homeland only

FENCING, -S n sport of fighting with swords

FEND, -ED, -ING, -S vb give support (to someone, esp oneself) ▷ n shift or effort

FENDER, -S n low metal frame in front of a fireplace

FENDERED adj having a fender

FENDERS ▸ fender

FENDIER ▸ fendy

FENDIEST ▸ fendy

FENDING ▸ fend

FENDS ▸ fend

FENDY, FENDIER, FENDIEST adj thrifty

FENESTRA n small opening in or between bones

FENI, -S n Goan alcoholic drink

FENING, -A, -S n small currency unit of Bosnia-Herzegovina

FENIS ▸ feni

FENITAR, -S variant of ▸ **fumitory**

FENKS n whale blubber

FENLAND, -S ▸ fen

FENMAN, FENMEN ▸ fen

FENNEC, -S n type of nocturnal desert fox

FENNEL, -S n fragrant plant

FENNIER ▸ fenny

FENNIES ▸ fenny

FENNIEST ▸ fenny

FENNING same as ▸ **fening**

FENNISH ▸ fen

FENNY, FENNIER, FENNIES, FENNIEST adj boggy or marshy ▷ n feni

FENS ▸ fen

FENT, -S n piece of waste fabric

FENTANYL n narcotic drug used in medicine to relieve pain

FENTHION n type of pesticide

FENTS ▸ fent

FENURON, -S n type of herbicide

FEOD, -S same as ▸ **feud**

FEODAL ▸ feod

FEODARY ▸ feod

FEODS ▸ feod

FEOFF, -ED, -ING, -S same as ▸ **fief**

FEOFFEE, -S n (in feudal society) a vassal granted a fief by their lord

FEOFFER, -S ▸ feoff

FEOFFING ▸ feoff

FEOFFOR, -S ▸ feoff

FEOFFS ▸ feoff

FER same as ▸ **far**

FERACITY ▸ feracious

FERAL, -S adj wild ▷ n person who displays such tendencies and appearance

FERBAM, -S n powder used as a fungicide

FERE, -R, -S, -ST n companion ▷ adj fierce

FERETORY n shrine, usually portable, for a saint's relics

FERIA, -E, -S n weekday on which no feast occurs

FERIAL adj of or relating to a feria

FERIAS ▸ feria

FERINE same as ▸ **feral**

FERITY, FERITIES ▸ feral

FERLIE same as ▸ **ferly**

FERLY, FERLIED, FERLIER, FERLIES, FERLIEST, -ING adj wonderful ▷ n wonder ▷ vb wonder

FERM, -S variant of ▸ **farm**

FERMATA, -S, FERMATE another word for ▸ **pause**

FERMENT, -S n any agent that causes fermentation ▷ vb (cause to) undergo fermentation

FERMI, -S n unit of length

FERMION, -S n type of particle

FERMIS ▸ fermi

FERMIUM, -S n chemical element

FERMS ▸ ferm

FERN, -S n flowerless plant with fine fronds

FERNALLY n seedless plant that is not a true fern

FERNBIRD n small brown and white New Zealand swamp bird with a fernlike tail

FERNERY n place where ferns are grown

FERNIER ▸ ferny

FERNIEST ▸ ferny

FERNING, -S n production of a fern-like pattern

FERNINST same as ▸ **fornenst**

FERNLESS ▸ fern

FERNLIKE ▸ fern

FERNS ▸ fern

FERNSHAW n fern thicket

FERNY, FERNIER, FERNIEST ▸ fern

FEROCITY ▸ ferocious

FERRATE, -S n type of salt

FERREL, -ED, -S variant of ▸ **ferrule**

FERREOUS adj containing or resembling iron

FERRET, -ED, -S n tamed polecat ▷ vb hunt with ferrets

FERRETER ▸ ferret

FERRETS ▸ ferret

FERRETY adj like a ferret

FERRIAGE n transportation by ferry

FERRIC adj of or containing iron

FERRIED ▸ ferry

FERRIES ▸ ferry

FERRITE, -S n type of ceramic compound

FERRITIC ▸ ferrite

FERRITIN n type of protein

FERROUS adj of or containing iron in the divalent state

FERRUGO, -S n disease affecting plants

FERRULE, -D, -S n metal cap to strengthen the end of a stick ▷ vb equip (a stick, etc) with a ferrule

FERRUM, -S Latin word for ▸ **iron**

FERRY, FERRIED, FERRIES, -ING n boat for transporting people and vehicles ▷ vb carry by ferry

FERRYMAN, FERRYMEN n someone who provides a ferry service

FERTILE, -R adj capable of producing young, crops, or vegetation

FERULA, -E, -S n large Mediterranean plant

FERULE, -D, -S, FERULING same as ▸ **ferrule**

FERVENCY another word for ▸ **fervour**

FERVENT adj intensely passionate and sincere

FERVID, -ER same as ▸ **fervent**

FERVIDLY ▸ fervid

FERVOR, -S same as ▸ **fervour**

FERVOUR, -S n intensity of feeling

FES ▸ fe

FESCUE, -S n pasture and lawn grass with stiff narrow leaves

FESS, -ED, -ING vb confess

FESSE, -S n horizontal band across a shield

FESSED ▸ fess

FESSES ▸ fesse

FESSING ▸ fess

FESSWISE adv in heraldry, with a horizontal band across the shield

FEST, -S n event at which the emphasis is on a particular activity

FESTA, -S n festival

FESTAL, -S adj festive ▷ n festivity

FESTALLY ▸ festal

FESTALS ▸ festal

FESTAS ▸ festa

FESTER, -ED, -S vb grow worse and increasingly hostile ▷ n small ulcer or sore containing pus

F

FESTIER ▸ **festy**

FESTIEST ▸ **festy**

FESTIVAL n organized series of special events or performances

FESTIVE adj of or like a celebration

FESTOON, -S vb hang decorations in loops ▹ n decorative chain

FESTS ▸ **fest**

FESTY, FESTIER, FESTIEST adj dirty

FET, -S, -TED, -TING vb fetch

FETA, -S n white salty Greek cheese

FETAL adj of, relating to, or resembling a fetus

FETAS ▸ **feta**

FETATION n state of pregnancy

FETCH, -ED, -ES vb go after and bring back ▹ n ghost or apparition of a living person

FETCHER, -S n person or animal that fetches

FETCHES ▸ **fetch**

FETCHING adj attractive

FETE, -D, -S, FETING n gala, bazaar, etc, usu held outdoors ▹ vb honour or entertain regally

FETERITA n type of sorghum

FETES ▸ **fete**

FETIAL, -ES, -S n ancient Roman herald

FETIALIS n priest in ancient Rome

FETIALS ▸ **fetial**

FETICH, -ES same as ▸ **fetish**

FETICHE variant of ▸ **fetich**

FETICHES ▸ **fetich**

FETICIDE n destruction of a fetus in the uterus

FETID, -ER, -EST adj stinking

FETIDITY ▸ **fetid**

FETIDLY ▸ **fetid**

FETING ▸ **fete**

FETISH, -ES n irrational devotion (to an object, activity, etc)

FETLOCK, -S n projection behind and above a horse's hoof

FETOLOGY n branch of medicine concerned with the fetus in the uterus

FETOR, -S n stale or putrid odour

FETS ▸ **fet**

FETT, -S variant of ▸ **fet**

FETTA, -S variant of ▸ **feta**

FETTED ▸ **fet**

FETTER, -ED, -S n chain or shackle for the foot ▹ vb restrict

FETTERER ▸ **fetter**

FETTERS ▸ **fetter**

FETTING ▸ **fet**

FETTLE, -D, -S same as ▸ **fettling**

FETTLER, -S n person employed to maintain railway tracks

FETTLES ▸ **fettle**

FETTLING n refractory material used to line the hearth of puddling furnaces

FETTS ▸ **fett**

FETUS, -ES n embryo of a mammal in the later stages of development

FETWA, -S variant of ▸ **fatwa**

FEU, -ED, -ING, -S n (in Scotland) type of rent ▹ vb grant land to a person who pays a feu

FEUAR, -S n tenant of a feu

FEUD, -ED, -S n long bitter hostility between two people or groups ▹ vb carry on a feud

FEUDAL adj of or like feudalism

FEUDALLY ▸ **feudal**

FEUDARY n holder of land through feudal right

FEUDED ▸ **feud**

FEUDING, -S ▸ **feud**

FEUDIST, -S n person who takes part in a feud or quarrel

FEUDS ▸ **feud**

FEUED ▸ **feu**

FEUING ▸ **feu**

FEUS ▸ **feu**

FEUTRE, -D, -S, FEUTRING vb place in a resting position

FEVER, -ING, -S n (illness causing) high body temperature ▹ vb affect with or as if with fever

FEVERED ▸ **fever**

FEVERFEW n bushy European plant with white flower heads, formerly used medicinally

FEVERING ▸ **fever**

FEVERISH adj suffering from fever

FEVEROUS same as ▸ **feverish**

FEVERS ▸ **fever**

FEW, -ER, -EST, -S adj not many ▹ n as in **the few** small number of people considered as a class

FEWMET, -S variant of ▸ **fumet**

FEWNESS ▸ **few**

FEWS ▸ **few**

FEWTER, -ED, -S variant of ▸ **feutre**

FEWTRILS n trifles, trivia

FEY, -ED, -ER, -EST, -ING, -S adj whimsically strange ▹ vb clean out

FEYLY ▸ **fey**

FEYNESS ▸ **fey**

FEYS ▸ **fey**

FEZ, -ES, -ZES n brimless tasselled cap, orig from Turkey

FEZZED adj wearing a fez

FEZZES ▸ **fez**

FEZZY ▸ **fez**

FIACRE, -S n small four-wheeled horse-drawn carriage

FIANCE, -S n man engaged to be married

FIANCEE, -S n woman who is engaged to be married

FIANCES ▸ **fiance**

FIAR, -S n property owner

FIARS n legally fixed price of corn

FIASCO, FIASCHI, -ES, -S n ridiculous or humiliating failure

FIAT, -ED, -ING, -S n arbitrary order ▹ vb issue a fiat

FIAUNT, -S n warrant issued to the Irish Court of Chancery

FIB, -BED, -BING, -S n trivial lie ▹ vb tell a lie

FIBBER, -S ▸ **fib**

FIBBERY ▸ **fib**

FIBBING ▸ **fib**

FIBER, -S same as ▸ **fibre**

FIBERED ▸ **fibre**

FIBERISE same as ▸ **fiberize**

FIBERIZE vb break into fibres

FIBERS ▸ **fiber**

FIBRANNE n synthetic fabric

FIBRATE, -S n drug used to lower fat levels in the body

FIBRE, -S n thread that can be spun into yarn

FIBRED ▸ **fibre**

FIBRES ▸ **fibre**

FIBRIL, -S n small fibre

FIBRILAR ▸ **fibril**

FIBRILLA same as ▸ **fibril**

FIBRILS ▸ **fibril**

FIBRIN, -S n white insoluble elastic protein

FIBRO, -S n mixture of cement and asbestos fibre

FIBROID, -S adj (of structures or tissues) containing or resembling fibres ▹ n benign tumour composed of fibrous connective tissue

FIBROIN, -S n tough elastic protein

FIBROMA, -S n type of benign tumour

FIBROS ▸ fibro

FIBROSE, -D, -S vb become fibrous

FIBROSIS n formation of an abnormal amount of fibrous tissue

FIBROTIC ▸ fibrosis

FIBROUS adj consisting of, containing, or resembling fibres

FIBS ▸ fib

FIBSTER, -S n fibber

FIBULA, -E, -S n slender outer bone of the lower leg

FIBULAR ▸ fibula

FIBULAS ▸ fibula

FICAIN, -S n cysteine proteinase isolated from the latex of figs

FICE, -S n small aggressive dog

FICHE, -S n film for storing publications in miniature

FICHU, -S n woman's shawl or scarf

FICIN, -S n enzyme

FICKLE, -D, -R, -S, -ST, FICKLING adj changeable, inconstant ▷ vb puzzle

FICKLY ▸ fickle

FICO, -ES, -S n worthless trifle

FICTILE adj moulded or capable of being moulded from clay

FICTION, -S n literary works of the imagination

FICTIVE adj of, relating to, or able to create fiction

FICTOR, -S n sculptor

FICUS, -ES n type of plant

FID, -S n spike for separating strands of rope in splicing

FIDDIOUS vb treat someone as Coriolanus, in the eponymous play, dealt with Aufidius

FIDDLE, -D, -S n violin ▷ vb play the violin

FIDDLER, -S n person who plays the fiddle

FIDDLES ▸ fiddle

FIDDLEY, -S n vertical space above a vessel's engine room

FIDDLIER ▸ fiddly

FIDDLING adj trivial ▷ n act of fiddling

FIDDLY, FIDDLIER adj awkward to do or use

FIDEISM, -S n theological doctrine

FIDEIST, -S ▸ fideism

FIDELITY n faithfulness

FIDES n faith or trust

FIDGE, -D, -S, FIDGING obsolete word for ▸ **fidget**

FIDGET, -ED, -S vb move about restlessly ▷ n person who fidgets

FIDGETER ▸ fidget

FIDGETS ▸ fidget

FIDGETY ▸ fidget

FIDGING ▸ fidge

FIDIBUS n spill for lighting a candle or pipe

FIDO, -S n generic term for a dog

FIDS ▸ fid

FIDUCIAL adj used as a standard of reference or measurement

FIE, -ST same as ▸ **fey**

FIEF, -S n land granted by a lord in return for war service

FIEFDOM, -S n (in Feudal Europe) the property owned by a lord

FIEFS ▸ fief

FIELD, -ED, -ING, -S n piece of land used for pasture or growing crops ▷ vb stop, catch, or return (the ball) as a fielder

FIELDER, -S n (in certain sports) player whose task is to field the ball

FIELDING ▸ field

FIELDS ▸ field

FIEND, -S n evil spirit

FIENDISH adj of or like a fiend

FIENDS ▸ fiend

FIENT, -S n fiend

FIER, -S same as ▸ **fere**

FIERCE, -R, -ST adj wild or aggressive

FIERCELY ▸ fierce

FIERCER ▸ fierce

FIERCEST ▸ fierce

FIERE, -S same as ▸ **fere**

FIERIER ▸ fiery

FIERIEST ▸ fiery

FIERILY ▸ fiery

FIERS ▸ fier

FIERY, FIERIER, FIERIEST adj consisting of or like fire

FIEST ▸ fie

FIESTA, -S n religious festival, carnival

FIFE, -D, -S, FIFING n small high-pitched flute ▷ vb play (music) on a fife

FIFER, -S ▸ fife

FIFES ▸ fife

FIFI, -S n mountaineering hook

FIFING ▸ fife

FIFIS ▸ fifi

FIFTEEN, -S n five and ten

FIFTH, -S n number five in a series ▷ adj of or being number five in a series

FIFTHLY adv in the fifth place or position

FIFTHS ▸ fifth

FIFTIES ▸ fifty

FIFTIETH adj being the number of fifty in order ▷ n one of 50 equal or parts

FIFTY, FIFTIES n five times ten

FIFTYISH ▸ fifty

FIG, -GED, -GING, -S n soft pear-shaped fruit ▷ vb dress (up) or rig (out)

FIGEATER n large beetle

FIGGED ▸ fig

FIGGERY n adornment, ornament

FIGGIER ▸ figgy

FIGGIEST ▸ figgy

FIGGING ▸ fig

FIGGY, FIGGIER, FIGGIEST adj tasting like figs

FIGHT, -ING, -S, FOUGHT, FOUGHTEN vb struggle (against) in battle or physical combat ▷ n aggressive conflict between two (groups of) people

FIGHTER, -S n boxer

FIGHTING ▸ fight

FIGHTS ▸ fight

FIGJAM, -S n very conceited person

FIGLIKE adj like a fig

FIGMENT, -S n fantastic notion, invention, or fabrication

FIGO, -S variant of ▸ **fico**

FIGS ▸ fig

FIGTREE, -S n tree that produces figs

FIGULINE adj of or resembling clay ▷ n article made of clay

FIGURAL adj composed of or relating to human or animal figures

FIGURANT n ballet dancer who does group work but no solo roles

FIGURATE adj exhibiting or produced by figuration

FIGURE, -S, FIGURING n numerical symbol ▷ vb calculate (sums or amounts)

FIGURED adj decorated with a design

FIGURER, -S ▸ figure

FIGURES ▸ figure

FIGURINE n statuette

FIGURING ▸ figure

FIGURIST n user of numbers

F

FIGWORT, -S n plant with small brown or greenish flowers

FIKE, -D, -S, FIKING vb fidget

FIKERY, FIKERIES n fuss

FIKES ▸ fike

FIKIER ▸ fiky

FIKIEST ▸ fiky

FIKING ▸ fike

FIKISH adj fussy

FIKY, FIKIER, FIKIEST adj fussy

FIL same as ▸ **fils**

FILA ▸ filum

FILABEG, -S variant of ▸ **filibeg**

FILACER, -S n formerly, English legal officer

FILAGREE same as ▸ **filigree**

FILAMENT n fine wire in a light bulb that gives out light

FILANDER n species of kangaroo

FILAR adj of thread

FILAREE, -S n type of storksbill, a weed

FILARIA, -E n type of parasitic nematode worm

FILARIAL ▸ filaria

FILARIAN ▸ filaria

FILARIID adj of or relating to a family of threadlike roundworms

FILASSE, -S n vegetable fibre such as jute

FILATORY n machine for making threads

FILATURE n act or process of spinning silk, etc, into threads

FILAZER, -S variant of ▸ **filacer**

FILBERD, -S variant of ▸ **filbert**

FILBERT, -S n hazelnut

FILCH, -ED, -ES, -ING vb steal (small amounts)

FILCHER, -S ▸ filch

FILCHES ▸ filch

FILCHING ▸ filch

FILE, -D, -S, FILING n box or folder used to keep documents in order ▷ vb place (a document) in a file

FILEABLE ▸ file

FILECARD n type of brush with sharp steel bristles, used for cleaning the teeth of a file

FILED ▸ file

FILEFISH n tropical fish with a narrow body

FILEMOT, -S n type of brown colour

FILENAME n codified name of a file a computer system

FILER, -S ▸ file

FILES ▸ file

FILET, -ED, -ING, -S variant of ▸ **fillet**

FILFOT, -S variant of ▸ **fylfot**

FILIAL adj of or befitting a son or daughter

FILIALLY ▸ filial

FILIATE, -D, -S vb fix judicially the paternity of (a child)

FILIBEG, -S n kilt worn by Scottish Highlanders

FILICIDE n act of killing one's own son or daughter

FILIFORM adj having the form of a thread

FILIGREE n delicate ornamental work of gold or silver wire ▷ adj made of filigree ▷ vb decorate with or as if with filigree

FILII ▸ filius

This plural of **filius**, a Latin word for son, is the only 5-letter word that lets you get rid of three Is!

FILING ▸ file

FILINGS pl n shavings removed by a file

FILIOQUE n theological term found in the Nicene Creed

FILISTER same as ▸ **fillister**

FILIUS, FILII n son

FILK, -S n parodic type of folk music with science fiction lyrics

FILL, -ED, -S vb make or become full

FILLABLE ▸ fill

FILLE, -S n girl

FILLED ▸ fill

FILLER, -S n substance that fills a gap or increases bulk

FILLES ▸ fille

FILLET, -ED, -S n boneless piece of meat or fish ▷ vb remove the bones from

FILLETER n person who fillets

FILLETS ▸ fillet

FILLIBEG same as ▸ **filibeg**

FILLIES ▸ filly

FILLING, -S n substance that fills a gap or cavity ▷ adj (of food) substantial and satisfying

FILLIP, -ED, -S n something that adds stimulation or enjoyment ▷ vb stimulate or excite

FILLO, -S variant of ▸ **filo**

FILLS ▸ fill

FILLY, FILLIES n young female horse

FILM, -ED, -S n projected images creating the illusion of movement ▷ vb photograph with a video camera ▷ adj connected with films or the cinema

FILMABLE ▸ film

FILMCARD n cinema loyalty card

FILMDOM, -S n cinema industry

FILMED ▸ film

FILMER, -S n film-maker

FILMFEST n film festival

FILMGOER n person who goes regularly to the cinema

FILMI adj of or relating to Indian films

FILMIC adj of or suggestive of films or the cinema

FILMIER ▸ filmy

FILMIEST ▸ filmy

FILMILY ▸ filmy

FILMING, -S n act of photographing with a video camera

FILMISH ▸ film

FILMLAND n cinema industry

FILMLESS ▸ film

FILMLIKE ▸ film

FILMS ▸ film

FILMSET, -S vb set (type matter) by filmsetting

FILMY, FILMIER, FILMIEST adj very thin, delicate

FILO, -S n type of flaky Greek pastry in very thin sheets

FILOSE adj resembling a thread or threadlike process

FILS n monetary unit of Bahrain, Iraq, Jordan, and Kuwait

FILTER, -ED, -S n device permitting fluid to pass but retaining solids ▷ vb remove impurities from (a substance) with a filter

FILTERER ▸ filter

FILTERS ▸ filter

FILTH, -S n disgusting dirt

FILTHIER ▸ filthy

FILTHILY ▸ filthy

FILTHS ▸ filth

FILTHY, FILTHIER adj characterized by or full of filth ▷ adv extremely

FILTRATE n filtered gas or liquid ▷ vb remove impurities with a filter

FILTRE adj as in **cafe filtre** a strong black filtered coffee

FILUM, FILA n any threadlike structure or part

FIMBLE, -S n male plant of the hemp

FIMBRIA, -E *n* fringe or fringelike margin or border
FIMBRIAL ▸ fimbria
FIN, -NED, -NING, -S *n* any of the appendages of some aquatic animals ▸ *vb* provide with fins
FINABLE *adj* liable to a fine
FINAGLE, -D, -S *vb* get or achieve by craftiness or trickery
FINAGLER ▸ finagle
FINAGLES ▸ finagle
FINAL *adj* at the end ▸ *n* deciding contest
FINALE, -S *n* concluding part of a performance
FINALIS *n* musical finishing note
FINALISE *same as* ▸ finalize
FINALISM *n* doctrine that final causes determine the course of all events
FINALIST *n* competitor in a final
FINALITY *n* condition or quality of being final or settled
FINALIZE *vb* put into final form
FINALLY *adv* after a long delay
FINALS *pl n* deciding part of a competition
FINANCE, -D, -S *vb* provide or obtain funds for ▸ *n* system of money, credit, and investment
FINBACK, -S *another name for* ▸ rorqual
FINCA, -S *n* Spanish villa
FINCH, -ES *n* small songbird with a short strong beak
FINCHED *adj* with streaks or spots on the back
FINCHES ▸ finch
FIND, -S *vb* discover by chance ▸ *n* person or thing found, esp when valuable
FINDABLE ▸ find
FINDER, -S *n* small telescope fitted to a larger one
FINDING, -S ▸ find
FINDRAM, -S *variant of* ▸ finnan
FINDS ▸ find
FINE, -D, -S *adj* very good ▸ *n* payment imposed as a penalty ▸ *vb* impose a fine on
FINEABLE *same as* ▸ finable
FINED ▸ fine
FINEER, -ED, -S *variant of* ▸ veneer
FINEISH ▸ fine
FINELESS ▸ fine

FINELY *adv* into small pieces
FINENESS *n* state or quality of being fine
FINER, -S ▸ fine
FINERIES ▸ finery
FINERS ▸ finer
FINERY, FINERIES *n* showy clothing
FINES ▸ fine
FINESPUN *adj* spun or drawn out to a fine thread
FINESSE, -D, -S *n* delicate skill ▸ *vb* bring about with finesse
FINESSER ▸ finesse
FINESSES ▸ finesse
FINEST, -S *n* (in the US) police of a particular city
FINFISH *n* fish with fins, as opposed to shellfish
FINFOOT, -S *n* type of aquatic bird
FINGAN, -S *variant of* ▸ finjan
FINGER, -S *n* one of the four long jointed parts of the hand ▸ *vb* touch or handle with the fingers
FINGERED *adj* marked or dirtied by handling
FINGERER ▸ finger
FINGERS ▸ finger
FINI *n* end; finish
FINIAL, -S *n* ornament at the apex of a gable or spire
FINIALED *adj* having a finial or finials
FINIALS ▸ finial
FINICAL *another word for* ▸ finicky
FINICKIN *variant of* ▸ finicky
FINICKY *adj* excessively particular, fussy
FINIKIN *variant of* ▸ finicky
FINIKING *variant of* ▸ finicky
FINING, -S *n* process of removing bubbles from molten glass
FINIS, -ES *n* end; finish
FINISH, -ES *vb* bring to an end, stop ▸ *n* end, last part
FINISHED *adj* perfected
FINISHER *n* craftsperson who carries out the final tasks in a manufacturing process
FINISHES ▸ finish
FINITE, -S *adj* having limits in space, time, or size ▸ *n* verb limited by person, number, tense or mood
FINITELY ▸ finite
FINITES ▸ finite
FINITISM *n* mathematical philosophy which rejects infinite quantities

FINITIST *n* one who believes in or advocates finitism
FINITO *adj* finished
FINITUDE ▸ finite
FINJAN, -S *n* small, handleless coffee cup
FINK, -ED, -ING, -S *n* strikebreaker ▸ *vb* inform (on someone), as to the police
FINLESS ▸ fin
FINLIKE ▸ fin
FINLIT, -S *n* understanding of the concepts associated with finance
FINMARK, -S *n* former monetary unit of Finland
FINNAC, -S *variant of* ▸ finnock
FINNACK, -S *variant of* ▸ finnock
FINNACS ▸ finnac
FINNAN, -S *n* smoked haddock
FINNED ▸ fin
FINNER, -S *another name for* ▸ rorqual
FINNESKO *n* reindeer-skin boot
FINNICKY *variant of* ▸ finicky
FINNIER ▸ finny
FINNIEST ▸ finny
FINNING ▸ fin
FINNMARK *n* former Finnish monetary unit
FINNOCK, -S *n* young sea trout on its first return to fresh water
FINNSKO *variant of* ▸ finnesko
FINNY, FINNIER, FINNIEST *adj* relating to or containing many fishes
FINO, -S *n* very dry sherry
FINOCHIO *same as* > finocchio
FINOS ▸ fino
FINS ▸ fin
FINSKO *variant of* ▸ finnesko
FINTECH, -S *n* financial services technology
FIORD, -S *same as* ▸ fjord
FIORIN, -S *n* type of temperate perennial grass
FIPPENCE *n* fivepence
FIPPLE, -S *n* wooden plug forming a flue in the end of a pipe
FIQH, -S *n* Islamic jurisprudence
FIQUE, -S *n* hemp
FIR, -S *n* pyramid-shaped tree
FIRE, -D, -S *n* state of combustion producing heat, flames, and smoke ▸ *vb*

operate (a weapon) so that a bullet or missile is released

FIREABLE ▶ **fire**

FIREARM, -S n rifle, pistol, or shotgun

FIREBACK n ornamental iron slab against the back wall of a hearth

FIREBALL n ball of fire at the centre of an explosion

FIREBASE n artillery base from which heavy fire is directed at the enemy

FIREBIRD n any of various songbirds having a bright red plumage, esp the Baltimore oriole

FIREBOAT n motor vessel with fire-fighting apparatus

FIREBOMB n bomb that is designed to cause fires ▷ vb detonate such a bomb

FIREBOX n furnace chamber of a boiler in a steam locomotive

FIREBRAT n type of small primitive wingless insect

FIREBUG, -S n person who deliberately sets fire to property

FIREBUSH n as in **Chilean firebush** South American shrub with scarlet flowers

FIRECLAY n heat-resistant clay used in the making of firebricks, furnace linings, etc

FIRED ▶ **fire**

FIREDAMP n explosive gas, composed mainly of methane, formed in mines

FIREDOG, -S n either of two metal stands supporting logs in a fire

FIREFANG vb become overheated through decomposition

FIREFLY n beetle that glows in the dark

FIREHALL n US and Canadian word for fire station

FIREHOSE n hose used to extinguish fires

FIRELESS ▶ **fire**

FIRELIT adj lit by firelight

FIRELOCK n obsolete type of gunlock with a priming mechanism ignited by sparks

FIREMAN, FIREMEN n a male firefighter

FIREMARK n plaque indicating that a building is insured

FIREMEN ▶ **fireman**

FIREPAN, -S n metal container for a fire in a room

FIREPINK n wildflower belonging to the pink family

FIREPIT, -S n hole dug in the ground for a fire

FIREPLUG n US and New Zealand name for a fire hydrant

FIREPOT, -S n Chinese fondue-like cooking pot

FIRER, -S ▶ **fire**

FIREREEL n fire engine

FIREROOM n stokehold

FIRERS ▶ **firer**

FIRES ▶ **fire**

FIRESHIP n vessel set alight and directed among enemy warships

FIRESIDE n hearth

FIRETRAP n building that would burn easily or one without fire escapes

FIREWALL n appliance that prevents unauthorized access to a computer network from the internet ▷ vb protect (a computer system) or block (unwanted access) with a firewall

FIREWEED n first vegetation growing in burnt-over areas

FIREWOOD n wood for burning

FIREWORK n device ignited to produce colourful sparks and explosions

FIREWORM n cranberry worm

FIRIE, -S n in Australian English, informal word for a firefighter

FIRING, -S n discharge of a firearm

FIRK, -ED, -ING, -S vb beat

FIRKIN, -S n small wooden barrel or similar container

FIRKING ▶ **firk**

FIRKINS ▶ **firkin**

FIRKS ▶ **firk**

FIRLOT, -S n unit of measurement for grain

FIRM, -ED, -EST, -ING, -S adj not soft or yielding ▷ adv in an unyielding manner ▷ vb make or become firm ▷ n business company

FIRMAN, -S n edict of a sultan

FIRMED ▶ **firm**

FIRMER, -S ▶ **firm**

FIRMEST ▶ **firm**

FIRMING ▶ **firm**

FIRMLESS adj unstable

FIRMLY ▶ **firm**

FIRMNESS ▶ **firm**

FIRMS ▶ **firm**

FIRMWARE n fixed form of software programmed into a read-only memory

FIRN, -S another name for ▶ **neve**

FIRRIER ▶ **firry**

FIRRIEST ▶ **firry**

FIRRING, -S n wooden battens used in building construction

FIRRY, FIRRIER, FIRRIEST adj of, relating to, or made from fir trees

FIRS ▶ **fir**

FIRST adj earliest in time or order ▷ n person or thing coming before all others ▷ adv before anything else

FIRSTLY adv coming before other points, questions, etc

FIRSTS pl n saleable goods of the highest quality

FIRTH, -S n narrow inlet of the sea, esp in Scotland

FIRWOOD, -S n wood of the fir tree

FISC, -S n state or royal treasury

FISCAL, -S adj of government finances, esp taxes ▷ n (in some countries) a public prosecutor

FISCALLY ▶ **fiscal**

FISCALS ▶ **fiscal**

FISCS ▶ **fisc**

FISGIG, -S variant of ▶ **fishgig**

FISH, -ED, -ES n cold-blooded vertebrate with gills, that lives in water ▷ vb try to catch fish

FISHABLE ▶ **fish**

FISHBALL n fried ball of flaked fish and mashed potato

FISHBOAT n boat used for fishing

FISHBOLT n bolt used for fastening a fishplate to a rail

FISHBONE n bone of a fish

FISHBOWL n goldfish bowl

FISHCAKE n mixture of flaked fish and mashed potatoes formed into a flat circular shape

FISHED ▶ **fish**

FISHER, -S n fisherman

FISHERY n area of the sea used for fishing

FISHES ▶ **fish**

FISHEYE, -S n type of lens

FISHFUL adj teeming with fish

FISHGIG, -S n pole with barbed prongs for impaling fish

FISHHOOK *n* sharp hook used in angling, esp one with a barb

FISHIER ▸ **fishy**

FISHIEST ▸ **fishy**

FISHIFY *vb* change into fish

FISHILY ▸ **fishy**

FISHING, -S *n* job or pastime of catching fish

FISHKILL *n* mass killing of fish by pollution

FISHLESS ▸ **fish**

FISHLIKE ▸ **fish**

FISHLINE *n* line used on a fishing-rod

FISHMEAL *n* ground dried fish used as feed for farm animals or as a fertilizer

FISHNET, -S *n* open mesh fabric resembling netting

FISHPOLE *n* boom arm for a microphone

FISHPOND ▸ **fish**

FISHSKIN *n* skin of a fish

FISHTAIL *n* nozzle placed over a Bunsen burner to produce a fanlike flame ▷ *vb* slow an aeroplane by swerving the tail

FISHWAY, -S *n* fish ladder

FISHWIFE *n* derogatory term for a coarse scolding woman

FISHWORM *n* worm used as fishing bait

FISHY, FISHIER, FISHIEST *adj* of or like fish

FISK, -ED, -ING, -S *vb* frisk

FISNOMIE *n* physiognomy

FISSATE ▸ **fissile**

FISSILE *adj* capable of undergoing nuclear fission

FISSION, -S *n* splitting

FISSIPED *adj* having toes separated from one another ▷ *n* fissiped animal

FISSIVE ▸ **fissile**

FISSLE, -D, -S, FISSLING *vb* rustle

FISSURAL ▸ **fissure**

FISSURE, -D, -S *n* long narrow cleft or crack ▷ *vb* crack or split apart

FIST, -ED, -S *n* clenched hand ▷ *vb* hit with the fist

FISTFUL, -S *n* quantity that can be held in a fist or hand

FISTIANA *n* world of boxing

FISTIC *adj* of or relating to fisticuffs or boxing

FISTICAL ▸ **fistic**

FISTIER ▸ **fisty**

FISTIEST ▸ **fisty**

FISTING, -S *n* act of fisting

FISTMELE *n* measurement of the height of the string of a braced bow

FISTNOTE *n* note in printed text preceded by the fist symbol

FISTS ▸ **fist**

FISTULA, -E, -S *n* long narrow ulcer

FISTULAR *same as* ▸ **fistulous**

FISTULAS ▸ **fistula**

FISTY, FISTIER, FISTIEST ▸ **fist**

FIT, -S, -TED, -TEST, -TING, -TINGS *vb* be appropriate or suitable for ▷ *adj* appropriate ▷ *n* way in which something fits

FITCH, -ES *n* fur of the polecat or ferret

FITCHE *adj* pointed

FITCHEE *variant of* ▸ **fitche**

FITCHES ▸ **fitch**

FITCHET, -S *same as* ▸ **fitch**

FITCHEW, -S *archaic name for* ▸ **polecat**

FITCHY *variant of* ▸ **fitche**

FITFUL *adj* occurring in irregular spells

FITFULLY ▸ **fitful**

FITLY, FITLIER, FITLIEST *adv* in a proper manner or place or at a proper time

FITMENT, -S *n* accessory attached to a machine

FITNA, -S *n* state of trouble or chaos

FITNESS *n* state of being fit

FITS ▸ **fit**

FITT, -S *n* song

FITTABLE ▸ **fit**

FITTE, -S *variant of* ▸ **fitt**

FITTED ▸ **fit**

FITTER, -S ▸ **fit**

FITTES ▸ **fitte**

FITTEST ▸ **fit**

FITTING ▸ **fit**

FITTINGS ▸ **fit**

FITTS ▸ **fitt**

FIVE *n* one more than four

FIVEFOLD *adj* having five times as many or as much ▷ *adv* by five times as many or as much

FIVEPIN ▸ **fivepins**

FIVEPINS *n* bowling game played esp in Canada

FIVER, -S *n* five-pound note

FIVES *n* ball game resembling squash

FIX, -ES *vb* make or become firm, stable, or secure ▷ *n* difficult situation

FIXABLE ▸ **fix**

FIXATE, -D, -S, FIXATING *vb* become or cause to become fixed

FIXATIF, -S *variant of* ▸ **fixative**

FIXATING ▸ **fixate**

FIXATION *n* obsessive interest in something

FIXATIVE *n* liquid used to preserve or hold things in place ▷ *adj* serving or tending to fix

FIXATURE *n* something that holds an object in place

FIXED *adj* attached or placed so as to be immovable

FIXEDLY ▸ **fixed**

FIXER, -S *n* solution used to make a photographic image permanent

FIXES ▸ **fix**

FIXING *n* means of attaching one thing to another

FIXINGS *pl n* apparatus or equipment

FIXIT, -S *n* solution to a complex problem ▷ *adj* that fixes things

FIXITIES ▸ **fixity**

FIXITS ▸ **fixit**

FIXITY, FIXITIES *n* state of being fixed

FIXIVE ▸ **fix**

FIXT *adj* fixed

FIXTURE, -S *n* permanently fitted piece of household equipment

FIXURE, -S *n* firmness

FIZ *variant of* ▸ **fizz**

FIZGIG, -S *vb* inform on someone to the police

FIZZ, -ED, -ES, -ING, -INGS *vb* make a hissing or bubbling noise ▷ *n* hissing or bubbling noise

FIZZEN, -S *variant of* ▸ **foison**

FIZZER, -S *n* anything that fizzes

FIZZES ▸ **fizz**

FIZZGIG, -S *variant of* ▸ **fishgig**

FIZZIER ▸ **fizzy**

FIZZIEST ▸ **fizzy**

FIZZILY *adv* in a fizzy manner

FIZZING ▸ **fizz**

FIZZINGS ▸ **fizz**

FIZZLE, -D, -S, FIZZLING *vb* make a weak hissing or bubbling sound ▷ *n* hissing or bubbling sound

FIZZY, FIZZIER, FIZZIEST ▸ **fizz**

FJELD, -S *n* high rocky plateau

FJORD, -S *n* long narrow inlet of the sea between cliffs

FJORDIC ▸ **fjord**

FJORDS ▸ **fjord**

FLAB, -S *n* unsightly body fat

FLABBIER ▸ **flabby**

FLABBILY ▸ **flabby**

FLABBY, FLABBIER adj having flabby flesh

FLABELLA ▸flabellum

FLABS ▸flab

FLACCID adj soft and limp

FLACK, -ED, -ING, -S vb flap

FLACKER, -S vb flap

FLACKERY ▸flack

FLACKET, -S n flagon ▹vb flap or flutter about

FLACKING ▸flack

FLACKS ▸flack

FLACON, -S n small stoppered bottle or flask

FLAFF, -ED, -ING, -S vb flap

FLAFFER, -S vb flutter

FLAFFING ▸flaff

FLAFFS ▸flaff

FLAG, -GED, -GING, -S n piece of cloth attached to a pole as an emblem or signal ▹vb mark with a flag or sticker

FLAGELLA ▸flagellum

FLAGGED ▸flag

FLAGGER, -S ▸flag

FLAGGIER ▸flaggy

FLAGGING ▸flag

FLAGGY, FLAGGIER adj drooping

FLAGLESS ▸flag

FLAGMAN, FLAGMEN n person who has charge of a flag

FLAGON, -S n wide bottle

FLAGPOLE n pole for a flag

FLAGRANT adj openly outrageous

FLAGS ▸flag

FLAGSHIP n admiral's ship

FLAIL, -ED, -ING, -S vb wave about wildly ▹n tool formerly used for threshing grain by hand

FLAIR, -S n natural ability

FLAK, -S n anti-aircraft fire

FLAKE, -D, -S, FLAKING n small thin piece, esp chipped off something ▹vb peel off in flakes

FLAKER, -S ▸flake

FLAKES ▸flake

FLAKEY same as ▸flaky

FLAKIER ▸flaky

FLAKIES pl n dandruff

FLAKIEST ▸flaky

FLAKILY ▸flaky

FLAKING ▸flake

FLAKS ▸flak

FLAKY, FLAKIER, FLAKIEST adj like or made of flakes

FLAM, -MED, -MING, -S n falsehood, deception, or sham ▹vb cheat or deceive

FLAMBE, -S vb cook or serve (food) in flaming brandy ▹adj (of food) served in flaming brandy

FLAMBEAU n burning torch, as used in night processions

FLAMBEE, -D, -S same as ▸flambe

FLAMBES ▸flambe

FLAME, -D, -S n luminous burning gas coming from burning material ▹vb burn brightly

FLAMELET ▸flame

FLAMEN, -S, FLAMINES n (in ancient Rome) type of priest

FLAMENCO n rhythmical Spanish dance accompanied by a guitar and vocalist

FLAMENS ▸flamen

FLAMEOUT n failure of an aircraft jet engine in flight due to extinction of the flame ▹vb (of a jet engine) to fail in flight or to cause (a jet engine) to fail in flight

FLAMER, -S ▸flame

FLAMES ▸flame

FLAMFEW, -S n fantastic trifle

FLAMIER ▸flamy

FLAMIEST ▸flamy

FLAMINES ▸flamen

FLAMING adj burning with flames ▹adv extremely

FLAMINGO n large pink wading bird with a long neck and legs

FLAMM, -S variant of ▸flam

FLAMMED ▸flam

FLAMMING ▸flam

FLAMMS ▸flamm

FLAMMULE n small flame

FLAMS ▸flam

FLAMY, FLAMIER, FLAMIEST ▸flame

FLAN, -S n open sweet or savoury tart

FLANCARD n armour covering a horse's flank

FLANCH, -ED, -ES variant of ▸flaunch

FLANE, -D, FLANING vb walk idly, saunter

FLANERIE n aimless strolling or lounging

FLANES ▸flane

FLANEUR, -S n idler or loafer

FLANGE, -S n projecting rim or collar ▹vb attach or provide (a component) with a flange

FLANGED ▸flange

FLANGER, -S ▸flange

FLANGES ▸flange

FLANGING n act of flanging

FLANING ▸flane

FLANK, -ED, -ING, -S n part of the side between the hips and ribs ▹vb be at or move along the side of

FLANKEN, -S n cut of beef

FLANKER, -S n one of a detachment of soldiers guarding the flanks

FLANKING ▸flank

FLANKS ▸flank

FLANNEL, -S n small piece of cloth for washing the face ▹vb talk evasively

FLANNEN, -S adj made of flannel

FLANNIE, -S same as ▸flanny

FLANNY n shirt made of flannel

FLANS ▸flan

FLAP, -PED, -PING, -S vb move back and forwards or up and down ▹n action or sound of flapping

FLAPERON n control flap on aircraft wing

FLAPJACK n chewy biscuit made with oats

FLAPLESS ▸flap

FLAPLIKE adj like a flap

FLAPPED ▸flap

FLAPPER, -S n (in the 1920s) an unconventional young woman

FLAPPIER ▸flappy

FLAPPING ▸flap

FLAPPY, FLAPPIER adj loose

FLAPS ▸flap

FLARE, -D, FLARING vb blaze with a sudden unsteady flame ▹n sudden unsteady flame

FLARES pl n trousers with legs that widen below the knee

FLAREUP, -S n outbreak of something

FLARIER ▸flary

FLARIEST ▸flary

FLARING ▸flare

FLARY, FLARIER, FLARIEST adj flare-like

FLASER, -S n type of sedimentary structure in rock

FLASH, -ED, -ES, -EST n sudden burst of light or flame ▹adj vulgarly showy ▹vb emit or reflect light suddenly or intermittently

FLASHER, -S ▸flash

FLASHES ▸flash

FLASHEST ▸flash

FLASHGUN n type of electronic flash for a camera

FLASHIER ▸flashy

FLASHILY ▸flashy

FLASHING n watertight material used to cover joins in a roof

FLASHY, FLASHIER adj showy in a vulgar way

FLASK, -S n flat bottle

FLASKET, -S n long shallow basket

FLASKS ▸ flask

FLAT, -S, -TED, -TEST, -TING adj level and horizontal ▷ adv in or into a flat position ▷ n flat surface ▷ vb live in a flat

FLATBACK n flat-backed ornament, designed for viewing from front

FLATBED, -S n type of printing machine

FLATBOAT n flat-bottomed boat for transporting goods on a canal

FLATBROD n flatbread made with rye

FLATCAP, -S n Elizabethan man's hat

FLATCAR, -S n railway goods wagon without raised sides

FLATETTE n very small flat

FLATFEET ▸ flatfoot

FLATFISH n sea fish, such as the sole, which has a flat body

FLATFOOT, FLATFEET n flattening of the instep arch

FLATFORM n thick, level sole on a shoe

FLATHEAD n common Australian flatfish

FLATIRON n (formerly) an iron for pressing clothes that was heated by being placed on a stove

FLATLAND n land notable for its levelness

FLATLET, -S n small flat

FLATLINE vb have a flat line displaying on medical equipment monitoring one's vital signs

FLATLING adv in a flat or prostrate position ▷ adj with the flat side, as of a sword

FLATLONG adv prostrate

FLATLY ▸ flat

FLATMATE n person with whom one shares a flat

FLATNESS ▸ flat

FLATPACK n pieces packed into a flat box for home assembly

FLATPICK vb play (a guitar, etc) by plucking individual strings with a plectrum

FLATS ▸ flat

FLATTED ▸ flat

FLATTEN, -S vb make or become flat or flatter

FLATTER, -S vb praise insincerely

FLATTERY n excessive or insincere praise

FLATTEST ▸ flat

FLATTIE, -S n flat tyre

FLATTING ▸ flat

FLATTISH adj somewhat flat

FLATTOP, -S n informal name for an aircraft carrier

FLATTY n flat shoe

FLATUOUS ▸ flatus

FLATUS, -ES n gas generated in the alimentary canal

FLATWARE n cutlery

FLATWASH n laundry that can be ironed mechanically

FLATWAYS adv with the flat or broad side down or in contact with another surface

FLATWISE same as ▸ flatways

FLATWORK n laundry that can be ironed mechanically

FLATWORM n worm, such as a tapeworm, with a flattened body

FLAUGHT, -S vb flutter

FLAUNCH n cement or mortar slope to throw off water ▷ vb cause to slope in this manner

FLAUNE, -S variant of ▸ flam

FLAUNT, -ED, -S vb display (oneself or one's possessions) arrogantly ▷ n act of flaunting

FLAUNTER ▸ flaunt

FLAUNTS ▸ flaunt

FLAUNTY adj characterized by or inclined to ostentatious display

FLAUTA, -S n tortilla rolled around a filling

FLAUTIST n flute player

FLAVA, -S n individual style

FLAVANOL n type of flavonoid

FLAVAS ▸ flava

FLAVIN, -S n heterocyclic ketone

FLAVINE, -S same as ▸ flavin

FLAVINS ▸ flavin

FLAVONE, -S n crystalline compound occurring in plants

FLAVONOL n flavonoid said to offer protection against heart disease

FLAVOR, -ED, -S same as ▸ flavour

FLAVORER ▸ flavor

FLAVORS ▸ flavor

FLAVORY adj flavoursome

FLAVOUR, -S n distinctive taste ▷ vb give flavour to

FLAVOURY adj flavoursome

FLAW, -ED, -ING, -S n imperfection or blemish ▷ vb make or become blemished, defective, or imperfect

FLAWIER ▸ flawy

FLAWIEST ▸ flawy

FLAWING ▸ flaw

FLAWLESS ▸ flaw

FLAWN, -S variant of ▸ flam

FLAWS ▸ flaw

FLAWY, FLAWIER, FLAWIEST ▸ flaw

FLAX, -ES n plant grown for its stem fibres and seeds

FLAXEN adj (of hair) pale yellow

FLAXES ▸ flax

FLAXIER ▸ flaxy

FLAXIEST ▸ flaxy

FLAXLIKE adj like flax

FLAXSEED n seed of the flax plant, which yields linseed oil

FLAXY, FLAXIER, FLAXIEST same as ▸ flaxen

FLAY, -ED, -ING, -S vb remove the skin from

FLAYER, -S ▸ flay

FLAYING ▸ flay

FLAYS ▸ flay

FLAYSOME adj frightening

FLEA, -S n small bloodsucking insect

FLEABAG, -S n dirty or unkempt person, esp a woman

FLEABANE n as in **Canadian fleabane** small plant thought to ward off fleas

FLEABITE n bite of a flea

FLEADH, -S n festival of Irish music, dancing, and culture

FLEAM, -S n lancet used for letting blood

FLEAPIT, -S n shabby cinema or theatre

FLEAS ▸ flea

FLEASOME adj having fleas

FLEAWORT n type of plant

FLECHE, -S n slender spire

FLECK, -ED, -ING, -S n small mark, streak, or speck ▷ vb speckle

FLECKER, -S same as ▸ fleck

FLECKIER ▸ flecky

FLECKING ▸ fleck

FLECKS ▸ fleck

FLECKY, FLECKIER ▸ fleck

FLECTION n act of bending or the state of being bent

FLED ▸ flee

FLEDGE, -D, -S, FLEDGING vb feed and care for (a young bird) until it is able to fly

FLEDGIER ▸ fledgy
FLEDGING ▸ fledge
FLEDGY, FLEDGIER adj feathery or feathered
FLEE, FLED, -ING, -S vb run away (from)
FLEECE, -D, -S, FLEECING n sheep's coat of wool ▷ vb defraud or overcharge
FLEECER, -S ▸ fleece
FLEECES ▸ fleece
FLEECH, -ED, -ES vb flatter
FLEECIE, -S n person who collects fleeces for baling
FLEECIER ▸ fleecy
FLEECIES ▸ fleecie
FLEECILY ▸ fleecy
FLEECING ▸ fleece
FLEECY, FLEECIER adj made of or like fleece ▷ n person who collects fleeces for baling
FLEEING ▸ flee
FLEEK n as in **on fleek** stylish, on trend
FLEEKS same as ▸ fleek
FLEER, -ED, -ING, -S vb grin or laugh at ▷ n derisory glance or grin
FLEERER, -S ▸ fleer
FLEERING ▸ fleer
FLEERS ▸ fleer
FLEES ▸ flee
FLEET, -ED, -EST, -S n number of warships organized as a unit ▷ adj swift in movement ▷ vb move rapidly
FLEETER, -S n person who sails with a fleet of ships
FLEETEST ▸ fleet
FLEETING adj rapid and soon passing
FLEETLY ▸ fleet
FLEETS ▸ fleet
FLEG, -GED, -GING, -S vb scare
FLEHMEN, -S vb (of mammal) grimace
FLEISHIG same as ▸ fleishik
FLEISHIK adj containing or derived from meat or meat products
FLEME, -D, -S, FLEMIT vb drive out
FLEMING n inhabitant of Flanders or a Flemish-speaking Belgian
FLEMISH vb stow (a rope) in a Flemish coil
FLEMIT ▸ fleme
FLENCH, -ED, -ES same as ▸ flense
FLENCHER ▸ flench
FLENCHES ▸ flench
FLENSE, -D, -S, FLENSING vb strip (a whale, seal, etc) of (its blubber or skin)
FLENSER, -S ▸ flense

FLENSES ▸ flense
FLENSING ▸ flense
FLESH, -ED, -ES, -ING n soft part of a human or animal body ▷ vb remove flesh from
FLESHER, -S n person or machine that fleshes hides or skins
FLESHES ▸ flesh
FLESHIER ▸ fleshy
FLESHILY ▸ fleshy
FLESHING ▸ flesh
FLESHLY adj fleshy; fat
FLESHPOT n pot in which meat is cooked
FLESHY, FLESHIER adj plump
FLETCH, -ED, -ES same as ▸ fledge
FLETCHER n person who makes arrows
FLETCHES ▸ fletch
FLETTON, -S n type of brick
FLEUR, -S n flower emblem used in heraldry
FLEURET, -S same as > fleurette
FLEURON, -S n decorative piece of pastry
FLEURS ▸ fleur
FLEURY same as ▸ flory
FLEW ▸ fly
FLEWED adj having large flews
FLEWS pl n upper lip of a bloodhound or similar dog
FLEX, -ED, -ES, -ING n flexible insulated electric cable ▷ vb bend
FLEXAGON n hexagon made from a single pliable strip of triangles
FLEXED ▸ flex
FLEXES ▸ flex
FLEXI, -S n fleximtime
FLEXIBLE adj easily bent
FLEXIBLY ▸ flexible
FLEXILE same as ▸ flexible
FLEXING ▸ flex
FLEXION, -S n act of bending a joint or limb
FLEXIS ▸ flexi
FLEXO, -S n flexography
FLEXOR, -S n type of muscle
FLEXOS ▸ flexo
FLEXTIME same as > flexitime
FLEXUOSE same as ▸ flexuous
FLEXUOUS adj full of bends or curves
FLEXURAL ▸ flexure
FLEXURE, -S n act of flexing or the state of being flexed
FLEXWING n collapsible fabric wing used in hang gliding

FLEY, -ED, -ING, -S vb be afraid or cause to be afraid
FLIBBERT n small piece or bit
FLIC, -S n French police officer
FLICHTER vb flutter
FLICK, -ED, -ING, -S vb touch or move in a quick movement ▷ n tap or quick stroke
FLICKER, -S vb shine unsteadily or intermittently ▷ n unsteady brief light
FLICKERY adj flickering
FLICKING ▸ flick
FLICKS ▸ flick
FLICS ▸ flic
FLIED ▸ fly
FLIER, -S ▸ fly
FLIES ▸ fly
FLIEST ▸ fly
FLIGHT, -ED, -S n journey by air ▷ vb cause (a ball, dart, etc) to float slowly or deceptively towards its target
FLIGHTY adj frivolous and fickle
FLIM, -S n five-pound note
FLIMFLAM n nonsense ▷ vb deceive
FLIMP, -ED, -ING, -S vb steal
FLIMS ▸ flim
FLIMSIER ▸ flimsy
FLIMSIES ▸ flimsy
FLIMSILY ▸ flimsy
FLIMSY, FLIMSIER, FLIMSIES adj not strong or substantial ▷ n thin paper used for making carbon copies
FLINCH, -ED, -ES vb draw back suddenly
FLINCHER ▸ flinch
FLINCHES ▸ flinch
FLINDER, -S n fragment ▷ vb scamper about flutteringly
FLING, -ING, -S, FLUNG vb throw, send, or move forcefully or hurriedly ▷ n spell of self-indulgent enjoyment
FLINGER, -S ▸ fling
FLINGING ▸ fling
FLINGS ▸ fling
FLINKITE n anhydrous phosphate
FLINT, -ED, -ING, -S n hard grey stone ▷ vb fit or provide with a flint
FLINTIER ▸ flinty
FLINTIFY vb turn to flint
FLINTILY ▸ flinty
FLINTING ▸ flint
FLINTS ▸ flint
FLINTY, FLINTIER adj cruel

FLIP, -PED, -PEST, -S vb throw (something small or light) carelessly ▷ n snap or tap ▷ adj flippant

FLIPBOOK n book of drawings made to seem animated by flipping pages

FLIPFLOP n rubber sandal

FLIPPANT adj treating serious things lightly

FLIPPED ▶ flip

FLIPPER, -S n limb of a sea animal adapted for swimming

FLIPPEST ▶ flip

FLIPPIER ▶ flippy

FLIPPING n act or instance of flipping

FLIPPY, FLIPPIER adj (of clothes) moving to and fro as the wearer walks

FLIPS ▶ flip

FLIPSIDE n reverse or opposite side

FLIR, -S n forward looking infrared radar

FLIRT, -ED, -ING, -S vb behave as if physically attracted to someone ▷ n person who flirts

FLIRTER, -S ▶ flirt

FLIRTIER ▶ flirty

FLIRTING ▶ flirt

FLIRTISH ▶ flirt

FLIRTS ▶ flirt

FLIRTY, FLIRTIER ▶ flirt

FLISK, -ED, -ING, -S vb skip

FLISKIER ▶ flisky

FLISKING ▶ flisk

FLISKS ▶ flisk

FLISKY, FLISKIER ▶ flisk

FLIT, -S, -TED, -TING vb move lightly and rapidly ▷ n act of flitting

FLITCH, -ED, -ES n side of pork salted and cured ▷ vb cut (a tree trunk) into pieces of timber

FLITE, -D, -S, FLITING vb scold or rail at ▷ n dispute or scolding

FLITS ▶ flit

FLITT, -S adj fleet ▷ vb to flit

FLITTED ▶ flit

FLITTER, -S ▶ flit

FLITTERN n bark of young oak tree

FLITTERS ▶ flitter

FLITTING ▶ flit

FLITTS ▶ flitt

FLIVVER, -S n old, cheap, or battered car

FLIX, -ED, -ES, -ING n fur ▷ vb have fur

FLIXWEED n plant of the mustard family

FLOAT, -ED vb rest on the surface of a liquid ▷ n object used to help someone or something float

FLOATAGE same as ▶ flotage

FLOATANT n substance used in fly-fishing, to help dry flies to float

FLOATCUT adj as in floatcut file file with rows of parallel teeth

FLOATED ▶ float

FLOATEL, -S same as ▶ flotel

FLOATER, -S n person or thing that floats

FLOATIER ▶ floaty

FLOATING adj moving about, changing

FLOATS pl n footlights

FLOATY, FLOATIER adj filmy and light

FLOB, -BED, -BING, -S vb spit

FLOC, -S same as ▶ flock

FLOCCED ▶ floc

FLOCCI ▶ floccus

FLOCCING ▶ floc

FLOCCOSE adj consisting of or covered with woolly tufts or hairs

FLOCCULE n small aggregate of flocculent material

FLOCCULI > flocculus

FLOCCUS, FLOCCI n downy or woolly covering ▷ adj (of a cloud) having the appearance of woolly tufts

FLOCK, -ED, -ING, -S n number of animals of one kind together ▷ vb gather in a crowd ▷ adj (of wallpaper) with a velvety raised pattern

FLOCKIER ▶ flocky

FLOCKING ▶ flock

FLOCKS ▶ flock

FLOCKY, FLOCKIER ▶ flock

FLOCS ▶ floc

FLOE, -S n sheet of floating ice

FLOG, -GED, -S vb beat with a whip or stick

FLOGGER, -S ▶ flog

FLOGGING ▶ flog

FLOGS ▶ flog

FLOKATI, -S n Greek hand-woven shaggy woollen rug

FLONG, -S n material used for making moulds in stereotyping

FLOOD, -ED, -S n overflow of water onto a normally dry area ▷ vb cover or become covered with water

FLOODER, -S ▶ flood

FLOODING n submerging of land under water

FLOODLIT adj illuminated with a floodlight

FLOODS ▶ flood

FLOODWAY n conduit for floodwater

FLOOEY adj awry

FLOOIE same as ▶ flooey

FLOOR, -ED, -ING, -S n lower surface of a room ▷ vb knock down

FLOORAGE n area of floor

FLOORED ▶ floor

FLOORER, -S n coup de grâce

FLOORING ▶ floor

FLOORPAN n bottom part of a motor vehicle's interior

FLOORS ▶ floor

FLOP, -PED, -PING, -S vb bend, fall, or collapse loosely or carelessly ▷ n failure

FLOPOVER n TV visual effect of page being turned

FLOPPED ▶ flop

FLOPPER, -S ▶ flop

FLOPPIER ▶ floppy

FLOPPIES ▶ floppy

FLOPPILY ▶ floppy

FLOPPING ▶ flop

FLOPPY, FLOPPIER, FLOPPIES adj hanging downwards, loose ▷ n floppy disk

FLOPS ▶ flop

FLOR, -S n type of yeast

FLORA, -E, -S n plants of a given place or time

FLORAL, -S adj consisting of or decorated with flowers ▷ n class of perfume

FLORALLY ▶ floral

FLORALS ▶ floral

FLORAS ▶ flora

FLOREAT, FLOREANT vb may (a person, institution, etc) flourish

FLORENCE n type of fennel

FLORET, -S n part of a composite flower head

FLORID, -ER adj with a red or flushed complexion

FLORIDLY ▶ florid

FLORIER ▶ flory

FLORIEST ▶ flory

FLORIGEN n hypothetical plant hormone

FLORIN, -S n former British and Australian coin

FLORIST, -S n seller of flowers

FLORS ▶ flor

FLORUIT, -S prep (he or she) flourished in ▷ n such a period in a person's life

FLORULA, -E n flora of a small single environment

FLORULE, -S same as ▶ florula

FLORY, FLORIER, FLORIEST adj containing a fleur-de-lys

FLOSCULE n floret

FLOSH, -ES n hopper-shaped box

FLOSS, -ED, -ES, -ING n fine silky fibres ▷ vb clean (between the teeth) with dental floss

FLOSSER, -S ▸ floss

FLOSSES ▸ floss

FLOSSIE variant of ▸ flossy

FLOSSIER ▸ flossy

FLOSSILY ▸ flossy

FLOSSING ▸ floss

FLOSSY, FLOSSIER adj consisting of or resembling floss

FLOTA, -S n formerly, Spanish commercial fleet

FLOTAGE, -S n act or state of floating

FLOTANT adj in heraldry, flying in the air

FLOTAS ▸ flota

FLOTE, -D, -S, FLOTING n aquatic perennial grass ▷ vb skim (eg milk)

FLOTEL, -S n (in the oil industry) rig or boat used as accommodation

FLOTES ▸ flote

FLOTILLA n small fleet or fleet of small ships

FLOTING ▸ flote

FLOTSAM, -S n floating wreckage

FLOUNCE, -D, -S vb go with emphatic movements ▷ n flouncing movement

FLOUNCY ▸ flounce

FLOUNDER vb move with difficulty, as in mud ▷ n edible flatfish

FLOUR, -ED, -ING, -S n powder made by grinding grain, esp wheat ▷ vb sprinkle with flour

FLOURIER ▸ floury

FLOURING ▸ flour

FLOURISH vb be active, successful, or widespread ▷ n dramatic waving motion

FLOURS ▸ flour

FLOURY, FLOURIER ▸ flour

FLOUSE, -D, -S, FLOUSING vb splash

FLOUSH, -ED, -ES variant of ▸ flouse

FLOUSING ▸ flouse

FLOUT, -ED, -ING, -S vb deliberately disobey (a rule, law, etc)

FLOUTER, -S ▸ flout

FLOUTING ▸ flout

FLOUTS ▸ flout

FLOW, -ED, -ING, -S vb (of liquid) move in a stream

▷ n act, rate, or manner of flowing

FLOWABLE adj capable of flowing

FLOWAGE, -S n act of overflowing or the state of having overflowed

FLOWED ▸ flow

FLOWER, -S n part of a plant that produces seeds ▷ vb produce flowers, bloom

FLOWERED adj decorated with a floral design

FLOWERER n plant that flowers at a specified time or in a specified way

FLOWERET another name for ▸ floret

FLOWERS ▸ flower

FLOWERY adj decorated with a floral design

FLOWING ▸ flow

FLOWN ▸ fly

FLOWS ▸ flow

FLOX adj as in flox silk type of silk

FLU, -S n any of various viral infections

FLUATE, -S n fluoride

FLUB, -BED, -BING, -S vb bungle

FLUBBER, -S ▸ flub

FLUBBING ▸ flub

FLUBDUB, -S n bunkum

FLUBS ▸ flub

FLUE, -S n passage or pipe for smoke or hot air

FLUED adj having a flue

FLUELLEN n type of plant

FLUELLIN same as ▸ fluellen

FLUENCE, -S n particle or energy density

FLUENCY n quality of being fluent

FLUENT, -S adj able to speak or write with ease ▷ n variable quantity in fluxions

FLUENTLY ▸ fluent

FLUENTS ▸ fluent

FLUERIC adj of or relating to fluidics

FLUERICS pl n fluidics

FLUES ▸ flue

FLUEWORK n collectively, organ stops

FLUEY, FLUIER, FLUIEST adj involved in, caused by, or like influenza

FLUFF, -ED, -ING, -S n soft fibres ▷ vb make or become soft and puffy

FLUFFER, -S n person employed on a railway to clear the tracks

FLUFFIER ▸ fluffy

FLUFFILY ▸ fluffy

FLUFFING ▸ fluff

FLUFFS ▸ fluff

FLUFFY, FLUFFIER adj of, resembling, or covered with fluff

FLUGEL, -S n grand piano or harpsichord

FLUID, -S n substance able to flow and change its shape ▷ adj able to flow or change shape easily

FLUIDAL ▸ fluid

FLUIDIC ▸ fluidics

FLUIDICS n study and use of the flow of fluids in tubes

FLUIDIFY vb make fluid

FLUIDISE same as ▸ fluidize

FLUIDITY n state of being fluid

FLUIDIZE vb make fluid

FLUIDLY ▸ fluid

FLUIDRAM n British imperial measure

FLUIDS ▸ fluid

FLUIER ▸ fluey

FLUIEST ▸ fluey

FLUISH ▸ flu

FLUKE, -D, -S, FLUKING n accidental stroke of luck ▷ vb gain, make, or hit by a fluke

FLUKEY same as ▸ fluky

FLUKIER ▸ fluky

FLUKIEST ▸ fluky

FLUKILY ▸ fluky

FLUKING ▸ fluke

FLUKY, FLUKIER, FLUKIEST adj done or gained by an accident

FLUME, -D, -S, FLUMING n narrow sloping channel for water ▷ vb transport (logs) in a flume

FLUMMERY n silly or trivial talk

FLUMMOX vb puzzle or confuse

FLUMP, -ED, -ING, -S vb move or fall heavily

FLUNG ▸ fling

FLUNK, -ED, -ING, -S vb fail ▷ n low grade below the pass standard

FLUNKER, -S ▸ flunk

FLUNKEY, -S same as ▸ flunky

FLUNKIE same as ▸ flunky

FLUNKIES ▸ flunky

FLUNKING ▸ flunk

FLUNKS ▸ flunk

FLUNKY, FLUNKIES n servile person

FLUOR, -S same as > fluorspar

FLUORENE n white insoluble crystalline solid

FLUORIC adj of, concerned with, or produced from fluorine or fluorspar

FLUFFING ▸ fluff

FLUFFS ▸ fluff

FLUORID, -S same as
▸fluoride
FLUORIDE n compound
containing fluorine
FLUORIDS ▸fluorid
FLUORIN, -S same as
▸fluorine
FLUORINE n toxic yellow
gas: most reactive of all the
elements
FLUORINS ▸fluorin
FLUORITE same as
> fluorspar
FLUORS ▸fluor
FLURR, -ED, -ING, -S vb
scatter
FLURRIED ▸flurry
FLURRIES ▸flurry
FLURRING ▸flurr
FLURRS ▸flurr
FLURRY, FLURRIED,
FLURRIES n sudden
commotion ▷ vb confuse
FLUS ▸flu
FLUSH, -ED, -ES, -EST vb
blush or cause to blush ▷ n
blush ▷ adj level with the
surrounding surface ▷ adv
so as to be level
FLUSHER, -S ▸flush
FLUSHES ▸flush
FLUSHEST ▸flush
FLUSHIER ▸flushy
FLUSHING n extra feeding
given to ewes before mating
to increase the lambing
percentage
FLUSHY, FLUSHIER adj
ruddy
FLUSTER, -S vb make
nervous or upset ▷ n
nervous or upset state
FLUSTERY adj flustered
FLUTE, -S n wind instrument
▷ vb utter in a high-pitched
tone
FLUTED adj having
decorative grooves
FLUTER, -S n craftsperson
who makes flutes or fluting
FLUTES ▸flute
FLUTEY, -ER, FLUTIER,
FLUTIEST adj resembling a
flute in sound
FLUTINA, -S n type of
accordion
FLUTING, -S n design of
decorative grooves
FLUTIST, -S same as
▸flautist
FLUTTER, -S vb flap ▷ n
flapping movement
FLUTTERY adj flapping
rapidly
FLUTY ▸flute
FLUVIAL adj of rivers

FLUX, -ED, -ES, -ING n
constant change or instability
▷ vb make or become fluid
FLUXGATE n type of
magnetometer
FLUXING ▸flux
FLUXION, -S n rate of
change of a function
FLUXIVE ▸flux
FLUYT, -S n Dutch sailing ship
FLY, FLEW, FLIED, FLIES,
FLIEST, FLOWN, -EST vb
move through the air on
wings or in an aircraft ▷ n
fastening at the front of
trousers ▷ adj sharp and
cunning
FLYABLE ▸fly
FLYAWAY, -S adj (of hair)
very fine and soft ▷ n person
who is frivolous or flighty
FLYBACK, -S n item of
electrical equipment
FLYBANE, -S n type of
campion
FLYBELT, -S n strip of
tsetse-infested land
FLYBLOW, FLYBLEW, -S vb
contaminate ▷ n egg or
young larva of a blowfly
FLYBLOWN adj covered with
blowfly eggs
FLYBLOWS ▸flyblow
FLYBOAT, -S n any small
swift boat
FLYBOOK, -S n small case or
wallet for storing artificial
flies
FLYBOY, -S n air force pilot
FLYBY, -S n flight past a
particular position or target
FLYER, -S ▸fly
FLYEST ▸fly
FLYHAND, -S n device on a
printing press
FLYING, -S ▸fly
FLYLEAF n blank leaf at the
beginning or end of a book
FLYLESS ▸fly
FLYLINE, -S n type of line
used in fly fishing
FLYMAKER n person who
makes fishing flies
FLYMAN, FLYMEN n
stagehand
FLYOFF, -S n all water
transferred from the earth to
the atmosphere
FLYOVER, -S n road passing
over another by a bridge
FLYPAPER n paper with a
sticky poisonous coating,
used to kill flies
FLYPAST, -S n ceremonial
flight of aircraft over a
given area

FLYPE, -D, -S, FLYPING vb
fold back
FLYPITCH n area for
unlicensed stalls at markets
FLYSCH, -ES n type of
marine sedimentary facies
FLYSHEET n part of tent
FLYSPECK n small speck of
the excrement of a fly ▷ vb
mark with flyspecks
FLYSPRAY n insecticide
sprayed from an aerosol
FLYTE, -D, -S same as ▸flite
FLYTIER, -S n person who
makes their own fishing flies
FLYTING, -S ▸flyte
FLYTRAP, -S n any of various
insectivorous plants
FLYWAY, -S n usual route
used by birds when migrating
FLYWHEEL n heavy wheel
regulating the speed of a
machine
FOAL, -ED, -S n young of a
horse or related animal ▷ vb
give birth to a foal
FOALFOOT n coltsfoot
FOALING, -S n act of giving
birth to a foal
FOALS ▸foal
FOAM, -ED, -S n mass of
small bubbles on a liquid
▷ vb produce foam
FOAMABLE ▸foam
FOAMED ▸foam
FOAMER, -S n (possibly
obsessive) enthusiast
FOAMIER ▸foamy
FOAMIEST ▸foamy
FOAMILY ▸foamy
FOAMING, -S ▸foam
FOAMLESS ▸foam
FOAMLIKE ▸foam
FOAMS ▸foam
FOAMY, FOAMIER,
FOAMIEST adj of,
resembling, consisting of, or
covered with foam
FOB, -BED, -BING, -S n short
watch chain ▷ vb cheat
FOCACCIA n flat Italian
bread made with olive oil
and yeast
FOCAL adj of or at a focus
FOCALISE same as ▸focalize
FOCALIZE less common word
for ▸focus
FOCALLY ▸focal
FOCUS, FOCI, -ED, -ES,
-ING, -SED, -SES n point at
which light or sound waves
converge ▷ vb bring or come
into focus
FOCUSER, -S ▸focus
FOCUSES ▸focus
FOCUSING ▸focus

F

FOCUSSED ▸focus

FOCUSSES ▸focus

FODDER, -ED, -S n feed for livestock ▷ vb supply (livestock) with fodder

FODDERER ▸fodder

FODDERS ▸fodder

FODGEL adj buxom

FOE, -S n enemy, opponent

FOEDARIE variant of ▸fedarie

FOEFIE adj as in **foefie slide** rope along which a person may traverse on a pulley

FOEHN, -S same as ▸fohn

FOEMAN, FOEMEN n enemy in war

FOEN same as ▸foe

FOES ▸foe

FOETAL same as ▸fetal

FOETID, -ER same as ▸fetid

FOETIDLY ▸foetid

FOETOR, -S same as ▸fetor

FOETUS, -ES same as ▸fetus

FOG, -GED, -S n mass of condensed water vapour in the lower air ▷ vb cover with steam

FOGASH, -ES n type of Hungarian pikeperch

FOGBOUND adj prevented from operating by fog

FOGBOW, -S n faint arc of light sometimes seen in a fog bank

FOGDOG, -S n spot sometimes seen in fog near the horizon

FOGEY, -S n old-fashioned person

FOGEYDOM ▸fogey

FOGEYISH ▸fogey

FOGEYISM ▸fogey

FOGEYS ▸fogey

FOGFRUIT n wildflower of the verbena family

FOGGAGE, -S n grass grown for winter grazing

FOGGED ▸fog

FOGGER, -S n device that generates a fog

FOGGIER ▸foggy

FOGGIEST ▸foggy

FOGGILY ▸foggy

FOGGING, -S n act of fogging

FOGGY, FOGGIER, FOGGIEST ▸fog

FOGHORN, -S n large horn sounded to warn ships in fog

FOGIE, -S variant of ▸fogey

FOGLE, -S n silk handkerchief

FOGLESS ▸fog

FOGLIGHT n motor-vehicle light used in fog

FOGMAN, FOGMEN n person in charge of railway fog-signals

FOGOU, -S n subterranean building found in Cornwall

FOGRAM, -S n fogey

FOGS ▸fog

FOGY same as ▸fogey

FOGYDOM, -S ▸fogy

FOGYISH ▸fogy

FOGYISM, -S ▸fogy

FOH interj expression of disgust

FOHN, -S n type of warm dry wind

FOIBLE, -S n minor weakness or slight peculiarity

FOID, -S n rock-forming mineral similar to feldspar

FOIL, -ED, -S vb ruin (someone's plan) ▷ n metal in a thin sheet, esp for wrapping food

FOILABLE ▸foil

FOILED ▸foil

FOILING, -S ▸foil

FOILIST, -S n person who fences with a foil

FOILS ▸foil

FOILSMAN, FOILSMEN n person who uses or specializes in using a foil

FOIN, -ED, -ING, -S n thrust or lunge with a weapon ▷ vb thrust with a weapon

FOISON, -S n plentiful supply or yield

FOIST, -ED, -ING, -S vb force or impose on

FOISTER, -S ▸foist

FOISTING ▸foist

FOISTS ▸foist

FOLACIN, -S n folic acid

FOLATE, -S n folic acid

FOLD, -ED, -ING, -S vb bend so that one part covers another ▷ n folded piece or part

FOLDABLE ▸fold

FOLDAWAY adj (of a bed) able to be folded and put away when not in use

FOLDBACK n (in multitrack recording) a process for returning a signal to a performer instantly

FOLDBOAT another name for ▸faltboat

FOLDED ▸fold

FOLDER, -S n piece of folded cardboard for holding loose papers

FOLDEROL same as ▸falderal

FOLDERS ▸folder

FOLDING, -S ▸fold

FOLDOUT, -S another name for ▸gatefold

FOLDS ▸fold

FOLDUP, -S n something that folds up

FOLEY, -S n footsteps editor

FOLIA ▸folium

FOLIAGE, -S n leaves

FOLIAGED adj having foliage

FOLIAGES ▸foliage

FOLIAR adj of or relating to a leaf or leaves

FOLIATE, -S adj relating to, possessing, or resembling leaves ▷ vb ornament with foliage or with leaf forms such as foils

FOLIATED adj ornamented with or made up of foliage or foils

FOLIATES ▸foliate

FOLIC adj as in **folic acid** any of a group of vitamins of the B complex

FOLIE, -S n madness

FOLIO, -ED, -ING, -S n sheet of paper folded in half to make two leaves of a book ▷ adj of or made in the largest book size ▷ vb number the leaves of (a book) consecutively

FOLIOLE, -S n part of a compound leaf

FOLIOS ▸folio

FOLIOSE adj leaf-bearing

FOLIOUS adj leaf-bearing

FOLIUM, FOLIA, -S n plane geometrical curve

FOLK, -S n people in general ▷ adj traditional to the common people of a country

FOLKIE, -R, -S, -ST n devotee of folk music ▷ adj of or relating to folk music

FOLKISH ▸folk

FOLKLAND n former type of land tenure

FOLKLIFE n traditional customs, arts, crafts, and other forms of cultural expression of a people

FOLKLIKE ▸folk

FOLKLORE n traditional beliefs and stories of a people

FOLKMOOT n (in early medieval England) an assembly of the people of a district, town, or shire

FOLKMOT, -S same as ▸folkmoot

FOLKMOTE same as ▸folkmoot

FOLKMOTS ▸folkmot

FOLKS ▸folk

FOLKSIER ▸folksy

FOLKSILY ▸folksy

FOLKSONG n traditional song

FOLKSY, FOLKSIER adj simple and unpretentious

FOLKTALE n tale or legend from an oral tradition

FOLKWAY singular form of ▸**folkways**

FOLKWAYS pl n traditional and customary ways of living

FOLKY same as ▸**folkie**

FOLLES ▸**follis**

FOLLICLE n small cavity in the body, esp one from which a hair grows

FOLLIED ▸**folly**

FOLLIES ▸**folly**

FOLLIS, FOLLES n Roman coin

FOLLOW, -ED, -S vb go or come after

FOLLOWER n disciple or supporter

FOLLOWS ▸**follow**

FOLLOWUP n further action

FOLLY, FOLLIED, FOLLIES, -ING n foolishness ▷ vb behave foolishly

FOMENT, -ED, -S vb encourage or stir up (trouble)

FOMENTER ▸**foment**

FOMENTS ▸**foment**

FOMES, FOMITES n any material that may harbour pathogens

FOMITE same as ▸**fomes**

FOMITES ▸**fomes**

FON, -NED, -NING, -S vb compel

FOND, -ED, -ER, -EST, -ING, -S adj tender, loving ▷ n background of a design, as in lace ▷ vb dote

FONDA, -S n Spanish hotel

FONDANT, -S n (sweet made from) flavoured paste of sugar and water ▷ adj (of a colour) soft

FONDAS ▸**fonda**

FONDED ▸**fond**

FONDER ▸**fond**

FONDEST ▸**fond**

FONDING ▸**fond**

FONDLE, -D, -S, FONDLING vb caress

FONDLER, -S ▸**fondle**

FONDLES ▸**fondle**

FONDLING ▸**fondle**

FONDLY ▸**fond**

FONDNESS ▸**fond**

FONDS ▸**fond**

FONDU, -S n ballet movement

FONDUE, -D, -S, FONDUING n Swiss dish ▷ vb cook and serve (food) as a fondue

FONDUS ▸**fondu**

FONE, -S n informal spelling of telephone

FONLY adv foolishly

FONNED ▸**fon**

FONNING ▸**fon**

FONS ▸**fon**

FONT, -S n bowl in a church for baptismal water

FONTAL ▸**font**

FONTANEL n soft membraneous gap in an infant's skull

FONTANGE n type of tall headdress

FONTINA, -S n mild Italian cheese

FONTLET, -S ▸**font**

FONTS ▸**font**

FOO, -S n temporary computer variable or file

FOOBAR same as ▸**fubar**

FOOD, -S n what one eats; solid nourishment

FOODBANK n charity which distributes food to the needy

FOODERY n restaurant

FOODFUL adj supplying abundant food

FOODIE, -S n gourmet

FOODISM, -S n enthusiasm for and interest in good food

FOODLAND n land on which food is produced

FOODLESS ▸**food**

FOODOIR, -S n book or blog that combines a personal memoir with recipes

FOODS ▸**food**

FOODSHED n the area through which food is transported from farm to consumer

FOODWAYS pl n customs and traditions relating to food and its preparation

FOODY same as ▸**foodie**

FOOFARAW n vulgar ornamentation

FOOL, -ED, -S n person lacking sense or judgment ▷ vb deceive (someone)

FOOLERY n foolish behaviour

FOOLFISH n orange filefish or winter flounder

FOOLING, -S ▸**fool**

FOOLISH adj unwise, silly, or absurd

FOOLS ▸**fool**

FOOLSCAP n size of paper, 34.3 × 43.2 centimetres

FOOS ▸**foo**

FOOSBALL n US and Canadian name for table football

FOOT, FEET, -ED n part of the leg below the ankle ▷ vb kick

FOOTAGE, -S n amount of film used

FOOTBAG, -S n sport of keeping a beanbag off the ground by kicking it

FOOTBALL n game played by two teams kicking a ball in an attempt to score goals

FOOTBAR, -S n any bar used by the foot

FOOTBATH n vessel for bathing the feet

FOOTBED, -S n insole in a boot or shoe

FOOTBOY, -S n boy servant

FOOTED ▸**foot**

FOOTER, -ED, -S n person who goes on foot ▷ vb potter

FOOTFALL n sound of a footstep

FOOTGEAR another name for ▸**footwear**

FOOTHILL n lower slope of a mountain or a relatively low hill at the foot of a mountain

FOOTHOLD n secure position from which progress may be made

FOOTIE, -S same as ▸**footy**

FOOTIER ▸**footy**

FOOTIES ▸**footie**

FOOTIEST ▸**footy**

FOOTING, -S n basis or foundation

FOOTLE, -D, -S vb loiter aimlessly ▷ n foolishness

FOOTLER, -S ▸**footle**

FOOTLES ▸**footle**

FOOTLESS ▸**foot**

FOOTLIKE ▸**foot**

FOOTLING adj trivial ▷ n trifle

FOOTLONG n type of extra-long frankfurter

FOOTMAN, FOOTMEN n male servant in uniform

FOOTMARK n mark or trace of mud, wetness, etc, left by a person's foot on a surface

FOOTMEN ▸**footman**

FOOTMUFF n muff used to keep the feet warm

FOOTNOTE n note printed at the foot of a page ▷ vb supply (a page, book, etc) with footnotes

FOOTPACE n normal or walking pace

FOOTPAD, -S n highwayman, on foot rather than horseback

FOOTPAGE n errand-boy

FOOTPATH n narrow path for walkers

FOOTPOST n post delivered on foot

FOOTPUMP n pump operated with the foot

FOOTRA, -S variant of ▸ foutra

FOOTRACE n race run on foot

FOOTRAS ▸ footra

FOOTREST n something that provides a support for the feet, such as a low stool, rail, etc

FOOTROPE n part of a boltrope to which the foot of a sail is stitched

FOOTRULE n rigid measure, one foot in length

FOOTS pl n sediment that accumulates at the bottom of a vessel

FOOTSAL, -S n type of indoor football with five players on each side

FOOTSIE, -S n flirtation involving the touching together of feet

FOOTSLOG vb march

FOOTSORE adj having sore or tired feet, esp from much walking

FOOTSTEP n step in walking

FOOTSY variant of ▸ footsie

FOOTWALL n rocks on the lower side of an inclined fault plane or mineral vein

FOOTWAY, -S n way or path for pedestrians

FOOTWEAR n anything worn to cover the feet

FOOTWELL n part of a car in which the foot pedals are located

FOOTWORK n skilful use of the feet, as in sport or dancing

FOOTWORN adj footsore

FOOTY, FOOTIER, FOOTIEST n football ▸ adj mean

FOOZLE, -D, -S, FOOZLING vb bungle (a shot) ▸ n bungled shot

FOOZLER, -S ▸ foozle

FOOZLES ▸ foozle

FOOZLING ▸ foozle

FOP, -PED, -PING, -S n man excessively concerned with fashion ▸ vb act like a fop

FOPLING, -S n vain affected dandy

FOPPED ▸ fop

FOPPERY n clothes, affectations, etc of or befitting a fop

FOPPING ▸ fop

FOPPISH ▸ fop

FOPS ▸ fop

FOR prep indicating benefit, receipt, timespan, distance, etc

FORA ▸ forum

FORAGE, -ED, -S, FORAGING vb search about (for) ▸ n food for cattle or horses

FORAGER, -S ▸ forage

FORAGES ▸ forage

FORAGING ▸ forage

FORAM, -S n marine protozoan

FORAMEN, -S, FORAMINA n natural hole

FORAMS ▸ foram

FORANE adj as in vicar forane type of Roman Catholic priest

FORAY, -ED, -ING, -S n brief raid or attack ▸ vb raid or ravage (a town, district, etc)

FORAYER, -S ▸ foray

FORAYING ▸ foray

FORAYS ▸ foray

FORB, -S n any herbaceous plant that is not a grass

FORBAD ▸ forbid

FORBADE ▸ forbid

FORBEAR, FORBARE, -S, FORBORNE vb cease or refrain (from doing something)

FORBID, FORBAD, FORBADE, -S vb prohibit, refuse to allow

FORBIDAL ▸ forbid

FORBIDS ▸ forbid

FORBODE, -D, -S vb obsolete word meaning forbid ▸ n obsolete word meaning forbidding

FORBORE past tense of ▸ forbear

FORBORNE ▸ forbear

FORBS ▸ forb

FORBY adv besides

FORBYE same as ▸ forby

FORCAT, -S n convict or galley slave

FORCE, -S, FORCING n strength or power ▸ vb compel, make (someone) do something

FORCED adj compulsory

FORCEDLY ▸ forced

FORCEFUL adj emphatic and confident

FORCEOUT n play in baseball in which a runner is forced to run to next base and is put out

FORCEPS, FORCIPES pl n surgical pincers

FORCER, -S ▸ force

FORCES ▸ force

FORCIBLE adj involving physical force or violence

FORCIBLY ▸ forcible

FORCING ▸ force

FORCIPES ▸ forceps

FORD, -ED, -ING, -S n shallow place where a river may be crossed ▸ vb cross (a river) at a ford

FORDABLE ▸ ford

FORDED ▸ ford

FORDID ▸ fordo

FORDING ▸ ford

FORDLESS ▸ ford

FORDO, FORDID, -ES, -ING, -NE vb destroy

FORDONNE vb as in from fordonne fordone

FORDS ▸ ford

FORE, -S adj in, at, or towards the front ▸ n front part ▸ interj golfer's shouted warning

FOREARM, -S n arm from the wrist to the elbow ▸ vb prepare beforehand

FOREBAY, -S n reservoir or canal

FOREBEAR n ancestor

FOREBITT n post at a ship's foremast for securing cables

FOREBODE vb warn of or indicate (an event, result, etc) in advance

FOREBODY n part of a ship forward of the foremast

FOREBOOM n boom of a foremast

FOREBY variant of ▸ forby

FOREBYE variant of ▸ forby

FORECAR, -S n vehicle attached to a motorcycle

FORECAST vb predict (weather, events, etc) ▸ n prediction

FOREDATE vb antedate

FOREDECK n deck between the bridge and the forecastle

FOREDO, FOREDID, -ES, -NE same as ▸ fordo

FOREDOOM vb doom or condemn beforehand

FOREFACE n muzzle of an animal

FOREFEEL, FOREFELT vb have a premonition of

FOREFEET ▸ forefoot

FOREFELT ▸ forefeel

FOREFEND same as ▸ forfend

FOREFOOT, FOREFEET n either of the front feet of an animal

FOREGO, -ES same as ▸ forgo

FOREGOER ▸ **forego**
FOREGOES ▸ **forego**
FOREGONE *adj* gone or completed
FOREGUT, -S *n* anterior part of the digestive tract of vertebrates
FOREHAND *n* stroke played with the palm of the hand facing forward ▷ *adj* (of a stroke) made with the wrist facing the direction of play ▷ *adv* with a forehand stroke ▷ *vb* play (a shot) forehand
FOREHEAD *n* part of the face above the eyebrows
FOREHENT *vb* seize in advance
FOREHOCK *n* foreleg cut of bacon or pork
FOREHOOF *n* front hoof
FOREIGN *adj* not of, or in, one's own country
FOREKING *n* previous king
FOREKNOW, FOREKNEW *vb* know in advance
FOREL, -LED, -S *vb* cover (a book) with parchment
FORELADY *n* forewoman of a jury
FORELAID ▸ **forelay**
FORELAIN ▸ **forelie**
FORELAND *n* headland, cape, or coastal promontory
FORELAY, FORELAID, -S *archaic word for* ▸ **ambush**
FORELEG, -S *n* either of the front legs of an animal
FORELEND, FORELENT *vb* give up
FORELIE, FORELAIN, -S *vb* lie in front of
FORELIFT *vb* lift up in front
FORELIMB *n* front or anterior limb
FORELLED ▸ **forel**
FORELOCK *n* lock of hair over the forehead ▷ *vb* secure (a bolt) by means of a forelock
FORELS ▸ **forel**
FOREMAN, FOREMEN *n* person in charge of a group of workers
FOREMAST *n* mast nearest the bow of a ship
FOREMEAN *vb* intend in advance
FOREMEN ▸ **foreman**
FOREMILK *n* first milk drawn from a cow's udder prior to milking
FOREMOST *adv* first in time, place, or importance ▷ *adj* first in time, place, or importance

FORENAME *n* first name
FORENOON *n* morning
FORENSIC *adj* used in or connected with courts of law
FOREPART *n* first or front part in place, order, or time
FOREPAST *adj* bygone
FOREPAW, -S *n* either of the front feet of a land mammal
FOREPEAK *n* interior part of a vessel that is furthest forward
FOREPLAN *vb* plan in advance
FORERAN ▸ **forerun**
FORERANK *n* first rank
FOREREAD *vb* foretell
FORERUN, FORERAN, -S *vb* serve as a herald for
FORES ▸ **fore**
FORESAID *less common word for* ▸ **aforesaid**
FORESAIL *n* main sail on the foremast of a ship
FORESAW ▸ **foresee**
FORESAY, -S *vb* foretell
FORESEE, FORESAW, -N, -S *vb* see or know beforehand
FORESEER ▸ **foresee**
FORESEES ▸ **foresee**
FORESHEW *variant of* ▸ **foreshow**
FORESHIP *n* fore part of a ship
FORESHOW *vb* indicate in advance
FORESIDE *n* front or upper side or part
FORESKIN *n* fold of skin covering the tip of the penis
FORESLOW *variant of* ▸ **forslow**
FOREST, -ED, -S *n* large area with a thick growth of trees ▷ *vb* create a forest (in)
FORESTAL ▸ **forest**
FORESTAY *n* adjustable stay used on ships
FORESTED ▸ **forest**
FORESTER *n* person skilled in forestry
FORESTRY *n* science of planting and caring for trees
FORESTS ▸ **forest**
FORETELL, FORETOLD *vb* tell or indicate beforehand
FORETIME *n* time already gone
FORETOLD ▸ **foretell**
FORETOP, -S *n* platform at the top of the foremast
FOREVER, -S *adv* without end ▷ *n* very long time
FOREWARD *n* vanguard ▷ *vb* guard (something) in front

FOREWARN *vb* warn beforehand
FOREWENT *past tense of* ▸ **forego**
FOREWIND *n* favourable wind
FOREWING *n* either wing of the anterior pair of an insect's two pairs of wings
FOREWORD *n* introduction to a book
FOREWORN *same as* ▸ **forworn**
FOREX, -ES *n* foreign exchange
FOREYARD *n* yard for supporting the foresail of a square-rigger
FORFAIR, -S *vb* perish
FORFAIRN *adj* worn out
FORFAIRS ▸ **forfair**
FORFAULT *variant of* ▸ **forfeit**
FORFEIT, -S *n* thing lost or given up as a penalty for a fault or mistake ▷ *vb* lose as a forfeit ▷ *adj* lost as a forfeit
FORFEND, -S *vb* protect or secure
FORFEX, -ES *n* pair of pincers, esp the paired terminal appendages of an earwig
FORGAT *past tense of* ▸ **forget**
FORGAVE ▸ **forgive**
FORGE, -D, -S *n* place where metal is worked, smithy ▷ *vb* make a fraudulent imitation of (something)
FORGEMAN, FORGEMEN ▸ **forge**
FORGER, -S ▸ **forge**
FORGERY *n* illegal copy of something
FORGES ▸ **forge**
FORGET, -S *vb* fail to remember
FORGING, -S *n* process of producing a metal component by hammering
FORGIVE, FORGAVE, -N, -S *vb* cease to blame or hold resentment against, pardon
FORGIVER ▸ **forgive**
FORGIVES ▸ **forgive**
FORGO, -ES, -ING, -NE *vb* do without or give up
FORGOER, -S ▸ **forgo**
FORGOES ▸ **forgo**
FORGOING ▸ **forgo**
FORGONE ▸ **forgo**
FORGOT *past tense of* ▸ **forget**
FORHAILE *vb* distress
FORHENT, -S *variant of* ▸ **forehent**

FORHOO, -ED, -S vb forsake

FORHOOIE variant of
▶**forhoo**

FORHOOS ▶**forhoo**

FORHOW, -ED, -S variant of
▶**forhoo**

FORINSEC adj foreign

FORINT, -S n standard
monetary unit of Hungary

FORJUDGE vb deprive of a
right by the judgment of a
court

FORK, -ING, -S, -SFUL n tool
for eating food ▷ vb pick up,
dig, etc with a fork

FORKBALL n method of
pitching in baseball

FORKED adj having a fork or
forklike parts

FORKEDLY ▶**forked**

FORKER, -S ▶**fork**

FORKFUL, -S ▶**fork**

FORKHEAD n forked head of
a rod

FORKIER ▶**forky**

FORKIEST ▶**forky**

FORKING ▶**fork**

FORKLESS ▶**fork**

FORKLIFT n vehicle for
loading goods on wooden
pallets

FORKLIKE ▶**fork**

FORKS ▶**fork**

FORKSFUL ▶**fork**

FORKTAIL n bird belonging
to the flycatcher family

**FORKY, FORKIER,
FORKIEST** adj forked

FORLANA, -S n Venetian
dance

FORLEND, -S, FORLENT
variant of ▶**forelend**

FORLESE, -S, FORLORE vb
lose, forsake

FORLORN, -S adj lonely and
unhappy ▷ n forsaken
person

FORM, -ED, -S n shape or
appearance ▷ vb give a
(particular) shape to or take
a (particular) shape

FORMABLE ▶**form**

FORMABLY ▶**form**

FORMAL, -S adj of or
characterized by
conventions of behaviour
▷ n woman's evening gown

FORMALIN n solution of
formaldehyde in water

FORMALLY ▶**formal**

FORMALS ▶**formal**

FORMANT, -S n any of
several frequency ranges

FORMAT, -ED, -S n size and
shape of a publication ▷ vb
arrange in a format

FORMATE, -S n type of salt
or ester of formic acid ▷ vb
fly aircraft in formation

FORMATED ▶**format**

FORMATES ▶**formate**

FORMATS ▶**format**

FORME, -S n type matter
assembled and ready for
printing

FORMED ▶**form**

FORMEE, -S n type of
heraldic cross

FORMER, -S adj of an earlier
time, previous ▷ n person or
thing that forms or shapes

FORMERLY adv in the past

FORMERS ▶**former**

FORMES ▶**forme**

FORMFUL adj imaginative

FORMIATE variant of
▶**formate**

FORMIC adj of, relating to,
or derived from ants

FORMICA, -S n tradename
for any of various laminated
plastic sheets

FORMING, -S ▶**form**

FORMLESS adj without a
definite shape or form

FORMOL, -S same as
▶**formalin**

FORMS ▶**form**

FORMULA, -E, -S n written
form of a scientific or
mathematical rule

FORMULAR adj of or
relating to formulas ▷ n
model or set form

FORMULAS ▶**formula**

FORMWORK n
arrangement of wooden
boards to shape concrete

FORMYL, -S n the
monovalent group CHO-

FORNENST prep situated
against or facing towards

FORNENT variant of
▶**fornenst**

FORNICAL ▶**fornix**

FORNIX, FORNICES n any
archlike structure

FORPET, -S n quarter of a
peck (measure)

FORPINE, -D, -S vb waste
away

FORPIT, -S variant of ▶**forpet**

FORRAD, -ER, -S adv Scots
word for forward ▷ n
forward

FORRAY, -ED, -S archaic
variant of ▶**foray**

FORREN adj old word for
foreign

FORRIT adv Scots word for
forward(s)

FORSAID ▶**forsay**

FORSAKE, -S vb withdraw
support or friendship from

FORSAKEN adj completely
deserted or helpless

FORSAKER ▶**forsake**

FORSAKES ▶**forsake**

FORSAY, FORSAID, -S vb
renounce

FORSLACK vb be neglectful

FORSLOE, -D, -S variant of
▶**forslow**

FORSLOW, -S vb hinder

FORSOOK past tense of
▶**forsake**

FORSOOTH adv indeed

FORSPEAK, FORSPOKE vb
bewitch

FORSPEND, FORSPENT vb
exhaust

FORSPOKE ▶**forspeak**

FORSWATT adj sweat-
covered

FORSWEAR, FORSWORE
vb renounce or reject

FORSWINK vb exhaust
through toil

FORSWORE ▶**forswear**

FORSWORN past participle of
▶**forswear**

FORSWUNK adj overworked

FORT, -ED, -ING, -S n
fortified building or place
▷ vb fortify

FORTE n thing at which a
person excels ▷ adv loudly

FORTED ▶**fort**

FORTES ▶**fortis**

FORTH adv forwards, out, or
away ▷ prep out of

FORTHINK vb regret

FORTHY adv old word for
therefore

FORTIES ▶**forty**

FORTIETH adj being the
number of forty in order ▷ n
one of 40 equal parts

FORTIFY vb make (a place)
defensible, as by building
walls

FORTING ▶**fort**

FORTIS, FORTES adj (of a
consonant) articulated with
considerable muscular
tension ▷ n type of
consonantal pronunciation

FORTLET, -S ▶**fort**

FORTRESS n large fort or
fortified town ▷ vb protect
with or as if with a fortress

FORTS ▶**fort**

FORTUITY n chance or
accidental occurrence

FORTUNE, -D, -S n luck, esp
when favourable ▷ vb befall

FORTY, FORTIES n four
times ten

FORTYISH ▶ **forty**
FORUM, FORA, -S *n*
meeting or medium for open
discussion or debate
FORWARD *same as*
▶ **forwards**
FORWARDS *adv* towards or
at a place further ahead in
space or time
FORWARN, -S *archaic word
for* ▶ **forbid**
FORWASTE *vb* lay waste
FORWEARY *vb* exhaust
FORWENT *past tense of*
▶ **forgo**
FORWHY *adv* for what
reason
FORWORN *adj* weary
FORZA, FORZE *n* force
FORZANDO, FORZANDI
another word for > **sforzando**
FORZATO, FORZATI, -S
variant of ▶ **forzando**
FORZE ▶ **forza**
FOSS *same as* ▶ **fosse**
FOSSA, -E, -S *n* anatomical
depression, trench, or
hollow area
FOSSATE *adj* having cavities
or depressions
FOSSE, -S *n* ditch or moat,
esp one dug as a fortification
FOSSED *adj* having a ditch or
moat
FOSSES ▶ **fosse**
FOSSETTE *n* small
depression or fossa, as in a
bone
FOSSICK, -S *vb* search, esp
for gold or precious stones
FOSSIL, -S *n* hardened
remains of an animal or
plant preserved in rock ▷ *adj*
of, like, or being a fossil
FOSSOR, -S *n* grave digger
FOSSULA, -E *n* small fossa
FOSTER, -ED, -S *vb* promote
the growth or development
of ▷ *adj* of or involved in
fostering a child
FOSTERER ▶ **foster**
FOSTERS ▶ **foster**
FOSTRESS *n* female fosterer
FOTHER, -ED, -S *vb* stop a
leak in a ship's hull
FOU, -ER, -EST, -S *adj* full ▷ *n*
bushel
FOUAT, -S *n* succulent
pink-flowered plant
FOUD, -S *n* sheriff in Orkney
and Shetland
FOUDRIE, -S *n* foud's district
or office
FOUDS ▶ **foud**
FOUER ▶ **fou**
FOUEST ▶ **fou**

FOUET, -S *n* archaic word for
a whip
FOUETTE, -S *n* step in ballet
FOUGADE, -S *n* booby-
trapped pit or type of mine
FOUGASSE *n* type of bread
made with olive oil
FOUGHT ▶ **fight**
FOUGHTEN ▶ **fight**
FOUGHTY *adj* musty
FOUL, -ED, -ER, -EST, -S *adj*
loathsome or offensive ▷ *n*
violation of the rules ▷ *vb*
make dirty or polluted
FOULARD, -S *n* soft light
fabric
FOULDER, -S *vb* flash like
lightning
FOULE, -S *n* type of woollen
cloth
FOULED ▶ **foul**
FOULER ▶ **foul**
FOULES ▶ **foule**
FOULEST ▶ **foul**
FOULIE, -S *n* bad mood
FOULING, -S ▶ **foul**
FOULLY ▶ **foul**
FOULMART *n* polecat
FOULNESS *n* state or quality
of being foul
FOULS ▶ **foul**
FOUMART, -S *former name for
the* ▶ **polecat**
FOUND, -ED, -ING, -S *vb* set
up or establish (an
institution, etc)
FOUNDER, -S *vb* break
down or fail ▷ *n* person who
establishes an institution,
etc
FOUNDING ▶ **found**
FOUNDRY *n* place where
metal is melted and cast
FOUNDS ▶ **found**
FOUNT, -S *same as* ▶ **font**
FOUNTAIN *n* jet of water
FOUNTFUL *adj* full of springs
FOUNTS ▶ **fount**
FOUR, -S *n* one more than
three
FOURBALL *n* type of golf
match for two pairs
FOURCHEE *n* type of
heraldic cross
FOUREYED *adj* wearing
spectacles
FOURFOLD *adj* having four
times as many or as much
▷ *adv* by four times as many
or as much
FOURGON, -S *n* long
covered wagon
FOURPLAY *n* supply of
television, internet, landline
and mobile phone services
by one provider

FOURPLEX *n* building that
contains four separate
dwellings
FOURS ▶ **four**
FOURSES *n* snack eaten at
four o'clock
FOURSOME *n* group of four
people
FOURTEEN *n* four and ten
FOURTH, -S *n* number four
in a series ▷ *adj* of or being
number four in a series
FOURTHLY *adv* in the fourth
place or position
FOURTHS ▶ **fourth**
FOUS ▶ **fou**
FOUSSA, -S *n* Madagascan
civet-like animal
FOUSTY, FOUSTIER *archaic
variant of* ▶ **fusty**
FOUTER, -ED, -S *same as*
▶ **footer**
FOUTH, -S *n* abundance
FOUTRA, -S *n* fig; expression
of contempt
FOUTRE, -D, -S, FOUTRING
same as ▶ **footer**
FOVEA, -E, -S *n* any small pit
in the surface of a bodily
organ or part
FOVEAL ▶ **fovea**
FOVEAS ▶ **fovea**
FOVEATE ▶ **fovea**
FOVEATED ▶ **fovea**
FOVEOLA, -E, -S *n* small fovea
FOVEOLAR ▶ **foveola**
FOVEOLAS ▶ **foveola**
FOVEOLE, -S *same as*
▶ **foveola**
FOVEOLET *same as*
▶ **foveola**
FOWL, -ED, -S *n* domestic
cock or hen ▷ *vb* hunt or
snare wild birds
FOWLER, -S ▶ **fowling**
FOWLING, -S *n* shooting or
trapping of birds for sport or
as a livelihood
FOWLPOX *n* viral infection
of poultry and other birds
FOWLS ▶ **fowl**
FOWTH, -S *variant of* ▶ **fouth**
FOX, -ED, -ES *n* reddish-
brown bushy-tailed animal
of the dog family ▷ *vb*
perplex or deceive
FOXBERRY *n* lingonberry
FOXED ▶ **fox**
FOXES ▶ **fox**
FOXFIRE, -S *n* glow emitted
by certain fungi
FOXFISH *n* type of shark
FOXGLOVE *n* tall plant with
purple or white flowers
FOXHOLE, -S *n* small pit dug
for protection

F

FOXHOUND n dog bred for hunting foxes

FOXHUNT, -S n hunting of foxes with hounds ▷ vb hunt foxes with hounds

FOXIE, -S n fox terrier

FOXIER ▶ foxy

FOXIES ▶ foxie

FOXIEST ▶ foxy

FOXILY ▶ foxy

FOXINESS ▶ foxy

FOXING, -S n piece of leather used on part of the upper of a shoe

FOXLIKE ▶ fox

FOXSHARK n thresher shark

FOXSHIP, -S n cunning

FOXSKIN, -S adj made from the skin of a fox ▷ n skin of a fox

FOXTAIL, -S n type of grass

FOXTROT, -S n ballroom dance with slow and quick steps ▷ vb perform this dance

FOXY, FOXIER, FOXIEST adj of or like a fox, esp in craftiness

FOY, -S n loyalty

This unusual word for loyalty can be a good scorer.

FOYBOAT, -S n small rowing boat

FOYER, -S n entrance hall in a theatre, cinema, or hotel

FOYLE, -D, -S, FOYLING variant of ▶ foil

FOYNE, -D, -S, FOYNING variant of ▶ foin

FOYS ▶ foy

FOZIER ▶ fozy

FOZIEST ▶ fozy

FOZINESS ▶ fozy

FOZY, FOZIER, FOZIEST adj spongy

FRA, -S n brother: a title given to an Italian monk or friar

FRAB, -BED, -BING, -S vb nag

FRABBIT adj peevish

FRABJOUS adj splendid

FRABS ▶ frab

FRACAS, -ES n noisy quarrel

FRACK, -ED, -S adj bold ▷ vb release oil or gas from rock by fracking

FRACKER, -S n individual or company which engages in fracking

FRACKING n method of releasing oil or gas from rock

FRACKS ▶ frack

FRACT, -ED, -ING, -S vb break

FRACTAL, -S n mathematically repeating structure ▷ adj relating to or involving fractals

FRACTED ▶ fract

FRACTI ▶ fractus

FRACTING ▶ fract

FRACTION n numerical quantity that is not a whole number ▷ vb divide

FRACTS ▶ fract

FRACTUR, -S variant of ▶ fraktur

FRACTURE n breaking, esp of a bone ▷ vb break

FRACTURS ▶ fractur

FRACTUS, FRACTI n ragged-shaped cloud formation

FRAE Scot word for ▶ from

FRAENUM, FRAENA, -S n fold of membrane or skin that supports an organ

FRAG, -GED, -S vb kill or wound (a fellow soldier or superior officer) deliberately

FRAGGING ▶ frag

FRAGILE, -R adj easily broken or damaged

FRAGMENT n piece broken off ▷ vb break into pieces

FRAGOR, -S n sudden sound

FRAGRANT adj sweet-smelling

FRAGS ▶ frag

FRAIL, -ER, -EST, -S adj physically weak ▷ n rush basket for figs or raisins

FRAILISH ▶ frail

FRAILLY ▶ frail

FRAILS ▶ frail

FRAILTEE variant of ▶ frailty

FRAILTY n physical or moral weakness

FRAIM, -S n stranger

FRAISE, -D, -S, FRAISING n neck ruff worn during the 16th century ▷ vb provide a rampart with a palisade

FRAKTUR, -S n style of typeface

FRAMABLE ▶ frame

FRAME, -D, -S n structure giving shape or support ▷ vb put together, construct

FRAMER, -S ▶ frame

FRAMES ▶ frame

FRAMING, -S n frame, framework, or system of frames

FRAMPAL same as ▶ frampold

FRAMPLER n quarrelsome person

FRAMPOLD adj peevish

FRANC, -S n monetary unit

FRANCISE same as ▶ francize

FRANCIUM n radioactive metallic element

FRANCIZE vb make French

FRANCO adj post-free

FRANCS ▶ franc

FRANION, -S n lover, paramour

FRANK, -ED, -EST, -ING, -S adj honest and straightforward in speech or attitude ▷ n official mark on a letter permitting delivery ▷ vb put such a mark on (a letter)

FRANKER, -S ▶ frank

FRANKEST ▶ frank

FRANKING ▶ frank

FRANKLIN n (in 14th- and 15th-century England) a landholder of free but not noble birth

FRANKLY adv in truth

FRANKS ▶ frank

FRANKUM, -S n spruce resin

FRANTIC adj distracted with rage, grief, joy, etc

FRANZY, FRANZIER adj irritable

FRAP, -PED, -PING, -S vb lash down or together

FRAPE adj tightly bound

FRAPPANT adj striking, vivid

FRAPPE, -S adj (of drinks) chilled ▷ n type of drink

FRAPPED ▶ frap

FRAPPEE same as ▶ frappe

FRAPPES ▶ frappe

FRAPPING ▶ frap

FRAPS ▶ frap

FRAS ▶ fra

FRASCATI n dry or semisweet white wine from the Lazio region of Italy

FRASS, -ES n refuse left by insects and insect larvae

FRAT, -S n member of a fraternity

FRATCH, -ES n quarrel

FRATCHY adj quarrelsome

FRATE, FRATI n friar

FRATER, -S n mendicant friar or a lay brother in a monastery or priory

FRATERY ▶ frater

FRATI ▶ frate

FRATRY, FRATRIES ▶ frater

FRATS ▶ frat

FRAU, -S n married German woman

FRAUD, -S n (criminal) deception, swindle

FRAUDFUL ▶ fraud

FRAUDS ▶ fraud

FRAUGHAN n small shrub

FRAUGHT, -S adj tense or anxious ▷ vb archaic word for load ▷ n archaic word for freight

FRAULEIN n unmarried German woman

FRAUS ▶ frau
FRAUTAGE n cargo
FRAWZEY, -S n celebration
FRAY, -ED, -S n noisy quarrel or conflict ▷ vb make or become ragged at the edge
FRAYING, -S ▶ fray
FRAYS ▶ fray
FRAZIL, -S n small pieces of ice that form in turbulently moving water
FRAZZLE, -D, -S n exhausted state ▷ vb tire out
FREAK, -ED, -ING, -S n abnormal person or thing ▷ adj abnormal ▷ vb streak with colour
FREAKERY n as in **control freakery** obsessive need to be in control of events
FREAKFUL variant of ▶ freakish
FREAKIER ▶ freaky
FREAKILY ▶ freaky
FREAKING ▶ freak
FREAKISH adj of, related to, or characteristic of a freak
FREAKOUT n heightened emotional state
FREAKS ▶ freak
FREAKY, FREAKIER adj weird, peculiar
FRECKLE, -S n small brown spot on the skin ▷ vb mark or become marked with freckles
FRECKLED ▶ freckle
FRECKLES ▶ freckle
FRECKLY ▶ freckle
FREDAINE n escapade
FREE, -D, -ING, -S, -ST adj able to act at will, not compelled or restrained ▷ vb release, liberate
FREEBEE, -S variant of ▶ freebie
FREEBIE, -S n something provided without charge ▷ adj without charge
FREEBOOT vb act as a freebooter
FREEBORN adj not born in slavery
FREED ▶ free
FREEDMAN, FREEDMEN n man freed from slavery
FREEDOM, -S n right of unrestricted use or access
FREEFALL adj as in **freefall parachuting** parachuting in which the jumper manoeuvres in free fall before opening the parachute
FREEFORM n irregular flowing shape, often used in industrial or fabric design

▷ adj freely flowing, spontaneous
FREEGAN, -S n person who avoids buying consumer goods
FREEHAND adj drawn without guiding instruments
FREEHOLD n tenure of land for life without restrictions ▷ adj of or held by freehold
FREEING ▶ free
FREEKEH, -S n type of cereal
FREELOAD vb act as a freeloader
FREELY ▶ free
FREEMAN, FREEMEN n person who has been given the freedom of a city
FREEMIUM n free service with paid additional options
FREENESS ▶ free
FREEPOST adj (of post) able to be posted without charge
FREER, -S n liberator
FREERIDE n extreme form of skiing, snowboarding, or mountain biking
FREERS ▶ freer
FREES ▶ free
FREESIA, -S n plant with fragrant tubular flowers
FREEST ▶ free
FREET, -S n omen or superstition
FREETIER ▶ freety
FREETS ▶ freet
FREETY, FREETIER adj superstitious
FREEWARE n computer software that may be distributed and used without payment
FREEWAY, -S n motorway
FREEWILL n apparent human ability to make choices that are not externally determined
FREEZE, -S, FREEZING, FROZE, FROZEN vb turn from liquid to solid by the reduction of temperature ▷ n period of very cold weather
FREEZER, -S n insulated cabinet for cold-storage of perishable foods
FREEZES ▶ freeze
FREEZING ▶ freeze
FREIGHT, -S n commercial transport of goods ▷ vb send by freight
FREIT, -S variant of ▶ freet
FREITIER ▶ freity
FREITS ▶ freit
FREITY, FREITIER adj superstitious

FREMD, -S n strange person or thing
FREMIT, -S same as ▶ fremd
FREMITUS n vibration felt by a hand placed on the body
FRENA ▶ frenum
FRENCH, -ED, -ES vb cut (food) into thin strips
FRENEMY n supposed friend who behaves in a treacherous manner
FRENETIC adj uncontrolled, excited ▷ n madman
FRENNE, -S variant of ▶ fremd
FRENULA ▶ frenulum
FRENULAR ▶ frenulum
FRENULUM, FRENULA n group of bristles on the hind wing of some moths
FRENUM, FRENA, -S same as ▶ fraenum
FRENZIED adj filled with or as if with frenzy
FRENZIES ▶ frenzy
FRENZILY ▶ frenzy
FRENZY, FRENZIES n wild excitement or agitation ▷ vb make frantic
FREON, -S n tradename for an aerosol refrigerant
FREQUENT adj happening often ▷ vb visit habitually
FRERE, -S n friar
FRESCADE n shady place or cool walk
FRESCO, -ED, -ES, -S n watercolour painting done on wet plaster ▷ vb paint a fresco
FRESCOER ▶ fresco
FRESCOES ▶ fresco
FRESCOS ▶ fresco
FRESH, -ED, -ES, -EST, -ING adj newly made, acquired, etc ▷ adv recently ▷ vb freshen
FRESHEN, -S vb make or become fresh or fresher
FRESHER, -S n first-year student
FRESHES ▶ fresh
FRESHEST ▶ fresh
FRESHET, -S n sudden overflowing of a river
FRESHIE, -S n (in Australia) freshwater crocodile
FRESHING ▶ fresh
FRESHISH ▶ fresh
FRESHLY ▶ fresh
FRESHMAN, FRESHMEN same as ▶ fresher
FRESNEL, -S n unit of frequency
FRET, -S, -TED, -TING vb be worried ▷ n worried state
FRETFUL adj irritable

FRETLESS ▸ fret

FRETS ▸ fret

FRETSAW, -S n fine saw with a narrow blade, used for fretwork

FRETSOME adj vexing

FRETTED ▸ fret

FRETTER, -S ▸ fret

FRETTIER ▸ fretty

FRETTING ▸ fret

FRETTY, FRETTIER adj decorated with frets

FRETWORK n decorative carving in wood

FRIABLE adj easily crumbled

FRIAND, -S n small almond cake

FRIANDE, -S variant of ▸ friand

FRIANDS ▸ friand

FRIAR, -S n member of a male Roman Catholic religious order

FRIARIES ▸ friary

FRIARLY ▸ friar

FRIARS ▸ friar

FRIARY, FRIARIES n house of friars

FRIB, -S n piece of wool removed from a fleece during classing

FRIBBLE, -D, -S vb fritter away ▷ n wasteful or frivolous person or action ▷ adj frivolous

FRIBBLER ▸ fribble

FRIBBLES ▸ fribble

FRIBS ▸ frib

FRICADEL variant of ▸ frikkadel

FRICANDO n larded and braised veal fillet

FRICHT, -ED, -S vb Scots word for frighten

FRICOT, -S n Acadian stew of potatoes and meat or fish

FRICTION n resistance met with by a body moving over another

FRIDGE, -D, -S, FRIDGING n apparatus in which food and drinks are kept cool ▷ vb archaic word for chafe

FRIED ▸ fry

FRIEND, -ED, -S n person whom one knows well and likes ▷ vb befriend

FRIENDLY adj showing or expressing liking ▷ n match played for its own sake and not as part of a competition

FRIENDS ▸ friend

FRIER, -S same as ▸ fryer

FRIES ▸ fry

FRIEZE, -D, -S, FRIEZING n ornamental band on a wall ▷ vb give a nap to (cloth)

FRIG, -ES, -GED, -GING, -S vb behave foolishly or aimlessly ▷ n fridge

FRIGATE, -S n medium-sized fast warship

FRIGES ▸ frig

FRIGGED ▸ frig

FRIGGER, -S ▸ frig

FRIGGING ▸ frig

FRIGHT, -ED, -S n sudden fear or alarm

FRIGHTEN vb scare or terrify

FRIGHTS ▸ fright

FRIGID, -ER adj formal or stiff in temperament

FRIGIDLY ▸ frigid

FRIGOT, -S variant of ▸ frigate

FRIGS ▸ frig

FRIJOL, -ES n variety of bean

FRIJOLE variant of ▸ frijol

FRIJOLES ▸ frijol

FRILL, -ED, -ING, -S n gathered strip of fabric attached at one edge ▷ vb adorn or fit with a frill or frills

FRILLER, -S ▸ frill

FRILLERY n fabric or clothing arranged in frills

FRILLIER ▸ frilly

FRILLIES pl n flimsy women's underwear

FRILLING ▸ frill

FRILLS ▸ frill

FRILLY, FRILLIER adj with a frill or frills

FRINGE, -D, -S n hair cut short and hanging over the forehead ▷ vb decorate with a fringe ▷ adj (of theatre) unofficial or unconventional

FRINGIER ▸ fringy

FRINGING n act of fringing

FRINGY, FRINGIER adj having a fringe

FRIPON, -S n rogue

FRIPPER, -S n dealer in old clothes

FRIPPERY n useless ornamentation

FRIPPET, -S n frivolous or flamboyant young woman

FRIS, -ES n fine frieze-like fabric

FRISBEE, -S n tradename of a light plastic disc for throwing in a game

FRISE n fabric with a long nap used for upholstery and rugs

FRISEE, -S n endive

FRISES ▸ fris

FRISETTE, -S n curly or frizzed fringe, often an artificial hairpiece, worn by women on the forehead

FRISEUR, -S n hairdresser

FRISK, -ED, -ING, -S vb move or leap playfully ▷ n playful movement

FRISKA, -S n (in Hungarian music) the fast movement of a piece

FRISKED ▸ frisk

FRISKER, -S ▸ frisk

FRISKET, -S n part of a hand printing press

FRISKFUL ▸ frisk

FRISKIER ▸ frisky

FRISKILY ▸ frisky

FRISKING ▸ frisk

FRISKS ▸ frisk

FRISKY, FRISKIER adj lively or high-spirited

FRISSON, -S n shiver of fear or excitement

FRIST, -ED, -ING, -S archaic word for ▸ postpone

FRISURE, -S n styling the hair into curls

FRIT, -S, -TED, -TING n basic materials for making glass, glazes for pottery, etc ▷ vb fuse (materials) in making frit

FRITES pl n chipped potatoes

FRITFLY n type of small black fly

FRITH, -S same as ▸ firth

FRITS ▸ frit

FRITT, -S same as ▸ frit

FRITTATA n flat thick Italian omelette

FRITTED ▸ frit

FRITTER, -S n piece of food fried in batter ▷ vb waste or squander

FRITTING ▸ frit

FRITTS ▸ fritt

FRITURE, -S archaic word for ▸ fritter

FRITZ, -ED, -ES, -ING n as in on the fritz in a state of disrepair ▷ vb (of an appliance, etc) become broken or start malfunctioning

FRIULANO n type of Italian cheese

FRIVOL, -ED, -S vb behave frivolously

FRIVOLER ▸ frivol

FRIVOLS ▸ frivol

FRIZ variant of ▸ frizz

FRIZADO, -S n fine frieze-like fabric

FRIZE, -D, -S, FRIZING n coarse woollen fabric ▷ vb freeze

FRIZER, -S n person who gives nap to cloth

FRIZES ▸ frize

FRIZETTE same as ▸ frisette

FRIZING ▸ frize

FRIZZ, -ED, -ES, -ING vb form (hair) into stiff wiry curls ▷ n hair that has been frizzed

FRIZZER, -S ▸ frizz

FRIZZES ▸ frizz

FRIZZIER ▸ frizzy

FRIZZIES pl n condition of having frizzy hair

FRIZZILY ▸ frizzy

FRIZZING ▸ frizz

FRIZZLE, -D, -S n dress ▷ vb cook or heat until crisp and shrivelled ▷ n tight curl

FRIZZLER ▸ frizzle

FRIZZLES ▸ frizzle

FRIZZLY ▸ frizzle

FRIZZY, FRIZZIER adj (of the hair) in tight crisp wiry curls

FRO, -S adv away ▷ n afro

FROCK, -ED, -S n dress ▷ vb invest (a person) with the office or status of a cleric

FROCKING n coarse material suitable for making frocks or work clothes

FROCKS ▸ frock

FROE, -S n cutting tool

FROG, -S n type of amphibian

FROGBIT, -S n floating aquatic Eurasian plant

FROGEYE, -S n plant disease

FROGEYED adj affected by frogeye

FROGEYES ▸ frogeye

FROGFISH n type of angler fish

FROGGED adj decorated with frogging

FROGGERY n place where frogs are kept

FROGGIER ▸ froggy

FROGGING n decorative fastening of looped braid on a coat

FROGGY, FROGGIER adj like a frog

FROGLET, -S n young frog

FROGLIKE ▸ frog

FROGLING n young frog

FROGMAN, FROGMEN n swimmer with equipment for working under water

FROGS ▸ frog

FROIDEUR n coldness

FROING, -S n as in **toing and froing** going back and forth

FROISE, -S n kind of pancake

FROLIC, -S vb run and play in a lively way ▷ n lively and merry behaviour ▷ adj full of merriment or fun

FROLICKY adj frolicsome

FROLICS ▸ frolic

FROM prep indicating the point of departure, source, etc

FROMAGE, -S n as in **fromage frais** low-fat soft cheese

FROMENTY same as ▸ frumenty

FROND, -S n long leaf or leaflike part of a fern, palm, or seaweed

FRONDAGE n fronds collectively

FRONDED adj having fronds

FRONDENT adj leafy

FRONDEUR n 17th-century French rebel

FRONDOSE adj leafy or like a leaf

FRONDOUS adj leafy or like a leaf

FRONDS ▸ frond

FRONS, FRONTES n plate on the head of some insects

FRONT, -ED, -EST, -ING, -S n fore part ▷ adj of or at the front ▷ vb face (onto)

FRONTAGE n facade of a building

FRONTAL, -S adj of, at, or in the front ▷ n decorative hanging for the front of an altar

FRONTED ▸ front

FRONTER, -S n front side

FRONTES ▸ frons

FRONTEST ▸ front

FRONTIER n area of a country bordering on another

FRONTING ▸ front

FRONTLET n small decorative loop worn on a woman's forehead

FRONTMAN, FRONTMEN n nominal leader who lacks real power or authority

FRONTON, -S n wall against which pelota or jai alai is played

FRONTOON variant of ▸ fronton

FRONTS ▸ front

FRORE adj very cold or frosty

FROREN variant of ▸ frore

FRORN variant of ▸ frore

FRORNE variant of ▸ frore

FRORY variant of ▸ frore

FROS ▸ fro

FROSH, -ES n freshman

FROST, -S n white frozen dew or mist ▷ vb become covered with frost

FROSTBIT > frostbite

FROSTED, -S adj (of glass) having a rough surface to make it opaque ▷ n type of ice cream dish

FROSTIER ▸ frosty

FROSTILY ▸ frosty

FROSTING n sugar icing

FROSTNIP n milder form of frostbite

FROSTS ▸ frost

FROSTY, FROSTIER adj characterized or covered by frost

FROTH, -ED, -S n mass of small bubbles ▷ vb foam

FROTHER, -S ▸ froth

FROTHERY n anything insubstantial, like froth

FROTHIER ▸ frothy

FROTHILY ▸ froth

FROTHING n act of frothing

FROTHS ▸ froth

FROTHY, FROTHIER ▸ froth

FROTTAGE n act or process of taking a rubbing from a rough surface for a work of art

FROUFROU n swishing sound, as made by a long silk dress

FROUGHY adj rancid

FROUNCE, -D, -S vb wrinkle

FROUZIER ▸ frouzy

FROUZILY adv in a frouzy manner

FROUZY, FROUZIER same as ▸ frowzy

FROW, -S same as ▸ froe

FROWARD adj obstinate

FROWARDS same as ▸ froward

FROWIE, -R, -ST variant of ▸ froughy

FROWN, -ED, -ING, -S vb wrinkle one's brows in worry, anger, or thought ▷ n frowning expression

FROWNER, -S ▸ frown

FROWNIER ▸ frowny

FROWNING ▸ frown

FROWNS ▸ frown

FROWNY, FROWNIER adj displaying a frown

FROWS ▸ frow

FROWSIER ▸ frowsy

FROWSILY adv in a frowsy manner

FROWST, -ED, -S n hot and stale atmosphere ▷ vb abandon oneself to such an atmosphere

FROWSTER ▸ frowst

FROWSTS ▸ frowst

FROWSTY adj stale or musty

FROWSY, FROWSIER same as ▸ frowzy

FROWY variant of ▸ froughy

FROWZIER ▸ frowzy

FROWZILY ▶ frowzy
FROWZY, FROWZIER adj dirty or unkempt
FROZE ▶ freeze
FROZEN ▶ freeze
FROZENLY ▶ freeze
FRUCTAN, -S n type of polymer of fructose
FRUCTED adj fruit-bearing
FRUCTIFY vb (cause to) bear fruit
FRUCTIVE adj fruitful
FRUCTOSE n crystalline sugar occurring in many fruits
FRUG, -GED, -GING, -S vb perform the frug, a 1960s dance
FRUGAL adj thrifty, sparing
FRUGALLY ▶ frugal
FRUGGED ▶ frug
FRUGGING ▶ frug
FRUGS ▶ frug
FRUICT, -S obsolete variant of ▶ fruit
FRUIT, -ED, -ING, -S n part of a plant containing seeds ▷ vb bear fruit
FRUITAGE n process, state, or season of producing fruit
FRUITED ▶ fruit
FRUITER, -S n fruit grower
FRUITERY n fruitage
FRUITFUL adj useful or productive
FRUITIER ▶ fruity
FRUITILY ▶ fruity
FRUITING ▶ fruit
FRUITION n fulfilment of something worked for or desired
FRUITIVE adj enjoying
FRUITLET n small fruit
FRUITS ▶ fruit
FRUITY, FRUITIER adj of or like fruit
FRUMENTY n kind of porridge made from hulled wheat boiled with milk, sweetened, and spiced
FRUMP, -ED, -ING, -S n dowdy person ▷ vb mock or taunt
FRUMPIER ▶ frumpy
FRUMPILY ▶ frumpy
FRUMPING ▶ frump
FRUMPISH same as ▶ frumpy
FRUMPLE, -D, -S vb wrinkle or crumple
FRUMPS ▶ frump
FRUMPY, FRUMPIER adj (of a person, clothes, etc) dowdy or unattractive
FRUSH, -ED, -ES, -ING vb break into pieces

FRUST, -S n fragment
FRUSTA ▶ frustum
FRUSTS ▶ frust
FRUSTULE n hard siliceous cell wall of a diatom
FRUSTUM, FRUSTA, -S n part of a solid between the base and a plane parallel to the base
FRUTEX, FRUTICES n shrub
FRUTIFY vb malapropism for notify
FRY, FRIED, FRIES vb cook or be cooked in fat or oil ▷ n dish of fried food
FRYABLE ▶ fry
FRYBREAD n Native American fried bread
FRYER, -S n person or thing that fries
FRYING, -S ▶ fry
FRYPAN, -S n long-handled shallow pan used for frying
FUB, -BED, -BING, -S vb
FUBAR adj irreparably damaged or bungled
FUBBED ▶ fub
FUBBERY n cheating
FUBBIER ▶ fubby
FUBBIEST ▶ fubby
FUBBING ▶ fub
FUBBY, FUBBIER, FUBBIEST adj short and stout
FUBS ▶ fub
FUBSY, FUBSIER, FUBSIEST adj short and stout
FUCHSIA, -S n ornamental shrub
FUCHSIN, -S n greenish crystalline substance
FUCHSINE same as ▶ fuchsin
FUCHSINS ▶ fuchsin
FUCHSITE n form of mica
FUCI ▶ fucus
FUCOID, -S n type of seaweed
FUCOIDAL adj of or relating to fucoid
FUCOIDS ▶ fucoid
FUCOSE, -S n aldose
FUCOUS same as ▶ fucoidal
FUCUS, FUCI, -ES n type of seaweed
FUCUSED adj archaic word meaning made up with cosmetics
FUCUSES ▶ fucus
FUD, -S n rabbit's tail
FUDDIER ▶ fuddy
FUDDIES ▶ fuddy
FUDDIEST ▶ fuddy
FUDDLE, -D, -S, FUDDLING vb cause to be intoxicated or confused ▷ n confused state

FUDDLER, -S ▶ fuddle
FUDDLES ▶ fuddle
FUDDLING ▶ fuddle
FUDDY, FUDDIER, FUDDIES, FUDDIEST n old-fashioned person ▷ adj old-fashioned
FUDGE, -D, -S, FUDGING n soft caramel-like sweet ▷ vb make (an issue) less clear deliberately ▷ interj mild exclamation of annoyance
FUDGIER ▶ fudgy
FUDGIEST ▶ fudgy
FUDGING ▶ fudge
FUDGY, FUDGIER, FUDGIEST adj resembling or containing fudge
FUDS ▶ fud
FUEHRER, -S n leader: applied esp to Adolf Hitler
FUEL, -ED, -ING, -LED, -LING, -S n substance burned or treated to produce heat or power ▷ vb provide with fuel
FUELER, -S ▶ fuel
FUELING ▶ fuel
FUELLED ▶ fuel
FUELLER, -S ▶ fuel
FUELLING ▶ fuel
FUELS ▶ fuel
FUELWOOD n any wood used as a fuel
FUERO, -S n Spanish code of laws
FUFF, -ED, -ING, -S vb puff
FUFFIER ▶ fuffy
FUFFIEST ▶ fuffy
FUFFING ▶ fuff
FUFFS ▶ fuff
FUFFY, FUFFIER, FUFFIEST adj puffy
FUG, -GED, -GING, -S n hot stale atmosphere ▷ vb sit in a fug
FUGACITY n property of a gas that expresses its tendency to escape or expand
FUGAL adj of, relating to, or in the style of a fugue
FUGALLY ▶ fugal
FUGATO, -S adj in the manner or style of a fugue ▷ n movement, section, or piece in this style
FUGGED ▶ fug
FUGGIER ▶ fuggy
FUGGIEST ▶ fuggy
FUGGILY ▶ fug
FUGGING ▶ fug
FUGGY, FUGGIER, FUGGIEST ▶ fug
FUGHETTA n short fugue
FUGIE, -S n runaway

FUGIO, -S *n* former US copper coin

FUGITIVE *n* person who flees, esp from arrest or pursuit ▷ *adj* fleeing

FUGLE, -D, -S, FUGLING *vb* act as a fugleman

FUGLEMAN, FUGLEMEN *n* (formerly) a soldier used as an example for those learning drill

FUGLES ▸ fugle

FUGLING ▸ fugle

FUGS ▸ fug

FUGU, -S *n* puffer fish

U is not normally a desirable letter to have on your rack unless you happen to have the Q, and two Us can be trouble. This Japanese fish can help you out.

FUGUE, -D, -S, FUGUING *n* type of musical composition ▷ *vb* be in a dreamlike, altered state of consciousness

FUGUIST, -S *n* composer of fugues

FUGUS ▸ fugu

FUHRER, -S *same as* ▸ fuehrer

FUJI, -S *n* type of African music

FULCRA ▸ fulcrum

FULCRATE ▸ fulcrum

FULCRUM, FULCRA, -S *n* pivot about which a lever turns

FULFIL, -S *vb* achieve (a desire or promise)

FULFILL, -S *same as* ▸ fulfil

FULFILS ▸ fulfil

FULGENCY ▸ fulgent

FULGENT *adj* shining brilliantly

FULGID *same as* ▸ fulgent

FULGOR, -S *n* brilliance

FULGOUR, -S *variant of* ▸ fulgor

FULGURAL > fulgurate

FULHAM, -S *n* loaded die

FULL, -ED, -EST, -ING, -S *adj* containing as much as or as many as possible ▷ *adv* completely ▷ *vb* clean, shrink, and press cloth

FULLAGE, -S *n* price charged for fulling cloth

FULLAM, -S *variant of* ▸ fulham

FULLAN, -S *variant of* ▸ fulham

FULLBACK *n* defensive player

FULLED ▸ full

FULLER, -ED, -S *n* person who fulls cloth for a living ▷ *vb* forge (a groove) or caulk (a riveted joint)

FULLERY *n* place where fulling is carried out

FULLEST ▸ full

FULLFACE *n* in printing, a letter that takes up full body size

FULLING ▸ full

FULLISH ▸ full

FULLNESS ▸ full

FULLS ▸ full

FULLY *adv* greatest degree or extent

FULMAR, -S *n* Arctic sea bird

FULMINE, -D, -S *vb* fulminate

FULMINIC *adj* as in **fulminic acid**, unstable volatile acid

FULNESS ▸ full

FULSOME, -R *adj* distastefully excessive or insincere

FULVID *variant of* ▸ fulvous

FULVOUS *adj* of a dull brownish-yellow colour

FUM, -S *n* phoenix, in Chinese mythology

FUMADO, -ES, -S *n* salted, smoked fish

FUMAGE, -S *n* tax on hearths

FUMARASE *n* enzyme

FUMARATE *n* salt of fumaric acid

FUMARIC *adj* as in **fumaric acid** colourless crystalline acid

FUMAROLE *n* vent in or near a volcano from which hot gases, esp steam, are emitted

FUMATORY *n* chamber where insects and fungi are destroyed by fumigation

FUMBLE, -D, -S, FUMBLING *vb* handle awkwardly ▷ *n* act of fumbling

FUMBLER, -S ▸ fumble

FUMBLES ▸ fumble

FUMBLING ▸ fumble

FUME, -S, FUMING *vb* be very angry

FUMED *adj* (of wood) having been exposed to ammonia fumes

FUMELESS ▸ fume

FUMELIKE ▸ fume

FUMER, -S ▸ fume

FUMEROLE *variant of* ▸ fumarole

FUMERS ▸ fumer

FUMES ▸ fume

FUMET, -S *n* liquor from cooking fish, meat, or game

FUMETTE, -S *variant of* ▸ fumet

FUMETTO, FUMETTI, -S *n* speech balloon in a comic or cartoon

FUMIER ▸ fumy

FUMIEST ▸ fumy

FUMIGANT *n* substance used for fumigating

FUMIGATE *vb* disinfect with fumes

FUMING ▸ fume

FUMINGLY ▸ fume

FUMITORY *n* chiefly European plant with spurred flowers, formerly used medicinally

FUMOSITY ▸ fume

FUMOUS ▸ fume

FUMS ▸ fum

FUMULUS, FUMULI *n* smokelike cloud

FUMY, FUMIER, FUMIEST ▸ fume

FUN, -NED, -NER, -NEST, -NING, -S *n* enjoyment or amusement ▷ *vb* trick ▷ *adj* providing amusement or entertainment

FUNBOARD *n* type of surfboard

FUNCKIA, -S *n* ornamental plant

FUNCTION *n* purpose something exists for ▷ *vb* operate or work

FUNCTOR, -S *n* performer of a function

FUND, -ED *n* stock of money for a special purpose ▷ *vb* provide money to

FUNDABLE ▸ fund

FUNDED ▸ fund

FUNDER, -S ▸ fund

FUNDI, -S *n* expert or boffin

FUNDIC ▸ fundus

FUNDIE, -S *n* fundamentalist

FUNDING, -S ▸ fund

FUNDIS ▸ fundi

FUNDLESS ▸ fund

FUNDS *pl n* money that is readily available

FUNDUS *n* base of an organ

FUNDY *n* fundamentalist

FUNEBRAL *variant of* > funebrial

FUNEBRE *adj* funereal or mournful

FUNERAL, -S *n* ceremony of burying or cremating a dead person

FUNERARY *adj* of or for a funeral

FUNEREAL *adj* gloomy or sombre

FUNEST *adj* lamentable

FUNFAIR, -S *n* entertainment with machines to ride on and stalls

FUNFEST, -S n enjoyable time

FUNG, -S same as ▸ **funk**

FUNGAL, -S adj of, derived from, or caused by a fungus or fungi ▸ n fungus or fungal infection

FUNGI ▸ **fungus**

FUNGIBLE n goods replaceable by similar goods of equal quantity or weight ▸ adj having the quality of fungibles

FUNGIC ▸ **fungus**

FUNGO, -ED, -ES, -ING, -S n in baseball, act of tossing and hitting the ball ▸ vb toss and hit a ball

FUNGOID, -S adj resembling a fungus

FUNGOING ▸ **fungo**

FUNGOS ▸ **fungo**

FUNGOUS adj appearing and spreading quickly like a fungus

FUNGS ▸ **fung**

FUNGUS, FUNGI, -ES n plant such as a mushroom or mould

FUNHOUSE n amusing place at fairground

FUNICLE, -S n stalk that attaches an ovule to the wall of the ovary

FUNICULI ▸ **funiculus**

FUNK, -ED, -ING, -S n style of dance music with a strong beat ▸ vb avoid (doing something) through fear

FUNKER, -S ▸ **funk**

FUNKHOLE n dugout

FUNKIA, -S n ornamental plant

FUNKIER ▸ **funky**

FUNKIEST ▸ **funky**

FUNKILY ▸ **funky**

FUNKING ▸ **funk**

FUNKS ▸ **funk**

FUNKSTER n performer or fan of funk music

FUNKY, FUNKIER, FUNKIEST adj (of music) having a strong beat

FUNNED ▸ **fun**

FUNNEL, -ED, -S n cone-shaped tube ▸ vb (cause to) move through or as if through a funnel

FUNNER ▸ **fun**

FUNNEST ▸ **fun**

FUNNIER ▸ **funny**

FUNNIES pl n comic strips in a newspaper

FUNNIEST ▸ **funny**

FUNNILY ▸ **funny**

FUNNING ▸ **fun**

FUNNY, FUNNIER, FUNNIEST adj comical, humorous ▸ n joke or witticism

FUNNYMAN, FUNNYMEN n comedian

FUNPLEX n large amusement centre

FUNS ▸ **fun**

FUNSTER, -S n funnyman or funnywoman

FUR, -S n soft hair of a mammal ▸ vb cover or become covered with fur

FURACITY > **furacious**

FURAL, -S same as ▸ **furfural**

FURAN, -S n colourless liquid used as a solvent

FURANE, -S variant of ▸ **furan**

FURANOSE n simple sugar containing a furan ring

FURANS ▸ **furan**

FURBALL, -S n ball of fur regurgitated by an animal

FURBELOW n flounce, ruffle, or other ornamental trim ▸ vb put a furbelow on (a garment)

FURBISH, vb smarten up

FURCA, -E n any forklike structure, esp in insects

FURCAL ▸ **furca**

FURCATE, -D, -S vb divide into two parts ▸ adj forked, branching

FURCRAEA n plant belonging to the Agave family

FURCULA, -E n any forklike part or organ

FURCULAR ▸ **furcula**

FURCULUM same as ▸ **furcula**

FURDER same as ▸ **further**

FUREUR, -S n rage or anger

FURFAIR, -S variant of ▸ **furfur**

FURFUR, -ES, -S n scurf or scaling of the skin

FURFURAL n colourless liquid used as a solvent

FURFURAN same as ▸ **furan**

FURFURES ▸ **furfur**

FURFUROL variant of ▸ **furfural**

FURFURS ▸ **furfur**

FURIBUND adj furious

FURIES ▸ **fury**

FURIOSO, -S adv in a frantically rushing manner ▸ n passage or piece to be performed in this way

FURIOUS adj very angry

FURKID, -S n companion animal

FURL, -ED, -ING, -S vb roll up and fasten (a sail, umbrella, or flag) ▸ n act or an instance of furling

FURLABLE ▸ **furl**

FURLANA, -S variant of ▸ **forlana**

FURLED ▸ **furl**

FURLER, -S ▸ **furl**

FURLESS ▸ **fur**

FURLIKE adj like fur

FURLING ▸ **furl**

FURLONG, -S n unit of length

FURLOUGH n leave of absence ▸ vb grant a furlough to

FURLS ▸ **furl**

FURMENTY same as ▸ **frumenty**

FURMETY same as ▸ **frumenty**

FURMITY same as ▸ **frumenty**

FURNACE, -D, -S n enclosed chamber containing a very hot fire ▸ vb burn in a furnace

FURNISH vb provide with furniture

FUROL, -S variant of ▸ **fural**

FUROLE, -S variant of ▸ **fural**

FUROLS ▸ **furol**

FUROR, -S same as ▸ **furore**

FURORE, -S n very excited or angry reaction

FURORS ▸ **furor**

FURPHY, FURPHIES n rumour or fictitious story

FURPIECE n item of clothing made of or decorated with fur

FURR, -S vb old word meaning furrow

FURRED same as ▸ **furry**

FURRIER, -S n dealer in furs

FURRIERY n occupation of a furrier

FURRIES ▸ **furry**

FURRIEST ▸ **furry**

FURRILY ▸ **furry**

FURRINER n dialect rendering of foreigner

FURRING, -S ▸ **fur**

FURROW, -ED, -S n trench made by a plough ▸ vb make or become wrinkled

FURROWER ▸ **furrow**

FURROWS ▸ **furrow**

FURROWY adj having furrows

FURRS ▸ **furr**

FURRY, FURRIES, FURRIEST adj like or covered with fur or something furlike ▸ n child's fur-covered toy animal

FURS ▸ fur

FURTH adv Scots word meaning out

FURTHER, -S adv in addition ▷ adj more distant ▷ vb promote

FURTHEST adv to the greatest degree ▷ adj most distant

FURTIVE adj sly and secretive

FURUNCLE technical name for ▸ boil

FURY, FURIES n wild anger

FURZE, -S n gorse

FURZY, FURZIER, FURZIEST ▸ furze

FUSAIN, -S n fine charcoal pencil

FUSARIUM, FUSARIA n type of fungus

FUSAROL, -S variant of ▸ fusarole

FUSAROLE n type of architectural moulding

FUSAROLS ▸ fusarol

FUSBALL, -S same as ▸ foosball

FUSC adj dark brown

FUSCOUS adj of a brownish-grey colour

FUSE, -D, -S, FUSING n cord containing an explosive for detonating a bomb ▷ vb (cause to) fail as a result of a blown fuse

FUSEE, -S n (in early clocks and watches) a spirally grooved spindle

FUSEL, -S n mixture of amyl alcohols, propanol, and butanol

FUSELAGE n body of an aircraft

FUSELESS ▸ fuse

FUSELIKE ▸ fuse

FUSELS ▸ fusel

FUSES ▸ fuse

FUSHION, -S n spirit

FUSIBLE adj capable of being melted

FUSIBLY ▸ fusible

FUSIDIC adj as in fusidic acid kind of acid

FUSIFORM adj elongated and tapering at both ends

FUSIL, -S n light flintlock musket

FUSILE adj easily melted

FUSILEER same as ▸ fusilier

FUSILIER n soldier of certain regiments

FUSILLI, -S n spiral-shaped pasta

FUSILS ▸ fusil

FUSING ▸ fuse

FUSION, -S n melting ▷ adj of a style of cooking

FUSIONAL ▸ fusion

FUSIONS ▸ fusion

FUSK, -ED, -ING, -S vb obtain data from (a website) by using hacking software

FUSKER, -ED, -S vb obtain data from (a website) by using hacking software

FUSKING ▸ fusk

FUSKS ▸ fusk

FUSS, -ED, -ES, -ING n needless activity or worry ▷ vb make a fuss

FUSSBALL same as ▸ foosball

FUSSED ▸ fuss

FUSSER, -S ▸ fuss

FUSSES ▸ fuss

FUSSIER ▸ fussy

FUSSIEST ▸ fussy

FUSSILY ▸ fussy

FUSSING ▸ fuss

FUSSPOT, -S n person who is difficult to please and complains often

FUSSY, FUSSIER, FUSSIEST adj inclined to fuss

FUST, -ED, -ING, -S vb become mouldy

FUSTET, -S n wood of the Venetian sumach shrub

FUSTIAN, -S n (formerly) a hard-wearing fabric of cotton mixed with flax or wool ▷ adj cheap

FUSTIC, -S n large tropical American tree

FUSTIER ▸ fusty

FUSTIEST ▸ fusty

FUSTILY ▸ fusty

FUSTING ▸ fust

FUSTOC, -S variant of ▸ fustic

FUSTS ▸ fust

FUSTY, FUSTIER, FUSTIEST adj stale-smelling

FUSUMA, -S n Japanese sliding door

FUTCHEL, -S n timber support in a carriage

FUTHARC, -S same as ▸ futhark

FUTHARK, -S n phonetic alphabet consisting of runes

FUTHORC, -S same as ▸ futhark

FUTHORK, -S same as ▸ futhark

FUTILE, -R, -ST adj unsuccessful or useless

FUTILELY ▸ futile

FUTILER ▸ futile

FUTILEST ▸ futile

FUTILITY n lack of effectiveness or success

FUTON, -S n Japanese-style bed

FUTSAL, -S n form of association football

FUTTOCK, -S n one of the ribs in the frame of a wooden vessel

FUTURAL adj relating to the future

FUTURE n time to come ▷ adj yet to come or be

FUTURES pl n type of commodity trading

FUTURISM n early 20th-century artistic movement

FUTURIST ▸ futurism

FUTURITY n future

FUTZ, -ED, -ES, -ING vb fritter time away

FUZE, -D, -S, FUZING same as ▸ fuse

FUZEE, -S same as ▸ fusee

FUZELESS adj without a fuze

FUZES ▸ fuze

FUZIL, -S variant of ▸ fusil

FUZING ▸ fuze

FUZZ, -ED, -ES, -ING n mass of fine or curly hairs or fibres ▷ vb make or become fuzzy

FUZZBALL n ball of fuzz

FUZZBOX n device that distorts sound

FUZZED ▸ fuzz

FUZZES ▸ fuzz

FUZZIER ▸ fuzzy

FUZZIEST ▸ fuzzy

FUZZILY ▸ fuzzy

FUZZING ▸ fuzz

FUZZLE, -D, -S, FUZZLING vb make drunk

FUZZTONE n device distorting electric guitar sound

FUZZY, FUZZIER, FUZZIEST adj of, like, or covered with fuzz

FY interj exclamation of disapproval

FYCE, -S variant of ▸ fice

FYKE, -D, -S, FYKING n fish trap ▷ vb catch fish in this manner

FYLE, -S variant of ▸ file

FYLFOT, -S rare word for ▸ swastika

FYNBOS, -ES n area of low-growing, evergreen vegetation

FYRD, -S n militia of an Anglo-Saxon shire

FYTTE, -S n section of a song

F

Gg

Only three two-letter words begin with **G** (**gi**, **go** and **gu**). Knowing these will save you worrying about other possibilities. There are quite a few short words beginning with **G** that use **Y**, which can prove very useful. These include **gay**, **gey** and **guy** (7 points each), as well as **gym** and **gyp** (9 points each). And don't forget the very useful **gox** for 11 points.

GAB, -BED, -BING, -S vb talk or chatter ▷ n mechanical device

GABBA, -S n type of electronic dance music

GABBARD, -S same as ▷ **gabbart**

GABBART, -S n Scottish sailing barge

GABBAS ▷ **gabba**

GABBED ▷ **gab**

GABBER, -S ▷ **gab**

GABBIER ▷ **gabby**

GABBIEST ▷ **gabby**

GABBING ▷ **gab**

GABBLE, -D, -S, GABBLING vb speak rapidly and indistinctly ▷ n rapid indistinct speech

GABBLER, -S ▷ **gabble**

GABBLES ▷ **gabble**

GABBLING ▷ **gabble**

GABBRO, -S n dark basic plutonic igneous rock

GABBROIC ▷ **gabbro**

GABBROID adj gabbro-like

GABBROS ▷ **gabbro**

GABBY, GABBIER, GABBIEST adj talkative

GABELLE, -S n salt tax levied until 1790

GABELLED ▷ **gabelle**

GABELLER n person who collects the gabelle

GABELLES ▷ **gabelle**

GABFEST, -S n prolonged gossiping or conversation

GABIES ▷ **gaby**

GABION, -S n cylindrical metal container filled with stones

GABIONED ▷ **gabion**

GABIONS ▷ **gabion**

GABLE, -S n triangular upper part of a wall between sloping roofs

GABLED ▷ **gable**

GABLES ▷ **gable**

GABLET, -S n small gable

GABLING ▷ **gable**

GABNASH n chatter

GABOON, -S n dark wood

GABS ▷ **gab**

GABY, GABIES n unintelligent person

GACH, -ED, -ES, -ING vb behave boastfully

GACHER, -S n person who boasts

GACHES ▷ **gach**

GACHING ▷ **gach**

GAD, -DED, -DING, -S vb go about in search of pleasure ▷ n carefree adventure

GADABOUT n pleasure-seeker

GADARENE adj headlong

GADDED ▷ **gad**

GADDER, -S ▷ **gad**

GADDI, -S n cushioned Indian throne

GADDING ▷ **gad**

GADDIS ▷ **gaddi**

GADE, -S same as ▷ **gad**

GADFLY, GADFLIES n fly that bites cattle

GADGE, -S n man

GADGET, -S n small mechanical device or appliance

GADGETRY n gadgets

GADGETS ▷ **gadget**

GADGETY adj characterized by gadgets

GADGIE, -S n fellow

GADI, -S n cushioned Indian throne

GADID, -S n type of marine fish

GADIS ▷ **gadi**

GADJE, -S same as ▷ **gadgie**

GADJO, -S same as ▷ **gorgio**

GADLING, -S n vagabond

GADMAN, GADMEN n person who drives animals

GADOID, -S adj of the cod family of marine fishes ▷ n gadoid fish

GADROON, -S n type of decorative moulding

GADS ▷ **gad**

GADSMAN, GADSMEN n person who drives animals

GADSO n archaic expression of surprise

GADWALL, -S n type of duck related to the mallard

GADZOOKS interj mild oath

GAE, -D, -ING, -N, -S Scot word for ▷ **go**

GAFF, -ED, -S n stick with an iron hook for landing large fish ▷ vb hook or land (a fish) with a gaff

GAFFE, -S n social blunder

GAFFED ▷ **gaff**

GAFFER, -S n foreman or boss

GAFFES ▷ **gaffe**

GAFFING, -S ▷ **gaff**

GAFFS ▷ **gaff**

GAFFSAIL n quadrilateral fore-and-aft sail on a sailing vessel

GAG, -GED, -GING, -S vb choke or retch ▷ n cloth etc put into or tied across the mouth

GAGA adj senile

GAGAKU, -S n type of traditional Japanese music

GAGE, -D, -S, GAGING vb gauge ▷ n (formerly) an object thrown down as a challenge to fight

GAGEABLE ▷ **gage**

GAGEABLY ▷ **gage**

GAGED ▷ **gage**

GAGER, -S same as ▷ **gauger**

GAGES ▷ **gage**

GAGGED ▸gag

GAGGER, -S n person or thing that gags

GAGGERY n practice of telling jokes

GAGGING ▸gag

GAGGLE, -D, -S, GAGGLING n disorderly crowd ▷vb (of geese) to cackle

GAGING ▸gage

GAGMAN, GAGMEN n person who writes gags for a comedian

GAGS ▸gag

GAGSTER, -S n standup comedian

GAHNITE, -S n dark green mineral

GAID, -S same as ▸gad

GAIETY, GAIETIES n cheerfulness

GAIJIN n (in Japan) a foreigner

GAILLARD same as ▸galliard

GAILY adv merrily

GAIN, -ED, -EST, -ING vb acquire or obtain ▷n profit or advantage ▷adj straight or near

GAINABLE ▸gain

GAINED ▸gain

GAINER, -S n person or thing that gains

GAINEST ▸gain

GAINFUL adj useful or profitable

GAINING ▸gain

GAININGS pl n profits or earnings

GAINLESS ▸gain

GAINLY, GAINLIER adj graceful or well-formed ▷adv conveniently or suitably

GAINS pl n profits or winnings

GAINSAY, GAINSAID, -S vb deny or contradict

GAINST short for ▸against

GAIR, -S n strip of green grass on a hillside

GAIRFOWL same as ▸garefowl

GAIRS ▸gair

GAIT, -ED, -ING, -S n manner of walking ▷vb teach (a horse) a particular gait

GAITA, -S n type of bagpipe

GAITED ▸gait

GAITER, -S n cloth or leather covering for the lower leg

GAITERED adj wearing gaiters

GAITERS ▸gaiter

GAITING ▸gait

GAITS ▸gait

GAITT, -S Scots word for ▸gate

GAJO, -S same as ▸gorgio

GAL, -S n girl

GALA, -S n festival

GALABEA, -S same as ▸djellaba

GALABEAH same as ▸djellaba

GALABEAS ▸galabea

GALABIA, -S same as ▸djellaba

GALABIAH same as ▸djellaba

GALABIAS ▸galabia

GALABIEH same as ▸djellaba

GALABIYA same as ▸djellaba

GALACTIC adj of the Galaxy or other galaxies

GALAGE, -S same as ▸galosh

GALAGO, -S another name for ▸bushbaby

GALAH, -S n Australian cockatoo

GALANGA, -S same as ▸galingale

GALANGAL same as ▸galingale

GALANGAS ▸galanga

GALANT, -S n 18th-century style of music

GALANTY n as in galanty show pantomime shadow play

GALAPAGO n tortoise

GALAS ▸gala

GALATEA, -S n strong twill-weave cotton fabric

GALAVANT same as ▸gallivant

GALAX, -ES n coltsfoot

GALAXY, GALAXIES n system of stars

GALBANUM n bitter aromatic gum resin

GALE, -D, -S, GALING n strong wind ▷vb be very stormy

GALEA, -E, -S n part or organ shaped like a helmet

GALEATE ▸galea

GALEATED ▸galea

GALED ▸gale

GALENA, -S n soft bluish-grey mineral

GALENIC ▸galena

GALENITE same as ▸galena

GALENOID adj pertaining to galena

GALERE, -S n group of people having a common interest

GALES ▸gale

GALETTE, -S n type of savoury pancake

GALILEE, -S n type of porch or chapel

GALING ▸gale

GALIOT, -S n small swift galley

GALIPOT, -S n resin obtained from several species of pine

GALIVANT same as ▸gallivant

GALL, -ED, -S n impudence ▷vb annoy

GALLABEA same as ▸djellaba

GALLABIA same as ▸djellaba

GALLANT, -S adj brave and noble ▷n man who tried to impress with fashionable clothes or daring acts ▷vb court or flirt (with)

GALLATE, -S n salt of gallic acid

GALLEASS n three-masted lateen-rigged galley

GALLED ▸gall

GALLEIN, -S n type of dyestuff

GALLEON, -S n large three-masted sailing ship

GALLERIA n central court through several storeys of a shopping centre

GALLERY n room or building for displaying works of art ▷vb tunnel; form an underground gallery

GALLET, -ED, -S vb use mixture to support a roof-slate

GALLETA, -S n low-growing, coarse grass

GALLETED ▸gallet

GALLETS ▸gallet

GALLEY, -S n kitchen of a ship or aircraft

GALLFLY n any of several small insects

GALLIARD n spirited dance in triple time for two persons, popular in the 16th and 17th centuries ▷adj lively

GALLIASS same as ▸galleass

GALLIC adj of or containing gallium

GALLICA, -S n variety of rose

GALLICAN adj favouring restriction of papal control of the French church

GALLICAS ▸gallica

GALLIED ▸gally

GALLIER ▸gally

GALLIES ▸gally

GALLIEST ▸gally

G

GALLING adj annoying or bitterly humiliating

GALLIOT, -S same as ▸ **galiot**

GALLIPOT same as ▸ **galipot**

GALLISE, -D, -S same as ▸ **gallize**

GALLIUM, -S n soft grey metallic element

GALLIVAT n armed vessel formerly used in Asian waters

GALLIZE, -D, -S vb add water and sugar to increase the quantity of wine produced

GALLNUT, -S n type of plant gall that resembles a nut

GALLOCK adj left-handed

GALLON, -S n liquid measure of eight pints, equal to 4.55 litres

GALLOON, -S n narrow band of cord, gold braid, etc

GALLOOT, -S same as ▸ **galoot**

GALLOP, -ED, -S n horse's fastest pace ▹ vb go or ride at a gallop

GALLOPER ▸ **gallop**

GALLOPS ▸ **gallop**

GALLOUS adj of or containing gallium in the divalent state

GALLOW, -ED vb frighten

GALLOWAY n breed of hornless beef cattle

GALLOWED ▸ **gallow**

GALLOWS n wooden structure used for hanging criminals

GALLS ▸ **gall**

GALLUMPH same as ▸ **galumph**

GALLUS adj bold

GALLUSED adj held up by galluses

GALLUSES pl n pair of straps worn over the shoulders for holding up the trousers

GALLY, GALLIED, GALLIER, GALLIES, GALLIEST, -ING vb frighten ▹ adj (of land) damp or barren

GALOCHE, -D, -S same as ▸ **galosh**

GALOOT, -S n clumsy or uncouth person

GALOP, -ED, -ING, -PED, -S n 19th-century dance in quick duple time ▹ vb dance a galop

GALOPADE same as ▸ **galop**

GALOPED ▸ **galop**

GALOPIN, -S n boy who ran errands for a cook

GALOPING ▸ **galop**

GALOPINS ▸ **galopin**

GALOPPED ▸ **galop**

GALOPS ▸ **galop**

GALORE, -S adj in abundance ▹ n abundance

GALOSH, -ED, -ES n waterproof overshoe ▹ vb cover with galoshes

GALOSHE same as ▸ **galosh**

GALOSHED ▸ **galosh**

GALOSHES ▸ **galosh**

GALOWSES Shakespearean plural for ▸ **gallows**

GALS ▸ **gal**

GALTONIA n type of bulbous plant with waxy white flowers and a fragrant scent

GALUMPH, -S vb leap or move about clumsily

GALUT, -S same as ▸ **galuth**

GALUTH, -S n exile of Jews from Palestine

GALUTS ▸ **galut**

GALVANIC adj of or producing an electric current generated by chemical means

GALVO, -S n instrument for measuring electric current

GALYAC, -S same as ▸ **galyak**

GALYAK, -S n smooth glossy fur

GAM, -MED, -MING, -S n school of whales ▹ vb (of whales) form a school

GAMA, -S n tall perennial grass

GAMASH, -ES n type of gaiter

GAMAY, -S n red grape variety

GAMB, -S n in heraldry, the whole foreleg of a beast

GAMBA, -S n second-largest member of the viol family

GAMBADE, -S same as ▸ **gambado**

GAMBADO, -S n leap or gambit; caper ▹ vb perform a gambado

GAMBAS ▸ **gamba**

GAMBE, -S same as ▸ **gamb**

GAMBESON n garment worn under mail in the Middle Ages

GAMBET, -S n tattler

GAMBETTA n redshank

GAMBIA, -S same as ▸ **gambier**

GAMBIER, -S n astringent resinous substance

GAMBIR, -S same as ▸ **gambier**

GAMBIST, -S n person who plays the (viola da) gamba

GAMBIT, -ED, -S n opening move intended to secure an advantage ▹ vb sacrifice a chess piece to gain a better position

GAMBLE, -D, -S vb play games of chance to win money ▹ n risky undertaking

GAMBLER, -S ▸ **gamble**

GAMBLES ▸ **gamble**

GAMBLING ▸ **gamble**

GAMBO, -ES, -S n farm cart

GAMBOGE, -S n gum resin

GAMBOGIC ▸ **gamboge**

GAMBOL, -ED, -S vb jump about playfully, frolic ▹ n frolic

GAMBOS ▸ **gambo**

GAMBREL, -S n hock of a horse or similar animal

GAMBROON n type of linen cloth

GAMBS ▸ **gamb**

GAMBUSIA n small fish that feeds on mosquito larvae

GAME, -D, -S, -ST n amusement or pastime ▹ vb play games ▹ adj brave

GAMEBAG, -S n bag for carrying hunted game birds

GAMEBOOK n book containing a range of possible strategies for a game

GAMECOCK n cock bred and trained for fighting

GAMED ▸ **game**

GAMEFISH n fish caught for sport

GAMEFOWL n cock bred for cockfighting

GAMELAN, -S n type of percussion orchestra

GAMELIKE ▸ **game**

GAMELY adv in a brave or sporting manner

GAMENESS n courage or bravery

GAMEPLAY n plot of a computer or video game or the way that it is played

GAMER, -S n person who plays computer games

GAMES ▸ **game**

GAMESHOW n TV show in which games are played by contestants

GAMESIER ▸ **gamesy**

GAMESMAN, GAMESMEN n one who practises gamesmanship

GAMESOME adj full of merriment

GAMEST ▸ **game**

GAMESTER n someone who plays games

GAMESY, GAMESIER adj sporty

GAMETAL ▸ gamete

GAMETE, -S n reproductive cell

GAMETIC ▸ gamete

GAMEY, GAMIER, GAMIEST adj having the smell or flavour of game

GAMGEE n as in gamgee tissue type of wound-dressing

GAMIC adj (esp of reproduction) requiring the fusion of gametes

GAMIER ▸ gamey

GAMIEST ▸ gamey

GAMIFY, GAMIFIED, GAMIFIES vb add gamelike elements to a task to encourage participation

GAMILY ▸ gamey

GAMIN, -S n street urchin

GAMINE, -S n slim boyish young woman

GAMINESS ▸ gamey

GAMING, -S n playing games

GAMMA, -S n third letter of the Greek alphabet

GAMMADIA > gammadion

GAMMAS ▸ gamma

GAMMATIA > gammation

GAMME, -S n musical scale

GAMMED ▸ gam

GAMMER, -S n dialect word for an old woman

GAMMES ▸ gamme

GAMMIER ▸ gammy

GAMMIEST ▸ gammy

GAMMING ▸ gam

GAMMOCK, -S vb clown around

GAMMON, -ED, -S n cured or smoked ham ▷ vb score a double victory in backgammon over

GAMMONER ▸ gammon

GAMMONS ▸ gammon

GAMMY, GAMMIER, GAMMIEST adj (of the leg) lame

GAMODEME n isolated breeding population

GAMONE, -S n chemical used by gametes

GAMP, -S n umbrella

GAMPISH adj bulging

GAMPS ▸ gamp

GAMS ▸ gam

GAMUT, -S n whole range or scale (of music, emotions, etc)

GAMY same as ▸ gamey

GAMYNESS ▸ gamy

GAN, -NED, -NING, -S vb go

GANACHE, -S n rich icing or filling

GANCH, -ED, -ES, -ING vb impale

GANDER, -ED, -S n male goose ▷ vb look

GANDY adj as in gandy dancer railway track maintenance worker

GANE ▸ go

GANEF, -S n unscrupulous opportunist

GANEV, -S same as ▸ ganef

GANG, -ED, -S n (criminal) group ▷ vb become or act as a gang

GANGBO, -S n order restricting the activities of a gang member

GANGED ▸ gang

GANGER, -S n foreman of a gang of labourers

GANGING, -S ▸ gang

GANGLAND n criminal underworld

GANGLE, -D, -S vb move awkwardly

GANGLIA ▸ ganglion

GANGLIAL ▸ ganglion

GANGLIAR ▸ ganglion

GANGLIER ▸ gangly

GANGLING adj lanky and awkward

GANGLION, GANGLIA n group of nerve cells

GANGLY, GANGLIER same as ▸ gangling

GANGPLOW n plough designed to produce parallel furrows

GANGREL, -S n wandering beggar

GANGRENE n decay of body tissue as a result of disease or injury ▷ vb become or cause to become affected with gangrene

GANGS ▸ gang

GANGSMAN, GANGSMEN n foreman

GANGSTA, -S n member of a street gang

GANGSTER n member of a criminal gang

GANGUE, -S n valueless material in an ore

GANGWAY, -S same as > gangplank

GANISTER n type of sedimentary rock

GANNED ▸ gan

GANNET, -S n large sea bird

GANNETRY n gannets' breeding-place

GANNETS ▸ gannet

GANNING ▸ gan

GANOF, -S same as ▸ ganef

GANOID, -S adj of the scales of certain fishes ▷ n ganoid fish

GANOIN, -S n outer layer of fish scales

GANOINE, -S same as ▸ ganoin

GANOINS ▸ ganoin

GANS ▸ gan

GANSEY, -S n jersey or pullover

GANT, -ED, -ING, -S vb yawn

GANTLET, -S n section of a railway where two tracks overlap ▷ vb make railway tracks form a gantlet

GANTLINE n line rove through a sheave for hoisting men or gear

GANTLOPE same as ▸ gauntlet

GANTRY, GANTRIES n structure supporting something

GANTS ▸ gant

GANYMEDE n potboy

GANZFELD n type of experiment used in parapsychology

GAOL, -ED, -ING, -S same as ▸ jail

GAOLBIRD n person who is or has been confined to gaol, esp repeatedly

GAOLED ▸ gaol

GAOLER, -S ▸ gaol

GAOLING ▸ gaol

GAOLLESS adj without a gaol

GAOLS ▸ gaol

GAP, -PED, -S n break or opening

GAPE, -D vb stare in wonder ▷ n act of gaping

GAPER, -S n person or thing that gapes

GAPES n disease of young domestic fowl

GAPESEED n person who stares, mouth agape, at something

GAPEWORM n type of parasitic worm that lives in the trachea of birds

GAPIER ▸ gapy

GAPIEST ▸ gapy

GAPING, -S adj wide open ▷ n state of having a gaping mouth

GAPINGLY ▸ gaping

GAPINGS ▸ gaping

GAPLESS ▸ gap

GAPO, -S n (in S America) forest near a river

GAPOSIS n gap between closed fastenings on a garment

GAPPED ▸ **gap**
GAPPER, -S n person taking a year out of education
GAPPIER ▸ **gappy**
GAPPIEST ▸ **gappy**
GAPPING, -S n the act of taking a gap year
GAPPY, GAPPIER, GAPPIEST ▸ **gap**
GAPS ▸ **gap**
GAPY, GAPIER, GAPIEST ▸ **gape**
GAR, -RED, -RING, -S vb Scots word meaning compel
GARAGE, -D, -S n building used to house cars ▸ vb put or keep a car in a garage
GARAGEY, GARAGIER adj (of music) in a garage style
GARAGING n accommodation for housing a motor vehicle
GARAGIST n person who runs a garage
GARB, -ED, -ING, -S n clothes ▸ vb clothe
GARBAGE, -S n rubbish
GARBAGEY ▸ **garbage**
GARBAGY adj like garbage
GARBANZO another name for ▸ **chickpea**
GARBE, -S n in heraldry, a wheat-sheaf
GARBED ▸ **garb**
GARBES ▸ **garbe**
GARBING ▸ **garb**
GARBLE, -S, GARBLING vb jumble (a story, quotation, etc), esp unintentionally ▸ n act of garbling
GARBLED adj (of a story etc) jumbled and confused
GARBLER, -S ▸ **garble**
GARBLES ▸ **garble**
GARBLESS ▸ **garb**
GARBLING ▸ **garble**
GARBO, -S n dustman
GARBOARD n bottommost plank of a vessel's hull
GARBOIL, -S n confusion or disturbance
GARBOS ▸ **garbo**
GARBS ▸ **garb**
GARBURE, -S n thick soup from France
GARCINIA n tropical tree
GARCON, -S n waiter
GARDA, -I n member of the Irish police force
GARDANT, -S same as ▸ **guardant**
GARDEN, -ED, -S n piece of land for growing flowers, fruit, or vegetables ▸ vb cultivate a garden

GARDENER n person who works in or takes care of a garden as an occupation or pastime
GARDENIA n large fragrant white waxy flower
GARDENS ▸ **garden**
GARDYLOO n act of throwing slops from a window
GARE, -S n filth ▸ adj greedy; covetous
GAREFOWL n great auk
GARES ▸ **gare**
GARFISH same as ▸ **garpike**
GARGANEY n small Eurasian duck, closely related to the mallard
GARGET, -S n inflammation of the mammary gland
GARGETY ▸ **garget**
GARGLE, -D, -S, GARGLING vb wash the throat ▸ n liquid used for gargling
GARGLER, -S ▸ **gargle**
GARGLES ▸ **gargle**
GARGLING ▸ **gargle**
GARGOYLE n waterspout carved in the form of a grotesque face, esp on a church ▸ vb provide with gargoyles
GARI, -S n thinly sliced pickled ginger
GARIAL, -S same as ▸ **gavial**
GARIGUE, -S n open shrubby vegetation of dry Mediterranean regions
GARIS ▸ **gari**
GARISH, -ED, -ES adj crudely bright or colourful ▸ vb heal
GARISHLY ▸ **garish**
GARJAN, -S same as ▸ **gurjun**
GARLAND, -S n wreath of flowers worn or hung as a decoration ▸ vb decorate with garlands
GARLIC, -S n pungent bulb of a plant of the onion family
GARLICKY adj containing or resembling the taste or odour of garlic
GARLICS ▸ **garlic**
GARMENT, -S n article of clothing ▸ vb cover or clothe
GARMS pl n clothing
GARNER, -ED, -S vb collect or store ▸ n place for storage or safekeeping
GARNET, -S n red semiprecious stone
GARNI adj garnished
GARNISH vb decorate (food) ▸ n decoration for food
GAROTE, -D, -S, GAROTING same as ▸ **garrotte**

GAROTTE, -D, -S same as ▸ **garrotte**
GAROTTER ▸ **garotte**
GAROTTES ▸ **garotte**
GAROUPA, -S same as ▸ **groper**
GARPIKE, -S n primitive freshwater bony fish
GARRAN, -S same as ▸ **garron**
GARRE, -S vb compel
GARRED ▸ **gar**
GARRES ▸ **garre**
GARRET, -S n attic in a house
GARRETED adj living in a garret
GARRETS ▸ **garret**
GARRIGUE same as ▸ **garigue**
GARRING ▸ **gar**
GARRISON n troops stationed in a town or fort ▸ vb station troops in
GARRON, -S n small sturdy pony
GARROT, -S n goldeneye duck
GARROTE, -D, -S same as ▸ **garrotte**
GARROTER ▸ **garrote**
GARROTES ▸ **garrote**
GARROTS ▸ **garrot**
GARROTTE n method of execution by strangling ▸ vb kill by this method
GARRYA, -S n catkin-bearing evergreen shrub
GARS ▸ **gar**
GART a past tense of ▸ **gar**
GARTER, -ED, -S n band used to hold up a sock or stocking ▸ vb secure with a garter
GARTH, -S n courtyard surrounded by a cloister
GARUDA, -S n Hindu god
GARUM, -S n fermented fish sauce
GARVEY, -S n small flat-bottomed yacht
GARVIE, -S n sprat
GARVOCK, -S n sprat
GAS, -ES, -SED, -SES n airlike substance that is not liquid or solid ▸ vb poison or render unconscious with gas
GASAHOL, -S n mixture of petrol and alcohol used as fuel
GASALIER same as ▸ **gasolier**
GASBAG, -S n person who talks too much ▸ vb talk in a voluble way
GASCON, -S n boaster

GASEITY n state of being gaseous

GASELIER same as ▸ gasolier

GASEOUS adj of or like gas

GASES ▸ gas

GASFIELD n area in which natural gas is found underground

GASH, -ED, -ER, -ES, -EST, -ING vb make a long deep cut in ▷ n long deep cut ▷ adj witty

GASHFUL adj full of gashes

GASHING ▸ gash

GASHLY, GASHLIER adv wittily ▷ adj hideous; ghastly

GASHOUSE n gasworks

GASIFIED ▸ gasify

GASIFIER ▸ gasify

GASIFIES ▸ gasify

GASIFORM adj in a gaseous form

GASIFY, GASIFIED, GASIFIES vb change into a gas

GASKET, -S n type of seal

GASKETED adj having a gasket

GASKETS ▸ gasket

GASKIN, -S n lower part of a horse's thigh

GASKING, -S same as ▸ gasket

GASKINS ▸ gaskin

GASLESS ▸ gas

GASLIGHT vb manipulate (a person) with lies until they doubt their sanity

GASLIT adj lit by gas

GASMAN, GASMEN n man employed by a gas company

GASOGENE n siphon bottle

GASOHOL, -S n mixture of petrol and alcohol used as fuel

GASOLENE same as ▸ gasoline

GASOLIER n branched hanging fitting for gaslights

GASOLINE n petrol

GASP, -ED, -S vb draw in breath sharply or with difficulty ▷ n convulsive intake of breath

GASPER, -S n person who gasps

GASPIER ▸ gaspy

GASPIEST ▸ gaspy

GASPING, -S ▸ gasp

GASPS ▸ gasp

GASPY, GASPIER, GASPIEST ▸ gasp

GASSED ▸ gas

GASSER, -S n drilling or well that yields natural gas

GASSES ▸ gas

GASSIER ▸ gassy

GASSIEST ▸ gassy

GASSILY ▸ gassy

GASSING, -S ▸ gas

GASSY, GASSIER, GASSIEST adj filled with gas

GAST, -ED, -ING, -S vb old word for frighten

GASTER, -ED, -S vb old word for frighten

GASTFULL adj dismal

GASTHAUS n guest house

GASTIGHT adj not allowing gas to enter or escape

GASTING ▸ gast

GASTNESS n dread

GASTRAEA n hypothetical primeval form posited by Haeckel

GASTRAL adj relating to the stomach

GASTREA, -S same as ▸ gastraea

GASTRIC adj of the stomach

GASTRIN, -S n polypeptide hormone

GASTRULA n saclike animal embryo

GASTS ▸ gast

GASWORKS n plant where coal gas is made

GAT, -S n pistol or revolver

GATCH, -ED, -ES, -ING vb behave boastfully

GATCHER, -S n person who boasts

GATCHES ▸ gatch

GATCHING ▸ gatch

GATE, -D, -S, GATING n movable barrier, usu hinged, in a wall or fence ▷ vb provide with a gate or gates

GATEAU, -S, -X n rich elaborate cake

GATED ▸ gate

GATEFOLD n oversize page in a book or magazine that is folded in

GATELEG, -S n table having hinged legs that swing out

GATELESS ▸ gate

GATELIKE ▸ gate

GATEMAN, GATEMEN n gatekeeper

GATEPOST n post on which a gate is hung

GATER, -S variant of ▸ gator

GATES ▸ gate

GATEWAY, -S n entrance with a gate

GATH n (in Indian music) second section of a raga

GATHER, -ED, -S vb assemble ▷ n act of gathering

GATHERER ▸ gather

GATHERS ▸ gather

GATHS ▸ gath

GATING, -S ▸ gate

GATLING n as in gatling gun kind of machine-gun

GATOR, -S short form of ▸ alligator

GATS ▸ gat

GATVOL adj in South African English, fed up

GAU, -S n district set up by the Nazi Party

GAUCH vb behave boastfully

GAUCHE, -D, -S, -ST, GAUCHING adj socially awkward ▷ vb make gauche

GAUCHELY ▸ gauche

GAUCHER, -S n gauche person

GAUCHES ▸ gauche

GAUCHEST ▸ gauche

GAUCHING ▸ gauche

GAUCHO, -S n S American cowboy

GAUCIE variant of ▸ gaucy

GAUCY, GAUCIER, GAUCIEST adj plump or jolly

GAUD, -ED, -ING, -S n article of cheap finery ▷ vb decorate gaudily

GAUDERY n cheap finery or display

GAUDGIE, -S same as ▸ gadgie

GAUDIER ▸ gaudy

GAUDIES ▸ gaudy

GAUDIEST ▸ gaudy

GAUDILY ▸ gaudy

GAUDING ▸ gaud

GAUDS ▸ gaud

GAUDY, GAUDIER, GAUDIES, GAUDIEST adj vulgarly bright or colourful ▷ n festival held at some schools and colleges

GAUFER, -S n wafer

GAUFFER, -S same as ▸ goffer

GAUFRE, -S same as ▸ gaufer

GAUGE, -D, -S vb estimate or judge ▷ n measuring instrument ▷ adj of a pressure measurement

GAUGER, -S n person or thing that gauges

GAUGES ▸ gauge

GAUGING, -S ▸ gauge

GAUJE, -S same as ▸ gadgie

GAULT, -S n stiff compact clay or thick heavy clayey soil

GAULTER, -S n person who digs gault

GAULTS ▸ gault
GAUM, -ED, -ING, -S vb understand
GAUMIER ▸ gaumy
GAUMIEST ▸ gaumy
GAUMING ▸ gaum
GAUMLESS variant spelling of ▸ **gormless**
GAUMS ▸ gaum
GAUMY, GAUMIER, GAUMIEST adj clogged
GAUN ▸ go
GAUNCH, -ED, -ES same as ▸ **ganch**
GAUNT, -ED, -ER, -EST, -ING, -S adj lean and haggard ▷ vb yawn
GAUNTLET n heavy glove with a long cuff ▷ vb run (or cause to run) the gauntlet
GAUNTLY ▸ gaunt
GAUNTREE same as ▸ **gantry**
GAUNTRY same as ▸ **gantry**
GAUNTS ▸ gaunt
GAUP, -ED, -ING, -S same as ▸ **gawp**
GAUPER, -S ▸ gaup
GAUPING ▸ gaup
GAUPS ▸ gaup
GAUPUS, -ES same as ▸ **gawpus**
GAUR, -S n large wild member of the cattle tribe
GAUS ▸ gau
GAUSS, -ES n unit of magnetic flux density
GAUSSIAN adj denoting the mathematical principles of K F Gauss
GAUZE, -S n transparent loosely woven fabric
GAUZIER ▸ gauzy
GAUZIEST ▸ gauzy
GAUZILY ▸ gauzy
GAUZY, GAUZIER, GAUZIEST adj resembling gauze
GAVAGE, -S n forced feeding by means of a tube
GAVE ▸ give
GAVEL, -ED, -ING, -LED, -S n small hammer banged on a table ▷ vb use a gavel to restore order
GAVELMAN, GAVELMEN n gavelkind tenant
GAVELOCK n iron crowbar
GAVELS ▸ gavel
GAVIAL, -S n as in **false gavial** small crocodile
GAVOT, -S same as ▸ **gavotte**
GAVOTTE, -D, -S n old formal dance ▷ vb dance a gavotte
GAW, -S n as in **weather gaw** partial rainbow

GAWCY, GAWCIER, GAWCIEST same as ▸ **gaucy**
GAWD, -S same as ▸ **gaud**
GAWK, -ED, -ING, -S vb stare stupidly
GAWKER, -S ▸ gawk
GAWKIER ▸ gawky
GAWKIES ▸ gawky
GAWKIEST ▸ gawky
GAWKILY ▸ gawky
GAWKING ▸ gawk
GAWKISH same as ▸ **gawky**
GAWKS ▸ gawk
GAWKY, GAWKIER, GAWKIES, GAWKIEST adj clumsy or awkward ▷ n clumsy or awkward person
GAWMOGE, -S n clownish person
GAWP, -ED, -ING, -S vb stare stupidly
GAWPER, -S ▸ gawp
GAWPING ▸ gawp
GAWPS ▸ gawp
GAWPUS, -ES n silly person
GAWS ▸ gaw
GAWSIE, -R, -ST same as ▸ **gaucy**
GAWSY same as ▸ **gaucy**
GAY, -ER, -EST, -S adj carefree and merry ▷ n homosexual person
GAYAL, -S n type of ox
GAYDAR, -S n supposed ability to recognize if another person is gay
GAYER ▸ gay
GAYEST ▸ gay
GAYETY, GAYETIES same as ▸ **gaiety**
GAYLY ▸ gay
GAYNESS ▸ gay
GAYS ▸ gay
GAYSOME adj. full of merriment
GAYWINGS n flowering wintergreen
GAZABO, -ES, -S n fellow or companion
GAZAL, -S same as ▸ **ghazal**
GAZANG, -ED, -S vb inconvenience a buyer by declining to sell a house just before the purchase is completed
GAZANIA, -S n S African plant
GAZAR, -S n type of silk cloth
GAZE, -D, -S vb look fixedly ▷ n fixed look
GAZEBO, -ES, -S n summerhouse with a good view
GAZED ▸ gaze
GAZEFUL adj gazing

GAZELLE, -S n small graceful antelope
GAZEMENT n view
GAZER, -S ▸ gaze
GAZES ▸ gaze
GAZETTE, -D, -S n official publication containing announcements ▷ vb announce or report (facts or an event) in a gazette
GAZIER ▸ gazy
GAZIEST ▸ gazy
GAZING ▸ gaze
GAZOGENE same as ▸ **gasogene**
GAZON, -S n sod used to cover a parapet in a fortification
GAZOO, -S n kazoo
GAZOOKA, -S same as ▸ **gazoo**
GAZOON, -S same as ▸ **gazon**
GAZOOS ▸ gazoo
GAZPACHO n Spanish soup made from tomatoes, peppers, etc, and served cold
GAZUMP, -ED, -S vb raise the price of a property after verbally agreeing it with (a prospective buyer) ▷ n act or an instance of gazumping
GAZUMPER ▸ gazump
GAZUMPS ▸ gazump
GAZUNDER vb reduce an offer on a property immediately before purchase ▷ n act or instance of gazundering
GAZY, GAZIER, GAZIEST adj prone to gazing
GEAL, -ED, -ING, -S vb congeal
GEALOUS Spenserian spelling of ▸ **jealous**
GEALOUSY Spenserian spelling of ▸ **jealousy**
GEALS ▸ geal
GEAN, -S n white-flowered tree
GEAR, -ED, -S n set of toothed wheels used to change direction or speed ▷ vb prepare or organize for something
GEARBOX n case enclosing a set of gears in a motor vehicle
GEARCASE n protective casing for gears
GEARE, -S Spenserian spelling of ▸ **jeer**
GEARED ▸ gear
GEARES ▸ geare
GEARHEAD n part in engine gear system

GEARING, -S n system of gears designed to transmit motion

GEARLESS ▶ gear

GEARS ▶ gear

GEASON adj wonderful

GEAT, -S n in casting, the channel which leads to a mould

GEBUR, -S n tenant farmer

GECK, -ED, -ING, -S vb beguile

GECKO, -ES, -S n small tropical lizard

GECKS ▶ geck

GED, -S Scots word for ▶ **pike**

GEDACT, -S n flutelike stopped metal diapason organ pipe

GEDDIT interj exclamation meaning do you understand it?

GEDECKT, -S same as ▶ **gedact**

GEDS ▶ ged

GEE, -D, -ING, -S interj mild exclamation of surprise, admiration, etc ▷ vb move (an animal, esp a horse) ahead

GEEBUNG, -S n Australian tree or shrub

GEECHEE, -S n speaker of a dialect found in an area of the southern US

GEED ▶ gee

GEEGAW, -S same as ▶ **gewgaw**

GEEING ▶ gee

GEEK, -S n person skilled in a specific subject

GEEKDOM, -S ▶ geek

GEEKED adj highly excited

GEEKERY n preoccupation with, or great knowledge about, a specialized subject

GEEKIER ▶ geeky

GEEKIEST ▶ geeky

GEEKISH adj of or like a geek

GEEKISM, -S n preoccupation with subjects generally considered unfashionable or boring

GEEKS ▶ geek

GEEKY, GEEKIER, GEEKIEST adj of or like a geek

GEELBEK, -S n edible marine fish

GEEP, -S n cross between a goat and a sheep

GEEPOUND another name for ▶ **slug**

GEEPS ▶ geep

GEES ▶ gee

GEESE ▶ goose

GEEST, -S n area of heathland in N Germany and adjacent areas

GEEZ interj expression of surprise

GEEZAH, -S variant spelling of ▶ **geezer**

GEEZER, -S n man

GEFILTE adj as in gefilte fish dish of fish stuffed with various ingredients

GEFUFFLE same as ▶ **kerfuffle**

GEFULLTE adj as in gefullte fish dish of fish stuffed with various ingredients

GEGGIE, -S Scottish slang word for ▶ **mouth**

GEISHA, -S n (in Japan) professional female companion for men

GEIST, -S n spirit

GEIT, -ED, -ING, -S n border on clothing ▷ vb put a border on (an article of clothing)

GEL, -LED, -LING, -S n jelly-like substance ▷ vb form a gel

GELABLE adj capable of forming a gel

GELADA, -S n NE African baboon

GELANDE adj as in gelande jump jump made in downhill skiing

GELANT, -S same as ▶ **gellant**

GELASTIC adj relating to laughter

GELATE, -D, -S, GELATING vb form a gel

GELATI, -S n layered dessert

GELATIN, -S same as ▶ **gelatine**

GELATINE n substance made by boiling animal bones

GELATING ▶ gelate

GELATINS ▶ gelatin

GELATION n act or process of freezing a liquid

GELATIS ▶ gelati

GELATO, -S n Italian ice cream

GELCAP, -S n medicine enclosed in gelatine

GELCOAT, -S n thin layer of gel or resin applied to a surface

GELD, -ED, -S vb emasculate; weaken ▷ n tax on land in Anglo-Saxon and Norman England

GELDER, -S ▶ geld

GELDING, -S ▶ geld

GELDS ▶ geld

GELEE, -S n jelly

GELID, -ER, -EST adj very cold, icy, or frosty

GELIDITY ▶ gelid

GELIDLY ▶ gelid

GELLANT, -S n substance that causes gelling

GELLED ▶ gel

GELLIES ▶ gelly

GELLING ▶ gel

GELLY, GELLIES same as ▶ **gelignite**

GELOSY, GELOSIES Spenserian spelling of ▶ **jealousy**

GELS ▶ gel

GELSEMIA ▶ gelsemium

GELT, -S n money

GEM, -MED, -MING, -S n precious stone or jewel ▷ vb set or ornament with gems

GEMATRIA n numerology of the Hebrew language and alphabet

GEMCLIP, -S n paperclip

GEMEL, -S n in heraldry, either of a pair of parallel bars

GEMFISH n Australian food fish with a delicate flavour

GEMINAL adj occurring in pairs

GEMINATE adj combined in pairs ▷ vb arrange or be arranged in pairs

GEMINI n expression of surprise

GEMINIES ▶ geminy

GEMINOUS adj in pairs

GEMINY, GEMINIES n pair

GEMLIKE ▶ gem

GEMMA, -E n reproductive structure in liverworts, mosses, etc

GEMMAN, GEMMEN dialect form of ▶ **gentleman**

GEMMATE, -D, -S adj (of some plants and animals) having gemmae ▷ vb produce or reproduce by gemmae

GEMMED ▶ gem

GEMMEN ▶ gemman

GEMMEOUS adj gem-like

GEMMERY n gems collectively

GEMMIER ▶ gemmy

GEMMIEST ▶ gemmy

GEMMILY ▶ gem

GEMMING ▶ gem

GEMMULE, -S n bud

GEMMY, GEMMIER, GEMMIEST ▶ gem

GEMOLOGY n branch of mineralogy that is concerned with gems and gemstones

GEMONY same as ▶ **jiminy**

G

GEMOT, -S n (in Anglo-Saxon England) a legal or administrative assembly

GEMOTE, -S same as ▶ gemot

GEMOTS ▶ gemot

GEMS ▶ gem

GEMSBOK, -S same as ▶ oryx

GEMSBUCK same as ▶ oryx

GEMSHORN n type of medieval flute

GEMSTONE n precious or semiprecious stone, esp one which has been cut and polished

GEN, -NED, -NING n information ▷ vb gain information

GENA, -S n cheek

GENAL ▶ gena

GENAPPE, -S n smooth worsted yarn used for braid, etc

GENAS ▶ gena

GENDARME n member of the French police force

GENDER, -ED, -S n state of being male or female in relation to social and cultural roles ▷ vb assign a gender to

GENE, -S n part of a cell

GENERA ▶ genus

GENERAL, -S adj common or widespread ▷ n very senior army officer ▷ vb act as a general

GENERALE singular form of > generalia

GENERALS ▶ general

GENERANT n something that generates

GENERATE vb produce or bring into being

GENERIC, -S adj of a class, group, or genus ▷ n drug, food product, etc that does not have a trademark

GENEROUS adj free in giving

GENES ▶ gene

GENESIS, GENESES n beginning or origin

GENET, -S n type of agile catlike mammal

GENETIC adj of genes or genetics

GENETICS n study of heredity and variation in organisms

GENETRIX n female progenitor

GENETS ▶ genet

GENETTE, -S same as ▶ genet

GENEVA, -S n gin

GENIAL adj cheerful and friendly

GENIALLY ▶ genial

GENIC adj of or relating to a gene or genes

GENIE, -S n (in fairy tales) magical wish-granting servant

GENII ▶ genius

GENIP, -S same as ▶ genipap

GENIPAP, -S n evergreen Caribbean tree

GENIPAPO n tropical American tree

GENIPAPS ▶ genipap

GENIPS ▶ genip

GENISTA, -S n any member of the broom family

GENITAL adj of the reproductive organs

GENITALS pl n external reproductive organs

GENITIVE n grammatical case indicating possession ▷ adj denoting such a grammatical case

GENITOR, -S n biological father

GENITRIX same as ▶ genetrix

GENITURE n birth

GENIUS, GENII, -ES n (person with) an exceptional ability

GENIZAH, -S, GENIZOT, GENIZOTH n repository for sacred objects which may not be destroyed

GENLOCK, -S n generator locking device ▷ vb activate a genlock

GENNAKER n type of sail for boats

GENNED ▶ gen

GENNEL, -S same as ▶ ginnel

GENNET, -S n female donkey or ass

GENNIES ▶ genny

GENNING ▶ gen

GENNY, GENNIES same as ▶ genoa

GENOA, -S n large triangular jib sail

GENOCIDE n deliberate killing of an ethnic group

GENOGRAM n expanded family tree

GENOISE, -S n rich sponge cake

GENOM, -S same as ▶ genome

GENOME, -S n all the genetic material in an organism

GENOMIC ▶ genome

GENOMICS n branch of molecular genetics concerned with the study of genomes

GENOMS ▶ genom

GENOTYPE n genetic constitution of an organism ▷ vb determine the genotype of

GENRE, -S n style of literary, musical, or artistic work

GENRO, -S n group of Japanese statesmen

GENS, GENTES n (in ancient Rome) a group of aristocratic families

GENSENG, -S same as ▶ ginseng

GENT n gentleman

GENTEEL adj affectedly proper and polite

GENTES ▶ gens

GENTIAN, -S n mountain plant with deep blue flowers

GENTIER ▶ genty

GENTIEST ▶ genty

GENTIL adj gentle

GENTILE, -S n non-Jewish person ▷ adj used to designate a place or the inhabitants of a place

GENTILIC adj tribal

GENTLE, -D, -R, -S, -ST, GENTLING adj mild or kindly ▷ vb tame or subdue (a horse) ▷ n maggot, esp when used as bait in fishing

GENTLY ▶ gentle

GENTOO, -S n grey-backed penguin

GENTRICE n high birth

GENTRIES ▶ gentry

GENTRIFY vb cause a neighbourhood to appeal to the middle classes

GENTRY, GENTRIES n term for people just below the nobility in social rank

GENTS n men's public toilet

GENTY, GENTIER, GENTIEST adj neat

GENU, -A n any knee-like bend in a structure or part

GENUINE adj not fake, authentic

GENUS, GENERA, -ES n group of animals or plants

GEO, -S n (esp in Shetland) a small fjord or gully

GEOCACHE vb search for hidden containers using GPS as a recreational activity

GEOCARPY n ripening of fruits below ground, as occurs in the peanut

GEOCODE, -D, -S vb assign geographical coordinates to a physical location using a digital code

GEODATA n information about geographical location held in a digital format

GEODE, -S n cavity within a rock mass or nodule

GEODESIC adj of the geometry of curved surfaces ▷ n shortest line between two points on a curve

GEODESY n study of the shape and size of the earth

GEODETIC same as ▷ geodesic

GEODIC ▷ geode

GEODUCK, -S n king clam

GEOFACT, -S n rock shaped by natural forces

GEOGENY same as ▷ geogony

GEOGNOST ▷ geognosy

GEOGNOSY n early form of geology

GEOGONIC ▷ geogony

GEOGONY n science of the earth's formation

GEOID, -S n hypothetical surface

GEOIDAL ▷ geoid

GEOIDS ▷ geoid

GEOLATRY n worship of the earth

GEOLOGER ▷ geology

GEOLOGIC ▷ geology

GEOLOGY n study of the earth

GEOMANCY n prophecy made from casting down a handful of earth

GEOMANT, -S n geomancer

GEOMETER n person who is practised in or who studies geometry

GEOMETRY n branch of mathematics dealing with points, lines, curves, and surfaces

GEOMYOID adj relating to burrowing rodents of the genus Geomys

GEOPHAGY n practice of eating earth, clay, chalk, etc, found in some primitive tribes

GEOPHONE n device for recording seismic movement

GEOPHYTE n perennial plant that propagates by means of buds below the soil surface

GEOPONIC adj of or relating to agriculture, esp as a science

GEOPROBE n probing device used for sampling soil

GEORGIC, -S adj agricultural ▷ n poem about rural or agricultural life

GEOS ▷ geo

GEOTAG, -S n geographical co-ordinates digitally applied to data ▷ vb apply a geotag to data

GEOTAXIS, GEOTAXES n movement of an organism in response to the stimulus of gravity

GEOTHERM n line or surface within or on the earth connecting points of equal temperature

GER, -S n portable Mongolian dwelling

GERAH, -S n ancient Hebrew unit of weight

GERANIAL n cis- isomer of citral

GERANIOL n type of alcohol with an odour of roses

GERANIUM n cultivated plant with red, pink, or white flowers

GERARDIA n any plant of the genus Gerardia

GERBE, -S same as ▷ garbe

GERBERA, -S n type of plant

GERBES ▷ gerbe

GERBIL, -S n burrowing desert rodent of Asia and Africa

GERBILLE same as ▷ gerbil

GERBILS ▷ gerbil

GERE, -S Spenserian spelling of ▷ gear

GERENT, -S n person who rules or manages

GERENUK, -S n slender antelope

GERES ▷ gere

GERLE, -S Spenserian spelling of ▷ girl

GERM, -ED, -ING, -S n microbe, esp one causing disease ▷ vb sprout

GERMAIN, -S same as ▷ germen

GERMAINE same as ▷ germen

GERMAINS ▷ germain

GERMAN, -S n type of dance ▷ adj having the same parents as oneself

GERMANE adj relevant

GERMANIC adj of or containing germanium in the tetravalent state

GERMANS ▷ german

GERMED ▷ germ

GERMEN, -S, GERMINA n cells that gives rise to the germ cells

GERMFREE ▷ germ

GERMIER ▷ germy

GERMIEST ▷ germy

GERMIN, -S same as ▷ germen

GERMINA ▷ germen

GERMINAL adj of or in the earliest stage of development

GERMING ▷ germ

GERMINS ▷ germin

GERMLIKE ▷ germ

GERMS ▷ germ

GERMY, GERMIER, GERMIEST adj full of germs

GERNE, -D, -S, GERNING vb grin

GERONIMO interj shout given by US paratroopers as they jump into battle

GERONTIC adj of or relating to the senescence of an organism

GEROPIGA n grape syrup used to sweeten inferior port wines

GERS ▷ ger

GERT adv in dialect, great or very big

GERTCHA interj get out of here!

GERUND, -S n noun formed from a verb

GESNERIA n S American plant grown for its bright flowers

GESSE, -D, -S, GESSING Spenserian spelling of ▷ guess

GESSO, -ED, -ES n plaster used for painting or in sculpture ▷ vb apply gesso to

GEST, -S n notable deed or exploit

GESTALT, -S n perceptual pattern or structure

GESTANT adj laden

GESTAPO, -S n any secret state police organization

GESTATE, -D, -S vb carry (young) in the uterus during pregnancy

GESTE, -S same as ▷ gest

GESTIC adj consisting of gestures

GESTICAL ▷ gestic

GESTS ▷ gest

GESTURAL ▷ gesture

GESTURE, -D, -S n movement to convey meaning ▷ vb gesticulate

GESTURER ▷ gesture

GESTURES ▷ gesture

GET, -S, GOT vb obtain or receive

GETA, -S n type of Japanese wooden sandal

GETABLE ▸ get

GETAS ▸ geta

GETAWAY, -S *n* used in escape

GETOUT, -S *n* excuse to get out of doing something

GETS ▸ get

GETTABLE ▸ get

GETTER, -ED, -S *n* person or thing that gets ▸ *vb* remove (a gas) by the action of a getter

GETTING, -S ▸ get

GETUP, -S *n* outfit

GEUM, -S *n* type of herbaceous plant

GEWGAW, -S *n* showy but valueless trinket ▸ *adj* showy and valueless

GEWGAWED *adj* decorated gaudily

GEWGAWS ▸ gewgaw

GEY, -ER, -EST *adv* extremely ▸ *adj* gallant

GEYAN *adv* somewhat

GEYER ▸ gey

GEYEST ▸ gey

GEYSER, -ED, -S *n* spring that discharges steam and hot water ▸ *vb* erupt like a geyser

GHARIAL, -S *same as* ▸ gavial

GHARRI, -S *same as* ▸ gharry

GHARRIES ▸ gharry

GHARRIS ▸ gharri

GHARRY, GHARRIES *n* (in India) horse-drawn vehicle

GHAST, -ED, -ING, -S *vb* terrify

GHASTFUL *adj* dismal

GHASTING ▸ ghast

GHASTLY *adj* unpleasant ▸ *adv* unhealthily

GHASTS ▸ ghast

GHAT, -S *n* (in India) set of steps leading down to a river

GHAUT, -S *n* small cleft in a hill

GHAZAL, -S *n* Arabic love poem

GHAZEL, -S *same as* ▸ ghazal

GHAZI, -ES, -S *n* Muslim fighter against infidels

GHEE, -S *n* (in Indian cookery) clarified butter

GHERAO, -ED, -ES, -S *n* form of industrial action in India ▸ *vb* trap an employer in his or her office, to indicate the workforce's discontent

GHERKIN, -S *n* small pickled cucumber

GHESSE, -D, -S, GHESSING, GHEST *Spenserian spelling of* ▸ guess

GHETTO, -ED, -ES, -S *n* slum area inhabited by a deprived minority ▸ *vb* ghettoize

GHI, -S *same as* ▸ ghee

GHIBLI, -S *n* fiercely hot wind of North Africa

GHILGAI, -S *same as* ▸ gilgai

GHILLIE, -D, -S *n* (in Scotland) attendant for hunting or fishing ▸ *vb* act as a ghillie

GHIS ▸ ghi

GHOST, -ED, -ING, -S *n* disembodied spirit of a dead person ▸ *vb* ghostwrite

GHOSTIER ▸ ghosty

GHOSTING ▸ ghost

GHOSTLY *adj* frightening in appearance or effect

GHOSTS ▸ ghost

GHOSTY, GHOSTIER *adj* pertaining to ghosts

GHOUL, -S *n* person with morbid interests

GHOULIE, -S *n* goblin

GHOULISH *adj* of or relating to ghouls

GHOULS ▸ ghoul

GHRELIN, -S *n* hormone that stimulates appetite

GHUBAR *adj* as in ghubar numeral type of numeral

GHYLL, -S *same as* ▸ gill

GI, -S *n* white suit worn in martial arts

GIAMBEUX *n* jambeaux; leg armour

GIANT, -S *n* mythical being of superhuman size ▸ *adj* huge

GIANTESS *same as* ▸ giant

GIANTISM *same as* > gigantism

GIANTLY *adj* giantlike

GIANTRY *n* collective term for giants

GIANTS ▸ giant

GIARDIA, -S *n* species of parasite

GIB, -BED, -BING, -S *n* metal wedge, pad, or thrust bearing ▸ *vb* fasten or supply with a gib

GIBBER, -ED, -S *vb* speak or utter rapidly and unintelligibly ▸ *n* boulder

GIBBET, -ED, -S *n* gallows for displaying executed criminals ▸ *vb* put to death by hanging on a gibbet

GIBBING ▸ gib

GIBBON, -S *n* agile tree-dwelling ape of S Asia

GIBBOSE *same as* ▸ gibbous

GIBBOUS *adj* (of the moon) between half and fully illuminated

GIBBSITE *n* mineral consisting of hydrated aluminium oxide

GIBE, -D, -S, GIBING *vb* make jeering or scoffing remarks (at) ▸ *n* derisive or provoking remark

GIBEL, -S *n* Prussian carp

GIBER, -S ▸ gibe

GIBES ▸ gibe

GIBING ▸ gibe

GIBINGLY ▸ gibe

GIBLET ▸ giblets

GIBLETS *pl n* gizzard, liver, heart, and neck of a fowl

GIBLI, -S *same as* ▸ ghibli

GIBS ▸ gib

GIBSON, -S *n* martini garnished with onion

GIBUS, -ES *n* collapsible top hat

GID, -S *n* disease of sheep

GIDDAP *interj* exclamation used to make a horse go faster

GIDDAY *interj* expression of greeting

GIDDIED ▸ giddy

GIDDIER ▸ giddy

GIDDIES ▸ giddy

GIDDIEST ▸ giddy

GIDDILY ▸ giddy

GIDDUP *same as* ▸ giddyup

GIDDY, GIDDIED, GIDDIER, GIDDIES, GIDDIEST, -ING *adj* having or causing a feeling of dizziness ▸ *vb* make giddy

GIDDYAP *same as* ▸ giddyup

GIDDYING ▸ giddy

GIDDYUP *interj* exclamation used to make a horse go faster

GIDGEE, -S *n* small acacia tree

GIDJEE, -S *same as* ▸ gidgee

GIDS ▸ gid

GIE, -D, -ING, -N, -S *Scot word for* ▸ give

GIF, -S *n* file held in GIF format

GIFT, -S *n* present ▸ *vb* make a present of

GIFTABLE *adj* suitable as gift ▸ *n* something suitable as gift

GIFTED *adj* talented

GIFTEDLY ▸ gifted

GIFTEE, -S *n* person given a gift

GIFTING, -S *n* act of gifting

GIFTLESS ▸ gift

GIFTS ▸ gift

GIFTSHOP *n* shop selling articles suitable for gifts

GIFTWARE *n* anything that may be given as a present

GIFTWRAP vb wrap (a gift) in decorative wrapping paper
GIG, -GED, -GING, -S n single performance by pop or jazz musicians ▷ vb play a gig or gigs
GIGA, -S, GIGHE same as ▶ gigue
GIGABIT, -S n unit of information in computing
GIGABYTE n one thousand and twenty-four megabytes
GIGAFLOP n measure of computer processing speed
GIGANTIC adj enormous
GIGAS ▶ giga
GIGATON, -S n unit of explosive force
GIGAVOLT n billion volts
GIGAWATT n unit of power equal to 1 billion watts
GIGGED ▶ gig
GIGGING ▶ gig
GIGGIT, -ED, -S vb move quickly
GIGGLE, -D, -S vb laugh nervously or foolishly ▷ n such a laugh
GIGGLER, -S ▶ giggle
GIGGLES ▶ giggle
GIGGLIER ▶ giggly
GIGGLING ▶ giggle
GIGGLY, GIGGLIER ▶ giggle
GIGHE ▶ giga
GIGLET, -S n flighty girl
GIGLOT, -S same as ▶ giglet
GIGMAN, GIGMEN n one who places great importance on respectability
GIGOT, -S n leg of lamb or mutton
GIGS ▶ gig
GIGUE, -S n piece of music incorporated into the classical suite
GILA, -S n large venomous brightly coloured lizard
GILBERT, -S n unit of magnetomotive force
GILCUP, -S same as ▶ giltcup
GILD, -ED, -S vb put a thin layer of gold on
GILDEN adj gilded
GILDER, -S ▶ gild
GILDHALL same as > guildhall
GILDING, -S ▶ gild
GILDS ▶ gild
GILDSMAN, GILDSMEN ▶ gild
GILET, -S n waist- or hip-length garment
GILGAI, -S n natural water hole

GILGIE, -S n type of freshwater crayfish
GILL, -ED, -ING n radiating structure beneath the cap of a mushroom ▷ vb catch (fish) or (of fish) to be caught in a gill net
GILLAROO n type of brown trout
GILLED ▶ gill
GILLER, -S ▶ gill
GILLET, -S n mare
GILLIE, -D, -S n (in Scotland) attendant for hunting or fishing ▷ vb act as a gillie
GILLING ▶ gill
GILLION, -S n (no longer in technical use) one thousand million
GILLNET, -S n net designed to catch fish by the gills ▷ vb fish using a gillnet
GILLS pl n breathing organs in fish and other water creatures
GILLY, -ING same as ▶ gillie
GILLYVOR n type of carnation
GILPEY, -S n mischievous, frolicsome boy or girl
GILPY, GILPIES same as ▶ gilpey
GILT, -S n young sow
GILTCUP, -S n buttercup
GILTHEAD n type of fish
GILTS ▶ gilt
GILTWOOD adj made of wood and gilded
GIMBAL, -ED vb support on gimbals
GIMBALS pl n set of pivoted rings
GIMCRACK adj showy but cheap ▷ n cheap showy trifle or gadget
GIMEL, -S n third letter of the Hebrew alphabet
GIMLET, -ED, -S n small tool ▷ adj penetrating or piercing ▷ vb make holes in (wood) using a gimlet
GIMMAL, -S n ring composed of interlocking rings ▷ vb provide with gimmals
GIMME, -S interj give me! ▷ n something easily obtained
GIMMER, -S n year-old ewe
GIMMES ▶ gimme
GIMMICK, -S n something designed to attract attention ▷ vb make gimmicky
GIMMICKY ▶ gimmick
GIMMIE, -S n very short putt in golf

GIMMOR, -S n mechanical device
GIMP, -ED, -ING, -S n tapelike trimming of silk, wool, or cotton, often stiffened with wire ▷ vb slang term for limp
GIMPIER ▶ gimpy
GIMPIEST ▶ gimpy
GIMPING ▶ gimp
GIMPS ▶ gimp
GIMPY, GIMPIER, GIMPIEST same as ▶ gammy
GIN, -NED, -S n spirit flavoured with juniper berries ▷ vb free (cotton) of seeds with an engine
GINCH, -ES same as ▶ gitch
GING, -S n child's catapult
GINGAL, -S n type of musket mounted on a swivel
GINGALL, -S same as ▶ gingal
GINGALS ▶ gingal
GINGE, -S n person with ginger hair
GINGELEY same as ▶ gingili
GINGELI, -S same as ▶ gingili
GINGELLI same as ▶ gingili
GINGELLY same as ▶ gingili
GINGELY same as ▶ gingili
GINGER, -ED, -S n root of a tropical plant, used as a spice ▷ adj light reddish-brown ▷ vb add the spice ginger to (a dish)
GINGERLY adv cautiously ▷ adj cautious
GINGERS ▶ ginger
GINGERY adj like or tasting of ginger
GINGES ▶ ginge
GINGHAM, -S n cotton cloth, usu checked or striped
GINGILI, -S n oil obtained from sesame seeds
GINGILLI same as ▶ gingili
GINGIVA, -E same as ▶ gum
GINGIVAL ▶ gingiva
GINGKO, -ES, -S same as ▶ ginkgo
GINGLE, -S same as ▶ jingle
GINGLYMI ▶ ginglymus
GINGS ▶ ging
GINHOUSE n building where cotton is ginned
GINK, -S n man or boy
GINKGO, -ES, -S n ornamental Chinese tree
GINKS ▶ gink
GINN same as ▶ jinn
GINNED ▶ gin
GINNEL, -S n narrow passageway between buildings
GINNER, -S ▶ gin

GINNERY another word for ▸ginhouse

GINNIER ▸ginny

GINNIEST ▸ginny

GINNING, -S ▸gin

GINNY, GINNIER, GINNIEST adj relating to the spirit gin

GINS ▸gin

GINSENG, -S n (root of) a plant

GINSHOP, -S n tavern

GIO, -S same as ▸geo

GIOCOSO adv (of music) to be expressed joyfully or playfully

GIOS ▸gio

GIP, -S vb clean fish before curing

GIPON, -S another word for ▸jupon

GIPPED ▸gip

GIPPER, -S ▸gip

GIPPIES ▸gippy

GIPPING ▸gip

GIPPY, GIPPIES n starling

GIPS ▸gip

GIPSEN, -S obsolete word for ▸gypsy

GIPSY, GIPSIED, GIPSIES, -ING n member of a nomadic people ▹vb live like a gipsy

GIPSYDOM ▸gipsy

GIPSYING ▸gipsy

GIPSYISH ▸gipsy

GIPSYISM n gipsy custom

GIRAFFE, -S n African ruminant mammal

GIRAFFID adj giraffe-like ▹n member of the Giraffidae family

GIRASOL, -S n type of opal

GIRASOLE same as ▸girasol

GIRASOLS ▸girasol

GIRD, -ED, -S vb put a belt round ▹n blow or stroke

GIRDER, -S n large metal beam

GIRDING, -S ▸gird

GIRDLE, -D, -S, GIRDLING n woman's elastic corset ▹vb surround or encircle

GIRDLER, -S n person or thing that girdles

GIRDLES ▸girdle

GIRDLING ▸girdle

GIRDS ▸gird

GIRKIN, -S same as ▸gherkin

GIRL, -S n female child

GIRLHOOD n state or time of being a girl

GIRLIE, -S adj suited to young women ▹n little girl

GIRLIER ▸girly

GIRLIES ▸girlie

GIRLIEST ▸girly

GIRLISH adj of or like a girl in looks, behaviour, etc

GIRLOND, -S obsolete word for ▸garland

GIRLS ▸girl

GIRLY, GIRLIER, GIRLIEST same as ▸girlie

GIRN, -ED, -ING, -S vb grimace or snarl

GIRNEL, -S n large chest for storing meal

GIRNER, -S ▸girn

GIRNIE, -R, -ST adj peevish

GIRNING ▸girn

GIRNS ▸girn

GIRO, -S n system of transferring money

GIROLLE, -S n chanterelle mushroom

GIRON, -S n part of a heraldic shield

GIRONIC ▸giron

GIRONNY adj divided into segments from the fesse point

GIRONS ▸giron

GIROS ▸giro

GIROSOL, -S same as ▸girasol

GIRR, -S same as ▸gird

GIRSH, -ES n currency unit of Saudi Arabia

GIRT, -ED, -ING, -S vb gird; bind

GIRTH, -ED, -ING, -S n measurement round something ▹vb fasten a girth on (a horse)

GIRTING ▸girt

GIRTLINE n gantline

GIRTS ▸girt

GIS ▸gi

GISARME, -S n long-shafted battle-axe

GISMO, -S same as ▸gizmo

GIST, -S n substance or main point of a matter

GIT, -S, -TED, -TING vb dialect version of get

GITANA, -S n Romany woman from Spain

GITANO, -S n Romany man from Spain

GITCH, -ES n underwear

GITE, -S n self-catering holiday cottage for let in France

GITS ▸git

GITTED ▸git

GITTERN, -S n obsolete medieval instrument ▹vb play the gittern

GITTIN n Jewish divorce

GITTING ▸git

GIUST, -ED, -ING, -S same as ▸joust

GIUSTO adv as observed strictly

GIUSTS ▸giust

GIVABLE ▸give

GIVE, GAVE, -S vb present (something) to another person ▹n resilience or elasticity

GIVEABLE ▸give

GIVEAWAY n something that reveals hidden feelings or intentions ▹adj very cheap or free

GIVEBACK n reduction in wages in return for some other benefit, in time of recession

GIVED same as ▸gyved

GIVEN, -S n assumed fact

GIVER, -S ▸give

GIVES ▸give

GIVING, -S ▸give

GIZMO, -S n device

GIZZ, -ES n wig

GIZZARD, -S n part of a bird's stomach

GIZZEN, -ED, -S vb (of wood) to warp

GIZZES ▸gizz

GJETOST, -S n type of Norwegian cheese

GJU, -S n type of violin used in Shetland

> This unusual word for a Shetland fiddle is great for disposing of awkward letters for a good score.

GLABELLA n elevation of the frontal bone above the nose

GLABRATE same as ▸glabrous

GLABROUS adj without hair or a similar growth

GLACE, -D, -ED, -ING, -S adj preserved in a thick sugary syrup ▹vb ice or candy (cakes, fruits, etc)

GLACIAL, -S adj of ice or glaciers ▹n ice age

GLACIATE vb cover or become covered with glaciers or masses of ice

GLACIER, -S n slow-moving mass of ice

GLACIS, -ES n slight incline

GLAD, -DED, -DER, -DEST, -DING, -S adj pleased and happy ▹vb become glad ▹n gladiolus

GLADDEN, -S vb make glad

GLADDER ▸glad

GLADDEST ▸glad

GLADDIE, -S n gladiolus

GLADDING ▸glad

GLADDON, -S n stinking iris

GLADE, -S n open space in a forest

GLADFUL adj full of gladness

GLADIATE adj shaped like a sword

GLADIER ▸ glady

GLADIEST ▸ glady

GLADIOLA same as > gladiolus

GLADIOLE same as > gladiolus

GLADIOLI > gladiolus

GLADIUS n short sword used by Roman legionaries

GLADLY, GLADLIER ▸ glad

GLADNESS ▸ glad

GLADS ▸ glad

GLADSOME adj joyous or cheerful

GLADWRAP n in New Zealand English, thin film for wrapping food ▷ vb cover with gladwrap

GLADY, GLADIER, GLADIEST ▸ glade

GLAIK, -S n prank

GLAIKET same as ▸ glaikit

GLAIKIT adj foolish

GLAIKS ▸ glaik

GLAIR, -ED, -ING, -S n white of egg ▷ vb apply glair to (something)

GLAIRE, -S same as ▸ glair

GLAIRED ▸ glair

GLAIRES ▸ glaire

GLAIRIER ▸ glairy

GLAIRIN, -S n viscous mineral deposit

GLAIRING ▸ glair

GLAIRINS ▸ glairin

GLAIRS ▸ glair

GLAIRY, GLAIRIER ▸ glair

GLAIVE, -S archaic word for ▸ sword

GLAIVED adj armed with a sword

GLAIVES ▸ glaive

GLAM, -MED, -MER, -MEST, -MING, -S n magical illusion ▷ vb make oneself look glamorous ▷ adj glamorous

GLAMMIER ▸ glammy

GLAMMING ▸ glam

GLAMMY, GLAMMIER adj glamorous

GLAMOR, -ED, -S same as ▸ glamour

GLAMOUR, -S n alluring charm or fascination ▷ vb bewitch

GLAMPING n camping with luxurious physical comforts

GLAMS ▸ glam

GLANCE, -D, -S, GLANCING vb look rapidly or briefly ▷ n brief look

GLANCER, -S n log or pole used to protect trees from damage

GLANCES ▸ glance

GLANCING ▸ glance

GLAND, -S n organ that produces and secretes substances

GLANDERS n highly infectious bacterial disease of horses, sometimes transmitted to humans

GLANDES ▸ glans

GLANDS ▸ gland

GLANDULE n small gland

GLANS, GLANDES n any small rounded body or glandlike mass

GLARE, -D, -S vb stare angrily ▷ n angry stare ▷ adj smooth and glassy

GLAREAL adj (of a plant) growing in cultivated land

GLARED ▸ glare

GLAREOUS adj resembling the white of an egg

GLARES ▸ glare

GLARIER ▸ glary

GLARIEST ▸ glary

GLARING adj conspicuous

GLARY, GLARIER, GLARIEST ▸ glare

GLASNOST n policy of openness and accountability, esp, formerly, in the USSR

GLASS, -ED, -ING n hard brittle substance ▷ vb cover with, enclose in, or fit with glass

GLASSEN adj glassy

GLASSES pl n pair of lenses for correcting faulty vision

GLASSFUL n amount held by a full glass

GLASSIE same as ▸ glassy

GLASSIER ▸ glassy

GLASSIES ▸ glassy

GLASSIFY vb turn into glass

GLASSILY ▸ glassy

GLASSINE n glazed translucent paper used for book jackets

GLASSING ▸ glass

GLASSMAN, GLASSMEN n man whose work is making or selling glassware

GLASSY, GLASSIER, GLASSIES adj like glass ▷ n glass marble

GLAUCOMA n eye disease

GLAUCOUS adj covered with a bluish waxy or powdery bloom

GLAUM, -ED, -ING, -S vb snatch

GLAUR, -S n mud or mire

GLAURIER ▸ glaury

GLAURS ▸ glaur

GLAURY, GLAURIER ▸ glaur

GLAZE, -D, -S vb fit or cover with glass ▷ n transparent coating

GLAZEN adj glazed

GLAZER, -S ▸ glaze

GLAZES ▸ glaze

GLAZIER, -S n person who fits windows with glass

GLAZIERY ▸ glazier

GLAZIEST ▸ glazy

GLAZILY ▸ glaze

GLAZING, -S n surface of a glazed object

GLAZY, GLAZIEST ▸ glaze

GLEAM, -ED, -S n small beam or glow of light ▷ vb emit a gleam

GLEAMER, -S n mirror used to cheat in card games

GLEAMIER ▸ gleamy

GLEAMING ▸ gleam

GLEAMS ▸ gleam

GLEAMY, GLEAMIER ▸ gleam

GLEAN, -ED, -ING, -S vb gather (facts etc) bit by bit

GLEANER, -S ▸ glean

GLEANING ▸ glean

GLEANS ▸ glean

GLEAVE, -S archaic word for ▸ sword

GLEBA, -E n mass of spores

GLEBE, -S n land granted to a member of the clergy

GLEBIER ▸ gleby

GLEBIEST ▸ gleby

GLEBOUS adj gleby

GLEBY, GLEBIER, GLEBIEST adj relating to a glebe

GLED, -S n red kite (bird)

GLEDE, -S same as ▸ gled

GLEDGE, -D, -S, GLEDGING vb glance sideways

GLEDS ▸ gled

GLEE, -ING, -S n triumph and delight ▷ vb be full of glee

GLEED, -S n burning ember or hot coal

GLEEFUL adj merry or joyful

GLEEING ▸ glee

GLEEK, -ED, -ING, -S vb jeer

GLEEMAN, GLEEMEN n minstrel

GLEENIE, -S n guinea fowl

GLEES ▸ glee

GLEESOME adj full of glee

GLEG, -GER, -GEST adj quick

GLEGLY ▸ gleg

GLEGNESS ▸ gleg

GLEI, -S same as ▸ gley

GLEN, -S n deep narrow valley, esp in Scotland

G

GLENLIKE ▶ glen
GLENOID, -S adj resembling or having a shallow cavity ▷ n shallow cavity
GLENS ▶ glen
GLENT, -ED, -ING, -S same as ▶ glint
GLEY, -ED, -S n bluish-grey compact sticky soil ▷ vb squint
GLEYING, -S ▶ gley
GLEYS ▶ gley
GLIA, -S n web of tissue that supports nerve cells
GLIADIN, -S n protein of cereals with a high proline content
GLIADINE same as ▶ gliadin
GLIADINS ▶ gliadin
GLIAL ▶ glia
GLIAS ▶ glia
GLIB, -BED, -BER, -BEST, -BING, -S adj fluent but insincere or superficial ▷ vb render glib, smooth, or slippery
GLIBBERY adj slippery
GLIBBEST ▶ glib
GLIBBING ▶ glib
GLIBLY ▶ glib
GLIBNESS ▶ glib
GLIBS ▶ glib
GLID, -DER, -DEST adj moving smoothly and easily
GLIDDERY adj slippery
GLIDDEST ▶ glid
GLIDE, -D, -S, GLODE vb move easily and smoothly ▷ n smooth easy movement
GLIDER, -S n flying phalanger
GLIDES ▶ glide
GLIDING, -S n sport of flying gliders
GLIFF, -ING, -S n slap
GLIFT, -S n moment
GLIKE, -S same as ▶ gleek
GLIM, -S n light or lamp
GLIME, -D, -S, GLIMING vb glance sideways
GLIMMER, -S vb shine faintly, flicker ▷ n faint gleam
GLIMMERY adj glimmering, shimmery
GLIMPSE, -D, -S n brief or incomplete view ▷ vb catch a glimpse of
GLIMPSER ▶ glimpse
GLIMPSES ▶ glimpse
GLIMS ▶ glim
GLINT, -ED, -ING, -S vb gleam brightly ▷ n bright gleam
GLINTIER ▶ glinty
GLINTING ▶ glint

GLINTS ▶ glint
GLINTY, GLINTIER ▶ glint
GLIOMA, -S, -TA n tumour of the brain and spinal cord
GLIOSIS, GLIOSES n process leading to scarring in the nervous system
GLISK, -S n glimpse
GLISSADE n gliding step in ballet ▷ vb perform a glissade
GLISSE, -S n type of dance step
GLISTEN, -S vb gleam by reflecting light ▷ n gleam or gloss
GLISTER, -S archaic word for ▶ glitter
GLIT, -S n slimy matter
GLITCH, -ES n small problem that stops something from working
GLITCHY ▶ glitch
GLITS ▶ glit
GLITTER, -S vb shine with bright flashes ▷ n sparkle or brilliance
GLITTERY ▶ glitter
GLITZ, -ED, -ES, -ING n ostentatious showiness ▷ vb make something more attractive
GLITZIER ▶ glitzy
GLITZILY ▶ glitzy
GLITZING ▶ glitz
GLITZY, GLITZIER adj showily attractive
GLOAM, -S n dusk
GLOAMING n twilight
GLOAMS ▶ gloam
GLOAT, -ED, -S vb regard one's own good fortune with pleasure ▷ n act of gloating
GLOATER, -S ▶ gloat
GLOATING n act of gloating
GLOATS ▶ gloat
GLOB, -S n rounded mass of thick fluid
GLOBAL adj worldwide
GLOBALLY ▶ global
GLOBATE adj shaped like a globe
GLOBATED same as ▶ globate
GLOBBY, GLOBBIER adj thick and lumpy
GLOBE, -D, -S, GLOBING n sphere with a map of the earth on it ▷ vb form or cause to form into a globe
GLOBI ▶ globus
GLOBIER ▶ globy
GLOBIEST ▶ globy
GLOBIN, -S n protein component of haemoglobin
GLOBING ▶ globe

GLOBINS ▶ globin
GLOBOID, -S adj shaped approximately like a globe ▷ n globoid body
GLOBOSE adj spherical or approximately spherical ▷ n globose object
GLOBOUS same as ▶ globose
GLOBS ▶ glob
GLOBULAR adj shaped like a globe or globule ▷ n globular star cluster
GLOBULE, -S n small round drop
GLOBULET n small globule
GLOBULIN n simple protein found in living tissue
GLOBUS, GLOBI n any spherelike structure
GLOBY, GLOBIER, GLOBIEST adj round
GLOCHID, -S n barbed spine on a plant
GLODE ▶ glide
GLOGG, -S n hot alcoholic mixed drink
GLOIRE, -S n glory
GLOM, -MED, -MING, -S vb attach oneself to or associate oneself with
GLOMERA ▶ glomus
GLOMMED ▶ glom
GLOMMING ▶ glom
GLOMS ▶ glom
GLOMUS, GLOMERA n small anastomosis in an artery or vein
GLONOIN, -S n nitroglycerin
GLOOM, -ED, -ING, -S n melancholy ▷ vb look sullen or unhappy
GLOOMFUL ▶ gloom
GLOOMIER ▶ gloomy
GLOOMILY ▶ gloomy
GLOOMING ▶ gloom
GLOOMS ▶ gloom
GLOOMY, GLOOMIER adj despairing or sad
GLOOP, -ED, -ING, -S vb cover with a viscous substance
GLOOPIER ▶ gloopy
GLOOPING ▶ gloop
GLOOPS ▶ gloop
GLOOPY, GLOOPIER ▶ gloop
GLOP, -PED, -PING, -S vb cover with a viscous substance
GLOPPIER ▶ gloppy
GLOPPING ▶ glop
GLOPPY, GLOPPIER ▶ glop
GLOPS ▶ glop
GLORIA, -S n silk, wool, cotton, or nylon fabric
GLORIED ▶ glory

GLORIES ▸ glory

GLORIFY vb make (something) seem more worthy than it is

GLORIOLE another name for a ▸ halo

GLORIOSA n bulbous African tropical plant

GLORIOUS adj brilliantly beautiful

GLORY, GLORIED, GLORIES, -ING n praise or honour ▷ vb triumph or exalt

GLOSS, -ED, -ES, -ING n surface shine or lustre ▷ vb make glossy

GLOSSA, -E, -S n paired tonguelike lobe in the labium of an insect

GLOSSAL ▸ glossa

GLOSSARY n list of special or technical words with definitions

GLOSSAS ▸ glossa

GLOSSED ▸ gloss

GLOSSEME n smallest meaningful unit of a language, such as stress, form, etc

GLOSSER, -S ▸ gloss

GLOSSES ▸ gloss

GLOSSIER ▸ glossy

GLOSSIES ▸ glossy

GLOSSILY ▸ glossy

GLOSSINA n tsetse fly

GLOSSING ▸ gloss

GLOSSIST same as ▸ glossator

GLOSSY, GLOSSIER, GLOSSIES adj smooth and shiny ▷ n expensively produced magazine

GLOST, -S n lead glaze used for pottery

GLOTTAL adj of the glottis

GLOTTIC adj of or relating to the tongue or the glottis

GLOTTIS n vocal cords and the space between them

GLOUT, -ED, -ING, -S vb look sullen

GLOVE, -S n covering for the hand

GLOVEBOX n small compartment in a car for miscellaneous articles

GLOVED ▸ glove

GLOVER, -S n person who makes or sells gloves

GLOVES ▸ glove

GLOVING, -S ▸ glove

GLOW, -ED, -S vb emit light and heat without flames ▷ n glowing light

GLOWER, -ED, -S n scowl ▷ vb stare angrily

GLOWFLY n firefly

GLOWING adj full of praise

GLOWLAMP n small light consisting of two or more electrodes in an inert gas

GLOWS ▸ glow

GLOWWORM n European beetle which produces a greenish light

GLOXINIA n tropical plant with large bell-shaped flowers

GLOZE, -D, -S vb explain away ▷ n flattery or deceit

GLOZING, -S ▸ gloze

GLUCAGON n hormone that releases glucose into the blood

GLUCAN, -S n any polysaccharide consisting of a polymer of glucose

GLUCINA, -S n oxide of glucinum

GLUCINIC > glucinium

GLUCINUM same as > glucinium

GLUCONIC adj as in gluconic acid acid that occurs naturally in fruit

GLUCOSE, -S n kind of sugar found in fruit

GLUCOSIC ▸ glucose

GLUE, -D, -ING, -S, GLUIER, GLUIEST, GLUING n natural or synthetic sticky substance ▷ vb fasten with glue

GLUEBALL n hypothetical composite subatomic particle

GLUED ▸ glue

GLUEING ▸ glue

GLUEISH same as ▸ gluish

GLUELIKE ▸ glue

GLUEPOT, -S n container for holding glue

GLUER, -S ▸ glue

GLUES ▸ glue

GLUEY ▸ glue

GLUG, -GED, -GING, -S n word representing a gurgling sound ▷ vb drink noisily, taking big gulps

GLUHWEIN n mulled wine

GLUIER ▸ glue

GLUIEST ▸ glue

GLUILY ▸ glue

GLUINESS ▸ glue

GLUING ▸ glue

GLUISH adj having the properties of glue

GLUM, -MER, -MEST adj sullen or gloomy

GLUME, -S n one of a pair of dry membranous bracts in grasses

GLUMELLA n palea

GLUMES ▸ glume

GLUMLY ▸ glum

GLUMMER ▸ glum

GLUMMEST ▸ glum

GLUMNESS ▸ glum

GLUMPIER ▸ glumpy

GLUMPILY ▸ glumpy

GLUMPISH ▸ glumpy

GLUMPS n state of sulking

GLUMPY, GLUMPIER adj sullen

GLUMS n gloomy feelings

GLUNCH, -ED, -ES vb look sullen

GLUON, -S n hypothetical particle

GLURGE, -S n stories supposed to be true but often fabricated

GLUT, -S, -TED, -TING n excessive supply ▷ vb oversupply

GLUTAEAL ▸ glutaeus

GLUTAEUS, GLUTAEI same as ▸ gluteus

GLUTAMIC adj as in glutamic acid nonessential amino acid that plays a part in nitrogen metabolism

GLUTCH, -ED, -ES vb swallow

GLUTE, -S same as ▸ gluteus

GLUTEAL ▸ gluteus

GLUTEI ▸ gluteus

GLUTELIN n water-insoluble plant protein found in cereals

GLUTEN, -S n protein found in cereal grain

GLUTENIN n type of protein

GLUTENS ▸ gluten

GLUTES ▸ glute

GLUTEUS, GLUTEI n any of the three muscles of the buttock

GLUTS ▸ glut

GLUTTED ▸ glut

GLUTTING ▸ glut

GLUTTON, -S n greedy person

GLUTTONY n practice of eating too much

GLYCAN, -S n polysaccharide

GLYCEMIA US spelling of > glycaemia

GLYCEMIC ▸ glycemia

GLYCERIA n manna grass

GLYCERIC adj of, containing, or derived from glycerol

GLYCERIN same as ▸ glycerol

GLYCEROL n colourless odourless syrupy liquid

GLYCERYL n (something) derived from glycerol

GLYCIN, -S same as ▸ glycine

GLYCINE, -S n nonessential amino acid

G

GLYCINS ▸ glycin

GLYCOGEN n starchlike carbohydrate stored in the liver and muscles of humans and animals

GLYCOL, -S n another name (not in technical usage) for a diol

GLYCOLIC ▸ glycol

GLYCOLS ▸ glycol

GLYCONIC n verse consisting of a spondee, choriamb and pyrrhic

GLYCOSE, -S n any of various monosaccharides

GLYCOSYL n glucose-derived radical

GLYCYL, -S n radical of glycine

GLYPH, -S n carved channel or groove

GLYPHIC ▸ glyph

GLYPHS ▸ glyph

GLYPTAL, -S n alkyd resin

GLYPTIC adj of or relating to engraving or carving

GLYPTICS n art of engraving precious stones

GNAMMA variant of ▸ namma

GNAR, -RED, -RING, -S same as ▸ gnarl

GNARL, -ING, -S n any knotty protuberance or swelling on a tree ▷ vb knot or cause to knot

GNARLED adj rough, twisted, and knobbly

GNARLIER ▸ gnarly

GNARLING ▸ gnarl

GNARLS ▸ gnarl

GNARLY, GNARLIER adj good

GNARR, -S same as ▸ gnarl

GNARRED ▸ gnar

GNARRING ▸ gnar

GNARRS ▸ gnarr

GNARS ▸ gnar

GNASH, -ED, -ES, -ING vb grind (the teeth) together ▷ n act of gnashing the teeth

GNASHER n tooth

GNASHERS pl n teeth, esp false ones

GNASHES ▸ gnash

GNASHING ▸ gnash

GNAT, -S n small biting two-winged fly

GNATHAL same as ▸ gnathic

GNATHIC adj of or relating to the jaw

GNATHION n lowest point of the midline of the lower jaw: a reference point in craniometry

GNATHITE n appendage of an arthropod that is specialized for grasping or chewing

GNATLIKE ▸ gnat

GNATLING n small gnat

GNATS ▸ gnat

GNATTY, GNATTIER adj infested with gnats

GNATWREN n small bird of the gnatcatcher family

GNAW, -ED, -N, -S vb bite or chew steadily ▷ n act or an instance of gnawing

GNAWABLE ▸ gnaw

GNAWED ▸ gnaw

GNAWER, -S ▸ gnaw

GNAWING, -S ▸ gnaw

GNAWN ▸ gnaw

GNAWS ▸ gnaw

GNEISS, -ES n coarse-grained metamorphic rock

GNEISSIC ▸ gneiss

GNOCCHI n dumplings

GNOME, GNOMAE, -S n imaginary creature like a little old man

GNOMIC adj of pithy sayings

GNOMICAL same as ▸ gnomic

GNOMISH ▸ gnome

GNOMIST, -S n writer of pithy sayings

GNOMON, -S n stationary arm on a sundial

GNOMONIC ▸ gnomon

GNOMONS ▸ gnomon

GNOSIS, GNOSES n supposedly revealed knowledge of spiritual truths

GNOSTIC, -S adj of, relating to, or possessing knowledge ▷ n one who knows

GNOW, -S n Australian wild bird

GNU, -S n ox-like S African antelope

GO, GANE, GAUN, -ES, -NE, -S vb move to or from a place ▷ n attempt

GOA, -S n Tibetan gazelle

GOAD, -ED, -ING, -S vb provoke (someone) to take some kind of action, usu in anger ▷ n spur or provocation

GOADLIKE ▸ goad

GOADS ▸ goad

GOADSMAN, GOADSMEN n person who uses a goad

GOADSTER n goadsman

GOAF, -S n waste left in old mine workings

GOAL, -ED, -ING, -S n posts through which the ball or

puck has to move to score ▷ vb in rugby, to convert a try into a goal

GOALBALL n game played with a ball that emits sound

GOALED ▸ goal

GOALIE, -S n goalkeeper

GOALING ▸ goal

GOALLESS ▸ goal

GOALPOST n one of the two posts marking the limit of a goal

GOALS ▸ goal

GOALWARD adv towards a goal

GOANNA, -S n large Australian lizard

GOARY variant spelling of ▸ gory

GOAS ▸ goa

GOAT, -S n sure-footed ruminant animal with horns

GOATEE, -S n pointed tuft-like beard

GOATEED ▸ goatee

GOATEES ▸ goatee

GOATFISH n red mullet

GOATHERD n person who looks after a herd of goats

GOATIER ▸ goaty

This means more like a goat: it may seem a silly sort of word but because it uses such common letters the chance to play it as a bonus comes up very frequently.

GOATIES ▸ goaty

GOATIEST ▸ goaty

GOATISH adj of, like, or relating to a goat

GOATLIKE ▸ goat

GOATLING n young goat

GOATS ▸ goat

GOATSE, -S n deliberately offensive image placed maliciously into a website

GOATSKIN n leather made from the skin of a goat

GOATWEED n plant of the genus Capraria

GOATY, GOATIER, GOATIES, GOATIEST n pointed tuft-like beard ▷ adj resembling a goat

GOB, -BED, -BING, -S n lump of a soft substance ▷ vb spit

GOBAN, -S n board on which go is played

GOBANG, -S n Japanese board-game

GOBANS ▸ goban

GOBAR adj as in **gobar numeral** kind of numeral

GOBBED ▸ gob

GOBBET, -S n lump, esp of food

GOBBI ▸ **gobbo**
GOBBIER ▸ **gobby**
GOBBIEST ▸ **gobby**
GOBBING ▸ **gob**
GOBBLE, -D, -S, GOBBLING
vb eat hastily and greedily
▸ n rapid gurgling cry of the
male turkey ▸ interj
imitation of this sound
GOBBLER, -S n turkey
GOBBLES ▸ **gobble**
GOBBLING ▸ **gobble**
GOBBO, GOBBI n
hunchback
**GOBBY, GOBBIER,
GOBBIEST** adj
loudmouthed and offensive
GOBI, -S n (in Indian
cookery) cauliflower
GOBIES ▸ **goby**
GOBIID, -S n small
spiny-finned fish
GOBIOID, -S n type of
spiny-finned fish
GOBIS ▸ **gobi**
GOBLET, -S n drinking cup
without handles
GOBLIN, -S n (in folklore)
small malevolent creature
GOBO, -ES, -S n shield
placed around a microphone
GOBONEE same as ▸ **gobony**
GOBONY adj in heraldry,
composed of a row of small,
alternately coloured,
squares
GOBOS ▸ **gobo**
GOBS ▸ **gob**
GOBURRA, -S n kookaburra
GOBY, GOBIES n small
spiny-finned fish
GOD, -DED, -DING, -S n
spirit or being worshipped as
having supernatural power
▸ vb deify
GODCHILD n child for whom
a person stands as
godparent
GODDED ▸ **god**
GODDEN, -S n evening
greeting
GODDESS n female divinity
GODDING ▸ **god**
GODET, -S n triangular piece
of material inserted into a
garment
GODETIA, -S n plant with
showy flowers
GODETS ▸ **godet**
GODHEAD, -S n essential
nature and condition of
being a god
GODHOOD, -S n state of
being divine
GODLESS adj wicked or
unprincipled

GODLIER ▸ **godly**
GODLIEST ▸ **godly**
GODLIKE adj resembling or
befitting a god or God
GODLILY ▸ **godly**
GODLING, -S n little god
**GODLY, GODLIER,
GODLIEST** adj devout or
pious
GODOWN, -S n (in East Asia
and India) a warehouse
GODROON, -S same as
▸ **gadroon**
GODS ▸ **god**
GODSEND, -S n something
unexpected but welcome
GODSHIP, -S n divinity
GODSO same as ▸ **gadso**
GODSON, -S n male
godchild
GODSPEED n expression of
one's good wishes for a
person's success and safety
GODWARD adv towards
God
GODWARDS same as
▸ **godward**
GODWIT, -S n shore bird
with long legs and an
upturned bill
GOE same as ▸ **go**
GOEL, -S n in Jewish law, a
blood-avenger
GOER, -S n person who
attends something regularly
GOES ▸ **go**
GOEST vb archaic 2nd person
sing present of go
GOETH vb archaic 3rd person
sing present of go
GOETHITE n black, brown,
or yellow mineral
GOETIC ▸ **goety**
GOETY, GOETIES n
witchcraft
GOEY, GOIER, GOIEST adj
go-ahead
GOFER, -S n employee or
assistant performing menial
tasks
GOFF, -ED, -ING, -S obsolete
variant of ▸ **golf**
GOFFER, -ED, -S vb press
pleats into (a frill) ▸ n
ornamental frill made by
pressing pleats
GOFFING ▸ **goff**
GOFFS ▸ **goff**
GOGGA, -S n any small
insect
GOGGLE, -D, -S, GOGGLING
vb (of the eyes) bulge ▸ n
fixed or bulging stare
GOGGLER, -S n big-eyed
scad
GOGGLES ▸ **goggle**

GOGGLIER ▸ **goggly**
GOGGLING ▸ **goggle**
GOGGLY, GOGGLIER
▸ **goggle**
GOGLET, -S n long-necked
water-cooling vessel
GOGO, -S n disco
GOHONZON n (in Nichiren
Buddhism) paper scroll to
which devotional chanting is
directed
GOIER ▸ **goey**
GOIEST ▸ **goey**
GOING, -S ▸ **go**
GOITER, -S same as ▸ **goitre**
GOITERED ▸ **goiter**
GOITERS ▸ **goiter**
GOITRE, -S n swelling of the
thyroid gland in the neck
GOITRED ▸ **goitre**
GOITRES ▸ **goitre**
GOITROUS ▸ **goitre**
GOJI, -S same as > **wolfberry**
GOLCONDA n source of
wealth or riches, esp a mine
GOLD, -ER, -EST, -S n yellow
precious metal ▸ adj made
of gold
GOLDARNS ▸ **goldarn**
GOLDBUG, -S n American
beetle with a bright metallic
lustre
GOLDEN, -ED, -ER, -S adj
made of gold ▸ vb gild
GOLDENLY ▸ **golden**
GOLDENS ▸ **golden**
GOLDER ▸ **gold**
GOLDEST ▸ **gold**
GOLDEYE, -S n N American
fish
GOLDFISH n orange fish
kept in ponds or aquariums
GOLDIER ▸ **goldy**
GOLDIES ▸ **goldy**
GOLDIEST ▸ **goldy**
GOLDISH ▸ **gold**
GOLDLESS ▸ **gold**
GOLDS ▸ **gold**
GOLDSIZE n adhesive used
to fix gold leaf to a surface
GOLDTAIL n as in **goldtail
moth** European moth with
white wings and a soft white
furry body with a yellow tail
tuft
GOLDTONE adj gold-
coloured ▸ n photographic
image printed on a
glass-plate with a painted
golden backing
GOLDURNS ▸ **goldurn**
GOLDWORK n gold objects
collectively
**GOLDY, GOLDIER,
GOLDIES, GOLDIEST** adj
gold-like ▸ n goldfinch

G

GOLE, -S obsolete spelling of ▸ goal

GOLEM, -S n (in Jewish legend) artificially created human

GOLES ▸ gole

GOLF, -ED, -S n outdoor sport ▷ vb play golf

GOLFER, -S n person who plays golf

GOLFIANA n collection of golfing memorabilia

GOLFING, -S ▸ golf

GOLFS ▸ golf

GOLGOTHA n place of burial

GOLIARD, -S n one of a number of wandering scholars

GOLIARDY ▸ goliard

GOLIAS, -ED, -ES vb behave outrageously

GOLIATH, -S n giant

GOLLAN, -S n yellow flower

GOLLAND, -S same as ▸ gollan

GOLLANS ▸ gollan

GOLLAR, -ED, -S same as ▸ goller

GOLLER, -ED, -S vb roar

GOLLIED ▸ golly

GOLLIES ▸ golly

GOLLOP, -ED, -S vb eat or drink (something) quickly or greedily

GOLLOPER ▸ gollop

GOLLOPS ▸ gollop

GOLLY, GOLLIED, GOLLIES, -ING interj exclamation of mild surprise ▷ vb spit

GOLOSH, -ED, -ES same as ▸ galosh

GOLOSHE same as ▸ galosh

GOLOSHED ▸ golosh

GOLOSHES ▸ golosh

GOLP, -S same as ▸ golpe

GOLPE, -S n in heraldry, a purple circle

GOLPS ▸ golp

GOMBEEN, -S n usury

GOMBO, -S same as ▸ gumbo

GOMBRO, -S same as ▸ gumbo

GOMBROON n Persian and Chinese pottery and porcelain wares

GOMBROS ▸ gombro

GOMER, -S n unwanted hospital patient

GOMERAL, -S same as ▸ gomeril

GOMEREL, -S same as ▸ gomeril

GOMERIL, -S n Scots word for a slow-witted person

GOMERS ▸ gomer

GOMOKU, -S another word for ▸ gobang

GOMPA, -S n Tibetan monastery

GOMUTI, -S n feather palm tree

GOMUTO, -S same as ▸ gomuti

GON, -S n geometrical grade

GONAD, -S n organ producing reproductive cells

GONADAL ▸ gonad

GONADIAL ▸ gonad

GONADIC ▸ gonad

GONADS ▸ gonad

GONCH, -ES same as ▸ gitch

GONDELAY same as ▸ gondola

GONDOLA, -S n long narrow boat used in Venice

GONE ▸ go

GONEF, -S same as ▸ ganef

GONENESS n faintness from hunger

GONER, -S n person or thing beyond help or recovery

GONFALON n banner hanging from a crossbar

GONFANON same as ▸ gonfalon

GONG, -ED, -ING, -S n rimmed metal disc ▷ vb sound a gong

GONGLIKE ▸ gong

GONGS ▸ gong

GONGSTER n person who strikes a gong

GONGYO, -S n Buddhist ceremony

GONIA ▸ gonion

GONIDIA ▸ gonidium

GONIDIAL ▸ gonidium

GONIDIC ▸ gonidium

GONIDIUM, GONIDIA n green algal cell in the thallus of a lichen

GONIF, -S same as ▸ ganef

GONIFF, -S same as ▸ ganef

GONIFS ▸ gonif

GONION, GONIA n point or apex of the angle of the lower jaw

GONIUM n immature reproductive cell

GONK, -S n stuffed toy, often used as a mascot

GONNA vb going to

GONOCYTE n any cell which may potentially undergo meiosis

GONODUCT n duct leading from a gonad to the exterior, through which gametes pass

GONOF, -S same as ▸ ganef

GONOPH, -S same as ▸ ganef

GONOPOD, -S n either of the reproductive organs of insects

GONOPORE n external pore in insects, earthworms, etc, through which the gametes are extruded

GONOSOME n individuals, collectively, in a colonial animal that are involved with reproduction

GONS ▸ gon

GONYS, -ES n lower outline of a bird's bill

GONZO, -S adj wild or crazy ▷ n wild or crazy person

GOO, -S n sticky substance

GOOBER, -S another name for ▸ peanut

GOOBY, GOOBIES n spittle

GOOD, -S adj giving pleasure ▷ n benefit

GOODBY, -S same as ▸ goodbye

GOODBYE, -S n expression used on parting ▷ interj expression used on parting ▷ sentence substitute farewell

GOODBYS ▸ goodby

GOODIE same as ▸ goody

GOODIER ▸ goody

GOODIES ▸ goody

GOODIEST ▸ goody

GOODISH ▸ good

GOODLY, GOODLIER adj considerable

GOODMAN, GOODMEN n husband

GOODNESS n quality of being good ▷ interj exclamation of surprise

GOODS ▸ good

GOODSIRE n grandfather

GOODTIME adj wildly seeking pleasure

GOODWIFE n mistress of a household

GOODWILL n kindly feeling

GOODY, GOODIER, GOODIES, GOODIEST n hero in a book or film ▷ interj child's exclamation of pleasure ▷ adj smug and sanctimonious

GOODYEAR n euphemistic term for the Devil

GOOEY, GOOIER, GOOIEST adj sticky and soft

GOOF, -ED, -ING, -S n mistake ▷ vb make a mistake

GOOFBALL n barbiturate sleeping pill

GOOFED ▸ goof

GOOFIER ▸ goofy

GOOFIEST ▸ goofy

GOOFILY ▶ goofy
GOOFING ▶ goof
GOOFS ▶ goof
GOOFUS, -ES *n* slow-witted or stupid person
GOOFY, GOOFIER, GOOFIEST *adj* silly or ridiculous
GOOG, -S *n* egg
GOOGLE, -D, -S, GOOGLING *vb* search on the internet using a search engine
GOOGLIES ▶ googly
GOOGLING ▶ google
GOOGLY, GOOGLIES *n* ball that spins unexpectedly on the bounce
GOOGOL, -S *n* number shown as one followed by 100 zeros
GOOGS ▶ goog
GOOIER ▶ gooey
GOOIEST ▶ gooey
GOOILY ▶ gooey
GOOINESS *n* quality of being gooey
GOOK, -S *n* sticky, messy substance
GOOKIER ▶ gooky
GOOKIEST ▶ gooky
GOOKS ▶ gook
GOOKY, GOOKIER, GOOKIEST *adj* sticky and messy
GOOL, -S *n* corn marigold
GOOLD, -S *Scots word for* ▶ gold
GOOLS ▶ gool
GOOMBAH, -S *n* patron or mentor
GOOMBAY, -S *n* Bahamian soft drink
GOON, -S *n* person hired to commit violent acts
GOONDA, -S *n* (in India) habitual criminal
GOONERY *n* behaviour typical of goons
GOONEY, -S *n* albatross
GOONIE, -S *Scots word for a* ▶ gown
GOONIER ▶ goony
GOONIES ▶ goonie
GOONIEST ▶ goony
GOONS ▶ goon
GOONY, GOONIER, GOONIEST ▶ goon
GOOP, -S *n* sticky or semiliquid substance
GOOPED *adj* as in gooped up sticky with goop
GOOPIER ▶ goopy
GOOPIEST ▶ goopy
GOOPS ▶ goop
GOOPY, GOOPIER, GOOPIEST ▶ goop

GOOR, -S *same as* ▶ gur
GOORAL, -S *same as* ▶ goral
GOORIE, -S *same as* ▶ kuri
GOOROO, -S *same as* ▶ guru
GOORS ▶ goor
GOORY *same as* ▶ kuri
GOOS ▶ goo
GOOSE, GEESE, -D, -S, GOOSING *n* web-footed bird like a large duck ▷ *vb* prod (someone) playfully in the bottom
GOOSEGOB *n* gooseberry
GOOSEGOG *n* gooseberry
GOOSERY *n* place for keeping geese
GOOSES ▶ goose
GOOSEY, -S *same as* ▶ goosy
GOOSIER ▶ goosy
GOOSIES ▶ goosy
GOOSIEST ▶ goosy
GOOSING ▶ goose
GOOSY, GOOSIER, GOOSIES, GOOSIEST *adj* of or like a goose ▷ *n* goose
GOPAK, -S *n* Russian peasant dance
GOPHER, -ED, -S *n* American burrowing rodent ▷ *vb* burrow
GOPIK, -S *n* money unit of Azerbaijan
GOPURA, -S *n* gateway tower of an Indian temple
GOPURAM, -S *same as* ▶ gopura
GOPURAS ▶ gopura
GOR, -S *interj* God! ▷ *n* seagull
GORA, -S *n* (in Indian English) White or fair-skinned male
GORAL, -S *n* small S Asian goat antelope
GORAMY, GORAMIES *same as* ▶ gourami
GORAS ▶ gora
GORBELLY *n* large belly
GORBLIMY *same as* > gorblimey
GORCOCK, -S *n* male of the red grouse
GORCROW, -S *n* carrion crow
GORDITA, -S *n* small thick tortilla
GORE, -D, -S *n* blood from a wound ▷ *vb* pierce with horns
GOREFEST *n* film featuring excessive depictions of bloodshed
GORES ▶ gore
GORGE, -D, -S, GORGING *n* deep narrow valley ▷ *vb* eat greedily

GORGEDLY ▶ gorge
GORGEOUS *adj* strikingly beautiful or attractive
GORGER, -S ▶ gorge
GORGERIN *another name for* ▶ necking
GORGERS ▶ gorger
GORGES ▶ gorge
GORGET, -S *n* collar-like piece of armour
GORGETED ▶ gorget
GORGETS ▶ gorget
GORGIA, -S *n* improvised sung passage
GORGING ▶ gorge
GORGIO, -S *n* word used by Roma people for a non-Roma
GORGON, -S *n* terrifying or repulsive woman
GORHEN, -S *n* female red grouse
GORI, -S *n* (in Indian English) White or fair-skinned female
GORIER ▶ gory
GORIEST ▶ gory
GORILLA, -S *n* largest of the apes, found in Africa
GORILY ▶ gory
GORINESS ▶ gory
GORING, -S ▶ gore
GORIS ▶ gori
GORM, -ED, -ING, -S *n* foolish person ▷ *vb* understand
GORMAND, -S *same as* ▶ gourmand
GORMED ▶ gorm
GORMIER ▶ gormy
GORMIEST ▶ gormy
GORMING ▶ gorm
GORMLESS *adj* stupid
GORMS ▶ gorm
GORMY, GORMIER, GORMIEST *adj* gormless
GORP, -ED, -ING, -S *same as* ▶ gawp
GORS ▶ gor
GORSE, -S *n* prickly yellow-flowered shrub
GORSEDD, -S *n* meeting held daily before an eisteddfod
GORSES ▶ gorse
GORSIER ▶ gorsy
GORSIEST ▶ gorsy
GORSOON, -S *n* young boy
GORSY, GORSIER, GORSIEST ▶ gorsy
GORY, GORIER, GORIEST *adj* horrific or bloodthirsty
GOS ▶ go
GOSH *interj* exclamation of mild surprise or wonder
GOSHAWK, -S *n* large hawk
GOSHT, -S *n* Indian meat dish**

GOSLET, -S n pygmy goose

GOSLING, -S n young goose

GOSPEL, -S n any of the first four books of the New Testament ▷ adj denoting a kind of religious music ▷ vb teach the gospel

GOSPELER same as > gospeller

GOSPELLY adj like gospel music

GOSPELS ▶ gospel

GOSPODA ▶ gospodin

GOSPODAR n hospodar

GOSPODIN, GOSPODA n Russian title of address, often indicating respect

GOSPORT, -S n aeroplane communication device

GOSS, -ED, -ING vb spit

GOSSAMER n very fine fabric

GOSSAN, -S n oxidized portion of a mineral vein in rock

GOSSE, -S variant of ▶ gorse

GOSSED ▶ goss

GOSSES ▶ gosse

GOSSIB, -S n gossip

GOSSING ▶ goss

GOSSIP, -ED, -S n idle talk, esp about other people ▷ vb engage in gossip

GOSSIPER ▶ gossip

GOSSIPRY n idle talk

GOSSIPS ▶ gossip

GOSSIPY adj tending to gossip

GOSSOON, -S n young boy

GOSSYPOL n toxic crystalline pigment that is a constituent of cottonseed oil

GOSTER, -ED, -S vb laugh uncontrollably

GOT ▶ get

GOTCH, -ES same as ▶ gitch

GOTCHA, -S adj as in gotcha lizard Australian name for a crocodile

GOTCHES ▶ gotch

GOTCHIES pl n underwear

GOTH, -S n aficionado of goth music and fashion

GOTHIC, -S adj relating to a literary style characterized by gloom and the supernatural ▷ n family of heavy script typefaces

GOTHIER ▶ gothy

GOTHIEST ▶ gothy

GOTHITE, -S same as ▶ goethite

GOTHS ▶ goth

GOTHY, GOTHIER, GOTHIEST adj characteristic of goth music and fashion

GOTTA vb got to

GOTTEN a past participle of ▶ get

GOUACHE, -S n (painting using) watercolours mixed with glue

GOUGE, -D, -S, GOUGING vb scoop or force out ▷ n hole or groove

GOUGER, -S n person or tool that gouges

GOUGERE, -S n choux pastry flavoured with cheese

GOUGERS ▶ gouger

GOUGES ▶ gouge

GOUGING ▶ gouge

GOUJEERS same as ▶ goodyear

GOUJON, -S n small strip of food

GOUK, -S same as ▶ gowk

GOULASH n rich stew seasoned with paprika

GOURA, -S n large, crested ground pigeon found in New Guinea

GOURAMI, -S n large SE Asian labyrinth fish

GOURAS ▶ goura

GOURD, -S n fleshy fruit of a climbing plant

GOURDE, -S n standard monetary unit of Haiti

GOURDFUL n as much as a gourd will hold

GOURDIER ▶ gourdy

GOURDS ▶ gourd

GOURDY, GOURDIER adj (of horses) swollen-legged

GOURMAND n person who is very keen on food and drink

GOURMET, -S n connoisseur of food and drink

GOUSTY, GOUSTIER adj dismal

GOUT, -S n drop or splash (of something)

GOUTFLY n fly whose larvae infect crops

GOUTIER ▶ gouty

GOUTIEST ▶ gouty

GOUTILY ▶ gouty

GOUTS ▶ gout

GOUTTE, -S n (in heraldry) the shape of a drop of liquid

GOUTWEED n Eurasian plant with white flowers and creeping underground stems

GOUTWORT n bishop's weed

GOUTY, GOUTIER, GOUTIEST adj having the disease gout

GOV, -S n boss

GOVERN, -ED, -S vb rule, direct, or control ▷ n ability to be governed

GOVERNOR n official governing a province or state

GOVERNS ▶ govern

GOVS ▶ gov

GOWAN, -S n any of various yellow or white field flowers

GOWANED ▶ gowan

GOWANS ▶ gowan

GOWANY ▶ gowan

GOWD, -ER, -EST, -S Scots word for ▶ gold

GOWF, -ED, -ING, -S vb strike

GOWFER, -S ▶ gowf

GOWFING ▶ gowf

GOWFS ▶ gowf

GOWK, -S n stupid person

GOWL, -ED, -ING, -S n substance in the corner of the eyes after sleep ▷ vb howl

GOWLAN, -S same as ▶ gollan

GOWLAND, -S same as ▶ gollan

GOWLANS ▶ gowlan

GOWLED ▶ gowl

GOWLING ▶ gowl

GOWLS ▶ gowl

GOWN, -ED, -ING, -S n woman's long formal dress ▷ vb supply with or dress in a gown

GOWNBOY, -S n foundationer schoolboy who wears a gown

GOWNED ▶ gown

GOWNING ▶ gown

GOWNMAN, GOWNMEN n professional person who wears a gown

GOWNS ▶ gown

GOWNSMAN, GOWNSMEN same as ▶ gownman

GOWPEN, -S n pair of cupped hands

GOX, -ES n gaseous oxygen

> **Gox** is gaseous oxygen, especially useful if you can use it to hit a bonus square.

GOYLE, -S n ravine

GOZZAN, -S same as ▶ gossan

GRAAL, -S n holy grail

GRAB, -BED, -BING, -S vb grasp suddenly, snatch ▷ n sudden snatch

GRABBER, -S ▶ grab

GRABBIER ▶ grabby

GRABBING ▶ grab

GRABBLE, -D, -S vb scratch or feel about with the hands

GRABBLER ▸ grabble
GRABBLES ▸ grabble
GRABBY, GRABBIER *adj* greedy or selfish
GRABEN, -S *n* elongated trough of land
GRABS ▸ grab
GRACE, -D, -S, GRACING *n* beauty and elegance ▷ *vb* honour
GRACEFUL *adj* having beauty of movement, style, or form
GRACES ▸ grace
GRACILE *adj* gracefully thin or slender
GRACILIS, GRACILES *n* thin muscle on the inner thigh
GRACING ▸ grace
GRACIOSO *n* clown in Spanish comedy
GRACIOUS *adj* kind and courteous ▷ *interj* expression of mild surprise or wonder
GRACKLE, -S *n* American songbird with a dark iridescent plumage
GRAD, -S *n* graduate
GRADABLE *adj* capable of being graded ▷ *n* word of this kind
GRADATE, -D, -S *vb* change or cause to change imperceptibly
GRADATIM *adv* step by step
GRADDAN, -S *vb* dress corn
GRADE, -D, -S, GRADING *n* place on a scale of quality, rank, or size ▷ *vb* arrange in grades
GRADELY *adj* fine
GRADER, -S *n* person or thing that grades
GRADES ▸ grade
GRADIENT *n* (degree of) slope ▷ *adj* sloping uniformly
GRADIN, -S *n* ledge above or behind an altar
GRADINE, -S *same as* ▸ gradin
GRADING, -S ▸ grade
GRADINO, GRADINI *n* work of art that decorates an altar gradin
GRADINS ▸ gradin
GRADS ▸ grad
GRADUAL, -S *adj* occurring or moving in small stages ▷ *n* antiphon or group of several antiphons
GRADUAND *n* person who is about to graduate
GRADUATE *vb* receive a degree or diploma ▷ *n* holder of a degree

GRADUS, -ES *n* book of études or other musical exercises
GRAECISE *same as* ▸ graecize
GRAECIZE *vb* make or become like the ancient Greeks
GRAFF, -ED, -ING, -S *same as* ▸ graft
GRAFFITI *pl n* words or drawings scribbled or sprayed on walls etc
GRAFFITO *n* instance of graffiti
GRAFFS ▸ graff
GRAFT, -ED, -S *n* surgical transplant of skin or tissue ▷ *vb* transplant (living tissue) surgically
GRAFTAGE *n* in horticulture, the art of grafting
GRAFTED ▸ graft
GRAFTER, -S ▸ graft
GRAFTING ▸ graft
GRAFTS ▸ graft
GRAHAM, -S *n* cracker made of graham flour
GRAIL, -S *n* any desired ambition or goal
GRAILE, -S *same as* ▸ grail
GRAILS ▸ grail
GRAIN, -ED, -S *n* seedlike fruit of a cereal plant ▷ *vb* paint in imitation of the grain of wood or leather
GRAINAGE *n* duty paid on grain
GRAINE, -S *n* eggs of the silkworm
GRAINED ▸ grain
GRAINER, -S ▸ grain
GRAINES ▸ graine
GRAINIER ▸ grainy
GRAINING *n* pattern or texture of the grain of wood, leather, etc
GRAINS ▸ grain
GRAINY, GRAINIER *adj* resembling, full of, or composed of grain
GRAIP, -S *n* long-handled gardening fork
GRAITH, -ED, -S *vb* clothe
GRAITHLY ▸ graith
GRAITHS ▸ graith
GRAKLE, -S *same as* ▸ grackle
GRALLOCH *n* entrails of a deer ▷ *vb* disembowel (a deer killed in a hunt)
GRAM, -S *n* metric unit of mass
GRAMA, -S *n* type of grass
GRAMARY *same as* ▸ gramarye

GRAMARYE *n* magic, necromancy, or occult learning
GRAMAS ▸ grama
GRAMASH *n* type of gaiter
GRAME, -S *n* sorrow
GRAMERCY *interj* many thanks
GRAMES ▸ grame
GRAMMA, -S *n* pasture grass of the South American plains
GRAMMAGE *n* weight of paper expressed as grams per square metre
GRAMMAR, -S *n* branch of linguistics
GRAMMAS ▸ gramma
GRAMME, -S *same as* ▸ gram
GRAMOCHE *same as* ▸ gramash
GRAMP, -S *n* grandfather
GRAMPA, -S *variant of* ▸ grandpa
GRAMPIES ▸ grampy
GRAMPS ▸ gramp
GRAMPUS *n* dolphin-like mammal
GRAMPY, GRAMPIES *n* grandfather
GRAMS ▸ gram
GRAN, -S *n* grandmother
GRANA ▸ granum
GRANARY *n* storehouse for grain
GRAND, -ER, -EST, -S *adj* large or impressive, imposing ▷ *n* thousand pounds or dollars
GRANDAD, -S *n* grandfather
GRANDAM, -S *n* archaic word for grandmother
GRANDAME *same as* ▸ grandam
GRANDAMS ▸ grandam
GRANDDAD *same as* ▸ grandad
GRANDDAM *same as* ▸ grandam
GRANDE *feminine form of* ▸ grand
GRANDEE, -S *n* Spanish nobleman of the highest rank
GRANDER ▸ grand
GRANDEST ▸ grand
GRANDEUR *n* magnificence
GRANDKID *n* grandchild
GRANDLY ▸ grand
GRANDMA, -S *n* grandmother
GRANDPA, -S *n* grandfather
GRANDS ▸ grand
GRANDSIR *same as* > grandsire
GRANDSON *n* male grandchild

G

GRANFER, -S *n* grandfather

GRANGE, -S *n* country house with farm buildings

GRANGER, -S *n* keeper or member of a grange

GRANGES ▸ **grange**

GRANITA, -S *n* Italian iced drink

GRANITE, -S *n* very hard igneous rock

GRANITIC ▸ **granite**

GRANNAM, -S *n* old woman

GRANNIE *same as* ▸ **granny**

GRANNIED ▸ **granny**

GRANNIES ▸ **granny**

GRANNOM, -S *n* type of caddis fly used as a bait by anglers

GRANNY, GRANNIED, GRANNIES *n* grandmother ▸ *vb* defeat without conceding a single point

GRANOLA, -S *n* muesli-like breakfast cereal

GRANS ▸ **gran**

GRANT, -ED, -ING, -S *vb* consent to fulfil (a request) ▸ *n* money provided by a government for a specific purpose

GRANTEE, -S *n* person to whom a grant is made

GRANTER, -S ▸ **grant**

GRANTING ▸ **grant**

GRANTOR, -S *n* person who makes a grant

GRANTS ▸ **grant**

GRANULAR *adj* of or like grains

GRANULE, -S *n* small grain

GRANUM, GRANA, -S *n* membrane layer in a chloroplast

GRAPE, -D, GRAPING *n* small juicy green or purple berry ▸ *vb* grope

GRAPERY *n* building where grapes are grown

GRAPES *n* abnormal growth on the fetlock of a horse

GRAPEY ▸ **grape**

GRAPH, -ED, -ING, -S *n* type of graph ▸ *vb* draw or represent in a graph

GRAPHEME *n* smallest meaningful contrastive unit in a writing system

GRAPHENE *n* layer of graphite one atom thick

GRAPHIC *adj* vividly descriptive

GRAPHICS *pl n* diagrams, graphs, etc, esp as used on a television programme or computer screen

GRAPHING ▸ **graph**

GRAPHITE *n* soft black form of carbon, used in pencil leads

GRAPHIUM *n* stylus (for writing)

GRAPHS ▸ **graph**

GRAPIER ▸ **grapy**

GRAPIEST ▸ **grapy**

GRAPING ▸ **grape**

GRAPLE, -S *same as* ▸ **grapple**

GRAPLIN, -S *same as* ▸ **grapnel**

GRAPLINE *same as* ▸ **grapnel**

GRAPLINS ▸ **graplin**

GRAPNEL, -S *n* device with several hooks

GRAPPA, -S *n* type of Italian brandy

GRAPPLE, -D, -S *vb* try to cope with (something difficult) ▸ *n* grapnel

GRAPPLER ▸ **grapple**

GRAPPLES ▸ **grapple**

GRAPY, GRAPIER, GRAPIEST ▸ **grape**

GRASP, -ED, -S *vb* grip something firmly ▸ *n* grip or clasp

GRASPER, -S ▸ **grasp**

GRASPING *adj* greedy or avaricious

GRASPS ▸ **grasp**

GRASS, -ED, -ES, -ING *n* common type of plant ▸ *vb* cover with grass

GRASSER, -S *n* police informant

GRASSES ▸ **grass**

GRASSIER ▸ **grassy**

GRASSILY ▸ **grassy**

GRASSING ▸ **grass**

GRASSUM, -S *n* in Scots law, sum paid when taking a lease

GRASSY, GRASSIER *adj* covered with, containing, or resembling grass

GRASTE *archaic past participle of* ▸ **grace**

GRAT ▸ **greet**

GRATE, -D, -S *vb* rub into small bits on a rough surface ▸ *n* framework of metal bars for holding fuel in a fireplace

GRATEFUL *adj* feeling or showing gratitude

GRATER, -S *n* tool with a sharp surface for grating food

GRATES ▸ **grate**

GRATIFY *vb* satisfy or please ▸ *adj* giving one satisfaction or pleasure

GRATIN, -S *n* crust of browned breadcrumbs

GRATINE *adj* cooked au gratin

GRATINEE *vb* cook au gratin

GRATING, -S *adj* harsh or rasping ▸ *n* framework of metal bars covering an opening

GRATINS ▸ **gratin**

GRATIS *adj* free, for nothing

GRATTOIR *n* scraper made of flint

GRATUITY *n* money given for services rendered, tip

GRAUNCH *vb* crush or destroy

GRAUPEL, -S *n* soft hail or snow pellets

GRAV, -S *n* unit of acceleration

GRAVAMEN *n* that part of an accusation weighing most heavily against an accused

GRAVE, -D, -N, -S, -ST *n* hole for burying a corpse ▸ *adj* causing concern ▸ *vb* cut, carve, sculpt, or engrave ▸ *adv* to be performed in a solemn manner

GRAVEL, -ED, -S *n* mixture of small stones and coarse sand ▸ *vb* cover with gravel

GRAVELLY *adj* like gravel

GRAVELS ▸ **gravel**

GRAVELY ▸ **grave**

GRAVEN ▸ **grave**

GRAVER, -S *n* tool for engraving

GRAVES ▸ **grave**

GRAVEST ▸ **grave**

GRAVID *adj* pregnant

GRAVIDA, -E, -S *n* pregnant woman

GRAVIDLY ▸ **gravid**

GRAVIES ▸ **gravy**

GRAVING, -S ▸ **grave**

GRAVIS *adj* as in **myasthenia gravis** chronic muscle-weakening disease

GRAVITAS *n* seriousness or solemnity

GRAVITON *n* postulated quantum of gravitational energy

GRAVITY *n* force of attraction

GRAVLAKS *same as* ▸ **gravlax**

GRAVLAX *n* dry-cured salmon

GRAVS ▸ **grav**

GRAVURE, -S *n* method of intaglio printing

GRAVY, GRAVIES *n* juices from meat in cooking

GRAWLIX n sequence of symbols used in text to replace profanity

GRAY, -ED, -ER, -EST, -ING, -S same as ▸ **grey**

GRAYBACK same as ▸ **greyback**

GRAYED ▸ **gray**

GRAYER ▸ **gray**

GRAYEST ▸ **gray**

GRAYFISH n dogfish

GRAYFLY n trumpet fly

GRAYHEAD n one with grey hair

GRAYHEN, -S n female of the black grouse

GRAYING ▸ **gray**

GRAYISH ▸ **gray**

GRAYLAG, -S same as ▸ **greylag**

GRAYLE, -S n holy grail

GRAYLING n fish of the salmon family

GRAYLIST vb hold (someone) in suspicion, without actually excluding him or her from a particular activity

GRAYLY ▸ **gray**

GRAYMAIL n tactic to avoid prosecution in an espionage case

GRAYNESS ▸ **grey**

GRAYOUT, -S n impairment of vision due to lack of oxygen

GRAYS ▸ **gray**

GRAZABLE ▸ **graze**

GRAZE, -D, -S vb feed on grass ▸ n slight scratch or scrape

GRAZER, -S ▸ **graze**

GRAZES ▸ **graze**

GRAZIER, -S n person who feeds cattle for market

GRAZING, -S n land on which grass for livestock is grown

GRAZIOSO adv (of music) to be played gracefully

GREASE, -D, -S, GREASING n soft melted animal fat ▸ vb apply grease to

GREASER, -S n mechanic, esp of motor vehicles

GREASES ▸ **grease**

GREASIER ▸ **greasy**

GREASIES ▸ **greasy**

GREASILY ▸ **greasy**

GREASING ▸ **grease**

GREASY, GREASIER, GREASIES adj covered with or containing grease ▸ n shearer

GREAT, -ER, -S adj large in size or number ▸ n distinguished person

GREATEN, -S vb make or become great

GREATER ▸ **great**

GREATEST n most outstanding individual in a given field

GREATLY ▸ **great**

GREATS ▸ **great**

GREAVE, GREAVING n piece of armour for the shin ▸ vb grieve

GREAVED ▸ **greave**

GREAVES pl n residue left after the rendering of tallow

GREAVING ▸ **greave**

GREBE, -S n diving water bird

GREBO, -ES, -S same as ▸ **greebo**

GRECE, -S n flight of steps

GRECIAN, -S same as ▸ **grece**

GRECISE, -D, -S same as ▸ **graecize**

GRECIZE, -D, -S same as ▸ **graecize**

GRECQUE, -S n ornament of Greek origin

GREE, -ING, -S n superiority or victory ▸ vb come or cause to come to agreement or harmony

GREEBO, -ES, -S n unkempt or dirty-looking rock music fan

GREECE, -S same as ▸ **grece**

GREED, -S n excessive desire for food, wealth, etc

GREEDIER ▸ **greedy**

GREEDILY ▸ **greedy**

GREEDS ▸ **greed**

GREEDY, GREEDIER adj having an excessive desire for something

GREEGREE same as ▸ **grigri**

GREEING ▸ **gree**

GREEK, -ED, -ING vb represent text as grey lines on a computer screen

GREEN, -ED, -EST, -S adj of a colour between blue and yellow ▸ n colour between blue and yellow ▸ vb make or become green

GREENBUG n common name for Schizaphis graminum

GREENED ▸ **green**

GREENER, -S n recent immigrant

GREENERY n vegetation

GREENEST ▸ **green**

GREENEYE n small slender fish with pale green eyes

GREENFLY n green aphid, a common garden pest

GREENIE, -S n conservationist

GREENIER ▸ **greeny**

GREENIES ▸ **greenie**

GREENING n process of making or becoming more aware of environmental considerations

GREENISH ▸ **green**

GREENLET n type of insectivorous songbird

GREENLIT adj given permission to proceed

GREENLY ▸ **green**

GREENS ▸ **green**

GREENTH, -S n greenness

GREENWAY n linear open space, with pedestrian and cycle paths

GREENY, GREENIER ▸ **green**

GREES ▸ **gree**

GREESE, -S, GREESING same as ▸ **grece**

GREET, GRAT, -ED, -S, GRUTTEN vb meet with expressions of welcome ▸ n weeping

GREETE, -S same as ▸ **greet**

GREETED ▸ **greet**

GREETER, -S n person who greets people

GREETES ▸ **greete**

GREETING n act or words of welcoming on meeting

GREETS ▸ **greet**

GREFFIER n registrar

GREGALE, -S n northeasterly wind occurring in the Mediterranean

GREGATIM adv in flocks or crowds

GREGE, -D, -S, GREGING vb make heavy

GREGO, -S n short, thick jacket

GREIGE, -S adj (of a fabric or material) not yet dyed ▸ n unbleached or undyed cloth or yarn

GREIN, -ED, -ING, -S vb desire fervently

GREISEN, -S n light-coloured metamorphic rock

GREISLY same as ▸ **grisly**

GREMIAL, -S n cloth spread on the lap of a bishop during Mass

GREMLIN, -S n imaginary being

GREMMIE, -S n young surfer

GREMMY same as ▸ **gremmie**

GREN, -NED, -NING, -S same as ▸ **grin**

GRENACHE n variety of grape

G

GRENADE, -S n small bomb

GRENNED ▸ **gren**

GRENNING ▸ **gren**

GRENS ▸ **gren**

GRESE, -S same as ▸ **grece**

GRESSING same as ▸ **grece**

GREVE, -S same as ▸ **greave**

GREW, -ED, -ING, -S vb shudder

GREWSOME archaic or US spelling of ▸ **gruesome**

GREX, -ES n group of plants

GREY, -ED, -ER, -EST, -S adj of a colour between black and white ▷ n grey colour ▷ vb become or make grey

GREYBACK n any of various animals having a grey back, such as the grey whale and the hooded crow

GREYED ▸ **grey**

GREYER ▸ **grey**

GREYEST ▸ **grey**

GREYHEAD n one having grey hair

GREYHEN, -S n female of the black grouse

GREYING, -S ▸ **grey**

GREYISH ▸ **grey**

GREYLAG, -S n large grey goose

GREYLIST vb hold (someone) in suspicion, without actually excluding him or her from a particular activity

GREYLY ▸ **grey**

GREYNESS ▸ **grey**

GREYS ▸ **grey**

GRIBBLE, -S n type of small marine crustacean

GRICE, -D, -S vb collect objects concerned with railways ▷ n object collected or place visited by a railway enthusiast

GRICER, -S ▸ **grice**

GRICES ▸ **grice**

GRICING, -S ▸ **grice**

GRID, -DED, -DING, -S n network of horizontal and vertical lines, bars, etc ▷ vb form a grid pattern

GRIDDER, -S n American football player

GRIDDING ▸ **grid**

GRIDDLE, -D, -S n flat iron plate for cooking ▷ vb cook (food) on a griddle

GRIDE, -D, -S, GRIDING vb grate or scrape harshly ▷ n harsh or piercing sound

GRIDELIN n greyish violet colour

GRIDES ▸ **gride**

GRIDING ▸ **gride**

GRIDIRON n frame of metal bars for grilling food ▷ vb cover with parallel lines

GRIDLOCK n situation where traffic is not moving ▷ vb (of traffic) to obstruct (an area)

GRIDS ▸ **grid**

GRIECE, -D, -S same as ▸ **grece**

GRIEF, -S n deep sadness

GRIEFER, -S n online gamer who spoils the game for others on purpose

GRIEFFUL adj stricken with grief

GRIEFS ▸ **grief**

GRIESIE same as ▸ **grisy**

GRIESLY same as ▸ **grisy**

GRIESY same as ▸ **grisy**

GRIEVANT n any person with a grievance

GRIEVE, -D, -S vb (cause to) feel grief ▷ n farm manager or overseer

GRIEVER, -S ▸ **grieve**

GRIEVES ▸ **grieve**

GRIEVING ▸ **grieve**

GRIEVOUS adj very severe or painful

GRIFF, -S n information

GRIFFE, -S n carved ornament at the base of a column

GRIFFIN, -S n mythical monster

GRIFFON, -S same as ▸ **griffin**

GRIFFS ▸ **griff**

GRIFT, -ED, -ING, -S vb swindle

GRIFTER, -S ▸ **grift**

GRIFTING ▸ **grift**

GRIFTS ▸ **grift**

GRIG, -GED, -GING, -S n young eel ▷ vb fish for grigs

GRIGRI, -S n African talisman, amulet, or charm

GRIGS ▸ **grig**

GRIKE, -S n fissure in rock

GRILL, -ING, -S n device on a cooker ▷ vb cook under a grill

GRILLADE n grilled food

GRILLAGE n arrangement of beams and crossbeams used as a foundation on soft ground

GRILLE, -S n grating over an opening

GRILLED adj cooked on a grill or gridiron

GRILLER, -S ▸ **grill**

GRILLERY n place where food is grilled

GRILLES ▸ **grille**

GRILLING ▸ **grill**

GRILLION n extremely large but unspecified number, quantity, or amount ▷ determiner amounting to a grillion

GRILLS ▸ **grill**

GRILSE, -S n salmon on its first return from the sea to fresh water

GRIM, -MER, -MEST adj stern

GRIMACE, -D, -S n ugly or distorted facial expression ▷ vb make a grimace

GRIMACER ▸ **grimace**

GRIMACES ▸ **grimace**

GRIME, -D, -S, GRIMING n ingrained dirt ▷ vb make very dirty

GRIMIER ▸ **grimy**

GRIMIEST ▸ **grimy**

GRIMILY ▸ **grime**

GRIMING ▸ **grime**

GRIMLY ▸ **grim**

GRIMMER ▸ **grim**

GRIMMEST ▸ **grim**

GRIMNESS ▸ **grim**

GRIMOIRE n textbook of sorcery and magic

GRIMY, GRIMIER, GRIMIEST ▸ **grime**

GRIN, -NED, -S vb smile broadly, showing the teeth ▷ n broad smile

GRINCH, -ES n person whose attitude has a dispiriting effect

GRIND, -ING, -S vb crush or rub to a powder ▷ n hard work

GRINDED obsolete past participle of ▸ **grind**

GRINDER, -S n device for grinding substances

GRINDERY n place in which tools and cutlery are sharpened

GRINDING ▸ **grind**

GRINDS ▸ **grind**

GRINNED ▸ **grin**

GRINNER, -S ▸ **grin**

GRINNING ▸ **grin**

GRINS ▸ **grin**

GRIOT, -S n (in W Africa) member of a caste recording tribal history

GRIP, -PED, -PING, -S n firm hold or grasp ▷ vb grasp or hold tightly

GRIPE, -D, -S vb complain persistently ▷ n complaint

GRIPER, -S ▸ **gripe**

GRIPES ▸ **gripe**

GRIPEY, GRIPIER, GRIPIEST adj causing gripes

GRIPING, -S n act of griping

GRIPLE same as ▶ **gripple**

GRIPMAN, GRIPMEN n cable-car operator

GRIPPE, -S former name for ▶ **influenza**

GRIPPED ▶ **grip**

GRIPPER, -S ▶ **grip**

GRIPPES ▶ **grippe**

GRIPPIER ▶ **grippy**

GRIPPING ▶ **grip**

GRIPPLE, -S adj greedy ▷ n hook

GRIPPY, GRIPPIER adj having grip

GRIPS ▶ **grip**

GRIPSACK n travel bag

GRIPT archaic variant of ▶ **gripped**

GRIPTAPE n rough tape for sticking to a surface to provide a greater grip

GRIPY same as ▶ **gripey**

GRIS same as ▶ **grece**

GRISE, -D, -S, GRISING vb shudder

GRISELY same as ▶ **grisly**

GRISEOUS adj streaked or mixed with grey

GRISES ▶ **grise**

GRISETTE n (formerly) a young French working-class woman

GRISGRIS same as ▶ **grigri**

GRISING ▶ **grise**

GRISKIN, -S n lean part of a loin of pork

GRISLED another word for ▶ **grizzled**

GRISLY, GRISLIER, GRISLIES adj horrifying or ghastly ▷ n large American bear

GRISON, -S n type of mammal

GRISSINI pl n thin crisp breadsticks

GRISSINO n Italian breadstick

GRIST, -S n grain for grinding

GRISTER, -S n device for grinding grain

GRISTLE, -S n tough stringy animal tissue found in meat

GRISTLY ▶ **gristle**

GRISTS ▶ **grist**

GRISY adj grim

GRIT, -S, -TED, -TEST n rough particles of sand ▷ vb spread grit on (an icy road etc) ▷ adj great

GRITH, -S n security or peace guaranteed for a period of time

GRITLESS ▶ **grit**

GRITS ▶ **grit**

GRITTED ▶ **grit**

GRITTER, -S n vehicle that spreads grit on the roads

GRITTEST ▶ **grit**

GRITTIER ▶ **gritty**

GRITTILY ▶ **gritty**

GRITTING n spreading grit on road surfaces

GRITTY, GRITTIER adj courageous and tough

GRIVET, -S n E African monkey

GRIZ, -ZES n grizzly bear

GRIZE, -S same as ▶ **grece**

GRIZZES ▶ **griz**

GRIZZLE, -S vb whine or complain ▷ n grey colour

GRIZZLED adj grey-haired

GRIZZLER ▶ **grizzle**

GRIZZLES ▶ **grizzle**

GRIZZLY n large American bear ▷ adj somewhat grey

GROAN, -ED, -S n deep sound of grief or pain ▷ vb utter a groan

GROANER, -S n person or thing that groans

GROANFUL adj sad

GROANING ▶ **groan**

GROANS ▶ **groan**

GROAT n fourpenny piece

GROATS pl n hulled and crushed grain of various cereals

GROCER, -S n shopkeeper selling foodstuffs

GROCERY n business or premises of a grocer

GROCKED same as ▶ **grokked**

GROCKING same as ▶ **grokking**

GROCKLE, -S n tourist in SW England

GRODY, GRODIER, GRODIEST adj unpleasant

GROG, -GED, -GING, -S n spirit, usu rum, and water ▷ vb drink grog

GROGGERY n grogshop

GROGGIER ▶ **groggy**

GROGGILY ▶ **groggy**

GROGGING ▶ **grog**

GROGGY, GROGGIER adj faint, shaky, or dizzy

GROGRAM, -S n coarse fabric

GROGS ▶ **grog**

GROGSHOP n drinking place, esp one of disreputable character

GROIN, -ED, -ING, -S n place where the legs join the abdomen ▷ vb construct with curved arrises

GROK, -ED, -ING, -KED, -KING, -S vb understand completely and intuitively

GROMA, -S n Roman surveying instrument

GROMET, -S same as ▶ **grommet**

GROMMET, -S n ring or eyelet

GROMWELL n hairy flowering plant

GRONE, -D, -S, GRONING obsolete word for ▶ **groan**

GROOF, -S n face, or front of the body

GROOLY, GROOLIER adj gruesome

GROOM, -ED, -S n person who looks after horses ▷ vb make or keep one's clothes and appearance neat and tidy

GROOMER, -S ▶ **groom**

GROOMING ▶ **groom**

GROOMS ▶ **groom**

GROOVE, -D, -S, GROOVING n long narrow channel in a surface

GROOVER, -S n device that makes grooves

GROOVES ▶ **groove**

GROOVIER ▶ **groovy**

GROOVILY ▶ **groovy**

GROOVING ▶ **groove**

GROOVY, GROOVIER adj attractive or exciting

GROPE, -D, -S, GROPING vb feel about or search uncertainly ▷ n instance of groping

GROPER, -S n type of large fish of warm and tropical seas

GROPES ▶ **grope**

GROPING ▶ **grope**

GROSBEAK n finch with a large powerful bill

GROSCHEN n former Austrian monetary unit worth one hundredth of a schilling

GROSER, -S n gooseberry

GROSERT, -S another word for ▶ **groser**

GROSET, -S another word for ▶ **groser**

GROSS, -ED, -ES, -EST, -ING adj flagrant ▷ n twelve dozen ▷ vb make as total revenue before deductions ▷ interj exclamation indicating disgust

GROSSART another word for ▶ **groser**

GROSSED ▶ **gross**

GROSSER, -S ▶ **gross**

GROSSES ▶ **gross**

GROSSEST ▶ **gross**

GROSSING ▶ **gross**

GROSSLY ▸ gross

GROSZ, -E, -Y n Polish monetary unit

GROT, -S n rubbish

GROTTIER ▸ grotty

GROTTO, -ES, -S n small picturesque cave

GROTTOED adj having a grotto

GROTTOES ▸ grotto

GROTTOS ▸ grotto

GROTTY, GROTTIER adj nasty or in bad condition

GROUCH, -ED, -ES vb grumble or complain ▷ n person who is always complaining

GROUCHY adj bad-tempered

GROUF, -S same as ▸ groof

GROUGH, -S n natural channel or fissure in a peat moor

GROUND, -S n surface of the earth ▷ adj on or of the ground ▷ vb base or establish

GROUNDED adj sensible and down-to-earth

GROUNDEN obsolete variant of ▸ ground

GROUNDER n (in baseball) ball that travels along the ground

GROUNDS ▸ ground

GROUP, -ED, -S n number of people or things regarded as a unit ▷ vb place or form into a group

GROUPAGE n gathering people or objects into a group or groups

GROUPED ▸ group

GROUPER, -S n large edible sea fish

GROUPIE, -S n ardent fan of a celebrity or of a sport or activity

GROUPING n set of people or organizations who act or work together to achieve a shared aim

GROUPIST n follower of a group

GROUPLET n small group

GROUPOID n magma

GROUPS ▸ group

GROUPY same as ▸ groupie

GROUSE, -D, -S, -ST, GROUSING n stocky game bird ▷ vb grumble or complain ▷ adj fine or excellent

GROUSER, -S ▸ grouse

GROUSES ▸ grouse

GROUSEST ▸ grouse

GROUSING ▸ grouse

GROUT, -ED, -ING n thin mortar ▷ vb fill up with grout

GROUTER, -S ▸ grout

GROUTIER ▸ grouty

GROUTING ▸ grout

GROUTS pl n sediment or grounds

GROUTY, GROUTIER adj sullen or surly

GROVE, -S n small group of trees

GROVED ▸ grove

GROVEL, -ED, -S vb behave humbly in order to win a superior's favour

GROVELER ▸ grovel

GROVELS ▸ grovel

GROVES ▸ grove

GROVET, -S n wrestling hold

GROVY, GROVIER, GROVIEST adj like a grove

GROW, -N, -S vb develop physically

GROWABLE adj able to be cultivated

GROWER, -S n person who grows plants

GROWING, -S ▸ grow

GROWL, -ED, -ING, -S vb make a low rumbling sound ▷ n growling sound

GROWLER, -S n person, animal, or thing that growls

GROWLERY n place to retreat to, alone, when ill-humoured

GROWLIER ▸ growly

GROWLING ▸ growl

GROWLS ▸ growl

GROWLY, GROWLIER ▸ growl

GROWN ▸ grow

GROWNUP, -S n adult

GROWS ▸ grow

GROWTH, -S n growing ▷ adj of or relating to growth

GROWTHY adj rapid-growing

GROYNE, -S n wall built out from the shore to control erosion

GROZING adj as in grozing iron iron for smoothing joints between lead pipes

GRR interj expressing anger or annoyance

GRRL, -S n as in riot grrl young woman who enjoys feminist punk rock

This slang term for a young woman who likes feminist punk can come in useful when you are short of vowels. And it can also be spelt **grrrl**.

GRRRL, -S same as ▸ grrl

GRUB, -BED, -BING, -S n legless insect larva ▷ vb search carefully for something

GRUBBER, -S n person who grubs

GRUBBIER ▸ grubby

GRUBBILY ▸ grubby

GRUBBING ▸ grub

GRUBBLE, -D, -S same as ▸ grabble

GRUBBY, GRUBBIER adj dirty

GRUBS ▸ grub

GRUBWORM another word for ▸ grub

GRUDGE, -D, -S vb be unwilling to give or allow ▷ n resentment ▷ adj planned or carried out in order to settle a grudge

GRUDGER, -S ▸ grudge

GRUDGES ▸ grudge

GRUDGING ▸ grudge

GRUE, -D, -ING, -S, GRUING n shiver or shudder ▷ vb shiver or shudder

GRUEL, -ED, -LED, -S n thin porridge ▷ vb subject to exhausting experiences

GRUELER, -S ▸ gruel

GRUELING same as > gruelling

GRUELLED ▸ gruel

GRUELLER ▸ gruel

GRUELS ▸ gruel

GRUES ▸ grue

GRUESOME adj causing horror and disgust

GRUFE, -S same as ▸ groof

GRUFF, -ED, -ER, -EST, -ING, -S adj rough or surly in manner or voice ▷ vb talk gruffly

GRUFFIER ▸ gruffy

GRUFFILY ▸ gruffy

GRUFFING ▸ gruff

GRUFFISH ▸ gruff

GRUFFLY ▸ gruff

GRUFFS ▸ gruff

GRUFFY, GRUFFIER adj gruff

GRUFTED adj dirty

GRUGRU, -S n tropical American palm

GRUIFORM adj relating to an order of birds, including cranes and bustards

GRUING ▸ grue

GRUM, -MER, -MEST adj surly

GRUMBLE, -D, -S vb complain ▷ n complaint

GRUMBLER ▸ grumble

GRUMBLES ▸ grumble

GRUMBLY ▸ **grumble**

GRUME, -S n clot

GRUMLY ▸ **grum**

GRUMMER ▸ **grum**

GRUMMEST ▸ **grum**

GRUMMET, -S same as ▸ **grommet**

GRUMNESS ▸ **grum**

GRUMOSE same as ▸ **grumous**

GRUMOUS adj (esp of plant parts) consisting of granular tissue

GRUMP, -ED, -ING, -S n surly or bad-tempered person ▷ vb complain or grumble

GRUMPH, -ED, -S vb grunt

GRUMPHIE n pig

GRUMPHS ▸ **grumph**

GRUMPHY same as ▸ **grumphie**

GRUMPIER ▸ **grumpy**

GRUMPIES ▸ **grumpy**

GRUMPILY ▸ **grumpy**

GRUMPING ▸ **grump**

GRUMPISH same as ▸ **grumpy**

GRUMPS ▸ **grump**

GRUMPY, GRUMPIER, GRUMPIES adj bad-tempered ▷ n bad-tempered person

GRUND n as in **grund mail** payment for right of burial

GRUNDIES pl n men's underpants

GRUNGE, -S n style of rock music with a distorted guitar sound

GRUNGER, -S n fan of grunge music

GRUNGES ▸ **grunge**

GRUNGEY adj messy or dirty

GRUNGY, GRUNGIER adj messy or dirty

GRUNION, -S n Californian marine fish that spawns on beaches

GRUNT, -ED, -ING, -S vb make a low short gruff sound, like a pig ▷ n pig's sound

GRUNTER, -S n person or animal that grunts, esp a pig

GRUNTING ▸ **grunt**

GRUNTLE, -D, -S vb grunt or groan

GRUNTS ▸ **grunt**

GRUSHIE adj healthy and strong

GRUTCH, -ED, -ES vb grudge

GRUTTEN ▸ **greet**

GRUYERE, -S n hard flat whole-milk cheese with holes

GRYCE, -S same as ▸ **grice**

GRYDE, -D, -S, GRYDING same as ▸ **gride**

GRYESY adj grey

GRYFON, -S same as ▸ **griffin**

GRYKE, -S same as ▸ **grike**

GRYPE, -S same as ▸ **gripe**

GRYPHON, -S same as ▸ **griffin**

GRYPT archaic form of ▸ **gripped**

GRYSBOK, -S n small antelope

GRYSELY same as ▸ **grisly**

GRYSIE same as ▸ **grisy**

GU, -S same as ▸ **gju**

GUACHARO another name for ▸ **oilbird**

GUACO, -S n any of several plants used as an antidote to snakebite

GUAIAC, -S same as ▸ **guaiacum**

GUAIACOL n yellowish creosote-like liquid

GUAIACS ▸ **guaiac**

GUAIACUM n tropical American evergreen tree

GUAIOCUM same as ▸ **guaiacum**

GUAN, -S n type of bird of Central and S America

GUANA, -S another word for ▸ **iguana**

GUANACO, -S n S American animal related to the llama

GUANAS ▸ **guana**

GUANASE, -S n type of enzyme

GUANAY, -S n type of cormorant

GUANGO, -S n rain tree

GUANIDIN same as ▸ **guanidine**

GUANIN, -S same as ▸ **guanine**

GUANINE, -S n white almost insoluble compound

GUANINS ▸ **guanin**

GUANO, -S n dried sea-bird manure

GUANS ▸ **guan**

GUANXI, -S n Chinese social concept

GUANYLIC adj as in **guanylic acid** nucleotide consisting of guanine, ribose or deoxyribose, and a phosphate group

GUAR, -S n Indian plant

GUARACHA same as ▸ **huarache**

GUARACHE same as ▸ **huarache**

GUARACHI same as ▸ **huarache**

GUARANA, -S n type of shrub native to Venezuela

GUARANI, -S n standard monetary unit of Paraguay

GUARANTY n pledge of responsibility for fulfilling another person's obligations in case of default

GUARD, -ING, -S vb watch over to protect or to prevent escape ▷ n person or group that guards

GUARDAGE n state of being in the care of a guardian

GUARDANT adj (of a beast) shown full face ▷ n guardian

GUARDDOG n dog trained to protect premises

GUARDED adj cautious or noncommittal

GUARDEE, -S n guardsman

GUARDER, -S ▸ **guard**

GUARDIAN n keeper or protector ▷ adj protecting or safeguarding

GUARDING ▸ **guard**

GUARDS ▸ **guard**

GUARISH vb heal

GUARS ▸ **guar**

GUAVA, -S n yellow-skinned tropical American fruit

GUAYULE, -S n bushy shrub of the southwestern US

GUB, -BED, -BING, -S n Scots word for mouth ▷ vb hit or defeat

GUBBAH, -S same as ▸ **gub**

GUBBED ▸ **gub**

GUBBING ▸ **gub**

GUBBINS n object of little or no value

GUBS ▸ **gub**

GUCK, -S n slimy matter

GUCKIER ▸ **gucky**

GUCKIEST ▸ **gucky**

GUCKS ▸ **guck**

GUCKY, GUCKIER, GUCKIEST adj slimy and mucky

GUDDLE, -D, -S, GUDDLING vb catch (fish) with the hands ▷ n muddle

GUDE Scots word for ▸ **good**

GUDEMAN, GUDEMEN n male householder

GUDES n goods

GUDESIRE n grandfather

GUDEWIFE n female householder

GUDGEON, -S n small freshwater fish ▷ vb trick or cheat

GUE, -S same as ▸ **gju**

GUELDER adj as in **guelder rose** kind of shrub

GUENON, -S n slender Old World monkey

GUERDON, -S n reward or payment ▷ vb give a guerdon to

GUEREZA, -S n handsome colobus monkey

GUERIDON n small ornately carved table

GUERILLA same as > guerrilla

GUERITE, -S n turret used by a sentry

GUERNSEY n seaman's knitted woollen sweater

GUES ▶ gue

GUESS, -ED, -ES, -ING vb estimate or draw a conclusion without proper knowledge ▷ n estimate or conclusion reached by guessing

GUESSER, -S ▶ guess

GUESSES ▶ guess

GUESSING ▶ guess

GUEST, -ED, -ING, -S n person entertained at another's expense ▷ vb appear as a visiting player or performer

GUESTEN, -S vb stay as a guest in someone's house

GUESTING ▶ guest

GUESTS ▶ guest

GUFF, -S n nonsense

GUFFAW, -ED, -S n crude noisy laugh ▷ vb laugh in this way

GUFFIE, -S Scots word for ▶ pig

GUFFS ▶ guff

GUGA, -S n gannet chick

GUGGLE, -D, -S, GUGGLING vb drink making a gurgling sound

GUGLET, -S same as ▶ goglet

GUICHET, -S n grating, hatch, or small opening in a wall

GUID Scot word for ▶ good

GUIDABLE ▶ guide

GUIDAGE, -S n guidance

GUIDANCE n leadership, instruction, or advice

GUIDE, -D, -S n person who conducts tour expeditions ▷ vb act as a guide for

GUIDER, -S ▶ guide

GUIDES ▶ guide

GUIDEWAY n track controlling the motion of something

GUIDING, -S ▶ guide

GUIDON, -S n small pennant

GUIDS pl n Scots word for possessions

GUILD, -S n organization or club

GUILDER, -S n former monetary unit of the Netherlands

GUILDRY n in Scotland, corporation of merchants

GUILDS ▶ guild

GUILE, -D, -S, GUILING n cunning or deceit ▷ vb deceive

GUILEFUL ▶ guile

GUILER, -S n deceiver

GUILES ▶ guile

GUILING ▶ guile

GUILT, -ED, -ING, -S n fact or state of having done wrong ▷ vb make (a person) feel guilty

GUILTIER ▶ guilty

GUILTILY ▶ guilty

GUILTING ▶ guilt

GUILTS ▶ guilt

GUILTY, GUILTIER adj responsible for an offence or misdeed

GUIMBARD n Jew's harp

GUIMP, -S same as ▶ guimpe

GUIMPE, -D, -S, GUIMPING n short blouse worn under a pinafore dress ▷ vb make with gimp

GUIMPS ▶ guimp

GUINEA, -S n former British monetary unit

GUINEP, -S n type of tropical American tree

GUIPURE, -S n heavy lace

GUIRO, -S n percussion instrument made from a hollow gourd

GUISARD, -S n guiser

GUISE, -D, -S n false appearance ▷ vb disguise or be disguised in fancy dress

GUISER, -S n mummer, esp at Christmas or Halloween revels

GUISES ▶ guise

GUISING, -S ▶ guise

GUITAR, -S n stringed instrument

GUITGUIT n bird belonging to the family Coerebidae

GUIZER, -S same as ▶ guiser

GUL, -S n design used in Turkoman carpets

GULA, -S n gluttony

GULAG, -S n forced-labour camp

GULAR, -S adj of or situated in the throat or oesophagus ▷ n throat or oesophagus

GULAS ▶ gula

GULCH, -ED, -ES, -ING n deep narrow valley ▷ vb swallow fast

GULDEN, -S same as ▶ guilder

GULE Scots word for ▶ marigold

GULES n red in heraldry

GULET, -S n wooden Turkish sailing boat

GULF, -ED, -ING, -S n large deep bay ▷ vb swallow up

GULFIER ▶ gulfy

GULFIEST ▶ gulfy

GULFING ▶ gulf

GULFLIKE ▶ gulf

GULFS ▶ gulf

GULFWEED n type of brown seaweed

GULFY, GULFIER, GULFIEST ▶ gulf

GULL, -ED, -ING, -S n long-winged sea bird ▷ vb cheat or deceive

GULLABLE same as ▶ gullible

GULLABLY ▶ gullable

GULLED ▶ gull

GULLER, -S n deceiver

GULLERY n breeding-place for gulls

GULLET, -S n muscular tube from the mouth to the stomach

GULLEY, -ED, -S same as ▶ gully

GULLIBLE adj easily tricked

GULLIBLY ▶ gullible

GULLIED ▶ gully

GULLIES ▶ gully

GULLING ▶ gull

GULLISH adj stupid

GULLS ▶ gull

GULLWING adj (of vehicle door) opening upwards

GULLY, GULLIED, GULLIES, -ING n channel cut by running water ▷ vb make (channels) in (the ground, sand, etc)

GULOSITY n greed or gluttony

GULP, -ED, -ING, -S vb swallow hastily ▷ n gulping

GULPER, -S ▶ gulp

GULPH, -S archaic word for ▶ gulf

GULPIER ▶ gulpy

GULPIEST ▶ gulpy

GULPING ▶ gulp

GULPS ▶ gulp

GULPY, GULPIER, GULPIEST ▶ gulp

GULS ▶ gul

GULY adj relating to gules

GUM, -MED, -S n firm flesh in which the teeth are set ▷ vb stick with gum

GUMBALL, -S n round piece of chewing gum

GUMBO, -S n soup or stew thickened with okra pods

GUMBOIL, -S n abscess on the gum

GUMBOOT, -S n long rubber boot

GUMBOS ▸ gumbo

GUMBOTIL n sticky clay formed by the weathering of glacial drift

GUMDROP, -S n hard jelly-like sweet

GUMLANDS pl n infertile land where kauri once grew

GUMLESS ▸ gum

GUMLIKE ▸ gum

GUMLINE, -S n line where gums meet teeth

GUMMA, -S, -TA n rubbery tumour

GUMMED ▸ gum

GUMMER, -S n punch-cutting tool

GUMMI, -S n gelatin-based flavoured sweet

GUMMIER ▸ gummy

GUMMIES ▸ gummy

GUMMIEST ▸ gummy

GUMMILY ▸ gummy

GUMMING, -S ▸ gum

GUMMIS ▸ gummi

GUMMITE, -S n orange or yellowish amorphous secondary mineral

GUMMOSE, -S same as ▸ gummous

GUMMOSIS n abnormal production of gum in trees

GUMMOUS adj resembling or consisting of gum

GUMMY, GUMMIER, GUMMIES, GUMMIEST adj toothless ▹ n type of small crustacean-eating shark

GUMNUT, -S n hardened seed container of the gumtree

GUMP, -ED, -ING, -S vb guddle

GUMPHION n funeral banner

GUMPING ▸ gump

GUMPS ▸ gump

GUMPTION n resourcefulness

GUMS ▸ gum

GUMSHOE, -D, -S n waterproof overshoe ▹ vb act stealthily

GUMTREE, -S n any of various trees that yield gum

GUMWEED, -S n any of several yellow-flowered plants

GUMWOOD, -S same as ▸ gumtree

GUN, -NED, -NEN, -S n weapon with a tube from

which missiles are fired ▹ vb cause (an engine) to run at high speed

GUNBOAT, -S n small warship

GUNDIES ▸ gundy

GUNDOG, -S n dog trained to work with a hunter or gamekeeper

GUNDY, GUNDIES n toffee

GUNFIGHT n fight between persons using firearms ▹ vb fight with guns

GUNFIRE, -S n repeated firing of guns

GUNFLINT n piece of flint in a flintlock's hammer used to strike the spark that ignites the charge

GUNG adj as in gung ho extremely or excessively enthusiastic about something

GUNGE, -D, -S, GUNGING n sticky unpleasant substance ▹ vb block or encrust with gunge

GUNGIER ▸ gungy

GUNGIEST ▸ gungy

GUNGING ▸ gunge

GUNGY, GUNGIER, GUNGIEST ▸ gunge

GUNHOUSE n on a warship, an armoured rotatable enclosure for guns

GUNITE, -S n mortar sprayed in a very dense concrete layer

GUNK, -ED, -ING, -S n slimy or filthy substance ▹ vb cover with gunk

GUNKHOLE vb make a series of short boat excursions

GUNKIER ▸ gunky

GUNKIEST ▸ gunky

GUNKING ▸ gunk

GUNKS ▸ gunk

GUNKY, GUNKIER, GUNKIEST ▸ gunk

GUNLAYER n person who aims a ship's gun

GUNLESS ▸ gun

GUNLOCK, -S n mechanism in some firearms

GUNMAKER n person who makes guns

GUNMAN, GUNMEN n armed criminal

GUNMETAL n alloy of copper, tin, and zinc ▹ adj dark grey

GUNNAGE, -S n number of guns carried by a warship

GUNNED ▸ gun

GUNNEL, -S same as ▸ gunwale

GUNNEN ▸ gun

GUNNER, -S n artillery soldier

GUNNERA, -S n type of herbaceous plant

GUNNERS ▸ gunner

GUNNERY n use or science of large guns

GUNNIES ▸ gunny

GUNNING, -S ▸ gun

GUNNY, GUNNIES n strong coarse fabric used for sacks

GUNNYBAG same as ▸ gunnysack

GUNPAPER n cellulose nitrate explosive made by treating paper with nitric acid

GUNPLAY, -S n use of firearms, as by criminals

GUNPOINT n muzzle of a gun

GUNPORT, -S n porthole or other opening for a gun

GUNROOM, -S n room where guns are stored

GUNS ▸ gun

GUNSEL, -S n criminal who carries a gun

GUNSHIP, -S n ship or helicopter armed with heavy guns

GUNSHOT, -S n shot or range of a gun

GUNSIGHT n device on a gun which helps the user to aim

GUNSMITH n person who manufactures or repairs firearms, esp portable guns

GUNSTICK n ramrod

GUNSTOCK n wooden handle to which the barrel of a rifle is attached

GUNSTONE n cannonball

GUNTER, -S n type of gaffing

GUNWALE, -S n top of a ship's side

GUNYAH, -S n hut or shelter in the bush

GUP, -S n gossip

GUPPY, GUPPIES n small colourful aquarium fish

GUPS ▸ gup

GUQIN, -S n type of Chinese zither

GUR, -S n unrefined cane sugar

GURAMI, -S same as ▸ gourami

GURDIES ▸ gurdy

GURDWARA n Sikh place of worship

GURDY, GURDIES n winch on a fishing boat

GURGE, -D, -S, GURGING vb swallow up

GURGLE, -D, -S n bubbling noise ▷ vb (of water) to make low bubbling noises when flowing

GURGLET, -S same as ▶ goglet

GURGLIER ▶ gurgly

GURGLING ▶ gurgle

GURGLY, GURGLIER adj making gurgling sounds

GURGOYLE same as ▶ gargoyle

GURJUN, -S n S or SE Asian tree that yields a resin

GURL, -ED, -ING, -S vb snarl

GURLET, -S n type of pickaxe

GURLIER ▶ gurly

GURLIEST ▶ gurly

GURLING ▶ gurl

GURLS ▶ gurl

GURLY, GURLIER, GURLIEST adj stormy

GURN, -ED, -ING, -S variant spelling of ▶ girn

GURNARD, -S n spiny armour-headed sea fish

GURNED ▶ gurn

GURNET, -S same as ▶ gurnard

GURNEY, -S n wheeled stretcher for transporting hospital patients

GURNING ▶ gurn

GURNS ▶ gurn

GURRAH, -S n type of coarse muslin

GURRIER, -S n tough, ill-mannered person

GURRY, GURRIES n dog-fight

GURS ▶ gur

GURSH, -ES n unit of currency in Saudi Arabia

GURU, -S n Hindu or Sikh religious teacher or leader

GURUDOM, -S n state of being a guru

GURUISM, -S ▶ guru

GURUS ▶ guru

GURUSHIP ▶ guru

GUS ▶ gu

GUSH, -ED, -ES, -ING vb flow out suddenly and profusely ▷ n sudden copious flow

GUSHER, -S n spurting oil well

GUSHES ▶ gush

GUSHIER ▶ gushy

GUSHIEST ▶ gushy

GUSHILY ▶ gushy

GUSHING ▶ gush

GUSHY, GUSHIER, GUSHIEST adj displaying excessive sentimentality

GUSLA, -S n Balkan single-stringed musical instrument

GUSLAR, -S n player of the gusla

GUSLAS ▶ gusla

GUSLE, -S same as ▶ gusla

GUSLI, -S n Russian harp-like musical instrument

GUSSET, -S n piece of material sewn into a garment to strengthen it ▷ vb put a gusset in (a garment)

GUSSETED ▶ gusset

GUSSETS ▶ gusset

GUSSIE n young pig

GUSSY, GUSSIED, GUSSIES, -ING vb dress elaborately

GUST, -ED, -ING, -S n sudden blast of wind ▷ vb blow in gusts

GUSTABLE n anything that can be tasted

GUSTED ▶ gust

GUSTFUL adj tasty

GUSTIE adj tasty

GUSTIER ▶ gusty

GUSTIEST ▶ gusty

GUSTILY ▶ gusty

GUSTING ▶ gust

GUSTLESS adj tasteless

GUSTO, -ES, -S n enjoyment or zest

GUSTS ▶ gust

GUSTY, GUSTIER, GUSTIEST adj windy and blustery

GUT, -TED, -TING n intestine ▷ vb remove the guts from ▷ adj basic or instinctive

GUTCHER, -S n grandfather

GUTFUL, -S n bellyful

GUTLESS adj cowardly

GUTLIKE ▶ gut

GUTROT, -S n upset stomach

GUTS, -ED, -ES, -ING vb devour greedily

GUTSER, -S n as in come a gutser fall heavily to the ground

GUTSES ▶ guts

GUTSFUL, -S n bellyful

GUTSIER ▶ gutsy

GUTSIEST ▶ gutsy

GUTSILY ▶ gutsy

GUTSING ▶ guts

GUTSY, GUTSIER, GUTSIEST adj courageous

GUTTA, -E, -S n small drop-like ornament

GUTTATE, -S adj covered with small drops or drop-like markings ▷ vb exude droplets of liquid

GUTTATED same as ▶ guttate

GUTTATES ▶ guttate

GUTTED ▶ gut

GUTTER, -ED, -S n shallow channel for carrying away water ▷ vb (of a candle) burn unsteadily

GUTTERY adj vulgar

GUTTIER ▶ gutty

GUTTIES ▶ gutty

GUTTIEST ▶ gutty

GUTTING ▶ gut

GUTTLE, -D, -S, GUTTLING vb eat greedily

GUTTLER, -S ▶ guttle

GUTTLES ▶ guttle

GUTTLING ▶ guttle

GUTTURAL adj (of a sound) produced at the back of the throat ▷ n guttural consonant

GUTTY, GUTTIER, GUTTIES, GUTTIEST n urchin or delinquent ▷ adj courageous

GUTZER, -S n bad fall

GUV, -S informal name for ▶ governor

GUY, -ED, -ING, -S n man or boy ▷ vb make fun of

GUYLE, -D, -S, GUYLING same as ▶ guile

GUYLER, -S ▶ guyle

GUYLES ▶ guyle

GUYLINE, -S n guy rope

GUYLINER n eyeliner worn by men

GUYLINES ▶ guyline

GUYLING ▶ guyle

GUYOT, -S n flat-topped submarine mountain

GUYS ▶ guy

GUYSE, -S same as ▶ guise

GUZZLE, -D, -S, GUZZLING vb eat or drink greedily

GUZZLER, -S n person or thing that guzzles

GUZZLES ▶ guzzle

GUZZLING ▶ guzzle

GWEDUC, -S same as ▶ geoduck

GWEDUCK, -S same as ▶ geoduck

GWEDUCS ▶ gweduc

GWINE dialect form of ▶ going

GWINIAD, -S n type of freshwater white fish

GWYNIAD, -S n type of freshwater white fish

GYAL, -S same as ▶ gayal

GYAN, -S n (in Indian English) knowledge

GYBE, -D, -S, GYBING vb (of a sail) swing suddenly from one side to the other ▷ n instance of gybing

GYELD, -S old form of ▶ guild

GYLDEN old form of ▸ **golden**
GYM, -S n gymnasium
GYMBAL, -S same as
▸ **gimbal**
GYMKHANA n horse-riding competition
GYMMAL, -S same as
▸ **gimmal**
GYMNASIA > **gymnasium**
GYMNASIC > **gymnasium**
GYMNAST, -S n expert in gymnastics
GYMNIC adj gymnastic
GYMP, -ED, -ING, -S same as
▸ **gimp**
GYMPIE, -S n tall tree with stinging hairs on its leaves
GYMPING ▸ **gymp**
GYMPS ▸ **gymp**
GYMS ▸ **gym**
GYMSLIP, -S n tunic or pinafore formerly worn by schoolgirls
GYMSUIT, -S n costume worn for gymnastics
GYNAE, -S adj gynaecological ▹ n gynaecology
GYNAECEA > **gynaeceum**
GYNAECIA > **gynaecium**
GYNAES ▸ **gynae**
GYNANDRY n hermaphroditism
GYNARCHY n government by women
GYNECIA ▸ **gynecium**
GYNECIC adj relating to the female sex
GYNECIUM, GYNECIA same as > **gynoecium**
GYNECOID same as
> **gynaecoid**
GYNIATRY n gynaecology: medicine concerned with diseases in women
GYNIE, -S n gynaecology
GYNNEY, -S n guinea hen

GYNNY, GYNNIES same as
▸ **gynney**
GYNO, -S n gynaecologist
GYNOECIA > **gynoecium**
GYNOS ▸ **gyno**
GYNY n gynaecology
GYOZA, -S n Japanese fried dumpling
GYP, -S n slang word for severe pain

This little word, meaning severe pain, can be useful when you are short of vowels.

GYPLURE, -S n synthetic version of a gypsy moth pheromone
GYPO, -S n small-scale independent logger
GYPPIE same as ▸ **gippy**
GYPPY, GYPPIES same as
▸ **gippy**
GYPS ▸ **gyp**
GYPSEIAN adj relating to gypsies
GYPSEOUS ▸ **gypsum**
GYPSIED ▸ **gypsy**
GYPSIES ▸ **gypsy**
GYPSUM, -S n chalklike mineral
GYPSY, GYPSIED, GYPSIES, -ING n member of a nomadic people ▹ vb live like a gypsy
GYPSYDOM ▸ **gypsy**
GYPSYING ▸ **gypsy**
GYPSYISH ▸ **gypsy**
GYPSYISM n state of being a gypsy
GYRAL adj having a circular, spiral, or rotating motion
GYRALLY ▸ **gyral**
GYRANT adj gyrating
GYRASE, -S n topoisomerase enzyme
GYRATE, -D, -S, GYRATING vb rotate or spiral about a

point or axis ▹ adj curved or coiled into a circle
GYRATION n act or process of gyrating
GYRATOR, -S n electronic circuit that inverts the impedance
GYRATORY ▸ **gyrate**
GYRE, -D, -S, GYRING n circular or spiral movement or path ▹ vb whirl
GYRENE, -S n nickname for a member of the US Marine Corps
GYRES ▸ **gyre**
GYRI ▸ **gyrus**
GYRING ▸ **gyre**
GYRO, -S n gyrocompass
GYROCAR, -S n two-wheeled car
GYRODYNE n aircraft with rotor
GYROIDAL adj spiral
GYROLITE n silicate
GYRON, -S same as
▸ **giron**
GYRONIC ▸ **gyron**
GYRONNY same as
▸ **gironny**
GYRONS ▸ **gyron**
GYROS ▸ **gyro**
GYROSE adj marked with sinuous lines
GYROSTAT same as
> **gyroscope**
GYROUS adj marked with sinuous lines
GYRUS, GYRI, -ES n convolution
GYTE, -S n Scots word for a spoilt child
GYTRASH n spirit that haunts lonely roads
GYTTJA, -S n sediment on a lake bottom
GYVE, -D, -S, GYVING vb shackle or fetter ▹ n fetter

Hh

H forms a two-letter word in front of every vowel except **U** (and you can make **uh** with **U**), making it a versatile tile when you want to form words in more than one direction. It also goes with **M** to make **hm**. As **H** is worth 4 points on its own, you can earn some very high scores by doing this: even **ha**, **he**, **hi** and **ho** will give 5 points each. There are lots of good short words beginning with **H**, like **haw**, **hew**, **how**, **hay**, **hey** and **hoy** (9 each), while **hyp** can be useful if you are short of vowels. More high-scoring words with **H** include **haj**, **hex** and **hox** for 13 points each, and never forget the invaluable **zho** for 15 points.

HA *interj* exclamation of triumph, surprise, or scorn

HAAF, -S *n* fishing ground off the Shetland and Orkney Islands

HAAR, -S *n* cold sea mist or fog off the North Sea

HABANERA *n* slow Cuban dance in duple time

HABANERO *n* variety of chilli pepper

HABDABS *n* highly nervous state

HABDALAH *n* prayer at end of Jewish sabbath

HABENDUM *n* part of a deed defining the limits of ownership

HABILE *adj* skilful

HABIT, -ING, -S *n* established way of behaving ▷ *vb* clothe

HABITAN, -S *same as* ▶ **habitant**

HABITANT *n* person who lives in a place

HABITAT, -S *n* natural home of an animal or plant

HABITED *adj* dressed in a habit

HABITING ▶ **habit**

HABITS ▶ **habit**

HABITUAL *adj* done regularly and repeatedly ▷ *n* person with a habit

HABITUDE *n* habit or tendency

HABITUE, -S *n* frequent visitor to a place

HABITUS *n* general physical state

HABLE *old form of* ▶ **able**

HABOOB, -S *n* sandstorm

HABU, -S *n* large venomous snake

HACEK, -S *n* pronunciation symbol in Slavonic language

HACHIS *n* hash (the dish)

HACHURE, -D, -S *n* shading drawn on a map to indicate steepness of a hill ▷ *vb* mark or show by hachures

HACIENDA *n* ranch or large estate in Latin America

HACK, -ED, -S *vb* cut or chop violently ▷ *n* (inferior) writer or journalist ▷ *adj* unoriginal or of a low standard

HACKABLE ▶ **hack**

HACKBOLT *n* shearwater

HACKBUT, -S *another word for* ▶ **arquebus**

HACKED ▶ **hack**

HACKEE, -S *n* chipmunk

HACKER, -S *n* computer enthusiast

HACKERY *n* journalism

HACKETTE *n* informal, derogatory term for female journalist

HACKIE, -S *n* US word meaning cab driver

HACKING, -S ▶ **hack**

HACKLE, -D, HACKLING *same as* ▶ **heckle**

HACKLER, -S ▶ **hackle**

HACKLES *pl n* hairs which rise in response to emotion

HACKLET, -S *n* kittiwake

HACKLIER ▶ **hackly**

HACKLING ▶ **hackle**

HACKLY, HACKLIER *adj* rough or jagged

HACKMAN, HACKMEN *n* taxi driver

HACKNEY, -S *n* taxi ▷ *vb* make commonplace and banal by too frequent use

HACKS ▶ **hack**

HACKSAW, -N, -S *n* small saw for cutting metal ▷ *vb* cut with a hacksaw

HACKWORK *n* dull repetitive work

HAD, -DEN, -DING, -S *vb* Scots form of hold

HADAL *adj* denoting very deep zones of the oceans

HADARIM ▶ **heder**

HADAWAY *sentence substitute* exclamation urging the hearer to refrain from delay

HADDEN ▶ **had**

HADDEST *same as* ▶ **hadst**

HADDIE, -S *n* finnan haddock

HADDING ▶ **had**

HADDOCK, -S *n* edible sea fish of N Atlantic

HADE, -D, -S, HADING *n* angle made to the vertical by the plane of a fault or vein ▷ *vb* incline from the vertical

HADEDAH, -S *n* large grey-green S African ibis

HADES ▶ **hade**

HADING ▶ **hade**

HADITH, -S *n* body of tradition about Muhammad and his followers

HADJ, -ES *same as* ▶ **hajj**

HADJEE, -S *same as* ▶ **hadji**

HADJES ▶ **hadj**

HADJI, -S *same as* ▶ **hajji**

HADROME, -S *n* part of xylem

HADRON, -S *n* type of elementary particle

HADRONIC ▶ **hadron**

HADRONS ▶ **hadron**

H

HADS ▸ had
HADST singular form of the past tense (indicative mood) of ▸ have
HAE, -D, -ING, -N, -S Scot variant of ▸ have
HAEM, -S n red organic pigment containing ferrous iron
HAEMAL adj of the blood
HAEMATAL same as ▸ haemal
HAEMATIC n agent that stimulates the production of red blood cells
HAEMATIN n dark bluish or brownish pigment
HAEMIC same as ▸ haematic
HAEMIN, -S n haematin chloride
HAEMOID same as > haematoid
HAEMONY n plant mentioned in Milton's poetry
HAEMS ▸ haem
HAEN ▸ hae
HAEREDES ▸ haeres
HAEREMAI interj Māori expression of welcome ▷ n act of saying 'haeremai'
HAERES, HAEREDES same as ▸ heres
HAES ▸ hae
HAET, -S n whit
HAFF, -S n lagoon
HAFFET, -S n side of head
HAFFIT, -S same as ▸ haffet
HAFFLIN, -S same as ▸ halfling
HAFFS ▸ haff
HAFIZ, -ES n title for a person who knows the Koran by heart
HAFNIUM, -S n metallic element found in zirconium ores
HAFT, -ED, -ING, -S n handle of an axe, knife, or dagger ▷ vb provide with a haft
HAFTARA, -S same as ▸ haftarah
HAFTARAH, HAFTAROS, HAFTAROT n short reading from the Prophets
HAFTARAS ▸ haftara
HAFTAROS ▸ haftarah
HAFTAROT ▸ haftarah
HAFTED ▸ haft
HAFTER, -S ▸ haft
HAFTING ▸ haft
HAFTORAH, HAFTOROS, HAFTOROT same as ▸ haftarah
HAFTS ▸ haft
HAG, -GED, -GING, -S n ugly old woman ▷ vb hack

HAGADIC same as ▸ haggadic
HAGADIST same as ▸ haggadist
HAGBERRY same as ▸ hackberry
HAGBOLT, -S same as ▸ hackbolt
HAGBORN adj born of a witch
HAGBUSH same as ▸ arquebus
HAGBUT, -S same as ▸ arquebus
HAGDEN, -S same as ▸ hackbolt
HAGDON, -S same as ▸ hackbolt
HAGDOWN, -S same as ▸ hackbolt
HAGFISH n any of various primitive eel-like vertebrates
HAGG, -S n boggy place
HAGGADA, -S same as ▸ haggadah
HAGGADAH, HAGGADOT n book containing the order of service of the traditional Jewish Passover meal
HAGGADAS ▸ haggada
HAGGADIC ▸ haggadah
HAGGADOT ▸ haggadah
HAGGARD, -S adj looking tired and ill ▷ n hawk that has reached maturity before being caught
HAGGED ▸ hag
HAGGING ▸ hag
HAGGIS, -ES n Scottish dish
HAGGISH ▸ hag
HAGGLE, -D, -S vb bargain or wrangle over a price
HAGGLER, -S ▸ haggle
HAGGLES ▸ haggle
HAGGLING n act of haggling
HAGGS ▸ hagg
HAGLET, -S same as ▸ hacklet
HAGLIKE ▸ hag
HAGRIDE, -S, HAGRODE vb torment or obsess
HAGRIDER ▸ hagride
HAGRIDES ▸ hagride
HAGRODE ▸ hagride
HAGS ▸ hag
HAH, -S same as ▸ ha
HAHA, -S n wall or other boundary marker that is set in a ditch
HAHNIUM, -S n transuranic element
HAHS ▸ hah
HAICK, -S same as ▸ haik
HAIDUK, -S n rural brigand
HAIK, -A, -S n Arab's outer garment
HAIKAI same as ▸ haiku

HAIKS ▸ haik
HAIKU, -S n Japanese verse form in 17 syllables
HAIL, -ED, -ING, -S n (shower of) small pellets of ice ▷ vb fall as or like hail ▷ sentence substitute exclamation of greeting
HAILER, -S ▸ hail
HAILIER ▸ haily
HAILIEST ▸ haily
HAILING ▸ hail
HAILS ▸ hail
HAILSHOT n small scattering shot
HAILY, HAILIER, HAILIEST ▸ hail
HAIMISH same as ▸ heimish
HAIN, -ED, -S vb Scots word meaning save
HAINCH, -ED, -ES Scots form of ▸ haunch
HAINED ▸ hain
HAINING, -S ▸ hain
HAINS ▸ hain
HAINT, -S same as ▸ haunt
HAIQUE, -S same as ▸ haik
HAIR, -ING, -S n threadlike growth on the skin ▷ vb provide with hair
HAIRBALL n mass of hair that forms in the stomach an animal
HAIRBAND n band worn around head to control hair
HAIRBELL same as ▸ harebell
HAIRCAP, -S n type of moss
HAIRCUT, -S n act or an instance of cutting the hair
HAIRDO, -S n hairstyle
HAIRED adj with hair
HAIRGRIP n small bent clasp used to fasten the hair
HAIRIER ▸ hairy
HAIRIEST ▸ hairy
HAIRIF, -S another name for ▸ cleavers
HAIRILY adv in a hairy manner
HAIRING ▸ hair
HAIRLESS adj having little or no hair ▷ n as in **Mexican hairless** small breed of hairless dog
HAIRLIKE ▸ hair
HAIRLINE n edge of hair at the top of the forehead ▷ adj very fine or narrow
HAIRLOCK n lock of hair
HAIRNET, -S n any of several kinds of light netting worn over the hair
HAIRPIN, -S n U-shaped wire used to hold the hair in place

HAIRS ▸ hair
HAIRST, -ED, -S *Scots form of* ▸ **harvest**
HAIRTAIL *n* spiny-finned fish
HAIRWING *n* fishing lure tied with hair
HAIRWORK *n* thing made from hair
HAIRWORM *n* any of various hairlike nematode worms
HAIRY, HAIRIER, HAIRIEST *adj* covered with hair
HAITH *interj* Scots oath
HAJ, -ES *same as* ▸ **hadj**

A **haj** is a Muslim pilgrimage to Mecca, and one of the key words to remember for using the J. It can also be spelt **hadj** or **hajj**, and one who makes a haj is called a **hadjee, hadji, haji** or **hajji**.

HAJI, -S *same as* ▸ **hajji**
HAJJ, -ES *n* pilgrimage a Muslim makes to Mecca
HAJJAH *n* Muslim woman who has made a pilgrimage to Mecca
HAJJES ▸ hajj
HAJJI, -S *n* Muslim who has made a pilgrimage to Mecca
HAKA, -S *n* ceremonial Māori dance with chanting
HAKAM, -S *n* text written by a rabbi
HAKARI, -S *n* Māori ritual feast
HAKAS ▸ haka
HAKE, -S *n* edible sea fish of N hemisphere
HAKEA, -S *n* Australian tree or shrub with hard woody fruit
HAKEEM, -S *same as* ▸ **hakim**
HAKES ▸ hake
HAKIM, -S *n* Muslim judge, ruler, or administrator
HAKU, -S *in New Zealand English, same as* ▸ **kingfish**
HALACHA, -S, HALACHOT *n* Jewish religious law
HALACHIC ▸ halacha
HALACHOT ▸ halacha
HALAKAH, -S *same as* ▸ **halacha**
HALAKHA, -S, HALAKHOT, HALAKOTH *same as* ▸ **halacha**
HALAKHAH *same as* ▸ **halacha**
HALAKHAS ▸ halakha
HALAKHIC ▸ halakhah
HALAKHOT ▸ halakha
HALAKIC ▸ halakha
HALAKIST ▸ halakha
HALAKOTH ▸ halakha

HALAL, -LED, -S *n* meat from animals slaughtered according to Muslim law ▷ *adj* of or relating to such meat ▷ *vb* kill (animals) in this way
HALALA, -S *n* money unit in Saudi Arabia
HALALAH, -S *same as* ▸ **halala**
HALALAS ▸ halala
HALALLED ▸ halal
HALALS ▸ halal
HALATION *n* bright ring surrounding a light source
HALAVAH, -S *same as* ▸ **halvah**
HALAZONE *n* type of disinfectant
HALBERD, -S *n* spear with an axe blade
HALBERT, -S *same as* ▸ **halberd**
HALCYON, -S *adj* peaceful and happy ▷ *n* mythological bird
HALE, -D, -S, -ST, HALING *adj* healthy, robust ▷ *vb* pull or drag
HALENESS ▸ hale
HALER, -S, -U *same as* ▸ **heller**
HALES ▸ hale
HALEST ▸ hale
HALF, -S *n* either of two equal parts ▷ *adj* denoting one of two equal parts ▷ *adv* to the extent of half
HALFA, -S *n* African grass
HALFBACK *n* position in some team sports
HALFBEAK *n* type of fish with a short upper jaw and a protruding lower jaw
HALFEN *same as* ▸ **half**
HALFLIFE *n* time taken for half of the atoms in a radioactive material to undergo decay
HALFLIN, -S *same as* ▸ **halfling**
HALFLING *n* person only half-grown
HALFLINS ▸ halflin
HALFNESS ▸ half
HALFPACE *n* landing on staircase
HALFPIPE *n* U-shaped object used in skateboarding stunts
HALFS ▸ half
HALFTIME *n* rest period between the two halves of a game
HALFTONE *n* illustration showing lights and shadows by means of very small dots ▷ *adj* relating to, used in, or made by halftone

HALFWAY *adj* at or to half the distance
HALFWIT, -S *n* foolish or stupid person
HALIBUT, -S *n* large edible flatfish of N Atlantic
HALICORE *n* dugong
HALID, -S *same as* ▸ **halide**
HALIDE, -S *n* binary compound
HALIDOM, -S *n* holy place or thing
HALIDOME *same as* ▸ **halidom**
HALIDOMS ▸ halidom
HALIDS ▸ halid
HALIER, -OV, -S *n* former currency unit of Slovakia
HALIMOT, -S *n* court held by lord
HALIMOTE *same as* ▸ **halimot**
HALIMOTS ▸ halimot
HALING ▸ hale
HALIOTIS *n* type of shellfish
HALITE, -S *n* colourless or white mineral
HALITOUS ▸ halitus
HALITUS *n* vapour
HALL, -S *n* entrance passage
HALLAH, -S, HALLOT *variant spelling of* ▸ **challah**
HALLAL, -S *same as* ▸ **halal**
HALLALI, -S *n* bugle call
HALLALOO *same as* ▸ **halloo**
HALLALS ▸ hallal
HALLAN, -S *n* partition in cottage
HALLEL, -S *n* (in Judaism) section of the liturgy
HALLIAN, -S *same as* ▸ **hallion**
HALLIARD *same as* ▸ **halyard**
HALLING, -S *n* Norwegian country dance
HALLION, -S *n* lout
HALLMARK *n* typical feature ▷ *vb* stamp with a hallmark
HALLO, -ED, -ES, -ING, -S *same as* ▸ **halloo**
HALLOA, -ED, -S *same as* ▸ **halloo**
HALLOED ▸ hallo
HALLOES ▸ hallo
HALLOING ▸ hallo
HALLOO, -ED, -S *interj* shout used to call hounds at a hunt ▷ *n* shout of 'halloo' ▷ *vb* shout (something) to (someone)
HALLOS ▸ hallo
HALLOT ▸ hallah
HALLOTH *same as* ▸ **challah**
HALLOUMI *n* salty white sheep's cheese from Greece

or Turkey, usually eaten grilled

HALLOW, -S vb consecrate or set apart as being holy

HALLOWED adj regarded as holy

HALLOWER ▸ hallow

HALLOWS ▸ hallow

HALLS ▸ hall

HALLUCAL ▸ hallux

HALLUX, HALLUCES n first digit on the hind foot of an animal

HALLWAY, -S n entrance area

HALLYON, -S same as ▸ hallion

HALM, -S same as ▸ haulm

HALMA, -S n board game

HALMS ▸ halm

HALO, -ED, -ES, -ING, -S n ring of light round the head of a sacred figure ▷ vb surround with a halo

HALOGEN, -S n any of a group of nonmetallic elements

HALOID, -S adj resembling or derived from a halogen ▷ n compound containing halogen atoms in its molecules

HALOING ▸ halo

HALOLIKE ▸ halo

HALON, -S n any of a class of chemical compounds

HALOS ▸ halo

HALOSERE n plant community that originates and develops in conditions of high salinity

HALOUMI, -S same as ▸ halloumi

HALSE, -D, -S, HALSING vb embrace

HALSER, -S ▸ halse

HALSES ▸ halse

HALSING ▸ halse

HALT, -ED, -S vb come or bring to a stop ▷ n temporary stop ▷ adj lame

HALTER, -ED, -S n strap round a horse's head with a rope to lead it with ▷ vb put a halter on (a horse)

HALTERE, -S n one of a pair of modified hind wings in dipterous insects

HALTERED ▸ halter

HALTERES ▸ haltere

HALTERS ▸ halter

HALTING, -S ▸ halt

HALTLESS ▸ halt

HALTS ▸ halt

HALUTZ, -IM variant spelling of ▸ chalutz

HALVA, -S same as ▸ halvah

HALVAH, -S n E Mediterranean, Middle Eastern, or Indian sweetmeat

HALVAS ▸ halva

HALVE, -D, -S vb divide in half

HALVER, -S ▸ halve

HALVES ▸ halve

HALVING, -S n act of halving

HALWA, -S n type of sweet Indian dish

HALYARD, -S n rope for raising a ship's sail or flag

HAM, -MED, -MING, -S n smoked or salted meat from a pig's thigh ▷ vb overact

HAMADA, -S n rocky plateau in desert

HAMAL, -S n (in Middle Eastern countries) a porter or servant

HAMARTIA n flaw in character which leads to the downfall of the protagonist in a tragedy

HAMATE, -S adj hook-shaped ▷ n small bone in the wrist

HAMATSA, -S n Native Canadian dance

HAMAUL, -S same as ▸ hamal

HAMBLE, -D, -S, HAMBLING vb mutilate

HAMBONE, -D, -S vb strike body to provide percussion

HAMBURG, -S same as > hamburger

HAME, -D, -S, HAMING n Scots word for home ▷ vb to home

HAMEWITH adv Scots word meaning homewards

HAMFAT, -S n mediocre performer

HAMING ▸ hame

HAMLET, -S n small village

HAMMADA, -S same as ▸ hamada

HAMMAL, -S same as ▸ hamal

HAMMAM, -S n bathing establishment

HAMMED ▸ ham

HAMMER, -ED, -S n tool ▷ vb hit (as if) with a hammer

HAMMERER ▸ hammer

HAMMERS ▸ hammer

HAMMIER ▸ hammy

HAMMIES ▸ hammy

HAMMIEST ▸ hammy

HAMMILY ▸ hammy

HAMMING ▸ ham

HAMMOCK, -S same as ▸ hummock

HAMMY, HAMMIER, HAMMIES, HAMMIEST adj (of an actor) overacting or tending to overact ▷ n hamstring

HAMOSE adj shaped like a hook

HAMOUS same as ▸ hamose

HAMPER, -ED, -S vb make it difficult for (someone or something) to move or progress ▷ n large basket with a lid

HAMPERER ▸ hamper

HAMPERS ▸ hamper

HAMPSTER same as ▸ hamster

HAMS ▸ ham

HAMSTER, -S n small rodent with a short tail and cheek pouches

HAMULAR ▸ hamulus

HAMULATE ▸ hamulus

HAMULI ▸ hamulus

HAMULOSE ▸ hamulus

HAMULOUS ▸ hamulus

HAMULUS, HAMULI n biological attribute

HAMZA, -S n sign used in Arabic to represent the glottal stop

HAMZAH, -S same as ▸ hamza

HAMZAS ▸ hamza

HAN archaic inflected form of ▸ have

HANAP, -S n medieval drinking cup

HANAPER, -S n small wickerwork basket

HANAPS ▸ hanap

HANCE, -S same as ▸ haunch

HANCH, -ED, -ES, -ING vb try to bite

HAND, -ED, -ING, -S n part of the body at the end of the arm ▷ vb pass, give

HANDAX, -ES n small axe held in one hand

HANDAXE same as ▸ handax

HANDAXES ▸ handax

HANDBAG n woman's small bag

HANDBAGS pl n incident in which people threaten to fight

HANDBALL n game in which two teams try to throw a ball into their opponent's goal ▷ vb pass (the ball) with a blow of the fist

HANDBELL n bell rung by hand, esp one of a tuned set used in musical performance

HANDBILL n small printed notice

HANDBOOK n small reference or instruction book

HANDCAR, -S n small railway vehicle

HANDCART n simple cart pushed or pulled by hand, used for transporting goods

HANDCLAP n act of clapping hands

HANDCUFF n one of a linked pair of metal rings for locking round wrists ▷ vb put handcuffs on

HANDED ▷ **hand**

HANDER, -S ▷ **hand**

HANDFAST n agreement, esp of marriage, confirmed by a handshake ▷ vb betroth or marry (two persons or another person) by joining the hands

HANDFEED, HANDFED vb feed (a person or an animal) by hand

HANDFUL, -S, HANDSFUL n amount that can be held in the hand

HANDGRIP n covering on the handle of a racket or club

HANDGUN, -S n firearm such as a pistol

HANDHELD adj held in position by the hand ▷ n computer that can be held in the hand

HANDHOLD n object, crevice, etc, that can be used as a grip or support, as in climbing

HANDICAP n hindrance or disadvantage ▷ vb make it difficult for (someone) to do something

HANDIER ▷ **handy**

HANDIEST ▷ **handy**

HANDILY adv in a handy way or manner

HANDING ▷ **hand**

HANDISM, -S n discrimination against left- or right-handed people

HANDJAR, -S n Persian dagger

HANDKNIT n garment knitted by hand

HANDLE, -D, -S n part of an object that is held so that it can be used ▷ vb hold, feel, or move with the hands

HANDLER, -S n person who controls an animal

HANDLES ▷ **handle**

HANDLESS ▷ **hand**

HANDLIKE ▷ **hand**

HANDLINE n hand-operated fishing line

HANDLING n act or an instance of picking up, turning over, or touching something

HANDLIST n rough list

HANDLOOM n weaving device operated by hand

HANDMADE adj made by hand, not by machine

HANDMAID n person or thing that serves as a useful but subordinate purpose

HANDOFF, -S n (in rugby) act of warding off an opposing player

HANDOUT, -S n clothing, food, or money given to a needy person

HANDOVER n transfer or surrender

HANDPASS vb pass the ball by striking it with the hand

HANDPICK vb choose or select with great care, as for a special job or purpose

HANDPLAY n fighting with fists

HANDRAIL n rail alongside a stairway, to provide support

HANDROLL n large dried-seaweed cone filled with cold rice and other ingredients

HANDS ▷ **hand**

HANDSAW, -S n any saw for use in one hand only

HANDSEL, -S n gift for good luck ▷ vb give a handsel to (a person)

HANDSET, -S n telephone mouth- and earpiece in a single unit

HANDSEWN adj sewn by hand

HANDSFUL ▷ **handful**

HANDSIER ▷ **handsy**

HANDSOME adj (esp of a man) good-looking ▷ n term of endearment for a beloved person

HANDSY, HANDSIER adj engaging in unwanted physical contact

HANDWORK n work done by hand rather than by machine

HANDWRIT ▷ **handwrite**

HANDY, HANDIER, HANDIEST adj convenient, useful

HANDYMAN, HANDYMEN n man who is good at making or repairing things

HANEPOOT n variety of muscat grape

HANG, -ED, -S, HUNG vb attach or be attached at the top with the lower part free

HANGABLE adj suitable for hanging

HANGAR, -ED, -S n large shed for storing aircraft ▷ vb put in a hangar

HANGBIRD n any bird, esp the Baltimore oriole, that builds a hanging nest

HANGDOG, -S adj guilty, ashamed ▷ n furtive or sneaky person

HANGED ▷ **hang**

HANGER, -S n curved piece of wood, wire, etc with a hook

HANGFIRE n failure to fire

HANGI, -S n Māori oven

HANGING, -S ▷ **hang**

HANGIS ▷ **hangi**

HANGMAN, HANGMEN n man who executes people by hanging

HANGNAIL n piece of skin partly torn away from the base or side of a fingernail

HANGNEST same as ▷ **hangbird**

HANGOUT, -S n place where one lives or that one frequently visits

HANGOVER n headache and nausea as a result of drinking too much alcohol

HANGRY, HANGRIER adj irritable as a result of feeling hungry

HANGS ▷ **hang**

HANGTAG, -S n attached label

HANGUL, -S n alphabetic scheme used in Korean

HANGUP, -S n emotional or psychological problem

HANIWA, -S n Japanese funeral offering

HANJAR, -S same as ▷ **handjar**

HANK, -ED, -ING, -S n coil, esp of yarn ▷ vb attach (a sail) to a stay by hanks

HANKER, -ED, -S vb desire intensely

HANKERER ▷ **hanker**

HANKERS ▷ **hanker**

HANKIE same as ▷ **hanky**

HANKIES ▷ **hanky**

HANKING ▷ **hank**

HANKS ▷ **hank**

HANKY, HANKIES n handkerchief

HANSA, -S same as ▷ **hanse**

HANSE, -S n medieval guild of merchants

HANSEL, -ED, -S same as ▷ **handsel**

HANSES ▷ **hanse**

HANSOM, -S *n* two-wheeled one-horse carriage

HANT, -ED, -ING, -S *same as* ▸ **haunt**

HANTLE, -S *n* good deal

HANTS ▸ **hant**

HANUKIAH *n* candelabrum having nine branches that is lit during the festival of Hanukkah

HANUMAN, -S *n* type of monkey

HAO, -S *n* monetary unit of Vietnam

HAOMA, -S *n* type of ritual drink

HAOS ▸ **hao**

HAP, -PED, -PING, -S *n* luck ▸ *vb* cover up

HAPAX, -ES *n* word that appears once in a work of literature

HAPHTARA *same as* ▸ **haftarah**

HAPKIDO, -S *n* Korean martial art

HAPLESS *adj* unlucky

HAPLITE, -S *variant of* ▸ **aplite**

HAPLITIC ▸ **haplite**

HAPLOID, -S *adj* denoting a cell or organism with unpaired chromosomes ▸ *n* haploid cell or organism

HAPLOIDY ▸ **haploid**

HAPLONT, -S *n* organism with a haploid number of chromosomes

HAPLOPIA *n* normal single vision

HAPLOSIS, HAPLOSES *n* production of a haploid number of chromosomes during meiosis

HAPLY *archaic word for* ▸ **perhaps**

HAPPED ▸ **hap**

HAPPEN, -ED, -S *vb* take place, occur

HAPPI, -S *n* type of loose Japanese coat

HAPPIED ▸ **happy**

HAPPIER ▸ **happy**

HAPPIES ▸ **happy**

HAPPIEST ▸ **happy**

HAPPILY ▸ **happy**

HAPPING ▸ **hap**

HAPPIS ▸ **happi**

HAPPOSHU *n* beer-like Japanese drink

HAPPY, HAPPIED, HAPPIER, HAPPIES, HAPPIEST, -ING *adj* feeling or causing joy ▸ *vb* make happy

HAPS ▸ **hap**

HAPTEN, -S *n* incomplete antigen

HAPTENE, -S *same as* ▸ **hapten**

HAPTENIC ▸ **haptene**

HAPTENS ▸ **hapten**

HAPTERON *n* organ of attachment in some aquatic plants

HAPTIC *adj* relating to or based on the sense of touch

HAPTICAL *same as* ▸ **haptic**

HAPTICS *n* science of sense of touch

HAPU, -S *n* subtribe

HAPUKA, -S *another name for* ▸ **groper**

HAPUKU, -S *same as* ▸ **hapuka**

HAPUS ▸ **hapu**

HAQUETON *same as* > **hacqueton**

HARAAM *same as* ▸ **haram**

HARAKEKE *in New Zealand English, another name for* ▸ **flax**

HARAM, -S *n* anything that is forbidden by Islamic law

HARAMBEE *n* work chant used on the E African coast ▸ *interj* cry of harambee

HARAMS ▸ **haram**

HARANGUE *vb* address angrily or forcefully ▸ *n* angry or forceful speech

HARASS, -ES *vb* annoy or trouble constantly

HARASSED ▸ **harass**

HARASSER ▸ **harass**

HARASSES ▸ **harass**

HARBOR, -ED, -S *same as* ▸ **harbour**

HARBORER ▸ **harbor**

HARBORS ▸ **harbor**

HARBOUR, -S *n* sheltered port ▸ *vb* maintain secretly in the mind

HARD, -ER, -EST *adj* firm, solid, or rigid ▸ *adv* with great energy or effort

HARDASS *n* tough person

HARDBACK *n* book with a stiff cover ▸ *adj* of or denoting a hardback

HARDBAG, -S *n* rigid container on a motorcycle

HARDBAKE *n* almond toffee

HARDBALL *n* as in **play hardball** act in a ruthless or uncompromising way

HARDBEAM *same as* ▸ **hornbeam**

HARDBODY *n* attractive person with a muscular physique

HARDBOOT *n* type of skiing boot

HARDCASE *n* tough person ▸ *adj* relating to a container that has a rigid structure

HARDCORE *n* style of rock music with short fast songs and little melody

HARDEDGE *n* style of painting in which vividly coloured subjects are clearly delineated ▸ *adj* of, relating to, or denoting this style of painting

HARDEN, -S *vb* make or become hard ▸ *n* rough fabric made from hards

HARDENED *adj* toughened by experience

HARDENER *n* person or thing that hardens

HARDENS ▸ **harden**

HARDER ▸ **hard**

HARDEST ▸ **hard**

HARDFACE *n* uncompromising person

HARDHACK *n* woody plant

HARDHAT, -S *n* hat made of a hard material for protection ▸ *adj* typical of construction workers

HARDHEAD *same as* > **hardheads**

HARDIER ▸ **hardy**

HARDIES ▸ **hardy**

HARDIEST ▸ **hardy**

HARDILY *adv* in a hardy manner

HARDISH ▸ **hard**

HARDLINE *adj* uncompromising

HARDLY *adv* scarcely or not at all

HARDMAN, HARDMEN *n* tough, ruthless, or violent man

HARDNESS *n* quality or condition of being hard

HARDNOSE *n* tough person

HARDOKE, -S *n* burdock

HARDPACK *n* rigid backpack

HARDPAN, -S *n* hard impervious layer of clay below the soil

HARDROCK *adj* concerned with extracting minerals other than coal ▸ *n* tough uncompromising man

HARDS *pl n* coarse fibres and other refuse from flax and hemp

HARDSET *adj* in difficulties

HARDSHIP *n* suffering

HARDTACK *n* kind of hard saltless biscuit, formerly eaten by sailors

HARDTAIL *n* mountain bike with no rear suspension

H

HARDTOP, -S *n* car equipped with a metal or plastic roof

HARDWARE *n* metal tools or implements

HARDWIRE *vb* instal permanently in computer

HARDWOOD *n* wood of a broad-leaved tree such as oak or ash

HARDY, HARDIER, HARDIES, HARDIEST *adj* able to stand difficult conditions ▷ *n* any blacksmith's tool made with a square shank

HARE, -D, -S, HARING *n* animal like a large rabbit, with longer ears and legs ▷ *vb* run (away) quickly

HAREBELL *n* blue bell-shaped flower

HARED ▶ **hare**

HARELD, -S *n* long-tailed duck

HARELIKE ▶ **hare**

HARES ▶ **hare**

HAREWOOD *n* sycamore wood that has been stained for use in furniture making

HARIANA, -S *n* Indian breed of cattle

HARICOT, -S *n* variety of French bean

HARIGALS *same as* > **harigalds**

HARIJAN, -S *n* member of an Indian caste

HARING ▶ **hare**

HARIRA, -S *n* Moroccan soup

HARISH *adj* like hare

HARISSA, -S *n* hot paste

HARK, -ED, -ING, -S *vb* listen

HARKEN, -ED, -S *same as* ▶ **hearken**

HARKENER ▶ **harken**

HARKENS ▶ **harken**

HARKING ▶ **hark**

HARKS ▶ **hark**

HARL, -ED, -S *same as* ▶ **herl**

HARLING, -S ▶ **harl**

HARLS ▶ **harl**

HARM, -ED, -ING, -S *vb* injure physically, mentally, or morally ▷ *n* physical, mental, or moral injury

HARMALA, -S *n* African plant

HARMALIN *n* chemical derived from harmala

HARMAN, -S *n* constable

HARMED ▶ **harm**

HARMEL, -S *same as* ▶ **harmala**

HARMER, -S ▶ **harm**

HARMFUL *adj* causing or tending to cause harm

HARMIN, -S *same as* ▶ **harmalin**

HARMINE, -S *same as* ▶ **harmalin**

HARMING ▶ **harm**

HARMINS ▶ **harmin**

HARMLESS *adj* safe to use, touch, or be near

HARMONIC *adj* of harmony ▷ *n* overtone of a musical note produced when that note is played

HARMONY *n* peaceful agreement and cooperation

HARMOST, -S *n* Spartan governor

HARMOSTY *n* office of a harmost

HARMS ▶ **harm**

HARN, -S *n* coarse linen

HARNESS *n* arrangement of straps for attaching a horse to a cart or plough ▷ *vb* put a harness on

HARNS ▶ **harn**

HARO, -S *interj* cry meaning alas ▷ *n* cry of 'haro'

HAROSET, -S *n* Jewish dish eaten at Passover

HAROSETH *same as* ▶ **haroset**

HAROSETS ▶ **haroset**

HARP, -ED, -ING, -S *n* large triangular stringed instrument ▷ *vb* play the harp

HARPER, -S ▶ **harp**

HARPIES ▶ **harpy**

HARPIN *n* type of protein

HARPING ▶ **harp**

HARPINGS *pl n* wooden members used for strengthening the bow of a vessel

HARPINS *same as* ▶ **harpings**

HARPIST, -S ▶ **harp**

HARPOON, -S *n* barbed spear attached to a rope for hunting whales ▷ *vb* spear with a harpoon

HARPS ▶ **harp**

HARPY, HARPIES *n* nasty or bad-tempered woman

HARRIDAN *n* nagging or vicious woman

HARRIED ▶ **harry**

HARRIER, -S *n* cross-country runner

HARRIES ▶ **harry**

HARROW, -ED, -S *n* implement used to break up lumps of soil ▷ *vb* draw a harrow over

HARROWER ▶ **harrow**

HARROWS ▶ **harrow**

HARRUMPH *vb* clear or make the noise of clearing the throat

HARRY, HARRIED, HARRIES, -ING *vb* keep asking (someone) to do something

HARSH, -ED, -ER, -ES, -EST, -ING *adj* severe and difficult to cope with ▷ *vb* ruin or end a state of elation

HARSHEN, -S *vb* make harsh

HARSHER ▶ **harsh**

HARSHES ▶ **harsh**

HARSHEST ▶ **harsh**

HARSHING ▶ **harsh**

HARSHLY ▶ **harsh**

HARSLET, -S *same as* ▶ **haslet**

HART, -S *n* adult male deer

HARTAL, -S *n* (in India) closing shops or suspending work

HARTBEES *same as* > **hartbeest**

HARTELY *archaic spelling of* ▶ **heartily**

HARTEN, -ED, -S *same as* ▶ **hearten**

HARTS ▶ **hart**

HARUMPH, -S *same as* ▶ **harrumph**

HARUSPEX *n* priest in ancient Rome

HARVEST, -S *n* (season for) the gathering of crops ▷ *vb* gather (a ripened crop)

HAS ▶ **have**

HASH, -ED, -ES, -ING *n* dish of diced cooked meat and vegetables reheated ▷ *vb* chop into small pieces

HASHEESH *same as* ▶ **hashish**

HASHES ▶ **hash**

HASHIER ▶ **hashy**

HASHIEST ▶ **hashy**

HASHING ▶ **hash**

HASHISH *n* illegal drug made from the cannabis plant

HASHMARK *n* character (#)

HASHTAG, -S *n* word or phrase used to denote the topic of a Twitter post

HASHY, HASHIER, HASHIEST ▶ **hash**

HASK, -S *n* archaic name for a basket for transporting fish

HASLET, -S *n* loaf of cooked minced pig's offal, eaten cold

HASP, -ED, -ING, -S *n* type of fastening ▷ *vb* secure (a door, window, etc) with a hasp

HASS, -ES *n* as in **white hass** oatmeal pudding made with sheep's gullet

HASSAR, -S n South American catfish

HASSEL, -S variant of ▸ **hassle**

HASSES ▸ **hass**

HASSIUM, -S n chemical element

HASSLE, -D, -S, HASSLING n trouble, bother ▷ vb bother or annoy

HASSOCK, -S n cushion for kneeling on in church

HASSOCKY adj full of hassocks

HAST singular form of the present tense (indicative mood) of ▸ **have**

HASTA Spanish for ▸ **until**

HASTATE adj shaped like a spear

HASTATED same as ▸ **hastate**

HASTE, -D, -S n (excessive) quickness ▷ vb hasten

HASTEFUL ▸ **haste**

HASTEN, -ED, -S vb (cause to) hurry

HASTENER ▸ **hasten**

HASTENS ▸ **hasten**

HASTES ▸ **haste**

HASTIER ▸ **hasty**

HASTIEST ▸ **hasty**

HASTILY ▸ **hasty**

HASTING, -S ▸ **haste**

HASTY, HASTIER, HASTIEST adj (too) quick

HAT, -S, -TED n covering for the head, often with a brim ▷ vb supply (a person) with a hat or put a hat on (someone)

HATABLE ▸ **hate**

HATBAND, -S n band or ribbon around a hat

HATBOX, -ES n box or case for a hat or hats

HATBRUSH n brush for hats

HATCH, -ED, -ES vb (cause to) emerge from an egg ▷ n hinged door covering an opening in a floor or wall

HATCHECK n cloakroom

HATCHED ▸ **hatch**

HATCHEL, -S same as ▸ **heckle**

HATCHER, -S ▸ **hatch**

HATCHERY n place where eggs are hatched under artificial conditions

HATCHES ▸ **hatch**

HATCHET, -S n small axe

HATCHETY adj like a hatchet

HATCHING ▸ **hatch**

HATCHWAY n opening in the deck of a ship

HATE, -D, -S, HATING vb dislike intensely ▷ n intense dislike

HATEABLE ▸ **hate**

HATED ▸ **hate**

HATEFUL adj causing or deserving hate

HATELESS ▸ **hate**

HATER, -S ▸ **hate**

HATERENT same as ▸ **hatred**

HATERS ▸ **hater**

HATES ▸ **hate**

HATFUL, -S, HATSFUL n amount a hat will hold

HATGUARD n string to keep a hat from blowing off

HATH form of the present tense (indicative mood) of ▸ **have**

HATHA n as in hatha yoga form of yoga

HATING ▸ **hate**

HATLESS ▸ **hat**

HATLIKE ▸ **hat**

HATMAKER n maker of hats

HATPEG, -S n peg to hang hat on

HATPIN, -S n pin used to secure a woman's hat to her hair

HATRACK, -S n rack for hanging hats on

HATRED, -S n intense dislike

HATS ▸ **hat**

HATSFUL ▸ **hatful**

HATSTAND n frame or pole equipped with hooks or arms for hanging up hats, coats, etc

HATTED ▸ **hat**

HATTER, -ED, -S n person who makes and sells hats ▷ vb annoy

HATTERIA n species of reptile

HATTERS ▸ **hatter**

HATTING, -S ▸ **hat**

HATTOCK, -S n small hat

HAUBERK, -S n long sleeveless coat of mail

HAUBOIS same as ▸ **hautboy**

HAUD, -ING, -S, HUDDEN Scot word for ▸ **hold**

HAUF, -S Scot word for ▸ **half**

HAUGH, -S n low-lying often alluvial riverside meadow

HAUGHT same as ▸ **haughty**

HAUGHTY adj proud, arrogant

HAUL, -ED, -S vb pull or drag with effort ▷ n hauling

HAULAGE, -S n (charge for) transporting goods

HAULBACK n (in lumbering) line used to bring a cable back

HAULD, -S Scots word for ▸ **hold**

HAULED ▸ **haul**

HAULER, -S same as ▸ **haulier**

HAULIER, -S n firm or person that transports goods by road

HAULING, -S n act of hauling

HAULM, -S n stalks of beans, peas, or potatoes collectively

HAULMIER ▸ **haulmy**

HAULMS ▸ **haulm**

HAULMY, HAULMIER adj having haulms

HAULOUT, -S n act of hauling a boat out of water

HAULS ▸ **haul**

HAULST same as ▸ **halse**

HAULT same as ▸ **haughty**

HAULYARD same as ▸ **halyard**

HAUN, -S n Scot word for hand

HAUNCH, -ED, -ES n human hip or fleshy hindquarter of an animal ▷ vb cause (an animal) to come down on its haunches

HAUNS ▸ **haun**

HAUNT, -S vb visit in the form of a ghost ▷ n place visited frequently

HAUNTED adj frequented by ghosts

HAUNTER, -S ▸ **haunt**

HAUNTING adj memorably beautiful or sad

HAUNTS ▸ **haunt**

HAURIANT adj rising

HAURIENT same as ▸ **hauriant**

HAUSE, -D, -S, HAUSING same as ▸ **halse**

HAUSEN, -S n variety of sturgeon

HAUSES ▸ **hause**

HAUSFRAU n German housewife

HAUSING ▸ **hause**

HAUT, -ER, -EST same as ▸ **haughty**

HAUTBOIS same as ▸ **hautboy**

HAUTBOY, -S n type of strawberry

HAUTE adj French word meaning high

HAUTER ▸ **haut**

HAUTEST ▸ **haut**

HAUTEUR, -S n haughtiness

HAUYNE, -S n blue mineral containing calcium

HAVARTI, -S n Danish cheese

HAVDALAH n ceremony at the end of the Sabbath

HAVDOLOH same as ▸ **havdalah**

HAVE, HAS, -S vb possess, hold ▷ n person possessing wealth, security, etc

H

HAVELOCK n cap flap covering the back of the neck

HAVEN, -ED, -ING, -S n place of safety ▷ vb secure or shelter in or as if in a haven

HAVEOUR, -S same as ▶ havior

HAVER, -ED, -ING, -S vb talk nonsense ▷ n nonsense

HAVEREL, -S n fool

HAVERING ▶ haver

HAVERS ▶ haver

HAVES ▶ have

HAVILDAR n noncommissioned officer in the Indian army, equivalent in rank to sergeant

HAVING, -S ▶ have

HAVIOR, -S same as ▶ haviour

HAVIOUR, -S n possession

HAVOC, -KED, -S n disorder and confusion ▷ vb lay waste

HAVOCKER ▶ havoc

HAVOCS ▶ havoc

HAW, -ED, -ING, -S n hawthorn berry ▷ vb make an inarticulate utterance

HAWALA, -S n Middle Eastern system of money transfer

HAWBUCK, -S n bumpkin

HAWEATER n resident of Manitoulin Island, Ontario

HAWED ▶ haw

HAWFINCH n European finch with a stout bill and brown plumage with black-and-white wings

HAWING ▶ haw

HAWK, -ED, -S n bird of prey ▷ vb offer (goods) for sale in the street or door-to-door

HAWKBELL n bell fitted to a hawk's leg

HAWKBILL same as > hawksbill

HAWKBIT, -S n any of three perennial plants

HAWKED ▶ hawk

HAWKER, -S n travelling salesperson

HAWKEY, -S same as ▶ hockey

HAWKEYED adj having extremely keen sight

HAWKEYS ▶ hawkey

HAWKIE, -S n cow with white stripe on face

HAWKING, -S another name for ▶ falconry

HAWKISH adj favouring the use of force rather than diplomacy

HAWKIT adj having a white streak

HAWKLIKE ▶ hawk

HAWKMOTH n narrow-winged moth

HAWKNOSE n hooked nose

HAWKS ▶ hawk

HAWKSHAW n private detective

HAWKWEED n hairy plant with clusters of dandelion-like flowers

HAWM, -ED, -ING, -S vb be idle and relaxed

HAWS ▶ haw

HAWSE, -D, -S, HAWSING vb of boats, pitch violently when at anchor

HAWSER, -S n large rope used on a ship

HAWSES ▶ hawse

HAWSING ▶ hawse

HAWTHORN n thorny shrub or tree

HAY, -ED, -S n grass cut and dried as fodder ▷ vb cut, dry, and store (grass, clover, etc) as fodder

HAYBAND, -S n rope made by twisting hay together

HAYBOX, -ES n airtight box used to keep partially cooked food warm

HAYCOCK, -S n pile of hay left until dry enough to move

HAYED ▶ hay

HAYER, -S n person who makes hay

HAYEY, HAYIER, HAYIEST ▶ hay

HAYFIELD n field of hay

HAYFORK, -S n long-handled fork

HAYIER ▶ hayey

HAYIEST ▶ hayey

HAYING, -S ▶ hay

HAYLAGE, -S n type of hay for animal fodder

HAYLE, -S n welfare

HAYLOFT, -S n loft for storing hay

HAYMAKER n person who helps to cut, turn, toss, spread, or carry hay

HAYMOW, -S n part of a barn where hay is stored

HAYRACK, -S n rack for holding hay for feeding to animals

HAYRAKE, -S n large rake used to collect hay

HAYRICK, -S same as ▶ haystack

HAYRIDE, -S n pleasure trip in hay wagon

HAYS ▶ hay

HAYSEED, -S n seeds or fragments of grass or straw

HAYSEL, -S n season for making hay

HAYSTACK n large pile of stored hay

HAYWARD, -S n parish officer in charge of enclosures and fences

HAYWIRE, -S adj (of things) not functioning properly ▷ n wire for binding hay

HAZAN, -IM, -S n man employed to lead services in a synagogue

HAZARD, -ED, -S n something that could be dangerous ▷ vb put in danger

HAZARDER ▶ hazard

HAZARDRY n taking of risks

HAZARDS ▶ hazard

HAZE, -D, -S n mist, often caused by heat ▷ vb make or become hazy

HAZEL, -S n small tree producing edible nuts ▷ adj (of eyes) greenish-brown

HAZELHEN n type of grouse

HAZELLY ▶ hazel

HAZELNUT n nut of a hazel shrub, which has a smooth shiny hard shell

HAZELS ▶ hazel

HAZER, -S ▶ haze

HAZES ▶ haze

HAZIER ▶ hazy

HAZIEST ▶ hazy

HAZILY ▶ hazy

HAZINESS ▶ hazy

HAZING, -S ▶ haze

HAZMAT, -S n hazardous material

HAZY, HAZIER, HAZIEST adj not clear, misty

HAZZAN, -IM, -S same as ▶ hazan

HE, -S pron male person or animal ▷ n male person or animal ▷ interj expression of amusement or derision

HEAD n upper or front part of the body ▷ adj chief, principal ▷ vb be at the top or front of

HEADACHE n continuous pain in the head

HEADACHY adj suffering from, caused by, or likely to cause a headache

HEADAGE, -S n payment to farmer based on animals owned

HEADBAND n ribbon or band worn around the head

HEADBANG vb nod one's head violently to the beat of loud rock music

HEADCASE n foolish or crazy person

HEADED adj having a head or heads

HEADEND, -S n facility from which cable television is transmitted

HEADER, -S n striking a ball with the head

HEADFAST n mooring rope at the bows of a ship

HEADFISH same as ▸ **sunfish**

HEADFUL, -S n amount head will hold

HEADGATE n gate used to control the flow of water at the upper end of a lock or conduit

HEADGEAR n hats collectively

HEADHUNT vb recruit employee from another company

HEADIER ▸ **heady**

HEADIEST ▸ **heady**

HEADILY ▸ **heady**

HEADING, -S same as ▸ **head**

HEADLAMP same as ▸ **headlight**

HEADLAND n area of land jutting out into the sea

HEADLESS adj without a head

HEADLIKE ▸ **head**

HEADLINE n title at the top of a newspaper article, esp on the front page

HEADLOCK n wrestling hold

HEADLONG adj with the head first ▹ adv with the head foremost

HEADMAN, HEADMEN n chief or leader

HEADMARK n characteristic

HEADMEN ▸ **headman**

HEADMOST less common word for ▸ **foremost**

HEADNOTE n note at book chapter head

HEADPIN, -S another word for ▸ **kingpin**

HEADPOND n artificial pond behind a dam

HEADRACE n channel that carries water to a water wheel, turbine, etc

HEADRAIL n end of a snooker table from which play is started

HEADREST n support for the head, as on a dentist's chair or car seat

HEADRIG, -S n edge of ploughed field

HEADRING n African head decoration

HEADROOM n space above person's head in a vehicle

HEADROPE n rope round an animal's head

HEADS adv with the side of a coin with a head on it uppermost

HEADSAIL n any sail set forward of the foremast

HEADSET, -S n pair of headphones

HEADSHIP n position or state of being a leader, esp the head teacher of a school

HEADSHOT n photo of person's head

HEADSMAN, HEADSMEN n (formerly) an executioner who beheaded condemned persons

HEADSTAY n rope from mast to bow on ship

HEADWALL n steep slope at the head of a glacial cirque

HEADWARD same as ▸ **headwards**

HEADWAY, -S same as ▸ **headroom**

HEADWIND n wind blowing against the course of an aircraft or ship

HEADWORD n key word placed at the beginning of a line, paragraph, etc, as in a dictionary entry

HEADWORK n intellectual labour

HEADY, HEADIER, HEADIEST adj intoxicating or exciting

HEAL, -ED, -S vb make or become well

HEALABLE ▸ **heal**

HEALD, -ED, -ING, -S same as ▸ **heddle**

HEALED ▸ **heal**

HEALEE, -S n person who is being healed

HEALER, -S ▸ **heal**

HEALING, -S ▸ **heal**

HEALS ▸ **heal**

HEALSOME Scots word for ▸ **wholesome**

HEALTH, -S n normal (good) condition of someone's body ▹ interj exclamation wishing someone good health as part of a toast

HEALTHY adj having good health

HEAME old form of ▸ **home**

HEAP, -ED, -S n pile of things one on top of another ▹ vb gather into a pile

HEAPER, -S ▸ **heap**

HEAPIER ▸ **heapy**

HEAPIEST ▸ **heapy**

HEAPING adj (of a spoonful) heaped

HEAPS ▸ **heap**

HEAPY, HEAPIER, HEAPIEST adj having many heaps

HEAR, -S vb perceive (a sound) by ear

HEARABLE ▸ **hear**

HEARD, -S same as ▸ **herd**

HEARE, -S old form of ▸ **hair**

HEARER, -S ▸ **hear**

HEARES ▸ **heare**

HEARIE old form of ▸ **hairy**

HEARING, -S ▸ **hear**

HEARKEN, -S vb listen

HEARS ▸ **hear**

HEARSAY, -S n gossip, rumour

HEARSE, -D, -S, HEARSING n funeral car used to carry a coffin ▹ vb put in hearse

HEARSIER ▸ **hearsy**

HEARSING ▸ **hearse**

HEARSY, HEARSIER adj like a hearse

HEART, -ED, -ING n organ that pumps blood round the body ▹ vb (of vegetables) form a heart

HEARTEN, -S vb encourage, make cheerful

HEARTH, -S n floor of a fireplace

HEARTIER ▸ **hearty**

HEARTIES ▸ **hearty**

HEARTILY adv thoroughly or vigorously

HEARTING ▸ **heart**

HEARTLET n little heart

HEARTLY adv vigorously

HEARTPEA same as ▸ **heartseed**

HEARTS n card game

HEARTY, HEARTIER, HEARTIES adj substantial, nourishing ▹ n comrade, esp a sailor

HEAST, -S same as ▸ **hest**

HEASTE, -S same as ▸ **hest**

HEASTS ▸ **heast**

HEAT, -S vb make or become hot ▹ n state of being hot

HEATABLE ▸ **heat**

HEATED adj angry and excited

HEATEDLY ▸ **heated**

HEATER, -S n device for supplying heat

HEATH, -S n area of open uncultivated land

HEATHEN, -S n person who does not believe in an established religion ▹ adj of or relating to heathen peoples

HEATHER, -S n low-growing plant ▷ adj of a heather colour
HEATHERY ▸ heather
HEATHIER ▸ heathy
HEATHS ▸ heath
HEATHY, HEATHIER ▸ heath
HEATING, -S n device or system for supplying heat
HEATLESS ▸ heat
HEATS ▸ heat
HEATSPOT n spot on skin produced by heat
HEATWAVE n prolonged period of unusually hot weather
HEAUME, -S n large helmet reaching the shoulders
HEAVE, -D, -S, HOVEN vb lift with effort ▷ n heaving
HEAVEN, -S n place believed to be the home of God
HEAVENLY adj of or like heaven
HEAVENS ▸ heaven
HEAVER, -S ▸ heave
HEAVES ▸ heave
HEAVIER ▸ heavy
HEAVIES ▸ heavy
HEAVIEST ▸ heavy
HEAVILY ▸ heavy
HEAVING, -S ▸ heave
HEAVY, HEAVIER, HEAVIES, HEAVIEST adj of great weight ▷ n person hired to threaten violence
HEAVYISH adj rather heavy
HEAVYSET adj stockily built
HEBDOMAD n number seven or a group of seven
HEBE, -S n any of various flowering shrubs
HEBEN, -S old form of ▸ ebony
HEBENON, -S n source of poison
HEBENS ▸ heben
HEBES ▸ hebe
HEBETANT adj causing dullness
HEBETATE adj (of plant parts) having a blunt or soft point ▷ vb make or become blunted
HEBETIC adj of or relating to puberty
HEBETUDE n mental dullness or lethargy
HEBONA, -S same as ▸ hebenon
HEBRAISE same as ▸ hebraize
HEBRAIZE vb become or cause to become Hebrew or Hebraic

HECATOMB n sacrifice of 100 oxen
HECH interj expression of surprise
HECHT, -ING, -S same as ▸ hight
HECK, -S interj mild exclamation of surprise, irritation, etc ▷ n frame for obstructing the passage of fish in a river
HECKLE, -D, -S, HECKLING vb interrupt with comments, questions, or taunts ▷ n instrument for combing flax or hemp
HECKLER, -S ▸ heckle
HECKLES ▸ heckle
HECKLING ▸ heckle
HECKS ▸ heck
HECKUVA adj heck of a
HECTARE, -S n one hundred ares
HECTIC, -S adj rushed or busy ▷ n hectic fever or flush
HECTICAL same as ▸ hectic
HECTICLY ▸ hectic
HECTICS ▸ hectic
HECTOR, -ED, -S vb bully ▷ n blustering bully
HECTORER ▸ hector
HECTORLY ▸ hector
HECTORS ▸ hector
HEDARIM same as ▸ hadarim
HEDDLE, -D, -S, HEDDLING n frame on a loom ▷ vb pass thread through a heddle
HEDER, HADARIM, -S variant spelling of ▸ cheder
HEDERA, -S n ivy
HEDERAL ▸ hedera
HEDERAS ▸ hedera
HEDERS ▸ heder
HEDGE, -D, -S n row of bushes forming a barrier or boundary ▷ vb be evasive or noncommittal
HEDGEHOG n small mammal with a protective covering of spines
HEDGEHOP vb (of an aircraft) to fly close to the ground, as in crop spraying
HEDGEPIG same as ▸ hedgehog
HEDGER, -S ▸ hedge
HEDGEROW n bushes forming a hedge
HEDGERS ▸ hedger
HEDGES ▸ hedge
HEDGIER ▸ hedgy
HEDGIEST ▸ hedgy
HEDGING, -S ▸ hedge
HEDGY, HEDGIER, HEDGIEST ▸ hedge

HEDONIC ▸ hedonism
HEDONICS n branch of psychology concerned with the study of pleasant and unpleasant sensations
HEDONISM n doctrine that pleasure is the most important thing in life
HEDONIST ▸ hedonism
HEED, -ED, -ING, -S n careful attention ▷ vb pay careful attention to
HEEDER, -S ▸ heed
HEEDFUL ▸ heed
HEEDIER ▸ heedy
HEEDIEST ▸ heedy
HEEDING ▸ heed
HEEDLESS adj taking no notice
HEEDS ▸ heed
HEEDY, HEEDIER, HEEDIEST adj heedful; attentive
HEEHAW, -ED, -S interj representation of the braying sound of a donkey ▷ vb make braying sound
HEEL, -ED, -S n back part of the foot ▷ vb repair the heel of (a shoe)
HEELBALL n mixture of beeswax and lampblack used by shoemakers
HEELBAR, -S n small shop where shoes are repaired
HEELED ▸ heel
HEELER, -S n dog that herds cattle by biting at their heels
HEELING, -S ▸ heel
HEELLESS ▸ heel
HEELPOST n post for carrying the hinges of a door or gate
HEELS ▸ heel
HEELTAP, -S n layer of leather, etc, in the heel of a shoe
HEEZE, -D, -S, HEEZING Scots word for ▸ hoist
HEEZIE, -S n act of lifting
HEEZING ▸ heeze
HEFT, -ED, -ING, -S vb assess the weight of (something) by lifting ▷ n weight
HEFTE same as ▸ heave
HEFTED ▸ heft
HEFTER, -S ▸ heft
HEFTIER ▸ hefty
HEFTIEST ▸ hefty
HEFTILY ▸ hefty
HEFTING ▸ heft
HEFTS ▸ heft
HEFTY, HEFTIER, HEFTIEST adj large, heavy, or strong
HEGARI, -S n African sorghum

HEGEMON, -S *n* person in authority

HEGEMONY *n* political domination

HEGIRA, -S *n* emigration escape or flight

HEGUMEN, -S *n* head of a monastery of the Eastern Church

HEGUMENE *n* head of Greek nunnery

HEGUMENS ▶ hegumen

HEGUMENY *n* office of hegumen

HEH, -S *interj* exclamation of surprise or inquiry

HEID, -S *Scot word for* **▶ head**

HEIDUC, -S *n* Hungarian guerilla warrior

HEIFER, -S *n* young cow

HEIGH *same as* **▶ hey**

HEIGHT, -S *n* distance from base to top

HEIGHTEN *vb* make or become higher or more intense

HEIGHTH, -S *obsolete form of* **▶ height**

HEIGHTS ▶ height

HEIL, -ED, -ING, -S *vb* give a German greeting

HEIMISH *adj* comfortable

HEINIE, -S *n* buttocks

HEINOUS *adj* evil and shocking

HEIR, -ED, -ING, -S *n* person entitled to inherit property or rank ▷ *vb* inherit

HEIRDOM, -S *n* succession by right of blood

HEIRED ▶ heir

HEIRESS *n* woman who inherits or expects to inherit great wealth

HEIRING ▶ heir

HEIRLESS ▶ heir

HEIRLOOM *n* object that has belonged to a family for generations

HEIRS ▶ heir

HEIRSHIP *n* state or condition of being an heir

HEISHI *n* Native American shell jewellery

HEIST, -ED, -ING, -S *n* robbery ▷ *vb* steal or burgle

HEISTER, -S ▶ heist

HEISTING ▶ heist

HEISTS ▶ heist

HEITIKI, -S *n* Māori neck ornament of greenstone

HEJAB, -S *same as* **▶ hijab**

HEJIRA, -S *same as* **▶ hegira**

HEJRA, -S *same as* **▶ hegira**

HEKETARA *n* small shrub that has flowers with white petals and yellow centres

HEKTARE, -S *same as* **▶ hectare**

HELCOID *adj* having ulcers

HELD ▶ hold

HELE, -D, -S, HELING *vb* as in **hele in** insert (cuttings, etc) into soil

HELENIUM *n* plant with daisy-like yellow or variegated flowers

HELES ▶ hele

HELIAC *same as* **▶ heliacal**

HELIACAL *adj* as in **heliacal rising** rising of a celestial object at approximately the same time as the rising of the sun

HELIAST, -S *n* ancient Greek juror

HELIBUS *n* helicopter carrying passengers

HELICAL *adj* spiral

HELICASE *n* enzyme vital to all living organisms

HELICES ▶ helix

HELICITY *n* projection of the spin of an elementary particle on the direction of propagation

HELICOID *adj* shaped like a spiral ▷ *n* any surface resembling that of a screw thread

HELICON, -S *n* bass tuba

HELICOPT *vb* transport using a helicopter

HELIDECK *n* landing deck for helicopters on ships, oil platforms, etc

HELILIFT *vb* transport by helicopter

HELIMAN, HELIMEN *n* helicopter pilot

HELING ▶ hele

HELIO, -S *n* instrument for sending messages in Morse code

HELIODOR *n* clear yellow form of beryl used as a gemstone

HELIOS ▶ helio

HELIOSIS, HELIOSES *n* bad effect of overexposure to the sun

HELIPAD, -S *n* place for helicopters to land and take off

HELIPORT *n* airport for helicopters

HELISKI, -S *vb* ski down a mountain after ascending it by helicopter

HELISTOP *n* landing place for helicopter

HELITACK *n* use of helicopters to extinguish a forest fire

HELIUM, -S *n* very light colourless odourless gas

HELIX, HELICES, -ES *n* spiral

HELL, -ED, -ING, -S *n* believed to be where wicked people go when they die ▷ *vb* act wildly

HELLBENT *adj* intent

HELLBOX *n* (in printing) container for broken type

HELLCAT, -S *n* spiteful fierce-tempered woman

HELLED ▶ hell

HELLER, -S *n* monetary unit of the Czech Republic

HELLERI, -S *n* Central American fish

HELLERS ▶ heller

HELLERY *n* wild or mischievous behaviour

HELLFIRE *n* torment of hell, imagined as eternal fire

HELLHOLE *n* unpleasant or evil place

HELLICAT *n* evil creature

HELLIER, -S *n* slater

HELLING ▶ hell

HELLION, -S *n* rough or rowdy person, esp a child

HELLISH *adj* very unpleasant ▷ *adv* (intensifier) extremely

HELLKITE *n* bird of prey from hell

HELLO, -ED, -ES, -ING, -S *interj* expression of greeting or surprise ▷ *n* act of saying 'hello' ▷ *sentence substitute* expression of greeting ▷ *vb* say hello

HELLOVA *same as* **▶ helluva**

HELLS ▶ hell

HELLUVA *adj* phonetic representation of 'hell of a'

HELLWARD *adj* towards hell

HELM, -ED, -ING, -S *n* tiller or wheel for steering a ship ▷ *vb* direct or steer

HELMER, -S *n* film director

HELMET, -S *n* hard hat worn for protection

HELMETED ▶ helmet

HELMETS ▶ helmet

HELMING ▶ helm

HELMINTH *n* any parasitic worm, esp a nematode or fluke

HELMLESS ▶ helm

HELMS ▶ helm

HELMSMAN, HELMSMEN *n* person at the helm who steers the ship

HELO, -S *n* helicopter

HELOT, -S *n* serf or slave

HELOTAGE *same as* **▶ helotism**

HELOTISM n condition or quality of being a helot

HELOTRY n serfdom or slavery

HELOTS ▷ helot

HELP, -ED, -S vb make something easier, better, or quicker for (someone) ▷ n assistance or support

HELPABLE ▷ help

HELPDESK n place where advice is given by telephone

HELPED ▷ help

HELPER, -S ▷ help

HELPFUL adj giving help

HELPING, -S n single portion of food

HELPLESS adj weak or incapable

HELPLINE n telephone line set aside for callers to contact an organization for help with a problem

HELPMATE n companion and helper, esp a spouse

HELPMEET less common word for ▷ helpmate

HELPS ▷ help

HELVE, -D, -S, HELVING n handle of a hand tool such as an axe or pick ▷ vb fit a helve to (a tool)

HEM, -MED, -MING, -S n bottom edge of a garment ▷ vb provide with a hem

HEMAGOG same as > hemagogue

HEMAL same as ▷ haemal

HEMATAL same as ▷ hemal

HEMATEIN same as > haematein

HEMATIC, -S same as ▷ haematic

HEMATIN same as ▷ haematin

HEMATINE n red dye

HEMATINS ▷ hematin

HEMATITE n red, grey, or black mineral

HEMATOID same as > haematoid

HEMATOMA same as > haematoma

HEME, -S same as ▷ haem

HEMIC same as ▷ haematic

HEMIN, -S same as ▷ haemin

HEMINA, -S n old liquid measure

HEMINS ▷ hemin

HEMIOLA, -S n rhythmic device

HEMIOLIA same as ▷ hemiola

HEMIOLIC ▷ hemiola

HEMIONE, -S ▷ hemionus

HEMIONUS n Asian wild ass

HEMIOPIA n defective vision seeing only halves of things

HEMIOPIC ▷ hemiopia

HEMIPOD, -S same as ▷ hemipode

HEMIPODE n button quail

HEMIPODS ▷ hemipod

HEMIPTER n insect with beaklike mouthparts

HEMLINE, -S n level to which the hem of a skirt hangs

HEMLOCK, -S n poisonous plant

HEMMED ▷ hem

HEMMER, -S n attachment on a sewing machine for hemming

HEMMING ▷ hem

HEMOCOEL same as > haemocoel

HEMOCYTE same as > haemocyte

HEMOID same as > haematoid

HEMOLYSE vb break down so that haemoglobin is released

HEMOLYZE vb undergo or make undergo hemolysis

HEMOSTAT same as > haemostat

HEMP, -S n Asian plant with tough fibres

HEMPEN ▷ hemp

HEMPIE variant of ▷ hempy

HEMPIER ▷ hempy

HEMPIEST ▷ hempy

HEMPLIKE ▷ hemp

HEMPS ▷ hemp

HEMPSEED n seed of hemp

HEMPWEED n climbing weed

HEMPY, HEMPIER, HEMPIES, HEMPIEST adj of or like hemp ▷ n rogue

HEMS ▷ hem

HEN, -NED, -NING, -S n female domestic fowl ▷ vb lose one's courage

HENBANE, -S n poisonous plant with sticky hairy leaves

HENBIT, -S n European plant with small dark red flowers

HENCE adv from this time ▷ interj begone! away!

HENCH, -ER, -EST adj fit and muscular

HENCHMAN, HENCHMEN n person employed by someone powerful to carry out orders

HENCOOP, -S n cage for poultry

HEND, -ED, -ING, -S vb seize

HENEQUEN n agave plant native to Yucatán

HENEQUIN same as ▷ henequen

HENGE, -S n monument from the Neolithic and Bronze Ages

HENHOUSE n coop for hens

HENIQUEN same as ▷ henequen

HENIQUIN same as ▷ heniquen

HENLEY, -S n type of sweater

HENLIKE ▷ hen

HENNA, -ED, -ING, -S n reddish dye made from a shrub or tree ▷ vb dye (the hair) with henna

HENNED ▷ hen

HENNER, -S n challenge

HENNERY n place or farm for keeping poultry

HENNIER ▷ henny

HENNIES ▷ henny

HENNIEST ▷ henny

HENNIN, -S n former women's hat

HENNING ▷ hen

HENNINS ▷ hennin

HENNISH ▷ hen

HENNY, HENNIER, HENNIES, HENNIEST adj like a hen ▷ n cock that looks like a hen

HENOTIC adj acting to reconcile

HENPECK, -S vb (of a woman) to harass or torment (a man)

HENRY, HENRIES, -S n unit of electrical inductance

HENS ▷ hen

HENT, -ED, -ING, -S vb seize ▷ n anything that has been grasped, esp by the mind

HEP, -PER, -PEST, -S adj aware of or following the latest trends ▷ n fact of being hep

HEPAR, -S n compound containing sulphur

HEPARIN, -S n polysaccharide present in most body tissues

HEPARS ▷ hepar

HEPATIC, -S adj of the liver ▷ n any of various drugs for use in treating diseases of the liver

HEPATICA n woodland plant with white, mauve, or pink flowers

HEPATICS ▷ hepatic

HEPATISE same as ▷ hepatize

HEPATITE n mineral containing sulphur
HEPATIZE vb turn into liver
HEPATOMA n cancer of liver
HEPCAT, -S n person who is hep
HEPPER ▸ hep
HEPPEST ▸ hep
HEPS ▸ hep
HEPSTER, -S same as ▸ hipster
HEPT archaic spelling of ▸ heaped
HEPTAD, -S n group or series of seven
HEPTAGON n geometric figure with seven sides
HEPTANE, -S n alkane found in petroleum
HEPTARCH > heptarchy
HEPTOSE, -S n any monosaccharide with seven carbon atoms per molecule
HER pron refers to anything personified as feminine ▷ adj belonging to her ▷ determiner of, belonging to, or associated with her
HERALD, -ED, -S n person who announces important news ▷ vb signal the approach of
HERALDIC adj of or relating to heraldry
HERALDRY n study of coats of arms and family trees
HERALDS ▸ herald
HERB, -S n plant used for flavouring in cookery, and in medicine
HERBAGE, -S n herbaceous plants collectively
HERBAGED adj with grass growing on it
HERBAGES ▸ herbage
HERBAL, -S adj of or relating to herbs, usually culinary or medicinal herbs ▷ n book describing and listing the properties of plants
HERBAR, -S same as ▸ herbary
HERBARIA > herbarium
HERBARS ▸ herbar
HERBARY n herb garden
HERBED adj flavoured with herbs
HERBELET same as ▸ herblet
HERBIER ▸ herby
HERBIEST ▸ herby
HERBIST, -S same as > herbalist
HERBLESS ▸ herb
HERBLET, -S n little herb
HERBLIKE ▸ herb
HERBOSE same as ▸ herbous

HERBOUS adj with abundance of herbs
HERBS ▸ herb
HERBY, HERBIER, HERBIEST adj abounding in herbs
HERCULES n as in hercules beetle very large tropical American beetle
HERD, -ED, -S n group of animals feeding and living together ▷ vb collect into a herd
HERDBOY, -S n boy who looks after herd
HERDED ▸ herd
HERDEN, -S n type of coarse cloth
HERDER, -S same as ▸ herdsman
HERDESS n female herder
HERDIC, -S n small horse-drawn carriage
HERDING, -S n act of herding
HERDLIKE ▸ herd
HERDMAN, HERDMEN same as ▸ herdsman
HERDS ▸ herd
HERDSMAN, HERDSMEN n man who looks after a herd of animals
HERDWICK n hardy breed of sheep
HERE adv in, at, or to this place or point
HEREAT adv because of this
HEREAWAY same as > hereabout
HEREBY adv by means of or as a result of this
HEREDES ▸ heres
HEREDITY n passing on of characteristics from one generation to another
HEREFROM adv from here
HEREIN adv in this place, matter, or document
HEREINTO adv into this place, circumstance, etc
HERENESS n state of being here
HEREOF adv of or concerning this
HEREON archaic word for ▸ hereupon
HERES, HEREDES n heir
HERESY, HERESIES n opinion contrary to accepted opinion or belief
HERETIC, -S n person who holds unorthodox opinions
HERETO adv this place, matter, or document
HERETRIX n in Scots law, female inheritor

HEREUNTO archaic word for ▸ hereto
HEREUPON adv following immediately after this
HEREWITH adv with this
HERIED ▸ hery
HERIES ▸ hery
HERIOT, -S n (in medieval England) a death duty paid to the lord
HERISSE adj with bristles
HERISSON n spiked beam used as fortification
HERITAGE n something inherited
HERITOR, -S n person who inherits
HERITRIX n female heritor
HERL, -S n barb or barbs of a feather
HERLING, -S n Scots word for a type of fish
HERLS ▸ herl
HERM, -S n (in ancient Greece) a stone head of Hermes
HERMA, -E, -I same as ▸ herm
HERMAEAN adj type of statue
HERMAI ▸ herma
HERMETIC adj sealed so as to be airtight
HERMIT, -S n person living in solitude, esp for religious reasons
HERMITIC ▸ hermit
HERMITRY n life as hermit
HERMITS ▸ hermit
HERMS ▸ herm
HERN, -S archaic or dialect word for ▸ heron
HERNIA, -E, -S n medical problem
HERNIAL ▸ hernia
HERNIAS ▸ hernia
HERNIATE n form a hernia
HERNS ▸ hern
HERNSHAW same as > heronshaw
HERO, -ES, -S n principal character in a film, book, etc
HEROIC adj courageous
HEROICAL same as ▸ heroic
HEROICLY ▸ heroic
HEROICS pl n extravagant behaviour
HEROIN, -S n highly addictive illegal drug derived from morphine
HEROINE, -S n principal female character in a novel, play, etc
HEROINS ▸ heroin
HEROISE, -D, -S same as ▸ heroize

H

HEROISM, -S *n* great courage and bravery

HEROIZE, -D, -S *vb* make into hero

HERON, -S *n* long-legged wading bird

HERONRY *n* colony of breeding herons

HERONS ▸ heron

HERONSEW *same as* **> heronshaw**

HEROON, -S *n* temple or monument dedicated to a hero

HEROS ▸ hero

HEROSHIP ▸ hero

HERPES, -ES *n* any of several inflammatory skin diseases

HERPETIC *adj* of or relating to herpes ▹ *n* person with herpes

HERPTILE *adj* denoting, relating to, or characterizing both reptiles and amphibians

HERRIED ▸ herry

HERRIES ▸ herry

HERRING, -S *n* important food fish of northern seas

HERRY, HERRIED, HERRIES, -ING *vb* harry

HERS *pron* something belonging to her

HERSALL, -S *n* rehearsal

HERSE, -S *n* harrow

HERSED *adj* arranged like a harrow

HERSELF *pron* feminine singular reflexive form

HERSES ▸ herse

HERSHIP, -S *n* act of plundering

HERSTORY *n* history from a female point of view or as it relates to women

HERTZ, -ES *n* unit of frequency

HERY, HERIED, HERIES, -ING *vb* praise

HERYE, -D, -S *same as* ▸ **hery**

HERYING ▸ hery

HES ▸ he

HESITANT *adj* undecided or wavering

HESITATE *vb* be slow or uncertain in doing something

HESP, -ED, -ING, -S *same as* ▸ **hasp**

HESPERID *n* species of butterfly

HESPING ▸ hesp

HESPS ▸ hesp

HESSIAN, -S *n* coarse jute fabric

HESSITE, -S *n* black or grey metallic mineral

HEST, -S *archaic word for* ▸ **behest**

HET *adj* Scots word for hot

HETAIRIA *n* society

HETE, -S, HETING *same as* ▸ **hight**

HETH, -S *n* eighth letter of the Hebrew alphabet

HETHER *same as* ▸ **hither**

HETHS ▸ heth

HETING ▸ hete

HETMAN, -S, HETMEN *another word for* ▸ **ataman**

HEUCH, -S *Scots word for* ▸ **crag**

HEUCHERA *n* N American plant with heart-shaped leaves and mostly red flowers

HEUCHS ▸ heuch

HEUGH, -S *same as* ▸ **heuch**

HEUREKA, -S *same as* ▸ **eureka**

HEURETIC *same as* **> heuristic**

HEURISM, -S *n* use of logic

HEVEA, -S *n* rubber-producing South American tree

HEW, -ED, -N, -S *vb* cut with an axe

HEWABLE ▸ hew

HEWED ▸ hew

HEWER, -S ▸ hew

HEWGH *interj* sound made to imitate the flight of an arrow

HEWING, -S ▸ hew

HEWN ▸ hew

HEWS ▸ hew

HEX, -ED, -ES *adj* of or relating to hexadecimal notation ▹ *n* evil spell ▹ *vb* bewitch

This word meaning to bewitch is a really useful one for using the X.

HEXACT, -S *n* part of a sponge with six rays

HEXAD, -S *n* group or series of six

HEXADE, -S *same as* ▸ **hexad**

HEXADIC ▸ hexad

HEXADS ▸ hexad

HEXAFOIL *n* pattern with six lobes

HEXAGLOT *n* book written in six languages

HEXAGON, -S *n* geometrical figure with six sides

HEXAGRAM *n* star formed by extending the sides of a regular hexagon to meet at six points

HEXAMINE *n* fuel for camping stoves

HEXANE, -S *n* liquid alkane existing in five isomeric forms

HEXANOIC *adj* as in **hexanoic acid** insoluble oily carboxylic acid found in coconut and palm oils and in milk

HEXAPLA, -S *n* edition of the Old Testament

HEXAPLAR ▸ hexapla

HEXAPLAS ▸ hexapla

HEXAPOD, -S *n* six-footed arthropod

HEXAPODY *n* verse measure consisting of six metrical feet

HEXARCH *adj* (of a plant) with six veins

HEXARCHY *n* alliance of six states

HEXED ▸ hex

HEXENE, -S *same as* ▸ **hexylene**

HEXER, -S ▸ hex

HEXEREI, -S *n* witchcraft

HEXERS ▸ hexer

HEXES ▸ hex

HEXING, -S ▸ hex

HEXONE, -S *n* colourless insoluble liquid ketone

HEXOSAN, -S *n* form of polysaccharide

HEXOSE, -S *n* monosaccharide, such as glucose

HEXYL, -S *n* chemical compound

HEXYLENE *n* chemical compound similar to ethylene

HEXYLIC ▸ hexyl

HEXYLS ▸ hexyl

HEY, -ED, -ING, -S *interj* expression of surprise or for catching attention ▹ *vb* perform a country dance

HEYDAY, -S *n* time of greatest success, prime

HEYDEY, -S *variant of* ▸ **heyday**

HEYDUCK, -S *same as* ▸ **haiduk**

HEYED ▸ hey

HEYING ▸ hey

HEYS ▸ hey

HI *interj* hello

HIANT *adj* gaping

HIATAL ▸ hiatus

HIATUS, -ES *n* pause or interruption in continuity

HIBACHI, -S *n* portable brazier for heating and cooking food

HIBERNAL *adj* of or occurring in winter**

HIBISCUS n tropical plant with large brightly coloured flowers

HIC interj representation of the sound of a hiccup

HICATEE, -S same as ▸ hiccatee

HICCATEE n tortoise native to the Caribbean

HICCOUGH same as ▸ hiccup

HICCUP, -ED, -S n spasm of the breathing organs ▸ vb make a hiccup

HICCUPY adj tending to hiccup

HICK, -ER, -EST, -S n unsophisticated country person ▸ adj unsophisticated

HICKEY, -S n object or gadget

HICKIE, -S same as ▸ hickey

HICKISH ▸ hick

HICKORY n N American nut-bearing tree

HICKS ▸ hick

HICKWALL n green woodpecker

HICKYMAL n titmouse

HID ▸ hide

HIDABLE ▸ hide

HIDAGE, -S n former tax on land

HIDALGA, -S n Spanish noblewoman

HIDALGO, -S n member of the lower nobility in Spain

HIDDEN ▸ hide

HIDDENLY ▸ hide

HIDDER, -S n young ram

HIDE, HID, HIDDEN, -D, -S vb put (oneself or an object) somewhere difficult to see or find ▸ n place of concealment, esp for a bird-watcher

HIDEAWAY n private place

HIDED ▸ hide

HIDELESS ▸ hide

HIDEOUS adj ugly, revolting

HIDEOUT, -S n hiding place

HIDER, -S ▸ hide

HIDES ▸ hide

HIDING, -S ▸ hide

HIDLING n hiding place

HIDLINGS adv in secret

HIDLINS same as ▸ hidlings

HIDROSIS, HIDROSES n any skin disease affecting the sweat glands

HIDROTIC ▸ hidrosis

HIE, -D, -ING, -S, HYING vb hurry

HIELAMAN n Aboriginal Australian shield

HIELAND adj characteristic of Highlanders

HIEMAL less common word for ▸ hibernal

HIEMS n winter

HIERARCH n person in a position of high-priestly authority

HIERATIC adj of or relating to priests ▸ n hieratic script of ancient Egypt

HIERURGY n performance of religious drama or music

HIES ▸ hie

HIGGLE, -D, -S, HIGGLING less common word for ▸ haggle

HIGGLER, -S ▸ higgle

HIGGLES ▸ higgle

HIGGLING ▸ higgle

HIGH, -ED, -EST, -ING, -S adj being a relatively great distance from top to bottom; tall ▸ adv at or to a height ▸ n high place or level ▸ vb hie

HIGHBALL n tall drink of whisky with soda water or ginger ale and ice ▸ vb move at great speed

HIGHBORN adj of noble or aristocratic birth

HIGHBOY, -S n tall chest of drawers in two sections

HIGHBRED adj of noble breeding

HIGHBROW n intellectual and serious person ▸ adj concerned with serious, intellectual subjects

HIGHBUSH adj (of bush) growing tall ▸ n tall-growing bush

HIGHED ▸ high

HIGHER, -ED, -S n advanced level of the Scottish Certificate of Education ▸ vb raise up

HIGHEST ▸ high

HIGHING ▸ high

HIGHISH ▸ high

HIGHJACK same as ▸ hijack

HIGHLAND n relatively high ground

HIGHLIFE n African music genre

HIGHLY adv extremely

HIGHMAN, HIGHMEN n dice weighted to make it fall in particular way

HIGHMOST adj highest

HIGHNESS n condition of being high or lofty

HIGHRISE n tall building

HIGHROAD n main road

HIGHS ▸ high

HIGHSPOT n highlight

HIGHT, -ED, -S, HOTE, HOTEN vb archaic word for name or call

HIGHTAIL vb go or move in a great hurry

HIGHTED ▸ hight

HIGHTH, -S old form of ▸ height

HIGHTING n oath

HIGHTOP, -S n top of ship's mast

HIGHTS ▸ hight

HIGHVELD n high-altitude grassland region of E South Africa

HIGHWAY, -S n main road

HIJAB, -S n covering for the head and face

HIJACK, -ED, -S vb seize control of (an aircraft or other vehicle) while travelling ▸ n instance of hijacking

HIJACKER ▸ hijack

HIJACKS ▸ hijack

HIJINKS n lively enjoyment

HIJRA, -S same as ▸ hijrah

HIJRAH, -S same as ▸ hegira

HIJRAS ▸ hijra

HIKE, -D, -S n long walk in the country, esp for pleasure ▸ vb go for a long walk

HIKER, -S ▸ hike

HIKES ▸ hike

HIKING, -S n sport of taking long walks in the country

HIKOI, -ED, -ING, -S n walk or march, esp a Māori protest march ▸ vb take part in such a march

HILA ▸ hilum

HILAR ▸ hilus

HILARITY n mirth and merriment

HILCH, -ED, -ES, -ING vb hobble

HILD same as ▸ hold

HILDING, -S n coward

HILI ▸ hilus

HILL, -ED, -ING, -S n raised part of the earth's surface ▸ vb form into a hill or mound

HILLER, -S ▸ hill

HILLFOLK n people living in the hills

HILLFORT n fortified hilltop

HILLIER ▸ hilly

HILLIEST ▸ hilly

HILLING, -S ▸ hill

HILLMEN same as ▸ hillfolk

HILLO, -ED, -ES, -ING, -S same as ▸ hello

HILLOA, -ED, -S same as ▸ halloa

HILLOCK, -S n small hill

HILLOCKY adj having hillocks

HILLOED ▸ hillo

H

HILLOES ▸ hillo

HILLOING ▸ hillo

HILLOS ▸ hillo

HILLS ▸ hill

HILLSIDE n side of a hill

HILLTOP, -S n top of hill

HILLY, HILLIER, HILLIEST ▸ hill

HILT, -ED, -ING, -S n handle of a sword or knife ▷ vb supply with a hilt

HILTLESS ▸ hilt

HILTS ▸ hilt

HILUM, HILA n scar on a seed

HILUS, HILI rare word for ▸ hilum

HIM, -S pron refers to a male person or animal ▷ n male person

HIMATION, HIMATIA n (in ancient Greece) a cloak draped around the body

HIMBO, -S n derogatory term for an attractive but empty-headed man

HIMS ▸ him

HIMSELF pron masculine singular reflexive form

HIN, -S n Hebrew unit of capacity

HINAHINA same as ▸ mahoe

HINAU, -S n New Zealand tree

HIND, -MOST, -S adj situated at the back ▷ n female deer

HINDCAST vb test (a mathematical model)

HINDER, -ED, -S vb get in the way of ▷ adj situated at the back

HINDERER ▸ hinder

HINDERS ▸ hinder

HINDFOOT, HINDFEET n back foot

HINDGUT, -S n part of the vertebrate digestive tract

HINDHEAD n back of head

HINDLEG, -S n back leg

HINDMILK n breast milk produced after the first part of feeding

HINDMOST ▸ hind

HINDS ▸ hind

HINDWARD adj at back

HINDWING n back wing

HING, -S n asafoetida

HINGE, -D, -S, HINGING n device for holding two parts so one can swing freely ▷ vb depend (on)

HINGER, -S n tool for making hinges

HINGES ▸ hinge

HINGING ▸ hinge

HINGS ▸ hing

HINKY, HINKIER, HINKIEST adj strange

HINNIE n sweetheart

HINNY, -IED, -S n indirect heart

HINNY, HINNIED, HINNIES, -ING n offspring of a male horse and a female donkey ▷ vb whinny

HINS ▸ hin

HINT, -ED, -S n indirect suggestion ▷ vb suggest indirectly

HINTER, -S ▸ hint

HINTING, -S ▸ hint

HINTS ▸ hint

HIOI, -S n New Zealand plant of the mint family

HIP, -PER, -PEST, -S n either side of the body between the pelvis and the thigh ▷ adj aware of or following the latest trends ▷ interj exclamation used to introduce cheers

HIPBONE, -S n either of the bones that form the sides of the pelvis

HIPLESS ▸ hip

HIPLIKE ▸ hip

HIPLINE, -S n widest part of a person's hips

HIPLY ▸ hip

HIPNESS ▸ hip

HIPPARCH n (in ancient Greece) a cavalry commander

HIPPED adj having a hip or hips

HIPPEN, -S n baby's nappy

HIPPER ▸ hip

HIPPEST ▸ hip

HIPPIC adj of horses

HIPPIE same as ▸ hippy

HIPPIER ▸ hippy

HIPPIES ▸ hippy

HIPPIEST ▸ hippy

HIPPIN, -S same as ▸ hippen

HIPPING, -S same as ▸ hippen

HIPPINS ▸ hippin

HIPPISH adj in low spirits

HIPPO, -S n hippopotamus

HIPPURIC adj as in hippuric acid crystalline solid excreted in the urine of mammals

HIPPUS, -ES n spasm of eye

HIPPY, HIPPIER, HIPPIES, HIPPIEST n person whose behaviour implies a rejection of values ▷ adj having large hips

HIPPYDOM ▸ hippy

HIPPYISH adj pertaining to or like a hippy

HIPS ▸ hip

HIPSHOT adj having a dislocated hip

HIPSTER n enthusiast of modern jazz

HIPSTERS pl n trousers cut so that the top encircles the hips

HIPT old form of ▸ hipped

HIRABLE ▸ hire

HIRAGANA n Japanese system of writing

HIRAGE, -S n fee for hiring

HIRCINE adj of or like a goat, esp in smell

HIRE, -D, -S vb pay to have temporary use of ▷ n hiring

HIREABLE ▸ hire

HIREAGE, -S same as ▸ hirage

HIRED ▸ hire

HIREE, -S n hired person

HIRELING n derogatory term for a person who works only for wages

HIRER, -S ▸ hire

HIRES ▸ hire

HIRING, -S ▸ hire

HIRLING, -S n Scots word for a type of fish

HIRPLE, -D, -S, HIRPLING vb limp ▷ n limping gait

HIRRIENT n trilled sound

HIRSEL, -ED, -S vb sort into groups

HIRSLE, -D, -S, HIRSLING vb wriggle or fidget

HIRSTIE adj dry

HIRSUTE adj hairy

HIRUDIN, -S n anticoagulant

HIS adj belonging to him

HISH, -ED, -ES, -ING same as ▸ hiss

HISN dialect form of ▸ his

HISPID adj covered with stiff hairs or bristles

HISS, -ED, -ES n sound like that of a long s (as an expression of contempt) ▷ vb utter a hiss ▷ interj exclamation of derision or disapproval

HISSELF dialect form of ▸ himself

HISSER, -S ▸ hiss

HISSES ▸ hiss

HISSIER ▸ hissy

HISSIES ▸ hissy

HISSIEST ▸ hissy

HISSING, -S ▸ hiss

HISSY, HISSIER, HISSIES, HISSIEST n temper tantrum ▷ adj having the sound of a hiss

HIST, -ED, -ING, -S interj exclamation used to attract

attention ▷ vb make hist sound

HISTAMIN variant of > histamine

HISTED ▸ hist

HISTIDIN variant of > histidine

HISTIE same as ▸ hirstie

HISTING ▸ hist

HISTIOID same as ▸ histoid

HISTOGEN n obsolete term for part of a plant stem

HISTOID adj (esp of a tumour)

HISTONE, -S n any of a group of proteins present in cell nuclei

HISTORIC adj famous or significant in history

HISTORY n (record or account of) past events

HISTRIO, -S n actor

HISTRION same as ▸ histrio

HISTRIOS ▸ histrio

HISTS ▸ hist

HIT, -S, -TING vb strike, touch forcefully ▷ n hitting

HITCH, -ED, -ES, -ING n minor problem ▷ vb obtain (a lift) by hitchhiking

HITCHER, -S ▸ hitch

HITCHES ▸ hitch

HITCHIER ▸ hitchy

HITCHILY ▸ hitch

HITCHING ▸ hitch

HITCHY, HITCHIER ▸ hitch

HITHE, -S n small harbour

HITHER, -ED, -S adv or towards this place ▷ vb come

HITHERTO adv until this time

HITHES ▸ hithe

HITLESS ▸ hit

HITMAKER n successful performer or producer of popular music

HITMAN, HITMEN n professional killer

HITS ▸ hit

HITTABLE ▸ hit

HITTER, -S n boxer who has a hard punch rather than skill or finesse

HITTING ▸ hit

HIVE, -D, HIVING n structure in which social bees live and rear their young ▷ vb cause (bees) to collect or (of bees) to collect inside a hive

HIVELESS ▸ hive

HIVELIKE ▸ hive

HIVEMIND n people who share their knowledge with one another, producing

either collective intelligence or conformity

HIVER, -S n person who keeps beehives

HIVES n allergic reaction

HIVEWARD adj towards hive

HIVING ▸ hive

HIYA sentence substitute informal term of greeting

HIZEN, -S n type of Japanese porcelain

HIZZ, -ED, -ES, -ING same as ▸ hiss

HIZZONER n nickname for mayor

HM interj sound made to express hesitation or doubt

HMM same as ▸ hm

This variant of **hm**, like its shorter form, can be useful when you have a shortage of vowels.

HMMM interj expressing thoughtful consideration

HO, -ING, -S interj imitation or representation of the sound of a deep laugh ▷ n cry of 'ho' ▷ vb halt

HOA, -ED, -ING, -S same as ▸ ho

HOACTZIN same as ▸ hoatzin

HOAED ▸ hoa

HOAGIE, -S n sandwich made with long bread roll

HOAGY same as ▸ hoagie

HOAING ▸ hoa

HOAR, -ED, -ING, -S adj covered with hoarfrost ▷ vb make hoary

HOARD, -ED, -S n store hidden away for future use ▷ vb save or store

HOARDER, -S ▸ hoard

HOARDING n large board for displaying advertisements

HOARDS ▸ hoard

HOARED ▸ hoar

HOARHEAD n person with white hair

HOARIER ▸ hoary

HOARIEST ▸ hoary

HOARILY ▸ hoary

HOARING ▸ hoar

HOARS ▸ hoar

HOARSE, -R, -ST adj (of a voice) rough and unclear

HOARSELY ▸ hoarse

HOARSEN, -S vb make or become hoarse

HOARSER ▸ hoarse

HOARSEST ▸ hoarse

HOARY, HOARIER, HOARIEST adj grey or white(-haired)

HOAS ▸ hoa

HOAST, -ED, -ING, -S n cough ▷ vb cough

HOASTMAN, HOASTMEN n shipper of coal

HOASTS ▸ hoast

HOATZIN, -S n South American bird

HOAX, -ED, -ES, -ING n deception or trick ▷ vb deceive or play a trick upon

HOAXER, -S ▸ hoax

HOAXES ▸ hoax

HOAXING ▸ hoax

HOB, -BED, -BING, -S n flat top part of a cooker ▷ vb cut or form with a hob

HOBBER, -S n machine used in making gears

HOBBIES ▸ hobby

HOBBING ▸ hob

HOBBISH adj like a clown

HOBBIT, -S n one of an imaginary race of half-size people

HOBBITRY ▸ hobbit

HOBBITS ▸ hobbit

HOBBLE, -D, -S, HOBBLING vb walk lamely ▷ n strap, rope, etc, used to hobble a horse

HOBBLER, -S ▸ hobble

HOBBLES ▸ hobble

HOBBLING ▸ hobble

HOBBY, HOBBIES n activity pursued in one's spare time

HOBBYISM ▸ hobby

HOBBYIST ▸ hobby

HOBDAY, -S vb alleviate a breathing problem in certain horses

HOBDAYED ▸ hobday

HOBDAYS ▸ hobday

HOBJOB, -S vb do odd jobs

HOBLIKE ▸ hob

HOBNAIL, -S n short nail with a large head for protecting soles ▷ vb provide with hobnails

HOBNOB, -S vb be on friendly terms (with)

HOBNOBBY adj tending to hobnob

HOBNOBS ▸ hobnob

HOBO, -ED, -ES, -ING, -S n tramp or vagrant ▷ vb live as hobo

HOBODOM, -S ▸ hobo

HOBOED ▸ hobo

HOBOES ▸ hobo

HOBOING ▸ hobo

HOBOISM, -S ▸ hobo

HOBOS ▸ hobo

HOBS ▸ hob

HOC adj Latin for this

HOCK, -ED, -ING, -S n joint in the leg of an animal

H

corresponding to a human ankle ▷ vb pawn
HOCKER, -S ▸ hock
HOCKEY, -S n team sport
HOCKING ▸ hock
HOCKLE, -D, -S, HOCKLING vb spit
HOCKS ▸ hock
HOCKSHOP n pawnshop
HOCUS, -ED, -ES, -ING, -SED, -SES vb take in
HOD, -DED, -DING, -S n open wooden box attached to a pole ▷ vb bob up and down
HODAD, -S n person who pretends to be a surfer
HODADDY same as ▸ hodad
HODADS ▸ hodad
HODDED ▸ hod
HODDEN, -S n coarse homespun cloth
HODDIN, -S same as ▸ hodden
HODDING ▸ hod
HODDINS ▸ hoddin
HODDLE, -D, -S, HODDLING vb waddle
HODJA, -S n respectful Turkish form of address
HODMAN, HODMEN n hod carrier
HODS ▸ hod
HOE, -D, -ING, -S n long-handled tool used for loosening soil or weeding ▷ vb scrape or weed with a hoe
HOECAKE, -S n maize cake
HOED ▸ hoe
HOEDOWN, -S n boisterous square dance
HOEING ▸ hoe
HOELIKE ▸ hoe
HOER, -S ▸ hoe
HOES ▸ hoe
HOG, -GED, -S n castrated male pig ▷ vb take more than one's share of
HOGAN, -S n wooden dwelling covered with earth
HOGBACK, -S n narrow ridge of steeply inclined rock strata
HOGEN, -S n strong alcoholic drink
HOGFISH n type of fish
HOGG, -S same as ▸ hog
HOGGED ▸ hog
HOGGER, -S ▸ hog
HOGGEREL n year-old sheep
HOGGERS ▸ hogger
HOGGERY n hogs collectively
HOGGET, -S n young sheep that has yet to be sheared

HOGGIN, -S n finely sifted gravel
HOGGING, -S same as ▸ hoggin
HOGGINS ▸ hoggin
HOGGISH adj selfish, gluttonous, or dirty
HOGGS ▸ hogg
HOGH, -S n ridge of land
HOGHOOD, -S n condition of being hog
HOGHS ▸ hogh
HOGLIKE ▸ hog
HOGMANAY n New Year's Eve
HOGMANE, -S n short stiff mane
HOGMENAY variant of ▸ hogmanay
HOGNOSE, -S n as in hognose snake puff adder
HOGNOSED adj as in hognosed skunk any of several American skunks having a broad snoutlike nose
HOGNOSES ▸ hognose
HOGNUT, -S another name for ▸ pignut
HOGS ▸ hog
HOGSHEAD n large cask
HOGTIE, -D, -S, HOGTYING vb tie together the legs or the arms and legs of
HOGWARD, -S n person looking after hogs
HOGWASH n nonsense
HOGWEED, -S n any of several umbelliferous plants
HOH, -ED, -ING, -S same as ▸ ho
HOHA adj bored or annoyed
HOHED ▸ hoh
HOHING ▸ hoh
HOHS ▸ hoh
HOI, -ED, -ING, -S same as ▸ hoy
HOICK, -ED, -ING vb raise abruptly and sharply
HOICKS, -ED, -ES interj cry used to encourage hounds to hunt ▷ vb shout hoicks
HOIDEN, -ED, -S same as ▸ hoyden
HOIED ▸ hoi
HOIING ▸ hoi
HOIK, -ED, -ING, -S same as ▸ hoick
HOING ▸ hoi
HOIS ▸ hoi
HOISE, -D, -S, HOISING same as ▸ hoist
HOISIN, -S n Chinese sweet spicy sauce
HOISING ▸ hoise
HOISINS ▸ hoisin

HOIST, -ED, -ING, -S vb raise or lift up ▷ n device for lifting things
HOISTER, -S ▸ hoist
HOISTING ▸ hoist
HOISTMAN, HOISTMEN n person operating a hoist
HOISTS ▸ hoist
HOISTWAY n shaft for a hoist
HOKA, -S n red cod
HOKE, -D, -S, HOKING vb overplay (a part, etc)
HOKEY, HOKIER, HOKIEST adj corny
HOKI, -S n fish of New Zealand waters
HOKIER ▸ hokey
HOKIEST ▸ hokey
HOKILY ▸ hokey
HOKINESS ▸ hokey
HOKING ▸ hoke
HOKIS ▸ hoki
HOKKU same as ▸ haiku
HOKONUI, -S n illicit whisky
HOKUM, -S n rubbish, nonsense
HOKYPOKY n trickery
HOLARCHY n system composed of interacting holons
HOLARD, -S n amount of water contained in soil
HOLD, HELD, -S vb keep or support in or with the hands or arms ▷ n act or way of holding
HOLDABLE ▸ hold
HOLDALL, -S n large strong travelling bag
HOLDBACK n part of a horse harness
HOLDDOWN n control function in a computer
HOLDEN past participle of ▸ hold
HOLDER, -S n person or thing that holds
HOLDFAST n act of gripping strongly
HOLDING, -S ▸ hold
HOLDOUT, -S n (in US English) person who refuses to change
HOLDOVER n official who continues in office after his or her term has expired
HOLDS ▸ hold
HOLDUP, -S n robbery, esp an armed one
HOLE, -D, -S n area hollowed out in a solid ▷ vb make holes in
HOLELESS ▸ hole
HOLES ▸ hole
HOLESOM same as ▸ holesome

HOLESOME *same as*
> **wholesome**

HOLEY, -ER, -EST *adj* full of holes

HOLIBUT, -S *same as*
> **halibut**

HOLIDAY, -S *n* time spent away from home for rest or recreation ▷ *vb* spend a holiday

HOLIER > **holy**

HOLIES > **holy**

HOLIEST > **holy**

HOLILY *adv* in a holy, devout, or sacred manner

HOLINESS *n* state of being holy

HOLING, -S > **hole**

HOLISM, -S *n* view that a whole is greater than the sum of its parts

HOLIST, -S > **holism**

HOLISTIC *adj* considering the complete person, physically and mentally

HOLISTS > **holist**

HOLK, -ED, -ING, -S *vb* dig

HOLLA, -ED, -ING, -S *same as*
> **hollo**

HOLLAND, -S *n* coarse linen cloth, used esp for furnishing

HOLLAS > **holla**

HOLLER, -ED, -S *n* shout, yell ▷ *vb* shout or yell

HOLLIDAM *same as*
> **halidom**

HOLLIES > **holly**

HOLLO, -ED, -ES, -ING, -S *interj* cry for attention, or of encouragement ▷ *vb* shout

HOLLOA, -ED, -S *same as*
> **hollo**

HOLLOED > **hollo**

HOLLOES > **hollo**

HOLLOING > **hollo**

HOLLOO, -ED, -S *same as*
> **halloo**

HOLLOS > **hollo**

HOLLOW, -ED, -ER, -S *adj* having a hole or space inside ▷ *n* cavity or space ▷ *vb* form a hollow in

HOLLOWLY > **hollow**

HOLLOWS > **hollow**

HOLLY, HOLLIES *n* evergreen tree with prickly leaves and red berries

HOLM, -S *n* island in a river, lake, or estuary

HOLME, -S *same as* > **holm**

HOLMIA, -S *n* oxide of holmium

HOLMIC *adj* of or containing holmium

HOLMIUM, -S *n* silver-white metallic element

HOLMS > **holm**

HOLO, -S *n* short for hologram

HOLOCENE *adj* of the most recent epoch of the Quaternary period

HOLOGAMY *n* condition of having gametes like ordinary cells

HOLOGRAM *n* three-dimensional photographic image

HOLOGYNY *n* inheritance of genetic traits through females only

HOLON, -S *n* autonomous self-reliant unit, esp in manufacturing

HOLONIC > **holon**

HOLONS > **holon**

HOLOPTIC *adj* with eyes meeting at the front

HOLOS > **holo**

HOLOTYPE *n* original specimen from which a description of a new species is made

HOLOZOIC *adj* (of animals) obtaining nourishment by feeding on plants or other animals

HOLP *past tense of* > **help**

HOLPEN *past participle of*
> **help**

HOLS *pl n* holidays

HOLSTEIN *n* breed of cattle

HOLSTER, -S *n* leather case for a pistol, hung from a belt ▷ *vb* return (a pistol) to its holster

HOLT, -S *n* otter's lair

HOLUBTSI *pl n* cabbage rolls

HOLY, HOLIER, HOLIES, HOLIEST *adj* of God or a god ▷ *n* sacred place

HOLYDAM, -S *same as*
> **halidom**

HOLYDAME *same as*
> **halidom**

HOLYDAMS > **holydam**

HOLYDAY, -S *n* day on which a religious festival is observed

HOLYTIDE *n* time for special religious observance

HOM, -S *n* sacred plant of the Parsees and ancient Persians

HOMA, -S *same as* > **hom**

HOMAGE, -D, -S, HOMAGING *n* show of respect or honour towards someone or something ▷ *vb* render homage to

HOMAGER, -S > **homage**

HOMAGES > **homage**

HOMAGING > **homage**

HOMALOID *n* geometrical plane

HOMAS > **homa**

HOMBRE, -S *slang word for*
> **man**

HOMBURG, -S *n* man's soft felt hat

HOME, -D, -S *n* place where one lives ▷ *adj* of one's home, birthplace, or native country ▷ *adv* to or at home ▷ *vb* direct towards (a point or target)

HOMEBIRD *n* person who is reluctant to leave their home

HOMEBODY *n* person whose life and interests are centred on the home

HOMEBOY, -S *n* close friend

HOMEBRED *adj* raised or bred at home ▷ *n* animal bred at home

HOMEBREW *n* home-made beer

HOMED > **home**

HOMEFELT *adj* felt personally

HOMEGIRL > **homeboy**

HOMELAND *n* country from which a person's ancestors came

HOMELESS *adj* having nowhere to live ▷ *pl n* people who have nowhere to live

HOMELIER > **homely**

HOMELIKE > **home**

HOMELILY > **homely**

HOMELY, HOMELIER *adj* simple, ordinary, and comfortable

HOMELYN, -S *n* species of ray

HOMEMADE *adj* made at home

HOMEOBOX *adj* of genes that regulate cell development

HOMEOSIS, HOMEOSES *n* process of one part coming to resemble another

HOMEOTIC > **homeosis**

HOMEPAGE *n* main page of website

HOMEPORT *n* port where vessel is registered

HOMER, -ED, -ING, -S *n* homing pigeon ▷ *vb* score a home run in baseball

HOMERIC *adj* grand or heroic

HOMERING > **homer**

HOMEROOM *n* common room at school

HOMERS > **homer**

HOMES ▸ **home**

HOMESICK adj sad because missing one's home and family

HOMESITE n site for building house

HOMESPUN adj (of philosophies or opinions) plain and unsophisticated ▷ n cloth made at home or made of yarn spun at home

HOMESTAY n period spent living as a guest in someone's home

HOMETOWN n town where one lives or was born

HOMEWARD adj going home ▷ adv towards home

HOMEWARE n crockery, furniture, and furnishings with which a house, room, etc, is furnished

HOMEWORK n school work done at home

HOMEY, -S same as ▸ **homy**

HOMICIDE n killing of a human being

HOMIE, -S short for ▸ **homeboy**

HOMIER ▸ **homy**

HOMIES ▸ **homie**

HOMIEST ▸ **homy**

HOMILIES ▸ **homily**

HOMILIST ▸ **homily**

HOMILY, HOMILIES n speech telling people how they should behave

HOMINES ▸ **homo**

HOMINESS ▸ **homy**

HOMING, -S adj relating to the ability to return home after travelling ▷ n ability to return home after travelling

HOMINIAN same as ▸ **hominid**

HOMINID, -S n humankind or any extinct forerunner of humankind ▷ adj of or belonging to this family

HOMINIES ▸ **hominy**

HOMININ, -S n member of a zoological family

HOMININE adj characteristic of humans

HOMININS ▸ **hominin**

HOMINISE same as ▸ **hominize**

HOMINIZE vb make suitable for humans

HOMINOID n humanlike animal ▷ adj of or like a human

HOMINY, HOMINIES n coarsely ground maize

HOMME, -S French word for ▸ **man**

HOMMOCK, -S same as ▸ **hummock**

HOMMOS, -ES same as ▸ **hummus**

HOMO, HOMINES, -S n homogenized milk

HOMODONT adj (of most nonmammalian vertebrates) having teeth that are all of the same type

HOMODYNE adj of strengthened radio waves

HOMOGAMY n simultaneous maturation of all the anthers and stigmas of a flower

HOMOGENY n similarity in structure of individuals or parts because of common ancestry

HOMOGONY n condition in a plant of having stamens and styles of the same length in all the flowers

HOMOLOG, -S same as ▸ **homologue**

HOMOLOGY n condition of being homologous

HOMONYM, -S n word that is spelt the same as another

HOMONYMY n the quality of being pronounced or spelt in the same way

HOMOS ▸ **homo**

HOMOTONY ▸ **homotonic**

HOMOTYPE n something with same structure as something else

HOMOTYPY ▸ **homotype**

HOMS ▸ **hom**

HOMUNCLE n homunculus

HOMY, HOMIER, HOMIEST adj like a home

HON, -S short for ▸ **honey**

HONAN, -S n silk fabric of rough weave

HONCHO, -ED, -ES, -S n person in charge ▷ vb supervise or be in charge of

HOND, -S old form of ▸ **hand**

HONDA, -S n loop used to make a lasso

HONDLE, -D, -S, HONDLING vb negotiate on price

HONDS ▸ **hond**

HONE, -D, -S, HONING vb sharpen ▷ n fine whetstone used for sharpening edged tools and knives

HONER, -S ▸ **hone**

HONES ▸ **hone**

HONEST, -ER adj truthful and moral

HONESTLY adv in an honest manner ▷ interj expression of disgust, surprise, etc

HONESTY n quality of being honest

HONEWORT n European plant that has clusters of small white flowers

HONEY, -ED, -ING, -S n edible substance made by bees; term of endearment ▷ vb sweeten with or as if with honey

HONEYBEE n bee widely domesticated as a source of honey and beeswax

HONEYBUN n term of endearment

HONEYDEW n sugary substance produced by aphids and similar insects

HONEYED ▸ **honey**

HONEYFUL adj full of honey

HONEYING ▸ **honey**

HONEYPOT n container for honey

HONEYS ▸ **honey**

HONG, -ING, -S n (in China) a factory, warehouse, etc ▷ vb archaic form of hang

HONGI, -ED, -ES, -ING, -S n Māori greeting in which people touch noses ▷ vb touch noses

HONGING ▸ **hong**

HONGIS ▸ **hongi**

HONGS ▸ **hong**

HONIED same as ▸ **honeyed**

HONIEDLY ▸ **honey**

HONING ▸ **hone**

HONK, -ED, -ING, -S n sound made by a car horn ▷ vb (cause to) make this sound

HONKER, -S n person or thing that honks

HONKING ▸ **honk**

HONKS ▸ **honk**

HONOR, -ED, -ING same as ▸ **honour**

HONORAND n person being honoured

HONORARY adj held or given only as an honour

HONORED ▸ **honor**

HONOREE, -S same as ▸ **honorand**

HONORER, -S ▸ **honour**

HONORING ▸ **honor**

HONORS same as ▸ **honours**

HONOUR, -ED, -S n sense of honesty and fairness ▷ vb give praise and attention to

HONOUREE n person who is honoured

HONOURER ▸ **honour**

HONOURS ▸ **honour**

HONS ▸ **hon**

HOO interj expression of joy, excitement, etc

HOOCH, -ES n alcoholic drink, esp illicitly distilled spirits
HOOCHIE, -S n immoral woman
HOOD, -ING, -S n head covering, often attached to a coat or jacket ▷ vb cover with or as if with a hood
HOODED adj (of a garment) having a hood
HOODIA, -S n any of several southern African succulent plants
HOODIE, -S n hooded sweatshirt
HOODIER ▸ hoody
HOODIES ▸ hoodie
HOODIEST ▸ hoody
HOODING ▸ hood
HOODLESS ▸ hood
HOODLIKE ▸ hood
HOODLUM, -S n violent criminal, gangster
HOODMAN, HOODMEN n man wearing a hood
HOODMOLD n moulding over door or window
HOODOO, -ED, -S n (cause of) bad luck ▷ vb bring bad luck to
HOODS ▸ hood
HOODWINK vb trick, deceive
HOODY, HOODIER, HOODIEST ▸ hood
HOOEY, -S n nonsense ▷ interj nonsense
HOOF, -ING, -S, HOOVES n horny covering of the foot of a horse, deer, etc ▷ vb kick or trample with the hooves
HOOFBEAT n sound made by hoof on the ground
HOOFED adj having a hoof or hoofs
HOOFER, -S n professional dancer
HOOFING ▸ hoof
HOOFLESS ▸ hoof
HOOFLIKE ▸ hoof
HOOFROT, -S n disease of hoof
HOOFS ▸ hoof
HOOK, -S n curved object used to hang, hold, or pull something ▷ vb fasten or catch (as if) with a hook
HOOKA, -S same as ▸ hookah
HOOKAH, -S n water-pipe for smoking tobacco
HOOKAS ▸ hooka
HOOKED adj bent like a hook
HOOKER, -S n person or thing that hooks

HOOKEY, -S same as ▸ hooky
HOOKIER ▸ hooky
HOOKIES ▸ hooky
HOOKIEST ▸ hooky
HOOKING, -S n act of hooking
HOOKLESS ▸ hook
HOOKLET, -S n little hook
HOOKLIKE ▸ hook
HOOKNOSE n nose with a pronounced outward and downward curve
HOOKS ▸ hook
HOOKUP, -S n contact of an aircraft with the hose of a tanker aircraft
HOOKWORM n blood-sucking worm with hooked mouthparts
HOOKY, HOOKIER, HOOKIES, HOOKIEST n truancy, usually from school ▷ adj hooklike
HOOLEY, -S n lively party
HOOLICAN same as > hoolachan
HOOLIE, -S same as ▸ hooley
HOOLIER ▸ hooly
HOOLIES ▸ hoolie
HOOLIEST ▸ hooly
HOOLIGAN n rowdy young person
HOOLOCK, -S n Indian gibbon
HOOLY, HOOLIER, HOOLIEST adj careful or gentle
HOON, -ED, -ING, -S n loutish youth who drives irresponsibly ▷ vb drive irresponsibly
HOOP, -ED, -ING, -S n rigid circular band ▷ vb surround with or as if with a hoop
HOOPER, -S rare word for ▸ cooper
HOOPING ▸ hoop
HOOPLA, -S n fairground game
HOOPLESS ▸ hoop
HOOPLIKE ▸ hoop
HOOPOE, -S n bird with a pinkish-brown plumage
HOOPOO, -S same as ▸ hoopoe
HOOPS ▸ hoop
HOOPSTER n basketball player
HOOR, -S n unpleasant or difficult thing
HOORAH, -ED, -S same as ▸ hurrah
HOORAY, -ED, -S same as ▸ hurrah
HOORD, -S same as ▸ hoard

HOOROO, -ED, -S n cheer of joy or victory ▷ vb shout 'hooroo'
HOORS ▸ hoor
HOOSEGOW slang word for ▸ jail
HOOSGOW, -S same as ▸ jail
HOOSH, -ED, -ES, -ING vb shoo away
HOOT, -ED, -ING n sound of a car horn ▷ vb sound (a car horn) ▷ interj exclamation of impatience or dissatisfaction
HOOTCH, -ES same as ▸ hooch
HOOTED ▸ hoot
HOOTER, -S n device that hoots
HOOTIER ▸ hooty
HOOTIEST ▸ hooty
HOOTING ▸ hoot
HOOTS same as ▸ hoot
HOOTY, HOOTIER, HOOTIEST ▸ hoot
HOOVE, -D, HOOVING same as ▸ heave
HOOVEN ▸ hoove
HOOVER, -ED, -S vb vacuum-clean (a carpet, furniture, etc)
HOOVES ▸ hoof
HOOVING ▸ hoove
HOP, -PED, -S vb jump on one foot ▷ n instance of hopping
HOPAK, -S n type of Ukrainian dance
HOPBIND, -S n stalk of the hop
HOPBINE, -S same as ▸ hopbind
HOPDOG, -S n species of caterpillar
HOPE, -D, -S, HOPING vb want (something) to happen or be true ▷ n expectation of something desired
HOPEFUL, -S adj having, expressing, or inspiring hope ▷ n person considered to be on the brink of success
HOPELESS adj having or offering no hope
HOPER, -S ▸ hope
HOPES ▸ hope
HOPFIELD n field where hops are grown
HOPING ▸ hope
HOPINGLY ▸ hope
HOPLITE, -S n (in ancient Greece) a heavily armed infantryman
HOPLITIC ▸ hoplite
HOPPED ▸ hop
HOPPER, -S n container for storing substances

HOPPIER ► hoppy

HOPPIEST ► hoppy

HOPPING, -S ► hop

HOPPLE, -D, -S, HOPPLING *same as* ► **hobble**

HOPPLER, -S ► hopple

HOPPLES ► hopple

HOPPLING ► hopple

HOPPUS *adj* as in **hoppus foot** unit of volume for round timber

HOPPY, HOPPIER, HOPPIEST *adj* tasting of hops

HOPS ► hop

HOPSACK, -S *n* roughly woven fabric

HOPTOAD, -S *n* toad

HORA, -S *n* traditional Israeli or Romanian circle dance

HORAH, -S *same as* ► **hora**

HORAL *less common word for* ► **hourly**

HORARY *adj* relating to the hours

HORAS ► hora

HORDE, -D, -S, HORDING *n* large crowd ▷ *vb* form, move in, or live in a horde

HORDEIN, -S *n* simple protein, rich in proline, that occurs in barley

HORDEOLA ► hordeolum

HORDES ► horde

HORDING ► horde

HORDOCK, -S *same as* ► **hardoke**

HORE *same as* ► **hoar**

HORIZON, -S *n* apparent line that divides the earth and the sky

HORK, -ED, -ING, -S *vb* spit

HORKEY, -S *same as* ► **hockey**

HORKING ► hork

HORKS ► hork

HORLICKS *n* as in **make a horlicks** make a mistake or a mess

HORME, -S *n* (in Jungian psychology) fundamental vital energy

HORMESES ► hormes

HORMESIS *n* beneficial effect of exposure to a very small amount of a toxic substance

HORMETIC *adj* relating to hormesis

HORMIC ► horme

HORMONAL ► hormone

HORMONE, -S *n* substance secreted by certain glands

HORMONIC ► hormone

HORN, -S *n* one of a pair of bony growths ▷ *vb* provide with a horn or horns

HORNBEAK *n* garfish

HORNBEAM *n* tree with smooth grey bark

HORNBILL *n* bird with a bony growth on its large beak

HORNBOOK *n* page of religious text with flattened cow horn over it

HORNBUG, -S *n* stag beetle

HORNED *adj* having a horn, horns, or hornlike parts

HORNER, -S *n* dealer in horn

HORNET, -S *n* large wasp with a severe sting

HORNFELS *n* hard fine-grained metamorphic rock

HORNFISH *n* fish of the needlefish family

HORNFUL, -S *n* amount a horn will hold

HORNGELD *n* feudal rent based on number of cattle

HORNIER ► horny

HORNIEST ► horny

HORNILY ► horny

HORNING, -S ► horn

HORNISH *adj* like horn

HORNIST, -S *n* horn player

HORNITO, -S *n* small vent in volcano

HORNLESS ► horn

HORNLET, -S *n* small horn

HORNLIKE ► horn

HORNPIPE *n* (music for) a solo dance, traditionally performed by sailors

HORNPOUT *n* catfish

HORNS ► horn

HORNTAIL *n* wasplike insect

HORNWORK *n* bastion in fortifications

HORNWORM *n* caterpillar of the hawk moth

HORNWORT *n* aquatic plant

HORNY, HORNIER, HORNIEST *adj* of or like horn

HOROEKA, -S *n* New Zealand tree

HOROKAKA *n* low-growing New Zealand plant with fleshy leaves and pink or white flowers

HOROLOGE *rare word for* > **timepiece**

HOROLOGY *n* art of making clocks and watches or of measuring time

HOROPITO *n* New Zealand plant

HOROPTER *n* locus of points in space that have the same disparity as fixation

HORRENT *adj* bristling

HORRIBLE *adj* disagreeable, unpleasant ▷ *n* horrible thing

HORRIBLY *adv* in a horrible manner

HORRID, -ER *adj* disagreeable, unpleasant

HORRIDLY ► horrid

HORRIFIC *adj* causing horror

HORRIFY *vb* cause to feel horror or shock

HORROR *n* (thing or person causing) terror or hatred ▷ *adj* having a frightening subject

HORRORS *pl n* fit of misery or anxiety ▷ *interj* expression of dismay, sometimes facetious

HORS *prep* as in **hors d'oeuvre** appetizer

HORSE, -D, -S *n* large animal with hooves, a mane, and a tail ▷ *vb* provide with a horse

HORSEBOX *n* trailer used for transporting horses

HORSECAR *n* streetcar drawn by horses

HORSED ► horse

HORSEFLY *n* large bloodsucking fly

HORSEMAN, HORSEMEN *n* person skilled in riding

HORSEPOX *n* viral infection of horses

HORSES ► horse

HORSEWAY *n* road for horses

HORSEY, HORSIER, HORSIEST *adj* very keen on horses

HORSIE, -S *n* child's word for a horse

HORSIER ► horsey

HORSIES ► horsie

HORSIEST ► horsey

HORSILY ► horsey

HORSING, -S ► horse

HORST, -S *n* ridge of land

HORSTE, -S *variant of* ► **horst**

HORSTS ► horst

HORSY *same as* ► **horsey**

HOS ► ho

HOSANNA, -S *interj* exclamation of praise to God ▷ *n* act of crying 'hosanna' ▷ *vb* cry hosanna

HOSANNAH *same as* ► **hosanna**

HOSANNAS ► hosanna

HOSE, -D, -N, -S, HOSING *n* flexible pipe for conveying liquid ▷ *vb* water with a hose

HOSEL, -S *n* socket in head of golf club

HOSELIKE ▸ **hose**

HOSELS ▸ **hosel**

HOSEMAN, HOSEMEN *n* firefighter in charge of a hose

HOSEN ▸ **hose**

HOSEPIPE *n* hose

HOSER, -S *n* person who swindles or deceives others

HOSES ▸ **hose**

HOSEY, -ED, -ING, -S *vb* claim possession

HOSIER, -S *n* person who sells stockings, etc

HOSIERY *n* stockings, socks, and tights collectively

HOSING ▸ **hose**

HOSPICE, -S *n* nursing home for the terminally ill

HOSPITAL *n* place where people who are ill are looked after and treated

HOSPITIA > **hospitium**

HOSPODAR *n* (formerly) the governor or prince of Moldavia or Wallachia under Ottoman rule

HOSS, -ES *n* horse

HOST, -ED, -S *n* person who entertains guests ▷ *vb* be the host of

HOSTA, -S *n* ornamental plant

HOSTAGE, -S *n* person who is illegally held prisoner

HOSTAS ▸ **hosta**

HOSTED ▸ **host**

HOSTEL, -ED, -S *n* building providing accommodation ▷ *vb* stay in hostels

HOSTELER *same as* > **hosteller**

HOSTELRY *n* inn, pub

HOSTELS ▸ **hostel**

HOSTESS *n* woman who receives and entertains guests ▷ *vb* act as hostess

HOSTIE, -S *n* informal Australian word for an air hostess

HOSTILE, -S *adj* unfriendly ▷ *n* hostile person

HOSTING, -S ▸ **host**

HOSTLER, -S *another name (esp Brit) for* ▸ **ostler**

HOSTLESS *adj* lacking a host

HOSTLY ▸ **host**

HOSTRY, HOSTRIES *n* lodging

HOSTS ▸ **host**

HOT, -S, -TED, -TEST *adj* having a high temperature ▷ *vb* make or become hot

HOTBED, -S *n* any place encouraging a particular activity

HOTBLOOD *n* type of horse

HOTBOX, -ES *n* container maintained at a high temperature to heat its contents

HOTCAKE, -S *n* pancake

HOTCH, -ED, -ES, -ING *vb* jog

HOTCHPOT *n* collecting of property so that it may be redistributed in equal shares

HOTDOG, -S *vb* perform a series of manoeuvres in skiing, etc

HOTE ▸ **hight**

HOTEL, -S *n* establishment providing lodging and meals

HOTELDOM *n* hotel business

HOTELIER *n* owner or manager of a hotel

HOTELING *n* office practice in which desk space is booked in advance by an employee as required

HOTELMAN, HOTELMEN *n* hotel owner

HOTELS ▸ **hotel**

HOTEN ▸ **hight**

HOTFOOT, -S *adv* quickly and eagerly ▷ *vb* move quickly

HOTHEAD, -S *n* excitable or fiery person

HOTHOUSE *n* greenhouse

HOTLINE, -S *n* direct telephone link for emergency use

HOTLINER *n* person running a phone-in radio programme

HOTLINES ▸ **hotline**

HOTLINK, -S *n* area on website connecting to another site

HOTLY ▸ **hot**

HOTNESS ▸ **hot**

HOTPLATE *n* heated metal surface on an electric cooker

HOTPOT, -S *n* casserole topped with potatoes

HOTPRESS *vb* subject (paper, cloth, etc) to heat and pressure

HOTROD, -S *n* car with a modified engine for increased power

HOTS ▸ **hot**

HOTSHOT, -S *n* important person or expert, esp when showy

HOTSPOT, -S *n* place where wireless broadband is provided

HOTSPUR, -S *n* impetuous or fiery person

HOTTED ▸ **hot**

HOTTER, -ED, -S *vb* simmer

HOTTEST ▸ **hot**

HOTTIE, -S *n* attractive person

HOTTING, -S *n* stealing fast cars to put on a show of skilful driving

HOTTISH *adj* fairly hot

HOTTY *same as* ▸ **hottie**

HOUDAH, -S *same as* ▸ **howdah**

HOUDAN, -S *n* breed of light domestic fowl

HOUF, -ED, -ING, -S *same as* ▸ **howf**

HOUFF, -ED, -ING, -S *same as* ▸ **howf**

HOUFING ▸ **houf**

HOUFS ▸ **houf**

HOUGH, -ED, -ING, -S *n* in Scotland, a cut of meat corresponding to shin ▷ *vb* hamstring (cattle, horses, etc)

HOUHERE, -S *n* small evergreen New Zealand tree

HOUMMOS *same as* ▸ **hummus**

HOUMOUS *same as* ▸ **hummus**

HOUMOUS, -ES *same as* ▸ **hummus**

HOUND, -ED, -ING, -S *n* hunting dog ▷ *vb* pursue relentlessly

HOUNDER, -S ▸ **hound**

HOUNDING ▸ **hound**

HOUNDS ▸ **hound**

HOUNGAN, -S *n* voodoo priest

HOUR *n* twenty-fourth part of a day, sixty minutes

HOURI, -S *n* any of the nymphs of paradise

HOURLIES ▸ **hourly**

HOURLONG *adj* lasting an hour

HOURLY, HOURLIES *adv* (happening) every hour ▷ *adj* of, occurring, or done once every hour ▷ *n* something that is done by the hour

HOURS *pl n* indefinite time

HOUSE, -D, -S *n* building used as a home ▷ *vb* give accommodation to

HOUSEBOY *n* male domestic servant

HOUSED ▸ **house**

HOUSEFLY *n* common fly often found in houses

HOUSEFUL *n* full amount or number that can be accommodated in a particular house

HOUSEL, -ED, -S *vb* give the Eucharist to (someone)

H

HOUSEMAN, HOUSEMEN *n*
junior hospital doctor

HOUSER, -S ▸ **house**

HOUSES ▸ **house**

HOUSESIT, HOUSESAT *vb*
live in and look after a house
during the absence of its
owner or owners

HOUSETOP *n* rooftop

**HOUSEY, HOUSIER,
HOUSIEST** *adj* of or like
house music

HOUSING, -S *n* (providing
of) houses

HOUSLING *adj* of sacrament
▸ *n* growing of the climbing
stem of the hop into a dense
mass

HOUT, -ED, -S *same as* ▸ **hoot**

HOUTING, -S *n* type of fish

HOUTS ▸ **hout**

HOVE, -D, -S, HOVING *vb* swell

HOVEA, -S *n* Australian
plant with purple flowers

HOVED ▸ **hove**

HOVEL, -ED, -ING, -LED, -S *n*
small dirty house or hut ▸ *vb*
shelter or be sheltered in a
hovel

HOVELLER *n* person
working on boat

HOVELS ▸ **hovel**

HOVEN ▸ **heave**

HOVER, -ED, -ING, -S *vb* (of
a bird etc) remain suspended
in one place in the air ▸ *n* act
of hovering

HOVERER, -S ▸ **hover**

HOVERFLY *n* hovering
wasp-like fly

HOVERING ▸ **hover**

HOVERS ▸ **hover**

HOVES ▸ **hove**

HOVING ▸ **hove**

HOW, -S *adv* in what way, by
what means ▸ *n* the way a
thing is done ▸ *sentence
substitute* supposed Native
American greeting

HOWBE *same as* ▸ **howbeit**

HOWBEIT *adv* in archaic
usage, however

HOWDAH, -S *n* canopied
seat on an elephant's back

HOWDIE *n* midwife

**HOWDY, HOWDIED,
HOWDIES, -ING** *vb* greet
someone

HOWE, -S *n* depression in
the earth's surface

HOWEVER *adv* nevertheless

HOWF, -ED, -ING, -S *n*
haunt, esp a public house
▸ *vb* visit a place frequently

HOWFF, -ED, -ING, -S *vb*
visit a place frequently

HOWFING ▸ **howf**

HOWFS ▸ **howf**

HOWITZER *n* large gun
firing shells at a steep angle

HOWK, -ED, -ING, -S *vb* dig
(out or up)

HOWKER, -S ▸ **howk**

HOWKING ▸ **howk**

HOWKS ▸ **howk**

HOWL, -ED, -S *n* loud
wailing cry ▸ *vb* utter a howl

HOWLBACK *same as*
> **howlround**

HOWLED ▸ **howl**

HOWLER, -S *n* stupid mistake

HOWLET, -S *another word for*
▸ **owl**

HOWLING, -S *adj* great ▸ *n*
act of wailing

HOWLS ▸ **howl**

HOWRE, -S *same as* ▸ **hour**

HOWS ▸ **how**

HOWSO *same as*
> **howsoever**

HOWZAT *interj* cry in cricket
appealing for dismissal of
batsman

HOWZIT *informal word for*
▸ **hello**

HOX, -ED, -ES, -ING *vb*
hamstring

This is a word found in
Shakespeare's plays, and it
means to cut a horse's
hamstring. It's one of the
many short words with X
that can get you a high
score.

HOY, -ED, -ING, -S *interj* cry
used to attract someone's
attention ▸ *n* freight barge
▸ *vb* drive animal with cry

HOYA, -S *n* any of various E
Asian or Australian plants

HOYDEN, -ED, -S *n* wild or
boisterous girl ▸ *vb* behave
like a hoyden

HOYED ▸ **hoy**

HOYING ▸ **hoy**

HOYLE, -S *n* archer's mark
used as a target

HOYS ▸ **hoy**

HRYVNA, -S *n* standard
monetary unit of Ukraine

HRYVNIA, -S *same as*
> **hryvna**

HRYVNYA, -S *same as*
> **hryvna**

HUANACO, -S *same as*
> **guanaco**

HUAQUERO *n* Central
American tomb robber

HUARACHE *n* Mexican
sandal

HUARACHO *same as*
▸ **huarache**

HUB, -S *n* centre of a wheel,
through which the axle
passes

HUBBIES ▸ **hubby**

HUBBLY, HUBBLIER *adj*
having an irregular surface

HUBBUB, -S *n* confused
noise of many voices

HUBBUBOO *same as*
▸ **hubbub**

HUBBUBS ▸ **hubbub**

HUBBY, HUBBIES *n*
husband

HUBCAP, -S *n* metal disc
that protects the hub of a
wheel

HUBLESS *adj* without a hub

HUBRIS, -ES *n* pride,
arrogance

HUBS ▸ **hub**

HUCK, -ED, -ING, -S *same as*
> **huckaback**

HUCKERY *adj* ugly

HUCKING ▸ **huck**

HUCKLE, -D, -S, HUCKLING
n hip or haunch ▸ *vb* force
out or arrest roughly

HUCKS ▸ **huck**

HUCKSTER *n* person using
aggressive methods of
selling ▸ *vb* peddle

HUDDEN ▸ **haud**

HUDDLE, -D, -S, HUDDLING
vb hunch (oneself) through
cold or fear ▸ *n* small group

HUDDLER, -S ▸ **huddle**

HUDDLES ▸ **huddle**

HUDDLING ▸ **huddle**

HUDDUP *interj* get up

HUDNA, -S *n* truce or
ceasefire for a fixed duration

HUDUD, -S *n* set of laws and
punishments in the Koran

HUE, -S *n* colour, shade

HUED *adj* having a hue or
colour as specified

HUELESS ▸ **hue**

HUER, -S *n* pilchard
fisherman

HUES ▸ **hue**

HUFF, -ED, -S *n* passing
mood of anger or
resentment ▸ *vb* blow or
puff heavily

HUFFER, -S ▸ **huffing**

HUFFIER ▸ **huffy**

HUFFIEST ▸ **huffy**

HUFFILY ▸ **huff**

HUFFING, -S *n* practice of
inhaling fumes for
intoxicating effects

HUFFISH ▸ **huff**

HUFFKIN, -S *n* type of muffin

HUFFS ▸ **huff**

**HUFFY, HUFFIER,
HUFFIEST** ▸ **huff**

HUG, -GED, -GING, -S *vb* clasp tightly in the arms, usu with affection ▷ *n* tight or fond embrace

HUGE, -R, -ST *adj* very big

HUGELY *adv* very much

HUGENESS ▷ **huge**

HUGEOUS *same as* ▷ **huge**

HUGER ▷ **huge**

HUGEST ▷ **huge**

HUGGABLE ▷ **hug**

HUGGED ▷ **hug**

HUGGER, -S ▷ **hug**

HUGGIER ▷ **huggy**

HUGGIEST ▷ **huggy**

HUGGING ▷ **hug**

HUGGY, HUGGIER, HUGGIEST *adj* sensitive and caring

HUGS ▷ **hug**

HUGY *same as* ▷ **huge**

HUH *interj* exclamation of derision or inquiry

HUHU, -S *n* type of hairy New Zealand beetle

HUI, -S *n* meeting of Māori people

HUIA, -S *n* extinct bird of New Zealand

HUIC *interj* in hunting, a call to hounds

HUIPIL, -ES, -S *n* Mayan woman's blouse

HUIS ▷ **hui**

HUISACHE *n* American tree

HUISSIER *n* doorkeeper

HUITAIN, -S *n* verse of eighteen lines

HULA, -S *n* swaying Hawaiian dance

HULE, -S *same as* ▷ **ule**

HULK, -ED, -S *n* body of an abandoned ship ▷ *vb* move clumsily

HULKIER ▷ **hulky**

HULKIEST ▷ **hulky**

HULKING *adj* bulky, unwieldy

HULKS ▷ **hulk**

HULKY, HULKIER, HULKIEST *same as* ▷ **hulking**

HULL, -ED, -ING, -S *n* main body of a boat ▷ *vb* remove the hulls from

HULLER, -S ▷ **hull**

HULLIER ▷ **hully**

HULLIEST ▷ **hully**

HULLING ▷ **hull**

HULLO, -ED, -ES, -ING, -S *same as* ▷ **hello**

HULLOA, -ED, -S *same as* ▷ **halloa**

HULLOED ▷ **hullo**

HULLOES ▷ **hullo**

HULLOING ▷ **hullo**

HULLOO, -ED, -S *same as* ▷ **halloo**

HULLOS ▷ **hullo**

HULLS ▷ **hull**

HULLY, HULLIER, HULLIEST *adj* having husks

HUM, -MED, -S *vb* make a low continuous vibrating sound ▷ *n* humming sound

HUMA, -S *n* mythical bird

HUMAN, -S *adj* of or typical of people ▷ *n* human being

HUMANE, -R, -ST *adj* kind or merciful

HUMANELY ▷ **humane**

HUMANER ▷ **humane**

HUMANEST ▷ **humane**

HUMANISE *same as* ▷ **humanize**

HUMANISM *n* belief in human effort rather than religion

HUMANIST ▷ **humanism**

HUMANITY *n* human race

HUMANIZE *vb* make human or humane

HUMANLY *adv* by human powers or means

HUMANOID *adj* resembling a human being in appearance ▷ *n* (in science fiction) a robot or creature resembling a human being

HUMANS ▷ **human**

HUMAS ▷ **huma**

HUMATE, -S *n* decomposed plants used as fertilizer

HUMBLE, -D, -S, -ST *adj* conscious of one's failings ▷ *vb* cause to feel humble, humiliate

HUMBLER, -S ▷ **humble**

HUMBLES ▷ **humble**

HUMBLEST ▷ **humble**

HUMBLING ▷ **humble**

HUMBLY ▷ **humble**

HUMBUG, -S *n* hard striped peppermint sweet ▷ *vb* cheat or deceive (someone)

HUMBUZZ *n* type of beetle

HUMDRUM, -S *adj* ordinary, dull ▷ *n* monotonous routine, task, or person

HUMECT, -ED, -S *vb* make moist

HUMEFY, HUMEFIED, HUMEFIES *same as* ▷ **humify**

HUMERAL, -S *adj* of or relating to the humerus ▷ *n* silk shawl worn by a priest at High Mass; humeral veil

HUMERUS, HUMERI *n* bone from the shoulder to the elbow

HUMF, -ED, -ING, -S *same as* ▷ **humph**

HUMHUM, -S *n* Indian cotton cloth

HUMIC *adj* of, derived from, or resembling humus

HUMICOLE *n* any plant that thrives on humus

HUMID, -ER, -EST *adj* damp and hot

HUMIDEX *n* system of measuring discomfort

HUMIDIFY *vb* make the air in (a room) more humid or damp

HUMIDITY *n* dampness

HUMIDLY ▷ **humid**

HUMIDOR, -S *n* humid place for storing cigars, tobacco, etc

HUMIFY, HUMIFIED, HUMIFIES *vb* convert or be converted into humus

HUMILITY *n* quality of being humble

HUMINT, -S *n* human intelligence

HUMITE, -S *n* mineral containing magnesium

HUMITURE *n* measure of both humidity and temperature

HUMLIE, -S *n* hornless cow

HUMMABLE ▷ **hum**

HUMMAUM, -S *same as* ▷ **hammam**

HUMMED ▷ **hum**

HUMMEL, -S *adj* (of cattle) hornless ▷ *vb* remove horns from

HUMMER, -S ▷ **hum**

HUMMING, -S ▷ **hum**

HUMMLE *adj* as in **hummle bonnet** type of Scottish cap

HUMMOCK, -S *n* very small hill ▷ *vb* form into a hummock or hummocks

HUMMOCKY *adj* having hummocks

HUMMUM, -S *same as* ▷ **hammam**

HUMMUS, -ES *n* creamy dip

HUMOGEN, -S *n* type of fertilizer

HUMOR, -ED, -ING, -S *same as* ▷ **humour**

HUMORAL *adj* denoting or relating to a type of immunity

HUMORED ▷ **humor**

HUMORESK *n* humorous musical composition

HUMORFUL ▷ **humor**

HUMORING ▷ **humor**

HUMORIST *n* writer or entertainer who uses humour in his or her work

HUMOROUS *adj* amusing, esp in a witty or clever way

HUMORS ▷ **humor**

H

HUMOUR, -ED, -S n ability to say or perceive things that are amusing ▷ vb be kind and indulgent to

HUMOUS, -ES same as ▷ humus

HUMP, -ED, -ING, -S n raised piece of ground ▷ vb carry or heave

HUMPBACK same as > hunchback

HUMPED ▷ hump

HUMPEN, -S n old German drinking glass

HUMPER, -S ▷ hump

HUMPH, -ED, -ING, -S interj exclamation of annoyance or scepticism ▷ vb exclaim humph

HUMPIER ▷ humpy

HUMPIES ▷ humpy

HUMPIEST ▷ humpy

HUMPING ▷ hump

HUMPLESS ▷ hump

HUMPLIKE ▷ hump

HUMPS ▷ hump

HUMPTY, HUMPTIES n low padded seat

HUMPY, HUMPIER, HUMPIES, HUMPIEST adj full of humps ▷ n primitive hut

HUMS ▷ hum

HUMSTRUM n medieval musical instrument

HUMUS, -ES n decomposing matter in the soil

HUMUSY, HUMUSIER adj like humus

HUMVEE, -S n military vehicle

HUN, -S n member of any of several nomadic peoples

HUNCH, -ED, -ES, -ING n feeling or suspicion not based on facts ▷ vb draw (one's shoulders) up or together

HUNDRED, -S n ten times ten ▷ adj amounting to a hundred

HUNG ▷ hang

HUNGAN, -S same as ▷ houngan

HUNGER, -ED, -S n discomfort or weakness from lack of food ▷ vb want very much

HUNGERLY adj hungry

HUNGERS ▷ hunger

HUNGOVER adj suffering from hangover

HUNGRIER ▷ hungry

HUNGRILY ▷ hungry

HUNGRY, HUNGRIER adj desiring food

HUNH same as ▷ huh

HUNK n large piece

HUNKER, -ED vb squat

HUNKERS pl n haunches

HUNKIER ▷ hunky

HUNKIEST ▷ hunky

HUNKS, -ES n grumpy person

HUNKY, HUNKIER, HUNKIEST adj excellent

HUNNISH ▷ hun

HUNS ▷ hun

HUNT, -S vb seek out and kill (wild animals) for food or sport ▷ n hunting

HUNTABLE ▷ hunt

HUNTAWAY n sheepdog trained to drive sheep by barking

HUNTED adj harassed and worn

HUNTEDLY ▷ hunt

HUNTER, -S n person or animal that hunts wild animals

HUNTING, -S n pursuit and killing or capture of wild animals

HUNTRESS n female hunter

HUNTS ▷ hunt

HUNTSMAN, HUNTSMEN n man who hunts wild animals, esp foxes

HUP, -PED, -PING, -S vb cry hup to get a horse to move

HUPIRO, -S n in New Zealand English, same as > stinkwood

HUPPAH, -S, HUPPOT variant spelling of ▷ chuppah

HUPPED ▷ hup

HUPPING ▷ hup

HUPPOT same as ▷ huppah

HUPPOTH same as ▷ huppot

HUPS ▷ hup

HURCHEON same as ▷ urchin

HURDEN, -S same as ▷ harden

HURDIES pl n buttocks or haunches

HURDLE, -D, -S, HURDLING n light barrier for jumping over in some races ▷ vb jump over (something)

HURDLER, -S ▷ hurdle

HURDLES ▷ hurdle

HURDLING ▷ hurdle

HURDS same as ▷ hards

HURL, -ED, -S vb throw or utter forcefully ▷ n act or an instance of hurling

HURLBAT, -S same as ▷ whirlbat

HURLED ▷ hurl

HURLER, -S ▷ hurl

HURLEY, -S n another word for the game of hurling

HURLIES ▷ hurly

HURLING, -S n Irish game like hockey

HURLS ▷ hurl

HURLY, HURLIES n wheeled barrow

HURRA, -ED, -ING, -S same as ▷ hurrah

HURRAH, -ED, -S interj exclamation of joy or applause ▷ n cheer of joy or victory ▷ vb shout 'hurrah'

HURRAING ▷ hurra

HURRAS ▷ hurra

HURRAY, -ED, -S same as ▷ hurrah

HURRIED adj done quickly or too quickly

HURRIER, -S ▷ hurry

HURRY, HURRIES vb (cause to) move or act very quickly ▷ n doing something or the need to do something quickly

HURRYING ▷ hurry

HURST, -S n wood

HURT, -ING, -S vb cause physical or mental pain to ▷ n physical or mental pain ▷ adj injured or pained

HURTER, -S ▷ hurt

HURTFUL adj unkind

HURTING ▷ hurt

HURTLE, -D, -S, HURTLING vb move quickly or violently

HURTLESS adj uninjured

HURTLING ▷ hurtle

HURTS ▷ hurt

HUSBAND, -S n man to whom one is married ▷ vb use economically

HUSH, -ES, -ING vb make or be silent ▷ n stillness or silence ▷ interj plea or demand for silence

HUSHABY interj used in quietening a baby or child to sleep ▷ n lullaby ▷ vb quieten to sleep

HUSHABYE same as ▷ hushaby

HUSHED ▷ hush

HUSHEDLY ▷ hush

HUSHER, -ED, -S same as ▷ usher

HUSHES ▷ hush

HUSHFUL adj quiet

HUSHIER ▷ hushy

HUSHIEST ▷ hushy

HUSHING ▷ hush

HUSHY, HUSHIER, HUSHIEST adj secret

HUSK, -ED, -S n outer covering of certain seeds and fruits ▷ vb remove the husk from

HUSKER, -S ▷ husk

HUSKIER ▷ husky

HUSKIES ▷ husky

HUSKIEST ▷ husky

HUSKILY ▸ husky
HUSKING, -S ▸ husk
HUSKLIKE ▸ husk
HUSKS ▸ husk
HUSKY, HUSKIER, HUSKIES, HUSKIEST adj slightly hoarse ▸ n Arctic sledge dog with thick hair and a curled tail
HUSO, -S n sturgeon
HUSS, -ES n flesh of the European dogfish
HUSSAR, -S n lightly armed cavalry soldier
HUSSES ▸ huss
HUSSIF, -S n sewing kit
HUSTINGS pl n political campaigns and speeches before an election
HUSTLE, -D, -S, HUSTLING vb push about, jostle ▸ n lively activity or bustle
HUSTLER, -S ▸ hustle
HUSTLES ▸ hustle
HUSTLING ▸ hustle
HUSWIFE, -S, HUSWIVES same as ▸ housewife
HUT, -S, -TED n small house, shelter, or shed ▸ vb equip with huts
HUTCH, -ED, -ES, -ING n cage for pet rabbits etc ▸ vb store or keep in or as if in a hutch
HUTCHIE, -S n temporary shelter
HUTCHING ▸ hutch
HUTIA, -S n rodent native to the Caribbean
HUTLIKE ▸ hut
HUTMENT, -S n number or group of huts
HUTS ▸ hut
HUTTED ▸ hut
HUTTING, -S ▸ hut
HUTZPA, -S same as ▸ hutzpah
HUTZPAH, -S variant spelling of ▸ chutzpah
HUTZPAS ▸ hutzpa
HUZOOR, -S n person of rank in India
HUZZA, -ED, -ING, -S same as ▸ huzzah
HUZZAH, -ED, -S archaic word for ▸ hurrah
HUZZAING ▸ huzza
HUZZAS ▸ huzza
HWAN another name for ▸ won
HWYL, -S n emotional fervour, as in the recitation of poetry

This Welsh word can come in very useful for dealing with a consonant-heavy rack.

HYACINE, -S same as ▸ hyacinth
HYACINTH n sweet-smelling spring flower that grows from a bulb
HYAENA, -S same as ▸ hyena
HYAENIC ▸ hyaena
HYALIN, -S n glassy translucent substance
HYALINE, -S adj clear and translucent, with no fibres or granules ▸ n glassy transparent surface
HYALINS ▸ hyalin
HYALITE, -S n clear and colourless variety of opal in globular form
HYALOGEN n insoluble substance in body structures
HYALOID, -S adj clear and transparent ▸ n delicate transparent membrane
HYBRID, -S n offspring of two plants or animals of different species ▸ adj of mixed origin
HYBRIS, -ES same as ▸ hubris
HYDATID, -S n cyst containing tapeworm larvae
HYDATOID adj watery
HYDRA, -E, -S n mythical many-headed water serpent
HYDRACID n acid, such as hydrochloric acid, that does not contain oxygen
HYDRAE ▸ hydra
HYDRAGOG n drug that removes water
HYDRANT, -S n outlet from a water main with a nozzle for a hose
HYDRANTH n polyp in a colony of hydrozoan coelenterates
HYDRANTS ▸ hydrant
HYDRAS ▸ hydra
HYDRASE, -S n enzyme that removes water
HYDRATE, -S n chemical compound of water with another substance ▸ vb treat or impregnate with water
HYDRATED adj (of a compound) chemically bonded to water molecules
HYDRATES ▸ hydrate
HYDRATOR ▸ hydrate
HYDREMIA same as > hydraemia
HYDRIA, -E n (in ancient Greece and Rome) a large water jar
HYDRIC adj of or containing hydrogen
HYDRID, -S same as ▸ hydroid

HYDRIDE, -S n compound of hydrogen with another element
HYDRIDS ▸ hydrid
HYDRILLA n aquatic plant used as an oxygenator in aquaria and pools
HYDRO, -S n hotel offering facilities for hydropathy ▸ adj short for hydroelectric
HYDROGEL n gel in which the liquid constituent is water
HYDROGEN n light flammable colourless gas that combines with oxygen to form water
HYDROID, -S adj of an order of colonial hydrozoan coelenterates ▸ n hydroid colony or individual
HYDROMA, -S same as ▸ hygroma
HYDROMEL n another word for mead (the drink)
HYDRONIC adj using hot water in heating system
HYDROPIC ▸ hydropsy
HYDROPS n anaemia in a fetus
HYDROPSY same as ▸ dropsy
HYDROS ▸ hydro
HYDROSKI n hydrofoil used on some seaplanes to provide extra lift when taking off
HYDROSOL n sol that has water as its liquid phase
HYDROUS adj containing water
HYDROXY adj of a type of chemical compound
HYDROXYL n the monovalent group −OH or the ion OH⁻
HYDROZOA > hydrozoon
HYDYNE, -S n type of rocket fuel
HYE, -D, -ING, -S same as ▸ hie
HYEN, -S same as ▸ hyena
HYENA, -S n scavenging doglike mammal of Africa and S Asia
HYENIC ▸ hyena
HYENINE adj of hyenas
HYENOID adj of or like hyenas
HYENS ▸ hyen
HYES ▸ hye
HYETAL adj of or relating to rain, rainfall, or rainy regions
HYGEIST, -S same as > hygienist
HYGGE, -S n Danish practice that promotes wellbeing
HYGIEIST same as > hygienist
HYGIENE, -S n principles of health and cleanliness
HYGIENIC adj promoting health or cleanliness

HYGROMA, -S *n* swelling soft tissue that occurs over a joint

HYING ▸ hie

HYKE, -S *same as* ▸ **haik**

HYLA, -S *n* type of tropical American tree frog

HYLDING, -S *same as* ▸ **hilding**

HYLE, -S *n* wood

HYLEG, -S *n* dominant planet when someone is born

HYLES ▸ hyle

HYLIC *adj* solid

HYLICISM *n* materialism

HYLICIST ▸ hylicism

HYLISM, -S *same as* ▸ **hylicism**

HYLIST, -S ▸ hylism

HYLOBATE *n* gibbon

HYLOIST, -S *n* materialist

HYLOZOIC ▸ hylozoism

HYMEN, -S *n* membrane partly covering the vaginal opening

HYMENAL ▸ hymen

HYMENEAL *adj* of or relating to marriage ▸ *n* wedding song or poem

HYMENEAN *n* wedding song

HYMENIA ▸ hymenium

HYMENIAL ▸ hymenium

HYMENIUM, HYMENIA *n* (in some fungi) a layer of cell-producing spores

HYMENS ▸ hymen

HYMN, -ED, -ING, -S *n* Christian song of praise sung to God or a saint ▸ *vb* express (praises, thanks, etc) by singing hymns

HYMNAL, -S *n* book of hymns ▸ *adj* of, relating to, or characteristic of hymns

HYMNARY *same as* ▸ **hymnal**

HYMNBOOK *n* book containing the words and music of hymns

HYMNED ▸ hymn

HYMNIC ▸ hymn

HYMNING ▸ hymn

HYMNIST, -S *n* person who composes hymns

HYMNLESS ▸ hymn

HYMNLIKE ▸ hymn

HYMNODY *n* composition or singing of hymns

HYMNS ▸ hymn

HYNDE, -S *same as* ▸ **hind**

HYOID, -S *adj* of or relating to the hyoid bone ▸ *n* horseshoe-shaped bone

HYOIDAL *adj* of or relating to the hyoid bone

HYOIDEAN *same as* ▸ **hyoidal**

HYOIDS ▸ hyoid

HYOSCINE *n* colourless viscous liquid alkaloid

HYP, -PED, -PING, -S *n* short for hypotenuse ▸ *vb* offend

HYPALGIA *n* reduced ability to feel pain

HYPATE, -S *n* string of lyre

HYPE, -D, -S *n* intensive or exaggerated publicity or sales promotion ▸ *vb* promote (a product) using intensive or exaggerated publicity

HYPER, -ER, -EST, -S *n* excitable person ▸ *adj* excitable

HYPERGOL *n* type of fuel

HYPERNYM *n* superordinate

HYPERON, -S *n* any baryon that is not a nucleon

HYPEROPE *n* person with hyperopia

HYPERS ▸ hyper

HYPES ▸ hype

HYPESTER *n* person who gives a product intense publicity

HYPHA, -E *n* any of the filaments in the mycelium of a fungus

HYPHAL ▸ hypha

HYPHEMIA *n* bleeding inside eye

HYPHEN, -ED, -S *n* punctuation mark (-) ▸ *vb* hyphenate

HYPHENIC ▸ hyphen

HYPHENS ▸ hyphen

HYPHY, HYPHIES *n* type of hip-hop music

HYPING, -S ▸ hype

HYPNIC, -S *n* sleeping drug

HYPNOID *adj* of or relating to a state resembling sleep

HYPNONE, -S *n* sleeping drug

HYPNOSIS, HYPNOSES *n* artificially induced state of relaxation

HYPNOTEE *n* person being hypnotized

HYPNOTIC *adj* of or (as if) producing hypnosis ▸ *n* drug that induces sleep

HYPNUM, -S *n* species of moss

HYPO, -ED, -ING, -S *vb* inject with a hypodermic syringe

HYPOACID *adj* abnormally acidic

HYPOBOLE *n* act of anticipating objection

HYPOCIST *n* type of juice

HYPODERM *n* layer of thick-walled tissue in some plants

HYPOED ▸ hypo

HYPOGAEA > hypogaeum

HYPOGEA ▸ hypogeum

HYPOGEAL *adj* occurring or living below the surface of the ground

HYPOGEAN ▸ hypogeum

HYPOGENE *adj* formed, taking place, or originating beneath the surface of the earth

HYPOGEUM, HYPOGEA *n* underground vault, esp one used for burials

HYPOGYNY *adj* having the gynoecium above the other floral parts

HYPOID, -S *adj* as in **hypoid gear** type of gear ▸ *n* hypoid gear

HYPOING ▸ hypo

HYPONEA, -S *same as* ▸ **hypopnea**

HYPONOIA *n* underlying meaning

HYPONYM, -S *n* word whose meaning is included as part of another

HYPONYMY ▸ hyponym

HYPOPNEA *same as* > **hypopnoea**

HYPOPYON *n* pus in eye

HYPOS ▸ hypo

HYPOTHEC *n* charge on property in favour of a creditor

HYPOXIA, -S *n* deficiency in oxygen delivery

HYPOXIC ▸ hypoxia

HYPPED ▸ hyp

HYPPING ▸ hyp

HYPS ▸ hyp

HYPURAL *adj* below the tail

HYRACES ▸ hyrax

HYRACOID ▸ hyrax

HYRAX, HYRACES, -ES *n* type of hoofed rodent-like animal of Africa and Asia

HYSON, -S *n* Chinese green tea

HYSSOP, -S *n* sweet-smelling herb used in folk medicine

HYSTERIA *n* state of uncontrolled excitement, anger, or panic

HYSTERIC *adj* of or suggesting hysteria

HYTE *adj* crazy

HYTHE, -S *same as* ▸ **hithe**

I i

The letter **I** can prove a difficult tile to use effectively in Scrabble. It's one of the most common tiles in the game, so you often end up with two or more on your rack, but it can be hard to get rid of. Where **I** does come in very useful, though, is in the number of everyday short words that can be formed from it, which are very helpful when you need to form short words in addition to the main word that you want to play. These words include **in**, **is**, **it** (2 points each), **id** (3) and **if** (5). Other handy words are **icy** (8), **ivy** (9) and **imp** (7). Don't forget the three-letter words that use **K**: **ilk**, **ink** and **irk** (7 each), while **iwi** for 6 points can be very useful in getting rid of a surplus of **I**s.

IAMB, -S *n* metrical foot of two syllables
IAMBI ▸ **iambus**
IAMBIC, -S *adj* written in a type of metrical unit ▷ *n* iambic foot, line, or stanza
IAMBIST, -S *n* one who writes iambs
IAMBS ▸ **iamb**
IAMBUS, IAMBI, -ES *same as* ▸ **iamb**
IANTHINE *adj* violet
IATRIC *adj* relating to medicine or physicians
IATRICAL *same as* ▸ **iatric**
IBADAH, IBADAT *n* following of Islamic beliefs and practices
IBERIS, -ES *n* plant with white or purple flowers
IBEX, -ES, IBICES *n* wild goat
IBIDEM *adv* in the same place
IBIS, -ES *n* large wading bird with long legs
IBOGAINE *n* dopamine blocker
IBRIK, -S *same as* ▸ **cezve**
ICE, -S *n* water in the solid state, formed by freezing liquid water ▷ *vb* form or cause to form ice
ICEBALL, -S *n* ball of ice
ICEBERG, -S *n* large floating mass of ice
ICEBLINK *n* yellowish-white reflected glare in the sky over an ice field
ICEBOAT, -S *n* boat that breaks up bodies of ice in water ▷ *vb* pilot an iceboat
ICEBOUND *adj* covered or made immobile by ice

ICEBOX, -ES *n* refrigerator
ICECAP, -S *n* mass of ice permanently covering an area
ICED *adj* covered with icing
ICEFALL, -S *n* part of a glacier
ICEFIELD *n* very large flat expanse of ice floating in the sea; large ice floe
ICEFISH *vb* fish through a hole in the ice on a lake
ICEHOUSE *n* building for storing ice
ICEKHANA *n* motor race on a frozen lake
ICELESS ▸ **ice**
ICELIKE ▸ **ice**
ICEMAKER *n* device for making ice
ICEMAN, ICEMEN *n* person who sells or delivers ice
ICEPACK, -S *n* bag or folded cloth containing ice
ICER, -S *n* person who ices cakes
ICES ▸ **ice**
ICESCAPE *n* landscape covered in ice
ICESTONE *n* cryolite
ICEWINE, -S *n* dessert wine made from grapes that have frozen before being harvested
ICEWORM, -S *n* small worm found in glaciers
ICH, -ED, -ES, -ING, -S *archaic form of* ▸ **eke**

A Shakespearean spelling of **eke**, this is a useful little word worth remembering because of its unusual combination of letters and relatively high score.

ICHABOD *interj* the glory has departed
ICHED ▸ **ich**
ICHES ▸ **ich**
ICHING ▸ **ich**
ICHNITE, -S *n* trace fossil
ICHOR, -S *n* fluid said to flow in the veins of the gods
ICHOROUS ▸ **ichor**
ICHORS ▸ **ichor**
ICHS ▸ **ich**
ICHTHIC *same as* ▸ **ichthyic**
ICHTHYIC *adj* of, relating to, or characteristic of fishes
ICHTHYS *n* early Christian emblem
ICICLE, -S *n* tapering spike of ice
ICICLED *adj* covered with icicles
ICICLES ▸ **icicle**
ICIER ▸ **icy**
ICIEST ▸ **icy**
ICILY *adv* in an icy or reserved manner
ICINESS *n* condition of being icy or very cold
ICING, -S *n* mixture used to decorate cakes
ICK, -S *interj* expression of disgust ▷ *n* something sticky

An interjection expressing disgust, this is one of the highest-scoring 3-letter words beginning with I. It can also take a Y to make **icky**.

ICKER, -S *n* ear of corn
ICKIER ▸ **icky**
ICKIEST ▸ **icky**
ICKILY ▸ **icky**

ICKINESS ▸icky
ICKLE, -R, -ST *ironically childish word for* ▸**little**
ICKS ▸ick
ICKY, ICKIER, ICKIEST *adj* sticky
ICON, -S *n* picture of Christ or another religious figure
ICONES *archaic form of* ▸icons
ICONIC *adj* relating to the character of an icon
ICONICAL *same as* ▸iconic
ICONIFY *vb* render as an icon
ICONISE, -D, -S *same as* ▸iconize
ICONIZE, -D, -S *vb* render as an icon
ICONS ▸icon
ICTAL ▸ictus
ICTERIC, -S ▸icterus
ICTERID, -S *n* bird of the oriole family
ICTERINE ▸icterid
ICTERUS *n* yellowing of plant leaves
ICTIC ▸ictus
ICTUS, -ES *n* metrical or rhythmic stress in verse feet
ICY, ICIER, ICIEST *adj* very cold
ID, -S *n* mind's instinctive unconscious energies
IDANT, -S *n* chromosome
IDE *n* silver orfe fish
IDEA, -S *n* plan or thought formed in the mind
IDEAED *adj* expressing a particular idea
IDEAL, -S *adj* most suitable ▸*n* conception of something that is perfect
IDEALESS ▸idea
IDEALISE *same as* ▸idealize
IDEALISM *n* tendency to seek perfection in everything
IDEALIST ▸idealism
IDEALITY ▸ideal
IDEALIZE *vb* regard or portray as perfect or nearly perfect
IDEALLY ▸ideal
IDEALOGY *corruption of* ▸ideology
IDEALS ▸ideal
IDEAS ▸idea
IDEATA ▸ideatum
IDEATE, -D, -S, IDEATING *vb* form or have an idea of
IDEATION ▸ideate
IDEATIVE ▸ideate
IDEATUM, IDEATA *n* objective reality
IDEE, -S *n* idea
IDEM *adj* same

IDENT, -S *n* short visual image that works as a logo
IDENTIC *adj* having the same intention regarding another power
IDENTIFY *vb* prove or recognize as being a certain person or thing
IDENTITY *n* state of being a specified person or thing
IDENTS ▸ident
IDEOGRAM *n* symbol that directly represents a concept or thing
IDEOLOGY *n* body of ideas and beliefs of a group, nation, etc
IDES *n* specific date of each month in the Roman calendar
IDIOCY, IDIOCIES *n* utter stupidity
IDIOGRAM *another name for* ▸**karyogram**
IDIOLECT *n* variety or form of a language used by an individual
IDIOM, -S *n* group of words with special meaning
IDIOT, -S *n* foolish or stupid person
IDIOTCY *same as* ▸idiocy
IDIOTIC *adj* of or resembling an idiot
IDIOTISH *same as* ▸idiotic
IDIOTISM *archaic word for* ▸idiocy
IDIOTS ▸idiot
IDIOTYPE *n* unique part of antibody
IDLE, -D, -S, -ST, IDLING *adj* not doing anything ▸*vb* spend (time) doing very little
IDLEHOOD ▸idle
IDLENESS ▸idle
IDLER, -S *n* person who idles
IDLES ▸idle
IDLESSE *poetic word for* ▸idleness
IDLEST ▸idle
IDLING ▸idle
IDLY ▸idle
IDOCRASE *n* green, brown, or yellow mineral
IDOL, -S *n* object of excessive devotion
IDOLA ▸idolum
IDOLATER ▸idolatry
IDOLATOR *n* one who worships idols
IDOLATRY *n* worship of idols
IDOLISE, -D, -S *same as* ▸idolize
IDOLISER ▸idolise
IDOLISES ▸idolise
IDOLISM, -S ▸idol

IDOLIST, -S ▸idolize
IDOLIZE, -D, -S *vb* love or admire excessively
IDOLIZER ▸idolize
IDOLIZES ▸idolize
IDOLON *n* mental picture
IDOLS ▸idol
IDOLUM, IDOLA *n* mental picture
IDONEITY ▸idoneous
IDONEOUS *adj* appropriate
IDS ▸id
IDYL, -S *same as* ▸idyll
IDYLIST, -S *same as* ▸idyllist
IDYLL, -S *n* scene or time of great peace and happiness
IDYLLIAN *same as* ▸idyllic
IDYLLIC *adj* of or relating to an idyll
IDYLLIST *n* writer of idylls
IDYLLS ▸idyll
IDYLS ▸idyl
IF, -S *n* uncertainty or doubt
IFF *conj* in logic, a shortened form of if and only if

This word is one of the highest-scoring 3-letter words beginning with I, and of course provides a useful extension to **if**.

IFFIER ▸iffy
IFFIEST ▸iffy
IFFILY *adv* in an iffy manner
IFFINESS ▸iffy
IFFY, IFFIER, IFFIEST *adj* doubtful, uncertain
IFS ▸if
IFTAR, -S *n* meal eaten by Muslims
IGAD *same as* ▸egad
IGAPO, -S *n* flooded forest
IGARAPE, -S *n* canoe route
IGG, -ED, -ING, -S *vb* antagonize
IGLOO, -S *n* Inuit house
IGLU, -S *same as* ▸igloo
IGNARO, -ES, -S *n* ignoramus
IGNATIA, -S *n* dried seed
IGNEOUS *adj* (of rock) formed as molten rock cools
IGNIFY, IGNIFIED, IGNIFIES *vb* turn into fire
IGNITE, -D, -S, IGNITING *vb* catch fire or set fire to
IGNITER, -S *n* person or thing that ignites
IGNITES ▸ignite
IGNITING ▸ignite
IGNITION *n* system that ignites the fuel-and-air mixture to start an engine
IGNITOR, -S *same as* ▸igniter
IGNITRON *n* mercury-arc rectifier controlled by a subsidiary electrode

IGNOBLE, -R *adj* dishonourable

IGNOBLY ▸ ignoble

IGNOMIES ▸ ignomy

IGNOMINY *n* humiliating disgrace

IGNOMY, IGNOMIES *Shakespearean variant of* ▸ **ignominy**

IGNORAMI > ignoramus

IGNORANT *adj* lacking knowledge ▷ *n* ignorant person

IGNORE, -D, -S, IGNORING *vb* refuse to notice, disregard deliberately ▷ *n* disregard

IGNORER, -S ▸ ignore

IGNORES ▸ ignore

IGNORING ▸ ignore

IGUANA, -S *n* large tropical American lizard

IGUANIAN ▸ iguana

IGUANID, -S *same as* ▸ **iguana**

IHRAM, -S *n* white robes worn by Muslim pilgrims to Mecca

IJTIHAD, -S *n* effort of deriving a legal ruling from the Koran

IKAN, -S *n* (in Malaysia) fish

IKAT, -S *n* method of creating patterns in fabric

IKEBANA, -S *n* Japanese art of flower arrangement

IKON, -S *same as* ▸ **icon**

ILEA ▸ ileum

This is the plural of **ileum**, part of the small intestine, and is often useful as a rack-balancing play when you have too many vowels.

ILEAC *adj* of or relating to the ileum

ILEAL *same as* ▸ **ileac**

ILEITIS *n* inflammation of the ileum

ILEUM, ILEA *n* lowest part of the small intestine

ILEUS, -ES *n* obstruction of the intestine

ILEX, -ES, ILICES *n* any of a genus of trees or shrubs that includes holly

ILIA ▸ ilium

ILIAC *adj* of or relating to the ilium

ILIACUS, ILIACI *n* muscle near the ilium

ILIAD, -S *n* epic poem

ILIAL ▸ ilium

ILICES ▸ ilex

ILIUM, ILIA *n* part of the hipbone

ILK, -S *n* type

ILKA *determiner* Scots word meaning each

ILKADAY, -S *n* Scots word for a weekday

ILKS ▸ ilk

ILL, -ER, -EST, -S *adj* not in good health ▷ *n* evil, harm ▷ *adv* badly

ILLAPSE, -D, -S *vb* slide in

ILLATION *rare word for* > **inference**

ILLATIVE *adj* of or relating to illation ▷ *n* illative case

ILLEGAL, -S *adj* against the law ▷ *n* person who entered or attempted to enter a country illegally

ILLER ▸ ill

ILLEST ▸ ill

ILLIAD, -S *n* wink

ILLICIT *adj* illegal

ILLINIUM *n* type of radioactive element

ILLIPE, -S *n* Asian tree

ILLIQUID *adj* (of an asset) not easily convertible into cash

ILLISION *n* act of striking against

ILLITE, -S *n* clay mineral of the mica group

ILLITIC ▸ illite

ILLNESS *n* disease or indisposition

ILLOGIC, -S *n* reasoning characterized by lack of logic

ILLS ▸ ill

ILLTH, -S *n* condition of poverty or misery

ILLUDE, -D, -S, ILLUDING *vb* trick or deceive

ILLUME, -D, -S, ILLUMING *vb* illuminate

ILLUMINE *vb* throw light in or into

ILLUMING ▸ illume

ILLUPI, -S *same as* ▸ **illipe**

ILLUSION *n* deceptive appearance or belief

ILLUSIVE *same as* ▸ **illusory**

ILLUSORY *adj* seeming to be true, but actually false

ILLUVIA ▸ illuvium

ILLUVIAL ▸ illuvium

ILLUVIUM, ILLUVIA *n* material washed down from one soil layer to a lower one

ILLY *adv* badly

ILMENITE *n* black mineral found in igneous rocks and in layered deposits and in veins

IMAGE, -D, -S *n* mental picture of someone or something ▷ *vb* picture in the mind

IMAGER, -S *n* device that produces images

IMAGERY *n* images collectively, esp in the arts

IMAGES ▸ image

IMAGINAL *adj* of, relating to, or resembling an imago

IMAGINE, -D *vb* form a mental image of ▷ *sentence substitute* exclamation of surprise

IMAGINER ▸ imagine

IMAGINES ▸ imago

IMAGING, -S ▸ image

IMAGISM, -S *n* poetic movement

IMAGIST, -S ▸ imagism

IMAGO, IMAGINES, -ES, -S *n* mature adult insect

IMAM, -S *n* leader of prayers in a mosque

IMAMATE, -S *n* region or territory governed by an imam

IMAMS ▸ imam

IMARET, -S *n* (in Turkey) a hospice for pilgrims or travellers

IMARI, -S *n* Japanese porcelain

IMAUM, -S *same as* ▸ **imam**

IMBALM, -ED, -S *same as* ▸ **embalm**

IMBALMER ▸ imbalm

IMBALMS ▸ imbalm

IMBAR, -RED, -S *vb* bar in

IMBARK, -ED, -S *vb* cover in bark

IMBARRED ▸ imbar

IMBARS ▸ imbar

IMBASE, -D, -S, IMBASING *vb* degrade

IMBATHE, -D, -S *vb* bathe

IMBECILE *n* stupid person ▷ *adj* stupid or senseless

IMBED, -DED, -S *same as* ▸ **embed**

IMBIBE, -D, -S, IMBIBING *vb* drink (alcoholic drinks)

IMBIBER, -S ▸ imbibe

IMBIBES ▸ imbibe

IMBIBING ▸ imbibe

IMBITTER *same as* ▸ **embitter**

IMBIZO, -S *n* meeting in S Africa

IMBLAZE, -D, -S *vb* depict heraldically

IMBODY, IMBODIED, IMBODIES *same as* ▸ **embody**

IMBOLDEN *same as* ▸ **embolden**

IMBORDER *vb* enclose in a border

IMBOSK, -ED, -S *vb* conceal

IMBOSOM, -S *vb* hold in one's heart

IMBOSS, -ED, -ES same as ▶ **emboss**

IMBOWER, -S vb enclose in a bower

IMBRAST Spenserian past participle of ▶ **embrace**

IMBREX, IMBRICES n curved tile

IMBROWN, -S vb make brown

IMBRUE, -D, -S, IMBRUING vb stain, esp with blood

IMBRUTE, -D, -S vb reduce to a bestial state

IMBUE, -D, -S, IMBUING vb fill or inspire with (ideals or principles)

IMBURSE, -D, -S vb pay

IMID, -S n immunomodulatory drug

IMIDE, -S n any of a class of organic compounds

IMIDIC ▶ **imide**

IMIDO ▶ **imide**

IMIDS ▶ **imid**

IMINE, -S n any of a class of organic compounds

IMINO ▶ **imine**

IMIPENEM n drug used to destroy bacteria

IMITABLE ▶ **imitate**

IMITANCY n tendency to imitate

IMITANT, -S same as > **imitation**

IMITATE, -D, -S vb take as a model

IMITATOR ▶ **imitate**

IMMANE adj monstrous

IMMANELY ▶ **immane**

IMMANENT adj present within and throughout something

IMMANITY ▶ **immane**

IMMANTLE vb cover with a mantle

IMMASK, -ED, -S vb disguise

IMMATURE n young animal ▷ adj not fully developed

IMMENSE, -R adj extremely large

IMMERGE, -D, -S archaic word for ▶ **immerse**

IMMERSE, -S vb involve deeply, engross

IMMERSED adj sunk or submerged

IMMERSER ▶ **immerse**

IMMERSES ▶ **immerse**

IMMESH, -ED, -ES variant of ▶ **enmesh**

IMMEW, -ED, -ING, -S vb confine

IMMIES ▶ **immy**

IMMINENT adj about to happen

IMMINGLE vb blend or mix together

IMMINUTE adj reduced

IMMIT, -S, -TED vb insert

IMMIX, -ED, -ES, -ING vb mix in

IMMOBILE adj not moving

IMMODEST adj behaving in an indecent or improper manner

IMMOLATE vb kill as a sacrifice

IMMOMENT adj of no value

IMMORAL adj morally wrong, corrupt

IMMORTAL adj living forever ▷ n person whose fame will last for all time

IMMOTILE adj not capable of moving spontaneously and independently

IMMUNE, -R, -S, -ST adj protected against a specific disease ▷ n immune person or animal

IMMUNISE same as ▶ **immunize**

IMMUNITY n ability to resist disease

IMMUNIZE vb make immune to a disease

IMMURE, -D, -S, IMMURING vb imprison

IMMY, IMMIES n image-orthicon camera

IMP, -ED, -S n (in folklore) creature with magical powers ▷ vb method of repairing the wing of a hawk or falcon

IMPACT, -ED, -S n strong effect ▷ vb have a strong effect on

IMPACTER ▶ **impact**

IMPACTOR ▶ **impact**

IMPACTS ▶ **impact**

IMPAINT, -S vb paint

IMPAIR, -ED, -S vb weaken or damage

IMPAIRER ▶ **impair**

IMPAIRS ▶ **impair**

IMPALA, -S n southern African antelope

IMPALE, -D, -S, IMPALING vb pierce with a sharp object

IMPALER, -S ▶ **impale**

IMPALES ▶ **impale**

IMPALING ▶ **impale**

IMPANATE adj embodied in bread

IMPANEL, -S variant spelling (esp US) of ▶ **empanel**

IMPANNEL same as ▶ **impanel**

IMPARITY less common word for > **disparity**

IMPARK, -ED, -S vb make into a park

IMPARL, -ED, -S vb parley

IMPART, -ED, -S vb communicate (information)

IMPARTER ▶ **impart**

IMPARTS ▶ **impart**

IMPASSE, -S n situation in which progress is impossible

IMPASTE, -D, -S vb apply paint thickly to

IMPASTO, -S n technique of applying paint thickly ▷ vb apply impasto

IMPAVE, -D, -S, IMPAVING vb set in a pavement

IMPAVID adj fearless

IMPAVING ▶ **impave**

IMPAWN, -ED, -S vb pawn

IMPEACH vb charge with a serious crime against the state

IMPEARL, -S vb adorn with pearls

IMPED ▶ **imp**

IMPEDE, -D, -S, IMPEDING vb hinder in action or progress

IMPEDER, -S ▶ **impede**

IMPEDES ▶ **impede**

IMPEDING ▶ **impede**

IMPEDOR, -S n component that offers impedance

IMPEL, -LED, -S vb push or force (someone) to do something

IMPELLER n vaned rotating disc of a centrifugal pump, compressor, etc

IMPELLOR same as ▶ **impeller**

IMPELS ▶ **impel**

IMPEND, -ED, -S vb be about to happen

IMPERIA ▶ **imperium**

IMPERIAL adj of or like an empire or emperor ▷ n wine bottle holding the equivalent of eight normal bottles

IMPERIL, -S vb put in danger

IMPERIUM, IMPERIA n supreme power of Roman consuls and emperors

IMPETIGO n contagious skin disease

IMPETUS n incentive, impulse

IMPHEE, -S n African sorghum plant

IMPI, -ES, -S n group of Zulu warriors

IMPIETY n lack of respect or religious reverence

IMPING, -S ▶ **imp**

IMPINGE, -D, -S vb affect or restrict

IMPINGER ▸ impinge

IMPINGES ▸ impinge

IMPINGS ▸ imping

IMPIOUS adj showing a lack of respect or reverence

IMPIS ▸ impi

IMPISH adj mischievous

IMPISHLY ▸ impish

IMPLANT, -S n something put into someone's body ▷ vb put (something) into someone's body

IMPLATE, -D, -S vb sheathe

IMPLEACH vb intertwine

IMPLEAD, -S vb sue or prosecute

IMPLED ▸ implead

IMPLEDGE vb pledge

IMPLETE, -D, -S vb fill

IMPLEX, -ES n part of an arthropod

IMPLICIT adj expressed indirectly

IMPLIED adj hinted at or suggested

IMPLIES ▸ imply

IMPLODE, -D, -S vb collapse inwards

IMPLORE, -D, -S vb beg earnestly

IMPLORER ▸ implore

IMPLORES ▸ implore

IMPLUNGE vb submerge

IMPLUVIA > impluvium

IMPLY, IMPLIES, -ING vb indicate by hinting, suggest

IMPOCKET vb put in a pocket

IMPOLDER vb make into a polder

IMPOLICY n act or an instance of being injudicious or impolitic

IMPOLITE adj showing bad manners

IMPONE, -D, -S, IMPONING vb impose

IMPONENT n person who imposes a duty, etc

IMPONES ▸ impone

IMPONING ▸ impone

IMPOROUS adj not porous

IMPORT, -ED, -S vb bring in (goods) from another country ▷ n something imported

IMPORTER ▸ import

IMPORTS ▸ import

IMPOSE, -D, -S vb force the acceptance of

IMPOSER, -S ▸ impose

IMPOSES ▸ impose

IMPOSEX n acquisition by female organisms of male characteristics

IMPOSING adj grand, impressive

IMPOST, -ED, -S n tax, esp a customs duty ▷ vb classify (imported goods) according to the duty payable on them

IMPOSTER ▸ impost

IMPOSTOR n person who cheats or swindles by pretending to be someone else

IMPOSTS ▸ impost

IMPOT, -S n slang term for the act of imposing

IMPOTENT adj powerless ▷ n one who is impotent

IMPOTS ▸ impot

IMPOUND, -S vb take legal possession of, confiscate

IMPOWER, -S less common spelling of ▸ empower

IMPREGN, -S vb impregnate

IMPRESA, -S n heraldic device

IMPRESE, -S same as ▸ impresa

IMPRESS vb affect strongly, usu favourably ▷ n impressing

IMPRESSE n heraldic device

IMPREST, -S n fund of cash used to pay incidental expenses

IMPRIMIS adv in the first place

IMPRINT, -S n mark made by printing or stamping ▷ vb produce (a mark) by printing or stamping

IMPRISON vb put in prison

IMPRO, -S n short for improvisation

IMPROPER adj indecent

IMPROS ▸ impro

IMPROV, -S n improvisational comedy

IMPROVE, -D, -S vb make or become better

IMPROVER ▸ improve

IMPROVES ▸ improve

IMPROVS ▸ improv

IMPS ▸ imp

IMPUDENT adj cheeky, disrespectful

IMPUGN, -ED, -S vb challenge the truth or validity of

IMPUGNER ▸ impugn

IMPUGNS ▸ impugn

IMPULSE, -D, -S vb give an impulse to ▷ n sudden urge to do something

IMPUNITY n exemption or immunity from punishment or recrimination

IMPURE, -R, -ST adj having dirty or unwanted substances mixed in

IMPURELY ▸ impure

IMPURER ▸ impure

IMPUREST ▸ impure

IMPURITY n impure element or thing

IMPURPLE vb colour purple

IMPUTE, -D, -S, IMPUTING vb attribute responsibility to

IMPUTER, -S ▸ impute

IMPUTES ▸ impute

IMPUTING ▸ impute

IMSHI interj go away!

IMSHY same as ▸ imshi

IN, -NED, -S prep indicating position inside, state or situation, etc ▷ adv indicating position inside, entry into, etc ▷ adj fashionable ▷ n way of approaching or befriending a person ▷ vb take in

INACTION n act of doing nothing

INACTIVE adj idle

INANE, -R, -S, -ST adj senseless, silly ▷ n something that is inane

INANELY ▸ inane

INANER ▸ inane

INANES ▸ inane

INANEST ▸ inane

INANGA, -S n common type of New Zealand grass tree

INANITY n lack of intelligence or imagination

INAPT, -ER, -EST adj not apt or fitting

INAPTLY ▸ inapt

INARABLE adj not arable

INARCH, -ED, -ES vb graft (a plant)

INARM, -ED, -ING, -S vb embrace

INASMUCH conj as in inasmuch as , in view of the fact that

INAURATE adj gilded ▷ vb cover in gold

INBEING, -S n existence in something else

INBENT adj bent inwards

INBOARD adj (of a boat's engine) inside the hull ▷ adv within the sides of or towards the centre of a vessel or aircraft

INBOARDS same as ▸ inboard

INBORN adj existing from birth, natural

INBOUND, -S vb pass into the playing area from outside it ▷ adj coming in

INBOX, -ES n folder which stores incoming email messages

INBREAK, -S n breaking in

INBRED, -S n inbred animal ▷ adj produced as a result of inbreeding

INBREED, -S vb breed from closely related individuals

INBRING, -S vb bring in

INBUILT adj present from the start

INBURST, -S n irruption ▷ vb burst in

INBY adv into the house or an inner room ▷ adj located near or nearest to the house

INBYE adv near the house

INCAGE, -D, -S, INCAGING vb confine in or as in a cage

INCANT, -ED, -S vb chant (a spell)

INCASE, -D, -S, INCASING variant spelling of ▶ encase

INCAVE, -D, -S, INCAVING vb hide

INCAVI ▶ incavo

INCAVING ▶ incave

INCAVO, INCAVI n incised part of a carving

INCEDE, -D, -S, INCEDING vb advance

INCENSE, -D, -S vb make very angry ▷ n substance that gives off a perfume when burned

INCENSER n incense burner

INCENSES ▶ incense

INCENSOR n incense burner

INCENT, -ED, -S vb provide incentive

INCENTER same as ▶ incentre

INCENTRE n centre of an inscribed circle

INCENTS ▶ incent

INCEPT, -ED, -S vb (of organisms) to ingest (food) ▷ n rudimentary organ

INCEPTOR ▶ incept

INCEPTS ▶ incept

INCH, -ED, -ES, -ING n unit of length ▷ vb move slowly and gradually

INCHASE, -D, -S same as ▶ enchase

INCHED ▶ inch

INCHER, -S n something measuring given amount of inches

INCHES ▶ inch

INCHING ▶ inch

INCHMEAL adv gradually

INCHOATE adj just begun and not yet properly developed ▷ vb begin

INCHPIN, -S n cervine sweetbread

INCHTAPE n measuring tape marked out in inches

INCHWORM n larva of a type of moth

INCIDENT n something that happens ▷ adj related (to) or dependent (on)

INCIPIT, -S n Latin introductory phrase

INCISAL adj relating to the cutting edge of incisors and cuspids

INCISE, -D, -S, INCISING vb cut into with a sharp tool

INCISION n cut, esp one made during a surgical operation

INCISIVE adj direct and forceful

INCISOR, -S n front tooth, used for biting into food

INCISORY ▶ incisor

INCISURE n incision or notch in an organ or part

INCITANT n something that incites

INCITE, -D, -S, INCITING vb stir up, provoke

INCITER, -S ▶ incite

INCITES ▶ incite

INCITING ▶ incite

INCIVIL archaic form of ▶ uncivil

INCIVISM n neglect of a citizen's duties

INCLASP, -S vb clasp

INCLE, -S same as ▶ inkle

INCLINE, -S vb lean, slope ▷ n slope

INCLINED adj having a disposition

INCLINER ▶ incline

INCLINES ▶ incline

INCLIP, -S vb embrace

INCLOSE, -D, -S less common spelling of ▶ enclose

INCLOSER ▶ inclose

INCLOSES ▶ inclose

INCLUDE, -S vb have as part of the whole

INCLUDED adj (of the stamens or pistils of a flower) not protruding beyond the corolla

INCLUDES ▶ include

INCOG, -S n incognito

INCOME, -S n amount of money earned

INCOMER, -S n person who comes to a place in which they were not born

INCOMES ▶ income

INCOMING adj coming in ▷ n act of coming in

INCONIE adj fine or delicate

INCONNU, -S n whitefish of Arctic waters

INCONNUE n unknown woman

INCONNUS ▶ inconnu

INCONY adj fine or delicate

INCORPSE vb incorporate

INCREASE vb make or become greater in size, number, etc ▷ n rise in number, size, etc

INCREATE adj (esp of gods) never having been created

INCROSS n variation produced by inbreeding ▷ vb produce by inbreeding

INCRUST, -S same as ▶ encrust

INCUBATE vb (of a bird) hatch (eggs) by sitting on them

INCUBI ▶ incubus

INCUBOUS adj having overlapping leaves

INCUBUS, INCUBI n (in folklore) type of demon

INCUDAL ▶ incus

INCUDATE ▶ incus

INCUDES ▶ incus

INCULT adj (of land) uncultivated

INCUMBER less common spelling of ▶ encumber

INCUR, -RED, -S vb cause (something unpleasant) to happen

INCURVE, -D, -S vb curve or cause to curve inwards

INCUS, INCUDES n bone in the ear of mammals

INCUSE, -D, -S, INCUSING n design stamped or hammered onto a coin ▷ vb impress (a design) in a coin ▷ adj stamped or hammered onto a coin

INCUT, -S adj cut or etched in ▷ n indent in rock used as a foothold

INDABA, -S n (among South Africans) a meeting to discuss a serious topic

INDAGATE vb investigate

INDAMIN, -S same as ▶ indamine

INDAMINE n organic base used in the production of the dye safranine

INDAMINS ▶ indamin

INDART, -ED, -S vb dart in

INDEBTED adj owing gratitude for help or favours

INDECENT adj morally offensive

INDEED adv really, certainly ▷ interj expression of indignation or surprise

INDEEDY interj indeed

INDENE, -S n colourless liquid hydrocarbon

INDENT, -ED, -S vb make a dent in

INDENTER ▸ indent

INDENTOR ▸ indent

INDENTS ▸ indent

INDEVOUT adj not devout

INDEW, -ED, -ING, -S same as ▸ indue

INDEX, -ED, -ES, -ING n alphabetical list of subjects dealt with in a book ▷ vb provide (a book) with an index

INDEXAL ▸ index

INDEXED ▸ index

INDEXER, -S ▸ index

INDEXES ▸ index

INDEXING ▸ index

INDIA, -S n code word for the letter I

INDICAN, -S n compound secreted in the urine

INDICANT n something that indicates

INDICATE vb be a sign or symptom of

INDICES plural of ▸ index

INDICIA ▸ indicium

INDICIAL ▸ indicium

INDICIUM, INDICIA n notice

INDICT, -ED, -S vb formally charge with a crime

INDICTEE ▸ indict

INDICTER ▸ indict

INDICTOR ▸ indict

INDICTS ▸ indict

INDIE, -S adj (of rock music) released by an independent record label ▷ n independent record company

INDIGEN, -S same as ▸ indigene

INDIGENE n indigenous person, animal, or thing

INDIGENS ▸ indigen

INDIGENT adj extremely poor ▷ n impoverished person

INDIGEST n undigested mass ▷ vb suffer indigestion

INDIGN adj undeserving

INDIGNLY ▸ indign

INDIGO, -ES, -S adj deep violet-blue ▷ n dye of this colour

INDIGOID adj of, concerned with, or resembling indigo or its blue colour ▷ n any of a number of synthetic dyes or pigments related in chemical structure to indigo

INDIGOS ▸ indigo

INDIRECT adj done or caused by someone or something else

INDITE, -D, -S, INDITING vb write

INDITER, -S ▸ indite

INDITES ▸ indite

INDITING ▸ indite

INDIUM, -S n soft silvery-white metallic element

INDOCILE adj difficult to discipline or instruct

INDOL, -S same as ▸ indole

INDOLE, -S n crystalline heterocyclic compound

INDOLENT adj lazy

INDOLES ▸ indole

INDOLS ▸ indol

INDOOR adj inside a building

INDOORS adv inside or into a building

INDORSE, -D, -S variant spelling of ▸ endorse

INDORSEE n the person to whom a note or bill is indorsed

INDORSER ▸ indorse

INDORSES ▸ indorse

INDORSOR ▸ indorse

INDOW, -ED, -ING, -S archaic variant of ▸ endow

INDOXYL, -S n water-soluble crystalline compound

INDRAFT, -S same as > indraught

INDRAWN adj drawn or pulled in

INDRENCH vb submerge

INDRI same as ▸ indris

INDRIS, -ES n large lemuroid primate

INDUCE, -D, -S, INDUCING vb persuade or influence

INDUCER, -S ▸ induce

INDUCES ▸ induce

INDUCIAE n time limit for a defendant to appear in court

INDUCING ▸ induce

INDUCT, -ED, -S vb formally install (someone) in office

INDUCTEE n military conscript

INDUCTOR n device designed to create inductance in an electrical circuit

INDUCTS ▸ induct

INDUE, -D, -S, INDUING variant spelling of ▸ endue

INDULGE, -D, -S vb allow oneself pleasure

INDULGER ▸ indulge

INDULGES ▸ indulge

INDULIN, -S same as ▸ induline

INDULINE n any of a class of blue dyes obtained from aniline and aminoazobenzene

INDULINS ▸ indulin

INDULT, -S n type of faculty granted by the Holy See

INDUNA, -S n (in South Africa) a Black African overseer

INDURATE vb make or become hard or callous ▷ adj hardened, callous, or unfeeling

INDUSIA ▸ indusium

INDUSIAL ▸ indusium

INDUSIUM, INDUSIA n outgrowth on the undersurface of fern leaves

INDUSTRY n manufacture of goods

INDUVIAE pl n withered leaves

INDUVIAL ▸ induviae

INDWELL, -S, INDWELT vb (of a spirit, principle, etc) to inhabit

INDYREF, -S n independence referendum

INEARTH, -S poetic word for ▸ bury

INEDIBLE adj not fit to be eaten

INEDIBLY ▸ inedible

INEDITA pl n unpublished writings

INEDITED adj not edited

INEPT, -ER, -EST adj clumsy, lacking skill

INEPTLY ▸ inept

INEQUITY n injustice or unfairness

INERM adj without thorns

INERMOUS same as ▸ inerm

INERRANT same as > inerrable

INERT, -ER, -EST, -S n inert thing ▷ adj without the power of motion or resistance

INERTIA, -E, -S n feeling of unwillingness to do anything

This is not the easiest of words to see in play, but its combination of common letters makes it one of the most frequently played 7-letter bonuses, while its plurals, which can be **inertiae** or **inertias**, are among the 8-letter bonus words that come up most often.

INERTIAL ▸ inertia

INERTIAS ▸ inertia

INERTLY ▸ inert

INERTS ▸ inert

INESSIVE n grammatical case in Finnish

INEXACT adj not exact or accurate

INEXPERT n unskilled person ▷ adj lacking skill

INFALL, -S vb move towards (something) under the influence of gravity

INFAME, -D, -S, INFAMING vb defame

INFAMIES ▸ infamy

INFAMING ▸ infame

INFAMISE same as ▸ infamize

INFAMIZE vb make infamous

INFAMOUS adj well-known for something bad

INFAMY, INFAMIES n state of being infamous

INFANCY n early childhood

INFANT, -S n very young child ▷ adj of, relating to, or designed for young children

INFANTA, -S n (formerly) daughter of a king of Spain or Portugal

INFANTE, -S n (formerly) any son of a king of Spain or Portugal, except the heir to the throne

INFANTRY n soldiers who fight on foot

INFANTS ▸ infant

INFARCT, -S n localized area of dead tissue ▷ vb obstruct the blood supply to part of a body

INFARE, -S vb enter

INFAUNA, -E, -S n fauna that lives in ocean and river beds

INFAUNAL ▸ infauna

INFAUNAS ▸ infauna

INFAUST adj unlucky

INFECT, -ED, -S vb affect with a disease ▷ adj contaminated or polluted with or as if with a disease

INFECTER ▸ infect

INFECTOR ▸ infect

INFECTS ▸ infect

INFECUND less common word for ▸ infertile

INFEED, -S n action of supplying a machine with a material

INFEFT, -ED, -S vb give possession of heritable property

INFELT adj heartfelt

INFEOFF, -S same as ▸ enfeoff

INFER, -RED, -S vb work out from evidence

INFERE adv together

INFERIAE pl n offerings made to the spirits of the dead

INFERIOR adj lower in quality, position, or status ▷ n person of lower position or status

INFERNAL adj of hell

INFERNO, -S n intense raging fire

INFERRED ▸ infer

INFERRER ▸ infer

INFERS ▸ infer

INFEST, -ED, -S vb inhabit or overrun in unpleasantly large numbers

INFESTER ▸ infest

INFESTS ▸ infest

INFICETE adj not witty

INFIDEL, -S n person with no religion ▷ adj of unbelievers or unbelief

INFIELD, -S n area of the field near the pitch

INFIGHT, -S, INFOUGHT vb box at close quarters

INFILL, -ED, -S vb fill in ▷ n act of filling or closing gaps in something

INFIMUM, INFIMA, -S n greatest lower bound

INFINITE adj without any limit or end ▷ n something without any limit or end

INFINITY n endless space, time, or number

INFIRM, -ED, -ER, -S vb make infirm ▷ adj physically or mentally weak

INFIRMLY ▸ infirm

INFIRMS ▸ infirm

INFIX, -ED, -ES, -ING vb fix firmly in ▷ n affix inserted into the middle of a word

INFIXION ▸ infix

INFLAME, -D, -S vb make angry or excited

INFLAMER ▸ inflame

INFLAMES ▸ inflame

INFLATE, -D, -S vb expand by filling with air or gas

INFLATER ▸ inflate

INFLATES ▸ inflate

INFLATOR ▸ inflate

INFLATUS n act of breathing in

INFLECT, -S vb change (the voice) in tone or pitch

INFLEXED adj curved or bent inwards and downwards towards the axis

INFLICT, -S vb impose (something unpleasant) on

INFLIGHT adj provided during flight in an aircraft

INFLOW, -S n something, such as liquid or gas, that flows in ▷ vb flow in

INFLUENT adj flowing in ▷ n something flowing in, esp a tributary

INFLUX, -ES n arrival or entry of many people or things

INFO, -S n information

INFOBAHN same as ▸ internet

INFOLD, -ED, -S variant spelling of ▸ enfold

INFOLDER ▸ infold

INFOLDS ▸ infold

INFORCE, -D, -S same as ▸ enforce

INFORM, -ED, -S vb tell ▷ adj without shape

INFORMAL adj relaxed and friendly

INFORMED ▸ inform

INFORMER n person who informs to the police

INFORMS ▸ inform

INFOS ▸ info

INFOTECH n information technology

INFOUGHT ▸ infight

INFRA adv (esp in textual annotation) below

INFRACT, -S vb violate or break (a law, an agreement, etc)

INFRARED adj of or using rays below the red end of the visible spectrum ▷ n infrared part of the spectrum

INFRINGE vb break (a law or agreement)

INFRUGAL adj wasteful

INFULA same as ▸ infulae

INFULAE pl n two ribbons hanging from a bishop's mitre

INFUSE, -D, -S, INFUSING vb fill (with an emotion or quality)

INFUSER, -S n any device used to make an infusion

INFUSES ▸ infuse

INFUSING ▸ infuse

INFUSION n infusing

INFUSIVE ▸ infusion

INFUSORY adj containing infusoria ▷ n infusorian, a tiny water-dwelling mammal

ING, -S n meadow near a river

INGAN, -S Scots word for ▸ onion

INGATE, -S n entrance

INGATHER vb gather together or in (a harvest)

INGENER, -S Shakespearean form of ▸ **engineer**

INGENIUM n genius

INGENU, -S n artless or inexperienced boy or young man

INGENUE, -S n inexperienced girl or young woman

INGENUS ▸ **ingenu**

INGEST, -ED, -S vb take (food or liquid) into the body

INGESTA pl n nourishment taken through the mouth

INGESTED ▸ **ingest**

INGESTS ▸ **ingest**

INGINE, -S n genius

INGLE, -S n fire in a room or a fireplace

INGLOBE, -D, -S vb shape as a sphere

INGO, -ES n revelation

INGOING, -S same as ▸ **ingo**

INGOT, -ED, -ING, -S n oblong block of cast metal ▹ vb shape (metal) into ingots

INGRAFT, -S variant spelling of ▸ **engraft**

INGRAIN, -S vb impress deeply on the mind or nature ▹ adj (of carpets) made of fibre that is dyed before being spun ▹ n carpet made from ingrained yarn

INGRAM, -S adj ignorant ▹ n ignorant person

INGRATE, -S n ungrateful person ▹ adj ungrateful

INGRESS n entrance

INGROOVE vb cut a groove into

INGROSS archaic form of ▸ **engross**

INGROUND adj sunk into ground ▹ vb fix (something) in the ground or in a foundation

INGROUP, -S n highly cohesive and relatively closed social group

INGROWN adj grown abnormally into the flesh

INGROWTH n act of growing inwards

INGRUM, -S adj ignorant ▹ n ignorant person

INGS ▸ **ing**

INGUINAL adj of or relating to the groin

INGULF, -ED, -S variant spelling of ▸ **engulf**

INGULPH, -S archaic form of ▸ **engulf**

INHABIT, -S vb live in

INHALANT n medical preparation inhaled to help breathing problems ▹ adj inhaled for its soothing or therapeutic effect

INHALE, -D, -S, INHALING vb breathe in (air, smoke, etc)

INHALER, -S n container for an inhalant

INHALES ▸ **inhale**

INHALING ▸ **inhale**

INHAUL, -S n line for hauling in a sail

INHAULER same as ▸ **inhaul**

INHAULS ▸ **inhaul**

INHAUST, -S vb drink in

INHEARSE vb bury

INHERCE, -D, -S same as ▸ **inhearse**

INHERE, -D, -S, INHERING vb be an inseparable part (of)

INHERENT adj existing as an inseparable part

INHERES ▸ **inhere**

INHERING ▸ **inhere**

INHERIT, -S vb receive (money etc) from someone who has died

INHESION less common word for ▸ **inherence**

INHIBIN, -S n peptide hormone

INHIBIT, -S vb restrain (an impulse or desire)

INHOLDER n inhabitant

INHOOP, -ED, -S vb confine

INHUMAN adj cruel or brutal

INHUMANE adj not humane

INHUMATE vb bury

INHUME, -D, -S, INHUMING vb inter

INHUMER, -S ▸ **inhume**

INHUMES ▸ **inhume**

INHUMING ▸ **inhume**

INIA ▸ **inion**

INIMICAL adj unfavourable or hostile

INION, INIA, -S n most prominent point at the back of the head

INIQUITY n injustice or wickedness

INISLE, -D, -S, INISLING vb put on or make into an island

INITIAL, -S adj first, at the beginning ▹ n first letter, esp a person's name ▹ vb sign with one's initials

INITIATE vb begin or set going ▹ n recently initiated person ▹ adj initiated

INJECT, -ED, -S vb put (a fluid) into the body with a syringe

INJECTOR ▸ **inject**

INJECTS ▸ **inject**

INJELLY vb place in jelly

INJERA, -S n white Ethiopian flatbread, similar to a crepe

INJOINT, -S vb join

INJUNCT, -S vb issue a legal injunction against (a person)

INJURE, -D, -S, INJURING vb hurt physically or mentally

INJURER, -S ▸ **injure**

INJURES ▸ **injure**

INJURIES ▸ **injury**

INJURING ▸ **injure**

INJURY, INJURIES n physical hurt

INK, -ED, -ING, -S n coloured liquid used for writing or printing ▹ vb mark in ink (something already marked in pencil)

INKBERRY n North American holly tree

INKBLOT, -S n abstract patch of ink

INKED ▸ **ink**

INKER, -S ▸ **ink**

INKHORN, -S n (formerly) a small portable container for ink

INKHOSI, AMAKHOSI, AMAKOSI, -S n Zulu clan chief

INKIER ▸ **inky**

INKIEST ▸ **inky**

INKINESS ▸ **inky**

INKING ▸ **ink**

INKJET, -S adj of a method of printing ▹ n inkjet printer

INKLE, -D, -S n kind of linen tape used for trimmings ▹ vb hint

INKLESS ▸ **ink**

INKLIKE ▸ **ink**

INKLING, -S n slight idea or suspicion

INKOSI, -S same as ▸ **inkhosi**

INKPAD, -S n pad used for rubber-stamping or fingerprinting

INKPOT, -S n ink-bottle

INKS ▸ **ink**

INKSPOT, -S n ink stain

INKSTAIN n stain made by ink

INKSTAND n stand or tray for holding writing tools and containers for ink

INKSTONE n stone used in making ink

INKWELL, -S n small container for ink

INKWOOD, -S n type of tree

INKY, INKIER, INKIEST adj dark or black

INLACE, -D, -S, INLACING variant spelling of ▸ **enlace**

INLAID ▸ **inlay**

INLAND, -S adv in or towards the interior of a country ▷ adj of or in the interior of a country or region ▷ n interior of a country or region

INLANDER ▸ **inland**

INLANDS ▸ **inland**

INLAY, INLAID, -ING, -S n inlaid substance or pattern ▷ vb decorate by inserting wooden pieces

INLAYER, -S ▸ **inlay**

INLAYING ▸ **inlay**

INLAYS ▸ **inlay**

INLET, -S n water extending from the sea into the land ▷ vb insert or inlay

INLIER, -S n outcrop of rocks surrounded by younger rocks

INLOCK, -ED, -S vb lock up

INLY adv inwardly

INLYING adj situated within or inside

INMATE, -S n person living in an institution such as a prison

INMESH, -ED, -ES variant spelling of ▸ **enmesh**

INMOST adj innermost

INN, -S n pub or small hotel, esp in the country ▷ vb stay at an inn

INNAGE, -S n type of measurement

INNARDS pl n internal organs

INNATE adj being part of someone's nature, inborn

INNATELY ▸ **innate**

INNATIVE adj native

INNED ▸ **in**

INNER, -S adj happening or located inside ▷ n red innermost ring on a target

INNERLY ▸ **inner**

INNERS ▸ **inner**

INNERVE, -D, -S vb supply with nervous energy

INNING, -S n division of baseball match

INNIT interj isn't it

INNLESS adj without inns

INNOCENT adj not guilty of a crime ▷ n innocent person, esp a child

INNOVATE vb introduce new ideas or methods

INNS ▸ **inn**

INNUENDO n indirect reference to something rude or unpleasant

INNYARD, -S n courtyard of an inn

INOCULUM, INOCULA n substance used in giving an inoculation

INORB, -ED, -ING, -S vb enclose in or as if in an orb

INORNATE adj simple

INOSINE, -S n type of molecule making up cell

INOSITE, -S same as ▸ **inositol**

INOSITOL n cyclic alcohol

INOTROPE n drug for controlling muscular contractions

INPHASE adj in the same phase

INPOUR, -ED, -S vb pour in

INPUT, -S, -TED n resources put into a project etc ▷ vb enter (data) in a computer

INPUTTER ▸ **input**

INQILAB, -S n (in India, Pakistan, etc) revolution

INQUERE, -D, -S Spenserian form of ▸ **inquire**

INQUEST, -S n official inquiry into a sudden death

INQUIET, -S vb disturb

INQUIRE, -D, -S vb seek information or ask (about)

INQUIRER ▸ **inquire**

INQUIRES ▸ **inquire**

INQUIRY n question

INRO n Japanese seal-box

INROAD, -S n invasion or hostile attack

INRUN, -S n slope down which ski jumpers ski

INRUSH, -ES n sudden and overwhelming inward flow

INS ▸ **in**

INSANE, -R, -ST adj severely mentally ill

INSANELY ▸ **insane**

INSANER ▸ **insane**

INSANEST ▸ **insane**

INSANIE, -S n insanity

INSANITY n state of being insane

INSCAPE, -S n essential inner nature of a person, etc

INSCIENT adj ignorant

INSCONCE vb fortify

INSCRIBE vb write or carve words on

INSCROLL vb write on a scroll

INSCULP, -S vb engrave

INSCULPT adj engraved

INSEAM, -ED, -S vb contain

INSECT, -S n small animal with six legs

INSECTAN ▸ **insect**

INSECTS ▸ **insect**

INSECURE adj anxious, not confident

INSEEM, -ED, -S vb cover with grease

INSERT, -S vb put inside or include ▷ n something inserted

INSERTED adj (of a muscle) attached to the bone that it moves

INSERTER ▸ **insert**

INSERTS ▸ **insert**

INSET, -S, -TED n small picture inserted within a larger one ▷ vb place in or within ▷ adj decorated with something inserted

INSETTER ▸ **inset**

INSHEATH vb sheathe

INSHELL, -S vb retreat, as into a shell

INSHIP, -S vb travel or send by ship

INSHORE adj close to the shore ▷ adv towards the shore

INSHRINE variant spelling of ▸ **enshrine**

INSIDE, -S prep in or to the interior of ▷ adj on or of the inside ▷ adv on, in, or to the inside, indoors ▷ n inner side, surface, or part

INSIDER, -S n someone who has privileged knowledge

INSIDES ▸ **inside**

INSIGHT, -S n deep understanding

INSIGNE same as ▸ **insignia**

INSIGNIA n badge or emblem of honour or office

INSINEW, -S vb connect or strengthen, as with sinews

INSIPID adj lacking interest, spirit, or flavour

INSIST, -ED, -S vb demand or state firmly

INSISTER ▸ **insist**

INSISTS ▸ **insist**

INSNARE, -D, -S less common spelling of ▸ **ensnare**

INSNARER ▸ **insnare**

INSNARES ▸ **insnare**

INSOFAR adv to the extent

INSOLATE vb expose to sunlight, as for bleaching

INSOLE, -S n inner sole of a shoe or boot

INSOLENT n insolent person ▷ adj rude and disrespectful

INSOLES ▸ **insole**

INSOMNIA n inability to sleep

INSOMUCH adv such an extent

INSOOTH adv indeed

INSOUL, -ED, -S variant of ▸ **ensoul**

INSOURCE vb subcontract work to a company under the same general ownership

INSPAN, -S vb harness (animals) to (a vehicle)

INSPECT, -S vb check closely or officially

INSPHERE variant spelling of ▸ **ensphere**

INSPIRE, -S vb fill with enthusiasm, stimulate

INSPIRED adj brilliantly creative

INSPIRER ▸ **inspire**

INSPIRES ▸ **inspire**

INSPIRIT vb fill with vigour

INSPO, -S n source of inspiration

INSTABLE less common word for ▸ **unstable**

INSTAL, -S same as ▸ **install**

INSTALL, -S vb put in and prepare (equipment) for use

INSTALS ▸ **instal**

INSTANCE n particular example ▷ vb mention as an example

INSTANCY n quality of being urgent or imminent

INSTANT, -S n very brief time ▷ adj happening at once

INSTAR, -S vb decorate with stars ▷ n stage in the development of an insect

INSTATE, -D, -S vb place in a position or office

INSTEAD adv as a replacement or substitute

INSTEP, -S n part of the foot

INSTIL, -S vb introduce (an idea etc) gradually into someone's mind

INSTILL, -S same as ▸ **instil**

INSTILS ▸ **instil**

INSTINCT n inborn tendency to behave in a certain way ▷ adj animated or impelled (by)

INSTRESS vb create or sustain

INSTROKE n inward stroke

INSTRUCT vb order to do something

INSUCKEN adj of a sucken

INSULA, -E n pyramid-shaped area of the brain

INSULANT n insulation

INSULAR, -S adj not open to new ideas, narrow-minded ▷ n islander

INSULATE vb reduce the transfer of electricity, heat, or sound by lining with nonconducting material

INSULIN, -S n hormone produced in the pancreas

INSULSE adj stupid

INSULT, -ED, -S vb behave rudely to, offend ▷ n insulting remark or action

INSULTER ▸ **insult**

INSULTS ▸ **insult**

INSURANT n holder of an insurance policy

INSURE, -S, INSURING vb protect by insurance

INSURED, -S adj covered by insurance ▷ n those covered by an insurance policy

INSURER, -S n person or company that sells insurance

INSURES ▸ **insure**

INSURING ▸ **insure**

INSWATHE vb bind or wrap

INSWEPT adj narrowed towards the front

INSWING, -S n type of movement of a bowled cricket ball

INTACT adj not changed or damaged in any way

INTACTLY ▸ **intact**

INTAGLIO, INTAGLI n (gem carved with) an engraved design

INTAKE, -S n amount or number taken in

INTARSIA n mosaic of inlaid wood

INTEGER, -S n positive or negative whole number or zero

INTEGRAL adj being an essential part of a whole ▷ n sum of a large number of very small quantities

INTEGRIN n protein that acts as a signal receptor between cells

INTEL, -S n US military intelligence

INTEND, -S vb propose or plan (to do something)

INTENDED adj planned or future ▷ n person whom one is to marry

INTENDER ▸ **intend**

INTENDS ▸ **intend**

INTENSE, -R adj of great strength or degree

INTENT, -S n intention ▷ adj paying close attention

INTENTLY ▸ **intent**

INTENTS ▸ **intent**

INTER, -RED, -S vb bury (a dead body)

INTERACT vb act on or in close relation with each other

INTERAGE adj between different ages

INTERBED vb lie between strata of different minerals

INTERCOM n internal communication system with loudspeakers

INTERCUT another word for ▸ **crosscut**

INTERESS vb interest

INTEREST n desire to know or hear more about something ▷ vb arouse the interest of

INTERIM, -S adj temporary, provisional, or intervening ▷ n intervening time ▷ adv meantime

INTERIOR n inside ▷ adj inside, inner

INTERLAP less common word for ▸ **overlap**

INTERLAY vb insert (layers) between ▷ n material, such as paper, placed between a printing plate and its base

INTERMAT n patch of seabed devoid of vegetation

INTERMIT vb suspend (activity) or (of activity) to be suspended temporarily or at intervals

INTERMIX vb mix together

INTERN, -ED, -S vb imprison, esp during a war ▷ n trainee doctor in a hospital

INTERNAL adj of or on the inside ▷ n medical examination of the inside of the body

INTERNE, -S same as ▸ **intern**

INTERNED ▸ **intern**

INTERNEE n person who is interned

INTERNES ▸ **interne**

INTERNET n worldwide computer network

INTERNS ▸ **intern**

INTERRED ▸ **inter**

INTERREX n person who governs during an interregnum

INTERROW adj occurring between rows

INTERS ▸ **inter**

INTERSEX n person with characteristics that are not uniquely male or female

INTERTIE n short roofing timber

INTERVAL n time between two particular moments or events

INTERWAR adj of or happening in the period between World War I and World War II

INTERWEB same as
▶ **internet**
INTHRAL, -S archaic form of
▶ **enthral**
INTHRALL archaic form of
▶ **enthral**
INTHRALS ▶ **inthral**
INTHRONE archaic form of
▶ **enthrone**
INTI, -S n former monetary
unit of Peru
INTIFADA n Palestinian
uprising against Israel in the
West Bank and Gaza Strip
INTIL Scot form of ▶ **into**
INTIMA, -E, -S n innermost
layer of an organ or part
INTIMACY n close or warm
friendship
INTIMAE ▶ **intima**
INTIMAL ▶ **intima**
INTIMAS ▶ **intima**
INTIMATE adj having a close
personal relationship ▷ n
close friend ▷ vb hint at or
suggest
INTIME adj intimate
INTIMISM n school of
impressionist painting
INTIMIST ▶ **intimism**
INTIMITY n intimacy
INTINE, -S n inner wall of a
pollen grain or a spore
INTIRE archaic form of
▶ **entire**
INTIS ▶ **inti**
INTITLE, -D, -S archaic form of
▶ **entitle**
INTITULE vb (in Britain) to
entitle (an act of parliament)
INTO prep indicating motion
towards the centre, result of
a change, etc
INTOED adj having
inward-turning toes
INTOMB, -ED, -S same as
▶ **entomb**
INTONACO n wet plaster
surface on which frescoes
are painted
INTONATE vb pronounce
with a rise and fall of the
voice
INTONE, -D, -S, INTONING
vb speak or recite in an
unvarying tone of voice
INTONER, -S ▶ **intone**
INTONES ▶ **intone**
INTONING ▶ **intone**
INTORT, -ED, -S vb twist
inward
INTOWN adj infield
INTRA prep within
INTRADA, -S n prelude
INTRADAY adj occurring
within one day

INTRADOS n inner curve or
surface of an arch or vault
INTRANET n internal
network that makes use of
internet technology
INTRANT, -S n one who
enters
INTREAT, -S archaic spelling of
▶ **entreat**
INTRENCH less common
spelling of ▶ **entrench**
INTREPID adj fearless, bold
INTRIGUE vb make
interested or curious ▷ n
secret plotting
INTRINCE adj intricate
INTRO, -S n introduction
INTROFY vb increase the
wetting properties
INTROIT, -S n short prayer
said or sung
INTROLD variant of ▶ **entrold**
INTROMIT vb enter or insert
or allow to enter or be
inserted
INTRON, -S n stretch of DNA
INTRONIC adj of or like an
intron
INTRONS ▶ **intron**
INTRORSE adj turned
inwards or towards the axis
INTROS ▶ **intro**
INTRUDE, -D, -S vb come in
or join in without being
invited
INTRUDER n person who
enters a place without
permission
INTRUDES ▶ **intrude**
INTRUST, -S same as
▶ **entrust**
INTUBATE vb insert a tube
or cannula into (a hollow
organ)
INTUIT, -ED, -S vb know or
discover by intuition
INTURN, -S n inward turn
INTURNED adj turned
inward
INTURNS ▶ **inturn**
INTUSE, -S n contusion
INTWINE, -D, -S less common
spelling of ▶ **entwine**
INTWIST, -S vb twist
together
INUKSHUK n stone used by
Inuit people to mark a
location
INUKSUK, INUKSUIT, -S
same as ▶ **inukshuk**
INULA, -S n plant of the
elecampane genus
INULASE, -S n enzyme
INULIN, -S n fructose
polysaccharide
INUNDANT ▶ **inundate**

INUNDATE vb flood
INURBANE adj not urbane
INURE, -D, -S, INURING vb
cause to accept or become
hardened to
INURN, -ED, -ING, -S vb
place (esp cremated ashes)
in an urn
INUST adj burnt in
INUSTION ▶ **inust**
INUTILE adj useless
INVADE, -D, -S, INVADING
vb enter (a country) by
military force
INVADER, -S ▶ **invade**
INVADES ▶ **invade**
INVADING ▶ **invade**
INVALID, -S n injured or
chronically ill person ▷ vb
dismiss from active service
because of illness or injury
▷ adj having no legal force
INVAR, -S n alloy made from
iron and nickel
INVASION n invading
INVASIVE adj of or relating
to an invasion, intrusion, etc
INVEAGLE archaic form of
▶ **inveigle**
INVECKED same as
▶ **invected**
INVECTED adj bordered with
small convex curves
INVEIGH, -S vb criticize
strongly
INVEIGLE vb coax by
cunning or trickery
INVENIT sentence substitute
(he or she) designed it
INVENT, -ED, -S vb think up
or create (something new)
INVENTER same as
▶ **inventor**
INVENTOR n person who
invents, esp as a profession
INVENTS ▶ **invent**
INVERITY n untruth
INVERSE, -D, -S vb make
something opposite or
contrary in effect ▷ adj
reversed in effect, sequence,
direction, etc ▷ n exact
opposite
INVERT, -ED, -S vb turn
upside down or inside out
INVERTER n any device for
converting a direct current
into an alternating current
INVERTIN same as
> **invertase**
INVERTOR same as
▶ **inverter**
INVERTS ▶ **invert**
INVEST, -ED, -S vb spend
(money, time, etc) with the
expectation of profit

INVESTOR ▶ invest
INVESTS ▶ invest
INVEXED adj concave
INVIABLE adj not viable, esp financially
INVIABLY ▶ inviable
INVIOUS adj without paths or roads
INVIRILE adj unmanly
INVISCID adj not viscid
INVITAL adj not vital
INVITE, -D, -S vb request the company of ▷ n invitation
INVITEE, -S n one who is invited
INVITER, -S ▶ invite
INVITES ▶ invite
INVITING adj tempting, attractive ▷ n old word for invitation
INVOCATE archaic word for ▶ invoke
INVOICE, -D, -S n bill for goods or services ▷ vb present (a customer) with an invoice
INVOKE, -D, -S, INVOKING vb put (a law or penalty) into operation
INVOKER, -S ▶ invoke
INVOKES ▶ invoke
INVOKING ▶ invoke
INVOLUTE adj complex, intricate, or involved ▷ n curve described by the free end of a thread as it is wound around another curve ▷ vb become involute
INVOLVE, -D, -S vb include as a necessary part
INVOLVER ▶ involve
INVOLVES ▶ involve
INWALL, -ED, -S vb surround with a wall
INWARD adj directed towards the middle ▷ adv towards the inside or middle ▷ n inward part
INWARDLY adv within the private thoughts or feelings
INWARDS adv towards the inside or middle of something
INWEAVE, -D, -S, INWOVE, INWOVEN vb weave together
INWICK, -ED, -S vb perform a type of curling stroke
INWIND, -S, INWOUND vb wind or coil around
INWIT, -S n conscience
INWITH adv within
INWITS ▶ inwit
INWORK, -ED, -S vb work in
INWORN adj worn in
INWOUND ▶ inwind

INWOVE ▶ inweave
INWOVEN ▶ inweave
INWRAP, -S, -T less common spelling of ▶ enwrap
INYALA, -S n antelope
IO, -S interj exclamation of triumph ▷ n cry of 'io'
IODATE, -D, -S, IODATING same as ▶ iodize
IODATION ▶ iodate
IODIC adj of or containing iodine
IODID, -S same as ▶ iodide
IODIDE, -S n chemical compound
IODIDS ▶ iodid
IODIN, -S same as ▶ iodine
IODINATE vb cause to combine with iodine
IODINE, -S n bluish-black element
IODINS ▶ iodin
IODISE, -D, -S, IODISING same as ▶ iodize
IODISER, -S ▶ iodise
IODISES ▶ iodise
IODISING ▶ iodise
IODISM, -S n poisoning caused by iodine or its compounds
IODIZE, -D, -S, IODIZING vb treat with iodine
IODIZER, -S ▶ iodize
IODIZES ▶ iodize
IODIZING ▶ iodize
IODOFORM n yellow crystalline insoluble volatile solid
IODOPHOR n substance in which iodine is combined with an agent that renders it soluble
IODOPSIN n violet light-sensitive pigment in the retina
IODOUS adj of or containing iodine
IODURET, -S n iodide
IODYRITE n silver iodide
IOLITE, -S n grey or violet-blue dichroic mineral
ION, -S n electrically charged atom
IONIC adj of or in the form of ions
IONICITY n ionic character
IONICS pl n study of ions
IONISE, -D, -S, IONISING same as ▶ ionize
IONISER, -S same as ▶ ionizer
IONISES ▶ ionise
IONISING ▶ ionise
IONIUM, -S n naturally occurring radioisotope of thorium

IONIZE, -D, -S, IONIZING vb change into ions
IONIZER, -S n person or thing that ionizes
IONIZES ▶ ionize
IONIZING ▶ ionize
IONOGEN, -S n compound that exists as ions when dissolved
IONOMER, -S n type of thermoplastic
IONONE, -S n yellowish liquid mixture
IONS ▶ ion
IOPANOIC adj as in iopanoic acid type of acid containing iodine
IOS ▶ io
IOTA, -S n ninth letter in the Greek alphabet

This word for a Greek letter is another of those that come in handy when you are trying to rid your rack of too many vowels.

IOTACISM n pronunciation tendency in Modern Greek
IOTAS ▶ iota
IPECAC, -S n type of S American shrub
IPOMOEA, -S n convolvulaceous plant
IPPON, -S n winning point awarded in a judo or karate competition
IRACUND adj easily angered
IRADE, -S n written edict of a Muslim ruler
IRATE, -R, -ST adj very angry
IRATELY ▶ irate
IRATER ▶ irate
IRATEST ▶ irate
IRE, -D, -S, IRING vb anger ▷ n anger
IREFUL ▶ ire
IREFULLY ▶ ire
IRELESS ▶ ire
IRENIC adj tending to conciliate or promote peace
IRENICAL same as ▶ irenic
IRENICON variant spelling of > eirenicon
IRENICS n branch of theology
IRES ▶ ire
IRID, -S n type of iris
IRIDAL ▶ irid
IRIDEAL ▶ irid
IRIDES ▶ iris
IRIDIAL ▶ irid
IRIDIAN ▶ irid
IRIDIC adj of or containing iridium

IRIDISE, -D, -S *vb* make iridescent

IRIDIUM, -S *n* very hard corrosion-resistant metal

IRIDIZE, -D, -S *vb* make iridescent

IRIDS ▸ irid

IRING ▸ ire

IRIS, IRIDES, -ED, -ES, -ING *n* part of the eye ▷ *vb* display iridescence

IRISATE, -D, -S *vb* make iridescent

IRISCOPE *n* instrument that displays the prismatic colours

IRISED ▸ iris

IRISES ▸ iris

IRISING ▸ iris

IRITIC ▸ iritis

IRITIS, -ES *n* inflammation of the iris of the eye

Since a plague of Is tends to afflict every Scrabble player's rack at regular intervals, it is well worth knowing words like this one, which use several of the wretched letter!

IRK, -ED, -ING, -S *vb* irritate, annoy

IRKSOME *adj* irritating, annoying

IROKO, -S *n* tropical African hardwood tree

IRON, -ED, -S *n* strong silvery-white metallic element ▷ *adj* made of iron ▷ *vb* smooth (clothes or fabric) with an iron

IRONBARK *n* Australian eucalyptus with hard rough bark

IRONCLAD *adj* covered or protected with iron ▷ *n* large wooden 19th-century warship with armoured plating

IRONE, -S *n* fragrant liquid

You may surprise your opponent by adding an E to **iron** if you know this word for a kind of aromatic oil.

IRONED ▸ iron

IRONER, -S ▸ iron

IRONES ▸ irone

IRONIC *adj* using irony

IRONICAL *same as* ▸ ironic

IRONIER ▸ irony

IRONIES ▸ irony

IRONIEST ▸ irony

IRONING, -S *n* clothes to be ironed

IRONISE, -D, -S *same as* ▸ ironize

IRONIST, -S ▸ ironize

IRONIZE, -D, -S *vb* use or indulge in irony

IRONLESS ▸ iron

IRONLIKE ▸ iron

IRONMAN, IRONMEN *n* very strong man

IRONNESS ▸ iron

IRONS ▸ iron

IRONSIDE *n* person with great stamina or resistance

IRONWARE *n* domestic articles made of iron

IRONWEED *n* plant with purplish leaves

IRONWOOD *n* any of various trees, such as hornbeam, with exceptionally hard wood

IRONWORK *n* work done in iron, esp decorative work

IRONY, IRONIER, IRONIES, IRONIEST *n* grammatical device ▷ *adj* of, resembling, or containing iron

IRREAL *adj* unreal

IRRIGATE *vb* supply (land) with water by artificial channels or pipes

IRRISION *n* mockery

IRRISORY *adj* mocking

IRRITANT *adj* causing irritation ▷ *n* something that annoys or irritates

IRRITATE *vb* annoy, anger

IRRUPT, -ED, -S *vb* enter forcibly or suddenly

IS *vb* form of the present tense of *be*

ISABEL, -S *n* brown yellow colour

ISABELLA *same as* ▸ isabel

ISABELS ▸ isabel

ISAGOGE, -S *n* academic introduction

ISAGOGIC > isagogics

ISARITHM *n* line on a map connecting places with the same population density

ISATIN, -S *n* yellowish-red crystalline compound

ISATINE, -S *same as* ▸ isatin

ISATINIC ▸ isatin

ISATINS ▸ isatin

ISBA, -S *n* log hut

ISCHEMIA *same as* > ischaemia

ISCHEMIC > ischaemia

ISCHIA ▸ ischium

ISCHIAL ▸ ischium

ISCHIUM, ISCHIA *n* part of the hipbone

ISCHURIA *n* retention of urine

ISH, -ES *n* issue

An **ish** is a word for an issue in Scots law. If you have I, S and H on your rack, remember that as well as adding **ish** to the end of many words, you can also play those letters as a word in its own right.

ISIT *sentence substitute* expression used in response to a statement

ISLAND, -ED, -S *n* piece of land surrounded by water ▷ *vb* cause to become an island

ISLANDER *n* person who lives on an island

ISLANDS ▸ island

ISLE, -D, -S, ISLING *vb* make an isle of ▷ *n* island

ISLELESS *adj* without islands

ISLEMAN, ISLEMEN *n* islander

ISLES ▸ isle

ISLESMAN, ISLESMEN *same as* ▸ isleman

ISLET, -S *n* small island

ISLETED *adj* having islets

ISLETS ▸ islet

ISLING ▸ isle

ISM, -S *n* doctrine, system, or practice

While **ism** can be added to the ends of many words as a suffix, it's worth remembering it as a word in its own right.

ISMATIC *adj* following fashionable doctrines

ISMS ▸ ism

ISNA *vb* is not

ISNAE *same as* ▸ isna

ISO, -S *n* short segment of film that can be replayed easily

ISOAMYL, -S *n* as in **isoamyl acetate** colourless volatile compound

ISOBAR, -S *n* line on a map connecting areas of equal atmospheric pressure

ISOBARE, -S *same as* ▸ isobar

ISOBARIC *adj* having equal atmospheric pressure

ISOBARS ▸ isobar

ISOBASE, -S *n* line connecting points of equal land upheaval

ISOBATH, -S *n* line on a map connecting points of equal depth of water

ISOBRONT *n* line connecting points of simultaneous storm development

ISOBUTYL *n* as in **methyl isobutyl ketone** colourless insoluble liquid ketone used as a solvent for organic compounds
ISOCHASM *n* line connecting points of equal aurorae frequency
ISOCHEIM *n* line on a map connecting places with the same mean winter temperature
ISOCHIME *same as* ▸isocheim
ISOCHOR, -S *n* line on a graph showing variation of a fluid's temperature and pressure
ISOCHORE *same as* ▸isochor
ISOCHORS ▸isochor
ISOCHRON *n* line on an isotope ratio diagram
ISOCLINE *same as* ▸isoclinal
ISOCRACY *n* form of government in which all people have equal powers
ISOCRYME *n* line connecting points of equal winter temperature
ISODICON, ISODICA *n* short anthem
ISODOMON, ISODOMA *n* masonry formed of uniform blocks, with courses are of equal height
ISODOMUM *same as* ▸isodomon
ISODONT, -S *n* animal in which the teeth are of similar size
ISODOSE, -S *n* dose of radiation applied in radiotherapy
ISOETES *n* quillwort
ISOFORM, -S *n* protein similar in function but not form to another
ISOGAMIC ▸isogamy
ISOGAMY *n* fusion of similar gametes
ISOGENIC *same as* ▸isogenous
ISOGENY ▸isogenous
ISOGLOSS *n* line drawn on a linguistic map
ISOGON, -S *n* equiangular polygon
ISOGONAL *same as* ▸isogonic
ISOGONE, -S *same as* ▸isogonic
ISOGONIC *adj* having, making, or involving equal angles ▷ *n* imaginary line

connecting points on the earth's surface having equal magnetic declination
ISOGONS ▸isogon
ISOGONY ▸isogonic
ISOGRAFT *vb* grafting tissue from a donor genetically identical to the recipient
ISOGRAM, -S *same as* ▸isopleth
ISOGRAPH *n* line connecting points of the same linguistic usage
ISOGRIV, -S *n* line on a map connecting points of equal angular bearing
ISOHEL, -S *n* line on a map connecting places with equal sunshine
ISOHYET, -S *n* line on a map connecting places with equal rainfall
ISOKONT, -S *same as* >isokontan
ISOLABLE ▸isolate
ISOLATE, -D, -S *vb* place apart or alone ▷ *n* isolated person or group
ISOLATOR ▸isolate
ISOLEAD, -S *n* line on a ballistic graph
ISOLEX, -ES *n* line on map showing where a particular word is used
ISOLINE, -S *same as* ▸isopleth
ISOLOG > isologous
ISOLOGS > isologous
ISOLOGUE > isologous
ISOMER, -S *n* compound that has the same molecular formula as another
ISOMERE, -S *same as* ▸isomer
ISOMERIC ▸isomer
ISOMERS ▸isomer
ISOMETRY *n* distance-preserving injective map between metric spaces
ISOMORPH *n* substance or organism that exhibits isomorphism
ISONOME, -S *n* line on a map showing equal abundance of a species
ISONOMIC ▸isonomy
ISONOMY *n* equality before the law of the citizens of a state
ISOPACH, -S *n* line on a map connecting places with equal rock thickness
ISOPHONE *n* isogloss marking off an area in which a particular feature of pronunciation is found

ISOPHOTE *n* line on a diagram of a celestial object joining points of equal brightness
ISOPLETH *n* line on a map connecting places with the same amount of some geographical phenomenon
ISOPOD, -S *n* type of crustacean ▷ *adj* of this type of crustacean
ISOPODAN ▸isopod
ISOPODS ▸isopod
ISOPRENE *n* colourless volatile liquid with a penetrating odour
ISOS ▸iso
ISOSPIN, -S *n* number used to classify elementary particles
ISOSPORY *n* condition of having spores of only one kind
ISOSTACY *n* state of balance in earth's crust
ISOSTASY *same as* ▸isostacy
ISOTACH, -S *n* line on a map connecting points of equal wind speed
ISOTHERE *n* line on a map linking places with the same mean summer temperature
ISOTHERM *n* line on a map connecting points of equal temperature
ISOTONE, -S *n* atom with same number of neutrons as another
ISOTONIC *adj* (of two or more muscles) having equal tension
ISOTOPE, -S *n* atom with same atomic number as another
ISOTOPIC ▸isotope
ISOTOPY ▸isotope
ISOTRON, -S *n* device for separating small quantities of isotopes
ISOTROPY > isotropic
ISOTYPE, -S *n* pictorial presentation of statistical information
ISOTYPIC ▸isotype
ISOZYME, -S *n* variant of an enzyme
ISOZYMIC ▸isozyme
ISSEI, -S *n* first-generation Japanese immigrant
ISSUABLE *adj* capable of issuing or being issued
ISSUABLY ▸issuable
ISSUANCE *n* act of issuing
ISSUANT *adj* emerging or issuing

ISSUE, -D, -S, ISSUING n topic of interest or discussion ▷ vb make (a statement etc) publicly

ISSUER, -S ▶ issue

ISSUES ▶ issue

ISSUING ▶ issue

ISTANA, -S n (in Malaysia) a royal palace

ISTHMI ▶ isthmus

ISTHMIAN n inhabitant of an isthmus ▷ adj relating to or situated in an isthmus

ISTHMIC ▶ isthmus

ISTHMOID ▶ isthmus

ISTHMUS, ISTHMI n narrow strip of land connecting two areas of land

ISTLE, -S n fibre obtained from various agave and yucca trees

IT pron refers to a nonhuman, animal, plant, or inanimate object ▷ n player whose turn it is to catch the others in children's games

ITA, -S n type of palm

ITACISM, -S n pronunciation of the Greek letter eta

ITACONIC adj as in itaconic acid white colourless crystalline carboxylic acid

ITALIC, -S adj (of printing type) sloping to the right ▷ n style of printing type

ITAS ▶ ita

ITCH, -ED, -ES n skin irritation causing a desire to scratch ▷ vb have an itch

ITCHIER ▶ itchy

ITCHIEST ▶ itchy

ITCHILY ▶ itch

ITCHING, -S ▶ itch

ITCHWEED n white hellebore

ITCHY, ITCHIER, ITCHIEST ▶ itch

ITEM, -ED, -ING, -S n single thing in a list or collection ▷ adv likewise ▷ vb itemize

ITEMISE, -D, -S same as ▶ itemize

ITEMISER ▶ itemise

ITEMISES ▶ itemise

ITEMIZE, -D, -S vb make a list of

ITEMIZER ▶ itemize

ITEMIZES ▶ itemize

ITEMS ▶ item

ITERANCE ▶ iterate

ITERANT ▶ iterate

ITERATE, -D, -S vb repeat

ITERUM adv again

ITHER Scot word for ▶ other

ITS pron belonging to it ▷ adj of or belonging to it

ITSELF pron reflexive form of it

IURE adv by law

IVIED adj covered with ivy

IVIES ▶ ivy

IVORIED ▶ ivory

IVORIER ▶ ivory

IVORIES pl n keys of a piano

IVORIEST ▶ ivory

IVORIST, -S n worker in ivory

IVORY, IVORIER, IVORIEST n bony substance forming the tusks of elephants ▷ adj yellowish-white

IVRESSE, -S n drunkenness

IVY, IVIES n evergreen climbing plant

IVYLEAF adj as in ivyleaf geranium type of geranium plant

IVYLIKE ▶ ivy

IWI n Māori tribe

This Māori word for a tribe is a great one for getting rid of an awkward combination of letters.

IWIS archaic word for ▶ certainly

IXIA, -S n southern African plant

IXNAY interj nix

IXODID, -S n hard-bodied tick

IXORA, -S n flowering shrub

IXTLE, -S same as ▶ istle

IZAR, -S n long garment worn by Muslim women

IZARD, -S n type of goat-antelope

IZARS ▶ izar

IZVESTIA n news

IZZARD, -S n letter Z

IZZAT, -S n honour or prestige

I

Jj

J, being worth 8 points on its own, is a good tile for scoring well with, especially as it combines well with **Z** to make **jiz** and with **X** to make great words like **jeux**, **jinx** and **jynx**. However, **J** is a difficult letter when it comes to making bonus words scoring that extra 50 points, so you will normally have to play it off fairly quickly. There are two two-letter words that begin with **J**: **ja** and **jo**. As **J** has such a high value, look out for double- and triple-letter squares when playing these. There are plenty of good three-letter words starting with **J**: **jab** (12 points), **jak** (14), **jam** (12), **jar** (10), **jaw** (13), **jay** (13), **jet** (10), **jib** (12), **jig** (11), **job** (12), **jog** (11), **jot** (10), **joy** (13), **jug** (11) and **jut** (10).

JA interj yes ▷ sentence substitute yes

JAB, -BED, -BING, -S vb poke sharply ▷ n quick punch or poke

JABBER, -ED, -S vb talk rapidly or incoherently ▷ n rapid or incoherent talk

JABBERER ▶ jabber

JABBERS ▶ jabber

JABBING ▶ jab

JABBLE, -D, -S, JABBLING vb ripple

JABERS interj Irish exclamation

JABIRU, -S n large white-and-black Australian stork

JABOT, -S n frill or ruffle on the front of a blouse or shirt

JABS ▶ jab

JACAL, -ES, -S n Mexican daub hut

JACAMAR, -S n tropical American bird with an iridescent plumage

JACANA, -S n long-legged long-toed bird

JACARE, -S another name for ▶ cayman

JACCHUS n small monkey

JACENT adj lying

JACINTH, -S another name for ▶ hyacinth

JACINTHE n hyacinth

JACINTHS ▶ jacinth

JACK, -ED n device for raising a motor vehicle or other heavy object ▷ vb lift or push (an object) with a jack

JACKAL, -S n doglike wild animal of Africa and Asia ▷ vb behave like a jackal

JACKAROO same as ▶ jackeroo

JACKASS n fool

JACKBOOT n high military boot ▷ vb oppress

JACKDAW, -S n Eurasian bird of the crow family

JACKED ▶ jack

JACKEEN, -S n slick self-assertive lower-class Dubliner

JACKER, -S n labourer

JACKEROO n young male management trainee on a sheep or cattle station ▷ vb work as a jackeroo

JACKERS ▶ jacker

JACKET, -S n short coat ▷ vb put a jacket on (someone or something)

JACKETED ▶ jacket

JACKETS ▶ jacket

JACKFISH n small pike fish

JACKIES ▶ jacky

JACKING, -S ▶ jack

JACKLEG, -S n unskilled worker

JACKLING n particular way of winning the ball in rugby

JACKMAN, JACKMEN n retainer

JACKPOT, -S n largest prize that may be won in a game ▷ vb accumulate stake money in a prize fund

JACKS n type of game

JACKSTAY n object to which a sail edge is fastened along a yard

JACKY, JACKIES n old slang word for gin

JACOBIN, -S n variety of fancy pigeon

JACOBUS n former English gold coin

JACONET, -S n light cotton fabric

JACQUARD n fabric in which the design is incorporated into the weave

JACULATE vb hurl

JACUZZI, -S n type of bath or pool

JADE, -S, JADING n semiprecious stone ▷ adj bluish-green ▷ vb exhaust or make exhausted from work or use

JADED adj tired and unenthusiastic

JADEDLY ▶ jaded

JADEITE, -S n usually green or white mineral

JADELIKE ▶ jade

JADERY, JADERIES n shrewishness

JADES ▶ jade

JADING ▶ jade

JADISH ▶ jade

JADISHLY ▶ jade

JADITIC ▶ jade

JAEGER, -S n German or Austrian marksman

JAFFA, -S n (in cricket) well-bowled ball

JAG, -GING, -S n period of uncontrolled indulgence in an activity ▷ vb cut unevenly

JAGA, -ED, -ING, -S n guard ▷ vb guard or watch

JAGER, -S same as ▶ jaeger

JAGG, -S same as ▶ jag

JAGGARY same as ▶ jaggery

JAGGED, -ER ►jag

JAGGEDLY ►jag

JAGGER, -S n pedlar

JAGGERY n coarse brown sugar

JAGGHERY same as ►jaggery

JAGGIER ►jaggy

JAGGIES ►jaggy

JAGGIEST ►jaggy

JAGGING ►jag

JAGGS ►jagg

JAGGY, JAGGIER, JAGGIES, JAGGIEST adj prickly ▷ n jagged computer image

JAGHIR, -S n Indian regional governance

JAGHIRE, -S n Indian regional governance

JAGHIRS ►jaghir

JAGIR, -S n Indian regional governance

JAGLESS ►jag

JAGRA, -S n Hindu festival

JAGS ►jag

JAGUAR, -S n large S American spotted cat

JAI interj victory (to)

JAIL, -ED, -ING, -S n prison ▷ vb send to prison

JAILABLE ►jail

JAILBIRD n person who has often been in prison

JAILED ►jail

JAILER, -S n person in charge of a jail

JAILING ►jail

JAILLESS ►jail

JAILOR, -S same as ►jailer

JAILS ►jail

JAK, -S same as ►jack

JAKE, -R, -ST adj slang word meaning all right

JAKES, -ES n toilet; lavatory

JAKEST ►jake

JAKEY, -S n derogatory Scots word for a homeless alcoholic person

JAKFRUIT same as > jackfruit

JAKS ►jak

JALABIB ►jilbab

JALAP, -S n Mexican convolvulaceous plant

JALAPENO n very hot type of green chilli pepper, used esp in Mexican cookery

JALAPIC ►jalap

JALAPIN, -S n purgative resin

JALAPS ►jalap

JALEBI, -S n type of Asian sweet fried snack

JALFREZI adj (in Indian cookery) stir-fried with green peppers, onions, and green chillies ▷ n curry made with green peppers, onions, and green chillies

JALLEBI, -S same as ►jalebi

JALOP, -S same as ►jalap

JALOPIES ►jalopy

JALOPPY same as ►jalopy

JALOPS ►jalop

JALOPY, JALOPIES n old car

JALOUSE, -D, -S vb suspect

JALOUSIE n window blind or shutter constructed from angled slats of wood, plastic, etc

JAM, -MED, -S vb pack tightly into a place ▷ n fruit preserve or hold-up of traffic

JAMAAT, -S n Islamic council

JAMADAR, -S n Indian army officer

JAMB, -ED, -ING, -S n side post of a door or window frame ▷ vb climb up a crack in rock

JAMBART, -S same as ►greave

JAMBE, -S same as ►jamb

JAMBEAU, -S, -X, JAMBEUX another word for ►greave

JAMBED ►jamb

JAMBEE, -S n light cane

JAMBER, -S same as ►greave

JAMBES ►jambe

JAMBEUX ►jambeau

JAMBIER, -S same as ►greave

JAMBING ►jamb

JAMBIYA, -S n curved dagger

JAMBIYAH same as ►jambiya

JAMBIYAS ►jambiya

JAMBO sentence substitute E African salutation

JAMBOK, -S same as ►sjambok

JAMBOLAN n Asian tree

JAMBONE, -S n type of play in the card game euchre

JAMBOOL, -S same as ►jambolan

JAMBOREE n large gathering or celebration

JAMBS ►jamb

JAMBU, -S same as ►jambolan

JAMBUL, -S same as ►jambolan

JAMBUS ►jambu

JAMDANI, -S n patterned muslin

JAMES, -ES n jemmy

JAMJAR, -S n container for preserves

JAMLIKE ►jam

JAMMABLE ►jam

JAMMED ►jam

JAMMER, -S ►jam

JAMMIER ►jammy

JAMMIES informal word for ►pyjamas

JAMMIEST ►jammy

JAMMING, -S ►jam

JAMMY, JAMMIER, JAMMIEST adj lucky

JAMON n as in jamon serrano cured ham from Spain

JAMPAN, -S n type of sedan chair used in India

JAMPANEE n jampan bearer

JAMPANI, -S same as ►jampanee

JAMPANS ►jampan

JAMPOT, -S n container for preserves

JAMS ►jam

JANE, -S n girl or woman

JANGLE, -D, -S, JANGLING vb (cause to) make a harsh ringing noise ▷ n harsh ringing noise

JANGLER, -S ►jangle

JANGLES ►jangle

JANGLIER ►jangly

JANGLING ►jangle

JANGLY, JANGLIER adj making a jangling sound

JANIFORM adj with two faces

JANISARY same as >janissary

JANITOR, -S n caretaker of a school or other building

JANITRIX n female janitor

JANIZAR, -S same as >janissary

This is an old word for a Turkish soldier, combining J and Z. If your opponent plays it, remember that you can add not only an S to it to form the plural, but also a Y, making the variant spelling **janizary**.

JANIZARY same as >janissary

JANKER, -S n device for transporting logs

JANN, -S n lesser jinn

JANNEY, -ED, -S vb act as a disguised reveller at Christmas

JANNIED ►janny

JANNIES ►janny

JANNOCK, -S same as ►jonnock

JANNS ►jann

JANNY, JANNIED, JANNIES, -ING n janitor ▷ vb work as a janitor

JANSKY, -S n unit of flux density**

JANTEE archaic version of ►**jaunty**

JANTY, JANTIER, JANTIES, JANTIEST n petty officer ▷ adj (in archaic usage) jaunty

JAPAN, -NED, -S n very hard varnish, usu black ▷ vb cover with this varnish ▷ adj relating to or varnished with japan

JAPANISE same as ►**japanize**

JAPANIZE vb make Japanese

JAPANNED ►**japan**

JAPANNER ►**japan**

JAPANS ►**japan**

JAPE, -D, -S n joke or prank ▷ vb joke or jest (about)

JAPER, -S ►**jape**

JAPERIES ►**japery**

JAPERS ►**japer**

JAPERY, JAPERIES ►**jape**

JAPES ►**jape**

JAPING, -S ►**jape**

JAPINGLY ►**jape**

JAPINGS ►**japing**

JAPONICA n shrub with red flowers

JAR, -RED, -S n wide-mouthed container ▷ vb have a disturbing or unpleasant effect

JARARACA n South American snake

JARARAKA same as ►**jararaca**

JARFUL, -S, JARSFUL same as ►**jar**

JARGON, -ED, -S n specialized technical language ▷ vb use or speak in jargon

JARGONEL n pear

JARGONS ►**jargon**

JARGONY adj full of jargon

JARGOON, -S same as ►**jargon**

JARHEAD, -S n US Marine

JARINA, -S n South American palm tree

JARK, -S n seal or pass

JARKMAN, JARKMEN n forger of passes or licences

JARKS ►**jark**

JARL, -S n Scandinavian chieftain or noble

JARLDOM, -S ►**jarl**

JARLS ►**jarl**

JAROOL, -S n Indian tree

JAROSITE n yellow to brown mineral

JAROVISE same as ►**jarovize**

JAROVIZE vb vernalize

JARP, -ED, -ING, -S vb strike or smash

JARRAH, -S n Australian eucalyptus yielding valuable timber

JARRED ►**jar**

JARRING, -S ►**jar**

JARS ►**jar**

JARSFUL ►**jarful**

JARTA, -S n heart

JARUL, -S variant of ►**jarool**

JARVEY, -S n hackney coachman

JARVIE, -S same as ►**jarvey**

JASEY, -S n wig

JASIES ►**jasy**

JASMIN, -S same as ►**jasmine**

JASMINE, -S n shrub with sweet-smelling yellow or white flowers

JASMINS ►**jasmin**

JASP, -S another word for ►**jasper**

JASPE, -S adj resembling jasper ▷ n subtly striped woven fabric

JASPER, -S n variety of quartz

JASPERY adj resembling jasper

JASPES ►**jaspe**

JASPIS, -ES archaic word for ►**jasper**

JASPS ►**jasp**

JASS, -ES obsolete variant of ►**jazz**

JASSID, -S n leafhopper

JASY, JASIES n wig

JATAKA, -S n text describing the birth of Buddha

JATO, -S n jet-assisted takeoff

JATROPHA n poisonous shrub of C America used primarily as a biofuel

JAUK, -ED, -ING, -S vb dawdle

JAUNCE, -D, -S, JAUNCING vb prance

JAUNDICE n disease marked by yellowness of the skin ▷ vb distort (the judgment, etc) adversely

JAUNSE, -D, -S, JAUNSING same as ►**jaunce**

JAUNT, -ED, -ING, -S n short journey for pleasure ▷ vb make such a journey

JAUNTEE old spelling of ►**jaunty**

JAUNTIE old spelling of ►**jaunty**

JAUNTIER ►**jaunty**

JAUNTIES ►**jaunty**

JAUNTILY ►**jaunty**

JAUNTING ►**jaunt**

JAUNTS ►**jaunt**

JAUNTY, JAUNTIER, JAUNTIES adj sprightly and cheerful ▷ n master-at-arms on a naval ship

JAUP, -ED, -ING, -S same as ►**jarp**

JAVA, -S n coffee or a variety of it

JAVEL, -S adj as in **javel water** bleach or disinfectant

JAVELIN, -S n light spear thrown in sports competitions ▷ vb spear with a javelin

JAVELINA n collared peccary

JAVELINS ►**javelin**

JAVELLE adj as in **javelle water** bleach or disinfectant

JAVELS ►**javel**

JAW, -ED, -S n one of the bones in which the teeth are set ▷ vb talk lengthily

JAWAN, -S n (in India) a soldier

JAWARI, -S n variety of sorghum

JAWBONE, -D, -S n lower jaw of a person or animal ▷ vb try to persuade by virtue of one's high office or position

JAWBONER ►**jawbone**

JAWBONES ►**jawbone**

JAWBOX, -ES n metal sink

This Scots word for a metal sink combines the J and X, and of course its plural **jawboxes**, earning an extra 50 points, would be even better.

JAWED ►**jaw**

JAWFALL, -S n dejection

JAWHOLE, -S n cesspit

JAWING, -S ►**jaw**

JAWLESS ►**jaw**

JAWLIKE ►**jaw**

JAWLINE, -S n outline of the jaw

JAWS ►**jaw**

JAY, -S n type of bird

JAYBIRD, -S n jay

JAYCEE, -S n member of a Junior Chamber of Commerce

JAYGEE, -S n lieutenant junior grade in the US army

JAYS ►**jay**

JAYVEE, -S n junior varsity sports team

JAYWALK, -S vb cross or walk in a street recklessly or illegally

JAZERANT n coat of metal plates sewn onto cloth

JAZY, JAZIES n wig
> This means a wig and is a wonderfully useful little word, combining J and Z for a high score.

JAZZ, -ED, -ES, -ING n kind of music ▷ vb play or dance to jazz music

JAZZBO, -S n jazz musician or fan

JAZZED ▸jazz

JAZZER, -S ▸jazz

JAZZES ▸jazz

JAZZIER ▸jazzy

JAZZIEST ▸jazzy

JAZZILY ▸jazzy

JAZZING ▸jazz

JAZZLIKE ▸jazz

JAZZMAN ▸jazz

JAZZMEN ▸jazz

JAZZY, JAZZIER, JAZZIEST adj flashy or showy

JEALOUS adj fearful of losing (something) to a rival

JEALOUSE vb be jealous of

JEALOUSY n state of or an instance of feeling jealous

JEAN n tough twill-weave cotton fabric

JEANED adj wearing jeans

JEANETTE n light jean cloth

JEANS pl n casual denim trousers

JEAT, -S n jet

JEBEL, -S n hill or mountain in an Arab country

JEDI, -S n person claiming to live according to the Jedi philosophy

JEE, -D, -ING, -S variant of ▸gee

JEEL, -ED, -ING, -S vb make into jelly

JEELIE same as ▸jeely

JEELIED ▸jeely

JEELIES ▸jeely

JEELING ▸jeel

JEELS ▸jeel

JEELY, JEELIED, JEELIES, -ING n jelly ▷ vb make into jelly

JEEP, -ED, -ING, -S n small military four-wheel drive road vehicle ▷ vb travel in a jeep

JEEPERS interj mild exclamation of surprise

JEEPING ▸jeep

JEEPNEY, -S n Filipino bus converted from a jeep

JEEPS ▸jeep

JEER, -ED, -S vb scoff or deride ▷ n cry of derision

JEERER, -S ▸jeer

JEERING, -S ▸jeer

JEERS ▸jeer

JEES ▸jee

JEESLY same as ▸jeezly

JEEZ interj expression of surprise or irritation

JEEZE same as ▸jeez

JEEZELY same as ▸jeezly

JEEZLY adj used as an intensifier

JEFE, -S n (in Spanish-speaking countries) a military or political leader

JEFF, -ED, -ING, -S vb downsize or close down (an organization)

JEGGINGS pl n women's leggings designed to look like tight denim jeans

JEHAD, -S same as ▸jihad

JEHADEEN same as ▸jihadeen

JEHADI, -S same as ▸jihadi

JEHADISM same as ▸jihadism

JEHADIST ▸jehadism

JEHADS ▸jehad

JEHU, -S n fast driver

JEJUNA ▸jejunum

JEJUNAL ▸jejunum

JEJUNE adj simple or naive

JEJUNELY ▸jejune

JEJUNITY ▸jejune

JEJUNUM, JEJUNA, -S n part of the small intestine

JELAB, -S same as ▸jellaba

JELL, -ED, -ING, -S vb form into a jelly-like substance

JELLABA, -S n loose robe with a hood

JELLABAH same as ▸jellaba

JELLABAS ▸jellaba

JELLED ▸jell

JELLIES ▸jelly

JELLIFY vb make into or become jelly

JELLING ▸jell

JELLO, -S n (in US English) type of dessert

JELLS ▸jell

JELLY, JELLIED, JELLIES, -ING n fruit-flavoured clear dessert set with gelatine ▷ vb jellify

JELUTONG n Malaysian tree

JEMADAR, -S n native officer serving as a mercenary in India

JEMBE, -S n hoe

JEMIDAR, -S same as ▸jemadar

JEMIMA, -S n boot with elastic sides

JEMMY, JEMMIED, JEMMIER, JEMMIES, JEMMIEST, -ING n short

steel crowbar used by burglars ▷ vb prise (something) open with a jemmy ▷ adj neat

JENNET, -S n female donkey or ass

JENNY, JENNIES same as ▸jennet

JEOFAIL, -S n oversight in legal pleading

JEON, -S n Korean pancake

JEOPARD, -S vb put in jeopardy

JEOPARDY n danger ▷ vb put in jeopardy

JERBIL, -S n variant spelling of ▸gerbil

JERBOA, -S n small mouselike rodent with long hind legs

JEREED, -S same as ▸jerid

JEREMIAD n long mournful complaint

JEREPIGO n sweet fortified wine similar to port

JERID, -S n wooden javelin

JERK, -ED, -S vb move or throw abruptly ▷ n sharp or abruptly stopped movement

JERKER, -S ▸jerk

JERKIER ▸jerky

JERKIES ▸jerky

JERKIEST ▸jerky

JERKILY ▸jerky

JERKIN, -S n sleeveless jacket

JERKING, -S ▸jerk

JERKINS ▸jerkin

JERKS ▸jerk

JERKY, JERKIER, JERKIES, JERKIEST adj characterized by jerks ▷ n type of cured meat

JEROBOAM n wine bottle holding the equivalent of four normal bottles

JERQUE, -D, -S, JERQUING vb search for contraband
> To **jerque** is to search a vessel for stolen goods, and if you have the right additional letters to make **jerqued, jerquer, jerques** or **jerquing**, using all your letters, you would get a really great score.

JERQUER, -S ▸jerque

JERQUES ▸jerque

JERQUING ▸jerque

JERREED, -S variant spelling of ▸jerid

JERRICAN n five-gallon fuel can

JERRID, -S n blunt javelin

JERRY, JERRIES short for ▸jeroboam

JERRYCAN n flat-sided can used for storing or transporting liquids, esp motor fuel

JERSEY, -S n knitted jumper

JERSEYED ▶ jersey

JERSEYS ▶ jersey

JESS, -ED, -ES, -ING n short leather strap used in falconry ▷ vb put jesses on (a hawk or falcon)

JESSAMY n fop

JESSANT adj emerging

JESSE same as ▶ jess

JESSED ▶ jess

JESSES ▶ jess

JESSING ▶ jess

JEST, -ED, -S vb joke ▷ n something done or said for amusement

JESTBOOK n book of amusing stories

JESTED ▶ jest

JESTEE, -S n person about whom a joke is made

JESTER, -S n professional clown at court

JESTFUL ▶ jest

JESTING, -S ▶ jest

JESTS ▶ jest

JESUS n French paper size

JET, -S, -TED, -TING n aircraft driven by jet propulsion ▷ vb fly by jet aircraft

JETBEAD, -S n ornamental shrub

JETE, -S n dance step

JETFOIL, -S n type of hydrofoil that is propelled by water jets

JETLAG, -S n tiredness caused by crossing timezones in jet flight

JETLIKE ▶ jet

JETLINER n commercial airliner powered by jet engines

JETON, -S n gambling chip

JETPACK, -S n wearable harness with jets, used for transport

JETPORT, -S n airport for jet planes

JETS ▶ jet

JETSAM, -S n goods thrown overboard to lighten a ship

JETSOM, -S same as ▶ jetsam

JETSON, -S archaic form of ▶ jetsam

JETTED ▶ jet

JETTIED ▶ jetty

JETTIER ▶ jetty

JETTIES ▶ jetty

JETTIEST ▶ jetty

JETTING ▶ jet

JETTISON vb abandon

JETTON, -S n counter or token

JETTY, JETTIED, JETTIER, JETTIES, JETTIEST, -ING n small pier ▷ adj of or resembling jet, esp in colour or polish ▷ vb equip with a cantilevered floor

JETWAY, -S n tradename of device used in airports

JEU, -X n game

Jeu is the French word for game or play. The plural form, **jeux**, is a great little word, using both J and X, particularly if you can play it on a double- or triple-word square.

JEUNE adj young

JEUX ▶ jeu

JEWEL, -ED, -ING, -LED, -S n precious or semiprecious stone ▷ vb fit or decorate with a jewel or jewels

JEWELER, -S same as ▶ jeweller

JEWELING ▶ jewel

JEWELLED ▶ jewel

JEWELLER n dealer in jewels

JEWELRY same as > jewellery

JEWELS ▶ jewel

JEWFISH n old-fashioned name for a type of freshwater catfish

JEWIE, -S n informal Australian word for a jewfish

JEZAIL, -S n Afghan musket

A **jezail** is a kind of Afghan musket, and if you have an S to go with it, earning the extra 50 points, so much the better.

JEZEBEL, -S n shameless or scheming woman

JHALA, -S n Indian musical style

JHATKA, -S n slaughter of animals for food according to Sikh law

JIAO, -S n Chinese currency unit

JIB, -S same as ▶ jibe

JIBB, -ED, -S same as ▶ jibe

JIBBA, -S n long, loose coat worn by Muslim men

JIBBAH, -S same as ▶ jubbah

JIBBAS ▶ jibba

JIBBED ▶ jibb

JIBBER, -ED, -S variant of ▶ gibber

JIBBING, -S ▶ jibb

JIBBONS pl n spring onions

JIBBOOM, -S n spar forming an extension of the bowsprit

JIBBS ▶ jibb

JIBE, -D, -S, JIBING vb taunt or jeer ▷ n insulting or taunting remark

JIBER, -S ▶ jibe

JIBES ▶ jibe

JIBING ▶ jibe

JIBINGLY ▶ jibe

JIBS ▶ jib

JICAMA, -S n pale brown turnip

JIFF, -S same as ▶ jiffy

JIFFIES ▶ jiffy

JIFFS ▶ jiff

JIFFY, JIFFIES n very short period of time

JIG, -GED, -S n type of lively dance ▷ vb dance a jig

JIGGER, -ED, -S n small whisky glass ▷ vb interfere or alter

JIGGIER ▶ jiggy

JIGGIEST ▶ jiggy

JIGGING, -S ▶ jig

JIGGISH ▶ jig

JIGGLE, -D, -S, JIGGLING vb move up and down with short jerky movements ▷ n short jerky motion

JIGGLIER ▶ jiggly

JIGGLING ▶ jiggle

JIGGLY, JIGGLIER ▶ jiggle

JIGGY, JIGGIER, JIGGIEST adj resembling jig

JIGLIKE ▶ jig

JIGOT, -S same as ▶ gigot

JIGS ▶ jig

JIGSAW, -ED, -N, -S n type of game ▷ vb cut with a jigsaw

JIHAD, -S n Islamic holy war against unbelievers

JIHADEEN pl n jihadists

JIHADI, -S n person who takes part in a jihad

JIHADISM n Islamic fundamentalist movement that favours jihads

JIHADIST ▶ jihadism

JIHADS ▶ jihad

JILBAB, JALABIB, -S n long robe worn by Muslim women

JILGIE, -S n freshwater crayfish

JILL, -S variant spelling of ▶ gill

JILLAROO n young female management trainee on a sheep or cattle station

JILLET, -S n flighty or capricious woman

JILLION, -S n extremely large number or amount

JILLS ▶ jill

JILT, -ED, -ING, -S vb leave or reject (one's lover) ▷ n woman who jilts a lover

JILTER, -S ▸jilt
JILTING ▸jilt
JILTS ▸jilt
JIMCRACK same as
▸gimcrack
JIMINY interj expression of
surprise
JIMJAMS, JIMJAM pl n state
of nervous tension,
excitement, or anxiety
JIMMIE same as ▸jimmy
JIMMIED ▸jimmy
JIMMIES ▸jimmy
JIMMINY interj expression of
surprise
JIMMY, JIMMIED, JIMMIES,
-ING same as ▸jemmy
JIMP, -ER, -EST adj
handsome
JIMPIER ▸jimpy
JIMPIEST ▸jimpy
JIMPLY adv neatly
JIMPNESS ▸jimp
JIMPSON same as ▸jimson
JIMPY, JIMPIER, JIMPIEST
adj neat and tidy
JIMSON, -S n as in jimson
weed type of poisonous
plant
JIN, -S n Chinese unit of
weight
JINGAL, -S n swivel-
mounted gun
JINGALL, -S same as ▸jingal
JINGALS ▸jingal
JINGBANG n entirety of
something
JINGKO, -ES same as
▸gingko
JINGLE, -D, -S, JINGLING n
catchy verse or song used in
an advert ▷ vb (cause to)
make a gentle ringing sound
JINGLER, -S ▸jingle
JINGLES ▸jingle
JINGLET, -S n sleigh-bell
clapper
JINGLIER ▸jingly
JINGLING ▸jingle
JINGLY, JINGLIER ▸jingle
JINGO, -ES n loud and
bellicose patriot; chauvinism
JINGOISH ▸jingo
JINGOISM n aggressive
nationalism
JINGOIST ▸jingoism
JINJILI, -S n type of sesame
JINK, -ED, -ING, -S vb move
quickly or jerkily in order to
dodge someone ▷ n jinking
movement
JINKER, -ED, -S n vehicle for
transporting timber ▷ vb
carry or transport in a jinker
JINKING ▸jink
JINKS ▸jink

JINN, -S n spirit in Muslim
mythology
JINNE interj South African
exclamation
JINNEE same as ▸jinni
JINNI, -S n spirit in Muslim
mythology
JINNS ▸jinn
JINS ▸jin
JINX, -ED, -ES, -ING n person
or thing bringing bad luck
▷ vb be or put a jinx on
JIPIJAPA n plant whose
leaves are used for making
panama hats
JIPYAPA, -S same as
▸jipijapa
JIRBLE, -D, -S, JIRBLING vb
pour carelessly
JIRD, -S n gerbil
JIRGA, -S n Afghan council
JIRKINET, -S n bodice
JIRRE same as ▸jinne
JITNEY, -S n small cheap bus
JITTER, -ED, -S vb be anxious
or nervous
JITTERY adj nervous
JIUJITSU variant spelling of
▸jujitsu
JIUJUTSU same as ▸jujutsu
JIVE, -D, -S, -ST, JIVING n
lively dance of the 1940s and
1950s ▷ vb dance the jive
▷ adj pertaining to or
indicative of jive
JIVEASS adj misleading or
phoney ▷ n person who
loves fun and excitement
JIVED ▸jive
JIVER, -S ▸jive
JIVES ▸jive
JIVEST ▸jive
JIVEY, JIVIER, JIVIEST adj
jazzy; lively
JIVING ▸jive
JIVY same as ▸jivey
JIZ n wig

When you find yourself with
J and Z but nothing else that
looks promising, there may
well be an I on the board
around which you can form
jiz, which means a wig.

JIZZ, -ES n term for the
characteristics that identify
a particular species of bird or
plant
JNANA, -S n type of yoga
JO n Scots word for
sweetheart
JOANNA, -S n piano
JOANNES same as
▸johannes
JOB, -BED, -S n occupation
or paid employment ▷ vb
work at casual jobs

JOBATION n scolding
JOBBED ▸job
JOBBER, -S n person who
jobs
JOBBERY n practice of
making private profit out of
a public office
JOBBIE, -S n referring to a
thing usually specified in the
preceding part of a sentence
JOBBING, -S adj doing
individual jobs for payment
▷ n act of seeking work
JOBE, -D, -S, JOBING vb
scold
JOBLESS pl n as in the
jobless unemployed people
▷ adj unemployed
JOBNAME, -S n title of
position
JOBS ▸job
JOBSHARE n arrangement
in which two people divide
the duties for one job
between them
JOCK, -S n athlete
JOCKDOM, -S n world of
male athletes
JOCKETTE n female athlete
JOCKEY, -ED, -S n person
who rides horses in races
▷ vb ride (a horse) in a race
JOCKIER ▸jocky
JOCKIEST ▸jocky
JOCKISH adj macho
JOCKNEY, -S n the Scots
dialect influenced by
cockney speech patterns
JOCKO, -S n chimpanzee
JOCKS ▸jock
JOCKY, JOCKIER, JOCKIEST
adj indicating or appropriate
to a male athlete
JOCO, -S adj relaxed ▷ n joke
JOCOSE, -R, -ST adj playful
or humorous
JOCOSELY ▸jocose
JOCOSER ▸jocose
JOCOSEST ▸jocose
JOCOSITY ▸jocose
JOCULAR adj fond of joking
JOCUND, -ER adj merry or
cheerful
JOCUNDLY ▸jocund
JODEL, -LED, -S same as
▸yodel
JODHPUR n as in jodhpur
boots ankle-length leather
riding boots
JODHPURS pl n riding
breeches
JOE, -S same as ▸jo
JOEY, -S n young kangaroo
JOG, -GED, -S vb run at a
gentle pace, esp for exercise
▷ n slow run

JOGGER, -S *n* person who runs at a jog for exercise

JOGGING, -S ▸ **jog**

JOGGLE, -D, -S, JOGGLING *vb* shake or move jerkily ▹ *n* act of joggling

JOGGLER, -S ▸ **joggle**

JOGGLES ▸ **joggle**

JOGGLING ▸ **joggle**

JOGPANTS *pl n* trousers worn for jogging

JOGS ▸ **jog**

JOGTROT, -S *n* easy bouncy gait ▹ *vb* move at a jogtrot

JOHANNES *n* Portuguese gold coin minted in the early 18th century

JOHN, -S *n* toilet

JOHNBOAT *n* small flat-bottomed boat

JOHNNIE *same as* ▸ **johnny**

JOHNNY, JOHNNIES *n* chap

JOHNS ▸ **john**

JOIN, -ED, -S *vb* become a member (of) ▹ *n* place where two things are joined

JOINABLE ▸ **join**

JOINDER, -S *n* act of joining, esp in legal contexts

JOINED ▸ **join**

JOINER, -S *n* maker of finished woodwork

JOINERY *n* joiner's work

JOINING, -S ▸ **join**

JOINS ▸ **join**

JOINT, -S *adj* shared by two or more ▹ *n* place where bones meet but can move ▹ *vb* divide meat into joints

JOINTED *adj* having a joint or joints

JOINTER, -S *n* tool for pointing mortar joints

JOINTING ▸ **joint**

JOINTLY ▸ **joint**

JOINTS ▸ **joint**

JOINTURE *n* provision made by a husband for his spouse after his death

JOIST, -ED, -ING, -S *n* horizontal beam ▹ *vb* construct (a floor, roof, etc) with joists

JOJOBA, -S *n* shrub of SW North America

JOKE, -D, -S *n* thing said or done to cause laughter ▹ *vb* make jokes

JOKER, -S *n* person who jokes

JOKES ▸ **joke**

JOKESOME ▸ **joke**

JOKESTER *n* person who makes jokes

JOKEY, JOKIER, JOKIEST *adj* intended as a joke

JOKILY ▸ **joke**

JOKINESS ▸ **joke**

JOKING, -S *n* act of joking

JOKINGLY ▸ **joke**

JOKINGS ▸ **joking**

JOKOL *Shetland word for* ▸ **yes**

JOKY *same as* ▸ **jokey**

JOL, -LED, -LING, -S *n* party ▹ *vb* have a good time

JOLE, -D, -S, JOLING *vb* knock

JOLL, -S *variant of* ▸ **jole**

JOLLED ▸ **jol**

JOLLER, -S *n* person who has a good time

JOLLEY, -S *same as* ▸ **jolly**

JOLLEYER ▸ **jolley**

JOLLEYS ▸ **jolley**

JOLLIED ▸ **jolly**

JOLLIER, -S *n* joker

JOLLIES ▸ **jolly**

JOLLIEST ▸ **jolly**

JOLLIFY *vb* be or cause to be jolly

JOLLILY ▸ **jolly**

JOLLING ▸ **jol**

JOLLITY *n* condition of being jolly

JOLLOF *adj* as in jollof rice W African dish made from rice and meat or fish

JOLLOP, -S *n* cream or unguent

JOLLS ▸ **joll**

JOLLY, JOLLIED, JOLLIES, JOLLIEST, -ING *adj* full of good humour ▹ *adv* extremely ▹ *vb* try to make or keep (someone) cheerful ▹ *n* festivity or celebration

JOLLYER, -S ▸ **jolly**

JOLLYING ▸ **jolly**

JOLS ▸ **jol**

JOLT, -ED, -S *n* unpleasant surprise or shock ▹ *vb* surprise or shock

JOLTER, -S ▸ **jolt**

JOLTHEAD *n* fool

JOLTIER ▸ **jolty**

JOLTIEST ▸ **jolty**

JOLTILY ▸ **jolt**

JOLTING, -S *n* act of jolting

JOLTS ▸ **jolt**

JOLTY, JOLTIER, JOLTIEST ▸ **jolt**

JOMO, -S *same as* ▸ **zo**

JOMON, -S *n* particular era in Japanese history

JOMOS ▸ **jomo**

JONCANOE *n* Jamaican ceremony

JONES, -ED, -ES, -ING *vb* desire

JONG, -S *n* friend, often used in direct address

JONGLEUR *n* (in medieval France) an itinerant minstrel

JONGS ▸ **jong**

JONNOCK *adj* genuine ▹ *adv* honestly

JONQUIL, -S *n* fragrant narcissus

JONTY, JONTIES *n* petty officer

JOOK, -ED, -ING, -S *vb* poke or puncture (the skin) ▹ *n* jab or the resulting wound

JOOKERY *n* mischief

JOOKING ▸ **jook**

JOOKS ▸ **jook**

JOR, -S *n* movement in Indian music

JORAM, -S *same as* ▸ **jorum**

JORDAN, -S *n* chamber pot

JORDELOO *same as* ▸ **gardyloo**

JORS ▸ **jor**

JORUM, -S *n* large drinking bowl or vessel or its contents

JOSEPH, -S *n* woman's floor-length riding coat

JOSH, -ED, -ES *vb* tease ▹ *n* teasing or bantering joke

JOSHER, -S ▸ **josh**

JOSHES ▸ **josh**

JOSHING, -S *n* act of joshing

JOSKIN, -S *n* bumpkin

JOSS, -ES *n* Chinese deity

JOSSER, -S *n* unintelligent person

JOSSES ▸ **joss**

JOSTLE, -D, -S, JOSTLING *vb* knock or push against ▹ *n* act of jostling

JOSTLER, -S ▸ **jostle**

JOSTLES ▸ **jostle**

JOSTLING ▸ **jostle**

JOT, -S, -TED *vb* write briefly ▹ *n* very small amount

JOTA, -S *n* Spanish dance

JOTS ▸ **jot**

JOTTED ▸ **jot**

JOTTER, -S *n* notebook

JOTTIER ▸ **jotty**

JOTTIEST ▸ **jotty**

JOTTING, -S ▸ **jot**

JOTTY, JOTTIER, JOTTIEST ▸ **jot**

JOTUN, -S *n* giant

JOTUNN, -S *same as* ▸ **jotun**

JOTUNS ▸ **jotun**

JOUAL, -S *n* nonstandard variety of Canadian French

JOUGS *pl n* iron ring for restraining an offender

JOUK, -ED, -ING, -S *vb* duck or dodge ▹ *n* sudden evasive movement

JOUKERY *same as* ▸ **jookery**

JOUKING ▸ **jouk**

JOUKS ▸ **jouk**

J

JOULE, -D, -S, JOULING n unit of work or energy ▷ vb knock

JOUNCE, -D, -S, JOUNCING vb shake or jolt or cause to shake or jolt ▷ n jolting movement

JOUNCIER ▸jouncy

JOUNCING ▸jounce

JOUNCY, JOUNCIER ▸jouncy

JOUR, -S n day

JOURNAL, -S n daily newspaper or magazine ▷ vb record in a journal

JOURNEY, -S n act of travelling from one place to another ▷ vb travel

JOURNO, -S n journalist

JOURS ▸jour

JOUST, -ED, -S n combat between two knights ▷ vb fight on horseback using lances

JOUSTER, -S ▸joust

JOUSTING n act of jousting

JOUSTS ▸joust

JOVIAL adj happy and cheerful

JOVIALLY ▸jovial

JOVIALTY ▸jovial

JOW, -ED, -ING, -S vb ring (a bell)

JOWAR, -S n variety of sorghum

JOWARI, -S same as ▸jowar

JOWARS ▸jowar

JOWED ▸jow

JOWING ▸jow

JOWL, -ING, -S n lower jaw ▷ vb knock

JOWLED ▸jowl

JOWLER, -S n dog with prominent jowls

JOWLIER ▸jowly

JOWLIEST ▸jowly

JOWLING ▸jowl

JOWLS ▸jowl

JOWLY, JOWLIER, JOWLIEST ▸jowl

JOWS ▸jow

JOY, -ED, -ING, -S n feeling of great delight or pleasure ▷ vb feel joy

JOYANCE, -S n joyous feeling or festivity

JOYED ▸joy

JOYFUL adj feeling or bringing great joy

JOYFULLY ▸joyful

JOYING ▸joy

JOYLESS adj feeling or bringing no joy

JOYOUS adj extremely happy and enthusiastic

JOYOUSLY ▸joyous

JOYPAD, -S n computer games console

JOYRIDE, -S, JOYRODE n drive in a car one has stolen ▷ vb take such a ride

JOYRIDER ▸joyride

JOYRIDES ▸joyride

JOYRODE ▸joyride

JOYS ▸joy

JOYSTICK n control device for an aircraft or computer

JUBA, -S n lively African-American dance

JUBATE adj possessing a mane

JUBBAH, -S n long loose outer garment with wide sleeves

JUBE, -S n part of a church or cathedral

JUBHAH, -S same as ▸jubbah

JUBILANT adj feeling or expressing great joy

JUBILATE vb have or express great joy

JUBILE, -S same as ▸jubilee

JUBILEE, -S n special anniversary, esp 25th or 50th

JUBILES ▸jubile

JUCO, -S n junior college in America

JUD, -S n large block of coal

JUDAS, -ES n peephole

JUDDER, -ED, -S vb vibrate violently ▷ n violent vibration

JUDDERY adj shaky

JUDGE, -D, -S n public official ▷ vb act as a judge

JUDGER, -S ▸judge

JUDGES ▸judge

JUDGEY adj tending to be judgmental

JUDGIER ▸judgy

JUDGIEST ▸judgy

JUDGING, -S n act of judging

JUDGMENT n opinion reached after careful thought

JUDGY, JUDGIER, JUDGIEST adj tending to be judgmental

JUDICARE n (in Canada) state-paid legal services

JUDICIAL adj of or by a court or judge

JUDIES ▸judy

JUDO, -S n type of sport

JUDOGI, -S n white two-piece cotton costume

JUDOIST, -S ▸judo

JUDOKA, -S n competitor or expert in judo

JUDOS ▸judo

JUDS ▸jud

JUDY, JUDIES n woman

JUG, -GED, -GING, -GINGS, -S n container for liquids ▷ vb stew or boil (meat, esp hare) in an earthenware container

JUGA ▸jugum

JUGAAD, -S n (in Indian English) problem-solving

JUGAL, -S adj of or relating to the zygomatic bone ▷ n cheekbone

JUGATE adj having parts arranged in pairs

JUGFUL, -S, JUGSFUL same as ▸jug

JUGGED ▸jug

JUGGING ▸jug

JUGGINGS ▸jug

JUGGINS n silly person

JUGGLE, -D, -S, JUGGLING vb throw and catch (objects) to keep them in the air ▷ n act of juggling

JUGGLER, -S n person who juggles, esp a professional entertainer

JUGGLERY ▸juggle

JUGGLES ▸juggle

JUGGLING ▸juggle

JUGHEAD, -S n clumsy person

JUGLET, -S n small jug

JUGS ▸jug

JUGSFUL ▸jugful

JUGULA ▸jugulum

JUGULAR, -S n one of three large veins of the neck

JUGULATE vb check (a disease) by extreme measures or remedies

JUGULUM, JUGULA n lower throat

JUGUM, JUGA, -S n part of an insect's forewing

JUICE, -D, -S, JUICING n liquid part of vegetables, fruit, or meat ▷ vb extract juice from fruits and vegetables

JUICER, -S n kitchen appliance

JUICES ▸juice

JUICIER ▸juicy

JUICIEST ▸juicy

JUICILY ▸juicy

JUICING ▸juice

JUICY, JUICIER, JUICIEST adj full of juice

JUJITSU, -S n Japanese martial art

JUJU, -S n W African magic charm or fetish

JUJUBE, -S n chewy sweet made of flavoured gelatine

JUJUISM, -S ▸juju

JUJUIST, -S ▸juju

JUJUS ▶juju

JUJUTSU, -S same as ▶jujitsu

JUKE, -D, -S, JUKING vb dance or play dance music

JUKEBOX n coin-operated music box

JUKED ▶juke

JUKES ▶juke

JUKING ▶juke

JUKSKEI, -S n type of game

JUKU, -S n Japanese martial art

JULEP, -S n sweet alcoholic drink

JULIENNE adj (of vegetables or meat) cut into thin shreds ▷ n clear soup containing thinly shredded vegetables ▷ vb cut into thin pieces

JULIET, -S n code word for the letter J

JUMAR, -ED, -ING, -RED, -S n climbing tool ▷ vb climb (up a fixed rope) using jumars

JUMART, -S n mythical offspring of a bull and a mare

JUMBAL, -S same as ▶jumble

JUMBIE, -S n Caribbean ghost

JUMBLE, -D, -S, JUMBLING n confused heap or state ▷ vb mix in a disordered way

JUMBLER, -S ▶jumble

JUMBLES ▶jumble

JUMBLIER ▶jumbly

JUMBLING ▶jumble

JUMBLY, JUMBLIER ▶jumble

JUMBO, -S adj very large ▷ n large jet airliner

JUMBOISE same as ▶jumboize

JUMBOIZE vb extend (a ship) by inserting a part between the bow and stern

JUMBOS ▶jumbo

JUMBUCK, -S n sheep

JUMBY n Caribbean ghost ·

JUMELLE, -S n paired objects

JUMP, -ED, -S vb leap or spring into the air using the leg muscles ▷ n act of jumping

JUMPABLE ▶jump

JUMPED ▶jump

JUMPER, -S n sweater or pullover

JUMPIER ▶jumpy

JUMPIEST ▶jumpy

JUMPILY ▶jumpy

JUMPING, -S ▶jump

JUMPOFF, -S n round in a showjumping contest

JUMPROPE n rope held in the hands and jumped over

JUMPS ▶jump

JUMPSHOT n type of shot in basketball in which a player jumps to reach the basket

JUMPSIES pl n game involving jumping over a straight rope

JUMPSUIT n one-piece garment of combined trousers and jacket or shirt

JUMPY, JUMPIER, JUMPIEST adj nervous

JUN variant of ▶chon

JUNCATE, -S same as ▶junket

JUNCO, -ES, -S n North American bunting

JUNCTION n place where routes, railway lines, or roads meet

JUNCTURE n point in time, esp a critical one

JUNCUS, -ES n type of rush

JUNGLE, -S n tropical forest of dense tangled vegetation

JUNGLED adj covered with jungle

JUNGLES ▶jungle

JUNGLI, -S n uncultured person

JUNGLIER ▶jungly

JUNGLIS ▶jungli

JUNGLIST n jungle-music enthusiast

JUNGLY, JUNGLIER ▶jungle

JUNIOR, -ED, -S adj of lower standing ▷ n junior person ▷ vb work as a junior

JUNIPER, -S n evergreen shrub with purple berries

JUNK, -ED, -ING, -S n discarded or useless objects ▷ vb discard as junk

JUNKANOO n Bahamian ceremony

JUNKED ▶junk

JUNKER, -S n (formerly) young German nobleman

JUNKET, -ED, -S n excursion by public officials ▷ vb (of a public official, committee, etc) to go on a junket

JUNKETER ▶junket

JUNKETS ▶junket

JUNKIE, -S n slang word for person addicted to something

JUNKIER ▶junky

JUNKIES ▶junkie

JUNKIEST ▶junky

JUNKING ▶junk

JUNKMAN, JUNKMEN n man who trades in discarded items

JUNKS ▶junk

JUNKY, JUNKIER, JUNKIEST adj of low quality

JUNKYARD n place where junk is stored or collected for sale

JUNTA, -S n military officers holding power in a country

JUNTO, -S same as ▶junta

JUPATI, -S n type of palm tree

JUPE, -S n sleeveless jacket

JUPON, -S n short sleeveless padded garment

JURA ▶jus

JURAL adj of or relating to law or to the administration of justice

JURALLY ▶jural

JURANT, -S n person taking oath

JURASSIC adj of the second period of the Mesozoic era

JURAT, -S n statement at the foot of an affidavit

JURATORY adj of, relating to, or expressed in an oath

JURATS ▶jurat

JURE, -S adv by legal right ▷ n legal right

JUREL, -S n edible fish

JURES ▶jure

JURIDIC same as > juridical

JURIED ▶jury

JURIES ▶jury

JURIST, -S n expert in law

JURISTIC adj of or relating to jurists

JURISTS ▶jurist

JUROR, -S n member of a jury

JURY, JURIED, JURIES, -ING n group of people sworn to deliver a verdict in a court of law ▷ adj makeshift ▷ vb evaluate by jury

JURYLESS ▶jury

JURYMAN, JURYMEN n member of a jury, esp a man

JURYMAST n replacement mast

JURYMEN ▶juryman

JUS, JURA n right, power, or authority

JUSSIVE, -S n mood of verbs used for giving orders; imperative

JUST, -ED, -EST, -ING adv very recently ▷ adj fair or impartial in action or judgment ▷ vb joust

JUSTER, -S ▶just

JUSTEST ▶just

JUSTICE, -S n quality of being just

JUSTICER n magistrate

JUSTICES ▶justice

J

J

JUSTIFY *vb* prove right or reasonable

JUSTING ▶ **just**

JUSTLE, -D, -S, JUSTLING *less common word for* ▶ **jostle**

JUSTLY ▶ **just**

JUSTNESS ▶ **just**

JUSTS *same as* ▶ **joust**

JUT, -S, -TED, -TING *vb* project or stick out ▷ *n* something that juts out

JUTE, -S *n* plant fibre, used for rope, canvas, etc

JUTELIKE ▶ **jute**

JUTES ▶ **jute**

JUTS ▶ **jut**

JUTTED ▶ **jut**

JUTTIED ▶ **jutty**

JUTTIER ▶ **jutty**

JUTTIES ▶ **jutty**

JUTTIEST ▶ **jutty**

JUTTING ▶ **jut**

JUTTY, JUTTIED, JUTTIER, JUTTIES, JUTTIEST, -ING *vb* project beyond ▷ *adj* characterized by jutting

JUVE, -S *same as* ▶ **juvenile**

JUVENAL, -S *variant spelling* (*esp US*) *of* ▶ **juvenile**

JUVENILE *adj* young ▷ *n* young person or child

JUVES ▶ **juve**

JUVIE, -S *n* juvenile detention centre

JYMOLD *adj* having a hinge

JYNX, -ES *n* wryneck

This unusual word, another name for the bird known as a wryneck, is unique in combining J, Y and X without using any vowels.

Kk

Worth 5 points, **K** is a valuable tile to have in your rack. However, it's not the most useful tile for forming bonus words scoring that extra 50 points, so, as with the **J**, you will normally want to play it off fairly quickly. There are four two-letter words beginning with **K**: **ka**, **ki**, **ko** and **ky**. When it comes to three-letter words, remember **keg** (8 points), **ken** (7), **key** (10), **kex** (14), **kid** (8), **kin** (7), **kip** (9) and **kit** (7). Other three-letter words with **K** well worth remembering are **jak** (14) and **zek** (16).

KA, -ING, -S *n* (in ancient Egypt) type of spirit ▷ *vb* (in archaic usage) help

KAAL *adj* naked

KAAMA, -S *n* large African antelope with lyre-shaped horns

KAAS *n* Dutch cabinet or wardrobe

KAB, -S *variant spelling of* ▶ **cab**

KABAB, -BED, -S *same as* ▶ **kebab**

KABAKA, -S *n* any of the former rulers of the Baganda people

KABALA, -S *same as* ▶ **kabbalah**

KABALISM ▶ **kabala**

KABALIST ▶ **kabala**

KABAR, -S *archaic form of* ▶ **caber**

KABAYA, -S *n* tunic

KABBALA, -S *same as* ▶ **kabbalah**

KABBALAH *n* ancient Jewish mystical tradition

KABBALAS ▶ **kabbala**

KABELE, -S *same as* ▶ **kebele**

KABELJOU *n* large fish that is an important food fish of South African waters

KABIKI, -S *n* fruit tree found in India

KABLOOEY *interj* expressing alarming or surprising abruptness

KABLOOIE *same as* ▶ **kablooey**

KABLOONA *n* (among Canadian Inuits) person who is not Inuit

KABOB, -BED, -S *same as* ▶ **kebab**

KABOCHA, -S *n* type of Japanese pumpkin

KABOODLE *same as* ▶ **caboodle**

KABOOM, -S *n* loud echoing explosive sound

KABS ▶ **kab**

KABUKI, -S *n* form of Japanese drama

KACCHA, -S *n* trousers worn traditionally by Sikhs

KACHA *adj* crude

KACHAHRI *n* Indian courthouse

KACHCHA *same as* ▶ **kacha**

KACHERI, -S *same as* ▶ **kachahri**

KACHINA, -S *n* type of supernatural being

KACHORI, -S *n* balls of fried dough with various fillings, eaten as a snack

KACK, -S *same as* ▶ **cack**

KADAI, -S *same as* ▶ **karahi**

KADDISH *n* ancient Jewish liturgical prayer

KADE, -S *same as* ▶ **ked**

KADI, -S *variant spelling of* ▶ **cadi**

KAE, -D, -ING, -S *n* dialect word for jackdaw or jay ▷ *vb* (in archaic usage) help

KAF, -S *n* letter of the Hebrew alphabet

KAFFIYAH *same as* ▶ **kaffiyeh**

KAFFIYEH *same as* ▶ **keffiyeh**

KAFILA, -S *n* caravan

KAFS ▶ **kaf**

KAFTAN, -S *n* long loose garment

KAFUFFLE *n* commotion or disorder

KAGO, -S *n* Japanese sedan chair

KAGOOL, -S *variant spelling of* ▶ **cagoule**

KAGOS ▶ **kago**

KAGOUL, -S *variant spelling of* ▶ **cagoule**

KAGOULE, -S *same as* ▶ **kagoul**

KAGOULS ▶ **kagoul**

KAGU, -S *n* crested nocturnal bird

KAHAL, -S *n* Jewish community

KAHAWAI, -S *n* food and game fish of New Zealand

KAHUNA, -S *n* Hawaiian priest, shaman, or expert

KAI, -S *n* food

KAIAK, -ED, -ING, -S *same as* ▶ **kayak**

KAID, -S *n* North African chieftain or leader

KAIE, -S *archaic form of* ▶ **key**

KAIF, -S *same as* ▶ **kif**

KAIK, -S *same as* ▶ **kainga**

KAIKA, -S *same as* ▶ **kainga**

KAIKAI, -S *n* food

KAIKAS ▶ **kaika**

KAIKS ▶ **kaik**

KAIL, -S *same as* ▶ **kale**

KAILYARD *same as* ▶ **kaleyard**

KAIM, -S *same as* ▶ **kame**

KAIMAKAM *n* Turkish governor

KAIMS ▶ **kaim**

KAIN, -S *variant spelling of* ▶ **cain**

KAING ▶ **ka**

KAINGA, -S *n* (in New Zealand) a Māori village or small settlement

KAINIT, -S *same as* ▶ **kainite**

KAINITE, -S n white mineral
KAINITS ▸ kainit
KAINS ▸ kain
KAIS ▸ kai
KAISER, -S n German or Austro-Hungarian emperor
KAISERIN n empress
KAISERS ▸ kaiser
KAIZEN, -S n type of philosophy
KAJAWAH, -S n type of seat or pannier used on a camel
KAJEPUT, -S n variety of Australian melaleuca
KAKA, -S n parrot of New Zealand
KAKAPO, -S n nocturnal New Zealand parrot
KAKARIKI n green-feathered New Zealand parrot
KAKAS ▸ kaka
KAKEMONO n Japanese wall hanging
KAKI, -S n Asian persimmon tree
KAKIEMON n type of 17th century Japanese porcelain
KAKIS ▸ kaki
KAKIVAK, -S n fish spear used by Inuit people
KAKODYL, -S variant spelling of ▸ cacodyl
KAKURO, -S n crossword-style puzzle with numbers
KALAM, -S n discussion and debate
KALAMATA n as in kalamata olive aubergine-coloured Greek olive
KALAMDAN n Persian box in which to keep pens
KALAMS ▸ kalam
KALE, -S n cabbage with crinkled leaves
KALENDAR variant form of ▸ calendar
KALENDS same as ▸ calends
KALES ▸ kale
KALEWIFE n Scots word for a female vegetable or cabbage seller
KALEYARD n vegetable garden
KALI, -S another name for ▸ saltwort
KALIAN, -S another name for ▸ hookah
KALIF, -S variant spelling of ▸ caliph
KALIFATE same as > caliphate
KALIFS ▸ kalif
KALIMBA, -S n musical instrument

KALINITE n alum
KALIPH, -S variant spelling of ▸ caliph
KALIS ▸ kali
KALIUM, -S n Latin for potassium
KALLIDIN n type of peptide
KALMIA, -S n evergreen ericaceous shrub
KALONG, -S n fruit bat
KALOOKI, -S n card game
KALOOKIE same as ▸ kalooki
KALOOKIS ▸ kalooki
KALOTYPE variant spelling of ▸ calotype
KALPA, -S n period in Hindu cosmology
KALPAC, -S variant spelling of ▸ calpac
KALPAK, -S variant spelling of ▸ calpac
KALPAS ▸ kalpa
KALPIS, -ES n Greek water jar
KALUKI, -S same as ▸ kalooki
KALUMPIT n type of Filipino fruit tree or its fruit
KALYPTRA n Greek veil
KAM Shakespearean word for ▸ crooked
KAMA, -S n large African antelope with lyre-shaped horns
KAMAAINA n Hawaiian local
KAMACITE n alloy of iron and nickel, occurring in meteorites
KAMAHI, -S n hardwood tree
KAMALA, -S n S Asian tree
KAMAS ▸ kama
KAME, -S n irregular mound of gravel, sand, etc
KAMEES, -ES same as ▸ kameez
KAMEEZ, -ES n long tunic
KAMELA, -S same as ▸ kamala
KAMERAD, -S interj shout of surrender ▷ vb surrender
KAMES ▸ kame
KAMI n divine being or spiritual force in Shinto
KAMICHI, -S n South American bird
KAMIK, -S n traditional Inuit boot
KAMIKAZE n Japanese pilot who performed a suicide mission ▷ adj undertaken in the knowledge that it will kill the person performing it
KAMIKS ▸ kamik
KAMILA, -S same as ▸ kamala

KAMIS, -ES same as ▸ kameez
KAMME same as ▸ kam
KAMOKAMO n kind of marrow found in New Zealand
KAMOTIK, -S n type of Inuit sledge
KAMOTIQ, -S same as ▸ kamotik
KAMPONG, -S n (in Malaysia) village
KAMSEEN, -S same as ▸ khamsin
KAMSIN, -S same as ▸ kamseen
KANA, -S n Japanese syllabary
KANAE, -S n grey mullet
KANAS ▸ kana
KANBAN, -S n just-in-time manufacturing process
KANDY, KANDIES same as ▸ candie
KANE, -S n Hawaiian man or boy
KANEH, -S n 6-cubit Hebrew measure
KANES ▸ kane
KANG, -S n Chinese heatable platform
KANGA, -S n piece of gaily decorated thin cotton cloth
KANGAROO n Australian marsupial ▷ vb (of a car) move forward with sudden jerks
KANGAS ▸ kanga
KANGHA, -S n comb traditionally worn by Sikhs
KANGS ▸ kang
KANJI, -S n Japanese writing system
KANS, -ES n Indian wild sugar cane
KANT, -ED, -ING, -S archaic spelling of ▸ cant
KANTAR, -S n unit of weight
KANTED ▸ kant
KANTELA, -S same as ▸ kantele
KANTELE, -S n Finnish stringed instrument
KANTEN, -S same as ▸ agar
KANTHA, -S n Bengali embroidered quilt
KANTIKOY vb dance ceremonially
KANTING ▸ kant
KANTS ▸ kant
KANUKA, -S n New Zealand myrtaceous tree
KANZU, -S n long garment
KAOLIANG n any of various E Asian varieties of sorghum
KAOLIN, -S n fine white clay

KAOLINE, -S *same as* ▶ **kaolin**
KAOLINIC ▶ **kaolin**
KAOLINS ▶ **kaolin**
KAON, -S *n* type of meson
KAONIC ▶ **kaon**
KAONS ▶ **kaon**
KAPA, -S *n* Hawaiian cloth made from beaten mulberry bark
KAPEYKA, KAPEEK *n* small currency unit of Belarus
KAPH, -S *n* 11th letter of the Hebrew alphabet
KAPOK, -S *n* fluffy fibre
KAPOW, -S *n* sharp explosive sound
KAPPA, -S *n* tenth letter in the Greek alphabet
KAPU, -S *n* (in Hawaii) system of rules for daily life
KAPUKA, -S *same as* > **broadleaf**
KAPUS ▶ **kapu**
KAPUT *adj* ruined or broken
KAPUTT *same as* ▶ **kaput**
KARA, -S *n* steel bangle traditionally worn by Sikhs
KARAHI, -S *n* type of wok
KARAISM, -S *n* beliefs and doctrines of a Jewish sect
KARAIT, -S *same as* ▶ **krait**
KARAKA, -S *n* New Zealand tree
KARAKIA, -S *n* prayer
KARAKUL, -S *n* sheep of central Asia
KARAMU, -S *n* small New Zealand tree
KARANGA, -S *n* call or chant of welcome, sung by a female elder ▷ *vb* perform a karanga
KARAOKE, -S *n* form of entertainment
KARAS ▶ **kara**
KARAT, -S *n* measure of the proportion of gold in an alloy
KARATE, -S *n* Japanese system of unarmed combat
KARATEKA *n* competitor or expert in karate
KARATES ▶ **karate**
KARATS ▶ **karat**
KAREAREA *n* New Zealand falcon
KARENGO, -S *n* edible type of Pacific seaweed
KARITE, -S *n* shea tree
KARK, -ED, -ING, -S *variant spelling of* ▶ **cark**
KARMA, -S *n* person's actions affecting his or her fate in the next reincarnation
KARMIC ▶ **karma**

KARN, -S *old word for* ▶ **cairn**
KARO, -S *n* small New Zealand tree or shrub
KAROO, -S *n* high arid plateau
KARORO, -S *n* large seagull
KAROS ▶ **karo**
KAROSHI, -S *n* (in Japan) death caused by overwork
KAROSS, -ES *n* type of blanket
KARRI, -S *n* Australian eucalypt
KARROO, -S *same as* ▶ **karoo**
KARSEY, -S *variant spelling of* ▶ **khazi**
KARSIES ▶ **karsy**
KARST, -S *n* characteristic scenery of a limestone region
KARSTIC ▶ **karst**
KARSTIFY *vb* become karstic
KARSTS ▶ **karst**
KARSY, KARSIES *variant spelling of* ▶ **khazi**
KART, -S *n* light low-framed vehicle
KARTER, -S ▶ **kart**
KARTING, -S ▶ **kart**
KARTS ▶ **kart**
KARYON, -S *n* nucleus of a cell
KARYOTIN *less common word for* > **chromatin**
KARZY, KARZIES *variant spelling of* ▶ **khazi**
KAS ▶ **ka**
KASBAH, -S *n* citadel of any of various North African cities
KASHA, -S *n* dish originating in Eastern Europe
KASHER, -ED, -S *vb* make fit for use
KASHMIR, -S *variant spelling of* ▶ **cashmere**
KASHRUS *same as* ▶ **kashruth**
KASHRUT, -S *same as* ▶ **kashruth**
KASHRUTH *n* condition of being fit for ritual use in general
KASHRUTS ▶ **kashrut**
KASME *interj* (in Indian English) I swear
KAT, -S *same as* ▶ **khat**
KATA, -S *n* form of exercise
KATAKANA *n* system of Japanese syllabic writing
KATAL, -S *n* SI unit of catalytic activity
KATANA, -S *n* Japanese samurai sword
KATAS ▶ **kata**

KATCHINA *variant spelling of* ▶ **kachina**
KATCINA, -S *variant spelling of* ▶ **kachina**
KATHAK, -S *n* form of dancing
KATHODAL ▶ **kathode**
KATHODE, -S *variant spelling of* ▶ **cathode**
KATHODIC ▶ **kathode**
KATHUMP, -S *n* sound of a dull heavy blow
KATI, -S *variant spelling of* ▶ **catty**
KATION, -S *variant spelling of* ▶ **cation**
KATIPO, -S *n* small poisonous New Zealand spider
KATIS ▶ **kati**
KATORGA, -S *n* type of labour camp
KATS ▶ **kat**
KATSINA, -M, -S *n* (among the Hopi) doll representing spirit messengers
KATSURA, -S *n* Asian tree
KATTI, -S *variant spelling of* ▶ **catty**
KATYDID, -S *n* large green grasshopper of N America
KAUGH, -S *same as* ▶ **kiaugh**
KAUMATUA *n* senior member of a tribe
KAUPAPA, -S *n* strategy, policy, or cause
KAURI, -S *n* large New Zealand conifer
KAURIES ▶ **kaury**
KAURIS ▶ **kauri**
KAURU, -S *n* edible stem of the cabbage tree
KAURY, KAURIES *variant spelling of* ▶ **kauri**
KAVA, -S *n* Polynesian shrub
KAVAKAVA *same as* ▶ **kava**
KAVAL, -S *n* type of flute played in the Balkans
KAVAS ▶ **kava**
KAVASS, -ES *n* armed Turkish constable
KAW, -ED, -ING, -S *variant spelling of* ▶ **caw**
KAWA, -S *n* protocol or etiquette
KAWAII, -S *n* (in Japan) quality of being lovable or cute
KAWAKAWA *n* aromatic shrub or small tree of New Zealand
KAWAS ▶ **kawa**
KAWAU, -S *n* New Zealand name for black shag
KAWED ▶ **kaw**
KAWING ▶ **kaw**

K

K

KAWS ▸ kaw
KAY, -S *n* name of the letter K
KAYAK, -ED, -S *n* Inuit canoe ▸ *vb* travel by kayak
KAYAKER, -S ▸ kayak
KAYAKING ▸ kayak
KAYAKS ▸ kayak
KAYLE *n* one of a set of ninepins
KAYLES *pl n* ninepins
KAYLIED *adj* intoxicated or drunk
KAYO, -ED, -ES, -S *another term for* ▸ **knockout**
KAYOING, -S ▸ kayo
KAYOS ▸ kayo
KAYS ▸ kay
KAZACHKI *same as* ▸ **kazachok**
KAZACHOC *n* Ukrainian folk dance
KAZACHOK *n* Russian folk dance
KAZATSKI *same as* ▸ **kazachok**
KAZATSKY *same as* ▸ **kazachok**
KAZATZKA *same as* ▸ **kazachok**
KAZI, -S *variant spelling of* ▸ **khazi**
KAZOO, -S *n* musical instrument
KBAR, -S *n* kilobar
KEA, -S *n* large brownish-green parrot of New Zealand
KEASAR, -S *archaic variant of* ▸ **kaiser**
KEAVIE, -S *n* archaic or dialect word for a type of crab
KEB, -BED, -BING, -S *vb* Scots word meaning miscarry or reject a lamb
KEBAB, -BED, -S *n* food grilled on a skewer ▸ *vb* skewer
KEBAR, -S *n* Scots word for beam or rafter
KEBBED ▸ keb
KEBBIE, -S *n* Scots word for shepherd's crook
KEBBING ▸ keb
KEBBOCK, -S *n* Scots word for a cheese
KEBBUCK, -S *same as* ▸ **kebbock**
KEBELE, -S *n* Ethiopian local council
KEBLAH, -S *same as* ▸ **kiblah**
KEBOB, -BED, -S *same as* ▸ **kebab**
KEBS ▸ keb
KECK, -ED, -ING *vb* retch or feel nausea

KECKLE, -D, -S *Scots variant of* ▸ **cackle**
KECKLING ▸ keckle
KECKS, -ES *n* trousers
KECKSY, KECKSIES *n* dialect word meaning hollow plant stalk
KED, -S *n* as in **sheep ked** sheep tick
KEDDAH, -S *same as* ▸ **kheda**
KEDGE, -D, -S, KEDGING *vb* move (a ship) using cable attached to an anchor ▸ *n* light anchor used for kedging
KEDGER, -S *n* small anchor
KEDGEREE *n* dish of fish with rice and eggs
KEDGERS ▸ kedger
KEDGES ▸ kedge
KEDGIER ▸ kedgy
KEDGIEST ▸ kedgy
KEDGING ▸ kedge
KEDGY, KEDGIER, KEDGIEST *adj* dialect word for happy or lively
KEDS ▸ ked
KEECH, -ES *n* old word for lump of fat
KEEF, -S *same as* ▸ **kif**
KEEK, -ED, -ING, -S *Scot word for* ▸ **peep**
KEEKER, -S ▸ keek
KEEKING ▸ keek
KEEKS ▸ keek
KEEL, -ED, -S *n* part of a ship ▸ *vb* mark with a stain
KEELAGE, -S *n* fee charged by certain ports
KEELBOAT *n* river boat with a shallow draught and a keel
KEELED ▸ keel
KEELER, -S *n* bargeman
KEELHALE *same as* ▸ **keelhaul**
KEELHAUL *vb* reprimand (someone) harshly
KEELIE, -S *n* kestrel
KEELING, -S ▸ keel
KEELLESS ▸ keel
KEELMAN, KEELMEN *n* bargeman
KEELS ▸ keel
KEELSON, -S *n* part of a ship
KEEMA, -S *n* (in Indian cookery) minced meat
KEEN, -ED, -EST, -S *adj* eager or enthusiastic ▸ *vb* wail over the dead ▸ *n* lament for the dead
KEENER, -S ▸ keen
KEENEST ▸ keen
KEENING, -S ▸ keen
KEENLY ▸ keen
KEENNESS ▸ keen
KEENO, -S *same as* ▸ **keno**

KEENS ▸ keen
KEEP, -S, KEPT *vb* have or retain possession of ▸ *n*. cost of food and everyday expenses
KEEPABLE ▸ keep
KEEPER, -S *n* person who looks after animals in a zoo
KEEPING, -S ▸ keep
KEEPNET, -S *n* cylindrical net used to keep fish alive
KEEPS ▸ keep
KEEPSAKE *n* gift treasured for the sake of the giver
KEEPSAKY *adj* superficially attractive
KEESHOND *n* breed of dog of the spitz type
KEESTER, -S *same as* ▸ **keister**
KEET, -S *short for* ▸ **parakeet**
KEEVE, -S *n* tub or vat
KEF, -S *same as* ▸ **kif**
KEFFEL, -S *dialect word for* ▸ **horse**
KEFFIYAH *same as* ▸ **kaffiyeh**
KEFFIYEH *n* cotton headdress worn by Arabs
KEFIR, -S *n* effervescent drink
KEFS ▸ kef
KEFTEDES *n* Greek dish of meatballs cooked with herbs and onions
KEFUFFLE *same as* > **kerfuffle**
KEG, -GED, -GING, -S *n* small metal beer barrel ▸ *vb* put in kegs
KEGELER, -S *same as* ▸ **kegler**
KEGGED ▸ keg
KEGGER, -S ▸ keg
KEGGING ▸ keg
KEGLER, -S *n* participant in a game of tenpin bowling
KEGLING, -S *n* bowling
KEGS ▸ keg
KEHUA, -S *n* ghost or spirit
KEIGHT ▸ ketch
KEIR, -S *same as* ▸ **kier**
KEIREN, -S *n* type of track cycling event
KEIRETSU *n* group of Japanese businesses
KEIRIN, -S *n* cycling race originating in Japan
KEIRS ▸ keir
KEISTER, -S *n* rump
KEITLOA, -S *n* type of rhinoceros
KEKENO, -S *n* New Zealand fur seal
KEKS *same as* ▸ **kecks**
KEKSYE, -S *same as* ▸ **kex**

KELEP, -S n large ant found in Central and South America

KELIM, -S same as ▸ **kilim**

KELL, -S dialect word for ▸ **hairnet**

KELLAUT, -S same as ▸ **khilat**

KELLIES ▸ **kelly**

KELLS ▸ **kell**

KELLY, KELLIES n part of a drill system

KELOID, -S n type of scar tissue

KELOIDAL ▸ **keloid**

KELOIDS ▸ **keloid**

KELP, -ED, -ING, -S n large brown seaweed ▷ vb burn seaweed to make a type of ash

KELPER, -S n Falkland Islander

KELPFISH n type of fish that lives among kelp

KELPIE, -S n Australian sheepdog

KELPING ▸ **kelp**

KELPS ▸ **kelp**

KELPY same as ▸ **kelpie**

KELSON, -S same as ▸ **keelson**

KELT, -S n salmon that has recently spawned

KELTER, -S same as ▸ **kilter**

KELTIE variant spelling of ▸ **kelty**

KELTIES ▸ **kelty**

KELTS ▸ **kelt**

KELTY, KELTIES n old Scots word for a drink imposed on someone not thought to be drinking enough

KELVIN, -S n SI unit of temperature

KEMB, -ED, -ING, -S old word for ▸ **comb**

KEMBLA, -S n small change

KEMBO, -ED, -ING, -S same as ▸ **kimbo**

KEMBS ▸ **kemb**

KEMP, -ED, -S n coarse hair or strand of hair ▷ vb dialect word meaning to compete or try to come first

KEMPER, -S ▸ **kemp**

KEMPIER ▸ **kempy**

KEMPIEST ▸ **kempy**

KEMPING, -S ▸ **kemp**

KEMPLE, -S n variable Scottish measure for hay or straw

KEMPS ▸ **kemp**

KEMPT adj (of hair) tidy

KEMPY, KEMPIER, KEMPIEST ▸ **kemp**

KEN, -NED, -S vb know ▷ n range of knowledge or perception

KENAF, -S another name for ▸ **ambary**

KENCH, -ES n bin for salting and preserving fish

KENDO, -S n Japanese sport of fencing using wooden staves

KENDOIST n person who practises kendo

KENDOS ▸ **kendo**

KENNED ▸ **ken**

KENNEL, -ED, -S n hutlike shelter for a dog ▷ vb put or go into a kennel

KENNER, -S ▸ **ken**

KENNET, -S n old word for a small hunting dog

KENNETT, -S vb spoil or destroy ruthlessly

KENNING, -S ▸ **ken**

KENO, -S n game of chance similar to bingo

KENOSIS, KENOSES n Christ's renunciation of certain divine attributes

KENOTIC, -S ▸ **kenosis**

KENOTRON n signal-amplifying device

KENS ▸ **ken**

KENSPECK adj Scots for easily seen or recognized

KENT, -ED, -ING, -S dialect word for ▸ **punt**

KENTE, -S n brightly coloured handwoven cloth

KENTED ▸ **kent**

KENTES ▸ **kente**

KENTIA, -S n plant name

KENTING ▸ **kent**

KENTS ▸ **kent**

KEP, -PED, -PEN, -PING, -PIT, -S, KIPPEN vb catch

KEPHALIC variant spelling of ▸ **cephalic**

KEPHALIN same as ▸ **cephalin**

KEPHIR, -S same as ▸ **kefir**

KEPI, -S n French military cap with a flat top and a horizontal peak

KEPPED ▸ **kep**

KEPPEN ▸ **kep**

KEPPING ▸ **kep**

KEPPIT ▸ **kep**

KEPS ▸ **kep**

KEPT ▸ **keep**

KERAMIC rare variant of ▸ **ceramic**

KERAMICS rare variant of ▸ **ceramics**

KERATIN, -S n fibrous protein found in the hair and nails

KERATOID adj resembling horn

KERATOMA n horny growth on the skin

KERATOSE adj (esp of certain sponges) having a horny skeleton

KERB, -ED, -S n edging to a footpath ▷ vb provide with or enclose with a kerb

KERBAYA, -S n blouse worn by Malay women

KERBED ▸ **kerb**

KERBING, -S n material used for a kerb

KERBS ▸ **kerb**

KERBSIDE n edge of a pavement where it drops to the level of the road

KERCHIEF n piece of cloth worn over the head or round the neck

KERCHOO interj atishoo

KEREL, -S n chap or fellow

KERERU, -S n New Zealand pigeon

KERF, -ED, -ING, -S n cut made by a saw, an axe, etc ▷ vb cut

KERKY, KERKIER, KERKIEST adj stupid

KERMA, -S n quantity of radiation

KERMES, -ES n dried bodies of female scale insects

KERMESS same as ▸ **kermis**

KERMESSE same as ▸ **kermis**

KERMIS, -ES n (formerly) annual country festival or carnival

KERMODE, -S n type of black bear found in Canada

KERN, -S n projection of a printed character ▷ vb furnish (a typeface) with a kern

KERNE, -D, -S same as ▸ **kern**

KERNEL, -ED, -S n seed of a nut, cereal, or fruit stone ▷ vb form kernels

KERNELLY adj with or like kernels

KERNELS ▸ **kernel**

KERNES ▸ **kerne**

KERNING, -S n provision of kerns in printing

KERNISH adj resembling an armed foot soldier or peasant

KERNITE, -S n light soft colourless or white mineral

KERNS ▸ **kern**

KERO, -S short for ▸ **kerosene**

KEROGEN, -S n material that produces hydrocarbons when heated

KEROS ▸ **kero**

KEROSENE n liquid mixture distilled from petroleum and used as a fuel or solvent

K

KEROSINE same as
▸ **kerosene**

KERPLUNK vb land noisily

KERRIA, -S n type of shrub
with yellow flowers

KERRY, KERRIES n breed of
dairy cattle

KERSEY, -S n smooth
woollen cloth

KERVE, -D, -S, KERVING
dialect word for ▸ **carve**

KERYGMA, -S n Christian
gospel

KESAR, -S old variant of
▸ **kaiser**

KESH, -ES n beard and uncut
hair traditionally worn by
Sikhs

KEST, -ING, -S old form of
▸ **cast**

KESTREL, -S n type of small
falcon

KESTS ▸ **kest**

KET, -S n dialect word for
carrion

KETA, -S n type of salmon

KETAINE adj in poor taste

KETAMINE n drug used in
medicine as an anaesthetic

KETAS ▸ **keta**

KETCH, KEIGHT, -ES, -ING n
two-masted sailing vessel
▹ vb (in archaic usage) catch

KETCHUP, -S n thick cold
sauce, usu made of
tomatoes

KETCHUPY adj like ketchup

KETE, -S n basket woven
from flax

KETENE, -S n colourless
irritating toxic gas

KETES ▸ **kete**

KETMIA, -S n as in **bladder
ketmia** plant with pale
yellow flowers

KETO adj as in **keto form**
form of tautomeric
compounds

KETOL, -S n nitrogenous
substance

KETONE, -S n type of organic
solvent

KETONIC ▸ **ketone**

KETOSE n any
monosaccharide that
contains a ketone group

KETOSIS, KETOSES n high
concentration of ketone
bodies in the blood

KETOTIC ▸ **ketosis**

KETOXIME n oxime formed
by reaction between
hydroxylamine and a ketone

KETS ▸ **ket**

KETTLE, -D, -S, KETTLING n
container used for boiling

water ▹ vb contain a public
protest in an enclosed space

**KETUBAH, -S, KETUBOT,
KETUBOTH** n Jewish
marriage contract

KEVEL, -S n strong bitt or
bollard for securing heavy
hawsers

KEVIL, -S old variant of
▸ **kevel**

KEWL, -ER, -EST nonstandard
variant spelling of ▸ **cool**

KEWPIE, -S n type of brightly
coloured doll

KEX, -ES n any of several
hollow-stemmed
umbelliferous plants

This is another of the great
high-scoring 3-letter words
that use X.

KEY, -ED, -EST n device for
operating a lock by moving a
bolt ▹ adj of great
importance ▹ vb enter (text)
using a keyboard

KEYBOARD n set of keys on
a piano, computer, etc ▹ vb
enter (text) using a keyboard

KEYBUGLE n bugle with
keys

KEYCARD, -S n electronic
card used as a key

KEYED ▸ **key**

KEYER, -S n device that keys
signals or information into a
device or computing system

KEYEST ▸ **key**

KEYFRAME n image used to
show the start and end of
animation sequence

KEYHOLE, -S n opening for
inserting a key into a lock

KEYING, -S ▸ **key**

KEYLESS ▸ **key**

KEYLINE, -S n outline image
on artwork or plans to show
where it is to be placed

KEYNOTE, -D, -S adj central
or dominating ▹ n dominant
idea of a speech etc ▹ vb
deliver a keynote address to
(a political convention, etc)

KEYNOTER n person
delivering a keynote address

KEYNOTES ▸ **keynote**

KEYPAD, -S n small panel
with a set of buttons

KEYPAL, -S n person one
regularly exchanges emails
with for fun

KEYPRESS n single
depression of a keyboard key

KEYPUNCH n keyboard
device to transfer data onto
punched cards ▹ vb transfer
(data) onto punched cards

KEYRING, -S n metal ring for
keeping keys together

KEYS interj children's cry for
truce

KEYSET, -S n set of computer
keys used for a particular
purpose

KEYSTER, -S same as
▸ **keister**

KEYSTONE n most
important part of a process,
organization, etc ▹ vb
project or provide with a
distorted image

KEYWAY, -S n engineering
device

KEYWORD, -S n word or
phrase used to find
something on a computer

KGOTLA, -S n (in South
African English) meeting
place

KHADDAR, -S n cotton cloth

KHADI, -S same as ▸ **khaddar**

KHAF, -S n letter of the
Hebrew alphabet

KHAKI, -S adj dull
yellowish-brown ▹ n fabric
of this colour used for
military uniforms

KHALAT, -S same as ▸ **khilat**

KHALIF, -S variant spelling of
▸ **caliph**

KHALIFA, -S same as ▸ **caliph**

KHALIFAH same as ▸ **caliph**

KHALIFAS ▸ **khalifa**

KHALIFAT same as
> **caliphate**

KHALIFS ▸ **khalif**

KHAMSEEN same as
▸ **khamsin**

KHAMSIN, -S n hot
southerly wind

KHAN, -S n title of respect in
Afghanistan and central Asia

KHANATE, -S n territory
ruled by a khan

KHANDA, -S n double-edged
sword

KHANGA, -S same as
▸ **kanga**

KHANJAR, -S n type of
dagger

KHANS ▸ **khan**

KHANSAMA same as
> **khansamah**

KHANUM, -S feminine form of
▸ **khan**

KHAPH, -S n letter of the
Hebrew alphabet

KHARIF, -S n crop harvested
at the beginning of winter

KHAT, -S n white-flowered
evergreen shrub

KHAYA, -S n type of
African tree

KHAYAL, -S n kind of Indian classical vocal music

KHAYAS ▸ khaya

KHAZEN, -IM, -S same as ▸ **chazan**

KHAZI, -S n lavatory

KHEDA, -S n enclosure used to capture wild elephants

KHEDAH, -S same as ▸ **kheda**

KHEDAS ▸ kheda

KHEDIVA, -S n khedive's wife

KHEDIVAL ▸ khedive

KHEDIVAS ▸ khedive

KHEDIVE, -S n viceroy of Egypt under Ottoman suzerainty

KHET, -S n Thai district

KHETH, -S same as ▸ **heth**

KHETS ▸ khet

KHI, -S n letter of the Greek alphabet

This is a letter of the Greek alphabet, also spelt **chi**. It is worth remembering as one of the higher-scoring 3-letter words starting with K.

KHILAFAT same as > **caliphate**

KHILAT, -S n (in the Middle East) gift given to someone as a mark of honour

KHILIM, -S same as ▸ **kilim**

KHIMAR, -S n type of headscarf worn by Muslim women

KHIRKAH, -S n dervish's woollen or cotton outer garment

KHIS ▸ khi

KHODJA, -S same as ▸ **khoja**

KHOJA, -S n teacher in a Muslim school

KHOR, -S n watercourse

KHOTBAH, -S same as ▸ **khutbah**

KHOTBEH, -S same as ▸ **khutbah**

KHOUM, -S n Mauritanian monetary unit

KHUD, -S n Indian ravine

KHURTA, -S same as ▸ **kurta**

KHUSKHUS n aromatic perennial Indian grass whose roots are woven into mats, fans, and baskets

KHUTBAH, -S n sermon in a Mosque, especially on a Friday

KI, -S n vital energy

KIAAT, -S n tropical African leguminous tree

KIACK, -S n N American fish of the herring family

KIANG, -S n variety of wild ass

KIAUGH, -S n (in Scots) anxiety

KIBBE, -S n Middle Eastern dish

KIBBEH, -S same as ▸ **kibbe**

KIBBES ▸ kibbe

KIBBI, -S same as ▸ **kibbe**

KIBBITZ same as ▸ **kibitz**

KIBBLE, -D, -S, KIBBLING n bucket used in wells or in mining for hoisting ▷ vb grind into small pieces

KIBBUTZ n communal farm or factory in Israel

KIBE, -S n chilblain

KIBEI, -S n someone of Japanese ancestry born in the US and educated in Japan

KIBES ▸ kibe

KIBIBYTE n two to the power of ten bytes

KIBITKA, -S n (in Russia) covered sledge or wagon

KIBITZ, -ED, -ES vb interfere or offer unwanted advice

KIBITZER ▸ kibitz

KIBITZES ▸ kibitz

KIBLA, -S same as ▸ **kiblah**

KIBLAH, -S n direction of Mecca

KIBLAS ▸ kibla

KIBOSH, -ED, -ES vb put a stop to

KICK, -ED, -S vb drive, push, or strike with the foot ▷ n thrust or blow with the foot

KICKABLE ▸ kick

KICKBACK n money paid illegally for favours done ▷ vb have a strong reaction

KICKBALL n children's ball game or the large ball used in it

KICKBOX vb box with hands and feet

KICKDOWN n method of changing gear in a car with automatic transmission

KICKED ▸ kick

KICKER, -S n person or thing that kicks

KICKFLIP n type of skateboarding manoeuvre ▷ vb perform a kickflip in skateboarding

KICKIER ▸ kicky

KICKIEST ▸ kicky

KICKING, -S n act of kicking

KICKOFF, -S n kick that starts a game of football

KICKOUT, -S n (in basketball) instance of kicking the ball

KICKS ▸ kick

KICKSHAW n valueless trinket

KICKUP, -S n fuss

KICKY, KICKIER, KICKIEST adj excitingly unusual and different

KID, -DED, -S n child ▷ vb tease or deceive (someone) ▷ adj younger

KIDDER, -S ▸ kid

KIDDIE same as ▸ **kiddy**

KIDDIED ▸ kiddy

KIDDIER, -S n old word for a market trader

KIDDIES ▸ kiddy

KIDDING, -S n act of kidding

KIDDISH ▸ kid

KIDDLE, -S n device for catching fish in a river or in the sea

KIDDO, -ES, -S n very informal term of address for a young person

KIDDUSH n (in Judaism) special blessing

KIDDY, KIDDIED, KIDDIES, -ING n affectionate word for a child ▷ vb tease or deceive

KIDEL, -S same as ▸ **kiddle**

KIDGE dialect word for ▸ **lively**

KIDGIE, -R, -ST adj dialect word for friendly and welcoming

KIDGLOVE adj overdelicate or overrefined

KIDLET, -S n humorous word for small child

KIDLIKE ▸ kid

KIDLING, -S n young kid

KIDLIT, -S n children's literature

KIDNAP, -ED, -S vb seize and hold (a person) to ransom

KIDNAPEE ▸ kidnap

KIDNAPER ▸ kidnap

KIDNAPS ▸ kidnap

KIDNEY, -S n either of the pair of organs that produce urine

KIDOLOGY n practice of bluffing or deception

KIDS ▸ kid

KIDSKIN, -S n soft smooth leather

KIDULT, -S n adult interested in entertainments intended for children ▷ adj aimed at or suitable for kidults, or both children and adults

KIDVID, -S n informal word for children's video or television

KIEF, -S same as ▸ **kif**

KIEKIE, -S n climbing bush plant of New Zealand

KIELBASA n Polish sausage

KIELBASI same as ▸ **kielbasa**

KIELBASY same as ▸ **kielbasa**

KIER, -S n vat in which cloth is bleached

KIERIE, -S n South African cudgel

KIERS ▸ kier

KIESTER, -S same as ▸ keister

KIEV, -S n type of chicken dish

KIEVE, -S same as ▸ keeve

KIEVS ▸ kiev

KIF, -S n marijuana

KIFF adj South African slang for excellent

KIFS ▸ kif

KIGHT, -S n archaic spelling of kite, the bird of prey

KIKOI, -S n piece of cotton cloth

KIKUMON, -S n emblem of the imperial family of Japan

KIKUYU, -S n type of grass

KILD old spelling of ▸ killed

KILERG, -S n 1000 ergs

KILEY, -S same as ▸ kylie

KILIKITI n Polynesian version of cricket

KILIM, -S n pileless woven rug

KILL, -ED, -S vb cause the death of ▹ n act of killing

KILLABLE ▸ kill

KILLADAR n fort commander or governor

KILLAS, -ES n Cornish clay slate

KILLCOW, -S n important person

KILLCROP n ever-hungry baby, thought to be a fairy changeling

KILLDEE, -S same as ▸ killdeer

KILLDEER n large brown-and-white North American plover with a noisy cry

KILLDEES ▸ killdee

KILLED ▸ kill

KILLER, -S n person or animal that kills, esp habitually

KILLICK, -S n small anchor, esp one made of a heavy stone

KILLIE, -S same as ▸ killifish

KILLING, -S adj very tiring ▹ n sudden financial success

KILLJOY, -S n person who spoils others' pleasure

KILLOCK, -S same as ▸ killick

KILLOGIE n sheltered place in front of a kiln

KILLS ▸ kill

KILLUT, -S same as ▸ khilat

KILN, -ED, -ING, -S n type of oven ▹ vb fire or process in a kiln

KILO, -S n code word for the letter k

KILOBAR, -S n 1000 bars

KILOBASE n unit of measurement for DNA and RNA equal to 1000 base pairs

KILOBAUD n 1000 baud

KILOBIT, -S n 1024 bits

KILOBYTE n 1024 units of information

KILOGRAM n one thousand grams

KILOGRAY n 1000 gray

KILOMOLE n 1000 moles

KILOPOND n informal unit of gravitational force

KILORAD, -S n 1000 rads

KILOS ▸ kilo

KILOTON, -S n one thousand tons

KILOVOLT n one thousand volts

KILOWATT n one thousand watts

KILP, -S dialect form of ▸ kelp

KILT, -S n knee-length pleated tartan skirt-like garment ▹ vb put pleats in (cloth)

KILTED ▸ kilt

KILTER, -S n working order or alignment

KILTIE, -S n someone wearing a kilt

KILTING, -S ▸ kilt

KILTLIKE ▸ kilt

KILTS ▸ kilt

KILTY same as ▸ kiltie

KIMBO, -ED, -ING, -S vb place akimbo

KIMCHEE, -S same as ▸ kimchi

KIMCHI, -S n Korean dish

KIMMER, -S same as ▸ cummer

KIMONO, -S n loose wide-sleeved Japanese robe

KIMONOED ▸ kimono

KIMONOS ▸ kimono

KIN, -S n person's relatives collectively ▹ adj related by blood

KINA, -S n standard monetary unit of Papua New Guinea

KINAKINA same as ▸ quinine

KINARA, -S n African candle holder

KINAS ▸ kina

KINASE, -S n type of enzyme

KINCHIN, -S old slang word for ▸ child

KINCOB, -S n fine silk fabric

KIND, -ED, -EST, -ING, -S adj considerate, friendly, and helpful ▹ n class or group with common characteristics ▹ vb old word for beget or father

KINDA adv very informal shortening of kind of

KINDED ▸ kind

KINDER, -S adj more kind ▹ n kindergarten or nursery school

KINDEST ▸ kind

KINDIE same as ▸ kindy

KINDIES ▸ kindy

KINDING ▸ kind

KINDLE, -D, -S vb set (a fire) alight

KINDLER, -S ▸ kindle

KINDLES ▸ kindle

KINDLESS adj heartless

KINDLIER ▸ kindly

KINDLILY ▸ kindly

KINDLING n dry wood or straw for starting fires

KINDLY, KINDLIER adj having a warm-hearted nature ▹ adv in a considerate way

KINDNESS n quality of being kind

KINDRED, -S adj having similar qualities ▹ n blood relationship

KINDS ▸ kind

KINDY, KINDIES n kindergarten

KINE, -S pl n cows or cattle ▹ n Japanese pestle

KINEMA, -S same as ▸ cinema

KINES ▸ kine

KINESES ▸ kinesis

KINESIC adj of or relating to kinesics

KINESICS n study of the role of body movements in communication

KINESIS, KINESES n movement of an organism

KINETIC adj relating to or caused by motion

KINETICS n branch of mechanics concerned with the study of bodies in motion

KINETIN, -S n plant hormone

KINFOLK, -S another word for ▸ kinsfolk

KING, -ED, -ING, -S n male ruler of a monarchy ▹ vb make king

KINGBIRD n any of several large American flycatchers

KINGBOLT n pivot bolt that connects the body of a horse-drawn carriage to the front axle

KINGCUP, -S n yellow-flowered plant

KINGDOM, -S n state ruled by a king or queen

KINGED ▷ **king**

KINGFISH n food and game fish occurring in warm American Atlantic coastal waters

KINGHOOD ▷ **king**

KINGING ▷ **king**

KINGKLIP n edible eel-like marine fish of S Africa

KINGLE, -S n Scots word for a type of hard rock

KINGLESS ▷ **king**

KINGLET, -S n king of a small or insignificant territory

KINGLIER ▷ **kingly**

KINGLIKE ▷ **king**

KINGLING n minor king

KINGLY, KINGLIER adj appropriate to a king ▷ adv in a manner appropriate to a king

KINGPIN, -S n most important person in an organization

KINGPOST n vertical post connecting the apex of a triangular roof truss to the tie beam

KINGS ▷ **king**

KINGSHIP n position or authority of a king

KINGSIDE n side of the chessboard on which a particular king is at the start of a game

KINGWOOD n hard fine-grained violet-tinted wood of a Brazilian leguminous tree

KININ, -S n type of polypeptide

KINK, -ED, -ING, -S n twist or bend in rope, wire, hair, etc ▷ vb form or cause to form a kink

KINKAJOU n arboreal mammal of Central and South America

KINKED ▷ **kink**

KINKIER ▷ **kinky**

KINKIEST ▷ **kinky**

KINKILY ▷ **kinky**

KINKING ▷ **kink**

KINKLE, -S n little kink

KINKS ▷ **kink**

KINKY, KINKIER, KINKIEST adj tightly curled or looped

KINLESS adj without any relatives

KINO, -S same as ▶ **keno**

KINONE, -S n benzoquinone

KINOS ▷ **kino**

KINRED, -S old form of ▶ **kindred**

KINS ▷ **kin**

KINSFOLK pl n one's family or relatives

KINSHIP, -S n blood relationship

KINSMAN, KINSMEN n relative

KIORE, -S n small brown rat native to New Zealand

KIOSK, -S n small booth

KIP, -PED, -PING, -S vb sleep ▷ n sleep or slumber

KIPE, -S n dialect word for a basket for catching fish

KIPP, -S uncommon variant of ▶ **kip**

KIPPA, -S n skullcap worn by male Jews

KIPPAGE, -S n Scots word for a state of anger or excitement

KIPPAH, -S same as ▶ **kippa**

KIPPAS ▶ **kippa**

KIPPED ▷ **kip**

KIPPEN ▷ **kep**

KIPPER, -S n cleaned, salted, and smoked herring ▷ vb cure (a herring) by salting and smoking it

KIPPERED adj (of fish, esp herring) having been cleaned, salted, and smoked

KIPPERER ▷ **kipper**

KIPPERS ▷ **kipper**

KIPPING ▷ **kip**

KIPPS ▷ **kipp**

KIPS ▷ **kip**

KIPSKIN, -S same as ▶ **kip**

KIPUNJI, -S n Tanzanian species of monkey

KIR, -S n drink made from dry white wine and cassis

KIRANA, -S n small family-owned shop in India

KIRBEH, -S n leather bottle

KIRBY n as in kirby grip type of hairgrip

KIRIGAMI, -S n art, originally Japanese, of folding and cutting paper into decorative shapes

KIRIMON, -S n Japanese imperial crest

KIRK, -ED, -S Scot word for ▶ **church**

KIRKING, -S ▷ **kirk**

KIRKMAN, KIRKMEN n member or strong upholder of the Kirk

KIRKS ▷ **kirk**

KIRKTON, -S n village or town with a parish church

KIRKWARD adv towards the church

KIRKYARD n churchyard

KIRMESS same as ▶ **kermis**

KIRN, -ED, -ING, -S dialect word for ▶ **churn**

KIRPAN, -S n short sword traditionally carried by Sikhs

KIRRI, -S n South African cudgel

KIRS ▷ **kir**

KIRSCH, -ES n cherry brandy

KIRTAN, -S n devotional singing

KIRTLE, -D, -S n woman's skirt or dress ▷ vb dress with a kirtle

KIS ▶ **ki**

KISAN, -S n peasant or farmer

KISH, -ES n graphite formed on the surface of molten iron

KISHKA, -S same as ▶ **kishke**

KISHKE, -S n stuffed beef or fowl intestine, boiled and roasted

KISKADEE n large flycatcher of tropical America

KISMAT, -S same as ▶ **kismet**

KISMET, -S n fate or destiny

KISMETIC ▶ **kismet**

KISMETS ▶ **kismet**

KISS, -ED, -ES, -ING vb touch with the lips in affection or greeting ▷ n touch with the lips

KISSABLE ▶ **kiss**

KISSABLY ▶ **kiss**

KISSED ▶ **kiss**

KISSEL, -S n Russian dessert

KISSER, -S n mouth or face

KISSES ▶ **kiss**

KISSIER ▶ **kissy**

KISSIEST ▶ **kissy**

KISSING, -S ▶ **kiss**

KISSY, KISSIER, KISSIEST adj showing exaggerated affection

KIST, -ED, -ING, -S n large wooden chest ▷ vb place in a coffin

KISTFUL, -S ▶ **kist**

KISTING ▶ **kist**

KISTS ▶ **kist**

KISTVAEN n stone tomb

KIT, -S, -TED, -TING n outfit or equipment for a specific purpose ▷ vb fit or provide

KITBAG, -S n bag for a soldier's or traveller's belongings

KITCHEN, -S n room used for cooking ▷ vb (in archaic usage) provide with food

KITE, -D, -S n light frame covered with a thin material ▷ vb soar and glide

KITELIKE ▶ **kite**

KITENGE, -S n thick cotton cloth

KITER, -S ▶ **kite**

KITES ▶ **kite**

K

KITH, -S *n* one's friends and acquaintances

KITHARA, -S variant of ▶ cithara

KITHE, -D, -S, KITHING same as ▶ kythe

KITHS ▶ kith

KITING, -S ▶ kite

KITLING, -S dialect word for ▶ kitten

KITS ▶ kit

KITSCH, -ES *n* tawdry or vulgarized art or literature with popular sentimental appeal ▷ *adj* having this quality

KITSCHY ▶ kitsch

KITSET, -S *n* New Zealand word for furniture supplied in pieces

KITTED ▶ kit

KITTEL, -S *n* white garment worn for certain Jewish rituals or burial

KITTEN, -ED, -S *n* young cat ▷ *vb* (of cats) give birth

KITTENY *adj* like a kitten

KITTIES ▶ kitty

KITTING ▶ kit

KITTLE, -D, -R, -S, -ST, KITTLING *adj* capricious and unpredictable ▷ *vb* be troublesome or puzzling to (someone)

KITTLIER ▶ kittly

KITTLING ▶ kittle

KITTLY, KITTLIER Scots word for ▶ ticklish

KITTUL, -S *n* type of palm from which jaggery sugar comes

KITTY, KITTIES *n* communal fund

KITUL, -S same as ▶ kittul

KIVA, -S *n* large room in a Pueblo village

KIWI, -S *n* New Zealand flightless bird with a long beak and no tail

KLANG, -S *n* (in music) kind of tone

KLAP, -PED, -PING, -S *vb* slap or spank

KLATCH, -ES *n* gathering, especially over coffee

KLATSCH same as ▶ klatch

KLAVERN, -S *n* local Ku Klux Klan group

KLAVIER, -S same as ▶ clavier

KLAXON, -ED, -S *n* loud horn used on emergency vehicles ▷ *vb* hoot with a klaxon

KLEAGLE, -S *n* person with a particular rank in the Ku Klux Klan

KLEENEX *n* tradename for a kind of tissue

KLEFTIKO *n* type of Greek lamb dish

KLEPHT, -S *n* group of Greeks

KLEPHTIC ▶ klepht

KLEPHTS ▶ klepht

KLEPTO, -S *n* compulsive thief

KLETT, -S *n* lightweight climbing boot

KLEZMER, -S *n* Jewish folk musician

KLICK, -S *n* kilometre

KLIEG, -S *n* as in klieg light intense carbon-arc light

KLIK, -S US military slang word for > kilometre

KLINKER, -S *n* type of brick used in paving

KLIPDAS *n* rock hyrax

KLISTER, -S *n* type of ski dressing for improving grip on snow

KLONDIKE same as ▶ klondyke

KLONDYKE *n* rich source of something ▷ *vb* transfer (bulk loads of fish) to factory ships at sea for processing

KLONG, -S *n* type of canal in Thailand

KLOOCH, -ES same as > kloochman

KLOOF, -S *n* mountain pass or gorge

KLOOTCH same as > kloochman

KLUDGE, -D, -S, KLUDGING *n* untidy solution ▷ *vb* cobble something together

KLUDGEY ▶ kludgy

KLUDGIER ▶ kludgy

KLUDGING ▶ kludge

KLUDGY, KLUDGIER ▶ kludge

KLUGE, -D, -S, KLUGING same as ▶ kludge

KLUTZ, -ES *n* clumsy or stupid person

KLUTZY, KLUTZIER ▶ klutz

KLYSTRON *n* electron tube for the amplification of microwaves

KNACK, -ING, -S *n* skilful way of doing something ▷ *vb* dialect word for crack or snap

KNACKED *adj* broken or worn out

KNACKER, -S *n* buyer of old horses for killing ▷ *vb* exhaust

KNACKERY *n* slaughterhouse for horses

KNACKIER ▶ knacky

KNACKING ▶ knack

KNACKISH *adj* old word meaning cunning or artful

KNACKS ▶ knack

KNACKY, KNACKIER *adj* old or dialect word for cunning or artful

KNAG, -S *n* knot in wood

KNAGGY, KNAGGIER *adj* knotty

KNAGS ▶ knag

KNAIDEL, -S same as ▶ kneidel

KNAP, -PED, -PING, -S *n* crest of a hill ▷ *vb* hit, hammer, or chip

KNAPPER, -S ▶ knap

KNAPPING ▶ knap

KNAPPLE, -D, -S old word for ▶ nibble

KNAPS ▶ knap

KNAPSACK *n* soldier's or traveller's bag worn strapped on the back

KNAPWEED *n* plant with purplish thistle-like flowers

KNAR, -RING, -S old spelling of ▶ gnar

KNARL, -S old spelling of ▶ gnarl

KNARLIER ▶ knarly

KNARLS ▶ knarl

KNARLY, KNARLIER same as ▶ gnarly

KNARRED ▶ knar

KNARRIER ▶ knarry

KNARRING ▶ knar

KNARRY, KNARRIER ▶ knar

KNARS ▶ knar

KNAUR, -S variant form of ▶ knur

KNAVE, -S *n* jack at cards

KNAVERY *n* dishonest behaviour

KNAVES ▶ knave

KNAVISH ▶ knave

KNAWE, -S same as ▶ knawel

KNAWEL, -S *n* type of Old World plant

KNAWES ▶ knawe

KNEAD, -ED, -ING, -S *vb* work (dough) into a smooth mixture with the hands

KNEADER, -S ▶ knead

KNEADING ▶ knead

KNEADS ▶ knead

KNEE, -D, -ING, -S *n* joint between thigh and lower leg ▷ *vb* strike or push with the knee

KNEECAP, -S *n* nontechnical name for ▶ patella

KNEED ▶ knee

KNEEHOLE *n* space for the knees, esp under a desk

KNEEING ▶ knee

KNEEJERK *adj* (of a reply or reaction) automatic and predictable

KNEEL, -ED, -ING, -S, KNELT *vb* fall or rest on one's knees ▷ *n* act or position of kneeling

KNEELER, -S ▶ kneel

KNEELIKE *adj* like a knee

KNEELING ▸ kneel

KNEELS ▸ kneel

KNEEPAD, -S n protective covering for the knee

KNEEPAN, -S another word for ▸ **patella**

KNEEROOM n space to put one's knees

KNEES ▸ knee

KNEESIES n flirtatious touching of knees under table

KNEESOCK n type of sock that comes up to the knee

KNEIDEL, -S n (in Jewish cookery) small dumpling

KNELL, -ED, -ING, -S n sound of a bell, esp at a funeral or death ▷ vb ring a knell

KNELT ▸ kneel

KNESSET, -S n parliament or assembly

KNEVELL, -S vb old Scots word meaning beat

KNEW ▸ know

KNICKER adj of or relating to knickers

KNICKERS pl n woman's or girl's undergarment

KNICKS pl n knickers

KNIFE, -D, -S, KNIVES n sharp-edged blade with a handle ▷ vb cut or stab with a knife

KNIFEMAN, KNIFEMEN n man who is armed with a knife

KNIFER, -S ▸ knife

KNIFES ▸ knife

KNIFING, -S ▸ knife

KNIGHT, -ED, -S n man who has been given a knighthood ▷ vb award a knighthood to

KNIGHTLY adj of, resembling, or appropriate for a knight

KNIGHTS ▸ knight

KNISH, -ES n type of dish

KNIT, -S, -TED, -TING vb make (a garment) by interlocking a series of loops in wool or other yarn ▷ n fabric made by knitting

KNITBONE n comfrey

KNITCH, -ES dialect word for ▸ **bundle**

KNITS ▸ knit

KNITTED ▸ knit

KNITTER, -S ▸ knit

KNITTING ▸ knit

KNITTLE, -S n old word for string or cord

KNITWEAR n knitted clothes, such as sweaters

KNIVE, -D, KNIVING rare variant of ▸ **knife**

KNIVES ▸ knife

KNIVING ▸ knive

KNOB, -BED, -BING, -S n rounded projection, such as a switch on a radio ▷ vb supply with knobs

KNOBBER, -S n two-year-old male deer

KNOBBIER ▸ knobby

KNOBBING ▸ knob

KNOBBLE, -S n small knob ▷ vb dialect word meaning strike

KNOBBLED same as ▸ **knobbly**

KNOBBLES ▸ knobble

KNOBBLY adj covered with small bumps

KNOBBY, KNOBBIER ▸ knob

KNOBLIKE ▸ knob

KNOBS ▸ knob

KNOCK, -ED, -ING, -S vb give a blow or push to ▷ n blow or rap

KNOCKER, -S n metal fitting for knocking on a door

KNOCKING ▸ knock

KNOCKOFF n informal word for a cheap, often illegal, copy of something

KNOCKOUT n blow that renders an opponent unconscious ▷ vb render (someone) unconscious

KNOCKS ▸ knock

KNOLL, -ED, -ING, -S n small rounded hill ▷ vb (in archaic or dialect usage) knell

KNOLLER, -S ▸ knoll

KNOLLIER ▸ knolly

KNOLLING ▸ knoll

KNOLLS ▸ knoll

KNOLLY, KNOLLIER ▸ knoll

KNOP, -S n knob, esp an ornamental one

KNOPPED ▸ knop

KNOPS ▸ knop

KNOSP, -S n budlike architectural feature

KNOT, -S, -TED, -TING n type of fastening ▷ vb tie with or into a knot

KNOTHEAD n stupid person

KNOTHOLE n hole in a piece of wood where a knot has been

KNOTLESS ▸ knot

KNOTLIKE ▸ knot

KNOTS ▸ knot

KNOTTED ▸ knot

KNOTTER, -S ▸ knot

KNOTTIER ▸ knotty

KNOTTILY ▸ knotty

KNOTTING ▸ knot

KNOTTY, KNOTTIER adj full of knots

KNOTWEED n type of plant with small flowers and jointed stems

KNOTWORK n ornamentation consisting of a mass of intertwined and knotted cords

KNOUT, -S, -ED, -ING, -S n stout whip ▷ vb whip

KNOW, KNEW, -S vb be or feel certain of the truth of (information etc)

KNOWABLE ▸ know

KNOWE, -S same as ▸ **knoll**

KNOWER, -S ▸ know

KNOWES ▸ knowe

KNOWHOW, -S n ingenuity, knack, or skill

KNOWING, -S ▸ know

KNOWN, -S n fact or something that is known

KNOWS ▸ know

KNUB, -S dialect word for ▸ **knob**

KNUBBIER ▸ knubby

KNUBBLE, -D, -S vb dialect word for beat or pound using one's fists

KNUBBLY adj having small lumps or protuberances

KNUBBY, KNUBBIER adj knub

KNUBS ▸ knub

KNUCKLE, -D, -S n bone at the finger joint ▷ vb rub with the knuckles

KNUCKLER n type of pitch in baseball

KNUCKLES ▸ knuckle

KNUCKLY ▸ knuckle

KNUR, -S n knot or protuberance in a tree trunk or in wood

KNURL, -ED, -ING, -S n small ridge, often one of a series ▷ vb impress with a series of fine ridges or serrations

KNURLIER ▸ knurly

KNURLING ▸ knurl

KNURLS ▸ knurl

KNURLY, KNURLIER rare word for ▸ **gnarled**

KNURR, -S same as ▸ **knur**

KNURS ▸ knur

KNUT, -S n dandy

KO n (in New Zealand) traditional digging tool

KOA, -S n Hawaiian leguminous tree

KOALA, -S n tree-dwelling Australian marsupial with dense grey fur

KOAN, -S n (in Zen Buddhism) problem that admits no logical solution

KOAS ▸ koa

KOB, -S n any of several species of antelope

K

KOBAN, -S n old oval-shaped Japanese gold coin

KOBANG, -S same as ▸ **koban**

KOBANS ▸ **koban**

KOBO, -S n Nigerian monetary unit

KOBOLD, -S n mischievous household sprite

KOBOS ▸ **kobo**

KOBS ▸ **kob**

KOCHIA, -S n any of several plants whose foliage turns dark red

KOEKOEA, -S n long-tailed cuckoo of New Zealand

KOEL, -S n any of several parasitic cuckoos

KOFF, -S n Dutch masted merchant vessel

KOFTA, -S n Indian dish

KOFTGAR, -S n (in India) person skilled at inlaying steel with gold

KOFTGARI n ornamental Indian metalwork

KOFTGARS ▸ **koftgar**

KOFTWORK same as ▸ **koftgari**

KOGAL, -S n (in Japan) trendy teenage girl

KOHA, -S n gift or donation, esp of cash

KOHANIM ▸ **kohen**

KOHAS ▸ **koha**

KOHEKOHE n New Zealand tree with large glossy leaves and reddish wood

KOHEN, KOHANIM n member of the Jewish priestly caste

KOHL, -S n cosmetic powder

KOHLRABI n type of cabbage with an edible stem

KOHLS ▸ **kohl**

KOI, -S n any of various ornamental forms of the common carp

KOINE, -S n common language among speakers of different languages

KOIS ▸ **koi**

KOJI, -S n Japanese steamed rice

KOKA, -S n former type of score in judo

KOKAKO, -S n type of crow

KOKAM, -S same as ▸ **kokum**

KOKANEE, -S n type of freshwater salmon

KOKAS ▸ **koka**

KOKER, -S n Guyanese sluice

KOKIRI, -S n type of rough-skinned New Zealand triggerfish

KOKOBEH adj (of certain fruit) having a rough skin

KOKOPU, -S n any of several small freshwater fish of New Zealand

KOKOWAI, -S n type of clay

KOKRA, -S n type of wood

KOKUM, -S n tropical tree

KOLA, -S n as in **kola nut** caffeine-containing seed used in medicine and soft drinks

KOLACKY n sweet bun with a fruit, jam, or nut filling

KOLAS ▸ **kola**

KOLBASI, -S same as ▸ **kolbassi**

KOLBASSA same as ▸ **kielbasa**

KOLBASSI n type of sausage

KOLHOZ, -ES, -Y same as ▸ **kolkhoz**

KOLINSKI same as ▸ **kolinsky**

KOLINSKY n Asian mink

KOLKHOS, -Y same as ▸ **kolkhoz**

KOLKHOZ, -Y n (formerly) collective farm in the Soviet Union

KOLKOZ, -ES, -Y same as ▸ **kolkhoz**

KOLO, -S n Serbian folk dance

KOMATIK, -S n type of sledge

KOMBU, -S n dark brown seaweed

KOMISSAR same as ▸ **commissar**

KOMITAJI n rebel or revolutionary

KOMONDOR n large powerful dog of an ancient Hungarian breed, originally used for sheep herding

KON, -D, -NING, -S old word for ▸ **know**

KONAKI, -S same as ▸ **koneke**

KONBU, -S same as ▸ **kombu**

KOND ▸ **kon**

KONDO, -S n (in Uganda) thief or armed robber

KONEKE, -S n type of farm vehicle

KONFYT, -S n South African fruit preserve

KONGONI n E African hartbeest

KONINI, -S n edible dark purple berry

KONK, -ED, -ING, -S same as ▸ **conk**

KONNING ▸ **kon**

KONS ▸ **kon**

KOODOO, -S same as ▸ **kudu**

KOOK, -ED, -ING, -S n eccentric person ▷ vb dialect word for vanish

KOOKIE same as ▸ **kooky**

KOOKIER ▸ **kooky**

KOOKIEST ▸ **kooky**

KOOKILY ▸ **kooky**

KOOKING ▸ **kook**

KOOKS ▸ **kook**

KOOKUM, -S same as ▸ **kokum**

KOOKY, KOOKIER, KOOKIEST adj crazy, eccentric, or foolish

KOOLAH, -S old form of ▸ **koala**

KOORI, -ES, -S n Aboriginal Australian

KOP, -S n prominent isolated hill or mountain in southern Africa

KOPECK, -S n former Russian monetary unit

KOPEK, -S same as ▸ **kopeck**

KOPH, -S n 19th letter in the Hebrew alphabet

KOPIYKA, -S, KOPIYKY, KOPIYOK n monetary unit of Ukraine

KOPJE, -S n small hill

KOPPA, -S n consonantal letter in the Greek alphabet

KOPPIE, -S same as ▸ **kopje**

KOPS ▸ **kop**

KOR, -S n ancient Hebrew unit of capacity

KORA, -S n West African instrument

KORAI ▸ **kore**

KORARI, -S n native New Zealand flax plant

KORAS ▸ **kora**

KORAT, -S n as in **korat cat** rare blue-grey breed of cat

KORE, KORAI, -S n ancient Greek statue of a young woman wearing clothes

KORERO, -ED, -S n talk or discussion ▷ vb speak or converse

KORES ▸ **kore**

KORFBALL n game similar to basketball, in which each team consists of six men and six women

KORIMAKO another name for ▸ **bellbird**

KORKIR, -S n variety of lichen used in dyeing

KORMA, -S n type of mild Indian dish

KORO, -S n elderly Māori man

KOROMIKO n flowering New Zealand shrub

KORORA, -S n small New Zealand penguin

KOROS ▸ **koro**

KOROWAI, -S n decorative woven cloak worn by a Māori chief

KORS ▸ **kor**

KORU, -S n stylized curved pattern used esp in carving

KORUNA, KORUN, -S, KORUNY *n* standard monetary unit of the Czech Republic

KORUS ▸ **koru**

KOS, -ES *n* Indian unit of distance

KOSHER, -ED, -S *adj* conforming to Jewish religious law ▷ *n* kosher food ▷ *vb* prepare in accordance with Jewish dietary rules

KOSMOS, -ES *variant form of* ▸ **cosmos**

KOSS, -ES *same as* ▸ **kos**

KOTARE, -S *n* small greenish-blue kingfisher

KOTCH, -ED, -ES, -ING *vb* South African slang for vomit

KOTO, -S *n* Japanese stringed instrument

KOTOW, -ED, -ING, -S *same as* ▸ **kowtow**

KOTOWER, -S ▸ **kotow**

KOTOWING ▸ **kotow**

KOTOWS ▸ **kotow**

KOTTABOS *same as* ▸ **cottabus**

KOTUKU, -S *n* type of white heron

KOTWAL, -S *n* senior police officer or magistrate in an Indian town

KOULAN, -S *same as* ▸ **kulan**

KOUMIS, -ES *same as* ▸ **kumiss**

KOUMISS *same as* ▸ **kumiss**

KOUMYS, -ES *same as* ▸ **kumiss**

KOUMYSS *same as* ▸ **kumiss**

KOUPREY, -S *n* large wild SE Asian ox

KOURA, -S *n* New Zealand freshwater crayfish

KOURBASH *same as* ▸ **kurbash**

KOUROS, KOUROI *n* ancient Greek statue of a young man

KOUSKOUS *same as* ▸ **couscous**

KOUSSO, -S *n* Abyssinian tree

KOW, -S *old variant of* ▸ **cow**

This old or dialect variant of **cow** scores well for a 3-letter word, and can be a good one to form when playing in more than one direction.

KOWHAI, -S *n* New Zealand tree

KOWS ▸ **kow**

KOWTOW, -ED, -S *vb* be servile (towards) ▷ *n* act of kowtowing

KOWTOWER ▸ **kowtow**

KOWTOWS ▸ **kowtow**

KRAAL, -ED, -ING, -S *n* S African village surrounded by a strong fence ▷ *adj* denoting or relating to the tribal aspects of the Black African way of life ▷ *vb* enclose (livestock) in a kraal

KRAB, -S *same as* ▸ **karabiner**

KRAFT, -S *n* strong wrapping paper

KRAI, -S *n* administrative division of Russia

KRAIT, -S *n* brightly coloured venomous snake of S and SE Asia

KRAKEN, -S *n* legendary sea monster

KRAMERIA *another name for* ▸ **rhatany**

KRANG, -S *n* dead whale from which the blubber has been removed

KRANS, -ES *n* sheer rock face

KRANTZ, -ES *same as* ▸ **krans**

KRANZ, -ES *same as* ▸ **krans**

KRATER, -S *same as* ▸ **crater**

KRAUT, -S *n* sauerkraut

KRAY, -S *same as* ▸ **krai**

KREASOTE *same as* ▸ **creosote**

KREATINE *same as* ▸ **creatine**

KREEP, -S *n* lunar substance

KREESE, -D, -S, KREESING *same as* ▸ **kris**

KREMLIN, -S *n* citadel of any Russian city

KRENG, -S *same as* ▸ **krang**

KREOSOTE *same as* ▸ **creosote**

KREPLACH *pl n* small filled dough casings usually served in soup

KREPLECH *same as* ▸ **kreplach**

KREUTZER *n* any of various former copper and silver coins of Germany or Austria

KREUZER, -S *same as* ▸ **kreutzer**

KREWE, -S *n* club taking part in New Orleans carnival parade

KRILL, -S *n* small shrimplike sea creature

KRIMMER, -S *n* tightly curled light grey fur

KRIS, -ED, -ES, -ING *n* type of Malayan and Indonesian knife ▷ *vb* stab or slash with a kris

KROMESKY *n* croquette consisting of a piece of bacon wrapped round minced meat or fish

KRONA, KRONOR, KRONUR *n* standard monetary unit of Sweden

KRONE, -N, -R *n* standard monetary unit of Norway and Denmark

KRONOR ▸ **krona**

KRONUR ▸ **krona**

KROON, -I, -S *n* former monetary unit of Estonia

KRUBI, -S *n* aroid plant with an unpleasant smell

KRUBUT, -S *same as* ▸ **krubi**

KRULLER, -S *variant spelling of* ▸ **cruller**

KRUMHORN *variant spelling of* ▸ **crumhorn**

KRUMKAKE *n* Scandinavian biscuit

KRUMPER, -S ▸ **krumping**

KRUMPING *n* type of aggressive dance

KRUNK, -S *n* style of hip-hop music

KRUNKED *same as* ▸ **crunked**

KRUNKS ▸ **krunk**

KRYOLITE *variant spelling of* ▸ **cryolite**

KRYOLITH *same as* ▸ **cryolite**

KRYPSIS, KRYPSES *n* idea that Christ made secret use of his divine attributes

KRYPTON, -S *n* colourless gas

KRYTRON, -S *n* type of fast electronic gas-discharge switch

KSAR, -S *old form of* ▸ **tsar**

KUBASA, -S *same as* ▸ **kielbasa**

KUBIE, -S *n* Ukrainian roll filled with kielbasa

KUCCHA, -S *same as* ▸ **kaccha**

KUCHCHA *same as* ▸ **kacha**

KUCHEN, -S *n* breadlike cake

KUDLIK, -S *n* Inuit soapstone seal-oil lamp

KUDO *variant of* ▸ **kudos**

KUDOS, -ES *n* fame or credit

KUDU, -S *n* African antelope with spiral horns

KUDZU, -S *n* hairy leguminous climbing plant

KUE, -S *n* name of the letter Q

KUEH *n* (in Malaysia) any cake of Malay, Chinese, or Indian origin

KUES ▸ **kue**

KUFI, -S *n* cap for Muslim man

KUFIYAH, -S *same as* ▸ **keffiyeh**

KUGEL, -S *n* baked pudding in traditional Jewish cooking

KUIA, -S *n* Māori female elder or elderly woman

KUKRI, -S n heavy, curved knife used by Gurkhas

KUKU, -S n mussel

KULA, -S n ceremonial gift exchange among islanders in the W Pacific

KULAK, -I, -S n (formerly) property-owning Russian peasant

KULAN, -S n Asiatic wild ass

KULAS ▸ **kula**

KULBASA, -S same as ▸ **kielbasa**

KULFI, -S n Indian dessert

KULTUR, -S n German civilization

KUMARA, -S n tropical root vegetable with yellow flesh

KUMARI, -S n (in Indian English) maiden

KUMBALOI pl n worry beads

KUMERA, -S same as ▸ **kumara**

KUMIKUMI same as ▸ **kamokamo**

KUMIS, -ES same as ▸ **kumiss**

KUMISS, -ES n drink made from fermented mare's or other milk

KUMITE, -S n freestyle sparring or fighting

KUMKUM, -S n red pigment used by Hindu women to make a mark on the forehead

KUMMEL, -S n German liqueur

KUMQUAT, -S n citrus fruit resembling a tiny orange

KUMYS, -ES same as ▸ **kumiss**

KUNA, KUNE n standard monetary unit of Croatia

KUNEKUNE n feral pig

KUNJOOS adj (in Indian English) mean or stingy

KUNKAR, -S n type of limestone

KUNKUR, -S same as ▸ **kunkar**

KUNZITE, -S n variety of the mineral spodumene

KURBASH vb whip with a hide whip

KURGAN, -S n Russian burial mound

KURI, -S n mongrel dog

KURRE, -S old variant of ▸ **cur**

KURSAAL, -S n public room at a health resort

KURTA, -S n long loose garment

KURTOSIS, KURTOSES n measure of the concentration of a distribution around its mean

KURU, -S n degenerative disease of the nervous system

This word for a kind of sickness found in New Guinea can give you something to play when you have two Us to dispose of.

KURUSH, -ES n small currency unit of Turkey

KURVEY, -ED, -S vb (in old South African English) transport goods by ox cart

KURVEYOR ▸ **kurvey**

KURVEYS ▸ **kurvey**

KUSSO, -S variant spelling of ▸ **kousso**

KUTA, -S n (in Indian English) male dog

KUTCH, -ES same as ▸ **catechu**

KUTCHA adj makeshift or not solid

KUTCHES ▸ **kutch**

KUTI, -S n (in Indian English) female dog

KUTU, -S n body louse

KUVASZ, -OK n breed of dog from Hungary

KUZU, -S same as ▸ **kudzu**

A Japanese climbing plant, this can be a great word for getting a high score out of a difficult rack.

KVAS, -ES same as ▸ **kvass**

KVASS, -ES n alcoholic drink

KVELL, -ED, -ING, -S vb US word meaning be happy

KVETCH, -ED, -ES vb complain or grumble

KVETCHER ▸ **kvetch**

KVETCHES ▸ **kvetch**

KVETCHY adj tending to grumble or complain

KWACHA, -S n standard monetary unit of Zambia

KWAITO, -S n type of South African pop music

KWANZA, -S n standard monetary unit of Angola

KWELA, -S n type of pop music

KY pl n Scots word for cows

KYACK, -S n type of pannier

KYAK, -S same as ▸ **kayak**

KYANG, -S same as ▸ **kiang**

KYANISE, -D, -S same as ▸ **kyanize**

KYANITE, -S n grey, green, or blue mineral

KYANITIC ▸ **kyanite**

KYANIZE, -D, -S vb treat (timber) with corrosive sublimate

KYAR, -S same as ▸ **coir**

KYAT, -S n standard monetary unit of Myanmar

KYBO, -S n temporary lavatory used when camping

KYBOSH, -ED, -ES same as ▸ **kibosh**

KYDST ▸ **kythe**

KYE, -S n Korean fundraising meeting

KYLE, -S n narrow strait or channel

KYLICES ▸ **kylix**

KYLIE, -S n type of boomerang

KYLIKES ▸ **kylix**

KYLIN, -S n (in Chinese art) mythical animal

KYLIX, KYLICES, KYLIKES, -ES n drinking vessel used in ancient Greece

KYLLOSIS, KYLLOSES n club foot

KYLOE, -S n breed of beef cattle

KYMOGRAM n image or other visual record created by a kymograph

KYND, -ED, -ING, -S old variant of ▸ **kind**

KYNDE, -S old variant of ▸ **kind**

KYNDED ▸ **kynd**

KYNDES ▸ **kynde**

KYNDING ▸ **kynd**

KYNDS ▸ **kynd**

KYNE pl n archaic word for cows

KYOGEN, -S n type of Japanese drama

KYPE, -S n hook on the lower jaw of a mature male salmon

KYPHOSIS, KYPHOSES n backward curvature of the thoracic spine

KYPHOTIC ▸ **kyphosis**

KYRIE, -S n type of prayer

KYRIELLE n verse form of French origin characterized by repeated lines or words

KYRIES ▸ **kyrie**

KYTE, -S n belly

KYTHE, KYDST, -D, -S, KYTHING vb appear

KYU, -S n (in judo) one of the five student grades

This means a novice grade in judo, and its unusual combination of letters makes it a useful word to remember when you have an unpromising set of letters on your rack.

LI

L can be a difficult letter to use well, especially when you need to play short words. Just three two-letter words begin with **L**: **la**, **li** and **lo**. Knowing this will save you valuable time in a game, especially when you are trying to fit words into a crowded board. There aren't very many three-letter words either, but don't forget common words like **lab** (5 points), **law** (6), **lay** (6), **low** (6) and **lye** (6). Try to remember the three-letter words that combine **L** with **X**: **lax**, **lex**, **lox** and **lux** (10 points each). These are particularly useful towards the end of a game if you have an **X** but little opportunity to play it. There is also the very useful **luz** for 12 points.

LA, -S *n* the sixth note of the musical scale
LAAGER, -ED, -S *n* (in Africa) a camp defended by a circular formation of wagons ▷ *vb* form (wagons) into a laager
LAARI, -S *same as* ▶ **lari**
LAB, -S *n* laboratory
LABARUM, LABARA, -S *n* standard carried in Christian processions
LABDA, -S *same as* ▶ **lambda**
LABDANUM *n* dark resinous juice obtained from various rockroses
LABDAS ▶ **labda**
LABEL, -ED, -ING, -LED, -S *n* piece of card fixed to an object ▷ *vb* give a label to
LABELER, -S ▶ **label**
LABELING ▶ **label**
LABELLA ▶ **labellum**
LABELLED ▶ **label**
LABELLER ▶ **label**
LABELLUM, LABELLA *n* lip-like part of certain plants
LABELS ▶ **label**
LABIA ▶ **labium**
LABIAL, -S *adj* of the lips ▷ *n* speech sound that involves the lips
LABIALLY ▶ **labial**
LABIALS ▶ **labial**
LABIATE, -S *n* plant with a two-lipped flower
LABIATED *adj* having a lip
LABIATES ▶ **labiate**
LABILE *adj* (of a compound) prone to chemical change
LABILITY ▶ **labile**
LABIS, -ES *n* spoon used to give the Eucharist to communicants

LABIUM, LABIA *n* lip or liplike structure
LABLAB, -S *n* twining leguminous plant
LABNEH, -S *n* Mediterranean soft cheese
LABOR, -ING, -S *same as* ▶ **labour**
LABORED *same as* ▶ **laboured**
LABORER, -S *same as* ▶ **labourer**
LABORING ▶ **labor**
LABORISM *same as* > **labourism**
LABORIST *same as* > **labourist**
LABORITE *n* adherent of the Labour party
LABORS ▶ **labor**
LABOUR, -S *n* physical work or exertion ▷ *vb* work hard
LABOURED *adj* uttered or done with difficulty
LABOURER *n* person who labours, esp someone doing manual work for wages
LABOURS ▶ **labour**
LABRA ▶ **labrum**
LABRADOR *n* large retriever dog with a usu gold or black coat
LABRAL *adj* of or like a lip
LABRET, -S *n* piece of bone or shell
LABRID, -S *same as* ▶ **labroid**
LABROID, -S *n* type of fish ▷ *adj* of or relating to such fish
LABROSE *adj* thick-lipped
LABRUM, LABRA, -S *n* lip or liplike part
LABRUSCA *n* grape variety

LABRYS, -ES *n* type of axe
LABS ▶ **lab**
LABURNUM *n* ornamental tree with yellow hanging flowers
LAC, -S *same as* ▶ **lakh**
LACE, -D, -S *n* delicate fabric ▷ *vb* fasten with shoelaces, cords, etc
LACEBARK *n* small evergreen tree
LACED ▶ **lace**
LACELESS ▶ **lace**
LACELIKE ▶ **lace**
LACER, -S ▶ **lace**
LACERANT *adj* painfully distressing
LACERATE *vb* tear (flesh) ▷ *adj* having edges that are jagged or torn
LACERS ▶ **lacer**
LACERTID *n* type of lizard
LACES ▶ **lace**
LACET, -S *n* braided work in lace
LACEWING *n* any of various neuropterous insects
LACEWOOD *n* wood of sycamore tree
LACEWORK *n* work made from lace
LACEY *same as* ▶ **lacy**
LACHES, -ES *n* unreasonable delay in pursuing a legal remedy
LACIER ▶ **lacy**
LACIEST ▶ **lacy**
LACILY ▶ **lacy**
LACINESS ▶ **lacy**
LACING, -S ▶ **lace**
LACINIA, -E *n* narrow fringe on petal

L

LACK, -ED, -ING, -S *n* shortage of something needed ▷ *vb* need

LACKADAY another word for ▶ alas

LACKED ▶ lack

LACKER, -ED, -S variant spelling of ▶ lacquer

LACKEY, -ED, -S *n* servile follower ▷ *vb* act as a lackey (to)

LACKING ▶ lack

LACKLAND *n* fool

LACKS ▶ lack

LACMUS, -ES *n* old form of litmus

LACONIC *adj* using only a few words, terse

LACONISM *n* economy of expression

LACQUER, -S *n* hard varnish for wood or metal ▷ *vb* apply lacquer to

LACQUEY, -S same as ▶ lackey

LACRIMAL *adj* of tears or the glands which produce them ▷ *n* bone near tear gland

LACROSSE *n* sport in which teams catch and throw a ball using long sticks with a pouched net

LACRYMAL same as ▶ lacrimal

LACS ▶ lac

LACTAM, -S *n* any of a group of inner amides

LACTARY *adj* relating to milk

LACTASE, -S *n* any of a group of enzymes that hydrolyse lactose to glucose and galactose

LACTATE, -D, -S *vb* secrete milk ▷ *n* ester or salt of lactic acid

LACTEAL, -S *adj* of or like milk ▷ *n* any of the lymphatic vessels that convey chyle from the small intestine to the blood

LACTEAN another word for ▶ lacteous

LACTEOUS *adj* milky

LACTIC *adj* of or derived from milk

LACTIFIC *adj* yielding milk

LACTITOL *n* type of artificial sweetener

LACTONE, -S *n* any of a class of organic compounds

LACTONIC ▶ lactone

LACTOSE, -S *n* white crystalline sugar found in milk

LACUNA, -E, -S *n* gap or missing part, esp in a document or series

LACUNAL ▶ lacuna

LACUNAR, -S *n* ceiling, soffit, or vault having coffers ▷ *adj* having a lacuna

LACUNARY ▶ lacuna

LACUNAS ▶ lacuna

LACUNATE ▶ lacuna

LACUNE, -S *n* hiatus

LACUNOSE ▶ lacuna

LACY, LACIER, LACIEST *adj* fine, like lace

LAD, -S *n* boy or young man

LADANUM, -S same as ▶ labdanum

LADDER, -ED, -S *n* frame of two poles connected by horizontal steps for climbing ▷ *vb* cause to have a line of undone stitches

LADDERY *adj* (of tights) laddered

LADDIE, -S *n* familiar term for a male, esp a young man

LADDIER ▶ laddy

LADDIES ▶ laddie

LADDIEST ▶ laddy

LADDISH *adj* behaving in a macho or immature manner

LADDISM, -S *n* laddish attitudes and behaviour

LADDY, LADDIER, LADDIEST *adj* laddish

LADE, -D, -S *vb* put cargo on board ▷ *n* watercourse

LADEN, -ED, -ING, -S *adj* loaded ▷ *vb* load with cargo

LADER, -S ▶ lade

LADES ▶ lade

LADETTE, -S *n* young woman who behaves in ways considered typical of young men

LADHOOD, -S ▶ lad

LADIES *n* women's public toilet

LADIFY, LADIFIED, LADIFIES same as ▶ ladyfy

LADING, -S ▶ lade

LADINO, -S *n* Italian variety of white clover

LADLE, -D, -S, LADLING *n* long-handled spoon with a large bowl ▷ *vb* serve out

LADLEFUL ▶ ladle

LADLER, -S *n* person who serves with a ladle

LADLES ▶ ladle

LADLING ▶ ladle

LADRON, -S same as ▶ ladrone

LADRONE, -S *n* thief

LADRONS ▶ ladron

LADS ▶ lad

LADY *n* woman ▷ *adj* female

LADYBIRD *n* small red beetle with black spots

LADYBUG, -S same as ▶ ladybird

LADYCOW, -S another word for ▶ ladybird

LADYFIED ▶ ladyfy

LADYFIES ▶ ladyfy

LADYFISH *n* type of game fish

LADYFLY another word for ▶ ladybird

LADYFY, LADYFIED, LADYFIES *vb* make a lady of (someone)

LADYHOOD ▶ lady

LADYISH ▶ lady

LADYISM, -S ▶ lady

LADYKIN, -S *n* endearing form of 'lady'

LADYLIKE *adj* polite and dignified

LADYLOVE *n* beloved woman

LADYNESS *n* state of being a lady

LADYPALM *n* small palm, grown indoors

LADYSHIP *n* title of a peeress

LAER, -ED, -ING, -S another word for ▶ laager

LAESIE old form of ▶ lazy

LAETARE, -S *n* fourth Sunday of Lent

LAETRILE *n* drug used to treat cancer

LAEVO *adj* on the left

LAEVULIN *n* polysaccharide occurring in the tubers of certain helianthus plants

LAG, -GED, -S *vb* go too slowly, fall behind ▷ *n* delay between events

LAGAN, -S *n* goods or wreckage on the sea bed

LAGENA, -S *n* bottle with a narrow neck

LAGEND, -S same as ▶ lagan

LAGER, -ED, -ING, -S *n* light-bodied beer ▷ *vb* ferment into lager

LAGGARD, -S *n* person who lags behind ▷ *adj* sluggish, slow

LAGGED ▶ lag

LAGGEN, -S *n* spar of a barrel

LAGGER, -S *n* person who lags pipes

LAGGIN, -S same as ▶ laggen

LAGGING, -S ▶ lag

LAGGINS ▶ laggin

LAGNAPPE same as ▷ lagniappe

LAGOON, -S *n* water cut off from the sea by reefs or sand bars

LAGOONAL ▶ lagoon

LAGOONS ▶ lagoon

LAGS ▶ lag

LAGUNA, -S n lagoon

LAGUNE, -S same as ▶ lagoon

LAH, -S n (in tonic sol-fa) sixth degree of any major scale

LAHAL, -S n game played by native peoples of the Pacific Northwest

LAHAR, -S n landslide of volcanic debris and water

LAHS ▶ lah

LAIC, -S adj laical ▷ n layman

LAICAL adj secular

LAICALLY ▶ laic

LAICH, -S n low-lying piece of land

LAICISE, -D, -S same as ▶ laicize

LAICISM, -S ▶ laic

LAICITY n state of being laical

LAICIZE, -D, -S vb remove ecclesiastical status from

LAICS ▶ laic

LAID, -ED, -ING, -S Scots form of ▶ load

LAIDLY, LAIDLIER adj very ugly

LAIDS ▶ laid

LAIGH, -ER, -EST, -S adj low-lying ▷ n area of low-lying ground

LAIK, -ED, -ING, -S vb play (a game, etc)

LAIKA, -S n type of small dog

LAIKED ▶ laik

LAIKER, -S ▶ laik

LAIKING ▶ laik

LAIKS ▶ laik

LAIN ▶ lay

LAIPSE, -D, -S, LAIPSING vb beat soundly

LAIR, -ED, -ING, -S n resting place of an animal ▷ vb retreat to or rest in a lair

LAIRAGE, -S n accommodation for farm animals

LAIRD, -S n Scottish landowner

LAIRDLY adj pertaining to lairds

LAIRDS ▶ laird

LAIRED ▶ lair

LAIRIER ▶ lairy

LAIRIEST ▶ lairy

LAIRING ▶ lair

LAIRISE, -D, -S same as ▶ lairize

LAIRIZE, -D, -S vb show off

LAIRS ▶ lair

LAIRY, LAIRIER, LAIRIEST adj gaudy or flashy

LAISSE, -S n type of rhyme scheme

LAITANCE n white film forming on drying concrete

LAITH Scots form of ▶ loath

LAITHLY same as ▶ laidly

LAITY, LAITIES n non-clergy

LAKE, -D, -S n expanse of water entirely surrounded by land ▷ vb take time away from work

LAKEBED, -S n bed of lake

LAKED ▶ lake

LAKEFILL n area of land on a filled lake

LAKEHEAD n shore of a lake farthest from the outlet

LAKELAND n countryside with a lot of lakes

LAKELET, -S n small lake

LAKELIKE ▶ lake

LAKEPORT n port on lake

LAKER, -S n lake cargo vessel

LAKES ▶ lake

LAKESIDE n area at edge of lake

LAKEVIEW adj having a view of a lake

LAKEWARD same as ▶ lakewards

LAKH, -S n (in India) 100 000, esp referring to this sum of rupees

LAKIER ▶ laky

LAKIEST ▶ laky

LAKIN, -S short form of ▶ ladykin

LAKING, -S ▶ lake

LAKINS ▶ lakin

LAKISH adj similar to poetry of Lake poets

LAKSA, -S n (in Malaysia) Chinese dish of rice noodles in curry or hot soup

LAKY, LAKIER, LAKIEST adj of the reddish colour of the pigment lake

LALANG, -S n coarse weedy Malaysian grass

LALDIE, -S n great gusto

LALDY same as ▶ laldie

LALIQUE, -S n ornamental glass

LALL, -ED, -S vb make imperfect 'l' or 'r' sounds

LALLAN, -S n literary version of the English spoken in Lowland Scotland

LALLAND, -S same as ▶ lallan

LALLANS ▶ lallan

LALLED ▶ lall

LALLING, -S ▶ lall

LALLS ▶ lall

LALLYGAG vb loiter aimlessly

LAM, -MED, -S vb attack vigorously

LAMA, -S n Buddhist priest in Tibet or Mongolia

LAMANTIN another word for ▶ manatee

LAMAS ▶ lama

LAMASERY n monastery of lamas

LAMB, -ED, -S n young sheep ▷ vb give birth to a lamb or lambs

LAMBADA, -S n type of Brazilian dance

LAMBAST, -S vb beat or thrash

LAMBASTE same as ▶ lambast

LAMBASTS ▶ lambast

LAMBDA, -S n 11th letter of the Greek alphabet

LAMBDOID adj having the shape of the Greek letter lambda

LAMBED ▶ lamb

LAMBENCY ▶ lambent

LAMBENT adj (of a flame) flickering softly

LAMBER, -S n person that attends to lambing ewes

LAMBERT, -S n cgs unit of illumination, equal to 1 lumen per square centimetre

LAMBIE, -S same as ▶ lambkin

LAMBIER ▶ lamby

LAMBIES ▶ lambie

LAMBIEST ▶ lamby

LAMBING, -S n birth of lambs at the end of winter

LAMBKILL n N American dwarf shrub

LAMBKIN, -S n young lamb

LAMBLIKE ▶ lamb

LAMBLING n small lamb

LAMBOYS n skirt-like piece of armour made from metal strips

LAMBS ▶ lamb

LAMBSKIN n skin of a lamb, usually with the wool still on, used to make coats, slippers, etc

LAMBY, LAMBIER, LAMBIEST adj lamb-like

LAME, -R, -S, -ST, LAMING adj having an injured or disabled leg or foot ▷ vb make lame ▷ n fabric interwoven with gold or silver threads

LAMED, -S n 12th letter in the Hebrew alphabet

LAMEDH, -S same as ▶ lamed

LAMEDS ▶ lamed

LAMELLA, -E, -S *n* thin layer, plate, etc, like the calcified layers of which bone is formed

LAMELLAR ▸ lamella

LAMELLAS ▸ lamella

LAMELY ▸ lame

LAMENESS ▸ lame

LAMENT, -S *vb* feel or express sorrow (for) ▹ *n* passionate expression of grief

LAMENTED *adj* grieved for

LAMENTER ▸ lament

LAMENTS ▸ lament

LAMER ▸ lame

LAMES ▸ lame

LAMEST ▸ lame

LAMETER, -S *Scots form of* ▸ lamiger

LAMIA, -E, -S *n* female monster with a snake's body and a woman's head

LAMIGER, -S *n* disabled person

LAMINA, -E, -S *n* thin plate, esp of bone or mineral

LAMINAL, -S *n* consonant articulated with blade of tongue

LAMINAR ▸ lamina

LAMINARY ▸ lamina

LAMINAS ▸ lamina

LAMINATE *vb* make (a sheet of material) by sticking together thin sheets ▹ *n* laminated sheet ▹ *adj* composed of lamina

LAMING ▸ lame

LAMININ, -S *n* type of protein

LAMINOSE ▸ lamina

LAMINOUS ▸ lamina

LAMISH *adj* rather lame

LAMISTER *n* fugitive

LAMITER, -S *same as* ▸ lameter

LAMMED ▸ lam

LAMMER, -S *Scots word for* ▸ amber

LAMMIE *same as* ▸ lammy

LAMMIES ▸ lammy

LAMMIGER *same as* ▸ lamiger

LAMMING, -S ▸ lam

LAMMY, LAMMIES *n* thick woollen jumper

LAMP, -ED, -S *n* device which produces light from electricity, oil, or gas ▹ *vb* go quickly with long steps

LAMPAD, -S *n* candlestick

LAMPAS, -ES *n* swelling of the mucous membrane of the hard palate of horses

LAMPASSE *same as* ▸ lampas

LAMPED ▸ lamp

LAMPER, -S *n* lamprey

LAMPERN, -S *n* migratory European lamprey

LAMPERS ▸ lamper

LAMPHOLE *n* hole in ground for lowering lamp into sewer

LAMPING, -S ▸ lamp

LAMPION, -S *n* oil-burning lamp

LAMPLESS *adj* without a lamp

LAMPLIT *adj* lit by lamps

LAMPOON, -S *n* humorous satire ridiculing someone ▹ *vb* satirize or ridicule

LAMPPOST *n* post supporting a lamp in the street

LAMPREY, -S *n* eel-like fish with a round sucking mouth

LAMPS ▸ lamp

LAMPUKA, -S *same as* ▸ lampuki

LAMPUKI, -S *n* type of fish

LAMPYRID *n* firefly

LAMS ▸ lam

LAMSTER, -S *n* fugitive

LANA, -S *n* wood from genipap tree

LANAI, -S *Hawaiian word for* ▸ veranda

LANAS ▸ lana

LANATE *adj* having or consisting of a woolly covering of hairs

LANATED *same as* ▸ lanate

LANCE, -D, -S, LANCING *n* long spear used by a mounted soldier ▹ *vb* pierce (a boil or abscess) with a lancet

LANCEGAY *n* kind of ancient spear

LANCELET *n* type of marine invertebrate

LANCER *n* formerly, cavalry soldier armed with a lance

LANCERS *n* quadrille for eight or sixteen couples

LANCES ▸ lance

LANCET, -S *n* pointed two-edged surgical knife

LANCETED *adj* having one or more lancet arches or windows

LANCETS ▸ lancet

LANCH, -ED, -ES, -ING *obsolete form of* ▸ launch

LANCIERS *pl n* type of dance

LANCING ▸ lance

LAND *n* solid part of the earth's surface ▹ *vb* come or bring to earth after a flight, jump, or fall

LANDAU, -S *n* four-wheeled carriage with two folding hoods

LANDDROS *n* sheriff

LANDE, -S *n* type of moorland in SW France

LANDED *adj* possessing or consisting of lands

LANDER, -S *n* spacecraft which lands on a planet or other body

LANDES ▸ lande

LANDFALL *n* ship's first landing after a voyage

LANDFAST *adj* (of ice) attached to the shore

LANDFILL *n* disposing of rubbish by covering it with earth

LANDFORM *n* any natural feature of the earth's surface, such as valleys and mountains

LANDGRAB *n* sudden attempt to establish ownership of something

LANDING, -S *n* floor area at the top of a flight of stairs

LANDLADY *n* woman who owns and leases property

LANDLER, -S *n* Austrian country dance

LANDLESS ▸ land

LANDLINE *n* telecommunications cable laid over land

LANDLORD *n* person who rents out land, houses, etc

LANDMAN, LANDMEN *n* person who lives and works on land

LANDMARK *n* prominent object in or feature of a landscape

LANDMASS *n* large continuous area of land

LANDMEN ▸ landman

LANDMINE *n* type of bomb laid on or just under the surface of the ground ▹ *vb* lay (an area) with landmines

LANDRACE *n* white very long-bodied lop-eared breed of pork pig

LANDRAIL *n* type of bird

LANDS *pl n* holdings in land

LANDSIDE *n* part of an airport farthest from the aircraft

LANDSKIP *another word for* ▸ landscape

LANDSLID ▸ landslide

LANDSLIP *same as* ▸ landslide

LANDSMAN, LANDSMEN *n* person who works or lives on

land, as distinguished from a seaman

LANDWARD *same as* ▸ **landwards**

LANDWASH *n* part of the shore between the high-water mark and the sea

LANDWIND *n* wind that comes from the land

LANE, -S *n* narrow road

LANELY *Scots form of* ▸ **lonely**

LANES ▸ **lane**

LANEWAY, -S *n* lane

LANG, -EST *Scot word for* ▸ **long**

LANGAHA, -S *n* type of Madagascan snake

LANGAR, -S *n* dining hall in a gurdwara

LANGER *adj* comparative form of **lang**

LANGERED *adj* drunk

LANGEST ▸ **lang**

LANGLAUF *n* cross-country skiing

LANGLEY, -S *n* unit of solar radiation

LANGRAGE *n* shot consisting of scrap iron packed into a case, formerly used in naval warfare

LANGREL, -S *same as* ▸ **langrage**

LANGSHAN *n* breed of chicken

LANGSPEL *n* type of Scandinavian stringed instrument

LANGSPIL *n* type of Scandinavian stringed instrument

LANGSYNE *adv* long ago ▷ *n* times long past, esp those fondly remembered

LANGUAGE *n* system of sounds, symbols, etc for communicating thought ▷ *vb* express in language

LANGUE, -S *n* language considered as an abstract system

LANGUED *adj* having a tongue

LANGUES ▸ **langue**

LANGUET, -S *n* anything resembling a tongue

LANGUID *adj* lacking energy

LANGUISH *vb* suffer neglect or hardship

LANGUOR, -S *n* dreamy relaxation

LANGUR, -S *n* type of arboreal Old World monkey

LANIARD, -S *same as* ▸ **lanyard**

LANIARY *adj* adapted for tearing ▷ *n* tooth adapted for tearing

LANITAL, -S *n* fibre used in production of synthetic wool

LANK, -ED, -ER, -EST, -ING, -S *adj* straight and limp ▷ *vb* become lank

LANKIER ▸ **lanky**

LANKIEST ▸ **lanky**

LANKILY ▸ **lanky**

LANKING ▸ **lank**

LANKLY ▸ **lank**

LANKNESS ▸ **lank**

LANKS ▸ **lank**

LANKY, LANKIER, LANKIEST *adj* tall and thin

LANNER, -S *n* large falcon

LANNERET *n* male or tercel of the lanner falcon

LANNERS ▸ **lanner**

LANOLIN, -S *n* grease from sheep's wool used in ointments etc

LANOLINE *same as* ▸ **lanolin**

LANOLINS ▸ **lanolin**

LANOSE *same as* ▸ **lanate**

LANOSITY ▸ **lanose**

LANT, -S *n* stale urine

LANTANA, -S *n* shrub with orange or yellow flowers

LANTERN, -S *n* light in a transparent protective case ▷ *vb* supply with a lantern

LANTHORN *archaic word for* ▸ **lantern**

LANTS ▸ **lant**

LANTSKIP *another word for* ▸ **landscape**

LANUGO, -S *n* layer of fine hairs, esp the covering of the human fetus before birth

LANX *n* dish; plate

LANYARD, -S *n* neck cord to hold a knife or whistle

LAOGAI, -S *n* forced labour camp in China

LAP, -PED, -S *n* part between the waist and knees when sitting ▷ *vb* overtake so as to be one or more circuits ahead

LAPBOARD *n* flat board that can be used on the lap as a makeshift table or desk

LAPDOG, -S *n* small pet dog

LAPEL, -S *n* part of the front of a coat or jacket folded back towards the shoulders

LAPELED ▸ **lapel**

LAPELLED ▸ **lapel**

LAPELS ▸ **lapel**

LAPFUL, -S *same as* ▸ **lap**

LAPHELD *adj* small enough to be used on one's lap

LAPIDARY *adj* of or relating to stones ▷ *n* person who cuts, polishes, sets, or deals in gemstones

LAPIDATE *vb* pelt with stones

LAPIDES ▸ **lapis**

LAPIDIFY *vb* change into stone

LAPIDIST *n* cutter and engraver of precious stones

LAPILLUS, LAPILLI *n* small piece of lava thrown from a volcano

LAPIN, -S *n* rabbit fur

LAPIS, LAPIDES, -ES *n* as in **lapis lazuli** brilliant blue mineral gemstone

LAPJE, -S *same as* ▸ **lappie**

LAPPED ▸ **lap**

LAPPEL, -S *same as* ▸ **lapel**

LAPPER, -ED, -S *n* one that laps ▷ *vb* curdle

LAPPET, -S *n* small hanging flap

LAPPETED ▸ **lappet**

LAPPETS ▸ **lappet**

LAPPIE, -S *n* rag

LAPPING, -S ▸ **lap**

LAPS ▸ **lap**

LAPSABLE ▸ **lapse**

LAPSANG, -S *n* Chinese tea

LAPSE, -D, -S, LAPSING *n* temporary drop in a standard ▷ *vb* drop in standard

LAPSER, -S ▸ **lapse**

LAPSES ▸ **lapse**

LAPSIBLE ▸ **lapse**

LAPSING ▸ **lapse**

LAPSTONE *n* device used by a cobbler on which leather is beaten

LAPSUS *n* lapse or error

LAPTOP, -S *adj* small enough to fit on a user's lap ▷ *n* small computer

LAPTRAY, -S *n* tray with a cushioned underside

LAPWING, -S *n* plover with a tuft of feathers on the head

LAPWORK, -S *n* work with lapping edges

LAR, -S *n* boy or young man

LARBOARD *n* port (side of a ship)

LARCENER ▸ **larceny**

LARCENY *n* theft

LARCH, -ES *n* deciduous coniferous tree

LARCHEN *adj* of larch

LARCHES ▸ **larch**

LARD, -ED, -ING, -S *n* soft white pig fat ▷ *vb* insert strips of bacon in before cooking

L

LARDER, -S *n* storeroom for food

LARDERER *n* person in charge of larder

LARDERS ▶ larder

LARDIER ▶ lardy

LARDIEST ▶ lardy

LARDING ▶ lard

LARDLIKE ▶ lard

LARDON, -S *n* strip or cube of fat or bacon used in larding meat

LARDOON, -S *same as* **▶ lardon**

LARDS ▶ lard

LARDY, LARDIER, LARDIEST *adj* fat

LARE, -S *another word for* **▶ lore**

LAREE, -S *n* Asian fish-hook

LARES ▶ lare

LARGANDO *adv* (music) growing slower and more marked

LARGE, -R, -S, -ST *adj* great in size, number ▷ *n* formerly, musical note

LARGELY *adv* principally

LARGEN, -ED, -S *another word for* **▶ enlarge**

LARGER ▶ large

LARGES ▶ large

LARGESS *same as* **▶ largesse**

LARGESSE *n* generous giving, esp of money

LARGEST ▶ large

LARGISH *adj* fairly large

LARGO, -S *adv* in a slow and dignified manner ▷ *n* performance piece in a slow manner

LARI, -S *n* monetary unit of Georgia

LARIAT, -ED, -S *n* lasso ▷ *vb* tether with lariat

LARIGAN, -S *n* type of tanned moccasin boot

LARINE *adj* of, relating to, or resembling a gull

LARIS ▶ lari

LARK, -ED, -ING, -S *n* small brown songbird ▷ *vb* frolic

LARKER, -S ▶ lark

LARKIER ▶ larky

LARKIEST ▶ larky

LARKING ▶ lark

LARKISH ▶ lark

LARKS ▶ lark

LARKSOME *adj* mischievous

LARKSPUR *n* plant with spikes of blue, pink, or white flowers with spurs

LARKY, LARKIER, LARKIEST *adj* frolicsome

LARMIER, -S *n* pouch under lower eyelid of deer

LARN, -ED, -ING, -S, -T *vb* learn

LARNAX, LARNAKES *n* terracotta coffin

LARNED ▶ larn

LARNEY, LARNIER, LARNIEST *n* South African word for a rich person ▷ *adj* (of clothes) smart

LARNING ▶ larn

LARNS ▶ larn

LARNT ▶ larn

LAROID *adj* relating to Larus genus of gull family

LARRIGAN *n* knee-high oiled leather moccasin boot worn by trappers, etc

LARRIKIN *n* mischievous or unruly person

LARRUP, -ED, -S *vb* beat or flog

LARRUPER ▶ larrup

LARRUPS ▶ larrup

LARS ▶ lar

LARUM, -S *n* archaic word for **▶ alarm**

LARVA, -E, -S *n* immature insect

LARVAL ▶ larva

LARVAS ▶ larva

LARVATE *adj* masked; concealed

LARVATED *same as* **▶ larvate**

LARYNGAL *adj* laryngeal ▷ *n* sound articulated in the larynx

LARYNX, LARYNGES, -ES *n* part of the throat containing the vocal cords

LAS ▶ la

LASAGNA, -S *same as* **▶ lasagne**

LASAGNE, -S *n* sheet pasta

LASCAR, -S *n* Indian or SE Asian sailor

LASE, -D, -S *vb* be capable of acting as a laser

LASER, -ED, -ING, -S *n* device producing a very narrow intense beam of light ▷ *vb* use a laser on (something), esp as part of medical treatment

LASES ▶ lase

LASH, -ED, -ES, -ING *n* eyelash ▷ *vb* hit with a whip

LASHER, -S ▶ lash

LASHES ▶ lash

LASHING ▶ lash

LASHINGS *pl n* great amount of

LASHINS *variant of* **▶ lashings**

LASHKAR, -S *n* troop of Indian men with weapons

LASHLESS *adj* (of a whip) without a lash

LASING, -S ▶ lase

LASKET, -S *n* loop at the foot of a sail onto which an extra sail may be fastened

LASQUE, -S *n* flat-cut diamond

LASS, -ES *n* girl or young woman

LASSI, -S *n* cold drink made of yoghurt or buttermilk, flavoured with sugar, salt, or spice

LASSIE, -S *n* little lass

LASSIS ▶ lassi

LASSLORN *adj* abandoned by a young woman

LASSO, -ED, -ES, -S *n* rope with a noose ▷ *vb* catch with a lasso

LASSOCK, -S *another word for* **▶ lass**

LASSOED ▶ lasso

LASSOER, -S ▶ lasso

LASSOES ▶ lasso

LASSOING *n* act of lassoing

LASSOS ▶ lasso

LASSU, -S *n* slow part of csárdás folk dance

LASSY *n* short for molasses

LAST, -ED, -S *adv* coming at the end or after all others ▷ *adj* only remaining ▷ *n* last person or thing ▷ *vb* continue

LASTAGE, -S *n* space for storing goods in ship

LASTBORN *n* last child to be born

LASTED ▶ last

LASTER, -S ▶ last

LASTING, -S *adj* remaining effective for a long time ▷ *n* strong durable fabric used for shoe uppers, etc

LASTLY *adv* at the end or at the last point

LASTS ▶ last

LAT, -I, -S *n* former coin of Latvia

LATAH, -S *n* psychological condition

LATAKIA, -S *n* Turkish tobacco

LATCH, -ED, -ES, -ING *n* fastening for a door with a bar and lever ▷ *vb* fasten with a latch

LATCHET, -S *n* shoe fastening

LATCHING ▶ latch

LATCHKEY *n* key for an outside door or gate, esp one that lifts a latch

LATE *adj* after the normal or expected time ▷ *adv* after the normal or expected time

LATED *archaic word for* ▷ **belated**

LATEEN, -S *adj* of a rig with a triangular sail bent to a yard hoisted to the head of a low mast

LATEENER *n* lateen-rigged ship

LATEENS ▷ **lateen**

LATELY *adv* in recent times

LATEN, -ED, -ING, -S *vb* become or cause to become late

LATENCE, -S ▷ **latent**

LATENCY ▷ **latent**

LATENED ▷ **laten**

LATENESS ▷ **late**

LATENING ▷ **laten**

LATENS ▷ **laten**

LATENT, -S *adj* hidden and not yet developed ▷ *n* fingerprint that is not visible to the eye

LATENTLY ▷ **latent**

LATENTS ▷ **latent**

LATER *adv* afterwards

LATERAD *adv* towards the side

LATERAL, -S *adj* of or relating to the side or sides ▷ *n* lateral object, part, passage, or movement ▷ *vb* pass laterally

LATERISE *same as* ▷ **laterize**

LATERITE *n* any of a group of deposits consisting of residual insoluble ferric and aluminium oxides

LATERIZE *vb* develop into a laterite

LATEST, -S *n* the most recent news

LATEWAKE *n* vigil held over a dead body

LATEWOOD *n* wood formed later in tree's growing season

LATEX, -ES, LATICES *n* milky fluid found in some plants

LATH, -S *n* thin strip of wood ▷ *vb* attach laths to

LATHE, -D, -S *n* machine for turning wood or metal while it is being shaped ▷ *vb* shape, bore, or cut a screw thread in or on (a workpiece) on a lathe

LATHEE, -S *same as* ▷ **lathi**

LATHEN *adj* covered with laths

LATHER, -ED, -S *n* froth of soap and water ▷ *vb* make frothy

LATHERER ▷ **lather**

LATHERS ▷ **lather**

LATHERY ▷ **lather**

LATHES ▷ **lathe**

LATHI, -S *n* long heavy wooden stick used as a weapon in India

LATHIER ▷ **lathy**

LATHIEST ▷ **lathy**

LATHING, -S ▷ **lathe**

LATHIS ▷ **lathi**

LATHLIKE ▷ **lath**

LATHS ▷ **lath**

LATHWORK *n* work made of laths

LATHY, LATHIER, LATHIEST *adj* resembling a lath, esp in being tall and thin

LATHYRUS *n* genus of climbing plant

LATI ▷ **lat**

LATICES ▷ **latex**

LATIGO, -ES, -S *n* strap on horse's saddle

LATILLA, -S *n* stick making up part of ceiling

LATINA, -S *n* American female citizen of Latin American origin

LATINISE *same as* ▷ **latinize**

LATINITY *n* facility in the use of Latin

LATINIZE *vb* translate into Latin

LATINO, -S *n* American male citizen of Latin American origin

LATISH *adv* rather late ▷ *adj* rather late

LATITANT *adj* concealed

LATITAT, -S *n* writ presuming that person accused was hiding

LATITUDE *n* angular distance measured in degrees N or S of the equator

LATKE, -S *n* crispy Jewish pancake

LATOSOL, -S *n* type of deep, well-drained soil

LATRANT *adj* barking

LATRIA, -S *n* adoration that may be offered to God alone

LATRINE, -S *n* toilet in a barracks

LATRON, -S *n* bandit

LATS ▷ **lat**

LATTE, -S *n* coffee with hot milk

LATTEN, -S *n* metal or alloy, esp brass, made in thin sheets

LATTER, -S *adj* second of two ▷ *n* second of two people or things

LATTERLY *adv* recently

LATTERS ▷ **latter**

LATTES ▷ **latte**

LATTICE, -S *n* framework of intersecting strips of wood ▷ *vb* adorn with a lattice

LATTICED ▷ **lattice**

LATTICES ▷ **lattice**

LATTIN, -S *n* brass alloy beaten into a thin sheet

LATU, -S *n* type of edible Asian seaweed

LAUAN, -S *n* type of wood used in furniture-making

LAUCH, -ING, -S, LEUCH, LEUCHEN, LEUGH, LEUGHEN *Scots form of* ▷ **laugh**

LAUD, -ED, -ING *vb* praise or glorify ▷ *n* praise or glorification

LAUDABLE *adj* praiseworthy

LAUDABLY ▷ **laudable**

LAUDANUM *n* opium-based sedative

LAUDATOR *n* one who praises highly

LAUDED ▷ **laud**

LAUDER, -S ▷ **laud**

LAUDING ▷ **laud**

LAUDS *n* traditional morning prayer of the Western Church

LAUF, -S *n* run in bobsleighing

LAUGH, -ED, -S *vb* make sounds with the voice expressing amusement ▷ *n* act of laughing

LAUGHER, -S ▷ **laugh**

LAUGHFUL ▷ **laugh**

LAUGHIER ▷ **laughy**

LAUGHING ▷ **laugh**

LAUGHS ▷ **laugh**

LAUGHTER *n* sound or action of laughing

LAUGHY, LAUGHIER *adj* laughing a lot

LAUNCE, -D, -S, LAUNCING *old form of* ▷ **lance**

LAUNCH, -ED, -ES *vb* put into the water for the first time ▷ *n* launching

LAUNCHER *n* device for launching projectiles

LAUNCHES ▷ **launch**

LAUNCING ▷ **launce**

LAUND, -S *n* open grassy space

LAUNDER, -S *vb* wash and iron ▷ *n* water trough

LAUNDRY *n* clothes for washing

LAUNDS ▷ **laund**

LAURA, -E, -S *n* group of monastic cells

L

LAUREATE adj crowned with laurel leaves as a sign of honour ▷ n person honoured with an award for art or science ▷ vb crown with laurel

LAUREL, -ED, -S n glossy-leaved shrub, bay tree ▷ vb crown with laurel

LAURIC adj as in **lauric acid** dodecanoic acid

LAURYL, -S n as in **lauryl alcohol** crystalline solid used to make detergents

LAUWINE, -S n avalanche

LAV, -S short for ▶ **lavatory**

LAVA, -S n molten rock thrown out by volcanoes

LAVABO, -ES, -S n ritual washing of priest's hands at Mass

LAVAFORM n in form of lava

LAVAGE, -S n washing out of a hollow organ

LAVAL adj of or relating to lava

LAVALAVA n draped skirtlike garment worn by Polynesians

LAVALIER n decorative pendant worn on chain

LAVALIKE ▶ **lava**

LAVANDIN n hybrid of two varieties of the lavender plant

LAVAS ▶ **lava**

LAVASH, -ES n Armenian flat bread

LAVATERA n type of plant closely resembling the mallow

LAVATION n act or process of washing

LAVATORY n toilet

LAVE, -D, -S, LAVING archaic word for ▶ **wash**

LAVEER, -ED, -S vb (in sailing) tack

LAVEMENT n washing with injections of water

LAVENDER n shrub with fragrant flowers ▷ adj bluish-purple

LAVER, -S n priest's basin for ritual ablutions

LAVEROCK n Scot and northern English dialect word for ▶ **skylark**

LAVERS ▶ **laver**

LAVES ▶ **lave**

LAVING ▶ **lave**

LAVISH, -ED, -ES adj prolific ▷ vb give or spend generously

LAVISHER ▶ **lavish**

LAVISHES ▶ **lavish**

LAVISHLY ▶ **lavish**

LAVOLT, -ED, -S same as ▶ **lavolta**

LAVOLTA, -S n old Italian dance ▷ vb dance the lavolta

LAVOLTED ▶ **lavolt**

LAVOLTS ▶ **lavolt**

LAVRA, -S same as ▶ **laura**

LAVROCK, -S same as ▶ **laverock**

LAVS ▶ **lav**

LAVVY, LAVVIES n lavatory

LAW, -ED, -ER, -EST, -S n rule binding on a community ▷ vb prosecute ▷ adj (in archaic usage) low

LAWBOOK, -S n book on subject of law

LAWCOURT n court of law

LAWED ▶ **law**

LAWER ▶ **law**

LAWEST ▶ **law**

LAWFARE, -S n use of the law by a country against its enemies

LAWFUL adj allowed by law

LAWFULLY ▶ **lawful**

LAWGIVER n giver of a code of laws

LAWIN, -S n bill or reckoning

LAWINE, -S n avalanche

LAWING, -S same as ▶ **lawin**

LAWINS ▶ **lawin**

LAWK interj used to show surprise

LAWKS same as ▶ **lawk**

LAWLAND, -S same as ▶ **lowland**

LAWLESS adj breaking the law

LAWLIKE ▶ **law**

LAWMAKER same as ▶ **lawgiver**

LAWMAN, LAWMEN n officer of the law

LAWN, -ING, -S n area of tended and mown grass ▷ vb create or make into a lawn

LAWNED adj having a lawn

LAWNIER ▶ **lawny**

LAWNIEST ▶ **lawny**

LAWNING ▶ **lawn**

LAWNS ▶ **lawn**

LAWNY, LAWNIER, LAWNIEST ▶ **lawn**

LAWS ▶ **law**

LAWSUIT, -S n court case

LAWYER, -ED, -S n professional legal expert ▷ vb act as lawyer

LAWYERLY adj like a lawyer

LAWYERS ▶ **lawyer**

LAX, -ED, -ER, -ES, -EST, -ING adj not strict ▷ vb make lax, loosen

LAXATION n act of making lax or the state of being lax

LAXATIVE adj (medicine) inducing the emptying of the bowels ▷ n medicine that induces the emptying of the bowels

LAXATOR, -S n muscle that loosens body part

LAXED ▶ **lax**

LAXER ▶ **lax**

LAXES ▶ **lax**

LAXEST ▶ **lax**

LAXING ▶ **lax**

LAXISM, -S ▶ **laxist**

LAXIST, -S n lenient or tolerant person

LAXITY, LAXITIES ▶ **lax**

LAXLY ▶ **lax**

LAXNESS ▶ **lax**

LAY, LAIN, -ED, -S vb put in horizontal position

LAYABOUT n lazy person ▷ vb hit out with violent and repeated blows in all directions

LAYAWAY, -S n merchandise reserved for future delivery

LAYBACK, -S n technique for climbing cracks ▷ vb use layback technique

LAYDEEZ pl n jocular spelling of ladies

LAYED ▶ **lay**

LAYER, -ED, -S n single thickness of some substance ▷ vb form a layer

LAYERAGE n covering stem or branch with soil to encourage new roots

LAYERED ▶ **layer**

LAYERING n act of arranging something in layers

LAYERS ▶ **layer**

LAYETTE, -S n clothes for a newborn baby

LAYIN, -S n basketball score

LAYING, -S ▶ **lay**

LAYINS ▶ **layin**

LAYLOCK, -S old form of ▶ **lilac**

LAYMAN, LAYMEN n person who is not a member of the clergy

LAYOFF, -S n act of suspending employees

LAYOUT, -S n arrangement, esp of printing matter

LAYOVER, -S n break in a journey

LAYS ▶ **lay**

LAYSHAFT n auxiliary shaft in a gearbox

LAYSTALL n place where waste is deposited

LAYTIME, -S *n* time allowed for loading cargo

LAYUP, -S *n* period of incapacity through illness

LAYWOMAN, LAYWOMEN *n* woman who is not a member of the clergy

LAZAR, -S *n* archaic word for a person with leprosy

LAZARET, -S *same as* ▸ **lazaretto**

LAZARS ▸ **lazar**

LAZE, -D, -S, LAZING *vb* be idle or lazy ▹ *n* time spent lazing

LAZIED ▸ **lazy**

LAZIER ▸ **lazy**

LAZIES ▸ **lazy**

LAZIEST ▸ **lazy**

LAZILY ▸ **lazy**

LAZINESS ▸ **lazy**

LAZING ▸ **laze**

LAZO, -ED, -ES, -ING, -S *another word for* ▸ **lasso**

LAZULI, -S *n* lapis lazuli

LAZULITE *n* blue mineral

LAZURITE *n* rare blue mineral consisting of a sodium-calcium-aluminium silicate

LAZY, LAZIED, LAZIER, LAZIES, LAZIEST, -ING *vb* laze ▹ *adj* not inclined to work or exert oneself

LAZYISH ▸ **lazy**

LAZZO, LAZZI *n* comic routine in the commedia dell'arte

LEA, -S *n* meadow

LEACH, -ED, -ES, -ING *vb* remove by passing a liquid through ▹ *n* act or process of leaching

LEACHATE *n* water that carries salts dissolved out of materials through which it has percolated

LEACHED ▸ **leach**

LEACHER, -S ▸ **leach**

LEACHES ▸ **leach**

LEACHIER ▸ **leachy**

LEACHING ▸ **leach**

LEACHY, LEACHIER *adj* porous

LEAD, -S, LED *vb* guide or conduct ▹ *n* first or most prominent place ▹ *adj* acting as a leader or lead

LEADABLE *adj* able to be led

LEADED *adj* (of windows) made from many small panes of glass held together by lead strips

LEADEN, -ED, -S *adj* heavy or sluggish ▹ *vb* become or cause to become leaden

LEADENLY ▸ **leaden**

LEADENS ▸ **leaden**

LEADER, -S *n* person who leads

LEADIER ▸ **leady**

LEADIEST ▸ **leady**

LEADING, -S ▸ **lead**

LEADLESS *adj* without lead

LEADMAN, LEADMEN *n* man who leads

LEADOFF, -S *n* initial move

LEADS ▸ **lead**

LEADSMAN, LEADSMEN *n* sailor who takes soundings with a lead line

LEADWORK *n* maintenance work involving lead pipes, etc

LEADWORT *n* type of tropical or subtropical shrub with red, blue, or white flowers

LEADY, LEADIER, LEADIEST *adj* like lead

LEAF, -ED, -ING, -S, LEAVES *n* flat usu green blade attached to the stem of a plant ▹ *vb* turn (pages) cursorily

LEAFAGE, -S *n* leaves of plants

LEAFBUD, -S *n* bud producing leaves rather than flowers

LEAFED ▸ **leaf**

LEAFERY *n* foliage

LEAFIER ▸ **leafy**

LEAFIEST ▸ **leafy**

LEAFING ▸ **leaf**

LEAFLESS ▸ **leaf**

LEAFLET, -S *n* sheet of printed matter for distribution ▹ *vb* distribute leaflets (to)

LEAFLIKE ▸ **leaf**

LEAFMOLD *n* fungus on decayed leaves

LEAFROLL *n* viral disease of potatoes

LEAFS ▸ **leaf**

LEAFWORM *n* cotton plant pest

LEAFY, LEAFIER, LEAFIEST *adj* covered with leaves

LEAGUE, -D, -S, LEAGUING *n* association promoting the interests of its members

LEAGUER, -S *vb* harass; beset ▹ *n* encampment, esp of besiegers

LEAGUES ▸ **league**

LEAGUING ▸ **league**

LEAK, -ED, -ING, -S *n* hole or defect that allows the escape or entrance of liquid, gas, radiation, etc ▹ *vb* let liquid etc in or out

LEAKAGE, -S *n* act or instance of leaking

LEAKED ▸ **leak**

LEAKER, -S ▸ **leak**

LEAKIER ▸ **leaky**

LEAKIEST ▸ **leaky**

LEAKILY ▸ **leaky**

LEAKING ▸ **leak**

LEAKLESS ▸ **leak**

LEAKS ▸ **leak**

LEAKY, LEAKIER, LEAKIEST *adj* leaking

LEAL, -ER, -EST *adj* loyal

LEALLY ▸ **leal**

LEALTY, LEALTIES ▸ **leal**

LEAM, -ED, -ING, -S *vb* shine

LEAN, -ED, -EST, -S, -T *vb* rest (against) ▹ *adj* thin but healthy-looking ▹ *n* lean part of meat

LEANER, -S ▸ **lean**

LEANEST ▸ **lean**

LEANING, -S ▸ **lean**

LEANLY ▸ **lean**

LEANNESS ▸ **lean**

LEANS ▸ **lean**

LEANT ▸ **lean**

LEANY *old form of* ▸ **lean**

LEAP, -ED, -ING, -S, -T *vb* make a sudden powerful jump ▹ *n* sudden powerful jump

LEAPER, -S ▸ **leap**

LEAPFROG *n* game in which a player vaults over another bending down ▹ *vb* play leapfrog

LEAPING ▸ **leap**

LEAPROUS *old form of* ▸ **leprous**

LEAPS ▸ **leap**

LEAPT ▸ **leap**

LEAR, -ED, -ING, -S *vb* instruct

LEARE, -S *same as* ▸ **lear**

LEARED ▸ **lear**

LEARES ▸ **leare**

LEARIER ▸ **leary**

LEARIEST ▸ **leary**

LEARING ▸ **lear**

LEARN, -ED, -ING, -S, -T *vb* gain skill or knowledge by study, practice, or teaching

LEARNER, -S *n* someone who is learning something

LEARNING ▸ **learn**

LEARNS ▸ **learn**

LEARNT ▸ **learn**

LEARS ▸ **lear**

LEARY, LEARIER, LEARIEST *same as* ▸ **leery**

LEAS ▸ **lea**

LEASABLE ▸ **lease**

LEASE, -D, -S *n* contract by which land or property is rented for a stated time ▹ *vb* let or rent by lease

L

LEASER, -S ▶ lease

LEASES ▶ lease

LEASH, -ED, -ES, -ING n lead for a dog ▷ vb control by a leash

LEASING, -S ▶ lease

LEASOW, -ED, -S vb pasture

LEASOWE, -S same as ▶ leasow

LEASOWED ▶ leasow

LEASOWES ▶ leasowe

LEASOWS ▶ leasow

LEAST, -S n smallest amount ▷ adj smallest ▷ n smallest one ▷ adv in the smallest degree

LEASURE, -S old form of ▶ leisure

LEAT, -S n trench or ditch that conveys water to a mill wheel

LEATHER, -S n material made from treated animal skins ▷ adj of leather ▷ vb beat or thrash

LEATHERN adj made of or resembling leather

LEATHERS ▶ leather

LEATHERY adj like leather, tough

LEATS ▶ leat

LEAVE, LEAVING vb go away from ▷ n permission to be absent

LEAVED adj with leaves

LEAVEN, -ED, -S n substance that causes dough to rise ▷ vb raise with leaven

LEAVENER n person or thing that leavens

LEAVENS ▶ leaven

LEAVER, -S ▶ leave

LEAVES ▶ leaf

LEAVIER ▶ leavy

LEAVIEST ▶ leavy

LEAVING ▶ leave

LEAVINGS pl n something remaining, such as refuse

LEAVY, LEAVIER, LEAVIEST same as ▶ leafy

LEAZE, -S same as ▶ lease

LEBBEK, -S n type of timber tree

LEBEN, -S n semiliquid food made from curdled milk

LECANORA n type of lichen

LECCY, LECCIES n electricity

LECHAIM, -S interj drinking toast ▷ n drink for a toast

LECHAYIM same as ▶ lechaim

LECHWE, -S n African antelope

LECITHIN n yellow-brown compound found in plant and animal tissues

LECTERN, -S n reading desk

LECTIN, -S n type of protein

LECTION, -S n variant reading of a passage in a text

LECTOR, -S n university lecturer

LECTRESS n female reader

LECTURE, -D, -S n informative talk ▷ vb give a talk

LECTURER n person who lectures, esp in a university or college

LECTURES ▶ lecture

LECTURN, -S old form of ▶ lectern

LECYTHI ▶ lecythus

LECYTHIS n genus of very tall trees

LECYTHUS, LECYTHI n (in ancient Greece) a vase with a narrow neck

LED ▶ lead

LEDDEN, -S n language; speech

LEDE, -S n introductory part of a news story

LEDGE, -S n narrow shelf

LEDGED ▶ ledge

LEDGER, -ED, -S n book of debit and credit accounts ▷ vb fish using a wire trace while the bait floats freely and the weight sinks

LEDGES ▶ ledge

LEDGY, LEDGIER, LEDGIEST ▶ ledge

LEDUM, -S n evergreen shrub

LEE, -D, -ING n sheltered side ▷ vb (Scots) lie

LEEAR, -S Scots form of ▶ liar

LEEBOARD n board lowered along the lee side of a vessel to reduce drift

LEECH, -ED, -ES, -ING n bloodsucking worm ▷ vb use leeches to suck the blood of

LEECHDOM n remedy

LEECHED ▶ leech

LEECHEE, -S same as ▶ litchi

LEECHES ▶ leech

LEECHING ▶ leech

LEED ▶ lee

LEEING ▶ lee

LEEK, -S n vegetable with a long bulb and thick stem

LEEP, -ED, -ING, -S vb boil; scald

LEER, -ED, -S vb look or grin at in a sneering manner ▷ n sneering look or grin

LEERIER ▶ leery

LEERIEST ▶ leery

LEERILY ▶ leery

LEERING, -S ▶ leer

LEERS ▶ leer

LEERY, LEERIER, LEERIEST adj suspicious or wary (of)

LEES pl n sediment of wine

LEESE, -S, LEESING old form of ▶ loose

LEET, -S n shortlist

LEETLE form of ▶ little

LEETS ▶ leet

LEEWARD n lee side ▷ adv towards this side ▷ adj towards where the wind blows

LEEWARDS adv towards the lee side

LEEWAY, -S n room for free movement within limits

LEEZE adj as in leeze me Scots for lief is me, an expression of affection

LEFT, -ER, -EST, -S adj on the opposite side from right ▷ n left side

LEFTE old past tense of ▶ lift

LEFTER ▶ left

LEFTEST ▶ left

LEFTIE same as ▶ lefty

LEFTIES ▶ lefty

LEFTISH ▶ left

LEFTISM, -S ▶ leftist

LEFTIST, -S adj of the political left ▷ n supporter of the political left

LEFTMOST ▶ left

LEFTOVER n unused portion of food or material ▷ adj left as an unused portion

LEFTS ▶ left

LEFTWARD same as ▶ leftwards

LEFTWING adj of or relating to the leftist faction of a party, etc

LEFTY, LEFTIES n left-winger

LEG, -S n limb on which a person or animal walks, runs, or stands

LEGACY, LEGACIES n thing left in a will

LEGAL, -S adj established or permitted by law ▷ n legal expert

LEGALESE n conventional language in which legal documents are written

LEGALISE same as ▶ legalize

LEGALISM n strict adherence to the letter of the law

LEGALIST ▶ legalism

LEGALITY n state or quality of being legal or lawful

LEGALIZE vb make legal

LEGALLY ▶ legal

LEGALS ▸ legal

LEGATARY n legatee

LEGATE, -D, -S, LEGATING n messenger or representative, esp from the Pope ▷ vb leave as legacy

LEGATEE, -S n recipient of a legacy

LEGATES ▸ legate

LEGATINE ▸ legate

LEGATING ▸ legate

LEGATION n diplomatic minister and his or her staff

LEGATO, -S adv smoothly ▷ n playing with no gaps between notes

LEGATOR, -S n person who gives a legacy or makes a bequest

LEGATOS ▸ legato

LEGEND, -S n traditional story

LEGENDRY ▸ legend

LEGENDS ▸ legend

LEGER, -ING, -S variant of ▸ ledger

LEGERITY n agility

LEGERS ▸ leger

LEGES ▸ lex

LEGGE, -S vb lighten or lessen

LEGGED ▸ leg

LEGGER, -S n person who moves barge through tunnel using legs

LEGGES ▸ legge

LEGGIE, -S n leg spin bowler

LEGGIER ▸ leggy

LEGGIERO adj light; delicate

LEGGIES ▸ leggie

LEGGIEST ▸ leggy

LEGGIN, -S same as ▸ legging

LEGGING, -S n extra outer covering for the lower leg

LEGGINS ▸ leggin

LEGGISM, -S n blacklegging

LEGGO sentence substitute let go!

LEGGY, LEGGIER, LEGGIEST adj having long legs

LEGHOLD, -S n type of animal trap that clamps down on the animal's leg

LEGHORN, -S n Italian wheat straw woven into hats

LEGIBLE adj easily read

LEGIBLY ▸ legible

LEGION, -S n large military force ▷ adj very large or numerous

LEGIONED adj arranged in legions

LEGIONS ▸ legion

LEGIST, -S n legal mind

LEGIT, -S n legitimate drama ▷ adj legitimate

LEGITIM, -S n inheritance due to children from father

LEGITS ▸ legit

LEGLAN, -S same as ▸ leglin

LEGLEN, -S same as ▸ leglin

LEGLESS adj without legs

LEGLET, -S n leg jewellery

LEGLIKE ▸ leg

LEGLIN, -S n milk-pail

LEGMAN, LEGMEN n newsman who reports from the scene

LEGONG, -S n Indonesian dance

LEGROOM, -S n space to put one's legs

LEGS ▸ leg

LEGSIDE, -S n part of a cricket field to the left of a right-handed batsman as they face the bowler

LEGUAAN, -S n S African lizard

LEGUAN, -S same as ▸ leguaan

LEGUME, -S n pod of a plant of the pea or bean family

LEGUMIN, -S n protein from leguminous plants

LEGWEAR, -S n clothing for legs

LEGWORK, -S n work that involves travelling on foot or as if on foot

LEHAIM, -S same as ▸ lechaim

LEHAYIM, -S same as ▸ lehaim

LEHR, -S n long tunnel-shaped oven used for annealing glass

LEHUA, -S n flower of Hawaii

LEI, -S n Hawaiian garland

LEIDGER, -S same as ▸ ledger

LEIGER, -S same as ▸ ledger

LEIPOA, -S n Australian bird

LEIR, -ED, -ING, -S same as ▸ lear

LEIS ▸ lei

LEISH, -ER, -EST adj agile

LEISLER, -S n small bat

LEISTER, -S n pronged fishing spear ▷ vb spear with a leister

LEISURE, -D, -S n time for relaxation or hobbies ▷ vb have leisure

LEK, -KED, -S, -U n bird display area ▷ vb gather at lek

LEKE old form of ▸ leak

LEKGOTLA n meeting place for village assemblies, court cases, and meetings of village leaders

LEKKED ▸ lek

LEKKER adj attractive or nice

LEKKING, -S ▸ lek

LEKS ▸ lek

LEKU ▸ lek

LEKVAR, -S n prune or apricot pie filling

LEKYTHOS, LEKYTHI, LEKYTHOI n Greek flask

LEKYTHUS same as ▸ lekythos

LEMAN, -S n beloved

LEME, -D, -S, LEMING same as ▸ leam

LEMEL, -S n metal filings

LEMES ▸ leme

LEMING ▸ leme

LEMMA, -S, -TA n word in its citation form

LEMME vb (short for) let me

LEMMING, -S n rodent of Arctic regions

LEMNISCI > lemniscus

LEMON, -ED, -ING, -S n yellow oval fruit ▷ adj pale-yellow ▷ vb flavour with lemon

LEMONADE n lemon-flavoured soft drink, often fizzy

LEMONED ▸ lemon

LEMONIER ▸ lemony

LEMONING ▸ lemon

LEMONISH ▸ lemon

LEMONS ▸ lemon

LEMONY, LEMONIER adj like a lemon

LEMPIRA, -S n monetary unit of Honduras

LEMUR, -S n animal like a small monkey

LEMURES pl n spirits of the dead

LEMURIAN same as ▸ lemuroid

LEMURINE same as ▸ lemuroid

LEMUROID adj relating to the superfamily which includes the lemurs ▷ n animal that resembles or is closely related to a lemur

LEMURS ▸ lemur

LEND, -S, LENT vb give temporary use of

LENDABLE ▸ lend

LENDER, -S ▸ lend

LENDING, -S ▸ lend

LENDS ▸ lend

LENES ▸ lenis

LENG, -ED, -ER, -EST, -ING, -S vb linger ▷ adj long

LENGTH, -S n extent or measurement from end to end

LENGTHEN vb make or become longer

LENGTHS ▸ length

LENGTHY adj very long

LENIENCE ▸ lenient

LENIENCY ▸ lenient

LENIENT, -S adj tolerant, not strict or severe ▷ n lenient person

LENIFY, LENIFIED, LENIFIES vb make lenient

LENIS, LENES adj pronounced with little muscular tension ▷ n consonant like this

LENITE, -D, -S, LENITING vb undergo lenition

LENITIES ▸ lenity

LENITING ▸ lenite

LENITION n weakening of consonant sound

LENITIVE adj soothing or alleviating of pain or distress ▷ n lenitive drug

LENITY, LENITIES n mercy or clemency

LENO, -S n weave in which the warp yarns are twisted in pairs between the weft

LENS, -ES n piece of glass or similar material with one or both sides curved

LENSE same as ▸ lens

LENSED adj incorporating a lens

LENSES ▸ lens

LENSING, -S n materials which colour and diffuse light

LENSLESS ▸ lens

LENSLIKE adj like a lens

LENSMAN, LENSMEN n camera operator

LENT ▸ lend

LENTANDO adv slowing down

LENTEN adj of or relating to Lent

LENTI ▸ lento

LENTIC adj of, relating to, or inhabiting still water

LENTICEL n any of numerous pores in the stem of a woody plant

LENTICLE n lens-shaped layer of mineral or rock embedded in a matrix of different constitution

LENTIGO technical name for a ▸ freckle

LENTIL, -S n edible seed

LENTISC, -S same as ▸ lentisk

LENTISK, -S n mastic tree

LENTO, LENTI, -S adv slowly ▷ n movement or passage performed slowly

LENTOID, -S adj lentiform ▷ n lentiform object

LENTOR, -S n lethargy

LENTOS ▸ lento

LENTOUS adj lethargic

LENVOY, -S another word for ▸ envoy

LEONE, -S n monetary unit of Sierra Leone

LEONINE adj like a lion

LEOPARD, -S n large spotted animal of the cat family

LEOTARD, -S n tight-fitting garment covering the upper body

LEP, -PED, -PING, -S, -T dialect word for ▸ leap

LEPER, -S n person who is ignored or despised

LEPID adj amusing

LEPIDOTE adj covered with scales, scaly leaves, or spots ▷ n lepidote person, creature, or thing

LEPORID, -S adj of the family of mammals including rabbits and hares ▷ n any animal belonging to this family

LEPORINE adj of, relating to, or resembling a hare

LEPPED ▸ lep

LEPPING ▸ lep

LEPRA, -S n leprosy

LEPROSE adj having or denoting a whitish scurfy surface

LEPROSY n disease attacking the nerves and skin

LEPROTIC adj relating to leprosy

LEPROUS adj having leprosy

LEPS ▸ lep

LEPT ▸ lep

LEPTA ▸ lepton

LEPTIN, -S n protein that regulates the amount of fat in the body

LEPTOME, -S n tissue of plant conducting food

LEPTON, LEPTA, -S n any of a group of elementary particles with weak interactions

LEPTONIC ▸ lepton

LEPTONS ▸ lepton

LEQUEAR, -S same as ▸ lacunar

LERE, -D, -S, LERING same as ▸ lear

LERNAEAN adj relating to Lerna, the swamp in which dwelt the Hydra

LERP, -S n crystallized honeydew

LESBIAN, -S n homosexual woman ▷ adj of homosexual women

LESBIC adj relating to lesbians

LESION, -ED, -S n change in an organ of the body caused by injury ▷ vb cause lesions

LESS, -ES n smaller amount ▷ adj smaller in extent, degree, or duration ▷ pron smaller part or quantity ▷ adv smaller extent or degree ▷ prep after deducting, minus

LESSEE, -S n person to whom a lease is granted

LESSEN, -ED, -S vb make or become smaller or not as much

LESSER adj not as great in quantity, size, or worth

LESSES ▸ less

LESSON, -ED, -S n class or single period of instruction in a subject ▷ vb censure or punish

LESSOR, -S n person who grants a lease of property

LEST, -ED, -ING, -S conj so as to prevent any possibility that ▷ vb listen

LESULA, -S n species of monkey inhabiting forests in DR Congo

LET, -S, -TED n act of letting property ▷ vb obstruct

LETCHED ▸ letch

LETCHES ▸ letch

LETCHING ▸ letch

LETDOWN, -S n disappointment

LETHAL, -S adj deadly ▷ n weapon, etc capable of causing death

LETHALLY ▸ lethal

LETHALS ▸ lethal

LETHARGY n sluggishness or dullness

LETHE, -S n forgetfulness

LETHEAN ▸ lethe

LETHEE, -S n life-blood

LETHES ▸ lethe

LETHIED adj forgetful

LETOUT, -S n circumstance that serves as an excuse not to do something

LETS ▸ let

LETTABLE ▸ let

LETTED ▸ let

LETTER n written message ▷ vb put letters on

LETTERED adj learned

LETTERER ▸ letter

LETTERN, -S another word for ▸ lectern

L

LETTERS pl n literary knowledge

LETTING, -S ▶let

LETTRE, -S n letter

LETTUCE, -S n plant with large green leaves used in salads

LETUP, -S n lessening or abatement

LEU n monetary unit of Romania

LEUCEMIA same as > leukaemia

LEUCEMIC adj of or like leucemia

LEUCH ▶lauch

LEUCHEN ▶lauch

LEUCIN, -S same as ▶leucine

LEUCINE, -S n essential amino acid

LEUCINS ▶leucin

LEUCISM, -S n condition causing pale discoloration of hair or skin

LEUCITE, -S n grey or white mineral

LEUCITIC ▶leucite

LEUCO n as in leuco base colourless compound

LEUCOMA, -S n white opaque scar of the cornea

LEUCON, -S n type of sponge

LEUCOSES ▶leucosis

LEUCOSIN n albumin in cereal grains

LEUCOSIS, LEUCOSES same as > leukaemia

LEUCOTIC adj of or relating to leucosis

LEUD, -ES, -S Scots word for ▶breadth

LEUGH ▶lauch

LEUGHEN ▶lauch

LEUKEMIA same as > leukaemia

LEUKEMIC ▶leukemia

LEUKOMA, -S same as ▶leucoma

LEUKON, -S n white blood cell count

LEUKOSIS, LEUKOSES n abnormal growth of white blood cells

LEUKOTIC ▶leukosis

LEV, -A, -S n monetary unit of Bulgaria

LEVANT, -ED, -S n leather made from the skins of goats, sheep, or seals ▷ vb bolt or abscond

LEVANTER n easterly wind in the W Mediterranean area, esp in the late summer

LEVANTS ▶levant

LEVATOR, -S n muscle that raises a part of the body

LEVE, -S same as ▶lief

LEVEE, -D, -ING, -S n natural or artificial river embankment ▷ vb go to the reception of

LEVEL, -ED, -ING, -LED, -S adj horizontal ▷ vb make even or horizontal ▷ n horizontal line or surface

LEVELER, -S same as ▶leveller

LEVELING ▶level

LEVELLED ▶level

LEVELLER n person or thing that levels

LEVELLY ▶level

LEVELS ▶level

LEVER, -ED, -ING, -S n handle used to operate machinery ▷ vb prise or move with a lever

LEVERAGE n action or power of a lever ▷ vb borrow capital required

LEVERED ▶lever

LEVERET, -S n young hare

LEVERING ▶lever

LEVERS ▶lever

LEVES ▶leve

LEVIABLE adj (of taxes, tariffs, etc) liable to be levied

LEVIED ▶levy

LEVIER, -S ▶levy

LEVIES ▶levy

LEVIGATE vb grind into a fine powder or a smooth paste ▷ adj having a smooth polished surface

LEVIN, -S archaic word for > lightning

LEVIRATE n practice, required by Old Testament law, of marrying the widow of one's brother

LEVIS pl n jeans

LEVITATE vb rise or cause to rise into the air

LEVITE, -S n Christian clergyman or clergywoman

LEVITIC ▶levite

LEVITY, LEVITIES n fickleness

LEVO adj anticlockwise

LEVODOPA n substance occurring naturally in the body and used to treat Parkinson's disease

LEVOGYRE n counterclockwise spiral

LEVIS ▶lev

LEVULIN, -S n substance obtained from certain bulbs

LEVULOSE n fructose

LEVY, LEVIED, LEVIES, -ING vb impose and collect (a tax) ▷ n imposition or collection of taxes

LEW adj tepid

LEWDSBY another word for ▶lewdster

LEWDSTER n lewd person

LEWIS, -ES n lifting device for heavy stone or concrete blocks

LEWISIA, -S n type of herb

LEWISITE n colourless oily poisonous liquid

LEWISSON same as ▶lewis

LEX, LEGES, -ES n system or body of laws

LEXEME, -S n minimal meaningful unit of language

LEXEMIC ▶lexeme

LEXES ▶lex

LEXICA ▶lexicon

LEXICAL adj relating to the vocabulary of a language

LEXICON, LEXICA, -S n dictionary

LEXIGRAM n figure or symbol that represents a word

LEXIS, -ES n totality of vocabulary in a language

LEY, -S n land under grass

LEYLANDI same as > leylandii

LEYS ▶ley

LI n Chinese measurement of distance

LIABLE adj legally obliged or responsible

LIAISE, -D, -S, LIAISING vb establish and maintain communication

LIAISON, -S n communication and contact between groups

LIANA, -S n climbing plant

LIANE, -S same as ▶liana

LIANG, -S n Chinese unit of weight

LIANOID ▶liana

LIAR, -S n person who tells lies

LIARD, -S adj grey ▷ n former small coin

LIARS ▶liar

LIART Scots form of ▶liard

LIAS, -ES n lowest series of rocks of the Jurassic system

LIASSIC adj relating to the earliest epoch of the Jurassic period

LIATRIS n North American plant with white flowers

LIB, -BED, -BING, -S n informal word for liberation ▷ vb geld

LIBANT adj touching lightly

LIBATE, -D, -S, LIBATING vb offer as gift to the gods

LIBATION n drink poured as an offering to the gods

LIBATORY ▸ libate

LIBBARD, -S another word for ▸ leopard

LIBBED ▸ lib

LIBBER, -S n liberationist

LIBBING ▸ lib

LIBECCIO n strong westerly or southwesterly wind blowing onto the W coast of Corsica

LIBEL, -ED, -ING, -LED, -S n published statement falsely damaging a person's reputation ▷ vb falsely damage the reputation of

LIBELANT same as ▸ libellant

LIBELED ▸ libel

LIBELEE, -S same as ▸ libellee

LIBELER, -S ▸ libel

LIBELING ▸ libel

LIBELIST ▸ libel

LIBELLED ▸ libel

LIBELLEE n person against whom a libel has been filed in an ecclesiastical court

LIBELLER ▸ libel

LIBELOUS ▸ libel

LIBELS ▸ libel

LIBER, -S, LIBRI n tome or book

LIBERAL, -S adj having social and political views that favour progress and reform ▷ n person with such views

LIBERATE vb set free

LIBERO, -S another name for ▸ sweeper

LIBERS ▸ liber

LIBERTY n freedom

LIBIDO, -S n psychic energy

LIBKEN, -S n lodging

LIBLAB, -S n 19th century British liberal

LIBRA, -E, -S n ancient Roman unit of weight

LIBRAIRE n bookseller

LIBRARY n room or building where books are kept

LIBRAS ▸ libra

LIBRATE, -D, -S vb oscillate or waver

LIBRETTO, LIBRETTI n words of an opera

LIBRI ▸ liber

LIBS ▸ lib

LICE ▸ louse

LICENCE, -D, -S n document giving official permission ▷ vb (in the US) give permission to

LICENCEE same as ▸ licensee

LICENCER ▸ licence

LICENCES ▸ licence

LICENSE, -D, -S vb grant or give a licence for

LICENSEE n holder of a licence

LICENSER ▸ license

LICENSES ▸ license

LICENSOR ▸ license

LICENTE adj permitted; allowed

LICH, -ES n dead body

LICHANOS n note played using forefinger

LICHEE, -S same as ▸ litchi

LICHEN, -S n small flowerless plant forming a crust on rocks, trees, etc ▷ vb cover with lichen

LICHENED ▸ lichen

LICHENIN n complex polysaccharide occurring in certain species of moss

LICHENS ▸ lichen

LICHES ▸ lich

LICHGATE n roofed gate to a churchyard

LICHI, -S same as ▸ litchi

LICHT, -ED, -ER, -EST, -ING, -S Scot word for ▸ light

LICHTLY vb Scots word meaning treat discourteously

LICHTS ▸ licht

LICHWAKE n night vigil over a dead body

LICHWAY, -S n path used to carry coffin into church

LICIT adj lawful, permitted

LICITLY ▸ licit

LICK, -ED, -S vb pass the tongue over ▷ n licking

LICKER, -S ▸ lick

LICKING, -S n beating

LICKS ▸ lick

LICKSPIT n flattering or servile person

LICORICE same as ▸ liquorice

LICTOR, -S n one of a group of ancient Roman officials

LID, -S n movable cover

LIDAR, -S n radar-type instrument

LIDDED ▸ lid

LIDDING, -S n lids

LIDGER, -S variant form of ▸ ledger

LIDLESS adj having no lid or top

LIDO, -S n open-air centre for swimming and water sports

LIDS ▸ lid

LIE, -S vb make a false statement ▷ n falsehood

LIED, -ER n setting for solo voice and piano of a poem

LIEF, -ER, -EST, -S adv gladly ▷ adj ready ▷ n beloved person

LIEFLY ▸ lief

LIEFS ▸ lief

LIEGE, -S adj bound to give or receive feudal service ▷ n lord

LIEGEDOM ▸ liege

LIEGEMAN, LIEGEMEN n (formerly) the subject of a sovereign or feudal lord

LIEGER, -S same as ▸ ledger

LIEGES ▸ liege

LIEN, -S n right to hold another's property until a debt is paid

LIENABLE adj that can be subject of a lien

LIENAL adj of or relating to the spleen

LIENEE, -S n person against whom a lien has been placed

LIENOR, -S n person who holds a lien

LIENS ▸ lien

LIENTERY n passage of undigested food in the faeces

LIER, -S n person who lies down

LIERNE, -S n short secondary rib that connects intersections of the primary ribs

LIERS ▸ lier

LIES ▸ lie

LIEU, -S n stead

LIEVE, -R, -S, -ST same as ▸ leve

LIFE, LIVES n state of living beings

LIFEBELT n ring filled with air, used to keep a person afloat when in danger of drowning

LIFEBOAT n boat used for rescuing people at sea

LIFEBUOY n any of various kinds of buoyant device for keeping people afloat

LIFECARE n care of person's health and welfare

LIFEFUL adj full of life

LIFEHACK n action that simplifies a task or reduces frustration in everyday life ▷ vb perform a lifehack

LIFEHOLD adj (of land) held while one is alive

LIFELESS adj dead

LIFELIKE adj closely resembling or representing life

LIFELINE n means of contact or support

LIFELONG *adj* lasting all of a person's life

LIFER, -S *n* prisoner sentenced to imprisonment for life

LIFES *pl n* as in **still lifes** paintings or drawings of inanimate objects

LIFESOME *adj* full of life

LIFESPAN *n* period of time during which a person or animal may be expected to live

LIFETIME *n* length of time a person is alive

LIFEWAY, -S *n* way of life

LIFEWORK *n* work to which a person has devoted their life

LIFT, -ED, -ING, -S *vb* move upwards in position, status, volume, etc ▷ *n* cage raised and lowered in a vertical shaft

LIFTABLE ▶ lift

LIFTBACK *n* hatchback

LIFTBOY, -S *n* person who operates a lift

LIFTED ▶ lift

LIFTER, -S ▶ lift

LIFTGATE *n* rear opening of hatchback

LIFTING ▶ lift

LIFTMAN, LIFTMEN *same as* ▶ liftboy

LIFTOFF, -S *n* moment a rocket leaves the ground ▷ *vb* (of a rocket) to leave its launch pad

LIFTS ▶ lift

LIFULL *obsolete form of* ▶ lifeful

LIG, -GED, -S *n* function with free entertainment and refreshments ▷ *vb* attend such a function

LIGAMENT *n* band of tissue joining bones

LIGAN, -S *same as* ▶ lagan

LIGAND, -S *n* atom, molecule, radical, or ion forming a complex with a central atom

LIGANS ▶ ligan

LIGASE, -S *n* any of a class of enzymes

LIGATE, -D, -S, LIGATING *vb* tie up or constrict (something) with a ligature

LIGATION ▶ ligate

LIGATIVE ▶ ligate

LIGATURE *n* link, bond, or tie ▷ *vb* bind with a ligature

LIGER, -S *n* hybrid offspring of a female tiger and a male lion

LIGGE, -S *obsolete form of* ▶ lie

LIGGED ▶ lig

LIGGER, -S ▶ lig

LIGGES ▶ ligge

LIGGING, -S ▶ lig

LIGHT, -ED, -EST, -ING, -S *n* electromagnetic radiation by which things are visible ▷ *adj* bright ▷ *vb* ignite ▷ *adv* with little luggage

LIGHTEN, -S *vb* make less dark

LIGHTER, -S *n* device for lighting cigarettes etc ▷ *vb* convey in a type of flat-bottomed barge

LIGHTEST ▶ light

LIGHTFUL *adj* full of light

LIGHTING ▶ light

LIGHTISH ▶ light

LIGHTLY *adv* in a light way ▷ *vb* belittle

LIGHTS ▶ light

LIGNAGE, -S *another word for* ▶ lineage

LIGNAN, -S *n* beneficial substance found in plants

LIGNE, -S *n* unit of measurement

LIGNEOUS *adj* of or like wood

LIGNES ▶ ligne

LIGNIFY *vb* become woody with the deposition of lignin in cell walls

LIGNIN, -S *n* complex polymer occurring in certain plant cell walls making the plant rigid

LIGNITE, -S *n* woody textured rock used as fuel

LIGNITIC ▶ lignite

LIGNOSE, -S *n* explosive compound

LIGNUM, -S *n* wood

LIGROIN, -S *n* volatile fraction of petroleum

LIGROINE *same as* ▶ ligroin

LIGROINS ▶ ligroin

LIGS ▶ lig

LIGULA, -E, -S *same as* ▶ ligule

LIGULAR ▶ ligula

LIGULAS ▶ ligula

LIGULATE *adj* having the shape of a strap

LIGULE, -S *n* membranous outgrowth between the leaf blade and sheath

LIGULOID ▶ ligula

LIGURE, -S *n* any of the 12 precious stones used in the breastplates of high priests

LIKABLE *adj* easy to like

LIKABLY ▶ likable

LIKE, -D, -S, -ST *adj* similar ▷ *vb* find enjoyable ▷ *n* favourable feeling, desire, or preference

LIKEABLE *same as* ▶ likable

LIKEABLY *same as* ▶ likably

LIKED ▶ like

LIKELY, LIKELIER *adj* tending or inclined ▷ *adv* probably

LIKEN, -ED, -ING, -S *vb* compare

LIKENESS *n* resemblance

LIKENING ▶ liken

LIKENS ▶ liken

LIKER, -S ▶ like

LIKES ▶ like

LIKEST ▶ like

LIKEWAKE *same as* ▶ lykewake

LIKEWALK *same as* ▶ lykewake

LIKEWISE *adv* similarly

LIKIN, -S *n* historically, Chinese tax

LIKING, -S *n* fondness

LIKINS ▶ likin

LIKUTA *n* coin in the former Zaïre

LILAC, -S *n* shrub with pale mauve flowers ▷ *adj* light-purple

LILIED *adj* decorated with lilies

LILIES ▶ lily

LILL, -ED, -ING, -S *obsolete form of* ▶ loll

LILLIPUT *adj* tiny ▷ *n* tiny person or being

LILLS ▶ lill

LILO, -S *n* inflatable mattress

LILT, -ED, -S *n* musical quality in speech ▷ *vb* speak with a lilt

LILTING ▶ lilt

LILTS ▶ lilt

LILY, LILIES *n* plant which has large, often white, flowers

LILYLIKE *adj* resembling a lily

LIMA, -S *n* type of edible bean

LIMACEL, -S *n* small shell inside some kinds of slug

LIMACES ▶ limax

LIMACINE *adj* relating to slugs

LIMACON, -S *n* heart-shaped curve

LIMAIL, -S *same as* ▶ lemel

LIMAN, -S *n* lagoon

LIMAS ▶ lima

LIMATION *n* polishing

LIMAX, LIMACES *n* slug

LIMB, -ED, -ING, -S *n* arm, leg, or wing ▷ *vb* dismember

LIMBA | 388

LIMBA, -S n type of African tree

LIMBATE adj having an edge or border of a different colour from the rest

LIMBEC, -S obsolete form of ▸ alembic

LIMBECK, -S obsolete form of ▸ alembic

LIMBECS ▸ limbec

LIMBED ▸ limb

LIMBER, -ED, -S vb loosen stiff muscles by exercising ▷ adj pliant or supple ▷ n part of a gun carriage

LIMBERER ▸ limber

LIMBERLY ▸ limber

LIMBERS ▸ limber

LIMBI ▸ limbus

LIMBIC ▸ limbus

LIMBIER ▸ limby

LIMBIEST ▸ limby

LIMBING ▸ limb

LIMBLESS ▸ limb

LIMBMEAL adv piece by piece

LIMBO, -ED, -ES, -ING, -S n region between Heaven and Hell for the unbaptized ▷ vb perform a Caribbean dance that entails passing under a bar while leaning backwards

LIMBOUS adj with overlapping edges

LIMBS ▸ limb

LIMBUS, LIMBI, -ES n border

LIMBY, LIMBIER, LIMBIEST adj with long legs, stem, branches, etc

LIME, -D n calcium compound used as a fertilizer or in making cement ▷ vb spread a calcium compound upon (land) ▷ adj having the flavour of lime fruit

LIMEADE, -S n drink made from sweetened lime juice and plain or carbonated water

LIMED ▸ lime

LIMEKILN n kiln in which calcium carbonate is burned to produce quicklime

LIMELESS ▸ lime

LIMELIT > limelight

LIMEN, -S, LIMINA another term for > threshold

LIMEPIT, -S n pit containing lime in which hides are placed to remove the hair

LIMERICK n humorous verse of five lines

LIMES, LIMITES n fortified boundary of the Roman Empire

LIMEWASH n mixture of lime and water used to whitewash walls, ceilings, etc

LIMEY, -S n British person ▷ adj British

LIMIER ▸ limy

LIMIEST ▸ limy

LIMINA ▸ limen

LIMINAL adj relating to the point beyond which a sensation becomes too faint to be experienced

LIMINESS ▸ limy

LIMING, -S ▸ lime

LIMIT, -ING, -S n ultimate extent, degree, or amount of something ▷ vb restrict or confine

LIMITARY adj of, involving, or serving as a limit

LIMITED, -S adj having a limit ▷ n limited train, bus, etc

LIMITER, -S n thing that limits something

LIMITES ▸ limes

LIMITING ▸ limit

LIMITS ▸ limit

LIMMA, -S n semitone

LIMMER, -S n scoundrel

LIMN, -ED, -ING, -S vb represent in drawing or painting

LIMNAEID n type of snail

LIMNED ▸ limn

LIMNER, -S ▸ limn

LIMNETIC adj of the open water of lakes down to the depth of light penetration

LIMNIC adj relating to lakes

LIMNING ▸ limn

LIMNS ▸ limn

LIMO, -S short for > limousine

LIMONENE n liquid optically active terpene with a lemon-like odour

LIMONITE n common brown, black, or yellow amorphous secondary mineral

LIMONIUM n sea plant with funnel-shaped flowers

LIMOS ▸ limo

LIMOSIS, LIMOSES n excessive hunger

LIMOUS adj muddy

LIMP, -ED, -EST, -S vb walk with an uneven step ▷ n limping walk ▷ adj without firmness or stiffness

LIMPA, -S n type of rye bread

LIMPED ▸ limp

LIMPER, -S ▸ limp

LIMPEST ▸ limp

LIMPET, -S n shellfish which sticks to rocks ▷ adj denoting weapons that are magnetically attached to their targets

LIMPID adj clear or transparent

LIMPIDLY ▸ limpid

LIMPING, -S ▸ limp

LIMPKIN, -S n rail-like wading bird

LIMPLY ▸ limp

LIMPNESS ▸ limp

LIMPS ▸ limp

LIMPSEY same as ▸ limpsy

LIMPSY, LIMPSIER adj limp

LIMULI ▸ limulus

LIMULOID n type of crab

LIMULUS, LIMULI n horseshoe crab

LIMY, LIMIER, LIMIEST adj of, like, or smeared with birdlime

LIN, -NED, -NING, -S vb cease

LINABLE ▸ line

LINAC, -S n linear accelerator

LINAGE, -S n number of lines in written or printed matter

LINALOL, -S same as ▸ linalool

LINALOOL n optically active colourless fragrant liquid

LINCH, -ES n ledge

LINCHET, -S another word for ▸ linch

LINCHPIN n pin to hold a wheel on its axle

LINCTURE n medicine taken by licking

LINCTUS n cough medicine

LIND, -S variant of ▸ linden

LINDANE, -S n white poisonous crystalline powder

LINDEN, -S n large tree with heart-shaped leaves and fragrant yellowish flowers

LINDIED ▸ lindy

LINDIES ▸ lindy

LINDS ▸ lind

LINDWORM n wingless serpent-like dragon

LINDY, LINDIED, LINDIES, -ING n lively dance ▷ vb perform the lindy

LINE, -D, -S n long narrow mark ▷ vb mark with lines

LINEABLE ▸ line

LINEAGE, -S n descent from an ancestor

LINEAL adj in direct line of descent

LINEALLY ▸ lineal

LINEAR adj of or in lines

LINEARLY ▶ linear
LINEATE adj marked with lines
LINEATED same as ▶ lineate
LINEBRED adj having an ancestor that is common to sire and dam
LINECUT, -S n method of relief printing
LINED ▶ line
LINELESS ▶ line
LINELIKE ▶ line
LINEMAN, LINEMEN same as ▶ linesman
LINEMATE n ice hockey player on the same line as another
LINEMEN ▶ lineman
LINEN, -S n cloth or thread made from flax
LINENIER ▶ lineny
LINENS ▶ linen
LINENY, LINENIER adj like linen
LINER, -S n large passenger ship
LINES ▶ line
LINESMAN, LINESMEN n (in some sports) an official who helps the referee or umpire
LINEUP, -S n row or arrangement of people or things
LINEY ▶ line
LING, -S n slender food fish
LINGA, -S same as ▶ lingam
LINGAM, -S n (in Sanskrit) masculine gender
LINGAS ▶ linga
LINGCOD, -S n type of food fish
LINGEL, -S n shoemaker's thread
LINGER, -ED, -S vb delay or prolong departure
LINGERER ▶ linger
LINGERIE n women's underwear or nightwear
LINGERS ▶ linger
LINGIER ▶ lingy
LINGIEST ▶ lingy
LINGLE, -S same as ▶ lingel
LINGO, -ES, -S n foreign or unfamiliar language or jargon
LINGOT, -S n ingot
LINGS ▶ ling
LINGSTER n person able to communicate with aliens
LINGUA, -E, -S n any tongue-like structure
LINGUAL, -S adj of the tongue ▷ n lingual consonant
LINGUAS ▶ lingua

LINGUICA n Portuguese sausage
LINGUINE n kind of pasta in the shape of thin flat strands
LINGUINI same as ▶ linguine
LINGUISA same as ▶ linguica
LINGUIST n person skilled in foreign languages
LINGULA, -E, -S n small tongue
LINGULAR ▶ lingula
LINGULAS ▶ lingula
LINGY, LINGIER, LINGIEST adj heather-covered
LINHAY, -S n farm building with an open front
LINIER ▶ liny
LINIEST ▶ liny
LINIMENT n medicated liquid rubbed on the skin to relieve pain or stiffness
LININ, -S n network of viscous material in the nucleus of a cell
LINING, -S n layer of cloth attached to the inside of a garment etc
LININS ▶ linin
LINISH, -ED, -ES vb polish metal
LINISHER ▶ linish
LINISHES ▶ linish
LINK, -ED, -ING, -S n any of the rings forming a chain ▷ vb connect with or as if with links
LINKABLE ▶ link
LINKAGE, -S n act of linking or the state of being linked
LINKBOY, -S n (formerly) a boy who carried a torch for pedestrians in dark streets
LINKED ▶ link
LINKER, -S n person or thing that links
LINKIER ▶ linky
LINKIEST ▶ linky
LINKING ▶ link
LINKMAN, LINKMEN same as ▶ linkboy
LINKROT, -S n state of having expired hyperlinks on a website
LINKS ▶ link
LINKSMAN, LINKSMEN same as ▶ linkboy
LINKSPAN n hinged bridge on a quay, used to move vehicles on or off a vessel
LINKSTER n interpreter
LINKUP, -S n establishing of a union between objects, groups, organizations, etc
LINKWORK n something made up of links

LINKY, LINKIER, LINKIEST adj (of countryside) consisting of links
LINN, -S n waterfall or a pool at the foot of it
LINNED ▶ lin
LINNET, -S n songbird of the finch family
LINNEY, -S same as ▶ linhay
LINNIES ▶ linny
LINNING ▶ lin
LINNS ▶ linn
LINNY, LINNIES same as ▶ linhay
LINO, -S same as ▶ linoleum
LINOCUT, -S n design cut in relief in lino mounted on a block of wood
LINOLEIC adj as in linoleic acid colourless oily essential fatty acid found in linseed
LINOLEUM n type of floor covering
LINOS ▶ lino
LINOTYPE n line of metal type produced by machine ▷ vb set as line of type
LINS ▶ lin
LINSANG, -S n any of several forest-dwelling viverrine mammals
LINSEED, -S n seed of the flax plant
LINSEY, -S n type of cloth
LINSTOCK n long staff holding a lighted match, formerly used to fire a cannon
LINT, -S n shreds of fibre, etc ▷ vb shed or remove lint
LINTED adj having lint
LINTEL, -S n horizontal beam at the top of a door or window
LINTELED adj (of a door or window) having a lintel
LINTELS ▶ lintel
LINTER, -S n machine for stripping the short fibres of ginned cotton seeds
LINTIE, -S Scot word for ▶ linnet
LINTIER ▶ linty
LINTIES ▶ lintie
LINTIEST ▶ linty
LINTING, -S n process of making lint
LINTLESS ▶ lint
LINTOL, -S same as ▶ lintel
LINTS ▶ lint
LINTSEED same as ▶ linseed
LINTY, LINTIER, LINTIEST ▶ lint
LINUM, -S n type of plant of temperate regions

LINURON, -S *n* type of herbicide

LINUX, -ES *n* nonproprietary computer operating system

LINY, LINIER, LINIEST ▸ line

LION, -S *n* large animal of the cat family

LIONCEL, -S *n* (in heraldry) small lion

LIONEL, -S *same as* ▸ **lioncel**

LIONESS *n* female lion

LIONET, -S *n* young lion

LIONFISH *n* any of various scorpion fishes of the Pacific

LIONHEAD *n* small breed of rabbit with long fur around the face

LIONISE, -D, -S *same as* ▸ **lionize**

LIONISER ▸ lionise

LIONISES ▸ lionise

LIONISM, -S *n* the condition of being treated as a celebrity

LIONIZE, -D, -S *vb* treat as a celebrity

LIONIZER ▸ lionize

LIONIZES ▸ lionize

LIONLIER ▸ lionly

LIONLIKE ▸ lion

LIONLY, LIONLIER *adj* like a lion

LIONS ▸ lion

LIP, -PED, -S *n* either of the fleshy edges of the mouth ▸ *vb* touch with the lips

LIPA, -S *n* monetary unit of Croatia

LIPAEMIA *n* abnormally large amount of fat in the blood

LIPARITE *n* type of igneous rock

LIPAS ▸ lipa

LIPASE, -S *n* any of a group of enzymes that digest fat

LIPE, -S *n* lurching or jerking movement

LIPEMIA, -S *same as* ▸ **lipaemia**

LIPES ▸ lipe

LIPGLOSS *n* cosmetic for the lips to give a sheen

LIPID, -S *n* any of a group of organic compounds including fats, oils, waxes, and sterols

LIPIDE, -S *same as* ▸ **lipid**

LIPIDIC ▸ lipid

LIPIDS ▸ lipid

LIPIN, -S *n* family of nuclear proteins

LIPLESS ▸ lip

LIPLIKE ▸ lip

LIPLINER *n* cosmetic used to outline the lips

LIPO, -S *n* liposuction

LIPOCYTE *n* fat-storing cell

LIPOGRAM *n* piece of writing in which all words containing a particular letter have been omitted

LIPOIC *adj* as in **lipoic acid** sulphur-containing fatty acid

LIPOID, -S *n* fatlike substance, such as wax

LIPOIDAL ▸ lipoid

LIPOIDS ▸ lipoid

LIPOMA, -S, -TA *n* benign tumour composed of fatty tissue

LIPOS ▸ lipo

LIPOSOME *n* particle formed by lipids

LIPOSUCK *vb* subject to liposuction

LIPPED ▸ lip

LIPPEN, -ED, -S *vb* trust

LIPPER, -ED, -S *Scots word for* ▸ **ripple**

LIPPIE *variant of* ▸ **lippy**

LIPPIER ▸ lippy

LIPPIES ▸ lippy

LIPPIEST ▸ lippy

LIPPING, -S ▸ lip

LIPPY, LIPPIER, LIPPIES, LIPPIEST *adj* insolent or cheeky ▸ *n* lipstick

LIPREAD, -S *vb* follow what someone says by watching their lips

LIPS ▸ lip

LIPSALVE *n* substance used to prevent or relieve chapped lips

LIPSTICK *n* cosmetic in stick form, for colouring the lips ▸ *vb* put lipstick on

LIPURIA, -S *n* presence of fat in the urine

LIQUABLE *adj* that can be melted

LIQUATE, -D, -S *vb* separate one component of by heating until the more fusible part melts

LIQUEFY *vb* become liquid

LIQUESCE *vb* become liquid

LIQUEUR, -S *n* flavoured and sweetened alcoholic spirit ▸ *vb* flavour with liqueur

LIQUID, -S *n* substance in a physical state which can change shape but not size ▸ *adj* of or being a liquid

LIQUIDLY ▸ liquid

LIQUIDS ▸ liquid

LIQUIDUS *n* line on graph above which a substance is in liquid form

LIQUIDY *adj* having the nature of liquid

LIQUIFY *same as* ▸ **liquefy**

LIQUITAB *n* soluble plastic capsule containing liquid detergent or medicine

LIQUOR, -ED, -S *n* alcoholic drink ▸ *vb* steep in warm water to form wort in brewing

LIRA, -S, LIRE, LIRI, LIROT, LIROTH *n* monetary unit of Turkey, Malta, and formerly of Italy

LIRIOPE, -S *n* grasslike plant

LIRIPIPE *n* tip of a graduate's hood

LIRIPOOP *same as* ▸ **liripipe**

LIRK, -ED, -ING, -S *vb* wrinkle

LIROT ▸ lira

LIROTH ▸ lira

LIS, -SES *n* fleur-de-lis

LISENTE ▸ sente

LISK, -S *Yorkshire dialect for* ▸ **groin**

LISLE, -S *n* strong fine cotton thread or fabric

LISP, -ED, -S *n* speech defect in which *s* and *z* are pronounced *th* ▸ *vb* speak or utter with a lisp

LISPER, -S ▸ lisp

LISPING, -S ▸ lisp

LISPOUND *n* unit of weight

LISPS ▸ lisp

LISPUND, -S *same as* ▸ **lispound**

LISSES ▸ lis

LISSOM *adj* supple, agile

LISSOME *same as* ▸ **lissom**

LISSOMLY ▸ lissom

LIST, -ED, -ETH *n* item-by-item record of names or things, usu written one below another ▸ *vb* make a list of

LISTABLE ▸ list

LISTBOX *n* small box on a computer screen, showing a list of options

LISTED ▸ list

LISTEE, -S *n* person on list

LISTEL, -S *another name for* ▸ **fillet**

LISTEN, -ED, -S *vb* concentrate on hearing something

LISTENER ▸ listen

LISTENS ▸ listen

LISTER, -S *n* plough that throws soil to the sides of a central furrow

LISTERIA *n* type of rodlike Gram-positive bacterium

LISTERS ▸ lister

LISTETH ► list
LISTFUL adj paying attention
LISTICLE n article which consists of a list
LISTING, -S n list or an entry in a list
LISTLESS adj lacking interest or energy
LISTS pl n field of combat in a tournament
LISTSERV n email service for those with similar interests
LIT, -S n archaic word for dye or colouring
LITAI ► litas
LITANY, LITANIES n prayer with responses from the congregation
LITAS, LITAI, LITU n monetary unit of Lithuania
LITCHI, -S n Chinese tree with round edible fruits
LITE, -D, -S, -ST, LITING same as ► light
LITENESS ► lite
LITER, -S same as ► litre
LITERACY n ability to read and write
LITERAL, -S adj according to the explicit meaning of a word or text ▷ n misspelling in a text
LITERARY adj of or knowledgeable about literature
LITERATE adj able to read and write ▷ n literate person
LITERATI, LITERATO pl n literary people
LITEROSE adj affectedly literary
LITERS ► liter
LITES ► lite
LITEST ► lite
LITH, -S n limb or joint
LITHARGE n lead monoxide
LITHATE, -S n salt of uric acid
LITHE, -D, -R, -S, -ST, LITHING adj flexible or supple, pliant ▷ vb listen
LITHELY ► lithe
LITHEMIA n gout
LITHEMIC ► lithemia
LITHER ► lithe
LITHERLY adj crafty; cunning
LITHES ► lithe
LITHEST ► lithe
LITHIA, -S n lithium present in mineral waters as lithium salts
LITHIC adj of stone
LITHIFY vb turn into rock
LITHING ► lithe

LITHITE, -S n part of cell with sensory element
LITHIUM, -S n chemical element, the lightest known metal
LITHO, -ED, -ES, -ING, -S n lithography ▷ vb print using lithography
LITHOID adj resembling rock
LITHOING ► litho
LITHOPS n fleshy-leaved plant
LITHOS ► litho
LITHOSOL n type of azonal soil
LITHS ► lith
LITIGANT n person involved in a lawsuit ▷ adj engaged in litigation
LITIGATE vb bring or contest a law suit
LITING ► lite
LITMUS, -ES n soluble powder obtained from lichens
LITORAL same as ► littoral
LITOTES n ironical understatement used for effect
LITOTIC ► litotes
LITRE, -S n unit of liquid measure
LITREAGE n volume in litres
LITRES ► litre
LITS ► lit
LITTEN adj lighted
LITTER, -ED, -S n untidy rubbish ▷ vb strew with litter
LITTERER n one who litters
LITTERS ► litter
LITTERY adj covered in litter
LITTLE, -R, -S, -ST adj small ▷ adv not a lot ▷ n small amount, extent, or duration
LITTLIE, -S n young child
LITTLIN, -S same as ► littling
LITTLING n child
LITTLINS ► littlin
LITTLISH adj rather small
LITTORAL adj of or by the seashore ▷ n coastal district
LITU ► litas
LITURGIC ► liturgy
LITURGY n prescribed form of public worship
LITUUS, -ES n curved trumpet
LIVABLE adj tolerable or pleasant to live (with)
LIVE, -D, -ST vb be alive ▷ adj living, alive ▷ adv in the form of a live performance
LIVEABLE same as ► livable
LIVEBLOG vb blog about (an event) as it happens

LIVED ► live
LIVEDO, -S n reddish discoloured patch on the skin
LIVELIER ► lively
LIVELILY ► lively
LIVELOD, -S n livelihood
LIVELONG adj long or seemingly long
LIVELOOD n livelihood
LIVELY, LIVELIER adj full of life or vigour
LIVEN, -ED, -ING, -S vb make or become lively
LIVENER, -S ► liven
LIVENESS n state of being alive
LIVENING ► liven
LIVENS ► liven
LIVER, -S n person who lives in a specified way
LIVERED adj having liver
LIVERIED adj wearing livery
LIVERIES ► livery
LIVERING n process of liquid becoming lumpy
LIVERISH adj having a disorder of the liver
LIVERS ► liver
LIVERY, LIVERIES n distinctive dress ▷ adj of or resembling liver
LIVES ► life
LIVEST ► live
LIVETRAP n box constructed to trap an animal without injuring it
LIVEWARE n personnel working in a computer system
LIVEWELL n container of water on a fishing boat used to store live fish
LIVEYER, -S n (in Newfoundland) a full-time resident
LIVEYERE same as ► liveyer
LIVEYERS ► liveyer
LIVID, -ER, -EST adj angry or furious
LIVIDITY n state of being livid
LIVIDLY ► livid
LIVIER, -S same as ► liveyer
LIVING, -S adj possessing life, not dead or inanimate ▷ n means whereby one lives
LIVINGLY ► living
LIVINGS ► living
LIVOR, -S another word for ► lividity
LIVRE, -S n former French unit of money of account
LIVYER, -S same as ► liveyer
LIXIVIA ► lixivium
LIXIVIAL > lixiviate

LIXIVIUM, LIXIVIA *n* alkaline solution obtained by leaching wood ash with water

LIZARD, -S *n* four-footed reptile with a long body and tail

LIZZIE, -S *n* as in **tin lizzie** old or decrepit car

LLAMA, -S *n* woolly animal of the camel family

LLANERO, -S *n* native of llanos

LLANO, -S *n* extensive grassy treeless plain

LO *interj* look!

LOACH, -ES *n* carplike fish

LOAD *n* burden or weight ▷ *vb* put a load on or into

LOADABLE *adj* able to be loaded

LOADED *adj* containing a hidden trap

LOADEN, -ED, -S *vb* load

LOADER, -S *n* person who loads a gun or other firearm

LOADING, -S *n* load or burden

LOADS *pl n* lots or a lot

LOADSTAR *same as* ▸ **lodestar**

LOAF, -ED, -S, LOAVES *n* shaped mass of baked bread ▷ *vb* idle, loiter

LOAFER, -S *n* idler

LOAFING, -S ▸ **loaf**

LOAFS ▸ **loaf**

LOAM, -ED, -ING, -S *n* fertile soil ▷ *vb* cover, treat, or fill with loam

LOAMIER ▸ **loamy**

LOAMIEST ▸ **loamy**

LOAMING ▸ **loam**

LOAMLESS ▸ **loam**

LOAMS ▸ **loam**

LOAMY, LOAMIER, LOAMIEST ▸ **loam**

LOAN, -ED, -ING, -S *n* money lent at interest ▷ *vb* lend

LOANABLE ▸ **loan**

LOANBACK *n* facility by which an individual can borrow from his or her pension fund ▷ *vb* make use of this facility

LOANED ▸ **loan**

LOANEE, -S *n* sportsperson who is loaned out

LOANER, -S ▸ **loan**

LOANING, -S ▸ **loan**

LOANS ▸ **loan**

LOANWORD *n* word adopted from one language into another

LOAST ▸ **lose**

LOATH, -EST *adj* unwilling or reluctant (to)

LOATHE, -D, -S *vb* hate

LOATHER, -S ▸ **loathe**

LOATHES ▸ **loathe**

LOATHEST ▸ **loath**

LOATHFUL *adj* causing loathing

LOATHING *n* strong disgust

LOATHLY *adj* loathsome

LOATHY *obsolete form of* > **loathsome**

LOAVE, -D, LOAVING *vb* form a loaf

LOAVES ▸ **loaf**

LOAVING ▸ **loave**

LOB, -BED, -BING, -S *n* ball struck in a high arc ▷ *vb* strike in a high arc

LOBAR *adj* of or affecting a lobe

LOBATE *adj* with or like lobes

LOBATED *same as* ▸ **lobate**

LOBATELY ▸ **lobate**

LOBATION *n* division into lobes

LOBBED ▸ **lob**

LOBBER, -S *n* one who lobs

LOBBIED ▸ **lobby**

LOBBIES ▸ **lobby**

LOBBING ▸ **lob**

LOBBY, LOBBIED, LOBBIES, -ING *n* corridor into which rooms open ▷ *vb* try to influence (legislators) in the formulation of policy

LOBBYER, -S ▸ **lobby**

LOBBYGOW *n* errand boy

LOBBYING ▸ **lobby**

LOBBYISM ▸ **lobbyist**

LOBBYIST *n* person who lobbies on behalf of a particular interest

LOBE, -S *n* rounded projection

LOBED ▸ **lobe**

LOBEFIN, -S *n* type of fish

LOBELESS *adj* having no lobes

LOBELET, -S *n* small lobe

LOBELIA, -S *n* garden plant

LOBELIKE *adj* like a lobe

LOBELINE *n* crystalline alkaloid extracted from the seeds of the Indian tobacco plant

LOBES ▸ **lobe**

LOBI ▸ **lobus**

LOBING, -S *n* formation of lobes

LOBIPED *adj* with lobed toes

LOBLOLLY *n* southern US pine tree

LOBO, -S *n* timber wolf

LOBOLA, -S *n* (in African custom) price paid by a bridegroom's family to his bride's family

LOBOLO, -S *same as* ▸ **lobola**

LOBOS ▸ **lobo**

LOBOSE *another word for* ▸ **lobate**

LOBOTOMY *n* surgical incision into a lobe of the brain to treat certain disorders

LOBS ▸ **lob**

LOBSTER, -S *n* shellfish ▷ *vb* fish for lobsters

LOBSTICK *n* tree used as landmark

LOBTAIL, -S *vb* (of a whale) hit a surface of water with the tail

LOBULAR ▸ **lobule**

LOBULATE ▸ **lobule**

LOBULE, -S *n* small lobe or a subdivision of a lobe

LOBULI ▸ **lobulus**

LOBULOSE ▸ **lobule**

LOBULUS, LOBULI *n* small lobe

LOBUS, LOBI *n* lobe

LOBWORM, -S *same as* ▸ **lugworm**

LOCA ▸ **locus**

LOCAL, -S *adj* of a particular place ▷ *n* person from a particular place

LOCALE, -S *n* scene of an event

LOCALISE *same as* ▸ **localize**

LOCALISM *n* pronunciation, phrase, etc, peculiar to a particular locality

LOCALIST ▸ **localism**

LOCALITE *n* resident of an area

LOCALITY *n* neighbourhood or area

LOCALIZE *vb* restrict to a particular place

LOCALLY *adv* within a particular area or place

LOCALS ▸ **local**

LOCATE, -D, -S, LOCATING *vb* discover the whereabouts of

LOCATER, -S ▸ **locate**

LOCATES ▸ **locate**

LOCATING ▸ **locate**

LOCATION *n* site or position

LOCATIVE *adj* (of a word or phrase) indicating place or direction ▷ *n* locative case

LOCATOR, -S *n* part of index that shows where to find information

LOCAVORE *n* person who prefers locally produced food

LOCH, -S *n* lake

LOCHAN, -S *n* small inland loch

LOCHE, -S *n* freshwater fish of the cod family

LOCHS ▸ **loch**

LOCI ▸ **locus**

LOCIE, -S *n* type of logging engine

LOCK, -ED, -S *n* appliance for fastening a door, case, etc ▸ *vb* fasten or become fastened securely

LOCKABLE ▸ **lock**

LOCKAGE, -S *n* system of locks in a canal

LOCKAWAY *n* investment intended to be held for a relatively long time

LOCKBOX *n* system of collecting funds from companies by banks

LOCKDOWN *n* device used to secure equipment, etc

LOCKED ▸ **lock**

LOCKER, -S *n* small cupboard with a lock

LOCKET, -S *n* small hinged pendant for a portrait etc

LOCKFAST *adj* securely fastened with a lock

LOCKFUL, -S *n* sufficient to fill a canal lock

LOCKING, -S ▸ **lock**

LOCKJAW, -S *n* tetanus

LOCKLESS *adj* having no lock

LOCKMAN, LOCKMEN *n* lock-keeper

LOCKNUT, -S *n* nut screwed down on a primary nut to stop it from loosening

LOCKOUT, -S *n* closing of a workplace by an employer to force workers to accept terms

LOCKPICK *another word for* ▸ **picklock**

LOCKRAM, -S *n* type of linen cloth

LOCKS ▸ **lock**

LOCKSET, -S *n* hardware used to lock door

LOCKSMAN, LOCKSMEN *same as* ▸ **lockman**

LOCKSTEP *n* method of marching in step as closely as possible

LOCKUP, -S *n* prison

LOCO, -ED, -ES, -ING, -S *n* locomotive ▸ *vb* poison with locoweed

LOCOFOCO *n* match

LOCOING ▸ **loco**

LOCOISM, -S *n* disease of cattle, sheep, and horses caused by eating locoweed

LOCOMAN, LOCOMEN *n* railwayman

LOCOMOTE *vb* move from one place to another

LOCOS ▸ **loco**

LOCOWEED *n* any of several perennial leguminous plants

LOCULAR *adj* divided into compartments by septa

LOCULATE *same as* ▸ **locular**

LOCULE, -S *n* any of the chambers of an ovary or anther

LOCULED *adj* having locules

LOCULES ▸ **locule**

LOCULUS, LOCULI *same as* ▸ **locule**

LOCUM, -S *n* temporary stand-in for a doctor, or clergyman or clergywoman

LOCUS, LOCA, LOCI *n* area or place where something happens

LOCUST, -ED, -S *n* destructive insect ▸ *vb* ravage, as locusts

LOCUSTA, -E *n* flower cluster unit in grasses

LOCUSTAL ▸ **locusta**

LOCUSTED ▸ **locust**

LOCUSTS ▸ **locust**

LOCUTION *n* manner or style of speech

LOCUTORY *adj* room intended for conversation

LOD, -S *n* type of logarithm

LODE, -S *n* vein of ore

LODEN, -S *n* thick waterproof, woollen cloth

LODES ▸ **lode**

LODESMAN, LODESMEN *n* pilot

LODESTAR *n* star used in navigation or astronomy as a point of reference

LODGE, -D, -S *n* gatekeeper's house ▸ *vb* live in another's house at a fixed charge

LODGER, -S *n* tenant

LODGES ▸ **lodge**

LODGING *n* temporary residence

LODGINGS *pl n* rented room or rooms in which to live, esp in another person's house

LODGMENT *n* act of lodging or the state of being lodged

LODICULA *n* delicate scale in grass

LODICULE *n* minute scale at the base of the ovary in grass flowers

LODS ▸ **lod**

LOERIE, -S *same as* ▸ **lourie**

LOESS, -ES *n* fine-grained soil

LOESSAL ▸ **loess**

LOESSES ▸ **loess**

LOESSIAL ▸ **loess**

LOESSIC *adj* relating to or consisting of loess

LOFT, -ED, -ING, -S *n* space between the top storey and roof of a building ▸ *vb* strike, throw, or kick (a ball) high into the air

LOFTER, -S *n* former type of golf club

LOFTIER ▸ **lofty**

LOFTIEST ▸ **lofty**

LOFTILY ▸ **lofty**

LOFTING ▸ **loft**

LOFTLESS ▸ **loft**

LOFTLIKE ▸ **loft**

LOFTS ▸ **loft**

LOFTSMAN, LOFTSMEN *n* person who reproduces in actual size a draughtsman's design for a ship or an aircraft

LOFTY, LOFTIER, LOFTIEST *adj* of great height

LOG, -GED, -S *n* portion of a felled tree stripped of branches ▸ *vb* saw logs from a tree

LOGAN, -S *another name for* ▸ **bogan**

LOGANIA, -S *n* type of Australian plant

LOGANS ▸ **logan**

LOGBOARD *n* board used for logging a ship's records

LOGBOOK, -S *n* book recording the details about a car or a ship's journeys

LOGE, -S *n* small enclosure or box in a theatre or opera house

LOGGAT, -S *n* small piece of wood

LOGGED ▸ **log**

LOGGER, -S *n* tractor or crane for handling logs

LOGGETS *n* old-fashioned game played with sticks

LOGGIA, -S, LOGGIE *n* covered gallery at the side of a building

LOGGIER ▸ **loggy**

LOGGIEST ▸ **loggy**

LOGGING, -S ▸ **log**

LOGGISH ▸ **log**

LOGGY, LOGGIER, LOGGIEST *adj* sluggish

LOGIA ▸ **logion**

LOGIC, -S *n* philosophy of reasoning

LOGICAL *adj* of logic

LOGICIAN *n* person who specializes in or is skilled at logic

LOGICISE same as ▸ **logicize**

LOGICISM n philosophical theory that all of mathematics can be deduced from logic

LOGICIST ▸ logicism

LOGICIZE vb present reasons for or against

LOGICS ▸ logic

LOGIE, -S n fireplace of a kiln

LOGIER ▸ logy

LOGIES ▸ logie

LOGIEST ▸ logy

LOGILY ▸ logy

LOGIN, -S n process by which a computer user logs on

LOGINESS ▸ logy

LOGINS ▸ login

LOGION, LOGIA, -S n saying of Christ regarded as authentic

LOGISTIC n uninterpreted calculus or system of symbolic logic ▷ adj (of a curve) having a particular form of equation

LOGJAM, -S n blockage of logs in a river ▷ vb cause a logjam

LOGJUICE n poor quality port wine

LOGLINE, -S n synopsis of screenplay

LOGLOG, -S n logarithm of a logarithm (in equations, etc)

LOGO same as ▸ **logotype**

LOGOED adj having a logo

LOGOFF, -S n process by which a computer user logs off

LOGOGRAM n single symbol representing an entire morpheme, word, or phrase

LOGOI ▸ logos

LOGOMACH n one who argues over words

LOGON, -S variant of ▸ login

LOGOS, LOGOI n reason expressed in words and things, argument, or justification

LOGOTYPE n piece of type with several uncombined characters cast on it

LOGOTYPY ▸ logotype

LOGOUT, -S variant of ▸ logoff

LOGROLL, -S vb procure the passage of (legislation) by trading votes

LOGS ▸ log

LOGWAY, -S another name for ▸ gangway

LOGWOOD, -S n tree of the Caribbean and Central America

LOGY, LOGIER, LOGIEST adj dull or listless

LOHAN, -S another word for ▸ arhat

LOIASIS, LOIASES n disease caused by a tropical eye worm

LOID, -ED, -ING, -S vb open (a lock) using a celluloid strip

LOIN n part of the body between the ribs and the hips

LOINS pl n hips and the inner surface of the legs

LOIPE, -N n cross-country skiing track

LOIR, -S n large dormouse

LOITER, -ED, -S vb stand or wait aimlessly or idly

LOITERER ▸ loiter

LOITERS ▸ loiter

LOKE, -S n track

LOKSHEN pl n noodles

LOLIGO, -S n type of squid

LOLIUM, -S n type of grass

LOLL, -ED, -ING, -S vb lounge lazily ▷ n act or instance of lolling

LOLLER, -S ▸ loll

LOLLIES ▸ lolly

LOLLING ▸ loll

LOLLIPOP n boiled sweet on a small wooden stick

LOLLOP, -ED, -S vb move clumsily

LOLLOPY adj moving with a lollop

LOLLS ▸ loll

LOLLY, LOLLIES n lollipop or ice lolly

LOLLYGAG same as ▸ lallygag

LOLLYPOP same as ▸ lollipop

LOLOG, -S same as ▸ loglog

LOLZ same as ▸ lulz

LOMA, -S, -TA n lobe

LOME, -S, LOMING n fertile soil ▷ vb cover with lome

LOMED ▸ lome

LOMEIN, -S n Chinese dish

LOMENT, -S n pod of certain leguminous plants

LOMENTA ▸ lomentum

LOMENTS ▸ loment

LOMENTUM, LOMENTA same as ▸ loment

LOMES ▸ lome

LOMING ▸ lome

LOMPISH another word for ▸ lumpish

LONE adj solitary

LONELIER ▸ lonely

LONELILY ▸ lonely

LONELY, LONELIER adj sad because alone

LONENESS ▸ lone

LONER, -S n solitary person

LONESOME adj lonely ▷ n own

LONG, -ED, -EST adj having length ▷ adv for a certain time ▷ vb have a strong desire (for)

LONGA, -S n long note

LONGAN, -S n sapindaceous tree of tropical and subtropical Asia

LONGAS ▸ longa

LONGBOAT n largest boat carried on a ship

LONGBOW, -S n large powerful bow

LONGCASE n as in longcase clock grandfather clock

LONGE, -ING, -S n rope used in training a horse ▷ vb train using a longe

LONGED ▸ long

LONGEING ▸ longe

LONGER, -S n line of barrels on a ship

LONGERON n main longitudinal structural member of an aircraft

LONGERS ▸ longer

LONGES ▸ longe

LONGEST ▸ long

LONGEVAL another word for ▸ longaeval

LONGFORM adj (of a text) long in form

LONGHAIR n cat with long hair

LONGHAND n ordinary writing, not shorthand or typing

LONGHEAD n person with long head

LONGHORN n British breed of beef cattle with long curved horns

LONGIES n long johns

LONGING, -S n yearning ▷ adj having or showing desire

LONGISH adj rather long

LONGJUMP n jumping contest decided by length

LONGLEAF n North American pine tree

LONGLINE n (tennis) straight stroke played down court

LONGLIST n initial list from which a shortlist is selected ▷ vb include (eg a candidate) on a longlist

LONGLY ▸ long

LONGNECK n US, Canadian and Australian word for a 330-ml beer bottle with a long narrow neck

LONGNESS ▸ long

LONGS pl n full-length trousers

LONGSHIP n narrow open boat with oars and a square sail, used by the Vikings

LONGSOME adj slow; boring

LONGSPUR n any of various Arctic and North American buntings

LONGTIME adj of long standing

LONGUEUR n period of boredom or dullness

LONGWALL n long face in coal mine

LONGWAYS adv lengthways

LONGWISE same as ▸ longways

LONGWORM n as in sea longworm kind of marine worm

LONICERA n honeysuckle

LOO, -ED, -ING, -S n toilet ▷ vb Scots word meaning love

LOOBIER ▸ looby

LOOBIES ▸ looby

LOOBIEST ▸ looby

LOOBILY ▸ looby

LOOBY, LOOBIER, LOOBIES, LOOBIEST adj foolish ▷ n foolish or stupid person

LOOED ▸ loo

LOOEY, -S n lieutenant

LOOF, -S, LOOVES n part of ship's side

LOOFA, -S same as ▸ loofah

LOOFAH, -S n sponge made from the dried pod of a gourd

LOOFAS ▸ loofa

LOOFFUL, -S n handful

LOOFS ▸ loof

LOOGIE, -S n lump of spit and phlegm

LOOIE, -S same as ▸ looey

LOOING ▸ loo

LOOK, -ED, -ING, -S vb direct the eyes or attention (towards) ▷ n instance of looking

LOOKDOWN n way paper appears when looked at under reflected light

LOOKED ▸ look

LOOKER, -S n person who looks

LOOKIE interj look (over here)

LOOKING ▸ look

LOOKISM, -S n discrimination because of appearance

LOOKIST, -S ▸ lookism

LOOKIT interj look at this

LOOKOUT, -S n act of watching for danger or for an opportunity ▷ vb be careful

LOOKOVER n inspection, esp a brief one

LOOKS ▸ look

LOOKSISM same as ▸ lookism

LOOKUP, -S n act of looking up information

LOOKY same as ▸ lookie

LOOM, -ED, -ING, -S n machine for weaving cloth ▷ vb appear dimly

LOON, -S n diving bird

LOONEY, -S same as ▸ loony

LOONIE n Canadian dollar coin

LOONIER ▸ loony

LOONIES ▸ loony

LOONIEST ▸ loony

LOONILY ▸ loony

LOONING, -S n cry of the loon

LOONS ▸ loon

LOONY, LOONIER, LOONIES, LOONIEST adj very foolish ▷ n very foolish person

LOOP, -ED, -S n round shape made by a curved line ▷ vb form with a loop

LOOPER, -S n person or thing that loops or makes loops

LOOPHOLE n means of evading a rule without breaking it ▷ vb provide with loopholes

LOOPIER ▸ loopy

LOOPIEST ▸ loopy

LOOPILY ▸ loopy

LOOPING, -S ▸ loop

LOOPLIKE adj like a loop

LOOPS ▸ loop

LOOPY, LOOPIER, LOOPIEST adj curly or twisted

LOOR a Scots form of ▸ lief

LOORD, -S obsolete word for ▸ lout

LOOS ▸ loo

LOOSE, -D, -R, -S, -ST adj not tight, fastened, fixed, or tense ▷ adv in a loose manner ▷ vb free

LOOSEBOX n enclosed stall with a door in which an animal can be kept

LOOSED ▸ loose

LOOSELY ▸ loose

LOOSEN, -ED, -S vb make loose

LOOSENER ▸ loosen

LOOSENS ▸ loosen

LOOSER ▸ loose

LOOSES ▸ loose

LOOSEST ▸ loose

LOOSIE n informal word for loose forward

LOOSIES pl n cigarettes sold individually

LOOSING, -S n celebration of one's 21st birthday

LOOT, -ED, -S, LUTTEN vb pillage ▷ n goods stolen during pillaging

LOOTEN Scots past form of ▸ let

LOOTER, -S ▸ loot

LOOTING, -S ▸ loot

LOOTS ▸ loot

LOOVES ▸ loof

LOP, -PED, -S vb cut away ▷ n part(s) lopped off

LOPE, -D, -S, LOPING vb run with long easy strides ▷ n loping stride

LOPER, -S ▸ lope

LOPES ▸ lope

LOPGRASS n smooth-bladed grass

LOPING ▸ lope

LOPINGLY adv in a loping manner

LOPOLITH n saucer- or lens-shaped body of intrusive igneous rock

LOPPED ▸ lop

LOPPER, -ED, -S n tool for lopping ▷ vb curdle

LOPPET, -S n long-distance cross-country ski race

LOPPIER ▸ loppy

LOPPIES ▸ loppy

LOPPIEST ▸ loppy

LOPPING, -S ▸ lop

LOPPY, LOPPIER, LOPPIES, LOPPIEST adj floppy ▷ n ranch hand

LOPS ▸ lop

LOPSIDED adj greater in height, weight, or size on one side

LOPSTICK variant of ▸ lobstick

LOQUAT, -S n ornamental evergreen rosaceous tree

LOQUITUR n stage direction meaning he or she speaks

LOR interj exclamation of surprise or dismay

LORAL adj of part of side of bird's head

LORAN, -S n radio navigation system operating over long distances

LORATE adj like a strap

LORCHA, -S n junk-rigged vessel

L

LORD, -ED, -S n person with power over others ▷ vb act in a superior way
LORDING, -S n gentleman
LORDKIN, -S n little lord
LORDLESS ▶ lord
LORDLIER ▶ lordly
LORDLIKE ▶ lord
LORDLING n young lord
LORDLY, LORDLIER adj imperious, proud ▷ adv in the manner of a lord
LORDOMA, -S same as ▶ lordosis
LORDOSIS, LORDOSES n forward curvature of the lumbar spine
LORDOTIC ▶ lordosis
LORDS ▶ lord
LORDSHIP n position or authority of a lord
LORDY interj exclamation of surprise or dismay
LORE, -S n body of traditions
LOREAL adj concerning or relating to lore
LOREL, -S another word for ▶ losel
LORES ▶ lore
LORGNON, -S n monocle or pair of spectacles
LORIC, -S same as ▶ lorica
LORICA, -E, -S n hard outer covering of rotifers, ciliate protozoans, and similar organisms
LORICATE ▶ lorica
LORICS ▶ loric
LORIES ▶ lory
LORIKEET n small brightly coloured Australian parrot
LORIMER, -S n (formerly) a person who made bits and spurs
LORINER, -S same as ▶ lorimer
LORING, -S n teaching
LORIOT, -S n golden oriole (bird)
LORIS, -ES n any of several prosimian primates
LORN, -ER, -EST adj forsaken or wretched
LORNNESS ▶ lorn
LORRELL, -S obsolete word for ▶ losel
LORRY, LORRIES n large vehicle for transporting loads by road
LORY, LORIES n small parrot of Australia and Indonesia
LOS n approval
LOSABLE ▶ lose
LOSE, LOAST, -D, -S vb part with

LOSEL, -S n worthless person ▷ vb worthless
LOSEN same as ▶ lose
LOSER, -S n person or thing that loses
LOSES ▶ lose
LOSH interj lord
LOSING adj unprofitable; failing
LOSINGLY ▶ lose
LOSINGS pl n losses
LOSS, -ES n losing
LOSSIER ▶ lossy
LOSSIEST ▶ lossy
LOSSLESS ▶ loss
LOSSY, LOSSIER, LOSSIEST adj designed to have a high attenuation
LOST adj missing
LOSTNESS ▶ lost
LOT, -S, -TED, -TING pron great number ▷ n collection of people or things ▷ vb draw lots for
LOTA, -S n globular water container
LOTAH, -S same as ▶ lota
LOTAS ▶ lota
LOTE, -S another word for ▶ lotus
LOTH, -ER, -EST same as ▶ loath
LOTHARIO n rake, libertine, or seducer
LOTHER ▶ loth
LOTHEST ▶ loth
LOTHFULL obsolete form of ▶ loathful
LOTHNESS ▶ loth
LOTHSOME same as > loathsome
LOTI n monetary unit of Lesotho
LOTIC adj of communities living in rapidly flowing water
LOTION, -S n medical or cosmetic liquid for use on the skin
LOTO same as ▶ lotto
LOTOS, -ES same as ▶ lotus
LOTS ▶ lot
LOTSA determiner lots of
LOTTA determiner lot of
LOTTE, -S n type of fish
LOTTED ▶ lot
LOTTER, -S n someone who works an allotment
LOTTERY n method of raising money by selling tickets that win prizes by chance
LOTTES ▶ lotte
LOTTING ▶ lot
LOTTO, -S n game of chance

LOTUS, -ES n legendary plant whose fruit induces forgetfulness
LOU, -ED, -ING, -S Scot word for ▶ love
LOUCHE, -R, -ST adj shifty
LOUCHELY ▶ louche
LOUCHER ▶ louche
LOUCHEST ▶ louche
LOUD, -ER, -EST adj noisy
LOUDEN, -ED, -S vb make louder
LOUDER ▶ loud
LOUDEST ▶ loud
LOUDISH adj fairly loud
LOUDLY, LOUDLIER ▶ loud
LOUDNESS ▶ loud
LOUED ▶ lou
LOUGH, -S n loch
LOUIE, -S same as ▶ looey
LOUING ▶ lou
LOUIS n former French gold coin
LOUMA, -S n market in developing countries
LOUN, -ED, -ING, -S same as ▶ lown
LOUND, -ED, -ING, -S same as ▶ lound
LOUNDER, -S vb beat severely
LOUNDING ▶ lound
LOUNDS ▶ lound
LOUNED ▶ loun
LOUNGE, -D, -S, LOUNGING n living room in a private house ▷ vb sit, lie, or stand in a relaxed manner
LOUNGER, -S n extending chair
LOUNGES ▶ lounge
LOUNGEY, LOUNGIER adj suggestive of a lounge bar or easy-listening music
LOUNGING ▶ lounge
LOUNGY adj casual; relaxed
LOUNING ▶ loun
LOUNS ▶ loun
LOUP, -ED, -EN, -ING, -IT, -S Scot word for ▶ leap
LOUPE, -S n magnifying glass used by jewellers, horologists, etc
LOUPED ▶ loup
LOUPEN ▶ loup
LOUPES ▶ loupe
LOUPING ▶ loup
LOUPIT ▶ loup
LOUPS ▶ loup
LOUR, -ED, -S vb be overcast ▷ n menacing scowl
LOURE, -S n slow, former French dance
LOURED ▶ lour
LOURES ▶ loure**

LOURIE, -S n type of African bird
LOURIER ▸ loury
LOURIES ▸ lourie
LOURIEST ▸ loury
LOURING, -S ▸ lour
LOURS ▸ lour
LOURY, LOURIER, LOURIEST adj sombre
LOUS ▸ lou
LOUSE, LICE, -D, -S n wingless parasitic insect ▷ vb ruin or spoil
LOUSER, -S n mean nasty person
LOUSES ▸ louse
LOUSIER ▸ lousy
LOUSIEST ▸ lousy
LOUSILY ▸ lousy
LOUSING, -S n act or instance of removing lice
LOUSY, LOUSIER, LOUSIEST adj mean or unpleasant
LOUT, -ED, -ING, -S n crude person ▷ vb bow or stoop
LOUTERY n crude or boorish behaviour
LOUTING ▸ lout
LOUTISH adj of a lout
LOUTS ▸ lout
LOUVAR, -S n large silvery whalelike scombroid fish
LOUVER, -S same as ▸ louvre
LOUVERED same as ▸ louvred
LOUVERS ▸ louver
LOUVRE, -S n one of a set of parallel slats slanted to admit air but not rain
LOUVRED adj having louvres
LOUVRES ▸ louvre
LOVABLE adj attracting or deserving affection
LOVABLY ▸ lovable
LOVAGE, -S n European plant used for flavouring food
LOVAT, -S n yellowish-or bluish-green mixture in tweeds
LOVE, -D, -S vb have a great affection for ▷ n great affection
LOVEABLE same as ▸ lovable
LOVEABLY ▸ lovable
LOVEBIRD n small parrot
LOVEBITE n temporary red mark left on a person's skin by someone biting or sucking it
LOVEBUG, -S n small US flying insect
LOVED ▸ love
LOVEFEST n event when people talk about loving one another

LOVELESS adj without love
LOVELIER ▸ lovely
LOVELIES ▸ lovely
LOVELILY ▸ lovely
LOVELOCK n long lock of hair worn on the forehead
LOVELORN adj miserable because of unhappiness in love
LOVELY, LOVELIER, LOVELIES adj very attractive ▷ n attractive woman
LOVER, -S n person who loves something or someone
LOVERED adj having a lover
LOVERLY adj like a lover
LOVERS ▸ lover
LOVES ▸ love
LOVESEAT n armchair for two people
LOVESICK adj pining or languishing because of love
LOVESOME adj full of love
LOVEVINE n leafless parasitic vine
LOVEY, -S, LOVIER, LOVIEST adj loving; affectionate ▷ n affectionate person
LOVIE, -S n beloved person
LOVIER ▸ lovey
LOVIES ▸ lovie
LOVIEST ▸ lovey
LOVING, -S adj affectionate, tender ▷ n state of being in love
LOVINGLY ▸ loving
LOVINGS ▸ loving
LOW, -ED, -EST, -S adj not high ▷ adv in a low position ▷ n low position ▷ vb moo
LOWAN, -S n type of Australian bird
LOWBALL, -S vb deliberately under-charge
LOWBORN adj of ignoble or common parentage
LOWBOY, -S n table fitted with drawers
LOWBRED same as ▸ lowborn
LOWBROW, -S adj with nonintellectual tastes and interests ▷ n person with nonintellectual tastes
LOWBUSH n type of blueberry bush
LOWDOWN, -S n inside info
LOWE, -S variant of ▸ low
LOWED ▸ low
LOWER, -ED, -S adj below one or more other things ▷ vb cause or allow to move down

LOWERIER ▸ lowery
LOWERING ▸ lower
LOWERS ▸ lower
LOWERY, LOWERIER adj sombre
LOWES ▸ lowe
LOWEST ▸ low
LOWING, -S ▸ low
LOWISH ▸ low
LOWLAND, -S n low-lying country ▷ adj of a lowland or lowlands
LOWLIER ▸ lowly
LOWLIEST ▸ lowly
LOWLIFE, -S, LOWLIVES n member or members of the underworld
LOWLIFER ▸ lowlife
LOWLIFES ▸ lowlife
LOWLIGHT n unenjoyable or unpleasant part of an event
LOWLILY ▸ lowly
LOWLIVES ▸ lowly
LOWLY, LOWLIER, LOWLIEST adj modest, humble ▷ adv in a low or lowly manner
LOWN, -ED, -ING, -S vb calm
LOWND, -ED, -ING, -S same as ▸ lown
LOWNE, -S same as ▸ loon
LOWNED ▸ lown
LOWNES ▸ lowne
LOWNESS ▸ low
LOWNING ▸ lown
LOWNS ▸ lown
LOWP, -ED, -ING, -S same as ▸ loup
LOWPASS adj (of a filter) transmitting frequencies below a certain value
LOWPED ▸ lowp
LOWPING ▸ lowp
LOWPS ▸ lowp
LOWRIDER n car with body close to ground
LOWRIE another name for ▸ lory
LOWRY, LOWRIES another name for ▸ lory
LOWS ▸ low
LOWSE, -D, -R, -S, -ST, LOWSING vb release or loose ▷ adj loose
LOWSIT ▸ lowse
LOWT, -ED, -ING, -S same as ▸ lout
LOWVELD, -S n low ground in S Africa
LOX, -ED, -ES, -ING vb load fuel tanks of spacecraft with liquid oxygen ▷ n kind of smoked salmon

A good word when you have an X to dispose of.

LOXYGEN, -S n liquid oxygen

L

LOY, -S *n* narrow spade with a single footrest

LOYAL, -ER, -EST, -LER *adj* faithful

LOYALISM ▸ **loyalist**

LOYALIST *n* patriotic supporter of the sovereign or government

LOYALLER ▸ **loyal**

LOYALLY ▸ **loyal**

LOYALTY *n* quality of being loyal

LOYS ▸ **loy**

LOZELL, -S *obsolete form of* ▸ **losel**

LOZEN, -S *n* window pane

LOZENGE, -S *n* medicated tablet

LOZENGED *adj* decorated with lozenges

LOZENGES ▸ **lozenge**

LOZENGY *adj* divided by diagonal lines to form a lattice

LOZENS ▸ **lozen**

LUACH, LUCHOT, LUCHOTH *n* Jewish calendar

LUAU, -S *n* feast of Hawaiian food

LUBBARD, -S *same as* ▸ **lubber**

LUBBER, -S *n* big, awkward, or stupid person

LUBBERLY *adj* big and awkward

LUBBERS ▸ **lubber**

LUBE, -D, -S, LUBING *n* lubricating oil ▹ *vb* lubricate with oil

LUBFISH *n* type of fish

LUBING ▸ **lube**

LUBRIC *adj* slippery

LUBRICAL *same as* ▸ **lubric**

LUCARNE, -S *n* type of dormer window

LUCE, -S *another name for* ▸ **pike**

LUCENCE, -S ▸ **lucent**

LUCENCY ▸ **lucent**

LUCENT *adj* brilliant

LUCENTLY ▸ **lucent**

LUCERN, -S *same as* ▸ **lucerne**

LUCERNE, -S *n* alfalfa

LUCERNS ▸ **lucern**

LUCES ▸ **luce**

LUCHOT ▸ **luach**

LUCHOTH ▸ **luach**

LUCID, -ER, -EST *adj* clear

LUCIDITY ▸ **lucid**

LUCIDLY ▸ **lucid**

LUCIFER, -S *n* friction match

LUCIGEN, -S *n* type of lamp

LUCITE, -S *n* type of transparent acrylic-based plastic

LUCK, -ED, -ING, -S *n* fortune, good or bad ▹ *vb* have good fortune

LUCKEN *adj* shut

LUCKIE *same as* ▸ **lucky**

LUCKIER ▸ **lucky**

LUCKIES ▸ **lucky**

LUCKIEST ▸ **lucky**

LUCKILY ▸ **lucky**

LUCKING ▸ **luck**

LUCKLESS *adj* having bad luck

LUCKS ▸ **luck**

LUCKY, LUCKIER, LUCKIES, LUCKIEST *adj* having or bringing good luck ▹ *n* old woman

LUCRE, -S *n* money or wealth

LUCULENT *adj* easily understood

LUCUMA, -S *n* S American tree

LUCUMO, -S *n* Etruscan king

LUD, -S *n* lord ▹ *interj* exclamation of dismay or surprise

LUDERICK *n* Australian fish, usu black or dark brown in colour

LUDIC *adj* playful

LUDO, -S *n* game played with dice and counters on a board

LUDS ▸ **lud**

LUDSHIP, -S ▸ **lud**

LUES *n* pestilence

LUETIC, -S ▸ **lues**

LUFF, -ED, -ING, -S *vb* sail (a ship) towards the wind ▹ *n* leading edge of a fore-and-aft sail

LUFFA, -S *same as* ▸ **loofah**

LUFFED ▸ **luff**

LUFFING ▸ **luff**

LUFFS ▸ **luff**

LUG, -GED, -GING, -S *vb* carry with great effort ▹ *n* projection serving as a handle

LUGE, -D, -S *n* racing toboggan ▹ *vb* ride on a luge

LUGEING, -S ▸ **luge**

LUGER, -S *n* pistol

LUGES ▸ **luge**

LUGGABLE *n* unwieldy portable computer

LUGGAGE, -S *n* suitcases, bags, etc

LUGGED ▸ **lug**

LUGGER, -S *n* small working boat with an oblong sail

LUGGIE, -S *n* wooden bowl

LUGGING ▸ **lug**

LUGHOLE, -S *informal word for* ▸ **ear**

LUGING, -S ▸ **luge**

LUGS ▸ **lug**

LUGSAIL, -S *n* four-sided sail

LUGWORM, -S *n* large worm used as bait

LUIT, -EN *Scots past form of* ▸ **let**

LUKE *variant of* ▸ **lukewarm**

LUKEWARM *adj* moderately warm, tepid

LULIBUB, -S *obsolete form of* ▸ **lollipop**

LULL, -ED, -ING, -S *vb* soothe (someone) by soft sounds or motions ▹ *n* brief time of quiet in a storm etc

LULLABY *n* quiet song ▹ *vb* quiet with a lullaby

LULLED ▸ **lull**

LULLER ▸ **lull**

LULLING ▸ **lull**

LULLS ▸ **lull**

LULU, -S *n* person or thing deemed to be outstanding

LULZ *pl n* laughs at someone else's or one's own expense

LUM, -S *n* chimney

LUMA, -S *n* monetary unit of Armenia

LUMBAGO, -S *n* pain in the lower back

LUMBANG, -S *n* type of tree

LUMBAR, -S *adj* of the part of the body between the lowest ribs and the hipbones ▹ *n* old-fashioned kind of ship

LUMBER, -ED, -S *n* unwanted disused household articles ▹ *vb* burden with something unpleasant

LUMBERER ▸ **lumber**

LUMBERLY *adj* heavy; clumsy

LUMBERS ▸ **lumber**

LUMBI ▸ **lumbus**

LUMBRICI > **lumbricus**

LUMBUS, LUMBI *n* part of the lower back and sides between the pelvis and the ribs

LUMEN, -S, LUMINA *n* derived SI unit of luminous flux

LUMENAL ▸ **lumen**

LUMENS ▸ **lumen**

LUMINA ▸ **lumen**

LUMINAL ▸ **lumen**

LUMINANT *n* something used to give light

LUMINARY *n* famous person ▹ *adj* of, involving, or characterized by light or enlightenment

LUMINE, -D, -S, LUMINING vb illuminate

LUMINISM n US artistic movement

LUMINIST ▸ luminism

LUMINOUS adj reflecting or giving off light

LUMME interj exclamation of surprise or dismay

LUMMIER ▸ lummy

LUMMIEST ▸ lummy

LUMMOX, -ES n clumsy person

LUMMY, LUMMIER, LUMMIEST interj exclamation of surprise ▷ adj excellent

LUMP, -ED, -ING, -S n shapeless mass ▷ vb consider as one group

LUMPEN, -S adj stupid or unthinking ▷ n member of underclass

LUMPENLY ▸ lumpen

LUMPENS ▸ lumpen

LUMPER, -S n stevedore

LUMPFISH n North Atlantic scorpaenoid fish

LUMPIA, -S n type of Indonesian spring roll

LUMPIER ▸ lumpy

LUMPIEST ▸ lumpy

LUMPILY ▸ lumpy

LUMPING ▸ lump

LUMPISH adj stupid or clumsy

LUMPKIN, -S n lout

LUMPS ▸ lump

LUMPY, LUMPIER, LUMPIEST adj full of lumps

LUMS ▸ lum

LUN, -S n sheltered spot

LUNA, -S n large American moth

LUNACY, LUNACIES n foolishness

LUNANAUT same as ▸ lunarnaut

LUNAR, -S adj relating to the moon ▷ n lunar distance

LUNARIAN n inhabitant of the moon

LUNARIES ▸ lunary

LUNARIST n one believing the moon influences weather

LUNARS ▸ lunar

LUNARY, LUNARIES n moonwort herb

LUNAS ▸ luna

LUNATE, -S adj shaped like a crescent ▷ n crescent-shaped bone forming part of the wrist

LUNATED variant of ▸ lunate

LUNATELY ▸ lunate

LUNATES ▸ lunate

LUNATIC, -S adj foolish ▷ n foolish person

LUNATION n period of time taken by the moon to go around the earth

LUNCH, -ED, -ES, -ING n meal at midday ▷ vb eat lunch

LUNCHBOX n container for carrying a packed lunch

LUNCHED ▸ lunch

LUNCHEON n formal lunch

LUNCHER, -S ▸ lunch

LUNCHES ▸ lunch

LUNCHING ▸ lunch

LUNE, -S same as ▸ lunette

LUNET, -S n small moon or satellite

LUNETTE, -S n anything that is shaped like a crescent

LUNG, -S n organ that allows an animal or bird to breathe air

LUNGAN, -S same as ▸ longan

LUNGE, -D, -ING, -S, LUNGING n sudden forward motion ▷ vb move with or make a lunge

LUNGEE, -S same as ▸ lungi

LUNGEING ▸ lunge

LUNGER, -S ▸ lunge

LUNGES ▸ lunge

LUNGFISH n freshwater bony fish with an air-breathing lung

LUNGFUL, -S ▸ lung

LUNGI, -S n cotton cloth worn as a loincloth, sash, or turban

LUNGIE, -S n guillemot

LUNGING ▸ lunge

LUNGIS ▸ lungi

LUNGLESS adj having no lungs

LUNGLIKE adj like a lung

LUNGS ▸ lung

LUNGWORM n type of parasitic worm occurring in the lungs of mammals

LUNGWORT n plant with spotted leaves

LUNGYI, -S same as ▸ lungi

LUNIER ▸ luny

LUNIES ▸ luny

LUNIEST ▸ luny

LUNINESS ▸ luny

LUNK, -S n awkward person

LUNKER, -S n very large fish

LUNKHEAD n stupid person

LUNKS ▸ lunk

LUNS ▸ lun

LUNT, -ED, -ING, -S vb produce smoke

LUNULA, -E n white area at base of the fingernail

LUNULAR same as ▸ lunulate

LUNULATE adj having markings shaped like crescents

LUNULE, -S same as ▸ lunula

LUNY, LUNIER, LUNIES, LUNIEST same as ▸ loony

LUNYIE, -S same as ▸ lungie

LUPIN, -S n garden plant

LUPINE, -S adj like a wolf ▷ n lupin

LUPINS ▸ lupin

LUPOID adj having lupus

LUPOUS adj relating to lupus

LUPPEN Scots past form of ▸ leap

LUPULIN, -S n resinous powder extracted from the hop plant

LUPULINE adj relating to lupulin

LUPULINS ▸ lupulin

LUPUS, -ES n ulcerous skin disease

LUR, -S n large bronze musical horn

LURCH, -ED, -ES vb tilt suddenly ▷ n lurching movement

LURCHER, -S n crossbred dog trained to hunt silently

LURCHES ▸ lurch

LURCHING ▸ lurch

LURDAN, -S n stupid or dull person ▷ adj dull or stupid

LURDANE, -S same as ▸ lurdan

LURDANS ▸ lurdan

LURDEN, -S same as ▸ lurdan

LURE, -D, -S, LURING vb tempt by promise of reward ▷ n person that lures

LURER, -S ▸ lure

LURES ▸ lure

LUREX, -ES n thin glittery thread

LURGI, -S same as ▸ lurgy

LURGIES ▸ lurgy

LURGIS ▸ lurgi

LURGY, LURGIES n any undetermined illness

LURID, -ER, -EST adj sensational

LURIDLY ▸ lurid

LURING, -S ▸ lure

LURINGLY ▸ lure

LURINGS ▸ luring

LURK, -ED, -S vb lie hidden

LURKER, -S ▸ lurk

LURKING, -S adj lingering

LURKS ▸ lurk

L

LURRY, LURRIES *n* confused jumble

LURS ▸ lur

LURVE, -S *n* love

LUSCIOUS *adj* extremely pleasurable to taste or smell

LUSER, -S *n* humorous term for computer user

LUSH, -ED, -ES, -EST, -ING *adj* growing thickly ▸ *n* alcoholic ▸ *vb* drink to excess

LUSHER, -S *adj* more lush ▸ *n* drunkard

LUSHES ▸ lush

LUSHEST ▸ lush

LUSHIER ▸ lushy

LUSHIES ▸ lushy

LUSHIEST ▸ lushy

LUSHING ▸ lush

LUSHLY ▸ lush

LUSHNESS ▸ lush

LUSHY, LUSHIER, LUSHIES, LUSHIEST *adj* slightly intoxicated ▸ *n* drunkard

LUSK, -ED, -ING, -S *vb* lounge around

LUSKISH *adj* lazy

LUSKS ▸ lusk

LUST, -ED, -ING, -S *n* strong desire ▸ *vb* have strong desire (for)

LUSTER, -ED, -S *same as* ▸ lustre

LUSTICK *obsolete word for* ▸ lusty

LUSTIER ▸ lusty

LUSTIEST ▸ lusty

LUSTILY ▸ lusty

LUSTING ▸ lust

LUSTIQUE *obsolete word for* ▸ lusty

LUSTLESS ▸ lust

LUSTRA ▸ lustrum

LUSTRAL *adj* of or relating to a ceremony of purification

LUSTRATE *vb* purify by means of religious rituals or ceremonies

LUSTRE, -D, -S *n* gloss, sheen ▸ *vb* make, be, or become lustrous

LUSTRINE *same as* ▸ lustring

LUSTRING *n* glossy silk cloth, formerly used for clothing, upholstery, etc

LUSTROUS ▸ lustre

LUSTRUM, LUSTRA, -S *n* period of five years

LUSTS ▸ lust

LUSTY, LUSTIER, LUSTIEST *adj* vigorous, healthy

LUSUS, -ES *n* freak, mutant

LUTANIST *same as* ▸ lutenist

LUTE, -D, -S *n* musical instrument r ▸ *vb* seal with cement and clay

LUTEA *adj* yellow

LUTEAL *adj* relating to the development of the corpus luteum

LUTECIUM *same as* ▸ lutetium

LUTED ▸ lute

LUTEFISK *n* Scandinavian fish dish

LUTEIN, -S *n* xanthophyll pigment

LUTELIKE *adj* like a lute

LUTENIST *n* person who plays the lute

LUTEOLIN *n* yellow crystalline compound found in many plants

LUTEOUS *adj* of a greenish-yellow colour

LUTER, -S *n* lute player

LUTES ▸ lute

LUTETIUM *n* silvery-white metallic element

LUTEUM *adj* yellow

LUTFISK, -S *same as* ▸ lutefisk

LUTHERN, -S *another name for* ▸ dormer

LUTHIER, -S *n* lute-maker

LUTING, -S *n* cement and clay

LUTIST, -S *same as* ▸ lutenist

LUTITE, -S *another name for* ▸ pelite

LUTTEN ▸ loot

LUTZ, -ES *n* skating jump

LUV, -S, -VED, -VING *n* love ▸ *vb* love

LUVVIE, -S *n* person who is involved in acting or the theatre

LUVVING ▸ luv

LUVVY *same as* ▸ luvvie

LUX, -ED, -ES, -ING *n* unit of illumination ▸ *vb* clean with a vacuum cleaner

> One of the key words using X.

LUXATE, -D, -S, LUXATING *vb* put (a shoulder, knee, etc) out of joint

LUXATION ▸ luxate

LUXE, -R, -ST *adj* luxurious

LUXED ▸ lux

LUXER ▸ luxe

LUXES ▸ lux

LUXEST ▸ luxe

LUXING ▸ lux

LUXMETER *n* device for measuring light

LUXURIES ▸ luxury

LUXURIST *n* person who loves luxurious things

LUXURY, LUXURIES *n* enjoyment of rich, very comfortable living ▸ *adj* of or providing luxury

LUZ, -ZES *n* supposedly indestructible bone of the human body

> This very unusual word is very useful for playing the Z.

LUZERN, -S *n* alfalfa

LUZZES ▸ luz

LWEI, -S *n* Angolan monetary unit

LYAM, -S *n* leash

LYARD *same as* ▸ liard

LYART *same as* ▸ liard

LYASE, -S *n* any enzyme that catalyses the separation of two parts of a molecule

LYCAENID *n* type of butterfly

LYCEA ▸ lyceum

LYCEE, -S *n* secondary school

LYCEUM, LYCEA, -S *n* public building for concerts

LYCH, -ES *same as* ▸ lich

LYCHEE, -S *same as* ▸ litchi

LYCHES ▸ lych

LYCHGATE *same as* ▸ lichgate

LYCHNIS *n* plant with red, pink, or white flowers

LYCOPENE *n* red pigment

LYCOPOD, -S *n* type of moss

LYCOPSID *n* type of club moss

LYCRA, -S *n* type of elastic fabric used for tight-fitting garments

LYDDITE, -S *n* explosive consisting chiefly of fused picric acid

LYE, -S *n* caustic solution

LYFULL *obsolete form of* ▸ lifeful

LYING, -S ▸ lie

LYINGLY ▸ lie

LYINGS ▸ lying

LYKEWAKE *n* watch held over a dead person, often with festivities

LYKEWALK *variant of* ▸ lykewake

LYM, -S *obsolete form of* ▸ lyam

LYME, -S *n* as in lyme grass type of perennial dune grass

LYMITER, -S *same as* ▸ limiter

LYMPH *n* colourless bodily fluid

LYMPHAD, -S *n* ancient rowing boat

LYMPHOID *adj* of or resembling lymph, or relating to the lymphatic system

LYMPHOMA *n* any form of cancer of the lymph nodes

LYMPHOUS *adj* resembling lymph

LYMPHS ▶ lymph
LYMS ▶ lym
LYNAGE, -S *obsolete form of* ▶ **lineage**
LYNCEAN *adj* of a lynx
LYNCH, -ED, -ES *vb* put to death without a trial
LYNCHER, -S ▶ lynch
LYNCHES ▶ lynch
LYNCHET, -S *n* ridge formed by ploughing a hillside
LYNCHING ▶ lynch
LYNCHPIN *same as* ▶ **linchpin**
LYNE, -S *n* flax
LYNX, -ES *n* animal of the cat family
LYNXLIKE ▶ lynx
LYOLYSIS, LYOLYSES *n* formation of an acid and a base from the interaction of a salt with a solvent
LYOPHIL *same as* > **lyophilic**
LYOPHILE *same as* > **lyophilic**
LYOPHOBE *same as* > **lyophobic**
LYRA *n* as in **lyra viol** lutelike musical instrument
LYRATE *adj* shaped like a lyre
LYRATED *same as* ▶ **lyrate**
LYRATELY ▶ lyrate
LYRE, -S *n* ancient musical instrument

LYREBIRD *n* Australian bird, the male of which spreads its tail into the shape of a lyre
LYRES ▶ lyre
LYRIC, -S *adj* expressing emotion in songlike style ▷ *n* short poem in a songlike style
LYRICAL *same as* ▶ **lyric**
LYRICISE *same as* ▶ **lyricize**
LYRICISM *n* quality or style of lyric poetry
LYRICIST *n* person who writes the words of songs or musicals
LYRICIZE *vb* write lyrics
LYRICON, -S *n* wind synthesizer
LYRICS ▶ lyric
LYRIFORM *adj* lyre-shaped
LYRISM, -S *n* art or technique of playing the lyre
LYRIST, -S *same as* ▶ **lyricist**
LYSATE, -S *n* material formed by lysis
LYSE, -D, LYSING *vb* undergo lysis
LYSERGIC *adj* as in **lysergic acid** crystalline compound used in medical research
LYSES ▶ lysis
LYSIN, -S *n* group of antibodies that dissolve cells

LYSINE, -S *n* essential amino acid that occurs in proteins
LYSING ▶ lyse
LYSINS ▶ lysin
LYSIS, LYSES *n* destruction of cells by a lysin
LYSOGEN, -S *n* lysis-inducing agent
LYSOGENY ▶ lysogen
LYSOL, -S *n* antiseptic solution
LYSOSOME *n* any of numerous small particles that are present in the cytoplasm of most cells
LYSOZYME *n* enzyme occurring in tears, certain body tissues, and egg white
LYSSA, -S *less common word for* ▶ **rabies**
LYTE, -D, -S, LYTING *vb* dismount
LYTHE, -S *n* type of fish
LYTHRUM, -S *n* genus of plants including loosestrife
LYTIC *adj* relating to, causing, or resulting from lysis
LYTING ▶ lyte
LYTTA, -E, -S *n* mass of cartilage under the tongue in carnivores

Mm

M is a very useful letter when you need to form short words as it starts a two-letter word with every vowel, as well as with **Y** and with another **M**. Remembering this allows you to use **M** effectively when you're forming a word parallel to, and in contact with, a word that is already on the board. **M** also combines well with **X** and **Z**, so there is a lot of potential for high-scoring words. Keep **max**, **mix** and **mux** (12 points each) in mind, as well as **miz** and **moz** (14 each). It's also worth remembering the three-letter words ending in **W**: **maw**, **mew** and **mow** (8 points each). **Myc** is another useful word to remember when you are short of vowels.

MA, -S n mother

MAA, -ED, -ING vb (of goats) bleat

MAAR, -E, -S n coneless volcanic crater

MAAS, -ES n thick soured milk

MAATJES n pickled herring

MABE, -S n type of pearl

MABELA, -S n ground sorghum

MABES ▶ mabe

MAC, -S n macintosh

MACA, -S n type of plant

MACABER same as ▶ macabre

MACABRE, -R adj strange and horrible, gruesome

MACACO, -S n type of lemur

MACADAM, -S n type of road surface

MACAHUBA n South American palm tree

MACALLUM n ice cream with raspberry sauce

MACAQUE, -S n monkey of Asia and Africa

MACARISE vb congratulate

MACARISM n blessing

MACARIZE same as ▶ macarise

MACARON, -S n small meringue cake

MACARONI n pasta in short tube shapes

MACARONS ▶ macaron

MACAROON n small biscuit or cake made with ground almonds

MACAS ▶ maca

MACASSAR n oily preparation formerly put on the hair to make it smooth and shiny

MACAW, -S n large tropical American parrot

MACCABAW same as ▶ maccaboy

MACCABOY n dark rose-scented snuff

MACCHIA, MACCHIE n thicket in Italy

MACCOBOY same as ▶ maccaboy

MACE, -D, -S, MACING n club ▷ vb use a mace

MACER, -S n macebearer, esp (in Scotland) an official who acts as usher in a court of law

MACERAL, -S n any of the organic units that constitute coal

MACERATE vb soften by soaking

MACERS ▶ macer

MACES ▶ mace

MACH, -S n ratio of the speed of a body in a particular medium to the speed of sound in that medium

MACHACA, -S n Mexican dish of shredded dried beef

MACHAIR, -S n (in the western Highlands of Scotland) a strip of sandy, grassy land

MACHAN, -S n (in India) a raised platform used in tiger hunting

MACHE, -S n papier-mâché

MACHER, -S n important or influential person

MACHES ▶ mache

MACHETE, -S n broad heavy knife used for cutting or as a weapon

MACHI n as in machi chips in Indian English, fish and chips

MACHINE, -D, -S n apparatus designed to perform a task ▷ vb make or produce by machine

MACHISMO n exaggerated or strong masculinity

MACHO, -S adj strongly masculine ▷ n strong masculinity

MACHOISM ▶ macho

MACHOS ▶ macho

MACHREE, -S n Irish form of address meaning my dear

MACHS ▶ mach

MACHZOR, -S n Jewish prayer book

MACING ▶ mace

MACK, -S same as ▶ mac

MACKEREL n edible sea fish

MACKINAW n thick short double-breasted plaid coat

MACKLE, -D, -S, MACKLING n blurred impression ▷ vb mend hurriedly or in a makeshift way

MACKS ▶ mack

MACLE, -S n crystal consisting of two parts

MACLED ▶ macle

MACLES ▶ macle

MACON, -S n wine from the Mâcon area

MACOYA, -S n South American tree

MACRAME, -S n ornamental work of knotted cord

MACRAMI, -S same as ▸ **macrame**

MACRO, -S n close-up lens

MACRON, -S n mark placed over a letter to represent a long vowel

MACROPOD n member of kangaroo family

MACROS ▸ **macro**

MACRURAL adj long-tailed

MACRURAN n type of decapod crustacean

MACS ▸ **mac**

MACULA, -E, -S n small spot like a freckle

MACULAR ▸ **macula**

MACULAS ▸ **macula**

MACULATE vb spot, stain, or pollute ▸ adj spotted or polluted

MACULE, -S, MACULING same as ▸ **mackle**

MACULED ▸ **macule**

MACULES ▸ **macule**

MACULING ▸ **macule**

MACULOSE adj having spots

MACUMBA, -S n religious cult in Brazil

MAD, -DED, -DEST, -DING, -S adj mentally deranged ▸ vb make mad

MADAFU, -S n coconut milk

MADAM, -ED, -ING, -S, MESDAMES n polite term of address for a woman ▸ vb call someone madam

MADAME, -S n French title equivalent to Mrs

MADAMED ▸ **madam**

MADAMES ▸ **madame**

MADAMING ▸ **madam**

MADAMS ▸ **madam**

MADCAP, -S adj foolish or reckless ▸ n impulsive or reckless person

MADDED ▸ **mad**

MADDEN, -ED, -S vb infuriate or irritate

MADDER, -S n type of rose

MADDEST ▸ **mad**

MADDING ▸ **mad**

MADDISH ▸ **mad**

MADDOCK, -S same as ▸ **mattock**

MADE ▸ **make**

MADEFY, MADEFIED, MADEFIES vb make moist

MADEIRA, -S n kind of rich sponge cake

MADERISE vb become reddish

MADERIZE same as ▸ **maderise**

MADEUPPY adj artificial or contrived in an obvious way

MADGE, -S n type of hammer

MADHOUSE n place filled with uproar or confusion

MADID adj wet

MADISON, -S n type of cycle relay race

MADLING, -S n foolish person

MADLY adv with great speed and energy

MADMAN, MADMEN n reckless man

MADNESS n insanity

MADONNA, -S n picture or statue of the Virgin Mary

MADOQUA, -S n Ethiopian antelope

MADRAS, -ES n medium-hot curry

MADRASA, -S same as ▸ **madrasah**

MADRASAH n educational institution, particularly for Islamic religious instruction

MADRASAS ▸ **madrasa**

MADRASES ▸ **madras**

MADRASSA same as ▸ **madrasah**

MADRE, -S Spanish word for ▸ **mother**

MADRIGAL n 16th–17th-century part song for unaccompanied voices

MADRONA, -S n N American evergreen tree or shrub

MADRONE, -S same as ▸ **madrona**

MADRONO, -S same as ▸ **madrona**

MADS ▸ **mad**

MADTOM, -S n species of catfish

MADURO, -S adj (of cigars) dark and strong ▸ n cigar of this type

MADWOMAN, MADWOMEN n reckless woman

MADWORT, -S n low-growing Eurasian plant with small blue flowers

MADZOON, -S same as ▸ **matzoon**

MAE, -S adj more

MAELID, -S n mythical spirit of apple tree

MAENAD, -ES, -S n female disciple of Dionysus

MAENADIC ▸ **maenad**

MAENADS ▸ **maenad**

MAERL, -S n type of red coralline algae

MAES ▸ **mae**

MAESTOSO adv be performed majestically ▸ n piece or passage directed to be played in this way

MAESTRO, MAESTRI, -S n outstanding musician or conductor

MAFFIA, -S same as ▸ **mafia**

MAFFICK, -S vb celebrate extravagantly and publicly

MAFFLED adj baffled

MAFFLIN, -S n half-witted person

MAFFLING same as ▸ **mafflin**

MAFFLINS ▸ **mafflin**

MAFIA, -S n international secret organization founded in Sicily

MAFIC, -S n minerals present in igneous rock

MAFIOSO, MAFIOSI, -S n member of the Mafia

MAFTED adj suffering under oppressive heat

MAFTIR, -S n final section of the weekly Torah reading

MAG, -GED, -GING, -S vb talk ▸ n talk

MAGAININ n substance with antibacterial properties

MAGALOG, -S same as > **magalogue**

MAGAZINE n periodical publication with articles by different writers

MAGE, -S archaic word for ▸ **magician**

MAGENTA, -S adj deep purplish-red ▸ n deep purplish red

MAGES ▸ **mage**

MAGESHIP ▸ **mage**

MAGG, -S same as ▸ **mag**

MAGGED ▸ **mag**

MAGGIE, -S n magpie

MAGGING ▸ **mag**

MAGGOT, -S n larva of an insect

MAGGOTY adj relating to, resembling, or ridden with maggots

MAGGS ▸ **magg**

MAGI ▸ **magus**

MAGIAN, -S ▸ **magus**

MAGIC, -KED, -S n supposed art of invoking supernatural powers to influence events ▸ vb transform or produce by or as if by magic ▸ adj of, using, or like magic

MAGICAL ▸ **magic**

MAGICIAN n conjuror

MAGICKED ▸ **magic**

MAGICS ▸ **magic**

MAGILP, -S same as ▸ **megilp**

MAGISM, -S ▸ **magus**

MAGISTER n person entitled to teach in medieval university

M

MAGLEV, -S *n* type of high-speed train

MAGMA, -S, -TA *n* molten rock inside the earth's crust

MAGMATIC ▸ **magma**

MAGNATE, -S *n* influential or wealthy person, esp in industry

MAGNES, -ES *n* magnetic iron ore

MAGNESIA *n* white tasteless substance used as an antacid and a laxative

MAGNESIC ▸ **magnesia**

MAGNET, -S *n* piece of iron or steel capable of attracting iron and pointing north when suspended

MAGNETAR *n* neutron star with intense magnetic field

MAGNETIC *adj* having the properties of a magnet

MAGNETO, -S *n* apparatus for ignition in an internal-combustion engine

MAGNETON *n* unit of magnetic moment

MAGNETOS ▸ **magneto**

MAGNETS ▸ **magnet**

MAGNIFIC *adj* magnificent, grandiose, or pompous

MAGNIFY *vb* increase in apparent size, as with a lens

MAGNOLIA *n* shrub or tree with showy white or pink flowers

MAGNON, -S *n* short for Cro-Magnon

MAGNOX, -ES *n* alloy used in fuel elements of some nuclear reactors

MAGNUM, -S *n* large wine bottle holding about 1.5 litres

MAGNUS *adj* as in **magnus hitch** knot similar to a clove hitch but having one more turn

MAGOT, -S *n* Chinese or Japanese figurine in a crouching position, usually grotesque

MAGPIE, -S *n* black-and-white bird

MAGS ▸ **mag**

MAGSMAN, MAGSMEN *n* raconteur

MAGUEY, -S *n* tropical American agave plant

MAGUS, MAGI *n* Zoroastrian priest of the ancient Medes and Persians

MAGYAR *adj* of or relating to a style of sleeve

MAHA *n* as in **maha yoga** form of yoga

MAHANT, -S *n* chief priest in a Hindu temple

MAHARAJA *same as* > **maharajah**

MAHARANI *n* wife of a maharaja

MAHATMA, -S *n* person revered for holiness and wisdom

MAHEWU, -S *n* (in South Africa) fermented liquid meal porridge

MAHIMAHI *n* Pacific fish

MAHJONG, -S *n* game of Chinese origin, using tiles

MAHJONGG *same as* ▸ **mahjong**

MAHJONGS ▸ **mahjong**

MAHMAL, -S *n* litter used in Muslim ceremony

MAHOE, -S *n* New Zealand tree

MAHOGANY *n* hard reddish-brown wood of several tropical trees ▷ *adj* reddish-brown

MAHONIA, -S *n* Asian and American evergreen shrub

MAHOUT, -S *n* (in India) elephant driver or keeper

MAHSEER, -S *n* large freshwater Indian fish

MAHSIR, -S *same as* ▸ **mahseer**

MAHUA, -S *n* Indian tree

MAHUANG, -S *n* herbal medicine from shrub

MAHUAS ▸ **mahua**

MAHWA, -S *same as* ▸ **mahua**

MAHZOR, -IM, -S *same as* ▸ **machzor**

MAIASAUR *same as* > **maiasaura**

MAID, -ED, -ING, -S *n* female servant ▷ *vb* work as maid

MAIDAN, -S *n* (in Pakistan, India, etc) open area

MAIDED ▸ **maid**

MAIDEN, -S *n* young unmarried woman ▷ *adj* unmarried

MAIDENLY *adj* modest

MAIDENS ▸ **maiden**

MAIDHOOD ▸ **maid**

MAIDING ▸ **maid**

MAIDISH ▸ **maid**

MAIDISM, -S *n* pellagra

MAIDLESS ▸ **maid**

MAIDS ▸ **maid**

MAIEUTIC *adj* of or relating to the Socratic method of eliciting knowledge by a series of questions and answers

MAIGRE, -S *adj* not containing meat ▷ *n* species of fish

MAIHEM, -S *same as* ▸ **mayhem**

MAIK, -S *n* old halfpenny

MAIKO, -S *n* apprentice geisha

MAIKS ▸ **maik**

MAIL, -ED, -ING, -S *n* letters and packages transported and delivered by the post office ▷ *vb* send by mail

MAILABLE ▸ **mail**

MAILBAG, -S *n* large bag for transporting or delivering mail

MAILBOAT *n* boat that carries mail

MAILBOX *n* box into which letters and parcels are delivered

MAILCAR, -S *same as* > **mailcoach**

MAILE, -S *n* halfpenny

MAILED ▸ **mail**

MAILER, -S *n* person who addresses or mails letters, etc

MAILES ▸ **maile**

MAILGRAM *n* telegram

MAILING, -S ▸ **mail**

MAILL, -S *n* Scots word meaning rent

MAILLESS ▸ **mail**

MAILLOT, -S *n* tights worn for ballet, gymnastics, etc

MAILLS ▸ **maill**

MAILMAN, MAILMEN *n* postman

MAILROOM *n* room where mail to and from building is dealt with

MAILS ▸ **mail**

MAILSACK *same as* ▸ **mailbag**

MAILSHOT *n* posting of advertising material to many selected people at once

MAILVAN, -S *n* vehicle used to transport post

MAIM, -ED, -S *vb* cripple or mutilate ▷ *n* injury or defect

MAIMER, -S ▸ **maim**

MAIMING, -S ▸ **maim**

MAIMS ▸ **maim**

MAIN, -ED, -ER, -EST, -ING, -S *adj* chief or principal ▷ *n* principal pipe or line carrying water, gas, or electricity ▷ *vb* lower sails

MAINBOOM *n* spar for mainsail

MAINDOOR *n* door from street into house

MAINED ▸ main

MAINER ▸ main

MAINEST ▸ main

MAINING ▸ main

MAINLAND n stretch of land which forms the main part of a country

MAINLINE n the trunk route between two points ▷ adj having an important position

MAINLY adv for the most part, chiefly

MAINMAST n chief mast of a ship

MAINOR, -S n act of doing something

MAINOUR, -S same as ▸ mainor

MAINS ▸ main

MAINSAIL n largest sail on a mainmast

MAINSTAY n chief support

MAINTAIN vb continue or keep in existence

MAINTOP, -S n top or platform at the head of the mainmast

MAINYARD n yard for a square mainsail

MAIOLICA same as ▸ majolica

MAIR, -S Scots form of ▸ more

MAIRE, -S n New Zealand tree

MAIREHAU n small aromatic shrub of New Zealand

MAIRES ▸ maire

MAIRS ▸ mair

MAISE, -S n measure of herring

MAIST, -S Scot word for ▸ most

MAISTER, -S Scots word for ▸ master

MAISTRY ▸ maister

MAISTS ▸ maist

MAIZE, -S n type of corn with spikes of yellow grains

MAJAGUA, -S same as ▸ mahoe

MAJESTIC adj beautiful, dignified, and impressive

MAJESTY n stateliness or grandeur

MAJLIS, -ES n (in Arab countries) an assembly

MAJOLICA n type of ornamented Italian pottery

MAJOR, -ED, -ING, -S adj greater in number, quality, or extent ▷ n middle-ranking army officer ▷ vb do one's principal study in (a particular subject)

MAJORAT, -S n estate, the right to which is that of the first born child of a family

MAJORED ▸ major

MAJORING ▸ major

MAJORITY n greater number

MAJORLY adv very

MAJORS ▸ major

MAK, -S Scot word for ▸ make

MAKABLE ▸ make

MAKAR, -S same as ▸ maker

MAKE, MADE, -S, MAKING vb create, construct, or establish ▷ n brand, type, or style

MAKEABLE n rough, unpolished stone

MAKEBATE n troublemaker

MAKEFAST n strong support to which a vessel is secured

MAKELESS ▸ make

MAKEOVER vb transfer the title of (property, etc) ▷ n alterations to improve a person's appearance

MAKER, -S n person or company that makes something

MAKES ▸ make

MAKEUP, -S n cosmetics applied to the face

MAKHANI, -S n Indian dish made with butter or ghee ▷ adj denoting such a dish

MAKI, -S n in Japanese cuisine, rice and other ingredients wrapped in a short seaweed roll

MAKIMONO n Japanese scroll

MAKING ▸ make

MAKINGS pl n potentials, qualities, or materials

MAKIS ▸ maki

MAKO, -S n powerful shark of the Atlantic and Pacific Oceans

MAKS ▸ mak

MAKUTA plural of ▸ likuta

MAKUTU, -ED, -S n Polynesian witchcraft ▷ vb cast a spell on

MAL, -S n illness

MALA, -S n string of beads or knots, used in praying and meditating

MALACCA, -S n stem of the rattan palm

MALACIA, -S n softening of an organ or tissue

MALADY, MALADIES n disease or illness

MALAISE, -S n something wrong which affects a

section of society or area of activity

MALAM, -S same as ▸ mallam

MALAMUTE n Alaskan sled dog of the spitz type, having a dense usually greyish coat

MALANDER same as ▸ malanders

MALANGA, -S same as ▸ cocoyam

MALAPERT adj saucy or impudent ▷ n saucy or impudent person

MALAPROP n word unintentionally confused with one of similar sound

MALAR, -S n cheekbone ▷ adj of or relating to the cheek or cheekbone

MALARIA, -S n infectious disease caused by mosquito bite

MALARIAL ▸ malaria

MALARIAN ▸ malaria

MALARIAS ▸ malaria

MALARKEY n nonsense or rubbish

MALARKY same as ▸ malarkey

MALAROMA n bad smell

MALARS ▸ malar

MALAS ▸ mala

MALATE, -S n any salt or ester of malic acid

MALAX, -ED, -ES, -ING vb soften

MALAXAGE ▸ malax

MALAXATE same as ▸ malax

MALAXED ▸ malax

MALAXES ▸ malax

MALAXING ▸ malax

MALE, -S adj of the sex which can fertilize reproductive cells ▷ n male person or animal

MALEATE, -S n any salt or ester of maleic acid

MALEDICT vb utter a curse against ▷ adj cursed or detestable

MALEFIC adj causing evil

MALEFICE n wicked deed

MALEIC adj as in **maleic acid** colourless soluble crystalline substance

MALEMIUT same as ▸ malamute

MALEMUTE same as ▸ malamute

MALENESS ▸ male

MALES ▸ male

MALFED adj having malfunctioned

MALGRADO prep in spite of

MALGRE, -D, -S, MALGRING same as ▸ maugre

MALI, -S n member of an Indian caste

MALIBU n as in **malibu board** lightweight surfboard

MALIC adj as in **malic acid** colourless crystalline compound occurring in apples

MALICE, -D, -S, MALICING n desire to cause harm to others ▷ vb wish harm to

MALICHO, -S n mischief

MALICING ▸ malice

MALIGN, -ED, -S vb slander or defame ▷ adj evil in influence or effect

MALIGNER ▸ malign

MALIGNLY ▸ malign

MALIGNS ▸ malign

MALIHINI n (in Hawaii) a foreigner or stranger

MALIK, -S n person of authority in India

MALINE, -S n stiff net

MALINGER vb feign illness to avoid work

MALIS ▸ mali

MALISM, -S n belief that evil dominates world

MALISON, -S archaic or poetic word for ▸ **curse**

MALIST ▸ malism

MALKIN, -S archaic or dialect name for a ▸ **cat**

MALL, -ED, -S n street or shopping area closed to vehicles ▷ vb maul

MALLAM, -S n (in W Africa) expert in the Koran

MALLARD, -S n wild duck

MALLCORE n type of rock music combining heavy metal and hip-hop

MALLEATE vb hammer

MALLECHO same as ▸ **malicho**

MALLED ▸ mall

MALLEE, -S n low-growing eucalypt in dry regions

MALLEI ▸ malleus

MALLEOLI ▸ malleolus

MALLET, -S n (wooden) hammer

MALLEUS, MALLEI n small bone in the middle ear

MALLING, -S ▸ mall

MALLOW, -S n plant with pink or purple flowers

MALLS ▸ mall

MALM, -S n soft greyish limestone that crumbles easily

MALMAG, -S n Asian monkey

MALMIER ▸ malmy

MALMIEST ▸ malmy

MALMS ▸ malm

MALMSEY, -S n sweet Madeira wine

MALMY, MALMIER, MALMIEST adj looking like malm

MALODOR, -S same as ▸ **malodour**

MALODOUR n unpleasant smell

MALONATE n salt of malonic acid

MALONIC adj as in **malonic acid** colourless crystalline compound

MALOTI plural of ▸ **loti**

MALPOSED adj in abnormal position

MALS ▸ mal

MALSTICK same as > **maulstick**

MALT, -S n grain, such as barley, dried in a kiln ▷ vb make into or make with malt

MALTASE, -S n enzyme that hydrolyses maltose to glucose

MALTED, -S n malted milk drink

MALTESE adj as in **maltese cross** cross-shaped part of a film projector

MALTHA, -S n any of various naturally occurring mixtures of hydrocarbons

MALTIER ▸ malty

MALTIEST ▸ malty

MALTING, -S n building in which malt is made or stored

MALTIPOO n cross between a Maltese and a poodle

MALTMAN, MALTMEN same as ▸ **maltster**

MALTOL, -S n food additive

MALTOSE, -S n sugar formed by the action of enzymes on starch

MALTREAT vb treat badly

MALTS ▸ malt

MALTSTER n person who makes or deals in malt

MALTWORM n heavy drinker

MALTY, MALTIER, MALTIEST adj of, like, or containing malt

MALUS, -ES n financial penalty incurred by an investor

MALVA, -S n mallow plant

MALVASIA n type of grape used to make malmsey

MALVESIE same as ▸ **malmsey**

MALWA, -S n Ugandan drink brewed from millet

MALWARE, -S n computer program designed to cause damage to a system

MALWAS ▸ malwa

MAM, -S same as ▸ **mother**

MAMA, -S n mother

MAMAGUY, -S vb deceive or tease ▷ n deception or flattery

MAMAKAU, -S same as ▸ **mamaku**

MAMAKO, -S same as ▸ **mamaku**

MAMAKU, -S n tall edible New Zealand tree fern

MAMALIGA same as ▸ **polenta**

MAMAS ▸ mama

MAMASAN, -S n (in Japan) woman in a position of authority

MAMATEEK n type of wigwam

MAMBA, -S n deadly S African snake

MAMBO, -ED, -ES, -ING, -S n Latin American dance resembling the rumba ▷ vb perform this dance

MAMEE, -S same as ▸ **mamey**

MAMELON, -S n small rounded hillock

MAMELUCO n Brazilian of mixed European and South American descent

MAMELUKE n member of a military class once ruling Egypt

MAMEY, -ES, -S n tropical tree

MAMIE, -S n tropical tree

MAMILLA, -E n nipple or teat

MAMILLAR adj of the breast

MAMLUK, -S same as ▸ **mameluke**

MAMMA, -E, -S n buxom and voluptuous woman

MAMMAL, -S n animal of the type that suckles its young

MAMMARY adj of the breasts or milk-producing glands ▷ n breast

MAMMAS ▸ mamma

MAMMATE adj having breasts

MAMMATUS, MAMMATI n breast-shaped cloud

MAMMEE, -S same as ▸ **mamey**

MAMMER, -ED, -S vb hesitate

MAMMET, -S same as ▸ **maumet**

MAMMETRY n worship of idols

MAMMETS ▶ mammet

MAMMEY, -S same as ▶ mamey

MAMMIE same as ▶ mammy

MAMMIES ▶ mammy

MAMMIFER same as ▶ mammal

MAMMILLA same as ▶ mamilla

MAMMITIS same as ▶ mastitis

MAMMOCK, -S n fragment ▷ vb tear or shred

MAMMON, -S n wealth regarded as a source of evil

MAMMOTH, -S n extinct elephant-like mammal ▷ adj colossal

MAMMY, MAMMIES same as ▶ mother

MAMPARA, -S n foolish person, idiot

MAMPOER, -S n home-distilled brandy

MAMS ▶ mam

MAMSELLE n mademoiselle

MAN, -D, -NED, -NING, -S, MEN n adult male ▷ vb supply with sufficient people for operation or defence

MANA, -S n authority, influence

MANACLE, -D, -S vb handcuff or fetter ▷ n metal ring or chain put round the wrists or ankles

MANAGE, -D, -S vb succeed in doing

MANAGER, -S n person in charge of a business, institution, actor, sports team, etc

MANAGES ▶ manage

MANAGING adj having administrative control or authority

MANAIA, -S n figure in Māori carving

MANAKIN, -S same as ▶ manikin

MANANA, -S n tomorrow ▷ adv tomorrow

MANAS ▶ mana

MANAT, -S n standard monetary unit of Azerbaijan

MANATEE, -S n large tropical plant-eating aquatic mammal

MANATI, -S same as ▶ manatee

MANATOID ▶ manatee

MANATS ▶ manat

MANATU, -S n large flowering deciduous New Zealand tree

MANAWA, -S in New Zealand, same as ▶ mangrove

MANBAG, -S n small handbag with a shoulder strap, carried by men

MANBAND, -S n boy band whose members have reached maturity

MANCALA, -S n African and Asian board game

MANCANDO adv musical direction meaning fading away

MANCHE, -S n long sleeve

MANCHEGO n Spanish cheese

MANCHES ▶ manche

MANCHET, -S n type of bread

MANCIPLE n steward who buys provisions, esp in a college, Inn of Court, or monastery

MANCUS, -ES n former English coin

MAND ▶ man

MANDALA, -S n circular design symbolizing the universe

MANDALIC same as ▶ mandala

MANDAMUS n order of a superior court

MANDARIN n high-ranking government official

MANDATE, -D, -S n official or authoritative command ▷ vb give authority to

MANDATOR ▶ mandate

MANDI, -S n (in India) a big market

MANDIBLE n lower jawbone or jawlike part

MANDIOC, -S same as ▶ manioc

MANDIOCA same as ▶ manioc

MANDIOCS ▶ mandioc

MANDIR, -S n Hindu or Jain temple

MANDIRA, -S same as ▶ mandir

MANDIRS ▶ mandir

MANDIS ▶ mandi

MANDOLA, -S n early type of mandolin

MANDOLIN n musical instrument with four pairs of strings

MANDOM, -S n mankind

MANDORA, -S n ancestor of mandolin

MANDORLA n area of light surrounding Christ in a painting

MANDRAKE n plant with a forked root

MANDREL, -S n shaft on which work is held in a lathe

MANDRIL, -S same as ▶ mandrel

MANDRILL n large blue-faced baboon

MANDRILS ▶ mandril

MANE n long hair on the neck of a horse, lion, etc

MANEB, -S n powdered fungicide

MANED ▶ mane

MANEGE, -D, -S, MANEGING n art of training horses and riders ▷ vb train horse

MANEH, -S same as ▶ mina

MANELESS ▶ mane

MANENT ▶ manet

MANES pl n spirits of the dead, often revered as minor deities

MANET, MANENT vb theatre direction, remain on stage

MANEUVER same as ▶ manoeuvre

MANFUL adj determined and brave

MANFULLY ▶ manful

MANG, -ED, -ING, -S vb speak

MANGA, -S n type of Japanese comic book

MANGABEY n large African monkey

MANGABY same as ▶ mangabey

MANGAL, -S n Turkish brazier

MANGANIC adj of or containing manganese in the trivalent state

MANGANIN n copper-based alloy

MANGAS ▶ manga

MANGE, -S n skin disease of domestic animals

MANGEAO, -S n small New Zealand tree with glossy leaves

MANGED ▶ mang

MANGEL, -S n Eurasian variety of the beet plant

MANGER, -S n eating trough in a stable or barn

MANGES ▶ mange

MANGEY same as ▶ mangy

MANGIER ▶ mangy

MANGIEST ▶ mangy

MANGILY ▶ mangy

MANGING ▶ mang

MANGLE, -D, -S, MANGLING vb destroy by crushing and twisting ▷ n machine with rollers for squeezing water from washed clothes

M

MANGLER, -S ▸ mangle

MANGLES ▸ mangle

MANGLING ▸ mangle

MANGO, -ES, -S n tropical fruit with sweet juicy yellow flesh

MANGOLD, -S n type of root vegetable

MANGONEL n war engine for hurling stones

MANGOS ▸ mango

MANGROVE n tropical tree with exposed roots, which grows beside water

MANGS ▸ mang

MANGY, MANGIER, MANGIEST adj having mange

MANHOLE, -S n hole with a cover, through which a person can enter a drain or sewer

MANHOOD, -S n state or quality of being a man or being manly

MANHUNT, -S n organized search, usu by police, for a wanted man

MANI n place to pray

MANIA, -S n extreme enthusiasm

MANIAC, -S n person acting wildly

MANIACAL adj characteristic of mania

MANIACS ▸ maniac

MANIAS ▸ mania

MANIC, -S adj extremely excited or energetic ▸ n person with mania

MANICURE n cosmetic care of the fingernails and hands ▸ vb care for (the fingernails and hands) in this way

MANIES ▸ many

MANIFEST adj easily noticed, obvious ▸ vb show plainly ▸ n list of cargo or passengers for customs

MANIFOLD adj numerous and varied ▸ n pipe with several outlets, esp in an internal-combustion engine ▸ vb duplicate (a page, book, etc)

MANIFORM adj like hand

MANIHOC, -S variation of ▸ manioc

MANIHOT, -S n tropical American plant

MANIKIN, -S n little man or dwarf

MANILA, -S n strong brown paper used for envelopes

MANILLA, -S n early currency in W Africa in the form of a small bracelet

MANILLE, -S n (in ombre and quadrille) the second best trump

MANIOC, -S same as ▸ cassava

MANIOCA, -S same as ▸ manioc

MANIOCS ▸ manioc

MANIPLE, -S n (in ancient Rome) a unit of 120 to 200 foot soldiers

MANIS, -ES n pangolin

MANITO, -S same as ▸ manitou

MANITOU, -S n Native American deified spirit or force

MANITU, -S same as ▸ manitou

MANJACK, -S n single individual

MANKIER ▸ manky

MANKIEST ▸ manky

MANKIND, -S n human beings collectively

MANKINI, -S n man's revealing swimming costume

MANKY, MANKIER, MANKIEST adj worthless, rotten, or in bad taste

MANLESS ▸ man

MANLIER ▸ manly

MANLIEST ▸ manly

MANLIKE adj resembling or befitting a man

MANLILY ▸ manly

MANLY, MANLIER, MANLIEST adj (possessing qualities) appropriate to a man

MANMADE adj made or produced by human beings

MANNA, -S n miraculous food which sustained the Israelites in the wilderness

MANNAN, -S n drug derived from mannose

MANNAS ▸ manna

MANNED ▸ man

MANNER n way a thing happens or is done

MANNERED adj affected

MANNERLY adj having good manners, polite ▸ adv with good manners

MANNERS pl n person's social conduct

MANNIKIN same as ▸ manikin

MANNING ▸ man

MANNISH adj like a man

MANNITE, -S same as ▸ mannitol

MANNITIC ▸ mannitol

MANNITOL n white crystalline water-soluble sweet-tasting substance

MANNOSE, -S n hexose sugar

MANO, -ES, -S n stone for grinding grain

MANOAO, -S n New Zealand shrub

MANOES ▸ mano

MANOR, -S n large country house and its lands

MANORIAL ▸ manor

MANORS ▸ manor

MANOS ▸ mano

MANPACK, -S n load carried by one person

MANPOWER n available number of workers

MANQUE, -S adj would-be ▸ n section on a roulette table

MANRED, -S n homage

MANRENT, -S same as ▸ manred

MANRIDER n train carrying miners in coal mine

MANROPE, -S n rope railing

MANS ▸ man

MANSARD, -S n type of sloping roof

MANSCAPE vb groom a man's bodily hair for aesthetics

MANSE, -S n house provided for a minister in some religious denominations

MANSHIFT n work done by one person in one shift

MANSION, -S n large house

MANSONRY n mansions collectively

MANSUETE adj gentle

MANSWORN adj perjured ▸ n someone who perjures

MANTA, -S n type of large ray with very wide winglike pectoral fins

MANTEAU, -S, -X n cloak or mantle

MANTEEL, -S n cloak

MANTEL, -S n structure round a fireplace ▸ vb construct a mantel

MANTELET n woman's short mantle, often lace-trimmed, worn in the mid-19th century

MANTELS ▸ mantel

MANTES ▸ mantis

MANTIC adj of or relating to divination and prophecy

MANTID, -S same as ▸ mantis

MANTIES ▸ manty

MANTILLA n (in Spain) a lace scarf covering a woman's head and shoulders

MANTIS, MANTES, -ES *n* carnivorous insect like a grasshopper

MANTISSA *n* part of a common logarithm consisting of the decimal point and the figures following it

MANTLE, -D, -S *same as* ▸ **mantel**

MANTLET, -S *same as* ▸ **mantelet**

MANTLING *n* drapery or scrollwork around a shield

MANTO, -ES, -S *same as* ▸ **manteau**

MANTRA, -S *n* any sacred word or syllable used as an object of concentration

MANTRAM, -S *same as* ▸ **mantra**

MANTRAP, -S *n* snare for catching people, esp trespassers

MANTRAS ▸ **mantra**

MANTRIC ▸ **mantra**

MANTUA, -S *n* loose gown of the 17th and 18th centuries

MANTY, MANTIES *Scots variant of* ▸ **mantua**

MANUAL, -S *adj* of or done with the hands ▸ *n* handbook

MANUALLY ▸ **manual**

MANUALS ▸ **manual**

MANUARY *same as* ▸ **manual**

MANUBRIA > **manubrium**

MANUCODE *n* bird of Paradise with blue-black plumage

MANUHIRI *n* visitor to a Māori marae

MANUKA, -S *n* New Zealand tree

MANUL, -S *n* Asian wildcat

MANUMEA, -S *n* pigeon of Samoa

MANUMIT, -S *vb* free from slavery

MANURE, -D, -S, MANURING *n* animal excrement used as a fertilizer ▸ *vb* fertilize (land) with this

MANURER, -S ▸ **manure**

MANURES ▸ **manure**

MANURIAL ▸ **manure**

MANURING ▸ **manure**

MANUS *n* wrist and hand

MANWARD *adv* towards humankind

MANWARDS *same as* ▸ **manward**

MANWISE *adv* in a human way

MANY, MANIES *adj* numerous ▸ *n* large number

MANYATA, -S *same as* ▸ **manyatta**

MANYATTA *n* settlement of Maasai people

MANYFOLD *adj* many in number

MANZELLO *n* instrument like saxophone

MAOMAO, -S *n* fish of New Zealand seas

MAORMOR, -S *same as* ▸ **mormaor**

MAP, -PED, -S *n* representation of the earth's surface or some part of it ▸ *vb* make a map of

MAPAU, -S *n* small New Zealand tree

MAPLE, -S *n* tree with broad leaves, a variety of which yields sugar

MAPLESS ▸ **map**

MAPLIKE ▸ **map**

MAPMAKER *n* person who draws maps

MAPPABLE ▸ **map**

MAPPED ▸ **map**

MAPPER, -S ▸ **map**

MAPPERY *n* making of maps

MAPPING, -S ▸ **map**

MAPPIST, -S ▸ **map**

MAPS ▸ **map**

MAPSTICK *same as* ▸ **mopstick**

MAPWISE *adv* like map

MAQUETTE *n* sculptor's small preliminary model or sketch

MAQUI *n* Chilean shrub

MAQUILA, -S *n* US-owned factory in Mexico

MAQUIS *n* French underground movement in World War II

MAR, -D, -RED, -RING, -S *vb* spoil or impair ▸ *n* disfiguring mark

MARA, -S *n* harelike S American rodent

MARABI, -S *n* kind of music popular in S African townships in the 1930s

MARABOU, -S *n* large black-and-white African stork

MARABOUT *n* Muslim holy man or hermit of North Africa

MARACA, -S *n* shaken percussion instrument

MARAE, -S *n* enclosed space in front of a Māori meeting house

MARAGING *adj* as in **maraging steel** strong low-carbon steel

MARAH, -S *n* bitterness

MARAKA ▸ **marka**

MARANTA, -S *n* tropical American plant

MARARI, -S *n* eel-like blennioid food fish

MARAS ▸ **mara**

MARASCA, -S *n* European cherry tree with red acid-tasting fruit

MARASMIC ▸ **marasmus**

MARASMUS *n* emaciation

MARATHON *n* long-distance race of 26 miles 385 yards (42.195 kilometres) ▸ *adj* of or relating to a race on foot of 26 miles 385 yards (42.195 kilometres)

MARAUD, -ED, -S *vb* wander or raid in search of plunder

MARAUDER ▸ **maraud**

MARAUDS ▸ **maraud**

MARAVEDI *n* any of various Spanish coins of copper or gold

MARBLE, -D *n* kind of limestone with a mottled appearance ▸ *vb* mottle with variegated streaks in imitation of marble

MARBLER, -S ▸ **marble**

MARBLES *n* game in which marble balls are rolled at one another

MARBLIER ▸ **marble**

MARBLING *n* mottled effect or pattern resembling marble

MARBLY ▸ **marble**

MARC, -S *n* remains of grapes or other fruit that have been pressed for wine-making

MARCATO, -S *adj* (of notes) heavily accented ▸ *adv* with each note heavily accented ▸ *n* heavily accented note

MARCEL, -S *n* hairstyle characterized by repeated regular waves ▸ *vb* make such waves in (the hair)

MARCELLA *n* type of fabric

MARCELS ▸ **marcel**

MARCH, -ED, -ES, -ING *vb* walk with a military step ▸ *n* action of marching

MARCHEN *n* German story

MARCHER, -S *n* person who marches

MARCHES ▸ **march**

MARCHESA *n* (in Italy) the wife or widow of a marchese

M

MARCHESE, MARCHESI n (in Italy) a nobleman ranking below a prince and above a count

MARCHING ▶ **march**

MARCHMAN, MARCHMEN n person living on border

MARCONI, -S vb communicate by wireless

MARCS ▶ **marc**

MARD ▶ **mar**

MARDY, MARDIED, MARDIER, MARDIES, MARDIEST, -ING adj (of a child) spoilt ▷ vb behave in mardy way

MARE, -S, MARIA n female horse or zebra

MAREMMA, -S, MAREMME n marshy unhealthy region near the shore, esp in Italy

MARENGO adj browned in oil and cooked with tomatoes, mushrooms, garlic, wine, etc

MARERO, -S n member of a C American organized criminal gang

MARES ▶ **mare**

MARG, -S short for > **margarine**

MARGARIC adj of or resembling pearl

MARGARIN n ester of margaric acid

MARGATE, -S n greyish fish of W Atlantic

MARGAY, -S n feline mammal of Central and S America

MARGE, -S n margarine

MARGENT, -S same as ▶ **margin**

MARGES ▶ **marge**

MARGIN, -ED, -S n edge or border ▷ vb provide with a margin

MARGINAL adj insignificant, unimportant ▷ n marginal constituency

MARGINED ▶ **margin**

MARGINS ▶ **margin**

MARGOSA, -S n Indian tree

MARGRAVE n (formerly) a German nobleman ranking above a count

MARGS ▶ **marg**

MARIA ▶ **mare**

MARIACHI n small ensemble of street musicians in Mexico

MARID, -S n spirit in Muslim mythology

MARIES ▶ **mary**

MARIGOLD n plant with yellow or orange flowers

MARIGRAM n graphic record of the tide levels at a particular coastal station

MARIMBA, -S n Latin American percussion instrument

MARINA, -S n harbour for yachts and other pleasure boats

MARINADE n seasoned liquid in which fish or meat is soaked before cooking

MARINARA n Italian pasta sauce

MARINAS ▶ **marina**

MARINATE vb soak in marinade

MARINE, -S adj of the sea or shipping ▷ n (esp in Britain and the US) soldier trained for land and sea combat

MARINER, -S n sailor

MARINERA n folk dance of Peru

MARINERS ▶ **mariner**

MARINES ▶ **marine**

MARIPOSA n plant of southwestern US and Mexico

MARISH, -ES n marsh

MARITAGE n right of a lord to choose the spouses of his wards

MARITAL adj relating to marriage

MARITIME adj relating to shipping

MARJORAM n aromatic herb used for seasoning food and in salads

MARK, -S n line, dot, scar, etc visible on a surface ▷ vb make a mark on

MARKA, MARAKA, -S n unit of currency introduced as an interim currency in Bosnia-Herzegovina

MARKDOWN n price reduction ▷ vb reduce in price

MARKED adj noticeable

MARKEDLY ▶ **marked**

MARKER, -S n object used to show the position of something

MARKET, -ED, -S n assembly or place for buying and selling ▷ vb offer or produce for sale

MARKETER ▶ **market**

MARKETS ▶ **market**

MARKHOOR same as ▶ **markhor**

MARKHOR, -S n large wild Himalayan goat

MARKING, -S n arrangement of colours on an animal or plant

MARKKA, -A, -S n former standard monetary unit of Finland

MARKMAN, MARKMEN n person owning land

MARKS ▶ **mark**

MARKSMAN, MARKSMEN n person skilled at shooting

MARKUP, -S n percentage added to the cost of something to give the seller a profit

MARL, -ED, -S n soil formed of clay and lime, used as fertilizer ▷ vb fertilize (land) with marl

MARLE, -S same as ▶ **marvel**

MARLED ▶ **marl**

MARLES ▶ **marle**

MARLIER ▶ **marly**

MARLIEST ▶ **marly**

MARLIN, -S same as ▶ **marline**

MARLINE, -S n light rope, usually tarred, made of two strands laid left-handed

MARLING, -S same as ▶ **marline**

MARLINS ▶ **marlin**

MARLITE, -S n type of marl that contains clay and calcium carbonate

MARLITIC ▶ **marlite**

MARLS ▶ **marl**

MARLY, MARLIER, MARLIEST adj marl-like

MARM, -S same as ▶ **madam**

MARMEM n as in marmem alloy type of alloy

MARMITE, -S n large cooking pot

MARMOSE, -S n South American opossum

MARMOSET n small bushy-tailed monkey

MARMOT, -S n burrowing rodent

MARMS ▶ **marm**

MAROCAIN n fabric of ribbed crepe

MARON, -S n freshwater crustacean

MAROON, -ED, -S adj reddish-purple ▷ vb abandon ashore, esp on an island ▷ n exploding firework or flare used as a warning signal

MAROONER ▶ **maroon**

MAROONS ▶ **maroon**

MAROQUIN n morocco leather

MAROR, -S n Jewish ceremonial dish of bitter herbs

MARPLOT, -S n person who spoils a plot

MARQUE, -S n brand of product, esp of a car

MARQUEE, -S n large tent used for a party or exhibition

MARQUES ▸ marque

MARQUESS n nobleman of the rank below a duke

MARQUIS n (in some European countries) nobleman of the rank above a count

MARQUISE same as ▸ marquee

MARRA, -S n (in N England) friend

MARRAM, -S n as in marram grass any of several grasses that grow on sandy shores

MARRANO, -S n Spanish or Portuguese Jew of the late Middle Ages who was converted to Christianity

MARRAS ▸ marra

MARRED ▸ mar

MARRELS same as ▸ merils

MARRER, -S ▸ mar

MARRI, -S n W Australian eucalyptus

MARRIAGE n state of being married

MARRIED ▸ marry

MARRIEDS pl n married people

MARRIER, -S ▸ marry

MARRIES ▸ marry

MARRING ▸ mar

MARRIS ▸ marri

MARRON, -S n large edible sweet chestnut

MARROW, -ED, -S n fatty substance inside bones ▷ vb be mate to

MARROWY adj full of marrow

MARRUM, -S same as ▸ marram

MARRY, MARRIED, MARRIES, -ING vb take as a spouse ▷ interj exclamation of surprise or anger

MARS ▸ mar

MARSALA, -S n dark sweet dessert wine made in Sicily

MARSE, -S same as ▸ master

MARSH, -ES n low-lying wet land

MARSHAL, -S n officer of the highest rank ▷ vb arrange in order

MARSHALL n shortened form of Marshall Plan

MARSHALS ▸ marshal

MARSHED adj having a marsh

MARSHES ▸ marsh

MARSHY, MARSHIER adj of, involving, or like a marsh

MARSPORT n spoilsport

MARSUPIA ▸ marsupium

MART, -ED, -ING, -S n market ▷ vb sell or trade

MARTAGON n Eurasian lily plant cultivated for its mottled purplish-red flowers

MARTED ▸ mart

MARTEL, -S n hammer-shaped weapon ▷ vb use such a weapon

MARTELLO n small circular tower for coastal defence, formerly much used in Europe

MARTELS ▸ martel

MARTEN, -S n weasel-like animal

MARTEXT, -S n preacher who makes many mistakes

MARTIAL adj of war, warlike

MARTIALS pl n as in court martials military courts that try people subject to military law

MARTIAN, -S n inhabitant of Mars

MARTIN, -S n bird with a slightly forked tail

MARTINET n person who maintains strict discipline

MARTING ▸ mart

MARTINI, -S n cocktail of vermouth and gin

MARTINS ▸ martin

MARTLET, -S n footless bird often found in coats of arms

MARTS ▸ mart

MARTYR, -ED, -S n person who dies or suffers for his or her beliefs ▷ vb make a martyr of

MARTYRIA ▸ martyrium

MARTYRLY ▸ martyr

MARTYRS ▸ martyr

MARTYRY n shrine or chapel erected in honour of a martyr

MARVEL, -ED, -S vb be filled with wonder ▷ n wonderful thing

MARVELER n (US) person who marvels

MARVELS ▸ marvel

MARVER, -ED, -S vb roll molten glass on slab

MARVY, MARVIER, MARVIEST shortened form of > marvelous

MARY, MARIES n woman

MARYBUD, -S n bud of marigold

MARYJANE n woman's shoe with strap over the top

MARZIPAN n paste of ground almonds, sugar, and egg whites ▷ vb cover with marzipan

MAS ▸ ma

MASA, -S n Mexican maize dough

MASALA, -S n mixture of spices ground into a paste ▷ adj spicy

MASAS ▸ masa

MASCARA, -S n cosmetic for darkening the eyelashes

MASCARON n in architecture, a face carved in stone or metal

MASCLE, -S n charge consisting of a lozenge with a lozenge-shaped hole in the middle

MASCLED ▸ mascle

MASCLES ▸ mascle

MASCON, -S n any of several lunar regions of high gravity

MASCOT, -S n person, animal, or thing supposed to bring good luck

MASCULY ▸ mascle

MASE, -D, -S, MASING vb function as maser

MASER, -S n device for amplifying microwaves

MASES ▸ mase

MASH, -ED, -ES n soft pulpy mass ▷ vb crush into a soft mass

MASHER, -S ▸ mash

MASHES ▸ mash

MASHGIAH same as > mashgiach

MASHIACH n messiah

MASHIE, -S n former golf club, used for approach shots

MASHIER ▸ mashy

MASHIES ▸ mashie

MASHIEST ▸ mashy

MASHING, -S ▸ mash

MASHLAM, -S same as ▸ maslin

MASHLIM, -S same as ▸ maslin

MASHLIN, -S same as ▸ maslin

MASHLOCH same as ▸ maslin

MASHLUM, -S same as ▸ maslin

MASHMAN, MASHMEN n brewery worker

MASHUA, -S n South American plant

M

MASHUP, -S n piece of music in which a producer or DJ blends together two or more tracks

MASHY, MASHIER, MASHIEST adj like mash

MASING ▸ mase

MASJID, -S same as ▸ mosque

MASK, -S n covering for the face, as a disguise or protection ▹ vb cover with a mask

MASKABLE ▸ mask

MASKED adj disguised or covered by or as if by a mask

MASKEG, -S n North American bog

MASKER, -S n person who wears a mask or takes part in a masque

MASKING, -S n act or practice of masking

MASKLIKE ▸ mask

MASKS ▸ mask

MASLIN, -S n mixture of wheat, rye or other grain

MASON, -ED, -ING, -S n person who works with stone ▹ vb construct or strengthen with masonry

MASONIC adj of, characteristic of, or relating to Freemasons

MASONING ▸ mason

MASONITE n tradename for a kind of dark brown hardboard used for partitions, lining, etc

MASONRY n stonework

MASONS ▸ mason

MASOOLAH n Indian boat used in surf

MASQUE, -S n 16th–17th-century form of dramatic entertainment

MASQUER, -S same as ▸ masker

MASQUES ▸ masque

MASS, -ING n coherent body of matter ▹ adj large-scale ▹ vb form into a mass

MASSA, -S old fashioned variant of ▸ master

MASSACRE n indiscriminate killing of large numbers of people ▹ vb kill in large numbers

MASSAGE, -D, -S n rubbing and kneading of parts of the body to reduce pain or stiffness ▹ vb give a massage to

MASSAGER ▸ massage

MASSAGES ▸ massage

MASSAS ▸ massa

MASSCULT n culture of masses

MASSE n billiard stroke that makes the ball move in a curve around another ball

MASSED ▸ mass

MASSEDLY ▸ mass

MASSES pl n body of common people

MASSETER n muscle of the cheek used in moving the jaw, esp in chewing

MASSEUR, -S n person who gives massages

MASSEUSE n woman who gives massages, esp as a profession

MASSICOT n yellow earthy secondary mineral

MASSIER ▸ massy

MASSIEST ▸ massy

MASSIF, -S n connected group of mountains

MASSING ▸ mass

MASSIVE, -S adj large and heavy ▹ n group of friends or associates

MASSLESS ▸ mass

MASSOOLA same as ▸ masoolah

MASSTIGE n impression of exclusivity in mass-produced goods

MASSY, MASSIER, MASSIEST literary word for ▸ massive

MAST, -ED, -ING, -S n tall pole for supporting something, esp a ship's sails ▹ vb equip with a mast

MASTABA, -S n mud-brick superstructure above tombs in ancient Egypt

MASTABAH same as ▸ mastaba

MASTABAS ▸ mastaba

MASTED ▸ mast

MASTER, -ED, -S n person in control, such as an owner of animals ▹ vb acquire knowledge of or skill in

MASTERLY adj showing great skill

MASTERS ▸ master

MASTERY n expertise

MASTFUL ▸ mast

MASTHEAD n head of a mast ▹ vb send (a sailor) to the masthead as a punishment

MASTIC, -S n gum obtained from certain trees

MASTICH, -S same as ▸ mastic

MASTICHE same as ▸ mastic

MASTICHS ▸ mastich

MASTICOT same as ▸ massicot

MASTICS ▸ mastic

MASTIER ▸ masty

MASTIEST ▸ masty

MASTIFF, -S n large dog

MASTING ▸ mast

MASTITIC ▸ mastitis

MASTITIS n inflammation of a breast or udder

MASTIX, -ES n type of gum

MASTLESS ▸ mast

MASTLIKE ▸ mast

MASTODON n extinct elephant-like mammal

MASTOID, -S n projection of the bone behind the ear ▹ adj shaped like a nipple or breast

MASTS ▸ mast

MASTY, MASTIER, MASTIEST ▸ mast

MASU, -S n Japanese salmon

MASULA, -S same as ▸ masoolah

MASURIUM n silver-grey metallic element

MASUS ▸ masu

MAT, -S, -TED n piece of fabric used as a floor covering or to protect a surface ▹ vb tangle or become tangled into a dense mass ▹ adj having a dull, lustreless, or roughened surface

MATACHIN n dancer with sword

MATADOR, -S n bullfighter who kills the bull

MATADORA n female matador

MATADORE n form of dominoes game

MATADORS ▸ matador

MATAI, -S n New Zealand tree, the wood of which is used for timber for building

MATAMATA (in Malaysia) a former name for ▸ police

MATATA, -S same as ▸ fernbird

MATATU, -S n type of shared taxi used in Kenya

MATCH, -ED, -ES n contest in a game or sport ▹ vb be exactly like, equal to, or in harmony with

MATCHA, -S n Japanese green tea

MATCHBOX n small box for holding matches

MATCHED ▸ match

MATCHER, -S ▸ match

MATCHES ▸ match

MATCHET, -S same as ▸ machete

MATCHING ▶ match

MATCHUP, -S n sports match

MATE, -D, -S n friend ▷ vb pair (animals) or (of animals) be paired for reproduction

MATELESS ▶ mate

MATELOT, -S n sailor

MATELOTE n fish served with a sauce of wine, onions, seasonings, and fish stock

MATELOTS ▶ matelot

MATER, -S, MATRES n mother: often used facetiously

MATERIAL n substance of which a thing is made ▷ adj of matter or substance

MATERIEL n materials and equipment of an organization, esp of a military force

MATERNAL adj of a mother

MATERS ▶ mater

MATES ▶ mate

MATESHIP n comradeship of friends, usually male, viewed as an institution

MATEY, -S, MATIER, MATIES, MATIEST adj friendly or intimate ▷ n friend or fellow: usually used in direct address

MATFELON n knapweed

MATGRASS n widespread European grass

MATH same as ▶ maths

MATHESIS, MATHESES n learning or wisdom

MATHS n science concerned with the study of numbers

MATICO, -S n Peruvian shrub

MATIER ▶ matey

MATIES ▶ matey

MATIEST ▶ matey

MATILDA, -S n bushman's swag

MATILY ▶ matey

MATIN adj of or relating to matins

MATINAL same as ▶ matin

MATINEE, -S n afternoon performance in a theatre or cinema

MATINESS ▶ maty

MATING, -S ▶ mate

MATINS pl n early morning church service

MATIPO, -S n New Zealand shrub

MATJES same as ▶ maatjes

MATLESS ▶ mat

MATLO, -S same as ▶ matelot

MATLOW, -S same as ▶ matelot

MATOKE, -S n (in Uganda) the flesh of bananas, boiled and mashed as a food

MATOOKE, -S same as ▶ matoke

MATRASS n long-necked glass flask

MATRES ▶ mater

MATRIC, -S n matriculation

MATRICE same as ▶ matrix

MATRICES ▶ matrix

MATRICS ▶ matric

MATRIX, MATRICES, -ES n substance or situation in which something originates, takes form, or is enclosed

MATRON, -S n staid or dignified married woman

MATRONAL ▶ matron

MATRONLY adj (of a woman) middle-aged and plump

MATRONS ▶ matron

MATROSS n gunner's assistant

MATS ▶ mat

MATSAH, -S same as ▶ matzo

MATSURI, -S n Japanese religious ceremony

MATT, -S adj dull, not shiny ▷ n dull surface

MATTE, -S same as ▶ matt

MATTED ▶ mat

MATTEDLY ▶ mat

MATTER, -ED, -S n substance of which something is made ▷ vb be of importance

MATTERY adj containing pus

MATTES ▶ matte

MATTIE, -S n young herring

MATTIFY vb make (the skin of the face) less oily or shiny using cosmetics

MATTIN same as ▶ matin

MATTING, -S ▶ mat

MATTINS same as ▶ matins

MATTOCK, -S n large pick with one of its blade ends flattened for loosening soil

MATTOID, -S n person displaying eccentric behaviour

MATTRASS same as ▶ matrass

MATTRESS n large stuffed flat case, often with springs, used on or as a bed

MATTS ▶ matt

MATURATE vb mature or bring to maturity

MATURE, -D, -S, -ST,

MATURING adj fully developed or grown-up ▷ vb make or become mature

MATURELY ▶ mature

MATURER, -S ▶ mature

MATURES ▶ mature

MATUREST ▶ mature

MATURING ▶ mature

MATURITY n state of being mature

MATUTINE same as > matutinal

MATWEED, -S n grass found on moors

MATY same as ▶ matey

MATZA, -S same as ▶ matzo

MATZAH, -S same as ▶ matzo

MATZAS ▶ matza

MATZO, -S, -T n large very thin biscuit of unleavened bread

MATZOH, -S, MATZOTH same as ▶ matzo

MATZOON, -S n fermented milk product similar to yogurt

MATZOS ▶ matzo

MATZOT ▶ matzo

MATZOTH ▶ matzoh

MAUBY, MAUBIES n Caribbean bittersweet drink

MAUD, -S n shawl or rug of grey wool plaid

MAUDLIN adj foolishly or tearfully sentimental

MAUDS ▶ maud

MAUGER same as ▶ maugre

MAUGRE, -D, -S, MAUGRING prep in spite of ▷ vb behave spitefully towards

MAUL, -ED, -S vb handle roughly ▷ n loose scrum

MAULER ▶ maul

MAULERS pl n hands

MAULGRE, -D, -S same as ▶ maugre

MAULING, -S n act of mauling

MAULS ▶ maul

MAULVI, -S n expert in Islamic law

MAUMET, -S n false god

MAUMETRY ▶ maumet

MAUMETS ▶ maumet

MAUN dialect word for ▶ must

MAUND, -ED, -ING, -S n unit of weight used in Asia ▷ vb beg

MAUNDER, -S vb talk or act aimlessly or idly

MAUNDIES ▶ maundy

MAUNDING ▶ maund

MAUNDS ▶ maund

M

MAUNDY, MAUNDIES *n* ceremonial washing of the feet of poor people

MAUNGY, MAUNGIER *adj* (esp of a child) sulky, bad-tempered, or peevish

MAUNNA *vb* Scots term meaning must not

MAURI, -S *n* soul

MAUSIER ▶ mausy

MAUSIEST ▶ mausy

MAUSOLEA > mausoleum

MAUSY, MAUSIER, MAUSIEST *adj* foggy; misty

MAUT, -S *same as* **▶ mahout**

MAUTHER, -S *n* girl or young woman

MAUTS ▶ maut

MAUVAIS *adj* bad

MAUVAISE *feminine form of* **▶ mauvais**

MAUVE, -R, -S, -ST *adj* pale purple ▷ *n* any of various pale purple colours

MAUVEIN, -S *same as* **▶ mauveine**

MAUVEINE *same as* **▶ mauve**

MAUVEINS ▶ mauvein

MAUVER ▶ mauve

MAUVES ▶ mauve

MAUVEST ▶ mauve

MAUVIN, -S *same as* **▶ mauveine**

MAUVINE, -S *same as* **▶ mauveine**

MAUVINS ▶ mauvin

MAUZY, MAUZIER, MAUZIEST *adj* foggy; misty

MAVEN, -S *n* expert or connoisseur

MAVERICK *adj* independent and unorthodox ▷ *n* person of independent or unorthodox views ▷ *vb* take illegally

MAVIE, -S *n* type of thrush

MAVIN, -S *same as* **▶ maven**

MAVIS, -ES *n* song thrush

MAW, -ED, -ING, -S *n* animal's mouth, throat, or stomach ▷ *vb* eat or bite

MAWBOUND *adj* (of cattle) constipated

MAWED ▶ maw

MAWGER *adj* (of persons or animals) thin or lean

MAWING ▶ maw

MAWK, -S *n* maggot

MAWKIER ▶ mawky

MAWKIEST ▶ mawky

MAWKISH *adj* foolishly sentimental

MAWKS ▶ mawk

MAWKY, MAWKIER, MAWKIEST ▶ mawk

MAWMET, -S *same as* **▶ maumet**

MAWMETRY ▶ mawmet

MAWMETS ▶ mawmet

MAWN, -S *n* measure of capacity

MAWPUS, -ES *same as* **▶ mopus**

MAWR, -S *same as* **▶ mauther**

MAWS ▶ maw

MAWSEED, -S *n* poppy seed

MAWTHER, -S *same as* **▶ mauther**

MAX, -ED, -ES, -ING *vb* reach the full extent

> **Max** is a short form of **maximum**, and can also be a verb giving **maxed**, **maxes** and **maxing**. Another of the key words using X, and it can be extended to **maxi**.

MAXI, -S *adj* (of a garment) very long ▷ *n* type of large racing yacht

MAXIBOAT *n* large racing yacht

MAXICOAT *n* long coat

MAXILLA, -E, -S *n* upper jawbone of a vertebrate

MAXILLAR ▶ maxilla

MAXILLAS ▶ maxilla

MAXIM, -S *n* general truth or principle

MAXIMA ▶ maximum

MAXIMAL, -S *adj* maximum ▷ *n* maximum

MAXIMAND *n* something that is to be maximized

MAXIMIN, -S *n* highest of a set of minimum values

MAXIMISE *same as* **▶ maximize**

MAXIMIST ▶ maxim

MAXIMITE *n* type of explosive

MAXIMIZE *vb* increase to a maximum

MAXIMS ▶ maxim

MAXIMUM, MAXIMA, -S *n* greatest possible (amount or number) ▷ *adj* of, being, or showing a maximum or maximums

MAXIMUS *n* method rung on twelve bells

MAXING ▶ max

MAXIS ▶ maxi

MAXIXE, -S *n* Brazilian dance in duple time

MAXWELL, -S *n* cgs unit of magnetic flux

MAY, -ED, -ING, -S, MIGHTEST, MIGHTST, MOUGHT *vb* used as an auxiliary to express possibility, permission, opportunity, etc ▷ *vb* gather may (hawthorn)

MAYA, -S *n* illusion, esp the material world of the senses regarded as illusory

MAYAN ▶ maya

MAYAPPLE *n* American plant

MAYAS ▶ maya

MAYBE, -S *adv* perhaps, possibly ▷ *sentence substitute* possibly ▷ *n* possibility

MAYBIRD, -S *n* American songbird

MAYBUSH *n* flowering shrub

MAYDAY, -S *n* international radiotelephone distress signal

MAYED ▶ may

MAYEST *same as* **▶ mayst**

MAYFISH *n* type of N American fish

MAYFLY, MAYFLIES *n* short-lived aquatic insect

MAYHAP *archaic word for* **▶ perhaps**

MAYHEM, -S *n* violent destruction or confusion

MAYING, -S ▶ may

MAYO, -S *n* mayonnaise

MAYOR, -S *n* head of a municipality

MAYORAL ▶ mayor

MAYORESS *n* female mayor

MAYORS ▶ mayor

MAYOS ▶ mayo

MAYPOLE, -S *n* pole set up for dancing round on the first day of May to celebrate spring

MAYPOP, -S *n* American wild flower

MAYS ▶ may

MAYST *singular form of the present tense of* **▶ may**

MAYSTER, -S *same as* **▶ master**

MAYVIN, -S *same as* **▶ maven**

MAYWEED, -S *n* widespread Eurasian weedy plant

MAZAEDIA > mazaedium

MAZARD, -S *same as* **▶ mazer**

MAZARINE *n* blue colour

MAZE, -D, -S, MAZING *n* complex network of paths or lines

MAZEDLY *adv* in a bewildered way

MAZEFUL ▶ maze

MAZELIKE ▶ maze

MAZELTOV *interj* congratulations

MAZEMENT ▸ maze

MAZER, -S *n* large hardwood drinking bowl

MAZES ▸ maze

MAZEY *adj* dizzy

MAZHBI, -S *n* low-caste Sikh

MAZIER ▸ mazy

MAZIEST ▸ mazy

MAZILY ▸ mazy

MAZINESS ▸ mazy

MAZING ▸ maze

MAZOURKA *same as* ▸ mazurka

MAZOUT, -S *same as* ▸ mazut

MAZUMA, -S *n* money

MAZURKA, -S *n* lively Polish dance

MAZUT, -S *n* residue left after distillation of petrol

MAZY, MAZIER, MAZIEST *adj* of or like a maze

MAZZARD, -S *same as* ▸ mazard

MBAQANGA *n* style of Black popular music of urban South Africa

MBIRA, -S *n* African musical instrument

ME, -S *n* (in tonic sol-fa) third degree of any major scale ▸ *pron* refers to the speaker or writer

MEACOCK, -S *n* timid person

MEAD, -S *n* alcoholic drink made from honey

MEADOW, -S *n* piece of grassland

MEADOWY *adj* consisting of meadows

MEADS ▸ mead

MEAGER, -ER *same as* ▸ meagre

MEAGERLY ▸ meagre

MEAGRE, -R, -S, -ST *adj* scanty or insufficient ▸ *n* Mediterranean fish

MEAGRELY ▸ meagre

MEAGRER ▸ meagre

MEAGRES ▸ meagre

MEAGREST ▸ meagre

MEAL, -ED, -ING, -S *n* occasion when food is served and eaten ▸ *vb* cover with meal

MEALER, -S *n* person eating but not lodging at boarding house

MEALIE, -S *n* maize

MEALIER ▸ mealy

MEALIES ▸ mealie

MEALIEST ▸ mealy

MEALING ▸ meal

MEALLESS ▸ meal

MEALS ▸ meal

MEALTIME *n* time for meal

MEALWORM *n* larva of various beetles which feeds on meal, flour, and similar stored foods

MEALY, MEALIER, MEALIEST *adj* resembling meal

MEALYBUG *n* plant-eating homopterous insect

MEAN, -EST, -S, -T *vb* intend to convey or express ▸ *adj* miserly, ungenerous, or petty ▸ *n* middle point between two extremes

MEANDER, -S *vb* follow a winding course ▸ *n* winding course

MEANE, -D, -S *vb* moan

MEANER, -S ▸ mean

MEANES ▸ meane

MEANEST ▸ mean

MEANIE, -S *n* unkind or miserly person

MEANING, -S *n* what something means

MEANLY ▸ mean

MEANNESS ▸ mean

MEANS ▸ mean

MEANT ▸ mean

MEANTIME *n* intervening period ▸ *adv* meanwhile

MEANY *same as* ▸ meanie

MEARE, -S *same as* ▸ mere

MEARING *adj* forming boundary

MEASE, -D, -S, MEASING *vb* assuage

MEASLE, MEASLING *vb* infect with measles

MEASLED *adj* (of cattle, sheep, or pigs) infested with tapeworm larvae

MEASLES *n* infectious disease producing red spots

MEASLIER ▸ measly

MEASLING ▸ measle

MEASLY, MEASLIER *adj* meagre

MEASURE *n* size or quantity ▸ *vb* determine the size or quantity of

MEASURED *adj* slow and steady

MEASURER ▸ measure

MEASURES *pl n* rock strata that contain a particular type of deposit

MEAT, -S *n* animal flesh as food

MEATAL ▸ meatus

MEATAXE, -S *n* meat cleaver

MEATBALL *n* minced beef, shaped into a ball before cooking

MEATED *adj* fattened

MEATH, -S *same as* ▸ mead

MEATHE, -S *same as* ▸ mead

MEATHEAD *n* stupid person

MEATHES ▸ meathe

MEATHOOK *n* hook on which to hang meat

MEATHS ▸ meath

MEATIER ▸ meaty

MEATIEST ▸ meaty

MEATILY ▸ meaty

MEATLESS ▸ meat

MEATLOAF *n* chopped meat served in loaf-shaped mass

MEATMAN, MEATMEN *n* meat seller

MEATS ▸ meat

MEATUS, -ES *n* natural opening or channel

MEATY, MEATIER, MEATIEST *adj* (tasting) of or like meat

MEAWES *same as* ▸ mews

MEAZEL, -S *same as* ▸ mesel

MEBIBYTE *n* 2^{20} bytes

MEBOS, -ES *n* South African dish of dried apricots

MECCA, -S *n* place that attracts many visitors

MECH, -S *n* mechanic

MECHANIC *n* person skilled in repairing or operating machinery

MECHITZA *n* screen in synagogue separating men and women

MECHOUI, -S *n* Canadian dish of meat roasted on a spit

MECHS ▸ mech

MECK, -S *same as* ▸ maik

MECONATE *n* salt of meconic acid

MECONIC *adj* derived from poppies

MECONIN, -S *n* substance found in opium

MECONIUM *n* dark green mucoid material that forms the first faeces of a newborn infant

MED, -S *n* doctor

MEDACCA, -S *n* Japanese freshwater fish

MEDAKA, -S *same as* ▸ medacca

MEDAL, -ED, -ING, -LED, -S *n* piece of metal with an inscription etc, given as a reward or memento ▸ *vb* honour with a medal

MEDALET, -S *n* small medal

MEDALING ▸ medal

MEDALIST *same as* > medallist

MEDALLED ▸ medal

M

MEDALLIC ▶ medal
MEDALS ▶ medal
MEDCINAL *same as*
  > medicinal
MEDDLE, -D, -S *vb* interfere
  annoyingly
MEDDLER, -S ▶ meddle
MEDDLES ▶ meddle
MEDDLING ▶ meddle
MEDEVAC, -S *n* evacuation
  of casualties ▷ *vb* transport
  (a wounded or sick person)
  to hospital
MEDFLY, MEDFLIES *n*
  Mediterranean fruit fly
MEDIA, -E, -S *n* medium of
  cultivation, conveyance, or
  expression
MEDIACY *n* quality or state
  of being mediate
MEDIAD *adj* situated near
  the median line or plane of
  an organism
MEDIAE ▶ media
MEDIAL, -S *adj* of or in the
  middle ▷ *n* speech sound
  between being fortis and
  lenis
MEDIALLY ▶ medial
MEDIALS ▶ medial
MEDIAN, -S *n* middle (point
  or line) ▷ *adj* of, relating to,
  situated in, or directed
  towards the middle
MEDIANLY ▶ median
MEDIANS ▶ median
MEDIANT, -S *n* third degree
  of a major or minor scale
MEDIAS ▶ media
MEDIATE, -D, -S *vb*
  intervene in a dispute to
  bring about agreement ▷ *adj*
  occurring as a result of or
  dependent upon mediation
MEDIATOR ▶ mediate
MEDIC, -S *n* doctor or
  medical student
MEDICAID *n* US federal
  health insurance
  programme for persons on
  low income
MEDICAL, -S *adj* of the
  science of medicine ▷ *n*
  medical examination
MEDICANT *n* medicinal
  substance
MEDICARE *n* US federal
  health insurance
  programme for older people
MEDICATE *vb* treat with a
  medicinal substance
MEDICIDE *n* suicide assisted
  by doctor
MEDICINE *n* substance used
  to treat disease ▷ *vb* treat
  with medicine

MEDICK, -S *n* type of small
  leguminous plant with
  yellow or purple flowers
MEDICO, -S *n* doctor or
  medical student
MEDICS ▶ medic
MEDIEVAL *adj* of the Middle
  Ages ▷ *n* person living in
  medieval times
MEDIGAP, -S *n* private
  health insurance
MEDII ▶ medius
MEDINA, -S *n* ancient
  quarter of North African
  city
MEDIOCRE *adj* average in
  quality
MEDITATE *vb* reflect deeply,
  esp on spiritual matters
MEDIUM *adj* midway
  between extremes, average
  ▷ *n* middle state, degree, or
  condition
MEDIUMS *pl n* medium-
  dated gilt-edged securities
MEDIUS, MEDII, -ES *n*
  middle finger
MEDIVAC, -S *variant spelling
  of* ▶ medevac
MEDLAR, -S *n* apple-like
  fruit of a small tree
MEDLE, -D, -S, MEDLING
  same as ▶ meddle
MEDLEY, -S *n* miscellaneous
  mixture ▷ *adj* of, being, or
  relating to a mixture or
  variety
MEDLING ▶ medle
MEDRESA, -S *same as*
  ▶ madrasah
MEDRESE, -S *same as*
  ▶ madrasah
MEDS ▶ med
MEDULLA, -E, -S *n* marrow,
  pith, or inner tissue
MEDULLAR ▶ medulla
MEDULLAS ▶ medulla
MEDUSA, -E, -S *n* jellyfish
MEDUSAL ▶ medusa
MEDUSAN, -S ▶ medusa
MEDUSAS ▶ medusa
MEDUSOID *same as*
  ▶ medusa
MEE, -S *n* Malaysian noodle
  dish
MEED, -S *n* recompense
MEEK, -ER, -EST *adj*
  submissive or humble
MEEKEN, -ED, -S *vb* make
  meek
MEEKER ▶ meek
MEEKEST ▶ meek
MEEKLY ▶ meek
MEEKNESS ▶ meek
MEEMIE, -S *n* attack of
  hysteria

MEER, -ED, -ING, -S *same as*
  ▶ mere
MEERCAT, -S *same as*
  ▶ meerkat
MEERED ▶ meer
MEERING ▶ meer
MEERKAT, -S *n* S African
  mongoose
MEERS ▶ meer
MEES ▶ mee
MEET, -EST, -S *vb* come
  together (with) ▷ *n*
  meeting, esp a sports
  meeting ▷ *adj* fit or suitable
MEETER, -S ▶ meet
MEETEST ▶ meet
MEETING, -S ▶ meet
MEETLY ▶ meet
MEETNESS *n* properness
MEETS ▶ meet
MEFF, -S *dialect word for*
  ▶ tramp
MEG, -S *short for*
  ▶ megabyte
MEGA *adj* extremely good,
  great, or successful
MEGABAR, -S *n* unit of
  million bars
MEGABIT, -S *n* one million
  bits
MEGABUCK *n* million
  dollars
MEGABYTE *n* 2^{20} or 1 048 576
  bytes
MEGACITY *n* city with over
  10 million inhabitants
MEGADEAL *n* very good deal
MEGADOSE *n* very large
  dose, as of a medicine,
  vitamin, etc
MEGADYNE *n* unit of million
  dynes
MEGAFLOP *n* measure of a
  computer's processing
  speed
MEGAFOG, -S *n* amplified
  fog signal
MEGAHIT, -S *n* great success
MEGALITH *n* great stone,
  esp as part of a prehistoric
  monument
MEGALOPS *n* crab in larval
  stage
MEGAMALL *n* very large
  shopping mall
MEGAPLEX *n* large cinema
  complex
MEGAPOD, -S *same as*
  ▶ megapode
MEGAPODE *n* bird of
  Australia, New Guinea, and
  adjacent islands
MEGAPODS ▶ megapod
MEGARA ▶ megaron
MEGARAD, -S *n* unit of
  million rads

MEGARON, MEGARA, -S *n* tripartite rectangular room, found in Bronze Age Greece and Asia Minor

MEGASS, -ES *another name for* ▶ **bagasse**

MEGASSE *same as* ▶ **megass**

MEGASSES ▶ **megass**

MEGASTAR *n* very well-known personality in the entertainment business

MEGATON, -S *n* explosive power equal to that of one million tons of TNT

MEGAVOLT *n* one million volts

MEGAWATT *n* one million watts

MEGILLA, -S *same as* ▶ **megillah**

MEGILLAH *n* scroll of the Book of Esther, read on the festival of Purim

MEGILLAS ▶ **megilla**

MEGILP, -S *n* oil-painting medium of linseed oil with mastic varnish or turpentine

MEGILPH, -S *same as* ▶ **megilp**

MEGILPS ▶ **megilp**

MEGOHM, -S *n* one million ohms

MEGRIM *n* caprice

MEGRIMS *n* period of low spirits

MEGS ▶ **meg**

MEH *interj* expression of indifference or boredom

MEHNDI, -S *n* (esp in India) the practice of painting designs on the hands, feet, etc using henna

MEIKLE *adj* Scots word meaning large

MEIN, -ED, -ING, -S *Scots word for* ▶ **moan**

MEINEY, -S *same as* ▶ **meiny**

MEINIE *same as* ▶ **meiny**

MEINIES ▶ **meiny**

MEINING ▶ **mein**

MEINS ▶ **mein**

MEINT *same as* ▶ **ming**

MEINY, MEINIES *n* retinue or household

MEIOCYTE *n* cell that divides by meiosis to produce four haploid spores

MEIONITE *n* mineral containing silica

MEIOSIS, MEIOSES *n* type of cell division

MEIOTIC ▶ **meiosis**

MEISHI, -S *n* business card in Japan

MEISTER, -S *n* person who excels at a particular activity

MEITH, -S *n* landmark

MEJLIS, -ES *same as* ▶ **majlis**

MEKKA, -S *same as* ▶ **mecca**

MEL, -S *n* pure form of honey

MELA, -S *n* Indian cultural or religious fair or festival

MELAENA, -S *n* medical condition

MELAMED, MELAMDIM *n* Hebrew teacher

MELAMINE *n* colourless crystalline compound used in making synthetic resins

MELANGE, -S *n* mixture

MELANIAN *n* freshwater mollusc

MELANIC, -S *adj* relating to melanism or melanosis ▷ *n* darker form of creature

MELANIN, -S *n* dark pigment found in the hair, skin, and eyes

MELANISE *same as* ▶ **melanize**

MELANISM *same as* > **melanosis**

MELANIST ▶ **melanism**

MELANITE *n* black variety of andradite garnet

MELANIZE *vb* turn into melanin

MELANO, -S *n* person with extremely dark skin

MELANOID *adj* resembling melanin ▷ *n* dark substance formed in urine

MELANOMA *n* tumour composed of dark-coloured cells, occurring in some skin cancers

MELANOS ▶ **melano**

MELANOUS *adj* having a dark complexion and black hair

MELAS ▶ **mela**

MELBA *adj* relating to a type of dessert sauce or toast

MELD, -ED, -ING, -S *vb* merge or blend ▷ *n* act of melding

MELDER, -S ▶ **meld**

MELDING ▶ **meld**

MELDS ▶ **meld**

MELEE, -S *n* noisy confused fight or crowd

MELENA, -S *n* excrement stained by blood

MELIC, -S *adj* (of poetry, esp ancient Greek lyric poems) intended to be sung ▷ *n* type of grass

MELICK, -S *n* either of two pale green perennial grasses

MELICS ▶ **melic**

MELIK, -S *same as* ▶ **malik**

MELILITE *n* mineral containing calcium

MELILOT, -S *n* plant with small white or yellow fragrant flowers

MELINITE *n* high explosive made from picric acid

MELISMA, -S *n* expressive vocal phrase or passage consisting of several notes sung to one syllable

MELITTIN *n* main toxic component in bee venom

MELL, -ED, -ING, -S *vb* mix

MELLAY, -S *same as* ▶ **melee**

MELLED ▶ **mell**

MELLIFIC *adj* forming or producing honey

MELLING ▶ **mell**

MELLITE, -S *n* soft yellow mineral

MELLITIC ▶ **mellite**

MELLOW, -ED, -ER, -S *adj* soft, not harsh ▷ *vb* make or become mellow

MELLOWLY ▶ **mellow**

MELLOWS ▶ **mellow**

MELLOWY *adj* mellow

MELLS ▶ **mell**

MELODEON *n* small accordion

MELODIA, -S *same as* ▶ **melodica**

MELODIC *adj* of melody

MELODICA *n* type of flute

MELODICS *n* study of melody

MELODIES ▶ **melody**

MELODION *same as* ▶ **melodeon**

MELODISE *same as* ▶ **melodize**

MELODIST *n* composer of melodies

MELODIZE *vb* provide with a melody

MELODY, MELODIES *n* series of musical notes which make a tune

MELOID, -S *n* type of long-legged beetle

MELON, -S *n* large round juicy fruit with a hard rind

MELONIER ▶ **melony**

MELONS ▶ **melon**

MELONY, MELONIER *adj* like a melon

MELS ▶ **mel**

MELT, -ED, -S, MOLTEN *vb* (cause to) become liquid by heat ▷ *n* act or process of melting

MELTABLE ▶ **melt**

MELTAGE, -S *n* process or result of melting or the amount melted

MELTDOWN *n* (in a nuclear reactor) melting of the fuel

M

rods, with the possible release of radiation

MELTED ▸ melt

MELTEMI, -S n northerly wind in the northeast Mediterranean

MELTER, -S ▸ melt

MELTIER ▸ melty

MELTIEST ▸ melty

MELTING, -S ▸ melt

MELTITH, -S n meal

MELTON, -S n heavy smooth woollen fabric with a short nap, used esp for overcoats

MELTS ▸ melt

MELTY, MELTIER, MELTIEST adj tending to melt

MEM, -S n 13th letter in the Hebrew alphabet, transliterated as m

MEMBER, -S n individual making up a body or society ▷ adj (of a country or group) belonging to an organization or alliance

MEMBERED adj having members

MEMBERS ▸ member

MEMBRAL adj of limbs

MEMBRANE n thin flexible tissue in a plant or animal body

MEME, -S n idea or element of social behaviour

MEMENTO, -S n thing serving to remind, souvenir

MEMES ▸ meme

MEMETIC adj of or relating to a meme

MEMETICS n study of genetic transmission of culture

MEMO, -S n memorandum

MEMOIR n biography or historical account based on personal knowledge

MEMOIRS pl n collection of reminiscences about a period or series of events

MEMORIAL n something serving to commemorate a person or thing ▷ adj serving as a memorial

MEMORIES ▸ memory

MEMORISE same as ▸ memorize

MEMORIZE vb commit to memory

MEMORY, MEMORIES n ability to remember

MEMOS ▸ memo

MEMS ▸ mem

MEMSAHIB n (formerly, in India) term of respect used for a European married woman

MEN ▸ man

MENACE, -D, -S, MENACING n threat ▷ vb threaten, endanger

MENACER, -S ▸ menace

MENACES ▸ menace

MENACING ▸ menace

MENAD, -S same as ▸ maenad

MENAGE, -D, -S, MENAGING old form of ▸ manage

MENARCHE n first occurrence of menstruation

MENAZON, -S n type of insecticide

MEND, -ED, -S vb repair or patch ▷ n mended area

MENDABLE ▸ mend

MENDED ▸ mend

MENDER, -S ▸ mend

MENDIGO, -S n Spanish beggar or vagrant

MENDING, -S n something to be mended, esp clothes

MENDS ▸ mend

MENE, -D, -S, MENING Scots form of ▸ moan

MENEER, -S n S African title of address

MENES ▸ mene

MENFOLK pl n men collectively, esp the men of a particular family

MENFOLKS same as ▸ menfolk

MENG, -ED, -ING, -S vb mix

MENGE, -S same as ▸ meng

MENGED ▸ meng

MENGES ▸ menge

MENGING ▸ meng

MENGS ▸ meng

MENHADEN n marine N American fish, source of fishmeal, fertilizer, and oil

MENHIR, -S n single upright prehistoric stone

MENIAL, -S adj involving boring work of low status ▷ n person with a menial job

MENIALLY ▸ menial

MENIALS ▸ menial

MENILITE n liver opal

MENING ▸ mene

MENINX, MENINGES n one of three membranes that envelop the brain and spinal cord

MENISCAL ▸ meniscus

MENISCUS, MENISCI n curved surface of a liquid

MENO adv musical instruction indicating 'less'

MENOLOGY n ecclesiastical calendar of the months

MENOMINI same as ▸ menominee

MENOPOME n American salamander

MENORAH, -S n seven-branched candelabrum used as an emblem of Judaism

MENSA, -S n faint constellation in the S hemisphere

MENSAE n star of the mensa constellation

MENSAL adj monthly

MENSAS ▸ mensa

MENSCH, -EN, -ES n decent person

MENSCHY adj decent

MENSE, -D, MENSING vb grace

MENSEFUL adj gracious

MENSES n menstruation

MENSH, -ED, -ES, -ING vb mention

MENSHEN n Chinese door god

MENSHES ▸ mensh

MENSHING ▸ mensh

MENSING ▸ mense

MENSTRUA > menstruum

MENSUAL same as ▸ mensal

MENSURAL adj of or involving measure

MENSWEAR n clothing for men

MENT same as ▸ ming

MENTA ▸ mentum

MENTAL adj of, in, or done by the mind

MENTALLY ▸ mental

MENTEE, -S n person trained by mentor

MENTHENE n liquid obtained from menthol

MENTHOL, -S n organic compound found in peppermint

MENTION, -S vb refer to briefly ▷ n brief reference

MENTO, -S n Jamaican song

MENTOR, -ED, -S n adviser or guide ▷ vb act as a mentor to (someone)

MENTOS ▸ mento

MENTUM, MENTA n chin

MENU, -S n list of dishes to be served, or from which to order

MENUDO, -S n Mexican soup

MENUS ▸ menu

MENYIE, -S same as ▸ meinie

MEOU, -ED, -ING, -S same as ▸ meow

MEOW, -ED, -ING, -S vb (of a cat) to make a characteristic crying sound ▷ interj imitation of this sound

MEPHITIC *adj* poisonous

MEPHITIS *n* foul-smelling discharge

MERANTI, -S *n* wood from any of several Malaysian trees

MERC, -ES, -S *n* mercenary

MERCADO, -S *n* market

MERCAPTO *adj* of a particular chemical group

MERCAT, -S *Scots word for* ▸ market

MERCER, -S *n* dealer in textile fabrics and fine cloth

MERCERY ▸ mercer

MERCES ▸ merc

MERCH, -ES *n* merchandise

MERCHANT *n* person engaged in trade, wholesale trader ▸ *adj* of ships involved in commercial trade or their crews ▸ *vb* conduct trade in

MERCHES ▸ merch

MERCHET, -S *n* type of fine paid by feudal tenant to his lord

MERCHILD *n* mythical creature with upper body of child and lower body of fish

MERCIES ▸ mercy

MERCIFUL *adj* compassionate

MERCIFY *vb* show mercy to

MERCS ▸ merc

MERCURIC *adj* of or containing mercury in the divalent state

MERCURY *n* silvery liquid metal

MERCY, MERCIES *n* compassionate treatment

MERDE, -S *French word for* > excrement

MERE, -R, -S, -ST, MERING *adj* nothing more than ▸ *n* lake ▸ *vb* old form of survey

MERED *adj* forming a boundary

MEREL, -S *same as* ▸ meril

MERELL *same as* ▸ meril

MERELLS *same as* ▸ merils

MERELS ▸ merel

MERELY *adv* only

MERENGUE *n* type of lively dance music

MERER ▸ mere

MERES ▸ mere

MERESMAN, MERESMEN *n* man who decides on boundaries

MEREST ▸ mere

MERFOLK, -S *n* mermaids and mermen

MERGE, -D, -S *vb* combine or blend

MERGEE, -S *n* business taken over by merger

MERGENCE ▸ merge

MERGER, -S *n* combination of business firms into one

MERGES ▸ merge

MERGING, -S ▸ merge

MERGUEZ *n* heavily spiced N African sausage

MERI, -S *n* Māori war club

MERICARP *n* part of plant fruit

MERIDIAN *n* imaginary circle of the earth passing through both poles ▸ *adj* along or relating to a meridian

MERIL *n* counter used in merils

MERILS *n* old board game

MERIMAKE *n* merrymaking

MERING, -S ▸ mere

MERINGUE *n* baked mixture of egg whites and sugar

MERINO, -S *n* breed of sheep with fine soft wool

MERIS ▸ meri

MERISIS, MERISES *n* growth by division of cells

MERISM, -S *n* duplication of biological parts

MERISTEM *n* plant tissue responsible for growth

MERISTIC *adj* of or relating to the number of organs or parts in an animal or plant body

MERIT, -ED, -ING, -S *n* excellence or worth ▸ *vb* deserve

MERK, -S *n* old Scots coin

MERL, -S *same as* ▸ merle

MERLE, -S *adj* (of a dog, esp a collie) having a bluish-grey coat with speckles or streaks of black ▸ *n* dog with this coat

MERLIN, -S *n* small falcon

MERLING, -S *n* whiting

MERLINS ▸ merlin

MERLON, -S *n* solid upright section in a crenellated battlement

MERLOT, -S *n* type of black grape

MERLS ▸ merl

MERMAID, -S *n* imaginary sea creature with the upper part of a woman and the lower part of a fish

MERMAN, MERMEN *n* male counterpart of the mermaid

MEROGONY *n* development of embryo from part of ovum

MEROME, -S *same as* ▸ merosome

MERONYM, -S *n* part of something used to refer to the whole

MERONYMY ▸ meronym

MEROPIA, -S *n* partial blindness

MEROPIC ▸ meropia

MEROSOME *n* segment in body of worm

MERRIE *adj* (archaic) merry

MERRIER ▸ merry

MERRIES ▸ merry

MERRIEST ▸ merry

MERRILY ▸ merry

MERRY, MERRIER, MERRIES, MERRIEST *adj* cheerful or jolly ▸ *n* type of cherry

MERRYMAN, MERRYMEN *n* jester

MERSALYL *n* salt of sodium

MERSE, -S *n* low level ground by a river or shore

MERSION, -S *n* dipping in water

MERYCISM *n* rumination

MES ▸ me

MESA, -S *n* flat-topped hill found in arid regions

MESAIL, -S *n* visor

MESAL *same as* ▸ mesial

MESALLY ▸ mesal

MESARAIC *adj* of mesentery

MESARCH *adj* having the first-formed xylem surrounded by that formed later

MESAS ▸ mesa

MESCAL, -S *n* spineless globe-shaped cactus

MESCALIN *same as* > mescaline

MESCALS ▸ mescal

MESCLUM, -S *same as* ▸ mesclun

MESCLUN, -S *n* type of green salad

MESDAMES ▸ madam

MESE, -S *n* middle string on lyre

MESEEMS, MESEEMED *vb* it seems to me

MESEL, -S *n* archaic word for a person with leprosy

MESELED *adj* archaic word meaning leprosy

MESELS ▸ mesel

MESES ▸ mese

MESETA, -S *n* plateau in Spain

MESH, -ED, -ES *n* network or net ▸ *vb* (of gear teeth) engage ▸ *adj* made from mesh

MESHIER ▸ meshy

MESHIEST ▸ meshy

MESHING, -S ▸ mesh

MESHUGA *n* crazy person

MESHUGAH *same as* ▸ meshuga

M

MESHUGAS *adj* crazy
MESHUGGA *same as*
► **meshuga**
MESHUGGE *same as*
► **meshuga**
MESHWORK *n* network
MESHY, MESHIER,
MESHIEST ► **mesh**
MESIAD *adj* relating to or
situated at the middle or
centre
MESIAL *another word for*
► **medial**
MESIALLY ► **mesial**
MESIAN *same as* ► **mesial**
MESIC ► **meson**
MESMERIC *adj* holding
(someone) as if spellbound
MESNALTY *n* lands of a
mesne lord
MESNE, -S *adj* (in law)
intermediate or intervening
MESOCARP *n* middle layer
of the pericarp of a fruit,
such as the flesh of a peach
MESODERM *n* middle germ
layer of an animal embryo
MESOGLEA *n* gelatinous
material found in jellyfish
MESOLITE *n* type of mineral
MESOMERE *n* cell in
fertilized ovum
MESON, -S *n* elementary
atomic particle
MESONIC ► **meson**
MESONS ► **meson**
MESOPHYL *same as*
> **mesophyll**
MESOSAUR *n* extinct
aquatic reptile
MESOSOME *n* part of
bacterial cell
MESOTRON *same as* ► **meson**
MESOZOAN *n* type of
parasite
MESOZOIC *adj* of, denoting,
or relating to an era of
geological time
MESPIL, -S *n* type of N
American tree
MESPRISE *same as*
► **misprise**
MESPRIZE *same as*
► **misprise**
MESQUIN *adj* mean
MESQUINE *same as*
► **mesquin**
MESQUIT, -S *same as*
► **mesquite**
MESQUITE *n* small tree
whose sugary pods are used
as animal fodder
MESQUITS ► **mesquit**
MESS, -ED, -ES, -ING *n*
untidy or dirty confusion
▷ *vb* muddle or dirty

MESSAGE, -D, -S *n*
communication sent ▷ *vb*
send as a message
MESSAN, -S *Scots word for*
► **dog**
MESSED ► **mess**
MESSES ► **mess**
MESSIAH, -S *n* exceptional
or hoped for liberator
MESSIAS *same as* ► **messiah**
MESSIER ► **messy**
MESSIEST ► **messy**
MESSILY ► **messy**
MESSING ► **mess**
MESSMAN, MESSMEN *n*
sailor working in ship's mess
MESSMATE *n* person with
whom one shares meals in a
mess, esp in the army
MESSMEN ► **messman**
MESSUAGE *n* house
together with outbuildings
and adjacent land
MESSY, MESSIER,
MESSIEST *adj* dirty,
confused, or untidy
MESTER, -S *n* master: used
as a term of address for a
man who is the head of a
house
MESTESO, -S *n* Spanish
music genre
MESTO *adj* sad
MESTOM, -S *same as*
► **mestome**
MESTOME, -S *n* conducting
tissue associated with
parenchyma
MESTOMS ► **mestom**
MET, -S *n* meteorology
META *adj* in a self-parodying
style
METABOLY *n* ability of some
cells, esp protozoans, to
alter their shape
METADATA *n* data which
accompanies digital data
METAFILE *n* (in computing)
file format that can hold
other types of file
METAGE, -S *n* official
measuring of weight or
contents
METAIRIE *n* area of land on
which farmer pays rent in
kind
METAL, -ED, -ING, -LED, -S *n*
malleable element able to
conduct heat and electricity
▷ *adj* made of metal ▷ *vb* fit
or cover with metal
METALISE *same as*
> **metallize**
METALIST *same as*
> **metallist**
METALIZE *same as* > **metallize**

METALLED ► **metal**
METALLIC *adj* of or
consisting of metal ▷ *n*
something metallic
METALLY *adj* like metal
METALS ► **metal**
METAMALE *n* sterile male
organism
METAMER, -S *n* any of two
or more isomeric
compounds exhibiting
metamerism
METAMERE *n* body segmen
of invertebrates
METAMERS ► **metamer**
METAMICT *adj* of the
amorphous state of a
substance that has lost its
crystalline structure
METANOIA *n* repentance
METAPHOR *n* type of figure
of speech
METAPLOT > **metapelet**
METASOMA *n* posterior par
of an arachnid's abdomen
(opisthosoma) that never
carries appendages
METATAG, -S *n* element of
HTML code used by search
engines to index pages
METATE, -S *n* stone for
grinding grain on
METAYAGE *n* farming in
which rent is paid in kind
METAYER, -S *n* farmer who
pays rent in kind
METAZOA ► **metazoan**
METAZOAL ► **metazoan**
METAZOAN, METAZOA *n*
animal having a body
composed of many cells
▷ *adj* of the metazoans
METAZOIC *adj* relating to
the group of multicellular
animals that includes all
animals except sponges
METAZOON *same as*
► **metazoan**
METCAST, -S *n* weather
forecast
METE, -D, -S, METING *vb*
deal out as punishment ▷ *n*
measure
METEOR, -S *n* small
fast-moving heavenly body
METEORIC *adj* of a meteor
METEORS ► **meteor**
METEPA, -S *n* type of
pesticide
METER, -ED, -ING, -S *same as*
► **metre**
METERAGE *n* act of
measuring
METERED ► **meter**
METERING ► **meter**
METERS ► **meter**

METES ▸ **mete**

METEWAND *same as* ▸ **metestick**

METEYARD *same as* ▸ **metestick**

METH *n* methylated spirits

METHADON *same as* ▸ **methadone**

METHANAL *n* colourless poisonous irritating gas

METHANE, -S *n* colourless inflammable gas

METHANOL *n* colourless poisonous liquid used as a solvent and fuel

METHINK *same as* ▸ **methinks**

METHINKS *vb* it seems to me

METHO, -S *n* methylated spirits

METHOD, -S *n* way or manner

METHODIC *same as* ▸ **method**

METHODS ▸ **method**

METHOS ▸ **metho**

METHOXY *n* steroid drug

METHOXYL *n* chemical compound of methyl and hydroxyl

METHS *n* methylated spirits

METHYL, -S *n* compound containing a saturated hydrocarbon group of atoms

METHYLAL *n* colourless volatile flammable liquid

METHYLIC ▸ **methyl**

METHYLS ▸ **methyl**

METHYSIS, METHYSES *n* drunkenness

METIC *n* (in ancient Greece) alien having some rights of citizenship

METICA, -S *n* former proposed monetary unit of Mozambique

METICAL, METICAIS, -S *n* money unit in Mozambique

METICAS ▸ **metica**

METICS ▸ **metic**

METIER, -S *n* profession or trade

METIF, -S *n* person of mixed ancestry

METING ▸ **mete**

METIS *n* person of mixed ancestry

METISSE, -S ▸ **metis**

METOL, -S *n* organic substance used as a photographic developer

METONYM, -S *n* word used in a metonymy

METONYMY *n* figure of speech in which one thing is

replaced by another associated with it

METOPE, METOPAE, -S *n* square space between two triglyphs in a Doric frieze

METOPIC *adj* of or relating to the forehead

METOPISM *n* congenital disfigurement of forehead

METOPON, -S *n* painkilling drug

METOPRYL *n* type of anaesthetic

METRAZOL *n* drug used to improve blood circulation

METRE, -D, -S, METRING *n* unit of length ▹ *vb* express in poetry

METRIC *adj* of the decimal system of weights and measures based on the metre

METRICAL *adj* of measurement

METRICS *n* art of using poetic metre

METRIFY *vb* render into poetic metre

METRING ▸ **metre**

METRIST, -S *n* person skilled in the use of poetic metre

METRITIS *n* inflammation of the uterus

METRO, -S *n* underground railway system, esp in Paris

METS ▸ **met**

METTLE, -S *n* courage or spirit

METTLED *adj* spirited, courageous, or valiant

METTLES ▸ **mettle**

METUMP, -S *n* band for carrying a load or burden

MEU, -S *another name for* ▸ **spignel**

MEUNIERE *adj* cooked in butter with lemon juice and parsley

MEUS ▸ **meu**

MEUSE, -D, -S, MEUSING *n* gap through which an animal passed ▹ *vb* go through this gap

MEVE, -D, -S, MEVING *same as* ▸ **move**

MEVROU, -S *n* S African title of address

MEW, -ED, -ING *n* cry of a cat ▹ *vb* utter this cry

MEWL, -ED, -ING, -S *vb* (esp of a baby) to cry weakly ▹ *n* weak or whimpering cry

MEWLER, -S ▸ **mewl**

MEWLING ▸ **mewl**

MEWLS ▸ **mewl**

MEWS, -ED, -ES, -ING *same as* ▸ **meuse**

MEYNT ▸ **ming**

MEZAIL, -S *same as* ▸ **mesail**

MEZCAL, -S *variant spelling of* ▸ **mescal**

MEZE, -S *n* type of hors d'oeuvre

MEZEREON *same as* ▸ **mezereum**

MEZEREUM *n* dried bark of certain shrubs, formerly used to treat arthritis

MEZES ▸ **meze**

MEZQUIT, -S *same as* ▸ **mesquite**

A **mezquit** is a kind of American tree, and makes a great bonus to play. Remember also that it takes an E to form the variant spelling **mezquite**.

MEZQUITE *same as* ▸ **mesquite**

MEZQUITS ▸ **mezquit**

MEZUZA, -S *same as* ▸ **mezuzah**

MEZUZAH, -S, MEZUZOT, MEZUZOTH *n* piece of parchment inscribed with biblical passages

MEZUZAS ▸ **mezuza**

MEZUZOT ▸ **mezuzah**

MEZUZOTH ▸ **mezuzah**

MEZZ *same as* ▸ **mezzanine**

MEZZE, -S *same as* ▸ **meze**

MEZZO, -S *adv* moderately ▹ *n* singer with voice between soprano and contralto

MGANGA, -S *n* witch doctor

MHO, -S *former name for* ▸ **siemens**

MHORR, -S *n* African gazelle

MHOS ▸ **mho**

MI, -S *n* (in tonic sol-fa) the third degree of any major scale

MIAOU, -ED, -ING, -S *same as* ▸ **meow**

MIAOW, -ED, -ING, -S *same as* ▸ **meow**

MIASM, -S *same as* ▸ **miasma**

MIASMA, -S, -TA *n* unwholesome or foreboding atmosphere

MIASMAL ▸ **miasma**

MIASMAS ▸ **miasma**

MIASMATA ▸ **miasma**

MIASMIC ▸ **miasma**

MIASMOUS ▸ **miasma**

MIASMS ▸ **miasm**

MIAUL, -ED, -ING, -S *same as* ▸ **meow**

MIB, -S *n* marble used in games

M

MIBUNA, -S n type of Japanese leafy vegetable

MIC, -S n microphone

MICA, -S n glasslike mineral used as an electrical insulator

MICATE, -D, -S, MICATING vb add mica to

MICAWBER n person who idles and trusts to fortune

MICE ▶ mouse

MICELL, -S same as ▶ micelle

MICELLA, -E, -S same as ▶ micelle

MICELLAR ▶ micelle

MICELLAS ▶ micella

MICELLE, -S n charged aggregate of molecules of colloidal size in a solution

MICELLS ▶ micell

MICH, -ED, -ES same as ▶ mitch

MICHAEL, -S n as in take the michael teasing

MICHE same as ▶ mich

MICHED ▶ mich

MICHER, -S ▶ mich

MICHES ▶ mich

MICHIGAN US name for > newmarket

MICHING, -S ▶ mich

MICHT, -S n Scots word for might

MICKERY n waterhole, esp in a dry riverbed

MICKEY, -S n young bull ▷ vb drug a person's drink

MICKIES ▶ micky

MICKLE, -R, -S, -ST adj large or abundant ▷ adv much ▷ n great amount

MICKY, MICKIES same as ▶ mickey

MICO, -S n marmoset

MICRA ▶ micron

MICRIFY vb make very small

MICRO, -S n small computer

MICROBAR n millionth of a bar of pressure

MICROBE, -S n minute organism, esp one causing disease

MICROBIC ▶ microbe

MICROBUS n small bus

MICROCAP adj (of investments) involving very small amounts of capital

MICROCAR n small car

MICRODOT n photographic copy of a document reduced to pinhead size

MICROHM, -S n millionth of an ohm

MICROJET n light jet-propelled aircraft

MICROLUX n millionth of a lux

MICROMHO n millionth of a mho

MICRON, MICRA, -S n unit of length equal to one millionth of a metre

MICROS ▶ micro

MICRURGY n manipulation and examination of single cells under a microscope

MICS ▶ mic

MICTION, -S n urination

MID, -S adj intermediate, middle ▷ n middle ▷ prep amid

MIDAIR, -S n some point above ground level, in the air

MIDBAND adj using a range of frequencies between narrowband and broadband

MIDBRAIN n part of the brain that develops from the middle portion of the embryonic neural tube

MIDCALF n garment reaching to middle of the calf

MIDCAP adj (of investments) involving medium-sized amounts of capital

MIDCULT, -S n middlebrow culture

MIDDAY, -S n noon

MIDDEN, -S n rubbish heap

MIDDEST adj in middle

MIDDIE same as ▶ middy

MIDDIES ▶ middy

MIDDLE, -D, -S adj equidistant from two extremes ▷ n middle point or part ▷ vb place in the middle

MIDDLER, -S n pupil in middle years at school

MIDDLES ▶ middle

MIDDLING adj mediocre ▷ adv moderately

MIDDY, MIDDIES n middle-sized glass of beer

MIDFIELD n area between the two opposing defences

MIDGE, -S n small mosquito-like insect

MIDGET, -S n very small thing ▷ adj much smaller than normal

MIDGIE, -S n informal word for a midge

MIDGIER ▶ midgy

MIDGIES ▶ midgie

MIDGIEST ▶ midgy

MIDGUT, -S n middle part of the digestive tract

MIDGY, MIDGIER, MIDGIEST adj characterized by midges

MIDI, -S adj (of a skirt, coat, etc) reaching to below the knee or midcalf ▷ n skirt, coat, etc reaching to below the knee or midcalf

MIDIBUS n medium-sized bus

MIDIRON, -S n golf club used for medium-length approach shots

MIDIS ▶ midi

MIDLAND, -S n middle part of a country

MIDLEG, -S n middle of leg

MIDLIFE, MIDLIVES n middle age

MIDLIFER n middle-aged person

MIDLINE, -S n line at middle of something

MIDLIST, -S n books in publisher's range that sell reasonably well

MIDLIVES ▶ midlife

MIDMONTH n middle of month

MIDMOST, -S adv in the middle or midst ▷ n the middle or midst

MIDNIGHT n twelve o'clock at night

MIDNOON, -S n noon

MIDPAY adj paying more than an unskilled job but less than a high-income one

MIDPOINT n point on a line equally distant from either end

MIDRANGE n part of loudspeaker

MIDRASH n homily on a Jewish scriptural passage

MIDRIB, -S n main vein of a leaf

MIDRIFF, -S n middle part of the body

MIDS ▶ mid

MIDSHIP adj in, of, or relating to the middle of a vessel ▷ n middle of a vessel

MIDSHIPS same as > amidships

MIDSHORE adj between the inshore and the offshore

MIDSIZE adj medium-sized

MIDSIZED same as ▶ midsize

MIDSOLE, -S n layer between the inner and the outer sole of a shoe

MIDSPACE n area in middle of space

MIDST, -S n middle

MIDSTORY n level of forest trees between smallest and tallest

MIDSTS ▶ midst

MIDTERM, -S n middle of a term in a school, university, etc

MIDTHIGH n garment reaching to the middle of the thigh

MIDTOWN, -S n centre of a town

MIDWATCH n naval watch period beginning at midnight

MIDWATER n middle part of a body of water

MIDWAY, -S adv halfway ▷ adj in or at the middle of the distance ▷ n place in a fair, carnival, etc, where sideshows are located

MIDWEEK, -S n middle of the week

MIDWIFE, -D, -S, MIDWIVES n trained person who assists at childbirth ▷ vb act as midwife

MIDWIVE, -D vb act as midwife

MIDWIVES ▶ midwife

MIDYEAR, -S n middle of the year

MIELIE, -S same as ▶ mealie

MIEN, -S n person's bearing, demeanour, or appearance

MIEVE, -D, -S, MIEVING same as ▶ move

MIFF, -ED, -ING, -S vb take offence or offend ▷ n petulant mood

MIFFIER ▶ miffy

MIFFIEST ▶ miffy

MIFFILY ▶ miffy

MIFFING ▶ miff

MIFFS ▶ miff

MIFFY, MIFFIER, MIFFIEST adj easily upset

MIFTY same as ▶ miffy

MIG, -S n marble used in games

MIGAWD interj interjection used to express surprise

MIGG, -S same as ▶ mig

MIGGLE, -S n US word for playing marble

MIGGS ▶ migg

MIGHT, -S n physical strength

MIGHTEST ▶ may

MIGHTFUL same as ▶ mighty

MIGHTIER ▶ mighty

MIGHTILY adv to a great extent, amount, or degree

MIGHTS ▶ might

MIGHTST ▶ may

MIGHTY, MIGHTIER adj powerful ▷ adv very

MIGNON, -S adj small and pretty ▷ n tender boneless cut of meat

MIGNONNE ▶ mignon

MIGNONS ▶ mignon

MIGRAINE n severe headache, often with nausea and visual disturbances

MIGRANT, -S n person or animal that moves from one place to another ▷ adj moving from one place to another

MIGRATE, -D, -S vb move from one place to settle in another

MIGRATOR ▶ migrate

MIGS ▶ mig

MIHA, -S n young fern frond which has not yet opened

MIHI, -ED, -ING, -S n Māori ceremonial greeting ▷ vb greet

MIHRAB, -S n niche in a mosque showing the direction of Mecca

MIJNHEER same as ▶ mynheer

MIKADO, -S n Japanese emperor

MIKE, -D, -S, MIKING n microphone ▷ vb supply with a microphone

MIKRON, MIKRA, -S same as ▶ micron

MIKVA, -S n place for ritual bathing by Orthodox Jews

MIKVAH, -S, MIKVOTH n pool used for ritual purification

MIKVAS ▶ mikva

MIKVEH, -S, MIKVOS, MIKVOT same as ▶ mikvah

MIKVOTH ▶ mikvah

MIL, -S n unit of length equal to one thousandth of an inch

MILADI, -S same as ▶ milady

MILADIES ▶ milady

MILADIS ▶ miladi

MILADY, MILADIES n (formerly) a continental title for an English gentlewoman

MILAGE, -S same as ▶ mileage

MILCH adj (of a cow) giving milk

MILCHIG same as ▶ milchik

MILCHIK adj containing or used in the preparation of milk products

MILD, -ED, -ER, -EST, -ING, -S adj not strongly flavoured ▷ n dark beer flavoured with fewer hops than bitter ▷ vb become gentle

MILDEN, -ED, -S vb make or become mild or milder

MILDER ▶ mild

MILDEST ▶ mild

MILDEW, -ED, -S same as ▶ mould

MILDEWY adj covered with mildew

MILDING ▶ mild

MILDISH adj rather mild

MILDLY ▶ mild

MILDNESS ▶ mild

MILDS ▶ mild

MILE, -S n unit of length equal to 1760 yards or 1.609 kilometres

MILEAGE, -S n distance travelled in miles

MILEPOST n signpost that shows the distance in miles to or from a place

MILER, -S n athlete, horse, etc, that specializes in races of one mile

MILES ▶ mile

MILESIAN adj Irish

MILESIMO n Spanish word meaning thousandth

MILFOIL, -S same as ▶ yarrow

MILIA ▶ milium

MILIARIA n acute itching eruption of the skin, caused by blockage of the sweat glands

MILIARY adj resembling or relating to millet seeds

MILIEU, -S, -X n environment or surroundings

MILING, -S n activity of running one mile

MILITANT adj aggressive or vigorous in support of a cause ▷ n militant person

MILITAR same as ▶ military

MILITARY adj of or for soldiers, armies, or war ▷ n armed services

MILITATE vb have a strong influence or effect

MILITIA, -S n military force of trained citizens

MILIUM, MILIA n pimple

MILK, -ED, -ING, -S n white fluid produced by female mammals to feed their young ▷ vb draw milk from

MILKEN adj of or like milk

MILKER, -S n cow, goat, etc, that yields milk

MILKFISH n type of large silvery tropical food and game fish

MILKIER ▶ milky

MILKIEST ▶ milky

M

MILKILY ► milky
MILKING, -S ► milk
MILKLESS ► milk
MILKLIKE ► milk
MILKMAID n (esp in former times) woman who milks cows
MILKMAN, MILKMEN n man who delivers milk to people's houses
MILKO, -S informal name for ► milkman
MILKS ► milk
MILKSHED n area where milk is produced
MILKSOP, -S n feeble man
MILKWEED n monarch butterfly
MILKWOOD n tree producing latex
MILKWORT n plant with small flowers
MILKY, MILKIER, MILKIEST adj of or like milk
MILL, -S n factory ▷ vb grind, press, or process in or as if in a mill
MILLABLE ► mill
MILLAGE, -S adj American tax rate calculated in thousandths per dollar
MILLCAKE n food for livestock
MILLDAM, -S n dam built to raise the water level to turn a millwheel
MILLE, -S French word for ► thousand
MILLED adj crushed or ground in a mill
MILLEPED same as > millepede
MILLER, -S n person who works in a mill
MILLES ► mille
MILLET, -S n type of cereal grass
MILLHAND n person who works in a mill
MILLIAMP n one thousandth of an ampere
MILLIARD n one thousand millions
MILLIARE n ancient Roman unit of distance
MILLIARY adj relating to or marking a distance equal to an ancient Roman mile of a thousand paces
MILLIBAR n unit of atmospheric pressure
MILLIE, -S n insulting name for a young working-class woman
MILLIEME n Tunisian monetary unit worth one thousandth of a dinar

MILLIER, -S n metric weight of million grams
MILLIES ► millie
MILLIGAL n unit of gravity
MILLILUX n thousandth of lux
MILLIME, -S same as ► millieme
MILLIMHO n thousandth of mho
MILLINE, -S n measurement of advertising space
MILLINER n maker or seller of women's hats
MILLINES ► milline
MILLING, -S n act or process of grinding, cutting, pressing, or crushing in a mill
MILLIOHM n thousandth of ohm
MILLION, -S n one thousand thousands
MILLIPED same as > millipede
MILLIREM n unit of radiation
MILLPOND n pool which provides water to turn a millwheel
MILLRACE n current of water that turns a millwheel
MILLRIND n iron support fitted across an upper millstone
MILLRUN, -S same as ► millrace
MILLS ► mill
MILLTAIL n channel carrying water away from mill
MILLWORK n work done in a mill
MILNEB, -S n type of pesticide
MILO, -S n variety of sorghum with heads of yellow or pinkish seeds
MILOR, -S same as ► milord
MILORD, -S n (formerly) a continental title used for an English gentleman
MILORS ► milor
MILOS ► milo
MILPA, -S n form of subsistence agriculture in Mexico
MILREIS n former monetary unit of Portugal and Brazil
MILS ► mil
MILSEY, -S n milk strainer
MILT, -ED, -ING, -S n reproductive fluid of male fish ▷ vb fertilize (the roe of a female fish) with milt
MILTER, -S n male fish that is mature and ready to breed
MILTIER ► milty

MILTIEST ► milty
MILTING ► milt
MILTONIA n tropical American orchid
MILTS ► milt
MILTY, MILTIER, MILTIEST adj full of milt
MILTZ, -ES same as ► milt
MILVINE adj of kites and related birds
MIM, -MER, -MEST adj prim, modest, or demure
MIMBAR, -S n pulpit in mosque
MIME, -D, -S, MIMING n acting without the use of words ▷ vb act in mime
MIMEO, -ED, -ING, -S vb mimeograph
MIMER, -S ► mime
MIMES ► mime
MIMESIS, MIMESES n imitative representation of nature or human behaviour
MIMESTER ► mime
MIMETIC adj imitating or representing something
MIMETITE n rare secondary mineral
MIMIC, -KED, -S vb imitate (a person or manner), esp for satirical effect ▷ n person or animal that is good at mimicking ▷ adj of, relating to, or using mimicry
MIMICAL ► mimic
MIMICKED ► mimic
MIMICKER ► mimic
MIMICRY n act or art of copying or imitating closely
MIMICS ► mimic
MIMING ► mime
MIMMER ► mim
MIMMEST ► mim
MIMMICK, -S same as ► minnick
MIMOSA, -E, -S n shrub with fluffy yellow flowers and sensitive leaves
MIMSEY same as ► mimsy
MIMSY, MIMSIER, MIMSIEST adj prim, underwhelming, and ineffectual
MIMULUS n plants cultivated for their yellow or red flowers
MINA, -E, -S n ancient unit of weight and money, used in Asia Minor
MINABLE ► mine
MINACITY ► minacious
MINAE ► mina
MINAR, -S n tower
MINARET, -S n tall slender tower of a mosque

MINARS ▸ minar

MINAS ▸ mina

MINATORY adj threatening or menacing

MINBAR, -S same as ▸ **mimbar**

MINCE, -D, -S vb cut or grind into very small pieces ▷ n minced meat

MINCER, -S n machine for mincing meat

MINCES ▸ mince

MINCEUR adj (of food) low-fat

MINCIER ▸ mincy

MINCIEST ▸ mincy

MINCING adj affectedly elegant in manner

MINCY, MINCIER, MINCIEST adj excessively particular or fussy

MIND, -S n thinking faculties ▷ vb take offence at

MINDED adj having an inclination as specified

MINDEDLY adv in the manner of a person with the kind of mind specified

MINDER, -S n aide or bodyguard

MINDFUL adj heedful

MINDING, -S ▸ mind

MINDLESS adj stupid

MINDS ▸ mind

MINDSET, -S n ideas and attitudes with which a person approaches a situation

MINE, -D, -S pron belonging to me ▷ n deep hole for digging out coal, ores, etc ▷ vb dig for minerals

MINEABLE ▸ mine

MINED ▸ mine

MINEOLA, -S same as ▸ **minneola**

MINER, -S n person who works in a mine

MINERAL, -S n naturally occurring inorganic substance, such as metal ▷ adj of, containing, or like minerals

MINERS ▸ miner

MINES ▸ mine

MINETTE, -S n type of rock

MINEVER, -S same as ▸ **miniver**

MING, MEYNT, -ED, -S vb mix

MINGER, -S n insulting word for an unattractive person

MINGIER ▸ mingy

MINGIEST ▸ mingy

MINGILY adv in a miserly manner

MINGING adj unattractive or unpleasant

MINGLE, -D, -S, MINGLING vb mix or blend

MINGLER, -S ▸ mingle

MINGLES ▸ mingle

MINGLING ▸ mingle

MINGS ▸ ming

MINGY, MINGIER, MINGIEST adj miserly

MINI, -S same as > **minidress**

MINIATE, -D, -S vb paint with minium

MINIBAR, -S n selection of drinks and confectionery provided in a hotel room

MINIBIKE n light motorcycle

MINIBUS n small bus

MINICAB, -S n ordinary car used as a taxi

MINICAM, -S n portable television camera

MINICAMP n period spent together in isolation by sports team

MINICAMS ▸ minicam

MINICAR, -S n small car

MINICOM, -S n device allowing typed telephone messages to be sent and received

MINIDISC n (esp formerly) small recordable compact disc

MINIDISH n small parabolic aerial for reception or transmission to a communications satellite

MINIDISK same as ▸ **minidisc**

MINIER ▸ miny

MINIEST ▸ miny

MINIFY, MINIFIED, MINIFIES vb minimize or lessen the size or importance of (something)

MINIGOLF n putting game played via various obstacles

MINIKIN, -S n small, dainty, or affected person or thing ▷ adj dainty, prim, or affected

MINILAB, -S n equipment for processing photographic film

MINIM, -S n note half the length of a semibreve ▷ adj very small

MINIMA ▸ minimum

MINIMAL, -S adj minimum ▷ n small surfboard

MINIMART n convenience store

MINIMAX n lowest of a set of maximum values ▷ vb make maximum as low as possible

MINIMENT same as ▸ **muniment**

MINIMILL n small mill

MINIMISE same as ▸ **minimize**

MINIMISM n desire to reduce to minimum

MINIMIST ▸ minimism

MINIMIZE vb reduce to a minimum

MINIMOTO n reduced-size replica motorcycle used for racing

MINIMS ▸ minim

MINIMUM, MINIMA, -S n least possible (amount or number) ▷ adj of, being, or showing a minimum or minimums

MINIMUS adj youngest: used after the surname of a schoolboy with elder brothers at the same school

MINING, -S n act, process, or industry of extracting coal or ores from the earth

MINION, -S n servile assistant ▷ adj dainty, pretty, or elegant

MINIPARK n small park

MINIS ▸ mini

MINISH, -ED, -ES vb diminish

MINISKI, -S n short ski

MINISODE n episode of a television series shortened for broadcast on the internet

MINISTER n head of a government department ▷ vb attend to the needs of

MINISTRY n profession or duties of a member of the clergy

MINIUM, -S n bright red poisonous insoluble oxide of lead

MINIVAN, -S n small van, esp one with seats in the back for carrying passengers

MINIVER, -S n white fur, used in ceremonial costumes

MINIVET, -S n brightly coloured tropical Asian cuckoo shrike

MINK, -S n stoat-like animal

MINKE, -S n as in **minke whale** type of small whalebone whale or rorqual

MINKS ▸ mink

MINNEOLA n juicy citrus fruit that is a cross between a tangerine and a grapefruit

MINNICK, -S vb behave in fussy way

MINNIE, -S n mother

MINNOCK, -S same as ▸ **minnick**

MINNOW, -S n small freshwater fish

MINNY same as ▸ **minnie**

MINO, -S same as ▸ **mynah**

MINOR, -ED, -ING, -S adj lesser ▷ n person regarded legally as a child ▷ vb take a minor

MINORCA, -S n breed of light domestic fowl

MINORED ▸ **minor**

MINORING ▸ **minor**

MINORITY n lesser number

MINORS ▸ **minor**

MINOS ▸ **mino**

MINOTAUR n as in **minotaur beetle** kind of dung-beetle

MINSHUKU n guesthouse in Japan

MINSTER, -S n cathedral or large church

MINSTREL n medieval singer or musician

MINT, -ED, -ING, -S n plant with aromatic leaves ▷ vb make (coins)

MINTAGE, -S n process of minting

MINTED ▸ **mint**

MINTER, -S ▸ **mint**

MINTIER ▸ **minty**

MINTIEST ▸ **minty**

MINTING ▸ **mint**

MINTLIKE adj like mint

MINTS ▸ **mint**

MINTY, MINTIER, MINTIEST ▸ **mint**

MINUEND, -S n number from which another number is to be subtracted

MINUET, -ED, -S n stately dance ▷ vb dance the minuet

MINUS, -ES adj indicating subtraction ▷ n sign (-) denoting subtraction or a number less than zero ▷ prep reduced by the subtraction of

MINUTE, -D, -R, -ST, MINUTING n 60th part of an hour or degree ▷ vb record in the minutes ▷ adj very small

MINUTELY adv in great detail ▷ adj occurring every minute

MINUTER ▸ **minute**

MINUTES pl n official record of the proceedings of a meeting or conference

MINUTEST ▸ **minute**

MINUTIA singular noun of ▸ **minutiae**

MINUTIAE pl n trifling or precise details

MINUTIAL ▸ **minutiae**

MINUTING ▸ **minute**

MINX, -ES n bold girl

MINXISH ▸ **minx**

MINY, MINIER, MINIEST adj of or like mines

MINYAN, -IM, -S n number of persons required by Jewish law to be present for a religious service

MIOCENE adj of, denoting, or formed in the fourth epoch of the Tertiary period

MIOMBO, -S n (in E Africa) a dry wooded area with sparse deciduous growth

MIOSIS, MIOSES, -ES n excessive contraction of the pupil of the eye

MIOTIC, -S ▸ **miosis**

MIPS n unit used to express the speed of a computer's central processing unit

MIQUELET n type of lock on old firearm

MIR, -I, -S n peasant commune in prerevolutionary Russia

MIRABLE adj wonderful

MIRACLE, -S n wonderful supernatural event

MIRADOR, -S n window, balcony, or turret

MIRAGE, -S n optical illusion, esp one caused by hot air

MIRBANE, -S n substance used in perfumes

MIRCHI Indian English word for ▸ **hot**

MIRE, -D, -S, MIRING n swampy ground ▷ vb sink or be stuck in a mire

MIREPOIX n mixture of sautéed root vegetables

MIRES ▸ **mire**

MIREX, -ES n type of insecticide

MIRI ▸ **mir**

MIRID, -S n variety of leaf bug

MIRIER ▸ **miry**

MIRIEST ▸ **miry**

MIRIFIC adj achieving wonderful things

MIRIN, -S n Japanese rice wine

MIRINESS ▸ **mire**

MIRING ▸ **mire**

MIRINS ▸ **mirin**

MIRITI, -S n South American palm

MIRK, -ER, -EST, -S same as ▸ **murk**

MIRKIER ▸ **mirky**

MIRKIEST ▸ **mirky**

MIRKILY ▸ **mirk**

MIRKS ▸ **mirk**

MIRKY, MIRKIER, MIRKIEST ▸ **mirk**

MIRLIER ▸ **mirly**

MIRLIEST ▸ **mirly**

MIRLITON another name (chiefly US) for ▸ **chayote**

MIRLY, MIRLIER, MIRLIEST same as ▸ **marly**

MIRO, -S n tall New Zealand tree

MIROMIRO n small New Zealand bird

MIROS ▸ **miro**

MIRROR, -ED, -S n coated glass surface for reflecting images ▷ vb reflect in or as if in a mirror

MIRS ▸ **mir**

MIRTH, -S n laughter, merriment, or gaiety

MIRTHFUL ▸ **mirth**

MIRTHS ▸ **mirth**

MIRV, -ED, -ING, -S n missile with several warheads ▷ vb arm with mirvs

MIRY, MIRIER, MIRIEST ▸ **mire**

MIRZA, -S n title of respect placed before the surname of a distinguished man

MIS ▸ **mi**

MISACT, -ED, -S vb act wrongly

MISADAPT vb adapt badly

MISADD, -ED, -S vb add badly

MISAGENT n bad agent

MISAIM, -ED, -S vb aim badly

MISALIGN vb align badly

MISALLOT vb allot wrongly

MISALLY vb form unsuitable alliance

MISALTER vb alter wrongly

MISANDRY n hatred of men

MISAPPLY vb use something for a purpose for which it is not intended or is not suited

MISARRAY n disarray

MISASSAY vb assay wrongly

MISATE ▸ **miseat**

MISATONE vb atone wrongly

MISAVER, -S vb claim wrongly

MISAWARD vb award wrongly

MISBEGIN, MISBEGAN, MISBEGUN vb begin badly

MISBIAS vb prejudice wrongly

MISBILL, -S vb present inaccurate bill

MISBIND, -S, MISBOUND vb
bind wrongly

MISBIRTH n abortion

MISBORN adj born
prematurely

MISBOUND ▸ misbind

MISBRAND vb put
misleading label on

MISBUILD, MISBUILT vb
build badly

MISCALL, -S vb call by the
wrong name

MISCARRY vb have a
miscarriage

MISCAST, -S vb cast (a role or
actor) inappropriately

MISCH adj as in **misch metal**
alloy of cerium and other
rare earth metals

MISCHIEF n annoying but
not malicious behaviour

MISCHOSE ▸ mischoose

MISCIBLE adj able to be
mixed

MISCITE, -D, -S vb cite
wrongly

MISCLAIM vb claim wrongly

MISCLASS vb class badly

MISCODE, -D, -S vb code
wrongly

MISCOIN, -S vb coin wrongly

MISCOLOR same as
▸ miscolour

MISCOOK, -S vb cook badly

MISCOPY vb copy badly

MISCOUNT vb count or
calculate incorrectly ▷ n
false count or calculation

MISCREED n false creed

MISCUE, -D, -S, MISCUING n
faulty stroke in snooker, etc
▷ vb make a miscue

MISCUT, -S vb cut wrongly

MISDATE, -D, -S vb date (a
letter, event, etc) wrongly

MISDEAL, -S, -T vb deal out
cards incorrectly ▷ n faulty
deal

MISDEED, -S n wrongful act

MISDEEM, -S, MISDEMPT vb
form bad opinion of

MISDIAL, -S vb dial
telephone number
incorrectly

MISDID ▸ misdo

MISDIET, -S n wrong diet
▷ vb diet or eat improperly

MISDIGHT adj done badly
▷ vb mismanage or treat
badly

MISDO, MISDID, -ES, -ING
vb do badly or wrongly

MISDOER, -S ▸ misdo

MISDOES ▸ misdo

MISDOING ▸ misdo

MISDONE adj done badly

MISDONNE same as
▸ misdone

MISDOUBT archaic word for
▸ doubt

**MISDRAW, -N, -S,
MISDREW** vb draw poorly

MISDREAD n fear of
approaching evil ▷ vb fear or
dread

MISDREW ▸ misdraw

MISDRIVE, MISDROVE vb
drive badly

MISE, -S n issue in the
obsolete writ of right

MISEASE, -S n unease

MISEAT, MISATE, -EN, -S vb
eat unhealthy food

MISEDIT, -S vb edit badly

MISENROL vb enrol wrongly

MISENTER vb enter wrongly

MISENTRY n wrong or
mistaken entry

MISER, -S n person who
hoards money and hates
spending it

MISERE, -S n call in solo
whist and other card games
declaring a hand that will
win no tricks

MISERERE n type of psalm

MISERES ▸ misere

MISERIES ▸ misery

MISERLY adj of or
resembling a miser

MISERS ▸ miser

MISERY, MISERIES n great
unhappiness

MISES ▸ mise

MISEVENT n mishap

MISFAITH n distrust

**MISFALL, -S, MISFALNE,
MISFELL** vb happen as
piece of bad luck

MISFARE, -D, -S vb get on
badly

MISFEED, MISFED, -S vb
feed wrongly

MISFEIGN vb feign with evil
motive

MISFELL ▸ misfall

MISFIELD vb fail to field
properly

MISFILE, -D, -S vb file
(papers, records, etc)
wrongly

MISFIRE, -D, -S vb (of a
firearm or engine) fail to fire
correctly ▷ n act or an
instance of misfiring

MISFIT, -S n person not
suited to his or her social
environment ▷ vb fail to fit
or be fitted

MISFOCUS n wrong or poor
focus

MISFOLD, -S vb fold wrongly

MISFORM, -S vb form badly

MISFRAME vb frame
wrongly

MISGAGE, -D, -S vb gage
wrongly

MISGAUGE vb gauge badly

MISGIVE, MISGAVE, -N, -S
vb make or be apprehensive
or suspicious

MISGO, -ES, -ING, -NE vb go
wrong way

MISGRADE vb grade
wrongly

MISGRAFF adj badly done

MISGRAFT vb graft wrongly

MISGROW, MISGREW, -N, -S
vb grow in unsuitable way

MISGUESS vb guess wrongly

MISGUIDE vb guide or direct
wrongly or badly

MISHAP, -S n minor accident
▷ vb happen as bad luck

MISHAPT same as
> misshapen

MISHEAR, -D, -S vb hear
(what someone says)
wrongly

MISHIT, -S n faulty shot,
kick, or stroke ▷ vb hit or
kick a ball with a faulty
stroke

MISHMASH n confused
collection or mixture

MISHMEE, -S n root of Asian
plant

MISHMI, -S n evergreen
perennial plant

MISHMOSH same as
▸ mishmash

MISHUGAS same as
> meshugaas

MISINFER vb infer wrongly

MISINTER vb bury wrongly

MISJOIN, -S vb join badly

MISJUDGE vb judge wrongly
or unfairly

MISKAL, -S n unit of weight
in Iran

MISKEEP, -S, MISKEPT vb
keep wrongly

MISKEN, -S, -T vb be
unaware of

MISKEPT ▸ miskeep

MISKEY, -ED, -S vb key
wrongly

MISKICK, -S vb fail to kick
properly

**MISKNOW, MISKNEW, -N,
-S** vb have wrong idea about

MISLABEL vb label badly

MISLABOR vb labour
wrongly

**MISLAY, MISLAID,
MISLAIN, -S** vb lose
(something) temporarily

MISLAYER ▸ mislay

M

M

MISLAYS ▶ mislay

MISLEAD, -S, MISLED vb give false or confusing information to

MISLEARN vb learn wrongly

MISLED ▶ mislead

MISLEEKE same as ▶ **mislike**

MISLETOE same as > **mistletoe**

MISLIE, -S, MISLYING vb lie wrongly

MISLIGHT, MISLIT vb use light to lead astray

MISLIKE, -D, -S vb dislike ▷ n dislike or aversion

MISLIKER ▶ mislike

MISLIKES ▶ mislike

MISLIT ▶ mislight

MISLIVE, -D, -S vb live wickedly

MISLODGE vb lodge wrongly

MISLUCK, -S vb have bad luck

MISLYING ▶ mislie

MISMAKE, MISMADE, -S vb make badly

MISMARK, -S vb mark wrongly

MISMARRY vb make unsuitable marriage

MISMATCH vb form an unsuitable partner, opponent, or set ▷ n unsuitable match

MISMATE, -D, -S vb mate wrongly

MISMEET, -S, MISMET vb fail to meet

MISMETRE vb fail to follow the metre of a poem

MISMOVE, -D, -S vb move badly

MISNAME, -D, -S vb name badly

MISNOMER n incorrect or unsuitable name ▷ vb apply a misnomer to

MISO, -S n thick brown salty paste made from soya beans

MISOGAMY n hatred of marriage

MISOGYNY n hatred of women

MISOLOGY n hatred of reasoning or reasoned argument

MISORDER vb order badly

MISOS ▶ miso

MISPAGE, -D, -S vb page wrongly

MISPAINT vb paint badly or wrongly

MISPARSE vb parse wrongly

MISPART, -S vb part wrongly

MISPATCH vb patch wrongly

MISPEN, -S vb write wrongly

MISPLACE vb mislay

MISPLAN, -S vb plan badly or wrongly

MISPLANT vb plant badly or wrongly

MISPLAY, -S vb play badly or wrongly in games or sports ▷ vb wrong or unskilful play

MISPLEAD, MISPLED vb plead incorrectly

MISPOINT vb punctuate badly

MISPOISE n lack of poise ▷ vb lack poise

MISPRICE vb give the wrong price to

MISPRINT n printing error ▷ vb print a letter incorrectly

MISPRISE same as ▶ **misprize**

MISPRIZE vb fail to appreciate the value of

MISPROUD adj undeservedly proud

MISQUOTE vb quote inaccurately

MISRAISE vb raise wrongly or excessively

MISRATE, -D, -S vb rate wrongly

MISREAD, -S vb misinterpret (a situation etc)

MISREFER vb refer wrongly

MISRELY vb rely wrongly

MISROUTE vb send wrong way

MISRULE, -D, -S vb govern inefficiently or unjustly ▷ n inefficient or unjust government

MISS, -ED, -ES vb fail to notice, hear, hit, reach, find, or catch ▷ n fact or instance of missing

MISSA, -E n Roman Catholic mass

MISSABLE ▶ miss

MISSAE ▶ missa

MISSAID ▶ missay

MISSAL, -S n book containing the prayers and rites of the Mass

MISSAW ▶ missee

MISSAY, MISSAID, -S vb say wrongly

MISSEAT, -S vb seat wrongly

MISSED ▶ miss

MISSEE, MISSAW, -N, -S vb see wrongly

MISSEEM, -S vb be unsuitable for

MISSEEN ▶ missee

MISSEES ▶ missee

MISSEL, -S adj as in **missel thrush** large European thrush

MISSELL, -S, MISSOLD vb sell (a product, esp a financial one) misleadingly

MISSELS ▶ missel

MISSEND, -S, MISSENT vb send wrongly

MISSENSE n type of genetic mutation ▷ vb give a wrong sense or meaning

MISSENT ▶ missend

MISSES ▶ miss

MISSET, -S vb set wrongly

MISSHAPE vb shape badly ▷ n something that is badly shaped

MISSHOD adj badly shod

MISSHOOD n state of being an unmarried woman

MISSIER ▶ missy

MISSIES ▶ missy

MISSIEST ▶ missy

MISSILE, -S n rocket with an exploding warhead

MISSILRY same as > **missilery**

MISSING adj lost or absent

MISSION, -S n specific task or duty ▷ vb direct a mission to or establish a mission in

MISSIS, -ES same as ▶ **missus**

MISSISH adj like a schoolgirl

MISSIVE, -S n letter ▷ adj sent or intended to be sent

MISSOLD ▶ missell

MISSORT, -S vb sort wrongly

MISSOUND vb sound wrongly

MISSOUT, -S n someone who has been overlooked

MISSPACE vb space out wrongly

MISSPEAK, MISSPOKE vb speak wrongly

MISSPELL, MISSPELT vb spell (a word) wrongly

MISSPEND, MISSPENT vb waste or spend unwisely

MISSPOKE ▶ misspeak

MISSTAMP vb stamp badly

MISSTART vb start wrongly

MISSTATE vb state incorrectly

MISSTEER vb steer badly

MISSTEP, -S n false step ▷ vb take a false step

MISSTOP, -S vb stop wrongly

MISSTYLE vb call by the wrong name

MISSUIT, -S vb be unsuitable for

MISSUS, -ES n one's wife or the wife of the person addressed or referred to

MISSY, MISSIER, MISSIES, MISSIEST n affectionate or disparaging form of address to a girl ▷ adj missish

MIST, -ED, -S n thin fog ▷ vb cover or be covered with mist

MISTAKE, -S n error or blunder ▷ vb misunderstand

MISTAKEN adj wrong in judgment or opinion

MISTAKER ▶ mistake

MISTAKES ▶ mistake

MISTAL, -S n cow shed

MISTBOW, -S same as ▶ fogbow

MISTEACH vb teach badly

MISTED ▶ mist

MISTELL, -S, MISTOLD vb tell wrongly

MISTEND, -S vb tend wrongly

MISTER, -ED, -S n informal form of address for a man ▷ vb call (someone) mister

MISTERM, -S vb term badly

MISTERS ▶ mister

MISTERY same as ▶ mystery

MISTEUK Scots variant of ▶ mistook

MISTFUL ▶ mist

MISTHINK vb have poor opinion of

MISTHROW, MISTHREW vb fail to throw properly

MISTICO, -S n small Mediterranean sailing ship

MISTIER ▶ misty

MISTIEST ▶ misty

MISTILY ▶ misty

MISTIME, -D, -S vb do (something) at the wrong time

MISTING, -S n application of a fake suntan by spray

MISTITLE vb name badly

MISTLE, -D, -S, MISTLING same as ▶ mizzle

MISTOLD ▶ mistell

MISTOOK past tense of ▶ mistake

MISTOUCH vb fail to touch properly

MISTRACE vb trace wrongly

MISTRAIN vb train wrongly

MISTRAL, -S n strong dry northerly wind of S France

MISTREAT vb treat (a person or animal) badly

MISTRESS n woman in a position of authority, ownership, or control ▷ vb become a mistress

MISTRIAL n trial made void because of some error

MISTRUST vb have doubts or suspicions about ▷ n lack of trust

MISTRUTH n something untrue

MISTRYST vb fail to keep an appointment with

MISTS ▶ mist

MISTUNE, -D, -S vb fail to tune properly

MISTUTOR vb instruct badly

MISTY, MISTIER, MISTIEST adj full of mist

MISTYPE, -D, -S vb type badly

MISUNION n wrong or bad union

MISUSAGE ▶ misuse

MISUSE, -D, -S, MISUSING, MISUST n incorrect, improper, or careless use ▷ vb use wrongly

MISUSER, -S n abuse of some right, privilege, office, etc

MISUSES ▶ misuse

MISUSING ▶ misuse

MISUST ▶ misuse

MISVALUE vb value badly

MISWEND, -S vb assess wrongly

MISWEND, -S, MISWENT vb become lost

MISWORD, -S vb word badly

MISWRITE, MISWRIT, MISWROTE vb write badly

MISYOKE, -D, -S vb join wrongly

MITCH, -ED, -ES, -ING vb play truant from school

MITE, -S n very small spider-like animal

MITER, -ED, -ING, -S same as ▶ mitre

MITERER, -S ▶ miter

MITERING ▶ miter

MITERS ▶ miter

MITES ▶ mite

MITHER, -ED, -S vb fuss over or moan about something

MITICIDE n any drug or agent that destroys mites

MITIER ▶ mity

MITIEST ▶ mity

MITIGANT adj acting to mitigate ▷ n means of easing, lessening, or assuaging

MITIGATE vb make less severe

MITIS, -ES n malleable iron

MITOGEN, -S n any agent that induces mitosis

MITOSIS, MITOSES n type of cell division

MITOTIC ▶ mitosis

MITRAL adj of or like a mitre

MITRE, -D, -S, MITRING n bishop's pointed headdress ▷ vb join with a mitre joint

MITSVAH, -S, MITSVOTH same as ▶ mitzvah

MITT, -S same as ▶ mitten

MITTEN, -S n glove with one section for the thumb and one for the four fingers together

MITTENED adj wearing mittens

MITTENS ▶ mitten

MITTIMUS n warrant of commitment to prison

MITTS ▶ mitt

MITUMBA, -S n used clothes imported for sale in African countries

MITY, MITIER, MITIEST adj having mites

MITZVAH, -S, MITZVOTH n commandment or precept, esp one found in the Bible

MIURUS, -ES n type of rhythm in poetry

MIX, -ES, -T vb combine or blend into one mass ▷ n mixture

MIXABLE ▶ mix

MIXDOWN, -S n (in sound recording) the transfer of a multitrack master mix to two-track stereo tape

MIXED adj formed or blended together by mixing

MIXEDLY ▶ mixed

MIXEN, -S n dunghill

MIXER, -S n kitchen appliance used for mixing foods

MIXES ▶ mix

MIXIBLE ▶ mix

MIXIER ▶ mixy

MIXIEST ▶ mixy

MIXING, -S n act of mixing

MIXOLOGY n art of mixing cocktails

MIXT ▶ mix

MIXTAPE, -S n compilation of songs from various sources

MIXTE adj of a type of bicycle frame

MIXTION, -S n amber-based mixture used in making gold leaf

MIXTURE, -S n something mixed

MIXUP, -S n something that is mixed up

MIXY, MIXIER, MIXIEST adj mixed

MIZ, -ZES shortened form of ▶ misery

Miz is an informal short form of **misery**, very useful as a Z word. But you'll need a blank tile for the second Z if you want to form the plural **mizzes**.

M

MIZEN, -S same as ▸ **mizzen**

MIZMAZE, -S n maze

MIZUNA, -S n Japanese variety of lettuce

MIZZ same as ▸ **miz**

MIZZEN, -S n sail set on a mizzenmast ▸ adj of or relating to any kind of gear used with a mizzenmast

MIZZES ▸ **miz**

MIZZLE, -D, -S, MIZZLING vb decamp

MIZZLIER ▸ **mizzly**

MIZZLING ▸ **mizzle**

MIZZLY, MIZZLIER ▸ **mizzle**

MIZZY adj as in **mizzy maze** dialect expression meaning state of confusion

MM interj expression of enjoyment of taste or smell

MMM interj interjection expressing agreement or enjoyment

MNA, -S same as ▸ **mina**

MNEME, -S n ability to retain memory

MNEMIC ▸ **mneme**

MNEMON, -S n unit of memory

MNEMONIC adj intended to help the memory ▸ n something, for instance a verse, intended to help the memory

MNEMONS ▸ **mnemon**

MO, -S n moment

MOA, -S n large extinct flightless New Zealand bird

MOAI n any of the gigantic carved stone figures found on Easter Island (Rapa Nui)

MOAN, -ED, -S n low cry of pain ▸ vb make or utter with a moan

MOANER, -S ▸ **moan**

MOANFUL ▸ **moan**

MOANING, -S ▸ **moan**

MOANS ▸ **moan**

MOAS ▸ **moa**

MOAT, -ED, -ING, -S n deep wide ditch, esp round a castle ▸ vb surround with or as if with a moat

MOATLIKE ▸ **moat**

MOATS ▸ **moat**

MOB, -BED, -S n disorderly crowd ▸ vb surround in a mob

MOBBER, -S ▸ **mob**

MOBBIE same as ▸ **mobby**

MOBBIES ▸ **mobby**

MOBBING, -S ▸ **mob**

MOBBISH ▸ **mob**

MOBBISM, -S n behaviour as mob

MOBBLE, -D, -S, MOBBLING same as ▸ **moble**

MOBBY, MOBBIES n (formerly) drink fermented from sweet potatoes or ginger

MOBCAP, -S n woman's 18th-century cotton cap

MOBCAST, -S vb create and upload a podcast directly from a mobile phone

MOBE, -S n mobile phone

MOBEY, -S same as ▸ **moby**

MOBIE same as ▸ **moby**

MOBIES ▸ **moby**

MOBILE, -S adj able to move ▸ n hanging structure designed to move in air currents

MOBILISE same as ▸ **mobilize**

MOBILITY n ability to move physically

MOBILIZE vb (of the armed services) prepare for active service

MOBISODE n episode of a TV show made for viewing on a mobile phone

MOBLE, -D, -S, MOBLING vb muffle

MOBLOG, -S n blog recorded in the form of mobile phone calls, text messages, and photographs

MOBOCRAT > **mobocracy**

MOBS ▸ **mob**

MOBSMAN, MOBSMEN n person in mob

MOBSTER, -S n member of a criminal organization

MOBY, MOBIES n mobile phone

MOC, -S shortening of ▸ **moccasin**

MOCCASIN same as ▸ **moccasin**

MOCCASIN n soft leather shoe

MOCCIES pl n informal Australian word for moccasins

MOCH, -ED, -ING, -S n spell of humid weather ▸ vb (of foods) become musty or spoiled

MOCHA, -S n kind of strong dark coffee

MOCHED ▸ **moch**

MOCHELL, -S same as ▸ **much**

MOCHI, -S n confection made with rice flour and sweetened bean paste

MOCHIE, -R, -ST adj damp or humid

MOCHILA, -S n South American shoulder bag

MOCHING ▸ **moch**

MOCHIS ▸ **mochi**

MOCHS ▸ **moch**

MOCHY same as ▸ **mochie**

MOCK, -ED, -S vb make fun of ▸ adj sham or imitation ▸ n act of mocking

MOCKABLE ▸ **mock**

MOCKADO n imitation velvet

MOCKAGE, -S same as ▸ **mockery**

MOCKED ▸ **mock**

MOCKER, -ED, -S vb dress up

MOCKERY n derision

MOCKING, -S ▸ **mock**

MOCKNEY, -S n person who affects a cockney accent ▸ adj denoting an affected cockney accent or a person who has one

MOCKS ▸ **mock**

MOCKTAIL n cocktail without alcohol

MOCKUP, -S n working full-scale model of a machine, apparatus, etc, for testing, research, etc

MOCOCK, -S n Native American birchbark container

MOCS ▸ **moc**

MOCUCK, -S same as ▸ **mocock**

MOCUDDUM same as ▸ **muqaddam**

MOD, -DED, -S n member of a group of fashionable young people, orig in the 1960s ▸ vb modify (a piece of software or hardware)

MODAL, -S adj of or relating to mode or manner ▸ n modal word

MODALISM n type of Christian doctrine

MODALIST ▸ **modalism**

MODALITY n condition of being modal

MODALLY ▸ **modal**

MODALS ▸ **modal**

MODDED ▸ **mod**

MODDER, -S n person who modifies a piece of hardware or software

MODDING, -S n practice of modifying a car to alter its appearance or performance

MODE, -S n method or manner

MODEL, -ED, -LED, -S n (miniature) representation ▸ adj excellent or perfect ▸ vb make a model of

MODELER, -S ▸ model
MODELING same as
> **modelling**
MODELIST same as
> **modellist**
MODELLED ▸ model
MODELLER ▸ model
MODELLO, MODELLI, -S n
artist's preliminary sketch or
model
MODELS ▸ model
MODEM, -ED, -ING, -S n
device for connecting two
computers by a telephone
line ▷ vb send or receive by
modem
MODENA, -S n popular
variety of domestic fancy
pigeon
MODER, -S n intermediate
layer in humus
MODERATE adj not extreme
▷ n person of moderate
views ▷ vb make or become
less violent or extreme
MODERATO adv at a
moderate speed ▷ n
moderato piece
MODERN, -ER, -S adj of
present or recent times ▷ n
contemporary person
MODERNE, -S n style of
architecture and design of
the late 1920s and 1930s
▷ adj of or relating to this
style of architecture and
design
MODERNER ▸ modern
MODERNES ▸ moderne
MODERNLY ▸ modern
MODERNS ▸ modern
MODERS ▸ moder
MODES ▸ mode
MODEST, -ER adj not vain or
boastful
MODESTLY ▸ modest
MODESTY n quality or
condition of being modest
MODGE, -D, -S, MODGING
vb do shoddily
MODI ▸ modus
MODICUM, MODICA, -S n
small quantity
MODIFIED ▸ modify
MODIFIER n word that
qualifies the sense of
another
**MODIFY, MODIFIED,
MODIFIES** vb change
slightly
MODII ▸ modius
MODIOLAR ▸ modiolus
MODIOLUS, MODIOLI n
central bony pillar of the
cochlea
MODISH adj in fashion

MODISHLY ▸ modish
MODIST, -S n follower of
fashion
MODISTE, -S n fashionable
dressmaker or milliner
MODISTS ▸ modist
MODIUS, MODII n ancient
Roman quantity measure
MODIWORT Scots variant of
> **mouldwarp**
MODS ▸ mod
MODULAR, -S adj of,
consisting of, or resembling
a module or modulus ▷ n
thing comprised of
modules
MODULATE vb vary in tone
MODULE, -S n self-
contained unit, section, or
component with a specific
function
MODULI ▸ modulus
MODULO adv with reference
to modulus
MODULUS, MODULI n
coefficient expressing a
specified property
MODUS, MODI n way of
doing something
MOE, -S adv more ▷ n wry
face
MOELLON, -S n rubble
MOES ▸ moe
MOFETTE, -S n opening in a
region of nearly extinct
volcanic activity, through
which gases pass
MOFFETTE same as
> **mofette**
MOFUSSIL n provincial area
in India
MOG, -GED, -GING, -S vb
go away
MOGGAN, -S n stocking
without foot
MOGGED ▸ mog
MOGGIE same as ▸ **moggy**
MOGGIES ▸ moggy
MOGGING ▸ mog
MOGGY, MOGGIES n cat
MOGHUL, -S same as
▸ **mogul**
MOGS ▸ mog
MOGUL, -S n important or
powerful person
MOGULED adj having
moguls
MOGULS ▸ mogul
MOHAIR, -S n fine hair of
the Angora goat
MOHALIM same as
▸ **mohelim**
MOHAWK, -S n half turn
from either edge of either
skate to the corresponding
edge of the other skate

MOHEL, -IM, -S n man
qualified to conduct
circumcisions
MOHICAN, -S n punk
hairstyle
MOHO, -S n boundary
between the earth's crust
and mantle
MOHR, -S same as
▸ **mhorr**
MOHUA, -S n small New
Zealand bird
MOHUR, -S n former Indian
gold coin worth 15 rupees
MOI pron (used facetiously)
me
MOIDER, -ED, -S same as
▸ **moither**
MOIDORE, -S n former
Portuguese gold coin
MOIETY, MOIETIES n half
MOIL, -ED, -ING, -S vb
moisten or soil or become
moist, soiled, etc ▷ n toil
MOILE, -S n type of rice
pudding made with almond
milk
MOILED ▸ moil
MOILER, -S ▸ moil
MOILES ▸ moile
MOILING ▸ moil
MOILS ▸ moil
MOINEAU, -S n small
fortification

Meaning a type of small
fortification, this is another
of those very useful 7-letter
vowel dumps.

MOIRA, -I n fate
MOIRE, -S adj having a
watered or wavelike pattern
▷ n any fabric that has such a
pattern
MOISER, -S n informer
**MOIST, -ED, -ER, -EST, -ING,
-S** adj slightly wet ▷ vb
moisten
MOISTEN, -S vb make or
become moist
MOISTER ▸ moist
MOISTEST ▸ moist
MOISTFUL adj full of
moisture
MOISTIFY vb moisten
MOISTING ▸ moist
MOISTLY ▸ moist
MOISTS ▸ moist
MOISTURE n liquid diffused
as vapour or condensed in
drops
MOIT, -S same as ▸ **mote**
MOITHER, -S vb bother or
bewilder
MOITS ▸ moit
MOJARRA, -S n tropical
American sea fish

M

MOJITO, -S n rum-based cocktail

MOJO, -ES, -S n charm or magic spell

MOKADDAM same as ▸ **muqaddam**

MOKE, -S n donkey

MOKI, -S n edible sea fish of New Zealand

MOKIHI, -S n Māori raft

MOKIS ▸ **moki**

MOKO, -S n Māori tattoo or tattoo pattern

MOKOMOKO n type of skink found in New Zealand

MOKOPUNA n grandchild or young person

MOKORO, -S n (in Botswana) the traditional dugout canoe of the people of the Okavango Delta

MOKOS ▸ **moko**

MOKSHA, -S n freedom from the endless cycle of transmigration into a state of bliss

MOL, -S n the SI unit mole

MOLA, -S another name for ▸ **sunfish**

MOLAL adj of a solution containing one mole of solute per thousand grams of solvent

MOLALITY n measure of solvent concentration

MOLAR, -S n large back tooth used for grinding ▸ adj of any of these teeth

MOLARITY n concentration

MOLARS ▸ **molar**

MOLAS ▸ **mola**

MOLASSE n sediment from the erosion of mountain ranges

MOLASSES n dark syrup, a by-product of sugar refining

MOLD, -ED, -S same as ▸ **mould**

MOLDABLE ▸ **mold**

MOLDED ▸ **mold**

MOLDER, -ED, -S same as ▸ **moulder**

MOLDIER ▸ **moldy**

MOLDIEST ▸ **moldy**

MOLDING, -S same as ▸ **moulding**

MOLDS ▸ **mold**

MOLDWARP same as > **mouldwarp**

MOLDY, MOLDIER, MOLDIEST same as ▸ **mouldy**

MOLE, -D, -S, MOLING n small dark raised spot on the skin ▸ vb as in **mole out** seek as if by burrowing

MOLECAST n molehill

MOLECULE n simplest freely existing chemical unit, composed of two or more atoms

MOLED ▸ **mole**

MOLEHILL n small mound of earth thrown up by a burrowing mole

MOLEHUNT n hunt for a mole

MOLELIKE adj like a mole

MOLES ▸ **mole**

MOLESKIN n dark grey dense velvety pelt of a mole, used as a fur

MOLEST, -ED, -S vb disturb or annoy

MOLESTER ▸ **molest**

MOLESTS ▸ **molest**

MOLIES ▸ **moly**

MOLIMEN, -S n effort needed to perform bodily function

MOLINE, -S adj (of a cross) having arms of equal length, forked and curved back at the ends ▸ n moline cross

MOLINET, -S n stick for whipping chocolate

MOLING ▸ **mole**

MOLL, -S n gangster's female accomplice

MOLLA, -S same as ▸ **mollah**

MOLLAH, -S same as ▸ **mullah**

MOLLAS ▸ **molla**

MOLLIE same as ▸ **molly**

MOLLIES ▸ **molly**

MOLLIFY vb pacify or soothe

MOLLS ▸ **moll**

MOLLUSC, -S n soft-bodied, usu hard-shelled, animal

MOLLUSCA n molluscs collectively

MOLLUSCS ▸ **mollusc**

MOLLUSK, -S same as ▸ **mollusc**

MOLLY, MOLLIES n American freshwater fish

MOLOCH, -S n spiny Australian desert-living lizard

MOLOSSUS, MOLOSSI n division of metre in poetry

MOLS ▸ **mol**

MOLT, -ED, -ING, -S same as ▸ **moult**

MOLTEN ▸ **melt**

MOLTENLY ▸ **melt**

MOLTER, -S ▸ **molt**

MOLTING ▸ **molt**

MOLTO adv very

MOLTS ▸ **molt**

MOLY, MOLIES, -S n mythical magic herb

MOLYBDIC adj of or containing molybdenum in the trivalent or hexavalent state

MOLYS ▸ **moly**

MOM, -S same as ▸ **mother**

MOME, -S n fool

MOMENT, -S n short space of time

MOMENTA ▸ **momentum**

MOMENTLY same as ▸ **moment**

MOMENTO, -S same as ▸ **memento**

MOMENTS ▸ **moment**

MOMENTUM, MOMENTA n impetus to go forward, develop, or get stronger

MOMES ▸ **mome**

MOMI same as ▸ **mom**

MOMISM, -S n excessive domination of a child by his or her mother

MOMMA, -S same as ▸ **mamma**

MOMMET, -S same as ▸ **mammet**

MOMMY, MOMMIES same as ▸ **mom**

MOMOIR, -S n memoir written by a woman about motherhood

MOMS ▸ **mom**

MOMUS, -ES n person who ridicules

MON, -S dialect variant of ▸ **man**

MONA n W African guenon monkey

MONACHAL less common word for ▸ **monastic**

MONACID, -S same as ▸ **monoacid**

MONACT, -S n sponge spicule with a single ray

MONAD, -S n any fundamental singular metaphysical entity

MONADAL ▸ **monad**

MONADES ▸ **monas**

MONADIC adj being or relating to a monad

MONADISM n doctrine that monads are the ultimate units of reality

MONADS ▸ **monad**

MONAL, -S n S Asian pheasant

MONAMINE n type of a mine

MONANDRY n custom of having only one male partner over a period of time

MONARCH, -S n sovereign ruler of a state

MONARCHY n government by or a state ruled by a sovereign

MONARDA, -S n mintlike N American plant

MONAS, MONADES, -ES same as ▸ **monad**

MONASTIC adj of monks, nuns, or monasteries ▸ n person who is committed to this way of life, esp a monk

MONAUL, -S same as ▸ **monal**

MONAURAL adj relating to, having, or hearing with only one ear

MONAXIAL another word for ▸ **uniaxial**

MONAXON, -S n type of sponge

MONAZITE n yellow to reddish-brown mineral

MONDAIN, -S n man who moves in fashionable society ▸ adj characteristic of fashionable society

MONDAINE n woman who moves in fashionable society ▸ adj characteristic of fashionable society

MONDAINS ▸ **mondain**

MONDE, -S n French word meaning world or society

MONDIAL adj of or involving the whole world

MONDO, -S n Buddhist questioning technique

MONECIAN same as > **monecious**

MONELLIN n sweet protein

MONEME, -S less common word for ▸ **morpheme**

MONER, -A n hypothetical simple organism

MONERAN, -S n type of bacterium

MONERON same as ▸ **moner**

MONETARY adj of money or currency

MONETH, -S same as ▸ **month**

MONETISE same as ▸ **monetize**

MONETIZE vb establish as the legal tender of a country

MONEY, -S, MONIES n medium of exchange, coins or banknotes

MONEYBAG n bag for money

MONEYBOX n box for keeping money in

MONEYED adj rich

MONEYER, -S n person who coins money

MONEYMAN, MONEYMEN n person supplying money

MONEYS ▸ **money**

MONG, -S n Australian shortening of mongrel

MONGCORN same as ▸ **maslin**

MONGEESE ▸ **mongoose**

MONGER, -ED, -S n trader or dealer ▸ vb deal in

MONGERY ▸ **monger**

MONGO, -S same as ▸ **mungo**

MONGOE, -S same as ▸ **mongo**

MONGOOSE, MONGEESE n stoat-like mammal of Asia and Africa that kills snakes

MONGOS ▸ **mongo**

MONGREL, -S n animal, esp a dog, of mixed breed ▸ adj of mixed breed or origin

MONGS ▸ **mong**

MONGST short for ▸ **amongst**

MONIAL, -S n mullion

MONIC adj denoting a type of polynomial

MONICKER same as ▸ **moniker**

MONIE Scots word for ▸ **many**

MONIED same as ▸ **moneyed**

MONIES ▸ **money**

MONIKER, -S n person's name or nickname

MONILIA, -E, -S n type of fungus

MONILIAL adj denoting a thrush infection caused by a fungus

MONILIAS ▸ **monilia**

MONIMENT same as ▸ **monument**

MONISH, -ED, -ES same as ▸ **admonish**

MONISM, -S n doctrine that reality consists of only one basic substance or element

MONIST, -S ▸ **monism**

MONISTIC ▸ **monism**

MONISTS ▸ **monist**

MONITION n warning or caution

MONITIVE adj reproving

MONITOR, -S n person or device that checks, controls, warns, or keeps a record of something ▸ vb watch and check on

MONITORY adj acting as or giving a warning ▸ n letter containing a monition

MONK, -S n member of an all-male religious community

MONKEY, -ED, -S n long-tailed primate ▸ vb meddle or fool

MONKFISH n type of fish

MONKHOOD n condition of being a monk

MONKISH adj of, relating to, or resembling a monk or monks

MONKS ▸ **monk**

MONO, -S n monophonic sound

MONOACID adj base which is capable of reacting with only one molecule of a monobasic acid

MONOAO, -S n New Zealand plant with rigid leaves

MONOBLOC adj made from a single piece of something

MONOBROW n appearance of a single eyebrow as a result of the eyebrows joining above a person's nose

MONOCARP n plant that is monocarpic

MONOCLE, -S n eyeglass for one eye only

MONOCLED ▸ **monocle**

MONOCLES ▸ **monocle**

MONOCOT, -S n type of flowering plant with a single embryonic seed leaf

MONOCRAT > **monocracy**

MONOCROP vb plant the same crop in a field every year

MONOCYTE n large phagocytic leucocyte with a spherical nucleus and clear cytoplasm

MONODIC ▸ **monody**

MONODIES ▸ **monody**

MONODIST ▸ **monody**

MONODONT adj (of certain animals, esp the male narwhal) having a single tooth throughout life

MONODY, MONODIES n (in Greek tragedy) an ode sung by a single actor

MONOECY same as > **monoecism**

MONOFIL, -S n synthetic thread or yarn composed of a single strand rather than twisted fibres

MONOFUEL n single type of fuel

MONOGAMY n custom of being married to one person at a time

MONOGENY n the hypothetical descent of all organisms from a single cell or organism

MONOGERM adj containing single seed

M

MONOGLOT n person speaking only one language

MONOGONY n asexual reproduction

MONOGRAM n design of combined letters, esp a person's initials ▷ vb decorate (clothing, stationery, etc) with a monogram

MONOGYNY n custom of having only one female partner over a period of time

MONOHULL n sailing vessel with a single hull

MONOKINE n type of protein

MONOKINI n bottom half of a bikini

MONOLINE adj as in **monoline insurer** insurer who pays the principal and interest on a bond in the event of a default

MONOLITH n large upright block of stone

MONOLOG, -S same as > monologue

MONOLOGY > monologue

MONOMARK n series of letters or figures to identify goods, personal articles, etc

MONOMER, -S n compound whose molecules can join together to form a polymer

MONOMIAL n expression consisting of a single term, such as 5ax ▷ adj consisting of a single algebraic term

MONOMODE adj denoting a type of optical fibre

MONONYM, -S n person who is famous enough to be known only by one name

MONOPOD, -S same as ▷ monopode

MONOPODE n tree stem which elongates from the tip and gives rise to lateral branches

MONOPODS ▷ monopod

MONOPODY n single-foot measure in poetry

MONOPOLE n magnetic pole considered in isolation

MONOPOLY n exclusive possession of or right to do something

MONORAIL n single-rail railway

MONOS ▷ mono

MONOSEMY n fact of having only a single meaning

MONOSES ▷ monosis

MONOSIES ▷ monosy

MONOSIS, MONOSES n abnormal separation

MONOSKI, -S n wide ski on which the skier stands with both feet ▷ vb ski on a monoski

MONOSOME n unpaired chromosome, esp an X-chromosome in an otherwise diploid cell

MONOSOMY n condition with a missing pair of chromosomes

MONOSY, MONOSIES same as ▷ monosis

MONOTASK vb perform only one task at a time

MONOTINT n black-and-white photograph or transparency

MONOTONE n unvaried pitch in speech or sound ▷ adj unvarying ▷ vb speak in monotone

MONOTONY n wearisome routine, dullness

MONOTYPE n single print made from a metal or glass plate on which a picture has been painted

MONOXIDE n oxide that contains one oxygen atom per molecule

MONS ▷ mon

MONSIEUR n French title of address equivalent to sir or Mr

MONSOON, -S n seasonal wind of SE Asia

MONSTER, -S n imaginary, usu frightening, beast ▷ adj huge ▷ vb criticize (a person or group) severely

MONSTERA n type of tropical climbing plant

MONSTERS ▷ monster

MONTAGE, -D, -S n (making of) a picture composed from pieces of others ▷ vb make as a montage

MONTAN adj as in **montan wax** hard wax obtained from lignite and peat

MONTANE, -S n area of mountain dominated by vegetation ▷ adj of or inhabiting mountainous regions

MONTANT, -S n vertical part in woodwork

MONTANTO n rising blow

MONTANTS ▷ montant

MONTARIA n Brazilian canoe

MONTE, -S n gambling card game of Spanish origin

MONTEITH n large ornamental bowl

MONTEM, -S n former money-raising practice at Eton school

MONTERO, -S n round cap with a flap at the back worn by hunters

MONTES ▷ monte

MONTH, -S n one of the twelve divisions of the calendar year

MONTHLY adj happening or payable once a month ▷ adv once a month ▷ n monthly magazine

MONTHS ▷ month

MONTICLE same as > monticule

MONTIES ▷ monty

MONTRE, -S n pipes of organ

MONTURE, -S n mount or frame

MONTY, MONTIES n complete form of something

MONUMENT n something, esp a building or statue, that commemorates something

MONURON, -S n type of weedkiller

MONY Scot word for ▷ many

MOO, -ED, -ING, -S n long deep cry of a cow ▷ vb make this noise ▷ interj instance or imitation of this sound

MOOCH, -ED, -ES, -ING vb loiter about aimlessly

MOOCHER, -S ▷ mooch

MOOCHES ▷ mooch

MOOCHING ▷ mooch

MOOD, -S n temporary (gloomy) state of mind

MOODIED ▷ moody

MOODIER ▷ moody

MOODIES ▷ moody

MOODIEST ▷ moody

MOODILY ▷ moody

MOODS ▷ mood

MOODY, MOODIED, MOODIER, MOODIES, MOODIEST, -ING adj sullen or gloomy ▷ vb flatter

MOOED ▷ moo

MOOI adj pleasing or nice

MOOING ▷ moo

MOOK, -S n person regarded with contempt, esp a stupid person

MOOKTAR, -S same as ▷ mukhtar

MOOL, -ED, -ING, -S same as ▷ mould

MOOLA, -S same as ▷ moolah

MOOLAH, -S slang word for ▷ money

MOOLAS ▷ moola

MOOLED ▶ mool
MOOLEY, -S same as ▶ mooly
MOOLI, -S n type of large white radish
MOOLIES ▶ mooly
MOOLING ▶ mool
MOOLIS ▶ mooli
MOOLOO, -S n person from the Waikato
MOOLS ▶ mool
MOOLVI, -S same as ▶ moolvie
MOOLVIE, -S n (esp in India) Muslim learned man
MOOLVIS ▶ moolvi
MOOLY, MOOLIES same as ▶ muley
MOON, -ING, -S n natural satellite of the earth ▷ vb be idle in a listless or dreamy way
MOONBEAM n ray of moonlight
MOONBOW, -S n rainbow made by moonlight
MOONCAKE n type of round Chinese cake
MOONCALF n person who idles time away
MOONDOG, -S n bright spot in the sky caused by moonlight
MOONDUST n dust on surface of moon
MOONED adj decorated with a moon
MOONER, -S ▶ moon
MOONEYE, -S n N American large-eyed freshwater fish
MOONFACE n big round face ▷ vb have a moon face
MOONFISH n type of tropical fish
MOONG n as in moong bean kind of bean
MOONGATE n circular gateway in a wall
MOONIER ▶ moony
MOONIES ▶ moony
MOONIEST ▶ moony
MOONILY ▶ moony
MOONING ▶ moon
MOONISH ▶ moon
MOONLESS ▶ moon
MOONLET, -S n small moon
MOONLIKE ▶ moon
MOONLIT adj illuminated by the moon
MOONPORT n place from which flights leave for moon
MOONRISE n moment when the moon appears above the horizon
MOONROCK n rock from moon

MOONROOF same as ▶ sunroof
MOONS ▶ moon
MOONSAIL n small sail high on a mast
MOONSEED n type of climbing plant with red or black fruits
MOONSET, -S n moment when the moon disappears below the horizon
MOONSHEE same as ▶ munshi
MOONSHIP n lunar module
MOONSHOT n launching of a spacecraft to the moon
MOONWALK n instance of walking on the moon
MOONWARD adj towards moon
MOONWORT n type of fern with crescent-shaped leaflets
MOONY, MOONIER, MOONIES, MOONIEST adj dreamy or listless ▷ n foolish person
MOOP, -ED, -ING, -S same as ▶ moup
MOOR, -ED, -S n tract of open uncultivated ground covered with grass and heather ▷ vb secure (a ship) with ropes etc
MOORAGE, -S n place for mooring a vessel
MOORBURN n practice of burning off old growth on a heather moor
MOORCOCK n male of the red grouse
MOORED ▶ moor
MOORFOWL n red grouse
MOORHEN, -S n small black water bird
MOORIER ▶ moory
MOORIEST ▶ moory
MOORILL, -S n disease of cattle on moors
MOORING n place for mooring a ship
MOORINGS pl n ropes and anchors used in mooring a vessel
MOORISH adj denoting a style of architecture in Spain
MOORLAND n area of moor
MOORLOG, -S n rotted wood below the surface of a moor
MOORMAN, MOORMEN n person living on a moor
MOORS ▶ moor
MOORVA, -S same as ▶ murva

MOORWORT n low-growing pink-flowered shrub that grows in peaty bogs
MOORY, MOORIER, MOORIEST ▶ moor
MOOS ▶ moo
MOOSE n large N American deer
MOOT, -ED, -EST, -S adj debatable ▷ vb bring up for discussion ▷ n (in Anglo-Saxon England) a local administrative assembly
MOOTABLE ▶ moot
MOOTED ▶ moot
MOOTER, -S ▶ moot
MOOTEST ▶ moot
MOOTING, -S ▶ moot
MOOTMAN, MOOTMEN n person taking part in a moot
MOOTNESS ▶ moot
MOOTS ▶ moot
MOOVE, -D, -S, MOOVING same as ▶ move
MOP, -PED, -PING, -S n long stick with twists of cotton or a sponge on the end, used for cleaning ▷ vb clean or soak up with or as if with a mop
MOPANE, -S same as ▶ mopani
MOPANI, -S n S African tree that is highly resistant to drought
MOPBOARD n wooden border fixed round the base of an interior wall
MOPE, -S, MOPING, MOPISHLY vb be gloomy and apathetic ▷ n gloomy person
MOPED, -S n light motorized cycle
MOPEHAWK same as ▶ mopoke
MOPER, -S ▶ mope
MOPERIES ▶ mopery
MOPERS ▶ moper
MOPERY, MOPERIES n gloominess
MOPES ▶ mope
MOPEY same as ▶ mopy
MOPHEAD, -S n person with shaggy hair
MOPIER ▶ mopy
MOPIEST ▶ mopy
MOPILY ▶ mopy
MOPINESS ▶ mopy
MOPING ▶ mope
MOPINGLY ▶ mope
MOPISH ▶ mope
MOPISHLY ▶ mope
MOPOKE, -S n species of owl
MOPPED ▶ mop

M

MOPPER, -S ▸ mop

MOPPET, -S same as ▸ **poppet**

MOPPIER ▸ moppy

MOPPIEST ▸ moppy

MOPPING ▸ mop

MOPPY, MOPPIER, MOPPIEST adj (of hair) thick, dishevelled

MOPS ▸ mop

MOPSIES ▸ mopsy

MOPSTICK n mop handle

MOPSY, MOPSIES n untidy or dowdy person

MOPUS, -ES n person who mopes

MOPY, MOPIER, MOPIEST ▸ mope

MOQUETTE n thick velvety fabric used for carpets and upholstery

MOR, -S n layer of acidic humus formed in cool moist areas

MORA, -E, -S n quantity of a short syllable in verse

MORAINAL ▸ moraine

MORAINE, -S n accumulated mass of debris deposited by a glacier

MORAINIC ▸ moraine

MORAL, -S adj concerned with right and wrong conduct ▷ n lesson to be obtained from a story or event ▷ vb moralize

MORALE, -S n degree of confidence or hope of a person or group

MORALISE same as ▸ **moralize**

MORALISM n habit or practice of moralizing

MORALIST n person with a strong sense of right and wrong

MORALITY n good moral conduct

MORALIZE vb make moral pronouncements

MORALL, -ED, -S same as ▸ **mural**

MORALLER ▸ moral

MORALLS ▸ morall

MORALLY ▸ moral

MORALS ▸ moral

MORAS ▸ mora

MORASS, -ES n marsh

MORASSY adj swampy

MORAT, -S n drink containing mulberry juice

MORATORY > moratoria

MORATS ▸ morat

MORAY, -S n large voracious eel

MORBID, -ER adj unduly interested in death or unpleasant events

MORBIDLY ▸ morbid

MORBIFIC adj causing disease

MORBILLI same as ▸ **measles**

MORBUS, -ES n disease

MORCEAU, -X n fragment or morsel

MORCHA, -S n (in India) hostile demonstration

MORDANCY ▸ mordant

MORDANT, -S adj sarcastic or scathing ▷ n substance used to fix dyes ▷ vb treat (a fabric, yarn, etc) with a mordant

MORDENT, -S n melodic ornament in music

MORE adj greater in amount or degree ▷ adv greater extent ▷ pron greater or additional amount or number

MOREEN, -S n heavy, usually watered, fabric of wool or wool and cotton

MOREISH adj (of food) causing a desire for more

MOREL, -S n edible mushroom with a pitted cap

MORELLE, -S n nightshade

MORELLO, -S n variety of small very dark sour cherry

MORELS ▸ morel

MORENDO, -S adv (in music) dying away ▷ n gentle decrescendo at the end of a musical strain

MORENESS ▸ more

MOREOVER adv in addition to what has already been said

MOREPORK same as ▸ **mopoke**

MORES pl n customs and conventions embodying the fundamental values of a community

MORESQUE adj (esp of decoration and architecture) of Moorish style ▷ n Moorish design or decoration

MORGAN, -S n American breed of small compact saddle horse

MORGAY, -S n small dogfish

MORGEN, -S n South African unit of area

MORGUE, -S same as ▸ **mortuary**

MORIA, -S n folly

MORIBUND adj without force or vitality

MORICHE, -S same as ▸ **miriti**

MORION, -S n 16th-century helmet with a brim and wide comb

MORISCO, -S n morris dance

MORISH same as ▸ **moreish**

MORKIN, -S n animal dying in accident

MORLING, -S n sheep killed by disease

MORMAOR, -S n former high-ranking Scottish nobleman

MORN, -S n morning

MORNAY, -S n dish served with a cheese sauce

MORNE, -D, -S same as ▸ **mourn**

MORNING, -S n part of the day before noon

MORNS ▸ morn

MOROCCO, -S n goatskin leather

MORON, -S n insulting term for a foolish or stupid person

MORONIC ▸ moron

MORONISM ▸ moron

MORONITY ▸ moron

MORONS ▸ moron

MOROSE, -R, -ST adj sullen or moody

MOROSELY ▸ morose

MOROSER ▸ morose

MOROSEST ▸ morose

MOROSITY ▸ morose

MORPH, -ED, -S n phonological representation of a morpheme ▷ vb undergo or cause to undergo morphing

MORPHEAN adj of or relating to Morpheus, the god of sleep and dreams

MORPHED ▸ morph

MORPHEME n speech element that cannot be subdivided

MORPHEW, -S n blemish on skin

MORPHIA, -S same as ▸ **morphine**

MORPHIC adj as in **morphic resonance** idea that an event can lead to similar events in the future through a telepathic effect

MORPHIN, -S variant form of ▸ **morphine**

MORPHINE n drug extracted from opium, used as an anaesthetic and sedative

MORPHING n one image changing to another by small gradual steps using computer animation

MORPHINS ▶ morphin

MORPHO, -S *n* type of butterfly

MORPHS ▶ morph

MORRA, -S *same as* **▶ mora**

MORRELL, -S *n* tall SW Australian eucalyptus with pointed buds

MORRHUA, -S *n* cod

MORRICE, -S *same as* **▶ morris**

MORRION, -S *same as* **▶ morion**

MORRIS, -ED, -ES *vb* perform morris dance

MORRO, -S *n* rounded hill or promontory

MORROW, -S *n* next day

MORS ▶ mor

MORSAL, -S *same as* **▶ morsel**

MORSE, -S *n* clasp or fastening on a cope

MORSEL, -ED, -S *n* small piece, esp of food ▷ *vb* divide into morsels

MORSES ▶ morse

MORSURE, -S *n* bite

MORT, -S *n* call blown on a hunting horn to signify the death of the animal hunted

MORTAL, -S *adj* subject to death ▷ *n* human being

MORTALLY ▶ mortal

MORTALS ▶ mortal

MORTAR, -ED, -S *n* small cannon with a short range ▷ *vb* fire on with mortars

MORTARY *adj* of or like mortar

MORTBELL *n* bell rung for funeral

MORTGAGE *n* conditional pledging of property as security for the repayment of a loan ▷ *vb* pledge (property) as security thus ▷ *adj* of or relating to a mortgage

MORTICE, -D, -S *same as* **▶ mortise**

MORTICER ▶ mortice

MORTICES ▶ mortice

MORTIFIC *adj* causing death

MORTIFY *vb* humiliate

MORTISE, -D, -S *n* slot cut into a piece of wood, stone, etc ▷ *vb* cut a slot in (a piece of wood, stone, etc)

MORTISER ▶ mortise

MORTISES ▶ mortise

MORTLING *n* dead body

MORTMAIN *n* status of lands held inalienably by a church

MORTS ▶ mort

MORTSAFE *n* cage placed over a grave to deter body snatchers

MORTUARY *n* building where corpses are kept before burial or cremation ▷ *adj* of or relating to death or burial

MORULA, -E, -S *n* solid ball of cells resulting from the splitting of a fertilized ovum

MORULAR ▶ morula

MORULAS ▶ morula

MORWONG, -S *n* food fish of Australasian coastal waters

MORYAH *interj* exclamation of annoyance, disbelief, etc

MOS ▶ mo

MOSAIC, -S *n* design or decoration using small pieces of coloured stone or glass

MOSASAUR *n* type of extinct Cretaceous giant marine lizard, typically with paddle-like limbs

MOSCATO, -S *n* type of sweet dessert wine

MOSCHATE *n* odour like musk

MOSE, -D, -S, MOSING *vb* have glanders

MOSELLE, -S *n* German white wine from the Moselle valley

MOSES ▶ mose

MOSEY, -ED, -ING, -S *vb* walk in a leisurely manner

MOSH, -ED, -ES *n* dance performed to loud rock music ▷ *vb* dance in this manner

MOSHAV, -IM *n* cooperative settlement in Israel

MOSHED ▶ mosh

MOSHER, -S ▶ mosh

MOSHES ▶ mosh

MOSHING, -S ▶ mosh

MOSING ▶ mose

MOSK, -S *same as* **▶ mosque**

MOSLINGS *pl n* shavings from animal skin being prepared

MOSQUE, -S *n* Muslim temple

MOSQUITO *n* blood-sucking flying insect

MOSS, -ED, -ES, -ING *n* small flowerless plant growing in masses on moist surfaces ▷ *vb* gather moss

MOSSBACK *n* old turtle, shellfish, etc, that has a growth of algae on its back

MOSSED ▶ moss

MOSSER, -S ▶ moss

MOSSES ▶ moss

MOSSIE, -S *n* common sparrow

MOSSIER ▶ mossy

MOSSIES ▶ mossie

MOSSIEST ▶ mossy

MOSSING ▶ moss

MOSSLAND *n* land covered in peat

MOSSLIKE ▶ moss

MOSSO *adv* to be performed with rapidity

MOSSY, MOSSIER, MOSSIEST ▶ moss

MOST, -S *n* greatest number or degree ▷ *adj* greatest in number or degree ▷ *adv* in the greatest degree

MOSTE ▶ mote

MOSTEST, -S ▶ most

MOSTLY *adv* for the most part, generally

MOSTS ▶ most

MOSTWHAT *adv* mostly

MOT, -S *n* girl or young woman, esp one's girlfriend

MOTE, MOSTE, -N, -S *n* tiny speck ▷ *vb* may or might

MOTED *adj* containing motes

MOTEL, -S *n* roadside hotel for motorists

MOTELIER *n* person running motel

MOTELS ▶ motel

MOTEN ▶ mote

MOTES ▶ mote

MOTET, -S *n* short sacred choral song

MOTETT, -S *same as* **▶ motet**

MOTEY, -S, MOTIER, MOTIEST *adj* containing motes ▷ *n* pigment made from earth

MOTH, -S *n* nocturnal insect like a butterfly

MOTHBALL *n* small ball of camphor or naphthalene used to repel moths from stored clothes ▷ *vb* store (something operational) for future use

MOTHED *adj* damaged by moths

MOTHER, -ED, -S *n* female parent ▷ *adj* native or inborn ▷ *vb* look after as a mother

MOTHERLY *adj* of or resembling a mother, esp in warmth, or protectiveness

MOTHERS ▶ mother

MOTHERY *adj* like mother of vinegar

MOTHIER ▶ mothy

MOTHIEST ▶ mothy

M

MOTHLIKE ▸ moth
MOTHS ▸ moth
MOTHY, MOTHIER, MOTHIEST adj ragged
MOTIER ▸ motey
MOTIEST ▸ motey
MOTIF, -S n (recurring) theme or design
MOTIFIC adj causing motion
MOTIFS ▸ motif
MOTILE, -S adj capable of independent movement ▷ n person whose mental imagery strongly reflects movement
MOTILITY ▸ motile
MOTION, -ED, -S n process, action, or way of moving ▷ vb direct (someone) by gesture
MOTIONAL ▸ motion
MOTIONED ▸ motion
MOTIONER ▸ motion
MOTIONS ▸ motion
MOTIVATE vb give incentive to
MOTIVE, -D, -S, MOTIVING n reason for a course of action ▷ adj causing motion ▷ vb motivate
MOTIVIC adj of musical motif
MOTIVING ▸ motive
MOTIVITY n power of moving or of initiating motion
MOTLEY, -ER, -S, MOTLIER, MOTLIEST adj miscellaneous ▷ n costume of a jester
MOTMOT, -S n tropical American bird with a long tail and blue and brownish-green plumage
MOTOR, -ED, -ING, -S n engine, esp of a vehicle ▷ vb travel by car ▷ adj of or relating to cars and other vehicles powered by engines
MOTORAIL n transport of cars by train
MOTORBUS n bus driven by an internal-combustion engine
MOTORCAR n self-propelled electric railway car
MOTORDOM n world of motor cars
MOTORED ▸ motor
MOTORIAL ▸ motor
MOTORIC, -S n person trained in the muscular causes of vocal changes ▷ adj pertaining to motion
MOTORING ▸ motor
MOTORISE same as ▸ motorize

MOTORIST n driver of a car
MOTORIUM n area of nervous system involved in movement
MOTORIZE vb equip with a motor
MOTORMAN, MOTORMEN n driver of an electric train
MOTORS ▸ motor
MOTORWAY n main road for fast-moving traffic
MOTORY ▸ motor
MOTS ▸ mot
MOTSER, -S n large sum of money, esp a gambling win
MOTT, -S n clump of trees
MOTTE, -S n mound on which a castle was built
MOTTIER ▸ motty
MOTTIES ▸ motty
MOTTIEST ▸ motty
MOTTLE, -D, -S, MOTTLING vb colour with streaks or blotches of different shades ▷ n mottled appearance, as of the surface of marble
MOTTLER, -S n paintbrush for mottled effects
MOTTLES ▸ mottle
MOTTLING ▸ mottle
MOTTO, -ES, -S n saying expressing an ideal or rule of conduct
MOTTOED adj having motto
MOTTOES ▸ motto
MOTTOS ▸ motto
MOTTS ▸ mott
MOTTY, MOTTIER, MOTTIES, MOTTIEST n target at which coins are aimed in pitch-and-toss ▷ adj containing motes
MOTUCA, -S n Brazilian fly
MOTZA, -S same as ▸ motser
MOU, -S Scots word for ▸ mouth
MOUCH, -ED, -ES, -ING same as ▸ mooch
MOUCHARD n police informer
MOUCHED ▸ mouch
MOUCHER, -S ▸ mouch
MOUCHES ▸ mouch
MOUCHING ▸ mouch
MOUCHOIR n handkerchief
MOUE, -S n disdainful or pouting look
MOUFFLON same as ▸ mouflon
MOUFLON, -S n wild mountain sheep of Corsica and Sardinia
MOUGHT ▸ may
MOUILLE adj palatalized, as in the sounds represented by Spanish ll or ñ

MOUJIK, -S same as ▸ muzhik
MOULAGE, -S n mould making
MOULD, -ED, -S n hollow container in which metal etc is cast ▷ vb shape
MOULDER, -S vb decay into dust ▷ n person who moulds or makes moulds
MOULDIER ▸ mouldy
MOULDING n moulded ornamental edging
MOULDS ▸ mould
MOULDY, MOULDIER adj stale or musty
MOULIN, -S n vertical shaft in a glacier
MOULINET n device for bending crossbow
MOULINS ▸ moulin
MOULS Scots word for ▸ mould
MOULT, -ED, -ING, -S vb shed feathers, hair, or skin to make way for new growth ▷ n process of moulting
MOULTEN adj having moulted
MOULTER, -S ▸ moult
MOULTING ▸ moult
MOULTS ▸ moult
MOUND, -ED, -ING, -S n heap, esp of earth or stones ▷ vb gather into a mound
MOUNSEER same as ▸ monsieur
MOUNT, -S vb climb or ascend ▷ n backing or support on which something is fixed
MOUNTAIN n hill of great size ▷ adj of, found on, or for use on a mountain or mountains
MOUNTANT n adhesive for mounting pictures
MOUNTED adj riding horses
MOUNTER, -S ▸ mount
MOUNTING same as ▸ mount
MOUNTS ▸ mount
MOUP, -ED, -ING, -S vb nibble
MOURN, -ED, -S vb feel or express sorrow for (a dead person or lost thing)
MOURNER, -S n person attending a funeral
MOURNFUL adj sad or dismal
MOURNING n grieving ▷ adj of or relating to mourning
MOURNS ▸ mourn
MOUS ▸ mou
MOUSAKA, -S same as ▸ moussaka

MOUSE, MICE, -D, -S *n* small long-tailed rodent ▷ *vb* stalk and catch mice

MOUSEKIN *n* little mouse

MOUSEMAT *n* piece of material on which a computer mouse is moved

MOUSEPAD *n* pad for computer mouse

MOUSER, -S *n* cat used to catch mice

MOUSERY *n* place infested with mice

MOUSES ▸ mouse

MOUSEY *same as* ▸ **mousy**

MOUSIE, -S *n* little mouse

MOUSIER ▸ mousy

MOUSIES ▸ mousie

MOUSIEST ▸ mousy

MOUSILY ▸ mousy

MOUSING, -S *n* device for closing off a hook

MOUSLE, -D, -S, MOUSLING *vb* handle roughly

MOUSME, -S *n* Japanese girl or young woman

MOUSMEE, -S *same as* ▸ **mousme**

MOUSMES ▸ mousme

MOUSSAKA *n* dish made with meat, aubergines, and tomatoes, topped with cheese sauce

MOUSSE, -D, -S, MOUSSING *n* dish of flavoured cream whipped and set ▷ *vb* apply mousse to

MOUSSEUX *n* type of sparkling wine

MOUSSING ▸ mousse

MOUST, -ED, -ING, -S *same as* ▸ **must**

MOUSY, MOUSIER, MOUSIEST *adj* like a mouse, esp in hair colour

MOUTAN, -S *n* variety of peony

MOUTER, -ED, -S *same as* ▸ **multure**

MOUTERER ▸ mouter

MOUTERS ▸ mouter

MOUTH, -ED, -ING, -S *n* opening in the head for eating and issuing sounds ▷ *vb* form (words) with the lips without speaking

MOUTHER, -S ▸ mouth

MOUTHFUL *n* amount of food or drink put into the mouth at any one time when eating or drinking

MOUTHIER ▸ mouthy

MOUTHILY ▸ mouthy

MOUTHING ▸ mouth

MOUTHS ▸ mouth

MOUTHY, MOUTHIER *adj* bombastic

MOUTON, -S *n* sheepskin processed to resemble the fur of another animal

MOVABLE, -S *adj* able to be moved or rearranged ▷ *n* movable article, esp a piece of furniture

MOVABLY ▸ movable

MOVANT, -S *n* person who applies to a court of law

MOVE, -D, -S *vb* change in place or position ▷ *n* moving

MOVEABLE *same as* ▸ **movable**

MOVEABLY ▸ moveable

MOVED ▸ move

MOVELESS *adj* immobile

MOVEMENT *n* action or process of moving

MOVER, -S *n* person or animal that moves in a particular way

MOVES ▸ move

MOVIE, -S *n* cinema film

MOVIEDOM *n* world of cinema

MOVIEOKE *n* entertainment in which people act out scenes from movies

MOVIEOLA *same as* ▸ **moviola**

MOVIES ▸ movie

MOVING *adj* arousing or touching the emotions

MOVINGLY ▸ moving

MOVIOLA, -S *n* viewing machine used in cutting and editing film

MOW, -ED, -N, -S *vb* cut (grass or crops) ▷ *n* part of a barn where hay, straw, etc, is stored

MOWA, -S *same as* ▸ **mahua**

MOWBURN, -S *vb* heat up in mow

MOWBURNT *adj* (of hay, straw, etc) damaged by overheating in a mow

MOWDIE, -S *Scots word for* ▸ **mole**

MOWED ▸ mow

MOWER, -S ▸ mow

MOWING, -S ▸ mow

MOWN ▸ mow

MOWRA, -S *same as* ▸ **mahua**

MOWS ▸ mow

MOXA, -S *n* downy material obtained from various plants

MOXIE, -S *n* courage, nerve, or vigour

MOY, -S *n* coin

MOYA, -S *n* mud emitted from a volcano

MOYITY, MOYITIES *same as* ▸ **moiety**

MOYL, -S *same as* ▸ **moyle**

MOYLE, -D, -S, MOYLING *vb* toil

MOYLS ▸ moyl

MOYS ▸ moy

MOZ, -ES *n* hex

This unusual word, Australian slang for bad luck, is another of the very useful short words that use the Z, and it can be extended to **moze** or **mozo**.

MOZE, -D, MOZING *vb* give nap to

MOZES ▸ moz

MOZETTA, -S, MOZETTE *same as* ▸ **mozzetta**

MOZING ▸ moze

MOZO, -S *n* porter in southwest USA

MOZZ, -ES *same as* ▸ **moz**

MOZZETTA, MOZZETTE *n* short hooded cape worn by the pope, cardinals, etc

MOZZIE, -S *same as* ▸ **mossie**

MOZZLE, -D, -S, MOZZLING *n* luck ▷ *vb* hamper or impede (someone)

MPRET, -S *n* former Albanian ruler

MRIDANG, -S *n* drum used in Indian music

MRIDANGA *same as* ▸ **mridang**

MRIDANGS ▸ mridang

MU, -S *n* twelfth letter in the Greek alphabet

MUCATE, -S *n* salt of mucic acid

MUCH, -ES *adj* large amount or degree of ▷ *n* large amount or degree ▷ *adv* great degree

MUCHACHA *n* (in Spain) young woman or female servant

MUCHACHO *n* (in Spain) young man or male servant

MUCHEL, -S *same as* ▸ **much**

MUCHELL, -S *same as* ▸ **much**

MUCHELS ▸ muchel

MUCHES ▸ much

MUCHLY ▸ much

MUCHNESS *n* magnitude

MUCHO *adv* Spanish for very

MUCIC *adj* as in **mucic acid** colourless crystalline solid carboxylic acid

MUCID *adj* mouldy, musty, or slimy

MUCIDITY ▸ mucid

MUCIGEN, -S *n* substance present in mucous cells that is converted into mucin

M

MUCILAGE n gum or glue

MUCIN, -S n any of a group of nitrogenous mucoproteins occurring in saliva, skin, tendon, etc

MUCINOID adj of or like mucin

MUCINOUS ▶ mucin

MUCINS ▶ mucin

MUCK, -ED, -ING, -S n dirt, filth

MUCKER, -ED, -S n person who shifts broken rock or waste ▷ vb hoard

MUCKHEAP n dunghill

MUCKIER ▶ mucky

MUCKIEST ▶ mucky

MUCKILY ▶ mucky

MUCKING ▶ muck

MUCKLE, -R, -S, -ST adj large

MUCKLUCK same as ▶ mukluk

MUCKRAKE n agricultural rake for spreading manure ▷ vb seek out and expose scandal, esp concerning public figures

MUCKS ▶ muck

MUCKWORM n any larva or worm that lives in mud

MUCKY, MUCKIER, MUCKIEST adj dirty or muddy

MUCLUC, -S same as ▶ mukluk

MUCOID, -S adj of the nature of or resembling mucin ▷ n substance like mucin

MUCOIDAL same as ▶ mucoid

MUCOIDS ▶ mucoid

MUCOR, -S n type of fungus

MUCOSA, -E, -S n mucus-secreting membrane that lines body cavities

MUCOSAL ▶ mucosa

MUCOSAS ▶ mucosa

MUCOSE same as ▶ mucous

MUCOSITY ▶ mucous

MUCOUS adj of, resembling, or secreting mucus

MUCRO, -NES, -S n short pointed projection from certain parts or organs

MUCULENT adj like mucus

MUCUS, -ES n slimy secretion of the mucous membranes

MUD, -DED, -DING, -S n wet soft earth ▷ vb cover in mud

MUDBANK, -S n sloping area of mud beside a body of water

MUDBATH, -S n medicinal bath in heated mud

MUDBUG, -S n crayfish

MUDCAP, -S vb use explosive charge in blasting

MUDCAT, -S n any of several large North American catfish

MUDDED ▶ mud

MUDDER, -S n horse that runs well in mud

MUDDIED ▶ muddy

MUDDIER ▶ muddy

MUDDIES ▶ muddy

MUDDIEST ▶ muddy

MUDDILY ▶ muddy

MUDDING ▶ mud

MUDDLE, -D, -S vb confuse ▷ n state of confusion

MUDDLER, -S n person who muddles or muddles through

MUDDLES ▶ muddle

MUDDLIER ▶ muddly

MUDDLING ▶ muddle

MUDDLY, MUDDLIER ▶ muddle

MUDDY, MUDDIED, MUDDIER, MUDDIES, MUDDIEST, -ING adj covered or filled with mud ▷ vb make muddy

MUDEJAR n Spanish Moor ▷ adj of or relating to a style of architecture

MUDEYE, -S n larva of the dragonfly

MUDFISH n fish that lives at the muddy bottoms of rivers, lakes, etc

MUDFLAP, -S n flap above wheel to deflect mud

MUDFLAT, -S n tract of low muddy land

MUDFLOW, -S n flow of soil mixed with water down a steep unstable slope

MUDGE, -D, -S, MUDGING vb speak vaguely

MUDGER, -S ▶ mudge

MUDGES ▶ mudge

MUDGING ▶ mudge

MUDGUARD n cover over a wheel to prevent mud or water being thrown up by it

MUDHEN, -S n water bird living in muddy place

MUDHOLE, -S n hole with mud at bottom

MUDHOOK, -S n anchor

MUDIR, -S n local governor

MUDIRIA, -S n province of mudir

MUDIRIEH same as ▶ mudiria

MUDIRS ▶ mudir

MUDLARK, -S n street urchin ▷ vb play in mud

MUDPACK, -S n cosmetic paste applied to the face

MUDPIE, -S n small mass of mud moulded into a pie shape

MUDPUPPY n type of salamander

MUDRA, -S n hand movement in Hindu religious dancing

MUDROCK, -S n type of sedimentary rock

MUDROOM, -S n room where muddy shoes may be left

MUDS ▶ mud

MUDSCOW, -S n boat for travelling over mudflats

MUDSILL, -S n support for building at or below ground

MUDSLIDE n landslide of mud

MUDSLING, MUDSLUNG vb make accusations against a rival candidate

MUDSTONE n dark grey clay rock similar to shale but with the lamination less well developed

MUDWORT, -S n plant growing in mud

MUEDDIN, -S same as ▶ muezzin

MUENSTER n whitish-yellow semihard whole milk cheese, often flavoured with caraway or aniseed

MUESLI, -S n mixture of grain, nuts, and dried fruit

MUEZZIN, -S n official who summons Muslims to prayer

MUFF, -ED, -ING, -S n tube-shaped covering to keep the hands warm ▷ vb bungle (an action)

MUFFIN, -S n light round flat yeast cake

MUFFING ▶ muff

MUFFINS ▶ muffin

MUFFISH ▶ muff

MUFFLE, -D, -S, MUFFLING vb wrap up for warmth or to deaden sound ▷ n something that muffles

MUFFLER, -S n scarf

MUFFLES ▶ muffle

MUFFLING ▶ muffle

MUFFS ▶ muff

MUFLON, -S same as ▶ moufflon

MUFTI, -S n civilian clothes worn by a person who usually wears a uniform

MUG, -GED, -S n large drinking cup ▷ vb attack in order to rob

MUGFUL, -S same as ▶ mug

MUGG, -S same as ▶ mug

MUGGA, -S n Australian eucalyptus tree

MUGGAR, -S same as ▸ mugger

MUGGAS ▸ mugga

MUGGED ▸ mug

MUGGEE, -S n mugged person

MUGGER, -S n person who commits robbery with violence

MUGGIER ▸ muggy

MUGGIEST ▸ muggy

MUGGILY ▸ muggy

MUGGING, -S ▸ mug

MUGGINS n stupid or gullible person

MUGGISH same as ▸ muggy

MUGGLE, -S n person who does not possess supernatural powers

MUGGS ▸ mugg

MUGGUR, -S same as ▸ mugger

MUGGY, MUGGIER, MUGGIEST adj (of weather) damp and stifling

MUGHAL, -S same as ▸ mogul

MUGS ▸ mug

MUGSHOT, -S n police photograph of person's face

MUGWORT, -S n N temperate herbaceous plant with aromatic leaves

MUGWUMP, -S n neutral or independent person

MUHLY, MUHLIES n American grass

MUID, -S n former French measure of capacity

MUIL, -S same as ▸ mule

MUIR, -S same as ▸ moor

MUIRBURN same as ▸ moorburn

MUIRS ▸ muir

MUIST, -ED, -ING, -S same as ▸ must

MUJIK, -S same as ▸ muzhik

MUKHTAR, -S n lawyer in India

MUKLUK, -S n soft boot, usually of sealskin

MUKTUK, -S n thin outer skin of the beluga, used as food

MULBERRY n tree whose leaves are used to feed silkworms ▷ adj dark purple

MULCH, -ED, -ES, -ING n mixture of wet straw, leaves, etc ▷ vb cover (land) with mulch

MULCT, -ED, -ING, -S vb cheat or defraud ▷ n fine or penalty

MULE, -D, MULING n offspring of a horse and a donkey ▷ vb strike coin with different die on each side

MULES, -ED, -ES, -ING vb surgically remove folds of skin from a sheep

MULETA, -S n small cape attached to a stick used by a matador

MULETEER n mule driver

MULEY, -S adj (of cattle) having no horns ▷ n any hornless cow

MULGA, -S n Australian acacia shrub growing in desert regions

MULIE, -S n type of N American deer

MULING ▸ mule

MULISH adj obstinate

MULISHLY ▸ mulish

MULL, -ED, -ING, -S vb think (over) or ponder ▷ n promontory or headland

MULLA, -S same as ▸ mullah

MULLAH, -S n Muslim scholar, teacher, or religious leader

MULLAHED same as ▸ mullered

MULLAHS ▸ mullah

MULLARKY same as ▸ malarkey

MULLAS ▸ mulla

MULLED ▸ mull

MULLEIN, -S n type of European plant

MULLEN, -S same as ▸ mullein

MULLER, -S n flat heavy implement used to grind material ▷ vb beat up or defeat thoroughly

MULLERED adj drunk

MULLERS ▸ muller

MULLET, -S n edible sea fish

MULLEY, -S same as ▸ muley

MULLIGAN n stew made from odds and ends of food

MULLING ▸ mull

MULLION, -S n vertical dividing bar in a window ▷ vb furnish with mullions

MULLITE, -S n colourless mineral

MULLOCK, -S n waste material from a mine

MULLOCKY adj like mullock

MULLOWAY n large Australian sea fish, valued for sport and food

MULLS ▸ mull

MULMUL, -S n muslin

MULMULL, -S same as ▸ mulmul

MULMULS ▸ mulmul

MULSE, -S n drink containing honey

MULSH, -ED, -ES, -ING same as ▸ mulch

MULTEITY n manifoldness

MULTIAGE adj involving different age groups

MULTICAR adj involving several cars

MULTIDAY adj involving more than one day

MULTIFID adj having or divided into many lobes or similar segments

MULTIFIL n fibre made up of many filaments

MULTIGYM n exercise apparatus incorporating a variety of weights, used for toning the muscles

MULTIJET adj involving more than one jet

MULTIPED adj having many feet ▷ n insect or animal having many feet

MULTIPLE adj having many parts ▷ n quantity which contains another an exact number of times

MULTIPLY vb increase in number or degree

MULTITON adj weighing several tons

MULTIUSE adj suitable for more than one use

MULTIWAY adj having several paths or routes

MULTUM, -S n substance used in brewing

MULTURE, -D, -S n fee formerly paid to a miller for grinding grain ▷ vb take multure

MULTURER ▸ multure

MULTURES ▸ multure

MUM, -MED, -S n mother ▷ vb act in a mummer's play

MUMBLE, -D, -S vb speak indistinctly, mutter ▷ n indistinct utterance

MUMBLER, -S ▸ mumble

MUMBLES ▸ mumble

MUMBLIER ▸ mumbly

MUMBLING ▸ mumble

MUMBLY, MUMBLIER ▸ mumble

MUMM, -S same as ▸ mum

MUMMED ▸ mum

MUMMER, -ED, -S n actor in a traditional English folk play ▷ vb perform as a mummer

MUMMERY n performance by mummers

MUMMIA, -S n mummified flesh used as medicine

M

MUMMIED ▶ mummy

MUMMIES ▶ mummy

MUMMIFY vb preserve a body as a mummy

MUMMING, -S ▶ mum

MUMMOCK, -S same as ▶ mammock

MUMMS ▶ mumm

MUMMY, MUMMIED, MUMMIES, -ING n body embalmed and wrapped for burial in ancient Egypt ▷ vb mummify

MUMP, -ED, -ING vb be silent

MUMPER, -S ▶ mump

MUMPING ▶ mump

MUMPISH ▶ mumps

MUMPS n infectious disease with swelling in the glands of the neck

MUMS ▶ mum

MUMSY, MUMSIER, MUMSIES, MUMSIEST adj (of a woman) wearing clothes that are old-fashioned and unflattering ▷ n mother

MUMU, -S n oven in Papua New Guinea

MUN, -S same as ▶ maun

MUNCH, -ED, -ES, -ING vb chew noisily and steadily

MUNCHER, -S ▶ munch

MUNCHES ▶ munch

MUNCHIE n small amount of food eaten between meals

MUNCHIER ▶ munchy

MUNCHIES pl n craving for food

MUNCHING ▶ munch

MUNCHKIN n undersized person or a child, esp an appealing one

MUNCHY, MUNCHIER adj suitable for snacking

MUNDANE, -R adj everyday

MUNDIC, -S n iron pyrites

MUNDIFY vb cleanse

MUNDUNGO n tripe in Spain

MUNG, -ED, -ING, -S vb process (computer data)

MUNGA, -S n army canteen

MUNGCORN n maslin

MUNGE, -S vb modify a password into an unguessable state

MUNGED ▶ mung

MUNGES ▶ munge

MUNGING ▶ mung

MUNGO, -ES, -S n cheap felted fabric made from waste wool

MUNGOOSE same as ▶ mongoose

MUNGOS ▶ mungo

MUNGS ▶ mung

MUNI, -S n municipal radio broadcast

MUNIFY, MUNIFIED, MUNIFIES vb fortify

MUNIMENT n means of defence

MUNIS ▶ muni

MUNITE, -D, -S, MUNITING vb strengthen

MUNITION vb supply with munitions

MUNNION, -S archaic word for ▶ mullion

MUNS ▶ mun

MUNSHI, -S n secretary in India

MUNSTER, -S variant of ▶ muenster

MUNTED adj destroyed or ruined

MUNTER, -S n insulting word for an unattractive person

MUNTIN, -S n supporting or strengthening bar

MUNTINED adj having a muntin

MUNTING, -S same as ▶ muntin

MUNTINS ▶ muntin

MUNTJAC, -S n small Asian deer

MUNTJAK, -S same as ▶ muntjac

MUNTRIE, -S n Australian shrub with green-red edible berries

MUON, -S n elementary particle with a mass 207 times that of an electron

MUONIC ▶ muon

MUONIUM, -S n form of hydrogen

MUONS ▶ muon

MUPPET, -S n stupid person

MUQADDAM n person of authority in India

MURA, -S n group of people living together in Japanese countryside

MURAENA, -S n moray eel

MURAENID n eel of moray family

MURAGE, -S n tax levied for the construction or maintenance of town walls

MURAL, -S n painting on a wall ▷ adj of or relating to a wall

MURALED same as ▶ muralled

MURALIST ▶ mural

MURALLED adj decorated with mural

MURALS ▶ mural

MURAS ▶ mura

MURDABAD interj down with

MURDER, -ED, -S n unlawful intentional killing of a human being ▷ vb kill in this way

MURDEREE n murder victim

MURDERER n person who murders someone

MURDERS ▶ murder

MURE, -D, -S, MURING archaic or literary word for ▶ immure

MUREIN, -S n polymer found in cells

MURENA, -S same as ▶ muraena

MURES ▶ mure

MUREX, -ES, MURICES n marine gastropod formerly used as a source of purple dye

MURGEON, -S vb grimace at

MURIATE, -S obsolete name for a ▶ chloride

MURIATED ▶ muriate

MURIATES ▶ muriate

MURIATIC adj as in muriatic acid former name for a strong acid used in many industrial processes

MURICATE adj having a surface roughened by numerous short points

MURICES ▶ murex

MURID, -S n animal of the mouse family

MURIFORM adj like mouse

MURINE, -S n animal belonging to the family that includes rats and mice

MURING ▶ mure

MURK, -ED, -ER, -EST, -ING, -S n thick darkness ▷ adj dark or gloomy ▷ vb murder (a person)

MURKIER ▶ murky

MURKIEST ▶ murky

MURKILY ▶ murky

MURKING ▶ murk

MURKISH ▶ murk

MURKLY ▶ murk

MURKS ▶ murk

MURKSOME ▶ murk

MURKY, MURKIER, MURKIEST adj dark or gloomy

MURL, -ED, -ING, -S vb crumble

MURLAIN, -S n type of basket

MURLAN, -S same as ▶ murlain

MURLED ▶ murl

MURLIER ▸ murly
MURLIEST ▸ murly
MURLIN, -S same as ▸ **murlain**
MURLING ▸ murl
MURLINS ▸ murlin
MURLS ▸ murl
MURLY, MURLIER, MURLIEST ▸ murl
MURMUR, -ED, -S vb speak or say in a quiet indistinct way ▸ n continuous low indistinct sound
MURMURER ▸ murmur
MURMURS ▸ murmur
MURPHY, MURPHIES dialect or informal word for ▸ **potato**
MURR, -S n former name for a cold
MURRA, -S same as ▸ **murrhine**
MURRAGH, -S n type of large caddis fly
MURRAIN, -S n cattle plague
MURRAM, -S n type of gravel
MURRAS ▸ murra
MURRAY, -S n large Australian freshwater fish
MURRE, -S n type of guillemot
MURREE, -S n native Australian
MURRELET n type of small diving bird related to the auks
MURREN, -S same as ▸ **murrain**
MURRES ▸ murre
MURREY, -S adj mulberry colour
MURRHA, -S same as ▸ **murra**
MURRHINE adj of or relating to an unknown substance used in ancient Rome to make vases, cups, etc ▸ n substance so used
MURRI, -S same as ▸ **murree**
MURRIES ▸ murry
MURRIN, -S same as ▸ **murrain**
MURRINE, -S same as ▸ **murrhine**
MURRINS ▸ murrin
MURRION, -S same as ▸ **murrain**
MURRIS ▸ murri
MURRS ▸ murr
MURRY, MURRIES same as ▸ **moray**
MURSHID, -S n Sufi master or guide
MURTHER, -S same as ▸ **murder**

MURTI, -S n image of a deity, which itself is considered divine
MURVA, -S n type of hemp
MUS ▸ mu
MUSANG, -S n catlike animal of Malaysia
MUSAR, -S n rabbinic literature concerned with ethics
MUSCA, -E n small constellation in the S hemisphere
MUSCADEL same as ▸ **muscatel**
MUSCADET n white grape, used for making wine
MUSCADIN n Parisian dandy
MUSCAE ▸ musca
MUSCAT, -S same as ▸ **muscatel**
MUSCATEL n rich sweet wine made from muscat grapes
MUSCATS ▸ muscat
MUSCID, -S n type of fly
MUSCLE, -D, -S, MUSCLING n tissue in the body which produces movement ▸ vb force one's way (in)
MUSCLEY adj of a muscular build
MUSCLIER ▸ muscly
MUSCLING ▸ muscle
MUSCLY, MUSCLIER same as ▸ **muscley**
MUSCOID, -S adj moss-like ▸ n moss-like plant
MUSCONE, -S same as ▸ **muskone**
MUSCOSE adj like moss
MUSCOVY adj as in **muscovy duck** a kind of duck
MUSCULAR adj with well-developed muscles
MUSE, -D, -S vb ponder quietly ▸ n state of abstraction
MUSEFUL ▸ muse
MUSER, -S ▸ muse
MUSES ▸ muse
MUSET, -S same as ▸ **musit**
MUSETTE, -S n type of bagpipe formerly popular in France
MUSEUM, -S n building where objects are exhibited and preserved
MUSH, -ED, -ES n soft pulpy mass ▸ interj order to dogs in a sled team to start up or go faster ▸ vb travel by or drive a dogsled
MUSHA interj Irish exclamation of surprise

MUSHED ▸ mush
MUSHER, -S ▸ mush
MUSHES ▸ mush
MUSHIE, -S n mushroom
MUSHIER ▸ mushy
MUSHIES ▸ mushie
MUSHILY ▸ mushy
MUSHING, -S n act of mushing
MUSHRAT same as ▸ **muskrat**
MUSHRATS same as ▸ **mushrat**
MUSHROOM n edible fungus with a stem and cap ▸ vb grow rapidly
MUSHY, MUSHIER, MUSHIEST adj soft and pulpy
MUSIC, -KED, -S n art form using a melodious and harmonious combination of notes ▸ vb play music
MUSICAL, -S adj of or like music ▸ n play or film with songs and dancing
MUSICALE n party or social evening with a musical programme
MUSICALS ▸ musical
MUSICIAN n person who plays or composes music, esp as a profession
MUSICK, -S same as ▸ **music**
MUSICKED ▸ music
MUSICKER ▸ music
MUSICKS ▸ musick
MUSICS ▸ music
MUSIMON, -S same as ▸ **moufflon**
MUSING, -S ▸ muse
MUSINGLY ▸ muse
MUSINGS ▸ musing
MUSIT, -S n gap in fence
MUSIVE adj mosaic
MUSJID, -S same as ▸ **masjid**
MUSK, -ED, -ING, -S n scent obtained from a gland of the musk deer or produced synthetically ▸ vb perfume with musk
MUSKEG, -S n area of undrained boggy land
MUSKET, -S n long-barrelled gun
MUSKETRY n (use of) muskets
MUSKETS ▸ musket
MUSKIE, -S n large North American freshwater game fish
MUSKIER ▸ musky
MUSKIES ▸ muskie
MUSKIEST ▸ musky
MUSKILY ▸ musky

M

MUSKING ▸ musk

MUSKIT, -S same as ▸ mesquite

MUSKLE, -S same as ▸ mussel

MUSKONE, -S n substance in musk

MUSKOX, -EN n large Canadian mammal

MUSKRAT, -S n N American beaver-like rodent

MUSKROOT same as > moschatel

MUSKS ▸ musk

MUSKY, MUSKIER, MUSKIEST adj smelling of musk

MUSLIN, -S n fine cotton fabric

MUSLINED adj wearing muslin

MUSLINET n coarse muslin

MUSLINS ▸ muslin

MUSMON, -S same as ▸ musimon

MUSO, -S n musician who is concerned with technique rather than content or expression

MUSPIKE, -S n Canadian freshwater fish

MUSQUASH same as ▸ muskrat

MUSROL, -S n part of bridle

MUSS, -ED, -ES, -ING vb make untidy ▹ n state of disorder

MUSSE same as ▸ muss

MUSSED ▸ muss

MUSSEL, -S n edible shellfish with a dark hinged shell

MUSSES ▸ muss

MUSSIER ▸ mussy

MUSSIEST ▸ mussy

MUSSILY ▸ mussy

MUSSING ▸ muss

MUSSY, MUSSIER, MUSSIEST adj untidy or disordered

MUST, -ED, -ING, -S vb used as an auxiliary to express obligation, certainty, or resolution ▹ n essential or necessary thing

MUSTACHE same as > moustache

MUSTANG, -S n wild horse of SW USA

MUSTARD, -S n paste made from the powdered seeds of a plant ▹ adj brownish-yellow

MUSTARDY adj like mustard

MUSTED ▸ must

MUSTELID n member of weasel family

MUSTER, -ED, -S vb summon up ▹ n assembly of military personnel

MUSTERER ▸ muster

MUSTERS ▸ muster

MUSTH, -S n state of frenzied excitement in the males of certain large mammals

MUSTIER ▸ musty

MUSTIEST ▸ musty

MUSTILY ▸ musty

MUSTING ▸ must

MUSTS ▸ must

MUSTY, MUSTIER, MUSTIEST adj smelling mouldy and stale

MUT, -S another word for ▸ em

MUTABLE adj liable to change

MUTABLY ▸ mutable

MUTAGEN, -S n any substance that can induce genetic mutation

MUTANDUM, MUTANDA n something to be changed

MUTANT, -S n mutated animal, plant, etc ▹ adj of or resulting from mutation

MUTASE, -S n type of enzyme

MUTATE, -D, -S, MUTATING vb (cause to) undergo mutation

MUTATION same as ▸ mutant

MUTATIVE ▸ mutate

MUTATOR, -S n something that causes a mutation

MUTATORY adj subject to change

MUTCH, -ED, -ES, -ING n close-fitting linen cap ▹ vb cadge

MUTCHKIN n Scottish unit of liquid measure equal to slightly less than one pint

MUTE, -R, -S, -ST, MUTING adj silent ▹ vb reduce the volume or soften the tone of a musical instrument

MUTED adj (of sound or colour) softened

MUTEDLY ▸ muted

MUTELY ▸ mute

MUTENESS ▸ mute

MUTER ▸ mute

MUTES ▸ mute

MUTEST ▸ mute

MUTI, -S n medicine, esp herbal medicine

MUTICATE same as ▸ muticous

MUTICOUS adj lacking an awn, spine, or point

MUTILATE vb deprive of a limb or other part

MUTINE, -D, -S, MUTINING vb mutiny

MUTINEER n person who mutinies

MUTINES ▸ mutine

MUTING ▸ mute

MUTINIED ▸ mutiny

MUTINIES ▸ mutiny

MUTINING ▸ mutine

MUTINOUS adj openly rebellious

MUTINY, MUTINIED, MUTINIES n rebellion against authority, esp by soldiers or sailors ▹ vb commit mutiny

MUTIS ▸ muti

MUTISM, -S n state of being mute

MUTON, -S n part of gene

MUTS ▸ mut

MUTT, -S n mongrel dog

MUTTER, -ED, -S vb utter or speak indistinctly ▹ n muttered sound or grumble

MUTTERER ▸ mutter

MUTTERS ▸ mutter

MUTTON, -S n flesh of sheep, used as food

MUTTONY adj like mutton

MUTTS ▸ mutt

MUTUAL, -S adj felt or expressed by each of two people about the other ▹ n mutual company

MUTUALLY ▸ mutual

MUTUALS ▸ mutual

MUTUCA, -S same as ▸ motuca

MUTUEL, -S n system of betting

MUTULAR ▸ mutule

MUTULE, -S n flat block in a Doric cornice

MUTUUM, -S n contract for loan of goods

MUUMUU, -S n loose brightly coloured dress worn by women in Hawaii

MUX, -ED, -ES, -ING vb spoil

> This word meaning to spoil or botch is very useful not only because it contains an X, but because its verb forms can enable you to clear your rack of unpromising letters.

MUZAK, -S n piped background music

MUZAKIER ▸ muzaky

MUZAKS ▸ muzak

MUZAKY, MUZAKIER adj having a bland sound

MUZHIK, -S n Russian peasant, esp under the tsars

MUZJIK, -S same as ▸ **muzhik**

Meaning a Russian peasant, this is a wonderful high-scoring word, combining Z, J and K, and if you can play the plural using all of your tiles, you'll get a bonus of 50 points.

MUZZ, -ED, -ES, -ING vb make (something) muzzy

MUZZIER ▸ **muzzy**

MUZZIEST ▸ **muzzy**

MUZZILY ▸ **muzzy**

MUZZING ▸ **muzz**

MUZZLE, -D, -S, MUZZLING n animal's mouth and nose ▸ vb prevent from being heard or noticed

MUZZLER, -S ▸ **muzzle**

MUZZLES ▸ **muzzle**

MUZZLING ▸ **muzzle**

MUZZY, MUZZIER, MUZZIEST adj confused or muddled

MVULE, -S n tropical African tree

MWAH interj representation of the sound of a kiss

MWALIMU, -S n teacher

MY adj belonging to me ▸ interj exclamation of surprise or awe

MYAL ▸ **myalism**

MYALGIA, -S n pain in a muscle or a group of muscles

MYALGIC ▸ **myalgia**

MYALISM, -S n kind of witchcraft

MYALIST, -S ▸ **myalism**

MYALL, -S n Australian acacia with hard scented wood

MYASIS, MYASES same as ▸ **myiasis**

MYC, -S n oncogene that aids the growth of tumorous cells

MYCELE, -S n microscopic spike-like structure in mucus

MYCELIA ▸ **mycelium**

MYCELIAL ▸ **mycelium**

MYCELIAN ▸ **mycelium**

MYCELIUM, MYCELIA n mass forming the body of a fungus

MYCELLA, -S n blue-veined Danish cream cheese

MYCELOID ▸ **mycelium**

MYCETES n fungus

MYCETOMA n chronic fungal infection

MYCOLOGY n study of fungi

MYCOSIS, MYCOSES n any infection or disease caused by fungus

MYCOTIC ▸ **mycosis**

MYCS ▸ **myc**

MYELIN, -S n white tissue forming an insulating sheath around certain nerve fibres

MYELINE, -S same as ▸ **myelin**

MYELINIC ▸ **myelin**

MYELINS ▸ **myelin**

MYELITIS, MYELITES n inflammation of the spinal cord or of the bone marrow

MYELOID adj of or relating to the spinal cord or the bone marrow

MYELOMA, -S n tumour of the bone marrow

MYELON, -S n spinal cord

MYGALE, -S n large American spider

MYIASIS, MYIASES n infestation of the body by the larvae of flies

MYLAR, -S n tradename for a kind of strong polyester film

MYLODON, -S n prehistoric giant sloth

MYLODONT same as ▸ **mylodon**

MYLONITE n fine-grained metamorphic rock

MYNA, -S same as ▸ **mynah**

MYNAH, -S n tropical Asian starling which can mimic human speech

MYNAS ▸ **myna**

MYNHEER, -S n Dutch title of address

MYOBLAST n cell from which muscle develops

MYOGEN, -S n albumin found in muscle

MYOGENIC adj originating in or forming muscle tissue

MYOGENS ▸ **myogen**

MYOGRAM, -S n tracings of muscular contractions

MYOGRAPH n instrument for recording tracings of muscular contractions

MYOID, -S adj like muscle ▸ n section of a retinal cone or rod which is sensitive to changes in light intensity

MYOLOGIC ▸ **myology**

MYOLOGY n study of the structure and diseases of muscles

MYOMA, -S, -TA n benign tumour composed of muscle tissue

MYOMANCY n divination through observing mice

MYOMAS ▸ **myoma**

MYOMATA ▸ **myoma**

MYOMERE, -S n part of a vertebrate embryo

MYOPATHY n any disease affecting muscles or muscle tissue

MYOPE, -S n a person with myopia

MYOPHILY n pollination of plants by flies

MYOPIA, -S n short-sightedness

MYOPIC, -S n shortsighted person

MYOPIES ▸ **myopy**

MYOPS, -ES same as ▸ **myope**

MYOPY, MYOPIES same as ▸ **myopia**

MYOSCOPE n electrical instrument for stimulating muscles

MYOSES ▸ **myosis**

MYOSIN, -S n protein found in muscle

MYOSIS, MYOSES, -ES same as ▸ **miosis**

MYOSITIS n inflammation of muscle

MYOSOTE, -S same as ▸ **myosotis**

MYOSOTIS n type of hairy-leaved flowering plant, such as the forget-me-not

MYOTIC, -S ▸ **miosis**

MYOTOME, -S n any segment of embryonic mesoderm that develops into skeletal muscle

MYOTONIA n lack of muscle tone, frequently including muscle spasm or rigidity

MYOTONIC ▸ **myotonia**

MYOTUBE, -S n cylindrical cell in muscle

MYRBANE, -S same as ▸ **mirbane**

MYRIAD, -S adj innumerable ▸ n large indefinite number

MYRIADTH ▸ **myriad**

MYRIAPOD n type of invertebrate with a long segmented body and many legs, such as a centipede

MYRICA, -S n dried root bark of the wax myrtle

MYRINGA, -S n eardrum

MYRIOPOD same as ▸ **myriapod**

MYRISTIC adj of nutmeg plant family

MYRMIDON n follower or henchperson

M

MYRRH, -S n aromatic gum used in perfume, incense, and medicine
MYRRHIC ▸ myrrh
MYRRHIER ▸ myrrhy
MYRRHINE ▸ murra
MYRRHOL, -S n oil of myrrh
MYRRHS ▸ myrrh
MYRRHY, MYRRHIER adj of or like myrrh
MYRTLE, -S n flowering evergreen shrub
MYSELF pron reflexive form of I or me
MYSID, -S n small shrimplike crustacean
MYSOST, -S n Norwegian cheese
MYSPACE, -D, -S vb search for (someone) on the MySpace website
MYSTAGOG n person instructing others in religious mysteries
MYSTERY n strange or inexplicable thing
MYSTIC, -S n person who seeks spiritual knowledge ▷ adj mystical
MYSTICAL adj having a spiritual or religious significance beyond human understanding
MYSTICLY ▸ mystic
MYSTICS ▸ mystic
MYSTIFY vb bewilder or puzzle
MYSTIQUE n aura of mystery or power
MYTH, -S n tale with supernatural characters
MYTHI ▸ mythus
MYTHIC same as ▸ **mythical**
MYTHICAL adj of or relating to myth
MYTHIER ▸ mythy
MYTHIEST ▸ mythy
MYTHISE, -D, -S same as ▸ **mythize**
MYTHISM, -S same as > **mythicism**
MYTHIST, -S ▸ mythism
MYTHIZE, -D, -S same as > **mythicize**
MYTHOS, MYTHOI n beliefs of a specific group or society
MYTHS ▸ myth
MYTHUS, MYTHI same as ▸ **mythos**
MYTHY, MYTHIER, MYTHIEST adj of or like myth
MYTILOID adj like mussel
MYXAMEBA same as > **myxamoeba**
MYXEDEMA same as > **myxoedema**
MYXO, -S n viral disease of rabbits
MYXOCYTE n cell in mucous tissue
MYXOID adj containing mucus
MYXOMA, -S, -TA n tumour composed of mucous connective tissue
MYXOS ▸ myxo
MZEE, -S n old person ▷ adj advanced in years
MZUNGU, -S n (in E Africa) White person

M

Nn

Along with **R** and **T**, **N** is one of the most common consonants in Scrabble. As you'll often have it on your rack, it's well worth learning what **N** can do in different situations. **N** is useful when you need short words, as it begins two-letter words with every vowel except **I**, and with **Y** as well. There are plenty of three-letter words starting with ▶**N**, but there aren't many high-scoring ones apart from **nix** for 10 points each, **nym** for 8 points and **nek** for 7 points. Remember words like **nab** (5 points), **nag** (4), **nap** (5), **nav** (6), **nay** (6), **new** (6), **nib** (5), **nob** (5), **nod** (4), **now** (6) and **nug** (4).

NA same as ▶ **nae**

NAAM, -S same as ▶ **nam**

NAAN, -S n slightly leavened flat Indian bread

NAARTJE, -S same as ▶ **naartjie**

NAARTJIE n tangerine

NAB, -BED, -BING, -S vb arrest (someone)

NABBER, -S n thief

NABBING ▶ **nab**

NABE, -S n Japanese hotpot

NABIS n Parisian art movement

NABK, -S n edible berry

NABLA, -S another name for ▶ **del**

NABOB, -S n rich, powerful, or important man

NABOBERY ▶ **nabob**

NABOBESS ▶ **nabob**

NABOBISH ▶ **nabob**

NABOBISM ▶ **nabob**

NABOBS ▶ **nabob**

NABS ▶ **nab**

NACARAT, -S n red-orange colour

NACELLE, -S n streamlined enclosure on an aircraft

NACH n Indian dance

NACHAS n pleasure

NACHE, -S n rump

NACHO, -S n snack of a piece of tortilla with a topping

NACKET, -S n light lunch, snack

NACRE, -S n mother of pearl

NACRED ▶ **nacre**

NACREOUS ▶ **nacre**

NACRES ▶ **nacre**

NACRITE, -S n mineral

NACROUS ▶ **nacre**

NADA, -S n nothing

NADIR, -S n point in the sky opposite the zenith

NADIRAL ▶ **nadir**

NADIRS ▶ **nadir**

NAE, -S Scot word for ▶ **no**

NAEBODY Scots variant of ▶ **nobody**

NAES ▶ **nae**

NAETHING Scots variant of ▶ **nothing**

NAEVE, -S n birthmark

NAEVI ▶ **naevus**

NAEVOID ▶ **naevus**

NAEVUS, NAEVI n birthmark or mole

NAFF, -ED, -ER, -EST, -ING, -S adj lacking quality or taste ▷ vb go away

NAFFLY ▶ **naff**

NAFFNESS ▶ **naff**

NAFFS ▶ **naff**

NAG, -GED, -GING, -S vb scold or find fault constantly ▷ n person who nags

NAGA, -S n cobra

NAGANA, -S n disease of all domesticated animals of central and southern Africa

NAGAPIE, -S n bushbaby

NAGARI, -S n scripts for writing several languages of India

NAGAS ▶ **naga**

NAGGED ▶ **nag**

NAGGER, -S ▶ **nag**

NAGGIER ▶ **naggy**

NAGGIEST ▶ **naggy**

NAGGING, -S ▶ **nag**

NAGGY, NAGGIER, NAGGIEST ▶ **nag**

NAGMAAL, -S n Communion

NAGOR, -S another name for ▶ **reedbuck**

NAGS ▶ **nag**

NAGWARE, -S n software that is initially free and then requires payment

NAH same as ▶ **no**

NAHAL, -S n agricultural settlement run by an Israeli military youth organization

NAIAD, -ES, -S n nymph living in a lake or river

NAIANT adj swimming

NAIF, -ER, -EST, -S less common word for ▶ **naive**

NAIFLY ▶ **naif**

NAIFNESS ▶ **naif**

NAIFS ▶ **naif**

NAIK, -S n chief

NAIL, -ED, -S n pointed piece of metal used to join two objects together ▷ vb attach (something) with nails

NAILER, -S ▶ **nail**

NAILERY n nail factory

NAILFILE n small metal file used to shape and smooth the nails

NAILFOLD n skin at base of fingernail

NAILHEAD n decorative device, as on tooled leather, resembling the round head of a nail

NAILING, -S ▶ **nail**

NAILLESS ▶ **nail**

NAILS ▶ **nail**

NAILSET, -S n punch for driving down the head of a nail

NAIN adj own

NAINSELL n own self

NAINSOOK n light soft plain-weave cotton fabric, used esp for babies' wear

N

NAIRA, -S *n* standard monetary unit of Nigeria, divided into 100 kobo

NAIRU, -S *n* Non-Accelerating Inflation Rate of Unemployment

NAISSANT *adj* (of a beast) having only the forepart shown above a horizontal division of a shield

NAIVE, -R, -S, -ST *adj* innocent and gullible ▷ *n* person who is naive, esp in artistic style

NAIVELY ▶ naive
NAIVER ▶ naive
NAIVES ▶ naive
NAIVEST ▶ naive
NAIVETE, -S *variant of* ▶ naivety
NAIVETY *n* state or quality of being naive
NAIVIST ▶ naive
NAKED, -ER, -EST *adj* without clothes
NAKEDLY ▶ naked
NAKER, -S *n* small kettledrum used in medieval music
NAKFA, -S *n* standard currency unit of Eritrea
NALA, -S *n* ravine
NALED, -S *n* type of insecticide
NALLA, -S *n* ravine
NALLAH, -S *same as* ▶ nalla
NALLAS ▶ nalla
NALOXONE *n* substance that counteracts opiates
NAM, -S *n* distraint
NAMABLE ▶ name
NAMASKAR *n* salutation used in India
NAMASTE, -S *n* Indian greeting
NAME, -D, -S *n* word by which a person or thing is known ▷ *vb* give a name to
NAMEABLE ▶ name
NAMED ▶ name
NAMELESS *adj* without a name
NAMELY *adv* that is to say
NAMER, -S ▶ name
NAMES ▶ name
NAMESAKE *n* person with the same name as another
NAMETAG, -S *n* identification badge
NAMETAPE *n* narrow cloth tape bearing the owner's name and attached to an article
NAMING, -S ▶ name
NAMMA *adj* as in namma hole Australian word for a natural well in rock

NAMS ▶ nam
NAMU, -S *n* black New Zealand sandfly
NAN, -S *n* grandmother
NANA, -S *same as* ▶ nan
NANDIN, -S *same as* ▶ nandina
NANDINA, -S *n* type of shrub
NANDINE, -S *n* African palm civet
NANDINS ▶ nandin
NANDOO, -S *same as* ▶ nandu
NANDU, -S *n* type of ostrich
NANE *Scot word for* ▶ none
NANG *adj* excellent; cool
NANISM, -S *n* dwarfism
NANITE, -S *n* microscopically small machine or robot
NANKEEN, -S *n* hard-wearing buff-coloured cotton fabric
NANKIN, -S *same as* ▶ nankeen
NANNA, -S *same as* ▶ nan
NANNIE *same as* ▶ nanny
NANNY, NANNIED, NANNIES *n* woman whose job is looking after young children ▷ *vb* be too protective towards
NANNYGAI *n* edible sea fish of Australia which is red in colour and has large prominent eyes
NANNYING *n* act of nannying
NANNYISH ▶ nanny
NANO, -S *n* science concerned with materials on a molecular scale
NANOBE, -S *n* microbe that is smaller than the smallest known bacterium
NANOBEE, -S *n* artificial nanoparticle
NANOBES ▶ nanobe
NANOBOT, -S *n* microscopically small robot
NANODOT, -S *n* microscopic cluster of atoms used to store data in a computer chip
NANOGRAM *n* unit of measurement
NANOOK, -S *n* polar bear
NANOPORE *n* microscopically small pore in an electrically insulating membrane
NANOS ▶ nano
NANOTECH *n* technology of very small objects
NANOTUBE *n* cylindrical molecule of carbon

NANOWATT *n* unit of measurement
NANOWIRE *n* microscopically thin wire
NANS ▶ nan
NANUA, -S *same as* ▶ moki
NAOS, NAOI, -ES *n* ancient classical temple
NAP, -PED, -PING, -S *n* short sleep ▷ *vb* have a short sleep
NAPA, -S *n* type of leather
NAPALM, -ED, -S *n* highly inflammable jellied petrol, used in bombs ▷ *vb* attack (people or places) with napalm
NAPAS ▶ napa
NAPE, -D, -S, NAPING *n* back of the neck ▷ *vb* attack with napalm
NAPERY, NAPERIES *n* household linen, esp table linen
NAPES ▶ nape
NAPHTHA, -S *n* liquid mixture used as a solvent and in petrol
NAPHTHOL *n* white crystalline solid used in dyes
NAPHTHYL *n* type of monovalent radical
NAPHTOL, -S *same as* ▶ naphthol
NAPIFORM *adj* shaped like a turnip
NAPING ▶ nape
NAPKIN, -S *same as* ▶ nappy
NAPLESS *adj* threadbare
NAPOLEON *n* former French gold coin worth 20 francs
NAPOO, -ED, -ING, -S *vb* military slang meaning kill
NAPPA, -S *n* soft leather
NAPPE, -S *n* mass of rock that has been thrust from its original position by earth movements
NAPPED ▶ nap
NAPPER, -S *n* person or thing that raises the nap on cloth
NAPPES ▶ nappe
NAPPIE *same as* ▶ nappy
NAPPIER ▶ nappy
NAPPIES ▶ nappy
NAPPIEST ▶ nappy
NAPPING ▶ nap
NAPPY, NAPPIER, NAPPIES, NAPPIEST *n* piece of absorbent material fastened round a baby's lower torso ▷ *adj* having a nap
NAPRON, -S *same as* ▶ apron
NAPROXEN *n* pain-killing drug
NAPS ▶ nap

NARAS, -ES same as ▶ **narras**

NARCEEN, -S same as ▶ **narceine**

NARCEIN, -S same as ▶ **narceine**

NARCEINE n narcotic alkaloid that occurs in opium

NARCEINS ▶ **narcein**

NARCISM, -S n exceptional admiration for oneself

NARCISSI ▶ **narcissus**

NARCIST, -S n narcissist

NARCOMA, -S n coma caused by intake of narcotic drugs

NARCOSE same as ▶ **narcosis**

NARCOSIS, NARCOSES n effect of a narcotic

NARCOTIC adj of a drug which produces numbness and drowsiness ▷ n such a drug

NARD, -ED, -ING, -S n any of several plants with aromatic roots ▷ vb anoint with nard oil

NARDINE ▶ **nard**

NARDING ▶ **nard**

NARDOO, -S n cloverlike fern which grows in swampy areas

NARDS ▶ **nard**

NARES, NARIS pl n nostrils

NARGHILE another name for ▶ **hookah**

NARGHILY same as ▶ **narghile**

NARGILE, -S same as ▶ **narghile**

NARGILEH same as ▶ **narghile**

NARGILES ▶ **nargile**

NARGILY same as ▶ **narghile**

NARIAL adj of or relating to the nares

NARIC ▶ **nares**

NARICORN n bird's nostril

NARINE same as ▶ **narial**

NARIS ▶ **nares**

NARK, -ED, -ING, -S vb annoy ▷ n informer or spy

NARKIER ▶ **narky**

NARKIEST ▶ **narky**

NARKING ▶ **nark**

NARKS ▶ **nark**

NARKY, NARKIER, NARKIEST adj irritable or complaining

NARQUOIS adj malicious

NARRAS, -ES n type of shrub

NARRATE, -D, -S vb tell (a story)

NARRATER same as ▶ **narrator**

NARRATES ▶ **narrate**

NARRATOR n person who tells a story or gives an account of something

NARRE adj nearer

NARROW, -ED, -ER adj small in breadth in comparison to length ▷ vb make or become narrow

NARROWLY ▶ **narrow**

NARROWS n narrow part of a strait, river, or current

NARTHEX n portico at the west end of a basilica or church

NARTJIE, -S same as ▶ **naartjie**

This word for a small sweet orange is one to look out for when you have the J with the good letters of 'retain'. And it has alternative spellings **naartje** and **naartjie**.

NARWAL, -S same as ▶ **narwhal**

NARWHAL, -S n Arctic whale with a long spiral tusk

NARWHALE same as ▶ **narwhal**

NARWHALS ▶ **narwhal**

NARY adv not

NAS vb has not

NASAL, -S adj of the nose ▷ n nasal speech sound, such as English m, n, or ng

NASALISE same as ▶ **nasalize**

NASALISM n nasal pronunciation

NASALITY ▶ **nasal**

NASALIZE vb pronounce nasally

NASALLY ▶ **nasal**

NASALS ▶ **nasal**

NASARD, -S n organ stop

NASCENCE ▶ **nascent**

NASCENCY ▶ **nascent**

NASCENT adj starting to grow or develop

NASHGAB, -S n chatter

NASHI, -S n fruit of the Japanese pear

NASIAL ▶ **nasion**

NASION, -S n craniometric point where the top of the nose meets the ridge of the forehead

NASSELLA n as in **nassella tussock** type of tussock grass

NASTALIK n type of script

NASTIC adj (of movement of plants) independent of the direction of the external stimulus

NASTIER ▶ **nasty**

NASTIES ▶ **nasty**

NASTIEST ▶ **nasty**

NASTILY ▶ **nasty**

NASTY, NASTIER, NASTIES, NASTIEST adj unpleasant ▷ n something unpleasant

NASUTE, -S n type of termite

NAT, -S n supporter of nationalism

NATAL adj of or relating to birth

NATALITY n birth rate in a given place

NATANT adj (of aquatic plants) floating on the water

NATANTLY adv in a floating manner

NATATION n swimming

NATATORY adj of or relating to swimming

NATCH, -ES sentence substitute naturally ▷ n notch

NATES, NATIS pl n buttocks

NATHEMO same as ▶ **nathemore**

NATHLESS same as ▶ **natheless**

NATIFORM adj resembling buttocks

NATION, -S n country and its social and political structures

NATIONAL adj of or serving a nation as a whole ▷ n citizen of a nation

NATIONS ▶ **nation**

NATIS ▶ **nates**

NATIVE, -S adj relating to a place where a person was born ▷ n person born in a place

NATIVELY ▶ **native**

NATIVES ▶ **native**

NATIVISM n policy of favouring the natives of a country over the immigrants

NATIVIST ▶ **nativism**

NATIVITY n birth or origin

NATRIUM, -S obsolete name for ▶ **sodium**

NATRON, -S n whitish or yellow mineral

NATS ▶ **nat**

NATTER, -ED, -S vb talk idly or chatter ▷ n long idle chat

NATTERER ▶ **natter**

NATTERS ▶ **natter**

NATTERY adj irritable

NATTIER ▶ **natty**

NATTIEST ▶ **natty**

NATTILY ▶ **natty**

NATTY, NATTIER, NATTIEST adj smart and spruce

NATURA, -E n nature

N

NATURAL, -S *adj* normal or to be expected ▷ *n* person with an inborn talent or skill

NATURE, -S *n* whole system of the physical world not controlled by human beings

NATURED *adj* having a certain disposition

NATURES ▶ **nature**

NATURING *adj* creative

NATURISM *n* nudism

NATURIST ▶ **naturism**

NAUCH, -ES *same as* ▶ **nautch**

NAUGHT, -S *n* nothing ▷ *adv* not at all

NAUGHTY *adj* disobedient or mischievous

NAUMACHY *same as* > **naumachia**

NAUNT, -S *n* aunt

NAUPLIAL *adj* of or like a nauplius, the larval form of certain crustaceans

NAUPLIUS, NAUPLII *n* larva of many crustaceans

NAUSEA, -S *n* feeling of being about to vomit

NAUSEANT *n* substance inducing nausea

NAUSEAS ▶ **nausea**

NAUSEATE *vb* make (someone) feel sick

NAUSEOUS *adj* as if about to vomit

NAUTCH, -ES *n* intricate traditional Indian dance

NAUTIC *same as* ▶ **nautical**

NAUTICAL *adj* of the sea or ships

NAUTICS *n* science of navigation

NAUTILUS, NAUTILI *n* shellfish with many tentacles

NAV, -S *n* (short for) navigation

NAVAID, -S *n* navigational aid

NAVAL *adj* of or relating to a navy or ships

NAVALISM *n* domination of naval interests

NAVALLY ▶ **naval**

NAVAR, -S *n* system of air navigation

NAVARCH, -S *n* admiral

NAVARCHY *n* navarch's term of office

NAVARHO, -S *n* aircraft navigation system

NAVARIN, -S *n* stew of mutton or lamb with root vegetables

NAVARS ▶ **navar**

NAVE, -S *n* long central part of a church

NAVEL, -S *n* hollow in the middle of the abdomen

NAVES ▶ **nave**

NAVETTE, -S *n* gem cut

NAVEW, -S *another name for* ▶ **turnip**

NAVICERT *n* certificate specifying the contents of a neutral ship's cargo

NAVICULA *n* incense holder

NAVIES ▶ **navy**

NAVIGATE *vb* direct or plot the path or position of a ship, aircraft, or car

NAVS ▶ **nav**

NAVVY, NAVVIED, NAVVIES, -ING *n* labourer employed on a road or a building site ▷ *vb* work as a navvy

NAVY, NAVIES *n* warships with their crews and organization ▷ *adj* navy-blue

NAW *same as* ▶ **no**

NAWAB, -S *n* (formerly) a Muslim ruler or landowner in India

NAY, -S *interj* no ▷ *n* person who votes against a motion ▷ *adv* used for emphasis ▷ *sentence substitute* no

NAYSAY, NAYSAID, -S *vb* say no

NAYSAYER ▶ **naysay**

NAYSAYS ▶ **naysay**

NAYTHLES *same as* > **natheless**

NAYWARD *n* as in **to the nayward** towards denial

NAYWARDS *same as* ▶ **nayward**

NAYWORD, -S *n* proverb

NAZE, -S *n* flat marshy headland

NAZI, -S *n* person who thinks or acts in a brutal or dictatorial way

NAZIFY, NAZIFIED, NAZIFIES *vb* make nazi in character

NAZIR, -S *n* Muslim official

NAZIS ▶ **nazi**

NDUJA, -S *n* spicy pork paste

NE *conj* nor

NEAFE, -S *same as* ▶ **nieve**

NEAFFE, -S *same as* ▶ **nieve**

NEAL, -ED, -ING, -S *same as* ▶ **anneal**

NEANIC *adj* of or relating to the early stages in a life cycle

NEAP, -ED, -ING, -S *adj* of, relating to, or constituting a neap tide ▷ *vb* be grounded by a neap tide

NEAR, -ED, -ER, -EST, -ING, -S *adj* indicating a place or time not far away ▷ *vb* draw close (to) ▷ *prep* at or to a place or time not far away from ▷ *adv* at or to a place or time not far away ▷ *n* left side of a horse or vehicle

NEARBY *adj* not far away ▷ *adv* close at hand

NEARED ▶ **near**

NEARER ▶ **near**

NEAREST ▶ **near**

NEARING ▶ **near**

NEARISH *adj* quite near

NEARLY, NEARLIER *adv* almost

NEARNESS ▶ **near**

NEARS ▶ **near**

NEARSIDE *n* side of a vehicle that is nearer the kerb

NEAT, -ER, -EST, -S *adj* tidy and clean ▷ *n* domestic bovine animal

NEATEN, -ED, -S *vb* make neat

NEATER ▶ **neat**

NEATEST ▶ **neat**

NEATH *short for* ▶ **beneath**

NEATHERD *n* cowherd

NEATLY ▶ **neat**

NEATNESS ▶ **neat**

NEATNIK, -S *n* very neat and tidy person

NEATS ▶ **neat**

NEB, -BED, -BING, -S *n* beak of a bird or the nose of an animal ▷ *vb* look around nosily

NEBBICH, -S *same as* ▶ **nebbish**

NEBBING ▶ **neb**

NEBBISH *n* timid person

NEBBISHE *same as* ▶ **nebbish**

NEBBISHY *adj* timid

NEBBUK, -S *n* type of shrub

NEBECK, -S *same as* ▶ **nebbuk**

NEBEK, -S *same as* ▶ **nebbuk**

NEBEL, -S *n* Hebrew musical instrument

NEBISH, -ES *same as* ▶ **nebbish**

NEBRIS, -ES *n* fawn-skin

NEBS ▶ **neb**

NEBULA, -E, -S *n* hazy cloud of particles and gases

NEBULAR ▶ **nebula**

NEBULAS ▶ **nebula**

NEBULE, -S *n* cloud

NEBULISE *same as* ▶ **nebulize**

NEBULIUM *n* element

NEBULIZE *vb* turn (a liquid) into a fine spray

NEBULOSE *same as* ▶ **nebulous**

NEBULOUS adj vague and unclear

NEBULY adj wavy

NECK, -ED, -S n part of the body joining the head to the shoulders ▷ vb kiss and cuddle

NECKATEE n piece of ornamental cloth worn around the neck

NECKBAND n band around the neck of a garment

NECKBEEF n cheap cattle flesh

NECKED ▷ neck

NECKER, -S ▷ neck

NECKGEAR n any neck covering

NECKING, -S n activity of kissing and embracing passionately

NECKLACE n decorative piece of jewellery worn around the neck

NECKLESS ▷ neck

NECKLET, -S n ornament worn round the neck

NECKLIKE ▷ neck

NECKLINE n shape or position of the upper edge of a dress or top

NECKS ▷ neck

NECKSHOT n shot in the neck of an animal

NECKTIE, -S same as ▷ tie

NECKWEAR n articles of clothing, such as ties, scarves, etc, worn around the neck

NECKWEED n type of plant

NECROPSY n postmortem examination ▷ vb carry out a necropsy

NECROSE, -D, -S vb cause or undergo necrosis

NECROSIS n death of cells in the body

NECROTIC ▷ necrosis

NECTAR, -S n sweet liquid collected from flowers by bees

NECTARED adj filled with nectar

NECTARS ▷ nectar

NECTARY n structure secreting nectar in a plant

NED, -S n derogatory name for an adolescent hooligan

NEDDIER ▷ neddy

NEDDIES ▷ neddy

NEDDIEST ▷ neddy

NEDDISH ▷ ned

NEDDY, NEDDIER, NEDDIES, NEDDIEST n donkey ▷ adj of or relating to neds

NEDETTE, -S n derogatory name for a female adolescent hooligan

NEDS ▷ ned

NEE prep indicating the maiden name of a married woman ▷ adj indicating the maiden name of a married woman

NEED, -ED, -ING vb require or be in want of ▷ n condition of lacking something

NEEDER, -S ▷ need

NEEDFIRE n beacon

NEEDFUL adj necessary or required

NEEDFULS n must-haves

NEEDIER ▷ needy

NEEDIEST ▷ needy

NEEDILY ▷ needy

NEEDING ▷ need

NEEDLE, -D, -S, NEEDLING n thin pointed piece of metal with an eye through which thread is passed for sewing ▷ vb goad or provoke

NEEDLER, -S n needle maker

NEEDLES ▷ needle

NEEDLESS adj unnecessary

NEEDLIER ▷ needly

NEEDLING ▷ needle

NEEDLY, NEEDLIER adj like or full of needles

NEEDMENT n a necessity

NEEDS adv necessarily ▷ pl n what is required

NEEDY, NEEDIER, NEEDIEST adj poor, in need of financial support

NEELD, -S same as ▷ needle

NEELE, -S same as ▷ needle

NEEM, -S n type of large Indian tree

NEEMB, -S same as ▷ neem

NEEMS ▷ neem

NEEP, -S dialect name for ▷ turnip

NEESE, -D, -S, NEESING same as ▷ neeze

NEEZE, -D, -S, NEEZING vb sneeze

NEF, -S n church nave

NEFAST adj wicked

NEFS ▷ nef

NEG, -S n photographic negative

NEGATE, -D, -S, NEGATING vb invalidate

NEGATER, -S ▷ negate

NEGATES ▷ negate

NEGATING ▷ negate

NEGATION n opposite or absence of something

NEGATIVE adj expressing a denial or refusal ▷ n negative word or statement

NEGATON, -S same as ▷ negatron

NEGATOR, -S ▷ negate

NEGATORY adj relating to the act of negation

NEGATRON obsolete word for ▷ electron

NEGLECT, -S vb take no care of ▷ n neglecting or being neglected

NEGLIGE, -S variant of ▷ negligee

NEGLIGEE n woman's lightweight usu lace-trimmed dressing gown

NEGLIGES ▷ neglige

NEGRONI, -S n type of cocktail

NEGS ▷ neg

NEGUS, -ES n hot drink of port and lemon juice

NEIF, -S same as ▷ nieve

NEIGH, -ED, -S n loud high-pitched sound made by a horse ▷ vb make this sound

NEIGHBOR same as > neighbour

NEIGHED ▷ neigh

NEIGHING n act of neighing

NEIGHS ▷ neigh

NEINEI, -S n type of plant

NEIST Scots variant of ▷ next

NEITHER pron not one nor the other ▷ adj not one nor the other (of two)

NEIVE, -S same as ▷ nieve

NEK, -S n mountain pass

NEKTON, -S n free-swimming animals in the middle depths of a sea or lake

NEKTONIC ▷ nekton

NEKTONS ▷ nekton

NELIES same as ▷ nelis

NELIS n type of pear

NELLIE, -S n type of albatross

NELLY n as in not on your nelly not under any circumstances

NELSON, -S n type of wrestling hold

NELUMBO, -S n type of aquatic plant

NEMA, -S n filament

NEMATIC, -S n substance having a mesomorphic state

NEMATODE n slender cylindrical unsegmented worm

NEMATOID ▷ nematode

NEMESES ▷ nemesis

NEMESIA, -S n type of southern African plant

N

NEMESIS, NEMESES n retribution or vengeance

NEMN, -ED, -ING, -S vb name

NEMORAL adj of a wood

NEMOROUS adj woody

NEMPT adj named

NENE, -S n rare black-and-grey short-winged Hawaiian goose

NENNIGAI same as ▸ **nannygai**

NENUPHAR n type of water lily

NEOBLAST n worm cell

NEOCON, -S n supporter of neoconservative politics

NEOGENE adj of, denoting, or formed during the Miocene and Pliocene epochs

NEOLITH, -S n Neolithic stone implement

NEOLOGIC > **neologism**

NEOLOGY same as > **neologism**

NEOMORPH n genetic component

NEOMYCIN n type of antibiotic obtained from a bacterium

NEON, -S n element used in illuminated signs and lights ▹ adj of or illuminated by neon

NEONATAL adj relating to the first few weeks of a baby's life

NEONATE, -S n newborn child

NEONED adj lit with neon

NEONS ▸ neon

NEOPAGAN n advocate of the revival of paganism

NEOPHILE n person who welcomes new things

NEOPHOBE > **neophobia**

NEOPHYTE n beginner or novice

NEOPLASM n any abnormal new growth of tissue

NEOPRENE n synthetic rubber used in waterproof products

NEOSOUL, -S n soul music combined with other genres

NEOTENIC ▸ **neoteny**

NEOTENY n persistence of larval or fetal features in the adult form of an animal

NEOTERIC adj belonging to a new fashion or trend ▹ n new writer or philosopher

NEOTOXIN n harmful agent

NEOTYPE, -S n specimen selected to replace a type

specimen that has been lost or destroyed

NEP, -S n catmint

NEPENTHE n drug that ancient writers referred to as a means of forgetting grief or trouble

NEPER, -S n unit expressing the ratio of two quantities

NEPETA, -S same as ▸ **catmint**

NEPHEW, -S n son of one's sister or brother

NEPHRIC adj renal

NEPHRISM n chronic kidney disease

NEPHRITE n tough fibrous amphibole mineral

NEPHROID adj kidney-shaped

NEPHRON, -S n urine-secreting tubule in the kidney

NEPIONIC adj of or relating to the juvenile period in the life cycle of an organism

NEPIT, -S n unit of information equal to 1.44 bits

NEPOTIC ▸ **nepotism**

NEPOTISM n favouritism in business shown to relatives and friends

NEPOTIST ▸ **nepotism**

NEPS ▸ nep

NERAL, -S n isomer of citral

NERD, -S n boring person obsessed with a particular subject

NERDIC, -S same as > **geekspeak**

NERDIER ▸ nerdy

NERDIEST ▸ nerdy

NERDISH ▸ nerd

NERDS ▸ nerd

NERDY, NERDIER, NERDIEST adj clumsy, socially inept

NEREID, -ES, -S n sea nymph in Greek mythology

NEREIS n type of marine worm

NERINE, -S n type of S African plant related to the amaryllis

NERITE, -S n type of sea snail

NERITIC adj of or formed in shallow seas near a coastline

NERK, -S n fool

NERKA, -S n type of salmon

NERKS ▸ nerk

NEROL, -S n scented liquid

NEROLI, -S n brown oil used in perfumery

NEROLS ▸ nerol

NERTS interj nuts

NERTZ same as ▸ **nerts**

NERVAL ▸ nerve

NERVATE adj (of leaves) with veins

NERVE, -D, -S n bundle of fibres that conducts impulses between the brain and body ▹ vb give courage to oneself

NERVELET n small nerve

NERVER, -S n someone or something which nerves

NERVES ▸ nerve

NERVIER ▸ nervy

NERVIEST ▸ nervy

NERVILY ▸ nervy

NERVINE, -S adj having a soothing effect upon the nerves ▹ n nervine drug or agent

NERVING, -S ▸ nerve

NERVOUS adj apprehensive or worried

NERVULAR adj relating to a nervule

NERVULE, -S n small vein

NERVURE, -S n stiff rod in an insect's wing

NERVY, NERVIER, NERVIEST adj excitable or nervous

NESCIENT > **nescience**

NESH, -ER, -EST adj sensitive to the cold

NESHNESS ▸ nesh

NESS, -ES n headland, cape

NEST, -ED, -S n place or structure in which birds or certain animals lay eggs or give birth to young ▹ vb make or inhabit a nest

NESTABLE ▸ nest

NESTED ▸ nest

NESTER, -S ▸ nest

NESTFUL, -S n the contents of a nest

NESTING, -S ▸ nest

NESTLE, -D, -S vb snuggle

NESTLER, -S ▸ nestle

NESTLES ▸ nestle

NESTLIKE ▸ nest

NESTLING n bird too young to leave the nest

NESTMATE n bird that shares a nest with another bird

NESTOR, -S n wise old man

NESTS ▸ nest

NET, -S, -TED n fabric of meshes of string, thread, or wire with many openings ▹ vb catch (a fish or animal) in a net ▹ adj left after all deductions

NETBALL, -S n team game in which a ball has to be thrown through a high net

NETBOOK, -S n type of small laptop computer

NETE, -S n lyre string

NETFUL, -S n the contents of a net

NETHEAD, -S n expert on the internet

NETHER adj lower

NETIZEN, -S n person who regularly uses the internet

NETLESS adj without a net

NETLIKE adj resembling a net

NETOP, -S n friend

NETROOT, -S n activist who promotes a cause via the internet

NETS ▸ net

NETSPEAK n jargon, abbreviations, and emoticons typically used by frequent internet users

NETSUKE, -S n (in Japan) a carved ornamental toggle

NETSURF, -S vb browse the internet for information

NETT, -S same as ▸ net

NETTABLE adj that can be netted

NETTED ▸ net

NETTER, -S n person that makes nets

NETTIE n enthusiastic user of the internet

NETTIER ▸ netty

NETTIES ▸ netty

NETTIEST ▸ netty

NETTING, -S ▸ net

NETTLE, -D, -S, NETTLING n plant with stinging hairs on the leaves ▹ vb bother or irritate

NETTLER, -S n one that nettles

NETTLES ▸ nettle

NETTLIER ▸ nettly

NETTLING ▸ nettle

NETTLY, NETTLIER adj like a nettle

NETTS ▸ nett

NETTY, NETTIER, NETTIES, NETTIEST n lavatory ▹ adj resembling a net

NETWORK, -S n system of intersecting lines, roads, etc ▹ vb broadcast (a programme) over a network

NEUK, -S Scot word for ▸ nook

NEUM, -S same as ▸ neume

NEUMATIC adj relating to a neume

NEUME, -S n notational symbol

NEUMIC ▸ neume

NEUMS ▸ neum

NEURAL adj of a nerve or the nervous system

NEURALLY ▸ neural

NEURAXON n biological cell component

NEURINE, -S n poisonous alkaloid

NEURISM, -S n nerve force

NEURITE, -S n biological cell component

NEURITIC ▸ neuritis

NEURITIS n inflammation of a nerve or nerves

NEUROID, -S adj resembling a nerve ▹ n either of the halves of a neural arch

NEUROMA, -S n any tumour composed of nerve tissue

NEURON, -S same as ▸ neurone

NEURONAL ▸ neurone

NEURONE, -S n cell specialized to conduct nerve impulses

NEURONIC ▸ neurone

NEURONS ▸ neuron

NEUROPIL n dense network of neurons and glia in the central nervous system

NEUROSAL adj relating to neurosis

NEUROSIS, NEUROSES n disorder producing anxiety or obsessive behaviour

NEUROTIC adj emotionally unstable ▹ n neurotic person

NEURULA, -S n stage of embryonic development

NEURULAE ▸ neurula

NEURULAR ▸ neurula

NEURULAS ▸ neurula

NEUSTIC, -S n part of a sentence that differs with mood

NEUSTON, -S n organisms that float on the surface of open water

NEUTER, -ED, -S adj belonging to a particular class of grammatical inflections in some languages ▹ vb castrate (an animal) ▹ n neuter gender

NEUTRAL, -S adj taking neither side in a war or dispute ▹ n neutral person or nation

NEUTRINO n elementary particle with no mass or electrical charge

NEUTRON, -S n electrically neutral elementary particle

NEVE, -S n mass of porous ice, formed from snow

NEVEL, -LED, -S vb beat with the fists

NEVER adv at no time ▹ sentence substitute at no time ▹ interj surely not!

NEVES ▸ neve

NEVI ▸ nevus

NEVOID ▸ naevus

NEVUS, NEVI same as ▸ naevus

NEW, -ED, -ER, -EST, -ING adj not existing before ▹ adv recently ▹ vb make new

NEWB, -S n newbie

NEWBIE, -S n person new to a job, club, etc

NEWBORN, -S adj recently or just born ▹ n newborn baby

NEWBS ▸ newb

NEWCOME adj recently arrived

NEWCOMER n recent arrival or participant

NEWED ▸ new

NEWEL, -S n post at the top or bottom of a flight of stairs

NEWELL, -S n new thing

NEWELLED ▸ newel

NEWELLS ▸ newell

NEWELS ▸ newel

NEWER ▸ new

NEWEST ▸ new

NEWFOUND adj newly or recently discovered

NEWIE, -S n fresh idea or thing

NEWING ▸ new

NEWISH adj fairly new

NEWISHLY ▸ newish

NEWLY adv recently

NEWLYWED n recently married person

NEWMOWN adj freshly cut

NEWNESS ▸ new

NEWS, -ED, -ES, -ING n important or interesting new happenings ▹ vb report

NEWSBEAT n particular area of news reporting

NEWSBOY, -S n boy who sells or delivers newspapers

NEWSCAST n radio or television broadcast of the news

NEWSCLIP n brief extract from news broadcast

NEWSDESK n news gathering and reporting department

NEWSED ▸ news

NEWSES ▸ news

NEWSFEED n service that provides news articles for distribution

N

NEWSGIRL n female newsreader or reporter

NEWSHAWK n newspaper reporter

NEWSIE same as ▸ newsy

NEWSIER ▸ newsy

NEWSIES ▸ newsy

NEWSIEST ▸ newsy

NEWSING ▸ news

NEWSLESS ▸ news

NEWSMAN, NEWSMEN n male newsreader or reporter

NEWSPEAK n deliberately ambiguous and misleading language of politicians and officials

NEWSREEL n short film giving news

NEWSROOM n room where news is received and prepared for publication or broadcasting

NEWSWIRE n electronic means of delivering up-to-the-minute news

NEWSY, NEWSIER, NEWSIES, NEWSIEST adj full of news ▷ n newsagent

NEWT, -S n small amphibious creature

NEWTON, -S n unit of force

NEWTS ▸ newt

NEWWAVER n member of new wave

NEXT, -S adv immediately following ▷ n next person or thing

NEXTDOOR adj in or at the adjacent house or building

NEXTLY ▸ next

NEXTNESS ▸ next

NEXTS ▸ next

NEXUS, -ES n connection or link

NGAI n clan or tribe

NGAIO, -S n small New Zealand tree

NGANA, -S same as ▸ nagana

NGARARA, -S n lizard found in New Zealand

NGATI, -S n (occurring as part of the tribe name) a tribe or clan

NGOMA, -S n type of drum

NGULTRUM n standard monetary unit of Bhutan, divided into 100 chetrum

NGWEE, -S n Zambian monetary unit

NHANDU, -S n type of spider

NIACIN, -S n vitamin of the B complex

NIAGARA, -S n deluge or outpouring

NIB, -BED, -BING, -S n writing point of a pen ▷ vb provide with a nib

NIBBLE, -D, -S, NIBBLING vb take little bites (of) ▷ n little bite

NIBBLER, -S n person, animal, or thing that nibbles

NIBBLES ▸ nibble

NIBBLIES ▸ nibbly

NIBBLING ▸ nibble

NIBBLY, NIBBLIES n small item of food

NIBLET, -S n very small piece of food

NIBLICK, -S n former golf club giving a great deal of lift

NIBLIKE ▸ nib

NIBS ▸ nib

NICAD, -S n rechargeable dry-cell battery

NICE, -R, -ST adj pleasant

NICEISH ▸ nice

NICELY ▸ nice

NICENESS ▸ nice

NICER ▸ nice

NICEST ▸ nice

NICETY, NICETIES n subtle point

NICHE, -D, -S, NICHING n hollow area in a wall ▷ adj of or aimed at a specialist group or market ▷ vb place (a statue) in a niche

NICHER, -ED, -S vb snigger

NICHES ▸ niche

NICHING ▸ niche

NICHROME n (tradename) alloy of nickel and chrome

NICHT, -S Scot word for ▸ night

NICISH ▸ nice

NICK, -ED, -ING, -S vb make a small cut in ▷ n small cut

NICKAR, -S n hard seed

NICKED ▸ nick

NICKEL, -ED, -S n silvery-white metal often used in alloys ▷ vb plate with nickel

NICKELIC adj of or containing metallic nickel

NICKELS ▸ nickel

NICKER, -ED, -S n pound sterling ▷ vb (of a horse) to neigh softly

NICKING ▸ nick

NICKLE, -D, -S, NICKLING same as ▸ nickel

NICKNACK n cheap ornament or trinket

NICKNAME n familiar name given to a person or place ▷ vb call by a nickname

NICKS ▸ nick

NICKUM, -S n mischievous person

NICOISE adj prepared with tomatoes, black olives, garlic and anchovies

NICOL, -S n device for producing plane-polarized light

NICOTIAN n tobacco user

NICOTIN same as ▸ nicotine

NICOTINE n poisonous substance found in tobacco

NICOTINS same as ▸ nicotin

NICTATE, -D, -S same as > nictitate

NID, -S same as ▸ nide

NIDAL ▸ nidus

NIDATE, -D, -S, NIDATING vb undergo nidation

NIDATION n implantation

NIDDICK, -S n nape of the neck

NIDE, -D, -S vb nest

NIDERING same as > niddering

NIDES ▸ nide

NIDGET, -ED, -S n type of hoe ▷ vb assist a woman in labour

NIDI ▸ nidus

NIDIFY, NIDIFIED, NIDIFIES vb (of a bird) to make or build a nest

NIDING, -S n coward

NIDOR, -S n cooking smell

NIDOROUS ▸ nidor

NIDORS ▸ nidor

NIDS ▸ nid

NIDUS, NIDI, -ES n nest in which insects or spiders deposit their eggs

NIE, -D, -S archaic spelling of ▸ nigh

NIECE, -S n daughter of one's sister or brother

NIED ▸ nie

NIEF, -S same as ▸ nieve

NIELLI ▸ niello

NIELLIST ▸ niello

NIELLO, NIELLI, -ED, -S n black compound of sulphur and silver, lead, or copper ▷ vb decorate or treat with niello

NIENTE adv softly fading away

NIES ▸ nie

NIEVE, -S n closed hand

NIEVEFUL n closed handful

NIEVES ▸ nieve

NIFE, -S n earth's core

NIFF, -ED, -ING, -S n stink ▷ vb stink

NIFFER, -ED, -S vb barter

NIFFIER ▸ niffy

NIFFIEST ▸ niffy

NIFFING ► niff
NIFFNAFF vb trifle
NIFFS ► niff
NIFFY, NIFFIER, NIFFIEST
► niff
NIFTIER ► nifty
NIFTIES ► nifty
NIFTIEST ► nifty
NIFTILY ► nifty
NIFTY, NIFTIER, NIFTIES,
NIFTIEST adj neat or smart
▷ n nifty thing
NIGELLA, -S n type of
Mediterranean plant
NIGGARD, -S n stingy
person ▷ adj miserly ▷ vb
act in a niggardly way
NIGGLE, -D, -S vb worry
slightly ▷ n small worry or
doubt
NIGGLER, -S ► niggle
NIGGLES ► niggle
NIGGLIER ► niggly
NIGGLING adj petty ▷ n act
or instance of niggling
NIGGLY, NIGGLIER ► niggle
NIGH, -ED, -ER, -EST, -ING,
-S prep near ▷ adv nearly
▷ adj near ▷ vb approach
NIGHLY ► nigh
NIGHNESS ► nigh
NIGHS ► nigh
NIGHT n time of darkness
between sunset and sunrise
▷ adj of, occurring, or
working at night
NIGHTCAP n drink taken just
before bedtime
NIGHTED adj darkened
NIGHTIE, -S n nightgown
NIGHTJAR n nocturnal bird
with a harsh cry
NIGHTLY adv (happening)
each night ▷ adj happening
each night
NIGHTS adv at night or on
most nights
NIGHTY same as ► nightie
NIGIRI, -S n small oval block
of cold rice, wasabi and fish
NIGRIFY vb blacken
NIGROSIN same as
> nigrosine
NIHIL, -S n nil
NIHILISM n rejection of all
established authority and
institutions
NIHILIST ► nihilism
NIHILITY n state or
condition of being nothing
NIHILS ► nihil
NIHONGA, -S n Japanese
form of painting
NIHONIUM n highly
radioactive element
NIKAB, -S same as ► niqab

NIKAH, -S n Islamic
marriage contract
NIKAU, -S n palm tree native
to New Zealand
NIL, -S n nothing, zero
NILGAI, -S n large Indian
antelope
NILGAU, -S same as
► nilghau
NILGHAI, -S same as ► nilgai
NILGHAU, -S same as
► nilgai
NILL, -ED, -ING, -S vb be
unwilling
NILS ► nil
NIM, -MED, -MING, -S n
game involving removing
one or more small items
from several rows or piles
▷ vb steal
NIMB, -S n halo
NIMBED ► nimb
NIMBI ► nimbus
NIMBLE, -R, -ST adj agile
and quick
NIMBLY ► nimble
NIMBS ► nimb
NIMBUS, NIMBI, -ES n dark
grey rain cloud
NIMBUSED ► nimbus
NIMBUSES ► nimbus
NIMBYISM n practice of
objecting to something that
will affect one or take place
in one's locality
NIMIETY rare word for
► excess
NIMIOUS ► nimiety
NIMMED ► nim
NIMMER, -S ► nim
NIMMING ► nim
NIMONIC adj as in nimonic
alloy type of nickel-based
alloy
NIMPS adj easy
NIMROD, -S n hunter
NIMS ► nim
NINCOM, -S same as
> nicompoop
NINCUM, -S same as
> nicompoop
NINE, -S n one more than
eight
NINEBARK n North
American shrub
NINEFOLD adj having nine
times as many or as much
▷ adv by nine times as much
or as many
NINEPIN n skittle used in
ninepins
NINEPINS n game of skittles
NINER, -S n (US) student in
the ninth grade
NINES ► nine
NINETEEN n ten and nine

NINETY, NINETIES n ten
times nine
NINJA, -S n person skilled in
ninjutsu
NINJITSU same as ► ninjutsu
NINJUTSU n Japanese
martial art
NINNY, NINNIES n stupid
person
NINNYISH ► ninny
NINON, -S n fine strong silky
fabric
NINTH, -S n number nine in a
series ▷ adj coming after the
eighth
NINTHLY adv in the ninth
place or position
NINTHS ► ninth
NIOBATE, -S n type of salt
crystal
NIOBIC adj of or containing
niobium in the pentavalent
state
NIOBITE, -S another name for
> columbite
NIOBIUM, -S n white
metallic element
NIOBOUS adj of or
containing niobium in the
trivalent state
NIP, -PED, -PING, -S vb hurry
▷ n pinch or light bite
NIPA, -S n palm tree of S and
SE Asia
NIPPED ► nip
NIPPER, -ED n small child
▷ vb secure with rope
NIPPERS pl n instrument or
tool for pinching or
squeezing
NIPPIER ► nippy
NIPPIEST ► nippy
NIPPILY ► nippy
NIPPING ► nip
NIPPLE, -D, -S, NIPPLING n
projection in the centre of a
breast ▷ vb provide with a
nipple
NIPPY, NIPPIER, NIPPIEST
adj frosty or chilly
NIPS ► nip
NIPTER, -S n type of religious
ceremony
NIQAAB, -S same as ► niqab
NIQAB, -S n type of veil worn
by some Muslim women

One of those invaluable
words allowing you to play
the Q without a U. It can
also be spelt **niqaab** or
nikab.

NIRAMIAI n sumo wrestling
procedure
NIRL, -ED, -ING, -IT, -S vb
shrivel
NIRLIE variant of ► nirly

N

NIRLIER ▶ nirly
NIRLIEST ▶ nirly
NIRLING ▶ nirl
NIRLIT ▶ nirl
NIRLS ▶ nirl
NIRLY, NIRLIER, NIRLIEST adj shrivelled
NIRVANA, -S n absolute spiritual enlightenment and bliss
NIRVANIC ▶ nirvana
NIS n friendly goblin
NISBERRY same as
> naseberry
NISEI, -S n native-born citizen of the US or Canada whose parents were Japanese
NISGUL, -S n smallest and weakest bird in a brood of chickens
NISH, -ES n nothing
NISI adj (of a court order) coming into effect on a specified date
NISSE, -S same as ▶ nis
NISUS n impulse towards or striving after a goal
NIT, -S n egg or larva of a louse
NITE, -S variant of ▶ night
NITER, -S same as ▶ nitre
NITERIE, -S n nightclub
NITERS ▶ niter
NITERY ▶ niter
NITES ▶ nite
NITHER, -ED, -S vb shiver
NITHING, -S n coward
NITID adj bright
NITINOL, -S n metal alloy
NITON, -S less common name for ▶ radon
NITPICK, -S vb criticize unnecessarily
NITPICKY ▶ nitpick
NITRATE, -D, -S n compound of nitric acid, used as a fertilizer ▷ vb treat with nitric acid or a nitrate
NITRATOR ▶ nitrate
NITRE, -S n potassium nitrate
NITREOUS adj as in **nitreous silica** another name for quartz glass
NITRES ▶ nitre
NITRIC adj of or containing nitrogen
NITRID, -S same as ▶ nitride
NITRIDE, -D, -S n compound of nitrogen ▷ vb make into a nitride
NITRIDS ▶ nitrid
NITRIFY vb treat or cause to react with nitrogen
NITRIL, -S same as ▶ nitrile

NITRILE, -S n any one of a particular class of organic compounds
NITRILS ▶ nitril
NITRITE, -S n salt or ester of nitrous acid
NITRO, -S n nitroglycerine
NITROGEN n colourless odourless gas that forms four fifths of the air
NITROLIC adj pertaining to a group of acids
NITROS ▶ nitro
NITROSO adj of a particular monovalent group
NITROSYL another word for ▶ nitroso
NITROUS adj derived from or containing nitrogen in a low valency state
NITROX, -ES n mixture of nitrogen and oxygen used in diving
NITROXYL n type of chemical
NITRY adj nitrous
NITRYL, -S n chemical compound
NITS ▶ nit
NITTY, NITTIER, NITTIEST adj infested with nits
NITWIT, -S n stupid person
NIVAL adj of or growing in or under snow
NIVATION n weathering of rock around a patch of snow by alternate freezing and thawing
NIVEOUS adj resembling snow, esp in colour
NIX, -ED, -ES, -ING sentence substitute be careful! watch out! ▷ n rejection or refusal ▷ vb veto, deny, reject, or forbid (plans, suggestions, etc)

This is a handy little word, combining X with two of the most common tiles in the game.

NIXE n water sprite
NIXED ▶ nix
NIXER, -S n spare-time job
NIXES ▶ nix
NIXIE, -S n female water sprite, usually unfriendly to humans
NIXING ▶ nix
NIXY same as ▶ nixie
NIZAM, -S n (formerly) a Turkish regular soldier
NIZAMATE n territory of the nizam
NIZAMS ▶ nizam
NKOSI, -S n term of address to a superior

NO, -ES, -S interj expresses denial, disagreement, or refusal ▷ adj not any, not a ▷ adv not at all ▷ n answer or vote of 'no'
NOAH, -S n shark
NOB, -S n person of wealth or social distinction
NOBBIER ▶ nobby
NOBBIEST ▶ nobby
NOBBILY ▶ nob
NOBBLE, -D, -S, NOBBLING vb attract the attention of
NOBBLER, -S ▶ nobble
NOBBLES ▶ nobble
NOBBLING ▶ nobble
NOBBUT adv nothing but
NOBBY, NOBBIER, NOBBIEST ▶ nob
NOBELIUM n artificially produced radioactive element
NOBILITY n quality of being noble
NOBLE, -R, -S, -ST adj showing or having high moral qualities ▷ n member of the nobility
NOBLEMAN, NOBLEMEN n man of noble rank
NOBLER ▶ noble
NOBLES ▶ noble
NOBLESSE n noble birth or condition
NOBLEST ▶ noble
NOBLY ▶ noble
NOBODY, NOBODIES pron no person ▷ n person of no importance
NOBS ▶ nob
NOCAKE, -S n Indian meal made from dried corn
NOCEBO, -S n harmless substance that causes harmful effects in patients who expect it to be harmful
NOCENT, -S n guilty person
NOCENTLY ▶ nocent
NOCENTS ▶ nocent
NOCHEL, -S same as ▶ notchel
NOCHELED same as > notcheled
NOCHELS ▶ nochel
NOCK, -ED, -ING, -S n notch on an arrow or a bow for the bowstring ▷ vb fit (an arrow) on a bowstring
NOCKET, -S same as ▶ nacket
NOCKING ▶ nock
NOCKS ▶ nock
NOCTILIO n type of bat
NOCTUA, -S n type of moth
NOCTUARY n nightly journal

N

NOCTUAS ▸ noctua
NOCTUID, -S n type of nocturnal moth ▹ adj of or relating to this type of moth
NOCTULE, -S n any of several large Old World insectivorous bats
NOCTUOID adj of or like a noctuid ▹ n member of the family of moths Noctuidae
NOCTURIA n excessive urination during the night
NOCTURN, -S n any of the main sections of the office of matins
NOCTURNE n short dreamy piece of music
NOCTURNS ▸ nocturn
NOCUOUS adj harmful
NOD, -DED, -S vb lower and raise (one's head) briefly in agreement or greeting ▹ n act of nodding
NODAL adj of or like a node
NODALISE same as ▸ nodalize
NODALITY ▸ nodal
NODALIZE vb make something nodal
NODALLY ▸ nodal
NODATED adj knotted
NODATION n knottiness
NODDED ▸ nod
NODDER, -S ▸ nod
NODDIER ▸ noddy
NODDIES ▸ noddy
NODDIEST ▸ noddy
NODDING, -S ▸ nod
NODDLE, -D, -S, NODDLING n head ▹ vb nod (the head), as through drowsiness
NODDY, NODDIER, NODDIES, NODDIEST n tropical tern with a dark plumage ▹ adj very easy to use or understand
NODE, -S n point on a plant stem from which leaves grow
NODI ▸ nodus
NODICAL adj of or relating to the nodes of a celestial body
NODOSE adj having nodes or knotlike swellings
NODOSITY ▸ nodose
NODOUS same as ▸ nodose
NODS ▸ nod
NODULAR ▸ nodule
NODULE, -S n small knot or lump
NODULED ▸ nodule
NODULES ▸ nodule
NODULOSE ▸ nodule
NODULOUS ▸ nodule

NODUS, NODI n problematic idea, situation, etc
NOEL, -S n Christmas
NOES ▸ no
NOESIS, NOESES, -ES n exercise of reason
NOETIC adj of or relating to the mind
NOG, -S same as ▸ nogging
NOGAKU n Japanese style of drama
NOGG, -S same as ▸ nog
NOGGED adj built with timber and brick
NOGGIN, -S n head
NOGGING, -S n short horizontal timber member
NOGGINS ▸ noggin
NOGGS ▸ nogg
NOGS ▸ nog
NOH n stylized classic drama of Japan
NOHOW adv under any conditions
NOHOWISH ▸ nohow
NOIL, -S n short or knotted fibres that are separated from the long fibres by combing
NOILIER ▸ noily
NOILIES ▸ noily
NOILIEST ▸ noily
NOILS ▸ noil
NOILY, NOILIER, NOILIES, NOILIEST n dry white vermouth drink from France ▹ adj resembling a noil
NOINT, -ED, -ING, -S vb anoint
NOINTER, -S n mischievous child
NOINTING ▸ noint
NOINTS ▸ noint
NOIR, -S adj (of a film) showing characteristics of a film noir, in plot or style ▹ n film noir
NOIRISH ▸ noir
NOIRS ▸ noir
NOISE, -D, -S, NOISING n sound, usu a loud or disturbing one ▹ vb spread (news or gossip)
NOISEFUL ▸ noise
NOISENIK n rock musician who performs loud harsh music
NOISES ▸ noise
NOISETTE n hazelnut chocolate ▹ adj flavoured or made with hazelnuts
NOISIER ▸ noisy
NOISIEST ▸ noisy
NOISILY ▸ noisy
NOISING ▸ noise

NOISOME adj (of smells) offensive
NOISY, NOISIER, NOISIEST adj making a lot of noise
NOLE, -S same as ▸ noll
NOLITION n unwillingness
NOLL, -S n head
NOLO, -S n as in nolo contendere plea indicating that the defendant does not wish to contest the case
NOM, -S n name
NOMA, -S n gangrenous inflammation of the mouth
NOMAD, -S n member of a tribe with no fixed dwelling place
NOMADE, -S same as ▸ nomad
NOMADIC adj relating to or characteristic of nomads
NOMADIES ▸ nomady
NOMADISE same as ▸ nomadize
NOMADISM ▸ nomad
NOMADIZE vb live as nomads
NOMADS ▸ nomad
NOMADY, NOMADIES n practice of living like nomads
NOMARCH, -S n head of an ancient Egyptian nome
NOMARCHY n any of the provinces of modern Greece
NOMAS ▸ noma
NOMBLES variant spelling of ▸ numbles
NOMBRIL, -S n point on a shield
NOME, -S n any of the former provinces of modern Greece
NOMEN, -S, NOMINA n ancient Roman's second name
NOMES ▸ nome
NOMIC adj normal or habitual
NOMINA ▸ nomen
NOMINAL, -S adj in name only ▹ n nominal element
NOMINATE vb suggest as a candidate ▹ adj having a particular name
NOMINEE, -S n candidate
NOMISM, -S n adherence to laws as a primary exercise of religion
NOMISTIC ▸ nomism
NOMOGENY n law of life originating as a natural process
NOMOGRAM n arrangement of two linear or logarithmic scales
NOMOI ▸ nomos**

N

NOMOLOGY n science of law and law-making

NOMOS, NOMOI n convention

NOMS ▸ nom

NON adv not

NONA n sleeping sickness

NONACID, -S adj not acid ▸ n nonacid substance

NONACTOR n person who is not an actor

NONADULT n person who is not an adult

NONAGE, -D, -S n state of being under full legal age

NONAGON, -S n geometric figure with nine sides

NONANE, -S n type of chemical compound

NONANOIC adj as in **nonanoic acid** colourless oily fatty acid with a rancid odour

NONARIES ▸ nonary

NONART, -S n something that does not constitute art

NONARY, NONARIES n set or group of nine

NONAS same as ▸ **nones**

NONAVIAN adj not relating to birds

NONBANK, -S n business or institution that is not a bank but provides similar services

NONBASIC adj not basic

NONBEING n philosophical problem relating to the question of existence

NONBLACK n person who is not Black

NONBODY n nonphysical nature of a person

NONBOOK, -S n book with little substance

NONBRAND adj not produced by a well-known company

NONCASH adj other than cash

NONCE, -S n present time or occasion

NONCLASS n lack of class

NONCLING adj not liable to stick

NONCOLA, -S n soft drink other than cola

NONCOLOR same as ▸ **noncolour**

NONCOM, -S n person not involved in combat

NONCORE adj not central or essential

NONCOUNT adj not capable of being counted

NONCRIME n incident that is not a crime

NONDAIRY adj not containing dairy products

NONDANCE n series of movements that do not constitute a dance

NONDRIP adj (of paint) specially formulated to minimize dripping during application

NONDRUG adj not involving the use of drugs

NONE pron not any

NONEGO, -S n everything that is outside one's conscious self

NONELECT n person not chosen

NONELITE adj not elite

NONEMPTY adj not empty

NONENTRY n failure to enter

NONEQUAL adj not equal ▸ n person who is not the equal of another person

NONES n (in the Roman calendar) the ninth day before the ides of each month

NONESUCH n matchless person or thing

NONET, -S n piece of music composed for a group of nine instruments

NONETTE, -S same as ▸ **nonet**

NONETTO, NONETTI, -S same as ▸ **nonet**

NONEVENT n disappointing or insignificant occurrence

NONFACT, -S n event or thing not provable

NONFAN, -S n person who is not a fan

NONFARM adj not connected with a farm

NONFAT adj fat free

NONFATAL adj not resulting in or capable of causing death

NONFATTY adj not fatty

NONFINAL adj not final

NONFLUID adj not fluid ▸ n something that is not a fluid

NONFOCAL adj not focal

NONFOOD, -S n item that is not food ▸ adj relating to items other than food

NONFUEL, -S adj not relating to fuel ▸ n energy not used for generating heat, power, or electricity

NONG, -S n stupid or incompetent person

NONGAME adj not pursued for competitive sport purposes

NONGAY, -S n person who is not gay

NONGLARE adj not causing glare ▸ n any of various nonglare materials

NONGREEN adj not green

NONGS ▸ nong

NONGUEST n person who is not a guest

NONGUILT n state of being innocent

NONHARDY adj fragile

NONHEME adj of dietary iron, obtained from vegetable foods

NONHERO n person who is not a hero

NONHOME adj not of the home

NONHUMAN n something not human

NONI, -S n tree of SE Asia and the Pacific islands

NONIDEAL adj not ideal

NONIMAGE n person who is not a celebrity

NONINERT adj not inert

NONIONIC adj not ionic

NONIRON adj not requiring ironing

NONIS ▸ noni

NONISSUE n matter of little importance

NONJUROR n person who refuses to take an oath, as of allegiance

NONJURY n trial without a jury

NONKIN, -S n those who are not related to a person

NONLABOR same as ▸ **nonlabour**

NONLEAFY adj not leafy

NONLEGAL adj not legal

NONLEVEL adj not level

NONLIFE, NONLIVES n matter which is not living

NONLOCAL adj not of, affecting, or confined to a limited area or part ▸ n person who is not local to an area

NONLOYAL adj not loyal

NONLYRIC adj without lyrics

NONMAJOR n student who is not majoring in a specified subject

NONMAN, NONMEN n being that is not a man

NONMEAT, -S n substance that does not contain meat ▸ adj not containing meat

NONMEN ▸ nonman

NONMETAL n chemical element that forms acidic oxides and is a poor conductor of heat and electricity

NONMETRO *adj* not metropolitan

NONMODAL *adj* not modal

NONMONEY *adj* not involving money

NONMORAL *adj* not involving morality

NONMUSIC *n* (unpleasant) noise

NONNASAL *adj* not nasal

NONNAVAL *adj* not belonging to the navy

NONNEWS *adj* not concerned with news

NONNIES ▶ nonny

NONNOBLE *adj* not noble

NONNOVEL *n* literary work that is not a novel

NONNY, NONNIES *n* meaningless word

NONOBESE *adj* not obese

NONOHMIC *adj* not having electrical resistance

NONOILY *adj* not oily

NONORAL *adj* not oral

NONOWNER *n* person who is not an owner

NONPAGAN *n* person who is not a pagan

NONPAID *adj* without payment

NONPAPAL *adj* not of the pope

NONPAR *adj* nonparticipating

NONPARTY *adj* not connected with a political party

NONPAST, -S *n* any grammatical tense that is not the past tense

NONPEAK, -S *n* period of low demand

NONPLAY, -S *n* social behaviour that is not classed as play

NONPLUS *vb* put at a loss ▷ *n* state of utter perplexity prohibiting action or speech

NONPOINT *adj* without a specific site

NONPOLAR *adj* not polar

NONPOOR, -S *adj* not poor ▷ *n* person who is not poor

NONPRINT *adj* published in a format other than print on paper

NONPROS *vb* enter a judgment of non prosequitur

NONQUOTA *adj* not included in a quota

NONRATED *adj* not rated

NONRIGID *adj* not rigid

NONRIVAL *n* person or thing not competing for success

NONROYAL *adj* not royal ▷ *n* person who is not a member of a royal family

NONRUN *adj* (of tights) not laddering

NONRURAL *adj* not rural

NONSELF *n* foreign molecule in the body

NONSENSE *n* something that has or makes no sense ▷ *interj* exclamation of disagreement

NONSKED, -S *n* non-scheduled aeroplane

NONSKID *adj* designed to reduce skidding

NONSKIER *n* person who does not ski

NONSLIP *adj* designed to prevent slipping

NONSOLAR *adj* not related to the sun

NONSOLID *n* substance that is not a solid

NONSTATE *adj* not relating to the state

NONSTICK *adj* coated with a substance that food will not stick to when cooked

NONSTOP, -S *adv* without a stop ▷ *adj* without a stop ▷ *n* nonstop flight

NONSTORY *n* story of little substance or importance

NONSTYLE *n* style that cannot be identified

NONSUCH same as ▶ **nonesuch**

NONSUGAR *n* substance that is not a sugar

NONSUIT, -S *n* order of a judge dismissing a suit ▷ *vb* order the dismissal of the suit of (a person)

NONTAX, -ES *n* tax that has little real effect

NONTIDAL *adj* not having a tide

NONTITLE *adj* without title

NONTONAL *adj* not written in a key

NONTONIC *adj* not tonic

NONTOXIC *n* substance which is not poisonous ▷ *adj* not poisonous

NONTRUMP *adj* not of the trump suit

NONTRUTH same as ▶ **untruth**

NONUNION *adj* (of a company) not employing trade union members ▷ *n* failure of broken bones or bone fragments to heal

NONUPLE, -S *adj* ninefold ▷ *n* ninefold number

NONUPLET *n* child born in a multiple birth of nine siblings

NONURBAN *adj* rural

NONUSE, -S *n* failure to use

NONUSER, -S ▶ nonuse

NONUSES ▶ nonuse

NONUSING ▶ nonuse

NONVALID *adj* not valid

NONVIRAL *adj* not caused by a virus

NONVITAL *adj* not vital

NONVOCAL *n* music track without singing

NONVOTER *n* person who does not vote

NONWAGE *adj* not part of wages

NONWAR, -S *n* state of nonviolence

NONWHITE *n* person who is not White

NONWOODY *adj* not woody

NONWOOL *adj* not wool

NONWORD, -S *n* series of letters not recognised as a word

NONWORK, -S *adj* not involving work ▷ *n* part of life which does not involve work

NONWOVEN *n* material made by a method other than weaving

NONYL, -S *n* type of chemical

NONZERO *adj* not equal to zero

NOO *n* type of Japanese musical drama

NOOB, -S same as ▶ **newbie**

NOODGE, -D, -S, NOODGING *vb* annoy persistently

NOODLE, -D, -S *n* ribbon-like strip of pasta ▷ *vb* improvise aimlessly on a musical instrument

NOODLING *n* aimless musical improvisation

NOOGIE, -S *n* act of inflicting pain by rubbing head hard

NOOIT *interj* South African exclamation of surprise

NOOK, -S *n* corner or recess

NOOKIER ▶ nooky

NOOKIEST ▶ nooky

NOOKLIKE ▶ nook

NOOKS ▶ nook

NOOKY, NOOKIER, NOOKIEST *adj* resembling a nook

NOOLOGY *n* study of intuition

N

NOOMETRY n mind measurement

NOON, -ED, -S n twelve o'clock midday ▷ vb take a rest at noon

NOONDAY, -S adj happening at noon ▷ n middle of the day

NOONED ▸ noon

NOONER, -S n event taking place in the middle of the day

NOONING, -S n midday break for rest or food

NOONS ▸ noon

NOONTIDE same as ▸ noontime

NOONTIME n middle of the day

NOOP, -S n point of the elbow

NOOSE, -D, -S, NOOSING n loop in the end of a rope, tied with a slipknot ▷ vb catch in a noose

NOOSER, -S n person who uses a noose

NOOSES ▸ noose

NOOSING ▸ noose

NOPAL, -ES, -S n type of cactus

NOPALITO n small cactus

NOPALS ▸ nopal

NOPE interj no

NOPLACE same as ▸ nowhere

NOR prep and not

NORDIC adj of competitions in cross-country racing and ski-jumping

NORI, -S n edible seaweed

NORIA, -S n water wheel with buckets attached to its rim

NORIMON, -S n Japanese passenger vehicle

NORIS ▸ nori

NORITE, -S n variety of igneous rock

NORITIC ▸ norite

NORLAND, -S n north part of a country or the earth

NORM, -S n standard that is regarded as normal

NORMA, -S n norm or standard

NORMAL, -S adj usual, regular, or typical ▷ n usual or regular state, degree or form

NORMALCY ▸ normal

NORMALLY adv as a rule

NORMALS ▸ normal

NORMAN, -S n post used for winding on a ship

NORMANDE n type of cattle

NORMANS ▸ norman

NORMAS ▸ norma

NORMCORE n deliberately normal style of dress

NORMED adj having been normalized

NORMLESS adj without a norm

NORMS ▸ norm

NORSEL, -S vb fit with short lines for fastening hooks

NORTENA, -S same as ▸ norteno

NORTENO, -S n type of Mexican music

NORTH, -ED, -S n direction towards the North Pole, opposite south ▷ adj in the north ▷ adv in, to, or towards the north ▷ vb move north

NORTHER, -S n wind or storm from the north ▷ vb move north

NORTHERN adj situated in or towards the north ▷ n person from the north

NORTHERS ▸ norther

NORTHING n movement or distance covered in a northerly direction

NORTHS ▸ north

NORWARD same as > northward

NORWARDS same as ▸ norward

NOS ▸ no

NOSE, -D, -S n organ of smell, used also in breathing ▷ vb move forward slowly and carefully

NOSEAN, -S n type of mineral

NOSEBAG, -S n bag containing feed fastened round a horse's head

NOSEBAND n part of a horse's bridle that goes around the nose

NOSED ▸ nose

NOSEDIVE, NOSEDOVE vb (of an aircraft) plunge suddenly with the nose pointing downwards

NOSEGAY, -S n small bunch of flowers

NOSELESS ▸ nose

NOSELIKE ▸ nose

NOSELITE same as ▸ nosean

NOSER, -S n strong headwind

NOSES ▸ nose

NOSEY, -S adj prying or inquisitive ▷ n nosey person

NOSH, -ED, -ES, -ING n food ▷ vb eat

NOSHER, -S ▸ nosh

NOSHERIE same as ▸ noshery

NOSHERS ▸ nosher

NOSHERY n restaurant or other place where food is served

NOSHES ▸ nosh

NOSHING ▸ nosh

NOSIER ▸ nosy

NOSIES ▸ nosy

NOSIEST ▸ nosy

NOSILY ▸ nosy

NOSINESS ▸ nosy

NOSING, -S n edge of a step or stair tread

NOSODE, -S n homeopathic remedy

NOSOLOGY n branch of medicine concerned with the classification of diseases

NOSTOC, -S n type of bacterium occurring in moist places

NOSTOS, NOSTOI n story of a return home

NOSTRIL, -S n one of the two openings at the end of the nose

NOSTRO adj as in nostro account bank account conducted by a British bank with a foreign bank

NOSTRUM, -S n quack medicine

NOSY, NOSIER, NOSIES, NOSIEST adj prying or inquisitive ▷ n inquisitive person

NOT adv expressing negation, refusal, or denial

NOTA ▸ notum

NOTABLE, -S adj worthy of being noted, remarkable ▷ n person of distinction

NOTABLY adv particularly or especially

NOTAEUM, -S n back of a bird's body

NOTAIRE, -S n (in France) notary

NOTAL ▸ notum

NOTANDUM, NOTANDA n notable fact

NOTARIAL ▸ notary

NOTARIES ▸ notary

NOTARISE same as ▸ notarize

NOTARIZE vb attest to or authenticate (a document, contract, etc), as a notary

NOTARY, NOTARIES n person authorized to witness legal documents

NOTATE, -D, -S, NOTATING vb write (esp music) in notation

NOTATION n representation of numbers or quantities in a system by a series of symbols

NOTATOR, -S n person who notates

NOTCH, -ED, -ES, -ING n V-shaped cut ▷ vb make a notch in

NOTCHEL, -S vb refuse to pay another person's debts

NOTCHER, -S n person who cuts notches

NOTCHES ▶ notch

NOTCHIER ▶ notchy

NOTCHING ▶ notch

NOTCHY, NOTCHIER adj (of a motor vehicle gear mechanism) requiring careful gear-changing

NOTE, -S, NOTING n short letter ▷ vb notice, pay attention to

NOTEBOOK n book for writing in

NOTECARD n greetings card with space to write note

NOTECASE same as ▶ wallet

NOTED adj well-known

NOTEDLY ▶ noted

NOTELESS ▶ note

NOTELET, -S n small folded card with a design on the front

NOTEPAD, -S n number of sheets of paper fastened together

NOTER, -S n person who takes notes

NOTES ▶ note

NOTHER same as ▶ other

NOTHING, -S pron not anything ▷ adv not at all ▷ n person or thing of no importance

NOTICE, -D, -S, NOTICING n observation or attention ▷ vb observe, become aware of

NOTICER, -S n person who takes notice

NOTICES ▶ notice

NOTICING ▶ notice

NOTIFIED ▶ notify

NOTIFIER ▶ notify

NOTIFY, NOTIFIED, NOTIFIES vb inform

NOTING ▶ note

NOTION, -S n idea or opinion

NOTIONAL adj speculative, imaginary, or unreal

NOTIONS ▶ notion

NOTITIA, -E, -S n register or list, esp of ecclesiastical districts

NOTORNIS n rare flightless rail of New Zealand

NOTOUR adj notorious

NOTT same as ▶ not

NOTTURNO, NOTTURNI n piece of music

NOTUM, NOTA n cuticular plate on an insect

NOUGAT, -S n chewy sweet containing nuts and fruit

NOUGHT, -S n figure o

NOUL, -S same as ▶ noll

NOULD vb would not

NOULDE same as ▶ nould

NOULE, -S same as ▶ noll

NOULS ▶ noul

NOUMENA ▶ noumenon

NOUMENAL ▶ noumenon

NOUMENON, NOUMENA n thing as it is in itself

NOUN, -S n word that refers to a person, place, or thing

NOUNAL ▶ noun

NOUNALLY ▶ noun

NOUNIER ▶ nouny

NOUNIEST ▶ nouny

NOUNLESS ▶ noun

NOUNS ▶ noun

NOUNY, NOUNIER, NOUNIEST adj like a noun

NOUP, -S n steep headland

NOURICE, -S n nurse

NOURISH vb feed

NOURSLE, -D, -S vb nurse

NOUS, -ES n common sense

NOUSELL vb foster

NOUSES ▶ nous

NOUSLE, -D, -S, NOUSLING vb nuzzle

NOUT same as ▶ nought

NOUVEAU adj having recently become the thing specified

NOUVEAUX same as ▶ nouveau

NOUVELLE n long short story

NOVA, -E, -S n type of star

NOVALIA n newly reclaimed land

NOVALIKE adj resembling a nova

NOVAS ▶ nova

NOVATE, -S, NOVATING vb substitute one thing in place of another

NOVATED adj as in novated lease Australian system of employer-aided car purchase

NOVATES ▶ novate

NOVATING ▶ novate

NOVATION n substitution of a new obligation for an old one by mutual agreement

NOVEL, -S n long fictitious story in book form ▷ adj fresh, new, or original

NOVELDOM n realm of fiction

NOVELESE n style of writing characteristic of poor novels

NOVELISE same as ▶ novelize

NOVELISH adj resembling a novel

NOVELISM n innovation

NOVELIST n writer of novels

NOVELIZE vb convert (a true story, film, etc) into a novel

NOVELLA, -E, -S, NOVELLE n short novel

NOVELLY ▶ novel

NOVELS ▶ novel

NOVELTY n newness

NOVEMBER n code word for the letter N

NOVENA, -E, -S n set of prayers or services on nine consecutive days

NOVENARY n set of nine

NOVENAS ▶ novena

NOVERCAL adj stepmotherly

NOVERINT n writ

NOVICE, -S n beginner

NOVICHOK n powerful nerve agent developed in the former USSR

NOVITY, NOVITIES n novelty

NOVUM, -S n game played with dice

NOW, -S adv at or for the present time ▷ n the present time

NOWADAYS adv in these times

NOWAY adv in no manner

NOWAYS same as ▶ noway

NOWCAST, -S n report on current weather conditions

NOWED adj knotted

NOWHENCE adv from no place

NOWHERE, -S adv not anywhere ▷ n nonexistent or insignificant place

NOWISE another word for ▶ noway

NOWL, -S n crown of the head

NOWN same as ▶ own

NOWNESS ▶ nown

NOWS ▶ now

NOWT, -S n nothing

NOWTIER ▶ nowty

NOWTIEST ▶ nowty

NOWTS ▶ nowt

NOWTY, NOWTIER, NOWTIEST adj bad-tempered

NOWY adj having a small projection at the centre (of a cross)

N

NOX, -ES n nitrogen oxide

Meaning nitrogen oxide, this is another of those very useful short words containing X.

NOXAL adj relating to damage done by something belonging to another

NOXES ▸ nox

NOXIOUS adj poisonous or harmful

NOY, -ED, -ING, -S vb harass

NOYADE, -S n execution by drowning

NOYANCE, -S n nuisance

NOYAU, -S, -X n brandy-based liqueur

NOYED ▸ noy

NOYES, -ES archaic form of ▸ noise

NOYING ▸ noy

NOYOUS ▸ noy

NOYS ▸ noy

NOYSOME ▸ noy

NOZZER, -S n new recruit (in the Navy)

NOZZLE, -S n projecting spout through which fluid is discharged

NTH adj of an unspecified number

A good word to remember for awkward situations on the board, as it's one of very few 3-letter words that doesn't contain a vowel.

NU, -S n 13th letter in the Greek alphabet

NUANCE, -D, -S, NUANCING n subtle difference in colour, meaning, or tone ▷ vb give subtle differences to

NUB, -BED, -S n point or gist (of a story etc) ▷ vb hang from the gallows

NUBBER, -S n weakly hit ball in baseball

NUBBIER ▸ nubby

NUBBIEST ▸ nubby

NUBBIN, -S n something small or undeveloped, esp a fruit or ear of corn

NUBBING, -S n act of hanging (a criminal)

NUBBINS ▸ nubbin

NUBBLE, -D, -S, NUBBLING n small lump ▷ vb dialect word for beat or pound using one's fists

NUBBLIER ▸ nubbly

NUBBLING ▸ nubble

NUBBLY, NUBBLIER ▸ nubble

NUBBY, NUBBIER, NUBBIEST adj having small lumps or protuberances

NUBECULA n small irregular galaxy near the S celestial pole

NUBIA, -S n fleecy scarf for the head, worn by women

NUBIFORM adj cloudlike

NUBILE adj (of a girl or woman) mature enough for marriage

NUBILITY ▸ nubile

NUBILOSE same as ▸ nubilous

NUBILOUS adj cloudy

NUBS ▸ nub

NUBUCK, -S n type of leather with a velvety finish

NUCELLAR ▸ nucellus

NUCELLUS, NUCELLI n central part of a plant ovule containing the embryo sac

NUCHA, -E n back or nape of the neck

NUCHAL, -S n scale on a reptile's neck

NUCLEAL ▸ nucleus

NUCLEAR adj of nuclear weapons or energy

NUCLEASE n any of a group of enzymes that hydrolyse nucleic acids to simple nucleotides

NUCLEATE adj having a nucleus ▷ vb form a nucleus

NUCLEI ▸ nucleus

NUCLEIC adj as in nucleic acid type of complex compound that is a vital constituent of living cells

NUCLEIDE same as ▸ nuclide

NUCLEIN, -S n protein that occurs in the nuclei of living cells

NUCLEOID n component of a bacterium

NUCLEOLE variant of > nucleolus

NUCLEOLI > nucleolus

NUCLEON, -S n proton or neutron

NUCLEUS, NUCLEI n centre, esp of an atom or cell

NUCLIDE, -S n species of atom characterized by its atomic number and its mass number

NUCLIDIC ▸ nuclide

NUCULE, -S n small seed

NUDATION n act of removing a covering

NUDDY, NUDDIES n as in in the nuddy in the nude

NUDE, -R, -S, -ST adj naked ▷ n naked figure in painting, sculpture, or photography

NUDELY ▸ nude

NUDENESS ▸ nude

NUDER ▸ nude

NUDES ▸ nude

NUDEST ▸ nude

NUDGE, -D, -S, NUDGING vb push gently, esp with the elbow ▷ n gentle push or touch

NUDGER, -S ▸ nudge

NUDGES ▸ nudge

NUDGING ▸ nudge

NUDICAUL adj (of plants) having stems without leaves

NUDISM, -S n practice of not wearing clothes

NUDIST, -S ▸ nudism

NUDITY, NUDITIES n state or fact of being nude

NUDNICK, -S same as ▸ nudnik

NUDNIK, -S n boring person

NUDZH, -ED, -ES, -ING same as ▸ nudge

NUFF, -S slang form of ▸ enough

NUFFIN, -S slang form of ▸ nothing

NUFFS ▸ nuff

NUG, -S n lump of wood sawn from a log

NUGAE pl n jests

NUGATORY adj of little value

NUGGAR, -S n sailing boat used to carry cargo on the Nile

NUGGET, -ED, -S n small lump of gold in its natural state ▷ vb polish footwear

NUGGETY adj of or resembling a nugget

NUGS ▸ nug

NUISANCE n something or someone that causes annoyance or bother

NUKE, -D, -S, NUKING vb attack with nuclear weapons ▷ n nuclear weapon

NULL, -S adj without legal force ▷ vb make negative

NULLA, -S same as ▸ nullah

NULLAH, -S n stream or drain

NULLAS ▸ nulla

NULLED ▸ null

NULLIFY vb make ineffective

NULLING, -S n knurling

NULLITY n state of being null

NULLNESS ▸ null

NULLS ▸ null

NUMB, -ED, -EST, -ING, -S adj without feeling, as through cold, shock, or fear ▷ vb make numb

NUMBAT, -S n small Australian marsupial

NUMBED ▷ numb

NUMBER, -ED, -S n sum or quantity ▷ vb count

NUMBERER n person who numbers

NUMBERS ▷ number

NUMBEST ▷ numb

NUMBFISH n any of several electric ray fish

NUMBHEAD n insulting word for a stupid person

NUMBING ▷ numb

NUMBLES pl n animal organs, cooked for food

NUMBLY ▷ numb

NUMBNESS ▷ numb

NUMBNUT n insulting word for a stupid person

NUMBNUTS n insulting word for a stupid person

NUMBS ▷ numb

NUMCHUCK same as ▷ nunchaku

NUMDAH, -S n coarse felt made esp in India

NUMEN n deity or spirit presiding over a thing or place

NUMERACY n ability to use numbers, esp in arithmetical operations

NUMERAL, -S n word or symbol used to express a sum or quantity ▷ adj of, consisting of, or denoting a number

NUMERARY adj of or relating to numbers

NUMERATE adj able to do basic arithmetic ▷ vb read (a numerical expression)

NUMERIC, -S n number or numeral

NUMEROUS adj existing or happening in large numbers

NUMINA plural of ▷ numen

NUMINOUS adj arousing religious or spiritual emotions ▷ n something that arouses religious or spiritual emotions

NUMMARY adj of or relating to coins

NUMMIER ▷ nummy

NUMMIEST ▷ nummy

NUMMULAR adj shaped like a coin

NUMMY, NUMMIER, NUMMIEST adj delicious

NUMNAH, -S same as ▷ numdah

NUMPKIN, -S n stupid person

NUMPTY, NUMPTIES n stupid person

NUMSKULL same as > numbskull

NUN, -S n female member of a religious order

NUNATAK, -S n isolated mountain peak projecting through glacial ice

NUNCHAKU, -S n throwing weapon used in martial arts

NUNCHEON n light snack

NUNCHUCK same as ▷ nunchuk

NUNCHUK, -S n throwing weapon used in martial arts

NUNCIO, -S n pope's ambassador

NUNCLE, -S archaic or dialect word for ▷ uncle

NUNDINAL n any of seven Roman letters indicating the days of the week

NUNDINE, -S n market day

NUNHOOD, -S n condition, practice, or character of a nun

NUNLIKE ▷ nun

NUNNERY n convent

NUNNISH ▷ nun

NUNNY n as in nunny bag small sealskin haversack used in Canada

NUNS ▷ nun

NUNSHIP, -S ▷ nun

NUPTIAL adj relating to marriage

NUPTIALS pl n wedding

NUR, -S n wooden ball

NURAGHE, NURAGHI n Sardinian round tower

NURAGHIC ▷ nuraghe

NURD, -S same as ▷ nerd

NURDIER ▷ nurdy

NURDIEST ▷ nurdy

NURDISH ▷ nerd

NURDLE, -D, -S, NURDLING vb score runs in cricket by soft deflections

NURDS ▷ nurd

NURDY, NURDIER, NURDIEST ▷ nurd

NURHAG, -S n Sardinian round tower

NURL, -ED, -ING, -S variant of ▷ knurl

NURR, -S n wooden ball

NURS ▷ nur

NURSE, -D, -S n person employed to look after sick people ▷ vb look after (a sick person)

NURSER, -S n person who treats something carefully

NURSERY n room where children sleep or play

NURSES ▷ nurse

NURSING, -S n practice or profession of caring for the sick and injured

NURSLE, -D, -S vb nuzzle

NURSLING n child or young animal that is being suckled, nursed, or fostered

NURTURAL ▷ nurture

NURTURE, -D, -S n act or process of promoting development ▷ vb promote or encourage development

NURTURER ▷ nurture

NURTURES ▷ nurture

NUS ▷ nu

NUT, -S, -TED n fruit consisting of a hard shell and a kernel ▷ vb gather nuts

NUTANT adj having the apex hanging down

NUTARIAN n person whose diet is based around nuts

NUTATE, -D, -S, NUTATING vb nod

NUTATION n periodic variation in the precession of the earth's axis

NUTBAR, -S n bar made from chopped nuts

NUTBROWN adj of a brownish colour, esp a reddish-brown

NUTCASE, -S n slang word for a foolish or reckless person

NUTGALL, -S n nut-shaped gall caused by gall wasps on the oak and other trees

NUTGRASS n type of plant

NUTHATCH n small songbird

NUTHIN n nothing

NUTJOB, -S n slang word for a foolish or reckless person

NUTLET, -S n portion of a fruit that fragments when mature

NUTLIKE ▷ nut

NUTLOAF n savoury loaf made from nuts

NUTMEAL, -S n type of grain

NUTMEAT, -S n kernel of a nut

NUTMEG, -S n spice made from the seed of a tropical tree ▷ vb kick or hit the ball between the legs of (an opposing player)

NUTMEGGY adj of or similar to nutmeg

NUTMEGS ▷ nutmeg

N

NUTPICK, -S n tool used to dig the meat from nuts

NUTRIA, -S n fur of the coypu

NUTRIENT n substance that provides nourishment ▷ adj providing nourishment

NUTS ▶ nut

NUTSEDGE same as ▶ nutgrass

NUTSHELL n shell around the kernel of a nut

NUTSIER ▶ nutsy

NUTSIEST ▶ nutsy

NUTSO, -S n slang word for a foolish or reckless person

NUTSY, NUTSIEST adj slang word for foolish or reckless

NUTTED ▶ nut

NUTTER, -S n slang word for a foolish or reckless person

NUTTERY n place where nut trees grow

NUTTIER ▶ nutty

NUTTIEST ▶ nutty

NUTTILY ▶ nutty

NUTTING, -S n act of gathering nuts

NUTTY, NUTTIER, NUTTIEST adj containing or resembling nuts

NUTWOOD, -S n any of various nut-bearing trees, such as walnut

NUZZER, -S n present given to a superior in India

NUZZLE, -D, -S, NUZZLING vb push or rub gently with the nose or snout

NUZZLER, -S n person or thing that nuzzles

NUZZLES ▶ nuzzle

NUZZLING ▶ nuzzle

NY, -S same as ▶ nigh

NYAFF, -ED, -ING, -S n small or contemptible person ▷ vb yelp like a small dog

NYAH interj interjection used to express contempt

NYALA, -S n spiral-horned southern African antelope

NYANZA, -S n (in E Africa) a lake

NYAS, -ES n young hawk

NYBBLE, -S n small byte

NYE, -D, -S, NYING n flock of pheasants ▷ vb near

NYLGHAI, -S same as ▶ nilgai

NYLGHAU, -S same as ▶ nilgai

NYLON n synthetic material used for clothing etc

NYLONED adj wearing nylons

NYLONS pl n stockings made of nylon

NYM adj as in nym war dispute about publishing material online under a pseudonym

NYMPH, -ED, -ING, -S n mythical spirit of nature, represented as a beautiful young woman ▷ vb fish with a particular type of fly on the hook

NYMPHA, -E n either one of the labia minora

NYMPHAEA n water lily

NYMPHAL ▶ nymph

NYMPHEAN ▶ nymph

NYMPHED ▶ nymph

NYMPHIC ▶ nymph

NYMPHING ▶ nymph

NYMPHISH ▶ nymph

NYMPHLY adj resembling a nymph

NYMPHS ▶ nymph

NYS ▶ ny

NYSSA, -S n type of tree

NYSTATIN n type of antibiotic obtained from a bacterium

N

Oo

With eight **O**s in the bag, you're likely to have at least one on your rack during a game. There are plenty of good two-letter words starting with **O**. It's worth knowing that **O** will form a two-letter word in front of every other vowel except **A**, as well as in front of **Y**. **O** also combines well with **X**, with **ox** (9 points) as the obvious starting point, and several words that refer to **oxygen** (17), including **oxo** (10) and **oxy** (13). Don't forget the short everyday words that begin with **O**. While **on** and **or** (2 each) won't earn you many points, they can be very helpful when you are trying to score in more than one direction at a time. **Ok** (6 points), and **of** and **oh** (5 each) can also prove very useful.

OAF, -S, OAVES n stupid or clumsy person

OAFISH ▶ oaf

OAFISHLY ▶ oaf

OAFS ▶ oaf

OAK, -S n deciduous forest tree

OAKED adj relating to wine that is stored for a time in oak barrels prior to bottling

OAKEN adj made of the wood of the oak

OAKER, -S same as ▶ ochre

OAKIER ▶ oaky

OAKIES ▶ oaky

OAKIEST ▶ oaky

OAKINESS n quality of being oaky

OAKLEAF n the leaf of the oak

OAKLIKE ▶ oak

OAKLING, -S n young oak

OAKMOSS n type of lichen

OAKS ▶ oak

OAKUM, -S n fibre obtained by unravelling old rope

OAKWOOD, -S n the wood of the oak

OAKY, OAKIER, OAKIES, OAKIEST adj hard like the wood of an oak ▷ n ice cream

OANSHAGH n foolish girl or woman

OAR, -ING, -S n pole with a broad blade, used for rowing a boat ▷ vb propel with oars

OARAGE, -S n use or number of oars

OARED adj equipped with oars

OARFISH n very long ribbonfish with long slender ventral fins

OARIER ▶ oary

OARIEST ▶ oary

OARING ▶ oar

OARLESS ▶ oar

OARLIKE ▶ oar

OARLOCK, -S n swivelling device that holds an oar in place

OARS ▶ oar

OARSMAN, OARSMEN n man who rows a boat

OARWEED, -S n type of brown seaweed

OARY, OARIER, OARIEST adj of or like an oar

OASIS, OASES n fertile area in a desert

OAST, -S n oven for drying hops

OAT, -S n hard cereal grown as food

OATCAKE, -S n thin flat biscuit of oatmeal

OATEN adj made of oats or oat straw

OATER, -S n film about the American Wild West

OATH, -S n solemn promise, esp to be truthful in court

OATHABLE adj able to take an oath

OATHS ▶ oath

OATIER ▶ oaty

OATIEST ▶ oaty

OATLIKE ▶ oat

OATMEAL, -S n coarse flour made from oats ▷ adj pale brownish-cream

OATS ▶ oat

OATY, OATIER, OATIEST adj of, like, or containing oats

OAVES ▶ oaf

OB, -S n expression of opposition

OBA, -S n (in W Africa) a Yoruba chief or ruler

OBANG, -S n former Japanese coin

OBAS ▶ oba

OBCONIC adj shaped like a cone and attached at the pointed end

OBDURACY ▶ obdurate

OBDURATE adj hardhearted or stubborn ▷ vb make obdurate

OBDURE, -D, -S, OBDURING vb make obdurate

OBE, -S n ancient Laconian village

OBEAH, -ED, -ING, -S vb cast spell on

OBEAHISM ▶ obeah

OBEAHS ▶ obeah

OBECHE, -S n African tree

OBEDIENT adj obeying or willing to obey

OBEISANT > obeisance

OBEISM, -S n belief in obeah

OBELI ▶ obelus

OBELIA, -S n type of jellyfish

OBELION n area of skull

OBELISE, -D, -S same as ▶ obelize

OBELISK, -S n stone column tapering to a pyramid at the top

OBELISM, -S n practice of marking passages in text

O

OBELIZE, -D, -S vb mark (a word or passage) with an obelus

OBELUS, OBELI n mark used to indicate spurious words or passages

OBENTO, -S n Japanese lunch box

OBES ▸ obe

OBESE, -R, -ST adj very fat

OBESELY ▸ obese

OBESER ▸ obese

OBESEST ▸ obese

OBESITY ▸ obese

OBESOGEN n agent causing obesity

OBEY, -ED, -ING, -S vb carry out instructions or orders

OBEYABLE ▸ obey

OBEYED ▸ obey

OBEYER, -S ▸ obey

OBEYING ▸ obey

OBEYS ▸ obey

OBI, -ED, -ING, -S n broad sash tied in a large flat bow at the back ▷ vb bewitch

OBIA, -S same as ▸ obeah

OBIED ▸ obi

OBIING ▸ obi

OBIISM, -S ▸ obi

OBIIT vb died

OBIS ▸ obi

OBIT, -S n memorial service

OBITAL adj of obits

OBITER adv by the way

OBITS ▸ obit

OBITUAL adj of obits

OBITUARY n announcement of someone's death, esp in a newspaper

OBJECT, -ED, -S n physical thing ▷ vb express disapproval

OBJECTOR ▸ object

OBJECTS ▸ object

OBJET, -S n object

OBJURE, -D, -S, OBJURING vb put on oath

OBLAST, -I, -S n administrative division of the constituent republics of Russia

OBLATE, -S adj (of a sphere) flattened at the poles ▷ n person dedicated to a monastic or religious life

OBLATELY ▸ oblate

OBLATES ▸ oblate

OBLATION n religious offering

OBLATORY ▸ oblation

OBLIGANT n person promising to pay a sum

OBLIGATE vb compel, constrain, or oblige morally

or legally ▷ adj compelled, bound, or restricted

OBLIGATO, OBLIGATI same as ▸ obbligato

OBLIGE, -D, -S vb compel (someone) morally or by law

OBLIGEE, -S n person in whose favour an obligation, contract, or bond is created

OBLIGER, -S ▸ oblige

OBLIGES ▸ oblige

OBLIGING adj ready to help other people

OBLIGOR, -S n person who binds themself by contract

OBLIQUE, -D, -R, -S adj slanting ▷ n symbol (/) ▷ vb take or have an oblique direction

OBLIQUID adj oblique

OBLIVION n state of being forgotten

OBLONG, -S adj having two long sides, two short sides, and four right angles ▷ n oblong figure

OBLONGLY ▸ oblong

OBLONGS ▸ oblong

OBLOQUY n verbal abuse

OBO, -S n ship carrying oil and ore

OBOE, -S n double-reeded woodwind instrument

OBOIST, -S ▸ oboe

OBOL, -S same as ▸ obolus

OBOLARY adj very poor

OBOLE, -S n former weight unit in pharmacy

OBOLI ▸ obolus

OBOLS ▸ obol

OBOLUS, OBOLI n Greek unit of weight

OBOS ▸ obo

OBOVATE adj shaped like the longitudinal section of an egg

OBOVOID adj (of a fruit) egg-shaped with the narrower end at the base

OBS ▸ ob

OBSCENE, -R adj indecent

OBSCURE, -D, -R, -S adj not well known ▷ vb make (something) obscure

OBSEQUIE same as ▸ obsequy

OBSEQUY singular of > obsequies

OBSERVE, -D, -S vb see or notice

OBSERVER n person who observes, esp one who watches someone or something carefully

OBSERVES ▸ observe

OBSESS, -ED, -ES vb preoccupy (someone) compulsively

OBSESSOR ▸ obsess

OBSIDIAN n dark glassy volcanic rock

OBSIGN, -ED, -S vb confirm

OBSOLETE adj no longer in use ▷ vb make obsolete

OBSTACLE n something that makes progress difficult

OBSTRUCT vb block with an obstacle

OBTAIN, -ED, -S vb acquire intentionally

OBTAINER ▸ obtain

OBTAINS ▸ obtain

OBTECT adj (of a pupa) encased in a hardened secretion

OBTECTED same as ▸ obtect

OBTEMPER vb comply (with)

OBTEND, -ED, -S vb put forward

OBTEST, -ED, -S vb beg (someone) earnestly

OBTRUDE, -D, -S vb push oneself or one's ideas on others

OBTRUDER ▸ obtrude

OBTRUDES ▸ obtrude

OBTUND, -ED, -S vb deaden or dull

OBTURATE vb stop up (an opening, esp the breech of a gun)

OBTUSE, -R, -ST adj not sharp or pointed

OBTUSELY ▸ obtuse

OBTUSER ▸ obtuse

OBTUSEST ▸ obtuse

OBTUSITY ▸ obtuse

OBVERSE, -S n opposite way of looking at an idea ▷ adj facing or turned towards the observer

OBVERT, -ED, -S vb deduce the obverse of (a proposition)

OBVIABLE ▸ obviate

OBVIATE, -D, -S vb make unnecessary

OBVIATOR ▸ obviate

OBVIOUS adj easy to see or understand, evident

OBVOLUTE adj (of leaves or petals in the bud) folded so that the margins overlap each other

OBVS adv obviously

OCA, -S n any of various South American herbaceous plants

OCARINA, -S n small oval wind instrument

OCAS ► oca

OCCAM, -S n computer programming language

OCCAMIES ► occamy

OCCAMS ► occam

OCCAMY, OCCAMIES n type of alloy

OCCASION n time at which a particular thing happens ▷ vb cause

OCCIDENT literary or formal word for ► west

OCCIES ► occy

OCCIPUT, OCCIPITA, -S n back of the head

OCCLUDE, -D, -S vb obstruct

OCCLUDER ► occlude

OCCLUDES ► occlude

OCCLUSAL ► occlusion

OCCLUSOR n muscle for closing opening

OCCULT, -ED, -S adj relating to the supernatural ▷ vb (of a celestial body) to hide (another celestial body) from view

OCCULTER n something that obscures

OCCULTLY ► occult

OCCULTS ► occult

OCCUPANT n person occupying a specified place

OCCUPATE same as ► occupy

OCCUPIED ► occupy

OCCUPIER n person who lives in a particular house, whether as owner or tenant

OCCUPY, OCCUPIED, OCCUPIES vb live or work in (a building)

OCCUR, -RED, -S vb happen

OCCY, OCCIES n as in all over the occy dialect expression meaning in every direction

OCEAN, -S n vast area of sea between continents

OCEANAUT n undersea explorer

OCEANIC adj of or relating to the ocean

OCEANID, -S n ocean nymph in Greek mythology

OCEANS ► ocean

OCELLAR ► ocellus

OCELLATE ► ocellus

OCELLUS, OCELLI n simple eye of insects and some other invertebrates

OCELOID adj of or like an ocelot

OCELOT, -S n American wild cat with a spotted coat

OCH interj expression of surprise, annoyance, or disagreement

OCHE, -S n (in darts) mark behind which a player must stand

OCHER, -ED, -ING, -S same as ► ochre

OCHERIER ► ochery

OCHERING ► ocher

OCHERISH adj (US) resembling ochre

OCHEROID adj (US) of or like ochre

OCHEROUS ► ocher

OCHERS ► ocher

OCHERY, OCHERIER same as ► ochry

OCHES ► oche

OCHIDORE n type of crab

OCHONE interj expression of sorrow or regret

OCHRE, -D, -S, OCHRING n brownish-yellow earth ▷ adj moderate yellow-orange to orange ▷ vb colour with ochre

OCHREA, -E, -S n cup-shaped structure that sheathes the stems of certain plants

OCHREATE same as ► ocreate

OCHRED ► ochre

OCHREOUS ► ochre

OCHRES ► ochre

OCHREY ► ochre

OCHRIER ► ochry

OCHRIEST ► ochry

OCHRING ► ochre

OCHROID ► ochre

OCHROUS ► ochre

OCHRY, OCHRIER, OCHRIEST adj containing or resembling ochre

OCICAT, -S n breed of cat with a spotted coat

OCKER, -S n uncultivated or boorish Australian

OCKERISM n Australian boorishness

OCKERS ► ocker

OCKODOLS pl n one's feet when wearing boots

OCOTILLO n cactus-like tree

OCREA, -E, -S same as ► ochrea

OCREATE adj possessing an ocrea

OCTA, -S same as ► okta

OCTAD, -S n group or series of eight

OCTADIC ► octad

OCTADS ► octad

OCTAGON, -S n geometric figure with eight sides

OCTAL, -S n number system with a base 8

OCTAN, -S n illness that occurs weekly

OCTANE, -S n hydrocarbon found in petrol

OCTANGLE same as ► octagon

OCTANOL, -S n alcohol containing eight carbon atoms

OCTANS ► octan

OCTANT, -S n any of the eight parts into which the three planes containing the Cartesian coordinate axes divide space

OCTANTAL ► octant

OCTANTS ► octant

OCTAPLA, -S n book with eight texts

OCTAPODY n line of verse with eight metrical feet

OCTARCHY n government by eight rulers

OCTAS ► octa

OCTAVAL ► octave

OCTAVE, -S n (interval between the first and) eighth note of a scale ▷ adj consisting of eight parts

OCTAVO, -S n book size in which the sheets are folded into eight leaves

OCTET, -S n group of eight performers

OCTETT, -S same as ► octet

OCTETTE, -S same as ► octet

OCTETTS ► octett

OCTOFID adj divided into eight

OCTONARY adj relating to or based on the number eight ▷ n stanza of eight lines

OCTOPI ► octopus

OCTOPOD, -S n type of mollusc ▷ adj of these molluscs

OCTOPOID adj of or like an octopus

OCTOPUS, OCTOPI n sea creature with a soft body and eight tentacles

OCTOPUSH n hockey-like game played underwater

OCTROI, -S n duty on various goods brought into certain European towns

OCTUOR, -S n octet

OCTUPLE, -D, -S n quantity or number eight times as great as another ▷ adj eight times as much or as many ▷ vb multiply by eight

OCTUPLET n one of eight offspring from one birth

OCTUPLEX n something made up of eight parts

OCTUPLY adv by eight times
OCTYL, -S n group of atoms
OCULAR, -S adj relating to the eyes or sight ▷ n lens in an optical instrument
OCULARLY ▸ ocular
OCULARS ▸ ocular
OCULATE adj possessing eyes
OCULATED same as ▸ oculate
OCULI ▸ oculus
OCULIST, -S n ophthalmologist
OCULUS, OCULI n round window
OD, -S n hypothetical force
ODA, -S n room or chamber
ODAH, -S same as ▸ oda
ODAL, -S same as ▸ udal
ODALLER, -S ▸ odal
ODALS ▸ odal
ODAS ▸ oda
ODD, -ER, -EST adj unusual
ODDBALL, -S n eccentric person ▷ adj strange or peculiar
ODDER ▸ odd
ODDEST ▸ odd
ODDISH ▸ odd
ODDITY, ODDITIES n odd person or thing
ODDLY ▸ odd
ODDMENT, -S n odd piece or thing
ODDNESS ▸ odd
ODDS pl n probability of something happening
ODDSMAN, ODDSMEN n umpire
ODE, -S n lyric poem, usu addressed to a particular subject
ODEA ▸ odeum
ODEON, -S same as ▸ odeum
ODES ▸ ode
ODEUM, ODEA, -S n ancient building for musical performances
ODIC ▸ od
ODIOUS adj offensive
ODIOUSLY ▸ odious
ODISM, -S ▸ od
ODIST, -S ▸ od
ODIUM, -S n widespread dislike
ODOGRAPH same as ▸ odometer
ODOMETER n device that records the number of miles that a bicycle or motor vehicle has travelled
ODOMETRY ▸ odometer
ODONATA pl n insects of an order that includes dragonflies

ODONATE, -S n dragonfly or related insect
ODONTIC adj of teeth
ODONTIST n dentist
ODONTOID adj toothlike ▷ n bone in the spine
ODONTOMA n tumour near teeth
ODOR, -S same as ▸ odour
ODORANT, -S n something with a strong smell
ODORATE adj having a strong smell
ODORED same as ▸ odoured
ODORFUL same as ▸ odourful
ODORISE, -D, -S same as ▸ odorize
ODORISER same as ▸ odorizer
ODORISES ▸ odorise
ODORIZE, -D, -S vb give an odour to
ODORIZER n something that odorizes
ODORIZES ▸ odorize
ODORLESS ▸ odor
ODOROUS adj having or emitting a characteristic smell
ODORS ▸ odor
ODOUR, -S n particular smell
ODOURED adj having an odour
ODOURFUL adj full of odour
ODOURS ▸ odour
ODS ▸ od
ODSO n cry of surprise
ODYL, -S same as ▸ od
ODYLE, -S same as ▸ od
ODYLISM, -S ▸ odyl
ODYLS ▸ odyl
ODYSSEAN adj of or like an odyssey
ODYSSEY, -S n long eventful journey
ODZOOKS interj cry of surprise
OE, -S n grandchild
OECIST, -S n colony founder
OECOLOGY less common spelling of ▸ ecology
OEDEMA, -S, -TA n abnormal swelling
OEDIPAL adj relating to a complex whereby a male child wants to replace his father
OEDIPEAN same as ▸ oedipal
OEILLADE n suggestive glance
OENOLOGY n study of wine
OENOMEL, -S n drink made of wine and honey

OENOPHIL same as ▸ oenophile
OERLIKON n type of cannon
OERSTED, -S n cgs unit of magnetic field strength
OES ▸ oe
OESTRAL ▸ oestrus
OESTRIN, -S obsolete term for ▸ oestrogen
OESTRIOL n weak oestrogenic hormone secreted by the mammalian ovary
OESTRONE n weak oestrogenic hormone secreted by the mammalian ovary
OESTROUS ▸ oestrus
OESTRUAL adj relating to oestrus
OESTRUM, -S same as ▸ oestrus
OESTRUS n regularly occurring period of fertility in female mammals
OEUVRE, -S n work of art, literature, music, etc
OF prep belonging to
OFF, -ED, -S prep away from ▷ adv away ▷ adj not operating ▷ n side of the field to which the batsman's feet point ▷ vb take off
OFFA prep off
OFFAL, -S n edible organs of an animal, such as liver or kidneys
OFFBEAT, -S adj unusual or eccentric ▷ n any of the normally unaccented beats in a bar
OFFCAST, -S n cast-off
OFFCUT, -S n piece remaining after the required parts have been cut out
OFFED ▸ off
OFFENCE, -S n (cause of) hurt feelings or annoyance
OFFEND, -ED, -S vb hurt the feelings of, insult
OFFENDER ▸ offend
OFFENDS ▸ offend
OFFENSE, -S same as ▸ offence
OFFER, -ED, -S vb present (something) for acceptance or rejection ▷ n something offered
OFFEREE, -S n person to whom an offer is made
OFFERER, -S ▸ offer
OFFERING n thing offered
OFFEROR, -S ▸ offer
OFFERS ▸ offer
OFFHAND adj casual, curt ▷ adv without preparation

OFFICE, -S *n* room or building where people work at desks

OFFICER, -S *n* person in authority in the armed services ▷ *vb* furnish with officers

OFFICES ▸ office

OFFICIAL *adj* of a position of authority ▷ *n* person who holds a position of authority

OFFIE, -S *n* off-licence

OFFING, -S *n* area of the sea visible from the shore

OFFISH *adj* aloof or distant in manner

OFFISHLY ▸ offish

OFFKEY *adj* out of tune

OFFLINE *adj* disconnected from a computer or the internet

OFFLOAD, -S *vb* pass responsibility to someone else

OFFPEAK *adj* relating to times outside periods of intensive use

OFFPRINT *n* separate reprint of an article that originally appeared in a larger publication ▷ *vb* reprint (an article taken from a larger publication) separately

OFFPUT, -S *n* act of putting off

OFFRAMP, -S *n* road allowing traffic to leave a motorway

OFFS ▸ off

OFFSCUM, -S *n* scum

OFFSET, -S *vb* cancel out ▷ *n* printing method

OFFSHOOT *n* something developed from something else

OFFSHORE *adv* away from or at some distance from the shore ▷ *adj* sited or conducted at sea ▷ *n* company operating abroad where the tax system is more advantageous than at home ▷ *vb* transfer (work) to another country where wages are lower

OFFSIDE *adv* (positioned) illegally ahead of the ball ▷ *n* side of a vehicle nearest the centre of the road

OFFSIDER *n* partner or assistant

OFFSIDES ▸ offside

OFFSTAGE *adv* out of the view of the audience ▷ *n* something that happens offstage

OFFTAKE, -S *n* act of taking off

OFFTRACK *adj* not at a racetrack

OFFY *same as* ▸ **offie**

OFLAG, -S *n* prisoner-of-war camp for officers in World War II

OFT, -ER, -EST *adv* often

OFTEN, -ER, -EST *adv* frequently, much of the time

OFTER ▸ oft

OFTEST ▸ oft

OFTTIMES *same as* ▸ **often**

OGAM, -S *same as* ▸ **ogham**

OGAMIC ▸ ogam

OGAMS ▸ ogam

OGDOAD, -S *n* group of eight

OGEE, -S *n* moulding having a cross section in the form of a letter S

OGEED *adj* (of an arch or moulding) having an ogee

OGEES ▸ ogee

OGGIN, -S *n* sea

OGHAM, -S *n* ancient writing system used by the Celts

OGHAMIC ▸ ogham

OGHAMIST ▸ ogham

OGHAMS ▸ ogham

OGIVAL ▸ ogive

OGIVE, -S *n* diagonal rib or groin of a Gothic vault

OGLE, -D, -S *vb* stare or gape at ▷ *n* flirtatious look

OGLER, -S ▸ ogle

OGLES ▸ ogle

OGLING, -S ▸ ogle

OGMIC ▸ ogam

OGRE, -S *n* giant that eats human flesh

OGREISH ▸ ogre

OGREISM, -S ▸ ogre

OGRES ▸ ogre

OGRESS, -ES ▸ ogre

OGRISH ▸ ogre

OGRISHLY ▸ ogre

OGRISM, -S ▸ ogre

OH, -ED, -ING, -S *interj* exclamation of surprise, pain, etc ▷ *vb* say 'oh'

OHIA, -S *n* Hawaiian plant

OHING ▸ oh

OHM, -S *n* unit of electrical resistance

OHMAGE, -S *n* electrical resistance in ohms

OHMIC *adj* of or relating to a circuit element

OHMMETER *n* instrument for measuring electrical resistance

OHMS ▸ ohm

OHO *interj* exclamation expressing surprise, exultation, or derision

OHONE *same as* ▸ **ochone**

OHS ▸ oh

OI, -S *interj* shout to attract attention ▷ *n* grey-faced petrel

OIDIA ▸ oidium

OIDIOID ▸ oidium

OIDIUM, OIDIA *n* type of fungal spore

OIK, -S *n* insulting word for person regarded as inferior because ignorant or lower-class

OIKIST, -S *same as* ▸ **oecist**

OIKS ▸ oik

OIL, -ED, -ING, -S *n* viscous liquid, insoluble in water and usu flammable ▷ *vb* lubricate (a machine) with oil

OILBIRD, -S *n* type of nocturnal gregarious cave-dwelling bird

OILCAMP, -S *n* camp for oil workers

OILCAN, -S *n* container with a long nozzle for applying oil to machinery

OILCLOTH *n* waterproof material

OILCUP, -S *n* cup-shaped oil reservoir in a machine providing continuous lubrication for a bearing

OILED ▸ oil

OILER, -S *n* person, device, etc, that lubricates or supplies oil

OILERIES ▸ oilery

OILERS ▸ oiler

OILERY, OILERIES *n* oil business

OILFIELD *n* area containing oil reserves

OILFIRED *adj* using oil as fuel

OILGAS, -ES *n* gaseous mixture of hydrocarbons used as a fuel

OILHOLE, -S *n* hole for oil

OILIER ▸ oily

OILIEST ▸ oily

OILILY ▸ oily

OILINESS ▸ oily

OILING ▸ oil

OILLET, -S *same as* ▸ **eyelet**

OILMAN, OILMEN *n* person who owns or operates oil wells

OILNUT, -S *n* nut from which oil is extracted

OILPAN, -S *n* sump

OILPAPER *n* oiled paper

O

OILPROOF adj resistant to oil

OILS ▸ oil

OILSEED, -S n seed from which oil is extracted

OILSKIN, -S n (garment made from) waterproof material

OILSTONE n stone with a fine grain lubricated with oil and used for sharpening cutting tools

OILTIGHT adj not allowing oil through

OILWAY, -S n channel for oil

OILY, OILIER, OILIEST adj soaked or covered with oil

OINK, -ED, -ING, -S n grunt of a pig or an imitation of this ▸ interj imitation or representation of the grunt of a pig ▸ vb make noise of pig

OINOLOGY same as ▸ oenology

OINOMEL, -S same as ▸ oenomel

OINT, -ED, -ING, -S vb anoint

OINTMENT n greasy substance used for healing skin or as a cosmetic

OINTS ▸ oint

OIS ▸ oi

OITICICA n South American tree

OJIME, -S n Japanese bead used to secure cords

OK interj expression of approval

OKA, -S n unit of weight used in Turkey

OKAPI, -S n African animal related to the giraffe but with a shorter neck

OKAS ▸ oka

OKAY, -ED, -ING, -S adj satisfactory ▸ vb approve or endorse ▸ n approval or agreement ▸ interj expression of approval

OKE, -S same as ▸ oka

OKEH, -S variant of ▸ okay

OKES ▸ oke

OKEYDOKE variant of ▸ okay

OKIMONO, -S n Japanese ornamental item

OKRA, -S n tropical plant with edible green pods

OKTA, -S n unit used in meteorology to measure cloud cover

OLD, -EST, -S adj having lived or existed for a long time ▸ n earlier or past time

OLDE adj old-world or quaint, used facetiously

OLDEN, -ED, -ING, -S adj old ▸ vb grow old

OLDER ▸ old

OLDEST ▸ old

OLDIE, -S n old but popular song or film

OLDISH ▸ old

OLDNESS ▸ old

OLDS ▸ old

OLDSQUAW n type of long-tailed sea duck

OLDSTER, -S n older person

OLDSTYLE n printing type style

OLDWIFE, OLDWIVES n any of various fishes, esp the menhaden or the alewife

OLDY same as ▸ oldie

OLE, -S interj exclamation of approval or encouragement customary at bullfights ▸ n cry of olé

OLEA ▸ oleum

OLEANDER n Mediterranean flowering evergreen shrub

OLEARIA, -S n daisy bush

OLEASTER n type of shrub with silver-white twigs and yellow flowers

OLEATE, -S n any salt or ester of oleic acid

OLEFIANT adj forming oil

OLEFIN, -S same as ▸ olefine

OLEFINE, -S another name for ▸ alkene

OLEFINIC ▸ olefine

OLEFINS ▸ olefin

OLEIC adj as in oleic acid colourless oily liquid used in making soap

OLEIN, -S another name for ▸ triolein

OLEINE, -S same as ▸ olein

OLEINS ▸ olein

OLENT adj having smell

OLEO, -S n as in oleo oil extracted from beef fat

OLES ▸ ole

OLESTRA, -S n trademark term for an artificial fat

OLEUM, OLEA, -S n type of sulphuric acid

OLFACT, -ED, -S vb smell something

OLIBANUM n frankincense

OLICOOK, -S n doughnut

OLID adj foul-smelling

OLIGARCH n member of an oligarchy

OLIGAEMIA same as ▸ oligaemia

OLIGEMIC ▸ oligaemia

OLIGIST, -S n type of iron ore

OLIGOMER n compound of relatively low molecular

weight containing up to five monomer units

OLIGURIA n excretion of an abnormally small volume of urine

OLIGURIC adj relating to oliguria

OLINGO, -S n South American mammal

OLIO, -S n dish of many different ingredients

OLIPHANT archaic variant of ▸ elephant

OLITORY n kitchen garden

OLIVARY adj shaped like an olive

OLIVE, -S n small green or black fruit used as food or pressed for its oil ▸ adj greyish-green

OLIVER, -S n as in Bath oliver type of unsweetened biscuit

OLIVES ▸ olive

OLIVET, -S n button shaped like olive

OLIVINE, -S n olive-green mineral of the olivine group

OLIVINIC adj containing olivine

OLLA, -S n cooking pot

OLLAMH, -S n old Irish term for a wise man

OLLAS ▸ olla

OLLAV, -S same as ▸ ollamh

OLLER, -S n waste ground

OLLIE, -D, -ING, -S n type of skateboarding jump ▸ vb perform an ollie

OLM, -S n pale blind eel-like salamander

OLOGIES ▸ ology

OLOGIST, -S n scientist

OLOGOAN, -S vb complain loudly without reason

OLOGY, OLOGIES n science or other branch of knowledge

OLOROSO, -S n golden-coloured sweet sherry

OLPE, OLPAE, -S n ancient Greek jug

OLYCOOK, -S same as ▸ olykoek

OLYKOEK, -S n American type of doughnut

OLYMPIAD n staging of the modern Olympic Games

OLYMPICS pl n modern revival of the ancient Greek games, featuring sporting contests

OM, -S n sacred syllable in Hinduism

OMA, -S n grandmother

OMADHAUN *n* foolish man or boy

OMAS ▸ **oma**

OMASA ▸ **omasum**

OMASAL ▸ **omasum**

OMASUM, OMASA *n* compartment in the stomach of a ruminant animal

OMBER, -S *same as* ▸ **ombre**

OMBRE, -S *n* 18th-century card game

OMBRELLA *old form of* ▸ **umbrella**

OMBRES ▸ **ombre**

OMBU, -S *n* South American tree

OMEGA, -S *n* last letter in the Greek alphabet

OMELET, -S *same as* ▸ **omelette**

OMELETTE *n* dish of eggs beaten and fried

OMEN, -ED, -ING, -S *n* happening or object thought to foretell success or misfortune ▹ *vb* portend

OMENTA ▸ **omentum**

OMENTAL ▸ **omentum**

OMENTUM, OMENTA, -S *n* double fold of the peritoneum

OMER, -S *n* ancient Hebrew unit of dry measure

OMERTA, -S *n* conspiracy of silence

OMICRON, -S *n* 15th letter in the Greek alphabet

OMIKRON, -S *same as* ▸ **omicron**

OMINOUS *adj* worrying, seeming to foretell misfortune

OMISSION *n* something that has been left out or passed over

OMISSIVE ▸ **omission**

OMIT, -S, -TED, -TING *vb* leave out

OMITTER, -S ▸ **omit**

OMITTING ▸ **omit**

OMLAH, -S *n* staff team in India

OMMATEUM, OMMATEA *n* insect eye

OMNEITY *n* state of being all

OMNIANA, -S *n* miscellaneous collection

OMNIARCH *n* ruler of everything

OMNIBUS *n* several books or TV or radio programmes made into one ▹ *adj* consisting of or dealing with several different things at once

OMNIETY *same as* ▸ **omneity**

OMNIFIC *adj* creating all things

OMNIFIED ▸ **omnify**

OMNIFIES ▸ **omnify**

OMNIFORM *adj* of all forms

OMNIFY, OMNIFIED, OMNIFIES *vb* make something universal

OMNIMODE *adj* of all functions

OMNIUM, -S *n* total value

OMNIVORA *n* group of omnivorous mammals

OMNIVORE *n* omnivorous animal

OMNIVORY *n* state of being omnivorous

OMOHYOID *n* muscle in shoulder

OMOPHAGY *same as* > **omophagia**

OMOPLATE *n* shoulder blade

OMOV, -S *n* voting system in which each voter has one vote to cast

OMPHALI ▸ **omphalos**

OMPHALIC ▸ **omphalos**

OMPHALOS, OMPHALI, OMPHALOI *n* (in the ancient world) a sacred conical object, esp a stone

OMRAH, -S *n* Muslim noble

OMS ▸ **om**

ON, -NED, -NING, -S *prep* indicating position above, attachment, closeness, etc ▹ *adv* in operation ▹ *adj* operating ▹ *n* side of the field on which the batsman stands ▹ *vb* go on

ONAGER, -S, ONAGRI *n* wild ass of Persia

ONBEAT, -S *n* first and third beats in a bar of four-four time

ONBOARD, -S *vb* incorporate (a person) into a group

ONCE, -S *adv* on one occasion ▹ *n* one occasion

ONCER, -S *n* (formerly) a one-pound note

ONCES ▸ **once**

ONCET *dialect form of* ▸ **once**

ONCIDIUM *n* American orchid

ONCOGEN, -S *n* substance causing tumours to form

ONCOGENE *n* gene that can cause cancer when abnormally activated

ONCOGENS ▸ **oncogen**

ONCOLOGY *n* branch of medicine concerned with the study, classification, and treatment of tumours

ONCOME, -S *n* act of coming on

ONCOMICE > **oncomouse**

ONCOMING *adj* approaching from the front ▹ *n* approach or onset

ONCOST, -S *same as* > **overheads**

ONCOTOMY *n* surgical cutting of a tumour

ONCUS *same as* ▸ **onkus**

ONDATRA, -S *same as* ▸ **musquash**

ONDINE, -S *same as* ▸ **undine**

ONDING, -S *Scots word for* ▸ **onset**

ONDOGRAM *n* record made by ondograph

ONE, -S *adj* single, lone ▹ *n* number or figure 1 ▹ *pron* any person

ONEFOLD *adj* simple

ONEIRIC *adj* of or relating to dreams

ONELY *same as* ▸ **only**

ONENESS *n* unity

ONER, -S *n* single continuous action

ONERIER ▸ **onery**

ONERIEST ▸ **onery**

ONEROUS *adj* (of a task) difficult to carry out

ONERS ▸ **oner**

ONERY, ONERIER, ONERIEST *same as* ▸ **ornery**

ONES ▸ **one**

ONESELF *pron* reflexive form of *one*

ONESIE, -S *n* one-piece garment combining a top with trousers

ONETIME *adj* at some time in the past

ONEYER, -S *old form of* ▸ **one**

ONEYRE, -S *same as* ▸ **oneyer**

ONFALL, -S *n* attack or onset

ONFLOW, -S *n* flowing on

ONGAONGA *n* New Zealand nettle with a severe or fatal sting

ONGOING *adj* in progress, continuing

ONGOINGS *pl n* things that are happening

ONIE *variant spelling of* ▸ **ony**

ONION, -ED, -ING, -S *n* strongly flavoured edible bulb ▹ *vb* add onion to

ONIONIER ▸ **oniony**

ONIONING ▸ **onion**

O

ONIONS ▶ onion

ONIONY, ONIONIER
▶ onion

ONIRIC same as ▶ oneiric

ONISCOID adj of or like
woodlice

ONIUM, -S n as in onium
compound type of chemical
salt

ONKUS adj bad

ONLAY, -S n artificial veneer
for a tooth

ONLIEST same as ▶ only

ONLINE adj connected to a
computer or the internet

ONLINER, -S n person who
uses the internet regularly

ONLOAD, -ED, -S vb load
files on to a computer

ONLOOKER n person who
watches without taking
part

ONLY adj alone of its kind
▷ adv exclusively

ONNED ▶ on

ONNING ▶ on

ONO, -S n Hawaiian fish

ONOMAST, -S n person who
studies proper names

ONOS ▶ ono

ONRUSH, -ES n forceful
forward rush or flow

ONS ▶ on

ONSCREEN adj appearing
on screen

ONSET, -S n beginning

ONSETTER n attacker

ONSHORE adv towards the
land

ONSIDE, -S adv (of a player in
various sports) in a legal
position ▷ adj taking one's
part or side ▷ n part of
cricket field where a
batsman stands

ONST same as ▶ once

ONSTAGE adj visible by
audience

ONSTEAD, -S Scots word for
> farmstead

ONSTREAM adj in operation

ONTIC adj having real
existence

ONTO prep a position on

ONTOGENY n entire
sequence of events involved
in the development of an
individual organism

ONTOLOGY n branch of
philosophy concerned with
existence

ONUS, -ES n responsibility
or burden

ONWARD same as
▶ onwards

ONWARDLY ▶ onward

ONWARDS adv at or
towards a point or position
ahead

ONY Scots word for ▶ any

ONYCHA, -S n part of
mollusc

ONYCHIA, -S n
inflammation of the nails or
claws of animals

ONYCHITE n type of stone

ONYCHIUM n part of insect
foot

ONYMOUS adj (of a book)
bearing its author's name

ONYX, -ES n type of quartz
with coloured layers

OO, -S Scots word for ▶ wool

OOBIT, -S n hairy caterpillar

OOCYST, -S n type of zygote

OOCYTE, -S n immature
female germ cell that gives
rise to an ovum

OODLES pl n great
quantities

OODLINS same as ▶ oodles

OOF, -S n money

OOFIER ▶ oofy

OOFIEST ▶ oofy

OOFS ▶ oof

OOFTISH n money

OOFY, OOFIER, OOFIEST
▶ oof

OOGAMETE n female
gamete

OOGAMIES ▶ oogamy

OOGAMOUS ▶ oogamy

OOGAMY, OOGAMIES n
type of reproduction

OOGENY, OOGENIES same
as ▶ oogenesis

OOGONIA ▶ oogonium

OOGONIAL ▶ oogonium

OOGONIUM, OOGONIA n
immature female germ cell
forming oocytes by repeated
divisions

OOH, -ED, -S interj
exclamation of surprise,
pleasure, pain, etc ▷ vb say
ooh

OOHING, -S n act of
exclaiming 'ooh'

OOHS ▶ ooh

OOIDAL adj shaped like an
egg

OOLACHAN same as
▶ eulachon

OOLAKAN, -S same as
▶ eulachon

OOLICHAN n north Pacific
candlefish

OOLITE, -S n limestone
made up of tiny grains of
calcium carbonate

OOLITH, -S n tiny spherical
grain of sedimentary rock

OOLITIC ▶ oolite

OOLOGIC ▶ oology

OOLOGIES ▶ oology

OOLOGIST ▶ oology

OOLOGY, OOLOGIES n
study of birds' eggs

OOLONG, -S n kind of dark
tea

OOM, -S n title of respect
used to refer to an elderly
man

OOMIAC, -S same as ▶ umiak

OOMIACK, -S same as
▶ umiak

OOMIACS ▶ oomiac

OOMIAK, -S same as
▶ umiak

OOMPAH, -ED, -S n
representation of the sound
made by a deep brass
instrument ▷ vb make the
noise of a brass instrument

OOMPH, -S n enthusiasm,
vigour, or energy

OOMS ▶ oom

OOMYCETE n organism
formerly classified as fungi

OON, -S Scots word for ▶ oven

OONT, -S n camel

OOP, -ED, -ING vb Scots
word meaning to bind

OOPHORON n ovary

OOPHYTE, -S n
gametophyte in mosses,
liverworts, and ferns

OOPHYTIC ▶ oophyte

OOPING ▶ oop

OOPS interj exclamation of
surprise or apology

OOR Scots form of ▶ our

OORALI, -S n member of
Indian people

OORIAL, -S n Himalayan
sheep

OORIE, -R, -ST adj Scots
word meaning shabby

This Scots word is one of the
classic 5-letter vowel
dumps. It has almost
equally useful variants
ourie and **owrie**.

OOS ▶ oo

OOSE, -S n dust

OOSIER ▶ oosy

OOSIEST ▶ oosy

OOSPERM, -S n fertilized
ovum

OOSPHERE n large female
gamete produced in the
oogonia of algae and fungi

OOSPORE, -S n thick-walled
spore developed from a
fertilized oosphere

OOSPORIC ▶ oospore

OOSY, OOSIER, OOSIEST
▶ oose

OOT, -S Scots word for ▶ out
OOTHECA, -E n capsule containing eggs
OOTHECAL ▶ ootheca
OOTID, -S n immature female gamete that develops into an ovum
OOTS ▶ oot
OOZE, -D, -S, OOZING vb flow slowly ▷ n sluggish flow
OOZIER ▶ oozy
OOZIEST ▶ oozy
OOZILY ▶ oozy
OOZINESS ▶ oozy
OOZING ▶ ooze
OOZY, OOZIER, OOZIEST adj moist or dripping
OP, -S n operation
OPA, -S n grandfather
OPACIFY vb become or make opaque
OPACITY n state or quality of being opaque
OPACOUS same as ▶ opaque
OPAH, -S n large soft-finned deep-sea fish
OPAL, -S n iridescent precious stone
OPALED adj made like opal
OPALESCE vb exhibit a milky iridescence
OPALINE, -S adj opalescent ▷ n opaque or semiopaque whitish glass
OPALISED same as ▶ opalized
OPALIZED adj made into opal
OPALS ▶ opal
OPAQUE, -D, -R, -S, -ST, OPAQUING adj not able to be seen through, not transparent ▷ n opaque pigment used to block out particular areas on a negative ▷ vb make opaque
OPAQUELY ▶ opaque
OPAQUER ▶ opaque
OPAQUES ▶ opaque
OPAQUEST ▶ opaque
OPAQUING ▶ opaque
OPAS ▶ opa
OPCODE, -S n computer code containing operating instructions
OPE, -D, -S, OPING archaic or poetic word for ▶ open
OPEN, -ED, -EST, -S adj not closed ▷ vb (cause to) become open ▷ n competition which all may enter
OPENABLE ▶ open
OPENCAST adj as in opencast mining mining by excavating from the surface

OPENED ▶ open
OPENER, -S n tool for opening cans and bottles
OPENEST ▶ open
OPENING, -S n beginning ▷ adj first
OPENLY ▶ open
OPENNESS ▶ open
OPENS ▶ open
OPENSIDE n in rugby, flanker who plays on the open side of the scrum
OPENWORK n ornamental work, as of metal or embroidery, having a pattern of openings or holes
OPEPE, -S n African tree
OPERA, -S n drama in which the text is sung to an orchestral accompaniment
OPERABLE adj capable of being treated by a surgical operation
OPERABLY ▶ operable
OPERAND, -S n quantity, variable, or function upon which an operation is performed
OPERANT, -S adj producing effects ▷ n person or thing that operates
OPERAS ▶ opera
OPERATE, -D, -S vb (cause to) work
OPERATIC adj of or relating to opera
OPERATOR n person who operates a machine or instrument
OPERCELE same as ▶ opercule
OPERCULA > operculum
OPERCULE n gill cover
OPERETTA n light-hearted comic opera
OPERON, -S n group of adjacent genes in bacteria
OPEROSE adj laborious
OPES ▶ ope
OPHIDIAN n reptile of the suborder which comprises the snakes
OPHITE, -S n any of several greenish mottled rocks
OPHITIC adj having small elongated feldspar crystals enclosed
OPHIURA, -S n sea creature like a starfish
OPHIURAN same as ▶ ophiura
OPHIURAS ▶ ophiura
OPHIURID same as ▶ ophiura
OPIATE, -D, -S, OPIATING n narcotic drug containing opium ▷ adj containing or

consisting of opium ▷ vb treat with an opiate
OPIFICER n craftsperson
OPINABLE adj thinkable
OPINE, -D, -S, OPINING vb express an opinion
OPING ▶ ope
OPINICUS n mythical monster
OPINING ▶ opine
OPINION, -S n personal belief or judgment
OPIOID, -S n substance that resembles morphine
OPIUM, -S n addictive narcotic drug made from poppy seeds
OPIUMISM n addiction to opium
OPIUMS ▶ opium
OPOPANAX n medical resin from plant
OPORICE, -S n former medicine made from fruit
OPOSSUM, -S n small marsupial of America or Australasia
OPPIDAN, -S adj of a town ▷ n person living in a town
OPPILANT ▶ oppilate
OPPILATE vb block (the pores, bowels, etc)
OPPO, -S n counterpart in another organization
OPPONENS n muscle of the thumb
OPPONENT n person one is working against in a contest, battle, or argument ▷ adj opposite, as in position
OPPOS ▶ oppo
OPPOSE, -D, -S vb work against
OPPOSER, -S ▶ oppose
OPPOSES ▶ oppose
OPPOSING ▶ oppose
OPPOSITE adj situated on the other side ▷ n person or thing that is opposite ▷ prep facing ▷ adv on the other side
OPPRESS vb control by cruelty or force
OPPUGN, -ED, -S vb call into question
OPPUGNER ▶ oppugn
OPPUGNS ▶ oppugn
OPS ▶ op
OPSIMATH n person who learns late in life
OPSIN, -S n type of protein
OPSONIC ▶ opsonin
OPSONIFY same as ▶ opsonize
OPSONIN, -S n constituent of blood serum

OPSONISE same as
▶ opsonize
OPSONIUM n relish eaten with bread
OPSONIZE vb subject (bacteria) to the action of opsonins
OPT, -ED, -ING, -S vb show a preference, choose
OPTANT, -S n person who opts
OPTATIVE adj indicating or expressing choice, preference, or wish ▷ n optative mood
OPTED ▶ opt
OPTER, -S ▶ opt
OPTIC adj relating to the eyes or sight
OPTICAL adj of or involving light or optics
OPTICIAN n person qualified to prescribe glasses
OPTICIST n optics expert
OPTICS n science of sight and light
OPTIMA ▶ optimum
OPTIMAL adj best or most favourable
OPTIMATE n Roman aristocrat
OPTIME, -S n mathematics student at Cambridge University
OPTIMISE same as ▶ optimize
OPTIMISM n tendency to take the most hopeful view
OPTIMIST ▶ optimism
OPTIMIZE vb make the most of
OPTIMUM, OPTIMA, -S n best possible conditions ▷ adj most favourable
OPTING ▶ opt
OPTION, -ED, -S n choice ▷ vb obtain an option on
OPTIONAL adj possible but not compulsory ▷ n optional thing
OPTIONED ▶ option
OPTIONEE n holder of a financial option
OPTIONS ▶ option
OPTOLOGY n science of sight
OPTRONIC adj relating to optronics
OPTS ▶ opt
OPULENCE ▶ opulent
OPULENCY ▶ opulent
OPULENT adj having or indicating wealth
OPULUS, -ES n flowering shrub
OPUNTIA, -S n type of cactus

OPUS, -ES n artistic creation, esp a musical work
OPUSCLE, -S same as
▶ opuscule
OPUSCULA > opusculum
OPUSCULE n small or insignificant artistic work
OPUSES ▶ opus
OQUASSA, -S n American trout
OR, -S prep before ▷ adj of the metal gold ▷ n gold
ORA ▶ os
ORACH same as ▶ orache
ORACHE, -S n type of plant
ORACIES ▶ oracy
ORACLE, -D, -S, ORACLING n shrine of an ancient god ▷ vb utter as an oracle
ORACULAR adj of or like an oracle
ORACY, ORACIES n capacity to use speech
ORAD adv towards the mouth
ORAGIOUS adj stormy
ORAL, -S adj spoken ▷ n spoken examination
ORALISM, -S n oral method of communicating with deaf people
ORALIST, -S ▶ oralism
ORALITY n state of being oral
ORALLY ▶ oral
ORALS ▶ oral
ORANG, -S n orangutan
ORANGE, -R, -S, -ST n reddish-yellow citrus fruit ▷ adj reddish-yellow
ORANGERY n greenhouse for growing orange trees
ORANGES ▶ orange
ORANGEST ▶ orange
ORANGEY ▶ orange
ORANGIER ▶ orangy
ORANGISH ▶ orangy
ORANGS ▶ orang
ORANGY, ORANGIER
▶ orange
ORANT, -S n artistic representation of worshipper
ORARIA ▶ orarium
ORARIAN, -S n person who lives on the coast
ORARION, -S n garment worn by Greek clergyman
ORARIUM, ORARIA n handkerchief
ORATE, -D, -S, ORATING vb make or give an oration
ORATION, -S n formal speech
ORATOR, -S n skilful public speaker

ORATORIO n musical composition for choir and orchestra
ORATORS ▶ orator
ORATORY n art of making speeches
ORATRESS n female orator
ORATRIX n female orator
ORATURE, -S n oral forms of literature
ORB, -ED, -ING, -S n ceremonial decorated sphere ▷ vb make or become circular or spherical
ORBIER ▶ orby
ORBIEST ▶ orby
ORBING ▶ orb
ORBIT, -ED, -ING, -S n curved path ▷ vb move in an orbit around
ORBITA, -S same as ▶ orbit
ORBITAL, -S adj of or denoting an orbit ▷ n region surrounding an atomic nucleus
ORBITAS ▶ orbita
ORBITED ▶ orbit
ORBITER, -S n spacecraft or satellite designed to orbit a planet without landing on it
ORBITIES ▶ orbity
ORBITING ▶ orbit
ORBITS ▶ orbit
ORBITY, ORBITIES n bereavement
ORBLESS ▶ orb
ORBLIKE adj like an orb
ORBS ▶ orb
ORBY, ORBIER, ORBIEST adj orb-shaped
ORC, -S n any of various whales, such as the killer and grampus
ORCA, -S n killer whale
ORCEIN, -S n brown crystalline material
ORCHARD, -S n area where fruit trees are grown
ORCHAT, -S same as
▶ orchard
ORCHEL, -S same as ▶ orchil
ORCHELLA same as ▶ orchil
ORCHELS ▶ orchel
ORCHESIS, ORCHESES n art of dance
ORCHID, -S n plant with flowers that have unusual lip-shaped petals
ORCHIL, -S n any of various lichens
ORCHILLA same as ▶ orchil
ORCHILS ▶ orchil
ORCHIS, -ES n type of orchid
ORCIN, -S same as ▶ orcinol
ORCINE, -S same as ▶ orcinol

O

ORCINOL, -S n colourless crystalline water-soluble solid

ORCINS ▸ orcin

ORCS ▸ orc

ORD, -S n pointed weapon

ORDAIN, -ED, -S vb make (someone) a member of the clergy

ORDAINER ▸ ordain

ORDAINS ▸ ordain

ORDALIAN adj of an ordeal

ORDALIUM same as ▸ ordeal

ORDEAL, -S n painful or difficult experience

ORDER, -ED, -ING, -S n instruction to be carried out ▷ vb give an instruction to

ORDERER, -S ▸ order

ORDERING ▸ order

ORDERLY adj well-organized ▷ n hospital attendant ▷ adv according to custom or rule

ORDERS ▸ order

ORDINAL, -S adj denoting a certain position in a sequence of numbers ▷ n book containing the forms of services for the ordination of ministers

ORDINAND n candidate for ordination

ORDINANT n person who ordains

ORDINAR, -S Scots word for ▸ ordinary

ORDINARY adj usual or normal

ORDINATE n vertical coordinate of a point in a two-dimensional system of coordinates ▷ vb ordain

ORDINEE, -S n person being ordained

ORDINES ▸ ordo

ORDNANCE n weapons and military supplies

ORDO, ORDINES, -S n religious order

ORDS ▸ ord

ORDURE, -S n excrement

ORDUROUS ▸ ordure

ORE, -S n (rock containing) a mineral which yields metal

OREAD, -ES, -S n mountain nymph

OREBODY n mass of ore in a mine

ORECTIC adj of or relating to the desires

ORECTIVE ▸ orexis

OREGANO, -S n sweet-smelling herb used in cooking

OREIDE, -S same as ▸ oroide

OREODONT n extinct prehistoric mammal

OREOLOGY same as ▸ orology

OREWEED, -S n seaweed

OREXIN, -S n hormone that promotes wakefulness and stimulates the appetite

OREXIS, -ES n appetite

ORF, -S n infectious disease of sheep

ORFE, -S n small slender European fish

ORFRAY, -S same as ▸ orphrey

ORFS ▸ orf

ORG, -S n organization

ORGAN, -S n part of an animal or plant that has a particular function

ORGANA ▸ organon

ORGANDIE n fine cotton fabric

ORGANDY same as ▸ organdie

ORGANIC, -S adj of or produced from animals or plants ▷ n substance that is derived from animal or vegetable matter

ORGANISE same as ▸ organize

ORGANISM n any living animal or plant

ORGANIST n organ player

ORGANITY same as ▸ organism

ORGANIZE vb make arrangements for

ORGANON, ORGANA, -S n system of logical or scientific rules

ORGANS ▸ organ

ORGANUM, -S same as ▸ organon

ORGANZA, -S n thin stiff fabric of silk, cotton, or synthetic fibre

ORGEAT, -S n drink made with orange flower water

ORGIA, -S same as ▸ orgy

ORGIAC ▸ orgy

ORGIAS ▸ orgia

ORGIAST, -S n person who indulges immoderately in an activity

ORGIC ▸ orgy

ORGIES ▸ orgy

ORGONE, -S n substance claimed to be needed for mental health

ORGS ▸ org

ORGUE, -S n number of stakes lashed together

ORGULOUS adj proud

ORGY, ORGIES n act of immoderate indulgence

ORIBATID n type of mite

ORIBI, -S n small African antelope

ORICHALC n type of alloy

ORIEL, -S n type of bay window

ORIELLED adj having an oriel

ORIELS ▸ oriel

ORIENCY n state of being iridescent

ORIENT, -ED, -S vb position (oneself) according to one's surroundings ▷ n eastern sky or the dawn ▷ adj eastern

ORIENTAL adj eastern ▷ n slender breed of cat

ORIENTED ▸ orient

ORIENTER ▸ orient

ORIENTS ▸ orient

ORIFEX, -ES same as ▸ orifice

ORIFICE, -S n opening or hole

ORIGAMI, -S n Japanese decorative art of paper folding

ORIGAN, -S another name for ▸ marjoram

ORIGANE, -S same as ▸ origan

ORIGANS ▸ origan

ORIGANUM n type of aromatic plant

ORIGIN, -S n point from which something develops

ORIGINAL adj first or earliest ▷ n first version, from which others are copied

ORIGINS ▸ origin

ORIHOU, -S n small New Zealand tree

ORILLION n part of bastion

ORINASAL adj pronounced with simultaneous oral and nasal articulation ▷ n orinasal speech sound

ORIOLE, -S n tropical or American songbird

ORISHA, -S n any of the minor gods or spirits of traditional Yoruba religion

ORISON, -S another word for ▸ prayer

ORIXA, -S same as ▸ orisha

ORLE, -S n border around a shield

ORLEANS n type of fabric

ORLES ▸ orle

ORLISTAT n drug used for slimming

ORLON, -S n crease-resistant acrylic fibre or fabric

O

ORLOP, -S n (in a vessel with four or more decks) the lowest deck

ORMER, -S n edible marine mollusc

ORMOLU, -S n gold-coloured alloy used for decoration

ORNAMENT n decorative object ▷ vb decorate

ORNATE, -R, -ST adj highly decorated, elaborate

ORNATELY ▶ ornate

ORNATER ▶ ornate

ORNATEST ▶ ornate

ORNERY, ORNERIER adj stubborn or vile-tempered

ORNIS, -ES less common word for ▶ avifauna

ORNITHES n birds in Greek myth

ORNITHIC adj of or relating to birds or a bird fauna

OROGEN, -S n part of earth subject to orogeny

OROGENIC ▶ orogeny

OROGENS ▶ orogen

OROGENY n formation of mountain ranges

OROIDE, -S n alloy containing copper, tin, and other metals

OROLOGY same as > orography

OROMETER n aneroid barometer with an altitude scale

ORONASAL adj of or relating to the mouth and nose

OROPESA, -S n float used in minesweeping

OROTUND adj (of the voice) resonant and booming

ORPHAN, -ED, -S n child whose parents are dead ▷ vb deprive of parents

ORPHIC adj mystical or occult

ORPHICAL same as ▶ orphic

ORPHISM, -S n style of abstract art

ORPHREY, -S n richly embroidered band or border

ORPIMENT n yellow mineral

ORPIN, -S same as ▶ orpine

ORPINE, -S n type of plant

ORPINS ▶ orpin

ORRA adj odd or unmatched

ORRAMAN, ORRAMEN n man who does odd jobs

ORRERY, ORRERIES n mechanical model of the solar system

ORRICE, -S same as ▶ orris

ORRIS, -ES n kind of iris

ORS ▶ or

ORSEILLE same as ▶ orchil

ORSELLIC ▶ orseille

ORT n fragment

ORTHIAN adj having high pitch

ORTHICON n type of television camera tube

ORTHO, -S n type of photographic plate

ORTHODOX adj conforming to established views

ORTHOEPY n study of correct or standard pronunciation

ORTHOPOD n surgeon

ORTHOS ▶ ortho

ORTHOSIS, ORTHOSES n artificial or mechanical aid to support a weak part of the body

ORTHOTIC > orthotics

ORTHROS n canonical hour in the Greek Church

ORTOLAN, -S n small European songbird eaten as a delicacy

ORTS pl n scraps or leavings

ORVAL, -S n plant of sage family

ORYX, -ES n large African antelope

ORZO, -S n pasta in small grain shapes

OS, ORA, -AR, -SA n mouth or mouthlike part or opening

OSCAR, -S n cash

OSCHEAL adj of the scrotum

OSCINE, -S n songbird ▷ adj of songbirds

OSCININE ▶ oscine

OSCITANT > oscitancy

OSCITATE vb yawn

OSCULA ▶ osculum

OSCULANT adj possessing some of the characteristics of two different taxonomic groups

OSCULAR adj of or relating to an osculum

OSCULATE vb kiss

OSCULE, -S n small mouth or opening

OSCULUM, OSCULA n mouthlike aperture

OSE, -S same as ▶ esker

OSETRA, -S n type of caviar

OSHAC, -S n plant smelling of ammonia

OSIER, -S n willow tree

OSIERED adj covered with osiers

OSIERIES ▶ osiery

OSIERS ▶ osier

OSIERY, OSIERIES n work done with osiers

OSMATE, -S n salt of osmic acid

OSMATIC adj relying on sense of smell

OSMIATE, -S same as ▶ osmate

OSMIC adj of or containing osmium in a high valence state

OSMICS n science of smell

OSMIOUS same as ▶ osmous

OSMIUM, -S n heaviest known metallic element

OSMOL, -S same as ▶ osmole

OSMOLAL ▶ osmole

OSMOLAR adj containing one osmole per litre

OSMOLE, -S n unit of osmotic pressure

OSMOLS ▶ osmol

OSMOSE, -D, -S, OSMOSING vb undergo or cause to undergo osmosis

OSMOSIS n movement of a liquid through a membrane

OSMOTIC ▶ osmosis

OSMOUS adj of or containing osmium in a low valence state

OSMUND, -S same as ▶ osmunda

OSMUNDA, -S n type of fern

OSMUNDS ▶ osmund

OSNABURG n coarse plain-woven cotton used for sacks, furnishings, etc

OSPREY, -S n large fish-eating bird of prey

OSSA ▶ os

OSSARIUM same as ▶ ossuary

OSSATURE n skeleton

OSSEIN, -S n protein that forms the organic matrix of bone

OSSELET, -S n growth on knee of horse

OSSEOUS adj consisting of or like bone

OSSETER, -S n sturgeon

OSSETRA, -S same as ▶ osetra

OSSIA, -S n alternate version or passage ▷ conj or

OSSICLE, -S n small bone, esp one of those in the middle ear

OSSIFIC adj making something turn to bone

OSSIFIED adj converted into bone

OSSIFIER ▶ ossify

OSSIFY, OSSIFIES vb (cause to) become bone, harden

OSSOBUCO n Italian dish of veal shank and vegetables stewed in wine

OSSUARY *n* any container for the burial of human bones, such as an urn or vault

OSTEAL *adj* of or relating to bone or to the skeleton

OSTEITIC ▸ **osteitis**

OSTEITIS *n* inflammation of a bone

OSTENT, -ED, -S *n* appearance ▸ *vb* display boastfully

OSTEOGEN *n* material from which bone forms

OSTEOID, -S *adj* of or resembling bone ▸ *n* bony deposit

OSTEOMA, -S *n* tumour composed of bone or bonelike tissue

OSTEOSIS, OSTEOSES *n* forming of bony tissue

OSTIA ▸ **ostium**

OSTIAL ▸ **ostium**

OSTIARY another word for ▸ **porter**

OSTIATE *adj* having ostium

OSTINATO, OSTINATI *n* persistently repeated phrase or rhythm

OSTIOLAR ▸ **ostiole**

OSTIOLE, -S *n* pore in the reproductive bodies of certain algae and fungi

OSTIUM, OSTIA *n* pore in sponges through which water enters the body

OSTLER, -S *n* stableman at an inn

OSTMARK, -S *n* currency of the former East Germany

OSTOMATE *n* person with an ostomy

OSTOMY, OSTOMIES *n* surgically made opening

OSTOSIS, OSTOSES *n* formation of bone

OSTRACA ▸ **ostracon**

OSTRACOD *n* type of minute crustacean

OSTRACON, OSTRACA *n* (in ancient Greece) a potsherd used for ostracizing

OSTRAKON, OSTRAKA same as ▸ **ostracon**

OSTREGER *n* keeper of hawks

OSTRICH *n* large African bird that runs fast but cannot fly

OTAKU, -S *n* Japanese computer geek

OTALGIA, -S technical name for ▸ **earache**

OTALGIC ▸ **otalgia**

OTALGY, OTALGIES same as ▸ **otalgia**

OTARID *adj* of or like an otary, an eared seal

OTARIES ▸ **otary**

OTARINE ▸ **otary**

This means like an otary or eared seal, and is perhaps the most commonly played of all 7-letter bonus words, so well worth learning for that extra 50 points it can give you.

OTARY, OTARIES *n* seal with ears

OTHER, -ED, -ING, -S *vb* regard (a person or people) as different from oneself or one's group

OTIC *adj* of or relating to the ear

OTIOSE *adj* not useful

OTIOSELY ▸ **otiose**

OTIOSITY ▸ **otiose**

OTITIC ▸ **otitis**

OTITIS, OTITIDES, -ES *n* inflammation of the ear

OTOCYST, -S *n* embryonic structure in vertebrates that develops into the inner ear

OTOLITH, -S *n* granule of calcium carbonate in the inner ear of vertebrates

OTOLOGIC *adj* relating to otology

OTOLOGY *n* branch of medicine concerned with the ear

OTOSCOPE another name for > **auriscope**

OTOSCOPY *n* examination of ear using otoscope

OTOTOXIC *adj* toxic to the ear

OTTAR, -S variant of ▸ **attar**

OTTAVA, -S *n* interval of an octave

OTTAVINO *n* piccolo

OTTER, -ED, -ING, -S *n* small brown freshwater mammal that eats fish ▸ *vb* fish using an otter board

OTTO, -S another name for ▸ **attar**

OTTOMAN, -S *n* storage chest with a padded lid for use as a seat

OTTOS ▸ **otto**

OU, -ENS, -S *interj* expressing concession ▸ *n* man, bloke, or chap

OUABAIN, -S *n* poisonous white crystalline glycoside

OUAKARI, -S *n* South American monkey

OUBAAS, -ES *n* man in authority

OUBIT, -S *n* hairy caterpillar

OUCH, -ED, -ES, -ING *interj* exclamation of sudden pain ▸ *n* brooch or clasp set with gems ▸ *vb* say ouch

OUCHT, -S Scots word for ▸ **anything**

OUD, -S *n* Arabic stringed musical instrument

OUENS ▸ **ou**

OUGHLY, OUGHLIED, OUGHLIES variant of ▸ **ugly**

OUGHT, -ED, -ING, -S *vb* have an obligation ▸ *n* zero

OUGIYA, -S *n* standard monetary unit of Mauritania

OUGLIE, -D, -S variant of ▸ **ugly**

OUGUIYA, -S *n* standard monetary unit of Mauritania

OUIJA, -S *n* tradename for a board through which spirits supposedly answer questions

OUISTITI *n* marmoset

OUK, -S Scots word for ▸ **week**

OULACHON same as ▸ **eulachon**

OULAKAN, -S same as ▸ **eulachon**

OULD, -ER, -EST Scots or Irish form of ▸ **old**

OULK, -S Scots form of ▸ **week**

OULONG, -S same as ▸ **oolong**

OUMA, -S *n* grandmother, often as a title with a surname

OUNCE, -S *n* unit of weight equal to one sixteenth of a pound

OUNDY, OUNDIER, OUNDIEST *adj* wavy

OUP, -ED, -ING, -S same as ▸ **oop**

OUPA, -S *n* grandfather, often as a title with a surname

OUPED ▸ **oup**

OUPH, -S same as ▸ **oaf**

OUPHE, -S same as ▸ **oaf**

OUPHS ▸ **ouph**

OUPING ▸ **oup**

OUPS ▸ **oup**

OUR *adj* belonging to us ▸ *determiner* of, belonging to, or associated in some way with us

OURALI, -S *n* plant from which curare comes

OURANG, -S same as ▸ **orang**

OURARI, -S same as ▸ **ourali**

OUREBI, -S same as ▸ **oribi**

OURIE, -R, -ST same as ▸ **oorie**

OURN dialect form of ▸ **our**

O

OUROLOGY same as ▸ **urology**

OURS pron thing(s) belonging to us

OURSELF pron formal word for myself used by monarchs

OUS ▸ **ou**

OUSEL, -S same as ▸ **ouzel**

OUST, -ED, -ING, -S vb force (someone) out, expel

OUSTER, -S n act of forcing someone out of a position

OUSTING ▸ **oust**

OUSTITI, -S n device for opening locked door

OUSTS ▸ **oust**

OUT, -ED, -S adj denoting movement or distance away from ▸ vb put or throw out

OUTA prep informal contraction of out of

OUTACT, -ED, -S vb surpass in acting

OUTADD, -ED, -S vb beat or surpass at adding

OUTAGE, -S n period of power failure

OUTARGUE vb defeat in argument

OUTASITE adj amazing, excellent

OUTASK, -ED, -S vb declare wedding banns

OUTATE ▸ **outeat**

OUTBACK, -S n remote bush country of Australia

OUTBAKE, -D, -S vb bake more or better than

OUTBAR, -S vb keep out

OUTBARK, -S vb bark more or louder than

OUTBARS ▸ **outbar**

OUTBAWL, -S vb bawl more or louder than

OUTBEAM, -S vb beam more or brighter than

OUTBEG, -S vb beg more or better than

OUTBID, -S vb offer a higher price than

OUTBITCH vb bitch more or better than

OUTBLAZE vb blaze more or hotter than

OUTBLEAT vb bleat more or louder than

OUTBLESS vb bless more than

OUTBLOOM vb bloom more or better than

OUTBLUFF vb surpass in bluffing

OUTBLUSH vb blush more than

OUTBOARD adj (of a boat's engine) portable, with its own propeller ▸ adv away from the centre line of a vessel or aircraft ▸ n outboard motor

OUTBOAST vb surpass in boasting

OUTBOUND adj going out

OUTBOX, -ED, -ES vb surpass in boxing

OUTBRAG, -S vb brag more or better than

OUTBRAVE vb surpass in bravery

OUTBRAWL vb defeat in a brawl

OUTBREAK, OUTBROKE n sudden occurrence (of something unpleasant) ▸ vb break out

OUTBREED, OUTBRED vb produce offspring outside a particular family or tribe

OUTBROKE ▸ **outbreak**

OUTBUILD, OUTBUILT vb exceed in building

OUTBULGE vb bulge outwards

OUTBULK, -S vb exceed in bulk

OUTBULLY vb exceed in bullying

OUTBURN, -S, -T vb burn longer or brighter than

OUTBURST n sudden expression of emotion ▸ vb burst out

OUTBUY, -S vb buy more than

OUTBY adv outside

OUTBYE same as ▸ **outby**

OUTCALL, -S n visit to customer's home by professional ▸ vb bid higher than another player in a card game

OUTCAPER vb exceed in capering

OUTCAST, -S n person rejected by a particular group ▸ adj rejected, abandoned, or discarded

OUTCASTE n person who has been expelled from a caste ▸ vb cause (someone) to lose his or her caste

OUTCASTS ▸ **outcast**

OUTCATCH vb catch more than

OUTCAVIL vb exceed in cavilling

OUTCHARM vb exceed in charming

OUTCHEAT vb exceed in cheating

OUTCHIDE, OUTCHID vb exceed in chiding

OUTCITY n anywhere outside a city's confines

OUTCLASS vb surpass in quality

OUTCLIMB, OUTCLOMB vb exceed in climbing

OUTCOACH vb exceed in coaching

OUTCOME, -S n result

OUTCOOK, -S vb cook more or better than

OUTCOUNT vb exceed in counting

OUTCRAWL vb crawl further or faster than

OUTCRIED ▸ **outcry**

OUTCRIES ▸ **outcry**

OUTCROP, -S n part of a rock formation that sticks out of the earth ▸ vb (of rock strata) to protrude through the surface of the earth

OUTCROSS vb breed (animals or plants of the same breed but different strains) ▸ n animal or plant produced as a result of outcrossing

OUTCROW, -S vb exceed in crowing

OUTCROWD vb have more crowd than

OUTCROWS ▸ **outcrow**

OUTCRY, OUTCRIED, OUTCRIES n vehement or widespread protest ▸ vb cry louder or make more noise than (someone or something)

OUTCURSE vb exceed in cursing

OUTCURVE n baseball thrown to curve away from batter

OUTDANCE vb surpass in dancing

OUTDARE, -D, -S vb be more brave than

OUTDATE, -S vb make or become old-fashioned or obsolete

OUTDATED adj old-fashioned

OUTDATES ▸ **outdate**

OUTDO, OUTDID, -ES, -ING, -NE vb surpass in performance

OUTDODGE vb surpass in dodging

OUTDOER, -S ▸ **outdo**

OUTDOES ▸ **outdo**

OUTDOING ▸ **outdo**

OUTDONE ▸ **outdo**

OUTDOOR adj taking place in the open air

OUTDOORS adv in(to) the open air ▷ n open air

OUTDRAG, -S vb beat in drag race

OUTRANK ▶ outdrink

OUTDRAW, -N, -S, OUTDREW vb draw (a gun) faster than

OUTDREAM vb exceed in dreaming

OUTDRESS vb dress better than

OUTDREW ▶ outdraw

OUTDRINK, OUTDRANK, OUTDRUNK vb drink more alcohol than

OUTDRIVE, OUTDROVE vb exceed in driving

OUTDROP, -S same as ▶ outcrop

OUTDROVE ▶ outdrive

OUTDRUNK ▶ outdrink

OUTDUEL, -S vb defeat in duel

OUTDURE, -D, -S vb last longer than

OUTDWELL, OUTDWELT vb live outside something

OUTEARN, -S vb earn more than

OUTEAT, OUTATE, -EN, -S vb eat more than

OUTECHO vb echo more than

OUTED ▶ out

OUTEDGE, -S n furthest limit

OUTER, -S adj on the outside ▷ n white outermost ring on a target

OUTFABLE vb exceed in creating fables

OUTFACE, -D, -S vb subdue or disconcert by staring

OUTFALL, -S n mouth of a river or drain

OUTFAST, -S vb fast longer than

OUTFAWN, -S vb exceed in fawning

OUTFEAST vb exceed in feasting

OUTFEEL, -S, OUTFELT vb exceed in feeling

OUTFENCE vb surpass at fencing

OUTFIELD n area far from the pitch

OUTFIGHT vb surpass in fighting

OUTFIND, -S, OUTFOUND vb exceed in finding

OUTFIRE, -D, -S vb exceed in firing

OUTFISH vb catch more fish than

OUTFIT, -S n matching set of clothes ▷ vb furnish or be furnished with an outfit

OUTFLANK vb get round the side of (an enemy army)

OUTFLASH vb be flashier than

OUTFLEW ▶ outfly

OUTFLIES ▶ outfly

OUTFLING, OUTFLUNG n cutting remark ▷ vb whip out

OUTFLOAT vb surpass at floating

OUTFLOW, -S n anything that flows out, such as liquid or money ▷ vb flow faster than

OUTFLOWN ▶ outfly

OUTFLOWS ▶ outflow

OUTFLUNG ▶ outfling

OUTFLUSH n burst of light

OUTFLY, OUTFLEW, OUTFLIES, OUTFLOWN vb fly better or faster than

OUTFOOL, -S vb be more foolish than

OUTFOOT, -S vb (of a boat) go faster than (another boat)

OUTFOUND ▶ outfind

OUTFOX, -ED, -ES vb defeat or foil by being more cunning

OUTFROWN vb dominate by frowning more than

OUTGAIN, -S vb gain more than

OUTGAS, -ES vb undergo the removal of adsorbed or absorbed gas from solids

OUTGATE, -S n way out

OUTGAVE ▶ outgive

OUTGAZE, -D, -S vb gaze beyond

OUTGIVE, OUTGAVE, -N, -S vb exceed in giving

OUTGLARE vb exceed in glaring

OUTGLEAM vb gleam more than

OUTGLOW, -S vb glow more than

OUTGNAW, -N, -S vb exceed in gnawing

OUTGO, -ES, -NE, OUTWENT vb exceed or outstrip ▷ n cost

OUTGOER, -S ▶ outgo

OUTGOES ▶ outgo

OUTGOING adj leaving ▷ n act of going out

OUTGONE ▶ outgo

OUTGREW ▶ outgrow

OUTGRIN, -S vb exceed in grinning

OUTGROSS vb earn more than

OUTGROUP n group of people outside one's own group of people

OUTGROW, OUTGREW, -N, -S vb become too large or too old for

OUTGUARD n guard furthest away from main party

OUTGUESS vb surpass in guessing

OUTGUIDE n folder in filing system ▷ vb beat or surpass at guiding

OUTGUN, -S vb surpass in fire power

OUTGUSH vb gush out

OUTHAUL, -S n line or cable for tightening the foot of a sail

OUTHEAR, -D, -S vb exceed in hearing

OUTHER same as ▶ other

OUTHIRE, -D, -S vb hire out

OUTHIT, -S vb hit something further than (someone else)

OUTHOMER vb score more home runs than

OUTHOUSE n building near a main building

OUTHOWL, -S vb exceed in howling

OUTHUMOR same as ▷ outhumour

OUTHUNT, -S vb exceed in hunting

OUTHYRE, -D, -S same as ▶ outhire

OUTING, -S n leisure trip

OUTJEST, -S vb exceed in jesting

OUTJET, -S n projecting part

OUTJINX vb exceed in jinxing

> If someone else plays **jinx**, you can outjinx them by adding O, U and T! And if you can form the whole word using all of your letters, you'll get a 50-point bonus.

OUTJUMP, -S vb jump higher or farther than

OUTJUT, -S vb jut out ▷ n projecting part

OUTKEEP, -S, OUTKEPT vb beat or surpass at keeping

OUTKICK, -S vb exceed in kicking

OUTKILL, -S vb exceed in killing

OUTKISS vb exceed in kissing

OUTLAID ▶ outlay

OUTLAIN ▶ outlie

OUTLAND, -S adj outlying or distant ▷ n outlying areas of a country or region

OUTLASH n sudden attack ▷ vb shed tears

OUTLAST, -S vb last longer than

OUTLAUGH vb laugh longer or louder than

OUTLAW, -ED, -S n criminal deprived of legal protection, bandit ▷ vb make illegal

OUTLAWRY n act of outlawing or the state of being outlawed

OUTLAWS ▷ outlaw

OUTLAY, OUTLAID, -S n expenditure ▷ vb spend (money)

OUTLEAD, -S, OUTLED vb be better leader than

OUTLEAP, -S, -T vb leap higher or farther than

OUTLEARN vb exceed in learning

OUTLED ▷ outlead

OUTLER, -S n farm animal kept out of doors

OUTLET, -S n means of expressing emotion

OUTLIE, OUTLAIN, -D, -S vb lie outside a particular place

OUTLIER, -S n outcrop of rocks that is entirely surrounded by older rocks

OUTLIES ▷ outlie

OUTLINE, -D, -S n short general explanation ▷ vb summarize

OUTLINER ▷ outline

OUTLINES ▷ outline

OUTLIVE, -D, -S vb live longer than

OUTLIVER ▷ outlive

OUTLIVES ▷ outlive

OUTLOOK, -S n attitude ▷ vb look out

OUTLOVE, -D, -S vb exceed in loving

OUTLYING adj distant from the main area

OUTMAN, -S vb surpass in manpower

OUTMARCH vb exceed in marching

OUTMATCH vb surpass or outdo (someone)

OUTMODE, -S vb make unfashionable

OUTMODED adj no longer fashionable or accepted

OUTMODES ▷ outmode

OUTMOST another word for > outermost

OUTMOVE, -D, -S vb move faster or better than

OUTNAME, -D, -S vb be more notorious than

OUTNESS n state or quality of being external

OUTNIGHT vb refer to night more often than

OUTPACE, -D, -S vb go faster than (someone)

OUTPAINT vb exceed in painting

OUTPART, -S n remote region

OUTPASS vb exceed in passing

OUTPEEP, -S vb peep out

OUTPEER, -S vb surpass

OUTPITCH vb exceed in pitching

OUTPITY vb exceed in pitying

OUTPLACE vb find job for ex-employee

OUTPLAN, -S vb exceed in planning

OUTPLAY, -S vb perform better than one's opponent

OUTPLOD, -S vb exceed in plodding

OUTPLOT, -S vb exceed in plotting

OUTPOINT vb score more points than

OUTPOLL, -S vb win more votes than

OUTPORT, -S n isolated fishing village, esp in Newfoundland

OUTPOST, -S n outlying settlement

OUTPOUR, -S n act of flowing or pouring out ▷ vb pour or cause to pour out freely or rapidly

OUTPOWER vb have more power than

OUTPRAY, -S vb exceed in praying

OUTPREEN vb exceed in preening

OUTPRESS vb exceed in pressing

OUTPRICE vb sell at better price than

OUTPRIZE vb prize more highly than

OUTPSYCH vb defeat by psychological means

OUTPULL, -S vb exceed in pulling

OUTPUNCH vb punch better than

OUTPUPIL n student sent to a different school to the one he or she would normally attend

OUTPUSH vb exceed in pushing

OUTPUT, -S n amount produced ▷ vb produce (data) at the end of a process

OUTQUOTE vb exceed in quoting

OUTRACE, -D, -S vb surpass in racing

OUTRAGE, -D, -S n great moral indignation ▷ vb offend morally

OUTRAISE vb raise more money than

OUTRAN ▷ outrun

OUTRANCE n furthest extreme

OUTRANG ▷ outring

OUTRANGE vb have a greater range than

OUTRANK, -S vb be of higher rank than (someone)

OUTRATE, -D, -S vb offer better rate than

OUTRAVE, -D, -S vb outdo in raving

OUTRE adj shockingly eccentric

OUTREACH vb surpass in reach ▷ n act or process of reaching out

OUTREAD, -S vb outdo in reading

OUTRED, -S vb be redder than

OUTREIGN vb reign for longer than

OUTREMER n land overseas

OUTRIDE, -S, OUTRODE vb outdo by riding faster, farther, or better than ▷ n extra unstressed syllable within a metrical foot

OUTRIDER n motorcyclist acting as an escort

OUTRIDES ▷ outride

OUTRIG, -S vb supply with outfit

OUTRIGHT adv absolute(ly) ▷ adj complete

OUTRIGS ▷ outrig

OUTRING, OUTRANG, -S, OUTRUNG vb exceed in ringing

OUTRIVAL vb surpass

OUTRO, -S n instrumental passage that concludes a piece of music

OUTROAR, -S vb roar louder than

OUTROCK, -S vb outdo in rocking

OUTRODE ▷ outride

OUTROLL, -S vb exceed in rolling

OUTROOP, -S n auction

OUTROOT, -S vb root out

OUTROPE, -S same as
▶ **outroop**
OUTROPER ▶ **outrope**
OUTROPES ▶ **outrope**
OUTROS ▶ **outro**
OUTROW, -ED, -S vb outdo
in rowing
OUTRUN, OUTRAN, -S vb
run faster than
OUTRUNG ▶ **outring**
OUTRUNS ▶ **outrun**
OUTRUSH n flowing or
rushing out ▷ vb rush out
OUTS ▶ **out**
OUTSAID ▶ **outsay**
OUTSAIL, -S vb sail better
than
OUTSANG ▶ **outsing**
OUTSAT ▶ **outsit**
OUTSAVOR same as
> **outsavour**
OUTSAW ▶ **outsee**
OUTSAY, OUTSAID, -S vb
say something out loud
OUTSCOLD vb outdo in
scolding
OUTSCOOP vb outdo in
achieving scoops
OUTSCORE vb score more
than
OUTSCORN vb defy with
scorn
OUTSEE, OUTSAW, -N, -S vb
exceed in seeing
OUTSELL, -S, OUTSOLD vb
be sold in greater quantities
than
OUTSERT, -S another word for
> **wraparound**
OUTSERVE vb serve better
at tennis than
OUTSET, -S n beginning
OUTSHAME vb greatly
shame
OUTSHINE, OUTSHONE vb
surpass (someone) in
excellence
OUTSHOOT vb surpass or
excel in shooting ▷ n thing
that projects or shoots out
OUTSHOT, -S n projecting
part
OUTSHOUT vb shout louder
than
OUTSIDE, -S adv indicating
movement to or position on
the exterior ▷ adj unlikely
▷ n external area or surface
OUTSIDER n person outside
a specific group
OUTSIDES ▶ **outside**
OUTSIGHT n power of seeing
OUTSIN, -S vb sin more than
**OUTSING, OUTSANG, -S,
OUTSUNG** vb sing better or
louder than

OUTSINS ▶ **outsin**
OUTSIT, OUTSAT, -S vb sit
longer than
OUTSIZE, -S adj larger than
normal ▷ n outsize garment
OUTSIZED same as
▶ **outsize**
OUTSIZES ▶ **outsize**
OUTSKATE vb skate better
than
OUTSKIRT singular of
> **outskirts**
OUTSLEEP, OUTSLEPT vb
sleep longer than
OUTSLICK vb outsmart
OUTSMART vb outwit
OUTSMELL, OUTSMELT vb
surpass in smelling
OUTSMILE vb outdo in
smiling
OUTSMOKE vb smoke more
than
OUTSNORE vb outdo in
snoring
OUTSOAR, -S vb fly higher
than
OUTSOLD ▶ **outsell**
OUTSOLE, -S n outermost
sole of a shoe
OUTSPAN, -S vb relax
OUTSPEAK, OUTSPOKE vb
speak better or louder than
OUTSPEED, OUTSPED vb
go faster than
OUTSPELL, OUTSPELT vb
exceed at spelling
OUTSPEND, OUTSPENT vb
spend more than
OUTSPOKE ▶ **outspeak**
OUTSPORT vb sport in
excess of
OUTSTAND, OUTSTOOD vb
be outstanding or excel
OUTSTARE vb stare longer
than
OUTSTART vb jump out ▷ n
outset
OUTSTATE vb surpass in
stating
OUTSTAY, -S vb overstay
OUTSTEER vb steer better
than
OUTSTEP, -S vb step farther
than
OUTSTOOD ▶ **outstand**
OUTSTRIP vb surpass
OUTSTUDY vb outdo in
studying
OUTSTUNT vb outdo in
performing stunts
OUTSULK, -S vb outdo in
sulking
OUTSUM, -S vb add up to
more than
OUTSUNG ▶ **outsing**
OUTSWAM ▶ **outswim**

**OUTSWEAR, OUTSWARE,
OUTSWORE, OUTSWORN**
vb swear more than
OUTSWEEP n outward
movement of arms in
swimming breaststroke
OUTSWELL vb exceed in
swelling
OUTSWEPT adj curving
outwards
**OUTSWIM, OUTSWAM, -S,
OUTSWUM** vb outdo in
swimming
OUTSWING n (in cricket)
movement of a ball from leg
to off through the air
OUTSWORE ▶ **outswear**
OUTSWORN ▶ **outswear**
OUTSWUM ▶ **outswim**
OUTSWUNG adj made to
curve outwards
OUTTA prep informal
contraction of out of
OUTTAKE, -N, -S, OUTTOOK
n unreleased take from a
recording session, film, or TV
programme ▷ vb take out
OUTTALK, -S vb talk more,
longer, or louder than
(someone)
OUTTASK, -S vb assign task
to staff outside organization
OUTTELL, -S, OUTTOLD vb
make known
OUTTHANK vb outdo in
thanking
OUTTHINK vb outdo in
thinking
OUTTHREW ▶ **outthrow**
OUTTHROB vb outdo in
throbbing
OUTTHROW, OUTTHREW
vb throw better than
OUTTOLD ▶ **outtell**
OUTTOOK ▶ **outtake**
OUTTOP, -S vb rise higher
than
OUTTOWER vb tower over
OUTTRADE vb surpass in
trading
OUTTRICK vb outdo in
trickery
OUTTROT, -S vb exceed at
trotting
OUTTRUMP vb count for
more than
OUTTURN, -S same as
▶ **output**
OUTVALUE vb surpass in
value
OUTVAUNT vb outdo in
boasting
OUTVENOM vb surpass in
venomousness
OUTVIE, -D, -S, OUTVYING
vb outdo in competition

O

OUTVOICE vb surpass in noise

OUTVOTE, -D, -S vb defeat by getting more votes than

OUTVOTER ▶ outvote

OUTVOTES ▶ outvote

OUTVYING ▶ outvie

OUTWAIT, -S vb wait longer than

OUTWALK, -S vb walk farther or longer than

OUTWAR, -S vb surpass or exceed in warfare

OUTWARD same as ▶ outwards

OUTWARDS adv towards the outside

OUTWARS ▶ outwar

OUTWASH n gravel carried and deposited by water from melting glaciers

OUTWASTE vb outdo in wasting

OUTWATCH vb surpass in watching

OUTWEAR, -S, OUTWORE vb use up or destroy by wearing

OUTWEARY vb exhaust

OUTWEED, -S vb root out

OUTWEEP, -S, OUTWEPT vb outdo in weeping

OUTWEIGH vb be more important, significant, or influential than

OUTWELL, -S vb pour out

OUTWENT ▶ outgo

OUTWEPT ▶ outweep

OUTWHIRL vb surpass at whirling

OUTWICK, -S vb move one curling stone by striking with another

OUTWILE, -D, -S vb surpass in cunning

OUTWILL, -S vb demonstrate stronger will than

OUTWIN, -S, OUTWON vb get out of

OUTWIND, -S, OUTWOUND vb unwind

OUTWING, -S vb surpass in flying

OUTWINS ▶ outwin

OUTWISH vb surpass in wishing

OUTWIT, -S vb get the better of (someone) by cunning

OUTWITH prep outside

OUTWITS ▶ outwit

OUTWON ▶ outwin

OUTWORE ▶ outwear

OUTWORK, -S n defences which lie outside main defensive works ▷ vb work better, harder, etc, than

OUTWORN adj no longer in use

OUTWORTH vb be more valuable than

OUTWOUND ▶ outwind

OUTWREST vb extort

OUTWRITE, OUTWRIT, OUTWROTE vb outdo in writing

OUTYELL, -S vb outdo in yelling

OUTYELP, -S vb outdo in yelping

OUTYIELD vb yield more than

OUVERT adj open

OUVERTE feminine form of ▶ ouvert

OUVRAGE, -S n work

OUVRIER, -S n worker

OUVRIERE feminine form of ▶ ouvrier

OUVRIERS ▶ ouvrier

OUZEL, -S n type of bird

OUZO, -S n strong aniseed-flavoured spirit from Greece

OVA ▶ ovum

OVAL, -S adj egg-shaped ▷ n anything that is oval in shape

OVALITY ▶ oval

OVALLY ▶ oval

OVALNESS ▶ oval

OVALS ▶ oval

OVARIAL ▶ ovary

OVARIAN ▶ ovary

OVARIES ▶ ovary

OVARIOLE n tube in insect ovary

OVARIOUS adj of eggs

OVARITIS n inflammation of an ovary

OVARY, OVARIES n female egg-producing organ

OVATE, -D, -S, OVATING adj shaped like an egg ▷ vb give ovation

OVATELY ▶ ovate

OVATES ▶ ovate

OVATING ▶ ovate

OVATION, -S n enthusiastic round of applause

OVATOR, -S ▶ ovate

OVEL, -S n mourner, esp during the first seven days after a death

OVEN, -ED, -ING, -S n heated compartment or container for cooking ▷ vb cook in an oven

OVENABLE adj (of food) suitable for cooking in an oven

OVENBIRD n type of small brownish South American bird

OVENED ▶ oven

OVENING ▶ oven

OVENLIKE ▶ oven

OVENS ▶ oven

OVENWARE n heat-resistant dishes in which food can be both cooked and served

OVENWOOD n pieces of wood for burning in an oven

OVER, -ED, -ING, -S adv indicating position on the top of, amount greater than, etc ▷ adj finished ▷ n (in cricket) series of six balls bowled from one end ▷ vb jump over

OVERABLE adj too able

OVERACT, -S vb act in an exaggerated way

OVERAGE, -S adj beyond a specified age ▷ n amount beyond given limit

OVERAGED adj very old

OVERAGES ▶ overage

OVERALL, -S adv in total ▷ n coat-shaped protective garment ▷ adj from one end to the other

OVERAPT adj tending excessively

OVERARCH vb form an arch over

OVERARM, -S adv with the arm above the shoulder ▷ adj bowled, thrown, or performed with the arm raised above the shoulder ▷ vb throw (a ball) overarm

OVERATE ▶ overeat

OVERAWE, -D, -S vb affect (someone) with an overpowering sense of awe

OVERBAKE vb bake too long

OVERBANK n sediment deposited on the flood plain of a river

OVERBEAR, OVERBORE, OVERBORN vb dominate or overcome

OVERBEAT vb beat too much

OVERBED adj fitting over bed

OVERBET, -S vb bet too much

OVERBID, -S vb bid for more tricks than one can expect to win ▷ n bid higher than someone else's bid

OVERBIG adj too big

OVERBILL vb charge too much money

OVERBITE n extension of the upper front teeth over the lower front teeth when the mouth is closed

OVERBLOW, OVERBLEW vb blow into (a wind instrument) with greater force than normal

OVERBOIL vb boil too much

OVERBOLD adj too bold

OVERBOOK vb accept too many bookings

OVERBOOT n protective boot worn over an ordinary boot or shoe

OVERBORE ▸ **overbear**

OVERBORN ▸ **overbear**

OVERBRED adj produced by too much selective breeding

OVERBRIM vb overflow

OVERBROW vb hang over

OVERBULK vb loom large over

OVERBURN vb (formerly) copy information onto CD

OVERBUSY adj too busy ▸ vb make too busy

OVERBUY, -S vb buy too much or too many

OVERBY adv Scots expression meaning over the road or across the way

OVERCALL n bid higher than the preceding one ▸ vb bid higher than (an opponent)

OVERCAME ▸ **overcome**

OVERCAST adj (of the sky) covered with clouds ▸ vb make or become overclouded or gloomy ▸ n covering, as of clouds or mist

OVERCLAD adj wearing too many clothes

OVERCLOY vb weary with excess

OVERCLUB vb (in golf) use a club which causes the shot to go too far

OVERCOAT n heavy coat

OVERCOLD adj too cold

OVERCOME, OVERCAME vb gain control over after an effort

OVERCOOK vb spoil food by cooking it for too long

OVERCOOL vb cool too much

OVERCOY adj too modest

OVERCRAM vb fill too full

OVERCRAW same as ▸ **overcrow**

OVERCROP vb exhaust (land) by excessive cultivation

OVERCROW vb crow over

OVERCURE vb take curing process too far

OVERCUT, -S vb cut too much

OVERDARE vb dare too much

OVERDEAR adj too dear

OVERDECK n upper deck

OVERDO, OVERDID, -ES, -NE vb do to excess

OVERDOER ▸ **overdo**

OVERDOES ▸ **overdo**

OVERDOG, -S n person or side in an advantageous position

OVERDONE ▸ **overdo**

OVERDOSE n excessive dose of a drug ▸ vb take an overdose

OVERDRAW, OVERDREW vb withdraw more money than is in (one's bank account)

OVERDRY vb dry too much

OVERDUB, -S vb add (new sounds) to an audio recording so that the old and the new sounds can be heard ▸ n sound or series of sounds added by this method

OVERDUE adj still due after the time allowed

OVERDUST vb dust too much

OVERDYE, -D, -S vb dye (a fabric, yarn, etc) excessively

OVERDYER ▸ **overdye**

OVERDYES ▸ **overdye**

OVEREASY adj too easy

OVEREAT, OVERATE, -S vb eat more than is necessary or healthy

OVERED ▸ **over**

OVEREDIT vb edit too much

OVEREGG, -S vb exaggerate absurdly

OVEREYE, -D, -S vb survey

OVERFALL, OVERFELL n turbulent stretch of water caused by marine currents over an underwater ridge ▸ vb fall over

OVERFAR adv too far

OVERFAST adj too fast

OVERFAT adj too fat

OVERFEAR vb fear too much

OVERFEED, OVERFED vb give (a person, plant, or animal) more food than is necessary or healthy

OVERFELL ▸ **overfall**

OVERFILL vb put more into (something) than there is room for

OVERFINE adj too fine

OVERFISH vb fish too much

OVERFIT adj too fit

OVERFLEW ▸ **overfly**

OVERFLOW vb flow over ▸ n something that overflows

OVERFLY, OVERFLEW vb fly over (a territory) or past (a point)

OVERFOLD n fold in which one or both limbs have been inclined more than 90°

OVERFOND adj excessively keen (on)

OVERFOUL adj too foul

OVERFREE adj too forward

OVERFULL adj excessively full

OVERFUND vb supply with too much money

OVERGALL vb make sore all over

OVERGANG vb dominate

OVERGAVE ▸ **overgive**

OVERGEAR vb cause (a company) to have too high a proportion of loan stock

OVERGET, -S, OVERGOT vb overtake

OVERGILD, OVERGILT vb gild too much

OVERGIRD, OVERGIRT vb gird too tightly

OVERGIVE, OVERGAVE vb give up

OVERGLAD adj too glad

OVERGO, -ES, -NE, OVERWENT vb go beyond

OVERGOAD vb goad too much

OVERGOES ▸ **overgo**

OVERGONE ▸ **overgo**

OVERGOT ▸ **overget**

OVERGROW, OVERGREW vb grow over or across (an area, path, lawn, etc)

OVERHAIR n outer coat of animal

OVERHALE same as ▸ **overhaile**

OVERHAND adj thrown or performed with the hand raised above the shoulder ▸ adv with the hand above the shoulder ▸ vb sew with the thread passing over two edges in one direction

OVERHANG, OVERHUNG vb project beyond something ▸ n overhanging part

OVERHARD adj too hard

OVERHATE vb hate too much

OVERHAUL vb examine and repair ▸ n examination and repair

OVERHEAD adj above one's head ▸ adv over or above head height ▸ n stroke in racket games played from above head height

OVERHEAP vb supply too much

OVERHEAR vb hear (a speaker or remark) unintentionally

O

OVERHEAT vb make or become excessively hot ▷ n condition of being overheated

OVERHELD ▸ overhold

OVERHENT vb overtake

OVERHIGH adj too high

OVERHIT, -S vb hit too strongly

OVERHOLD, OVERHELD vb value too highly

OVERHOLY adj too holy

OVERHOPE vb hope too much

OVERHOT adj too hot

OVERHUNG ▸ overhang

OVERHUNT vb hunt too much

OVERHYPE vb hype too much

OVERIDLE adj too idle

OVERING ▸ over

OVERJOY, -S vb give great delight to

OVERJUMP vb jump too far

OVERJUST adj too just

OVERKEEN adj too keen

OVERKEEP, OVERKEPT vb keep too long

OVERKEST same as ▸ overcast

OVERKILL n treatment that is greater than required

OVERKIND adj too kind

OVERKING n supreme king

OVERKNEE adj reaching to above knee

OVERLADE vb overburden

OVERLAID ▸ overlay

OVERLAIN ▸ overlie

OVERLAND adv by land ▷ vb drive (cattle or sheep) overland

OVERLAP, -S vb share part of the same space or period of time (as) ▷ n area overlapping

OVERLARD vb cover with lard

OVERLATE adj too late

OVERLAX adj too lax

OVERLAY, OVERLAID, -S vb cover with a thin layer ▷ n something that is laid over something else

OVERLEAF adv on the back of the current page

OVERLEAP vb leap too far

OVERLEND, OVERLENT vb lend too much

OVERLET, -S vb let to too many

OVERLEWD adj too lewd

OVERLIE, OVERLAIN, -S vb lie on or cover (something or someone)

OVERLIER ▸ overlie

OVERLIES ▸ overlie

OVERLIT > overlight

OVERLIVE vb live longer than (another person)

OVERLOAD vb put too large a load on or in ▷ n excessive load

OVERLOCK vb sew fabric with interlocking stitch

OVERLONG adj too or excessively long

OVERLOOK vb fail to notice ▷ n high place affording a view

OVERLORD n supreme lord or master

OVERLOUD adj too loud

OVERLOVE vb love too much

OVERLUSH adj too lush

OVERLY adv excessively

OVERMAN, -S, OVERMEN vb provide with too many workers ▷ n man who oversees others

OVERMANY adj too many ▷ n excess of people

OVERMAST vb provide mast that is too big

OVERMEEK adj too meek

OVERMELT vb melt too much

OVERMEN ▸ overman

OVERMILD adj too mild

OVERMILK vb milk too much

OVERMINE vb mine too much

OVERMIX vb mix too much

OVERMUCH adj too much ▷ n excessive amount

OVERNAME vb repeat (someone's) name

OVERNEAR adj too near

OVERNEAT adj too neat

OVERNET, -S vb cover with net

OVERNEW adj too new

OVERNICE adj too fastidious, precise, etc

OVERPACK vb pack too much

OVERPAGE same as ▸ overleaf

OVERPAID ▸ overpay

OVERPART vb give an actor too difficult a role

OVERPASS, OVERPAST vb pass over, through, or across

OVERPAY, OVERPAID, -S vb pay (someone) at too high a rate

OVERPEER vb look down over

OVERPERT adj too insolent

OVERPLAN vb plan excessively

OVERPLAY same as ▸ overact

OVERPLOT vb plot onto existing graph or map

OVERPLUS n surplus or excess quantity

OVERPLY vb ply too much

OVERPOST vb hurry over

OVERPUMP vb pump too much

OVERRACK vb strain too much

OVERRAKE vb rake over

OVERRAN ▸ overrun

OVERRANK adj too rank ▷ vb assign an unnecessarily high rank to

OVERRASH adj too rash

OVERRATE vb have too high an opinion of

OVERREAD vb read over

OVERRED, -S vb paint over in red

OVERREN, -S same as ▸ overrun

OVERRICH adj (of food) excessively flavoursome or fatty

OVERRIDE, OVERRODE vb overrule ▷ n device or system that can override an automatic control

OVERRIFE adj too rife

OVERRIPE adj (of a fruit or vegetable) so ripe that it has started to decay

OVERRODE ▸ override

OVERRUDE adj very rude

OVERRUFF vb defeat trump card by playing higher trump

OVERRULE vb reverse the decision of (a person with less power)

OVERRUN, OVERRAN, -S vb conquer rapidly ▷ n act or an instance of overrunning

OVERS ▸ over

OVERSAD adj too sad

OVERSAIL vb project beyond

OVERSALE n selling of more than is available

OVERSALT vb put too much salt in

OVERSAVE vb put too much money in savings

OVERSAW ▸ oversee

OVERSEA same as ▸ overseas

OVERSEAS adj to, of, or from a distant country ▷ adv across the sea ▷ n foreign country or foreign countries collectively

OVERSEE, OVERSAW, -N, -S vb watch over from a position of authority

OVERSEED vb plant too much seed in

OVERSEEN ▷ oversee

OVERSEER n person who oversees others, esp work ers

OVERSEES ▷ oversee

OVERSELL, OVERSOLD vb exaggerate the merits or abilities of

OVERSET, -S vb disturb or upset

OVERSEW, -N, -S vb sew (two edges) with stitches that pass over them both

OVERSHOE n protective shoe worn over an ordinary shoe

OVERSHOT adj (of a water wheel) driven by a flow of water that passes over the wheel ▷ n type of fishing rod

OVERSICK adj too sick

OVERSIDE adv over the side (of a ship) ▷ n top side

OVERSIZE adj larger than the usual size ▷ n size larger than the usual or proper size

OVERSKIP vb skip over

OVERSLIP vb slip past

OVERSLOW adj too slow

OVERSMAN, OVERSMEN n overseer

OVERSOAK vb soak too much

OVERSOFT adj too soft

OVERSOLD ▷ oversell

OVERSOON adv too soon

OVERSOUL n universal divine essence

OVERSOW, -N, -S vb sow again after first sowing

OVERSPIN n forward spinning motion

OVERSTAY vb stay beyond the limit or duration of

OVERSTEP vb go beyond (a certain limit)

OVERSTIR vb stir too much

OVERSUDS vb produce too much lather

OVERSUP, -S vb sup too much

OVERSURE adj too sure

OVERSWAM ▷ overswim

OVERSWAY vb overrule

OVERSWIM, OVERSWAM, OVERSWUM vb swim across

OVERT adj open, not hidden

OVERTAKE, OVERTOOK vb move past (a vehicle or person) travelling in the same direction

OVERTALK vb talk over

OVERTAME adj too tame

OVERTART adj too bitter

OVERTASK vb impose too heavy a task upon

OVERTAX vb put too great a strain on

OVERTEEM vb be too full of something

OVERTHIN vb make too thin

OVERTIME adv in addition to one's normal working hours ▷ n work at a regular job done in addition to regular working hours ▷ vb exceed the required time for (a photographic exposure)

OVERTIP, -S vb give too much money as a tip

OVERTIRE vb make too tired

OVERTLY ▷ overt

OVERTOIL vb work too hard

OVERTONE n additional meaning

OVERTOOK ▷ overtake

OVERTOP, -S vb exceed in height

OVERTRIM vb trim too much

OVERTRIP vb tread lightly over

OVERTURE n orchestral introduction ▷ vb make or present an overture to

OVERTURN vb turn upside down ▷ n act of overturning or the state of being overturned

OVERTYPE vb type over existing text

OVERURGE vb urge too strongly

OVERUSE, -D, -S vb use excessively ▷ n excessive use

OVERVEIL vb cover over

OVERVIEW n general survey

OVERVOTE vb vote more times than is allowed

OVERWARM vb make too warm

OVERWARY adj excessively wary

OVERWASH n act of washing over something

OVERWEAK adj too weak

OVERWEAR, OVERWORE, OVERWORN vb wear out

OVERWEEN vb think too highly of

OVERWENT ▷ overgo

OVERWET, -S vb make too wet

OVERWIDE adj too wide

OVERWILY adj too crafty

OVERWIND vb wind (a watch) beyond the proper limit

OVERWING vb fly above

OVERWISE adj too wise

OVERWORD n repeated word or phrase

OVERWORE ▷ overwear

OVERWORK vb work too much ▷ n excessive work

OVERWORN ▷ overwear

OVERWRAP vb cover with a wrapping

OVERYEAR vb keep for later year

OVERZEAL n excess of zeal

OVIBOS, -ES n type of ox

OVICIDAL ▷ ovicide

OVICIDE, -S n killing of sheep

OVIDUCAL ▷ oviduct

OVIDUCT, -S n tube through which eggs are conveyed

OVIFORM adj shaped like an egg

OVINE, -S adj of or like a sheep ▷ n member of sheep family

OVIPARA n all oviparous animals

OVIPOSIT vb (of insects and fishes) to deposit eggs through an ovipositor

OVISAC, -S n capsule or sac in which egg cells are produced

OVIST, -S n person believing ovum contains all subsequent generations

OVOID, -S adj egg-shaped ▷ n something that is ovoid

OVOIDAL, -S adj ovoid ▷ n something that is ovoid

OVOIDS ▷ ovoid

OVOLO, OVOLI, -S n type of convex moulding

Two Os on your rack can normally be dealt with; three is a bit much, but this word for a moulding can handle them. Note that the plural can be **ovolos** or **ovoli**.

OVONIC adj using particular electronic storage batteries

OVONICS n science of ovonic equipment

OVULAR ▷ ovule

OVULARY ▷ ovule

OVULATE, -D, -S vb produce or release an egg cell from an ovary

OVULE, -S n plant part that contains the egg cell

OVUM, OVA n unfertilized egg cell

OW interj exclamation of pain

OWCHE, -S same as ▷ ouch

OWE, -D, -S, OWING *vb* be obliged to pay (a sum of money) to (a person)
OWELTY, OWELTIES *n* equality, esp in financial transactions
OWER *Scots word for* ▶ **over**
OWERBY *adv* over there
OWERLOUP *n* Scots word meaning encroachment
OWES ▶ **owe**
OWIE, -S *n* minor injury
OWING ▶ **owe**
OWL, -ED, -ING, -S *n* night bird of prey ▷ *vb* act like an owl
OWLER, -S *n* smuggler
OWLERIES ▶ **owlery**
OWLERS ▶ **owler**
OWLERY, OWLERIES *n* place where owls live
OWLET, -S *n* young or nestling owl
OWLIER ▶ **owly**
OWLIEST ▶ **owly**
OWLING ▶ **owl**
OWLISH *adj* like an owl
OWLISHLY ▶ **owlish**
OWLLIKE ▶ **owl**
OWLS ▶ **owl**
OWLY, OWLIER, OWLIEST *same as* ▶ **owlish**
OWN, -ED, -ING, -S *adj* used to emphasize possession ▷ *pron* thing(s) belonging to a particular person ▷ *vb* possess
OWNABLE *adj* able to be owned
OWNED ▶ **own**
OWNER, -S *n* person who owns
OWNING ▶ **own**
OWNS ▶ **own**
OWNSOME, -S *n* solitary state
OWRE, -S *same as* ▶ **ower**
OWRECAME, OWRECAME *n* chorus of song ▷ *vb* overcome
OWRELAY, -S *Scots form of* ▶ **overlay**
OWRES ▶ **owre**
OWREWORD *variant of* ▶ **overword**
OWRIE, -R, -ST *same as* ▶ **oorie**
OWSE *Scots form of* ▶ **ox**
OWSEN *Scots word for* ▶ **oxen**
OWT, -S *dialect word for* ▶ **anything**
OX, -EN, -ES *n* castrated bull
OXALATE, -D, -S *n* salt or ester of oxalic acid ▷ *vb* treat with oxalate

OXALIC *adj* as in **oxalic acid** poisonous acid found in many plants
OXALIS, -ES *n* type of plant
OXAZEPAM *n* drug used to relieve anxiety
OXAZINE, -S *n* type of chemical compound
OXAZOLE, -S *n* type of liquid chemical compound
OXBLOOD, -S *n* dark reddish-brown colour ▷ *adj* of this colour
OXBOW, -S *n* piece of wood fitted around the neck of a harnessed ox
OXCART, -S *n* cart pulled by ox
OXEN ▶ **ox**
OXER, -S *n* high fence
OXES ▶ **ox**
OXEYE, -S *n* daisy-like flower
OXFORD, -S *n* type of stout laced shoe with a low heel
OXGANG, -S *n* old measure of farmland
OXGATE, -S *same as* ▶ **oxgang**
OXHEAD, -S *n* head of an ox
OXHEART, -S *n* heart-shaped cherry
OXHERD, -S *n* person who tends oxen
OXHIDE, -S *n* leather made from the hide of an ox
OXIC *adj* involving oxygen
OXID, -S *same as* ▶ **oxide**
OXIDABLE *adj* able to undergo oxidation
OXIDANT, -S *n* substance that acts or is used as an oxidizing agent
OXIDASE, -S *n* enzyme that brings about oxidation
OXIDASIC ▶ **oxidase**
OXIDATE, -D, -S *another word for* ▶ **oxidize**
OXIDE, -S *n* compound of oxygen and one other element
OXIDIC ▶ **oxide**
OXIDISE, -D, -S *same as* ▶ **oxidize**
OXIDISER *same as* ▶ **oxidizer**
OXIDISES ▶ **oxidise**
OXIDIZE, -D, -S *vb* combine chemically with oxygen
OXIDIZER *same as* ▶ **oxidant**
OXIDIZES ▶ **oxidize**
OXIDS ▶ **oxid**
OXIES ▶ **oxy**
OXIM, -S *same as* ▶ **oxime**
OXIME, -S *n* type of chemical compound
OXIMETER *n* instrument for measuring oxygen in blood

OXIMETRY ▶ **oximeter**
OXIMS ▶ **oxim**
OXLAND, -S *same as* ▶ **oxgang**
OXLIKE ▶ **ox**
OXLIP, -S *n* type of woodland plant
OXO *n* as in **oxo acid** acid that contains oxygen
OXONIUM, -S *n* as in **oxonium compound** type of salt derived from an organic ether
OXPECKER *n* type of African starling
OXSLIP, -S *same as* ▶ **oxlip**
OXTAIL, -S *n* tail of an ox, used in soups and stews
OXTER, -ED, -ING, -S *n* armpit ▷ *vb* grip under arm
OXTONGUE *n* type of plant
OXY, OXIES ▶ **ox**
OXYACID, -S *n* any acid that contains oxygen
OXYANION *n* anion containing oxygen atoms
OXYGEN, -S *n* gaseous element essential to life and combustion
OXYGENIC ▶ **oxygen**
OXYGENS ▶ **oxygen**
OXYMEL, -S *n* mixture of vinegar and honey
OXYMORON, OXYMORA *n* figure of speech that combines two apparently contradictory ideas
OXYNTIC *adj* of or denoting stomach cells that secrete acid
OXYPHIL, -S *n* type of cell found in glands
OXYPHILE *same as* ▶ **oxyphil**
OXYPHILS ▶ **oxyphil**
OXYSALT, -S *n* any salt of an oxyacid
OXYSOME, -S *n* group of molecules
OXYTOCIC *adj* accelerating childbirth by stimulating uterine contractions ▷ *n* oxytocic drug or agent
OXYTOCIN *n* hormone that stimulates the ejection of milk in mammals
OXYTONE, -S *adj* having an accent on the final syllable ▷ *n* oxytone word
OXYTONIC *adj* (of a word) having the stress or acute accent on the last syllable
OXYTROPE *n* type of flowering plant
OY, -S *n* grandchild
OYE *same as* ▶ **oy**

OYER, -S *n* (in the 13th century) an assize

OYES, -ES, -SES *same as* ▸ **oyez**

OYEZ, -ES *interj* shouted three times by a public crier calling for attention ▸ *n* such a cry

OYS ▸ **oy**

OYSTER, -ED, -S *n* edible shellfish ▸ *vb* dredge for, gather, or raise oysters

OYSTERER *n* person fishing for oysters

OYSTERS ▸ **oyster**

OYSTRIGE *archaic variant of* ▸ **ostrich**

OZAENA, -S *n* inflammation of nasal mucous membrane

OZALID, -S *n* method of duplicating writing or illustrations

OZEKI, -S *n* sumo wrestling champion

OZONATE, -D, -S *vb* add ozone to

OZONE, -S *n* strong-smelling form of oxygen

OZONIC ▸ **ozone**

OZONIDE, -S *n* type of unstable explosive compound

OZONISE, -D, -S *same as* ▸ **ozonize**

OZONISER ▸ **ozonise**

OZONISES ▸ **ozonise**

OZONIZE, -D, -S *vb* convert (oxygen) into ozone

OZONIZER ▸ **ozonize**

OZONIZES ▸ **ozonize**

OZONOUS ▸ **ozone**

OZZIE, -S *n* hospital

O

Pp

P forms a two-letter word in front of every vowel except U, which makes it very useful for joining a new word to one already on the board. It also forms several three-letter words with X: **pax**, **pix**, **pox** (12 points each) and **pyx** (15). Other three-letter words with P well worth remembering are **zap**, **zep** and **zip** for 14 points each and **jap** for 12 points.

PA n (formerly) fortified Māori settlement

PAAL, -S n stake driven into the ground

PAAN, -S n leaf of the betel tree

PABLUM, -S same as ▸ pabulum

PABOUCHE n soft shoe

PABULAR ▸ pabulum

PABULOUS ▸ pabulum

PABULUM, -S n food

PAC, -S n soft shoe

PACA, -S n large burrowing rodent

PACABLE adj easily appeased

PACAS ▸ paca

PACATION n act of making peace

PACE, -D, -S n single step in walking ▸ vb walk up and down, esp in anxiety ▸ prep with due respect to: used to express polite disagreement

PACEMAN, PACEMEN n (in cricket) fast bowler

PACER, -S n horse trained to move at a special gait, esp for racing

PACES ▸ pace

PACEWAY, -S n racecourse for trotting and pacing

PACEY adj fast-moving, quick, lively

PACHA, -S same as ▸ pasha

PACHADOM n rank of pacha

PACHAK, -S n fragrant roots of Asian plant

PACHALIC n jurisdiction of pasha

PACHAS ▸ pacha

PACHINKO n Japanese game similar to pinball

PACHISI, -S n Indian game resembling backgammon

PACHOULI same as > patchouli

PACHUCO, -S n young Mexican living in the US

PACIER ▸ pacy

PACIEST ▸ pacy

PACIFIC adj tending to bring peace

PACIFIED ▸ pacify

PACIFIER n baby's dummy

PACIFIES ▸ pacify

PACIFISM n belief that violence is unjustifiable

PACIFIST n person who refuses on principle to take part in war ▸ adj advocating, relating to, or characterized by pacifism

PACIFY, PACIFIED, PACIFIES vb soothe, calm

PACING, -S n act of pacing

PACK, -S vb put (clothes etc) together in a suitcase or bag ▸ n bag carried on a person's or animal's back

PACKABLE ▸ pack

PACKAGE, -D, -S same as ▸ packet

PACKAGER n independent firm specializing in design and production

PACKAGES ▸ package

PACKED adj completely filled

PACKER, -S n person or company who packs goods

PACKET, -ED, -S n small container (and contents) ▸ vb wrap up in a packet or as a packet

PACKFONG n Chinese alloy

PACKING, -S n material, such as paper or plastic, used to protect packed goods

PACKMAN, PACKMEN n man carrying a pack

PACKMULE n mule used to carry burdens

PACKNESS ▸ pack

PACKS ▸ pack

PACKSACK n bag carried strapped on the back or shoulder

PACKWAX n neck ligament

PACKWAY, -S n path for pack animals

PACO, -S n S American mammal

PACS ▸ pac

PACT, -S n formal agreement

PACTA ▸ pactum

PACTION, -S vb concur with

PACTS ▸ pact

PACTUM, PACTA n pact

PACY, PACIER, PACIEST same as ▸ pacey

PACZKI, -S n round filled doughnut

PAD, -DED, -S n piece of soft material used for protection, support, absorption of liquid, etc ▸ vb protect or fill with soft material

PADANG, -S n (in Malaysia) playing field

PADAUK, -S n tropical African or Asian tree

PADDED ▸ pad

PADDER, -S n highwayman who robs on foot

PADDIES ▸ paddy

PADDING, -S ▸ pad

PADDLE, -D, -S, PADDLING n short oar with a broad blade at one or each end ▸ vb move (a canoe etc) with a paddle

PADDLER, -S ▸ paddle

PADDLES ▸ paddle

PADDLING ▸ paddle

PADDOCK, -S n small field or enclosure for horses ▸ vb place (a horse) in a paddock

PADDY, PADDIES n fit of temper

PADELLA, -S n type of candle

PADERERO same as
▸**paterero**

PADI, -S same as ▸**paddy**

PADISHAH n Iranian ruler

PADKOS n snacks and
provisions for a journey

PADLE, -S another name for
▸**lumpfish**

PADLOCK, -S n detachable
lock with a hinged hoop ▷vb
fasten (something) with a
padlock

PADMA, -S n type of lotus

PADNAG, -S n ambling
horse

PADOUK, -S same as
▸**paduak**

PADRE, -S, PADRI n
chaplain to the armed forces

PADRONA, -S n female boss
or employer

PADRONE, -S, PADRONI n
owner or proprietor of an
inn, esp in Italy

PADS ▸**pad**

PADSAW, -S n small narrow
saw used for cutting curves

PADSHAH, -S same as
▸**padishah**

PADUASOY n rich strong silk
fabric used for hangings,
vestments, etc

PAEAN, -S n song of triumph
or thanksgiving

PAEANISM ▸**paean**

PAEANS ▸**paean**

PAELLA, -S n Spanish dish of
rice, chicken, shellfish, and
vegetables

PAENULA, -E, -S n ancient
Roman cloak

PAEON, -S n metrical foot of
four syllables

PAEONIC, -S ▸**paeon**

PAEONIES ▸**paeony**

PAEONS ▸**paeon**

PAEONY, PAEONIES same as
▸**peony**

PAESAN, -S n fellow
countryman

PAESANO, PAESANI, -S n
Italian-American man

PAESANS ▸**paesan**

PAGAN, -S adj not belonging
to one of the world's main
religions ▷n pagan person

PAGANDOM ▸**pagan**

PAGANISE same as
▸**paganize**

PAGANISH ▸**pagan**

PAGANISM ▸**pagan**

PAGANIST ▸**pagan**

PAGANIZE vb become
pagan, render pagan, or
convert to paganism

PAGANS ▸**pagan**

PAGE, -D, -S n (one side of)
sheet of paper forming a
book etc ▷vb summon
(someone) by bleeper or
loudspeaker

PAGEANT, -S n parade or
display of people in costume

PAGEBOY, -S n type of
hairstyle

PAGED ▸**page**

PAGEFUL, -S n amount (of
text, etc) that a page will hold

PAGEHOOD n state of being
a page

PAGER, -S n small electronic
device, capable of receiving
short messages

PAGES ▸**page**

PAGEVIEW n electronic page
of information displayed at
the request of a user

PAGINAL adj page-for-page

PAGINATE vb number the
pages of (a book, manuscript,
etc) in sequence

PAGING, -S ▸**page**

PAGLE, -S same as ▸**paigle**

PAGOD, -S same as ▸**pagoda**

PAGODA, -S n pyramid-
shaped Asian temple or
tower

PAGODITE n type of soft
mineral used for carving

PAGODS ▸**pagod**

PAGRI, -S n type of turban

PAGURIAN n type of
decapod crustacean of the
family which includes the
hermit crabs

PAGURID, -S same as
▸**pagurian**

PAH, -S same as ▸**pa**

PAHAUTEA same as
> **kaikawaka**

PAHLAVI, -S n former
Iranian coin

PAHOEHOE n hardened lava

PAHS ▸**pah**

PAID ▸**pay**

PAIDLE, -S Scots variant of
▸**paddle**

PAIGLE, -S n cowslip

PAIK, -ED, -ING, -S vb thump
or whack

PAIL, -S n bucket

PAILFUL, -S, PAILSFUL same
as ▸**pail**

PAILLARD n thin slice of meat

PAILLON, -S n thin leaf of
metal

PAILS ▸**pail**

PAILSFUL ▸**pailful**

PAIN, -ING n physical or
mental suffering ▷vb cause
(someone) mental or
physical suffering

PAINCH, -ES Scots variant of
▸**paunch**

PAINED adj having or
suggesting pain or distress

PAINFUL adj causing pain or
distress

PAINIM, -S n heathen or
pagan

PAINING ▸**pain**

PAINLESS adj not causing
pain or distress

PAINS pl n care or trouble

PAINT, -ED, -S n coloured
substance, spread on a
surface with a brush or roller
▷vb colour or coat with
paint

PAINTBOX n box containing
a tray of dry watercolour
paints

PAINTED ▸**paint**

PAINTER, -S n rope at the
front of a boat, for tying it up

PAINTIER ▸**painty**

PAINTING n picture
produced by using paint

PAINTPOT n pot for holding
paint

PAINTS ▸**paint**

PAINTURE n art of painting

PAINTY, PAINTIER ▸**paint**

PAIOCK, -S obsolete word for
▸**peacock**

PAIOCKE, -S obsolete word for
▸**peacock**

PAIOCKS ▸**paiock**

PAIR, -ED, -ER, -EST, -S n set
of two things matched for
use together ▷vb group or
be grouped in twos

PAIRE, -S obsolete spelling of
▸**pair**

PAIRED ▸**pair**

PAIRER ▸**pair**

PAIRES ▸**paire**

PAIREST ▸**pair**

PAIRIAL, -S variant of
▸**prial**

PAIRING, -S ▸**pair**

PAIRS ▸**pair**

PAIRWISE adv in pairs

PAIS n country

PAISA, -S, PAISE n monetary
unit of Bangladesh, Bhutan,
India, Nepal, and Pakistan

PAISAN, -S n fellow
countryman

PAISANA, -S n female
peasant

PAISANO, -S n friend

PAISANS ▸**paisan**

PAISAS ▸**paisa**

PAISE ▸**paisa**

PAISLEY, -S n pattern of
small curving shapes with
intricate detailing

P

PAITRICK Scots word for
> partridge
PAJAMA, -S same as > **pyjama**
PAJAMAED adj wearing
pajamas
PAJAMAS ▶ **pajama**
PAJOCK, -S obsolete word for
▶ **peacock**
PAJOCKE, -S obsolete word for
▶ **peacock**
PAJOCKS ▶ **pajock**
PAK, -S n pack
PAKAHI, -S n acid land that
is unsuitable for cultivation
PAKAPOO, -S n Chinese
lottery
PAKEHA, -S n person of
European descent, as
distinct from a Māori
PAKFONG, -S same as
▶ **packfong**
PAKIHI, -S n area of swampy
infertile land
PAKKA variant of ▶ **pukka**
PAKOKO, -S n small
freshwater fish
PAKORA, -S n fried battered
pieces of vegetable, chicken,
etc
PAKS ▶ **pak**
PAKTHONG n white alloy
containing copper, zinc, and
nickel
PAKTONG, -S same as
▶ **pakthong**
PAL, -S n friend ▷ vb
associate as friends
PALABRA, -S n word
PALACE, -S n residence of a
king, bishop, etc
PALACED adj having palaces
PALACES ▶ **palace**
PALADIN, -S n knight who
did battle for a monarch
PALAGI, -S n (in Samoa)
European
PALAIS n dance hall
PALAMA, -E n webbing on
bird's feet
PALAMATE ▶ **palama**
PALAMINO same as
▶ **palomino**
PALAPA, -S n open-sided
tropical building
PALAS, -ES n East Indian tree
PALATAL, -S adj of or
relating to the palate ▷ n
bony plate that forms the
palate
PALATE, -D, -S, PALATING n
roof of the mouth ▷ vb
perceive by taste
PALATIAL adj like a palace,
magnificent
PALATINE same as ▶ **palatal**
PALATING ▶ **palate**

PALAVER, -S n time-wasting
fuss ▷ vb (often used
humorously) have a
conference
PALAY, -S n type of rubber
PALAZZO, PALAZZI, -S n
Italian palace
PALE, -D, -R, -S, -ST adj
light, whitish ▷ vb become
pale ▷ n wooden or metal
post used in fences
PALEA, -E n bract in a grass
spikelet
PALEAL ▶ **palea**
PALEATE adj having scales
PALEBUCK n small African
antelope
PALED ▶ **pale**
PALELY ▶ **pale**
PALENESS ▶ **pale**
PALEOCON n extremely
right-wing conservative
PALEOSOL n ancient soil
horizon
PALER ▶ **pale**
PALES ▶ **pale**
PALEST ▶ **pale**
PALESTRA same as
> **palaestra**
PALET, -S n perpendicular
band on escutcheon
PALETOT, -S n loose outer
garment
PALETS ▶ **palet**
PALETTE, -S n artist's flat
board for mixing colours on
PALEWAYS same as
▶ **palewise**
PALEWISE adv by
perpendicular lines
PALFREY, -S n light saddle
horse, esp ridden by women
PALI, -S n cliff in Hawaii
PALIER ▶ **paly**
PALIEST ▶ **paly**
PALIFORM adj resembling
coral
PALIKAR, -S n Greek soldier
PALIMONY n alimony
awarded to a nonmarried
partner after the break-up of
a long-term relationship
PALING, -S n wooden or
metal post used in fences
PALINKA, -S n type of
apricot brandy
PALINODE n poem in which
the poet recants something
he or she has said in a former
poem
PALINODY ▶ **palinode**
PALIS ▶ **pali**
PALISADE n fence made of
wooden posts driven into
the ground ▷ vb enclose
with a palisade

PALISADO same as
▶ **palisade**
PALISH adj rather pale
PALKEE, -S n (formerly, in S
Asia) covered litter carried
on the shoulders
PALKI, -S same as ▶ **palkee**
PALL, -ED, -ING, -S n cloth
spread over a coffin ▷ vb
become boring
PALLA, -E n ancient Roman
cloak
PALLADIA > **palladium**
PALLADIC adj of or
containing palladium in the
trivalent or tetravalent state
PALLAE ▶ **palla**
PALLAH, -S n S African
antelope
PALLED ▶ **pall**
PALLET, -ED, -S same as
▶ **palette**
PALLETTE n armpit plate of a
suit of armour
PALLIA ▶ **pallium**
PALLIAL adj relating to
cerebral cortex
PALLIARD n person who
begs
PALLIATE vb lessen the
severity of (something)
without curing it
PALLID, -ER adj pale, esp
because ill or weak
PALLIDLY ▶ **pallid**
PALLIED ▶ **pally**
PALLIER ▶ **pally**
PALLIES ▶ **pally**
PALLIEST ▶ **pally**
PALLING ▶ **pall**
PALLIUM, PALLIA, -S n
garment worn by men in
ancient Greece or Rome
PALLONE, -S n Italian ball
game
PALLOR, -S n paleness of
complexion
PALLS ▶ **pall**
**PALLY, PALLIED, PALLIER,
PALLIES, PALLIEST, -ING**
adj on friendly terms ▷ vb as
in **pally up** become friends
with
PALM, -ED, -ING, -S n inner
surface of the hand ▷ vb
conceal in or about the
hand, as in sleight-of-hand
tricks
PALMAR adj of or relating to
the palm of the hand
PALMARY adj worthy of
praise
PALMATE adj shaped like an
open hand
PALMATED same as
▶ **palmate**

PALMBALL n baseball pitched from the palm and thumb

PALMED ▸ palm

PALMER, -S n medieval pilgrim

PALMETTE n ornament or design resembling the palm leaf

PALMETTO n small palm tree with fan-shaped leaves

PALMFUL, -S n amount that can be held in the palm of a hand

PALMIE, -S n palmtop computer

PALMIER, -S n type of French pastry

PALMIES ▸ palmie

PALMIEST ▸ palmy

PALMIET, -S n South African rush

PALMING ▸ palm

PALMIPED n web-footed bird

PALMIST > palmistry

PALMISTS > palmistry

PALMITIC adj as in palmitic acid white crystalline solid that is a saturated fatty acid

PALMITIN n colourless glyceride of palmitic acid

PALMLIKE ▸ palm

PALMS ▸ palm

PALMTOP, -S adj small enough to be held in the hand ▷ n computer small enough to be held in the hand

PALMY, PALMIEST adj successful, prosperous and happy

PALMYRA, -S n tall tropical Asian palm

PALOLO, -S n polychaete worm of the S Pacific Ocean

PALOMINO, -S n gold-coloured horse with a white mane and tail

PALOOKA, -S n stupid or clumsy boxer or other person

PALP, -ED, -ING, -S n sensory appendage in crustaceans and insects ▷ vb feel

PALPABLE adj obvious

PALPABLY ▸ palpable

PALPAL ▸ palp

PALPATE, -D, -S vb examine (an area of the body) by touching ▷ adj of, relating to, or possessing a palp or palps

PALPATOR n type of beetle

PALPEBRA n eyelid

PALPED ▸ palp

PALPI ▸ palpus

PALPING ▸ palp

PALPS ▸ palp

PALPUS, PALPI, -ES same as ▸ palp

PALS ▸ pal

PALSA, -S n landform of subarctic regions

PALSHIP, -S n state of being pals

PALSIED ▸ palsy

PALSIER ▸ palsy

PALSIES ▸ palsy

PALSIEST ▸ palsy

PALSTAFF variant of ▸ palstave

PALSTAVE n chisel made to fit into a split wooden handle

PALSY, PALSIER, PALSIES, PALSIEST, -ING n paralysis ▷ vb paralyse ▷ adj friendly

PALTER, -ED, -S vb act or talk insincerely

PALTERER ▸ palter

PALTERS ▸ palter

PALTRIER ▸ paltry

PALTRILY ▸ paltry

PALTRY, PALTRIER adj insignificant

PALUDAL adj of, relating to, or produced by marshes

PALUDIC adj of malaria

PALUDINE adj relating to marsh

PALUDISM rare word for ▸ malaria

PALUDOSE adj growing or living in marshes

PALUDOUS adj marshy

PALY, PALIER, PALIEST adj vertically striped

PAM, -S n knave of clubs

PAMPA n grassland area

PAMPAS, -ES pl n vast grassy plains in S America

PAMPEAN, -S ▸ pampas

PAMPER, -ED, -S vb treat (someone) with great indulgence, spoil

PAMPERER ▸ pamper

PAMPERO, -S n dry cold wind in South America

PAMPERS ▸ pamper

PAMPHLET n thin paper-covered booklet ▷ vb produce pamphlets

PAMPHREY n cabbage

PAMPOEN, -S n pumpkin

PAMS ▸ pam

PAN, -NED, -S n wide long-handled metal container used in cooking ▷ vb sift gravel from (a river) in a pan to search for gold

PANACEA, -S n remedy for all diseases or problems

PANACEAN ▸ panacea

PANACEAS ▸ panacea

PANACHE, -S n confident elegant style

PANADA, -S n mixture used as a thickening in cookery

PANAMA, -S n hat made of plaited leaves

PANARY, PANARIES n storehouse for bread

PANATELA same as > panatella

PANAX, -ES n genus of perennial herbs

PANBROIL vb broil in a pan

PANCAKE, -D, -S n thin flat circle of fried batter ▷ vb cause (an aircraft) to make a pancake landing

PANCE, -S n pansy

PANCETTA n lightly spiced cured bacon from Italy

PANCHAX n brightly coloured tropical Asian cyprinodont fish

PANCHEON n shallow bowl

PANCHION same as ▸ pancheon

PANCREAS n large gland behind the stomach that produces insulin and helps digestion

PAND, -S n valance

PANDA, -S n large black-and-white bearlike mammal from China

PANDAN, -S n type of palm of S E Asia

PANDANI, -S n tropical tree

PANDANS ▸ pandan

PANDANUS n Old World tropical palmlike plant

PANDAR, -ED, -S rare variant of ▸ pander

PANDAS ▸ panda

PANDECT, -S n treatise covering all aspects of a particular subject

PANDEMIA n epidemic affecting everyone

PANDEMIC adj (of a disease) occurring over a wide area ▷ n pandemic disease

PANDER, -ED, -S vb indulge (a person in his or her desires) ▷ n someone who indulges a person in his or her desires

PANDERER n someone who indulges a person in his or her desires

PANDERLY ▸ pander

PANDERS ▸ pander

PANDIED ▸ pandy

PANDIES ▸ pandy

P

PANDIT, -S same as ▸ **pundit**
PANDOOR, -S same as ▸ **pandour**
PANDORA, -S n handsome red sea bream
PANDORE, -S another word for ▸ **bandore**
PANDOUR, -S n one of an 18th-century force of Croatian soldiers
PANDOWDY n deep-dish pie made from fruit, esp apples, with a cake topping
PANDROP, -S n hard mint-flavoured sweet
PANDS ▸ **pand**
PANDURA, -S n ancient stringed instrument
PANDY, PANDIED, PANDIES, -ING n (in schools) stroke on the hand with a strap as a punishment ▷ vb punish with such strokes
PANE, -D, -S, PANING n sheet of glass in a window or door ▷ adj (of fish, meat, etc) dipped or rolled in breadcrumbs before cooking
PANEER, -S n soft white cheese, used in Indian cookery
PANEGYRY n formal public commendation; panegyric
PANEITY n state of being bread
PANEL, -ED, -LED, -S n flat distinct section of a larger surface, for example in a door ▷ vb cover or decorate with panels ▷ adj of a group acting as a panel
PANELESS ▸ **pane**
PANELING same as > **panelling**
PANELIST same as > **panellist**
PANELLED ▸ **panel**
PANELS ▸ **panel**
PANES ▸ **pane**
PANETELA same as ▸ **panatela**
PANFISH n small food fish ▷ vb fish for panfish
PANFORTE n hard spicy cake
PANFRY, PANFRIED, PANFRIES vb fry in a pan
PANFUL, -S n the contents of a pan
PANG, -ED, -ING, -S n sudden sharp feeling of pain or sadness ▷ vb cause pain
PANGA, -S n broad heavy knife of E Africa, used as a tool or weapon

PANGAMIC adj relating to pangamy
PANGAMY n unrestricted mating
PANGAS ▸ **panga**
PANGED ▸ **pang**
PANGEN, -S same as ▸ **pangene**
PANGENE, -S n hypothetical particle of protoplasm
PANGENS ▸ **pangen**
PANGING ▸ **pang**
PANGLESS adj without pangs
PANGOLIN n mammal with very long snout
PANGRAM, -S n sentence incorporating all the letters of the alphabet
PANGS ▸ **pang**
PANHUMAN adj relating to all humanity
PANIC, -KED, -S n sudden overwhelming fear ▷ vb feel or cause to feel panic ▷ adj of or resulting from such terror
PANICK, -S old word for ▸ **panic**
PANICKED ▸ **panic**
PANICKS ▸ **panick**
PANICKY ▸ **panic**
PANICLE, -S n loose, irregularly branched cluster of flowers
PANICLED ▸ **panicle**
PANICLES ▸ **panicle**
PANICS ▸ **panic**
PANICUM, -S n type of grass
PANIER, -S same as ▸ **pannier**
PANIM, -S n heathen or pagan
PANING ▸ **pane**
PANINO, PANINI n Italian sandwich
PANISC, -S n faun; attendant of Pan
PANISK, -S same as ▸ **panisc**
PANISLAM n all of Islam or the Muslim world
PANKO, -S n flaky breadcrumbs used in Japanese cookery
PANLIKE adj resembling a pan
PANMIXES ▸ **panmixis**
PANMIXIA n (in population genetics) random mating within an interbreeding population
PANMIXIS, PANMIXES same as ▸ **panmixia**
PANNAGE, -S n pasturage for pigs, esp in a forest
PANNE, -S n lightweight velvet fabric

PANNED ▸ **pan**
PANNER, -S ▸ **pan**
PANNES ▸ **panne**
PANNI ▸ **pannus**
PANNICK, -S old spelling of the noun ▸ **panic**
PANNICLE n thin layer of body tissue
PANNIER, -S n bag fixed on the back of a cycle
PANNIKEL n skull
PANNIKIN n small metal cup or pan
PANNING, -S ▸ **pan**
PANNIST, -S n person who plays a steel drum
PANNOSE adj like felt
PANNUS, PANNI, -ES n inflammatory fleshy lesion on the surface of the eye
PANOCHA, -S n coarse grade of sugar made in Mexico
PANOCHE, -S n type of dark sugar
PANOPLY n magnificent array
PANOPTIC adj taking in all parts, aspects, etc, in a single view
PANORAMA n wide unbroken view of a scene
PANPIPE, -S n wind instrument
PANS ▸ **pan**
PANSIED adj covered with pansies
PANSIES ▸ **pansy**
PANSOPHY n universal knowledge
PANSTICK n type of cosmetic in stick form
PANSY, PANSIES n small garden flower
PANT, -ED vb breathe quickly and noisily during or after exertion ▷ n act of panting
PANTABLE n soft shoe
PANTALET same as > **pantalets**
PANTALON n keyboard instrument
PANTED ▸ **pant**
PANTER, -S n person who pants
PANTHEON n (in ancient Greece and Rome) temple built to honour all the gods
PANTHER, -S n leopard, esp a black one
PANTIE same as ▸ **panty**
PANTIES pl n women's underpants
PANTILE, -D, -S n roofing tile with an S-shaped cross section ▷ vb tile roof with pantiles

PANTINE, -S n pasteboard puppet

PANTING, -S ▸ **pant**

PANTLEG, -S n leg part of a pair of trousers

PANTLER, -S n pantry servant

PANTO, -S same as > **pantomime**

PANTOFLE n kind of slipper

PANTON, -S n type of horseshoe

PANTOS ▸ **panto**

PANTOUM, -S n verse form

PANTRY, PANTRIES n small room or cupboard for storing food

PANTS pl n undergarment for the lower part of the body

PANTSUIT n woman's suit of a jacket or top and trousers

PANTUN, -S n Malayan poetry

PANTY n woman's undergarment

PANZER, -S n German tank

PAOLO, PAOLI n former Italian coin

PAP, -PED, -PING, -S n soft or semiliquid food ▷ vb (of the paparazzi) to follow and photograph (a famous person)

PAPA, -S n father

PAPABLE adj suitable for papacy

PAPACY, PAPACIES n position or term of office of a pope

PAPADAM, -S variant of ▸ **poppadom**

PAPADOM, -S variant of ▸ **poppadom**

PAPADUM, -S variant of ▸ **poppadom**

PAPAIN, -S n enzyme in the unripe fruit of the papaya

PAPAL adj of the pope

PAPALISE same as ▸ **papalize**

PAPALISM n papal system

PAPALIST n supporter of a pope

PAPALIZE vb make papal

PAPALLY ▸ **papal**

PAPAS ▸ **papa**

PAPASAN, -S n bowl-shaped chair

PAPAUMA, -S n New Zealand word for broadleaf

PAPAVER, -S n genus of poppies

PAPAW, -S same as ▸ **papaya**

PAPAYA, -S n large sweet tropical fruit

PAPAYAN ▸ **papaya**

PAPAYAS ▸ **papaya**

PAPE, -S n spiritual father

PAPER, -ED, -ING, -S n material made in sheets from wood pulp or other fibres ▷ vb cover (walls) with wallpaper

PAPERBOY n boy employed to deliver newspapers to people's homes

PAPERED ▸ **paper**

PAPERER, -S ▸ **paper**

PAPERIER ▸ **papery**

PAPERING ▸ **paper**

PAPERS ▸ **paper**

PAPERY, PAPERIER adj like paper, esp in thinness, flimsiness, or dryness

PAPES ▸ **pape**

PAPILIO, -S n butterfly

PAPILLA, -E n small projection of tissue

PAPILLAR ▸ **papilla**

PAPILLON n breed of toy spaniel with large ears

PAPOOSE, -S n Native American child

PAPPADAM same as ▸ **poppadom**

PAPPADOM same as ▸ **poppadom**

PAPPADUM n thin circle of dough fried in oil until crisp

PAPPED ▸ **pap**

PAPPI ▸ **pappus**

PAPPIER ▸ **pappy**

PAPPIES ▸ **pappy**

PAPPIEST ▸ **pappy**

PAPPING ▸ **pap**

PAPPOOSE same as ▸ **papoose**

PAPPOSE ▸ **pappus**

PAPPOUS ▸ **pappus**

PAPPUS, PAPPI, -ES n ring of hairs surrounding the fruit in composite plants

PAPPY, PAPPIER, PAPPIES, PAPPIEST adj resembling pap

PAPRICA, -S same as ▸ **paprika**

PAPRIKA n mild powdered seasoning

PAPRIKAS same as > **paprikash**

PAPS ▸ **pap**

PAPULA, -E, -S same as ▸ **papule**

PAPULAR ▸ **papule**

PAPULAS ▸ **papula**

PAPULE, -S n small solid usually round elevation of the skin

PAPULOSE ▸ **papule**

PAPULOUS ▸ **papule**

PAPYRAL ▸ **papyrus**

PAPYRI ▸ **papyrus**

PAPYRIAN ▸ **papyrus**

PAPYRINE ▸ **papyrus**

PAPYRUS, PAPYRI n tall water plant

PAR, -RED, -RING, -S n usual or average condition ▷ vb play (a golf hole) in par

PARA, -S n paratrooper

PARABEMA n architectural feature

PARABEN, -S n carcinogenic ester

PARABLE, -D, -S n story that illustrates a religious teaching ▷ vb write a parable

PARABOLA n regular curve resembling the course of an object thrown forward and up

PARABOLE n similitude

PARACHOR n quantity constant over range of temperatures

PARACME, -S n phase where fever lessens

PARADE, -D, -S, PARADING n procession or march ▷ vb display or flaunt

PARADER, -S ▸ **parade**

PARADES ▸ **parade**

PARADIGM n example or model

PARADING ▸ **parade**

PARADISE n heaven

PARADOR, -S n state-run hotel in Spain

PARADOS n bank behind a trench or other fortification

PARADOX n person or thing made up of contradictory elements

PARADOXY n state of being paradoxical

PARADROP n delivery of personnel or equipment from an aircraft by parachute

PARAE n type of fish

PARAFFIN n liquid mixture distilled from petroleum and used as a fuel or solvent ▷ vb treat with paraffin or paraffin wax

PARAFFLE n extravagant display

PARAFLE, -S same as ▸ **paraffle**

PARAFOIL n airfoil used on a paraglider

PARAFORM n paraformaldehyde

PARAGE, -S n type of feudal land tenure

P

PARAGOGE n addition of a sound or a syllable to the end of a word

PARAGON, -S n model of perfection ▷ vb equal or surpass

PARAGRAM n pun

PARAKEET n small long-tailed parrot

PARAKITE n series of linked kites

PARALLAX n apparent change in an object's position due to a change in the observer's position

PARALLEL adj separated by an equal distance at every point ▷ n line separated from another by an equal distance at every point ▷ vb correspond to

PARALOGY n anatomical similarity

PARALYSE vb affect with paralysis

PARALYZE same as ▶ paralyse

PARAMENT n ecclesiastical vestment or decorative hanging

PARAMESE n note in ancient Greek music

PARAMO, -S n high plateau in the Andes

PARAMOUR n lover

PARANETE n note in ancient Greek music

PARANG, -S n knife used by the Dyaks of Borneo

PARANOEA same as ▶ paranoia

PARANOIA n disorder causing delusions of grandeur or persecution

PARANOIC ▶ paranoia

PARANOID adj of, characterized by, or resembling paranoia ▷ n person who shows the behaviour associated with paranoia

PARANYM, -S n euphemism

PARAPARA n small carnivorous New Zealand tree

PARAPET, -S n low wall or railing along the edge of a balcony or roof ▷ vb provide with a parapet

PARAPH, -ED, -S n flourish after a signature ▷ vb embellish signature

PARAQUAT n yellow extremely poisonous soluble solid used in solution as a weedkiller

PARAQUET n long-tailed parrot

PARAS ▶ para

PARASAIL vb glide through air on parachute towed by boat

PARASANG n Persian unit of distance equal to about 5.5 kilometres or 3.4 miles

PARASHAH, PARASHOT n section of the Torah read in the synagogue

PARASITE n animal or plant living in or on another

PARASOL, -S n umbrella-like sunshade

PARATHA, -S n (in Indian cookery) flat unleavened bread

PARAVAIL adj lowest

PARAVANE n device that cuts the anchors of moored mines

PARAVANT adv pre-eminently ▷ n pre-eminent person or thing

PARAWING n paraglider

PARAXIAL adj (of a light ray) parallel to the axis of an optical system

PARAZOAN, PARAZOA n sea sponge

PARAZOON n parasitic animal

PARBAKE, -D, -S vb partially bake

PARBOIL, -S vb boil until partly cooked

PARBREAK vb vomit

PARCEL, -ED, -S n something wrapped up, package ▷ vb wrap up

PARCENER n person who takes an equal share with another or others

PARCH, -ED, -ES, -ING vb make very hot and dry

PARCHESI same as > parcheesi

PARCHING ▶ parch

PARCHISI same as > parcheesi

PARCLOSE n screen or railing in a church separating off an altar, chapel, etc

PARD, -S n leopard or panther

PARDAH, -S same as ▶ purdah

PARDAL, -S variant spelling of ▶ pardale

PARDALE, -S n leopard

PARDALIS n leopard

PARDALS ▶ pardal

PARDED adj having spots

PARDEE adv certainly

PARDI same as ▶ pardee

PARDIE same as ▶ pardee

PARDINE adj spotted

PARDNER, -S n friend or partner: used as a term of address

PARDON, -ED, -S vb forgive, excuse ▷ n forgiveness ▷ interj sorry ▷ sentence substitute sorry

PARDONER n (before the Reformation) person licensed to sell ecclesiastical indulgences

PARDONS ▶ pardon

PARDS ▶ pard

PARDY same as ▶ pardee

PARE, -D, -S vb cut off the skin or top layer of

PARECISM n state of having male and female organs close together

PARED ▶ pare

PAREIRA, -S n root of a South American climbing plant

PARELLA, -S n type of lichen

PARELLE, -S same as ▶ parella

PAREN, -S n parenthesis

PARENT, -ED, -S n father or mother ▷ vb raise offspring

PARENTAL adj of or relating to a parent or parenthood

PARENTED ▶ parent

PARENTS ▶ parent

PAREO, -S same as ▶ pareu

PARER, -S ▶ pare

PARERA, -S n New Zealand duck

PARERGON, PARERGA n work that is not one's main employment

PARERS ▶ parer

PARES ▶ pare

PARESIS, PARESES n incomplete or slight paralysis of motor functions

PARETIC, -S ▶ paresis

PAREU, -S n Polynesian skirt or loincloth

PAREV adj containing neither meat nor milk products

PAREVE same as ▶ parev

PARFAIT, -S n dessert consisting of layers of ice cream, fruit, and sauce

PARFLESH same as > parfleche

PARFOCAL adj with focal points in the same plane

PARGANA, -S n Indian sub-district

PARGE, -D, -S vb coat with plaster

PARGET, -ED, -S n plaster, mortar, etc, used to line chimney flues or cover walls ▷ vb cover or decorate with parget

PARGETER n one who pargets

PARGETS ▶ parget

PARGING, -S ▶ parge

PARGO, -ES, -S n sea bream

PARHELIA ▶ parhelion

PARHELIC ▷ parhelion

PARIAH, -S n social outcast

PARIAL, -S n pair royal of playing cards

PARIAN, -S n type of marble or porcelain

PARIES, PARIETES n wall of an organ or bodily cavity

PARIETAL adj of the walls of a body cavity such as the skull ▷ n parietal bone

PARIETES ▶ paries

PARING, -S n piece pared off

PARIS, -ES n type of herb

PARISH, -ES n area that has its own church and a priest or pastor

PARISHAD n Indian assembly

PARISHEN n member of parish

PARISHES ▶ parish

PARISON, -S n unshaped mass of glass

PARITIES ▶ parity

PARITOR, -S n official who summons witnesses

PARITY, PARITIES n equality or equivalence

PARK, -ED, -S n area of open land for recreational use by the public ▷ vb stop and leave (a vehicle) temporarily

PARKA, -S n large waterproof jacket with a hood

PARKADE, -S n building used as a car park

PARKAS ▶ parka

PARKED ▶ park

PARKEE, -S n Inuit outer garment

PARKER, -S ▶ park

PARKETTE n small public car park

PARKI, -S variant of ▶ parka

PARKIE, -S n park keeper

PARKIER ▶ parky

PARKIES ▶ parkie

PARKIEST ▶ parky

PARKIN, -S n moist spicy ginger cake

PARKING, -S ▶ park

PARKINS ▶ parkin

PARKIS ▶ parki

PARKISH adj like a park

PARKLAND n grassland with scattered trees

PARKLIKE ▶ park

PARKLY adj having many parks or resembling a park

PARKOUR, -S n sport of running in urban areas over obstacles

PARKS ▶ park

PARKWARD adv towards a park

PARKWAY, -S n wide road planted with trees, turf, etc

PARKY, PARKIER, PARKIEST adj (of the weather) chilly

PARLANCE n particular way of speaking, idiom

PARLANDO adv to be performed as though speaking

PARLANTE same as ▶ parlando

PARLAY, -ED, -S vb stake (winnings from one bet) on a subsequent wager ▷ n bet in which winnings are parlayed

PARLE, -D, -S, PARLING vb speak

PARLEY, -ED, -S n meeting between opponents to discuss terms ▷ vb have a parley

PARLEYER ▶ parley

PARLEYS ▶ parley

PARLIES pl n small Scottish biscuits

PARLING ▶ parle

PARLOR, -S same as ▶ parlour

PARLOUR, -S n living room for receiving visitors

PARLOUS adj dire ▷ adv extremely

PARLY n short form of parliament

PARMA, -S n breaded chicken dish

PARMESAN n Italian hard cheese

PAROCHIN n old Scottish parish

PARODIC ▶ parody

PARODIED ▶ parody

PARODIES ▶ parody

PARODIST ▶ parody

PARODOI n path leading to Greek theatre

PARODOS n ode sung by Greek chorus

PARODY, PARODIED, PARODIES n exaggerated and amusing imitation of someone else's style ▷ vb make a parody of

PAROEMIA n proverb

PAROL, -S n (formerly) pleadings in an action when presented by word of mouth ▷ adj (of a contract, lease, etc) not made under seal

PAROLE, -D, -S, PAROLING n early freeing of a prisoner on condition that he or she behaves well ▷ vb put on parole

PAROLEE, -S ▶ parole

PAROLES ▶ parole

PAROLING ▶ parole

PAROLS ▶ parol

PARONYM, -S n cognate word

PARONYMY ▶ paronym

PAROQUET n small long-tailed parrot

PARORE, -S n type of fish found around Australia and New Zealand

PAROSMIA n any disorder of the sense of smell

PAROTIC adj situated near the ear

PAROTID, -S adj relating to or situated near the parotid gland ▷ n parotid gland

PAROTIS n parotid gland

PAROTOID n poison gland on certain toads and salamanders ▷ adj resembling a parotid gland

PAROUS adj having given birth

PAROUSIA n Second Coming

PAROXYSM n uncontrollable outburst of rage, delight, etc

PARP, -ED, -ING, -S vb make a honking sound

PARPANE, -S n parapet on bridge

PARPED ▶ parp

PARPEN, -S same as ▶ parpend

PARPEND, -S same as ▶ perpend

PARPENS ▶ parpen

PARPENT, -S n parapet on bridge

PARPING ▶ parp

PARPOINT n parapet on bridge

PARPS ▶ parp

PARQUET, -S n floor covering made of wooden blocks ▷ vb cover with parquet

PARR, -S n salmon up to two years of age

PARRA, -S n tourist or non-resident on a beach

P

PARRAL, -S same as ▸ **parrel**

PARRAS ▸ **parra**

PARRED ▸ **par**

PARREL, -S n ring that holds the jaws of a boom to the mast

PARRIDGE Scottish variant of ▸ **porridge**

PARRIED ▸ **parry**

PARRIER, -S ▸ **parry**

PARRIES ▸ **parry**

PARRING ▸ **par**

PARRITCH Scottish variant of ▸ **porridge**

PARROCK, -S vb put (an animal) in a small field

PARROKET n small long-tailed parrot

PARROT, -ED, -S n tropical bird with a short hooked beak ▸ vb repeat (someone else's words) without thinking

PARROTER n person who repeats what is said

PARROTRY ▸ **parrot**

PARROTS ▸ **parrot**

PARROTY adj like a parrot; chattering

PARRS ▸ **parr**

PARRY, PARRIED, PARRIES, -ING vb ward off (an attack) ▸ n parrying

PARS ▸ **par**

PARSABLE ▸ **parse**

PARSE, -D, -S vb analyse (a sentence) in terms of grammar

PARSEC, -S n unit of astronomical distance

PARSED ▸ **parse**

PARSER, -S n program that interprets input to a computer

PARSES ▸ **parse**

PARSING, -S ▸ **parse**

PARSLEY, -S, PARSLIED n herb used for seasoning and decorating food ▸ vb garnish with parsley

PARSNEP, -S same as ▸ **parsnip**

PARSNIP, -S n long tapering cream-coloured root vegetable

PARSON, -S n Anglican parish priest

PARSONIC ▸ **parson**

PARSONS ▸ **parson**

PART n one of the pieces that make up a whole ▸ vb divide or separate

PARTAKE, -N, -S, PARTOOK vb take (food or drink)

PARTAKER ▸ **partake**

PARTAKES ▸ **partake**

PARTAN, -S Scottish word for ▸ **crab**

PARTED adj divided almost to the base

PARTER, -S n thing that parts

PARTERRE n formally patterned flower garden

PARTERS ▸ **parter**

PARTI, -S n concept of architectural design

PARTIAL, -S adj not complete ▸ n any of the component tones of a single musical sound ▸ vb remove (a factor) from a set of statistics

PARTIBLE adj (esp of property or an inheritance) divisible

PARTICLE n extremely small piece or amount

PARTIED ▸ **party**

PARTIER, -S n person who parties

PARTIES ▸ **party**

PARTIEST ▸ **party**

PARTIM adv in part

PARTING, -S same as ▸ **part**

PARTIS ▸ **parti**

PARTISAN n strong supporter of a party or group ▸ adj prejudiced or one-sided

PARTITA, -S n type of suite

PARTITE adj composed of or divided into a specified number of parts

PARTIZAN same as ▸ **partisan**

PARTLET, -S n woman's garment

PARTLY adv not completely

PARTNER, -S n either member of a couple in a relationship or activity ▸ vb be the partner of

PARTON, -S n hypothetical elementary particle

PARTOOK ▸ **partake**

PARTS pl n abilities or talents

PARTURE, -S n departure

PARTWAY adv some of the way

PARTWORK n series of magazines issued at regular intervals

PARTY, PARTIED, PARTIES, PARTIEST n social gathering for pleasure ▸ vb celebrate, have fun ▸ adj divided into different colours

PARTYER, -S n person who parties

PARTYING n act of partying

PARTYISM n devotion to a political party

PARULIS another name for ▸ **gumboil**

PARURA, -S same as ▸ **parure**

PARURE, -S n set of jewels or other ornaments

PARVE same as ▸ **parev**

PARVENU, -S n person newly risen to a position of power or wealth ▸ adj of or characteristic of a parvenu

PARVENUE n woman newly risen to a position of power or wealth ▸ adj of a parvenue

PARVENUS ▸ **parvenu**

PARVIS n court or portico in front of a building, esp a church

PARVISE, -S same as ▸ **parvis**

PARVO, -S n disease of cattle and dogs

PARVOLIN n substance resulting from the putrefaction of flesh

PARVOS ▸ **parvo**

PAS n dance step or movement, esp in ballet

PASCAL, -S n unit of pressure

PASCHAL, -S adj of the Passover or Easter ▸ n Passover or Easter

PASCUAL, -S adj relating to pasture ▸ n plant that grows in pasture

PASE, -S n movement of the cape or muleta by a matador

PASEAR, -ED, -S vb go for a rambling walk

PASELA, -S same as ▸ **bonsela**

PASEO, -S n bullfighters' procession

PASES ▸ **pase**

PASH, -ED, -ES, -ING n infatuation ▸ vb throw or be thrown and break or be broken to bits

PASHA, -S n high official of the Ottoman Empire

PASHADOM n territory of a pasha

PASHALIC same as ▸ **pashalik**

PASHALIK n province or jurisdiction of a pasha

PASHAS ▸ **pasha**

PASHED ▸ **pash**

PASHES ▸ **pash**

PASHIM, -S same as ▸ **pashm**

PASHING ▸ **pash**

PASHKA, -S n rich Russian dessert

PASHM, -S n underfur of various Tibetan animals, esp goats, used for cashmere shawls

PASHMINA n type of cashmere scarf or shawl made from the underfur of Tibetan goats

PASHMS ▸ pashm

PASKA, -S same as ▸ paskha

PASKHA, -S n Russian dessert eaten at Easter

PASPALUM n type of grass with wide leaves

PASPY, PASPIES n piece of music in triple time

PASQUIL, -S n abusive lampoon or satire ▷ vb ridicule with pasquil

PASS, -ED, -ES vb go by, past, or through ▷ n successful result in a test or examination

PASSABLE adj (just) acceptable

PASSABLY adv fairly

PASSADE, -S n act of moving back and forth in the same place

PASSADO, -S n forward thrust with sword

PASSAGE, -D, -S n channel or opening providing a way through ▷ vb move or cause to move at a passage

PASSAGER as in **passager hawk** young hawk or falcon caught while on migration

PASSAGES ▸ passage

PASSANT adj (of a heraldic beast) walking

PASSATA, -S n sauce made from sieved tomatoes

PASSBAND n frequency band within which signals are transmitted by a filter

PASSBOOK n record of a person's bank transactions

PASSCODE n password composed of digits

PASSE adj out-of-date

PASSED ▸ pass

PASSEE adj out-of-date

PASSEL, -S n group or quantity of no fixed number

PASSER, -S n person or thing that passes

PASSERBY n person that is passing or going by, esp on foot

PASSERS ▸ passer

PASSES ▸ pass

PASSIBLE adj susceptible to emotion or suffering

PASSIBLY ▸ passible

PASSIM adv everywhere, throughout

PASSING, -S adj brief or transitory ▷ n death

PASSION, -S n intense love ▷ vb give passionate character to

PASSIVE, -S adj not playing an active part ▷ n passive form of a verb

PASSKEY, -S n private key

PASSLESS adj having no pass

PASSMAN, PASSMEN n student who passes without honours

PASSMENT same as ▹ passement

PASSOUT, -S n (in ice hockey) pass by an attacking player from behind the opposition goal line

PASSOVER n lamb eaten during Passover

PASSPORT n official document of nationality granting permission to travel abroad ▷ vb (in the European Economic Area) award a firm the right to do business in every member state

PASSUS, -ES n division or section of a poem, story, etc

PASSWORD n secret word or phrase that ensures admission

PAST, -S adj of the time before the present ▷ n period of time before the present ▷ adv ago ▷ prep beyond

PASTA, -S n type of food that is made from flour and water

PASTANCE n activity that passes time

PASTAS ▸ pasta

PASTE, -D, -S n moist soft mixture, such as toothpaste ▷ vb fasten with paste

PASTEL, -S n coloured chalk crayon for drawing ▷ adj pale and delicate in colour

PASTER, -S n person or thing that pastes

PASTERN, -S n part of a horse's foot

PASTERS ▸ paster

PASTES ▸ paste

PASTEUP, -S n material pasted on a sheet of paper or board

PASTICCI > pasticcio

PASTICHE n work of art that mixes styles or copies the style of another artist

PASTIER ▸ pasty

PASTIES ▸ pasty

PASTIEST ▸ pasty

PASTIL, -S same as ▸ pastille

PASTILLE n small fruit-flavoured and sometimes medicated sweet

PASTILS ▸ pastil

PASTILY ▸ pasty

PASTIME, -S n activity that makes time pass pleasantly

PASTINA, -S n small pieces of pasta

PASTING, -S n heavy defeat

PASTIS, -ES n anise-flavoured alcoholic drink

PASTITSO n Greek dish of baked pasta

PASTLESS adj having no past

PASTNESS n quality of being past

PASTOR, -ED, -S n member of the clergy in charge of a congregation ▷ vb act as a pastor

PASTORAL adj of or depicting country life ▷ n poem or picture portraying country life

PASTORED ▸ pastor

PASTORLY adj like a pastor

PASTORS ▸ pastor

PASTRAMI n highly seasoned smoked beef

PASTRIES ▸ pastry

PASTROMI same as ▸ pastrami

PASTRY, PASTRIES n baking dough made of flour, fat, and water

PASTS ▸ past

PASTURAL adj of pasture

PASTURE, -D, -S n grassy land for farm animals to graze on ▷ vb cause (livestock) to graze

PASTURER n person who tends cattle

PASTURES ▸ pasture

PASTY, PASTIER, PASTIES, PASTIEST adj (of a complexion) pale and unhealthy ▷ n round of pastry folded over a savoury filling

PAT, -S, -TED, -TEST, -TING vb tap lightly ▷ n gentle tap or stroke ▷ adj quick, ready, or glib

PATACA, -S n monetary unit of Macao

PATAGIA ▸ patagium

PATAGIAL ▸ patagium

PATAGIUM, PATAGIA n web of skin acting as wings in bats

PATAKA, -S n building on stilts, used for storing provisions

P

PATAMAR, -S n type of boat
PATBALL, -S n game like squash but using hands
PATCH, -ED, -ES, -ING n piece of material sewn on a garment ▷ vb mend with a patch
PATCHER, -S ▶ patch
PATCHERY n bungling work
PATCHES ▶ patch
PATCHIER ▶ patchy
PATCHILY ▶ patchy
PATCHING ▶ patch
PATCHY, PATCHIER adj of uneven quality or intensity
PATE, -S n head
PATED ▶ pate
PATELLA, -E, -S n kneecap
PATELLAR ▶ patella
PATELLAS ▶ patella
PATEN, -S n plate used for the bread at Communion
PATENCY n condition of being obvious
PATENS ▶ paten
PATENT, -ED, -S n document giving the exclusive right to make or sell an invention ▷ adj open to public inspection ▷ vb obtain a patent for
PATENTEE n person, group, company, etc, that has been granted a patent
PATENTLY adv obviously
PATENTOR n person who or official body that grants a patent or patents
PATENTS ▶ patent
PATER, -S n father
PATERA, -E n shallow ancient Roman bowl
PATERERO n type of cannon
PATERNAL adj fatherly
PATERS ▶ pater
PATES ▶ pate
PATH, -ED, -ING, -S n surfaced walk or track ▷ vb make a path
PATHETIC adj causing feelings of pity or sadness ▷ pl n pathetic sentiments ▷ n pathetic person
PATHIC, -S n person who suffers ▷ adj of or relating to suffering
PATHING ▶ path
PATHLESS ▶ path
PATHNAME n description of where a file is found in a hierarchy of directories
PATHOGEN n thing that causes disease
PATHOS, -ES n power of arousing pity or sadness
PATHS ▶ path

PATHWAY, -S n path
PATIBLE adj endurable
PATIENCE n quality of being patient
PATIENT, -S adj enduring difficulties or delays calmly ▷ n person receiving medical treatment ▷ vb make calm
PATIKI, -S n New Zealand sand flounder or dab
PATIN, -S same as ▶ paten
PATINA, -E, -S n fine layer on a surface
PATINAED adj having a patina
PATINAS ▶ patina
PATINATE vb coat with patina
PATINE, -D, -S, PATINING vb cover with patina
PATINISE same as ▶ patinize
PATINIZE vb coat with patina
PATINS ▶ patin
PATIO, -S n paved area adjoining a house
PATKA, -S n head covering worn by Sikh men
PATLY adv fitly
PATNESS n appropriateness
PATOIS n regional dialect, esp of French
PATONCE adj (of cross) with limbs which broaden from centre
PATOOT, -S same as ▶ patootie
PATOOTIE n person's bottom
PATOOTS ▶ patoot
PATRIAL, -S n (in Britain, formerly) person with a right to live in the United Kingdom
PATRIATE vb bring under the authority of an autonomous country
PATRICK, -S n former Irish coin
PATRICO, -S n fraudulent priest
PATRIOT, -S n person who loves his or her country
PATROL, -S n regular circuit by a guard ▷ vb go round on guard, or reconnoitring
PATRON, -S n person who gives financial support
PATRONAL > patroness
PATRONLY adj like a patron
PATRONNE n woman who owns or manages a hotel, restaurant, or bar
PATRONS ▶ patron
PATROON, -S n Dutch land-holder in New Netherland and New York

PATS ▶ pat
PATSY, PATSIES n person who is easily cheated, victimized, etc
PATTAMAR n Indian courier
PATTE, -S n band keeping belt in place
PATTED ▶ pat
PATTEE adj (of a cross) having triangular arms widening outwards
PATTEN, -ED, -S n wooden clog or sandal ▷ vb wear pattens
PATTER, -ED, -S vb make repeated soft tapping sounds ▷ n quick succession of taps
PATTERER ▶ patter
PATTERN, -S n arrangement of repeated parts or decorative designs ▷ vb model
PATTERS ▶ patter
PATTES ▶ patte
PATTEST ▶ pat
PATTIE same as ▶ patty
PATTIES ▶ patty
PATTING ▶ pat
PATTLE, -S dialect for ▶ paddle
PATTRESS n box for the space behind electrical sockets and switches
PATTY, PATTIES n small flattened cake of minced food
PATTYPAN n small round flattish squash
PATU, -S n short Māori club, now used ceremonially
PATULENT adj spreading widely
PATULIN, -S n toxic antibiotic
PATULOUS adj spreading widely or expanded
PATUS ▶ patu
PATUTUKI n blue cod
PATY adj (of cross) having arms of equal length
PATZER, -S n novice chess player
PAUA, -S n edible shellfish of New Zealand
PAUCAL, -S n grammatical number for words in contexts where a few of their referents are described ▷ adj relating to or inflected for this number
PAUCITY n scarcity
PAUGHTY Scots word for ▶ haughty
PAUL, -S same as ▶ pawl

PAULDRON n either of two metal plates worn with armour to protect the shoulders

PAULIN, -S n tarpaulin

PAULS ▶ paul

PAUNCE, -S n pansy

PAUNCH, -ED, -ES n protruding belly ▷ vb stab in the stomach

PAUNCHY adj having a protruding belly or abdomen

PAUPER, -ED, -S n very poor person ▷ vb reduce to beggary

PAURAQUE n type of long-tailed nocturnal bird

PAUROPOD n minute myriapod

PAUSAL ▶ pause

PAUSE, -D, -S vb stop for a time ▷ n stop or rest in speech or action

PAUSEFUL adj taking pauses

PAUSER, -S ▶ pause

PAUSES ▶ pause

PAUSING, -S ▶ pause

PAV, -S short for ▶ pavlova

PAVAGE, -S n tax towards paving streets

PAVAN, -S same as ▶ pavane

PAVANE, -S n slow and stately dance

PAVANS ▶ pavan

PAVE, -D, -S vb form (a surface) with stone or brick ▷ n paved surface, esp an uneven one

PAVEED adj (of jewels) set close together

PAVEMENT n paved path for pedestrians ▷ vb provide with pavement

PAVEN, -S same as ▶ pavane

PAVER, -S ▶ pave

PAVES ▶ pave

PAVID adj fearful

PAVILION n building on a playing field etc ▷ vb place or set in or as if in a pavilion

PAVILLON n bell of wind instrument

PAVIN, -S same as ▶ pavane

PAVING, -S n paved surface ▷ adj of or for a paved surface or pavement

PAVINS ▶ pavin

PAVIOR, -S same as ▶ paviour

PAVIOUR, -S n person who lays paving

PAVIS n large square shield

PAVISE, -S same as ▶ pavis

PAVISER, -S n soldier holding a pavis

PAVISES ▶ pavise

PAVISSE, -S same as ▶ pavis

PAVLOVA, -S n meringue cake topped with whipped cream and fruit

PAVONE, -S n peacock

PAVONIAN same as ▶ pavonine

PAVONINE adj of or resembling a peacock or the colours, design, or iridescence of a peacock's tail

PAVS ▶ pav

PAW, -ED, -ING, -S n animal's foot with claws and pads ▷ vb scrape with the paw or hoof

PAWA, -S old word for ▶ peacock

PAWAW, -ED, -ING, -S vb recite N American incantation

PAWED ▶ paw

PAWER, -S n person or animal that paws

PAWING ▶ paw

PAWK, -S Scots word for ▶ trick

PAWKIER ▶ pawky

PAWKIEST ▶ pawky

PAWKILY ▶ pawky

PAWKS ▶ pawk

PAWKY, PAWKIER, PAWKIEST adj having or characterized by a dry wit

PAWL, -S n pivoted lever shaped to engage with a ratchet

PAWN, -ED, -ING, -S vb deposit (an article) as security for money borrowed ▷ n chessman of the lowest value

PAWNABLE ▶ pawn

PAWNAGE, -S ▶ pawn

PAWNCE, -S old word for ▶ pansy

PAWNED ▶ pawn

PAWNEE, -S n one who accepts goods in pawn

PAWNER, -S n one who pawns his or her possessions

PAWNING ▶ pawn

PAWNOR, -S same as ▶ pawner

PAWNS ▶ pawn

PAWNSHOP n premises of a pawnbroker

PAWPAW, -S same as ▶ papaw

PAWS ▶ paw

PAX, -ES n peace ▷ interj call signalling a desire to end hostilities

Latin for peace, this is yet another of those very useful short words containing X.

PAXIUBA, -S n tropical tree

PAXWAX, -ES n strong ligament in the neck of many mammals

PAY, PAID, -ED, -S vb give money etc in return for goods or services ▷ n wages or salary

PAYABLE, -S adj due to be paid ▷ n debt to be paid

PAYABLY ▶ payable

PAYBACK, -S n return on an investment

PAYCHECK n payment for work done

PAYDAY, -S n day on which wages or salaries are paid

PAYDOWN, -S n reduction of debt through repayment

PAYED ▶ pay

PAYEE, -S n person to whom money is paid or due

PAYER, -S n person who pays

PAYESS pl n uncut sideburns worn by some Jewish men

PAYFONE, -S US spelling of ▶ payphone

PAYGRADE n military rank

PAYING, -S ▶ pay

PAYLIST, -S n list of people to be paid

PAYLOAD, -S n passengers or cargo of an aircraft

PAYMENT, -S n act of paying

PAYNIM, -S n heathen or pagan

PAYNIMRY n state of being heathen

PAYNIMS ▶ paynim

PAYOFF, -S n final settlement, esp in retribution

PAYOLA, -S n bribe to promote a commercial product

PAYOR, -S same as ▶ payer

PAYOUT, -S n sum of money paid out

PAYPHONE n coin-operated telephone

PAYROLL, -S n list of employees who receive regular pay

PAYS ▶ pay

PAYSAGE, -S n landscape

PAYSD Spenserian form of ▶ poised

PAYSLIP, -S n note of payment given to employee

PAYWALL, -S n system that denies access to a website unless a payment is made

PAZAZZ, -ES same as ▶ pizzazz

PAZZAZZ same as ▶ pizzazz

PE n 17th letter of the Hebrew alphabet, transliterated as *p*

PEA, -S n climbing plant with seeds growing in pods

PEABERRY n coffee berry containing one seed

PEABRAIN n stupid person

PEACE, -D, -S, PEACING n calm, quietness

PEACEFUL adj not in a state of war or disagreement

PEACENIK n activist who opposes war

PEACES ▸ peace

PEACH, -ED, -ES, -ING n soft juicy fruit ▷ adj pinkish-orange ▷ vb inform against an accomplice

PEACHER, -S ▸ peach

PEACHES ▸ peach

PEACHICK n young peafowl

PEACHIER ▸ peachy

PEACHILY ▸ peachy

PEACHING ▸ peach

PEACHY, PEACHIER adj of or like a peach, esp in colour or texture

PEACING ▸ peace

PEACOAT, -S n woollen jacket

PEACOCK, -S n large male bird with a brilliantly coloured fanlike tail ▷ vb display (oneself) proudly

PEACOCKY ▸ peacock

PEACOD, -S same as ▸ peascod

PEAFOWL, -S n peacock or peahen

PEAG, -S n (formerly) money used by Native Americans

PEAGE, -S same as ▸ peag

PEAGS ▸ peag

PEAHEN, -S ▸ peacock

PEAK, -S n pointed top, esp of a mountain ▷ vb form or reach a peak ▷ adj of or at the point of greatest demand

PEAKED adj having a peak

PEAKIER ▸ peaky

PEAKIEST ▸ peaky

PEAKING, -S n act of peaking

PEAKISH adj sickly

PEAKLESS adj without a peak

PEAKLIKE ▸ peak

PEAKS ▸ peak

PEAKY, PEAKIER, PEAKIEST ▸ peak

PEAL, -ED, -ING, -S n long loud echoing sound, esp of bells or thunder ▷ vb sound with a peal or peals

PEALIKE ▸ pea

PEALING ▸ peal

PEALS ▸ peal

PEAN, -ED, -ING, -S same as ▸ peen

PEANUT, -S n pea-shaped nut that ripens underground

PEANUTTY adj having the taste of peanuts

PEAPOD, -S n pod of the pea plant

PEAR, -S n sweet juicy fruit with a narrow top and rounded base

PEARCE, -D, -S, PEARCING old spelling of ▸ pierce

PEARE, -S obsolete spelling of ▸ pear

PEARL, -ED, -ING, -S same as ▸ purl

PEARLASH n granular crystalline form of potassium carbonate

PEARLED ▸ pearl

PEARLER, -S n person who dives for or trades in pearls ▷ adj excellent

PEARLIER ▸ pearly

PEARLIES ▸ pearly

PEARLIN n type of lace used to trim clothes

PEARLING ▸ pearl

PEARLINS n type of lace

PEARLITE same as ▸ perlite

PEARLS ▸ pearl

PEARLY, PEARLIER, PEARLIES adj resembling a pearl, esp in lustre ▷ n London costermonger who wears pearl buttons

PEARMAIN n any of several varieties of apple having a red skin

PEARS ▸ pear

PEARST archaic variant of ▸ pierced

PEART, -ER, -EST adj lively

PEARTLY ▸ peart

PEARWOOD n wood from pear tree

PEAS ▸ pea

PEASANT, -S n person working on the land

PEASANTY adj having qualities ascribed to traditional country life or people

PEASCOD, -S n pod of a pea plant

PEASE, -D, -S, PEASING n archaic or dialect word for pea ▷ vb appease

PEASECOD n pod of a pea plant

PEASED ▸ pease

PEASEN obsolete plural of ▸ pease

PEASES ▸ pease

PEASING ▸ pease

PEASON obsolete plural of ▸ pease

PEAT, -S n decayed vegetable material found in bogs

PEATARY n area covered with peat

PEATERY same as ▸ peatary

PEATIER ▸ peaty

PEATIEST ▸ peaty

PEATLAND n area of land consisting of peat bogs

PEATMAN, PEATMEN n person who collects peat

PEATS ▸ peat

PEATSHIP n ship carrying peat

PEATY, PEATIER, PEATIEST ▸ peat

PEAVEY, -S n wooden lever used for handling logs

PEAVY, PEAVIES same as ▸ peavey

PEAZE, -D, -S, PEAZING same as ▸ pease

PEBA, -S n type of armadillo

PEBBLE, -D, -S n small roundish stone ▷ vb cover with pebbles

PEBBLIER ▸ pebbly

PEBBLING n (in curling) act of spraying the rink with drops of hot water to slow down the stone

PEBBLY, PEBBLIER ▸ pebble

PEBIBYTE n two to the power of fifty bytes

PEBRINE, -S n disease of silkworms

PEC n pectoral muscle

PECAN, -S n edible nut of a N American tree

PECCABLE adj liable to sin

PECCANCY ▸ peccant

PECCANT adj guilty of an offence

PECCARY n piglike animal of American forests

PECCAVI, -S n confession of guilt

PECH, -ED, -ING, -S Scottish word for ▸ pant

PECHAN, -S Scots word for ▸ stomach

PECHED ▸ pech

PECHING ▸ pech

PECHS ▸ pech

PECK, -ED, -S vb strike or pick up with the beak ▷ n pecking movement

PECKE, -S n quarter of bushel

PECKED ▸ peck

PECKER, -S n short for woodpecker

PECKES ▸ pecke

PECKIER ▸ pecky

PECKIEST ▸ pecky
PECKING, -S ▸ peck
PECKISH adj slightly hungry
PECKS ▸ peck
PECKY, PECKIER, PECKIEST adj discoloured
PECORINO, PECORINI n Italian cheese made from ewes' milk
PECS pl n pectoral muscles
PECTASE, -S n enzyme occurring in certain ripening fruits
PECTATE, -S n salt or ester of pectic acid
PECTEN, -S, PECTINES n comblike structure in the eye of birds and reptiles
PECTIC ▸ pectin
PECTIN, -S n substance in fruit that makes jam set
PECTINAL adj resembling a comb ▸ n fish with bones or a spine resembling a comb
PECTINEI > pectineus
PECTINES ▸ pecten
PECTINS ▸ pectin
PECTISE, -D, -S same as ▸ pectize
PECTIZE, -D, -S vb change into a jelly
PECTORAL adj of the chest or thorax ▸ n pectoral muscle or fin
PECTOSE, -S n insoluble carbohydrate found in unripe fruit
PECULATE vb embezzle (public money)
PECULIA ▸ peculium
PECULIAR adj strange ▸ n special sort, esp an accented letter
PECULIUM, PECULIA n property that a father or master allowed his child or slave to hold as his own
PED, -S n pannier
PEDAGOG, -S same as > pedagogue
PEDAGOGY n principles, practice, or profession of teaching
PEDAL, -ED, -ING, -LED, -S n foot-operated lever ▸ vb propel (a bicycle) by using its pedals ▸ adj of or relating to the foot or the feet
PEDALCAR n child's vehicle that is operated by pedals
PEDALED ▸ pedal
PEDALER, -S ▸ pedal
PEDALFER n type of zonal soil deficient in lime but containing deposits of aluminium and iron

PEDALIER n pedal piano
PEDALING ▸ pedal
PEDALLED ▸ pedal
PEDALLER n person who pedals
PEDALO, -ES, -S n pedal-operated pleasure craft
PEDALS ▸ pedal
PEDANT, -S n person who is excessively concerned with details and rules
PEDANTIC adj of, relating to, or characterized by pedantry
PEDANTRY n practice of being a pedant, esp in the minute observance of petty rules or details
PEDANTS ▸ pedant
PEDATE adj (of a plant leaf) divided into several lobes arising at a common point
PEDATELY ▸ pedate
PEDDER, -S old form of ▸ pedlar
PEDDLE, -D, -S, PEDDLING vb sell (goods) from door to door
PEDDLER, -S same as ▸ pedlar
PEDDLERY n business of peddler
PEDDLES ▸ peddle
PEDDLING ▸ peddle
PEDERERO n type of cannon
PEDES ▸ pes
PEDESIS, PEDESES n random motion of small particles
PEDESTAL n base supporting a column, statue, etc
PEDETIC adj of feet
PEDI, -S n pedicure
PEDICAB, -S n pedal-operated tricycle, available for hire
PEDICEL, -S n stalk bearing a single flower of an inflorescence
PEDICLE, -S n any small stalk
PEDICLED ▸ pedicle
PEDICLES ▸ pedicle
PEDICULI > pediculus
PEDICURE n medical or cosmetic treatment of the feet ▸ vb give a pedicure
PEDIFORM adj shaped like a foot
PEDIGREE n register of ancestors, esp of a purebred animal
PEDIMENT n triangular part over a door etc
PEDIPALP n either member of the second pair of head appendages of arachnids

PEDIS ▸ pedi
PEDLAR, -S n person who sells goods from door to door
PEDLARY same as ▸ pedlery
PEDLER, -S same as ▸ pedlar
PEDLERY n business of pedler
PEDOCAL, -S n type of soil that is rich in lime
PEDOLOGY same as > paedology
PEDRAIL, -S n device replacing wheel on rough surfaces
PEDRERO, -S n type of cannon
PEDRO, -S n card game
PEDS ▸ ped
PEDUNCLE same as ▸ pedicel
PEDWAY, -S n walkway for pedestrians only
PEE, -D, -ING, -S vb urinate ▸ n urine
PEEBEEN, -S n type of large evergreen
PEECE, -S obsolete variant of ▸ piece
PEED ▸ pee
PEEING ▸ pee
PEEK, -ED, -ING, -S n peep or glance ▸ vb glance quickly or secretly
PEEKABO, -S same as ▸ peekaboo
PEEKABOO n game in which one person hides his or her face and suddenly reveals it ▸ adj made of fabric that is almost transparent
PEEKABOS ▸ peekabo
PEEKAPOO n cross between a Pekingese and a poodle
PEEKED ▸ peek
PEEKING ▸ peek
PEEKS ▸ peek
PEEL, -ED, -S vb remove the skin or rind of (a vegetable or fruit) ▸ n rind or skin
PEELABLE ▸ peel
PEELED ▸ peel
PEELER, -S n device for peeling vegetables, fruit, etc
PEELING, -S n strip that has been peeled off
PEELS ▸ peel
PEEN, -ED, -S n end of a hammer head opposite the striking face ▸ vb strike with the peen of a hammer
PEENGE, -D, -S, PEENGING vb complain
PEENING, -S n act of peening
PEENS ▸ peen
PEEOY, -S n homemade firework

P

PEEP, -ED, -ING, -S vb look slyly or quickly ▷ n peeping look

PEEPBO, -S n game of peekaboo

PEEPE old spelling of ▷ **pip**

PEEPED ▷ **peep**

PEEPER, -S n person who peeps

PEEPES archaic spelling of ▷ **peeps**

PEEPHOLE n small aperture for observation

PEEPING ▷ **peep**

PEEPS ▷ **peep**

PEEPSHOW n box containing a series of pictures that can be seen through a small hole

PEEPTOE adj of a shoe in which the toe is not covered

PEEPUL, -S n Indian moraceous tree

PEER, -ED, -ING, -S n (in Britain) member of the nobility ▷ vb look closely and intently

PEERAGE, -S n whole body of peers

PEERED ▷ **peer**

PEERESS n (in Britain) woman holding the rank of a peer

PEERIE, -R, -S, -ST n spinning top ▷ adj small

PEERING ▷ **peer**

PEERLESS adj unequalled, unsurpassed

PEERS ▷ **peer**

PEERY n child's spinning top

PEES ▷ **pee**

PEESWEEP n early spring storm

PEETWEET n spotted sandpiper

PEEVE, -S, PEEVING vb irritate or annoy ▷ n something that irritates

PEEVED ▷ **peeve**

PEEVER, -S n hopscotch

PEEVES ▷ **peeve**

PEEVING ▷ **peeve**

PEEVISH adj fretful or irritable

PEEWEE, -S same as ▷ **pewee**

PEEWIT, -S same as ▷ **lapwing**

PEG, -GED, -S n pin or clip for joining, fastening, marking, etc ▷ vb fasten with pegs

PEGASUS n winged horse

PEGBOARD n board with holes into which pegs can be fitted

PEGBOX, -ES n part of stringed instrument that holds tuning pegs

PEGGED ▷ **peg**

PEGGIER ▷ **peggy**

PEGGIES ▷ **peggy**

PEGGIEST ▷ **peggy**

PEGGING, -S ▷ **peg**

PEGGY, PEGGIER, PEGGIES, PEGGIEST n type of small warbler ▷ adj resembling a peg

PEGH, -ED, -ING, -S variant of ▷ **pech**

PEGLESS ▷ **peg**

PEGLIKE ▷ **peg**

PEGS ▷ **peg**

PEGTOP, -S n type of spinning top

PEH, -S same as ▷ **pe**

PEIGNOIR n woman's light dressing gown

PEIN, -ED, -ING, -S same as ▷ **peen**

PEINCT, -ED, -S vb paint

PEINED ▷ **pein**

PEINING ▷ **pein**

PEINS ▷ **pein**

PEISE, -D, -S, PEISING same as ▷ **peize**

PEISHWA, -S n Indian leader

PEISHWAH same as ▷ **peishwa**

PEISHWAS ▷ **peishwa**

PEISING ▷ **peise**

PEIZE, -D, -S, PEIZING vb weight or poise

PEJORATE vb change for the worse

PEKAN, -S n large North American marten

PEKE, -S n Pekingese dog

PEKEPOO, -S same as ▷ **pekapoo**

PEKES ▷ **peke**

PEKIN, -S n silk fabric

PEKOE, -S n high-quality tea

PEL, -S n pixel

PELA, -S n insect living on wax

PELAGE, -S n coat of a mammal, consisting of hair, wool, fur, etc

PELAGIAL adj of the open sea ▷ n open body of water such as a lake or the sea

PELAGIAN adj of or inhabiting the open sea ▷ n pelagic creature

PELAGIC, -S adj of or relating to the open sea ▷ n any pelagic creature

PELAS ▷ **pela**

PELAU, -S n dish made with meat, rice, and pigeon peas

PELE, -S Spenserian variant of ▷ **peal**

PELERINE n woman's narrow cape with long pointed ends in front

PELES ▷ **pele**

PELF, -S n money or wealth

PELHAM, -S n horse's bit for a double bridle

PELICAN, -S n large water bird with a pouch beneath its bill

PELISSE, -S n cloak or loose coat which is usually fur-trimmed

PELITE, -S n any argillaceous rock such as shale

PELITIC ▷ **pelite**

PELL, -ED, -ING, -S n hide of an animal ▷ vb hit violently

PELLACH, -S same as ▷ **pellack**

PELLACK, -S n porpoise

PELLAGRA n disease caused by lack of vitamin B

PELLED ▷ **pell**

PELLET, -ED, -S n small ball of something ▷ vb strike with pellets

PELLETAL ▷ **pellet**

PELLETED ▷ **pellet**

PELLETS ▷ **pellet**

PELLICLE n thin skin or film

PELLING ▷ **pell**

PELLMELL n disorder

PELLOCK, -S n porpoise

PELLS ▷ **pell**

PELLUCID adj very clear

PELLUM, -S n dust

PELMA, -S n sole of the foot

PELMATIC ▷ **pelma**

PELMET, -S n ornamental drapery or board, concealing a curtain rail

PELOID, -S n mud used therapeutically

PELOLOGY n study of therapeutic uses of mud

PELON, -S adj hairless ▷ n hairless person or animal

PELORIA, -S n abnormal production of flowers in a plant

PELORIAN ▷ **peloria**

PELORIAS ▷ **peloria**

PELORIC ▷ **peloria**

PELORIES ▷ **pelory**

PELORISM n floral mutation

PELORUS n sighting device

PELORY, PELORIES n floral mutation

PELOTA, -S n game where players propel a ball against a wall

PELOTON, -S n main field of riders in a bicycle road race

PELS ▷ **pel**

PELT, -ED, -S vb throw missiles at ▷ n skin of a fur-bearing animal

PELTA, -E, -S n small ancient shield

PELTAST, -S n (in ancient Greece) lightly armed foot soldier

PELTATE adj (of leaves) having the stalk attached to the centre of the lower surface

PELTED ▸ pelt

PELTER, -ED, -S vb rain heavily

PELTING, -S ▸ pelt

PELTLESS ▸ pelt

PELTRY, PELTRIES n pelts of animals collectively

PELTS ▸ pelt

PELVES ▸ pelvis

PELVIC, -S adj of, near, or relating to the pelvis ▷ n pelvic bone

PELVIS, PELVES, -ES n framework of bones at the base of the spine

PEMBINA, -S n type of cranberry

PEMBROKE n small table

PEMICAN, -S same as ▸ pemmican

PEMMICAN n pressed cake of meat with fat and berries or dried fruits

PEMOLINE n mild stimulant

PEMPHIGI > pemphigus

PEMPHIX n type of crustacean

PEN, -NED, -NING, -S n instrument for writing in ink ▷ vb write or compose

PENAL adj of or used in punishment

PENALISE same as ▸ penalize

PENALITY ▸ penal

PENALIZE vb impose a penalty on

PENALLY ▸ penal

PENALTY n punishment for a crime or offence

PENANCE, -D, -S n voluntary self-punishment ▷ vb impose a penance upon (a sinner)

PENANG, -S variant of ▸ pinang

PENATES pl n household gods

PENCE ▸ penny

PENCEL, -S n small pennon

PENCHANT n inclination or liking

PENCIL, -ED, -S n thin cylindrical instrument for writing or drawing ▷ vb draw, write, or mark with a pencil

PENCILER ▸ pencil

PENCILS ▸ pencil

PENCRAFT n skill in writing

PEND, -ED, -S vb await judgment or settlement ▷ n archway or vaulted passage

PENDANT, -S n ornament worn on a chain round the neck

PENDED ▸ pend

PENDENCY ▸ pendent

PENDENT, -S adj hanging ▷ n pendant

PENDICLE n something dependent on another

PENDING prep while waiting for ▷ adj not yet decided or settled

PENDS ▸ pend

PENDU adj in informal Indian English, culturally backward

PENDULAR adj pendulous

PENDULE, -S n type of climbing manoeuvre

PENDULUM same as ▸ pendule

PENE, -D, PENING variant of ▸ peen

PENES ▸ penis

PENFOLD, -S same as ▸ pinfold

PENFUL, -S n contents of pen

PENGO, -S n former monetary unit of Hungary

PENGUIN, -S n flightless black-and-white sea bird

PENI old spelling of ▸ penny

PENIAL ▸ penis

PENICIL, -S n small pad for wounds

PENIE, -S old spelling of ▸ penny

PENILE adj of or relating to the penis

PENILL > penillion

PENING ▸ pene

PENIS, PENES, -ES n organ of copulation and urination in male mammals

PENITENT adj feeling sorry for having done wrong ▷ n someone who is penitent

PENK, -S n small fish

PENKNIFE n small knife with a blade that folds into the handle

PENKS ▸ penk

PENLIGHT n small thin flashlight

PENLIKE adj like a pen

PENLITE, -S same as ▸ penlight

PENMAN, PENMEN n person skilled in handwriting

PENNA, -E n large feather

PENNAL, -S n first-year student of Protestant university

PENNAME, -S n author's pseudonym

PENNANT, -S same as ▸ pendant

PENNATE adj having feathers, wings, or winglike structures

PENNATED same as ▸ pennate

PENNE, -S n pasta in the form of short tubes

PENNED ▸ pen

PENNEECH n card game

PENNEECK same as ▸ penneech

PENNER, -S n person who writes

PENNES ▸ penne

PENNI, -A, -S n former Finnish monetary unit

PENNIED adj having money

PENNIES ▸ penny

PENNILL n stanza in a Welsh poem

PENNINE, -S n mineral found in the Pennine Alps

PENNING ▸ pen

PENNIS ▸ penni

PENNON, -S n triangular or tapering flag

PENNONED adj equipped with a pennon

PENNONS ▸ pennon

PENNY, PENCE, PENNIES n coin worth one hundredth of a pound

PENNYBOY n employee whose duties include menial tasks, such as running errands

PENNYFEE n small payment

PENOCHE, -S n type of fudge

PENOLOGY n study of punishment and prison management

PENONCEL n small narrow flag

PENPOINT n tip of pen

PENS ▸ pen

PENSEE, -S n thought put down on paper

PENSEL, -S same as ▸ pencel

PENSIL, -S same as ▸ pencel

PENSILE adj designating or building a hanging nest

PENSILS ▸ pensil

PENSION, -S n regular payment to people above a certain age, etc ▷ vb grant a pension to

PENSIONE, PENSIONI n Italian boarding house

PENSIONS ▸ pension

PENSIVE adj deeply thoughtful, often with a tinge of sadness

PENSTER, -S n writer

PENSTOCK n conduit that supplies water to a hydroelectric power plant

PENSUM, -S n school exercise

PENT, -S n penthouse

PENTACLE same as
> pentagram

PENTACT, -S n sponge spicule with five rays

PENTAD, -S n group or series of five

PENTADIC ▸ pentad

PENTADS ▸ pentad

PENTAGON n geometric figure with five sides

PENTANE, -S n alkane hydrocarbon with three isomers

PENTANOL n colourless oily liquid

PENTARCH n member of pentarchy

PENTEL, -S n type of pen

PENTENE, -S n colourless flammable liquid alkene

PENTHIA, -S n child born fifth

PENTICE, -D, -S vb accommodate in a penthouse

PENTISE, -D, -S same as
▸ pentice

PENTITO, PENTITI n criminal who offers information to the police

PENTODE, -S n electronic valve having five electrodes

PENTOMIC adj denoting the subdivision of an army division into five battle groups

PENTOSAN n polysaccharide occurring in plants, humus, etc

PENTOSE, -S n monosaccharide containing five atoms of carbon per molecule

PENTROOF n lean-to

PENTS ▸ pent

PENTYL, -S n one of a particular chemical group

PENUCHE, -S same as
▸ panocha

PENUCHI, -S same as
▸ panocha

PENUCHLE same as
▸ pinochle

PENUCKLE same as
▸ penuchle

PENULT, -S n last syllable but one in a word

PENUMBRA, -S n (in an eclipse) partially shadowed region which surrounds the full shadow

PENURY, PENURIES n extreme poverty

PENWIPER n something for cleaning the ink from a pen

PENWOMAN, PENWOMEN n female writer

PEON, -ES, -S n Spanish-American farm labourer or unskilled worker

PEONAGE, -S n state of being a peon

PEONES ▸ peon

PEONIES ▸ peony

PEONISM, -S same as
▸ peonage

PEONS ▸ peon

PEONY, PEONIES n garden plant

PEOPLE, -D, -S, PEOPLING pl n persons generally ▷ vb provide with inhabitants

PEOPLER, -S n settler

PEOPLES ▸ people

PEOPLING ▸ people

PEP, -PED, -PING, -S n high spirits, energy, or enthusiasm ▷ vb liven by imbuing with new vigour

PEPERINO n type of volcanic rock

PEPERONI same as
> pepperoni

PEPFUL adj full of vitality

PEPINO, -S n purple-striped yellow fruit

PEPITA, -S n edible dried seed of a squash

PEPLA ▸ peplum

PEPLOS, -ES n part of a woman's attire in ancient Greece

PEPLUM, PEPLA, -S same as
▸ peplos

PEPLUMED ▸ peplum

PEPLUMS ▸ peplum

PEPLUS, -ES same as
▸ peplos

PEPO, -S n fruit such as the melon, squash, cucumber, or pumpkin

PEPONIDA variant of ▸ pepo

PEPONIUM variant of ▸ pepo

PEPOS ▸ pepo

PEPPED ▸ pep

PEPPER, -ED, -S n sharp hot condiment ▷ vb season with pepper

PEPPERER ▸ pepper

PEPPERS ▸ pepper

PEPPERY adj tasting of pepper

PEPPIER ▸ peppy

PEPPIEST ▸ peppy

PEPPILY ▸ peppy

PEPPING ▸ pep

PEPPY, PEPPIER, PEPPIEST adj full of vitality

PEPS ▸ pep

PEPSI, -S n (tradename) brand of soft drink

PEPSIN, -S n enzyme produced in the stomach

PEPSINE, -S same as ▸ pepsin

PEPSINS ▸ pepsin

PEPSIS ▸ pepsi

PEPTALK, -S n talk meant to inspire ▷ vb give a peptalk to

PEPTIC, -S adj relating to digestion or the digestive juices ▷ n substance that aids digestion

PEPTID, -S variant of
▸ peptide

PEPTIDE, -S n organic chemical compound

PEPTIDIC adj of peptides

PEPTIDS ▸ peptid

PEPTISE, -D, -S same as
▸ peptize

PEPTISER ▸ peptise

PEPTISES ▸ peptise

PEPTIZE, -D, -S vb disperse into a colloidal state

PEPTIZER ▸ peptize

PEPTIZES ▸ peptize

PEPTONE, -S n any of a group of organic compounds

PEPTONIC ▸ peptone

PEQUISTE n in Canada, member or supporter of the Parti Québécois

PER prep for each

PERACID, -S n acid in which the element forming the acid radical exhibits its highest valency

PERACUTE adj very acute

PERAEON, PERAEA, -S same as ▸ pereion

PERAI, -S another name for
▸ piranha

PERBORIC adj as in perboric acid, a hypothetical acid

PERC, -S n perchloride

PERCALE, -S n close-textured woven cotton fabric

PERCASE adv perchance

PERCE, -D, -N, -S, PERCING obsolete word for ▸ pierce

PERCEANT adj piercing

PERCED ▸ perce

PERCEIVE vb become aware of (something) through the senses

PERCEN ▸ perce

PERCENT, -S n percentage or proportion

PERCEPT, -S n concept that depends on recognition of some external object or phenomenon

PERCES ▸ perce

PERCH, -ED, -ES, -ING n resting place for a bird ▸ vb alight, rest, or place on or as if on a perch

PERCHER, -S ▸ perch

PERCHERY n barn in which hens are allowed to move without restriction

PERCHES ▸ perch

PERCHING ▸ perch

PERCID, -S n type of freshwater fish

PERCINE, -S adj of perches ▸ n type of perch-like fish

PERCING ▸ perce

PERCOCT, -S adj well-cooked ▸ vb cook thoroughly

PERCOID, -S n type of spiny-finned teleost fish

PERCOLIN n pain-relieving drug

PERCS ▸ perc

PERCUSS vb strike sharply, rapidly, or suddenly

PERDENDO adj (of music) getting gradually quieter and slower

PERDIE adv certainly

PERDU, -S adj (of a soldier) placed on hazardous sentry duty ▸ n soldier placed on hazardous sentry duty

PERDUE, -S same as ▸ perdu

PERDURE, -D, -S vb last for long time

PERDUS ▸ perdu

PERDY adv certainly

PERE, -S n addition to a French surname to specify the father

PEREA ▸ pereon

PEREGAL, -S adj equal ▸ n equal

PEREGRIN variant spelling of ▸ peregrine

PEREION, PEREIA, -S n thorax of some crustaceans

PEREIRA, -S n bark of a South American apocynaceous tree

PERENTIE n large dark-coloured Australian monitor lizard

PERENTY same as ▸ perentie

PEREON, PEREA, -S same as ▸ pereion

PEREOPOD same as ▸ pereiopod

PERES ▸ pere

PERFAY interj by my faith

PERFECT, -S adj having all the essential elements ▸ n perfect tense ▸ vb improve

PERFECTA n bet on the order of the first and second in a race

PERFECTI n ascetic group of elite Cathars

PERFECTO n large cigar that is tapered from both ends

PERFECTS ▸ perfect

PERFET obsolete variant of ▸ perfect

PERFIDY n perfidious act

PERFIN, -S former name for ▸ spif

PERFING, -S n practice of taking early retirement from the police force

PERFINS ▸ perfin

PERFORCE adv of necessity

PERFORM, -S vb carry out (an action)

PERFUME, -D, -S n liquid cosmetic worn for its pleasant smell ▸ vb give a pleasant smell to

PERFUMER n person who makes or sells perfume

PERFUMES ▸ perfume

PERFUMY adj like perfume

PERFUSE, -D, -S vb permeate through or over

PERGOLA, -S n framework of trellis supporting climbing plants

PERHAPS adv possibly, maybe ▸ sentence substitute it may happen, be so, etc ▸ n something that might have happened

PERI, -S n (in Persian folklore) one of a race of beautiful supernatural beings

PERIAGUA n dugout canoe

PERIANTH n outer part of a flower

PERIAPT, -S n charm or amulet

PERIBLEM n layer of meristematic tissue in stems and roots that gives rise to the cortex

PERIBOLI ▸ peribolos

PERICARP n part of a fruit enclosing the seed that develops from the wall of the ovary

PERICON n Argentinian dance

PERICOPE n selection from a book, esp a passage from the Bible read at religious services

PERIDERM n outer corky protective layer of woody stems and roots

PERIDIA ▸ peridium

PERIDIAL ▸ peridium

PERIDIUM, PERIDIA n distinct outer layer of the spore-bearing organ in many fungi

PERIDOT, -S n pale green transparent gemstone

PERIDOTE same as ▸ peridot

PERIDOTS ▸ peridot

PERIGEAL ▸ perigee

PERIGEAN ▸ perigee

PERIGEE, -S n point in the orbit of the moon or a satellite that is nearest the earth

PERIGON, -S n angle of 360°

PERIGONE n part enclosing the essential organs of a flower

PERIGONS ▸ perigon

PERIGYNY n condition of having the stamens and other floral parts at the same level as the carpels

PERIL, -ED, -ING, -LED, -S n great danger ▸ vb expose to danger

PERILLA, -S n type of mint

PERILLED ▸ peril

PERILOUS adj very hazardous or dangerous

PERILS ▸ peril

PERILUNE n point in a lunar orbit when a spacecraft launched from the moon is nearest the moon

PERINEA ▸ perineum

PERINEAL ▸ perineum

PERINEUM, PERINEA n region of the body between the anus and the genitals

PERIOD, -ED, -S n particular portion of time ▸ adj (of furniture, dress, a play, etc) dating from or in the style of an earlier time ▸ vb divide into periods

PERIODIC adj recurring at intervals

PERIODID n kind of iodide

PERIODS ▸ period

PERIOST, -S n thick fibrous two-layered membrane covering the surface of bones

PERIOTIC adj of or relating to the structures situated around the internal ear ▸ n periotic bone

PERIPETY n abrupt turn of events or reversal of circumstances

P

PERIPLUS n circumnavigation

PERIPTER n type of ancient temple

PERIQUE, -S n strong highly flavoured tobacco

PERIS ▸ peri

PERISARC n outer chitinous layer secreted by colonial hydrozoan coelenterates

PERISH, -ES vb be destroyed or die

PERISHED adj (of a person, part of the body, etc) extremely cold

PERISHER n mischievous person

PERISHES ▸ perish

PERITUS, PERITI n Catholic theology consultant

PERIWIG, -S same as ▸ peruke

PERJINK adj prim or finicky

PERJURE, -S vb render (oneself) guilty of perjury

PERJURED adj having sworn falsely

PERJURER ▸ perjure

PERJURES ▸ perjure

PERJURY n act or crime of lying while under oath in a court

PERK, -ED, -ING, -S n incidental benefit gained from a job, such as a company car ▷ adj pert ▷ vb (of coffee) percolate

PERKIER ▸ perky

PERKIEST ▸ perky

PERKILY ▸ perky

PERKIN, -S same as ▸ parkin

PERKING ▸ perk

PERKINS ▸ perkin

PERKISH adj perky

PERKS ▸ perk

PERKY, PERKIER, PERKIEST adj lively or cheerful

PERLITE, -S n variety of obsidian

PERLOUS same as ▸ perilous

PERM, -ED, -ING, -S n long-lasting curly hairstyle ▷ vb give (hair) a perm

PERMATAN n permanent tan, esp artificial

PERMEANT > permeance

PERMEASE n carrier protein

PERMEATE vb pervade or pass through the whole of (something)

PERMED ▸ perm

PERMIAN adj of, denoting, or formed in the last period of the Palaeozoic era

PERMIE, -S n person, esp an office worker, employed by a firm on a permanent basis

PERMING ▸ perm

PERMIT, -S vb give permission, allow ▷ n document giving permission to do something

PERMS ▸ perm

PERMUTE, -D, -S vb change the sequence of

PERN, -ED, -ING, -S n type of buzzard ▷ vb spin

PERNANCY n receiving of rents

PERNED ▸ pern

PERNING ▸ pern

PERNIO n chilblain

PERNOD, -S n aniseed-flavoured aperitif from France

PERNS ▸ pern

PEROG, -EN, -S same as ▸ pirog

PEROGI, -ES, -S n type of Polish dumpling

PEROGIE same as ▸ perogi

PEROGIES ▸ perogi

PEROGIS ▸ perogi

PEROGS ▸ perog

PEROGY same as ▸ perogi

PERONE, -S n fibula

PERONEAL adj of or relating to the fibula or the outer side of the leg

PERONEI ▸ peroneus

PERONES ▸ perone

PERONEUS, PERONEI n lateral muscle of the leg

PERORAL adj administered through mouth

PERORATE vb speak at length, esp in a formal manner

PEROXID, -S variant of ▸ peroxide

PEROXIDE n hydrogen peroxide used as a hair bleach ▷ adj bleached with or resembling peroxide ▷ vb bleach (the hair) with peroxide

PEROXIDS ▸ peroxid

PEROXO n type of acid

PEROXY adj containing the peroxide group

PERP, -S n someone who has committed a crime

PERPEND, -S n large stone that passes through a wall from one side to the other ▷ vb ponder

PERPENT, -S same as ▸ perpend

PERPLEX vb puzzle, bewilder

PERPS ▸ perp

PERRADII > perradius

PERRIER, -S n short mortar

PERRIES ▸ perry

PERRON, -S n external flight of steps

PERRUQUE old spelling of ▸ peruke

PERRY, PERRIES n alcoholic drink made from fermented pears

PERSALT, -S n any salt of a peracid

PERSANT adj piercing

PERSAUNT adj piercing

PERSE, -S, PERSING old variant of ▸ pierce

PERSEITY n quality of having substance independently of real objects

PERSES ▸ perse

PERSICO, -S same as ▸ persicot

PERSICOT n cordial made from apricots

PERSING ▸ perse

PERSIST, -S vb continue to be or happen, last

PERSON, -S n human being

PERSONA, -E, -S n someone's personality as presented to others

PERSONAL adj individual or private ▷ n item of movable property

PERSONAS ▸ persona

PERSONS ▸ person

PERSPEX n any of various clear acrylic resins

PERSPIRE vb sweat

PERSPIRY adj perspiring

PERST adj perished

PERSUADE vb make (someone) do something by argument, charm, etc

PERSUE, -D, -S, PERSUING obsolete form of ▸ pursue

PERSWADE obsolete form of ▸ persuade

PERT, -ER, -EST, -S adj saucy and cheeky ▷ n pert person

PERTAIN, -S vb belong or be relevant (to)

PERTAKE, -N, -S, PERTOOK obsolete form of ▸ partake

PERTER ▸ pert

PERTEST ▸ pert

PERTHITE n type of feldspar

PERTLY ▸ pert

PERTNESS ▸ pert

PERTOOK ▸ pertake

PERTS ▸ pert

PERTURB, -S vb disturb greatly

PERTUSE adj having holes

PERTUSED adj having holes

PERUKE, -S n wig for men worn in the 17th and 18th centuries

PERUKED adj wearing wig

PERUKES ▸ peruke

PERUSAL, -S ▸ peruse

PERUSE, -D, -S, PERUSING vb read in a careful or leisurely manner

PERUSER, -S ▸ peruse

PERUSES ▸ peruse

PERUSING ▸ peruse

PERVADE, -D, -S vb spread right through (something)

PERVADER ▸ pervade

PERVADES ▸ pervade

PERVERSE adj deliberately doing something different from what is thought normal or proper

PERVERT, -S vb use or alter for a wrong purpose

PERVIATE vb perforate or burrow

PERVIOUS adj able to be penetrated, permeable

PES, PEDES n animal part corresponding to the foot

PESADE, -S n position in which the horse stands on the hind legs with the forelegs in the air

PESANT, -S obsolete spelling of ▸ peasant

PESANTE adv to be performed clumsily

PESANTS ▸ pesant

PESAUNT, -S obsolete spelling of ▸ peasant

PESETA, -S n former monetary unit of Spain

PESEWA, -S n Ghanaian monetary unit

PESHWA, -S same as ▸ peishwa

PESKIER ▸ pesky

PESKIEST ▸ pesky

PESKILY ▸ pesky

PESKY, PESKIER, PESKIEST adj troublesome

PESO, -S n monetary unit of Argentina, Mexico, etc

PESSIMA n lowest point

PESSIMAL adj (of animal's environment) least favourable for survival

PESSIMUM same as ▸ pessimal

PEST, -S n annoying person

PESTER, -ED, -S vb annoy or nag continually

PESTERER ▸ pester

PESTERS ▸ pester

PESTFUL adj causing annoyance

PESTHOLE n breeding ground for disease

PESTIER ▸ pesty

PESTIEST ▸ pesty

PESTLE, -D, -S, PESTLING n club-shaped implement for grinding ▷ vb pound with or as if with a pestle

PESTO, -S n sauce for pasta

PESTS ▸ pest

PESTY, PESTIER, PESTIEST adj persistently annoying

PET, -S, -TED n animal kept for pleasure and companionship ▷ adj kept as a pet ▷ vb treat as a pet

PETABYTE n in computing, 10^{15} or 2^{50} bytes

PETAFLOP n (in computing) unit of processing speed

PETAL, -S n one of the brightly coloured outer parts of a flower

PETALED ▸ petal

PETALINE ▸ petal

PETALISM n ostracism in ancient Syracuse

PETALLED ▸ petal

PETALODY n condition in which stamens or other flower parts assume the form and function of petals

PETALOID adj resembling a petal, esp in shape

PETALOUS adj bearing or having petals

PETALS ▸ petal

PETANQUE n French game similar to bowls

PETAR, -S obsolete variant of ▸ petard

PETARA, -S n clothes basket

PETARD, -S n device containing explosives

PETARIES ▸ petary

PETARS ▸ petar

PETARY, PETARIES n weapon for hurling stones

PETASOS same as ▸ petasus

PETASUS n broad-brimmed hat worn by the ancient Greeks

PETCHARY n type of kingbird

PETCOCK, -S n small valve

PETECHIA n small discoloured spot on the skin

PETER, -ED, -ING, -S vb fall (off) in volume, intensity, etc, and finally cease ▷ n act of petering

PETERMAN, PETERMEN n burglar skilled in safe-breaking

PETERS ▸ peter

PETHER, -S old variant of ▸ pedlar

PETIOLAR ▸ petiole

PETIOLE, -S n stalk which attaches a leaf to a plant

PETIOLED ▸ petiole

PETIOLES ▸ petiole

PETIT adj of little or lesser importance

PETITE, -S adj (of a woman) small and dainty ▷ n clothing size for small women

PETITIO, -S n as in petitio principii, a form of fallacious reasoning

PETITION n formal request, esp one signed by many people and presented to parliament ▷ vb present a petition to

PETITIOS ▸ petitio

PETITORY adj soliciting

PETNAP, -S vb steal pet

PETNAPER ▸ petnap

PETNAPS ▸ petnap

PETRALE, -S n type of sole

PETRARY n weapon for hurling stones

PETRE, -S same as > saltpetre

PETREL, -S n sea bird with a hooked bill and tubular nostrils

PETRES ▸ petre

PETRI n as in petri dish shallow glass dish used for cultures of bacteria

PETRIFIC adj petrifying

PETRIFY vb frighten severely

PETROL, -S n flammable liquid obtained from petroleum ▷ vb supply with petrol

PETROLIC adj of, relating to, containing, or obtained from petroleum

PETROLS ▸ petrol

PETRONEL n obsolete cavalry firearm

PETROSAL adj of the dense part of the temporal bone that surrounds the inner ear ▷ n petrosal bone

PETROUS adj denoting the dense part of the temporal bone around the inner ear

PETS ▸ pet

PETSAI, -S n Chinese cabbage

PETTABLE ▸ pet

PETTED ▸ pet

PETTEDLY ▸ pet

PETTER, -S ▸ pet

PETTI, -ES, -S n petticoat

PETTIER ▸ petty

PETTIES ▸ petti

PETTIEST ▸ petty

P

PETTIFOG vb quibble or fuss over details
PETTILY ▶ petty
PETTING, -S ▶ pet
PETTIS ▶ petti
PETTISH adj peevish or fretful
PETTLE, -D, -S, PETTLING vb pat animal
PETTO n breast of an animal
PETTY, PETTIER, PETTIEST adj unimportant, trivial
PETULANT adj childishly irritable or peevish
PETUNIA, -S n garden plant with funnel-shaped flowers
PETUNTSE n fusible feldspathic mineral used in hard-paste porcelain
PETUNTZE same as ▶ petuntse
PEW, -S n fixed benchlike seat in a church
PEWEE, -S n small N American flycatcher
PEWIT, -S another name for ▶ lapwing
PEWS ▶ pew
PEWTER, -S n greyish metal made of tin and lead
PEWTERER ▶ pewter
PEWTERS ▶ pewter
PEWTERY adj of or like pewter
PEYOTE, -S another name for ▶ mescal
PEYOTISM n ritual use of peyote
PEYOTIST n person who uses peyote
PEYOTL, -S same as ▶ peyote
PEYSE, -D, -S, PEYSING vb weight or poise
PEYTRAL, -S same as ▶ peytrel
PEYTREL, -S n breastplate of horse's armour
PEZANT, -S obsolete spelling of ▶ peasant
PEZIZOID adj having cup-like form
PFENNIG, -E, -S n former German monetary unit
PFENNING old variant of ▶ pfennig
PFFT interj sound indicating sudden disappearance of something
PFUI interj phooey
PHABLET, -S n type of handheld personal computer
PHACELIA n plant grown for its large, deep blue bell flowers
PHACOID adj lentil- or lens-shaped

PHAEIC adj (of animals) having dusky coloration
PHAEISM, -S ▶ phaeic
PHAETON, -S n light four-wheeled horse-drawn carriage
PHAGE, -S n parasitic virus that destroys its host
PHALANGE another name for ▶ phalanx
PHALANX n closely grouped mass of people
PHALLI ▶ phallus
PHALLIC adj of or resembling a penis
PHALLIN, -S n poisonous substance from mushroom
PHALLOID adj resembling a penis
PHALLUS, PHALLI n penis
PHANG, -ED, -ING, -S old variant spelling of ▶ fang
PHANTASM n unreal vision, illusion
PHANTAST same as ▶ fantast
PHANTASY same as ▶ fantasy
PHANTOM, -S n ghost ▷ adj deceptive or unreal
PHANTOMY adj of phantoms
PHARAOH, -S n ancient Egyptian king
PHARE, -S n beacon tower
PHARISEE n self-righteous or hypocritical person
PHARM, -ED, -S vb redirect (a website user) to another, bogus website
PHARMA, -S n pharmaceutical companies considered together as an industry
PHARMACY n preparation and dispensing of drugs and medicines
PHARMAS ▶ pharma
PHARMED ▶ pharm
PHARMER, -S n person who pharms
PHARMING n rearing or growing genetically modified animals or plants in order to develop pharmaceuticals
PHARMS ▶ pharm
PHAROS, -ES n lighthouse
PHARYNX n cavity forming the back part of the mouth
PHASE, -D, -S n distinct or characteristic stage in a development or chain of events ▷ vb arrange or carry out in stages
PHASEAL ▶ phase

PHASED ▶ phase
PHASEOUT n gradual reduction
PHASER, -S n type of science-fiction weapon
PHASES ▶ phase
PHASIC ▶ phase
PHASING, -S n effect achieved by varying the phase relationship of two similar audio signals
PHASIS another word for ▶ phase
PHASMID, -S n stick insect or leaf insect
PHASOR, -S n rotating vector representing a quantity that varies sinusoidally
PHAT, -TER, -TEST adj terrific
PHATIC adj (of speech) used to express sociability rather than specific meaning
PHATTER ▶ phat
PHATTEST ▶ phat
PHEASANT n game bird with bright plumage
PHEAZAR, -S old variant of ▶ vizier
PHEER, -S same as ▶ fere
PHEERE, -S same as ▶ fere
PHEERS ▶ pheer
PHEESE, -D, -S, PHEESING vb worry
PHEEZE, -D, -S, PHEEZING same as ▶ pheese
PHELLEM, -S technical name for ▶ cork
PHELLOID adj like cork
PHELONIA > phelonion
PHENATE, -S n ester or salt of phenol
PHENAZIN same as > phenazine
PHENE, -S n genetically determined characteristic of organism
PHENETIC > phenetics
PHENETOL same as > phenetole
PHENGITE n type of alabaster
PHENIC adj of phenol
PHENIX, -ES same as ▶ phoenix
PHENOGAM same as > phaenogam
PHENOL, -S n chemical used in disinfectants and antiseptics
PHENOLIC adj of, containing, or derived from phenol ▷ n derivative of phenol
PHENOLS ▶ phenol

PHENOM, -S n person or thing of outstanding abilities

PHENOME, -S n full complement of phenotypical traits of an organism, species, etc

PHENOMS ▶ phenom

PHENOXY modifier as in **phenoxy resin** any of a class of resins derived from polyhydroxy ethers

PHENYL, -S n chemical substance

PHENYLIC ▶ phenyl

PHENYLS ▶ phenyl

PHEON, -S n barbed iron head of dart

PHERESIS, PHERESES n specialized form of blood donation

PHESE, -D, -S, PHESING same as **▶ pheese**

PHEW interj exclamation of relief, surprise, etc

PHI, -S n 21st letter in the Greek alphabet

PHIAL, -LED, -S n small bottle for medicine etc ▷ vb put in phial

PHILABEG same as **▶ filibeg**

PHILAMOT variant of **▶ filemot**

PHILIBEG variant spelling of **▶ filibeg**

PHILOMEL n nightingale

PHILOMOT n colour of dead leaf

PHILTER, -S same as **▶ philtre**

PHILTRA ▶ philtrum

PHILTRE, -D, -S n magic drink supposed to arouse love in the person who drinks it ▷ vb mix with love potion

PHILTRUM, PHILTRA n indentation above the upper lip

PHINNOCK variant spelling of **▶ finnock**

PHIS ▶ phi

PHISH, -ED, -ES vb engage in phishing

PHISHER, -S n person who phishes

PHISHES ▶ phish

PHISHING n internet fraud to extract personal and financial details

PHISNOMY n physiognomy

PHIZ, -ES, -ZES n face or a facial expression

PHIZOG, -S same as **▶ phiz**

PHIZZ n face

PHIZZES ▶ phiz

PHLEGM, -S n thick yellowish substance formed in the nose and throat during a cold

PHLEGMON n inflammatory mass that may progress to abscess

PHLEGMS ▶ phlegm

PHLEGMY ▶ phlegm

PHLOEM, -S n plant tissue that acts as a path for the distribution of food

PHLOMIS n plant of Phlomis genus

PHLOX, -ES n flowering garden plant

PHO, -S n Vietnamese noodle soup

PHOBIA, -S n intense and unreasoning fear or dislike

PHOBIC, -S adj of, relating to, or arising from a phobia ▷ n person with a phobia

PHOBISM, -S n phobia

PHOBIST, -S ▶ phobism

PHOCA, -E, -S n genus of seals

PHOCINE adj of, relating to, or resembling a seal

PHOEBE, -S n greyish-brown North American flycatcher

PHOEBUS n sun

PHOENIX n legendary bird said to set fire to itself and rise anew from its ashes

PHOH variant of **▶ foh**

PHOLAS, PHOLADES n type of bivalve mollusc

PHON, -S n unit of loudness

PHONAL adj relating to voice

PHONATE, -D, -S vb articulate speech sounds

PHONE, -D, -S, PHONING vb telephone ▷ n single uncomplicated speech sound

PHONECAM n digital camera incorporated in a mobile phone

PHONED ▶ phone

PHONEME, -S n one of the set of speech sounds in a language

PHONEMIC adj of or relating to the phoneme

PHONER, -S n person making a telephone call

PHONES ▶ phone

PHONETIC adj of speech sounds

PHONEY, -ED, -S adj not genuine ▷ n phoney person or thing ▷ vb fake

PHONIC ▶ phonics

PHONICS n method of teaching people to read

PHONIED ▶ phony

PHONIER ▶ phony

PHONIES ▶ phony

PHONIEST ▶ phony

PHONILY ▶ phony

PHONING ▶ phone

PHONO, -S n phonograph

PHONON, -S n quantum of vibrational energy

PHONOS ▶ phono

PHONS ▶ phon

PHONY, PHONIED, PHONIER, PHONIES, PHONIEST, -ING vb fake

PHOOEY interj exclamation of scorn or contempt

PHORATE, -S n type of insecticide

PHORESY n association in which one animal clings to another to ensure movement from place to place

PHORETIC adj relating to phoresy

PHORMINX n ancient Greek stringed instrument

PHORMIUM n New Zealand plant

PHORONID n small wormlike marine animal

PHOS ▶ pho

PHOSGENE n poisonous gas used in warfare

PHOSPHID same as **> phosphide**

PHOSPHIN same as **> phosphine**

PHOSPHOR n synthetic fluorescent or phosphorescent substance

PHOSSY adj as in **phossy jaw** gangrenous condition of the lower jawbone

PHOT, -S n unit of illumination

PHOTIC adj of or concerned with light

PHOTICS n science of light

PHOTINIA n genus of garden plants

PHOTINO, -S n hypothetical elementary particle

PHOTISM, -S n sensation of light or colour caused by stimulus of another sense

PHOTO, -ED, -ING, -S n photograph ▷ vb take a photograph of

PHOTOFIT n combining of photographs of facial features into a composite picture of a face

PHOTOG, -S n photograph

P

PHOTOGEN same as
▸ **photogene**
PHOTOGS ▸ **photog**
PHOTOING ▸ **photo**
PHOTOMAP n map
constructed by adding grid
lines, place names, etc, to
aerial photographs ▷ vb
map (an area) using aerial
photography
PHOTON, -S n quantum of
electromagnetic radiation
energy
PHOTONIC ▸ **photon**
PHOTONS ▸ **photon**
PHOTOPIA n normal
adaptation of the eye to
light
PHOTOPIC ▸ **photopia**
PHOTOPSY same as
▸ **photopsia**
PHOTOS ▸ **photo**
PHOTOSET vb set (type
matter) by photosetting
PHOTS ▸ **phot**
PHPHT interj expressing
irritation or reluctance
PHRASAL adj of, relating to,
or composed of phrases
PHRASE, -D, -S n group of
words forming a unit of
meaning, esp within a
sentence ▷ vb express in
words
PHRASER, -S ▸ **phrase**
PHRASES ▸ **phrase**
PHRASIER ▸ **phrasy**
PHRASING n exact words
used to say or write
something
PHRASY, PHRASIER adj
containing phrases
PHRATRAL ▸ **phratry**
PHRATRIC ▸ **phratry**
PHRATRY n group of people
within a tribe who have a
common ancestor
PHREAK, -ED, -S vb hack
into a telecommunications
system
PHREAKER ▸ **phreak**
PHREAKS ▸ **phreak**
PHREATIC adj of or relating
to ground water occurring
below the water table
PHRENIC, -S adj of or
relating to the diaphragm
▷ n (a nerve, blood vessel,
etc) located in the
diaphragm
PHRENISM n belief in
non-physical life force
PHRENSY obsolete spelling of
▸ **frenzy**
PHRYGANA another name for
▸ **garigue**

PHT same as ▸ **phpht**
It is easy to overlook this
little word, that may offer a
way out when your rack
seems hopelessly clogged
with consonants.
PHTHALIC adj as in phthalic
anhydride white crystalline
substance used mainly in
producing dyestuffs
PHTHALIN n colourless
compound formed by
reduction of phthalein
PHTHISES ▸ **phthisis**
PHTHISIC adj relating to or
affected with phthisis ▷ n
person with phthisis
PHTHISIS, PHTHISES n any
disease that causes wasting
of the body, esp pulmonary
tuberculosis
PHUT, -S, -TED, -TING vb
make muffled explosive
sound
PHWOAH same as ▸ **phwoar**
PHWOAR interj expression
of attraction
PHYLA ▸ **phylum**
PHYLAE ▸ **phyle**
PHYLAR ▸ **phylum**
PHYLARCH n chief of tribe
PHYLAXIS n protection
against infection
PHYLE, PHYLAE n tribe or
clan of an ancient Greek
people
PHYLESIS, PHYLESES n
evolutionary events that
modify taxon without
causing speciation
PHYLETIC adj of or relating
to the evolution of a species
or group of organisms
PHYLIC ▸ **phyle**
PHYLLARY n bract
subtending flower head of
composite plant
PHYLLID, -S n leaf of a
liverwort or moss
PHYLLITE n compact
lustrous metamorphic
rock
PHYLLO, -S variant of
▸ **filo**
PHYLLODE n flattened
leafstalk that resembles and
functions as a leaf
PHYLLODY n abnormal
development of leaves from
parts of flower
PHYLLOID adj resembling a
leaf ▷ n leaf-like organ
PHYLLOME n leaf or a
leaflike organ
PHYLLOS ▸ **phyllo**
PHYLON n tribe

PHYLUM, PHYLA n major
taxonomic division of
animals and plants
PHYSALIA n Portuguese
man-of-war
PHYSALIS n strawberry
tomato
PHYSED, -S n physical
education
PHYSES ▸ **physis**
PHYSETER n machine for
filtering
PHYSIC n medicine or drug,
esp a cathartic or purge ▷ vb
treat (a patient) with
medicine
PHYSICAL adj of the body, as
contrasted with the mind or
spirit
PHYSICKY ▸ **physic**
PHYSICS n science of the
properties of matter and
energy
PHYSIO, -S n
physiotherapist
PHYSIQUE n person's bodily
build and muscular
development
PHYSIS, PHYSES n part of
bone responsible for
lengthening
PHYTANE, -S n hydrocarbon
found in fossilised plant
remains
PHYTIN, -S n substance
from plants used as an
energy supplement
PHYTOID adj resembling
plant
PHYTOL, -S n alcohol used
to synthesize some vitamins
PHYTON, -S n unit of plant
structure
PHYTONIC ▸ **phyton**
PHYTONS ▸ **phyton**
PHYTOSIS, PHYTOSES n
disease caused by vegetable
parasite
PI, -ED, -ING, -S n sixteenth
letter in the Greek alphabet
▷ vb spill and mix (set type)
indiscriminately
PIA, -S n innermost of the
three membranes that cover
the brain and the spinal cord
PIACULAR adj making
expiation for a sacrilege
PIAFFE, -D, -S, PIAFFING n
passage done on the spot
▷ vb strut on the spot
PIAFFER, -S ▸ **piaffe**
PIAFFES ▸ **piaffe**
PIAFFING ▸ **piaffe**
PIAL adj relating to pia mater
PIAN, -S n contagious
tropical skin disease

PIANETTE n small piano

PIANI ▶ piano

PIANIC adj of piano

PIANINO, -S n small upright piano

PIANISM, -S n technique, skill, or artistry in playing the piano

PIANIST, -S n person who plays the piano

PIANISTE variant of ▶ pianist

PIANISTS ▶ pianist

PIANO, PIANI, -S n musical instrument with strings which are struck by hammers worked by a keyboard ▷ adv quietly

PIANOLA, -S n type of player piano

PIANOS ▶ piano

PIANS ▶ pian

PIARIST, -S n member of a Roman religious order

PIAS ▶ pia

PIASABA, -S same as ▶ piassava

PIASAVA, -S same as ▶ piassava

PIASSABA same as ▶ piassava

PIASSAVA n South American palm tree

PIASTER, -S same as ▶ piastre

PIASTRE, -S n fractional monetary unit of Egypt, Lebanon, Sudan, South Sudan, and Syria

PIAZZA, -S, PIAZZE n square or marketplace, esp in Italy

PIAZZIAN ▶ piazza

PIBAL, -S n method of measuring wind

PIBROCH, -S n form of bagpipe music

PIC, -S n photograph or illustration

PICA, -S n abnormal craving to ingest substances

PICACHO, -S n pointed solitary mountain

PICADOR, -S n mounted bullfighter with a lance

PICAL adj relating to pica

PICAMAR, -S n hydrocarbon extract of beechwood tar

PICANTE adj spicy

PICARA, -S n female adventurer

PICARIAN n tree-haunting bird

PICARO, -S n roguish adventurer

PICAROON n adventurer or rogue

PICAROS ▶ picaro

PICAS ▶ pica

PICAYUNE adj of small value or importance ▷ n any coin of little value, such as a five-cent piece

PICCATA, -S adj sautéed and served in a lemon sauce ▷ n dish of food sautéed and served in a lemon sauce

PICCIES ▶ piccy

PICCOLO, -S n small flute

PICCY, PICCIES n picture or photograph

PICE n former Indian coin worth one sixty-fourth of a rupee

PICENE, -S n type of hydrocarbon

PICEOUS adj of, relating to, or resembling pitch

PICHURIM n S American laurel tree

PICIFORM adj relating to certain tree-haunting birds

PICINE adj relating to woodpeckers

PICK, -ED, -ING, -S vb choose ▷ n choice

PICKABLE ▶ pick

PICKADIL same as ▶ piccadill

PICKAX same as ▶ pickaxe

PICKAXE, -D, -S n large pick ▷ vb use a pickaxe on (earth, rocks, etc)

PICKBACK vb carry by piggyback

PICKED ▶ pick

PICKEER, -S vb make raid for booty

PICKER, -S n person or thing that picks

PICKEREL n North American freshwater game fish

PICKERS ▶ picker

PICKERY n petty theft

PICKET, -ED, -S n person or group standing outside a workplace during a strike ▷ vb form a picket outside (a workplace)

PICKETER ▶ picket

PICKETS ▶ picket

PICKIER ▶ picky

PICKIEST ▶ picky

PICKILY ▶ picky

PICKIN, -S n small child

PICKING ▶ pick

PICKINGS pl n money easily acquired

PICKINS ▶ pickin

PICKLE, -S, PICKLING n food preserved in vinegar or salt water ▷ vb preserve in vinegar or salt water

PICKLED adj (of food) preserved

PICKLER, -S ▶ pickle

PICKLES ▶ pickle

PICKLING ▶ pickle

PICKLOCK n person who picks locks, esp one who gains unlawful access to premises by this means

PICKMAW, -S n type of gull

PICKOFF, -S n baseball play

PICKS ▶ pick

PICKUP, -S n small truck with an open body and low sides

PICKWICK n tool for raising the short wick of an oil lamp

PICKY, PICKIER, PICKIEST adj fussy

PICLORAM n type of herbicide

PICNIC, -S n informal meal out of doors ▷ vb have a picnic

PICNICKY adj like a picnic

PICNICS ▶ picnic

PICOGRAM n trillionth of gram

PICOLIN, -S variant of ▶ picoline

PICOLINE n liquid derivative of pyridine found in bone oil and coal tar

PICOLINS ▶ picolin

PICOMOLE n trillionth of a mole

PICONG, -S n any teasing or satirical banter

PICOT, -ED, -ING, -S n any of pattern of small loops, as on lace ▷ vb decorate material with small loops

PICOTE adj (of material) picoted

PICOTED ▶ picot

PICOTEE, -S n type of carnation

PICOTING ▶ picot

PICOTITE n dark-brown mineral

PICOTS ▶ picot

PICOWAVE vb treat food with gamma waves

PICQUET, -S vb provide early warning of attack

PICRA, -S n powder of aloes and canella

PICRATE, -S n any salt or ester of picric acid

PICRATED adj containing picrate

PICRATES ▶ picrate

PICRIC adj as in picric acid toxic sparingly soluble crystalline yellow acid

PICRITE, -S n coarse-grained ultrabasic igneous rock

PICRITIC ▶ picrite

PICS ▸ pic

PICTURAL n picture

PICTURE, -D, -S n drawing or painting ▹ vb visualize, imagine

PICUL, -S n unit of weight, used in China, Japan, and SE Asia

PICULET, -S n small tropical woodpecker with a short tail

PICULS ▸ picul

PIDDLE, -D, -S vb urinate

PIDDLER, -S ▸ piddle

PIDDLES ▸ piddle

PIDDLIER ▸ piddly

PIDDLING adj small or unimportant

PIDDLY, PIDDLIER adj trivial

PIDDOCK, -S n marine bivalve that bores into rock, clay, or wood

PIDGEON, -S variant of ▸ pidgin

PIDGIN, -S n language made up of elements of other languages

PIE, -S n dish of meat, fruit, etc baked in pastry

PIEBALD, -S adj (horse) with irregular black-and-white markings ▹ n black-and-white horse

PIECE, -D, -S n separate bit or part

PIECEN, -ED, -S vb join broken threads

PIECENER ▸ piecen

PIECENS ▸ piecen

PIECER, -S n person who mends, repairs, or joins something

PIECES ▸ piece

PIECING, -S ▸ piece

PIECRUST n pastry used for making pies

PIED ▸ pi

PIEDFORT n coin thicker than normal

PIEDISH n container for baking pies

PIEDMONT adj (of glaciers, plains, etc) formed or situated at the foot of a mountain or mountain range ▹ n gentle slope leading from mountains to flat land

PIEDNESS n state of being pied

PIEFORT, -S same as ▸ piedfort

PIEHOLE, -S n person's mouth

PIEING, -S n act of pushing a pie into a person's face

PIEMAN, PIEMEN n seller of pies

PIEND, -S n salient angle

PIEPLANT n rhubarb

PIER, -S n platform on stilts sticking out into the sea

PIERAGE, -S n accommodation for ships at piers

PIERCE, -D, -S vb make a hole in or through with a sharp instrument

PIERCER, -S ▸ pierce

PIERCES ▸ pierce

PIERCING adj (of a sound) shrill and high-pitched ▹ n art or practice of piercing body parts for the insertion of jewellery

PIERHEAD n end of a pier farthest from the shore

PIERID, -S n type of butterfly

PIERIS, -ES n American or Asiatic shrub

PIEROG, -EN, same as ▸ pirog

PIEROGI n Polish dumpling

PIEROGS ▸ pierog

PIERROT, -S n male clown or masquerader with a whitened face

PIERS ▸ pier

PIERST archaic spelling of ▸ pierced

PIERT, -S n small plant with small greenish flowers

PIES ▸ pie

PIET, -S n magpie

PIETA, -S n sculpture, painting, or drawing of the dead Christ, supported by the Virgin Mary

PIETIES ▸ piety

PIETISM, -S n exaggerated piety

PIETIST, -S ▸ pietism

PIETS ▸ piet

PIETY, PIETIES n deep devotion to God and religion

PIEZO adj piezoelectric

PIFFERO, -S n small rustic flute

PIFFLE, -D, -S n nonsense ▹ vb talk or behave feebly

PIFFLER, -S n talker of nonsense

PIFFLES ▸ piffle

PIFFLING adj worthless

PIG, -GED, -S n mammal with a long head and movable snout ▹ vb eat greedily

PIGBOAT, -S n submarine

PIGEON, -ED, -S n bird with a heavy body and short legs ▹ vb pigeonhole

PIGEONRY n loft for keeping pigeons

PIGEONS ▸ pigeon

PIGFACE, -S n creeping succulent plant

PIGFEED, -S n food for pigs

PIGFISH n grunting fish of the North American Atlantic coast

PIGGED ▸ pig

PIGGERY n place for keeping and breeding pigs

PIGGIE same as ▸ piggy

PIGGIER ▸ piggy

PIGGIES ▸ piggy

PIGGIEST ▸ piggy

PIGGIN, -S n small wooden bucket or tub

PIGGING, -S ▸ pig

PIGGINS ▸ piggin

PIGGISH adj like a pig, esp in appetite or manners

PIGGY, PIGGIER, PIGGIES, PIGGIEST n child's word for a pig ▹ adj like a pig

PIGHT, -ED, -ING, -S vb pierce

PIGHTLE, -S n small enclosure

PIGHTS ▸ pight

PIGLET, -S n young pig

PIGLIKE ▸ pig

PIGLING, -S n young pig

PIGMAEAN same as ▸ pygmaean

PIGMAN, PIGMEN n male pig farmer

PIGMEAN same as ▸ pygmaean

PIGMEAT, -S less common name for ▸ pork

PIGMEN ▸ pigman

PIGMENT, -S n colouring matter, paint or dye ▹ vb colour with pigment

PIGMIES ▸ pigmy

PIGMOID, -S adj of pygmies ▹ n pygmy

PIGMY, PIGMIES same as ▸ pygmy

PIGNOLI, -S same as ▸ pignolia

PIGNOLIA n edible seed of nut pine

PIGNOLIS ▸ pignoli

PIGNUS, PIGNORA n pawn or pledge

PIGNUT, -S n bitter nut of hickory trees

PIGOUT, -S n binge

PIGPEN, -S same as ▸ pigsty

PIGS ▸ pig

PIGSKIN, -S n skin of the domestic pig ▹ adj made of pigskin

PIGSNEY, -S same as ▸ pigsny

PIGSNIE, -S same as ▸ pigsny

PIGSNY n archaic pet name for a girl or woman

PIGSTICK, PIGSTUCK vb (esp in India) hunt and spear wild boar, esp from horseback

PIGSTIES ▸ pigsty

PIGSTUCK ▸ pigstick

PIGSTY, PIGSTIES n enclosure for pigs

PIGSWILL n waste food or other edible matter fed to pigs

PIGTAIL, -S n plait of hair hanging from the back or either side of the head

PIGWASH n wet feed for pigs

PIGWEED, -S n coarse North American weed

PIHOIHOI n variety of New Zealand pipit

PIING ▸ pi

PIKA, -S n burrowing mammal

PIKAKE, -S n type of Asian vine

PIKAS ▸ pika

PIKAU, -S n pack, knapsack, or rucksack

PIKE, -D, -S n large predatory freshwater fish ▸ vb stab or pierce using a pike ▸ adj (of the body position of a diver) bent at the hips but with the legs straight

PIKELET, -S n small thick pancake

PIKELIKE adj like a pike

PIKEMAN, PIKEMEN n (formerly) soldier armed with a pike

PIKER, -S n shirker

PIKES ▸ pike

PIKI, -S n bread made from blue cornmeal

PIKING, -S ▸ pike

PIKIS ▸ piki

PIKUL, -S same as ▸ picul

PILA, -E n pillar-like anatomical structure

PILAF, -S same as ▸ pilau

PILAFF, -S same as ▸ pilau

PILAFS ▸ pilaf

PILAO, -S same as ▸ pilau

PILAR adj relating to hair

PILASTER n square column, usu set in a wall

PILAU, -S n Middle Eastern dish

PILAW, -S same as ▸ pilau

PILCH, -ES n outer garment, originally one made of skin

PILCHARD n small edible sea fish of the herring family

PILCHER, -S n scabbard for sword

PILCHES ▸ pilch

PILCORN, -S n type of oat

PILCROW, -S n paragraph mark

PILE, -D n number of things lying on top of each other ▸ vb collect into a pile

PILEA, -S n plant which releases a cloud of pollen when shaken

PILEATE adj (of birds) having a crest

PILEATED same as ▸ pileate

PILED ▸ pile

PILEI ▸ pileus

PILELESS ▸ pile

PILEOUS adj hairy

PILER, -S n placer of things on pile

PILES pl n swollen veins in the rectum, haemorrhoids

PILEUM n top of a bird's head

PILEUP, -S n multiple collision of vehicles

PILEUS, PILEI n upper cap-shaped part of a mushroom

PILEWORK n construction built from heavy stakes or cylinders

PILEWORT n plant used to treat piles

PILFER, -ED, -S vb steal in small quantities

PILFERER ▸ pilfer

PILFERS ▸ pilfer

PILFERY n theft

PILGRIM, -S n person who journeys to a holy place ▸ vb travel as a pilgrim

PILI, -S, PILUS n Philippine tree with edible seeds resembling almonds

PILIER ▸ pily

PILIEST ▸ pily

PILIFORM adj resembling a long hair

PILING, -S n act of driving piles

PILINUT, -S n type of nut found in the Philippines

PILIS ▸ pili

PILL, -ED, -S n small ball of medicine swallowed whole ▸ vb peel or skin (something)

PILLAGE, -D, -S vb steal property by violence in war ▸ n violent seizure of goods, esp in war

PILLAGER ▸ pillage

PILLAGES ▸ pillage

PILLAR, -ED, -S n upright post, usu supporting a roof ▸ vb provide or support with pillars

PILLAU, -S same as ▸ pilau

PILLBOX n small box for pills

PILLBUG, -S n type of woodlouse

PILLED ▸ pill

PILLIE, -S n pilchard

PILLING, -S ▸ pill

PILLION, -S n seat for a passenger behind the rider of a motorcycle ▸ adv on a pillion ▸ vb ride pillion

PILLOCK, -S n stupid or annoying person

PILLORY n frame in which an offender was locked and exposed to public abuse ▸ vb ridicule publicly

PILLOW, -ED, -S n stuffed cloth bag for supporting the head in bed ▸ vb rest as if on a pillow

PILLOWY adj like a pillow

PILLS ▸ pill

PILLWORM n worm that rolls up spirally

PILLWORT n small Eurasian water fern

PILOSE adj covered with fine soft hairs

PILOSITY ▸ pilose

PILOT, -ED, -S n person qualified to fly an aircraft or spacecraft ▸ adj experimental and preliminary ▸ vb act as the pilot of

PILOTAGE n act of piloting an aircraft or ship

PILOTED ▸ pilot

PILOTING n navigational handling of a ship near land

PILOTIS pl n posts raising a building up from the ground

PILOTMAN, PILOTMEN n railway worker who directs trains through hazardous stretches of track

PILOTS ▸ pilot

PILOUS same as ▸ pilose

PILOW, -S same as ▸ pilau

PILSENER same as ▸ pilsner

PILSNER, -S n type of pale beer with a strong flavour of hops

PILULA, -E, -S n pill

PILULAR ▸ pilule

PILULAS ▸ pilula

PILULE, -S n small pill

PILUM n ancient Roman javelin

PILUS ▸ pili

PILY, PILIER, PILIEST adj like wool or pile

PIMA, -S n type of cotton

PIMENT, -S n wine flavoured with spices

PIMENTO, -S *same as*
▶ **pimiento**
PIMENTON *n* smoked chilli
powder
PIMENTOS ▶ **pimento**
PIMENTS ▶ **piment**
PIMIENTO *n* Spanish pepper
with a red fruit used as a
vegetable
PIMP, -ED, -S *vb* embellish
PIMPING, -S *n*
embellishment
PIMPLE, -S *n* small pus-filled
spot on the skin
PIMPLED ▶ **pimple**
PIMPLES ▶ **pimple**
PIMPLY, PIMPLIER ▶ **pimple**
PIMPS ▶ **pimp**
PIN, -NED, -S *n* short thin
piece of stiff wire with a
point and head, for fastening
things ▷ *vb* fasten with a pin
PINA, -S *n* cone of silver
amalgam
PINACOID *n* pair of opposite
parallel faces of crystal
PINAFORE *n* apron
PINAKOID *same as*
▶ **pinacoid**
PINANG, -S *n* areca tree
PINAS ▶ **pina**
PINASTER *n* Mediterranean
pine tree
PINATA, -S *n* papier-mâché
party decoration filled with
sweets
PINBALL, -S *vb* ricochet
PINBOARD *n* cork board for
pinning notices, messages
etc on
PINBONE, -S *n* part of sirloin
PINCASE, -S *n* case for
holding pins
PINCER, -ED *vb* grip with
pincers
PINCERS *pl n* tool consisting
of two hinged arms, for
gripping
PINCH, -ED, -ES, -ING *vb*
squeeze between finger and
thumb ▷ *n* act of pinching
PINCHBUG *n* type of crab
PINCHECK *n* small check
woven into fabric
PINCHED ▶ **pinch**
PINCHER, -S ▶ **pinch**
PINCHES ▶ **pinch**
PINCHGUT *n* miserly person
PINCHING ▶ **pinch**
PINCURL, -S *n* curl secured
by a hairpin
PINDAN, -S *n* desert region
of Western Australia
PINDAREE *same as* ▶ **pindari**
PINDARI, -S *n* former
irregular Indian horseman

PINDER, -S *n* person who
impounds
PINDLING *adj* peevish or
fractious
PINDOWN, -S *n* wrestling
manoeuvre
PINE, -D, -S, PINING *n*
evergreen coniferous tree
▷ *vb* feel great longing (for)
PINEAL, -S *adj* resembling a
pine cone ▷ *n* pineal gland
PINECONE *n* seed-
producing structure of a pine
tree
PINED ▶ **pine**
PINELAND *n* area covered
with pine forest
PINELIKE ▶ **pine**
PINENE, -S *n* isomeric
terpene found in many
essential oils
PINERY, PINERIES *n* place,
esp a hothouse, where
pineapples are grown
PINES ▶ **pine**
PINESAP *n* red herb of N
America
PINETUM, PINETA *n* area of
land where pine trees are
grown
PINEWOOD *n* wood of pine
trees
PINEY ▶ **pine**
PINFALL, -S *another name for*
▶ **fall**
PINFISH *n* small porgy of the
Atlantic
PINFOLD, -S *n* pound for
stray cattle ▷ *vb* gather or
confine in or as if in a pinfold
PING, -ED, -S *n* short
high-pitched sound ▷ *vb*
make such a noise
PINGER, -S *n* device, esp a
timer, that makes a pinging
sound
PINGING ▶ **ping**
PINGLE, -D, -S, PINGLING *vb*
enclose small area of ground
PINGLER, -S ▶ **pingle**
PINGLES ▶ **pingle**
PINGLING ▶ **pingle**
PINGO, -ES, -S *n* mound of
earth or gravel formed in
Arctic regions
PINGPONG *n* Australian
football
PINGRASS *n* weed with
fernlike leaves
PINGS ▶ **ping**
PINGUEFY *vb* become
greasy or fat
PINGUID *adj* fatty, oily, or
greasy
PINGUIN, -S *same as*
▶ **penguin**

PINHEAD, -S *n* head of a pin
PINHOLE, -S *n* small hole
made with or as if with a pin
PINIER ▶ **piny**
PINIES ▶ **piny**
PINIEST ▶ **piny**
PINING ▶ **pine**
PINION, -ED, -S *n* bird's wing
▷ *vb* immobilize (someone)
by tying or holding his or her
arms
PINITE, -S *n* greyish-green or
brown mineral
PINITOL, -S *n* compound
found in pinewood
PINK, -ED, -EST, -S *n* pale
reddish colour ▷ *adj* of the
colour pink ▷ *vb* (of an
engine) make a metallic
noise because not working
properly
PINKEN, -ED, -S *vb* turn pink
PINKER, -S *n* something
that pinks
PINKEST ▶ **pink**
PINKEY, -S *n* type of ship
PINKEYE, -S *n* acute
inflammation of the
conjunctiva of the eye
PINKEYS ▶ **pinkey**
PINKIE, -S *n* little finger
PINKIER ▶ **pinky**
PINKIES ▶ **pinkie**
PINKIEST ▶ **pinky**
PINKING, -S ▶ **pink**
PINKISH ▶ **pink**
PINKLY ▶ **pink**
PINKNESS ▶ **pink**
PINKO, -ES, -S *n* person
regarded as mildly left-wing
PINKROOT *n* plant with
red-and-yellow flowers and
pink roots
PINKS ▶ **pink**
PINKY, PINKIER, PINKIEST
adj of a pink colour
PINLESS *adj* without a pin
PINNA, -E, -S *n* external part
of the ear
PINNACE, -S *n* ship's boat
PINNACLE *n* highest point of
fame or success ▷ *vb* set on
or as if on a pinnacle
PINNAE ▶ **pinna**
PINNAL ▶ **pinna**
PINNAS ▶ **pinna**
PINNATE *adj* (of compound
leaves) having leaflets
growing opposite each other
in pairs
PINNATED *same as*
▶ **pinnate**
PINNED ▶ **pin**
PINNER, -S *n* person or thing
that pins
PINNET, -S *n* pinnacle

PINNIE, -S *same as* ▸ **pinny**

PINNING, -S ▸ **pin**

PINNIPED, -S *n* aquatic placental mammal such as the seal, sea lion, walrus, etc

PINNOCK, -S *n* small bird

PINNOED *adj* held or bound by the arms

PINNULA, -E, -S *same as* ▸ **pinnule**

PINNULAR ▸ **pinnule**

PINNULAS ▸ **pinnula**

PINNULE, -S *n* lobe of a leaflet of a pinnate compound leaf

PINNY *informal or child's name for* ▸ **pinafore**

PINOCHLE *n* card game for two to four players similar to bezique

PINOCLE, -S *same as* ▸ **pinochle**

PINOLE, -S *n* flour made in the southwestern United States

PINON, -ES, -S *n* low-growing pine

PINOT, -S *n* any of several grape varieties

PINOTAGE *n* variety of red grape

PINOTS ▸ **pinot**

PINPOINT *vb* locate or identify exactly ▸ *adj* exact ▸ *n* insignificant or trifling thing

PINPRICK *n* small irritation or annoyance ▸ *vb* puncture with or as if with a pin

PINS ▸ **pin**

PINSCHER *n* breed of dog

PINSPOT, -S *vb* illuminate with a small spotlight

PINSWELL *n* small boil

PINT, -S *n* liquid measure, 1/8 gallon (.568 litre)

PINTA, -S *n* pint of milk

PINTABLE *n* pinball machine

PINTADA, -S *same as* ▸ **pintado**

PINTADO, -S *n* species of seagoing petrel

PINTAIL, -S *n* greyish-brown duck with a pointed tail

PINTANO, -S *n* tropical reef fish

PINTAS ▸ **pinta**

PINTLE, -S *n* pin or bolt forming the pivot of a hinge

PINTO, -ES, -S *adj* marked with patches of white ▸ *n* pinto horse

PINTS ▸ **pint**

PINTSIZE *same as* ▸ **pintsized**

PINTUCK, -S *vb* tuck with a narrow fold of fabric

PINUP, -S *n* picture of a physically attractive person

PINWALE, -S *n* fabric with narrow ridges

PINWEED, -S *n* herb with tiny flowers

PINWHEEL *n* cogwheel whose teeth are formed by small pins

PINWORK, -S *n* (in needlepoint lace) fine raised stitches

PINWORM, -S *n* parasitic nematode worm

PINXIT *vb* (he or she) painted (it)

PINY, PINIER, PINIES, PINIEST *variant of* ▸ **peony**

PINYIN, -S *n* system of romanized spelling for the Chinese language

PINYON, -S *n* low-growing pine

PIOLET, -S *n* type of ice axe

PION, -S *n* type of subatomic particle

PIONED *adj* abounding in marsh marigolds

PIONEER, -S *n* explorer or early settler of a new country ▸ *vb* be the pioneer or leader of

PIONER, -S *obsolete spelling of* ▸ **pioneer**

PIONEY, -S *same as* ▸ **peony**

PIONIC ▸ **pion**

PIONIES ▸ **piony**

PIONING, -S *n* work of pioneers

PIONS ▸ **pion**

PIONY, PIONIES *same as* ▸ **peony**

PIOPIO, -S *n* New Zealand thrush, thought to be extinct

PIOSITY *n* grandiose display of piety

PIOTED *adj* pied

PIOUS *adj* deeply religious, devout

PIOUSLY ▸ **pious**

PIOY, -S *variant of* ▸ **peeoy**

PIOYE, -S *variant of* ▸ **peeoy**

PIOYS ▸ **pioy**

PIP, -PED, -PING, -S *n* small seed in a fruit ▸ *vb* chirp

PIPA, -S *n* tongueless S American toad

PIPAGE, -S *n* pipes collectively

PIPAL, -S *same as* ▸ **peepul**

PIPAS ▸ **pipa**

PIPE, -D, -S *n* tube for conveying liquid or gas ▸ *vb* play on a pipe

PIPEAGE, -S *same as* ▸ **pipage**

PIPECLAY *n* fine white clay used in tobacco pipes ▸ *vb* whiten with pipeclay

PIPED ▸ **pipe**

PIPEFISH, -S *n* fish with a long tubelike snout and an elongated body

PIPEFUL, -S *n* as much tobacco, etc as will fill a pipe

PIPELESS ▸ **pipe**

PIPELIKE ▸ **pipe**

PIPELINE *n* long pipe for transporting oil, water, etc

PIPER, -S *n* player on a pipe or bagpipes

PIPERIC ▸ **piperine**

PIPERINE *n* crystalline insoluble alkaloid that is the active ingredient of pepper

PIPERS ▸ **piper**

PIPES ▸ **pipe**

PIPESTEM *n* hollow stem of pipe

PIPET, -S *same as* ▸ **pipette**

PIPETTE, -D, -S *n* slender glass tube used to transfer or measure fluids ▸ *vb* transfer or measure out (a liquid) using a pipette

PIPEWORK *n* stops and flues on pipe organ

PIPEWORT *n* perennial plant with a twisted flower stalk and a greenish-grey scaly flower head

PIPI, -S *n* edible mollusc often used as bait

PIPIER ▸ **pipy**

PIPIEST ▸ **pipy**

PIPINESS *n* material's suitability for use as pipe

PIPING, -S *n* system of pipes

PIPINGLY ▸ **piping**

PIPINGS ▸ **piping**

PIPIS ▸ **pipi**

PIPIT, -S *n* small brownish songbird

PIPKIN, -S *same as* ▸ **piggin**

PIPLESS ▸ **pip**

PIPPED ▸ **pip**

PIPPIER ▸ **pippy**

PIPPIEST ▸ **pippy**

PIPPIN, -S *n* type of eating apple

PIPPING ▸ **pip**

PIPPINS ▸ **pippin**

PIPPY, PIPPIER, PIPPIEST *adj* containing many pips

PIPS ▸ **pip**

PIPUL, -S *n* Indian fig tree

PIPY, PIPIER, PIPIEST ▸ **pipe**

PIQUANCE *same as* ▸ **piquant**

PIQUANCY ▸ **piquant**

PIQUANT *adj* having a pleasant spicy taste

P

PIQUE, -D, -S, PIQUING *n* feeling of hurt pride, baffled curiosity, or resentment ▷ *vb* hurt the pride of

PIQUET, -ED, -S *n* card game for two ▷ *vb* play game of piquet

PIQUILLO *n* variety of sweet red pepper

PIQUING ▶ pique

PIR, -S *n* Sufi master

PIRACY, PIRACIES *n* robbery on the seas

PIRAGUA, -S *same as* **▶ pirogue**

PIRAI, -S *n* large S American fish

PIRANA, -S *same as* **▶ piranha**

PIRANHA, -S *n* fierce fish of tropical America

PIRARUCU *n* large S American food fish

PIRATE, -D, -S *n* sea robber ▷ *vb* sell or reproduce (artistic work etc) illegally

PIRATIC ▶ pirate

PIRATING *n* act of pirating

PIRAYA, -S *same as* **▶ pirai**

PIRIFORM *adj* shaped like pear

PIRL, -S *n* ripple in water

PIRLICUE *same as* **▶ purlicue**

PIRLS ▶ pirl

PIRN, -S *n* reel or bobbin

PIRNIE, -S *n* stripy nightcap

PIRNIT *adj* striped

PIRNS ▶ pirn

PIROG, -HI, -I, -IES *n* type of large Russian pie

PIROGEN *n* turnovers made from kneaded dough

PIROGHI ▶ pirog

PIROGI ▶ pirog

PIROGIES ▶ pirog

PIROGUE, -S *n* any of various kinds of dugout canoes

PIROJKI *same as* **▶ piroshki**

PIROQUE, -S *same as* **▶ pirogue**

PIROSHKI *same as* **▶ pirozhki**

PIROZHOK, PIROZHKI *n* small triangular pastry filled with meat, vegetables, etc

PIRS ▶ pir

PIS ▶ pi

PISCARY *n* place where fishing takes place

PISCATOR *n* fisherman

PISCINA, -E, -S *n* stone basin where water used at Mass is poured away

PISCINAL ▶ piscina

PISCINAS ▶ piscina

PISCINE, -S *n* pond or pool

PISCO, -S *n* S American brandy

PISE, -S *n* rammed earth or clay used to make floors or walls

PISH, -ED, -ES, -ING *interj* exclamation of impatience or contempt ▷ *vb* make this exclamation at (someone or something)

PISHEOG, -S *same as* **▶ pishogue**

PISHER, -S *n* Yiddish term for small boy

PISHES ▶ pish

PISHING ▶ pish

PISHOGE, -S *same as* **▶ pishogue**

PISHOGUE *n* sorcery

PISIFORM *adj* resembling a pea ▷ *n* small pealike bone on the ulnar side of the carpus

PISKY, PISKIES *n* Cornish fairy

PISMIRE, -S *archaic or dialect word for* **▶ ant**

PISO, -S *n* peso of the Philippines

PISOLITE *n* sedimentary rock

PISOLITH *same as* **▶ pisolite**

PISOS ▶ piso

PISTACHE *n* tree yielding pistachio nut

PISTE, -S *n* ski slope

PISTED *adj* marked off into pistes

PISTES ▶ piste

PISTIL, -S *n* seed-bearing part of a flower

PISTOL, -ED, -S *n* short-barrelled handgun ▷ *vb* shoot with a pistol

PISTOLE, -S *n* gold coin formerly used in Europe

PISTOLED ▶ pistol

PISTOLES ▶ pistole

PISTOLET *n* small pistol

PISTOLS ▶ pistol

PISTON, -S *n* cylindrical part in an engine that slides to and fro in a cylinder

PISTOU, -S *n* French sauce

PIT, -S, -TED *n* deep hole in the ground ▷ *vb* mark with small dents or scars

PITA, -S *n* any of several agave plants yielding a strong fibre

PITAHAYA *n* any giant cactus of Central America and the SW United States

PITAPAT, -S *adv* with quick light taps ▷ *n* such taps ▷ *vb* make quick light taps or beats

PITARA, -S *variant of* **▶ petara**

PITARAH, -S *variant of* **▶ petara**

PITARAS ▶ pitara

PITAS ▶ pita

PITAYA, -S *same as* **▶ pitahaya**

PITCH, -ED, -ES, -ING *vb* throw, hurl ▷ *n* area marked out for playing sport

PITCHER, -S *n* large jug with a narrow neck

PITCHES ▶ pitch

PITCHIER ▶ pitchy

PITCHILY ▶ pitchy

PITCHING ▶ pitch

PITCHMAN, PITCHMEN *n* itinerant pedlar of small merchandise who operates from a stand at a fair, etc

PITCHOUT *n* type of baseball pitch

PITCHY, PITCHIER *adj* full of or covered with pitch

PITEOUS *adj* arousing pity

PITFALL, -S *n* hidden difficulty or danger

PITH, -ED, -ING, -S *n* soft white lining of the rind of oranges etc ▷ *vb* destroy the brain and spinal cord of a laboratory animal

PITHBALL *n* type of conductor

PITHEAD, -S *n* top of a mine shaft and the buildings and hoisting gear around it

PITHED ▶ pith

PITHFUL ▶ pith

PITHIER ▶ pithy

PITHIEST ▶ pithy

PITHILY ▶ pithy

PITHING ▶ pith

PITHLESS ▶ pith

PITHLIKE ▶ pith

PITHOS, PITHOI *n* large ceramic container for oil or grain

PITHS ▶ pith

PITHY, PITHIER, PITHIEST *adj* short and full of meaning

PITIABLE *adj* arousing or deserving pity or contempt

PITIABLY ▶ pitiable

PITIED ▶ pity

PITIER, -S ▶ pity

PITIES ▶ pity

PITIETH *vb* as in **it pitieth me** archaic inflection of 'pity'

PITIFUL *adj* arousing pity

PITIKINS *n* as in **ods pitikins** mild oath

PITILESS *adj* feeling no pity or mercy

PITLIKE *adj* like a pit

PITMAN, -S, PITMEN *n* coal miner ▷ *n* connecting rod (in a machine)

PITON, -S *n* metal spike used in climbing to secure a rope

PITOT, -S *n* tube used to measure the pressure of a liquid stream

PITPROP, -S *n* support beam in mine shaft

PITS ▷ pit

PITSAW, -S *n* large saw formerly used for cutting logs into planks

PITTA, -S *n* small brightly coloured ground-dwelling tropical bird

PITTANCE *n* very small amount of money

PITTAS ▷ pitta

PITTED ▷ pit

PITTEN *adj* having been put

PITTER, -ED, -S *vb* make pattering sound

PITTING, -S ▷ pit

PITTITE, -S *n* occupant of a theatre pit

PITUITA, -S *n* thick nasal secretion

PITUITE, -S *n* mucus

PITURI, -S *n* Australian solanaceous shrub

PITY, PITIED, PITIES *n* sympathy or sorrow for others' suffering ▷ *vb* feel pity for

PITYING ▷ pity

PITYROID *adj* resembling bran

PIU *adv* more (quickly, softly, etc)

PIUM, -S *n* stinging insect

PIUPIU, -S *n* skirt worn by Māoris on ceremonial occasions

PIVOT, -ED, -ING, -S *n* central shaft on which something turns ▷ *vb* provide with or turn on a pivot

PIVOTAL *adj* of crucial importance

PIVOTED ▷ pivot

PIVOTER, -S ▷ pivot

PIVOTING ▷ pivot

PIVOTMAN, PIVOTMEN *n* person in rank around whom others wheel

PIVOTS ▷ pivot

PIX, -ES *less common spelling of* ▷ **pyx**

PIXEL, -S *n* any of a number of very small picture elements

PIXELATE *vb* divide an image into pixels

PIXELS ▷ pixel

PIXES ▷ pix

PIXIE *n* (in folklore) fairy

PIXIEISH ▷ pixie

PIXIES ▷ pixy

PIXILATE *same as* ▷ **pixelate**

PIXINESS ▷ pixie

PIXY, PIXIES *same as* ▷ **pixie**

PIXYISH ▷ pixy

PIZAZZ, -ES *same as* ▷ **pizzazz**

PIZAZZY *adj* exciting and lively

PIZE, -D, -S, PIZING *vb* strike (someone a blow)

PIZZA, -S *n* flat disc of dough covered with a wide variety of savoury toppings and baked

PIZZAZ, -ES *same as* ▷ **pzazz**

PIZZAZZ *n* attractive combination of energy and style

PIZZAZZY *same as* ▷ **pizazzy**

PIZZELLE *n* Italian sweet wafer

PIZZERIA *n* place where pizzas are made, sold, or eaten

PIZZLE, -S *n* archaic word for the penis of an animal

PLAAS, -ES *n* farm

PLACABLE *adj* easily placated or appeased

PLACABLY ▷ placable

PLACARD, -S *n* notice that is carried or displayed in public ▷ *vb* attach placards to

PLACATE, -D, -S *vb* make (someone) stop feeling angry or upset

PLACATER ▷ placate

PLACATES ▷ placate

PLACCAT, -S *variant of* ▷ **placket**

PLACCATE *variant of* ▷ **placket**

PLACCATS ▷ placcat

PLACE, -D, -S *n* particular part of an area or space ▷ *vb* put in a particular place

PLACEBO, -S *n* pill given to a patient instead of an active drug

PLACED ▷ place

PLACEMAN, PLACEMEN *n* person who holds a public office as a reward for political support

PLACEMAT *n* table mat for a person to put their plate on

PLACEMEN ▷ placeman

PLACENTA *n* organ formed in the womb during pregnancy, providing nutrients for the fetus

PLACER, -S *n* surface sediment containing particles of gold or some other valuable mineral

PLACES ▷ place

PLACET, -S *n* vote or expression of assent

PLACID, -ER *adj* not easily excited or upset, calm

PLACIDLY ▷ placid

PLACING, -S *n* method of issuing securities to the public using an intermediary

PLACIT, -S *n* decree or dictum

PLACITA ▷ placitum

PLACITS ▷ placit

PLACITUM, PLACITA *n* court or assembly in Middle Ages

PLACK, -S *n* small former Scottish coin

PLACKET, -S *n* opening at the waist of a dress or skirt

PLACKS ▷ plack

PLACOID, -S *adj* platelike or flattened ▷ *n* fish with placoid scales

PLAFOND, -S *n* ceiling, esp one having ornamentation

PLAGAL *adj* (of a cadence) progressing from the subdominant to the tonic chord

PLAGE, -S *n* bright patch in the sun's chromosphere

PLAGIARY *n* person who plagiarizes or a piece of plagiarism

PLAGIUM, -S *n* crime of kidnapping

PLAGUE, -D, -S, PLAGUING *n* fast-spreading fatal disease ▷ *vb* trouble or annoy continually

PLAGUER, -S ▷ plague

PLAGUES ▷ plague

PLAGUEY, PLAGUIER *same as* ▷ **plaguy**

PLAGUILY ▷ plaguy

PLAGUING ▷ plague

PLAGUY *adj* disagreeable or vexing ▷ *adv* disagreeably or annoyingly

PLAICE, -S *n* edible European flatfish

PLAID, -ED, -ING, -S *n* long piece of tartan cloth worn as part of Highland dress ▷ *vb* weave cloth into plaid

PLAIDMAN, PLAIDMEN *n* wearer of plaid

PLAIDS ▷ plaid

PLAIN, -ED, -ER, -EST, -ING *adj* easy to see or understand ▷ *n* large stretch of level

P

country ▷ *adv* clearly or simply ▷ *vb* complain
PLAINANT *n* plaintiff
PLAINED ▶ **plain**
PLAINER ▶ **plain**
PLAINEST ▶ **plain**
PLAINFUL *adj* apt to complain
PLAINING ▶ **plain**
PLAINISH ▶ **plain**
PLAINLY ▶ **plain**
PLAINS *pl n* extensive tracts of flat treeless countryside
PLAINT, -S *n* complaint or lamentation
PLAISTER *n* plaster
PLAIT, -ED, -ING, -S *n* intertwined length of hair ▷ *vb* intertwine separate strands in a pattern
PLAITER, -S ▶ **plait**
PLAITING ▶ **plait**
PLAITS ▶ **plait**
PLAN, -NED, -NING, -S *n* way thought out to do or achieve something ▷ *vb* arrange beforehand
PLANAR *adj* of or relating to a plane
PLANARIA *n* type of flatworm
PLANATE *adj* having been flattened
PLANCH, -ED, -ES *vb* cover with planks
PLANCHE *same as* ▶ **planch**
PLANCHED ▶ **planch**
PLANCHES ▶ **planch**
PLANCHET *n* piece of metal ready to be stamped as a coin, medal, etc
PLANE, -D, -S, PLANING *n* aeroplane ▷ *adj* perfectly flat or level ▷ *vb* glide or skim
PLANER, -S *n* machine with a cutting tool that makes repeated horizontal strokes
PLANES ▶ **plane**
PLANET, -S *n* large body in space that revolves round the sun or another star
PLANETIC ▶ **planet**
PLANETS ▶ **planet**
PLANFORM *n* outline or silhouette of an object, esp an aircraft, as seen from above
PLANGENT *adj* (of sounds) mournful and resounding
PLANING ▶ **plane**
PLANISH *vb* give a smooth surface to (a metal)
PLANK, -ED, -S *n* long flat piece of sawn timber ▷ *vb* cover or provide (an area) with planks

PLANKING *n* number of planks
PLANKS ▶ **plank**
PLANKTER *n* organism in plankton
PLANKTIC *adj* relating to plankton
PLANKTON *n* minute animals and plants floating in the surface water of a sea or lake
PLANLESS *adj* having no plan
PLANNED ▶ **plan**
PLANNER, -S *n* person who makes plans
PLANNING ▶ **plan**
PLANOSOL *n* soil of humid or subhumid uplands
PLANS ▶ **plan**
PLANT, -ED, -ING, -S *n* living organism that grows in the ground and has no power to move ▷ *vb* put in the ground to grow
PLANTA, -E, -S *n* sole of foot
PLANTAGE *n* plants
PLANTAIN *n* low-growing wild plant with broad leaves
PLANTAR *adj* of, relating to, or occurring on the sole of the foot
PLANTAS ▶ **planta**
PLANTED ▶ **plant**
PLANTER, -S *n* owner of a plantation
PLANTING ▶ **plant**
PLANTLET *n* small plant
PLANTS ▶ **plant**
PLANTULE *n* embryo in act of germination
PLANULA, -E *n* free-swimming larva of hydrozoan coelenterates
PLANULAR ▶ **planula**
PLANURIA *n* expulsion of urine from abnormal opening
PLANURY *another name for* ▶ **planuria**
PLANXTY *n* Celtic melody for harp
PLAP, -PED, -PING, -S *same as* ▶ **plop**
PLAQUE, -S *n* inscribed commemorative stone or metal plate
PLASH, -ED, -ES, -ING *same as* ▶ **pleach**
PLASHER, -S *n* type of farm tool
PLASHES ▶ **plash**
PLASHET, -S *n* small pond
PLASHIER ▶ **plashy**
PLASHING ▶ **plash**
PLASHY, PLASHIER *adj* wet or marshy

PLASM, -S *same as* ▶ **plasma**
PLASMA, -S *n* clear liquid part of blood
PLASMIC ▶ **plasma**
PLASMID, -S *n* small circle of bacterial DNA
PLASMIN, -S *n* proteolytic enzyme that causes fibrinolysis in blood clots
PLASMOID *n* section of a plasma having a characteristic shape
PLASMON, -S *n* sum total of plasmagenes in a cell
PLASMS ▶ **plasm**
PLAST *archaic past participle of* ▶ **place**
PLASTE *archaic past participle of* ▶ **place**
PLASTER, -S *n* mixture of lime, sand, etc for coating walls ▷ *vb* cover with plaster
PLASTERY *adj* like plaster
PLASTIC, -S *n* synthetic material that can be moulded when soft but sets in a hard long-lasting shape ▷ *adj* made of plastic
PLASTID, -S *n* small particle in the cells of plants and some animals
PLASTRAL ▶ **plastron**
PLASTRON *n* bony plate forming the ventral part of the shell of a tortoise or turtle
PLASTRUM *variant of* ▶ **plastron**
PLAT, -S, -TED, -TING *n* small area of ground
PLATAN, -S *n* plane tree
PLATANE, -S *same as* ▶ **platan**
PLATANNA *n* S African frog
PLATANS ▶ **platan**
PLATBAND *n* border of flowers in garden
PLATE, -S *n* shallow dish for holding food ▷ *vb* cover with a thin coating of gold, silver, or other metal
PLATEASM *n* talking with mouth open too wide
PLATEAU, -S, -X *n* area of level high land ▷ *vb* remain stable for a long period
PLATED *adj* coated with a layer of metal
PLATEFUL *same as* ▶ **plate**
PLATELET *n* minute particle occurring in blood of vertebrates and involved in clotting of blood
PLATEMAN, PLATEMEN *n* one of crew of steam train

PLATEN, -S *n* roller of a typewriter, against which the paper is held

PLATER, -S *n* person or thing that plates

PLATES ▸ plate

PLATFORM *n* raised floor

PLATIER ▸ platy

PLATIES ▸ platy

PLATIEST ▸ platy

PLATINA, -S *n* alloy of platinum and several other metals

PLATING, -S *n* coating of metal

PLATINIC *adj* of or containing platinum, esp in the tetravalent state

PLATINUM *n* valuable silvery-white metal

PLATONIC *adj* (of a relationship) friendly or affectionate but not romantic ▷ *n* platonic friend

PLATOON, -S *n* smaller unit within a company of soldiers ▷ *vb* organise into platoons

PLATS ▸ plat

PLATT *adj* as in **scale and platt** denoting a straight staircase with landings, as opposed to a spiral staircase

PLATTED ▸ plat

PLATTER, -S *n* large dish

PLATTING ▸ plat

PLATY, PLATIER, PLATIES, PLATIEST, -S *adj* of or designating rocks the constituents of which occur in flaky layers ▷ *n* brightly coloured freshwater fish

PLATYPUS, PLATYPI *n* Australian egg-laying amphibious mammal

PLATYS ▸ platy

PLATYSMA *n* muscle located on side of neck

PLAUDIT, -S *n* expression of enthusiastic approval

PLAUDITE *interj* give a round of applause!

PLAUDITS ▸ plaudit

PLAUSIVE *adj* expressing praise or approval

PLAY, -ED, -S *vb* occupy oneself in (a game or recreation) ▷ *n* story performed on stage or broadcast

PLAYA, -S *n* (in the US) temporary lake in a desert basin

PLAYABLE ▸ play

PLAYACT, -S *vb* pretend or make believe

PLAYAS ▸ playa

PLAYBACK *n* reproducing of a recording, esp formerly on magnetic tape ▷ *vb* listen to or watch (something recorded)

PLAYBILL *n* poster or bill advertising a play

PLAYBOOK *n* book containing a range of possible set plays

PLAYBOY, -S *n* rich man who lives only for pleasure

PLAYBUS *n* mobile playground in a bus

PLAYDATE *n* gathering of children at house for play

PLAYDAY, -S *n* day given to play

PLAYDOWN *same as* **▸ playoff**

PLAYED ▸ play

PLAYER, -S *n* person who plays a game or sport

PLAYFUL *adj* lively

PLAYGIRL *n* rich woman devoted to pleasure

PLAYGOER *n* person who goes often to the theatre

PLAYING, -S *n* act of playing

PLAYLAND *n* playground

PLAYLESS ▸ play

PLAYLET, -S *n* short play

PLAYLIKE ▸ play

PLAYLIST *n* list of songs chosen for playing, such as on a radio station ▷ *vb* put (a song) on a playlist

PLAYMATE *n* companion in play

PLAYOFF, -S *n* extra contest to decide the winner when two or more competitors are tied

PLAYPEN, -S *n* small portable enclosure in which a young child can safely be left to play

PLAYROOM *n* recreation room, esp for children

PLAYS ▸ play

PLAYSET, -S *n* outdoor equipment for children to play on

PLAYSLIP *n* form used to select numbers in a lottery draw

PLAYSOME *adj* playful

PLAYSUIT *n* woman's or child's outfit, usually comprising shorts and a top

PLAYTIME *n* time for play or recreation, such as a school break

PLAYWEAR *n* clothes suitable for playing in

PLAZA, -S *n* open space or square

PLEA, -ED, -ING, -S *n* serious or urgent request, entreaty ▷ *vb* entreat

PLEACH, -ED, -ES *vb* interlace the stems or boughs of (a tree or hedge)

PLEAD, -ED, -ING, -S, PLED *vb* ask urgently or with deep feeling

PLEADER, -S ▸ plead

PLEADING ▸ plead

PLEADS ▸ plead

PLEAED ▸ plea

PLEAING ▸ plea

PLEAS ▸ plea

PLEASANT *adj* pleasing, enjoyable

PLEASE, -S *vb* give pleasure or satisfaction to ▷ *adv* polite word of request

PLEASED ▸ please

PLEASER, -S ▸ please

PLEASES ▸ please

PLEASETH *obsolete inflection of* **▸ please**

PLEASING *adj* giving pleasure or satisfaction ▷ *n* act of giving pleasure

PLEASURE *n* feeling of happiness and satisfaction ▷ *vb* give pleasure to or take pleasure (in)

PLEAT, -ED, -S *n* fold made by doubling material back on itself ▷ *vb* arrange (material) in pleats

PLEATER, -S *n* attachment on a sewing machine that makes pleats

PLEATHER *n* synthetic leather

PLEATING *n* act of pleating

PLEATS ▸ pleat

PLEB *n* common vulgar person

PLEBBY, PLEBBIER *adj* common or vulgar

PLEBE, -S *n* member of the lowest class at the US Naval Academy or Military Academy

PLEBEAN *old variant of* **▸ plebeian**

PLEBEIAN *adj* of the lower social classes ▷ *n* member of the lower social classes

PLEBES ▸ plebe

PLEBIFY *vb* make plebeian

PLEBS *n* common people

PLECTRA ▸ plectrum

PLECTRE, -S *variant of* **▸ plectrum**

PLECTRON *same as* **▸ plectrum**

P

PLECTRUM, PLECTRA n small implement for plucking the strings of a guitar etc

PLED ▸ plead

PLEDGE, -D, -S, PLEDGING n solemn promise ▷ vb promise solemnly

PLEDGEE, -S n person to whom a pledge is given

PLEDGEOR same as ▸ pledgor

PLEDGER, -S same as ▸ pledgor

PLEDGES ▸ pledge

PLEDGET, -S n small flattened pad of wool, cotton, etc

PLEDGING ▸ pledge

PLEDGOR, -S n person who gives or makes a pledge

PLEIAD, -ES, -S n brilliant or talented group, esp one with seven members

PLENA ▸ plenum

PLENARTY n state of endowed church office when occupied

PLENARY adj (of a meeting) attended by all members ▷ n book read at the Eucharist

PLENCH, -ES n tool combining wrench and pliers

PLENIPO, -S n plenipotentiary diplomat

PLENISH vb fill, stock, or resupply

PLENISM, -S n philosophical theory

PLENIST, -S ▸ plenism

PLENTY, PLENTIES n large amount or number ▷ adj very many ▷ adv more than adequately

PLENUM, PLENA, -S n enclosure containing gas at a high pressure

PLEON, -S n abdomen of crustacean

PLEONAL adj of the abdomen of a crustacean

PLEONASM n use of more words than necessary

PLEONAST n person using more words than necessary

PLEONIC ▸ pleon

PLEONS ▸ pleon

PLEOPOD, -S another name for > swimmeret

PLERION, -S n filled-centre supernova remnant

PLEROMA, -S n abundance

PLEROME, -S n central column in growing stem or root

PLESH, -ES n small pool

PLESSOR, -S same as ▸ plexor

PLETHORA n excess

PLEUCH, -ED, -S same as ▸ pleugh

PLEUGH, -ED, -S Scottish word for ▸ plough

PLEURA, -E, -S n membrane covering the lungs

PLEURAL ▸ pleura

PLEURAS ▸ pleura

PLEURISY n inflammation of the membrane covering the lungs

PLEURON n part of the cuticle of arthropods

PLEUSTON n mass of small organisms, esp algae, floating at the surface of shallow pools

PLEW, -S n (formerly in Canada) beaver skin used as a standard unit of value in the fur trade

PLEX, -ED, -ES, -ING n shortening of multiplex ▷ vb make a plexus

PLEXAL ▸ plexus

PLEXED ▸ plex

PLEXES ▸ plex

PLEXING ▸ plex

PLEXOR, -S n small hammer with a rubber head

PLEXURE, -S n act of weaving together

PLEXUS, -ES n complex network of nerves or blood vessels

PLIABLE adj easily bent

PLIABLY ▸ pliable

PLIANCY ▸ pliant

PLIANT adj pliable

PLIANTLY ▸ pliant

PLICA, -E, -S n folding over of parts, such as a fold of skin, muscle, peritoneum, etc

PLICAL ▸ plica

PLICAS ▸ plica

PLICATE, -D, -S adj having or arranged in parallel folds or ridges ▷ vb arrange into parallel folds

PLIE n classic ballet practice posture with back erect and knees bent

PLIED ▸ ply

PLIER n person who plies a trade

PLIERS pl n tool with hinged arms and jaws for gripping

PLIES ▸ ply

PLIGHT, -ED, -S vb pledge

PLIGHTER ▸ plight

PLIGHTS ▸ plight

PLIM, -MED, -MING, -S vb swell with water

PLIMSOL, -S same as ▸ plimsoll

PLIMSOLE same as ▸ plimsoll

PLIMSOLL n light rubber-soled canvas shoe worn for various sports

PLIMSOLS ▸ plimsol

PLING, -ED, -ING, -S n (in computer jargon) an exclamation mark ▷ vb beg from

PLINK, -ED, -S n short sharp often metallic sound ▷ vb make such a noise

PLINKER, -S ▸ plink

PLINKIER ▸ plinky

PLINKING ▸ plink

PLINKS ▸ plink

PLINKY, PLINKIER adj (of a sound) short, sharp, and often metallic

PLINTH, -S n slab forming the base of a statue, column, etc

PLIOCENE adj of the Pliocene geological time period

PLIOFILM n transparent plastic material

PLIOSAUR n type of dinosaur

PLIOTRON n type of vacuum tube

PLISKIE, -R, -S n practical joke ▷ adj tricky or mischievous

PLISKY same as ▸ pliskie

PLISSE, -S n fabric with a wrinkled finish, achieved by treatment involving caustic soda

PLOAT, -ED, -ING, -S vb thrash

PLOD, -DED, -S vb walk with slow heavy steps ▷ n act of plodding

PLODDER, -S n person who plods

PLODDING ▸ plod

PLODGE, -D, -S, PLODGING vb wade in water, esp the sea ▷ n act of wading

PLODS ▸ plod

PLOGGING n picking up litter while jogging

PLOIDY, PLOIDIES n number of copies of set of chromosomes in cell

PLONG, -D, -S obsolete variant of ▸ plunge

PLONGE, -D, -S, PLONGING same as ▸ plunge

PLONGS ▸ plong

P

PLONK, -ED, -ING, -S vb put (something) down heavily and carelessly ▷ n act of plonking ▷ interj exclamation imitative of this sound

PLONKER, -S n stupid person

PLONKIER ▸ plonky

PLONKING ▸ plonk

PLONKO, -S n alcoholic, esp one who drinks wine

PLONKS ▸ plonk

PLONKY, PLONKIER ▸ plonk

PLOOK, -S same as ▸ plouk

PLOOKIE same as ▸ plouky

PLOOKIER ▸ plooky

PLOOKS ▸ plook

PLOOKY, PLOOKIER ▸ plook

PLOP, -PED, -PING, -S n sound of an object falling into water without a splash ▷ vb make this sound ▷ interj exclamation imitative of this sound

PLOSION, -S n sound of an abrupt break or closure, esp the audible release of a stop

PLOSIVE, -S adj pronounced with a sudden release of breath ▷ n plosive consonant

PLOT, -S, -TED, -TING n secret plan to do something illegal or wrong ▷ vb plan secretly, conspire

PLOTFUL ▸ plot

PLOTLESS ▸ plot

PLOTLINE n literary or dramatic plot

PLOTS ▸ plot

PLOTTAGE n land that makes up plot

PLOTTED ▸ plot

PLOTTER, -S same as ▸ plouter

PLOTTIE, -S n hot spiced drink

PLOTTIER ▸ plotty

PLOTTIES ▸ plottie

PLOTTING ▸ plot

PLOTTY, PLOTTIER adj intricately plotted

PLOTZ, -ED, -ES, -ING vb faint or collapse

PLOUGH, -ED, -S n agricultural tool for turning over soil ▷ vb turn over (earth) with a plough

PLOUGHER ▸ plough

PLOUGHS ▸ plough

PLOUK, -S n pimple

PLOUKIE ▸ plouk

PLOUKIER ▸ plouky

PLOUKS ▸ plouk

PLOUKY, PLOUKIER ▸ plouk

PLOUTER, -S same as ▸ plowter

PLOVER, -S n shore bird with a straight bill and long pointed wings

PLOVERY adj characterized by plovers

PLOW, -ED, -S same as ▸ plough

PLOWABLE ▸ plow

PLOWBACK n reinvestment of profits

PLOWBOY, -S same as > ploughboy

PLOWED ▸ plow

PLOWER, -S ▸ plow

PLOWHEAD n draught iron of plow

PLOWING, -S > ploughing

PLOWLAND n land plowed

PLOWMAN, PLOWMEN same as ▸ ploughman

PLOWS ▸ plow

PLOWTAIL n the end of a plough where the handles are

PLOWTER, -S vb work or play in water or mud ▷ n act of plowtering

PLOWWISE adv as in ploughing

PLOY, -ED, -ING, -S n manoeuvre designed to gain an advantage ▷ vb form a column from a line of troops

PLOYE, -S n buckwheat pancake

PLOYED ▸ ploy

PLOYES ▸ ploye

PLOYING ▸ ploy

PLOYS ▸ ploy

PLU same as ▸ plew

PLUCK, -ED, -ING, -S vb pull or pick off ▷ n courage

PLUCKER, -S ▸ pluck

PLUCKIER ▸ plucky

PLUCKILY ▸ plucky

PLUCKING ▸ pluck

PLUCKS ▸ pluck

PLUCKY, PLUCKIER adj brave

PLUE, -S same as ▸ plew

PLUFF, -ED, -ING, -S vb expel in puffs

PLUFFIER ▸ pluffy

PLUFFING ▸ pluff

PLUFFS ▸ pluff

PLUFFY, PLUFFIER ▸ pluff

PLUG, -GED, -GING, -S n thing fitting into and filling a hole ▷ vb block or seal (a hole or gap) with a plug

PLUGGER, -S ▸ plug

PLUGGING ▸ plug

PLUGHOLE n hole at the bottom of a bath or sink which can be closed with a plug

PLUGLESS ▸ plug

PLUGOLA, -S n plugging of products on television

PLUGS ▸ plug

PLUGUGLY n city tough; ruffian

PLUM, -MER, -MEST, -S n oval usu dark red fruit with a stone in the middle ▷ adj dark purplish-red

PLUMAGE, -S n bird's feathers

PLUMAGED ▸ plumage

PLUMAGES ▸ plumage

PLUMATE adj of, relating to, or possessing one or more feathers or plumes

PLUMB, -ED, -S vb understand (something obscure) ▷ adv exactly ▷ n weight suspended at the end of a line

PLUMBAGO n plant of warm regions with clusters of blue, white, or red flowers

PLUMBATE n compound formed from lead oxide

PLUMBED ▸ plumb

PLUMBER, -S n person who fits and repairs pipes and fixtures for water and drainage systems

PLUMBERY same as ▸ plumbing

PLUMBIC adj of or containing lead in the tetravalent state

PLUMBING n pipes and fixtures used in water and drainage systems

PLUMBISM n chronic lead poisoning

PLUMBITE n substance containing lead oxide

PLUMBOUS adj of or containing lead in the divalent state

PLUMBS ▸ plumb

PLUMBUM, -S n obsolete name for lead (the metal)

PLUMCAKE n cake with raisins in it

PLUMCOT, -S n hybrid of apricot and plum

PLUME, -D, -S, PLUMING n feather, esp one worn as an ornament ▷ vb adorn or decorate with feathers or plumes

PLUMELET n small plume

P

PLUMERIA n tropical tree with candelabra-like branches

PLUMERY n plumes collectively

PLUMES ▶ plume

PLUMIER ▶ plumy

PLUMIEST ▶ plumy

PLUMING ▶ plume

PLUMIPED n bird with feathered feet

PLUMIST, -S n person who makes plumes

PLUMLIKE ▶ plum

PLUMMER ▶ plum

PLUMMEST ▶ plum

PLUMMET, -S vb plunge downward ▷ n weight on a plumb line or fishing line

PLUMMY, PLUMMIER adj of, full of, or like plums

PLUMOSE same as ▶ plumate

PLUMOUS adj having plumes or feathers

PLUMP, -ED, -EST, -ING, -S adj moderately or attractively fat ▷ vb sit or fall heavily and suddenly ▷ n heavy abrupt fall or the sound of this ▷ adv suddenly or heavily

PLUMPEN, -S vb make or become plump

PLUMPER, -S n pad carried in the mouth by actors to round out the cheeks

PLUMPEST ▶ plump

PLUMPIE same as ▶ plumpy

PLUMPIER ▶ plumpy

PLUMPING ▶ plump

PLUMPISH adj on the plump side

PLUMPLY ▶ plump

PLUMPS ▶ plump

PLUMPY, PLUMPIER adj plump

PLUMS ▶ plum

PLUMULA, -E n down feather

PLUMULAR ▶ plumule

PLUMULE, -S n embryonic shoot of seed-bearing plants

PLUMY, PLUMIER, PLUMIEST adj like a feather

PLUNDER, -S vb take by force, esp in time of war ▷ n things plundered, spoils

PLUNGE, -D, -S, PLUNGING vb put or throw forcibly or suddenly (into) ▷ n plunging dive

PLUNGER, -S n rubber suction cup used to clear blocked pipes

PLUNGES ▶ plunge

PLUNGING ▶ plunge

PLUNK, -ED, -ING, -S vb pluck the strings of (a banjo etc) to produce a twanging sound ▷ n act or sound of plunking ▷ interj exclamation imitative of the sound of something plunking ▷ adv exactly

PLUNKER, -S ▶ plunk

PLUNKIER ▶ plunky

PLUNKING ▶ plunk

PLUNKS ▶ plunk

PLUNKY, PLUNKIER adj sounding like plucked banjo string

PLUOT, -S n hybrid fruit of the plum and apricot

PLURAL, -S adj of or consisting of more than one ▷ n word indicating more than one

PLURALLY ▶ plural

PLURALS ▶ plural

PLURISIE same as ▶ pleurisy

PLURRY euphemism for ▶ bloody

PLUS, -ED, -ES, -ING, -SED, -SES, -SING vb make or become greater in value

PLUSAGE, -S same as ▶ plussage

PLUSED ▶ plus

PLUSES ▶ plus

PLUSH, -ER, -ES, -EST n fabric with long velvety pile ▷ adj luxurious

PLUSHED adj showily luxurious

PLUSHER ▶ plush

PLUSHES ▶ plush

PLUSHEST ▶ plush

PLUSHIER ▶ plushy

PLUSHILY ▶ plushy

PLUSHLY ▶ plush

PLUSHY, PLUSHIER same as ▶ plush

PLUSING ▶ plus

PLUSSAGE n amount over and above another amount

PLUSSED ▶ plus

PLUSSES ▶ plus

PLUSSING ▶ plus

PLUTEAL ▶ pluteus

PLUTEUS, PLUTEI n larva of sea urchin

PLUTO, -ED, -ES, -ING, -S vb reduce in importance

PLUTOID, -S n dwarf planet whose orbit is beyond Neptune's

PLUTOING ▶ pluto

PLUTON, -S n any mass of igneous rock that has solidified below the surface of the earth

PLUTONIC adj formed from molten rock that has solidified below the earth's surface

PLUTONS ▶ pluton

PLUTOS ▶ pluto

PLUVIAL, -S n period of high rainfall

PLUVIAN, -S n crocodile bird

PLUVIOSE same as ▶ pluvious

PLUVIOUS adj of or relating to rain

PLUVIUS adj as in pluvius insurance insurance against rain

PLY, PLIED, PLIES, -ING vb work at (a job or trade) ▷ n thickness of wool, fabric, etc

PLYER, -S n person who plies trade

PLYING ▶ ply

PLYINGLY ▶ ply

PLYWOOD, -S n board made of thin layers of wood glued together

PNEUMA, -S n person's vital spirit, soul, or creative energy

PO, -S n chamberpot

POA, -S n type of grass

POACEOUS adj relating to the plant family which comprises grasses

POACH, -ED, -ES, -ING vb catch (animals) illegally on someone else's land

POACHER, -S n person who catches animals illegally on someone else's land

POACHES ▶ poach

POACHIER ▶ poachy

POACHING ▶ poach

POACHY, POACHIER adj (of land) wet and soft

POAKA, -S n type of stilt (bird) native to New Zealand

POAKE, -S n waste matter from tanning of hides

POAS ▶ poa

POBLANO, -S n variety of chilli pepper

POBOY, -S n New Orleans sandwich

POCHARD, -S n European diving duck

POCHAY, -ED, -S n closed horse-drawn four-wheeled coach ▷ vb transport by pochay

POCHETTE n envelope-shaped handbag

POCHOIR, -S n print made from stencils

POCK, -ED, -ING, -S n pus-filled blister resulting

from smallpox ▷ vb mark
with scars

POCKARD, -S variant of
▶ pochard

POCKED ▶ pock

POCKET, -ED, -S n small bag
sewn into clothing for
carrying things ▷ vb put into
one's pocket ▷ adj small

POCKETER ▶ pocket

POCKETS ▶ pocket

POCKIER ▶ pocky

POCKIES pl n woollen mittens

POCKIEST ▶ pocky

POCKILY ▶ pock

POCKING ▶ pock

POCKMARK n pitted scar
left on the skin after the
healing of a smallpox or
similar pustule ▷ vb scar or
pit (a surface) with
pockmarks

POCKPIT, -S n mark left on
skin after a pock has gone

POCKS ▶ pock

**POCKY, POCKIER,
POCKIEST** ▶ pock

POCO adv little

POCOSEN, -S same as
▶ pocosin

POCOSIN, -S n swamp in US
upland coastal region

POCOSON, -S same as
▶ pocosin

POD, -DED, -DING, -S n long
narrow seed case of peas,
beans, etc ▷ vb remove the
pod from

PODAGRA, -S n gout of the
foot or big toe

PODAGRAL ▶ podagra

PODAGRAS ▶ podagra

PODAGRIC ▶ podagra

PODAL adj relating to feet

PODALIC adj relating to feet

PODARGUS n bird of SE Asia
and Australia

PODCAST, -S n audio file
able to be downloaded and
listened to on a computer or
MP3 player ▷ vb make
available in this format

PODDED ▶ pod

PODDIE n user of or
enthusiast for the iPod, a
portable digital music player

PODDIER ▶ poddy

PODDIES ▶ poddy

PODDIEST ▶ poddy

PODDING ▶ pod

PODDLE, -D, -S, PODDLING
vb move or travel in a
leisurely manner

**PODDY, PODDIER,
PODDIES, PODDIEST** n
handfed calf or lamb ▷ adj fat

PODESTA, -S n (in modern
Italy) subordinate
magistrate in some towns

PODEX, -ES n posterior

PODGE, -S n chubby person

PODGIER ▶ podgy

PODGIEST ▶ podgy

PODGILY ▶ podgy

**PODGY, PODGIER,
PODGIEST** adj chubby

PODIA ▶ podium

PODIAL ▶ podium

PODIATRY another word for
> chiropody

PODITE, -S n crustacean leg

PODITIC adj similar to the
limb segment of an
arthropod

PODIUM, PODIA, -ED, -S n
small raised platform for a
conductor or speaker ▷ vb
finish in the top three places
in a sporting competition

PODLEY, -S n young coalfish

PODLIKE ▶ pod

PODOCARP n stem
supporting fruit

PODOLOGY n study of feet

PODOMERE n segment of
limb of arthropod

PODS ▶ pod

PODSOL, -S same as
▶ podzol

PODSOLIC ▶ podzol

PODSOLS ▶ podsol

PODUNK, -S adj small or
unimportant ▷ n small or
unimportant thing

PODZOL, -S n type of soil
characteristic of coniferous
forest regions

PODZOLIC ▶ podzol

PODZOLS ▶ podzol

POECHORE n dry region

POEM, -S n imaginative
piece of writing in rhythmic
lines

POEMATIC adj of poetry

POEMS ▶ poem

POEP, -ED, -ING, -S n
emission of gas from the
anus ▷ vb break wind

**POESY, POESIED, POESIES,
-ING** n poetry ▷ vb write
poems

POET, -S n writer of poems

POETESS n female poet

POETIC adj of or like poetry

POETICAL adj poetic ▷ n
poet

POETICS n principles and
forms of poetry or the study
of these

POETISE, -D, -S same as
> poeticize

POETISER ▶ poetise

POETISES ▶ poetise

POETIZE, -D, -S same as
> poeticize

POETIZER ▶ poetize

POETIZES ▶ poetize

POETLESS ▶ poet

POETLIKE ▶ poet

POETRY, POETRIES n
poems

POETS ▶ poet

POETSHIP n state of being
poet

POFFLE, -S n small piece of
land

POGEY, -S n financial or
other relief given to the
unemployed by the
government

POGGE, -S n European
marine scorpaenoid fish

POGIES ▶ pogy

POGO, -ED, -ES, -ING, -S vb
jump up and down on one
spot

POGOER, -S ▶ pogo

POGOES ▶ pogo

POGOING ▶ pogo

POGONIA, -S n orchid with
pink or white fragrant
flowers

POGONIP, -S n icy winter fog

POGOS ▶ pogo

POGROM, -ED, -S n
organized persecution and
massacre ▷ vb carry out a
pogrom

POGY, POGIES same as
▶ pogey

POH, -ED, -ING, -S interj
exclamation expressing
contempt or disgust ▷ vb
reject contemptuously

POHIRI, -S variant spelling of
▶ powhiri

POHS ▶ poh

POI, -S n ball of woven flax
swung rhythmically by
Māori women during poi
dances

POIGNADO old variant of
▶ poniard

POIGNANT adj sharply
painful to the feelings

POILU, -S n infantryman in
the French Army

POINADO old variant of
▶ poniard

POIND, -ED, -ING, -S vb take
(property of a debtor) in
execution or by way of
distress

POINDER, -S ▶ point

POINDING ▶ poind

POINDS ▶ poind

POINT, -S n main idea in a
discussion ▷ vb show the

P

position of something by extending a finger towards it

POINTE, -S n tip of the toe

POINTED adj having a sharp end

POINTEL, -S n engraver's tool

POINTER, -S n helpful hint

POINTES ▸ pointe

POINTIER ▸ pointy

POINTING n insertion of mortar between the joints in brickwork

POINTMAN, POINTMEN n soldier who walks at the front of an infantry patrol in combat

POINTS ▸ point

POINTY, POINTIER adj having a sharp point or points

POIS ▸ poi

POISE, -S, POISING n calm dignified manner ▹ vb be balanced or suspended

POISED adj absolutely ready

POISER, -S n balancing organ of some insects

POISES ▸ poise

POISHA, -S n monetary unit of Bangladesh

POISING ▸ poise

POISON, -ED, -S n substance that kills or injures when swallowed or absorbed ▹ vb give poison to

POISONER ▸ poison

POISONS ▸ poison

POISSON, -S n fish

POITIN, -S variant spelling of ▸ poteen

POITREL, -S n breastplate of horse's armour

POITRINE n woman's bosom

POKABLE ▸ poke

POKAL, -S n tall drinking cup

POKE, -D, -S, POKING vb jab or prod with one's finger, a stick, etc ▹ n poking

POKEFUL, -S n contents of small bag

POKER, -S n metal rod for stirring a fire

POKERISH adj stiff like poker

POKEROOT same as ▸ pokeweed

POKERS ▸ poker

POKES ▸ poke

POKEWEED n plant with a poisonous root used medicinally

POKEY, -S same as ▸ pokie

POKIE n poker machine

POKIER ▸ poky

POKIES ▸ poky

POKIEST ▸ poky

POKILY ▸ poky

POKINESS ▸ poky

POKING ▸ poke

POKY, POKIER, POKIES, POKIEST adj small and cramped

POL, -S n political campaigner

POLACCA, -S same as ▸ polacre

POLACRE, -S n three-masted sailing vessel

POLAR, -S adj of or near either of the earth's poles ▹ n type of line in geometry

POLARISE same as ▸ polarize

POLARITY n state of having two directly opposite tendencies or opinions

POLARIZE vb form or cause to form into groups with directly opposite views

POLARON, -S n kind of electron

POLARS ▸ polar

POLDER, -ED, -S n land reclaimed from the sea, esp in the Netherlands ▹ vb reclaim land from the sea

POLE, -D, -S n long rounded piece of wood etc ▹ vb strike or push with a pole

POLEAX same as ▸ poleaxe

POLEAXE, -D, -S vb hit or stun with a heavy blow ▹ n axe formerly used in battle or used by a butcher

POLECAT, -S n small animal of the weasel family

POLED ▸ pole

POLEIS ▸ polis

POLELESS ▸ pole

POLEMIC n fierce attack on or defence of a particular opinion, belief, etc ▹ adj of or involving dispute or controversy

POLEMICS n art of dispute

POLEMISE same as ▸ polemize

POLEMIST ▸ polemic

POLEMIZE vb engage in controversy

POLENTA, -S n thick porridge made in Italy, usually from maize

POLER, -S n person or thing that poles, esp a punter

POLES ▸ pole

POLESTAR n guiding principle, rule, standard, etc

POLEWARD adv towards a pole

POLEY, -S adj (of cattle) hornless or polled ▹ n animal with horns removed

POLEYN, -S n piece of armour for protecting the knee

POLEYS ▸ poley

POLICE, -D, -S, POLICING n organized force in a state which keeps law and order ▹ vb control or watch over with police or a similar body

POLICER, -S n computer device controlling use

POLICES ▸ police

POLICIER n film featuring police investigating crimes

POLICIES ▸ policy

POLICING ▸ police

POLICY, POLICIES n plan of action adopted by a person, group, or state

POLIES ▸ poly

POLING, -S ▸ pole

POLIO, -S n acute viral disease

POLIS, POLEIS, -ES n ancient Greek city-state

POLISH, -ES vb make smooth and shiny by rubbing ▹ n substance used for polishing

POLISHED adj accomplished

POLISHER ▸ polish

POLISHES ▸ polish

POLITE, -R, -ST adj showing consideration for others in one's manners, speech, etc

POLITELY ▸ polite

POLITER ▸ polite

POLITEST ▸ polite

POLITIC adj wise and likely to prove advantageous

POLITICK vb engage in politics

POLITICO n politician

POLITICS n winning and using of power to govern society

POLITY, POLITIES n politically organized state, church, or society

POLJE, -S n large elliptical depression in karst regions

POLK, -ED, -ING, -S vb dance a polka

POLKA, -ED, -ING, -S n lively 19th-century dance ▹ vb dance a polka

POLKED ▸ polk

POLKING ▸ polk

POLKS ▸ polk

POLL, -S n questioning of a random sample of people to find out general opinion ▹ vb receive (votes)

POLLACK, -S n food fish related to the cod, found in northern seas**

POLLAN, -S *n* whitefish that occurs in lakes in Northern Ireland

POLLARD, -S *n* animal that has shed its horns or has had them removed ▷ *vb* cut off the top of (a tree) to make it grow bushy

POLLAXE, -D, -S *same as* ▶ **poleaxe**

POLLED *adj* (of animals, esp cattle) having the horns cut off or being naturally hornless

POLLEE, -S ▶ **poll**

POLLEN, -ED, -S *n* fine dust produced by flowers to fertilize other flowers ▷ *vb* collect pollen

POLLENT *adj* strong

POLLER, -S ▶ **poll**

POLLEX, POLLICES *n* first digit of the forelimb of amphibians, reptiles, birds, and mammals

POLLICAL ▶ **pollex**

POLLICES ▶ **pollex**

POLLICIE *obsolete spelling of* ▶ **policy**

POLLICY *obsolete spelling of* ▶ **policy**

POLLIES ▶ **polly**

POLLING, -S *n* casting or registering of votes at an election

POLLINIA > **pollinium**

POLLINIC ▶ **pollen**

POLLIST, -S *n* one advocating the use of polls

POLLIWIG *same as* ▶ **polliwog**

POLLIWOG *n* sailor who has not crossed the equator

POLLMAN, POLLMEN *n* one passing a degree without honours

POLLOCK, -S *same as* ▶ **pollack**

POLLS ▶ **poll**

POLLSTER *n* person who conducts opinion polls

POLLUTE, -S *vb* contaminate with something poisonous or harmful

POLLUTED *adj* made unclean or impure

POLLUTER ▶ **pollute**

POLLUTES ▶ **pollute**

POLLY, POLLIES *n* politician

POLLYWIG *same as* ▶ **polliwog**

POLLYWOG *same as* ▶ **polliwog**

POLO, -S *n* game like hockey played by teams of players on horseback

POLOIDAL *adj* relating to a type of magnetic field

POLOIST, -S *n* devotee of polo

POLONIE *same as* ▶ **polony**

POLONIES ▶ **polony**

POLONISE *same as* ▶ **polonize**

POLONISM ▶ **polonise**

POLONIUM *n* radioactive element that occurs in trace amounts in uranium ores

POLONIZE *vb* make Polish

POLONY, POLONIES *n* bologna sausage

POLOS ▶ **polo**

POLT, -ED, -ING, -S *n* thump or blow ▷ *vb* strike

POLTFOOT, POLTFEET *adj* having a club foot ▷ *n* club foot

POLTING ▶ **polt**

POLTROON *n* utter coward

POLTS ▶ **polt**

POLY, POLIES, -S *n* polytechnic

POLYACID *adj* having two or more hydroxyl groups ▷ *n* compound made up of two or more hydroxyl groups

POLYACT *adj* (of a sea creature) having many tentacles or limb-like protrusions

POLYADIC *adj* (of a relation, operation, etc) having several argument places

POLYARCH *n* member of polyarchy

POLYAXON *n* nerve cell with multiple branches

POLYBAG, -S *vb* put into a polythene bag

POLYBRID *n* hybrid plant with more than two parental groups

POLYCOT, -S *n* plant that has or appears to have more than two cotyledons

POLYDRUG *adj* relating to using several drugs together

POLYENE, -S *n* organic chemical compound

POLYENIC ▶ **polyene**

POLYGALA *n* herbaceous plant or small shrub

POLYGAM, -S *n* plant of the Polygamia class

POLYGAMY *n* practice of having more than one husband or wife at the same time

POLYGENE *n* any of a group of genes that each produce a small effect on a particular

characteristic of the phenotype

POLYGENY > **polygenic**

POLYGLOT *adj* able to speak or write several languages ▷ *n* person who can speak many languages

POLYGON, -S *n* geometrical figure with three or more angles and sides

POLYGONY ▶ **polygon**

POLYGYNE *adj* (of a colony of insects) having more than one egg-laying queen

POLYGYNY *n* practice of having more than one female partner at the same time

POLYMATH *n* person of great and varied learning

POLYMER, -S *n* chemical compound with large molecules made of simple molecules of the same kind

POLYMERY ▶ **polymer**

POLYNYA, -S *same as* ▶ **polynya**

POLYNYA, -S, POLYNYI *n* stretch of open water surrounded by ice

POLYOL, -S *n* type of alcohol

POLYOMA, -S *n* type of tumour caused by virus

POLYONYM *n* object with many names

POLYP, -S *n* small simple sea creature with a hollow cylindrical body

POLYPARY *n* common base and connecting tissue of a colony of coelenterate polyps, esp coral

POLYPE, -S *variant of* ▶ **polyp**

POLYPED, -S *same as* ▶ **polypod**

POLYPES ▶ **polype**

POLYPHON *n* musical instrument resembling a lute

POLYPI ▶ **polypus**

POLYPIDE *n* polyp forming part of a colonial animal

POLYPILL *n* pill containing a number of medicines that all treat the same condition

POLYPINE *adj* of or relating to polyps

POLYPITE *same as* ▶ **polypide**

POLYPNEA *n* rapid breathing

POLYPOD, -S *adj* (esp of insect larvae) having many legs or similar appendages ▷ *n* animal of this type

P

POLYPODY n fern with deeply divided leaves and round naked sori

POLYPOID ▸ polyp

POLYPORE n type of fungi

POLYPOUS ▸ polyp

POLYPS ▸ polyp

POLYPUS, POLYPI same as ▸ polyp

POLYS ▸ poly

POLYSEME n word with many meanings

POLYSEMY n existence of several meanings in a single word

POLYSOME n assemblage of ribosomes associated with a messenger RNA molecule

POLYSOMY ▸ polysome

POLYTENE adj denoting a type of giant-size chromosome

POLYTENY ▸ polytene

POLYTYPE n crystal occurring in more than one form ▷ vb produce by use of a polytype

POLYURIA n state of discharging abnormally large quantities of urine

POLYURIC ▸ polyuria

POLYZOA n small mosslike aquatic creatures

POLYZOAN another word for ▸ bryozoan

POLYZOIC adj (of certain colonial animals) having many zooids or similar polyps

POLYZOON n individual zooid within polyzoan

POM, -S same as ▸ pommy

POMACE, -S n apple pulp left after pressing for juice

POMADE, -D, -S, POMADING n perfumed oil put on the hair to make it smooth and shiny ▷ vb put pomade on

POMANDER n mixture of sweet-smelling petals, herbs, etc

POMATO, -ES n hybrid of tomato and potato

POMATUM, -S n pomade ▷ vb put pomatum on

POMBE, -S n any alcoholic drink

POME, -S n fleshy fruit of the apple and related plants

POMELIKE adj like a pome

POMELO, -S n edible yellow fruit, like a grapefruit

POMEROY, -S n bullet used to down airships

POMES ▸ pome

POMFRET, -S n small black rounded liquorice sweet

POMMEE adj (of cross) having end of each arm ending in disk

POMMEL, -ED, -S same as ▸ pummel

POMMELE adj having a pommel

POMMELED ▸ pommel

POMMELS ▸ pommel

POMMETTY adj having a pommel

POMMIE same as ▸ pommy

POMMY, POMMIES n word used by Australians and New Zealanders for a British person

POMO, -S n postmodernist

POMOLOGY n branch of horticulture that is concerned with the study and cultivation of fruit

POMOS ▸ pomo

POMP, -S n stately display or ceremony

POMPANO, -S n deep-bodied carangid food fish

POMPELO, -S n large Asian citrus fruit

POMPEY, -ED, -S vb mollycoddle

POMPIER, -S adj slavishly conventional ▷ n conventional or imitative artist

POMPILID n spider-hunting wasp

POMPION, -S n pumpkin

POMPOM, -S n decorative ball of tufted wool, silk, etc

POMPON, -S same as ▸ pompom

POMPOON, -S variant of ▸ pompom

POMPOSO adj (of music) to be played in a ceremonial manner

POMPOUS adj foolishly serious and grand, self-important

POMPS ▸ pomp

POMROY, -S variant of ▸ pomeroy

POMS ▸ pom

POMWATER n kind of apple

PONCE, -D, -S, PONCING vb act stupidly or waste time

PONCEAU, -S, -X n scarlet red

PONCED ▸ ponce

PONCES ▸ ponce

PONCEY, PONCIER, PONCIEST adj ostentatious or pretentious

PONCHO, -S n loose circular cloak with a hole for the head

PONCHOED adj wearing poncho

PONCHOS ▸ poncho

PONCIER ▸ poncey

PONCIEST ▸ poncey

PONCING ▸ ponce

PONCY same as ▸ poncey

POND, -ED, -ING, -S n small area of still water ▷ vb hold back (flowing water)

PONDAGE, -S n water held in reservoir

PONDED ▸ pond

PONDER, -ED, -S vb think thoroughly or deeply (about)

PONDERAL adj relating to weight

PONDERED ▸ ponder

PONDERER ▸ ponder

PONDERS ▸ ponder

PONDING ▸ pond

PONDOK, -S n (in southern Africa) crudely made house or shack

PONDS ▸ pond

PONDWEED n plant that grows in ponds

PONE, -S n bread made of maize

PONENT, -S adj westerly ▷ n the west

PONES ▸ pone

PONEY, -S same as ▸ pony

PONG, -ED, -ING, -S n strong unpleasant smell ▷ vb give off a strong unpleasant smell

PONGA, -S n tall New Zealand tree fern

PONGAL, -S n Indian dish of cooked rice

PONGAS ▸ ponga

PONGED ▸ pong

PONGEE, -S n thin plain-weave silk fabric

PONGID, -S n primate of the family which includes the gibbons and the great apes

PONGIER ▸ pongy

PONGIEST ▸ pongy

PONGING ▸ pong

PONGO, -ES, -S n anthropoid ape, esp an orang-utan or (formerly) a gorilla

PONGS ▸ pong

PONGY, PONGIER, PONGIEST ▸ pong

PONIARD, -S n small slender dagger ▷ vb stab with a poniard

PONIED ▸ pony

PONIES ▸ pony

PONK, -ED, -ING, -S n evil spirit ▷ vb stink

PONS, PONTES n bridge of connecting tissue

PONT, -S n (in South Africa) river ferry

PONTAGE, -S n tax paid for repairing bridge

PONTAL adj of or relating to the pons

PONTES ▸ pons

PONTIC adj of or relating to the pons

PONTIE same as ▸ ponty

PONTIES ▸ ponty

PONTIFEX n (in ancient Rome) any of the senior members of the Pontifical College

PONTIFF, -S n Pope

PONTIFIC ▸ pontiff

PONTIFY vb speak or behave in a pompous or dogmatic manner

PONTIL, -S same as ▸ punty

PONTILE, -S adj relating to pons ▷ n metal bar used in glass-making

PONTILS ▸ pontil

PONTINE adj of or relating to bridges

PONTON, -S variant of ▸ pontoon

PONTOON, -S n floating platform supporting a temporary bridge ▷ vb cross a river using pontoons

PONTS ▸ pont

PONTY, PONTIES n rod used for shaping molten glass

PONY, PONIED, PONIES, -ING n small horse ▷ vb settle bill or debt

PONYSKIN n leather from pony hide

PONYTAIL n long hair tied in one bunch at the back of the head

PONZU, -S n type of Japanese dipping sauce

POO, -ED, -ING, -S vb defecate

POOBAH, -S n influential person

POOCH, -ED, -ES, -ING n slang word for dog ▷ vb bulge or protrude

POOD, -S n unit of weight, used in Russia

POODLE, -S n dog with curly hair often clipped fancifully

POODS ▸ pood

POOED ▸ poo

POOGYE, -S n Hindu nose-flute

POOH, -ED, -ING, -S interj exclamation of disdain, contempt, or disgust ▷ vb make such an exclamation

POOING ▸ poo

POOJA, -S variant of ▸ puja

POOJAH, -S variant of ▸ puja

POOJAS ▸ pooja

POOK, -ING, -IT, -S vb pluck

POOKA, -S n malevolent Irish spirit

POOKING ▸ pook

POOKIT ▸ pook

POOKS ▸ pook

POOL, -ED, -ING n small body of still water ▷ vb put in a common fund

POOLER, -S n person taking part in pool

POOLHALL n room containing pool tables

POOLING ▸ pool

POOLROOM n hall or establishment where pool, billiards, etc, are played

POOLS pl n organized nationwide gambling pool

POOLSIDE n area surrounding swimming pool

POON, -S n SE Asian tree

POONAC, -S n coconut residue

POONCE, -D, -S, POONCING vb act stupidly or waste time

POONS ▸ poon

POOP, -ED, -ING, -S n raised part at the back of a sailing ship ▷ vb (of a wave or sea) break over the stern of (a vessel)

POOPER, -S n as in **party pooper** person who spoils other people's enjoyment

POOPIER ▸ poopy

POOPIEST ▸ poopy

POOPING ▸ poop

POOPS ▸ poop

POOPY, POOPIER, POOPIEST adj stupid or ineffectual

POOR, -ER, -EST adj having little money and few possessions

POORBOX n box used for the collection of money for the poor

POORER ▸ poor

POOREST ▸ poor

POORI, -S n unleavened Indian bread

POORISH ▸ poor

POORLY, POORLIER adv in a poor manner ▷ adj not in good health

POORNESS ▸ poor

POORT, -S n (in South Africa) steep narrow mountain pass

POORTITH same as ▸ puirtith

POORTS ▸ poort

POORWILL n bird of N America

POOS ▸ poo

POOT, -ED, -ERS, -ING, -S vb break wind

POOTER, -ED vb hurry away

POOTERS ▸ poot

POOTING ▸ poot

POOTLE, -D, -S, POOTLING vb travel or go in a relaxed or leisurely manner

POOTS ▸ poot

POP, -PED, -PING, -S vb make or cause to make a small explosive sound ▷ n small explosive sound ▷ adj popular

POPADUM, -S same as ▸ poppadom

POPCORN, -S n grains of maize heated until they puff up and burst

POPE, -S n bishop of Rome as head of the Roman Catholic Church

POPEDOM, -S n office or dignity of a pope

POPEHOOD ▸ pope

POPELESS ▸ pope

POPELIKE ▸ pope

POPERA, -S n pop music drawing on opera or classical music

POPERIN, -S n kind of pear

POPES ▸ pope

POPESEYE adj denoting a cut of steak

POPESHIP ▸ pope

POPETTE, -S n young female fan or performer of pop music

POPEYED adj staring in astonishment

POPGUN, -S n toy gun that fires a pellet or cork by means of compressed air

POPINAC, -S n type of thorny shrub

POPINACK same as ▸ popinac

POPINACS ▸ popinac

POPINJAY n conceited, foppish, or overly talkative person

POPJOY, -ED, -S vb amuse oneself

POPLAR, -S n tall slender tree

POPLIN, -S n ribbed cotton material

POPLITEI > popliteus

P

POPLITIC same as
> **popliteal**
POPOUT, -S n type of out in baseball
POPOVER, -S n individual Yorkshire pudding, often served with roast beef
POPPA, -S same as ▸ **papa**
POPPADOM n thin round crisp Indian bread
POPPADUM same as
▸ **poppadom**
POPPAS ▸ **poppa**
POPPED ▸ **pop**
POPPER, -S n press stud
POPPET, -S n term of affection for a small child or sweetheart
POPPIED adj covered with poppies
POPPIER ▸ **poppy**
POPPIES ▸ **poppy**
POPPIEST ▸ **poppy**
POPPING ▸ **pop**
POPPISH adj like pop music
POPPIT, -S n bead used to form necklace
POPPLE, -D, -S, POPPLING vb (of boiling water or a choppy sea) to heave or toss
POPPLIER ▸ **popply**
POPPLING ▸ **popple**
POPPLY, POPPLIER adj covered in small bumps
POPPY, POPPIER, POPPIES, POPPIEST n plant with a large red flower ▸ adj reddish-orange
POPRIN same as ▸ **poperin**
POPS ▸ **pop**
POPSICLE n tradename for a kind of ice lolly
POPSIE same as ▸ **popsy**
POPSIES ▸ **popsy**
POPSOCK, -S n women's knee-length nylon stocking
POPSTER, -S n pop star
POPSTREL n young, attractive female pop star
POPSY, POPSIES n attractive young woman
POPULACE n ordinary people
POPULAR, -S adj widely liked and admired ▸ n cheap newspapers with mass circulation
POPULATE vb live in, inhabit
POPULISM n political strategy based on an appeal to the prejudices of ordinary people
POPULIST adj appealing to the interests or prejudices of ordinary people ▸ n person who appeals to the interests

or prejudices of ordinary people
POPULOUS adj densely populated
PORAE, -S n large edible sea fish of New Zealand waters
PORAL adj relating to pores
PORANGI adj crazy
PORCH, -ES n covered approach to the entrance of a building
PORCHED adj having a porch
PORCHES ▸ **porch**
PORCINE adj of or like a pig
PORCINO, PORCINI n edible woodland fungus
PORE, -D, -S, PORING n tiny opening in the skin or in the surface of a plant ▸ vb make a close intent examination or study
PORER, -S n person who pores
PORES ▸ **pore**
PORGE, -D, -S, PORGING vb cleanse (slaughtered animal) ceremonially
PORGIE same as ▸ **porgy**
PORGIES ▸ **porgy**
PORGING ▸ **porge**
PORGY, PORGIES n any of various sparid fishes
PORIER ▸ **pory**
PORIEST ▸ **pory**
PORIFER, -S n type of invertebrate
PORIN, -S n protein through which molecules can pass
PORINA, -S n moth the larva of which causes damage to grassland
PORINESS ▸ **pory**
PORING ▸ **pore**
PORINS ▸ **porin**
PORISM, -S n type of mathematical proposition
PORISTIC ▸ **porism**
PORK, -ED, -ING, -S vb eat ravenously ▸ n the flesh of pigs used as food
PORKER, -S n pig raised for food
PORKIER ▸ **porky**
PORKIES ▸ **porky**
PORKIEST ▸ **porky**
PORKING ▸ **pork**
PORKLING n pig
PORKPIE, -S n hat with a round flat crown and a brim that can be turned up or down
PORKS ▸ **pork**
PORKWOOD n wood of small American tree

PORKY, PORKIER, PORKIES, PORKIEST adj of or like pork ▸ n lie
PORLOCK, -S vb interrupt or intrude at an awkward moment
POROGAMY n fertilization of seed plants
POROSE adj pierced with small pores
POROSIS, POROSES n porous condition of bones
POROSITY n state or condition of being porous
POROUS adj allowing liquid to pass through gradually
POROUSLY ▸ **porous**
PORPESS n type of fish
PORPESSE same as
▸ **porpoise**
PORPHYRY n reddish rock with large crystals in it
PORPOISE n fishlike sea mammal ▸ vb (of an aeroplane) nose-dive during landing
PORRECT, -S adj extended forwards ▸ vb stretch forward
PORRIDGE n breakfast food made of oatmeal cooked in water or milk
PORRIDGY adj having the consistency of porridge
PORRIGO, -S n disease of the scalp
PORT, -ED, -ING, -S vb turn (a boat) towards its left side
PORTA, -S n aperture in an organ
PORTABLE adj easily carried ▸ n article designed to be easily carried, such as a television or typewriter
PORTABLY ▸ **portable**
PORTAGE, -D, -S n (route for) transporting boats overland ▸ vb transport (boats) in this way
PORTAGUE n former Portuguese gold coin
PORTAL, -S n large imposing doorway or gate
PORTALED ▸ **portal**
PORTALS ▸ **portal**
PORTANCE n person's bearing
PORTAPAK same as
> **portapack**
PORTAS ▸ **porta**
PORTASES variant of
▸ **portesse**
PORTATE adj diagonally athwart escutcheon
PORTED ▸ **port**
PORTEND, -S vb be a sign of

PORTENT, -S n sign of a future event

PORTEOUS variant of ▸portesse

PORTER, -ED, -S n person who carries luggage ▷ vb carry luggage

PORTERLY adj like a porter

PORTERS ▸ porter

PORTESS variant of ▸portesse

PORTESSE n prayer book

PORTFIRE n slow-burning fuse formerly used in fireworks

PORTHOLE n small round window in a ship or aircraft

PORTHORS same as ▸portesse

PORTHOS same as ▸portesse

PORTICO, -S n porch or covered walkway with columns supporting the roof

PORTIER ▸ porty

PORTIERE n curtain hung in a doorway

PORTIEST ▸ porty

PORTIGUE same as ▸portague

PORTING ▸ port

PORTION, -S n part or share ▷ vb divide (something) into shares

PORTLAND n type of rose

PORTLAST n gunwale of ship

PORTLESS ▸ port

PORTLY, PORTLIER adj rather fat

PORTMAN, PORTMEN n inhabitant of a port

PORTOISE same as ▸portlast

PORTOLAN n book of sailing charts

PORTOUS variant of ▸portesse

PORTRAIT n picture of a person ▷ adj (of a publication or an illustration in a publication) of greater height than width

PORTRAY, -S vb describe or represent by artistic means, as in writing or film

PORTRESS n female porter, esp a doorkeeper

PORTS ▸ port

PORTSIDE adj beside port

PORTULAN same as ▸portolan

PORTY, PORTIER, PORTIEST adj like port

PORY, PORIER, PORIEST adj containing pores

POS ▸ po

POSABLE ▸ pose

POSADA, -S n inn in a Spanish-speaking country

POSAUNE, -S n organ chorus reed

POSE, -D, -S vb place in or take up a particular position to be photographed or drawn ▷ n position while posing

POSEABLE adj able to be manipulated into poses

POSED ▸ pose

POSER, -S n puzzling question

POSERISH same as ▸ posey

POSERS ▸ poser

POSES ▸ pose

POSEUR, -S n person who behaves in an affected way to impress others

POSEUSE, -S n female poseur

POSEY adj (of a place) for, characteristic of, or full of posers

POSH, -ED, -ER, -ES, -EST, -ING adj smart, luxurious ▷ adv in a manner associated with the upper class ▷ vb make posh

POSHLY ▸ posh

POSHNESS ▸ posh

POSHO, -S n corn meal

POSHTEEN same as ▸ posteen

POSIER ▸ posy

POSIES ▸ posy

POSIEST ▸ posy

POSING, -S ▸ pose

POSINGLY ▸ pose

POSINGS ▸ posing

POSIT, -ED, -ING, -S vb lay down as a basis for argument ▷ n fact, idea, etc, that is posited

POSITIF, -S n (on older organs) manual controlling soft stops

POSITING ▸ posit

POSITION n place ▷ vb place

POSITIVE same as ▸ plus

POSITON, -S n part of chromosome

POSITRON n particle with same mass as electron but positive charge

POSITS ▸ posit

POSNET, -S n small basin or dish

POSOLE, -S n Central American stew

POSOLOGY n branch of medicine concerned with appropriate doses of drugs

POSS, -ED, -ING vb wash (clothes) by agitating them with a long rod, pole, etc

POSSE, -S n group of people organized to maintain law and order

POSSED ▸ poss

POSSER, -S n short stick used for stirring clothes in a washtub

POSSES ▸ posse

POSSESS vb have as one's property

POSSET, -ED, -S n drink of hot milk curdled with ale, beer, etc, flavoured with spices ▷ vb treat with a posset

POSSIBLE adj able to exist, happen, or be done ▷ n person or thing that might be suitable or chosen

POSSIBLY adv perhaps, not necessarily

POSSIE, -S n place

POSSING ▸ poss

POSSUM, -ED, -S vb pretend to be dead, asleep, ignorant, etc

POST, -ED, -S n official system of delivering letters and parcels ▷ vb send by post

POSTAGE, -S n charge for sending a letter or parcel by post

POSTAL, -S adj of a Post Office or the mail-delivery service ▷ n postcard

POSTALLY ▸ postal

POSTALS ▸ postal

POSTANAL adj behind the anus

POSTBAG, -S n postperson's bag

POSTBASE n morpheme used as a suffix on a root word

POSTBOX n box into which mail is put for collection by the postal service

POSTBOY, -S n man or boy who brings the post round to offices

POSTBURN adj after injury from burns

POSTBUS n vehicle carrying the mail that also carries passengers

POSTCARD n card for sending a message by post without an envelope

POSTCAVA n inferior vena cava

POSTCODE n system of letters and numbers used to

P

aid the sorting of mail ▷ *vb* put a postcode on a letter

POSTCOUP *adj* after a coup

POSTDATE *vb* write a date on (a cheque) that is later than the actual date

POSTDIVE *adj* following a dive

POSTDOC, -S *n* postdoctoral degree

POSTDRUG *adj* of time after drug has been taken

POSTED ▷ **post**

POSTEEN, -S *n* Afghan leather jacket

POSTER, -ED, -S *n* large picture or notice stuck on a wall ▷ *vb* cover with posters

POSTERN, -S *n* small back door or gate ▷ *adj* situated at the rear or the side

POSTERS ▷ **poster**

POSTFACE *n* note added to the end of a text

POSTFACT *adj* relating to a culture in which appeals to the emotions prevail over facts

POSTFIRE *adj* of the period after a fire

POSTFIX *vb* add or append at the end of something

POSTFORM *vb* mould or shape (plastic) while it hot from reheating

POSTGAME *adj* of period after sports match

POSTGRAD *n* graduate taking further degree

POSTHEAT *n* industrial heating process ▷ *vb* heat a material after welding to relieve stresses

POSTHOLE *n* hole dug in ground to hold fence post

POSTICAL *adj* (of the position of plant parts) behind another part

POSTICHE *adj* (of architectural ornament) inappropriately applied ▷ *n* imitation, counterfeit, or substitute

POSTIE, -S *n* postman or postwoman

POSTIL, -ED, -S *n* commentary or marginal note, as in a Bible ▷ *vb* annotate (a biblical passage)

POSTIN, -S *variant of* ▷ **posteen**

POSTING, -S *n* job to which someone is assigned

POSTINS ▷ **postin**

POSTIQUE *variant of* ▷ **postiche**

POSTLIKE *adj* like a post

POSTLUDE *n* final or concluding piece or movement

POSTMAN, POSTMEN *n* man who collects and delivers post

POSTMARK *n* official mark stamped on letters showing place and date of posting ▷ *vb* put such a mark on (mail)

POSTMEN ▷ **postman**

POSTNATI *pl n* those born in Scotland after its union with England

POSTOP, -S *n* person recovering from surgery

POSTORAL *adj* situated at the back of the mouth

POSTPAID *adj* with the postage prepaid

POSTPONE *vb* put off to a later time

POSTPOSE *vb* place (word or phrase) after other constituents in sentence

POSTPUNK *adj* (of pop music) belonging to a style that followed punk rock ▷ *n* musician of the musical trend after punk

POSTRACE *adj* of the period after a race

POSTRIOT *adj* of the period after a riot

POSTS ▷ **post**

POSTSHOW *adj* of the period after a show

POSTSYNC *vb* add a sound recording to (and synchronize with) an existing video or film recording

POSTTAX *adj* of the period after tax is being

POSTTEEN *n* young adult

POSTTEST *n* test taken after a lesson

POSTURAL ▷ **posture**

POSTURE, -D, -S *n* position or way in which someone stands, walks, etc ▷ *vb* behave in an exaggerated way to get attention

POSTURER ▷ **posture**

POSTURES ▷ **posture**

POSTWAR *adj* occurring or existing after a war

POSY, POSIER, POSIES, POSIEST *n* small bunch of flowers

POT, -S, -TED, -TING *n* round deep container ▷ *vb* plant in a pot

POTABLE, -S *adj* drinkable ▷ *n* something fit to drink

POTAE, -S *n* hat

POTAGE, -S *n* thick soup

POTAGER, -S *n* small kitchen garden

POTAGES ▷ **potage**

POTALE, -S *n* residue from a grain distillery, used as animal feed

POTAMIC *adj* of or relating to rivers

POTASH, -ED, -ES *n* white powdery substance obtained from ashes and used as fertilizer ▷ *vb* treat with potash

POTASS, -ES *abbreviated form of* ▷ **potassium**

POTASSA, -S *n* potassium oxide

POTASSES ▷ **potass**

POTASSIC ▷ **potassium**

POTATION *n* act of drinking

POTATO, -ES *n* roundish starchy vegetable that grows underground

POTATORY *adj* of, relating to, or given to drinking

POTBELLY *n* bulging belly

POTBOIL, -S *vb* boil in a pot

POTBOUND *adj* (of plant) unable to grow because pot is too small

POTBOY, -S *n* (esp formerly) youth or man employed at a public house to serve beer, etc

POTCH, -ES *n* inferior quality opal used in jewellery for mounting precious opals

POTCHE, -D, POTCHING *vb* stab

POTCHER, -S ▷ **potche**

POTCHES ▷ **potch**

POTCHING ▷ **potche**

POTE, -D, -S, POTING *vb* push

POTEEN, -S *n* (in Ireland) illegally made alcoholic drink

POTENCE, -S *same as* ▷ **potency**

POTENCY *n* state or quality of being potent

POTENT *adj* having great power or influence ▷ *n* potentate or ruler

POTENTLY ▷ **potent**

POTENTS ▷ **potent**

POTES ▷ **pote**

POTFUL, -S *n* amount held by a pot

POTGUN, -S *n* pot-shaped mortar

POTHEEN, -S *n* rare variant of ▷ **poteen**

POTHER, -ED, -S *n* fuss or commotion ▷ *vb* make or be troubled or upset

POTHERB, -S n plant whose leaves, flowers, or stems are used in cooking
POTHERED ▸ pother
POTHERS ▸ pother
POTHERY adj stuffy
POTHOLE, -D, -S n hole in the surface of a road
POTHOLER > potholing
POTHOLES ▸ pothole
POTHOOK, -S n S-shaped hook for suspending a pot over a fire
POTHOS, -ES n climbing plant
POTHOUSE n (formerly) small tavern or pub
POTICARY obsolete spelling of > pothecary
POTICHE, -S n tall vase or jar that narrows towards the neck
POTIN, -S n bronze alloy with high tin content
POTING ▸ pote
POTINS ▸ potin
POTION, -S n dose of medicine or poison
POTJIE, -S n three-legged iron pot used for cooking
POTLACH same as ▸ potlatch
POTLACHE same as ▸ potlatch
POTLATCH n competitive ceremonial activity among certain Native American tribes
POTLIKE ▸ pot
POTLINE, -S n row of electrolytic cells for reducing metals
POTLUCK, -S n whatever food happens to be available without special preparation
POTMAN, POTMEN same as ▸ potboy
POTOO, -S n nocturnal tropical bird
POTOROO, -S n Australian leaping rodent
POTPIE, -S n meat and vegetable stew with a pie crust on top
POTS ▸ pot
POTSHARD same as ▸ potsherd
POTSHARE same as ▸ potsherd
POTSHERD n broken fragment of pottery
POTSHOP, -S n public house
POTSHOT, -S n shot taken without careful aim
POTSIE same as ▸ potsy
POTSIES ▸ potsy

POTSTONE n impure massive variety of soapstone, formerly used for making cooking vessels
POTSY, POTSIES n hopscotch
POTT, -S old variant of ▸ pot
POTTABLE adj (esp of a snooker ball) easily potted
POTTAGE, -S n thick soup or stew
POTTED ▸ pot
POTTEEN, -S same as ▸ poteen
POTTER, -ED, -S same as ▸ putter
POTTERER ▸ potter
POTTERS ▸ potter
POTTERY n articles made from baked clay
POTTIER ▸ potty
POTTIES ▸ potty
POTTIEST ▸ potty
POTTING ▸ pot
POTTLE, -S n liquid measure equal to half a gallon
POTTO, -S n short-tailed prosimian primate
POTTS ▸ pott
POTTY, POTTIER, POTTIES, POTTIEST adj silly or eccentric ▷ n bowl used by a small child as a toilet
POTZER, -S same as ▸ patzer
POUCH, -ED, -ES, -ING n small bag ▷ vb place in or as if in a pouch
POUCHFUL n amount a pouch will hold
POUCHIER ▸ pouchy
POUCHING ▸ pouch
POUCHY, POUCHIER ▸ pouch
POUDER, -S obsolete spelling of ▸ powder
POUDRE, -S old spelling of ▸ powder
POUF, -ED, -ING, -S n large solid cushion used as a seat ▷ vb pile up hair into rolled puffs
POUFF, -S same as ▸ pouf
POUFFE, -D, -S, POUFFING same as ▸ pouf
POUFFIER ▸ pouffy
POUFFING ▸ pouffe
POUFFS ▸ pouff
POUFFY, POUFFIER adj (of hair) puffed out
POUFING ▸ pouf
POUFS ▸ pouf
POUK, -ING, -S Scots variant of ▸ poke
POUKE, -S n mischievous spirit
POUKING ▸ pouk
POUKIT ▸ pouk

POUKS ▸ pouk
POULAINE n tapering toe of shoe
POULARD, -S n hen that has been spayed for fattening
POULARDE same as ▸ poulard
POULARDS ▸ poulard
POULDER, -S obsolete spelling of ▸ powder
POULDRE, -S archaic spelling of ▸ powder
POULDRON same as ▸ pauldron
POULE, -S n fowl suitable for slow stewing
POULP, -S n octopus
POULPE, -S variant of ▸ poulp
POULPS ▸ poulp
POULT, -S n young of a gallinaceous bird
POULTER, -S n poultry dealer
POULTICE n moist dressing, often heated, applied to inflamed skin ▷ vb apply poultice to
POULTRY n domestic fowls
POULTS ▸ poult
POUNCE, -D, -S, POUNCING vb spring upon suddenly to attack or capture ▷ n pouncing
POUNCER, -S ▸ pounce
POUNCES ▸ pounce
POUNCET, -S n box with a perforated top used for perfume
POUNCING ▸ pounce
POUND, -ED, -ING, -S n monetary unit of Britain and some other countries ▷ vb hit heavily and repeatedly
POUNDAGE n charge of so much per pound of weight or sterling
POUNDAL, -S n fps unit of force
POUNDED ▸ pound
POUNDER, -S ▸ pound
POUNDING ▸ pound
POUNDS ▸ pound
POUPE, -D, -S, POUPING, POUPT vb make sudden blowing sound
POUR, -ED, -S vb flow or cause to flow out in a stream
POURABLE ▸ pour
POURED ▸ pour
POURER, -S ▸ pour
POURIE, -S n jug
POURING, -S ▸ pour
POURS ▸ pour
POURSEW, -S obsolete spelling of ▸ pursue

P

POURSUE, -D, -S obsolete spelling of ▸ **pursue**

POURSUIT same as ▸ **pursuit**

POURTRAY obsolete spelling of ▸ **portray**

POUSADA, -S n traditional Portuguese hotel

POUSSE, -S same as ▸ **pease**

POUSSIE, -S old variant of ▸ **pussy**

POUSSIN, -S n young chicken reared for eating

POUT, -ED, -S vb thrust out one's lips, look sulky ▹ n pouting look

POUTER, -S n pigeon that can puff out its crop

POUTFUL adj tending to pout

POUTHER, -S Scots variant of ▸ **powder**

POUTIER ▸ **pouty**

POUTIEST ▸ **pouty**

POUTINE, -S n dish of chipped potatoes topped with cheese and sauce

POUTING, -S ▸ **pout**

POUTS ▸ **pout**

POUTY, POUTIER, POUTIEST ▸ **pout**

POVERTY n state of being without enough food or money

POW, -S interj exclamation to indicate that a collision or explosion has taken place ▹ n head or a head of hair

POWAN, -S n type of freshwater whitefish occurring in some Scottish lakes

POWDER, -ED, -S n substance in the form of tiny loose particles ▹ vb apply powder to

POWDERER ▸ **powder**

POWDERS ▸ **powder**

POWDERY ▸ **powder**

POWER, -ED, -ING, -S n ability to do or act ▹ vb give or provide power to

POWERFUL adj having great power or influence ▹ adv extremely

POWERING ▸ **power**

POWERS ▸ **power**

POWHIRI, -S n Māori ceremony of welcome, esp to a marae

POWIN, -S n peacock

POWN, -S variant of ▸ **powin**

POWND, -ED, -ING, -S obsolete spelling of ▸ **pound**

POWNEY, -S old Scots spelling of ▸ **pony**

POWNIE, -S old Scots spelling of ▸ **pony**

POWNS ▸ **pown**

POWNY old Scots spelling of ▸ **pony**

POWRE, -D, -S, POWRING obsolete spelling of ▸ **power**

POWS ▸ **pow**

POWSOWDY same as > **pousowdie**

POWTER, -ED, -S vb scrabble about

POWWAW interj expression of disbelief or contempt

POWWOW, -ED, -S n talk or conference ▹ vb hold a powwow

POX, -ED, -ES, -ING n disease in which skin pustules form ▹ vb infect with pox

POXIER ▸ **poxy**

POXIEST ▸ **poxy**

POXING ▸ **pox**

POXVIRUS n virus such as smallpox

POXY, POXIER, POXIEST adj of poor quality; rotten

POYNANT old variant of ▸ **poignant**

POYNT, -ED, -ING, -S obsolete spelling of ▸ **point**

POYOU, -S n type of armadillo

POYSE, -D, -S, POYSING obsolete variant of ▸ **poise**

POYSON, -ED, -S obsolete spelling of ▸ **poison**

POZ adj positive

Poz is an old-fashioned short form of **positive**, and one of the most frequently played short Z words.

POZOLE, -S same as ▸ **posole**

POZZ adj positive

POZZIES ▸ **pozzy**

POZZOLAN same as > **pozzolana**

POZZY, POZZIES same as ▸ **possie**

PRAAM, -S same as ▸ **pram**

PRABBLE, -S variant of ▸ **brabble**

PRACTIC, -S adj practical ▹ n practice ▹ vb put (a theory) into practice

PRACTICE same as ▸ **practise**

PRACTICK obsolete word for ▸ **practice**

PRACTICS ▸ **practic**

PRACTISE vb do repeatedly so as to gain skill

PRACTIVE obsolete word for ▸ **active**

PRAD, -S n horse

PRADHAN, -S n (in India) chief or leader

PRADS ▸ **prad**

PRAECIPE n written request addressed to court

PRAEDIAL adj of or relating to land, farming, etc ▹ n slave attached to a farm

PRAEFECT same as ▸ **prefect**

PRAELECT same as ▸ **prelect**

PRAESES n Roman governor

PRAETOR, -S n (in ancient Rome) senior magistrate ranking just below the consuls

PRAHU, -S same as ▸ **proa**

PRAIRIE, -S n large treeless area of grassland

PRAIRIED ▸ **prairie**

PRAIRIES ▸ **prairie**

PRAISE, -D, -S, PRAISING vb express approval of (someone or something) ▹ n something said or written to show approval

PRAISER, -S ▸ **praise**

PRAISES ▸ **praise**

PRAISING ▸ **praise**

PRAJNA, -S n wisdom or understanding

PRALINE, -S n sweet made of nuts and caramelized sugar

PRAM, -S n four-wheeled carriage for a baby, pushed by hand

PRANA, -S n cosmic energy believed to come from the sun

PRANCE, -D, -S, PRANCING vb walk with exaggerated bouncing steps ▹ n act of prancing

PRANCER, -S ▸ **prance**

PRANCES ▸ **prance**

PRANCING ▸ **prance**

PRANCK, -ED, -S obsolete variant of ▸ **prank**

PRANCKE, -S obsolete variant of ▸ **prank**

PRANCKED ▸ **prancke**

PRANCKES ▸ **prancke**

PRANCKS ▸ **pranck**

PRANDIAL adj of or relating to a meal

PRANG, -ED, -ING, -S n crash in a car or aircraft ▹ vb crash or damage (an aircraft or car)

PRANK, -ED, -ING, -S n mischievous trick ▹ vb dress or decorate showily or gaudily

PRANKFUL ▸ **prank**

PRANKIER ▸ **pranky**

PRANKING ▶ prank
PRANKISH ▶ prank
PRANKLE, -D, -S *obsolete variant of* ▶ prance
PRANKS ▶ prank
PRANKY, PRANKIER ▶ prank
PRAO, -S *same as* ▶ proa
PRASE, -S *n* light green translucent variety of chalcedony
PRAT, -S *n* stupid person
PRATE, -D, -S *vb* talk idly and at length ▷ *n* chatter
PRATER, -S ▶ prate
PRATES ▶ prate
PRATFALL, PRATFELL *vb* fall upon one's buttocks
PRATIE, -S *n* potato
PRATING, -S ▶ prate
PRATIQUE *n* formal permission given to a vessel to use a foreign port
PRATS ▶ prat
PRATT, -ED, -ING, -S *n* buttocks ▷ *vb* hit on the buttocks
PRATTLE, -D, -S *vb* chatter in a childish or foolish way ▷ *n* childish or foolish talk
PRATTLER ▶ prattle
PRATTLES ▶ prattle
PRATTS ▶ pratt
PRATY *obsolete variant of* ▶ pretty
PRAU, -S *same as* ▶ proa
PRAUNCE, -D, -S *obsolete variant of* ▶ prance
PRAUS ▶ prau
PRAVITY *n* moral degeneracy
PRAWLE, -S *n* Shakespearian spelling of 'brawl'
PRAWLIN, -S *variant of* ▶ praline
PRAWN, -ED, -ING, -S *n* edible shellfish like a large shrimp ▷ *vb* catch prawns
PRAWNER, -S ▶ prawn
PRAWNING ▶ prawn
PRAWNS ▶ prawn
PRAXIS, PRAXES, -ES *n* practice as opposed to theory
PRAY, -ED, -S *vb* say prayers ▷ *adv* I beg you ▷ *interj* I beg you
PRAYER, -S *n* thanks or appeal addressed to one's God
PRAYING, -S ▶ pray
PRAYS ▶ pray
PRE *prep* before
PREACE, -D, -S, PREACING *obsolete variant of* ▶ press

PREACH, -ED, -ES *vb* give a talk on a religious theme as part of a church service
PREACHER *n* person who preaches, esp in church
PREACHES ▶ preach
PREACHY *adj* inclined to or marked by preaching
PREACING ▶ preace
PREACT, -ED, -S *vb* act beforehand
PREADAPT *vb* adapt beforehand
PREADMIT *vb* prepare patient prior to treatment
PREADOPT *vb* adopt in advance
PREADULT *n* animal or person who has not reached adulthood
PREAGED *adj* treated to appear older
PREALLOT *vb* allot beforehand
PREALTER *vb* alter beforehand
PREAMBLE *n* introductory part to something said or written ▷ *vb* write a preamble
PREAMP, -S *n* electronic amplifier
PREANAL *adj* situated in front of anus
PREAPPLY *vb* apply beforehand
PREARM, -ED, -S *vb* arm beforehand
PREASE, -D, -S, PREASING *vb* crowd or press
PREASSE, -D, -S *obsolete spelling of* ▶ press
PREAUDIT *n* examination of contracts before a transaction
PREAVER, -S *vb* aver in advance
PREAXIAL *adj* situated or occurring in front of the axis of the body
PREBADE ▶ prebid
PREBAKE, -D, -S *vb* bake before further cooking
PREBASAL *adj* in front of a base
PREBEND, -S *n* allowance paid to a canon or member of the cathedral chapter
PREBID, PREBADE, -S *vb* bid beforehand
PREBILL, -S *vb* issue an invoice before the service has been provided
PREBIND, -S, PREBOUND *vb* bind a book in a hard-wearing binding

PREBIRTH *n* period of life before birth
PREBLESS *vb* bless a couple before they marry
PREBOARD *vb* board an aircraft before other passengers
PREBOIL, -S *vb* boil beforehand
PREBOOK, -S *vb* book well in advance
PREBOOM *adj* of the period before an economic boom
PREBORN *adj* unborn
PREBOUND ▶ prebind
PREBUILD, PREBUILT *vb* build beforehand
PREBUY, -S *vb* buy in advance
PRECAST, -S *adj* cast in a particular form before being used ▷ *vb* cast (concrete) in a particular form before use
PRECAVA, -E *n* superior vena cava
PRECAVAL *n* type of vein
PRECEDE, -D, -S *vb* go or be before
PRECEESE *Scots variant of* ▶ precise
PRECENT, -S *vb* issue a command or law
PRECEPIT *old word for* ▶ precipice
PRECEPT, -S *n* rule of behaviour
PRECES *pl n* prayers
PRECESS *vb* undergo or cause to undergo precession
PRECHECK *vb* check beforehand
PRECHILL *vb* chill beforehand
PRECHOSE ▶ prechoose
PRECIEUX *n* pretentious male
PRECINCT *n* area in a town closed to traffic
PRECIOUS *adj* of great value and importance ▷ *adv* very
PRECIP, -S *n* precipitation
PRECIPE, -S *n* type of legal document
PRECIPS ▶ precip
PRECIS, -ED, -ES *n* short written summary of a longer piece ▷ *vb* make a precis of
PRECISE, -R *adj* exact, accurate in every detail
PRECISED ▶ precis
PRECISER ▶ precise
PRECISES ▶ precis
PRECITED *adj* cited previously
PRECLEAN *vb* clean beforehand

P

PRECLEAR vb approve in advance

PRECLUDE vb make impossible to happen

PRECODE, -D, -S vb code beforehand

PRECOOK, -S vb cook (food) beforehand

PRECOOL, -S vb cool in advance

PRECOUP adj of the period before a coup

PRECRASH adj of the period before a crash

PRECURE, -D, -S vb cure in advance

PRECURSE n forerunning ▷ vb be a precursor of

PRECUT, -S vb cut in advance

PRECYCLE vb preemptive approach to waste reduction involving minimal use of packaging

PREDATE, -D, -S vb occur at an earlier date than

PREDATOR n predatory animal

PREDAWN, -S n period before dawn

PREDEATH n period immediately before death

PREDELLA, PREDELLE n series of small paintings or sculptures in a long narrow strip on an altarpiece

PREDIAL, -S same as ▶ praedial

PREDICT, -S vb tell about in advance, prophesy

PREDIED ▶ predy

PREDIES ▶ predy

PREDIVE adj happening before a dive

PREDOOM, -S vb pronounce (someone or something's) doom beforehand

PREDRAFT adj before a draft ▷ n preliminary draft prior to an official draft

PREDRIED ▶ predry

PREDRIES ▶ predry

PREDRILL vb drill in advance

PREDRY, PREDRIED, PREDRIES vb dry beforehand

PREDUSK, -S n period before dusk

PREDY, PREDIED, PREDIES, -ING vb prepare for action

PREE, -D, -ING, -S vb try or taste

PREEDIT, -S vb edit beforehand

PREEING ▶ pree

PREELECT vb elect beforehand

PREEMIE, -S n premature infant

PREEMPT, -S vb acquire in advance of or to the exclusion of others

PREEN, -ED, -ING, -S vb (of a bird) clean or trim (feathers) with the beak ▷ n pin, esp a decorative one

PREENACT vb enact beforehand

PREENED ▶ preen

PREENER, -S ▶ preen

PREENING ▶ preen

PREENS ▶ preen

PREERECT vb erect beforehand

PREES ▶ pree

PREEVE, -D, -S, PREEVING old form of ▶ prove

PREEXIST vb exist beforehand

PREFAB, -S n prefabricated house ▷ vb manufacture sections of (building) in factory

PREFACE, -D, -S n introduction to a book ▷ vb serve as an introduction to (a book, speech, etc)

PREFACER ▶ preface

PREFACES ▶ preface

PREFADE, -D, -S vb fade beforehand

PREFARD vb old form of preferred

PREFECT, -S n senior pupil in a school, with limited power over others

PREFER, -S vb like better

PREFIGHT adj of the period before a boxing match

PREFILE, -D, -S vb file beforehand

PREFIRE, -D, -S vb fire beforehand

PREFIX, -ED, -ES n letters put at the beginning of a word to make a new word ▷ vb put as an introduction or prefix (to)

PREFIXAL ▶ prefix

PREFIXED ▶ prefix

PREFIXES ▶ prefix

PREFLAME adj of the period before combustion

PREFOCUS vb focus in advance

PREFORM, -S vb form beforehand

PREFRANK vb frank in advance

PREFROZE > prefreeze

PREFUND, -S vb pay for in advance

PREGAME, -D, -S vb consume alcoholic drinks before going to a social gathering

PREGGERS informal word for ▶ pregnant

PREGGIER ▶ preggy

PREGGO adj slang word for pregnant

PREGGY, PREGGIER informal word for ▶ pregnant

PREGNANT adj carrying a fetus in the womb

PREGUIDE vb give guidance in advance

PREHAB, -S n any programme of training designed to prevent sports injury

PREHEAT, -S vb heat (an oven, grill, pan, etc) beforehand

PREHEND, -S vb take hold of

PREHNITE n green mineral

PREHUMAN n hominid that predates human beings

PREIF, -S old form of ▶ proof

PREIFE, -S old form of ▶ proof

PREIFS ▶ preif

PREJINK variant of ▶ perjink

PREJUDGE vb judge beforehand without sufficient evidence

PRELACY n office or status of a prelate

PRELATE, -S n bishop or other churchman of high rank

PRELATIC ▶ prelate

PRELATY n prelacy

PRELAW adj before taking up study of law

PRELECT, -S vb lecture or discourse in public

PRELEGAL adj of the period before the start of a law course

PRELIFE, PRELIVES n life lived before one's life on earth

PRELIM n event which precedes another

PRELIMIT vb limit beforehand

PRELIMS pl n pages of a book which come before the main text

PRELIVES ▶ prelife

PRELOAD, -S vb load beforehand

PRELOVED adj previously owned or used

PRELUDE, -D, -S n introductory movement in music ▷ vb act as a prelude to (something)

PRELUDER ▶ prelude

PRELUDES ▶ prelude

PRELUDIO, PRELUDI n musical prelude

PRELUNCH adj of the period before lunch

PREM, -S n informal word for a premature infant

PREMADE adj made in advance

PREMAKE, -S vb make beforehand

PREMAN, PREMEN n hominid

PREMEAL adj of the period before a meal

PREMED, -S n premedical student

PREMEDIC same as ▶ premed

PREMEDS ▶ premed

PREMEET adj happening before a meet

PREMEN ▶ preman

PREMIA ▶ premium

PREMIE, -S same as ▶ preemie

PREMIER, -S n prime minister ▷ adj chief, leading

PREMIERE n first performance of a play, film, etc ▷ vb give, or (of a film, play, or opera) be, a premiere

PREMIERS ▶ premier

PREMIES ▶ premie

PREMISE, -D, -S n statement used as the basis of reasoning ▷ vb state or assume (a proposition) as a premise

PREMISS same as ▶ premise

PREMIUM, PREMIA, -S n additional sum of money, as on a wage or charge

PREMIX, -ED, -ES, -T vb mix beforehand

PREMOLAR n tooth between the canine and first molar in adult humans ▷ adj situated before a molar tooth

PREMOLD, -S same as ▶ premould

PREMOLT same as ▶ premoult

PREMORAL adj not governed by sense of right and wrong

PREMORSE adj appearing as though the end had been bitten off

PREMOTOR adj relating to a part of the frontal lobe of the brain

PREMOULD vb mould in advance

PREMOULT adj happening in the period before an animal moults

PREMOVE, -D, -S vb prompt to action

PREMS ▶ prem

PREMUNE adj having immunity to a disease as a result of latent infection

PREMY variant of ▶ preemie

PRENAME, -S n forename

PRENASAL n bone in the front of the nose

PRENATAL adj before birth, during pregnancy ▷ n prenatal examination

PRENEED adj arranged in advance of eventual requirements

PRENOMEN less common spelling of ▶ praenomen

PRENOON adj of the period before noon

PRENT, -ED, -ING, -S Scots variant of ▶ print

PRENTICE vb bind as an apprentice

PRENTING ▶ prent

PRENTS ▶ prent

PRENUP, -S n prenuptial agreement

PRENZIE adj Shakespearian word supposed by some to mean 'princely'

PREON, -S n (in particle physics) hypothetical subcomponent of a quark

PREOP, -S n patient being prepared for surgery

PREORAL adj situated in front of mouth

PREORDER vb order in advance

PREOWNED adj second-hand

PREP, -PED, -PING, -S vb prepare

PREPACK, -S vb pack in advance of sale

PREPAID ▶ prepay

PREPARE, -D, -S vb make or get ready

PREPARER ▶ prepare

PREPARES ▶ prepare

PREPASTE vb paste in advance

PREPAVE, -D, -S vb pave beforehand

PREPAY, PREPAID, -S vb pay for in advance

PREPENSE adj (usually in legal contexts) arranged in advance ▷ vb consider beforehand

PREPLACE vb place in advance

PREPLAN, -S vb plan beforehand

PREPLANT adj planted in advance

PREPONE, -D, -S vb bring forward to an earlier time

PREPOSE, -D, -S vb place before

PREPPED ▶ prep

PREPPIE same as ▶ preppy

PREPPIER ▶ preppy

PREPPIES ▶ preppy

PREPPILY ▶ preppy

PREPPING ▶ prep

PREPPY, PREPPIER, PREPPIES adj denoting a fashion style of neat, understated clothes ▷ n person exhibiting such style

PREPREG, -S n material already impregnated with synthetic resin

PREPRESS adj before printing

PREPRICE vb price in advance

PREPRINT vb print in advance

PREPS ▶ prep

PREPUBIS, PREPUBES n animal hip bone

PREPUCE, -S n foreskin

PREPUNCH vb pierce with holes in advance

PREPUPA, -E, -S n insect in stage of life before pupa

PREPUPAL adj of the period between the larval and pupal stages

PREPUPAS ▶ prepupa

PREQUEL, -S n film or book about an earlier stage of a story

PRERACE adj of the period before a race

PRERADIO adj before the invention of radio

PRERENAL adj anterior to kidney

PRERINSE vb treat before rinsing

PRERIOT adj of the period before a riot

PREROCK adj of the era before rock music

PRERUPT adj abrupt

PRESA, PRESE n musical sign or symbol to indicate the entry of a part

PRESAGE, -D, -S vb be a sign or warning of ▷ n omen

PRESAGER ▶ presage

PRESAGES ▶ presage

PRESALE, -S n practice of arranging the sale of a product before it is available

PRESBYTE n person with presbyopy

PRESCIND vb withdraw attention (from something)

PRESCORE vb record (the score of a film) before shooting

PRESCUTA > **prescutum**

PRESE ▸ **presa**

PRESELL, -S, PRESOLD vb promote in advance of appearance

PRESENCE n fact of being in a specified place

PRESENT adj being in a specified place ▸ n present time or tense ▸ vb introduce formally or publicly

PRESENTS pl n used in a deed or document to refer to itself

PRESERVE vb keep from being damaged, changed, or ended ▸ n area of interest restricted to a particular person or group

PRESES variant of ▸ **praeses**

PRESET, -S vb set a timer so that equipment starts to work at a specific time ▸ adj (of equipment) with the controls set in advance ▸ n control that is used to set initial conditions

PRESHAPE vb shape beforehand

PRESHIP, -S vb ship in advance

PRESHOW, -N, -S vb show in advance

PRESIDE, -D, -S vb be in charge, esp of a meeting

PRESIDER ▸ **preside**

PRESIDES ▸ **preside**

PRESIDIA > **presidium**

PRESIDIO n military post or establishment, esp in countries formerly under Spanish control

PRESIFT, -S vb sift beforehand

PRESLEEP adj of the period before sleep

PRESLICE vb slice in advance

PRESOAK, -S vb soak beforehand

PRESOLD ▸ **presell**

PRESOLVE vb solve beforehand

PRESONG adj of the period before a song is sung

PRESORT, -S vb sort in advance

PRESPLIT adj of the period prior to a split

PRESS, -ED, -ES vb apply force or weight to ▸ n printing machine

PRESSER, -S ▸ **press**

PRESSES ▸ **press**

PRESSFAT n wine vat

PRESSFUL ▸ **press**

PRESSIE, -S informal word for ▸ **present**

PRESSING adj urgent ▸ n large number of gramophone records produced at one time

PRESSION n act of pressing

PRESSMAN, PRESSMEN n man who works for the press

PRESSOR, -S n something that produces an increase in blood pressure

PRESSRUN n number of books printed at one time

PRESSURE n force produced by pressing ▸ vb persuade forcefully

PRESSY same as ▸ **pressie**

PREST, -ED, -ING, -S adj prepared for action or use ▸ n loan of money ▸ vb give as a loan

PRESTAMP vb stamp in advance

PRESTED ▸ **prest**

PRESTER, -S ▸ **prest**

PRESTIGE n high status or respect resulting from success or achievements

PRESTING ▸ **prest**

PRESTO, -S adv very quickly ▸ n passage to be played very quickly

PRESTORE vb store in advance

PRESTOS ▸ **presto**

PRESTS ▸ **prest**

PRESUME, -D, -S vb suppose to be the case

PRESUMER ▸ **presume**

PRESUMES ▸ **presume**

PRETAPE, -D, -S vb (formerly) tape in advance

PRETASTE vb taste in advance

PRETAX adj before tax

PRETEEN, -S n boy or girl approaching his or her teens

PRETELL, -S, PRETOLD vb predict

PRETENCE n behaviour intended to deceive, pretending

PRETEND, -S vb claim (something untrue) ▸ adj fanciful

PRETENSE same as ▸ **pretence**

PRETERIT same as > **preterite**

PRETERM, -S n premature baby

PRETEST, -S vb test (something) before presenting it ▸ n act or instance of pretesting

PRETEXT, -S n false reason given to hide the real one ▸ vb get personal information under false pretences

PRETOLD ▸ **pretell**

PRETONIC adj relating to the syllable before the one bearing the primary stress in a word

PRETOR, -S same as ▸ **praetor**

PRETRAIN vb train in advance

PRETREAT vb treat in advance

PRETRIAL n hearing prior to a trial

PRETRIM, -S vb trim in advance

PRETTIED ▸ **pretty**

PRETTIER ▸ **pretty**

PRETTIES ▸ **pretty**

PRETTIFY vb make pretty

PRETTILY ▸ **pretty**

PRETTY, PRETTIED, PRETTIER, PRETTIES adj pleasing to look at ▸ adv fairly, moderately ▸ vb pretty

PRETYPE, -D, -S vb type in advance

PRETZEL, -S n brittle salted biscuit ▸ vb bend or twist

PREUNION n early form of trade union

PREUNITE vb unite in advance

PREVAIL, -S vb gain mastery

PREVALUE vb value beforehand

PREVE, -D, -S, PREVING vb prove

PREVENE, -D, -S vb come before

PREVENT, -S vb keep from happening or doing

PREVERB, -S n particle preceding root of verb

PREVES ▸ **preve**

PREVIEW, -S n advance showing of a film or exhibition before it is shown to the public ▸ vb view in advance

PREVING ▸ **preve**

PREVIOUS adj coming or happening before

PREVISE, -D, -S vb predict or foresee

PREVISIT vb visit beforehand

PREVISOR ▸ previse

PREVUE, -D, -S, PREVUING same as ▸ **preview**

PREWAR adj relating to the period before a war, esp before World War I or II

PREWARM, -S vb warm beforehand

PREWARN, -S vb warn in advance

PREWASH vb give a preliminary wash to (clothes) ▹ n preliminary wash

PREWEIGH vb weigh beforehand

PREWIRE, -D, -S vb wire beforehand

PREWORK, -S vb work in advance

PREWORN adj (of clothes) second-hand

PREWRAP, -S vb wrap in advance

PREWRITE, PREWROTE vb write beforehand

PREWYN, -S obsolete spelling of ▸ **prune**

PREX, -ES same as ▸ **prexy**

PREXIE same as ▸ **prexy**

PREXY, PREXIES n US college president

PREY, -ED, -ING, -S n animal hunted and killed for food by another animal ▹ vb hunt or seize food by killing other animals

PREYER, -S ▸ prey

PREYFUL adj rich in prey

PREYING ▸ prey

PREYS ▸ prey

PREZ, -ES n president

PREZZIE, -S same as ▸ **pressie**

PRIAL, -S n pair royal of cards

PRIAPEAN same as ▸ **priapic**

PRIAPI ▸ priapus

PRIAPIC adj phallic

PRIAPUS, PRIAPI n representation of the penis

PRIBBLE, -S variant of ▸ **prabble**

PRICE, -D, -S n amount of money for which a thing is bought or sold ▹ vb fix or ask the price of

PRICER, -S ▸ price

PRICES ▸ price

PRICEY adj expensive

PRICIER ▸ pricy

PRICIEST ▸ pricy

PRICILY ▸ pricey

PRICING, -S ▸ price

PRICK, -ED, -ING, -S vb pierce lightly with a sharp point ▹ n sudden sharp pain caused by pricking

PRICKER, -S n person or thing that pricks

PRICKET, -S n male deer in the second year of life

PRICKIER ▸ pricky

PRICKING ▸ prick

PRICKLE, -D, -S n thorn or spike on a plant ▹ vb have a tingling or pricking sensation

PRICKLY adj having prickles

PRICKS ▸ prick

PRICKY, PRICKIER adj covered with pricks

PRICY, PRICIER, PRICIEST same as ▸ **pricey**

PRIDE, -D, -S, PRIDING n feeling of pleasure and satisfaction when one has done well

PRIDEFUL ▸ pride

PRIDES ▸ pride

PRIDIAN adj relating to yesterday

PRIDING ▸ pride

PRIED ▸ pry

PRIEDIEU n piece of furniture for use when kneeling to pray

PRIEF, -S obsolete variant of ▸ **proof**

PRIEFE, -S obsolete variant of ▸ **proof**

PRIEFS ▸ prief

PRIER, -S n person who pries

PRIES ▸ pry

PRIEST, -ED, -S n (in the Christian church) person who can administer the sacraments and preach ▹ vb make a priest

PRIESTLY adj of, relating to, characteristic of, or befitting a priest

PRIESTS ▸ priest

PRIEVE, -D, -S, PRIEVING obsolete variant of ▸ **proof**

PRIG, -GED, -GING, -S n self-righteous person who acts as if superior to others

PRIGGER, -S n thief

PRIGGERY ▸ prig

PRIGGING ▸ prig

PRIGGISH ▸ prig

PRIGGISM ▸ prig

PRIGS ▸ prig

PRILL, -ED, -ING, -S vb convert (a material) into a granular free-flowing form ▹ n prilled material

PRIM, -MED, -MEST, -MING, -S adj formal, proper, and rather prudish ▹ vb make prim

PRIMA, -S same as ▸ **primo**

PRIMACY n state of being first in rank, grade, etc

PRIMAGE, -S n tax added to customs duty

PRIMAL adj of basic causes or origins

PRIMALLY ▸ primal

PRIMARY adj chief, most important ▹ n person or thing that is first in position, time, or importance

PRIMAS ▸ prima

PRIMATAL n primate

PRIMATE, -S n member of an order of mammals including monkeys and humans

PRIMATIC ▸ primate

PRIME, -D, -S adj main, most important ▹ n time when someone is most vigorous ▹ vb give (someone) information in advance

PRIMELY ▸ prime

PRIMER, -S n special paint applied to bare wood etc before the main paint

PRIMERO, -S n 16th- and 17th-century card game

PRIMERS ▸ primer

PRIMES ▸ prime

PRIMEUR, -S n anything (esp fruit) produced early

PRIMEVAL adj of the earliest age of the world

PRIMI ▸ primo

PRIMINE, -S n integument surrounding an ovule or the outer of two such integuments

PRIMING, -S same as ▸ **primer**

PRIMLY ▸ prim

PRIMMED ▸ prim

PRIMMER, -S n elementary textbook

PRIMMEST ▸ prim

PRIMMING ▸ prim

PRIMNESS ▸ prim

PRIMO, PRIMI, -S n upper or right-hand part in a piano duet

PRIMP, -ED, -ING, -S vb tidy (one's hair or clothes) fussily

PRIMROSE n pale yellow spring flower ▹ adj pale yellow

PRIMROSY adj abounding in primroses

PRIMS ▸ prim

PRIMSIE, -R Scots variant of ▸ **prim**

P

PRIMULA, -S *n* type of primrose with brightly coloured flowers

PRIMUS, -ES *n* presiding bishop in the Synod

PRIMY *adj* prime

PRINCE, -D, -S, PRINCING *n* son of a king or queen ▷ *vb* act like a prince

PRINCELY *adj* of or like a prince ▷ *adv* in a princely manner

PRINCES ▶ **prince**

PRINCESS *n* female member of a royal family, esp the daughter of the king or queen

PRINCING ▶ **prince**

PRINCIPE, PRINCIPI *n* prince

PRINCOCK *same as* ▶ **princox**

PRINCOX *n* pert youth

PRINK, -ED, -ING, -S *vb* dress (oneself) finely

PRINKER, -S ▶ **prink**

PRINKING ▶ **prink**

PRINKS ▶ **prink**

PRINT, -ED, -S *vb* reproduce (a newspaper, book, etc) in large quantities by mechanical or electronic means ▷ *n* printed words etc

PRINTER, -S *n* person or company engaged in printing

PRINTERY *n* establishment in which printing is carried out

PRINTING *n* process of producing printed matter

PRINTOUT *n* printed information produced by a computer output device

PRINTS ▶ **print**

PRION, -S *n* dovelike petrel with a serrated bill

PRIOR, -S *adj* earlier ▷ *n* head monk in a priory

PRIORATE *n* office, status, or term of office of a prior

PRIORESS *n* deputy head nun in a convent

PRIORIES ▶ **priory**

PRIORITY *n* most important thing that must be dealt with first

PRIORLY ▶ **prior**

PRIORS ▶ **prior**

PRIORY, PRIORIES *n* place where certain orders of monks or nuns live

PRISAGE, -S *n* customs duty levied until 1809 upon wine imported into England

PRISE, -D, -S, PRISING *same as* ▶ **pry**

PRISER, -S ▶ **prise**

PRISERE, -S *n* primary sere or succession from bare ground to the community climax

PRISERS ▶ **priser**

PRISES ▶ **prise**

PRISING ▶ **prise**

PRISM, -S *n* transparent block used to disperse light into a spectrum

PRISMOID *n* prism-like geometrical shape

PRISMS ▶ **prism**

PRISMY ▶ **prism**

PRISON, -ED, -S *n* building where criminals and accused people are held ▷ *vb* imprison

PRISONER *n* person held captive

PRISONS ▶ **prison**

PRISS, -ED, -ES, -ING *n* prissy person ▷ *vb* act prissily

PRISSIER ▶ **prissy**

PRISSIES ▶ **prissy**

PRISSILY ▶ **prissy**

PRISSING ▶ **priss**

PRISSY, PRISSIER, PRISSIES *adj* prim, correct, and easily shocked ▷ *n* prissy person

PRISTANE *n* colourless combustible liquid

PRISTINE *adj* clean, new, and unused

PRITHEE *interj* pray thee

PRIVACY *n* condition of being private

PRIVADO, -S *n* close friend

PRIVATE, -R, -S *adj* for the use of one person or group only ▷ *n* soldier of the lowest rank

PRIVET, -S *n* bushy evergreen shrub used for hedges

PRIVIER ▶ **privy**

PRIVIES ▶ **privy**

PRIVIEST ▶ **privy**

PRIVILY *adv* in a secret way

PRIVITY *n* legally recognized relationship between two parties

PRIVY, PRIVIER, PRIVIES, PRIVIEST *adj* sharing knowledge of something secret ▷ *n* toilet, esp an outside one

PRIZABLE *adj* of worth

PRIZE, -D, -S, PRIZING *n* reward given for success in a competition etc ▷ *adj* winning or likely to win a prize ▷ *vb* value highly

PRIZEMAN, PRIZEMEN *n* man who wins a prize

PRIZER, -S *n* contender for prize

PRIZES ▶ **prize**

PRIZING ▶ **prize**

PRO, -S *prep* in favour of ▷ *n* professional ▷ *adv* in favour of a motion etc

PROA, -S *n* canoe-like boat used in the South Pacific

PROB, -S *n* problem

PROBABLE *adj* likely to happen or be true ▷ *n* person who is likely to be chosen for a team, event, etc

PROBABLY *adv* in all likelihood ▷ *sentence substitute* I believe such a thing or situation may be the case

PROBALL *adj* believable

PROBAND, -S *n* first patient to be investigated in a family study

PROBANG, -S *n* long flexible rod used to apply medication

PROBATE, -D, -S *n* process of proving the validity of a will ▷ *vb* establish officially the authenticity and validity of (a will)

PROBE, -D, -S *vb* search into or examine closely ▷ *n* surgical instrument used to examine a wound, cavity, etc

PROBER, -S ▶ **probe**

PROBES ▶ **probe**

PROBING, -S *n* act of making a thorough enquiry

PROBIT, -S *n* statistical measurement

PROBITY *n* honesty, integrity

PROBLEM, -S *n* something difficult to deal with or solve ▷ *adj* of a literary work that deals with difficult moral questions

PROBS ▶ **prob**

PROCAINE *n* colourless or white crystalline water-soluble substance

PROCARP, -S *n* female reproductive organ in red algae

PROCEED *vb* start or continue doing

PROCEEDS *pl n* money obtained from an event or activity

PROCESS *n* series of actions or changes ▷ *vb* handle or prepare by a special method of manufacture

PROCHAIN *variant of* ▶ **prochein**

PROCHEIN adj next or nearest

PROCINCT n state of preparedness

PROCLAIM vb declare publicly

PROCLIVE adj prone

PROCTAL adj relating to the rectum

PROCTOR, -S n university worker who enforces discipline ▷ vb invigilate (an examination)

PROCURAL ▶ procure

PROCURE, -D, -S vb get, provide

PROCURER n person who provides something

PROCURES ▶ procure

PROD, -DED, -S vb poke with something pointed ▷ n prodding

PRODDER, -S ▶ prod

PRODDING n act of prodding

PRODIGAL adj recklessly extravagant, wasteful ▷ n person who spends lavishly or squanders money

PRODIGY n person with some marvellous talent

PRODITOR n traitor

PRODNOSE vb make uninvited inquiries (about someone else's business, for example)

PRODROMA n symptom that signals the onset of a disease

PRODROME, PRODROMI n any symptom that signals the impending onset of a disease

PRODRUG, -S n compound that is metabolized in the body to produce an active drug

PRODS ▶ prod

PRODUCE, -D, -S vb bring into existence ▷ n food grown for sale

PRODUCER n person with control over the making of a film, record, etc

PRODUCES ▶ produce

PRODUCT, -S n something produced

PROEM, -S n introduction or preface

PROEMIAL ▶ proem

PROEMS ▶ proem

PROETTE, -S n female golfing professional

PROF, -S short for > professor

PROFACE interj much good may it do you

PROFANE, -D, -S adj showing disrespect for religion or holy things ▷ vb treat (something sacred) irreverently, desecrate

PROFANER ▶ profane

PROFANES ▶ profane

PROFESS vb state or claim (something as true), sometimes falsely

PROFFER, -S vb offer ▷ n act of proffering

PROFILE, -D, -S n outline, esp of the face, as seen from the side ▷ vb draw, write, or make a profile of

PROFILER n device that creates a profile

PROFILES ▶ profile

PROFIT, -ED, -S n money gained ▷ vb gain or benefit

PROFITER ▶ profit

PROFITS ▶ profit

PROFORMA n invoice issued before an order is placed

PROFOUND adj showing or needing great knowledge ▷ n great depth

PROFS ▶ prof

PROFUSE adj plentiful

PROFUSER ▶ profuse

PROG, -GED, -GING, -S vb prowl about for or as if for food or plunder ▷ n food obtained by begging

PROGENY n children

PROGERIA n premature old age in children

PROGGED ▶ prog

PROGGER, -S n fan of progressive rock

PROGGING ▶ prog

PROGGINS n proctor

PROGNOSE vb predict course of disease

PROGRADE vb (of beach) advance towards sea

PROGRAM, -S n sequence of coded instructions for a computer ▷ vb write a computer program

PROGRESS n improvement, development ▷ vb become more advanced or skilful

PROGS ▶ prog

PROGUN adj in favour of public owning firearms

PROHIBIT vb forbid or prevent from happening

PROIGN, -ED, -S same as ▶ proin

PROIN, -ED, -ING, -S vb trim or prune

PROINE, -S same as ▶ proin

PROINED ▶ proin

PROINES ▶ proine

PROINING ▶ proin

PROINS ▶ proin

PROJECT, -S n planned scheme to do or examine something over a period ▷ vb make a forecast based on known data

PROJET, -S n draft of a proposed treaty

PROKE, -D, -S, PROKING vb thrust or poke

PROKER, -S ▶ proke

PROKES ▶ proke

PROKING ▶ proke

PROLABOR adj favouring the Labor party

PROLAMIN same as > prolamine

PROLAN, -S n constituent of human pregnancy urine

PROLAPSE n slipping down of an internal organ of the body from its normal position ▷ vb (of an internal organ) slip from its normal position

PROLATE, -D, -S adj having a polar diameter which is longer than the equatorial diameter ▷ vb pronounce or utter

PROLE, -D, -S, PROLING old form of ▶ prowl

PROLEG, -S n appendage on abdominal segment of a caterpillar

PROLER, -S n prowler

PROLES ▶ prole

PROLIFIC adj very productive

PROLINE, -S n nonessential amino acid that occurs in protein

PROLING ▶ prole

PROLIX adj (of speech or a piece of writing) overlong and boring

PROLIXLY ▶ prolix

PROLL, -ED, -ING, -S vb prowl or search

PROLLER, -S ▶ proll

PROLLING ▶ proll

PROLLS ▶ proll

PROLLY adv probably

PROLOG, -ED, -S same as ▶ prologue

PROLOGUE n introduction to a play or book ▷ vb introduce or preface with or as if with a prologue

PROLONG, -S vb make (something) last longer

PROLONGE n (formerly) rope used as part of the towing equipment of a gun carriage

P

PROLONGS ▸ prolong

PROM, -S n formal dance held at a high school or college

PROMETAL n type of cast iron

PROMINE, -S n substance promoting cell growth

PROMISE, -D, -S vb say that one will definitely do or not do something ▷ n undertaking to do or not to do something

PROMISEE n person to whom a promise is made

PROMISER ▸ promise

PROMISES ▸ promise

PROMISOR n person who makes a promise

PROMMER, -S n spectator at promenade concert

PROMO, -ED, -ING, -S vb promote (something)

PROMOTE, -D, -S vb help to make (something) happen or increase

PROMOTER n person who organizes or finances an event etc

PROMOTES ▸ promote

PROMOTOR variant of
▸ **promoter**

PROMPT, -ED, -S vb cause (an action) ▷ adj done without delay ▷ adv exactly ▷ n anything that serves to remind

PROMPTER n person offstage who prompts actors

PROMPTLY ▸ prompt

PROMPTS ▸ prompt

PROMS ▸ prom

PROMULGE vb bring to public knowledge

PRONAOS, PRONAOI n inner area of the portico of a classical temple

PRONATE, -D, -S vb turn (a limb, hand, or foot) so that the palm or sole is directed downwards

PRONATOR n any muscle whose contractions produce or affect pronation

PRONE, -R, -S, -ST n sermon ▷ adj sloping downwards

PRONELY ▸ prone

PRONER ▸ prone

PRONES ▸ prone

PRONEST ▸ prone

PRONEUR, -S n flatterer

PRONG, -ED, -ING, -S n one spike of a fork or similar instrument ▷ vb prick or spear with or as if with a prong

PRONK, -ED, -ING, -S vb jump straight up

PRONOTA ▸ pronotum

PRONOTAL ▸ pronotum

PRONOTUM, PRONOTA n notum of the prothorax of an insect

PRONOUN, -S n word, such as she or it, used to replace a noun

PRONTO adv at once

PROO interj (to a horse) stop!

PROOF, -ED, -ING, -S n evidence that shows that something is true or has happened ▷ adj able to withstand ▷ vb take a proof from (type matter)

PROOFER, -S n reader of proofs

PROOFING ▸ proof

PROOFS ▸ proof

PROOTIC, -S n bone in front of ear

PROP, -PED, -PING, -S vb support (something) so that it stays upright or in place ▷ n pole, beam, etc used as a support

PROPAGE, -D, -S vb propagate

PROPALE, -D, -S vb publish (something)

PROPANE, -S n flammable gas found in petroleum and used as a fuel

PROPANOL n colourless alcohol

PROPEL, -S vb cause to move forward

PROPENAL n type of aldehyde used as a herbicide and tear gas

PROPEND, -S vb be inclined or disposed

PROPENE, -S n colourless gaseous alkene obtained by cracking petroleum

PROPENOL n liquid used to make allylic alcohol

PROPENSE adj inclining forward

PROPENYL n three-carbon radical

PROPER, -ER, -S adj real or genuine ▷ n service or psalm regarded as appropriate to a specific day, season, etc

PROPERLY ▸ proper

PROPERS ▸ proper

PROPERTY same as
▸ **proprium**

PROPHAGE n type of virus in a bacterial cell

PROPHASE n first stage of mitosis

PROPHECY n prediction

PROPHESY vb foretell

PROPHET, -S n person chosen by God to spread His word

PROPHYLL n leaf-shaped plant structure

PROPINE, -D, -S vb drink a toast to

PROPJET, -S another name for
▸ **turboprop**

PROPMAN, PROPMEN n member of the stage crew in charge of the stage props

PROPOLIS n resinous aromatic substance collected by bees from trees

PROPONE, -D, -S vb propose or put forward, esp before a court

PROPOSAL n act of proposing

PROPOSE, -D, -S vb put forward for consideration

PROPOSER ▸ propose

PROPOSES ▸ propose

PROPOUND vb put forward for consideration

PROPPANT n material used in the oil extraction process

PROPPED ▸ prop

PROPPING ▸ prop

PROPRIUM, PROPRIA n attribute that is not essential to a species but is common and peculiar to it

PROPS ▸ prop

PROPYL, -S n type of monovalent radical

PROPYLA ▸ propylon

PROPYLIC ▸ propyl

PROPYLON, PROPYLA n portico, esp one that forms the entrance to a temple

PROPYLS ▸ propyl

PROPYNE, -S n type of gaseous methyl acetylene

PRORATE, -D, -S vb divide, assess, or distribute (something) proportionately

PRORE, -S n forward part of ship

PROROGUE vb suspend (parliament) without dissolving it

PROS ▸ pro

PROSAIC adj lacking imagination, dull

PROSAISM n prosaic quality or style

PROSAIST ▸ prosaism

PROSE, -D, -S n ordinary speech or writing in contrast to poetry ▷ vb speak or write in a tedious style

PROSECCO n Italian sparkling white wine

PROSECT, -S *vb* dissect a cadaver for a public demonstration

PROSED ▶ prose

PROSEMAN, PROSEMEN *n* writer of prose

PROSER, -S *n* writer of prose

PROSES ▶ prose

PROSIER ▶ prosy

PROSIEST ▶ prosy

PROSIFY *vb* write prose

PROSILY ▶ prosy

PROSING, -S ▶ prose

PROSIT *interj* good health! cheers!

PROSO, -S *n* millet

PROSODIC ▶ prosody

PROSODY *n* study of poetic metre and techniques

PROSOMA, -S *n* head and thorax of an arachnid

PROSOMAL ▶ prosoma

PROSOMAS ▶ prosoma

PROSOPON *n* (in Christianity) manifestation of any of the persons of the Trinity

PROSOS ▶ proso

PROSPECT *n* something anticipated ▷ *vb* explore, esp for gold

PROSPER, -S *vb* be successful

PROST *same as* ▶ **prosit**

PROSTATE *n* gland in male mammals that surrounds the neck of the bladder ▷ *adj* of or relating to the prostate gland

PROSTYLE *adj* (of a building) having a row of columns in front ▷ *n* prostyle building, portico, etc

PROSUMER *n* amateur user of electronic equipment suitable for professionals

PROSY, PROSIER, PROSIEST *adj* dull and long-winded

PROTAMIN *same as* ▶ **protamine**

PROTASIS, PROTASES *n* antecedent of a conditional statement

PROTATIC ▶ protasis

PROTEA, -S *n* African shrub with showy flowers

PROTEAN, -S *adj* constantly changing ▷ *n* creature that can change shape

PROTEAS ▶ protea

PROTEASE *n* any enzyme involved in proteolysis

PROTECT, -S *vb* defend from trouble, harm, or loss

PROTEGE, -S *n* person who is protected and helped by another

PROTEGEE *n* woman or girl who is protected and helped by another

PROTEGES ▶ protege

PROTEI ▶ proteus

PROTEID, -S *n* protein

PROTEIDE *variant of* ▶ **proteid**

PROTEIDS ▶ proteid

PROTEIN, -S *n* any of a group of complex organic compounds that are essential for life

PROTEND, -S *vb* hold out or stretch

PROTENSE *n* extension

PROTEOME *n* full complement of proteins that occur within a cell, tissue, or organism

PROTEOSE *n* compound formed during proteolysis

PROTEST, -S *n* declaration or demonstration of objection ▷ *vb* object, disagree

PROTEUS, PROTEI *n* aerobic bacterium

PROTHYL, -S *variant of* ▶ **protyle**

PROTIST, -S *n* organism belonging to the protozoans, unicellular algae, and simple fungi

PROTIUM, -S *n* most common isotope of hydrogen

PROTO *adj* as in **proto team** team of people trained to deal with underground rescues, etc

PROTOCOL *n* rules of behaviour for formal occasions

PROTON, -S *n* positively charged particle in the nucleus of an atom

PROTONIC *adj* (of a solvent, such as water) able to donate hydrogen ions to solute molecules

PROTONS ▶ proton

PROTOPOD *n* part of crustacean's leg

PROTORE, -S *n* primary mineral deposit

PROTOXID *variant of* ▶ **protoxide**

PROTOZOA ▶ protozoan

PROTRACT *vb* lengthen or extend (a situation etc)

PROTRADE *adj* in favour of trade

PROTRUDE *vb* stick out, project

PROTURAN *n* any of an order of white wingless insects

PROTYL, -S *same as* ▶ **protyle**

PROTYLE, -S *n* hypothetical primitive substance

PROTYLS ▶ protyl

PROUD, -ER, -EST *adj* feeling pleasure and satisfaction

PROUDFUL *adj* full of pride

PROUDISH *adj* rather proud

PROUDLY ▶ proud

PROUL, -ED, -ING, -S *variant of* ▶ **prowl**

PROULER, -S *Scots variant of* ▶ **prowler**

PROULING ▶ proul

PROULS ▶ proul

PROUNION *adj* in favour of or supporting the constitutional union between two or more countries

PROVABLE ▶ prove

PROVABLY ▶ prove

PROVAND, -S *n* food

PROVANT, -S *adj* supplied with provisions ▷ *vb* supply with provisions

PROVE, -D, -N, -S *vb* establish the validity of

PROVEDOR *variant of* > **provedore**

PROVEN ▶ prove

PROVEND, -S *same as* ▶ **provand**

PROVENLY ▶ prove

PROVER, -S ▶ prove

PROVERB, -S *n* short saying that expresses a truth or gives a warning ▷ *vb* utter or describe (something) in the form of a proverb

PROVERS ▶ prover

PROVES ▶ prove

PROVIANT *variant of* ▶ **provand**

PROVIDE, -D, -S *vb* make available

PROVIDER ▶ provide

PROVIDES ▶ provide

PROVIDOR *variant of* > **provedore**

PROVINCE *n* area governed as a unit of a country or empire

PROVINE, -D, -S *vb* plant branch of vine in ground for propagation

PROVING, -S ▶ prove

PROVIRAL ▶ provirus

PROVIRUS *n* inactive form of a virus in a host cell

PROVISO, -S *n* condition, stipulation**

P

PROVISOR n person who receives provision

PROVISOS ▸ proviso

PROVOKE, -D, -S vb deliberately anger

PROVOKER ▸ provoke

PROVOKES ▸ provoke

PROVOST, -S n head of certain university colleges in Britain

PROW, -ER, -EST, -S n bow of a vessel ▷ adj gallant

PROWAR adj in favour of or supporting war

PROWER ▸ prow

PROWESS n superior skill or ability

PROWEST ▸ prow

PROWL, -ED, -ING, -S vb move stealthily around a place as if in search of prey or plunder ▷ n prowling

PROWLER, -S ▸ prowl

PROWLING ▸ prowl

PROWLS ▸ prowl

PROWS ▸ prow

PROXEMIC > proxemics

PROXIES ▸ proxy

PROXIMAL same as > proximate

PROXIMO adv in or during the next or coming month

PROXY, PROXIES n person authorized to act on behalf of someone else

PROYN, -ED, -ING, -S obsolete spelling of ▸ prune

PROYNE, -S obsolete spelling of ▸ prune

PROYNED ▸ proyn

PROYNES ▸ proyne

PROYNING ▸ proyn

PROYNS ▸ proyn

PRUDE, -S n person who is excessively modest, prim, or proper

PRUDENCE n caution in practical affairs

PRUDENT adj cautious, discreet, and sensible

PRUDERY ▸ prude

PRUDES ▸ prude

PRUDISH ▸ prude

PRUH variant of ▸ proo

PRUINA, -S n woolly white covering on some lichens

PRUINE, -S obsolete spelling of ▸ prune

PRUINOSE adj coated with a powdery or waxy bloom

PRUNABLE ▸ prune

PRUNE, -D, -S n dried plum ▷ vb cut off dead parts or excessive branches from (a tree or plant)

PRUNELLA n strong fabric, esp a twill-weave worsted, used for gowns and the uppers of some shoes

PRUNELLE same as ▸ prunella

PRUNELLO same as ▸ prunella

PRUNER, -S ▸ prune

PRUNES ▸ prune

PRUNEY, PRUNIER, PRUNIEST adj resembling a prune

PRUNING, -S ▸ prune

PRUNT, -S n glass ornamentation

PRUNTED ▸ prunt

PRUNTS ▸ prunt

PRUNUS, -ES n type of ornamental tree or shrub

PRURIGO, -S n chronic inflammatory disease of the skin

PRURITIC ▸ pruritus

PRURITUS n any intense sensation of itching

PRUSIK, -ED, -S n sliding knot used in climbing ▷ vb climb (up a rope) using prusiks

PRUSSIAN adj as in prussian blue colour pigment, discovered in Berlin

PRUSSIC adj as in prussic acid weakly acidic extremely poisonous aqueous solution of hydrogen cyanide

PRUTA same as ▸ prutah

PRUTAH, PRUTOT, PRUTOTH n former Israeli coin

PRY, PRIED, PRIES vb make an impertinent or uninvited inquiry into a private matter ▷ n act of prying

PRYER, -S same as ▸ prier

PRYING, -S ▸ pry

PRYINGLY ▸ pry

PRYINGS ▸ prying

PRYS old variant of ▸ price

PRYSE, -D, -S, PRYSING old variant of ▸ price

PRYTANEA > prytaneum

PRYTHEE same as ▸ prithee

PSALM, -ED, -ING, -S n sacred song ▷ vb sing a psalm

PSALMIC ▸ psalm

PSALMING ▸ psalm

PSALMIST n writer of psalms

PSALMODY n singing of sacred music

PSALMS ▸ psalm

PSALTER, -S n book containing a version of Psalms

PSALTERY n ancient instrument played by plucking strings

PSALTRY same as ▸ psaltery

PSAMMITE rare name for > sandstone

PSAMMON, -S n microscopic life forms living between grains of sand

PSCHENT, -S n ancient Egyptian crown

PSELLISM n stammering

PSEPHISM n proposition adopted by a majority vote

PSEPHITE n any rock that consists of large fragments embedded in a finer matrix

PSEUD, -S n pretentious person

PSEUDERY n pretentious talk

PSEUDISH ▸ pseud

PSEUDO, -S n pretentious person

PSEUDS ▸ pseud

PSHAW, -ED, -ING, -S n exclamation of disgust, impatience, disbelief, etc ▷ vb make this exclamation

PSI, -S n 23rd letter of the Greek alphabet

PSILOCIN n hallucinogenic substance

PSILOSIS, PSILOSES n disease of the small intestine

PSILOTIC ▸ psilosis

PSION, -S n type of elementary particle

PSIONIC ▸ psionics

PSIONICS n study of the practical use of psychic powers

PSIONS ▸ psion

PSIS ▸ psi

PSOAS, PSOAE, PSOAI, -ES n either of two muscles of the loins that aid in flexing and rotating the thigh

PSOATIC ▸ psoas

PSOCID, -S n tiny wingless insect

PSORA, -S n itching skin complaint

PSORALEA n type of tropical and subtropical plant with curly leaves and white or purple flowers

PSORALEN n treatment for some skin diseases

PSORAS ▸ psora

PSORIC ▸ psora

PSST interj sound made to attract someone's attention

PST interj sound made to attract someone's attention

You would need to be fairly desperate to use good letters to play this exclamation, but sometimes with no vowels on your rack things can be that desperate.

PSYCH, -ED, -ES, -ING, -S vb psychoanalyse

PSYCHE same as ▸ **psych**

PSYCHED ▸ **psych**

PSYCHES ▸ **psych**

PSYCHIC, -S adj having mental powers which cannot be explained by natural laws ▷ n person with psychic powers

PSYCHING ▸ **psych**

PSYCHISM n belief in a universal soul

PSYCHIST ▸ **psychism**

PSYCHOID n name for an animal's innate impetus to perform actions

PSYCHS ▸ **psych**

PSYLLA, -S same as ▸ **psyllid**

PSYLLID, -S n type of insect of the family which comprises the jumping plant lice

PSYLLIUM n grain, the husks of which are used as a laxative

PSYOP, -S n psychological operation

PSYWAR, -S n psychological warfare

PTARMIC, -S n material that causes sneezing

PTERIA ▸ **pterion**

PTERIN, -S n compound such as folic acid

PTERION, PTERIA n point on the side of the skull where a number of bones meet

PTEROIC adj as in **pteroic acid** a kind of acid found in spinach

PTEROPOD n small marine gastropod mollusc

PTERYGIA > **pterygium**

PTERYLA, -E n any of the tracts of skin that bear contour feathers

PTILOSIS, PTILOSES n falling out of eye lashes

PTISAN, -S n grape juice drained off without pressure

PTOMAIN, -S same as ▸ **ptomaine**

PTOMAINE n any of a group of poisonous alkaloids found in decaying matter

PTOMAINS ▸ **ptomain**

PTOOEY interj imitation of the sound of spitting

PTOSIS, PTOSES n prolapse or drooping of a part, esp the eyelid

PTOTIC ▸ **ptosis**

PTUI same as ▸ **ptooey**

PTYALIN, -S n amylase secreted in the saliva of human beings and other animals

PTYALISE same as ▸ **ptyalize**

PTYALISM n excessive secretion of saliva

PTYALIZE vb expel saliva from the mouth

PTYXIS, PTYXES, -ES n folding of a leaf in a bud

PUB, -BED, -BING, -S n building with a bar licensed to sell alcoholic drinks ▷ vb visit a pub or pubs

PUBBINGS ▸ **pubbing**

PUBCO, -S n company operating a chain of pubs

PUBERAL adj relating to puberty

PUBERTAL ▸ **puberty**

PUBERTY n period at the beginning of adolescence

PUBIC adj of the lower abdomen

PUBIS, -ES n one of the three sections of the hipbone that forms part of the pelvis

PUBLIC, -S adj of or concerning the people as a whole ▷ n community, people in general

PUBLICAN n person who owns or runs a pub

PUBLICLY adv in a public manner

PUBLICS ▸ **public**

PUBLISH vb produce and issue (printed matter) for sale

PUBS ▸ **pub**

PUCAN, -S n traditional Connemara open sailing boat

PUCCOON, -S n N American plant that yields a red dye

PUCE, -R, -S, -ST adj purplish-brown ▷ n colour varying from deep red to dark purplish-brown

PUCELAGE n state of being a maid or girl

PUCELLE, -S n maid or girl

PUCER ▸ **puce**

PUCES ▸ **puce**

PUCEST ▸ **puce**

PUCK, -ED, -ING, -S n mischievous or evil spirit ▷ vb strike (the ball) in hurling

PUCKA same as ▸ **pukka**

PUCKED ▸ **puck**

PUCKER, -ED, -S vb gather into wrinkles ▷ n wrinkle or crease

PUCKERER ▸ **pucker**

PUCKERS ▸ **pucker**

PUCKERY adj tending to pucker ▷ n puckishness

PUCKFIST n puffball

PUCKING ▸ **puck**

PUCKISH ▸ **puck**

PUCKLE, -S n early type of machine gun

PUCKOUT, -S n (in hurling) free hit made by the goalkeeper

PUCKS ▸ **puck**

PUCKSTER n hockey player

PUD, -S short for ▸ **pudding**

PUDDEN, -S dialect spelling of ▸ **pudding**

PUDDER, -ED, -S vb make bother or fuss

PUDDIER ▸ **puddy**

PUDDIES ▸ **puddy**

PUDDIEST ▸ **puddy**

PUDDING, -S n dessert, esp a cooked one served hot

PUDDINGY adj having the consistency of a pudding

PUDDLE, -D, -S n small pool of water, esp of rain ▷ vb make (clay etc) into puddle

PUDDLER, -S ▸ **puddle**

PUDDLES ▸ **puddle**

PUDDLIER ▸ **puddly**

PUDDLING n process for converting pig iron into wrought iron

PUDDLY, PUDDLIER ▸ **puddle**

PUDDOCK, -S same as ▸ **paddock**

PUDDY, PUDDIER, PUDDIES, PUDDIEST n paw ▷ adj short and podgy

PUDENCY n modesty, shame, or prudishness

PUDENDA ▸ **pudendum**

PUDENDAL ▸ **pudendum**

PUDENDUM, PUDENDA n human external genital organs collectively, esp female

PUDENT adj lacking in ostentation; humble

PUDEUR, -S n sense of shame or embarrassment

PUDGE, -S same as ▸ **podge**

PUDGIER ▸ **pudgy**

PUDGIEST ▸ **pudgy**

PUDGILY ▸ **pudgy**

PUDGY, PUDGIER, PUDGIEST adj podgy

PUDIBUND adj prudish

P

PUDIC adj relating to the pudenda

PUDICITY n modesty

PUDOR, -S n sense of shame

PUDS ▶ pud

PUDSEY variant of ▶ pudsy

PUDSY, PUDSIER, PUDSIES, PUDSIEST adj plump ▷ n plump person

PUDU, -S n diminutive Andean antelope

PUEBLO, -S n communal village of flat-roofed houses

PUER, -ED, -ING, -S vb steep hides in an alkaline substance from the dung of dogs

PUERILE adj silly and childish

PUERING ▶ puer

PUERPERA n woman who has recently given birth

PUERS ▶ puer

PUFF, -ED, -S n (sound of) short blast of breath, wind, etc ▷ vb blow or breathe in short quick draughts

PUFFA adj type of quilted and padded jacket

PUFFBACK n type of small African bird

PUFFBALL n ball-shaped fungus

PUFFBIRD n brownish tropical American bird with a large head

PUFFED ▶ puff

PUFFER, -S n person or thing that puffs

PUFFERY n exaggerated praise, esp in publicity or advertising

PUFFIER ▶ puffy

PUFFIEST ▶ puffy

PUFFILY ▶ puffy

PUFFIN, -S n sea bird with a brightly coloured beak

PUFFING, -S ▶ puff

PUFFINS ▶ puffin

PUFFS ▶ puff

PUFFY, PUFFIER, PUFFIEST adj short of breath

PUG, -GED, -S n small snub-nosed dog ▷ vb mix or knead (clay) with water to form a malleable mass or paste

PUGAREE, -S same as ▶ puggree

PUGGAREE same as ▶ puggree

PUGGED ▶ pug

PUGGERY same as ▶ puggree

PUGGIE, -S n Scottish word for fruit machine

PUGGIER ▶ puggy

PUGGIES ▶ puggie

PUGGIEST ▶ puggy

PUGGING, -S ▶ pug

PUGGISH ▶ pug

PUGGLE, -D, -S, PUGGLING vb stir up by poking

PUGGREE, -S n scarf, usually pleated, around the crown of some hats, esp sun helmets

PUGGRY, PUGGRIES same as ▶ puggree

PUGGY, PUGGIER, PUGGIEST adj sticky, claylike ▷ n term of endearment

PUGH interj exclamation of disgust

PUGIL, -S n pinch or small handful

PUGILISM n art, practice, or profession of fighting with the fists

PUGILIST ▶ pugilism

PUGILS ▶ pugil

PUGMARK, -S n trail of an animal

PUGREE, -S same as ▶ puggree

PUGS ▶ pug

PUH interj exclamation expressing contempt or disgust

PUHA, -S n sow thistle

PUIR, -ER, -EST Scottish word for ▶ poor

PUIRTITH n poverty

PUISNE, -S adj (esp of a subordinate judge) of lower rank ▷ n judge of lower rank

PUISNY adj younger or inferior

PUISSANT adj powerful

PUJA, -S n ritual in honour of the gods, performed either at home or in the mandir (temple)

PUJAH, -S same as ▶ puja

PUJARI, -S n Hindu priest

PUJAS ▶ puja

PUKA, -S in New Zealand English, same as ▶ broadleaf

PUKATEA, -S n aromatic New Zealand tree

PUKE, -D, -S, PUKING vb vomit ▷ n act of vomiting

PUKEKO, -S n brightly coloured New Zealand wading bird

PUKER, -S n person who vomits

PUKES ▶ puke

PUKEY, PUKIER, PUKIEST adj of or like vomit

PUKING ▶ puke

PUKKA adj properly done, constructed, etc

PUKKAH adj genuine

PUKU, -S n belly or stomach

PUKY same as ▶ pukey

PUL, -IK, -S n Afghan monetary unit

PULA, -S n standard monetary unit of Botswana

PULAO, -S same as ▶ pilau

PULAS ▶ pula

PULDRON, -S same as ▶ pauldron

PULE, -D, -S vb whine or whimper

PULER, -S ▶ pule

PULES ▶ pule

PULI, -S n Hungarian sheepdog

PULICENE adj flea-ridden

PULICIDE n flea-killing substance

PULIER ▶ puly

PULIEST ▶ puly

PULIK ▶ pul

PULING, -S ▶ pule

PULINGLY ▶ pule

PULINGS ▶ puling

PULIS ▶ puli

PULK, -S same as ▶ pulka

PULKA, -S n reindeer-drawn sleigh

PULKHA, -S same as ▶ pulka

PULKS ▶ pulk

PULL, -ED, -ING, -S vb exert force on (an object) to move it towards the source of the force ▷ n act of pulling

PULLBACK n act of pulling back

PULLED ▶ pull

PULLER, -S ▶ pull

PULLET, -S n young hen

PULLEY, -ED, -S n device for lifting weights by a downward pull ▷ vb lift with a pulley

PULLI ▶ pullus

PULLIES ▶ pully

PULLING ▶ pull

PULLMAN, -S n luxurious railway coach, esp a sleeping car

PULLORUM n as in **pullorum disease** acute serious bacterial disease of very young birds

PULLOUT, -S n removable section of a magazine, etc

PULLOVER n sweater that is pulled on over the head

PULLS ▶ pull

PULLUP, -S n exercise in which the body is raised by the arms pulling on a horizontal bar

PULLUS, PULLI n technical term for a chick or young bird

PULLY, PULLIES n pullover

PULMO, -NES n lung

PULMONIC adj of or relating to the lungs ▷ n person with lung disease

PULMOTOR n apparatus for pumping oxygen into the lungs during artificial respiration

PULP, -ED, -S n soft wet substance made from crushed or beaten matter ▷ vb reduce to pulp

PULPAL ▶ pulp

PULPALLY ▶ pulp

PULPED ▶ pulp

PULPER, -S ▶ pulp

PULPIER ▶ pulpy

PULPIEST ▶ pulpy

PULPIFY vb reduce to pulp

PULPILY ▶ pulpy

PULPING, -S n act of pulping

PULPIT, -S n raised platform for a preacher

PULPITAL ▶ pulpit

PULPITED ▶ pulpit

PULPITER n preacher

PULPITRY n art of delivering sermons

PULPITS ▶ pulpit

PULPITUM n stone screen dividing nave and choir

PULPLESS ▶ pulp

PULPMILL n mill making raw material for paper

PULPOUS adj soft and yielding

PULPS ▶ pulp

PULPWOOD n pine, spruce, or any other soft wood used to make paper

PULPY, PULPIER, PULPIEST adj having a soft or soggy consistency

PULQUE, -S n light alcoholic drink from Mexico

PULS ▶ pul

PULSANT adj vibrant

PULSAR, -S n small dense star which emits regular bursts of radio waves

PULSATE, -D, -S vb throb, quiver

PULSATOR n device that stimulates rhythmic motion of a body

PULSE, -D, -S, PULSING n regular beating of blood through the arteries at each heartbeat ▷ vb beat, throb, or vibrate

PULSEJET n type of ramjet engine

PULSER, -S n thing that pulses

PULSES ▶ pulse

PULSIDGE archaic word for ▶ pulse

PULSIFIC adj causing the pulse to increase

PULSING ▶ pulse

PULSION, -S n act of driving forward

PULSOJET same as ▶ pulsejet

PULTAN, -S n native Indian regiment

PULTON, -S same as ▶ pultan

PULTOON, -S same as ▶ pultan

PULTRUDE vb produce reinforced plastic process by pultrusion

PULTUN, -S same as ▶ pultan

PULTURE, -S n food and drink claimed by foresters

PULU, -S n substance used for stuffing cushions

PULVER, -ED, -S vb make into powder

PULVIL, -S vb apply perfumed powder

PULVILIO n perfumed powder

PULVILLE same as ▶ pulvil

PULVILLI > pulvillus

PULVILS ▶ pulvil

PULVINAR n part of the thalamus

PULVINUS, PULVINI n swelling at the base of a leafstalk

PULWAR, -S n light Indian river boat

PULY, PULIER, PULIEST adj whiny

PUMA, -S n large American wild cat with a greyish-brown coat

PUMELO, -S same as ▶ pomelo

PUMICATE vb pound fruit with pumice to make juice

PUMICE, -D, -S, PUMICING n light porous stone used for scouring ▷ vb rub or polish with pumice

PUMICER, -S ▶ pumice

PUMICES ▶ pumice

PUMICING ▶ pumice

PUMICITE n fine-grained variety of pumice

PUMIE, -S n small stone

PUMMEL, -ED, -S vb strike repeatedly with or as if with the fists

PUMMELO, -S same as ▶ pomelo

PUMMELS ▶ pummel

PUMP, -ED, -ING, -S n machine used to force a liquid or gas to move in a particular direction ▷ vb raise or drive with a pump

PUMPABLE adj capable of being pumped

PUMPED ▶ pump

PUMPER, -S ▶ pump

PUMPHOOD n cover for the upper wheel of a chain pump

PUMPING, -S ▶ pump

PUMPION, -S archaic word for ▶ pumpkin

PUMPJACK n pumping apparatus at an oil well

PUMPKIN, -S n large round fruit with an orange rind

PUMPKING n programmer with authority to change the master source code

PUMPKINS ▶ pumpkin

PUMPLESS ▶ pump

PUMPLIKE ▶ pump

PUMPS ▶ pump

PUMY adj large and round

PUN, -NED, -S n use of words to exploit double meanings for humorous effect ▷ vb make puns

PUNA, -S n high cold dry plateau, esp in the Andes

PUNALUA, -S n marriage between the sisters of one family to the brothers of another

PUNALUAN ▶ punalua

PUNALUAS ▶ punalua

PUNAS ▶ puna

PUNCE, -D, -S, PUNCING n kick ▷ vb kick

PUNCH, -ED, -ES, -ING vb strike at with a clenched fist ▷ n blow with a clenched fist

PUNCHBAG n stuffed bag punched for boxing training

PUNCHED ▶ punch

PUNCHEON n large cask of variable capacity, usually between 70 and 120 gallons

PUNCHER, -S ▶ punch

PUNCHES ▶ punch

PUNCHIER ▶ punchy

PUNCHILY ▶ punchy

PUNCHING ▶ punch

PUNCHOUT n fist fight

PUNCHY, PUNCHIER adj forceful

PUNCING ▶ punce

PUNCTA ▶ punctum

PUNCTATE adj having or marked with minute spots, holes, or depressions

PUNCTO, -S n tip of a fencing sword

PUNCTUAL adj arriving or taking place at the correct time

PUNCTULE n very small opening

PUNCTUM, PUNCTA, -S *n* tip or small point

PUNCTURE *n* small hole made by a sharp object, esp in a tyre ▷ *vb* pierce a hole in

PUNDIT, -S *n* expert who speaks publicly on a subject

PUNDITIC *adj* of or relating to pundits

PUNDITRY *n* expressing of expert opinions

PUNDITS ▷ **pundit**

PUNDONOR *n* point of honour

PUNG, -S *n* horse-drawn sleigh with a boxlike body on runners

PUNGA, -S *variant spelling of* ▷ **ponga**

PUNGENCE *n* pungency

PUNGENCY ▷ **pungent**

PUNGENT *adj* having a strong sharp bitter flavour

PUNGLE, -D, -S, PUNGLING *vb* make payment

PUNGS ▷ **pung**

PUNIER ▷ **puny**

PUNIEST ▷ **puny**

PUNILY ▷ **puny**

PUNINESS ▷ **puny**

PUNISH, -ED, -ES *vb* cause (someone) to suffer or undergo a penalty for some wrongdoing

PUNISHER ▷ **punish**

PUNISHES ▷ **punish**

PUNITION *n* punishment

PUNITIVE *adj* relating to punishment

PUNITORY *same as* ▷ **punitive**

PUNJI, -ED, -ES, -ING, -S *n* sharpened bamboo stick ▷ *vb* fortify with punjis

PUNK, -ER, -ERS, -EST, -S *n* style of rock music of the late 1970s ▷ *adj* relating to the punk movement

PUNKA, -S *n* fan made of a palm leaf or leaves

PUNKAH, -S *same as* ▷ **punka**

PUNKAS ▷ **punka**

PUNKER ▷ **punk**

PUNKERS ▷ **punk**

PUNKEST ▷ **punk**

PUNKETTE *n* female follower of punk music

PUNKEY, -S *n* small winged insect

PUNKIE, -S *same as* ▷ **punkey**

PUNKIER ▷ **punky**

PUNKIES ▷ **punkie**

PUNKIEST ▷ **punky**

PUNKIN, -S *same as* ▷ **pumpkin**

PUNKISH ▷ **punk**

PUNKS ▷ **punk**

PUNKY, PUNKIER, PUNKIEST *adj* of punk music

PUNNED ▷ **pun**

PUNNER, -S ▷ **pun**

PUNNET, -S *n* small basket for fruit

PUNNIER ▷ **punny**

PUNNIEST ▷ **punny**

PUNNING, -S ▷ **pun**

PUNNY, PUNNIER, PUNNIEST *adj* of puns

PUNS ▷ **pun**

PUNSTER, -S *n* person who is fond of making puns

PUNT, -ED, -ING, -S *n* open flat-bottomed boat propelled by a pole ▷ *vb* travel in a punt

PUNTEE, -S *same as* ▷ **punty**

PUNTER, -S *n* informal word for a member of the public

PUNTIES ▷ **punty**

PUNTING ▷ **punt**

PUNTO, -S *n* hit in fencing

PUNTS ▷ **punt**

PUNTSMAN, PUNTSMEN *n* man in charge of a river punt

PUNTY, PUNTIES *n* long iron rod used in the finishing process of glass-blowing

PUNY, PUNIER, PUNIEST *adj* small and feeble

PUP, -PED, -PING, -S *n* young of certain animals, such as dogs and seals ▷ *vb* (of dogs, seals, etc) to give birth to pups

PUPA, -E, -S *n* insect at the stage of development between a larva and an adult

PUPAL ▷ **pupa**

PUPARIA ▷ **puparium**

PUPARIAL ▷ **puparium**

PUPARIUM, PUPARIA *n* case enclosing the pupae of certain insects

PUPAS ▷ **pupa**

PUPATE, -D, -S, PUPATING *vb* (of an insect larva) to develop into a pupa

PUPATION ▷ **pupate**

PUPFISH *n* type of small fish

PUPIL, -S *n* person who is taught by a teacher

PUPILAGE *same as* > **pupillage**

PUPILAR ▷ **pupil**

PUPILARY *same as* > **pupillary**

PUPILLAR ▷ **pupil**

PUPILS ▷ **pupil**

PUPPED ▷ **pup**

PUPPET, -S *n* small doll or figure moved by strings or by the operator's hand

PUPPETRY *n* art of making and manipulating puppets and presenting puppet shows

PUPPETS ▷ **puppet**

PUPPIED ▷ **puppy**

PUPPIES ▷ **puppy**

PUPPING ▷ **pup**

PUPPODUM *same as* ▷ **poppadom**

PUPPY, PUPPIED, PUPPIES, -ING *n* young dog ▷ *vb* have puppies

PUPPYDOM *n* state of being a puppy

PUPPYING ▷ **puppy**

PUPPYISH ▷ **puppy**

PUPPYISM *n* impudence

PUPS ▷ **pup**

PUPU, -S *n* Hawaiian dish

PUPUNHA, -S *n* fruit of a type of palm tree

PUPUS ▷ **pupu**

PUR, -S *same as* ▷ **purr**

PURANA, -S *n* type of Sanskrit sacred writing

PURANIC ▷ **purana**

PURBLIND *adj* partly or nearly blind

PURCHASE *vb* obtain by payment ▷ *n* thing that is bought

PURDA, -S *same as* ▷ **purdah**

PURDAH, -S *n* Muslim and Hindu custom of keeping women in seclusion

PURDAHED ▷ **purdah**

PURDAHS ▷ **purdah**

PURDAS ▷ **purda**

PURE, -D, -R, -S, -ST, PURING *adj* unmixed, untainted ▷ *vb* make pure

PUREBRED *adj* denoting a pure strain obtained through many generations of controlled breeding ▷ *n* purebred animal

PURED ▷ **pure**

PUREE, -D, -ING, -S *n* smooth thick pulp of cooked and sieved fruit, vegetables, meat, or fish ▷ *vb* make (cooked foods) into a puree

PURELY *adv* in a pure manner

PURENESS ▷ **pure**

PURER ▷ **pure**

PURES ▷ **pure**

PUREST ▷ **pure**

PURFLE, -D, -S *n* ruffled or curved ornamental band ▷ *vb* decorate with such a band or bands

PURFLER, -S ▸ purfle

PURFLES ▸ purfle

PURFLING same as ▸ **purfle**

PURFLY ▸ purfle

PURGE, -D, -S n rid (a thing or place) of (unwanted things or people) ▷ n purging

PURGER, -S ▸ purge

PURGES ▸ purge

PURGING, -S ▸ purge

PURI, -S n unleavened flaky Indian bread, that is deep-fried in ghee and served hot

PURIFIED ▸ purify

PURIFIER n device or substance that frees something of extraneous, contaminating, or debasing matter

PURIFY, PURIFIED, PURIFIES vb make or become pure

PURIN, -S same as ▸ **purine**

PURINE, -S n colourless crystalline solid that can be prepared from uric acid

PURING ▸ pure

PURINS ▸ purin

PURIRI, -S n forest tree of New Zealand

PURIS ▸ puri

PURISM, -S n strict insistence on the correct usage or style

PURIST, -S ▸ purism

PURISTIC ▸ purism

PURISTS ▸ purist

PURITAN, -S n person who follows strict moral or religious principles ▷ adj of or like a puritan

PURITY, PURITIES n state or quality of being pure

PURL, -ED, -S n stitch made by knitting a plain stitch backwards ▷ vb knit in purl

PURLER, -S n headlong or spectacular fall

PURLICUE vb finish a pen stroke with a flourish

PURLIEU, -S, -X n land on the edge of a royal forest

PURLIN, -S n horizontal beam that supports the rafters of a roof

PURLINE, -S same as ▸ **purlin**

PURLING, -S ▸ purl

PURLINS ▸ purlin

PURLOIN, -S vb steal

PURLS ▸ purl

PURPIE, -S old Scots word for ▸ **purslane**

PURPLE, -D, -R, -S, -ST, PURPLING n colour between red and blue ▷ adj of a colour between red and blue ▷ vb make purple

PURPLIER ▸ purply

PURPLING ▸ purple

PURPLISH ▸ purple

PURPLY, PURPLIER ▸ purple

PURPORT, -S vb claim (to be or do something) ▷ n apparent meaning, significance

PURPOSE, -D, -S n reason for which something is done or exists ▷ vb intend to do (something)

PURPURA, -S n blood disease causing purplish spots

PURPURE, -S n purple

PURPURIC ▸ purpura

PURPURIN n red crystalline compound used as a stain for biological specimens

PURPY variant of ▸ **purpie**

PURR, -ED, -S vb (of cats) make low vibrant sound, usu when pleased ▷ n this sound

PURRING, -S ▸ purr

PURRS ▸ purr

PURS ▸ pur

PURSE, -D, -S, PURSING n small bag for money ▷ vb draw (one's lips) together into a small round shape

PURSEFUL n that which can be contained in purse

PURSER, -S n ship's officer who keeps the accounts

PURSES ▸ purse

PURSEW, -ED, -S archaic spelling of ▸ **pursue**

PURSIER ▸ pursy

PURSIEST ▸ pursy

PURSILY ▸ pursy

PURSING ▸ purse

PURSLAIN same as ▸ **purslane**

PURSLANE n weedy plant used in salads

PURSUAL, -S n act of pursuit

PURSUANT adj in agreement or conformity

PURSUE, -D, -S, PURSUING vb chase

PURSUER, -S ▸ pursue

PURSUES ▸ pursue

PURSUING ▸ pursue

PURSUIT, -S n pursuing

PURSY, PURSIER, PURSIEST adj short-winded

PURTIER ▸ purty

PURTIEST ▸ purty

PURTRAID variant of ▸ **purtrayd**

PURTRAYD adj archaic spelling of portrayed

PURTY, PURTIER, PURTIEST adj pretty

PURULENT adj of or containing pus

PURVEY, -ED, -S vb supply (provisions) ▷ n food and drink laid on at a wedding reception, etc

PURVEYOR n person, organization, etc, that supplies food and provisions

PURVEYS ▸ purvey

PURVIEW, -S n scope or range of activity or outlook

PUS, -ES n yellowish matter produced by infected tissue

PUSH, -ES vb move or try to move by steady force ▷ n act of pushing

PUSHBACK n negative or unfavourable response

PUSHBALL n game in which two teams try to push a heavy ball towards opposite goals

PUSHBIKE n pedal-driven bicycle

PUSHCART n handcart, typically having two wheels and a canvas roof, used esp by street vendors

PUSHDOWN n list in which the last item added is at the top

PUSHED adj short of

PUSHER, -S n person who or thing that pushes

PUSHES ▸ push

PUSHFUL ▸ push

PUSHIER ▸ pushy

PUSHIEST ▸ pushy

PUSHILY ▸ pushy

PUSHING prep almost or nearly (a certain age, speed, etc) ▷ adj aggressively ambitious ▷ adv almost or nearly (a certain age, speed, etc)

PUSHOVER n something easily achieved

PUSHPIN, -S n pin with a small ball-shaped head

PUSHPIT, -S n safety rail at the stern of a boat

PUSHROD, -S n metal rod transmitting motion in an engine

PUSHUP, -S n exercise in which the body is raised and lowered to the floor by the arms

P

PUSHY, PUSHIER, PUSHIEST adj too assertive or ambitious

PUSLE, -D, -S, PUSLING old spelling of ▸ **puzzle**

PUSLEY, -S same as ▸ **purslane**

PUSLIKE ▸ **pus**

PUSLING ▸ **pusle**

PUSS, -ES same as ▸ **pussy**

PUSSEL, -S n maid or girl

PUSSER, -S n naval purser

PUSSES ▸ **puss**

PUSSIER ▸ **pussy**

PUSSIES ▸ **pussy**

PUSSIEST ▸ **pussy**

PUSSLEY, -S n weedy trailing herb

PUSSLIES ▸ **pussly**

PUSSLIKE ▸ **puss**

PUSSLY, PUSSLIES variant of ▸ **pussley**

PUSSY, PUSSIER, PUSSIES, PUSSIEST n cat ▸ adj containing or full of pus

PUSSYCAT same as ▸ **pussy**

PUSTULAR ▸ **pustule**

PUSTULE, -S n pimple containing pus

PUSTULED ▸ **pustule**

PUSTULES ▸ **pustule**

PUT, -S vb cause to be (in a position, state, or place) ▸ n throw in putting the shot

PUTAMEN, -S, PUTAMINA n hard endocarp or stone of fruit

PUTATIVE adj reputed, supposed

PUTCHEON n trap for catching salmon

PUTCHER, -S n trap for catching salmon

PUTCHOCK same as ▸ **pachak**

PUTCHUK, -S same as ▸ **pachak**

PUTDOWN, -S n snub or insult

PUTEAL, -S n enclosure around a well

PUTELI, -S n (in India) type of boat

PUTID adj having an unpleasant odour

PUTLOCK, -S same as ▸ **putlog**

PUTLOG, -S n short horizontal beam that with others supports the floor planks of a scaffold

PUTOFF, -S n pretext or delay

PUTOIS n brush to paint pottery

PUTON, -S n hoax or piece of mockery

PUTOUT, -S n baseball play in which the batter or runner is put out

PUTREFY vb rot and produce an offensive smell

PUTRID, -ER adj rotten and foul-smelling

PUTRIDLY ▸ **putrid**

PUTS ▸ **put**

PUTSCH, -ES n sudden violent attempt to remove a government from power

PUTT, -ED, -S n stroke on the putting green to roll the ball into or near the hole ▸ vb strike (the ball) in this way

PUTTEE, -S n strip of cloth worn around the leg

PUTTEN old Scots past participle of ▸ **put**

PUTTER, -ED, -S n golf club for putting ▸ vb busy oneself in a desultory though agreeable manner

PUTTERER ▸ **putter**

PUTTERS ▸ **putter**

PUTTI ▸ **putto**

PUTTIE same as ▸ **puttee**

PUTTIED ▸ **putty**

PUTTIER, -S n glazier

PUTTIES ▸ **putty**

PUTTING, -S ▸ **put**

PUTTO, PUTTI n representation of a small boy

PUTTOCK, -S n type of bird of prey

PUTTS ▸ **putt**

PUTTY, PUTTIED, PUTTIES, -ING n stiff paste of whiting and linseed oil ▸ vb fill, fix, or coat with putty

PUTURE, -S n claim of foresters for food

PUTZ, -ED, -ES, -ING n despicable or stupid person ▸ vb waste time

PUY, -S n small volcanic cone

PUZEL, -S same as ▸ **pucelle**

PUZZEL, -S same as ▸ **pucelle**

PUZZLE, -D, -S vb perplex and confuse or be perplexed or confused ▸ n problem that cannot be easily solved

PUZZLER, -S n person or thing that puzzles

PUZZLES ▸ **puzzle**

PUZZLING ▸ **puzzle**

PWN, -ED, -ING, -S vb defeat (an opponent) in conclusive and humiliating fashion

PYA, -S n monetary unit of Myanmar worth one hundredth of a kyat

PYAEMIA, -S n type of blood poisoning

PYAEMIC ▸ **pyaemia**

PYAS ▸ **pya**

PYAT, -S n magpie ▸ adj pied

PYCNIC same as ▸ **pyknic**

PYCNIDIA > pycnidium

PYCNITE, -S n variety of topaz

PYCNON, -S old word for ▸ **semitone**

PYCNOSIS, PYCNOSES n process of shrinking in a cell nucleus

PYCNOTIC ▸ **pycnosis**

PYE, -ING, -S same as ▸ **pie**

PYEBALD, -S same as ▸ **piebald**

PYEING ▸ **pye**

PYELITIC ▸ **pyelitis**

PYELITIS n inflammation of the pelvis of the kidney

PYEMIA, -S same as ▸ **pyaemia**

PYEMIC ▸ **pyaemia**

PYENGADU variant of ▸ **pyinkado**

PYES ▸ **pye**

PYET, -S same as ▸ **pyat**

PYGAL, -S n rear part

PYGARG, -S n type of horned mammal

PYGARGUS n white-tailed bird of prey

PYGIDIA ▸ **pygidium**

PYGIDIAL ▸ **pygidium**

PYGIDIUM, PYGIDIA n terminal division in certain invertebrates

PYGMAEAN ▸ **pygmy**

PYGMEAN ▸ **pygmy**

PYGMIES ▸ **pygmy**

PYGMOID, -S adj of or like pygmies ▸ n pygmy

PYGMY, PYGMIES n something that is a very small example of its type ▸ adj very small

PYGMYISH ▸ **pygmy**

PYGMYISM ▸ **pygmy**

PYIC adj relating to pus

PYIN, -S n constituent of pus

PYINKADO n leguminous tree native to India and Myanmar

PYINS ▸ **pyin**

PYJAMA same as ▸ **pyjamas**

PYJAMAED ▸ **pyjamas**

PYJAMAS pl n loose-fitting trousers and top worn in bed

PYKNIC, -S adj characterized by a broad squat fleshy physique ▸ n person with this physical type

PYKNOSIS, PYKNOSES n thickening of a cell

PYKNOTIC ▶ pyknosis
PYLON, -S *n* steel tower-like structure supporting electrical cables
PYLORI ▶ pylorus
PYLORIC ▶ pylorus
PYLORUS, PYLORI *n* small circular opening at the base of the stomach
PYNE, -D, -S, PYNING *archaic variant of* ▶ **pine**
PYODERMA *n* any skin eruption characterized by pustules or the formation of pus
PYOGENIC *adj* of or relating to the formation of pus
PYOID *adj* resembling pus
PYONER, -S *old variant of* ▶ **pioneer**
PYONINGS *n* old term for the work of pioneers
PYORRHEA *same as* > **pyorrhoea**
PYOSIS, PYOSES *n* formation of pus
PYOT, -S *same as* ▶ **pyat**
PYRAL ▶ pyre
PYRALID, -S *n* tropical moth
PYRALIS *same as* ▶ **pyralid**
PYRAMID, -S *n* solid figure with a flat base and triangular sides sloping upwards to a point ▷ *vb* build up or be arranged in the form of a pyramid
PYRAMIS *n* pyramid-shaped structure
PYRAN, -S *n* unsaturated heterocyclic organic compound
PYRANOID ▶ pyran
PYRANOSE *n* structure in many sugars
PYRANS ▶ pyran
PYRAZOLE *n* crystalline soluble basic heterocyclic compound
PYRE, -S *n* pile of wood for burning a corpse on
PYRENE, -S *n* solid polynuclear aromatic hydrocarbon extracted from coal tar
PYRENOID *n* any of various small protein granules that occur in certain algae
PYRES ▶ pyre
PYRETIC *adj* of, relating to, or characterized by fever

PYREX, -ES *n* tradename for glass used in cookery and chemical apparatus
PYREXIA, -S *technical name for* ▶ **fever**
PYREXIAL ▶ pyrexia
PYREXIAS ▶ pyrexia
PYREXIC ▶ pyrexia
PYRIC *adj* of or relating to burning
PYRIDIC ▶ pyridine
PYRIDINE *n* colourless hygroscopic liquid with a characteristic odour
PYRIFORM *adj* (esp of organs of the body) pear-shaped
PYRITE *n* yellow mineral consisting of iron sulphide in cubic crystalline form
PYRITES *same as* ▶ **pyrite**
PYRITIC ▶ pyrite
PYRITISE *same as* ▶ **pyritize**
PYRITIZE *vb* convert into pyrites
PYRITOUS ▶ pyrite
PYRO, -S *n* pyromaniac
PYROGEN, -S *n* any of a group of substances that cause a rise in temperature in an animal body
PYROGY, PYROGIES *same as* ▶ **pierogi**
PYROHY, PYROHIES *same as* ▶ **perogi**
PYROLA, -S *n* evergreen perennial
PYROLISE *same as* ▶ **pyrolize**
PYROLIZE *vb* subject to pyrolysis
PYROLOGY *n* study of heat
PYROLYSE *vb* subject to pyrolysis
PYROLYZE *same as* ▶ **pyrolyse**
PYRONE, -S *n* type of heterocyclic compound
PYRONIN, -S *n* red dye used as a biological stain
PYRONINE *same as* ▶ **pyronin**
PYRONINS ▶ pyronin
PYROPE, -S *n* deep yellowish-red garnet used as a gemstone
PYROPUS *variant of* ▶ **pyrope**
PYROS ▶ pyro
PYROSIS, PYROSES *technical name for* > **heartburn**

PYROSOME *n* tube-shaped glowing marine creature
PYROSTAT *n* device that activates an alarm or extinguisher in the event of a fire
PYROXENE *n* silicate mineral
PYROXYLE *same as* > **pyroxylin**
PYRRHIC, -S *n* metrical foot of two short or unstressed syllables ▷ *adj* of or relating to such a metrical foot
PYRRHOUS *adj* ruddy or reddish
PYRROL, -S *same as* ▶ **pyrrole**
PYRROLE, -S *n* colourless insoluble toxic liquid
PYRROLIC ▶ pyrrole
PYRROLS ▶ pyrrol
PYRUVATE *n* ester or salt of pyruvic acid
PYRUVIC *adj* as in **pyruvic acid** colourless pleasant-smelling liquid
PYSANKA, PYSANKY *n* hand-painted Ukrainian Easter egg
PYTHIUM, -S *n* type of fungi
PYTHON, -S *n* large nonpoisonous snake that crushes its prey
PYTHONIC ▶ python
PYTHONS ▶ python
PYURIA, -S *n* any condition characterized by the presence of pus in the urine
PYX, -ED, -ES, -ING *n* any receptacle for the Eucharistic Host ▷ *vb* put (something) in a pyx

This word can also be spelt **pix**. It's a great word to know as it can earn a good score from a rack that is short of vowels.

PYXIDES ▶ pyxis
PYXIDIUM, PYXIDIA *n* dry fruit of such plants as the plantain
PYXIE, -S *n* creeping evergreen shrub of the eastern US
PYXING ▶ pyx
PYXIS, PYXIDES *same as* ▶ **pyxidium**
PZAZZ, -ES *same as* ▶ **pizzazz**

P

Qq

With a value of 10 points, **Q** can help you to achieve some good scores, but it can also be a very awkward tile, making it difficult to get bonus words scoring that extra 50 points, and you will normally want to play it off quickly. Often you will not have a **U** to go with it, so it's a good idea to remember the short words beginning with **Q** that don't need a **U**. This is easy, as there's only one two-letter word starting with **Q**: **qi** (11 points). There are four three-letter words, only one of which needs a **U**: **qua** (12). The other three are **qat**, **qin** and **qis** (12 each). If you do have a **U**, remember **quiz** (22), which is a very useful word, and can take an **S** at the front to make **squiz**. Don't forget **quartz** (24) either, or the useful **suq** (12 points) that is easily overlooked.

QABALA, -S *same as*
▶ **kabbalah**
QABALAH, -S *same as*
▶ **kabbalah**
QABALAS ▶ **qabala**
QABALISM ▶ **qabalah**
QABALIST ▶ **qabalah**
QADI, -S *variant spelling of*
▶ **cadi**
QAID, -S *n* chief

An Arabic word, this and its variant **qadi** are two of the most frequently played words in Scrabble. There are also alternative spellings **cadi, caid, kadi** and **kaid**.

QAIMAQAM *n* Turkish officer or official
QAJAQ, -S *n* kayak
QALAMDAN *n* writing case
QAMUTIK, -S *n* sledge with wooden runners
QANAT, -S *n* underground irrigation channel

This word comes up many times as one of the words allowing you to play the Q without a U.

QAPIK, -S *n* monetary unit of Azerbaijan
QASIDA, -S *n* Arabic verse form
QAT, -S *variant spelling of*
▶ **khat**

The leaves of this shrub are chewed as a stimulant, and it's certainly been a stimulus for Scrabble, being one of the three 3-letter words that

can be played without a U: the others are **qin** and **qis**.

QAWWAL, -S *n* qawwali singer
QAWWALI, -S *n* Islamic religious song, esp in Asia
QAWWALS ▶ **qawwal**
QI, -S *n* vital energy
QIBLA, -S *variant of* ▶ **kiblah**

The direction in which Muslims turn to pray, a useful word allowing the Q to be played without the U. It can also be spelt **keblah, kibla** and **kiblah**.

QIGONG, -S *n* system of breathing and exercise
QIN, -S *n* Chinese stringed instrument related to the zither

This Chinese musical instrument is another indispensable word as, like **qat**, it combines Q with two of the most common letters in the game.

QINDAR, -KA, -S *n* Albanian monetary unit
QINS ▶ **qin**
QINTAR, -KA, -S *same as*
▶ **qindar**
QIS ▶ **qi**
QIVIUT, -S *n* soft muskox wool
QOPH, -S *variant of* ▶ **koph**

A letter of the Hebrew alphabet, also spelt **koph**. The Hebrew alphabet, like the Greek alphabet, is well

worth studying from the Scrabble point of view, as it gives you many other useful short words like **ayin, beth, heth, kaph** and **lamedh**.

QORMA, -S *variant spelling of*
▶ **korma**
QUA *prep* in the capacity of

This is the only three-letter word beginning with Q that needs a U. It is played so often that it is well worth mastering all the hooks to this: it takes A at the front to make **aqua** and D, G, I, T and Y at the back to make **quad, quag, quai, quat** and **quay**.

QUAALUDE *n* methaqualone
QUACK, -ED, -ING, -S *vb* (of a duck) utter a harsh guttural sound ▷ *n* unqualified person who claims medical knowledge
QUACKER, -S ▶ **quack**
QUACKERY *n* activities or methods of a quack
QUACKIER ▶ **quacky**
QUACKING ▶ **quack**
QUACKISH ▶ **quack**
QUACKISM *same as*
▶ **quackery**
QUACKLE, -D, -S *same as*
▶ **quack**
QUACKS ▶ **quack**
QUACKY, QUACKIER
▶ **quack**
QUAD, -S *n* quadrangle
QUADDED *adj* formed of multiple quads

QUADDING n birdwatching in a specified area

QUADPLAY same as ▸fourplay

QUADPLEX n apartment on four floors

QUADRANS n Roman coin

QUADRANT n quarter of a circle

QUADRAT, -S n area marked out for the study of plants

QUADRATE n cube or square, or a square or cubelike object ▷ vb make square or rectangular ▷ adj square or rectangular

QUADRATI > quadratus

QUADRATS ▸quadrat

QUADRIC, -S adj having or characterized by an equation of the second degree ▷ n quadric curve or surface

QUADRIGA n (in the classical world) a two-wheeled chariot drawn by four horses abreast

QUADS ▸quad

QUAERE, -D, -S n query or question ▷ interj ask or inquire to ask

QUAESTOR n any of several magistrates of ancient Rome, usually a financial administrator

QUAFF, -ED, -ING, -S vb drink heartily or in one draught

QUAFFER, -S ▸quaff

QUAFFING ▸quaff

QUAFFS ▸quaff

QUAG, -S another word for ▸quagmire

QUAGGA, -S n recently extinct zebra

QUAGGY, QUAGGIER adj resembling a marsh or quagmire

QUAGMIRE n soft wet area of land ▷ vb bog down

QUAGMIRY ▸quagmire

QUAGS ▸quag

QUAHAUG, -S same as ▸quahog

QUAHOG, -S n edible clam

QUAI, -S same as ▸quay

QUAICH, -ES, -S n small shallow drinking cup

QUAIGH same as ▸quaich

QUAIL, -ED, -ING, -S n small game bird of the partridge family ▷ vb shrink back with fear

QUAINT, -ER adj attractively unusual, esp in an old-fashioned style

QUAINTLY ▸quaint

QUAIR, -S n book

QUAIS ▸quai

QUAKE, -D, -S, QUAKING, QUAKINGS vb shake or tremble with or as if with fear ▷ n earthquake

QUAKER, -S ▸quake

QUAKES ▸quake

QUAKIER ▸quaky

QUAKIEST ▸quaky

QUAKILY ▸quaky

QUAKING ▸quake

QUAKINGS ▸quake

QUAKY, QUAKIER, QUAKIEST adj inclined to quake

QUALE, QUALIA n essential property or quality

QUALIFY vb provide or be provided with the abilities necessary

QUALITY n degree or standard of excellence ▷ adj excellent or superior

QUALM, -S n pang of conscience

QUALMIER ▸qualmy

QUALMING adj having a qualm ▷ n state of having a qualm

QUALMISH ▸qualm

QUALMS ▸qualm

QUALMY, QUALMIER ▸qualm

QUAMASH another name for ▸camass

QUANDANG same as ▸quandong

QUANDARY n difficult situation or dilemma

QUANDONG n small Australian tree with edible fruit and nuts used in preserves

QUANGO, -S n partly independent official body set up by a government

QUANNET, -S n flat file with handle at one end

QUANT, -ED, -ING, -S n long pole for propelling a boat ▷ vb propel (a boat) with a quant

QUANTA ▸quantum

QUANTAL adj of or relating to a quantum or an entity that is quantized

QUANTED ▸quant

QUANTIC, -S n mathematical function

QUANTIFY vb discover or express the quantity of

QUANTILE n element of a division

QUANTING ▸quant

QUANTISE same as ▸quantize

QUANTITY n specified or definite amount or number

QUANTIZE vb restrict (a physical quantity) to one of a set of values characterized by quantum numbers

QUANTONG same as ▸quandong

QUANTS ▸quant

QUANTUM, QUANTA, -S n desired or required amount ▷ adj of or designating a major breakthrough

QUARE, -R, -ST adj remarkable or strange

QUARK, -S n subatomic particle thought to be the fundamental unit of matter

> This subatomic particle appears in the Scrabble cloud-chamber fairly often, and when it does, remember that you can put an S on the front of it to make **squark**.

QUARREL, -S n angry disagreement ▷ vb have a disagreement or dispute

QUARRIAN n cockatiel of scrub and woodland regions of inland Australia

QUARRIED ▸quarry

QUARRIER another word for > quarryman

QUARRIES ▸quarry

QUARRION same as ▸quarrian

QUARRY, QUARRIED, QUARRIES n place where stone is dug from the surface of the earth ▷ vb extract (stone) from a quarry

QUART, -S n unit of liquid measure equal to two pints (1.136 litres)

QUARTAN, -S adj (esp of a malarial fever) occurring every third day ▷ n quartan malaria

QUARTE, -S n fourth of eight basic positions from which a parry or attack can be made in fencing

QUARTER n one of four equal parts of something ▷ vb divide into four equal parts ▷ adj being or consisting of one of four equal parts

QUARTERN n fourth part of certain weights or measures, such as a peck or a pound

QUARTERS pl n accommodation, esp as

Q

provided for military personnel

QUARTES ▶ **quarte**

QUARTET, -S *n* group of four performers

QUARTETT *same as* ▶ **quartet**

QUARTIC, -S *n* biquadratic equation

QUARTIER *n* city district

QUARTILE *n* one of three values of a variable dividing its distribution into four groups with equal frequencies ▷ *adj* of a quartile

QUARTO, -S *n* book size in which the sheets are folded into four leaves

QUARTS ▶ **quart**

QUARTZ, -ES *n* hard glossy mineral

QUARTZY ▶ **quartz**

QUASAR, -S *n* extremely distant starlike object that emits powerful radio waves

QUASH, -ED, -ES, -ING *vb* annul or make void

QUASHER, -S ▶ **quash**

QUASHES ▶ **quash**

QUASHING ▶ **quash**

QUASI *adv* as if

QUASS, -ES *variant of* ▶ **kvass**

QUASSIA, -S *n* tropical American tree

QUASSIN, -S *n* bitter crystalline substance

QUAT, -S, -TED, -TING *n* spot ▷ *vb* beat down or squash

QUATCH, -ED, -ES *vb* move

QUATE, -S *n* fortune

QUATORZE *n* cards worth 14 points in piquet

QUATRAIN *n* stanza or poem of four lines

QUATRE, -S *n* playing card with four pips

QUATS ▶ **quat**

QUATTED ▶ **quat**

QUATTING ▶ **quat**

QUAVER, -ED, -S *vb* (of a voice) quiver or tremble ▷ *n* note half the length of a crotchet

QUAVERER ▶ **quaver**

QUAVERS ▶ **quaver**

QUAVERY ▶ **quaver**

QUAY, -S *n* wharf built parallel to the shore

QUAYAGE, -S *n* system of quays

QUAYD *archaic past participle of* ▶ **quail**

Meaning daunted, this Spenserian word makes a surprising hook for **quay**.

QUAYLIKE ▶ **quay**

QUAYS ▶ **quay**

QUAYSIDE *n* edge of a quay along the water

QUAZZY, QUAZZIER *adj* unwell

QUBIT, -S *n* quantum bit

QUBYTE, -S *n* unit of eight qubits

QUEACH, -ES *n* thicket

QUEACHY *adj* unwell

QUEAN, -S *n* Scots word for a young unmarried woman

QUEASIER ▶ **queasy**

QUEASILY ▶ **queasy**

QUEASY, QUEASIER *adj* having the feeling that one is about to vomit

QUEAZY, QUEAZIER *same as* ▶ **queasy**

QUEBEC, -S *n* code word for the letter Q

QUEECHY *same as* ▶ **queachy**

QUEEN, -ED, -ING, -S *n* female sovereign who is the official ruler or head of state ▷ *vb* crown as queen

QUEENCUP *n* type of flowering plant

QUEENDOM *n* territory, state, people, or community ruled over by a queen

QUEENED ▶ **queen**

QUEENIE, -S *n* scallop

QUEENIER ▶ **queeny**

QUEENIES ▶ **queenie**

QUEENING ▶ **queen**

QUEENITE *n* supporter of a queen

QUEENLET *n* queen of a small realm

QUEENLY *adj* resembling or appropriate to a queen ▷ *adv* in a manner appropriate to a queen

QUEENS ▶ **queen**

QUEENY, QUEENIER *adj* resembling a queen

QUEER, -ED, -ER, -EST, -ING, -S *adj* not normal or usual ▷ *vb* spoil or thwart

QUEERISH ▶ **queer**

QUEERITY ▶ **queer**

QUEERLY ▶ **queer**

QUEERS ▶ **queer**

QUEEST, -S *n* wood pigeon

QUEINT *same as* ▶ **quaint**

QUELCH, -ED, -ES *same as* ▶ **squelch**

QUELEA, -S *n* East African weaver bird

QUELL, -ED, -ING, -S *vb* suppress

QUELLER, -S ▶ **quell**

QUELLING ▶ **quell**

QUELLS ▶ **quell**

QUEME, -D, -S, QUEMING *vb* please

QUENA, -S *n* Andean flute

QUENCH, -ED, -ES *vb* satisfy (one's thirst)

QUENCHER ▶ **quench**

QUENCHES ▶ **quench**

QUENELLE *n* finely sieved mixture of cooked meat or fish shaped into various forms

QUEP *interj* expression of derision

QUERCINE *adj* of or relating to oak trees

QUERIDA, -S *n* sweetheart

QUERIED ▶ **query**

QUERIER, -S ▶ **query**

QUERIES ▶ **query**

QUERIST, -S *n* person who makes inquiries or queries

QUERN, -S *n* stone hand mill for grinding corn

QUERY, QUERIED, QUERIES, -ING *n* question, esp one raising doubt ▷ *vb* express uncertainty, doubt, or an objection

QUEST, -ED, -S *n* long and difficult search ▷ *vb* go in search of

QUESTANT *n* one who quests

QUESTED ▶ **quest**

QUESTER, -S ▶ **quest**

QUESTING ▶ **quest**

QUESTION *n* form of words addressed to a person in order to obtain an answer ▷ *vb* put a question or questions to (a person)

QUESTOR, -S *same as* ▶ **quaestor**

QUESTS ▶ **quest**

QUETCH, -ED, -ES *vb* move

QUETHE, -S, QUETHING *vb* say

QUETSCH *n* plum brandy

QUETZAL, -S *n* crested bird of Central and N South America

This is a great word if you can get the tiles for it, so it's well worth remembering both spellings – it can also be **quezal** – and the four plural forms, which are **quetzals** or **quetzales** and **quezals** or **quezales**.

QUEUE, -D, -ING, -S, QUEUING, QUEUINGS *n* line of people or vehicles waiting for something ▷ *vb* form or remain in a line while waiting

QUEUER, -S ▸ queue
QUEUES ▸ queue
QUEUING ▸ queue
QUEUINGS ▸ queue
QUEY, -S n young cow
QUEYN, -S n girl or young woman
QUEYNIE, -S same as ▸ queyn
QUEYNS ▸ queyn
QUEYS ▸ quey
QUEZAL, -ES, -S same as ▸ quetzal
QUIBBLE, -D, -S vb make trivial objections ▷ n trivial objection
QUIBBLER ▸ quibble
QUIBBLES ▸ quibble
QUIBLIN, -S same as ▸ quibble
QUICH, -ED, -ING vb move
QUICHE, -S n savoury flan with an egg custard filling
QUICHED ▸ quich
QUICHES ▸ quiche
QUICHING ▸ quich
QUICK, -ER, -EST, -S adj speedy, fast ▷ n area of sensitive flesh under a nail ▷ adv in a rapid manner
QUICKEN, -S vb make or become faster ▷ n rowan tree
QUICKER ▸ quick
QUICKEST ▸ quick
QUICKIE, -S n anything done or made hurriedly ▷ adj made or done rapidly
QUICKLY ▸ quick
QUICKS ▸ quick
QUICKSET adj (of plants or cuttings) planted so as to form a hedge ▷ n hedge composed of such plants
QUICKY same as ▸ quickie
QUID, -S n pound (sterling)
QUIDAM, -S n specified person
QUIDDANY n quince jelly ▷ vb make into quince jelly
QUIDDIT, -S same as ▸ quiddity
QUIDDITY n essential nature of something
QUIDDLE, -D, -S vb waste time
QUIDDLER ▸ quiddle
QUIDDLES ▸ quiddle
QUIDNUNC n person eager to learn news and scandal
QUIDS ▸ quid
QUIESCE, -D, -S vb quieten
QUIET, -ED, -ER, -ERS, -EST, -ING, -S adj with little noise ▷ n quietness ▷ vb make or become quiet

QUIETEN, -S vb make or become quiet
QUIETER ▸ quiet
QUIETERS ▸ quiet
QUIETEST ▸ quiet
QUIETING ▸ quiet
QUIETISM n passivity and calmness of mind towards external events
QUIETIST ▸ quietism
QUIETIVE n sedative drug
QUIETLY ▸ quiet
QUIETS ▸ quiet
QUIETUDE n quietness, peace, or tranquillity
QUIETUS n release from life
QUIFF, -S n tuft of hair brushed up above the forehead
QUIFFED adj having a quiff
QUIFFS ▸ quiff
QUIGHT, -ED, -S vb quit
QUILL, -ED, -S n pen made from the feather of a bird's wing or tail ▷ vb wind (thread, yarn, etc) onto a spool or bobbin
QUILLAI, -S another name for ▸ soapbark
QUILLAIA same as ▸ quillai
QUILLAIS ▸ quillai
QUILLAJA same as ▸ quillai
QUILLED ▸ quill
QUILLET, -S n quibble or subtlety
QUILLING n craftwork in which material is formed into small bands that form the basis of a design
QUILLMAN, QUILLMEN n clerk
QUILLON, -S n either half of the extended crosspiece of a sword or dagger
QUILLOW, -S n quilt folded to make a pillow
QUILLS ▸ quill
QUILT, -ED, -S n padded covering for a bed ▷ vb stitch together two layers of (fabric) with padding between them
QUILTER, -S ▸ quilt
QUILTING n material used for making a quilt
QUILTS ▸ quilt
QUIN, -S n short for quintuplet
QUINA, -S n quinine
QUINARY adj consisting of fives or by fives ▷ n set of five
QUINAS ▸ quina
QUINATE adj arranged in or composed of five parts
QUINCE, -S n acid-tasting pear-shaped fruit

QUINCHE, -D, -S vb move
QUINCUNX n five objects arranged in the shape of a rectangle with the fifth in the centre
QUINE, -S variant of ▸ quean
QUINELA, -S same as ▸ quinella
QUINELLA n form of betting in which the punter bets on selecting the first and second place-winners in any order
QUINES ▸ quine
QUINIC adj as in quinic acid white crystalline soluble optically active carboxylic acid
QUINIE, -S n girl or young woman
QUINIELA same as ▸ quinella
QUINIES ▸ quinie
QUININ, -S same as ▸ quinine
QUININA, -S same as ▸ quinine
QUININE, -S n bitter drug used as a tonic and formerly to treat malaria
QUININS ▸ quinin
QUINNAT, -S n Pacific salmon
QUINO, -S same as ▸ keno
QUINOA, -S n type of grain high in nutrients
QUINOID, -S same as > quinonoid
QUINOL, -S n white crystalline soluble phenol used as a photographic developer
QUINOLIN same as > quinoline
QUINOLS ▸ quinol
QUINONE, -S n yellow crystalline water-soluble unsaturated ketone
QUINOS ▸ quino
QUINS ▸ quin
QUINSIED ▸ quinsy
QUINSY, QUINSIES n inflammation of the throat or tonsils
QUINT, -S same as ▸ quin
QUINTA, -S n Portuguese vineyard where grapes for wine or port are grown
QUINTAIN n post or target set up for tilting exercises for mounted knights or foot soldiers
QUINTAL, -S n unit of weight
QUINTAN, -S adj (of a fever) occurring every fourth day ▷ n quintan fever

Q

QUINTAR, -S n Albanian unit of currency

QUINTAS ▸ quinta

QUINTE, -S n fifth of eight basic positions from which a parry or attack can be made in fencing

QUINTET, -S n group of five performers

QUINTETT same as ▸ quintet

QUINTIC, -S adj of or relating to the fifth degree ▹ n mathematical function

QUINTILE n aspect of 72° between two heavenly bodies

QUINTIN, -S same as ▸ quintain

QUINTS ▸ quint

QUINZE, -S n card game where players aim to score 15

Deriving from the French word for fifteen, this makes a high-scoring word that you may well get to play, and if you can use all your tiles to form the plural, you'll get a 50-point bonus.

QUINZHEE n shelter made from hollowed-out snow

QUINZIE, -S same as ▸ quinzhee

QUIP, -PED, -PING, -S n witty saying ▹ vb make a quip

QUIPO, -S same as ▸ quipu

QUIPPED ▸ quip

QUIPPER, -S ▸ quip

QUIPPIER ▸ quippy

QUIPPING ▸ quip

QUIPPISH ▸ quip

QUIPPU, -S same as ▸ quipu

QUIPPY, QUIPPIER ▸ quip

QUIPS ▸ quip

QUIPSTER n person inclined to make sarcastic or witty remarks

QUIPU, -S n device of the Incas used to record information using knotted cords

QUIRE, -D, -S, QUIRING n set of 24 or 25 sheets of paper ▹ vb arrange in quires

QUIRK, -ED, -ING, -S n peculiarity of character ▹ vb quip

QUIRKIER ▸ quirky

QUIRKILY ▸ quirk

QUIRKING ▸ quirk

QUIRKISH ▸ quirk

QUIRKS ▸ quirk

QUIRKY, QUIRKIER ▸ quirk

QUIRT, -ED, -ING, -S n whip with a leather thong at one end ▹ vb strike with a quirt

QUISLING n traitor who aids an occupying enemy force

QUIST, -S n wood pigeon

QUIT, -S, -TED, -TING vb stop (doing something) ▹ adj free (from)

QUITCH, -ED, -ES vb move

QUITE, -D, -S, QUITING archaic form of ▸ quit

QUITRENT n former rent payable by a freeholder to their lord that released them from performing services

QUITS ▸ quit

QUITTAL, -S n repayment of an action with a similar action

QUITTED ▸ quit

QUITTER, -S n person who lacks perseverance

QUITTING ▸ quit

QUITTOR, -S n infection of the cartilages on the side of a horse's foot

QUIVER, -ED, -S vb shake with a tremulous movement ▹ n shaking or trembling

QUIVERER ▸ quiver

QUIVERS ▸ quiver

QUIVERY ▸ quiver

QUIXOTE, -S n impractical idealist

Using the Q and X, this word for an impractical dreamer has a reasonable chance of coming up, so keeping an eye open for it is not that quixotic!

QUIXOTIC adj romantic and unrealistic

QUIXOTRY ▸ quixote

QUIZ, -ZED, -ZES, -ZING n entertainment in which the knowledge of the players is tested by a series of questions ▹ vb investigate by close questioning

QUIZZER, -S ▸ quiz

QUIZZERY ▸ quiz

QUIZZES ▸ quiz

QUIZZIFY ▸ quiz

QUIZZING ▸ quiz

QULLIQ, -S n type of oil lamp used by Inuit people

QUOAD adv as far as

QUOD, -DED, -DING, -S n jail ▹ vb say

QUODLIN, -S n cooking apple

QUODS ▸ quod

QUOHOG, -S n edible clam

QUOIF, -ED, -ING, -S vb arrange (the hair)

QUOIN, -ED, -ING, -S n external corner of a building ▹ vb wedge

QUOIST, -S n wood pigeon

QUOIT, -ED, -ING n large ring used in the game of quoits ▹ vb throw as a quoit

QUOITER, -S ▸ quoit

QUOITING ▸ quoit

QUOITS n game in which quoits are tossed at a stake in the ground

QUOKKA, -S n small Australian wallaby

QUOLL, -S n Australian catlike carnivorous marsupial

QUOMODO, -S n manner

QUONDAM adj of an earlier time

QUONK, -ED, -ING, -S vb make an accidental noise while broadcasting

QUOOKE archaic past participle of ▸ quake

QUOP, -PED, -PING, -S vb pulsate or throb

QUORATE adj having or being a quorum

QUORUM, -S n minimum number of people required to be present at a meeting

QUOTA, -S n share that is due from, due to, or allocated to a group or person

QUOTABLE adj apt or suitable for quotation

QUOTABLY ▸ quotable

QUOTAS ▸ quota

QUOTE, -D, -S, QUOTING vb repeat (words) exactly ▹ n quotation ▹ interj expression used to indicate that the words that follow form a quotation

QUOTER, -S ▸ quote

QUOTES ▸ quote

QUOTH vb said

QUOTHA interj expression of mild sarcasm, used in picking up a word or phrase used by someone else

QUOTIENT n result of the division of one number or quantity by another

QUOTING ▸ quote

QUOTUM, -S same as ▸ quota

QURSH, -ES same as ▸ qurush

QURUSH, -ES n former Saudi Arabian currency unit

QUYTE, -D, -S, QUYTING same as ▸ quit

QWERTY, QWERTIES, -S n standard English-language typewriter or computer keyboard

Q

Rr

R is one of the most common consonants in Scrabble, along with **N** and **T**. Despite this, however, there is only one two-letter word beginning with **R**: **re** (2 points). This is worth remembering, as you won't need to waste time trying to think of others. There are some good three-letter words with **R**, however, some of which are quite unusual: **raj**, **rax** and **rex** (10 each), and **rez** and **riz** (12 each). Also, don't forget common words like **raw**, **ray** and **row** (6 each).

RABANNA, -S n Madagascan woven raffia

RABASKA, -S n large canoe

RABAT, -S, -TED vb rotate so that the plane rotated coincides with another

RABATINE n type of collar

RABATO, -ES, -S n wired or starched collar

RABATS ▸ rabat

RABATTE, -S same as ▸ rabat

RABATTED ▸ rabat

RABATTES ▸ rabatte

RABBET, -ED, -S n recess cut into a surface ▷ vb cut or form a rabbet in (timber)

RABBI, -ES, -S n Jewish spiritual leader

RABBIN, -S same as ▸ rabbi

RABBINIC adj of or relating to rabbis

RABBINS ▸ rabbin

RABBIS ▸ rabbi

RABBIT, -ED, -S n small burrowing mammal with long ears ▷ vb talk too much

RABBITER n person who traps and sells rabbits

RABBITO, -S same as ▸ rabbitoh

RABBITOH n (formerly) an itinerant seller of rabbits for eating

RABBITOS ▸ rabbito

RABBITRY n place where tame rabbits are kept and bred

RABBITS ▸ rabbit

RABBITY adj like a rabbit

RABBLE, -D, -S, RABBLING n disorderly crowd of noisy people ▷ vb stir, mix, or skim (the molten charge) in a roasting furnace

RABBLER, -S n device for stirring, mixing, or skimming a molten charge in a furnace

RABBLES ▸ rabble

RABBLING ▸ rabble

RABBONI, -S n very respectful Jewish title or form of address

RABI, -S n (in Pakistan, India, etc) a crop that is harvested at the end of winter

RABIC ▸ rabies

RABID, -ER, -EST adj fanatical

RABIDITY ▸ rabid

RABIDLY ▸ rabid

RABIES n usu fatal viral disease transmitted by dogs and certain other animals

RABIETIC ▸ rabies

RABIS ▸ rabi

RABONA, -S n method of kicking a football

RACA adj biblical word meaning worthless or empty-headed

RACAHOUT n acorn flour or drink made from it

RACCOON, -S n small N American mammal with a long striped tail

RACE, -D, -S n contest of speed ▷ vb compete with in a race

RACEABLE adj fit for racing

RACECARD n card providing information about a race meeting

RACED ▸ race

RACEGOER n one who attends a race meeting, esp a habitual frequenter of race meetings

RACEMATE n racemic compound

RACEME, -S n cluster of flowers along a central stem, as in the foxglove

RACEMED adj with or in racemes

RACEMES ▸ raceme

RACEMIC adj being a mixture of equal amounts of enantiomers

RACEMISE same as ▸ racemize

RACEMISM ▸ racemic

RACEMIZE vb change or cause to change into a racemic mixture

RACEMOID adj resembling a raceme

RACEMOSE adj being or resembling a raceme

RACEMOUS same as ▸ racemose

RACEPATH same as > racetrack

RACER, -S n person, animal, or machine that races

RACES ▸ race

RACEWALK vb race by walking fast rather than running

RACEWAY, -S n racetrack, esp one for banger racing

RACH, -ES n scent hound

RACHE same as ▸ rach

RACHES ▸ rach

RACHET, -ED, -S same as ▸ ratchet

RACHIAL ▸ rachis

RACHIDES ▸ rachis

RACHILLA n (in grasses) the short stem of a spikelet that bears the florets

RACHIS, RACHIDES, -ES n main axis or stem of an inflorescence or compound leaf

RACHITIC ▸ rachitis

RACHITIS another name for ▸ rickets

R

RACIAL adj relating to the division of the human species into races

RACIALLY ▸ racial

RACIER ▸ racy

RACIEST ▸ racy

RACILY ▸ racy

RACINESS ▸ racy

RACING, -S adj denoting or associated with horse races ▸ n practice of engaging in contests of speed

RACINO, -S n combined racetrack and casino

RACISM, -S n discrimination against people of races other than one's own

RACIST, -S ▸ racism

RACK, -ED, -ING, -INGS, -S n framework for holding particular articles, such as coats or luggage ▸ vb cause great suffering to

RACKER, -S ▸ rack

RACKET, -ED, -S n bat with strings stretched in an oval frame, used in tennis etc ▸ vb strike with a racket

RACKETEER n someone making a racket

RACKETRY n noise and commotion

RACKETS ▸ racket

RACKETT, -S n early double-reeded wind instrument

RACKETY adj involving noise, commotion and excitement

RACKFUL, -S ▸ rack

RACKING ▸ rack

RACKINGS ▸ rack

RACKLE, -S n (Scot) chain

RACKS ▸ rack

RACKWORK n mechanism with a rack and pinion

RACLETTE n Swiss dish of melted cheese served on boiled potatoes

RACLOIR, -S n scraper

RACON, -S n radar beacon

RACOON, -S same as ▸ raccoon

RACQUET, -S same as ▸ racket

RACY, RACIER, RACIEST adj slightly shocking

RAD, -DED, -DER, -DEST, -DING, -S n former unit of absorbed ionizing radiation dose ▸ vb fear ▸ adj slang term for great

RADAR, -S n device for tracking distant objects

RADDED ▸ rad

RADDER ▸ rad

RADDEST ▸ rad

RADDING ▸ rad

RADDLE, -S, RADDLING same as ▸ ruddle

RADDLED adj (of a person) unkempt or run-down in appearance

RADDLES ▸ raddle

RADDLING ▸ raddle

RADDOCKE same as ▸ ruddock

RADE (in Scots dialect) past tense of ▸ ride

RADGE, -R, -S, -ST adj angry or uncontrollable ▸ n person acting in such a way

RADIABLE adj able to be X-rayed

RADIAL, -S adj spreading out from a common central point ▸ n radial-ply tyre

RADIALE, RADIALIA n bone in the wrist

RADIALLY ▸ radial

RADIALS ▸ radial

RADIAN, -S n unit for measuring angles, equal to 57.296°

RADIANCE n quality or state of being radiant

RADIANCY same as ▸ radiance

RADIANS ▸ radian

RADIANT, -S adj looking happy ▸ n point or object that emits radiation

RADIATA, -S n type of pine tree

RADIATE, -D, -S vb spread out from a centre ▸ adj having rays or a radial structure

RADIATOR n arrangement of pipes containing hot water or steam to heat a room

RADICAL, -S adj fundamental ▸ n person advocating fundamental (political) change

RADICAND n number from which a root is to be extracted

RADICANT adj forming roots from the stem

RADICATE vb root or cause to take root

RADICEL, -S n very small root

RADICES ▸ radix

RADICLE, -S n small or developing root

RADICULE same as ▸ radicle

RADII ▸ radius

RADIO, -ED, -ING, -S n use of electromagnetic waves for broadcasting, communication, etc ▸ vb transmit (a message) by radio ▸ adj of, relating to, or using radio

RADIOES less common spelling of ▸ radios

RADIOING ▸ radio

RADIOMAN, RADIOMEN n radio operator

RADIOS ▸ radio

RADISH, -ES n small hot-flavoured root vegetable eaten raw in salads

RADIUM, -S n radioactive metallic element

RADIUS, RADII, -ED, -ES n (length of) a straight line from the centre to the circumference of a circle ▸ vb give a round shape

RADIX, RADICES, -ES n any number that is the base of a number system or of a system of logarithms

RADOME, -S n protective housing for a radar antenna

RADON, -S n radioactive gaseous element

RADS ▸ rad

RADULA, -E, -S n horny tooth-bearing strip on the tongue of molluscs

RADULAR ▸ radula

RADULAS ▸ radula

RADULATE ▸ radula

RADWASTE n radioactive waste

RAFALE, -S n burst of artillery fire

RAFF, -S n rubbish

RAFFIA, -S n prepared palm fibre for weaving mats etc

RAFFISH adj slightly disreputable

RAFFLE, -D, -S, RAFFLING n lottery with goods as prizes ▸ vb offer as a prize in a raffle

RAFFLER, -S ▸ raffle

RAFFLES ▸ raffle

RAFFLING ▸ raffle

RAFFS ▸ raff

RAFT, -ED, -S n floating platform of logs, planks, etc ▸ vb convey on or travel by raft, or make a raft from

RAFTER, -ED, -S n one of the main beams of a roof ▸ vb fit with rafters

RAFTING ▸ raft

RAFTMAN, RAFTMEN same as ▸ raftsman

RAFTS ▸ raft

RAFTSMAN, RAFTSMEN *n* someone who does rafting

RAG, -S *n* fragment of cloth ▷ *vb* tease ▷ *adj* of various charitable events at a British university

RAGA, -S *n* pattern of melody and rhythm in Indian music

RAGBAG, -S *n* confused assortment, jumble

RAGBOLT, -S *n* bolt that has angled projections on it

RAGDE *archaic past form of* ▶ **rage**

RAGDOLL, -S *n* breed of cat

RAGE, -D, -S *n* violent anger or passion ▷ *vb* speak or act with fury

RAGEE, -S *same as* ▶ **ragi**

RAGEFUL ▶ **rage**

RAGER, -S ▶ **rage**

RAGES ▶ **rage**

RAGG, -S *same as* ▶ **ragstone**

RAGGA, -S *n* dance-oriented style of reggae

RAGGED, -ER *adj* tattered

RAGGEDLY ▶ **ragged**

RAGGEDY *adj* somewhat ragged

RAGGEE, -S *same as* ▶ **ragi**

RAGGERY *n* rags

RAGGIER ▶ **raggy**

RAGGIES ▶ **raggy**

RAGGIEST ▶ **raggy**

RAGGING, -S ▶ **rag**

RAGGLE, -D, -S, RAGGLING *n* thin groove cut in stone or brickwork ▷ *vb* cut a raggle in

RAGGS ▶ **ragg**

RAGGY, RAGGIER, RAGGIES, RAGGIEST *adj* ragged ▷ *n* cereal grass cultivated in Africa and Asia for its edible grain

RAGI, -S *n* cereal grass cultivated in Africa and Asia for its edible grain

RAGING, -S ▶ **rage**

RAGINGLY ▶ **rage**

RAGINGS ▶ **raging**

RAGINI, -S *n* Indian musical form related to a raga

RAGIS ▶ **ragi**

RAGLAN, -S *adj* (of a sleeve) joined to a garment from the neck to the underarm ▷ *n* coat with sleeves that continue to the collar

RAGMAN, -S, RAGMEN *n* rag-and-bone man

RAGMENT, -S *n* statute, roll, or list

RAGOUT, -ED, -S *n* richly seasoned stew of meat and vegetables ▷ *vb* make into a ragout

RAGS ▶ **rag**

RAGSTONE *n* hard sandstone or limestone, esp when used for building

RAGTAG, -S *n* disparaging term for common people

RAGTAIL *adj* ragged; shabby

RAGTIME, -S *n* style of jazz piano music

RAGTIMER ▶ **ragtime**

RAGTIMES ▶ **ragtime**

RAGTOP, -S *n* informal word for a car with a folding or removable roof

RAGU, -S *n* Italian meat and tomato sauce

RAGULED *same as* ▶ **raguly**

RAGULY *adj* (in heraldry) having toothlike projections

RAGUS ▶ **ragu**

RAGWEED, -S *n* any of several plants

RAGWHEEL *n* toothed wheel

RAGWORK, -S *n* weaving or needlework using rags

RAGWORM, -S *n* type of worm that lives chiefly in burrows in sand or mud

RAGWORT, -S *n* plant with ragged leaves and yellow flowers

RAH, -ED, -ING, -S *informal US word for* ▶ **cheer**

RAHUI, -S *n* Māori prohibition

RAI, -S *n* type of Algerian popular music

RAIA, -S *same as* ▶ **rayah**

RAID, -ED, -S *n* sudden surprise attack or search ▷ *vb* make a raid on

RAIDER, -S ▶ **raid**

RAIDING, -S ▶ **raid**

RAIDS ▶ **raid**

RAIK, -ED, -ING, -S *n* wander ▷ *vb* wander

RAIL, -ED, -ING, -S *n* horizontal bar, esp as part of a fence or track ▷ *vb* complain bitterly or loudly

RAILAGE, -S *n* cost of transporting goods by rail

RAILBED, -S *n* ballast layer supporting the sleepers of a railway track

RAILBIRD *n* racing aficionado

RAILBUS *n* bus-like vehicle for use on railway lines

RAILCAR, -S *n* passenger-carrying railway vehicle consisting of a single coach

RAILCARD *n* card entitling the holder to cheaper rail travel

RAILCARS ▶ **railcar**

RAILE, -S *archaic spelling of* ▶ **rail**

RAILED ▶ **rail**

RAILER, -S ▶ **rail**

RAILES ▶ **raile**

RAILHEAD *n* terminal of a railway

RAILING, -S *n* fence made of rails supported by posts

RAILLERY *n* teasing or joking

RAILLESS ▶ **rail**

RAILLY, RAILLIES *old word for* ▶ **mock**

RAILMAN, RAILMEN *n* railway employee

RAILROAD *same as* ▶ **railway**

RAILS ▶ **rail**

RAILWAY, -S *n* track of iron rails on which trains run

RAIMENT, -S *n* clothing

RAIN, -ED, -ING, -S *n* water falling in drops from the clouds ▷ *vb* fall or pour down as rain

RAINBAND *n* dark band in the solar spectrum caused by water in the atmosphere

RAINBIRD *n* bird whose call is believed to be a sign of impending rain

RAINBOW, -S *n* arch of colours in the sky

RAINBOWY *adj* resembling a rainbow

RAINCOAT *n* water-resistant overcoat

RAINDATE *n* US term for an alternative date in case of rain

RAINDROP *n* water droplet that falls from the sky when it is raining

RAINE, -S *archaic spelling of* ▶ **reign**

RAINED ▶ **rain**

RAINES ▶ **raine**

RAINFALL *n* amount of rain

RAINIER ▶ **rainy**

RAINIEST ▶ **rainy**

RAINILY ▶ **rainy**

RAINING ▶ **rain**

RAINLESS ▶ **rain**

RAINOUT, -S *n* radioactive fallout or atmospheric pollution carried to the earth by rain

RAINS ▶ **rain**

RAINSUIT *n* waterproof jacket and trousers

RAINWASH n action of rain ▷ vb erode or wet as a result of rain

RAINWEAR n protective garments intended for use in wet weather

RAINY, RAINIER, RAINIEST adj characterized by a large rainfall

RAIRD, -S same as ▶ reird

RAIS ▶ rai

RAISABLE ▶ raise

RAISE, -D, -S vb lift up ▷ n increase in pay

RAISER, -S ▶ raise

RAISES ▶ raise

RAISIN, -S n dried grape

RAISING, -S n rule that moves a constituent from an embedded clause into the main clause

RAISINS ▶ raisin

RAISINY adj tasting of raisins

RAISONNE adj carefully thought out

RAIT, -ED, -ING, -S same as ▶ ret

RAITA, -S n Indian dish of chopped cucumber, mint, etc in yogurt

RAITED ▶ rait

RAITING ▶ rait

RAITS ▶ rait

RAIYAT, -S same as ▶ ryot

RAJ, -ES n (in India) government

This Indian word for rule or empire is one of the essential short words that use a J. Remember that it can be extended to **raja**.

RAJA, -S same as ▶ rajah

RAJAH, -S n Indian ruler

RAJAS ▶ raja

RAJASHIP ▶ raja

RAJES ▶ raj

RAKE, -D, -S n tool used for smoothing earth or gathering leaves, hay, etc ▷ vb gather or smooth with a rake

RAKEE, -S same as ▶ raki

RAKELIKE adj like a rake

RAKEOFF, -S n share of profits, esp one that is illegal or given as a bribe

RAKER, -S n person who rakes

RAKERIES ▶ rakery

RAKERS ▶ raker

RAKERY, RAKERIES n rakish behaviour

RAKES ▶ rake

RAKI, -S n strong spirit distilled from grain

RAKIA, -S n strong fruit-based alcoholic drink popular in the Balkans

RAKIJA, -S same as ▶ rakia

RAKING, -S n (in rugby) offence of scraping an opponent with the studs

RAKIS ▶ raki

RAKISH adj dashing or jaunty

RAKISHLY ▶ rakish

RAKSHAS same as ▶ rakshasa

RAKSHASA n Hindu demon

RAKU, -S n type of Japanese pottery

RALE, -S n abnormal coarse crackling sound heard on auscultation of the chest

RALLIED ▶ rally

RALLIER, -S ▶ rally

RALLIES ▶ rally

RALLINE adj relating to a family of birds that includes the rails, crakes, and coots

RALLY, RALLIED, RALLIES, -ING n large gathering of people for a meeting ▷ vb bring or come together after dispersal or for a common cause

RALLYE, -S US variant of ▶ rally

RALLYING ▶ rally

RALLYIST ▶ rally

RALPH, -ED, -ING, -S vb slang word meaning vomit

RAM, -MED, -MING, -S n male sheep ▷ vb strike against with force

RAMADA, -S n outdoor eating area with roof but open sides

RAMAKIN, -S same as ▶ ramekin

RAMAL adj relating to a branch or branches

RAMATE adj with branches

RAMBLA, -S n dried-up riverbed

RAMBLE, -D, -S vb walk without a definite route ▷ n walk, esp in the country

RAMBLER, -S n person who rambles

RAMBLES ▶ ramble

RAMBLING adj large and irregularly shaped ▷ n activity of going for long walks in the country

RAMBUTAN n SE Asian tree that has bright red edible fruit

RAMCAT, -S n dialect word for a male cat

RAMEAL same as ▶ ramal

RAMEE, -S same as ▶ ramie

RAMEKIN, -S n small ovenproof dish for a single serving of food

RAMEN, -S n Japanese dish consisting of a clear broth containing thin white noodles

RAMENTUM, RAMENTA n any of the thin brown scales that cover the stems and leaves of young ferns

RAMEOUS same as ▶ ramal

RAMEQUIN same as ▶ ramekin

RAMET, -S n any of the individuals in a group of clones

RAMI, -S same as ▶ ramie

RAMIE, -S n woody Asian shrub with broad leaves

RAMIFIED ▶ ramify

RAMIFIES ▶ ramify

RAMIFORM adj having a branchlike shape

RAMIFY, RAMIFIED, RAMIFIES vb become complex

RAMILIE, -S same as ▶ ramillie

RAMILLIE n wig with a plait at the back fashionable in the 18th century

RAMIN, -S n swamp-growing tree found in Malaysia and Indonesia

RAMIS ▶ rami

RAMJET, -S n type of jet engine

RAMMED ▶ ram

RAMMEL, -S n discarded or waste matter

RAMMER, -S ▶ ram

RAMMIER ▶ rammy

RAMMIES ▶ rammy

RAMMIEST ▶ rammy

RAMMING ▶ ram

RAMMISH adj like a ram, esp in being foul-smelling

RAMMLE, -S n collection of items saved in case they become useful

RAMMY, RAMMIER, RAMMIES, RAMMIEST n Scots word for a noisy disturbance or free-for-all ▷ adj like a ram

RAMONA, -S same as > sagebrush

RAMOSE adj having branches

RAMOSELY ▶ ramose

RAMOSITY ▶ ramose

RAMOUS same as ▶ ramose

RAMOUSLY ▶ ramose

RAMP, -ED, -S n slope joining two level surfaces ▷vb (esp of animals) to rush around in a wild excited manner

RAMPAGE, -D, -S vb dash about violently

RAMPAGER ▸ rampage

RAMPAGES ▸ rampage

RAMPANCY ▸ rampant

RAMPANT adj growing or spreading uncontrollably

RAMPART, -S n mound or wall for defence ▷vb provide with a rampart

RAMPAUGE Scots variant of ▸ rampage

RAMPED ▸ ramp

RAMPER, -S ▸ ramp

RAMPICK, -S same as ▸ rampike

RAMPIKE, -S n US or dialect word for a dead tree

RAMPING, -S ▸ ramp

RAMPION, -S n European and Asian plant

RAMPIRE, -S archaic variant of ▸ rampart

RAMPIRED ▸ rampire

RAMPIRES ▸ rampire

RAMPOLE, -S same as ▸ rampike

RAMPS ▸ ramp

RAMPSMAN, RAMPSMEN n mugger

RAMROD, -S n long thin rod used for cleaning the barrel of a gun ▷ adj (of someone's posture) very straight and upright ▷vb drive

RAMS ▸ ram

RAMSHORN n any of various freshwater snails

RAMSON, -S n type of garlic

RAMSTAM adv headlong ▷ adj headlong

RAMTIL, -S n African plant grown in India esp for its oil

RAMTILLA same as ▸ ramtil

RAMTILS ▸ ramtil

RAMULAR adj relating to a branch or branches

RAMULI ▸ ramulus

RAMULOSE adj (of the parts or organs of animals and plants) having many small branches

RAMULOUS same as ▸ ramulose

RAMULUS, RAMULI n small branch

RAMUS n barb of a bird's feather

RAN ▸ run

RANA, -S n genus of frogs

RANARIAN adj of or relating to frogs

RANARIUM n place for keeping frogs

RANAS ▸ rana

RANCE, -D, -S, RANCING Scots word for ▸ prop

RANCEL, -S vb (in Shetland and Orkney) carry out a search

RANCES ▸ rance

RANCH, -ED, -ES, -ING n large cattle farm in the American West ▷vb run a ranch

RANCHER, -S n person who owns, manages, or works on a ranch

RANCHERA n type of Mexican country music

RANCHERO another word for ▸ rancher

RANCHERS ▸ rancher

RANCHES ▸ ranch

RANCHING ▸ ranch

RANCHMAN, RANCHMEN n man who owns, manages, or works on a ranch

RANCHO, -S n hut or group of huts for housing ranch workers

RANCID, -ER adj (of butter, bacon, etc) stale and having an offensive smell

RANCIDLY ▸ rancid

RANCING ▸ rance

RANCOR, -S same as ▸ rancour

RANCORED ▸ rancor

RANCORS ▸ rancor

RANCOUR, -S n deep bitter hate

RAND, -ED, -ING, -S n leather strip on the heel of a shoe ▷vb cut into rands

RANDAN, -S n boat rowed by three people

RANDED ▸ rand

RANDEM, -S adv with three horses harnessed together as a team ▷n carriage or team of horses so driven

RANDIE same as ▸ randy

RANDIER ▸ randy

RANDIES ▸ randy

RANDIEST ▸ randy

RANDILY ▸ randy

RANDING ▸ rand

RANDLORD n mining magnate during the 19th-century gold boom in Johannesburg

RANDOM, -S adj made or done by chance or without a plan ▷n (in mining) the course of a vein of ore

RANDOMLY ▸ random

RANDOMS ▸ random

RANDON, -S old variant of ▸ random

RANDS ▸ rand

RANDY, RANDIER, RANDIES, RANDIEST adj rude or reckless ▷n rude or reckless person

RANEE, -S same as ▸ rani

RANG, -S n (Scot) rank

RANGE, -D, -S n limits of effectiveness or variation ▷vb vary between one point and another

RANGER, -S n official in charge of a nature reserve etc

RANGES ▸ range

RANGI, -S n sky

RANGIER ▸ rangy

RANGIEST ▸ rangy

RANGILY ▸ rangy

RANGING, -S ▸ range

RANGIORA n evergreen New Zealand shrub or small tree

RANGIS ▸ rangi

RANGOLI, -S n traditional Indian ground decoration

RANGS ▸ rang

RANGY, RANGIER, RANGIEST adj having long slender limbs

RANI, -S n wife or widow of a rajah

RANID, -S n frog

RANIFORM adj froglike

RANINE adj relating to frogs

RANIS ▸ rani

RANK, -ED, -EST, -S n relative place or position ▷vb have a specific rank or position ▷ adj complete or absolute

RANKE, -S archaic variant of ▸ rank

RANKED ▸ rank

RANKER, -S n soldier in the ranks

RANKES ▸ ranke

RANKEST ▸ rank

RANKING, -S adj prominent ▷n position on a scale

RANKISH adj old word meaning rather rank

RANKISM, -S n discrimination against people on the grounds of rank

RANKIST, -S n person who discriminates on the grounds of rank

RANKLE, -D, -S, RANKLING vb continue to cause resentment or bitterness

RANKLESS ▸ rank
RANKLING ▸ rankle
RANKLY ▸ rank
RANKNESS ▸ rank
RANKS ▸ rank
RANPIKE, -S same as
▸ rampike
RANSACK, -S vb search
thoroughly
RANSEL, -S same as ▸ rancel
RANSOM, -ED, -S n money
demanded for the release of
a kidnapped person ▷ vb pay
money to obtain the release
of a captive
RANSOMER ▸ ransom
RANSOMS ▸ ransom
RANT, -ED, -S vb talk in a
loud and excited way ▷ n
loud excited speech
RANTER, -S ▸ rant
RANTING, -S ▸ rant
RANTS ▸ rant
RANULA, -S n saliva-filled
cyst that develops under the
tongue
RANULAR adj of a cyst
under the tongue
RANULAS ▸ ranula
RANZEL, -S same as ▸ rancel
RAOULIA, -S n flowering
plant of New Zealand
RAP, -PED, -S vb hit with a
sharp quick blow ▷ n quick
sharp blow
RAPACITY > rapacious
RAPE n plant with bright
yellow flowers
RAPESEED n seed of the
oilseed rape plant
RAPHAE ▸ raphe
RAPHANIA n type of
ergotism possibly resulting
from consumption of radish
seeds
RAPHE, RAPHAE, -S n
elongated ridge of
conducting tissue along the
side of certain seeds
RAPHIA, -S same as ▸ raffia
RAPHIDE, -S n needle-
shaped crystal that occurs in
many plant cells
RAPHIS same as ▸ raphide
RAPID, -ER, -EST adj quick,
swift
RAPIDITY ▸ rapid
RAPIDLY ▸ rapid
RAPIDS pl n part of a river
with a fast, turbulent
current
RAPIER, -S n fine-bladed
sword
RAPIERED adj carrying a
rapier
RAPIERS ▸ rapier

RAPINE, -S n pillage or
plundering
RAPINI, -S n type of leafy
vegetable
RAPLOCH, -S n Scots word
for homespun woollen
material ▷ adj Scots word
meaning coarse or
homemade
RAPPAREE n Irish irregular
soldier of the late 17th
century
RAPPE, -S n Arcadian dish of
grated potatoes and pork or
chicken
RAPPED ▸ rap
RAPPEE, -S n moist English
snuff of the 18th and 19th
centuries
RAPPEL, -ED, -S n (formerly)
a drumbeat to call soldiers to
arms ▷ vb abseil
RAPPEN n Swiss coin equal
to one hundredth of a franc
RAPPER, -S n something
used for rapping, such as a
knocker on a door
RAPPES ▸ rappe
RAPPING, -S ▸ rap
RAPPINI same as ▸ rapini
RAPPORT, -S n harmony or
agreement
RAPS ▸ rap
RAPT adj engrossed or
spellbound
RAPTLY ▸ rapt
RAPTNESS ▸ rapt
RAPTOR, -S n any bird of prey
RAPTURE, -D, -S n ecstasy
▷ vb entrance
RARE, -D, -R, -S, -ST adj
uncommon ▷ vb rear
RAREBIT, -S n as in **Welsh
rarebit** dish made from
melted cheese served on
toast
RARED ▸ rare
RAREE n as in **raree show**
street show or carnival
RAREFIED adj highly
specialized, exalted
RAREFIER ▸ rarefy
RAREFY, RAREFIES vb
make or become rarer or less
dense
RARELY adv seldom
RARENESS ▸ rare
RARER ▸ rare
RARERIPE adj ripening early
▷ n fruit or vegetable that
ripens early
RARES ▸ rare
RAREST ▸ rare
RARIFIED same as ▸ rarefied
RARIFY, RARIFIES same as
▸ rarefy

RARING adj ready
RARITY, RARITIES n
something that is valuable
because it is unusual
RARK, -ED, -ING, -S vb as in
rark up informal New
Zealand expression meaning
reprimand severely
RAS n headland
RASBORA, -S n often
brightly coloured tropical fish
RASCAL, -S n rogue ▷ adj
belonging to the mob or
rabble
RASCALLY adj dishonest or
mean ▷ adv in a dishonest or
mean fashion
RASCALS ▸ rascal
RASCASSE n any of various
fishes with venomous spines
on the fins
RASCHEL, -S n type of
loosely knitted fabric
RASE, -D, -S, RASING same
as ▸ raze
RASER, -S ▸ rase
RASES ▸ rase
RASH, -ED, -ES, -EST, -ING
adj hasty, reckless, or
incautious ▷ n eruption of
spots or patches on the skin
▷ vb (in old usage) cut
RASHER, -S n thin slice of
bacon
RASHES ▸ rash
RASHEST ▸ rash
RASHIE, -S n protective shirt
worn by surfers
RASHING ▸ rash
RASHLIKE ▸ rash
RASHLY ▸ rash
RASHNESS ▸ rash
RASING ▸ rase
RASMALAI n Indian dessert
made from cheese, milk, and
almonds
RASORIAL adj (of birds such
as domestic poultry)
adapted for scratching the
ground for food
RASP, -ED, -S n harsh
grating noise ▷ vb speak in a
grating voice
RASPER, -S ▸ rasp
RASPIER ▸ raspy
RASPIEST ▸ raspy
RASPING adj (esp of a noise)
harsh or grating
RASPINGS pl n browned
breadcrumbs for coating fish
and other foods before
frying, baking, etc
RASPISH ▸ rasp
RASPS ▸ rasp
RASPY, RASPIER, RASPIEST
same as ▸ rasping

RASSE, -S n small S Asian civet

RASSLE, -D, -S, RASSLING dialect variant of ▸ **wrestle**

RASSLER, -S n wrestler

RASSLES ▸ **rassle**

RASSLING ▸ **rassle**

RAST archaic past form of ▸ **race**

RASTA adj rastafarian

RASTER, -ED, -S n image consisting of rows of pixel information ▸ vb turn a digital image into a large picture

RASTRUM, -S n pen for drawing the five lines of a musical stave simultaneously

RASURE, -S n scraping

RAT, -S, -TED n small rodent ▸ vb inform (on)

RATA, -S n New Zealand hardwood forest tree

RATABLE adj able to be rated or evaluated ▸ n something that can be rated or evaluated

RATABLES pl n property that is liable to rates

RATABLY ▸ **ratable**

RATAFEE, -S same as ▸ **ratafia**

RATAFIA, -S n liqueur made from fruit

RATAL, -S n amount on which rates are assessed ▸ adj of or relating to rates (local taxation)

RATAN, -S same as ▸ **rattan**

RATANIES ▸ **ratany**

RATANS ▸ **ratan**

RATANY, RATANIES n flowering desert shrub

RATAPLAN n drumming sound ▸ vb drum

RATAS ▸ **rata**

RATATAT, -S n sound of knocking on a door

RATBAG, -S n insulting term for an eccentric or unreliable person

RATBITE n as in **ratbite fever** acute infectious disease that can be caught from rats

RATCH, -ED, -ES, -ING same as ▸ **ratchet**

RATCHET, -S n set of teeth on a bar or wheel allowing motion in one direction only ▸ vb move using or as if using a ratchet system

RATCHING ▸ **ratch**

RATE, -D n degree of speed or progress ▸ vb consider or value

RATEABLE same as ▸ **ratable**

RATEABLY ▸ **rateable**

RATED ▸ **rate**

RATEEN, -S same as ▸ **ratine**

RATEL, -S n large African and S Asian musteline mammal

RATER, -S ▸ **rate**

RATES pl n (in some countries) a tax on property levied by a local authority

RATFINK, -S n contemptible or undesirable person

RATFISH n deep-sea fish with a whiplike tail

RATH, -S same as ▸ **rathe**

RATHA, -S n (in India) a four-wheeled carriage drawn by horses or bullocks

RATHE adj blossoming or ripening early in the season

RATHER adv to some extent ▸ interj expression of strong affirmation, often in answer to a question

RATHEST adv dialect or archaic word meaning soonest

RATHOLE, -S n rat's hiding place or burrow

RATHRIPE adj dialect word meaning mature or ripe ahead of time ▸ n variety of apple or other fruit that is quick to ripen

RATHS ▸ **rath**

RATICIDE n rat poison

RATIFIED ▸ **ratify**

RATIFIER ▸ **ratify**

RATIFY, RATIFIED, RATIFIES vb give formal approval to

RATINE, -S n coarse loosely woven cloth

RATING, -S n valuation or assessment

RATIO, -S n relationship between two numbers or amounts expressed as a proportion

RATION, -ED n fixed allowance of food etc ▸ vb limit to a certain amount per person

RATIONAL adj reasonable, sensible ▸ n rational number

RATIONED ▸ **ration**

RATIONS pl n fixed daily allowance of food

RATIOS ▸ **ratio**

RATITE, -S adj (of flightless birds) having a breastbone that lacks a keel ▸ n bird that belongs to this group

RATLIKE ▸ **rat**

RATLIN, -S same as ▸ **ratline**

RATLINE, -S n light line tied across the shrouds of a sailing vessel

RATLING, -S n young rat

RATLINS ▸ **ratlin**

RATO, -S n rocket-assisted take-off

RATOO, -S same as ▸ **ratu**

RATOON, -ED, -S n new shoot that grows from near the root or crown of crop plants ▸ vb propagate by such a growth

RATOONER n plant that spreads by ratooning

RATOONS ▸ **ratoon**

RATOOS ▸ **ratoo**

RATOS ▸ **rato**

RATPACK, -S n members of the press who pursue celebrities

RATPROOF adj impenetrable by rats

RATS ▸ **rat**

RATSBANE n rat poison, esp arsenic oxide

RATTAIL, -S n type of fish

RATTAN, -S n climbing palm with jointed stems used for canes

RATTED ▸ **rat**

RATTEEN, -S same as ▸ **ratine**

RATTEN, -ED, -S vb sabotage or steal tools in order to disrupt the work of

RATTENER ▸ **ratten**

RATTENS ▸ **ratten**

RATTER, -S n dog or cat that catches and kills rats

RATTERY n rats' dwelling area

RATTIER ▸ **ratty**

RATTIEST ▸ **ratty**

RATTILY ▸ **ratty**

RATTING, -S ▸ **rat**

RATTISH adj of, resembling, or infested with rats

RATTLE, -D, -S vb give out a succession of short sharp sounds ▸ n short sharp sound

RATTLER, -S n something that rattles

RATTLES ▸ **rattle**

RATTLIER ▸ **rattly**

RATTLIN, -S same as ▸ **ratline**

RATTLINE same as ▸ **ratline**

RATTLING adv exceptionally, very ▸ n succession of short sharp sounds

RATTLINS ▸ **rattlin**

RATTLY, RATTLIER adj having a rattle

R

RATTON, -S n dialect word for a little rat

RATTOON, -S same as ►ratoon

RATTRAP, -S n device for catching rats

RATTY, RATTIER, RATTIEST adj bad-tempered, irritable

RATU, -S n title used by Fijian chiefs or nobles

RAUCID adj raucous

RAUCITY ►raucous

RAUCLE, -R, -ST adj Scots word for rough or tough

RAUCOUS adj hoarse or harsh

RAUGHT archaic past form of ►reach

RAUN, -S n fish roe or spawn

RAUNCH, -ED, -ES n lack of polish or refinement ▷ vb behave in a raunchy manner

RAUNCHY adj earthy, sexy

RAUNGE, -D, -S, RAUNGING archaic word for ►range

RAUNS ►raun

RAUPATU, -S n confiscation or seizure of land

RAUPO, -S n New Zealand bulrush

RAURIKI, -S n any of various plants with prickly leaves

RAV, -S n Hebrew word for rabbi

RAVAGE, -D, -S, RAVAGING vb cause extensive damage to ▷ n destructive action

RAVAGER, -S ►ravage

RAVAGES ►ravage

RAVAGING ►ravage

RAVE, -D, -S vb talk wildly or with enthusiasm ▷ n enthusiastically good review

RAVEL, -ED, -ING, -LED, -S vb tangle or become entangled ▷ n tangle or complication

RAVELER, -S ►ravel

RAVELIN, -S n outwork having two embankments at a salient angle

RAVELING ►ravel

RAVELINS ►ravelin

RAVELLED ►ravel

RAVELLER ►ravel

RAVELLY adj tangled

RAVELS ►ravel

RAVEN, -ED, -EST, -S n black bird like a large crow ▷ adj (of hair) shiny black ▷ vb seize or seek (plunder, prey, etc)

RAVENER, -S ►raven

RAVENEST ►raven

RAVENING adj (of animals) hungrily searching for prey

RAVENOUS adj very hungry

RAVER, -S n person who leads a wild or uninhibited social life

RAVES ►rave

RAVEY, RAVIER, RAVIEST adj characteristic of a rave

RAVIGOTE n rich white sauce with herbs and shallots

RAVIN, -ED, -ING, -S archaic spelling of ►raven

RAVINE, -S n narrow steep-sided valley worn by a stream

RAVINED ►ravine

RAVINES ►ravine

RAVING, -S adj delirious ▷ n frenzied, irrational, or wildly extravagant talk or utterances

RAVINGLY ►raving

RAVINGS ►raving

RAVINING ►ravin

RAVINS ►ravin

RAVIOLI, -S n small squares of pasta with a savoury filling

RAVISH, -ED, -ES vb enrapture

RAVISHER ►ravish

RAVISHES ►ravish

RAVS ►rav

RAW, -ER, -EST, -S n as in **in the raw** without clothes ▷ adj uncooked

RAWARU, -S n New Zealand name for blue cod

RAWBONE archaic variant of ►rawboned

RAWBONED adj having a lean bony physique

RAWER ►raw

RAWEST ►raw

RAWHEAD, -S n bogeyman

RAWHIDE, -D, -S n untanned hide ▷ vb whip

RAWIN, -S n monitoring of winds in the upper atmosphere using radar and a balloon

RAWING, -S (in dialect) same as ►rowen

RAWINS ►rawin

RAWISH ►raw

RAWLY ►raw

RAWMAISH n Irish word for foolish or exaggerated talk

RAWN, -S (in dialect) same as ►rowen

RAWNESS ►raw

RAWNS ►rawn

RAWS ►raw

RAX, -ED, -ES, -ING vb stretch or extend ▷ n act of stretching or straining

A dialect word meaning to stretch or strain, and one of the essential short words to know for using the X.

RAY, -ED, -ING, -S n single line or narrow beam of light ▷ vb (of an object) to emit (light) in rays or (of light) to issue in the form of rays

RAYA, -S same as ►rayah

RAYAH, -S n (formerly) a non-Muslim subject of the Ottoman Empire

RAYAS ►raya

RAYED ►ray

RAYGRASS same as ►ryegrass

RAYING ►ray

RAYLE, -D, -S, RAYLING archaic spelling of ►rail

RAYLESS adj dark

RAYLET, -S n small ray

RAYLIKE adj resembling a ray

RAYLING ►rayle

RAYNE, -S archaic spelling of ►reign

RAYON, -S n (fabric made of) a synthetic fibre

RAYS ►ray

RAZE, -D, -S, RAZING vb destroy (buildings or a town) completely

RAZEE, -D, -ING, -S n sailing ship that has had its upper deck or decks removed ▷ vb remove the upper deck or decks of (a sailing ship)

RAZER, -S ►raze

RAZES ►raze

RAZING ►raze

RAZMATAZ n noisy or showy fuss or activity

RAZOO, -S n imaginary coin

RAZOR, -ED, -ING, -S n sharp instrument for shaving ▷ vb cut or shave with a razor

RAZURE, -S same as ►rasure

RAZZ, -ED, -ES vb make fun of

RAZZIA, -S n raid for plunder or slaves

RAZZING, -S n act of making fun of someone

RAZZLE, -S n as in **on the razzle** out enjoying oneself or celebrating

RE prep concerning ▷ n the second note of the musical scale

REABSORB vb absorb again

REACCEDE vb accede again

REACCENT vb accent again

REACCEPT vb accept again

REACCUSE vb accuse again

REACH, -ED, -ES, -ING vb arrive at ▷ n distance that one can reach

REACHER, -S ▷ reach

REACHES ▷ reach

REACHING ▷ reach

REACT, -ED, -ING, -S vb act in response (to)

REACTANT n substance that participates in a chemical reaction

REACTED ▷ react

REACTING ▷ react

REACTION n physical or emotional response to a stimulus

REACTIVE adj chemically active

REACTOR, -S n apparatus in which a nuclear reaction is controlled to produce energy

REACTS ▷ react

READ, -S vb look at and understand or take in (written or printed matter) ▷ n matter suitable for reading

READABLE adj enjoyable to read

READABLY ▷ readable

READAPT, -S vb adapt again

READD, -ED, -ING, -S vb add again

READDICT vb cause to become addicted again

READDING ▷ readd

READDS ▷ readd

READER, -S n person who reads

READERLY adj pertaining to or suitable for a reader

READERS ▷ reader

READIED ▷ ready

READIER ▷ ready

READIES pl n ready money

READIEST ▷ ready

READILY adv promptly

READING, -S ▷ read

READJUST vb adapt to a new situation

README, -S n document which accompanies computer files or software

READMIT, -S vb let (a person, country, etc) back into a place or organization

READOPT, -S vb adopt again

READORN, -S vb adorn again

READOUT, -S n act of retrieving information from a computer memory or storage device

READS ▷ read

READVISE vb advise again

READY, READIED, READIER, READIEST, -ING adj prepared for use or action ▷ vb prepare

REAEDIFY vb rebuild

REAFFIRM vb state again, confirm

REAFFIX vb affix again

REAGENCY ▷ reagent

REAGENT, -S n chemical substance that reacts with another

REAGIN, -S n type of antibody that is formed against an allergen

REAGINIC ▷ reagin

REAGINS ▷ reagin

REAIS ▷ real

REAK, -ED, -ING, -S same as ▷ reck

REAL, REAIS, -ER, -ES, -EST, -S adj existing in fact ▷ n standard monetary unit of Brazil

REALGAR, -S n rare orange-red soft mineral

REALIA pl n real-life facts and material used in teaching

REALIGN, -S vb change or put back to a new or former place or position

REALISE, -D, -S same as ▷ realize

REALISER ▷ realise

REALISES ▷ realise

REALISM, -S n awareness or acceptance of things as they are

REALIST, -S n person who accepts events, etc as they are

REALITY n state of things as they are

REALIZE, -D, -S vb become aware or grasp the significance of

REALIZER ▷ realize

REALIZES ▷ realize

REALLIE old or dialect variant of ▷ really

REALLIED ▷ really

REALLIES ▷ really

REALLOT, -S vb allot again

REALLY, REALLIED, REALLIES adv very ▷ interj exclamation of dismay, doubt, or surprise ▷ vb (in archaic usage) rally

REALM, -S n kingdom

REALNESS ▷ real

REALO, -S n member of the German Green party with moderate views

A **realo** is a member of the less radical section of the German Green party. It is important to know not because it scores well, but because it provides an easily overlooked hook by allowing you to add O to **real**.

REALS ▷ real

REALTER, -S vb alter again

REALTIE n archaic word meaning sincerity

REALTIES ▷ realty

REALTIME adj (of a data-processing system) constantly updating to reflect the latest changes in data

REALTONE n audio clip of an original recording, used as a mobile phone ringtone

REALTOR, -S n estate agent

REALTY, REALTIES n immovable property

REAM, -ED, -ING, -S n twenty quires of paper, generally 500 sheets ▷ vb enlarge (a hole) by use of a reamer

REAME, -S archaic variant of ▷ realm

REAMED ▷ ream

REAMEND, -S vb amend again

REAMER, -S n tool used for smoothing the bores of holes accurately to size

REAMES ▷ reame

REAMIER ▷ reamy

REAMIEST ▷ reamy

REAMING ▷ ream

REAMS ▷ ream

REAMY, REAMIER, REAMIEST Scots for ▷ creamy

REAN, -S same as ▷ reen

REANNEX vb annex again

REANOINT vb anoint again

REANS ▷ rean

REANSWER vb answer again

REAP, -ED, -S vb cut and gather (a harvest)

REAPABLE ▷ reap

REAPED ▷ reap

REAPER, -S n person who reaps or machine for reaping

REAPHOOK n sickle

REAPING, -S n act of reaping

REAPPEAR vb appear again

REAPPLY vb put or spread (something) on again

REAPS ▷ reap

REAR, -ED, -S n back part ▷ vb care for and educate (children)

R

REARER, -S ▸ rear

REARGUE, -D, -S vb argue again

REARING, -S n act of rearing

REARISE, -N, -S, REAROSE vb arise again

REARLY old word for ▸ **early**

REARM, -ED, -ING, -S vb arm again

REARMICE > rearmouse

REARMING ▸ rearm

REARMOST adj nearest the back

REARMS ▸ rearm

REAROSE ▸ rearise

REAROUSE vb arouse again

REARREST vb arrest again

REARS ▸ rear

REARWARD adj in the rear ▷ adv towards the rear ▷ n position in the rear, esp the rear division of a military formation

REASCEND vb ascend again

REASCENT n new ascent

REASON, -S n cause or motive ▷ vb think logically in forming conclusions

REASONED adj well thought out or well presented

REASONER ▸ reason

REASONS ▸ reason

REASSAIL vb assail again

REASSERT vb assert (rights, claims, etc) again

REASSESS vb reconsider the value or importance of

REASSIGN vb move (personnel, resources, etc) to a new post, department, location, etc

REASSORT vb assort again

REASSUME vb assume again

REASSURE vb restore confidence to

REAST, -ED, -ING, -S same as ▸ **reest**

REASTIER ▸ reasty

REASTING ▸ reast

REASTS ▸ reast

REASTY, REASTIER adj (in dialect) rancid

REATA, -S n lasso

REATE, -S n type of crowfoot

REATTACH vb attach again

REATTACK vb attack again

REATTAIN vb attain again

REAVAIL, -S vb avail again

REAVE, -D, -S, REAVING, REFT vb carry off (property, prisoners, etc) by force

REAVER, -S ▸ reave

REAVES ▸ reave

REAVING ▸ reave

REAVOW, -ED, -S vb avow again

REAWAKE, -D, -S, REAWOKE, REAWOKEN vb awake again

REAWAKEN vb emerge or rouse from sleep

REAWAKES ▸ reawake

REAWOKE ▸ reawake

REAWOKEN ▸ reawake

REB, -S n Confederate soldier in the American Civil War

REBACK, -ED, -S vb provide with a new back, backing, or lining

REBADGE, -D, -S vb relaunch (a product) under a new name, brand, or logo

REBAIT, -ED, -S vb bait again

REBAR, -S n rod providing reinforcement in concrete structures

REBASE, -D, -S, REBASING vb set on a new foundation

REBATE, -D, -S, REBATING n discount or refund ▷ vb cut a rabbet in

REBATER, -S ▸ rebate

REBATES ▸ rebate

REBATING ▸ rebate

REBATO, -ES, -S same as ▸ **rabato**

REBBE, -S n individual's chosen spiritual mentor

REBEC, -S n medieval stringed instrument resembling the violin

REBECK, -S same as ▸ **rebec**

REBECS ▸ rebec

REBEGIN, REBEGAN, -S, REBEGUN vb begin again

REBEL, -LED, -S vb revolt against the ruling power ▷ n person who rebels ▷ adj rebelling

REBELDOM ▸ rebel

REBELLED ▸ rebel

REBELLER ▸ rebel

REBELLOW vb reecho loudly

REBELS ▸ rebel

REBID, -DEN, -S vb bid again

REBILL, -ED, -S vb bill again

REBIND, -S vb bind again

REBIRTH, -S n revival or renaissance

REBITE, REBIT, -S, REBITING, REBITTEN vb (in printing) to give another application of acid

REBLEND, -S vb blend again

REBLENT same as ▸ **reblend**

REBLOOM, -S vb bloom again

REBOANT adj resounding or reverberating

REBOARD, -S vb board again

REBODY, REBODIED, REBODIES vb give a new body to

REBOIL, -ED, -S vb boil again

REBOOK, -ED, -S vb book again

REBOOT, -ED, -S vb shut down and then restart (a computer system)

REBOP, -S same as ▸ **bebop**

REBORE, -D, -S, REBORING n boring of a cylinder to restore its true shape ▷ vb carry out this process

REBORN adj active again after a period of inactivity

REBORROW vb borrow again

REBOTTLE vb bottle again

REBOUGHT ▸ rebuy

REBOUND, -S vb spring back ▷ n act of rebounding

REBOZO, -S n long scarf covering the shoulders and head

REBRACE, -D, -S vb brace again

REBRANCH vb branch again

REBRAND, -S vb change or update the image of (an organization or product)

REBREED, REBRED, -S vb breed again

REBS ▸ reb

REBUFF, -ED, -S vb reject or snub ▷ n blunt refusal, snub

REBUILD, -S, REBUILT vb build (a building or town) again, after severe damage

REBUKE, -D, -S, REBUKING vb scold sternly ▷ n stern scolding

REBUKER, -S ▸ rebuke

REBUKES ▸ rebuke

REBUKING ▸ rebuke

REBURIAL ▸ rebury

REBURY, REBURIED, REBURIES vb bury again

REBUS, -ES n puzzle consisting of pictures and symbols representing words or syllables

REBUT, -S, -TED vb prove that (a claim) is untrue

REBUTTAL ▸ rebut

REBUTTED ▸ rebut

REBUTTER n defendant's pleading in reply to a claimant's surrejoinder

REBUTTON vb button again

REBUY, REBOUGHT, -ING, -S vb buy again

REC, -S n short for recreation

RECAL, -S same as ▸ **recall**

RECALL, -ED, -S vb recollect or remember ▷ n ability to remember

RECALLER ▸ recall

RECALLS ▸ recall

RECALS ▸ recal

RECAMIER n shade of pink

RECANE, -D, -S, RECANING vb cane again

RECANT, -ED, -S vb withdraw (a statement or belief) publicly

RECANTER ▸ recant

RECANTS ▸ recant

RECAP, -PED, -S vb recapitulate ▷ n recapitulation

RECAPTOR ▸ recapture

RECARPET vb replace one carpet with another

RECARRY vb carry again

RECAST, -S vb organize or set out in a different way

RECATCH, RECAUGHT vb catch again

RECCE, -D, -ED, -ING, -S vb reconnoitre ▷ n reconnaissance

RECCIED ▸ reccy

RECCIES ▸ reccy

RECCO, -S same as ▸ recce

RECCY, RECCIED, RECCIES, -ING same as ▸ recce

RECEDE, -D, -S, RECEDING vb move to a more distant place

RECEIPT, -S n written acknowledgment of money or goods received ▷ vb acknowledge payment of (a bill), as by marking it

RECEIVAL n act of receiving or state of being received

RECEIVE, -S vb take, accept, or get

RECEIVED adj generally accepted

RECEIVER n part of telephone that is held to the ear

RECEIVES ▸ receive

RECEMENT vb cement again

RECENCY ▸ recent

RECENSE, -D, -S vb revise

RECENSOR vb censor again

RECENT, -ER adj having happened lately

RECENTLY ▸ recent

RECENTRE vb centre again

RECEPT, -S n idea or image formed in the mind by repeated experience

RECEPTOR n sensory nerve ending that changes specific stimuli into nerve impulses

RECEPTS ▸ recept

RECESS, -ED, -ES n niche or alcove ▷ vb place or set (something) in a recess

RECHANGE vb change again

RECHARGE vb cause (a battery etc) to take in and store electricity again

RECHART, -S vb chart again

RECHATE, -S same as ▸ recheat

RECHEAT n (in a hunt) sounding of the horn to call back the hounds ▷ vb sound the horn to call back the hounds

RECHECK, -S vb check again

RECHEW, -ED, -S vb chew again

RECHIE adj smoky

RECHIP, -S vb put a new chip into (a stolen mobile phone) so it can be reused

RECHOOSE, RECHOSE, RECHOSEN vb choose again

RECIPE, -S n directions for cooking a dish

RECIRCLE vb circle again

RECISION n act of cancelling or rescinding

RECIT, -S n narrative

RECITAL, -S n musical performance by a soloist or soloists

RECITE, -D, -S, RECITING vb repeat (a poem, story, etc) aloud to an audience

RECITER, -S ▸ recite

RECITES ▸ recite

RECITING ▸ recite

RECITS ▸ recit

RECK, -ED, -ING, -S vb mind or care about (something)

RECKAN, -S adj strained, tormented, or twisted ▷ n chain or hook for hanging a pot over a fire

RECKED ▸ reck

RECKING ▸ reck

RECKLESS adj heedless of danger

RECKLING dialect word for ▸ runt

RECKON, -ED, -S vb consider or think

RECKONER n any of various devices or tables used to facilitate reckoning, esp a ready reckoner

RECKONS ▸ reckon

RECKS ▸ reck

RECLAD, -S vb cover in a different substance

RECLAIM, -S vb regain possession of ▷ n act of reclaiming or state of being reclaimed

RECLAME, -S n public acclaim or attention

RECLASP, -S vb clasp again

RECLEAN, -S vb clean again

RECLIMB, -S vb climb again

RECLINE, -D, -S vb rest in a leaning position

RECLINER n armchair with adjustable back

RECLINES ▸ recline

RECLOSE, -D, -S vb close again

RECLOTHE vb clothe again

RECLUSE, -S n person who avoids other people ▷ adj solitary

RECOAL, -ED, -S vb supply or be supplied with fresh coal

RECOAT, -ED, -S vb coat again

RECOCK, -ED, -S vb cock again

RECODE, -D, -S, RECODING vb put into a new code

RECODIFY vb codify again

RECODING ▸ recode

RECOIL, -ED, -S vb jerk or spring back ▷ n backward jerk

RECOILER ▸ recoil

RECOILS ▸ recoil

RECOIN, -ED, -S vb coin again

RECOLLET n member of a particular Franciscan order

RECOLOR, -S same as ▸ recolour

RECOLOUR vb give a new colour to

RECOMB, -ED, -S vb comb again

RECOMMIT vb send (a bill) back to a committee for further consideration

RECON, -NED, -S vb make a preliminary survey

RECONFER vb confer again

RECONNED ▸ recon

RECONS ▸ recon

RECONVEY vb convey again

RECOOK, -ED, -S vb cook again

RECOPY, RECOPIED, RECOPIES vb copy again

RECORD, -ED, -S n document or other thing that preserves information ▷ vb put in writing

RECORDER n person or machine that records, esp audio or video material

RECORDS ▸ record

RECORK, -ED, -S vb cork again

RECOUNT, -S vb tell in detail

RECOUP, -ED, -S vb regain or make good (a loss)

R

RECOUPE, -S vb (in law) keep back or withhold

RECOUPED ▸ recoup

RECOUPES ▸ recoupe

RECOUPLE vb couple again

RECOUPS ▸ recoup

RECOURE, -D, -S archaic variant of ▸ recover

RECOURSE archaic word for ▸ return

RECOVER, -S vb become healthy again

RECOVERY n act of recovering from sickness, a shock, or a setback

RECOWER, -S archaic variant of ▸ recover

RECOYLE, -D, -S archaic spelling of ▸ recoil

RECRATE, -D, -S vb crate again

RECREANT n disloyal or cowardly person ▷ adj cowardly

RECREATE vb amuse (oneself or someone else)

RECROSS vb move or go across (something) again

RECROWN, -S vb crown again

RECRUIT, -S vb enlist (new soldiers, members, etc) ▷ n newly enlisted soldier

RECS ▸ rec

RECTA ▸ rectum

RECTAL adj of the rectum

RECTALLY ▸ rectal

RECTI ▸ rectus

RECTIFY vb put right, correct

RECTION, -S n (in grammar) the determination of the form of one word by another word

RECTITIC ▸ rectitis

RECTITIS n inflammation of the rectum

RECTO, -S n right-hand page of a book

RECTOR, -S n member of the clergy in charge of a parish

RECTORAL adj of or relating to God's rule or to a rector

RECTORS ▸ rector

RECTORY n rector's house

RECTOS ▸ recto

RECTRESS same as ▸ rectoress

RECTRIX n any of the large stiff feathers of a bird's tail

RECTUM, RECTA, -S n final section of the large intestine

RECTUS, RECTI n straight muscle

RECUILE, -D, -S archaic variant of ▸ recoil

RECULE, -D, -S, RECULING archaic variant of ▸ recoil

RECUR, -RED, -S vb happen again

RECURE, -D, -S, RECURING vb archaic word for cure or recover

RECURRED ▸ recur

RECURS ▸ recur

RECURVE, -D, -S vb curve or bend (something) back or down

RECUSAL, -S n withdrawal of a judge from a case

RECUSANT n Roman Catholic who did not attend the services of the Church of England ▷ adj (formerly, of Catholics) refusing to attend services of the Church of England

RECUSE, -D, -S, RECUSING vb (in law) object to or withdraw (a judge)

RECUT, -S vb cut again

RECYCLE, -D, -S vb reprocess (used materials) for further use ▷ n repetition of a fixed sequence of events

RECYCLER ▸ recycle

RECYCLES ▸ recycle

RED, -DEST, -S adj of a colour varying from crimson to orange and seen in blood, fire, etc ▷ n red colour

REDACT, -ED, -S vb compose or draft (an edict, proclamation, etc)

REDACTOR ▸ redact

REDACTS ▸ redact

REDAMAGE vb damage again

REDAN, -S n fortification of two parapets at a salient angle

REDARGUE vb archaic word for disprove or refute

REDATE, -D, -S, REDATING vb change date of

REDBACK, -S n small venomous Australian spider

REDBAIT, -S vb harass those with leftwing leanings

REDBAY, -S n type of tree

REDBELLY n any of various animals having red underparts

REDBIRD, -S n type of bird, the male of which has bright red plumage

REDBONE, -S n type of American dog

REDBRICK n provincial British university of relatively recent foundation

REDBUD, -S n American tree with heart-shaped leaves

REDBUG, -S another name for ▸ chigger

REDCAP, -S n member of the military police

REDCOAT, -S n (formerly) a British soldier

REDD, -ED, -S vb bring order to ▷ n act or an instance of redding

REDDEN, -ED, -S vb make or become red

REDDENDA > reddendum

REDDENDO n Scottish legal clause specifying what duties are required in exchange for something

REDDENED ▸ redden

REDDENS ▸ redden

REDDER, -S ▸ redd

REDDEST ▸ red

REDDIER ▸ reddy

REDDIEST ▸ reddy

REDDING, -S ▸ redd

REDDISH adj somewhat red

REDDLE, -D, -S, REDDLING same as ▸ ruddle

REDDS ▸ redd

REDDY, REDDIER, REDDIEST adj reddish

REDE, -D, -S, REDING n advice or counsel ▷ vb advise

REDEAL, -S, -T vb deal again

REDEAR, -S n variety of sunfish with a red flash above the gills

REDECIDE vb decide again

REDED ▸ rede

REDEEM, -ED, -S vb make up for

REDEEMER ▸ redeem

REDEEMS ▸ redeem

REDEFEAT vb defeat again

REDEFECT vb defect back or again

REDEFIED ▸ redefy

REDEFIES ▸ redefy

REDEFINE vb define (something) again or differently

REDEFY, REDEFIED, REDEFIES vb defy again

REDELESS ▸ rede

REDEMAND vb demand again

REDENY, REDENIED, REDENIES vb deny again

REDEPLOY vb assign to a new position or task

REDES ▸ rede

REDESIGN vb change the design of (something) ▷ n something that has been redesigned

REDEYE, -S n inferior whiskey

REDFIN, -S *n* any of various small fishes with reddish fins that are popular aquarium fishes

REDFISH *n* male salmon that has recently spawned

REDFOOT, -S *n* fatal disease of newborn lambs

REDHEAD, -S *n* person with reddish hair

REDHORSE *n* type of fish

REDIA, -E, -S *n* parasitic larva of flukes

REDIAL, -ED, -S *vb* dial (a telephone number) again

REDIAS ▸ redia

REDID ▸ redo

REDIGEST *vb* digest again

REDING ▸ rede

REDIP, -PED, -S *vb* dip again

REDIPT *archaic past form of* ▸ redip

REDIRECT *vb* send in a new direction or course

REDISTIL *vb* distil again

REDIVIDE *vb* divide again

REDLEG, -S *n* bird with red legs

REDLINE, -D, -S *vb* refuse a loan to (a person or country) because of the presumed risks involved

REDLINER ▸ redline

REDLINES ▸ redline

REDLY ▸ red

REDNESS ▸ red

REDO, REDID, -ES, -ING, -NE, -S *vb* do over again in order to improve ▸ *n* instance of redoing something

REDOCK, -ED, -S *vb* dock again

REDOES ▸ redo

REDOING ▸ redo

REDOLENT *adj* reminiscent (of)

REDON, -NED, -S *vb* don again

REDONE ▸ redo

REDONNED ▸ redon

REDONS ▸ redon

REDOS ▸ redo

REDOUBLE *vb* increase, multiply, or intensify ▸ *n* act of redoubling

REDOUBT, -S *n* small fort defending a hilltop or pass ▸ *vb* fear

REDOUND, -S *vb* cause advantage or disadvantage (to)

REDOUT, -S *n* reddened vision caused by a rush of blood to the head

REDOWA, -S *n* Bohemian folk dance similar to the waltz

REDOX, -ES *n* chemical reaction in which one substance is reduced and the other is oxidized

REDPOLL, -S *n* mostly grey-brown finch with a red crown and pink breast

REDRAFT, -S *vb* write a second copy of (a letter, proposal, essay, etc) ▸ *n* second draft

REDRAW, -N, -S, REDREW *vb* draw or draw up (something) again or differently

REDRAWER ▸ redraw

REDRAWN ▸ redraw

REDRAWS ▸ redraw

REDREAM, -S, -T *vb* dream again

REDRESS *vb* make amends for ▸ *n* compensation or amends

REDREW ▸ redraw

REDRIED ▸ redry

REDRIES ▸ redry

REDRILL, -S *vb* drill again

REDRIVE, -N, -S, REDROVE *vb* drive again

REDROOT, -S *n* yellow-flowered bog plant whose roots yield a red dye

REDROVE ▸ redrive

REDRY, REDRIED, REDRIES, -ING *vb* dry again

REDS ▸ red

REDSEAR *same as* ▸ redshort

REDSHANK *n* large Eurasian sandpiper with red legs

REDSHARE *n* red algae

REDSHIFT *n* shift in the lines of the spectrum of an astronomical object

REDSHIRE *same as* ▸ redshare

REDSHIRT *vb* take a year out of a sports team

REDSHORT *vb* become brittle at red-hot temperatures

REDSTART *n* European bird of the thrush family

REDTAIL, -S *n* variety of bird with red colouring on its tail

REDTOP, -S *n* sensationalist tabloid newspaper

REDUB, -BED, -S *vb* fix or repair

REDUCE, -D, -S, REDUCING *vb* bring down, lower

REDUCER, -S *n* chemical solution used to lessen the density of a negative or print

REDUCES ▸ reduce

REDUCING ▸ reduce

REDUCTOR *n* apparatus in which substances can be reduced

REDUIT, -S *n* fortified part from which a garrison may fight on once an enemy has taken outworks

REDUVIID *n* type of insect

REDUX *adj* brought back or returned

REDWARE, -S *another name for* ▸ kelp

REDWATER *n* tick-borne disease of cattle

REDWING, -S *n* small European thrush

REDWOOD, -S *n* giant Californian conifer with reddish bark

REDYE, -D, -ING, -S *vb* dye again

REE, -S *n* Scots word for walled enclosure

REEARN, -ED, -S *vb* earn again

REEBOK, -S *same as* ▸ rhebok

REECH, -ED, -ES, -ING *vb* (in dialect) smoke

REECHIE *same as* ▸ reechy

REECHIER ▸ reechy

REECHING ▸ reech

REECHO, -ED, -ES *vb* echo again

REECHY, REECHIER *adj* (in dialect) smoky

REED, -ED, -S *n* tall grass that grows in swamps and shallow water

REEDBED, -S *n* area of wetland with reeds growing in it

REEDBIRD *n* any of several birds that frequent reed beds, esp (in the US and Canada) the bobolink

REEDBUCK *n* buff-coloured African antelope with inward-curving horns

REEDE, -S *obsolete variant of* ▸ red

REEDED ▸ reed

REEDEN *adj* of or consisting of reeds

REEDER, -S *n* thatcher

REEDES ▸ reede

REEDIER ▸ reedy

REEDIEST ▸ reedy

REEDIFY *vb* edify again or rebuild

REEDILY ▸ reedy

REEDING, -S *n* set of small semicircular architectural mouldings**

REEDIT, -ED, -S vb edit again

REEDLIKE adj resembling a reed

REEDLING n tawny titlike Eurasian songbird common in reed beds

REEDMAN, REEDMEN n musician who plays a wind instrument that has a reed

REEDS ▸ reed

REEDSTOP n organ stop that controls a rank of reed pipes

REEDY, REEDIER, REEDIEST adj harsh and thin in tone

REEF, -ED, -S n ridge of rock or coral near the surface of the sea ▸ vb roll up part of a sail

REEFABLE ▸ reef

REEFED ▸ reef

REEFER, -S n short thick jacket worn esp by sailors

REEFIER ▸ reefy

REEFIEST ▸ reefy

REEFING, -S ▸ reef

REEFS ▸ reef

REEFY, REEFIER, REEFIEST adj with reefs

REEJECT, -S vb eject again

REEK, -ED, -S vb smell strongly ▸ n strong unpleasant smell

REEKER, -S ▸ reek

REEKIE same as ▸ **reeky**

REEKIER ▸ reeky

REEKIEST ▸ reeky

REEKING ▸ reek

REEKS ▸ reek

REEKY, REEKIER, REEKIEST adj steamy or smoky

REEL, -ED, -S n cylindrical object on which film, tape, thread, or wire is wound ▸ vb stagger, sway, or whirl

REELABLE ▸ reel

REELECT, -S vb elect again

REELED ▸ reel

REELER, -S ▸ reel

REELING, -S ▸ reel

REELMAN, REELMEN n (formerly) member of a beach life-saving team operating a winch

REELS ▸ reel

REEMBARK vb embark again

REEMBODY vb embody again

REEMERGE vb emerge again

REEMIT, -S vb emit again

REEMPLOY vb employ again

REEN, -S n ditch, esp a drainage channel

REENACT, -S vb enact again

REENDOW, -S vb endow again

REENGAGE vb engage again

REENJOY, -S vb enjoy again

REENLIST vb enlist again

REENROLL vb enrol again

REENS ▸ reen

REENTER, -S vb enter again

REENTRY n return of a spacecraft into the earth's atmosphere

REEQUIP, -S vb equip again

REERECT, -S vb erect again

REES ▸ ree

REEST, -ED, -ING, -S vb (esp of horses) to be noisily uncooperative

REESTIER ▸ reesty

REESTING ▸ reest

REESTS ▸ reest

REESTY, REESTIER same as ▸ **reasty**

REEVE, -D, -S, REEVING n local representative of the king in a shire until the early 11th century ▸ vb pass (a rope or cable) through an eye or other narrow opening

REEVOKE, -D, -S vb evoke again

REEXPEL, -S vb expel again

REEXPORT vb export again

REEXPOSE vb expose again

REF, -FED, -S n referee in sport ▸ vb referee

REFACE, -D, -S, REFACING vb repair or renew the facing of (a wall)

REFALL, -EN, -S, REFELL vb fall again

REFASTEN vb fasten again

REFECT, -ED, -S vb archaic word for restore or refresh with food and drink

REFEED, REFED, -S vb feed again

REFEEL, -S, REFELT vb feel again

REFEL, -LED, -S vb refute

REFELL ▸ refall

REFELLED ▸ refel

REFELS ▸ refel

REFELT ▸ refeel

REFENCE, -D, -S vb fence again

REFER, -RED, -S vb allude (to)

REFEREE, -D, -S n umpire in sports, esp soccer or boxing ▸ vb act as referee of

REFERENT n object or idea to which a word or phrase refers

REFERRAL ▸ refer

REFERRED ▸ refer

REFERRER ▸ refer

REFERS ▸ refer

REFFED ▸ ref

REFFING, -S n act or instance of refereeing a sports match

REFI, -S n refinancing of a debt

REFIGHT, -S, REFOUGHT vb fight again ▸ n second or new fight

REFIGURE vb figure again

REFILE, -D, -S, REFILING vb file again

REFILL, -ED, -S vb fill again ▸ n second or subsequent filling

REFILM, -ED, -S vb film again

REFILTER vb filter again

REFIND, -S vb find again

REFINE, -S, REFINING vb purify

REFINED adj cultured or polite

REFINER, -S n person, device, or substance that removes impurities, etc

REFINERY n place where sugar, oil, etc is refined

REFINES ▸ refine

REFINING ▸ refine

REFINISH vb finish again

REFIRE, -D, -S, REFIRING vb fire again

REFIS ▸ refi

REFIT, -S, -TED vb make ready for use again by repairing or reequipping ▸ n repair or reequipping for further use

REFIX, -ED, -ES, -ING vb fix again

REFLAG, -S vb flag again

REFLATE, -D, -S vb inflate or be inflated again

REFLECT, -S vb throw back, esp rays of light, heat, etc

REFLET, -S n iridescent glow or lustre, as on ceramic ware

REFLEW ▸ refly

REFLEX, -ED, -ES n involuntary response to a stimulus or situation ▸ adj (of a muscular action) involuntary ▸ vb bend, turn, or reflect backwards

REFLEXLY ▸ reflex

REFLIES ▸ refly

REFLOAT, -S vb float again

REFLOOD, -S vb flood again

REFLOW, -ED, -S vb flow again

REFLOWER vb flower again

REFLOWN ▸ refly

REFLOWS ▸ reflow

REFLUENT adj flowing back

REFLUX, -ED, -ES vb boil in a vessel attached to a

condenser, so that the vapour condenses and flows back in ▷ n act of refluxing

REFLY, REFLEW, REFLIES, REFLOWN, -ING vb fly again

REFOCUS vb focus again or anew

REFOLD, -ED, -S vb fold again

REFOOT, -ED, -S vb foot again

REFOREST vb replant (an area that was formerly forested) with trees

REFORGE, -D, -S vb forge again

REFORM, -ED, -S n improvement ▷ vb improve

REFORMAT vb format again

REFORMED ▸ reform

REFORMER ▸ reform

REFORMS ▸ reform

REFOUGHT ▸ refight

REFOUND, -S vb found again

REFRACT, -S vb change the course of (light etc) passing from one medium to another

REFRAIN, -S n frequently repeated part of a song ▷ vb abstain (from action)

REFRAME, -D, -S vb support or enclose (a picture, photograph, etc) in a new or different frame

REFREEZE, REFROZE, REFROZEN vb freeze or be frozen again after having defrosted

REFRESH vb revive or reinvigorate, as through food, drink, or rest

REFRIED ▸ refry

REFRIES ▸ refry

REFRINGE formerly used to mean ▸ refract

REFRONT, -S vb put a new front on

REFROZE ▸ refreeze

REFROZEN ▸ refreeze

REFRY, REFRIED, REFRIES, -ING vb fry again

REFS ▸ ref

REFT ▸ reave

REFUEL, -ED, -S vb supply or be supplied with fresh fuel

REFUGE, -D, -S, REFUGING n (source of) shelter or protection ▷ vb take refuge or give refuge to

REFUGEE, -S n person who seeks refuge, esp in a foreign country

REFUGES ▸ refuge

REFUGIA ▸ refugium

REFUGING ▸ refuge

REFUGIUM, REFUGIA n region that has remained unaltered by a climatic change affecting surrounding regions

REFUND, -ED, -S vb pay back ▷ n return of money

REFUNDER ▸ refund

REFUNDS ▸ refund

REFURB, -ED, -S vb refurbish ▷ n (act or instance of) refurbishment

REFUSAL, -S n denial of anything demanded or offered

REFUSE, -D, -S, REFUSING vb decline, deny, or reject ▷ n rubbish or useless matter

REFUSER, -S ▸ refuse

REFUSES ▸ refuse

REFUSING ▸ refuse

REFUSION n new or further fusion

REFUSNIK same as > refusenik

REFUTAL, -S n act or process of refuting

REFUTE, -D, -S, REFUTING vb disprove

REFUTER, -S ▸ refute

REFUTES ▸ refute

REFUTING ▸ refute

REG, -S n large expanse of stony desert terrain

REGAIN, -ED, -S vb get back or recover ▷ n process of getting something back, esp lost weight

REGAINER ▸ regain

REGAINS ▸ regain

REGAL, -S adj of or like a king or queen ▷ n portable organ equipped only with small reed pipes

REGALE, -D, -S, REGALING vb entertain (someone) with stories etc ▷ n feast

REGALER, -S ▸ regale

REGALES ▸ regale

REGALIA, -S pl n ceremonial emblems of royalty or high office

REGALIAN adj royal

REGALIAS ▸ regalia

REGALING ▸ regale

REGALISM n principle that the sovereign has supremacy in church affairs

REGALIST ▸ regalism

REGALITY n state or condition of being royal

REGALLY ▸ regal

REGALS ▸ regal

REGAR, -S same as ▸ regur

REGARD, -ED, -S vb consider ▷ n respect or esteem

REGARDER ▸ regard

REGARDS ▸ regard

REGARS ▸ regar

REGATHER vb gather again

REGATTA, -S n meeting for yacht or boat races

REGAUGE, -D, -S vb gauge again

REGAVE ▸ regive

REGEAR, -ED, -S vb readjust

REGELATE vb undergo or cause to undergo regelation, a type of refreezing

REGENCE, -S old variant of ▸ regency

REGENCY n status or period of office of a regent

REGENT, -S n ruler of a kingdom during the absence, childhood, or illness of its monarch ▷ adj ruling as a regent

REGENTAL ▸ regent

REGENTS ▸ regent

REGES ▸ rex

REGEST, -ED, -S n archaic word for register ▷ vb register

REGGAE, -S n style of Jamaican popular music with a strong beat

REGGO, -S same as ▸ rego

REGICIDE n killing of a king

REGIE, -S n government-directed management or government monopoly

REGIFT, -ED, -S vb give (a previously received gift) to someone else

REGIFTER n person who regifts something

REGIFTS ▸ regift

REGILD, -ED, -S vb gild again

REGILT archaic past form of ▸ regild

REGIME, -S n system of government

REGIMEN, -S n prescribed system of diet etc

REGIMENT n organized body of troops as a unit of the army ▷ vb force discipline or order on, esp in a domineering manner

REGIMES ▸ regime

REGINA, -E, -S n queen

REGINAL adj queenly

REGINAS ▸ regina

REGION, -S n administrative division of a country

REGIONAL adj of, characteristic of, or limited to a region ▷ n regional heat of a competition

R

R

REGIONS ▶ region

REGISTER n (book containing) an official list or record of things ▷ vb enter in a register or set down in writing

REGISTRY n place where official records are kept

REGIUS adj as in **regius professor** Crown-appointed holder of a university chair

REGIVE, REGAVE, -N, -S, REGIVING vb give again or back

REGLAZE, -D, -S vb glaze again

REGLET, -S n flat narrow architectural moulding

REGLOSS vb gloss again or give a new gloss to

REGLOW, -ED, -S vb glow again

REGLUE, -D, -S, REGLUING vb glue again

REGMA, -TA n type of fruit with cells that break open and break away when ripe

REGMAKER n drink taken to relieve the symptoms of a hangover

REGMATA ▶ regma

REGNA ▶ regnum

REGNAL adj of a sovereign, reign, or kingdom

REGNANCY ▶ regnant

REGNANT adj reigning

REGNUM, REGNA n reign or rule

REGO, -S n registration of a motor vehicle

REGOLITH n layer of loose material covering the bedrock of the earth and moon

REGORGE, -D, -S vb vomit up

REGOS ▶ rego

REGOSOL, -S n type of azonal soil

REGRADE, -D, -S vb grade again

REGRAFT, -S vb graft again

REGRANT, -S vb grant again

REGRATE, -D, -S vb buy up (commodities) in advance so as to raise their price for resale

REGRATER ▶ regrate

REGRATES ▶ regrate

REGRATOR ▶ regrate

REGREDE, -D, -S vb go back

REGREEN, -S vb green again

REGREET, -S vb greet again or return greetings of

REGRESS vb revert to a former worse condition ▷ n

return to a former and worse condition

REGRET, -S vb feel sorry about ▷ n feeling of repentance, guilt, or sorrow

REGREW ▶ regrow

REGRIND, -S, REGROUND vb grind again

REGROOM, -S vb groom again

REGROOVE vb groove again

REGROUND ▶ regrind

REGROUP, -S vb reorganize (military forces) after an attack or a defeat

REGROW, REGREW, -N, -S vb grow or be grown again after having been cut or having died or withered

REGROWTH n growing back of hair, plants, etc

REGS ▶ reg

REGULA, -E n rule

REGULAR, -S adj normal, customary, or usual ▷ n regular soldier

REGULATE vb control, esp by rules

REGULI ▶ regulus

REGULINE ▶ regulus

REGULISE variant spelling of ▶ regulize

REGULIZE vb turn into regulus

REGULO, -S n any of a number of temperatures to which a gas oven may be set

REGULUS, REGULI n impure metal forming beneath the slag during the smelting of ores

REGUR, -S n black loamy Indian soil

REH, -S n (in India) salty surface crust on the soil

REHAB, -BED, -S vb help (a person) to readapt to society or a new job ▷ n treatment or help given to an addict, etc

REHABBER ▶ rehab

REHABS ▶ rehab

REHAMMER vb hammer again

REHANDLE vb handle again

REHANG, -ED, -S, REHUNG vb hang again

REHARDEN vb harden again

REHASH, -ED, -ES vb rework or reuse ▷ n old ideas presented in a new form

REHEAR, -D, -S vb hear again

REHEARSE vb practise (a play, concert, etc)

REHEAT, -ED, -S vb heat or be heated again

REHEATER ▶ reheat

REHEATS ▶ reheat

REHEEL, -ED, -S vb put a new heel or new heels on

REHEM, -MED, -S vb hem again

REHINGE, -D, -S vb put a new hinge or new hinges on

REHIRE, -D, -S, REHIRING vb hire again

REHOBOAM n wine bottle holding the equivalent of six normal bottles (approximately 156 ounces)

REHOME, -D, -S vb find a new home for (esp a pet)

REHOMING n act of rehoming

REHOUSE, -D, -S vb provide with a new (and better) home

REHS ▶ reh

REHUNG ▶ rehang

REI n name for a former Portuguese coin

REIF, -S n Scots word meaning robbery or plunder

REIFIED ▶ reify

REIFIER, -S ▶ reify

REIFIES ▶ reify

REIFS ▶ reif

REIFY, REIFIED, REIFIES, -ING vb consider or make (an abstract idea or concept) real or concrete

REIGN, -ED, -ING, -S n period of a sovereign's rule ▷ vb rule (a country)

REIGNITE vb catch fire or cause to catch fire again

REIGNS ▶ reign

REIK, -S Scots word for ▶ smoke

REIKI, -S n form of therapy to encourage healing or restore wellbeing

REIKS ▶ reik

REILLUME vb relight

REIMAGE, -D, -S vb image again

REIMPORT vb import (goods manufactured from exported raw materials) ▷ n act of reimporting

REIMPOSE vb establish previously imposed laws, controls, etc again

REIN, -ED, -ING vb check or manage with reins

REINCITE vb incite again

REINCUR, -S vb incur again

REINDEER n deer of Arctic regions with large branched antlers

REINDEX vb index again

REINDICT vb indict again

REINDUCE vb induce again

REINDUCT vb induct again

REINED ▶ rein

REINETTE n variety of apple

REINFECT vb infect or contaminate again

REINFORM vb inform again

REINFUND vb archaic word for pour in again

REINFUSE vb infuse again

REINING ▶ rein

REINJECT vb inject again

REINJURE vb injure again

REINJURY n further injury

REINK, -ED, -ING, -S vb ink again

REINLESS ▶ rein

REINS pl n narrow straps attached to a bit to guide a horse

REINSERT vb insert again

REINSMAN, REINSMEN n driver in a trotting race

REINSTAL same as ▶ reinstall

REINSURE vb insure again

REINTER, -S vb inter again

REINVADE vb invade again

REINVENT vb replace (a product, etc) with an entirely new version

REINVEST vb put back profits from a previous investment into the same enterprise

REINVITE vb invite again

REINVOKE vb invoke again

REIRD, -S Scots word for ▶ din

REIS, -ES n small branch

REISHI, -S n type of mushroom with a shiny cap

REISSUE, -D, -S n book, record, etc, that is released again after being unavailable ▷ vb release (a book, record, etc) again after a period of unavailability

REISSUER ▶ reissue

REISSUES ▶ reissue

REIST, -ED, -ING, -S same as ▶ reest

REITBOK, -S same as ▶ reedbuck

REITER, -ED, -S n soldier in the German cavalry ▷ vb repeat something

REIVE, -D, -S vb go on a plundering raid

REIVER, -S ▶ reive

REIVES ▶ reive

REIVING, -S n act of going on a plundering raid

REJACKET vb put a new jacket on

REJECT, -ED, -S vb refuse to accept or believe ▷ n person or thing rejected as not up to standard

REJECTEE n someone who has been rejected

REJECTER ▶ reject

REJECTOR ▶ reject

REJECTS ▶ reject

REJIG, -GED, -S vb reequip (a factory or plant) ▷ n act or process of rejigging

REJIGGER ▶ rejig

REJIGS ▶ rejig

REJOICE, -D, -S vb feel or express great happiness

REJOICER ▶ rejoice

REJOICES ▶ rejoice

REJOIN, -ED, -S vb join again

REJON, -ES n bullfighting lance

REJONEO, -S n bullfighting activity in which a mounted bullfighter spears the bull with lances

REJONES ▶ rejon

REJOURN, -S vb archaic word meaning postpone or adjourn

REJUDGE, -D, -S vb judge again

REJUGGLE vb juggle again

REKE, -D, -S, REKING same as ▶ reck

REKEY, -ED, -ING, -S vb key again

REKINDLE vb arouse former emotions or interests

REKING ▶ reke

REKNIT, -S vb knit again

REKNOT, -S vb knot again

RELABEL, -S vb label again

RELACE, -D, -S, RELACING vb lace again

RELACHE, -S n break

RELACING ▶ relace

RELAID ▶ relay

RELAND, -ED, -S vb land again

RELAPSE, -D, -S vb fall back into bad habits, illness, etc ▷ n return of bad habits, illness, etc

RELAPSER ▶ relapse

RELAPSES ▶ relapse

RELATA ▶ relatum

RELATE, -S, RELATING vb establish a relation between

RELATED adj linked by kinship or marriage

RELATER, -S ▶ relate

RELATES ▶ relate

RELATING ▶ relate

RELATION n connection between things

RELATIVE adj true to a certain degree or extent ▷ n person connected by blood or marriage

RELATOR, -S n person who relates a story

RELATUM, RELATA n one of the objects between which a relation is said to hold

RELAUNCH vb launch again ▷ n another launching, or something that is relaunched

RELAX, -ES, -ING vb make or become looser, less tense, or less rigid

RELAXANT n drug or agent that relaxes, esp one that relaxes tense muscles ▷ adj of, relating to, or tending to produce relaxation

RELAXED ▶ relax

RELAXER, -S n person or thing that relaxes

RELAXES ▶ relax

RELAXIN, -S n hormone secreted during pregnancy

RELAXING ▶ relax

RELAXINS ▶ relaxin

RELAY, RELAID, -ED, -ING, -S n fresh set of people or animals relieving others ▷ vb pass on (a message)

RELEARN, -S, -T vb learn (something previously known) again

RELEASE, -D, -S vb set free ▷ n setting free

RELEASEE n someone to whom an estate is released or someone released from captivity

RELEASER ▶ release

RELEASES ▶ release

RELEASOR n someone releasing an estate to someone else

RELEGATE vb put in a less important position

RELEND, -S vb lend again

RELENT, -ED, -S vb give up a harsh intention, become less severe

RELET, -S vb let again

RELETTER vb redo lettering of

RELEVANT adj connected with the matter in hand

RELEVE, -S n dance move in which heels are off the ground

RELIABLE adj able to be trusted, dependable ▷ n something or someone believed to be reliable

RELIABLY ▶ reliable

RELIANCE n dependence, confidence, or trust

RELIANT ▶ reliance

RELIC, -S n something that has survived from the past

R

RELICT, -S n relic

RELIDE archaic past form of ▸ rely

RELIE archaic spelling of ▸ rely

RELIED ▸ rely

RELIEF, -S n gladness at the end or removal of pain, distress, etc

RELIER, -S ▸ rely

RELIES ▸ rely

RELIEVE, -S vb bring relief to

RELIEVED adj experiencing relief, esp from worry or anxiety

RELIEVER n person or thing that relieves

RELIEVES ▸ relieve

RELIEVO, -S same as ▸ relief

RELIGHT, -S, RELIT vb ignite or cause to ignite again

RELIGION n system of belief in and worship of a supernatural power or god

RELINE, -D, -S, RELINING vb line again or anew

RELINK, -ED, -S vb link again

RELIQUE, -S archaic spelling of ▸ relic

RELISH, -ED, -ES vb enjoy, like very much ▸ n liking or enjoyment

RELIST, -ED, -S vb list again

RELISTEN vb listen again

RELISTS ▸ relist

RELIT ▸ relight

RELIVE, -D, -S, RELIVING vb experience (a sensation etc) again, esp in the imagination

RELIVER, -S vb deliver up again

RELIVES ▸ relive

RELIVING ▸ relive

RELLENO, -S n Mexican dish of stuffed vegetable

RELLIE, -S n informal word for a relative

RELLISH (in music) variant of ▸ relish

RELLO, -S n informal Australian word for a relative

RELOAD, -ED, -S vb put fresh ammunition into (a firearm)

RELOADER ▸ reload

RELOADS ▸ reload

RELOAN, -ED, -S vb loan again

RELOCATE vb move to a new place to live or work

RELOCK, -ED, -S vb lock again

RELOOK, -ED, -S vb look again

RELUCENT adj bright

RELUCT, -ED, -S vb struggle or rebel

RELUME, -D, -S, RELUMING vb light or brighten again

RELUMINE same as ▸ relume

RELUMING ▸ relume

RELY, RELIED, RELIES, -ING vb depend (on)

REM, -S n dose of ionizing radiation

REMADE, -S n object that has been reconstructed from original materials

REMAIL, -ED, -S vb mail again

REMAILER n internet service that forwards emails anonymously

REMAILS ▸ remail

REMAIN, -ED vb continue

REMAINER n person who remains

REMAINS pl n relics, esp of ancient buildings

REMAKE, -S, REMAKING vb make again in a different way ▸ n new version of an old film

REMAKER, -S ▸ remake

REMAKES ▸ remake

REMAKING ▸ remake

REMAN, -NED, -S vb man again or afresh

REMAND, -ED, -S vb send back into custody or put on bail before trial

REMANENT adj remaining or left over ▸ n archaic word meaning remainder

REMANET, -S n something left over

REMANIE, -S n fragments and fossils of older origin found in a more recent deposit

REMANNED ▸ reman

REMANS ▸ reman

REMAP, -PED, -S vb map again

REMARK, -ED, -S vb make a casual comment (on) ▸ n observation or comment

REMARKER ▸ remark

REMARKET vb market again

REMARKS ▸ remark

REMARQUE n printing mark in the margin of a plate

REMARRY vb marry again

REMASTER vb make a new master audio recording from an earlier recording

REMATCH n second or return game or contest between two players ▸ vb match (two contestants) again

REMATE, -D, -S, REMATING vb mate (animals) again ▸ n finishing pass in bullfighting

REMBLAI, -S n earth used for an embankment or rampart

REMBLE, -D, -S, REMBLING dialect word for ▸ remove

REMEAD, -ED, -S archaic or dialect word for ▸ remedy

REMEDE, -D, -S, REMEDING archaic or dialect word for ▸ remedy

REMEDIAL adj intended to correct or cure

REMEDIAT archaic word for ▸ remedial

REMEDIED ▸ remedy

REMEDIES ▸ remedy

REMEDING ▸ remede

REMEDY, REMEDIED, REMEDIES n means of curing pain or disease ▸ vb put right

REMEET, -S, REMET vb meet again

REMEID, -ED, -S archaic or dialect word for ▸ remedy

REMELT, -ED, -S vb melt again

REMEMBER vb retain in or recall to one's memory

REMEN, -S n ancient Egyptian measurement unit

REMEND, -ED, -S vb mend again

REMENS ▸ remen

REMERCY vb archaic word for thank

REMERGE, -D, -S vb merge again

REMET ▸ remeet

REMEX, REMIGES n any of the large flight feathers of a bird's wing

REMIGATE vb row

REMIGES ▸ remex

REMIGIAL ▸ remex

REMIND, -ED, -S vb cause to remember

REMINDER n something that recalls the past

REMINDS ▸ remind

REMINT, -ED, -S vb mint again

REMISE, -D, -S, REMISING vb give up or relinquish (a right, claim, etc) ▸ n second thrust made on the same lunge after the first has missed

REMISS adj negligent or careless

REMISSLY ▸ remiss

REMIT, -S, -TED vb send (money) for goods, services, etc, esp by post ▸ n area of competence or authority

REMITTAL ▸ remit

REMITTED ▸ remit
REMITTEE n recipient of a remittance
REMITTER n person who remits
REMITTOR same as ▸ remitter
REMIX, -ED, -ES, -ING vb change the relative prominence of each performer's part of (a recording) ▷ n remixed version of a recording
REMIXER, -S n person who remixes a recording
REMIXES ▸ remix
REMIXING ▸ remix
REMIXT informal past form of ▸ remix
REMNANT, -S n small piece, esp of fabric, left over ▷ adj remaining
REMODEL, -S vb give a different shape or form to ▷ n something that has been remodelled
REMODIFY vb modify again
REMOLADE same as > remoulade
REMOLD, -ED, -S US spelling of ▸ remould
REMORA, -S n spiny-finned fish
REMORID ▸ remora
REMORSE, -S n feeling of sorrow and regret for something one did
REMOTE, -R, -S, -ST adj far away, distant ▷ n (in informal usage) remote control
REMOTELY ▸ remote
REMOTER ▸ remote
REMOTES ▸ remote
REMOTEST ▸ remote
REMOTION n removal
REMOUD Spenserian variant of ▸ removed
REMOULD, -S vb change completely ▷ n renovated tyre
REMOUNT, -S vb get on (a horse, bicycle, etc) again ▷ n fresh horse
REMOVAL, -S n act of removing, esp changing residence
REMOVE, -S, REMOVING vb take away or off ▷ n degree of difference
REMOVED adj very different or distant
REMOVER, -S ▸ remove
REMOVES ▸ remove
REMOVING ▸ remove
REMS ▸ rem

REMUAGE, -S n process of turning wine bottles to let the sediment out
REMUDA, -S n stock of horses enabling riders to change mounts
REMUEUR, -S n person carrying out remuage
REMURMUR vb murmur again or murmur in reply
REN, -NED, -S archaic variant of ▸ run
RENAGUE, -D, -S same as ▸ renege
RENAIL, -ED, -S vb nail again
RENAL adj of the kidneys
**RENAME, -D, -S,
RENAMING** vb change the name of (someone or something)
RENATURE vb return to natural state
RENAY, -ED, -ING, -S vb archaic word meaning renounce
REND, -ED, -ING, -S vb tear or wrench apart
RENDANG, -S n spicy Indonesian meat dish
RENDED ▸ rend
RENDER, -ED, -S vb cause to become ▷ n first thin coat of plaster applied to a surface
RENDERER ▸ render
RENDERS ▸ render
RENDIBLE ▸ rend
RENDING ▸ rend
RENDS ▸ rend
RENDZINA n dark soil found in grassy or formerly grassy areas of moderate rainfall
RENEAGUE same as ▸ renege
RENEGADE n person who deserts a cause ▷ vb become a renegade
RENEGADO archaic word for ▸ renegade
RENEGATE old variant of ▸ renegade
RENEGE, -ED, -S, RENEGING vb go back (on a promise etc)
RENEGER, -S ▸ renege
RENEGES ▸ renege
RENEGING ▸ renege
RENEGUE, -D, -S same as ▸ renege
RENEGUER ▸ renege
RENEGUES ▸ renege
RENEST, -ED, -S vb nest again or form a new nest
RENEW, -ED, -ING, -S vb begin again
RENEWAL, -S n act of renewing or state of being renewed

RENEWED ▸ renew
RENEWER, -S ▸ renew
RENEWING ▸ renew
RENEWS ▸ renew
RENEY, -ED, -ING, -S same as ▸ renay
RENFORCE, RENFORST vb archaic word for reinforce
RENGA, -S n type of collaborative poetry found in Japan
RENIED ▸ reny
RENIES ▸ reny
RENIFORM adj having the shape or profile of a kidney
RENIG, -GED, -S same as ▸ renege
RENIN, -S n enzyme secreted by the kidneys
RENITENT adj reluctant
RENK, -ER, -EST adj unpleasant
RENMINBI same as ▸ yuan
RENNASE, -S same as ▸ rennin
RENNE, -S archaic variant of ▸ run
RENNED ▸ ren
RENNES ▸ renne
RENNET, -S n substance for curdling milk to make cheese
RENNIN, -S n enzyme that occurs in gastric juice
RENNING, -S ▸ ren
RENNINS ▸ rennin
RENO, -S n renovated house
RENOGRAM n X-ray kidney image
RENOS ▸ reno
RENOTIFY vb notify again
RENOUNCE vb give up (a belief, habit, etc) voluntarily ▷ n failure to follow suit in a card game
RENOVATE vb restore to good condition
RENOWN, -S n widespread good reputation ▷ vb make famous
RENOWNED adj famous
RENOWNER n renown giver
RENOWNS ▸ renown
RENS ▸ ren
RENT, -ED, -S n payment made by a tenant to a landlord or owner of a property ▷ vb grant the right to use one's property for payment
RENTABLE ▸ rend
RENTAL, -S n sum payable as rent ▷ adj of or relating to rent
RENTE, -S n annual income from capital investment

RENTED ▸ rent

RENTER, -S n person who lets his or her property in return for rent

RENTES ▸ rente

RENTIER, -S n person who lives off unearned income such as rents or interest

RENTING, -S ▸ rent

RENTS ▸ rent

RENUMBER vb number again or afresh

RENVERSE, RENVERST vb archaic word meaning overturn

RENVOI, -S n referring of a dispute to a jurisdiction other than that in which it arose

RENVOY, -S old variant of ▸ renvoi

RENY, RENIED, RENIES, -ING same as ▸ renay

REO, -S n New Zealand language

REOBJECT vb object again

REOBTAIN vb obtain again

REOCCUPY vb occupy (a building, area, etc) again

REOCCUR, -S vb happen, take place, or come about again

REOFFEND vb commit another offence

REOFFER, -S vb offer again

REOIL, -ED, -ING, -S vb oil again

REOPEN, -ED, -S vb open again after a period of being closed or suspended

REOPENER n clause in a legal document allowing for an issue to be revisited at a subsequent date

REOPENS ▸ reopen

REOPPOSE vb oppose again

REORDAIN vb ordain again

REORDER, -S vb change the order of

REORG, -ED, -ING, -S vb reorganize

REORIENT vb adjust or align (something) in a new or different way

REOS ▸ reo

REOUTFIT vb outfit again

REOVIRUS n type of virus

REP, -PED, -S n sales representative ▸ vb work as a representative

REPACIFY vb pacify again

REPACK, -ED, -S vb place or arrange (articles) again or in a different way

REPAID ▸ repay

REPAINT, -S vb apply a new or fresh coat of paint

REPAIR, -ED, -S vb restore to good condition, mend ▸ n act of repairing

REPAIRER ▸ repair

REPAIRS ▸ repair

REPAND adj having a wavy margin

REPANDLY ▸ repand

REPANEL, -S vb panel again or anew

REPAPER, -S vb paper again or afresh

REPARK, -ED, -S vb park again

REPARTEE n interchange of witty retorts ▸ vb retort

REPASS, -ED, -ES vb pass again

REPAST, -ED, -S n meal ▸ vb feed (on)

REPATCH vb patch again

REPAVE, -D, -S, REPAVING vb pave again

REPAY, REPAID, -ING, -S vb pay back, refund

REPEAL, -ED, -S vb cancel (a law) officially ▸ n act of repealing

REPEALER ▸ repeal

REPEALS ▸ repeal

REPEAT, -S vb say or do again ▸ n act or instance of repeating

REPEATED adj done, made, or said again and again

REPEATER n firearm that may be discharged many times without reloading

REPEATS ▸ repeat

REPEG, -GED, -S vb peg again

REPEL, -LED, -S vb be disgusting to

REPELLER ▸ repel

REPELS ▸ repel

REPENT, -ED, -S vb feel regret for (a deed or omission) ▸ adj lying or creeping along the ground

REPENTER ▸ repent

REPENTS ▸ repent

REPEOPLE vb people again

REPEREPE n New Zealand word for the elephant fish

REPERK, -ED, -S vb perk again

REPERUSE vb peruse again

REPETEND n digit or series of digits in a recurring decimal that repeats itself

REPHRASE vb express in different words

REPIN, -NED, -S vb pin again

REPINE, -D, -S, REPINING vb fret or complain

REPINER, -S ▸ repine

REPINES ▸ repine

REPINING ▸ repine

REPINNED ▸ repin

REPINS ▸ repin

REPIQUE, -D, -S n score of 30 in the card-game piquet ▸ vb score a repique against (someone)

REPLA ▸ replum

REPLACE, -D, -S vb substitute for

REPLACER ▸ replace

REPLACES ▸ replace

REPLAN, -S vb plan again

REPLANT, -S vb plant again

REPLATE, -D, -S vb plate again

REPLAY, -ED, -S n immediate reshowing on TV of an incident in sport ▸ vb play (a match, recording, etc) again

REPLEAD, -S, REPLED vb plead again

REPLEDGE vb pledge again

REPLETE, -D, -S adj filled or gorged ▸ vb fill again

REPLEVIN n recovery of goods unlawfully taken

REPLEVY vb recover possession of (goods) by replevin

REPLICA, -S n exact copy

REPLICON n region of a DNA molecule that is replicated from a single origin

REPLIED ▸ reply

REPLIER, -S ▸ reply

REPLIES ▸ reply

REPLOT, -S vb plot again

REPLOUGH vb plough again

REPLOW, -ED, -S vb plow again

REPLUM, REPLA n internal separating wall in some fruits

REPLUMB, -S vb plumb again

REPLUNGE vb plunge again

REPLY, REPLIED, REPLIES, -ING vb answer or respond ▸ n answer or response

REPO, -S n act of repossessing

REPOINT, -S vb repair the joints of (brickwork, masonry, etc) with mortar or cement

REPOLISH vb polish again

REPOLL, -ED, -S vb poll again

REPOMAN, REPOMEN n man employed to repossess goods in cases of non-payment

REPONE, -D, -S, REPONING vb restore (someone) to his or her former status, office, etc

REPORT, -ED, -S vb give an account of ▷ n account or statement

REPORTER n person who gathers news for a newspaper, TV, etc

REPORTS ▸ report

REPOS ▸ repo

REPOSAL, -S n repose

REPOSALL archaic spelling of ▸ reposal

REPOSALS ▸ reposal

REPOSE, -D, -S, REPOSING n peace ▷ vb lie or lay at rest

REPOSER, -S ▸ repose

REPOSES ▸ repose

REPOSING ▸ repose

REPOSIT, -S vb put away, deposit, or store up

REPOST, -ED, -S vb post again

REPOSURE old word for ▸ repose

REPOT, -S, -TED vb put (a house plant) into a new usually larger pot

REPOUR, -ED, -S vb pour back or again

REPOUSSE adj raised in relief ▷ n design or surface made in this way

REPOWER, -S vb put new engine in

REPP, -S same as ▸ rep

REPPED ▸ rep

REPPING, -S ▸ rep

REPPS ▸ repp

REPREEVE archaic spelling of ▸ reprieve

REPRESS vb keep (feelings) in check

REPRICE, -D, -S vb price again

REPRIEFE n (in archaic usage) reproof

REPRIEVE vb postpone the execution of (a condemned person) ▷ n (document granting) postponement or cancellation of a punishment

REPRIME, -D, -S vb prime again

REPRINT, -S vb print further copies of (a book) ▷ n reprinted copy

REPRISAL n retaliation

REPRISE, -D, -S n repeating of an earlier theme ▷ vb repeat an earlier theme

REPRIVE, -D, -S archaic spelling of ▸ reprieve

REPRIZE, -D, -S archaic spelling of ▸ reprise

REPRO, -S n imitation or facsimile of a work of art; reproduction

REPROACH vb blame, rebuke

REPROBE, -D, -S vb probe again

REPROOF, -S n severe blaming of someone for a fault ▷ vb treat (a coat, jacket, etc) so as to renew its texture, etc

REPROS ▸ repro

REPROVAL same as ▸ reproof

REPROVE, -D, -S vb speak severely to (someone) about a fault

REPROVER ▸ reprove

REPROVES ▸ reprove

REPRYVE, -D, -S archaic spelling of ▸ reprieve

REPS ▸ rep

REPTANT adj creeping, crawling, or lying along the ground

REPTILE, -S n cold-blooded egg-laying vertebrate with horny scales or plates ▷ adj creeping, crawling, or squirming

REPTILIA ▸ reptilium

REPUBLIC n government in which the people possess the supreme power

REPUGN, -ED, -S vb oppose or conflict (with)

REPULP, -ED, -S vb pulp again

REPULSE, -D, -S vb be disgusting to ▷ n act of driving back

REPULSER ▸ repulse

REPULSERS ▸ repulse

REPUMP, -ED, -S vb pump again

REPUNIT, -S n any number that consists entirely of the same repeated digits

REPURE, -D, -S, REPURING vb archaic word meaning make pure again

REPURIFY vb purify again

REPURING ▸ repure

REPURSUE vb pursue again

REPUTE, -S, REPUTING n reputation ▷ vb consider (a person or thing) to be as specified

REPUTED adj supposed

REPUTES ▸ repute

REPUTING ▸ repute

REQUERE, -D, -S archaic variant of ▸ require

REQUEST, -S vb ask ▷ n asking

REQUIEM, -S n Mass celebrated for the dead

REQUIGHT archaic spelling of ▸ requite

REQUIN, -S vb type of shark

REQUINTO n type of small guitar

REQUIRE, -D, -S vb want or need

REQUIRER ▸ require

REQUIRES ▸ require

REQUIT, -S vb quit again

REQUITAL n act or an instance of requiting

REQUITE, -D, -S vb return to someone (the same treatment or feeling as received)

REQUITER ▸ requite

REQUITES ▸ requite

REQUITS ▸ requit

REQUOTE, -D, -S vb quote again

REQUOYLE archaic spelling of ▸ recoil

RERACK, -ED, -S vb rack again

RERAIL, -ED, -S vb put back on a railway line

RERAISE, -D, -S vb raise again

RERAN ▸ rerun

REREAD, -S vb read (something) again

RERECORD vb record again

REREDOS n ornamental screen behind an altar

REREMAI, -S n New Zealand word for the basking shark

REREMICE > reremouse

REREMIND vb remind again

RERENT, -ED, -S vb rent again

REREPEAT vb repeat again

REREVIEW vb review again

REREVISE vb revise again

REREWARD archaic spelling of ▸ rearward

RERIG, -GED, -S vb rig again

RERISE, -N, -S, RERISING, REROSE vb rise again

REROLL, -ED, -S vb roll again

REROLLER ▸ reroll

REROLLS ▸ reroll

REROOF, -ED, -S vb put a new roof or roofs on

REROSE ▸ rerise

REROUTE, -S vb send or direct by a different route

RERUN, RERAN, -S n film or programme that is broadcast again, repeat ▷ vb put on (a film or programme) again

R

RES, -ES informal word for
▸ **residence**
RESADDLE vb saddle again
RESAID ▸ **resay**
RESAIL, -ED, -S vb sail again
RESALE, -S n selling of
something purchased earlier
RESALGAR archaic variant of
▸ **realgar**
RESALUTE vb salute back or
again
RESAMPLE vb (in graphics or
digital photography) change
the size or resolution of
RESAT ▸ **resit**
RESAW, -ED, -ING, -N, -S vb
saw again
RESAY, RESAID, -ING, -S vb
say again or in response
RESCALE, -D, -S vb resize
RESCHOOL vb retrain
RESCIND, -S vb annul or
repeal
RESCORE, -D, -S vb score
afresh
RESCREEN vb screen again
RESCRIPT n ordinance
taking the form of a reply by
the Roman emperor to a
point of law
RESCUE, -D, -S, RESCUING
vb deliver from danger or
trouble, save ▸ n act of
rescuing
RESCUEE, -S n person who is
rescued
RESCUER, -S ▸ **rescue**
RESCUES ▸ **rescue**
RESCUING ▸ **rescue**
RESCULPT vb sculpt again
RESEAL, -ED, -S vb close or
secure tightly again
RESEARCH n systematic
investigation to discover
facts or collect information
▸ vb carry out investigations
RESEASON vb season again
RESEAT, -ED, -S vb show (a
person) to a new seat
RESEAU, -S, -X n mesh
background to a lace or
other pattern
RESECT, -ED, -S vb cut out
part of (a bone, an organ, or
other structure or part)
RESECURE vb secure again
RESEDA, -S n plant that has
small spikes of grey-green
flowers ▸ adj of a
greyish-green colour
RESEE, -ING, -N, -S vb see
again
RESEED, -ED, -S vb form
seed and reproduce
naturally, forming a
constant plant population

RESEEING ▸ **resee**
RESEEK, -S, RESOUGHT vb
seek again
RESEEN ▸ **resee**
RESEES ▸ **resee**
RESEIZE, -D, -S vb seize
again
RESELECT vb choose
(someone or something)
again
RESELL, -S, RESOLD vb sell
(something) one has
previously bought
RESELLER ▸ **resell**
RESELLS ▸ **resell**
RESEMBLE vb be or look like
RESEND, -S vb send again
RESENT, -ED, -S vb feel bitter
about
RESENTER ▸ **resent**
RESENTS ▸ **resent**
RESERVE, -S vb set aside,
keep for future use ▸ n
something, esp money
or troops, kept for
emergencies
RESERVED adj not showing
one's feelings, lacking
friendliness
RESERVER ▸ **reserve**
RESERVES ▸ **reserve**
RESES ▸ **res**
RESET, -S vb set again (a
broken bone, matter in type,
a gemstone, etc) ▸ n act or
an instance of setting again
RESETTED same as ▸ **reset**
RESETTER ▸ **reset**
RESETTLE vb settle to live in
a different place
RESEW, -ED, -ING, -N, -S vb
sew again
RESH, -ES n 20th letter of
the Hebrew alphabet
RESHAPE, -D, -S vb shape
(something) again or
differently
RESHAPER ▸ **reshape**
RESHAPES ▸ **reshape**
RESHAVE, -D, -N, -S vb
shave again
RESHES ▸ **resh**
RESHINE, -D, -S, RESHONE
vb shine again
RESHIP, -S vb ship again
RESHOE, RESHOD, -D, -S vb
put a new shoe or shoes on
RESHONE ▸ **reshine**
RESHOOT, -S, RESHOT vb
shoot again
RESHOW, -ED, -N, -S vb
show again
RESHOWER vb have
another shower
RESHOWN ▸ **reshow**
RESHOWS ▸ **reshow**

RESIANCE archaic word for
▸ **residence**
RESIANT, -S archaic word for
▸ **resident**
RESID, -S n residual oil left
over from the petroleum
distillation process
RESIDE, -D, -S, RESIDING vb
dwell permanently
RESIDENT n person who
lives in a place ▸ adj living in
a place
RESIDER, -S ▸ **reside**
RESIDES ▸ **reside**
RESIDING ▸ **reside**
RESIDS ▸ **resid**
RESIDUA ▸ **residuum**
RESIDUAL adj of or being a
remainder ▸ n something
left over as a residue
RESIDUE, -S n what is left,
remainder
RESIDUUM, RESIDUA n
residue
RESIFT, -ED, -S vb sift again
RESIGHT, -S vb sight again
RESIGN, -S vb give up office,
a job, etc
RESIGNED adj content to
endure
RESIGNER ▸ **resign**
RESIGNS ▸ **resign**
RESILE, -D, -S, RESILING vb
spring or shrink back
RESILIN, -S n substance
found in insect bodies
RESILING ▸ **resile**
RESILINS ▸ **resilin**
RESILVER vb silver again
RESIN, -ED, -ING, -S n sticky
substance from plants, esp
pines ▸ vb treat or coat with
resin
RESINATA n type of wine
RESINATE vb impregnate
with resin
RESINED ▸ **resin**
RESINER, -S n applier or
collector of resin
RESINIER ▸ **resiny**
RESINIFY vb become or
cause to be resinous
RESINING ▸ **resin**
RESINISE variant spelling of
▸ **resinize**
RESINIZE vb apply resin to
RESINOID adj resembling,
characteristic of, or
containing resin ▸ n any
resinoid substance, esp a
synthetic compound
RESINOUS ▸ **resin**
RESINS ▸ **resin**
RESINY, RESINIER adj
resembling, containing or
covered with resin

R

RESIST, -ED, -S vb withstand or oppose ▷ n substance used to protect something

RESISTER ▶ resist

RESISTOR n component of an electrical circuit producing resistance

RESISTS ▶ resist

RESIT, RESAT, -S vb take (an exam) again ▷ n exam that has to be taken again

RESITE, -D, -S, RESITING vb move to a different site

RESITS ▶ resit

RESIZE, -D, -S, RESIZING vb change size of

RESKETCH vb sketch again

RESKEW, -ED, -S archaic spelling of ▶ rescue

RESKILL, -S vb train (workers) to acquire new skills

RESKIN, -S vb replace the outermost layer of an aircraft

RESKUE, -D, -S, RESKUING archaic spelling of ▶ rescue

RESLATE, -D, -S vb slate again

RESMELT, -S vb smelt again

RESMOOTH vb smooth again

RESOAK, -ED, -S vb soak again

RESOD, -DED, -S vb returf

RESOFTEN vb soften again

RESOJET, -S n type of jet engine

RESOLD ▶ resell

RESOLDER vb solder again

RESOLE, -D, -S, RESOLING vb put a new sole or new soles on

RESOLUTE adj firm in purpose ▷ n someone resolute

RESOLVE, -S vb decide with an effort of will ▷ n absolute determination

RESOLVED adj determined

RESOLVER ▶ resolve

RESOLVES ▶ resolve

RESONANT adj resounding or reechoing ▷ n type of unobstructed speech sound

RESONATE vb resound or cause to resound

RESORB, -ED, -S vb absorb again

RESORCIN n substance used principally in dyeing

RESORT, -ED, -S vb have recourse (to) for help etc ▷ n place for holidays

RESORTER ▶ resort

RESORTS ▶ resort

RESOUGHT ▶ reseek

RESOUND, -S vb echo or ring with sound

RESOURCE n thing resorted to for support ▷ vb provide funding or other resources for

RESOW, -ED, -ING, -N, -S vb sow again

RESPACE, -D, -S vb change the spacing of

RESPADE, -D, -S vb dig over

RESPEAK, -S, RESPOKE, RESPOKEN vb speak further

RESPECT, -S n consideration ▷ vb treat with esteem

RESPELL, -S, RESPELT vb spell again

RESPIRE, -D, -S vb breathe

RESPITE, -D, -S n pause, interval of rest ▷ vb grant a respite to

RESPLEND vb be resplendent

RESPLICE vb splice again

RESPLIT, -S vb split again

RESPOKE ▶ respeak

RESPOKEN ▶ respeak

RESPOND, -S vb answer ▷ n pilaster or an engaged column that supports an arch or a lintel

RESPONSA n that part of rabbinic literature concerned with written rulings in answer to questions

RESPONSE n answer

RESPOOL, -S vb rewind onto spool

RESPOT, -S vb (in billiards) replace (a ball) on one of the spots

RESPRANG ▶ respring

RESPRAY, -S n new coat of paint applied to a car, van, etc ▷ vb spray (a car, wheels, etc) with a new coat of paint

RESPREAD vb spread again

RESPRING, RESPRANG, RESPRUNG vb put new springs in

RESPROUT vb sprout again

RESPRUNG ▶ respring

REST, -ED, -S n freedom from exertion etc ▷ vb take a rest

RESTABLE vb put in stable again or elsewhere

RESTACK, -S vb stack again

RESTAFF, -S vb staff again

RESTAGE, -D, -S vb produce or perform a new production of (a play)

RESTAMP, -S vb stamp again

RESTART, -S vb commence (something) or set

(something) in motion again ▷ n act or an instance of starting again

RESTATE, -D, -S vb state or affirm (something) again or in a different way

RESTED ▶ rest

RESTEM, -S vb stem again

RESTER, -S ▶ rest

RESTFUL adj relaxing or soothing

RESTIER ▶ resty

RESTIEST ▶ resty

RESTIFF same as ▶ restive

RESTING, -S ▶ rest

RESTITCH vb stitch again

RESTIVE adj restless or impatient

RESTLESS adj bored or dissatisfied

RESTO, -S n restored antique, vintage car, etc

RESTOCK, -S vb replenish stores or supplies

RESTOKE, -D, -S vb stoke again

RESTORAL n restoration

RESTORE, -D, -S vb return (a building, painting, etc) to its original condition

RESTORER ▶ restore

RESTORES ▶ restore

RESTOS ▶ resto

RESTRAIN vb hold (someone) back from action

RESTRESS vb stress again or differently

RESTRICT vb confine to certain limits

RESTRIKE, RESTRUCK vb strike again

RESTRING, RESTRUNG vb string again or anew

RESTRIVE, RESTROVE vb strive again

RESTROOM n room in a public building having lavatories and washing facilities

RESTROVE ▶ restrive

RESTRUCK ▶ restrike

RESTRUNG ▶ restring

RESTS ▶ rest

RESTUDY vb study again

RESTUFF, -S vb put new stuffing in

RESTUMP, -S vb provide with new stumps

RESTY, RESTIER, RESTIEST adj restive

RESTYLE, -D, -S vb style again

RESUBMIT vb submit again

RESULT, -ED, -S n outcome or consequence ▷ vb be the outcome or consequence (of)

R

RESUME, -D, -S, RESUMING vb begin again ▷ n summary

RESUMER, -S ▶ resume

RESUMES ▶ resume

RESUMING ▶ resume

RESUMMON vb summon again

RESUPINE adj lying on the back

RESUPPLY vb provide (with something) again

RESURGE, -D, -S vb rise again from or as if from the dead

RESURVEY vb survey again

RESUS, -ES, -SES n (short for) resuscitation room

RET, -S, -TED, -TING vb moisten or soak (flax, hemp, jute, etc) to facilitate separation of fibres

RETABLE, -S n ornamental screenlike structure above and behind an altar

RETABLO, -S n shelf for panels behind an altar

RETACK, -ED, -S vb tack again

RETACKLE vb tackle again

RETACKS ▶ retack

RETAG, -GED, -S vb tag again

RETAIL, -ED, -S n selling of goods individually or in small amounts to the public ▷ adj of or engaged in such selling ▷ adv by retail ▷ vb sell or be sold retail

RETAILER ▶ retail

RETAILOR vb tailor afresh

RETAILS ▶ retail

RETAIN, -ED, -S vb keep in one's possession

Perhaps the most important word in Scrabble, because its letters combine with every other letter apart from A, Q, V, X, Y and Z to form a 7-letter bonus word that will score you an extra 50 points, so if you have these six letters on your rack you know that a bonus is either available or very close. And if you have an S as well, so much the better, because not only does this rack offer you 11 different words to choose from, but if none of these can be fitted in then **retains** combines with every other letter except for Q, V, X, Y and Z to form at least one 8-letter word.

RETAINER n fee to retain someone's services

RETAINS ▶ retain

RETAKE, -N, -S, RETAKING, RETOOK vb recapture ▷ n act of rephotographing a scene

RETAKER, -S ▶ retake

RETAKES ▶ retake

RETAKING ▶ retake

RETALLY vb count up again

RETAMA, -S n type of shrub

RETAPE, -D, -S, RETAPING vb tape again

RETARD, -ED, -S vb delay or slow (progress or development)

RETARDER n substance that slows down chemical change

RETARDS ▶ retard

RETARGET vb target afresh or differently

RETASTE, -D, -S vb taste again

RETAUGHT ▶ reteach

RETAX, -ED, -ES, -ING vb tax again

RETCH, -ED, -ES vb try to vomit ▷ n involuntary spasm of the stomach

RETCHING n act of retching

RETE, RETIA n any network of nerves or blood vessels

RETEACH, RETAUGHT vb teach again

RETEAM, -ED, -S vb team up again

RETEAR, -S, RETORE, RETORN vb tear again

RETELL, -S, RETOLD vb relate (a story, etc) again or differently

RETELLER ▶ retell

RETELLS ▶ retell

RETEM, -S n type of shrub

RETEMPER vb temper again

RETEMS ▶ retem

RETENE, -S n yellow crystalline hydrocarbon found in tar oils

RETEST, -ED, -S vb test (something) again or differently

RETHINK, -S vb consider again, esp with a view to changing one's tactics ▷ n act or an instance of thinking again

RETHREAD vb thread again

RETIA ▶ rete

RETIAL ▶ rete

RETIARII ▶ retiarius

RETIARY adj of, relating to, or resembling a net or web

RETICENT adj uncommunicative, reserved

RETICLE, -S n network of fine lines, wires, etc, used in optical instruments

RETICULA > reticulum

RETICULE same as ▶ reticle

RETIE, -D, -ING, -S, RETYING vb tie again

RETIFORM adj netlike

RETILE, -D, -S, RETILING vb put new tiles in or on

RETIME, -D, -S, RETIMING vb time again or alter time of

RETINA, -E, -S n light-sensitive membrane at the back of the eye

RETINAL, -S adj of or relating to the retina ▷ n aldehyde form of the polyene retinol

RETINAS ▶ retina

RETINE, -S n chemical found in body cells that slows cell growth and division

RETINENE n aldehyde form of the polyene retinol

RETINES ▶ retine

RETINITE n any of various resins of fossil origin, esp one derived from lignite

RETINOIC adj containing or derived from retinoid

RETINOID adj resinlike ▷ n derivative of vitamin A

RETINOL, -S n another name for vitamin A and rosin oil

RETINT, -ED, -S vb tint again or change tint of

RETINUE, -S n band of attendants

RETINUED ▶ retinue

RETINUES ▶ retinue

RETINULA n part of the compound eye in certain arthropods

RETIRACY n (in US English) retirement

RETIRAL, -S n act of retiring from office, one's work, etc

RETIRANT n (in US English) retired person

RETIRE, -S vb (cause to) give up office or work, esp through age

RETIRED adj having retired from work etc

RETIREE, -S n person who has retired from work

RETIRER, -S ▶ retire

RETIRES ▶ retire

RETIRING adj shy

RETITLE, -D, -S vb give a new title to

RETOLD ▶ retell

RETOOK ▸ retake

RETOOL, -ED, -S vb replace, reequip, or rearrange the tools in (a factory, etc)

RETORE ▸ retear

RETORN ▸ retear

RETORT, -ED, -S vb reply quickly, wittily, or angrily ▷ n quick, witty, or angry reply

RETORTER ▸ retort

RETORTS ▸ retort

RETOTAL, -S vb add up again

RETOUCH vb restore or improve by new touches, esp of paint ▷ n art or practice of retouching

RETOUR, -ED, -S vb (in Scottish law) to return as heir

RETOX, -ED, -ES, -ING vb embark on a binge of something unhealthy after a period of abstinence

RETRACE, -D, -S vb go back over (a route etc) again

RETRACER ▸ retrace

RETRACES ▸ retrace

RETRACK vb track again

RETRACT, -S vb withdraw (a statement etc)

RETRAICT archaic form of ▸ retreat

RETRAIN, -S vb train to do a new or different job

RETRAIT, -S archaic form of ▸ retreat

RETRAITE archaic form of ▸ retreat

RETRAITS ▸ retrait

RETRAITT n archaic word meaning portrait

RETRAL adj at, near, or towards the back

RETRALLY ▸ retral

RETRATE, -D, -S archaic form of ▸ retreat

RETREAD, -S, RETROD n remould ▷ vb remould

RETREAT, -S vb move back from a position, withdraw ▷ n act of or military signal for retiring or withdrawal

RETREE, -S n imperfectly made paper

RETRENCH vb reduce expenditure, cut back

RETRIAL, -S n second trial of a case or defendant in a court of law

RETRIED ▸ retry

RETRIES ▸ retry

RETRIEVE vb fetch back again ▷ n chance of being retrieved

RETRIM, -S vb trim again

RETRO, -S adj associated with or revived from the past ▷ n a retro style of art

RETROACT vb act in opposition

RETROD ▸ retread

RETROFIT vb equip (a piece of equipment) with new parts after manufacture

RETRONYM n word coined for existing thing to distinguish it from new thing

RETRORSE adj (esp of plant parts) pointing backwards or in a direction opposite to normal

RETROS ▸ retro

RETRY, RETRIED, RETRIES, -ING vb try again (a case already determined)

RETS ▸ ret

RETSINA, -S n Greek wine flavoured with resin

RETTED ▸ ret

RETTERY n flax-retting place

RETTING ▸ ret

RETUND, -ED, -S vb weaken or blunt

RETUNE, -D, -S, RETUNING vb tune (a musical instrument) differently or again

RETURF, -ED, -S vb turf again

RETURN, -ED, -S vb go or come back ▷ n returning ▷ adj of or being a return

RETURNEE n person who returns to his or her native country, esp after war service

RETURNER n person or thing that returns

RETURNIK n someone returning to the former Soviet Union

RETURNS ▸ return

RETUSE adj having a rounded apex and a central depression

RETWEET, -S vb post (another user's post) on the Twitter website for one's own followers

RETWIST, -S vb twist again

RETYING ▸ retie

RETYPE, -D, -S, RETYPING vb type again

REUNIFY vb bring together again something previously divided

REUNION, -S n meeting of people who have been apart

REUNITE, -D, -S vb bring or come together again after a separation

REUNITER ▸ reunite

REUNITES ▸ reunite

REUPTAKE, REUPTOOK vb absorb again ▷ n act of reabsorbing

REURGE, -D, -S, REURGING vb urge again

REUSABLE adj able to be used more than once

REUSE, -D, -S, REUSING vb use again ▷ n act of using something again

REUTTER, -S vb utter again

REV, -S, -VED, -VING n revolution (of an engine) ▷ vb increase the speed of revolution of (an engine)

REVALUE, -D, -S vb adjust the exchange value of (a currency) upwards

REVAMP, -ED, -S vb renovate or restore ▷ n something that has been renovated or revamped

REVAMPER ▸ revamp

REVAMPS ▸ revamp

REVANCHE n revenge

REVEAL, -ED, -S vb make known ▷ n vertical side of an opening in a wall

REVEALER ▸ reveal

REVEALS ▸ reveal

REVEHENT adj (in anatomy) carrying back

REVEILLE n morning bugle call to waken soldiers

REVEL, -ED, -ING, -LED, -S vb take pleasure (in) ▷ n occasion of noisy merrymaking

REVELER, -S ▸ revel

REVELING ▸ revel

REVELLED ▸ revel

REVELLER ▸ revel

REVELRY n festivity

REVELS ▸ revel

REVENANT n something, esp a ghost, that returns

REVENGE, -D, -S n retaliation for wrong done ▷ vb make retaliation for

REVENGER ▸ revenge

REVENGES ▸ revenge

REVENUAL ▸ revenue

REVENUE, -S n income, esp of a state

REVENUED ▸ revenue

REVENUER n revenue officer or cutter

REVENUES ▸ revenue

REVERB, -ED, -S n electronic device that creates artificial acoustics ▷ vb reverberate

REVERE, -D, -S, REVERING vb be in awe of and respect greatly

R

REVEREND adj worthy of reverence ▷ n member of the clergy

REVERENT adj showing reverence

REVERER, -S ▸ revere

REVERES ▸ revere

REVERIE, -S n absent-minded daydream

REVERIFY vb verify again

REVERING ▸ revere

REVERIST n someone given to reveries

REVERS n turned back part of a garment, such as a lapel

REVERSAL n act or an instance of reversing

REVERSE, -D, -S vb turn upside down or the other way round ▷ n opposite ▷ adj opposite or contrary

REVERSER ▸ reverse

REVERSES ▸ reverse

REVERSI n game played on a draughtboard

REVERSIS n type of card game

REVERSO, -S another name for ▸ verso

REVERT, -ED, -S vb return to a former state

REVERTER ▸ revert

REVERTS ▸ revert

REVERY same as ▸ reverie

REVEST, -S, -TED vb restore (former power, authority, status, etc, to a person)

REVESTRY same as ▸ vestry

REVESTS ▸ revest

REVET, -S, -TED vb face (a wall or embankment) with stones

REVEUR, -S n daydreamer

REVEUSE, -S n female daydreamer

REVIE, -D, -S, REVYING vb archaic cards term meaning challenge by placing a larger stake

REVIEW, -ED, -S n critical assessment of a book, concert, etc ▷ vb hold or write a review of

REVIEWAL same as ▸ review

REVIEWED ▸ review

REVIEWER ▸ review

REVIEWS ▸ review

REVILE, -D, -S, REVILING vb be abusively scornful of

REVILER, -S ▸ revile

REVILES ▸ revile

REVILING ▸ revile

REVISAL, -S ▸ revise

REVISE, -D, -S, REVISING vb change or alter ▷ n act, process, or result of revising

REVISER, -S ▸ revise

REVISES ▸ revise

REVISING ▸ revise

REVISION n act of revising

REVISIT, -S vb visit again

REVISOR, -S ▸ revise

REVISORY adj of or having the power of revision

REVIVAL, -S n reviving or renewal

REVIVE, -D, -S vb bring or come back to life, vigour, use, etc

REVIVER, -S ▸ revive

REVIVES ▸ revive

REVIVIFY vb give new life to

REVIVING ▸ revive

REVIVOR, -S n means of reviving a lawsuit that has been suspended

REVOICE, -D, -S vb utter again

REVOKE, -D, -S, REVOKING vb cancel (a will, agreement, etc) ▷ n act of revoking

REVOKER, -S ▸ revoke

REVOKES ▸ revoke

REVOKING ▸ revoke

REVOLT, -ED, -S n uprising against authority ▷ vb rise in rebellion

REVOLTER ▸ revolt

REVOLTS ▸ revolt

REVOLUTE adj (esp of the margins of a leaf) rolled backwards and downwards

REVOLVE, -D, -S vb turn round, rotate ▷ n circular section of a stage that can be rotated

REVOLVER n repeating pistol

REVOLVES ▸ revolve

REVOTE, -D, -S, REVOTING vb decide or grant again by a new vote

REVS ▸ rev

REVUE, -S n theatrical entertainment with topical sketches and songs

REVUIST, -S ▸ revue

REVULSED adj filled with disgust

REVVED ▸ rev

REVVING ▸ rev

REVYING ▸ revie

REW, -S archaic spelling of ▸ rue

REWAKE, -D, -S, REWAKING, REWOKE, REWOKEN vb awaken again

REWAKEN, -S vb awaken again

REWAKES ▸ rewake

REWAKING ▸ rewake

REWAN archaic past form of ▸ rewin

REWARD, -ED, -S n something given in return for a service ▷ vb pay or give something to (someone) for a service, information, etc

REWARDER ▸ reward

REWARDS ▸ reward

REWAREWA n New Zealand tree

REWARM, -ED, -S vb warm again

REWASH, -ED, -ES vb wash again

REWATER, -S vb water again

REWAX, -ED, -ES, -ING vb wax again

REWEAR, -S, REWORE, REWORN vb wear again

REWEAVE, -D, -S, REWOVE, REWOVEN vb weave again

REWED, -DED, -S vb wed again

REWEIGH, -S vb weigh again

REWELD, -ED, -S vb weld again

REWET, -S, -TED vb wet again

REWIDEN, -S vb widen again

REWILD, -ED, -S vb return areas of land to a wild state

REWIN, -S, REWON vb win again

REWIND, -ED, -S, REWOUND vb wind again

REWINDER ▸ rewind

REWINDS ▸ rewind

REWINS ▸ rewin

REWIRE, -D, -S vb provide (a house, engine, etc) with new wiring

REWIRING n act of rewiring

REWOKE ▸ rewake

REWOKEN ▸ rewake

REWON ▸ rewin

REWORD, -ED, -S vb alter the wording of

REWORE ▸ rewear

REWORK, -ED, -S vb improve or bring up to date

REWORN ▸ rewear

REWOUND ▸ rewind

REWOVE ▸ reweave

REWOVEN ▸ reweave

REWRAP, -S, -T vb wrap again

REWRITE, -S, REWROTE vb write again in a different way ▷ n something rewritten

REWRITER ▸ rewrite

REWRITES ▸ rewrite

REWROTE ▸ rewrite

REWS ▸ rew

REWTH, -S archaic variant of ▸ ruth

R

REX, REGES, -ES *n* king

> **Rex** is a Latin word for **king**, a very commonly played X word.

REXINE, -S *n* tradename for a form of artificial leather
REYNARD, -S *n* fox
REZ, -ES, -ZES *n* informal word for an instance of reserving; reservation

> **Rez** is a short informal word for **reservation**, and is one of the most commonly played Z words.

REZERO, -ED, -ES, -S *vb* reset to zero
REZES ► rez
REZONE, -D, -S *vb* zone again
REZONING *n* act of changing the land use classification of an area
REZZES ► rez
RHABDOID *adj* rod-shaped ▷ *n* rod-shaped structure found in cells of some plants and animals
RHABDOM, -S *n* rodlike structure found in the eye of insects
RHABDOME *same as* ► **rhabdom**
RHABDOMS ► rhabdom
RHABDUS *n* sponge spicule
RHACHIAL ► rachis
RHACHIS *same as* ► **rachis**
RHAGADES *pl n* cracks found in the skin
RHAMNOSE *n* type of plant sugar
RHAMNUS *n* buckthorn
RHAPHE, RHAPHAE, -S *same as* ► **raphe**
RHAPHIDE *same as* ► **raphide**
RHAPHIS *same as* ► **raphide**
RHAPSODE *n* (in ancient Greece) professional reciter of poetry
RHAPSODY *n* freely structured emotional piece of music
RHATANY *n* S American leguminous shrub
RHEA, -S *n* S American three-toed ostrich
RHEBOK, -S *n* woolly brownish-grey southern African antelope
RHEMATIC *adj* of or relating to word formation
RHEME, -S *n* constituent of a sentence that adds most new information

RHENIUM, -S *n* silvery-white metallic element with a high melting point
RHEOBASE *n* minimum nerve impulse required to elicit a response from a tissue
RHEOCORD *same as* > **rheochord**
RHEOLOGY *n* branch of physics concerned with the flow and change of shape of matter
RHEOPHIL *adj* liking flowing water
RHEOSTAT *n* instrument for varying the resistance of an electrical circuit
RHEOTOME *n* interrupter
RHESUS, -ES *n* macaque monkey
RHETOR, -S *n* teacher of rhetoric
RHETORIC *n* art of effective speaking or writing
RHETORS ► rhetor
RHEUM, -S *n* watery discharge from the eyes or nose
RHEUMED *adj* rheumy
RHEUMIC *adj* of or relating to rheum
RHEUMIER ► rheumy
RHEUMS ► rheum
RHEUMY, RHEUMIER *adj* of the nature of rheum
RHEXIS, RHEXES, -ES *n* rupture
RHIES ► rhy
RHIME, -S *old spelling of* ► **rhyme**
RHINAL *adj* of or relating to the nose
RHINE, -S *n* dialect word for a ditch
RHINITIC ► rhinitis
RHINITIS *n* inflammation of the mucous membrane that lines the nose
RHINO, -S *n* rhinoceros
RHIZIC *adj* of or relating to the root of an equation
RHIZINE, -S *same as* ► **rhizoid**
RHIZOBIA > rhizobium
RHIZOID, -S *n* hairlike structure in mosses, ferns, and related plants
RHIZOMA *same as* ► **rhizome**
RHIZOME, -S *n* thick underground stem producing new plants
RHIZOMIC ► rhizome
RHIZOPI ► rhizopus
RHIZOPOD *n* type of protozoan of the phylum which includes the amoebas

RHIZOPUS, RHIZOPI *n* type of fungus
RHO, -S *n* 17th letter in the Greek alphabet

> It's useful to remember words that start with RH, as they can come in useful. If you or someone else plays **rho**, which is a Greek letter, remember that it can be expanded to, for example, **rhody, rhomb, rhodium, rhombus** or **rhomboid**.

RHODAMIN *same as* > **rhodamine**
RHODANIC *adj* of or relating to thiocyanic acid
RHODIC *adj* of or containing rhodium, esp in the tetravalent state
RHODIE *same as* ► **rhody**
RHODIES ► rhody
RHODINAL *n* substance with a lemon-like smell found esp in citronella and certain eucalyptus oils
RHODIUM, -S *n* hard metallic element
RHODORA, -S *n* type of shrub
RHODOUS *adj* of or containing rhodium (but proportionally more than a rhodic compound)
RHODY, RHODIES *n* rhododendron
RHOMB, -S *same as* ► **rhombus**
RHOMBI ► rhombus
RHOMBIC *adj* relating to or having the shape of a rhombus
RHOMBOI ► rhombos
RHOMBOID *n* parallelogram with adjacent sides of unequal length ▷ *adj* having such a shape
RHOMBOS, RHOMBOI *n* wooden slat attached to a thong that makes a roaring sound when the thong is whirled
RHOMBS ► rhomb
RHOMBUS, RHOMBI *n* diamond-shaped figure
RHONCHAL ► rhonchus
RHONCHUS, RHONCHI *n* respiratory sound resembling snoring
RHONCUS *n* respiratory sound resembling snoring
RHONE, -S *same as* ► **rone**
RHOPALIC *adj* (of verse) with each word having one more syllable than the word before

R

RHOS ▶ rho
RHOTIC adj denoting or speaking a dialect of English in which postvocalic rs are pronounced
RHUBARB, -S n garden plant with fleshy stalks ▷ interj noise made by actors to simulate conversation ▷ vb simulate conversation in this way
RHUBARBY adj tasting of rhubarb
RHUMB, -S n imaginary line on the surface of a sphere that intersects all meridians at the same angle
RHUMBA, -ED, -S same as ▶ rumba
RHUMBS ▶ rhumb
RHUS, -ES n genus of shrubs and small trees
RHY, RHIES archaic spelling of ▶ rye

This alternative spelling of **rye** can come in useful when you are short of vowels.

RHYME, -D, -S, RHYMING n sameness of the final sounds at the ends of lines of verse, or in words ▷ vb make a rhyme
RHYMER, -S same as > **rhymester**
RHYMES ▶ rhyme
RHYMING ▶ rhyme
RHYMIST, -S ▶ rhyme
RHYNE, -S same as ▶ **rhine**
RHYOLITE n fine-grained igneous rock
RHYTA ▶ rhyton
RHYTHM, -S n any regular movement or beat
RHYTHMAL adj rhythmic
RHYTHMED ▶ rhythm
RHYTHMI ▶ rhythmus
RHYTHMIC adj of, relating to, or characterized by rhythm, as in movement or sound
RHYTHMS ▶ rhythm
RHYTHMUS, RHYTHMI n rhythm
RHYTINA, -S n type of sea cow
RHYTON, RHYTA, -S n (in ancient Greece) horn-shaped drinking vessel
RIA, -S n long narrow inlet of the seacoast
RIAD, -S n traditional Moroccan house with an interior garden
RIAL, -S n standard monetary unit of Iran

RIALTO, -S n market or exchange
RIANCY, RIANCIES ▶ riant
RIANT adj laughing
RIANTLY ▶ riant
RIAS ▶ ria
RIATA, -S same as ▶ **reata**
RIB, -BED, -S n one of the curved bones forming the framework of the upper part of the body ▷ vb provide or mark with ribs
RIBA, -S n (in Islam) interest or usury
RIBALD, -ER, -S adj humorously or mockingly rude ▷ n ribald person
RIBALDLY ▶ ribald
RIBALDRY n ribald language or behaviour
RIBALDS ▶ ribald
RIBAND, -S n ribbon awarded for some achievement
RIBAS ▶ riba
RIBAUD, -S archaic variant of ▶ **ribald**
RIBAUDRY archaic variant of ▶ **ribaldry**
RIBAUDS ▶ ribaud
RIBBAND, -S same as ▶ **riband**
RIBBED ▶ rib
RIBBER, -S n someone who ribs
RIBBIE, -S n baseball run batted in
RIBBIER ▶ ribby
RIBBIES ▶ ribbie
RIBBIEST ▶ ribby
RIBBING, -S ▶ rib
RIBBIT, -S n sound a frog makes
RIBBON, -ED, -S n narrow band of fabric used for trimming, tying, etc ▷ vb adorn with a ribbon or ribbons
RIBBONRY n ribbons or ribbon work
RIBBONS ▶ ribbon
RIBBONY adj resembling ribbons
RIBBY, RIBBIER, RIBBIEST adj with noticeable ribs
RIBCAGE, -S n bony structure of ribs enclosing the lungs
RIBES n genus of shrubs that includes currants
RIBEYE, -S n beefsteak cut from the outer side of the rib section
RIBGRASS same as ▶ **ribwort**
RIBIBE, -S n rebeck
RIBIBLE, -S same as ▶ **ribibe**

RIBIER, -S n variety of grape
RIBLESS ▶ rib
RIBLET, -S n small rib
RIBLIKE ▶ rib
RIBOSE, -S n pentose sugar that occurs in RNA and riboflavin
RIBOSOME n any of numerous minute particles in the cytoplasm of cells
RIBOZYME n RNA molecule capable of catalysing a chemical reaction
RIBS ▶ rib
RIBSTON, -S n variety of apple
RIBSTONE same as ▶ **ribston**
RIBSTONS ▶ ribston
RIBULOSE n type of sugar
RIBWORK, -S n work or structure involving ribs
RIBWORT, -S n Eurasian plant with lancelike ribbed leaves
RICE, -D, -S, RICING n cereal plant grown on wet ground in warm countries ▷ vb sieve (vegetables) to a coarse mashed consistency
RICEBIRD n any of various birds frequenting rice fields, esp the Java sparrow
RICED ▶ rice
RICER, -S n kitchen utensil through which soft foods are pressed to form a coarse mash
RICERCAR same as > **ricercare**
RICERS ▶ ricer
RICES ▶ rice
RICEY adj resembling or containing rice
RICH, -ED, -ER, -EST, -ING adj owning a lot of money or property, wealthy ▷ vb (in archaic usage) enrich
RICHEN, -ED, -S vb enrich
RICHER ▶ rich
RICHES pl n wealth
RICHESSE n wealth or richness
RICHEST ▶ rich
RICHING ▶ rich
RICHLY adv elaborately
RICHNESS n state or quality of being rich
RICHT, -ED, -ER, -EST, -ING, -S Scots variant of ▶ **right**
RICHWEED n type of plant
RICIER ▶ ricy
RICIEST ▶ ricy
RICIN, -S n highly toxic protein, a lectin, derived from castor-oil seeds
RICING ▶ rice

RICINS ▸ ricin

RICINUS n genus of plants

RICK, -ED, -ING, -S n stack of hay etc ▷ vb wrench or sprain (a joint)

RICKER, -S n young kauri tree of New Zealand

RICKET n mistake

RICKETS n disease of children marked by softening of the bones, bow legs, etc

RICKETTY same as ▸ rickety

RICKETY adj shaky or unstable

RICKEY, -S n cocktail consisting of gin or vodka, lime juice, and soda water, served iced

RICKING ▸ rick

RICKLE, -S n unsteady or shaky structure

RICKLY, RICKLIER adj archaic word for run-down or rickety

RICKRACK n zigzag braid used for trimming

RICKS ▸ rick

RICKSHA, -S same as ▸ rickshaw

RICKSHAW n light two-wheeled vehicle pulled by one or two people

RICKYARD n place where hayricks are put

RICOCHET vb (of a bullet) rebound from a solid surface ▷ n such a rebound

RICOTTA, -S n soft white unsalted Italian cheese made from sheep's milk

RICRAC, -S same as ▸ rickrack

RICTAL ▸ rictus

RICTUS, -ES n gape or cleft of an open mouth or beak

RICY, RICIER, RICIEST same as ▸ ricey

RID, -DED, -DING, -S vb clear or relieve (of)

RIDABLE ▸ ride

RIDDANCE n act of getting rid of something undesirable or unpleasant

RIDDED ▸ rid

RIDDEN ▸ ride

RIDDER, -S ▸ rid

RIDDING ▸ rid

RIDDLE, -D, -S, RIDDLING n question made puzzling to test one's ingenuity ▷ vb speak in riddles

RIDDLER, -S ▸ riddle

RIDDLES ▸ riddle

RIDDLING ▸ riddle

RIDE, RIDDEN, -S vb sit on and control or propel (a horse, bicycle, etc) ▷ n journey on a horse etc

RIDEABLE ▸ ride

RIDENT adj laughing, smiling, or happy

RIDER, -S n person who rides

RIDERED ▸ rider

RIDERS ▸ rider

RIDES ▸ ride

RIDGE, -D, -S n long narrow hill ▷ vb form into a ridge or ridges

RIDGER, -S n plough used to form furrows and ridges

RIDGES ▸ ridge

RIDGETOP n summit of ridge

RIDGEWAY n road or track along a ridge, esp one of great antiquity

RIDGIER ▸ ridgy

RIDGIEST ▸ ridgy

RIDGING, -S ▸ ridge

RIDGY, RIDGIER, RIDGIEST ▸ ridge

RIDIC adj ridiculous

RIDICULE n treatment of a person or thing as ridiculous ▷ vb laugh at, make fun of

RIDING, -S ▸ ride

RIDLEY, -S n marine turtle

RIDOTTO, -S n entertainment with music and dancing, often in masquerade

RIDS ▸ rid

RIEL, -S n standard monetary unit of Cambodia

RIEM, -S n strip of hide

RIEMPIE, -S n leather thong or lace used mainly to make chair seats

RIEMS ▸ riem

RIESLING n type of white wine

RIEVE, -D, -S, RIEVING vb archaic word for rob or plunder

RIEVER, -S n archaic word for robber or plunderer

RIEVES ▸ rieve

RIEVING ▸ rieve

RIF, -S vb lay off

RIFAMPIN n drug used in the treatment of tuberculosis, meningitis, and leprosy

RIFE, -R, -ST adj widespread or common

RIFELY ▸ rife

RIFENESS ▸ rife

RIFER ▸ rife

RIFEST ▸ rife

RIFF, -ED, -ING, -S n short repeated melodic figure ▷ vb play or perform riffs in jazz or rock music

RIFFAGE, -S n (in jazz or rock music) act or an instance of playing a short series of chords

RIFFED ▸ riff

RIFFING ▸ riff

RIFFLE, -D, -S, RIFFLING vb flick through (pages etc) quickly ▷ n rapid in a stream

RIFFLER, -S n file with a curved face for filing concave surfaces

RIFFLES ▸ riffle

RIFFLING ▸ riffle

RIFFOLA, -S n use of an abundance of dominant riffs

RIFFRAFF n rabble, disreputable people

RIFFS ▸ riff

RIFLE, -D, -S n firearm with a long barrel ▷ vb cut spiral grooves inside the barrel of a gun

RIFLEMAN, RIFLEMEN n person skilled in the use of a rifle, esp a soldier

RIFLER, -S ▸ rifle

RIFLERY n rifle shots

RIFLES ▸ rifle

RIFLING, -S n cutting of spiral grooves on the inside of a firearm's barrel

RIFLIP, -S n genetic difference between two individuals

RIFS ▸ rif

RIFT, -ED, -ING, -S n break in friendly relations ▷ vb burst or cause to burst open

RIFTE archaic word for ▸ rift

RIFTED ▸ rift

RIFTIER ▸ rifty

RIFTIEST ▸ rifty

RIFTING ▸ rift

RIFTLESS ▸ rift

RIFTS ▸ rift

RIFTY, RIFTIER, RIFTIEST ▸ rift

RIG, -GED, -S vb arrange in a dishonest way ▷ n apparatus for drilling for oil and gas

RIGADOON n old Provençal dance in lively duple time

RIGATONI n macaroni in the form of short ridged often slightly curved pieces

RIGAUDON same as ▸ rigadoon

RIGG, -S n type of fish

RIGGALDS ▸ riggald

RIGGED ▸ rig

RIGGER, -S n person who rigs vessels, etc

R

RIGGING, -S ▸ rig
RIGGS ▸ rigg
RIGHT, -ED, -EST, -ING, -S adj just ▷ adv correctly ▷ n claim, title, etc allowed or due ▷ vb bring or come back to a normal or correct state
RIGHTEN, -S vb set right
RIGHTER, -S ▸ right
RIGHTEST ▸ right
RIGHTFUL adj in accordance with what is right
RIGHTIER ▸ righty
RIGHTIES ▸ righty
RIGHTING ▸ right
RIGHTISH adj somewhat right, esp politically
RIGHTISM ▸ rightist
RIGHTIST adj on the political right ▷ n supporter of the political right
RIGHTLY adv in accordance with the true facts or justice
RIGHTO interj expression of agreement or compliance
RIGHTS ▸ right
RIGHTY, RIGHTIER, RIGHTIES n right-handed person ▷ adj right-handed
RIGID, -ER, -EST, -S adj inflexible or strict ▷ adv completely or excessively ▷ n strict and unbending person
RIGIDIFY vb make or become rigid
RIGIDISE same as ▸ rigidize
RIGIDITY ▸ rigid
RIGIDIZE vb make or become rigid
RIGIDLY ▸ rigid
RIGIDS ▸ rigid
RIGLINGS ▸ rigling
RIGLINS ▸ riglin
RIGOL, -S n (in dialect) ditch or gutter
RIGOLL, -S same as ▸ rigol
RIGOLS ▸ rigol
RIGOR, -S same as ▸ rigour
RIGORISM n strictness in judgment or conduct
RIGORIST ▸ rigorism
RIGOROUS adj harsh, severe, or stern
RIGORS ▸ rigor
RIGOUR, -S n harshness, severity, or strictness
RIGOUT, -S n person's clothing
RIGS ▸ rig
RIKISHA, -S same as ▸ rickshaw
RIKISHI n sumo wrestler
RIKSHAW, -S same as ▸ rickshaw
RILE, -D, -S, RILING vb anger or annoy

RILEY, RILIER, RILIEST adj cross or irritable
RILIEVO, RILIEVI same as ▸ relief
RILING ▸ rile
RILL, -ED, -ING, -S n small stream ▷ vb trickle
RILLE, -S same as ▸ rill
RILLED ▸ rill
RILLES ▸ rille
RILLET, -S n little rill
RILLING ▸ rill
RILLMARK n mark left by the trickle of a rill
RILLS ▸ rill
RIM, -MED, -S n edge or border ▷ vb put a rim on (a pot, cup, wheel, etc)
RIMA, -E n long narrow opening
RIMAYE, -S n crevasse at the head of a glacier
RIME, -D, -S, RIMING same as ▸ rhyme
RIMELESS ▸ rhyme
RIMER, -S same as > rhymester
RIMES ▸ rime
RIMESTER same as > rhymester
RIMFIRE, -S adj (of a cartridge) having the primer in the rim of the base ▷ n cartridge of this type
RIMIER ▸ rimy
RIMIEST ▸ rimy
RIMINESS ▸ rimy
RIMING ▸ rime
RIMLAND, -S n area situated on the outer edges of a region
RIMLESS ▸ rim
RIMMED ▸ rim
RIMMER, -S n tool for shaping the edge of something
RIMMING, -S ▸ rim
RIMOSE adj (esp of plant parts) having the surface marked by a network of intersecting cracks
RIMOSELY ▸ rimose
RIMOSITY ▸ rimose
RIMOUS same as ▸ rimose
RIMPLE, -D, -S, RIMPLING vb crease or wrinkle
RIMROCK, -S n rock forming the boundaries of a sandy or gravelly alluvial deposit
RIMS ▸ rim
RIMSHOT, -S n deliberate simultaneous striking of skin and rim of drum
RIMU, -S n New Zealand tree
RIMY, RIMIER, RIMIEST adj coated with rime

RIN, -NING, -S Scots variant of ▸ run
RIND, -ED, -ING, -S n tough outer coating of fruits, cheese, or bacon ▷ vb take the bark off
RINDIER ▸ rindy
RINDIEST ▸ rindy
RINDING ▸ rind
RINDLESS ▸ rind
RINDS ▸ rind
RINDY, RINDIER, RINDIEST adj with a rind or rindlike skin
RINE, -S archaic variant of ▸ rind
RING, -ED, -S vb give out a clear resonant sound, as a bell ▷ n instance of ringing
RINGBARK vb cut away a circular strip of bark from a tree or branch
RINGBIT, -S n type of bit worn by a horse
RINGBOLT, -S n bolt with a ring fitted through an eye attached to the bolt head
RINGBONE n abnormal bony growth affecting the pastern of a horse, often causing lameness
RINGDOVE n large Eurasian pigeon with white patches on the wings and neck
RINGED ▸ ring
RINGENT adj (of the corolla of plants) consisting of two gaping lips
RINGER, -S n person or thing apparently identical to another
RINGETTE n team sport played on ice, using straight sticks to control a rubber ring
RINGGIT, -S n standard monetary unit of Malaysia
RINGHALS n variety of cobra
RINGING, -S ▸ ring
RINGLESS ▸ ring
RINGLET, -S n curly lock of hair
RINGLETY adj resembling a ringlet
RINGLIKE ▸ ring
RINGMAN, RINGMEN n (in dialect) ring finger
RINGNECK n any bird that has ringlike markings round its neck
RINGS ▸ ring
RINGSIDE n row of seats nearest a boxing or circus ring ▷ adj providing a close uninterrupted view

RINGSTER n member of a ring controlling a market in antiques, art treasures, etc

RINGTAIL n possum with a curling tail used to grip branches while climbing

RINGTAW, -S n game in which the aim is to knock marbles out of a ring

RINGTONE n musical tune played by a mobile phone when a call is received

RINGTOSS n game in which participants try to throw hoops onto an upright stick

RINGWAY, -S n bypass

RINGWISE adj used to being in the ring and able to respond appropriately

RINGWOMB n complication at lambing resulting from failure of the cervix to open

RINGWORK n circular earthwork

RINGWORM n fungal skin disease in circular patches

RINK, -ED, -ING, -S n sheet of ice for skating or curling ▷ vb skate on a rink

RINKHALS n S African cobra that can spit venom

RINKING ▶ rink

RINKS ▶ rink

RINKSIDE n area at the side of a rink

RINNING ▶ rin

RINS ▶ rin

RINSABLE ▶ rinse

RINSE, -D, -S vb remove soap from (washed clothes, hair, etc) by applying clean water ▷ n act of rinsing

RINSER, -S ▶ rinse

RINSES ▶ rinse

RINSIBLE ▶ rinse

RINSING, -S ▶ rinse

RIOJA, -S n red or white Spanish wine with a vanilla bouquet and flavour

RIOT, -ED, -S n disorderly unruly disturbance ▷ vb take part in a riot

RIOTER, -S ▶ riot

RIOTING, -S ▶ riot

RIOTISE, -S n archaic word for riotous behaviour and excess

RIOTIZE, -S same as ▶ riotise

RIOTOUS adj unrestrained

RIOTRY, RIOTRIES n riotous behaviour

RIOTS ▶ riot

RIP, -PED, -PING, -S vb tear violently ▷ n split or tear

RIPARIAL ▶ riparian

RIPARIAN adj of or on the banks of a river ▷ n person who owns land on a riverbank

RIPCORD, -S n cord pulled to open a parachute

RIPE, -D, -S, -ST, RIPING adj ready to be reaped, eaten, etc ▷ vb ripen

RIPECK, -S same as ▶ ryepeck

RIPED ▶ ripe

RIPELY ▶ ripe

RIPEN, -ED, -ING, -S vb grow ripe

RIPENER, -S ▶ ripen

RIPENESS ▶ ripe

RIPENING ▶ ripen

RIPENS ▶ ripen

RIPER, -S adj more ripe ▷ n old Scots word meaning plunderer

RIPES ▶ ripe

RIPEST ▶ ripe

RIPIENO, RIPIENI, -S n (in baroque concertos and concerti grossi) the full orchestra

RIPING ▶ ripe

RIPOFF, -S n grossly overpriced article

RIPOST, -S same as ▶ riposte

RIPOSTE, -D, -S n verbal retort ▷ vb make a riposte

RIPOSTS ▶ ripost

RIPP, -S n old Scots word for a handful of grain

RIPPABLE ▶ rip

RIPPED ▶ rip

RIPPER, -S n person who rips

RIPPIER, -S n archaic word for fish seller

RIPPING, -S ▶ rip

RIPPLE, -D, -S n slight wave or ruffling of a surface ▷ vb flow or form into little waves (on)

RIPPLER, -S ▶ ripple

RIPPLES ▶ ripple

RIPPLET, -S n tiny ripple

RIPPLIER ▶ ripply

RIPPLING ▶ ripple

RIPPLY, RIPPLIER ▶ ripple

RIPPS ▶ ripp

RIPRAP, -S vb deposit broken stones in or on

RIPS ▶ rip

RIPSAW, -ED, -N, -S n handsaw for cutting along the grain of timber ▷ vb saw with a ripsaw

RIPSTOP, -S n tear-resistant cloth

RIPT archaic past form of ▶ rip

RIPTIDE, -S n stretch of turbulent water in the sea

RIRORIRO n small New Zealand bush bird

RISALDAR n Indian cavalry officer

RISE, -N, -S vb get up from a lying, sitting, or kneeling position ▷ n act of rising

RISER, -S n person who rises, esp from bed

RISES ▶ rise

RISHI, -S n Indian seer or sage

RISIBLE adj causing laughter, ridiculous

RISIBLES pl n sense of humour

RISIBLY ▶ risible

RISING, -S ▶ rise

RISK, -ED, -ING, -S n chance of disaster or loss ▷ vb act in spite of the possibility of (injury or loss)

RISKER, -S ▶ risk

RISKFUL ▶ risk

RISKIER ▶ risky

RISKIEST ▶ risky

RISKILY ▶ risky

RISKING ▶ risk

RISKLESS ▶ risk

RISKS ▶ risk

RISKY, RISKIER, RISKIEST adj full of risk, dangerous

RISOLUTO adj musical term meaning firm and decisive ▷ adv firmly and decisively

RISORIUS, RISORII n facial muscle responsible for smiling

RISOTTO, -S n dish of rice cooked in stock with vegetables, meat, etc

RISP, -ED, -S vb Scots word meaning rasp

RISPETTO, RISPETTI n kind of folk song

RISPING, -S ▶ risp

RISPS ▶ risp

RISQUE, -S same as ▶ risk

RISSOLE, -S n cake of minced meat, coated with breadcrumbs and fried

RISTRA, -S n string of dried chilli peppers

RISUS, -ES n involuntary grinning expression

RIT, -S, -TED, -TING vb Scots word for cut or slit

RITARD, -S n (in music) a slowing down

RITE, -S n formal practice or custom, esp religious

RITELESS ▶ rite

RITENUTO adv held back momentarily ▷ n (in music) a slowing down

RITES ▶ rite

R

RITORNEL n (in music) orchestral passage

RITS ▸ rit

RITT, -S same as ▸ rit

RITTED ▸ rit

RITTER, -S n knight or horseman/horsewoman

RITTING ▸ rit

RITTS ▸ ritt

RITUAL, -S n prescribed order of rites ▷ adj concerning rites

RITUALLY ▸ ritual

RITUALS ▸ ritual

RITZ, -ES n ostentatious display

RITZIER ▸ ritzy

RITZIEST ▸ ritzy

RITZILY ▸ ritzy

RITZY, RITZIER, RITZIEST adj luxurious or elegant

RIVA, -S n rock cleft

RIVAGE, -S n bank, shore, or coast

RIVAL, -ED, -ING, -LED, -S n person or thing that competes with another ▷ adj in the position of a rival ▷ vb (try to) equal

RIVALESS n female rival

RIVALING ▸ rival

RIVALISE same as ▸ rivalize

RIVALITY ▸ rival

RIVALIZE vb become a rival

RIVALLED ▸ rival

RIVALRY n keen competition

RIVALS ▸ rival

RIVAS ▸ riva

RIVE, -D, -N, -S, RIVING vb split asunder

RIVEL, -LED, -S vb archaic word meaning wrinkle

RIVEN ▸ rive

RIVER, -S n large natural stream of water

RIVERAIN same as ▸ riparian

RIVERBED n bed of a river

RIVERED adj with a river or rivers

RIVERET, -S n archaic word for rivulet or stream

RIVERIER ▸ rivery

RIVERINE same as ▸ riparian

RIVERMAN, RIVERMEN n boatman or man earning his living working on a river

RIVERS ▸ river

RIVERWAY n river serving as a waterway

RIVERY, RIVERIER adj riverlike

RIVES ▸ rive

RIVET, -ED, -ING, -S, -TED n bolt for fastening metal plates ▷ vb fasten with rivets

RIVETER, -S ▸ rivet

RIVETING ▸ rivet

RIVETS ▸ rivet

RIVETTED ▸ rivet

RIVIERA, -S n coastline resembling the Mediterranean Riviera

RIVIERE, -S n necklace of diamonds which gradually increase in size

RIVING ▸ rive

RIVLIN, -S Scots word for rawhide shoe

RIVO interj (in the past) an informal toast

RIVULET, -S n small stream

RIVULOSE adj having meandering lines

RIVULUS n type of small tropical American fish

RIYAL, -S n standard monetary unit of Qatar, divided into 100 dirhams

RIZ (in some dialects) past form of ▸ rise

This unusual past tense of **rise** is one of the essential Z words.

RIZA, -S n partial icon cover made from precious metal

RIZARD, -S n redcurrant

RIZAS ▸ riza

RIZZAR, -ED, -S n Scots word for redcurrant ▷ vb Scots word for sun-dry

RIZZART, -S n Scots word for redcurrant

RIZZER, -ED, -S same as ▸ rizzar

RIZZOR, -ED, -S vb dry

ROACH, -ES, -ING n Eurasian freshwater fish ▷ vb clip (mane) short so that it stands upright

ROACHED adj arched convexly, as the back of certain breeds of dog, such as the whippet

ROACHES ▸ roach

ROACHING ▸ roach

ROAD, -S n way prepared for passengers, vehicles, etc

ROADBED, -S n material used to make a road

ROADEO, -S n competition testing driving skills

ROADHOG, -S n selfish or aggressive driver

ROADIE, -S n person who transports and sets up equipment for a band

ROADING, -S n road building

ROADKILL n remains of an animal or animals killed on the road by motor vehicles

ROADLESS ▸ road

ROADMAN, ROADMEN n someone involved in road repair or construction

ROADS ▸ road

ROADSHOW n radio show broadcast live from a place being visited by a touring disc jockey

ROADSIDE n side of a road ▷ adj situated beside a road

ROADSMAN, ROADSMEN same as ▸ roadman

ROADSTER n open car with only two seats

ROADWAY, -S n part of a road used by vehicles

ROADWORK n sports training by running along roads

ROAM, -ED, -S vb wander about ▷ n act of roaming

ROAMER, -S ▸ roam

ROAMING, -S ▸ roam

ROAMS ▸ roam

ROAN, -S adj (of a horse) having a brown or black coat sprinkled with white hairs ▷ n roan horse

ROANPIPE n Scots word for a drainpipe leading down from a gutter

ROANS ▸ roan

ROAR, -ED, -S vb make or utter a loud deep hoarse sound like that of a lion ▷ n such a sound

ROARER, -S ▸ roar

ROARIE Scots word for ▸ noisy

ROARIER ▸ roary

ROARIEST ▸ roary

ROARING, -S ▸ roar

ROARMING adj severe

ROARS ▸ roar

ROARY, ROARIER, ROARIEST adj sounding like a roar or tending to roar

ROAST, -ED, -S vb cook by dry heat, as in an oven ▷ n roasted joint of meat ▷ adj roasted

ROASTER, -S n person or thing that roasts

ROASTIE, -S n roast potato

ROASTING adj extremely hot ▷ n severe criticism or scolding

ROASTS ▸ roast

ROATE, -D, -S, ROATING archaic form of ▸ rote

ROB, -BED, -BING, -S vb steal from

ROBALO, -S n tropical fish

ROBAND, -S n piece of marline used for fastening a sail to a spar

ROBATA, -S n grill used for Japanese cooking

ROBBED ▸ rob

ROBBER, -S ▸ rob

ROBBERY n stealing of property from a person by using or threatening to use force

ROBBIN, -S same as ▸ **roband**

ROBBING ▸ rob

ROBBINS ▸ robbin

ROBE, -D, -S n long loose outer garment ▹ vb put a robe on

ROBELIKE adj like a robe

ROBES ▸ robe

ROBIN, -S n small brown bird with a red breast

ROBING, -S ▸ robe

ROBINIA, -S n type of leguminous tree

ROBINS ▸ robin

ROBLE, -S n oak tree

ROBOCALL n automated telephone call that delivers a message to a large number of people

ROBORANT adj tending to fortify or increase strength ▹ n drug or agent that increases strength

ROBOT, -S n automated machine, esp one performing functions in a human manner

ROBOTIC ▸ robot

ROBOTICS n science of designing and using robots

ROBOTISE same as ▸ **robotize**

ROBOTISM ▸ robot

ROBOTIZE vb automate

ROBOTRY ▸ robot

ROBOTS ▸ robot

ROBS ▸ rob

ROBURITE n flameless explosive

ROBUST, -ER adj very strong and healthy

ROBUSTA, -S n species of coffee tree

ROBUSTER ▸ robust

ROBUSTLY ▸ robust

ROC, -S n monstrous bird of Arabian mythology

ROCAILLE n decorative rock or shell work

ROCH, -ES same as ▸ **rotch**

ROCHET, -S n white surplice with tight sleeves, worn by Church dignitaries

ROCK, -ED, -S n hard mineral substance that makes up part of the earth's crust, stone ▹ vb (cause to) sway to and fro ▹ adj of or relating to rock music

ROCKABLE ▸ rock

ROCKABY same as ▸ **rockabye**

ROCKABYE n lullaby or rocking motion used with a baby during lullabies

ROCKAWAY n four-wheeled horse-drawn carriage, usually with two seats and a hard top

ROCKED ▸ rock

ROCKER, -S n rocking chair

ROCKERY n garden featuring rocks

ROCKET, -ED, -S n self-propelling device powered by the burning of explosive contents ▹ vb move fast, esp upwards

ROCKETER n bird that launches itself into the air like a rocket when flushed

ROCKETRY n science and technology of the design and operation of rockets

ROCKETS ▸ rocket

ROCKFALL n instance of rocks breaking away and falling from an outcrop

ROCKFISH n any of various fishes that live among rocks

ROCKIER, -S n archaic or dialect word for rock pigeon

ROCKIEST ▸ rocky

ROCKILY ▸ rocky

ROCKING, -S ▸ rock

ROCKLAY, -S same as ▸ **rokelay**

ROCKLESS ▸ rock

ROCKLIKE ▸ rock

ROCKLING n any of various small sea fishes having an elongated body and barbels around the mouth

ROCKOON, -S n rocket fired from a balloon at high altitude

ROCKROSE n any of various shrubs or herbaceous plants cultivated for their roselike flowers

ROCKS ▸ rock

ROCKWEED n any of various seaweeds that grow on rocks exposed at low tide

ROCKWOOL n mineral wool used for insulation

ROCKWORK n structure made of rock

ROCKY, ROCKIEST adj having many rocks

ROCOCO, -S adj (of furniture, architecture, etc) having much elaborate decoration ▹ n style of architecture and decoration characterized by elaborate ornamentation

ROCQUET, -S n another name for the salad plant rocket

ROCS ▸ roc

ROD, -DED, -S n slender straight bar, stick ▹ vb clear with a rod

RODDING, -S ▸ rod

RODE, -D, -S vb (of the male woodcock) to perform a display flight

RODENT, -S n animal with teeth specialized for gnawing

RODEO, -ED, -ING, -S n display of skill by cowboys, such as bareback riding ▹ vb take part in a rodeo

RODES ▸ rode

RODEWAY, -S archaic spelling of ▸ **roadway**

RODING, -S ▸ rode

RODLESS ▸ rod

RODLIKE ▸ rod

RODMAN, RODMEN n someone who uses or fishes with a rod

RODNEY, -S n type of small fishing boat used in Canada

RODS ▸ rod

RODSMAN, RODSMEN same as ▸ **rodman**

RODSTER, -S n angler

ROE, -S n mass of eggs in a fish, sometimes eaten as food

ROEBUCK, -S n male of the roe deer

ROED adj with roe inside

ROEMER, -S n drinking glass, typically having an ovoid bowl on a short stem

ROENTGEN n unit measuring a radiation dose

ROES ▸ roe

ROESTI, -S same as ▸ **rosti**

ROESTONE same as ▸ **oolite**

ROGALLO, -S n flexible fabric delta wing

ROGATION n solemn supplication, esp in a form of ceremony prescribed by the Church

ROGATORY adj (esp in legal contexts) seeking or authorized to seek information

ROGER, -ED, -ING, -S interj (used in signalling) message received ▹ vb acknowledge a received message

ROGNON, -S n isolated rock outcrop on a glacier

R

ROGUE, -D, -ING, -S, ROGUING *n* dishonest or unprincipled person ▷ *adj* (of a wild beast) living apart from the herd ▷ *vb* rid (a field or crop) of inferior or unwanted plants

ROGUER, -S *n* rogue

ROGUERY *n* dishonest or immoral behaviour

ROGUES ▶ rogue

ROGUIER ▶ roguy

ROGUIEST ▶ roguy

ROGUING ▶ rogue

ROGUISH *adj* dishonest or unprincipled

ROGUY, ROGUIER, ROGUIEST *adj* roguish

ROHE, -S *n* territory of a Māori tribal group

ROID, -S *n* short form of steroid

ROIL, -ED, -ING, -S *vb* make (a liquid) cloudy or turbid by stirring up dregs or sediment

ROILIER ▶ roily

ROILIEST ▶ roily

ROILING ▶ roil

ROILS ▶ roil

ROILY, ROILIER, ROILIEST *adj* cloudy or muddy

ROIN, -ED, -ING, -S *same as* ▶ royne

ROINISH *same as* ▶ roynish

ROINS ▶ roin

ROIST, -ED, -ING, -S *archaic variant of* ▶ roister

ROISTER, -S *vb* make merry noisily or boisterously

ROISTING ▶ roist

ROISTS ▶ roist

ROJAK, -S *n* (in Malaysia) a salad dish served in chilli sauce

ROJI, -S *n* Japanese tea garden or its path of stones

ROK, -S *same as* ▶ roc

Rok is an alternative spelling of **roc**, the mythical bird. Other spellings are **ruc** and **rukh**.

ROKE, -D, -S, ROKING *vb* (in dialect) steam or smoke

ROKELAY, -S *n* type of cloak

ROKER, -S *n* variety of ray

ROKES ▶ roke

ROKIER ▶ roky

ROKIEST ▶ roky

ROKING ▶ roke

ROKKAKU *n* hexagonal Japanese kite

ROKS ▶ rok

ROKY, ROKIER, ROKIEST *adj* (in dialect) steamy or smoky

ROLAG, -S *n* roll of carded wool ready for spinning

ROLAMITE *n* type of bearing using two rollers and a moving flexible band

ROLE, -S *n* task or function

ROLF, -ED, -ING, -INGS, -S *vb* massage following a particular technique

ROLFER, -S ▶ rolf

ROLFING ▶ rolf

ROLFINGS ▶ rolf

ROLFS ▶ rolf

ROLL, -ED, -S *vb* move by turning over and over ▷ *n* act of rolling over or from side to side

ROLLABLE ▶ roll

ROLLAWAY *n* mounted on rollers so as to be easily moved, esp to be stored away after use

ROLLBACK *n* reduction to a previous price

ROLLBAR, -S *n* bar that reinforces the frame of a car

ROLLED ▶ roll

ROLLER, -S *n* rotating cylinder

ROLLICK, -S *vb* behave in a boisterous manner ▷ *n* boisterous or carefree escapade

ROLLICKY *adj* rollicking

ROLLIE, -S *n* hand-rolled cigarette

ROLLING, -S ▶ roll

ROLLMOP, -S *n* herring fillet rolled round onion slices and pickled

ROLLNECK *adj* (of a garment) having a high neck that is worn rolled over ▷ *n* rollneck sweater or other garment

ROLLOCK, -S *same as* ▶ rowlock

ROLLOUT, -S *n* presentation to the public of a new aircraft, product, etc; launch

ROLLOVER *n* instance of a prize continuing in force for an additional period

ROLLS ▶ roll

ROLLTOP *n* as in **rolltop desk** desk having a slatted wooden panel that can be pulled down over the writing surface

ROLLUP, -S *n* something rolled into a tube shape

ROLLWAY, -S *n* incline down which logs are rolled

ROM, -S *n* member of a European nomadic people

ROMA *n* member of a European nomadic people

ROMAGE, -S *archaic variant of* ▶ rummage

ROMAIKA, -S *n* Greek dance

ROMAINE, -S *n* cos (lettuce)

ROMAJI, -S *n* Roman alphabet as used to write Japanese

ROMAL, -S *same as* ▶ rumal

ROMAN, -S *adj* in or relating to the vertical style of printing type used for most printed matter ▷ *n* roman type

ROMANCE, -D, -S *n* love affair ▷ *vb* exaggerate or fantasize

ROMANCER ▶ romance

ROMANCES ▶ romance

ROMANISE *same as* ▶ romanize

ROMANIZE *vb* impart a Roman Catholic character to (a ceremony, practice, etc)

ROMANO, -S *n* hard light-coloured sharp-tasting cheese

ROMANS ▶ roman

ROMANTIC *adj* of or dealing with love ▷ *n* romantic person or artist

ROMANZA, -S *n* short instrumental piece of song-like character

ROMAUNT, -S *n* verse romance

ROMCOM, -S *n* comedy based around the romantic relationships of the characters

ROMEO, -S *n* male sweetheart

ROMNEYA, -S *n* bushy type of poppy

ROMP, -ED, -ING, -S *vb* play wildly and joyfully ▷ *n* boisterous activity

ROMPER *n* playful or boisterous child

ROMPERS *pl n* child's overalls

ROMPING ▶ romp

ROMPISH *adj* inclined to romp

ROMPS ▶ romp

ROMS ▶ rom

RONCADOR *n* any of several types of fish

RONDACHE *n* round shield

RONDAVEL *n* circular building, often thatched

RONDE, -S *n* round dance

RONDEAU, -X *n* poem with the opening words of the first line used as a refrain

RONDEL, -S n rondeau with a two-line refrain appearing twice or three times

RONDELET n brief rondeau, having five or seven lines and a refrain taken from the first line

RONDELLE n type of bead

RONDELS ▶ **rondel**

RONDES ▶ **ronde**

RONDINO, -S n short rondo

RONDO, -S n piece of music with a leading theme continually returned to

RONDURE, -S n circle or curve

RONE, -S n Scots word for a gutter carrying rainwater from a roof

RONEO, -ED, -ING, -S vb duplicate (a document) from a stencil ▷ n document reproduced by this process

RONEPIPE same as ▶ **rone**

RONES ▶ **rone**

RONG archaic past participle of ▶ **ring**

RONGGENG n Malay traditional dance

RONIN, -S n lordless samurai, esp one whose feudal lord has been deprived of his territory

RONNE, RONNING archaic form of ▶ **run**

RONNEL, -S n type of pesticide

RONNIE, -S n Dublin slang word for moustache

RONNING ▶ **ronne**

RONT, -S archaic variant of ▶ **runt**

RONTE, -S archaic variant of ▶ **runt**

RONTGEN, -S variant spelling of ▶ **roentgen**

RONTS ▶ **ront**

RONZ n rest of New Zealand (in relation to Auckland)

RONZER, -S n New Zealander not from Auckland

ROO, -S n kangaroo

ROOD, -S n crucifix

ROOF, -ED, -S n outside upper covering of a building, car, etc ▷ vb put a roof on

ROOFER, -S ▶ **roof**

ROOFIE, -S n tablet of sedative drug

ROOFIER ▶ **roofy**

ROOFIES ▶ **roofie**

ROOFIEST ▶ **roofy**

ROOFING, -S n material used to build a roof

ROOFLESS ▶ **roof**

ROOFLIKE ▶ **roof**

ROOFLINE n uppermost edge of a roof

ROOFS ▶ **roof**

ROOFTOP, -S n outside part of the roof of a building

ROOFTREE same as ▷ **ridgepole**

ROOFY, ROOFIER, ROOFIEST adj with roofs

ROOIBOS n tea prepared from the dried leaves of an African plant

ROOIKAT, -S n South African lynx

ROOK, -ED, -ING, -S n Eurasian bird of the crow family ▷ vb swindle

ROOKERY n colony of rooks, penguins, or seals

ROOKIE, -S n new recruit

ROOKIER ▶ **rooky**

ROOKIES ▶ **rookie**

ROOKIEST ▶ **rooky**

ROOKING ▶ **rook**

ROOKISH ▶ **rook**

ROOKS ▶ **rook**

ROOKY, ROOKIER, ROOKIEST adj abounding in rooks

ROOM, -ED, -ING, -S n enclosed area in a building ▷ vb occupy or share a room

ROOMER, -S ▶ **room**

ROOMETTE n self-contained compartment in a railway sleeping carriage

ROOMFUL, -S, ROOMSFUL n number or quantity sufficient to fill a room

ROOMIE, -S n roommate

ROOMIER ▶ **roomy**

ROOMIES ▶ **roomie**

ROOMIEST ▶ **roomy**

ROOMILY ▶ **roomy**

ROOMING ▶ **room**

ROOMMATE n person with whom one shares a room or apartment

ROOMS ▶ **room**

ROOMSFUL ▶ **roomful**

ROOMSOME adj archaic word meaning roomy

ROOMY, ROOMIER, ROOMIEST adj spacious

ROON, -S n Scots word for shred or strip

ROOP, -ED, -ING, -S same as ▶ **roup**

ROOPIER ▶ **roopy**

ROOPIEST ▶ **roopy**

ROOPING ▶ **roop**

ROOPIT same as ▶ **roopy**

ROOPS ▶ **roop**

ROOPY, ROOPIER, ROOPIEST adj (in dialect) hoarse

ROORBACH same as ▶ **roorback**

ROORBACK n false or distorted report or account, used to obtain political advantage

ROOS ▶ **roo**

ROOSA, -S n type of grass

ROOSE, -D, -S, ROOSING vb flatter

ROOSER, -S ▶ **roose**

ROOSES ▶ **roose**

ROOSING ▶ **roose**

ROOST, -ED, -ING, -S n perch for fowls ▷ vb perch

ROOSTER, -S n domestic cock

ROOSTING ▶ **roost**

ROOSTS ▶ **roost**

ROOT, -ED n part of a plant that grows down into the earth obtaining nourishment ▷ vb establish a root and start to grow

ROOTAGE, -S n root system

ROOTBALL n mass of the roots of a plant

ROOTCAP, -S n layer of cells at root tip

ROOTED ▶ **root**

ROOTEDLY ▶ **root**

ROOTER, -S ▶ **root**

ROOTHOLD ▶ **root**

ROOTIER ▶ **rooty**

ROOTIES ▶ **rooty**

ROOTIEST ▶ **rooty**

ROOTING, -S ▶ **root**

ROOTKIT, -S n set of programs used to gain unauthorized access to a computer system

ROOTLE, -D, -S, ROOTLING vb search unsystematically

ROOTLESS adj having no sense of belonging

ROOTLET, -S n small root or branch of a root

ROOTLIKE ▶ **root**

ROOTLING ▶ **rootle**

ROOTS adj (of popular music) going back to the origins of a style

ROOTSY, ROOTSIER ▶ **roots**

ROOTWORM n beetle larva feeding on roots

ROOTY, ROOTIER, ROOTIES, ROOTIEST adj rootlike ▷ n (in military slang) bread

ROPABLE adj capable of being roped

ROPE, -D, -S n thick cord ▷ vb bind or fasten with rope

ROPEABLE same as ▶ **ropable**

R

ROPED ▶ rope

ROPELIKE ▶ rope

ROPER, -S n someone who makes ropes

ROPERIES ▶ ropery

ROPERS ▶ roper

ROPERY, ROPERIES n place where ropes are made

ROPES ▶ rope

ROPEWALK n long narrow usually covered path or shed where ropes are made

ROPEWAY, -S n type of aerial lift

ROPEWORK n making, mending, or tying ropes

ROPEY adj inferior or inadequate

ROPIER ▶ ropy

ROPIEST ▶ ropy

ROPILY ▶ ropey

ROPINESS ▶ ropey

ROPING, -S ▶ rope

ROPY, ROPIER, ROPIEST same as ▶ ropey

ROQUE, -S n game developed from croquet

ROQUET, -ED, -S vb drive one's ball against (another person's ball) in croquet ▷ n act of roqueting

ROQUETTE n another name for the salad plant rocket

RORAL archaic word for ▶ dewy

RORE, -S archaic spelling of ▶ roar

RORIC same as ▶ roral

RORID same as ▶ roral

RORIE same as ▶ roary

RORIER ▶ rory

RORIEST ▶ rory

RORQUAL, -S n toothless whale with a dorsal fin

RORT, -ED, -ING, -S n dishonest scheme ▷ vb take unfair advantage of something

RORTER, -S n small-scale confidence trickster

RORTIER ▶ rorty

RORTIEST ▶ rorty

RORTING, -S ▶ rort

RORTS ▶ rort

RORTY, RORTIER, RORTIEST ▶ rort

RORY, RORIER, RORIEST adj dewy

ROSACE, -S another name for ▶ rosette

ROSACEA, -S n chronic inflammatory disease affecting the skin of the face

ROSACES ▶ rosace

ROSAKER, -S archaic word for ▶ realgar

ROSALIA, -S n melody which is repeated but at a higher pitch each time

ROSARIA ▶ rosarium

ROSARIAN n person who cultivates roses, esp professionally

ROSARIES ▶ rosary

ROSARIUM, ROSARIA n rose garden

ROSARY, ROSARIES n series of prayers

ROSBIF, -S n term used in France for an English person

ROSCID adj dewy

ROSCOE, -S slang word for ▶ gun

ROSE, -D, -S, ROSING n flowering plant ▷ vb cause to redden

ROSEAL adj rosy or roselike

ROSEATE adj rose-coloured

ROSEBAY, -S n perennial plant with spikes of deep pink flowers

ROSEBED, -S n part of a garden where roses grow

ROSEBOWL n bowl for displaying roses or other flowers

ROSEBUD, -S n rose which has not yet fully opened

ROSEBUSH n flowering shrub

ROSED ▶ rose

ROSEFISH n red food fish of North Atlantic coastal waters

ROSEHIP, -S n berry-like fruit of a rose plant

ROSELESS ▶ rise

ROSELIKE ▶ rise

ROSELLA, -S n type of Australian parrot

ROSELLE, -S n Indian flowering plant

ROSEMARY n fragrant flowering shrub

ROSEOLA, -S n feverish condition of young children caused by a virus

ROSEOLAR ▶ roseola

ROSEOLAS ▶ roseola

ROSERIES ▶ rosery

ROSEROOT n Eurasian mountain plant

ROSERY, ROSERIES n bed or garden of roses

ROSES ▶ rose

ROSESLUG n one of various types of pest that feed on roses

ROSET, -ED, -ING, -S, -TED Scots word meaning rosin ▷ vb rub rosin on

ROSETTE, -S n rose-shaped ornament

ROSETTED ▶ roset

ROSETTES ▶ rosette

ROSETTY ▶ roset

ROSETY ▶ roset

ROSEWOOD n fragrant wood used to make furniture

ROSHAMBO n the game of rock-paper-scissors

ROSHI, -S n teacher of Zen Buddhism

ROSIED ▶ rosy

ROSIER, -S archaic word for ▶ rosebush

ROSIERE, -S archaic word for ▶ rosebush

ROSIERS ▶ rosier

ROSIES ▶ rosy

ROSIEST ▶ rosy

ROSILY ▶ rosy

ROSIN, -ED, -ING, -S n resin used for treating the bows of violins etc ▷ vb apply rosin to

ROSINATE n chemical compound

ROSINED ▶ rosin

ROSINER, -S n strong alcoholic drink

ROSINESS ▶ rosy

ROSING ▶ rose

ROSINIER ▶ rosiny

ROSINING ▶ rosin

ROSINOL, -S n yellowish fluorescent oily liquid obtained from certain resins

ROSINOUS adj rosiny

ROSINS ▶ rosin

ROSINY, ROSINIER adj resembling rosin

ROSIT, -ED, -ING, -S same as ▶ roset

ROSOGLIO same as ▶ rosolio

ROSOLIO, -S n type of cordial

ROSSER, -S n bark-removing machine

ROST, -ED, -ING, -S archaic spelling of ▶ roast

ROSTELLA > rostellum

ROSTER, -ED, -S n list of people and their turns of duty ▷ vb place on a roster

ROSTI, -S n Swiss dish of fried grated potato

ROSTING ▶ rost

ROSTIS ▶ rosti

ROSTRA ▶ rostrum

ROSTRAL adj of or like a beak or snout

ROSTRATE adj having a beak or beaklike process

ROSTRUM, ROSTRA, -S n platform or stage

ROSTS ▶ rost

ROSULA, -S n rosette

ROSULATE adj in the form of a rose

ROSY, ROSIED, ROSIES, ROSIEST, -ING adj pink-coloured ▷ vb redden or make pink

ROT, -S, -TED, -TING vb decompose or decay ▷ n decay

ROTA, -S n list of people who take it in turn to do a particular task

ROTAL adj of or relating to wheels or rotation

ROTAN, -S another name for ▶ rattan

ROTARY, ROTARIES adj revolving ▷ n traffic roundabout

ROTAS ▶ rota

ROTATE, -D, -S vb (cause to) move round a centre or on a pivot

ROTATING adj revolving around a central axis, line, or point

ROTATION n act of rotating

ROTATIVE same as ▶ rotatory

ROTATOR, -S n person, device, part, or muscle that rotates or causes rotation

ROTATORY adj of, relating to, possessing, or causing rotation

ROTAVATE same as ▶ rotovate

ROTCH, -ES n little auk

ROTCHE same as ▶ rotch

ROTCHES ▶ rotch

ROTCHIE, -S same as ▶ rotch

ROTE, -D, -S, ROTING n mechanical repetition ▷ vb learn by rote

ROTELY adv by rote

ROTENONE n white odourless crystalline substance

ROTES ▶ rote

ROTGRASS n type of grass blamed for sheeprot

ROTGUT, -S n alcoholic drink of inferior quality

ROTHER, -S dialect word for ▶ ox

ROTI, -S n (in India and the Caribbean) a type of unleavened bread

ROTIFER, -S n minute aquatic multicellular invertebrate

ROTIFORM adj in the shape of a wheel

ROTING ▶ rote

ROTINI, -S n type of small spiral-shaped pasta

ROTIS ▶ roti

ROTL, -S n unit of weight used in Muslim countries

ROTO, -S n printing process using a cylinder etched with many small recesses in a rotary press

ROTOLO, ROTOLI, -S n (in Italian cuisine) a roll

ROTON, -S n quantum of vortex motion

ROTOR, -S n revolving portion of a dynamo, motor, or turbine

ROTOS ▶ roto

ROTOTILL vb break up soil using a machine with revolving blades

ROTOVATE vb break up (the surface of the earth, or an area of ground) using a rotavator

ROTPROOF adj proof against rot

ROTS ▶ rot

ROTTAN, -S n (in dialect) a rat

ROTTE, -S n ancient stringed instrument

ROTTED ▶ rot

ROTTEN, -ER, -S adj decaying ▷ n (in dialect) a rat

ROTTENLY ▶ rotten

ROTTENS ▶ rotten

ROTTER, -S n despicable person

ROTTES ▶ rotte

ROTTING ▶ rot

ROTULA, -E, -S n kneecap

ROTUND, -ED, -ER, -S adj round and plump ▷ vb make round

ROTUNDA, -S n circular building or room, esp with a dome

ROTUNDED ▶ rotund

ROTUNDER ▶ rotund

ROTUNDLY ▶ rotund

ROTUNDS ▶ rotund

ROTURIER n freeholder or ordinary person

ROUBLE, -S n monetary unit of Russia, Belarus, and Tajikistan

ROUCHE, -S same as ▶ ruche

ROUCHED adj trimmed with a rouche

ROUCHES ▶ rouche

ROUCHING n lace trimming

ROUCOU, -S another name for ▶ annatto

ROUE, -S n man given to immoral living

ROUEN, -S n breed of duck

ROUES ▶ roue

ROUGE, -D, -S, ROUGING n red cosmetic used to colour the cheeks ▷ vb apply rouge to

ROUGH, -ED, -EST, -S adj uneven or irregular ▷ vb make rough ▷ n rough state or area

ROUGHAGE n indigestible constituents of food which aid digestion

ROUGHDRY vb dry (clothes or linen) without smoothing

ROUGHED ▶ rough

ROUGHEN, -S vb make or become rough

ROUGHER, -S n person that does the rough preparatory work on something ▷ adj more rough

ROUGHEST ▶ rough

ROUGHHEW vb cut or hew (timber, stone, etc) roughly without finishing the surface

ROUGHIE, -S n small food fish found in Australian waters

ROUGHING n (in ice hockey) excessive use of force

ROUGHISH adj somewhat rough

ROUGHLEG n any of several kinds of large hawk with feathered legs

ROUGHLY adv without being exact or fully authenticated

ROUGHOUT n unfinished roughly shaped artefact

ROUGHS ▶ rough

ROUGHT archaic past form of ▶ reach

ROUGHY spelling variant of ▶ roughie

ROUGING ▶ rouge

ROUILLE, -S n kind of sauce

ROUL, -S archaic form of ▶ roll

ROULADE, -S n slice of meat rolled and cooked

ROULE, -S archaic form of ▶ roll

ROULEAU, -S, -X n roll of paper containing coins

ROULES ▶ roule

ROULETTE n gambling game played with a revolving wheel and a ball ▷ vb use a toothed wheel on (something), as in engraving, making stationery, etc

ROULS ▶ roul

ROUM, -S archaic spelling of ▶ room

ROUMING, -S n portion of common pastureland

R

ROUMS ▸ roum

ROUNCE, -S n handle that is turned to move paper and plates on a printing press

ROUNCY, ROUNCIES archaic word for ▸ horse

ROUND, -EST, -S adj spherical, cylindrical, circular, or curved ▷ prep indicating an encircling movement, presence on all sides, etc ▷ vb move round ▷ n round shape

ROUNDED adj round or curved

ROUNDEL, -S same as ▸ roundelay

ROUNDER n run round all four bases after one hit in rounders

ROUNDERS n bat-and-ball team game

ROUNDEST ▸ round

ROUNDING n process in which a number with a fraction is approximated as the closest number up or down

ROUNDISH adj somewhat round

ROUNDLE, -S same as ▸ roundel

ROUNDLET n small circle

ROUNDLY adv thoroughly

ROUNDS ▸ round

ROUNDUP, -S n act of gathering together

ROUNDURE n archaic word meaning roundness

ROUP, -ED, -ING, -S n any of various chronic respiratory diseases of birds, esp poultry ▷ vb sell by auction

ROUPET adj Scots word meaning hoarse or croaky

ROUPIER ▸ roupy

ROUPIEST ▸ roupy

ROUPILY ▸ roup

ROUPING ▸ roup

ROUPIT same as ▸ roupet

ROUPS ▸ roup

ROUPY, ROUPIER, ROUPIEST ▸ roup

ROUSABLE adj capable of being roused

ROUSANT adj (in heraldry) rising

ROUSE, -D, -S vb provoke or excite

ROUSER, -S n person or thing that rouses people

ROUSES ▸ rouse

ROUSING adj lively, vigorous

ROUSSEAU n pemmican fried in its own fat

ROUST, -ED, -ING, -S vb rout or stir, as out of bed

ROUSTER, -S n unskilled labourer on an oil rig

ROUSTING ▸ roust

ROUSTS ▸ roust

ROUT, -S n overwhelming defeat ▷ vb defeat and put to flight

ROUTE, -D, -ING, -S n roads taken to reach a destination ▷ vb send by a particular route

ROUTEMAN, ROUTEMEN n (in US English) delivery man or salesman doing a particular round

ROUTER, -S n device that allows data to be moved between points on a network

ROUTES ▸ route

ROUTEWAY n track, road, or waterway, etc, used as a route to somewhere

ROUTH, -S n abundance ▷ adj abundant

ROUTHIE, -R adj abundant, plentiful, or well filled

ROUTHS ▸ routh

ROUTINE, -S n usual or regular method of procedure ▷ adj ordinary or regular

ROUTING, -S ▸ rout

ROUTOUS ▸ rout

ROUTS ▸ rout

ROUX n fat and flour cooked together as a basis for sauces

ROVE, -D, -N, -S, ROVING, ROVINGS vb wander about

ROVER, -S n wanderer, traveller

ROVES ▸ rove

ROVING ▸ rove

ROVINGLY ▸ rove

ROVINGS ▸ rove

ROW, -ED, -S n straight line of people or things ▷ vb propel (a boat) by oars

ROWABLE ▸ row

ROWAN, -S n tree producing bright red berries; mountain ash

ROWBOAT, -S n small boat propelled by one or more pairs of oars

ROWDEDOW same as ▸ rowdydow

ROWDIER ▸ rowdy

ROWDIES ▸ rowdy

ROWDIEST ▸ rowdy

ROWDILY ▸ rowdy

ROWDY, ROWDIER, ROWDIES, ROWDIEST adj disorderly, noisy, and rough ▷ n person like this

ROWDYDOW n hullabaloo ▷ vb make noise

ROWDYISH ▸ rowdy

ROWDYISM n rowdy behaviour or tendencies or a habitual pattern of rowdy behaviour

ROWED ▸ row

ROWEL, -ED, -ING, -LED, -S n small spiked wheel on a spur ▷ vb goad (a horse) using a rowel

ROWEN, -S another word for > aftermath

ROWER, -S ▸ row

ROWIE, -S n Scottish bread roll made with butter and fat

ROWING, -S ▸ row

ROWLOCK, -S n device on a boat that holds an oar in place

ROWME, -S archaic variant of ▸ room

ROWND, -ED, -ING, -S archaic variant of ▸ round

ROWNDELL archaic variant of ▸ roundel

ROWNDING ▸ rownd

ROWNDS ▸ rownd

ROWOVER, -S n act of winning a rowing race unopposed

ROWS ▸ row

ROWT, -ED, -ING, -S archaic variant of ▸ rout

ROWTH, -S same as ▸ routh

ROWTING ▸ rowt

ROWTS ▸ rowt

ROYAL, -LER, -S adj of, befitting, or supported by a king or queen ▷ n member of a royal family

ROYALET, -S n minor king

ROYALISE same as ▸ royalize

ROYALISM n royalist

ROYALIST n supporter of monarchy ▷ adj of or relating to royalists

ROYALIZE vb make royal

ROYALLER ▸ royal

ROYALLY ▸ royal

ROYALS ▸ royal

ROYALTY n royal people

ROYNE, -D, -S, ROYNING archaic word for ▸ gnaw

ROYNISH archaic word for ▸ mangy

ROYST, -ED, -ING, -S same as ▸ roist

ROYSTER, -S same as ▸ roister

ROYSTING ▸ royst

ROYSTS ▸ royst

ROZELLE same as ▸ roselle

ROZET, -ED, -ING, -S same as ▸ roset

ROZIT, -ED, -ING, -S same as ▶ roset

ROZZER, -S n slang word for a police officer

RUANA, -S n woollen wrap resembling a poncho

RUB, -BED, -S vb apply pressure with a circular or backwards-and-forwards movement ▷ n act of rubbing

RUBABOO, -S n soup or stew made by boiling pemmican

RUBACE, -S same as ▶ rubasse

RUBAI, -S n verse form of Persian consisting of four-line stanzas

RUBAIYAT n (in Persian poetry) a verse form consisting of four-line stanzas

RUBASSE, -S n type of quartz containing red haematite

RUBATO, RUBATI, -S n expressive flexibility of tempo ▷ adv with a flexible tempo

RUBBABOO same as ▶ rubaboo

RUBBED ▶ rub

RUBBER, -ED, -S n strong waterproof elastic material ▷ adj made of or producing rubber ▷ vb provide with rubber coating

RUBBERY adj having the texture of or resembling rubber, esp in flexibility or toughness

RUBBET old Scots past form of ▶ rob

RUBBIDY same as ▶ rubbity

RUBBIES ▶ rubby

RUBBING, -S ▶ rub

RUBBISH n waste matter ▷ vb criticize

RUBBISHY adj worthless, of poor quality, or useless

RUBBIT old Scots past form of ▶ rob

RUBBITY n pub

RUBBLE, -D, -S, RUBBLING n fragments of broken stone, brick, etc ▷ vb turn into rubble

RUBBLIER ▶ rubbly

RUBBLING ▶ rubble

RUBBLY, RUBBLIER ▶ rubble

RUBBOARD n board for scrubbing clothes on

RUBBY, RUBBIES n slang word for rubbing alcohol

RUBBYDUB n person who drinks cheap alcohol mixtures

RUBDOWN, -S n act of drying or cleaning vigorously

RUBE, -S n unsophisticated countryman

RUBEFY, RUBEFIED, RUBEFIES vb make red

RUBEL, -S n currency unit of Belarus

RUBELLA, -S n mild contagious viral disease

RUBELLAN n red-coloured mineral

RUBELLAS ▶ rubella

RUBELS ▶ rubel

RUBEOLA, -S technical name for ▶ measles

RUBEOLAR ▶ rubeola

RUBEOLAS ▶ rubeola

RUBES ▶ rube

RUBICON, -S n point of no return ▷ vb (in bezique) to beat before the loser has managed to gain as many as 1000 points

RUBICUND adj ruddy

RUBIDIC ▶ rubidium

RUBIDIUM n soft highly reactive radioactive element

RUBIED ▶ ruby

RUBIER ▶ ruby

RUBIES ▶ ruby

RUBIEST ▶ ruby

RUBIFY, RUBIFIED, RUBIFIES same as ▶ rubefy

RUBIN, -S archaic word for ▶ ruby

RUBINE, -S archaic word for ▶ ruby

RUBINS ▶ rubin

RUBIOUS adj of the colour ruby

RUBLE, -S, RUBLI same as ▶ rouble

RUBOFF, -S n resulting effect on something else; consequences

RUBRIC, -S n set of rules for behaviour ▷ adj written, printed, or marked in red

RUBRICAL ▶ rubric

RUBRICS ▶ rubric

RUBS ▶ rub

RUBSTONE n stone used for sharpening or smoothing, esp a whetstone

RUBUS, -ES n fruit-bearing genus of shrubs

RUBY, RUBIED, RUBIER, RUBIES, RUBIEST, -ING n red precious gemstone ▷ adj deep red ▷ vb redden

RUBYLIKE ▶ ruby

RUC, -S same as ▶ roc

RUCHE, -D, -S n pleat or frill of lace etc as a decoration ▷ vb put a ruche on

RUCHING, -S n material used for a ruche

RUCK, -ED, -ING, -S n rough crowd of common people ▷ vb wrinkle or crease

RUCKLE, -D, -S, RUCKLING another word for ▶ ruck

RUCKMAN, RUCKMEN n person who plays in a ruck

RUCKS ▶ ruck

RUCKSACK n large pack carried on the back

RUCKSEAT n seat fixed to or forming part of a rucksack

RUCKUS, -ES n uproar

RUCOLA, -S n another name for the salad plant rocket

RUCS ▶ ruc

RUCTION, -S n uproar

RUCTIOUS adj tending or likely to cause ructions

RUD, -DED, -DING, -S n red or redness ▷ vb redden

RUDAS, -ES n Scots word for a coarse, rude old woman

RUDD, -S n European freshwater fish

RUDDED ▶ rud

RUDDER, -S n device for steering a boat or aircraft

RUDDIED ▶ ruddy

RUDDIER ▶ ruddy

RUDDIES ▶ ruddy

RUDDIEST ▶ ruddy

RUDDILY ▶ ruddy

RUDDING ▶ rud

RUDDLE, -D, -S, RUDDLING n red ochre, used esp to mark sheep ▷ vb mark (sheep) with ruddle

RUDDOCK, -S dialect name for the ▶ robin

RUDDS ▶ rudd

RUDDY, RUDDIED, RUDDIER, RUDDIES, RUDDIEST, -ING adj of a fresh healthy red colour ▷ adv bloody ▷ vb redden

RUDE, -R, -S, -ST adj insulting or impolite ▷ n archaic spelling of rood (crucifix)

RUDELY ▶ rude

RUDENESS ▶ rude

RUDER ▶ rude

RUDERAL, -S n plant that grows on waste ground ▷ adj growing in waste places

RUDERY, RUDERIES ▶ rude

RUDES ▶ rude

RUDESBY n archaic word for rude person

RUDEST ▶ rude

RUDI, -S same as ▸ **rudie**

RUDIE, -S n member of a youth movement originating in the 1960s

RUDIMENT n first principle or elementary stage of a subject

RUDIS ▸ **rudi**

RUDISH adj somewhat rude

RUDIST, -S n cone-shaped extinct mollusc

RUDISTID same as ▸ **rudist**

RUDISTS ▸ **rudist**

RUDS ▸ **rud**

RUDY same as ▸ **rudie**

RUE, -D, -S vb feel regret for ▸ n plant with evergreen bitter leaves

RUEDA, -S n type of Cuban round dance

RUEFUL adj regretful or sorry

RUEFULLY ▸ **rueful**

RUEING, -S ▸ **rue**

RUELLE, -S n area between bed and wall

RUELLIA, -S n genus of plants

RUER, -S ▸ **rue**

RUES ▸ **rue**

RUFF, -ED, -ING, -S n circular pleated, gathered, or fluted collar ▸ vb trump

RUFFE, -S n European freshwater fish

RUFFED ▸ **ruff**

RUFFES ▸ **ruffe**

RUFFIAN, -S n violent lawless person ▸ vb act like a ruffian

RUFFIN, -S archaic name for ▸ **ruffe**

RUFFING ▸ **ruff**

RUFFINS ▸ **ruffin**

RUFFLE, -D, -S, RUFFLING vb disturb the calm of ▸ n frill or pleat

RUFFLER, -S n person or thing that ruffles

RUFFLES ▸ **ruffle**

RUFFLIER ▸ **ruffly**

RUFFLIKE ▸ **ruff**

RUFFLING ▸ **ruffle**

RUFFLY, RUFFLIER adj ruffled

RUFFS ▸ **ruff**

RUFIYAA, -S n standard monetary unit of the Maldives

RUFOUS, -ES n reddish-brown colour

RUG, -S n small carpet ▸ vb (in dialect) tug

RUGA, -E n fold, wrinkle, or crease

RUGAL adj (in anatomy) with ridges or folds

RUGALACH same as ▸ **rugelach**

RUGATE same as ▸ **rugose**

RUGBY, RUGBIES n form of football played with an oval ball which may be handled by the players

RUGELACH n fruit and nut pastry shaped like a croissant

RUGGED, -ER adj rocky or steep

RUGGEDLY ▸ **rugged**

RUGGER, -S same as ▸ **rugby**

RUGGIER ▸ **ruggy**

RUGGIEST ▸ **ruggy**

RUGGING, -S ▸ **rug**

RUGGY, RUGGIER, RUGGIEST adj (in dialect) rough or rugged

RUGLIKE ▸ **rug**

RUGOLA, -S n another name for the salad plant rocket

RUGOSA, -S n any of various shrubs descended from a particular type of wild rose

RUGOSE adj wrinkled

RUGOSELY ▸ **rugose**

RUGOSITY ▸ **rugose**

RUGOUS same as ▸ **rugose**

RUGRAT, -S n informal word for a young child

RUGS ▸ **rug**

RUGULOSE adj with little wrinkles

RUIN, -ED, -S vb destroy or spoil completely ▸ n destruction or decay

RUINABLE ▸ **ruin**

RUINATE, -D, -S vb archaic word for bring or come to ruin

RUINED ▸ **ruin**

RUINER, -S ▸ **ruin**

RUING, -S ▸ **rue**

RUINING, -S ▸ **ruin**

RUINOUS adj causing ruin

RUINS ▸ **ruin**

RUKH, -S same as ▸ **roc**

RULABLE ▸ **rule**

RULE, -D, -S n statement of what is allowed, for example in a game or procedure ▸ vb govern

RULELESS ▸ **rule**

RULER, -ED, -ING, -S n person who governs ▸ vb punish by hitting with a ruler

RULES ▸ **rule**

RULESSE adj archaic word meaning ruleless or without rules

RULIER ▸ **ruly**

RULIEST ▸ **ruly**

RULING, -S n formal decision ▸ adj controlling or exercising authority

RULLION, -S n Scots word for rawhide shoe

RULLOCK, -S same as ▸ **rowlock**

RULY, RULIER, RULIEST adj orderly

RUM, -MEST, -S n alcoholic drink distilled from sugar cane ▸ adj odd, strange

RUMAKI, -S n savoury of chicken liver and sliced water chestnut wrapped in bacon

RUMAL, -S n handkerchief or type of cloth

RUMBA, -ED, -ING, -S n lively ballroom dance of Cuban origin ▸ vb dance the rumba

RUMBELOW n nonsense word used in the refrain of certain sea shanties

RUMBLE, -D, -S vb make a low continuous noise ▸ n deep resonant sound

RUMBLER, -S ▸ **rumble**

RUMBLES ▸ **rumble**

RUMBLIER ▸ **rumbly**

RUMBLING ▸ **rumble**

RUMBLY, RUMBLIER adj rumbling or liable to rumble

RUMBO, -S n rum-based cocktail

RUMDUM, -S n alcoholic

RUME, -S archaic form of ▸ **rheum**

RUMEN, -S, RUMINA n first compartment of the stomach of ruminants

RUMES ▸ **rume**

RUMINA ▸ **rumen**

RUMINAL ▸ **rumen**

RUMINANT n cud-chewing (animal, such as a cow, sheep, or deer) ▸ adj of ruminants

RUMINATE vb chew the cud

RUMKIN, -S n archaic term for a drinking vessel

RUMLY ▸ **rum**

RUMMAGE, -D, -S vb search untidily at length ▸ n untidy search through a collection of things

RUMMAGER ▸ **rummage**

RUMMAGES ▸ **rummage**

RUMMER, -S n drinking glass

RUMMEST ▸ **rum**

RUMMIER ▸ **rummy**

RUMMIES ▸ **rummy**

RUMMIEST ▸ **rummy**

RUMMILY ▸ **rummy**

RUMMISH adj rather strange, peculiar, or odd ▸ vb roar or protest

RUMMY, RUMMIER, RUMMIES, RUMMIEST *n* card game in which players try to collect sets or sequences ▷ *adj* of or like rum in taste or smell

RUMNESS ▸ rum

RUMOR, -ED, -ING, -S same as ▸ rumour

RUMORER, -S *n* person given to spreading rumours

RUMORING ▸ rumor

RUMOROUS *adj* involving or containing rumours

RUMORS ▸ rumor

RUMOUR, -ED, -S *n* unproved statement ▷ *vb* pass around or circulate in the form of a rumour

RUMOURER *n* someone given to spreading rumours

RUMOURS ▸ rumour

RUMP, -ED, -ING, -S *n* buttocks ▷ *vb* turn back on

RUMPIER ▸ rumpy

RUMPIES ▸ rumpy

RUMPIEST ▸ rumpy

RUMPING ▸ rump

RUMPLE, -D, -S, RUMPLING *vb* make untidy, crumpled, or dishevelled ▷ *n* wrinkle, fold, or crease

RUMPLESS ▸ rump

RUMPLIER ▸ rumply

RUMPLING ▸ rumple

RUMPLY, RUMPLIER ▸ rumple

RUMPOT, -S *n* alcoholic

RUMPS ▸ rump

RUMPUS, -ES *n* noisy commotion

RUMPY, RUMPIER, RUMPIES, RUMPIEST *n* tailless Manx cat ▷ *adj* with a large or noticeable rump

RUMS ▸ rum

RUN, RAN, -S *vb* move with a more rapid gait than walking ▷ *n* act or spell of running

RUNABOUT *n* small car used for short journeys ▷ *vb* move busily from place to place

RUNAGATE *n* vagabond, fugitive, or renegade

RUNANGA, -S *n* Māori assembly or council

RUNAWAY, -S *n* person or animal that runs away

RUNBACK, -S *n* (in tennis) the areas behind the baselines of the court

RUNCH, -ES *n* another name for white charlock

RUNCIBLE *adj* as in runcible spoon forklike utensil with two prongs and one sharp curved prong

RUND, -S same as ▸ roon

RUNDALE, -S *n* system of land tenure in Ireland

RUNDLE, -S *n* rung of a ladder

RUNDLED *adj* rounded

RUNDLES ▸ rundle

RUNDLET, -S *n* liquid measure, generally about 15 gallons

RUNDOWN, -S *adj* tired; exhausted ▷ *n* brief review, résumé, or summary

RUNDS ▸ rund

RUNE, -S *n* any character of the earliest Germanic alphabet

RUNED *adj* with runes on

RUNELIKE *adj* resembling a rune or runes

RUNES ▸ rune

RUNFLAT, -S *adj* having a safety feature that prevents tyres becoming dangerous when flat

RUNG, -S *n* crosspiece on ladder

RUNGED *adj* having rungs

RUNGLESS ▸ rung

RUNGS ▸ rung

RUNIC ▸ rune

RUNKLE, -D, -S, RUNKLING *vb* (in dialect) crease or wrinkle

RUNLESS ▸ run

RUNLET, -S *n* cask for wine, beer, etc

RUNNABLE ▸ run

RUNNEL, -S *n* small brook

RUNNER, -S *n* competitor in a race

RUNNET, -S *dialect word for* ▸ rennet

RUNNIER ▸ runny

RUNNIEST ▸ runny

RUNNING, -S ▸ run

RUNNY, RUNNIER, RUNNIEST *adj* tending to flow

RUNOFF, -S *n* extra race to decide the winner after a tie

RUNOUT, -S *n* dismissal of a batsman by running them out

RUNOVER, -S *n* incident in which someone is run over by a vehicle

RUNPROOF *adj* (of stockings or tights) designed to be especially resistant to being ripped

RUNRIG, -S same as ▸ rundale

RUNROUND same as ▸ runaround

RUNS ▸ run

RUNT, -S *n* smallest animal in a litter

RUNTED *adj* stunted

RUNTIER ▸ runty

RUNTIEST ▸ runty

RUNTISH ▸ runt

RUNTS ▸ runt

RUNTY, RUNTIER, RUNTIEST ▸ runt

RUNWAY, -S *n* hard level roadway where aircraft take off and land

RUPEE, -S *n* monetary unit of India and Pakistan

RUPIA, -S *n* type of skin eruption

RUPIAH, -S *n* standard monetary unit of Indonesia

RUPIAS ▸ rupia

RUPTURE, -D, -S *n* breaking, breach ▷ *vb* break, burst, or sever

RURAL, -S *adj* in or of the countryside ▷ *n* country dweller

RURALISE same as ▸ ruralize

RURALISM ▸ rural

RURALIST ▸ rural

RURALITE ▸ rural

RURALITY ▸ rural

RURALIZE *vb* make rural in character, appearance, etc

RURALLY ▸ rural

RURALS ▸ rural

RURBAN *adj* part country, part urban

RURP, -S *n* very small piton

RURU, -S another name for ▸ mopoke

RUSA, -S *n* type of deer with a mane

RUSALKA, -S *n* water nymph or spirit

RUSAS ▸ rusa

RUSCUS, -ES *n* type of shrub

RUSE, -S *n* stratagem or trick

RUSH, -ED *vb* move or do very quickly ▷ *n* sudden quick or violent movement ▷ *adj* done with speed, hasty

RUSHEE, -S *n* someone interested in gaining fraternity or sorority membership

RUSHEN *adj* made of rushes

RUSHER, -S ▸ rush

RUSHES *pl n* (in film-making) the initial prints of a scene or scenes before editing

RUSHIER ▸ rushy

RUSHIEST ▸ rushy

R

RUSHING, -S ▶ **rush**
RUSHLIKE ▶ **rush**
**RUSHY, RUSHIER,
RUSHIEST** adj full of rushes
RUSINE adj of or relating to
rusa deer
RUSK, -S n hard brown crisp
biscuit, used esp for feeding
babies
RUSMA, -S n Turkish
depilatory
RUSSE adj as in **charlotte
russe** cold dessert made
from cream, etc, surrounded
by sponge fingers
RUSSEL, -S n type of woollen
fabric
RUSSET, -ED, -S adj
reddish-brown ▷ n apple
with rough reddish-brown
skin ▷ vb become
russet-coloured
RUSSETY adj of a russet
colour
RUSSIA, -S n Russia leather
RUSSIFY vb cause to
become Russian in character
RUSSULA, -E, -S n type of
fungus, typically of
toadstool shape
RUST, -ED, -S n reddish-
brown coating formed on
iron etc that has been
exposed to moisture ▷ adj
reddish-brown ▷ vb become
coated with rust
RUSTABLE adj liable to rust
RUSTED ▶ **rust**
RUSTIC, -S adj of or
resembling country people
▷ n person from the country
RUSTICAL n rustic
RUSTICLY ▶ **rustic**
RUSTICS ▶ **rustic**
RUSTIER ▶ **rusty**
RUSTIEST ▶ **rusty**
RUSTILY ▶ **rusty**
RUSTING, -S ▶ **rust**

RUSTLE, -D, -S n low
whispering sound ▷ vb steal
(cattle)
RUSTLER, -S n cattle thief
RUSTLES ▶ **rustle**
RUSTLESS ▶ **rust**
RUSTLING ▶ **rustle**
RUSTRE, -S n (in heraldry)
lozenge with a round hole in
the middle showing the
background colour
RUSTRED ▶ **rustre**
RUSTRES ▶ **rustre**
RUSTS ▶ **rust**
**RUSTY, RUSTIER,
RUSTIEST** adj coated with
rust
RUT, -S, -TED n furrow
made by wheels ▷ vb make
ruts in
RUTABAGA n plant with a
bulbous edible root
RUTH, -S n pity
RUTHENIC adj of or
containing ruthenium, esp
in a high valency state
RUTHER adv rather
RUTHFUL adj full of or
causing sorrow or pity
RUTHLESS adj pitiless,
merciless
RUTHS ▶ **ruth**
RUTILANT adj of a reddish
colour or glow
RUTILE, -S n black,
yellowish, or reddish-brown
mineral
RUTIN, -S n bioflavonoid
found in various plants
including rue
RUTS ▶ **rut**
RUTTED ▶ **rut**
RUTTER, -S n (in history)
type of cavalry soldier
RUTTIER ▶ **rutty**
RUTTIEST ▶ **rutty**
RUTTILY ▶ **rutty**
RUTTING, -S ▶ **rut**

RUTTISH adj (of an animal)
in a condition of rut
**RUTTY, RUTTIER,
RUTTIEST** adj full of ruts or
holes
RYA, -S n type of rug
originating in Scandinavia
RYAL, -S n one of several old
coins
RYAS ▶ **rya**
RYBAT, -S n polished stone
piece forming the side of a
window or door
RYE, -S n kind of grain used
for fodder and bread
RYEBREAD n bread made
from rye flour
RYEFLOUR n flour made
from rye
RYEGRASS n type of grass,
widely cultivated as a forage
crop
RYEPECK, -S n punt-
mooring pole
RYES ▶ **rye**
RYFE archaic variant of ▶ **rife**
RYKE, -D, -S, RYKING Scots
variant of ▶ **reach**
RYMME, -D, -S, RYMMING
same as ▶ **rim**
RYND, -S n (in milling)
crossbar piece forming part
of the support structure of
the upper millstone
RYOKAN, -S n traditional
Japanese inn
RYOT, -S n (in India) a
peasant or tenant farmer
RYOTWARI n (in India)
system of land tenure in
which land taxes are paid to
the state
RYPE, -R n ptarmigan
RYPECK, -S same as
▶ **ryepeck**
RYPER ▶ **rype**
RYU, -S n school of Japanese
martial arts

R

Ss

S begins only four two-letter words, **sh** (5 points), **si**, **so** and **st** (2 each). These are easy to remember, and it's worth noting that two of them, **sh** and **st**, don't use any vowels. Interestingly, there are quite a few three-letter words beginning with **S** that don't contain vowels, some of which give good scores. These are **shh** (9), **shy** (9), **sky** (10), **sly** (6), **sny** (6), **spy** (8), **sty** (6), **swy** (9) and **syn** (6). **S** also forms a number of three-letter words with **X**. These are easy to remember as they use every vowel except **U**: **sax**, **sex**, **six** and **sox** (10 each). When it comes to **Z**, you will find **saz**, **sez** and **soz** (12 each) very useful, and the same applies to **suq** (12 points).

SAAG, -S n (in Indian cookery) spinach

SAB, -BED, -BING, -S n person engaged in direct action to prevent a targeted activity taking place ▷ vb take part in such action

SABAL, -S n variety of palm tree

SABATON, -S n foot covering in suit of armour

SABAYON, -S n dessert or sweet sauce made with egg yolks, sugar, and wine

SABBAT, -S n midnight meeting of witches

SABBATH, -S n period of rest

SABBATIC n period of leave granted to university staff

SABBATS ▸ sabbat

SABBED ▸ sab

SABBING, -S ▸ sab

SABE, -D, -ING, -S n very informal word meaning sense or savvy ▷ vb very informal word meaning know or savvy

SABELLA, -S n marine worm

SABER, -ED, -ING, -S same as ▸ sabre

SABES ▸ sabe

SABHA, -S n set of Muslim prayer beads

SABICU, -S n type of Caribbean tree

SABIN, -S n unit of acoustic absorption

SABINE, -S variant of ▸ savin

SABINS ▸ sabin

SABIR, -S n member of ancient Turkic people

SABKHA, -S n flat coastal plain with a salt crust, common in Arabia

SABKHAH, -S n sabkha

SABKHAS ▸ sabkha

SABKHAT, -S n sabkha

SABLE, -D, -R, -S, -ST, SABLING n dark fur from a small weasel-like Arctic animal ▷ adj black

SABOT, -S n wooden shoe traditionally worn by peasants in France

SABOTAGE n intentional damage done to machinery, systems, etc ▷ vb damage intentionally

SABOTED adj wearing sabots

SABOTEUR n person who commits sabotage

SABOTIER n wearer of wooden clogs

SABOTS ▸ sabot

SABRA, -S n native-born Israeli Jew

SABRE, -D, -S, SABRING n curved cavalry sword ▷ vb injure or kill with a sabre

SABREUR, -S n person wielding sabre

SABRING ▸ sabre

SABS ▸ sab

SABULINE same as ▸ sabulous

SABULOSE same as ▸ sabulous

SABULOUS adj like sand in texture

SABURRA, -S n granular deposit

SABURRAL ▸ saburra

SABURRAS ▸ saburra

SAC, -S n pouchlike structure in an animal or plant

SACATON, -S n coarse grass of the southwestern US and Mexico

SACBUT, -S n medieval trombone

SACCADE, -S n movement of the eye when it makes a sudden change of fixation, as in reading

SACCADIC ▸ saccade

SACCATE adj in the form of a sac

SACCOS, SACCOI, -ES n bishop's garment in the Orthodox Church

SACCULAR adj of or resembling a sac

SACCULE, -S n small sac

SACCULUS, SACCULI same as ▸ saccule

SACELLUM, SACELLA n tomb within a church

SACHEM, -S same as ▸ sagamore

SACHEMIC ▸ sachem

SACHEMS ▸ sachem

SACHET, -S n small envelope or bag containing a single portion

SACHETED adj contained in a sachet

SACHETS ▸ sachet

SACK, -ED, -S n large bag made of coarse material ▷ vb dismiss

SACKABLE adj of an offence that is sufficiently serious to warrant dismissal from a job

S

SACKAGE, -D, -S n act of sacking a place ▷ vb sack or plunder

SACKBUT, -S n medieval form of trombone

SACKED ▶ sack

SACKER, -S ▶ sack

SACKFUL, -S, SACKSFUL ▶ sack

SACKING, -S n rough woven material used for sacks

SACKLESS adj old word meaning innocent

SACKLIKE ▶ sack

SACKLOAD n amount of something that a sack contains

SACKS ▶ sack

SACKSFUL ▶ sackful

SACLESS adj old word meaning unchallengeable

SACLIKE ▶ sac

SACQUE, -S same as ▶ sack

SACRA ▶ sacrum

SACRAL, -S adj of or associated with sacred rites ▷ n sacral vertebra

SACRARIA ▶ sacrarium

SACRED, -ER adj holy

SACREDLY ▶ sacred

SACRIFY vb old form of sacrifice

SACRING, -S n act or ritual of consecration

SACRIST, -S same as > sacristan

SACRISTY n room in a church where sacred objects are kept

SACRUM, SACRA, -S n wedge-shaped bone at the base of the spine

SACS ▶ sac

SAD, -DED, -DER, -DEST, -DING, -S adj sorrowful, unhappy ▷ vb New Zealand word meaning express sadness or displeasure strongly

SADDEN, -ED, -S vb make (someone) sad

SADDER ▶ sad

SADDEST ▶ sad

SADDHU, -S same as ▶ sadhu

SADDIE, -S same as ▶ saddo

SADDING ▶ sad

SADDISH ▶ sad

SADDLE, -D, -S, SADDLING n rider's seat on a horse or bicycle ▷ vb put a saddle on (a horse)

SADDLER, -S n maker or seller of saddles

SADDLERY n saddles and harness for horses collectively

SADDLES ▶ saddle

SADDLING ▶ saddle

SADDO, -ES, -S vb make sad ▷ n socially inadequate or pathetic person

SADE, -S same as ▶ sadhe

SADHANA, -S n one of a number of spiritual practices which lead to perfection

SADHE, -S n 18th letter in the Hebrew alphabet

SADHU, -S n Hindu wandering holy man

SADI, -S variant of ▶ sadhe

SADIRON, -S n heavy iron pointed at both ends, for pressing clothes

SADIS ▶ sadi

SADISM, -S n gaining of pleasure from inflicting suffering

SADIST, -S ▶ sadism

SADISTIC ▶ sadism

SADISTS ▶ sadist

SADLY ▶ sad

SADNESS ▶ sad

SADO, -S variant of ▶ chado

SADS ▶ sad

SADZA, -S n southern African porridge

SAE Scot word for ▶ so

SAECULUM, SAECULA n age in astronomy

SAETER, -S n upland pasture in Norway

SAFARI, -ED, -S n expedition to hunt or observe wild animals, esp in Africa ▷ vb go on safari

SAFARIST n person on safari

SAFE, -D, -R, -S, -ST, SAFING adj secure, protected ▷ n strong lockable container ▷ vb make safe

SAFELY ▶ safe

SAFENESS ▶ safe

SAFER ▶ safe

SAFES ▶ safe

SAFEST ▶ safe

SAFETY, SAFETIED, SAFETIES n state of being safe ▷ vb make safe

SAFFIAN, -S n leather tanned with sumach and usually dyed a bright colour

SAFFRON, -S n orange-coloured flavouring obtained from a crocus ▷ adj orange

SAFFRONY adj like saffron

SAFING ▶ safe

SAFRANIN same as > safranine

SAFROL, -S n oily liquid obtained from sassafras

SAFROLE, -S n colourless or yellowish oily water-insoluble liquid

SAFROLS ▶ safrol

SAFRONAL n oily liquid derived from saffron

SAFT, -ER, -EST Scot word for ▶ soft

SAG, -GED, -S vb sink in the middle ▷ n droop

SAGA, -S n legend of Norse heroes

SAGACITY n foresight, discernment, or keen perception

SAGAMAN, SAGAMEN n person reciting Norse sagas

SAGAMORE n (among some Native Americans) a chief or eminent man

SAGANASH n Algonquian term for an Englishman

SAGAS ▶ saga

SAGATHY n type of light fabric

SAGBUT, -S n medieval trombone

SAGE, -R, -S, -ST n very wise person ▷ adj wise

SAGEHOOD n state of being wise

SAGELY ▶ sage

SAGENE, -S n fishing net

SAGENESS ▶ sage

SAGENITE n mineral found in crystal form

SAGER ▶ sage

SAGES ▶ sage

SAGEST ▶ sage

SAGGAR, -ED, -S n box in which fragile ceramic wares are placed for protection ▷ vb put in a saggar

SAGGARD, -S n saggar

SAGGARED ▶ saggar

SAGGARS ▶ saggar

SAGGED ▶ sag

SAGGER, -ED, -S same as ▶ saggar

SAGGIER ▶ saggy

SAGGIEST ▶ saggy

SAGGING, -S ▶ sag

SAGGY, SAGGIER, SAGGIEST adj tending to sag

SAGIER ▶ sagy

SAGIEST ▶ sagy

SAGINATE vb fatten livestock

SAGITTA, -S n sine of an arc

SAGITTAL adj resembling an arrow

SAGITTAS ▶ sagitta

SAGO, -S n starchy cereal from the powdered pith of the sago palm tree

SAGOIN, -S n South American monkey

SAGOS ▶ sago

SAGOUIN, -S n South American monkey

SAGRADA adj as in **cascara sagrada** dried bark of the cascara buckthorn

SAGS ▶ sag

SAGUARO, -S n giant cactus of desert regions

SAGUIN, -S n South American monkey

SAGUM n Roman soldier's cloak

SAGY, SAGIER, SAGIEST adj like or containing sage

SAHEB, -S same as ▶ **sahib**

SAHIB, -S n Indian term of address placed after a man's name as a mark of respect

SAHIBA, -S n respectful Indian term of address for woman

SAHIBAH, -S n sahiba

SAHIBAS ▶ sahiba

SAHIBS ▶ sahib

SAHIWAL, -S n breed of cattle in India

SAHUARO, -S same as ▶ **saguaro**

SAI, -S n South American monkey

SAIBLING n freshwater fish

SAIC, -S n boat of eastern Mediterranean

SAICE, -S same as ▶ **syce**

SAICK, -S n boat of eastern Mediterranean

SAICS ▶ saic

SAID, -S same as ▶ **sayyid**

SAIDEST ▶ say

SAIDS ▶ said

SAIDST ▶ say

SAIGA, -S n either of two antelopes of the plains of central Asia

SAIKEI, -S n Japanese ornamental miniature landscape

SAIKLESS old Scots word for ▶ **innocent**

SAIL, -ED, -S n sheet of fabric stretched to catch the wind for propelling a sailing boat ▷ vb travel by water

SAILABLE ▶ sail

SAILBOAT n boat propelled chiefly by sail

SAILED ▶ sail

SAILER, -S n vessel, esp one equipped with sails, with specified sailing characteristics

SAILFISH n large tropical game fish, with a long sail-like fin on its back

SAILING, -S n practice, art, or technique of sailing a vessel

SAILLESS ▶ sail

SAILOR, -S n member of a ship's crew

SAILORLY adj like a sailor

SAILORS ▶ sailor

SAILPAST n sailing of ships past a particular place

SAILROOM n space on ship for storing sails

SAILS ▶ sail

SAIM, -S Scots word for ▶ **lard**

SAIMIN, -S n Hawaiian dish of noodles

SAIMIRI, -S n South American monkey

SAIMS ▶ saim

SAIN, -ED, -ING, -S vb make the sign of the cross over so as to bless or protect from evil or sin

SAINE vb old form of say

SAINED ▶ sain

SAINFOIN n Eurasian plant with pink flowers, widely grown as feed for grazing farm animals

SAINING ▶ sain

SAINS ▶ sain

SAINT, -ING, -S n person venerated after death as specially holy ▷ vb canonize

SAINTDOM ▶ saint

SAINTED adj formally recognized by a Christian Church as a saint

SAINTESS n female saint

SAINTING ▶ saint

SAINTISH ▶ saint

SAINTISM n quality of being saint

SAINTLY adj behaving in a very good, patient, or holy way

SAINTS ▶ saint

SAIQUE, -S n boat in eastern Mediterranean

SAIR, -ED, -ER, -EST, -ING, -S Scot word for ▶ **sore**

SAIS ▶ sai

SAIST ▶ say

SAITH, -S form of the present tense (indicative mood) of ▶ **say**

SAITHE, -S n dark-coloured food fish found in northern seas

SAITHS ▶ saith

SAIYID, -S n Muslim descended from Muhammad's grandson

SAJOU, -S n South American monkey

SAKE, -S n benefit

SAKER, -S n large falcon of E Europe and central Asia

SAKERET, -S n male saker

SAKERS ▶ saker

SAKES ▶ sake

SAKI, -S n small arboreal monkey

SAKIA, -S n water wheel in Middle East

SAKIEH, -S same as ▶ **sakia**

SAKIS ▶ saki

SAKIYEH, -S same as ▶ **sakia**

SAKKOS, SAKKOI, -ES n bishop's garment in Orthodox Church

SAKSAUL, -S n Asian tree

SAKTI, -S n wife of a Hindu god

SAL, -S pharmacological term for ▶ **salt**

SALAAM, -ED, -S n low bow of greeting among Muslims ▷ vb make a salaam

SALABLE same as ▶ **saleable**

SALABLY ▶ saleably

SALAD, -S n dish of raw vegetables, eaten as a meal or part of a meal

SALADANG n variety of ox

SALADE, -S same as ▶ **sallet**

SALADING n ingredients for salad

SALADS ▶ salad

SALAL, -S n North American shrub

SALAMI, -S n highly spiced sausage

SALAMON, -S n word used in old oaths

SALARIAT n salary-earning class

SALARIED adj earning or providing a salary

SALARY, SALARIES n fixed regular payment, usu monthly, to an employee ▷ vb pay a salary to

SALAT, -S n obligatory series of Islamic prayers facing towards Mecca

SALBAND, -S n coating of mineral

SALCHOW, -S n type of figure-skating jump

SALE, -S n exchange of goods for money

SALEABLE adj fit or likely to be sold

SALEABLY ▶ saleable

SALEP, -S n dried ground starchy tubers of various orchids

SALERING n enclosed area for livestock at market

SALEROOM n place where goods are sold by auction

SALES ▸ sale

SALESMAN, SALESMEN n man who sells goods

SALET, -S same as ▸ sallet

SALEWD ▸ salue

SALEYARD n area with pens for holding animals before auction

SALFERN, -S n plant of borage family

SALIC adj (of rocks and minerals) having a high content of silica and alumina

SALICES ▸ salix

SALICET, -S n soft-toned organ stop

SALICETA ▸ saliceta

SALICETS ▸ salicet

SALICIN, -S n colourless or white crystalline water-soluble glucoside

SALICINE same as ▸ salicin

SALICINS ▸ salicin

SALIENCE ▸ salient

SALIENCY n quality of being prominent

SALIENT, -S adj prominent, noticeable ▸ n projecting part of a front line

SALIFY, -IED, -IES, SALIFIES vb treat, mix with, or cause to combine with a salt

SALIGOT, -S n water chestnut

SALINA, -S n salt marsh, lake, or spring

SALINE, -S adj containing salt ▸ n solution of sodium chloride and water

SALINISE same as ▸ salinize

SALINITY ▸ saline

SALINIZE vb treat with salt

SALIVA, -S n liquid that forms in the mouth, spittle

SALIVAL ▸ saliva

SALIVARY ▸ saliva

SALIVAS ▸ saliva

SALIVATE vb produce saliva

SALIX, SALICES n plant or tree of willow family

SALL archaic form of ▸ shall

SALLAD, -S old spelling of ▸ salad

SALLAL, -S n North American shrub

SALLE, -S n hall

SALLEE, -S n SE Australian eucalyptus

SALLES ▸ salle

SALLET, -S n light round helmet

SALLIED ▸ sally

SALLIER, -S ▸ sally

SALLIES ▸ sally

SALLOW, -ED, -ER, -S adj of an unhealthy pale or yellowish colour ▸ vb make sallow ▸ n any of several small willow trees

SALLOWLY ▸ sallow

SALLOWS ▸ sallow

SALLOWY adj full of sallows

SALLY, SALLIED, SALLIES, -ING n violent excursion ▸ vb set or rush out

SALMI n ragout of game stewed in a rich brown sauce

SALMIS same as ▸ salmi

SALMON, -S n large fish with orange-pink flesh valued as food ▸ adj orange-pink

SALMONET n young salmon

SALMONID n type of soft-finned fish of the family which includes the salmon

SALMONS ▸ salmon

SALMONY adj of or like a salmon

SALOL, -S n white sparingly soluble crystalline compound

SALON, -S n commercial premises of a hairdresser, beautician, etc

SALOON, -S n closed car with four or more seats

SALOOP, -S n infusion of aromatic herbs or other plant parts formerly used as a tonic or cure

SALOP, -S variant of ▸ saloop

SALOPIAN ▸ saloop

SALOPS ▸ salop

SALP, -S n minute animal floating in sea

SALPA, -E, -S n any of various minute floating animals of warm oceans

SALPIAN, -S n minute animal floating in sea

SALPICON n mixture of chopped fish, meat, or vegetables in a sauce

SALPID, -S n minute animal floating in sea

SALPINX n Fallopian tube or Eustachian tube

SALPS ▸ salp

SALS ▸ sal

SALSA, -ED, -ING, -S n lively Puerto Rican dance ▸ vb dance the salsa

SALSE, -S n volcano expelling mud

SALSIFY n Mediterranean plant with a long white edible root

SALSILLA n tropical American vine

SALT, -EST, -S n white crystalline substance used to season food ▸ vb season or preserve with salt

SALTANDO n staccato piece of violin playing

SALTANT, -S adj (of an organism) differing from others of its species because of a saltation ▸ n saltant organism

SALTATE, -D, -S vb go through saltation

SALTATO, -S n staccato piece of violin playing

SALTBOX n box for salt with a sloping lid

SALTBUSH n shrub that grows in alkaline desert regions

SALTCAT, -S n salty medicine for pigeons

SALTED adj seasoned, preserved, or treated with salt

SALTER, -S n person who deals in or manufactures salt

SALTERN, -S n place where salt is obtained from pools of evaporated sea water

SALTERS ▸ salter

SALTERY n factory where fish is salted for storage

SALTEST ▸ salt

SALTFISH n salted cod

SALTIE, -S n saltwater crocodile

SALTIER, -S same as ▸ saltire

SALTIES ▸ saltie

SALTIEST ▸ salty

SALTILY ▸ salty

SALTINE, -S n salty biscuit

SALTING, -S n area of low ground regularly inundated with salt water

SALTIRE, -S n diagonal cross on a shield

SALTISH ▸ salt

SALTLESS ▸ salt

SALTLIKE ▸ salt

SALTLY ▸ salt

SALTNESS ▸ salt

SALTO, -ED, -ING, -S n daring jump ▸ vb perform a daring jump

SALTPAN, -S n shallow basin containing salt from an evaporated salt lake

SALTS ▸ salt

SALTUS, -ES n break in the continuity of a sequence

SALTWORK n place where salt is refined

SALTWORT n any of several chenopodiaceous plants

SALTY, SALTIEST adj of, tasting of, or containing salt

SALUE, SALEWD, -D, -S, SALUING vb old word meaning salute

SALUKI, -S n type of tall hound with a smooth coat

SALUT interj cheers!

SALUTARY adj producing a beneficial result

SALUTE, -D, -S, SALUTING n motion of the arm as a formal military sign of respect ▷ vb greet with a salute

SALUTER, -S ▶ salute

SALUTES ▶ salute

SALUTING ▶ salute

SALVABLE adj capable of or suitable for being saved or salvaged

SALVABLY ▶ salvable

SALVAGE, -D, -S n saving of a ship or other property from destruction ▷ vb save from destruction or waste

SALVAGEE n rope on sailing ship

SALVAGER ▶ salvage

SALVAGES ▶ salvage

SALVE, -D, -S n healing or soothing ointment ▷ vb soothe or appease

SALVER, -S same as ▶ salvor

SALVES ▶ salve

SALVETE, -S n Latin greeting

SALVIA, -S n plant with blue or red flowers

SALVIFIC adj acting to salve

SALVING, -S ▶ salve

SALVO, -ED, -ES, -ING, -S n simultaneous discharge of guns etc ▷ vb attack with a salvo

SALVOR, -S n person instrumental in salvaging a vessel or its cargo

SALVOS ▶ salvo

SALWAR, -S n pair of loose-fitting trousers narrowing around the ankles

SAM, -MED, -MING, -S vb collect

SAMA, -S n Japanese title of respect

SAMAAN, -S n South American tree

SAMADHI, -S n state of deep meditative contemplation

SAMAN, -S n South American tree

SAMARA, -S n dry indehiscent one-seeded fruit

SAMARIUM n silvery metallic element

SAMAS ▶ sama

SAMBA, -ED, -ING, -S n lively Brazilian dance ▷ vb perform such a dance

SAMBAL, -S n Malaysian dish

SAMBAR, -S n S Asian deer with three-tined antlers

SAMBAS ▶ samba

SAMBHAR, -S n Indian dish

SAMBHUR, -S n Asian deer

SAMBO, -ES, -S n type of wrestling based on judo

SAMBUCA, -S n Italian liqueur

SAMBUKE, -S n ancient Greek stringed instrument

SAMBUR, -S same as ▶ sambar

SAME, -S adj identical, not different, unchanged ▷ n something identical

SAMECH, -S n letter in Hebrew alphabet

SAMEK, -S variant of ▶ samekh

SAMEKH, -S n 15th letter in the Hebrew alphabet

SAMEKS ▶ samek

SAMEL adj of brick, not sufficiently fired

SAMELY adj the same

SAMEN old Scots form of ▶ same

SAMENESS n state or quality of being the same

SAMES ▶ same

SAMEY, SAMIER, SAMIEST adj monotonous

SAMFOO, -S n style of casual dress worn by Chinese women

SAMFU, -S same as ▶ samfoo

SAMIEL, -S same as ▶ simoom

SAMIER ▶ samey

SAMIEST ▶ samey

SAMISEN, -S n Japanese plucked stringed instrument with a long neck

SAMITE, -S n heavy fabric of silk used in the Middle Ages

SAMITHI, -S same as ▶ samiti

SAMITI, -S n (in India) an association, esp one formed to organize political activity

SAMIZDAT n system of secret printing and distribution of banned literature in the former USSR

SAMLET, -S n young salmon

SAMLOR, -S n motor vehicle in Thailand

SAMMED ▶ sam

SAMMIE n sandwich

SAMMIES ▶ sammy

SAMMING ▶ sam

SAMMY, SAMMIES n (in South Africa) an Indian fruit and vegetable vendor

SAMNITIS n poisonous plant mentioned by Spenser

SAMOSA, -S n (in Indian cookery) a small fried triangular spiced meat or vegetable pasty

SAMOVAR, -S n Russian tea urn

SAMOYED, -S n Siberian breed of dog with a tightly curled tail

SAMP, -S n crushed maize used for porridge

SAMPAN, -S n small boat with oars used in China

SAMPHIRE n plant found on rocks by the seashore

SAMPI, -S n old Greek number character

SAMPIRE, -S n samphire

SAMPIS ▶ sampi

SAMPLE, -D, -S n part taken as representative of a whole ▷ vb take and test a sample of

SAMPLER, -S n piece of embroidery showing the embroiderer's skill

SAMPLERY n making of samplers

SAMPLES ▶ sample

SAMPLING n process of selecting a random sample

SAMPS ▶ samp

SAMS ▶ sam

SAMSARA, -S n endless cycle of birth, death, and rebirth

SAMSARIC adj relating to the eternal cycle of birth, suffering, death and rebirth in Indian religions

SAMSHOO, -S same as ▶ samshu

SAMSHU, -S n alcoholic drink made from fermented rice

SAMSKARA n Hindu purification ceremony

SAMURAI, -S n member of an ancient Japanese warrior caste

SAN n sanatorium

SANATIVE less common word for ▶ curative

SANATORY adj healing

SANCAI, -S n glaze in Chinese pottery

SANCHO, -S n African stringed instrument

SANCTA ▶ sanctum

SANCTIFY vb make holy

S

SANCTION n permission, authorization ▷ vb allow, authorize

SANCTITY n sacredness, inviolability

SANCTUM, SANCTA, -S n sacred place

SAND, -ED, -S n substance consisting of small grains of rock, esp on a beach or in a desert ▷ vb smooth with sandpaper

SANDABLE ▶ sand

SANDAL, -S n light shoe consisting of a sole attached by straps ▷ vb put sandals on

SANDALED ▶ sandal

SANDALS ▶ sandal

SANDARAC n either of two coniferous trees having hard fragrant dark wood

SANDBAG, -S n bag filled with sand, used as protection against flood water ▷ vb protect with sandbags

SANDBANK n bank of sand below the surface of a river or sea

SANDBAR, -S n ridge of sand in a river or sea, often exposed at low tide

SANDBOX n container on a locomotive from which sand is released onto the rails

SANDBOY, -S n as in **happy as a sandboy** very happy or high-spirited

SANDBUR, -S n variety of wild grass

SANDBURR n variety of wild grass

SANDBURS ▶ sandbur

SANDDAB, -S n type of small Pacific flatfish

SANDED ▶ sand

SANDEK, -S n man who holds a baby being circumcised

SANDER, -S n power tool for smoothing surfaces

SANDFISH n burrowing Pacific fish

SANDFLY n any of various small mothlike flies

SANDHEAP n heap of sand

SANDHI, -S n modification of a word under the influence of an adjacent word

SANDHILL n hill of sand

SANDHIS ▶ sandhi

SANDHOG, -S n person who works in underground or underwater construction projects

SANDIER ▶ sandy

SANDIEST ▶ sandy

SANDING, -S ▶ sand

SANDIVER n scum forming on molten glass

SANDLESS ▶ sand

SANDLIKE ▶ sand

SANDLING n sand eel

SANDLOT, -S n area of vacant ground used for children's games

SANDMAN, SANDMEN n (in folklore) a magical person supposed to put children to sleep

SANDPEEP n small sandpiper

SANDPILE n pile of sand

SANDPIT, -S n shallow pit or container holding sand for children to play in

SANDPUMP n pump for wet sand

SANDS ▶ sand

SANDSHOE n light canvas shoe with a rubber sole

SANDSOAP n gritty general-purpose soap

SANDSPIT n small point of land created by sand dunes

SANDSPUR n American wild grass

SANDWICH n two slices of bread with a layer of food between ▷ vb insert between two other things

SANDWORM n any of various polychaete worms that live in burrows on sandy shores, esp the lugworm

SANDWORT n any of numerous caryophyllaceous plants

SANDY, SANDIER, SANDIEST adj covered with sand

SANDYISH adj somewhat sandy or covered with sand

SANE, -D, -R, -S, -ST, SANING adj of sound mind ▷ vb heal

SANELY ▶ sane

SANENESS ▶ sane

SANER ▶ sane

SANES ▶ sane

SANEST ▶ sane

SANG, -S Scots word for ▶ song

SANGA, -S n Ethiopian ox

SANGAR, -S n breastwork of stone or sods

SANGAREE n spiced drink similar to sangria

SANGARS ▶ sangar

SANGAS ▶ sanga

SANGEET, -S n Indian pre-wedding celebration

SANGER, -S n sandwich

SANGH, -S n Indian union or association

SANGHA, -S n Buddhist monastic order or community

SANGHAT, -S n local Sikh community or congregation

SANGHS ▶ sangh

SANGLIER n wild boar

SANGO, -S same as ▶ sanger

SANGOMA, -S n witch doctor or herbalist

SANGOS ▶ sango

SANGRAIL n legendary cup used by Christ at the Last Supper

SANGREAL same as ▶ sangrail

SANGRIA, -S n Spanish drink of red wine and fruit

SANGS ▶ sang

SANGUIFY vb turn into blood

SANGUINE adj cheerful, optimistic ▷ n red pencil containing ferric oxide, used in drawing

SANICLE, -S n type of plant with clusters of small white flowers

SANIDINE n alkali feldspar that is found in lavas

SANIES n thin greenish foul-smelling discharge from a wound, etc

SANIFY, SANIFIED, SANIFIES vb make healthy

SANING ▶ sane

SANIOUS ▶ sanies

SANITARY adj promoting health by getting rid of dirt and germs

SANITATE vb make sanitary

SANITIES ▶ sanity

SANITISE same as ▶ sanitize

SANITIZE vb omit unpleasant details to make (news) more acceptable

SANITY, SANITIES n state of having a normal healthy mind

SANJAK, -S n (in the Turkish Empire) a subdivision of a vilayet

SANK ▶ sink

SANKO, -S n African stringed instrument

SANNIE, -S Scots word for ▶ sandshoe

SANNOP, -S n Native American married man

SANNUP, -S n Native American married man

SANNYASI n Brahman who having attained the last

stage of life as a beggar will not be reborn

SANPAN, -S n sampan

SANPRO, -S n sanitary-protection products collectively

SANS archaic word for ▸ **without**

SANSA, -S n African musical instrument

SANSAR, -S n name of a wind that blows in Iran

SANSAS ▸ sansa

SANSEI, -S n American whose parents were Japanese immigrants

SANSERIF n style of printer's typeface

SANT, -S n devout person in India

SANTAL, -S n sandalwood

SANTALIC adj of sandalwood

SANTALIN n substance giving sandalwood its colour

SANTALOL n liquid from sandalwood used in perfume

SANTALS ▸ santal

SANTERA, -S n priestess of santeria

SANTERIA n Caribbean religious cult

SANTERO, -S n priest of santeria

SANTIM, -I, -S, -U n former money unit in Latvia

SANTIR, -S n Middle Eastern stringed instrument

SANTO, -S n saint or representation of one

SANTOKU, -S n type of Japanese knife

SANTOL, -S n fruit from Southeast Asia

SANTON, -S n French figurine

SANTONIN n soluble substance extracted from santonica

SANTONS ▸ santon

SANTOOR, -S same as ▸ **santir**

SANTOS ▸ santo

SANTOUR, -S n Middle Eastern stringed instrument

SANTS ▸ sant

SANTUR, -S n Middle Eastern stringed instrument

SANYASI, -S same as ▸ **sannyasi**

SAOLA, -S n small, very rare bovine mammal of Vietnam and Laos

SAOUARI, -S n tropical American tree

SAP, -PED, -S n moisture that circulates in plants ▸ vb undermine

SAPAJOU, -S n capuchin monkey

SAPAN, -S n tropical tree

SAPEGO, -ES n skin disease

SAPELE, -S n type of W African tree

SAPFUL adj full of sap

SAPHEAD, -S n idiot or fool

SAPHENA, -E, -S n either of two large superficial veins of the legs

SAPID, -ER, -EST adj having a pleasant taste

SAPIDITY ▸ sapid

SAPIENCE ▸ sapient

SAPIENCY ▸ sapient

SAPIENS adj relating to or like modern human beings

SAPIENT, -S adj wise, shrewd ▸ n wise person

SAPLESS ▸ sap

SAPLING, -S n young tree

SAPONIFY vb convert (a fat) into a soap by treatment with alkali

SAPONIN, -S n any of a group of plant glycosides

SAPONINE ▸ saponin

SAPONINS ▸ saponin

SAPONITE n type of clay mineral

SAPOR, -S n quality in a substance that is perceived by the sense of taste

SAPOROUS ▸ sapor

SAPORS ▸ sapor

SAPOTA, -S same as ▸ **sapodilla**

SAPOTE, -S n Central American tree

SAPOUR, -S variant of ▸ **sapor**

SAPPAN, -S n tropical tree

SAPPED ▸ sap

SAPPER, -S n soldier in an engineering unit

SAPPHIC, -S adj lesbian ▸ n verse written in a particular form

SAPPHIRE n blue precious stone ▸ adj deep blue

SAPPHISM n lesbianism

SAPPHIST n lesbian

SAPPIER ▸ sappy

SAPPIEST ▸ sappy

SAPPILY ▸ sappy

SAPPING, -S n act of sapping

SAPPLE, -D, -S, SAPPLING vb Scots word meaning wash in water

SAPPY, SAPPIER, SAPPIEST adj (of plants) full of sap

SAPREMIA American spelling of > **sapraemia**

SAPREMIC ▸ sapremia

SAPROBE, -S n organism that lives on decaying organisms

SAPROBIC ▸ saprobe

SAPROPEL n decomposed remains of aquatic organisms at the bottoms of lakes and oceans

SAPS ▸ sap

SAPSAGO, -S n hard greenish Swiss cheese

SAPUCAIA n Brazilian tree

SAPWOOD, -S n soft wood, just beneath the bark in tree trunks, that consists of living tissue

SAR, -ED, -ING, -S n marine fish ▸ vb Scots word meaning savour

SARABAND same as > **sarabande**

SARAFAN, -S n Russian woman's cloak

SARAN, -S n any one of a class of thermoplastic resins

SARANGI, -S n stringed instrument of India played with a bow

SARANS ▸ saran

SARAPE, -S n serape

SARCASM, -S n (use of) bitter or wounding ironic language

SARCENET n fine soft silk fabric formerly from Italy and used for clothing, ribbons, etc

SARCINA, -E, -S n type of bacterium

SARCODE, -S n material making up living cell

SARCODIC ▸ sarcode

SARCOID, -S adj of, relating to, or resembling flesh ▸ n tumour resembling a sarcoma

SARCOMA, -S n malignant tumour beginning in connective tissue

SARCONET n type of silk

SARCOUS adj (of tissue) muscular or fleshy

SARD, -S n orange, red, or brown variety of chalcedony

SARDANA, -S n Catalan dance

SARDAR, -S n title used before the name of Sikh men

SARDEL, -S n small fish

SARDELLE n small fish

SARDELS ▸ sardel

SARDINE, -D, -S n small fish of the herring family ▸ vb cram together

S

SARDIUS same as ▶ **sard**

SARDONIC adj mocking or scornful

SARDONYX n brown-and-white gemstone

SARDS ▶ **sard**

SARED ▶ **sar**

SAREE, -S same as ▶ **sari**

SARGASSA > **sargassum**

SARGASSO same as > **sargassum**

SARGE, -S n sergeant

SARGO same as ▶ **sargus**

SARGOS, -ES variant of ▶ **sargus**

SARGUS, -ES n species of sea fish

SARI, -S n long piece of cloth draped around the body and over one shoulder

SARIN, -S n chemical used in warfare as a lethal nerve gas producing asphyxia

SARING ▶ **sar**

SARINS ▶ **sarin**

SARIS ▶ **sari**

SARK, -S n shirt or (formerly) chemise

SARKIER ▶ **sarky**

SARKIEST ▶ **sarky**

SARKILY ▶ **sarky**

SARKING, -S n flat planking supporting the roof cladding of a building

SARKS ▶ **sark**

SARKY, SARKIER, SARKIEST adj sarcastic

SARMENT, -S n thin twig

SARMENTA > **sarmentum**

SARMENTS ▶ **sarment**

SARMIE, -S n sandwich

SARNEY, -S n sandwich

SARNIE, -S n sandwich

SAROD, -S n Indian stringed musical instrument

SARODE, -S n Indian stringed instrument

SARODIST n sarod player

SARODS ▶ **sarod**

SARONG, -S n long piece of cloth tucked around the waist or under the armpits

SARONIC ▶ **saros**

SAROS, -ES n cycle in which eclipses of the sun and moon occur in the same sequence

SARPANCH n head of a panchayat

SARRASIN n buckwheat

SARRAZIN same as ▶ **sarrasin**

SARS ▶ **sar**

SARSAR, -S same as ▶ **sansar**

SARSDEN, -S n sarsen

SARSEN, -S n boulder of silicified sandstone

SARSENET same as ▶ **sarcenet**

SARSENS ▶ **sarsen**

SARSNET, -S n type of silk

SARTOR, -S humorous or literary word for ▶ **tailor**

SARTORII > **sartorius**

SARTORS ▶ **sartor**

SARUS, -ES n Indian bird of crane family

SASANQUA n type of camellia

SASARARA n scolding

SASER, -S n device for amplifying ultrasound

SASH, -ED, -ES, -ING n decorative strip of cloth worn round the waist or over one shoulder ▷ vb furnish with a sash, sashes, or sash windows

SASHAY, -ED, -S vb move or walk in a casual or a showy manner

SASHED ▶ **sash**

SASHES ▶ **sash**

SASHIMI, -S n Japanese dish of thin fillets of raw fish

SASHING ▶ **sash**

SASHLESS ▶ **sash**

SASIN, -S another name for > **blackbuck**

SASINE, -S n granting of legal possession of feudal property

SASINS ▶ **sasin**

SASS, -ED, -ES, -ING n insolent or impudent talk or behaviour ▷ vb talk or answer back in such a way

SASSABY n African antelope of grasslands and semideserts

SASSE n old word meaning canal lock

SASSED ▶ **sass**

SASSES ▶ **sass**

SASSIER ▶ **sassy**

SASSIES ▶ **sassy**

SASSIEST ▶ **sassy**

SASSILY ▶ **sassy**

SASSING ▶ **sass**

SASSOLIN n boric acid

SASSWOOD same as > **sassy**

SASSY, SASSIER, SASSIES, SASSIEST adj insolent, impertinent ▷ n W African leguminous tree with poisonous bark

SASTRA, -S same as ▶ **shastra**

SASTRUGA, SASTRUGI n ridge on a snow-covered plain

SAT ▶ **sit**

SATAI, -S same as ▶ **satay**

SATANG, -S n monetary unit of Thailand worth one hundredth of a baht

SATANIC adj of Satan

SATANISM n worship of the devil

SATANIST ▶ **satanism**

SATANITY n quality of being satanic

SATARA, -S n type of cloth

SATAY, -S n Indonesian and Malaysian dish

SATCHEL, -S n bag, usu with a shoulder strap, for carrying books

SATCOM, -S n satellite communications

SATE, -D, -S, SATING vb satisfy (a desire or appetite) fully

SATEEN, -S n glossy linen or cotton fabric, woven in such a way that it resembles satin

SATELESS adj old word meaning insatiable

SATELLES n species of bacteria

SATEM adj denoting or belonging to a particular group of Indo-European languages

SATES ▶ **sate**

SATI, -S n Indian widow suicide

SATIABLE adj capable of being satiated

SATIABLY ▶ **satiable**

SATIATE, -D, -S vb provide with more than enough, so as to disgust

SATIETY n feeling of having had too much

SATIN, -ED, -ING, -S n silky fabric with a glossy surface on one side ▷ adj like satin in texture ▷ vb cover with satin

SATINET, -S n thin or imitation satin

SATING ▶ **sate**

SATINIER ▶ **satiny**

SATINING ▶ **satin**

SATINPOD n honesty (the plant)

SATINS ▶ **satin**

SATINY, SATINIER adj like satin

SATIRE, -S n use of ridicule to expose vice or folly

SATIRIC same as > **satirical**

SATIRISE same as ▶ **satirize**

SATIRIST n writer of satire

SATIRIZE vb ridicule by means of satire

SATIS ▶ **sati**

SATISFY vb please, content

SATIVE adj old word meaning cultivated

SATNAV, -S n satellite navigation system

SATORI, -S n state of sudden indescribable intuitive enlightenment

SATRAP, -S n (in ancient Persia) a provincial governor or subordinate ruler

SATRAPAL ▷ satrap

SATRAPS ▷ satrap

SATRAPY n province, office, or period of rule of a satrap

SATSANG, -S n sacred gathering in Hinduism

SATSUMA, -S n kind of small orange

SATURANT n substance that causes a solution, etc, to be saturated ▷ adj (of a substance) causing saturation

SATURATE vb soak thoroughly

SATURNIC adj poisoned by lead

SATYR, -S n woodland god, part man, part goat

SATYRA, -S n female satyr

SATYRAL, -S n mythical beast in heraldry

SATYRAS ▷ satyra

SATYRE, -S n as in sea satyre sea creature mentioned in Spenser's poetry

SATYRESS n female satyr

SATYRIC ▷ satyr

SATYRID, -S n butterfly with typically brown or dark wings with paler markings

SATYRISK n small satyr

SATYRS ▷ satyr

SAU archaic past tense of ▷ see

SAUBA, -S n South American ant

SAUCE, -D, -S, SAUCING n liquid added to food to enhance flavour ▷ vb prepare (food) with sauce

SAUCEBOX n saucy person

SAUCED ▷ sauce

SAUCEPAN n cooking pot with a long handle

SAUCEPOT n cooking pot with lid

SAUCER, -S n small round dish put under a cup

SAUCES ▷ sauce

SAUCH, -S n sallow or willow

SAUCIER, -S n chef who makes sauces

SAUCIEST ▷ saucy

SAUCILY ▷ saucy

SAUCING ▷ sauce

SAUCISSE n type of explosive fuse

SAUCY, SAUCIEST adj impudent

SAUFGARD old form of ▷ safeguard

SAUGER, -S n small North American pikeperch

SAUGH, -S same as ▷ sauch

SAUGHY adj Scots word meaning made of willow

SAUL, -S Scots word for ▷ soul

SAULGE, -S n old word for sage plant

SAULIE, -S n Scots word meaning professional mourner

SAULS ▷ saul

SAULT, -S n waterfall in Canada

SAUNA, -ED, -ING, -S n Finnish-style steam bath ▷ vb have a sauna

SAUNT, -ED, -ING, -S Scots form of ▷ saint

SAUNTER, -S vb walk in a leisurely manner, stroll ▷ n leisurely walk

SAUNTING ▷ saunt

SAUNTS ▷ saunt

SAUREL, -S n type of mackerel

SAURIAN, -S n lizard

SAURIES ▷ saury

SAUROID, -S adj like a lizard ▷ n type of fish

SAUROPOD n type of herbivorous dinosaur including the brontosaurus and the diplodocus

SAURY, SAURIES n type of fish of tropical and temperate seas

SAUSAGE, -S n minced meat in an edible tube-shaped skin

SAUT, -ED, -ING, -S Scot word for ▷ salt

SAUTE, -ED, -ING, -S vb fry quickly in a little fat ▷ n dish of sautéed food ▷ adj sautéed until lightly brown

SAUTED ▷ saut

SAUTEED ▷ saute

SAUTEING ▷ saute

SAUTERNE n sauternes

SAUTES ▷ saute

SAUTING ▷ saut

SAUTOIR, -S n long necklace or pendant

SAUTOIRE variant of ▷ sautoir

SAUTOIRS ▷ sautoir

SAUTS ▷ saut

SAV, -S short for ▷ saveloy

SAUCING ▷ sauce

SAUCISSE n type of explosive fuse

SAVABLE ▷ save

SAVAGE, -D, -R, -S, -ST, SAVAGING adj wild, untamed ▷ n uncivilized person ▷ vb attack ferociously

SAVAGELY ▷ savage

SAVAGER ▷ savage

SAVAGERY n viciousness and cruelty

SAVAGES ▷ savage

SAVAGEST ▷ savage

SAVAGING ▷ savage

SAVAGISM ▷ savage

SAVANNA, -S n open grasslands of tropical Africa

SAVANNAH same as ▷ savanna

SAVANNAS ▷ savanna

SAVANT, -S n learned person

SAVANTE, -S ▷ savant

SAVANTS ▷ savant

SAVARIN, -S n type of cake

SAVASANA n type of pose in yoga

SAVATE, -S n form of boxing in which blows may be delivered with the feet

SAVE, -D, -S vb rescue or preserve from harm, protect ▷ n act of preventing a goal ▷ prep except

SAVEABLE ▷ save

SAVED ▷ save

SAVEGARD vb old word meaning protect

SAVELOY, -S n spicy smoked sausage

SAVER, -S ▷ save

SAVES ▷ save

SAVEY, -ED, -ING, -S vb understand

SAVIN, -S n small spreading juniper bush of Europe, N Asia, and North America

SAVINE, -S same as ▷ savin

SAVING, -S n economy ▷ prep except ▷ adj tending to save or preserve

SAVINGLY ▷ saving

SAVINGS ▷ saving

SAVINS ▷ savin

SAVIOR, -S same as ▷ saviour

SAVIOUR, -S n person who rescues another

SAVOR, -ED, -ING, -S same as ▷ savour

SAVORER, -S ▷ savor

SAVORIER ▷ savory

SAVORIES ▷ savory

SAVORILY ▷ savour

SAVORING ▷ savor

SAVOROUS ▷ savour

SAVORS ▷ savor

S

SAVORY, SAVORIER, SAVORIES same as ▸savoury

SAVOUR, -ED, -S vb enjoy, relish ▷ n characteristic taste or odour

SAVOURER ▸savour

SAVOURLY adv old word meaning refreshingly

SAVOURS ▸savour

SAVOURY adj salty or spicy ▷ n savoury dish served before or after a meal

SAVOY, -S n variety of cabbage

SAVOYARD n person keenly interested in the operettas of Gilbert and Sullivan

SAVOYS ▸savoy

SAVS ▸sav

SAVVEY, -ED, -S vb understand

SAVVIED ▸savvy

SAVVIER ▸savvy

SAVVIES ▸savvy

SAVVIEST ▸savvy

SAVVILY ▸savvy

SAVVY, SAVVIED, SAVVIER, SAVVIES, SAVVIEST, -ING vb understand ▷ n understanding, intelligence ▷ adj shrewd

SAW, -ED, -S n hand tool for cutting wood and metal ▷ vb cut with a saw

SAWAH, -S n paddy field

SAWBILL, -S n type of hummingbird

SAWBLADE n blade of a saw

SAWBONES n surgeon or doctor

SAWBUCK, -S n structure for supporting wood that is being sawn

SAWDER, -ED, -S n flattery ▷ vb flatter

SAWDUST, -S n fine wood fragments made in sawing ▷ vb cover with sawdust

SAWDUSTY adj covered in sawdust

SAWED ▸saw

SAWER, -S ▸saw

SAWFISH n fish with a long toothed snout

SAWFLY, SAWFLIES n any of various hymenopterous insects

SAWGRASS n type of sedge with serrated leaves

SAWHORSE n structure for supporting wood that is being sawn

SAWING, -S ▸saw

SAWLIKE ▸saw

SAWLOG, -S n log suitable for sawing

SAWMILL, -S n mill where timber is sawn into planks

SAWN past participle of ▸saw

SAWNEY, -S n derogatory word for a fool

SAWPIT, -S n pit above which a log is sawn into planks

SAWS ▸saw

SAWSHARK n shark with long sawlike snout

SAWTOOTH, SAWTEETH n one of the teeth of a saw

SAWYER, -S n person who saws timber for a living

SAX, -ES same as > saxophone

SAXATILE adj living among rocks

SAXAUL, -S n Asian tree

SAXE adj as in saxe blue light greyish-blue colour

SAXES ▸sax

SAXHORN, -S n valved brass instrument used chiefly in brass and military bands

SAXICOLE variant of ▸saxatile

SAXIST, -S n saxophone player

SAXMAN, SAXMEN n saxophone player

SAXONIES ▸saxony

SAXONITE n igneous rock

SAXONY, SAXONIES n fine three-ply yarn

SAXTUBA, -S n bass saxhorn

SAY, SAIDEST, SAIDST, SAIST, -EST, -NE, -S, -ST vb speak or utter ▷ n right or chance to speak

SAYABLE, -S n anything that can be said

SAYED, -S same as ▸sayyid

SAYER, -S ▸say

SAYEST ▸say

SAYID, -S same as ▸sayyid

SAYING, -S ▸say

SAYNE ▸say

SAYON, -S n type of tunic

SAYONARA n Japanese farewell

SAYONS ▸sayon

SAYS ▸say

SAYST ▸say

SAYYID, -S n Muslim descended from Muhammad's grandson

SAZ, -ES, -ZES n Middle Eastern stringed instrument

This musical instrument is one of the most frequently played Z words.

SAZERAC, -S n mixed drink of whisky, Pernod, syrup, bitters, and lemon

SAZES ▸saz

SAZHEN, -S n Russian measure of length

SAZZES ▸saz

SBIRRO, SBIRRI n Italian police officer

SCAB, -BED, -BING, -S n crust formed over a wound ▷ vb become covered with a scab

SCABBARD n sheath for a sword or dagger

SCABBED ▸scab

SCABBIER ▸scabby

SCABBILY ▸scabby

SCABBING ▸scab

SCABBLE, -D, -S vb shape (stone) roughly

SCABBY, SCABBIER adj covered with scabs

SCABIES n itchy skin disease

SCABIOSA n flowering plant

SCABIOUS n plant with showy blue, red, or whitish dome-shaped flower heads ▷ adj having or covered with scabs

SCABLAND n barren rocky land

SCABLIKE ▸scab

SCABRID adj having a rough or scaly surface

SCABROUS adj rough and scaly

SCABS ▸scab

SCAD n any of various carangid fishes

SCADS pl n large amount or number

SCAFF, -ED, -ING, -S n Scots word meaning food ▷ vb ask for (food) in a mean or rude manner

SCAFFIE, -S n Scots word meaning street cleaner

SCAFFIER ▸scaffy

SCAFFIES ▸scaffie

SCAFFING ▸scaff

SCAFFOLD n temporary platform for builders or other tradespeople ▷ vb provide with a scaffold

SCAFFS ▸scaff

SCAFFY, SCAFFIER adj having little value, cheap

SCAG, -GED, -GING, -S n tear in a garment or piece of cloth ▷ vb make a tear in (cloth)

SCAGLIA, -S n type of limestone

SCAGS ▸scag

SCAIL, -ED, -ING, -S vb Scots word meaning disperse

SCAITH, -ED, -S vb old word meaning injure

SCALA, -E n passage inside the cochlea

SCALABLE adj capable of being scaled or climbed

SCALABLY ▸ scalable

SCALADE, -S short for ▸ escalade

SCALADO, -S same as ▸ scalade

SCALAE ▸ scala

SCALAGE, -S n percentage deducted from the price of goods liable to shrink or leak

SCALAR, -S adj having magnitude but no direction ▸ n quantity that has magnitude but not direction

SCALARE, -S another name for > angelfish

SCALARS ▸ scalar

SCALAWAG same as > scallywag

SCALD, -ED, -S vb burn with hot liquid ▸ n (in ancient Scandinavia) a bard or minstrel

SCALDER, -S ▸ scald

SCALDIC ▸ scald

SCALDING n instance of burning with hot liquid

SCALDINO, SCALDINI n Italian brazier

SCALDS ▸ scald

SCALE, -D, -S n one of the thin overlapping plates covering fishes and reptiles ▸ vb remove scales from

SCALENE, -S n triangle with three unequal sides

SCALENUS, SCALENI n any one of the three muscles situated on each side of the neck

SCALEPAN n part of scales holding weighed object

SCALER, -S n person or thing that scales

SCALES ▸ scale

SCALEUP, -S n increase

SCALIER ▸ scaly

SCALIEST ▸ scaly

SCALING, -S ▸ scale

SCALL, -S n disease of the scalp characterized by itching and scab formation

SCALLED ▸ scall

SCALLIES ▸ scally

SCALLION same as ▸ shallot

SCALLOP, -S n edible shellfish with two fan-shaped shells ▸ vb decorate (an edge) with scallops

SCALLS ▸ scall

SCALLY, SCALLIES n rascal

SCALP, -ED, -S n skin and hair on top of the head ▸ vb cut off the scalp of

SCALPEL, -S n small surgical knife

SCALPER, -S ▸ scalp

SCALPING n process in which the top portion of a metal ingot is machined away before use

SCALPINS n small stones

SCALPRUM n large scalpel

SCALPS ▸ scalp

SCALY, SCALIER, SCALIEST adj resembling or covered in scales

SCAM, -MED, -MING, -S n dishonest scheme ▸ vb swindle (someone) by means of a trick

SCAMBLE, -D, -S vb scramble

SCAMBLER ▸ scamble

SCAMBLES ▸ scamble

SCAMEL, -S n Shakespearian word of uncertain meaning

SCAMMED ▸ scam

SCAMMER, -S n person who perpetrates a scam

SCAMMING ▸ scam

SCAMMONY n twining Asian convolvulus plant

SCAMP, -ED, -ING, -S n mischievous child ▸ vb perform without care

SCAMPER, -S vb run about hurriedly or in play ▸ n scampering

SCAMPI, -ES, -S pl n large prawns

SCAMPING ▸ scamp

SCAMPIS ▸ scampi

SCAMPISH ▸ scamp

SCAMPS ▸ scamp

SCAMS ▸ scam

SCAMSTER same as ▸ scammer

SCAMTO, -S n argot of urban Black people in South Africa

SCAN, -D, -NED, -NING, -S vb scrutinize carefully ▸ n scanning

SCANDAL, -S n disgraceful action or event ▸ vb disgrace

SCANDENT adj (of plants) having a climbing habit

SCANDIA, -S n scandium oxide

SCANDIC adj of or containing scandium

SCANDIUM n rare silvery-white metallic element

SCANNED ▸ scan

SCANNER, -S n electronic device used for scanning

SCANNING ▸ scan

SCANS ▸ scan

SCANSION n metrical scanning of verse

SCANT, -ED, -ER, -EST, -ING, -S adj barely sufficient, meagre ▸ vb limit in size or quantity ▸ adv scarcely

SCANTIER ▸ scanty

SCANTIES pl n women's underwear

SCANTILY ▸ scanty

SCANTING ▸ scant

SCANTITY n quality of being scant

SCANTLE, -D, -S vb stint

SCANTLY ▸ scant

SCANTS ▸ scant

SCANTY, SCANTIER adj barely sufficient or not sufficient

SCAPA, -ED, -ING, -S variant of ▸ scarper

SCAPE, -D, -S, SCAPING n leafless stalk in plants ▸ vb archaic word for escape

SCAPHOID obsolete word for > navicular

SCAPI ▸ scapus

SCAPING ▸ scape

SCAPOSE ▸ scape

SCAPPLE, -D, -S vb shape roughly

SCAPULA, -E, -S n shoulder blade

SCAPULAR adj of the scapula ▸ n loose sleeveless garment worn by monks over their habits

SCAPULAS ▸ scapula

SCAPUS, SCAPI n flower stalk

SCAR, -RED, -RING, -S n mark left by a healed wound ▸ vb mark or become marked with a scar

SCARAB, -S n sacred beetle of ancient Egypt

SCARABEE n old word for scarab beetle

SCARABS ▸ scarab

SCARCE, -R, -ST adj insufficient to meet demand

SCARCELY adv hardly at all

SCARCER ▸ scarce

SCARCEST ▸ scarce

SCARCITY n inadequate supply

SCARE, -DER, -S, SCARING vb frighten or be frightened ▸ n fright, sudden panic ▸ adj causing (needless) fear or alarm

SCARED ▸ scare

S

SCAREDER ▸ scare

SCAREDY n someone who is easily frightened

SCARER, -S ▸ scare

SCARES ▸ scare

SCAREY adj frightening

SCARF, -ED, -ING, -S, SCARVES n piece of material worn round the neck, head, or shoulders ▸ vb join

SCARFER, -S ▸ scarf

SCARFING ▸ scarf

SCARFISH n type of fish

SCARFPIN n decorative pin securing a scarf

SCARFS ▸ scarf

SCARIER ▸ scary

SCARIEST ▸ scary

SCARIFY vb scratch or cut slightly all over

SCARILY ▸ scary

SCARING ▸ scare

SCARIOSE same as ▸ scarious

SCARIOUS adj (of plant parts) membranous, dry, and brownish in colour

SCARLESS ▸ scar

SCARLET, -S n brilliant red ▸ adj bright red ▸ vb make scarlet

SCARMOGE n old form of skirmish

SCARP, -ED, -ING, -S n steep slope ▸ vb wear or cut so as to form a steep slope

SCARPA, -ED, -S vb run away

SCARPED ▸ scarp

SCARPER, -S vb run away ▸ n hasty departure

SCARPH, -ED, -S vb join with scarf joint

SCARPING ▸ scarp

SCARPS ▸ scarp

SCARRE, -S n Shakespearian word of unknown meaning

SCARRED ▸ scar

SCARRES ▸ scarre

SCARRIER ▸ scarry

SCARRING ▸ scar

SCARRY, SCARRIER ▸ scar

SCARS ▸ scar

SCART, -ED, -ING, -S vb scratch or scrape ▸ n scratch or scrape

SCARTH, -S Scots word for > cormorant

SCARTING ▸ scart

SCARTS ▸ scart

SCARVED adj wearing a scarf

SCARVES ▸ scarf

SCARY, SCARIER, SCARIEST adj frightening

SCAT, -S, -TED, -TING vb go away ▸ n jazz singing using improvised vocal sounds instead of words

SCATBACK n American football player

SCATCH, -ES same as ▸ stilt

SCATH, -S vb old word meaning injure

SCATHE, -D, -S vb attack with severe criticism ▸ n harm

SCATHING adj harshly critical

SCATHS ▸ scath

SCATOLE, -S n substance found in coal

SCATS ▸ scat

SCATT, -S n old word meaning tax ▸ vb tax

SCATTED ▸ scat

SCATTER, -S vb throw about in various directions ▸ n scattering

SCATTERY adj dispersed

SCATTIER ▸ scatty

SCATTILY ▸ scatty

SCATTING ▸ scat

SCATTS ▸ scatt

SCATTY, SCATTIER adj empty-headed

SCAUD, -ED, -ING, -S Scot word for ▸ scald

SCAUP, -ED, -ING, -S variant of ▸ scalp

SCAUPER, -S same as ▸ scorper

SCAUPING ▸ scaup

SCAUPS ▸ scaup

SCAUR, -ED, -ING, -S same as ▸ scar

SCAURIES ▸ scaury

SCAURING ▸ scaur

SCAURS ▸ scaur

SCAURY, SCAURIES n young seagull

SCAVAGE, -D, -S n old word meaning toll ▸ vb scavenge

SCAVAGER ▸ scavage

SCAVAGES ▸ scavage

SCAVENGE vb search for (anything usable) among discarded material

SCAW, -S n headland

SCAWTITE n mineral containing calcium

SCAZON, -S n metre in poetry

SCEAT, -S, -TAS, -TS n Anglo-Saxon coin

SCEATT same as ▸ sceat

SCEATTAS ▸ sceat

SCEATTS ▸ sceat

SCEDULE, -D, -S old spelling of ▸ schedule

SCELERAT n villain

SCENA, -S n scene in an opera, usually longer than a single aria

SCENARIO n summary of the plot of a play or film

SCENARY n scenery

SCENAS ▸ scena

SCEND, -ED, -ING, -S vb (of a vessel) to surge upwards in a heavy sea ▸ n upward heaving of a vessel pitching

SCENE, -D, -S, SCENING n place of action of a real or imaginary event ▸ vb set in a scene

SCENEMAN, SCENEMEN n person shifting stage scenery

SCENERY n natural features of a landscape

SCENES ▸ scene

SCENIC, -S adj picturesque ▸ n something scenic

SCENICAL ▸ scene

SCENICS ▸ scenic

SCENING ▸ scene

SCENT, -ING, -S n pleasant smell ▸ vb detect by smell

SCENTED ▸ scent

SCENTFUL adj old word meaning having scent

SCENTING ▸ scent

SCENTS ▸ scent

SCEPSIS n doubt

SCEPTER, -S same as ▸ sceptre

SCEPTIC, -S n person who habitually doubts generally accepted beliefs ▸ adj of or relating to sceptics

SCEPTRAL adj royal

SCEPTRE, -S n ornamental rod symbolizing royal power ▸ vb invest with authority

SCEPTRED ▸ sceptre

SCEPTRES ▸ sceptre

SCEPTRY adj having sceptre

SCERNE, -D, -S, SCERNING vb old word meaning discern

SCHANSE, -S ▸ schantze

SCHANTZE n stones heaped to shelter soldier in battle

SCHANZE, -S same as ▸ schantze

SCHAPPE, -D, -S n yarn or fabric made from waste silk

SCHAPSKA n cap worn by lancer

SCHAV, -S n Polish soup

SCHEDULE n plan of procedure for a project ▸ vb plan to occur at a certain time

SCHELLUM n Scots word meaning rascal

SCHELLY n freshwater whitefish of the English Lake District

SCHELM, -S n South African word meaning rascal

SCHEMA, -S, -TA n overall plan or diagram

SCHEME, -D, -S n systematic plan ▷ vb plan in an underhand manner

SCHEMER, -S ▸ scheme

SCHEMES ▸ scheme

SCHEMIE, -S n insulting Scots word for a resident of a housing scheme

SCHEMING adj given to making plots ▷ n intrigues

SCHERZO, SCHERZI, -S n brisk lively piece of music

SCHIEDAM n type of gin produced in the Netherlands

SCHILLER n unusual iridescent or metallic lustre in some minerals

SCHIMMEL n roan horse

SCHISM, -S n (group resulting from) division in an organization

SCHISMA, -S n short musical interval of half a comma

SCHISMS ▸ schism

SCHIST, -S n crystalline rock which splits into layers

SCHIZOID adj relating to a disorder characterized by self-absorption

SCHIZONT n cell formed from a trophozoite during the life cycle of sporozoan protozoans

SCHLAGER n German duelling sword

SCHLEP, -S vb drag or lug (oneself or an object) with difficulty ▷ n arduous journey or procedure

SCHLEPP, -S vb schlep

SCHLEPPY same as ▸ shleppy

SCHLEPS ▸ schlep

SCHLICH, -S n finely crushed ore

SCHLIERE n (in physics or geology) streak of different density or composition from surroundings

SCHLOCK, -S n goods of cheap or inferior quality ▷ adj cheap, inferior, or trashy

SCHLOCKY adj of poor quality

SCHLOSS n German castle

SCHLUB, -S n coarse or contemptible person

SCHLUMP, -S vb move in lazy way

SCHLUMPY ▸ schlump

SCHMALTZ n excessive sentimentality

SCHMALZ same as ▸ schmaltz

SCHMALZY adj schmaltzy

SCHMATTE same as > schmutter

SCHMEAR, -S n situation, matter, or affair ▷ vb spread or smear

SCHMECK, -S n taste ▷ vb taste good

SCHMEER, -S same as ▸ schmear

SCHMELZ n ornamental glass

SCHMELZE variant of ▸ schmelz

SCHMICK adj (in Australia) excellent, elegant, or stylish

SCHMO, -S n dull, stupid, or boring person

SCHMOCK, -S n stupid person

SCHMOE, -S same as ▸ schmo

SCHMOOS variant of ▸ schmoose

SCHMOOSE vb chat

SCHMOOZ n chat

SCHMOOZE vb chat or gossip ▷ n trivial conversation

SCHMOOZY ▸ schmooze

SCHMOS ▸ schmo

SCHMUCK, -S n stupid or contemptible person ▷ vb act as a schmuck

SCHMUCKY adj foolish

SCHMUTZ n dirt; grime

SCHNAPPS n strong alcoholic spirit

SCHNAPS same as ▸ schnapps

SCHNECKE > schnecken

SCHNEID, -S n succession of losses

SCHNELL adj German word meaning quick

SCHNOOK, -S n stupid or gullible person

SCHNORR, -S vb beg

SCHNOZ, -ES n nose

SCHNOZZ n nose

SCHOLAR, -S n learned person

SCHOLIA ▸ scholium

SCHOLION n scholarly annotation

SCHOLIUM, SCHOLIA n commentary or annotation, esp on a classical text

SCHOOL, -ED, -S n place where children are taught or instruction is given in a subject ▷ vb educate or train

SCHOOLE, -S n old form of shoal

SCHOOLED ▸ school

SCHOOLER n pupil at a school of a specified kind

SCHOOLES ▸ schoole

SCHOOLIE n schoolteacher or a high-school student

SCHOOLS ▸ school

SCHOONER n sailing ship rigged fore-and-aft

SCHORL, -S n type of black tourmaline

SCHOUT, -S n council officer in Netherlands

SCHRIK, -S variant of ▸ skrik

SCHROD, -S n young cod

SCHTICK, -S same as ▸ shtick

SCHTIK, -S n schtick

SCHTOOK, -S n trouble

SCHTOOM adj silent

SCHTUCK, -S n trouble

SCHTUM adj silent

SCHUIT, -S n Dutch boat with flat bottom

SCHUL, -N, -S same as ▸ shul

SCHUSS, -ED, -ES n straight high-speed downhill run ▷ vb perform a schuss

SCHUSSER ▸ schuss

SCHUSSES ▸ schuss

SCHUYT, -S n Dutch boat with flat bottom

SCHVITZ same as ▸ shvitz

SCHWA, -S n vowel representing the sound in unstressed syllables

SCHWAG, -S n promotional material given away for free

SCHWAS ▸ schwa

SCIAENID adj of or relating to a family of mainly tropical and subtropical marine percoid fishes ▷ n any of these fish

SCIARID, -S n small fly

SCIATIC, -S adj of the hip ▷ n sciatic part of the body

SCIATICA n severe pain in the large nerve in the back of the leg

SCIATICS ▸ sciatic

SCIENCE, -S n systematic study and knowledge of natural or physical phenomena

SCIENCED adj old word meaning learned

SCIENCES ▸ science

SCIENT adj old word meaning scientific

SCIENTER adv knowingly

SCILICET adv namely

SCILLA, -S n plant with small bell-shaped flowers

SCIMETAR n scimitar

S

SCIMITAR n curved sword
SCIMITER n scimitar
SCINCOID adj of, relating to, or resembling a skink ▷ n any animal, esp a lizard, resembling a skink
SCIOLISM n practice of opinionating on subjects of which one has only superficial knowledge
SCIOLIST ▸ sciolism
SCIOLOUS ▸ sciolism
SCIOLTO adv musical direction meaning freely
SCION, -S n descendant or heir
SCIROC, -S ▸ scirocco
SCIROCCO n hot Mediterranean wind
SCIROCS ▸ sciroc
SCIRRHUS, SCIRRHI n hard cancerous growth composed of fibrous tissues
SCISSEL, -S n waste metal left over from sheet metal after discs have been punched out of it
SCISSIL, -S n scissel
SCISSILE adj capable of being cut or divided
SCISSILS ▸ scissil
SCISSION n act or an instance of cutting, splitting, or dividing
SCISSOR vb cut (an object) with scissors
SCISSORS pl n cutting instrument with two crossed pivoted blades
SCISSURE n longitudinal cleft
SCIURID, -S n squirrel or related rodent
SCIURINE adj relating to a family of rodents that includes squirrels, marmots, and chipmunks ▷ n any squirrel-like animal
SCIUROID adj (of an animal) resembling a squirrel
SCLAFF, -ED, -S vb cause (the club) to hit (the ground behind the ball) when making a stroke ▷ n sclaffing stroke or shot
SCLAFFER ▸ sclaff
SCLAFFS ▸ sclaff
SCLATE, -D, -S, SCLATING vb (Scots) slate ▷ n (Scots) slate
SCLAVE, -S n old form of slave
SCLERA, -E, -S n tough white substance that forms the outer covering of the eyeball

SCLERAL ▸ sclera
SCLERAS ▸ sclera
SCLERE, -S n supporting anatomical structure
SCLEREID n type of biological cell
SCLEREMA n condition in which body tissues harden
SCLERES ▸ sclere
SCLERITE n any of the hard chitinous plates that make up the exoskeleton of an arthropod
SCLEROID adj (of organisms and their parts) hard or hardened
SCLEROMA n any small area of abnormally hard tissue, esp in a mucous membrane
SCLEROSE vb affect with sclerosis
SCLEROUS adj hard
SCLIFF, -S n Scots word for small piece
SCLIM, -MED, -S vb Scots word meaning climb
SCODY, SCODIER, SCODIEST adj unkempt
SCOFF, -ED, -S vb express derision ▷ n mocking expression
SCOFFER, -S ▸ scoff
SCOFFING ▸ scoff
SCOFFLAW n person who habitually flouts or violates the law
SCOFFS ▸ scoff
SCOG, -GED, -GING, -S vb shelter
SCOINSON n part of door or window frame
SCOLD, -ED, -S vb find fault with, reprimand ▷ n person who scolds
SCOLDER, -S ▸ scold
SCOLDING ▸ scold
SCOLDS ▸ scold
SCOLECES ▸ scolex
SCOLECID n variety of worm
SCOLEX, SCOLECES, SCOLICES n headlike part of a tapeworm
SCOLIA ▸ scolion
SCOLICES ▸ scolex
SCOLIOMA n condition with abnormal curvature of spine
SCOLION, SCOLIA n ancient Greek drinking song
SCOLLOP, -S variant of ▸ scallop
SCOLYTID n type of beetle
SCOMBRID n fish of mackerel family
SCOMFISH vb Scots word meaning stifle

SCONCE, -D, -S, SCONCING n bracket on a wall for holding candles or lights ▷ vb challenge (a fellow student) to drink a large quantity of beer
SCONE, -S n small plain cake baked in an oven or on a griddle
SCONTION n part of door or window frame
SCOOBY, SCOOBIES n slang for a clue, notion
SCOOCH, -ED, -ES vb compress one's body into smaller space
SCOOG, -ED, -ING, -S vb shelter
SCOOP, -ED, -ING, -S n shovel-like tool for ladling or hollowing out ▷ vb take up or hollow out with or as if with a scoop
SCOOPER, -S ▸ scoop
SCOOPFUL ▸ scoop
SCOOPING ▸ scoop
SCOOPS ▸ scoop
SCOOSH, -ED, -ES vb squirt ▷ n squirt or rush of liquid
SCOOT, -ED, -ING, -S vb leave or move quickly ▷ n act of scooting
SCOOTCH same as ▸ scooch
SCOOTED ▸ scoot
SCOOTER, -S n child's vehicle propelled by pushing on the ground with one foot ▷ vb go on a scooter
SCOOTING ▸ scoot
SCOOTS ▸ scoot
SCOP, -S n (in Anglo-Saxon England) a bard or minstrel
SCOPA, -E, -S n tuft of hairs on the abdomen or hind legs of a bee
SCOPATE adj having tuft-type hairs
SCOPE, -D, -S, SCOPING n opportunity for using abilities ▷ vb look at or examine carefully
SCOPELID n deep-sea fish
SCOPES ▸ scope
SCOPING ▸ scope
SCOPS ▸ scop
SCOPULA, -E, -S n small tuft of dense hairs on the legs and chelicerae of some spiders
SCORCH, -ED, -ES vb burn on the surface ▷ n slight burn
SCORCHER n very hot day
SCORCHES ▸ scorch
SCORDATO adj musical term meaning out of tune

SCORE, -D, -S n points gained in a game or competition ▷ vb gain (points) in a game

SCOREPAD n pad for recording score in game

SCORER, -S ▶ score

SCORES ▶ score

SCORIA, -E n mass of solidified lava containing many cavities

SCORIAC ▶ scoria

SCORIAE ▶ scoria

SCORIFY vb remove (impurities) from metals by forming scoria

SCORING, -S n act or practice of scoring

SCORIOUS ▶ scoria

SCORN, -ED, -ING, -S n open contempt ▷ vb despise

SCORNER, -S ▶ scorn

SCORNFUL ▶ scorn

SCORNING ▶ scorn

SCORNS ▶ scorn

SCORPER, -S n kind of fine chisel with a square or curved tip

SCORPION n small lobster-shaped animal with a sting at the end of a jointed tail

SCORSE, -D, -S, SCORSING vb exchange

SCORSER, -S ▶ scorse

SCORSES ▶ scorse

SCORSING ▶ scorse

SCOT, -S n payment or tax

SCOTCH, -ED, -ES vb put an end to ▷ n gash

SCOTER, -S n type of sea duck

SCOTIA, -S n deep concave moulding

SCOTOMA, -S n blind spot

SCOTOMIA n dizziness

SCOTOMY n dizziness

SCOTOPIA n ability of the eye to adjust for night vision

SCOTOPIC ▶ scotopia

SCOTS ▶ scot

SCOTTIE, -S n type of small sturdy terrier

SCOUG, -ED, -ING, -S vb shelter

SCOUP, -ED, -ING, -S vb Scots word meaning jump

SCOUR, -ED, -ING, -S vb clean or polish by rubbing with something rough ▷ n scouring

SCOURER, -S ▶ scour

SCOURGE, -D, -S n person or thing causing severe suffering ▷ vb cause severe suffering to

SCOURGER ▶ scourge

SCOURGES ▶ scourge

SCOURIE, -S n young seagull

SCOURING ▶ scour

SCOURS ▶ scour

SCOURSE, -D, -S vb exchange

SCOUSE, -S n stew made from left-over meat

SCOUSER, -S n inhabitant of Liverpool

SCOUSES ▶ scouse

SCOUT, -ED, -ING, -S n person sent out to reconnoitre ▷ vb act as a scout

SCOUTER, -S ▶ scout

SCOUTH, -S n Scots word meaning plenty of room

SCOUTHER vb Scots word meaning scorch

SCOUTHS ▶ scouth

SCOUTING ▶ scout

SCOUTS ▶ scout

SCOW, -ED, -ING, -S n unpowered barge used for carrying freight ▷ vb transport by scow

SCOWDER, -S vb Scots word meaning scorch

SCOWED ▶ scow

SCOWING ▶ scow

SCOWL, -ED, -ING, -S vb have an angry or sullen expression

SCOWLER, -S n person who scowls

SCOWLING ▶ scowl

SCOWLS ▶ scowl

SCOWP, -ED, -ING, -S vb Scots word meaning jump

SCOWRER, -S n old word meaning hooligan

SCOWRIE, -S n young seagull

SCOWS ▶ scow

SCOWTH, -S n Scots word meaning plenty of scope

SCOWTHER vb Scots word meaning scorch

SCOWTHS ▶ scowth

SCOZZA, -S n rowdy person, esp one who drinks a lot of alcohol

SCRAB, -BED, -S vb scratch

SCRABBLE vb scrape at with the hands, feet, or claws ▷ n board game in which words are formed by letter tiles

SCRABBLY adj covered with stunted trees

SCRABS ▶ scrab

SCRAE, -S Scots word for ▶ scree

SCRAG, -GED, -S n thin end of a neck of mutton ▷ vb wring the neck of

SCRAGGLY adj untidy or irregular

SCRAGGY adj thin, bony

SCRAGS ▶ scrag

SCRAICH, -S vb Scots word meaning scream

SCRAIGH, -S same as ▶ scraich

SCRAM, -MED, -S vb go away quickly ▷ n emergency shutdown of a nuclear reactor

SCRAMB, -ED, -S vb scratch with nails or claws

SCRAMBLE vb climb or crawl hastily or awkwardly ▷ n scrambling

SCRAMBS ▶ scramb

SCRAMJET n type of jet engine

SCRAMMED ▶ scram

SCRAMS ▶ scram

SCRAN, -S n food

SCRANCH vb crunch

SCRANNEL adj thin ▷ n thin person or thing

SCRANNY adj scrawny

SCRANS ▶ scran

SCRAP, -PED, -S n small piece ▷ vb discard as useless

SCRAPE, -D, -S vb rub with something rough or sharp ▷ n act or sound of scraping

SCRAPER, -S ▶ scrape

SCRAPES ▶ scrape

SCRAPIE, -S n disease of sheep and goats

SCRAPING n act of scraping

SCRAPPED ▶ scrap

SCRAPPER n person who scraps

SCRAPPLE n scraps of pork cooked with cornmeal and formed into a loaf

SCRAPPY adj fragmentary, disjointed

SCRAPS ▶ scrap

SCRAT, -S, -TED vb scratch

SCRATCH vb mark or cut with anything rough or sharp ▷ n wound, mark, or sound made by scratching ▷ adj put together at short notice

SCRATCHY ▶ scratch

SCRATS ▶ scrat

SCRATTED ▶ scrat

SCRATTLE vb dialect word meaning scratch

SCRAUCH, -S vb squawk

SCRAUGH, -S vb squawk

SCRAVEL, -S vb move quickly

SCRAW, -S n sod from the surface of a peat bog or from a field

SCRAWB | 612

SCRAWB, -ED, -S *same as*
▸**scrob**

SCRAWL, -ED, -S *vb* write
carelessly or hastily ▸ *n*
scribbled writing

SCRAWLER ▸**scrawl**

SCRAWLS ▸**scrawl**

SCRAWLY ▸**scrawl**

SCRAWM, -ED, -S *vb* dialect
word meaning scratch

SCRAWNY *adj* thin and bony

SCRAWP, -ED, -S *vb* scratch
(the skin) to relieve itching

SCRAWS ▸**scraw**

SCRAY, -S *n* tern

SCRAYE, -S *n* tern

SCRAYS ▸**scray**

SCREAK, -ED, -S *vb* screech
or creak ▸ *n* screech or creak

SCREAKY ▸**screak**

SCREAM, -ED, -S *vb* utter a
piercing cry, esp of fear or
pain ▸ *n* shrill piercing cry

SCREAMER *n* person or
thing that screams

SCREAMO, -S *n* type of emo
music featuring screaming
vocals

SCREAMS ▸**scream**

SCREE, -S *n* slope of loose
shifting stones

SCREECH *n* shrill cry ▸ *vb*
utter a shrill cry

SCREECHY *adj* loud and
shrill

SCREED, -ED, -S *n* long
tedious piece of writing ▸ *vb*
rip

SCREEDER ▸**screed**

SCREEDS ▸**screed**

SCREEN, -ED, -S *n* surface of
a television set, VDU, etc
▸ *vb* shelter or conceal with
or as if with a screen

SCREENER ▸**screen**

SCREENIE *n* informal
Australian word for
screensaver

SCREENS ▸**screen**

SCREES ▸**scree**

SCREET, -ED, -S *vb* shed
tears ▸ *n* act or sound of
crying

SCREEVE, -D, -S *vb* write

SCREEVER ▸**screeve**

SCREEVES ▸**screeve**

SCREICH, -S *same as* ▸**screigh**

SCREIGH, -S *Scot word for*
▸**screech**

SCREW, -ING, -S *n* metal pin
with a spiral ridge along its
length ▸ *vb* turn (a screw)

SCREWED *adj* fastened by a
screw or screws

SCREWER, -S ▸**screw**

SCREWIER ▸**screwy**

SCREWING ▸**screw**

SCREWS ▸**screw**

SCREWTOP *n* lid with a
threaded rim that is turned
to close it securely

SCREWUP, -S *n* something
done badly

SCREWY, SCREWIER *adj*
odd or eccentric

SCRIBAL ▸**scribe**

SCRIBBLE *vb* write hastily or
illegibly ▸ *n* something
scribbled

SCRIBBLY ▸**scribble**

SCRIBE, -D, -S, SCRIBING *n*
person who copies
documents ▸ *vb* score a line
with a pointed instrument

SCRIBER, -S *n* pointed steel
tool used to score materials
as a guide to cutting, etc

SCRIBES ▸**scribe**

SCRIBING ▸**scribe**

SCRIBISM ▸**scribe**

SCRIECH, -S *vb* Scots word
meaning screech

SCRIED ▸**scry**

SCRIENE, -S *n* old form of
screen

SCRIES ▸**scry**

SCRIEVE, -D, -S *vb* Scots
word meaning write

SCRIGGLE *vb* wriggle

SCRIGGLY ▸**scriggle**

SCRIKE, -D, -S, SCRIKING *vb*
old word meaning shriek

SCRIM, -S *n* open-weave
muslin or hessian fabric

SCRIMP, -ED, -S *vb* be very
economical

SCRIMPER ▸**scrimp**

SCRIMPIT *adj* Scots word
meaning ungenerous

SCRIMPLY *adv* sparingly

SCRIMPS ▸**scrimp**

SCRIMPY ▸**scrimp**

SCRIMS ▸**scrim**

SCRIMURE *old word for*
▸**fencer**

SCRINE, -S *n* old form of
shrine

SCRIP, -S *n* certificate
representing a claim to
stocks or shares

SCRIPT, -ED, -S *n* text of a
film, play, or TV programme
▸ *vb* write a script for

SCRIPTER *n* person who
writes scripts for films, play,
or television dramas

SCRIPTS ▸**script**

SCRITCH *vb* screech

SCRIVE, -D, -S, SCRIVING
Scots word for ▸**write**

SCROB, -BED, -S *vb* scrape
with claws

SCROBBLE *vb* record a
person's music preferences
in order to recommend
similar music

SCROBE, -S *n* groove

SCROBS ▸**scrob**

SCROD, -S *n* young cod or
haddock

SCROFULA *n* tuberculosis of
the lymphatic glands

SCROG, -S *n* Scots word
meaning small tree

SCROGGIE *adj* having scrogs
upon it

SCROGGIN *n* mixture of nuts
and dried fruits

SCROGGY *variant of*
▸**scroggie**

SCROGS ▸**scrog**

SCROLL, -ED, -S *n* roll of
parchment or paper ▸ *vb*
move (text) up or down on a
VDU screen

SCROLLER *n* person or thing
that scrolls

SCROLLS ▸**scroll**

SCROME, -D, -S, SCROMING
vb crawl or climb

SCROOCH *vb* scratch (the
skin) to relieve itching

SCROOGE, -D, -S *variant of*
▸**scrouge**

SCROOP, -ED, -S *vb* emit a
grating or creaking sound
▸ *n* such a sound

SCROOTCH *vb* hunch up

SCRORP, -S *n* deep scratch
or weal

SCROTA ▸**scrotum**

SCROTAL ▸**scrotum**

SCROTUM, SCROTA, -S *n*
pouch of skin containing the
testicles

SCROUGE, -D, -S *vb* crowd
or press

SCROUGER *n* American
word meaning whopper

SCROUGES ▸**scrouge**

SCROUNGE *vb* get by
cadging or begging

SCROUNGY *adj* shabby

SCROW, -S *n* scroll

SCROWDGE *vb* squeeze

SCROWL, -ED, -S *vb* old form
of scroll

SCROWLE, -S *vb* old form of
scroll

SCROWLED ▸**scrowl**

SCROWLES ▸**scrowle**

SCROWLS ▸**scrowl**

SCROWS ▸**scrow**

SCROYLE, -S *n* old word
meaning wretch

SCRUB, -BED, -S *vb* clean by
rubbing, often with a hard
brush and water ▸ *n*

instance of scrubbing ▷ *adj* stunted or inferior

SCRUBBER *n* person or thing that scrubs

SCRUBBY *adj* covered with scrub

SCRUBS ▶ scrub

SCRUFF, -ED, -S same as ▶ scum

SCRUFFY *adj* unkempt or shabby

SCRUM, -MED, -S *n* restarting of play in rugby ▷ *vb* form a scrum

SCRUMMIE *n* informal word for a scrum half

SCRUMMY *adj* delicious

SCRUMP, -ED, -S *vb* steal (apples) from an orchard or garden

SCRUMPLE *vb* crumple or crush

SCRUMPOX *n* skin infection spread among players in scrum

SCRUMPS ▶ scrump

SCRUMPY *n* rough dry cider

SCRUMS ▶ scrum

SCRUNCH *vb* crumple or crunch or be crumpled or crunched ▷ *n* act or sound of scrunching

SCRUNCHY *adj* crunchy

SCRUNT, -S *n* Scots word meaning stunted thing

SCRUNTY ▶ scrunt

SCRUPLE, -D, -S *n* doubt produced by one's conscience or morals ▷ *vb* have doubts on moral grounds

SCRUPLER ▶ scruple

SCRUPLES ▶ scruple

SCRUTINY *n* close examination

SCRUTO, -S *n* trapdoor on stage

SCRUZE, -D, -S, SCRUZING *vb* old word meaning squeeze

SCRY, SCRIED, SCRIES, -DE *vb* divine, esp by crystal gazing

SCRYER, -S ▶ scry

SCRYING, -S ▶ scry

SCRYNE, -S *n* old form of shrine

SCUBA, -ED, -ING, -S *n* apparatus used in diving ▷ *vb* dive using scuba equipment

SCUCHIN, -S *n* old form of scutcheon

SCUD, -DED, -DING, -S *vb* move along swiftly ▷ *n* act of scudding

SCUDDER, -S ▶ scud

SCUDDING ▶ scud

SCUDDLE, -D, -S *vb* scuttle

SCUDI ▶ scudo

SCUDLER, -S *n* Scots word meaning leader of festivities

SCUDO, SCUDI *n* any of several former Italian coins

SCUDS ▶ scud

SCUFF, -ED, -ING, -S *vb* drag (the feet) while walking ▷ *n* mark caused by scuffing

SCUFFER, -S *n* type of sandal

SCUFFING ▶ scuff

SCUFFLE, -D, -S *vb* fight in a disorderly manner ▷ *n* disorderly struggle

SCUFFLER ▶ scuffle

SCUFFLES ▶ scuffle

SCUFFS ▶ scuff

SCUFT, -S *n* dialect word meaning nape of neck

SCUG, -GED, -GING, -S *vb* shelter

SCUL, -S *n* old form of school

SCULCH, -ES *n* rubbish

SCULK, -ED, -ING, -S *vb* old form of skulk

SCULKER, -S ▶ sculk

SCULKING ▶ sculk

SCULKS ▶ sculk

SCULL, -ED, -ING, -S *n* small oar ▷ *vb* row (a boat) using sculls

SCULLE, -S *n* old form of school

SCULLED ▶ scull

SCULLER, -S ▶ scull

SCULLERY *n* small room where washing-up and other kitchen work is done

SCULLES ▶ sculle

SCULLING ▶ scull

SCULLION *n* servant employed to do the hard work in a kitchen

SCULLS ▶ scull

SCULP, -ED, -ING, -S *variant of* ▶ sculpture

SCULPIN, -S *n* type of fish of the family which includes bullheads and sea scorpions

SCULPING ▶ sculp

SCULPINS ▶ sculpin

SCULPS ▶ sculp

SCULPSIT *vb* (he or she) sculptured it: used formerly on sculptures next to a sculptor's name

SCULPT, -ED, -S same as ▶ sculpture

SCULPTOR *n* person who makes sculptures

SCULPTS ▶ sculpt

SCULS ▶ scul

SCULTCH same as ▶ sculch

SCUM, -MED, -MING, -S *n* impure or waste matter on the surface of a liquid ▷ *vb* remove scum from

SCUMBER, -S *vb* old word meaning defecate

SCUMBLE, -D, -S *vb* soften or blend (an outline or colour) with a thin upper coat of opaque colour ▷ *n* upper layer of colour applied in this way

SCUMFISH *vb* Scots word meaning disgust

SCUMLESS ▶ scum

SCUMLIKE ▶ scum

SCUMMED ▶ scum

SCUMMER, -S ▶ scum

SCUMMIER ▶ scummy

SCUMMILY ▶ scummy

SCUMMING ▶ scum

SCUMMY, SCUMMIER *adj* of, resembling, consisting of, or covered with scum

SCUMS ▶ scum

SCUNGE, -D, -S, SCUNGING *vb* borrow ▷ *n* dirty or worthless person

SCUNGIER ▶ scungy

SCUNGILE same as ▶ scungille

SCUNGILI same as ▶ scungilli

SCUNGING ▶ scunge

SCUNGY, SCUNGIER *adj* sordid or dirty

SCUNNER, -S *vb* Scot word meaning to feel aversion ▷ *n* strong aversion

SCUP, -S *n* common sparid fish of American coastal regions of the Atlantic

SCUPPAUG *n* sea fish

SCUPPER, -S *vb* defeat or ruin ▷ *n* drain in the side of a ship

SCUPS ▶ scup

SCUR, -RED, -RING, -S *n* small unattached growth of horn at the site of a normal horn in cattle

SCURF, -S *n* flaky skin on the scalp

SCURFIER ▶ scurfy

SCURFS ▶ scurf

SCURFY, SCURFIER ▶ scurf

SCURRED ▶ scur

SCURRIED ▶ scurry

SCURRIER *n* old word meaning scout

SCURRIES ▶ scurry

SCURRIL *adj* old word meaning vulgar

SCURRILE *adj* old word meaning vulgar

SCURRING ▶ scur

S

SCURRY, SCURRIED, SCURRIES vb move hastily ▷ n act or sound of scurrying

SCURS ▶ scur

SCURVIER ▶ scurvy

SCURVIES ▶ scurvy

SCURVILY ▶ scurvy

SCURVY, SCURVIER, SCURVIES n disease caused by lack of vitamin C ▷ adj mean and despicable

SCUSE, -D, -S, SCUSING shortened form of ▶ excuse

SCUT, -S n short tail of the hare, rabbit, or deer

SCUTA ▶ scutum

SCUTAGE, -S n payment to a lord from his vassal in lieu of military service

SCUTAL ▶ scute

SCUTATE adj (of animals) having or covered with large bony or horny plates

SCUTCH, -ED, -ES vb separate the fibres from the woody part of (flax) by pounding ▷ n tool used for this

SCUTCHER same as ▶ scutch

SCUTCHES ▶ scutch

SCUTE, -S n horny or chitinous plate that makes up part of the exoskeleton in armadillos, etc

SCUTELLA > scutellum

SCUTES ▶ scute

SCUTIGER n species of centipede

SCUTS ▶ scut

SCUTTER, -S informal word for ▶ scurry

SCUTTLE, -D, -S n fireside container for coal ▷ vb run with short quick steps

SCUTTLER ▶ scuttle

SCUTTLES ▶ scuttle

SCUTUM, SCUTA n middle of three plates into which the notum of an insect's thorax is divided

SCUTWORK n menial or dull work

SCUZZ, -ES n dirt

SCUZZY, SCUZZIER adj unkempt, dirty, or squalid

SCYBALUM, SCYBALA n hard faeces in stomach

SCYE, -S n Scots word meaning sleeve-hole

SCYPHATE adj shaped like cup

SCYPHUS, SCYPHI n ancient Greek two-handled drinking cup

SCYTALE, -S n coded message in ancient Sparta

SCYTHE, -D, -S, SCYTHING n long-handled tool with a curved blade for cutting grass ▷ vb cut with a scythe

SCYTHER, -S ▶ scythe

SCYTHES ▶ scythe

SCYTHING ▶ scythe

SDAINE, -D, -S, SDAINING vb old form of disdain

SDAYN, -ED, -ING, -S vb old form of disdain

SDEIGN, -ED, -S vb old form of disdain

SDEIGNE, -S vb old form of disdain

SDEIGNED ▶ sdeign

SDEIGNES ▶ sdeign

SDEIGNS ▶ sdeign

SDEIN, -ED, -ING, -S vb old form of disdain

SEA, -S n mass of salt water covering three quarters of the earth's surface

SEABAG, -S n canvas bag for holding a sailor's belongings

SEABANK, -S n sea shore

SEABEACH n beach at seaside

SEABED, -S n bottom of sea

SEABIRD, -S n bird that lives on the sea

SEABLITE n prostrate annual plant of the goosefoot family

SEABOARD n coast

SEABOOT, -S n sailor's waterproof boot

SEABORNE adj carried on or by the sea

SEABREAM n type of food fish of European seas

SEACOAST, -S n land bordering on the sea

SEACOCK, -S n valve in the hull of a vessel below the water line

SEACRAFT n skill of a sailor

SEACUNNY n steersman on an Indian ship

SEADOG, -S n another word for ▶ fogbow

SEADROME n aerodrome floating on sea

SEAFARER n traveller who goes by sea

SEAFLOOR n bottom of the sea

SEAFOAM, -S n foam formed on the sea

SEAFOLK, -S n people who sail the sea

SEAFOOD, -S n edible saltwater fish or shellfish

SEAFOWL, -S n seabird

SEAFRONT, -S n built-up area facing the sea

SEAGIRT adj surrounded by the sea

SEAGOING adj built for travelling on the sea

SEAGRASS n grass which grows by or in the sea

SEAGULL, -S n gull

SEAHAWK, -S n skua

SEAHOG, -S n porpoise

SEAHORSE n marine fish with a horselike head that swims upright

SEAHOUND n dogfish

SEAKALE, -S n European coastal plant

SEAL, -S n piece of wax, etc attached to a document as a mark of authentication ▷ vb close with or as if with a seal

SEALABLE ▶ seal

SEALANT, -S n any substance used for sealing

SEALCH, -S Scots word for ▶ seal

SEALED adj (of a road) having a hard surface

SEALER, -S n person or thing that seals

SEALERY n occupation of hunting seals

SEALGH, -S Scots word for ▶ seal

SEALIFT, -S vb transport by ship

SEALINE, -S n company running regular sailings

SEALING, -S ▶ seal

SEALLIKE adj resembling a seal

SEALS ▶ seal

SEALSKIN n skin or prepared fur of a seal, used to make coats

SEALWAX n sealing wax

SEALYHAM n type of short-legged terrier

SEAM, -ED, -ING, -S n line where two edges are joined, as by stitching ▷ vb mark with furrows or wrinkles

SEAMAID, -S n mermaid

SEAMAN, SEAMEN n sailor

SEAMANLY adj like or appropriate to a seaman

SEAMARK, -S n conspicuous object on a shore used as a guide

SEAME, -S n old word meaning grease

SEAMED ▶ seam

SEAMEN ▶ seaman

SEAMER, -S n bowler who makes the ball bounce on its seam

SEAMES ▶ seame

SEAMFREE adj having no seam

SEAMIER ▸ seamy

SEAMIEST ▸ seamy

SEAMING, -S ▸ seam

SEAMLESS adj (of a garment) without seams

SEAMLIKE ▸ seam

SEAMOUNT n submarine mountain rising more than 1000 metres above the surrounding ocean floor

SEAMS ▸ seam

SEAMSET, -S n tool for flattening seams in metal

SEAMSTER n person who sews

SEAMY, SEAMIER, SEAMIEST adj sordid

SEAN, -ED, -ING, -S vb fish with seine net

SEANCE, -S n meeting at which spiritualists attempt to communicate with the dead

SEANED ▸ sean

SEANING ▸ sean

SEANS ▸ sean

SEAPIECE n artwork depicting sea

SEAPLANE n aircraft designed to take off from and land on water

SEAPORT, -S n town or city with a harbour for boats and ships

SEAQUAKE n agitation and disturbance of the sea caused by an earthquake at the sea bed

SEAR, -ED, -ER, -EST, -S vb scorch, burn the surface of ▸ n mark caused by searing ▸ adj dried up

SEARAT, -S n pirate

SEARCE, -D, -S, SEARCING vb sift

SEARCH, -ED, -ES vb examine closely in order to find something ▸ n instance of searching

SEARCHER ▸ search

SEARCHES ▸ search

SEARCING ▸ searce

SEARE adj old word meaning dry and withered

SEARED ▸ sear

SEARER ▸ sear

SEAREST ▸ sear

SEARING, -S ▸ sear

SEARNESS ▸ sear

SEAROBIN n type of American gurnard

SEARS ▸ sear

SEAS ▸ sea

SEASCAPE n picture of a scene at sea

SEASCOUT n member of seagoing scouts

SEASE, -D, -S, SEASING vb old form of seize

SEASHELL n empty shell of a mollusc

SEASHORE n land bordering on the sea

SEASICK adj suffering from nausea caused by the motion of a ship

SEASIDE, -S n area, esp a holiday resort, on the coast

SEASING ▸ sease

SEASON, -S n one of four divisions of the year ▸ vb flavour with salt, herbs, etc

SEASONAL adj depending on or varying with the seasons ▸ n seasonal thing

SEASONED ▸ season

SEASONER ▸ season

SEASONS ▸ season

SEASPEAK n language used by sailors

SEASURE, -S n old form of seizure

SEAT, -ED, -S n thing designed or used for sitting on ▸ vb cause to sit

SEATBACK n back of seat

SEATBELT n safety belt in vehicle

SEATED ▸ seat

SEATER, -S n person or thing that seats

SEATING, -S n supply or arrangement of seats ▸ adj of or relating to the provision of places to sit

SEATLESS ▸ seat

SEATMATE n person sitting in next seat

SEATRAIN n ship that can carry a train

SEATROUT n trout living in the sea

SEATS ▸ seat

SEATWORK n school work done at pupils' desks

SEAWALL, -S n wall built to prevent encroachment or erosion by the sea

SEAWAN, -S n shell beads used by certain Native Americans as money

SEAWANT, -S n Native American name for silver coins

SEAWARD same as ▸ seawards

SEAWARDS adv towards the sea

SEAWARE, -S n any of numerous large coarse seaweeds

SEAWATER n water from sea

SEAWAY, -S n waterway giving access to an inland port

SEAWEED, -S n plant growing in the sea

SEAWEEDY adj full of seaweed

SEAWIFE, SEAWIVES n variety of sea fish

SEAWOMAN, SEAWOMEN n sailor

SEAWORM, -S n marine worm

SEAZE, -D, -S, SEAZING vb old form of seize

SEBACIC adj derived from sebacic acid, a white crystalline acid

SEBASIC same as ▸ sebacic

SEBATE, -S n salt of sebacic acid

SEBESTEN n Asian tree

SEBIFIC adj producing fat

SEBUM, -S n oily substance secreted by the sebaceous glands

SEBUNDY n irregular soldier in India

SEC, -S same as ▸ secant

SECALOSE n type of sugar

SECANT, -S n the ratio of the length of the hypotenuse to the length of the adjacent side

SECANTLY ▸ secant

SECANTS ▸ secant

SECATEUR n secateurs

SECCO, -S n wall painting done on dried plaster with tempera

SECEDE, -D, -S, SECEDING vb withdraw formally from a political alliance or federation

SECEDER, -S ▸ secede

SECEDES ▸ secede

SECEDING ▸ secede

SECERN, -ED, -S vb (of a gland or follicle) to secrete

SECESH, -ES n secessionist in US Civil War

SECESHER n secessionist in US Civil War

SECESHES ▸ secesh

SECH, -S n hyperbolic secant

SECKEL, -S variant of ▸ seckle

SECKLE, -S n type of pear

SECLUDE, -S vb keep (a person) from contact with others

SECLUDED adj private, sheltered

SECLUDES ▸ seclude

SECO adj (of wine) dry

S

SECODONT n animal with cutting back teeth

SECONAL, -S n tradename for secobarbital

SECOND, -ED, -S adj coming directly after the first ▷ n person or thing coming second ▷ vb express formal support for (a motion proposed in a meeting)

SECONDE, -S n second of eight positions from which a parry or attack can be made in fencing

SECONDED ▶ **second**

SECONDEE n person who is seconded

SECONDER ▶ **second**

SECONDES ▶ **seconde**

SECONDI ▶ **secondo**

SECONDLY adv in the second place or position

SECONDO, SECONDI n left-hand part in a piano duet

SECONDS ▶ **second**

SECPAR, -S n distance unit in astronomy

SECRECY n state of being secret

SECRET, -ER, -S adj kept from the knowledge of others ▷ n something kept secret

SECRETA n secretions

SECRETE, -D, -S vb (of an organ, gland, etc) produce and release (a substance)

SECRETER ▶ **secret**

SECRETES ▶ **secrete**

SECRETIN n peptic hormone secreted by the mucosae of the duodenum and jejunum

SECRETLY ▶ **secret**

SECRETOR ▶ **secrete**

SECRETS ▶ **secret**

SECS ▶ **sec**

SECT, -S n subdivision of a religious or political group

SECTARY n member of a sect

SECTATOR n member of sect

SECTILE adj able to be cut smoothly

SECTION, -S n part cut off ▷ vb cut or divide into sections

SECTOR, -ED, -S n part or subdivision of a nation ▷ vb divide into sectors

SECTORAL ▶ **sector**

SECTORED ▶ **sector**

SECTORS ▶ **sector**

SECTS ▶ **sect**

SECULA ▶ **seculum**

SECULAR, -S adj worldly, as opposed to sacred ▷ n member of the secular clergy

SECULUM, SECULA, -S n age in astronomy

SECUND adj having or designating parts arranged on or turned to one side of the axis

SECUNDLY ▶ **secund**

SECUNDUM adj according to

SECURE, -D, -S, -ST, SECURING adj free from danger ▷ vb obtain

SECURELY ▶ **secure**

SECURER, -S ▶ **secure**

SECURES ▶ **secure**

SECUREST ▶ **secure**

SECURING ▶ **secure**

SECURITY n precautions against theft, espionage, or other danger

SED old spelling of ▶ **said**

SEDAN, -S same as ▶ **saloon**

SEDATE, -D, -R, -S, -ST, SEDATING adj calm and dignified ▷ vb give a sedative drug to

SEDATELY ▶ **sedate**

SEDATER ▶ **sedate**

SEDATES ▶ **sedate**

SEDATEST ▶ **sedate**

SEDATING ▶ **sedate**

SEDATION n state of calm, esp when brought about by sedatives

SEDATIVE adj having a soothing or calming effect ▷ n sedative drug

SEDENT adj seated

SEDER, SEDARIM, -S n Jewish ceremonial meal held on the first night or first two nights of Passover

SEDERUNT n sitting of an ecclesiastical assembly, court, etc

SEDES Latin word for ▶ **seat**

SEDGE, -S n coarse grasslike plant growing on wet ground

SEDGED adj having sedge

SEDGES ▶ **sedge**

SEDGY, SEDGIER, SEDGIEST ▶ **sedge**

SEDILE n seat for clergy in church

SEDILIA n group of three seats where the celebrant and ministers sit during High Mass

SEDILIUM n seat for clergy in church

SEDIMENT n matter which settles to the bottom of a liquid

SEDITION n speech or action encouraging rebellion against the government

SEDUCE, -D, -S, SEDUCING vb win over or attract

SEDUCER, -S n person who entices, allures, or seduces

SEDUCES ▶ **seduce**

SEDUCING ▶ **seduce**

SEDUCIVE adj seductive

SEDUCTOR n person who seduces

SEDULITY ▶ **sedulous**

SEDULOUS adj diligent or persevering

SEDUM, -S n rock plant

SEE, -N, -S vb perceive with the eyes or mind ▷ n diocese of a bishop

SEEABLE ▶ **see**

SEECATCH n male seal in Aleutians

SEED, -ED, -S n mature fertilized grain of a plant ▷ vb sow with seed

SEEDBED, -S n area of soil prepared for the growing of seedlings before they are transplanted

SEEDBOX n part of plant that contains seeds

SEEDCAKE n sweet cake flavoured with caraway seeds and lemon rind or essence

SEEDCASE n part of a fruit enclosing the seeds

SEEDED ▶ **seed**

SEEDER, -S n person or thing that seeds

SEEDHEAD n seed-containing part of a plant

SEEDIER ▶ **seedy**

SEEDIEST ▶ **seedy**

SEEDILY ▶ **seedy**

SEEDING, -S ▶ **seed**

SEEDLESS ▶ **seed**

SEEDLIKE ▶ **seed**

SEEDLING n young plant raised from a seed

SEEDLIP, -S n basket holding seeds to be sown

SEEDMAN, SEEDMEN n seller of seeds

SEEDNESS n old word meaning sowing of seeds

SEEDPOD, -S n carpel enclosing the seeds of a flowering plant

SEEDS ▶ **seed**

SEEDSMAN, SEEDSMEN n seller of seeds

SEEDTIME n season when seeds are sown

SEEDY, SEEDIER, SEEDIEST adj shabby

SEEING, -S ▶ **see**

SEEK, -ING, -S, SOUGHT vb try to find or obtain

SEEKER, -S ▸ seek

SEEKING ▸ seek

SEEKS ▸ seek

SEEL, -ED, -S vb sew up the eyelids of (a hawk or falcon) so as to render it tame

SEELD adj old word meaning rare

SEELED ▸ seel

SEELIE pl n good benevolent fairies

SEELIER ▸ seely

SEELIEST ▸ seely

SEELING, -S ▸ seel

SEELS ▸ seel

SEELY, SEELIER, SEELIEST adj old word meaning happy

SEEM, -ED, -S vb appear to be

SEEMER, -S ▸ seem

SEEMING, -S adj apparent but not real ▷ n outward or false appearance

SEEMLESS adj old word meaning unseemly

SEEMLY, SEEMLIER adj proper or fitting ▷ adv properly or decorously

SEEMS ▸ seem

SEEN ▸ see

SEEP, -ED, -ING, -S vb trickle through slowly, ooze ▷ n small spring or place where water, oil, etc, has oozed through the ground

SEEPAGE, -S n act or process of seeping

SEEPED ▸ seep

SEEPIER ▸ seepy

SEEPIEST ▸ seepy

SEEPING ▸ seep

SEEPS ▸ seep

SEEPY, SEEPIER, SEEPIEST adj tending to seep

SEER, -S n person who sees

SEERESS ▸ seer

SEERS ▸ seer

SEES ▸ see

SEESAW, -ED, -S n plank balanced in the middle so that two people seated on either end ride up and down alternately ▷ vb move up and down

SEETHE, -D, -S vb be very agitated ▷ n act or state of seething

SEETHER, -S ▸ seethe

SEETHES ▸ seethe

SEETHING adj boiling or foaming as if boiling

SEEWING, -S n suing

SEFER, SIFREI n scrolls of the Law

SEG, -S n metal stud on shoe sole

SEGAR, -S n cigar

SEGETAL adj (of weeds) growing amongst crops

SEGGAR, -S n box in which pottery is baked

SEGHOL, -S n pronunciation mark in Hebrew

SEGMENT, -S n one of several sections into which something may be divided ▷ vb divide into segments

SEGNO, SEGNI, -S n sign at the beginning or end of a section directed to be repeated

SEGO, -S n American variety of lily

SEGOL, -S variant of ▸ seghol

SEGOLATE variant of > segholate

SEGOLS ▸ segol

SEGOS ▸ sego

SEGREANT adj having raised wings in heraldry

SEGS ▸ seg

SEGUE, -D, -ING, -S vb proceed from one section or piece of music to another without a break ▷ n practice or an instance of playing music in this way

SEGUGIO, -S n Italian breed of dog

SEHRI, -S n meal eaten before sunrise by Muslims fasting during Ramadan

SEI, -S n type of rorqual

SEICENTO n 17th century with reference to Italian art and literature

SEICHE, -S n periodic oscillation of the surface of an enclosed or partially enclosed body of water

SEIDEL, -S n vessel for drinking beer

SEIF, -S n long ridge of blown sand in a desert

SEIGNEUR n feudal lord

SEIGNIOR n (in England) the lord of a seigniory

SEIGNORY n lordship

SEIK, -ER, -EST Scot word for ▸ sick

SEIL, -ED, -ING, -S vb dialect word meaning strain

SEINE, -D, -S n large fishing net that hangs vertically from floats ▷ vb catch (fish) using this net

SEINER, -S ▸ seine

SEINES ▸ seine

SEINING, -S ▸ seine

SEIR, -S n fish of Indian seas

SEIS ▸ sei

SEISABLE ▸ seise

SEISE, -D, -S vb put into legal possession of (property, etc)

SEISER, -S ▸ seise

SEISES ▸ seise

SEISIN, -S n feudal possession of an estate in land

SEISING, -S ▸ seise

SEISINS ▸ seisin

SEISM, -S n earthquake

SEISMAL adj of earthquakes

SEISMIC adj relating to earthquakes

SEISMISM n occurrence of earthquakes

SEISMS ▸ seism

SEISOR, -S n person who takes seisin

SEISURE, -S n act of seisin

SEITAN, -S same as ▸ seiten

SEITEN, -S n gluten from wheat

SEITY, SEITIES n selfhood

SEIZA, -S n traditional Japanese kneeling position

SEIZABLE ▸ seize

SEIZAS ▸ seiza

SEIZE, -D, -S vb take hold of forcibly or quickly

SEIZER, -S ▸ seize

SEIZES ▸ seize

SEIZIN, -S same as ▸ seisin

SEIZING, -S n binding used for holding together two ropes, two spars, etc

SEIZINS ▸ seizin

SEIZOR, -S n person who takes seisin

SEIZURE, -S n sudden violent attack of an illness

SEJANT adj (of a beast) shown seated

SEJEANT same as ▸ sejant

SEKOS, -ES n holy place

SEKT, -S n German sparkling wine

SEL, -S Scot word for ▸ self

SELADANG n Malaysian tapir

SELAH, -S n Hebrew word of unknown meaning occurring in the Old Testament psalms

SELAMLIK n men's quarters in Turkish house

SELCOUTH adj old word meaning strange

SELD adj old word meaning rare

SELDOM adv not often, rarely

SELDOMLY ▸ seldom

SELDSEEN adj old word meaning seldom seen

SELE, -S n old word meaning happiness

S

SELECT, -ED, -S vb pick out or choose ▷ adj chosen in preference to others

SELECTA, -S n disc jockey

SELECTED ▶ select

SELECTEE n person who is selected, esp for military service

SELECTLY ▶ select

SELECTOR n person or thing that selects

SELECTS ▶ select

SELENATE n any salt or ester formed by replacing one or both of the hydrogens of selenic acid with metal ions or organic groups

SELENIAN adj of the moon

SELENIC adj of or containing selenium, esp in the hexavalent state

SELENIDE n compound containing selenium

SELENITE n colourless glassy variety of gypsum

SELENIUM n nonmetallic element with photoelectric properties

SELENOUS same as > selenious

SELES ▶ sele

SELF, -ED, -S, SELVES n distinct individuality or identity of a person or thing ▷ pron myself, yourself, himself, or herself ▷ vb reproduce by oneself

SELFDOM, -S n selfhood

SELFED ▶ self

SELFHEAL n low-growing European herbaceous plant

SELFHOOD n state of having a distinct identity

SELFIE, -S n photograph taken by pointing a camera at oneself

SELFING, -S ▶ self

SELFISH adj caring too much about oneself and not enough about others

SELFISM, -S n emphasis on self

SELFIST, -S ▶ selfism

SELFLESS adj unselfish

SELFNESS n egotism

SELFS ▶ self

SELFSAME adj very same

SELFWARD adj toward self

SELICTAR n Turkish sword-bearer

SELKIE, -S same as ▶ silkie

SELL, -S vb exchange (something) for money ▷ n manner of selling

SELLA, -E, -S n area of bone in body

SELLABLE ▶ sell

SELLAE ▶ sella

SELLAS ▶ sella

SELLE, -S n old word meaning seat

SELLER, -S n person who sells

SELLES ▶ selle

SELLING, -S n providing goods or services to customers in exchange for money

SELLOFF, -S n act of selling cheaply

SELLOUT, -S n performance of a show etc for which all the tickets are sold

SELLS ▶ sell

SELS ▶ sel

SELSYN, -S same as ▶ synchro

SELTZER, -S n natural effervescent water containing minerals

SELVA, -S n dense equatorial forest

SELVAGE, -D, -S n edge of cloth, woven so as to prevent unravelling ▷ vb edge or border

SELVAGEE n rope used as strap

SELVAGES ▶ selvage

SELVAS ▶ selva

SELVEDGE same as ▶ selvage

SELVES ▶ self

SEMANTIC adj relating to the meaning of words

SEMANTRA > semantron

SEMATIC adj acting as a warning, esp to potential predators

SEMBLANT n semblance

SEMBLE, -D, -S, SEMBLING vb seem

SEME, -S adj dotted (with)

SEMEE variant of ▶ seme

SEMEED adj seme

SEMEION, SEMEIA n unit of metre in ancient poetry

SEMEME, -S n meaning of a morpheme

SEMEMIC ▶ sememe

SEMEN, -S, SEMINA n sperm-carrying fluid produced by male animals

SEMES ▶ seme

SEMESTER vb organize the academic year into two divisions

SEMI n semidetached house

SEMIARID adj denoting land that lies on the edges of a desert but has a slightly higher rainfall

SEMIBALD adj partly bald

SEMIBOLD adj denoting a weight of typeface between medium and bold face ▷ n semibold type

SEMIBULL n papal bull issued before coronation

SEMICOMA n condition similar to a coma

SEMIDEAF adj partly deaf

SEMIDOME n half-dome, esp one used to cover a semicircular apse

SEMIDRY adj partly dry

SEMIE, -S n historical name for a student in second year at a Scottish university

SEMIFIT adj not fully fit

SEMIGALA adj characterized by quite a lot of celebration and fun ▷ n occasion that is festive but not to the degree of a gala

SEMIHARD adj partly hard

SEMIHIGH adj moderately high

SEMIHOBO n person looking almost like hobo

SEMILLON n grape used to make wine

SEMILOG adj semilogarithmic

SEMILUNE n half-moon shape

SEMIMAT adj semimatt

SEMIMATT adj with surface midway between matt and gloss

SEMIMILD adj somewhat mild

SEMINA ▶ semen

SEMINAL adj original and influential

SEMINAR, -S n meeting of a group of students for discussion

SEMINARY n college for priests

SEMINATE vb sow

SEMINUDE adj partly nude

SEMIOPEN adj half-open

SEMIOSIS, SEMIOSES n action involving establishing a relationship between signs

SEMIOTIC adj relating to signs and symbols, esp spoken or written signs

SEMIOVAL adj shaped like half of an oval

SEMIPED, -S n measure in poetic metre

SEMIPRO, -S n semiprofessional

SEMIRAW adj not fully cooked or processed

SEMIS, -ES n ancient Roman coin

SEMISOFT adj partly soft

SEMITAR, -S old spelling of ▶scimitar

SEMITAUR old spelling of ▶scimitar

SEMITIST n student of Semitic languages and culture

SEMITONE n smallest interval between two notes in Western music

SEMIWILD adj not fully domesticated

SEMMIT, -S n Scots word meaning a vest

SEMOLINA n hard grains of wheat left after the milling of flour, used to make puddings and pasta

SEMPER adv Latin word meaning always

SEMPLE, -R, -ST adj Scots word meaning simple

SEMPLICE adv performed in a simple manner

SEMPRE adv (preceding a tempo or dynamic marking) always

SEMPSTER n person who sews

SEMSEM, -S n sesame

SEMUNCIA n ancient Roman coin

SEN, -S n monetary unit of Brunei, Cambodia, Indonesia, and Malaysia

SENA, -S n (in India) the army

SENARIES ▶senary

SENARIUS, SENARII n type of poem

SENARY, SENARIES adj of or relating to the number six

SENAS ▶sena

SENATE, -S n main governing body at some universities

SENATOR, -S n member of a senate

SEND, -S vb cause (a person or thing) to go to or be taken or transmitted to a place

SENDABLE ▶send

SENDAL, -S n fine silk fabric used for ceremonial clothing, etc

SENDED vb old word meaning sent

SENDER, -S ▶send

SENDING, -S ▶send

SENDOFF, -S n demonstration of good wishes at a person's departure ▷ vb dispatch (something, such as a letter)

SENDS ▶send

SENDUP, -S n parody or imitation

SENE, -S n money unit in Samoa

SENECA, -S variant of ▶senega

SENECIO, -S n type of plant of the genus which includes groundsels and ragworts

SENEGA, -S n milkwort plant of the eastern US

SENES ▶sene

SENESCE, -D, -S vb grow old

SENGI, -S n African shrew

SENGREEN n house leek

SENHOR, -ES, -S n Portuguese term of address for man

SENHORA, -S n Portuguese term of address for woman

SENHORES ▶senhor

SENHORS ▶senhor

SENILE, -S adj mentally or physically weak because of old age ▷ n senile person

SENILELY adv ▶senile

SENILES ▶senile

SENILITY ▶senile

SENIOR, -S adj superior in rank or standing ▷ n senior person

SENITI, -S n money unit in Tonga

SENNA, -S n tropical plant

SENNET, -S n fanfare: used as a stage direction in Elizabethan drama

SENNIGHT archaic word for ▶week

SENNIT, -S n flat braided cordage used on ships

SENOPIA, -S n short-sightedness in old age

SENOR, -ES, -S n Spanish term of address equivalent to sir or Mr

SENORA, -S n Spanish term of address equivalent to madam or Mrs

SENORES ▶senor

SENORITA n Spanish term of address equivalent to madam or Miss

SENORS ▶senor

SENRYU n Japanese short poem

SENS ▶sen

SENSA ▶sensum

SENSATE, -D, -S adj perceived by the senses ▷ vb make sensate

SENSE, -D, -S n any of the faculties of perception or feeling ▷ vb perceive

SENSEFUL adj full of sense

SENSEI, -S n martial arts teacher

SENSES ▶sense

SENSI, -S same as ▶sensei

SENSIBLE adj having or showing good sense ▷ n sensible thing or person

SENSIBLY ▶sensible

SENSILE adj capable of feeling

SENSILLA > sensillum

SENSING, -S ▶sense

SENSIS ▶sensi

SENSISM, -S n theory that ideas spring from senses

SENSIST, -S ▶sensism

SENSOR, -S n device that detects or measures the presence of something, such as radiation

SENSORIA > sensorium

SENSORS ▶sensor

SENSORY adj of the senses or sensation

SENSUAL adj giving pleasure to the body and senses rather than the mind

SENSUM, SENSA n sensation detached from the information it conveys

SENSUOUS adj pleasing to the senses

SENT, -ED, -I, -ING, -S n former monetary unit of Estonia ▷ vb old spelling of scent

SENTE n money unit in Lesotho

SENTED ▶sent

SENTENCE n sequence of words capable of standing alone as a statement, question, or command ▷ vb pass sentence on (a convicted person)

SENTI ▶sent

SENTIENT adj capable of feeling ▷ n sentient person or thing

SENTIMO, -S n money unit in Philippines

SENTINEL n sentry ▷ vb guard as a sentinel

SENTING ▶sent

SENTRY, SENTRIES n soldier on watch

SENTS ▶sent

SENVY, SENVIES n mustard

SENZA prep without

SEPAD, -DED, -S vb suppose

SEPAL, -S n leaflike division of the calyx of a flower

SEPALED ▶sepal

SEPALINE same as ▶sepaloid

SEPALLED ▶sepal

SEPALODY n changing of a flower part into a sepal

SEPALOID adj (esp of petals) resembling a sepal in structure and function

S

SEPALOUS adj with sepals

SEPALS ▶ sepal

SEPARATA > separatum

SEPARATE vb act as a barrier between ▷ adj not the same, different ▷ n item of clothing that only covers half the body

SEPHEN, -S n stingray

SEPIA, -S n reddish-brown pigment ▷ adj dark reddish-brown

SEPIC adj of sepia

SEPIMENT n hedge

SEPIOST, -S n cuttlefish bone

SEPIUM, -S n cuttlefish bone

SEPMAG adj designating a film, etc for which the sound is recorded on separate magnetic material

SEPOY, -S n (formerly) Indian soldier in the service of the British

SEPPUKU, -S n Japanese ritual suicide

SEPS n species of lizard

SEPSIS, SEPSES n poisoning caused by pus-forming bacteria

SEPT, -S n clan, esp in Ireland or Scotland

SEPTA ▶ septum

SEPTAGE, -S n waste removed from septic tank

SEPTAL adj of or relating to a septum

SEPTARIA > septarium

SEPTATE adj divided by septa

SEPTET, -S n group of seven performers

SEPTETTE same as ▶ septet

SEPTIC, -S adj (of a wound) infected ▷ n infected wound

SEPTICAL ▶ septic

SEPTICS ▶ septic

SEPTIMAL adj of number seven

SEPTIME, -S n seventh of eight basic positions from which a parry can be made in fencing

SEPTLEVA n gambling term from old card game

SEPTORIA n any of various parasitic fungi

SEPTS ▶ sept

SEPTUM, SEPTA, -S n dividing partition between two cavities in the body

SEPTUOR, -S n group of seven musicians

SEPTUPLE vb multiply by seven ▷ adj seven times as much or as many ▷ n quantity or number seven times as great as another

SEQUEL, -S n novel, play, or film that continues the story of an earlier one

SEQUELA, -E n disease related to or arising from a pre-existing disease

SEQUELS ▶ sequel

SEQUENCE n arrangement of two or more things in successive order ▷ vb arrange in a sequence

SEQUENCY n number of changes in a mathematical list

SEQUENT, -S adj following in order or succession ▷ n something that follows

SEQUIN, -ED, -S n small ornamental metal disc on a garment ▷ vb apply sequins

SEQUITUR n conclusion that follows from the premises

SEQUOIA, -S n giant Californian coniferous tree

This word for a redwood tree is one of the most frequently played bonuses using the Q, a great one to remember as it also clears out a surplus of vowels.

SER, -S n unit of weight used in India

SERA ▶ serum

SERAC, -S n pinnacle of ice among crevasses on a glacier, usually on a steep slope

SERAFILE n line of soldiers

SERAFIN, -S n old silver coin of Goa

SERAGLIO n sultan's palace

SERAI, -S n caravanserai or inn

SERAIL, -S same as ▶ seraglio

SERAIS ▶ serai

SERAL ▶ sere

SERANG, -S n captain of a crew of sailors in SE Asia

SERAPE, -S n blanket-like shawl often of brightly-coloured wool

SERAPH, -IM, -S n member of the highest order of angels

SERAPHIC adj of or resembling a seraph

SERAPHIM ▶ seraph

SERAPHIN n angel

SERAPHS ▶ seraph

SERDAB, -S n secret chamber in an ancient Egyptian tomb

SERE, -D, -R, -S, -ST, SERING adj dried up or withered ▷ n

series of changes occurring in the ecological succession of a particular community ▷ vb sear

SEREIN, -S n fine rain falling from a clear sky after sunset

SERENADE n music played or sung to a person by an admirer ▷ vb sing or play a serenade to (someone)

SERENATA n 18th-century cantata, often dramatic in form

SERENATE n old form of serenade ▷ vb make serene

SERENE, -D, -R, -S, -ST, SERENING adj calm, peaceful ▷ vb make serene

SERENELY ▶ serene

SERENER ▶ serene

SERENES ▶ serene

SERENEST ▶ serene

SERENING ▶ serene

SERENITY n state or quality of being serene

SERER ▶ sere

SERES ▶ sere

SEREST ▶ sere

SERF, -S n medieval farm labourer who could not leave the land they worked on

SERFAGE, -S ▶ serf

SERFDOM, -S ▶ serf

SERFHOOD ▶ serf

SERFISH ▶ serf

SERFLIKE ▶ serf

SERFS ▶ serf

SERFSHIP ▶ serf

SERGE, -S n strong woollen fabric

SERGEANT n noncommissioned officer in the army

SERGED adj with sewn seam

SERGER, -S n sewing machine attachment for finishing seams

SERGES ▶ serge

SERGING, -S n type of sewing

SERIAL, -S n story or play produced in successive instalments ▷ adj of or forming a series

SERIALLY ▶ serial

SERIALS ▶ serial

SERIATE, -D, -S adj forming a series ▷ vb form into a series

SERIATIM adv in a series

SERIC adj of silk

SERICIN, -S n gelatinous protein found on the fibres of raw silk

SERICITE n type of mica

SERICON, -S n solution used in alchemy

SERIEMA, -S n either of two cranelike South American birds

SERIES n group or succession of related things, usu arranged in order

SERIF, -S n small line at the extremities of a main stroke in a type character

SERIFED adj having serifs

SERIFFED adj having serifs

SERIFS ▶ serif

SERIN, -S n any of various small yellow-and-brown finches

SERINE, -S n sweet-tasting amino acid

SERING ▶ sere

SERINGA, -S n any of several trees that yield rubber

SERINS ▶ serin

SERIOUS adj giving cause for concern

SERIPH, -S same as ▶ serif

SERJEANT same as ▶ sergeant

SERK, -S Scots word for ▶ shirt

SERKALI, -S n government in Africa

SERKS ▶ serk

SERMON, -ED, -S n speech on a religious or moral subject ▷ vb deliver a sermon

SERMONER variant of > sermoneer

SERMONET n short sermon

SERMONIC ▶ sermon

SERMONS ▶ sermon

SEROLOGY n science concerned with serums

SEROMA, -S n abnormal pocket of clear fluid in the body

SERON, -S n crate

SEROON, -S n crate

SEROPUS n liquid consisting of serum and pus

SEROSA, -E, -S n one of the thin membranes surrounding the embryo in an insect's egg

SEROSAL ▶ serosa

SEROSAS ▶ serosa

SEROSITY ▶ serous

SEROTINE adj produced, flowering, or developing late in the season ▷ n either of two insectivorous bats

SEROTINY n state of being serotinous

SEROTYPE n category into which material is placed

based on its serological activity ▷ vb class according to serotype

SEROUS adj of, containing, or like serum

SEROVAR, -S n subdivision of species

SEROW, -S n either of two antelopes of mountainous regions of S and SE Asia

SERPENT, -S n snake

SERPIGO, -S n any progressive skin eruption

SERPULA, -E, -S n type of marine mollusc

SERPULID n marine polychaete worm

SERR, -S vb press close together

SERRA, -E, -S n sawlike part or organ

SERRAN, -S n species of fish

SERRANID n type of marine fish of the family which includes the sea bass and sea perch

SERRANO, -S n type of Spanish ham

SERRANS ▶ serran

SERRAS ▶ serra

SERRATE, -S adj (of leaves) having a margin of forward pointing teeth ▷ vb make serrate

SERRATED adj having a notched or sawlike edge

SERRATES ▶ serrate

SERRATUS, SERRATI n muscle in thorax

SERRE, -D, -S, SERRING vb press close together

SERRIED adj in close formation

SERRIES ▶ serry

SERRING ▶ serre

SERRS ▶ serr

SERRY, SERRIES, -ING vb close together

SERS ▶ ser

SERUEWE, -D, -S vb old word meaning survey

SERUM, SERA, -S n watery fluid left after blood has clotted

SERUMAL ▶ serum

SERUMS ▶ serum

SERVABLE ▶ serve

SERVAL, -S n feline African mammal

SERVANT, -S n person employed to do household work for another ▷ vb work as a servant

SERVE, -D, -S vb work for (a person, community, or cause) ▷ n act of serving the ball

SERVER, -S n player who serves in racket games

SERVERY n room from which food is served

SERVES ▶ serve

SERVEWE, -D, -S vb old word meaning survey

SERVICE, -D, -S n serving ▷ adj serving the public rather than producing goods ▷ vb provide a service or services to

SERVICER ▶ service

SERVICES ▶ service

SERVIENT adj subordinate

SERVILE, -S adj too eager to obey people, fawning ▷ n servile person

SERVING, -S n portion of food

SERVITOR n servant or attendant

SERVLET, -S n small program that runs on a web server

SERVO, -S n servomechanism ▷ adj of a servomechanism

SERVQUAL n provision of high-quality products backed by a high level of customer service

SESAME, -S n plant cultivated for its seeds and oil

SESAMOID adj of or relating to various small bones formed in tendons ▷ n sesamoid bone

SESE interj exclamation found in Shakespeare

SESELI, -S n garden plant

SESEY interj exclamation found in Shakespeare

SESH, -ES short for ▶ session

SESS, -ED, -ES, -ING n old word meaning tax ▷ vb assess or impose (a tax)

SESSA interj exclamation found in Shakespeare

SESSED ▶ sess

SESSES ▶ sess

SESSILE adj (of flowers or leaves) having no stalk

SESSING ▶ sess

SESSION, -S n period spent in an activity

SESSPOOL n cesspool

SESTERCE n silver or, later, bronze coin of ancient Rome worth a quarter of a denarius

SESTET, -S n last six lines of a sonnet

SESTETT, -S n group of six

SESTETTE n group of six

S

SESTETTO n composition for six musicians

SESTETTS ▸ **sestett**

SESTINA, -S n elaborate verse form of Italian origin

SESTINE, -S n poem of six lines

SESTON, -S n type of plankton

SET, -S vb put in a specified position or state ▷ n setting or being set ▷ adj fixed or established beforehand

SETA, -E n bristle or bristle-like appendage

SETAL ▸ **seta**

SETBACK, -S n anything that delays progress

SETENANT n pair of postage stamps of different values joined together

SETIFORM adj shaped like a seta

SETLINE, -S n any of various types of fishing line

SETNESS ▸ **set**

SETOFF, -S n counterbalance

SETON, -S n surgical thread inserted below the skin

SETOSE adj covered with setae

SETOUS ▸ **seta**

SETOUT, -S n beginning or outset

SETS ▸ **set**

SETSCREW n screw that fits into the boss or hub of a wheel

SETT, -S n badger's burrow

SETTEE, -S n couch

SETTER, -ED, -S n long-haired gun dog ▷ vb treat with a piece of setterwort

SETTING, -S ▸ **set**

SETTLE, -D, -S, SETTLING vb arrange or put in order ▷ n long wooden bench with high back and arms

SETTLER, -S n colonist

SETTLES ▸ **settle**

SETTLING ▸ **settle**

SETTLOR, -S n person who settles property on someone

SETTS ▸ **sett**

SETUALE, -S n valerian

SETULE, -S n small bristle

SETULOSE ▸ **setule**

SETULOUS ▸ **setule**

SETUP, -S n way in which anything is organized or arranged

SETWALL, -S n valerian

SEV, -S n Indian snack of deep-fried noodles

SEVEN n one more than six

SEVENISH adj about seven

SEVENS n Rugby Union match or series of matches played with seven players on each side

SEVENTH, -S n number seven in a series ▷ adj coming after the sixth and before the eighth

SEVENTY n ten times seven

SEVER, -ED, -ING, -S vb cut through or off

SEVERAL, -S adj some, a few ▷ n individual person

SEVERE, -R, -ST adj strict or harsh

SEVERED ▸ **sever**

SEVERELY ▸ **severe**

SEVERER ▸ **severe**

SEVEREST ▸ **severe**

SEVERIES ▸ **severy**

SEVERING ▸ **sever**

SEVERITY ▸ **severe**

SEVERS ▸ **sever**

SEVERY, SEVERIES n part of vaulted ceiling

SEVICHE, -S n Mexican fish dish

SEVRUGA, -S n species of sturgeon

SEVS ▸ **sev**

SEW, -ED, -N, -S vb join with thread repeatedly passed through with a needle

SEWABLE ▸ **sew**

SEWAGE, -S n waste matter carried away in sewers

SEWAN, -S same as ▸ **seawan**

SEWAR, -S n Asian dagger

SEWED ▸ **sew**

SEWEL, -S n scarecrow

SEWELLEL n mountain beaver

SEWELS ▸ **sewel**

SEWEN, -S same as ▸ **sewin**

SEWER, -ED, -ING, -S n drain to remove waste water and sewage ▷ vb provide with sewers

SEWERAGE n system of sewers

SEWERED ▸ **sewer**

SEWERING ▸ **sewer**

SEWERS ▸ **sewer**

SEWIN, -S n sea trout

SEWING, -S ▸ **sew**

SEWINS ▸ **sewin**

SEWN ▸ **sew**

SEWS ▸ **sew**

SEX, -ED, -ES, -ING n state of being biologically male or female ▷ vb find out the sex of

SEXER, -S n person who determines the sex of chickens

SEXES ▸ **sex**

SEXFID adj split into six

SEXFOIL, -S n flower with six petals or leaves

SEXIER ▸ **sexy**

SEXIEST ▸ **sexy**

SEXILY ▸ **sexy**

SEXINESS ▸ **sexy**

SEXING, -S ▸ **sex**

SEXISM, -S n discrimination on the basis of a person's gender

SEXIST, -S ▸ **sexism**

SEXLESS adj neither male nor female

SEXTAIN, -S same as ▸ **sestina**

SEXTAN adj (of a fever) marked by paroxysms that recur after an interval of five days

SEXTANS n ancient Roman coin

SEXTANT, -S n navigator's instrument for measuring angles

SEXTARII ▸ **sextarius**

SEXTET, -S n group of six performers

SEXTETT, -S n sextet

SEXTETTE same as ▸ **sextet**

SEXTETTS ▸ **sextett**

SEXTILE, -S n value of a variable dividing its distribution into six groups with equal frequencies

SEXTO, -S same as ▸ **sixmo**

SEXTOLET n group of six musical notes

SEXTON, -S n official in charge of a church and churchyard

SEXTOS ▸ **sexto**

SEXTUOR, -S n sextet

SEXTUPLE vb multiply by six ▷ adj six times as much or as many ▷ n quantity or number six times as great as another

SEXTUPLY ▸ **sextuple**

SEXUAL adj of or characterized by sex

SEXUALLY ▸ **sexual**

SEXY, SEXIER, SEXIEST adj exciting or attractive

SEY, -S n Scots word meaning part of a cow carcase

SEYEN, -S n old form of scion

SEYS ▸ **sey**

SEYSURE, -S n old form of seizure

SEZ vb informal spelling of 'says'

Sez is a short informal form of **says**, very useful for disposing of the Z.

SFERICS same as ▸ **spherics**

SFORZATO, SFORZATI same as > **sforzando**

SFUMATO, -S n gradual transition between areas of different colour in painting

SH interj hush

SHA interj be quiet

SHABASH interj (in Indian English) bravo or well done

SHABBIER ▸ **shabby**

SHABBILY ▸ **shabby**

SHABBLE, -S n Scots word meaning old sword

SHABBY, SHABBIER adj worn or dilapidated in appearance

SHABRACK n saddlecloth of a cavalry horse

SHACK, -ED, -ING, -S n rough hut ▷ vb evade (work or responsibility)

SHACKIER ▸ **shacky**

SHACKING ▸ **shack**

SHACKLE, -D, -S n metal ring for securing a person's wrists or ankles ▷ vb fasten with shackles

SHACKLER ▸ **shackle**

SHACKLES ▸ **shackle**

SHACKO, -ES, -S same as ▸ **shako**

SHACKS ▸ **shack**

SHACKY, SHACKIER adj resembling a shack; dilapidated

SHAD, -S n herring-like fish

SHADBLOW n type of shrub

SHADBUSH n type of N American tree or shrub

SHADCHAN n Jewish marriage broker

SHADDOCK another name for ▸ **pomelo**

SHADDUP interj shut up

SHADE, -D n relative darkness ▷ vb screen from light

SHADER, -S ▸ **shade**

SHADES pl n gathering darkness at nightfall

SHADFLY American name for ▸ **mayfly**

SHADIER ▸ **shady**

SHADIEST ▸ **shady**

SHADILY ▸ **shady**

SHADING, -S n graded areas of tone indicating light and dark in a painting or drawing

SHADKHAN same as ▸ **shadchan**

SHADOOF, -S n mechanism for raising water

SHADOW, -ED, -S n dark shape cast on a surface when something stands between

a light and the surface ▷ vb cast a shadow over

SHADOWER ▸ **shadow**

SHADOWS ▸ **shadow**

SHADOWY adj (of a place) full of shadows

SHADRACH n lump of iron that has not been melted in the furnace

SHADS ▸ **shad**

SHADUF, -S same as ▸ **shadoof**

SHADY, SHADIER, SHADIEST adj situated in or giving shade

SHAFT, -ED, -S n long narrow straight handle of a tool or weapon ▷ vb treat badly

SHAFTER, -S ▸ **shaft**

SHAFTING n assembly of rotating shafts for transmitting power

SHAFTS ▸ **shaft**

SHAG, -GING, -S n cormorant ▷ adj (of a carpet) having a long pile ▷ vb make shaggy

SHAGBARK n North American hickory tree

SHAGGED adj shaggy

SHAGGIER ▸ **shaggy**

SHAGGILY ▸ **shaggy**

SHAGGING ▸ **shag**

SHAGGY, SHAGGIER adj covered with rough hair or wool

SHAGPILE adj (of carpet) having long fibres

SHAGREEN n sharkskin

SHAGROON n nineteenth-century Australian settler in Canterbury

SHAGS ▸ **shag**

SHAH, -S n formerly, ruler of Iran

SHAHADA, -S n Islamic declaration of faith

SHAHADAH same as ▸ **shahada**

SHAHADAS ▸ **shahada**

SHAHDOM, -S ▸ **shah**

SHAHEED, -S same as ▸ **shahid**

SHAHID, -S n Muslim martyr

SHAHS ▸ **shah**

SHAIKH, -S n sheikh

SHAIRD, -S n Scots word meaning shred

SHAIRN, -S Scots word for ▸ **dung**

SHAITAN, -S n (in Muslim countries) an evil spirit

SHAKABLE ▸ **shake**

SHAKE, -N, -S n move quickly up and down or back and forth ▷ n act of shaking

SHAKED vb old form of shook

SHAKEN ▸ **shake**

SHAKEOUT n process of reducing the number of people in a workforce

SHAKER, -S n container in which drinks are mixed or from which powder is shaken

SHAKES ▸ **shake**

SHAKEUP, -S n radical reorganization

SHAKIER ▸ **shaky**

SHAKIEST ▸ **shaky**

SHAKILY ▸ **shaky**

SHAKING, -S ▸ **shake**

SHAKO, -ES, -S n tall cylindrical peaked military hat with a plume

SHAKT vb old form of shook

SHAKUDO, -S n Japanese alloy of copper and gold

SHAKY, SHAKIER, SHAKIEST adj unsteady

SHALE, -D, -S, SHALING n flaky sedimentary rock

SHALEY ▸ **shale**

SHALIER ▸ **shaly**

SHALIEST ▸ **shaly**

SHALING ▸ **shale**

SHALL, SHOULD vb used as an auxiliary to make the future tense

SHALLI, -S n type of fabric

SHALLON, -S n American shrub

SHALLOON n light twill-weave woollen fabric used chiefly for coat linings, etc

SHALLOP, -S n light boat used for rowing in shallow water

SHALLOT, -S n kind of small onion

SHALLOW, -S adj not deep ▷ n shallow place in a body of water ▷ vb make or become shallow

SHALM, -S n old woodwind instrument

SHALOM, -S n Jewish greeting meaning 'peace be with you'

SHALOT, -S n shallot

SHALT singular form of the present tense (indicative mood) of ▸ **shall**

SHALWAR, -S n pair of loose-fitting trousers narrowing around the ankles

SHALY, SHALIER, SHALIEST ▸ **shale**

S

SHAM, -MED, -MING, -S n thing or person that is not genuine ▷ adj not genuine ▷ vb fake, feign

SHAMA, -S n Indian songbird

SHAMABLE ▶ shame

SHAMABLY ▶ shame

SHAMAL, -S n hot northwesterly wind

SHAMAN, -S n priest of shamanism

SHAMANIC ▶ shaman

SHAMANS ▶ shaman

SHAMAS ▶ shama

SHAMBA, -S n (in E Africa) any field used for growing crops

SHAMBLE, -D vb walk in a shuffling awkward way ▷ n awkward or shuffling walk

SHAMBLES n disorderly event or place

SHAMBLY ▶ shamble

SHAME, -D, -S n painful emotion caused by awareness of having done something foolish ▷ vb cause to feel shame

SHAMEFUL adj causing or deserving shame

SHAMER, -S n cause of shame

SHAMES ▶ shame

SHAMIANA n tent in India

SHAMINA, -S n wool blend of pashm and shahtoosh

SHAMING, -S n act or attempt to embarrass someone

SHAMISEN n Japanese stringed instrument

SHAMMAS same as ▶ shammes

SHAMMASH same as ▶ shammes

SHAMMED ▶ sham

SHAMMER, -S ▶ sham

SHAMMES n official acting as the beadle, sexton, and caretaker of a synagogue

SHAMMIED ▶ shammy

SHAMMIES ▶ shammy

SHAMMING ▶ sham

SHAMMOS same as ▶ shammes

SHAMMY, SHAMMIED, SHAMMIES n piece of chamois leather ▷ vb rub with a shammy

SHAMOIS n chamois ▷ vb clean with shamois

SHAMOS same as ▶ shammes

SHAMOY, -ED, -S n chamois ▷ vb rub with a shamoy

SHAMPOO, -S n liquid soap for washing hair, carpets, or upholstery ▷ vb wash with shampoo

SHAMROCK n clover leaf, esp as the Irish emblem

SHAMS ▶ sham

SHAMUS, -ES n police or private detective

SHAN, -S variant of ▶ shand

SHAND, -S n old word meaning fake coin

SHANDIES ▶ shandy

SHANDRY n light horse-drawn cart

SHANDS ▶ shand

SHANDY, SHANDIES n drink made of beer and lemonade

SHANGHAI vb force or trick (someone) into doing something ▷ n catapult

SHANK, -ED, -ING, -S n lower leg ▷ vb (of fruits, roots, etc) to show disease symptoms

SHANNY, SHANNIES n European blenny of rocky coastal waters

SHANS ▶ shan

SHANTEY, -S same as ▶ shanty

SHANTI, -S n peace

SHANTIES ▶ shanty

SHANTIH, -S same as ▶ shanti

SHANTIS ▶ shanti

SHANTUNG, -S n soft Chinese silk with a knobbly surface

SHANTY, SHANTIES n shack or crude dwelling

SHAPABLE ▶ shape

SHAPE, -D, -S n outward form of an object ▷ vb form or mould

SHAPELY adj having an attractive shape

SHAPEN, -ED, -S vb shape

SHAPER, -S ▶ shape

SHAPES ▶ shape

SHAPEUP, -S n system of hiring dockers for a day's work

SHAPING, -S ▶ shape

SHAPS n leather over-trousers worn by cowboys

SHARABLE ▶ share

SHARD, -S n broken piece of pottery or glass

SHARDED adj old word meaning hidden under dung

SHARDS ▶ shard

SHARE, -D, -S n part of something that belongs to or is contributed by a person ▷ vb give or take a share of (something)

SHAREMAN, SHAREMEN n member of a fishing-boat crew who shares profits

SHARER, -S ▶ share

SHARES ▶ share

SHARIA, -S n body of doctrines that regulate the lives of Muslims

SHARIAH, -S same as ▶ sharia

SHARIAS ▶ sharia

SHARIAT, -S n Islamic religious law

SHARIF, -S same as ▶ sherif

SHARING, -S ▶ share

SHARK, -ED, -ING, -S n large usu predatory sea fish ▷ vb obtain (something) by cheating or deception

SHARKER, -S n shark hunter

SHARKING ▶ shark

SHARKISH adj resembling or behaving like a shark

SHARKS ▶ shark

SHARN, -S Scots word for ▶ dung

SHARNIER ▶ sharny

SHARNIES ▶ sharny

SHARNS ▶ sharn

SHARNY, SHARNIER, SHARNIES n (Scot) person who cleans a cow-house ▷ adj (Scot) covered in dung

SHARON n as in sharon fruit persimmon

SHARP, -ED, -EST, -ING, -S adj having a keen cutting edge or fine point ▷ adv promptly ▷ n symbol raising a note one semitone above natural pitch ▷ vb make sharp

SHARPEN, -S vb make or become sharp or sharper

SHARPER, -S n person who cheats

SHARPEST ▶ sharp

SHARPIE, -S n member of a teenage group having short hair and distinctive clothes

SHARPING ▶ sharp

SHARPISH adj fairly sharp ▷ adv promptly

SHARPLY ▶ sharp

SHARPS ▶ sharp

SHARPY n swindler

SHASH, -ED, -ES, -ING vb old form of sash

SHASHLIK n type of kebab

SHASLIK, -S n type of kebab

SHASTA, -S n plant of the daisy family

SHASTER, -S same as ▶ shastra

SHASTRA, -S n any of the sacred writings of Hinduism

SHATOOSH same as > **shahtoosh**

SHATTER, -S vb break into pieces ▷ n fragment

SHATTERY adj liable to shatter

SHAUCHLE vb Scots word meaning shuffle

SHAUCHLY ▸ **shauchle**

SHAUGH, -S n old word meaning small wood

SHAUL, -ED, -ING, -S vb old form of shawl

SHAVABLE ▸ **shave**

SHAVE, -D, -S vb remove (hair) from (the face, head, or body) with a razor or shaver ▷ n act of shaving

SHAVEN adj closely shaved or tonsured

SHAVER, -S n electric razor

SHAVES ▸ **shave**

SHAVIE, -S n Scots word meaning trick

SHAVING, -S ▸ **shave**

SHAW, -ED, -ING, -S n small wood ▷ vb show

SHAWARMA n strips of lamb, usu served in a pitta

SHAWED ▸ **shaw**

SHAWING ▸ **shaw**

SHAWL, -ED, -ING, -S n piece of cloth worn over a woman's shoulders or wrapped around a baby ▷ vb cover with a shawl

SHAWLEY, -S same as ▸ **shawlie**

SHAWLIE, -S n insulting term for a working-class woman who wears a shawl

SHAWLING ▸ **shawl**

SHAWLS ▸ **shawl**

SHAWM, -S n medieval form of the oboe with a conical bore and flaring bell

SHAWN variant of ▸ **shawm**

SHAWS ▸ **shaw**

SHAY, -S dialect word for ▸ **chaise**

SHAYA, -S n Indian plant

SHAYKH, -S same as ▸ **sheikh**

SHAYS ▸ **shay**

SHAZAM interj magic slogan

SHCHI, -S n Russian cabbage soup

SHE, -S pron female person or animal previously mentioned ▷ n female person or animal

SHEA, -S n tropical African tree

SHEADING n any of the six subdivisions of the Isle of Man

SHEAF, -ED, -ING, -S, SHEAVES n bundle of papers ▷ vb tie into a sheaf

SHEAFIER ▸ **sheafy**

SHEAFING ▸ **sheafy**

SHEAFS ▸ **sheaf**

SHEAFY, SHEAFIER ▸ **sheaf**

SHEAL, -ED, -ING, -S vb old word meaning shell

SHEAR, -ED, -ING, -S vb clip hair or wool from ▷ n breakage caused through strain or twisting

SHEARER, -S ▸ **shear**

SHEARING ▸ **shear**

SHEARLEG n one spar of shearlegs

SHEARMAN, SHEARMEN n person who trims cloth

SHEARS ▸ **shear**

SHEAS ▸ **shea**

SHEATH, -S n close-fitting cover, esp for a knife or sword

SHEATHE, -D, -S vb put into a sheath

SHEATHER ▸ **sheathe**

SHEATHES ▸ **sheathe**

SHEATHS ▸ **sheath**

SHEATHY ▸ **sheathe**

SHEAVE, -D, SHEAVING vb gather or bind into sheaves ▷ n wheel with a grooved rim

SHEAVES ▸ **sheaf**

SHEAVING ▸ **sheave**

SHEBANG, -S n situation, matter, or affair

SHEBEAN, -S same as ▸ **shebeen**

SHEBEEN, -S n place where alcohol is sold illegally ▷ vb run a shebeen

SHECHITA n Jewish method of killing animals for food

SHED, -DED, -S n building used for storage or shelter or as a workshop ▷ vb get rid of

SHEDABLE ▸ **shed**

SHEDDED ▸ **shed**

SHEDDER, -S n person or thing that sheds

SHEDDING ▸ **shed**

SHEDFUL, -S n quantity or amount contained in a shed

SHEDHAND n labourer working in a shearing shed

SHEDLIKE ▸ **shed**

SHEDLOAD n very large amount or number

SHEDS ▸ **shed**

SHEEL, -ED, -ING, -S vb old word meaning shell

SHEEN, -ED, -ING, -S n glistening brightness on the surface of something ▷ adj shining and beautiful ▷ vb give a sheen to

SHEENFUL ▸ **sheen**

SHEENIER ▸ **sheeny**

SHEENING ▸ **sheen**

SHEENS ▸ **sheen**

SHEENY, SHEENIER ▸ **sheen**

SHEEP n ruminant animal bred for wool and meat

SHEEPCOT n sheepcote

SHEEPDOG n dog used for herding sheep

SHEEPIER ▸ **sheepy**

SHEEPISH adj embarrassed because of feeling foolish

SHEEPLE, -S n group of people who follow the majority in matters of opinion, taste, etc

SHEEPMAN, SHEEPMEN n person who keeps sheep

SHEEPO, -S n person employed to bring sheep to the catching pen in a shearing shed

SHEEPY, SHEEPIER ▸ **sheep**

SHEER, -ED, -ER, -EST, -ING, -S adj absolute, complete ▷ adv steeply ▷ vb change course suddenly ▷ n any transparent fabric used for making garments

SHEERLEG n one spar of sheerlegs

SHEERLY ▸ **sheer**

SHEERS ▸ **sheer**

SHEESH interj exclamation of surprise or annoyance

SHEESHA, -S n water-pipe for smoking tobacco

SHEET, -ED, -S n large piece of cloth used as an inner bed cover ▷ vb provide with, cover, or wrap in a sheet

SHEETER, -S ▸ **sheet**

SHEETFED adj printing on separate sheets of paper

SHEETIER ▸ **sheety**

SHEETING n material from which sheets are made

SHEETS ▸ **sheet**

SHEETY, SHEETIER ▸ **sheet**

SHEEVE, -S n part of mine winding gear

SHEHITAH, -S n slaughter of animals according to Jewish religious law

SHEHITAH same as ▸ **shehita**

SHEHITAS ▸ **shehita**

SHEHNAI, -S n Indian wind instrument

SHEIK, -S same as ▸ **sheikh**

SHEIKDOM same as > **sheikhdom**

SHEIKH, -S n Arab chief

SHEIKHA, -S *n* chief wife of a sheikh

SHEIKHS ▶ sheikh

SHEIKS ▶ sheik

SHEILA, -S *n* girl or woman

SHEILING *n* hut used by shepherds

SHEITAN, -S *n* Muslim demon

SHEITEL, -S *n* traditional wig worn by Orthodox Jewish women

SHEKEL, SHEKALIM, -IM, -S *n* monetary unit of Israel

SHELDUCK *n* large brightly coloured wild duck of Europe and Asia

SHELF, -ED, -ING, -S, SHELVES *n* board fixed horizontally to something ▷ *vb* put on a shelf

SHELFFUL ▶ shelf

SHELFIER ▶ shelfy

SHELFING ▶ shelf

SHELFS ▶ shelf

SHELFY, SHELFIER ▶ shelf

SHELL, -ED, -ING, -S *n* hard outer covering of an egg, nut, or certain animals ▷ *vb* take the shell from

SHELLAC, -S *n* resin used in varnishes ▷ *vb* coat with shellac

SHELLAC *vb* shellac

SHELLACS ▶ shellac

SHELLED ▶ shell

SHELLER, -S ▶ shell

SHELLFUL ▶ shell

SHELLIER ▶ shelly

SHELLING ▶ shell

SHELLS ▶ shell

SHELLY, SHELLIER ▶ shell

SHELTA, -S *n* secret language used by some travelling people in Britain and Ireland

SHELTER, -S *n* structure providing protection from danger or the weather ▷ *vb* give shelter to

SHELTERY *adj* giving shelter

SHELTIE *n* small dog similar to a collie

SHELTY, SHELTIES *same as* **▶ sheltie**

SHELVE, -D *vb* put aside or postpone

SHELVER, -S ▶ shelve

SHELVES ▶ shelf

SHELVIER ▶ shelvy

SHELVING *n* (material for) shelves

SHELVY, SHELVIER *adj* having shelves

SHEN *n* (in Chinese thought) spiritual element of the psyche

SHENAI, -S *same as* **▶ shehnai**

SHEND, -ING, -S, SHENT *vb* put to shame

SHEOL, -S *n* hell

SHEPHERD *n* person who tends sheep ▷ *vb* guide or watch over (people)

SHEQALIM *n* plural of sheqel

SHEQEL, -S *same as* **▶ shekel**

SHERANG, -S *n* person in charge

SHERBERT *same as* **▶ sherbet**

SHERBET, -S *n* fruit-flavoured fizzy powder

SHERD, -S *same as* **▶ shard**

SHERE *old spelling of* **▶ sheer**

SHEREEF, -S *same as* **▶ sherif**

SHERIA, -S *same as* **▶ sharia**

SHERIAT, -S *n* Muslim religious law

SHERIF, -S *n* descendant of Muhammad through his daughter Fatima

SHERIFF, -S *n* (in the US) chief law enforcement officer of a county

SHERIFS ▶ sherif

SHERLOCK *n* detective ▷ *vb* investigate (something)

SHERO, -ES *n* woman considered a hero

SHEROOT, -S *n* cheroot

SHERPA, -S *n* official who assists at a summit meeting

SHERRIED *adj* flavoured with sherry

SHERRIES ▶ sherry

SHERRIS *n* old form of sherry

SHERRY, SHERRIES *n* pale or dark brown fortified wine

SHERWANI *n* long coat closed up to the neck, worn by men in India

SHES ▶ she

SHET, -S, -TING *vb* old form of shut

SHETLAND *n* type of wool spun in the Shetland islands

SHETS ▶ shet

SHETTING ▶ shet

SHEUCH, -ED, -S *n* ditch or trough ▷ *vb* dig

SHEUGH, -ED, -S *same as* **▶ sheuch**

SHEVA, -S *n* mark in Hebrew writing

SHEW, -ED, -ING, -N, -S *archaic spelling of* **▶ show**

SHEWEL, -S *n* old word meaning scarecrow

SHEWER, -S ▶ shew

SHEWING ▶ shew

SHEWN ▶ shew

SHEWS ▶ shew

SHH *interj* sound made to ask for silence

SHHH *interj* used to request quietness

SHIAI, -S *n* judo contest

SHIATSU, -S *n* type of massage

SHIATZU, -S *n* shiatsu

SHIBAH, -S *n* Jewish period of mourning

SHICKER, -S *n* alcoholic drink

SHIDDER, -S *n* old word meaning a female animal

SHIDDUCH *n* arranged marriage

SHIED ▶ shy

SHIEL, -ED, -S *vb* sheal

SHIELD, -ED, -S *n* piece of armour carried on the arm to protect the body from blows or missiles ▷ *vb* protect

SHIELDER ▶ shield

SHIELDS ▶ shield

SHIELED ▶ shiel

SHIELING *n* rough hut or shelter used by people tending cattle on high or remote ground

SHIELS ▶ shiel

SHIER, -S *n* horse that shies habitually

SHIES ▶ shy

SHIEST ▶ shy

SHIFT, -ED, -ING, -S *vb* move ▷ *n* shifting

SHIFTER, -S ▶ shift

SHIFTIER ▶ shifty

SHIFTILY ▶ shifty

SHIFTING ▶ shift

SHIFTS ▶ shift

SHIFTY, SHIFTIER *adj* evasive or untrustworthy

SHIGELLA *n* type of rod-shaped Gram-negative bacterium

SHIITAKE *n* kind of mushroom widely used in East Asian cookery

SHIKAR, -S *n* hunting, esp big-game hunting ▷ *vb* hunt (game, esp big game)

SHIKARA, -S *n* (in Kashmir) light, flat-bottomed boat

SHIKAREE *same as* **▶ shikari**

SHIKARI, -S *n* (in India) a hunter

SHIKARS ▶ shikar

SHIKKER, -S *n* Yiddish term for drunk person

SHIKRA, -S *n* small Asian sparrowhawk

SHILINGI *n* money unit in Tanzania

SHILL, -ED, -S *n* confidence trickster's assistant ▷ *vb* act as a shill

SHILLALA n short Irish club or cudgel

SHILLED ▸ shill

SHILLING n former British coin

SHILLS ▸ shill

SHILPIT adj puny

SHILY ▸ shy

SHIM, -MED, -MING, -S n thin strip of material placed between two close surfaces to fill a gap ▷ vb fit or fill up with a shim

SHIMAAL, -S n hot Middle Eastern wind

SHIMMED ▸ shim

SHIMMER, -S n faint unsteady light ▷ vb shine with a faint unsteady light

SHIMMERY adj shining with a glistening or tremulous light

SHIMMEY, -S n chemise

SHIMMIED ▸ shimmy

SHIMMIES ▸ shimmy

SHIMMING ▸ shim

SHIMMY, SHIMMIED, SHIMMIES n American ragtime dance ▷ vb dance the shimmy

SHIMS ▸ shim

SHIN, -NED, -NING, -S n front of the lower leg ▷ vb climb by using the hands or arms and legs

SHINBONE n tibia

SHINDIES ▸ shindy

SHINDIG, -S n noisy party

SHINDY, SHINDIES, -S n quarrel or commotion

SHINE, -D, -S, SHINING, SHONE vb give out or reflect light; cause to gleam ▷ n brightness or lustre

SHINER, -S n black eye

SHINES ▸ shine

SHINESS ▸ shy

SHINGLE, -D n wooden roof tile ▷ vb cover (a roof) with shingles

SHINGLER ▸ shingle

SHINGLES n disease causing a rash of small blisters along a nerve

SHINGLY ▸ shingle

SHINIER ▸ shiny

SHINIES ▸ shiny

SHINIEST ▸ shiny

SHINILY ▸ shiny

SHINING ▸ shine

SHINKIN, -S n worthless person

SHINLEAF n wintergreen

SHINNE, -S n old form of chin

SHINNED ▸ shin

SHINNERY n American oak tree

SHINNES ▸ shinne

SHINNEY, -S vb climb with hands and legs

SHINNIED ▸ shinny

SHINNIES ▸ shinny

SHINNING ▸ shin

SHINNY, SHINNIED, SHINNIES same as ▸ shinty

SHINOLA, -S n tradename of a kind of boot polish

SHINS ▸ shin

SHINTY, SHINTIED, SHINTIES n game like hockey ▷ vb play shinty

SHINY, SHINIER, SHINIES, SHINIEST adj bright and polished

SHIP, -PED, -PING, -S n large seagoing vessel ▷ vb send or transport by carrier, esp a ship

SHIPFUL, -S n amount carried by ship

SHIPLAP, -S n method of constructing ship hull

SHIPLESS ▸ ship

SHIPLOAD n quantity carried by a ship

SHIPMAN, SHIPMEN n master or captain of a ship

SHIPMATE n sailor serving on the same ship as another

SHIPMEN ▸ shipman

SHIPMENT n act of shipping cargo

SHIPPED ▸ ship

SHIPPEN, -S n dialect word for cattle shed

SHIPPER, -S n person or company that ships

SHIPPING ▸ ship

SHIPPO, -S n Japanese enamel work

SHIPPON, -S n dialect word for cattle shed

SHIPPOS ▸ shippo

SHIPS ▸ ship

SHIPSIDE n part of wharf next to ship

SHIPTIME n arrival time of a supply ship

SHIPWAY, -S n structure on which a vessel is built, then launched

SHIPWORM n type of wormlike marine bivalve mollusc

SHIPYARD n place where ships are built

SHIR, -S n gathering in material

SHIRALEE n swag

SHIRAZ, -ES n variety of black grape used for wine

SHIRE, -D, -S, SHIRING n county ▷ vb refresh or rest

SHIREMAN, SHIREMEN n sheriff

SHIRES ▸ shire

SHIRING ▸ shire

SHIRK, -ED, -ING, -S vb avoid (duty or work) ▷ n person who shirks

SHIRKER, -S ▸ shirk

SHIRKING ▸ shirk

SHIRKS ▸ shirk

SHIRR, -ED, -ING, -S vb gather (fabric) into parallel rows to decorate a dress, etc ▷ n series of gathered rows decorating a dress, etc

SHIRRA, -S old Scots word for ▸ sheriff

SHIRRED ▸ shirr

SHIRRING ▸ shirr

SHIRRS ▸ shirr

SHIRS ▸ shir

SHIRT, -ED, -S n garment for the upper part of the body ▷ vb put a shirt on

SHIRTIER ▸ shirty

SHIRTILY ▸ shirty

SHIRTING n fabric used in making men's shirts

SHIRTS ▸ shirt

SHIRTY, SHIRTIER adj bad-tempered or annoyed

SHISH adj as in shish kebab dish of meat and vegetables grilled on skewers

SHISHA, -S n water-pipe for smoking tobacco

SHISO, -S n Asian plant with aromatic leaves

SHIST, -S n schist

SHITAKE, -S same as ▸ shiitake

SHITTAH, -S, SHITTIM n tree mentioned in the Old Testament

SHITZU, -S n breed of small dog with long, silky fur

SHIUR, -IM n lesson in which a passage of the Talmud is studied

SHIV, -S, -VED, -VING variant spelling of ▸ chiv

SHIVA, -S variant of ▸ shivah

SHIVAH, -S n Jewish period of formal mourning

SHIVAREE n discordant mock serenade to newlyweds, made with pans, kettles, etc

SHIVAS ▸ shiva

SHIVE, -S n flat cork or bung for wide-mouthed bottles

SHIVER, -ED, -S vb tremble, as from cold or fear ▷ n shivering

S

SHIVERER ▸ shiver

SHIVERS ▸ shiver

SHIVERY adj inclined to shiver or tremble

SHIVES ▸ shive

SHIVITI, -S n Jewish decorative plaque with religious message

SHIVOO, -S n Australian word meaning rowdy party

SHIVS ▸ shiv

SHIVVED ▸ shiv

SHIVVING ▸ shiv

SHIZZLE, -S n form of US rap slang

SHLEMIEL same as > schlemiel

SHLEP, -PED, -S vb schlep

SHLEPP, -S vb schlep

SHLEPPED ▸ shlep

SHLEPPER ▸ shlep

SHLEPPS ▸ shlepp

SHLEPPY adj dingy, shabby, or rundown

SHLEPS ▸ shlep

SHLOCK, -S n something of poor quality

SHLOCKY ▸ shlock

SHLOSHIM n period of thirty days' deep mourning following a death

SHLUB, -S same as ▸ schlub

SHLUMP, -ED, -S vb move in lazy way

SHLUMPY ▸ shlump

SHMALTZ n schmaltz

SHMALTZY ▸ shmaltz

SHMATTE, -S n rag

SHMEAR, -ED, -S same as ▸ schmear

SHMEER, -ED, -S same as ▸ schmear

SHMEK, -S n smell

SHMO, -ES same as ▸ schmo

SHMOCK, -S n despicable person

SHMOE same as ▸ schmoe

SHMOES ▸ shmo

SHMOOSE, -D, -S variant of ▸ schmooze

SHMOOZE, -D, -S variant of ▸ schmooze

SHMOOZER same as > schmoozer

SHMOOZES ▸ shmooze

SHMOOZY adj talking casually, gossipy

SHMUCK, -S n despicable person

SHMUCKY same as ▸ schmucky

SHNAPPS same as ▸ schnapps

SHNAPS n schnaps

SHNOOK, -S n stupid person

SHNORRER same as > schnorrer

SHO adj sure, as pronounced in southern US

SHOAL, -ED, -ER, -EST, -ING, -S n large number of fish swimming together ▷ vb make or become shallow ▷ adj (of the draught of a vessel) drawing little water

SHOALIER ▸ shoaly

SHOALING ▸ shoal

SHOALS ▸ shoal

SHOALY, SHOALIER adj shallow

SHOAT, -S n piglet that has recently been weaned

SHOCHET, -S n (in Judaism) a person licensed to slaughter animals and birds

SHOCHU, -S n type of Japanese alcoholic spirit

SHOCK, -ED, -S vb horrify, disgust, or astonish ▷ n sudden violent emotional disturbance ▷ adj bushy

SHOCKER, -S n person or thing that shocks or horrifies

SHOCKING adj causing horror, disgust, or astonishment

SHOCKS ▸ shock

SHOD ▸ shoe

SHODDEN vb old form of shod

SHODDIER ▸ shoddy

SHODDIES ▸ shoddy

SHODDILY ▸ shoddy

SHODDY, SHODDIER, SHODDIES adj made or done badly ▷ n yarn or fabric made from wool waste or clippings

SHODER, -S n skins used in making gold leaf

SHOE, SHOD, -D, -S n outer covering for the foot, ending below the ankle ▷ vb fit with a shoe or shoes

SHOEBILL n large wading bird of tropical E African swamps

SHOEBOX n cardboard box for shoes

SHOED ▸ shoe

SHOEHORN n smooth curved implement inserted at the heel of a shoe to ease the foot into it ▷ vb cram (people or things) into a very small space

SHOEING, -S ▸ shoe

SHOELACE n cord for fastening shoes

SHOELESS ▸ shoe

SHOEPAC, -S n waterproof boot

SHOEPACK n waterproof boot

SHOEPACS ▸ shoepac

SHOER, -S n person who shoes horses

SHOES ▸ shoe

SHOETREE n piece of metal, wood, or plastic inserted in a shoe to keep its shape

SHOFAR, -S, SHOFROTH n ram's horn sounded in Jewish synagogue

SHOG, -GED, -GING, -S vb shake

SHOGGLE, -D, -S vb shake

SHOGGLY ▸ shoggle

SHOGI, -S n Japanese chess

SHOGS ▸ shog

SHOGUN, -S n Japanese chief military commander

SHOGUNAL ▸ shogun

SHOGUNS ▸ shogun

SHOJI, -S n Japanese rice-paper screen in a sliding wooden frame

SHOJO n genre of Japanese comics intended for girls

SHOLA, -S n Indian plant

SHOLOM, -S n Hebrew greeting

SHONE ▸ shine

SHONEEN, -S n Irishman who imitates English ways

SHONKY, SHONKIER adj unreliable or unsound

SHOO, -ED, -ING, -S interj go away! ▷ vb drive away as by saying 'shoo'

SHOOFLY n as in shoofly pie US dessert similar to treacle tart

SHOOGIE, -D, -S vb Scots word meaning swing

SHOOGLE, -D, -S vb shake, sway, or rock back and forth ▷ n rocking motion

SHOOGLY ▸ shoogle

SHOOING ▸ shoo

SHOOK, -S n set of parts ready for assembly

SHOOL, -ED, -ING, -S dialect word for ▸ shovel

SHOOLE, -S dialect word for ▸ shovel

SHOOLED ▸ shool

SHOOLES ▸ shoole

SHOOLING ▸ shool

SHOOLS ▸ shool

SHOON plural of ▸ shoe

SHOORA, -S same as ▸ shura

SHOOS ▸ shoo

SHOOSH, -ED, -ES vb make a rushing sound when moving

SHOOT, -ING, -S vb hit, wound, or kill with a missile fired from a weapon ▷ n new branch or sprout of a plant

SHOOTER, -S n person or thing that shoots

SHOOTIE, -S n type of shoe that covers the ankle

SHOOTING ▸ **shoot**

SHOOTIST n person who shoots

SHOOTOUT n conclusive gunfight

SHOOTS ▸ **shoot**

SHOP, -PED, -PING, -S n place for sale of goods and services ▷ vb visit a shop or shops to buy goods

SHOPBOT, -S n price-comparison website

SHOPBOY, -S n boy working in shop

SHOPE n old form of shape

SHOPFUL, -S n amount stored in shop

SHOPGIRL n young woman working in a shop

SHOPHAR, -S same as ▸ **shofar**

SHOPLESS adj (of an area) having no shops

SHOPLIFT vb steal from shop

SHOPMAN, SHOPMEN n man working in shop

SHOPPE, -S old-fashioned spelling of ▸ **shop**

SHOPPED ▸ **shop**

SHOPPER, -S n person who buys goods in a shop

SHOPPES ▸ **shoppe**

SHOPPIER ▸ **shoppy**

SHOPPIES ▸ **shoppy**

SHOPPING ▸ **shop**

SHOPPY, SHOPPIER, SHOPPIES adj of a shop ▷ n shop assistant

SHOPS ▸ **shop**

SHOPTALK n conversation about one's work, carried on outside working hours

SHOPWORN adj worn or faded from being displayed in a shop

SHORAN, -S n short-range radar system

SHORE, -D, -S n edge of a sea or lake ▷ vb prop or support

SHOREMAN, SHOREMEN n person who lives on the shore

SHORER, -S ▸ **shore**

SHORES ▸ **shore**

SHORING, -S ▸ **shore**

SHORL, -S n black mineral

SHORN past participle of ▸ **shear**

SHORT, -ED, -ER, -EST, -ING adj not long ▷ adv abruptly

▷ n drink of spirits ▷ vb short-circuit

SHORTAGE n deficiency

SHORTARM adj (of a punch) with the arm bent

SHORTCUT n route that is shorter than the usual one

SHORTED ▸ **short**

SHORTEN, -S vb make or become shorter

SHORTER ▸ **short**

SHORTEST ▸ **short**

SHORTIA, -S n American flowering plant

SHORTIE, -S n person or thing that is extremely short

SHORTING ▸ **short**

SHORTISH ▸ **short**

SHORTLY adv soon

SHORTS pl n trousers reaching the top of the thigh or partway to the knee

SHORTY same as ▸ **shortie**

SHOT, -S, -TED, -TING vb load with shot

SHOTE, -S same as ▸ **shoat**

SHOTGUN, -S n gun for firing a charge of shot at short range ▷ adj involving coercion or duress ▷ vb shoot or threaten with or as if with a shotgun

SHOTHOLE n drilled hole into which explosive is put for blasting

SHOTS ▸ **shot**

SHOTT, -S n shallow temporary salt lake or marsh in the North African desert

SHOTTE, -S n old form of shoat

SHOTTED ▸ **shot**

SHOTTEN adj (of fish, esp herring) having recently spawned

SHOTTES ▸ **shotte**

SHOTTING ▸ **shot**

SHOTTLE, -S n small drawer

SHOTTS ▸ **shott**

SHOUGH, -S n old word meaning lapdog

SHOULD ▸ **shall**

SHOULDER n part of the body to which an arm, foreleg, or wing is attached ▷ vb bear (a burden or responsibility)

SHOULDST form of the past tense of ▸ **shall**

SHOUSE, -S n toilet ▷ adj unwell or in poor spirits

SHOUT, -ED, -ING, -S n loud cry ▷ vb cry out loudly

SHOUTER, -S ▸ **shout**

SHOUTHER Scots form of ▸ **shoulder**

SHOUTIER ▸ **shouty**

SHOUTING ▸ **shout**

SHOUTOUT n public greeting, esp one broadcast via television or radio

SHOUTS ▸ **shout**

SHOUTY, SHOUTIER adj characterized by or involving shouting

SHOVE, -D, -S vb push roughly ▷ n rough push

SHOVEL, -ED, -S n tool for lifting or moving loose material ▷ vb lift or move as with a shovel

SHOVELER n type of duck

SHOVELS ▸ **shovel**

SHOVER, -S ▸ **shove**

SHOVES ▸ **shove**

SHOVING, -S n act of pushing hard

SHOW, -ED, -N, -S vb make, be, or become noticeable or visible ▷ n public exhibition

SHOWABLE ▸ **show**

SHOWBIZ n entertainment industry including theatre, films, and TV

SHOWBOAT n paddle-wheel river steamer with a theatre and a repertory company ▷ vb perform or behave in a showy and flamboyant way

SHOWBOX n box containing showman's material

SHOWCASE n situation in which something is displayed to best advantage ▷ vb exhibit or display ▷ adj displayed or meriting display as in a showcase

SHOWD, -ED, -ING, -S vb rock or sway to and fro ▷ n rocking motion

SHOWDOWN n confrontation that settles a dispute

SHOWDS ▸ **showd**

SHOWED ▸ **show**

SHOWER, -ED, -S n kind of bath in which a person stands while being sprayed with water ▷ vb wash in a shower

SHOWERER ▸ **shower**

SHOWERS ▸ **shower**

SHOWERY ▸ **shower**

SHOWGHE, -S n old word meaning lapdog

SHOWGIRL n young woman who appears in shows, esp as a singer or dancer

SHOWGOER n member of the audience of a play, film, or show

SHOWIER ▸ **showy**

SHOWIEST ▸ showy

SHOWILY ▸ showy

SHOWING, -S ▸ show

SHOWJUMP vb take part in a showjumping competition

SHOWMAN, SHOWMEN n man skilled at presenting anything spectacularly

SHOWN ▸ show

SHOWOFF, -S n person who makes a vain display of himself or herself

SHOWRING n area where animals are displayed for sale or competition

SHOWROOM n room in which goods for sale are on display

SHOWS ▸ show

SHOWTIME n time when show begins

SHOWY, SHOWIER, SHOWIEST adj gaudy

SHOWYARD n yard where cattle are displayed

SHOYU, -S n Japanese variety of soy sauce

SHRADDHA n Hindu offering to an ancestor

SHRANK ▸ shrink

SHRAPNEL n artillery shell filled with pellets which scatter on explosion

SHRED, -DED, -S n long narrow strip torn from something ▷ vb tear to shreds

SHREDDER ▸ shred

SHREDDY ▸ shred

SHREDS ▸ shred

SHREEK, -ED, -S old spelling of ▸ shriek

SHREIK, -ED, -S old spelling of ▸ shriek

SHREW, -ED, -ING, -S n small mouselike animal ▷ vb curse or damn

SHREWD, -ER adj clever and perceptive

SHREWDIE n shrewd person

SHREWDLY ▸ shrewd

SHREWED ▸ shrew

SHREWING ▸ shrew

SHREWISH adj bad-tempered and nagging

SHREWS ▸ shrew

SHRI, -S n Indian title of respect

SHRIECH old spelling of ▸ shriek

SHRIEK, -ED, -S n shrill cry ▷ vb utter (with) a shriek

SHRIEKER ▸ shriek

SHRIEKS ▸ shriek

SHRIEKY ▸ shriek

SHRIEVAL adj of or relating to a sheriff

SHRIEVE, -D, -S archaic word for ▸ sheriff

SHRIFT, -S n act or an instance of shriving or being shriven

SHRIGHT, -S n old word meaning shriek

SHRIKE, -D, -S, SHRIKING n songbird with a heavy hooked bill ▷ vb archaic word for shriek

SHRILL, -ED, -ER, -S adj (of a sound) sharp and high-pitched ▷ vb utter shrilly

SHRILLY ▸ shrill

SHRIMP, -ED, -S n small edible shellfish ▷ vb fish for shrimps

SHRIMPER ▸ shrimp

SHRIMPS ▸ shrimp

SHRIMPY ▸ shrimp

SHRINAL ▸ shrine

SHRINE, -D, -S, SHRINING n place of worship associated with a sacred person or object ▷ vb enshrine

SHRINK, SHRANK, -S, SHRUNK vb become or make smaller ▷ n psychiatrist

SHRINKER ▸ shrink

SHRINKS ▸ shrink

SHRIS ▸ shri

SHRITCH vb old word meaning shriek

SHRIVE, -D, -N, -S, SHRIVING vb hear the confession of (a penitent)

SHRIVEL, -S vb shrink and wither

SHRIVEN ▸ shrive

SHRIVER, -S ▸ shrive

SHRIVES ▸ shrive

SHRIVING ▸ shrive

SHROFF, -ED, -S n (in China and Japan) expert employed to identify counterfeit money ▷ vb test (money) and separate out the counterfeit and base

SHROUD, -ED, -S n piece of cloth used to wrap a dead body ▷ vb conceal

SHROUDY ▸ shroud

SHROVE, -D, -S, SHROVING vb dialect word meaning to observe Shrove-tide

SHROW, -ED, -ING, -S vb old form of shrew

SHROWD adj old form of shrewd

SHROWED ▸ shrow

SHROWING ▸ shrow

SHROWS ▸ shrow

SHRUB, -BED, -S n woody plant smaller than a tree ▷ vb plant shrubs

SHRUBBY adj consisting of, planted with, or abounding in shrubs

SHRUBS ▸ shrub

SHRUG, -GED, -S vb raise and then drop (the shoulders) as a sign of indifference or doubt ▷ n shrugging

SHRUNK ▸ shrink

SHRUNKEN adj reduced in size

SHTCHI, -S n Russian cabbage soup

SHTETEL, -S same as ▸ shtetl

SHTETL, -S n Jewish community in Eastern Europe

SHTICK, -S n comedian's routine

SHTICKY ▸ shtick

SHTIK, -S ▸ shtick

SHTOOK, -S n trouble

SHTOOM, -ER adj silent

SHTUCK, -S n trouble

SHTUM adj silent

SHTUMM, -ER adj silent

SHUCK, -ED, -ING n outer covering of something ▷ vb remove the shucks from

SHUCKER, -S ▸ shuck

SHUCKING ▸ shuck

SHUCKS pl n something of little value ▷ interj exclamation of disappointment, annoyance, etc

SHUDDER, -S vb shake or tremble violently, esp with horror ▷ n instance of shaking or trembling

SHUDDERY adj shuddering

SHUFFLE, -D, -S vb walk without lifting the feet ▷ n act of shuffling

SHUFFLER ▸ shuffle

SHUFFLES ▸ shuffle

SHUFTI, -S same as ▸ shufty

SHUFTIES ▸ shufty

SHUFTIS ▸ shufty

SHUFTY, SHUFTIES n look

SHUGGY, SHUGGIES n swing, as at a fairground

SHUL, -N, -S Yiddish word for > synagogue

SHULE, -D, -S, SHULING vb saunter

SHULN ▸ shul

SHULS ▸ shul

SHUMAI pl n (in Japan) small stuffed dumplings

SHUN, -NED, -NING, -S vb avoid

SHUNLESS adj old word meaning not to be shunned

SHUNNED ▸ shun

SHUNNER, -S ▸ shun

SHUNNING ▸ shun

SHUNPIKE vb take side road to avoid toll at turnpike

SHUNS ▸ shun

SHUNT, -ED, -ING, -S vb move (objects or people) to a different position ▹ n shunting

SHUNTER, -S n small railway locomotive used for manoeuvring coaches

SHUNTING ▸ shunt

SHUNTS ▸ shunt

SHURA, -S n consultative council or assembly

SHURIKEN n Japanese weapon with blades or points, thrown by hand

SHUSH, -ED, -ES, -ING interj be quiet! ▹ vb quiet by saying 'shush'

SHUSHER, -S ▸ shush

SHUSHES ▸ shush

SHUSHING ▸ shush

SHUT, -S, -TING vb bring together or fold, close

SHUTDOWN n closing of a factory, shop, or other business ▹ vb discontinue operations permanently

SHUTE, -D, -S, SHUTING variant of ▸ chute

SHUTEYE, -S n sleep

SHUTING ▸ shute

SHUTOFF, -S n device that shuts something off

SHUTOUT, -S n game in which the opposing team does not score

SHUTS ▸ shut

SHUTTER, -S n hinged doorlike cover for closing off a window ▹ vb close or equip with a shutter

SHUTTING ▸ shut

SHUTTLE, -D, -S n bobbin-like device used in weaving ▹ vb move by or as if by a shuttle

SHUTTLER ▸ shuttle

SHUTTLES ▸ shuttle

SHVITZ, -ED, -ES vb sweat

SHWA, -S same as ▸ schwa

SHWANPAN same as ▸ swanpan

SHWAS ▸ shwa

SHWESHWE n African cotton print fabric

SHY, SHIED, SHIES, SHIEST, -EST, -ING adj not at ease in company ▹ vb start back in fear ▹ n throw

SHYER, -S ▸ shy

SHYEST ▸ shy

SHYING ▸ shy

SHYISH ▸ shy

SHYLOCK, -S vb lend money at an exorbitant rate of interest

SHYLY ▸ shy

SHYNESS ▸ shy

SHYPOO, -S n liquor of poor quality

SHYSTER, -S n person who uses discreditable or unethical methods

SI same as ▸ te

SIAL, -S n silicon-rich and aluminium-rich rocks of the earth's continental upper crust

SIALIC ▸ sial

SIALID, -S n species of fly

SIALIDAN ▸ sialid

SIALIDS ▸ sialid

SIALOID adj resembling saliva

SIALON, -S n type of ceramic

SIALS ▸ sial

SIAMANG, -S n large black gibbon

SIAMESE, -D, -S variant of ▸ siameze

SIAMEZE, -D, -S vb join together

SIB, -S n blood relative

SIBB, -S n sib

SIBILANT adj hissing ▹ n consonant pronounced with a hissing sound

SIBILATE vb pronounce or utter (words or speech) with a hissing sound

SIBILOUS ▸ sibilant

SIBLING, -S n brother or sister

SIBS ▸ sib

SIBSHIP, -S n group of children of the same parents

SIBYL, -S n (in ancient Greece and Rome) prophetess

SIBYLIC ▸ sibyl

SIBYLLIC ▸ sibyl

SIBYLS ▸ sibyl

SIC, -CED, -CING, -S adv thus ▹ vb attack

SICARIO, -S n hired gunman, esp in Latin America

SICCAN adj Scots word meaning such

SICCAR adj sure

SICCED ▸ sic

SICCING ▸ sic

SICCITY n dryness

SICE, -S same as ▸ syce

SICH adj old form of such

SICHT, -ED, -ING, -S Scot word for ▸ sight

SICK, -ED, -ER, -EST, -ING, -S adj vomiting or likely to vomit ▹ n vomit ▹ vb vomit

SICKBAY, -S n room for the treatment of sick people

SICKBED, -S n bed where sick person lies

SICKED ▸ sick

SICKEE, -S n person off work through illness

SICKEN, -ED, -S vb make nauseated or disgusted

SICKENER n something that induces sickness or nausea

SICKENS ▸ sicken

SICKER ▸ sick

SICKERLY adv Scots word meaning surely

SICKEST ▸ sick

SICKIE, -S n day of sick leave from work

SICKING ▸ sick

SICKISH ▸ sick

SICKLE, -D, -S, SICKLING n tool with a curved blade for cutting grass or grain ▹ vb cut with a sickle

SICKLIED ▸ sickly

SICKLIER ▸ sickly

SICKLIES ▸ sickly

SICKLILY ▸ sickly

SICKLING ▸ sickle

SICKLY, SICKLIED, SICKLIER, SICKLIES adj unhealthy, weak ▹ adv suggesting sickness ▹ vb make sickly

SICKNESS n particular illness or disease

SICKOUT, -S n industrial action in which all workers report sick simultaneously

SICKROOM n room to which a person who is ill is confined

SICKS ▸ sick

SICKY n day off work due to illness

SICLIKE adj Scots word meaning suchlike

SICS ▸ sic

SIDA, -S n Australian hemp plant

SIDALCEA n type of perennial N American plant

SIDAS ▸ sida

SIDDHA, -S n (in Hinduism) person who has achieved perfection

SIDDHI, -S n (in Hinduism) power attained with perfection

SIDDUR, -IM, -S n Jewish prayer book

SIDE, -D, -S n line or surface that borders anything ▹ adj at or on the side

S

SIDEARM, -S n weapon worn on belt ▷ vb provide with a sidearm

SIDEBAND n frequency band either above or below the carrier frequency

SIDEBAR, -S n small newspaper article beside larger one

SIDEBONE n damage to the cartilage in a horse's hoof

SIDEBURN n strip of whiskers down one side of the face

SIDECAR, -S n small passenger car on the side of a motorcycle

SIDED ▷ side

SIDEDLY adv pertaining to given number of sides

SIDEHILL n side of hill

SIDEKICK n close friend or associate

SIDELESS adj without sides

SIDELINE n subsidiary interest or source of income ▷ vb prevent (a player) from taking part in a game

SIDELING adj to one side ▷ adv sideways ▷ n slope, esp on the side of a road

SIDELOCK n long lock of hair on side of head

SIDELONG adj sideways ▷ adv obliquely

SIDEMAN, SIDEMEN n member of a dance band or a jazz group other than the leader

SIDEMEAT n meat from the side of a pig

SIDEMEN ▷ sideman

SIDENOTE n note written in margin

SIDEPATH n minor path

SIDER, -S n one who sides with another

SIDERAL adj from the stars

SIDERATE vb strike violently

SIDEREAL adj of or determined with reference to the stars

SIDERITE n pale yellow to brownish-black mineral

SIDEROAD n (esp in Ontario) a road going at right angles to concession roads

SIDERS ▷ sider

SIDES ▷ side

SIDESHOW n entertainment offered along with the main show

SIDESLIP same as ▷ slip

SIDESMAN, SIDESMEN n man elected to help the parish church warden

SIDESPIN n horizontal spin put on ball

SIDESTEP vb dodge (an issue) ▷ n movement to one side, such as in dancing or boxing

SIDEWALK n paved path for pedestrians, at the side of a road

SIDEWALL n either of the sides of a pneumatic tyre between the tread and the rim

SIDEWARD adj directed or moving towards one side ▷ adv towards one side

SIDEWAY variant of ▷ sideways

SIDEWAYS adv or from the side ▷ adj moving or directed to or from one side

SIDEWISE adv sideways

SIDH pl n fairy people

SIDHA, -S n (in Hinduism) person who has achieved perfection

SIDHE pl n inhabitants of fairyland

SIDHUISM n contrived metaphor or simile

SIDING, -S n short stretch of railway track on which trains are shunted from the main line

SIDLE, -D, -S, SIDLING vb walk in a furtive manner ▷ n sideways movement

SIDLER, -S ▷ sidle

SIDLES ▷ sidle

SIDLING ▷ sidle

SIECLE, -S n century, period, or era

SIEGE, -D, -S, SIEGING n surrounding and blockading of a place ▷ vb lay siege to

SIEGER, -S n person who besieges

SIEGES ▷ siege

SIEGING ▷ siege

SIELD adj (archaic) provided with a ceiling

SIEMENS n SI unit of electrical conductance

SIEN, -S n old word meaning scion

SIENITE, -S n type of igneous rock

SIENNA, -S n reddish- or yellowish-brown pigment made from natural earth

SIENS ▷ sien

SIENT, -S n old word meaning scion

SIEROZEM n type of soil

SIERRA, -S n range of mountains in Spain or America with jagged peaks

SIERRAN ▷ sierra

SIERRAS ▷ sierra

SIES interj in South Africa, an exclamation of disgust

SIESTA, -S n afternoon nap, taken in hot countries

SIETH, -S n old form of scythe

SIEUR, -S n French word meaning lord

SIEVE, -D, -S, SIEVING n utensil with mesh through which a substance is sifted or strained ▷ vb sift or strain through a sieve

SIEVERT, -S n derived SI unit of dose equivalent, equal to 1 joule per kilogram

SIEVES ▷ sieve

SIEVING ▷ sieve

SIF adj South African slang for disgusting

SIFAKA, -S n either of two large rare arboreal lemuroid primates

SIFFLE, -D, -S, SIFFLING vb whistle

SIFFLEUR n male professional whistler

SIFFLING ▷ siffle

SIFREI ▷ sefer

SIFT, -ED, -ING, -S vb remove the coarser particles from a substance with a sieve

SIFTER, -S ▷ sift

SIFTING ▷ sift

SIFTINGS pl n material or particles separated out by or as if by a sieve

SIFTS ▷ sift

SIG, -S n short for signature

SIGANID, -S n tropical fish

SIGH, -ED, -S n long audible breath expressing sadness, tiredness, relief, or longing ▷ vb utter a sigh

SIGHER, -S ▷ sigh

SIGHFUL ▷ sigh

SIGHING, -S n act of sighing

SIGHLESS ▷ sigh

SIGHLIKE ▷ sigh

SIGHS ▷ sigh

SIGHT, -ING, -S n ability to see ▷ vb catch sight of

SIGHTED adj not blind

SIGHTER, -S n any of six practice shots allowed to each competitor in a tournament

SIGHTING ▷ sight

SIGHTLY adj pleasing or attractive to see

SIGHTS ▷ sight

SIGHTSEE, SIGHTSAW vb visit the famous or interesting sights of (a place)

SIGIL, -S n seal or signet

SIGLA, -S n list of symbols used in a book

SIGLOS, SIGLOI n silver coin of ancient Persia

SIGLUM n symbol used in book

SIGMA, -S n 18th letter in the Greek alphabet

SIGMATE, -D, -S adj shaped like the Greek letter sigma or the Roman S ▷ n sigmate thing ▷ vb add a sigma

SIGMATIC ▷ sigmate

SIGMOID, -S adj shaped like the letter S ▷ n S-shaped bend in the final portion of the large intestine

SIGN, -ED, -S n indication of something not immediately or outwardly observable ▷ vb write (one's name) on (a document or letter) to show its authenticity

SIGNA pl n symbols

SIGNABLE ▷ sign

SIGNAGE, -S n signs collectively

SIGNAL, -ED, -S n sign or gesture to convey information ▷ adj very important ▷ vb convey (information) by signal

SIGNALER ▷ signal

SIGNALLY adv conspicuously or especially

SIGNALS ▷ signal

SIGNARY n set of symbols

SIGNED ▷ sign

SIGNEE, -S n person signing document

SIGNER, -S n person who signs something

SIGNET, -ED, -S n small seal used to authenticate documents ▷ vb stamp or authenticate with a signet

SIGNEUR old spelling of ▷ **senior**

SIGNIEUR n old word meaning lord

SIGNIFY vb indicate or suggest

SIGNING, -S n system of communication using hand and arm movements

SIGNIOR, -I, -S same as ▷ **signor**

SIGNIORY n old word meaning lordship

SIGNLESS ▷ sign

SIGNOR, -S n Italian term of address equivalent to sir or Mr

SIGNORA, -S n Italian term of address equivalent to madam or Mrs

SIGNORE, -S, SIGNORI n Italian man: a title of respect equivalent to sir

SIGNORIA n government of Italian city

SIGNORS ▷ signor

SIGNORY same as ▷ **seigniory**

SIGNPOST n post bearing a sign that shows the way ▷ vb mark with signposts

SIGNS ▷ sign

SIGS ▷ sig

SIJO, -S n Korean poem

SIK adj excellent

SIKA, -S n Japanese forest-dwelling deer

SIKE, -S n small stream

SIKER adj old spelling of sicker

SIKES ▷ sike

SIKORSKY n type of helicopter

SIKSIK, -S n Arctic ground squirrel

SILAGE, -D, -S, SILAGING n fodder crop harvested while green and partially fermented in a silo ▷ vb make silage

SILANE, -S n gas containing silicon

SILASTIC n tradename for a type of flexible silicone rubber

SILD, -S n any of various small young herrings

SILE, -D, -S, SILING vb pour with rain

SILEN, -S n god of woodland

SILENCE, -S n absence of noise or speech ▷ vb make silent

SILENCED adj (of a member of the clergy) forbidden to preach or perform clerical functions

SILENCER n device to reduce the noise of an engine exhaust or gun

SILENCES ▷ silence

SILENE, -S n type of plant with mostly red or pink flowers, often grown as a garden plant

SILENI ▷ silenus

SILENS ▷ silen

SILENT, -ER, -S adj tending to speak very little ▷ n silent film

SILENTLY ▷ silent

SILENTS ▷ silent

SILENUS, SILENI n woodland deity

SILER, -S n strainer

SILES ▷ sile

SILESIA, -S n twill-weave fabric of cotton or other fibre

SILEX, -ES n type of heat-resistant glass made from fused quartz

SILICA, -S n hard glossy mineral found as quartz and in sandstone

SILICATE n compound of silicon, oxygen, and a metal

SILICIC adj of, concerned with, or containing silicon or an acid obtained from silicon

SILICIDE n any one of a class of binary compounds formed between silicon and certain metals

SILICIFY vb convert or be converted into silica

SILICIUM rare name for ▷ **silicon**

SILICLE, -S same as ▷ **silicula**

SILICON, -S n brittle nonmetallic element ▷ adj denoting an area that contains much high-technology industry

SILICONE n tough synthetic substance made from silicon and used in lubricants

SILICONS ▷ silicon

SILICULA n short broad siliqua occurring in cruciferous plants

SILICULE same as ▷ **silicula**

SILING ▷ sile

SILIQUA, -E, -S n long dry dehiscent fruit of cruciferous plants such as the wallflower

SILIQUE, -S same as ▷ **siliqua**

SILK, -ED, -ING, -S n fibre made by the larva of a certain moth ▷ vb (of maize) develop long hairlike styles

SILKEN, -ED, -S adj made of silk ▷ vb make like silk

SILKIE, -S n Scots word for a seal

SILKIER ▷ silky

SILKIES ▷ silky

SILKIEST ▷ silky

SILKILY ▷ silky

SILKING ▷ silk

SILKLIKE ▷ silk

SILKS ▷ silk

SILKTAIL n waxwing

SILKWEED another name for ▷ **milkweed**

SILKWORM n caterpillar that spins a cocoon of silk

SILKY, SILKIER, SILKIEST adj of or like silk

SILL, -S n ledge at the bottom of a window or door

SILLABUB same as ▷ **syllabub**

S

SILLADAR n Indian irregular cavalryman

SILLER, -S n silver ▷ adj silver

SILLIBUB n syllabub

SILLIER ▶ silly

SILLIES ▶ silly

SILLIEST ▶ silly

SILLILY ▶ silly

SILLOCK, -S n young coalfish

SILLS ▶ sill

SILLY, SILLIER, SILLIES, SILLIEST adj foolish ▷ n foolish person

SILO, -ED, -ING, -S n pit or airtight tower for storing silage or grains ▷ vb put in a silo

SILOXANE n any of a class of compounds containing alternate silicon and oxygen atoms

SILPHIUM, SILPHIA n American flowering wild plant

SILT, -ED, -ING, -S n mud deposited by moving water ▷ vb fill or be choked with silt

SILTIER ▶ silty

SILTIEST ▶ silty

SILTING ▶ silt

SILTS ▶ silt

SILTY, SILTIER, SILTIEST ▶ silt

SILURIAN adj formed in the third period of the Palaeozoic

SILURID, -S n type of freshwater fish of the family which includes catfish

SILURIST n member of ancient Silurian tribe

SILUROID n freshwater fish

SILVA, -E, -S same as ▶ sylva

SILVAN, -S same as ▶ sylvan

SILVAS ▶ silva

SILVATIC adj wild, not domestic

SILVER, -ED, -S n white precious metal ▷ adj made of or of the colour of silver ▷ vb coat with silver

SILVERER ▶ silver

SILVERLY adv like silver

SILVERN adj silver

SILVERS ▶ silver

SILVERY adj like silver

SILVEX, -ES n type of weedkiller

SILVICAL adj of trees

SILVICS n study of trees

SIM, -S n computer game that simulates an activity

SIMA, -S n silicon-rich and magnesium-rich rocks of the earth's oceanic crust

SIMAR, -S variant spelling of ▶ cymar

SIMARRE, -S n woman's loose gown

SIMARS ▶ simar

SIMARUBA same as ▶ simarouba

SIMAS ▶ sima

SIMATIC ▶ sima

SIMAZINE n organic weedkiller

SIMBA, -S E African word for ▶ lion

SIMCHA, -S n Jewish celebration or festival

SIMI, -S n East African sword

SIMIAL adj of apes

SIMIAN, -S n monkey or ape ▷ adj of or resembling a monkey or ape

SIMILAR adj alike but not identical

SIMILE, -S n figure of speech comparing one thing to another, using 'as' or 'like'

SIMILISE same as ▶ similize

SIMILIZE vb use similes

SIMILOR, -S n alloy used in cheap jewellery

SIMIOID adj of apes

SIMIOUS adj of apes

SIMIS ▶ simi

SIMITAR, -S same as ▶ scimitar

SIMKIN, -S word used in India for > champagne

SIMLIN, -S n American variety of squash plant

SIMMER, -ED, -S vb cook gently at just below boiling point ▷ n state of simmering

SIMNEL, -S n fruit cake with marzipan eaten at Easter

SIMOLEON n American slang for dollar

SIMONIAC n person who is guilty of practising simony

SIMONIES ▶ simony

SIMONISE same as ▶ simonize

SIMONIST ▶ simony

SIMONIZE vb polish with wax

SIMONY, SIMONIES n practice of buying or selling Church benefits

SIMOOM, -S n hot suffocating sand-laden desert wind

SIMOON, -S same as ▶ simoom

SIMORG, -S n bird in Persian myth

SIMP, -S short for > simpleton

SIMPAI, -S n Indonesian monkey

SIMPER, -ED, -S vb smile in a silly or affected way ▷ n simpering smile

SIMPERER ▶ simper

SIMPERS ▶ simper

SIMPKIN, -S word used in India for > champagne

SIMPLE, -D, -S, -ST, SIMPLING adj easy to understand or do ▷ vb archaic word meaning to look for medicinal herbs

SIMPLER, -S ▶ simple

SIMPLES ▶ simple

SIMPLEST ▶ simple

SIMPLEX adj permitting the transmission of signals in only one direction in a radio circuit ▷ n simple not a compound word

SIMPLIFY vb make less complicated

SIMPLING ▶ simple

SIMPLISM n quality of being extremely naive

SIMPLIST n old word meaning expert in herbal medicine

SIMPLY adv in a simple manner

SIMPS ▶ simp

SIMS ▶ sim

SIMUL, -S adj simultaneous ▷ n simultaneous broadcast

SIMULANT adj simulating ▷ n simulant thing

SIMULAR, -S n person or thing that simulates or imitates ▷ adj fake

SIMULATE vb make a pretence of ▷ adj assumed or simulated

SIMULIUM n tropical fly

SIMULS ▶ simul

SIMURG, -S same as ▶ simurgh

SIMURGH, -S n bird in Persian myth

SIMURGS ▶ simurg

SIN, -NED, -NING, -S n offence or transgression ▷ vb commit a sin

SINAPISM n mixture of black mustard seeds and an adhesive, applied to the skin

SINCE prep during the period of time after ▷ adv from that time

SINCERE, -R adj without pretence or deceit

SINCIPUT n forward upper part of the skull

SIND, -ED, -S variant of ▶ syne

SINDING, -S ▶ sind

SINDON, -S n type of cloth

SINDS ▶ sind

SINE, -D, -S, SINING same as ▶ **syne**

SINECURE n paid job with minimal duties

SINED ▶ sine

SINES ▶ sine

SINEW, -ING, -S n tough fibrous tissue joining muscle to bone ▷ vb make strong

SINEWED adj having sinews

SINEWIER ▶ sinewy

SINEWING ▶ sinew

SINEWS ▶ sinew

SINEWY, SINEWIER adj lean and muscular

SINFONIA, SINFONIE n symphony orchestra

SINFUL adj guilty of sin

SINFULLY ▶ sinful

SING, -S, SUNG vb make musical sounds with the voice ▷ n act or performance of singing

SINGABLE ▶ sing

SINGE, -D, -ING, -S vb burn the surface of ▷ n superficial burn

SINGER, -S n person who sings, esp professionally

SINGES ▶ singe

SINGING, -S ▶ sing

SINGLE, -D, -S, SINGLING adj one only ▷ n single thing ▷ vb pick out from others

SINGLET, -S n sleeveless vest

SINGLING ▶ single

SINGLY adv one at a time

SINGS ▶ sing

SINGSONG n informal singing session ▷ adj (of the voice) repeatedly rising and falling in pitch

SINGULAR adj (of a word or form) denoting one person or thing ▷ n singular form of a word

SINGULT, -S n old word meaning sob

SINH, -S n hyperbolic sine

SINICAL ▶ sine

SINICISE same as ▶ **sinicize**

SINICIZE vb make Chinese

SINING ▶ sine

SINISTER adj threatening or suggesting evil or harm

SINK, SANK, -S vb submerge (in liquid) ▷ n fixed basin with a water supply and drainage pipe

SINKABLE ▶ sink

SINKAGE, -S n act of sinking or degree to which something sinks or has sunk

SINKER, -S n weight for a fishing line

SINKFUL, -S n amount that can be held in a sink

SINKHOLE n depression in the ground surface where a stream disappears underground

SINKIER ▶ sinky

SINKIEST ▶ sinky

SINKING, -S ▶ sink

SINKS ▶ sink

SINKY, SINKIER, SINKIEST adj giving underfoot

SINLESS adj free from sin or guilt

SINNED ▶ sin

SINNER, -ED, -S n person that sins ▷ vb behave like a sinner

SINNET, -S n braided rope

SINNING ▶ sin

SINOLOGY n study of Chinese culture, etc

SINOPIA, -S, SINOPIE n pigment made from iron ore

SINOPIS n pigment made from iron ore

SINOPITE n iron ore

SINS ▶ sin

SINSYNE adv Scots word meaning since

SINTER, -ED, -S n whitish porous incrustation deposited from hot springs ▷ vb form large particles from (powders) by heating or pressure

SINTERY adj consisting of sinter

SINUATE, -S vb wind

SINUATED same as ▶ **sinuate**

SINUATES ▶ sinuate

SINUITIS variant of > sinusitis

SINUOSE adj sinuous

SINUOUS adj full of turns or curves

SINUS, -ES n hollow space in a bone, esp an air passage opening into the nose

SINUSOID n blood vessel in certain organs ▷ adj resembling a sinus

SIP, -PED, -PING, -S vb drink in small mouthfuls ▷ n amount sipped

SIPE, -D, -S, SIPING vb soak

SIPHON, -ED, -S n bent tube which uses air pressure to draw liquid from a container ▷ vb draw off thus

SIPHONAL adj like a siphon

SIPHONED ▶ siphon

SIPHONET n sucking tube on an aphid

SIPHONIC same as ▶ **siphonal**

SIPHONS ▶ siphon

SIPING ▶ sipe

SIPPABLE adj able to be sipped

SIPPED ▶ sip

SIPPER, -S ▶ sip

SIPPET, -S n small piece of toast eaten with soup or gravy

SIPPING ▶ sip

SIPPLE, -D, -S, SIPPLING vb sip

SIPPY adj as in **sippy cup** infant's drinking cup with a tight-fitting lid and perforated spout

SIPS ▶ sip

SIR, -RED, -RING, -S n polite term of address for a man ▷ vb call someone 'sir'

SIRCAR, -S n government in India

SIRDAR, -S same as ▶ **sardar**

SIRE, -D, -S, SIRING n male parent of a horse or other domestic animal ▷ vb father

SIREE, -S emphasized form of ▶ **sir**

SIREN, -S n device making a loud wailing noise as a warning

SIRENIAN n animal such as the dugong and manatee

SIRENIC ▶ siren

SIRENISE variant of ▶ **sirenize**

SIRENIZE vb bewitch

SIRENS ▶ siren

SIRES ▶ sire

SIRGANG, -S n Asian bird

SIRI, -S n betel

SIRIASIS, SIRIASES n sunstroke

SIRIH, -S n betel

SIRING, -S ▶ sire

SIRIS ▶ siri

SIRKAR, -S n government in India

SIRLOIN, -S n prime cut of loin of beef

SIRNAME, -D, -S vb old form of surname

SIROC, -S n sirocco

SIROCCO, -S n hot wind blowing from N Africa into S Europe

SIROCS ▶ siroc

SIRONISE same as ▶ **sironize**

SIRONIZE vb treat (a woollen fabric) chemically to prevent it wrinkling after being washed

SIROSET adj of the chemical treatment of woollen fabrics to give a permanent-press effect

S

SIRRA, -S *disrespectful form of* ▸ **sir**

SIRRAH, -S *n* contemptuous term used in addressing a man or boy

SIRRAS ▸ **sirra**

SIRRED ▸ **sir**

SIRREE, -S *n* form of 'sir' used for emphasis

SIRRING ▸ **sir**

SIRS ▸ **sir**

SIRTUIN, -S *n* protein that regulates cell metabolism and ageing

SIRUP, -ED, -ING, -S *same as* ▸ **syrup**

SIRUPIER ▸ **sirupy**

SIRUPING ▸ **sirup**

SIRUPS ▸ **sirup**

SIRUPY, SIRUPIER ▸ **sirup**

SIRVENTE *n* verse form employed by the troubadours of Provence to satirize political themes

SIS, -ES *n* sister

SISAL, -S *n* (fibre of) plant used in making ropes

SISERARY *n* scolding

SISES ▸ **sis**

SISKIN, -S *n* yellow-and-black finch

SISS, -ES *shortening of* ▸ **sister**

SISSIER ▸ **sissy**

SISSIES ▸ **sissy**

SISSIEST ▸ **sissy**

SISSOO, -S *n* Indian tree

SISSY, SISSIER, SISSIES, SISSIEST *n* derogatory word for a weak or cowardly (person) ▹ *adj* weak or cowardly

SISSYISH ▸ **sissy**

SIST, -ED, -ING, -S *vb* Scottish law term meaning stop

SISTER, -ED, -S *n* girl or woman with the same parents as another person ▹ *adj* closely related, similar ▹ *vb* be or be like a sister

SISTERLY *adj* of or like a sister

SISTERS ▸ **sister**

SISTING ▸ **sist**

SISTRA ▸ **sistrum**

SISTROID *adj* contained between the convex sides of two intersecting curves

SISTRUM, SISTRA, -S *n* musical instrument of ancient Egypt consisting of a metal rattle

SISTS ▸ **sist**

SIT, SAT, -S *vb* rest one's body upright on the buttocks

SITAR, -S *n* Indian stringed musical instrument

SITARIST ▸ **sitar**

SITARS ▸ **sitar**

SITCOM, -S *n* situation comedy

SITE, -D, -S *n* place where something is, was, or is intended to be located ▹ *vb* provide with a site

SITELLA, -S *n* type of small generally black-and-white bird

SITES ▸ **site**

SITFAST, -S *n* sore on a horse's back caused by rubbing of the saddle

SITH *archaic word for* ▸ **since**

SITHE, -D, -S, SITHING *vb* old form of scythe

SITHEE *interj* look here! listen!

SITHEN *adv* old word meaning since

SITHENCE *adv* old word meaning since

SITHENS *adv* old word meaning since

SITHES ▸ **sithe**

SITHING ▸ **sithe**

SITING, -S *n* act of siting

SITKA *modifier* as in **sitka spruce** tall North American spruce tree

SITKAMER *n* sitting room

SITOLOGY *n* scientific study of food, diet, and nutrition

SITREP, -S *n* military situation report

SITS ▸ **sit**

SITTAR, -S *n* sitar

SITTELLA *variant spelling of* ▸ **sitella**

SITTEN *adj* dialect word for in the saddle

SITTER, -S *n* baby-sitter

SITTINE, -S *adj* of nuthatch bird family ▹ *n* type of nuthatch

SITTING, -S ▸ **sit**

SITUATE, -D, -S *vb* place ▹ *adj* (now used esp in legal contexts) situated

SITULA, -E *n* bucket-shaped container

SITUP, -S *n* exercise in which the body is brought into a sitting position

SITUS, -ES *n* position or location

SITZ *n* as in **sitz bath** bath in which the buttocks and hips are immersed in hot water

SITZMARK *n* depression in the snow where a skier has fallen

SIVER, -S *same as* ▸ **syver**

SIWASH, -ED, -ES *vb* (in the Pacific Northwest) to camp out with only natural shelter

SIX, -ES *n* one more than five

SIXAIN, -S *n* stanza or poem of six lines

SIXAINE, -S *n* six-line stanza of poetry

SIXAINS ▸ **sixain**

SIXER, -S *same as* ▸ **six**

SIXES ▸ **six**

SIXFOLD *adj* having six times as many or as much ▹ *adv* by six times as many or as much

SIXISH *adj* around six years of age

SIXMO, -S *n* book size resulting from folding a sheet of paper into six leaves

SIXPENCE *n* former British and Australian coin worth six pennies

SIXPENNY *adj* (of a nail) two inches in length

SIXSCORE *n* hundred and twenty

SIXTE, -S *n* sixth of eight basic positions from which a parry or attack can be made in fencing

SIXTEEN, -S *n* six and ten

SIXTES ▸ **sixte**

SIXTH, -S *n* number six in a series ▹ *adj* coming after the fifth and before the seventh in numbering order

SIXTHLY *adv* in the sixth place or position

SIXTHS ▸ **sixth**

SIXTIES ▸ **sixty**

SIXTIETH *adj* being the ordinal number of *sixty* in numbering order ▹ *n* one of 60 approximately equal parts of something

SIXTY, SIXTIES *n* six times ten

SIXTYISH ▸ **sixty**

SIZABLE *adj* quite large

SIZABLY ▸ **sizable**

SIZAR, -S *n* undergraduate receiving a maintenance grant from the college

SIZE, -S *n* dimensions, bigness ▹ *vb* arrange according to size

SIZEABLE *same as* ▸ **sizable**

SIZEABLY ▸ **sizable**

SIZED *adj* of a specified size

SIZEISM, -S *n* discrimination on the basis of a person's size

SIZEIST, -S ▸ **sizeism**

SIZEL, -S *n* scrap metal clippings

SIZER, -S ▸ **size**

SIZES ▸ **size**

SIZIER ▸ sizy
SIZIEST ▸ sizy
SIZINESS ▸ size
SIZING, -S ▸ size
SIZISM, -S *n* discrimination against people because of weight
SIZIST, -S ▸ sizism
SIZY, SIZIER, SIZIEST ▸ size
SIZZLE, -D, -S *vb* make a hissing sound like frying fat ▷ *n* hissing sound
SIZZLER, -S *n* something that sizzles
SIZZLES ▸ sizzle
SIZZLING *adj* extremely hot
SJAMBOK, -S *n* whip or riding crop made of hide ▷ *vb* beat with a sjambok
SJOE *interj* South African exclamation of surprise, admiration, exhaustion, etc
SKA, -S *n* type of Jamaican pop music of the 1960s
SKAG, -S *same as* ▸ scag
SKAIL, -ED, -ING, -S *vb* Scots word meaning disperse
SKAITH, -ED, -S *vb* Scots word meaning injure
SKALD, -S *n* (in ancient Scandinavia) a bard or minstrel
SKALDIC ▸ skald
SKALDS ▸ skald
SKANGER, -S *n* insulting Irish word for a young working-class person who wears casual sports clothes
SKANK, -ED, -ING, -S *n* fast dance to reggae music ▷ *vb* perform this dance
SKANKER, -S ▸ skank
SKANKIER ▸ skanky
SKANKING ▸ skank
SKANKS ▸ skank
SKANKY, SKANKIER *adj* dirty or unattractive
SKART, -S *Scots word for* > cormorant
SKARTH, -S *Scots word for* > cormorant
SKARTS ▸ skart
SKAS ▸ ska
SKAT, -S *n* three-handed card game using 32 cards
SKATE, -D, -S *n* boot with a steel blade or sets of wheels attached to the sole ▷ *vb* glide on or as if on skates
SKATER, -S *n* person who skates
SKATES ▸ skate
SKATING, -S ▸ skate
SKATOL, -S *n* skatole
SKATOLE, -S *n* white or brownish crystalline solid

SKATOLS ▸ skatol
SKATS ▸ skat
SKATT, -S *n* dialect word meaning throw
SKAW, -S *variant of* ▸ scaw
SKEAN, -S *n* kind of double-edged dagger
SKEANE, -S *same as* ▸ skein
SKEANS ▸ skean
SKEAR, -ED, -ING, -S *dialect form of* ▸ scare
SKEARIER ▸ skeary
SKEARING ▸ skear
SKEARS ▸ skear
SKEARY, SKEARIER *dialect form of* ▸ scary
SKED, -DED, -DING, -S *vb* short for schedule
SKEE, -D, -ING, -S *variant spelling of* ▸ ski
SKEECHAN *n* old Scots type of beer
SKEED ▸ skee
SKEEF *adj* South African slang for at an oblique angle
SKEEING ▸ skee
SKEELY, SKEELIER *adj* Scots word meaning skilful
SKEEN, -S *n* type of ibex
SKEER, -ED, -ING, -S *dialect form of* ▸ scare
SKEERIER ▸ skeery
SKEERING ▸ skeer
SKEERS ▸ skeer
SKEERY, SKEERIER *dialect form of* ▸ scary
SKEES ▸ skee
SKEET, -S *n* form of clay-pigeon shooting
SKEETER, -S *informal word for* ▸ mosquito
SKEETS ▸ skeet
SKEEVY, SKEEVIER *adj* repulsive
SKEG, -S *n* reinforcing brace between the after end of a keel and the rudderpost
SKEGG, -S *n* skeg
SKEGGER, -S *n* young salmon
SKEGGS ▸ skegg
SKEGS ▸ skeg
SKEIGH, -ER *adj* Scots word meaning shy
SKEIN, -ED, -ING, -S *n* yarn wound in a loose coil ▷ *vb* wind into a skein
SKELDER, -S *vb* beg
SKELETAL ▸ skeleton
SKELETON *n* framework of bones inside a person's or animal's body ▷ *adj* reduced to a minimum
SKELF, -S *n* splinter of wood, esp when embedded accidentally in the skin

SKELL, -S *n* homeless person
SKELLIE *adj* skelly
SKELLIED ▸ skelly
SKELLIER ▸ skelly
SKELLIES ▸ skelly
SKELLOCH *n* Scots word meaning scream
SKELLS ▸ skell
SKELLUM, -S *n* rogue
SKELLY, SKELLIED, SKELLIER, SKELLIES *n* whitefish of certain lakes in the Lake District ▷ *vb* look sideways or squint ▷ *adj* cross-eyed
SKELM, -S *n* villain or crook
SKELP, -ED, -ING, -S *vb* slap ▷ *n* slap
SKELPIT *vb* Scots word meaning skelped
SKELPS ▸ skelp
SKELTER, -S *vb* scurry
SKELUM, -S *n* Scots word meaning rascal
SKEN, -NED, -NING, -S *vb* squint or stare
SKENE, -S *n* Scots word meaning dagger
SKENNED ▸ sken
SKENNING ▸ sken
SKENS ▸ sken
SKEO, -ES, -S *n* Scots dialect word meaning hut
SKEP, -PED, -PING, -S *n* beehive, esp one constructed of straw ▷ *vb* gather into a hive
SKEPFUL, -S *n* amount skep will hold
SKEPPED ▸ skep
SKEPPING ▸ skep
SKEPS ▸ skep
SKEPSIS *n* doubt
SKEPTIC, -S *same as* ▸ sceptic
SKER, -RED, -RING, -S *vb* scour
SKERRICK *n* small fragment or amount
SKERRIES ▸ skerry
SKERRING ▸ sker
SKERRY, SKERRIES *n* rocky island or reef
SKERS ▸ sker
SKET, -S, -TED, -TING *vb* splash (water)
SKETCH, -ED, -ES *n* rough drawing ▷ *vb* make a sketch (of)
SKETCHER ▸ sketch
SKETCHES ▸ sketch
SKETCHY *adj* incomplete or inadequate
SKETS ▸ sket
SKETTED ▸ sket
SKETTING ▸ sket

S

SKEW, -ED, -EST, -ING, -S vb make slanting or crooked ▷ adj slanting or crooked ▷ n slanting position

SKEWBACK n sloping surface on both sides of a segmental arch that takes the thrust

SKEWBALD adj (horse) marked with patches of white and another colour ▷ n horse with this marking

SKEWED ▶ **skew**

SKEWER, -ED, -S n pin to hold meat together during cooking ▷ vb fasten with a skewer

SKEWEST ▶ **skew**

SKEWING ▶ **skew**

SKEWNESS n quality or condition of being skew

SKEWS ▶ **skew**

SKI, -S n one of a pair of long runners fastened to boots for gliding over snow or water ▷ vb travel on skis

SKIABLE ▶ **ski**

SKIAGRAM n picture made from shadows

SKIATRON n type of cathode ray tube

SKIBOB, -S n vehicle made of two short skis for gliding down snow slopes

SKID, -DED, -S vb (of a moving vehicle) slide sideways uncontrollably ▷ n skidding

SKIDDER, -S ▶ **skid**

SKIDDIER ▶ **skiddy**

SKIDDING n act of skidding

SKIDDOO, -S vb go away quickly

SKIDDY, SKIDDIER ▶ **skid**

SKIDLID, -S n crash helmet

SKIDMARK n mark left by a skid

SKIDOO, -ED, -S n snowmobile ▷ vb travel on a skidoo

SKIDOOER n person who rides a skidoo

SKIDOOS ▶ **skidoo**

SKIDPAD, -S n area of road used to test skidding

SKIDPAN, -S n area made slippery so that vehicle drivers can practise controlling skids

SKIDS ▶ **skid**

SKIDWAY, -S n platform on which logs ready for sawing are piled

SKIED ▶ **sky**

SKIER, -S ▶ **ski**

SKIES ▶ **sky**

SKIEY, -ER, -EST adj of the sky

SKIFF, -ED, -ING, -S n small boat ▷ vb travel in a skiff

SKIFFLE, -D, -S n style of popular music of the 1950s ▷ vb play this style of music

SKIFFS ▶ **skiff**

SKIING, -S ▶ **ski**

SKIJORER > **skijoring**

SKILFUL adj having or showing skill

SKILFULL less common spelling of ▶ **skilful**

SKILL, -S n special ability or expertise

SKILLED adj possessing or demonstrating skill, or special training

SKILLESS ▶ **skill**

SKILLET, -S n small frying pan or shallow cooking pot

SKILLFUL same as ▶ **skilful**

SKILLIER ▶ **skilly**

SKILLIES ▶ **skilly**

SKILLING n former Scandinavian coin of low denomination

SKILLION n part of a building having a lower, esp sloping, roof

SKILLS ▶ **skill**

SKILLY, SKILLIER, SKILLIES n thin soup or gruel ▷ adj skilled

SKIM, -MED, -MING, -S vb remove floating matter from the surface of (a liquid) ▷ n act or process of skimming

SKIMMER, -S n person or thing that skims

SKIMMIA, -S n shrub of S and SE Asia

SKIMMING ▶ **skim**

SKIMP, -ED, -ING, -S vb not invest enough time, money, material, etc

SKIMPIER ▶ **skimpy**

SKIMPILY ▶ **skimpy**

SKIMPING ▶ **skimp**

SKIMPS ▶ **skimp**

SKIMPY, SKIMPIER adj scanty or insufficient

SKIMS ▶ **skim**

SKIN, -NED, -NING, -S n outer covering of the body ▷ vb remove the skin of

SKINCARE n use of cosmetics in taking care of skin

SKINFOOD n cosmetic cream for the skin

SKINFUL, -S n sufficient alcoholic drink to make one drunk

SKINHEAD n youth with very short hair

SKINK, -ED, -ING, -S n type of lizard with reduced limbs and smooth scales ▷ vb serve a drink

SKINKER, -S ▶ **skink**

SKINKING ▶ **skink**

SKINKS ▶ **skink**

SKINLESS ▶ **skin**

SKINLIKE ▶ **skin**

SKINNED ▶ **skin**

SKINNER, -S n person who prepares or deals in animal skins

SKINNIER ▶ **skinny**

SKINNIES ▶ **skinny**

SKINNING ▶ **skin**

SKINNY, SKINNIER, SKINNIES adj thin ▷ n information

SKINS ▶ **skin**

SKINSUIT n skintight one-piece garment worn by cyclists to reduce friction

SKINT, -ER, -EST adj having no money

SKIO, -ES, -S n Scots dialect word meaning hut

SKIORER, -S n one who engages in the sport of skioring

SKIORING n sport of being towed on skis by horse

SKIOS ▶ **skio**

SKIP, -PED, -PING, -S vb leap lightly from one foot to the other ▷ n skipping

SKIPJACK n important food fish of tropical seas

SKIPLANE n aircraft fitted with skis to enable it to land on and take off from snow

SKIPPED ▶ **skip**

SKIPPER, -S vb captain ▷ n captain of a ship or aircraft

SKIPPET, -S n small round box for preserving a document or seal

SKIPPIER ▶ **skippy**

SKIPPING ▶ **skip**

SKIPPY, SKIPPIER adj in high spirits

SKIPS ▶ **skip**

SKIRL, -ED, -ING, -S n sound of bagpipes ▷ vb (of bagpipes) to give out a shrill sound

SKIRMISH n brief or minor fight or argument ▷ vb take part in a skirmish

SKIRR, -ED, -ING, -S vb move, run, or fly rapidly ▷ n whirring or grating sound, as of the wings of birds in flight

SKIRRET, -S n umbelliferous Old World plant

SKIRRING ▸ skirr

SKIRRS ▸ skirr

SKIRT, -ED, -S n woman's garment hanging from the waist ▷ vb border

SKIRTER, -S n person who skirts fleeces

SKIRTING n border fixed round the base of an interior wall to protect it from kicks, dirt, etc

SKIRTS ▸ skirt

SKIS ▸ ski

SKIT, -S n brief satirical sketch

SKITCH, -ED, -ES vb (of a dog) to attack

SKITE, -D, -S, SKITING n boast ▷ vb boast

SKITS ▸ skit

SKITTER, -S vb move or run rapidly or lightly

SKITTERY adj moving lightly and rapidly

SKITTISH adj playful or lively

SKITTLE, -D, -S n bottle-shaped object used as a target in some games ▷ vb play skittles

SKIVE, -D, -S vb evade work or responsibility

SKIVER, -ED, -S n tanned outer layer split from a skin ▷ vb cut leather

SKIVES ▸ skive

SKIVIE, -R, -ST adj old Scots word meaning disarranged

SKIVING, -S ▸ skive

SKIVVY, SKIVVIED, SKIVVIES n female servant who does menial work ▷ vb work as a skivvy

SKIVY ▸ skive

SKIWEAR, -S n clothes for skiing in

SKLATE, -D, -S, SKLATING Scots word for ▸ slate

SKLENT, -ED, -S Scots word for ▸ slant

SKLIFF, -ED, -S n Scots word meaning little piece ▷ vb shuffle (the feet)

SKLIM, -MED, -S vb Scots word meaning climb

SKOAL, -ED, -ING, -S same as ▸ skol

SKODY, SKODIER, SKODIEST adj dirty, unkempt

SKOFF, -ED, -ING, -S vb eat greedily

SKOG, -GED, -GING, -S same as ▸ scog

SKOKIAAN n (in South Africa) a potent alcoholic beverage

SKOL, -ED, -ING, -LED, -LING, -S sentence substitute good health! (a drinking toast) ▷ vb down (an alcoholic drink) in one go

SKOLIA ▸ skolion

SKOLING ▸ skol

SKOLION, SKOLIA n ancient Greek drinking song

SKOLLED ▸ skol

SKOLLIE same as ▸ skolly

SKOLLIES ▸ skolly

SKOLLING ▸ skol

SKOLLY, SKOLLIES n hooligan, usually one of a gang

SKOLS ▸ skol

SKOOKUM, -S adj strong or brave ▷ n strong or brave person

SKOOL, -S childish spelling of ▸ school

SKOOSH, -ED, -ES vb Scots word meaning squirt

SKORT, -S n pair of shorts with a front panel which gives the appearance of a skirt

SKOSH, -ES n little bit

SKRAN, -S n food

SKREEGH, -S same as ▸ skreigh

SKREEN, -S n screen

SKREIGH, -S vb Scots word meaning screech

SKRIECH, -S same as ▸ skreigh

SKRIED ▸ skry

SKRIEGH, -S same as ▸ skreigh

SKRIES ▸ skry

SKRIK, -S n South African word meaning fright

SKRIKE, -D, -S, SKRIKING vb cry

SKRIKS ▸ skrik

SKRIMP, -ED, -S vb steal apples

SKRONK, -S n type of dissonant, grating popular music

SKRUMP, -ED, -S vb steal apples

SKRY, SKRIED, SKRIES, -ING vb try to tell future

SKRYER, -S ▸ skry

SKRYING ▸ skry

SKUA, -S n large predatory gull

SKUDLER, -S n Scots word meaning leader of festivities

SKUG, -GED, -GING, -S vb shelter

SKULK, -ED, -ING, -S vb move stealthily ▷ n person who skulks

SKULKER, -S ▸ skulk

SKULKING ▸ skulk

SKULKS ▸ skulk

SKULL, -ED, -ING, -S n bony framework of the head ▷ vb strike on the head

SKULLCAP n close-fitting brimless cap

SKULLED ▸ skull

SKULLING ▸ skull

SKULLS ▸ skull

SKULPIN, -S n North American fish

SKUMMER, -S same as ▸ scumber

SKUNK, -ED, -ING, -S n small mammal which emits a foul-smelling fluid when attacked ▷ vb defeat overwhelmingly in a game

SKUNKIER ▸ skunky

SKUNKING ▸ skunk

SKUNKS ▸ skunk

SKUNKY, SKUNKIER ▸ skunk

SKURRY, SKURRIED, SKURRIES vb scurry

SKUTTLE, -D, -S vb scuttle

SKY, SKIED, SKIES, -ED, -ING n upper atmosphere as seen from the earth ▷ vb hit high in the air

SKYBOARD n small board used for skysurfing

SKYBORN adj born in heaven

SKYBORNE adj flying through sky

SKYBOX, -ES n luxurious suite high up in the stand of a sports stadium

SKYCAP, -S n luggage porter at American airport

SKYCLAD adj naked

SKYDIVE, -D, -S, SKYDOVE vb take part in skydiving

SKYDIVER ▸ skydive

SKYDIVES ▸ skydive

SKYDOVE ▸ skydive

SKYED ▸ sky

SKYER, -S n cricket ball hit up into air

SKYEY, -ER, -EST, SKYIER, SKYIEST adj of the sky

SKYF, -ED, -ING, -S n South African slang for a cigarette or substance for smoking ▷ vb smoke a cigarette

SKYGLOW, -S n glow in the night sky caused by urban lights

SKYHOME, -S n Australian word for a sub-penthouse flat in a tall building

SKYHOOK, -S n hook hung from a helicopter

SKYIER ▸ skyey
SKYIEST ▸ skyey
SKYING ▸ sky
SKYISH ▸ sky
SKYJACK, -S vb hijack (an aircraft)
SKYLAB, -S n orbiting space station
SKYLARK, -S n lark that sings while soaring at a great height ▷ vb play or frolic
SKYLESS adj having no sky
SKYLIGHT n window in a roof or ceiling
SKYLIKE ▸ sky
SKYLINE, -S n outline of buildings, trees, etc against the sky
SKYLIT adj having skylight
SKYMAN, SKYMEN n paratrooper
SKYPHOS, SKYPHOI n ancient Greek drinking cup
SKYR, -S n Scandinavian cheese
SKYRE, -D, -S, SKYRING vb Scots word meaning shine
SKYRMION n (in theoretical physics) mathematical model used to model baryons
SKYRS ▸ skyr
SKYSAIL, -S n square sail set above the royal on a square-rigger
SKYSCAPE n painting, drawing, photograph, etc, representing or depicting the sky
SKYSURF, -S vb perform freefall aerobatics
SKYTE, -D, -S, SKYTING vb Scots word meaning slide
SKYWALK, -S n tightrope walk at great height
SKYWARD adj towards the sky ▷ adv towards the sky
SKYWARDS same as ▸ skyward
SKYWATCH vb watch the sky in search of celestial bodies or aircraft
SKYWAY, -S n air route
SKYWRITE, SKYWROTE vb write message in sky with smoke from aircraft
SLAB, -BED, -BIER, -S n broad flat piece ▷ vb cut or make into a slab or slabs
SLABBER, -S vb dribble from the mouth
SLABBERY ▸ slabber
SLABBIER ▸ slab
SLABBIES ▸ slabby
SLABBING n act of slabbing

SLABBY, SLABBIES n person who works with slabs of timber
SLABLIKE ▸ slab
SLABS ▸ slab
SLACK, -ED, -EST, -ING same as ▸ slake
SLACKEN, -S vb make or become slack
SLACKER, -S n person who evades work or duty
SLACKEST ▸ slack
SLACKING ▸ slack
SLACKLY ▸ slack
SLACKS pl n casual trousers
SLADANG, -S n Malayan tapir
SLADE, -S n little valley
SLAE, -S Scots word for ▸ sloe
SLAG, -GED, -S n waste left after metal is smelted ▷ vb criticize
SLAGGIER ▸ slaggy
SLAGGING ▸ slag
SLAGGY, SLAGGIER ▸ slag
SLAGHEAP n heap of slag waste
SLAGS ▸ slag
SLAHAL, -S same as ▸ lahal
SLAID, -S vb (Scot) sledge
SLAIN ▸ slay
SLAINTE interj cheers!
SLAIRG, -ED, -S Scots word for ▸ spread
SLAISTER vb cover with a sloppy mess ▷ n sloppy mess
SLAKABLE ▸ slake
SLAKE, -D, -S, SLAKING vb satisfy (thirst or desire)
SLAKER, -S ▸ slake
SLAKES ▸ slake
SLAKING ▸ slake
SLALOM, -ED, -S n skiing or canoeing race over a winding course ▷ vb take part in a slalom
SLALOMER ▸ slalom
SLALOMS ▸ slalom
SLAM, -MED, -MING, -S vb shut, put down, or hit violently and noisily ▷ n act or sound of slamming
SLAMMER, -S n prison
SLAMMING ▸ slam
SLAMS ▸ slam
SLANDER, -S n false and malicious statement about a person ▷ vb utter slander about
SLANE, -S n spade for cutting turf
SLANG, -ED, -ING, -S n very informal language ▷ vb use insulting language to (someone)
SLANGER, -S n street vendor

SLANGIER ▸ slangy
SLANGILY ▸ slang
SLANGING ▸ slang
SLANGISH ▸ slang
SLANGS ▸ slang
SLANGY, SLANGIER ▸ slang
SLANK dialect word for ▸ lank
SLANT, -ED, -S vb lean at an angle, slope ▷ n slope
SLANTER, -S same as ▸ slinter
SLANTIER ▸ slanty
SLANTING ▸ slant
SLANTLY ▸ slant
SLANTS ▸ slant
SLANTY, SLANTIER adj slanting
SLAP, -PED, -S n blow with the open hand or a flat object ▷ vb strike with the open hand or a flat object
SLAPDASH adj careless and hasty ▷ adv carelessly or hastily ▷ n slapdash activity or work ▷ vb do in a hurried and careless manner
SLAPHEAD n derogatory term for a bald person
SLAPJACK n simple card game
SLAPPED ▸ slap
SLAPPER, -S ▸ slap
SLAPPING ▸ slap
SLAPS ▸ slap
SLAPSHOT n hard, fast, often wild, shot executed with a powerful downward swing
SLART, -ED, -ING, -S vb spill (something)
SLASH, -ED, -ES vb cut with a sweeping stroke ▷ n sweeping stroke
SLASHER, -S n machine used for cutting scrub or undergrowth in the bush
SLASHES ▸ slash
SLASHING adj aggressively critical ▷ n act of slashing
SLAT, -S, -TED, -TING n narrow strip of wood or metal ▷ vb provide with slats
SLATCH, -ES n slack part of rope
SLATE, -D, -S n rock which splits easily into thin layers ▷ vb cover with slates ▷ adj dark grey
SLATER, -S n person trained in laying roof slates
SLATES ▸ slate
SLATEY adj slightly mad
SLATHER, -S vb spread quickly or lavishly
SLATIER ▸ slaty

SLATIEST ▸ **slaty**
SLATING, -S n act or process of laying slates
SLATS ▸ **slat**
SLATTED ▸ **slat**
SLATTER, -S vb be slovenly
SLATTERY adj slovenly
SLATTING ▸ **slat**
SLATY, SLATIER, SLATIEST adj consisting of or resembling slate
SLAVE, -D, -S, SLAVING n person legally owned by another and forced to work for them ▷ vb work like a slave
SLAVER, -ED, -S n person or ship engaged in the slave trade ▷ vb dribble saliva from the mouth
SLAVERER ▸ **slaver**
SLAVERS ▸ **slaver**
SLAVERY n state or condition of being a slave
SLAVES ▸ **slave**
SLAVEY, -S n female general servant
SLAVING ▸ **slave**
SLAVISH adj of or like a slave
SLAW, -S short for ▸ **coleslaw**
SLAY, SLAIN, -ED, -S vb kill
SLAYABLE ▸ **slay**
SLAYED ▸ **slay**
SLAYER, -S ▸ **slay**
SLAYING, -S n act of slaying
SLAYS ▸ **slay**
SLEAVE, -D, -S, SLEAVING n tangled thread ▷ vb disentangle (twisted thread, etc)
SLEAZE, -D, -S, SLEAZING n behaviour considered dishonest or disreputable ▷ vb behave in a sleazy manner
SLEAZIER ▸ **sleazy**
SLEAZILY ▸ **sleazy**
SLEAZING ▸ **sleaze**
SLEAZY, SLEAZIER adj run-down or sordid
SLEB, -S n celebrity
SLED, -DED, -DING, -ED, -S same as ▸ **sledge**
SLEDDER, -S ▸ **sled**
SLEDDING ▸ **sled**
SLEDED ▸ **sled**
SLEDGE, -D, -S, SLEDGING n carriage on runners for sliding on snow ▷ vb travel by sledge
SLEDGER, -S ▸ **sledge**
SLEDGES ▸ **sledge**
SLEDGING ▸ **sledge**
SLEDS ▸ **sled**
SLEE, -R, -ST Scots word for ▸ **sly**

SLEECH, -ES n slippery mud
SLEECHY ▸ **sleech**
SLEEK, -ED, -EST, -ING, -S adj glossy, smooth, and shiny ▷ vb make smooth and glossy, as by grooming, etc
SLEEKEN, -S vb make sleek
SLEEKER, -S ▸ **sleek**
SLEEKEST ▸ **sleek**
SLEEKIER ▸ **sleeky**
SLEEKING ▸ **sleek**
SLEEKIT adj smooth
SLEEKLY ▸ **sleek**
SLEEKS ▸ **sleek**
SLEEKY, SLEEKIER ▸ **sleek**
SLEEP, -ING, -S, SLEPT n state of rest characterized by unconsciousness ▷ vb be in or as if in a state of sleep
SLEEPER, -S n railway car fitted for sleeping in
SLEEPERY Scots word for ▸ **sleepy**
SLEEPIER ▸ **sleepy**
SLEEPILY ▸ **sleepy**
SLEEPING ▸ **sleep**
SLEEPOUT n small building for sleeping in
SLEEPRY Scots word for ▸ **sleepy**
SLEEPS ▸ **sleep**
SLEEPY, SLEEPIER adj needing sleep
SLEER ▸ **slee**
SLEEST ▸ **slee**
SLEET, -ED, -ING, -S n rain and snow or hail falling together ▷ vb fall as sleet
SLEETIER ▸ **sleety**
SLEETING ▸ **sleet**
SLEETS ▸ **sleet**
SLEETY, SLEETIER ▸ **sleet**
SLEEVE, -D, -S n part of a garment which covers the arm
SLEEVEEN n sly obsequious smooth-tongued person
SLEEVER, -S n old beer measure
SLEEVES ▸ **sleeve**
SLEEVING n tubular flexible insulation into which bare wire can be inserted
SLEEZY, SLEEZIER adj sleazy
SLEIDED adj old word meaning separated
SLEIGH, -ED, -S same as ▸ **sledge**
SLEIGHER ▸ **sleigh**
SLEIGHS ▸ **sleigh**
SLEIGHT, -S n skill or cunning
SLENDER adj slim
SLENTER, -S same as ▸ **slinter**

SLEPT ▸ **sleep**
SLEUTH, -ED, -S n detective ▷ vb track or follow
SLEW, -ED, -ING, -S vb twist sideways, esp awkwardly
SLEY, -S n weaver's tool for separating threads
SLICE, -D, -S n thin flat piece cut from something ▷ vb cut into slices
SLICER, -S ▸ **slice**
SLICES ▸ **slice**
SLICING, -S ▸ **slice**
SLICK, -ED, -EST, -ING, -S adj persuasive and glib ▷ n patch of oil on water ▷ vb make smooth or sleek
SLICKEN, -S vb make smooth
SLICKER, -S n sly or untrustworthy person
SLICKEST ▸ **slick**
SLICKING ▸ **slick**
SLICKLY ▸ **slick**
SLICKS ▸ **slick**
SLID ▸ **slide**
SLIDABLE ▸ **slide**
SLIDDEN ▸ **slide**
SLIDDER, -S vb slip
SLIDDERY adj slippery
SLIDE, SLID, SLIDDEN, -D, -S vb slip smoothly along (a surface) ▷ n act of sliding
SLIDER, -S ▸ **slide**
SLIDES ▸ **slide**
SLIDEWAY n sloping channel down which things are slid
SLIDING, -S ▸ **slide**
SLIER ▸ **sly**
SLIEST ▸ **sly**
SLIEVE, -S n Irish mountain
SLIGHT, -ED, -ER, -S adj small in quantity or extent ▷ n snub ▷ vb insult (someone) by behaving rudely
SLIGHTLY adv in small measure or degree
SLIGHTS ▸ **slight**
SLILY ▸ **sly**
SLIM, -MED, -MEST, -MING, -S adj not heavy or stout, thin ▷ vb make or become slim by diet and exercise
SLIMDOWN n instance of an organization cutting staff
SLIME, -D, -S, SLIMING n unpleasant thick slippery substance ▷ vb cover with slime
SLIMIER ▸ **slimy**
SLIMIEST ▸ **slimy**
SLIMILY ▸ **slimy**
SLIMING ▸ **slime**
SLIMLINE adj slim

S

SLIMLY ► slim
SLIMMED ► slim
SLIMMER, -S ► slim
SLIMMEST ► slim
SLIMMING ► slim
SLIMMISH ► slim
SLIMNESS ► slim
SLIMPSY *adj* thin and flimsy
SLIMS ► slim
SLIMSY, SLIMSIER *adj* frail
SLIMY, SLIMIER, SLIMIEST *adj* of, like, or covered with slime
SLING, -ING, -S, SLUNG *n* bandage hung from the neck to support an injured hand or arm ▷ *vb* throw
SLINGER, -S ► sling
SLINGIER ► slingy
SLINGING ► sling
SLINGS ► sling
SLINGY, SLINGIER *adj* resembling the act of using a sling
SLINK, -ED, -ING, -S, SLUNK *vb* move furtively or guiltily ▷ *n* animal, esp a calf, born prematurely
SLINKER, -S ► slink
SLINKIER ► slinky
SLINKILY ► slinky
SLINKING ► slink
SLINKS ► slink
SLINKY, SLINKIER *adj* (of clothes) figure-hugging
SLINTER, -S *n* dodge, trick, or stratagem
SLIOTAR, -S *n* ball used in hurling
SLIP, -PED, -PING, -S *vb* lose balance by sliding ▷ *n* slipping
SLIPCASE *n* protective case for a book
SLIPE, -D, -S, SLIPING *n* wool removed from the pelt of a slaughtered sheep ▷ *vb* remove skin
SLIPFORM *n* mould used in building
SLIPING ► slipe
SLIPKNOT *n* knot tied so that it will slip along the rope round which it is made
SLIPLESS ► slip
SLIPOUT, -S *n* instance of slipping out
SLIPOVER *adj* of or denoting a garment that can be put on easily over the head ▷ *n* such a garment, esp a sleeveless pullover
SLIPPAGE *n* act or an instance of slipping
SLIPPED ► slip

SLIPPER, -S *n* light shoe for indoor wear ▷ *vb* hit or beat with a slipper
SLIPPERY *adj* so smooth or wet as to cause slipping or be difficult to hold
SLIPPIER ► slippy
SLIPPILY ► slippy
SLIPPING ► slip
SLIPPY, SLIPPIER *adj* slippery
SLIPRAIL *n* rail in a fence that can be slipped out of place to make an opening
SLIPS ► slip
SLIPSHOD *adj* (of an action) careless
SLIPSLOP *n* weak or unappetizing food or drink
SLIPSOLE *n* separate sole on shoe
SLIPT *vb* old form of slipped
SLIPUP, -S *n* mistake or mishap
SLIPWARE *n* pottery that has been decorated with clay
SLIPWAY, -S *n* launching slope on which ships are built or repaired
SLISH, -ES *n* old word meaning cut
SLIT, -S, -TED, -TING *n* long narrow cut or opening ▷ *vb* make a long straight cut in
SLITHER, -S *vb* slide unsteadily ▷ *n* slithering movement
SLITHERY *adj* moving with a slithering motion
SLITLESS ► slit
SLITLIKE ► slit
SLITS ► slit
SLITTED ► slit
SLITTER, -S ► slit
SLITTIER ► slitty
SLITTING ► slit
SLITTY, SLITTIER ► slit
SLIVE, -D, -N, -S, SLIVING, SLOVE *vb* slip
SLIVER, -ED, -S *n* small thin piece ▷ *vb* cut into slivers
SLIVERER ► sliver
SLIVERS ► sliver
SLIVES ► slive
SLIVING ► slive
SLIVOVIC *n* plum brandy
SLOAN, -S *n* severe telling-off
SLOB, -BED, -BING, -S *n* lazy and untidy person ▷ *vb* behave like a slob
SLOBBER, -S *vb* dribble or drool ▷ *n* liquid or saliva spilt from the mouth
SLOBBERY ► slobber

SLOBBIER ► slobby
SLOBBING ► slob
SLOBBISH ► slob
SLOBBY, SLOBBIER ► slob
SLOBLAND *n* muddy ground
SLOBS ► slob
SLOCKEN, -S *vb* Scots word meaning slake
SLOE, -S *n* sour blue-black fruit
SLOEBUSH *n* bush on which sloes grow
SLOES ► sloe
SLOETREE *n* sloe plant
SLOG, -GED, -GING, -S *vb* work hard and steadily ▷ *n* long and exhausting work or walk
SLOGAN, -S *n* catchword or phrase used in politics or advertising
SLOGANED *adj* having a slogan
SLOGANS ► slogan
SLOGGED ► slog
SLOGGER, -S ► slog
SLOGGING ► slog
SLOGS ► slog
SLOID, -S *n* Swedish woodwork
SLOJD, -S *same as* ► sloid
SLOKEN, -ED, -S *vb* Scots word meaning slake
SLOMMOCK *vb* walk assertively with a hip-rolling gait
SLOMO, -S *n* slow-motion sequence in a film
SLOOM, -ED, -ING, -S *vb* slumber
SLOOMIER ► sloomy
SLOOMING ► sloom
SLOOMS ► sloom
SLOOMY, SLOOMIER ► sloom
SLOOP, -S *n* small single-masted ship
SLOOSH, -ED, -ES *vb* wash with water
SLOOT, -S *n* ditch for irrigation or drainage
SLOP, -PED, -PING, -S *vb* splash or spill ▷ *n* spilt liquid
SLOPE, -D, -S *vb* slant ▷ *n* sloping surface
SLOPER, -S ► slope
SLOPES ► slope
SLOPIER ► slopy
SLOPIEST ► slopy
SLOPING ► slope
SLOPPED ► slop
SLOPPIER ► sloppy
SLOPPILY ► sloppy
SLOPPING ► slop
SLOPPY, SLOPPIER *adj* careless or untidy

SLOPS ▸ slop

SLOPWORK n manufacture of cheap shoddy clothing or the clothes so produced

SLOPY, SLOPIER, SLOPIEST ▸ slope

SLORM, -ED, -ING, -S vb wipe carelessly

SLOSH, -ED, -ES, -ING vb pour carelessly ▷ n splashing sound

SLOSHIER ▸ sloshy

SLOSHING ▸ slosh

SLOSHY, SLOSHIER ▸ slosh

SLOT, -S, -TED, -TING n narrow opening for inserting something ▷ vb make a slot or slots in

SLOTBACK n American football player

SLOTH, -ED, -ING, -S n slow-moving animal of tropical America ▷ vb be lazy

SLOTHFUL adj lazy or idle

SLOTHING ▸ sloth

SLOTHS ▸ sloth

SLOTS ▸ slot

SLOTTED ▸ slot

SLOTTER, -S ▸ slot

SLOTTING ▸ slot

SLOUCH, -ED, -ES vb sit, stand, or move with a drooping posture ▷ n drooping posture

SLOUCHER ▸ slouch

SLOUCHES ▸ slouch

SLOUCHY adj slouching

SLOUGH, -ED, -S n bog ▷ vb (of a snake) shed (its skin)

SLOUGHI, -S n N African breed of dog resembling a greyhound

SLOUGHS ▸ slough

SLOUGHY ▸ slough

SLOVE ▸ slive

SLOVEN, -S n habitually dirty or untidy person

SLOVENLY adj dirty or untidy ▷ adv in a slovenly manner

SLOVENRY n quality of being slovenly

SLOVENS ▸ sloven

SLOW, -ED, -ER, -EST, -S adj taking a longer time than is usual or expected ▷ adv slowly ▷ vb reduce the speed (of)

SLOWBACK n lazy person

SLOWDOWN n any slackening of pace

SLOWED ▸ slow

SLOWER ▸ slow

SLOWEST ▸ slow

SLOWING, -S ▸ slow

SLOWISH ▸ slow

SLOWLY ▸ slow

SLOWNESS ▸ slow

SLOWPOKE same as
> slowcoach

SLOWS ▸ slow

SLOWWORM n small legless lizard

SLOYD, -S n Swedish woodwork

SLUB, -BED, -BEST, -BING, -S n lump in yarn or fabric ▷ vb draw out and twist (a sliver of fibre) before spinning ▷ adj (of material) having an irregular appearance

SLUBB, -S same as ▸ slub

SLUBBED ▸ slub

SLUBBER, -S vb smear

SLUBBEST ▸ slub

SLUBBIER ▸ slubby

SLUBBING ▸ slub

SLUBBS ▸ slubb

SLUBBY, SLUBBIER ▸ slub

SLUBS ▸ slub

SLUDGE, -D, -S, SLUDGING n thick mud ▷ vb convert into sludge

SLUDGIER ▸ sludgy

SLUDGING ▸ sludge

SLUDGY, SLUDGIER adj consisting of, containing, or like sludge

SLUE, -D, -ING, -S, SLUING same as ▸ slew

SLUFF, -ED, -ING, -S same as ▸ slough

SLUG, -GED, -GING, -S n land snail with no shell ▷ vb hit hard

SLUGABED n person who remains in bed through laziness

SLUGFEST n fist fight

SLUGGARD n lazy person ▷ adj lazy

SLUGGED ▸ slug

SLUGGER, -S n (esp in boxing, baseball, etc) a person who strikes hard

SLUGGING ▸ slug

SLUGGISH adj slow-moving, lacking energy

SLUGHORN same as
▸ slogan

SLUGLIKE adj like a slug

SLUGS ▸ slug

SLUICE, -D, -S, SLUICING n channel that carries a rapid current of water ▷ vb drain water by means of a sluice

SLUICIER ▸ sluicy

SLUICING ▸ sluice

SLUICY, SLUICIER ▸ sluice

SLUING ▸ slue

SLUIT, -S n water channel in South Africa

SLUM, -MED, -MING, -S n squalid overcrowded house or area ▷ vb experience poorer places or conditions than usual

SLUMBER, -S n sleep ▷ vb sleep

SLUMBERY adj sleepy

SLUMBRY same as
▸ slumbery

SLUMGUM, -S n material left after wax is extracted from honeycomb

SLUMISM, -S n existence of slums

SLUMLORD n absentee landlord of slum property, esp one who profiteers

SLUMMED ▸ slum

SLUMMER, -S ▸ slum

SLUMMIER ▸ slummy

SLUMMING ▸ slum

SLUMMOCK vb move slowly and heavily

SLUMMY, SLUMMIER
▸ slum

SLUMP, -ED, -ING, -S vb (of prices or demand) decline suddenly ▷ n sudden decline in prices or demand

SLUMPIER ▸ slumpy

SLUMPING ▸ slump

SLUMPS ▸ slump

SLUMPY, SLUMPIER adj boggy

SLUMS ▸ slum

SLUNG ▸ sling

SLUNK ▸ slink

SLUR, -RED, -RING, -S vb pronounce or utter (words) indistinctly ▷ n slurring of words

SLURB, -S n suburban slum

SLURBAN ▸ slurb

SLURBS ▸ slurb

SLURP, -ED, -ING, -S vb eat or drink noisily ▷ n slurping sound

SLURPER, -S ▸ slurp

SLURPIER ▸ slurpy

SLURPING ▸ slurp

SLURPS ▸ slurp

SLURPY, SLURPIER adj making a slurping noise

SLURRED ▸ slur

SLURRIED ▸ slurry

SLURRIES ▸ slurry

SLURRING ▸ slur

SLURRY, SLURRIED, SLURRIES n muddy liquid mixture ▷ vb spread slurry

SLURS ▸ slur

SLURVE, -S n pitch in baseball combining elements of the slider and the curveball

S

SLUSE, -S same as ▶ **sluice**

SLUSH, -ED, -ES, -ING n watery muddy substance ▷ vb make one's way through or as if through slush

SLUSHIER ▶ **slushy**

SLUSHIES ▶ **slushy**

SLUSHILY ▶ **slushy**

SLUSHING ▶ **slush**

SLUSHY, SLUSHIER, SLUSHIES adj of, resembling, or consisting of slush ▷ n unskilled kitchen assistant

SLUTCH, -ES n mud

SLUTCHY ▶ **slutch**

SLY, SLIER, SLIEST, -ER, -EST adj crafty

SLYBOOTS pl n person who is sly

SLYER ▶ **sly**

SLYEST ▶ **sly**

SLYISH ▶ **sly**

SLYLY ▶ **sly**

SLYNESS ▶ **sly**

SLYPE, -S n covered passageway in a church

SMA Scots word for ▶ **small**

SMAAK, -ED, -ING, -S vb South African slang for like or love

SMACK, -ED, -S vb slap sharply ▷ n sharp slap ▷ adv squarely or directly

SMACKER, -S n loud kiss

SMACKING adj brisk

SMACKS ▶ **smack**

SMAIK, -S n Scots word meaning rascal

SMALL, -ED, -ER, -EST, -ING, -S adj not large in size, number, or amount ▷ n narrow part of the lower back ▷ adv into small pieces ▷ vb make small

SMALLAGE n wild celery

SMALLBOY n steward's assistant or deputy steward in European households in W Africa

SMALLED ▶ **small**

SMALLER ▶ **small**

SMALLEST ▶ **small**

SMALLING ▶ **small**

SMALLISH ▶ **small**

SMALLPOX n contagious disease with blisters that leave scars

SMALLS ▶ **small**

SMALLSAT n small communications satellite

SMALM, -ED, -ING, -S same as ▶ **smarm**

SMALMIER ▶ **smalmy**

SMALMILY ▶ **smalmy**

SMALMING ▶ **smalm**

SMALMS ▶ **smalm**

SMALMY, SMALMIER same as ▶ **smarmy**

SMALT, -S n type of silica glass coloured deep blue with cobalt oxide

SMALTI ▶ **smalto**

SMALTINE n mineral containing cobalt

SMALTITE n silver-white to greyish mineral

SMALTO, SMALTI, -S n coloured glass, etc, used in mosaics

SMALTS ▶ **smalt**

SMARAGD, -S n any green gemstone, such as the emerald

SMARAGDE same as ▶ **smaragd**

SMARAGDS ▶ **smaragd**

SMARM, -ED, -ING, -S vb bring (oneself) into favour (with) ▷ n obsequious flattery

SMARMIER ▶ **smarmy**

SMARMILY ▶ **smarmy**

SMARMING ▶ **smarm**

SMARMS ▶ **smarm**

SMARMY, SMARMIER adj unpleasantly suave or flattering

SMART, -ED, -ER, -EST, -ING adj well-kept and neat ▷ vb feel or cause stinging pain ▷ n stinging pain ▷ adv in a smart manner

SMARTEN, -S vb make or become smart

SMARTER ▶ **smart**

SMARTEST ▶ **smart**

SMARTIE same as ▶ **smarty**

SMARTIES ▶ **smarty**

SMARTING ▶ **smart**

SMARTISH ▶ **smart**

SMARTLY ▶ **smart**

SMARTS pl n know-how, intelligence, or wits

SMARTY, SMARTIES n would-be clever person

SMASH, -ED, -ES vb break violently and noisily ▷ n act or sound of smashing ▷ adv with a smash

SMASHER, -S n attractive person or thing

SMASHES ▶ **smash**

SMASHING adj excellent

SMASHUP, -S n bad collision of cars

SMATCH, -ED, -ES less common word for ▶ **smack**

SMATTER, -S n smattering ▷ vb prattle

SMAZE, -S n smoky haze, less damp than fog

SMEAR, -ED, -ING, -S vb spread with a greasy or sticky substance ▷ n dirty mark or smudge

SMEARER, -S ▶ **smear**

SMEARIER ▶ **smeary**

SMEARILY ▶ **smeary**

SMEARING ▶ **smear**

SMEARS ▶ **smear**

SMEARY, SMEARIER adj smeared, dirty

SMEATH, -S n duck

SMECTIC adj (of a substance) existing in state in which the molecules are oriented in layers

SMECTITE n type of clay mineral

SMEDDUM, -S n any fine powder

SMEE, -S n duck

SMEECH, -ED, -ES Southwest English dialect form of ▶ **smoke**

SMEEK, -ED, -ING, -S vb smoke

SMEES ▶ **smee**

SMEETH, -ED, -ING, -S n duck ▷ vb make smooth

SMEGMA, -S n whitish sebaceous secretion that accumulates beneath the prepuce

SMEIK, -ED, -S same as ▶ **smeke**

SMEIKING same as ▶ **smeking**

SMEIKS ▶ **smeik**

SMEKE, -D, -S, SMEKING n smoke ▷ vb smoke

SMELL, -ED, -ING, -S vb perceive (a scent or odour) by means of the nose ▷ n ability to perceive odours by the nose

SMELLER, -S ▶ **smell**

SMELLIER ▶ **smelly**

SMELLIES pl n pleasant-smelling products such as perfumes, body lotions, bath salts, etc

SMELLING ▶ **smell**

SMELLS ▶ **smell**

SMELLY, SMELLIER adj having a nasty smell

SMELT, -ED, -ING, -S vb extract metal from an ore

SMELTER, -S n industrial plant where smelting is carried out

SMELTERY variant of ▶ **smelter**

SMELTING ▶ **smelt**

SMELTS ▶ **smelt**

SMERK, -ED, -ING, -S same as ▶ **smirk**

SMEUSE, -S n way through hedge

SMEW, -S n duck of N Europe and Asia

SMICKER, -S vb smirk

SMICKET, -S n smock

SMIDDY, SMIDDIED, SMIDDIES Scots word for ▶ smithy

SMIDGE, -S n very small amount or part

SMIDGEN, -S n very small amount or part

SMIDGEON same as ▶ smidgen

SMIDGES ▶ smidge

SMIDGIN, -S same as ▶ smidgen

SMIGHT, -S same as ▶ smite

SMILAX, -ES n type of climbing shrub

SMILE, -D, -S n turning up of the corners of the mouth to show pleasure or friendliness ▷ vb give a smile

SMILEFUL adj full of smiles

SMILER, -S ▶ smile

SMILES ▶ smile

SMILET, -S n little smile

SMILEY, -S, SMILIER, SMILIES, SMILIEST n symbol depicting a smile or other facial expression ▷ adj cheerful

SMILING, -S ▶ smile

SMILODON n extinct sabre-toothed tiger

SMIR, -S n drizzly rain ▷ vb drizzle lightly

SMIRCH, -ED, -ES n stain ▷ vb disgrace

SMIRCHER ▶ smirch

SMIRCHES ▶ smirch

SMIRK, -ED, -S n smug smile ▷ vb give a smirk

SMIRKER, -S ▶ smirk

SMIRKIER ▶ smirky

SMIRKILY ▶ smirk

SMIRKING ▶ smirk

SMIRKS ▶ smirk

SMIRKY, SMIRKIER ▶ smirk

SMIRR, -ED, -ING, -S same as ▶ smir

SMIRRIER ▶ smirry

SMIRRING ▶ smirr

SMIRRS ▶ smirr

SMIRRY, SMIRRIER ▶ smirr

SMIRS ▶ smir

SMIRTING n flirting amongst those smoking outside a non-smoking office, pub, etc

SMISHING n phishing via text messages

SMITE, SMIT, -S, SMITING, SMITTEN, SMOTE vb strike hard

SMITER, -S ▶ smite

SMITES ▶ smite

SMITH, -ED, -S n worker in metal ▷ vb work in metal

SMITHERS pl n little shattered pieces

SMITHERY n trade or craft of a blacksmith

SMITHIED ▶ smithy

SMITHIES ▶ smithy

SMITHING n act of working as a smith

SMITHS ▶ smith

SMITHY, SMITHIED, SMITHIES n blacksmith's workshop ▷ vb work as a smith

SMITING ▶ smite

SMITS ▶ smit

SMITTED ▶ smit

SMITTEN ▶ smite

SMITTING ▶ smit

SMITTLE adj infectious

SMOCK, -ED, -S n loose overall ▷ vb gather (material) by sewing in a honeycomb pattern

SMOCKING n ornamental needlework used to gather material

SMOCKS ▶ smock

SMOG, -S n mixture of smoke and fog

SMOGGY, SMOGGIER ▶ smog

SMOGLESS ▶ smog

SMOGS ▶ smog

SMOILE, -D, -S, SMOILING same as ▶ smile

SMOKABLE ▶ smoke

SMOKE, -D, -S, SMOKING n cloudy mass that rises from something burning ▷ vb give off smoke or treat with smoke

SMOKEBOX n part of a steam engine or boiler

SMOKED ▶ smoke

SMOKEHO, -S same as ▶ smoko

SMOKEPOT n device for producing smoke

SMOKER, -S n person who habitually smokes tobacco

SMOKES ▶ smoke

SMOKEY, -S ▶ smoky

SMOKIE n smoked haddock

SMOKIER ▶ smoky

SMOKIES ▶ smoky

SMOKIEST ▶ smoky

SMOKILY ▶ smoky

SMOKING, -S ▶ smoke

SMOKO, -S n short break from work for tea or a cigarette

SMOKY, SMOKIER, SMOKIES, SMOKIEST adj filled with or giving off smoke, sometimes excessively ▷ n haddock that has been smoked

SMOLDER, -S same as ▶ smoulder

SMOLT, -S n young salmon at the stage when it migrates to the sea

SMOOCH, -ED, -ES vb kiss and cuddle ▷ n smooching

SMOOCHER ▶ smooch

SMOOCHES ▶ smooch

SMOOCHY adj romantic

SMOODGE, -D, -S same as ▶ smooch

SMOOGE, -D, -S, SMOOGING same as ▶ smooch

SMOOR, -ED, -ING, -S vb Scots word meaning put out fire

SMOOSH, -ED, -ES vb paint to give softened look

SMOOT, -ED, -ING, -S vb work as printer

SMOOTH, -ED, -ES, -S adj even in surface, texture, or consistency ▷ vb make smooth ▷ adv in a smooth manner ▷ n smooth part of something

SMOOTHE same as ▶ smooth

SMOOTHED ▶ smooth

SMOOTHEN vb make or become smooth

SMOOTHER ▶ smooth

SMOOTHES ▶ smooth

SMOOTHIE n smooth thick drink made with fruit and milk and sometimes ice cream

SMOOTHLY ▶ smooth

SMOOTHS ▶ smooth

SMOOTHY same as ▶ smoothie

SMOOTING ▶ smoot

SMOOTS ▶ smoot

SMORBROD n Danish hors d'oeuvre

SMORE, -D, -S, SMORING same as ▶ smoor

SMORG, -S n short for smorgasbord

SMORING ▶ smore

SMORZATO same as > smorzando

SMOTE ▶ smite

SMOTHER, -S vb suffocate or stifle ▷ n anything, such as a cloud of smoke, that stifles

SMOTHERY adj tending to smother

S

SMOUCH, -ED, -ES vb kiss
SMOULDER vb burn slowly with smoke but no flame ▷ n dense smoke, as from a smouldering fire
SMOULDRY adj smouldering
SMOUSE, -D, -S, SMOUSING vb South African word meaning peddle
SMOUSER, -S ▸ smouse
SMOUSES ▸ smouse
SMOUSING ▸ smouse
SMOUT, -ED, -ING, -S n child or undersized person ▷ vb creep or sneak
SMOWT, -S same as **▸ smout**
SMOYLE, -D, -S, SMOYLING same as **▸ smile**
SMRITI, -S n class of Hindu sacred literature
SMUDGE, -D, -S, SMUDGING vb make or become smeared or soiled ▷ n dirty mark
SMUDGER, -S ▸ smudge
SMUDGES ▸ smudge
SMUDGIER ▸ smudgy
SMUDGILY ▸ smudgy
SMUDGING ▸ smudge
SMUDGY, SMUDGIER adj smeared, blurred, or soiled, or likely to become so
SMUG, -GED, -GER, -GEST, -GING, -S adj self-satisfied ▷ vb make neat
SMUGGERY n condition or an instance of being smug
SMUGGEST ▸ smug
SMUGGING ▸ smug
SMUGGLE, -D, -S vb import or export (goods) secretly and illegally
SMUGGLER ▸ smuggle
SMUGGLES ▸ smuggle
SMUGLY ▸ smug
SMUGNESS ▸ smug
SMUGS ▸ smug
SMUR, -RED, -RING, -S same as **▸ smir**
SMURFING n intentionally overwhelming a computer network with messages
SMURRED ▸ smur
SMURRIER ▸ smurry
SMURRING ▸ smur
SMURRY, SMURRIER ▸ smur
SMURS ▸ smur
SMUSH, -ED, -ES, -ING vb crush
SMUT, -S, -TED, -TING n small dark smudge or stain ▷ vb mark or become marked or smudged
SMUTCH, -ED, -ES vb smudge ▷ n mark

SMUTCHY ▸ smutch
SMUTS ▸ smut
SMUTTED ▸ smut
SMUTTIER ▸ smutty
SMUTTILY ▸ smut
SMUTTING ▸ smut
SMUTTY, SMUTTIER ▸ smut
SMYTRIE, -S n Scots word meaning collection
SNAB, -S same as **▸ snob**
SNABBLE, -D, -S same as **▸ snaffle**
SNABS ▸ snab
SNACK, -ED, -ING, -S n light quick meal ▷ vb eat a snack
SNACKER, -S ▸ snack
SNACKIER ▸ snacky
SNACKING ▸ snack
SNACKS ▸ snack
SNACKY, SNACKIER adj of the nature of a snack
SNAFFLE, -D, -S n jointed bit for a horse ▷ vb steal
SNAFU, -ED, -ING, -S n confusion or chaos regarded as the normal state ▷ adj confused or muddled up, as usual ▷ vb throw into chaos
SNAG, -GED, -GING, -S n difficulty or disadvantage ▷ vb catch or tear on a point
SNAGGER, -S n type of fishing hook
SNAGGIER ▸ snaggy
SNAGGING ▸ snag
SNAGGLE, -S n tangled mass
SNAGGY, SNAGGIER adj having sharp protuberances
SNAGLIKE ▸ snag
SNAGS ▸ snag
SNAIL, -ED, -ING, -S n slow-moving mollusc with a spiral shell ▷ vb move slowly
SNAILERY n place where snails are bred
SNAILIER ▸ snaily
SNAILING ▸ snail
SNAILS ▸ snail
SNAILY, SNAILIER ▸ snail
SNAKE, -D, -S, SNAKING n long thin scaly limbless reptile ▷ vb move in a winding course like a snake
SNAKEBIT adj bitten by snake
SNAKED ▸ snake
SNAKEPIT n pit filled with snakes
SNAKES ▸ snake
SNAKEY same as **▸ snaky**
SNAKIER ▸ snaky
SNAKIEST ▸ snaky
SNAKILY ▸ snaky
SNAKING ▸ snake
SNAKISH ▸ snake

SNAKY, SNAKIER, SNAKIEST adj twisted or winding
SNAP, -PED, -PING, -S vb break suddenly ▷ n act or sound of snapping ▷ adj made on the spur of the moment ▷ adv with a snap
SNAPBACK n sudden rebound or change in direction
SNAPLESS ▸ snap
SNAPLINK n metal link used in mountaineering
SNAPPED ▸ snap
SNAPPER, -S n food fish of Australia and New Zealand ▷ vb stumble
SNAPPIER ▸ snappy
SNAPPILY ▸ snappy
SNAPPING ▸ snap
SNAPPISH same as **▸ snappy**
SNAPPY, SNAPPIER adj irritable
SNAPS ▸ snap
SNAPSHOT n informal photograph
SNAPTIN, -S n container for food
SNAPWEED n impatiens
SNAR, -RED, -RING, -S same as **▸ snarl**
SNARE, -D, -S n trap with a noose ▷ vb catch in or as if in a snare
SNARER, -S ▸ snare
SNARES ▸ snare
SNARF, -ED, -ING, -S vb eat or drink greedily
SNARFLE, -D, -S vb (of an animal) grunt and snort while rooting for food
SNARFS ▸ snarf
SNARIER ▸ snary
SNARIEST ▸ snary
SNARING, -S ▸ snare
SNARK, -S n imaginary creature in Lewis Carroll's poetry
SNARKIER ▸ snarky
SNARKILY ▸ snarky
SNARKS ▸ snark
SNARKY, SNARKIER adj unpleasant and scornful
SNARL, -ED, -S vb (of an animal) growl with bared teeth ▷ n act or sound of snarling
SNARLER, -S ▸ snarl
SNARLIER ▸ snarly
SNARLING ▸ snarl
SNARLS ▸ snarl
SNARLY, SNARLIER ▸ snarl
SNARRED ▸ snar
SNARRING ▸ snar
SNARS ▸ snar

SNARY, SNARIER, SNARIEST ▸ snare

SNASH, -ED, -ES, -ING *vb* Scots word meaning speak cheekily

SNASTE, -S *n* candle wick

SNATCH, -ED, -ES *vb* seize or try to seize suddenly ▷ *n* snatching

SNATCHER ▸ snatch

SNATCHES ▸ snatch

SNATCHY *adj* disconnected or spasmodic

SNATH, -S *n* handle of a scythe

SNATHE, -S *same as* ▸ snath

SNATHS ▸ snath

SNAW, -ED, -ING, -S Scots variant of ▸ snow

SNAZZIER ▸ snazzy

SNAZZILY ▸ snazzy

SNAZZY, SNAZZIER *adj* stylish and flashy

SNEAD, -S *n* scythe handle

SNEAK, -ED, -S *vb* move furtively ▷ *n* cowardly or underhand person ▷ *adj* without warning

SNEAKBOX *n* small camouflaged boat, used for wildfowl hunting

SNEAKED ▸ sneak

SNEAKER *n* canvas shoe with rubber sole

SNEAKERS ▸ sneaker

SNEAKEUP *n* sneaky person

SNEAKIER ▸ sneaky

SNEAKILY ▸ sneak

SNEAKING *adj* slight but persistent

SNEAKISH *adj* typical of a sneak

SNEAKS ▸ sneak

SNEAKSBY *n* sneak

SNEAKY, SNEAKIER *adj* ▸ sneak

SNEAP, -ED, -ING, -S *vb* nip

SNEATH, -S *same as* ▸ snath

SNEB, -BED, -BING, -S *same as* ▸ snib

SNEBBE, -S *same as* ▸ snub

SNEBBED ▸ sneb

SNEBBES ▸ snebbe

SNEBBING ▸ sneb

SNEBS ▸ sneb

SNECK, -ED, -ING, -S *n* small squared stone used in a rubble wall to fill spaces between stones ▷ *vb* fasten (a latch)

SNED, -DED, -DING, -S *vb* prune or trim

SNEE, -D, -ING, -S *vb* cut

SNEER, -ED, -S *n* contemptuous expression or remark ▷ *vb* show contempt by a sneer

SNEERER, -S ▸ sneer

SNEERFUL ▸ sneer

SNEERIER ▸ sneery

SNEERING ▸ sneer

SNEERS ▸ sneer

SNEERY, SNEERIER *adj* contemptuous or scornful

SNEES ▸ snee

SNEESH, -ED, -ES *n* Scots word meaning pinch of snuff ▷ *vb* take snuff

SNEESHAN *n* Scots word meaning pinch of snuff

SNEESHED ▸ sneesh

SNEESHES ▸ sneesh

SNEESHIN *same as* ▸ sneeshan

SNEEZE, -D, -S, SNEEZING *vb* expel air from the nose suddenly, involuntarily, and noisily ▷ *n* act or sound of sneezing

SNEEZER, -S ▸ sneeze

SNEEZES ▸ sneeze

SNEEZIER ▸ sneezy

SNEEZING ▸ sneeze

SNEEZY, SNEEZIER ▸ sneeze

SNELL, -ED, -ER, -EST, -ING, -S *adj* biting ▷ *vb* attach hook to fishing line

SNELLY ▸ snell

SNIB, -BED, -BING, -S *n* catch of a door or window ▷ *vb* bolt or fasten (a door)

SNICK, -ED, -ING, -S *n* small cut or notch ▷ *vb* make a small cut or notch in (something)

SNICKER, -S *same as* ▸ snigger

SNICKERY *adj* tending to snicker

SNICKET, -S *n* passageway between walls or fences

SNICKING ▸ snick

SNICKS ▸ snick

SNIDE, -D, -R, -S, -ST, SNIDING *adj* critical in an unfair and nasty way ▷ *n* sham jewellery ▷ *vb* fill or load

SNIDELY ▸ snide

SNIDER ▸ snide

SNIDES ▸ snide

SNIDEST ▸ snide

SNIDEY, SNIDIER, SNIDIEST *same as* ▸ snide

SNIDING ▸ snide

SNIES ▸ sny

SNIFF, -ED, -S *vb* inhale through the nose in short audible breaths ▷ *n* act or sound of sniffing

SNIFFER, -S *n* device for detecting hidden substances such as drugs

SNIFFIER ▸ sniffy

SNIFFILY ▸ sniffy

SNIFFING ▸ sniff

SNIFFISH *adj* disdainful

SNIFFLE, -D, -S *vb* sniff repeatedly, as when suffering from a cold ▷ *n* slight cold

SNIFFLER ▸ sniffle

SNIFFLES ▸ sniffle

SNIFFLY ▸ sniffle

SNIFFS ▸ sniff

SNIFFY, SNIFFIER *adj* contemptuous or scornful

SNIFT, -ED, -ING, -S *same as* ▸ sniff

SNIFTER, -S *n* small quantity of alcoholic drink ▷ *vb* sniff

SNIFTIER ▸ snifty

SNIFTING ▸ snift

SNIFTS ▸ snift

SNIFTY, SNIFTIER *adj* slang word meaning excellent

SNIG, -GED, -GING, -S *vb* drag (a felled log) by a chain or cable

SNIGGER, -S *n* sly laugh ▷ *vb* laugh slyly

SNIGGING ▸ snig

SNIGGLE, -D, -S *vb* fish for eels by dangling or thrusting a baited hook into cavities ▷ *n* baited hook used for sniggling eels

SNIGGLER ▸ sniggle

SNIGGLES ▸ sniggle

SNIGLET, -S *n* invented word

SNIGS ▸ snig

SNIP, -PED, -PING, -S *vb* cut in small quick strokes with scissors or shears ▷ *n* bargain ▷ *interj* representation of the sound of scissors or shears closing

SNIPE, -D, -S *n* wading bird with a long straight bill ▷ *vb* shoot at (a person) from cover

SNIPER, -S *n* person who shoots at someone from cover

SNIPES ▸ snipe

SNIPIER ▸ snipy

SNIPIEST ▸ snipy

SNIPING, -S ▸ snipe

SNIPPED ▸ snip

SNIPPER, -S ▸ snip

SNIPPET, -S *n* small piece

SNIPPETY ▸ snippet

SNIPPIER ▸ snippy

SNIPPILY ▸ snippy

SNIPPING ▸ snip

SNIPPY, SNIPPIER *adj* scrappy

SNIPS ▸ snip

S

SNIPY, SNIPIER, SNIPIEST adj like a snipe

SNIRT, -ED, -ING, -S n Scots word meaning suppressed laugh ▷ vb to snigger

SNIRTLE, -D, -S vb Scots word meaning snicker

SNIRTS ▶ snirt

SNIT, -S n fit of temper

SNITCH, -ED, -ES vb act as an informer ▷ n informer

SNITCHER ▶ snitch

SNITCHES ▶ snitch

SNITCHY adj bad-tempered or irritable

SNITS ▶ snit

SNITTY, SNITTIER adj cross or irritable

SNIVEL, -ED, -S vb cry in a whining way ▷ n act of snivelling

SNIVELER ▶ snivel

SNIVELLY adj tending to snivel

SNIVELS ▶ snivel

SNIVELY adj tending to snivel

SNOB, -S n person who judges others by social rank

SNOBBERY ▶ snob

SNOBBIER ▶ snobby

SNOBBILY ▶ snob

SNOBBISH ▶ snob

SNOBBISM ▶ snob

SNOBBY, SNOBBIER ▶ snob

SNOBLING n little snob

SNOBS ▶ snob

SNOCOACH n bus-like vehicle for travelling on snow

SNOD, -DED, -DER, -DEST, -DING, -DIT, -S adj Scots word meaning tidy ▷ vb make tidy

SNOEK, -S n edible marine fish

SNOEP adj mean or tight-fisted

SNOG, -GED, -GING, -S vb kiss and cuddle ▷ n act of kissing and cuddling

SNOGGER, -S n person who snogs

SNOGGING ▶ snog

SNOGS ▶ snog

SNOKE, -D, -ING, -S, SNOKING same as ▶ snook

SNOOD, -ED, -ING, -S n pouch loosely holding the hair at the back ▷ vb hold (the hair) in a snood

SNOOK, -ED, -ING, -S n any of several large game fishes ▷ vb lurk

SNOOKER, -S n game played on a billiard table ▷ vb leave

(a snooker opponent) unable to hit the target ball

SNOOKING ▶ snook

SNOOKS ▶ snook

SNOOL, -ED, -ING, -S vb Scots word meaning dominate

SNOOP, -ED, -ING, -S vb pry ▷ n snooping

SNOOPER, -S n person who snoops

SNOOPIER ▶ snoopy

SNOOPILY ▶ snoop

SNOOPING ▶ snoop

SNOOPS ▶ snoop

SNOOPY, SNOOPIER ▶ snoop

SNOOSE, -S n snuff

SNOOT, -ED, -ING, -S n nose ▷ vb look contemptuously at

SNOOTFUL n enough alcohol to make someone drunk

SNOOTIER ▶ snooty

SNOOTILY ▶ snooty

SNOOTING ▶ snoot

SNOOTS ▶ snoot

SNOOTY, SNOOTIER adj haughty

SNOOZE, -D, -S, SNOOZING vb take a brief light sleep ▷ n brief light sleep

SNOOZER, -S ▶ snooze

SNOOZES ▶ snooze

SNOOZIER ▶ snoozy

SNOOZING ▶ snooze

SNOOZLE, -D, -S vb cuddle and sleep

SNOOZY, SNOOZIER ▶ snooze

SNORE, -D, -S vb make snorting sounds while sleeping ▷ n sound of snoring

SNORER, -S ▶ snore

SNORES ▶ snore

SNORING, -S ▶ snore

SNORKEL, -S n tube allowing a swimmer to breathe ▷ vb swim using a snorkel

SNORT, -ED, -S vb exhale noisily through the nostrils ▷ n act or sound of snorting

SNORTER, -S n person or animal that snorts

SNORTIER ▶ snorty

SNORTING ▶ snort

SNORTS ▶ snort

SNORTY, SNORTIER ▶ snort

SNOT, -S, -TED, -TING n mucus from the nose ▷ vb blow one's nose

SNOTRAG, -S n handkerchief

SNOTS ▶ snot

SNOTTED ▶ snot

SNOTTER, -S vb breathe through obstructed nostrils

SNOTTERY ▶ snot

SNOTTIE n midshipman

SNOTTIER ▶ snotty

SNOTTIES ▶ snotty

SNOTTILY ▶ snotty

SNOTTING ▶ snot

SNOTTY, SNOTTIER, SNOTTIES adj covered with mucus from the nose

SNOUT, -ING, -S n animal's projecting nose and jaws ▷ vb have or give a snout

SNOUTED ▶ snout

SNOUTIER ▶ snouty

SNOUTING ▶ snout

SNOUTISH ▶ snout

SNOUTS ▶ snout

SNOUTY, SNOUTIER ▶ snout

SNOW, -ED, -ING, -S n frozen vapour falling from the sky in flakes ▷ vb fall as or like snow

SNOWBALL n snow pressed into a ball for throwing ▷ vb increase rapidly

SNOWBANK n bank of snow

SNOWBELL n Asian shrub

SNOWBELT n northern states of USA

SNOWBIRD n bird of Arctic regions

SNOWBOOT n boot for walking in snow

SNOWBUSH n North American plant

SNOWCAP, -S n cap of snow on top of a mountain

SNOWCAT, -S n tracked vehicle for travelling over snow

SNOWDOME n leisure centre with facilities for skiing, skating, etc

SNOWDROP n small white bell-shaped spring flower

SNOWED ▶ snow

SNOWFALL n fall of snow

SNOWFLEA n wingless insect that lives on or in snow

SNOWIER ▶ snowy

SNOWIEST ▶ snowy

SNOWILY ▶ snowy

SNOWING ▶ snow

SNOWISH adj like snow

SNOWK, -ED, -ING, -S same as ▶ snook

SNOWLAND n area where snow lies

SNOWLESS ▶ snow

SNOWLIKE ▶ snow

SNOWLINE n limit of permanent snow

SNOWMAN, SNOWMEN n figure shaped out of snow

SNOWMELT n melting of snow in spring

SNOWMEN ▸ snowman

SNOWMOLD same as > snowmould

SNOWPACK n body of hard-packed snow

SNOWPLOW n implement or vehicle for clearing snow away

SNOWS ▸ snow

SNOWSHED n shelter built over an exposed section of railway track

SNOWSHOE n racket-shaped frame with a network of thongs stretched across it for walking on snow ▹vb walk using snowshoes

SNOWSLIP n small snow avalanche

SNOWSUIT n one-piece winter outer garment for child

SNOWY, SNOWIER, SNOWIEST adj covered with or abounding in snow

SNUB, -BED, -BEST, -S vb insult deliberately ▹n deliberate insult ▹adj (of a nose) short and blunt

SNUBBE, -S n stub

SNUBBED ▸ snub

SNUBBER, -S ▸ snub

SNUBBES ▸ snubbe

SNUBBEST ▸ snub

SNUBBIER ▸ snubby

SNUBBING ▸ snub

SNUBBISH ▸ snub

SNUBBY, SNUBBIER ▸ snub

SNUBFIN adj as in snubfin dolphin Australian dolphin with a small dorsal fin

SNUBNESS ▸ snub

SNUBS ▸ snub

SNUCK past tense and past participle of ▸ sneak

SNUDGE, -D, -S, SNUDGING vb be miserly

SNUFF, -ED, -ING, -S n powdered tobacco for sniffing up the nostrils ▹vb extinguish (a candle)

SNUFFBOX n small container for holding snuff

SNUFFED ▸ snuff

SNUFFER, -S ▸ snuff

SNUFFIER ▸ snuffy

SNUFFILY ▸ snuffy

SNUFFING ▸ snuff

SNUFFLE, -D vb breathe noisily or with difficulty ▹n act or the sound of snuffling

SNUFFLER ▸ snuffle

SNUFFLES same as ▸ sniffles

SNUFFLY ▸ snuffle

SNUFFS ▸ snuff

SNUFFY, SNUFFIER adj of, relating to, or resembling snuff

SNUG, -GED, -GER, -GEST, -GING, -S adj warm and comfortable ▹n small peg that stops a bolt from turning ▹vb make or become comfortable and warm

SNUGGERY n cosy and comfortable place or room

SNUGGEST ▸ snug

SNUGGIES pl n specially warm underwear

SNUGGING ▸ snug

SNUGGLE, -D, -S vb nestle into a person or thing for warmth or from affection ▹n act of snuggling

SNUGGLY adj comfortably warm and suitable for snuggling

SNUGLY ▸ snug

SNUGNESS ▸ snug

SNUGS ▸ snug

SNUSH, -ED, -ES, -ING vb take snuff

SNUZZLE, -D, -S vb root in ground

SNY, SNIES same as ▸ snye

A side channel of a river, that can be useful when you are short of vowels. And note that it can be extended to form **snye**.

SNYE, -S n side channel of a river

SO, -S adv such an extent ▹interj exclamation of surprise, triumph, or realization ▹n the fifth note of the musical scale

SOAK, -ED, -EN, -S vb make wet ▹n soaking

SOAKAGE, -S n process or a period in which a permeable substance is soaked in a liquid

SOAKAWAY n pit filled with rubble, etc, into which rain or waste water drains

SOAKED ▸ soak

SOAKEN ▸ soak

SOAKER, -S ▸ soak

SOAKING, -S ▸ soak

SOAKS ▸ soak

SOAP, -ED, -ING, -S n compound of alkali and fat, used with water as a cleaning agent ▹vb apply soap to

SOAPBARK n W South American rosaceous tree

SOAPBOX n crate used as a platform for speech-making ▹vb deliver a speech from a soapbox

SOAPDISH n dish for holding soap

SOAPED ▸ soap

SOAPER, -S n soap opera

SOAPFISH n tropical fish with toxic mucus

SOAPIE, -S n soap opera

SOAPIER ▸ soapy

SOAPIES ▸ soapie

SOAPIEST ▸ soapy

SOAPILY ▸ soapy

SOAPING ▸ soap

SOAPLESS ▸ soap

SOAPLIKE ▸ soap

SOAPROOT n plant with roots used as soap substitute

SOAPS ▸ soap

SOAPSUDS pl n foam or lather produced when soap is mixed with water

SOAPWORT n Eurasian plant with clusters of fragrant pink or white flowers

SOAPY, SOAPIER, SOAPIEST adj covered with soap

SOAR, -ED, -S vb rise or fly upwards ▹n act of soaring

SOARAWAY adj exceedingly successful

SOARE, -S n young hawk

SOARED ▸ soar

SOARER, -S ▸ soar

SOARES ▸ soare

SOARING, -S ▸ soar

SOARS ▸ soar

SOAVE, -S n dry white Italian wine

SOB, -BED, -S vb weep with convulsive gasps ▹n act or sound of sobbing

SOBA, -S n (in Japanese cookery) noodles made from buckwheat flour

SOBBED ▸ sob

SOBBER, -S ▸ sob

SOBBING, -S ▸ sob

SOBEIT conj provided that

SOBER, -ED, -ER, -EST, -S adj not drunk ▹vb make or become sober

SOBERING ▸ sober

SOBERISE same as ▸ soberize

SOBERIZE vb make sober

SOBERLY ▸ sober

SOBERS ▸ sober

SOBFUL adj tearful

S

SOBOLE, -S n creeping underground stem that produces roots and buds
SOBRIETY n state of being sober
SOBS ▶ sob
SOC, -ES, -S n feudal right to hold court
SOCA, -S n mixture of soul and calypso music
SOCAGE, -S n tenure of land by certain services
SOCAGER, -S ▶ socage
SOCAGES ▶ socage
SOCAS ▶ soca
SOCCAGE, -S same as ▶ socage
SOCCER, -S n football played by two teams of eleven kicking a spherical ball
SOCES ▶ soc
SOCIABLE adj friendly or companionable ▷ n type of open carriage with two seats facing each other
SOCIABLY ▶ sociable
SOCIAL, -S adj living in a community ▷ n informal gathering
SOCIALLY ▶ social
SOCIALS ▶ social
SOCIATE, -S n associate
SOCIETAL adj of or relating to society, esp human society or social relations
SOCIETY n human beings considered as a group
SOCK, -ED, -ING, -S n knitted covering for the foot ▷ vb hit hard
SOCKET, -ED, -S n hole or recess into which something fits ▷ vb furnish with or place into a socket
SOCKETTE n sock not covering ankle
SOCKEYE, -S n Pacific salmon with red flesh
SOCKING ▶ sock
SOCKLESS ▶ sock
SOCKMAN, SOCKMEN same as ▶ socman
SOCKO adj excellent
SOCKS ▶ sock
SOCLE, -S another name for ▶ plinth
SOCMAN, SOCMEN n tenant holding land by socage
SOCS ▶ soc
SOD, -DED, -S n (piece of) turf ▷ vb cover with sods
SODA, -S n compound of sodium
SODAIC adj containing soda
SODAIN same as ▶ sudden

SODAINE same as ▶ sudden
SODALESS ▶ soda
SODALIST n member of sodality
SODALITE n blue, grey, yellow, or colourless mineral
SODALITY n religious or charitable society
SODAMIDE n white crystalline compound used as a dehydrating agent
SODAS ▶ soda
SODDED ▶ sod
SODDEN, -ED, -S adj soaked ▷ vb make or become sodden
SODDENLY ▶ sodden
SODDENS ▶ sodden
SODDIE, -S n house made of sod
SODDIER ▶ soddy
SODDIES ▶ soddie
SODDIEST ▶ soddy
SODDING ▶ sod
SODDY, SODDIER, SODDIEST adj covered with turf
SODGER, -ED, -S dialect variant of ▶ soldier
SODIC adj containing sodium
SODICITY ▶ sodic
SODIUM, -S n silvery-white metallic element
SODS ▶ sod
SOEVER adv in any way at all
SOFA, -S n couch
SOFABED, -S n sofa that converts into a bed
SOFAR, -S n system for determining a position at sea
SOFAS ▶ sofa
SOFFIONI pl n holes in volcano that emit steam
SOFFIT, -S n underside of a part of a building or a structural component
SOFT, -ED, -ER, -EST, -ING, -S adj easy to shape or cut ▷ vb soften
SOFTA, -S n Muslim student of divinity and jurisprudence
SOFTBACK n paperback
SOFTBALL n game similar to baseball, played using a larger softer ball
SOFTED ▶ soft
SOFTEN, -ED, -ES vb make or become soft or softer
SOFTENER n substance added to another substance to increase its softness
SOFTENS ▶ soften
SOFTER ▶ soft
SOFTEST ▶ soft

SOFTHEAD n insulting word for a stupid person
SOFTIE, -S n person who is easily upset
SOFTIES ▶ softy
SOFTING ▶ soft
SOFTISH ▶ soft
SOFTLING n weakling
SOFTLY ▶ soft
SOFTNESS n quality or an instance of being soft
SOFTS ▶ soft
SOFTWARE n computer programs
SOFTWOOD n wood of a coniferous tree
SOFTY, SOFTIES same as ▶ softie
SOG, -GED, -S vb soak
SOGER, -S same as ▶ sodger
SOGGED ▶ sog
SOGGIER ▶ soggy
SOGGIEST ▶ soggy
SOGGILY ▶ soggy
SOGGING, -S ▶ sog
SOGGY, SOGGIER, SOGGIEST adj soaked
SOGS ▶ sog
SOH, -S n (in tonic sol-fa) fifth degree of any major scale
SOHO interj exclamation announcing the sighting of a hare
SOHS ▶ soh
SOHUR, -S same as ▶ suhur
SOIGNE adj well-groomed, elegant
SOIGNEE variant of ▶ soigne
SOIL, -ED, -S n top layer of earth ▷ vb make or become dirty
SOILAGE, -S n green fodder
SOILED ▶ soil
SOILIER ▶ soily
SOILIEST ▶ soily
SOILING, -S ▶ soil
SOILLESS ▶ soil
SOILS ▶ soil
SOILURE, -S n act of soiling or the state of being soiled
SOILY, SOILIER, SOILIEST ▶ soil
SOIREE, -S n evening party or gathering
SOJA, -S same as ▶ soya
SOJOURN, -S n temporary stay ▷ vb stay temporarily
SOJU, -S n type of Korean vodka
SOKAH, -S same as ▶ soca
SOKAIYA n Japanese extortionist
SOKE, -S n right to hold a local court

SOKEMAN, SOKEMEN same as ▸ **socman**

SOKEN, -S n feudal district

SOKES ▸ **soke**

SOKOL, -S n Czech gymnastic association

SOL, -S n liquid colloidal solution

SOLA, -S n Indian plant

SOLACE, -D, -S, SOLACING vb comfort in distress ▷ n comfort in misery or disappointment

SOLACER, -S ▸ **solace**

SOLACES ▸ **solace**

SOLACING ▸ **solace**

SOLAH, -S n Indian plant

SOLAN, -S archaic name for ▸ **gannet**

SOLAND, -S n solan goose

SOLANDER n box for specimens, maps, etc, in the form of a book with a lid

SOLANDS ▸ **soland**

SOLANIN, -S same as ▸ **solanine**

SOLANINE n poisonous alkaloid found in various solanaceous plants

SOLANINS ▸ **solanin**

SOLANO, -S n hot wind in Spain

SOLANS ▸ **solan**

SOLANUM, -S n any plant of the genus that includes the potato

SOLAR, -S adj of the sun ▷ n upper room

SOLARIA ▸ **solarium**

SOLARISE same as ▸ **solarize**

SOLARISM n explanation of myths in terms of the movements and influence of the sun

SOLARIST ▸ **solarism**

SOLARIUM, SOLARIA n place with beds and ultraviolet lights used for acquiring an artificial suntan

SOLARIZE vb treat by exposure to the sun's rays

SOLARS ▸ **solar**

SOLAS ▸ **sola**

SOLATE, -D, -S, SOLATING vb change from gel to liquid

SOLATIA ▸ **solatium**

SOLATING ▸ **solate**

SOLATION n liquefaction of a gel

SOLATIUM, SOLATIA n compensation awarded for injury to the feelings

SOLD, -S n obsolete word for salary

SOLDADO, -S n soldier

SOLDAN, -S archaic word for ▸ **sultan**

SOLDE, -S n wages

SOLDER, -ED, -S n soft alloy used to join two metal surfaces ▷ vb join with solder

SOLDERER ▸ **solder**

SOLDERS ▸ **solder**

SOLDES ▸ **solde**

SOLDI ▸ **soldo**

SOLDIER, -S n member of an army ▷ vb serve in an army

SOLDIERY n soldiers collectively

SOLDO, SOLDI n former Italian copper coin

SOLDS ▸ **sold**

SOLE, -D, -S, SOLING adj one and only ▷ n underside of the foot ▷ vb provide (a shoe) with a sole

SOLECISE variant of ▸ **solecize**

SOLECISM n minor grammatical mistake

SOLECIST ▸ **solecism**

SOLECIZE vb commit a solecism

SOLED ▸ **sole**

SOLEI ▸ **soleus**

SOLEIN same as ▸ **sullen**

SOLELESS ▸ **sole**

SOLELY adv only, completely

SOLEMN, -ER adj serious, deeply sincere

SOLEMNLY ▸ **solemn**

SOLENESS ▸ **sole**

SOLENOID n coil of wire magnetized by passing a current through it

SOLER, -S same as ▸ **sole**

SOLERA, -S n system for ageing sherry and other fortified wines

SOLERET, -S n armour for foot

SOLERS ▸ **soler**

SOLES ▸ **sole**

SOLEUS, SOLEI, -ES n muscle in calf of leg

SOLFEGE, -S variant of > **solfeggio**

SOLFEGGI > **solfeggio**

SOLGEL adj changing between sol and gel

SOLI adv to be performed by or with soloists

SOLICIT, -S vb request

SOLICITY n act of making a request

SOLID, -ER, -EST, -S adj (of a substance) keeping its shape ▷ n three-dimensional shape

SOLIDAGO n chiefly American plant of the genus which includes the goldenrods

SOLIDARE n old coin

SOLIDARY adj marked by unity of interests, responsibilities, etc

SOLIDATE vb consolidate

SOLIDER ▸ **solid**

SOLIDEST ▸ **solid**

SOLIDI ▸ **solidus**

SOLIDIFY vb make or become solid or firm

SOLIDISH ▸ **solid**

SOLIDISM n belief that diseases spring from damage to solid parts of body

SOLIDIST ▸ **solidism**

SOLIDITY ▸ **solid**

SOLIDLY ▸ **solid**

SOLIDS ▸ **solid**

SOLIDUM, -S n part of pedestal

SOLIDUS, SOLIDI same as ▸ **slash**

SOLING ▸ **sole**

SOLION, -S n amplifier used in chemistry

SOLIPED, -S n animal whose hooves are not cloven

SOLIQUID n semi-solid, semi-liquid solution

SOLITARY adj alone, single ▷ n hermit

SOLITO adv musical instruction meaning play in usual manner

SOLITON, -S n type of isolated particle-like wave

SOLITUDE n state of being alone

SOLIVE, -S n type of joist

SOLLAR, -ED, -S n archaic word meaning attic ▷ vb put in a sollar

SOLLER, -S same as ▸ **sollar**

SOLLERET n protective covering for the foot consisting of riveted plates of armour

SOLLERS ▸ **soller**

SOLO, -ED, -ES, -ING, -S n music for one performer ▷ adj done alone ▷ adv by oneself, alone ▷ vb undertake a venture alone

SOLOIST, -S n person who performs a solo

SOLON, -S n US congressperson

SOLONETS same as ▸ **solonetz**

SOLONETZ n type of intrazonal soil with a high

S

saline content characterized by leaching

SOLONS ▶ solon

SOLOS ▶ solo

SOLPUGID n venomous arachnid

SOLS ▶ sol

SOLSTICE n either the shortest (in winter) or longest (in summer) day of the year

SOLUBLE, -S adj able to be dissolved ▷ n soluble substance

SOLUBLY ▶ soluble

SOLUM, -S n upper layers of the soil profile

SOLUNAR adj relating to sun and moon

SOLUS, -ES n advert printed or published separately from others

SOLUTAL adj relating to a solute

SOLUTE, -S n substance in a solution that is dissolved ▷ adj loose or unattached

SOLUTION n answer to a problem

SOLUTIVE adj dissolving ▷ n solvent or laxative

SOLVABLE adj capable of being solved

SOLVATE, -D, -S vb undergo, cause to undergo, or partake in solvation

SOLVE, -D, -S, SOLVING vb find the answer to (a problem)

SOLVENCY n ability to pay all debts

SOLVENT, -S adj having enough money to pay one's debts ▷ n liquid capable of dissolving other substances

SOLVER, -S ▶ solve

SOLVES ▶ solve

SOLVING ▶ solve

SOM, -S, -Y n currency of Kyrgyzstan and Uzbekistan

SOMA, -S, -TA n body of an organism as distinct from the germ cells

SOMAN, -S n compound developed as a nerve gas

SOMAS ▶ soma

SOMATA ▶ soma

SOMATIC adj of the body, as distinct from the mind

SOMATISM n materialism

SOMATIST ▶ somatism

SOMBER, -ED, -ER, -S adj (in the US) sombre ▷ vb (in the US) make sombre

SOMBERLY ▶ somber

SOMBERS ▶ somber

SOMBRE, -D, -R, -S, -ST, SOMBRING adj dark, gloomy ▷ vb make sombre

SOMBRELY ▶ sombre

SOMBRER ▶ sombre

SOMBRERO n wide-brimmed Mexican hat

SOMBRES ▶ sombre

SOMBREST ▶ sombre

SOMBRING ▶ sombre

SOMBROUS ▶ sombre

SOME pron certain unknown or unspecified people or things ▷ adv approximately

SOMEBODY pron some person ▷ n important person

SOMEDAY adv at some unspecified time in the future

SOMEDEAL adv to some extent ▷ n some part of something

SOMEDELE same as ▶ somedeal

SOMEGATE adv Scots word meaning somehow

SOMEHOW adv in some unspecified way

SOMEONE, -S pron somebody ▷ n significant or important person

SOMERSET n somersault

SOMETIME adv at some unspecified time ▷ adj former

SOMEWAY adv in some unspecified manner

SOMEWAYS same as ▶ someway

SOMEWHAT adv some extent, rather ▷ n vague amount

SOMEWHEN adv at some time

SOMEWHY adv for some reason

SOMEWISE adv in some way or to some degree

SOMITAL ▶ somite

SOMITE, -S n segment of mesoderm in vertebrate embryos

SOMITIC ▶ somite

SOMNIAL adj of dreams

SOMNIATE vb dream

SOMNIFIC adj inducing sleep

SOMONI, -S n monetary unit of Tajikistan

SOMS ▶ som

SOMY ▶ som

SON, -S n male offspring

SONANCE, -S ▶ sonant

SONANCY ▶ sonant

SONANT, -S n voiced sound able to form a syllable or syllable nucleus ▷ adj denoting a voiced sound like this

SONANTAL ▶ sonant

SONANTIC ▶ sonant

SONANTS ▶ sonant

SONAR, -S n device for detecting underwater objects by the reflection of sound waves

SONARMAN, SONARMEN n sonar operator

SONARS ▶ sonar

SONATA, -S n piece of music in several movements for one instrument

SONATINA n short sonata

SONATINE same as ▶ sonatina

SONCE, -S n Scots word meaning good luck

SONDAGE, -S n deep trial trench for inspecting stratigraphy

SONDE, -S n rocket, balloon, or probe used for observing in the upper atmosphere

SONDELI, -S n Indian shrew

SONDER, -S n yacht category

SONDES ▶ sonde

SONE, -S n subjective unit of loudness

SONERI, -S n Indian cloth of gold

SONES ▶ sone

SONG, -S n music for the voice

SONGBIRD n any bird with a musical call

SONGBOOK n book of songs

SONGFEST n event with many songs

SONGFUL adj tuneful

SONGKOK, -S n (in Malaysia and Indonesia) a kind of oval brimless hat, resembling a skull

SONGLESS ▶ song

SONGLIKE ▶ song

SONGMAN, SONGMEN n singer

SONGS ▶ song

SONGSTER n singer

SONHOOD, -S ▶ son

SONIC adj of or producing sound

SONICATE vb subject to sound waves

SONICS n study of mechanical vibrations in matter

SONLESS ▶ son

SONLIER ▶ sonly

SONLIEST ▸ sonly

SONLIKE ▸ son

SONLY, SONLIER, SONLIEST adj like a son

SONNE, -S same as ▸ son

SONNET, -ED, -S n fourteen-line poem ▹ vb compose sonnets

SONNY, SONNIES n term of address to a boy

SONOBUOY n buoy equipped to detect underwater noises and transmit them by radio

SONOGRAM n three-dimensional representation of a sound signal

SONORANT n type of frictionless continuant or nasal

SONORITY ▸ sonorous

SONOROUS adj (of sound) deep or resonant

SONOVOX n device used to alter sound of human voice in music recordings

SONS ▸ son

SONSE, -S same as ▸ sonce

SONSHIP, -S ▸ son

SONSIE same as ▸ sonsy

SONSY, SONSIER, SONSIEST adj plump

SONTAG, -S n type of knitted women's cape

SONTIES n Shakespearian oath

SOOCHONG same as ▸ souchong

SOOEY interj call used to summon pigs

SOOGEE, -D, -S vb clean a ship using a special solution

SOOGIE, -D, -S same as ▸ soogee

SOOJEY, -S same as ▸ soogee

SOOK, -ED, -ING, -S n baby ▹ vb suck

SOOKIER ▸ sooky

SOOKIEST ▸ sooky

SOOKING ▸ sook

SOOKS ▸ sook

SOOKY, SOOKIER, SOOKIEST adj tending to complain peevishly

SOOL, -ED, -ING, -S vb incite (a dog) to attack

SOOLE, -S same as ▸ sool

SOOLED ▸ sool

SOOLER, -S n person who incites a dog to attack

SOOLES ▸ soole

SOOLING ▸ sool

SOOLS ▸ sool

SOOM, -ED, -ING, -S Scots word for ▸ swim

SOON adv in a short time

SOONER, -S adv rather ▹ n idler or shirker

SOONEST adv as soon as possible

SOONISH adj somewhat soon

SOOP, -ED, -S Scots word for ▸ sweep

SOOPING, -S ▸ soop

SOOPS ▸ soop

SOOT, -ED, -ES, -S n black powder formed by the incomplete burning of an organic substance ▹ vb cover with soot

SOOTE n sweet

SOOTED ▸ soot

SOOTES ▸ soot

SOOTH, -EST, -S n truth or reality ▹ adj true or real

SOOTHE, -D, -S vb make calm

SOOTHER, -S vb flatter

SOOTHES ▸ soothe

SOOTHEST ▸ sooth

SOOTHFUL adj truthful

SOOTHING adj having a calming, assuaging, or relieving effect

SOOTHLY ▸ sooth

SOOTHS ▸ sooth

SOOTHSAY vb predict the future

SOOTIER ▸ sooty

SOOTIEST ▸ sooty

SOOTILY ▸ sooty

SOOTING, -S n state of becoming covered with soot

SOOTLESS ▸ soot

SOOTS ▸ soot

SOOTY, SOOTIER, SOOTIEST adj covered with soot

SOP, -PED, -S n concession to pacify someone ▹ vb mop up or absorb (liquid)

SOPH, -S shortened form of > sophomore

SOPHERIC ▸ sopherim

SOPHERIM n Jewish scribes

SOPHIES ▸ sophy

SOPHISM, -S n argument that seems reasonable but is actually false and misleading

SOPHIST, -S n person who uses clever but invalid arguments

SOPHS ▸ soph

SOPHY, SOPHIES n title of the Persian monarchs

SOPITE, -D, -S, SOPITING vb lull to sleep

SOPOR, -S n abnormally deep sleep

SOPOROSE adj sleepy

SOPOROUS same as ▸ soporose

SOPORS ▸ sopor

SOPPED ▸ sop

SOPPIER ▸ soppy

SOPPIEST ▸ soppy

SOPPILY ▸ soppy

SOPPING, -S ▸ sop

SOPPY, SOPPIER, SOPPIEST adj over-sentimental

SOPRA adv musical instruction meaning above

SOPRANO, SOPRANI, -S n singer with the highest female or boy's voice ▹ adj of a musical instrument that is the highest or second highest pitched in its family

SOPS ▸ sop

SORA, -S n North American rail with a yellow bill

SORAGE, -S n first year in hawk's life

SORAL ▸ sorus

SORAS ▸ sora

SORB, -ED, -ING, -S n any of various related trees, esp the mountain ash ▹ vb absorb or adsorb

SORBABLE ▸ sorb

SORBARIA n Asian shrub

SORBATE, -S n salt of sorbic acid

SORBED ▸ sorb

SORBENT, -S ▸ sorb

SORBET, -S same as ▸ sherbet

SORBIC ▸ sorb

SORBING ▸ sorb

SORBITAN n any of a group of compounds derived from sorbitol

SORBITE, -S n mineral found in steel

SORBITIC ▸ sorbite

SORBITOL n white water-soluble crystalline alcohol with a sweet taste

SORBO n as in sorbo rubber spongy form of rubber

SORBOSE, -S n sugar derived from the berries of the mountain ash

SORBS ▸ sorb

SORBUS, -ES n rowan or related tree

SORCERER n magician

SORCERY n witchcraft or magic

SORD, -ED, -ING, -S n flock of mallard ducks ▹ vb ascend in flight

SORDA n deaf woman

SORDED ▸ sord

SORDES pl n dark incrustations on the lips and teeth of patients with prolonged fever

SORDID, -ER adj dirty, squalid

SORDIDLY ▶ sordid

SORDINE, -S same as ▶ sordino

SORDING ▶ sord

SORDINO, SORDINI n mute for a stringed or brass musical instrument

SORDO n deaf man

SORDOR, -S n sordidness

SORDS ▶ sord

SORE, -D, -R, -S, -ST adj painful ▷ n painful area on the body ▷ adv greatly ▷ vb make sore

SOREDIA ▶ soredium

This is the plural of **soredium**, a reproductive body in lichens. It is a very frequently played bonus, and it has a 'twin': **roadies**. It is a good idea to become familiar with at least the higher probability twin sevens and eights, since the thought of one will often prompt the other, and it may well be that one twin will fit on the board where the other would not.

SOREDIAL ▶ soredium

SOREDIUM, SOREDIA n organ of vegetative reproduction in lichens

SOREE, -S same as ▶ sora

SOREHEAD n peevish or disgruntled person

SOREHON, -S n old Irish feudal right

SOREL, -S variant of ▶ sorrel

SORELL, -S same as ▶ sorrel

SORELS ▶ sorel

SORELY adv greatly

SORENESS ▶ sore

SORER ▶ sore

SORES ▶ sore

SOREST ▶ sore

SOREX, -ES n shrew or related animal

SORGHO, -S same as ▶ sorgo

SORGHUM, -S n kind of grass cultivated for grain

SORGO, -S n any of several varieties of sorghum that have sweetly sweet juice

SORI ▶ sorus

SORICINE adj of or resembling a shrew

SORICOID same as ▶ soricine

SORING, -S ▶ sore

SORITES n type of syllogism in which only the final conclusion is stated

SORITIC ▶ sorites

SORN, -ED, -S vb obtain food, etc, from another person by presuming on his or her generosity

SORNER, -S ▶ sorn

SORNING, -S ▶ sorn

SORNS ▶ sorn

SOROBAN, -S n Japanese abacus

SOROCHE, -S n altitude sickness

SORORAL adj of sister

SORORATE n custom in some societies of a widower marrying his deceased wife's younger sister

SORORIAL same as ▶ sororal

SORORISE same as ▶ sororize

SORORITY n society for female students

SORORIZE vb socialize in sisterly way

SOROSIS, SOROSES n fleshy multiple fruit

SORPTION n process in which one substance takes up or holds another

SORPTIVE ▶ sorption

SORRA, -S Irish word for ▶ sorrow

SORREL, -S n bitter-tasting plant

SORRIER ▶ sorry

SORRIEST ▶ sorry

SORRILY ▶ sorry

SORROW, -ED, -S n grief or sadness ▷ vb grieve

SORROWER ▶ sorrow

SORROWS ▶ sorrow

SORRY, SORRIER, SORRIEST adj feeling pity or regret ▷ interj exclamation expressing apology or asking someone to repeat what he or she has said

SORRYISH ▶ sorry

SORT, -S n group all sharing certain qualities or characteristics ▷ vb arrange according to kind

SORTA adv phonetic representation of 'sort of'

SORTABLE ▶ sort

SORTABLY ▶ sort

SORTAL, -S n type of logical or linguistic concept

SORTANCE n suitableness

SORTED interj exclamation of satisfaction, approval, etc ▷ adj having been corrected or made ready

SORTER, -S ▶ sort

SORTES pl n divination by opening book at random

SORTIE, -D, -S n relatively short return trip ▷ vb make a sortie

SORTING, -S ▶ sort

SORTMENT n assortment

SORTS ▶ sort

SORUS, SORI n cluster of sporangia on the undersurface of certain fern leaves

SOS ▶ so

SOSATIE, -S n skewer of curried meat pieces

SOSS, -ED, -ES vb make dirty or muddy

SOSSING, -S ▶ soss

SOT, -S, -TED n habitual drunkard ▷ adv indeed: used to contradict a negative statement ▷ vb be a drunkard

SOTERIAL adj of salvation

This means pertaining to salvation, and is one of the most important 8-letter words to know because the chance to play it as a bonus comes up so often.

SOTH, -S archaic variant of ▶ sooth

SOTOL, -S n American plant related to agave

SOTS ▶ sot

SOTTED ▶ sot

SOTTEDLY ▶ sot

SOTTING, -S ▶ sot

SOTTISH ▶ sot

SOU, -S n former French coin

SOUARI, -S n tree of tropical America

SOUBISE, -S n purée of onions mixed into a thick white sauce and served over eggs, fish, etc

SOUCAR, -S n Indian banker

SOUCE, -D, -S, SOUCING, SOUCT same as ▶ souse

SOUCHONG n black tea with large leaves

SOUCING ▶ souce

SOUCT ▶ souce

SOUDAN, -S obsolete variant of ▶ sultan

SOUFFLE, -S n light fluffy dish made with beaten egg whites ▷ adj made light and puffy

SOUFFLED ▶ souffle

SOUFFLES ▶ souffle

SOUGH, -ED, -ING, -S vb (of the wind) make a sighing sound ▷ n soft continuous murmuring sound

SOUGHT ▶ seek

SOUK, -ED, -ING, -S same as ▶ sook

SOUKOUS n style of African popular music

SOUKS ▶ souk

SOUL, -S n spiritual and immortal part of a human being

SOULDAN, -S same as ▶ soldan

SOULDIER same as ▶ soldier

SOULED adj having soul

SOULFUL adj full of emotion

SOULLESS adj lacking human qualities, mechanical

SOULLIKE adj resembling a soul

SOULMATE n person with whom one has most affinity

SOULS ▶ soul

SOULSTER n soul music singer

SOUM, -ED, -S vb decide how many animals can graze particular pasture

SOUMING, -S ▶ soum

SOUMS ▶ soum

SOUND, -ED, -EST, -S n something heard, noise ▷ vb make or cause to make a sound ▷ adj in good condition ▷ adv soundly

SOUNDBAR n long, slender speaker

SOUNDBOX n resonating chamber of the hollow body of a violin, guitar, etc

SOUNDED ▶ sound

SOUNDER, -S n device formerly used to convert electric signals into sounds

SOUNDEST ▶ sound

SOUNDING adj resounding

SOUNDLY ▶ sound

SOUNDMAN, SOUNDMEN n sound recorder in television crew

SOUNDS ▶ sound

SOUP, -ED, -ING, -S n liquid food made from meat, vegetables, etc ▷ vb give soup to

SOUPCON, -S n small amount

SOUPED ▶ soup

SOUPER, -S n person dispensing soup

SOUPFIN, -S n Pacific requiem shark valued for its fins

SOUPIER ▶ soupy

SOUPIEST ▶ soupy

SOUPILY adv in a soupy manner

SOUPING ▶ soup

SOUPLE, -D, -S, SOUPLING same as ▶ supple

SOUPLESS ▶ soup

SOUPLIKE ▶ soup

SOUPLING ▶ souple

SOUPS ▶ soup

SOUPY, SOUPIER, SOUPIEST adj having the appearance or consistency of soup

SOUR, -ED, -ER, -EST, -S adj sharp-tasting ▷ vb make or become sour

SOURBALL n tart-flavoured boiled sweet

SOURCE, -D, -S, SOURCING n origin or starting point ▷ vb establish a supplier of (a product, etc)

SOURDINE n soft stop on an organ or harmonium

SOURED ▶ sour

SOURER ▶ sour

SOUREST ▶ sour

SOURGUM, -S n tree of eastern N America

SOURING, -S ▶ sour

SOURISH ▶ sour

SOURLY ▶ sour

SOURNESS ▶ sour

SOUROCK, -S n Scots word for sorrel plant

SOURPUSS n person who is always gloomy, pessimistic, or bitter

SOURS ▶ sour

SOURSE, -S same as ▶ source

SOURSOP, -S n small tropical American tree

SOURVELD n grazing field with long coarse grass

SOURWOOD n sorrel tree

SOUS ▶ sou

SOUSE, -D, -S vb plunge (something) into liquid ▷ n liquid used in pickling

SOUSER, -S n person who frequently gets drunk

SOUSES ▶ souse

SOUSING, -S ▶ souse

SOUSLIK, -S same as ▶ suslik

SOUT, -S same as ▶ soot

SOUTACHE n narrow braid used as a decorative trimming

SOUTANE, -S n Roman Catholic priest's cassock

SOUTAR, -S same as ▶ souter

SOUTER, -S n shoemaker or cobbler

SOUTERLY ▶ souter

SOUTERS ▶ souter

SOUTH, -ED, -S n direction towards the South Pole, opposite north ▷ adj in the south ▷ adv in, to, or towards the south ▷ vb turn south

SOUTHER, -S n strong wind or storm from the south ▷ vb turn south

SOUTHERN adj situated in or towards the south ▷ n southerner

SOUTHERS ▶ souther

SOUTHING n movement, deviation, or distance covered in a southerly direction

SOUTHPAW n left-handed person, esp a boxer ▷ adj left-handed

SOUTHRON n southerner

SOUTHS ▶ south

SOUTHSAY same as ▶ soothsay

SOUTS ▶ sout

SOUVENIR n keepsake, memento ▷ vb steal or keep (something, esp a small article) for one's own use

SOUVLAKI same as ▶ souvlakia

SOV, -S shortening of ▶ sovereign

SOVIET, -S n formerly, elected council in the USSR ▷ adj of the former USSR

SOVIETIC ▶ soviet

SOVIETS ▶ soviet

SOVKHOZ, -Y n large mechanized farm in former USSR

SOVRAN, -S literary word for ▶ sovereign

SOVRANLY ▶ sovran

SOVRANS ▶ sovran

SOVRANTY ▶ sovran

SOVS ▶ sov

SOW, -ED, -N, -S vb scatter or plant (seed) in or on (the ground) ▷ n female adult pig

SOWABLE ▶ sow

SOWANS same as ▶ sowens

SOWAR, -S n Indian cavalryman

SOWARREE n Indian mounted escort

SOWARRY same as ▶ sowarree

SOWARS ▶ sowar

SOWBACK, -S another name for ▶ hogback

SOWBELLY n salt pork from pig's belly

SOWBREAD n S European primulaceous plant

SOWBUG, -S n (in N America) woodlouse

SOWCAR, -S same as ▶ soucar

SOWCE, -D, -S, SOWCING same as ▶ souse

SOWDER, -S same as ▶ sawder

S

SOWED ▶ sow

SOWENS n pudding made from oatmeal husks steeped and boiled

SOWER, -S ▶ sow

SOWF, -ED, -ING, -S same as ▶ sowth

SOWFF, -ED, -ING, -S same as ▶ sowth

SOWFING ▶ sowf

SOWFS ▶ sowf

SOWING, -S ▶ sow

SOWL, -ED, -ING, -S same as ▶ sole

SOWLE, -S same as ▶ sole

SOWLED ▶ sowl

SOWLES ▶ sowle

SOWLING ▶ sowl

SOWLS ▶ sowl

SOWM, -ED, -ING, -S same as ▶ soum

SOWN ▶ sow

SOWND, -ED, -ING, -S vb wield

SOWNE, -S same as ▶ sound

SOWP, -ED, -ING, -S n spoonful ▷ vb soak

SOWS ▶ sow

SOWSE, -D, -S, SOWSING same as ▶ souse

SOWSSE, -D, -S, SOWSSING same as ▶ souse

SOWTER, -S same as ▶ souter

SOWTH, -ED, -ING, -S vb Scots word meaning whistle

SOX pl n informal spelling of 'socks'

This informal word for **socks** is one of the key short words to remember for using the X.

SOY, -S n soya bean

SOYA, -S n plant whose edible bean is used for food and as a source of oil

SOYBEAN, -S n soya bean

SOYLE, -D, -S, SOYLING n body ▷ vb elucidate

SOYMEAL, -S n foodstuff made from soybeans

SOYMILK, -S n milk substitute made from soya

SOYS ▶ soy

SOYUZ, -ES n Russian spacecraft

SOZ interj (slang) sorry

SOZIN, -S n form of protein

SOZINE, -S same as ▶ sozin

SOZINS ▶ sozin

SOZZLE, -S, SOZZLING vb make wet

SOZZLED adj drunk

SOZZLES ▶ sozzle

SOZZLIER ▶ sozzly

SOZZLING ▶ sozzle

SOZZLY, SOZZLIER adj wet

SPA, -S n resort with a mineral-water spring ▷ vb visit a spa

SPACE, -D, -S n unlimited expanse in which all objects exist and move ▷ vb place at intervals

SPACELAB n laboratory in space where scientific experiments are performed

SPACEMAN, SPACEMEN n man who travels in space

SPACER, -S n piece of material used to create or maintain a space between two things

SPACES ▶ space

SPACEY, SPACIER, SPACIEST adj vague and dreamy

SPACIAL same as ▶ spatial

SPACIER ▶ spacey

SPACIEST ▶ spacey

SPACING, -S n arrangement of letters, words, etc, on a page in order to achieve legibility

SPACIOUS adj having a large capacity or area

SPACKLE, -D, -S vb fill holes in plaster

SPACY same as ▶ spacey

SPADE, -D, -S, SPADING n tool for digging

SPADEFUL n amount spade will hold

SPADEMAN, SPADEMEN n man who works with spade

SPADER, -S ▶ spade

SPADES ▶ spade

SPADGER, -S n sparrow

SPADICES ▶ spadix

SPADILLE n (in ombre and quadrille) the ace of spades

SPADILLO same as ▶ spadille

SPADING ▶ spade

SPADIX, SPADICES, -ES n spike of small flowers on a fleshy stem

SPADO, -ES, -NES, -S n neutered animal

SPADROON n type of sword

SPAE, -D, -S vb foretell (the future)

SPAEING, -S ▶ spae

SPAEMAN, SPAEMEN n man who can supposedly foretell the future

SPAER, -S ▶ spae

SPAES ▶ spae

SPAETZLE n German noodle dish

SPAEWIFE n woman who can supposedly foretell the future

SPAG, -GED, -GING, -S vb (of a cat) to scratch (a person) with the claws

SPAGERIC same as ▶ spagyric

SPAGGED ▶ spag

SPAGGING ▶ spag

SPAGIRIC same as ▶ spagyric

SPAGS ▶ spag

SPAGYRIC adj of or relating to alchemy ▷ n alchemist

SPAHEE, -S same as ▶ spahi

SPAHI, -S n (formerly) an irregular cavalryman in the Turkish armed forces

SPAIL, -S Scots word for ▶ spall

SPAIN, -ED, -ING, -S variant of ▶ spane

SPAING, -S ▶ spa

SPAINING ▶ spain

SPAINS ▶ spain

SPAIRGE, -D, -S Scots word for ▶ sparge

SPAIT, -S same as ▶ spate

SPAKE past tense of ▶ speak

SPALD, -S same as ▶ spauld

SPALDEEN n ball used in street game

SPALDS ▶ spald

SPALE, -S Scots word for ▶ spall

SPALL, -ED, -ING, -S n splinter or chip of ore, rock, or stone ▷ vb split or cause to split into such fragments

SPALLE, -S same as ▶ spauld

SPALLED ▶ spall

SPALLER, -S ▶ spall

SPALLES ▶ spalle

SPALLING ▶ spall

SPALLS ▶ spall

SPALPEEN n itinerant seasonal labourer

SPALT, -ED, -ING, -S vb split

SPAM, -MED, -MING, -S vb send unsolicited email simultaneously to a number of newsgroups on the internet ▷ n unsolicited electronic mail or text messages sent in this way

SPAMBOT, -S n computer program that sends spam

SPAMMED ▶ spam

SPAMMER, -S ▶ spam

SPAMMIE, -S n love bite

SPAMMIER ▶ spammy

SPAMMIES ▶ spammie

SPAMMING ▶ spam

SPAMMY, SPAMMIER adj bland

SPAMS ▶ spam

SPAN, -NED, -NING, -S n space between two points ▷ vb stretch or extend across

SPANCEL, -S *n* length of rope for hobbling an animal ▷ *vb* hobble (an animal) with a loose rope

SPANDEX *n* type of synthetic stretch fabric made from polyurethane fibre

SPANDREL *n* triangular surface bounded by the outer curve of an arch and the adjacent wall

SPANDRIL *same as* ▷ **spandrel**

SPANE, -D, -S, SPANING *vb* Scots word meaning wean

SPANG, -ED, -ING, -S *adv* exactly, firmly, or straight ▷ *vb* dash

SPANGHEW *vb* throw in air

SPANGING ▷ **spang**

SPANGLE, -D, -S *n* small shiny metallic ornament ▷ *vb* decorate with spangles

SPANGLER ▷ **spangle**

SPANGLES ▷ **spangle**

SPANGLET *n* little spangle

SPANGLY ▷ **spangle**

SPANGS ▷ **spang**

SPANIEL, -S *n* dog with long ears and silky hair

SPANING ▷ **spane**

SPANK, -ED, -S *vb* slap with the open hand, on the buttocks or legs ▷ *n* such a slap

SPANKER, -S *n* fore-and-aft sail or a mast that is aftermost in a sailing vessel

SPANKING *adj* outstandingly fine or smart ▷ *n* series of spanks, usually as a punishment for children

SPANKS ▷ **spank**

SPANLESS *adj* impossible to span

SPANNED ▷ **span**

SPANNER, -S *n* tool for gripping and turning a nut or bolt

SPANNING ▷ **span**

SPANS ▷ **span**

SPANSPEK *n* cantaloupe melon

SPANSULE *n* modified-release capsule of a drug

SPANWORM *n* larva of a type of moth

SPAR, -RED, -RING, -S *n* pole used as a ship's mast, boom, or yard ▷ *vb* box or fight using light blows for practice

SPARABLE *n* small nail with no head, used for fixing the soles and heels of shoes

SPARAXIS *n* type of plant with dainty spikes of star-shaped purple, red, or orange flowers

SPARE, SPARD, -D, -S, -ST *adj* extra ▷ *n* duplicate kept in case of damage or loss ▷ *vb* refrain from punishing or harming

SPARELY ▷ **spare**

SPARER, -S ▷ **spare**

SPARERIB *n* cut of pork ribs with most of the meat trimmed off

SPARERS ▷ **sparer**

SPARES ▷ **spare**

SPAREST ▷ **spare**

SPARGE, -D, -S, SPARGING *vb* sprinkle or scatter (something)

SPARGER, -S ▷ **sparge**

SPARGES ▷ **sparge**

SPARGING ▷ **sparge**

SPARID, -S *n* type of marine percoid fish ▷ *adj* of or belonging to this family of fish

SPARING *adj* economical

SPARK, -ED, -ING *n* fiery particle thrown out from a fire or caused by friction ▷ *vb* give off sparks

SPARKE, -S *n* weapon

SPARKED ▷ **spark**

SPARKER, -S ▷ **spark**

SPARKES ▷ **sparke**

SPARKIE, -S *n* electrician

SPARKIER ▷ **sparky**

SPARKIES ▷ **sparkie**

SPARKILY ▷ **sparky**

SPARKING ▷ **spark**

SPARKISH ▷ **spark**

SPARKLE, -D, -S *vb* glitter with many points of light ▷ *n* sparkling points of light

SPARKLER *n* hand-held firework that emits sparks

SPARKLES ▷ **sparkle**

SPARKLET *n* little spark

SPARKLY *adj* sparkling ▷ *n* sparkling thing

SPARKS *n* electrician

SPARKY, SPARKIER *adj* lively

SPARLIKE ▷ **spar**

SPARLING *n* European smelt

SPAROID, -S *same as* ▷ **sparid**

SPARRE, -S *same as* ▷ **spar**

SPARRED ▷ **spar**

SPARRER, -S ▷ **spar**

SPARRES ▷ **sparre**

SPARRIER ▷ **sparry**

SPARRING ▷ **spar**

SPARROW, -S *n* small brownish bird

SPARRY, SPARRIER *adj* (of minerals) containing, relating to, or resembling spar

SPARS ▷ **spar**

SPARSE, -R, -ST *adj* thinly scattered

SPARSELY ▷ **sparse**

SPARSER ▷ **sparse**

SPARSEST ▷ **sparse**

SPARSITY ▷ **sparse**

SPART, -S *n* esparto

SPARTAN, -S *adj* strict and austere ▷ *n* disciplined or brave person

SPARTH, -S *n* type of battle-axe

SPARTHE, -S *same as* ▷ **sparth**

SPARTHS ▷ **sparth**

SPARTINA *n* grass growing in salt marshes

SPARTS ▷ **spart**

SPAS ▷ **spa**

SPASM, -ED, -ING, -S *n* involuntary muscular contraction ▷ *vb* go into spasm

SPASMIC ▷ **spasm**

SPASMING ▷ **spasm**

SPASMS ▷ **spasm**

SPASTIC *adj* affected by spasms

SPAT, -S, -TED, -TING *vb* have a quarrel

SPATE, -S *n* large number of things happening within a period of time

SPATFALL *n* mass of larvae on sea bed

SPATHAL ▷ **spathe**

SPATHE, -S *n* large sheathlike leaf enclosing a flower cluster

SPATHED ▷ **spathe**

SPATHES ▷ **spathe**

SPATHIC *adj* (of minerals) resembling spar

SPATHOSE *same as* ▷ **spathic**

SPATIAL *adj* of or in space

SPATLESE *n* type of German wine, usu white

SPATS ▷ **spat**

SPATTED ▷ **spat**

SPATTEE, -S *n* type of gaiter

SPATTER, -S *vb* scatter or be scattered in drops over (something) ▷ *n* spattering sound

SPATTING ▷ **spat**

SPATULA, -S *n* utensil with a broad flat blade for spreading or stirring

SPATULAR ▷ **spatula**

SPATULAS ▷ **spatula**

SPATULE, -S *n* spatula

S

SPATZLE, -S *same as*
▶ **spaetzle**
SPAUL, -S *same as* ▶ **spauld**
SPAULD, -S *n* shoulder
SPAULS ▶ **spaul**
SPAVIE, -S *Scots variant of*
▶ **spavin**
SPAVIET *adj* Scots word
meaning spavined
SPAVIN, -S *n* enlargement of
the hock of a horse by a bony
growth
SPAVINED *adj* affected with
spavin
SPAVINS ▶ **spavin**
SPAW, -S *same as* ▶ **spa**
SPAWL, -ED, -ING, -S *vb* spit
SPAWN, -ED, -ING, -S *n*
jelly-like mass of eggs of fish,
frogs, or molluscs ▷ *vb* (of
fish, frogs, or molluscs) lay
eggs
SPAWNER, -S ▶ **spawn**
SPAWNIER ▶ **spawny**
SPAWNING ▶ **spawn**
SPAWNS ▶ **spawn**
SPAWNY, SPAWNIER *adj*
like spawn
SPAWS ▶ **spaw**
SPAY, -ED, -ING, -S *vb*
remove the ovaries from (a
female animal)
SPAYAD, -S *n* male deer
SPAYD, -S *same as* ▶ **spayad**
SPAYED ▶ **spay**
SPAYING ▶ **spay**
SPAYS ▶ **spay**
SPAZA *adj* as in spaza shop
South African slang for a
small shop in a township
SPEAK, -ING, -S, SPOKEN *vb*
say words, talk
SPEAKER, -S *n* person who
speaks, esp at a formal
occasion
SPEAKING ▶ **speak**
SPEAKOUT *n* firm or brave
statement of one's beliefs
SPEAKS ▶ **speak**
SPEAL, -S *same as* ▶ **spule**
SPEAN, -ED, -ING, -S *same as*
▶ **spane**
SPEAR, -ED, -S *n* weapon
consisting of a long shaft with
a sharp point ▷ *vb* pierce
with or as if with a spear
SPEARER, -S ▶ **spear**
SPEARGUN *n* device for
shooting spears underwater
SPEARIER ▶ **speary**
SPEARING *n* act of spearing
SPEARMAN, SPEARMEN *n*
soldier armed with a spear
SPEARS ▶ **spear**
SPEARY, SPEARIER ▶ **spear**
SPEAT, -S *same as* ▶ **spate**

SPEC, -CED, -CING *vb* set
specifications
SPECCIER ▶ **speccy**
SPECCIES ▶ **speccy**
SPECCING ▶ **speccy**
**SPECCY, SPECCIER,
SPECCIES** *n* person wearing
spectacles ▷ *adj* wearing
spectacles
SPECIAL, -S *adj*
distinguished from others of
its kind ▷ *n* product,
programme, etc which is
only available at a certain
time ▷ *vb* advertise and sell
(an item) at a reduced price
SPECIATE *vb* form or develop
into a new biological species
SPECIE *n* coins as distinct
from paper money
SPECIES *n* group of plants or
animals that are related
closely enough to interbreed
naturally
SPECIFIC *adj* particular,
definite ▷ *n* drug used to
treat a particular disease
SPECIFY *vb* refer to or state
specifically
SPECIMEN *n* individual or
part typifying a whole
SPECIOUS *adj* apparently
true, but actually false
SPECK, -ED, -ING, -S *n* small
spot or particle ▷ *vb* mark
with specks or spots
SPECKIER ▶ **specky**
SPECKIES ▶ **specky**
SPECKING ▶ **speck**
SPECKLE, -S *n* small spot
▷ *vb* mark with speckles
SPECKLED ▶ **speckle**
SPECKLES ▶ **speckle**
SPECKS ▶ **speck**
**SPECKY, SPECKIER,
SPECKIES** *same as* ▶ **speccy**
SPECS *pl n* spectacles
SPECT, -ED, -ING, -S *vb*
expect
SPECTATE *vb* watch
SPECTED ▶ **spect**
SPECTER, -S *same as*
▶ **spectre**
SPECTING ▶ **spect**
SPECTRA ▶ **spectrum**
SPECTRAL *adj* of or like a
spectre
SPECTRE, -S *n* ghost
SPECTRIN *n* any one of a
class of fibrous proteins
found in the membranes of
red blood cells
SPECTRUM, SPECTRA *n*
range of different colours,
radio waves, etc in order of
their wavelengths

SPECTS ▶ **spect**
SPECULA ▶ **speculum**
SPECULAR *adj* of, relating
to, or having the properties
of a mirror
SPECULUM, SPECULA *n*
medical instrument for
examining body cavities
SPED ▶ **speed**
SPEECH, -ED, -ES *n* act,
power, or manner of
speaking ▷ *vb* make a
speech
SPEED, SPED, -ED, -ING, -S *n*
swiftness ▷ *vb* go quickly
SPEEDER, -S ▶ **speed**
SPEEDFUL ▶ **speed**
SPEEDIER ▶ **speedy**
SPEEDILY ▶ **speedy**
SPEEDING ▶ **speed**
SPEEDO, -S *n* speedometer
SPEEDS ▶ **speed**
SPEEDUP, -S *n* acceleration
SPEEDWAY *n* track for
motorcycle racing
SPEEDY, SPEEDIER *adj*
prompt
SPEEL, -ED, -ING, -S *n*
splinter of wood ▷ *vb* Scots
word meaning climb
SPEELER, -S ▶ **speel**
SPEELING ▶ **speel**
SPEELS ▶ **speel**
SPEER, -ED, -ING, -S *same as*
▶ **speir**
SPEIL, -ED, -ING, -S *n* dialect
word for ▶ **climb**
SPEIR, -ED, -ING, -S *vb* ask
SPEISE, -S *same as* ▶ **speiss**
SPEISS, -ES *n* compounds
formed when ores
containing arsenic and
antimony are smelted
SPEK, -S *n* bacon, fat, or
fatty pork used for larding
venison or other game
SPEKBOOM *n* South African
shrub
SPEKS ▶ **spek**
SPELAEAN *adj* of, found in,
or inhabiting caves
SPELD, -ED, -S *vb* Scots word
meaning spread
SPELDER, -S *same as* ▶ **speld**
SPELDIN, -S *n* fish split and
dried
SPELDING *same as* ▶ **speldin**
SPELDINS ▶ **speldin**
SPELDRIN *same as* ▶ **speldin**
SPELDS ▶ **speld**
SPELEAN *same as*
▶ **spelaean**
SPELK, -S *n* splinter of wood
SPELL, -ED, -ING, -S *vb* give
in correct order the letters
that form (a word) ▷ *n*

S

formula of words supposed to have magic power

SPELLER, -S *n* person who spells words in the manner specified

SPELLFUL *adj* magical

SPELLING ▸ **spell**

SPELLS ▸ **spell**

SPELT, -S *n* wheat variety

SPELTER, -S *n* impure zinc, usually containing about 3 per cent of lead and other impurities

SPELTS ▸ **spelt**

SPELTZ, -ES *n* wheat variety

SPELUNK, -S *vb* explore caves

SPENCE, -S *n* larder or pantry

SPENCER, -S *n* short fitted coat or jacket

SPENCES ▸ **spence**

SPEND, -ING, -S, SPENT *vb* pay out (money)

SPENDALL *n* spendthrift

SPENDER, -S *n* person who spends money in a manner specified

SPENDIER ▸ **spendy**

SPENDING ▸ **spend**

SPENDS ▸ **spend**

SPENDY, SPENDIER *adj* expensive

SPENSE, -S *same as* ▸ **spence**

SPENT ▸ **spend**

SPEOS, -ES *n* (esp in ancient Egypt) a temple or tomb cut into a rock face

SPERLING *same as* ▸ **sparling**

SPERM, -S *n* male reproductive cell

SPERMARY *n* any organ in which sperm are produced

SPERMIC *same as* > **spermatic**

SPERMINE *n* colourless basic water-soluble amine

SPERMOUS *same as* > **spermatic**

SPERMS ▸ **sperm**

SPERRE, -D, -S, SPERRING *vb* bolt

SPERSE, -D, -S, SPERSING, SPERST *vb* disperse

SPERTHE, -S *same as* ▸ **sparth**

SPET, -S, -TING *same as* ▸ **spit**

SPETCH, -ED, -ES *n* piece of animal skin

SPETS ▸ **spet**

SPETSNAZ *n* Soviet intelligence force

SPETTING ▸ **spet**

SPETZNAZ *same as* ▸ **spetsnaz**

SPEUG, -S *n* Scots word for sparrow

SPEW, -ED, -ING, -S *vb* vomit ▹ *n* something ejected from the mouth

SPEWER, -S ▸ **spew**

SPEWIER ▸ **spewy**

SPEWIEST ▸ **spewy**

SPEWING ▸ **spew**

SPEWS ▸ **spew**

SPEWY, SPEWIER, SPEWIEST *adj* marshy

SPHAER, -S *same as* ▸ **sphere**

SPHAERE, -S *same as* ▸ **sphere**

SPHAERS ▸ **sphaer**

SPHAGNUM *n* moss found in bogs

SPHAIREE *n* game resembling tennis played with wooden bats and a perforated plastic ball

SPHEAR, -S *same as* ▸ **sphere**

SPHEARE, -S *same as* ▸ **sphere**

SPHEARS ▸ **sphear**

SPHENE, -S *n* brown, yellow, green, or grey lustrous mineral

SPHENIC *adj* having the shape of a wedge

SPHENOID *adj* wedge-shaped ▹ *n* wedge-shaped thing

SPHERAL *adj* of or shaped like a sphere

SPHERE, -D, -S, SPHERING *n* perfectly round solid object ▹ *vb* surround or encircle

SPHERIC *same as* > **spherical**

SPHERICS *n* geometry and trigonometry of figures on the surface of a sphere

SPHERIER ▸ **sphery**

SPHERING ▸ **sphere**

SPHEROID *n* solid figure that is almost but not exactly a sphere

SPHERULE *n* very small sphere or globule

SPHERY, SPHERIER *adj* resembling a sphere

SPHINGES ▸ **sphinx**

SPHINGID *n* hawk moth

SPHINX, SPHINGES, -ES *n* huge statue built by the ancient Egyptians

SPHYGMIC *adj* of or relating to the pulse

SPHYGMUS *n* person's pulse

SPHYNX, -ES *n* breed of cat

SPIAL, -S *n* observation

SPICA, -E, -S *n* spiral bandage formed by a series of overlapping figure-of-eight turns

SPICATE *adj* having, arranged in, or relating to spikes

SPICATED *same as* ▸ **spicate**

SPICCATO *n* style of playing a stringed instrument in which the bow bounces lightly off the strings

SPICE, -D, -S, SPICING *n* aromatic substance used as flavouring ▹ *vb* flavour with spices

SPICER, -S ▸ **spice**

SPICERY *n* spices collectively

SPICES ▸ **spice**

SPICEY *same as* ▸ **spicy**

SPICIER ▸ **spicy**

SPICIEST ▸ **spicy**

SPICILY ▸ **spicy**

SPICING ▸ **spice**

SPICKNEL *same as* ▸ **spignel**

SPICULA, -E *same as* ▸ **spiculum**

SPICULAR ▸ **spiculum**

SPICULE, -S *n* small slender pointed structure or crystal

SPICULUM *same as* ▸ **spicule**

SPICY, SPICIER, SPICIEST *adj* flavoured with spices

SPIDE, -S *n* insulting Irish word for a young working-class man who dresses in casual sports clothes

SPIDER, -ED, -S *n* small eight-legged creature which spins a web to catch insects for food ▹ *vb* follow internet links to gather information

SPIDERY *adj* thin and angular like a spider's legs

SPIDES ▸ **spide**

SPIE *same as* ▸ **spy**

SPIED ▸ **spy**

SPIEGEL, -S *n* manganese-rich pig iron

SPIEL, -ED, -ING, -S *n* speech made to persuade someone to do something ▹ *vb* deliver a prepared spiel

SPIELER, -S ▸ **spiel**

SPIELING ▸ **spiel**

SPIELS ▸ **spiel**

SPIER, -ED, -ING, -S *variant of* ▸ **speir**

SPIES ▸ **spy**

SPIF, -S *n* postage stamp perforated with the initials of a firm to avoid theft by employees

SPIFF, -ED, -S *vb* make smart

SPIFFIED ▸ **spiffy**

SPIFFIER ▸ **spiffy**

SPIFFIES ▸ **spiffy**

SPIFFILY ▸ **spiffy**

SPIFFING *adj* excellent

S

SPIFFS ▶ spiff

SPIFFY, SPIFFIED, SPIFFIER, SPIFFIES adj smart ▷ n smart thing or person ▷ vb smarten

SPIFS ▶ spif

SPIGHT, -ED, -S same as ▶ spite

SPIGNEL, -S n European umbelliferous plant

SPIGOT, -S n stopper for, or tap fitted to, a cask

SPIKE, -D, -S, SPIKING n sharp point ▷ vb put spikes on

SPIKELET n unit of a grass inflorescence

SPIKER, -S ▶ spike

SPIKERY n High-Church Anglicanism

SPIKES ▶ spike

SPIKEY same as ▶ spiky

SPIKIER ▶ spiky

SPIKIEST ▶ spiky

SPIKILY ▶ spiky

SPIKING ▶ spike

SPIKY, SPIKIER, SPIKIEST adj resembling a spike

SPILE, -D, -S n heavy timber stake or pile ▷ vb provide or support with a spile

SPILIKIN same as > **spillikin**

SPILING, -S ▶ spile

SPILITE, -S n type of igneous rock

SPILITIC ▶ spilite

SPILL, -ED, -ING, -S, SPILT vb pour from or as if from a container ▷ n fall

SPILLAGE n instance or the process of spilling

SPILLED ▶ spill

SPILLER, -S ▶ spill

SPILLING ▶ spill

SPILLS ▶ spill

SPILLWAY n channel that carries away surplus water, as from a dam

SPILT ▶ spill

SPILTH, -S n something spilled

SPIM, -S n spam sent and received via an instant-messaging system

SPIMMER, -S n person who sends spam via an instant-messaging system

SPIMMING n the sending of spam via an instant-messaging system

SPIMS ▶ spim

SPIN, -NING, -S, SPUN vb revolve or cause to revolve rapidly ▷ n revolving motion

SPINA, -E, -S n spine

SPINACH n dark green leafy vegetable

SPINACHY adj tasting of spinach

SPINAE ▶ spina

SPINAGE, -S same as ▶ spinach

SPINAL, -S adj of the spine ▷ n anaesthetic administered in the spine

SPINALLY ▶ spinal

SPINALS ▶ spinal

SPINAR, -S n fast-spinning star

SPINAS ▶ spina

SPINATE adj having a spine

SPINDLE, -D, -S n rotating rod that acts as an axle ▷ vb form into a spindle or equip with spindles

SPINDLER ▶ spindle

SPINDLES ▶ spindle

SPINDLY adj long, slender, and frail

SPINE, -S n backbone

SPINED ▶ spine

SPINEL, -S n any of a group of hard glassy minerals of variable colour

SPINELLE same as ▶ spinel

SPINELS ▶ spinel

SPINES ▶ spine

SPINET, -S n small harpsichord

SPINETTE same as ▶ spinet

SPINIER ▶ spiny

SPINIEST ▶ spiny

SPINIFEX n coarse spiny Australian grass

SPINK, -ED, -ING, -S n finch ▷ vb (of a finch) chirp

SPINLESS ▶ spin

SPINNER, -S n bowler who makes the ball change direction when it bounces

SPINNERY n spinning mill

SPINNET, -S same as ▶ spinet

SPINNEY, -S n small wood

SPINNIER ▶ spinny

SPINNIES ▶ spinny

SPINNING ▶ spin

SPINNY, SPINNIER, SPINNIES adj crazy

SPINODE, -S another name for ▶ cusp

SPINOFF, -S n development derived incidentally from an existing enterprise

SPINONE, SPINONI n as in **Italian spinone** wiry-coated gun dog

SPINOR, -S n type of mathematical object

SPINOSE adj (esp of plants) bearing many spines

SPINOUS adj resembling a spine or thorn

SPINOUT, -S n spinning skid that causes a car to run off the road

SPINS ▶ spin

SPINSTER n unmarried woman

SPINTEXT n preacher

SPINTO, -S n lyrical singing voice

SPINULA, -E n small spine

SPINULE, -S n very small spine, thorn, or prickle

SPINY, SPINIER, SPINIEST adj covered with spines

SPIRACLE n small blowhole for breathing through, such as that of a whale

SPIRAEA, -S n plant with small white or pink flowers

SPIRAL, -ED, -S n continuous curve formed by a point winding about a central axis ▷ vb move in a spiral ▷ adj having the form of a spiral

SPIRALLY ▶ spiral

SPIRALS ▶ spiral

SPIRANT, -S n fricative consonant

SPIRATED adj twisted in spiral

SPIRE, -D, -S, SPIRING n pointed part of a steeple ▷ vb assume the shape of a spire

SPIREA, -S same as ▶ spiraea

SPIRED ▶ spire

SPIRELET another name for ▶ fleche

SPIREM, -S same as ▶ spireme

SPIREME, -S n tangled mass of chromatin threads

SPIREMS ▶ spirem

SPIRES ▶ spire

SPIRIC, -S n type of curve

SPIRIER ▶ spiry

SPIRIEST ▶ spiry

SPIRILLA > **spirillum**

SPIRING ▶ spire

SPIRIT, -S n nonphysical aspect of a person concerned with profound thoughts ▷ vb carry away mysteriously

SPIRITED adj lively

SPIRITS ▶ spirit

SPIRITUS n spirit

SPIRITY adj spirited

SPIRLING same as ▶ sparling

SPIROID adj resembling a spiral or displaying a spiral form

SPIRT, -ED, -ING, -S same as ▶ spurt

SPIRTLE, -S same as ▶ spurtle**

SPIRTS ▸ spirt

SPIRULA, -E, -S n tropical cephalopod mollusc

SPIRY, SPIRIER, SPIRIEST ▸ spire

SPIT, -S, -TED, -TEN, -TING vb eject (saliva or food) from the mouth ▷ n saliva

SPITAL, -S n obsolete word for hospital

SPITBALL n small missile made from chewed paper ▷ vb make suggestions

SPITCHER adj doomed ▷ vb be doomed

SPITE, -D, -S, SPITING n deliberate nastiness ▷ vb annoy or hurt from spite

SPITEFUL adj full of or motivated by spite

SPITES ▸ spite

SPITFIRE n person with a fiery temper

SPITING ▸ spite

SPITS ▸ spit

SPITTED ▸ spit

SPITTEN ▸ spit

SPITTER, -S ▸ spit

SPITTIER ▸ spitty

SPITTING ▸ spit

SPITTLE, -S n fluid produced in the mouth, saliva

SPITTLY adj covered with spittle

SPITTOON n bowl to spit into

SPITTY, SPITTIER adj covered with saliva

SPITZ, -ES n stockily built dog with a tightly curled tail

SPIV, -S n smartly dressed man who makes a living by shady dealings

SPIVVERY n behaviour of spivs

SPIVVIER ▸ spivvy

SPIVVISH adj characteristic of a spiv

SPIVVY, SPIVVIER ▸ spiv

SPLAKE, -S n type of hybrid trout bred by Canadian zoologists

SPLASH, -ED, -ES vb scatter liquid on (something) ▷ n splashing sound

SPLASHER n anything used for protection against splashes

SPLASHES ▸ splash

SPLASHY adj having irregular marks

SPLAT, -S, -TED n wet slapping sound ▷ vb make wet slapping sound

SPLATCH vb splash

SPLATS ▸ splat

SPLATTED ▸ splat

SPLATTER n splash ▷ vb splash (something or someone) with small blobs

SPLAY, -ED, -ING, -S vb spread out, with ends spreading in different directions ▷ adj spread out ▷ n surface of a wall that forms an oblique angle to the main flat surfaces

SPLEEN, -S n abdominal organ which filters bacteria from the blood

SPLEENY ▸ spleen

SPLENDID adj excellent

SPLENDOR same as ▸ splendour

SPLENIA ▸ splenium

SPLENIAL ▸ splenius

SPLENIC adj of, relating to, or in the spleen

SPLENII ▸ splenius

SPLENIUM, SPLENIA n structure in brain

SPLENIUS, SPLENII n either of two flat muscles situated at the back of the neck

SPLENT, -S same as ▸ splint

SPLICE, -D, -S, SPLICING vb join by interweaving or overlapping ends

SPLICER, -S ▸ splice

SPLICES ▸ splice

SPLICING ▸ splice

SPLINE, -D, -S, SPLINING n type of narrow key around a shaft that fits into a corresponding groove ▷ vb provide (a shaft, part, etc) with splines

SPLINT, -ED, -S n rigid support for a broken bone ▷ vb apply a splint to (a broken arm, etc)

SPLINTER n thin sharp piece broken off, esp from wood ▷ vb break into fragments

SPLINTS ▸ splint

SPLISH, -ED, -ES vb splash

SPLIT, -S, -TED vb break into separate pieces ▷ n splitting

SPLITTER ▸ split

SPLODGE, -D, -S n large uneven spot or stain ▷ vb mark (something) with a splodge or splodges

SPLODGY ▸ splodge

SPLOG, -S n spam blog

SPLOOSH vb splash or cause to splash about uncontrollably ▷ n instance or sound of splooshing

SPLORE, -S n revel

SPLOSH, -ED, -ES vb scatter (liquid) vigorously about in

blobs ▷ n instance or sound of sploshing

SPLOTCH vb splash, daub

SPLOTCHY ▸ splotch

SPLURGE, -D, -S vb spend money extravagantly ▷ n bout of extravagance

SPLURGER ▸ splurge

SPLURGES ▸ splurge

SPLURGY ▸ splurge

SPLURT, -ED, -S vb gush out

SPLUTTER vb utter with spitting or choking sounds ▷ n spluttering

SPOD, -S adj boring, unattractive, or overly studious

SPODDY, SPODDIER ▸ spod

SPODE, -S n type of English china or porcelain

SPODIUM, -S n black powder

SPODOSOL n ashy soil

SPODS ▸ spod

SPOFFISH adj officious

SPOFFY same as ▸ spoffish

SPOIL, -ED, -ING, -S, -T vb damage

SPOILAGE n amount of material that has been spoilt

SPOILED ▸ spoil

SPOILER, -S n device on an aircraft or car to increase drag

SPOILFUL adj taking spoils

SPOILING ▸ spoil

SPOILS ▸ spoil

SPOILT ▸ spoil

SPOKE, -D, -S, SPOKING n radial member of a wheel ▷ vb equip with spokes

SPOKEN ▸ speak

SPOKES ▸ spoke

SPOKING ▸ spoke

SPOLIATE less common word for ▸ despoil

SPONDAIC adj of, relating to, or consisting of spondees ▷ n spondaic line

SPONDEE, -S n metrical foot of two long syllables

SPONDYL, -S n vertebra

SPONGE, -D, -S, SPONGING n sea animal with a porous absorbent skeleton ▷ vb wipe with a sponge

SPONGER, -S n person who sponges on others

SPONGES ▸ sponge

SPONGIER ▸ spongy

SPONGILY ▸ spongy

SPONGIN, -S n fibrous horny protein in sponges

SPONGING ▸ sponge

SPONGINS ▸ spongin

SPONGOID ▸ sponge

SPONGY, SPONGIER adj of or resembling a sponge

SPONSAL n marriage

SPONSING same as ▶ sponson

SPONSION n act or process of becoming surety

SPONSON, -S n outboard support for a gun enabling it to fire fore and aft

SPONSOR, -S n person who promotes something ▷ vb act as a sponsor for

SPONTOON n infantry weapon used in the 18th and 19th centuries

SPOOF, -ED, -ING, -S n mildly satirical parody ▷ vb fool (a person) with a trick or deception

SPOOFER, -S ▶ spoof

SPOOFERY ▶ spoof

SPOOFIER ▶ spoofy

SPOOFING ▶ spoof

SPOOFS ▶ spoof

SPOOFY, SPOOFIER ▶ spoof

SPOOK, -ED, -ING, -S n ghost ▷ vb frighten

SPOOKERY n spooky events

SPOOKIER ▶ spooky

SPOOKILY ▶ spooky

SPOOKING ▶ spook

SPOOKISH ▶ spook

SPOOKS ▶ spook

SPOOKY, SPOOKIER adj ghostly or eerie

SPOOL, -ED, -ING, -S n cylinder round which something can be wound ▷ vb wind or be wound onto a spool or reel

SPOOLER, -S ▶ spool

SPOOLING ▶ spool

SPOOLS ▶ spool

SPOOM, -ED, -ING, -S vb sail fast before wind

SPOON, -ED, -ING, -S n shallow bowl attached to a handle for eating, stirring, or serving food ▷ vb lift with a spoon

SPOONER, -S n person who engages in spooning

SPOONEY, -S same as ▶ spoony

SPOONFED adj having been given someone else's opinions

SPOONFUL n amount that a spoon is able to hold

SPOONIER ▶ spoony

SPOONIES ▶ spoony

SPOONILY ▶ spoony

SPOONING ▶ spoon

SPOONS ▶ spoon

SPOONY, SPOONIER, SPOONIES adj foolishly or stupidly in love ▷ n fool or silly person, esp one in love

SPOOR, -ED, -ING, -S n trail of an animal ▷ vb track (an animal) by following its trail

SPOORER, -S ▶ spoor

SPOORING ▶ spoor

SPOORS ▶ spoor

SPOOT, -S n razor shell

SPORADIC adj intermittent, scattered

SPORAL ▶ spore

SPORE, -D, -S, SPORING n minute reproductive body of some plants ▷ vb produce, carry, or release spores

SPORIDIA > sporidium

SPORING ▶ spore

SPORK, -S n spoon-shaped piece of cutlery with tines like a fork

SPOROID adj of or like a spore

SPOROZOA n class of microscopic creature

SPORRAN, -S n pouch worn in front of a kilt

SPORT, -ED n activity for pleasure, competition, or exercise ▷ vb wear proudly

SPORTER, -S ▶ sport

SPORTFUL ▶ sport

SPORTIER ▶ sporty

SPORTIES ▶ sporty

SPORTIF, -S adj sporty ▷ n sporty person

SPORTILY ▶ sporty

SPORTING adj of sport

SPORTIVE adj playful

SPORTS adj of or used in sports ▷ n meeting held at a school or college for competitions in athletic events

SPORTY, SPORTIER, SPORTIES adj (of a person) interested in sport ▷ n young person who takes an interest in sport and fitness

SPORULAR ▶ sporule

SPORULE, -S n spore, esp a very small spore

SPOSH, -ES n slush

SPOSHY, SPOSHIER ▶ sposh

SPOT, -S, -TED, -TING n small mark on a surface ▷ vb notice

SPOTLESS adj absolutely clean

SPOTLIT > spotlight

SPOTS ▶ spot

SPOTTED ▶ spot

SPOTTER, -S n person who notes numbers or types of trains or planes

SPOTTIE, -S n young deer of up to three months of age

SPOTTIER ▶ spotty

SPOTTIES ▶ spottie

SPOTTILY ▶ spotty

SPOTTING ▶ spot

SPOTTY, SPOTTIER adj with spots

SPOUSAGE n marriage

SPOUSAL, -S n marriage ceremony ▷ adj of or relating to marriage

SPOUSE, -D, -S, SPOUSING n person to whom one is married ▷ vb marry

SPOUT, -ED, -S vb pour out in a stream or jet ▷ n projecting tube or lip for pouring liquids

SPOUTER, -S ▶ spout

SPOUTIER ▶ spouty

SPOUTING n rainwater downpipe on the outside of a building

SPOUTS ▶ spout

SPOUTY, SPOUTIER ▶ spout

SPRACK adj vigorous

SPRACKLE vb clamber

SPRAD ▶ spread

SPRADDLE n disease of fowl preventing them from standing

SPRAG, -GED, -S n device used to prevent a vehicle from running backwards on an incline ▷ vb use sprag to prevent vehicle from moving

SPRAID vb chapped

SPRAIN, -ED, -S vb injure (a joint) by a sudden twist ▷ n such an injury

SPRAINT, -S n piece of otter's dung

SPRANG, -S n branch

SPRANGLE vb sprawl

SPRANGS ▶ sprang

SPRAT, -S n small sea fish

SPRATTLE vb scramble

SPRAUNCY adj smart

SPRAWL, -ED, -S vb lie or sit with the limbs spread out ▷ n part of a city that has spread untidily over a large area

SPRAWLER ▶ sprawl

SPRAWLS ▶ sprawl

SPRAWLY ▶ sprawl

SPRAY, -ED, -IER, -ING, -S n (device for producing) fine drops of liquid ▷ vb scatter in fine drops

SPRAYER, -S ▶ spray

SPRAYEY ▶ spray

SPRAYIER ▶ spray

SPRAYING ▶ spray

SPRAYS ▸ spray

SPREAD, SPRAD, -S vb open out or be displayed to the fullest extent ▷ n spreading ▷ adj extended or stretched out, esp to the fullest extent

SPREADER n machine or device used for scattering bulk materials over a relatively wide area

SPREADS ▸ spread

SPREAGH, -S n cattle raid

SPREATHE vb chap

SPREAZE, -S same as ▸ spreathe

SPREAZED same as > spreathed

SPREAZES ▸ spreaze

SPRED, -S same as ▸ spread

SPREDD, -S same as ▸ spread

SPREDDE, -N, -S same as ▸ spread

SPREDDS ▸ spredd

SPREDS ▸ spred

SPREE, -D, -ING, -S n session of overindulgence, usu in drinking or spending money ▷ vb go on a spree

SPREETHE same as ▸ spreathe

SPREEZE, -D, -S same as ▸ spreathe

SPRENT, -ED, -S adj sprinkled ▷ vb leap forward in an agile manner

SPREW, -S same as ▸ sprue

SPRIER ▸ spry

SPRIEST ▸ spry

SPRIG, -GED, -S n twig or shoot ▷ vb fasten or secure with sprigs

SPRIGGER ▸ sprig

SPRIGGY ▸ sprig

SPRIGHT, -S same as ▸ sprite

SPRIGS ▸ sprig

SPRING, -S, SPRONG, SPRUNG vb move suddenly upwards or forwards in a single motion, jump ▷ n season between winter and summer

SPRINGAL n young man

SPRINGE, -D, -S n type of snare for catching small wild animals or birds ▷ vb set such a snare

SPRINGER n small spaniel

SPRINGES ▸ springe

SPRINGLE same as ▸ springe

SPRINGS ▸ spring

SPRINGY adj elastic

SPRINKLE vb scatter (liquid or powder) in tiny drops or particles over (something) ▷ n act or an instance of sprinkling or a quantity that is sprinkled

SPRINT, -ED, -S n short race run at top speed ▷ vb run a short distance at top speed

SPRINTER ▸ sprint

SPRINTS ▸ sprint

SPRIT, -S n small spar set diagonally across a sail to extend it

SPRITE, -S n elf

SPRITELY same as > sprightly

SPRITES ▸ sprite

SPRITS ▸ sprit

SPRITZ, -ED, -ES vb spray liquid

SPRITZER n tall drink of wine and soda water

SPRITZES ▸ spritz

SPRITZIG adj (of wine) sparkling ▷ n sparkling wine

SPRITZY adj fizzy

SPROCKET n wheel with teeth on the rim, that drives or is driven by a chain

SPROD, -S n young salmon

SPROG, -S n child

SPROGLET n small child

SPROGS ▸ sprog

SPRONG ▸ spring

SPROUT, -ED, -S vb put forth shoots ▷ n shoot

SPRUCE, -D, -R, -S, -ST, SPRUCING n kind of fir ▷ adj neat and smart

SPRUCELY ▸ spruce

SPRUCER ▸ spruce

SPRUCES ▸ spruce

SPRUCEST ▸ spruce

SPRUCIER ▸ sprucy

SPRUCING ▸ spruce

SPRUCY, SPRUCIER ▸ spruce

SPRUE, -S n vertical channel in a mould

SPRUG, -S n sparrow

SPRUIK, -ED, -S vb old word meaning speak in public

SPRUIKER ▸ spruik

SPRUIKS ▸ spruik

SPRUIT, -S n small tributary stream or watercourse

SPRUNG ▸ spring

SPRUSH, -ED, -ES Scots form of ▸ spruce

SPRY, SPRIER, SPRIEST, -ER, -EST adj active or nimble

SPRYLY ▸ spry

SPRYNESS ▸ spry

SPUD, -DED, -DING, -S n potato ▷ vb remove (bark) or eradicate (weeds) with a spud

SPUDDER, -S same as ▸ spud

SPUDDIER ▸ spuddy

SPUDDING ▸ spud

SPUDDLE, -S n feeble movement

SPUDDY, SPUDDIER adj short and fat

SPUDGEL, -S n bucket on a long handle

SPUDS ▸ spud

SPUE, -D, -ING, -S, SPUING same as ▸ spew

SPUER, -S ▸ spue

SPUES ▸ spue

SPUG, -S same as ▸ spuggy

SPUGGY, SPUGGIES n house sparrow

SPUGS ▸ spug

SPUILZIE vb plunder

SPUING ▸ spue

SPULE, -S Scots word for ▸ shoulder

SPULYE, -D, -S same as ▸ spuilzie

SPULYIE, -D, -S same as ▸ spuilzie

SPULZIE, -D, -S same as ▸ spuilzie

SPUMANTE n Italian sparkling wine

SPUME, -D, -S, SPUMING vb froth ▷ n foam or froth on the sea

SPUMIER ▸ spumy

SPUMIEST ▸ spumy

SPUMING ▸ spume

SPUMONE, -S n creamy Italian ice cream

SPUMONI, -S same as ▸ spumone

SPUMOUS ▸ spume

SPUMY, SPUMIER, SPUMIEST ▸ spume

SPUN ▸ spin

SPUNGE, -S same as ▸ sponge

SPUNK, -ED, -ING, -S n courage, spirit ▷ vb catch fire

SPUNKIE, -S n will-o'-the-wisp

SPUNKIER ▸ spunky

SPUNKIES ▸ spunkie

SPUNKILY ▸ spunk

SPUNKING ▸ spunk

SPUNKS ▸ spunk

SPUNKY, SPUNKIER ▸ spunk

SPUNYARN n small stuff made from rope yarns twisted together

SPUR, -RED, -RING, -S n stimulus or incentive ▷ vb urge on, incite (someone)

SPURDOG, -S n the dogfish

SPURGALL vb prod with spur

SPURGE, -S n plant with milky sap

S

SPURIAE n type of bird feathers

SPURIOUS adj not genuine

SPURLESS ▸ spur

SPURLIKE adj like a spur

SPURLING same as ▸ sparling

SPURN, -ED, -ING, -S vb reject with scorn ▷ n instance of spurning

SPURNE, -S vb spur

SPURNED ▸ spurn

SPURNER, -S ▸ spurn

SPURNES ▸ spurne

SPURNING ▸ spurn

SPURNS ▸ spurn

SPURRED ▸ spur

SPURRER, -S ▸ spur

SPURREY, -S n any of several low-growing European plants

SPURRIER n maker of spurs

SPURRIES ▸ spurry

SPURRING ▸ spur

SPURRY, SPURRIES n spurrey ▷ adj resembling a spur

SPURS ▸ spur

SPURT, -ED, -ING, -S vb gush or cause to gush out in a jet ▷ n short sudden burst of activity or speed

SPURTER, -S ▸ spurt

SPURTING ▸ spurt

SPURTLE, -S n wooden spoon for stirring porridge

SPURTS ▸ spurt

SPURWAY, -S n path used by riders

SPUTA ▸ sputum

SPUTNIK, -S n early Soviet artificial satellite

SPUTTER, -S n splutter ▷ vb splutter

SPUTTERY adj sputtering

SPUTUM, SPUTA, -S n mass of spittle ejected from the mouth

SPY, SPIED, SPIES n person employed to obtain secret information ▷ vb act as a spy

SPYAL, -S n spy

SPYCAM, -S n camera used for covert surveillance

SPYGLASS n small telescope

SPYHOLE, -S n small hole in a door, etc through which one may watch secretly

SPYING, -S ▸ spy

SPYPLANE n military aeroplane used to spy on enemy

SPYRE, -S same as ▸ spire

SPYWARE, -S n software used to gain information about a computer user

SQUAB, -BED, -BER, -S n young bird yet to leave the nest ▷ adj (of birds) recently hatched and still unfledged ▷ vb fall

SQUABASH vb crush

SQUABBED ▸ squab

SQUABBER ▸ squab

SQUABBLE n petty or noisy quarrel ▷ vb quarrel over a small matter

SQUABBY ▸ squab

SQUABS ▸ squab

SQUACCO, -S n S European heron

SQUAD, -DED, -S n small group of people working or training together ▷ vb set up squads

SQUADDIE n private soldier

SQUADDY same as ▸ squaddie

SQUADRON n division of an air force, fleet, or cavalry regiment ▷ vb assign to squadrons

SQUADS ▸ squad

SQUAIL, -ED, -S vb throw sticks at

SQUAILER ▸ squail

SQUAILS ▸ squail

SQUALENE n terpene first found in the liver of sharks

SQUALID adj dirty and unpleasant

SQUALL, -ED, -S n sudden strong wind ▷ vb cry noisily, yell

SQUALLER ▸ squall

SQUALLS ▸ squall

SQUALLY ▸ squall

SQUALOID adj of or like a shark

SQUALOR, -S n disgusting dirt and filth

SQUAMA, -E n scale or scalelike structure

SQUAMATE ▸ squama

SQUAME, -S same as ▸ squama

SQUAMOSE same as ▸ squamous

SQUAMOUS adj (of epithelium) consisting of one or more layers of flat platelike cells

SQUAMULA same as > squamella

SQUAMULE same as > squamula

SQUANDER vb waste (money or resources) ▷ n extravagance or dissipation

SQUARE, -D, -S, -ST, SQUARING n geometric figure with four equal sides and four right angles ▷ adj square in shape ▷ vb multiply (a number) by itself ▷ adv directly

SQUARELY adv in a direct way

SQUARER, -S ▸ square

SQUARES ▸ square

SQUAREST ▸ square

SQUARIAL n type of square dish for receiving satellite television

SQUARING ▸ square

SQUARISH ▸ square

SQUARK, -S n hypothetical boson partner of a quark

SQUARSON n member of the clergy who is also a landowner

SQUASH, -ED, -ES vb crush flat ▷ n sweet fruit drink diluted with water

SQUASHER ▸ squash

SQUASHES ▸ squash

SQUASHY adj soft and easily squashed

SQUAT, -S, -TED vb crouch with the knees bent and the weight on the feet ▷ n place where squatters live ▷ adj short and broad

SQUATLY ▸ squat

SQUATS ▸ squat

SQUATTED ▸ squat

SQUATTER n illegal occupier of unused premises ▷ vb splash along

SQUATTLE vb squat

SQUATTY adj short and broad

SQUAWK, -ED, -S n loud harsh cry ▷ vb utter a squawk

SQUAWKER ▸ squawk

SQUAWKS ▸ squawk

SQUAWKY ▸ squawk

SQUEAK, -ED, -S n short shrill cry or sound ▷ vb make or utter a squeak

SQUEAKER ▸ squeak

SQUEAKS ▸ squeak

SQUEAKY ▸ squeak

SQUEAL, -ED, -S n long shrill cry or sound ▷ vb make or utter a squeal

SQUEALER ▸ squeal

SQUEALS ▸ squeal

SQUEEGEE n tool with a rubber blade for clearing water from a surface ▷ vb remove (water or other liquid) from (something) by use of a squeegee

SQUEEZE, -D, -S vb grip or press firmly ▷ n squeezing

SQUEEZER ▸ squeeze

SQUEEZES ▸ squeeze

SQUEEZY ▸ squeeze

SQUEG, -GED, -S vb oscillate

SQUEGGER ▸ squeg

SQUEGS ▸ squeg

SQUELCH vb make a wet sucking sound, as by walking through mud ▷ n squelching sound

SQUELCHY ▸ squelch

SQUIB, -BED, -S n small firework that hisses before exploding

SQUIBBER n (in baseball) ground ball that becomes a base hit

SQUIBS ▸ squib

SQUID, -DED, -S n sea creature with tentacles ▷ vb (of a parachute) to assume an elongated shape

SQUIDGE, -D, -S vb squash

SQUIDGY adj soft, moist, and squashy

SQUIDS ▸ squid

SQUIER, -S same as ▸ squire

SQUIFF same as ▸ squiffy

SQUIFFED same as ▸ squiffy

SQUIFFER n concertina

SQUIFFY adj slightly drunk

SQUIGGLE, -D, -S n wavy line ▷ vb wriggle

SQUIGGLY ▸ squiggle

SQUILGEE same as ▸ squeegee

SQUILL, -S n Mediterranean plant of the lily family

SQUILLA, -E, -S n type of mantis shrimp

SQUILLS ▸ squill

SQUINCH n small arch across an internal corner of a tower ▷ vb squeeze

SQUINIED ▸ squiny

SQUINIES ▸ squiny

SQUINNY vb squint ▷ adj squint

SQUINT, -ED, -S vb have eyes which face in different directions ▷ n squinting condition of the eye ▷ adj crooked

SQUINTER ▸ squint

SQUINTS ▸ squint

SQUINTY ▸ squint

SQUINY, SQUINIED, SQUINIES same as ▸ squinny

SQUIRAGE n body of squires

SQUIRE, -D, -S, SQUIRING n country gentleman, usu the main landowner in a community ▷ vb (of a man) escort (a woman)

SQUIREEN n petty squire

SQUIRELY ▸ squire

SQUIRES ▸ squire

SQUIRESS n wife of squire

SQUIRING ▸ squire

SQUIRISH ▸ squire

SQUIRL, -S n decorative flourish in handwriting

SQUIRM, -ED, -S vb wriggle, writhe ▷ n wriggling movement

SQUIRMER ▸ squirm

SQUIRMS ▸ squirm

SQUIRMY adj moving with a wriggling motion

SQUIRR, -ED, -S same as ▸ skirr

SQUIRREL n small bushy-tailed tree-living animal ▷ vb store for future use

SQUIRRS ▸ squirr

SQUIRT, -ED, -S vb force (a liquid) or (of a liquid) be forced out of a narrow opening ▷ n jet of liquid

SQUIRTER ▸ squirt

SQUIRTS ▸ squirt

SQUISH, -ED, -ES n soft squelching sound ▷ vb crush (something) with a soft squelching sound

SQUISHY adj soft and yielding to the touch

SQUIT, -S n insignificant person

SQUITCH n couch grass

SQUITS ▸ squit

SQUIZ, -ZES n look or glance, esp an inquisitive one

The word **quiz** comes up surprisingly often, so it is useful to remember that you can put an S on the front of it to form this Australian slang word for a quick look.

SQUOOSH vb squash

SQUOOSHY ▸ squoosh

SQUUSH, -ED, -ES same as ▸ squoosh

SRADDHA, -S n Hindu offering to ancestor

SRADHA, -S same as ▸ sraddha

SRI, -S n title of respect used when addressing a Hindu

SRIRACHA n type of spicy sauce

SRIS ▸ sri

ST interj exclamation to attract attention

STAB, -BED, -BING, -S vb pierce with something pointed ▷ n instance of stabbing

STABBER, -S ▸ stab

STABBING ▸ stab

STABILE, -S n stationary abstract construction, usually of wire, metal, wood, etc ▷ adj fixed

STABLE, -D, -S, -ST n building in which horses are kept ▷ vb put or keep (a horse) in a stable ▷ adj firmly fixed or established

STABLER, -S n stable owner

STABLES ▸ stable

STABLEST ▸ stable

STABLING n stable buildings or accommodation

STABLISH archaic variant of > establish

STABLY ▸ stable

STABS ▸ stab

STACCATO, STACCATI adv with the notes sharply separated ▷ adj consisting of short abrupt sounds ▷ n staccato note

STACHYS n type of plant of the genus which includes lamb's ears and betony

STACK, -ED, -S n ordered pile ▷ vb pile in a stack

STACKER, -S ▸ stack

STACKET, -S n fence of wooden posts

STACKING n arrangement of aircraft traffic in busy flight lanes

STACKS ▸ stack

STACKUP, -S n number of aircraft waiting to land

STACTE, -S n one of several sweet-smelling spices used in incense

STADDA, -S n type of saw

STADDLE, -S n type of support or prop

STADE, -S same as ▸ stadium

STADIA, -S n instrument used in surveying

STADIAL, -S n stage in development of glacier

STADIAS ▸ stadia

STADIUM, -S n sports arena with tiered seats for spectators

STAFF, -ED, -S n people employed in an organization ▷ vb supply with personnel

STAFFAGE n ornamentation in work of art

STAFFED ▸ staff

STAFFER, -S n member of staff, esp, in journalism, of editorial staff

STAFFING n act of hiring employees

STAFFMAN, STAFFMEN n person who holds the

S

levelling staff when a survey is being made

STAFFS ▸ staff

STAG, -GED, -GING, -S n adult male deer ▸ vb without a female escort ▸ adv apply for (shares) with the intention of selling them for quick profit

STAGE, -D, -S n step or period of development ▸ vb put (a play) on stage

STAGEFUL n amount that can appear on stage

STAGER, -S n person of experience

STAGERY n theatrical effects or techniques

STAGES ▸ stage

STAGETTE n young unmarried professional woman

STAGEY same as ▸ stagy

STAGGARD n male red deer in the fourth year of life

STAGGART same as ▸ staggard

STAGGED ▸ stag

STAGGER vb walk unsteadily ▸ n staggering

STAGGERS n disease of horses and other domestic animals that causes staggering

STAGGERY adj tending to stagger

STAGGIE, -S n little stag

STAGGIER ▸ staggy

STAGGIES ▸ staggie

STAGGING ▸ stag

STAGGY, STAGGIER ▸ stag

STAGHORN n type of fern with fronds that resemble antlers

STAGIER ▸ stagy

STAGIEST ▸ stagy

STAGILY ▸ stagy

STAGING, -S n temporary support used in building

STAGNANT adj (of water or air) stale from not moving

STAGNATE vb be stagnant

STAGS ▸ stag

STAGY, STAGIER, STAGIEST adj too theatrical or dramatic

STAID, -ER, -EST adj sedate, serious, and rather dull

STAIDLY ▸ staid

STAIG, -S Scots variant of ▸ stag

STAIN, -ED, -ING, -S vb discolour, mark ▸ n discoloration or mark

STAINER, -S ▸ stain

STAINING ▸ stain

STAINS ▸ stain

STAIR n one step in a flight of stairs

STAIRED adj having stairs

STAIRS pl n flight of steps between floors, usu indoors

STAIRWAY n staircase

STAITH, -S same as ▸ staithe

STAITHE, -S n wharf

STAITHS ▸ staith

STAKE, -D, -S, STAKING n pointed stick or post driven into the ground as a support or marker ▸ vb support or mark out with stakes

STAKEOUT n police surveillance of an area or house ▸ vb keep an area or house under surveillance

STAKER, -S n person who marks off an area with stakes

STAKES ▸ stake

STAKING ▸ stake

STALAG, -S n German prisoner-of-war camp

STALAGMA n stalagmite

STALAGS ▸ stalag

STALE, -D, -R, -S, -ST, STALING adj not fresh ▸ vb make or become stale ▸ n urine of horses or cattle

STALELY ▸ stale

STALER ▸ stale

STALES ▸ stale

STALEST ▸ stale

STALING ▸ stale

STALK, -ED, -ING, -S n plant's stem ▸ vb follow or approach stealthily

STALKER, -S ▸ stalk

STALKIER ▸ stalky

STALKILY ▸ stalky

STALKING ▸ stalk

STALKO, -ES, -S n idle gentleman

STALKS ▸ stalk

STALKY, STALKIER adj like a stalk

STALL, -ED, -ING, -S n small stand for the display and sale of goods ▸ vb (of a motor vehicle or engine) stop accidentally

STALLAGE n rent paid for market stall

STALLED ▸ stall

STALLING ▸ stall

STALLION n uncastrated male horse

STALLMAN, STALLMEN n keeper of a stall

STALLS ▸ stall

STALWART adj strong and sturdy ▸ n stalwart person

STAMEN, -S n pollen-producing part of a flower

STAMENED adj having stamen

STAMENS ▸ stamen

STAMINA, -S n enduring energy and strength

STAMINAL ▸ stamina

STAMINAS ▸ stamina

STAMMEL, -S n coarse woollen cloth in former use for undergarments

STAMMER, -S vb speak or say with involuntary pauses or repetition of syllables ▸ n tendency to stammer

STAMNOS, STAMNOI n ancient Greek jar

STAMP, -ED, -ING, -S n piece of gummed paper stuck to an envelope or parcel ▸ vb bring (one's foot) down forcefully

STAMPEDE n sudden rush of frightened animals or of a crowd ▸ vb (cause to) take part in a stampede

STAMPEDO same as ▸ stampede

STAMPER, -S ▸ stamp

STAMPING ▸ stamp

STAMPS ▸ stamp

STANCE, -S n attitude

STANCH, -ED, -ES vb stem the flow of (a liquid, esp blood) ▸ adj loyal and dependable

STANCHEL same as > stanchion

STANCHER ▸ stanch

STANCHES ▸ stanch

STANCHLY ▸ stanch

STANCK adj faint

STAND, -EN, -ING, -S, STOOD, STOODEN, STUDDEN vb be in, rise to, or place in an upright position ▸ n stall for the sale of goods

STANDARD n level of quality ▸ adj usual, regular, or average

STANDBY, -S n person or thing that is ready for use

STANDEE, -S n person who stands

STANDEN ▸ stand

STANDER, -S ▸ stand

STANDING ▸ stand

STANDISH n stand, usually of metal, for pens, ink bottles, etc

STANDOFF n act or an instance of standing off or apart ▸ vb stay at a distance

STANDOUT n distinctive or outstanding person or thing

STANDPAT n (in poker) refusal to change one's card

STANDS ▸ **stand**

STANDUP, -S n comedian who performs solo

STANE, -D, -S, STANING Scot word for ▸ **stone**

STANG, -ED, -ING, -S vb sting

STANHOPE n light one-seater carriage with two or four wheels

STANIEL, -S n kestrel

STANINE, -S n scale of nine levels

STANING ▸ **stane**

STANK, -ED, -ING, -S vb dam

STANNARY n place or region where tin is mined or worked

STANNATE n salt of stannic acid

STANNEL, -S same as ▸ **staniel**

STANNIC adj of or containing tin, esp in the tetravalent state

STANNITE n grey metallic mineral

STANNOUS adj of or containing tin, esp in the divalent state

STANNUM, -S n tin (the metal)

STANOL, -S n drug taken to prevent heart disease

STANYEL, -S same as ▸ **staniel**

STANZA, -S n verse of a poem

STANZAED ▸ **stanza**

STANZAIC ▸ **stanza**

STANZAS ▸ **stanza**

STANZE, -S same as ▸ **stanza**

STANZO, -ES, -S same as ▸ **stanza**

STAP, -PED, -PING, -S same as ▸ **stop**

STAPEDES ▸ **stapes**

STAPEDII > **stapedius**

STAPELIA n fleshy cactus-like leafless African plant

STAPES, STAPEDES n stirrup-shaped bone in the middle ear of mammals

STAPH, -S n staphylococcus

STAPLE, -D, -S n U-shaped piece of metal used to fasten papers ▷ vb fasten with staples ▷ adj of prime importance

STAPLER, -S n small device for fastening papers together

STAPLES ▸ **staple**

STAPLING n as in **stomach stapling** surgical treatment for obesity

STAPPED ▸ **stap**

STAPPING ▸ **stap**

STAPPLE, -S same as ▸ **stopple**

STAPS ▸ **stap**

STAR, -RED, -RING, -S n hot gaseous mass in space, visible in the night sky as a point of light ▷ vb feature or be featured as a star ▷ adj leading, famous

STARAGEN n tarragon

STARCH, -ED, -ES n carbohydrate forming the main food element in bread, potatoes, etc ▷ vb stiffen (fabric) with starch ▷ adj (of a person) formal

STARCHER ▸ **starch**

STARCHES ▸ **starch**

STARCHY adj containing starch

STARDOM, -S n status of a star in the entertainment or sports world

STARDUST n dusty material found between the stars

STARE, -D, -S vb look or gaze fixedly (at) ▷ n fixed gaze

STARER, -S ▸ **stare**

STARES ▸ **stare**

STARETS, STARTSY n Russian holy man

STARETZ same as ▸ **starets**

STARFISH n star-shaped sea creature

STARGAZE vb observe the stars

STARING, -S ▸ **stare**

STARK, -ED, -ER, -EST, -ING, -S adj harsh, unpleasant, and plain ▷ adv completely ▷ vb stiffen

STARKEN, -S vb become or make stark

STARKER ▸ **stark**

STARKERS adj completely naked

STARKEST ▸ **stark**

STARKING ▸ **stark**

STARKLY ▸ **stark**

STARKS ▸ **stark**

STARLESS ▸ **star**

STARLET, -S n young actress presented as a future star

STARLIKE ▸ **star**

STARLING n songbird with glossy black speckled feathers

STARLIT same as > **starlight**

STARN, -ED, -ING, -S same as ▸ **stern**

STARNIE, -S n Scots word for little star

STARNING ▸ **starn**

STARNOSE n American mole with starlike nose

STARNS ▸ **starn**

STAROSTA n headman of Russian village

STAROSTY n estate of Polish nobleman

STARR, -S n (in Judaism) release from a debt

STARRED ▸ **star**

STARRIER ▸ **starry**

STARRILY ▸ **starry**

STARRING ▸ **star**

STARRS ▸ **starr**

STARRY, STARRIER adj full of or like stars

STARS ▸ **star**

STARSHIP n spacecraft in science fiction

STARSPOT n dark patch on surface of star

START, -ED, -ING, -S vb take the first step, begin ▷ n first part of something

STARTER, -S n first course of a meal

STARTFUL adj tending to start

STARTING ▸ **start**

STARTISH same as ▸ **startful**

STARTLE, -D, -S vb slightly surprise or frighten

STARTLER ▸ **startle**

STARTLES ▸ **startle**

STARTLY adj (of a horse) prone to starting

STARTS ▸ **start**

STARTSY ▸ **starets**

STARTUP, -S n business enterprise that has been launched recently

STARVE, -D, -S, STARVING vb die or suffer or cause to die or suffer from hunger

STARVER, -S ▸ **starve**

STARVES ▸ **starve**

STARVING ▸ **starve**

STARWORT n plant with star-shaped flowers

STASES ▸ **stasis**

STASH, -ED, -ES, -ING vb store in a secret place ▷ n secret store

STASHIE, -S same as ▸ **stushie**

STASHING ▸ **stash**

STASIMON, STASIMA n ode sung in Greek tragedy

STASIS, STASES n stagnation in the normal flow of bodily fluids

STAT, -S n statistic

STATABLE ▸ **state**

STATAL adj of a federal state

S

STATANT adj (of an animal) in profile with all four feet on the ground

STATE, -S, STATING n condition of a person or thing ▷ adj of or concerning the State ▷ vb express in words

STATED adj (esp of a sum) determined by agreement

STATEDLY ▸ stated

STATELET n small state

STATELY adj dignified or grand ▷ adv in a stately manner

STATER, -S n any of various usually silver coins of ancient Greece

STATES ▸ state

STATIC adj stationary or inactive ▷ n crackling sound or speckled picture caused by interference in radio or TV reception

STATICAL ▸ static

STATICE, -S n plant name formerly used for both thrift and sea lavender

STATICKY adj characterized by static

STATICS n study of the forces producing a state of equilibrium

STATIM adv right away

STATIN, -S n type of drug that lowers the levels of low-density lipoproteins in the blood

STATING ▸ state

STATINS ▸ statin

STATION, -S n place where trains stop for passengers ▷ vb assign (someone) to a particular place

STATISM, -S n theory or practice of concentrating economic and political power in the state

STATIST, -S n advocate of statism ▷ adj of, characteristic of, advocating, or relating to statism

STATIVE, -S adj denoting a verb describing a state rather than an activity, act, or event ▷ n stative verb

STATOR, -S n stationary part of a rotary machine or device

STATS ▸ stat

STATTO, -S n person preoccupied with the facts and figures of a subject

STATUA, -S same as ▸ statue

STATUARY n statues collectively ▷ adj of, relating to, or suitable for statues

STATUAS ▸ statua

STATUE, -S n large sculpture of a human or animal figure

STATUED adj decorated with or portrayed in a statue or statues

STATUES ▸ statue

STATURE, -S n person's height

STATURED adj having stature

STATURES ▸ stature

STATUS, -ES n social position

STATUSY adj conferring or having status

STATUTE, -S n written law

STAUMREL n stupid person

STAUN, -ING, -S Scot word for ▸ stand

STAUNCH same as ▸ stanch

STAUNING ▸ staun

STAUNS ▸ staun

STAVE, -D, -S, STAVING same as ▸ staff

STAW, -ED, -ING, -S Scots form of ▸ stall

STAY, -ED, -ING vb remain in a place or condition ▷ n period of staying in a place

STAYAWAY n strike in South Africa

STAYED ▸ stay

STAYER, -S n person or thing that stays

STAYING ▸ stay

STAYLESS adj with no stays or support

STAYNE, -D, -S, STAYNING same as ▸ stain

STAYRE, -S same as ▸ stair

STAYS pl n old-fashioned corsets with bones in them

STAYSAIL n sail fastened on a stay

STEAD, -ED, -S n place or function that should be taken by another ▷ vb help or benefit

STEADIED ▸ steady

STEADIER ▸ steady

STEADIES ▸ steady

STEADILY ▸ steady

STEADING n farmstead

STEADS ▸ stead

STEADY, STEADIED, STEADIES adj not shaky or wavering ▷ vb make steady ▷ adv in a steady manner

STEAK, -S n thick slice of meat, esp beef

STEAL, -ED, -ING, -S, -T, STOLEN, STOLN, STOWN vb take unlawfully or without permission

STEALAGE n theft

STEALE, -S n handle

STEALED ▸ steal

STEALER, -S n person who steals something

STEALES ▸ steale

STEALING ▸ steal

STEALS ▸ steal

STEALT ▸ steal

STEALTH, -S n moving carefully and quietly ▷ adj (of technology) able to render an aircraft almost invisible to radar ▷ vb approach undetected

STEALTHY adj characterized by great caution, secrecy, etc

STEAM, -ED, -S n vapour into which water changes when boiled ▷ vb give off steam

STEAMER, -S n steam-propelled ship ▷ vb travel by steamer

STEAMIE, -S n public wash house

STEAMIER ▸ steamy

STEAMIES ▸ steamie

STEAMILY ▸ steamy

STEAMING adj very hot ▷ n robbery by a large gang of youths

STEAMS ▸ steam

STEAMY, STEAMIER adj full of steam

STEAN, -S n earthenware vessel

STEANE, -D, -S, STEANING same as ▸ steen

STEANS ▸ stean

STEAPSIN n pancreatic lipase

STEAR, -D, -ING, -S same as ▸ steer

STEARAGE same as ▸ steerage

STEARATE n any salt or ester of stearic acid

STEARD ▸ stear

STEARE, -D, -S same as ▸ steer

STEARIC adj of or relating to suet or fat

STEARIN, -S n colourless crystalline ester of glycerol and stearic acid

STEARINE same as ▸ stearin

STEARING ▸ stear

STEARINS ▸ stearin

STEARS ▸ stear

STEATITE same as ▸ soapstone

STEATOMA n tumour of sebaceous gland

STED, -DED, -DING, -S same as ▸ stead

STEDD, -S same as ▸ stead

STEDDE, -S same as ▶ **stead**
STEDDED ▶ **sted**
STEDDES ▶ **stedde**
STEDDIED ▶ **steddy**
STEDDIES ▶ **steddy**
STEDDING ▶ **sted**
STEDDS ▶ **stedd**
STEDDY, STEDDIED, STEDDIES same as ▶ **steady**
STEDE, -D, -S, STEDING same as ▶ **stead**
STEDFAST same as > **steadfast**
STEDING ▶ **stede**
STEDS ▶ **sted**
STEED, -ED, -ING, -S same as ▶ **stead**
STEEDIED ▶ **steedy**
STEEDIES ▶ **steedy**
STEEDING ▶ **steed**
STEEDS ▶ **steed**
STEEDY, STEEDIED, STEEDIES same as ▶ **steady**
STEEK, -ED, -ING, -IT, -S vb Scots word meaning shut
STEEL, -D, -ED, -ING n hard malleable alloy of iron and carbon ▷ vb prepare (oneself) for something unpleasant
STEELBOW n material lent to tenant by landlord
STEELD ▶ **steel**
STEELED ▶ **steel**
STEELIE, -S n steel ball bearing used as marble
STEELIER ▶ **steely**
STEELIES ▶ **steelie**
STEELING ▶ **steel**
STEELMAN, STEELMEN n man working in the steel industry
STEELS pl n shares and bonds of steel companies
STEELY, STEELIER ▶ **steel**
STEEM, -ED, -ING, -S variant of ▶ **esteem**
STEEN, -ED, -ING, -S vb line with stone
STEENBOK n small antelope of central and southern Africa
STEENED ▶ **steen**
STEENING ▶ **steen**
STEENS ▶ **steen**
STEEP, -ED, -EST, -ING, -S adj sloping sharply ▷ vb soak or be soaked in liquid ▷ n instance or the process of steeping
STEEPEN, -S vb become steep or steeper
STEEPER, -S ▶ **steep**
STEEPEST ▶ **steep**
STEEPEUP adj very steep
STEEPIER ▶ **steepy**

STEEPING ▶ **steep**
STEEPISH ▶ **steep**
STEEPLE, -S same as ▶ **spire**
STEEPLED ▶ **steeple**
STEEPLES ▶ **steeple**
STEEPLY ▶ **steep**
STEEPS ▶ **steep**
STEEPUP adj very steep
STEEPY, STEEPIER same as ▶ **steep**
STEER, -ED, -ING, -S vb direct the course of (a vehicle or ship) ▷ n castrated male ox
STEERAGE n cheapest accommodation on a passenger ship
STEERED ▶ **steer**
STEERER, -S ▶ **steer**
STEERIER ▶ **steery**
STEERIES ▶ **steery**
STEERING ▶ **steer**
STEERS ▶ **steer**
STEERY, STEERIER, STEERIES n commotion ▷ adj busy or bustling
STEEVE, -D, -R, -S, -ST, STEEVING n spar having a pulley block at one end ▷ vb stow (cargo) securely in the hold of a ship
STEEVELY ▶ **steeve**
STEEVER ▶ **steeve**
STEEVES ▶ **steeve**
STEEVEST ▶ **steeve**
STEEVING ▶ **steeve**
STEGODON n mammal of Pliocene to Pleistocene times, similar to the mastodon
STEIL, -S same as ▶ **steal**
STEIN, -ED, -ING, -S same as ▶ **steen**
STEINBOK same as ▶ **steenbok**
STEINED ▶ **stein**
STEINING ▶ **stein**
STEINS ▶ **stein**
STELA, -E, -I same as ▶ **stele**
STELAR ▶ **stele**
STELE, -S n upright stone slab or column decorated with figures or inscriptions
STELENE ▶ **stele**
STELES ▶ **stele**
STELIC ▶ **stele**
STELL, -ED, -ING, -S n shelter for cattle or sheep built on moorland or hillsides ▷ vb position or place
STELLA, -S n star or something star-shaped
STELLAR adj of stars
STELLAS ▶ **stella**
STELLATE adj resembling a star in shape
STELLED ▶ **stell**

STELLIFY vb change or be changed into a star
STELLING ▶ **stell**
STELLIO n as in **stellio lizard** type of lizard
STELLION n Mediterranean lizard
STELLITE n alloy containing cobalt, chromium, carbon, tungsten, and molybdenum
STELLS ▶ **stell**
STEM, -MED, -MING, -S vb stop (the flow of something) ▷ n main axis of a plant, which bears the leaves, axillary buds, and flowers
STEMBOK, -S same as ▶ **steenbok**
STEMBUCK same as ▶ **steenbok**
STEME, -D, -S, STEMING same as ▶ **steam**
STEMHEAD n head of the stem of a vessel
STEMING ▶ **steme**
STEMLESS ▶ **stem**
STEMLET, -S n little stem
STEMLIKE ▶ **stem**
STEMMA, -S, -TA n family tree
STEMME, -S archaic variant of ▶ **stem**
STEMMED ▶ **stem**
STEMMER, -S ▶ **stem**
STEMMERY n tobacco factory
STEMMES ▶ **stemme**
STEMMIER ▶ **stemmy**
STEMMING ▶ **stem**
STEMMY, STEMMIER adj (of wine) young and raw
STEMPEL, -S n timber support
STEMPLE, -S same as ▶ **stempel**
STEMS ▶ **stem**
STEMSON, -S n curved timber at the bow of a wooden vessel
STEMWARE n collective term for glasses, goblets, etc with stems
STEN, -NED, -NING, -S vb stride
STENCH, -ED, -ES n foul smell ▷ vb cause to smell
STENCHY ▶ **stench**
STENCIL, -S n thin sheet through which ink passes to form a pattern on the surface below ▷ vb make (a pattern) with a stencil
STEND, -ED, -ING, -S vb Scots word meaning bound
STENGAH, -S same as ▶ **stinger**

STENLOCK n fish of northern seas

STENNED ▸ sten

STENNING ▸ sten

STENO, -S n stenographer

STENOKY n survival dependent on conditions remaining within a narrow range of variables

STENOS ▸ steno

STENOSED adj abnormally contracted

STENOSIS, STENOSES n abnormal narrowing of a bodily canal or passage

STENOTIC ▸ stenosis

STENS ▸ sten

STENT, -ED, -ING, -S n surgical implant used to keep an artery open ▷ vb assess

STENTOR, -S n person with an unusually loud voice

STENTOUR n tax assessor

STENTS ▸ stent

STEP, -PED, -PING, -S, -T vb move and set down the foot, as when walking ▷ n stepping

STEPDAD, -S n stepfather

STEPDAME n old word for a stepmother

STEPHANE n ancient Greek headdress

STEPLESS adj without steps

STEPLIKE ▸ step

STEPMOM, -S n stepmother

STEPNEY, -S n spare wheel

STEPOVER n (in football) instance of raising the foot over the ball as a feint

STEPPE, -S n extensive grassy plain usually without trees

STEPPED ▸ step

STEPPER, -S n person who or animal that steps, esp a horse or a dancer

STEPPES ▸ steppe

STEPPING ▸ step

STEPS ▸ step

STEPSON, -S n son of one's spouse by an earlier relationship

STEPT ▸ step

STEPWISE adj arranged in the manner of or resembling steps ▷ adv with the form or appearance of steps

STERANE, -S n any of a class of hydrocarbons found in crude oils

STERE, -S n unit used to measure volumes of stacked timber

STEREO, -ED, -S n stereophonic record player ▷ adj feeding two loudspeakers through separate channels ▷ vb make stereophonic

STEREOME n tissue of a plant that provides mechanical support

STEREOS ▸ stereo

STERES ▸ stere

STERIC adj of or caused by the spatial arrangement of atoms in a molecule

STERICAL same as ▸ steric

STERIGMA n minute stalk bearing a spore or chain of spores in certain fungi

STERILE adj free from germs

STERLET, -S n small sturgeon of N Asia and E Europe

STERLING n British money system ▷ adj genuine and reliable

STERN, -ED, -ER, -EST, -ING, -S adj severe, strict ▷ n rear part of a ship ▷ vb row boat backward

STERNA ▸ sternum

STERNAGE n sterns

STERNAL ▸ sternum

STERNED ▸ stern

STERNER ▸ stern

STERNEST ▸ stern

STERNING ▸ stern

STERNITE n part of an arthropod

STERNLY ▸ stern

STERNS ▸ stern

STERNSON n timber bolted to the sternpost and keelson at the stern of a wooden vessel

STERNUM, STERNA, -S n long flat bone to which most of the ribs are attached

STERNWAY n movement of a vessel sternforemost

STEROID, -S n organic compound containing a carbon ring system

STEROL, -S n natural insoluble alcohol such as cholesterol and ergosterol

STERTOR, -S n laborious or noisy breathing

STERVE, -D, -S, STERVING same as ▸ starve

STET, -S, -TED, -TING interj instruction to ignore an alteration previously made ▷ vb indicate to a printer that deleted matter is to be kept ▷ n mark indicating that deleted matter is to be kept

STETSON, -S n cowboy hat

STETTED ▸ stet

STETTING ▸ stet

STEVEN, -S n voice

STEVIA, -S n any of a genus of plant with sweet leaves

STEW, -S n food cooked slowly in a closed pot ▷ vb cook slowly in a closed pot

STEWABLE ▸ stew

STEWARD, -S n person who looks after passengers on a ship or aircraft ▷ vb act as a steward (of)

STEWED adj (of food) cooked by stewing

STEWER, -S ▸ stew

STEWIER ▸ stewy

STEWIEST ▸ stewy

STEWING, -S ▸ stew

STEWPAN, -S n pan used for making stew

STEWPOND n fishpond

STEWPOT, -S n pot used for making stew

STEWS ▸ stew

STEWY, STEWIER, STEWIEST ▸ stew

STEY, -ER, -EST, -S adj (Scots) steep ▷ n ladder

STHENIA, -S n abnormal strength

STHENIC adj abounding in energy or bodily strength

STIBBLE, -S Scots form of ▸ stubble

STIBBLER n horse allowed to eat stubble

STIBBLES ▸ stibble

STIBIAL ▸ stibium

STIBINE, -S n colourless slightly soluble poisonous gas

STIBIUM, -S obsolete name for ▸ antimony

STIBNITE n soft greyish mineral

STICCADO n type of xylophone

STICCATO same as ▸ sticcado

STICH, -S n line of poetry

STICHERA > sticheron

STICHIC ▸ stich

STICHOS, STICHOI n line of poem

STICHS ▸ stich

STICK, -ED, -ING, -S n long thin piece of wood ▷ vb push (a pointed object) into (something)

STICKER, -S n adhesive label or sign ▷ vb put stickers on

STICKFUL ▸ stick

STICKIE, -S n notepaper with an adhesive strip

S

STICKIED ▸ sticky
STICKIER ▸ sticky
STICKIES ▸ stickie
STICKILY ▸ sticky
STICKING ▸ stick
STICKIT *Scots form of* ▸ **stuck**
STICKJAW *n* stodgy food
STICKLE, -D, -S *vb* dispute stubbornly, esp about minor points
STICKLER *n* person who insists on something
STICKLES ▸ stickle
STICKMAN, STICKMEN *n* human figure drawn in thin strokes
STICKOUT *n* conspicuous person or thing
STICKPIN *n* tiepin
STICKS ▸ stick
STICKUM, -S *n* adhesive
STICKUP, -S *n* robbery at gun-point
STICKY, STICKIED, STICKIER *adj* covered with an adhesive substance ▸ *vb* make sticky ▸ *n* inquisitive look or stare
STICTION *n* frictional force to be overcome to set one object in motion when it is in contact with another
STIDDIE, -D, -S *same as* ▸ **stithy**
STIE *same as* ▸ **sty**
STIED ▸ sty
STIES ▸ sty
STIEVE, -R, -ST *same as* ▸ **steeve**
STIEVELY ▸ stieve
STIEVER ▸ stieve
STIEVEST ▸ stieve
STIFF, -ED, -ER, -EST, -ING, -S *adj* not easily bent or moved ▸ *n* loser or failure ▸ *adv* completely or utterly ▸ *vb* fail completely
STIFFEN, -S *vb* make or become stiff
STIFFER ▸ stiff
STIFFEST ▸ stiff
STIFFING ▸ stiff
STIFFISH ▸ stiff
STIFFLY ▸ stiff
STIFFS ▸ stiff
STIFLE, -D, -S *vb* suppress ▸ *n* joint in the hind leg of a horse, dog, etc
STIFLER, -S ▸ stifle
STIFLES ▸ stifle
STIFLING *adj* uncomfortably hot and stuffy
STIGMA, -S, -TA *n* mark of social disgrace
STIGMAL *adj* of part of insect wing

STIGMAS ▸ stigma
STIGMATA ▸ stigma
STIGME, -S *n* dot in Greek punctuation
STILB, -S *n* unit of luminance
STILBENE *n* colourless or slightly yellow crystalline hydrocarbon used in the manufacture of dyes
STILBITE *n* white or yellow zeolite mineral
STILBS ▸ stilb
STILE, -D, -S, STILING *same as* ▸ **style**
STILET, -S *same as* ▸ **stylet**
STILETTO *n* small narrow dagger ▸ *vb* stab with a stiletto
STILING ▸ stile
STILL, -ED, -EST, -ING, -S *adv* now or in the future as before ▸ *adj* motionless ▸ *n* calmness; apparatus for distillation ▸ *vb* make still
STILLAGE *n* frame or stand for keeping things off the ground, such as casks in a brewery
STILLED ▸ still
STILLER, -S ▸ still
STILLEST ▸ still
STILLIER ▸ stilly
STILLING ▸ still
STILLION *n* stand for cask
STILLMAN, STILLMEN *n* someone involved in the operation of a still
STILLS ▸ still
STILLSON *n* type of wrench
STILLY, STILLIER *adv* quietly or calmly ▸ *adj* still, quiet, or calm
STILT, -ING, -S *n* either of a pair of long poles with footrests for walking raised from the ground ▸ *vb* raise or place on or as if on stilts
STILTED *adj* stiff and formal in manner
STILTER, -S ▸ stilt
STILTIER ▸ stilty
STILTING ▸ stilt
STILTISH ▸ stilt
STILTS ▸ stilt
STILTY, STILTIER ▸ stilt
STIM, -S *n* very small amount
STIME, -D, -S, STIMING *same as* ▸ **styme**
STIMIE, -D, -S *same as* ▸ **stymie**
STIMING ▸ stime
STIMS ▸ stim
STIMULUS, STIMULI *n* something that rouses a person or thing to activity

STIMY, -ING *same as* ▸ **stymie**
STING, -ED, -S, STONG, STUNG *vb* (of certain animals or plants) wound by injecting with poison ▸ *n* wound or pain caused by or as if by stinging
STINGE, -S *n* stingy or miserly person
STINGED ▸ sting
STINGER, -S *n* person, plant, animal, etc, that stings or hurts
STINGES ▸ stinge
STINGIER ▸ stingy
STINGIES ▸ stingy
STINGILY ▸ stingy
STINGING ▸ sting
STINGO, -S *n* strong alcohol
STINGRAY *n* flatfish capable of inflicting painful wounds
STINGS ▸ sting
STINGY, STINGIER, STINGIES *adj* mean or miserly ▸ *n* stinging nettle
STINK, -ING, -S, STUNK *n* strong unpleasant smell ▸ *vb* give off a strong unpleasant smell
STINKARD *n* smelly person
STINKBUG *n* type of insect that releases an unpleasant odour
STINKER, -S *n* difficult or unpleasant person or thing
STINKIER ▸ stinky
STINKING ▸ stink
STINKO *adj* drunk
STINKPOT *n* thing that stinks
STINKS ▸ stink
STINKY, STINKIER *adj* having a foul smell
STINT, -ED, -ING, -S *vb* be miserly with (something) ▸ *n* allotted amount of work
STINTER, -S ▸ stint
STINTIER ▸ stinty
STINTING ▸ stint
STINTS ▸ stint
STINTY, STINTIER ▸ stint
STIPA, -S *n* variety of grass
STIPE *n* stalk in plants that bears reproductive structures
STIPED *same as* > **stipitate**
STIPEL, -S *n* small paired leaflike structure at the base of certain leaflets
STIPEND, -S *n* regular allowance or salary
STIPES, STIPITES *n* second maxillary segment in insects and crustaceans

S

STIPPLE, -D, -S vb paint, draw, or engrave using dots ▷ n technique of stippling
STIPPLER ▶ stipple
STIPPLES ▶ stipple
STIPULAR ▶ stipule
STIPULE, -S n small paired usually leaflike outgrowth occurring at the base of a leaf or its stalk
STIPULED ▶ stipule
STIPULES ▶ stipule
STIR, -RED, -RING, -S vb mix up (a liquid) by moving a spoon etc around in it ▷ n stirring
STIRE, -D, -S, STIRING same as ▶ steer
STIRK, -S n heifer of 6 to 12 months old
STIRLESS ▶ stir
STIRP same as ▶ stirps
STIRPS, STIRPES n line of descendants from an ancestor
STIRRA, -S same as ▶ sirra
STIRRAH, -S same as ▶ sirrah
STIRRAS ▶ stirra
STIRRE, -S same as ▶ steer
STIRRED ▶ stir
STIRRER, -S n person who deliberately causes trouble
STIRRES ▶ stirre
STIRRING ▶ stir
STIRRUP, -S n metal loop attached to a saddle for supporting a rider's foot
STIRS ▶ stir
STISHIE, -S same as ▶ stushie
STITCH, -ED, -ES n link made by drawing thread through material with a needle ▷ vb sew
STITCHER ▶ stitch
STITCHES ▶ stitch
STITHY, STITHIED, STITHIES n forge or anvil ▷ vb forge on an anvil
STIVE, -D, -S, STIVING vb stifle
STIVER, -S n former Dutch coin
STIVES ▶ stive
STIVIER ▶ stivy
STIVIEST ▶ stivy
STIVING ▶ stive
STIVY, STIVIER, STIVIEST adj stuffy
STOA, -E, -I, -S n covered walk that has a colonnade on one or both sides
STOAT, -S n small mammal of the weasel family
STOB, -BED, -BING, -S same as ▶ stab

STOBIE adj as in **stobie pole** steel and concrete pole for supporting electricity wires
STOBS ▶ stob
STOCCADO n fencing thrust
STOCCATA same as ▶ stoccado
STOCIOUS same as ▶ stotious
STOCK, -ED n total amount of goods available for sale in a shop ▷ adj kept in stock, standard ▷ vb keep for sale or future use
STOCKADE n enclosure or barrier made of stakes ▷ vb surround with a stockade
STOCKAGE n livestock put to graze on crops
STOCKCAR n car that has been strengthened for a form of racing in which the cars often collide
STOCKED ▶ stock
STOCKER, -S ▶ stock
STOCKIER ▶ stocky
STOCKILY ▶ stocky
STOCKING n close-fitting covering for the foot and leg
STOCKISH adj stupid or dull
STOCKIST n dealer who stocks a particular product
STOCKMAN, STOCKMEN n man engaged in the rearing or care of farm livestock, esp cattle
STOCKPOT n pot in which stock for soup is made
STOCKS pl n instrument of punishment in which an offender was locked
STOCKY, STOCKIER adj (of a person) broad and sturdy
STODGE, -D, -S, STODGING n heavy starchy food ▷ vb stuff (oneself or another) with food
STODGER, -S n dull person
STODGES ▶ stodge
STODGIER ▶ stodgy
STODGILY ▶ stodgy
STODGING ▶ stodge
STODGY, STODGIER adj (of food) heavy and starchy
STOEP, -S n verandah
STOGEY, -S same as ▶ stogy
STOGIE same as ▶ stogy
STOGY, STOGIES n any long cylindrical inexpensive cigar
STOIC, -S n person who suffers hardship without showing his or her feelings ▷ adj suffering hardship without showing one's feelings

STOICAL adj suffering great difficulties without showing one's feelings
STOICISM n indifference to pleasure and pain
STOICS ▶ stoic
STOIT, -ED, -ING, -S vb bounce
STOITER, -S vb stagger
STOITING ▶ stoit
STOITS ▶ stoit
STOKE, STOKING vb feed and tend (a fire or furnace)
STOKED adj very pleased
STOKER, -S n person employed to tend a furnace on a ship or train powered by steam
STOKES n cgs unit of kinematic viscosity
STOKESIA n American flowering plant
STOKING ▶ stoke
STOKVEL, -S n (in S Africa) informal savings pool or syndicate
STOLE, -S n long scarf or shawl
STOLED adj wearing a stole
STOLEN ▶ steal
STOLES ▶ stole
STOLID, -ER adj showing little emotion or interest
STOLIDLY ▶ stolid
STOLLEN, -S n rich sweet bread containing nuts, raisins, etc
STOLN ▶ steal
STOLON, -S n long horizontal stem that grows along the surface of the soil
STOLONIC ▶ stolon
STOLONS ▶ stolon
STOLPORT n airport for short take-off aircraft
STOMA, -S, -TA n pore in a plant leaf that controls the passage of gases
STOMACH, -S n organ in the body which digests food ▷ vb put up with
STOMACHY adj having a large belly
STOMACK, -S n as in **have a stomack** (in E Africa) be pregnant
STOMAL ▶ stoma
STOMAS ▶ stoma
STOMATA ▶ stoma
STOMATAL adj of, relating to, or possessing stomata or a stoma
STOMATE, -S n opening on leaf through which water evaporates

STOMATIC adj of or relating to a mouth or mouthlike part

STOMIUM, STOMIA, -S n part of the sporangium of ferns that ruptures to release the spores

STOMODEA ▶ stomodeum

STOMP, -ED, -ING, -S vb tread heavily ▷ n rhythmic stamping jazz dance

STOMPER, -S n song with a strong beat

STOMPIE, -S n cigarette butt

STOMPIER ▶ stompy

STOMPIES ▶ stompie

STOMPING ▶ stomp

STOMPS ▶ stomp

STOMPY, STOMPIER adj (of music) encouraging stomping of the feet

STONABLE ▶ stone

STOND, -S same as ▶ stand

STONE, -D, -S n material of which rocks are made ▷ vb throw stones at

STONECUT n (print made from) a carved block of stone

STONED ▶ stone

STONEFLY n type of insect whose larvae are aquatic

STONEN adj of stone

STONER, -S n device for removing stones from fruit

STONERAG n type of lichen

STONERAW same as ▶ stonerag

STONERN same as ▶ stonen

STONERS ▶ stoner

STONES ▶ stone

STONEY same as ▶ stony

STONG ▶ sting

STONIED ▶ stony

STONIER ▶ stony

STONIES ▶ stony

STONIEST ▶ stony

STONILY ▶ stony

STONING, -S ▶ stone

STONISH same as ▶ astonish

STONK, -ED, -ING, -S vb bombard (soldiers, buildings, etc) with artillery ▷ n concentrated bombardment

STONKER, -S vb destroy

STONKING ▶ stonk

STONKS ▶ stonk

STONN, -ING, -S same as ▶ stun

STONNE, -D, -S same as ▶ stun

STONNING ▶ stonn

STONNS ▶ stonn

STONY, STONIED, STONIER, STONIES, STONIEST, -ING adj of or like stone ▷ vb astonish

STOOD ▶ stand

STOODEN ▶ stand

STOOGE, -D, -S, STOOGING n actor who feeds lines to a comedian ▷ vb act as a stooge

STOOK, -ED, -S n number of sheaves set upright in a field to dry ▷ vb set up (sheaves) in stooks

STOOKER, -S ▶ stook

STOOKIE, -S n stucco

STOOKING n act of stooking

STOOKS ▶ stook

STOOL, -ED, -ING, -S n chair without arms or back ▷ vb (of a plant) send up shoots from the base of the stem

STOOLIE, -S n police informer

STOOLING ▶ stool

STOOLS ▶ stool

STOOLY n (US) informant for the police

STOOP, -ED, -S vb bend forward and downward

STOOPE, -S same as ▶ stoup

STOOPED ▶ stoop

STOOPER, -S ▶ stoop

STOOPES ▶ stoope

STOOPING ▶ stoop

STOOPS ▶ stoop

STOOR, -S same as ▶ stour

STOOSHIE same as ▶ stushie

STOOZE, -D, -S, STOOZING vb borrow money cheaply and invest it to make a profit

STOOZER, -S n person who stoozes

STOOZES ▶ stooze

STOOZING ▶ stooze

STOP, -PED, -PING, -S, -T vb cease or cause to cease from doing (something) ▷ n stopping or being stopped

STOPBAND n band of frequencies stopped by a filter

STOPBANK n embankment to prevent flooding

STOPCOCK n valve to control or stop the flow of fluid in a pipe

STOPE, -D, -S n steplike excavation made in a mine to extract ore ▷ vb mine (ore, etc) by cutting stopes

STOPER, -S n drill used in mining

STOPES ▶ stope

STOPGAP, -S n temporary substitute

STOPING, -S n process by which country rock is broken up and engulfed by magma

STOPLESS ▶ stop

STOPOFF, -S n break in a journey

STOPOVER n short break in a journey ▷ vb make a stopover

STOPPAGE n act of stopping something or the state of being stopped

STOPPED ▶ stop

STOPPER, -S n plug for closing a bottle etc ▷ vb close or fit with a stopper

STOPPING ▶ stop

STOPPLE, -D, -S same as ▶ stopper

STOPS ▶ stop

STOPT ▶ stop

STOPWORD n common word not used in computer search engines

STORABLE ▶ store

STORAGE, -S n storing

STORAX, -ES n type of tree or shrub with white flowers

STORE, -D, -S, STORING vb collect and keep (things) for future use ▷ n shop

STOREMAN, STOREMEN n man looking after storeroom

STORER, -S ▶ store

STORES pl n supply of food and essentials for a journey

STOREY, -S n floor or level of a building

STOREYED adj having a storey or storeys

STOREYS ▶ storey

STORGE, -S n affection

STORIED ▶ story

STORIES ▶ story

STORING ▶ store

STORK, -S n large wading bird

STORM, -ED, -S n violent weather with wind, rain, or snow ▷ vb attack or capture (a place) suddenly

STORMER, -S n outstanding example of its kind

STORMFUL ▶ storm

STORMIER ▶ stormy

STORMILY ▶ stormy

STORMING adj characterized by or displaying dynamism, speed, and energy

STORMS ▶ storm

STORMY, STORMIER adj characterized by storms

STORY, STORIED, STORIES, -ING n narration of a chain of events ▷ vb decorate with scenes from history

STOSS, -ES adj (of the side of a hill) facing the onward flow of a glacier ▷ n hillside facing glacier flow

S

STOT, -S, -TED, -TING n bullock ▷ vb bounce or cause to bounce

STOTIN, -OV, -S n former monetary unit of Slovenia

STOTINKA, STOTINKI n monetary unit of Bulgaria, worth one hundredth of a lev

STOTINOV ▶ stotin

STOTINS ▶ stotin

STOTIOUS adj drunk

STOTS ▶ stot

STOTT, -S same as ▶ stot

STOTTED ▶ stot

STOTTER, -S same as ▶ stot

STOTTIE, -S n wedge of bread cut from a flat round loaf

STOTTING ▶ stot

STOTTS ▶ stott

STOTTY same as ▶ stottie

STOUN, -ING, -S same as ▶ stun

STOUND, -ED, -S n short while ▷ vb ache

STOUNING ▶ stoun

STOUNS ▶ stoun

STOUP, -S n small basin for holy water

STOUR, -S n turmoil or conflict

STOURE, -S same as ▶ stour

STOURIE same as ▶ stoury

STOURIER ▶ stoury

STOURS ▶ stour

STOURY, STOURIER adj dusty

STOUSH, -ED, -ES vb hit or punch (someone) ▷ n fighting or violence

STOUSHIE same as ▶ stushie

STOUT, -ER, -EST, -S adj fat ▷ n strong dark beer

STOUTEN, -S vb make or become stout

STOUTER ▶ stout

STOUTEST ▶ stout

STOUTH, -S n Scots word meaning theft

STOUTISH ▶ stout

STOUTLY ▶ stout

STOUTS ▶ stout

STOVAINE n anaesthetic drug

STOVE, -D, -S n apparatus for cooking or heating ▷ vb process (ceramics, metalwork, etc) by heating in a stove

STOVER, -S n fodder

STOVES ▶ stove

STOVETOP US word for ▶ hob

STOVIES pl n potatoes stewed with onions

STOVING, -S ▶ stove

STOW, -ED, -S vb pack or store

STOWABLE ▶ stow

STOWAGE, -S n space or charge for stowing goods

STOWAWAY n person who hides on a ship or aircraft in order to travel free ▷ vb travel in such a way

STOWDOWN n packing of ship's hold

STOWED ▶ stow

STOWER, -S ▶ stow

STOWING, -S ▶ stow

STOWLINS adv stealthily

STOWN ▶ steal

STOWND, -ED, -S same as ▶ stound

STOWP, -S same as ▶ stoup

STOWRE, -S same as ▶ stour

STOWS ▶ stow

STRABISM n abnormal alignment of one or both eyes

STRACK vb archaic past tense form of strike

STRAD, -S n violin made by Stradivarius

STRADDLE vb have one leg or part on each side of (something) ▷ n act or position of straddling

STRADIOT n Venetian cavalryman

STRADS ▶ strad

STRAE, -S Scots form of ▶ straw

STRAFE, -D, -S vb attack (an enemy) with machine guns from the air ▷ n act or instance of strafing

STRAFER, -S ▶ strafe

STRAFES ▶ strafe

STRAFF, -ED, -S same as ▶ strafe

STRAFING n act of strafing

STRAG, -S n straggler

STRAGGLE vb go or spread in a rambling or irregular way

STRAGGLY ▶ straggle

STRAGS ▶ strag

STRAICHT Scots word for ▶ straight

STRAIGHT adj not curved or crooked ▷ adv in a straight line ▷ n straight part, esp of a racetrack ▷ vb tighten

STRAIK, -ED, -S Scots word for ▶ stroke

STRAIN, -S vb subject to mental tension ▷ n tension or tiredness

STRAINED adj not natural, forced

STRAINER n sieve

STRAINS ▶ strain

STRAINT, -S n pressure

STRAIT, -ED, -ER, -S n narrow channel connecting two areas of sea ▷ adj (of spaces, etc) affording little room ▷ vb tighten

STRAITEN vb embarrass or distress, esp financially

STRAITER ▶ strait

STRAITLY ▶ strait

STRAITS ▶ strait

STRAK vb archaic past tense form of strike

STRAKE, -S n curved metal plate forming part of the metal rim on a wooden wheel

STRAKED adj having a strake

STRAKES ▶ strake

STRAMASH n uproar ▷ vb destroy

STRAMMEL same as ▶ strummel

STRAMONY n former asthma medicine made from the dried leaves and flowers of the thorn apple

STRAMP, -ED, -S Scots variant of ▶ tramp

STRAND, -ED, -S vb run aground ▷ n shore

STRANDER ▶ strand

STRANDS ▶ strand

STRANG dialect variant of ▶ strong

STRANGE, -S adj odd or unusual ▷ n odd or unfamiliar person or thing

STRANGER n person who is not known or is new to a place or experience

STRANGES ▶ strange

STRANGLE vb kill by squeezing the throat

STRAP, -PED, -S n strip of flexible material for lifting or holding in place ▷ vb fasten with a strap or straps

STRAPPER n strapping person

STRAPPY adj having straps

STRAPS ▶ strap

STRASS, -ES another word for ▶ paste

STRATA ▶ stratum

STRATAL ▶ stratum

STRATEGY n overall plan

STRATH, -S n flat river valley

STRATI ▶ stratus

STRATIFY vb form or be formed in layers or strata

STRATOSE adj formed in strata

STRATOUS adj of stratus

STRATUM, STRATA, -S n layer, esp of rock

STRATUS, STRATI n grey layer cloud

STRAUCHT Scots word for ▶ **stretch**

STRAUGHT same as ▶ **straucht**

STRAUNGE same as ▶ **strange**

STRAVAGE same as ▶ **stravaig**

STRAVAIG vb wander aimlessly

STRAW, -ED, -ING, -S n dried stalks of grain ▷ vb spread around

STRAWEN adj of straw

STRAWHAT adj of summer dramatic performance

STRAWIER ▶ **strawy**

STRAWING ▶ **straw**

STRAWN ▶ **strew**

STRAWS ▶ **straw**

STRAWY, STRAWIER adj containing straw, or like straw in colour or texture

STRAY, -ED, -ING, -S vb wander ▷ adj having strayed ▷ n stray animal

STRAYER, -S ▶ **stray**

STRAYING ▶ **stray**

STRAYS ▶ **stray**

STRAYVE, -D, -S vb wander aimlessly

STREAK, -ED, -S n long band of contrasting colour or substance ▷ vb mark with streaks

STREAKER ▶ **streak**

STREAKS ▶ **streak**

STREAKY adj marked with streaks

STREAM, -ED, -S n small river ▷ vb flow steadily

STREAMER n strip of coloured paper that unrolls when tossed

STREAMS ▶ **stream**

STREAMY adj (of an area, land, etc) having many streams

STREEK, -ED, -S Scots word for ▶ **stretch**

STREEKER ▶ **streek**

STREEKS ▶ **streek**

STREEL, -ED, -S vb trail

STREET, -ED, -S n public road, usu lined with buildings ▷ vb lay out a street or streets

STREETY adj of streets

STREIGHT same as ▶ **strait**

STREIGNE same as ▶ **strain**

STRELITZ n former Russian soldier

STRENE, -S same as ▶ **strain**

STRENGTH n quality of being strong

STREP, -S n streptococcus

STREPENT adj noisy

STREPS ▶ **strep**

STRESS, -ED, -ES n tension or strain ▷ vb emphasize

STRESSOR n event, experience, etc, that causes stress

STRESSY adj characterized by stress

STRETCH vb extend or be extended ▷ n stretching

STRETCHY adj characterized by elasticity

STRETTA, -S, STRETTE same as ▶ **stretto**

STRETTO, STRETTI, -S n (in a fugue) the close overlapping of two parts or voices

STREUSEL n crumbly topping for rich pastries

STREW, STRAWN, -ED, -ING, -N, -S vb scatter (things) over a surface

STREWAGE ▶ **strew**

STREWED ▶ **strew**

STREWER, -S ▶ **strew**

STREWING ▶ **strew**

STREWN ▶ **strew**

STREWS ▶ **strew**

STREWTH interj expression of surprise or alarm

STRIA, -E n scratch or groove on the surface of a rock crystal

STRIATA ▶ **striatum**

STRIATAL adj relating to the corpus striatum in the brain

STRIATE, -S adj marked with striae ▷ vb mark with striae

STRIATED adj having a pattern of scratches or grooves

STRIATES ▶ **striate**

STRIATUM, STRIATA n part of brain

STRICH, -ES n screech owl

STRICK, -S n any bast fibres preparatory to being made into slivers

STRICKEN adj seriously affected by disease, grief, pain, etc

STRICKLE n board used for sweeping off excess material in a container ▷ vb level, form, or sharpen with a strickle

STRICKS ▶ **strick**

STRICT, -ER adj stern or severe

STRICTLY ▶ **strict**

STRIDDEN ▶ **stride**

STRIDDLE same as ▶ **straddle**

STRIDE, STRIDDEN, -S, STRIDING, STRODE vb walk with long steps ▷ n long step

STRIDENT adj loud and harsh

STRIDER, -S ▶ **stride**

STRIDES ▶ **stride**

STRIDING ▶ **stride**

STRIDOR, -S n high-pitched whistling sound made during respiration

STRIFE, -S n conflict, quarrelling

STRIFT, -S n struggle

STRIG, -GED, -S vb remove stalk from

STRIGA, -E same as ▶ **stria**

STRIGATE adj streaked

STRIGGED ▶ **strig**

STRIGIL, -S n curved blade used to scrape the body after bathing

STRIGINE adj of or like owl

STRIGOSE adj bearing stiff hairs or bristles

STRIGS ▶ **strig**

STRIKE, -S, STRIKING, STROKEN, STROOK, STRUCK vb cease work as a protest ▷ n stoppage of work as a protest

STRIKER, -S n striking worker

STRIKES ▶ **strike**

STRIKING ▶ **strike**

STRIM, -MED, -S vb cut (grass) using an electric trimmer

STRINE, -S n informal name for Australian English

STRING, -S, STRUNG n thin cord used for tying ▷ vb provide with a string or strings

STRINGED adj (of a musical instrument) having strings that are plucked or played with a bow

STRINGER n journalist retained by a newspaper to cover a particular town or area

STRINGS ▶ **string**

STRINGY adj like string

STRINKLE Scots variant of ▶ **sprinkle**

STRIP, -PED, -S, -T vb take (the covering or clothes) off ▷ n act of stripping

STRIPE, -S, STRIPING n long narrow band of contrasting colour or substance ▷ vb mark (something) with stripes

S

STRIPED *adj* marked or decorated with stripes

STRIPER, -S *n* officer who has a stripe or stripes on his or her uniform

STRIPES ▸ stripe

STRIPEY *same as* ▸ **stripy**

STRIPIER ▸ stripy

STRIPING ▸ stripe

STRIPPED ▸ strip

STRIPPER *n* device or substance for removing paint etc

STRIPS ▸ strip

STRIPT ▸ strip

STRIPY, STRIPIER *adj* marked by or with stripes

STRIVE, -D, -N, -S, STRIVING, STROVE *vb* make a great effort

STRIVER, -S ▸ strive

STRIVES ▸ strive

STRIVING ▸ strive

STROAM, -ED, -S *vb* wander

STROBE, -D, -S, STROBING *n* high intensity flashing beam of light ▷ *vb* give the appearance of slow motion by using a strobe

STROBIC *adj* spinning or appearing to spin

STROBIL, -S *n* scaly multiple fruit

STROBILA *n* body of a tapeworm, consisting of a string of similar segments

STROBILE *same as* > strobilus

STROBILI ▸ strobilus

STROBILS ▸ strobil

STROBING ▸ strobe

STRODDLE *same as* ▸ **straddle**

STRODE ▸ stride

STRODLE, -D, -S *same as* ▸ **straddle**

STROKE, -D, -S, STROKING *vb* touch or caress lightly with the hand ▷ *n* light touch or caress with the hand

STROKEN ▸ strike

STROKER, -S ▸ stroke

STROKES ▸ stroke

STROKING ▸ stroke

STROLL, -ED, -S *vb* walk in a leisurely manner ▷ *n* leisurely walk

STROLLER *n* chair-shaped carriage for a baby

STROLLS ▸ stroll

STROMA, -TA *n* gel-like matrix of chloroplasts and certain cells

STROMAL ▸ stroma

STROMATA ▸ stroma

STROMB, -S *n* shellfish like a whelk

STROMBUS *same as* ▸ **stromb**

STROND, -S *same as* ▸ **strand**

STRONG, -ER *adj* having physical power

STRONGLY ▸ strong

STRONGYL *same as* > strongyle

STRONTIA > strontium

STRONTIC > strontium

STROOK ▸ strike

STROOKE, -S *n* stroke

STROOKEN *same as* ▸ **stricken**

STROOKES ▸ strooke

STROP, -PED, -S *n* leather strap for sharpening razors ▷ *vb* sharpen (a razor, etc) on a strop

STROPHE, -S *n* movement made by chorus during a choral ode

STROPHIC *adj* of, relating to, or employing a strophe or strophes

STROPPED ▸ strop

STROPPER ▸ strop

STROPPY *adj* angry or awkward

STROPS ▸ strop

STROUD, -S *n* coarse woollen fabric

STROUP, -S *Scots word for* ▸ **spout**

STROUPAN *same as* > stroupach

STROUPS ▸ stroup

STROUT, -ED, -S *vb* bulge

STROVE ▸ strive

STROW, -ED, -ING, -N, -S *archaic variant of* ▸ **strew**

STROWER, -S ▸ strow

STROWING ▸ strow

STROWN ▸ strow

STROWS ▸ strow

STROY, -ED, -ING, -S *archaic variant of* ▸ **destroy**

STROYER, -S ▸ stroy

STROYING ▸ stroy

STROYS ▸ stroy

STRUCK ▸ strike

STRUCKEN *same as* ▸ **stricken**

STRUDEL, -S *n* thin sheet of filled dough rolled up and baked

STRUGGLE *vb* work, strive, or make one's way with difficulty ▷ *n* striving

STRUM, -MED, -S *vb* play (a guitar, etc) by sweeping the thumb across the strings

STRUMA, -E, -S *n* abnormal enlargement of the thyroid gland

STRUMMED ▸ strum

STRUMMEL *n* straw

STRUMMER ▸ strum

STRUMOSE ▸ struma

STRUMOUS ▸ struma

STRUMS ▸ strum

STRUNG ▸ string

STRUNT, -ED, -S *Scots word for* ▸ **strut**

STRUT, -S, -TED *vb* walk pompously, swagger ▷ *n* bar supporting a structure

STRUTTER ▸ strut

STUB, -BED, -BING, -S *n* short piece left after use ▷ *vb* strike (the toe) painfully against an object

STUBBIE *same as* ▸ **stubby**

STUBBIER ▸ stubby

STUBBIES ▸ stubby

STUBBILY ▸ stubby

STUBBING ▸ stub

STUBBLE, -S *n* short stalks of grain left in a field after reaping

STUBBLED *adj* having the stubs of stalks left after a crop has been cut and harvested

STUBBLES ▸ stubble

STUBBLY ▸ stubble

STUBBORN *adj* refusing to agree or give in ▷ *vb* make stubborn

STUBBY, STUBBIER, STUBBIES *adj* short and broad ▷ *n* small bottle of beer

STUBS ▸ stub

STUCCO, -ED, -ES, -S *n* plaster used for coating or decorating walls ▷ *vb* apply stucco to (a building)

STUCCOER ▸ stucco

STUCCOES ▸ stucco

STUCCOS ▸ stucco

STUCK, -S *n* thrust

STUD, -DED, -DING, -S *n* small piece of metal attached to a surface for decoration ▷ *vb* set with studs

STUDBOOK *n* written record of the pedigree of a purebred stock, esp of racehorses

STUDDED ▸ stud

STUDDEN ▸ stand

STUDDIE, -S *Scots word for* ▸ **anvil**

STUDDING ▸ stud

STUDDLE, -S *n* post

STUDE *vb* past tense and past participle of staun (Scots form of stand)

STUDENT, -S *n* person who studies a subject, esp at university

STUDENTY adj denoting the characteristics believed typical of a student
STUDFARM n farm where horses are bred
STUDFISH n American minnow
STUDIED adj carefully practised
STUDIER, -S ▸ study
STUDIES ▸ study
STUDIO, -S n workroom of an artist or photographer
STUDIOUS adj fond of study
STUDLIER ▸ studly
STUDLIKE adj like a stud
STUDLY, STUDLIER adj strong and virile
STUDS ▸ stud
STUDWORK n work decorated with studs
STUDY, STUDIES, -ING vb be engaged in learning (a subject) ▷ n act or process of studying
STUFF, -ED, -S n substance or material ▷ vb pack, cram, or fill completely
STUFFER, -S ▸ stuff
STUFFIER ▸ stuffy
STUFFILY ▸ stuffy
STUFFING n seasoned mixture with which food is stuffed
STUFFS ▸ stuff
STUFFY, STUFFIER adj lacking fresh air
STUGGY, STUGGIER adj stout
STUIVER, -S same as ▸ stiver
STUKKEND adj South African slang for broken or wrecked
STULL, -S n timber prop or platform in a stope
STULM, -S n shaft
STULTIFY vb dull (the mind) by boring routine
STUM, -MED, -MING, -S n partly fermented wine added to fermented wine as a preservative ▷ vb preserve (wine) by adding stum
STUMBLE, -D, -S vb trip and nearly fall ▷ n stumbling
STUMBLER ▸ stumble
STUMBLES ▸ stumble
STUMBLY adj tending to stumble
STUMER, -S n forgery or cheat
STUMM same as ▸ shtoom
STUMMED ▸ stum
STUMMEL, -S n bowl of a smoker's pipe
STUMMING ▸ stum

STUMP, -ED, -ING, -S n base of a tree left when the main trunk has been cut away ▷ vb baffle
STUMPAGE n standing timber or its value
STUMPED ▸ stump
STUMPER, -S ▸ stump
STUMPIER ▸ stumpy
STUMPIES ▸ stumpy
STUMPILY ▸ stumpy
STUMPING ▸ stump
STUMPS ▸ stump
STUMPY, STUMPIER, STUMPIES adj short and thick ▷ n stumpy thing
STUMS ▸ stum
STUN, -NED, -NING, -S vb shock or overwhelm ▷ n state or effect of being stunned
STUNG ▸ sting
STUNK ▸ stink
STUNKARD adj sulky
STUNNED ▸ stun
STUNNER, -S n beautiful person or thing
STUNNING ▸ stun
STUNS ▸ stun
STUNSAIL n type of light auxiliary sail
STUNT, -ING, -S vb prevent or impede the growth of ▷ n acrobatic or dangerous action
STUNTED ▸ stunt
STUNTING ▸ stunt
STUNTMAN, STUNTMEN n man who performs dangerous acts in a film, etc in place of an actor
STUNTS ▸ stunt
STUPA, -S n domed edifice housing Buddhist or Jain relics
STUPE, -D, -S, STUPING n hot damp cloth applied to the body to relieve pain ▷ vb treat with a stupe
STUPEFY vb make insensitive or lethargic
STUPENT adj astonished
STUPES ▸ stupe
STUPID, -ER, -S adj lacking intelligence ▷ n stupid person
STUPIDLY ▸ stupid
STUPIDS ▸ stupid
STUPING ▸ stupe
STUPOR, -S n dazed or unconscious state
STUPRATE vb ravish
STURDIED ▸ sturdy
STURDIER ▸ sturdy
STURDIES ▸ sturdy
STURDILY ▸ sturdy

STURDY, STURDIER, STURDIES adj healthy and robust ▷ n disease of sheep
STURE same as ▸ stoor
STURGEON n fish from which caviar is obtained
STURMER, -S n type of eating apple with pale green skin
STURNINE ▸ sturnus
STURNOID ▸ sturnus
STURNUS n bird of starling family
STURT, -ED, -ING, -S vb bother
STUSHIE, -S n commotion, rumpus, or row
STUTTER, -S vb speak with repetition of initial consonants ▷ n tendency to stutter
STY, STIED, STIES, -ING vb climb
STYE, -D, -S n inflammation at the base of an eyelash
STYGIAN adj dark, gloomy, or hellish
STYING ▸ sty
STYLAR ▸ stylus
STYLATE adj having style
STYLE, -D, -S n shape or design ▷ vb shape or design
STYLEE, -S same as ▸ style
STYLER, -S ▸ style
STYLES ▸ style
STYLET, -S n wire to stiffen a flexible cannula or catheter
STYLI ▸ stylus
STYLIE, -R, -ST adj fashion-conscious
STYLING, -S ▸ style
STYLISE, -D, -S same as ▸ stylize
STYLISER ▸ stylise
STYLISES ▸ stylise
STYLISH adj smart, elegant, and fashionable
STYLIST, -S n hairdresser
STYLITE, -S n one of a class of recluses who in ancient times lived on the top of high pillars
STYLITIC ▸ stylite
STYLIZE, -D, -S vb cause to conform to an established stylistic form
STYLIZER ▸ stylize
STYLIZES ▸ stylize
STYLO, -S n type of fountain pen
STYLOID, -S adj resembling a stylus ▷ n spiny growth
STYLOPES ▸ stylops
STYLOPID n type of parasitic insect

S

STYLOPS, STYLOPES n type of insect that lives as a parasite in other insects

STYLOS ▸ **stylo**

STYLUS, STYLI, -ES n needle-like device on a record player

STYME, -D, -S, STYMING vb peer

STYMIE vb hinder or thwart

STYMIED ▸ **stymy**

STYMIES ▸ **stymy**

STYMING ▸ **styme**

STYMY, STYMIED, STYMIES, -ING same as ▸ **stymie**

STYPSIS n action, application, or use of a styptic

STYPTIC, -S adj (drug) used to stop bleeding ▷ n styptic drug

STYRAX, -ES n type of tropical or subtropical tree

STYRE, -D, -S, STYRING same as ▸ **stir**

STYRENE, -S n colourless flammable liquid

STYRES ▸ **styre**

STYRING ▸ **styre**

STYTE, -D, -S, STYTING vb bounce

SUABLE adj liable to be sued in a court

SUABLY ▸ **suable**

SUASIBLE ▸ **suasion**

SUASION, -S n persuasion

SUASIVE ▸ **suasion**

SUASORY ▸ **suasion**

SUAVE, -R, -ST adj smooth and sophisticated in manner

SUAVELY ▸ **suave**

SUAVER ▸ **suave**

SUAVEST ▸ **suave**

SUAVITY ▸ **suave**

SUB, -BED, -S n subeditor ▷ vb act as a substitute

SUBA, -S n shepherd's cloak

SUBABBOT n abbot who is subordinate to another abbot

SUBACID adj (esp of some fruits) moderately acid or sour

SUBACRID adj slightly acrid

SUBACT, -ED, -S vb subdue

SUBACUTE adj intermediate between acute and chronic

SUBADAR, -S n chief native officer of a company of Indian soldiers in the British service

SUBADULT n animal not quite at adult stage

SUBAGENT n agent who is subordinate to another agent

SUBAH, -S same as ▸ **subadar**

SUBAHDAR same as ▸ **subadar**

SUBAHS ▸ **subah**

SUBALAR adj below a wing

SUBAQUA adj of or relating to underwater sport

SUBAREA, -S n area within a larger area

SUBARID adj receiving slightly more rainfall than arid regions

SUBAS ▸ **suba**

SUBATOM, -S n part of an atom

SUBAUDIO adj (of sound) low frequency

SUBAURAL adj below the ear

SUBAXIAL adj below an axis of the body

SUBBASAL ▸ **subbase**

SUBBASE, -S same as ▸ **subbass**

SUBBASIN n geographical basin within larger basin

SUBBASS another name for ▸ **bourdon**

SUBBED ▸ **sub**

SUBBIE, -S n subcontractor

SUBBING, -S ▸ **sub**

SUBBLOCK n part of mathematical matrix

SUBBREED n breed within a larger breed

SUBBY same as ▸ **subbie**

SUBCASTE n subdivision of a caste

SUBCAUSE n factor less important than a cause

SUBCELL, -S n cell within a larger cell

SUBCHIEF n chief below the main chief

SUBCHORD n part of a curve

SUBCLAIM n claim that is part of a larger claim

SUBCLAN, -S n clan within a larger clan

SUBCLASS n principal subdivision of a class ▷ vb assign to a subclass

SUBCLERK n clerk who is subordinate to another clerk

SUBCODE, -S n computer tag identifying data

SUBCOOL, -S vb make colder

SUBCOSTA n vein in insect wing

SUBCRUST n secondary crust below main crust

SUBCULT, -S n cult within larger cult

SUBCUTIS, SUBCUTES n layer of tissue beneath outer skin

SUBDEAN, -S n deputy of dean

SUBDEB, -S n young woman who is not yet a debutante

SUBDEPOT n depot within a larger depot

SUBDEW, -ED, -S same as ▸ **subdue**

SUBDUAL, -S ▸ **subdue**

SUBDUCE, -D, -S vb withdraw

SUBDUCT, -S vb draw or turn (the eye, etc) downwards

SUBDUE, -S, SUBDUING vb overcome

SUBDUED adj cowed, passive, or shy

SUBDUER, -S ▸ **subdue**

SUBDUES ▸ **subdue**

SUBDUING ▸ **subdue**

SUBDUPLE adj in proportion of one to two

SUBDURAL adj between the dura mater and the arachnoid

SUBDWARF n star smaller than a dwarf star

SUBECHO n echo resonating more quietly than another echo

SUBEDAR, -S same as ▸ **subadar**

SUBEDIT, -S vb edit and correct (written or printed material)

SUBENTRY n entry within another entry

SUBEPOCH n epoch within another epoch

SUBEQUAL adj not quite equal

SUBER, -S n cork

SUBERATE n salt of suberic acid

SUBERECT adj not quite erect

SUBERIC same as ▸ **suberose**

SUBERIN, -S n fatty or waxy substance that is present in the walls of cork cells

SUBERISE same as ▸ **suberize**

SUBERIZE vb impregnate (cell walls) with suberin during the formation of corky tissue

SUBEROSE adj relating to, resembling, or consisting of cork

SUBEROUS same as ▸ **suberose**

SUBERS ▸ **suber**

SUBFEU, -ED, -S vb grant feu or land rights to a vassal

SUBFIELD n subdivision of a field

SUBFILE, -S n file within another file

SUBFIX, -ES n suffix

SUBFLOOR n rough floor that forms a base for a finished floor

SUBFLUID adj viscous

SUBFRAME n frame on which car body is built

SUBFUSC, -S adj devoid of brightness or appeal ▷ n (at Oxford University) formal academic dress

SUBFUSK, -S same as ▸ subfusc

SUBGENRE n genre within a larger genre

SUBGENUS n taxonomic group that is a subdivision of a genus but of higher rank than a species

SUBGOAL, -S n secondary goal

SUBGRADE n ground beneath a roadway or pavement

SUBGRAPH n graph sharing vertices of other graph

SUBGROUP n small group that is part of a larger group

SUBGUM, -S n Chinese dish

SUBHA n string of beads used in praying and meditating

SUBHEAD, -S n heading of a subsection in a printed work

SUBHUMAN adj less than human

SUBHUMID adj not wet enough for trees to grow

SUBIDEA, -S n secondary idea

SUBIMAGO n first winged stage of the mayfly

SUBINDEX same as > subscript

SUBITEM, -S n item that is less important than another item

SUBITISE same as ▸ subitize

SUBITIZE vb perceive the number of (a group of items) at a glance and without counting

SUBITO adv (preceding or following a dynamic marking, etc) suddenly

SUBJECT, -S n person or thing being dealt with or studied ▷ adj being under the rule of a monarch or government ▷ vb cause to undergo

SUBJOIN, -S vb add or attach at the end of something spoken, written, etc

SUBLATE, -D, -S vb deny

SUBLEASE n lease of property made by a person who is a lessee of that property ▷ vb grant a sublease of (property)

SUBLET, -S vb rent out (property rented from someone else) ▷ n sublease

SUBLEVEL n subdivision of a level

SUBLIME, -D, -S adj of high moral, intellectual, or spiritual value ▷ vb change from a solid to a vapour without first melting

SUBLIMER ▸ sublime

SUBLIMES ▸ sublime

SUBLIMIT n limit on a subcategory

SUBLINE, -S n secondary headline

SUBLOT, -S n subdivision of a lot

SUBLUNAR same as > sublunary

SUBMAN, SUBMEN n primitive form of human

SUBMENTA > submentum

SUBMENU, -S n further list of options within computer menu

SUBMERGE vb put or go below the surface of water or other liquid

SUBMERSE same as ▸ submerge

SUBMISS adj old word meaning docile or submissive

SUBMIT, -S vb surrender

SUBNASAL adj beneath nose

SUBNET, -S n part of network

SUBNICHE n subdivision of a niche

SUBNODAL adj below the level of a node

SUBOCEAN adj beneath the ocean

SUBOPTIC adj below the eye

SUBORAL adj not quite oral

SUBORDER n taxonomic group that is a subdivision of an order

SUBORN, -ED, -S vb bribe or incite (a person) to commit a wrongful act

SUBORNER ▸ suborn

SUBORNS ▸ suborn

SUBOVAL adj not quite oval

SUBOVATE adj almost egg-shaped

SUBOXIDE n oxide of an element containing less oxygen than the common oxide formed by the element

SUBPANEL n panel that is part of larger panel

SUBPAR adj not up to standard

SUBPART, -S n part within another part

SUBPENA, -S same as ▸ subpoena

SUBPHASE n subdivision of a phase

SUBPHYLA > subphylum

SUBPLOT, -S n secondary plot in a novel, play, or film

SUBPOENA n writ requiring a person to appear before a lawcourt ▷ vb summon (someone) with a subpoena

SUBPOLAR adj of the areas south of the Arctic and north of the Antarctic

SUBPRIME n loan made to a borrower with a poor credit rating

SUBPRIOR n monk junior to a prior

SUBPUBIC adj beneath the pubic bone

SUBRACE, -S n subdivision of a race

SUBRENT, -S n rent paid to renter who rents to another ▷ vb rent out (a property that is already rented)

SUBRING, -S n mathematical ring that is a subset of another ring

SUBRULE, -S n rule within another rule

SUBS ▸ sub

SUBSALE, -S n sale carried out within the process of a larger sale

SUBSCALE, -S n scale within a scale

SUBSEA adj undersea

SUBSECT, -S n sect within a larger sect

SUBSENSE n definition that is a division of a wider definition

SUBSERE, -S n secondary sere arising when the progress of a sere has been interrupted

SUBSERVE vb be helpful or useful to

SUBSET, -S n mathematical set contained within a larger set

SUBSHAFT n secondary shaft in a mine

SUBSHELL n part of a shell of an atom

SUBSHRUB n small bushy plant that is woody except for the tips of the branches

SUBSIDE, -D, -S vb become less intense

SUBSIDER ▸ subside

SUBSIDES ▸ subside

SUBSIDY n financial aid

SUBSIST, -S vb manage to live

SUBSITE, -S n location within a website

SUBSIZAR n type of undergraduate at Cambridge

SUBSKILL n element of a wider skill

SUBSOIL, -S n earth just below the surface soil ▷ vb plough (land) to a depth below the normal ploughing level

SUBSOLAR adj (of a point on the earth) directly below the sun

SUBSONG, -S n subdued form of birdsong modified from the full territorial song

SUBSONIC adj moving at a speed less than that of sound

SUBSPACE n part of a mathematical matrix

SUBSTAGE n part of a microscope below the stage

SUBSTATE n subdivision of state

SUBSTORM n disturbance in the magnetic field of a planet

SUBSTYLE n line on a dial

SUBSUME, -D, -S vb include (an idea, case, etc) under a larger classification or group

SUBTACK, -S Scots word for ▸ sublease

SUBTALAR adj beneath the ankle-bone

SUBTASK, -S n task that is part of a larger task

SUBTAXON, SUBTAXA n supplementary piece of identifying information in plant or animal scientific name

SUBTEEN, -S n young person who has not yet become a teenager

SUBTEND, -S vb be opposite (an angle or side)

SUBTENSE n line that subtends

SUBTEST, -S n test that is part of larger test

SUBTEXT, -S n underlying theme in a piece of writing

SUBTHEME n secondary theme

SUBTIDAL adj below the level of low tide

SUBTIL same as ▸ subtle

SUBTILE, -R rare spelling of ▸ subtle

SUBTILIN n antibiotic drug

SUBTILTY ▸ subtilte

SUBTITLE n secondary title of a book ▷ vb provide with a subtitle or subtitles

SUBTLE, -R, -ST adj not immediately obvious

SUBTLETY n fine distinction

SUBTLY ▸ subtle

SUBTONE, -S n subdivision of a tone

SUBTONIC n seventh degree of a major or minor scale

SUBTOPIA n suburban development that encroaches on rural areas

SUBTOPIC n topic within a larger topic

SUBTOTAL n total made up by a column of figures, forming part of the total made up by a larger group ▷ vb work out a subtotal for (a group)

SUBTRACT vb take (one number or quantity) from another

SUBTRADE n (in N America) specialist hired by a building contractor

SUBTREND n minor trend

SUBTRIBE n tribe within a larger tribe

SUBTRIST adj slightly sad

SUBTRUDE vb intrude stealthily

SUBTUNIC adj below membrane ▷ n garment worn under a tunic

SUBTWEET vb post a negative tweet about someone without naming them

SUBTYPE, -S n secondary or subordinate type or genre

SUBUCULA n ancient Roman man's undergarment

SUBULATE adj (esp of plant parts) tapering to a point

SUBUNIT, -S n distinct part or component of something larger

SUBURB, -S n residential area on the outskirts of a city

SUBURBAN adj mildly derogatory term for inhabiting a suburb ▷ n

mildly derogatory term for a person who lives in a suburb

SUBURBED ▸ suburb

SUBURBIA n suburbs and their inhabitants

SUBURBS ▸ suburb

SUBVENE, -D, -S vb happen in such a way as to be of assistance

SUBVERSE, SUBVERST same as ▸ subvert

SUBVERT, -S vb overthrow the authority of

SUBVICAR n assistant to a vicar

SUBVIRAL adj of, caused by, or denoting a part of the structure of a virus

SUBVIRUS n organism smaller than a virus

SUBVOCAL adj formed in mind without being spoken aloud

SUBWAY, -ED, -S n passage under a road or railway ▷ vb travel by subway

SUBWORLD n underworld

SUBZERO adj lower than zero

SUBZONAL ▸ subzone

SUBZONE, -S n subdivision of a zone

SUCCADE, -S n piece of candied fruit

SUCCAH, -S same as ▸ sukkah

SUCCEED, -S vb accomplish an aim

SUCCES French word for ▸ success

SUCCESS n achievement of something attempted

SUCCI ▸ succus

SUCCINCT adj brief and clear

SUCCINIC adj of, relating to, or obtained from amber

SUCCINYL n constituent of succinic acid

SUCCISE adj ending abruptly, as if cut off

SUCCOR, -ED, -S same as ▸ succour

SUCCORER ▸ succor

SUCCORS ▸ succor

SUCCORY another name for ▸ chicory

SUCCOS same as ▸ succoth

SUCCOSE ▸ succus

SUCCOT same as ▸ sukkoth

SUCCOTH variant of ▸ sukkoth

SUCCOUR, -S n help in distress ▷ vb give aid to (someone in time of difficulty)

SUCCOUS ▸ succus

SUCCUMB, -S vb give way (to something overpowering)

SUCCUS, SUCCI n fluid

SUCCUSS vb shake (a patient) to detect the sound of fluid in a cavity

SUCH adj of the kind specified ▷ pron such things

SUCHLIKE pron such or similar things ▷ n such or similar things ▷ adj of such a kind

SUCHNESS ▸ such

SUCHWISE ▸ such

SUCK, -S vb draw (liquid or air) into the mouth ▷ n sucking

SUCKEN, -S Scots word for ▸ district

SUCKENER n tenant

SUCKENS ▸ sucken

SUCKER, -ED, -S n person who is easily deceived or swindled ▷ vb strip off the suckers from (a plant)

SUCKET, -S same as ▸ succade

SUCKFISH n type of spiny-finned marine fish

SUCKHOLE n sycophant ▷ vb behave in a sycophantic manner

SUCKIER ▸ sucky

SUCKIEST ▸ sucky

SUCKING, -S adj not yet weaned

SUCKLE, -D, -S vb feed at the breast

SUCKLER, -S ▸ suckle

SUCKLES ▸ suckle

SUCKLESS ▸ suck

SUCKLING n unweaned baby or young animal

SUCKS interj expression of disappointment

SUCKY, SUCKIER, SUCKIEST adj despicable

SUCRASE, -S another name for > invertase

SUCRE, -S n former standard monetary unit of Ecuador

SUCRIER, -S n small container for sugar at table

SUCROSE, -S same as ▸ sugar

SUCTION, -S n sucking ▷ vb subject to suction

SUCURUJU n anaconda

SUD singular of ▸ suds

SUDAMEN, -S, SUDAMINA n small cavity in the skin

SUDARIA ▸ sudarium

SUDARIES ▸ sudary

SUDARIUM, SUDARIA n room in a Roman bathhouse

where sweating is induced by heat

SUDARY, SUDARIES same as ▸ sudarium

SUDATE, -D, -S, SUDATING vb sweat

SUDATION ▸ sudate

SUDATORY ▸ sudate

SUDD, -S n floating masses of reeds and weeds on the White Nile

SUDDEN, -S adj done or occurring quickly and unexpectedly

SUDDENLY adv quickly and without warning

SUDDENS ▸ sudden

SUDDENTY n suddenness

SUDDER, -S n supreme court in India

SUDDS ▸ sudd

SUDOKU, -S n type of puzzle in which numbers must be arranged in a grid according to certain rules

SUDOR, -S technical name for ▸ sweat

SUDORAL ▸ sudor

SUDOROUS ▸ sudor

SUDORS ▸ sudor

SUDS, -ED, -ES, -ING pl n froth of soap and water, lather ▷ vb wash in suds

SUDSER, -S n soap opera

SUDSES ▸ suds

SUDSIER ▸ sudsy

SUDSIEST ▸ sudsy

SUDSING ▸ suds

SUDSLESS ▸ suds

SUDSY, SUDSIER, SUDSIEST ▸ suds

SUE, -D, -S vb start legal proceedings against

SUEABLE ▸ sue

SUED ▸ sue

SUEDE, -D, -S, SUEDING n leather with a velvety finish on one side ▷ vb give a suede finish to

SUEDETTE n imitation suede fabric

SUEDING ▸ suede

SUENT adj smooth

SUER, -S ▸ sue

SUES ▸ sue

SUET, -S n hard fat obtained from sheep and cattle

SUETE, -S n southeasterly wind in Cape Breton Island

SUETIER ▸ suety

SUETIEST ▸ suety

SUETS ▸ suet

SUETTY, SUETTIER ▸ suet

SUETY, SUETIER, SUETIEST ▸ suet

SUFFARI, -S same as ▸ safari

SUFFECT, -S adj additional ▷ n additional consul in ancient Rome

SUFFER, -ED, -S vb undergo or be subjected to

SUFFERER ▸ suffer

SUFFERS ▸ suffer

SUFFETE, -S n official in ancient Carthage

SUFFICE, -D, -S vb be enough for a purpose

SUFFICER ▸ suffice

SUFFICES ▸ suffice

SUFFIX, -ED, -ES n letters added to the end of a word to form another word ▷ vb add (letters) to the end of a word to form another word

SUFFIXAL ▸ suffix

SUFFIXED ▸ suffix

SUFFIXES ▸ suffix

SUFFLATE archaic word for ▸ inflate

SUFFRAGE n right to vote in public elections

SUFFUSE, -D, -S vb spread through or over (something)

SUG, -GED, -S vb sell a product while pretending to conduct market research

SUGAN, -S n straw rope

SUGAR, -S n carbohydrate used to sweeten food and drinks ▷ vb sweeten or cover with sugar

SUGARED adj made sweeter or more appealing with or as with sugar

SUGARER, -S ▸ sugary

SUGARIER ▸ sugary

SUGARING n method of removing unwanted body hair

SUGARS ▸ sugar

SUGARY, SUGARIER adj of, like, or containing sugar

SUGGED ▸ sug

SUGGEST, -S vb put forward (an idea) for consideration

SUGGING, -S n practice of selling products under the pretence of conducting market research

SUGH, -ED, -ING, -S same as ▸ sough

SUGO, -S n Italian pasta sauce

SUGS ▸ sug

SUHUR, -S n meal eaten before sunrise by Muslims fasting during Ramadan

SUI adj of itself

SUICIDAL adj tending towards suicide

SUICIDE, -D, -S n killing oneself intentionally ▷ vb die by suicide

S

SUID, -S n pig or related animal

SUIDIAN, -S ▸ suid

SUIDS ▸ suid

SUILLINE adj of or like a pig

SUING, -S ▸ sue

SUINT, -S n water-soluble substance found in the fleece of sheep

SUIPLAP, -S n South African slang for a drunkard

SUIT, -ED, -S n set of clothes designed to be worn together ▷ vb be appropriate for

SUITABLE adj appropriate or proper

SUITABLY ▸ suitable

SUITCASE n portable travelling case for clothing

SUITE, -S n set of connected rooms in a hotel

SUITED ▸ suit

SUITER, -S n piece of luggage for carrying suits and dresses

SUITES ▸ suite

SUITING, -S n fabric used for suits

SUITLIKE ▸ suit

SUITOR, -ED, -S n person who is courting someone ▷ vb act as a suitor

SUITRESS n female suitor

SUITS ▸ suit

SUIVANTE n lady's maid

SUIVEZ vb musical direction meaning follow

SUJEE, -S same as ▸ soogee

SUK, -S same as ▸ suq

SUKH, -S same as ▸ suq

SUKIYAKI n Japanese dish consisting of sliced meat and vegetables

SUKKAH, -S n structure in which orthodox Jews eat and sleep during Sukkoth

SUKKOS same as ▸ sukkoth

SUKKOT same as ▸ sukkoth

SUKKOTH n eight-day Jewish harvest festival

SUKS ▸ suk

SUKUK, -S n financial certificate conforming to Islam lending principles

SULCAL ▸ sulcus

SULCATE adj marked with longitudinal parallel grooves

SULCATED same as ▸ sulcate

SULCUS, SULCI n linear groove, furrow, or slight depression

SULDAN, -S same as ▸ sultan

SULFA, -S same as ▸ sulpha

SULFATE, -D, -S same as ▸ sulphate

SULFATIC adj relating to sulphate

SULFID, -S same as ▸ sulphide

SULFIDE, -S same as ▸ sulphide

SULFIDS ▸ sulfid

SULFINYL same as > sulphinyl

SULFITE, -S same as ▸ sulphite

SULFITIC ▸ sulfite

SULFO same as > sulphonic

SULFONE, -S same as ▸ sulphone

SULFONIC ▸ sulfone

SULFONYL same as > sulphuryl

SULFUR, -ED, -S variant of ▸ sulphur

SULFURET same as > sulphuret

SULFURIC ▸ sulfur

SULFURS ▸ sulfur

SULFURY adj containing sulfur

SULFURYL same as > sulphuryl

SULK, -ED, -ING, -S vb be silent and sullen because of resentment or bad temper ▷ n resentful or sullen mood

SULKER, -S same as ▸ sulk

SULKIER ▸ sulky

SULKIES ▸ sulky

SULKIEST ▸ sulky

SULKILY ▸ sulky

SULKING ▸ sulk

SULKS ▸ sulk

SULKY, SULKIER, SULKIES, SULKIEST adj moody or silent because of anger or resentment ▷ n light two-wheeled vehicle for one person

SULLAGE, -S n filth or waste, esp sewage

SULLEN, -ER, -S adj unwilling to talk or be sociable ▷ n sullen mood

SULLENLY ▸ sullen

SULLENS ▸ sullen

SULLY, SULLIED, SULLIES, -ING vb ruin (someone's reputation) ▷ n stain

SULPHA, -S n any of a group of sulphonamides that prevent the growth of bacteria

SULPHATE n salt or ester of sulphuric acid ▷ vb treat with a sulphate or convert into a sulphate

SULPHID, -S same as ▸ sulphide

SULPHIDE n compound of sulphur with another element

SULPHIDS ▸ sulphid

SULPHITE n salt or ester of sulphurous acid

SULPHONE n type of organic compound

SULPHUR, -S n pale yellow nonmetallic element ▷ vb treat with sulphur

SULPHURY adj containing sulphur

SULTAN, -S n sovereign of a Muslim country

SULTANA, -S n kind of raisin

SULTANIC ▸ sultan

SULTANS ▸ sultan

SULTRIER ▸ sultry

SULTRILY ▸ sultry

SULTRY, SULTRIER adj (of weather or climate) hot and humid

SULU, -S n type of sarong worn in Fiji

SUM, -MED, -S n result of addition, total ▷ vb add or form a total of (something)

SUMAC, -S same as ▸ sumach

SUMACH, -S n type of temperate or subtropical shrub or small tree

SUMACS ▸ sumac

SUMATRA, -S n violent storm blowing from the direction of Sumatra

SUMI, -S n type of black ink used in Japan

SUMLESS adj uncountable

SUMMA, -E, -S n compendium of theology, philosophy, or canon law

SUMMABLE ▸ sum

SUMMAE ▸ summa

SUMMAND, -S n number or quantity forming part of a sum

SUMMAR Scots variant of ▸ summer

SUMMARY n brief account giving the main points of something ▷ adj done quickly, without formalities

SUMMAS ▸ summa

SUMMAT, -S pron something ▷ n impressive or important person or thing

SUMMATE, -D, -S vb add up

SUMMATS ▸ summat

SUMMED ▸ sum

SUMMER, -ED, -S n warmest season of the year ▷ vb spend the summer (at a place)

SUMMERLY adj like summer

SUMMERS ▸ summer

SUMMERY ▸ summer

SUMMING, -S ▸ sum

SUMMIST, -S *n* writer of summae

SUMMIT, -ED, -S *n* top of a mountain or hill ▷ *vb* reach summit

SUMMITAL ▸ summit

SUMMITED ▸ summit

SUMMITRY *n* practice of conducting international negotiations by summit conferences

SUMMITS ▸ summit

SUMMON, -ED *vb* order (someone) to come

SUMMONER ▸ summon

SUMMONS *n* command summoning someone ▷ *vb* order (someone) to appear in court

SUMO, -S *n* Japanese style of wrestling

SUMOIST, -S ▸ sumo

SUMOS ▸ sumo

SUMOTORI *n* sumo wrestler

SUMP, -S *n* container in an internal-combustion engine into which oil can drain

SUMPH, -S *n* stupid person

SUMPHISH ▸ sumph

SUMPHS ▸ sumph

SUMPIT, -S *n* Malay blowpipe

SUMPITAN *same as* ▸ **sumpit**

SUMPITS ▸ sumpit

SUMPS ▸ sump

SUMPTER, -S *n* packhorse, mule, or other beast of burden

SUMPWEED *n* American weed

SUMS ▸ sum

SUMY *pl n* the monetary units of Uzbekistan

SUN, -NED, -NING, -S *n* star around which the earth and other planets revolve ▷ *vb* expose (oneself) to the sun's rays

SUNBACK *adj* (of dress) cut low at back

SUNBAKE, -S *vb* sunbathe, esp in order to become tanned ▷ *n* period of sunbaking

SUNBAKED *adj* (esp of roads, etc) dried or cracked by the sun's heat

SUNBAKES ▸ sunbake

SUNBATH, -S *n* exposure of the body to the sun to get a suntan

SUNBATHE *vb* lie in the sunshine in order to get a suntan

SUNBATHS ▸ sunbath

SUNBEAM, -S *n* ray of sun

SUNBEAMY *adj* full of sunbeams

SUNBEAT *adj* exposed to sun

SUNBED, -S *n* machine for giving an artificial tan

SUNBELT, -S *n* southern states of the US

SUNBERRY *n* red fruit like the blackberry

SUNBIRD, -S *n* type of small songbird with a bright plumage in the males

SUNBLIND *n* blind that shades a room from the sun's glare

SUNBLOCK *n* cream applied to the skin to protect it from the sun's rays

SUNBOW, -S *n* bow of colours produced when sunlight shines through spray

SUNBURN, -S, -T *n* painful reddening of the skin caused by overexposure to the sun ▷ *vb* become sunburnt

SUNBURST *n* burst of sunshine, as through a break in the clouds

SUNCARE, -S *n* use of products in protecting skin from the sun

SUNCHOKE *n* Jerusalem artichoke

SUNDAE, -S *n* ice cream topped with fruit etc

SUNDARI, -S *n* Indian tree

SUNDECK, -S *n* upper open deck on a passenger ship

SUNDER, -ED, -S *vb* break apart

SUNDERER ▸ sunder

SUNDERS ▸ sunder

SUNDEW, -S *n* type of bog plant with leaves covered in sticky hairs

SUNDIAL, -S *n* device showing the time by means of a pointer that casts a shadow

SUNDOG, -S *n* small rainbow or halo near the horizon

SUNDOWN, -S *same as* ▸ **sunset**

SUNDRA, -S *same as* ▸ **sundari**

SUNDRESS *n* strapped dress worn in hot weather

SUNDRI, -S *same as* ▸ **sundari**

SUNDRIES ▸ sundry

SUNDRILY ▸ sundry

SUNDRIS ▸ sundri

SUNDROPS *pl n* any of various American primroses

SUNDRY, SUNDRIES *adj* several, various

SUNFAST *adj* not fading in sunlight

SUNFISH *n* large sea fish with a rounded body

SUNG ▸ sing

SUNGAR, -S *same as* ▸ **sangar**

SUNGAZER *n* person who practises sungazing

SUNGLASS *n* convex lens used to focus the sun's rays and thus produce heat or ignition

SUNGLOW, -S *n* pinkish glow often seen in the sky before sunrise or after sunset

SUNGREBE *another name for* ▸ **finfoot**

SUNHAT, -S *n* hat that shades the face and neck from the sun

SUNI, -S *n* S African dwarf antelope

SUNK, -S *n* bank or pad

SUNKEN *adj* unhealthily hollow

SUNKER, -S *n* rock (partially) submerged in shallow water

SUNKET, -S *n* something good to eat

SUNKIE, -S *n* little stool

SUNKS ▸ sunk

SUNLAMP, -S *n* lamp that generates ultraviolet rays

SUNLAND, -S *n* sunny area

SUNLESS *adj* without sun or sunshine

SUNLIGHT *n* light that comes from the sun

SUNLIKE ▸ sun

SUNLIT ▸ sunlight

SUNN, -S *n* tropical leguminous plant

SUNNA, -S *n* body of traditional Islamic law

SUNNAH, -S *same as* ▸ **sunna**

SUNNAS ▸ sunna

SUNNED ▸ sun

SUNNIER ▸ sunny

SUNNIES *pl n* pair of sunglasses

SUNNIEST ▸ sunny

SUNNILY ▸ sunny

SUNNING ▸ sun

SUNNS ▸ sunn

SUNNY, SUNNIER, SUNNIEST *adj* full of or exposed to sunlight

SUNPORCH *n* porch for sunbathing on

S

SUNPROOF ▸ sun

SUNRAY, -S n ray of light from the sun

SUNRISE, -S n daily appearance of the sun above the horizon

SUNROOF, -S n panel in the roof of a car that opens to let in air

SUNROOM, -S n room or glass-enclosed porch designed to display beautiful views

SUNS ▸ sun

SUNSCALD n sun damage on tomato plants

SUNSET, -S vb phase out

SUNSHADE n anything used to shade people from the sun, such as a parasol or awning

SUNSHINE n light and warmth from the sun

SUNSHINY adj sunny

SUNSPECS pl n sunglasses

SUNSPOT, -S n dark patch appearing temporarily on the sun's surface

SUNSTAR, -S n type of starfish with up to 13 arms

SUNSTONE n type of translucent feldspar with reddish-gold speckles

SUNSUIT, -S n child's outfit consisting of a brief top and shorts or a short skirt

SUNTAN, -S n browning of the skin caused by exposure to the sun

SUNTRAP, -S n very sunny sheltered place

SUNUP, -S same as ▸ sunrise

SUNWARD same as ▸ sunwards

SUNWARDS adv towards the sun

SUNWISE adv moving in the same direction as the sun

SUP, -PED, -PING, -S same as ▸ supine

SUPAWN, -S same as ▸ suppawn

SUPE, -S n superintendent

SUPER, -ED, -ING, -S adj excellent ▷ n superannuation ▷ interj enthusiastic expression of approval or assent ▷ vb. work as superintendent

SUPERADD vb add (something) to something that has already been added

SUPERATE vb overcome

SUPERB, -ER adj excellent, impressive, or splendid

SUPERBAD adj exceptionally bad

SUPERBER ▸ superb

SUPERBLY ▸ superb

SUPERBUG n bacterium resistant to antibiotics

SUPERCAR n very expensive fast or powerful car with a centrally located engine

SUPERCOP n high-ranking police officer

SUPERCOW n dairy cow that produces a very high milk yield

SUPERED ▸ super

SUPEREGO n that part of the unconscious mind that governs ideas about what is right and wrong

SUPERFAN n very devoted fan

SUPERFIT adj highly fit

SUPERFIX n linguistic feature distinguishing the meaning of one word from another

SUPERFLY adj pretentiously flamboyant

SUPERGUN n large powerful gun

SUPERHET n type of radio receiver

SUPERHIT n very popular hit

SUPERHOT adj very hot

SUPERING ▸ super

SUPERIOR adj greater in quality, quantity, or merit ▷ n person of greater rank or status

SUPERJET n supersonic aircraft

SUPERLIE, SUPERLAY vb lie above

SUPERLOO n automated public toilet

SUPERMAN, SUPERMEN n man with great physical or mental powers

SUPERMAX n jail or other facility having the very highest levels of security

SUPERMEN ▸ superman

SUPERMOM n very capable and busy mother

SUPERNAL adj of or from the world of the divine

SUPERPRO n person regarded as a real professional

SUPERS ▸ super

SUPERSET n set containing all the members of another set plus other members

SUPERSEX n in genetics, type of sterile organism

SUPERSPY n highly accomplished spy

SUPERTAX n extra tax on incomes above a certain level

SUPES ▸ supe

SUPINATE vb turn (the hand and forearm) so that the palm faces up or forwards

SUPINE, -S adj lying flat on one's back ▷ n noun form derived from a verb in Latin

SUPINELY ▸ supine

SUPINES ▸ supine

SUPLEX, -ES n type of wrestling hold

SUPPAWN, -S n kind of porridge

SUPPEAGO same as ▸ serpigo

SUPPED ▸ sup

SUPPER, -ED, -S n light evening meal ▷ vb eat supper

SUPPING ▸ sup

SUPPLANT vb take the place of, oust

SUPPLE, -D, -R, -S, -ST, SUPPLING adj (of a person) moving and bending easily and gracefully ▷ vb make or become supple

SUPPLELY same as ▸ supply

SUPPLER ▸ supple

SUPPLES ▸ supple

SUPPLEST ▸ supple

SUPPLIAL n instance of supplying

SUPPLIED ▸ supply

SUPPLIER ▸ supply

SUPPLIES ▸ supply

SUPPLING ▸ supple

SUPPLY, SUPPLIED, SUPPLIES vb provide with something required ▷ n supplying ▷ adj acting as a temporary substitute ▷ adv in a supple manner

SUPPORT, -S vb bear the weight of ▷ n supporting

SUPPOSAL n supposition

SUPPOSE, -S vb presume to be true

SUPPOSED adj presumed to be true without proof, doubtful

SUPPOSER ▸ suppose

SUPPOSES ▸ suppose

SUPPRESS vb put an end to

SUPRA adv above, esp referring to earlier parts of a book etc

SUPREMA ▸ supremum

SUPREME, -R, -S adj highest in authority, rank, or degree ▷ n rich sauce made with a base of veal or chicken stock

SUPREMO, -S n person in overall authority

SUPREMUM, SUPREMA n (in maths) smallest quantity

greater than or equal to each of a set or subset

SUPS ▸ **sup**

SUQ, -S n open-air marketplace

This unusual word for an Arab marketplace is easy to overlook because we tend not to think of words ending in Q. It can also be spelt **sook, souk, suk** or **sukh**.

SUR prep above

SURA, -S n any of the 114 chapters of the Koran

SURAH, -S n twill-weave fabric of silk or rayon, used for dresses, blouses, etc

SURAL adj of or relating to the calf of the leg

SURAMIN, -S n drug used in treating sleeping sickness

SURANCE, -S same as ▷ assurance

SURAS ▸ **sura**

SURAT, -S n cotton fabric from Surat in India

SURBAHAR n Indian string instrument

SURBASE, -S n uppermost part, such as a moulding, of a pedestal, base, or skirting

SURBASED adj having a surbase

SURBASES ▸ **surbase**

SURBATE, -D, -S, SURBET vb make feet sore through walking

SURBED, -S vb put something on its edge

SURBET ▸ **surbate**

SURCEASE n cessation or intermission ▷ vb desist from (some action)

SURCOAT, -S n tunic worn by a knight over their armour

SURCULUS, SURCULI n sucker on plant

SURD, -S n number that cannot be expressed in whole numbers ▷ adj of or relating to a surd

SURDITY n deafness

SURDS ▸ **surd**

SURE, -D, -R, -S, -ST, SURING adj free from uncertainty or doubt ▷ interj certainly ▷ vb archaic form of sewer

SUREFIRE adj certain to succeed

SURELY adv it must be true that

SURENESS ▸ **sure**

SURER ▸ **sure**

SURES ▸ **sure**

SUREST ▸ **sure**

SURETY, SURETIED, SURETIES n person who takes responsibility for the fulfilment of another's obligation ▷ vb be surety for

SURF, -ED, -S n foam caused by waves breaking on the shore ▷ vb take part in surfing

SURFABLE ▸ **surf**

SURFACE, -D, -S n outside or top of an object ▷ vb become apparent

SURFACER ▸ **surface**

SURFACES ▸ **surface**

SURFBIRD n American shore bird

SURFBOAT n boat with a high bow and stern and flotation chambers

SURFED ▸ **surf**

SURFEIT, -S n excessive amount ▷ vb supply or feed excessively

SURFER, -S ▸ **surfing**

SURFFISH n fish of American coastal seas

SURFIE, -S n young person whose main interest is in surfing

SURFIER ▸ **surfy**

SURFIES ▸ **surfie**

SURFIEST ▸ **surfy**

SURFING, -S n sport of riding on a board on the crest of a wave

SURFLIKE ▸ **surf**

SURFMAN, SURFMEN n sailor skilled in sailing through surf

SURFRIDE, SURFRODE vb ride on surf

SURFS ▸ **surf**

SURFSIDE adj next to the sea

SURFY, SURFIER, SURFIEST ▸ **surf**

SURGE, -D, -S n sudden powerful increase ▷ vb increase suddenly

SURGEFUL ▸ **surge**

SURGENT ▸ **surge**

SURGEON, -S n doctor who specializes in surgery

SURGER, -S ▸ **surge**

SURGERY n treatment in which the patient's body is cut open in order to treat the affected part

SURGES ▸ **surge**

SURGICAL adj involving or used in surgery

SURGIER ▸ **surgy**

SURGIEST ▸ **surgy**

SURGING, -S ▸ **surge**

SURGY, SURGIER, SURGIEST ▸ **surge**

SURICATE n type of meerkat

SURIMI, -S n blended seafood product made from precooked fish

SURING ▸ **sure**

SURLIER ▸ **surly**

SURLIEST ▸ **surly**

SURLILY ▸ **surly**

SURLOIN, -S same as ▸ **sirloin**

SURLY, SURLIER, SURLIEST adj ill-tempered and rude

SURMISAL ▸ **surmise**

SURMISE, -D, -S n guess, conjecture ▷ vb guess (something) from incomplete or uncertain evidence

SURMISER ▸ **surmise**

SURMISES ▸ **surmise**

SURMOUNT vb overcome (a problem)

SURNAME, -D, -S n family name ▷ vb furnish with or call by a surname

SURNAMER ▸ **surname**

SURNAMES ▸ **surname**

SURPASS vb be greater than or superior to

SURPLICE n loose white robe worn by members of the clergy and choristers

SURPLUS n amount left over in excess of what is required ▷ adj extra ▷ vb be left over in excess of what is required

SURPRINT vb print (additional matter) over something already printed ▷ n marks, printed matter, etc, that have been surprinted

SURPRISE n unexpected event ▷ vb cause to feel amazement or wonder

SURPRIZE same as ▸ **surprise**

SURQUEDY same as ▷ **surquedry**

SURRA, -S n tropical febrile disease of animals

SURREAL, -S adj bizarre ▷ n atmosphere or qualities evoked by surrealism

SURREBUT vb give evidence to support the surrebutter

SURREY, -S n light horse-drawn carriage

SURROUND vb be, come, or place all around (a person or thing) ▷ n border or edging

SURROYAL n high point on stag's horns

S

SURTAX, -ED, -ES n extra tax on incomes above a certain level ▷ vb assess for liability to surtax

SURTITLE n printed translation of the libretto of an opera in a language foreign to the audience

SURTOUT, -S n man's overcoat resembling a frock coat

SURUCUCU n South American snake

SURVEIL, -S same as > **surveille**

SURVEY, -ED, -S vb view or consider in a general way ▷ n surveying

SURVEYAL ▶ **survey**

SURVEYED ▶ **survey**

SURVEYOR n person whose occupation is to survey land or buildings

SURVEYS ▶ **survey**

SURVIEW, -S vb survey

SURVIVAL n condition of having survived ▷ adj of, relating to, or assisting the act of surviving

SURVIVE, -D, -S vb continue to live or exist after (a difficult experience)

SURVIVER same as ▶ **survivor**

SURVIVES ▶ **survive**

SURVIVOR n person or thing that survives

SUS, -ED, -ES, -ING same as ▶ **suss**

SUSHI, -S n Japanese dish of small cakes of cold rice with a topping of raw fish

SUSING ▶ **sus**

SUSLIK, -S n central Eurasian ground squirrel

SUSPECT, -S vb believe (someone) to be guilty without having any proof ▷ adj not to be trusted ▷ n person who is suspected

SUSPENCE same as ▶ **suspense**

SUSPEND, -S vb hang from a high place

SUSPENS same as ▶ **suspense**

SUSPENSE n state of uncertainty while awaiting news, an event, etc

SUSPIRE, -D, -S vb sigh or utter with a sigh

SUSS, -ED, -ES, -ING vb attempt to work out (a situation, etc), using one's intuition ▷ n sharpness of mind

SUSTAIN, -S vb maintain or prolong ▷ n prolongation of a note, by playing technique or electronics

SUSU, -S n (in the Caribbean) savings fund shared by friends

SUSURRUS > **susurrate**

SUSUS ▶ **susu**

SUTILE adj involving sewing

SUTLER, -S n merchant who accompanied an army in order to sell provisions

SUTLERY ▶ **sutler**

SUTOR, -S n cobbler

SUTORIAL ▶ **sutor**

SUTORIAN ▶ **sutor**

SUTORS ▶ **sutor**

SUTRA, -S n Sanskrit sayings or collections of sayings

SUTTA, -S n Buddhist scripture

SUTTEE, -S n custom whereby a widow burnt herself on her husband's funeral pyre

SUTTLE, -D, -S, SUTTLING vb work as a sutler

SUTTLY ▶ **subtle**

SUTURAL ▶ **suture**

SUTURE, -D, -S, SUTURING n stitch joining the edges of a wound ▷ vb join (the edges of a wound, etc) by means of sutures

SUZERAIN n state or sovereign with limited authority over another self-governing state

SVARAJ, -ES same as ▶ **swaraj**

SVASTIKA same as ▶ **swastika**

SVEDBERG n unit used in physics

SVELTE, -R, -ST adj attractively or gracefully slim

SVELTELY ▶ **svelte**

SVELTER ▶ **svelte**

SVELTEST ▶ **svelte**

SWAB, -BED, -BING, -S n small piece of cotton wool used to apply medication, clean a wound, etc ▷ vb clean (a wound) with a swab

SWABBER, -S n person who uses a swab

SWABBIE same as ▶ **swabby**

SWABBIES ▶ **swabby**

SWABBING ▶ **swab**

SWABBY, SWABBIES n seaman

SWABS ▶ **swab**

SWACHH adj (in Indian English) clean

SWACK, -ED, -ING, -S adj flexible ▷ vb strike

SWAD, -S n loutish person

SWADDIE same as ▶ **swaddy**

SWADDIES ▶ **swaddy**

SWADDLE, -D, -S vb wrap (a baby) in swaddling clothes ▷ n swaddling clothes

SWADDLER ▶ **swaddle**

SWADDLES ▶ **swaddle**

SWADDY, SWADDIES n private soldier

SWADS ▶ **swad**

SWAG, -GED, -GING, -S n stolen property ▷ vb sway from side to side

SWAGE, -D, -S, SWAGING n shaped tool or die used in forming cold metal by hammering ▷ vb form (metal) with a swage

SWAGER, -S ▶ **swage**

SWAGES ▶ **swage**

SWAGGED ▶ **swag**

SWAGGER, -S vb walk or behave arrogantly ▷ n arrogant walk or manner ▷ adj elegantly fashionable

SWAGGIE, -S same as ▶ **swagger**

SWAGGING ▶ **swag**

SWAGING ▶ **swage**

SWAGMAN, SWAGMEN n tramp who carries their belongings in a bundle on their back

SWAGS ▶ **swag**

SWAGSHOP n shop selling cheap goods

SWAGSMAN, SWAGSMEN same as ▶ **swagman**

SWAIL, -S same as ▶ **swale**

SWAIN, -S n suitor

SWAINING n acting as suitor

SWAINISH ▶ **swain**

SWAINS ▶ **swain**

SWALE, -D, -S n moist depression in a tract of land ▷ vb sway

SWALIER ▶ **swaly**

SWALIEST ▶ **swaly**

SWALING, -S ▶ **swale**

SWALLET, -S n hole where water goes underground

SWALLIES ▶ **swally**

SWALLOW, -S vb cause to pass down one's throat ▷ n swallowing

SWALLY, SWALLIES n alcoholic drink

SWALY, SWALIER, SWALIEST ▶ **swale**

SWAM ▶ **swim**

SWAMI, -ES, -S n Hindu religious teacher

SWAMP, -ED, -ING, -S *n* watery area of land, bog ▷ *vb* cause (a boat) to fill with water and sink

SWAMPER, -S *n* person who lives or works in a swampy region

SWAMPIER ▶ swampy

SWAMPING ▶ swamp

SWAMPISH ▶ swamp

SWAMPS ▶ swamp

SWAMPY, SWAMPIER ▶ swamp

SWAMY *same as* ▶ swami

SWAN, -NED, -NING, -S *n* large usu white water bird with a long graceful neck ▷ *vb* wander about idly

SWANG ▶ swing

SWANHERD *n* person who herds swans

SWANK, -ED, -EST, -ING, -S *vb* show off or boast ▷ *n* showing off or boasting

SWANKER, -S ▶ swank

SWANKEST ▶ swank

SWANKEY, -S *same as* ▶ swanky

SWANKIE *same as* ▶ swanky

SWANKIER ▶ swanky

SWANKIES ▶ swanky

SWANKILY ▶ swanky

SWANKING ▶ swank

SWANKPOT *same as* ▶ swank

SWANKS ▶ swank

SWANKY, SWANKIER, SWANKIES *adj* expensive and showy, stylish ▷ *n* lively person

SWANLIKE ▶ swan

SWANNED ▶ swan

SWANNERY *n* place where swans are kept and bred

SWANNIE, -S *n* (in New Zealand) type of heavy woollen shirt

SWANNIER ▶ swanny

SWANNIES ▶ swannie

SWANNING ▶ swan

SWANNY, SWANNIER *adj* swanlike

SWANPAN, -S *n* Chinese abacus

SWANS ▶ swan

SWANSKIN *n* skin of a swan with the feathers attached

SWANSONG *n* beautiful song fabled to be sung by a swan before it dies

SWAP, -PED, -PING, -S, -T *vb* exchange (something) for something else ▷ *n* exchange

SWAPFILE *n* computer file which provides space for transferred programs

SWAPPED ▶ swap

SWAPPER, -S ▶ swap

SWAPPING ▶ swap

SWAPS ▶ swap

SWAPT ▶ swap

SWAPTION *another name for* ▶ swap

SWARAJ, -ES *n* (in British India) self-government

SWARD, -ED, -ING, -S *n* stretch of short grass ▷ *vb* cover or become covered with grass

SWARDIER ▶ swardy

SWARDING ▶ sward

SWARDS ▶ sward

SWARDY, SWARDIER *adj* covered with sward

SWARE ▶ swear

SWARF, -ED, -ING, -S, SWARVED, SWARVES, SWARVING *n* material removed by cutting tools in the machining of metals, stone, etc ▷ *vb* faint

SWARM, -ED, -ING, -S *n* large group of bees or other insects ▷ *vb* move in a swarm

SWARMER, -S ▶ swarm

SWARMING ▶ swarm

SWARMS ▶ swarm

SWART *adj* swarthy

SWARTH, -S *same as* ▶ swart

SWARTHY *adj* dark-complexioned

SWARTY, SWARTIER *adj* swarthy

SWARVE *same as* ▶ swarf

SWARVED ▶ swarf

SWARVES ▶ swarf

SWARVING ▶ swarf

SWASH, -ED, -ES, -ING *n* rush of water up a beach following each break of the waves ▷ *vb* wash or move with noisy splashing

SWASHER, -S *n* braggart

SWASHES ▶ swash

SWASHIER ▶ swashy

SWASHING ▶ swash

SWASHY, SWASHIER *adj* slushy

SWASTICA *same as* ▶ swastika

SWASTIKA *n* primitive religious symbol in the shape of a Greek cross

SWAT, -S, -TED, -TING *vb* strike or hit sharply ▷ *n* swatter

SWATCH, -ES *n* sample of cloth

SWATH, -S *n* width of one sweep of a scythe or of the blade of a mowing machine

SWATHE, -D, -S *vb* bandage or wrap completely ▷ *n* bandage or wrapping

SWATHER, -S ▶ swathe

SWATHES ▶ swathe

SWATHIER ▶ swathy

SWATHING *n* act of enveloping (with a garment, bandage, etc)

SWATHS ▶ swath

SWATHY, SWATHIER ▶ swath

SWATS ▶ swat

SWATTED ▶ swat

SWATTER, -S *n* device for killing insects ▷ *vb* splash

SWATTIER *same as* ▶ swottier

SWATTING ▶ swat

SWATTY *same as* ▶ swotty

SWAY, -ED, -S *vb* swing to and fro or from side to side ▷ *n* power or influence

SWAYABLE ▶ sway

SWAYBACK *n* abnormal sagging in the spine of older horses

SWAYED ▶ sway

SWAYER, -S ▶ sway

SWAYFUL ▶ sway

SWAYING, -S ▶ sway

SWAYL, -ED, -ING, -S *same as* ▶ sweal

SWAYS ▶ sway

SWAZZLE, -S *n* small metal instrument used to produce a shrill voice

SWEAL, -ED, -ING, -S *vb* scorch

SWEAR, SWARE, -ING, -S, SWORE, SWORN *vb* use obscene or blasphemous language

SWEARD, -S *same as* ▶ sword

SWEARER, -S ▶ swear

SWEARIER ▶ sweary

SWEARING ▶ swear

SWEARS ▶ swear

SWEARY, SWEARIER *adj* using swear-words

SWEAT, -ING, -S *n* salty liquid given off through the pores of the skin ▷ *vb* have sweat coming through the pores

SWEATBOX *n* device for causing tobacco leaves, fruit, or hides to sweat

SWEATED *adj* made by exploited labour

SWEATER, -S *n* (woollen) garment for the upper part of the body

SWEATIER ▶ sweaty

SWEATILY ▶ sweaty

SWEATING ▸ sweat

SWEATS ▸ sweat

SWEATY, SWEATIER adj covered with sweat

SWEDE, -S n kind of turnip

SWEDGER, -S n Scots dialect word for sweet

SWEE, -D, -ING, -S vb sway

SWEEL, -ED, -ING, -S same as ▸ sweal

SWEENEY, -S n police flying squad

SWEENY, SWEENIES n wasting of the shoulder muscles of a horse

SWEEP, -ING, -S, SWEPT vb remove dirt from (a floor) with a broom ▷ n sweeping

SWEEPER, -S n device used to sweep carpets

SWEEPIER ▸ sweepy

SWEEPING ▸ sweep

SWEEPS ▸ sweep

SWEEPY, SWEEPIER ▸ sweep

SWEER, -ED, -ING, -S variant of ▸ sweir

SWEERT variant of ▸ sweer

SWEES ▸ swee

SWEET, -ED, -ER, -EST, -S adj tasting of or like sugar ▷ n shaped piece of food consisting mainly of sugar ▷ vb sweeten

SWEETEN, -S vb make (food or drink) sweet or sweeter

SWEETER ▸ sweet

SWEETEST ▸ sweet

SWEETIE, -S n lovable person

SWEETING n variety of sweet apple

SWEETISH ▸ sweet

SWEETLIP n type of Australian fish with big lips

SWEETLY ▸ sweet

SWEETMAN, SWEETMEN n (in the Caribbean) a man kept by a woman

SWEETS ▸ sweet

SWEETSOP n small tropical American tree

SWEETY same as ▸ sweetie

SWEIR, -ED, -ER, -EST, -ING, -S vb swear ▷ adj lazy

SWEIRT variant of ▸ sweir

SWELCHIE n whirlpool in Orkney

SWELL, -ED, -EST, -ING, -S, SWOLLEN, SWOLN vb expand or increase ▷ n swelling or being swollen ▷ adj excellent or fine

SWELLDOM n fashionable society

SWELLED ▸ swell

SWELLER, -S ▸ swell

SWELLEST ▸ swell

SWELLING ▸ swell

SWELLISH ▸ swell

SWELLS ▸ swell

SWELT, -ED, -ING, -S vb die

SWELTER, -S vb feel uncomfortably hot ▷ n hot and uncomfortable condition

SWELTING ▸ swelt

SWELTRY adj sultry

SWELTS ▸ swelt

SWEPT ▸ sweep

SWERF, -ED, -ING, -S same as ▸ swarf

SWERVE, -D, -S, SWERVING vb turn aside from a course sharply or suddenly ▷ n swerving

SWERVER, -S ▸ swerve

SWERVES ▸ swerve

SWERVING ▸ swerve

SWEVEN, -S n vision or dream

SWEY, -ED, -ING, -S same as ▸ swee

SWIDDEN, -S n area of land where slash-and-burn techniques have been used

SWIES ▸ swy

SWIFT, -ED, -EST, -ING, -S adj moving or able to move quickly ▷ n fast-flying bird with pointed wings ▷ adv swiftly or quickly ▷ vb make tight

SWIFTER, -S n line run around the ends of capstan bars

SWIFTEST ▸ swift

SWIFTIE n trick, ruse, or deception

SWIFTIES ▸ swifty

SWIFTING ▸ swift

SWIFTLET n type of small Asian swift

SWIFTLY ▸ swift

SWIFTS ▸ swift

SWIFTY, SWIFTIES same as ▸ swiftie

SWIG, -GED, -GING, -S n large mouthful of drink ▷ vb drink in large mouthfuls

SWIGGER, -S ▸ swig

SWIGGING ▸ swig

SWIGS ▸ swig

SWILE, -S n seal (the marine animal)

SWILER, -S n (in Newfoundland) a seal hunter

SWILES ▸ swile

SWILING, -S n practice of hunting seals

SWILL, -ED, -ING, -S vb drink greedily ▷ n sloppy mixture containing waste food, fed to pigs

SWILLER, -S ▸ swill

SWILLING ▸ swill

SWILLS ▸ swill

SWIM, SWAM, -MING, -S, SWUM vb move along in water by movements of the limbs ▷ n act or period of swimming

SWIMMER ▸ swim

SWIMMERS pl n swimming costume

SWIMMIER ▸ swimmy

SWIMMILY ▸ swimmy

SWIMMING ▸ swim

SWIMMY, SWIMMIER adj dizzy

SWIMS ▸ swim

SWIMSUIT n woman's swimming garment that leaves the arms and legs bare

SWIMWEAR n swimming costumes

SWINDGE, -D, -S same as ▸ swinge

SWINDLE, -D, -S vb cheat (someone) out of money ▷ n instance of swindling

SWINDLER ▸ swindle

SWINDLES ▸ swindle

SWINE, -S n contemptible person

SWINEPOX n acute infectious viral disease of pigs

SWINERY n pig farm

SWINES ▸ swine

SWING, SWANG, -S, SWUNG vb move to and fro, sway ▷ n swinging

SWINGARM n main part of the rear suspension on a motorcycle

SWINGBIN n rubbish bin with a lid that swings shut after being opened

SWINGBY, -S n act of spacecraft passing close to planet

SWINGE, -D, -S vb beat, flog, or punish

SWINGER, -S n person regarded as being modern and lively

SWINGES ▸ swinge

SWINGIER ▸ swingy

SWINGING adj lively and modern

SWINGISM n former resistance to use of agricultural machines

SWINGLE, -D, -S n flat-bladed wooden instrument used for beating and scraping flax ▷ vb use a swingle on

SWINGMAN, SWINGMEN n musician specializing in swing music

SWINGS ▶ swing

SWINGY, SWINGIER adj lively and modern

SWINISH ▶ swine

SWINK, -ED, -ING, -S vb toil or drudge ▷ n toil or drudgery

SWINKER, -S ▶ swink

SWINKING ▶ swink

SWINKS ▶ swink

SWINNEY, -S variant of ▶ sweeny

SWIPE, -D, SWIPING vb strike (at) with a sweeping blow ▷ n hard blow

SWIPER, -S ▶ swipe

SWIPES pl n beer, esp when poor or weak

SWIPEY, SWIPIER, SWIPIEST adj drunk

SWIPING ▶ swipe

SWIPLE, -S same as ▶ swipple

SWIPPLE, -S n part of a flail that strikes the grain

SWIRE, -S n neck

SWIRL, -ED, -S vb turn with a whirling motion ▷ n whirling motion

SWIRLIER ▶ swirly

SWIRLING ▶ swirl

SWIRLS ▶ swirl

SWIRLY, SWIRLIER ▶ swirl

SWISH, -ED, -ES, -EST vb move with a whistling or hissing sound ▷ n whistling or hissing sound ▷ adj fashionable, smart

SWISHER, -S ▶ swish

SWISHES ▶ swish

SWISHEST ▶ swish

SWISHIER ▶ swishy

SWISHING ▶ swish

SWISHY, SWISHIER adj moving with a swishing sound

SWISS, -ES n type of muslin

SWISSING n method of treating cloth

SWITCH, -ED, -ES n device for opening and closing an electric circuit ▷ vb change abruptly

SWITCHEL n type of beer

SWITCHER ▶ switch

SWITCHES ▶ switch

SWITCHY ▶ switch

SWITH adv swiftly

SWITHE same as ▶ swith

SWITHER, -S vb hesitate or be indecisive ▷ n state of hesitation or uncertainty

SWITHLY ▶ swith

SWITS, -ES same as ▶ switch

SWIVEL, -ED, -S vb turn on a central point ▷ n coupling device that allows an attached object to turn freely

SWIVET, -S n nervous state

SWIZ n swindle or disappointment

SWIZZ, -ED, -ES, -ING same as ▶ swiz

SWIZZLE, -D, -S vb cheat or con ▷ n act of cheating or conning

SWIZZLER ▶ swizzle

SWIZZLES ▶ swizzle

SWOB, -BED, -BING, -S less common word for ▶ swab

SWOBBER, -S ▶ swob

SWOBBING ▶ swob

SWOBS ▶ swob

SWOFFER, -S ▶ swoffing

SWOFFING n sport of saltwater fly-fishing

SWOLE, -R, -ST adj muscular from weight training

SWOLLEN ▶ swell

SWOLN ▶ swell

SWOON, -ED, -S n faint ▷ vb faint because of shock or strong emotion

SWOONER, -S ▶ swoon

SWOONIER ▶ swoony

SWOONING ▶ swoon

SWOONS ▶ swoon

SWOONY, SWOONIER adj romantic

SWOOP, -ED, -ING, -S vb sweep down or pounce on suddenly ▷ n swooping

SWOOPER, -S ▶ swoop

SWOOPIER ▶ swoopy

SWOOPING ▶ swoop

SWOOPS ▶ swoop

SWOOPY, SWOOPIER ▶ swoop

SWOOSH, -ED, -ES vb make a swirling or rustling sound when moving or pouring out ▷ n swirling or rustling sound or movement

SWOP, -PED, -PING, -S, -T same as ▶ swap

SWOPPER, -S ▶ swop

SWOPPING ▶ swop

SWOPS ▶ swop

SWOPT ▶ swop

SWORD, -ED, -ING, -S n weapon with a long sharp blade ▷ vb bear a sword

SWORDER, -S n fighter with sword

SWORDING ▶ sword

SWORDMAN, SWORDMEN same as > swordsman

SWORDS ▶ sword

SWORE ▶ swear

SWORN ▶ swear

SWOT, -S, -TED, -TING vb study (a subject) intensively ▷ n person who studies hard

SWOTTER, -S same as ▶ swot

SWOTTIER ▶ swotty

SWOTTING ▶ swot

SWOTTY, SWOTTIER adj given to studying hard, esp to the exclusion of other activities

SWOUN, -S same as ▶ swoon

SWOUND, -ED same as ▶ swoon

SWOUNDS less common spelling of ▶ zounds

SWOUNE, -D, -S, SWOUNING same as ▶ swoon

SWOUNS ▶ swoun

SWOWND, -S same as ▶ swoon

SWOWNE, -S same as ▶ swoon

SWOZZLE, -S same as ▶ swazzle

SWUM ▶ swim

SWUNG ▶ swing

SWY, SWIES n Australian gambling game involving two coins

> A type of card game, this word can be useful in helping you to clear a difficult rack.

SYBARITE n lover of luxury ▷ adj luxurious

SYBBE, -S same as ▶ sib

SYBIL, -S same as ▶ sibyl

SYBO n spring onion

SYBOE, -S same as ▶ sybo

SYBOTIC adj of a swineherd

SYBOTISM ▶ sybotic

SYBOW, -S same as ▶ sybo

SYCAMINE n mulberry tree mentioned in the Bible, thought to be the black mulberry

SYCAMORE n tree with five-pointed leaves and two-winged fruits

SYCE, -S n (formerly, in India) a servant employed to look after horses, etc

SYCEE, -S n silver ingots formerly used as a medium of exchange in China

SYCES ▶ syce

SYCOMORE same as ▶ sycamore

SYCON, -S n type of sponge

SYCONIUM, SYCONIA n fleshy fruit of the fig

S

SYCONOID adj of or like a sycon

SYCONS ▶ sycon

SYCOSIS, SYCOSES n chronic inflammation of the hair follicles

SYE, -D, -ING, -S vb strain

SYEN, -S same as ▶ scion

SYENITE, -S n light-coloured coarse-grained plutonic igneous rock

SYENITIC ▶ syenite

SYENS ▶ syen

SYES ▶ sye

SYKE, -S same as ▶ sike

SYKER adv surely

SYKES ▶ syke

SYLI, -S n Finnish unit of volume

SYLLABI ▶ syllabus

SYLLABIC adj of or relating to syllables ▷ n syllabic consonant

SYLLABLE n part of a word pronounced as a unit

SYLLABUB n dessert of beaten cream, sugar, and wine

SYLLABUS, SYLLABI n list of subjects for a course of study

SYLLOGE, -S n collection or summary

SYLPH, -S n slender, graceful girl or woman

SYLPHIC ▶ sylph

SYLPHID, -S n little sylph

SYLPHIDE same as ▶ sylphid

SYLPHIDS ▶ sylphid

SYLPHIER ▶ sylphy

SYLPHINE ▶ sylph

SYLPHISH ▶ sylph

SYLPHS ▶ sylph

SYLPHY, SYLPHIER ▶ sylph

SYLVA, -E, -S n trees growing in a particular region

SYLVAN, -S adj relating to woods and trees ▷ n inhabitant of the woods, esp a spirit

SYLVANER n German variety of grape

SYLVANS ▶ sylvan

SYLVAS ▶ sylva

SYLVATIC adj growing, living, or occurring in a wood or beneath a tree

SYLVIA, -S n songbird

SYLVIINE ▶ sylvia

SYLVIN, -S same as ▶ sylvite

SYLVINE, -S same as ▶ sylvite

SYLVINS ▶ sylvin

SYLVITE, -S n soluble colourless, white, or coloured mineral

SYMAR, -S same as ▶ cymar

SYMBION, -S same as ▶ symbiont

SYMBIONT n organism living in a state of symbiosis

SYMBIOT, -S same as ▶ symbiont

SYMBIOTE same as ▶ symbiont

SYMBIOTS ▶ symbiot

SYMBOL, -ED, -S n sign or thing that stands for something else ▷ vb be a symbol

SYMBOLE, -S same as ▶ cymbal

SYMBOLED ▶ symbol

SYMBOLES ▶ symbole

SYMBOLIC adj of or relating to a symbol or symbols

SYMBOLS ▶ symbol

SYMITAR, -S same as ▶ scimitar

SYMITARE same as ▶ scimitar

SYMITARS ▶ symitar

SYMMETRY n state of having two halves that are mirror images of each other

SYMPATHY n compassion for someone's pain or distress

SYMPATRY n existing of organisms together without interbreeding

SYMPHILE n insect that lives in the nests of social insects and is fed and reared by the inmates

SYMPHILY n presence of different kinds of animal in ants'nests

SYMPHONY n composition for orchestra, with several movements

SYMPLAST n continuous system of protoplasts, linked by plasmodesmata and bounded by the cell wall

SYMPLOCE n word repetition in successive clauses

SYMPODIA > sympodium

SYMPOSIA > symposium

SYMPTOM, -S n sign indicating the presence of an illness

SYN Scots word for ▶ since

SYNAGOG, -S same as > synagogue

SYNANGIA > synangium

SYNANON, -S n type of therapy given to drug addicts

SYNANTHY n abnormal joining between flowers

SYNAPHEA n continuity in metre of verses of poem

SYNAPSE, -D n gap where nerve impulses pass between two nerve cells ▷ vb create a synapse

SYNAPSES ▶ synapsis

SYNAPSID n prehistoric mammal-like reptile

SYNAPSIS, SYNAPSES n association in pairs of homologous chromosomes at the start of meiosis

SYNAPTE, -S n litany in Greek Orthodox Church

SYNAPTIC adj of or relating to a synapse

SYNARCHY n joint rule

SYNASTRY n coincidence of astrological influences

SYNAXIS, SYNAXES n early Christian meeting

SYNC, -ED, -ING, -S n synchronization ▷ vb synchronize

SYNCARP, -S n fleshy multiple fruit

SYNCARPY n quality of consisting of united carpels

SYNCED ▶ sync

SYNCH, -ED, -ING, -S same as ▶ sync

SYNCHRO, -S n type of electrical device

SYNCHS ▶ synch

SYNCING ▶ sync

SYNCLINE n downward slope of stratified rock

SYNCOM, -S n communications satellite in stationary orbit

SYNCOPAL ▶ syncope

SYNCOPE, -S n omission of one or more sounds or letters from the middle of a word

SYNCOPIC ▶ syncope

SYNCS ▶ sync

SYNCYTIA > syncytium

SYND, -ED, -S same as ▶ syne

SYNDESES ▶ syndesis

SYNDESIS, SYNDESES n use of syndetic constructions

SYNDET, -S n synthetic detergent

SYNDETIC adj denoting a grammatical construction in which two clauses are connected by a conjunction

SYNDETON n syndetic construction

SYNDETS ▶ syndet

SYNDIC, -S n business or legal agent of some institutions

SYNDICAL adj relating to the theory that syndicates of

workers should seize the means of production

SYNDICS ▶ syndic

SYNDING, -S ▶ synd

SYNDROME *n* combination of symptoms indicating a particular disease

SYNDS ▶ synd

SYNE, -D, -S, SYNING *vb* rinse ▷ *n* rinse ▷ *adv* since

SYNECHIA *n* abnormality of the eye

SYNECTIC > synectics

SYNED ▶ syne

SYNEDRIA > synedrion

SYNERGIA *same as* ▶ synergy

SYNERGIC ▶ synergy

SYNERGID *n* type of cell in embryo

SYNERGY *n* collective effect that is greater than the sum of individual effects

SYNES ▶ syne

SYNESIS, SYNESES *n* grammatical construction in which the form of a word is conditioned by the meaning

SYNFUEL, -S *n* synthetic fuel

SYNGAMIC ▶ syngamy

SYNGAMY *n* reproduction involving the fusion of male and female gametes

SYNGAS, -ES *n* mixture of carbon monoxide and hydrogen

SYNGENIC *same as* > syngeneic

SYNGRAPH *n* document signed by several parties

SYNING ▶ syne

SYNKARYA > synkaryon

SYNOD, -S *n* church council

SYNODAL, -S *adj* of or relating to a synod ▷ *n* money paid to a bishop by less senior members of the clergy at a synod

SYNODIC *adj* involving conjunction of the same star, planet, or satellite

SYNODS ▶ synod

SYNONYM, -S *n* word with the same meaning as another

SYNONYME *same as* ▶ synonym

SYNONYMS ▶ synonym

SYNONYMY *n* study of synonyms

SYNOPSIS, SYNOPSES *n* summary or outline

SYNOPTIC *adj* of or relating to a synopsis ▷ *n* any of the three synoptic Gospels

SYNOVIA, -S *n* clear thick fluid that lubricates the body joints

SYNOVIAL *adj* of or relating to the synovia

SYNOVIAS ▶ synovia

SYNROC, -S *n* titanium-ceramic substance that can incorporate nuclear waste in its crystals

SYNTAGM, -S *same as* ▶ syntagma

SYNTAGMA *n* syntactic unit or a word or phrase forming a syntactic unit

SYNTAGMS ▶ syntagm

SYNTAN, -S *n* synthetic tanning substance

SYNTAX, -ES *n* way in which words are arranged to form phrases and sentences

SYNTENIC ▶ synteny

SYNTENY *n* presence of two or more genes on the same chromosome

SYNTEXIS *n* liquefaction

SYNTH, -S *n* type of electrophonic musical instrument operated by a keyboard and pedals

SYNTHASE *n* enzyme that catalyses a synthesis process

SYNTHON, -S *n* molecule used in synthesis

SYNTHPOP *n* pop music using synthesizers

SYNTHS ▶ synth

SYNTONE, -S *n* person who is syntonic

SYNTONIC *adj* emotionally in harmony with one's environment

SYNTONIN *n* substance in muscle

SYNTONY *n* matching of frequencies

SYNTYPE, -S *n* original specimen by which a new species is described

SYNURA, -E *n* variety of microbe

SYPE, -D, -S, SYPING *same as* ▶ sipe

SYPHER, -ED, -S *vb* lap (a chamfered edge) in order to form a flush surface

SYPHON, -ED, -S *same as* ▶ siphon

SYPHONAL *same as* ▶ siphonal

SYPHONED ▶ syphon

SYPHONIC *same as* ▶ siphonic

SYPHONS ▶ syphon

SYPING ▶ sype

SYRAH, -S *n* type of French red wine

SYREN, -S *same as* ▶ siren

SYRETTE, -S *n* small disposable syringe

SYRINGA, -S *n* mock orange or lilac

SYRINGE, -D *n* device for withdrawing or injecting fluids ▷ *vb* wash out or inject with a syringe

SYRINX, SYRINGES, -ES *n* vocal organ of a bird

SYRPHIAN *same as* ▶ syrphid

SYRPHID, -S *n* type of fly

SYRTIS, SYRTES *n* area of quicksand

SYRUP, -ED, -ING, -S *n* solution of sugar in water ▷ *vb* bring to the consistency of syrup

SYRUPIER ▶ syrupy

SYRUPING ▶ syrup

SYRUPS ▶ syrup

SYRUPY, SYRUPIER *adj* thick and sweet

SYSADMIN *n* computer system administrator

SYSOP, -S *n* person who runs a system or network

SYSSITIA *n* ancient Spartan communal meal

SYSTEM, -S *n* method or set of methods

SYSTEMED *adj* having system

SYSTEMIC *adj* affecting the entire animal or body ▷ *n* systemic pesticide, fungicide, etc

SYSTEMS ▶ system

SYSTOLE, -S *n* regular contraction of the heart as it pumps blood

SYSTOLIC ▶ systole

SYSTYLE, -S *n* building with different types of columns

SYTHE, -S *same as* ▶ sith

SYVER, -S *n* street drain or the grating over it

SYZYGAL ▶ syzygy

SYZYGIAL ▶ syzygy

SYZYGY, SYZYGIES *n* position of a celestial body when sun, earth, and the body are in line

S

Tt

T is one of the most common consonants in Scrabble. There are only four two-letter words that begin with **T**, but they are easy to remember as there is one for every vowel except **U**. Like **S**, **T** begins a number of three-letter words that don't use vowels, which are well worth remembering. These are: **thy** (6 points), **try** (6), **tsk** (7), **twp** (8) and **tyg** (7). There are also some useful three-letter words using **X**: **tax**, **tex**, **tix** and **tux** (10 each). If you have an **X** during a game, remember words like **text** (11), **texts** (12), **textile** (14), **textual** (14) and **texture** (14), **textism** (16) and **thanx** (15). Some of these have seven letters, and so will earn you 50-point bonuses if you use all your tiles to form them. Other threes well worth remembering are **tiz** (12) and **taj** (10).

TA, -S interj thank you ▷ n thank you

TAAL, -S n language: usually, by implication, Afrikaans

TAATA, -S n (in E Africa) father

This East African word for a father is one of those short words that can help you dispose of a surplus of As.

TAB, -BED, -S n small flap or projecting label ▷ vb supply with a tab

TABANID, -S n stout-bodied fly

TABARD, -S n short sleeveless tunic decorated with a coat of arms, worn in medieval times

TABARDED adj wearing a tabard

TABARDS ▸ tabard

TABARET, -S n hard-wearing fabric of silk or similar cloth with stripes of satin or moire

TABASHIR same as > tabasheer

TABBED ▸ tab

TABBIED ▸ tabby

TABBIER ▸ tabby

TABBIES ▸ tabby

TABBIEST ▸ tabby

TABBINET same as ▸ tabinet

TABBING, -S n act of supplying with tabs

TABBIS, -ES n silken cloth

TABBOULI same as > tabbouleh

TABBY, TABBIED, TABBIER, TABBIES, TABBIEST, -ING vb make (a material) appear wavy ▷ n female domestic cat ▷ adj brindled

TABEFY, TABEFIED, TABEFIES vb emaciate or become emaciated

TABER, -ED, -ING, -S old variant of ▸ tabor

TABERD, -S same as ▸ tabard

TABERDAR n holder of a scholarship at Queen's College, Oxford

TABERDS ▸ taberd

TABERED ▸ taber

TABERING ▸ taber

TABERS ▸ taber

TABES n wasting of a bodily organ or part

TABETIC, -S ▸ tabes

TABI, -S n thick-soled Japanese sock, worn with sandals

TABID adj emaciated

TABINET, -S n type of tabbied fabric

TABIS ▸ tabi

TABLA, -S n one of a pair of Indian drums played with the hands

TABLE, -D, -S n piece of furniture with a flat top supported by legs ▷ vb submit (a motion) for discussion by a meeting

TABLEAU, -S, -X n silent motionless group arranged to represent some scene

TABLED ▸ table

TABLEFUL ▸ table

TABLEMAT n small mat used for protecting the surface of a table from hot dishes

TABLES ▸ table

TABLET, -ED, -S n medicinal pill ▷ vb make (something) into a tablet

TABLETOP n upper surface of a table

TABLETS ▸ tablet

TABLIER, -S n (formerly) part of a dress resembling an apron

TABLING, -S ▸ table

TABLOID, -S n small-sized newspaper with many photographs

TABLOIDY adj characteristic of a tabloid newspaper; trashy

TABOGGAN same as ▸ toboggan

TABOO, -ED, -ING, -S n prohibition resulting from religious or social conventions ▷ adj forbidden by a taboo ▷ vb place under a taboo

TABOOLEY variant of > tabbouleh

TABOOS ▸ taboo

TABOR, -ED, -ING, -S n small drum ▷ vb play the tabor

TABORER, -S ▸ tabor

TABORET, -S n low stool, originally in the shape of a drum

TABORIN, -S same as ▸ taboret

TABORINE same as
▸**taborin**
TABORING ▸**tabor**
TABORINS ▸**taborin**
TABORS ▸**tabor**
TABOULEH variant of
> **tabbouleh**
TABOULI, -S same as
> **tabbouleh**
TABOUR, -ED, -S same as
▸**tabor**
TABOURER ▸**tabour**
TABOURET same as
▸**taboret**
TABOURIN same as
▸**taboret**
TABOURS ▸**tabour**
TABRERE, -S same as ▸**tabor**
TABRET, -S n smaller version
of a tabor
TABS ▸**tab**
TABU, -ED, -ING, -S same as
▸**taboo**
TABULA, -E n tablet for
writing on
TABULAR adj arranged in a
table
TABULATE vb arrange
(information) in a table ▹ adj
having a flat surface
TABULI, -S variant of
> **tabbouleh**
TABUN, -S n organic
compound used as a lethal
nerve gas
TABUS ▸**tabu**
TACAHOUT n abnormal
outgrowth on the tamarisk
plant
TACAN, -S n electronic
ultrahigh-frequency
navigation system for
aircraft
TACE, -S same as ▸**tasset**
TACET adv (in a musical
direction) indicating that an
instrument or singer does
not take part
TACH, -S n device for
measuring speed
TACHE, -S n buckle, clasp, or
hook
TACHINA n as in **tachina fly**
bristly face
TACHINID n type of fly
TACHISM, -S same as
▸**tachisme**
TACHISME n type of action
painting evolved in France
TACHISMS ▸**tachism**
TACHIST, -S ▸**tachism**
TACHISTE ▸**tachisme**
TACHISTS ▸**tachist**
TACHO, -S same as
> **tachogram**
TACHS ▸**tach**

TACHYON, -S n hypothetical
elementary particle
TACIT adj implied but not
spoken
TACITLY ▸**tacit**
TACITURN adj habitually
uncommunicative
TACK, -ED, -S n short nail
with a large head ▹ vb fasten
with tacks
TACKER, -S ▸**tack**
TACKET, -S n nail, esp a
hobnail
TACKETY adj studded with
tackets
TACKEY same as ▸**tacky**
TACKIER ▸**tacky**
TACKIES pl n S African word
for plimsolls
TACKIEST ▸**tacky**
TACKIFY vb give (eg rubber)
a sticky feel
TACKILY ▸**tacky**
TACKING, -S ▸**tack**
TACKLE, -D, -S, TACKLING
vb deal with (a task) ▹ n act
of tackling an opposing
player
TACKLER, -S ▸**tackle**
TACKLES ▸**tackle**
TACKLESS ▸**tack**
TACKLING ▸**tackle**
TACKS ▸**tack**
TACKSMAN, TACKSMEN n
leaseholder, esp a tenant in
the Highlands who sublets
TACKY, TACKIER, TACKIEST
adj slightly sticky
TACNODE, -S n point at
which two branches of a
curve have a common
tangent
TACO, -S n tortilla fried until
crisp, served with a filling
TACONITE, -S n fine-grained
sedimentary rock
TACOS ▸**taco**
TACRINE, -S n drug used to
treat Alzheimer's disease
TACT, -S n skill in avoiding
giving offence
TACTFUL ▸**tact**
TACTIC n method or plan to
achieve an end
TACTICAL adj of or
employing tactics
TACTICS n art of directing
military forces in battle
TACTILE adj of or having the
sense of touch
TACTION, -S n act of
touching
TACTISM, -S another word for
▸**taxis**
TACTLESS ▸**tact**
TACTS ▸**tact**

TACTUAL adj caused by
touch
TAD, -S n small bit or piece
TADDIE, -S short for
▸**tadpole**
TADPOLE, -S n limbless
tailed larva of a frog or toad
TADS ▸**tad**
TAE, -D, -ING, -S Scots form of
▸**toe**
TAEDIUM, -S archaic spelling
of ▸**tedium**
TAEING ▸**tae**
TAEL, -S n unit of weight,
used in East Asia
TAENIA, -E, -S n (in ancient
Greece) a narrow fillet or
headband for the hair
TAENIATE adj ribbon-like
TAENIOID adj ribbon-like
TAENITE, -S n nickel-iron
alloy found in meteorites
TAES ▸**tae**
TAFFAREL same as ▸**taffrail**
TAFFEREL same as ▸**taffrail**
TAFFETA n shiny silk or
rayon fabric
TAFFETAS same as ▸**taffeta**
TAFFETY adj made of taffeta
TAFFIA, -S same as ▸**tafia**
TAFFIES ▸**taffy**
TAFFRAIL n rail at the back
of a ship or boat
TAFFY, TAFFIES same as
▸**toffee**
TAFIA, -S n type of rum, esp
from Guyana or the
Caribbean
**TAG, -GED, -GING, -GINGS,
-S** n label bearing
information ▹ vb attach a
tag to
TAGALONG n one who trails
behind, esp uninvited; a
hanger-on
TAGAREEN n junk shop
TAGBOARD n sturdy form of
cardboard
TAGETES n any of a genus of
plants with yellow or orange
flowers
TAGGANT, -S n microscopic
material added to substance
to identify it
TAGGED ▸**tag**
TAGGEE, -S n one who has
been made to wear a tag
TAGGER, -S n one who
marks with a tag
TAGGIER ▸**taggy**
TAGGIEST ▸**taggy**
TAGGING ▸**tag**
TAGGINGS ▸**tag**
TAGGY, TAGGIER, TAGGIEST
adj (of wool, hair, etc)
matted

T

TAGHAIRM n form of divination once practised in the Highlands of Scotland

TAGINE, -S n large, heavy N African cooking pot

TAGLESS adj having no tag

TAGLIKE adj resembling a tag

TAGLINE, -S n funny line of a joke

TAGLIONI n type of coat

TAGMA, -TA n distinct region of the body of an arthropod

TAGMEME, -S n class of speech elements all of which may fulfil the same grammatical role

TAGMEMIC ▶tagmeme

TAGRAG, -S same as ▶ ragtag

TAGS ▶tag

TAGUAN, -S n nocturnal flying squirrel

TAHA, -S n type of South African bird

TAHINA, -S same as ▶tahini

TAHINI, -S n paste made from ground sesame seeds

TAHR, -S n goatlike mammal of mountainous regions of S and SW Asia

TAHSIL, -S n administrative division of a zila in certain states in India

TAI, -S n type of sea bream

TAIAHA, -S n carved weapon in the form of a staff, now used in Māori ceremonial oratory

TAIGA, -S n belt of coniferous forest

TAIGLACH same as ▶teiglach

TAIGLE, -D, -S, TAIGLING vb entangle or impede

TAIHOA, -ED, -S vb in New Zealand English, wait

TAIKO, -S n large Japanese drum

TAIL, -ED n rear part of an animal's body, usu having a flexible appendage ▷ adj at the rear ▷ vb follow (someone) secretly

TAILARD, -S n one having a tail

TAILBACK n queue of traffic stretching back from an obstruction

TAILBONE nontechnical name for ▶ coccyx

TAILCOAT n man's black coat with a tapering tail

TAILED ▶tail

TAILER, -S n one that tails

TAILERON n aileron located on the tailplane of an aircraft

TAILERS ▶tailer

TAILFAN, -S n fanned structure at the hind end of a lobster

TAILFIN, -S n decorative projection at the back of a car

TAILFLY n in angling, the lowest fly on a wet-fly cast

TAILGATE n door at the rear of a hatchback vehicle ▷ vb drive very close behind (a vehicle)

TAILHOOK n hook on an aircraft that catches a braking cable

TAILING n part of a beam, rafter, projecting brick or stone, etc, embedded in a wall

TAILINGS pl n waste left over after milling processes

TAILLAMP n rear light

TAILLE, -S n (in France before 1789) a tax levied by a king or overlord on his subjects

TAILLESS ▶tail

TAILLEUR n woman's suit

TAILLIE, -S n (in Scots law) the limitation of an estate or interest to a person and their heirs

TAILLIKE adj resembling a tail

TAILOR, -ED, -S n person who makes men's clothes ▷ vb cut or style (a garment) to specific requirements

TAILPIPE vb attach an object, esp a tin can, to the tail of an animal

TAILRACE n channel that carries water away from a water wheel, turbine, etc

TAILS adv with the side of a coin that does not have a portrait of a head on it uppermost

TAILSKID n runner under the tail of an aircraft

TAILSPIN, TAILSPUN n uncontrolled spinning dive of an aircraft ▷ vb go into a tailspin

TAILWIND n wind coming from the rear

TAILYE, -S same as ▶taillie

TAILZIE, -S same as ▶taillie

TAIN, -S n tinfoil used in backing mirrors

TAINT, -ED, -ING, -S vb spoil with a small amount of decay or other bad quality ▷ n something that taints

TAINTURE n contamination; staining

TAIPAN, -S n large poisonous Australian snake

TAIRA, -S same as ▶ tayra

TAIS ▶tai

TAISCH, -ES n (in Scotland) apparition of a person whose death is imminent

TAISH, -ES same as ▶taisch

TAIT, -S same as ▶tate

TAIVER, -ED, -S same as ▶taver

TAIVERT adj Scots word meaning confused or bewildered

TAJ, -ES n tall conical cap worn as a mark of distinction by Muslims

This is one of the key words to remember for using the J.

TAJINE, -S same as ▶ tagine

TAK, -S Scots variant spelling of ▶take

TAKA, -S n standard monetary unit of Bangladesh, divided into 100 paise

TAKABLE ▶take

TAKAHE, -S n very rare flightless New Zealand bird

TAKAMAKA same as > tacamahac

TAKAS ▶taka

TAKE, -N, -S, TOOK vb remove from a place ▷ n one of a series of recordings from which the best will be used

TAKEABLE ▶take

TAKEAWAY adj (of food) sold for consumption away from the premises ▷ n shop or restaurant selling meals for eating elsewhere

TAKEDOWN n disassembly

TAKEN ▶take

TAKEOFF, -S n act or process of making an aircraft airborne

TAKEOUT, -S n shop or restaurant that sells such food

TAKEOVER n act of taking control of a company by buying a large number of its shares

TAKER, -S n person who agrees to take something that is offered

TAKES ▶take

TAKEUP, -S n claiming or acceptance of something that is due or available

TAKHI, -S n type of wild Mongolian horse

TAKI, -S same as ▶takhi

TAKIER ▸taky
TAKIEST ▸taky
TAKIN, -S n bovid mammal of mountainous regions of S Asia
TAKING, -S ▸take
TAKINGLY ▸take
TAKINGS ▸taking
TAKINS ▸takin
TAKIS ▸taki
TAKKIES ▸takky
TAKKY n S African word for plimsoll
TAKS ▸tak
TAKY, TAKIER, TAKIEST adj appealing
TALA, -S n standard monetary unit of Samoa, divided into 100 sene
TALAK, -S same as ▸talaq
TALANT, -S old variant of ▸talon
TALAPOIN n smallest of the guenon monkeys
TALAQ, -S n Muslim form of divorce

In Islamic law, a word for divorce: easy to miss because one tends not to think of words ending in Q.

TALAR, -S n ankle-length robe
TALARIA pl n winged sandals, such as those worn by Hermes
TALARS ▸talar
TALAS ▸tala
TALAUNT, -S old variant of ▸talon
TALAYOT, -S n ancient Balearic stone tower
TALBOT, -S n ancient breed of large hound
TALC, -ED, -ING, -KED, -KING, -S n talcum powder ▷ vb apply talc to ▷ adj of, or relating to, talc
TALCIER ▸talcy
TALCIEST ▸talcy
TALCING ▸talc
TALCKED ▸talc
TALCKIER ▸talcky
TALCKING ▸talc
TALCKY, TALCKIER same as ▸talcy
TALCOSE ▸talc
TALCOUS ▸talc
TALCS ▸talc
TALCUM, -ED, -S n white, grey, brown, or pale green mineral ▷ vb apply talcum to
TALCY, TALCIER, TALCIEST adj like, containing, or covered in talc
TALE n story

TALEA, -E n rhythmic pattern in certain mediaeval choral compositions
TALEFUL adj having many tales
TALEGGIO n Italian cheese
TALENT, -S n natural ability
TALENTED ▸talent
TALENTS ▸talent
TALER, -S same as ▸thaler
TALES n group of persons summoned to fill vacancies on a jury panel
TALESMAN, TALESMEN ▸tales
TALEYSIM ▸tallith
TALI ▸talus
TALION, -S n principle of making punishment correspond to the crime
TALIONIC adj of or relating to talion
TALIONS ▸talion
TALIPAT, -S same as ▸talipot
TALIPED, -S adj having a club foot ▷ n club-footed person
TALIPES n congenital deformity of the foot by which it is twisted in any of various positions
TALIPOT, -S n palm tree of East India
TALISMAN n object believed to have magic power
TALK, -ED, -S vb express ideas or feelings by means of speech ▷ n speech or lecture
TALKABLE ▸talk
TALKBACK n broadcast in which telephone comments or questions from the public are transmitted live
TALKBOX n voice box
TALKED ▸talk
TALKER, -S ▸talk
TALKFEST n lengthy discussion
TALKIE, -S n early film with a soundtrack
TALKIER ▸talky
TALKIES ▸talkie
TALKIEST ▸talky
TALKING, -S n speech; the act of speaking
TALKS ▸talk
TALKTIME n length of time a mobile phone can be used before its battery runs out
TALKY, TALKIER, TALKIEST adj containing too much dialogue or inconsequential talk
TALL, -ER, -EST, -S adj higher than average

TALLAGE, -D, -S n tax levied on Crown lands and royal towns ▷ vb levy a tax (upon)
TALLAT, -S same as ▸tallet
TALLBOY, -S n high chest of drawers
TALLENT, -S n archaic word meaning abundance
TALLER ▸tall
TALLEST ▸tall
TALLET, -S n loft
TALLIATE vb levy a tax
TALLIED ▸tally
TALLIER, -S ▸tally
TALLIES ▸tally
TALLIS, -ES, -IM variant of ▸tallith
TALLISH adj quite tall
TALLISIM ▸tallis
TALLIT, -ES, -IM, -OT, -S variant of ▸tallith
TALLITH, TALEYSIM, -S n shawl worn by Jewish males during religious services
TALLITIM ▸tallit
TALLITOT ▸tallit
TALLITS ▸tallit
TALLNESS ▸tall
TALLOL, -S n oily liquid used for making soaps, lubricants, etc
TALLOT, -S same as ▸tallet
TALLOW, -ED, -S n hard animal fat used to make candles ▷ vb cover or smear with tallow
TALLOWY adj like tallow
TALLS ▸tall
TALLY, TALLIED, TALLIES, -ING vb (of two things) correspond ▷ n record of a debt or score
TALLYHO, -S n cry to encourage hounds when the quarry is sighted ▷ vb make the cry of tallyho
TALLYING ▸tally
TALLYMAN, TALLYMEN n male scorekeeper or recorder
TALMA, -S n short cloak
TALMUD, -S n primary source of Jewish religious law, consisting of the Mishnah and the Gemara
TALMUDIC ▸talmud
TALMUDS ▸talmud
TALON, -S n bird's hooked claw
TALONED ▸talon
TALONS ▸talon
TALOOKA, -S same as ▸taluk
TALPA, -E, -S n sebaceous cyst
TALUK, -S n subdivision of a district

TALUKA, -S same as ▸**taluk**

TALUKDAR n person in charge of a taluk

TALUKS ▸**taluk**

TALUS, TALI, -ES n bone of the ankle that articulates with the leg bones to form the ankle joint

TALWEG, -S same as ▸**thalweg**

TAM, -S n type of hat

TAMABLE ▸**tame**

TAMAL, -S same as ▸**tamale**

TAMALE, -S n Mexican dish of minced meat wrapped in maize husks and steamed

TAMALS ▸**tamal**

TAMANDU, -S same as ▸**tamandua**

TAMANDUA n small arboreal edentate mammal

TAMANDUS ▸**tamandu**

TAMANOIR n anteater

TAMANU, -S n poon tree

TAMARA, -S n powder consisting of cloves, cinnamon, fennel, coriander, etc

TAMARACK n North American larch

TAMARAO, -S same as ▸**tamarau**

TAMARAS ▸**tamara**

TAMARAU, -S n small rare member of a cattle tribe in the Philippines

TAMARI, -S n Japanese variety of soy sauce

TAMARIN, -S n small monkey of South and Central America

TAMARIND n tropical tree

TAMARINS ▸**tamarin**

TAMARIS ▸**tamari**

TAMARISK n evergreen shrub with slender branches and feathery flower clusters

TAMASHA, -S n (in India) a show

TAMBAC, -S same as ▸**tombac**

TAMBAK, -S same as ▸**tombac**

TAMBALA, -S n unit of Malawian currency

TAMBER, -S same as ▸**timbre**

TAMBOUR, -S n embroidery frame consisting of two hoops ▷ vb embroider (fabric or a design) on a tambour

TAMBOURA n stringed instrument used in Indian music

TAMBOURS ▸**tambour**

TAMBUR, -S n old Turkish stringed instrument

TAMBURA, -S n Middle-Eastern stringed instrument with a long neck

TAMBURIN n Spenserian form of 'tambourine'

TAMBURS ▸**tambur**

TAME, -D, -S, -ST adj (of animals) brought under human control ▷ vb make tame

TAMEABLE ▸**tame**

TAMED ▸**tame**

TAMEIN, -S n Burmese skirt

TAMELESS ▸**tame**

TAMELY ▸**tame**

TAMENESS ▸**tame**

TAMER, -S ▸**tame**

TAMES ▸**tame**

TAMEST ▸**tame**

TAMIN, -S n thin woollen fabric

TAMINE, -S same as ▸**tamin**

TAMING, -S n act of making (something) tame

TAMINS ▸**tamin**

TAMIS, -ES same as ▸**tammy**

TAMISE n type of thin cloth

TAMISES ▸**tamis**

TAMMAR, -S n small scrub wallaby

TAMMIE, -S n short for tam-o'shanter, a traditional Scottish hat

TAMMIED ▸**tammy**

TAMMIES ▸**tammie**

TAMMY, TAMMIED, -ING n glazed woollen or mixed fabric ▷ vb strain (sauce, soup, etc) through a tammy

TAMP, -ED, -S vb pack down by repeated taps

TAMPALA, -S n Asian plant, eaten as food

TAMPAN, -S n biting mite

TAMPED ▸**tamp**

TAMPER, -ED, -S vb interfere ▷ n person or thing that tamps

TAMPERER ▸**tamper**

TAMPERS ▸**tamper**

TAMPING, -S adj very angry ▷ n act or instance of tamping

TAMPION, -S n plug placed in a gun's muzzle to keep out moisture and dust

TAMPON, -ED, -S n plug of cotton wool inserted into a wound or body cavity to absorb blood ▷ vb use a tampon

TAMPS ▸**tamp**

TAMS ▸**tam**

TAMWORTH n any of a hardy rare breed of long-bodied reddish pigs

TAN, -NED, -NEST, -S n brown coloration of the skin from exposure to sunlight ▷ vb (of skin) go brown from exposure to sunlight ▷ adj yellowish-brown

TANA, -S n small Madagascan lemur

TANADAR, -S n commanding officer of an Indian police station

TANAGER, -S n American songbird with a short thick bill

TANAGRA, -S n type of tanager

TANAISTE n deputy prime minister of the Republic of Ireland

TANAS ▸**tana**

TANBARK, -S n bark of certain trees, esp the oak and hemlock, used as a source of tannin

TANDEM, -S n bicycle for two riders, one behind the other

TANDOOR, -S n type of Indian clay oven

TANDOORI adj (of food) cooked in an Indian clay oven ▷ n Indian method of cooking meat or vegetables on a spit in a clay oven

TANDOORS ▸**tandoor**

TANE old Scottish variant of ▸**taken**

TANG, -ED, -ING, -S n strong taste or smell ▷ vb cause to ring

TANGA, -S n triangular loincloth worn by indigenous peoples in tropical America

TANGED ▸**tang**

TANGELO, -S n hybrid produced by crossing a tangerine tree with a grapefruit tree

TANGENCE n touching

TANGENCY ▸**tangent**

TANGENT, -S n line that touches a curve without intersecting it

TANGHIN, -S n poison formerly used in Madagascar to determine the guilt of crime suspects

TANGI, -S n Māori funeral ceremony

TANGIBLE adj able to be touched ▷ n tangible thing or asset

TANGIBLY ▸ tangible

TANGIE, -S *n* water spirit of Orkney, appearing as a figure draped in seaweed, or as a seahorse

TANGIER ▸ tangy

TANGIES ▸ tangie

TANGIEST ▸ tangy

TANGING ▸ tang

TANGIS ▸ tangi

TANGLE, -D, -S *n* confused mass or situation ▷ *vb* twist together in a tangle

TANGLER, -S ▸ tangle

TANGLES ▸ tangle

TANGLIER ▸ tangly

TANGLING *n* act or condition of tangling

TANGLY, TANGLIER ▸ tangle

TANGO, -ED, -ES, -ING, -S *n* S American dance ▷ *vb* dance a tango

TANGOIST ▸ tango

TANGOS ▸ tango

TANGRAM, -S *n* type of Chinese puzzle

TANGS ▸ tang

TANGUN, -S *n* small and sturdy Tibetan pony

TANGY, TANGIER, TANGIEST *adj* having a pungent, fresh, or briny flavour or aroma

TANH, -S *n* hyperbolic tangent

TANIST, -S *n* heir apparent of a Celtic chieftain

TANISTRY ▸ tanist

TANISTS ▸ tanist

TANIWHA, -S *n* mythical Māori monster that lives in water

TANK, -ED, -S *n* container for liquids or gases ▷ *vb* put or keep in a tank

TANKA, -S *n* Japanese verse form consisting of five lines

TANKAGE, -S *n* capacity or contents of a tank or tanks

TANKARD, -S *n* large beer-mug, often with a hinged lid

TANKAS ▸ tanka

TANKED ▸ tank

TANKER, -ED, -S *n* ship or truck for carrying liquid in bulk ▷ *vb* transport by means of a tanker

TANKFUL, -S *n* quantity contained in a tank

TANKIA, -S *n* type of boat used in Canton

TANKIES ▸ tanky

TANKING, -S *n* heavy defeat

TANKINI, -S *n* swimming costume consisting of a camisole top and bikini briefs

TANKLESS ▸ tank

TANKLIKE ▸ tank

TANKS ▸ tank

TANKSHIP *same as* ▸ **tanker**

TANKY, TANKIES *n* die-hard communist

TANLING, -S *n* suntanned person

TANNA, -S *n* Indian police station or army base

TANNABLE ▸ tan

TANNAGE, -S *n* act or process of tanning

TANNAH, -S *same as* ▸ **tanna**

TANNAS ▸ tanna

TANNATE, -S *n* any salt or ester of tannic acid

TANNED ▸ tan

TANNER, -S ▸ tan

TANNERY *n* place where hides are tanned

TANNEST ▸ tan

TANNIC *adj* of, containing, or produced from tannin or tannic acid

TANNIE, -S *n* in S Africa, title of respect used to refer to an elderly woman

TANNIN, -S *n* vegetable substance used in tanning

TANNING, -S ▸ tan

TANNINS ▸ tannin

TANNISH ▸ tan

TANNOY, -ED, -S *n* sound-amplifying apparatus used as a public-address system ▷ *vb* announce (something) using a Tannoy system

TANREC, -S *same as* ▸ **tenrec**

TANS ▸ tan

TANSY, TANSIES *n* yellow-flowered plant

TANTALIC *adj* of or containing tantalum, esp in the pentavalent state

TANTALUM *n* hard greyish-white metallic element

TANTALUS *n* case in which bottles of drink are locked with their contents tantalizingly visible

TANTARA, -S *n* blast, as on a trumpet or horn

TANTI *adj* old word for worthwhile

TANTIES ▸ tanty

TANTIVY *adv* at full speed ▷ *n* hunting cry, esp at full gallop

TANTO, -S *adv* too much ▷ *n* type of Japanese sword

TANTONY *n* runt

TANTOS ▸ tanto

TANTRA, -S *n* sacred books of Tantrism

TANTRIC ▸ tantra

TANTRISM *n* teaching of tantra

TANTRIST *n* person who practises or teaches tantrism

TANTRUM, -S *n* childish outburst of temper

TANTY, TANTIES *n* tantrum

TANUKI, -S *n* animal similar to a raccoon, found in Japan

TANYARD, -S *n* part of a tannery

TAO, -S *n* (in Confucian philosophy) the correct course of action

TAONGA, -S *n* New Zealand word meaning treasure

TAOS ▸ tao

TAP, -PED, -PING, -PINGS, -S *vb* knock lightly and usu repeatedly ▷ *n* light knock

TAPA *n* inner bark of the paper mulberry

TAPACOLO *n* small bird of Chile and Argentina

TAPACULO *same as* ▸ **tapacolo**

TAPADERA *n* leather covering for the stirrup on an American saddle

TAPADERO *same as* ▸ **tapadera**

TAPALO, -S *n* Latin American scarf, often patterned and brightly coloured

TAPAS *pl n* (in Spanish cookery) light snacks or appetizers

TAPE, -D, -S *n* narrow long strip of material ▷ *vb* (formerly) record on magnetic tape

TAPEABLE ▸ tape

TAPED ▸ tape

TAPELESS ▸ tape

TAPELIKE ▸ tape

TAPELINE *n* tape used for measuring and fitting garments

TAPEN *adj* made of tape

TAPENADE *n* savoury paste made from capers, olives, and anchovies, with olive oil and lemon juice

TAPER, -ED, -S ▸ tape

TAPERER, -S ▸ tape

TAPERING ▸ tape

TAPERS ▸ taper

TAPES ▸ tape

TAPESTRY n fabric decorated with coloured woven designs ▷ vb portray in tapestry

TAPET, -ED, -ING, -S n example of tapestry ▷ vb decorate with tapestries

TAPETA ▶ **tapetum**

TAPETAL ▶ **tapetum**

TAPETED ▶ **tapet**

TAPETI, -S n forest rabbit of Brazil

TAPETING ▶ **tapet**

TAPETIS ▶ **tapeti**

TAPETS ▶ **tapet**

TAPETUM, TAPETA, -S n layer of nutritive cells that surrounds developing spore cells

TAPEWORM n long flat parasitic worm living in the intestines of vertebrates

TAPHOLE, -S n hole in a furnace for running off molten metal or slag

TAPHOUSE n inn or bar

TAPING, -S n act of taping

TAPIOCA, -S n beadlike starch made from cassava root

TAPIR, -S n piglike mammal of tropical America and SE Asia, with a long snout

TAPIROID ▶ **tapir**

TAPIRS ▶ **tapir**

TAPIS, -ES n tapestry or carpeting

TAPIST, -S n person who records printed matter in an audio format

TAPLASH n dregs of beer

TAPLESS adj without a tap

TAPPA, -S same as ▶ **tapa**

TAPPABLE ▶ **tap**

TAPPAS ▶ **tappa**

TAPPED ▶ **tap**

TAPPER, -S n person who taps

TAPPET, -S n short steel rod in an engine, transferring motion from one part to another

TAPPICE, -D, -S vb hide

TAPPING ▶ **tap**

TAPPINGS ▶ **tap**

TAPPIT adj crested; topped

TAPROOM, -S n public bar in a hotel or pub

TAPROOT, -S n main root of a plant, growing straight down

TAPS ▶ **tap**

TAPSMAN, TAPSMEN n old word for a barman

TAPSTER, -S n bartender

TAPSTRY adj relating to tapestry ▷ n taproom in a public house

TAPU, -ED, -ING, -S adj sacred ▷ n Māori religious or superstitious restriction on something ▷ vb put a tapu on something

TAQUERIA n restaurant specializing in tacos

TAR, -RED, -RING, -RINGS, -S n thick black liquid distilled from coal etc ▷ vb coat with tar

TARA, -S same as ▶ **taro**

TARABISH n type of card game

TARAIRE, -S n type of New Zealand tree

TARAKIHI n common edible sea fish of New Zealand waters

TARAMA, -S n cod roe

TARAMEA, -S n variety of New Zealand speargrass

TARAND, -S n northern animal of legend, now supposed to have been the reindeer

TARANTAS same as > **tarantass**

TARAS ▶ **tara**

TARBOOSH n brimless cap formerly worn by Muslim men

TARBOUSH same as ▶ **tarboosh**

TARBOY, -S n boy who applies tar to the skin of sheep cut during shearing

TARBUSH same as ▶ **tarboosh**

TARCEL, -S same as ▶ **tercel**

TARDIED ▶ **tardy**

TARDIER ▶ **tardy**

TARDIES ▶ **tardy**

TARDIEST ▶ **tardy**

TARDILY ▶ **tardy**

TARDIVE adj tending to develop late

TARDO adj (of music) slow; to be played slowly

TARDY, TARDIED, TARDIER, TARDIES, TARDIEST, -ING adj slow or late ▷ vb delay or impede (something or someone)

TARDYON, -S n particle travelling more slowly than the speed of light

TARE, -D, -S, TARING, TARINGS n weight of the wrapping or container of goods ▷ vb weigh (a package, etc) in order to calculate the amount of tare

TARGA, -S n as in **targa top** denotes removable hard roof on a car

TARGE, -D, -S, TARGING vb interrogate

TARGET, -ED, -S n object or person a missile is aimed at ▷ vb aim for direct

TARGING ▶ **targe**

TARIFF, -ED, -S n tax levied on imports ▷ vb impose punishment for a criminal offence

TARING ▶ **tare**

TARINGS ▶ **tare**

TARLATAN n open-weave cotton fabric, used for stiffening garments

TARLETAN same as ▶ **tarlatan**

TARMAC, -S same as ▶ **macadam**

TARN, -S n small mountain lake

TARNAL adj damned ▷ adv extremely

TARNALLY ▶ **tarnal**

TARNISH vb make or become stained or less bright ▷ n discoloration or blemish

TARNS ▶ **tarn**

TARO, -S n plant with a large edible rootstock

TAROC, -S old variant of ▶ **tarot**

TAROK, -S old variant of ▶ **tarot**

TAROS ▶ **taro**

TAROT, -S n special pack of cards used mainly in fortune-telling ▷ adj relating to tarot cards

TARP, -S informal word for > **tarpaulin**

TARPAN, -S n European wild horse common in prehistoric times

TARPAPER n paper coated or impregnated with tar

TARPON, -S n large silvery clupeoid game fish found in warm Atlantic waters

TARPS ▶ **tarp**

TARRAGON n aromatic herb

TARRAS, -ES same as ▶ **trass**

TARRE, -S vb old word meaning to provoke or goad

TARRED ▶ **tar**

TARRES ▶ **tarre**

TARRIED ▶ **tarry**

TARRIER, -S ▶ **tarry**

TARRIES ▶ **tarry**

TARRIEST ▶ **tarry**

TARRING ▶ **tar**

TARRINGS ▶ **tar**

TARROCK, -S *n* seabird

TARROW, -ED, -S *vb* exhibit reluctance

TARRY, TARRIED, TARRIES, TARRIEST, -ING *vb* linger or delay ▷ *adj* covered in or resembling tar

TARS ▸ **tar**

TARSAL, -S *adj* of the tarsus or tarsi ▷ *n* tarsal bone

TARSEAL, -S *n* bitumen surface of a road

TARSEL, -S *same as* ▸ **tercel**

TARSI ▸ **tarsus**

TARSIA, -S *another term for* ▸ **intarsia**

TARSIER, -S *n* small nocturnal primate

TARSIOID *adj* resembling a tarsier ▷ *n* type of fossil

TARSIPED *n* generic term for a number of marsupials

TARSUS, TARSI *n* bones of the heel and ankle collectively

TART, -ED, -ER, -EST, -ING, -S *n* pie or flan with a sweet filling ▷ *adj* sharp or bitter ▷ *vb* (of food, drink, etc) become tart (sour)

TARTAN, -S *n* design of straight lines crossing at right angles

TARTANA, -S *n* small Mediterranean sailing boat

TARTANE, -S *same as* ▸ **tartana**

TARTANED ▸ **tartan**

TARTANES ▸ **tartane**

TARTANRY *n* excessive use of Scottish imagery to produce a distorted sentimental view of Scotland

TARTANS ▸ **tartan**

TARTAR, -S *n* hard deposit on the teeth

TARTARE, -S *n* mayonnaise sauce mixed with hard-boiled egg yolks, herbs, etc

TARTARIC *adj* of or derived from tartar or tartaric acid

TARTARLY *adj* resembling a tartar

TARTARS ▸ **tartar**

TARTED ▸ **tart**

TARTER ▸ **tart**

TARTEST ▸ **tart**

TARTINE, -S *n* slice of bread with butter or jam spread on it

TARTING ▸ **tart**

TARTISH ▸ **tart**

TARTLET, -S *n* individual pastry case with a filling of

fruit or other sweet or savoury mixture

TARTLY ▸ **tart**

TARTNESS ▸ **tart**

TARTRATE *n* any salt or ester of tartaric acid

TARTS ▸ **tart**

TARTUFE, -S *same as* ▸ **tartuffe**

TARTUFFE *n* person who hypocritically pretends to be deeply pious

TARTUFO, TARTUFI, -S *n* Italian mousse-like chocolate dessert

TARWEED, -S *n* resinous Californian plant

TARWHINE *n* bream of E Australia, silver in colour with gold streaks

TARZAN, -S *n* man with great physical strength

TAS ▸ **ta**

TASAR, -S *same as* ▸ **tussore**

TASBIH, -S *n* form of Islamic prayer

TASE, -D, -S, TASING *vb* stun with a taser gun

TASER, -ED, -ING, -S *vb* use a taser stun gun on (someone)

TASES ▸ **tase**

TASH, -ED, -ES, -ING *vb* stain or besmirch

TASING ▸ **tase**

TASK, -ED, -ING, -INGS, -S *n* piece of work to be done ▷ *vb* give someone a task to do

TASKBAR, -S *n* area of computer screen showing what programs are running

TASKED ▸ **task**

TASKER, -S ▸ **task**

TASKING ▸ **task**

TASKINGS ▸ **task**

TASKLESS ▸ **task**

TASKS ▸ **task**

TASKWORK *n* hard or unpleasant work

TASLET, -S *same as* ▸ **tasset**

TASS *n* cup, goblet, or glass

TASSA, -S *n* type of Indian kettledrum

TASSE, -S *same as* ▸ **tasset**

TASSEL, -ED, -S *n* decorative fringed knot of threads ▷ *vb* adorn with a tassel or tassels

TASSELL, -S *same as* ▸ **tassel**

TASSELLY *adj* adorned with tassels

TASSELS ▸ **tassel**

TASSELY *adj* decorated with tassels

TASSES ▸ **tasse**

TASSET, -S *n* piece of armour to protect the thigh

TASSIE, -S *same as* ▸ **tass**

TASSO, -S *n* spicy cured pork cut into strips

TASSWAGE *vb* archaic contraction of 'to assuage'

TASTABLE ▸ **taste**

TASTE, -D, -S, TASTING, TASTINGS *n* sense by which the flavour of a substance is distinguished ▷ *vb* distinguish the taste of (a substance)

TASTEFUL *adj* having or showing good taste

TASTER, -S *n* person employed to test the quality of food or drink by tasting it

TASTES ▸ **taste**

TASTEVIN *n* small shallow cup for wine tasting

TASTIER ▸ **tasty**

TASTIEST ▸ **tasty**

TASTILY ▸ **tasty**

TASTING ▸ **taste**

TASTINGS ▸ **taste**

TASTY, TASTIER, TASTIEST *adj* pleasantly flavoured

TAT, -S, -TED *n* tatty or tasteless articles ▷ *vb* make (something) by tatting

TATAHASH *n* stew containing potatoes and cheap cuts of meat

TATAMI, -S *n* thick rectangular mat of woven straw

TATAR, -S *n* brutal person

TATE, -S *n* small tuft of fibre

TATER, -S *n* potato

TATES ▸ **tate**

TATH, -ED, -ING, -S *vb* (of cattle) to defecate

TATHATA, -S *n* (in Buddhism) ultimate nature of things

TATHED ▸ **tath**

TATHING ▸ **tath**

TATHS ▸ **tath**

TATIE, -S *same as* ▸ **tattie**

TATLER, -S *old variant of* ▸ **tattler**

TATOU, -S *n* armadillo

TATOUAY, -S *n* large armadillo of South America

TATOUS ▸ **tatou**

TATS ▸ **tat**

TATSOI, -S *n* variety of Chinese cabbage

TATT, -S *same as* ▸ **tat**

TATTED ▸ **tat**

TATTER, -ED, -S *vb* make or become torn

TATTERY *adj* ragged

TATTIE, -S *Scot or dialect word for* ▸ **potato**

TATTIER ▸ **tatty**

TATTIES ▸ **tattie**

TATTIEST ▸ **tatty**

TATTILY ▸ tatty

TATTING, -S ▸ tat

TATTLE, -D, -S, TATTLING n gossip or chatter ▷ vb gossip or chatter

TATTLER, -S n person who tattles

TATTLES ▸ tattle

TATTLING ▸ tattle

TATTOO, -ED, -S n pattern made on the body by pricking the skin and staining it with indelible inks ▷ vb make such a pattern on the skin

TATTOOER, -S ▸ tattoo

TATTOOS ▸ tattoo

TATTOW, -ED, -S old variant of ▸ tattoo

TATTS ▸ tatt

TATTY, TATTIER, TATTIEST adj worn out, shabby, tawdry, or unkempt

TATU, -ED, -ING, -S old variant of ▸ tattoo

TAU, -S n 19th letter in the Greek alphabet

TAUBE, -S n type of obsolete German aeroplane

TAUGHT ▸ teach

TAUHINU, -S New Zealand name for ▸ poplar

TAUHOU, -S same as > silvereye

TAUIWI, -S n Māori term for the non-Māori people of New Zealand

TAULD vb old Scots variant of told

TAUNT, -ED, -S vb tease with jeers ▷ n jeering remark ▷ adj (of the mast or masts of a sailing vessel) unusually tall

TAUNTER, -S ▸ taunt

TAUNTING ▸ taunt

TAUNTS ▸ taunt

TAUON, -S n negatively charged elementary particle

TAUPATA, -S n New Zealand shrub or tree

TAUPE, -S adj brownish-grey ▷ n brownish-grey colour

TAUPIE, -S same as ▸ tawpie

TAUREAN adj born under or characteristic of Taurus

TAURIC same as ▸ taurean

TAURINE, -S adj of, relating to, or resembling a bull ▷ n substance obtained from the bile of animals

TAUS ▸ tau

TAUT, -ED, -ER, -EST, -ING, -S adj drawn tight ▷ vb Scots word meaning to tangle

TAUTAUG, -S same as ▸ tautog

TAUTED ▸ taut

TAUTEN, -ED, -S vb make or become taut

TAUTER ▸ taut

TAUTEST ▸ taut

TAUTING ▸ taut

TAUTIT adj Scots word meaning tangled

TAUTLY ▸ taut

TAUTNESS ▸ taut

TAUTOG, -S n large dark-coloured wrasse, used as a food fish

TAUTOMER n either of the two forms of a chemical compound that exhibits tautomerism

TAUTONYM n taxonomic name in which the generic and specific components are the same

TAUTS ▸ taut

TAV, -S n 23rd and last letter in the Hebrew alphabet

TAVA, -S n thick Indian frying pan

TAVAH, -S variant of ▸ tava

TAVAS ▸ tava

TAVER, -ED, -ING, -S vb wander about

TAVERN, -S n pub

TAVERNA, -S n Greek restaurant

TAVERNER n keeper of a tavern

TAVERNS ▸ tavern

TAVERS ▸ taver

TAVERT adj bewildered or confused

TAVS ▸ tav

TAW, -ED, -ING, -INGS vb convert skins into leather

TAWA, -S n tall timber tree from New Zealand

TAWAI, -S n New Zealand beech

TAWAS ▸ tawa

TAWDRIER ▸ tawdry

TAWDRIES ▸ tawdry

TAWDRILY ▸ tawdry

TAWDRY, TAWDRIER, TAWDRIES adj cheap, showy, and of poor quality ▷ n gaudy finery of poor quality

TAWED ▸ taw

TAWER, -S ▸ taw

TAWERIES ▸ tawery

TAWERS ▸ tawer

TAWERY, TAWERIES n place where tawing is carried out

TAWHAI, -S same as ▸ tawai

TAWHIRI, -S n small New Zealand tree with wavy green glossy leaves

TAWIE, -R, -ST adj easily persuaded or managed

TAWING ▸ taw

TAWINGS ▸ taw

TAWNEY, -S same as ▸ tawny

TAWNIER ▸ tawny

TAWNIES ▸ tawny

TAWNIEST ▸ tawny

TAWNILY ▸ tawny

TAWNY, TAWNIER, TAWNIES, TAWNIEST adj yellowish-brown ▷ n light brown to brownish-orange colour

TAWPIE, -S n Scottish word for a foolish young woman

TAWS same as ▸ tawse

TAWSE, -D, -S, TAWSING n leather strap with one end cut into thongs ▷ vb punish (someone) with or as if with a tawse

TAWT, -ED, -IER, -IEST, -ING, -S same as ▸ taut

TAWTIE ▸ tawt

TAWTIER ▸ tawt

TAWTIEST ▸ tawt

TAWTING ▸ tawt

TAWTS ▸ tawt

TAX, -ED, -ES, -INGS n compulsory payment levied by a government on income, property, etc to raise revenue ▷ vb levy a tax on

TAXA ▸ taxon

TAXABLE, -S adj capable of being taxed ▷ n person, income, property, etc, that is subject to tax

TAXABLY ▸ taxable

TAXATION n levying of taxes

TAXATIVE ▸ taxation

TAXED ▸ tax

TAXEME, -S n any element of speech that may differentiate meaning

TAXEMIC ▸ taxeme

TAXER, -S ▸ tax

TAXES ▸ tax

TAXI, -ED, -ES, -ING, TAXYING n car with a driver that may be hired ▷ vb (of an aircraft) run along the ground

TAXIARCH n (in ancient Greece) soldier in charge of troops

TAXICAB, -S same as ▸ taxi

TAXIED ▸ taxi

TAXIES ▸ taxi

TAXIING ▸ taxi

TAXIMAN, TAXIMEN n taxi driver

TAXING adj demanding, onerous

TAXINGLY ▸ taxing

TAXINGS ▸ tax

TAXIS, -ES n movement of a cell or organism in response to an external stimulus

TAXITE, -S n type of volcanic rock

TAXITIC ▸ taxite

TAXIWAY, -S n marked path along which aircraft taxi to or from a runway, parking area, etc

TAXLESS ▸ tax

TAXMAN, TAXMEN n collector of taxes

TAXOL, -S n trademarked anti-cancer drug

TAXON, TAXA, -S n any taxonomic group or rank

TAXONOMY n classification of plants and animals into groups

TAXONS ▸ taxon

TAXOR, -S ▸ tax

TAXPAID adj having had the applicable tax paid already

TAXPAYER n person or organization that pays taxes

TAXUS n genus of conifers

TAXWISE adv regarding tax

TAXYING ▸ taxi

TAY, -S Irish dialect word for ▸ tea

TAYBERRY n hybrid shrub produced by crossing a blackberry, raspberry, and loganberry

TAYRA, -S n large arboreal mammal of Central and South America

TAYS ▸ tay

TAZZA, -S, TAZZE n cup with a shallow bowl and a circular foot

TCHICK, -ED, -S vb make a clicking noise with the tongue

TE, -S n (in tonic sol-fa) seventh degree of any major scale

TEA, -ED, -ING, -S n drink made from infusing the dried leaves of an Asian bush in boiling water ▹ vb take tea

TEABAG, -S n porous bag of tea leaves for infusion

TEABERRY n berry of the wintergreen

TEABOARD n tea tray

TEABOWL, -S n small bowl used (instead of a teacup) for serving tea

TEABOX, -ES n box for storing tea

TEABREAD n loaf-shaped cake with dried fruit which has been steeped in tea before baking

TEACAKE, -S n flat bun, usually eaten toasted and buttered

TEACART, -S n trolley from which tea is served

TEACH, TAUGHT, -ES, -ING vb tell or show (someone) how to do something

TEACHER, -S n person who teaches, esp in a school

TEACHES ▸ teach

TEACHIE old form of ▸ tetchy

TEACHING ▸ teach

TEACUP, -S n cup out of which tea may be drunk

TEAD, -S old word for ▸ torch

TEADE, -S same as ▸ tead

TEADS ▸ tead

TEAED ▸ tea

TEAGLE, -D, -S, TEAGLING vb raise or hoist using a tackle

TEAHOUSE n restaurant, esp in Japan or China, where tea and light refreshments are served

TEAING ▸ tea

TEAK, -S n very hard wood of a tropical tree

TEAKWOOD another word for ▸ teak

TEAL, -S n kind of small duck

TEALIGHT n small candle

TEALIKE adj resembling tea

TEALS ▸ teal

TEAM, -ED, -S n group of people forming one side in a game ▹ vb make or cause to make a team

TEAMAKER n person or thing that makes tea

TEAMED ▸ team

TEAMER, -S ▸ team

TEAMING, -S ▸ team

TEAMMATE n fellow member of a team

TEAMS ▸ team

TEAMSTER n (in N America) truck driver

TEAMWISE adv in respect of a team; in the manner of a team

TEAMWORK n cooperative work by a team

TEAPOT, -S n container for making and serving tea

TEAPOY, -S n small table or stand with a tripod base

TEAR, -ED, -ING, -S, TORN n drop of fluid appearing in and falling from the eye ▹ vb rip a hole in

TEARABLE ▸ tear

TEARAWAY n wild or unruly person

TEARDOWN n demolition; disassembly

TEARDROP same as ▸ tear

TEARED ▸ tear

TEARER, -S ▸ tear

TEARFUL adj weeping or about to weep

TEARGAS n gas or vapour that makes the eyes smart and water ▹ vb deploy teargas against

TEARIER ▸ teary

TEARIEST ▸ teary

TEARILY ▸ teary

TEARING ▸ tear

TEARLESS ▸ tear

TEARLIKE adj like a tear

TEAROOM, -S same as ▸ teashop

TEARS ▸ tear

TEARY, TEARIER, TEARIEST adj characterized by, covered with, or secreting tears

TEAS ▸ tea

TEASABLE ▸ tease

TEASE, -D, -S vb make fun of (someone) in a provoking or playful way ▹ n person who teases

TEASEL, -ED, -S n plant with prickly leaves and flowers ▹ vb tease (a fabric)

TEASELER ▸ teasel

TEASELS ▸ teasel

TEASER, -S n annoying or difficult problem

TEASES ▸ tease

TEASHOP, -S n restaurant where tea and light refreshments are served

TEASING, -S ▸ tease

TEASPOON n small spoon for stirring tea

TEAT, -S n nipple of a breast or udder

TEATED ▸ teat

TEATIME, -S n late afternoon

TEATS ▸ teat

TEAWARE, -S n implements for brewing and serving tea

TEAZE, -D, -S, TEAZING old variant of ▸ tease

TEAZEL, -ED, -S same as ▸ teasel

TEAZES ▸ teaze

TEAZING ▸ teaze

TEAZLE, -D, -S, TEAZLING same as ▸ teasel

TEBBAD, -S n sandstorm

T

TEBIBYTE n 2^{40} bytes

TEC, -S short for > **detective**

TECH, -S n technical college

TECHED adj slightly mad

TECHIE, -S n person who is skilled in the use of technology ▷ adj relating to or skilled in the use of technology

TECHIER ▸ techy

TECHIES ▸ techie

TECHIEST ▸ techy

TECHILY ▸ techy

TECHNIC another word for > **technique**

TECHNICS n study or theory of industry and industrial arts

TECHNO, -S n type of electronic dance music with a very fast beat

TECHNOID n technician

TECHNOS ▸ techno

TECHS ▸ tech

TECHY, TECHIER, TECHIEST same as ▸ techie

TECKEL, -S n dachshund

TECS ▸ tec

TECTA ▸ tectum

TECTAL ▸ tectum

TECTITE, -S same as ▸ tektite

TECTONIC adj denoting or relating to construction or building

TECTRIX n small feather on a bird's wing or tail

TECTUM, TECTA, -S n any roof-like structure in the body

TED, -DED, -DING, -S vb shake out (hay), so as to dry it

TEDDER, -ED, -S n machine equipped with a series of small rotating forks for tedding hay

TEDDIE same as ▸ teddy

TEDDIES ▸ teddy

TEDDING ▸ ted

TEDDY, TEDDIES n teddy bear

TEDIER ▸ tedy

TEDIEST ▸ tedy

TEDIOUS adj causing fatigue or boredom

TEDISOME old Scottish variant of ▸ tedious

TEDIUM, -S n monotony

TEDS ▸ ted

TEDY, TEDIER, TEDIEST same as ▸ tedious

TEE, -D, -ING, -S n small peg from which a golf ball can be played at the start of each hole ▷ vb position (the ball) ready for striking, on or as if on a tee

TEEK adj in Indian English, well

TEEL, -S same as ▸ sesame

TEEM, -ED, -ING, -S vb be full of

TEEMER, -S ▸ teem

TEEMFUL ▸ teem

TEEMING ▸ teem

TEEMLESS ▸ teem

TEEMS ▸ teem

TEEN, -ED, -ING, -S n teenager ▷ vb set alight

TEENAGE, -S adj (of a person) aged between 13 and 19 ▷ n this period of time

TEENAGED adj (of a person) aged between 13 and 19

TEENAGER n person aged between 13 and 19

TEENAGES ▸ teenage

TEEND, -ED, -ING, -S same as ▸ tind

TEENDOM, -S n state of being a teenager

TEENDS ▸ teend

TEENE, -S n affliction or woe

TEENED ▸ teen

TEENER, -S ▸ teen

TEENES ▸ teene

TEENFUL adj troublesome or harmful

TEENIER ▸ teeny

TEENIEST ▸ teeny

TEENING ▸ teen

TEENS ▸ teen

TEENSY, TEENSIER same as ▸ teeny

TEENTIER ▸ teeny

TEENTSY same as ▸ teeny

TEENTY, TEENTIER same as ▸ teeny

TEENY, TEENIER, TEENIEST adj extremely small

TEENYBOP adj of or relating to a teenager who avidly follows fashions in pop music and clothes

TEEPEE, -S same as ▸ tepee

TEER, -ED, -ING, -S vb smear; daub

TEES ▸ tee

TEETER, -ED, -S vb wobble or move unsteadily

TEETH ▸ tooth

TEETHE, -D, -S, TEETHING vb (of a baby) grow his or her first teeth

TEETHER, -S n object for an infant to bite on during teething

TEETHES ▸ teethe

TEETHING ▸ teethe

TEETOTAL adj drinking no alcohol ▷ vb advocate total abstinence from alcohol

TEETOTUM n spinning top bearing letters of the alphabet on its four sides

TEEVEE, -S n television

TEF, -S n annual grass, of NE Africa, grown for its grain

TEFF, -S same as ▸ tef

TEFILLAH, TEFILLIN n either of the pair of blackened square cases worn by Jewish men during weekday morning prayers

TEFLON, -S n substance used in nonstick cooking vessels

TEFS ▸ tef

TEG, -S n two-year-old sheep

TEGG, -S same as ▸ teg

TEGMEN, TEGMINA n either of the leathery forewings of the cockroach and related insects

TEGMENTA > tegmentum

TEGMINA ▸ tegmen

TEGMINAL ▸ tegmen

TEGS ▸ teg

TEGU, -S n large South American lizard

TEGUA, -S n type of moccasin

TEGUEXIN same as ▸ tegu

TEGULA, -E n one of a pair of coverings of the forewings of certain insects

TEGULAR adj of, relating to, or resembling a tile or tiles

TEGUMEN, TEGUMINA same as ▸ tegmen

TEGUMENT n protective layer around an ovule

TEGUMINA ▸ tegumen

TEGUS ▸ tegu

TEHR, -S same as ▸ tahr

TEHSIL, -S n administrative region in some S Asian countries

TEIGLACH pl n morsels of dough boiled in honey, eaten as a dessert

TEIID, -S n member of the Teiidae family of lizards

TEIL, -S n lime tree

TEIN, -S n monetary unit of Kazakhstan

TEIND, -ED, -ING, -S Scot and northern English word for ▸ tithe

TEINS ▸ tein

TEKKIE, -S variant of ▸ techie

TEKTITE, -S n small dark glassy object found in several areas around the world

TEKTITIC ▸ tektite

TEL, -S same as ▸ tell

TELA, -E *n* any delicate tissue or weblike structure

TELAMON, -S *n* column in the form of a male figure

TELARY *adj* capable of spinning a web

TELCO, -S *n* telecommunications company

TELD *same as* ▸ **tauld**

TELE, -S *same as* ▸ **telly**

TELECAST *vb* broadcast by television ▸ *n* television broadcast

TELECHIR *n* robot arm controlled by a human operator

TELECINE *n* apparatus for producing a television signal from cinematograph film

TELECOM *n* telecommunications

TELECOMM *n* telecommunication

TELECOMS *same as* ▸ **telecom**

TELECON, -S *n* (short for) teleconference

TELECOPY *n* message or document sent by fax

TELEDU, -S *n* badger of SE Asia and Indonesia

TELEFAX *another word for* ▸ **fax**

TELEFILM *n* film made for TV

TELEGA, -S *n* rough four-wheeled cart used in Russia

TELEGONY *n* supposed influence of a previous sire on offspring borne by a female to other sires

TELEGRAM *n* formerly, a message sent by telegraph ▸ *vb* send a telegram

TELEMAN, TELEMEN *n* noncommissioned officer in the US navy

TELEMARK *n* turn in which one ski is placed far forward of the other and turned gradually inwards ▸ *vb* perform a telemark turn

TELEMEN ▸ **teleman**

TELEOST, -S *n* bony fish with rayed fins and a swim bladder ▸ *adj* of, relating to, or belonging to this type of fish

TELEPATH *n* person who is telepathic ▸ *vb* practise telepathy

TELEPIC, -S *n* feature-length film made for television

TELEPLAY *n* play written for television

TELEPORT *vb* (in science fiction) to transport (a person or object) across a distance instantaneously

TELERAN, -S *n* electronic navigational aid

TELERGIC ▸ **telergy**

TELERGY *n* name for the form of energy supposedly transferred during telepathy

TELES ▸ **tele**

TELESALE > **telesales**

TELESEME *n* old-fashioned electric signalling system

TELESES ▸ **telesis**

TELESHOP *vb* buy goods by telephone or internet

TELESIS, TELESES *n* purposeful use of natural and social processes to obtain specific social goals

TELESM, -S *n* talisman

TELESTIC *adj* relating to a hierophant

TELETEX *n* international means of communicating text between a variety of terminals

TELETEXT *n* system which shows information and news on television screens

TELETHON *n* lengthy television programme to raise charity funds, etc

TELETRON *n* system for showing enlarged televisual images, eg in sports stadiums

TELETYPE *vb* send typed message by telegraph

TELEVIEW *vb* watch television

TELEVISE *vb* broadcast on television

TELEWORK *vb* work from home, communicating by computer, telephone etc

TELEX, -ED, -ES, -ING *n* (formerly) international communication service using teleprinters ▸ *vb* (formerly) transmit by telex

TELFER, -ED, -S *n* overhead transport system

TELFERIC ▸ **telfer**

TELFERS ▸ **telfer**

TELFORD, -S *n* road built using a method favoured by Thomas Telford

TELIA ▸ **telium**

TELIAL ▸ **telium**

TELIC *adj* directed or moving towards some goal

TELICITY *n* quality of being telic

TELIUM, TELIA *n* spore-producing body of some rust fungi in which the teliospores are formed

TELL, -ING, -INGS, -S, TOLD *vb* make known in words ▸ *n* large mound resulting from the accumulation of rubbish

TELLABLE ▸ **tell**

TELLAR, -ED, -S *same as* ▸ **tiller**

TELLEN, -S *same as* ▸ **tellin**

TELLER, -ED, -S *n* narrator ▸ *vb* (of a plant) to produce tillers

TELLIES ▸ **telly**

TELLIN, -S *n* slim marine bivalve molluscs that live in intertidal sand

TELLING ▸ **tell**

TELLINGS ▸ **tell**

TELLINS ▸ **tellin**

TELLS ▸ **tell**

TELLTALE *n* person who reveals secrets ▸ *adj* revealing

TELLURAL *adj* of or relating to the earth

TELLURIC *adj* of, relating to, or originating on or in the earth or soil

TELLUS, -ES *n* earth

TELLY, TELLIES, -S *n* television

TELNET, -ED, -S *n* system allowing remote access to other computers on the same network ▸ *vb* use a telnet system

TELOGEN, -S *n* phase of hair growth

TELOI ▸ **telos**

TELOME, -S *n* fundamental unit of a plant's structure

TELOMERE *n* either of the ends of a chromosome

TELOMES ▸ **telome**

TELOMIC ▸ **telome**

TELOS, TELOI *n* objective; ultimate purpose

TELPHER, -S *same as* > **telferage**

TELS ▸ **tel**

TELSON, -S *n* segment of the body of crustaceans and arachnids

TELSONIC ▸ **telson**

TELSONS ▸ **telson**

TELT *same as* ▸ **tauld**

TEMBLOR, -S *n* earthquake or earth tremor

TEME, -D, -S *old variant of* ▸ **team**

TEMENOS, TEMENE *n* sacred area, esp one surrounding a temple

T

TEMERITY n boldness or audacity

TEMEROUS ▶temerity

TEMES ▶teme

TEMP, -ED, -S vb work for an employer on a temporary basis

TEMPEH, -S n fermented soya beans

TEMPER, -S n outburst of anger ▷ vb make less extreme

TEMPERA, -S n painting medium for powdered pigments

TEMPERED adj having the frequency differences between notes adjusted in accordance with the system of equal temperament

TEMPERER ▶temper

TEMPERS ▶temper

TEMPEST, -S n violent storm ▷ vb agitate or disturb violently

TEMPI ▶tempo

TEMPING, -S n act of working temporarily for an employer

TEMPLAR, -S n lawyer who has chambers in the Inner or Middle Temple in London

TEMPLATE n pattern used to cut out shapes accurately

TEMPLE, -S n building for worship

TEMPLED ▶temple

TEMPLES ▶temple

TEMPLET, -S same as ▶template

TEMPO, TEMPI, -S n rate or pace

TEMPORAL adj of time ▷ n any body part relating to or near the temple or temples

TEMPORE adv in the time of

TEMPOS ▶tempo

TEMPS ▶temp

TEMPT, -ED, -S vb entice (a person) to do something wrong

TEMPTER, -S ▶tempt

TEMPTING adj attractive or inviting

TEMPTS ▶tempt

TEMPURA, -S n Japanese dish of seafood or vegetables dipped in batter and deep-fried

TEMS same as ▶temse

TEMSE, -D, -S, TEMSING vb sieve

TEMULENT > temulence

TEN, -S n one more than nine

TENABLE adj able to be upheld or maintained

TENABLY ▶tenable

TENACE, -S n holding of two nonconsecutive high cards of a suit, such as the ace and queen

TENACITY > tenacious

TENACULA ▶tenaculum

TENAIL, -S same as ▶tenaille

TENAILLE n low outwork in the main ditch between two bastions

TENAILS ▶tenail

TENANCY n temporary possession of property owned by somebody else

TENANT, -ED, -S n person who rents land or a building ▷ vb hold (land or property) as a tenant

TENANTRY n tenants collectively

TENANTS ▶tenant

TENCH, -ES n freshwater game fish of the carp family

TEND, -ED, -ING, -S vb be inclined

TENDANCE n care and attention

TENDED ▶tend

TENDENCE same as ▶tendency

TENDENCY n inclination to act in a certain way

TENDENZ same as ▶tendency

TENDER, -ED, -S adj not tough ▷ vb offer ▷ n such an offer

TENDERER ▶tender

TENDERLY ▶tender

TENDERS ▶tender

TENDING ▶tend

TENDON, -S n strong tissue attaching a muscle to a bone

TENDRE, -S n care

TENDRIL, -S n slender stem by which a climbing plant clings

TENDRON, -S n shoot

TENDS ▶tend

TENDU, -S n position in ballet

TENE, -S same as ▶teen

TENEBRAE n darkness

TENEBRIO n type of small mealworm

TENEMENT n (esp in Scotland or the US) building divided into several flats

TENENDUM, TENENDA n part of a deed that specifies the terms of tenure

TENES ▶tene

TENESI n monetary unit of Turkmenistan

TENESMIC ▶tenesmus

TENESMUS n bowel disorder

TENET, -S n doctrine or belief

TENFOLD, -S n one tenth

TENGE, -S n standard monetary unit of Kazakhstan

TENIA, -E, -S same as ▶taenia

TENIASIS, TENIASES same as > taeniasis

TENIOID ▶tenia

TENNE, -S n tawny colour

TENNER, -S n ten-pound note

TENNES ▶tenne

TENNESI same as ▶tenesi

TENNIES ▶tenny

TENNIS, -ES n game in which players use rackets to hit a ball back and forth over a net

TENNIST, -S n tennis player

TENNO, -S n formal title of the Japanese emperor

TENNY, TENNIES same as ▶tenne

TENON, -ED, -ING, -S n projecting end on a piece of wood fitting into a slot in another ▷ vb form a tenon on (a piece of wood)

TENONER, -S ▶tenon

TENONING ▶tenon

TENONS ▶tenon

TENOR, -S n (singer with) the second highest male voice ▷ adj (of a voice or instrument) between alto and baritone

TENORINO, TENORINI n high tenor

TENORIST n musician playing any tenor instrument

TENORITE n black mineral found in copper deposits

TENORMAN, TENORMEN n person who plays tenor saxophone

TENOROON n tenor bassoon

TENORS ▶tenor

TENOTOMY n surgical division of a tendon

TENOUR, -S old variant of ▶tenor

TENPENCE n sum of money equivalent to ten pennies

TENPENNY adj (of a nail) three inches in length

TENPIN, -S n one of the pins used in tenpin bowling

TENREC, -S n small mammal resembling hedgehogs or shrews

TENS ▶ten

TENSE, -D, -R, -S, -ST, TENSING adj emotionally strained ▷ vb make or become tense ▷ n form of a verb showing the time of action

TENSELY ▸ tense

TENSER ▸ tense

TENSES ▸ tense

TENSEST ▸ tense

TENSIBLE adj capable of being stretched

TENSIBLY ▸ tensible

TENSILE adj of tension

TENSING ▸ tense

TENSION, -S n hostility or suspense ▷ vb tighten

TENSITY rare word for ▸ tension

TENSIVE adj of or causing tension or strain

TENSON, -S n type of French lyric poem

TENSOR, -S n any muscle that can cause a part to become firm or tense

TENT, -ING, -INGS, -S n portable canvas shelter ▷ vb camp in a tent

TENTACLE n flexible organ of many invertebrates, used for grasping, feeding, etc

TENTAGE n tents collectively

TENTED ▸ tent

TENTER, -ED, -S ▸ tent

TENTFUL, -S n number of people or objects that can fit in a tent

TENTH, -S n number ten in a series ▷ adj coming after the ninth in numbering or counting order, position, time, etc

TENTHLY adv in the tenth place or position

TENTHS ▸ tenth

TENTIE, -R, -ST adj wary

TENTING ▸ tent

TENTINGS ▸ tent

TENTLESS ▸ tent

TENTLIKE ▸ tent

TENTORIA > tentorium

TENTPOLE n film whose high earnings offset the cost of less high earnings of less popular ones

TENTS ▸ tent

TENTWISE adv in the manner of a tent

TENTY same as ▸ tentie

TENUE n deportment

TENUES ▸ tenuis

TENUIOUS same as ▸ tenuous

TENUIS, TENUES n (in the grammar of classical Greek) any of the voiceless stops

TENUITY ▸ tenuous

TENUOUS adj slight or flimsy

TENURE, -S, TENURING n (period of) the holding of an office or position ▷ vb assign a tenured position to

TENURED adj having tenure of office

TENURES ▸ tenure

TENURIAL ▸ tenure

TENURING ▸ tenure

TENUTO, TENUTI, -S adv (of a note) to be held for or beyond its full time value ▷ n note sustained thus

TENZON, -S same as ▸ tenson

TEOCALLI n any of various truncated pyramids built by the Aztecs as bases for their temples

TEOPAN, -S n enclosure surrounding a teocalli

TEOSINTE n tall Central American annual grass

TEPA, -S n type of tree native to South America

TEPACHE, -S n type of Mexican soft drink

TEPAL, -S n subdivisions of a perianth

TEPAS ▸ tepa

TEPEE, -S n cone-shaped tent, formerly used by Native Americans

TEPEFY, TEPEFIED, TEPEFIES vb make or become tepid

TEPHRA, -S n solid matter ejected during a volcanic eruption

TEPHRITE n variety of basalt

TEPID, -ER, -EST adj slightly warm

TEPIDITY ▸ tepid

TEPIDLY ▸ tepid

TEPOY, -S same as ▸ teapoy

TEQUILA, -S n Mexican alcoholic drink

TEQUILLA same as ▸ tequila

TERABYTE n large unit of computer memory

TERAFLOP n large unit of computer processing speed

TERAGLIN n edible marine fish of Australia which has fine scales and is blue in colour

TERAI, -S n felt hat with a wide brim worn in subtropical regions

TERAKIHI same as ▸ tarakihi

TERAOHM, -S n unit of resistance

TERAPH, -IM n household god or image venerated by ancient Semitic peoples

TERAS, TERATA n monstrosity; teratism

TERATISM n malformed animal or human, esp in the fetal stage

TERATOID adj resembling a monster

TERATOMA n tumour or group of tumours composed of tissue foreign to the site of growth

TERAWATT n unit of power equal to one million megawatts

TERBIA, -S n amorphous white insoluble powder

TERBIC ▸ terbium

TERBIUM, -S n rare metallic element

TERCE, -S n third of the seven canonical hours of the divine office

TERCEL, -S n male falcon or hawk, esp as used in falconry

TERCELET same as ▸ tercel

TERCELS ▸ tercel

TERCES ▸ terce

TERCET, -S n group of three lines of verse that rhyme together

TERCIO, -S n regiment of Spanish or Italian infantry

TEREBENE n mixture of hydrocarbons prepared from oil of turpentine and sulphuric acid

TEREBIC adj as in **terebic acid** white crystalline carboxylic acid produced by the action of nitric acid on turpentine

TEREBRA, -E, -S n ancient Roman device used for boring holes in defensive walls

TEREDO, -S n marine mollusc that bores into and destroys submerged timber

TEREFA same as ▸ tref

TEREFAH same as ▸ tref

TEREK, -S n type of sandpiper

TERES, -ES, TERETES n shoulder muscle

TERETE adj (esp of plant parts) smooth and usually cylindrical and tapering

TERETES ▸ teres

TERF, -S old variant of ▸ turf

TERFE, -S old variant of ▸ turf

TERFS ▸ terf

TERGA ▸ tergum

TERGAL ▸ tergum

T

TERGITE, -S n constituent part of a tergum

TERGUM, TERGA n cuticular plate covering the dorsal surface of a body segment of an arthropod

TERIYAKI adj basted with soy sauce and rice wine and broiled over an open fire ▷ n dish prepared in this way

TERM, -ED, -ING, -S n word or expression ▷ vb name or designate

TERMER, -S same as ▷ **termor**

TERMINAL adj (of an illness) ending in death ▷ n place where people or vehicles begin or end a journey

TERMINER n person or thing that limits or determines

TERMING ▶ **term**

TERMINUS, TERMINI n railway or bus station at the end of a line

TERMITE, -S n white antlike insect that destroys timber

TERMITIC ▶ **termite**

TERMLESS adj without limit or boundary

TERMLY, TERMLIES n publication issued once a term

TERMOR, -S n person who holds an estate for a term of years or until he or she dies

TERMS ▶ **term**

TERMTIME n time during a term, esp a school or university term

TERN, -S n gull-like sea bird with a forked tail and pointed wings

TERNAL ▶ **tern**

TERNARY adj consisting of three parts ▷ n group of three

TERNATE adj (esp of a leaf) consisting of three leaflets or other parts

TERNE, -D, -S, TERNING n alloy of lead containing tin and antimony ▷ vb coat with this alloy

TERNION, -S n group of three

TERNS ▶ **tern**

TERPENE, -S n unsaturated hydrocarbon found in the essential oils of many plants

TERPENIC ▶ **terpene**

TERPINE, -S n type of expectorant

TERPINOL same as > **terpineol**

TERRA, -E n (in legal contexts) earth or land

TERRACE, -D, -S n row of houses built as one block ▷ vb form into or provide with a terrace

TERRAE ▶ **terra**

TERRAIN, -S same as ▶ **terrane**

TERRANE, -S n series of rock formations

TERRAPIN n small turtle-like reptile

TERRARIA > **terrarium**

TERRAS, -ES same as ▶ **trass**

TERRASSE n paved area alongside a café

TERRAZZO n floor of marble chips set in mortar and polished

TERREEN, -S old variant of ▶ **tureen**

TERRELLA n magnetic globe designed to simulate and demonstrate the earth's magnetic fields

TERRENE, -S adj of or relating to the earth ▷ n land

TERRET, -S n ring on a harness saddle through which the reins are passed

TERRIBLE adj very serious ▷ n something terrible

TERRIBLY adv in a terrible manner

TERRIER, -S n any of various breeds of small active dog

TERRIES ▶ **terry**

TERRIFIC adj great or intense

TERRIFY vb fill with fear

TERRINE, -S n earthenware dish with a lid

TERRIT, -S same as ▶ **terret**

TERROIR, -S n combination of factors that gives a wine its distinctive character

TERROR, -S n great fear

TERRY, TERRIES n fabric with small loops covering both sides

TERSE, -R, -ST adj neat and concise

TERSELY ▶ **terse**

TERSER ▶ **terse**

TERSEST ▶ **terse**

TERSION, -S n action of rubbing or wiping

TERTIA, -S same as ▶ **tercio**

TERTIAL, -S same as ▶ **tertiary**

TERTIAN, -S adj (of a fever or the symptoms of a disease) occurring every other day ▷ n tertian fever or symptoms

TERTIARY adj third in degree, order, etc ▷ n any of the tertiary feathers

TERTIAS ▶ **tertia**

TERTIUM adj as in **tertium quid** unknown or indefinite thing related in some way to two known or definite things, but distinct from both

TERTIUS n third (in a group)

TERTS n card game using 32 cards

TERYLENE n tradename for a synthetic polyester fibre based on terephthalic acid

TERZETTA n tercet

TERZETTO, TERZETTI n trio, esp a vocal one

TES ▶ **te**

TESLA, -S n derived SI unit of magnetic flux density

TESSELLA n little tessera

TESSERA, -E n small square tile used in mosaics

TESSERAL ▶ **tessera**

TEST, -ED, -S vb try out to ascertain the worth, capability, or endurance of ▷ n critical examination

TESTA, -E n hard outer layer of a seed

TESTABLE ▶ **test**

TESTACY ▶ **testate**

TESTAE ▶ **testa**

TESTAMUR n certificate proving an examination has been passed

TESTATA ▶ **testatum**

TESTATE, -S adj having left a valid will ▷ n person who dies and leaves a legally valid will

TESTATOR n maker of a will

TESTATUM, TESTATA n part of a purchase deed

TESTE n witness

TESTED ▶ **test**

TESTEE, -S n person subjected to a test

TESTER, -S n person or thing that tests or is used for testing

TESTERN, -S vb give (someone) a teston

TESTERS ▶ **tester**

TESTES ▶ **testis**

TESTICLE n either of the two male reproductive glands

TESTIER ▶ **testy**

TESTIEST ▶ **testy**

TESTIFY vb give evidence under oath

TESTILY ▶ **testy**

TESTING, -S ▶ **test**

TESTIS, TESTES same as ▸ **testicle**

TESTON, -S n French silver coin of the 16th century

TESTOON, -S same as ▸ **teston**

TESTRIL, -S same as ▸ **testrill**

TESTRILL n sixpence

TESTRILS ▸ **testril**

TESTS ▸ **test**

TESTUDO, -S n protective cover used by the ancient Roman army

TESTY, TESTIER, TESTIEST adj irritable or touchy

TET, -S same as ▸ **teth**

TETANAL ▸ **tetanus**

TETANIC, -S adj of, relating to, or producing tetanus ▹ n tetanic drug or agent

TETANIES ▸ **tetany**

TETANISE same as ▸ **tetanize**

TETANIZE vb induce tetanus in (a muscle)

TETANOID ▸ **tetanus**

TETANUS n acute infectious disease producing muscular spasms and convulsions

TETANY, TETANIES n abnormal increase in the excitability of nerves and muscles

TETCHED same as ▸ **teched**

TETCHIER ▸ **tetchy**

TETCHILY ▸ **tetchy**

TETCHY, TETCHIER adj cross and irritable

TETE, -S n elaborate hairstyle

TETH, -S n ninth letter of the Hebrew alphabet

TETHER, -ED, -S n rope or chain for tying an animal to a spot ▹ vb tie up with rope

TETHS ▸ **teth**

TETOTUM, -S same as ▸ **teetotum**

TETRA, -S n brightly coloured tropical freshwater fish

TETRACID adj (of a base) capable of reacting with four molecules of a monobasic acid ▹ n tetracid base

TETRACT, -S n sponge spicule with four rays

TETRAD, -S n group or series of four

TETRADIC ▸ **tetrad**

TETRADS ▸ **tetrad**

TETRAGON n figure with four angles and four sides

TETRAMER n four-molecule polymer

TETRAPLA n book containing versions of the same text in four languages

TETRAPOD n any vertebrate that has four limbs

TETRARCH n ruler of one fourth of a country

TETRAS ▸ **tetra**

TETRAXON n four-pointed spicule

TETRI, -S n currency unit of Georgia

TETRODE, -S n electronic valve having four electrodes

TETRONAL n sedative drug

TETROSE, -S n type of sugar

TETROXID same as > **tetroxide**

TETRYL, -S n yellow crystalline explosive solid used in detonators

TETS ▸ **tet**

TETTER, -ED, -S n blister or pimple ▹ vb cause a tetter to erupt (on)

TETTIX, -ES n cicada

TEUCH, -ER, -EST Scots variant of ▸ **tough**

TEUCHAT, -S Scots variant of ▸ **tewit**

TEUCHER ▸ **teuch**

TEUCHEST ▸ **teuch**

TEUCHTER n in Scotland, derogatory word used by Lowlanders for a Highlander

TEUGH, -ER, -EST same as ▸ **teuch**

TEUGHLY ▸ **teugh**

TEVATRON n machine used in nuclear research

TEW, -ED, -ING, -S vb work hard

TEWART, -S same as ▸ **tuart**

TEWED ▸ **tew**

TEWEL, -S n horse's rectum

TEWHIT, -S same as ▸ **tewit**

TEWING ▸ **tew**

TEWIT, -S n lapwing

TEWS ▸ **tew**

TEX, -ES n unit of weight used to measure yarn density

TEXAS, -ES n structure on the upper deck of a paddle-steamer

TEXES ▸ **tex**

TEXT, -ED, -ING, -S n main body of a book as distinct from illustrations etc ▹ vb send a text message to (someone)

TEXTBOOK n standard book on a particular subject ▹ adj perfect

TEXTED ▸ **text**

TEXTER, -S n person who communicates by text messaging

TEXTILE, -S n fabric or cloth, esp woven ▹ adj of (the making of) fabrics

TEXTING, -S ▸ **text**

TEXTISM, -S n word typically used in a text message

TEXTLESS ▸ **text**

TEXTONYM n one of two or more words that can be created by pressing the same combination of numbers on a mobile phone

TEXTS ▸ **text**

TEXTUAL adj of, based on, or relating to, a text or texts

TEXTUARY adj of, relating to, or contained in a text ▹ n textual critic

TEXTURAL ▸ **texture**

TEXTURE, -D, -S n structure, feel, or consistency ▹ vb give a distinctive texture to (something)

THACK, -ED, -ING, -S Scots word for ▸ **thatch**

THAE Scots word for ▸ **those**

THAGI, -S same as ▸ **thuggee**

THAIM Scots variant of ▸ **them**

THAIRM, -S n catgut

THALAMI ▸ **thalamus**

THALAMIC ▸ **thalamus**

THALAMUS, THALAMI n mass of grey matter at the base of the brain

THALE n as in **thale** cress cruciferous wall plant

THALER, -S n former German, Austrian, or Swiss silver coin

THALI, -S n Indian meal consisting of several small dishes

THALIAN adj of or relating to comedy

THALIS ▸ **thali**

THALLI ▸ **thallus**

THALLIC adj of or containing thallium

THALLINE n type of chemical used in medicine

THALLIUM n highly toxic metallic element

THALLOID ▸ **thallus**

THALLOUS adj of or containing thallium, esp in the monovalent state

THALLUS, THALLI n undifferentiated vegetative body of algae, fungi, and lichens

THALWEG, -S n longitudinal outline of a riverbed from source to mouth

THAN, -S prep used to introduce the second

T

element of a comparison ▷ n old variant of 'then' (that time)

THANA, -S same as ▸ **tana**

THANADAR same as ▸ **tanadar**

THANAGE, -S n state of being a thane

THANAH, -S same as ▸ **tana**

THANAS ▸ **thana**

THANATOS n Greek personification of death

THANE, -S n Anglo-Saxon or medieval Scottish nobleman

THANEDOM ▸ **thane**

THANES ▸ **thane**

THANG, -S n thing

THANGKA, -S n (in Tibetan Buddhism) a religious painting on a scroll

THANGS ▸ **thang**

THANK, -ED, -ING vb express gratitude to

THANKEE interj thank you

THANKER, -S ▸ **thank**

THANKFUL adj grateful

THANKING ▸ **thank**

THANKIT adj as in **be thankit** thank God

THANKS pl n words of gratitude ▷ interj polite expression of gratitude

THANKYOU n conventional expression of gratitude

THANNA, -S same as ▸ **tana**

THANNAH, -S same as ▸ **tana**

THANNAS ▸ **thanna**

THANS ▸ **than**

THANX interj informal spelling of 'thanks'

THAR, -S same as ▸ **tahr**

THARM, -S n stomach

THARS ▸ **thar**

THAT pron used to refer to something already mentioned or familiar, or further away

THATAWAY adv that way

THATCH, -ED, -ES n roofing material of reeds or straw ▷ vb roof (a house) with reeds or straw

THATCHER ▸ **thatch**

THATCHES ▸ **thatch**

THATCHT old variant of ▸ **thatched**

THATCHY ▸ **thatch**

THATNESS n state or quality of being 'that'

THAW, -ED, -ING, -INGS, -S vb make or become unfrozen ▷ n thawing

THAWER, -S ▸ **thaw**

THAWIER ▸ **thawy**

THAWIEST ▸ **thawy**

THAWING ▸ **thaw**

THAWINGS ▸ **thaw**

THAWLESS ▸ **thaw**

THAWS ▸ **thaw**

THAWY, THAWIER, THAWIEST adj tending to thaw

THE determiner definite article, used before a noun

THEANINE n amino acid found in tea leaves

THEARCHY n rule or government by God or gods

THEATER, -S same as ▸ **theatre**

THEATRAL adj of or relating to the theatre

THEATRE, -S n place where plays etc are performed

THEATRIC adj of or relating to the theatre

THEAVE, -S n young ewe

THEBAINE n poisonous white crystalline alkaloid, found in opium but without opioid actions

THEBE, -S n monetary unit of Botswana

THECA, -E n enclosing organ, cell, or spore case

THECAL ▸ **theca**

THECATE ▸ **theca**

THEE, -D, -ING, -S pron refers to the person addressed ▷ vb use the word 'thee'

THEEK, -ED, -ING, -S Scots variant of ▸ **thatch**

THEELIN, -S trade name for ▸ **estrone**

THEELOL, -S n estriol

THEES ▸ **thee**

THEFT, -S n act or an instance of stealing

THEGN, -S same as ▸ **thane**

THEGNLY adj like a thegn

THEGNS ▸ **thegn**

THEIC, -S n person who drinks excessive amounts of tea

THEIN, -S old variant of ▸ **thane**

THEINE, -S another name for ▸ **caffeine**

THEINS ▸ **thein**

THEIR determiner of, belonging to, or associated in some way with them

THEIRS pron something belonging to them

THEISM, -S n belief in a God or gods

THEIST, -S ▸ **theism**

THEISTIC ▸ **theism**

THEISTS ▸ **theist**

THELF, THELVES n old contraction of 'the elf'

THELITIS n inflammation of the nipple

THELVES ▸ **thelf**

THEM pron refers to people or things other than the speaker or those addressed

THEMA, -TA n theme

THEMATIC adj of, relating to, or consisting of a theme or themes ▷ n thematic vowel

THEME, -D, -S, THEMING n main idea or subject being discussed ▷ vb design, decorate, arrange, etc, in accordance with a theme

THEMSELF pron reflexive form of one, whoever, anybody

THEN, -S adv at that time ▷ pron that time ▷ adj existing or functioning at that time ▷ n that time

THENAGE, -S old variant of ▸ **thanage**

THENAL adj of or relating to the thenar

THENAR, -S n palm of the hand ▷ adj of or relating to the palm or the region at the base of the thumb

THENCE adv from that place or time

THENS ▸ **then**

THEOCON, -S n person who believes that religion should play a greater role in politics

THEOCRAT > **theocracy**

THEODICY n branch of theology concerned with defending the attributes of God

THEOGONY n origin and descent of the gods

THEOLOG, -S same as > **theologue**

THEOLOGY n study of religions and religious beliefs

THEONOMY n state of being governed by God

THEORBO, -S n obsolete form of the lute, having two necks

THEOREM, -S n proposition that can be proved by reasoning

THEORIC, -S n theory; conjecture

THEORIES ▸ **theory**

THEORISE same as ▸ **theorize**

THEORIST n originator of a theory

THEORIZE vb form theories, speculate

THEORY, THEORIES n set of ideas to explain something

THEOSOPH n proponent of theosophy

THEOW, -S n slave in Anglo-Saxon Britain

THERAPY n curing treatment

THERBLIG n basic unit of work in an industrial process

THERE, -S adv in or to that place ▷ n that place

THEREAT adv at that point or time

THEREBY adv by that means

THEREFOR adv for this, that, or it

THEREIN adv in or into that place or thing

THEREMIN n musical instrument played by moving the hands through electromagnetic fields

THEREOF adv of or concerning that or it

THEREON archaic word for > thereupon

THEREOUT another word for > therefrom

THERES ▶ there

THERETO adv to that or it

THERIAC, -S n ointment or potion used as an antidote to a poison

THERIACA same as ▶ theriac

THERIACS ▶ theriac

THERIAN, -S n animal of the class Theria, a subclass of mammals

THERM, -S n unit of measurement of heat

THERMAE pl n public baths or hot springs, esp in ancient Greece or Rome

THERMAL, -S adj of heat ▷ n rising current of warm air

THERME, -S old variant of ▶ therm

THERMEL, -S n type of thermometer using thermoelectric current

THERMES ▶ therme

THERMIC same as ▶ thermal

THERMION n electron or ion emitted by a body at high temperature

THERMIT, -S variant of ▶ thermite

THERMITE adj as in thermite process process for reducing metallic oxides

THERMITS ▶ thermit

THERMOS n trademark for a stoppered vacuum flask

THERMS ▶ therm

THEROID adj of, relating to, or resembling a beast

THEROPOD n bipedal carnivorous saurischian dinosaur with strong hind legs and grasping hands

THESAURI > thesaurus

THESE determiner form of this used before a plural noun

THESIS, THESES n written work submitted for a degree

THESP, -S short for ▶ thespian

THESPIAN adj of or relating to drama and the theatre ▷ n actor or actress

THESPS ▶ thesp

THETA, -S n eighth letter of the Greek alphabet

THETCH, -ED, -ES old variant spelling of ▶ thatch

THETE, -S n member of the lowest order of freeman in ancient Athens

THETHER old variant of ▶ thither

THETIC adj (in classical prosody) of, bearing, or relating to a metrical stress

THETICAL another word for ▶ thetic

THETRI, -S n currency unit of Georgia

THEURGIC ▶ theurgy

THEURGY n intervention of a divine or supernatural agency in the affairs of human beings

THEW, -ES, -S n muscle, esp if strong or well-developed

THEWED adj strong; muscular

THEWES ▶ thew

THEWIER ▶ thewy

THEWIEST ▶ thewy

THEWLESS ▶ thew

THEWS ▶ thew

THEWY, THEWIER, THEWIEST ▶ thew

THEY pron people or things other than the speaker or people addressed

THIAMIN, -S same as ▶ thiamine

THIAMINE n vitamin found in the outer coat of rice and other grains

THIAMINS ▶ thiamin

THIASUS n people gathered to sing and dance in honour of a god

THIAZIDE n diuretic drug

THIAZIN, -S same as ▶ thiazine

THIAZINE n organic compound containing a ring system composed of four carbon atoms, a sulphur atom, and a nitrogen atom

THIAZINS ▶ thiazin

THIAZOL, -S same as ▶ thiazole

THIAZOLE n colourless liquid with a pungent smell

THIAZOLS ▶ thiazol

THIBET, -S n coloured woollen cloth

THIBLE, -S n stick for stirring porridge

THICK, -ED, -ER, -EST, -ING, -S adj of great or specified extent from one side to the other ▷ vb thicken

THICKEN, -S vb make or become thick or thicker

THICKER ▶ thick

THICKEST ▶ thick

THICKET, -S n dense growth of small trees

THICKETY adj covered in thickets

THICKIE same as ▶ thicko

THICKIES ▶ thicky

THICKING ▶ thick

THICKISH ▶ thick

THICKLY ▶ thick

THICKO, -ES, -S n insulting word for a stupid person

THICKS ▶ thick

THICKSET adj stocky in build ▷ n thicket

THICKY, THICKIES same as ▶ thicko

THIEF n person who steals

THIEVE, -D, -S vb steal

THIEVERY ▶ thieve

THIEVES ▶ thieve

THIEVING adj given to stealing other people's possessions

THIEVISH ▶ thief

THIG, -GED, -GING, -S vb beg

THIGGER, -S ▶ thig

THIGGING ▶ thig

THIGGIT Scots inflection of ▶ thig

THIGH, -S n upper part of the human leg

THIGHED adj having thighs

THIGHS ▶ thigh

THIGS ▶ thig

THILK pron that same

THILL, -S another word for ▶ shaft

THILLER, -S n horse that goes between the thills of a cart

THILLS ▶ thill

THIMBLE, -D, -S n cap protecting the end of the finger when sewing ▷ vb use a thimble

THIN, -NED, -NEST, -NING, -S adj not thick ▷ vb make or become thin ▷ adv in order to produce something thin

THINCLAD n track-and-field athlete

THINDOWN n reduction in the amount of particles of very high energy penetrating the earth's atmosphere

THINE adj of or associated with you (thou) ▷ pron something belonging to you (thou)

THING, -S n material object

THINGAMY n person or thing whose name is temporarily forgotten

THINGIER ▶ thingy

THINGIES ▶ thingy

THINGO, -S n thing the name of which is temporarily forgotten

THINGS ▶ thing

THINGY, THINGIER, THINGIES adj existing in reality; actual ▷ n person or thing whose name is temporarily forgotten

THINK, -ING, -S vb consider, judge, or believe

THINKER, -S ▶ think

THINKING ▶ think

THINKS ▶ think

THINLY ▶ thin

THINNED ▶ thin

THINNER, -S ▶ thin

THINNESS ▶ thin

THINNEST ▶ thin

THINNING ▶ thin

THINNISH ▶ thin

THINS ▶ thin

THIO adj of, or relating to, sulphur

THIOL, -S n any of a class of sulphur-containing organic compounds

THIOLIC ▶ thiol

THIOLS ▶ thiol

THIONATE n any salt or ester of thionic acid

THIONIC adj of, relating to, or containing sulphur

THIONIN, -S same as ▶ thionine

THIONINE n crystalline derivative of thiazine used as a violet dye to stain microscope specimens

THIONINS ▶ thionin

THIONYL, -S n the divalent group SO

THIOPHEN n colourless liquid heterocyclic compound found in the benzene fraction of coal tar

THIOPHIL adj having an attraction to sulphur

THIOTEPA n drug used in chemotherapy

THIOUREA n white water-soluble crystalline substance with a bitter taste

This word for a type of chemical compound is a good example of the kind of vowel-rich 8-letter word which takes a lot of practice to spot in actual play but is very likely to come up. Good players spend a lot of time mastering these!

THIR Scots word for ▶ these

THIRAM, -S n antifungal agent

THIRD, -ED, -ING, -S adj of number three in a series ▷ n one of three equal parts ▷ vb divide (something) by three

THIRDLY adv in the third place or position

THIRDS ▶ third

THIRL, -ED, -ING, -S vb bore or drill

THIRLAGE n obligation imposed upon tenants requiring them to have their grain ground at a specified mill

THIRLED ▶ thirl

THIRLING ▶ thirl

THIRLS ▶ thirl

THIRST, -ED, -ER, -S n desire to drink ▷ vb feel thirst

THIRSTY adj feeling a desire to drink

THIRTEEN n three and ten

THIRTY, THIRTIES n three times ten

THIS pron used to refer to a thing or person nearby, just mentioned, or about to be mentioned ▷ adj used to refer to the present time

THISAWAY adv this way

THISNESS n state or quality of being this

THISTLE, -S n prickly plant with dense flower heads

THISTLY ▶ thistle

THITHER adv or towards that place

THIVEL, -S same as ▶ thible

THLIPSIS, THLIPSES n compression, esp of part of the body

THO short for ▶ though

THOFT, -S n bench (in a boat) upon which a rower sits

THOLE, -D, -S, THOLING n wooden pin set in the side of a rowing boat to serve as a fulcrum for rowing ▷ vb bear or put up with

THOLEPIN same as ▶ thole

THOLES ▶ thole

THOLI ▶ tholus

THOLING ▶ thole

THOLOS, THOLOI n beehive-shaped tomb associated with Mycenaean Greece

THOLUS, THOLI n domed tomb

THON Scot word for ▶ yon

THONDER Scot word for ▶ yonder

THONG, -ING, -S n thin strip of leather etc ▷ vb decorate with a thong or thongs

THONGED adj fastened with a thong

THONGIER ▶ thongy

THONGING ▶ thong

THONGS ▶ thong

THONGY, THONGIER adj resembling a thong

THORACAL another word for ▶ thoracic

THORACES ▶ thorax

THORACIC adj of, near, or relating to the thorax

THORAX, THORACES, -ES n part of the body between the neck and the abdomen

THORIA, -S n insoluble white powder

THORIC ▶ thorium

THORITE, -S n yellow, brownish, or black radioactive mineral

THORIUM, -S n radioactive metallic element

THORN, -ED, -ING, -S n prickle on a plant ▷ vb jag or prick (something) as if with a thorn

THORNIER ▶ thorny

THORNILY ▶ thorny

THORNING ▶ thorn

THORNS ▶ thorn

THORNSET adj set with thorns

THORNY, THORNIER adj covered with thorns

THORO (nonstandard) variant spelling of ▶ thorough

THORON, -S n radioisotope of radon that is a decay product of thorium

THOROUGH adj complete ▷ n passage

THORP, -S n small village

THORPE, -S same as ▸ **thorp**

THORPS ▸ **thorp**

THOSE determiner form of that used before a plural noun

THOTHER pron old contraction of the other

THOU, -ED, -ING, -S pron used when talking to one person ▷ n one thousandth of an inch ▷ vb use the word thou

THOUGH adv nevertheless

THOUGHT, -S n concept or opinion

THOUING ▸ **thou**

THOUS ▸ **thou**

THOUSAND n ten hundred ▷ adj amounting to a thousand ▷ determiner amounting to a thousand

THOWEL, -S old variant of ▸ **thole**

THOWL, -S old variant of ▸ **thole**

THOWLESS adj lacking in vigour

THOWLS ▸ **thowl**

THRAE same as ▸ **frae**

THRALDOM same as ▸ **thrall**

THRALL, -ED, -S n state of being in the power of another person ▷ vb enslave or dominate

THRANG, -ED, -S n throng ▷ vb throng ▷ adj crowded

THRAPPLE n throat or windpipe ▷ vb throttle

THRASH, -ED, -ES vb beat, esp with a stick or whip ▷ n party

THRASHER same as ▸ **thresher**

THRASHES ▸ **thrash**

THRASHY adj relating to thrash punk

THRAVE, -S n twenty-four sheaves of corn

THRAW, -ED, -ING, -S vb twist (something); make something thrawn

THRAWARD adj contrary or stubborn

THRAWART same as ▸ **thraward**

THRAWED ▸ **thraw**

THRAWING ▸ **thraw**

THRAWN adj crooked or twisted

THRAWNLY ▸ **thrawn**

THRAWS ▸ **thraw**

THREAD, -ED n fine strand or yarn ▷ vb pass thread through

THREADEN adj made of thread

THREADER ▸ **thread**

THREADS slang word for ▸ **clothes**

THREADY adj of, relating to, or resembling a thread or threads

THREAP, -ED, -S vb scold

THREAPER ▸ **threap**

THREAPIT variant past participle of ▸ **threap**

THREAPS ▸ **threap**

THREAT, -ED, -S n declaration of intent to harm

THREATEN vb make or be a threat to

THREATS ▸ **threat**

THREAVE, -S same as ▸ **thrave**

THREE, -S n one more than two

THREEP, -ED, -S same as ▸ **threap**

THREEPER ▸ **threap**

THREEPIT variant past participle of ▸ **threep**

THREEPS ▸ **threep**

THREES ▸ **three**

THRENE, -S n dirge; threnody

THRENODE same as ▸ **threnody**

THRENODY n lament for the dead

THRENOS n threnody; lamentation

THRESH, -ED, -ES vb beat (wheat etc) to separate the grain from the husks and straw ▷ n act of threshing

THRESHEL n flail

THRESHER n large shark of tropical and temperate seas

THRESHES ▸ **thresh**

THRETTY nonstandard variant of ▸ **thirty**

THREW ▸ **throw**

THRICE adv three times

THRID, -DED, -S old variant of ▸ **thread**

THRIDACE n sedative made from lettuce juice

THRIDDED ▸ **thrid**

THRIDS ▸ **thrid**

THRIFT, -S n wisdom and caution with money

THRIFTY adj not wasteful with money

THRILL, -ED, -S n sudden feeling of excitement ▷ vb (cause to) feel a thrill

THRILLER n book, film, etc with an atmosphere of mystery or suspense

THRILLS ▸ **thrill**

THRILLY adj causing thrills

THRIMSA, -S same as ▸ **thrymsa**

THRIP same as ▸ **thrips**

THRIPS, -ES n small slender-bodied insect with piercing mouthparts that feeds on plant sap

THRISSEL Scots variant of ▸ **thistle**

THRIST, -ED, -S old variant of ▸ **thirst**

THRISTLE Scots variant of ▸ **thistle**

THRISTS ▸ **thrist**

THRISTY ▸ **thrist**

THRIVE, -D, -N, -S, THROVE vb flourish or prosper

THRIVER, -S ▸ **thrive**

THRIVES ▸ **thrive**

THRIVING ▸ **thrive**

THRO same as ▸ **through**

THROAT, -ED, -S n passage from the mouth and nose to the stomach and lungs ▷ vb vocalize in the throat

THROATY adj (of the voice) hoarse

THROB, -BED, -S vb pulsate repeatedly ▷ n throbbing

THROBBER ▸ **throb**

THROBS ▸ **throb**

THROE, -D, -ING n pang or pain ▷ vb endure throes

THROES pl n violent pangs or pains

THROMBI ▸ **thrombus**

THROMBIN n enzyme that acts on fibrinogen in blood, causing it to clot

THROMBUS, THROMBI n clot of coagulated blood that remains at the site of its formation

THRONE, -D, -S, THRONING n ceremonial seat of a monarch or bishop ▷ vb place or be placed on a throne

THRONG, -ED, -S vb crowd ▷ n great number of people or things crowded together ▷ adj busy

THRONING ▸ **throne**

THRONNER n person who is good at doing odd jobs

THROPPLE vb strangle or choke

THROSTLE n song thrush

THROTTLE n device controlling the amount of fuel entering an engine ▷ vb control the flow of fluid in an engine by using the throttle

T

THROUGH prep from end to end or side to side of ▷ adj finished

THROVE ▸ thrive

THROW, THREW, -ING, -N, -S vb hurl through the air ▷ n instance of throwing

THROWE, -S old variant of ▸ throe

THROWER, -S ▸ throw

THROWES ▸ throwe

THROWING ▸ throw

THROWN ▸ throw

THROWS ▸ throw

THRU same as ▸ through

THRUM, -MED, -S vb strum rhythmically but without expression ▷ n in textiles, unwoven ends of warp thread

THRUMMER ▸ thrum

THRUMMY adj made of thrums

THRUMS ▸ thrum

THRUPUT, -S n quantity of raw material or information processed in a given period

THRUSH, -ES n brown songbird

THRUST, -ED, -S vb push forcefully ▷ n forceful stab

THRUSTER n person or thing that thrusts

THRUSTOR variant of ▸ thruster

THRUSTS ▸ thrust

THRUTCH n narrow, fast-moving stream ▷ vb thrust

THRUWAY, -S n thoroughfare

THRYMSA, -S n gold coin used in Anglo-Saxon England

THUD, -DED, -S n dull heavy sound ▷ vb make such a sound

THUDDING n act of thudding

THUDS ▸ thud

THUG, -S n violent person, esp a criminal

THUGGEE, -S n (formerly) the methods of thugs in India

THUGGERY ▸ thug

THUGGISH ▸ thug

THUGGISM ▸ thug

THUGGO, -S n tough and violent person

THUGS ▸ thug

THUJA, -S n coniferous tree of North America and East Asia

THULIA, -S n oxide of thulium

THULITE, -S n rose-coloured zoisite sometimes incorporated into jewellery

THULIUM, -S n malleable ductile silvery-grey element

THUMB, -ED, -ING, -S n short thick finger set apart from the others ▷ vb touch or handle with the thumb

THUMBIER ▸ thumby

THUMBING ▸ thumb

THUMBKIN n thumbscrew

THUMBNUT n nut with projections enabling it to be turned by the thumb and forefinger

THUMBPOT n tiny flowerpot

THUMBS ▸ thumb

THUMBY, THUMBIER adj clumsy; uncoordinated

THUMP, -ED, -S n (sound of) a dull heavy blow ▷ vb strike heavily

THUMPER, -S ▸ thump

THUMPING adj huge or excessive

THUMPS ▸ thump

THUNDER, -S n loud noise accompanying lightning ▷ vb rumble with thunder

THUNDERY ▸ thunder

THUNK, -ED, -ING, -S another word for ▸ thud

THURIBLE same as ▸ censer

THURIFER n person appointed to carry the censer at religious ceremonies

THURIFY vb burn incense near or before an altar, shrine, etc

THURL, -S same as ▸ thirl

THUS, -ES adv in this manner ▷ n aromatic gum resin

THUSLY adv in such a way; thus

THUSNESS n state or quality of being thus

THUSWISE adv in this way; thus

THUYA, -S same as ▸ thuja

THWACK, -ED, -S n whack ▷ vb beat with something flat ▷ interj exclamation imitative of this sound

THWACKER ▸ thwack

THWACKS ▸ thwack

THWAITE, -S n piece of land cleared from forest or reclaimed from wasteland

THWART, -ED, -S vb foil or frustrate ▷ n seat across a boat ▷ adj passing or being situated across ▷ adv across

THWARTER ▸ thwart

THWARTLY ▸ thwart

THWARTS ▸ thwart

THY adj of or associated with you (thou) ▷ determiner belonging to or associated in some way with you (thou)

THYINE adj of relating to the sandarac tree

THYLOSE old variant of ▸ tylosis

THYLOSIS, THYLOSES same as ▸ tylosis

THYME, -S n aromatic herb

THYMEY ▸ thyme

THYMI ▸ thymus

THYMIC adj of or relating to the thymus

THYMIER ▸ thymy

THYMIEST ▸ thymy

THYMINE, -S n white crystalline pyrimidine base found in DNA

THYMOL, -S n substance obtained from thyme

THYMOMA, -S n type of tumour

THYMOSIN n hormone secreted by the thymus

THYMUS, THYMI, -ES n small gland at the base of the neck

THYMY, THYMIER, THYMIEST ▸ thyme

THYREOID same as ▸ thyroid

THYROID, -S n gland in the neck controlling body growth ▷ adj of or relating to the thyroid gland

THYROXIN same as > thyroxine

THYRSE, -S n type of inflorescence, occurring in the lilac and grape

THYRSI ▸ thyrsus

THYRSOID ▸ thyrse

THYRSUS, THYRSI same as ▸ thyrse

THYSELF pron reflexive form of thou

TI, -S same as ▸ te

TIAN, -S n traditional French vegetable stew or earthenware dish it is cooked in

TIAR, -S same as ▸ tiara

TIARA, -S n semicircular jewelled headdress

TIARAED ▸ tiara

TIARAS ▸ tiara

TIARS ▸ tiar

TIBIA, -E, -S n inner bone of the lower leg

TIBIAL ▸ tibia

TIBIALIS, TIBIALES n muscle in the calf of the leg

TIBIAS ▸ tibia

TIC, -CED, -CING, -S n spasmodic muscular twitch ▷ vb move in a spasmodic twitch

TICAL, -S n former standard monetary unit of Thailand

TICCA adj acquired for temporary use in exchange for payment

TICCED ► tic

TICCING ► tic

TICE, -D, -S, TICING vb tempt or allure; entice

TICH, -ES same as ► titch

TICHY, TICHIER, TICHIEST same as ► titchy

TICING ► tice

TICK, -ED, -S n mark used to check off or indicate the correctness of something ▷ vb mark with a tick

TICKEN, -S same as ► ticking

TICKER, -S n heart

TICKET, -ED n card or paper entitling the holder to admission, travel, etc ▷ vb attach or issue a ticket to

TICKETS pl n death or ruin

TICKEY, -S n former South African threepenny piece

TICKIES ► ticky

TICKING, -S n strong material for mattress covers

TICKLACE n (in Newfoundland) a kittiwake

TICKLE, -D, -S, TICKLING vb touch or stroke (a person) to produce laughter ▷ n tickling

TICKLER, -S n difficult or delicate problem

TICKLES ► tickle

TICKLIER ► tickly

TICKLING ► tickle

TICKLISH adj sensitive to tickling

TICKLY, TICKLIER ► tickle

TICKS ► tick

TICKSEED another name for > coreopsis

TICKTACK n sound made by a clock ▷ vb make a ticking sound

TICKTOCK n ticking sound made by a clock ▷ vb make a ticking sound

TICKY, TICKIES same as ► tickey

TICS ► tic

TICTAC, -S same as ► ticktack

TICTOC, -S same as ► ticktock

TID, -S n mood or humour

TIDAL adj (of a river, lake, or sea) having tides

TIDALLY ► tidal

TIDBIT, -S same as ► titbit

TIDDIER ► tiddy

TIDDIES ► tiddy

TIDDIEST ► tiddy

TIDDLE, -D, -S, TIDDLING vb busy oneself with inconsequential tasks

TIDDLER, -S n very small fish

TIDDLES ► tiddle

TIDDLEY, -S same as ► tiddly

TIDDLIER ► tiddly

TIDDLIES ► tiddly

TIDDLING ► tiddle

TIDDLY, TIDDLIER, TIDDLIES adj tiny ▷ n alcoholic beverage

TIDDY, TIDDIER, TIDDIES, TIDDIEST n four of trumps in the card game gleek

TIDE, -D, -S, TIDING n rise and fall of the sea caused by the gravitational pull of the sun and moon ▷ vb carry or be carried with or as if with the tide

TIDELAND n land between high-water and low-water marks

TIDELESS ► tide

TIDELIKE ► tide

TIDELINE n high-water mark left by the retreating tide

TIDEMARK n mark left by the highest or lowest point of a tide

TIDEMILL n watermill powered by the force of the tide

TIDERIP, -S same as ► riptide

TIDES ► tide

TIDESMAN, TIDESMEN n customs official at a port

TIDEWAVE n undulation of the earth's water levels as the tide moves around it

TIDEWAY, -S n strong tidal current or its channel, esp the tidal part of a river

TIDIED ► tidy

TIDIER ► tidy

TIDIERS ► tidy

TIDIES ► tidy

TIDIEST ► tidy

TIDILY ► tidy

TIDINESS ► tidy

TIDING ► tide

TIDINGS pl n news

TIDIVATE same as ► titivate

TIDS ► tid

TIDY, TIDIED, TIDIER, TIDIERS, TIDIES, TIDIEST, -ING adj neat and orderly ▷ vb put in order ▷ n small container for odds and ends

TIDYTIPS n herb with flowers resembling those of the daisy

TIE, -D, -S, TYING vb fasten or be fastened with string, rope, etc ▷ n long narrow piece of material worn knotted round the neck

TIEBACK, -S n length of cord, ribbon, or other fabric used for tying a curtain to one side

TIEBREAK n deciding game in drawn match

TIECLASP n clip, often ornamental, which holds a tie in place against a shirt

TIED ► tie

TIEING same as ► tie

TIELESS ► tie

TIEPIN, -S n ornamental pin used to pin the two ends of a tie to a shirt

TIER, -ED, -ING, -S n one of a set of rows placed one above and behind the other ▷ vb be or arrange in tiers

TIERCE, -S same as ► terce

TIERCED adj (of a shield) divided into three sections of similar size but different colour

TIERCEL, -S same as ► tercel

TIERCES ► tierce

TIERCET, -S same as ► tercet

TIERED ► tier

TIERING ► tier

TIERS ► tier

TIES ► tie

TIETAC, -S n fastener for holding a tie in place

TIETACK, -S same as ► tietac

TIETACS ► tietac

TIFF, -ED, -ING, -INGS, -S n petty quarrel ▷ vb have or be in a tiff

TIFFANY n sheer fine gauzy fabric

TIFFED ► tiff

TIFFIN, -ED, -S n (in India) a light meal, esp at midday ▷ vb take tiffin

TIFFING ► tiff

TIFFINGS ► tiff

TIFFINS ► tiffin

TIFFS ► tiff

TIFO, -S n organized fan display during a football match

TIFOSO, TIFOSI, -S n (in sport) a fanatical fan

TIFT, -ED, -ING, -S Scots variant of ► tiff

TIG, -GED, -GING, -S n child's game

TIGE, -S n trunk of an architectural column

TIGER, -S n large yellow-and-black striped Asian cat

TIGEREYE n golden brown silicified variety of crocidolite, used as an ornamental stone

TIGERIER ▸ tigery

TIGERISH ▸ tiger

TIGERISM n arrogant and showy manner

TIGERLY adj of or like a tiger

TIGERS ▸ tiger

TIGERY, TIGERIER adj like a tiger

TIGES ▸ tige

TIGGED ▸ tig

TIGGER, -ED, -S vb damage beyond repair by tinkering

TIGGING ▸ tig

TIGHT, -ER, -EST adj stretched or drawn taut ▸ adv in a close, firm, or secure way

TIGHTEN, -S vb make or become tight or tighter

TIGHTER ▸ tight

TIGHTEST ▸ tight

TIGHTISH ▸ tight

TIGHTLY ▸ tight

TIGHTS pl n one-piece clinging garment covering the body from the waist to the feet

TIGHTWAD n stingy person

TIGLIC adj as in tiglic acid syrupy liquid or crystalline colourless unsaturated carboxylic acid

TIGLON, -S same as ▸ tigon

TIGNON, -S n type of cloth headdress

TIGON, -S n hybrid offspring of a male tiger and a female lion

TIGRESS n female tiger

TIGRIDIA n type of tropical American plant

TIGRINE adj of, characteristic of, or resembling a tiger

TIGRISH ▸ tiger

TIGROID adj resembling a tiger

TIGS ▸ tig

TIKA, -S same as ▸ tikka

TIKANGA, -S n Māori ways or customs

TIKAS ▸ tika

TIKE, -S same as ▸ tyke

TIKI, -ED, -ING, -S n small carving of a grotesque person worn as a pendant ▸ vb take a scenic tour around an area

TIKKA, -S adj marinated in spices and dry-roasted ▸ n coloured spot or mark worn by Hindus

TIL, -S another name for ▸ sesame

TILAK, -S n coloured spot or mark worn by Hindus

TILAPIA, -S n type of fish

TILBURY n light two-wheeled horse-drawn open carriage

TILDE, -S n mark used in Spanish to indicate pronunciation

TILE, -D, -S n flat piece of ceramic, plastic, etc used to cover a roof, floor, or wall ▸ vb cover with tiles

TILEFISH n large brightly coloured deep-sea percoid food fish

TILELIKE adj like a tile

TILER, -S ▸ tile

TILERIES ▸ tilery

TILERS ▸ tiler

TILERY, TILERIES n place where tiles are produced

TILES ▸ tile

TILING, -S n tiles collectively

TILL, -ED, -ING, -INGS, -S prep until ▸ vb cultivate (land) ▸ n drawer for money, usu in a cash register

TILLABLE ▸ till

TILLAGE, -S n act, process, or art of tilling

TILLED ▸ till

TILLER, -ED, -S n on boats, a handle fixed to the top of a rudderpost to serve as a lever in steering ▸ vb use a tiller

TILLICUM n (in the Pacific Northwest) a friend

TILLIER ▸ tilly

TILLIEST ▸ tilly

TILLING ▸ till

TILLINGS ▸ till

TILLITE, -S n rock formed from hardened till

TILLS ▸ till

TILLY, TILLIER, TILLIEST ▸ till

TILS ▸ til

TILT, -ED, -ING, -INGS, -S vb slant at an angle ▸ n slope

TILTABLE ▸ tilt

TILTED ▸ tilt

TILTER, -S ▸ tilt

TILTH, -S n (condition of) land that has been tilled

TILTING ▸ tilt

TILTINGS ▸ tilt

TILTS ▸ tilt

TILTYARD n (formerly) an enclosed area for jousting

TIMARAU, -S same as ▸ tamarau

TIMARIOT n one holding a fief in feudal Turkey

TIMBAL, -S n type of kettledrum

TIMBALE, -S n mixture of meat, fish, etc, in a rich sauce

TIMBALS ▸ timbal

TIMBER, -S n wood as a building material ▸ adj made out of timber ▸ vb provide with timbers ▸ interj lumberjack's shouted warning when a tree is about to fall

TIMBERED adj made of or containing timber or timbers

TIMBERS ▸ timber

TIMBERY adj like timber

TIMBO, -S n Amazonian vine from which a useful insecticide can be derived

TIMBRAL adj relating to timbre

TIMBRE, -S n distinctive quality of sound of a voice or instrument

TIMBREL, -S n tambourine

TIMBRES ▸ timbre

TIME, -D, -S n past, present, and future as a continuous whole ▸ vb note the time taken by

TIMEBOMB n bomb containing a timing mechanism that determines the time it will detonate

TIMECARD n card used with a time clock

TIMED ▸ time

TIMELESS adj unaffected by time

TIMELIER ▸ timely

TIMELINE n graphic representation showing the passage of time as a line

TIMELY, TIMELIER adj at the appropriate time ▸ adv at the right or an appropriate time

TIMEOUS adj in good time

TIMEOUT, -S n short, interruption in play during which players rest, etc

TIMEPASS n way of passing the time ▸ vb pass the time

TIMER, -S n device for measuring time

TIMES ▸ time

TIMEWORK n work paid for by the length of time taken, esp by the hour or the day

TIMEWORN adj showing the adverse effects of overlong use or of old age

TIMID, -ER, -EST adj easily frightened

TIMIDITY ▶ timid

TIMIDLY ▶ timid

TIMING, -S n ability to judge when to do or say something so as to make the best effect

TIMIST, -S n one concerned with time

TIMOLOL, -S n relaxant medicine used (for example) to reduce blood pressure

TIMON, -S n apparatus by which a vessel is steered

TIMONEER n helmsman; tillerman

TIMONS ▶ timon

TIMOROUS adj timid

TIMOTHY n perennial grass of temperate regions

TIMOUS same as ▶ timeous

TIMOUSLY ▶ timous

TIMPANA, -S n traditional Maltese baked pasta and pastry dish

TIMPANI pl n set of kettledrums

TIMPANO n kettledrum

TIMPANUM same as ▶ tympanum

TIMPS same as ▶ timpani

TIN, -NED, -NING, -NINGS, -S n soft metallic element ▷ vb put (food) into tins

TINAJA, -S n large jar for cooling water

TINAMOU, -S n type of bird of Central and S America

TINCAL, -S another name for ▶ borax

TINCHEL, -S n in Scotland, a circle of deer hunters who gradually close in on their quarry

TINCT, -ED, -ING, -S vb tint ▷ adj tinted or coloured

TINCTURE n medicinal extract in a solution of alcohol ▷ vb give a tint or colour to

TIND, -ED, -ING, -S vb set alight

TINDAL, -S n petty officer

TINDED ▶ tind

TINDER, -S n dry easily burning material used to start a fire

TINDERY adj like tinder

TINDING ▶ tind

TINDS ▶ tind

TINE, -S, TINING n prong of a fork or antler ▷ vb lose

TINEA, -S n any fungal skin disease, esp ringworm

TINEAL ▶ tinea

TINEAS ▶ tinea

TINED ▶ tine

TINEID, -S n type of moth of the family which includes the clothes moths

TINES ▶ tine

TINFOIL, -S n paper-thin sheet of metal, used for wrapping foodstuffs

TINFUL, -S n contents of a tin or the amount a tin will hold

TING, -S same as ▶ thing

TINGE, -D, -ING, -S, TINGING n slight tint ▷ vb give a slight tint or trace to

TINGLE, -D, -S n prickling or stinging sensation ▷ vb feel a mild prickling or stinging sensation, as from cold or excitement

TINGLER, -S ▶ tingle

TINGLES ▶ tingle

TINGLIER ▶ tingly

TINGLING ▶ tingle

TINGLISH adj exciting

TINGLY, TINGLIER ▶ tingle

TINGS ▶ ting

TINHORN, -S n cheap pretentious person ▷ adj cheap and showy

TINIER ▶ tiny

TINIES pl n small children

TINIEST ▶ tiny

TINILY ▶ tiny

TININESS ▶ tiny

TINING ▶ tine

TINK, -ED, -ING, -S vb make short sound like a bell

TINKER, -ED, -S n (formerly) travelling mender of pots and pans ▷ vb fiddle with (an engine etc) in an attempt to repair it

TINKERER ▶ tinker

TINKERS ▶ tinker

TINKING ▶ tink

TINKLE, -D, -S vb ring with a high tinny sound like a small bell ▷ n this sound or action

TINKLER, -S same as ▶ tinker

TINKLES ▶ tinkle

TINKLIER ▶ tinkly

TINKLING ▶ tinkle

TINKLY, TINKLIER ▶ tinkle

TINKS ▶ tink

TINLIKE ▶ tin

TINMAN, TINMEN n one who works with tin or tin plate

TINNED ▶ tin

TINNER, -S n tin miner

TINNIE same as ▶ tinny

TINNIER ▶ tinny

TINNIES ▶ tinny

TINNIEST ▶ tinny

TINNILY ▶ tinny

TINNING ▶ tin

TINNINGS ▶ tin

TINNITUS n ringing or hissing sensation in one or both ears

TINNY, TINNIER, TINNIES, TINNIEST adj (of sound) thin and metallic ▷ n can of beer

TINPLATE n thin steel sheet coated with tin ▷ vb coat (a metal or object) with a layer of tin

TINPOT, -S adj worthless or unimportant ▷ n pot made of tin

TINS ▶ tin

TINSEL, -ED, -S n decorative metallic strips or threads ▷ adj made of or decorated with tinsel ▷ vb decorate with or as if with tinsel

TINSELLY adj adorned with tinsel

TINSELRY n tinsel-like material

TINSELS ▶ tinsel

TINSELY adj (US) like tinsel

TINSEY, -S old variant of ▶ tinsel

TINSMITH n person who works with tin or tin plate

TINSNIPS pl n metal cutters

TINSTONE n black or brown stone

TINT, -ED, -ING, -INGS, -S n (pale) shade of a colour ▷ vb give a tint to

TINTACK, -S n tin-plated tack

TINTED ▶ tint

TINTER, -S ▶ tint

TINTIER ▶ tinty

TINTIEST ▶ tinty

TINTING ▶ tint

TINTINGS ▶ tint

TINTLESS ▶ tint

TINTS ▶ tint

TINTY, TINTIER, TINTIEST adj having many tints

TINTYPE, -S another name for > ferrotype

TINWARE, -S n objects made of tin plate

TINWORK n objects made of tin

TINWORKS n place where tin is mined, smelted, or rolled

TINY, TINIER, TINIEST adj very small

T

TIP, -PED, -PING, -PINGS, -S, -T n narrow or pointed end of anything ▷ vb put a tip on

TIPCART, -S n cart that can be tipped to empty out its contents

TIPCAT, -S n game in which a piece of wood is tipped in the air with a stick

TIPI, -S variant spelling of ▷ **tepee**

TIPLESS ▷ **tip**

TIPOFF, -S n warning or hint, esp given confidentially

TIPPABLE ▷ **tip**

TIPPED ▷ **tip**

TIPPEE, -S n person who receives a tip, esp regarding share prices

TIPPER, -S n person who gives or leaves a tip

TIPPET, -S n fur cape for the shoulders

TIPPIER ▷ **tippy**

TIPPIEST ▷ **tippy**

TIPPING ▷ **tip**

TIPPINGS ▷ **tip**

TIPPLE, -D, -S, TIPPLING vb drink alcohol habitually, esp in small quantities ▷ n alcoholic drink

TIPPLER, -S ▷ **tipple**

TIPPLES ▷ **tipple**

TIPPLING ▷ **tipple**

TIPPY, TIPPIER, TIPPIEST adj extremely fashionable or stylish

TIPPYTOE same as ▷ **tiptoe**

TIPS ▷ **tip**

TIPSHEET n list of advice or instructions

TIPSIER ▷ **tipsy**

TIPSIEST ▷ **tipsy**

TIPSIFY vb make tipsy

TIPSILY ▷ **tipsy**

TIPSTAFF n court official

TIPSTER, -S n person who sells tips about races

TIPSTOCK n detachable section of a gunstock, usually gripped by the left hand of the user

TIPSY, TIPSIER, TIPSIEST adj slightly drunk

TIPT ▷ **tip**

TIPTOE, -D, -S vb walk quietly with the heels off the ground

TIPTOP, -S adj of the highest quality or condition ▷ n best in quality

TIPULA, -S n crane fly

TIPUNA, -S n ancestor

TIRADE, -S n long angry speech

TIRAGE, -S n drawing of wine from a barrel prior to bottling

TIRAMISU n Italian coffee-flavoured dessert

TIRASSE, -S n mechanism in an organ connecting two pedals

TIRE, -S vb reduce the energy of, as by exertion

TIRED, -ER, -EST adj exhausted

TIREDLY ▷ **tired**

TIRELESS adj energetic and determined

TIRELING n fatigued person or animal

TIRES ▷ **tire**

TIRESOME adj boring and irritating

TIRING, -S ▷ **tire**

TIRITI, -S n another name for the Treaty of Waitangi

> A Māori word for treaty. Any 6-letter word that lets you get rid of three Is can't be bad!

TIRL, -ED, -ING, -S vb turn

TIRO, -ES, -S same as ▷ **tyro**

TIRONIC variant of ▷ **tyronic**

TIROS ▷ **tiro**

TIRR, -ED, -ING, -S vb strip or denude

TIRRIT, -S n panic; scare

TIRRIVEE n Scots word for an outburst of bad temper

TIRRIVIE same as ▷ **tirrivee**

TIRRS ▷ **tirr**

TIS ▷ **ti**

TISANE, -S n infusion of dried or fresh leaves or flowers

TISICK, -S n splutter; cough

TISSUAL adj relating to tissue

TISSUE, -D, -S, TISSUING n substance of an animal body or plant ▷ vb weave into tissue

TISSUEY, TISSUIER adj like tissue

TISSUING ▷ **tissue**

TISSULAR adj relating to tissue

TISWAS, -ES n state of anxiety or excitement

TIT, -S, -TED, -TING n any of various small songbirds ▷ vb jerk or tug

TITAN, -S n person who is huge, strong, or very important

TITANATE n any salt or ester of titanic acid

TITANESS n woman who is huge, strong, or very important

TITANIA, -S n titanium dioxide

TITANIC adj huge or very important

TITANIS n large predatory flightless prehistoric bird

TITANISM n titanic power

TITANITE another name for ▷ **sphene**

TITANIUM n strong light metallic element used to make alloys

TITANOUS adj of or containing titanium, esp in the trivalent state

TITANS ▷ **titan**

TITBIT, -S n tasty piece of food

TITCH, -ES n small person

TITCHIE same as ▷ **titchy**

TITCHY, TITCHIER adj very small

TITE adj immediate

TITELY adv immediately

TITER, -S same as ▷ **titre**

TITFER, -S n hat

TITHABLE adj (until 1936) liable to pay tithes

TITHE, -D, -S, TITHING n esp formerly, one tenth of one's income or produce paid to the church as a tax ▷ vb charge or pay a tithe

TITHER, -S ▷ **tithe**

TITHES ▷ **tithe**

TITHING, -S ▷ **tithe**

TITHONIA n Central American herb with flowers resembling sunflowers

TITI, -S n small omnivorous monkey

TITIAN, -S n reddish gold colour

TITIS ▷ **titi**

TITIVATE vb smarten up

TITLARK, -S another name for ▷ **pipit**

TITLE, -S, TITLING n name of a book, film, etc ▷ vb give a title to

TITLED adj aristocratic

TITLER, -S n one who writes titles

TITLES ▷ **title**

TITLIKE adj like a tit

TITLING, -S ▷ **title**

TITLIST, -S n titleholder

TITMAN, TITMEN n (of pigs) the runt of a litter

TITMICE ▷ **titmouse**

TITMOSE old spelling of ▷ **titmouse**

TITMOUSE, TITMICE n any small active songbird

TITOKI, -S n New Zealand evergreen tree with a

spreading crown and glossy green leaves

TITRABLE ▶ titrate

TITRANT, -S *n* solution in a titration that is added to a measured quantity of another solution

TITRATE, -D, -S *vb* measure the volume or concentration of (a solution) by titration

TITRATOR *n* device used to perform titration

TITRE, -S *n* concentration of a solution as determined by titration

TITS ▶ tit

TITTED ▶ tit

TITTER, -ED, -S *vb* laugh in a suppressed way ▷ *n* suppressed laugh

TITTERER ▶ titter

TITTERS ▶ titter

TITTIE, -S *n* dialect word for a sister or young woman

TITTING ▶ tit

TITTISH *adj* testy

TITTLE, -D, -S, TITTLING *n* very small amount ▷ *vb* chatter; tattle

TITTUP, -ED, -S *vb* prance or frolic ▷ *n* caper

TITTUPPY *same as* ▶ **tittupy**

TITTUPS ▶ tittup

TITTUPY *adj* sprightly; lively

TITTY *same as* ▶ **tittie**

TITUBANT *adj* staggering

TITUBATE *vb* stagger

TITULAR, -S *adj* in name only ▷ *n* bearer of a title

TITULARY *same as* ▶ **titular**

TITULE, -D, -S, TITULING *same as* ▶ **title**

TITULI ▶ titulus

TITULING ▶ titule

TITULUS, TITULI *n* sign attached to the top of the cross during crucifixion

TITUP, -ED, -ING, -PED, -S *same as* ▶ **tittup**

TITUPIER ▶ titupy

TITUPING ▶ titup

TITUPPED ▶ titup

TITUPS ▶ titup

TITUPY, TITUPIER *same as* ▶ **tittupy**

TIVY *same as* ▶ **tantivy**

TIX *pl n* tickets

Tix is an informal word for **tickets** and one of the key short words for using the X.

TIYIN, -S *n* monetary unit of Uzbekistan and Kyrgyzstan

TIYN, -S *same as* ▶ **tiyin**

TIZ, -ES *n* state of confusion

TIZWAS, -ES *same as* ▶ **tiswas**

TIZZ, -ES *same as* ▶ **tizzy**

TIZZY, TIZZIES *n* confused or agitated state

TJANTING *n* pen-like tool used in batik for applying molten wax to fabric

TMESIS, TMESES *n* interpolation of a word between the parts of a compound word

TO *prep* indicating movement towards, equality or comparison, etc ▷ *adv* a closed position

TOAD, -S *n* animal like a large frog

TOADFISH *n* spiny-finned fish with a wide mouth

TOADFLAX *n* plant with narrow leaves and yellow-orange flowers

TOADIED ▶ toady

TOADIES ▶ toady

TOADISH ▶ toad

TOADLESS *adj* having no toads

TOADLET, -S *n* small toad

TOADLIKE ▶ toad

TOADRUSH *n* annual rush growing in damp lowlands

TOADS ▶ toad

TOADY, TOADIED, TOADIES *n* ingratiating person ▷ *vb* be ingratiating

TOADYING *n* act of toadying

TOADYISH ▶ toady

TOADYISM ▶ toady

TOAST, -ED, -ING, -S *n* sliced bread browned by heat ▷ *vb* brown (bread) by heat

TOASTER, -S ▶ toast

TOASTIE *same as* ▶ **toasty**

TOASTIER ▶ toasty

TOASTIES ▶ toasty

TOASTING ▶ toast

TOASTS ▶ toast

TOASTY, TOASTIER, TOASTIES *n* toasted sandwich ▷ *adj* tasting or smelling like toast

TOAZE, -D, -S, TOAZING *variant spelling of* ▶ **toze**

TOBACCO, -S *n* plant with large leaves dried for smoking

TOBIES ▶ toby

TOBOGGAN *n* narrow sledge for sliding over snow ▷ *vb* ride a toboggan

TOBOGGIN *variant spelling of* ▶ **toboggan**

TOBY, TOBIES *n* water stopcock at the boundary of a street and house section

TOC, -S *n* in communications code, signal for letter t

TOCCATA, -S, TOCCATE *n* rapid piece of music for a keyboard instrument

TOCHER, -ED, -S *n* dowry ▷ *vb* give a dowry to

TOCK, -ED, -ING, -S *n* sound made by a clock ▷ *vb* (of a clock) make such a sound

TOCKIER ▶ tocky

TOCKIEST ▶ tocky

TOCKING ▶ tock

TOCKS ▶ tock

TOCKY, TOCKIER, TOCKIEST *adj* muddy

TOCO, -S *n* punishment

TOCOLOGY *n* branch of medicine concerned with childbirth

TOCOS ▶ toco

TOCS ▶ toc

TOCSIN, -S *n* warning signal

TOD, -DED, -DING, -S *n* unit of weight, used for wool, etc ▷ *vb* produce a tod

TODAY, -S *n* this day ▷ *adv* on this day

TODDE, -S *same as* ▶ **tod**

TODDED ▶ tod

TODDES ▶ todde

TODDIES ▶ toddy

TODDING ▶ tod

TODDLE, -D, -S, TODDLING *vb* walk with short unsteady steps ▷ *n* act or an instance of toddling

TODDLER, -S *n* child beginning to walk

TODDLES ▶ toddle

TODDLING ▶ toddle

TODDY, TODDIES *n* sweetened drink of spirits and hot water

TODIES ▶ tody

TODS ▶ tod

TODY, TODIES *n* small bird of the Caribbean

TOE, -D, -ING, -S *n* digit of the foot ▷ *vb* touch or kick with the toe

TOEA, -S *n* monetary unit of Papua New Guinea

This monetary unit of Papua New Guinea is very often played to rid the rack of a surplus of vowels.

TOEBIE, -S *n* South African slang for sandwich

TOECAP, -S *n* strengthened covering for the toe of a shoe

TOECLIP, -S *n* clip on a bicycle pedal for the toes

TOED ▶ toe

TOEHOLD, -S *n* small space on a mountain for supporting the toe of the foot in climbing

T

TOEIER ▷ toey

> This is the comparative of **toey**, Australian slang for nervous or edgy, and can come in useful for dumping a surplus of vowels.

TOEIEST ▷ toey
TOEING ▷ toe
TOELESS adj not having toes
TOELIKE ▷ toe
TOENAIL, -S n thin hard clear plate covering part of the upper surface of the end of each toe ▷ vb join (beams) by driving nails obliquely
TOEPIECE n part of a shoe that covers the toes
TOEPLATE n metal reinforcement of the part of the sole of a shoe or boot underneath the toes
TOERAG, -S n contemptible person
TOES ▷ toe
TOESHOE, -S n ballet pump with padded toes
TOETOE, -S same as ▷ **toitoi**
TOEY, TOEIER, TOEIEST adj (of a person) nervous or anxious
TOFF n well-dressed or upper-class person
TOFFEE, -S n chewy sweet made of boiled sugar
TOFFIER ▷ toffy
TOFFIES ▷ toffy
TOFFIEST ▷ toffy
TOFFISH adj belonging to or characteristic of the upper class
TOFFS adj like a toff
TOFFY, TOFFIER, TOFFIES, TOFFIEST same as ▷ **toffee**
TOFORE prep before
TOFT, -S n homestead
TOFU, -S n soft food made from soya-bean curd
TOFUTTI, -S n tradename for nondairy, soya-based food products
TOG, -GED, -GING, -S n unit for measuring the insulating power of duvets ▷ vb dress oneself
TOGA, -E, -S n garment worn by citizens of ancient Rome ▷ vb wear a toga
TOGAED ▷ toga
TOGAS ▷ toga
TOGATE adj clad in a toga
TOGATED same as ▷ **togate**
TOGE, -S old variant of ▷ **toga**
TOGED ▷ toge
TOGES ▷ toge
TOGETHER adv in company ▷ adj organized

TOGGED ▷ tog
TOGGER, -ED, -S vb play football ▷ n football player
TOGGERY n clothes
TOGGING ▷ tog
TOGGLE, -D, -S, TOGGLING n small bar-shaped button inserted through a loop for fastening ▷ vb supply or fasten with a toggle or toggles
TOGGLER, -S ▷ toggle
TOGGLES ▷ toggle
TOGGLING ▷ toggle
TOGROG, -S n unit of currency in Mongolia
TOGS ▷ tog
TOGUE, -S n large North American freshwater game fish
TOHEROA, -S n large edible mollusc of New Zealand
TOHO, -S n (to a hunting dog) an instruction to stop
TOHUNGA, -S n Māori priest
TOIL, -ED, -ING, -INGS, -S n hard work ▷ vb work hard
TOILE, -S n transparent linen or cotton fabric
TOILED ▷ toil
TOILER, -S ▷ toil
TOILES ▷ toile
TOILET, -ED, -S n bowl connected to a drain for receiving and disposing of urine and faeces ▷ vb go to the toilet
TOILETRY n object or cosmetic used to clean or groom oneself
TOILETS ▷ toilet
TOILETTE same as ▷ **toilet**
TOILFUL same as ▷ **toilsome**
TOILINET n type of fabric with a woollen weft and a cotton or silk warp
TOILING ▷ toil
TOILINGS ▷ toil
TOILLESS ▷ toil
TOILS ▷ toil
TOILSOME adj requiring hard work
TOILWORN adj fatigued, wearied by work
TOING, -S n as in **toing and froing** state of going back and forth
TOISE, -S n obsolete French unit of length roughly equal to 2 metres
TOISEACH n ancient Celtic nobleman
TOISECH, -S same as ▷ **toiseach**
TOISES ▷ toise
TOISON, -S n fleece

TOIT, -ED, -ING, -S vb walk or move in an unsteady manner, as from old age
TOITOI, -S n tall grasses with feathery fronds
TOITS ▷ toit
TOKAMAK, -S n reactor used in thermonuclear experiments
TOKAY, -S n small gecko of S and SE Asia, having a retractile claw at the tip of each digit
TOKEN, -ED, -ING, -S n sign or symbol ▷ adj nominal or slight ▷ vb act as a symbol
TOKENISM n policy of making only a token effort, esp to comply with a law
TOKENS ▷ token
TOKO, -S same as ▷ **toco**
TOKOLOGY same as ▷ **tocology**
TOKOMAK, -S variant spelling of ▷ **tokamak**
TOKONOMA n recess off a living room in a Japanese house
TOKOS ▷ toko
TOKOTOKO n ceremonial carved Māori walking stick
TOLA, -S n unit of weight, used in India
TOLAN, -S n white crystalline derivative of acetylene
TOLANE, -S same as ▷ **tolan**
TOLANS ▷ tolan
TOLAR, -JEV, -JI, -S n former monetary unit of Slovenia
TOLAS ▷ tola
TOLBOOTH same as > **tollbooth**
TOLD ▷ tell
TOLE, -D, -S, TOLING, TOLINGS same as ▷ **toll**
TOLEDO, -S n type of sword originally made in Toledo
TOLERANT adj able to tolerate the beliefs, actions, opinions, etc, of others
TOLERATE vb allow to exist or happen
TOLES ▷ tole
TOLEWARE n enamelled or lacquered metalware, usually gilded
TOLIDIN, -S same as ▷ **tolidine**
TOLIDINE n compound used in dyeing and chemical analysis
TOLIDINS ▷ tolidin
TOLING ▷ tole
TOLINGS ▷ tole

TOLL, -ED, -ING, -INGS, -S *vb* ring (a bell) slowly and regularly ▷ *n* instance of tolling

TOLLABLE ▶ **toll**

TOLLAGE, -S *same as* ▶ **toll**

TOLLBAR, -S *n* bar blocking passage of a thoroughfare, raised on payment of a toll

TOLLDISH *n* dish used to measure out the portion of grain given to a miller as payment for their work

TOLLED ▶ **toll**

TOLLER, -S ▶ **toll**

TOLLEY, -S *n* large shooting marble used in a game of marbles

TOLLGATE *n* gate across a toll road or bridge at which travellers must pay

TOLLIE *same as* ▶ **tolly**

TOLLIES ▶ **tolly**

TOLLING ▶ **toll**

TOLLINGS ▶ **toll**

TOLLMAN, TOLLMEN *n* man who collects tolls

TOLLS ▶ **toll**

TOLLWAY, -S *n* road on which users must pay tolls to travel

TOLLY, TOLLIES *n* castrated calf

TOLSEL, -S *n* tolbooth

TOLSEY, -S *n* tolbooth

TOLT, -S *n* type of obsolete English writ

TOLTER, -ED, -S *vb* struggle or move with difficulty, as in mud

TOLTS ▶ **tolt**

TOLU, -S *n* sweet-smelling balsam obtained from a South American tree

TOLUATE, -S *n* any salt or ester of any of the three isomeric forms of toluic acid

TOLUENE, -S *n* colourless volatile flammable liquid obtained from petroleum and coal tar

TOLUIC *adj* as in **toluic acid** white crystalline derivative of toluene

TOLUID, -S *n* white crystalline derivative of glycocoll

TOLUIDE, -S *variant of* ▶ **toluid**

TOLUIDIN *n* type of dye

TOLUIDS ▶ **toluid**

TOLUOL, -S *another name for* ▶ **toluene**

TOLUOLE, -S *another name for* ▶ **toluene**

TOLUOLS ▶ **toluol**

TOLUS ▶ **tolu**

TOLUYL, -S *n* any of three groups derived from a toluic acid

TOLYL, -S *n* type of monovalent radical

TOLZEY, -S *n* tolbooth

TOM, -S *n* male cat ▷ *adj* (of an animal) male

TOMAHAWK *n* fighting axe of the Native Americans

TOMALLEY *n* fat from a lobster, eaten as a delicacy

TOMAN, -S *n* gold coin formerly issued in Persia

TOMATO, -ES *n* red fruit used in salads and as a vegetable

TOMATOEY *adj* tasting of tomato

TOMB, -ED, -ING, -S *n* grave ▷ *vb* place in a tomb

TOMBAC, -S *n* any of various brittle alloys containing copper and zinc

TOMBACK, -S *variant spelling of* ▶ **tombac**

TOMBACS ▶ **tombac**

TOMBAK, -S *same as* ▶ **tombac**

TOMBAL *adj* like or relating to a tomb

TOMBED ▶ **tomb**

TOMBIC *adj* of or relating to tombs

TOMBING ▶ **tomb**

TOMBLESS ▶ **tomb**

TOMBLIKE ▶ **tomb**

TOMBOC, -S *n* weapon

TOMBOLA, -S *n* lottery with tickets drawn from a revolving drum

TOMBOLO, -S *n* narrow bar linking a small island with another island or the mainland

TOMBOY, -S *n* girl who acts or dresses in a traditionally boyish way

TOMBS ▶ **tomb**

TOMCAT, -S *n* male cat

TOMCOD, -S *n* small fish resembling the cod

TOME, -S *n* large heavy book

TOMENTUM, TOMENTA *n* feltlike covering of downy hairs on leaves and other plant parts

TOMES ▶ **tome**

TOMFOOL, -S *n* fool ▷ *vb* act the fool

TOMIA ▶ **tomium**

TOMIAL ▶ **tomium**

TOMIUM, TOMIA *n* sharp edge of a bird's beak

TOMMY, TOMMIED,

TOMMIES, -ING *n* private in the British Army ▷ *vb* (formerly) to exploit workers by paying them in goods rather than in money

TOMMYCOD *n* type of cod

TOMMYING ▶ **tommy**

TOMMYROT *n* utter nonsense

TOMO, -S *n* shaft formed by the action of water on limestone or volcanic rock

TOMOGRAM *n* X-ray photograph of a selected plane section of a solid object

TOMORROW *n* the day after today ▷ *adv* on the day after today

TOMOS ▶ **tomo**

TOMPION, -S *same as* ▶ **tampion**

TOMPON, -ED, -S *same as* ▶ **tampon**

TOMPOT *adj* as in **tompot blenny** variety of blenny with tentacles over its eyes

TOMS ▶ **tom**

TOMTIT, -S *n* small European bird that eats insects and seeds

TON, -S *n* unit of weight

TONAL *adj* written in a key

TONALITE *n* igneous rock found in the Italian Alps

TONALITY *n* presence of a musical key in a composition

TONALLY ▶ **tonal**

TONANT *adj* very loud

TONDI ▶ **tondo**

TONDINO, TONDINI, -S *n* small tondo

TONDO, TONDI, -S *n* circular easel painting or relief carving

TONE, -D, -S, TONING, TONINGS *n* sound with reference to its pitch, volume, etc ▷ *vb* harmonize (with)

TONEARM, -S *same as* ▶ **pickup**

TONED ▶ **tone**

TONELESS *adj* having no tone

TONEME, -S *n* phoneme that is distinguished from another phoneme only by its tone

TONEMIC ▶ **toneme**

TONEPAD, -S *n* keypad used to transmit information

TONER, -S *n* cosmetic applied to the skin to reduce oiliness

TONES ▶ **tone**

T

TONETIC adj (of a language) distinguishing words by tone as well as by other sounds

TONETICS pl n area of linguistics concentrating on the use of tone to distinguish words semantically

TONETTE, -S n small musical instrument resembling a recorder

TONEY variant spelling of ▶ tony

TONG, -ED, -ING vb gather or seize with tongs ▷ n (formerly) a Chinese secret society

TONGA, -S n light two-wheeled vehicle used in rural areas of India

TONGED ▶ tong

TONGER, -S n one who uses tongs to gather oysters

TONGING ▶ tong

TONGMAN, TONGMEN another word for ▶ tonger

TONGS pl n large pincers for grasping and lifting

TONGSTER n tong member

TONGUE, -D, -S, TONGUING n muscular organ in the mouth, used in speaking and tasting ▷ vb use the tongue

TONIC, -S n medicine to improve body tone ▷ adj invigorating

TONICITY n state, condition, or quality of being tonic

TONICS ▶ tonic

TONIER ▶ tony

TONIES ▶ tony

TONIEST ▶ tony

TONIFY, TONIFIED, TONIFIES vb give tone to

TONIGHT, -S n the night or evening of this day ▷ adv in or during the night or evening of this day

TONING ▶ tone

TONINGS ▶ tone

TONISH adj stylish or fashionable

TONISHLY ▶ tonish

TONITE, -S n explosive used in quarrying

TONK, -ED, -ING, -S vb strike with a heavy blow

TONKA n as in **tonka bean** tall leguminous tree of tropical America

TONKED ▶ tonk

TONKER, -S ▶ tonk

TONKING ▶ tonk

TONKS ▶ tonk

TONLET, -S n skirt of a suit of armour, consisting of overlapping metal bands

TONNAG, -S n type of (usually tartan) shawl

TONNAGE, -S n weight capacity of a ship

TONNAGS ▶ tonnag

TONNE, -S same as ▶ ton

TONNEAU, -S, -X n detachable cover to protect the rear part of an open car

TONNELL, -S old spelling of ▶ tunnel

TONNER, -S n something that weighs one ton

TONNES ▶ tonne

TONNISH adj stylish or fashionable

TONS ▶ ton

TONSIL, -S n small gland in the throat

TONSILAR ▶ tonsil

TONSILS ▶ tonsil

TONSOR, -S n barber

TONSURE, -S n shaving of all or the top of the head as a religious or monastic practice ▷ vb shave the head of

TONSURED ▶ tonsure

TONSURES ▶ tonsure

TONTINE, -S n type of annuity scheme

TONTINER n subscriber to a tontine

TONTINES ▶ tontine

TONUS, -ES n normal tension of a muscle at rest

TONY, TONIER, TONIES, TONIEST adj stylish or distinctive ▷ n stylish or distinctive person

TOO adv also, as well

TOOART, -S variant spelling of ▶ tuart

TOODLE, -D, -S, TOODLING vb tootle

TOOK ▶ take

TOOL, -ED, -S n implement used by hand ▷ vb work on with a tool

TOOLBAG, -S n bag for storing or carrying tools

TOOLBAR, -S n row or column of selectable buttons displayed on a computer screen

TOOLBOX n box for storing or carrying tools

TOOLCASE n case for tools

TOOLED ▶ tool

TOOLER, -S ▶ tool

TOOLHEAD n adjustable attachment for a machine tool that holds the tool in position

TOOLIE, -S n adult who gatecrashes social events for school leavers

TOOLING, -S n any decorative work done with a tool

TOOLKIT, -S n set of tools designed to be used together or for a particular purpose

TOOLLESS adj having no tools

TOOLMAN, TOOLMEN n person who works with tools

TOOLPUSH n worker who directs the drilling on an oil rig

TOOLROOM n room, as in a machine shop, where tools are made or stored

TOOLS ▶ tool

TOOLSET, -S n set of tools associated with a computer application

TOOLSHED n small shed used for storing tools

TOOLTIP, -S n temporary window containing information about a tool on a computer application

TOOM, -ED, -EST, -ING, -S vb empty (something) ▷ adj empty

TOOMER ▶ toom

TOOMEST ▶ toom

TOOMING ▶ toom

TOOMS ▶ toom

TOON, -S n large tree of East Asia and Australia

TOONIE, -S n Canadian two-dollar coin

TOONS ▶ toon

TOORIE, -S n tassel or bobble on a bonnet

TOOSHIE, -R adj angry

TOOT, -ED, -ING n short hooting sound ▷ vb (cause to) make such a sound

TOOTER, -S ▶ toot

TOOTH, TEETH, -ING, -S n bonelike projection in the jaws of most vertebrates for biting and chewing

TOOTHED adj having a tooth or teeth

TOOTHFUL n little (esp alcoholic) drink

TOOTHIER ▶ toothy

TOOTHILY ▶ toothy

TOOTHING ▶ tooth

TOOTHS ▶ tooth

TOOTHY, TOOTHIER adj having or showing numerous, large, or prominent teeth

TOOTING ▶ toot

TOOTLE, -D, -S, TOOTLING vb hoot softly or repeatedly

▷ *n* soft hoot or series of hoots

TOOTLER, -S ▸ tootle

TOOTLES ▸ tootle

TOOTLING ▸ tootle

TOOTS, -ED, -ES, -ING *Scots version of* ▸ tut

TOOTSIE *same as* ▸ tootsy

TOOTSIES ▸ tootsy

TOOTSING ▸ toots

TOOTSY, TOOTSIES *n* (in US English) darling or sweetheart

TOP, -PED, -S *n* highest point or part ▷ *adj* at or of the top ▷ *vb* form a top on

TOPALGIA *n* pain restricted to a particular spot: a neurotic or hysterical symptom

TOPARCH, -S *n* ruler of a small state or realm

TOPARCHY ▸ toparch

TOPAZ, -ES *n* semiprecious stone in various colours

TOPAZINE *adj* like topaz

TOPCOAT, -S *n* overcoat

TOPCROSS *n* class of hybrid

TOPE, -D, -S, TOPING *vb* drink alcohol regularly ▷ *n* small European shark

TOPEE, -S *n* lightweight hat worn in tropical countries

TOPEK, -S *same as* ▸ tupik

TOPER, -S ▸ tope

TOPES ▸ tope

TOPFUL *variant spelling of* ▸ topfull

TOPFULL *adj* full to the top

TOPH, -S *n* variety of sandstone

TOPHE, -S *variant spelling of* ▸ toph

TOPHI ▸ tophus

TOPHS ▸ toph

TOPHUS, TOPHI *n* deposit of sodium urate in the helix of the ear or surrounding a joint

TOPI, -S *same as* ▸ topee

TOPIARY *n* art of trimming trees and bushes into decorative shapes ▷ *adj* of or relating to topiary

TOPIC, -S *n* subject of a conversation, book, etc

TOPICAL, -S *adj* relating to current events ▷ *n* type of anaesthetic

TOPICS ▸ topic

TOPING ▸ tope

TOPIS ▸ topi

TOPKICK, -S *n* (formerly) sergeant

TOPKNOT, -S *n* crest, tuft, decorative bow, etc, on the top of the head

TOPLESS *adj* having no top

TOPLINE, -D, -S *vb* headline; be the main focus of a newspaper story

TOPLINER ▸ topline

TOPLINES ▸ topline

TOPLOFTY *adj* haughty or pretentious

TOPMAKER *n* wool dealer

TOPMAN, TOPMEN *n* sailor positioned in the rigging of the topsail

TOPMAST, -S *n* mast next above a lower mast on a sailing vessel

TOPMEN ▸ topman

TOPMOST *adj* highest or best

TOPNOTCH *adj* excellent

TOPO *n* picture of a mountain with details of climbing routes superimposed on it

TOPOI ▸ topos

TOPOLOGY *n* geometry of the properties of a shape which are unaffected by continuous distortion

TOPONYM, -S *n* name of a place

TOPONYMY *n* study of place names

TOPOS, TOPOI *n* basic theme or concept

TOPOTYPE *n* specimen plant or animal taken from an area regarded as the typical habitat

TOPPED ▸ top

TOPPER, -S *n* top hat

TOPPIER ▸ toppy

TOPPIEST ▸ toppy

TOPPING, -S ▸ top

TOPPLE, -D, -S, TOPPLING *vb* (cause to) fall over

TOPPY, TOPPIER, TOPPIEST *adj* (of audio reproduction) having too many high-frequency sounds

TOPRAIL, -S *n* top rail on something such as a piece of furniture

TOPS ▸ top

TOPSAIL, -S *n* square sail carried on a yard set on a topmast

TOPSCORE *vb* score the highest in a sports match or competition

TOPSIDE, -S *n* lean cut of beef from the thigh

TOPSIDER *n* person in charge

TOPSIDES ▸ topside

TOPSMAN, TOPSMEN *n* chief drover

TOPSOIL, -S *n* surface layer of soil ▷ *vb* spread topsoil on (land)

TOPSPIN, -S *n* spin imparted to make a ball bounce or travel exceptionally far, high, or quickly

TOPSTONE *n* stone forming the top of something

TOPWATER *adj* floating on the top of the water

TOPWORK, -S *vb* graft shoots or twigs onto the main branches of (a tree)

TOQUE, -S *same as* ▸ tuque

TOQUET, -S *same as* ▸ toque

TOQUILLA *another name for* ▸ jipijapa

TOR, -S *n* high rocky hill

TORA, -S *variant spelling of* ▸ torah

TORAH, -S, TOROT, TOROTH *n* whole body of traditional Jewish teaching

TORAN, -S *n* (in Indian architecture) an archway

TORANA, -S *same as* ▸ toran

TORANS ▸ toran

TORAS ▸ tora

TORC, -S *same as* ▸ torque

TORCH, -ED, -ES, -ING *n* small portable battery-powered lamp ▷ *vb* deliberately set (a building) on fire

TORCHER, -S ▸ torch

TORCHERE *n* tall narrow stand for holding a candelabrum

TORCHERS ▸ torcher

TORCHES ▸ torch

TORCHIER *n* standing lamp with a bowl for casting light upwards

TORCHING ▸ torch

TORCHLIT *adj* lit by torches

TORCHON, -S *n* coarse linen or cotton lace with a simple openwork pattern

TORCHY *adj* sentimental; maudlin; characteristic of a torch song

TORCS ▸ torc

TORCULAR *n* tourniquet

TORDION, -S *n* old triple-time dance for two people

TORE, -S *same as* ▸ torus

TOREADOR *n* bullfighter

TORERO, -S *n* bullfighter, esp one on foot

TORES ▸ tore

TOREUTIC > toreutics

TORGOCH, -S *n* type of char

TORI ▸ torus

T

TORIC, -S adj of, relating to, or having the form of a torus

TORIES ▸ tory

TORII n gateway, esp one at the entrance to a Japanese Shinto temple

TORMENT, -S vb cause (someone) great suffering ▷ n great suffering

TORMENTA > tormentum

TORMENTS ▸ torment

TORMINA pl n severe stomach pains

TORMINAL ▸ tormina

TORN ▸ tear

TORNADE, -S same as ▸ tornado

TORNADIC ▸ tornado

TORNADO, -S n violent whirlwind

TORNILLO n shrub found in Mexico and some southwestern states of the US

TORO, -S n bull

TOROID, -S n surface generated by rotating a closed plane curve about a coplanar line that does not intersect it

TOROIDAL ▸ toroid

TOROIDS ▸ toroid

TOROS ▸ toro

TOROSE adj (of a cylindrical part) having irregular swellings

TOROSITY ▸ torose

TOROT ▸ torah

TOROTH ▸ torah

TOROUS same as ▸ torose

TORPEDO, -S n self-propelled underwater missile ▷ vb attack or destroy with or as if with torpedoes

TORPEFY vb make torpid

TORPID adj sluggish and inactive

TORPIDLY ▸ torpid

TORPIDS pl n series of boat races held at Oxford University

TORPOR, -S n torpid state

TORQUATE ▸ torques

TORQUE, -D, TORQUING n force causing rotation ▷ vb apply torque to (something)

TORQUER, -S ▸ torque

TORQUES n distinctive band of hair, feathers, skin, or colour around the neck of an animal

TORQUEY, TORQUIER adj providing torque

TORQUING ▸ torque

TORR, -S n unit of pressure

TORREFY vb dry (ores, etc) by subjection to intense heat

TORRENT, -S n rushing stream ▷ adj like or relating to a torrent

TORRET, -S same as ▸ terret

TORRID, -ER adj very hot and dry

TORRIDLY ▸ torrid

TORRIFY same as ▸ torrefy

TORRS ▸ torr

TORS ▸ tor

TORSADE, -S n ornamental twist or twisted cord, as on hats

TORSE, -S same as ▸ torso

TORSEL, -S n wooden beam along the top of a wall

TORSES ▸ torse

TORSI ▸ torso

TORSION, -S n twisting of a part by equal forces being applied at both ends but in opposite directions

TORSIVE adj twisted

TORSK, -S n fish with a single long dorsal fin

TORSO, TORSI, -S n trunk of the human body

TORT, -S n civil wrong or injury for which damages may be claimed

TORTA n (in mining) a flat circular pile of silver ore

TORTE, -N, -S n rich cake, originating in Austria

TORTELLI pl n type of stuffed pasta

TORTEN ▸ torte

TORTES ▸ torte

TORTIE, -S n tortoiseshell cat

TORTILE adj twisted or coiled

TORTILLA n thin Mexican pancake

TORTIOUS adj having the nature of or involving a tort

TORTIVE adj twisted

TORTOISE n slow-moving land reptile with a dome-shaped shell

TORTONI, -S n rich ice cream often flavoured with sherry

TORTRIX n type of moth

TORTS ▸ tort

TORTUOUS adj winding or twisting

TORTURE, -S vb cause (someone) severe pain or mental anguish ▷ n severe physical or mental pain

TORTURED ▸ torture

TORTURER ▸ torture

TORTURES ▸ torture

TORULA, -E, -S n any of various species of fungal microorganisms

TORULI ▸ torulus

TORULIN, -S n vitamin found in yeast

TORULOSE adj (of something cylindrical) alternately swollen and pinched along its length

TORULUS, TORULI n socket in an insect's head in which its antenna is attached

TORUS, TORI, -ES n large convex moulding approximately semicircular in cross section

TORY, TORIES n conservative or reactionary person ▷ adj conservative or reactionary

TOSA, -S n large reddish dog, originally bred for fighting

TOSE, -D, -S, TOSING same as ▸ toze

TOSH, -ED, -ES, -ING n nonsense ▷ vb tidy or trim

TOSHACH, -S n military leader of a clan

TOSHED ▸ tosh

TOSHER, -S ▸ tosh

TOSHES ▸ tosh

TOSHIER ▸ toshy

TOSHIEST ▸ toshy

TOSHING ▸ tosh

TOSHY, TOSHIER, TOSHIEST adj neat; trim

TOSING ▸ tose

TOSS, -ED, -ES, -ING, -INGS vb throw lightly ▷ n instance of tossing

TOSSEN old past participle of ▸ toss

TOSSES ▸ toss

TOSSIER ▸ tossy

TOSSIEST ▸ tossy

TOSSILY ▸ tossy

TOSSING ▸ toss

TOSSINGS ▸ toss

TOSSPOT, -S n habitual drinker

TOSSUP, -S n instance of tossing up a coin

TOSSY, TOSSIER, TOSSIEST adj impudent

TOST old past participle of ▸ toss

TOSTADA, -S n crispy deep-fried tortilla topped with meat, cheese, and refried beans

TOSTADO, -S same as ▸ tostada

TOSTONE, -S n Mexican dish of fried plantains

TOT, -S, -TED n small child
▷ vb total

TOTABLE ▸ tote

TOTAL, -ED, -ING, -LED, -S n whole, esp a sum of parts ▷ adj complete ▷ vb amount to

TOTALISE same as ▸ totalize

TOTALISM n practice of a one-party state that regulates every area of life

TOTALIST ▸ totalism

TOTALITY n whole amount

TOTALIZE vb combine or make into a total

TOTALLED ▸ total

TOTALLY ▸ total

TOTALS ▸ total

TOTANUS another name for ▸ redshank

TOTARA, -S n tall coniferous forest tree of New Zealand

TOTE, -D, -S, TOTING vb carry (a gun etc) ▷ n act of or an instance of toting

TOTEABLE ▸ tote

TOTED ▸ tote

TOTEM, -S n tribal badge or emblem

TOTEMIC ▸ totem

TOTEMISM n belief in kinship of groups or individuals having a common totem

TOTEMIST ▸ totemism

TOTEMITE ▸ totemism

TOTEMS ▸ totem

TOTER, -S ▸ tote

TOTES ▸ tote

TOTHER, -S n other ▷ adj the other

TOTIENT, -S n quantity of numbers less than, and sharing no common factors with, a number

TOTING ▸ tote

TOTITIVE n number less than, and having no common factors with, a given number

TOTS ▸ tot

TOTTED ▸ tot

TOTTER, -ED, -S vb move unsteadily ▷ n act or an instance of tottering

TOTTERER ▸ totter

TOTTERS ▸ totter

TOTTERY adj tending to totter

TOTTIE adj very small

TOTTIER ▸ totty

TOTTIES ▸ totty

TOTTIEST ▸ totty

TOTTING, -S ▸ tot

TOTTRING adj Shakespearian word meaning ragged

TOTTY, TOTTIER, TOTTIES, TOTTIEST n small child ▷ adj very small

TOUCAN, -S n tropical American bird with a large bill

TOUCANET n type of small toucan

TOUCANS ▸ toucan

TOUCH, -ES vb come into contact with ▷ n sense by which an object's qualities are perceived when they come into contact with part of the body ▷ adj of a non-contact version of a particular sport

TOUCHE interj acknowledgment of a remark or witty reply

TOUCHED adj emotionally moved

TOUCHER, -S ▸ touch

TOUCHES ▸ touch

TOUCHIER ▸ touchy

TOUCHILY ▸ touchy

TOUCHING adj emotionally moving ▷ prep relating to or concerning ▷ n instance of touching

TOUCHPAD n part of laptop computer functioning like a mouse

TOUCHUP, -S n renovation or retouching, as of a painting

TOUCHY, TOUCHIER adj easily offended

TOUGH, -ED, -ER, -EST, -ING, -S adj strong or resilient ▷ n rough violent person ▷ vb stand firm, hold out

TOUGHEN, -S vb make or become tough or tougher

TOUGHER ▸ tough

TOUGHEST ▸ tough

TOUGHIE, -S n person who is tough

TOUGHING ▸ tough

TOUGHISH ▸ tough

TOUGHLY ▸ tough

TOUGHS ▸ tough

TOUGHY same as ▸ toughie

TOUK, -ED, -ING, -S same as ▸ tuck

TOULADI, -S same as ▸ tuladi

TOUN, -S n Scots word for a town

TOUPEE, -S n small wig

TOUPEED adj wearing a toupee

TOUPEES ▸ toupee

TOUPET, -S same as ▸ toupee

TOUPIE, -S n round boneless smoked ham

TOUR, -ED, -S n journey visiting places of interest along the way ▷ vb make a tour (of)

TOURACO, -S n brightly coloured crested arboreal African bird

TOURED ▸ tour

TOURER, -S n large open car with a folding top

TOURIE, -S same as ▸ toorie

TOURING, -S ▸ tour

TOURISM, -S n tourist travel as an industry

TOURIST, -S n person travelling for pleasure ▷ adj of or relating to tourists or tourism

TOURISTA variant of ▸ tourist

TOURISTS ▸ tourist

TOURISTY adj informal term for full of tourists or tourist attractions

TOURNEY, -S n knightly tournament ▷ vb engage in a tourney

TOURNURE n outline or contour

TOURS ▸ tour

TOUSE, -D, -S, TOUSING, TOUSINGS vb tangle, ruffle, or disarrange; treat roughly

TOUSER, -S ▸ touse

TOUSES ▸ touse

TOUSIER ▸ tousy

TOUSIEST ▸ tousy

TOUSING ▸ touse

TOUSINGS ▸ touse

TOUSLE, -D, -S, TOUSLING vb make (hair or clothes) ruffled and untidy ▷ n disorderly, tangled, or rumpled state

TOUSTIE, -R adj irritable; testy

TOUSY, TOUSIER, TOUSIEST adj tousled

TOUT, -ED, -ING, -S vb seek business in a persistent manner ▷ n person who sells tickets for a popular event at inflated prices

TOUTER, -S ▸ tout

TOUTIE, -R, -ST adj childishly irritable or sullen

TOUTING ▸ tout

TOUTON, -S n deep-fried round of bread dough

TOUTS ▸ tout

TOUZE, -D, -S, TOUZING variant spelling of ▸ touse

TOUZIER ▸ touzy

TOUZIEST ▸ touzy

TOUZING ▸touze

TOUZLE, -D, -S, TOUZLING rare spelling of ▸tousle

TOUZY, TOUZIER, TOUZIEST variant spelling of ▸tousy

TOVARICH same as > tovarisch

TOVARISH same as > tovarisch

TOW, -ED, -ING, -INGS, -S vb drag, esp by means of a rope ▷ n instance of towing

TOWABLE ▸tow

TOWAGE, -S n charge made for towing

TOWARD same as ▸towards

TOWARDLY adj compliant

TOWARDS prep in the direction of

TOWAWAY, -S n vehicle which has been towed away

TOWBAR, -S n metal bar on a car for towing vehicles

TOWBOAT, -S n another word for tug (the boat)

TOWED ▸tow

TOWEL, -ED, -LED, -S n cloth for drying things ▷ vb dry or wipe with a towel

TOWELING same as > towelling

TOWELLED ▸towel

TOWELS ▸towel

TOWER, -S n tall structure, often forming part of a larger building ▷ vb rise like a tower

TOWERED adj having a tower or towers

TOWERIER ▸towery

TOWERING adj very tall or impressive

TOWERS ▸tower

TOWERY, TOWERIER adj with towers

TOWHEAD, -S n person with blond or yellowish hair

TOWHEE, -S n N American brownish-coloured sparrow

TOWIE, -S n truck used for towing

TOWIER ▸towy

TOWIES ▸towie

TOWIEST ▸towy

TOWING ▸tow

TOWINGS ▸tow

TOWKAY, -S n sir

TOWLINE, -S same as ▸towrope

TOWMON, -S same as ▸towmond

TOWMOND, -S n old word for year

TOWMONS ▸towmon

TOWMONT, -S same as ▸towmond

TOWN, -S n group of buildings larger than a village

TOWNEE, -S same as ▸townie

TOWNFOLK same as > townsfolk

TOWNHALL adj of a variety of the Asian plant moschatel

TOWNHOME another word for > townhouse

TOWNIE n resident of a town

TOWNIER ▸towny

TOWNIES ▸towny

TOWNIEST ▸town

TOWNLAND n division of land of various sizes

TOWNLESS ▸town

TOWNLET, -S n small town

TOWNLIER ▸townly

TOWNLING n person who lives in a town

TOWNLY, TOWNLIER adj characteristic of a town

TOWNS ▸town

TOWNSHIP n small town

TOWNSITE n site of a town

TOWNSKIP n old term for a mischievous and roguish child who frequents city streets

TOWNSMAN, TOWNSMEN n inhabitant of a town

TOWNWARD adv in the direction of a town

TOWNWEAR n clothes suitable for wearing while pursuing activities usually associated with towns

TOWNY, TOWNIER, TOWNIES, TOWNIEST adj characteristic of a town

TOWPATH, -S n path beside a canal or river

TOWPLANE n aeroplane that tows gliders

TOWROPE, -S n rope or cable used for towing a vehicle or vessel

TOWS ▸tow

TOWSACK, -S n sack made from tow

TOWSE, -D, -S, TOWSING same as ▸touse

TOWSER, -S ▸towse

TOWSES ▸towse

TOWSIER ▸towsy

TOWSIEST ▸towsy

TOWSING ▸towse

TOWSY, TOWSIER, TOWSIEST same as ▸tousy

TOWT, -ED, -ING, -S vb sulk

TOWY, TOWIER, TOWIEST ▸tow

TOWZE, -D, -S, TOWZING same as ▸touse

TOWZIER ▸towzy

TOWZIEST ▸towzy

TOWZING ▸towze

TOWZY, TOWZIER, TOWZIEST same as ▸tousy

TOXAEMIA n blood poisoning

TOXAEMIC ▸toxaemia

TOXEMIA, -S same as ▸toxaemia

TOXEMIC ▸toxaemia

TOXIC, -S adj poisonous ▷ n toxic substance

TOXICAL adj toxic

TOXICANT n toxic substance ▷ adj poisonous

TOXICITY n degree of strength of a poison

TOXICS ▸toxic

TOXIN, -S n poison of bacterial origin

TOXINE, -S nonstandard variant spelling of ▸toxin

TOXINS ▸toxin

TOXOCARA n parasitic worm infesting the intestines of cats and dogs

TOXOID, -S n toxin that has been treated to reduce its toxicity

TOY, -ED, -ING, -INGS, -S n something designed to be played with ▷ adj designed to be played with ▷ vb play, fiddle, or flirt

TOYBOX, -ES n box for toys

TOYCHEST n chest for toys

TOYED ▸toy

TOYER, -S ▸toy

TOYETIC adj (of a film or television franchise) able to generate revenue via spin-off toys

TOYING ▸toy

TOYINGS ▸toy

TOYISH adj resembling a toy

TOYISHLY ▸toyish

TOYLAND, -S n toy industry

TOYLESS ▸toy

TOYLIKE ▸toy

TOYLSOM old spelling of ▸toilsome

TOYMAN, TOYMEN n man who sells toys

TOYO, -S n Japanese straw-like material made out of rice paper and used to make hats

TOYON, -S n shrub related to the rose

TOYOS ▸toyo

TOYS ▸toy

TOYSHOP, -S n shop selling toys

TOYSOME adj playful

TOYTOWN, -S adj having an unreal and picturesque appearance ▷ n place with an unreal and picturesque appearance

TOYWOMAN, TOYWOMEN n woman who sells toys

TOZE, -D, -S, TOZING vb tease out; (of wool, etc) card

TOZIE, -S n type of shawl

TOZING ▸ toze

TRABEATE same as > trabeated

TRABS pl n training shoes

TRACE, -D, -S vb locate or work out (the cause of something) ▷ n track left by something

TRACER, -S n projectile which leaves a visible trail

TRACERY n pattern of interlacing lines

TRACES ▸ trace

TRACEUR, -S n parkour participant

TRACHEA, -E, -S n windpipe

TRACHEAL ▸ trachea

TRACHEAS ▸ trachea

TRACHEID n element of xylem tissue

TRACHLE, -D, -S vb Scots word meaning make (hair, clothing, etc) untidy

TRACHOMA n chronic contagious disease of the eye

TRACHYTE n light-coloured fine-grained volcanic rock

TRACING, -S n traced copy

TRACK, -ED, -S n rough road or path ▷ vb follow the trail or path of

TRACKAGE n collective term for railway tracks

TRACKBED n foundation on which railway tracks are laid

TRACKED ▸ track

TRACKER, -S ▸ track

TRACKIE adj resembling or forming part of a tracksuit

TRACKIES pl n loose-fitting trousers with elasticated cuffs

TRACKING n act or process of following something or someone

TRACKMAN, TRACKMEN n labourer who lays and maintains railway track

TRACKPAD same as ▸ touchpad

TRACKS ▸ track

TRACKWAY n path or track

TRACT, -ED, -ING, -S n wide area ▷ vb track

TRACTATE n short tract

TRACTED ▸ tract

TRACTILE adj capable of being drawn out

TRACTING ▸ tract

TRACTION n pulling, esp by engine power

TRACTIVE ▸ traction

TRACTOR, -S n motor vehicle with large rear wheels for pulling farm machinery

TRACTRIX n (in geometry) type of curve

TRACTS ▸ tract

TRACTUS n anthem sung in some RC masses

TRAD, -S n traditional jazz, as revived in the 1950s

TRADABLE ▸ trade

TRADE, -D, -S n buying, selling, or exchange of goods ▷ vb buy and sell ▷ adj intended for or available only to people in industry or business

TRADEFUL adj (of shops, for example) full of trade

TRADEOFF n exchange, esp as a compromise

TRADER, -S n person who engages in trade

TRADES ▸ trade

TRADIE, -S n tradesperson

TRADING, -S ▸ trade

TRADITOR n Christian who betrayed fellow Christians at the time of the Roman persecutions

TRADS ▸ trad

TRADUCE, -D, -S vb slander

TRADUCER ▸ traduce

TRADUCES ▸ traduce

TRAFFIC, -S n vehicles coming and going on a road ▷ vb trade

TRAGAL ▸ tragus

TRAGEDY n shocking or sad event

TRAGI ▸ tragus

TRAGIC, -S adj of or like a tragedy ▷ n tragedian

TRAGICAL same as ▸ tragic

TRAGICS ▸ tragic

TRAGOPAN n pheasant of S and SE Asia

TRAGULE, -S n mouse deer

TRAGUS, TRAGI n fleshy projection that partially covers the entrance to the external ear

TRAHISON n treason

TRAIK, -ED, -ING, -IT, -S vb Scots word for trudge

TRAIL, -ED, -S n path, track, or road ▷ vb drag along the ground

TRAILER, -S n vehicle designed to be towed by another vehicle ▷ vb use a trailer to advertise (something)

TRAILING adj (of a plant) having a long stem which spreads over the ground or hangs loosely

TRAILS ▸ trail

TRAIN, -ED, -S vb instruct in a skill ▷ n line of railway coaches or wagons drawn by an engine

TRAINEE, -S n person being trained ▷ adj (of a person) undergoing training

TRAINER n person who trains an athlete or sportsperson

TRAINERS pl n shoes in the style of those used for sports training

TRAINFUL n quantity of people or cargo that would be capable of filling a train

TRAINING n process of bringing a person to an agreed standard of proficiency by instruction

TRAINMAN, TRAINMEN n man who works on a train

TRAINS ▸ train

TRAINWAY n railway track; channel in a built-up area through which a train passes

TRAIPSE, -D, -S vb walk wearily ▷ n long or tiring walk

TRAIT, -S n characteristic feature

TRAITOR, -S n person guilty of treason or treachery

TRAITS ▸ trait

TRAJECT, -S vb transport or transmit

TRAM, -MED, -MING, -S n electric public transport vehicle ▷ vb adjust (a mechanism) to a fine degree

TRAMCAR, -S same as ▸ tram

TRAMEL, -ED, -S vb hinder or restrain

TRAMELL, -S old variant of ▸ trammel

TRAMELS ▸ tramel

TRAMLESS ▸ tram

TRAMLINE n tracks on which a tram runs

TRAMMED ▸ tram

TRAMMEL, -S n hindrance to free action or movement ▷ vb hinder or restrain

T

TRAMMIE, -S n conductor or driver of a tram

TRAMMING ▸ tram

TRAMP, -ED, -S vb travel on foot, hike ▷ n homeless person who travels on foot

TRAMPER, -S n person who tramps

TRAMPET, -S variant spelling of ▸ trampette

TRAMPIER ▸ trampy

TRAMPING ▸ tramp

TRAMPISH ▸ tramp

TRAMPLE, -D, -S vb tread on and crush ▷ n action or sound of trampling

TRAMPLER ▸ trample

TRAMPLES ▸ trample

TRAMPS ▸ tramp

TRAMPY, TRAMPIER adj like or characteristic of a tramp

TRAMROAD same as ▸ tramway

TRAMS ▸ tram

TRAMWAY, -S same as ▸ tramline

TRANCE, -D, -S, TRANCING n unconscious or dazed state ▷ vb put into or as into a trance

TRANCEY, TRANCIER adj (of music) characteristic of the trance sub-genre

TRANCHE, -S n portion of something large

TRANCHET n Stone Age cutting tool

TRANCIER ▸ trancey

TRANCING ▸ trance

TRANECT, -S n ferry

TRANGAM, -S n bauble or trinket

TRANGLE, -S n (in heraldry) a small fesse

TRANKUM, -S same as ▸ trangam

TRANQUIL adj calm and quiet

TRANS n short form of translation

TRANSACT vb conduct or negotiate (a business deal)

TRANSE, -S n way through; passage

TRANSECT n sample strip of land used to monitor plant distribution and animal populations ▷ vb cut or divide crossways

TRANSEPT n either of the two shorter wings of a cross-shaped church

TRANSES ▸ transe

TRANSFER vb move or send from one person or place to another ▷ n instance of transferring

TRANSFIX vb astound or stun

TRANSHIP same as ▸ transship

TRANSIRE n document allowing goods to pass through customs

TRANSIT, -S n passage or conveyance of goods or people ▷ vb make a transit

TRANSMAN, TRANSMEN n transgender man

TRANSMEW old variant of ▸ transmute

TRANSMIT vb pass (something) from one person or place to another

TRANSOM, -S n horizontal bar across a window

TRANSUDE vb (of a fluid) ooze or pass through interstices, pores, or small holes

TRANSUME vb make an official transcription of

TRANT, -ED, -ING, -S vb travel from place to place selling goods

TRANTER, -S ▸ trant

TRANTING ▸ trant

TRANTS ▸ trant

TRAP, -PED, -PING, -S n device for catching animals ▷ vb catch

TRAPAN, -S same as ▸ trepan

TRAPBALL n obsolete ball game

TRAPDOOR n door in a floor or roof

TRAPE, -D, TRAPING same as ▸ traipse

TRAPES, -ED, -ES same as ▸ traipse

TRAPEZE, -D, -S n horizontal bar suspended from two ropes, used by circus acrobats ▷ vb swing on a trapeze

TRAPEZIA > trapezium

TRAPEZII > trapezius

TRAPFALL n trapdoor that opens under the feet

TRAPING ▸ trape

TRAPLIKE ▸ trap

TRAPLINE n line of traps

TRAPNEST n nest that holds the eggs of a single hen

TRAPPEAN adj of, relating to, or consisting of igneous rock, esp a basalt

TRAPPED ▸ trap

TRAPPER, -S n person who traps animals for their fur

TRAPPIER ▸ trappy

TRAPPING ▸ trap

TRAPPOSE adj of or relating to traprock

TRAPPOUS same as ▸ trappose

TRAPPY, TRAPPIER adj having many traps

TRAPROCK n igneous rock, esp a basalt

TRAPS ▸ trap

TRAPSE, -D, -S, TRAPSING vb traipse

TRAPT old past participle of ▸ trap

TRAPUNTO n type of quilting that is only partly padded in a design

TRASH, -ED, -ES, -ING n anything worthless ▷ vb attack or destroy maliciously

TRASHCAN n dustbin

TRASHED ▸ trash

TRASHER, -S ▸ trash

TRASHERY ▸ trash

TRASHES ▸ trash

TRASHIER ▸ trashy

TRASHILY ▸ trashy

TRASHING ▸ trash

TRASHMAN, TRASHMEN n (in US English) binman

TRASHY, TRASHIER adj cheap, worthless, or badly made

TRASS, -ES n variety of the volcanic rock tuff

TRAT, -S n type of fishing line holding a series of baited hooks

TRATT, -S short for ▸ trattoria

TRAUCHLE vb Scots word meaning walk or work slowly and wearily

TRAUMA, -S, -TA n emotional shock

TRAVAIL, -S n labour or toil ▷ vb suffer or labour painfully

TRAVE, -S n stout wooden cage in which difficult horses are shod

TRAVEL, -S vb go from one place to another, through an area, or for a specified distance ▷ n act of travelling, esp as a tourist

TRAVELED same as ▸ travelled

TRAVELER same as ▸ traveller

TRAVELOG n film, lecture, or brochure on travel

TRAVELS ▸ travel

TRAVERSE vb pass or go over

TRAVES ▸ **trave**

TRAVESTY n grotesque imitation or mockery ▷ vb make or be a travesty of

TRAVIS, -ES same as ▸ **treviss**

TRAVOIS n sledge used for dragging logs

TRAVOISE same as ▸ **travois**

TRAWL, -ED, -ING, -S n net dragged at deep levels behind a fishing boat ▷ vb fish with such a net

TRAWLER, -S n trawling boat

TRAWLEY, -S same as ▸ **trolley**

TRAWLING ▸ **trawl**

TRAWLNET n large net used by trawlers

TRAWLS ▸ **trawl**

TRAY, -S n flat board, usu with a rim, for carrying things

TRAYBAKE n flat cake which is baked in a tray and cut into small squares

TRAYBIT, -S n threepenny bit

TRAYF adj not prepared according to Jewish law

TRAYFUL, -S n as many or as much as will fit on a tray

TRAYNE, -D, -S, TRAYNING old spelling of ▸ **train**

TRAYS ▸ **tray**

TREACHER n traitor; treacherous person

TREACLE, -D, -S n thick dark syrup produced when sugar is refined ▷ vb add treacle to

TREACLY ▸ **treacle**

TREAD, -ED, -ING, -S, TRODDEN vb set one's foot on ▷ n way of walking or dancing

TREADER, -S ▸ **tread**

TREADING ▸ **tread**

TREADLE, -D, -S n lever worked by the foot to turn a wheel ▷ vb work (a machine) with a treadle

TREADLER ▸ **treadle**

TREADLES ▸ **treadle**

TREADS ▸ **tread**

TREAGUE, -S n agreement to stop fighting

TREASON, -S n betrayal of one's sovereign or country

TREASURE n collection of wealth, esp gold or jewels ▷ vb prize or cherish

TREASURY n storage place for treasure

TREAT, -ED, -ING, -S vb deal with or regard in a certain manner ▷ n pleasure, entertainment, etc given or paid for by someone else

TREATER, -S ▸ **treat**

TREATIES ▸ **treaty**

TREATING ▸ **treat**

TREATISE n formal piece of writing on a particular subject

TREATS ▸ **treat**

TREATY, TREATIES n signed contract between states

TREBLE, -D, -S adj triple ▷ n (singer with or part for) a soprano voice ▷ vb increase three times

TREBLIER ▸ **trebly**

TREBLING n act of trebling

TREBLY, TREBLIER adj (of music) tinny

TRECENTO n 14th century, esp with reference to Italian art and literature

TRECK, -ED, -ING, -S same as ▸ **trek**

TREDDLE, -D, -S variant spelling of ▸ **treadle**

TREDILLE same as > **tredrille**

TREE, -D, -ING, -S n large perennial plant with a woody trunk ▷ vb drive or force up a tree

TREELAWN n narrow band of grass between a road and a pavement, usually planted with trees

TREELESS ▸ **tree**

TREELIKE ▸ **tree**

TREELINE n line marking the altitude above which trees will not grow

TREEN, -S adj made of wood ▷ n art of making treenware

TREENAIL n dowel used for pinning planks or timbers together

TREENS ▸ **treen**

TREES ▸ **tree**

TREESHIP n state of being a tree

TREETOP, -S n top of a tree

TREEWARE n reading materials that are printed on paper as opposed to a digital format

TREEWAX n any wax secreted by a tree

TREF adj in Judaism, ritually unfit to be eaten

TREFA same as ▸ **tref**

TREFAH same as ▸ **tref**

TREFOIL, -S n plant with a three-lobed leaf

TREHALA, -S n edible sugary substance from the cocoon of an Asian weevil

TREIF same as ▸ **tref**

TREIFA same as ▸ **tref**

TREILLE, -S another word for ▸ **trellis**

TREK, -KED, -S n long difficult journey, esp on foot ▷ vb make such a journey

TREKKER, -S ▸ **trek**

TREKKING n as in pony trekking the act of riding ponies cross-country

TREKS ▸ **trek**

TRELLIS n framework of horizontal and vertical strips of wood ▷ vb interweave (strips of wood, etc) to make a trellis

TREM, -S n lever for producing a tremolo on a guitar

TREMA, -S n mark placed over vowel to indicate it is to be pronounced separately

TREMATIC adj relating to the gills

TREMBLE, -D vb shake or quiver ▷ n instance of trembling

TREMBLER n device that vibrates to make or break an electrical circuit

TREMBLES n disease of cattle and sheep

TREMBLOR n earth tremor

TREMBLY ▸ **tremble**

TREMIE, -S n metal hopper and pipe used to distribute freshly mixed concrete underwater

TREMOLO, -S n quivering effect in singing or playing

TREMOR, -ED, -S n involuntary shaking ▷ vb tremble

TREMS ▸ **trem**

TRENAIL, -S same as ▸ **treenail**

TRENCH, -ED, -ES n long narrow ditch, esp one used as a shelter in war ▷ adj of or involving military trenches ▷ vb make a trench in (a place)

TRENCHER n wooden plate for serving food

TRENCHES ▸ **trench**

TREND, -ED, -ING, -S n general tendency or direction ▷ vb take a certain trend

TRENDIER ▸ **trendy**

TRENDIES ▸ **trendy**

TRENDIFY vb render fashionable

TRENDILY ▸ **trendy**

TRENDING ▸ **trend**

T

TRENDOID n follower of trends

TRENDS ▸ trend

TRENDY, TRENDIER, TRENDIES n consciously fashionable person ▷ adj consciously fashionable

TRENISE, -S n one of the figures in a quadrille

TRENTAL, -S n mass said in remembrance of a person 30 days after his or her death

TREPAN, -S same as ▸ trephine

TREPANG, -S n any of various large sea cucumbers

TREPANS ▸ trepan

TREPHINE n surgical instrument for removing circular sections of bone ▷ vb remove a circular section of bone from

TREPID adj trembling

TRES adv very

TRESPASS vb go onto another's property without permission ▷ n act of trespassing

TRESS, -ES, -ING n lock of hair, esp a long lock of woman's hair ▷ vb arrange in tresses

TRESSED adj having a tress or tresses

TRESSEL, -S variant spelling of ▸ trestle

TRESSES ▸ tress

TRESSIER ▸ tressy

TRESSING ▸ tress

TRESSOUR same as ▸ tressure

TRESSURE n narrow inner border on a shield, usually decorated with fleurs-de-lys

TRESSY, TRESSIER ▸ tress

TREST, -S old variant of ▸ trestle

TRESTLE, -S n board fixed on pairs of spreading legs, used as a support

TRESTS ▸ trest

TRET, -S n (formerly) allowance granted for waste due to transportation

TREVALLY n any of various food and game fishes

TREVET, -S same as ▸ trivet

TREVIS, -ES variant spelling of ▸ treviss

TREVISS n partition in a stable for keeping animals apart

TREW old variant spelling of ▸ true

TREWS pl n close-fitting tartan trousers

TREWSMAN, TREWSMEN n Highlander

TREY, -S n any card or dice throw with three spots

TREYBIT, -S same as ▸ traybit

TREYF adj not prepared according to Jewish law

TREYFA same as ▸ treyf

TREYS ▸ trey

TREZ, -ES same as ▸ trey

TRIABLE adj liable to be tried judicially

TRIAC, -S n device for regulating the amount of electric current reaching a circuit

TRIACID, -S adj (of a base) capable of reacting with three molecules of a monobasic acid

TRIACS ▸ triac

TRIACT, -S adj having three rays ▷ n sponge spicule with three rays

TRIACTOR n type of bet

TRIACTS ▸ triact

TRIAD, -S n group of three

TRIADIC, -S adj characteristic of a triad ▷ n something that has the characteristics of a triad

TRIADISM ▸ triad

TRIADIST ▸ triad

TRIADS ▸ triad

TRIAGE, -D, -S, TRIAGING n sorting emergency patients into categories of priority ▷ vb sort (patients) into categories of priority

TRIAL, -ED, -ING, -LED, -S n investigation of a case before a judge ▷ vb test or try out

TRIALISM n belief that humans consist of body, soul, and spirit

TRIALIST same as ▸ triallist

TRIALITY ▸ trialism

TRIALLED ▸ trial

TRIALS ▸ trial

TRIANGLE n geometric figure with three sides

TRIAPSAL adj (of a church) having three apses

TRIARCH, -S n one of three rulers of a triarchy

TRIARCHY n government by three people

TRIASSIC adj of, denoting, or formed in the first period of the Mesozoic era

TRIATIC, -S n rope between a ship's mastheads

TRIAXIAL adj having three axes ▷ n sponge spicule with three axes

TRIAXON, -S another name for ▸ triaxial

TRIAZIN, -S same as ▸ triazine

TRIAZINE n any of three azines that contain three nitrogen atoms in their molecules

TRIAZINS ▸ triazin

TRIAZOLE n heterocyclic compound

TRIBAL, -S adj of or denoting a tribe or tribes ▷ n member of a tribal community

TRIBALLY ▸ tribal

TRIBALS ▸ tribal

TRIBASIC adj (of an acid) containing three replaceable hydrogen atoms in the molecule

TRIBBLE, -S n frame for drying paper

TRIBE, -S n group of clans or families believed to have a common ancestor

TRIBLET, -S n spindle or mandrel used in making rings, tubes, etc

TRIBRACH n metrical foot of three short syllables

TRIBUNAL n board appointed to inquire into a specific matter

TRIBUNE, -S n people's representative, esp in ancient Rome

TRIBUTE, -S n sign of respect or admiration

TRIBUTER n miner

TRIBUTES ▸ tribute

TRICAR, -S n car with three wheels

TRICE, -D, -S, TRICING n moment ▷ vb haul up or secure

TRICEP same as ▸ triceps

TRICEPS n muscle at the back of the upper arm

TRICES ▸ trice

TRICHINA n parasitic nematode worm

TRICHITE n any of various needle-shaped crystals that occur in some glassy volcanic rocks

TRICHOID adj resembling a hair

TRICHOME n any hairlike outgrowth from the surface of a plant

TRICHORD n musical instrument with three strings

TRICING ▸ trice

TRICITY n area that comprises three adjoining cities

TRICK, -ED, -ING, -S n deceitful or cunning action or plan ▷ vb cheat or deceive

TRICKER, -S ▶ **trick**

TRICKERY n practice or an instance of using tricks

TRICKIE Scots form of ▶ **tricky**

TRICKIER ▶ **tricky**

TRICKILY ▶ **tricky**

TRICKING ▶ **trick**

TRICKISH same as ▶ **tricky**

TRICKLE, -D, -S vb (cause to) flow in a thin stream or drops ▷ n gradual flow

TRICKLET n tiny trickle

TRICKLY ▶ **trickle**

TRICKS ▶ **trick**

TRICKSY adj playing tricks habitually

TRICKY, TRICKIER adj difficult, needing careful handling

TRICLAD, -S n type of worm having a tripartite intestine

TRICOLOR same as > **tricolour**

TRICORN, -S n cocked hat with opposing brims turned back and caught in three places ▷ adj having three horns or corners

TRICORNE same as ▶ **tricorn**

TRICORNS ▶ **tricorn**

TRICOT, -S n thin rayon or nylon fabric knitted or resembling knitting, used for dresses, etc

TRICTRAC n game similar to backgammon

TRICYCLE n three-wheeled cycle ▷ vb ride a tricycle

TRIDACNA n giant clam

TRIDARN, -S n sideboard with three levels

TRIDE old spelling of the past tense of ▶ **try**

TRIDENT, -S n three-pronged spear ▷ adj having three prongs

TRIDUAN adj three days long

TRIDUUM, -S n period of three days for prayer before a feast

TRIE old spelling of ▶ **try**

TRIED ▶ **try**

TRIELLA, -S n bet on the winners of three nominated horse races

TRIENE, -S n chemical compound containing three double bonds

TRIENNIA > **triennium**

TRIENS, TRIENTES n Byzantine gold coin worth one third of a solidus

TRIER, -S n person or thing that tries

TRIES ▶ **try**

TRIETHYL adj consisting of three groups of ethyls

TRIFECTA n form of betting in which the better selects the first three place-winners in a horse race in the correct order

TRIFF, -ER, -EST adj terrific; very good indeed

TRIFFIC adj terrific; very good indeed

TRIFFID, -S n fictional plant that could kill humans

TRIFFIDY adj resembling a triffid

TRIFID adj divided or split into three parts or lobes

TRIFLE, -D, -S n insignificant thing or amount ▷ vb deal (with) as if worthless

TRIFLER, -S ▶ **trifle**

TRIFLES ▶ **trifle**

TRIFLING adj insignificant

TRIFOCAL adj having three focuses

TRIFOLD less common word for ▶ **triple**

TRIFOLIA > **trifolium**

TRIFOLY same as ▶ **trefoil**

TRIFORIA > **triforium**

TRIFORM adj having three parts

TRIG, -GED, -GEST, -GING, -S adj neat or spruce ▷ vb make or become spruce

TRIGAMY n condition of having three spouses

TRIGGED ▶ **trig**

TRIGGER, -S n small lever releasing a catch on a gun or machine ▷ vb set (an action or process) in motion

TRIGGEST ▶ **trig**

TRIGGING ▶ **trig**

TRIGLOT, -S n person who can speak three languages

TRIGLY ▶ **trig**

TRIGLYPH n stone block in a Doric frieze, having three vertical channels

TRIGNESS ▶ **trig**

TRIGO, -S n wheat field

TRIGON, -S n (in classical Greece or Rome) a triangular harp or lyre

TRIGONAL adj triangular

TRIGONIC ▶ **trigon**

TRIGONS ▶ **trigon**

TRIGOS ▶ **trigo**

TRIGRAM, -S n three-letter inscription

TRIGRAPH n combination of three letters used to represent a single speech sound

TRIGS ▶ **trig**

TRIHEDRA > **trihedron**

TRIJET, -S n jet with three engines

TRIKE, -S n tricycle

TRILBIED adj wearing a trilby

TRILBY, TRILBIES, -S n soft felt hat

TRILD old past tense of ▶ **trill**

TRILEMMA n quandary posed by three alternative courses of action

TRILITH, -S same as > **trilithon**

TRILL, -ED, -ING, -S n rapid alternation between two notes ▷ vb play or sing a trill

TRILLER, -S ▶ **trill**

TRILLING ▶ **trill**

TRILLION n one million million ▷ adj amounting to a trillion

TRILLIUM n plant of Asia and North America

TRILLO, -ES n (in music) a trill

TRILLS ▶ **trill**

TRILOBAL ▶ **trilobe**

TRILOBE, -S n three-lobed thing

TRILOBED adj having three lobes

TRILOBES ▶ **trilobe**

TRILOGY n series of three related books, plays, etc

TRIM, -MED, -MEST, -MING, -S adj neat and smart ▷ vb cut or prune into good shape ▷ n decoration

TRIMARAN n three-hulled boat

TRIMER, -S n polymer or a molecule of a polymer consisting of three identical monomers

TRIMERIC ▶ **trimer**

TRIMERS ▶ **trimer**

TRIMETER n verse line consisting of three metrical feet ▷ adj designating such a line

TRIMIX, -ES n gas mixture of nitrogen, helium and oxygen used by deep-sea divers

TRIMLY ▶ **trim**

TRIMMED ▶ **trim**

TRIMMER, -S ▶ **trim**

TRIMMEST ▶ **trim**

TRIMMING ▶ **trim**

TRIMNESS ▶ **trim**

TRIMORPH n substance, esp a mineral, that exists in three distinct forms

T

TRIMOTOR n vehicle with three motors

TRIMPOT, -S n small instrument for adjusting resistance or voltage

TRIMS ▸ trim

TRIMTAB, -S n small control surface to enable the pilot to balance an aircraft

TRIN, -S n triplet

TRINAL ▸ trine

TRINARY adj made up of three parts

TRINDLE, -D, -S vb move heavily on (or as if on) wheels

TRINE, -D, -S, TRINING n aspect of 120° between two planets, an orb of 8° being allowed ▷ adj of or relating to a trine ▷ vb put in a trine aspect

TRINGLE, -S n slim rod

TRINING ▸ trine

TRINITY n group of three

TRINKET, -S n small or worthless ornament or piece of jewellery ▷ vb ornament with trinkets

TRINKUM, -S n trinket or bauble

TRINODAL adj having three nodes

TRINS ▸ trin

TRIO, -S n group of three

TRIODE, -S n electronic valve having three electrodes, a cathode, an anode, and a grid

TRIOL, -S n any of a class of alcohols that have three hydroxyl groups per molecule

TRIOLEIN n naturally occurring glyceride of oleic acid, found in fats and oils

TRIOLET, -S n verse form of eight lines

TRIOLS ▸ triol

TRIONES pl n seven stars of the constellation Ursa Major

TRIONYM, -S another name for > trinomial

TRIOR, -S old form of ▸ trier

TRIOS ▸ trio

TRIOSE, -S n simple monosaccharide produced by the oxidation of glycerol

TRIOXID, -S same as ▸ trioxide

TRIOXIDE n any oxide that contains three oxygen atoms per molecule

TRIOXIDS ▸ trioxid

TRIP, -PED, -PING, -S n journey to a place and back,

esp for pleasure ▷ vb (cause to) stumble

TRIPACK, -S n pack of three

TRIPART adj composed of three parts

TRIPE, -S n stomach of a cow used as food

TRIPEDAL adj having three feet

TRIPERY n place where tripe is prepared

TRIPES ▸ tripe

TRIPEY ▸ tripe

TRIPHASE adj having three phases

TRIPHONE n group of three phonemes

TRIPIER ▸ tripy

TRIPIEST ▸ tripy

TRIPLANE n aeroplane having three wings arranged one above the other

TRIPLE, -D, -S, TRIPLING adj having three parts ▷ vb increase three times ▷ n something that is, or contains, three times as much as normal

TRIPLET, -S n one of three babies born at one birth

TRIPLEX n building divided into three separate dwellings ▷ vb separate into three parts

TRIPLIED ▸ triply

TRIPLIES ▸ triply

TRIPLING ▸ triple

TRIPLITE n brownish-red phosphate

TRIPLOID adj having or relating to three times the haploid number of chromosomes ▷ n triploid organism

TRIPLY, TRIPLIED, TRIPLIES vb give a reply to a duply

TRIPMAN, TRIPMEN n man working on a trip

TRIPOD, -S n three-legged stand, stool, etc

TRIPODAL ▸ tripod

TRIPODIC ▸ tripod

TRIPODS ▸ tripod

TRIPODY n metrical unit consisting of three feet

TRIPOLI, -S n lightweight porous siliceous rock

TRIPOS, -ES n final examinations for an honours degree at Cambridge University

TRIPPANT adj (in heraldry) in the process of tripping

TRIPPED ▸ trip

TRIPPER, -S n tourist

TRIPPERY adj like a tripper

TRIPPET, -S n any mechanism that strikes or is struck at regular intervals, as by a cam

TRIPPIER ▸ trippy

TRIPPING ▸ trip

TRIPPLE, -D, -S vb canter

TRIPPLER ▸ tripple

TRIPPLES ▸ tripple

TRIPPY, TRIPPIER adj suggestive of or resembling the effect produced by a hallucinogenic drug

TRIPS ▸ trip

TRIPSIS, TRIPSES n act of kneading the body to promote circulation, suppleness, etc

TRIPTAN, -S n drug used to treat migraine

TRIPTANE n colourless highly flammable liquid

TRIPTANS ▸ triptan

TRIPTOTE n word that has only three cases

TRIPTYCA variant of ▸ triptych

TRIPTYCH n painting or carving on three hinged panels, often forming an altarpiece

TRIPUDIA > tripudium

TRIPWIRE n wire that activates a trap, mine, etc when tripped over

TRIPY, TRIPIER, TRIPIEST ▸ tripe

TRIREME, -S n ancient Greek warship with three rows of oars on each side

TRISCELE variant spelling of ▸ triskele

TRISECT, -S vb divide into three parts, esp three equal parts

TRISEME, -S n metrical foot of a length equal to three short syllables

TRISEMIC ▸ triseme

TRISHAW, -S another name for ▸ rickshaw

TRISKELE n three-limbed symbol

TRISMIC ▸ trismus

TRISMUS n state of being unable to open the mouth

TRISOME, -S n chromosome occurring three times (rather than twice) in a cell

TRISOMIC ▸ trisomy

TRISOMY n condition of having one chromosome represented three times

TRIST variant spelling of ▸ triste

TRISTATE adj (of a digital computer chip) having high,

low, and floating output states

TRISTE *adj* sad

TRISTEZA *n* disease affecting citrus trees

TRISTFUL *same as* ▶ **triste**

TRISTICH *n* poem, stanza, or strophe that consists of three lines

TRISUL, -S *n* trident symbol of Siva

TRISULA, -S *same as* ▶ **trisul**

TRISULS ▶ **trisul**

TRITE, -R, -S, -ST *adj* (of a remark or idea) commonplace and unoriginal ▷ *n* (on a lyre) the third string from the highest in pitch

TRITELY ▶ **trite**

TRITER ▶ **trite**

TRITES ▶ **trite**

TRITEST ▶ **trite**

TRITHING *n* tripartition

TRITIATE *vb* replace normal hydrogen atoms in (a compound) by those of tritium

TRITICAL *adj* trite; hackneyed

TRITICUM *n* type of cereal grass of the genus which includes the wheats

TRITIDE, -S *n* tritium compound

TRITIUM, -S *n* radioactive isotope of hydrogen

TRITOMA, -S *another name for* ▶ **kniphofia**

TRITON, -S *n* any of various chiefly tropical marine gastropod molluscs

TRITONE, -S *n* musical interval consisting of three whole tones

TRITONIA *n* type of plant with typically scarlet or orange flowers

TRITONS ▶ **triton**

TRIUMPH, -S *n* (happiness caused by) victory or success ▷ *vb* be victorious or successful

TRIUMVIR *n* (esp in ancient Rome) a member of a triumvirate

TRIUNE, -S *adj* constituting three things in one ▷ *n* group of three

TRIUNITY ▶ **triune**

TRIVALVE *n* animal having three valves

TRIVET, -S *n* metal stand for a pot or kettle

TRIVIA *pl n* trivial things or details

TRIVIAL *adj* of little importance

TRIVIUM, -S *n* (in medieval learning) the lower division of the seven liberal arts

TRIZONAL ▶ **trizone**

TRIZONE, -S *n* area comprising three zones

TROAD, -S *same as* ▶ **trod**

TROADE, -S *same as* ▶ **trod**

TROADS ▶ **troad**

TROAK, -ED, -ING, -S *old form of* ▶ **truck**

TROAT, -ED, -ING, -S *vb* (of a rutting buck) to call or bellow

TROCAR, -S *n* surgical instrument for removing fluid from bodily cavities

TROCHAIC *adj* of, relating to, or consisting of trochees ▷ *n* verse composed of trochees

TROCHAL *adj* shaped like a wheel

TROCHAR, -S *old variant spelling of* ▶ **trocar**

TROCHE, -S *another name for* ▶ **lozenge**

TROCHEE, -S *n* metrical foot of one long and one short syllable

TROCHES ▶ **troche**

TROCHI ▶ **trochus**

TROCHIL, -S *same as* ▶ **trochilus**

TROCHILI ▶ **trochilus**

TROCHILS ▶ **trochil**

TROCHISK *another word for* ▶ **troche**

TROCHITE *n* joint of a crinoid

TROCHLEA *n* any bony or cartilaginous part with a grooved surface

TROCHOID *n* curve described by a fixed point on the radius or extended radius of a circle as the circle rolls along a straight line ▷ *adj* rotating about a central axis

TROCHUS, TROCHI *n* hoop (used in exercise)

TROCK, -ED, -ING, -S *same as* ▶ **truck**

TROCKEN *adj* dry (used of wine)

TROCKING ▶ **trock**

TROCKS ▶ **trock**

TROD, -S *vb* past participle of tread ▷ *n* path

TRODDEN ▶ **tread**

TRODE, -S *same as* ▶ **trod**

TRODS ▶ **trod**

TROELIE, -S *same as* ▶ **troolie**

TROELY *same as* ▶ **troolie**

TROFFER, -S *n* fixture for holding and reflecting light from a fluorescent tube

TROG, -GED, -GING, -S *vb* walk, esp aimlessly or heavily

TROGGS *n* Scots word meaning fidelity, loyalty

TROGON, -S *n* bird of tropical and subtropical America, Africa, and Asia

TROGS ▶ **trog**

TROIKA, -S *n* Russian vehicle drawn by three horses abreast

TROILITE *n* iron sulphide present in most meteorites

TROILUS *n* type of large butterfly

TROIS *Scots form of* ▶ **troy**

TROJAN, -S *n* bug inserted into a computer program

TROKE, -D, -S, TROKING *same as* ▶ **truck**

TROLAND, -S *n* unit of light intensity in the eye

TROLL, -ED, -ING, -S *n* giant or dwarf in Scandinavian folklore ▷ *vb* fish by dragging a lure through the water

TROLLER, -S ▶ **troll**

TROLLEY, -S *n* small wheeled table for food and drink ▷ *vb* transport on a trolley

TROLLIED ▶ **trolly**

TROLLIES ▶ **trolly**

TROLLING ▶ **troll**

TROLLISH *adj* like a troll

TROLLIUS *n* plant with globe-shaped flowers

TROLLS ▶ **troll**

TROLLY, TROLLIED, TROLLIES *same as* ▶ **trolley**

TROMBONE *n* brass musical instrument with a sliding tube

TROMINO, -S *n* shape made from three squares, each joined to the next along one full side

TROMMEL, -S *n* revolving cylindrical sieve used to screen crushed ore

TROMP, -ED, -ING, -S *vb* trample

TROMPE, -S *n* apparatus for supplying the blast of air in a forge

TROMPED ▶ **tromp**

TROMPES ▶ **trompe**

TROMPING ▶ **tromp**

T

TROMPS ▸ tromp

TRON, -S n public weighing machine

TRONA, -S n greyish mineral that occurs in salt deposits

TRONC, -S n pool into which waiters, waitresses, hotel workers, etc pay their tips

TRONE, -S same as ▸ tron

TRONK, -S n jail

TRONS ▸ tron

TROOLIE, -S n large palm leaf

TROOP, -ED, -ING, -S n large group ▹ vb move in a crowd

TROOPER, -S n cavalry soldier

TROOPIAL same as ▸ troupial

TROOPING ▸ troop

TROOPS ▸ troop

TROOZ same as ▸ trews

TROP adv too, too much

TROPARIA ▸ troparion

TROPE, -D, -S, TROPING n figure of speech ▹ vb use tropes

TROPHESY n disorder of the nerves relating to nutrition

TROPHI pl n collective term for the mandibles and other parts of an insect's mouth

TROPHIC adj of or relating to nutrition

TROPHY, TROPHIED, TROPHIES n cup, shield, etc given as a prize ▹ adj regarded as a highly desirable symbol of wealth or success ▹ vb award a trophy to (someone)

TROPIC, -S n either of two lines of latitude at 23½°N or 23½°S

TROPICAL adj of or in the tropics ▹ n tropical thing or place

TROPICS ▸ tropic

TROPIN, -S n adrenal androgen

TROPINE, -S n white crystalline poisonous alkaloid

TROPING ▸ trope

TROPINS ▸ tropin

TROPISM, -S n tendency of a plant or animal to turn in response to an external stimulus

TROPIST, -S ▸ tropism

TROPONIN n muscle-tissue protein involved in the controlling of muscle contraction

TROPPO adv too much ▹ adj mentally affected by a tropical climate

TROSSERS old form of ▸ trousers

TROT, -S, -TED, -TING vb (of a horse) move at a medium pace, lifting the feet in diagonal pairs ▹ n act of trotting

TROTH, -ED, -ING, -S n pledge of devotion, esp a betrothal ▹ vb promise to marry (someone)

TROTHFUL ▸ troth

TROTHING ▸ troth

TROTHS ▸ troth

TROTLINE n line suspended across a stream to which shorter hooked and baited lines are attached

TROTS ▸ trot

TROTTED ▸ trot

TROTTER, -S n pig's foot

TROTTING ▸ trot

TROTTOIR n pavement

TROTYL, -S n yellow solid used chiefly as a high explosive

TROU pl n trousers

TROUBLE, -S n (cause of) distress or anxiety ▹ vb (cause to) worry

TROUBLED ▸ trouble

TROUBLER ▸ trouble

TROUBLES ▸ trouble

TROUCH, -ES n rubbish

TROUGH, -ED, -S n long open container, esp for animals' food or water ▹ vb eat, consume, or take greedily

TROULE, -D, -S, TROULING old variant of ▸ troll

TROUNCE, -D, -S vb defeat utterly

TROUNCER ▸ trounce

TROUNCES ▸ trounce

TROUPE, -D, -S, TROUPING n company of performers ▹ vb (esp of actors) to move or travel in a group

TROUPER, -S n member of a troupe

TROUPES ▸ troupe

TROUPIAL n any of various American orioles

TROUPING ▸ troupe

TROUSE, -S pl n close-fitting breeches worn in Ireland

TROUSER vb take (something, esp money), often surreptitiously or unlawfully

TROUSERS pl n two-legged outer garment with legs reaching usu to the ankles

TROUSES ▸ trouse

TROUT, -ING, -S n game fish related to the salmon ▹ vb fish for trout

TROUTER, -S ▸ trout

TROUTFUL adj (of a body of water) full of trout

TROUTIER ▸ trouty

TROUTING ▸ trout

TROUTLET n small trout

TROUTS ▸ trout

TROUTY, TROUTIER ▸ trout

TROUVERE n poet of N France during the 12th and 13th centuries

TROUVEUR same as ▸ trouvere

TROVE, -S n as in **treasure-trove** valuable articles found hidden in the earth

TROVER, -S n act of assuming proprietary rights over goods or property belonging to another

TROVES ▸ trove

TROW, -ED, -ING, -S vb think, believe, or trust

TROWEL, -ED, -S n hand tool with a wide blade ▹ vb use a trowel on (plaster, soil, etc)

TROWELER ▸ trowel

TROWELS ▸ trowel

TROWING ▸ trow

TROWS ▸ trow

TROWSERS old spelling of ▸ trousers

TROWTH, -S variant spelling of ▸ troth

TROY, -S n system of weights used for precious metals and gemstones

TRUANCY ▸ truant

TRUANT, -ED, -S n pupil who stays away from school without permission ▹ adj being or relating to a truant ▹ vb play truant

TRUANTLY ▸ truant

TRUANTRY ▸ truant

TRUANTS ▸ truant

TRUCAGE, -S n art forgery

TRUCE, -D, -S, TRUCING n temporary agreement to stop fighting ▹ vb make a truce

TRUCHMAN, TRUCHMEN n interpreter; translator

TRUCIAL ▸ truce

TRUCING ▸ truce

TRUCK, -ED, -S n railway goods wagon ▹ vb exchange (goods); barter

TRUCKAGE n conveyance of cargo by truck

TRUCKED ▸ truck

TRUCKER, -S n truck driver

TRUCKFUL n amount of something that can be conveyed in a truck

TRUCKIE, -S n truck driver

TRUCKING n transportation of goods by lorry

TRUCKLE, -D, -S vb yield weakly or give in ▷ n small wheel

TRUCKLER ▸ truckle

TRUCKLES ▸ truckle

TRUCKMAN, TRUCKMEN n truck driver

TRUCKS ▸ truck

TRUDGE, -D, -S, TRUDGING vb walk heavily or wearily ▷ n long tiring walk

TRUDGEN, -S n type of swimming stroke

TRUDGEON nonstandard variant of ▸ trudgen

TRUDGER, -S ▸ trudge

TRUDGES ▸ trudge

TRUDGING ▸ trudge

TRUE, -D, -ING, -R, -S, -ST, TRUING adj in accordance with facts

TRUEBLUE n staunch royalist or Conservative

TRUEBORN adj being such by birth

TRUEBRED adj thoroughbred

TRUED ▸ true

TRUEING ▸ true

TRUELOVE n person that one loves

TRUEMAN, TRUEMEN n honest person

TRUENESS ▸ true

TRUER ▸ true

TRUES ▸ true

TRUEST ▸ true

TRUFFE, -S rare word for ▸ truffle

TRUFFLE, -D, -S n edible underground fungus ▷ vb hunt for truffles

TRUG, -S n long shallow basket used by gardeners

TRUGO, -S n game similar to croquet

TRUGS ▸ trug

TRUING ▸ true

TRUISM, -S n self-evident truth

TRUISTIC ▸ truism

TRULY adv in a true manner

TRUMEAU, -X n section of a wall or pillar between two openings

TRUMP, -ED, -ING, -S adj (in card games) of the suit outranking the others ▷ vb play a trump card on (another card)

TRUMPERY n something useless or worthless ▷ adj useless or worthless

TRUMPET, -S n valved brass instrument with a flared tube ▷ vb proclaim loudly

TRUMPING ▸ trump

TRUMPS ▸ trump

TRUNCAL adj of or relating to the trunk

TRUNCATE vb cut short ▷ adj cut short

TRUNDLE, -D, -S vb move heavily on wheels ▷ n act or an instance of trundling

TRUNDLER n golf or shopping trolley

TRUNDLES ▸ trundle

TRUNK, -ED n main stem of a tree ▷ vb lop or truncate

TRUNKFUL ▸ trunk

TRUNKING n cables that take a common route through an exchange building linking ranks of selectors

TRUNKS pl n shorts worn by a man for swimming

TRUNNEL, -S same as ▸ treenail

TRUNNION n one of a pair of coaxial projections attached to opposite sides of a cannon

TRUQUAGE variant of ▸ trucage

TRUQUEUR n art forger

TRUSS, -ED, -ES vb tie or bind up ▷ n device for holding a hernia, etc in place

TRUSSER, -S ▸ truss

TRUSSES ▸ truss

TRUSSING n system of trusses, esp for strengthening or reinforcing a structure

TRUST, -ED, -S vb believe in and rely on ▷ n confidence in the truth, reliability, etc of a person or thing ▷ adj of or relating to a trust or trusts

TRUSTEE, -D, -S n person holding property on another's behalf ▷ vb act as a trustee

TRUSTER, -S ▸ trust

TRUSTFUL adj inclined to trust others

TRUSTIER ▸ trusty

TRUSTIES ▸ trusty

TRUSTILY ▸ trusty

TRUSTING same as ▸ trustful

TRUSTOR, -S n person who sets up a trust

TRUSTS ▸ trust

TRUSTY, TRUSTIER, TRUSTIES adj faithful or reliable ▷ n trustworthy convict to whom special privileges are granted

TRUTH, -S n state of being true

TRUTHER, -S n person who does not believe official accounts of the 9/11 attacks on the US

TRUTHFUL adj honest

TRUTHIER ▸ truthy

TRUTHS ▸ truth

TRUTHY, TRUTHIER adj truthful

TRY, TRIED, TRIES, -ING, -INGS vb make an effort or attempt ▷ n attempt or effort

TRYE adj very good; select

TRYER, -S variant of ▸ trier

TRYING ▸ try

TRYINGLY ▸ try

TRYINGS ▸ try

TRYKE, -S variant spelling of ▸ trike

TRYMA, -TA n drupe produced by the walnut and similar plants

TRYOUT, -S n trial or test, as of an athlete or actor

TRYP, -S n parasitic protozoan

TRYPAN modifier as in trypan blue dye used for staining cells in biological research

TRYPS ▸ tryp

TRYPSIN, -S n enzyme occurring in pancreatic juice

TRYPTIC ▸ trypsin

TRYSAIL, -S n small fore-and-aft sail on a sailing vessel

TRYST, -ED, -ING, -S n arrangement to meet ▷ vb meet at or arrange a tryst

TRYSTE, -S variant spelling of ▸ tryst

TRYSTED ▸ tryst

TRYSTER, -S ▸ tryst

TRYSTES ▸ tryste

TRYSTING ▸ tryst

TRYSTS ▸ tryst

TRYWORKS n furnace for rendering blubber

TSADDIK, -S variant of ▸ zaddik

TSADDIQ, -S variant of ▸ zaddik

TSADE, -S variant spelling of ▸ sadhe

TSADI, -S variant of ▸ **sadhe**
TSADIK, -S same as ▸ **zaddik**
TSADIS ▸ **tsadi**
TSAMBA, -S n Tibetan dish made from roasted barley and tea
TSANTSA, -S n shrunken head of an enemy kept as a trophy
TSAR, -S n Russian emperor
TSARDOM, -S ▸ **tsar**
TSAREVNA n daughter of a tsar
TSARINA, -S n wife of a tsar
TSARISM, -S n system of government by a tsar
TSARIST, -S n supporter of a tsar
TSARITSA n wife of a tsar
TSARITZA variant spelling of ▸ **tsaritsa**
TSARS ▸ **tsar**
TSATSKE, -S variant of > **tchotchke**
TSESSEBE South African variant of ▸ **sassaby**
TSETSE, -S n any of various bloodsucking African flies
TSIGANE, -S variant of ▸ **tzigane**
TSIMMES variant spelling of ▸ **tzimmes**
TSITSITH n tassels or fringes of thread attached to the four corners of the tallith
TSK, -ED, -ING, -S vb utter the sound 'tsk', usu in disapproval

This can occasionally be useful because it enables you to play K without using vowels.

TSKTSK, -ED, -S same as ▸ **tsk**
TSOORIS variant of ▸ **tsuris**
TSORES variant of ▸ **tsuris**
TSORIS variant of ▸ **tsuris**
TSORRISS variant of ▸ **tsuris**
TSOTSI, -S n (in South Africa) an urban thug or gang member
TSOURIS variant of ▸ **tsuris**
TSUBA, -S n sword guard of a Japanese sword
TSUBO, -S n unit of area
TSUNAMI, -S n tidal wave, usu caused by an earthquake under the sea
TSUNAMIC ▸ **tsunami**
TSUNAMIS ▸ **tsunami**
TSURIS, -ES n grief or strife
TSUTSUMU n Japanese art of wrapping gifts
TUAN, -S n lord
TUART, -S n eucalyptus tree of Australia

TUATARA, -S n large lizard-like New Zealand reptile
TUATERA, -S variant spelling of ▸ **tuatara**
TUATH, -S n territory of an ancient Irish tribe
TUATUA, -S n edible marine bivalve of New Zealand waters
TUB, -BED, -BING, -BINGS, -S n open, usu round container ▷ vb wash (oneself or another) in a tub
TUBA, -E, -S n valved low-pitched brass instrument
TUBAGE, -S n insertion of a tube
TUBAIST, -S ▸ **tuba**
TUBAL adj of or relating to a tube
TUBAR another word for ▸ **tubular**
TUBAS ▸ **tuba**
TUBATE less common word for ▸ **tubular**
TUBBABLE ▸ **tub**
TUBBED ▸ **tub**
TUBBER, -S ▸ **tub**
TUBBIER ▸ **tubby**
TUBBIEST ▸ **tubby**
TUBBING ▸ **tub**
TUBBINGS ▸ **tub**
TUBBISH adj fat
TUBBY, TUBBIER, TUBBIEST adj (of a person) short and fat
TUBE, -D, -S n hollow cylinder
TUBEFUL, -S n quantity (of something) that a tube can hold
TUBELESS adj without a tube
TUBELIKE adj resembling a tube
TUBENOSE n seabird with tubular nostrils on its beak
TUBER, -S n fleshy underground root of a plant such as a potato
TUBERCLE n small rounded swelling
TUBEROID adj resembling a tuber ▷ n fleshy root resembling a tuber
TUBEROSE same as ▸ **tuberous**
TUBEROUS adj (of plants) forming, bearing, or resembling a tuber or tubers
TUBERS ▸ **tuber**
TUBES ▸ **tube**
TUBEWELL n type of water well

TUBEWORK n collective term for tubes or tubing
TUBEWORM n undersea worm
TUBFAST, -S n period of fasting and sweating in a tub, intended as a cure for disease
TUBFISH another name for ▸ **gurnard**
TUBFUL, -S n amount a tub will hold
TUBICOLE n tube-dwelling creature
TUBIFEX n type of small reddish freshwater worm
TUBIFORM same as ▸ **tubular**
TUBING, -S n length of tube
TUBIST, -S ▸ **tuba**
TUBLIKE ▸ **tub**
TUBS ▸ **tub**
TUBULAR, -S adj of or shaped like a tube ▷ n type of tyre
TUBULATE vb form or shape into a tube
TUBULE, -S n any small tubular structure
TUBULIN, -S n protein forming the basis of microtubules
TUBULOSE adj tube-shaped; consisting of tubes
TUBULOUS adj tube-shaped
TUBULURE n tube leading into a retort or other receptacle
TUCHIS, -ES n buttocks
TUCHUN, -S n (formerly) a Chinese military governor or warlord
TUCHUS, -ES same as ▸ **tuchis**
TUCK, -ED, -S vb push or fold into a small space ▷ n stitched fold
TUCKAHOE n type of edible root
TUCKBOX n box used for carrying food to school
TUCKED ▸ **tuck**
TUCKER, -ED, -S n food ▷ vb weary or tire completely
TUCKET, -S n flourish on a trumpet
TUCKING, -S n act of tucking
TUCKS ▸ **tuck**
TUCKSHOP n shop, esp one in or near a school, where food such as cakes and sweets are sold
TUCOTUCO n colonial burrowing South American rodent

TUCUTUCO variant spelling of ▸tucotuco

TUCUTUCU same as ▸tucotuco

TUFA, -S n porous rock formed as a deposit from springs

TUFF, -S n porous rock formed from volcanic dust or ash

TUFFE, -S old form of ▸tuft

TUFFET, -S n small mound or seat

TUFFS ▸tuff

TUFOLI, -S n type of tubular pasta

TUFT, -ING, -INGS, -S n bunch of feathers, grass, hair, etc held or growing together at the base ▷ vb provide or decorate with a tuft or tufts

TUFTED adj having a tuft or tufts

TUFTER, -S ▸tuft

TUFTIER ▸tufty

TUFTIEST ▸tufty

TUFTILY ▸tuft

TUFTING ▸tuft

TUFTINGS ▸tuft

TUFTS ▸tuft

TUFTY, TUFTIER, TUFTIEST ▸tuft

TUG, -GED, -GING, -GINGS, -S vb pull hard ▷ n hard pull

TUGBOAT, -S n boat used for towing barges, ships, etc

TUGGED ▸tug

TUGGER, -S ▸tug

TUGGING ▸tug

TUGGINGS ▸tug

TUGHRA, -S n Turkish Sultan's official emblem

TUGHRIK, -S same as ▸tugrik

TUGLESS ▸tug

TUGRA, -S variant of ▸tughra

TUGRIK, -S n standard monetary unit of Mongolia

TUGS ▸tug

TUI, -S n New Zealand honeyeater that mimics human speech and the songs of other birds

TUILE, -S n type of almond-flavoured dessert biscuit

TUILLE, -S n (in a suit of armour) hanging plate protecting the thighs

TUILYIE, -D, -S vb fight

TUILZIE, -D, -S variant form of ▸tuilyie

TUINA, -S n form of massage originating in China

TUIS ▸tui

TUISM, -S n practice of putting the interests of another before one's own

TUITION, -S n instruction, esp received individually or in a small group

TUKTOO, -S same as ▸tuktu

TUKTU, -S (in Canada) another name for ▸caribou

TULADI, -S n large trout found in Canada and the northern US

TULBAN, -S old form of ▸turban

TULCHAN, -S n skin of a calf placed next to a cow to induce it to give milk

TULE, -S n type of bulrush found in California

TULIP, -S n plant with bright cup-shaped flowers

TULIPANT n turban

TULIPS ▸tulip

TULLE, -S n fine net fabric of silk etc

TULLIBEE n cisco of the Great Lakes of Canada

TULPA, -S n being or object created through willpower and visualization techniques

TULSI, -S n type of basil

TULWAR, -S n Indian sabre

TUM, -S informal or childish word for ▸stomach

TUMBLE, -D, -S, TUMBLING vb (cause to) fall, esp awkwardly or violently ▷ n fall

TUMBLER, -S n stemless drinking glass

TUMBLES ▸tumble

TUMBLING ▸tumble

TUMBREL, -S n farm cart for carrying manure

TUMBRIL, -S same as ▸tumbrel

TUMEFY, TUMEFIED, TUMEFIES vb make or become tumid

TUMESCE, -D, -S vb swell

TUMID adj (of an organ or part of the body) enlarged or swollen

TUMIDITY ▸tumid

TUMIDLY ▸tumid

TUMMIES ▸tummy

TUMMLER, -S n entertainer employed to encourage audience participation

TUMMY, TUMMIES n stomach

TUMOR, -S same as ▸tumour

TUMORAL ▸tumour

TUMOROUS ▸tumour

TUMORS ▸tumor

TUMOUR, -S n abnormal growth in or on the body

TUMP, -ED, -ING, -S n small mound or clump ▷ vb make a tump around

TUMPHY, TUMPHIES n dolt; fool

TUMPIER ▸tumpy

TUMPIEST ▸tumpy

TUMPING ▸tump

TUMPLINE n band strung across the forehead or chest and attached to a pack in order to support it

TUMPS ▸tump

TUMPY, TUMPIER, TUMPIEST ▸tump

TUMS ▸tum

TUMSHIE, -S n turnip

TUMULAR adj of, relating to, or like a mound

TUMULARY same as ▸tumular

TUMULI ▸tumulus

TUMULOSE adj abounding in small hills or mounds

TUMULOUS same as ▸tumulose

TUMULT, -ED, -S n uproar or commotion ▷ vb stir up a commotion

TUMULUS, TUMULI n burial mound

TUN, -NED, -NING, -NINGS, -S n large beer cask ▷ vb put into or keep in tuns

TUNA, -S n large marine food fish

TUNABLE adj able to be tuned

TUNABLY ▸tunable

TUNAS ▸tuna

TUNBELLY n large round belly

TUND, -ED, -ING, -S vb beat; strike

TUNDISH n type of funnel

TUNDRA, -S n vast treeless Arctic region with permanently frozen subsoil

TUNDS ▸tund

TUNDUN, -S n wooden instrument used by Aboriginal Australians in religious rites

TUNE, -D, -S n (pleasing) sequence of musical notes ▷ vb adjust (a musical instrument) so that it is in tune

TUNEABLE same as ▸tunable

TUNEABLY ▸tuneable

TUNEAGE, -S n music

TUNED ▸tune

TUNEFUL *adj* having a pleasant tune

TUNELESS *adj* having no melody or tune

TUNER, -S *n* part of a radio or television receiver for selecting channels

TUNES ▸ tune

TUNEUP, -S *n* adjustments made to an engine to improve its performance

TUNG, -S *n* fast-drying oil obtained from the seeds of a central Asian tree

TUNGSTEN *n* greyish-white metal

TUNGSTIC *adj* of or containing tungsten, esp in a high valence state

TUNIC, -S *n* close-fitting jacket forming part of some uniforms

TUNICA, -E *n* tissue forming a layer or covering of an organ or part

TUNICATE *n* minute primitive marine chordate animal ▷ *adj* of, relating to this animal ▷ *vb* wear a tunic

TUNICIN, -S *n* cellulose-like substance found in tunicates

TUNICKED *adj* wearing a tunic

TUNICLE, -S *n* vestment worn at High Mass and other religious ceremonies

TUNICS ▸ tunic

TUNIER ▸ tuny

TUNIEST ▸ tuny

TUNING, -S *n* set of pitches to which the open strings of a guitar, violin, etc are tuned

TUNKET, -S *n* hell

TUNNAGE, -S *same as* ▸ **tonnage**

TUNNED ▸ tun

TUNNEL, -ED, -S *n* underground passage ▷ *vb* make a tunnel (through)

TUNNELER ▸ tunnel

TUNNELS ▸ tunnel

TUNNIES ▸ tunny

TUNNING ▸ tun

TUNNINGS ▸ tun

TUNNY, TUNNIES *same as* ▸ **tuna**

TUNS ▸ tun

TUNY, TUNIER, TUNIEST *adj* having an easily discernable melody

TUP, -PED, -S *n* male sheep ▷ *vb* cause (a ram) to mate with a ewe

TUPEK, -S *same as* ▸ **tupik**

TUPELO, -S *n* large tree of deep swamps and rivers of the southern US

TUPIK, -S *n* tent of seal or caribou skin used for shelter by Inuit people in summer

TUPLE, -S *n* row of values in a relational database

TUPPED ▸ tup

TUPPENCE *same as* ▸ **twopence**

TUPPENNY *same as* ▸ **twopenny**

TUPPING, -S *n* act of sheep mating

TUPS ▸ tup

TUPUNA, -S *same as* ▸ **tipuna**

TUQUE, -S *n* knitted cap with a long tapering end

TURACIN, -S *n* red pigment found in touraco feathers

TURACO, -S *same as* ▸ **touraco**

TURACOU, -S *variant of* ▸ **touraco**

TURBAN, -S *n* Muslim, Hindu, or Sikh man's head covering

TURBAND, -S *old variant of* ▸ **turban**

TURBANED ▸ turban

TURBANS ▸ turban

TURBANT, -S *old variant of* ▸ **turban**

TURBARY *n* land where peat or turf is cut or has been cut

TURBETH, -S *variant of* ▸ **turpeth**

TURBID *adj* muddy, not clear

TURBIDLY ▸ turbid

TURBINAL *same as* > **turbinate**

TURBINE, -S *n* machine or generator driven by gas, water, etc turning blades

TURBINED *adj* having a turbine

TURBINES ▸ turbine

TURBIT, -S *n* crested breed of domestic pigeon

TURBITH, -S *variant of* ▸ **turpeth**

TURBITS ▸ turbit

TURBO, -S *n* compressor in an engine

TURBOCAR *n* car driven by a gas turbine

TURBOFAN *n* engine in which a fan driven by a turbine forces air rearwards to increase thrust

TURBOJET *n* gas turbine in which the exhaust gases provide the propulsive thrust to drive an aircraft

TURBOND, -S *old variant of* ▸ **turban**

TURBOS ▸ turbo

TURBOT, -S *n* large European edible flatfish

TURD, -S *n* slang word for a piece of excrement

TURDINE *adj* of, relating to, or characteristic of thrushes

TURDION, -S *variant of* ▸ **tordion**

TURDOID *same as* ▸ **turdine**

TURDS ▸ turd

TUREEN, -S *n* serving dish for soup

TURF, -ED, -ING, -INGS, -S, TURVES *n* short thick even grass ▷ *vb* cover with turf

TURFEN *adj* made of turf

TURFIER ▸ turfy

TURFIEST ▸ turfy

TURFING ▸ turf

TURFINGS ▸ turf

TURFITE, -S *same as* ▸ **turfman**

TURFLESS ▸ turf

TURFLIKE ▸ turf

TURFMAN, TURFMEN *n* person devoted to horse racing

TURFS ▸ turf

TURFSKI, -S *n* ski down a grassy hill on skis modified with integral wheels

TURFY, TURFIER, TURFIEST *adj* of, covered with, or resembling turf

TURGENCY ▸ turgent

TURGENT *obsolete word for* ▸ **turgid**

TURGID, -ER *adj* (of language) pompous

TURGIDLY ▸ turgid

TURGITE, -S *n* red or black mineral consisting of hydrated ferric oxide

TURGOR, -S *n* normal rigid state of a cell

TURION, -S *n* perennating bud produced by many aquatic plants

TURISTA, -S *n* traveller's diarrhoea

TURK, -S *n* as in **young turk** person who agitates for radical reform

TURKEY, -S *n* large bird bred for food

TURKIES *old form of* > **turquoise**

TURKIS, -ES *old form of* > **turquoise**

TURKOIS *old form of* > **turquoise**

TURKS ▸ turk

TURLOUGH n seasonal lake or pond

TURM, -S n troop of horsemen

TURME, -S variant of ▸turm

TURMERIC n yellow spice obtained from the root of an Asian plant

TURMES ▸turme

TURMOIL, -S n agitation or confusion ▷ vb make or become turbulent

TURMS ▸turm

TURN, -ED, -S vb change the position or direction (of) ▷ n turning

TURNABLE ▸turn

TURNBACK n one who turns back (from a challenge, for example)

TURNCOAT n person who deserts one party or cause to join another

TURNCOCK n (formerly) official employed to turn on the water for the mains supply

TURNDOWN adj capable of being or designed to be folded or doubled down ▷ n instance of turning down

TURNDUN, -S another name for ▸tundun

TURNED ▸turn

TURNER, -S n person or thing that turns

TURNERY n objects made on a lathe

TURNHALL n building in which gymnastics is taught and practised

TURNING, -S n road or path leading off a main route

TURNIP, -ED, -S n root vegetable with orange or white flesh ▷ vb sow (a field) with turnips

TURNIPY adj like a turnip

TURNKEY, -S n jailer ▷ adj denoting a project in which a single contractor has responsibility for the complete job

TURNOFF, -S n road or other way branching off from the main

TURNOUT, -S n number of people appearing at a gathering

TURNOVER n total sales made by a business over a certain period

TURNPIKE n road where a toll is collected at barriers

TURNS ▸turn

TURNSKIN n old name for a werewolf

TURNSOLE n any of various plants having flowers that are said to turn towards the sun

TURNSPIT n servant whose job was to turn the spit on which meat was roasting

TURNT adj slang word for intoxicated

TURNUP, -S n the turned-up fold at the bottom of some trouser legs

TURPETH, -S n convolvulaceous plant of India, having roots with purgative properties

TURPS n colourless, flammable liquid

TURQUOIS variant of > turquoise

TURR, -S n Newfoundland name for the guillemot

TURRET, -S n small tower

TURRETED adj having or resembling a turret or turrets

TURRETS ▸turret

TURRICAL adj of, relating to, or resembling a turret

TURRS ▸turr

TURTLE, -D, -S n sea tortoise ▷ vb catch turtles

TURTLER, -S ▸turtle

TURTLES ▸turtle

TURTLING n act of catching turtles

TURVES ▸turf

TUSCHE, -S n substance used in lithography for drawing the design

TUSH, -ED, -ES, -ING interj exclamation of disapproval or contempt ▷ n small tusk ▷ vb utter the interjection 'tush'

TUSHERY n use of affectedly archaic language in novels, etc

TUSHES ▸tush

TUSHIE, -S n pair of buttocks

TUSHING ▸tush

TUSHKAR, -S variant of ▸tuskar

TUSHKER, -S variant of ▸tuskar

TUSHY variant of ▸tushie

TUSK, -ED, -INGS, -S n long pointed tooth of an elephant, walrus, etc ▷ vb stab, tear, or gore with the tusks

TUSKAR, -S n peat-cutting spade

TUSKED ▸tusk

TUSKER, -S n any animal with prominent tusks, esp a wild boar or elephant

TUSKIER ▸tusky

TUSKIEST ▸tusky

TUSKING ▸tusk

TUSKINGS ▸tusk

TUSKLESS ▸tusk

TUSKLIKE ▸tusk

TUSKS ▸tusk

TUSKY, TUSKIER, TUSKIEST ▸tusk

TUSSAC modifier as in tussac grass kind of grass

TUSSAH, -S same as ▸tussore

TUSSAL ▸tussis

TUSSAR, -S variant of ▸tussore

TUSSEH, -S variant of ▸tussore

TUSSER, -S same as ▸tussore

TUSSIS, TUSSES, -ES technical name for a ▸cough

TUSSIVE ▸tussis

TUSSLE, -D, -S, TUSSLING vb fight or scuffle ▷ n energetic fight, struggle, or argument

TUSSOCK, -S n tuft of grass

TUSSOCKY adj covered with tussocks

TUSSOR, -S variant of ▸tussore

TUSSORE, -S n strong coarse brownish Indian silk

TUSSORS ▸tussor

TUSSUCK, -S variant of ▸tussock

TUSSUR, -S variant of ▸tussore

TUT, -TED, -TING, -TINGS interj exclamation of mild disapproval, or surprise ▷ vb express disapproval by the exclamation of 'tut-tut' ▷ n payment system based on measurable work done

TUTANIA, -S n alloy of low melting point used mostly for decorative purposes

TUTEE, -S n one who is tutored, esp in a university

TUTELAGE n instruction or guidance, esp by a tutor

TUTELAR, -S same as ▸tutelary

TUTELARY adj having the role of guardian or protector ▷ n tutelary person, deity, or saint

TUTENAG, -S n zinc alloy

TUTMAN, TUTMEN n one who does tutwork

TUTOR, -ED, -ING, -S n person teaching individuals

or small groups ▷ *vb* act as a tutor to

TUTORAGE ▸ **tutor**

TUTORED ▸ **tutor**

TUTORESS *n* female tutor

TUTORIAL *n* period of instruction with a tutor ▷ *adj* of or relating to a tutor

TUTORING ▸ **tutor**

TUTORISE *variant spelling of* ▸ **tutorize**

TUTORISM ▸ **tutor**

TUTORIZE *vb* tutor

TUTORS ▸ **tutor**

TUTOYED *adj* addressed in a familiar way

TUTOYER, -S *vb* speak to someone on familiar terms

TUTRESS *same as* ▸ **tutoress**

TUTRIX, TUTRICES, -ES *n* female tutor; tutoress

TUTS, -ED, -ES, -ING *Scots version of* ▸ **tut**

TUTSAN, -S *n* woodland shrub of Europe and W Asia

TUTSED ▸ **tuts**

TUTSES ▸ **tuts**

TUTSING ▸ **tuts**

TUTTED ▸ **tut**

TUTTI, -S *adv* to be performed by the whole orchestra or choir ▷ *n* piece of tutti music

TUTTIES ▸ **tutty**

TUTTING ▸ **tut**

TUTTINGS ▸ **tut**

TUTTIS ▸ **tutti**

TUTTY, TUTTIES *n* finely powdered impure zinc oxide

TUTU, -S *n* short stiff skirt worn by ballerinas

TUTUED *adj* wearing tutu

TUTUS ▸ **tutu**

TUTWORK, -S *n* work paid using a tut system

TUX, -ES *short for* ▸ **tuxedo**

Tux is a short form of **tuxedo**, and is a very commonly played X word.

TUXEDO, -ES, -S *n* dinner jacket

TUXEDOED *adj* wearing a tuxedo

TUXEDOES ▸ **tuxedo**

TUXEDOS ▸ **tuxedo**

TUXES ▸ **tux**

TUYER, -S *variant of* ▸ **tuyere**

TUYERE, -S *n* water-cooled nozzle through which air is blown into a cupola, blast furnace, or forge

TUYERS ▸ **tuyer**

TUZZ, -ES *n* tuft or clump of hair

TWA, -S *Scots word for* ▸ **two**

TWADDLE, -D, -S *n* silly or pretentious talk or writing ▷ *vb* talk or write in a silly or pretentious way

TWADDLER ▸ **twaddle**

TWADDLES ▸ **twaddle**

TWADDLY ▸ **twaddle**

TWAE, -S *same as* ▸ **twa**

TWAFALD *Scots variant of* ▸ **twofold**

TWAIN, -S *n* two

TWAITE, -S *n* herring-like food fish

TWAL, -S *n* Scots word meaning twelve

TWANG, -ED, -ING, -S *n* sharp ringing sound ▷ *vb* (cause to) make a twang

TWANGER, -S ▸ **twang**

TWANGIER ▸ **twangy**

TWANGING ▸ **twang**

TWANGLE, -D, -S *vb* make a continuous loose twanging sound

TWANGLER ▸ **twangle**

TWANGLES ▸ **twangle**

TWANGS ▸ **twang**

TWANGY, TWANGIER ▸ **twang**

TWANK, -ED, -ING, -S *vb* make a sharply curtailed twang

TWANKAY, -S *n* variety of Chinese green tea

TWANKED ▸ **twank**

TWANKIES ▸ **twanky**

TWANKING ▸ **twank**

TWANKS ▸ **twank**

TWANKY, TWANKIES *same as* ▸ **twankay**

TWAS ▸ **twa**

TWASOME, -S *same as* ▸ **twosome**

TWATTLE, -D, -S *rare word for* ▸ **twaddle**

TWATTLER ▸ **twattle**

TWATTLES ▸ **twattle**

TWAY, -S *old variant of* ▸ **twain**

TWEAK, -ED, -ING, -S *vb* pinch or twist sharply ▷ *n* instance of tweaking

TWEAKER, -S *n* engineer's small screwdriver

TWEAKIER ▸ **tweaky**

TWEAKING ▸ **tweak**

TWEAKS ▸ **tweak**

TWEAKY, TWEAKIER ▸ **tweak**

TWEE, -ST *adj* too sentimental, sweet, or pretty

TWEED, -S *n* thick woollen cloth

TWEEDIER ▸ **tweedy**

TWEEDILY *adv* in a manner characteristic of upper-class people who live in the country

TWEEDLE, -D, -S *vb* improvise aimlessly on a musical instrument

TWEEDLER ▸ **tweedle**

TWEEDLES ▸ **tweedle**

TWEEDS ▸ **tweed**

TWEEDY, TWEEDIER *adj* of or made of tweed

TWEEL, -ED, -ING, -S *variant of* ▸ **twill**

TWEELY ▸ **twee**

TWEEN, -S *same as* ▸ **between**

TWEENAGE *adj* (of a child) between about eight and fourteen years old

TWEENER, -S *same as* > **tweenager**

TWEENESS ▸ **twee**

TWEENIE *same as* ▸ **tweeny**

TWEENIES ▸ **tweeny**

TWEENS ▸ **tween**

TWEENY, TWEENIES *n* maid who assists both cook and housemaid

TWEEP, -S *n* person who uses Twitter

TWEEPLE *pl n* people who communicate via the Twitter website

TWEEPS ▸ **tweep**

TWEER, -ED, -ING, -S *variant of* ▸ **twire**

TWEEST ▸ **twee**

TWEET, -ED, -ING, -S *vb* chirp ▷ *interj* imitation of the thin chirping sound made by small birds

TWEETER, -S *n* loudspeaker reproducing high-frequency sounds

TWEETING ▸ **tweet**

TWEETS ▸ **tweet**

TWEETUP, -S *n* online meeting of individuals arranged on the social networking website Twitter

TWEEZE, -D, -S, TWEEZING *vb* take hold of or pluck (hair, small objects, etc) with or as if with tweezers

TWEEZER *same as* ▸ **tweezers**

TWEEZERS *pl n* small pincer-like tool

TWEEZES ▸ **tweeze**

TWEEZING ▸ **tweeze**

TWELFTH, -S *n* number twelve in a series ▷ *adj* of or being number twelve in a series

TWELVE, -S n two more than ten

TWELVEMO another word for > duodecimo

TWELVES ▸ twelve

TWENTY, TWENTIES n two times ten

TWERK, -ED, -S vb dance provocatively by moving the hips rapidly back and forth

TWERKING n type of dance involving rapid hip movement

TWERKS ▸ twerk

TWERP, -S n silly person

TWERPIER ▸ twerpy

TWERPS ▸ twerp

TWERPY, TWERPIER ▸ twerp

TWIBIL, -S same as ▸ twibill

TWIBILL, -S n mattock with a blade shaped like an adze at one end and like an axe at the other

TWIBILS ▸ twibil

TWICE adv two times

TWICER, -S n someone who does something twice

TWICHILD n old word for a person in his or her dotage

TWIDDLE, -D, -S vb fiddle or twirl in an idle way ▷ n act or instance of twiddling

TWIDDLER ▸ twiddle

TWIDDLES ▸ twiddle

TWIDDLY ▸ twiddle

TWIER, -S variant of ▸ tuyere

TWIFOLD variant of ▸ twofold

TWIG, -GED, -GING, -S n small branch or shoot ▷ vb realize or understand

TWIGGEN adj made of twigs

TWIGGER, -S ▸ twig

TWIGGIER ▸ twiggy

TWIGGING ▸ twig

TWIGGY, TWIGGIER adj of or relating to a twig or twigs

TWIGHT, -ED, -S old variant of ▸ twit

TWIGLESS ▸ twig

TWIGLET, -S n small twig

TWIGLIKE ▸ twig

TWIGLOO, -S n temporary shelter made from twigs, branches, leaves, etc

TWIGS ▸ twig

TWIGSOME adj covered with twigs; twiggy

TWILIGHT n soft dim light just after sunset ▷ adj of or relating to the period towards the end of the day

TWILIT ▸ twilight

TWILL, -ED, -ING, -S n fabric woven to produce parallel ridges ▷ adj of a weave in which the weft yarns are worked around two or more warp yarns ▷ vb weave in this fashion

TWILLIES ▸ twilly

TWILLING ▸ twill

TWILLS ▸ twill

TWILLY, TWILLIES n machine having revolving spikes for opening and cleaning raw textile fibres

TWILT, -ED, -ING, -S variant of ▸ quilt

TWIN, -NED, -S n one of a pair, esp of two children born at one birth ▷ vb pair or be paired

TWINBORN adj born as a twin

TWINE, -D, -S, TWINING, TWININGS n string or cord ▷ vb twist or coil round

TWINER, -S ▸ twine

TWINES ▸ twine

TWINGE, -D, -S, TWINGING n sudden sharp pain or emotional pang ▷ vb have or cause to have a twinge

TWINIER ▸ twiny

TWINIEST ▸ twiny

TWINIGHT adj (of a baseball double-header) held in the late afternoon and evening

TWINING ▸ twine

TWININGS ▸ twine

TWINJET, -S n jet aircraft with two engines

TWINK, -ED, -ING, -S n white correction fluid for deleting written text ▷ vb twinkle

TWINKIE, -S n stupid person

TWINKING ▸ twink

TWINKLE, -D, -S vb shine brightly but intermittently ▷ n flickering brightness

TWINKLER ▸ twinkle

TWINKLES ▸ twinkle

TWINKLY adj sparkling

TWINKS ▸ twink

TWINKY n stupid person

TWINLING old name for ▸ twin

TWINNED ▸ twin

TWINNING ▸ twin

TWINS ▸ twin

TWINSET, -S n matching jumper and cardigan

TWINSHIP n condition of being a twin or twins

TWINTER, -S n animal that is two years old

TWINY, TWINIER, TWINIEST ▸ twine

TWIRE, -D, -S, TWIRING vb look intently at (with (or as if with) difficulty

TWIRL, -ED, -ING, -S vb turn or spin around quickly ▷ n whirl or twist

TWIRLER, -S ▸ twirl

TWIRLIER ▸ twirly

TWIRLING ▸ twirl

TWIRLS ▸ twirl

TWIRLY, TWIRLIER ▸ twirl

TWIRP, -S same as ▸ twerp

TWIRPIER ▸ twirpy

TWIRPS ▸ twirp

TWIRPY, TWIRPIER ▸ twirp

TWISCAR, -S variant of ▸ tuskar

TWIST, -ED, -S vb turn out of the natural position ▷ n twisting

TWISTER, -S n swindler

TWISTIER ▸ twist

TWISTING ▸ twist

TWISTOR, -S n variable corresponding to the coordinates of a point in space and time

TWISTS ▸ twist

TWISTY ▸ twist

TWIT, -S, -TED, -TING vb poke fun at (someone) ▷ n foolish person

TWITCH, -ED, -ES vb move spasmodically ▷ n nervous muscular spasm

TWITCHER n bird-watcher who tries to spot as many rare varieties as possible

TWITCHES ▸ twitch

TWITCHY adj nervous, worried, and ill-at-ease

TWITE, -S n N European finch with a brown streaked plumage

TWITS ▸ twit

TWITTED ▸ twit

TWITTEN, -S n narrow alleyway

TWITTER, -S vb (of birds) utter chirping sounds ▷ n act or sound of twittering

TWITTERY adj making a chirping sound

TWITTING ▸ twit

TWITTISH adj silly; foolish

TWIXT same as ▸ betwixt

TWIZZLE, -D, -S vb spin around

TWO, -S n one more than one

TWOCCER, -S ▸ twoccing

TWOCCING n act of breaking into a motor vehicle and driving it away

TWOCKER, -S ▸ twoccing

T

TWOCKING same as
▶ twoccing

TWOER, -S n (in a game)
something that scores two

TWOFER, -S n single ticket
allowing the buyer entrance
to two events

TWOFOLD, -S adj having
twice as many or as much
▷ adv by twice as many or as
much ▷ n folding piece of
theatrical scenery

TWONESS n state or
condition of being two

TWONIE, -S same as
▶ toonie

TWOONIE, -S variant of
▶ toonie

TWOPENCE n sum of two
pennies

TWOPENNY adj cheap or
tawdry

TWOS ▶ two

TWOSOME, -S n group of
two people

TWP adj Welsh dialect word
meaning stupid

This Welsh word for stupid is
useful because it contains
no vowels, and can help
you when you have an awkward
rack full of consonants.

TWYER, -S same as ▶ tuyere

TWYERE, -S variant of
▶ tuyere

TWYERS ▶ twyer

TWYFOLD adj twofold

TYCHISM, -S n theory that
chance is an objective reality
at work in the universe

TYCOON, -S n powerful
wealthy businessperson;
shogun

TYDE old variant of the past
participle of ▶ tie

TYE, -D, -ING, -S n trough
used in mining to separate
valuable material from dross
▷ vb (in mining) isolate
valuable material from dross
using a tye

TYEE, -S n large northern
Pacific salmon

TYEING ▶ tye

TYER, -S ▶ tye

TYES ▶ tye

TYG, -S n mug with two
handles

This old word for a
two-handled drinking cup is
another key word to know
for situations when you are
short of vowels.

TYIN variant of ▶ tyiyn

TYING ▶ tie

TYIYN, -S n money unit of
Kyrgyzstan

TYKE, -S n dog

TYKISH ▶ tyke

TYLER, -S variant of ▶ tiler

TYLOPOD, -S n mammal
with padded feet, such as a
camel or llama

TYLOSES ▶ tylosis

TYLOSIN, -S n broad
spectrum antibiotic

TYLOSIS, TYLOSES n
bladder-like outgrowth
from certain cells in woody
tissue

TYLOTE, -S n knobbed
sponge spicule

TYMBAL, -S same as
▶ timbal

TYMP, -S n blast furnace
outlet through which
molten metal flows

TYMPAN, -S same as
▶ tympanum

TYMPANA ▶ tympanum

TYMPANAL adj relating to
the tympanum

TYMPANI, TYMPANO same
as ▶ timpani

TYMPANIC adj of, relating
to, or having a tympanum
▷ n part of the temporal
bone in the mammalian
skull that surrounds the
auditory canal

TYMPANO ▶ tympani

TYMPANS ▶ tympan

TYMPANUM, TYMPANA n
cavity of the middle ear

TYMPANY n distention of
the abdomen

TYMPS ▶ tymp

TYND variant of ▶ tind

TYNDE variant of ▶ tind

TYNE, -D, -S, TYNING variant
of ▶ tine

TYPABLE ▶ type

TYPAL rare word for ▶ typical

TYPE, -D, -S n class or
category ▷ vb print with a
typewriter or word
processor

TYPEABLE ▶ type

TYPEBAR, -S n one of the
bars in a typewriter that
carry the type and are
operated by keys

TYPECASE n
compartmental tray for
storing printer's type

TYPECAST vb continually
cast (an actor or actress) in
similar roles

TYPED ▶ type

TYPEFACE n style of the type

TYPES ▶ type

TYPESET, -S vb set (text for
printing) in type

TYPEY variant of ▶ typy

TYPHOID, -S adj of or
relating to typhoid fever ▷ n
typhoid fever

TYPHON, -S n whirlwind

TYPHONIC ▶ typhoon

TYPHONS ▶ typhon

TYPHOON, -S n violent
tropical storm

TYPHOSE adj relating to
typhoid

TYPHOUS ▶ typhus

TYPHUS, -ES n infectious
feverish disease

TYPIC same as ▶ typical

TYPICAL adj true to type,
characteristic

TYPIER ▶ typy

TYPIEST ▶ typy

TYPIFIED ▶ typify

TYPIFIER ▶ typify

TYPIFY, TYPIFIED, TYPIFIES
vb be typical of

TYPING, -S n work or activity
of using a typewriter or word
processor

TYPIST, -S n person who
types with a typewriter or
word processor

TYPO, -S n typographical
error

TYPOLOGY n study of
types

TYPOS ▶ typo

TYPP, -S n unit of thickness
of yarn

TYPTO, -ED, -ING, -S vb
learn Greek conjugations

TYPY, TYPIER, TYPIEST adj
(of an animal) typifying the
breed

TYRAMINE n colourless
crystalline amine derived
from phenol

TYRAN, -ED, -ING, -S vb act
as a tyrant

TYRANNE, -D, -S variant of
▶ tyran

TYRANNIC ▶ tyranny

TYRANNIS n tyrannical
government

TYRANNY n tyrannical
rule

TYRANS ▶ tyran

TYRANT, -ED, -S n
oppressive or cruel ruler
▷ vb act the tyrant

TYRE, -D, -S, TYRING n
rubber ring, usu inflated,
over the rim of a vehicle's
wheel to grip the road ▷ vb
fit a tyre or tyres to (a wheel,
vehicle, etc)

TYRELESS ▶ tyre

TYRES ▸ tyre
TYRING ▸ tyre
TYRO, -ES, -NES, -S n novice
or beginner
TYRONIC ▸ tyro
TYROPITA n Greek cheese
pie
TYROS ▸ tyro
TYROSINE n aromatic
nonessential amino acid
TYSTIE, -S n black guillemot
TYTE variant spelling of
▸ tite
TYTHE, -D, -S, TYTHING
variant of ▸ tithe
TZADDI, -S same as ▸ sadhe
TZADDIK, -S variant of
▸ zaddik
TZADDIQ, -S variant of
▸ zaddik

An unlikely word from
Judaism, meaning a person
of great piety, but offering a
great score played as a
bonus.

TZADDIS ▸ tzaddi
TZADIK, -S same as
▸ zaddik
TZAR, -S same as ▸ tsar
TZARDOM, -S ▸ tzar
TZAREVNA variant of
▸ tsarevna
TZARINA, -S variant of
▸ tsarina
TZARISM, -S variant of
▸ tsarism
TZARIST, -S variant of
▸ tsarist
TZARITZA variant of
▸ tsaritsa

TZARS ▸ tzar
TZATZIKI n Greek dip made
from yogurt, chopped
cucumber, and mint
TZEDAKAH n charitable
donations as a Jewish moral
obligation
TZETSE, -S variant of ▸ tsetse
TZETZE, -S variant of ▸ tsetse
TZIGANE, -S n Romany
dance
TZIGANY variant of
▸ tzigane
TZIMMES n traditional
Jewish stew
TZITZIS variant of ▸ tsitsith
TZITZIT variant of ▸ tsitsith
TZITZITH variant of ▸ tsitsith
TZURIS, -ES variant of
▸ tsuris

T

Uu

U can be a difficult tile to use effectively. Although there are quite a few two-letter words beginning with **U**, most of them are quite unusual, and so difficult to remember. Only **up** (4 points) and **us** (2) are immediately obvious, so it's well worth learning words like **ug** (3), **uh** (5), **um** (4), and **un** and **ut** (2 each). Three-letter words beginning with **U** can also be difficult to remember. If you are trying to use a **Q**, **X** or **Z**, bear in mind that there aren't any valid three-letter words with these letters that start with **U**. Knowing this can save you valuable time. It's also helpful to remember that there aren't any particularly high-scoring two- or three-letter words starting with **U**, the best being **uke** (7 points), **uva** (6 points) and **ume** (5 points). If you have a surplus of **U**s, it is well worth remembering **ulu**, **umu** and **utu**, which score only 3 points but should improve your rack.

UAKARI, -S n type of monkey

UBEROUS adj abundant

UBERTY, UBERTIES n abundance

UBIETY, UBIETIES n condition of being in a particular place

UBIQUE adv everywhere

UBIQUITY n state of apparently being everywhere at once; omnipresence

UBUNTU, -S n quality of compassion and humanity

UCKERS n type of naval game

UDAL, -S n form of freehold possession of land used in Orkney and Shetland

UDALLER, -S n person possessing a udal

UDALS ▸ udal

UDDER, -S n large baglike milk-producing gland of cows, sheep, or goats

UDDERED ▸ udder

UDDERFUL n capacity of an udder

UDDERS ▸ udder

UDO, -S n stout perennial plant of Japan and China

UDOMETER n archaic term for an instrument for measuring rainfall or snowfall

UDOMETRY ▸ udometer

UDON, -S n (in Japanese cookery) large noodles made of wheat flour

UDOS ▸ udo

UDS interj God's or God save

UEY, -S n U-turn

UFO, -S n flying saucer

UFOLOGY n study of UFOs

UFOS ▸ ufo

UG, -GED, -GING, -S vb hate

UGALI, -S n type of stiff porridge

UGGED ▸ ug

UGGING ▸ ug

UGH, -S interj exclamation of disgust ▸ n sound made to indicate disgust

> Together with **uke**, this is the highest-scoring 3-letter word starting with U.

UGLIED ▸ ugly

UGLIER ▸ ugly

UGLIES ▸ ugly

UGLIEST ▸ ugly

UGLIFIED ▸ uglify

UGLIFIER ▸ uglify

UGLIFY, UGLIFIED, UGLIFIES vb make or become ugly or more ugly

UGLILY ▸ ugly

UGLINESS ▸ ugly

UGLY, UGLIED, UGLIER, UGLIES, UGLIEST, -ING adj of unpleasant appearance ▸ vb make ugly

UGS ▸ ug

UGSOME adj loathsome

UH interj used to express hesitation

UHLAN, -S n member of a body of lancers first employed in the Polish army

UHURU, -S n national independence

> You won't often have three Us on your rack, but when you do, this Swahili word for freedom may get you out of trouble. The only other 5-letter word containing three Us is **urubu**, a kind of vulture.

UILLEAN adj as in **uillean pipes** bagpipes developed in Ireland

UILLEANN same as ▸ **uillean**

UINTAITE n variety of asphalt

UJAMAA, -S n communally organized village in Tanzania

UKASE, -S n (in imperial Russia) a decree from the tsar

UKE, -S short form of ▸ **ukulele**

> Together with **ugh**, this is the highest-scoring 3-letter word starting with U.

UKELELE, -S same as ▸ **ukulele**

UKES ▸ uke

UKULELE, -S n small guitar with four strings

ULAMA, -S n body of Muslim scholars or religious leaders

ULAN, -S same as ▸ **uhlan**

ULCER, -ED, -ING, -S n open sore on the surface of the skin or mucous membrane. ▹ vb make or become ulcerous

ULCERATE vb make or become ulcerous

ULCERED ▸ ulcer

ULCERING ▸ ulcer

ULCEROUS adj of, like, or characterized by ulcers

ULCERS ▸ ulcer

ULE, -S n rubber tree

ULEMA, -S same as ▸ ulama

ULES ▸ ule

ULEX, -ES, ULICES n variety of shrub

ULEXITE, -S n type of mineral

ULICES ▸ ulex

ULICON, -S same as ▸ eulachon

ULIKON, -S same as ▸ eulachon

ULITIS, -ES n gingivitis

ULLAGE, -S, ULLAGING n volume by which a liquid container falls short of being full ▹ vb create ullage in

ULLAGED ▸ ullage

ULLAGES ▸ ullage

ULLAGING ▸ ullage

ULLING, -S n process of filling

ULMIN, -S n substance found in decaying vegetation

ULNA, -E, -S n inner and longer of the two bones of the human forearm

ULNAD adv towards the ulna

ULNAE ▸ ulna

ULNAR ▸ ulna

ULNARE, ULNARIA n bone in the wrist

ULNAS ▸ ulna

ULOSIS, ULOSES n formation of a scar

ULPAN, -IM n Israeli study centre

ULSTER, -S n man's heavy double-breasted overcoat

ULSTERED adj wearing an ulster

ULSTERS ▸ ulster

ULTERIOR adj (of an aim, reason, etc) concealed or hidden

ULTIMA, -S n final syllable of a word

ULTIMACY ▸ ultimate

ULTIMAS ▸ ultima

ULTIMATA > ultimatum

ULTIMATE adj final in a series or process ▹ n most significant, highest, furthest, or greatest thing ▹ vb end

ULTIMO adv in or during the previous month

ULTION, -S n vengeance

ULTISOL, -S n reddish-yellow acid soil

ULTRA, -S n person who has extreme or immoderate beliefs or opinions ▹ adj extreme or immoderate, esp in beliefs or opinions

ULTRADRY adj extremely dry

ULTRAHIP adj extremely trendy

ULTRAHOT adj extremely hot

ULTRAISM n extreme philosophy, belief, or action

ULTRAIST ▸ ultraism

ULTRALOW adj extremely low

ULTRARED obsolete word for ▸ infrared

ULTRAS ▸ ultra

ULU, -S n type of knife

ULULANT ▸ ululate

ULULATE, -D, -S vb howl or wail

ULUS ▸ ulu

ULVA, -S n genus of seaweed

ULYIE, -S Scots variant of ▸ oil

ULZIE, -S Scots variant of ▸ oil

UM, -MED, -MING, -S interj representation of a common sound made when hesitating in speech ▹ vb hesitate while speaking

UMAMI, -S n savoury flavour

UMANGITE n type of mineral

UMBEL, -S n umbrella-like flower cluster

UMBELED same as ▸ umbelled

UMBELLAR ▸ umbel

UMBELLED adj having umbels

UMBELLET same as > umbellule

UMBELS ▸ umbel

UMBELULE n secondary umbel

UMBER, -S adj dark brown to reddish-brown ▹ n type of dark brown earth containing ferric oxide (rust) ▹ vb stain with umber

UMBERED ▸ umber

UMBERIER ▸ umbery

UMBERING ▸ umber

UMBERS ▸ umber

UMBERY, UMBERIER adj like umber

UMBILICI > umbilicus

UMBLE adj as in umble pie (formerly) a pie made from the heart, entrails, etc of a deer

UMBLES another term for ▸ numbles

UMBO, -NES, -S n small hump projecting from the centre of the cap in certain mushrooms

UMBONAL ▸ umbo

UMBONATE ▸ umbo

UMBONES ▸ umbo

UMBONIC ▸ umbo

UMBOS ▸ umbo

UMBRA, -E, -S n shadow, esp the shadow cast by the moon onto the earth during a solar eclipse

UMBRAGE, -S n displeasure or resentment ▹ vb shade

UMBRAGED ▸ umbrage

UMBRAGES ▸ umbrage

UMBRAL ▸ umbra

UMBRAS ▸ umbra

UMBRATED adj shown in a faint manner

UMBRATIC ▸ umbra

UMBRE, -S same as ▸ umbrette

UMBREL, -S n umbrella

UMBRELLA n portable device used for protection against rain ▹ adj containing many different organizations

UMBRELLO same as ▸ umbrella

UMBRELS ▸ umbrel

UMBRERE, -S n helmet visor

UMBRES ▸ umbre

UMBRETTE n African wading bird

UMBRIERE same as ▸ umbrere

UMBRIL, -S same as ▸ umbrere

UMBROSE same as ▸ umbrous

UMBROUS adj shady

UME, -S n sour Japanese fruit

UMEBOSHI n dried and pickled ume

UMES ▸ ume

UMFAZI, -S n African married woman

UMIAC, -S variant of ▸ umiak

UMIACK, -S variant of ▸ umiak

UMIACS ▸ umiac

UMIAK, -S n Inuit boat made of skins

U

UMIAQ, -S *same as* ▸ **umiak**

An Inuit word for a type of canoe: easy to miss because one tends automatically to put the Q after the U and not think of a word ending in Q. The many variant spellings of this word include **umiac** and **umiak**.

UMLAUT, -ED, -S *n* mark (¨) placed over a vowel, esp in German, to indicate a change in its sound ▸ *vb* modify by umlaut

UMM *same as* ▸ **um**

UMMA, -S *n* Muslim community

UMMAH, -S *same as* ▸ **umma**

UMMAS ▸ **umma**

UMMED ▸ **um**

UMMING ▸ **um**

UMP, -ED, -ING, -S *short for* ▸ **umpire**

UMPH, -S *same as* ▸ **humph**

UMPIE *informal word for* ▸ **umpire**

UMPIES ▸ **umpy**

UMPING ▸ **ump**

UMPIRAGE ▸ **umpire**

UMPIRE, -D, -S, UMPIRING *n* official who rules on the playing of a game ▸ *vb* act as umpire in (a game)

UMPS ▸ **ump**

UMPTEEN *adj* very many

UMPTIER ▸ **umpty**

UMPTIEST ▸ **umpty**

UMPTIETH *same as* > **umpteenth**

UMPTY, UMPTIER, UMPTIEST *adj* very many

UMPY, UMPIES *same as* ▸ **umpie**

UMQUHILE *adv* formerly

UMRA, -S *n* pilgrimage to Mecca that can be made at any time of the year

UMRAH, -S *same as* ▸ **umra**

UMRAS ▸ **umra**

UMS ▸ **um**

UMTEENTH *same as* > **umpteenth**

UMU, -S *n* type of oven

UMWELT, -S *n* environmental factors that affect the behaviour of an animal or individual

UMWHILE *same as* ▸ **umquhile**

UN, -S *pron* spelling of 'one' intended to reflect a dialectal or informal pronunciation

UNABATED *adv* without any reduction in force ▸ *adj* not losing any original force or violence

UNABLE *adj* lacking the necessary power, ability, or authority (to do something)

UNABUSED *adj* not abused

UNACHING *adj* not aching

UNACIDIC *adj* not acidic

UNACTED *adj* not acted or performed

UNACTIVE *adj* inactive ▸ *vb* make (a person) inactive

UNADDED *adj* not added

UNADEPT, -S *adj* not adept ▸ *n* person who is not adept

UNADORED *adj* not adored

UNADULT *adj* not mature

UNAFRAID *adj* not frightened or nervous

UNAGED *adj* not old

UNAGEING *adj* not ageing

UNAGILE *adj* not agile

UNAGING *same as* ▸ **unageing**

UNAGREED *adj* not agreed

UNAI, -S *same as* ▸ **unau**

UNAIDED *adv* without any help or assistance ▸ *adj* not having received any help

UNAIMED *adj* not aimed or specifically targeted

UNAIRED *adj* not aired

UNAIS ▸ **unai**

UNAKIN *adj* not related

UNAKING *Shakespearean form of* ▸ **unaching**

UNAKITE, -S *n* type of mineral

UNALIKE *adj* not similar

UNALIST, -S *n* priest holding only one benefice

UNALIVE *adj* unaware

UNALLIED *adj* not allied

UNAMAZED *adj* not greatly surprised

UNAMUSED *adj* not entertained, diverted, or laughing

UNANCHOR *vb* remove anchor

UNANELED *adj* not having received extreme unction

UNAPT *adj* not suitable or qualified

UNAPTLY ▸ **unapt**

UNARCHED *adj* not arched

UNARGUED *adj* not debated

UNARISEN *adj* not having risen

UNARM, -ING, -S *less common word for* ▸ **disarm**

UNARMED *adj* without weapons

UNARMING ▸ **unarm**

UNARMS ▸ **unarm**

UNARTFUL *adj* not artful

UNARY *adj* consisting of, or affecting, a single element or component

UNASKED *adv* without being asked to do something ▸ *adj* (of a question) not asked, although sometimes implied

UNATONED *adj* not atoned for

UNAU, -S *n* two-toed sloth

UNAVOWED *adj* not openly admitted

UNAWAKE *adj* not awake

UNAWAKED *adj* not aroused

UNAWARE *adj* not aware or conscious ▸ *adv* by surprise

UNAWARES *adv* by surprise

UNAWED *adj* not awed

UNAXED *adj* not axed

UNBACKED *adj* (of a book, chair, etc) not having a back

UNBAG, -S *vb* take out of a bag

UNBAGGED ▸ **unbag**

UNBAGS ▸ **unbag**

UNBAITED *adj* not baited

UNBAKED *adj* not having been baked

UNBALE, -D, -S, UNBALING *vb* remove from bale

UNBAN, -NED, -S *vb* stop banning or permit again

UNBANDED *adj* not fastened with a band

UNBANKED *adj* not having been banked

UNBANNED ▸ **unban**

UNBANS ▸ **unban**

UNBAR, -RED, -S *vb* take away a bar or bars from

UNBARBED *adj* without barbs

UNBARE, -D, -S, UNBARING *vb* expose

UNBARK, -ED, -S *vb* strip bark from

UNBARRED ▸ **unbar**

UNBARS ▸ **unbar**

UNBASED *adj* not having a base

UNBASTED *adj* not basted

UNBATED *adj* (of a sword, lance, etc) not covered with a protective button

UNBATHED *adj* unwashed

UNBE, -EN *vb* make non-existent

UNBEAR, -ED, -S *vb* release (horse) from the bearing rein

UNBEATEN *adj* having suffered no defeat

UNBED, -DED, -S *vb* remove from bed

UNBEEN ▸ **unbe**

UNBEGET, -S *vb* deprive of existence

UNBEGGED *adj* not obtained by begging

UNBEGOT adj unbegotten
UNBEGUN adj not commenced
UNBEING, -S n non-existence
UNBELIEF n disbelief or rejection of belief
UNBELT, -ED, -S vb unbuckle the belt of (a garment)
UNBEND, -ED, -S vb become less strict or more informal in one's attitudes or behaviour
UNBENIGN adj not benign
UNBENT adj not bent or bowed
UNBEREFT adj not bereft
UNBESEEM vb be unbefitting to
UNBIAS, -ES vb free from prejudice
UNBIASED adj not having or showing prejudice or favouritism
UNBIASES ▸ unbias
UNBID same as ▸ **unbidden**
UNBIDDEN adj not ordered or asked
UNBILLED adj not having been billed
UNBIND, -S vb set free from bonds or chains
UNBISHOP vb remove from the position of bishop
UNBITT, -ED, -S vb remove (cable) from the bitts
UNBITTEN adj not having been bitten
UNBITTER adj not bitter
UNBITTS ▸ unbitt
UNBLAMED adj not blamed
UNBLENT same as > **unblended**
UNBLESS vb deprive of a blessing
UNBLEST same as > **unblessed**
UNBLIND, -S vb rid of blindness
UNBLOCK, -S vb remove a blockage from
UNBLOODY adj not covered with blood
UNBLOWED same as ▸ **unblown**
UNBLOWN adj (of a flower) still in the bud
UNBOBBED adj not bobbed
UNBODIED adj having no body
UNBODING adj having no presentiment
UNBOILED adj not boiled
UNBOLT, -S vb unfasten a bolt of (a door)
UNBOLTED adj (of grain, meal, or flour) not sifted

UNBOLTS ▸ unbolt
UNBONDED adj not bonded
UNBONE, -S, UNBONING vb remove bone from
UNBONED adj (of meat, fish, etc) not having had the bones removed
UNBONES ▸ unbone
UNBONING ▸ unbone
UNBONNET vb remove the bonnet from
UNBOOKED adj not reserved
UNBOOT, -S vb remove boots from
UNBOOTED ▸ unboot
UNBOOTS ▸ unboot
UNBORE adj unborn
UNBORN adj not yet born
UNBORNE adj not borne
UNBOSOM, -S vb relieve (oneself) of (secrets or feelings) by telling someone
UNBOTTLE vb allow out of bottle
UNBOUGHT adj not purchased
UNBOUNCY adj not bouncy
UNBOUND adj (of a book) not bound within a cover
UNBOWED adj not giving in or submitting
UNBOWING adj not bowing
UNBOX, -ED, -ES, -ING vb empty a box
UNBRACE, -D, -S vb remove tension or strain from
UNBRAID, -S vb remove braids from
UNBRAKE, -D, -S vb stop reducing speed by releasing brake
UNBRASTE archaic past form of ▸ **unbrace**
UNBRED adj not taught or instructed
UNBREECH vb remove breech from
UNBRIDLE vb remove the bridle from (a horse)
UNBRIGHT adj not bright
UNBROKE same as ▸ **unbroken**
UNBROKEN adj complete or whole
UNBRUSED same as > **unbruised**
UNBUCKLE vb undo the buckle or buckles of
UNBUDDED adj not having buds
UNBUILD, -S, UNBUILT vb destroy
UNBULKY adj not bulky
UNBUNDLE vb separate (hardware from software) for sales purposes

UNBURDEN vb relieve (one's mind or oneself) of a worry by confiding in someone
UNBURIED ▸ unbury
UNBURIES ▸ unbury
UNBURNED same as ▸ **unburnt**
UNBURNT adj not burnt
UNBURROW vb remove from a burrow
UNBURY, UNBURIED, UNBURIES vb unearth
UNBUSIED ▸ unbusy
UNBUSIER ▸ unbusy
UNBUSIES ▸ unbusy
UNBUSTED adj unbroken
UNBUSY, UNBUSIED, UNBUSIER, UNBUSIES adj not busy ▷ vb make less busy
UNBUTTON vb undo by unfastening the buttons of (a garment)
UNCAGE, -S, UNCAGING vb release from a cage
UNCAGED adj at liberty
UNCAGES ▸ uncage
UNCAGING ▸ uncage
UNCAKE, -D, -S, UNCAKING vb remove compacted matter from
UNCALLED adj not called
UNCANDID adj not frank
UNCANDOR n lack of candor
UNCANNED adj not canned
UNCANNY adj weird or mysterious
UNCAP, -PED, -S vb remove a cap or top from (a container)
UNCAPE, -D, -S, UNCAPING vb remove the cape from
UNCAPPED ▸ uncap
UNCAPS ▸ uncap
UNCARDED adj not carded
UNCARED adj as in **uncared for** not cared (for)
UNCARING adj thoughtless
UNCART, -ED, -S vb remove from a cart
UNCARVED adj not carved
UNCASE, -D, -S, UNCASING vb display
UNCASHED adj not cashed
UNCASING ▸ uncase
UNCASKED adj removed from a cask
UNCAST, -ED, -S adj not cast ▷ vb undo the process of casting
UNCATCHY adj not catchy
UNCATE same as ▸ **uncinate**
UNCAUGHT adj not caught
UNCAUSED adj not brought into existence by any cause

U

UNCE, -S same as ▸ **ounce**
UNCEDED adj not ceded
UNCES ▸ **unce**
UNCHAIN, -S vb remove a chain or chains from
UNCHAIR, -S vb unseat from chair
UNCHANCY adj unlucky, ill-omened, or dangerous
UNCHARGE vb unload
UNCHARM, -S vb disenchant
UNCHARY adj not cautious
UNCHASTE adj not chaste
UNCHECK, -S vb remove check mark from
UNCHEWED adj not chewed
UNCHIC adj not chic
UNCHICLY ▸ **unchic**
UNCHILD, -S vb deprive of children
UNCHOKE, -D, -S vb unblock
UNCHOSEN adj not chosen
UNCHURCH vb excommunicate
UNCI ▸ **uncus**
UNCIA, -E n twelfth part
UNCIAL, -S adj of a writing style used in manuscripts of the third to ninth centuries ▸ n uncial letter or manuscript
UNCIALLY ▸ **uncial**
UNCIALS ▸ **uncial**
UNCIFORM adj having the shape of a hook ▸ n any hook-shaped structure or part, esp a small bone of the wrist
UNCINAL same as ▸ **uncinate**
UNCINATE adj shaped like a hook
UNCINUS, UNCINI n small hooked structure
UNCIPHER vb decode
UNCITED adj not quoted
UNCIVIL adj impolite, rude or bad-mannered
UNCLAD adj having no clothes on
UNCLAMP, -S vb remove clamp from
UNCLASP, -S vb unfasten the clasp of (something)
UNCLASSY adj not classy
UNCLAWED adj not clawed
UNCLE, -S, UNCLING n brother of one's father or mother ▸ vb refer to as uncle
UNCLEAN adj lacking moral, spiritual, or physical cleanliness
UNCLEAR adj confusing or hard to understand

UNCLED ▸ **uncle**
UNCLEFT adj not cleft
UNCLENCH vb relax from a clenched position
UNCLES ▸ **uncle**
UNCLEW, -ED, -S vb undo
UNCLINCH same as ▸ **unclench**
UNCLING ▸ **uncle**
UNCLIP, -S vb remove clip from
UNCLIPT archaic past form of ▸ **unclip**
UNCLOAK, -S vb remove cloak from
UNCLOG, -S vb remove an obstruction from (a drain, etc)
UNCLONED adj not cloned
UNCLOSE, -D, -S vb open or cause to open
UNCLOTHE vb take off garments from
UNCLOUD, -S vb clear clouds from
UNCLOUDY adj not cloudy
UNCLOVEN adj not cleaved
UNCLOYED adj not cloyed
UNCLUTCH vb open from tight grip
UNCO, -ER, -ES, -EST, -S adj Scots word meaning unfamiliar or strange ▸ n remarkable person or thing
UNCOATED adj not covered with a layer
UNCOCK, -ED, -S vb remove from a cocked position
UNCODED adj not coded
UNCOER ▸ **unco**
UNCOES ▸ **unco**
UNCOEST ▸ **unco**
UNCOFFIN vb take out of a coffin
UNCOIL, -ED, -S vb unwind or untwist
UNCOINED adj (of a metal) not made into coin
UNCOLT, -ED, -S vb divest of a horse
UNCOMBED adj not combed
UNCOMELY adj not attractive
UNCOMFY adj not comfortable
UNCOMIC adj not comical
UNCOMMON adj not happening or encountered often
UNCOOKED adj raw
UNCOOL adj unsophisticated
UNCOOLED adj not cooled
UNCOPE, -D, -S, UNCOPING vb unmuzzle

UNCORD, -ED, -S vb release from cords
UNCORK, -ED, -S vb remove the cork from (a bottle)
UNCOS ▸ **unco**
UNCOSTLY adj inexpensive
UNCOUPLE vb disconnect or become disconnected
UNCOUTH adj lacking in good manners, refinement, or grace
UNCOVER, -S vb reveal or disclose
UNCOWL, -ED, -S vb remove hood from
UNCOY adj not modest
UNCOYNED same as ▸ **uncoined**
UNCRATE, -D, -S vb remove from a crate
UNCRAZY adj not crazy
UNCREATE vb unmake
UNCREWED adj not crewed
UNCROSS vb cease to cross
UNCROWN, -S vb take the crown from
UNCTION, -S n act of anointing with oil in a sacramental ceremony
UNCTUOUS adj pretending to be kind and concerned
UNCUFF, -ED, -S vb remove handcuffs from
UNCULLED adj not culled
UNCURB, -ED, -S vb remove curbs from (a horse)
UNCURED adj not cured
UNCURL, -ED, -S vb move or cause to move out of a curled or rolled up position
UNCURSE, -D, -S vb remove curse from
UNCURVED adj not curved
UNCUS, UNCI n hooked part or process, as in the human cerebrum
UNCUT adj not shortened or censored
UNCUTE adj not cute
UNDAM, -MED, -S vb free from a dam
UNDAMNED adj not damned
UNDAMPED adj (of an oscillating system) having unrestricted motion
UNDAMS ▸ **undam**
UNDARING adj not daring
UNDASHED adj not dashed
UNDATE, -S, UNDATING vb remove date from
UNDATED adj (of a manuscript, letter, etc) not having an identifying date
UNDATES ▸ **undate**
UNDATING ▸ **undate**

UNDAZZLE vb recover from a daze

UNDE same as ▶ **undee**

UNDEAD adj alive

UNDEAF, -ED, -S vb restore hearing to

UNDEALT adj not dealt (with)

UNDEAR adj not dear

UNDECENT same as ▶ **indecent**

UNDECK, -ED, -S vb remove decorations from

UNDEE adj wavy

UNDEEDED adj not transferred by deed

UNDEFIDE same as ▶ **undefied**

UNDEFIED adj not challenged

UNDEIFY vb strip of the status of a deity

UNDELETE vb restore (a deleted computer file or text)

UNDENIED adj not denied

UNDENTED adj not dented

UNDER adv indicating movement to or position beneath the underside or base ▷ prep less than

UNDERACT vb play (a role) without adequate emphasis

UNDERAGE adj below the required or standard age ▷ n shortfall

UNDERARM adj denoting a style of throwing in which the hand is swung below shoulder level ▷ adv in an underarm style ▷ n armpit

UNDERATE ▶ **undereat**

UNDERBID vb submit a bid lower than that of (others)

UNDERBIT > **underbite**

UNDERBUD vb produce fewer buds than expected

UNDERBUY vb buy (stock in trade) in amounts lower than required

UNDERCUT vb charge less than (a competitor) to obtain trade ▷ n act or an instance of cutting underneath

UNDERDO, UNDERDID vb do (something) inadequately

UNDERDOG n person or team in a weak or underprivileged position

UNDEREAT, UNDERATE vb not eat enough

UNDERFED > **underfeed**

UNDERFUR n layer of dense soft fur occurring beneath

the outer coarser fur in certain mammals

UNDERGO vb experience, endure, or sustain

UNDERGOD n subordinate god

UNDERJAW n lower jaw

UNDERLAP vb project under the edge of

UNDERLAY n felt or rubber laid beneath a carpet to increase insulation and resilience ▷ vb place (something) under or beneath

UNDERLET vb let for a price lower than expected or justified

UNDERLIE vb lie or be placed under

UNDERLIP n lower lip

UNDERLIT adj lit from beneath

UNDERMAN, UNDERMEN vb supply with insufficient staff ▷ n subordinate man

UNDERN, -S n time between sunrise and noon

UNDERPAD n layer of soft foam laid under carpeting

UNDERPAY vb pay someone insufficiently

UNDERPIN vb give strength or support to

UNDERRUN, UNDERRAN vb run beneath

UNDERSAY vb say by way of response

UNDERSEA adv below the surface of the sea

UNDERSET n ocean undercurrent ▷ vb support from underneath

UNDERSKY n lower sky

UNDERSOW vb sow a later-growing crop on already-seeded land

UNDERTAX vb tax insufficiently

UNDERTOW n strong undercurrent flowing in a different direction from the surface current

UNDERUSE vb use less than normal

UNDERWAY adj in progress ▷ adv in progress

UNDERWIT n halfwit

UNDESERT n lack of worth

UNDEVOUT adj not devout

UNDID ▶ **undo**

UNDIES pl n underwear, esp women's

UNDIGHT, -S vb remove

UNDIMMED adj (of eyes, light, etc) still bright or shining

UNDINE, -S n female water spirit

UNDINISM n obsession with water

UNDINTED adj not dinted

UNDIPPED adj not dipped

UNDIVINE adj not divine

UNDO, UNDID, -ES, -S vb open, unwrap ▷ n instance of undoing something

UNDOABLE adj impossible

UNDOCILE adj not docile

UNDOCK, -ED, -S vb take out of a dock

UNDOER, -S ▶ **undo**

UNDOES ▶ **undo**

UNDOING, -S n cause of someone's downfall

UNDONE adj not done or completed

UNDOOMED adj not doomed

UNDOS ▶ **undo**

UNDOTTED adj not dotted

UNDOUBLE vb stretch out

UNDRAPE, -D, -S vb remove drapery from

UNDRAW, -N, -S, UNDREW vb open (curtains)

UNDREAMT same as > **undreamed**

UNDRESS vb take off clothes from (oneself or another) ▷ n partial or complete nakedness ▷ adj characterized by or requiring informal or normal working dress or uniform

UNDREST same as > **undressed**

UNDREW ▶ **undraw**

UNDRIED adj not dried

UNDRIVEN adj not driven

UNDROSSY adj pure

UNDRUNK adj not drunk

UNDUBBED adj (of a film, etc) not dubbed

UNDUE adj greater than is reasonable; excessive

UNDUG adj not having been dug

UNDULANT adj resembling waves

UNDULAR ▶ **undulate**

UNDULATE vb move in waves ▷ adj having a wavy or rippled appearance, margin, or form

UNDULLED adj not dulled

UNDULOSE same as ▶ **undulous**

UNDULOUS adj undulate

UNDULY adv excessively

UNDY same as ▶ **undee**

UNDYED adj not dyed

UNDYING adj never ending, eternal

U

UNEAGER *adj* nonchalant

UNEARED *adj* not ploughed

UNEARNED *adj* not deserved

UNEARTH, -S *vb* reveal or discover by searching

UNEASE, -S ▸ **uneasy**

UNEASIER ▸ **uneasy**

UNEASILY ▸ **uneasy**

UNEASY, UNEASIER *adj* (of a person) anxious or apprehensive

UNEATEN *adj* (of food) not having been consumed

UNEATH, -ES *adv* not easily

UNEDGE, -D, -S, UNEDGING *vb* take the edge off

UNEDIBLE *variant of* ▸ **inedible**

UNEDITED *adj* not edited

UNELATED *adj* not elated

UNENDED *adj* without end

UNENDING *adj* not showing any signs of ever stopping

UNENVIED *adj* not envied

UNEQUAL, -S *adj* not equal in quantity, size, rank, value, etc ▹ *n* person who is not equal

UNERASED *adj* not rubbed out

UNERRING *adj* never mistaken, consistently accurate

UNESPIED *adj* unnoticed

UNETH *same as* ▸ **uneath**

UNEVADED *adj* not evaded

UNEVEN, -ER *adj* not level or flat

UNEVENLY ▸ **uneven**

UNEXOTIC *adj* not exotic

UNEXPERT *same as* ▸ **inexpert**

UNEYED *adj* unseen

UNFABLED *adj* not fictitious

UNFACT, -S *n* event or thing not provable

UNFADED *adj* not faded

UNFADING *adj* not fading

UNFAIR, -ED, -ER, -S *adj* not right, fair, or just ▹ *vb* disfigure

UNFAIRLY ▸ **unfair**

UNFAIRS ▸ **unfair**

UNFAITH, -S *n* lack of faith

UNFAKED *adj* not faked

UNFALLEN *adj* not fallen

UNFAMED *adj* not famous

UNFAMOUS *adj* not famous

UNFANCY *vb* consider (a sportsperson or team) unlikely to win or succeed ▹ *adj* not fancy

UNFANNED *adj* not fanned

UNFASTEN *vb* undo, untie, or open or become undone, untied, or opened

UNFAULTY *adj* not faulty

UNFAZED *adj* not disconcerted

UNFEARED *adj* unafraid

UNFED *adj* not fed

UNFEED *adj* unpaid

UNFELLED *adj* not cut down

UNFELT *adj* not felt

UNFELTED *adj* not felted

UNFENCE, -S *vb* remove a fence from

UNFENCED *adj* not enclosed by a fence

UNFENCES ▸ **unfence**

UNFETTER *vb* release from fetters, bonds, etc

UNFEUDAL *adj* not feudal

UNFEUED *adj* not feued

UNFILDE *archaic form of* ▸ **unfiled**

UNFILED *adj* not filed

UNFILIAL *adj* not filial

UNFILLED *adj* (of a container, receptacle, etc) not having become or been made full

UNFILMED *adj* not filmed

UNFINE *adj* not fine

UNFIRED *adj* not fired

UNFIRM *adj* soft or unsteady

UNFISHED *adj* not used for fishing

UNFIT, -S, -TER *adj* unqualified or unsuitable ▹ *vb* make unfit

UNFITLY *adv* in an unfit way

UNFITS ▸ **unfit**

UNFITTED *adj* unsuitable

UNFITTER ▸ **unfit**

UNFIX, -ES, -ING *vb* unfasten, detach, or loosen

UNFIXED *adj* not fixed

UNFIXES ▸ **unfix**

UNFIXING ▸ **unfix**

UNFIXITY *n* instability

UNFIXT *variant of* ▸ **unfixed**

UNFLASHY *adj* not flashy

UNFLAWED *adj* perfect

UNFLESH *vb* remove flesh from

UNFLEXED *adj* unbent

UNFLUSH *vb* lose the colour caused by flushing

UNFLUTED *adj* not fluted

UNFOILED *adj* not thwarted

UNFOLD, -ED, -S *vb* open or spread out from a folded state

UNFOLDER ▸ **unfold**

UNFOLDS ▸ **unfold**

UNFOLLOW *vb* stop following a person on a social networking site

UNFOND *adj* not fond

UNFONDLY *adv* in an unfond manner

UNFOOL, -ED, -S *vb* undeceive

UNFOOTED *adj* untrodden

UNFORBID *adj* archaic word meaning unforbidden

UNFORCED *adj* not forced or having been forced

UNFORGED *adj* genuine

UNFORGOT *adj* archaic word meaning unforgotten

UNFORKED *adj* not forked

UNFORM, -S *vb* make formless

UNFORMAL *same as* ▸ **informal**

UNFORMED *adj* in an early stage of development

UNFORMS ▸ **unform**

UNFOUGHT *adj* not fought

UNFOUND *adj* not found

UNFRAMED *adj* not framed

UNFREE, -D, -S *vb* remove freedom from

UNFREEZE, UNFROZE, UNFROZEN *vb* thaw or cause to thaw

UNFRIEND *vb* remove someone from one's list of friends on a social networking site

UNFROCK, -S *vb* deprive (a priest in holy orders) of his or her priesthood

UNFROZE ▸ **unfreeze**

UNFROZEN ▸ **unfreeze**

UNFUMED *adj* not fumigated

UNFUNDED *adj* not funded

UNFUNNY *adj* not funny

UNFURL, -ED, -S *vb* unroll or unfold

UNFURRED *adj* not adorned with fur

UNFUSED *adj* not fused

UNFUSSED *adj* not fussed

UNFUSSY *adj* not characterized by overelaborate detail

UNGAG, -GED, -S *vb* restore freedom of speech to

UNGAIN *adj* inconvenient

UNGAINLY *adj* lacking grace when moving ▹ *adv* clumsily

UNGALLED *adj* not annoyed

UNGARBED *adj* undressed

UNGATED *adj* without a gate

UNGAUGED *adj* not measured

UNGAZED *adj* as in **ungazed at/ungazed upon** not gazed (at or upon)

UNGAZING *adj* not gazing

UNGEAR, -ED, -S *vb* disengage

UNGELDED *adj* not gelded

UNGENIAL adj unfriendly

UNGENTLE adj not gentle

UNGENTLY ▶ ungentle

UNGET, -S vb get rid of

UNGIFTED adj not talented

UNGILD, -ED, -S, UNGILT vb remove gilding from

UNGIRD, -ED, -S vb remove belt from

UNGIRT adj not belted

UNGIRTH, -S vb release from a girth

UNGIVING adj inflexible

UNGLAD adj not glad

UNGLAZED adj not glazed

UNGLITZY adj not glitzy

UNGLOVE, -D, -S vb remove a glove or gloves

UNGLUE, -D, -S, UNGLUING vb remove adhesive from

UNGOD, -DED, -S vb remove status of being a god from

UNGODLY adj unreasonable or outrageous

UNGODS ▶ ungod

UNGORD same as ▶ ungored

UNGORED adj not gored

UNGORGED same as ▶ ungored

UNGOT same as ▶ ungotten

UNGOTTEN adj not obtained or won

UNGOWN, -ED, -S vb remove a gown from

UNGRACED adj not graced

UNGRADED adj not graded

UNGRAZED adj not grazed

UNGREEDY adj not greedy

UNGREEN adj not environmentally friendly

UNGROUND adj not crushed

UNGROUP, -S vb separate from a group

UNGROWN adj not fully developed

UNGUAL adj of, relating to, or affecting the fingernails or toenails

UNGUARD, -S vb expose (to attack)

UNGUENT, -S n ointment

UNGUENTA > unguentum

UNGUENTS ▶ unguent

UNGUES ▶ unguis

UNGUIDED adj not having a flight path controlled internally or externally

UNGUILTY adj innocent

UNGUIS, UNGUES n nail, claw, or hoof, or the part of the digit giving rise to it

UNGULA, -E n truncated cone, cylinder, etc

UNGULAR ▶ ungula

UNGULATE n hoofed mammal

UNGULED adj hoofed

UNGUM, -MED, -S vb remove adhesive from

UNGYVE, -D, -S, UNGYVING vb release from shackles

UNHABLE same as ▶ unable

UNHACKED adj not hacked

UNHAILED adj not hailed

UNHAIR, -ED, -S vb remove the hair from (a hide)

UNHAIRER ▶ unhair

UNHAIRS ▶ unhair

UNHALLOW vb desecrate

UNHALSED adj not hailed

UNHALVED adj not divided in half

UNHAND, -ED, -S vb release from one's grasp

UNHANDY adj not skilful with one's hands

UNHANG, -S, UNHUNG vb take down from hanging position

UNHANGED adj not executed by hanging

UNHANGS ▶ unhang

UNHAPPEN vb become as though never having happened

UNHAPPY adj sad, miserable ▷ vb make unhappy

UNHARDY adj fragile

UNHARMED adj not hurt or damaged in any way

UNHASP, -ED, -S vb unfasten

UNHASTY adj not speedy

UNHAT, -S, -TED vb doff one's hat

UNHEAD, -S vb remove the head from

UNHEADED adj not having a heading

UNHEADS ▶ unhead

UNHEAL, -S vb expose

UNHEALED adj not having healed physically, mentally, or emotionally

UNHEALS ▶ unheal

UNHEALTH n illness

UNHEARD adj not listened to

UNHEARSE vb remove from a hearse

UNHEART, -S vb discourage

UNHEATED adj not having been warmed up

UNHEDGED adj unprotected

UNHEEDED adj noticed but ignored

UNHEEDY adj not heedful

UNHELE, -D, -S, UNHELING same as ▶ unheal

UNHELM, -ED, -S vb remove the helmet of (oneself or another)

UNHELPED adj without help

UNHEMMED adj not hemmed

UNHEPPEN adj awkward

UNHEROIC adj not heroic

UNHERST archaic past form of ▶ unhearse

UNHEWN adj not hewn

UNHIDDEN adj not hidden

UNHINGE, -D, -S vb derange or unbalance (a person or his or her mind)

UNHIP, -PER adj not at all fashionable or up to date

UNHIRED adj not hired

UNHITCH vb unfasten or detach

UNHIVE, -D, -S, UNHIVING vb remove from a hive

UNHOARD, -S vb remove from a hoard

UNHOLIER ▶ unholy

UNHOLILY ▶ unholy

UNHOLPEN same as ▶ unhelped

UNHOLY, UNHOLIER adj immoral or wicked

UNHOMELY adj not homely

UNHONEST same as > dishonest

UNHOOD, -ED, -S vb remove a hood from

UNHOOK, -ED, -S vb unfasten the hooks of (a garment)

UNHOOP, -ED, -S vb remove a hoop from

UNHOPED adj not anticipated

UNHORSE, -D, -S vb knock or throw from a horse

UNHOUSE, -D, -S vb remove from a house

UNHUMAN adj inhuman or not human

UNHUNG ▶ unhang

UNHUNTED adj not hunted

UNHURT adj not injured in an accident, attack, etc

UNHUSK, -ED, -S vb remove the husk from

UNI, -S n (in informal English) university

UNIALGAL adj containing only one species of alga

UNIAXIAL adj (esp of plants) having an unbranched main axis

UNIBODY adj of a vehicle in which the frame and body are one unit ▷ n vehicle in which the frame and body are one unit

UNIBROW, -S n informal word for eyebrows that meet above the nose

U

UNICA ▶ **unicum**
UNICED adj noticed
UNICITY n oneness
UNICOLOR same as > **unicolour**
UNICOM, -S n designated radio frequency at some airports
UNICORN, -S n imaginary horselike creature with one horn growing from its forehead
UNICUM, UNICA n unique example or specimen
UNICYCLE n one-wheeled vehicle driven by pedals, used in a circus ▷ vb ride a unicycle
UNIDEAED adj not having ideas
UNIDEAL adj not ideal
UNIFACE, -S n type of tool
UNIFIC adj unifying
UNIFIED ▶ **unify**
UNIFIER, -S ▶ **unify**
UNIFIES ▶ **unify**
UNIFILAR adj composed of, having, or using only one wire, thread, filament, etc
UNIFORM, -S n special set of clothes for the members of an organization ▷ adj regular and even throughout, unvarying ▷ vb fit out (a body of soldiers, etc) with uniforms
UNIFY, UNIFIED, UNIFIES, -ING vb make or become one
UNILOBAR adj having one lobe
UNILOBED same as ▶ **unilobar**
UNIMBUED adj not imbued
UNIMODAL adj having or involving one mode
UNINSTAL same as > **uninstall**
UNINURED adj unaccustomed
UNION, -S n act of uniting or being united ▷ adj of a trade union
UNIONISE same as ▶ **unionize**
UNIONISM n principles of trade unions
UNIONIST n member or supporter of a union ▷ adj of or relating to a union or unionism
UNIONIZE vb organize (workers) into a trade union
UNIONS ▶ **union**
UNIPED, -S n person or thing with one foot

UNIPOD, -S n one-legged support, as for a camera
UNIPOLAR adj of, concerned with, or having a single magnetic or electric pole
UNIQUE, -R, -S, -ST adj being the only one of a particular type ▷ n person or thing that is unique
UNIQUELY ▶ **unique**
UNIQUER ▶ **unique**
UNIQUES ▶ **unique**
UNIQUEST ▶ **unique**
UNIRONED adj not ironed
UNIRONIC adj not ironic
UNIS ▶ **uni**
UNISEX, -ES adj not associated with a specific gender ▷ n style not associated with a specific gender
UNISIZE adj in one size only
UNISON, -S n complete agreement
UNISONAL ▶ **unison**
UNISONS ▶ **unison**
UNISSUED adj not issued
UNIT, -S n single undivided entity or whole
UNITAGE, -S ▶ **unit**
UNITAL ▶ **unit**
UNITARD, -S n all-in-one skintight suit
UNITARY adj consisting of a single undivided whole
UNITE, -S vb make or become an integrated whole ▷ n English gold coin minted in the Stuart period
UNITED adj produced by two or more people or things in combination
UNITEDLY ▶ **united**
UNITER, -S ▶ **unite**
UNITES ▶ **unite**
UNITIES ▶ **unity**
UNITING, -S ▶ **unite**
UNITION, -S n joining
UNITISE, -D, -S same as ▶ **unitize**
UNITISER same as ▶ **unitizer**
UNITISES ▶ **unitise**
UNITIVE adj tending to unite or capable of uniting
UNITIZE, -D, -S vb convert (an investment trust) into a unit trust
UNITIZER n person or thing that arranges units into batches
UNITIZES ▶ **unitize**
UNITRUST n type of income-producing trust fund
UNITS ▶ **unit**
UNITY, UNITIES n state of being one

UNIVALVE adj relating to a mollusc shell that consists of a single piece (valve) ▷ n gastropod mollusc or its shell
UNIVERSE n whole of all existing matter, energy, and space
UNIVOCAL adj unambiguous or unmistakable ▷ n word or term that has only one meaning
UNJADED adj not jaded
UNJAM, -MED, -S vb remove blockage from
UNJOINED adj not joined
UNJOINT, -S vb disjoint
UNJOYFUL adj not joyful
UNJOYOUS adj not joyous
UNJUDGED adj not judged
UNJUST, -ER adj not fair or just
UNJUSTLY ▶ **unjust**
UNKED adj alien
UNKEELED adj without a keel
UNKEMPT adj (of the hair) not combed
UNKEND same as ▶ **unkenned**
UNKENNED adj unknown
UNKENNEL vb release from a kennel
UNKENT same as ▶ **unkenned**
UNKEPT adj not kept
UNKET same as ▶ **unked**
UNKID same as ▶ **unked**
UNKIND, -ER adj unsympathetic or cruel
UNKINDLY ▶ **unkind**
UNKING, -ED, -S vb strip of sovereignty
UNKINGLY adj not kingly
UNKINGS ▶ **unking**
UNKINK, -ED, -S vb straighten out
UNKISS, -ES vb cancel (a previous action) with a kiss
UNKISSED adj not kissed
UNKISSES ▶ **unkiss**
UNKNIGHT vb strip of knighthood
UNKNIT, -S vb make or become undone, untied, or unravelled
UNKNOT, -S vb disentangle or undo a knot or knots in
UNKNOWN, -S adj not known ▷ n unknown person, quantity, or thing
UNKOSHER adj not conforming to Jewish religious law

UNLACE, -S, UNLACING vb loosen or undo the lacing of (shoes, garments, etc)
UNLACED adj not laced
UNLACES ▸ unlace
UNLACING ▸ unlace
UNLADE, -D, -S, UNLADING less common word for ▸ **unload**
UNLADEN adj not laden
UNLADES ▸ unlade
UNLADING ▸ unlade
UNLAID ▸ unlay
UNLASH, -ED, -ES vb untie or unfasten
UNLAST archaic variant of ▸ **unlaced**
UNLASTE archaic variant of ▸ **unlaced**
UNLATCH vb open or unfasten by the lifting or release of a latch
UNLAW, -ED, -ING, -S vb penalize
UNLAWFUL adj not permitted by law
UNLAWING ▸ unlaw
UNLAWS ▸ unlaw
UNLAY, UNLAID, -ING, -S vb untwist (a rope or cable) to separate its strands
UNLEAD, -S vb strip off lead
UNLEADED adj (of petrol) containing less tetraethyl lead ▸ n petrol containing a reduced amount of tetraethyl lead
UNLEADS ▸ unlead
UNLEAL adj treacherous
UNLEARN, -S vb try to forget something learnt or to discard accumulated knowledge
UNLEARNT adj denoting knowledge or skills innately present rather than learnt
UNLEASED adj not leased
UNLEASH vb set loose or cause (something bad)
UNLED adj not led
UNLESS conj except under the circumstances that ▸ prep except
UNLET adj not rented
UNLETHAL adj not deadly
UNLETTED adj unimpeded
UNLEVEL, -S adj not level ▸ vb make unbalanced
UNLEVIED adj not levied
UNLICH Spenserian form of ▸ **unlike**
UNLICKED adj not licked
UNLID, -DED, -S vb remove lid from
UNLIKE, -S adj dissimilar or different ▸ prep not like or

typical of ▸ n person or thing that is unlike another
UNLIKED adj not liked
UNLIKELY adj improbable
UNLIKES ▸ unlike
UNLIMBER vb disengage (a gun) from its limber
UNLIME, -D, -S, UNLIMING vb detach
UNLINE, -S, UNLINING vb remove the lining from
UNLINEAL adj not lineal
UNLINED adj not having any lining
UNLINES ▸ unline
UNLINING ▸ unline
UNLINK, -ED, -S vb undo the link or links between
UNLISTED adj not entered on a list
UNLIT adj (of a fire, cigarette, etc) not lit and therefore not burning
UNLIVE, -D, -S, UNLIVING vb live so as to nullify, undo, or live down (past events or times)
UNLIVELY adj lifeless
UNLIVES ▸ unlive
UNLIVING ▸ unlive
UNLOAD, -ED, -S vb remove (cargo) from (a ship, truck, or plane)
UNLOADER ▸ unload
UNLOADS ▸ unload
UNLOBED adj without lobes
UNLOCK, -S vb unfasten (a lock or door)
UNLOCKED adj not locked
UNLOCKS ▸ unlock
UNLOOKED adj not looked (at)
UNLOOSE, -D, -S vb set free or release
UNLOOSEN same as ▸ **unloose**
UNLOOSES ▸ unloose
UNLOPPED adj not chopped off
UNLORD, -ED, -S vb remove from position of being lord
UNLORDLY adv not in a lordlike manner
UNLORDS ▸ unlord
UNLOST adj not lost
UNLOVE, -S vb stop loving
UNLOVED adj not loved by anyone
UNLOVELY adj unpleasant in appearance or character
UNLOVES ▸ unlove
UNLOVING adj not feeling or showing love and affection
UNLUCKY adj having bad luck, unfortunate
UNMACHO adj not macho

UNMADE adj (of a bed) with the bedclothes not smoothed and tidied
UNMAILED adj not sent by post
UNMAIMED adj not injured
UNMAKE, -S, UNMAKING vb undo or destroy
UNMAKER, -S ▸ unmake
UNMAKES ▸ unmake
UNMAKING ▸ unmake
UNMAN, -S vb cause to lose courage or nerve
UNMANFUL adj unmanly
UNMANLY adj not masculine
UNMANNED adj having no personnel or crew
UNMANS ▸ unman
UNMANTLE vb remove mantle from
UNMAPPED adj not charted
UNMARD same as ▸ **unmarred**
UNMARKED adj having no signs of damage or injury
UNMARRED adj not marred
UNMARRY vb divorce
UNMASK, -ED, -S vb remove the mask or disguise from
UNMASKER ▸ unmask
UNMASKS ▸ unmask
UNMATED adj not mated
UNMATTED adj not matted
UNMEANT adj unintentional
UNMEEK adj not submissive
UNMEET adj not meet
UNMEETLY ▸ unmeet
UNMELLOW adj not mellow
UNMELTED adj not melted
UNMENDED adj not mended
UNMERRY adj not merry
UNMESH, -ED, -ES vb release from mesh
UNMET adj unfulfilled
UNMETED adj unmeasured
UNMEW, -ED, -ING, -S vb release from confinement
UNMILKED adj not milked
UNMILLED adj not milled
UNMINDED adj disregarded
UNMINED adj not mined
UNMINGLE vb separate
UNMIRY, UNMIRIER adj not swampy
UNMISSED adj unnoticed
UNMITER, -S same as ▸ **unmitre**
UNMITRE, -D, -S vb divest of a mitre
UNMIX, -ED, -ES, -ING vb separate
UNMIXT same as ▸ **unmix**
UNMOANED adj unmourned

U

UNMODISH adj passé

UNMOLD, -ED, -S same as
▸ **unmould**

UNMOLTEN adj not molten

UNMONIED same as
> **unmoneyed**

UNMOOR, -ED, -S vb weigh
the anchor or drop the
mooring of (a vessel)

UNMORAL adj outside
morality

UNMOULD, -S vb change
the shape of

UNMOUNT, -S vb dismount

UNMOVED adj not affected
by emotion, indifferent

UNMOVING adj still and
motionless

UNMOWN adj not mown

UNMUFFLE vb remove a
muffle or muffles from

UNMUZZLE vb take the
muzzle off (a dog, etc)

UNNAIL, -ED, -S vb unfasten
by removing nails

UNNAMED adj not
mentioned by name

UNNANELD same as
▸ **unaneled**

UNNATIVE adj not native
▷ vb no longer be a native of
a place

UNNEATH adj archaic word
for underneath

UNNEEDED adj not needed

UNNERVE, -D, -S vb cause
to lose courage, confidence,
or self-control

UNNEST, -ED, -S vb remove
from a nest

UNNETHES same as
▸ **unneath**

UNNETTED adj not having or
not enclosed in a net

UNNOBLE, -D, -S vb strip of
nobility

UNNOISY adj quiet

UNNOTED adj not noted

UNOAKED adj (of wine) not
matured in an oak barrel

UNOBEYED adj not obeyed

UNOFTEN adv infrequently

UNOILED adj not lubricated
with oil

UNOPEN adj not open

UNOPENED adj closed,
barred, or sealed

UNORDER, -S vb cancel an
order

UNORNATE same as
▸ **inornate**

UNOWED same as
▸ **unowned**

UNOWNED adj not owned

UNPACED adj without the
aid of a pacemaker

UNPACK, -ED, -S vb remove
the contents of (a suitcase,
trunk, etc)

UNPACKER ▸ **unpack**

UNPACKS ▸ **unpack**

UNPADDED adj not padded

UNPAGED adj (of a book)
having no page numbers

UNPAID adj without a salary
or wage

UNPAINED adj not suffering
pain

UNPAINT, -S vb remove
paint from

UNPAIRED adj not paired up

UNPANEL, -S vb unsaddle

UNPANGED adj without
pain or sadness

UNPANNEL same as
▸ **unpanel**

UNPAPER, -S vb remove
paper from

UNPARED adj not pared

UNPARTED adj not parted

UNPATHED adj not having a
path

UNPAVED adj not covered in
paving

UNPAY, -ING, -S vb undo

UNPEELED adj not peeled

UNPEERED adj unparalleled

UNPEG, -GED, -S vb remove
a peg or pegs from, esp to
unfasten

UNPEN, -NED, -S vb release
from a pen

UNPENT archaic past form of
▸ **unpen**

UNPEOPLE vb empty of
people

UNPERCH vb remove from a
perch

UNPERSON n person whose
existence is officially denied
or ignored

UNPICK, -S vb undo (the
stitches) of (a piece of
sewing)

UNPICKED adj (of knitting,
sewing, etc) having been
unravelled or picked out

UNPICKS ▸ **unpick**

UNPILE, -D, -S, UNPILING vb
remove from a pile

UNPIN, -NED, -S vb remove
a pin or pins from

UNPINKED adj not
decorated with a perforated
pattern

UNPINKT same as
▸ **unpinked**

UNPINNED ▸ **unpin**

UNPINS ▸ **unpin**

UNPITIED adj not pitied

UNPITTED adj not having
had pits removed

UNPLACE, -S same as
▸ **displace**

UNPLACED adj not given
or put in a particular
place

UNPLACES ▸ **unplace**

UNPLAIT, -S vb remove
plaits from

UNPLAYED adj not played

UNPLIANT adj not pliant

UNPLOWED adj not
ploughed

UNPLUG, -S vb disconnect
(a piece of electrical
equipment)

UNPLUMB, -S vb remove
lead from

UNPLUME, -D, -S vb remove
feathers from

UNPOETIC adj not poetic

UNPOISED adj not poised

UNPOISON vb extract
poison from

UNPOLISH vb remove polish
from

UNPOLITE same as
▸ **impolite**

UNPOLLED adj not included
in an opinion poll

UNPOPE, -D, -S, UNPOPING
vb strip of popedom

UNPOSED adj not posed

UNPOSTED adj not sent by
post

UNPOTTED adj not planted
in a pot

UNPOURED adj not poured

UNPRAISE vb withhold
praise from

UNPRAY, -ED, -S vb
withdraw (a prayer)

UNPREACH vb retract (a
sermon)

UNPRETTY adj unattractive

UNPRICED adj having no
fixed or marked price

UNPRIEST vb strip of
priesthood

UNPRIMED adj not primed

UNPRISON vb release from
prison

UNPRIZED adj not treasured

UNPROBED adj not
examined

UNPROP, -S vb remove
support from

UNPROPER same as
▸ **improper**

UNPROPS ▸ **unprop**

UNPROVED adj not having
been established as true,
valid, or possible

UNPROVEN adj not
established as true by
evidence or demonstration

UNPRUNED adj not pruned

UNPUCKER vb remove wrinkles from

UNPULLED adj not pulled

UNPURE same as ▶ impure

UNPURELY ▶ unpure

UNPURGED adj not purged

UNPURSE, -D, -S vb relax (lips) from pursed position

UNPUZZLE vb figure out

UNQUEEN, -S vb depose from the position of queen

UNQUIET, -S adj anxious or uneasy ▷ n state of unrest ▷ vb disquiet

UNQUOTE, -D, -S interj expression used to indicate the end of a quotation ▷ vb close (a quotation), esp in printing

UNRACED adj not raced

UNRACKED adj not stretched

UNRAISED adj not raised

UNRAKE, -S, UNRAKING vb unearth through raking

UNRAKED adj not raked

UNRAKES ▶ unrake

UNRAKING ▶ unrake

UNRANKED adj not ranked

UNRATED adj not rated

UNRAVEL, -S vb reduce (something knitted or woven) to separate strands

UNRAZED adj not razed

UNREAD adj (of a book or article) not yet read

UNREADY adj not ready or prepared

UNREAL adj (as if) existing only in the imagination

UNREALLY ▶ unreal

UNREAPED adj not reaped

UNREASON n irrationality or madness ▷ vb deprive of reason

UNREAVE, -D, -S vb unwind

UNRECKED adj disregarded

UNRED same as ▶ unread

UNREDY same as ▶ unready

UNREEL, -ED, -S vb unwind from a reel

UNREELER n machine that unwinds something from a reel

UNREELS ▶ unreel

UNREEVE, -D, -S, UNROVE, UNROVEN vb withdraw (a rope) from a block, thimble, etc

UNREIN, -ED, -S vb free from reins

UNRENT adj not torn

UNRENTED adj not rented

UNREPAID adj not repaid

UNREPAIR less common word for > disrepair

UNREST, -S n rebellious state of discontent

UNRESTED adj not rested

UNRESTS ▶ unrest

UNRETIRE vb resume work after retiring

UNRHYMED adj not rhymed

UNRIBBED adj not ribbed

UNRID adj unridden

UNRIDDEN adj not or never ridden

UNRIDDLE vb solve or puzzle out

UNRIDGED adj not ridged

UNRIFLED adj (of a firearm or its bore) not rifled

UNRIG, -GED, -S vb strip (a vessel) of standing and running rigging

UNRIGHT, -S n wrong ▷ adj not right or fair ▷ vb make wrong

UNRIGS ▶ unrig

UNRIMED same as ▶ unrhymed

UNRINGED adj not having or wearing a ring

UNRINSED adj not rinsed

UNRIP, -PED, -S vb rip open

UNRIPE, -R, -ST adj not fully matured

UNRIPELY ▶ unripe

UNRIPER ▶ unripe

UNRIPEST ▶ unripe

UNRIPPED ▶ unrip

UNRIPS ▶ unrip

UNRISEN adj not risen

UNRIVEN adj not torn apart

UNRIVET, -S vb remove rivets from

UNROBE, -D, -S, UNROBING same as ▶ disrobe

UNROLL, -ED, -S vb open out or unwind (something rolled or coiled)

UNROOF, -ED, -S vb remove the roof from

UNROOST, -S vb remove from a perch

UNROOT, -ED, -S less common word for ▶ uproot

UNROPE, -D, -S, UNROPING vb release from a rope

UNROTTED adj not rotted

UNROTTEN adj not rotten

UNROUGED adj not coloured with rouge

UNROUGH adj not rough

UNROUND, -S vb release (lips) from a rounded position

UNROUSED adj not roused

UNROVE ▶ unreeve

UNROVEN ▶ unreeve

UNROYAL adj not royal

UNRUBBED adj not rubbed

UNRUDE adj not rude

UNRUFFE same as ▶ unrough

UNRUFFLE vb calm

UNRULE, -S n lack of authority

UNRULED adj not ruled

UNRULES ▶ unrule

UNRULY, UNRULIER adj difficult to control or organize

UNRUSHED adj unhurried

UNRUSTED adj not rusted

UNS ▶ un

UNSADDLE vb remove the saddle from (a horse)

UNSAFE, -R, -ST adj dangerous

UNSAFELY ▶ unsafe

UNSAFER ▶ unsafe

UNSAFEST ▶ unsafe

UNSAFETY n lack of safety

UNSAID adj not said or expressed

UNSAILED adj not sailed

UNSAINED adj not blessed

UNSAINT, -S vb remove status of being a saint from

UNSALTED adj not seasoned, preserved, or treated with salt

UNSAPPED adj not undermined

UNSASHED adj not furnished with a sash

UNSATED adj not sated

UNSATING adj not satisfying

UNSAVED adj not saved

UNSAVORY same as > unsavoury

UNSAW ▶ unsee

UNSAWED same as ▶ unsawn

UNSAWN adj not cut with a saw

UNSAY, -ING, -S vb retract or withdraw (something said or written)

UNSCALE, -D, -S same as ▶ descale

UNSCARY adj not scary

UNSCREW, -S vb loosen (a screw or lid) by turning it

UNSEAL, -ED, -S vb remove or break the seal of

UNSEAM, -ED, -S vb open or undo the seam of

UNSEARED adj not seared

UNSEASON vb affect unfavourably

UNSEAT, -ED, -S vb throw or displace from a seat or saddle

UNSECRET adj not secret ▷ vb inform or make aware

U

UNSEE, UNSAW, -S vb undo the act of seeing something

UNSEEDED adj not given a top player's ranking in a tournament

UNSEEING adj not noticing or looking at anything

UNSEEL, -ED, -S vb undo seeling

UNSEELIE pl n evil malevolent fairies ▷ adj of or belonging to the unseelie

UNSEELS ▶ unseel

UNSEEMLY adj not according to expected standards of behaviour ▷ adv in an unseemly manner

UNSEEN, -S adj hidden or invisible ▷ adv without being seen ▷ n passage given to students for translation without them having seen it in advance

UNSEES ▶ unsee

UNSEIZED adj not seized

UNSELDOM adv frequently

UNSELF, -ED, -S, UNSELVES vb remove self-centredness from ▷ n lack of self

UNSELL, -S vb speak unfavourably and off-puttingly of (something or someone)

UNSELVES ▶ unself

UNSENSE, -D, -S vb remove sense from

UNSENT adj not sent

UNSERVED adj not served

UNSET, -S adj not yet solidified or firm ▷ vb displace

UNSETTLE vb change or become changed from a fixed or settled condition

UNSEW, -ED, -ING, -N, -S vb undo stitching of

UNSEX, -ED, -ES, -ING vb deprive (a person) of the attributes of his or her sex

UNSEXIER ▶ unsexy

UNSEXILY adv in an unsexy manner

UNSEXING ▶ unsex

UNSEXIST adj not sexist

UNSEXUAL adj not sexual

UNSEXY, UNSEXIER adj not exciting or attractive

UNSHADED adj not shaded

UNSHADOW vb remove shadow from

UNSHAKED same as ▶ unshaken

UNSHAKEN adj (of faith or feelings) not having been weakened

UNSHALE, -D, -S vb expose

UNSHAMED same as ▶ unashamed

UNSHAPE, -D, -S vb make shapeless

UNSHAPEN adj having no definite shape

UNSHAPES ▶ unshape

UNSHARED adj not shared

UNSHARP adj not sharp

UNSHAVED adj not shaved

UNSHAVEN adj having a stubbled chin

UNSHED adj not shed

UNSHELL, -S vb remove from a shell

UNSHENT adj undamaged

UNSHEWN adj unshown

UNSHIFT, -S vb release the shift key on a keyboard

UNSHIP, -S vb be or cause to be unloaded, discharged, or disembarked from a ship

UNSHOD adj not wearing shoes

UNSHOE, -S vb remove shoes from

UNSHOED same as ▶ unshod

UNSHOES ▶ unshoe

UNSHOOT, -S Shakespearean variant of ▶ unshout

UNSHORN adj not cut

UNSHOT, -S adj not shot ▷ vb remove shot from

UNSHOUT, -S vb revoke (an earlier statement) by shouting a contrary one

UNSHOWN adj not shown

UNSHOWY adj not showy

UNSHROUD vb uncover

UNSHRUBD adj old word meaning not having shrubs

UNSHRUNK adj not shrunk

UNSHUT, -S vb open

UNSICKER adj old Scottish word meaning unsettled

UNSIFTED adj not strained

UNSIGHT, -S vb obstruct vision of

UNSIGNED adj (of a letter etc) anonymous

UNSILENT adj not silent

UNSINEW, -S vb weaken

UNSINFUL adj without sin

UNSIZED adj not made or sorted according to size

UNSLAIN adj not killed

UNSLAKED adj not slaked

UNSLICED adj not sliced

UNSLICK adj not slick

UNSLING, -S, UNSLUNG vb remove or release from a slung position

UNSLUICE vb let flow

UNSLUNG ▶ unsling

UNSMART adj not smart

UNSMOKED adj not smoked

UNSMOOTH vb roughen

UNSMOTE same as ▶ unsmitten

UNSNAG, -S vb remove snags from

UNSNAP, -S vb unfasten (the snap or catch) of (something)

UNSNARL, -S vb free from a snarl or tangle

UNSNECK, -S vb unlatch

UNSOAKED adj not soaked

UNSOAPED adj not rubbed with soap

UNSOBER, -S adj not sober ▷ vb make unrefined in manners

UNSOCIAL adj avoiding the company of other people

UNSOCKET vb remove from a socket

UNSOD same as ▶ unsodden

UNSODDEN adj not soaked

UNSOFT adj hard

UNSOILED adj not soiled

UNSOLD adj not sold

UNSOLDER vb remove soldering from

UNSOLEMN adj unceremonious

UNSOLID adj not solid

UNSOLVED adj not having been solved or explained

UNSONCY same as ▶ unsonsy

UNSONSIE same as ▶ unsonsy

UNSONSY adj unfortunate

UNSOOTE adj not sweet

UNSORTED adj not sorted

UNSOUGHT adj not sought after

UNSOUL, -ED, -S vb cause to be soulless

UNSOUND adj unhealthy or unstable

UNSOURED adj not soured

UNSOWED same as ▶ unsown

UNSOWN adj not sown

UNSPAR, -S vb open

UNSPARED adj not spared

UNSPARS ▶ unspar

UNSPEAK, -S, UNSPOKE obsolete word for ▶ unsay

UNSPED adj not achieved

UNSPELL, -S vb release from a spell

UNSPENT adj not spent

UNSPHERE vb remove from its, one's, etc sphere or place

UNSPIDE same as ▶ unspied

UNSPIED adj unnoticed

UNSPILT adj not spilt

UNSPLIT adj not split

UNSPOILT *same as*
> **unspoiled**
UNSPOKE ▶ **unspeak**
UNSPOKEN *adj* not openly
expressed
UNSPOOL, -S *vb* unwind
from spool
UNSPRUNG *adj* without
springs
UNSPUN *adj* not spun
UNSTABLE *adj* lacking
stability or firmness
UNSTABLY ▶ **unstable**
UNSTACK, -S *vb* remove
from a stack
UNSTAGED *adj* not staged
UNSTAID *adj* not staid
UNSTARCH *vb* remove
starch from
UNSTARRY *adj* not
resembling or characteristic
of a star from the
entertainment world
UNSTATE, -S *vb* deprive of
state
UNSTATED *adj* not having
been articulated or uttered
UNSTATES ▶ **unstate**
UNSTAYED *adj* unhindered
UNSTEADY *adj* not securely
fixed ▷ *vb* make unsteady
UNSTEEL, -S *vb* make (the
heart, feelings, etc) more
gentle or compassionate
UNSTEP, -S *vb* remove (a
mast) from its step
UNSTICK, -S *vb* free or
loosen (something stuck)
UNSTITCH *vb* remove
stitching from
UNSTOCK, -S *vb* remove
stock from
UNSTONED *adj* not stoned
UNSTOP, -S *vb* remove the
stop or stopper from
UNSTOW, -ED, -S *vb* remove
from storage
UNSTRAP, -S *vb* undo the
straps fastening
(something) in position
UNSTRESS *n* weak syllable
▷ *vb* become less stressed
UNSTRING *vb* remove the
strings of
UNSTRIP, -S *vb* strip
UNSTRUCK *adj* not struck
UNSTRUNG *adj* emotionally
distressed
UNSTUCK *adj* freed from
being stuck, glued, fastened,
etc
UNSTUFFY *adj* well-
ventilated
UNSTUFT *same as*
> **unstuffed**
UNSTUNG *adj* not stung

UNSUBTLE *adj* not subtle
UNSUBTLY ▶ **unsubtle**
UNSUCKED *adj* not sucked
UNSUIT, -S *vb* make
unsuitable
UNSUITED *adj* not
appropriate for a particular
task or situation
UNSUITS ▶ **unsuit**
UNSUMMED *adj* not
calculated
UNSUNG *adj* not acclaimed
or honoured
UNSUNK *adj* not sunken
UNSUNNED *adj* not
subjected to sunlight
UNSUNNY *adj* not sunny
UNSUPPLE *adj* rigid
UNSURE, -R, -ST *adj* lacking
assurance or self-confidence
UNSURED *adj* not assured
UNSURELY ▶ **unsure**
UNSURER ▶ **unsure**
UNSUREST ▶ **unsure**
UNSWATHE *vb* unwrap
UNSWAYED *adj* not swayed
**UNSWEAR, -S, UNSWORE,
UNSWORN** *vb* retract or
revoke (a sworn oath)
UNSWEET *adj* not sweet
UNSWEPT *adj* not swept
UNSWORE ▶ **unswear**
UNSWORN ▶ **unswear**
UNTACK, -ED, -S *vb* remove
saddle and harness, etc
from
UNTACKLE *vb* remove tackle
from
UNTACKS ▶ **untack**
UNTAGGED *adj* without a
label
UNTAILED *adj* tailless
UNTAKEN *adj* not taken
UNTAME, -S, UNTAMING *vb*
undo the taming of
UNTAMED *adj* not brought
under human control
UNTAMES ▶ **untame**
UNTAMING ▶ **untame**
UNTANGLE *vb* free from
tangles or confusion
UNTANNED *adj* not tanned
UNTAPPED *adj* not yet used
UNTARRED *adj* not coated
with tar
UNTASTED *adj* not tasted
UNTAUGHT *adj* without
training or education
UNTAX, -ES, -ING *vb* stop
taxing
UNTAXED *adj* not subject to
taxation
UNTAXES ▶ **untax**
UNTAXING ▶ **untax**
UNTEACH *vb* cause to
disbelieve (teaching)

UNTEAM, -ED, -S *vb* disband
a team
UNTEMPER *vb* soften
UNTENANT *vb* remove (a
tenant)
UNTENDED *adj* not cared for
or attended to
UNTENDER *adj* not tender
UNTENT, -ED, -S *vb* remove
from a tent
UNTENTY *adj* inattentive
UNTESTED *adj* not having
been tested or examined
UNTETHER *vb* untie
UNTHATCH *vb* remove the
thatch from
UNTHAW, -S *same as* ▶ **thaw**
UNTHAWED *adj* not thawed
UNTHAWS ▶ **unthaw**
UNTHINK, -S *vb* reverse
one's opinion about
UNTHREAD *vb* draw out the
thread or threads from (a
needle, etc)
UNTHRIFT *n* unthrifty
person
UNTHRONE *less common
word for* ▶ **dethrone**
UNTIDIED ▶ **untidy**
UNTIDIER ▶ **untidy**
UNTIDIES ▶ **untidy**
UNTIDILY ▶ **untidy**
**UNTIDY, UNTIDIED,
UNTIDIER, UNTIDIES** *adj*
messy and disordered ▷ *vb*
make untidy
UNTIE, -D, -ING, -S *vb* open
or free (something that is
tied)
UNTIL *prep* in or throughout
the period before
UNTILE, -D, -S, UNTILING *vb*
strip tiles from
UNTILLED *adj* not tilled
UNTILTED *adj* not tilted
UNTIMED *adj* not timed
UNTIMELY *adj* occurring
before the expected or
normal time ▷ *adv*
prematurely or
inopportunely
UNTIN, -NED, -S *vb* remove
tin from
UNTINGED *adj* not tinged
UNTINNED ▶ **untin**
UNTINS ▶ **untin**
UNTIPPED *adj* not tipped
UNTIRED *adj* not tired
UNTIRING *adj* continuing
without declining in
strength
UNTITLED *adj* without a title
UNTO *prep* to
UNTOLD *adj* incapable of
description
UNTOMB, -ED, -S *vb* exhume

U

UNTONED adj not toned

UNTOOLED adj not tooled

UNTORN adj not torn

UNTOWARD adj causing misfortune or annoyance

UNTRACE, -S vb remove traces from

UNTRACED adj not traced

UNTRACES ▸ untrace

UNTRACK, -S vb remove from a track

UNTRADED adj not traded

UNTREAD, -S, UNTROD vb retrace (a course, path, etc)

UNTRENDY adj not trendy

UNTRIDE same as ▸ untried

UNTRIED adj not yet used, done, or tested

UNTRIM, -S vb deprive of elegance or adornment

UNTROD ▸ untread

UNTRUE, -R, -ST adj incorrect or false

UNTRUISM n something that is false

UNTRULY ▸ untrue

UNTRUSS vb release from or as if from a truss

UNTRUST, -S n mistrust

UNTRUSTY adj not trusty

UNTRUTH, -S n statement that is not true, lie

UNTUCK, -ED, -S vb become or cause to become loose or not tucked in

UNTUFTED adj not having tufts

UNTUNE, -D, -S, UNTUNING vb make out of tune

UNTURBID adj clear

UNTURF, -ED, -S vb remove turf from

UNTURN, -S vb turn in a reverse direction

UNTURNED adj not turned

UNTURNS ▸ unturn

UNTWINE, -D, -S vb untwist, unravel, and separate

UNTWIST, -S vb twist apart and loosen

UNTYING, -S ▸ untie

UNUNBIUM n chemical element

UNUNITED adj separated

UNURGED adj not urged

UNUSABLE adj not in good enough condition to be used

UNUSABLY ▸ unusable

UNUSED adj not being or never having been used

UNUSEFUL adj useless

UNUSUAL adj uncommon or extraordinary

UNVAIL, -ED, -ES, -S same as ▸ unveil

UNVAILE same as ▸ unveil

UNVAILED ▸ unvail

UNVAILES ▸ unvail

UNVAILS ▸ unvail

UNVALUED adj not appreciated or valued

UNVARIED adj not varied

UNVEIL, -ED, -S vb ceremonially remove the cover from (a new picture, plaque, etc)

UNVEILER n person who removes a veil

UNVEILS ▸ unveil

UNVEINED adj without veins

UNVENTED adj not vented

UNVERSED adj not versed

UNVESTED adj not vested

UNVETTED adj not thoroughly examined

UNVEXED adj not annoyed

UNVEXT same as ▸ unvexed

UNVIABLE adj not capable of succeeding, esp financially

UNVIEWED adj not viewed

UNVIRTUE n state of having no virtue

UNVISOR, -S vb remove a visor from

UNVITAL adj not vital

UNVIZARD same as ▸ unvisor

UNVOCAL adj not vocal

UNVOICE, -S vb pronounce without vibration of the vocal cords

UNVOICED adj not expressed or spoken

UNVOICES ▸ unvoice

UNVULGAR adj not vulgar

UNWAGED adj (of a person) not having a paid job

UNWAKED same as > unwakened

UNWALLED adj not surrounded by walls

UNWANING adj not waning

UNWANTED adj not wanted or welcome

UNWARDED adj not warded

UNWARE same as ▸ unaware

UNWARELY ▸ unware

UNWARES same as ▸ unawares

UNWARIE same as ▸ unwary

UNWARIER ▸ unwary

UNWARILY ▸ unwary

UNWARMED adj not warmed

UNWARNED adj not warned

UNWARPED adj not warped

UNWARY, UNWARIER adj not careful or cautious and therefore likely to be harmed

UNWASHED n ordinary people collectively

UNWASHEN same as ▸ unwashed

UNWASTED adj not wasted

UNWATER, -S vb dry out

UNWATERY adj not watery

UNWAXED adj not treated with wax

UNWAYED adj having no routes

UNWEAL, -S n ill or sorrow

UNWEANED adj not weaned

UNWEAPON vb disarm

UNWEARY adj not weary ▹ vb refresh or energize

UNWEAVE, -S, UNWOVE, UNWOVEN vb undo or unravel

UNWEBBED adj not webbed

UNWED adj not wed

UNWEDDED adj not wedded

UNWEEDED adj not weeded

UNWEENED adj unknown

UNWEIGHT vb remove weight from

UNWELDED adj not welded

UNWELDY same as ▸ unwieldy

UNWELL adj not healthy, ill

UNWEPT adj not wept for or lamented

UNWET adj not wet

UNWETTED same as ▸ unwet

UNWHIPT same as > unwhipped

UNWHITE adj not white

UNWIELDY adj too heavy, large, or awkward to be easily handled

UNWIFELY adj not like a wife

UNWIGGED adj without a wig

UNWILFUL adj complaisant

UNWILL, -S vb will the reversal of (something that has already occurred)

UNWILLED adj not intentional

UNWILLS ▸ unwill

UNWIND, -S vb relax after a busy or tense time

UNWINDER ▸ unwind

UNWINDS ▸ unwind

UNWINGED adj without wings

UNWIPED adj not wiped

UNWIRE, -D, -S, UNWIRING vb remove wiring from

UNWISDOM n imprudence

UNWISE, -R, -ST adj foolish

UNWISELY ▸ unwise

UNWISER ▶ **unwise**

UNWISEST ▶ **unwise**

UNWISH, -ES vb retract or revoke (a wish)

UNWISHED adj not desired

UNWISHES ▶ **unwish**

UNWIST adj unknown

UNWIT, -S, -TED vb divest of wit

UNWITCH vb release from witchcraft

UNWITS ▶ **unwit**

UNWITTED ▶ **unwit**

UNWITTY adj not clever and amusing

UNWIVE, -D, -S, UNWIVING vb remove a wife from

UNWOMAN, -S vb remove womanly qualities from

UNWON adj not won

UNWONT adj unaccustomed

UNWONTED adj out of the ordinary

UNWOODED adj not wooded

UNWOOED adj not wooed

UNWORDED adj not expressed in words

UNWORK, -S vb destroy (work previously done)

UNWORKED adj not worked

UNWORKS ▶ **unwork**

UNWORMED adj not rid of worms

UNWORN adj not having deteriorated through use or age

UNWORTH, -S n lack of value

UNWORTHY adj not deserving or worthy

UNWOUND past tense and past participle of ▶ **unwind**

UNWOVE ▶ **unweave**

UNWOVEN ▶ **unweave**

UNWRAP, -S vb remove the wrapping from (something)

UNWRITE, -S, UNWROTE vb cancel (what has been written)

UNWRUNG adj not twisted

UNYEANED adj not having given birth

UNYOKE, -D, -S, UNYOKING vb release (an animal, etc) from a yoke

UNYOUNG adj not young

UNZIP, -PED, -S vb unfasten the zip of (a garment)

UNZONED adj not divided into zones

UP, -PED, -S adv indicating movement to or position at a higher place ▷ adj of a high or higher position ▷ vb increase or raise

UPADAISY same as ▷ **upsadaisy**

UPALONG, -S n location away from a place

UPALONG, -S n location away from a place

UPAS, -ES n large Javan tree with whitish bark and poisonous milky sap

UPBEAR, -ER, -S, UPBORE vb sustain

UPBEAT, -S adj cheerful and optimistic ▷ n unaccented beat

UPBIND, -S vb bind up

UPBLOW, UPBLEW, -N, -S vb inflate

UPBOIL, -ED, -S vb boil up

UPBORE ▶ **upbear**

UPBORNE adj held up

UPBOUND adj travelling upwards

UPBOW, -S n stroke of the bow from its tip to its nut on a stringed instrument

UPBRAID, -S vb scold or reproach

UPBRAST same as ▶ **upburst**

UPBRAY, -ED, -S vb shame

UPBREAK, -S, UPBROKE, UPBROKEN vb escape upwards

UPBRING, -S vb rear

UPBROKE ▶ **upbreak**

UPBROKEN ▶ **upbreak**

UPBUILD, -S, UPBUILT vb build up

UPBURST, -S vb burst upwards

UPBY same as ▶ **upbye**

UPBYE adv yonder

UPCAST, -S n material cast or thrown up ▷ adj directed or thrown upwards ▷ vb throw or cast up

UPCATCH, UPCAUGHT vb catch up

UPCHEER, -S vb cheer up

UPCHUCK, -S vb vomit

UPCLIMB, -S vb ascend

UPCLOSE, -D, -S vb close up

UPCOAST adv up the coast

UPCOIL, -ED, -S vb make into a coil

UPCOME, -S vb come up

UPCOMING adj coming soon

UPCOURT adv (in basketball) away from one's own basket

UPCURL, -ED, -S vb curl up

UPCURVE, -D, -S vb curve upwards

UPCYCLE, -D, -S vb recycle a disposable product into an object of greater value

UPDART, -ED, -S vb dart upwards

UPDATE, -D, -S, UPDATING vb bring up to date ▷ n act of updating or something that is updated

UPDATER, -S ▶ **update**

UPDATES ▶ **update**

UPDATING ▶ **update**

UPDIVE, -D, -S, UPDIVING, UPDOVE vb leap upwards

UPDO, -S n type of hairstyle

UPDOMING n expansion of a rock upwards into a dome shape

UPDOS ▶ **updo**

UPDOVE ▶ **updive**

UPDRAFT, -S n upward air current

UPDRAG, -S vb drag up

UPDRAW, -N, -S, UPDREW vb draw up

UPDRY, UPDRIED, UPDRIES, -ING vb dry up

UPEND, -ED, -ING, -S vb turn or set (something) on its end

UPFIELD adj in sport, away from the defending team's goal

UPFILL, -ED, -S vb fill up

UPFLING, -S, UPFLUNG vb throw upwards

UPFLOW, -ED, -S vb flow upwards

UPFLUNG ▶ **upfling**

UPFOLD, -ED, -S vb fold up

UPFOLLOW vb follow

UPFRONT adj open and frank ▷ adv (of money) paid out at the beginning of a business arrangement

UPFURL, -ED, -S vb roll up

UPGANG, -S n climb

UPGATHER vb draw together

UPGAZE, -D, -S, UPGAZING vb gaze upwards

UPGIRD, -ED, -S vb support or hold up

UPGIRT, -ED, -S same as ▶ **upgird**

UPGO, -ES, -ING, -INGS, -NE, UPWENT vb ascend

UPGRADE, -D, -S vb promote (a person or job) to a higher rank

UPGRADER ▶ **upgrade**

UPGRADES ▶ **upgrade**

UPGROW, UPGREW, -N, -S vb grow up

UPGROWTH n process of developing or growing upwards

UPGUSH, -ED, -ES vb flow upwards

UPHAND adj lifted by hand

U

UPHANG, -S, UPHUNG *vb* hang up

UPHAUD, -S, UPHUDDEN *Scots variant of* ▶ **uphold**

UPHEAP, -ED, -S *vb* heap or pile up

UPHEAVAL *n* strong, sudden, or violent disturbance

UPHEAVE, -D, -R, -S, UPHOVE *vb* heave or rise upwards

UPHELD ▶ **uphold**

UPHILD *archaic past form of* ▶ **uphold**

UPHILL, -S *adj* sloping or leading upwards ▷ *adv* up a slope ▷ *n* difficulty

UPHOARD, -S *vb* hoard up

UPHOIST, -S *vb* raise

UPHOLD, UPHELD, -S *vb* maintain or defend against opposition

UPHOLDER ▶ **uphold**

UPHOLDS ▶ **uphold**

UPHOORD, -S *vb* heap up

UPHOVE ▶ **upheave**

UPHROE, -S *variant spelling of* ▶ **euphroe**

UPHUDDEN ▶ **uphaud**

UPHUNG ▶ **uphang**

UPHURL, -ED, -S *vb* throw upwards

UPJET, -S, -TED *vb* stream upwards

UPKEEP, -S *n* act, process, or cost of keeping something in good repair

UPKNIT, -S *vb* bind

UPLAID ▶ **uplay**

UPLAND, -S *adj* of or in an area of high or relatively high ground ▷ *n* area of high or relatively high ground

UPLANDER *n* person hailing from the uplands

UPLANDS ▶ **upland**

UPLAY, UPLAID, -ING, -S *vb* stash

UPLEAD, -S, UPLED *vb* lead upwards

UPLEAN, -ED, -S, -T *vb* lean on something

UPLEAP, -ED, -S, -T *vb* jump upwards

UPLED ▶ **uplead**

UPLIFT, -ED, -S *vb* raise or lift up ▷ *n* act or process of improving moral, social, or cultural conditions

UPLIFTER ▶ **uplift**

UPLIFTS ▶ **uplift**

UPLIGHT, -S, UPLIT *n* lamp or wall light designed or positioned to cast its light upwards ▷ *vb* light in an upward direction

UPLINK, -ED, -S *n* transmitter that sends signals up to a communications satellite ▷ *vb* send (data) to a communications satellite

UPLIT ▶ **uplight**

UPLOAD, -ED, -S *vb* transfer (data or a program) into the memory of another computer

UPLOCK, -ED, -S *vb* lock up

UPLOOK, -ED, -S *vb* look up

UPLYING *adj* raised

UPMAKE, UPMADE, -S, UPMAKING *vb* make up

UPMAKER, -S ▶ **upmake**

UPMAKES ▶ **upmake**

UPMAKING ▶ **upmake**

UPMARKET *adj* expensive and of superior quality ▷ *vb* make something upmarket

UPMOST *another word for* > **uppermost**

UPO *prep* upon

UPON *prep* on

UPPED ▶ **up**

UPPER, -S *adj* higher or highest in physical position, wealth, rank, or status ▷ *n* part of a shoe above the sole

UPPERCUT *n* short swinging upward punch delivered to the chin ▷ *vb* hit (an opponent) with an uppercut

UPPERS ▶ **upper**

UPPILE, -D, -S, UPPILING *vb* pile up

UPPING, -S ▶ **up**

UPPISH *adj* snobbish, arrogant, or presumptuous

UPPISHLY ▶ **uppish**

UPPITY, UPPITIER *adj* snobbish, arrogant, or presumptuous

UPPROP, -S *vb* support

UPRAISE, -D, -S *vb* lift up

UPRAISER ▶ **upraise**

UPRAISES ▶ **upraise**

UPRAN ▶ **uprun**

UPRATE, -D, -S, UPRATING *vb* raise the value, rate, or size of, upgrade

UPREACH *vb* reach up

UPREAR, -ED, -S *vb* lift up

UPREST, -S *n* uprising

UPRIGHT, -S *adj* vertical or erect ▷ *adv* vertically or in an erect position ▷ *n* vertical support, such as a post ▷ *vb* make upright

UPRISAL, -S ▶ **uprise**

UPRISE, -N, -S, UPROSE *vb* rise up

UPRISER, -S ▶ **uprise**

UPRISES ▶ **uprise**

UPRISING *n* rebellion or revolt

UPRIST, -S *same as* ▶ **uprest**

UPRIVER, -S *adv* towards or near the source of a river ▷ *n* area located upstream

UPROAR, -ED, -S *n* disturbance characterized by loud noise and confusion ▷ *vb* cause an uproar

UPROLL, -ED, -S *vb* roll up

UPROOT, -ED, -S *vb* pull up by or as if by the roots

UPROOTAL ▶ **uproot**

UPROOTED ▶ **uproot**

UPROOTER ▶ **uproot**

UPROOTS ▶ **uproot**

UPROSE ▶ **uprise**

UPROUSE, -D, -S *vb* rouse or stir up

UPRUN, UPRAN, -S *vb* run up

UPRUSH, -ED, -ES *n* upward rush, as of consciousness ▷ *vb* rush upwards

UPRYST *same as* ▶ **uprest**

UPS ▶ **up**

UPSCALE, -D, -S *adj* of or for the upper end of an economic or social scale ▷ *vb* upgrade

UPSEE, -S *n* drunken revel

UPSELL, -S, UPSOLD *vb* persuade a customer to buy a more expensive or additional item

UPSEND, -S, UPSENT *vb* send up

UPSET, -S *adj* emotionally or physically disturbed or distressed ▷ *vb* tip over ▷ *n* unexpected defeat or reversal

UPSETTER ▶ **upset**

UPSEY, -S *same as* ▶ **upsee**

UPSHIFT, -S *vb* move up (a gear)

UPSHOOT, -S *vb* shoot upwards

UPSHOT, -S *n* final result or conclusion

UPSIDE, -S *n* upper surface or part

UPSIES ▶ **upsy**

UPSILON, -S *n* 20th letter in the Greek alphabet

UPSIZE, -D, -S, UPSIZING *vb* increase in size

UPSKILL, -S *vb* improve the aptitude for work of (a person)

UPSLOPE, -S *adv* up a slope ▷ *n* upward slope

UPSOAR, -ED, -S *vb* soar up

UPSOLD ▶ **upsell**

UPSPEAK, UPSPAKE, -S, UPSPOKE, UPSPOKEN *vb* speak with rising intonation

UPSPEAR, -S *vb* grow upwards in a spear-like manner

UPSPOKE ▶ **upspeak**

UPSPOKEN ▶ **upspeak**

UPSPRING, UPSPRANG, UPSPRUNG *vb* spring up or come into existence ▷ *n* leap forwards or upwards

UPSTAGE, -D, -S *adj* at the back half of the stage ▷ *vb* draw attention to oneself from (someone else) ▷ *adv* on, at, or to the rear of the stage ▷ *n* back half of the stage

UPSTAGER ▶ **upstage**

UPSTAGES ▶ **upstage**

UPSTAIR *same as* ▶ **upstairs**

UPSTAIRS *adv* to or on an upper floor of a building ▷ *n* upper floor ▷ *adj* situated on an upper floor

UPSTAND, -S, UPSTOOD *vb* rise

UPSTARE, -D, -S *vb* stare upwards

UPSTART, -S *n* person who has risen suddenly to a position of power and behaves arrogantly ▷ *vb* start up, as in surprise, etc

UPSTATE, -S *adv* towards, in, from, or relating to the outlying or northern sections of a state ▷ *n* outlying, esp northern, sections of a state

UPSTATER ▶ **upstate**

UPSTATES ▶ **upstate**

UPSTAY, -ED, -S *vb* support

UPSTEP, -S *n* type of vocal intonation

UPSTIR, -S *vb* stir up ▷ *n* commotion

UPSTOOD ▶ **upstand**

UPSTREAM *adj* in or towards the higher part of a stream ▷ *vb* stream upwards

UPSTROKE *n* upward stroke or movement, as of a pen or brush

UPSURGE, -D, -S *n* rapid rise or swell ▷ *vb* surge up

UPSWARM, -S *vb* rise or send upwards in a swarm

UPSWAY, -ED, -S *vb* swing in the air

UPSWEEP, -S, UPSWEPT *n* curve or sweep upwards ▷ *vb* sweep, curve, or brush be swept, curved, or brushed upwards

UPSWELL, -S *vb* swell up or cause to swell up

UPSWEPT ▶ **upsweep**

UPSWING, -S, UPSWUNG *n* recovery period in a trade cycle ▷ *vb* swing or move up

UPSY, UPSIES *same as* ▶ **upsee**

UPTA *same as* ▶ **upter**

UPTAK, -S *same as* ▶ **uptake**

UPTAKE, -N, -S, UPTAKING, UPTOOK *n* numbers taking up something such as an offer or the act of taking it up ▷ *vb* take up

UPTAKS ▶ **uptak**

UPTALK, -ED, -S *n* style of speech in which every sentence ends with a rising tone ▷ *vb* talk in this manner

UPTEAR, -S, UPTORE, UPTORN *vb* tear up

UPTEMPO, -S *adj* fast ▷ *n* uptempo piece

UPTER *adj* of poor quality

UPTHROW, UPTHREW, -N, -S *n* upward movement of rocks on one side of a fault plane relative to rocks on the other side ▷ *vb* throw upwards

UPTHRUST *n* upward push

UPTICK, -S *n* rise or increase

UPTIE, -D, -S, UPTYING *vb* tie up

UPTIGHT *adj* nervously tense, irritable, or angry

UPTILT, -ED, -S *vb* tilt up

UPTIME, -S *n* time during which a machine, such as a computer, actually operates

UPTOOK ▶ **uptake**

UPTORE ▶ **uptear**

UPTORN ▶ **uptear**

UPTOSS, -ED, -ES *vb* throw upwards

UPTOWN, -S *adv* towards or in a part of a town that is away from the centre ▷ *n* such a part of town, esp a residential part

UPTOWNER ▶ **uptown**

UPTOWNS ▶ **uptown**

UPTRAIN, -S *vb* train up

UPTREND, -S *n* upward trend

UPTURN, -ED, -S *n* upward trend or improvement ▷ *vb* turn or cause to turn over or upside down

UPTYING ▶ **uptie**

UPVALUE, -D, -S *vb* raise the value of

UPVOTE, -D, -S, UPVOTING *vb* publicly approve of a social media post

UPWAFT, -ED, -S *vb* waft upwards

UPWARD *same as* ▶ **upwards**

UPWARDLY ▶ **upward**

UPWARDS *adv* from a lower to a higher place, level, condition, etc

UPWELL, -ED, -S *vb* well up

UPWENT ▶ **upgo**

UPWHIRL, -S *vb* spin upwards

UPWIND, -S, UPWOUND *adv* into or against the wind ▷ *adj* going against the wind ▷ *vb* wind up

UPWRAP, -S *vb* wrap up

UR *interj* hesitant utterance used to fill gaps in talking

URACHUS, URACHI *n* cord of tissue connected to the bladder

URACIL, -S *n* pyrimidine present in all living cells

URAEI ▶ **uraeus**

This plural of **uraeus**, an Egyptian symbol of kingship, is very useful for dumping a surplus of vowels.

URAEMIA, -S *n* accumulation of waste products in the blood

URAEMIC ▶ **uraemia**

URAEUS, URAEI, -ES *n* sacred serpent of ancient Egypt

URALI, -S *n* type of plant

URALITE, -S *n* mineral that replaces pyroxene in some rocks

URALITIC ▶ **uralite**

URANIA, -S *n* uranium dioxide

URANIAN *adj* heavenly

URANIAS ▶ **urania**

URANIC *adj* of or containing uranium, esp in a high valence state

URANIDE, -S *n* any element having an atomic number greater than that of protactinium

URANIN, -S *n* type of alkaline substance

URANISCI ▶ **uraniscus**

URANISM, -S *n* old word for homosexuality

URANITE, -S *n* any of various minerals containing uranium, esp torbernite or autunite

URANITIC ▶ **uranite**

URANIUM, -S *n* radioactive silvery-white metallic element

U

URANOUS *adj* of or containing uranium, esp in a low valence state

URANYL, -S *n* type of divalent form

URANYLIC ▸ **uranyl**

URANYLS ▸ **uranyl**

URAO, -S *n* type of mineral

URARE, -S *same as* ▸ **urali**

URARI, -S *same as* ▸ **urali**

URASE, -S *same as* ▸ **urease**

URATE, -S *n* any salt or ester of uric acid

URATIC ▸ **urate**

URB, -S *n* urban area

URBAN *adj* of or living in a city or town

URBANE, -R, -ST *adj* characterized by courtesy, elegance, and sophistication

URBANELY ▸ **urbane**

URBANER ▸ **urbane**

URBANEST ▸ **urbane**

URBANISE *same as* ▸ **urbanize**

URBANISM *n* character of city life

URBANIST *n* person who studies towns and cities

URBANITE *n* resident of an urban community

URBANITY *n* quality of being urbane

URBANIZE *vb* make (a rural area) more industrialized and urban

URBEX, -ES *n* short for urban exploration, the hobby of exploring derelict urban structures

URBIA, -S *n* urban area

URBS ▸ **urb**

URCEOLUS, URCEOLI *n* organ of a plant

URCHIN, -S *n* mischievous child

URD, -S *n* type of plant with edible seeds

URDE *adj* (in heraldry) having points

URDEE *same as* ▸ **urde**

URDS ▸ **urd**

URDY *n* heraldic line pattern

URE, -S *same as* ▸ **aurochs**

UREA, -S *n* white soluble crystalline compound found in urine

UREAL ▸ **urea**

UREAS ▸ **urea**

UREASE, -S *n* enzyme that converts urea to ammonium carbonate

UREDIA ▸ **uredium**

UREDIAL ▸ **uredium**

UREDINE, -S ▸ **uredo**

UREDINIA > **uredinium**

UREDIUM, UREDIA *n* spore-producing body of some rust fungi in which uredospores are formed

UREDO, -S *less common name for* > **urticaria**

UREIC ▸ **urea**

UREIDE, -S *n* any of a class of organic compounds derived from urea

UREMIA, -S *same as* ▸ **uraemia**

UREMIC ▸ **uremia**

URENA, -S *n* plant genus

URENT *adj* burning

URES ▸ **ure**

URESIS, URESES *n* urination

URETER, -S *n* tube that conveys urine from the kidney to the bladder

URETERAL ▸ **ureter**

URETERIC ▸ **ureter**

URETERS ▸ **ureter**

URETHAN, -S *same as* ▸ **urethane**

URETHANE *n* short for the synthetic material polyurethane ▷ *vb* treat with urethane

URETHANS ▸ **urethan**

URETHRA, -E, -S *n* canal that carries urine from the bladder out of the body

URETHRAL ▸ **urethra**

URETHRAS ▸ **urethra**

URETIC *adj* of or relating to urine

URGE, -D, -S *n* strong impulse, inner drive, or yearning ▷ *vb* plead with or press (a person to do something)

URGENCE, -S ▸ **urgent**

URGENCY ▸ **urgent**

URGENT *adj* requiring speedy action or attention

URGENTLY ▸ **urgent**

URGER, -S ▸ **urge**

URGES ▸ **urge**

URGING, -S ▸ **urge**

URGINGLY ▸ **urge**

URGINGS ▸ **urging**

URIAL, -S *n* type of sheep

URIC *adj* of or derived from urine

URICASE, -S *n* type of enzyme

URIDINE, -S *n* nucleoside present in all living cells in a combined form, esp in RNA

URIDYLIC *adj* as in **uridylic acid** nucleotide consisting of uracil, ribose, and a phosphate group

URINAL, -S *n* sanitary fitting used by men for urination

URINANT *adj* having the head downwards

URINARY *adj* of urine or the organs that secrete and pass urine ▷ *n* reservoir for urine

URINATE, -D, -S *vb* discharge urine

URINATOR ▸ **urinate**

URINE, -D, -S, URINING *n* pale yellow fluid passed as waste from the body ▷ *vb* urinate

URINEMIA *same as* ▸ **uremia**

URINEMIC ▸ **urinemia**

URINES ▸ **urine**

URINING ▸ **urine**

URINOSE *same as* ▸ **urinous**

URINOUS *adj* of, resembling, or containing urine

URITE, -S *n* part of the abdomen

URMAN, -S *n* forest

URN, -ED, -S *n* vase used as a container for the ashes of the dead ▷ *vb* put in an urn

URNAL ▸ **urn**

URNED ▸ **urn**

URNFIELD *n* cemetery full of individual cremation urns ▷ *adj* characterized by cremation in urns

URNFUL, -S *n* capacity of an urn

URNLIKE ▸ **urn**

URNS ▸ **urn**

UROBILIN *n* brownish pigment found in faeces and sometimes in urine

UROBORIC *adj* of or like a uroboros

UROBOROS *same as* > **ouroboros**

UROCHORD *n* notochord of a larval tunicate, typically confined to the tail region

URODELAN ▸ **urodele**

URODELE, -S *n* amphibian of the order which includes the salamanders and newts

UROGRAM, -S *n* X-ray of the urinary tract

UROLITH, -S *n* calculus in the urinary tract

UROLOGIC ▸ **urology**

UROLOGY *n* branch of medicine concerned with the urinary system and its diseases

UROMERE, -S *n* part of the abdomen

UROPOD, -S *n* paired appendage that forms part of the tailfan in lobsters

UROPODAL ▸ **uropod**

UROPODS ▸ **uropod**

UROPYGIA > **uropygium**

UROSCOPY n examination of urine

UROSIS, UROSES n urinary disease

UROSOME, -S n abdomen of arthropods

UROSTEGE n part of a serpent's tail

UROSTOMY n type of urinary surgery

UROSTYLE n bony rod forming the last segment of the vertebral column of frogs and toads

URP, -ED, -ING, -S dialect word for ▸ **vomit**

URSA, -E n she-bear

URSID, -S n meteor

URSIFORM adj bear-shaped or bearlike in form

URSINE adj of or like a bear

URSON, -S n type of porcupine

URTEXT, -S n earliest form of a text

URTEXTE same as ▸ **urtexts**

URTEXTS ▸ **urtext**

URTICA, -S n type of nettle

URTICANT n something that causes itchiness and irritation

URTICAS ▸ **urtica**

URTICATE adj characterized by the presence of weals ▸ vb sting

URUBU, -S n type of bird

URUS, -ES another name for the ▸ **aurochs**

URUSHIOL n poisonous pale yellow liquid occurring in poison ivy and the lacquer tree

URVA, -S n Indian mongoose

US pron refers to the speaker or writer and another person or other people

USABLE adj able to be used

USABLY ▸ **usable**

USAGE, -S n regular or constant use

USAGER, -S n person who has the use of something in trust

USAGES ▸ **usage**

USANCE, -S n period of time permitted for the redemption of foreign bills of exchange

USAUNCE, -S same as ▸ **usance**

USE, -S, USING vb put into service or action ▸ n using or being used

USEABLE same as ▸ **usable**

USEABLY ▸ **usable**

USED adj second-hand

USEFUL, -S adj able to be used advantageously or for several different purposes ▸ n odd-job man or general factotum

USEFULLY ▸ **useful**

USEFULS ▸ **useful**

USELESS adj having no practical use

USER, -S n continued exercise, use, or enjoyment of a right, esp in property

USERNAME n name given by computer user to gain access

USERS ▸ **user**

USES ▸ **use**

USHER, -ED, -ING, -S n official who shows people to their seats, as in a church ▸ vb conduct or escort

USHERESS n female usher

USHERING ▸ **usher**

USHERS ▸ **usher**

USING ▸ **use**

USNEA, -S n type of lichen

USQUABAE n whisky

USQUE, -S n whisky

USQUEBAE same as ▸ **usquabae**

USQUES ▸ **usque**

USTION, -S n burning

USTULATE adj charred ▸ vb give a charred appearance to

USUAL, -S adj of the most normal, frequent, or regular type ▸ n ordinary or commonplace events

USUALLY adv most often, in most cases

USUALS ▸ **usual**

USUCAPT ▸ **usucapion**

USUCAPTS > **usucapion**

USUFRUCT n right to use and derive profit from a piece of property belonging to another

USURE, -D, -S, USURING vb be involved in usury

USURER, -S n person who lends funds at an exorbitant rate of interest

USURES ▸ **usure**

USURESS n female usurer

USURIES ▸ **usury**

USURING ▸ **usure**

USURIOUS ▸ **usury**

USUROUS ▸ **usury**

USURP, -ED, -ING, -S vb seize (a position or power) without authority

USURPER, -S ▸ **usurp**

USURPING ▸ **usurp**

USURPS ▸ **usurp**

USURY, USURIES n practice of lending money at an extremely high rate of interest

USWARD adv towards us

USWARDS same as ▸ **usward**

UT, -S n syllable used in the fixed system of solmization for the note C

UTA n side-blotched lizard

UTAS, -ES n eighth day of a festival

UTE, -S n small truck with low sides

UTENSIL, -S n tool or container for practical use

UTERI ▸ **uterus**

UTERINE adj of or affecting the womb

UTERITIS n inflammation of the womb

UTERUS, UTERI, -ES n womb

UTES ▸ **ute**

UTILE, -S n W African tree

UTILIDOR n above-ground insulated casing for pipes in permafrost regions

UTILISE, -D, -S same as ▸ **utilize**

UTILISER ▸ **utilise**

UTILISES ▸ **utilise**

UTILITY n usefulness ▸ adj designed for use rather than beauty

UTILIZE, -D, -S vb make practical use of

UTILIZER ▸ **utilize**

UTILIZES ▸ **utilize**

UTIS, -ES n uproar

UTMOST, -S n the greatest possible degree or amount ▸ adj of the greatest possible degree or amount

UTOPIA, -S n real or imaginary society, place, state, etc considered to be perfect or ideal

UTOPIAN, -S adj of or relating to a perfect or ideal existence ▸ n idealistic social reformer

UTOPIAS ▸ **utopia**

UTOPIAST ▸ **utopia**

UTOPISM, -S ▸ **utopia**

UTOPIST, -S ▸ **utopia**

UTRICLE, -S n larger of the two parts of the membranous labyrinth of the internal ear

UTRICULI > **utriculus**

UTS ▸ **ut**

UTTER, -ED, -ER, -ERS, -EST, -ING, -S vb express (something) in sounds or words ▸ adj total or absolute

UTTERLY adv extremely

U

UTTERS ▸ utter
UTU, -S n reward
UVA, -E, -S n grape or fruit resembling this
UVEA, -S n part of the eyeball consisting of the iris, ciliary body, and choroid
UVEAL ▸ uvea
UVEAS ▸ uvea
UVEITIC ▸ uveitis

UVEITIS n inflammation of the uvea
UVEOUS ▸ uvea
UVULA, -E, -S n small fleshy part of the soft palate that hangs in the back of the throat
UVULAR, -S adj of or relating to the uvula ▸ n uvular consonant

UVULARLY ▸ uvular
UVULARS ▸ uvular
UVULAS ▸ uvula
UVULITIS n inflammation of the uvula
UXORIAL adj of or relating to a wife
UXORIOUS adj excessively fond of or dependent on one's wife

U

Vv

If you have a **V** on your rack, the first thing to remember is that there are no valid two-letter words beginning with **V**. In fact, there are no two-letter words that end in **V** either, so you can't form any two-letter words using **V**. Remembering this will stop you wasting time trying to think of some. While **V** is useless for two-letter words, it does start some good three-letter words. **Vax**, **vex** and **vox** (13 points each) are the best of these, while **vaw**, **vow** and **vly** (9 each) are also useful.

VAC, -KED, -KING, -S vb clean with a vacuum cleaner

> Meaning to clean with a vacuum cleaner, this can be a useful short word for dealing with that awkward letter V.

VACANCE, -S n vacant period

VACANCY n unfilled job

VACANT adj (of a toilet, room, etc) unoccupied

VACANTLY ▶ vacant

VACATE, -D, -S, VACATING vb cause (something) to be empty by leaving

VACATION n time when universities and law courts are closed ▷ vb take a vacation

VACATUR, -S n annulment

VACCINA, -S same as ▶ vaccinia

VACCINAL adj of or relating to vaccination

VACCINAS ▶ vaccina

VACCINE, -S n substance designed to make a person immune to a disease

VACCINEE n person who has been vaccinated

VACCINES ▶ vaccine

VACCINIA technical name for ▶ cowpox

VACHERIN n soft cheese made from cows' milk

VACKED ▶ vac

VACKING ▶ vac

VACS ▶ vac

VACUA ▶ vacuum

VACUATE, -S vb empty

VACUATED ▶ vacuate

VACUATES ▶ vacuate

VACUIST, -S n person believing in the existence of vacuums in nature

VACUITY n absence of intelligent thought or ideas

VACUOLAR ▶ vacuole

VACUOLE, -S n fluid-filled cavity in the cytoplasm of a cell

VACUOUS adj not expressing intelligent thought

VACUUM, VACUA, -ED, -S n empty space from which all or most air or gas has been removed ▷ vb clean with a vacuum cleaner

VADE, -S vb fade

VADED ▶ vade

VADES ▶ vade

VADING ▶ vade

VADOSE adj of or derived from water occurring above the water table

VAE, -S same as ▶ voe

VAG, -GED, -GING, -S n informal Australian word for a vagrant ▷ vb arrest someone for vagrancy

VAGABOND n person with no fixed home, esp a beggar

VAGAL adj of, relating to, or affecting the vagus nerve

VAGALLY ▶ vagal

VAGARIES ▶ vagary

VAGARISH ▶ vagary

VAGARY, VAGARIES n unpredictable change

VAGGED ▶ vag

VAGGING ▶ vag

VAGI ▶ vagus

VAGILE adj able to move freely

VAGILITY ▶ vagile

VAGINA, -E, -S n (in female mammals) passage from the womb to the external genitals

VAGINAL ▶ vagina

VAGINANT adj (of a leaf) sheathing its stem with its base

VAGINAS ▶ vagina

VAGINATE adj (esp of plant parts) having a sheath

VAGINULA n little sheath

VAGINULE same as ▶ vaginula

VAGITUS n newborn baby's cry

VAGOTOMY n surgical division of the vagus nerve

VAGRANCY n state or condition of being a vagrant

VAGRANT, -S n person with no settled home ▷ adj wandering

VAGROM same as ▶ vagrant

VAGS ▶ vag

VAGUE, -R, -S, -ST adj not clearly explained ▷ vb wander

VAGUED ▶ vague

VAGUELY ▶ vague

VAGUER ▶ vague

VAGUES ▶ vague

VAGUEST ▶ vague

VAGUING ▶ vague

VAGUISH adj rather vague

VAGUS, VAGI n tenth cranial nerve, which supplies the heart, lungs, and viscera

VAHANA, -S n vehicle

VAHINE, -S n Polynesian woman

VAIL, -ED, -ING, -S vb lower (something, such as a

V

weapon), esp as a sign of deference or submission

VAIN, -ER, -EST *adj* excessively proud, esp of one's appearance

VAINESSE *n* vainness

VAINEST ▸ vain

VAINLY ▸ vain

VAINNESS ▸ vain

VAIR, -S *n* fur used to trim robes in the Middle Ages

VAIRE *adj* of Russian squirrel fur

VAIRIER ▸ vairy

VAIRIEST ▸ vairy

VAIRS ▸ vair

VAIRY, VAIRIER, VAIRIEST ▸ vair

VAIVODE, -S *n* Slavic governor

VAKAS, -ES *n* Armenian priestly collar

VAKASS, -ES *n* Armenian priestly collar

VAKEEL, -S *n* (in India) ambassador

VAKIL, -S *same as* ▸ vakeel

VALANCE, -S *n* piece of drapery round the edge of a bed ▷ *vb* provide with a valance

VALANCED ▸ valance

VALANCES ▸ valance

VALE, -S *n* valley ▷ *sentence substitute* farewell

VALENCE, -S *same as* ▸ valency

VALENCIA *n* type of fabric

VALENCY *n* power of an atom to make molecular bonds

VALERATE *n* salt of valeric acid

VALERIAN *n* herb used as a sedative

VALERIC *adj* of, relating to, or derived from valerian

VALES ▸ vale

VALET, -ED, -ING, -S *n* man's personal male servant ▷ *vb* act as a valet (for)

VALETA, -S *n* old-time dance in triple time

VALETE, -S *n* farewell

VALETED ▸ valet

VALETES ▸ valete

VALETING ▸ valet

VALETS ▸ valet

VALGOID ▸ valgus

VALGOUS *same as* ▸ valgus

VALGUS, -ES *adj* denoting a deformity of a limb ▷ *n* abnormal position of a limb

VALI, -S *n* Turkish civil governor

VALIANCE ▸ valiant

VALIANCY ▸ valiant

VALIANT, -S *adj* brave or courageous ▷ *n* brave person

VALID, -ER, -EST *adj* soundly reasoned

VALIDATE *vb* make valid

VALIDER ▸ valid

VALIDEST ▸ valid

VALIDITY ▸ valid

VALIDLY ▸ valid

VALINE, -S *n* essential amino acid

VALIS ▸ vali

VALISE, -S *n* small suitcase

VALIUM, -S *n* as in valium picnic refers to a day on the New York Stock Exchange when business is slow

VALKYR, -S *variant of* ▸ valkyrie

VALKYRIE *n* Norse maiden who collects dead warriors to take to Valhalla

VALKYRS ▸ valkyr

VALLAR, -S *adj* pertaining to a rampart ▷ *n* gold Roman crown awarded to the first soldier who broke into the enemy's camp

VALLARY *same as* ▸ vallar

VALLATE *adj* surrounded with a wall

VALLEY, -S *n* low area between hills, often with a river running through it

VALLEYED *adj* having a valley

VALLEYS ▸ valley

VALLHUND *n* Swedish breed of dog

VALLONIA *same as* ▸ valonia

VALLUM, -S *n* Roman rampart or earthwork

VALONEA, -S *same as* ▸ valonia

VALONIA, -S *n* acorn cups and unripe acorns of a particular oak

VALOR, -S *same as* ▸ valour

VALORISE *same as* ▸ valorize

VALORIZE *vb* fix and maintain an artificial price for (a commodity) by governmental action

VALOROUS ▸ valour

VALORS ▸ valor

VALOUR, -S *n* bravery; brave person

VALPROIC *adj* as in valproic acid synthetic crystalline compound, used as an anticonvulsive

VALSE, -D, -S, VALSING *another word for* ▸ waltz

VALUABLE *adj* having great worth ▷ *n* valuable article of personal property, esp jewellery

VALUABLY ▸ valuable

VALUATE, -D, -S *vb* value or evaluate

VALUATOR *n* person who estimates the value of objects, paintings, etc

VALUE, -D, -S, VALUING *n* importance, usefulness ▷ *vb* assess the worth or desirability of

VALUER, -S ▸ value

VALUES ▸ value

VALUING ▸ value

VALUTA, -S *n* value of one currency in terms of its exchange rate with another

VALVAL *same as* ▸ valvular

VALVAR *same as* ▸ valvular

VALVATE *adj* furnished with a valve or valves

VALVE, -S *n* device to control the movement of fluid through a pipe ▷ *vb* provide with a valve

VALVED ▸ valve

VALVELET *same as* ▸ valvule

VALVES ▸ valve

VALVING ▸ valve

VALVULA, -E *same as* ▸ valvule

VALVULAR *adj* of or having valves

VALVULE, -S *n* small valve or a part resembling one

VAMBRACE *n* piece of armour used to protect the arm

VAMOOSE, -D, -S *vb* leave a place hurriedly

VAMOSE, -S *same as* ▸ vamoose

VAMOSED ▸ vamose

VAMOSES ▸ vamose

VAMOSING ▸ vamose

VAMP, -ED, -S *n* attractive woman who exploits men ▷ *vb* exploit (a man) in the fashion of a vamp

VAMPER, -S ▸ vamp

VAMPIER ▸ vampy

VAMPIEST ▸ vampy

VAMPING, -S ▸ vamp

VAMPIRE, -D, -S *n* (in folklore) corpse that rises at night to drink the blood of the living ▷ *vb* assail

VAMPIRIC ▸ vampire

VAMPISH ▸ vamp

VAMPLATE *n* piece of metal mounted on a lance to protect the hand

VAMPS ▸ vamp

VAMPY, VAMPIER, VAMPIEST ▸ vamp

VAN, -S n motor vehicle for transporting goods ▷ vb send in a van

VANADATE n any salt or ester of a vanadic acid

VANADIC adj of or containing vanadium, esp in a trivalent or pentavalent state

VANADIUM n metallic element, used in steel

VANADOUS adj of or containing vanadium

VANDA, -S n type of orchid

VANDAL, -S n person who deliberately damages property

VANDALIC ▸ vandal

VANDALS ▸ vandal

VANDAS ▸ vanda

VANDYKE, -D, -S n short pointed beard ▷ vb cut with deep zigzag indentations

VANE, -S n flat blade on a rotary device such as a weathercock or propeller

VANED ▸ vane

VANELESS ▸ vane

VANES ▸ vane

VANESSA, -S n type of butterfly

VANESSID n type of butterfly ▷ adj relating to this butterfly

VANG, -S n type of rope or tackle on a sailing ship

VANGUARD n unit of soldiers leading an army

VANILLA, -S n seed pod of a tropical climbing orchid, used for flavouring ▷ adj flavoured with vanilla

VANILLIC adj of, resembling, containing, or derived from vanilla or vanillin

VANILLIN n white crystalline aldehyde found in vanilla

VANISH, -ED, -ES vb disappear suddenly or mysteriously ▷ n second and weaker of the two vowels in a falling diphthong

VANISHER ▸ vanish

VANISHES ▸ vanish

VANITAS n type of Dutch painting

VANITIED adj with vanity units or mirrors

VANITIES ▸ vanity

VANITORY n vanity unit

VANITY, VANITIES n (display of) excessive pride

VANLIKE adj like a van

VANLOAD, -S n amount van will carry

VANMAN, VANMEN n man in control of a van

VANNED ▸ van

VANNER, -S n horse used to pull delivery vehicles

VANNING, -S ▸ van

VANPOOL, -S n van-sharing group

VANQUISH vb defeat (someone) utterly

VANS ▸ van

VANT, -S archaic word for ▸ vanguard

VANTAGE, -D, -S n state, position, or opportunity offering advantage ▷ vb benefit

VANTS ▸ vant

VANWARD adv in or towards the front

VAPE, -D, -S vb inhale nicotine vapour (from an electronic cigarette)

VAPER, -S n one who inhales nicotine vapour from an electronic cigarette

VAPES ▸ vape

VAPID, -ER, -EST adj lacking character, dull

VAPIDITY ▸ vapid

VAPIDLY ▸ vapid

VAPING, -S n the practice of inhaling nicotine vapour (from an electronic cigarette)

VAPOR, -ED, -ING, -S same as ▸ vapour

VAPORER, -S ▸ vapor

VAPORIER ▸ vapory

VAPORING ▸ vapor

VAPORISE same as ▸ vaporize

VAPORISH ▸ vapor

VAPORIZE vb change into a vapour

VAPOROUS same as > vaporific

VAPORS ▸ vapor

VAPORY, VAPORIER same as ▸ vapoury

VAPOUR, -ED, -S n moisture suspended in air as steam or mist ▷ vb evaporate

VAPOURER ▸ vapour

VAPOURS ▸ vapour

VAPOURY adj full of vapours

VAPULATE vb strike

VAQUERO, -S n cattle-hand

VAR, -S n unit of reactive power of an alternating current

VARA, -S n unit of length used in Spain, Portugal, and South America

VARACTOR n semiconductor diode that acts as a voltage-dependent capacitor

VARAN, -S n type of lizard

VARAS ▸ vara

VARDY, VARDIES n verdict

VARE, -S n rod

VAREC, -S n ash obtained from kelp

VARECH, -S same as ▸ varec

VARECS ▸ varec

VARENYKE pl n Ukrainian stuffed dumplings

VARES ▸ vare

VAREUSE, -S n type of coat

VARGUENO n type of Spanish cabinet

VARIA, -S n collection or miscellany, esp of literary works

VARIABLE adj not always the same, changeable ▷ n something that is subject to variation

VARIABLY ▸ variable

VARIANCE n act of varying

VARIANT, -S adj differing from a standard or type ▷ n something that differs from a standard or type

VARIAS ▸ varia

VARIATE, -D, -S n random variable or a numerical value taken by it ▷ vb vary

VARICEAL adj relating to a varix

VARICES ▸ varix

VARICOID same as ▸ cirsoid

VARICOSE adj of or resulting from varicose veins

VARIED ▸ vary

VARIEDLY ▸ vary

VARIER, -S n person who varies

VARIES ▸ vary

VARIETAL adj of or forming a variety, esp a biological variety ▷ n wine labelled with the name of the grape from which it is pressed

VARIETY n state of being diverse or various

VARIFORM adj varying in form or shape

VARIOLA, -S n smallpox

VARIOLAR ▸ variola

VARIOLAS ▸ variola

VARIOLE, -S n any of the rounded masses that make up the rock variolite

VARIORUM adj containing notes by various scholars or critics or various versions of the text ▷ n edition or text of this kind

V

VARIOUS adj of several kinds

VARISTOR n type of semiconductor device

VARITYPE vb produce (copy) on a Varityper ▷ n copy produced on a Varityper

VARIX, VARICES n tortuous dilated vein

VARLET, -S n menial servant

VARLETRY n varlets collectively

VARLETS ▷ varlet

VARLETTO same as ▷ varlet

VARMENT, -S same as ▷ varmint

VARMINT, -S n irritating or obnoxious person or animal

VARNA, -S n any of the four Hindu castes

VARNISH n solution of oil and resin, put on a surface to make it hard and glossy ▷ vb apply varnish to

VARNISHY adj like varnish

VAROOM same as ▷ vroom

VAROOMED same as ▷ varoom

VAROOMS same as ▷ varoom

VARROA, -S n small parasite

VARS ▷ var

VARSAL adj universal

VARSITY n university

VARTABED n position in the Armenian church

VARUS, -ES adj denoting a deformity of a limb ▷ n abnormal position of a limb

VARVE, -S n typically thin band of sediment deposited annually in glacial lakes

VARVED adj having layers of sedimentary deposit

VARVEL, -S n piece of falconry equipment

VARVES ▷ varve

VARY, VARIED, VARIES vb change

VARYING, -S ▷ vary

VAS, -A n vessel or tube that carries a fluid

VASAL ▷ vas

VASCULA ▷ vasculum

VASCULAR adj relating to vessels

VASCULUM, VASCULA n metal box used by botanists in the field for carrying botanical specimens

VASE, -S n ornamental jar, esp for flowers

VASEFUL, -S n contents of a vase

VASELIKE ▷ vase

VASELINE n translucent gelatinous substance

obtained from petroleum ▷ vb apply vaseline to

VASES ▷ vase

VASIFORM ▷ vas

VASOTOMY n surgery on the vas deferens

VASSAIL, -S archaic variant of ▷ vassal

VASSAL, -S n man given land by a lord in return for military service ▷ adj of or relating to a vassal ▷ vb vassalize

VASSALRY n vassalage

VASSALS ▷ vassal

VAST, -ER, -EST, -S adj extremely large ▷ n immense or boundless space

VASTIER ▷ vasty

VASTIEST ▷ vasty

VASTITY ▷ vast

VASTLY ▷ vast

VASTNESS ▷ vast

VASTS ▷ vast

VASTY, VASTIER, VASTIEST archaic or poetic word for ▷ vast

VAT, -S, -TED, -TING n large container for liquids ▷ vb place, store, or treat in a vat

VATABLE adj subject to VAT

VATFUL, -S n amount enough to fill a vat

VATIC adj of or characteristic of a prophet

VATICAL same as ▷ vatic

VATICIDE n murder of a prophet

VATMAN, VATMEN n Customs and Excise employee

VATS ▷ vat

VATTED ▷ vat

VATTER, -S n person who works with vats; blender

VATTING ▷ vat

VATU, -S n standard monetary unit of Vanuatu

VAU, -S same as ▷ vav

VAUCH, -ED, -ES, -ING vb move fast

VAUDOO, -S same as ▷ voodoo

VAUDOUX same as ▷ voodoo

VAULT, -ED, -S n secure room for storing valuables ▷ vb jump over (something) by resting one's hand(s) on it

VAULTAGE n group of vaults

VAULTED ▷ vault

VAULTER, -S ▷ vault

VAULTIER ▷ vaulty

VAULTING n arrangement of ceiling vaults in a building ▷ adj excessively confident

VAULTS ▷ vault

VAULTY, VAULTIER adj arched

VAUNCE, -D, -S, VAUNCING same as ▷ advance

VAUNT, -ED, -S, -ING vb describe or display (success or possessions) boastfully ▷ n boast

VAUNTAGE archaic variant of ▷ vantage

VAUNTED ▷ vaunt

VAUNTER, -S ▷ vaunt

VAUNTERY n bravado

VAUNTFUL ▷ vaunt

VAUNTIE same as ▷ vaunty

VAUNTIER ▷ vaunty

VAUNTING ▷ vaunt

VAUNTS ▷ vaunt

VAUNTY, VAUNTIER adj proud

VAURIEN, -S n rascal

VAUS ▷ vau

VAUT, -S same as ▷ vault

VAUTE, -D, -S, VAUTING same as ▷ vault

VAUTS ▷ vaut

VAV, -S n sixth letter of the Hebrew alphabet

It is surprising how often one wants to get rid of two Vs, and when one does, this word, the name of a Hebrew letter, fits the bill nicely. It has an equally useful variant **vaw**.

VAVASOR, -S n (in feudal society) vassal who also has their own vassals

VAVASORY n lands held by a vavasor

VAVASOUR same as ▷ vavasor

VAVASSOR same as ▷ vavasor

VAVS ▷ vav

VAW, -S same as ▷ vav

VAWARD, -S n vanguard

VAWNTIE, -R ▷ vaunt

VAWS ▷ vaw

VAWTE, -D, -S, VAWTING same as ▷ vault

VAX, -ES n vaccination

VEAL, -ED, -ING, -S n calf meat ▷ vb rear (calves) for use as veal

VEALE, -S Spenserian word for ▷ veil

VEALED ▷ veal

VEALER, -S n young bovine animal of up to 14 months old grown for veal

VEALES ▷ veale

VEALIER ▷ vealy

VEALIEST ▷ vealy

VEALING ▷ veal

VEALS ▷ veal

VEALY, VEALIER, VEALIEST ▸ veal

VECTOR, -ED, -S n quantity that has size and direction, such as force ▸ vb direct or guide (a pilot) by directions transmitted by radio

VEDALIA, -S n Australian ladybird which is a pest of citrus fruits

VEDETTE, -S n small patrol vessel

VEDUTA, -S, VEDUTE n painting of a town or city

VEE, -S n letter 'v'

VEEJAY, -S n video jockey

VEENA, -S same as ▸ vina

VEEP, -S n vice president

VEEPEE, -S n vice president

VEEPS ▸ veep

VEER, -ED, -ING, -INGS, -S vb change direction suddenly ▸ n change of course or direction

VEERIES ▸ veery

VEERING ▸ veer

VEERINGS ▸ veer

VEERS ▸ veer

VEERY, VEERIES n tawny brown North American thrush

VEES ▸ vee

VEG, -ES, -GED, -GES, -GING n vegetable or vegetables ▸ vb relax

> **Veg** is a short form of **vegetable**. If someone plays this, remember that you can add an A or O to it to form **vega** or **vego**.

VEGA, -S n tobacco plantation

VEGAN, -S n person who eats no meat, fish, eggs, or dairy products ▸ adj suitable for a vegan

VEGANIC adj farmed without the use of animal products or byproducts

VEGANISM ▸ vegan

VEGANS ▸ vegan

VEGAS ▸ vega

VEGELATE n type of chocolate

VEGEMITE n informal Australian word for a child

VEGES ▸ veg

VEGETAL, -S adj of or relating to plant life ▸ n vegetable

VEGETANT adj causing growth

VEGETATE vb live a dull boring life with no mental stimulation

VEGETE adj lively

VEGETIST n vegetable cultivator or enthusiast

VEGETIVE adj dull or passive ▸ n vegetable

VEGGED ▸ veg

VEGGES ▸ veg

VEGGIE, -R, -S, -ST n vegetable ▸ adj vegetarian

VEGGING ▸ veg

VEGIE, -R, -S, -ST n vegetable ▸ adj vegetarian

VEGO, -S adj vegetarian ▸ n vegetarian

VEHEMENT adj expressing strong feelings

VEHICLE, -S n machine for carrying people or objects

VEHM, -E n type of medieval German court

VEHMIC ▸ vehm

VEHMIQUE ▸ vehm

VEIL, -S n piece of thin cloth covering the head or face ▸ vb cover with or as if with a veil

VEILED adj disguised

VEILEDLY ▸ veiled

VEILER, -S ▸ veil

VEILIER ▸ veily

VEILIEST ▸ veily

VEILING, -S n veil or the fabric used for veils

VEILLESS ▸ veil

VEILLIKE ▸ veil

VEILS ▸ veil

VEILY, VEILIER, VEILIEST ▸ veil

VEIN, -ED, -S n tube that takes blood to the heart ▸ vb diffuse over or cause to diffuse over in streaked patterns

VEINAL ▸ vein

VEINED ▸ vein

VEINER, -S n wood-carving tool

VEINIER ▸ veiny

VEINIEST ▸ veiny

VEINING, -S n pattern or network of veins or streaks

VEINLESS ▸ vein

VEINLET, -S n any small vein or venule

VEINLIKE ▸ vein

VEINOUS ▸ vein

VEINS ▸ vein

VEINULE, -S less common spelling of ▸ venule

VEINULET same as ▸ veinlet

VEINY, VEINIER, VEINIEST ▸ vein

VELA ▸ velum

VELAMEN, VELAMINA n thick layer of dead cells that covers the aerial roots of certain orchids

VELAR, -S adj of, relating to, or attached to a velum ▸ n velar sound

VELARIA ▸ velarium

VELARIC ▸ velar

VELARISE same as ▸ velarize

VELARIUM, VELARIA n awning used to protect the audience in ancient Roman theatres and amphitheatres

VELARIZE vb supplement the pronunciation of (a speech sound) with articulation at the soft palate

VELARS ▸ velar

VELATE adj having or covered with velum

VELATED same as ▸ velate

VELATURA n overglaze

VELCRO, -S n tradename for a fastening of two strips of nylon fabric pressed together

VELD, -S n high grassland in southern Africa

VELDT, -S same as ▸ veld

VELE, -S same as ▸ veil

VELETA, -S same as ▸ valeta

VELIGER, -S n free-swimming larva of many molluscs

VELITES pl n light-armed troops in ancient Rome, drawn from the poorer classes

VELL, -S n salted calf's stomach, used in cheese making

VELLEITY n weakest level of desire or volition

VELLET, -S n velvet

VELLON, -S n silver and copper alloy used in old Spanish coins

VELLS ▸ vell

VELLUM, -S n fine calfskin parchment ▸ adj made of or resembling vellum

VELLUS n as in **vellus hair** short fine unpigmented hair covering the human body

VELOCE adv to be played rapidly

VELOCITY n speed of movement in a given direction

VELOUR n fabric similar to velvet

VELOURS same as ▸ velour

VELOUTE, -S n rich white sauce or soup made from stock, egg yolks, and cream

VELSKOEN n leather ankle boot

V

VELUM, VELA n any of various membranous structures

VELURE, -S n velvet or a similar fabric ▷ vb cover with velure

VELURED ▶ velure

VELURES ▶ velure

VELURING ▶ velure

VELVERET n type of velvet-like fabric

VELVET, -ED, -S n fabric with a thick soft pile ▷ vb cover with velvet

VELVETY ▶ velvet

VENA, -E n vein in the body

VENAL adj easily bribed

VENALITY ▶ venal

VENALLY ▶ venal

VENATIC adj of, relating to, or used in hunting

VENATION n arrangement of the veins in a leaf or in the wing of an insect

VENATOR, -S n hunter

VEND, -ED, -S vb sell

VENDABLE ▶ vend

VENDACE, -S n either of two small whitefish occurring in lakes in Scotland and NW England

VENDAGE, -S n vintage

VENDANGE same as ▶ vendage

VENDED ▶ vend

VENDEE, -S n person to whom something, esp real property, is sold

VENDER, -S same as ▶ vendor

VENDETTA n long-lasting quarrel between people in which they attempt to harm each other

VENDEUSE n female salesperson

VENDIBLE adj saleable or marketable ▷ n saleable object

VENDIBLY ▶ vendible

VENDING, -S ▶ vend

VENDIS, -ES same as ▶ vendace

VENDISS same as ▶ vendace

V   **VENDOR, -S** n person who sells goods such as newspapers or hamburgers from a stall or cart

VENDS ▶ vend

VENDUE, -S n public sale

VENEER, -ED, -S n thin layer of wood etc covering a cheaper material ▷ vb cover (a surface) with a veneer

VENEERER ▶ veneer

VENEERS ▶ veneer

VENEFIC adj having poisonous effects

VENENATE vb poison

VENENE, -S n medicine from snake venom

VENENOSE adj poisonous

VENERATE vb hold (a person) in deep respect

VENEREAL adj of or involving the genitals

VENERER, -S n hunter

VENETIAN n Venetian blind

VENEWE, -S same as ▶ venue

VENEY, -S n thrust

VENGE, -D, -S, VENGING vb avenge

VENGEFUL adj wanting revenge

VENGER, -S ▶ venge

VENGES ▶ venge

VENGING ▶ venge

VENIAL adj (of a sin or fault) easily forgiven

VENIALLY ▶ venial

VENIDIUM n genus of flowering plants

VENIN, -S n any of the poisonous constituents of animal venoms

VENINE, -S same as ▶ venin

VENINS ▶ venin

VENIRE, -S n list from which jurors are selected

VENISON, -S n deer meat

VENITE, -S n musical setting for the 95th psalm

VENNEL, -S n lane

VENOGRAM n X-ray of a vein

VENOLOGY n study of veins

VENOM, -ED, -ING, -S n malice or spite ▷ vb poison

VENOMER, -S ▶ venom

VENOMING ▶ venom

VENOMOUS ▶ venom

VENOMS ▶ venom

VENOSE adj having veins

VENOSITY n excessive quantity of blood in the venous system or in an organ or part

VENOUS adj of veins

VENOUSLY ▶ venous

VENT, -ED, -ING, -INGS, -S n outlet releasing fumes or fluid ▷ vb express (an emotion) freely

VENTAGE, -S n small opening

VENTAIL, -S n (in medieval armour) a covering for the lower part of the face

VENTAILE same as ▶ ventail

VENTAILS ▶ ventail

VENTANA, -S n window

VENTAYLE same as ▶ ventail

VENTED ▶ vent

VENTER, -S ▶ vent

VENTIGE, -S same as ▶ ventage

VENTIL, -S n valve on a musical instrument

VENTING ▶ vent

VENTINGS ▶ vent

VENTLESS ▶ vent

VENTOSE, -S adj full of wind ▷ n apparatus sometimes used to assist the delivery of a baby

VENTOUSE n ventose

VENTRAL, -S adj relating to the front of the body ▷ n ventral fin

VENTRE, -S same as ▶ venture

VENTRED ▶ ventre

VENTRES ▶ ventre

VENTRING ▶ ventre

VENTROUS ▶ ventre

VENTS ▶ vent

VENTURE, -D, -S n risky undertaking, esp in business ▷ vb do something risky

VENTURER ▶ venture

VENTURES ▶ venture

VENTURI, -S n tube used to control the flow of fluid

VENUE, -S n place where an organized gathering is held

VENULAR ▶ venule

VENULE, -S n any of the small branches of a vein

VENULOSE ▶ venule

VENULOUS ▶ venule

VENUS, -ES n type of marine bivalve mollusc

VENVILLE n type of parish tenure

VERA adj as in aloe vera plant substance used in skin and hair preparations

VERACITY n truthfulness

VERANDA, -S n porch or portico along the outside of a building

VERANDAH same as ▶ veranda

VERANDAS ▶ veranda

VERATRIA same as > veratrine

VERATRIN same as > veratrine

VERATRUM n genus of herbs

VERB, -S n word that expresses the idea of action, happening, or being

VERBAL, -S adj spoken ▷ n abuse or invective ▷ vb implicate (someone) in a crime by quoting an alleged admission of guilt in court

VERBALLY ▶ verbal

VERBALS ▶ verbal

VERBATIM adj word for word ▷ adv using exactly the same words

VERBENA, -S n plant with sweet-smelling flowers

VERBIAGE n excessive use of words

VERBID, -S n any nonfinite form of a verb or any nonverbal word derived from a verb

VERBIFY another word for ▶ verbalize

VERBILE, -S n person who is best stimulated by words

VERBING, -S n use of nouns as verbs

VERBLESS ▶ verb

VERBOSE, -R adj speaking at tedious length

VERBOTEN adj forbidden

VERBS ▶ verb

VERD n as in verd antique dark green mottled impure variety of serpentine marble

VERDANCY ▶ verdant

VERDANT adj covered in green vegetation

VERDELHO n type of grape

VERDERER n officer responsible for the maintenance of law and order in the royal forests

VERDEROR same as ▶ verderer

VERDET, -S n type of verdigris

VERDICT, -S n decision of a jury

VERDIN, -S n small W North American tit having grey plumage with a yellow head

VERDIT, -S same as ▶ verdict

VERDITE, -S n type of rock used in jewellery

VERDITER n blue-green pigment made from copper

VERDITES ▶ verdite

VERDITS ▶ verdit

VERDOY, -S n floral or leafy shield decoration

VERDURE, -S n flourishing green vegetation

VERDURED ▶ verdure

VERDURES ▶ verdure

VERECUND adj shy or modest

VERGE, -D, -S, VERGING n grass border along a road ▷ vb move in a specified direction

VERGENCE n inward or outward turning movement

of the eyes in convergence or divergence

VERGENCY adj inclination

VERGER, -S n church caretaker

VERGES ▶ verge

VERGING ▶ verge

VERGLAS n thin film of ice on rock

VERIDIC same as ▶ veridical

VERIER ▶ very

VERIEST ▶ very

VERIFIED ▶ verify

VERIFIER ▶ verify

VERIFY, VERIFIED, VERIFIES vb check the truth or accuracy of

VERILY adv in truth

VERISM, -S n extreme naturalism in art or literature

VERISMO, -S n school of composition that originated in Italian opera

VERISMS ▶ verism

VERIST, -S ▶ verism

VERISTIC ▶ verism

VERISTS ▶ verist

VERITAS n truth

VERITE, -S adj involving a high degree of realism or naturalism ▷ n this kind of realism in film

VERITY, VERITIES n true statement or principle

VERJUICE n acid juice of unripe grapes, apples, or crab apples ▷ vb make sour

VERJUS, -ES n acid juice of unripe grapes, apples, or crab apples

VERKRAMP adj bigoted or illiberal

VERLAN, -S n variety of French slang in which the syllables are inverted

VERLIG adj enlightened

VERLIGTE n (during apartheid) a White political liberal

VERMAL ▶ vermis

VERMEIL, -S n gilded silver, bronze, or other metal, used esp in the 19th century ▷ vb decorate with vermeil ▷ adj vermilion

VERMELL, -S same as ▶ vermeil

VERMES ▶ vermis

VERMIAN ▶ vermis

VERMIL, -S same as ▶ vermeil

VERMILY ▶ vermeil

VERMIN, -S n small animals collectively that are

troublesome to humans or domestic animals

VERMINED adj plagued with vermin

VERMINS ▶ vermin

VERMINY adj full of vermin

VERMIS, VERMES n middle lobe connecting the two halves of the cerebellum

VERMOULU adj worm-eaten

VERMOUTH n wine flavoured with herbs

VERMUTH, -S same as ▶ vermouth

VERNACLE same as ▶ vernicle

VERNAL adj occurring in spring

VERNALLY ▶ vernal

VERNANT ▶ vernal

VERNICLE n veronica

VERNIER, -S n movable scale on a measuring instrument for taking readings in fractions

VERNIX, -ES n white substance covering the skin of a foetus

VERONAL, -S n long-acting barbiturate used medicinally

VERONICA n plant with small blue, pink, or white flowers

VERQUERE n type of backgammon game

VERQUIRE variant of ▶ verquere

VERRA Scot word for ▶ very

VERREL, -S n ferrule

VERREY same as ▶ vair

VERRINE, -S n starter, dessert, or other dish served in a glass

VERRUCA, -E, -S n wart, usu on the foot

VERRUGA, -S same as ▶ verruca

VERRY same as ▶ vair

VERS n verse

VERSAL, -S n embellished letter

VERSANT, -S n side or slope of a mountain or mountain range

VERSE, -S n group of lines forming part of a song or poem ▷ vb write verse

VERSED adj thoroughly knowledgeable (about)

VERSELET n small verse

VERSEMAN, VERSEMEN n man who writes verse

VERSER, -S n versifier

VERSES ▶ verse

VERSET, -S n short, often sacred, verse
VERSICLE n short verse
VERSIFY vb write in verse
VERSIN, -S same as ▸ **versine**
VERSINE, -S n trigonometric function
VERSING, -S ▸ **verse**
VERSINS ▸ **versin**
VERSION, -S n form of something, with some differences from other forms ▸ vb keep track of the changes made to a computer file at different stages
VERSO, -S n left-hand page of a book
VERST, -S n unit of length used in Russia
VERSTE, -S same as ▸ **verst**
VERSTS ▸ **verst**
VERSUS prep in opposition to or in contrast with
VERSUTE adj cunning
VERT, -ED, -ING, -S n right to cut green wood in a forest ▸ vb turn
VERTEBRA n one of the bones that form the spine
VERTED ▸ **vert**
VERTEX, -ES, VERTICES n point on a geometric figure where the sides form an angle
VERTICAL adj straight up and down ▸ n vertical direction
VERTICES ▸ **vertex**
VERTICIL n circular arrangement of parts about an axis, esp leaves around a stem
VERTIGO, -S n dizziness, usu when looking down from a high place
VERTING ▸ **vert**
VERTISOL n type of clayey soil
VERTS ▸ **vert**
VERTU, -S same as ▸ **virtu**
VERTUE, -S same as ▸ **virtu**
VERTUOUS ▸ **vertu**
VERTUS ▸ **vertu**
VERVAIN, -S n plant with spikes of blue, purple, or white flowers
VERVE, -S n enthusiasm or liveliness
VERVEL, -S same as ▸ **varvel**
VERVEN, -S same as ▸ **vervain**
VERVES ▸ **verve**
VERVET, -S n variety of South African guenon monkey

VERY, VERIER, VERIEST adv more than usually, extremely ▸ adj absolute, exact
VESICA, -E, -S n bladder
VESICAL adj of or relating to a vesica, esp the urinary bladder
VESICANT n any substance that causes blisters ▸ adj acting as a vesicant
VESICAS ▸ **vesica**
VESICATE vb blister
VESICLE, -S n sac or small cavity
VESICULA n vesicle
VESPA, -S n type of wasp
VESPER n evening prayer, service, or hymn
VESPERAL n liturgical book containing the prayers, psalms, and hymns used at vespers
VESPERS pl n service of evening prayer
VESPIARY n nest or colony of social wasps or hornets
VESPID, -S n insect of the family that includes the common wasp and hornet ▸ adj of or belonging to this family
VESPINE adj of, relating to, or resembling a wasp or wasps
VESPOID adj like a wasp
VESSAIL, -S archaic variant of ▸ **vessel**
VESSEL, -ED, -S n container or ship ▸ adj contained in a vessel
VEST, -S n undergarment worn on the top half of the body ▸ vb give (authority) to (someone)
VESTA, -S n short friction match, usually of wood
VESTAL, -S adj pure, chaste ▸ n chaste woman
VESTALLY ▸ **vestal**
VESTALS ▸ **vestal**
VESTAS ▸ **vesta**
VESTED adj having an existing right to the immediate or future possession of property
VESTEE, -S n person having a vested interest in something
VESTIARY n room for storing clothes or dressing in, such as a vestry ▸ adj of or relating to clothes
VESTIGE, -S n small amount or trace
VESTIGIA > **vestigium**

VESTING, -S ▸ **vest**
VESTLESS ▸ **vest**
VESTLIKE ▸ **vest**
VESTMENT n garment or robe, esp one denoting office, authority, or rank
VESTRAL ▸ **vestry**
VESTRY, VESTRIES n room in a church used as an office by the priest or minister
VESTS ▸ **vest**
VESTURAL ▸ **vesture**
VESTURE, -D, -S n garment or something that seems like a garment ▸ vb clothe
VESTURER n person in charge of church vestments
VESTURES ▸ **vesture**
VESUVIAN n match for lighting cigars
VET, -S, -TED vb check the suitability of ▸ n military veteran
VETCH, -ES n climbing plant with a beanlike fruit used as fodder
VETCHY, VETCHIER adj consisting of vetches
VETERAN, -S n person with long experience in a particular activity ▸ adj long-serving
VETIVER, -S n tall hairless grass of tropical and subtropical Asia
VETIVERT n oil from the vetiver
VETKOEK, -S n South African cake
VETO, -ED, -ES, -ING n official power to cancel a proposal ▸ vb enforce a veto against
VETOER, -S ▸ **veto**
VETOES ▸ **veto**
VETOING ▸ **veto**
VETOLESS ▸ **veto**
VETS ▸ **vet**
VETTED ▸ **vet**
VETTER, -S ▸ **vet**
VETTING, -S n act of checking the suitability of someone or something
VETTURA, -S n Italian mode of transport
VEX, -ES vb frustrate, annoy
VEXATION n something annoying
VEXATORY ▸ **vex**
VEXED adj annoyed and puzzled
VEXEDLY ▸ **vexed**
VEXER, -S ▸ **vex**
VEXES ▸ **vex**
VEXIL, -S same as ▸ **vexillum**
VEXILLA ▸ **vexillum**

VEXILLAR ▶ vexillum

VEXILLUM, VEXILLA n vane of a feather

VEXILS ▶ vexil

VEXING, -S ▶ vex

VEXINGLY ▶ vex

VEXINGS ▶ vexing

VEXT same as ▶ **vexed**

VEZIR, -S same as ▶ **vizier**

VIA, -E, -S prep by way of ▷ n road

VIABLE adj able to be put into practice

VIABLY ▶ viable

VIADUCT, -S n bridge over a valley

VIAE ▶ via

VIAL, -ED, -ING, -LED, -LING, -S n small bottle for liquids ▷ vb put into a vial

VIALFUL, -S ▶ vial

VIALING ▶ vial

VIALLED ▶ vial

VIALLING ▶ vial

VIALS ▶ vial

VIAMETER n device to measure distance travelled

VIAND, -S n type of food, esp a delicacy

VIAS ▶ via

VIATIC same as ▶ **viatical**

VIATICA ▶ viaticum

VIATICAL adj of a road or a journey ▷ n purchase of a terminal patient's life assurance policy so that he or she may make use of the proceeds

VIATICUM, VIATICA n Holy Communion given to a person who is dying or in danger of death

VIATOR, -ES, -S n traveller

VIBE n feeling or flavour of the kind described

VIBES pl n vibrations

VIBEX, VIBICES n mark under the skin

VIBEY, VIBIER, VIBIEST adj lively and vibrant

VIBICES ▶ vibex

VIBIER ▶ vibey

VIBIEST ▶ vibey

VIBIST, -S n person who plays a vibraphone in a jazz band or group

VIBRANCE n vibrancy

VIBRANCY ▶ vibrant

VIBRANT, -S adj vigorous in appearance, energetic ▷ n trilled or rolled speech sound

VIBRATE, -D, -S vb move back and forth rapidly

VIBRATO, -S n rapid fluctuation in the pitch of a note

VIBRATOR n device that produces vibratory motion

VIBRATOS ▶ vibrato

VIBRIO, -S n curved or spiral rodlike bacterium

VIBRIOID ▶ vibrio

VIBRION, -S same as ▶ **vibrio**

VIBRIOS ▶ vibrio

VIBRISSA n any of the bristle-like sensitive hairs on the face of many mammals

VIBRONIC adj of, concerned with, or involving both electronic and vibrational energy levels of a molecule

VIBS pl n type of climbing shoes

VIBURNUM n subtropical shrub with white flowers and berry-like fruits

VICAR, -S n member of the clergy in charge of a parish

VICARAGE n vicar's house

VICARATE same as > **vicariate**

VICARESS n rank of nun

VICARIAL adj of or relating to a vicar, vicars, or a vicariate

VICARIES ▶ vicary

VICARLY adj like a vicar

VICARS ▶ vicar

VICARY, VICARIES n office of a vicar

VICE, -D, -S, VICING n immoral or evil habit or action ▷ adj serving in place of ▷ vb grip (something) with or as if with a vice ▷ prep instead of

VICELESS ▶ vice

VICELIKE ▶ vice

VICENARY adj relating to or consisting of 20

VICEROY, -S n governor of a colony who represented the monarch

VICES ▶ vice

VICHY, VICHIES n French mineral water

VICIATE, -S same as ▶ **vitiate**

VICIATED ▶ viciate

VICIATES ▶ viciate

VICINAGE n residents of a particular neighbourhood

VICINAL adj neighbouring

VICING ▶ vice

VICINITY n surrounding area

VICIOUS adj cruel and violent

VICOMTE, -S n French nobleman

VICTIM, -S n person or thing harmed or killed

VICTOR, -S n person who has defeated an opponent, esp in war or in sport

VICTORIA n large sweet plum, red and yellow in colour

VICTORS ▶ victor

VICTORY n winning of a battle or contest

VICTRESS n female victor

VICTRIX same as ▶ **victress**

VICTROLA n gramophone

VICTUAL vb supply with or obtain victuals

VICTUALS pl n food and drink

VICUGNA, -S same as ▶ **vicuna**

VICUNA, -S n S American animal like the llama

VID, -S same as ▶ **video**

VIDALIA, -S n type of sweet onion

VIDAME, -S n French nobleman

VIDE interj look

VIDENDUM, VIDENDA n that which is to be seen

VIDEO, -ED, -ING, -S vb record (a TV programme or event) on video ▷ adj relating to or used in producing television images ▷ n recording and showing of films and events

VIDEOCAM n camera for recording video footage

VIDEOED ▶ video

VIDEOFIT n computer-generated picture of a person sought by the police

VIDEOING ▶ video

VIDEOS ▶ video

VIDEOTEX n information system that displays data from a distant computer on a screen

VIDETTE, -S same as ▶ **vedette**

VIDICON, -S n small television camera tube used in closed-circuit television

VIDIMUS n inspection

VIDIOT, -S n person who watches a lot of low-quality television

VIDS ▶ vid

VIDUAGE, -S n widows collectively

VIDUAL adj widowed

VIDUITY n widowhood

VIDUOUS adj empty

VIE, -D, -S vb compete (with someone)

VIELLE, -S n stringed musical instrument

VIENNA n as in **vienna loaf**, **vienna steak** associated with Vienna

VIER, -S ▶ vie

VIES ▶ vie

VIEW, -ED, -S n opinion or belief ▷ vb think of (something) in a particular way

VIEWABLE ▶ view

VIEWBOOK n promotional booklet for a college or university

VIEWDATA n interactive form of videotext

VIEWED ▶ view

VIEWER, -S n person who watches television

VIEWIER ▶ viewy

VIEWIEST ▶ viewy

VIEWING, -S n act of watching television

VIEWLESS adj (of windows, etc) not affording a view

VIEWLY adj pleasant on the eye

VIEWPORT n viewable area on a computer display

VIEWS ▶ view

VIEWSHED n natural environment visible from a specific point

VIEWY, VIEWIER, VIEWIEST adj having fanciful opinions or ideas

VIFDA, -S same as ▶ vivda

VIFF, -ED, -ING, -S vb (of an aircraft) change direction abruptly

VIG, -S n interest on a loan that is paid to a moneylender

VIGA, -S n rafter

VIGIA, -S n navigational hazard whose existence has not been confirmed

VIGIL, -S n night-time period of staying awake to look after a sick person, pray, etc

VIGILANT adj watchful in case of danger

VIGILS ▶ vigil

VIGNERON n person who grows grapes for winemaking

VIGNETTE n small illustration placed at the beginning or end of a chapter or book ▷ vb portray in a vignette

VIGOR, -S same as ▶ vigour

VIGORISH n type of commission

VIGORO, -S n women's game similar to cricket

VIGOROSO adv in music, emphatically

VIGOROUS adj having physical or mental energy

VIGORS ▶ vigor

VIGOUR, -S n physical or mental energy

VIGS ▶ vig

VIHARA, -S n type of Buddhist temple

VIHUELA, -S n obsolete plucked stringed instrument of Spain

VIKING, -S n Dane, Norwegian, or Swede who raided by sea between the 8th and 11th centuries

VILAYET, -S n major administrative division of Turkey

VILD same as ▶ vile

VILDE same as ▶ vile

VILDLY ▶ vild

VILDNESS ▶ vild

VILE, -R, -ST adj very wicked

VILELY ▶ vile

VILENESS ▶ vile

VILER ▶ vile

VILEST ▶ vile

VILIACO, -S n coward

VILIAGO, -S same as ▶ viliaco

VILIFIED ▶ vilify

VILIFIER ▶ vilify

VILIFY, VILIFIED, VILIFIES vb attack the character of

VILIPEND vb treat or regard with contempt

VILL, -S n township

VILLA, -E, -S n large house with gardens

VILLADOM ▶ villa

VILLAE ▶ villa

VILLAGE, -S n small group of houses in a country area

VILLAGER n inhabitant of a village

VILLAGES ▶ village

VILLAGEY adj of or like a village

VILLAGIO same as ▶ viliaco

VILLAIN, -S n wicked person

VILLAINY n evil or vicious behaviour

VILLAN, -S same as ▶ villein

VILLANY same as ▶ villainy

VILLAR ▶ vill

VILLAS ▶ villa

VILLATIC adj of or relating to a villa, village, or farm

VILLEIN, -S n peasant bound in service to their lord

VILLI ▶ villus

VILLIACO n coward

VILLIAGO same as ▶ viliaco

VILLOSE same as ▶ villous

VILLOUS adj (of plant parts) covered with long hairs

VILLS ▶ vill

VILLUS, VILLI n one of the finger-like projections in the small intestine of many vertebrates

VIM, -S n force, energy

This word can be helpful when you're stuck with unpromising letters, and gives a reasonable score for a three-letter word.

VIMANA, -S n Indian mythological chariot of the gods

VIMEN, VIMINA n long flexible shoot that occurs in certain plants

VIMINAL ▶ vimen

VIMS ▶ vim

VIN, -S n French wine

VINA, -S n stringed musical instrument related to the sitar

VINAL, -S n type of manmade fibre

VINAS ▶ vina

VINASSE, -S n residue left in a still after distilling spirits, esp brandy

VINCA, -S n type of trailing plant with blue flowers

VINCIBLE adj capable of being defeated or overcome

VINCIBLY ▶ vincible

VINCULA ▶ vinculum

VINCULAR adj of or like a vinculum

VINCULUM, VINCULA n horizontal line drawn above a group of mathematical terms

VINDALOO n type of very hot Indian curry

VINE, -S n climbing plant, esp one producing grapes ▷ vb form like a vine

VINEAL adj relating to wines

VINED ▶ vine

VINEGAR, -S n acid liquid made from wine, beer, or cider ▷ vb apply vinegar to

VINEGARY adj containing vinegar

VINELESS ▶ vine

VINELIKE ▶ vine

VINER, -S n vinedresser

VINERIES ▶ vinery

VINERS ▶ viner

VINERY, VINERIES n hothouse for growing grapes

VINES ▶ vine

VINEW, -ED, -ING, -S vb become mouldy

VINEYARD n plantation of grape vines

VINIC adj of, relating to, or contained in wine

VINIER ▶ viny

VINIEST ▶ viny

VINIFERA n species of vine

VINIFY, VINIFIED, VINIFIES vb convert into wine

VINING ▶ vine

VINO, -S n wine

VINOLENT adj drunken

VINOLOGY n scientific study of vines

VINOS ▶ vino

VINOSITY n distinctive and essential quality and flavour of wine

VINOUS adj of or characteristic of wine

VINOUSLY ▶ vinous

VINS ▶ vin

VINT, -ED, -ING, -S vb sell (wine)

VINTAGE, -D, -S n wine from a particular harvest of grapes ▷ adj best and most typical ▷ vb gather (grapes) or make (wine)

VINTAGER n grape harvester

VINTAGES ▶ vintage

VINTED ▶ vint

VINTING ▶ vint

VINTNER, -S n dealer in wine

VINTRY, VINTRIES n place where wine is sold

VINTS ▶ vint

VINY, VINIER, VINIEST ▶ vine

VINYL, -S n type of plastic, used in mock leather and records ▷ adj of or containing a particular group of atoms

VINYLIC ▶ vinyl

VINYLS ▶ vinyl

VIOL, -S n early stringed instrument preceding the violin

VIOLA, -S n stringed instrument lower in pitch than a violin

VIOLABLE ▶ violate

VIOLABLY ▶ violate

VIOLAS ▶ viola

VIOLATE, -D, -S vb break (a law or agreement) ▷ adj violated or dishonoured

VIOLATER ▶ violate

VIOLATES ▶ violate

VIOLATOR ▶ violate

VIOLD archaic or poetic past form of ▶ vial

VIOLENCE n use of physical force, usu intended to cause injury or destruction

VIOLENT, -S adj using physical force with the intention of causing injury ▷ vb coerce

VIOLER, -S n person who plays the viol

VIOLET, -S n plant with bluish-purple flowers ▷ adj bluish-purple

VIOLIN, -S n small four-stringed musical instrument played with a bow

VIOLIST, -S n person who plays the viola

VIOLONE, -S n double-bass member of the viol family

VIOLS ▶ viol

VIOMYCIN n type of antibiotic

VIPER, -S n poisonous snake

VIPERINE same as ▶ viperous

VIPERISH same as ▶ viperous

VIPEROUS adj of, relating to, or resembling a viper

VIPERS ▶ viper

VIRAEMIA n condition in which virus particles circulate and reproduce in the bloodstream

VIRAEMIC ▶ viraemia

VIRAGO, -ES, -S n aggressive woman

VIRAL, -S adj of or caused by a virus ▷ n video, image, etc that spreads quickly on the internet

VIRALITY n the state of being viral

VIRALLY ▶ viral

VIRALS ▶ viral

VIRANDA, -S same as ▶ veranda

VIRANDO, -S same as ▶ veranda

VIRE, -D, -S, VIRING vb turn

VIRELAI, -S same as ▶ virelay

VIRELAY, -S n old French verse form

VIREMENT n administrative transfer of funds from one part of a budget to another

VIREMIA, -S same as ▶ viraemia

VIREMIC ▶ viremia

VIRENT adj green

VIREO, -S n American songbird

VIRES ▶ vire

VIRETOT, -S n as in on the viretot in a rush

VIRGA, -E, -S n wisps of rain or snow that evaporate before reaching the earth

VIRGATE, -S adj long, straight, and thin ▷ n obsolete measure of land area

VIRGE, -S n rod

VIRGER, -S n rod-bearer

VIRGES ▶ virge

VIRGIN, -S n person who has not had sexual intercourse ▷ adj chaste ▷ vb behave like a virgin

VIRGINAL adj like a virgin ▷ n early keyboard instrument like a small harpsichord

VIRGINED ▶ virgin

VIRGINIA n type of flue-cured tobacco grown originally in Virginia

VIRGINLY ▶ virgin

VIRGINS ▶ virgin

VIRGULE, -S another name for ▶ slash

VIRICIDE n substance that destroys viruses

VIRID adj verdant

VIRIDIAN n green pigment consisting of a hydrated form of chromic oxide

VIRIDITE n greenish mineral

VIRIDITY n quality or state of being green

VIRILE adj having traditional male characteristics

VIRILELY ▶ virile

VIRILISE same as ▶ virilize

VIRILITY ▶ virile

VIRILIZE vb cause male characteristics to appear in a female

VIRING ▶ vire

VIRINO, -S n entity postulated to be the causative agent of BSE

VIRION, -S n virus in infective form, consisting of an RNA particle within a protein covering

VIRL, -S same as ▶ ferrule

VIROGENE n type of viral gene

VIROID, -S n any of various infective RNA particles

VIROLOGY n study of viruses

VIROSE adj poisonous

VIROSIS, VIROSES n viral disease

VIROUS same as ▶ virose

VIRTU, -S n taste or love for curios or works of fine art

VIRTUAL adj having the effect but not the form of

VIRTUE, -S n moral goodness

VIRTUOSA, VIRTUOSE n female virtuoso

V

VIRTUOSO, VIRTUOSI *n* person with impressive esp musical skill ▷ *adj* showing exceptional skill or brilliance

VIRTUOUS *adj* morally good

VIRTUS ▶ **virtu**

VIRUCIDE *same as* ▶ **viricide**

VIRULENT *adj* extremely bitter or hostile

VIRUS, -ES *n* microorganism that causes disease in humans, animals, and plants

VIRUSOID *n* small plant virus

VIS *n* power, force, or strength

VISA, -ED, -ING, -S *n* permission to enter a country, shown by a stamp on the passport ▷ *vb* enter a visa into (a passport)

VISAGE, -S *n* face

VISAGED ▶ **visage**

VISAGES ▶ **visage**

VISAGIST *same as* > **visagiste**

VISAING ▶ **visa**

VISARD, -S *same as* ▶ **vizard**

VISAS ▶ **visa**

VISCACHA *n* South American rodent

VISCARIA *n* type of perennial plant

VISCERA *pl n* large abdominal organs

VISCERAL *adj* instinctive

VISCID *adj* sticky

VISCIDLY ▶ **viscid**

VISCIN, -S *n* sticky substance found on plants

VISCOID *adj* (of a fluid) somewhat viscous

VISCOSE, -S *same as* ▶ **viscous**

VISCOUNT *n* British nobleman ranking between an earl and a baron

VISCOUS *adj* thick and sticky

VISCUM, -S *n* shrub genus

VISCUS *n* internal organ

VISE, -D, -ING, -S, VISING *n* (in US English) vice ▷ *vb* (in US English) hold in a vice ▷ *vb* award a visa to

VISEED ▶ **vise**

VISEING ▶ **vise**

VISELIKE ▶ **vice**

VISES ▶ **vise**

VISHING, -S *n* telephone scam used to gain access to credit card numbers or bank details

VISIBLE, -S *adj* able to be seen ▷ *n* visible item of trade

VISIBLY ▶ **visible**

VISIE, -D, -ING, -S *same as* ▶ **vizy**

VISIER, -S ▶ **visie**

VISIES ▶ **visie**

VISILE, -S *n* person best stimulated by vision

VISING ▶ **vise**

VISION, -ED, -S *n* ability to see ▷ *vb* see or show in or as if in a vision

VISIONAL *adj* of, relating to, or seen in a vision, apparition, etc

VISIONED ▶ **vision**

VISIONER *n* visionary

VISIONS ▶ **vision**

VISIT, -ED, -ING, -S *vb* go or come to see ▷ *n* instance of visiting

VISITANT *n* ghost or apparition ▷ *adj* paying a visit

VISITE, -S *n* type of cape

VISITED ▶ **visit**

VISITEE, -S *n* person who is visited

VISITER, -S *variant of* ▶ **visitor**

VISITES ▶ **visite**

VISITING ▶ **visit**

VISITOR, -S *n* person who visits a particular place

VISITS ▶ **visit**

VISIVE *adj* visual

VISNE, -S *n* neighbourhood

VISNOMIE *same as* ▶ **visnomy**

VISNOMY *n* method of judging character from facial features

VISON, -S *n* type of mink

VISOR, -ED, -ING, -S *n* transparent part of a helmet that pulls down over the face ▷ *vb* cover, provide, or protect with a visor

VISTA, -ING, -S *n* (beautiful) extensive view ▷ *vb* make into vistas

VISTAED ▶ **vista**

VISTAING ▶ **vista**

VISTAL ▶ **vista**

VISTAS ▶ **vista**

VISTO, -S *same as* ▶ **vista**

VISUAL, -S *adj* done by or used in seeing ▷ *n* sketch to show the proposed layout of an advertisement

VISUALLY ▶ **visual**

VISUALS ▶ **visual**

VITA, -E, -S *n* curriculum vitae

VITAL *adj* essential or highly important

VITALISE *same as* ▶ **vitalize**

VITALISM *n* philosophical doctrine that the phenomena of life cannot be explained in purely mechanical terms

VITALIST ▶ **vitalism**

VITALITY *n* physical or mental energy

VITALIZE *vb* fill with life or vitality

VITALLY ▶ **vital**

VITALS *pl n* bodily organs that are necessary to maintain life

VITAMER, -S *n* type of chemical

VITAMIN, -S *n* one of a group of substances that are essential in the diet

VITAMINE *same as* ▶ **vitamin**

VITAMINS ▶ **vitamin**

VITAS ▶ **vita**

VITATIVE *adj* fond of life

VITE *adv* musical direction

VITELLI ▶ **vitellus**

VITELLIN *n* phosphoprotein that is the major protein in egg yolk

VITELLUS, VITELLI *n* yolk of an egg

VITESSE, -S *n* speed

VITEX, -ES *n* type of herb

VITIABLE ▶ **vitiate**

VITIATE, -D, -S *vb* spoil the effectiveness of

VITIATOR ▶ **vitiate**

VITICETA > **viticetum**

VITICIDE *n* vine killer

VITILIGO *n* area of skin that is white from albinism or loss of melanin pigmentation

VITIOUS *adj* mistaken

VITRAGE, -S *n* light fabric

VITRAIL, VITRAUX *n* stained glass

VITRAIN, -S *n* type of coal

VITRAUX ▶ **vitrail**

VITREOUS *adj* like or made from glass

VITREUM, -S *n* vitreous body

VITRIC *adj* of, relating to, resembling, or having the nature of glass

VITRICS *pl n* glass products

VITRIFY *vb* change or be changed into glass or a glassy substance

VITRINE, -S *n* glass display case or cabinet for works of art, curios, etc

VITRIOL, -S *n* language expressing bitterness and hatred ▷ *vb* injure with or as if with vitriol (sulphuric acid)

VITRO n as in **in vitro** (of processes) made to occur in an artificial environment

VITTA, -E n tubelike cavity containing oil that occurs in the fruits of certain plants

VITTATE ▸ vitta

VITTLE, -D, VITTLING obsolete or dialect spelling of ▸ victual

VITTLES obsolete or dialect spelling of ▸ victuals

VITTLING ▸ vittle

VITULAR same as ▸ vituline

VITULINE adj of or resembling a calf or veal

VIVA, -ED, -ING, -S interj long live (a person or thing) ▷ n examination in the form of an interview ▷ vb examine (a candidate) in a spoken interview

VIVACE, -S adv in a lively manner ▷ n piece of music to be performed in this way

VIVACITY n quality of being vivacious

VIVAED ▸ viva

VIVAING ▸ viva

VIVARIA ▸ vivarium

VIVARIES ▸ vivary

VIVARIUM, VIVARIA n place where animals are kept in natural conditions

VIVARY, VIVARIES same as ▸ vivarium

VIVAS ▸ viva

VIVAT, -S interj long live ▷ n expression of acclamation

VIVDA, -S n method of drying meat

VIVE interj long live

VIVELY adv in a lively manner

VIVENCY n physical or mental energy

VIVER, -S n fish pond

VIVERRA, -S n civet genus

VIVERRID > viverrine

VIVERS ▸ viver

VIVES n disease found in horses

VIVID, -ER, -EST adj very bright

VIVIDITY ▸ vivid

VIVIDLY ▸ vivid

VIVIFIC adj giving life

VIVIFIED ▸ vivify

VIVIFIER ▸ vivify

VIVIFY, VIVIFIED, VIVIFIES vb animate, inspire

VIVIPARA pl n animals that produce offspring that develop as embryos within the female parent

VIVIPARY n act of giving birth producing offspring that have developed as embryos

VIVISECT vb practise vivisection

VIVO adv with life and vigour

VIVRES pl n provisions

VIXEN, -S n female fox

VIXENISH ▸ vixen

VIXENLY ▸ vixen

VIXENS ▸ vixen

VIZAMENT n consultation

VIZARD, -ED, -S n means of disguise ▷ vb conceal by means of a disguise

VIZCACHA same as ▸ viscacha

VIZIED ▸ vizy

VIZIER, -S n high official in certain Muslim countries

VIZIES ▸ vizy

VIZIR, -S same as ▸ vizier

VIZIRATE ▸ vizir

VIZIRIAL ▸ vizir

VIZIRS ▸ vizir

VIZOR, -ING, -S same as ▸ visor

VIZORED ▸ vizor

VIZORING ▸ vizor

VIZORS ▸ vizor

VIZSLA, -S n breed of Hungarian hunting dog

VIZY, VIZIED, VIZIES, -ING vb look

VIZZIE, -D, -S same as ▸ vizy

VLEI, -S n area of low marshy ground

VLIES ▸ vly

VLOG, -GED, -S n video blog ▷ vb make and upload a vlog

VLOGGER, -S n person who keeps a video blog

VLOGGING n action of keeping a video blog

VLOGS ▸ vlog

VLY, VLIES same as ▸ vlei

> This word for low-lying wet ground can be useful when you are short of vowels. It can also be spelt **vlei**.

VOAR, -S n spring

VOCAB, -S n vocabulary

VOCABLE, -S n word regarded as a sequence of letters or sounds ▷ adj capable of being uttered

VOCABLY ▸ vocable

VOCABS ▸ vocab

VOCAL, -S adj relating to the voice ▷ n piece of jazz or pop music that is sung

VOCALESE n style of jazz singing

VOCALIC adj of, relating to, or containing a vowel or vowels

VOCALICS n non-verbal aspects of voice

VOCALION n type of musical instrument

VOCALISE same as ▸ vocalize

VOCALISM n exercise of the voice, as in singing or speaking

VOCALIST n singer

VOCALITY ▸ vocal

VOCALIZE vb express with the voice

VOCALLY ▸ vocal

VOCALS ▸ vocal

VOCATION n profession or trade

VOCATIVE n (in some languages) case of nouns used when addressing a person ▷ adj relating to, used in, or characterized by calling

VOCES ▸ vox

VOCODER, -S n type of synthesizer that uses the human voice as an oscillator

VOCULAR ▸ vocule

VOCULE, -S n faint noise made when articulating certain sounds

VODCAST, -S vb podcast with video

VODDY, VODDIES n informal word for vodka

VODKA, -S n (Russian) spirit distilled from potatoes or grain

VODOU, -S variant of ▸ voodoo

> This word for a kind of black magic may indeed work magic on an unpromising rack. And it has a host of variants, though few people will remember them all: **vaudoo, vaudoux, vodoun, vodun, voudon, voudou** and **voudoun**!

VODOUN, -S same as ▸ vodun

VODOUS ▸ vodou

VODUN, -S n voodoo

VOE, -S n (in Orkney and Shetland) a small bay or narrow creek

VOEMA, -S n vigour or energy

VOES ▸ voe

VOG, -S n air pollution caused by volcanic dust

VOGIE, -R, -ST adj conceited

VOGS ▸ vog

VOGUE, -S, VOGUIER, VOGUIEST n popular style

V

▷ adj popular or fashionable ▷ vb bring into vogue

VOGUED ▸ vogue

VOGUEING n dance style of the late 1980s

VOGUER, -S ▸ vogue

VOGUES ▸ vogue

VOGUEY ▸ vogue

VOGUIER ▸ vogue

VOGUIEST ▸ vogue

VOGUING, -S same as ▸ vogueing

VOGUISH ▸ vogue

VOICE, -S n (quality of) sound made when speaking or singing ▷ vb express verbally

VOICED adj articulated with accompanying vibration of the vocal cords

VOICEFUL ▸ voice

VOICER, -S ▸ voice

VOICES ▸ voice

VOICING, -S ▸ voice

VOID, -ING, -INGS, -S adj not legally binding ▷ n feeling of deprivation ▷ vb make invalid

VOIDABLE adj capable of being voided

VOIDANCE n annulment, as of a contract

VOIDED adj (of a design) with a hole in the centre of the same shape as the design

VOIDEE, -S n light meal eaten before bed

VOIDER, -S ▸ void

VOIDING ▸ void

VOIDINGS ▸ void

VOIDNESS ▸ void

VOILA interj word used to express satisfaction

VOILE, -S n light semitransparent fabric

VOIP, -S n voice over internet protocol

VOITURE, -S n type of vehicle

VOIVODE, -S n Slavic governor

VOL, -S n heraldic wings

VOLA, -E n palm of hand or sole of foot

VOLABLE adj quick-witted

VOLAE ▸ vola

VOLAGE adj changeable

VOLANT adj in a flying position

VOLANTE, -S n Spanish horse carriage

VOLAR adj of or relating to the palm of the hand or the sole of the foot

VOLARY, VOLARIES n large bird enclosure

VOLATIC, -S adj flying ▷ n creature with wings

VOLATILE adj liable to sudden change, esp in behaviour ▷ n volatile substance

VOLCANIC adj of or relating to volcanoes

VOLCANO, -S n mountain with a vent through which lava is ejected

VOLE, -S n small rodent ▷ vb win by taking all the tricks in a deal

VOLED ▸ vole

VOLELIKE adj like a vole

VOLENS adj as in nolens volens whether willing or unwilling

VOLERY, VOLERIES same as ▸ volary

VOLES ▸ vole

VOLET, -S n type of veil

VOLING ▸ vole

VOLITANT adj flying or moving about rapidly

VOLITATE vb flutter

VOLITION n ability to decide things for oneself

VOLITIVE adj of, relating to, or emanating from the will ▷ n (in some languages) a verb form or mood used to express a wish or desire

VOLK, -S n people or nation, esp the nation of Afrikaners

VOLLEY, -ED, -S n simultaneous discharge of ammunition ▷ vb discharge (ammunition) in a volley

VOLLEYER ▸ volley

VOLLEYS ▸ volley

VOLOST, -S n (in the former Soviet Union) a rural soviet

VOLPINO, -S n Italian breed of dog

VOLPLANE vb glide in an aeroplane

VOLS ▸ vol

VOLT, -ED, -ING, -S n unit of electric potential ▷ vb (in fencing) make a quick movement to avoid a thrust

VOLTA n quick-moving Italian dance

VOLTAGE, -S n electric potential difference expressed in volts

VOLTAIC adj producing an electric current

VOLTAISM another name for > galvanism

VOLTE, -S same as ▸ volt

VOLTED ▸ volt

VOLTES ▸ volte

VOLTI, -S n musical direction meaning turn the page

VOLTING ▸ volt

VOLTIS ▸ volti

VOLTS ▸ volt

VOLUBIL same as ▸ voluble

VOLUBLE adj talking easily and at length

VOLUBLY ▸ voluble

VOLUME, -D, -S, VOLUMING n size of the space occupied by something ▷ vb billow or surge in volume

VOLUMISE same as ▸ volumize

VOLUMIST n author

VOLUMIZE vb create volume in something

VOLUSPA, -S n Icelandic mythological poem

VOLUTE, -S n spiral or twisting turn, form, or object ▷ adj having the form of a volute

VOLUTED ▸ volute

VOLUTES ▸ volute

VOLUTIN, -S n granular substance found in cells

VOLUTION n rolling, revolving, or spiral form or motion

VOLUTOID ▸ volute

VOLVA, -E, -S n cup-shaped structure that sheathes the base of the stalk of certain mushrooms

VOLVATE ▸ volva

VOLVE, -D, -S, VOLVING vb turn over

VOLVOX, -ES n freshwater protozoan

VOLVULUS, VOLVULI n abnormal twisting of the intestines causing obstruction

VOM, -MED, -MING, -S vb vomit

VOMER, -S n thin flat bone separating the nasal passages in mammals

VOMERINE ▸ vomer

VOMERS ▸ vomer

VOMICA, -E, -S n pus-containing cavity

VOMIT, -ED, -ING, -S vb eject (the contents of the stomach) through the mouth ▷ n matter vomited

VOMITER, -S ▸ vomit

VOMITIER ▸ vomity

VOMITING ▸ vomit

VOMITIVE same as ▸ vomitory

VOMITO, -S n form of yellow fever
VOMITORY adj causing vomiting ▷ n vomitory agent
VOMITOS ▶ vomito
VOMITOUS adj arousing feelings of disgust
VOMITS ▶ vomit
VOMITUS n matter that has been vomited
VOMITY, VOMITIER adj resembling or smelling of vomit
VOMMED ▶ vom
VOMMING ▶ vom
VOMS ▶ vom
VONGOLE pl n (in Italian cookery) clams
VOODOO, -ED, -S n religion involving ancestor worship and witchcraft ▷ adj of or relating to voodoo ▷ vb affect by or as if by the power of voodoo
VOORSKOT n (in South Africa) advance payment made to a farmer for crops
VOR, -RED, -RING, -S vb (in dialect) warn
VORACITY > voracious
VORAGO, -ES, -S n chasm
VORANT adj devouring
VORLAGE, -S n skiing position
VORPAL adj sharp
VORRED ▶ vor
VORRING ▶ vor
VORS ▶ vor
VORTEX, -ES, VORTICES n whirlpool
VORTICAL ▶ vortex
VORTICES ▶ vortex
VOSTRO adj as in vostro account bank account held by a foreign bank with a British bank
VOTABLE ▶ vote
VOTARESS n female votary
VOTARIES ▶ votary
VOTARIST variant of ▶ votary
VOTARY, VOTARIES n person dedicated to a religion or to a cause ▷ adj ardently devoted to a deity
VOTE, -D, -S n choice made by a participant in a shared decision ▷ vb make a choice by a vote
VOTEABLE ▶ vote
VOTED ▶ vote
VOTEEN, -S n devotee
VOTELESS ▶ vote
VOTER, -S n person who can or does vote

VOTES ▶ vote
VOTING, -S ▶ vote
VOTIVE, -S adj done or given to fulfil a vow ▷ n votive offering
VOTIVELY ▶ votive
VOTIVES ▶ votive
VOTRESS ▶ votaress
VOUCH, -ED, -ES, -ING vb give personal assurance ▷ n act of vouching
VOUCHEE, -S n person summoned to court to defend a title
VOUCHER, -S n ticket used instead of money to buy specified goods ▷ vb summon someone to court as a vouchee
VOUCHES ▶ vouch
VOUCHING ▶ vouch
VOUDON, -S variant of ▶ voodoo
VOUDOU, -S same as ▶ voodoo
VOUDOUED ▶ voudou
VOUDOUN, -S variant of ▶ voodoo
VOUDOUS ▶ voudou
VOUGE, -S n form of pike used by foot soldiers in the 14th century and later
VOULGE, -S n type of medieval weapon
VOULU adj deliberate
VOUSSOIR n wedge-shaped stone or brick that is used with others to construct an arch
VOUTSAFE same as > vouchsafe
VOUVRAY, -S n dry white French wine
VOW, -ED, -ING, -S n solemn and binding promise ▷ vb promise solemnly
VOWEL, -LED, -S n speech sound made without obstructing the flow of breath ▷ vb say as a vowel
VOWELED adj having vowels
VOWELISE same as ▶ vowelize
VOWELIZE vb mark the vowel points in (a Hebrew word or text)
VOWELLED ▶ vowel
VOWELLY adj marked by vowels
VOWELS ▶ vowel
VOWER, -S ▶ vow
VOWESS, -ES n nun
VOWING ▶ vow
VOWLESS ▶ vow
VOWS ▶ vow
VOX, VOCES n voice or sound

Along with **vex**, this Latin word for voice is the highest-scoring 3-letter word beginning with V.

VOXEL, -S n any of a number of very small elements in a 3D image
VOYAGE, -D, -S n long journey by sea or in space ▷ vb make a voyage
VOYAGER, -S ▶ voyage
VOYAGES ▶ voyage
VOYAGEUR n French canoeman who transported furs from trading posts in N America
VOYAGING n act of voyaging
VOYEUR, -S n person abnormally interested in other people's distress
VOZHD, -S n Russian leader

This unlikely looking word is Russian for a chief or leader, and may provide a great score from an apparently difficult rack.

VRAIC, -S n type of seaweed
VRAICKER n person who gathers vraic
VRAICS ▶ vraic
VRIL, -S n life force
VROOM, -ED, -ING, -S interj exclamation imitative of a car engine revving up ▷ vb move noisily and at high speed
VROT adj South African slang for rotten
VROU, -S n South African word for a woman or wife
VROUW, -S n Afrikaner woman

The heart of any Scrabble player sinks to see a combination of U, V and W on the rack, as there are relatively few words that use even two of these letters. But **vrouw**, a word of Dutch origin for a woman or wife, may get you out of the mess.

VROW, -S same as ▶ vrouw
VUG, -S n small cavity in a rock or vein, usually lined with crystals

This unusual word of Cornish origin, meaning a cavity in rock, is another that can be useful when you have an uninspiring combination of letters. And it has a variant **vugh** and can be extended to **vuggy** or **vughy**.

V

VUGG, -S *same as* ▶ **vug**
VUGGIER ▶ **vuggy**
VUGGIEST ▶ **vuggy**
VUGGS ▶ **vugg**
**VUGGY, VUGGIER,
VUGGIEST** ▶ **vug**
VUGH, -IER, -IEST, -S *same as*
▶ **vug**
VUGHY ▶ **vug**
VUGS ▶ **vug**
VUGULAR *adj* relating to
vugs
VULCAN, -S *n* blacksmith
VULCANIC *same as*
▶ **volcanic**
VULCANS ▶ **vulcan**
VULGAR, -ER, -S *adj*
showing lack of good taste,
decency, or refinement ▷ *n*
common and ignorant
person
VULGARLY ▶ **vulgar**
VULGARS ▶ **vulgar**
VULGATE, -S *n* commonly
recognized text or version
VULGO *adv* generally
VULGUS, -ES *n* the common
people
VULN, -ED, -S *vb* wound
VULNING ▶ **vuln**
VULNS ▶ **vuln**
VULPINE *adj* of or like a fox
VULSELLA *n* forceps
VULTURE, -S *n* large bird
that feeds on the flesh of
dead animals

VULTURN, -S *n* type of
turkey
VULVA, -E, -S *n* female
external genitals
VULVAL ▶ **vulva**
VULVAR ▶ **vulva**
VULVAS ▶ **vulva**
VULVATE ▶ **vulva**
VUM, -MED, -MING, -S *vb*
swear
VUTTY, VUTTIER, VUTTIEST
adj dirty
VUVUZELA *n* South African
instrument blown by
football fans
VYING, -S ▶ **vie**
VYINGLY ▶ **vie**
VYINGS ▶ **vying**

V

Ww

W, like **V**, can be an awkward tile to handle, but at least there are two two-letter words that begin with **W**: **we** and **wo** (5 points each). There are three that end with **W**: **aw**, **ew** and **ow** (5 points each). There are lots of everyday three-letter words that earn good scores: **wiz** (15), **wax** (13) with its two old-fashioned variants **wex** and **wox** (also 13 each) and **way**, **who**, **why**, **wow** and **wry** (9 each). Don't forget **wok** (10) either, which can be as useful on the Scrabble board as in the kitchen!

WAAC, -S n (formerly) member of the Women's Auxiliary Army Corp

WAAH interj interjection used to express wailing

WAB, -S n skin web between the digits of certain animals

WABAIN, -S same as ▶ ouabain

WABBIT adj Scots word meaning weary

WABBLE, -D, -S, WABBLING same as ▶ wobble

WABBLER, -S ▶ wabble

WABBLES ▶ wabble

WABBLIER ▶ wabbly

WABBLING ▶ wabble

WABBLY, WABBLIER ▶ wabble

WABOOM, -S another word for ▶ wagenboom

WABS ▶ wab

WABSTER, -S Scots form of ▶ webster

WACK, -EST, -S n friend ▷ adj bad or inferior

WACKE, -S n any of various soft earthy rocks that resemble or are derived from basaltic rocks

WACKED adj exhausted

WACKER, -S same as ▶ wack

WACKES ▶ wacke

WACKEST ▶ wack

WACKIER ▶ wacky

WACKIEST ▶ wacky

WACKILY ▶ wacky

WACKO, -ES, -S n odd or eccentric person

WACKS ▶ wack

WACKY, WACKIER, WACKIEST adj eccentric or funny

WACONDA, -S n supernatural force in Sioux belief

WAD, -DED, -DING, -DINGS, -S n black earthy ore of manganese ▷ n small mass of soft material ▷ vb form (something) into a wad

WADABLE ▶ wade

WADD, -S same as ▶ wad

WADDED ▶ wad

WADDER, -S ▶ wad

WADDIE same as ▶ waddy

WADDIED ▶ waddy

WADDIES ▶ waddy

WADDING ▶ wad

WADDINGS ▶ wad

WADDLE, -D, -S, WADDLING vb walk with short swaying steps ▷ n swaying walk

WADDLER, -S ▶ waddle

WADDLES ▶ waddle

WADDLIER ▶ waddly

WADDLING ▶ waddle

WADDLY, WADDLIER ▶ waddle

WADDS ▶ wadd

WADDY, WADDIED, WADDIES, -ING n heavy wooden club used by Aboriginal Australians ▷ vb hit with a waddy

WADE, -D, -S, WADING, WADINGS vb walk with difficulty through water or mud ▷ n act or an instance of wading

WADEABLE ▶ wade

WADED ▶ wade

WADER n long-legged water bird

WADERS pl n long waterproof boots which completely cover the legs

WADES ▶ wade

WADGE, -S n large or roughly cut portion

WADI, -S n (in N Africa and Arabia) river which is dry except in the wet season

WADIES ▶ wady

WADING ▶ wade

WADINGS ▶ wade

WADIS ▶ wadi

WADMAAL, -S same as ▶ wadmal

WADMAL, -S n coarse thick woollen fabric, formerly woven for outer garments

WADMEL, -S same as ▶ wadmal

WADMOL, -S same as ▶ wadmal

WADMOLL, -S same as ▶ wadmal

WADMOLS ▶ wadmol

WADS ▶ wad

WADSET, -S vb pledge or mortgage

WADSETT, -S same as ▶ wadset

WADT, -S same as ▶ wad

WADY, WADIES same as ▶ wadi

WAE, -S old form of ▶ woe

WAEFUL old form of ▶ woeful

WAENESS n sorrow

WAES ▶ wae

WAESOME adj sorrowful

WAESUCK interj Scots word meaning alas

WAESUCKS interj alas

WAFER, -ED, -ING, -S n thin crisp biscuit ▷ vb seal, fasten, or attach with a wafer

WAFERIER ▶ wafery

WAFERING ▶ wafer

W

WAFERS ▸ wafer
WAFERY, WAFERIER adj like wafer; thin
WAFF, -ED, -ING, -S n gust or puff of air ▷ vb flutter or cause to flutter
WAFFIE, -S n person regarded as having little worth to society
WAFFING ▸ waff
WAFFLE, -D, -S vb speak or write in a vague wordy way ▷ n vague wordy talk or writing
WAFFLER, -S ▸ waffle
WAFFLES ▸ waffle
WAFFLIER ▸ waffly
WAFFLING ▸ waffle
WAFFLY, WAFFLIER ▸ waffle
WAFFS ▸ waff
WAFT, -ED, -S vb drift or carry gently through the air ▷ n something wafted
WAFTAGE, -S ▸ waft
WAFTED ▸ waft
WAFTER, -S n device that causes a draught
WAFTING, -S ▸ waft
WAFTS ▸ waft
WAFTURE, -S n act of wafting or waving
WAG, -GED, -GING, -S vb move rapidly from side to side ▷ n wagging movement
WAGE, -D, -S, WAGING n payment for work done, esp when paid weekly ▷ vb engage in (an activity)
WAGELESS ▸ wage
WAGER, -ED, -S vb bet on the outcome of something ▷ n bet on the outcome of an event or activity
WAGERER, -S ▸ wager
WAGERING n act of wagering
WAGERS ▸ wager
WAGES ▸ wage
WAGGA, -S n blanket or bed covering made out of sacks stitched together
WAGGED ▸ wag
WAGGER, -S ▸ wag
WAGGERY n quality of being humorous
WAGGING ▸ wag
WAGGISH adj jocular or humorous
WAGGLE, -D, -S, WAGGLING vb move with a rapid shaking or wobbling motion ▷ n rapid shaking or wobbling motion
WAGGLER, -S n float only the bottom of which is attached to the fishing line

WAGGLES ▸ waggle
WAGGLIER ▸ waggly
WAGGLING ▸ waggle
WAGGLY, WAGGLIER ▸ waggle
WAGGON, -ED, -S same as ▸ wagon
WAGGONER same as ▸ wagoner
WAGGONS ▸ waggon
WAGING ▸ wage
WAGMOIRE obsolete word for ▸ quagmire
WAGON, -ED, -ING, -S n four-wheeled vehicle for heavy loads ▷ vb transport by wagon
WAGONAGE n money paid for transport by wagon
WAGONED ▸ wagon
WAGONER, -S n person who drives a wagon
WAGONFUL ▸ wagon
WAGONING ▸ wagon
WAGONS ▸ wagon
WAGS ▸ wag
WAGSOME another word for ▸ waggish
WAGTAIL, -S n small long-tailed bird
WAGYU, -S n Japanese breed of beef cattle
WAHCONDA n (in Native American culture) supreme being
WAHINE, -S n Māori woman, esp a wife
WAHOO, -S n food and game fish of tropical seas
WAI, -S n in New Zealand, water
WAIATA, -S n Māori song
WAID ▸ weigh
WAIDE ▸ weigh
WAIF, -ED, -ING, -S n young person who is, or seems, homeless or neglected ▷ vb treat as a waif
WAIFISH ▸ waif
WAIFLIKE ▸ waif
WAIFS ▸ waif
WAIFT, -S n piece of lost property found by someone other than the owner
WAIL, -ED, -S vb cry out in pain or misery ▷ n mournful cry
WAILER, -S ▸ wail
WAILFUL ▸ wail
WAILING, -S ▸ wail
WAILS ▸ wail
WAILSOME ▸ wail
WAIN, -ED, -ING, -S vb transport ▷ n farm wagon
WAINAGE, -S n carriages etc for transportation of goods

WAINED ▸ wain
WAINING ▸ wain
WAINS ▸ wain
WAINSCOT n wooden lining of the lower part of the walls of a room ▷ vb line (a wall of a room) with a wainscot
WAIR, -ED, -ING, -S vb spend
WAIRSH, -ER variant spelling of ▸ wersh
WAIRUA, -S n in New Zealand, spirit or soul
WAIS ▸ wai
WAIST, -S n part of the trunk between the ribs and the hips
WAISTED adj having a waist or waistlike part
WAISTER, -S n sailor performing menial duties
WAISTING n act of wasting
WAISTS ▸ waist
WAIT, -ED, -ING, -INGS, -S vb remain inactive in expectation (of something) ▷ n act or period of waiting
WAITE, -S old form of ▸ wait
WAITED ▸ wait
WAITER, -ED, -S n person who serves in a restaurant etc ▷ vb serve at table
WAITES ▸ waite
WAITING ▸ wait
WAITINGS ▸ wait
WAITLIST n waiting list
WAITRESS n woman who serves people with food and drink in a restaurant ▷ vb work as a waitress
WAITRON, -S n waiter or waitress
WAITS ▸ wait
WAIVE, -D, -S, WAIVING vb refrain from enforcing (a law, right, etc)
WAIVER, -S n act or instance of voluntarily giving up a claim, right, etc
WAIVES ▸ waive
WAIVING ▸ waive
WAIVODE, -S same as ▸ voivode
WAIWODE, -S same as ▸ voivode
WAKA, -S n Māori canoe
WAKAME, -S n edible seaweed
WAKANDA, -S n supernatural quality in Native American belief system
WAKANE, -S n type of seaweed
WAKAS ▸ waka

W

WAKE, -D, -S, WOKEN vb rouse from sleep or inactivity ▷ n vigil beside a body the night before the funeral

WAKEFUL adj unable to sleep

WAKELESS adj (of sleep) deep or unbroken

WAKEMAN, WAKEMEN n watchman

WAKEN, -ED, -ING, -S vb wake

WAKENER, -S ▸ waken

WAKENING ▸ waken

WAKENS ▸ waken

WAKER, -S ▸ wake

WAKERIFE adj watchful

WAKERS ▸ waker

WAKES ▸ wake

WAKF, -S same as ▸ **waqf**

WAKIKI, -S n Melanesian shell currency

WAKING, -S ▸ wake

WALD, -S Scots form of ▸ **weld**

WALDHORN n organ reed stop

WALDO, -ES, -S n gadget for manipulating objects by remote control

WALDRAPP n type of ibis

WALDS ▸ wald

WALE, -D, -R, -RS, -S, WALING same as ▸ **weal**

WALI, -S same as ▸ **vali**

WALIE adj robust or strong

WALIER ▸ waly

WALIES ▸ waly

WALIEST ▸ waly

WALING ▸ wale

WALIS ▸ wali

WALISE, -S same as ▸ **valise**

WALK, -ED, -S vb move on foot with at least one foot always on the ground ▷ n short journey on foot, usu for pleasure

WALKABLE ▸ walk

WALKAWAY n easily achieved victory

WALKED ▸ walk

WALKER, -S n person who walks

WALKIES pl n as in go **walkies** a walk

WALKING, -S adj (of a person) considered to possess the qualities of something inanimate as specified ▷ n act of walking

WALKMILL same as > **waulkmill**

WALKOUT, -S n strike

WALKOVER n easy victory

WALKS ▸ walk

WALKUP, -S n building with stairs to upper floors

WALKWAY, -S n path designed for use by pedestrians

WALKYRIE variant of ▸ **valkyrie**

WALL, -ER, -ERS, -S n structure of brick, stone, etc used to enclose, divide, or support ▷ vb enclose or seal with a wall or walls

WALLA, -S same as ▸ **wallah**

WALLABA, -S n type of S American tree

WALLABY n marsupial like a small kangaroo

WALLAH, -S n person involved with or in charge of a specified thing

WALLAROO n large stocky Australian kangaroo of rocky regions

WALLAS ▸ walla

WALLED ▸ wall

WALLER ▸ wall

WALLERS ▸ wall

WALLET, -S n small folding case for paper money, documents, etc

WALLEY, -S n type of jump in figure skating

WALLEYE, -S n fish with large staring eyes

WALLEYED ▸ walleye

WALLEYES ▸ walleye

WALLEYS ▸ walley

WALLFISH n snail

WALLIE same as ▸ **wally**

WALLIER ▸ wally

WALLIES ▸ wally

WALLIEST ▸ wally

WALLING, -S ▸ wall

WALLOP, -ED, -S vb hit hard ▷ n hard blow

WALLOPER n person or thing that wallops

WALLOPS ▸ wallop

WALLOW, -ED, -S vb revel in an emotion ▷ n act or instance of wallowing

WALLOWER ▸ wallow

WALLOWS ▸ wallow

WALLS ▸ wall

WALLSEND n type of coal

WALLWORT n type of plant

WALLY, WALLIER, WALLIES, WALLIEST n stupid person ▷ adj fine, pleasing, or splendid

WALNUT, -S n edible nut with a wrinkled shell ▷ adj made from the wood of a walnut tree

WALRUS, -ES n large sea mammal with long tusks

WALTY, WALTIER, WALTIEST adj (of a ship) likely to roll over

WALTZ, -ED, -ES, -ING n ballroom dance ▷ vb dance a waltz

WALTZER, -S n person who waltzes

WALTZES ▸ waltz

WALTZING ▸ waltz

WALY, WALIER, WALIES, WALIEST same as ▸ **wally**

WAMBLE, -D, -S, WAMBLING vb move unsteadily ▷ n unsteady movement

WAMBLIER ▸ wambly

WAMBLING ▸ wamble

WAMBLY, WAMBLIER ▸ wamble

WAME, -S n belly, abdomen, or womb

WAMED ▸ wame

WAMEFOU, -S Scots variant of ▸ **wameful**

WAMEFUL, -S n bellyful

WAMES ▸ wame

WAMMUL, -S n dog

WAMMUS, -ES same as ▸ **wamus**

WAMPEE, -S n type of Asian fruit tree

WAMPISH vb wave

WAMPUM, -S n shells woven together, formerly used by Native Americans as money

WAMPUS, -ES same as ▸ **wamus**

WAMUS, -ES n type of cardigan or jacket

WAN, -NED, -NER, -NEST, -NING, -S adj pale and sickly looking ▷ vb make or become wan

WAND, -S n thin rod, esp one used in performing magic tricks

WANDER, -ED, -S vb move about without a definite destination or aim ▷ n act or instance of wandering

WANDERER ▸ wander

WANDEROO n macaque of India and Sri Lanka

WANDERS ▸ wander

WANDLE, -D, -S, WANDLING adj supple ▷ vb walk haltingly

WANDLIKE ▸ wand

WANDLING ▸ wandle

WANDOO, -S n eucalyptus tree of W Australia, having white bark and durable wood

WANDS ▸ wand

W

WANE, -D, -S vb decrease gradually in size or strength

WANEY ▸ wane

WANG, -S n cheekbone

WANGAN, -S same as ▸ wanigan

WANGLE, -D, -S, WANGLING vb get by devious methods ▸ n act or an instance of wangling

WANGLER, -S ▸ wangle

WANGLES ▸ wangle

WANGLING ▸ wangle

WANGS ▸ wang

WANGUN, -S same as ▸ wanigan

WANHOPE, -S n delusion

WANIER ▸ wany

WANIEST ▸ wany

WANIGAN, -S n provisions for camp

WANING, -S ▸ wane

WANION, -S n vehemence

WANKLE adj unstable

WANLE same as ▸ wandle

WANLY ▸ wan

WANNA vb spelling of 'want to' intended to reflect a dialectal or informal pronunciation

WANNABE, -S adj wanting to be, or be like, a particular person or thing ▸ n person who wants to be, or be like, a particular person or thing

WANNABEE same as ▸ wannabe

WANNABES ▸ wannabe

WANNED ▸ wan

WANNEL same as ▸ wandle

WANNER ▸ wan

WANNESS ▸ wan

WANNEST ▸ wan

WANNIGAN same as ▸ wanigan

WANNING ▸ wan

WANNION, -S same as ▸ wanion

WANNISH adj rather wan

WANS ▸ wan

WANT, -ED, -S vb need or long for ▸ n act or instance of wanting

WANTAGE, -S n shortage

WANTAWAY n footballer who wants to transfer to another club

WANTED ▸ want

WANTER, -S ▸ want

WANTHILL n molehill

WANTIES ▸ wanty

WANTING adj lacking ▸ prep without

WANTON, -ED, -S adj without motive, provocation, or justification ▸ n playful or capricious person ▸ vb squander or waste

WANTONER ▸ wanton

WANTONLY ▸ wanton

WANTONS ▸ wanton

WANTS ▸ want

WANTY, WANTIES n belt

WANWORDY adj without merit

WANWORTH n inexpensive purchase

WANY, WANIER, WANIEST ▸ wane

WANZE, -D, -S, WANZING vb wane

WAP, -PED, -PING, -S vb strike

WAPITI, -S n large N American deer

WAPPED ▸ wap

WAPPEND adj tired

WAPPER, -ED, -S vb blink

WAPPING ▸ wap

WAPS ▸ wap

WAQF, -S n endowment in Muslim law

An Arabic word meaning the donation of land, property or money for charitable purposes. As one of the Q words without a U, this comes up surprisingly often. It can also be spelt **wakf**.

WAR, -RED, -RING, -S n fighting between nations ▸ adj of, like, or caused by war ▸ vb conduct a war

WARAGI, -S n Ugandan alcoholic drink made from bananas

WARATAH, -S n Australian shrub with crimson flowers

WARB, -S n dirty or insignificant person

WARBIER ▸ warby

WARBIEST ▸ warby

WARBIRD, -S n vintage military aeroplane

WARBLE, -D, -S, WARBLING vb sing in a trilling voice ▸ n act or an instance of warbling

WARBLER, -S n any of various small songbirds

WARBLES ▸ warble

WARBLIER ▸ warbly

WARBLING ▸ warble

WARBLY, WARBLIER adj said in a quavering manner

WARBOT, -S n any robot or unmanned vehicle or device designed for and used in warfare

WARBS ▸ warb

WARBY, WARBIER, WARBIEST ▸ warb

WARCRAFT n skill in warfare

WARD, -ED, -S n room in a hospital for patients needing a similar kind of care ▸ vb guard or protect

WARDCORN n payment of corn

WARDED ▸ ward

WARDEN, -ED, -S n person in charge of a building and its occupants ▸ vb act as a warden

WARDENRY ▸ warden

WARDENS ▸ warden

WARDER, -ED, -S vb guard ▸ n prison officer

WARDIAN n as in wardian case type of glass container for housing delicate plants

WARDING, -S ▸ ward

WARDLESS ▸ ward

WARDMOTE n assembly of the citizens or liverymen of an area

WARDOG, -S n veteran warrior

WARDRESS n female officer in charge of prisoners in a jail

WARDROBE n cupboard for hanging clothes in

WARDROOM n officers' quarters on a warship

WARDROP, -S obsolete form of ▸ wardrobe

WARDS ▸ ward

WARDSHIP n state of being a ward

WARE, -D, WARING n articles of a specified type or material ▸ vb spend or squander

WAREHOU, -S n any of several edible saltwater New Zealand fish

WARELESS adj careless

WAREROOM n storeroom

WARES pl n goods for sale

WAREZ pl n illegally copied computer software

WARFARE, -D, -S vb engage in war ▸ n fighting or hostilities

WARFARER ▸ warfare

WARFARES ▸ warfare

WARFARIN n crystalline compound, used as a medical anticoagulant

WARGAME, -D, -S vb engage in simulated military conflicts

WARGAMER n person who takes part in wargames

WARGAMES ▸ wargame

WARHABLE adj able to fight in war

WARHEAD, -S n explosive front part of a missile

WARHORSE n (formerly) a horse used in battle

WARIER ▸ wary

WARIEST ▸ wary

WARILY ▸ wary

WARIMENT n caution

WARINESS ▸ wary

WARING ▸ ware

WARISON, -S n (esp formerly) a bugle note used as an order to a military force to attack

WARK, -ED, -ING, -S Scots form of ▸ work

WARLESS ▸ war

WARLIKE adj of or relating to war

WARLING, -S n one who is not liked

WARLOCK, -S n man who practises black magic

WARLORD, -S n military leader of a nation or part of a nation

WARM, -ED, -EST, -ING, -INGS, -S adj moderately hot ▷ vb make or become warm ▷ n warm place or area

WARMAKER n one who wages war

WARMAN, WARMEN n one experienced in warfare

WARMED ▸ warm

WARMEN ▸ warman

WARMER, -S ▸ warm

WARMEST ▸ warm

WARMING ▸ warm

WARMINGS ▸ warm

WARMISH ▸ warm

WARMIST, -S n person who believes global warming results from human activity

WARMLY ▸ warm

WARMNESS ▸ warm

WARMOUTH n type of fish

WARMS ▸ warm

WARMTH, -S n mild heat

WARMUP, -S n preparatory exercise routine

WARN, -ED, -S vb make aware of possible danger or harm

WARNER, -S ▸ warn

WARNING, -S n something that warns ▷ adj giving or serving as a warning

WARNS ▸ warn

WARP, -ED, -S vb twist out of shape ▷ n state of being warped

WARPAGE, -S ▸ warp

WARPAINT n paint used to decorate the face and body before battle

WARPATH, -S n route taken by Native Americans on a warlike expedition

WARPED ▸ warp

WARPER, -S ▸ warp

WARPING, -S ▸ warp

WARPLANE n any aircraft designed for and used in warfare

WARPOWER n ability to wage war

WARPS ▸ warp

WARPWISE adv (weaving) in the direction of the warp

WARRAGAL same as ▸ warrigal

WARRAGLE same as ▸ warrigal

WARRAGUL same as ▸ warrigal

WARRAN, -ED, -S same as ▸ warrant

WARRAND, -S same as ▸ warrant

WARRANED ▸ warran

WARRANS ▸ warran

WARRANT, -S n (document giving) official authorization ▷ vb make necessary

WARRANTY n (document giving) a guarantee

WARRAY, -ED, -S vb wage war on

WARRE same as ▸ war

WARRED ▸ war

WARREN, -S n series of burrows in which rabbits live

WARRENER n gamekeeper or keeper of a warren

WARRENS ▸ warren

WARREY, -ED, -S same as ▸ warray

WARRIGAL n dingo ▷ adj wild

WARRING ▸ war

WARRIOR, -S n person who fights in a war

WARRISON same as ▸ warison

WARS ▸ war

WARSAW, -S n type of grouper fish

WARSHIP, -S n ship designed and equipped for naval combat

WARSLE, -D, -S, WARSLING dialect word for ▸ wrestle

WARSLER, -S ▸ warsle

WARSLES ▸ warsle

WARSLING ▸ warsle

WARST obsolete form of ▸ worst

WARSTLE, -D, -S dialect form of ▸ wrestle

WARSTLER ▸ warstle

WARSTLES ▸ warstle

WART, -S n small hard growth on the skin

WARTED ▸ wart

WARTHOG, -S n wild African pig with wartlike lumps on the face

WARTIER ▸ warty

WARTIEST ▸ warty

WARTIME, -S n time of war ▷ adj of or in a time of war

WARTLESS ▸ wart

WARTLIKE ▸ wart

WARTS ▸ wart

WARTWEED n type of plant

WARTWORT another word for ▸ wartweed

WARTY, WARTIER, WARTIEST ▸ wart

WARWOLF n Roman engine of war

WARWORK, -S n work contributing to war effort

WARWORN adj worn down by war

WARY, WARIER, WARIEST adj watchful or cautious

WARZONE, -S n area where a war is taking place or there is some other violent conflict

WAS vb form of the past tense of be

WASABI, -S n Japanese cruciferous plant cultivated for its thick green pungent root

WASE, -S n pad to relieve pressure of load carried on head

WASH, -ED, -EN, -ES vb clean (oneself, clothes, etc) with water and usu soap ▷ n act or process of washing

WASHABLE n thing that can be washed ▷ adj (esp of fabrics or clothes) capable of being washed without deteriorating

WASHAWAY another word for ▸ washout

WASHBAG, -S n small bag for carrying toiletries when travelling

WASHBALL n ball of soap

WASHBOWL same as > washbasin

WASHDAY, -S n day on which clothes and linen are washed, often the same day each week

WASHDOWN n the act of washing (oneself or something) down

WASHED ▸ wash

WASHEN ▸ wash

WASHER, -ED, -S n ring put under a nut or bolt or in a tap

W

as a seal ▷ *vb* fit with a washer

WASHERY *n* plant where liquid is used to remove dirt from a mineral

WASHES ▷ **wash**

WASHFAST *adj* not fading when washed

WASHHAND *n* as in **washhand basin, washhand stand** for the washing of hands

WASHIER ▷ **washy**

WASHIEST ▷ **washy**

WASHILY ▷ **washy**

WASHIN, -S *n* increase in the angle of attack of an aircraft wing towards the wing tip

WASHING, -S *n* clothes to be washed

WASHINS ▷ **washin**

WASHLAND *n* frequently flooded plain

WASHOUT, -S *n* complete failure

WASHPOT, -S *n* pot for washing things in

WASHRAG, -S *same as* > **washcloth**

WASHROOM *n* toilet

WASHTUB, -S *n* tub or large container used for washing anything, esp clothes

WASHUP, -S *n* outcome of a process

WASHWIPE *n* windscreen spray-cleaning mechanism

WASHY, WASHIER, WASHIEST *adj* overdiluted or weak

WASM, -S *n* obsolete belief; an out-of-fashion 'ism'

WASP, -S *n* stinging insect with a slender black-and-yellow striped body

WASPIE, -S *n* tight-waisted corset

WASPIER ▷ **waspy**

WASPIES ▷ **waspie**

WASPIEST ▷ **waspy**

WASPILY ▷ **wasp**

WASPISH *adj* bad-tempered

WASPLIKE ▷ **wasp**

WASPNEST *n* nest of wasps

WASPS ▷ **wasp**

WASPY, WASPIER, WASPIEST ▷ **wasp**

WASSAIL, -S *n* formerly, festivity when much drinking took place ▷ *vb* drink health of (a person) at a wassail

WASSUP *sentence substitute* what is happening?

WAST, -S *singular form of the past tense of* ▷ **be**

WASTABLE ▷ **waste**

WASTAGE, -S *n* loss by wear or waste

WASTE, -D, -S, WASTINGS *vb* use pointlessly or thoughtlessly ▷ *n* act of wasting or state of being wasted ▷ *adj* rejected as worthless or surplus to requirements

WASTEBIN *n* bin for rubbish

WASTED ▷ **waste**

WASTEFUL *adj* extravagant

WASTEL, -S *n* fine bread or cake

WASTELOT *n* piece of waste ground in a city

WASTELS ▷ **wastel**

WASTER, -ED, -S *vb* waste ▷ *n* layabout

WASTERIE *same as* > **wastery**

WASTERS ▷ **waster**

WASTERY *n* extravagance

WASTES ▷ **waste**

WASTEWAY *n* open ditch

WASTFULL *obsolete form of* ▷ **wasteful**

WASTING *adj* reducing the vitality and strength of the body

WASTINGS ▷ **waste**

WASTNESS *same as* > **wasteness**

WASTREL, -S *n* lazy or worthless person

WASTRIE, -S *same as* ▷ **wastery**

WASTRIFE *n* wastefulness

WASTRY *n* wastefulness

WASTS ▷ **wast**

WAT, -S, -TER, -TEST *adj* wet

WATAP, -S *n* stringy thread made by Native Americans from the roots of conifers

WATAPE, -S *same as* ▷ **watap**

WATAPS ▷ **watap**

WATCH, -ED, -ES, -ING *vb* look at closely ▷ *n* portable timepiece for the wrist or pocket

WATCHA *interj* greeting meaning 'what are you?'

WATCHBOX *n* sentry's box

WATCHCRY *n* slogan used to rally support

WATCHDOG *n* dog kept to guard property

WATCHED ▷ **watch**

WATCHER, -S *n* person who watches

WATCHES ▷ **watch**

WATCHET, -S *n* shade of blue

WATCHEYE *n* eye with a light-coloured iris

WATCHFUL *adj* vigilant or alert

WATCHING ▷ **watch**

WATCHMAN, WATCHMEN *n* man employed to guard a building or property

WATCHOUT *n* lookout

WATE ▷ **wit**

WATER, -ED, -ING, -S *n* clear colourless tasteless liquid that falls as rain and forms rivers etc ▷ *vb* put water on or into

WATERAGE *n* transportation of cargo by means of ships, or the charges for such transportation

WATERBED *n* watertight mattress filled with water

WATERBUS *n* boat offering a regular transport service

WATERDOG *n* dog trained to hunt in water

WATERED ▷ **water**

WATERER, -S ▷ **water**

WATERHEN *another name for* > **gallinule**

WATERIER ▷ **watery**

WATERILY ▷ **watery**

WATERING ▷ **water**

WATERISH ▷ **water**

WATERJET *n* jet of water

WATERLOG *vb* flood with water

WATERLOO *n* total defeat

WATERMAN, WATERMEN *n* skilled boatman

WATERPOX *n* chickenpox

WATERS ▷ **water**

WATERSKI *vb* ski on water towed behind motorboat

WATERWAY *n* river, canal, or other navigable channel used as a means of travel or transport

WATERY, WATERIER *adj* of, like, or containing water

WATS ▷ **wat**

WATT, -S *n* unit of power

WATTAGE, -S *n* electrical power expressed in watts

WATTAPE, -S *same as* ▷ **watap**

WATTER ▷ **wat**

WATTEST ▷ **wat**

WATTHOUR *n* unit of energy equal to the power of one watt operating for an hour

WATTLE, -S, WATTLING *n* branches woven over sticks to make a fence ▷ *adj* made of, formed by, or covered with wattle ▷ *vb* construct from wattle

WATTLED ▸ wattle
WATTLES ▸ wattle
WATTLESS ▸ watt
WATTLING ▸ wattle
WATTS ▸ watt
WAUCHT, -ED, -S same as ▸ waught
WAUFF, -ED, -ING, -S same as ▸ waff
WAUGH, -ED, -ING, -S vb bark
WAUGHT, -ED, -S vb drink in large amounts
WAUK, -ED, -ING, -S vb full (cloth)
WAUKER, -S ▸ wauk
WAUKING ▸ wauk
WAUKMILL same as > waulkmill
WAUKRIFE variant of ▸ waulkrife
WAUKS ▸ wauk
WAUL, -ED, -S vb cry or wail plaintively like a cat
WAULING, -S ▸ waul
WAULK, -ED, -ING, -S same as ▸ wauk
WAULKER, -S ▸ waulk
WAULKING ▸ waulk
WAULKS ▸ waulk
WAULS ▸ waul
WAUR, -ED, -ING, -S, -ST obsolete form of ▸ war
WAVE, -D, -S vb move the hand to and fro as a greeting or signal ▷ n moving ridge on water
WAVEBAND n range of wavelengths or frequencies used for a particular type of radio transmission
WAVED ▸ wave
WAVEFORM n shape of the graph of a wave or oscillation obtained by plotting the value of some changing quantity against time
WAVELESS ▸ wave
WAVELET, -S n small wave
WAVELIKE ▸ wave
WAVEOFF, -S n signal or instruction to an aircraft not to land
WAVER, -ED, -S vb hesitate or be irresolute ▷ n act or an instance of wavering
WAVERER, -S ▸ waver
WAVERIER ▸ wavery
WAVERING ▸ wavery
WAVEROUS same as ▸ wavery
WAVERS ▸ waver
WAVERY, WAVERIER adj lacking firmness
WAVES ▸ wave

WAVESON, -S n goods floating on waves after shipwreck
WAVEY, -S n snow goose or other wild goose
WAVICLE, -S n origin of wave
WAVIER ▸ wavy
WAVIES ▸ wavy
WAVIEST ▸ wavy
WAVILY ▸ wavy
WAVINESS ▸ wavy
WAVING, -S ▸ wave
WAVY, WAVIER, WAVIES, WAVIEST adj having curves ▷ n snow goose or other wild goose
WAW, -S another name for ▸ vav
WAWA, -ED, -ING, -S n speech ▷ vb speak
WAWE, -S same as ▸ waw
WAWL, -ED, -S same as ▸ waul
WAWLING, -S ▸ wawl
WAWLS ▸ wawl
WAWS ▸ waw
WAX, -ED, -ES, WOX, WOXEN n solid fatty or oily substance used for sealing, making candles, etc ▷ vb coat or polish with wax
WAXABLE ▸ wax
WAXBERRY n waxy fruit of the wax myrtle or the snowberry
WAXBILL, -S n any of various chiefly African finchlike weaverbirds
WAXCLOTH another name for ▸ oilcloth
WAXED ▸ wax
WAXEN adj made of or like wax
WAXER, -S ▸ wax
WAXES ▸ wax
WAXEYE, -S n small New Zealand bird
WAXIER ▸ waxy
WAXIEST ▸ waxy
WAXILY ▸ waxy
WAXINESS ▸ waxy
WAXING, -S ▸ wax
WAXLIKE ▸ wax
WAXPLANT n climbing shrub of E Asia and Australia
WAXWEED, -S n type of wild flower
WAXWING, -S n type of songbird
WAXWORK, -S n lifelike wax model of a (famous) person
WAXWORM, -S n wax moth larva
WAXY, WAXIER, WAXIEST adj resembling wax in

colour, appearance, or texture
WAY, -ED, -ING, -S n manner or method ▷ vb travel
WAYANG, -S n type of Indonesian performance with dancers or puppets
WAYBACK, -S n area in the rear of a vehicle
WAYBILL, -S n document stating the nature, origin, and destination of goods being transported
WAYBOARD n thin geological seam separating larger strata
WAYBREAD n plantain
WAYED ▸ way
WAYFARE, -D, -S vb travel
WAYFARER n traveller
WAYFARES ▸ wayfare
WAYGOING n leaving
WAYGONE adj travel-weary
WAYGOOSE same as > wayzgoose
WAYING ▸ way
WAYLAY, WAYLAID, -S vb lie in wait for and accost or attack
WAYLAYER ▸ waylay
WAYLAYS ▸ waylay
WAYLEAVE n access to property granted by a landowner for payment
WAYLEGGO interj away here! let go!
WAYLESS ▸ way
WAYMARK, -S n symbol or signpost marking the route of a footpath ▷ vb mark out with waymarks
WAYMENT, -S vb express grief
WAYPOINT n stopping point on route
WAYPOST, -S n signpost
WAYS ▸ way
WAYSIDE, -S n side of a road
WAYWARD adj erratic, selfish, or stubborn
WAYWISER n device for measuring distance
WAYWODE, -S n Slavic governor
WAYWORN adj worn or tired by travel
WAZ same as ▸ wazz
WAZIR, -S another word for ▸ vizier
WAZOO, -S n slang word for person's bottom
WAZZ, -ED, -ES, -ING vb urinate ▷ n act of urinating
WAZZOCK, -S n foolish or annoying person

W

WE *pron* speaker or writer and one or more others

WEAK, -ER, -EST *adj* lacking strength

WEAKEN, -ED, -S *vb* make or become weak

WEAKENER ▸ **weaken**

WEAKENS ▸ **weaken**

WEAKER ▸ **weak**

WEAKEST ▸ **weak**

WEAKFISH *n* any of several sea trouts

WEAKISH ▸ **weak**

WEAKLIER ▸ **weakly**

WEAKLING *n* feeble person or animal

WEAKLY, WEAKLIER *adv* feebly ▸ *adj* weak or sickly

WEAKNESS *n* deficiency or failing

WEAKON, -S *n* subatomic particle

WEAKSIDE *n* (in basketball) side of court away from ball

WEAL, -S *n* raised mark left on the skin by a blow

WEALD, -S *n* open or forested country

WEALS ▸ **weal**

WEALSMAN, WEALSMEN *n* statesman

WEALTH, -S *n* state of being rich

WEALTHY *adj* possessing wealth

WEAMB, -S *same as* ▸ **wame**

WEAN, -ED, -S *vb* accustom (a baby or young mammal) to food other than mother's milk

WEANEL, -S *n* recently weaned child or animal

WEANER, -S *n* person or thing that weans

WEANING, -S ▸ **wean**

WEANLING *n* child or young animal recently weaned

WEANS ▸ **wean**

WEAPON, -S *vb* arm ▸ *n* object used in fighting

WEAPONED ▸ **weapon**

WEAPONRY *n* weapons collectively

WEAPONS ▸ **weapon**

WEAR, -ED, -INGS, -S, WORE, WORN *vb* have on the body as clothing or ornament ▸ *n* clothes suitable for a particular time or purpose

WEARABLE *adj* suitable for wear or able to be worn ▸ *n* any garment that can be worn

WEARED ▸ **wear**

WEARER, -S ▸ **wear**

WEARIED ▸ **weary**

WEARIER ▸ **weary**

WEARIES ▸ **weary**

WEARIEST ▸ **weary**

WEARIFUL *same as* ▸ **wearisome**

WEARILY ▸ **weary**

WEARING *adj* tiring ▸ *n* act of wearing

WEARINGS ▸ **wear**

WEARISH *adj* withered

WEARS ▸ **wear**

WEARY, WEARIED, WEARIER, WEARIES, WEARIEST *adj* tired or exhausted ▸ *vb* make or become weary

WEARYING ▸ **weary**

WEASAND, -S *former name for the* ▸ **trachea**

WEASEL, -ED, -S *n* small carnivorous mammal with a long body and short legs ▸ *vb* use ambiguous language to avoid speaking directly or honestly

WEASELER ▸ **weasel**

WEASELLY *adj* devious, cunning

WEASELS ▸ **weasel**

WEASELY *adj* devious, cunning

WEASON, -S *Scots form of* ▸ **weasand**

WEATHER, -S *n* day-to-day atmospheric conditions of a place ▸ *vb* (cause to) be affected by the weather

WEAVE, -D, -S, WOVE *vb* make (fabric) by interlacing (yarn) on a loom

WEAVER, -S *n* person who weaves, esp as a means of livelihood

WEAVES ▸ **weave**

WEAVING, -S ▸ **weave**

WEAZAND, -S *same as* ▸ **weasand**

WEAZEN, -ED, -S *same as* ▸ **wizen**

WEB, -BED, -S *n* net spun by a spider ▸ *vb* cover with or as if with a web

WEBAPP, -S *n* application program that is accessed on the internet

WEBBED ▸ **web**

WEBBIE, -S *n* person who is well versed in the use of the World Wide Web

WEBBIER ▸ **webby**

WEBBIES ▸ **webbie**

WEBBIEST ▸ **webby**

WEBBING, -S *n* anything that forms a web

WEBBY, WEBBIER, WEBBIEST *adj* of, relating to, resembling, or consisting of a web

WEBCAM, -S *n* camera that transmits images over the internet

WEBCAST, -S *n* broadcast of an event over the internet ▸ *vb* make such a broadcast

WEBCHAT, -S *vb* exchange messages via the internet

WEBER, -S *n* SI unit of magnetic flux

WEBFED *adj* (of printing press) printing from rolls of paper

WEBFOOT, WEBFEET *n* foot having the toes connected by folds of skin

WEBHEAD, -S *n* person who uses the internet a lot

WEBIFY, WEBIFIED, WEBIFIES *vb* convert (information) for display on the internet

WEBINAR, -S *n* interactive seminar conducted over the World Wide Web

WEBISODE *n* episode (of a television series) intended for online viewing

WEBLESS ▸ **web**

WEBLIKE ▸ **web**

WEBLISH *n* shorthand form of English that is used in text messaging, chatrooms, etc

WEBLOG, -S *n* person's online journal

WEBMAIL, -S *n* system of electronic mail accessed via the internet

WEBPAGE, -S *n* page on a website

WEBRING, -S *n* group of websites organized in a circular structure

WEBS ▸ **web**

WEBSITE, -S *n* group of connected pages on the World Wide Web

WEBSPACE *n* storage space on a web server

WEBSTER, -S *archaic word for* ▸ **weaver**

WEBWHEEL *n* wheel containing a plate or web instead of spokes

WEBWORK, -S *n* work done using the World Wide Web

WEBWORM, -S *n* type of caterpillar

WEBZINE, -S *n* magazine published on the internet

WECHT, -ED, -ING, -S *n* agricultural tool ▸ *vb* winnow (corn)

WED, -DED, -DING, -S vb marry

WEDDER, -ED, -S dialect form of ▸ **weather**

WEDDING, -S ▸ **wed**

WEDEL, -ED, -ING, -S variant of ▸ **wedeln**

WEDELN, -ED, -S n succession of high-speed turns performed in skiing ▸ vb perform a wedeln

WEDELS ▸ **wedel**

WEDGE, -D, -S n piece of material thick at one end and thin at the other ▸ vb fasten or split with a wedge

WEDGIE, -S n wedge-heeled shoe

WEDGIER ▸ **wedgy**

WEDGIES ▸ **wedgie**

WEDGIEST ▸ **wedgy**

WEDGING, -S ▸ **wedge**

WEDGY, WEDGIER, WEDGIEST ▸ **wedge**

WEDLOCK, -S n marriage

WEDS ▸ **wed**

WEE, -ING, -R, -S, -ST adj small or short ▸ n instance of urinating ▸ vb urinate

WEED, -ED n plant growing where undesired ▸ vb clear of weeds

WEEDBED, -S n body of water having lots of weeds

WEEDED ▸ **weed**

WEEDER, -S ▸ **weed**

WEEDERY n weed-ridden area

WEEDIER ▸ **weedy**

WEEDIEST ▸ **weedy**

WEEDILY ▸ **weedy**

WEEDING, -S ▸ **weed**

WEEDLESS ▸ **weed**

WEEDLIKE ▸ **weed**

WEEDLINE n edge of a weedbed

WEEDS pl n widow's mourning clothes

WEEDY, WEEDIER, WEEDIEST adj (of a person) thin and weak

WEEING ▸ **wee**

WEEJUNS pl n moccasin-style shoes for casual wear

WEEK, -S n period of seven days, esp one beginning on a Sunday ▸ adv seven days before or after a specified day

WEEKDAY, -S n any day of the week except Saturday or Sunday

WEEKE, -S same as ▸ **wick**

WEEKEND n Saturday and Sunday ▸ vb spend or pass a weekend

WEEKENDS adv at the weekend, esp regularly or during every weekend

WEEKES ▸ **weeke**

WEEKLIES ▸ **weekly**

WEEKLONG adj lasting a week

WEEKLY, WEEKLIES adv happening, done, etc once a week ▸ n newspaper or magazine published once a week ▸ adj happening once a week or every week

WEEKS ▸ **week**

WEEL, -S Scot word for ▸ **well**

WEEM, -S n underground home

WEEN, -ED, -ING, -S vb think or imagine (something)

WEENIE, -S adj very small ▸ n wiener

WEENIER ▸ **weeny**

WEENIES ▸ **weenie**

WEENIEST ▸ **weeny**

WEENING ▸ **ween**

WEENS ▸ **ween**

WEENSY, WEENSIER same as ▸ **weeny**

WEENY, WEENIER, WEENIEST adj very small

WEEP, -S, WEPT vb shed tears ▸ n spell of weeping

WEEPER, -S n person who weeps, esp a hired mourner

WEEPHOLE n small drain hole in wall

WEEPIE same as ▸ **weepy**

WEEPIER ▸ **weepy**

WEEPIES ▸ **weepy**

WEEPIEST ▸ **weepy**

WEEPILY ▸ **weepy**

WEEPING, -S adj (of plants) having slender hanging branches

WEEPS ▸ **weep**

WEEPY, WEEPIER, WEEPIES, WEEPIEST adj liable to cry ▸ n sentimental film or book

WEER ▸ **wee**

WEES ▸ **wee**

WEEST ▸ **wee**

WEET, -ER, -EST, -ING, -S dialect form of ▸ **wet**

WEETE, -D same as ▸ **wit**

WEETEN same as ▸ **wit**

WEETER ▸ **weet**

WEETEST ▸ **weet**

WEETING ▸ **weet**

WEETLESS obsolete variant of ▸ **witless**

WEETS ▸ **weet**

WEEVER, -S n type of small fish

WEEVIL, -S n small beetle that eats grain etc

WEEVILED same as ▸ **weevilled**

WEEVILLY adj full of weevils

WEEVILS ▸ **weevil**

WEEVILY adj full of weevils

WEEWEE, -D, -S vb urinate

WEFT, -ED, -ING, -S n cross threads in weaving ▸ vb form weft

WEFTAGE, -S n texture

WEFTE, -S n forsaken child

WEFTED ▸ **weft**

WEFTES ▸ **wefte**

WEFTING ▸ **weft**

WEFTS ▸ **weft**

WEFTWISE adv in the direction of the weft

WEID, -S n sudden illness

WEIGELA, -S n type of shrub

WEIGELIA same as ▸ **weigela**

WEIGH, WAID, WAIDE, -ED, -ING, -S vb have a specified weight

WEIGHAGE n duty paid for weighing goods

WEIGHED ▸ **weigh**

WEIGHER, -S ▸ **weigh**

WEIGHING ▸ **weigh**

WEIGHMAN, WEIGHMEN n person responsible for weighing goods

WEIGHS ▸ **weigh**

WEIGHT, -ED, -S n heaviness of an object ▸ vb add weight to

WEIGHTER ▸ **weight**

WEIGHTS ▸ **weight**

WEIGHTY adj important or serious

WEIL, -S n whirlpool

WEINER, -S same as ▸ **wiener**

WEIR, -ED, -ING, -S vb ward off ▸ n river dam

WEIRD, -ED, -ER, -EST, -ING, -S adj strange or bizarre ▸ vb warn beforehand

WEIRDIE, -S same as ▸ **weirdo**

WEIRDING ▸ **weird**

WEIRDLY ▸ **weird**

WEIRDO, -ES, -S n peculiar person

WEIRDS ▸ **weird**

WEIRDY n weird person

WEIRED ▸ **weir**

WEIRING ▸ **weir**

WEIRS ▸ **weir**

WEISE, -D, -S, WEISING same as ▸ **wise**

WEIZE, -D, -S, WEIZING same as ▸ **wise**

WEKA, -S n flightless New Zealand rail

WELAWAY same as ▸ **wellaway**

W

WELCH, -ED, -ES, -ING *same as* ► **welsh**

WELCHER, -S ► **welch**

WELCHES ► **welch**

WELCHING ► **welch**

WELCOME, -D, -S *vb* greet with pleasure ▷ *n* kindly greeting ▷ *adj* received gladly

WELCOMER ► **welcome**

WELCOMES ► **welcome**

WELD, -ED, -S *vb* join (pieces of metal or plastic) by softening with heat ▷ *n* welded joint

WELDABLE ► **weld**

WELDED ► **weld**

WELDER, -S ► **weld**

WELDING, -S ► **weld**

WELDLESS ► **weld**

WELDMENT *n* unit composed of welded pieces

WELDMESH *n* type of fencing consisting of wire mesh reinforced by welding

WELDOR, -S ► **weld**

WELDS ► **weld**

WELFARE, -S *n* wellbeing

WELK, -ED, -ING, -S *vb* wither; dry up

WELKE, -S *obsolete form of* ► **welk**

WELKED ► **welk**

WELKES ► **welke**

WELKIN, -S *n* sky, heavens, or upper air

WELKING ► **welk**

WELKINS ► **welkin**

WELKS ► **welk**

WELKT *adj* twisted

WELL, -ED, -ING, -INGS, -S *adv* satisfactorily ▷ *adj* in good health ▷ *interj* exclamation of surprise, interrogation, etc ▷ *n* hole sunk into the earth to reach water, oil, or gas ▷ *vb* flow upwards or outwards

WELLADAY *interj* alas

WELLAWAY *interj* alas

WELLBORN *adj* having been born into a wealthy family

WELLCURB *n* stone surround at top of well

WELLDOER *n* moral person

WELLED ► **well**

WELLHEAD *n* source of a well or stream

WELLHOLE *n* well shaft

WELLIE *n* wellington boot

WELLIES ► **welly**

WELLING ► **well**

WELLINGS ► **well**

WELLNESS *n* state of being in good physical and mental health

WELLS ► **well**

WELLSITE *n* site of well

WELLY, WELLIES *n* energy or commitment

WELS *n* type of catfish

WELSH, -ED, -ES, -ING *vb* fail to pay a debt or fulfil an obligation

WELSHER, -S ► **welsh**

WELSHES ► **welsh**

WELSHING ► **welsh**

WELT, -ED, -S *same as* ► **weal**

WELTER, -ED, -S *n* jumbled mass ▷ *vb* roll about, writhe, or wallow

WELTING, -S ► **welt**

WELTS ► **welt**

WEM, -S *same as* ► **wame**

WEMB, -S *same as* ► **wame**

WEMS ► **wem**

WEN, -S *n* cyst on the scalp

WENA *pron* South African word for you

WENCH, -ES *n* old word for a female servant

WEND, -ED, -ING, -S *vb* go or travel

WENDIGO, -S *n* evil spirit or cannibal

WENDING ► **wend**

WENDS ► **wend**

WENGE, -S *n* type of tree found in central and West Africa

WENNIER ► **wenny**

WENNIEST ► **wenny**

WENNISH ► **wen**

WENNY, WENNIER, WENNIEST ► **wen**

WENS ► **wen**

WENT, -S *n* path

WEPT ► **weep**

WERE *vb* form of the past tense of *be*

WEREGILD *same as* ► **wergild**

WEREWOLF *n* (in folklore) person who can turn into a wolf

WERGELD, -S *same as* ► **wergild**

WERGELT, -S *same as* ► **wergeld**

WERGILD, -S *n* price set on a person's life, to be paid as compensation by their slayer

WERO, -S *n* challenge made by an armed Māori warrior to a visitor to a marae

WERRIS, -ES *Australian slang word for* ► **urination**

WERSH, -ER, -EST *adj* tasteless

WERT *singular form of the past tense of* ► **be**

WERWOLF *same as* ► **werewolf**

WESAND, -S *same as* ► **weasand**

WESKIT, -S *informal word for* > **waistcoat**

WESSAND, -S *same as* ► **weasand**

WEST, -ED, -S *n* part of the horizon where the sun sets ▷ *adj* in the west ▷ *adv* in, to, or towards the west ▷ *vb* move in westerly direction

WESTER, -ED, -S *vb* move or appear to move towards the west ▷ *n* strong wind or storm from the west

WESTERLY *adj* of or in the west ▷ *adv* towards the west ▷ *n* wind blowing from the west

WESTERN, -S *adj* of or in the west ▷ *n* film or story about cowboys in the western US

WESTERS ► **wester**

WESTIE, -S *n* insulting word for a young working-class person from the western suburbs of Sydney

WESTING, -S *n* movement, deviation, or distance covered in a westerly direction

WESTLIN *Scots word for* ► **western**

WESTLINS *adv* to or in west

WESTMOST *adj* most western

WESTS ► **west**

WESTWARD *adv* towards the west ▷ *n* westward part or direction ▷ *adj* moving, facing, or situated in the west

WET, -S, -TED, -TEST, -TING, -TINGS *adj* covered or soaked with water or another liquid ▷ *n* moisture or rain ▷ *vb* make wet

WETA, -S *n* type of wingless insect

WETHER, -S *n* male sheep

WETLAND, -S *n* area of marshy land

WETLY ► **wet**

WETNESS *n* the state of being wet

WETPROOF *adj* waterproof

WETS ► **wet**

WETSUIT, -S *n* body suit for diving

WETTABLE ► **wet**

WETTED ► **wet**

WETTER, -S ► **wet**

WETTEST ► **wet**

WETTIE, -S *n* wetsuit

W

WETTING ▶ wet
WETTINGS ▶ wet
WETTISH ▶ wet
WETWARE, -S n the brain, as opposed to computers
WEX, -ED, -ES, -ING obsolete form of ▶ wax

Wex is an old word for wax, in the sense of grow. It gives a very good score for a 3-letter word, and can be extended to wexe.

WEXE obsolete form of ▶ wax
WEXED ▶ wex
WEXES ▶ wex
WEXING ▶ wex
WEY, -S n measurement of weight
WEYARD obsolete form of ▶ weird
WEYS ▶ wey
WEYWARD obsolete form of ▶ weird
WEZAND, -S obsolete form of ▶ weasand
WHA Scot word for ▶ who
WHACK, -ED, -S vb strike with a resounding blow ▷ n such a blow
WHACKER, -S ▶ whack
WHACKIER ▶ whacky
WHACKING adj huge ▷ n severe beating ▷ adv extremely
WHACKO, -ES, -S n odd or eccentric person
WHACKS ▶ whack
WHACKY, WHACKIER variant spelling of ▶ wacky
WHAE same as ▶ wha
WHAISLE, -D, -S Scots form of ▶ wheeze
WHAIZLE, -D, -S same as ▶ whaisle
WHAKAIRO n art of carving
WHALE, -D, -S n large fish-shaped sea mammal ▷ vb hunt for whales
WHALEMAN, WHALEMEN n person employed in whaling
WHALER, -S n ship or person involved in whaling
WHALERY n whaling
WHALES ▶ whale
WHALING, -S n hunting of whales for food and oil ▷ adv extremely
WHALLY adj (of eyes) with light-coloured irises
WHAM, -MED, -MING, -S interj expression indicating suddenness or forcefulness ▷ n forceful blow or impact ▷ vb strike or cause to strike with great force

WHAMMIES ▶ whammy
WHAMMING ▶ wham
WHAMMO, -S n sound of a sudden collision
WHAMMY, WHAMMIES n devastating setback
WHAMO same as ▶ whammo
WHAMPLE, -S n strike
WHAMS ▶ wham
WHANAU, -S n (in Māori societies) a family, esp an extended family
WHANG, -ED, -ING, -S vb strike or be struck so as to cause a resounding noise ▷ n resounding noise produced by a heavy blow
WHANGAM, -S n imaginary creature
WHANGED ▶ whang
WHANGEE, -S n tall woody grass grown for its stems, which are used for bamboo canes
WHANGING ▶ whang
WHANGS ▶ whang
WHAP, -PED, -PING, -S same as ▶ whop
WHAPPER, -S same as ▶ whopper
WHAPPING ▶ whap
WHAPS ▶ whap
WHARE, -S n Māori hut or dwelling place
WHARENUI n (in New Zealand) meeting house
WHARES ▶ whare
WHARF, -ED, -ING, -S n platform at a harbour for loading and unloading ships ▷ vb put (goods, etc) on a wharf
WHARFAGE n accommodation for ships at wharves
WHARFED ▶ wharf
WHARFIE, -S n person employed to load and unload ships
WHARFING ▶ wharf
WHARFS ▶ wharf
WHARVE, -S n wooden disc or wheel on a shaft serving as a flywheel or pulley
WHAT, -S pron which thing ▷ interj exclamation of anger, surprise, etc ▷ adv in which way, how much ▷ n part; portion
WHATA, -S n building on stilts or a raised platform for storing provisions
WHATCHA interj greeting meaning 'what are you?'
WHATEN adj what; what kind of

WHATEVER pron everything or anything that ▷ determiner intensive form of what
WHATEVS interj whatever
WHATNA another word for ▶ whaten
WHATNESS n what something is
WHATNOT, -S n similar unspecified things
WHATS ▶ what
WHATSIS US form of ▶ whatsit
WHATSIT, -S n person or thing the name of which is temporarily forgotten
WHATSO adj of whatever kind
WHATTEN same as ▶ whaten
WHAUP, -S n curlew
WHAUR, -S Scot word for ▶ where
WHEAL, -S same as ▶ weal
WHEAR obsolete variant of ▶ where
WHEARE obsolete variant of ▶ where
WHEAT, -S n grain used in making flour, bread, and pasta
WHEATEAR n small songbird
WHEATEN, -S n type of dog ▷ adj made of the grain or flour of wheat
WHEATIER ▶ wheaty
WHEATS ▶ wheat
WHEATY, WHEATIER adj having a wheat-like taste
WHEE interj exclamation of joy, thrill, etc
WHEECH, -ED, -S vb Scots word meaning move quickly
WHEEDLE, -D, -S vb coax or cajole
WHEEDLER ▶ wheedle
WHEEDLES ▶ wheedle
WHEEL, -ING, -S n disc that revolves on an axle ▷ vb push or pull (something with wheels)
WHEELED adj having or equipped with a wheel or wheels
WHEELER, -S n horse or other draught animal nearest the wheel
WHEELIE, -S n manoeuvre on a bike in which the front wheel is raised off the ground
WHEELIER ▶ wheely
WHEELIES ▶ wheelie
WHEELING ▶ wheel
WHEELMAN, WHEELMEN n helmsman

W

WHEELS ▸ wheel
WHEELY, WHEELIER adj resembling a wheel
WHEEN, -S n few
WHEENGE, -D, -S Scots form of ▸ **whinge**
WHEENS ▸ wheen
WHEEP, -ED, -ING, -S vb fly quickly and lightly
WHEEPLE, -D, -S vb whistle weakly
WHEEPS ▸ wheep
WHEESH, -ED, -ES vb Scots word meaning silence (a person, noise, etc)
WHEESHT, -S same as ▸ **wheesh**
WHEEZE, -D, -S, WHEEZING vb breathe with a hoarse whistling noise ▷ n wheezing sound
WHEEZER, -S ▸ wheeze
WHEEZES ▸ wheeze
WHEEZIER ▸ wheezy
WHEEZILY ▸ wheezy
WHEEZING ▸ wheeze
WHEEZLE, -D, -S vb make hoarse breathing sound
WHEEZY, WHEEZIER ▸ **wheeze**
WHEFT, -S same as ▸ **waft**
WHELK, -S n edible snail-like shellfish
WHELKED adj having or covered with whelks
WHELKIER ▸ whelky
WHELKS ▸ whelk
WHELKY, WHELKIER ▸ **whelk**
WHELM, -ED, -ING, -S vb engulf entirely with or as if with water
WHELP, -ED, -ING, -S n pup or cub ▷ vb (of an animal) give birth
WHEMMLE, -D, -S vb overturn
WHEN, -S adv at what time? ▷ pron at which time ▷ n question of when
WHENAS conj while; inasmuch as
WHENCE, -S n point of origin ▷ adv from what place or source ▷ pron from what place, cause, or source
WHENEVER adv at whatever time
WHENS ▸ when
WHENUA, -S n land
WHENWE, -S n White immigrant to South Africa from Zimbabwe
WHERE, -S adv in, at, or to what place? ▷ pron in, at, or to which place ▷ n question

as to the position, direction, or destination of something
WHEREAS n testimonial introduced by whereas
WHEREAT adv at or to which place
WHEREBY pron by which ▷ adv how? by what means?
WHEREFOR adv for which ▷ n explanation or reason
WHEREIN adv in what place or respect? ▷ pron in which place or thing
WHEREOF adv of what or which person or thing? ▷ pron of which person or thing
WHEREON adv on what thing or place? ▷ pron on which thing, place, etc
WHEREOUT adv out of which
WHERES ▸ where
WHERESO adv in or to an unspecified place
WHERETO adv towards what (place, end, etc)? ▷ pron to which
WHEREVER adv at whatever place ▷ pron at, in, or to every place or point which
WHERRET, -S vb strike (someone) a blow ▷ n blow, esp a slap on the face
WHERRIED ▸ wherry
WHERRIES ▸ wherry
WHERRIT, -S vb worry or cause to worry
WHERRY, WHERRIED, WHERRIES n any of certain kinds of half-decked commercial boats ▷ vb travel in a wherry
WHERVE, -S same as ▸ **wharve**
WHET, -S, -TED, -TING vb sharpen (a tool) ▷ n act of whetting
WHETHER conj used to introduce any indirect question
WHETS ▸ whet
WHETTED ▸ whet
WHETTER, -S ▸ whet
WHETTING ▸ whet
WHEUGH, -ED, -S same as ▸ **whew**
WHEW, -ED, -ING, -S interj exclamation expressing relief, delight, etc ▷ vb express relief
WHEY, -IER, -IEST, -S n watery liquid that separates from the curd when milk is clotted

WHEYEY ▸ whey
WHEYFACE n pale bloodless face
WHEYIER ▸ whey
WHEYIEST ▸ whey
WHEYISH ▸ whey
WHEYLIKE ▸ whey
WHEYS ▸ whey
WHICH pron used to request or refer to a choice from different possibilities ▷ adj used with a noun in requesting that a particular thing is further identified or distinguished
WHICKER, -S vb (of a horse) to whinny or neigh
WHID, -DED, -DING, -S vb move quickly
WHIDAH, -S same as ▸ **whydah**
WHIDDED ▸ whid
WHIDDER, -S vb move with force
WHIDDING ▸ whid
WHIDS ▸ whid
WHIFF, -ED, -ING, -S n puff of air or odour ▷ vb come, convey, or go in whiffs
WHIFFER, -S ▸ whiff
WHIFFET, -S n insignificant person
WHIFFIER ▸ whiffy
WHIFFING ▸ whiff
WHIFFLE, -D, -S vb think or behave in an erratic or unpredictable way
WHIFFLER n person who whiffles
WHIFFLES ▸ whiffle
WHIFFS ▸ whiff
WHIFFY, WHIFFIER adj smelly
WHIFT, -S n brief emission of air
WHIG, -GED, -GING, -S vb go quickly
WHILE, -D, WHILING n period of time ▷ vb pass time idly and pleasantly
WHILERE adv a while ago
WHILES adv at times
WHILEVER conj as long as
WHILING ▸ while
WHILK archaic and dialect word for ▸ **which**
WHILLY, WHILLIED, WHILLIES vb influence by flattery
WHILOM adv formerly ▷ adj one-time
WHILST same as ▸ **while**
WHIM, -MED, -MING, -S n sudden fancy ▷ vb have a whim

WHIMBREL n small European curlew with a striped head

WHIMMED ► whim

WHIMMIER ► whimmy

WHIMMING ► whim

WHIMMY, WHIMMIER adj having whims

WHIMPER, -S vb cry in a soft whining way ▷ n soft plaintive whine

WHIMPLE, -D, -S same as ► wimple

WHIMS ► whim

WHIMSEY, -S same as ► whimsy

WHIMSIED ► whimsy

WHIMSIER ► whimsy

WHIMSIES ► whimsy

WHIMSILY ► whimsy

WHIMSY, WHIMSIER, WHIMSIES n capricious idea ▷ adj quaint, comical, or unusual

WHIN, -S n gorse

WHINCHAT n type of songbird

WHINE, -D, -S n high-pitched plaintive cry ▷ vb make such a sound

WHINER, -S ► whine

WHINES ► whine

WHINEY same as ► whiny

WHINGE, -D, -S, WHINGING vb complain ▷ n complaint

WHINGER, -S ► whinge

WHINGES ► whinge

WHINGIER ► whingy

WHINGING ► whinge

WHINGY, WHINGIER adj complaining peevishly, whining

WHINIARD same as ► whinyard

WHINIER ► whiny

WHINIEST ► whiny

WHINING, -S ► whine

WHINNY, WHINNIED, WHINNIER, WHINNIES vb neigh softly ▷ n soft neigh ▷ adj covered in whin

WHINS ► whin

WHINY, WHINIER, WHINIEST adj high-pitched and plaintive

WHINYARD n sword

WHIO, -S n New Zealand mountain duck with blue plumage

WHIP, -PED, -PING, -S n cord attached to a handle, used for beating animals or people ▷ vb strike with a whip, strap, or cane

WHIPBIRD n any of several birds having a whistle ending in a whipcrack note

WHIPCAT, -S n tailor

WHIPCORD, -S n strong worsted or cotton fabric with a diagonally ribbed surface

WHIPJACK n beggar imitating a sailor

WHIPLASH n quick lash of a whip

WHIPLESS adj without a whip

WHIPLIKE ► whip

WHIPPED ► whip

WHIPPER, -S ► whip

WHIPPET, -S n racing dog like a small greyhound

WHIPPIER ► whippy

WHIPPING ► whip

WHIPPIT, -S n small canister of nitrous oxide

WHIPPY, WHIPPIER adj springy

WHIPRAY, -S n stingray

WHIPS ► whip

WHIPSAW, -N, -S n any saw with a flexible blade, such as a bandsaw ▷ vb saw with a whipsaw

WHIPSTER n insignificant but pretentious or cheeky person, esp a young one

WHIPT old past tense of ► whip

WHIPTAIL n type of lizard

WHIPWORM n parasitic worm living in the intestines of mammals

WHIR, -RED, -RING, -S n prolonged soft swish or buzz ▷ vb make or cause to make a whir

WHIRL, -ED, -S vb spin or revolve ▷ n whirling movement

WHIRLBAT n medieval weapon

WHIRLED ► whirl

WHIRLER, -S ► whirl

WHIRLIER ► whirly

WHIRLIES n illness induced by excessive use of alcohol

WHIRLING ► whirl

WHIRLS ► whirl

WHIRLY, WHIRLIER adj characterized by whirling

WHIRR, -S same as ► whir

WHIRRA interj exclamation of sorrow or deep concern

WHIRRED ► whir

WHIRRET, -S vb strike with sharp blow

WHIRRIED ► whirry

WHIRRIER ► whirry

WHIRRIES ► whirry

WHIRRING ► whir

WHIRRS ► whirr

WHIRRY, WHIRRIED, WHIRRIER, WHIRRIES vb move quickly ▷ adj characteristic of a whir

WHIRS ► whir

WHIRTLE, -S same as ► wortle

WHISH, -ED, -ES, -ING less common word for ► swish

WHISHT, -ED, -S interj hush!, be quiet! ▷ adj silent or still ▷ vb make or become silent

WHISK, -ED, -ING, -S vb move or remove quickly ▷ n quick movement

WHISKER, -S n any of the long stiff hairs on the face of a cat or other mammal

WHISKERY adj having whiskers

WHISKET, -S same as ► wisket

WHISKEY, -S n Irish or American whisky

WHISKIES ► whisky

WHISKING ► whisk

WHISKS ► whisk

WHISKY, WHISKIES n spirit distilled from fermented cereals

WHISPER, -S vb speak softly, without vibration of the vocal cords ▷ n soft voice

WHISPERY adj like a whisper

WHISS, -ED, -ES, -ING vb hiss

WHIST, -ED, -ING, -S same as ► whisht

WHISTLE, -D, -S vb produce a shrill sound ▷ n whistling sound

WHISTLER n person or thing that whistles

WHISTLES ► whistle

WHISTS ► whist

WHIT, -S n smallest particle

WHITE, -R, -ST adj of the colour of snow ▷ n colour of snow

WHITECAP n wave with a white broken crest

WHITED adj as in **whited sepulchre** hypocrite

WHITEFLY n tiny whitish insect that is harmful to greenhouse plants

WHITELY ► white

WHITEN, -ED, -S vb make or become white or whiter

WHITENER n substance that makes something white or whiter

WHITENS ► whiten

WHITEOUT n atmospheric condition in which blizzards

W

W

or low clouds make it very difficult to see

WHITEPOT *n* custard or milk pudding

WHITER ▸ white

WHITES *pl n* white clothes, as worn for playing cricket

WHITEST ▸ white

WHITEY *same as* ▸ whity

WHITHER, -S *same as* ▸ wuther

WHITIER ▸ whity

WHITIEST ▸ whity

WHITING, -S *n* edible sea fish

WHITISH ▸ white

WHITLING *n* type of trout

WHITLOW, -S *n* inflamed sore on a finger or toe, esp round a nail

WHITRACK *n* weasel or stoat

WHITRET, -S *same as* ▸ whittret

WHITRICK *n* dialect word for a male weasel

WHITS ▸ whit

WHITSTER *n* person who whitens clothes

WHITTAW, -S *same as* > whittawer

WHITTER, -S *variant spelling of* ▸ witter

WHITTLE, -D, -S *vb* cut or carve (wood) with a knife ▷ *n* knife, esp a large one

WHITTLER ▸ whittle

WHITTLES ▸ whittle

WHITTRET *n* male weasel

WHITY, WHITIER, WHITIEST *adj* of a white colour

WHIZ *same as* ▸ whizz

WHIZBANG *n* small-calibre shell

WHIZZ, -ED, -ES, -ING *vb* make a loud buzzing sound ▷ *n* loud buzzing sound

WHIZZER, -S ▸ whizz

WHIZZES ▸ whizz

WHIZZIER ▸ whizzy

WHIZZING ▸ whizz

WHIZZO *same as* ▸ whizzy

WHIZZY, WHIZZIER *adj* using sophisticated technology

WHO *pron* which person

WHOA *interj* command used to stop or slow down

WHODUNIT *same as* > whodunnit

WHOEVER *pron* any person who

WHOLE, -S *adj* containing all the elements or parts ▷ *n* complete thing or system

WHOLISM, -S *same as* ▸ holism

WHOLIST, -S *same as* ▸ holist

WHOLLY *adv* completely or totally

WHOLPHIN *n* whale-dolphin hybrid

WHOM *pron* objective form of *who*

WHOMBLE, -D, -S *same as* ▸ whemmle

WHOMEVER *pron* objective form of *whoever*

WHOMMLE, -D, -S *same as* ▸ whemmle

WHOMP, -ED, -ING, -S *vb* strike; thump

WHOMSO *pron* whom; whomever

WHOOBUB, -S *same as* ▸ hubbub

WHOOF, -ED, -ING, -S *same as* ▸ woof

WHOOMP, -S *n* sudden loud sound

WHOOMPH, -S *same as* ▸ whoomp

WHOOMPS ▸ whoomp

WHOOP, -ED, -ING *n* shout or cry to express excitement ▷ *vb* emit a whoop

WHOOPEE, -S *n* cry of joy

WHOOPER, -S *n* type of swan

WHOOPIE, -S *same as* ▸ whoopee

WHOOPING ▸ whoop

WHOOPLA, -S *n* commotion; fuss

WHOOPS *interj* exclamation of surprise or of apology

WHOOPSIE *n* animal excrement

WHOOSH, -ED, -ES *n* hissing or rushing sound ▷ *vb* make or move with a hissing or rushing sound

WHOOSIS *n* thingamajig

WHOOT, -ED, -ING, -S *obsolete variant of* ▸ hoot

WHOP, -PED, -S *vb* strike, beat, or thrash

WHOPPER, -S *n* anything unusually large

WHOPPING *n* beating as punishment ▷ *adj* unusually large ▷ *adv* extremely

WHOPS ▸ whop

WHORL, -ING, -S *n* ring of leaves or petals ▷ *vb* form a whorl or whorls

WHORLBAT *same as* ▸ whirlbat

WHORLED ▸ whorl

WHORLING ▸ whorl

WHORLS ▸ whorl

WHORT, -S *n* small shrub bearing blackish edible sweet berries

WHORTLE, -S *n* whortleberry

WHORTS ▸ whort

WHOSE *pron* of whom or of which ▷ *determiner* of whom or of which

WHOSESO *adj* possessive form of whoso

WHOSEVER *pron* belonging to whoever

WHOSIS, -ES *n* thingamajig

WHOSIT, -S *n* object or person whose name is not known

WHOSO *archaic word for* ▸ whoever

WHOT *obsolete variant of* ▸ hot

WHOW, -ED, -ING, -S *interj* wow ▷ *vb* to wow

WHUMMLE, -D, -S *same as* ▸ whemmle

WHUMP, -ED, -ING, -S *vb* make a dull thud ▷ *n* dull thud

WHUP, -PED, -PING, -S *vb* defeat totally

WHY, -S *adv* for what reason ▷ *pron* because of which ▷ *n* reason, purpose, or cause of something

WHYDA, -S *same as* ▸ whydah

WHYDAH, -S *n* type of black African bird

WHYDAS ▸ whyda

WHYDUNIT *same as* > whydunnit

WHYDAS ▸ whyda

WHYEVER *adv* for whatever reason

WHYS ▸ why

WIBBLE, -D, -S, WIBBLING *vb* wobble

WICCA, -S *n* cult or practice of witchcraft

WICCAN, -S *n* practitioner of wicca

WICCAS ▸ wicca

WICE *Scots form of* ▸ wise

WICH, -ES *n* variant of wych

WICK, -S *n* cord through a lamp or candle which carries fuel to the flame ▷ *adj* lively or active ▷ *vb* (of a material) draw in (water, fuel, etc)

WICKAPE, -S *same as* ▸ wicopy

WICKED, -ER, -S *adj* morally bad ▷ *n* wicked person

WICKEDLY ▸ wicked

WICKEDS ▸ wicked

WICKEN, -S *same as* ▸ quicken

WICKER, -S adj made of woven cane ⊳ n slender flexible twig or shoot, esp of willow

WICKERED ▸ wicker

WICKERS ▸ wicker

WICKET, -S n set of three cricket stumps and two bails

WICKIES ▸ wicky

WICKING, -S ▸ wick

WICKIUP, -S n crude shelter made of brushwood, mats, or grass and having an oval frame

WICKLESS ▸ wick

WICKS ▸ wick

WICKY, WICKIES same as ▸ quicken

WICKYUP, -S same as ▸ wickiup

WICOPY, WICOPIES n any of various North American trees, shrubs, or herbaceous plants

WIDDER, -S same as ▸ widow

WIDDIE same as ▸ widdy

WIDDIES ▸ widdy

WIDDLE, -D, -S, WIDDLING vb urinate ⊳ n urine

WIDDY, WIDDIES vb rope made of twigs

WIDE, -R, -S, -ST adj large from side to side ⊳ adv the full extent ⊳ n (in cricket) a ball outside a batsman's reach

WIDEBAND n wide bandwidth transmission medium ⊳ adj capable of transmitting on a wide bandwidth

WIDEBODY n aircraft with a wide fuselage

WIDELY ▸ wide

WIDEN, -ED, -S vb make or become wider

WIDENER, -S ▸ widen

WIDENESS ▸ wide

WIDENING n act of widening

WIDENS ▸ widen

WIDEOUT, -S n (in American football) player who catches passes from the quarterback

WIDER ▸ wide

WIDES ▸ wide

WIDEST ▸ wide

WIDGEON, -S same as ▸ wigeon

WIDGET, -S n any small device, the name of which is unknown or forgotten

WIDGIE, -S n Australian word for a female hooligan

WIDISH ▸ wide

WIDOW, -ED, -ING, -S n woman whose spouse is dead and who has not remarried ⊳ vb cause to become a widow

WIDOWER, -S n man whose spouse is dead and who has not remarried

WIDOWING ▸ widow

WIDOWMAN, WIDOWMEN n widower

WIDOWS ▸ widow

WIDTH, -S n distance from side to side

WIDTHWAY adj across the width

WIEL, -S same as ▸ weel

WIELD, -ED, -ING, -S vb hold and use (a weapon)

WIELDER, -S ▸ wield

WIELDIER ▸ wieldy

WIELDING ▸ wield

WIELDS ▸ wield

WIELDY, WIELDIER adj easily handled, used, or managed

WIELS ▸ wiel

WIENER, -S n kind of smoked beef or pork sausage, similar to a frankfurter

WIENIE, -S same as ▸ wiener

WIFE, -D, -S, WIFING, WIVES n woman to whom one is married ⊳ vb marry

WIFEDOM, -S n state of being a wife

WIFEHOOD ▸ wife

WIFELESS ▸ wife

WIFELIER ▸ wifely

WIFELIKE ▸ wife

WIFELY, WIFELIER ▸ wife

WIFES ▸ wife

WIFEY, -S n wife

WIFIE, -S n woman

WIFING ▸ wife

WIFTY, WIFTIER, WIFTIEST adj scatterbrained

WIG, -GING, -GINGS, -S n artificial head of hair ⊳ vb furnish with a wig

WIGAN, -S n stiff fabric

WIGEON, -S n duck found in marshland

WIGGED ▸ wig

WIGGERY n wigs

WIGGIER ▸ wiggy

WIGGIEST ▸ wiggy

WIGGING ▸ wig

WIGGINGS ▸ wig

WIGGLE, -D, -S, WIGGLING vb move jerkily from side to side ⊳ n wiggling movement

WIGGLER, -S ▸ wiggle

WIGGLES ▸ wiggle

WIGGLIER ▸ wiggly

WIGGLING ▸ wiggle

WIGGLY, WIGGLIER ▸ wiggle

WIGGY, WIGGIER, WIGGIEST adj eccentric

WIGHT, -ED, -ING, -S vb blame ⊳ n human being ⊳ adj strong and brave

WIGHTLY adv swiftly

WIGHTS ▸ wight

WIGLESS ▸ wig

WIGLET, -S n small wig

WIGLIKE ▸ wig

WIGMAKER n person who makes wigs

WIGS ▸ wig

WIGWAG, -S vb move (something) back and forth ⊳ n system of communication by flag semaphore

WIGWAM, -S n Native American's tent

WIKI, -S n website consisting mainly of user-generated content

WIKIUP, -S same as ▸ wickiup

WILCO interj expression indicating that the message just received will be complied with

WILD, -ED, -EST, -S same as ▸ wield

WILDCARD n person given entry to a competition without qualifying

WILDCAT, -S n European wild animal like a large domestic cat ⊳ adj risky and financially unsound ⊳ vb drill for petroleum or natural gas in an area having no known reserves

WILDED ▸ wild

WILDER, -ED, -S vb lead or be led astray

WILDEST ▸ wild

WILDFIRE n highly flammable material, such as Greek fire, formerly used in warfare

WILDFOWL n wild bird that is hunted for sport or food

WILDING, -S n uncultivated plant

WILDISH ▸ wild

WILDLAND n land which has not been cultivated

WILDLIFE n wild animals and plants collectively

WILDLING same as ▸ wilding

WILDLY ▸ wild

WILDMAN, WILDMEN n man who lives in the wild

WILDNESS ▸ wild

W

WILDS ▶ wild

WILDWOOD n wood or forest growing in a natural uncultivated state

WILE, -D, -S, WILING n trickery, cunning, or craftiness ▷ vb lure, beguile, or entice

WILEFUL adj deceitful

WILES ▶ wile

WILFUL adj headstrong or obstinate

WILFULLY ▶ wilful

WILGA, -S n small drought-resistant tree of Australia

WILI, -S n spirit

WILIER ▶ wily

WILIEST ▶ wily

WILILY ▶ wily

WILINESS ▶ wily

WILING ▶ wile

WILIS ▶ wili

WILJA, -S same as ▶ wiltja

WILL, -EST, -S, WOULD vb used as an auxiliary to form the future tense or to indicate intention, ability, or expectation ▷ n strong determination

WILLABLE adj able to be wished or determined by the will

WILLED adj having a will as specified

WILLER, -S ▶ will

WILLEST ▶ will

WILLET, -S n large American shore bird

WILLEY, -ED, -S same as ▶ willy

WILLFUL same as ▶ wilful

WILLIAM, -S n as in **sweet william** flowering plant

WILLIE n informal word for a penis

WILLIED ▶ willy

WILLIES ▶ willy

WILLING adj ready or inclined (to do something)

WILLIWAU same as ▶ williwaw

WILLIWAW n sudden strong gust of cold wind blowing offshore from a mountainous coast

WILLOW, -S n tree with thin flexible branches ▷ vb open and clean (fibres) with rotating spikes

WILLOWED ▶ willow

WILLOWER n willow

WILLOWS ▶ willow

WILLOWY adj slender and graceful

WILLS ▶ will

WILLY, WILLIED, WILLIES, -ING vb clean in a willowing-machine

WILLYARD adj timid

WILLYART same as ▶ willyard

WILLYING ▶ willy

WILLYWAW same as ▶ williwaw

WILT, -ED, -ING, -S vb (cause to) become limp or lose strength ▷ n act of wilting or state of becoming wilted

WILTJA, -S n Aboriginal Australian shelter

WILTS ▶ wilt

WILY, WILIER, WILIEST adj crafty or sly

WIMBLE, -D, -S, WIMBLING n any of a number of hand tools used for boring holes ▷ vb bore (a hole) with or as if with a wimble

WIMBREL, -S same as ▶ whimbrel

WIMMIN pl n intentional non-standard spelling of 'women'

WIMP, -ED, -ING, -S n feeble ineffectual person ▷ vb as in **wimp out** fail to complete something through fear

WIMPIER ▶ wimpy

WIMPIEST ▶ wimpy

WIMPING ▶ wimp

WIMPISH ▶ wimp

WIMPLE, -D, -S, WIMPLING n garment framing the face, worn by medieval women and now by nuns ▷ vb ripple or cause to ripple or undulate

WIMPS ▶ wimp

WIMPY, WIMPIER, WIMPIEST ▶ wimp

WIN, -NED, -S vb come first in (a competition, fight, etc) ▷ vb dry (grain, hay, etc) by exposure to sun and air ▷ n victory, esp in a game

WINCE, -D, -S vb draw back, as if in pain ▷ n wincing

WINCER, -S ▶ wince

WINCES ▶ wince

WINCEY, -S n plain- or twill-weave cloth

WINCH, -ED, -ES, -ING n machine for lifting or hauling using a cable or chain wound round a drum ▷ vb lift or haul using a winch

WINCHER, -S ▶ winch

WINCHES ▶ winch

WINCHING ▶ winch

WINCHMAN, WINCHMEN n man who operates a winch

WINCING, -S ▶ wince

WIND, -ED, -ING, -INGS, -S n current of air ▷ vb render short of breath

WINDABLE adj able to be wound

WINDAC, -S same as ▶ windas

WINDAGE, -S n deflection of a projectile as a result of the effect of the wind

WINDAS, -ES n windlass

WINDBAG, -S n person who talks much but uninterestingly

WINDBELL n light bell made to be sounded by wind

WINDBILL n bill of exchange cosigned by a guarantor

WINDBLOW n uprooting of trees by wind

WINDBURN n irritation and redness of the skin caused by exposure to wind

WINDED ▶ wind

WINDER, -S n person or device that winds, as an engine for hoisting the cages in a mine shaft

WINDFALL n unexpected good luck

WINDFLAW n squall

WINDGALL n soft swelling in the area of the fetlock joint of a horse

WINDGUN, -S n air gun

WINDIER ▶ windy

WINDIEST ▶ windy

WINDIGO, -S same as ▶ wendigo

WINDILY ▶ windy

WINDING ▶ wind

WINDINGS ▶ wind

WINDLASS n winch worked by a crank ▷ vb raise or haul (a weight, etc) by means of a windlass

WINDLE, -D, -S, WINDLING vb wind something round continuously

WINDLESS ▶ wind

WINDLING ▶ windle

WINDLOAD n force on a structure from wind

WINDMILL n machine for grinding or pumping driven by sails turned by the wind ▷ vb move or cause to move like the arms of a windmill

WINDOCK, -S same as ▶ winnock

WINDORE, -S n window

WINDOW, -ED, -S n opening in a wall to let in light or air ▷ vb furnish with windows

WINDOWY adj having many windows

WINDPACK n snow that has been compacted by the wind

WINDPIPE n tube linking the throat and the lungs

WINDRING adj winding

WINDROW, -S n long low ridge or line of hay or a similar crop ▷ vb put (hay or a similar crop) into windrows

WINDS ▶ wind

WINDSAIL n sail rigged as an air scoop over a hatch or companionway

WINDSES pl n ventilation shafts within mines

WINDSHIP n ship propelled by wind

WINDSLAB n crust formed on soft snow by the wind

WINDSOCK n cloth cone on a mast at an airfield to indicate wind direction

WINDSURF vb sail standing on a board equipped with a mast, sail, and boom

WINDUP, -S n prank or hoax

WINDWARD n direction from which the wind is blowing ▷ adj of or in the direction from which the wind blows ▷ adv towards the wind

WINDWAY, -S n part of wind instrument

WINDY, WINDIER, WINDIEST adj denoting a time or conditions in which there is a strong wind

WINE, -D, -S, WINING n alcoholic drink made from fermented grapes ▷ adj of a dark purplish-red colour ▷ vb give wine to

WINELESS ▶ wine

WINERY, WINERIES n place where wine is made

WINES ▶ wine

WINESAP, -S n variety of apple

WINESHOP n shop where wine is sold

WINESKIN n skin of a sheep or goat sewn up and used as a holder for wine

WINESOP, -S n old word for an alcoholic

WINEY adj having the taste or qualities of wine

WING, -ING, -S n one of the limbs or organs of a bird, insect, or bat that are used for flying ▷ vb fly

WINGBACK n position in some team sports

WINGBEAT n complete cycle of moving the wing by a bird in flight

WINGBOW, -S n distinctive band of colour marking the wing of a bird

WINGDING n noisy lively party or festivity

WINGE, -ING, -S same as ▶ whinge

WINGED adj furnished with wings

WINGEDLY ▶ winged

WINGEING ▶ winge

WINGER, -S n player positioned on a wing

WINGES ▶ winge

WINGIER ▶ wingy

WINGIEST ▶ wingy

WINGING ▶ wing

WINGLESS adj having no wings or vestigial wings

WINGLET, -S n small wing

WINGLIKE ▶ wing

WINGMAN, WINGMEN n player in the wing position in Australian Rules

WINGNUT, -S n nut with projections for gripping with the thumb and finger

WINGOVER n manoeuvre for reversing the direction of flight of an aircraft

WINGS ▶ wing

WINGSPAN n distance between the wing tips of an aircraft, bird, or insect

WINGSUIT n type of skydiving suit

WINGTIP, -S n outermost edge of a wing

WINGY, WINGIER, WINGIEST adj having wings

WINIER ▶ winy

WINIEST ▶ winy

WINING ▶ wine

WINISH ▶ wine

WINK, -ED, -S vb close and open (an eye) quickly as a signal ▷ n winking

WINKER, -S n person or thing that winks

WINKING, -S ▶ wink

WINKLE, -D, -S, WINKLING n shellfish with a spiral shell ▷ vb extract or prise out

WINKLER, -S n one who forces a person or thing out

WINKLES ▶ winkle

WINKLING ▶ winkle

WINKS ▶ wink

WINLESS adj not having won anything

WINN, -S n penny

WINNA vb will not

WINNABLE ▶ win

WINNARD, -S n heron

WINNED ▶ win

WINNER, -S n person or thing that wins

WINNING adj (of a person) charming, attractive, etc

WINNINGS pl n money or prizes won

WINNLE, -S n machine for winding thread or yarn

WINNOCK, -S n window

WINNOW, -ED, -S vb separate (chaff) from (grain) ▷ n device for winnowing

WINNOWER ▶ winnow

WINNOWS ▶ winnow

WINNS ▶ winn

WINO, -ES, -S n destitute person who habitually drinks cheap wine

WINS ▶ win

WINSEY, -S same as ▶ wincey

WINSOME, -R adj charming or winning

WINTER, -ED, -S n coldest season ▷ vb spend the winter

WINTERER ▶ winter

WINTERLY adj like winter

WINTERS ▶ winter

WINTERY same as ▶ wintry

WINTLE, -D, -S, WINTLING vb reel; stagger

WINTRIER ▶ wintry

WINTRILY ▶ wintry

WINTRY, WINTRIER adj of or like winter

WINY, WINIER, WINIEST same as ▶ winey

WINZE, -S n steeply inclined shaft, as for ventilation between levels

WIPE, -D, -S vb clean or dry by rubbing ▷ n act of wiping

WIPEABLE adj able to be wiped

WIPED ▶ wipe

WIPEOUT, -S n instance of wiping out

WIPER, -S n any piece of cloth, such as a handkerchief, towel, etc, used for wiping

WIPES ▶ wipe

WIPING, -S ▶ wipe

WIPPEN, -S n part of the hammer action in a piano

WIRABLE adj that can be wired

WIRE, -S n thin flexible strand of metal ▷ vb fasten with wire

WIRED adj excited or nervous

W

WIREDRAW, WIREDREW vb convert (metal) into wire by drawing through successively smaller dies

WIREHAIR n type of terrier

WIRELESS adj (of a computer network) connected by radio rather than by cables or fibre optics ▷ n old-fashioned name for radio ▷ vb send by wireless

WIRELIKE ▶ wire

WIRELINE n telegraph or telephone line

WIREMAN, WIREMEN n person who installs and maintains electric wiring, cables, etc

WIRER, -S n person who sets or uses wires to snare rabbits and similar animals

WIRES ▶ wire

WIRETAP, -S vb obtain information secretly via telegraph or telephone

WIREWAY, -S n tube for electric wires

WIREWORK n functional or decorative work made of wire

WIREWORM n destructive wormlike beetle larva

WIREWOVE adj woven out of wire

WIRIER ▶ wiry

WIRIEST ▶ wiry

WIRILDA, -S n SE Australian acacia tree with edible seeds

WIRILY ▶ wiry

WIRINESS ▶ wiry

WIRING, -S n system of wires ▷ adj used in wiring

WIRRA interj exclamation of sorrow or deep concern

WIRRAH, -S n Australian saltwater fish with bright blue spots

WIRRICOW same as ▶ worricow

WIRY, WIRIER, WIRIEST adj lean and tough

WIS, -SED, -SES, -SING vb know or suppose (something)

WISARD, -S obsolete spelling of ▶ wizard

WISDOM, -S n good sense and judgment

WISE, -D, -R, -S, -ST, WISING vb guide ▷ adj having wisdom ▷ n manner

WISEACRE n person who wishes to seem wise

WISED ▶ wise

WISEGUY, -S n person who wants to seem clever

WISELIER ▶ wisely

WISELING n one who claims to be wise

WISELY, WISELIER ▶ wise

WISENESS ▶ wise

WISENT, -S n European bison

WISER ▶ wise

WISES ▶ wise

WISEST ▶ wise

WISH, -ED, -ES vb want or desire ▷ n expression of a desire

WISHA interj expression of surprise

WISHBONE n V-shaped bone above the breastbone of a fowl

WISHED ▶ wish

WISHER, -S ▶ wish

WISHES ▶ wish

WISHFUL adj too optimistic

WISHING, -S ▶ wish

WISHLESS ▶ wish

WISHT variant of ▶ whisht

WISING ▶ wise

WISKET, -S n basket

WISP, -ED, -ING, -S n light delicate streak ▷ vb move or act like a wisp

WISPIER ▶ wispy

WISPIEST ▶ wispy

WISPILY ▶ wispy

WISPING ▶ wisp

WISPISH ▶ wisp

WISPLIKE ▶ wisp

WISPS ▶ wisp

WISPY, WISPIER, WISPIEST adj thin, fine, or delicate

WISS vb urinate

WISSED ▶ wis

WISSES ▶ wis

WISSING ▶ wis

WIST, -ED, -ING, -S vb know

WISTARIA same as ▶ wisteria

WISTED ▶ wist

WISTERIA n climbing shrub with blue or purple flowers

WISTFUL adj sadly longing

WISTING ▶ wist

WISTITI, -S n marmoset

WISTLY adv intently

WISTS ▶ wist

WIT, WATE, -S vb be aware of; know ▷ n ability to use words or ideas in a clever and amusing way

WITAN, -S n Anglo-Saxon assembly that met to counsel the king

WITBLITS n illegally distilled strong alcoholic drink

WITCH, -ED, -ES n person, usu female, who practises (black) magic ▷ vb cause or change by or as if by witchcraft

WITCHEN, -S n rowan tree

WITCHERY n practice of witchcraft

WITCHES ▶ witch

WITCHIER ▶ witchy

WITCHING adj relating to or appropriate for witchcraft ▷ n witchcraft

WITCHY, WITCHIER adj like a witch

WITE, -D, -S, WITING vb blame

WITELESS adj witless

WITES ▶ wite

WITGAT, -S n type of S African tree

WITH, -S prep indicating presence alongside, possession, means of performance, characteristic manner, etc ▷ n division between flues in chimney

WITHAL adv as well

WITHDRAW, WITHDREW vb take or move out or away

WITHE, -D, -S, WITHING n strong flexible twig suitable for binding things together ▷ vb bind with withes

WITHER vb wilt or dry up

WITHERED ▶ wither

WITHERER ▶ wither

WITHEROD n American shrub

WITHERS pl n ridge between a horse's shoulder blades

WITHES ▶ withe

WITHHOLD, WITHHELD vb refrain from giving

WITHIER ▶ withy

WITHIES ▶ withy

WITHIEST ▶ withy

WITHIN, -S adv in or inside ▷ prep in or inside ▷ n something that is within

WITHING ▶ withe

WITHINS ▶ within

WITHOUT, -S prep not accompanied by, using, or having ▷ adv outside ▷ n person who is without

WITHS ▶ with

WITHWIND n bindweed

WITHY, WITHIER, WITHIES, WITHIEST n willow tree, esp an osier ▷ adj (of people) tough and agile

WITING ▶ wite

WITLESS adj foolish

WITLING, -S n person who thinks themself witty

WITLOOF, -S n chicory

WITNESS n person who has seen something happen ▷ vb see at first hand

WITNEY, -S n type of blanket; heavy cloth

WITS ▸ wit

WITTED adj having wit

WITTER, -ED, -S vb chatter pointlessly or at unnecessary length ▷ n pointless chat

WITTIER ▸ witty

WITTIEST ▸ witty

WITTILY ▸ witty

WITTING, -S adj deliberate ▷ n act of becoming aware

WITTY, WITTIER, WITTIEST adj clever and amusing

WITWALL, -S n golden oriole

WIVE, -D, WIVING vb marry (a woman)

WIVEHOOD obsolete variant of ▸ wifehood

WIVER, -S another word for ▸ wivern

WIVERN, -S same as ▸ wyvern

WIVERS ▸ wiver

WIVES ▸ wife

WIVING ▸ wive

WIZ, -ES, -ZES shortened form of ▸ wizard

> Wiz is a short form of wizard. This is the highest-scoring 3-letter word beginning with W, and can be especially useful when there isn't much room to manoeuvre.

WIZARD, -ER, -S n magician ▷ adj superb

WIZARDLY adj like a wizard

WIZARDRY n magic or sorcery

WIZARDS ▸ wizard

WIZEN, -ER, -EST, -ING, -S vb make or become shrivelled ▷ n archaic word for 'weasand' (the gullet) ▷ adj wizened

WIZENED adj shrivelled or wrinkled

WIZENER ▸ wizen

WIZENEST ▸ wizen

WIZENING ▸ wizen

WIZENS ▸ wizen

WIZES ▸ wiz

WIZIER, -S same as ▸ vizier

WIZZEN, -S same as ▸ wizen

WIZZES ▸ wiz

WO, -S archaic spelling of ▸ woe

WOAD, -S n blue dye obtained from a plant

WOADED adj coloured blue with woad

WOADS ▸ woad

WOADWAX same as > woadwaxen

WOAH same as ▸ whoa

WOALD, -S same as ▸ weld

WOBBLE, -D, -S, WOBBLING vb move unsteadily ▷ n wobbling movement or sound

WOBBLER, -S ▸ wobble

WOBBLES ▸ wobble

WOBBLIER ▸ wobbly

WOBBLIES ▸ wobbly

WOBBLING ▸ wobble

WOBBLY, WOBBLIER, WOBBLIES adj unsteady ▷ n temper tantrum

WOBEGONE same as > woebegone

WOCK, -S same as ▸ wok

WODGE, -S n thick lump or chunk

WOE, -S n grief

WOEFUL adj extremely sad

WOEFULLY ▸ woeful

WOENESS ▸ woe

WOES ▸ woe

WOESOME adj woeful

WOF, -S n fool

WOFUL, -LER same as ▸ woeful

WOFULLY ▸ woful

WOGGLE, -S n ring of leather through which a Scout neckerchief is threaded

WOIWODE, -S same as ▸ voivode

WOJUS adj (Irish) of a poor quality

WOK, -S n bowl-shaped Chinese cooking pan, used for stir-frying

WOKE, -R, -ST adj alert to social and political injustice

WOKEN ▸ wake

WOKER ▸ woke

WOKEST ▸ woke

WOKKA modifier as in wokka board piece of fibreboard used as a musical instrument

WOKS ▸ wok

WOLD, -S same as ▸ weld

WOLF, -ED, -S, WOLVES n wild predatory canine mammal ▷ vb eat ravenously

WOLFER, -S same as ▸ wolver

WOLFFISH n type of large northern deep-sea fish with large sharp teeth

WOLFING, -S ▸ wolf

WOLFISH ▸ wolf

WOLFKIN, -S n young wolf

WOLFLIKE ▸ wolf

WOLFLING n young wolf

WOLFRAM, -S another name for ▸ tungsten

WOLFS ▸ wolf

WOLFSKIN n skin of wolf used for clothing, etc

WOLLY, WOLLIES n pickled cucumber or olive

WOLVE, -D vb hunt for wolves

WOLVER, -S n person who hunts wolves

WOLVES ▸ wolf

WOLVING, -S ▸ wolve

WOLVISH same as ▸ wolfish

WOMAN, -ED, -ING, -NED, -S, WOMEN n adult human female ▷ adj female ▷ vb provide with a woman or women

WOMANISH adj effeminate

WOMANISM n feminism among Black women

WOMANIST ▸ womanism

WOMANLY adj having qualities traditionally associated with a woman

WOMANNED ▸ woman

WOMANS ▸ woman

WOMB, -ING, -S vb enclose ▷ n hollow organ in female mammals where babies develop

WOMBAT, -S n small heavily built burrowing Australian marsupial

WOMBED ▸ womb

WOMBIER ▸ womby

WOMBIEST ▸ womby

WOMBING ▸ womb

WOMBLIKE ▸ womb

WOMBS ▸ womb

WOMBY, WOMBIER, WOMBIEST adj hollow; spacious

WOMEN ▸ woman

WOMERA, -S same as ▸ woomera

WOMMERA, -S same as ▸ woomera

WOMMIT, -S n foolish person

WOMYN n intentional non-standard spelling of 'women'

WON, -NED, -S n standard monetary unit of North Korea ▷ vb live or dwell

WONDER, -ED, -S vb be curious about ▷ n wonderful thing ▷ adj spectacularly successful

WONDERER ▸ wonder

WONDERS ▸ wonder

WONDRED adj splendid

WONDROUS adj wonderful

WONGA, -S n money

WONGI, -ED, -ING, -S vb talk informally

WONING, -S ▸ won

W

WONK, -S n person who is obsessively interested in a specified subject

WONKERY n activities of a wonk

WONKIER ▶ wonky

WONKIEST ▶ wonky

WONKILY adv in a wonky manner

WONKISH adj like a wonk

WONKS ▶ wonk

WONKY, WONKIER, WONKIEST adj shaky or unsteady

WONNED ▶ won

WONNER, -S ▶ won

WONNING, -S ▶ won

WONS ▶ won

WONT, -ING, -S adj accustomed ▷ n custom ▷ vb become or cause to become accustomed

WONTED adj accustomed or habituated (to doing something)

WONTEDLY ▶ wonted

WONTING ▶ wont

WONTLESS ▶ wont

WONTON, -S n dumpling filled with spiced minced pork

WONTS ▶ wont

WOO, -ED, -S vb seek the love or affection of

WOOABLE adj able to be wooed

WOOBUT, -S same as ▶ woubit

WOOD, -ING n substance trees are made of, used in carpentry and as fuel ▷ adj made of or using wood ▷ vb (of land) plant with trees

WOODBIN, -S n box for firewood

WOODBIND same as ▶ woodbine

WOODBINE n honeysuckle

WOODBINS ▶ woodbin

WOODBOX n box for firewood

WOODCHAT n European and N African songbird

WOODCHIP n textured wallpaper

WOODCHOP n wood-chopping competition

WOODCOCK n game bird

WOODCUT, -S n (print made from) an engraved block of wood

WOODED adj covered with trees

WOODEN, -ED, -ER, -S adj made of wood ▷ vb fell or kill (a person or animal)

WOODENLY ▶ wooden

WOODENS ▶ wooden

WOODFERN n type of evergreen fern

WOODFREE adj (of paper) made from pulp that has been treated to remove impurities

WOODHEN, -S another name for ▶ weka

WOODHOLE n store area for wood

WOODIE, -S n gallows rope

WOODIER ▶ woody

WOODIES ▶ woodie

WOODIEST ▶ woody

WOODING ▶ wood

WOODLAND n forest ▷ adj living in woods

WOODLARK n type of Old World lark

WOODLESS ▶ wood

WOODLICE > woodlouse

WOODLORE n woodcraft skills

WOODLOT, -S n area restricted to the growing of trees

WOODMAN, WOODMEN same as ▶ woodsman

WOODMEAL n sawdust powder

WOODMEN ▶ woodman

WOODMICE > woodmouse

WOODNESS ▶ wood

WOODNOTE n natural musical note or song, like that of a wild bird

WOODPILE n heap of firewood

WOODRAT, -S n pack-rat

WOODROOF same as ▶ woodruff

WOODRUFF n plant with small sweet-smelling white flowers and sweet-smelling leaves

WOODRUSH n plant with grasslike leaves and small brown flowers

WOODS pl n closely packed trees forming a forest or wood

WOODSHED n small outbuilding where firewood, garden tools, etc are stored

WOODSIA, -S n type of small fern with tufted rhizomes and wiry fronds

WOODSIER ▶ woodsy

WOODSKIN n canoe made of bark

WOODSMAN, WOODSMEN n person who lives in a wood or who is skilled at woodwork or carving

WOODSY, WOODSIER adj of, reminiscent of, or connected with woods

WOODTONE n colour matching that of wood

WOODWALE n green woodpecker

WOODWARD n person in charge of a forest or wood

WOODWASP n large wasplike insect

WOODWAX same as > woadwaxen

WOODWIND n type of wind instrument made of wood ▷ adj of or denoting a type of wind instrument, such as the oboe

WOODWORK n parts of a room or building made of wood

WOODWORM n insect larva that bores into wood

WOODWOSE n hairy wildman of the woods

WOODY, WOODIER, WOODIEST adj (of a plant) having a very hard stem

WOODYARD n place where timber is cut and stored

WOOED ▶ woo

WOOER, -S ▶ woo

WOOF, -ED, -ING, -S vb (of dogs) bark

WOOFER, -S n loudspeaker reproducing low-frequency sounds

WOOFIER ▶ woofy

WOOFIEST ▶ woofy

WOOFING ▶ woof

WOOFS ▶ woof

WOOFY, WOOFIER, WOOFIEST adj with close, dense texture

WOOHOO interj expression of joy, approval, etc

WOOING, -S ▶ woo

WOOINGLY ▶ woo

WOOINGS ▶ wooing

WOOL, -S n soft hair of sheep, goats, etc

WOOLD, -ED, -ING, -S vb wind (rope)

WOOLDER, -S n stick for winding rope

WOOLDING ▶ woold

WOOLDS ▶ woold

WOOLED same as ▶ woolled

WOOLEN, -S same as ▶ woollen

WOOLER, -S same as ▶ woolder

WOOLFAT, -S same as ▶ lanolin

WOOLFELL *n* skin of a sheep or similar animal with the fleece still attached

WOOLHAT, -S *n* hat made of wool

WOOLIE *n* wool garment

WOOLIER ▸ wooly

WOOLIES ▸ wooly

WOOLIEST ▸ wooly

WOOLILY ▸ wooly

WOOLLED *adj* (of animals) having wool

WOOLLEN, -S *adj* relating to or consisting partly or wholly of wool ▷ *n* garment or piece of cloth made of wool

WOOLLIER ▸ woolly

WOOLLIES ▸ woolly

WOOLLIKE ▸ wool

WOOLLILY ▸ woolly

WOOLLY, WOOLLIER, WOOLLIES *adj* of or like wool ▷ *n* knitted woollen garment

WOOLMAN, WOOLMEN *n* wool trader

WOOLPACK *n* cloth or canvas wrapping used to pack a bale of wool

WOOLS ▸ wool

WOOLSACK *n* sack containing or intended to contain wool

WOOLSEY, -S *n* cotton and wool blend

WOOLSHED *n* large building in which sheep shearing takes place

WOOLSKIN *n* sheepskin with wool still on

WOOLWARD *adv* with woollen side touching the skin

WOOLWORK *n* embroidery with wool

WOOLY, WOOLIER, WOOLIES, WOOLIEST *same as* ▸ **woolly**

WOOMERA, -S *n* notched stick used by Aboriginal Australians to aid the propulsion of a spear

WOON, -ED, -ING, -S *same as* ▸ **won**

WOONERF, -S *n* (in the Netherlands) road primarily for cyclists and pedestrians

WOONING ▸ woon

WOONS ▸ woon

WOOPIE, -S *n* well-off older person

WOOPS, -ED, -ES, -ING *vb* (esp of small child) vomit

WOOPY *n* well-off older person

WOORALI, -S *less common name for* ▸ **curare**

WOORARA, -S *same as* ▸ **wourali**

WOORARI, -S *same as* ▸ **wourali**

WOOS ▸ woo

WOOSE, -S *same as* ▸ **wuss**

WOOSEL, -S *same as* ▸ **ouzel**

WOOSELL, -S *same as* ▸ **ouzel**

WOOSELS ▸ woosel

WOOSES ▸ woose

WOOSH, -ED, -ES, -ING *same as* ▸ **whoosh**

WOOT *interj* (esp used by players in online games) shout of joy, victory, etc

WOOTZ, -ES *n* Middle-Eastern steel

WOOZIER ▸ woozy

WOOZIEST ▸ woozy

WOOZILY ▸ woozy

WOOZY, WOOZIER, WOOZIEST *adj* weak, dizzy, and confused

WOP, -PED, -PING, -S *vb* strike, beat, or thrash

WORD, -ED, -S *n* smallest single meaningful unit of speech or writing ▷ *vb* express in words

WORDAGE, -S *n* words considered collectively, esp a quantity of words

WORDBOOK *n* book containing words, usually with their meanings

WORDED ▸ word

WORDGAME *n* any game involving the formation, discovery, or alteration of a word or words

WORDIE, -S *n* person who loves words

WORDIER ▸ wordy

WORDIES ▸ wordie

WORDIEST ▸ wordy

WORDILY ▸ wordy

WORDING, -S *n* choice and arrangement of words

WORDISH *adj* talkative

WORDLESS *adj* inarticulate or silent

WORDLORE *n* knowledge about words

WORDPLAY *n* verbal wit based on the meanings and ambiguities of words

WORDS ▸ word

WORDWRAP *n* word-processing function that shifts a word at the end of a line to a new line to keep within preset margins

WORDY, WORDIER, WORDIEST *adj* using too many words

WORE ▸ wear

WORK, -S *n* physical or mental effort directed to making or doing something ▷ *adj* of or for work ▷ *vb* (cause to) do work

WORKABLE *adj* able to operate efficiently

WORKABLY ▸ workable

WORKADAY *n* working day ▷ *adj* ordinary

WORKBAG, -S *n* container for implements, tools, or materials

WORKBOAT *n* boat used for tasks

WORKBOOK *n* exercise book or textbook used for study, esp a textbook with spaces for answers

WORKBOOT *n* type of sturdy leather boot

WORKBOX *same as* ▸ **workbag**

WORKDAY, -S *another word for* ▸ **workaday**

WORKED *adj* made or decorated with evidence of workmanship

WORKER, -S *n* person who works in a specified way

WORKFARE *n* scheme in which unemployed people are required to do community work or job training in return for payments

WORKFLOW *n* rate of progress of work

WORKFOLK *pl n* working people, esp labourers on a farm

WORKFUL *adj* hardworking

WORKGIRL *n* young female manual worker

WORKHOUR *n* time set aside for work

WORKING, -S *n* operation or mode of operation of something ▷ *adj* relating to or concerned with a person or thing that works

WORKLESS ▸ work

WORKLOAD *n* amount of work to be done, esp in a specified period

WORKMAN, WORKMEN *n* manual worker

WORKMATE *n* person who works with another person

WORKMEN ▸ workman

WORKOUT, -S *n* session of physical exercise for training or fitness

W

WORKROOM n room in which work, usually manual labour, is done

WORKS ▶ work

WORKSAFE adj (of an internet link) suitable for viewing in the workplace

WORKSHOP n room or building for a manufacturing process ▷ vb perform (a play) with no costumes, set, or musical accompaniment

WORKSHY adj not inclined to work

WORKSITE n area where work is done

WORKSOME adj hardworking

WORKSONG n song sung while doing physical work

WORKTOP, -S n surface used for food preparation

WORKUP, -S n medical examination

WORKWEAR n clothes, such as overalls, as worn for work in a factory, shop, etc

WORKWEEK n number of hours or days in a week actually or officially allocated to work

WORLD, -S n planet earth ▷ adj of the whole world

WORLDED adj incorporating worlds

WORLDER, -S n person who belongs to a specified class or domain

WORLDIE, -S n world-class performance, achievement, person, etc

WORLDLY adj not spiritual ▷ adv in a worldly manner

WORLDS ▶ world

WORM, -ED, -ING n small limbless invertebrate animal ▷ vb rid of worms

WORMCAST n coil of earth excreted by a burrowing worm

WORMED ▶ worm

WORMER, -S ▶ worm

WORMERY n piece of apparatus in which worms are kept for study

WORMFLY n type of lure dressed on a double hook

WORMGEAR n gear with screw thread

WORMHOLE n hole made by a worm in timber, plants, or fruit

WORMIER ▶ wormy

WORMIEST ▶ wormy

WORMIL, -S n burrowing larva of type of fly

WORMING ▶ worm

WORMISH ▶ worm

WORMLIKE ▶ worm

WORMROOT n plant used to cure worms

WORMS n disease caused by parasitic worms living in the intestines

WORMSEED n any of various plants used to treat worm infestation

WORMWOOD n bitter plant

WORMY, WORMIER, WORMIEST adj infested with or eaten by worms

WORN ▶ wear

WORNNESS n quality or condition of being worn

WORRAL, -S n type of lizard

WORREL, -S same as ▶ worral

WORRICOW n frightening creature

WORRIED ▶ worry

WORRIER, -S ▶ worry

WORRIES ▶ worry

WORRIT, -ED, -S vb tease or worry

WORRY, WORRIED, WORRIES vb (cause to) be anxious or uneasy ▷ n (cause of) anxiety or concern

WORRYCOW same as ▶ worricow

WORRYING ▶ worry

WORSE, -D, -S, WORSING vb defeat

WORSEN, -ED, -S vb make or grow worse

WORSER archaic or nonstandard word for ▶ worse

WORSES ▶ worse

WORSET, -S n worsted fabric

WORSHIP, -S vb show religious devotion to ▷ n act or instance of worshipping

WORSING ▶ worse

WORST, -ING, -S n worst thing ▷ vb defeat

WORSTED, -S n type of woollen yarn or fabric

WORSTING ▶ worst

WORSTS ▶ worst

WORT, -S n any of various plants formerly used to cure diseases

WORTH, -ED, -ING, -S prep having a value of ▷ n value or price ▷ vb happen or betide

WORTHFUL adj worthy

WORTHIED ▶ worthy

WORTHIER ▶ worthy

WORTHIES ▶ worthy

WORTHILY ▶ worthy

WORTHING ▶ worth

WORTHS ▶ worth

WORTHY, WORTHIED, WORTHIER, WORTHIES adj deserving admiration or respect ▷ n notable person ▷ vb make worthy

WORTLE, -S n plate with holes for drawing wire through

WORTS ▶ wort

WOS ▶ wo

WOST form of the second person singular of ▶ wit

WOT, -S, -TED, -TEST, -TETH, -TING form of the present tense of ▶ wit

WOTCHA same as ▶ wotcher

WOTCHER sentence substitute slang term of greeting

WOTS ▶ wot

WOTTED ▶ wot

WOTTEST ▶ wot

WOTTETH ▶ wot

WOTTING ▶ wot

WOUBIT, -S n type of caterpillar

WOULD ▶ will

WOULDEST same as ▶ wouldst

WOULDS same as ▶ wouldst

WOULDST singular form of the past tense of ▶ will

WOUND, -S vb injure ▷ n injury

WOUNDED adj suffering from wounds

WOUNDER, -S ▶ wound

WOUNDIER ▶ woundy

WOUNDILY ▶ woundy

WOUNDING ▶ wound

WOUNDS ▶ wound

WOUNDY, WOUNDIER adj extreme

WOURALI, -S n plant from which curare is obtained

WOVE ▶ weave

WOVEN, -S n article made from woven cloth

WOW, -ED, -ING, -S interj exclamation of astonishment ▷ n astonishing person or thing ▷ vb be a great success with

WOWEE stronger form of ▶ wow

WOWF, -ER, -EST adj mad

This is a Scots word meaning crazy: you are not likely to get the chance to play this very often, but if your opponent plays **wow** and you have an F, you would be wowf to miss the opportunity of the hook!

WOWING ▶ wow

WOWS ▶ wow

WOWSER, -S n puritanical person

WOX ▸ wax

> **Wox** is an old past tense of the verb **wax**, to grow, and is another of the key words using X.

WOXEN ▸ wax

WRACK, -ED, -ING, -S n seaweed ▷ vb strain or shake (something) violently

WRACKFUL adj ruinous

WRACKING ▸ wrack

WRACKS ▸ wrack

WRAITH, -S n ghost

WRANG, -ED, -ING, -S Scot word for ▸ wrong

WRANGLE, -D, -S vb argue noisily ▷ n noisy argument

WRANGLER n one who wrangles

WRANGLES ▸ wrangle

WRANGS ▸ wrang

WRAP, -PED, -PING, -S vb fold (something) round (a person or thing) so as to cover ▷ n garment wrapped round the shoulders

WRAPOVER adj (of a garment) worn wrapped round the body and fastened so that the open edges overlap ▷ n such a garment

WRAPPAGE n material for wrapping

WRAPPED ▸ wrap

WRAPPER, -S vb cover with wrapping ▷ n cover for a product

WRAPPING ▸ wrap

WRAPS ▸ wrap

WRAPT same as ▸ rapt

WRASSE, -S n colourful sea fish

WRASSLE, -D, -S same as ▸ wrestle

WRAST, -ED, -ING, -S same as ▸ wrest

WRASTLE, -D, -S same as ▸ wrestle

WRASTS ▸ wrast

WRATE ▸ write

WRATH, -ED, -ING, -S n intense anger ▷ adj incensed ▷ vb make angry

WRATHFUL adj full of wrath

WRATHIER ▸ wrathy

WRATHILY ▸ wrathy

WRATHING ▸ wrath

WRATHS ▸ wrath

WRATHY, WRATHIER same as ▸ wrathful

WRAWL, -ED, -ING, -S vb howl

WRAXLE, -D, -S, WRAXLING vb wrestle

WREAK, -ED, -ING, -S, WROKE, WROKEN vb inflict (vengeance, etc) or cause (chaos, etc)

WREAKER, -S ▸ wreak

WREAKFUL adj seeking revenge

WREAKING ▸ wreak

WREAKS ▸ wreak

WREATH, -S n twisted ring or band of flowers or leaves used as a memorial or tribute

WREATHE, -D, -S vb form into or take the form of a wreath by twisting together

WREATHEN adj twisted into a wreath

WREATHER ▸ wreathe

WREATHES ▸ wreathe

WREATHS ▸ wreath

WREATHY adj twisted into wreath

WRECK, -ED, -ING, -S vb destroy ▷ n remains of something that has been destroyed or badly damaged

WRECKAGE n wrecked remains

WRECKED ▸ wreck

WRECKER, -S n formerly, person who lured ships onto the rocks in order to plunder them

WRECKFUL adj causing wreckage

WRECKING ▸ wreck

WRECKS ▸ wreck

WREN, -S n small brown songbird

WRENCH, -ED, -ES vb twist or pull violently ▷ n violent twist or pull

WRENCHER ▸ wrench

WRENCHES ▸ wrench

WRENS ▸ wren

WRENTIT, -S n type of long-tailed North American bird

WREST, -ED, -ING, -S vb twist violently ▷ n act or an instance of wresting

WRESTER, -S ▸ wrest

WRESTING ▸ wrest

WRESTLE, -D, -S vb fight by grappling with an opponent ▷ n act of wrestling

WRESTLER ▸ wrestle

WRESTLES ▸ wrestle

WRESTS ▸ wrest

WRETCH, -ES n despicable person

WRETCHED adj miserable or unhappy

WRETCHES ▸ wretch

WRETHE, -D, -S, WRETHING same as ▸ wreathe

WRICK, -ED, -ING, -S variant spelling (chiefly Brit) of ▸ rick

WRIED ▸ wry

WRIER ▸ wry

WRIES ▸ wry

WRIEST ▸ wry

WRIGGLE, -D, -S vb move with a twisting action ▷ n wriggling movement

WRIGGLER ▸ wriggle

WRIGGLES ▸ wriggle

WRIGGLY ▸ wriggle

WRIGHT, -S n maker

WRING, -ED, -ING, -S, WRUNG vb twist, esp to squeeze liquid out of

WRINGER, -S same as ▸ mangle

WRINGING ▸ wring

WRINGS ▸ wring

WRINKLE, -D, -S n slight crease, esp one in the skin due to age ▷ vb make or become slightly creased

WRINKLIE n derogatory word for an old person

WRINKLY ▸ wrinkle

WRIST, -ED, -ING, -S n joint between the hand and the arm ▷ vb hit an object with a twist of the wrist

WRISTER, -S n type of shot in hockey

WRISTIER ▸ wristy

WRISTING ▸ wrist

WRISTLET n band or bracelet worn around the wrist

WRISTS ▸ wrist

WRISTY, WRISTIER adj characterized by considerable movement of the wrist

WRIT, -S n written legal command

WRITABLE ▸ write

WRITE, WRATE, -S, WRITING, WRITINGS, WRITTEN, WROTE vb mark paper etc with symbols or words

WRITEOFF n uncollectible debt that is cancelled

WRITER, -S n author

WRITERLY adj of or characteristic of a writer

WRITERS ▸ writer

WRITES ▸ write

WRITHE, -D, -S, WRITHING vb twist or squirm in or as if in pain ▷ n act or an instance of writhing

WRITHEN adj twisted

WRITHER, -S ▸ writhe

W

WRITHES ▸ writhe
WRITHING ▸ writhe
WRITHLED *adj* wrinkled
WRITING ▸ write
WRITINGS ▸ write
WRITS ▸ writ
WRITTEN ▸ write
WRIZLED *adj* wrinkled
WROATH, -S *n* unforeseen trouble
WROKE ▸ wreak
WROKEN ▸ wreak
WRONG, -ED, -EST, -ING, -S *adj* incorrect or mistaken ▷ *adv* in a wrong manner ▷ *n* something immoral or unjust ▷ *vb* treat unjustly
WRONGER, -S ▸ wrong
WRONGEST ▸ wrong
WRONGFUL *adj* unjust or illegal
WRONGING ▸ wrong
WRONGLY ▸ wrong
WRONGOUS *adj* unfair
WRONGS ▸ wrong
WROOT, -ED, -ING, -S *obsolete form of* ▸ root
WROTE ▸ write
WROTH *adj* angry
WROTHFUL *same as* ▸ wrathful
WROUGHT *adj* (of metals) shaped by hammering or beating
WRUNG ▸ wring
WRY, WRIED, WRIER, WRIES, WRIEST, -ER, -EST, -ING *adj* drily humorous ▷ *vb* twist or contort
WRYBILL, -S *n* New Zealand plover whose bill is bent to one side
WRYER ▸ wry

WRYEST ▸ wry
WRYING ▸ wry
WRYLY ▸ wry
WRYNECK, -S *n* woodpecker that has a habit of twisting its neck round
WRYNESS ▸ wry
WRYTHEN *adj* twisted
WUD, -DED, -DING, -S *Scots form of* ▸ wood

> W and U are a horrible combination to have on your rack, so this Scots word for wood can be a godsend. And remember that it can also be a verb, meaning to load with wood, so you have **wuds, wudding** and **wudded**.

WUDDIES ▸ wuddy
WUDDING ▸ wud
WUDDY, WUDDIES *n* loop at the end of a rope
WUDS ▸ wud
WUDU, -S *n* Muslim practice of ritual washing before daily prayer
WULL, -ED, -ING, -S *obsolete form of* ▸ will
WUNNER, -S *same as* ▸ oner
WURLEY, -S *n* Aboriginal Australian hut
WURLIE, -S *same as* ▸ wurley
WURST, -S *n* large sausage, esp of a type made in Germany, Austria, etc
WURTZITE *n* zinc sulphide
WURZEL, -S *n* root
WUS, -ES *n* Welsh dialect term of address
WUSHU, -S *n* Chinese martial arts
WUSS, -ES *n* feeble person

WUSSY, WUSSIER, WUSSIES, WUSSIEST *adj* feeble ▷ *n* feeble person
WUTHER, -ED, -S *vb* (of wind) blow and roar
WUXIA, -S *n* Chinese fiction concerning the adventures of sword-wielding heroes

> This Chinese word for a genre of fiction may get you a decent score from a very difficult-looking rack.

WUZ *vb* nonstandard spelling of was
WUZZLE, -D, -S, WUZZLING *vb* mix up
WYCH, -ES *n* type of tree having flexible branches
WYE, -S *n* Y-shaped pipe

> If you have W and Y on your rack, look for an E on the board that will allow you to play this name for the letter Y, especially if you can land on a bonus square as a result.

WYLE, -D, -S, WYLING *vb* entice
WYN, -S *n* rune equivalent to English 'w'
WYND, -S *n* narrow lane or alley
WYNN, -S *same as* ▸ wyn
WYNS ▸ wyn
WYSIWYG *adj* denoting a computer screen display showing exactly what will print out
WYTE, -D, -S, WYTING *vb* blame
WYVERN, -S *n* heraldic beast

W

Xx

Worth 8 points on its own, **X** is one of the best tiles in the game. It doesn't, however, start many two- and three-letter words. There are only two valid two-letter words, **xi** and **xu** (9 points each) beginning with **X**, and only two three-letter words, **xed** and **xis**. Therefore, if you have an **X** on your rack and need to play short words, you're probably better off thinking of words that end in **X** or have **X** in them rather than those that start with **X**. Particularly good to remember are **zax**, **zex** (19 points each), **kex** (14 points) and **vax** (13 points).

XANTHAM, -S n acacia gum
XANTHAN, -S same as
▸ **xantham**
XANTHATE n any salt or ester of xanthic acid
XANTHEIN n soluble part of the yellow pigment that is found in the cell sap of some flowers
XANTHENE n yellowish crystalline heterocyclic compound used as a fungicide
XANTHIC adj of, containing, or derived from xanthic acid
XANTHIN, -S n any of a group of yellow or orange carotene derivatives
XANTHINE n crystalline compound found in urine, blood, certain plants, and certain animal tissues
XANTHINS ▸ **xanthin**
XANTHISM n condition of skin, fur, or feathers in which yellow coloration predominates
XANTHOMA n presence in the skin of fatty yellow or brownish plaques or nodules
XANTHONE n crystalline compound
XANTHOUS adj yellow-coloured
XEBEC, -S n small three-masted Mediterranean vessel

A kind of small boat, and a good high-scoring word that can easily be missed, as we tend to be slow to consider words beginning with X.

XED adj having a cross against
XENIA, -S n influence of pollen upon the form of the fruit developing after pollination
XENIAL ▸ **xenia**
XENIAS ▸ **xenia**
XENIC adj denoting the presence of bacteria
XENIUM n diplomatic gift
XENOGAMY n fertilization by the fusion of male and female gametes from different individuals of the same species
XENOGENY n offspring unlike either parent
XENOLITH n fragment of rock differing in origin, structure, etc from the igneous rock enclosing it
XENON, -S n colourless odourless gas
XENOPHYA pl n parts of shell or skeleton formed by foreign bodies
XENOPUS n African frog
XENOTIME n yellow-brown mineral
XENURINE adj relating to a type of armadillo ▸ n type of armadillo
XERAFIN, -S n Indian coin
XERANSIS, XERANSES n gradual loss of tissue moisture
XERANTIC ▸ **xeransis**
XERAPHIN same as ▸ **xerafin**
XERARCH adj (of a sere) having its origin in a dry habitat

XERASIA, -S n dryness of the hair
XERIC adj of, relating to, or growing in dry conditions
XEROMA, -S, -TA n excessive dryness of the cornea
XEROSERE n sere that originates in dry surroundings
XEROSIS, XEROSES n abnormal dryness of bodily tissues
XEROTES same as ▸ **xerosis**
XEROTIC ▸ **xerosis**
XEROX, -ED, -ES, -ING n trade name for a machine employing a xerographic copying process ▸ vb produce a copy (of a document, etc) using such a machine
XERUS, -ES n ground squirrel
XI, -S n 14th letter in the Greek alphabet
XIPHOID, -S adj shaped like a sword ▸ n part of the sternum
XIS ▸ **xi**
XOANON, XOANA n primitive image of a god supposed to have fallen from heaven

One of the few words starting with X. But be careful: the plural is **xoana** not **xoanons**.

X

XRAY, -S n code word for the letter X
XU n Vietnamese currency unit

XYLAN, -S *n* yellow polysaccharide consisting of xylose units

XYLEM, -S *n* plant tissue that conducts water and minerals from the roots to all other parts

XYLENE, -S *n* type of hydrocarbon

XYLENOL, -S *n* synthetic resin made from xylene

XYLIC ▸ **xylem**

XYLIDIN, -S *same as* ▸ **xylidine**

XYLIDINE *n* mixture of six isomeric amines derived from xylene and used in dyes

XYLIDINS ▸ **xylidin**

XYLITOL, -S *n* crystalline alcohol used as a sweetener

XYLOCARP *n* fruit, such as a coconut, having a hard woody pericarp

XYLOGEN, -S *same as* ▸ **xylem**

XYLOID *adj* of, relating to, or resembling wood

XYLOIDIN *n* type of explosive

XYLOL, -S *another name (not in technical usage) for* ▸ **xylene**

XYLOLOGY *n* study of the composition of wood

XYLOLS ▸ **xylol**

XYLOMA, -S, -TA *n* hard growth in fungi

XYLONIC *adj* denoting an acid formed from xylose

XYLONITE *n* type of plastic

XYLOSE, -S *n* white crystalline sugar found in wood and straw

XYLOTOMY *n* preparation of sections of wood for examination by microscope

XYLYL, -S *n* group of atoms

XYST, -S *n* long portico, esp one used in ancient Greece for athletics

A kind of court used by ancient Greek athletes for exercises, this is a lovely high-scoring word to play. And if your opponent plays it, remember that you can put an I on it to make **xysti**, as well as an S to make **xysts**.

XYSTER, -S *n* surgical instrument for scraping bone

XYSTOI ▸ **xystus**

XYSTOS, XYSTOI *same as* ▸ **xyst**

XYSTS ▸ **xyst**

XYSTUS, XYSTI *same as* ▸ **xyst**

Yy

Y can be a useful tile to have on your rack, particularly if you are short of vowels, but it can make it difficult to find bonus words scoring that extra 50 points, and you will normally want to play it off as soon as a good score offers itself. There are only four two-letter words beginning with **Y**, but these are easy to remember as there's one for every vowel except **I**: **ya**, **ye**, **yo** and **yu** (5 points each). There are quite a few useful three-letter words: **yez** (15), **yew** (9) and **yob** (8). Remember that **yob** was originally **boy** backwards: if you can't fit in **yob**, you may be able to use **boy** instead. And while his half-brother the **zo** (or **dzo** or **dso** or **zho**) gets all the attention, don't forget that the **yak** (10) earns quite a decent score!

YA, -S n type of Chinese pear

YAAR, -S n in informal Indian English, a friend

YABA, -S n informal word for 'yet another bloody acronym'

YABBA, -S n form of methamphetamine

YABBER, -ED, -S vb talk or jabber ▷ n talk or jabber

YABBIE same as ▶ **yabby**

YABBY, YABBIED, YABBIES, -ING n small freshwater crayfish ▷ vb go out to catch yabbies

YACCA, -S n Australian plant with a woody stem

YACHT, -ED, -S n large boat with sails or an engine ▷ vb sail in a yacht

YACHTER, -S ▶ **yacht**

YACHTIE, -S n yachtsman

YACHTING n sport or practice of sailing a yacht

YACHTMAN, YACHTMEN same as > **yachtsman**

YACHTS ▶ **yacht**

YACK, -ED, -ING, -S same as ▶ **yak**

YACKA, -S same as ▶ **yacca**

YACKED ▶ **yack**

YACKER, -S same as ▶ **yakka**

YACKING ▶ **yack**

YACKS ▶ **yack**

YAD, -S n hand-held pointer used for reading the sefer torah

YAE same as ▶ **ae**

YAFF, -ED, -ING, -S vb bark

YAFFLE, -S n woodpecker with a green back and wings

YAFFS ▶ **yaff**

YAG, -S n artificial crystal

YAGE, -S n tropical vine of the Amazon region

YAGER, -S same as ▶ **jaeger**

YAGES ▶ **yage**

YAGGER, -S n pedlar

YAGI, -S n type of highly directional aerial

YAGS ▶ **yag**

YAH, -S interj exclamation of derision or disgust ▷ n affected upper-class person

YAHOO, -S n crude coarse person

YAHOOISM ▶ **yahoo**

YAHOOS ▶ **yahoo**

YAHRZEIT n (in Judaism) the anniversary of the death of a close relative

YAHS ▶ **yah**

YAIRD, -S Scots form of ▶ **yard**

YAK, -KED, -KING, -S n Tibetan ox with long shaggy hair ▷ vb talk continuously about unimportant matters

YAKHDAN, -S n box for carrying ice on a pack animal

YAKIMONO n (in Japan) grilled or fried food

YAKITORI n Japanese dish consisting of small pieces of chicken skewered and grilled

YAKKA, -S n informal Australian word for work

YAKKED ▶ **yak**

YAKKER, -S same as ▶ **yakka**

YAKKING ▶ **yak**

YAKOW, -S n animal bred from a male yak and a domestic cow

YAKS ▶ **yak**

YAKUZA n Japanese criminal organization

YALD adj vigorous

YALE, -S n mythical beast with the body of an antelope (or similar animal) and swivelling horns

YAM, -S n tropical root vegetable

YAMALKA, -S same as ▶ **yarmulke**

YAMEN, -S n (in imperial China) the office or residence of a public official

YAMMER, -ED, -S vb whine in a complaining manner ▷ n yammering sound

YAMMERER ▶ **yammer**

YAMMERS ▶ **yammer**

YAMPY, YAMPIES n foolish person

YAMS ▶ **yam**

YAMULKA, -S same as ▶ **yarmulke**

YAMUN, -S same as ▶ **yamen**

YANG, -S n (in Chinese philosophy) one of two complementary principles maintaining harmony in the universe

YANK, -ED, -ING, -S vb pull or jerk suddenly ▷ n sudden pull or jerk

YANKEE, -S n code word for the letter Y

YANKER, -S ▶ **yank**

YANKIE, -S n impudent woman

YANKING ▶ **yank**

YANKS ▶ **yank**

YANQUI, -S n slang word for American

YANTRA, -S n diagram used in meditation

YAOURT, -S n yoghurt

YAP, -PED, -S vb bark with a high-pitched sound ▷ n high-pitched bark ▷ interj imitation or representation of the sound of a dog yapping

YAPOCK, -S same as ▷ **yapok**

YAPOK, -S n type of opossum

YAPON, -S same as ▷ **yaupon**

YAPP, -S n type of book binding

YAPPED ▷ **yap**

YAPPER, -S ▷ **yap**

YAPPIE, -S n young aspiring professional

YAPPIER ▷ **yappy**

YAPPIES ▷ **yappie**

YAPPIEST ▷ **yappy**

YAPPING, -S n act of yapping

YAPPS ▷ **yapp**

YAPPY, YAPPIER, YAPPIEST ▷ **yap**

YAPS ▷ **yap**

YAPSTER, -S ▷ **yap**

YAQONA, -S n Polynesian shrub

YAR adj nimble

YARAK, -S n fit condition for hunting

YARCO, -S n insulting word for a young working-class person who wears casual sports clothes

YARD, -ED, -S n unit of length ▷ vb draft (animals), esp to a saleyard

YARDAGE, -S n length measured in yards

YARDANG, -S n ridge formed by wind erosion

YARDARM, -S n outer end of a ship's yard

YARDBIRD n inexperienced or clumsy soldier

YARDED ▷ **yard**

YARDER, -S n one who drafts animals to a sale yard

YARDING, -S n group of animals displayed for sale

YARDLAND n archaic unit of land

YARDMAN, YARDMEN n farm overseer

YARDS ▷ **yard**

YARDWAND same as > **yardstick**

YARDWORK n garden work

YARE, -R, -ST adj ready, brisk, or eager ▷ adv readily or eagerly

YARELY ▷ **yare**

YARER ▷ **yare**

YAREST ▷ **yare**

YARFA, -S n peat

YARK, -ED, -ING, -S vb make ready

YARMELKE same as ▷ **yarmulke**

YARMULKA same as ▷ **yarmulke**

YARMULKE n skullcap worn by Jewish men

YARN, -ED, -ING, -S n thread used for knitting or making cloth ▷ vb thread with yarn

YARNER, -S ▷ **yarn**

YARNING ▷ **yarn**

YARNS ▷ **yarn**

YARPHA, -S n peat

YARR, -ED, -ING, -S n wild white flower ▷ vb growl or snarl

YARRAMAN, YARRAMEN n Australian word for a horse

YARRAN, -S n type of small hardy tree of inland Australia

YARRED ▷ **yarr**

YARRING ▷ **yarr**

YARROW, -S n wild plant with flat clusters of white flowers

YARRS ▷ **yarr**

YARTA, -S Shetland word for ▷ **heart**

YARTO, -S same as ▷ **yarta**

YAS ▷ **ya**

YASHMAC, -S same as ▷ **yashmak**

YASHMAK, -S n veil worn by a Muslim woman in public

YASMAK, -S same as ▷ **yashmak**

YATAGAN, -S same as ▷ **yataghan**

YATAGHAN n Turkish sword with a curved single-edged blade

YATE, -S n type of small eucalyptus tree yielding a very hard timber

YATTER, -ED, -S vb talk at length ▷ n continuous chatter

YAUD, -S Scots word for ▷ **mare**

YAULD adj alert or nimble

YAUP, -ED, -ING, -S variant spelling of ▷ **yawp**

YAUPER, -S ▷ **yaup**

YAUPING ▷ **yaup**

YAUPON, -S n southern US evergreen holly shrub

YAUPS ▷ **yaup**

YAUTIA, -S n Caribbean plant cultivated for its edible leaves and underground stems

YAW, -ED, -ING vb (of an aircraft or ship) turn to one side or from side to side while moving ▷ n act or movement of yawing

YAWEY ▷ **yaws**

YAWIER ▷ **yawy**

YAWIEST ▷ **yawy**

YAWING ▷ **yaw**

YAWL, -ED, -ING, -S n two-masted sailing boat ▷ vb howl, weep, or scream harshly

YAWMETER n instrument for measuring an aircraft's yaw

YAWN, -ED, -S vb open the mouth wide and take in air deeply, often when sleepy or bored ▷ n act of yawning

YAWNER, -S ▷ **yawn**

YAWNIER ▷ **yawny**

YAWNIEST ▷ **yawny**

YAWNING, -S ▷ **yawn**

YAWNS ▷ **yawn**

YAWNSOME adj boring

YAWNY, YAWNIER, YAWNIEST ▷ **yawn**

YAWP, -ED, -ING, -INGS, -S vb gape or yawn, esp audibly ▷ n shout, bark, yelp, or cry

YAWPER, -S ▷ **yawp**

YAWPING ▷ **yawp**

YAWPINGS ▷ **yawp**

YAWPS ▷ **yawp**

YAWS n infectious tropical skin disease

YAWY, YAWIER, YAWIEST adj having or resembling yaws

YAY, -S interj exclamation indicating approval or triumph ▷ n cry of approval

YBET archaic past participle of ▷ **beat**

YBLENT archaic past participle of ▷ **blend**

YBORE archaic past participle of ▷ **bear**

YBOUND archaic past participle of ▷ **bind**

YBOUNDEN archaic past participle of ▷ **bind**

YBRENT archaic past participle of ▷ **burn**

YCLAD archaic past participle of ▷ **clothe**

YCLED archaic past participle of ▷ **clothe**

YCLEEPE, -D, -S archaic form of ▷ **clepe**

YCLEPED same as ▷ **yclept**

YCLEPT adj having the name of

YCOND archaic past participle of ▷ **con**

YDRAD *archaic past participle of* ▷ **dread**

YDRED *archaic past participle of* ▷ **dread**

YE *pron* you ▷ *adj* the

YEA, -S *interj* yes ▷ *adv* indeed or truly ▷ *n* cry of agreement

YEAD, -ING, -S, YODE *vb* proceed

YEAH, -S *n* answer of yes

YEALDON, -S *n* fuel

YEALING, -S *n* person of the same age as oneself

YEALM, -ED, -ING, -S *vb* prepare for thatching

YEAN, -ED, -ING, -S *vb* (of a sheep or goat) to give birth to (offspring)

YEANLING *n* young of a goat or sheep

YEANS ▷ **yean**

YEAR, -S *n* time taken for the earth to make one revolution around the sun, about 365 days

YEARBOOK *n* reference book published annually containing details of the previous year's events

YEARD, -ED, -ING, -S *vb* bury

YEAREND, -S *n* end of the year

YEARLIES ▷ **yearly**

YEARLING *n* animal between one and two years old ▷ *adj* being a year old

YEARLONG *adj* throughout a whole year

YEARLY, YEARLIES *adv* every year or once a year ▷ *adj* occurring once a year or every year ▷ *n* publication, event, etc that occurs once a year

YEARN, -ED, -S *vb* want (something) very much

YEARNER, -S ▷ **yearn**

YEARNING *n* intense or overpowering longing, desire, or need

YEARNS ▷ **yearn**

YEARS ▷ **year**

YEAS ▷ **yea**

YEASAYER *n* person who usually agrees with proposals

YEAST, -ED, -ING, -S *n* fungus used to make bread rise ▷ *vb* froth or foam

YEASTIER ▷ **yeasty**

YEASTILY ▷ **yeasty**

YEASTING ▷ **yeasty**

YEASTS ▷ **yeasty**

YEASTY, YEASTIER *adj* of, resembling, or containing yeast

YEBO *interj* yes

YECCH, -S *same as* ▷ **yech**

YECH, -S *n* expression of disgust

YECHIER ▷ **yechy**

YECHIEST ▷ **yechy**

YECHS ▷ **yech**

YECHY, YECHIER, YECHIEST ▷ **yech**

YEDE, -S, YEDING *same as* ▷ **yead**

YEED, -ING, -S *same as* ▷ **yead**

YEELIN, -S *n* person of the same age as oneself

YEESH *interj* used to express frustration

YEGG, -S *n* burglar or safe-breaker

YEGGMAN, YEGGMEN *same as* ▷ **yegg**

YEGGS ▷ **yegg**

YEH *same as* ▷ **yeah**

YELD *adj* (of an animal) barren or too young to bear young

YELDRING *n* yellowhammer (bird)

YELDROCK *same as* ▷ **yeldring**

YELK, -S *n* yolk of an egg

YELL, -ED, -ING, -INGS, -S *vb* shout or scream in a loud or piercing way ▷ *n* loud cry of pain, anger, or fear

YELLER, -S ▷ **yell**

YELLING ▷ **yell**

YELLINGS ▷ **yell**

YELLOCH, -S *vb* yell

YELLOW, -ED, -ER *n* colour of gold, a lemon, etc ▷ *adj* of this colour ▷ *vb* make or become yellow

YELLOWLY ▷ **yellow**

YELLOWS *n* any of various fungal or viral diseases of plants

YELLOWY ▷ **yellow**

YELLS ▷ **yell**

YELM, -ED, -ING, -S *same as* ▷ **yealm**

YELP, -ED, -ING, -INGS, -S *n* short sudden cry ▷ *vb* utter a sharp or high-pitched cry of pain

YELPER, -S ▷ **yelp**

YELPING ▷ **yelp**

YELPINGS ▷ **yelp**

YELPS ▷ **yelp**

YELT, -S *n* young sow

YEMMER, -S *southwest English form of* ▷ **ember**

YEN, -NED, -NING, -S *n* monetary unit of Japan ▷ *vb* have a longing

YENTA, -S *n* meddlesome woman

YENTE, -S *same as* ▷ **yenta**

YEOMAN, YEOMEN *n* farmer owning and farming his own land

YEOMANLY *adj* of or like a yeoman ▷ *adv* in a yeomanly manner, as in being brave or loyal

YEOMANRY *n* yeomen

YEOMEN ▷ **yeoman**

YEOW *interj* used to express pain

YEP, -S *n* answer of yes

YER *adj* informal spelling of 'your'

YERBA, -S *n* stimulating South American drink made from dried leaves

YERD, -ED, -ING, -S *vb* bury

YERK, -ED, -ING, -S *vb* tighten stitches

YERSINIA *n* plague bacterium

YES, -ES, -SED, -SES, -SING *interj* expresses consent, agreement, or approval ▷ *n* answer or vote of yes ▷ *vb* reply in the affirmative

YESHIVA, -S, YESHIVOT *n* traditional Jewish school

YESHIVAH *same as* ▷ **yeshiva**

YESHIVAS ▷ **yeshiva**

YESHIVOT ▷ **yeshiva**

YESK, -ED, -ING, -S *vb* hiccup

YESSED ▷ **yes**

YESSES ▷ **yes**

YESSING ▷ **yes**

YESSIR *interj* expression of assent to a man

YESSIREE *interj* expression of assent

YESSUM *interj* expression of assent to a woman

YEST, -S *archaic form of* ▷ **yeast**

YESTER *adj* of or relating to yesterday

YESTERN *same as* ▷ **yester**

YESTREEN *n* yesterday evening

YESTS ▷ **yest**

YESTY *archaic form of* ▷ **yeasty**

YET *adv* up until then or now

YETI, -S *n* large legendary manlike creature alleged to inhabit the Himalayan Mountains

YETT, -S *n* gate or door

YETTIE, -S *n* young, entrepreneurial, and technology-based (person)

YETTS ▷ **yett**

YEUK, -ED, -ING, -S *vb* itch

Y

YEUKIER ▸ yeuky
YEUKIEST ▸ yeuky
YEUKING ▸ yeuk
YEUKS ▸ yeuk
YEUKY, YEUKIER, YEUKIEST ▸ yeuk
YEVE, -N, -S, YEVING vb give
YEW, -S n evergreen tree with needle-like leaves and red berries
YEWEN adj made of yew
YEWS ▸ yew
YEX, -ED, -ES, -ING vb hiccup

This word meaning to hiccup gives you a good score, and the verb forms offer the chance to expand it if someone else plays it, or if you get the chance later on.

YEZ interj yes
YFERE, -S adv together ▷ n friend or associate
YGLAUNST archaic past participle of ▸ glance
YGO archaic past participle of ▸ go
YGOE archaic past participle of ▸ go
YIBBLES adv Scots word meaning perhaps
YICKER, -ED, -S vb squeal or squeak
YIDAKI, -S n long wooden wind instrument played by some Australian Aboriginal peoples
YIELD, -ED, -S vb produce or bear ▷ n amount produced
YIELDER, -S ▸ yield
YIELDING adj submissive
YIELDS ▸ yield
YIKE, -D, YIKING n argument, squabble, or fight ▷ vb argue, squabble, or fight
YIKES interj expression of surprise, fear, or alarm
YIKING ▸ yike
YIKKER, -ED, -S vb squeal or squeak
YILL, -ED, -ING, -S n ale ▷ vb entertain with ale
YIN, -S Scots word for ▸ one
YINCE Scots form of ▸ once
YINDIE, -S n person who combines a lucrative career with non-mainstream tastes
YINGYANG n two opposing but complementary principles in Chinese philosophy
YINS ▸ yin
YIP, -PED, -PING, -S vb emit a high-pitched bark
YIPE same as ▸ yipes

YIPES interj expression of surprise, fear, or alarm
YIPPED ▸ yip
YIPPEE interj exclamation of joy or pleasure
YIPPER, -S n golfer who has a failure of nerve
YIPPIE, -S n young person sharing hippy ideals
YIPPING ▸ yip
YIPPY same as ▸ yippie
YIPS ▸ yip
YIRD, -ED, -ING, -S vb bury
YIRK, -ED, -ING, -S same as ▸ yerk
YIRR, -ED, -ING, -S vb snarl, growl, or yell
YIRTH, -S n earth
YITE, -S n European bunting with a yellowish head and body and brown streaked wings and tail
YITIE, -S same as ▸ yite
YITTEN adj frightened
YLEM, -S n original matter from which the basic elements are said to have been formed
YLIKE Spenserian form of ▸ alike
YLKE, -S archaic spelling of ▸ ilk
YMOLT Spenserian past participle of ▸ melt
YMOLTEN Spenserian past participle of ▸ melt
YMPE, -S, YMPING, YMPT Spenserian form of ▸ imp
YNAMBU, -S n South American bird
YO interj expression used as a greeting
YOB, -S n bad-mannered aggressive youth
YOBBERY n behaviour typical of aggressive surly youths
YOBBIER ▸ yobby
YOBBIEST ▸ yobby
YOBBISH adj typical of aggressive surly youths
YOBBISM, -S ▸ yob
YOBBO, -ES, -S same as ▸ yob
YOBBY, YOBBIER, YOBBIEST adj like a yob
YOBS ▸ yob
YOCK, -ED, -ING, -S vb chuckle
YOD, -S n tenth letter in the Hebrew alphabet
YODE ▸ yead
YODEL, -ED, -LED, -S vb sing with abrupt changes between a normal and a falsetto voice ▷ n act or sound of yodelling

YODELER, -S ▸ yodel
YODELING > yodelling
YODELLED ▸ yodel
YODELLER, -S ▸ yodel
YODELS ▸ yodel
YODH, -S same as ▸ yod
YODLE, -D, -S, YODLING variant spelling of ▸ yodel
YODLER, -S ▸ yodle
YODLES ▸ yodle
YODLING ▸ yodle
YODS ▸ yod
YOGA, -S n Hindu method of exercise and discipline
YOGEE, -S same as ▸ yogi
YOGH, -S n character used in Old and Middle English to represent a palatal fricative
YOGHOURT variant form of ▸ yogurt
YOGHS ▸ yogh
YOGHURT, -S same as ▸ yogurt
YOGI, -S n person who practises yoga
YOGIC ▸ yoga
YOGIN, -S same as ▸ yogi
YOGINI, -S ▸ yogi
YOGINS ▸ yogin
YOGIS ▸ yogi
YOGISM, -S ▸ yogi
YOGOURT, -S same as ▸ yogurt
YOGURT, -S n slightly sour custard-like food made from milk that has had bacteria added
YOHIMBE, -S n bark used in herbal medicine
YOICK, -ED, -ING vb urge on foxhounds
YOICKS, -ED, -ES interj cry used by huntsmen to urge on the hounds ▷ vb urge on foxhounds
YOJAN, -S n Indian unit of distance
YOJANA, -S same as ▸ yojan
YOJANS ▸ yojan
YOK, -KED, -KING, -S vb chuckle

A useful short word meaning to laugh, with an alternative spelling **yuk**.

YOKE, -D, -RS, -S, YOKING, YOKINGS n wooden bar put across the necks of two animals to hold them together ▷ vb put a yoke on
YOKEL, -S n simple person who lives in the country
YOKELESS ▸ yoke
YOKELISH ▸ yokel
YOKELS ▸ yokel
YOKEMATE n colleague
YOKER, -ED, -ING vb spit

YOKERS ▶ yoke

YOKES ▶ yoke

YOKING ▶ yoke

YOKINGS ▶ yoke

YOKKED ▶ yok

YOKKING ▶ yok

YOKOZUNA n grand champion sumo wrestler

YOKS ▶ yok

YOKUL Shetland word for ▶ yes

YOLD archaic past participle of ▶ yield

YOLDRING n yellowhammer (bird)

YOLK, -S n yellow part of an egg that provides food for the developing embryo

YOLKED ▶ yolk

YOLKIER ▶ yolky

YOLKIEST ▶ yolky

YOLKLESS ▶ yolk

YOLKS ▶ yolk

YOLKY, YOLKIER, YOLKIEST ▶ yolk

YOM, -IM n day

YOMP, -ED, -ING, -S vb walk or trek laboriously

YON adj that or those over there ▷ adv yonder ▷ pron that person or thing

YOND same as ▶ yon

YONDER, -S adv over there ▷ adj situated over there ▷ determiner being at a distance, either within view or as if within view ▷ n person

YONDERLY ▶ yonder

YONDERS ▶ yonder

YONI, -S n female genitalia

YONIC adj resembling a vulva

YONIS ▶ yoni

YONKER, -S same as ▶ younker

YONKS pl n very long time

YONNIE, -S n stone

YONT same as ▶ yon

YOOF, -S n non-standard spelling of youth

YOOP, -S n sob

YOPPER, -S n young person employed on a former UK government training programme

YORE, -S n time long past ▷ adv in the past

YORK, -ED, -ING, -S vb bowl or try to bowl (a batsman) by pitching the ball under or just beyond the bat

YORKER, -S n (in cricket) ball that pitches just under the bat

YORKIE, -S n Yorkshire terrier

YORKING ▶ york

YORKS ▶ york

YORLING, -S n as in yellow yorling yellowhammer

YORP, -ED, -ING, -S vb shout

YOU pron person or people addressed ▷ n personality of the person being addressed

YOUK, -ED, -ING, -S vb itch

YOUNG, -ER, -EST, -S adj in an early stage of life or growth ▷ n young people in general; offspring

YOUNGERS pl n young people

YOUNGEST ▶ young

YOUNGISH ▶ young

YOUNGLY adv youthfully

YOUNGS ▶ young

YOUNGTH, -S n youth

YOUNKER, -S n young man

YOUPON, -S same as ▶ yaupon

YOUR adj of, belonging to, or associated with you

YOURN dialect form of ▶ yours

YOURS pron something belonging to you

YOURSELF pron reflexive form of you

YOURT, -S same as ▶ yurt

YOUS pron dialect form of 'you' when referring to more than one person

YOUSE same as ▶ yous

YOUTH, -S n time of being young

YOUTHEN, -S vb render more youthful-seeming

YOUTHFUL adj vigorous or active

YOUTHIER ▶ youthy

YOUTHLY adj young

YOUTHS ▶ youth

YOUTHY, YOUTHIER Scots word for ▶ young

YOW, -ED, -ING, -S vb howl

YOWE, -S Scot word for ▶ ewe

YOWED ▶ yow

YOWES ▶ yowe

YOWIE, -S n legendary Australian apelike creature

YOWING ▶ yow

YOWL, -ED, -S n loud mournful cry ▷ vb produce a loud mournful wail or cry

YOWLER, -S ▶ yowl

YOWLEY, -S n yellowhammer (bird)

YOWLING, -S ▶ yowl

YOWLS ▶ yowl

YOWS ▶ yow

YOWZA interj exclamation of enthusiasm

YPERITE, -S n mustard gas

YPIGHT archaic past participle of ▶ pitch

YPLAST archaic past participle of ▶ place

YPLIGHT archaic past participle of ▶ plight

YPSILOID ▶ ypsilon

YPSILON, -S same as ▶ upsilon

YRAPT Spenserian form of ▶ rapt

YRENT archaic past participle of ▶ rend

YRIVD archaic past participle of ▶ rive

YRNEH, -S n unit of reciprocal inductance

YSAME Spenserian word for ▶ together

YSHEND, -S, YSHENT Spenserian form of ▶ shend

YSLAKED archaic past participle of ▶ slake

YTOST archaic past participle of ▶ toss

YTTERBIA n colourless hygroscopic substance used in certain alloys and ceramics

YTTERBIC > ytterbium

YTTRIA, -S n insoluble solid used mainly in incandescent mantles

YTTRIC ▶ yttrium

YTTRIOUS ▶ yttrium

YTTRIUM, -S n silvery metallic element used in various alloys

YU, -S n jade

YUAN, -S n standard monetary unit of the People's Republic of China

YUCA, -S same as ▶ yucca

YUCCA, -S n tropical plant with lancelike leaves

YUCCH interj expression of disgust

YUCH interj expression of disgust

YUCK, -ED, -ING, -S interj exclamation indicating contempt, dislike, or disgust ▷ vb chuckle

YUCKER, -S ▶ yuck

YUCKIER ▶ yucky

YUCKIEST ▶ yucky

YUCKING ▶ yuck

YUCKO adj disgusting ▷ interj exclamation of disgust

YUCKS ▶ yuck

YUCKY, YUCKIER, YUCKIEST adj disgusting, nasty

YUFT, -S n Russia leather

YUG, -S same as ▶ yuga

YUGA, -S n (in Hindu cosmology) one of the four ages of mankind

YUGARIE, -S variant spelling of ▶ **eugarie**

YUGAS ▶ **yuga**

YUGS ▶ **yug**

YUK, -KED, -KING, -S same as ▶ **yuck**

YUKATA, -S n light kimono

YUKE, -D, -S, YUKING vb itch

YUKIER ▶ **yuky**

YUKIEST ▶ **yuky**

YUKING ▶ **yuke**

YUKKED ▶ **yuk**

YUKKIER ▶ **yukky**

YUKKIEST ▶ **yukky**

YUKKING ▶ **yuk**

YUKKY, YUKKIER, YUKKIEST same as ▶ **yucky**

YUKO, -S n score of five points in judo

YUKS ▶ **yuk**

YUKY, YUKIER, YUKIEST adj itchy

YULAN, -S n Chinese magnolia with white flowers

YULE, -S n Christmas

YULETIDE n Christmas season

YUM interj expression of delight

YUMBERRY n purple-red edible fruit of an E Asian tree

YUMMIER ▶ **yummy**

YUMMIES ▶ **yummy**

YUMMIEST ▶ **yummy**

YUMMO adj tasty ▷ interj exclamation of delight or approval

YUMMY, YUMMIER, YUMMIES, YUMMIEST adj delicious ▷ interj exclamation indicating pleasure or delight ▷ n delicious food item

YUMP, -ED, -ING, -S vb leave the ground when driving over a ridge

YUMPIE, -S n young upwardly mobile person

YUMPING ▶ **yump**

YUMPS ▶ **yump**

YUNX, -ES n wryneck

YUP, -S n answer of yes

YUPON, -S same as ▶ **yaupon**

YUPPIE n young highly paid professional person ▷ adj typical of or reflecting the values of yuppies

YUPPIFY vb make yuppie in nature

YUPPY, YUPPIES same as ▶ **yuppie**

YUPPYDOM n state of being a yuppie

YUPS ▶ **yup**

YUPSTER, -S same as ▶ **yindie**

YURT, -S n circular tent

YURTA, -S same as ▶ **yurt**

YURTS ▶ **yurt**

YUS ▶ **yu**

YUTZ, -ES n Yiddish word meaning fool

YUZU, -S n type of citrus fruit

YWIS adv archaic word meaning certainly

YWROKE archaic past participle of ▶ **wreak**

Zz

Scoring the same as **Q** but easier to use, **Z** is normally a good tile to have, but it is not the best when it comes to making bonus words scoring that extra 50 points, so you will normally want to play it off as soon as a good score offers itself. There are three two-letter words beginning with **Z**, **za** and **ze** and **zo** (11 points). There are also some very good three-letter words starting with **Z**. These include another variant of **zo**, **zho** (15), as well as **zax** and **zex** (19 each), **zap** (14), **zep** (14), **zip** (14) and **zoo** (12).

ZA, -S n pizza
ZABAIONE n light foamy dessert
ZABAJONE same as ▶ zabaione
ZABETA, -S n tariff
ZABRA, -S n small sailing vessel
ZABTIEH, -S n Turkish police officer
ZACATON, -S n coarse grass
ZACK, -S n Australian five-cent piece
ZADDICK, -S adj righteous ▷ n Hasidic Jewish spiritual leader
ZADDIK, -IM, -S n Hasidic Jewish leader
ZAFFAR, -S same as ▶ zaffer
ZAFFER, -S n impure cobalt oxide, used to impart a blue colour to enamels
ZAFFIR, -S same as ▶ zaffer
ZAFFRE, -S same as ▶ zaffer
ZAFTIG adj ripe or curvaceous
ZAG, -GED, -GING, -S vb change direction sharply
ZAIBATSU n group or combine comprising a few wealthy families that controls industry, business, and finance in Japan
ZAIDA, -S n grandfather
ZAIDEH, -S same as ▶ zaida
ZAIDY, ZAIDIES same as ▶ zaida
ZAIKAI, -S n Japanese business community
ZAIRE, -S n currency used in the former Zaïre
ZAITECH, -S n investment in financial markets by a company to supplement its main income

ZAKAT, -S n annual tax on Muslims to aid the poor in the Muslim community
ZAKOUSKI, ZAKOUSKA same as ▶ zakuski
ZAKUSKI, ZAKUSKA pl n Russian hors d'oeuvres consisting of tiny sandwiches
ZAMAN, -S n tropical tree
ZAMANG, -S same as ▶ zaman
ZAMANS ▶ zaman
ZAMARRA, -S n sheepskin coat
ZAMARRO, -S same as ▶ zamarra
ZAMBOMBA n drum-like musical instrument
ZAMBUCK, -S n informal word for a St John ambulance attendant
ZAMBUK, -S same as ▶ zambuck
ZAMIA, -S n type of plant of tropical and subtropical America
ZAMINDAR n (in India) the owner of an agricultural estate
ZAMOUSE, -S n West African buffalo
ZAMPOGNA n Italian bagpipes
ZAMPONE, ZAMPONI n sausage made from pig's trotters
ZAMZAWED adj dialect word describing tea left in the pot to stew
ZANANA, -S same as ▶ zenana
ZANDER, -S n European freshwater pikeperch, valued as a food fish

ZANELLA, -S n twill fabric
ZANIED ▶ zany
ZANIER ▶ zany
ZANIES ▶ zany
ZANIEST ▶ zany
ZANILY ▶ zany
ZANINESS ▶ zany
ZANJA, -S n irrigation canal

An irrigation canal in Spanish America, notable for combining the J and Z.

ZANJERO, -S n irrigation supervisor

Someone who supervises the distribution of water in a **zanja** or irrigation canal. This has a fair chance of coming up in actual play, and would make a great bonus.

ZANTE, -S n type of wood
ZANY, ZANIED, ZANIER, ZANIES, ZANIEST, -ING adj comical in an endearing way ▷ n clown or buffoon who imitated other performers ▷ vb clown
ZANYISH ▶ zany
ZANYISM, -S ▶ zany
ZANZA, -S same as ▶ zanze
ZANZE, -S n African musical instrument
ZAP, -PED, -PING, -S vb move quickly ▷ n energy, vigour, or pep ▷ interj exclamation used to express sudden or swift action
ZAPATA adj (of a moustache) drooping
ZAPATEO, -S n Cuban folk dance
ZAPPED ▶ zap

Z

ZAPPER, -S n remote control for a television, etc
ZAPPIER ► zappy
ZAPPIEST ► zappy
ZAPPING ► zap
ZAPPY, ZAPPIER, ZAPPIEST adj energetic
ZAPS ► zap
ZAPTIAH, -S same as ► zaptieh
ZAPTIEH, -S n Turkish police officer

Watch out for this Turkish police officer, who can also be spelt **zabtieh** or **zaptiah**.

ZARAPE, -S n blanket-like shawl
ZARATITE n green amorphous mineral
ZAREBA, -S n (in NE Africa) enclosure of thorn bushes around a village or campsite
ZAREEBA, -S same as ► zareba
ZARF, -S n (esp in the Middle East) a holder, usually ornamental, for a hot coffee cup
ZARI, -S n thread made from fine gold or silver wire
ZARIBA, -S same as ► zareba
ZARIS ► zari
ZARNEC, -S n sulphide of arsenic
ZARNICH, -S same as ► zarnec
ZARZUELA n type of Spanish vaudeville or operetta, usually satirical in nature
ZAS ► za
ZASTRUGA, ZASTRUGI variant spelling of ► sastruga
ZATI, -S n type of macaque
ZAX, -ES n tool for cutting roofing slate

A chopper for trimming slate, and a great word combining X and Z. It has a variant **zex**.

ZAYIN, -S n seventh letter of the Hebrew alphabet
ZAZEN, -S n deep meditation undertaken whilst sitting upright with legs crossed
ZE pron gender-neutral pronoun
ZEA, -S n corn silk
ZEAL, -S n great enthusiasm or eagerness
ZEALANT, -S archaic variant of ► zealot
ZEALFUL ► zeal
ZEALLESS ► zeal
ZEALOT, -S n fanatic or extreme enthusiast

ZEALOTRY n extreme or excessive zeal or devotion
ZEALOTS ► zealot
ZEALOUS adj extremely eager or enthusiastic
ZEALS ► zeal
ZEAS ► zea
ZEATIN, -S n cytokinin derived from corn
ZEBEC, -S variant spelling of ► xebec
ZEBECK, -S same as ► zebec
ZEBECS ► zebec
ZEBRA, -S n black-and-white striped African animal of the horse family
ZEBRAIC adj like a zebra
ZEBRANO, -S n type of striped wood
ZEBRAS ► zebra
ZEBRASS n offspring of a male zebra and a female ass
ZEBRINA, -S n trailing herbaceous plant
ZEBRINE, -S ► zebra
ZEBRINNY n offspring of a male horse and a female zebra
ZEBROID ► zebra
ZEBRULA, -S n offspring of a male zebra and a female horse
ZEBRULE, -S same as ► zebrula
ZEBU, -S n Asian ox with a humped back and long horns
ZEBUB, -S n large African fly
ZEBUS ► zebu
ZECCHIN, -S same as ► zecchino
ZECCHINE same as ► zecchino
ZECCHINO, ZECCHINI n former gold coin
ZECCHINS ► zecchin
ZECHIN, -S same as ► zecchino
ZED, -S n British and New Zealand spoken form of the letter z

A name for the letter Z, and one of the most commonly played Z words.

ZEDA, -S n grandfather
ZEDOARY n dried rhizome of a tropical Asian plant
ZEDS ► zed
ZEE, -S the US word for ► zed

This word can be very useful because E is the most common tile in Scrabble, so keep it in mind if you draw a Z. Zee scores 12 points.

ZEIN, -S n protein occurring in maize
ZEK, -S n Soviet prisoner
ZEL, -S n Turkish cymbal
ZELANT, -S alternative form of ► zealant
ZELATOR, -S same as ► zelatrix
ZELATRIX n nun who monitors the behaviour of younger nuns
ZELKOVA, -S n type of elm tree
ZELOSO adv with zeal
ZELS ► zel
ZEMINDAR n (in India) the owner of an agricultural estate
ZEMSTVO, ZEMSTVA, -S n council in Tsarist Russia
ZEN, -S n calm meditative state
ZENAIDA, -S n dove
ZENANA, -S n part of a Muslim or Hindu home reserved for women and girls
ZENDIK, -S n (in Islam) unbeliever or heretic
ZENDO, -S n place where Zen Buddhists study
ZENITH, -S n highest point of success or power
ZENITHAL ► zenith
ZENITHS ► zenith
ZENS ► zen
ZEOLITE, -S n any of a large group of glassy secondary minerals
ZEOLITIC ► zeolite
ZEP, -S n type of long sandwich
ZEPHYR, -S n soft gentle breeze
ZEPPELIN n large cylindrical airship
ZEPPOLE, -S, ZEPPOLI n Italian fritter
ZEPS ► zep
ZERDA, -S n fennec
ZEREBA, -S same as ► zareba
ZERIBA, -S same as ► zareba
ZERK, -S n part of a mechanical joint into which grease can be inserted
ZERO, -ED, -ES, -ING, -S n (symbol representing) the number o ▷ adj having no measurable quantity or size ▷ vb adjust (an instrument or scale) so as to read zero ▷ determiner no (thing) at all
ZEROTH adj denoting a term in a series that precedes the term otherwise regarded as the first term

ZERUMBET n plant stem used as a stimulant and condiment

ZEST, -ED, -ING, -S n enjoyment or excitement ▷ vb give flavour, interest, or piquancy to

ZESTER, -S n kitchen utensil used to scrape fine shreds of peel from citrus fruits

ZESTFUL ▶ zest

ZESTIER ▶ zesty

ZESTIEST ▶ zesty

ZESTILY ▶ zest

ZESTING ▶ zest

ZESTLESS ▶ zest

ZESTS ▶ zest

ZESTY, ZESTIER, ZESTIEST ▶ zest

ZETA, -S n sixth letter in the Greek alphabet

ZETETIC, -S adj proceeding by inquiry ▷ n investigation

ZEUGMA, -S n figure of speech in which a word is used with two words although appropriate to only one of them

ZEUXITE, -S n ferriferous mineral

This mineral, a kind of tourmaline, makes an excellent bonus.

ZEX, -ES n tool for cutting roofing slate

ZEZE, -S n stringed musical instrument

ZHO, -S same as ▶ zo

A cross between a yak and a cow; the other forms are **dso, dzo, dzho** and **zo**, and it's worth remembering all of them.

ZHOMO, -S n female zho

ZHOOSH, -ED, -ES vb make more exciting or attractive

ZHOS ▶ zho

ZIBELINE n sable or the fur of this animal ▷ adj of, relating to, or resembling a sable

ZIBET, -S n large civet of S and SE Asia

ZIBETH, -S same as ▶ zibet

ZIBETS ▶ zibet

ZIFF, -S n beard

ZIFFIUS n sea monster

ZIFFS ▶ ziff

ZIG, -GED, -GING, -S same as ▶ zag

ZIGAN, -S n Romany dance

ZIGANKA, -S n Russian dance

ZIGANS ▶ zigan

ZIGGED ▶ zig

ZIGGING ▶ zig

ZIGGURAT n (in ancient Mesopotamia) a temple in the shape of a pyramid

ZIGS ▶ zig

ZIGZAG, -S n line or course having sharp turns in alternating directions ▷ vb move in a zigzag ▷ adj formed in or proceeding in a zigzag ▷ adv in a zigzag manner

ZIGZAGGY adj having sharp turns

ZIGZAGS ▶ zigzag

ZIKKURAT same as ▶ ziggurat

ZIKURAT, -S same as ▶ ziggurat

ZILA, -S n administrative district in India

ZILCH, -ES n nothing

ZILL, -S n finger cymbal

ZILLA, -S same as ▶ zila

ZILLAH, -S same as ▶ zila

ZILLAS ▶ zilla

ZILLION, -S n extremely large but unspecified number

ZILLS ▶ zill

ZIMB, -S same as ▶ zebub

ZIMBI, -S n cowrie shell used as money

ZIMBS ▶ zimb

ZIMOCCA, -S n bath sponge

ZIN, -S short form of ▷ zinfandel

ZINC, -ED, -ING, -KED, -KING, -S, ZINKED, ZINKING n bluish-white metallic element ▷ vb coat with zinc

ZINCATE, -S n any of a class of salts derived from the amphoteric hydroxide of zinc

ZINCED ▶ zinc

ZINCIC ▶ zinc

ZINCIER ▶ zincy

ZINCIEST ▶ zincy

ZINCIFY vb coat with zinc

ZINCING ▶ zinc

ZINCITE, -S n red or yellow mineral

ZINCKED ▶ zinc

ZINCKIER ▶ zincky

ZINCKIFY same as ▶ zincify

ZINCKING ▶ zinc

ZINCKY, ZINCKIER ▶ zinc

ZINCO, -S n printing plate made from zincography

ZINCODE, -S n positive electrode

ZINCOID ▶ zinc

ZINCOS ▶ zinco

ZINCOUS ▶ zinc

ZINCS ▶ zinc

ZINCY, ZINCIER, ZINCIEST ▶ zinc

ZINDABAD interj long live: used as part of a slogan in India, Pakistan, etc

ZINE, -S n magazine or fanzine

ZINEB, -S n organic insecticide

ZINES ▶ zine

ZING, -ED, -ING, -S n quality in something that makes it lively or interesting ▷ vb make or move with or as if with a high-pitched buzzing sound

ZINGANO, ZINGANI n Romany man

ZINGARA, ZINGARE n Romany woman

ZINGARO, ZINGARI n Romany man

ZINGED ▶ zing

ZINGEL, -S n small freshwater perch

ZINGER, -S ▶ zing

ZINGIBER n ginger plant

ZINGIER ▶ zingy

ZINGIEST ▶ zingy

ZINGING ▶ zing

ZINGS ▶ zing

ZINGY, ZINGIER, ZINGIEST adj vibrant

ZINKE, -S n cornett

ZINKED ▶ zinc

ZINKES ▶ zinke

ZINKIER ▶ zinky

ZINKIEST ▶ zinky

ZINKIFY vb coat with zinc

ZINKING ▶ zinc

ZINKY, ZINKIER, ZINKIEST ▶ zinc

ZINNIA, -S n plant of tropical and subtropical America

ZINS ▶ zin

ZIP, -PED, -PING, -S n fastening device operating by means of two rows of metal or plastic teeth ▷ vb fasten with a zip

ZIPLESS ▶ zip

ZIPLINE, -S n cable used for transportation across a river, gorge, etc

ZIPLOCK, -S adj fastened with interlocking plastic strips ▷ vb seal (a ziplock storage bag)

ZIPOLA, -S n nothing

ZIPPED ▶ zip

ZIPPER, -S same as ▶ zip

ZIPPERED adj provided or fastened with a zip

ZIPPERS ▶ zipper

ZIPPIER ▶ zippy

ZIPPIEST ▶ zippy

Z

ZIPPILY *adv* in a zippy manner

ZIPPING ▸ zip

ZIPPO, -S *n* nothing

ZIPPY, ZIPPIER, ZIPPIEST *adj* full of energy

ZIPS ▸ zip

ZIPTOP *adj* (of a bag) closed with a zip

ZIPWIRE, -S *same as* **▸ zipline**

ZIRAM, -S *n* industrial fungicide

ZIRCALOY *same as* **> zircalloy**

ZIRCON, -S *n* mineral used as a gemstone and in industry

ZIRCONIA *n* white oxide of zirconium, used as a pigment for paints, a catalyst, and an abrasive

ZIRCONIC > zirconium

ZIRCONS ▸ zircon

ZIT, -S *n* spot or pimple

This little word for a pimple can be very useful for disposing of the Z.

ZITE *same as* **▸ ziti**

ZITHER, -S *n* musical instrument consisting of strings stretched over a flat box

ZITHERN, -S *same as* **▸ zither**

ZITHERS ▸ zither

ZITI, -S *n* type of pasta

Another very useful word for disposing of the Z, **ziti** is a type of pasta. It has a variant **zite**. Remember that **ziti** takes an S to form **zitis**, but **zite** does not take an S.

ZITS ▸ zit

ZIZ *same as* **▸ zizz**

ZIZANIA, -S *n* aquatic grass

ZIZEL, -S *n* chipmunk

ZIZIT *same as* **▸ zizith**

ZIZITH *variant spelling of* **▸ tsitsith**

ZIZYPHUS *n* jujube tree

ZIZZ, -ED, -ING *n* short sleep ▷ *vb* take a short sleep, snooze

ZIZZLE, -D, -S, ZIZZLING *vb* sizzle

ZLOTY, ZLOTE, ZLOTIES, -S *n* monetary unit of Poland

ZLOTYCH *same as* **▸ zloty**

ZLOTYS ▸ zloty

ZO, -S *n* Tibetan breed of cattle

ZOA ▸ zoon

ZOAEA, -E, -S *same as* **▸ zoea**

ZOARIA ▸ zoarium

ZOARIAL ▸ zoarium

ZOARIUM, ZOARIA *n* colony of zooids

ZOBO, -S *same as* **▸ zo**

ZOBU, -S *same as* **▸ zo**

ZOCALO, -S *n* plaza in Mexico

ZOCCO, -S *n* plinth

ZOCCOLO, -S *same as* **▸ zocco**

ZOCCOS ▸ zocco

ZODIAC, -S *n* imaginary belt in the sky within which the sun, moon, and planets appear to move

ZODIACAL ▸ zodiac

ZODIACS ▸ zodiac

ZOEA, -E, -S *n* free-swimming larva of a crab or related crustacean

One of the most frequently played words in Scrabble, along with its friends **zoaea** and **zooea** and the various inflections: remember that these words can take an E in the plural as well as S, giving **zoeae**, **zoaeae** and **zooeae**.

ZOEAL ▸ zoea

ZOEAS ▸ zoea

ZOECIUM, ZOECIA *same as* **▸ zooecium**

ZOEFORM ▸ zoea

ZOETIC *adj* pertaining to life

ZOETROPE *n* cylinder-shaped toy with a sequence of pictures on its inner surface which produce an illusion of animation when it is rotated

ZOFTIG *adj* ripe or curvaceous

ZOIATRIA *n* veterinary surgery

ZOIC *adj* relating to or having animal life

ZOISITE, -S *n* grey, brown, or pink mineral

ZOISM, -S *n* belief in magical animal powers

ZOIST, -S ▸ zoism

ZOLPIDEM *n* drug used to treat insomnia

ZOMBI, -S *same as* **▸ zombie**

ZOMBIE, -S *n* corpse that has been reanimated by a supernatural spirit

ZOMBIFY *vb* turn into a zombie

ZOMBIISM ▸ zombie

ZOMBIS ▸ zombi

ZOMBOID *adj* like a zombie

ZOMBORUK *n* small swivelling cannon mounted on a camel's back

ZONA, -E *n* zone or belt

ZONAL *adj* of, relating to, or of the nature of a zone

ZONALLY ▸ zonal

ZONARY *same as* **▸ zonal**

ZONATE *adj* marked with, divided into, or arranged in zones

ZONATED *same as* **▸ zonate**

ZONATION *n* arrangement in zones

ZONDA, -S *n* South American wind

ZONE, -D, -S *n* area with particular features or properties ▷ *vb* divide into zones

ZONELESS ▸ zone

ZONER, -S *n* something which divides other things into zones

ZONES ▸ zone

ZONETIME *n* standard time of the time zone in which a ship is located at sea

ZONING, -S ▸ zone

ZONK, -ED, -ING, -S *vb* strike resoundingly

ZONOID, -S *adj* resembling a zone ▷ *n* finite vector sum of line segments

ZONULA, -E, -S *n* small zone or belt

ZONULAR ▸ zonule

ZONULAS ▸ zonula

ZONULE, -S *n* small zone, band, or area

ZONULET, -S *n* small belt

ZONURE, -S *n* lizard with a ringed tail

ZOO, -IER, -IEST, -S *n* place where live animals are kept for show

ZOOBLAST *n* animal cell

ZOOCHORE *n* plant with spores or seeds that are dispersed by animals

ZOOCHORY ▸ zoochore

ZOOCYTIA > zoocytium

ZOOEA, -E, -S *same as* **▸ zoea**

ZOOEAL ▸ zooea

ZOOEAS ▸ zooea

ZOOECIUM, ZOOECIA *n* part of a polyzoan colony that houses the feeding zooids

ZOOEY ▸ zoo

ZOOGAMY *n* reproduction involving zoosperm

ZOOGENIC *adj* produced from animals

ZOOGENY *n* doctrine of the formation of animals

ZOOGLEA, -E, -S *same as* **▸ zoogloea**

ZOOGLEAL ▸ zooglea

ZOOGLEAS ▸ zooglea
ZOOGLOEA n mass of bacteria adhering together by a jelly-like substance derived from their cell walls
ZOOGONY same as ▸ zoogeny
ZOOGRAFT n animal tissue grafted onto a human body
ZOOID, -S n any independent animal body, such as an individual of a coral colony
ZOOIDAL ▸ zooid
ZOOIDS ▸ zooid
ZOOIER ▸ zoo
ZOOIEST ▸ zoo
ZOOKS short form of ▸ gadzooks
ZOOLATER ▸ zoolatry
ZOOLATRY n worship of animals
ZOOLITE, -S n fossilized animal
ZOOLITH, -S n fossilized animal
ZOOLITIC ▸ zoolite
ZOOLOGIC ▸ zoology
ZOOLOGY n study of animals
ZOOM, -ED, -ING, -S vb move or rise very rapidly ▷ n sound or act of zooming
ZOOMABLE adj capable of being viewed at various levels of magnification
ZOOMANCY n divination through observing the actions of animals
ZOOMANIA n extreme or excessive devotion to animals
ZOOMED ▸ zoom
ZOOMETRY n study of the relative size of the different parts of an animal or animals
ZOOMING ▸ zoom
ZOOMORPH n representation of an animal form
ZOOMS ▸ zoom
ZOON, ZOA, -ED, -ING, -S vb zoom ▷ n zooid
ZOONAL ▸ zoon
ZOONED ▸ zoon
ZOONIC adj concerning animals
ZOONING ▸ zoon
ZOONITE, -S n segment of an articulated animal
ZOONITIC ▸ zoonite
ZOONOMIA same as ▸ zoonomy
ZOONOMIC ▸ zoonomy
ZOONOMY n science of animal life

ZOONOSIS, ZOONOSES n any infection or disease that is transmitted to humans from lower vertebrates
ZOONOTIC ▸ zoonosis
ZOONS ▸ zoon
ZOOPATHY n science of animal diseases
ZOOPERAL ▸ zoopery
ZOOPERY n experimentation on animals
ZOOPHAGY n eating other animals
ZOOPHILE n person who is devoted to animals and their protection
ZOOPHOBE > zoophobia
ZOOPHORI > zoophorus
ZOOPHYTE n any animal resembling a plant, such as a sea anemone
ZOOS ▸ zoo
ZOOSCOPY n condition causing hallucinations of animals
ZOOSPERM n gamete that can move independently
ZOOSPORE n asexual spore of some algae and fungi that moves by means of flagella
ZOOT n as in zoot suit man's suit consisting of baggy trousers and a long jacket
ZOOTAXY n science of the classification of animals

The science of classifying animals. An unlikely word to appear on your rack, but you never know, and it would make an impressive bonus!

ZOOTHOME n group of zooids
ZOOTIER ▸ zooty
ZOOTIEST ▸ zooty
ZOOTOMIC ▸ zootomy
ZOOTOMY n branch of zoology concerned with the dissection and anatomy of animals
ZOOTOXIC ▸ zootoxin
ZOOTOXIN n toxin, such as snake venom, that is produced by an animal
ZOOTROPE same as ▸ zoetrope
ZOOTY, ZOOTIER, ZOOTIEST adj showy
ZOOTYPE, -S n animal figure used as a symbol
ZOOTYPIC ▸ zootype
ZOOZOO, -S n wood pigeon
ZOPILOTE n small American vulture
ZOPPA adj syncopated
ZOPPO same as ▸ zoppa

ZORBING, -S n activity of travelling downhill inside a large air-filled ball
ZORGITE, -S n copper-lead selenide
ZORI, -S n Japanese sandal
ZORIL, -S same as ▸ zorilla
ZORILLA, -S n skunk-like African musteline mammal having a long black-and-white coat
ZORILLE, -S same as ▸ zorilla
ZORILLO, -S same as ▸ zorilla
ZORILS ▸ zoril
ZORINO, -S n skunk fur
ZORIS ▸ zori
ZORRO, -S n hoary fox
ZOS ▸ zo
ZOSTER, -S n shingles; herpes zoster
ZOUAVE, -S n (formerly) member of a body of French infantry composed of Algerian recruits
ZOUK, -S n style of dance music that combines African and Latin American rhythms
ZOUNDS interj archaic mild oath indicating surprise
ZOWEE same as ▸ zowie
ZOWIE interj expression of pleasurable surprise
ZOYSIA, -S n type of grass with short stiffly pointed leaves, often used for lawns
ZUCCHINI n courgette
ZUCHETTA same as > zucchetto
ZUCHETTO same as > zucchetto
ZUFFOLO, ZUFFOLI same as ▸ zufolo
ZUFOLO, ZUFOLI, -S n small flute
ZUGZWANG n (in chess) position in which one player can move only with loss or severe disadvantage ▷ vb manoeuvre (one's opponent) into a zugzwang
ZULU, -S n (in the NATO phonetic alphabet) used to represent z
ZUPA, -S n confederation of Serbian villages
ZUPAN, -S n head of a zupa
ZUPAS ▸ zupa
ZUPPA, -S n Italian soup
ZURF, -S same as ▸ zarf
ZUZ, -IM, -ZIM n ancient Hebrew silver coin
ZWIEBACK n small type of rusk
ZYDECO, -S n type of Black Cajun music
ZYGA ▸ zygon

Z

ZYGAENID adj of the burnet moth genus

ZYGAL ▸ zygon

ZYGANTRA > zygantrum

ZYGODONT adj possessing paired molar cusps

ZYGOID same as ▸ diploid

ZYGOMA, -S, -TA n slender arch of bone on each side of the skull of mammals

ZYGON, ZYGA n brain fissure

ZYGOSE, -S ▸ zygosis

ZYGOSIS n direct transfer of DNA between two cells that are temporarily joined

ZYGOSITY ▸ zygosis

ZYGOTE, -S n fertilized egg cell

ZYGOTENE n second stage of the prophase of meiosis

ZYGOTES ▸ zygote

ZYGOTIC ▸ zygote

ZYLONITE variant spelling of ▸ xylonite

ZYMASE, -S n mixture of enzymes that is obtained as an extract from yeast and ferments sugars

ZYME, -S n ferment

ZYMIC ▸ zyme

ZYMITE, -S n priest who uses leavened bread during communion

ZYMOGEN, -S n any of various inactive precursors of enzymes activated by a kinase

ZYMOGENE same as ▸ zymogen

ZYMOGENS ▸ zymogen

ZYMOGRAM n band of an electrophoretic medium showing a pattern of enzymes following electrophoresis

ZYMOID adj relating to a ferment

ZYMOLOGY n chemistry of fermentation

ZYMOME, -S n glutinous substance that is insoluble in alcohol

ZYMOSAN, -S n insoluble carbohydrate found in yeast

ZYMOSIS, ZYMOSES same as > zymolysis

ZYMOTIC, -S adj of, relating to, or causing fermentation ▷ n disease caused by an enzyme

ZYMURGY n study of fermentation processes

ZYTHUM, -S n ancient Egyptian beer

ZYZZYVA, -S n American weevil

ZZZ, -S n informal word for sleep

Z